The National Hockey League

Official Guide & Record Book

1993-94

Published by the National Hockey League.
Compiled by the NHL Communications Group
and the 26 NHL Club Public Relations Directors.
Copyright © 1993 by the National Hockey League

THE NATIONAL HOCKEY LEAGUE
Official Guide & Record Book/1993-94

Staff:
For the NHL: Michael Berger; Supervising Editor: Greg Inglis; Statistician: Benny Ercolani; Editorial Staff: Susan Elliott, David Keon, Michele Romanin, Sherry McKeown

Managing Editors: Ralph Dinger, James Duplacey

Contributing Editor: Igor Kuperman, Will Sutton

European Editor: Tom Ratschunas

Contributors:
Thomas H. Ahearn, David J. Candy, Edmond F. Coutu, Luca Del-Vita, Gregg Drinnan, Gene Dupras, Ronald Finston, Mel Foster, Jay Foundas, Gennady Fyodorov, Manon Gagnon (QMJHL), Claus Glenning, Glenn S. Grinter, Jeremy Hoegg, Paul Katz, Mike Kaiser, Derek Knee, Dana Lapierre, Gordon MacDonald, Ross McKeon, Mike Meyers (IHL), Robert P. Mitchell, Moncton Hawk's Booster Club, Herb Morell (OHL), NHL Broadcasters' Association, NHL Central Registry, NHL Players' Association, Guy Parent, David Rendall, Renato Rossi, Hellen M. Schroeder (AHL), Steven Steinsaltz, Jeff Weiss (CCHA), Michel Vigneault.

Consulting Publisher: Dan Diamond

Photo Credits:
Historical and special event photos: Bruce Bennett, David Bier, Graphic Artists Collection, New York Rangers, Rice Studio, Robert Shaver, Imperial Oil Turofsky Collection, Hockey Hall of Fame, Public Archives of Canada, Western Canada Pictorial Index.

Current photos: Graig Abel, Toronto; Joe Angeles, St. Louis; Steve Babineau, Boston; Sol Benjamin, Chicago; Bruce Bennett, NY Islanders; Tony Biegun, Winnipeg, Denis Brodeur, Montreal; Mark Buckner, St. Louis; Denny Cavanaugh, Pittsburgh; Steve Crandall, New Jersey; Bill Cunningham, Vancouver; Willie Dagenais, Montreal; Edmonton Northlands; Bob Fisher, Montreal; Ray Grabowski, Chicago; John Hartman, Detroit; J. Henson Photographics, Washington; The Ice Age, Toronto; George Kalinsky, NY Rangers; Deborah King, Washington; Jim Mackey, Detroit; Doug MacLellan; McElligott-Teckles Sports Focus Imaging, Ottawa; Bill McKeown, Edmonton; Jack Murray, Vancouver; Tim Parker, St. Louis; Photography Ink, Los Angeles; Andre Pichette, Montreal and Quebec; Richard Pilling, New Jersey; Len Redkoles, Philadelphia; Wen Roberts, Los Angeles, Al Ruelle, Boston; Harry Scull, Jr., Buffalo; Don Smith, San Jose; Diane Sobolewski, Hartford; Gerry Thomas, Edmonton; Jim Turner, New Jersey; Brad Watson, Calgary; Westfile, Edmonton; Rocky Widner, San Jose; Bill Wippert, Buffalo.

Canadian representatives:
North 49 Books, 193 Bartley Drive, Toronto, Ontario M4A 1E6
416/750-7777; FAX 416/750-2049
NHL Publishing, 194 Dovercourt Road, Toronto, Ontario M6J 3C8
416/531-6535; FAX 416/531-3939

U.S. representatives: Triumph Books,
644 South Clark Street, Chicago, Illinois 60605   312/939-3330; FAX 312/663-3557

International representatives: Barkers Worldwide Publications,
155 Maybury Road, Woking, Surrey, England GU21 5JR
Tel. and FAX: 011/44/483/776-141

Data Management and Typesetting: Caledon Data Management, Caledon, Ontario
Additional Typesetting: Moveable Type, Toronto, Ontario
Film Output and Process Camera: Stafford Graphics, Toronto, Ontario
Text Printing: Web Offset Publications, Pickering, Ontario
Cover Printing: Thorn Press, Don Mills, Ontario
Production Management: Dan Diamond and Associates, Inc., Toronto, Ontario

9 8 7 6 5 4 3 2 1
Digit on the right indicates the number of this printing.

ISBN 0-920445-30-6

The National Hockey League
1800 McGill College Ave., suite 2600, Montreal, Quebec H3A 3J6
650 Fifth Avenue, 33rd floor, New York, New York 10019-6108
75 International Boulevard, suite 300, Toronto, Ontario M9W 6L9

Table of Contents

Introduction	**5**
NHL Directory	**6**
Referees and Linesmen	**8**

11 CLUBS   records, rosters, management

Mighty Ducks of Anaheim	11
Boston Bruins	13
Buffalo Sabres	17
Calgary Flames	21
Chicago Blackhawks	25
Dallas Stars	29
Detroit Red Wings	33
Edmonton Oilers	37
Florida Panthers	41
Hartford Whalers	43
Los Angeles Kings	47
Montreal Canadiens	51
New Jersey Devils	55
New York Islanders	59
New York Rangers	63
Ottawa Senators	67
Philadelphia Flyers	71
Pittsburgh Penguins	75
Quebec Nordiques	79
St. Louis Blues	83
San Jose Sharks	87
Tampa Bay Lightning	91
Toronto Maple Leafs	95
Vancouver Canucks	99
Washington Capitals	103
Winnipeg Jets	107

111 FINAL STATISTICS 1992-93

Standings	111
Individual Leaders	112
Rookie Leaders	113
Three-or-More Goal Games	114
Goaltending Leaders	115
Team Statistics	116
Penalty and Power-Play Statistics	117
Regular Season Overtime	118
Penalty Shots	119

Table of Contents *continued*

119 NHL RECORD BOOK

All-Time Standings of NHL Teams	119
Year-by-year Final Standings and Leading Scorers	119
NHL History	132
Major Rule Changes	133
TEAM RECORDS	
Winning and Losing Streaks	135
Team Goaltending Records	136
Team Scoring Records	137
INDIVIDUAL RECORDS	**141**
Top 100 Scoring Leaders	151
All-Time Games Played Leaders	154
Goaltending Records	156
Coaching Records	158
One Season Scoring Records	159
Active Players' Three-or-More Goal Games	161
Rookie Scoring Records	162
50-Goal Seasons	163
100-Point Seasons	165
Five-or-more Goal Games	167
500th Goal, 1,000th Point	168
Trophies and Awards	**169**
AMATEUR AND ENTRY DRAFT	
First Selections	176
Summary by Player Sources	176
Detailed Draft Breakdown, OHL, WHL, QMJHL	177
Detailed Draft Breakdown, NCAA	178
Detailed Draft Breakdown, International	179
Analysis by Origin, Position, Age	179
Notes on 1993 First Round Selections	181
1993 Expansion Draft	182
1993 Entry Draft	182
First two rounds, 1992-69	184
NHL ALL-STARS	
All-Star Selection Records	188
All-Star Teams	189
All-Star Game Results	192
All-Star Game Records	193
HOCKEY HALL OF FAME	**196**

199 STANLEY CUP GUIDE & RECORD BOOK

1993 STANLEY CUP PLAYOFFS	
Results	199
Playoff Leaders	200
Team Statistics	201
STANLEY CUP RECORD BOOK	
Championship Trophy Winners	202
Stanley Cup Winners — rosters and final series scores	203
All-Time Playoff Format History	211
Playoff Records	212
Leading Playoff Scorers	223
Three-or-More-Goal Playoff Games	224
Leading Scorers and Playoff Standings, 1918-93	225
Overtime Games since 1918	226
Stanley Cup Coaching Records	228
Stanley Cup Penalty Shots, Longest Overtime Games	229

231 PLAYER REGISTER

Year-by-year records of forwards and defensemen	231
Late Additions to Player Register	381
Retired NHL Player Index	**383**

409 GOALTENDING REGISTER

Year-by-year records of goaltenders	409
Retired NHL Goaltender Index	**427**

430 1992-93 NHL PLAYER TRANSACTIONS

(1993-94 NHL Schedule begins inside front cover)

Introduction

Continued Growth

WELCOME TO *THE NHL OFFICIAL GUIDE & RECORD BOOK FOR 1993-94. THE CONTINUING* evolution of today's National Hockey League is reflected throughout this 62nd edition of the game's most comprehensive statistical annual. The Mighty Ducks of Anaheim and the Florida Panthers have been added to the club section at the beginning the book. Players drafted and signed as free agents by Anaheim can be found on page 11. Florida's roster is on page 41. Detailed career stats for these players are also included in the Player and Goaltender Registers which, in this year's biggest-ever 432-page edition, begin on page 231 for players and page 409 for goaltenders.

The League's renamed Conferences and Divisions and its new playoff structure are described on the inside front cover.

The book's Player and Goaltender Registers have been updated with the addition of players drafted in the first six rounds of the 1993 Entry Draft and in rounds seven through 11 of the 1992 Entry Draft. The later rounds of the 1993 Entry Draft have also been examined, enabling us to include several Eastern Europe prospects who will be attending training camp with the NHL club that selected them in the Entry Draft. These players along with a list of late free agent signings can be found on page 381. Continuing a procedure initiated last year, an analysis of each club's free agent signings and reserve list has resulted in numerous additions and deletions to the Registers. As well, more than 100 phonetic pronunciations of players' names have been added. Together, these changes combine to produce our most comprehensive listing of current and prospective NHL players and goaltenders.

European hockey receives expanded coverage in the *Guide's* Entry Draft section. Beginning on page 179, players drafted from the four major European hockey nations – Sweden, Russia/C.I.S., Czech Republic and Slovakia, and Finland – are listed by club and draft year. These tables reveal that CSKA Moscow (Red Army) has contributed 39 players to the NHL. Moscow Dynamo is second with 28 draftees, Czech club Dukla Jihlava is in third spot with 22 players drafted.

Twenty-six regular-season games are scheduled for non-NHL cities in 1993-94. These games and their locations are included in the overall NHL Schedule that begins on the inside cover of this edition and are also listed in each team's schedule panel found in the book's club section that begins on page 11.

This is the tenth edition of the *Official Guide & Record Book* published in this form. Beginning with this edition, advances in printing result in improved readability and photo reproduction. As always, our thanks to readers and members of the media who take the time to comment on the *Guide & Record Book*. Thanks as well to the people working in the communications departments of the NHL's member clubs and to their counterparts in the AHL, IHL, ECHL, Central, Colonial and junior leagues as well as in college athletic conferences and European hockey federations.

Best wishes for an enjoyable 1993-94 NHL season.

ACCURACY REMAINS THE *GUIDE & RECORD BOOK*'S TOP PRIORITY.
We appreciate comments and clarification from our readers. Please direct these to:

Michael Berger   40th floor, 1633 Broadway, New York, NY 10019 . . . or . . .

Greg Inglis   75 International Blvd., suite 300, Rexdale, Ontario M9W 6L9.

Your involvement makes a better book.

 # National Hockey League

Organized November 22, 1917

Board of Governors

Chairman – Bruce McNall

Mighty Ducks of Anaheim
(Disney Sports Enterprises, Inc.)
Michael D. Eisner – Governor
Tony Tavares – Alternate Governor
Jack Ferreira – Alternate Governor

Boston Bruins
(Boston Professional Hockey Association, Inc.)
Jeremy Jacobs – Governor
Louis Jacobs – Alternate Governor
Harry J. Sinden – Alternate Governor

Buffalo Sabres
(Niagara Frontier Hockey, L.P.)
Seymour H. Knox III – Governor
Seymour H. Knox IV – Alternate Governor
Gerard M. Meehan – Alternate Governor
Robert O. Swados – Alternate Governor

Calgary Flames
(Calgary Flames Hockey Club)
Harley N. Hotchkiss – Governor
William C. Hay – Alternate Governor
Byron J. Seaman – Alternate Governor

Chicago Blackhawks
(Chicago Blackhawk Hockey Team, Inc.)
William W. Wirtz – Governor
Gene Gozdecki – Alternate Governor
Arthur M. Wirtz Jr. – Alternate Governor
Thomas N. Ivan – Alternate Governor
Robert Pulford – Alternate Governor
W. Rockwell Wirtz – Alternate Governor

Dallas Stars
(Dallas Stars Hockey Club)
Norman Green – Governor
John W.G. Donahue – Alternate Governor
James R. Lites – Alternate Governor

Detroit Red Wings
(Detroit Red Wings, Inc.)
Michael Ilitch – Governor
Jay A. Bielfield – Alternate Governor
Jim Devellano – Alternate Governor
John A. Ziegler, Jr. – Alternate Governor

Edmonton Oilers
(Edmonton Oilers Hockey Corp.)
Peter Pocklington – Governor
Lorne J. Ruzicka – Alternate Governor
Glen Sather – Alternate Governor

Florida Panthers
(Florida Panthers Hockey Club)
William A. Torrey – Governor
Bob Clarke – Alternate Governor
Dean Jordan – Alternate Governor

Hartford Whalers
(Hartford Whalers Hockey Club, L.P.)
Richard H. Gordon – Governor

Los Angeles Kings
(L.A. Kings, Ltd.)
Bruce McNall – Governor
Roy Mlakar – Alternate Governor
Rogie Vachon – Alternate Governor

Montreal Canadiens
(Le Club de Hockey Canadien, Inc.)
Ronald L. Corey – Governor
A. Barry Joslin – Alternate Governor
Serge Savard – Alternate Governor

New Jersey Devils
(Meadowlanders, Inc.)
Dr. John J. McMullen – Governor
Louis A. Lamoriello – Alternate Governor
Peter McMullen – Alternate Governor

New York Islanders
(New York Islanders Hockey Club, L.P.)
Robert Rosenthal – Governor
John H. Krumpe – Alternate Governor
Don Maloney – Alternate Governor
Ralph Palleschi – Alternate Governor
Steve Walsh – Alternate Governor

New York Rangers
(New York Rangers Hockey Club)
Stanley R. Jaffe – Governor
Robert M. Gutkowski – Alternate Governor
Kenneth W. Munoz – Alternate Governor
Neil Smith – Alternate Governor

Ottawa Senators
(Ottawa Senators Hockey Club)
Roderick M. Bryden – Governor
Cyril Leeder – Alternate Governor
Randy J. Sexton – Alternate Governor

Philadelphia Flyers
(Philadelphia Flyers Limited Partnership)
Jay T. Snider – Governor
Russ W. Farwell – Alternate Governor
Ronald K. Ryan – Alternate Governor
Edward M. Snider – Alternate Governor

Pittsburgh Penguins
(Pittsburgh Hockey Associates)
Howard L. Baldwin – Governor
Morris Belzberg – Alternate Governor
John H. Kelley – Alternate Governor
J. Paul Martha – Alternate Governor
Craig Patrick – Alternate Governor
Thomas V. Ruta – Alternate Governor

Quebec Nordiques
(Le Club de Hockey les Nordiques)
Marcel Aubut – Governor
Gilles Leger – Alternate Governor
Pierre Page – Alternate Governor

St. Louis Blues
(St. Louis Blues Hockey Club, L.P.)
Michael F. Shanahan – Governor
Ron Caron – Alternate Governor
Thomas J. Guilfoil – Alternate Governor
Jack Quinn – Alternate Governor

San Jose Sharks
(San Jose Sharks)
George Gund III – Governor
Gordon Gund – Alternate Governor
Irvin A. Leonard – Alternate Governor
Arthur L. Savage – Alternate Governor

Tampa Bay Lightning
(Lightning Partners, Inc.)
David E. LeFevre – Governor
Phil Esposito – Alternate Governor
Mel Lowell – Alternate Governor

Toronto Maple Leafs
(Maple Leaf Gardens, Limited)
Steve A. Stavro – Governor
Brian P. Bellmore – Alternate Governor
Cliff Fletcher – Alternate Governor

Vancouver Canucks
(Vancouver Hockey Club, Ltd.)
Arthur R. Griffiths – Governor
Frank A. Griffiths – Alternate Governor
Frank W. Griffiths – Alternate Governor
J.B. Patrick Quinn – Alternate Governor

Washington Capitals
(Washington Hockey Limited Partnership)
Abe Pollin – Governor
Richard M. Patrick – Alternate Governor
David R. Poile – Alternate Governor

Winnipeg Jets
(8 Jets Hockey Ventures, Inc.)
Barry L. Shenkarow – Governor
Bill Davis – Alternate Governor
Michael A. Smith – Alternate Governor

League Offices

MONTREAL
1800 McGill College Ave.
Suite 2600
Montreal, Que. H3A 3J6
  Phone: 514/288-9220
  FAX: 514/284-0300

NEW YORK
33rd Floor, 650 Fifth Avenue
New York, NY, 10019-6108
  Phone: 212/398-1100
  FAX: 212/245-8221

TORONTO
75 International Blvd., Suite 300
Rexdale, Ont., M9W 6L9
  Phone: 416/798-0809
  General FAX: 416/798-0819
  Communications FAX: 416/798-0852

League Departments

NEW YORK

Gary B. Bettman – Commissioner
Stephen J. Solomon – Sr. Vice President &
  Chief Operating Officer
Jeffrey Pash – Sr. Vice President & General Counsel
Brian P. Burke – Sr. Vice President &
  Director of Hockey Operations
David Zimmerman – Associate General Counsel
Debbie Walsh – Executive Assistant to the Commissioner

Broadcasting

Glenn Adamo – Vice President, Broadcasting
Ellis T. "Skip" Prince III – Vice President, Television &
  Team Services

Communications

Arthur Pincus – Vice President, Public Relations
Bernadette Mansur – Vice President, Corporate
  Communications

Finance

Pat Cooper – Assistant Controller

Security

Dennis Cunningham – Director of Security

TORONTO

Jim Gregory – Vice President, Hockey Operations
Bryan Lewis – Director of Officiating
Wally Harris – Assistant Director of Officiating
Will Norris – Coordinator of Development
Frank Bonello – Director of Central Scouting
John Andersen – Central Scouting Administration
Al Wiseman – Assistant Director of Security
Chris Edwards – Video Coordinator

Officiating Supervisory Staff

Dave Newell, Matt Pavelich, Jim Christison,
John D'Amico, Bob Nadin, Sam Sisco,
Charlie Banfield, Ron Ego, Art Skov,
Dutch Van Deelen, Mark Rudolph

Central Scouting Staff

Jack Barzee, Gerry Blair, Chris Bordeleau,
Pat Carmichael, Mike Donaldson, Gary Eggleston,
Laurence Ferguson, Rolland Faubert,
Ralph Goldhirsch, Paul Goulet, Tom Martin,
Rob Pulford, Dan Reinisch, Jack Timmins,
Barry Trapp,

Communications Group

Gary Meagher – Executive Director of Communications
Susan Elliott – Director of Information and Editorial
  Services
Benny Ercolani – Statistician/Information Officer
Greg Inglis – Information Officer
Michele Romanin – Communications Assistant
David Keon – Communications Assistant

MONTREAL

Administration

Phil Scheuer – Director of Administration
Steve Hatzepetros – Assistant Director

Central Registry

Garry Lovegrove – Director of Central Registry
Madeleine Supino – Assistant Director

Consulting Services

Brian F. O'Neill – Director

Information Systems

Mario Carangi – Director
Luc Coulombe – Assistant Director

Finance

Joseph DeSousa – Controller
Olivia Pietrantonio – Assistant Controller

Pension

Yvon Chamberland – Director
Mary Skiadopoulos – Controller, Pension

NHL Enterprises, Inc.

1633 Broadway
40th Floor
New York, NY 10019
Phone: 212/767-4600
FAX: 212/767-4646

Steve Ryan – President
Lucia Ripi Benke – Assistant to the President

Legal

Richard Zahnd – Senior Vice President, General Counsel
Adam Helfant – Associate General Counsel

Finance

Walter Luby – Vice President, Financial
Mary C. McCarthy – Assistant Controller

Sponsorship Division

Steve Flatow – Vice President
Sarah Galvin – Director, Sponsor Services

Retail Licensing – U.S. & International

Fred Scalera – Vice President
Ilene Kent – Licensing & Marketing Director, Collectibles
Judy Salsberg – Director, Non-Apparel Products
Tina Ellis – Director, Children's Licensing
Brian Jennings – National Sales Director
William Tighe – Senior Regional Sales Manager
Brendan McQuillan – Eastern Regional Sales Manager

International

William Short – Managing Director
Barbara Balser – Administrative Manager

Event Marketing

Frank Supovitz – General Manager
Karen Hovsepian – Director
Lori Boesch – Director, Special Events

Publishing

Michael A. Berger – General Manager

Administration

Janet A. Meyers – Director of Administration
Andrew Crawford – Office Services Assistant

NHL Enterprises Canada, Inc.

75 International Blvd. Suite 301
Rexdale, Ont. M9W 6L9
Phone: 416/798-9388
FAX: 416/798-9395

Bob McLaughlin – Managing Director, Canadian Licensing
Angie Andreou – Administrative Co-ordinator
Karen Hanson – Licensing Manager
Fiona Hastie – Licensing Operations Manager
Barry Monaghan – Retail Merchandising Manager

NHL All–Star Weekend

1633 Broadway
40th Floor
New York, NY 10019
Phone: 212/767-4600
FAX: 212/767-4646

Frank Supovitz – General Manager
Lori Boesch – Director
Ann Devney – Manager
Anne Grotefeld – Manager
Mike Santos – Manager

Hockey Hall of Fame and Museum

BCE Place
30 Yonge Street
Toronto, Ont. M6K 3C3
Phone: 416/360-7735
FAX: 416/360-1501

Ian "Scotty" Morrison – Chairman
David Taylor – President
Phil Denyes – Director of Marketing and Communications
Jeff Denomme – Director of Finance and Operations
Ray Paquet – Director of Facility Systems and Exhibit
  Development
Philip Pritchard – Director of Information and Acquisitions
Ron Ellis – Education and Group Program Co-ordinator
Sue Bolender – Manager, Facilites Sales
Scott North – Manager, Special Events
Christine Simpson – Marketing Manager
Andy Yemen – Retail and Merchandise Manager

National Hockey League Players' Association

One Dundas Street West
Suite 2406
Toronto, Ontario
M5G 1Z3
Phone: 416/408-4040
FAX: 416/408-3685

Bob Goodenow – Executive Director
Sam Simpson – Director of Operations
Ian Pulver – Associate Counsel
Michael Humes – Director of Special Projects
Ted Saskin – Director of Licensing
Chris Malone – Associate Director, Licensing and
  Business Development.

League Commissioner and Presidents

Gary B. Bettman

Gary B. Bettman took office as the NHL's first
Commissioner on February 1, 1993. Since the
League was formed in 1917, five men have
served as League President. Here are the NHL's
Presidents listed with their years in office.

NHL President	Years in office
Frank Calder	1917 to 1943
Mervyn "Red" Dutton	1943 to 1946
Clarence Campbell	1946 to 1977
John A. Ziegler, Jr.	1977 to 1992
Gil Stein	1992 to 1993

Referees and Linesmen

DON ADAM . . . Referee . . . Born: Oct. 30, 1964 in Boulder, Colorado . . . Worked 1991 IIHF World Championships and 1992 Winter Olympics . . . Runs power-skating camps in the off-season. Enjoys travel, hiking, tennis and golf . . . He is single.

BLAINE ANGUS . . . Referee . . . Born: Sept. 25, 1961 in Shawville, Que. . . . Hired by the NHL in 1991, Angus worked his first NHL game Oct. 17, 1992. Total NHL games: 6 . . . enjoys golf, running and carpentry in the off-season . . . is a registered x-ray technologist . . . resides in Barrie, Ontario with his wife and two children.

RON ASSELSTINE . . . Linesman . . . Born: Nov. 6, 1946 in Toronto, Ont. . . . First NHL game: Oct. 10, 1979 . . . Total NHL games: 1,103 . . . Worked 1,000th NHL game on January 4, 1992 at New Jersey. Ron is very active in his community as chairman of the "Make-A-Wish" Foundation. He is married and has two children.

WAYNE BONNEY . . . Linesman . . . Born: May 27, 1953 in Ottawa, Ont. . . . First NHL game: Oct. 10, 1979 . . . Total NHL games: 1,073 . . . Joined the NHL in 1979. Bonney worked the 1989 All-Star Game in Edmonton and the Stanley Cup championship series in 1990, 1991 and 1993. He currently resides in Redwood, WA., with his wife and daughter. He is an avid baseball player.

RYAN BOZAK . . . Linesman . . . Born: Jan. 3, 1947 in Swift Current, Sask. . . . First NHL game: 1972 . . . Total NHL games: 1,528 . . . Joined the NHL in 1972 and worked his 1,500th NHL game in Jan. 17, 1993. He was selected to officiate in the 1983 and 1993 All-Star Games. During the off-season he enjoys golf and tennis and resides in San Diego, CA. Bozak has two children.

GORD BROSEKER . . . Linesman . . . Born: July 8, 1950 in Baltimore, MD . . . First NHL game: Jan 14, 1975 . . . Total NHL games: 1,343 . . . Joined the NHL in 1973 and officiated in his 1,250th NHL game in 1991-92. Before beginning his officiating career, he played baseball in the Texas Rangers' organization. Broseker was selected to officiate in the 1991 Stanley Cup championship series. He currently resides in Richmond, VA, with his wife and daughter.

PIERRE CHAMPOUX . . . Linesman . . . Born: Apr. 18, 1963 in Ville St. Pierre, Que. . . . First NHL game: Oct. 8, 1988 . . . Total NHL games: 316 . . . Began officiating minor league games at the age of 12 in the Quebec pee wee league. Since then he has worked in two international competitions, having officiated in an exhibition game between the United States and Canada at the Forum and in Canada Cup 1987. During the off-season, Champoux enjoys golf, tennis and cycling. Champoux is single.

KEVIN COLLINS . . . Linesman . . . Born: Dec. 15,1950 in Springfield, MA . . . First NHL game: Oct. 13, 1977 . . . Total NHL games: 1,275 . . . Joined the NHL in 1977. He was selected to officiate in the 1993 NHL All-Star Game and officiated in the 1993 Stanley Cup finals. Currently residing in Springfield, MA, Collins is married and has three children.

MICHAEL CVIK . . . Linesman . . . Born: July 6, 1962 in Calgary, Alta. . . . First NHL game: Oct. 8, 1987 . . . Total NHL games: 424 . . . The tallest of the officials at 6'9", began his officiating career in the AAHA in 1978. After working his way through the WHL, he joined the NHL in 1987. During the off-season, Mike is an instructor at the WHL School of Officiating. Sells real estate in the off-season. He enjoys weightlifting, cycling, music, reading, yoga and golf. He is single.

PAT DAPUZZO . . . Linesman . . . Born: Dec. 29, 1958 in Hoboken, NJ . . . First NHL game: Dec. 5, 1984 . . . Total NHL games: 649 . . . Officiated in his first NHL game on Dec. 5, 1984, in Madison Square Garden. He worked six games in the 1991 Canada Cup. Pat resides in North Bergen, NJ. He is married and has one child. He is an avid weightlifter and karate enthusiast.

BERNARD DEGRACE . . . Linesman . . . Born: May 1, 1967 in Lameque, N.B. . . . First NHL game: Oct. 15, 1991 . . . Total NHL games: 105 . . . Worked the 1992 Calder Cup Finals . . . During the off-season he enjoys golf, tennis and waterskiing . . . He is single.

GREG DEVORSKI . . . Linesman . . . Born: Aug. 3, 1969 in Guelph, Ont . . . Worked 1993 Memorial Cup and CIAU finals . . . Worked in AHL in 1993 . . . Continuing his education in the off-season. Enjoys swimming and hiking. He is single.

PAUL DEVORSKI . . . Referee . . . Born: Aug. 18, 1958 in Guelph, Ont. . . . Joined the NHL in 1987 . . . Total NHL games: 145 . . . Devorski enjoys golf and mountain biking. He is single.

SCOTT DRISCOLL . . . Linesman . . . Born: May 2, 1968 in Seaforth, Ont. . . . Hired by the NHL in 1991 . . . Began refereeing minor hockey at the age of 13 . . . First NHL game: Oct. 10, 1992 . . . Total NHL games: 46 . . . Worked 1993 AHL finals . . . Enjoys playing several sports in the off-season . . . He is married.

MARK FAUCETTE . . . Referee . . . Born: June 9, 1958 in Springfield, MA . . . First NHL game: 1985 . . . Total NHL games: 269 . . . Joined the NHL in 1985. First playoff game was 6-5 overtime win by Los Angeles over Vancouver in 1991. Enjoys boating. He is single.

RON FINN . . . Linesman . . . Born: Dec. 1, 1940 in Toronto, Ont. . . . First NHL game: October 11, 1969 . . . Total NHL games: 1,831 . . . Has worked in more games than any other active official. . . . A resident of Brampton, Ont. He has worked in two All-Star Games including 1977 (Vancouver) and 1982 (Washington, D.C.). He also worked during Rendez-Vous '87 in Quebec City. Finn set an NHL playoff record for officials by working in his 252nd career playoff game on April 23, 1991. He is an instructor at various officiating schools in Ontario. Ron is married and has four children.

KERRY FRASER . . . Referee . . . Born: June 30, 1952 in Sarnia, Ont. . . . Total NHL games: 825 . . . After playing minor league hockey as a youngster, attended the NHL training camp for officials in 1972. Fraser has become one of the League's most experienced and respected referees, as proven by his selection to referee five Stanley Cup championship series (1985, 1986, 1989-91). During the off-season, Fraser assists in numerous charitable fundraisers, does Public relations work for a financial institution and works with amateur hockey officials' groups. Fraser enjoys sailing and golf. He is married and has seven children.

GERARD GAUTHIER . . . Linesman . . . Born: Sept. 5, 1948 in Montreal, Que. . . . First NHL game: Oct. 16, 1971 . . . Total NHL games: 1,677 . . . Attended his first NHL training camp in 1971 after two years in junior hockey. He has been selected to work at two NHL All-Star Games in his career; Los Angeles (1981) and Calgary (1985). In addition, he has worked in the 1984 Canada Cup and in four Stanley Cup Championship series. On January 25, 1991, Gauthier became the fifth linesman in NHL history to reach 1,500 career games. During the off-season, Gauthier enjoys golfing and tennis. He is married and has two children.

TERRY GREGSON . . . Referee . . . Born: Nov. 7 1953 in Guelph, Ont. . . . First NHL game: Dec. 19, 1981 . . . Total NHL games: 696 . . . Joined the NHL in 1979. Gregson was selected to officiate his second career All-Star Game in 1991 at Chicago. Worked the 1992 and 1993 Stanley Cup Championship. President of the National Hockey League Officials' Association, Gregson also organizes the NHLOA's Golf Classic for the Children's Wish Foundation. During the off-season he is an avid traveller. Gregson is married.

SHANE HEYER . . . Referee . . . Born: Feb. 7,1964 in Summerland, B.C. . . . First NHL game: Oct. 5, 1988 . . . Total NHL games: 373 . . . Began officiating in Penticton, B.C., at the age of 10 and was invited to join the NHL program in 1988. In his first year of service, Heyer was selected to work in the December 31 game between the Los Angeles Kings and the Dynamo Riga club during Super Series '88-89. Heyer is single and enjoys softball, tennis and golf.

BOB HODGES . . . Linesman . . . Born: Aug. 16, 1944 in Hespeler, Ont. . . . First NHL game: Oct. 14, 1972 . . . Total NHL games: 1,485 . . . Hired by the NHL in 1972-73 season at the age of 28, Hodges is one of the NHL's senior officials. He has been chosen to work in the Stanley Cup Finals three times (1982, 1986 and 1987) and officiated at the All-Star Game in Calgary (1985) and Pittsburgh (1990). During the off-season he works with various charities and enjoys gardening, hunting, fishing and golf. Hodges is married and has two children.

RON HOGGARTH . . . Referee . . . Born: Apr. 12, 1948 in Barrie, Ont. . . . First NHL game: Oct. 16, 1971 . . . Total NHL games: 1,114 . . . Began officiating while still a student at McMaster University. He joined the NHL in 1971. Worked his 1,000th game December 21, 1991. During the summer, Hoggarth owns and operates KoHo pools in Barrie and is active in golf and tennis. He is married and has two daughters.

DAVE JACKSON . . . Referee . . . Born: Nov. 28, 1964 in Montreal, Que. . . . Total NHL games: 27 . . . One of two officials to join the NHL in 1989, he was an NHL trainee at the age of 21. He made his first NHL appearance in the 1990-91 season. Worked Calder Cup finals in 1993. During the off-season, he enjoys golf, softball, biking, carpentry, reading and cooking. Jackson is married and has one child.

GREG KIMERLY . . . Referee . . . Born: Dec. 8, 1964 in North York, Ont . . . Began officiating at age 16 . . . NHL trainee since 1990 . . . Ten years experience in minor hockey . . . Three years experience in OHL . . . He is married.

SWEDE KNOX . . . Linesman . . . Born: Mar. 2, 1948 in Edmonton, Alta. . . . First NHL game: Oct. 14, 1972 . . . Total NHL games: 1,624 . . . Joined the NHL in 1971. In 1982, he was selected to work in the NHL All-Star Gamê in Washington, D.C. He has also worked in five Stanley Cup championship series. Worked his 1,500th game October 26, 1991. A full-time resident of Edmonton, Swede is married and has two children. He enjoys squash and golf during the off-season.

DON KOHARSKI . . . Referee . . . Born: Dec. 2, 1955 in Halifax, N.S. . . . First NHL game: Oct. 14, 1977 . . . Total NHL games: 812 (163 as a linesman) . . . Hired as an official in the WHA at the age of 18. He joined the NHL in 1977 as a linesman, becoming a referee after 163 games. Koharski gained international experience in Canada Cup 1987 and has worked in six Stanley Cup Finals (1986-88, 1990-92). He refereed his first NHL All-Star Game in 1992. He is married and has two sons.

DENNIS LaRUE . . . Referee . . . Born: July 14, 1959 in Savannah, GA . . . Total NHL games: 22 . . . Attended the USA Hockey Referee Development Camp in 1983 and joined the NHL in 1988. He made his NHL debut on March 26, 1991. During the off-season he is a youth baseball coach and an instructor at the USA Hockey Referee Development Camp. He is an avid golfer. Dennis is married and has two children.

BRAD LAZAROWICH . . . Linesman . . . Born: Aug. 4, 1962 in Vancouver, B.C. . . . First NHL game: Oct. 9, 1986 . . . Total NHL games: 512 . . . Joined the NHL in 1986. Worked his 500th NHL game in March, 1993. During the off-season, studies business management and is an instructor at an officiating school. He is an avid bicyclist, golfer and weightlifter. He is married and has a daughter.

DAN MAROUELLI . . . Referee . . . Born: July 16, 1955 in Edmonton, Alta. . . . First NHL game: Nov. 2, 1984 . . . Total NHL games: 545 . . . Began his officiating career at the age of 13 with the Knights of Columbus. He joined the NHL in 1982. During the summer, Marouelli works at a number of refereeing schools and owns a small construction business in addition to participating in many charity fundraising events. He is an avid golfer. Dan is married and has three children.

ROB MARTELL . . . Referee . . . Born: October 21, 1963 in Winnipeg, Man. . . . First NHL game: Mar. 14, 1984 . . . Began officiating minor hockey at the age of 14 . . . During the off-season he works in a landscaping business and drives tractor trailers . . . Enjoys golf,biking and summer hockey . . . He is married.

ANDY McELMAN . . . Linesman . . . Born: Feb. 24, 1961 in Chicago Heights, IL . . . Graduate of USA Hockey Officiating Program . . . Worked two U.S. National Junior Championships, one IIHF World Junior Championship . . . Also worked IHL All-Star Game in Atlanta . . . Designs printed circuit boards in the off-season . . . Plays volleyball, ball hockey. He is married and has a son.

DAN McCOURT . . . Linesman . . . Born: Aug. 14, 1954 in Falconbridge, Ont. . . . First NHL game: Dec. 27, 1980 . . . Total NHL games: 886 . . . Joined the NHL in 1979. . . . Worked the 1990 All-Star Game in Pittsburgh. During the off-season, he works with the Easter Seals Society. He enjoys golf, baseball, boating and waterskiing. McCourt is married and has two daughters.

BILL McCREARY . . . Referee . . . Born: Nov. 17, 1955 in Guelph, Ont. . . . First NHL game: Nov. 3, 1984 . . . Total NHL games: 565 . . . Joined the NHL in 1982. He was selected to referee in 1991 Canada Cup. During the off-season also enjoys golfing and fishing. He is married and has two sons and a daughter.

MIKE McGEOUGH . . . Referee . . . Born: June 20, 1957 in Regina, Sask. . . . Total NHL games: 150 . . . Began his NHL career in 1987. During the off-season, McGeough enjoys golf and horseback riding. He instructs at various refereeing schools. He is married and has three children.

RANDY MITTON . . . Linesman . . . Born: Sept. 22, 1950 in Fredericton, N.B. . . . First NHL game: Dec. 26, 1973 . . . Total NHL games: 1,426 . . . Became involved in NHL officiating in 1972 after working in the WHL and AHL for two years. He gained international experience as a linesman for the 1987 Canada Cup and was selected to officiate in the 1988 NHL All-Star Game in St. Louis. During the off-season, Mitton teaches at a number of officiating schools in Western Canada. He is married and has two children.

DENIS MOREL . . . Referee . . . Born: Dec. 13, 1948 in Quebec City, Que. . . . First NHL game: Jan. 18, 1976 . . . Total NHL games: 1,080 . . . Began officiating in Quebec minor leagues before joining the NHL in 1976. Morel has worked in two Stanley Cup Championship series — 1988 and 1989. Worked 1,000th game, March 14, 1992. During the summer, he is a motivational speaker, instructs at officiating schools and hosts an annual charity golf tournament. He enjoys golf, running, fishing and art. He is married and has two children.

JEAN MORIN . . . Linesman . . . Born: August 10, 1963 in Sorel, Que. . . . First NHL game: Oct. 5, 1991 . . . Total NHL games: 107. Worked three games during the 1991-92 series between the U.S. or Canadian National Team and NHL teams . . . Enjoys golf, reading, softball and volleyball . . . He is married and has one child.

BRIAN MURPHY . . . Linesman . . . Born: Dec. 13, 1964 in Dover, NH . . . First NHL game: Oct. 7, 1988 . . . Total NHL games: 326 . . . Joined the League in 1988-89 after graduating from the University of New Hampshire with a degree in Business Administration. During his years at University, he worked in the NCAA officiating ranks, including the 1988 NCAA Division I National Championship Game in Lake Placid. During the off-season, Murphy enjoys golf and landscaping. Murphy is married and has one child.

TIM NOWAK . . . Linesman . . . Born: Sept. 6, 1967 in Buffalo, N.Y. . . . On-ice official since age 12 . . . Four years in AHL semi-finals . . . In the off-season he is an instructor for USA Hockey's referee development program. He enjoys golf and collecting sports cards. He is single.

DAN O'HALLORAN . . . Referee . . . Born: March 25, 1964 in Leamington, Ont. . . . Worked the 1992 IHL All-Star Game and the 1992 Turner Cup Finals . . . Enjoys carpentry, golf and cooking . . . He is married and has one child.

MARK PARE . . . Linesman . . . Born: July 26, 1957 in Windsor, Ont. . . . First NHL game: Oct. 11, 1979 . . . Total NHL games: 1,088 . . . Joined the NHL in 1979 after working minor leagues in Windsor. Pare worked his 1,000th game in 1991-92. He made his NHL All-Star Game debut in 1992. He enjoys golfing. Pare is married and has three children.

JERRY PATEMAN . . . Linesman . . . Born: Jan. 12, 1958 in The Hague, Netherlands . . . First NHL game: Nov. 10, 1982 . . . Total NHL games: 502 . . . The only NHL official not born in North America, Pateman started refereeing minor hockey in Chatham, Ont. at the age of 14. He joined the NHL in 1982 and officiated in the 1991 All-Star Game in Chicago. During the summer, Pateman works in a construction business, coaches baseball and enjoys gardening and golf. Pateman now resides in Aliquippa, PA. with his wife and two children.

PIERRE RACICOT . . . Linesman . . . Born: Feb. 15, 1967 in Verdun, Que . . . On-ice official since age 14 . . . Worked QMJHL finals in 1992 and 1993 and CIAU finals in 1993 . . . Works with young offenders in the off-season . . . Hobbies include softball, golf and computers . . . He is single.

LANCE ROBERTS . . . Referee . . . Born: May 28, 1957 in Edmonton, Alta. . . . Total NHL games: 57 . . . Began his career at the age of 15 in the minor leagues of Alberta. Worked AHL finals in 1992 and 1993. Roberts takes business courses during the summer and works in real estate. He is married with two daughters and enjoys golf and baseball.

RAY SCAPINELLO . . . Linesman . . . Born: Nov. 5, 1946 in Guelph, Ont. . . . First NHL Game in 1971 in Buffalo . . . Total NHL games: 1,764. . . . Joined NHL in 1971 . . . Has worked three All-Star Games, 12 consecutive Stanley Cup Finals plus the Canada Cup, Challenge Cup and Rendez-Vous 87 . . . In the off-season, Ray is a two-handicap golfer and works with the "Make-A-Wish" chapter in Guelph . . . He is married and has a son.

DAN SCHACHTE . . . Linesman . . . Born: July 13, 1958 in Madison, WI . . . First NHL game: October 8, 1982 . . . Total NHL games: 810 . . . Joined the NHL in 1982. He was chosen to officiate in the 1991 All-Star Game in Chicago. Also worked in the 1991 Canada Cup. He enjoys hunting, fishing and boating. He is married and has three children.

LYLE SEITZ . . . Linesman . . . Born: Jan. 22, 1969 in Brooks, Alta. . . . Began officiating minor hockey at the age of 9 . . . First NHL game: Oct. 6, 1992 . . . Total NHL games: 40 . . . Worked AHL finals, 1993 . . . Worked the 1991 WHL All-Star Game and the 1992 Memorial Cup Finals . . . Off-season activities include cattle and grain farming . . . Enjoys racquet sports, golf, cycling and weightlifting. He is single.

JAY SHARRERS . . . Linesman . . . Born: July 3, 1967 in New Westminster, B.C. . . . Joined the NHL in 1990 . . . First NHL game: Oct. 6, 1990 . . . Total NHL games: 184 . . . Has also worked Canadian college games and, in 1985-86, a tournament involving college teams from the U.S., Canada and Japan . . . Teaches at an officiating school. Enjoys camping, fishing, baseball and golf. He is single.

ROB SHICK . . . Referee . . . Born: Dec. 4, 1957, in Port Alberni, B.C. . . . First NHL game: Apr. 6, 1986 . . . Total NHL games: 383 . . . Joined the NHL in 1984. He is married. Instructs at a referees' school in the off-season. Enjoys golf, fishing and travelling.

PAUL STEWART . . . Referee . . . Born: Mar. 21, 1955 in Boston, MA . . . First NHL game: Mar. 27, 1987 . . . Total NHL games: 390 . . . Joined the NHL in 1985. Worked 1987 and 1991 Canada Cup. Stewart is the only former NHL player on the active officiating staff. During the off-season, Stewart is involved in a clothing company and assists several charities. Stewart is single and enjoys model trains, World War II history and golf.

LEON STICKLE . . . Linesman . . . Born: Apr. 20, 1948 in Toronto, Ont. . . . First NHL game: Oct. 17, 1970 . . . Total NHL games: 1,727 . . . Joined the NHL in 1969 after four years in the minor leagues. In his career, he has worked in three NHL All-Star Games (Montreal, 1975; Buffalo,1978 and Long Island, 1983). He also was selected as an official for the Canada Cup tournament in 1981 and 1984. He has worked in the Stanley Cup Finals six times (1977, 1978, 1980, 1981, 1984 and 1985). During the off-season, Stickle is active with the Ontario and Canadian Special Olympics, hosting a summer golf tournament. He is married and has three children.

RICHARD TROTTIER . . . Referee . . . Born: Feb. 28, 1957 in Laval, Que. . . . First NHL game: Dec 13, 1989 . . . Total NHL games: 69 . . . During his career, he has served as the executive vice-president for the Quebec Esso Cup in 1987-88 and 1988-89 and has been the referee-in-chief for the Quebec Ice Hockey Federation since 1986. He has worked CIAU, Memorial Cup and World Junior tournaments. During the off-season, he enjoys golf.

ANDY vanHELLEMOND . . . Referee . . . Born: Feb. 16, 1948 in Winnipeg, Man. . . . First NHL game: Nov. 22, 1972 . . . Total NHL games: 1,327 . . . Joined the NHL in 1971 and has become one of the senior NHL officials. He worked in two Stanley Cup Final series 17 consecutive years since 1977. During the summer, vanHellemond enjoys hiking, gardening and horseback riding.

DON VAN MASSENHOVEN . . . Referee . . . Born: July 17, 1960 in London, Ont. . . . Began officiating at the age of 15 . . . Worked the 1990 Memorial Cup Final in Hamilton. Also worked OHL finals 1991 and 1992. Is a police officer in the off-season. He is married and has two children. Coaches minor baseball in off-season.

MARK VINES . . . Linesman . . . Born: Dec. 3, 1960 in Elmira, Ont. . . . First NHL game: Oct. 13, 1984 . . . Total NHL games: 714 . . . Joined the NHL in 1984. Worked the 1991 Canada Cup and at the 1992 NHL All-Star game in Philadelphia. He attends university during the off-season and is single.

STEPHEN WALKOM . . . Referee . . . Born: Aug. 8, 1963 in North Bay, Ontario. . . . First NHL game: Oct. 18, 1992 . . . Total NHL games: 6 . . . Has also worked OHL, minor pro, Canadian college, Northern OHA, senior and junior B . . . Honors degree in Commerce from Laurentian U . . . Lives in Kitchener, Ont. . . . Enjoys running, cycling, racquet sports and sailing . . . Power-skating instructor.

BRAD WATSON . . . Referee . . . Born: Oct. 4, 1961 in Regina, Sask . . . Officiated junior hockey since 1984 . . . Worked 1989 IIHF World Junior Championships, 1991 Izvestia Tournament, 1991 Canada Cup exhibition game and 1992 Spengler Cup . . . He is married.

MARK WHELER . . . Linesman . . . Born: Sept. 20, 1965 in North Battleford, Sask. . . . First NHL game: Oct. 10, 1992 . . . Total NHL games: 70 . . . Began officiating at the age of 12. Worked the 1989 and 1992 Memorial Cup Finals. He works as an instructor at the WHL's officiating schools. Has Bachelor of Commerce degree. Enjoys playing golf, cycling and other outdoor activities. He is married and has one son.

NHL Attendance

| Season | Regular Season | | Playoffs | | Total |
	Games	Attendance	Games	Attendance	Attendance
1960-61	210	2,317,142	17	242,000	2,559,142
1961-62	210	2,435,424	18	277,000	2,712,424
1962-63	210	2,590,574	16	220,906	2,811,480
1963-64	210	2,732,642	21	309,149	3,041,791
1964-65	210	2,822,635	20	303,859	3,126,494
1965-66	210	2,941,164	16	249,000	3,190,184
1966-67	210	3,084,759	16	248,336	3,333,095
1967-68[1]	444	4,938,043	40	495,089	5,433,132
1968-69	456	5,550,613	33	431,739	5,982,352
1969-70	456	5,992,065	34	461,694	6,453,759
1970-71[2]	546	7,257,677	43	707,633	7,965,310
1971-72	546	7,609,368	36	582,666	8,192,034
1972-73[3]	624	8,575,651	38	624,637	9,200,288
1973-74	624	8,640,978	38	600,442	9,241,420
1974-75[4]	720	9,521,536	51	784,181	10,305,717
1975-76	720	9,103,761	48	726,279	9,830,040
1976-77	720	8,563,890	44	646,279	9,210,169
1977-78	720	8,526,564	45	686,634	9,213,198
1978-79	680	7,758,053	45	694,521	8,452,574
1979-80[5]	840	10,533,623	63	976,699	11,510,322
1980-81	840	10,726,198	68	966,390	11,692,588
1981-82	840	10,710,894	71	1,058,948	11,769,842
1982-83	840	11,020,610	66	1,088,222	12,028,832
1983-84	840	11,359,386	70	1,107,400	12,466,786
1984-85	840	11,633,730	70	1,107,500	12,741,230
1985-86	840	11,621,000	72	1,152,503	12,773,503
1986-87	840	11,855,880	87	1,383,967	13,239,847
1987-88	840	12,117,512	83	1,336,901	13,454,413
1988-89	840	12,417,969	83	1,327,214	13,745,183
1989-90	840	12,579,651	85	1,355,593	13,935,244
1990-91	840	12,343,897	92	1,442,203	13,786,100
1991-92[6]	880	12,769,676	86	1,327,920	14,097,596
1992-93[7]	1,008	14,158,177[8]	83	1,346,034	15,504,211

[1] First expansion: Los Angeles, Pittsburgh, California (Cleveland), Philadelphia, St. Louis and Minnesota
[2] Second expansion: Buffalo and Vancouver
[3] Third expansion: Atlanta (Calgary) and New York Islanders
[4] Fourth expansion: Kansas City (Colorado, New Jersey) and Washington
[5] Fifth expansion: Edmonton, Hartford, Quebec and Winnipeg
[6] Sixth expansion: San Jose
[7] Seventh expansion: Ottawa and Tampa Bay
[8] Includes 24 neutral site games

Notes

Mighty Ducks of Anaheim

First NHL Season: 1993-94

The Mighty Ducks of Anaheim for 1993-94 have been built through free agent signings, and the NHL Entry and Expansion Drafts. Top goaltending prospect Guy Hebert, left, was acquired from St. Louis in the Expansion Draft. Alexei Kasatonov, right, a 12-year veteran of Moscow's Central Red Army team, spent the last four seasons with the New Jersey Devils. He was the first defenseman taken by Anaheim in the Expansion Draft.

Schedule

Home			Away		
Oct.	Fri.	8 Detroit	**Oct.**	Tues.	19 NY Rangers
	Sun.	10 NY Islanders		Wed.	20 New Jersey
	Wed.	13 Edmonton		Sat.	23 Montreal
	Fri.	15 Boston		Mon.	25 Ottawa
	Sun.	17 Calgary		Thur.	28 San Jose
	Fri.	29 Washington	**Nov.**	Thur.	11 Calgary
	Sun.	31 San Jose		Sun.	14 Vancouver
Nov.	Wed.	3 Dallas		Fri.	19 Vancouver
	Fri.	5 New Jersey		Sun.	21 Edmonton
	Sun.	7 Pittsburgh		Mon.	22 Calgary
	Tues.	9 Dallas		Wed.	24 Winnipeg
		(at Phoenix)		Sat.	27 San Jose*
	Wed.	17 Toronto	**Dec.**	Thur.	2 Los Angeles
	Fri.	26 San Jose*		Tues.	14 Detroit
Dec.	Wed.	1 Winnipeg		Wed.	15 Toronto
	Sun.	5 Tampa Bay		Fri.	17 Dallas
	Tues.	7 Florida		Sun.	19 Chicago
	Sun.	12 St Louis		Mon.	20 Winnipeg
	Wed.	22 Dallas		Tues.	28 NY Islanders
	Sun.	26 Los Angeles		Thur.	30 Washington
Jan.	Mon.	10 Detroit	**Jan.**	Sat.	1 Florida*
	Wed.	12 San Jose		Sun.	2 Tampa Bay
	Fri.	14 Hartford			(at Orlando)
	Sun.	16 Vancouver		Thur.	6 Chicago
	Mon.	24 St Louis		Sat.	8 St Louis
	Wed.	26 Winnipeg		Tues.	18 Toronto
	Fri.	28 NY Rangers		Wed.	19 Detroit
Feb.	Wed.	2 Calgary		Sat.	29 Los Angeles
	Fri.	4 Vancouver	**Feb.**	Sun.	13 Edmonton*
	Sun.	6 Chicago*		Sun.	20 St Louis
	Fri.	11 Los Angeles		Wed.	23 Buffalo
	Wed.	16 Philadelphia		Thur.	24 Pittsburgh
	Fri.	18 Quebec		Sat.	26 Quebec
Mar.	Wed.	2 Montreal	**Mar.**	Sun.	6 San Jose*
	Fri.	4 Edmonton		Tues.	8 Chicago
	Wed.	9 Buffalo			(at Phoenix)
	Fri.	11 Chicago		Tues.	22 Dallas
	Sun.	13 Ottawa*		Thur.	24 Boston
	Wed.	16 Los Angeles		Sat.	26 Hartford
	Thur.	31 Edmonton		Sun.	27 Philadelphia
Apr.	Sat.	2 Toronto		Wed.	30 Los Angeles
	Mon.	11 Calgary	**Apr.**	Wed.	6 Calgary
	Wed.	13 Vancouver		Fri.	8 Edmonton
				Sat.	9 Vancouver

* Denotes afternoon game.

Home Starting Times:

Weeknights	7:35 p.m.
Sundays	7:05 p.m.
Matinees	1:05 p.m.
Except Fri. Feb. 11	6:05 p.m.
Sat. Apr. 2	5:05 p.m.

Franchise date: June 15, 1993

PACIFIC DIVISION

1st NHL Season

WESTERN CONFERENCE

1993-94 Player Personnel

FORWARDS	HT	WT	S	Place of Birth	Date	1992-93 Club
AALTO, Antti	6-2	185	L	Lappeenranta, Finland	3/4/75	TPS Turku
BAWA, Robin	6-2	214	R	Chemainus, B.C.	3/26/66	San Jose
CARNBACK, Patrick	6-0	187	L	Goteborg, Sweden	2/1/68	Fredericton
CORKUM, Bob	6-2	212	R	Salisbury, MA	12/18/67	Buffalo
DOURIS, Peter	6-1	195	R	Toronto, Ont.	2/19/66	Boston-Providence
EWEN, Todd	6-2	220	R	Saskatoon, Sask.	3/22/66	Montreal
GRIMSON, Stu	6-5	227	L	Kamloops, B.C.	5/20/65	Chicago
HALVERSON, Trevor	6-1	195	L	White River, Ont.	4/6/71	Baltimore
KARIYA, Paul	5-11	175	L	Vancouver, B.C.	10/16/74	U. of Maine
KARPOV, Valery	5-10	176	L	Chelyabinsk, USSR	8/5/71	Traktor Chelyabinsk
KING, Steven	6-0	195	R	Greenwich, RI	7/22/69	NY Rangers
KOZEL, Vitali	6-3	183	L	Minsk, USSR	5/26/75	Dynamo Minsk
LAMBERT, Denny	5-11	200	L	Wawa, Ont.	1/7/70	San Diego
LOACH, Lonnie	5-10	181	L	New Liskeard, Ont.	4/14/68	Los Angeles
LONEY, Troy	6-3	209	L	Bow Island, Alta.	9/21/63	Pittsburgh
McKAY, Scott	5-11	200	R	Burlington, Ont.	1/26/72	London
PENNEY, David	6-1	175	L	Easton, MA	5/16/74	Worchester Acad.
SACCO, Joe	6-1	195	L	Medford, MA	2/4/69	Toronto
SEMENOV, Anatoli	6-2	190	L	Moscow, USSR	3/5/62	Vancouver
SKALDE, Jarrod	6-0	170	L	Niagara Falls, Ont.	2/26/71	Utica
SWEENEY, Tim	5-11	185	L	Boston, MA	4/12/67	Providence
THOMSON, Jim	6-1	205	R	Edmonton, Alta.	12/30/65	Los Angeles
VAN ALLEN, Shaun	6-1	200	L	Shaunavon, Sask.	8/29/67	Edm.-Cape Breton
YAKE, Terry	5-11	175	R	New Westminst'r, B.C.	10/22/68	Hartford

DEFENSEMEN						
CHARTIER, Scott	6-1	200	R	St. Lazare, Man.	1/19/72	W. Michigan
DeSANTIS, Mark	6-0	205	R	Brampton, Ont.	1/12/72	Newmarket
DOLLAS, Bobby	6-2	212	L	Montreal, Que.	1/31/65	Adirondack
FEDOTOV, Anatoli	5-11	178	L	Saratov, USSR	5/11/66	Moncton
FERNER, Mark	6-0	193	L	Regina, Sask.	9/5/65	New Haven
HILL, Sean	6-0	195	R	Duluth, MN	2/14/70	Montreal
HOULDER, Bill	6-3	218	L	Thunder Bay, Ont.	3/11/67	Buffalo
KASATONOV, Alexei	6-1	215	L	Leningrad, USSR	10/14/59	New Jersey
LADOUCEUR, Randy	6-2	220	L	Brockville, Ont.	5/30/60	Hartford
O'CONNER, Myles	5-11	190	L	Calgary, Alta.	4/2/67	New Jersey-Utica
PETERSON, Matt	6-1	190	L	St. Louis Park, MN	2/15/75	Osseo
THOMPSON, Pat	6-2	190	R	Halifax, N.S.	1/16/72	Brown U.
TSULYGIN, Nikolai	6-3	196	R	Ufa, USSR	6/29/75	Salavat Yulayev Ufa
WILLIAMS, David	6-2	195	R	Plainfield, NJ	8/25/67	San Jose

GOALTENDERS	HT	WT	C	Place of Birth	Date	1992-93 Club
ASKEY, Tom	6-2	185	L	Kenmore, NY	10/4/74	Ohio State
GAGNON, Joel	6-0	194	L	Hearst, Ont.	3/14/75	Oshawa
HEBERT, Guy	5-11	180	L	Troy, NY	1/7/67	St. Louis
SHTALENKOV, Mikhail	6-2	180	L	Moscow, USSR	10/20/65	Milwaukee
TUGNUTT, Ron	5-11	155	L	Scarborough, Ont.	10/22/67	Edmonton

Entry Draft Selections 1993

1993
Pick

Pick	Player
4	Paul Kariya
30	Nikolai Tsulygin
56	Valeri Karpov
82	Joel Gagnon
108	Mikhail Shtalenkov
134	Antti Aalto
160	Matt Peterson
186	Tom Askey
212	Vitaly Kozel
238	Anatoli Fedotov
264	David Penney

© Disney

Coach

WILSON, RON
Head Coach, The Mighty Ducks of Anaheim.
Born in Windsor, Ont., May 28, 1955.

Ron Wilson was named the first-ever head coach of the Mighty Ducks on June 30, 1993, His playing and coaching experience includes professional, amateur and international hockey, including serving the past three full seasons as an assistant head coach with the Vancouver Canucks.

Wilson played an instrumental role last season in aiding Vancouver head coach Pat Quinn and the Canucks to a 46-29-9 record (.601) and a second-straight Smythe Division title. During Wilson's three seasons with Vancouver, the club posted a 116-98-30 record (.537) while making the playoffs in each of those years.

Prior to coaching in Vancouver, Wilson was an assistant coach with Vancouver's affiliate in Milwaukee of the International Hockey League under Ron Lapointe during the 1989-90 season.

Drafted out of Providence College by the Toronto Maple Leafs (132nd overall) in 1975, Wilson began his pro hockey career in 1976-77 with the Dallas Blackhawks in the now defunct Central Hockey League (CHL).

The Windsor, Ontario native began his NHL career in 1977-78, playing 13 games for the Maple Leafs. Wilson then moved to Switzerland in 1980-81 and competed with the Swiss teams Kloten and Davos for the next six seasons.

In 1984, Wilson signed as a free agent with the Minnesota North Stars where he finished out his professional career in 1987-88. Wilson's NHL career totals were 26-67-93 with 68 penalty minutes in 177 professional contests. His career playoff totals include four goals and 13 assists in 20 contests.

Wilson's father, Larry, played six NHL seasons with both the Detroit Red Wings and Chicago Blackhawks.

General Manager

FERREIRA, JACK
General Manager, The Mighty Ducks of Anaheim.
Born in Providence, R.I., June 9, 1944.

In his role as the first general manager in the history of The Mighty Ducks of Anaheim, Jack Ferreira brings with him more than 20 years of professional hockey experience, including vital experience in assembling an expansion team.

Following a four-year college hockey career as a goaltender at Boston University, where he received All-American honors while earning a bachelor's degree in history, Ferreira began his coaching career at Princeton University, serving as the school's assistant hockey coach in 1969. From 1970 to 1972 he was assistant hockey coach at Brown University.

His professional career began in 1972 with the New England Whalers of the World Hockey Association, where he served as head scout, assistant coach and assistant general manager through 1977.

From 1977 to 1980 he was a New England scout for the National Hockey League Central Scouting Service, and from 1980 to 1986 he was a U.S. and college scout for the Calgary Flames.

From there he took a post as director of player development for the New York Rangers, serving in that capacity from 1986 to 1988. From 1988 to 1990 he was vice president and general manager of the Minnesota North Stars and in 1990 he helped start the San Jose Sharks expansion franchise as that team's executive vice president and general manager.

Prior to joining The Mighty Ducks of Anaheim, he was director of pro scouting for the Montreal Canadiens, where he kept tabs on talent in the NHL, the International Hockey League and the American Hockey League throughout the 1992-93 season.

Ferreira was a member of the USA Hockey Committee for the 1992 Winter Olympics and served as general manager for the U.S. team at the 1991 World Hockey Championship in Finland.

Club Directory

Disney Sports Enterprises Inc.
The Pond of Anaheim
2695 Katella Ave.
P.O. Box 61077
Anaheim, CA 92803
Phone **714/704-2700**
FAX 714/704-2753
Capacity: 17,250

Management
Governor	Michael Eisner
President and Alternate Governor	Tony Tavares
Administrative Assistant to the President	Susan Jackson
Vice President of Finance/Administration	Andy Roundtree
Vice President of Sales and Marketing	Ken Wilson
Sales and Marketing Administrative Assistant	Janet Conley

Hockey Department
General Manager	Jack Ferreira
Assistant General Manager	Pierre Gauthier
Head Coach	Ron Wilson
Director of Player Personnel	David McNab
Director of Hockey Operations	Kevin Gilmore
Assistant Coaches	Al Sims, Tim Army
Trainer	Blynn DeNiro
Equipment Manager	Mark O'Neill
Assistant Equipment Manager	John Allaway
Pro Scout	Paul Fenton
Midwest Regional Scout	Al Godfrey
Northeast Regional Scout	Richard Green
Coordinator of Computer Scouting and Video	Angela Gorgone
Administrative Assistant to the General Manager	Barbara Potts
Administrative Assistant to Hockey Operations	Debbie Blanchard

Front Office Staff
Director of Sales and Marketing	Bill Holford
Director of Public Relations	Bill Robertson
Public Relations Assistant	Rob Scichili
Controller	Marc Serrio
Senior Accountant	Angela Wergechik
Manager of Marketing Services	Monica Spoelstra
Manager of Administration/Ticket Box Office	Jenny Price
Season Ticket Manager	Don Boudreau
Manager of Premium Ticketing Services	Anne McNiff
Merchandise Manager	Shelley Gartner
Managers, Sponsorship Sales	Jim Holtz and Mark Sowinski
Sponsorship Sales Assistant	Debra Cross
Ticket Sales Account Executives	Michelle Amiro, Patti Conklin and Jeanice Scott
Ticket Sales Assistant	Debbie Nielander
Administrative Assistant	Cindy Williams
Receptionist	Shelly Baker
Medical staff, broadcasters	TBA
Minor League Affiliations	San Diego Gulls (IHL) and Greensboro Monarchs (ECHL)
Television	KCAL and Prime Ticket
Rink Dimensions	200 feet by 85 feet
Team colors	Purple, jade, silver and white

Randy Ladouceur, left, is an 11-year veteran who has manned the blueline for Detroit and Hartford. Leftwinger Stu Grimson, right, was acquired by the Mighty Ducks from the Chicago Blackhawks.

Coaching History

Ron Wilson, 1993-94.

General Managers' History

Jack Ferreira, 1993-94.

Boston Bruins

1992-93 Results: 51w-26L-7T 109PTS. First, Adams Division

Steve Leach, far left, finished fifth in team scoring for the Bruins, collecting 26 goals and 25 assists in 79 games. The Bruins acquired goaltender Jon Casey, left, from Dallas on June 25, 1993 for Andy Moog.

Schedule

Home		Away	
Oct. Thur. 7 Buffalo		Oct. Tues. 5 NY Rangers	
Sat. 9 Quebec		Fri. 15 Anaheim	
Mon. 11 Montreal*		Sat. 16 San Jose	
Thur. 28 Ottawa		Tues. 19 Vancouver	
Sat. 30 St Louis		Fri. 22 Edmonton	
Nov. Thur. 4 Calgary		Sat. 23 Calgary	
Sat. 6 Tampa Bay		Nov. Tues. 2 Detroit	
Thur. 11 Edmonton*		Sun. 7 Buffalo	
Thur. 18 San Jose		Sat. 13 NY Islanders	
Sat. 20 Philadelphia		Wed. 17 Hartford	
Fri. 26 Florida*		Wed. 24 Pittsburgh	
Dec. Thur. 2 NY Islanders		Sat. 27 Toronto	
Sat. 4 Montreal		Tues. 30 Quebec	
Thur. 9 Vancouver		Dec. Sun. 5 Buffalo	
Sat. 11 Chicago		Wed. 15 New Jersey	
Sun. 12 Hartford		Sat. 18 Tampa Bay	
Thur. 23 Pittsburgh		Sun. 19 Florida	
Fri. 31 Philadelphia		Mon. 27 Ottawa	
(at Minnesota)		Jan. Tues. 11 Pittsburgh	
Jan. Sun. 2 Washington*		Thur. 13 Philadelphia	
Thur. 6 Winnipeg		Wed. 19 Montreal	
Sat. 8 Florida		Mon. 24 Hartford	
Mon. 10 Toronto		Tues. 25 Washington	
Sat. 15 Detroit		Fri. 28 NY Islanders	
Mon. 17 Hartford*		Feb. Sun. 6 Florida	
Sat. 29 NY Islanders		Tues. 8 Quebec	
Mon. 31 Quebec		Mon. 14 Los Angeles	
Feb. Thur. 3 NY Rangers		Wed. 16 Dallas	
Sat. 5 Philadelphia*		Fri. 18 St Louis	
Thur. 10 Buffalo		Sun. 20 Tampa Bay	
Sat. 12 New Jersey*		Wed. 23 NY Rangers	
Mar. Thur. 3 Los Angeles		Fri. 25 Winnipeg	
Sat. 5 Ottawa		Sun. 27 Chicago*	
Mon. 7 Washington		Mar. Tues. 8 Pittsburgh	
Thur. 10 NY Rangers		Sat. 12 New Jersey*	
Thur. 17 Pittsburgh		Mon. 14 Montreal	
Sat. 19 New Jersey*		Tues. 22 Quebec	
Thur. 24 Anaheim		Sun. 27 Washington*	
Sat. 26 Montreal*		Apr. Fri. 1 Buffalo	
Thur. 31 Dallas		Sun. 3 Pittsburgh*	
Apr. Thur. 7 Ottawa		(at Cleveland)	
Sat. 9 Tampa Bay*		Sun. 10 Philadelphia*	
Thur. 14 Hartford		Wed. 13 Ottawa	

* Denotes afternoon game.

Home Starting Times:
Weeknights .... 7:35 p.m.
Saturdays and Sundays .... 7:05 p.m.
Matinees .... 1:35 p.m.
Except Mon. Jan. 17 .... 5:05 p.m.

Franchise date: November 1, 1924

NORTHEAST DIVISION

70th NHL Season

EASTERN CONFERENCE

Year-by-Year Record

		Home			Road			Overall							
Season	GP	W	L	T	W	L	T	W	L	T	GF	GA	Pts.	Finished	Playoff Result
1992-93	84	29	10	3	22	16	4	51	26	7	332	268	109	1st, Adams Div.	Lost Div. Semi-Final
1991-92	80	23	11	6	13	21	6	36	32	12	270	275	84	2nd, Adams Div.	Lost Conf. Championship
1990-91	80	26	9	5	18	15	7	44	24	12	299	264	100	1st, Adams Div.	Lost Conf. Championship
1989-90	80	23	13	4	23	12	5	46	25	9	289	232	101	1st, Adams Div.	Lost Final
1988-89	80	17	15	8	20	14	6	37	29	14	289	256	88	2nd, Adams Div.	Lost Div. Final
1987-88	80	24	13	3	20	17	3	44	30	6	300	251	94	2nd, Adams Div.	Lost Final
1986-87	80	25	11	4	14	23	3	39	34	7	301	276	85	3rd, Adams Div.	Lost Div. Semi-Final
1985-86	80	24	9	7	13	22	5	37	31	12	311	288	86	3rd, Adams Div.	Lost Div. Semi-Final
1984-85	80	21	15	4	15	19	6	36	34	10	303	287	82	4th, Adams Div.	Lost Div. Semi-Final
1983-84	80	25	12	3	24	13	3	49	25	6	336	261	104	1st, Adams Div.	Lost Div. Semi-Final
1982-83	80	28	6	6	22	14	4	50	20	10	327	228	110	1st, Adams Div.	Lost Conf. Championship
1981-82	80	24	12	4	19	15	6	43	27	10	323	285	96	2nd, Adams Div.	Lost Div. Final
1980-81	80	26	10	4	11	20	9	37	30	13	316	272	87	2nd, Adams Div.	Lost Prelim. Round
1979-80	80	27	9	4	19	12	9	46	21	13	310	234	105	2nd, Adams Div.	Lost Quarter-Final
1978-79	80	25	10	5	18	13	9	43	23	14	316	270	100	1st, Adams Div.	Lost Semi-Final
1977-78	80	29	6	5	22	12	6	51	18	11	333	218	113	1st, Adams Div.	Lost Final
1976-77	80	27	7	6	22	16	2	49	23	8	312	240	106	1st, Adams Div.	Lost Final
1975-76	80	27	5	8	21	10	9	48	15	17	313	237	113	1st, Adams Div.	Lost Semi-Final
1974-75	80	29	5	6	11	21	8	40	26	14	345	245	94	2nd, Adams Div.	Lost Prelim. Round
1973-74	78	33	4	2	19	13	7	52	17	9	349	221	113	1st, East Div.	Lost Final
1972-73	78	27	10	2	24	12	3	51	22	5	330	235	107	2nd, East Div.	Lost Quarter-Final
1971-72	78	28	4	7	26	9	4	54	13	11	330	204	119	1st, East Div.	Won Stanley Cup
1970-71	78	33	4	2	24	10	5	57	14	7	399	207	121	1st, East Div.	Lost Quarter-Final
1969-70	76	27	3	8	13	14	11	40	17	19	277	216	99	2nd, East Div.	Won Stanley Cup
1968-69	76	29	3	6	13	15	10	42	18	16	303	221	100	2nd, East Div.	Lost Semi-Final
1967-68	74	22	9	6	15	18	4	37	27	10	259	216	84	3rd, East Div.	Lost Quarter-Final
1966-67	70	10	21	4	7	22	6	17	43	10	182	253	44	6th,	Out of Playoffs
1965-66	70	15	17	3	6	26	3	21	43	6	174	275	48	5th,	Out of Playoffs
1964-65	70	12	17	6	9	26	0	21	43	6	166	253	48	6th,	Out of Playoffs
1963-64	70	13	15	7	5	25	5	18	40	12	170	212	48	6th,	Out of Playoffs
1962-63	70	7	18	10	7	21	7	14	39	17	198	281	45	6th,	Out of Playoffs
1961-62	70	9	22	4	6	25	4	15	47	8	177	306	38	6th,	Out of Playoffs
1960-61	70	13	17	5	2	25	8	15	42	13	176	254	43	6th,	Out of Playoffs
1959-60	70	21	11	3	7	23	5	28	34	8	220	241	64	5th,	Out of Playoffs
1958-59	70	21	11	3	11	18	6	32	29	9	205	215	73	2nd,	Lost Semi-Final
1957-58	70	15	14	6	12	14	9	27	28	15	199	194	69	4th,	Lost Final
1956-57	70	20	9	6	14	15	6	34	24	12	195	174	80	3rd,	Lost Final
1955-56	70	14	14	7	9	20	6	23	34	13	147	185	59	5th,	Out of Playoffs
1954-55	70	16	10	9	7	16	12	23	26	21	169	188	67	4th,	Lost Semi-Final
1953-54	70	22	8	5	10	20	5	32	28	10	177	181	74	4th,	Lost Semi-Final
1952-53	70	19	10	6	9	19	7	28	29	13	152	172	69	3rd,	Lost Final
1951-52	70	15	12	8	10	17	8	25	29	16	162	176	66	4th,	Lost Semi-Final
1950-51	70	13	12	10	9	18	8	22	30	18	178	197	62	4th,	Lost Semi-Final
1949-50	70	15	12	8	7	20	8	22	32	16	198	228	60	5th,	Out of Playoffs
1948-49	60	18	10	2	11	13	6	29	23	8	178	163	66	2nd,	Lost Semi-Final
1947-48	60	12	8	10	11	16	3	23	24	13	167	168	59	3rd,	Lost Semi-Final
1946-47	60	18	7	5	8	16	6	26	23	11	190	175	63	3rd,	Lost Semi-Final
1945-46	50	11	5	4	13	13	4	24	18	8	167	156	56	2nd,	Lost Final
1944-45	50	11	12	2	5	18	2	16	30	4	179	219	36	4th,	Lost Semi-Final
1943-44	50	15	8	2	4	18	3	19	26	5	223	268	43	5th,	Out of Playoffs
1942-43	50	17	3	5	7	14	4	24	17	9	195	176	57	2nd,	Lost Final
1941-42	48	17	4	3	8	13	3	25	17	6	160	118	56	3rd,	Lost Semi-Final
1940-41	48	15	4	5	12	4	8	27	8	13	168	102	67	1st,	Won Stanley Cup
1939-40	48	20	3	1	11	9	4	31	12	5	170	98	67	1st,	Lost Semi-Final
1938-39	48	20	2	2	16	8	0	36	10	2	156	76	74	1st,	Won Stanley Cup
1937-38	48	18	3	3	12	8	4	30	11	7	142	89	67	1st, Amn. Div.	Lost Semi-Final
1936-37	48	9	11	4	14	7	3	23	18	7	120	110	53	2nd, Amn. Div.	Lost Quarter-Final
1935-36	48	15	8	1	7	12	5	22	20	6	92	83	50	2nd, Amn. Div.	Lost Quarter-Final
1934-35	48	17	7	0	9	9	6	26	16	6	129	112	58	1st, Amn. Div.	Lost Semi-Final
1933-34	48	11	11	2	7	14	3	18	25	5	111	130	41	4th, Amn. Div.	Out of Playoffs
1932-33	48	20	2	3	5	13	5	25	15	8	124	88	58	1st, Amn. Div.	Lost Semi-Final
1931-32	48	11	10	3	4	11	9	15	21	12	122	117	42	4th, Amn. Div.	Out of Playoffs
1930-31	44	17	1	5	11	9	1	28	10	6	143	90	62	1st, Amn. Div.	Lost Semi-Final
1929-30	44	23	1	0	15	4	1	38	5	1	179	98	77	1st, Amn. Div.	Lost Final
1928-29	44	16	6	1	10	7	4	26	13	5	89	52	57	1st, Amn. Div.	Won Stanley Cup
1927-28	44	13	4	5	7	9	6	20	13	11	77	70	51	1st, Amn. Div.	Lost Semi-Final
1926-27	44	15	7	0	6	13	3	21	20	3	97	89	45	2nd, Amn. Div.	Lost Final
1925-26	36	10	7	1	7	8	3	17	15	4	92	85	38	4th,	Out of Playoffs
1924-25	30	3	12	0	3	12	0	6	24	0	49	119	12	6th,	Out of Playoffs

1993-94 Player Personnel

FORWARDS	HT	WT	S	Place of Birth	Date	1992-93 Club
BANKS, Darren	6-2	215	L	Toronto, Ont.	3/18/66	Boston-Providence
DONATO, Ted	5-10	170	L	Dedham, MA	4/28/69	Boston
HEINZE, Steve	5-11	180	R	Lawrence, MA	1/30/70	Boston
HUGHES, Brent	5-11	185	L	New Westminster, B.C.	4/5/66	Boston
JUNEAU, Joe	6-0	175	R	Pont-Rouge, Que.	1/5/68	Boston
KNIPSCHEER, Fred	5-11	185	L	Ft. Wayne, IN	9/3/69	St. Cloud State
KVARTALNOV, Dmitri	5-11	180	L	Voskresensk, USSR	11/13/72	Khimik-Boston
LEACH, Steve	5-11	200	R	Cambridge, MA	1/16/66	Boston
LINDSAY, Scott	6-2	205	R	Red Deer, Alta.	8/29/72	Seattle
MAJOR, Mark	6-3	223	L	Toronto, Ont.	3/20/70	Cleveland
MAROIS, Daniel	6-0	190	R	Montreal, Que.	10/3/68	NY Islanders-C. District
McKIM, Andrew	5-8	175	R	St. John, N.B.	7/6/70	Boston-Providence
MURRAY, Glen	6-2	200	R	Bridgewater, N.S.	11/1/72	Boston-Providence
NEELY, Cam	6-1	210	R	Comox, B.C.	6/6/65	Boston
OATES, Adam	5-11	190	R	Weston, Ont.	8/27/62	Boston
PANTELEEV, Grigori	5-9	185	L	Gastello, USSR	11/13/72	Boston-Providence
REID, Dave	6-1	205	L	Toronto, Ont.	5/15/64	Boston
SMOLINSKI, Bryan	6-1	200	R	Toledo, OH	12/27/71	Michigan State-Boston
STUMPEL, Jozef	6-1	190	R	Nitra, Czechoslovakia	6/20/72	Boston-Providence
ZHOLTOK, Sergei	6-0	185	L	Riga, Latvia	12/2/72	Boston-Providence
DEFENSEMEN						
ARMSTRONG, Bill	6-5	220	L	Richmond Hill, Ont.	5/18/70	Hershey
BOURQUE, Ray	5-11	210	L	Montreal, Que.	12/28/60	Boston
CHERVYAKOV, Denis	6-0	185	L	St. Petersburg, Russia	4/20/70	Boston-Providence
FEATHERSTONE, Glen	6-4	215	L	Toronto, Ont.	7/8/68	Boston-Providence
HUSCROFT, Jamie	6-2	200	R	Creston, B.C.	1/9/67	Providence
KRYS, Mark	6-0	185	R	Timmins, Ont.	5/29/69	Prov.-John.-Cin.
MASTAD, Milt	6-3	205	L	Regina, Sask.	5/5/75	Seattle
MURPHY, Daniel	6-1	185	L	Needham, MA	5/13/70	Maine
PAQUETTE, Charles	6-1	193	L	Lachute, Que.	6/17/75	Sherbrooke
ROBERTS, Gord	6-0	190	L	Detroit, MI	10/2/57	Boston
ROHLOFF, Jon	5-11	200	R	Mankato, MN	10/3/69	Minnesota-Duluth
SEHER, Kurt	6-1	180	L	Lethbridge, Alta.	4/15/73	Seattle
SHAW, David	6-2	204	R	St. Thomas, Ont.	5/25/64	Boston
STOLK, Darren	6-4	210	L	Taber, Alta.	7/22/68	Salt Lake
SWEENEY, Don	5-10	185	L	St. Stephen, N.B.	8/17/66	Boston
TATARINOV, Mikhail	5-10	194	L	Irkutsk, Russia	7/16/66	Quebec
WESLEY, Glen	6-1	195	L	Red Deer, Alta.	10/2/68	Boston
WIEMER, Jim	6-4	210	L	Sudbury, Ont.	1/9/61	Boston-Providence

GOALTENDERS	HT	WT	C	Place of Birth	Date	1992-93 Club
BAILEY, Scott	6-0	195	L	Calgary, Alta.	5/2/72	Johnstown
BALES, Mike	6-1	180	L	Prince Albert, Sask.	8/6/71	Boston-Providence
BLUE, John	5-10	185	L	Huntington Beach, CA	2/19/66	Boston-Providence
CASEY, Jon	5-10	155	L	Grand Rapids, MN	3/29/62	Minnesota
LITTMAN, David	6-0	183	L	Cranston, RI	6/13/67	Tampa Bay-Atlanta
PERSSON, Joakim	5-11	172	L	Stockholm, Sweden	4/5/70	Hammarby

General Managers' History

Arthur H. Ross, 1924-25 to 1953-54; Lynn Patrick, 1954-55 to 1964-65; Leighton "Hap" Emms, 1965-66 to 1966-67; Milt Schmidt, 1967-68 to 1971-72; Harry Sinden, 1972-73 to date.

Coaching History

Arthur H. Ross, 1924-25 to 1927-28; Cy Denneny, 1928-29; Arthur H. Ross, 1929-30 to 1933-34; Frank Patrick, 1934-35 to 1935-36; Arthur H. Ross, 1936-37 to 1938-39; Ralph (Cooney) Weiland, 1939-40 to 1940-41; Arthur H. Ross, 1941-42 to 1944-45; Aubrey V. (Dit) Clapper, 1945-46 to 1948-49; George (Buck) Boucher, 1949-50; Lynn Patrick, 1950-51 to 1953-54; Lynn Patrick and Milt Schmidt, 1954-55; Milt Schmidt, 1955-56 to 1960-61; Phil Watson, 1961-62; Phil Watson and Milt Schmidt, 1962-63; Milt Schmidt, 1963-64 to 1965-66; Harry Sinden, 1966-67 to 1969-70; Tom Johnson, 1970-71 to 1971-72; Tom Johnson and Bep Guidolin, 1972-73; Bep Guidolin, 1973-74; Don Cherry, 1974-75 to 1978-79; Fred Creighton and Harry Sinden, 1979-80; Gerry Cheevers, 1980-81 to 1983-84; Gerry Cheevers and Harry Sinden, 1984-85; Butch Goring, 1985-86; Butch Goring and Terry O'Reilly, 1986-87; Terry O'Reilly, 1987-88 to 1988-89; Mike Milbury, 1989-90 to 1990-91; Rick Bowness, 1991-92; Brian Sutter, 1992-93 to date.

Captains' History

No Captain, 1924-25 to 1926-27; Lionel Hitchman, 1927-28 to 1930-31; George Owen, 1931-32; Dit Clapper, 1932-33 to 1937-38; Cooney Weiland, 1938-39; Dit Clapper, 1939-40 to 1945-46; Dit Clapper, John Crawford, 1946-47; John Crawford 1947-48 to 1949-50; Milt Schmidt, 1950-51 to 1953-54; Milt Schmidt, Ed Sanford, 1954-55; Fern Flaman, 1955-56 to 1960-61; Don McKenney, 1961-62, 1962-63; Leo Boivin, 1963-64 to 1965-66; John Bucyk, 1966-67; no captain, 1967-68 to 1972-73; John Bucyk, 1973-74 to 1976-77; Wayne Cashman, 1977-78 to 1982-83; Terry O'Reilly, 1983-84, 1984-85; Ray Bourque, Rick Middleton (co-captains) 1985-86 to 1987-88; Ray Bourque, 1988-89 to date.

Retired Numbers

2	Eddie Shore	1926-1940
3	Lionel Hitchman	1925-1934
4	Bobby Orr	1966-1976
5	Dit Clapper	1927-1947
7	Phil Esposito	1967-1975
9	John Bucyk	1957-1978
15	Milt Schmidt	1936-1955

1992-93 Scoring

Regular Season

Pos	#	Player	Team	GP	G	A	Pts	+/-	PIM	PP	SH	GW	GT	S	%
C	12	Adam Oates	BOS	84	45	97	142	15	32	24	1	11	0	254	17.7
C	49*	Joe Juneau	BOS	84	32	70	102	23	33	9	0	3	0	229	14.0
D	77	Ray Bourque	BOS	78	19	63	82	38	40	8	0	7	0	330	5.8
L	10	Dmitri Kvartalnov	BOS	73	30	42	72	9	16	11	0	4	2	226	13.3
R	27	Stephen Leach	BOS	79	26	25	51	6–	126	9	0	4	1	256	10.2
C	19	Dave Poulin	BOS	84	16	33	49	29	62	0	5	0	0	112	14.3
C	38	Vladimir Ruzicka	BOS	60	19	22	41	6–	38	7	0	2	0	146	13.0
L	17	Dave Reid	BOS	65	20	16	36	12	10	1	5	2	0	116	17.2
C	21*	Ted Donato	BOS	82	15	20	35	2	61	3	2	5	0	118	12.7
D	32	Don Sweeney	BOS	84	7	27	34	34	68	0	1	0	0	107	6.5
D	26	Glen Wesley	BOS	64	8	25	33	2–	47	4	1	0	0	183	4.4
R	23*	Stephen Heinze	BOS	73	18	13	31	20	24	0	2	4	0	146	12.3
D	34	David Shaw	BOS	77	10	14	24	10	108	1	1	1	0	122	8.2
R	8	Cam Neely	BOS	13	11	7	18	4	25	6	0	1	0	45	24.4
D	28	Gord Murphy	BOS	49	5	12	17	13–	62	3	0	2	0	68	7.4
D	14	Gordie Roberts	BOS	65	5	12	17	23	105	0	0	1	0	40	12.5
L	13*	Grigori Panteleev	BOS	39	8	6	14	6–	12	2	0	1	0	45	17.8
R	18*	C.J. Young	CGY	28	3	2	5	7–	20	1	0	0	0	21	14.3
			BOS	15	4	5	9	1	12	0	0	1	0	22	18.2
			TOTAL	43	7	7	14	6–	32	1	0	1	0	43	16.3
R	29	Darin Kimble	BOS	55	7	3	10	4	177	0	0	0	0	20	35.0
D	6	Glen Featherstone	BOS	34	5	5	10	6	102	1	0	0	0	33	15.2
L	42	Brent Hughes	BOS	62	5	4	9	4–	191	0	0	0	0	54	9.3
R	16	Peter Douris	BOS	19	4	4	8	5	4	0	1	0	0	33	12.1
L	41	Tim Sweeney	BOS	14	1	7	8	1	6	0	0	0	0	15	6.7
R	44*	Glen Murray	BOS	27	3	4	7	6–	8	2	0	1	0	28	10.7
D	36	Jim Wiemer	BOS	28	1	6	7	1	48	0	0	0	0	39	2.6
D	25	Stephane Richer	T.B.	3	0	0	0	3–	0	0	0	0	0	2	.0
			BOS	21	1	4	5	6–	18	0	0	1	0	22	4.5
			TOTAL	24	1	4	5	9–	18	0	0	1	0	24	4.2
C	45*	Andrew McKim	BOS	7	1	3	4	2	0	0	0	0	0	12	8.3
C	20*	Bryan Smolinski	BOS	9	1	3	4	3	0	0	0	0	0	10	10.0
R	22*	Jozef Stumpel	BOS	13	1	3	4	3–	4	0	0	0	0	8	12.5
L	56	Darren Banks	BOS	16	2	1	3	5	64	0	0	0	0	15	13.3
G	39	John Blue	BOS	23	0	2	2	0	6	0	0	0	0	0	.0
R	11*	Sergei Zholtok	BOS	1	0	1	1	1	0	0	0	0	0	2	.0
D	37	Dominic Lavoie	OTT	2	0	1	1	0	0	0	0	0	0	8	.0
			BOS	2	0	0	0	1–	2	0	0	0	0	7	.0
			TOTAL	4	0	1	1	1–	2	0	0	0	0	15	.0
R	40*	Chris Winnes	BOS	5	0	1	1	1	0	0	0	0	0	2	.0
G	35	Andy Moog	BOS	55	0	1	1	0	14	0	0	0	0	0	.0
G	30*	Mike Bales	BOS	1	0	0	0	0	0	0	0	0	0	0	.0
L	61*	Bill Huard	BOS	2	0	0	0	0	0	0	0	0	0	0	.0
D	43*	Denis Cheruyakov	BOS	2	0	0	0	1–	2	0	0	0	0	2	.0
G	1	Rejean Lemelin	BOS	10	0	0	0	0	4	0	0	0	0	0	.0

Goaltending

No.	Goaltender	GPI	Mins	Avg	W	L	T	EN	SO	GA	SA	S%
30	*Mike Bales	1	25	2.40	0	0	0	1	0	1	10	.900
39	John Blue	23	1322	2.90	9	8	4	1	1	64	597	.893
35	Andy Moog	55	3194	3.16	37	14	3	1	3	168	1357	.876
1	Rejean Lemelin	10	542	3.43	5	4	0	1	0	31	225	.862
	Totals	**84**	**5096**	**3.16**	**51**	**26**	**7**	**4**	**4**	**268**	**2193**	**.878**

Playoffs

Pos	#	Player	Team	GP	G	A	Pts	+/-	PIM	PP	SH	GW	GT	S	%
C	12	Adam Oates	BOS	4	0	9	9	0	4	0	0	0	0	11	.0
C	49*	Joe Juneau	BOS	4	2	4	6	1–	6	2	0	0	0	7	28.6
R	8	Cam Neely	BOS	4	4	1	5	0	4	1	0	0	0	16	25.0
R	27	Stephen Leach	BOS	4	1	1	2	0	2	0	0	0	0	18	5.6
C	19	Dave Poulin	BOS	4	1	1	2	3–	10	0	1	0	0	6	16.7
R	23*	Stephen Heinze	BOS	4	1	1	2	1–	2	0	0	0	0	6	16.7
D	77	Ray Bourque	BOS	4	1	0	1	2–	2	1	0	0	0	20	5.0
R	16	Peter Douris	BOS	4	1	0	1	3–	0	0	0	0	0	12	8.3
C	20*	Bryan Smolinski	BOS	4	1	0	1	1–	2	0	0	0	0	3	33.3
D	34	David Shaw	BOS	4	0	1	1	3–	6	0	0	0	0	6	.0
C	21*	Ted Donato	BOS	4	0	1	1	7–	0	0	0	0	0	9	.0
L	42	Brent Hughes	BOS	1	0	0	0	0	2	0	0	0	0	0	.0
D	36	Jim Wiemer	BOS	1	0	0	0	1–	4	0	0	0	0	0	.0
G	39	John Blue	BOS	2	0	0	0	0	0	0	0	0	0	0	.0
G	35	Andy Moog	BOS	3	0	0	0	0	0	0	0	0	0	0	.0
L	41	Tim Sweeney	BOS	3	0	0	0	0	0	0	0	0	0	0	.0
D	25	Stephane Richer	BOS	3	0	0	0	2–	0	0	0	0	0	0	.0
R	29	Darin Kimble	BOS	4	0	0	0	0	2	0	0	0	0	0	.0
D	14	Gordie Roberts	BOS	4	0	0	0	2–	6	0	0	0	0	0	.0
D	32	Don Sweeney	BOS	4	0	0	0	1–	4	0	0	0	0	5	.0
D	26	Glen Wesley	BOS	4	0	0	0	2–	0	0	0	0	0	12	.0
L	10	Dmitri Kvartalnov	BOS	4	0	0	0	0	0	0	0	0	0	5	.0

Goaltending

No.	Goaltender	GPI	Mins	Avg	W	L	EN	SO	GA	SA	S%
39	John Blue	2	96	3.13	0	1	0	0	5	49	.898
35	Andy Moog	3	161	5.22	0	3	0	0	14	67	.791
	Totals	**4**	**257**	**4.44**	**0**	**4**	**0**	**0**	**19**	**116**	**.836**

Club Records

Team

(Figures in brackets for season records are games played; records for fewest points, wins, ties, losses, goals, goals against are for 70 or more games)

Most Points	121	1970-71 (78)
Most Wins	57	1970-71 (78)
Most Ties	21	1954-55 (70)
Most Losses	47	1961-62 (70)
Most Goals	399	1970-71 (78)
Most Goals Against	306	1961-62 (70)
Fewest Points	38	1961-62 (70)
Fewest Wins	14	1962-63 (70)
Fewest Ties	5	1972-73 (78)
Fewest Losses	13	1971-72 (78)
Fewest Goals	147	1955-56 (70)
Fewest Goals Against	172	1952-53 (70)

Longest Winning Streak
- Over-all ... 14 — Dec. 3/29-Jan. 9/30
- Home ... *20 — Dec. 3/29-Mar. 18/30
- Away ... 8 — Feb. 17-Mar. 8/72; Mar. 15-Apr. 14/93

Longest Undefeated Streak
- Over-all ... 23 — Dec. 22/40-Feb. 23/41 (15 wins, 8 ties)
- Home ... 27 — Nov. 22/70-Mar. 20/71 (26 wins, 1 tie)
- Away ... 15 — Dec. 22/40-Mar. 16/41 (9 wins, 6 ties)

Longest Losing Streak
- Over-all ... 11 — Dec. 3/24-Jan. 5/25
- Home ... *11 — Dec. 8/24-Feb. 17/25
- Away ... 14 — Dec. 27/64-Feb. 21/65

Longest Winless Streak
- Over-all ... 20 — Jan. 28-Mar. 11/62 (16 losses, 4 ties)
- Home ... 11 — Dec. 8/24-Feb. 17/25 (11 losses)
- Away ... 14 — Three times

Most Shutouts, Season	15	1927-28 (44)
Most PIM, Season	2,443	1987-88 (80)
Most Goals, Game	14	Jan. 21/45 (NYR 3 at Bos. 14)

Individual

Most Seasons	21	John Bucyk
Most Games	1,436	John Bucyk
Most Goals, Career	545	John Bucyk
Most Assists, Career	806	Ray Bourque
Most Points, Career	1,339	John Bucyk (545 goals, 794 assists)
Most PIM, Career	2,095	Terry O'Reilly
Most Shutouts, Career	74	Tiny Thompson

Longest Consecutive Games Streak ... 418 — John Bucyk (Jan. 23/69-Mar. 2/75)

Most Goals, Season	76	Phil Esposito (1970-71)
Most Assists, Season	102	Bobby Orr (1970-71)
Most Points, Season	152	Phil Esposito (1970-71) (76 goals, 76 assists)
Most PIM, Season	304	Jay Miller (1987-88)

Most Points, Defenseman
Season ... *139 — Bobby Orr (1970-71) (37 goals, 102 assists)

Most Points, Center
Season ... 152 — Phil Esposito (1970-71) (76 goals, 76 assists)

Most Points, Right Wing
Season ... 105 — Ken Hodge (1970-71) (43 goals, 62 assists)

Ken Hodge (1973-74) (50 goals, 55 assists)
Rick Middleton (1983-84) (47 goals, 58 assists)

Most Points, Left Wing
Season ... 116 — John Bucyk (1970-71) (51 goals, 65 assists)

Most Points, Rookie
Season ... 102 — Joe Juneau (1992-93) (32 goals, 70 assists)

Most Shutouts, Season ... 15 — Hal Winkler (1927-28)

Most Goals, Game	4	Several players
Most Assists, Game	6	Ken Hodge (Feb. 9/71) Bobby Orr (Jan. 1/73)
Most Points, Game	7	Bobby Orr (Nov. 15/73) Phil Esposito (Dec. 19/74) Barry Pederson (Apr. 4/82) Cam Neely (Oct. 16/88)

* NHL Record.

All-time Record vs. Other Clubs

Regular Season

	At Home							On Road							Total						
	GP	W	L	T	GF	GA	PTS	GP	W	L	T	GF	GA	PTS	GP	W	L	T	GF	GA	PTS
Buffalo	79	47	23	9	330	243	103	79	26	39	14	250	299	66	158	73	62	23	580	542	169
Calgary	38	23	10	5	132	104	51	37	20	15	2	137	141	42	75	43	25	7	269	245	93
Chicago	275	159	84	32	999	773	350	277	92	141	44	741	896	228	552	251	225	76	1740	1669	578
Detroit	278	151	84	43	984	736	345	277	76	149	52	698	924	204	555	227	233	95	1682	1660	549
Edmonton	22	16	4	2	102	62	34	21	10	8	3	73	75	23	43	26	12	5	175	137	57
Hartford	52	37	11	4	217	138	78	51	21	23	7	186	185	49	103	58	34	11	403	323	127
Los Angeles	53	40	10	3	255	145	83	52	29	18	5	200	183	63	105	69	28	8	455	328	146
Minnesota	52	38	6	8	237	123	84	52	28	13	11	195	145	67	104	66	19	19	432	268	151
Montreal	306	141	113	52	903	824	334	306	84	178	44	706	1044	212	612	225	291	96	1609	1867	546
New Jersey	34	22	9	3	151	107	47	31	18	5	8	118	84	44	65	40	14	11	269	191	91
NY Islanders	38	20	9	9	148	108	49	39	20	15	4	134	127	44	77	40	24	13	282	235	93
NY Rangers	276	150	87	39	1007	769	336	280	104	122	54	782	851	262	556	254	209	93	1789	1620	601
Ottawa	4	4	0	0	20	10	8	3	3	0	0	11	5	6	7	7	0	0	31	15	14
Philadelphia	53	35	12	6	221	156	76	51	24	21	6	158	169	54	104	59	33	12	379	325	130
Pittsburgh	54	40	8	6	254	153	86	54	26	17	11	210	173	63	108	66	25	17	464	326	149
Quebec	51	27	16	8	209	160	62	52	31	16	5	235	193	67	103	58	32	13	444	353	129
St. Louis	50	33	10	7	224	136	73	51	22	20	9	180	160	53	101	55	30	16	404	296	126
San Jose	2	2	0	0	11	9	4	2	2	0	0	12	3	4	4	4	0	0	23	12	8
Tampa Bay	1	1	0	0	5	3	2	1	0	1	0	3	3	1	2	1	1	0	8	6	3
Toronto	279	151	81	47	924	751	349	279	86	146	47	726	949	219	558	237	227	94	1650	1695	568
Vancouver	42	35	3	4	192	93	74	43	22	13	8	183	144	52	85	57	16	12	375	237	126
Washington	34	21	9	4	142	98	46	34	17	9	8	131	105	42	68	38	18	12	273	203	88
Winnipeg	21	15	3	3	100	66	33	22	11	9	2	79	77	24	43	26	12	5	179	143	57
Defunct Clubs	164	112	39	13	525	306	237	164	79	67	18	496	440	176	328	191	106	31	1021	746	413
Totals	**2258**	**1320**	**631**	**307**	**8292**	**6073**	**2944**	**2258**	**851**	**1044**	**363**	**6644**	**7375**	**2065**	**4516**	**2171**	**1675**	**670**	**14936**	**13442**	**5012**

Playoffs

	Series	W	L	GP	W	L	T	GF	GA	Last Mtg.	Round	Result
Buffalo	6	5	1	33	19	14	0	132	113	1993	DSF	L 0-4
Chicago	6	5	1	22	16	5	1	97	63	1978	QF	W 4-0
Detroit	7	4	3	33	19	14	0	96	98	1957	SF	W 4-1
Edmonton	2	0	2	9	1	8	0	20	41	1990	F	L 1-4
Hartford	2	2	0	13	8	5	0	24	17	1991	DSF	W 4-2
Los Angeles	2	2	0	13	8	5	0	56	38	1977	QF	W 4-2
Minnesota	1	0	1	3	0	3	0	13	20	1981	PR	L 0-3
Montreal	27	6	21	132	48	84	0	317	410	1992	DF	W 4-0
New Jersey	1	1	0	7	4	3	0	30	19	1988	CF	W 4-3
NY Islanders	2	0	2	11	3	8	0	35	49	1983	CF	L 2-4
NY Rangers	9	6	3	42	22	18	2	114	104	1973	QF	L 1-4
Philadelphia	4	2	2	20	11	9	0	60	57	1978	SF	W 4-1
Pittsburgh	4	2	2	19	9	10	0	62	67	1992	CF	L 0-4
Quebec	2	1	1	11	6	5	0	37	36	1983	DSF	W 3-1
St. Louis	2	2	0	8	4	4	0	48	15	1972	SF	W 4-0
Toronto	13	5	8	62	30	31	1	153	150	1974	QF	W 4-0
Washington	1	1	0	4	4	0	0	15	6	1990	CF	W 4-0
Defunct Clubs	3	1	2	11	4	5	2	20	20			
Totals	**94**	**45**	**49**	**453**	**220**	**227**	**6**	**1345**	**1344**			

Playoff Results 1993-89

Year	Round	Opponent	Result	GF	GA
1993	DSF	Buffalo	L 0-4	12	19
1992	CF	Pittsburgh	L 0-4	7	19
	DF	Montreal	W 4-0	14	8
	DSF	Buffalo	W 4-3	19	24
1991	CF	Pittsburgh	L 2-4	18	27
	DF	Montreal	W 4-3	18	18
	DSF	Hartford	W 4-2	24	17
1990	F	Edmonton	L 1-4	8	20
	CF	Washington	W 4-0	15	6
	DF	Montreal	W 4-1	16	12
	DSF	Hartford	W 4-3	23	21
1989	DF	Montreal	L 1-4	13	16
	DSF	Buffalo	W 4-1	16	14

Abbreviations: Round: F – Final;
CF – conference final; **DF** – division final;
DSF – division semi-final; **SF** – semi-final;
QF – quarter-final; **PR** – preliminary round.
GA – goals against; **GF** – goals for.

1992-93 Results

	Home				Away	
Oct. 8	Hartford	3-2	Oct. 15	San Jose	8-2
10	NY Islanders	3-3	17	Los Angeles	6-8
12	Ottawa	6-3	22	Calgary	4-2
29	Los Angeles	8-3	23	Edmonton	6-3
31	Chicago	2-3	25	Vancouver*	5-3
Nov. 5	Quebec	6-4	Nov. 11	Buffalo	2-7
7	NY Rangers	2-2	16	Montreal	3-6
12	Calgary	5-3	23	Ottawa	3-2
14	Toronto	1-4	25	Washington	2-6
19	NY Islanders	5-2	28	Hartford	3-4
21	Philadelphia	4-3	30	Quebec	4-3
27	Hartford*	5-4	Dec. 5	New Jersey*	4-2
Dec. 3	Montreal	4-3	6	Philadelphia	7-1
10	Ottawa	4-2	9	Buffalo	2-5
15	Buffalo	2-3	12	Montreal	1-5
19	Washington	4-3	18	Detroit	1-6
22	Tampa Bay	5-3	26	Hartford	9-4
Jan. 2	Hartford	3-2	27	NY Rangers	5-6
7	Quebec	2-3	29	Winnipeg	4-5
9	New Jersey	2-6	31	Minnesota	3-5
12	Buffalo	5-2	Jan. 5	Pittsburgh	2-6
14	Pittsburgh	7-0	19	NY Islanders	2-2
16	Philadelphia	4-5	21	Philadelphia	5-4
18	San Jose*	4-3	25	Montreal	2-3
23	New Jersey	7-5	26	Quebec	4-4
28	Winnipeg	6-2	30	NY Islanders	6-5
Feb. 2	Edmonton	3-4	Feb. 3	Quebec	4-1
25	Minnesota	3-3	8	Pittsburgh	0-4
27	Washington*	5-4	9	St. Louis	6-1
Mar. 1	Montreal	2-5	11	Chicago	3-6
4	Vancouver	4-3	14	Tampa Bay	3-3
6	St. Louis*	4-3	17	Montreal	5-2
11	Montreal	5-2	20	Toronto	4-4
13	Ottawa*	6-3	Mar. 9	Pittsburgh	2-3
16	New Jersey	3-1	15	NY Rangers	3-1
20	Detroit*	4-7	18	Ottawa	4-1
22	Hartford	5-4	24	Buffalo	2-0
25	Montreal	2-0	30	Hartford	3-1
27	Pittsburgh*	3-5	Apr. 4	Buffalo*	3-0
Apr. 3	Buffalo*	3-1	6	Quebec	7-1
8	Quebec	6-2	10	Montreal	5-1
11	Ottawa	4-2	14	Ottawa	4-2

*Denotes afternoon game

Entry Draft
Selections 1993-79

1993
Pick
25	Kevyn Adams
51	Matt Alvey
88	Charles Paquette
103	Shawn Bates
129	Andrei Sapozhnikov
155	Milt Mastad
181	Ryan Golden
207	Hal Gill
233	Joel Prpic
259	Joakim Persson

1992
Pick
16	Dmitri Kvartalnov
55	Sergei Zholtok
112	Scott Bailey
133	Jiri Dopita
136	Grigori Panteleev
184	Kurt Seher
208	Mattias Timander
232	Chris Crombie
256	Denis Chervyakov
257	Evgeny Pavlov

1991
Pick
18	Glen Murray
40	Jozef Stumpel
62	Marcel Cousineau
84	Brad Tiley
106	Mariusz Czerkawski
150	Gary Golczewski
172	John Moser
194	Daniel Hodge
216	Steve Norton
238	Stephen Lombardi
260	Torsten Kienass

1990
Pick
21	Bryan Smolinski
63	Cameron Stewart
84	Jerome Buckley
105	Mike Bales
126	Mark Woolf
147	Jim Mackey
168	John Gruden
189	Darren Wetherill
210	Dean Capuano
231	Andy Bezeau
252	Ted Miskolczi

1989
Pick
17	Shayne Stevenson
38	Mike Parson
57	Wes Walz
80	Jackson Penney
101	Mark Montanari
122	Stephen Foster
143	Otto Hascak
164	Rick Allain
185	James Lavish
206	Geoff Simpson
227	David Franzosa

1988
Pick
18	Robert Cimetta
60	Stephen Heinze
81	Joe Juneau
102	Daniel Murphy
123	Derek Geary
165	Mark Krys
186	Jon Rohloff
228	Eric Reisman
249	Doug Jones

1987
Pick
3	Glen Wesley
14	Stephane Quintal
56	Todd Lalonde
67	Darwin McPherson
77	Matt Delguidice
98	Ted Donato
119	Matt Glennon
140	Rob Cheevers
161	Chris Winnes
182	Paul Ohman
203	Casey Jones
224	Eric Lemarque
245	Sean Gorman

1986
Pick
13	Craig Janney
34	Pekka Tirkkonen
76	Dean Hall
97	Matt Pesklewis
118	Garth Premak
139	Paul Beraldo
160	Brian Ferreira
181	Jeff Flaherty
202	Greg Hawgood
223	Staffan Malmqvist
244	Joel Gardner

1985
Pick
31	Alain Cote
52	Bill Ranford
73	Jaime Kelly
94	Steve Moore
115	Gord Hynes
136	Per Martinelle
157	Randy Burridge
178	Gord Cruickshank
199	Dave Buda
210	Bob Beers
220	John Byce
241	Marc West

1984
Pick
19	Dave Pasin
40	Ray Podloski
61	Jeff Cornelius
82	Robert Joyce
103	Mike Bishop
124	Randy Oswald
145	Mark Thietke
166	Don Sweeney
186	Kevin Heffernan
207	J.D. Urbanic
227	Bill Kopecky
248	Jim Newhouse

1983
Pick
21	Nevin Markwart
42	Greg Johnston
62	Greg Puhalski
82	Alain Larochelle
102	Allen Pederson
122	Terry Taillefer
142	Ian Armstrong
162	Francois Olivier
182	Harri Laurilla
202	Paul Fitzsimmons
222	Norm Foster
242	Greg Murphy

1982
Pick
1	Gord Kluzak
22	Brian Curran
39	Lyndon Byers
60	Dave Reid
102	Bob Nicholson
123	Bob Sweeney
144	John Meulenbroeks
165	Tony Fiore
186	Doug Kostynski
207	Tony Gilliard
228	Tommy Lehmann
249	Bruno Campese

1981
Pick
14	Normand Leveille
35	Luc Dufour
77	Scott McLellan
98	Joe Mantione
119	Bruce Milton
140	Mats Thelin
161	Armel Parisee
182	Don Sylvestri
203	Richard Bourque

1980
Pick
18	Barry Pederson
60	Tom Fergus
81	Steve Kasper
102	Randy Hillier
123	Steve Lyons
144	Tony McMurchy
165	Mike Moffat
186	Michael Thelven
207	Jens Ohling

1979
Pick
8	Ray Bourque
15	Brad McCrimmon
36	Doug Morrison
57	Keith Crowder
78	Larry Melnyk
99	Marco Baron
120	Mike Krushelnyski

Club Directory

Boston Garden
150 Causeway Street
Boston, Massachusetts 02114
Phone **617/227-3206**
FAX 617/523-7184
Capacity: 14,448

Executive
Owner and Governor	Jeremy M. Jacobs
Alternative Governor	Louis Jacobs
Alternative Governor, President and General Manager	Harry Sinden
Vice President	Tom Johnson
Assistant General Manager	Mike Milbury
Assistant to the President	Nate Greenberg
General Counsel	Barbara Macon
Director of Administration	Dale Hamilton
Administrative Assistant	Carol Gould
Receptionist	Karen Leonard

Coaching Staff
Coach	Brian Sutter
Assistant Coach	Tom McVie
Coach, Providence Bruins	Mike O'Connell
Coach, Charlotte Checkers	John Marks

Scouting Staff
Director of Player Evaluation	Bart Bradley
Director of Scouting	Bob Tindall
Director of European Scouting	Svenake Svenson
Assistant Directors of Scouting	Jim Morrison, Gordie Clark
Scouting Staff	Andre Lachapelle, Don Saatzer, Joe Lyons, Harvey Keck, Jean Ratelle, Yuri Agureikin & Dmitry Yeryomin, Pertti Hassanen, Zbenek Kusy, Jiri Hamel, Marcel Pelletier

Communications Staff
Director of Media Relations	Heidi Holland
Director of Community Relations, Marketing Services	Sue Byrne
Assistant Director of Community Relations & Marketing Services	Kevin Lyons
Media Relations Assistant	Jeff Gorton
Director of Alumni Relations	John Bucyk
Administrative Assistant	Mal Viola
Video Producer	Joe Curnane

Medical and Training Staff
Athletic Trainer	Don Del Negro
Assistant Athletic Trainer	Mike Murphy
Equipment Manager	Ken Fleger
Assistant Equipment Manager	Keith Robinson
Team Physicians	Dr. Bertram Zarins, Dr. Ashby Moncure, Dr. John J. Boyle
Team Dentists	Dr. John Kelly and Dr. Bruce Donoff
Team Psychologist	Dr. Fred Neff

Ticketing and Finance Staff
Director of Ticket Operations	Matt Brennan
Assistant Director of Ticket Operations	Jim Foley
Receptionist	Linda Bartlett
Controller	Bob Vogel
Accounting Manager	Richard McGlinchey
Accounts Payable	Barbara Johnson

Television and Radio
Broadcasters (WSBK-TV 38)	Fred Cusick and Derek Sanderson
Broadcasters (NESN)	Fred Cusick, Derek Sanderson and Dave Shea
Broadcasters (Radio)	Bob Wilson and John Bucyk
TV Channels	New England Sports Network (NESN) and WSBK-TV 38
Radio Station	WEEI (590 AM) and Bruins Radio Network
Seating Capacity	14,448
Dimensions of Rink	191 feet by 83 feet
Club Colors	Gold, Black and White

General Manager

SINDEN, HARRY JAMES
President and General Manager, Boston Bruins.
Born in Collins Bay, Ont., September 14, 1932.

Harry Sinden never played a game in the NHL but stepped into the Bruins' organization with an impressive coaching background in minor professional hockey and his continued excellence has earned him a place in the Hockey Hall of Fame as one of the true builders in hockey history. In 1965-66 as playing-coach of Oklahoma City Blazers in the CPHL, Sinden led the club to second place in the regular standings and then to eight straight playoff victories for the Jack Adams Trophy. After five years in OHA Senior hockey — including 1958 with the World Amateur Champion Whitby Dunlops — Sinden was named playing-coach in the old Eastern Professional League and its successor, the Central Professional League. Under his guidance, the Bruins of 1967-68 made the playoffs for the first time in nine seasons, finishing third in the East Division, and were nosed out of first place in 1968-69 by Montreal. In 1969-70, Sinden led the Bruins to their first Stanley Cup win since 1940-41. The following season he went into private business but returned to the hockey scene in the summer of 1972 when he was appointed coach of Team Canada. He moulded that group of NHL stars into a powerful unit and led them into an exciting eight-game series against the Soviet national team in September of 1972. Team Canada emerged the winner by a narrow margin with a record of four wins, three losses and one tie. Sinden then returned to the Bruins organization early in the 1972-73 season. Sinden last took over as the Bruins' coach in February 1985, after replacing Gerry Cheevers. Boston finished 11-10-3 with Sinden behind the bench before being defeated by Montreal in five games in the Adams Division semi-finals.

NHL Coaching Record

			Regular Season				Playoffs			
Season	Team	Games	W	L	T	%	Games	W	L	%
1966-67	Boston	70	17	43	10	.314				
1967-68	Boston	74	37	27	10	.568	4	0	4	.000
1968-69	Boston	76	42	18	16	.658	10	6	4	.600
1969-70	Boston	76	40	17	19	.651	14	12	2	.857*
1979-80	Boston	10	4	6	0	.400	9	4	5	.444
1984-85	Boston	24	11	10	3	.521	5	2	3	.400
	NHL Totals	330	151	121	58	.545	42	24	18	.571

* Stanley Cup win.

Coach

SUTTER, BRIAN
Coach, Boston Bruins. Born in Viking, Alta., October 7, 1956.

In his first season as coach of the Boston Bruins, Brian Sutter guided the team to a first place finish in the Adams Division. Brian Sutter became the 20th coach in the history of the Boston Bruins, joining the organization after four successful seasons as head coach of the St. Louis Blues. Sutter, who received the Jack Adams Trophy as the NHL's Coach of the Year in 1990-91 after directing the Blues to a club-record 47 wins, led the Blues to an above-.500 record in three of his four seasons behind the St. Louis bench. A second round draft selection in 1976, Sutter spent his entire playing career with the Blues, and ranks second in franchise history in games (779), goals (303), assists (333) and points (636).

Coaching Record

			Regular Season				Playoffs			
Season	Team	Games	W	L	T	%	Games	W	L	%
1988-89	St. Louis (NHL)	80	33	35	12	.488	10	5	5	.500
1989-90	St. Louis (NHL)	80	37	34	9	.519	12	7	5	.583
1990-91	St. Louis (NHL)	80	47	22	11	.656	13	6	7	.462
1991-92	St. Louis (NHL)	80	36	33	11	.519	6	2	4	.333
1992-93	Boston (NHL)	84	51	26	7	.649	4	0	4	.000
	NHL Totals	404	204	150	50	.567	45	20	25	.444

Buffalo Sabres

1992-93 Results: 38w-36L-10T 86PTS. Fourth, Adams Division

Schedule

Home		Away	
Oct.	Sun. 10 Hartford	**Oct.**	Thur. 7 Boston
	Fri. 15 NY Rangers		Sat. 9 Montreal
	Mon. 18 Detroit		Tues. 12 Philadelphia
	Fri. 22 Pittsburgh		Sat. 16 Washington
Nov.	Wed. 3 Pittsburgh		Sat. 23 Hartford
	(at Sacramento)		Wed. 27 Calgary
	Sun. 7 Boston		Fri. 29 Edmonton
	Wed. 10 Philadelphia		Sat. 30 Vancouver
	Fri. 19 Winnipeg	**Nov.**	Sat. 13 Philadelphia*
	Sun. 21 San Jose		Wed. 17 New Jersey
	Wed. 24 New Jersey		Mon. 22 Ottawa
	Fri. 26 Ottawa		Sat. 27 Quebec
Dec.	Sun. 5 Boston		Mon. 29 Toronto
	Fri. 10 Calgary	**Dec.**	Wed. 1 Tampa Bay
	Fri. 17 Los Angeles		Thur. 2 Florida
	Sun. 19 Tampa Bay		Wed. 8 Ottawa
	Thur. 23 Montreal		Sat. 11 Hartford
	Mon. 27 Philadelphia		Mon. 13 NY Rangers
	Fri. 31 NY Rangers		Thur. 16 Pittsburgh
Jan.	Sun. 2 Toronto		Sun. 26 NY Islanders
	Fri. 7 Pittsburgh	**Jan.**	Tues. 11 Chicago
	Sun. 9 Vancouver		Wed. 12 Winnipeg
	Wed. 19 Edmonton		Sat. 15 St Louis
	Thur. 27 Washington		Sun. 16 Dallas
	Sun. 30 Florida*		Mon. 24 Tampa Bay
Feb.	Sun. 6 NY Islanders		(at Orlando)
	Fri. 11 Montreal		Sat. 29 Montreal*
	Sun. 13 Dallas*	**Feb.**	Wed. 2 New Jersey
	Fri. 18 Florida		Fri. 4 Florida
	Mon. 21 Quebec		Tues. 8 NY Islanders
	Wed. 23 Anaheim		Thur. 10 Boston
	Fri. 25 Chicago		Wed. 16 Hartford
Mar.	Fri. 4 Pittsburgh		Sun. 20 Washington*
	Thur. 17 New Jersey		Sat. 26 Pittsburgh
	Sun. 20 Ottawa*	**Mar.**	Tues. 1 Quebec
	Wed. 23 St Louis		Wed. 2 Ottawa
	Fri. 25 Hartford		Sun. 6 Detroit
	Sun. 27 NY Islanders*		Tues. 8 San Jose
	Wed. 30 Tampa Bay		Wed. 9 Anaheim
Apr.	Fri. 1 Boston		Sat. 12 Los Angeles
	Fri. 8 Montreal		Fri. 18 NY Islanders
	Sun. 10 Quebec*		(at Minnesota)
	Thur. 14 Washington	**Apr.**	Sat. 2 Quebec
			Tues. 12 NY Rangers

* Denotes afternoon game.

Home Starting Times:

Weeknights	7:35 p.m.
Sundays	7:05 p.m.
Matinees	2:05 p.m.
Except Sun. Jan. 30	1:05 p.m.

Franchise date: May 22, 1970

NORTHEAST DIVISION

24th NHL Season

EASTERN CONFERENCE

Dale Hawerchuk, who registered 80 assists in 1992-93, has compiled at least 50 assists in each of his 12 NHL seasons.

Year-by-Year Record

		Home			Road			Overall							
Season	GP	W	L	T	W	L	T	W	L	T	GF	GA	Pts.	Finished	Playoff Result
1992-93	84	25	15	2	13	21	8	38	36	10	335	297	86	4th, Adams Div.	Lost Div. Final
1991-92	80	22	13	5	9	24	7	31	37	12	289	299	74	3rd, Adams Div.	Lost Div. Semi-Final
1990-91	80	15	13	12	16	17	7	31	30	19	292	278	81	3rd, Adams Div.	Lost Div. Semi-Final
1989-90	80	27	11	2	18	16	6	45	27	8	286	248	98	2nd, Adams Div.	Lost Div. Semi-Final
1988-89	80	25	12	3	13	23	4	38	35	7	291	299	83	3rd, Adams Div.	Lost Div. Semi-Final
1987-88	80	19	14	7	18	18	4	37	32	11	283	305	85	3rd, Adams Div.	Lost Div. Semi-Final
1986-87	80	18	18	4	10	26	4	28	44	8	280	308	64	5th, Adams Div.	Out of Playoffs
1985-86	80	23	16	1	14	21	5	37	37	6	296	291	80	5th, Adams Div.	Out of Playoffs
1984-85	80	23	10	7	15	18	7	38	28	14	290	237	90	3rd, Adams Div.	Lost Div. Semi-Final
1983-84	80	25	9	6	23	16	1	48	25	7	315	257	103	2nd, Adams Div.	Lost Div. Semi-Final
1982-83	80	25	7	8	13	22	5	38	29	13	318	285	89	3rd, Adams Div.	Lost Div. Final
1981-82	80	23	8	9	16	18	6	39	26	15	307	273	93	3rd, Adams Div.	Lost Div. Semi-Final
1980-81	80	21	7	12	18	13	9	39	20	21	327	250	99	1st, Adams Div.	Lost Quarter-Final
1979-80	80	27	5	8	20	12	8	47	17	16	318	201	110	1st, Adams Div.	Lost Semi-Final
1978-79	80	19	13	8	17	15	8	36	28	16	280	263	88	2nd, Adams Div.	Lost Prelim. Round
1977-78	80	25	7	8	19	12	9	44	19	17	288	215	105	2nd, Adams Div.	Lost Quarter-Final
1976-77	80	27	8	5	21	16	3	48	24	8	301	220	104	2nd, Adams Div.	Lost Quarter-Final
1975-76	80	28	7	5	18	14	8	46	21	13	339	240	105	2nd, Adams Div.	Lost Quarter-Final
1974-75	80	28	6	6	21	10	9	49	16	15	354	240	113	1st, Adams Div.	Lost Final
1973-74	78	23	10	6	9	24	6	32	34	12	242	250	76	5th, East Div.	Out of Playoffs
1972-73	78	30	6	3	7	21	11	37	27	14	257	219	88	4th, East Div.	Lost Quarter-Final
1971-72	78	11	19	9	5	24	10	16	43	19	203	289	51	6th, East Div.	Out of Playoffs
1970-71	78	16	13	10	8	26	5	24	39	15	217	291	63	5th, East Div.	Out of Playoffs

1993-94 Player Personnel

FORWARDS	HT	WT	S	Place of Birth	Date	1992-93 Club
AMBROZIAK, Peter	6-0	206	L	Toronto, Ont.	9/15/71	Rochester
AUDETTE, Donald	5-8	175	R	Laval, Que.	9/23/69	Buffalo-Rochester
BARNABY, Matthew	6-0	170	L	Ottawa, Ont.	5/4/73	Buffalo-Vic.
BARRIE, Mike	6-1	170	R	Kelowna, B.C.	3/16/74	Victoria
CIAVAGLIA, Peter	5-10	173	L	Albany, NY	7/15/69	Buffalo-Rochester
CLANCY, Chris	6-2	198	L	Kitchener, Ont.	11/28/72	Belleville
DAWE, Jason	5-10	195	L	Scarborough, Ont.	5/29/73	Peterborough
GAGE, Jody	6-0	190	R	Toronto, Ont.	11/29/59	Rochester
GORDIOUK, Viktor	5-10	176	R	Moscow, USSR	4/11/70	Buffalo-Rochester
HANNAN, Dave	5-10	185	L	Sudbury, Ont.	11/26/61	Buffalo
HAWERCHUK, Dale	5-11	190	L	Toronto, Ont.	4/4/63	Buffalo
IOB, Tony	5-11	206	L	Renfrew, Ont.	1/2/71	Rochester-Erie
KHMYLEV, Yuri	6-1	189	R	Moscow, USSR	8/9/64	Buffalo
LaFONTAINE, Pat	5-10	177	R	St. Louis, MO	2/22/65	Buffalo
MACDONALD, Doug	6-0	192	L	Port Moody, B.C.	2/8/69	Buffalo-Rochester
MAY, Brad	6-0	200	L	Toronto, Ont.	11/29/71	Buffalo
MOGILNY, Alexander	5-11	187	L	Khabarovsk, USSR	2/18/69	Buffalo
MOORE, Barrie	5-11	175	L	London, Ont.	5/22/75	Sudbury
NICHOL, Scott	5-8	160	R	Calgary, Alta.	12/31/74	Portland
PETRENKO, Sergei	5-11	167	L	Kharkov, USSR	9/10/68	Dynamo Moscow
PHILPOTT, Ethan	6-4	230	R	Rochester, MN	2/11/75	P.A. Academy
PRESLEY, Wayne	5-11	180	R	Detroit, MI	3/23/65	Buffalo
RAY, Rob	6-0	203	L	Stirling, Ont.	6/8/68	Buffalo
RUBACHUK, Brad	5-11	185	L	Winnipeg, Man.	6/11/70	Rochester
RUSHFORTH, Paul	6-0	189	R	Prince George, B.C.	4/22/74	North Bay-Belleville
SAFARIK, Richard	6-3	194	L	Nova Zausky	2/26/75	Nitra
SAVAGE, Joel	5-11	205	R	Surrey, B.C.	12/25/69	Rochester-Ft. Wayne
SIMON, Todd	5-10	188	R	Toronto, Ont.	4/21/72	Rochester
SIMPSON, Craig	6-2	195	R	London, Ont.	2/15/67	Edmonton
SWEENEY, Bob	6-3	200	R	Concord, MA	1/25/64	Buffalo
THOMAS, Scott	6-2	195	R	Buffalo, NY	1/18/70	Buffalo-Rochester
TILTGEN, Dean	5-11	175	L	Ponoka, Alta.	2/3/74	Red Deer
WINCH, Jason	6-1	215	L	Listowel, Ont.	5/23/71	Roch.-Ft. Wayne-Erie
WOOD, Randy	6-0	195	L	Princeton, NJ	10/12/63	Buffalo
YOUNG, Jason	5-10	197	L	Sudbury, Ont.	12/16/72	Rochester
DEFENSEMEN						
BODGER, Doug	6-2	213	L	Chemainus, B.C.	6/18/66	Buffalo
BOUCHER, Philippe	6-2	188	R	St. Apollinaire, Que.	3/24/73	Buf.-Roch.-Lav.
BROWN, Greg	6-0	185	R	Hartford, CT	3/7/68	Buffalo-Rochester
CARNEY, Keith	6-2	205	L	Providence, RI	2/3/70	Buffalo-Rochester
COOPER, David	6-2	204	L	Ottawa, Ont.	11/2/73	Medicine Hat
DI VITA, David	6-2	195	L	St. Clair Shores, MI	2/3/69	Rochester
DONNELLY, Gord	6-1	202	R	Montreal, Que.	4/5/62	Buffalo
MELANSON, Dean	5-11	211	R	Antigonish, N.S.	11/19/73	Rochester-St-Hyacinthe
MOLLER, Randy	6-2	207	R	Red Deer, Alta.	8/23/63	Buffalo-Rochester
O'DONNELL, Sean	6-2	224	L	Ottawa, Ont.	10/13/71	Rochester
PASCALL, Brad	6-2	192	L	Coquitlan, B.C.	7/29/70	Rochester-Erie
POZZO, Kevin	6-1	176	R	Calgary, Alta.	10/11/74	Moose Jaw
SHOEBOTTOM, Bruce	6-2	200	L	Windsor, Ont.	8/20/65	Rochester
SMEHLIK, Richard	6-3	208	L	Ostrava, Czech.	1/23/70	Buffalo
SUTTON, Ken	6-0	198	L	Edmonton, Alta.	5/11/69	Buffalo
SVOBODA, Petr	6-1	175	L	Most, Czech.	2/14/66	Buffalo
TSYGUROV, Denis	6-3	198	L	Togliatti	2/26/71	Lada Togliatti

GOALTENDERS	HT	WT	C	Place of Birth	Date	1992-93 Club
DAVIS, Chris	6-3	177	L	Calgary, Alta.	12/1/74	Calgary Royals
DRAPER, Tom	5-11	185	L	Outremont, Que.	11/20/66	Buffalo
FUHR, Grant	5-9	190	R	Spruce Grove, Alta.	9/28/62	Toronto-Buffalo
HASEK, Dominik	5-11	168	R	Pardubice, Czech.	1/29/65	Buffalo
KETTERER, Markus	5-11	165	L	Helsinki, Finland	8/23/67	Jokerit
PYE, Bill	5-9	180	L	Canton, MI	4/9/69	Rochester

Coaching History

"Punch" Imlach, 1970-71; "Punch" Imlach, Floyd Smith and Joe Crozier, 1971-72; Joe Crozier, 1972-73 to 1973-74; Floyd Smith, 1974-75 to 1976-77; Marcel Pronovost, 1977-78; Marcel Pronovost and Bill Inglis, 1978-79; Scott Bowman, 1979-80; Roger Neilson, 1980-81; Jim Roberts and Scott Bowman, 1981-82; Scott Bowman 1982-83 to 1984-85; Jim Schoenfeld and Scott Bowman, 1985-86; Scott Bowman, Craig Ramsay and Ted Sator, 1986-87; Ted Sator, 1987-88 to 1988-89; Rick Dudley, 1989-90 to 1990-91; Rick Dudley and John Muckler, 1991-92; John Muckler, 1992-93 to date.

Captains' History

Floyd Smith, 1970-71; Gerry Meehan, 1971-72 to 1973-74; Gerry Meehan and Jim Schoenfeld, 1974-75; Jim Schoenfeld, 1975-76 to 1976-77; Danny Gare, 1977-78 to 1980-81; Danny Gare and Gil Perreault, 1981-82; Gil Perreault, 1982-83 to 1985-86; Gil Perreault and Lindy Ruff, 1986-87; Lindy Ruff, 1987-88; Lindy Ruff and Mike Foligno, 1988-89; Mike Foligno, 1989-90. Mike Foligno and Mike Ramsey, 1990-91; Mike Ramsey, 1991-92; Mike Ramsey and Pat LaFontaine, 1992-93; Pat LaFontaine, 1993-94.

General Managers' History

George "Punch" Imlach, 1970-71 to 1977-78; John Anderson (acting), 1978-79; Scott Bowman, 1979-80 to 1985-86; Scott Bowman and Gerry Meehan, 1986-87; Gerry Meehan, 1987-88 to 1992-93; John Muckler, 1993-94.

Retired Numbers

11 Gilbert Perreault 1970-1987

1992-93 Scoring

Regular Season

Pos	#	Player	Team	GP	G	A	Pts	+/-	PIM	PP	SH	GW	GT	S	%
C	16	Pat LaFontaine	BUF	84	53	95	148	11	63	20	2	7	1	306	17.3
R	89	Alexander Mogilny	BUF	77	76	51	127	7	40	27	0	11	0	360	21.1
C	10	Dale Hawerchuk	BUF	81	16	80	96	17–	52	8	0	2	0	259	6.2
D	8	Doug Bodger	BUF	81	9	45	54	14	87	6	0	0	1	154	5.8
C	20	Bob Sweeney	BUF	80	21	26	47	2	118	4	3	3	0	120	17.5
L	19	Randy Wood	BUF	82	18	25	43	6	77	3	2	2	0	176	10.2
L	13	Yuri Khmylev	BUF	68	20	19	39	6	28	0	3	3	0	122	16.4
R	18	Wayne Presley	BUF	79	15	17	32	5	96	0	1	2	0	97	15.5
D	42*	Richard Smehlik	BUF	80	4	27	31	9	59	0	0	0	0	82	4.9
L	27	Brad May	BUF	82	13	13	26	3	242	0	0	1	0	114	11.4
D	7	Petr Svoboda	BUF	40	2	24	26	3	59	1	0	1	0	61	3.3
D	41	Ken Sutton	BUF	63	8	14	22	3–	30	1	0	2	1	77	10.4
C	14	Dave Hannan	BUF	55	5	15	20	8	43	0	0	0	0	43	11.6
R	28	Donald Audette	BUF	44	12	7	19	8–	51	2	0	0	0	92	13.0
L	12	Bob Errey	PIT	54	8	6	14	2–	76	0	0	2	0	79	10.1
			BUF	8	1	3	4	2	4	0	0	0	0	9	11.1
			TOTAL	62	9	9	18	0	80	0	0	2	0	88	10.2
D	3	Grant Ledyard	BUF	50	2	14	16	2–	45	1	0	0	0	79	2.5
D	34	Gord Donnelly	BUF	60	3	8	11	5	221	0	0	0	0	38	7.9
R	29	Bob Corkum	BUF	68	6	4	10	3–	38	0	1	1	0	69	8.7
R	9*	Viktor Gordiouk	BUF	16	3	6	9	4	0	0	0	0	0	24	12.5
D	24	Randy Moller	BUF	35	2	7	9	6	83	0	0	0	0	25	8.0
D	23	Bill Houlder	BUF	15	3	5	8	5	6	0	0	0	1	29	10.3
R	17	Colin Patterson	BUF	36	4	2	6	2–	22	0	1	0	0	30	13.3
D	6*	Keith Carney	BUF	30	2	4	6	3	55	0	0	1	0	26	7.7
L	32	Rob Ray	BUF	68	3	2	5	3–	211	1	0	0	0	28	10.7
D	4*	Philippe Boucher	BUF	18	0	4	4	1	14	0	0	0	0	28	.0
R	21*	Scott Thomas	BUF	7	1	1	2	2	15	0	0	0	0	4	25.0
L	36*	Matthew Barnaby	BUF	2	1	0	1	0	10	1	0	0	0	8	12.5
L	44*	Doug Macdonald	BUF	5	1	0	1	0	2	0	0	0	0	1	100.0
D	15	Greg Brown	BUF	10	0	1	1	5–	6	0	0	0	0	10	.0
G	35	Tom Draper	BUF	11	0	1	1	0	2	0	0	0	0	0	.0
C	12*	Pete Ciavaglia	BUF	3	0	0	0	0	0	0	0	0	0	2	.0
G	39	Dominik Hasek	BUF	28	0	0	0	0	0	0	0	0	0	0	.0
G	31	Grant Fuhr	TOR	29	0	0	0	0	0	0	0	0	0	0	.0
			BUF	29	0	0	0	0	10	0	0	0	0	0	.0
			TOTAL	58	0	0	0	0	10	0	0	0	0	0	.0

Goaltending

No.	Goaltender	GPI	Mins	Avg	W	L	T	EN	SO	GA	SA	S%
39	Dominik Hasek	28	1429	3.15	11	10	4	1	0	75	720	.896
31	Grant Fuhr	29	1694	3.47	11	15	2	3	0	98	903	.891
1	Daren Puppa	24	1306	3.58	11	5	4	0	0	78	706	.890
35	Tom Draper	11	664	3.70	5	6	0	1	0	41	344	.881
	Totals	**84**	**5104**	**3.49**	**38**	**36**	**10**	**5**	**0**	**297**	**2678**	**.889**

Playoffs

Pos	#	Player	Team	GP	G	A	Pts	+/-	PIM	PP	SH	GW	GT	S	%
C	10	Dale Hawerchuk	BUF	8	5	9	14	0	2	3	0	0	0	31	16.1
C	16	Pat LaFontaine	BUF	7	2	10	12	0	0	1	0	0	0	13	15.4
R	89	Alexander Mogilny	BUF	7	7	3	10	2	6	2	0	0	0	35	20.0
L	13	Yuri Khmylev	BUF	8	4	3	7	3	4	1	0	1	1	17	23.5
D	8	Doug Bodger	BUF	8	2	3	5	3	0	2	0	0	0	25	8.0
L	19	Randy Wood	BUF	8	1	4	5	0	4	1	0	0	0	17	5.9
D	41	Ken Sutton	BUF	8	3	1	4	3	8	0	0	0	0	16	18.8
R	28	Donald Audette	BUF	8	2	2	4	1	6	0	0	0	0	18	11.1
C	20	Bob Sweeney	BUF	8	2	2	4	2	8	0	0	1	1	18	11.1
D	42*	Richard Smehlik	BUF	8	0	4	4	3	2	0	0	0	0	11	.0
D	6*	Keith Carney	BUF	8	0	3	3	1	6	0	0	0	0	2	.0
C	14	Dave Hannan	BUF	8	1	1	2	1	18	0	0	0	0	5	20.0
L	27	Brad May	BUF	8	1	1	2	0	14	0	0	1	1	8	12.5
D	23	Bill Houlder	BUF	8	0	2	2	1	4	0	0	0	0	11	.0
R	18	Wayne Presley	BUF	8	1	0	1	2–	6	0	1	1	0	12	8.3
L	36*	Matthew Barnaby	BUF	1	0	1	1	1	4	0	0	0	0	0	.0
L	12	Bob Errey	BUF	4	0	1	1	1–	10	0	0	0	0	4	.0
R	17	Colin Patterson	BUF	8	0	1	1	0	2	0	0	0	0	2	.0
G	39	Dominik Hasek	BUF	1	0	0	0	0	0	0	0	0	0	0	.0
R	29	Bob Corkum	BUF	5	0	0	0	1	2	0	0	0	0	1	.0
G	31	Grant Fuhr	BUF	8	0	0	0	0	2	0	0	0	0	0	.0
D	3	Grant Ledyard	BUF	8	0	0	0	5–	8	0	0	0	0	12	.0

Goaltending

No.	Goaltender	GPI	Mins	Avg	W	L	EN	SO	GA	SA	S%
39	Dominik Hasek	1	45	1.33	1	0	0	0	1	24	.958
31	Grant Fuhr	8	474	3.42	3	4	0	1	27	216	.875
	Totals	**8**	**520**	**3.23**	**4**	**4**	**0**	**1**	**28**	**240**	**.883**

Club Records

Team

(Figures in brackets for season records are games played; records for fewest points, wins, ties, losses, goals, goals against are for 70 or more games)

Most Points	113	1974-75 (80)
Most Wins	49	1974-75 (80)
Most Ties	21	1980-81 (80)
Most Losses	44	1986-87 (80)
Most Goals	354	1974-75 (80)
Most Goals Against	308	1986-87 (80)
Fewest Points	51	1971-72 (78)
Fewest Wins	16	1971-72 (78)
Fewest Ties	6	1985-86 (80)
Fewest Losses	16	1974-75 (80)
Fewest Goals	203	1971-72 (78)
Fewest Goals Against	201	1979-80 (80)

Longest Winning Streak
Over-all .... 10 Jan. 4-23/84
Home .... 12 Nov. 12/72-
              Jan. 7/73
              Oct. 13-
              Dec. 10/89
Away .... 10 Dec. 10/83-
              Jan. 23/84

Longest Undefeated Streak
Over-all .... 14 March 6-
              April 6/80
              (8 wins, 6 ties)
Home .... 21 Oct. 8/72-
              Jan. 7/73
              (18 wins, 3 ties)
Away .... 10 Dec. 10/83-
              Jan. 23/84
              (10 wins)

Longest Losing Streak
Over-all .... 7 Oct. 25-
              Nov. 8/70;
              Apr. 3-15/93
Home .... 5 Feb. 15-Mar. 3/85
              Dec. 29/89-
              Jan. 26/90
Away .... 7 Oct. 14-
              Nov. 7/70
              Feb. 6-27/71

Longest Winless Streak
Over-all .... 12 Nov. 23-
              Dec. 20/91
              (8 losses, 4 ties)
Home .... 12 Jan. 27-
              Mar. 10/91
              (7 losses, 5 ties)
Away .... 23 Oct. 30/71-
              Feb. 19/72
              (15 losses, 8 ties)
Most Shutouts, Season 7 1974-75 (80)
Most PIM, Season 2,712 1991-92 (80)
Most Goals, Game .... 14 Jan. 21/75
              (Wsh. 2 at Buf. 14)
              Mar. 19/81
              (Tor. 4 at Buf. 14)

Individual

Most Seasons	17	Gilbert Perreault
Most Games	1,191	Gilbert Perreault
Most Goals, Career	512	Gilbert Perreault
Most Assists, Career	814	Gilbert Perreault
Most Points, Career	1,326	Gilbert Perreault
Most PIM, Career	1,450	Mike Foligno
Most Shutouts, Career	14	Don Edwards

Longest Consecutive
Games Streak .... 776 Craig Ramsay
              (Mar. 27/73-Feb. 10/83)
Most Goals, Season .... 76 Alexander Mogilny
              (1992-93)
Most Assists, Season ...... 95 Pat LaFontaine
              (1992-93)
Most Points, Season ...... 148 Pat LaFontaine
              (1992-93)
              (53 goals, 95 assists)
Most PIM, Season .... 354 Rob Ray
              (1991-92)

Most Points, Defenseman
Season .... 81 Phil Housley
              (1989-90)
              (21 goals, 60 assists)
Most Points, Center
Season .... 148 Pat LaFontaine
              (1992-93)
              (53 goals, 95 assists)
Most Points, Right Wing
Season .... 127 Alexander Mogilny
              (1992-93)
              (76 goals, 51 assists)

Most Points, Left Wing
Season .... 95 Richard Martin
              (1974-75)
              (52 goals, 43 assists)
Most Points, Rookie
Season .... 74 Richard Martin
              (1971-72)
              (44 goals, 30 assists)
Most Shutouts, Season .... 5 Don Edwards
              (1977-78)
              Tom Barrasso
              (1984-85)
Most Goals, Game .... 5 Dave Andreychuk
              (Feb. 6/86)
Most Assists, Game .... 5 Gilbert Perreault
              (Feb. 1/76;
              Mar. 9/80;
              Jan. 4/84)
              Dale Hawerchuk
              (Jan. 15/92);
              Pat LaFontaine
              (Dec. 31/92; Feb. 10/93)
Most Points, Game .... 7 Gilbert Perreault
              (Feb. 1/76)

All-time Record vs. Other Clubs

Regular Season

			At Home							On Road							Total			
	GP	W	L	T	GF	GA	PTS	GP	W	L	T	GF	GA	PTS	GP	W	L	T	GF	GA	PTS
Boston	79	39	26	14	299	250	92	79	23	47	9	243	330	55	158	62	73	23	542	580	147
Calgary	37	21	12	4	154	113	46	37	14	13	10	128	134	38	74	35	25	14	282	247	84
Chicago	44	28	10	6	173	113	62	42	14	22	6	115	136	34	86	42	32	12	288	249	96
Detroit	44	31	6	7	205	118	69	46	17	24	5	142	174	39	90	48	30	12	347	292	108
Edmonton	22	9	9	4	94	89	22	21	3	16	2	53	94	8	43	12	25	6	147	183	30
Hartford	52	28	17	7	221	171	63	53	26	19	8	168	162	60	105	54	36	15	389	333	123
Los Angeles	44	21	15	8	181	141	50	45	20	17	8	157	155	48	89	41	32	16	338	296	98
Minnesota	44	23	11	10	165	119	56	45	19	20	6	140	142	44	89	42	31	16	305	261	100
Montreal	74	33	23	18	233	220	84	75	20	47	8	222	314	48	149	53	70	26	455	534	132
New Jersey	32	24	4	4	155	94	52	33	19	7	7	135	104	45	65	43	11	11	290	198	97
Ottawa	2	1	0	1	11	10	3	1	0	1	0	5	7	0	3	1	1	1	16	17	3
NY Islanders	39	22	13	4	145	117	48	39	17	15	7	116	115	41	78	39	28	11	261	232	89
NY Rangers	47	30	11	6	219	149	66	46	16	19	11	135	160	43	93	46	30	17	354	309	109
Philadelphia	42	21	15	6	152	129	48	45	10	27	8	118	168	28	87	31	42	14	270	297	76
Pittsburgh	45	23	8	14	205	125	60	46	15	19	12	165	179	42	91	38	27	26	370	304	102
Quebec	52	29	15	8	212	170	66	51	17	26	8	163	197	42	103	46	41	16	375	367	108
St. Louis	43	29	10	4	184	133	62	42	12	24	6	113	159	30	85	41	34	10	297	292	92
San Jose	3	2	1	0	12	13	4	2	0	2	0	9	12	0	5	2	3	0	21	25	4
Tampa Bay	1	1	0	0	5	4	2	1	1	0	0	3	1	2	2	2	0	0	8	5	4
Toronto	49	31	16	2	209	142	64	48	22	18	8	180	152	52	97	53	34	10	389	294	116
Vancouver	44	22	14	8	159	127	52	43	12	21	10	140	165	34	87	34	35	18	299	292	86
Washington	35	26	5	4	156	93	56	34	21	7	6	140	95	48	69	47	12	10	296	188	104
Winnipeg	21	18	1	2	98	53	38	21	11	8	2	80	68	24	42	29	9	4	178	121	62
Defunct Clubs	23	13	5	5	94	63	31	23	12	8	3	97	76	27	46	25	13	8	191	139	58
Totals	**918**	**525**	**247**	**146**	**3741**	**2756**	**1196**	**918**	**341**	**427**	**150**	**2967**	**3299**	**832**	**1836**	**866**	**674**	**296**	**6708**	**6055**	**2028**

Playoffs

	Series	W	L	GP	W	L	T	GF	GA	Last Mtg.	Round	Result
Boston	6	1	5	33	14	19	0	113	132	1993	DSF	W 4-0
Chicago	2	2	0	9	8	1	0	36	17	1980	QF	W 4-0
Minnesota	2	1	1	7	3	4	0	28	26	1981	QF	L 1-4
Montreal	6	2	4	31	13	18	0	94	114	1993	DF	L 0-4
NY Islanders	3	0	3	16	4	12	0	45	59	1980	SF	L 2-4
NY Rangers	1	1	0	3	2	1	0	11	6	1978	PR	W 2-1
Philadelphia	2	0	2	11	3	8	0	23	35	1978	QF	L 1-4
Pittsburgh	1	0	1	3	1	2	0	9	9	1979	PR	L 1-2
Quebec	2	0	2	8	2	6	0	27	35	1985	DSF	L 2-3
St. Louis	1	1	0	3	2	1	0	7	8	1976	PR	W 2-1
Vancouver	2	2	0	7	6	1	0	28	14	1981	PR	W 3-0
Totals	**28**	**10**	**18**	**131**	**58**	**73**	**0**	**421**	**448**			

Playoff Results 1993-89

Year	Round	Opponent	Result	GF	GA
1993	DF	Montreal	L 0-4	12	16
	DSF	Boston	W 4-0	19	12
1992	DSF	Boston	L 3-4	24	19
1991	DSF	Montreal	L 2-4	24	29
1990	DSF	Montreal	L 2-4	13	17
1989	DSF	Boston	L 1-4	14	16

Abbreviations: Round: F – Final;
CF – conference final; **DF** – division final;
DSF – division semi-final; **PR** – preliminary
round. **GA** – goals against; **GF** – goals for.

1992-93 Results

	Home				Away	
Oct. 8	Quebec	4-5	**Oct.** 10	Hartford	5-2
11	Montreal	8-2	13	Pittsburgh	5-6
16	Tampa Bay	5-4	17	Washington	4-6
21	Chicago	4-1	28	Toronto	4-4
23	San Jose	5-4	31	Ottawa	2-2
30	Ottawa	12-3	**Nov.** 2	NY Rangers	6-7
Nov. 11	Boston	7-2	5	San Jose	5-7
13	Hartford	8-2	7	Los Angeles	2-5
21	Minnesota	3-4	14	NY Islanders	5-7
25	Quebec	1-1	17	Pittsburgh	2-4
27	Ottawa	4-1	18	New Jersey	2-3
Dec. 4	NY Islanders	5-5	22	Philadelphia	4-4
6	New Jersey	3-7	29	Ottawa	5-2
9	Boston	5-2	30	Montreal	0-3
11	Hartford	9-3	**Dec.** 7	Quebec	3-4
20	Toronto	5-4	12	Hartford	1-1
23	Washington	4-1	15	Boston	3-2
27	Pittsburgh*	2-4	19	Montreal	2-4
31	NY Rangers	11-6	**Jan.** 2	Ottawa	7-2
Jan. 3	St. Louis	6-5	6	Hartford	3-1
8	NY Islanders	6-5	12	Boston	2-5
10	Calgary	5-3	15	Vancouver	1-4
22	Quebec	6-2	17	Edmonton	2-3
27	Washington	4-3	19	Calgary	3-2
29	NY Rangers	6-4	23	Quebec	3-4
31	Edmonton*	4-5	26	Philadelphia	4-3
Feb. 3	Hartford	3-2	**Feb.** 8	Ottawa	2-4
12	Vancouver	1-3	10	Winnipeg	6-2
14	Pittsburgh	7-4	17	Hartford	5-3
24	Detroit	10-7	19	New Jersey	3-3
26	Montreal	4-6	27	Montreal	4-8
Mar. 1	Vancouver	2-5	**Mar.** 3	NY Rangers	2-2
5	Hartford	2-4	10	Quebec	7-4
7	Winnipeg	2-1	13	Hartford*	3-3
15	Los Angeles	2-4	16	St. Louis	2-2
24	Boston	0-2	20	Tampa Bay*	3-1
28	Ottawa	3-1	22	Montreal	8-3
31	New Jersey	5-2	25	Chicago	6-4
Apr. 4	Boston*	0-3	30	Washington	1-4
11	Quebec	1-3	**Apr.** 3	Boston*	2-3
13	Montreal	2-3	6	Minnesota	1-3
15	Philadelphia	4-7	10	Detroit*	5-6

*Denotes afternoon game

Entry Draft Selections 1993-79

1993

Pick	
38	Denis Tsygurov
64	Ethan Philpott
116	Richard Safarik
142	Kevin Pozzo
168	Sergei Petrenko
194	Mike Barrie
220	Barrie Moore
246	Chris Davis
272	Scott Nichol

1992

Pick	
11	David Cooper
35	Jozef Cierny
59	Ondrej Steiner
80	Dean Melanson
83	Matthew Barnaby
107	Markus Ketterer
108	Yuri Khmylev
131	Paul Rushforth
179	Dean Tiltgen
203	Todd Simon
227	Rick Kowalsky
251	Chris Clancy

1991

Pick	
13	Philippe Boucher
35	Jason Dawe
57	Jason Young
72	Peter Ambroziak
101	Steve Shields
123	Sean O'Donnell
124	Brian Holzinger
145	Chris Snell
162	Jiri Kuntos
189	Tony Iob
211	Spencer Meany
233	Mikhail Volkov
255	Michael Smith

1990

Pick	
14	Brad May
82	Brian McCarthy
97	Richard Smehlik
100	Todd Bojcun
103	Brad Pascall
142	Viktor Gordiyuk
166	Milan Nedoma
187	Jason Winch
208	Sylvain Naud
229	Kenneth Martin
250	Brad Rubachuk

1989

Pick	
14	Kevin Haller
56	John (Scott) Thomas
77	Doug MacDonald
98	Ken Sutton
107	Bill Pye
119	Mike Barkley
161	Derek Plante
183	Donald Audette
194	Mark Astley
203	John Nelson
224	Todd Henderson
245	Michael Bavis

1988

Pick	
13	Joel Savage
55	Darcy Loewen
76	Keith E. Carney
89	Alexander Mogilny
97	Robert Ray
106	David Di Vita
118	Mike McLaughlin
139	Mike Griffith
160	Daniel Ruoho
181	Wade Flaherty
223	Thomas Nieman
244	Robert Wallwork

1987

Pick	
1	Pierre Turgeon
22	Brad Miller
53	Andrew MacVicar
84	John Bradley
85	David Pergola
106	Chris Marshall
127	Paul Flanagan
148	Sean Dooley
153	Tim Roberts
169	Grant Tkachuk
190	Ian Herbers
211	David Littman
232	Allan MacIsaac

1986

Pick	
5	Shawn Anderson
26	Greg Brown
47	Bob Corkum
56	Kevin Kerr
68	David Baseggio
89	Larry Rooney
110	Miguel Baldris
131	Mike Hartman
152	Francois Guay
173	Shawn Whitham
194	Kenton Rein
215	Troy Arndt

1985

Pick	
14	Calle Johansson
35	Benoit Hogue
56	Keith Gretzky
77	Dave Moylan
98	Ken Priestlay
119	Joe Reekie
140	Petri Matikainen
161	Trent Kaese
182	Jiri Sejba
203	Boyd Sutton
224	Guy Larose
245	Ken Baumgartner

1984

Pick	
18	Mikael Andersson
39	Doug Trapp
60	Ray Sheppard
81	Bob Halkidis
102	Joey Rampton
123	James Gasseau
144	Darcy Wakaluk
165	Orvar Stambert
206	Brian McKinnon
226	Grant Delcourt
247	Sean Baker

1983

Pick	
5	Tom Barrasso
10	Normand Lacombe
11	Adam Creighton
31	John Tucker
34	Richard Hajdu
74	Daren Puppa
94	Jayson Meyer
114	Jim Hofford
134	Christian Ruuttu
154	Don McSween
174	Tim Hoover
194	Mark Ferner
214	Uwe Krupp
234	Marc Hamelin
235	Kermit Salfi

1982

Pick	
6	Phil Housley
9	Paul Cyr
16	Dave Andreychuk
26	Mike Anderson
30	Jens Johansson
68	Timo Jutila
79	Jeff Hamilton
100	Bob Logan
111	Jeff Parker
121	Jacob Gustavsson
142	Allen Bishop
163	Claude Verret
184	Rob Norman
205	Mike Craig
226	Jim Plankers

1981

Pick	
17	Jiri Dudacek
38	Hannu Virta
59	Jim Aldred
60	Colin Chisholm
80	Jeff Eatough
83	Anders Wikberg
101	Mauri Eivola
122	Ali Butorac
143	Heikki Leime
164	Gates Orlando
185	Venci Sebek
206	Warren Harper

1980

Pick	
20	Steve Patrick
41	Mike Moller
56	Sean McKenna
62	Jay North
83	Jim Wiemer
104	Dirk Rueter
125	Daniel Naud
146	Jari Paavola
167	Randy Cunneyworth
188	Dave Beckon
209	John Bader

1979

Pick	
11	Mike Ramsey
32	Lindy Ruff
53	Mark Robinson
55	Jacques Cloutier
74	Gilles Hamel
95	Alan Haworth
116	Rick Knickle

Coach and General Manager

MUCKLER, JOHN
Coach and General Manager, Buffalo Sabres.
Born in Midland, Ont., April 3, 1934.

John Muckler, added the title of General Manager on July 30 this past summer to go along with his head coaching duties. Muckler joined the Buffalo organization in May of 1991 as Director of Hockey Operations. He replaced Rick Dudley as head coach midway through the 1991-92 season, finishing the year with a 22-22-8 record. This past season Muckler guided the Sabres to the Adams Division Finals, the first time in ten seasons that Buffalo had ventured past the first round of the playoffs. One of the NHL's most experienced coaches, Muckler has been named as Coach of the Year in three different leagues; the EHL, AHL and the CHL. Muckler, who started his professional coaching career in 1959, joined the Edmonton Oilers in 1981 as coach of their Wichita farm affiliate and was eventually named as co-coach of the NHL squad in 1986. In 1988-89, he was hired as only the third coach in Oilers' history and promptly led the team to their fifth Stanley Cup championship.

Coaching Record

		Regular Season					Playoffs			
Season	Team	Games	W	L	T	%	Games	W	L	%
1964-65	Long Island (EHL)	72	42	29	1	.590	15	11	4	.733
1965-66	Long Island (EHL)	72	46	23	3	.660	12	7	5	.583
1968-69	**Minnesota (NHL)**	**35**	**6**	**23**	**6**	**.257**	....	....	....	....
1971-72	Cleveland (AHL)	76	32	34	10	.487	6	2	4	.333
1972-73	*Cleveland (AHL)	76	23	44	9	.362	....	....	....	....
1973-74	Providence (AHL)	76	38	26	12	.579	15	9	6	.600
1974-75	Providence (AHL)	76	43	21	12	.645	6	2	4	.333
1975-76	Providence (AHL)	76	34	34	8	.500	3	0	3	.000
1976-77	Providence (AHL)	53	21	30	2	.415	....	....	....	....
1978-79	Dallas (CHL)	76	45	28	3	.612	9	8	1	.889
1981-82	Wichita (CHL)	80	44	33	3	.569	7	3	4	.423
1989-90	**Edmonton (NHL)**	**80**	**38**	**28**	**14**	**.563**	**22**	**16**	**6**	**.727******
1990-91	**Edmonton (NHL)**	**80**	**37**	**37**	**6**	**.500**	**18**	**9**	**9**	**.500**
1991-92	**Buffalo (NHL)**	**52**	**22**	**22**	**8**	**.500**	**7**	**3**	**4**	**.429**
1992-93	**Buffalo (NHL)**	**84**	**38**	**36**	**10**	**.512**	**8**	**4**	**4**	**.500**
	NHL Totals	**331**	**141**	**146**	**44**	**.492**	**55**	**32**	**23**	**.582**

* Club moved to Jacksonville during regular season. ** Stanley Cup Win.

Club Directory

Memorial Auditorium
Buffalo, NY 14202
Phone **716/856-7300**
Outside Buffalo: **800/333-PUCK**
GM FAX 716/856-7350
Capacity: 16,284

Board of Directors	
Chairman of the Board and President	Seymour H. Knox, III
Vice-Chairman of the Board and Counsel	Robert O. Swados
Vice-Chairman of the Board	Robert E. Rich, Jr.
Treasurer	Joseph T.J. Stewart
Board of Directors	Edwin C. Andrews
Niagara Frontier Hockey, L.P. (includes above listed officers)	Peter C. Andrews, George L. Collins, Jr. M.D. John B. Fisher, John Houghton, Richard Rupp Howard T. Saperston, Jr., Paul A. Schoellkopf George Strawbridge, Jr.
Administration	
Assistant to the President	Seymour H. Knox, IV
Senior Vice-President/Finance	Robert W. Pickel
Senior Vice-President/Administration	George Bergantz
Executive Vice-President of Sports Operations	Gerry Meehan
Controller	Dan DiPofi
Consultant	Northrup R. Knox
Consultant/Administration	Mitchell Owen
Administrative Assistants:	
General Manager	Debbie Bonner
Finance	Elaine Burzynski
President	Carol McHugh
Administration	Verna B. Wojcik
Receptionists	Olive Anticola, Evelyn Battleson
Hockey Department	
General Manager/Head Coach	John Muckler
Director of Player Personnel	Don Luce
Assistant Coach	Don Lever
Assistant Coach	John Tortorella
Goaltender Consultant	Mitch Korn
Director of Scouting	Rudy Migay
Scouting Staff	Don Barrie, Jack Bowman, Larry Carriere, Baris Janicek, Dennis McIvor, Paul Merritt, Mike Racicot, Gleb Tchistyakov, Frank Zywiec
Professional Scout	Joe Crozier
Information Manager	Ken Bass
Administrative Assistant	Cyndi Dyll
Training/Medical	
Head Athletic Trainer	Jim Pizzutelli
Trainer	Rip Simonick
Club Doctor	John L. Butsch, M.D.
Orthopedic Consultant	Peter James, M.D.
Club Dentist	Donald DeRose, D.D.S.
Public Relations	
Director of Public Relations	Steve Rossi
Coordinator of Community Relations	Mary Beth Romano
Public Relations Assistant	Bruce R. Wawrzyniak
Media Relations Assistant	Jeff Holbrook
Administrative Assistant	Barb Blendowski
Team Photographer	Bill Wippert
Sales & Marketing	
Director of Sales & Marketing	Randy Scott
Sponsorship Sales Managers	Bob Russell, Jim DiMino, Tim Jehle, Heidi Puff
Director of Ticket Sales	Tom Pokel
Ticket Sales Coordinator	Anne Robillard
Ticket Sales Representative	Craig Cieplinski, Jim Meissner, Andrew White
Account Executive	David Aston
Marketing Associate	Andrew DiBlasi
Executive Sales/Marketing Administrative Assts.	Cheryl Schoenthaler, Ann Miller
Sales & Marketing Administrative Assistant	Sue Smith
Event Sales	
Director of Event Sales	Jeffrey D. Pickel
Director of Ticket Operations	John R. Sinclair
Ticket Administrators	Carm Glebe, Jennifer Glowny, Rose Thompson
Merchandise Manager	Mike Kaminska
Operations & Promotions	
Director of Operations	Stan Makowski
Director of Corporate Relations	Larry Playfair
Promotions Manager	Matt Rabinowitz
Staff Assistant	Gerry Magill
Public Address Announcer	Milt Ellis
Finance	
Accounting Manager	Chris Ivansitz
Finance Assistants	Robert M. Dahar, Birgid Haensel, Mary Jones, Melissa Kreuzer, Sally Lippert, Terese Melber
Aud Club	
Director of Food Service Operations & Facilities	Dave Boldt
General Manager	George Peddle
Executive Chef	Greyt Thuerck
Receptionist/Secretary	Jennifer Pawlowski
Crossroads Arena Corporation	
Executive Vice-President	Larry Quinn
Director of Suite Sales	Karen Marsch
Administrative Assistant	Deidre Daniels
TV & Radio	
Director of Communications	Paul Wieland
Television Producer	Joe Guarnieri
TV Stations - Home	TBA
Away	WUTV Fox 29
TV Broadcast Team	John Gurtler, Jim Lorentz
Radio Flagship Station	WGR AM-550
Radio Broadcast Team	Rick Jeanneret, Larry Playfair, Barry Beutel
General Information	
Dimensions of Rink	193 feet by 84 feet
Location of Press Box	Suspended from ceiling on west side
Club Colors	Blue, Gold & White
Training Camp/Practice Site	Sabreland/Wheatfield, NY
AHL Affiliate	Rochester Americans

Calgary Flames

1992-93 Results: 43w-30L-11T 97PTS. Second, Smythe Division

Schedule

Home		Away	
Oct.	Tues. 5 NY Islanders	**Oct.**	Sat. 9 Vancouver
	Thur. 7 San Jose		Thur. 14 San Jose
	Thur. 21 Vancouver		Sat. 16 Los Angeles
	Sat. 23 Boston		Sun. 17 Anaheim
	Mon. 25 Washington		Wed. 20 Edmonton
	Wed. 27 Buffalo		Sun. 31 Winnipeg
	Sat. 30 Edmonton	**Nov.**	Wed. 3 Hartford
Nov.	Tues. 9 Los Angeles		Thur. 4 Boston
	Thur. 11 Anaheim		Sat. 6 Montreal
	Sat. 13 Vancouver		Thur. 18 St Louis
	Mon. 15 Winnipeg		Sat. 20 Dallas
	Mon. 22 Anaheim	**Dec.**	Mon. 6 Ottawa
	Wed. 24 Toronto		Tues. 7 Quebec
	Fri. 26 Chicago		Fri. 10 Buffalo
	Tues. 30 Dallas		Sat. 11 Toronto
Dec.	Sat. 4 Philadelphia		Wed. 22 Edmonton
	Tues. 14 Vancouver		Thur. 23 Vancouver
	Fri. 17 St Louis		(at Saskatoon)
	Sat. 18 Winnipeg		Tues. 28 San Jose
	Mon. 20 Los Angeles	**Jan.**	Sun. 2 St Louis
	Thur. 30 Edmonton		Wed. 5 NY Rangers
	Fri. 31 Montreal		Fri. 7 NY Islanders
Jan.	Tues. 11 Quebec		Sat. 8 Pittsburgh
	Sat. 15 Ottawa		Mon. 17 San Jose*
	Mon. 24 Los Angeles		Wed. 19 Vancouver
	(at Phoenix)	**Feb.**	Wed. 2 Anaheim
	Wed. 26 Dallas		Sat. 5 Los Angeles
	Fri. 28 New Jersey		Wed. 9 Edmonton
	Sat. 29 St Louis		Fri. 18 Dallas
Feb.	Mon. 7 Edmonton		Sun. 20 Winnipeg*
	Fri. 11 Hartford		Tues. 22 Vancouver
	Sat. 12 Toronto	**Mar.**	Tues. 1 Detroit
	Mon. 14 Chicago		Thur. 3 Chicago
	Thur. 24 Tampa Bay		Sat. 5 New Jersey*
	Sat. 26 Los Angeles		Sun. 6 Washington*
Mar.	Wed. 9 Detroit		Tues. 15 Tampa Bay
	Fri. 11 Florida		Wed. 16 Florida
	Sat. 12 San Jose		Sun. 20 Toronto*
	Tues. 22 NY Rangers		Thur. 31 Philadelphia
	Sat. 26 Pittsburgh	**Apr.**	Sat. 2 Detroit*
Apr.	Wed. 6 Anaheim		Sun. 3 Chicago
	Fri. 8 San Jose		Mon. 11 Anaheim
	Sat. 9 Detroit		Wed. 13 Los Angeles

* Denotes afternoon game.

Home Starting Times:
Weeknights . . . . 7:35 p.m.
Saturdays . . . . 6:05 p.m.
Except Fri. Dec. 31 . . . . 6:05 p.m.

Franchise date: June 24, 1980. Transferred from Atlanta to Calgary.

PACIFIC DIVISION

22nd NHL Season

WESTERN CONFERENCE

Year-by-Year Record

		Home			Road			Overall						
Season	GP	W	L	T	W	L	T	W	L	T	GF	GA	Pts.	Finished	Playoff Result
1992-93	84	23	14	5	20	16	6	43	30	11	322	282	97	2nd, Smythe Div.	Lost Div. Semi-Final
1991-92	80	19	14	7	12	23	5	31	37	12	296	305	74	5th, Smythe Div.	Out of Playoffs
1990-91	80	29	8	3	17	18	5	46	26	8	344	263	100	2nd, Smythe Div.	Lost Div. Semi-Final
1989-90	80	28	7	5	14	16	10	42	23	15	348	265	99	1st, Smythe Div.	Lost Div. Semi-Final
1988-89	**80**	**32**	**4**	**4**	**22**	**13**	**5**	**54**	**17**	**9**	**354**	**226**	**117**	**1st, Smythe Div.**	**Won Stanley Cup**
1987-88	80	26	11	3	22	12	6	48	23	9	397	305	105	1st, Smythe Div.	Lost Div. Final
1986-87	80	25	13	2	21	18	1	46	31	3	318	289	95	2nd, Smythe Div.	Lost Div. Semi-Final
1985-86	80	23	11	6	17	20	3	40	31	9	354	315	89	2nd, Smythe Div.	Lost Final
1984-85	80	23	11	6	18	16	6	41	27	12	363	302	94	3rd, Smythe Div.	Lost Div. Semi-Final
1983-84	80	22	11	7	12	21	7	34	32	14	311	314	82	2nd, Smythe Div.	Lost Div. Final
1982-83	80	21	12	7	11	22	7	32	34	14	321	317	78	2nd, Smythe Div.	Lost Div. Final
1981-82	80	20	11	9	9	23	8	29	34	17	334	345	75	3rd, Smythe Div.	Lost Div. Semi-Final
1980-81	80	25	5	10	14	22	4	39	27	14	329	298	92	3rd, Patrick Div.	Lost Semi-Final
1979-80	80	18	15	7	17	17	6	35	32	13	282	269	83	4th, Patrick Div.	Lost Prelim. Round
1978-79	80	25	11	4	16	20	4	41	31	8	327	280	90	4th, Patrick Div.	Lost Prelim. Round
1977-78	80	20	13	7	14	14	12	34	27	19	274	252	87	3rd, Patrick Div.	Lost Prelim. Round
1976-77	80	22	11	7	12	23	5	34	34	12	264	265	80	3rd, Patrick Div.	Lost Prelim. Round
1975-76	80	19	14	7	16	19	5	35	33	12	262	237	82	3rd, Patrick Div.	Lost Prelim. Round
1974-75	80	24	9	7	10	22	8	34	31	15	243	233	83	4th, Patrick Div.	Out of Playoffs
1973-74	78	17	15	7	13	19	7	30	34	14	214	238	74	4th, West Div.	Lost Quarter-Final
1972-73	78	16	16	7	9	22	8	25	38	15	191	239	65	7th, West Div.	Out of Playoffs

Robert Reichel, top left, had his finest NHL season in 1992-93, collecting 40 goals and 48 assists for the Calgary Flames. Theo Fleury, top right, reached the 100-point plateau for the second time in his career in 1992-93 with 34 goals and 66 assists. Gary Roberts, left, is one of the NHL's finest all-round performers. He led the Flames with a plus/minus rating of +32.

1993-94 Player Personnel

FORWARDS	HT	WT	S	Place of Birth	Date	1992-93 Club
BEZEAU, Andy	5-11	180	L	St. John, NB	3/30/70	Brantford-Moncton
BOHONOS, Lonnie	5-11	180	R	Winnipeg, MB	5/20/73	Portland
BUCZKOWSKI, Paul	5-11	190	L	Saskatoon, SK	3/20/75	Saskatoon
DRURY, Ted	6-1	190	R	Boston, MA	9/13/71	Harvard
FLEURY, Theoren	5-6	160	R	Oxbow, Sask.	6/29/68	Calgary
FREER, Mark	5-10	180	L	Peterborough, ON	7/14/68	Ottawa
GILLINGHAM, Todd	6-2	200	L	Labrador City, Nfld.	1/31/70	Salt Lake
HAAS, David	6-0	200	L	Toronto, ON	6/23/68	Cape Breton
HARKINS, Todd	6-3	210	R	Cleveland, OH	10/8/68	Salt Lake-Calgary
HARRIS, Tim	6-2	190	R	Uxbridge, Ont.	10/16/67	Salt Lake
KEARNEY, Toby	6-2	190	L	Newburyport, MA	9/2/70	U of Vermont
KISIO, Kelly	5-9	183	R	Peace River, Alta.	9/18/59	San Jose
KRUSE, Paul	6-0	202	L	Merritt, B.C.	3/15/70	Salt Lake-Calgary
KUSHNER, Dale	6-1	195	L	Terrace, BC	6/13/66	Hershey
LaFRANCE, Darryl	5-11	180	R	Sudbury, ON	3/20/74	Oshawa
McCARTHY, Sandy	6-3	224	R	Toronto, Ont.	6/15/72	Salt Lake
MURRAY, Marty	5-9	170	L	Deloraine, MB	2/16/75	Brandon
NEILSON, David	6-3	210	L	Long Island, NY	1/25/71	U of Sask.
NIEUWENDYK, Joe	6-1	195	L	Oshawa, Ont.	9/10/66	Calgary
NIKOLIC, Alex	6-1	200	L	Sudbury, Ont.	3/1/70	Salt Lake
OTTO, Joel	6-4	220	R	Elk River, Man.	10/29/61	Calgary
PASLAWSKI, Greg	5-11	190	R	Kindersley, Sask.	8/25/61	Philadelphia-Calgary
RANHEIM, Paul	6-0	195	R	St. Louis, MO	1/25/66	Calgary
REICHEL, Robert	5-10	185	L	Litvinov, Czech.	6/25/71	Calgary
ROBERTS, Gary	6-1	190	L	North York, Ont.	5/23/66	Calgary
ST. PIERRE, David	6-0	180	R	Montreal, Que.	3/22/72	Salt Lake
SMITH, Damian	5-11	180	L	Durham, England	8/10/71	Durham
SOCHA, Gary	6-3	190	L	North Attleboro, MA	12/30/69	Providence-Salt Lake
STERN, Ron	6-0	195	R	Ste. Agathe, Que.	1/11/67	Calgary
STEVENS, Mike	5-11	196	L	Kitchener, ON	12/30/65	Binghamton
STILLMAN, Cory	6-0	180	L	Peterborough, Ont.	12/20/73	Peterborough
STRUCH, David	5-10	180	L	Flin Flon, Man.	2/11/71	Salt Lake
SUNDBLAD, Niklas	6-1	200	R	Stockholm, Sweden	1/3/73	AIK
SYLVESTER, Derek	6-2	215	R	Columbus, OH	5/15/75	Niagara Falls
VIITAKOSKI, Vesa	6-3	210	L	Lappeenranta, Finland	2/13/71	Tappara
WALZ, Wes	5-10	185	R	Calgary, AB	5/15/70	Hershey
DEFENSEMEN						
ALLISON, Jamie	6-1	190	L	Lindsay, ON	5/13/75	Detroit (OHL)
BONVIE, Dennis	6-1	220	R	Antigonish, NS	7/23/73	North Bay
BOUCHARD, Joel	6-0	180	L	Montreal, Que.	1/23/74	Verdun
DAHL, Kevin	5-11	190	R	Regina, Sask.	12/30/68	Calgary
DAHLQUIST, Chris	6-1	195	L	Fridley, MN	12/14/62	Calgary
ESAU, Leonard	6-3	190	R	Meadow Lake, SK	6/3/68	Halifax
GROLEAU, Francois	6-0	193	L	Longueuil, Que.	1/23/73	St. Jean
HOLDEN, Paul	6-3	210	L	Kitchener, Ont.	3/15/70	Phoenix-Salt Lake
HORVATH, Jason	5-11	190	L	Ituna, SK	11/30/74	Swift Current
MacINNIS, Al	6-2	196	R	Inverness, N.S.	7/11/63	Calgary
MILLER, Kris	6-0	200	L	Bemidji, MN	3/30/69	Raleigh
MUSIL, Frank	6-3	215	L	Pardubice, Czech.	12/17/64	Calgary
PETIT, Michel	6-1	205	R	St. Malo, Que.	2/12/64	Calgary
PEACOCK, Shane	5-10	200	R	Edmonton, AB	7/7/73	Lethbridge
SCHLEGEL, Brad	5-10	190	R	Kitchener, Ont.	7/22/68	Washington-Baltimore
SUTER, Gary	6-0	190	L	Madison, WI	6/24/64	Calgary
WORTMAN, Kevin	6-0	200	R	Sagus, MA	2/22/69	Salt Lake
YAWNEY, Trent	6-3	195	L	Hudson Bay, Sask.	9/29/65	Calgary

GOALTENDERS	HT	WT	C	Place of Birth	Date	1992-93 Club
KIDD, Trevor	6-2	190	L	Dugald, Man.	3/29/72	Salt Lake
MUZZATTI, Jason	6-1	190	L	Toronto, Ont.	2/3/70	Cgy.-T.C.-Ind.-S.L.
REESE, Jeff	5-9	170	L	Brantford, Ont.	3/24/66	Calgary
TREFILOV, Andrei	6-0	180	L	Kirovo. Chepetsk, USSR	8/31/69	Calgary-Salt Lake
VERNON, Mike	5-9	170	L	Calgary, Alta.	2/24/63	Calgary
WALKER, Mike	5-9	170	L	Beaverlodge, AB	12/22/74	Saskatoon

Coaching History

Bernie Geoffrion, 1972-73 to 1973-74; Bernie Geoffrion and Fred Creighton, 1974-75; Fred Creighton, 1975-76 to 1978-79; Al MacNeil, 1979-80 (Atlanta); 1980-81 to 1981-82 (Calgary); Bob Johnson, 1982-83 to 1986-87; Terry Crisp, 1987-88 to 1989-90; Doug Risebrough, 1990-91; Doug Risebrough and Guy Charron, 1991-92; Dave King, 1992-93 to date.

Captains' History

Keith McCreary, 1972-73 to 1974-75; Pat Quinn, 1975-76, 1976-77; Tom Lysiak, 1977-78, 1978-79; Jean Pronovost, 1979-80; Brad Marsh, 1980-81; Phil Russell, 1981-82, 1982-83; Lanny McDonald, Doug Risebrough (co-captains), 1983-84; Lanny McDonald, Doug Risebrough, Jim Peplinski (tri-captains), 1984-85 to 1986-87; Lanny McDonald, Jim Peplinski (co-captains), 1987-88; Lanny McDonald, Jim Peplinski, Tim Hunter (tri-captains), 1988-89; Brad McCrimmon, 1989-90; no captain, 1990-91; Joe Nieuwendyk, 1991-92 to date.

General Managers' History

Cliff Fletcher, 1972-73 to 1990-91; Doug Risebrough, 1991-92 to date.

Retired Numbers

9	Lanny McDonald	1981-1989

1992-93 Scoring

Regular Season

Pos	#	Player	Team	GP	G	A	Pts	+/-	PIM	PP	SH	GW	GT	S	%
R	14	Theoren Fleury	CGY	83	34	66	100	14	88	12	2	4	0	250	13.6
C	26	Robert Reichel	CGY	80	40	48	88	25	54	12	0	5	0	238	16.8
D	20	Gary Suter	CGY	81	23	58	81	1–	112	10	1	2	1	263	8.7
L	10	Gary Roberts	CGY	58	38	41	79	32	172	8	3	4	2	166	22.9
C	25	Joe Nieuwendyk	CGY	79	38	37	75	9	52	14	0	6	0	208	18.3
R	42	Sergei Makarov	CGY	71	18	39	57	0	40	5	0	3	0	105	17.1
D	2	Al MacInnis	CGY	50	11	43	54	15	61	7	0	4	0	201	5.5
C	29	Joel Otto	CGY	75	19	33	52	2	150	6	1	4	1	115	16.5
L	28	Paul Ranheim	CGY	83	21	22	43	4–	26	3	4	1	0	179	11.7
R	23	Greg Paslawski	PHI	60	14	19	33	0	12	4	0	0	0	90	15.6
			CGY	13	4	5	9	3	0	0	0	1	0	19	21.1
			TOTAL	73	18	24	42	3	12	4	0	1	0	109	16.5
R	22	Ronnie Stern	CGY	70	10	15	25	4	207	0	0	1	0	82	12.2
L	15	Brent Ashton	BOS	26	2	2	4	0	11	0	0	0	0	26	7.7
			CGY	32	8	11	19	11	41	0	2	1	0	58	13.8
			TOTAL	58	10	13	23	11	52	0	2	1	0	84	11.9
L	11*	Chris Lindberg	CGY	62	9	12	21	3–	18	1	0	1	0	74	12.2
D	34	Roger Johansson	CGY	77	4	16	20	13	62	1	0	0	0	101	4.0
D	18	Trent Yawney	CGY	63	1	16	17	9	67	0	0	0	0	61	1.6
D	3	Frank Musil	CGY	80	6	10	16	28	131	0	0	1	0	87	6.9
C	39	Brian Skrudland	MTL	23	5	3	8	1	55	0	2	1	0	29	17.2
			CGY	16	2	4	6	3	10	0	0	0	0	22	9.1
			TOTAL	39	7	7	14	4	65	0	2	1	0	51	13.7
L	16	Craig Berube	CGY	77	4	8	12	6–	209	0	0	2	0	58	6.9
D	7	Michel Petit	CGY	35	3	9	12	5–	54	2	0	0	0	58	5.2
C	33	Carey Wilson	CGY	22	4	7	11	10	8	1	2	0	0	30	13.3
D	4*	Kevin Dahl	CGY	61	2	9	11	9	56	1	0	0	0	40	5.0
D	5	Chris Dahlquist	CGY	74	3	7	10	0	66	0	0	1	0	64	4.7
D	21	Alexander Godynyuk	CGY	27	3	4	7	6	19	0	0	0	0	35	8.6
R	19*	Todd Harkins	CGY	15	2	3	5	4–	22	0	0	0	0	17	11.8
L	12*	Paul Kruse	CGY	27	2	3	5	2	41	0	0	0	0	17	11.8
G	35	Jeff Reese	CGY	26	0	4	4	0	4	0	0	0	0	0	.0
D	6	Greg Smyth	CGY	35	1	2	3	2	95	1	0	0	0	14	7.1
R	27	Tomas Forslund	CGY	6	0	2	2	0	0	0	0	0	0	3	.0
G	30	Mike Vernon	CGY	64	0	2	2	0	42	0	0	0	0	0	.0
L	38*	Patrick Lebeau	CGY	1	0	0	0	0	0	0	0	0	0	0	.0
C	13*	Shawn Heaphy	CGY	1	0	0	0	0	0	0	0	0	0	2	.0
G	1*	Andrei Trefilov	CGY	1	0	0	0	0	2	0	0	0	0	0	.0

Goaltending

No.	Goaltender	GPI	Mins	Avg	W	L	T	EN	SO	GA	SA	S%
35	Jeff Reese	26	1311	3.20	14	4	1	0	1	70	629	.889
30	Mike Vernon	64	3732	3.26	29	26	9	4	2	203	1804	.887
1	*Andrei Trefilov	1	65	4.62	0	0	1	0	0	5	39	.872
	Totals	**84**	**5120**	**3.30**	**43**	**30**	**11**	**4**	**3**	**282**	**2476**	**.886**

Playoffs

Pos	#	Player	Team	GP	G	A	Pts	+/-	PIM	PP	SH	GW	GT	S	%
R	14	Theoren Fleury	CGY	6	5	7	12	7–	27	3	1	0	0	21	23.8
C	25	Joe Nieuwendyk	CGY	6	3	6	9	4–	10	1	0	0	0	21	14.3
L	10	Gary Roberts	CGY	5	1	6	7	2–	43	1	0	0	0	4	25.0
D	2	Al MacInnis	CGY	6	1	6	7	4–	10	1	0	0	0	25	4.0
C	29	Joel Otto	CGY	6	4	2	6	1	4	0	1	1	0	14	28.6
C	26	Robert Reichel	CGY	6	2	4	6	6–	2	2	0	0	0	18	11.1
D	18	Trent Yawney	CGY	6	3	2	5	3–	6	1	0	0	0	16	18.8
D	20	Gary Suter	CGY	6	2	3	5	9–	8	0	1	0	0	13	15.4
D	5	Chris Dahlquist	CGY	6	3	1	4	1	4	0	0	0	0	12	25.0
R	23	Greg Paslawski	CGY	6	3	0	3	1–	0	0	0	1	0	12	25.0
L	15	Brent Ashton	CGY	6	0	3	3	6–	2	0	0	0	0	11	.0
C	39	Brian Skrudland	CGY	6	0	3	3	0	12	0	0	0	0	5	.0
D	3	Frank Musil	CGY	6	1	1	2	2	7	0	0	0	0	10	10.0
D	4*	Kevin Dahl	CGY	6	0	2	2	3–	8	0	0	0	0	5	.0
L	11*	Chris Lindberg	CGY	2	0	1	1	2–	2	0	0	0	0	2	.0
D	34	Roger Johansson	CGY	5	0	1	1	1–	2	0	0	0	0	4	.0
L	16	Craig Berube	CGY	6	0	1	1	2–	21	0	0	0	0	3	.0
L	28	Paul Ranheim	CGY	6	0	1	1	1–	0	0	0	0	0	7	.0
G	35	Jeff Reese	CGY	4	0	0	0	0	0	0	0	0	0	0	.0
G	30	Mike Vernon	CGY	4	0	0	0	0	2	0	0	0	0	0	.0
R	22	Ronnie Stern	CGY	6	0	0	0	5–	43	0	0	0	0	6	.0

Goaltending

No.	Goaltender	GPI	Mins	Avg	W	L	EN	SO	GA	SA	S%
35	Jeff Reese	4	209	4.88	1	3	1	0	17	91	.813
30	Mike Vernon	4	150	6.00	1	1	0	0	15	81	.815
	Totals	**6**	**360**	**5.50**	**2**	**4**	**1**	**0**	**33**	**173**	**.809**

Club Records

Team

(Figures in brackets for season records are games played; records for fewest points, wins, ties, losses, goals, goals against are for 70 or more games)

Most Points	117	1988-89 (80)
Most Wins	54	1988-89 (80)
Most Ties	19	1977-78 (80)
Most Losses	38	1972-73 (78)
Most Goals	397	1987-88 (80)
Most Goals Against	345	1981-82 (80)
Fewest Points	65	1972-73 (78)
Fewest Wins	25	1972-73 (78)
Fewest Ties	3	1986-87 (80)
Fewest Losses	17	1988-89 (80)
Fewest Goals	191	1972-73 (78)
Fewest Goals Against	226	1988-89 (80)

Longest Winning Streak
Overall .... 10 Oct. 14-
Nov. 3/78

Home .... 9 Oct. 17-
Nov. 15/78
Jan. 3-
Feb. 5/89
Mar. 3-
Apr. 1/90
Feb. 21-
Mar. 14/91

Away .... 7 Nov. 10-
Dec. 4/88

Longest Undefeated Streak
Over-all .... 13 Nov. 10-
Dec. 8/88
(12 wins, 1 tie)

Home .... 18 Dec. 29/90-
Mar. 14/91
(17 wins, 1 tie)

Away .... 9 Feb. 20-
Mar. 21/88
(6 wins, 3 ties)
Nov. 11-
Dec. 16/90
(6 wins, 3 ties)

Longest Losing Streak
Over-all .... 11 Dec. 14/85-
Jan. 7/86

Home .... 4 Seven times
Away .... 9 Dec. 1/85-
Jan. 12/86

Longest Winless Streak
Over-all .... 11 Dec. 14/85-
Jan. 7/86
(11 losses)
Jan. 5-26/93
(9 losses, 2 ties)

Home .... 6 Nov. 25-Dec. 18/82
(5 losses, 1 tie)

Away .... 13 Feb. 3-
Mar. 29/73
(10 losses, 3 ties)

Most Shutouts, Season 8 1974-75 (80)
Most PIM, Season 2,655 1991-92 (80)
Most Goals, Game .... 13 Feb. 10/93
(San Jose 1 at Calgary 13)

Individual

Most Seasons .... 10 Jim Peplinski, Al MacInnis
Most Games .... 728 Al MacInnis
Most Goals, Career ...... 257 Joe Nieuwendyk
Most Assists, Career ..... 555 Al MacInnis
Most Points, Career ..... 740 Al MacInnis
(185 goals, 555 assists)
Most PIM, Career ..... 2,405 Tim Hunter
Most Shutouts, Career ..... 20 Dan Bouchard
Longest Consecutive
Games Streak .... 257 Brad Marsh
(Oct. 11/78-
Nov. 10/81)
Most Goals, Season .... 66 Lanny McDonald
(1982-83)
Most Assists, Season ..... 82 Kent Nilsson
(1980-81)
Most Points, Season ...... 131 Kent Nilsson
(1980-81)
(49 goals, 82 assists)
Most PIM, Season .... 375 Tim Hunter
(1988-89)
Most Points, Defenseman
Season .... 103 Al MacInnis
(1990-91)
(28 goals, 75 assists)

Most Points, Center
Season .... 131 Kent Nilsson
(1980-81)
(49 goals, 82 assists)
Most Points, Right Wing
Season .... 110 Joe Mullen
(1988-89)
(51 goals, 59 assists)
Most Points, Left Wing
Season .... 90 Gary Roberts
(1991-92)
(53 goals, 37 assists)
Most Points, Rookie
Season .... 92 Joe Nieuwendyk
(1987-88)
(51 goals, 41 assists)
Most Shutouts, Season ..... 5 Dan Bouchard
(1973-74)
Phil Myre
(1974-75)
Most Goals, Game .... 5 Joe Nieuwendyk
(Jan. 11/89)
Most Assists, Game .... 6 Guy Chouinard
(Feb. 25/81)
Gary Suter
(Apr. 4/86)
Most Points, Game .... 7 Sergei Makarov
(Feb. 25/90)

All-time Record vs. Other Clubs

Regular Season

			At Home							On Road							Total				
	GP	W	L	T	GF	GA	PTS	GP	W	L	T	GF	GA	PTS	GP	W	L	T	GF	GA	PTS
Boston	37	15	20	2	141	137	32	38	10	23	5	104	132	25	75	25	43	7	245	269	57
Buffalo	37	13	14	10	134	128	36	37	12	21	4	113	154	28	74	25	35	14	247	282	64
Chicago	41	20	14	7	137	123	47	39	12	18	9	121	143	33	80	32	32	16	258	266	80
Detroit	38	23	10	5	173	122	51	37	12	19	6	123	145	30	75	35	29	11	296	267	81
Edmonton	51	26	19	6	239	193	58	51	16	27	8	183	220	40	102	42	46	14	422	413	98
Hartford	21	16	4	1	114	74	33	21	11	7	3	84	72	25	42	27	11	4	198	146	58
Los Angeles	67	42	17	8	327	257	92	66	25	35	6	245	265	56	133	67	52	14	572	492	148
Minnesota	40	26	4	10	169	107	62	40	16	19	5	132	150	37	80	42	23	15	301	257	99
Montreal	36	11	20	5	118	130	27	37	10	21	6	90	132	26	73	21	41	11	208	262	53
New Jersey	35	27	4	4	170	91	58	36	23	10	3	141	103	49	71	50	14	7	311	194	107
NY Islanders	42	18	13	11	152	133	47	42	10	23	9	112	172	29	84	28	36	20	264	305	76
NY Rangers	42	24	10	8	192	130	56	43	19	19	5	156	155	43	85	43	29	13	348	285	99
Ottawa	1	1	0	0	8	4	2	1	0	1	0	1	1	1	2	1	0	1	9	5	3
Philadelphia	44	22	13	9	182	148	53	43	11	30	2	116	179	24	87	33	43	11	298	327	77
Pittsburgh	37	21	9	7	158	111	49	37	10	18	9	123	137	29	74	31	27	16	281	248	78
Quebec	22	12	4	6	102	72	30	21	9	7	5	86	89	23	43	21	11	11	188	161	53
St. Louis	40	21	16	3	145	116	45	41	18	17	6	132	145	42	81	39	33	9	277	261	87
San Jose	7	5	2	0	42	18	10	9	8	1	0	38	25	16	16	13	3	0	80	43	26
Tampa Bay	1	1	0	0	3	2	2	2	1	1	0	9	10	2	3	2	1	0	12	12	4
Toronto	40	24	12	4	181	135	52	38	16	15	7	153	151	39	78	40	27	11	334	286	91
Vancouver	68	48	11	9	309	188	105	68	29	25	14	231	247	72	136	77	36	23	540	435	177
Washington	31	21	6	4	137	75	46	32	13	15	4	117	123	30	63	34	21	8	254	198	76
Winnipeg	49	32	10	7	235	156	71	48	18	22	8	176	202	44	97	50	32	15	411	358	115
Defunct Clubs	13	8	4	1	51	34	17	13	7	3	3	43	33	17	26	15	7	4	94	67	34
Totals	**840**	**477**	**236**	**127**	**3619**	**2654**	**1081**	**840**	**316**	**396**	**128**	**2829**	**3185**	**760**	**1680**	**793**	**632**	**255**	**6448**	**5839**	**1841**

Playoffs

	Series	W	L	GP	W	L	T	GF	GA	Last Mtg.	Round	Result
Chicago	2	2	0	8	7	1	0	30	17	1989	CF	W 4-1
Detroit	1	0	1	2	0	2	0	5	8	1978	PR	L 0-2
Edmonton	5	1	4	30	11	19	0	96	132	1991	DSF	L 3-4
Los Angeles	6	2	4	26	13	13	0	102	105	1993	DSF	L 2-4
Minnesota	1	0	1	6	2	4	0	18	25	1981	SF	L 2-4
Montreal	2	1	1	11	5	6	0	32	31	1989	F	W 4-2
NY Rangers	1	0	1	4	1	3	0	8	14	1980	PR	L 1-3
Philadelphia	2	1	1	11	4	7	0	28	43	1981	QF	W 4-3
St. Louis	1	1	0	7	4	3	0	28	22	1986	CF	W 4-3
Toronto	1	0	1	2	0	2	0	5	9	1979	PR	L 0-2
Vancouver	4	3	1	18	10	8	0	62	57	1989	DSF	W 4-3
Winnipeg	3	1	2	13	6	7	0	43	45	1987	DSF	L 2-4
Totals	**29**	**12**	**17**	**138**	**63**	**75**	**0**	**467**	**508**			

Playoff Results 1993-89

Year	Round	Opponent	Result	GF	GA
1993	DSF	Los Angeles	L 2-4	28	33
1991	DSF	Edmonton	L 3-4	20	22
1990	DSF	Los Angeles	L 2-4	24	29
1989	**F**	**Montreal**	**W 4-2**	**19**	**16**
	CF	Chicago	W 4-1	15	8
	DF	Los Angeles	W 4-0	22	11
	DSF	Vancouver	W 4-3	26	20

Abbreviations: Round: F – Final;
CF – conference final; **DF** – division final;
DSF – division semi-final; **SF** – semi-final;
QF – quarter-final; **PR** – preliminary round.
GA – goals against; **GF** – goals for.

1992-93 Results

		Home				Away	
Oct.	6	Los Angeles	4-5	Oct.	13	Minnesota	4-3
	8	Edmonton	7-2		15	Los Angeles	0-4
	10	Toronto	3-2		17	San Jose	6-2
	20	Los Angeles	6-2		25	Edmonton	4-0
	22	Boston	2-4		28	Winnipeg	7-5
	30	Washington	1-3	Nov.	4	Vancouver	5-5
	31	Minnesota	5-3		8	Quebec*	5-5
Nov.	2	Vancouver	5-3		11	Montreal	2-5
	5	Ottawa	8-4		11	Hartford	4-3
	19	Vancouver	4-3		12	Boston	3-5
	21	NY Islanders	3-4		14	Tampa Bay	5-3
	25	San Jose	3-4	Dec.	8	Edmonton	1-3
	27	Tampa Bay	3-2		11	Toronto	6-3
	28	Chicago	2-5		12	Ottawa	1-1
Dec.	2	Winnipeg	3-3		14	Detroit	3-0
	4	St. Louis	5-3		15	NY Rangers	3-0
	7	Edmonton	6-3		23	Winnipeg	4-3
	19	Los Angeles	5-3		27	Edmonton	7-3
	21	Edmonton	3-2	Jan.	7	St. Louis	2-3
	31	Montreal	2-3		9	Pittsburgh*	2-3
Jan.	2	Philadelphia	7-3		10	Buffalo	3-5
	5	Winnipeg	2-4		12	NY Islanders	2-8
	19	Buffalo	2-3		14	Philadelphia	4-4
	22	Winnipeg	4-4		16	Minnesota	3-4
	23	Pittsburgh	3-4		28	Los Angeles	2-1
	26	Detroit	1-9		30	San Jose	5-4
Feb.	10	San Jose	13-1	Feb.	2	Washington	6-4
	12	Quebec	4-4		3	New Jersey	5-4
	13	Hartford	4-4		17	Toronto	2-4
	16	Philadelphia	4-4		19	Detroit	3-3
	26	NY Rangers	4-4		21	Chicago*	3-4
	27	San Jose	5-4		23	San Jose	6-3
Mar.	11	Detroit	6-3	Mar.	2	Los Angeles	2-6
	13	New Jersey	4-3		4	St. Louis	1-2
	14	Vancouver	3-2		6	Tampa Bay	4-7
	16	Chicago	0-1		21	Winnipeg*	2-4
	24	St. Louis	2-4		29	Vancouver	3-1
	28	Toronto	0-4	Apr.	3	San Jose*	3-2
	30	Winnipeg	4-5		4	San Jose	4-3
Apr.	1	Minnesota	5-3		6	Los Angeles	3-3
	9	Vancouver	8-1		11	Vancouver*	3-6
	15	San Jose	7-3		13	Edmonton	4-2

*Denotes afternoon game

Entry Draft Selections 1993-79

1993

Pick	
18	Jesper Mattsson
44	Jamie Allison
70	Dan Tompkins
95	Jason Smith
96	Marty Murray
121	Darryl Lafrance
122	John Emmons
148	Andreas Karlsson
200	Derek Sylvester
252	German Titov
278	Burke Murphy

1992

Pick	
6	Cory Stillman
30	Chris O'Sullivan
54	Mathias Johansson
78	Robert Svehla
102	Sami Helenius
126	Ravil Yakubov
129	Joel Bouchard
150	Pavel Rajnoha
174	Ryan Mulhern
198	Brandon Carper
222	Jonas Hoglund
246	Andrei Potaichuk

1991

Pick	
19	Niklas Sundblad
41	Francois Groleau
52	Sandy McCarthy
63	Brian Caruso
85	Steven Magnusson
107	Jerome Butler
129	Bobby Marshall
140	Matt Hoffman
151	Kelly Harper
173	David St. Pierre
195	David Struch
217	Sergei Zolotov
239	Marko Jantunen
261	Andrei Trefilov

1990

Pick	
11	Trevor Kidd
26	Nicolas P. Perreault
32	Vesa Viitakoski
41	Etienne Belzile
62	Glen Mears
83	Paul Kruse
125	Chris Tschupp
146	Dmitri Frolov
167	Shawn Murray
188	Mike Murray
209	Rob Sumner
230	invalid claim
251	Leo Gudas

1989

Pick	
24	Kent Manderville
42	Ted Drury
50	Veli-Pekka Kautonen
63	Corey Lyons
70	Robert Reichel
84	Ryan O'Leary
105	F. (Toby) Kearney
147	Alex Nikolic
168	Kevin Wortman
189	Sergei Gomolyako
210	Dan Sawyer
231	Alexander Yudin
252	Kenneth Kennholt

1988

Pick	
21	Jason Muzzatti
42	Todd Harkins
84	Gary Socha
85	Thomas Forslund
90	Scott Matusovich
126	Jonas Bergqvist
147	Stefan Nilsson
168	Troy Kennedy
189	Brett Peterson
210	Guy Darveau
231	Dave Tretowicz
252	Sergei Priakhan

1987

Pick	
19	Bryan Deasley
25	Stephane Matteau
40	Kevin Grant
61	Scott Mahoney
70	Tim Harris
103	Tim Corkery
124	Joe Aloi
145	Peter Ciavaglia
166	Theoren Fleury
187	Mark Osiecki
208	William Sedergren
229	Peter Hasselblad
250	Magnus Svensson

1986

Pick	
16	George Pelawa
37	Brian Glynn
79	Tom Quinlan
100	Scott Bloom
121	John Parker
142	Rick Lessard
163	Mark Olsen
184	Warren Sharples
205	Doug Pickell
226	Anders Lindstrom
247	Antonin Stavjana

1985

Pick	
17	Chris Biotti
27	Joe Nieuwendyk
38	Jeff Wenaas
59	Lane MacDonald
80	Roger Johansson
101	Esa Keskinen
122	Tim Sweeney
143	Stu Grimson
164	Nate Smith
185	Darryl Olsen
206	Peter Romberg
227	Alexander Kozhevnikov
248	Bill Gregoire

1984

Pick	
12	Gary Roberts
33	Ken Sabourin
38	Paul Ranheim
75	Petr Rosol
96	Joel Paunio
117	Brett Hull
138	Kevan Melrose
159	Jiri Hrdina
180	Gary Suter
200	Petr Rucka
221	Stefan Jonsson
241	Rudolf Suchanek

1983

Pick	
13	Dan Quinn
51	Brian Bradley
55	Perry Berezan
66	John Bekkers
71	Kevan Guy
77	Bill Claviter
91	Igor Liba
111	Grant Blair
131	Jeff Hogg
151	Chris MacDonald
171	Rob Kivell
191	Tom Pratt
211	Jaroslav Benak
231	Sergei Makarov

1982

Pick	
29	Dave Reierson
37	Richard Kromm
51	Jim Laing
65	Dave Meszaros
72	Mark Lamb
93	Lou Kiriakou
114	Jeff Vaive
118	Mats Kihlstrom
135	Brad Ramsden
156	Roy Myllari
177	Ted Pearson
198	Jim Uens
219	Rick Erdall
240	Dale Thompson

1981

Pick	
15	Allan MacInnis
56	Mike Vernon
78	Peter Madach
99	Mario Simioni
120	Todd Hooey
141	Rick Heppner
162	Dale Degray
183	George Boudreau
204	Bruce Eakin

1980

Pick	
13	Denis Cyr
31	Tony Curtale
32	Kevin LaVallee
39	Steve Konroyd
76	Marc Roy
97	Randy Turnbull
118	John Multan
139	Dave Newsom
160	Claude Drouin
181	Hakan Loob
202	Steve Fletcher

1979

Pick	
12	Paul Reinhart
23	Mike Perovich
33	Pat Riggin
54	Tim Hunter
75	Jim Peplinski
96	Brad Kempthorne
117	Glenn Johnson

Club Directory

Olympic Saddledome
P.O. Box 1540 Station M
Calgary, Alberta T2P 3B9
Phone **403/261-0475**
FAX 403/261-0470
Capacity: 20,230

Owners Harley N. Hotchkiss, Norman L. Kwong, Sonia Scurfield, Byron J. Seaman, Daryl K. Seaman

Management
President / Alternate Governor . . . . . W.C. (Bill) Hay
Vice-President, General Manager . . . . . Doug Risebrough
Vice-President, Business and Finance . . . . . Clare Rhyasen
Vice-President, Marketing . . . . . Lanny McDonald
Vice-President, Broadcasting . . . . . Leo Ornest

Hockey Club Personnel
Director of Hockey Operations . . . . . Al MacNeil
Assistant General Manager . . . . . Al Coates
Head Coach . . . . . Dave King
Assistant Coaches . . . . . Guy Charron, Jamie Hislop, Slavomir Lener
Goaltending Consultant . . . . . Glenn Hall
St. John Head Coach . . . . . Bob Francis
St. John Assistant Coach . . . . . Rick Carriere
Scouts . . . . . Ray Clearwater, Jiri Hrdina, Guy Lapointe, Ian McKenzie
Director of Pro Scouting . . . . . Nick Polano
Scouting Staff . . . . . Ron Ferguson, Glen Giovanucci, Larry Popein, Tom Thompson, Ernie Vargas, Paul McIntosh, Jarmo Tolvanen
Secretary to President and Finance . . . . . Yvette Mutcheson
Secretary to General Manager . . . . . June Yeates
Secretary to Head Coach and Hockey Operations . . . . . Brenda Koyich

Administration
Controller . . . . . Lynne Tosh
Assistant Controller . . . . . Dorothy Stuart
Accounting Clerk . . . . . Lynn Horton
Receptionist . . . . . Karla Piper

Marketing
Manager, Marketing and Special Events . . . . . TBA
Manager, Publications and Advertising . . . . . Pat Halls
Assistant, VP Marketing . . . . . Judy Shupe
Retail Stores Manager . . . . . Mark Mason
Retail Operations Assistants . . . . . Mike Vacey, Linda Carrigan

Public Relations
Director of Public Relations . . . . . Rick Skaggs
Assistant Public Relations Director . . . . . Mike Burke
Secretary to Public Relations and Broadcasting . . Bernie Doenz

Ticketing
Ticket Manager . . . . . Ann-Marie Malarchuk
Assistant Ticket Manager . . . . . Linda Forrest

Medical/Training Staff
Head Trainer . . . . . Jim (Bearcat) Murray
Physiotherapist and Fitness Coordinator . . . . . James Gattinger
Equipment Manager . . . . . Bobby Stewart
Director of Medicine . . . . . Dr. Terry Groves
Orthopedic Surgeon . . . . . Dr. Lowell Van Zuiden
Team Dentist . . . . . Dr. Bill Blair

Facility
Home Ice . . . . . Olympic Saddledome
Capacity 20,230
Location of Press Boxes . . . . . Print – north side, Radio – south side, TV – concourse
Dimensions of Rink . . . . . 200 feet by 85 feet

Broadcast Stations
Radio . . . . . 66 CFR Radio (660 AM)
Television . . . . . Channels 2 & 7

General Manager

RISEBROUGH, DOUG
General Manager, Calgary Flames. Born in Guelph, Ont., January 29, 1954.

Doug Risebrough enters his third full NHL season as general manager of the Calgary Flames. After ending his 14-year NHL playing career with the Flames in 1987, Risebrough was named an assistant coach with Calgary and joined Terry Crisp behind the bench. Risebrough was appointed head coach of the Flames on May 18, 1990 and on May 16, 1991, he also assumed the role of general manager. Late in the 1991-92 campaign he handed the coaching responsibilities over to Guy Charron for the balance of the season.

During his first season as an NHL head coach, Risebrough led the Flames to a fourth place overall finish in the NHL standings. Risebrough was Montreal's first selection, seventh overall, in the 1974 Amateur Draft. During his nine years with the Canadiens, he helped his club to four consecutive Stanley Cup championships between 1976 and 1979. He joined the Flames just prior to the start of the club's 1982 training camp. During his NHL career, his clubs have won five Stanley Cups (1976-1979 and 1989 with Calgary) and two Presidents' Trophies (1987-88 and 1988-89).

NHL Coaching Record

		Regular Season					Playoffs			
Season	Team	Games	W	L	T	%	Games	W	L	%
1990-91	Calgary	80	46	26	8	.625	7	3	4	.429
1991-92	Calgary	64	25	30	9	.461	....	....	....	....
	NHL Totals	**144**	**71**	**56**	**17**	**.522**	**7**	**3**	**4**	**.429**

Coach

KING, DAVE
Coach, Calgary Flames. Born in Saskatoon, Sask., December 22, 1947.

Dave King, who is entering his 22nd season as a coach, brings a wealth of experience to the Calgary Flames' organization. Long respected for his outstanding contribution to the Canadian National Team program, King started his coaching career with the University of Saskatchewan in 1972-73, eventually moving on to the WHL before returning to Saskatchewan and leading the Huskies to the CIAU title in 1983. King first attracted nation-wide attention when he led the Canadian National Junior Team to the gold medal at the 1982 World Junior Championships. Since that time, he has directed the National and Olympic Teams in both the World Championships and the Olympics. Under his Guidance, Canada captured the silver medal at the 1992 Games, the country's first Olympic hockey medal since 1968.

Coaching Record

		Regular Season or World Championships					Playoffs or Olympics				
Year	Team	Games	W	L	T	%	Games	W	L	T	%
1984	Canadian National	....	....	....	....	....	7	4	3	0	.571
1987	Canadian National	10	3	5	2	.400	....	....	....	....	....
1988	Canadian National	....	....	....	....	....	8	5	2	1	.688
1989	Canadian National	10	7	3	0	.700	....	....	....	....	....
1990	Canadian National	10	6	3	1	.650	....	....	....	....	....
1991	Canadian National	10	5	2	3	.650	....	....	....	....	....
1992	Canadian National	6	2	3	1	.417	8	6	2	0	.750
1992-93	**Calgary (NHL)**	**84**	**43**	**30**	**11**	**.577**	**6**	**2**	**4**	**0**	**.333**
	NHL Totals	**84**	**43**	**30**	**11**	**.577**	**6**	**2**	**4**	**0**	**.333**

Chicago Blackhawks

1992-93 Results: 47W-25L-12T 106PTS. First, Norris Division

Schedule

Home				Away			
Oct.	Wed.	6	Florida	Oct.	Sat.	9	Toronto
	Sun.	10	Winnipeg		Tues.	12	Dallas
	Thur.	14	Hartford		Sat.	16	Winnipeg
	Mon.	18	Dallas		Sat.	30	Pittsburgh
	Thur.	21	Quebec	Nov.	Sat.	13	Toronto
	Sat.	23	Detroit		Thur.	18	Florida
	Tues.	26	St Louis		Sat.	20	Tampa Bay
	Thur.	28	Toronto		Wed.	24	Edmonton
	Sun.	31	Philadelphia		Fri.	26	Calgary
Nov.	Thur.	4	NY Islanders		Mon.	29	Vancouver
	Sun.	7	Edmonton	Dec.	Sat.	4	New Jersey
	Thur.	11	Pittsburgh		Tues.	7	St Louis
	Sun.	14	Dallas		Sat.	11	Boston
Dec.	Sun.	12	San Jose		Wed.	15	Dallas
	Sun.	19	Anaheim		Sat.	18	Philadelphia*
	Thur.	23	San Jose		Tues.	21	Detroit
	Mon.	27	Toronto		Sun.	26	St Louis
	Fri.	31	Dallas		Wed.	29	Winnipeg
Jan.	Sun.	2	Winnipeg	Jan.	Tues.	4	Dallas
	Thur.	6	Anaheim		Sat.	8	Washington*
	Sun.	9	Edmonton		Sat.	15	NY Islanders
	Tues.	11	Buffalo		Tues.	25	Detroit
	Thur.	13	Tampa Bay		Mon.	31	Ottawa
	Sun.	16	NY Rangers	Feb.	Wed.	2	Vancouver
	Thur.	27	Detroit		Fri.	4	Edmonton
	Sat.	29	Ottawa		Sun.	6	Anaheim*
Feb.	Thur.	17	Vancouver		Tues.	8	San Jose
	Sun.	20	New Jersey*		(at Sacramento)		
	Thur.	24	Winnipeg		Wed.	9	Los Angeles
	Sun.	27	Boston*		Fri.	11	San Jose
Mar.	Thur.	3	Calgary		Sun.	13	San Jose*
	Sun.	6	Los Angeles*		Mon.	14	Calgary
	Tues.	8	Anaheim		Fri.	18	Winnipeg
	(at Phoenix)				Fri.	25	Buffalo
	Sun.	13	Vancouver*	Mar.	Wed.	9	Los Angeles
	Sun.	20	St Louis*		Fri.	11	Anaheim
	Thur.	24	Montreal		Mon.	14	Quebec
	Sun.	27	Detroit*		Wed.	16	Montreal
	Thur.	31	Washington		Fri.	18	NY Rangers
Apr.	Sun.	3	Calgary		Tues.	22	Detroit
	Fri.	8	St Louis		Wed.	30	Hartford
	Sun.	10	Los Angeles*	Apr.	Tues.	5	St Louis
	Thur.	14	Toronto		Tues.	12	Toronto

* Denotes afternoon game.

Home Starting Times:

All games .... 7:35 p.m.
Except Matinees .... 1:35 p.m.

Franchise date: September 25, 1926

CENTRAL DIVISION

WESTERN CONFERENCE

68th NHL Season

Year-by-Year Record

		Home			Road			Overall							
Season	GP	W	L	T	W	L	T	W	L	T	GF	GA	Pts.	Finished	Playoff Result
1992-93	84	25	11	6	22	14	6	47	25	12	279	230	106	1st, Norris Div.	Lost Div. Semi-Final
1991-92	80	23	9	8	13	20	7	36	29	15	257	236	87	2nd, Norris Div.	Lost Final
1990-91	80	28	8	4	21	15	4	49	23	8	284	211	106	1st, Norris Div.	Lost Div. Semi-Final
1989-90	80	25	13	2	16	20	4	41	33	6	316	294	88	1st, Norris Div.	Lost Conf. Championship
1988-89	80	16	14	10	11	27	2	27	41	12	297	335	66	4th, Norris Div.	Lost Conf. Championship
1987-88	80	21	17	2	9	24	7	30	41	9	284	326	69	3rd, Norris Div.	Lost Div. Semi-Final
1986-87	80	18	13	9	11	24	5	29	37	14	290	310	72	3rd, Norris Div.	Lost Div. Semi-Final
1985-86	80	23	12	5	16	21	3	39	33	8	351	349	86	1st, Norris Div.	Lost Div. Semi-Final
1984-85	80	22	16	2	16	19	5	38	35	7	309	299	83	2nd, Norris Div.	Lost Conf. Championship
1983-84	80	25	13	2	5	29	6	30	42	8	277	311	68	4th, Norris Div.	Lost Div. Semi-Final
1982-83	80	29	8	3	18	15	7	47	23	10	338	268	104	1st, Norris Div.	Lost Conf. Championship
1981-82	80	20	13	7	10	25	5	30	38	12	332	363	72	4th, Norris Div.	Lost Conf. Championship
1980-81	80	21	11	8	10	22	8	31	33	16	304	315	78	2nd, Smythe Div.	Lost Prelim. Round
1979-80	80	21	12	7	13	15	12	34	27	19	241	250	87	1st, Smythe Div.	Lost Quarter-Final
1978-79	80	18	12	10	11	24	5	29	36	15	244	277	73	1st, Smythe Div.	Lost Quarter-Final
1977-78	80	20	9	11	12	20	8	32	29	19	230	220	83	1st, Smythe Div.	Lost Quarter-Final
1976-77	80	19	16	5	7	27	6	26	43	11	240	298	63	3rd, Smythe Div.	Lost Prelim. Round
1975-76	80	17	15	8	15	15	10	32	30	18	254	261	82	1st, Smythe Div.	Lost Quarter-Final
1974-75	80	24	12	4	13	23	4	37	35	8	268	241	82	3rd, Smythe Div.	Lost Quarter-Final
1973-74	78	20	6	13	21	8	10	41	14	23	272	164	105	2nd, West Div.	Lost Semi-Final
1972-73	78	26	9	4	16	18	5	42	27	9	284	225	93	1st, West Div.	Lost Final
1971-72	78	28	3	8	18	14	7	46	17	15	256	166	107	1st, West Div.	Lost Semi-Final
1970-71	78	30	6	3	19	14	6	49	20	9	277	184	107	1st, West Div.	Lost Final
1969-70	76	26	7	5	19	15	4	45	22	9	250	170	99	1st, East Div.	Lost Semi-Final
1968-69	76	20	14	4	14	19	5	34	33	9	280	246	77	6th, East Div.	Out of Playoffs
1967-68	74	20	13	4	12	13	12	32	26	16	212	222	80	4th, East Div.	Lost Semi-Final
1966-67	70	24	5	6	17	12	6	41	17	12	264	170	94	1st,	Lost Semi-Final
1965-66	70	21	8	6	16	17	2	37	25	8	240	187	82	2nd,	Lost Semi-Final
1964-65	70	20	13	2	14	15	6	34	28	8	224	176	76	3rd,	Lost Final
1963-64	70	26	4	5	10	18	7	36	22	12	218	169	84	2nd,	Lost Semi-Final
1962-63	70	17	9	9	15	12	8	32	21	17	194	178	81	2nd,	Lost Semi-Final
1961-62	70	20	10	5	11	16	8	31	26	13	217	186	75	3rd,	Lost Final
1960-61	**70**	20	6	9	9	18	8	**29**	**24**	**17**	**198**	**180**	**75**	**3rd,**	**Won Stanley Cup**
1959-60	70	18	11	6	10	18	7	28	29	13	191	180	69	3rd,	Lost Semi-Final
1958-59	70	14	12	9	14	17	4	28	29	13	197	208	69	3rd,	Lost Semi-Final
1957-58	70	15	17	3	9	22	4	24	39	7	163	202	55	5th,	Out of Playoffs
1956-57	70	12	15	8	4	24	7	16	39	15	169	225	47	6th,	Out of Playoffs
1955-56	70	9	19	7	10	20	5	19	39	12	155	216	50	6th,	Out of Playoffs
1954-55	70	6	21	8	7	19	9	13	40	17	161	235	43	6th,	Out of Playoffs
1953-54	70	8	21	6	4	30	1	12	51	7	133	242	31	6th,	Out of Playoffs
1952-53	70	14	11	10	13	17	5	27	28	15	169	175	69	4th,	Lost Semi-Final
1951-52	70	9	19	7	8	25	2	17	44	9	158	241	43	6th,	Out of Playoffs
1950-51	70	8	22	5	5	25	5	13	47	10	171	280	36	6th,	Out of Playoffs
1949-50	70	13	18	4	9	20	6	22	38	10	203	244	54	6th,	Out of Playoffs
1948-49	60	13	12	5	8	19	3	21	31	8	173	211	50	5th,	Out of Playoffs
1947-48	60	10	17	3	10	17	3	20	34	6	195	225	46	6th,	Out of Playoffs
1946-47	60	10	17	3	9	20	1	19	37	4	193	274	42	6th,	Out of Playoffs
1945-46	50	15	5	5	8	15	2	23	20	7	200	178	53	3rd,	Lost Semi-Final
1944-45	50	9	14	2	4	16	5	13	30	7	141	194	33	5th,	Out of Playoffs
1943-44	50	15	6	4	7	17	1	22	23	5	178	187	49	4th,	Lost Final
1942-43	50	14	3	8	3	15	7	17	18	15	179	180	49	5th,	Out of Playoffs
1941-42	48	15	8	1	7	15	2	22	23	3	145	155	47	4th,	Lost Quarter-Final
1940-41	48	11	10	3	5	15	4	16	25	7	112	139	39	5th,	Lost Semi-Final
1939-40	48	15	7	2	8	12	4	23	19	6	112	120	52	4th,	Lost Quarter-Final
1938-39	48	5	13	6	7	15	2	12	28	8	91	132	32	7th,	Out of Playoffs
1937-38	**48**	10	10	4	4	15	5	**14**	**25**	**9**	**97**	**139**	**37**	**3rd, Amn. Div.**	**Won Stanley Cup**
1936-37	48	8	13	3	6	14	4	14	27	7	99	131	35	4th, Amn. Div.	Out of Playoffs
1935-36	48	15	7	2	6	12	6	21	19	8	93	92	50	3rd, Amn. Div.	Lost Quarter-Final
1934-35	48	12	9	3	14	8	2	26	17	5	118	88	57	2nd, Amn. Div.	Lost Quarter-Final
1933-34	**48**	13	4	7	7	13	4	**20**	**17**	**11**	**88**	**83**	**51**	**2nd, Amn. Div.**	**Won Stanley Cup**
1932-33	48	12	7	5	4	13	7	16	20	12	88	101	44	4th, Amn. Div.	Out of Playoffs
1931-32	48	13	5	6	5	14	5	18	19	11	86	101	47	2nd, Amn. Div.	Lost Quarter-Final
1930-31	44	14	7	1	10	10	2	24	17	3	108	78	51	2nd, Amn. Div.	Lost Final
1929-30	44	12	9	1	9	9	4	21	18	5	117	111	47	2nd, Amn. Div.	Lost Quarter-Final
1928-29	44	3	13	6	4	16	2	7	29	8	33	85	22	5th, Amn. Div.	Out of Playoffs
1927-28	44	2	18	2	5	16	1	7	34	3	68	134	17	5th, Amn. Div.	Out of Playoffs
1926-27	44	12	8	2	7	14	1	19	22	3	115	116	41	3rd, Amn. Div.	Lost Quarter-Final

Coaching History

Pete Muldoon, 1926-27; Barney Stanley and Hugh Lehman, 1927-28; Herb Gardiner, 1928-29; Tom Shaughnessy and Bill Tobin, 1929-30; Dick Irvin, 1930-31; Dick Irvin and Bill Tobin, 1931-32; Godfrey Matheson, Emil Iverson and Tommy Gorman, 1932-33; Tommy Gorman, 1933-34; Clem Loughlin, 1934-35 to 1936-37; Bill Stewart, 1937-38; Bill Stewart and Paul Thompson, 1938-39; Paul Thompson, 1939-40 to 1943-44; Paul Thompson and Johnny Gottselig, 1944-45; Johnny Gottselig, 1945-46 to 1946-47; Johnny Gottselig and Charlie Conacher, 1947-48; Charlie Conacher, 1948-49 to 1949-50; Ebbie Goodfellow, 1950-51 to 1951-52; Sid Abel, 1952-53 to 1953-54; Frank Eddolls, 1954-55; Dick Irvin, 1955-56; Tommy Ivan, 1956-57; Tommy Ivan and Rudy Pilous, 1957-58; Rudy Pilous, 1958-59 to 1962-63; Billy Reay, 1963-64 to 1975-76; Billy Reay and Bill White, 1976-77; Bob Pulford, 1977-78 to 1978-79; Eddie Johnston, 1979-80; Keith Magnuson, 1980-81; Keith Magnuson and Bob Pulford, 1981-82; Orval Tessier, 1982-83 to 1983-84; Orval Tessier and Bob Pulford, 1984-85; Bob Pulford, 1985-86 to 1986-87; Bob Murdoch, 1987-88; Mike Keenan, 1988-89 to 1991-92; Darryl Sutter, 1992-93 to date.

Captains' History

Dick Irvin, 1926-27 to 1928-29; Duke Dutkowski, 1929-30; Ty Arbour, 1930-31 Cy Wentworth, 1931-32; Helge Bostrom, 1932-33; Chuck Gardiner, 1933-34; no captain, 1934-35; Johnny Gottselig, 1935-36 to 1939-40; Earl Seibert, 1940-41, 1941-42; Doug Bentley, 1942-43, 1943-44; Clint Smith 1944-45; John Mariucci, 1945-46; Red Hamill, 1946-47; John Mariucci, 1947-48; Gaye Stewart, 1948-49; Doug Bentley, 1949-50; Jack Stewart, 1950-51, 1951-52; Bill Gadsby, 1952-53, 1953-54; Gus Mortson, 1954-55 to 1956-57; no captain, 1957-58; Eddie Litzenberger, 1958-59 to 1960-61; Pierre Pilote, 1961-62 to 1967-68, no captain, 1968-69; Pat Stapleton, 1969-70; no captain, 1970-71 to 1974-75; Stan Mikita, Pit Martin, 1975-76; Stan Mikita, Pit Martin, Keith Magnuson, 1976-77; Keith Magnuson, 1977-78, 1978-79; Keith Magnuson, Terry Ruskowski, 1979-80; Terry Ruskowski, 1980-81, 1981-82; Darryl Sutter, 1982-83 to 1986-87; Keith Brown, Troy Murray, Denis Savard, 1987-88; Dirk Graham, 1988-89 to date.

1993-94 Player Personnel

FORWARDS	HT	WT	S	Place of Birth	Date	1992-93 Club
ANDRIYEVSKI, Alexander	6-5	211	R	Minsk, USSR	8/10/68	Indianapolis-Chicago
BELANGER, Hugo	6-1	190	L	St. Herbert, Que.	5/28/70	Clarkson U.
BOYER, Zac	6-1	185	R	Inuvik, N.W.T.	10/25/71	Indianapolis
BYRAM, Shawn	6-2	204	L	Neepawa, Man.	9/12/68	Indianapolis
CHRISTIAN, Dave	5-11	195	R	Warroad, MN	5/12/59	Chicago
CONN, Rob	6-2	200	R	Calgary, Alta.	9/3/68	Indianapolis
CROWLEY, Joe	6-2	195	L	Concord, MA	2/29/72	Indianapolis
DUBINSKY, Steve	6-0	190	L	Montreal, Que.	7/9/70	Clarkson U.
ELVENES, Stefan	6-1	183	L	Lund, Sweden	3/30/70	Rogle
GOULET, Michel	6-1	195	L	Peribonka, Que.	4/21/60	Chicago
GRAHAM, Dirk	5-11	190	R	Regina, Sask.	7/29/59	Chicago
GROSSI, Dino	6-0	195	R	Toronto, Ont.	6/25/70	Northeastern
HORACEK, Tony	6-4	215	L	Vancouver, B.C.	2/3/67	Indianapolis
HOUSE, Bobby	6-1	200	R	Whitehorse, Yukon	1/7/73	Brandon
HYMOVITZ, David	5-11	170	L	Boston, MA	5/30/74	Thayer Acad.
KIRTON, Scott	6-4	215	R	Penetanguishene, Ont.	10/4/71	U.N. Dakota
KLIMOVICH, Sergei	6-2	189	R	Novosibirsk, USSR	3/8/74	Dynamo Moscow
KRIVAKRASOV, Sergei	5-11	175	L	Angarsk, USSR	4/15/74	Indianapolis
LARMER, Steve	5-10	189	L	Peterborough, Ont.	6/16/61	Chicago
LeCOMPTE, Eric	6-4	190	L	Montreal, Que.	4/4/75	Hull
LEMIEUX, Jocelyn	5-10	200	L	Mont-Laurier, Que.	11/18/67	Chicago
MacINTYRE, Andy	6-1	190	L	Thunder Bay, Ont.	4/16/74	Saskatoon
MANLOW, Eric	6-0	190	L	Belleville, Ont.	4/7/75	Kitchener-Saskatoon
MATTEAU, Stephane	6-3	195	L	Rouyn Noranda, Que.	9/2/69	Chicago
MURPHY, Joe	6-1	190	L	London, Ont.	10/16/67	Chicago
MURRAY, Troy	5-11	195	R	Calgary, Alta.	7/31/62	Winnipeg-Chicago
NOONAN, Brian	6-1	180	R	Boston, MA	5/29/65	Chicago
PETERSON, Erik	6-0	185	L	Boston, MA	4/31/72	Providence
PETROV, Sergei	5-11	185	L	St. Petersburg, CIS	1/22/75	Cloquet
POMICHTER, Mike	6-2	200	L	New Haven, CT	9/10/73	Boston U.
PROKOPEC, Mike	6-1	175	R	Toronto, Ont.	5/17/74	Guelph
PULLOLA, Tommi	6-5	202	L	Vaasa, Finland	5/18/71	Lukko
ROENICK, Jeremy	6-0	170	R	Boston, MA	1/17/70	Chicago
ROLAND, Layne	6-1	215	R	Vernon, B.C.	2/6/74	Portland
RUUTTU, Christian	5-11	194	L	Lappeenranta, Finland	2/20/64	Chicago
SANDSTROM, Ulf	5-11	180	L	Fagerstad, Sweden	4/24/67	Lulea
SHANTZ, Jeff	6-0	184	R	Duchess, Alta.	10/10/73	Regina
St. JACQUES, Kevin	5-11	190	R	Edmonton, Alta.	2/25/71	Indianapolis
STICKNEY, Brett	6-5	205	L	Hanover, NH	5/26/72	Boston Coll.
SUTTER, Brent	5-11	180	R	Viking, Alta.	6/10/62	Chicago
TOPOROWSKI, Kerry	6-2	212	R	Prince Albert, Sask.	4/9/71	Indianapolis
TUCKER, Chris	5-11	183	L	White Plains, NY	2/9/72	U. of Wisconsin

DEFENSEMEN						
BALKOVEC, Maco	6-2	190	L	N. Westminster, B.C.	1/17/71	U. Wisconsin
BENNETT, Adam	6-4	206	R	Georgetown, Ont.	3/30/71	Indianapolis-Chicago
BROWN, Keith	6-1	195	R	Cornerbrook, Nfld.	5/6/60	Chicago
CHELIOS, Chris	6-1	192	R	Chicago, IL	1/25/62	Chicago
DROPPA, Ivan	6-3	209	L	Czechoslovakia	2/1/72	Indianapolis
DYKHUIS, Karl	6-3	200	L	Sept-Iles, Que.	7/8/72	Indianapolis-Chicago
HAKSTOL, Dave	6-1	200	R	Warberg, Alta.	7/30/68	Indianapolis
HOGAN, Tim	6-2	180	L	Oshawa, Ont.	1/7/74	U. Michigan
KELLOGG, Bob	6-4	210	L	Springfield, MA	2/16/71	Northeastern
KUCERA, Frantisek	6-2	205	R	Prague, Czech.	2/3/68	Chicago
LARKIN, Mike	6-1	180	L	Boston, MA	3/15/73	U. Vermont
MacDONALD, Scott	6-3	202	R	Brockton, MA	9/13/72	U. Vermont
MARCHMENT, Bryan	6-1	198	L	Scarborough, Ont.	5/1/69	Chicago
MUNI, Craig	6-3	200	L	Toronto, Ont.	7/19/62	Edmonton-Chicago
RAYMOND, Richard	6-1	187	R	Sudbury, Ont.	4/4/74	Kingston
RUSSELL, Cam	6-4	175	L	Halifax, N.S.	1/12/69	Chicago
SKRYPEC, Gerry	5-11	186	L	Kitchener, Ont.	6/21/74	Newmarket
SMITH, Steve	6-4	215	L	Glasgow, Scotland	4/30/63	Chicago
SPEER, Michael	6-2	202	L	Toronto, Ont.	3/26/71	Indianapolis
WILKINSON, Neil	6-3	190	R	Selkirk, Man.	8/15/67	San Jose

GOALTENDERS	HT	WT	C	Place of Birth	Date	1992-93 Club
BELFOUR, Ed	5-11	182	L	Carman, Man.	4/21/65	Chicago
HACKETT, Jeff	6-0	185	L	London, Ont.	6/1/68	San Jose
LeBLANC, Ray	5-10	170	R	Fitchburg, MA	10/24/64	Indianapolis
ROGLES, Chris	5-11	175	L	St. Louis, MO	1/22/69	Clarkson
SOUCY, Christian	5-11	160	L	Gatineau, Que.	9/14/70	Vermont

1992-93 Scoring

Regular Season

Pos	#	Player	Team	GP	G	A	Pts	+/-	PIM	PP	SH	GW	GT	S	%
C	27	Jeremy Roenick	CHI	84	50	57	107	15	86	22	3	3	3	255	19.6
D	7	Chris Chelios	CHI	84	15	58	73	14	282	8	0	2	0	290	5.2
R	28	Steve Larmer	CHI	84	35	35	70	23	48	14	4	6	1	228	15.4
D	5	Steve Smith	CHI	78	10	47	57	12	214	7	1	2	0	212	4.7
C	12	Brent Sutter	CHI	65	20	34	54	10	67	8	2	3	0	151	13.2
C	22	Christian Ruuttu	CHI	84	17	37	54	14	134	3	1	6	0	187	9.1
L	16	Michel Goulet	CHI	63	23	21	44	10	43	10	0	5	0	125	18.4
R	33	Dirk Graham	CHI	84	20	17	37	0	139	1	2	5	1	187	10.7
L	32	Stephane Matteau	CHI	79	15	18	33	6	98	2	0	4	0	95	15.8
L	14	Greg Gilbert	CHI	77	13	19	32	5	57	0	1	2	0	72	18.1
L	26	Jocelyn Lemieux	CHI	81	10	21	31	5	111	1	0	2	1	117	8.5
R	10	Brian Noonan	CHI	63	16	14	30	3	82	5	0	3	0	129	12.4
D	2	Bryan Marchment	CHI	78	5	15	20	15	313	1	0	1	0	75	6.7
D	6	Frantisek Kucera	CHI	71	5	14	19	7	59	1	0	1	0	117	4.3
R	25	Dave Christian	CHI	60	4	14	18	6	12	1	0	1	0	75	5.3
R	17	Joe Murphy	CHI	19	7	10	17	3-	18	5	0	1	0	43	16.3
C	19	Troy Murray	WPG	29	3	4	7	15-	34	1	0	0	0	45	6.7
			CHI	22	1	3	4	0	25	1	0	0	0	32	3.1
			TOTAL	51	4	7	11	15-	59	2	0	0	0	77	5.2
D	3	Craig Muni	EDM	72	0	11	11	15-	67	0	0	0	0	51	.0
			CHI	9	0	0	0	1	8	0	0	0	0	9	.0
			TOTAL	81	0	11	11	14-	75	0	0	0	0	60	.0
D	4	Keith Brown	CHI	33	2	6	8	3	39	0	0	0	0	47	4.3
R	44	Rob Brown	CHI	15	1	6	7	6	33	0	0	0	0	16	6.3
D	8	Cam Russell	CHI	67	2	4	6	5	151	0	0	0	0	49	4.1
D	45*	Karl Dykhuis	CHI	12	0	5	5	2	0	0	0	0	0	10	.0
G	30	Ed Belfour	CHI	71	0	3	3	0	28	0	0	0	0	0	.0
L	23	Stu Grimson	CHI	78	1	1	2	2	193	1	0	0	0	14	7.1
D	47*	Adam Bennett	CHI	16	0	2	2	2-	8	0	0	0	0	15	.0
R	15	Brad Lauer	CHI	7	0	1	1	1-	2	0	0	0	0	8	.0
D	43*	Milan Tichy	CHI	13	0	1	1	7	30	0	0	0	0	12	.0
D	42*	Steve Bancroft	CHI	1	0	0	0	0	0	0	0	0	0	0	.0
R	68*	Steve Tepper	CHI	1	0	0	0	0	0	0	0	0	0	0	.0
R	56*	Alex Andriyevski	CHI	1	0	0	0	0	0	0	0	0	0	0	.0
D	17	Rod Buskas	CHI	4	0	0	0	2	26	0	0	0	0	3	.0
R	59*	Sergei Krivakrasov	CHI	4	0	0	0	2-	2	0	0	0	0	6	.0
G	29	Jim Waite	CHI	20	0	0	0	0	0	0	0	0	0	0	.0

Goaltending

No.	Goaltender	GPI	Mins	Avg	W	L	T	EN	SO	GA	SA	S%
30	Ed Belfour	71	4106	2.59	41	18	11	1	7	177	1880	.906
29	Jim Waite	20	996	2.95	6	7	1	3	2	49	411	.881
	Totals	84	5108	2.70	47	25	12	4	9	230	2295	.900

Playoffs

Pos	#	Player	Team	GP	G	A	Pts	+/-	PIM	PP	SH	GW	GT	S	%
R	10	Brian Noonan	CHI	4	3	0	3	0	4	1	0	0	0	13	23.1
C	27	Jeremy Roenick	CHI	4	1	2	3	0	2	0	0	0	0	16	6.3
R	28	Steve Larmer	CHI	4	0	3	3	1	0	0	0	0	0	16	.0
C	12	Brent Sutter	CHI	4	1	1	2	0	4	0	0	0	0	9	11.1
D	7	Chris Chelios	CHI	4	0	2	2	1-	14	0	0	0	0	18	.0
L	26	Jocelyn Lemieux	CHI	4	1	0	1	0	2	0	0	0	0	7	14.3
L	16	Michel Goulet	CHI	3	0	1	1	1-	0	0	0	0	0	1	.0
L	32	Stephane Matteau	CHI	3	0	1	1	1-	2	0	0	0	0	4	.0
D	4	Keith Brown	CHI	4	0	1	1	1	2	0	0	0	0	3	.0
R	25	Dave Christian	CHI	1	0	0	0	0	0	0	0	0	0	1	.0
L	23	Stu Grimson	CHI	2	0	0	0	0	4	0	0	0	0	2	.0
L	14	Greg Gilbert	CHI	3	0	0	0	0	0	0	0	0	0	2	.0
G	30	Ed Belfour	CHI	4	0	0	0	0	2	0	0	0	0	0	.0
R	33	Dirk Graham	CHI	4	0	0	0	1-	0	0	0	0	0	10	.0
D	2	Bryan Marchment	CHI	4	0	0	0	1	12	0	0	0	0	6	.0
D	3	Craig Muni	CHI	4	0	0	0	0	2	0	0	0	0	5	.0
R	17	Joe Murphy	CHI	4	0	0	0	2-	8	0	0	0	0	9	.0
C	19	Troy Murray	CHI	4	0	0	0	0	0	0	0	0	0	3	.0
D	8	Cam Russell	CHI	4	0	0	0	0	0	0	0	0	0	3	.0
C	22	Christian Ruuttu	CHI	4	0	0	0	1-	2	0	0	0	0	7	.0
D	5	Steve Smith	CHI	4	0	0	0	2-	10	0	0	0	0	9	.0

Goaltending

No.	Goaltender	GPI	Mins	Avg	W	L	EN	SO	GA	SA	S%
30	Ed Belfour	4	249	3.13	0	4	0	0	13	97	.866
	Totals	4	251	3.11	0	4	0	0	13	97	.866

Club Records

Team

(Figures in brackets for season records are games played; records for fewest points, wins, ties, losses, goals, goals against are for 70 or more games)

Most Points	107	1970-71 (78)
		1971-72 (78)
Most Wins	49	1970-71 (78)
		1990-91 (80)
Most Ties	23	1973-74 (78)
Most Losses	51	1953-54 (70)
Most Goals	351	1985-86 (80)
Most Goals Against	363	1981-82 (80)
Fewest Points	31	1953-54 (70)
Fewest Wins	12	1953-54 (70)
Fewest Ties	6	1989-90 (80)
Fewest Losses	14	1973-74 (78)
Fewest Goals	*133	1953-54 (70)
Fewest Goals Against	164	1973-74 (78)

Longest Winning Streak

Over-all	8	Dec. 9-26/71
		Jan. 4-21/81
Home	13	Nov. 11-
		Dec. 20/70
Away	7	Dec. 9-29/64

Longest Undefeated Streak

Over-all	15	Jan. 14-
		Feb. 16/67
		(12 wins, 3 ties)
Home	18	Oct. 11-
		Dec. 20/70
		(16 wins, 2 ties)
Away	12	Oct. 29-
		Dec. 3/75
		(6 wins, 9 ties)

Longest Losing Streak

Over-all	13	Feb. 25-
		Oct. 11/51
Home	11	Feb. 8-
		Nov. 22/28
Away	17	Jan. 2-
		Oct. 7/54

Longest Winless Streak

Over-all	21	Dec. 17/50-
		Jan. 28/51
		(18 losses, 3 ties)

Home	*15	Dec. 16/28-
		Feb. 28/29
		(11 losses, 4 ties)
Away	23	Dec. 19/50-
		Oct. 11/51
		(15 losses, 8 ties)
Most Shutouts, Season	15	1969-70 (76)
Most PIM, Season	2,663	1991-92 (80)
Most Goals, Game	12	Jan. 30/69
		(Chi. 12 at Phil. 0)

Individual

Most Seasons	22	Stan Mikita
Most Games	1,394	Stan Mikita
Most Goals, Career	604	Bobby Hull
Most Assists, Career	926	Stan Mikita
Most Points, Career	1,467	Stan Mikita
		(541 goals, 926 assists)
Most PIM, Career	1,442	Keith Magnuson
Most Shutouts, Career	74	Tony Esposito
Longest Consecutive Games Streak	884	Steve Larmer
		(1982-83 to present)
Most Goals, Season	58	Bobby Hull
		(1968-69)
Most Assists, Season	87	Denis Savard (81-82, 87-88)
Most Points, Season	131	Denis Savard
		(1987-88)
		(44 goals, 87 assists)
Most PIM, Season	408	Mike Peluso
		(1991-92)
Most Points, Defenseman Season	85	Doug Wilson
		(1981-82)
		(39 goals, 46 assists)
Most Points, Center, Season	131	Denis Savard
		(1987-88)
		(44 goals, 87 assists)
Most Points, Right Wing, Season	101	Steve Larmer
		(1990-91)
		(44 goals, 57 assists)
Most Points, Left Wing, Season	107	Bobby Hull
		(1968-69)
		(58 goals, 49 assists)

Most Points, Rookie, Season	90	Steve Larmer
		(1982-83)
		(43 goals, 47 assists)
Most Shutouts, Season	15	Tony Esposito
		(1969-70)
Most Goals, Game	5	Grant Mulvey
		(Feb. 3/82)
Most Assists, Game	6	Pat Stapleton
		(Mar. 30/69)
Most Points, Game	7	Max Bentley
		(Jan. 28/43)
		Grant Mulvey
		(Feb. 3/82)

* NHL Record.

General Managers' History

Major Frederic McLaughlin, 1926-27 to 1941-42; Bill Tobin, 1942-43 to 1953-54; Tommy Ivan, 1954-55 to 1976-77; Bob Pulford, 1977-78 to 1989-90; Mike Keenan, 1990-91 to 1991-92; Mike Keenan and Bob Pulford, 1992-93; Bob Pulford, 1993-94.

Retired Numbers

1	Glenn Hall	1957-1967
9	Bobby Hull	1957-1972
21	Stan Mikita	1958-1980
35	Tony Esposito	1969-1984

All-time Record vs. Other Clubs

Regular Season

	At Home							On Road							Total						
	GP	W	L	T	GF	GA	PTS	GP	W	L	T	GF	GA	PTS	GP	W	L	T	GF	GA	PTS
Boston	277	141	92	44	896	741	326	275	84	159	32	773	999	200	552	225	251	76	1669	1740	526
Buffalo	42	22	14	6	136	115	50	44	10	28	6	113	173	26	86	32	42	12	249	288	76
Calgary	39	18	12	9	143	121	45	41	14	20	7	123	137	35	80	32	32	16	266	258	80
Detroit	306	143	115	48	927	844	334	306	90	188	28	755	1054	208	612	233	303	76	1682	1898	542
Edmonton	22	11	8	3	96	97	25	23	8	14	1	87	110	17	45	19	22	4	183	207	42
Hartford	21	13	5	3	97	58	29	22	11	9	2	78	77	24	43	24	14	5	175	135	53
Los Angeles	53	27	19	7	209	164	61	52	23	23	6	177	181	52	105	50	42	13	386	345	113
Minnesota	84	56	18	10	353	217	122	85	36	38	11	284	296	83	169	92	56	21	637	513	205
Montreal	266	91	121	54	717	742	236	266	51	167	48	626	1032	150	532	142	288	102	1343	1774	386
New Jersey	38	23	9	6	162	111	52	37	14	15	8	113	112	36	75	37	24	14	275	223	88
NY Islanders	40	19	16	5	131	141	43	38	11	16	11	113	137	33	78	30	32	16	244	278	76
NY Rangers	277	125	110	42	847	772	292	278	107	117	54	783	824	268	555	232	227	96	1630	1596	560
Ottawa	1	1	0	0	4	2	2	1	1	0	0	4	2	2	2	2	0	0	8	4	4
Philadelphia	52	24	18	10	185	141	66	53	15	28	10	143	176	40	105	39	38	28	328	317	106
Pittsburgh	51	34	8	9	217	143	77	50	22	23	5	167	177	49	101	56	31	14	384	320	126
Quebec	22	13	7	2	91	72	28	21	9	8	4	88	89	22	43	22	15	6	179	161	50
St. Louis	88	53	24	11	352	273	117	85	28	41	16	266	296	72	173	81	65	27	618	569	189
San Jose	3	2	0	1	16	8	5	3	2	1	0	8	8	4	6	4	1	1	24	16	9
Tampa Bay	4	2	0	2	15	9	6	3	2	1	0	12	10	4	7	4	1	2	27	19	10
Toronto	296	151	106	39	916	767	341	296	87	158	51	761	1021	225	592	238	264	90	1677	1788	566
Vancouver	49	32	12	5	185	115	69	50	15	23	12	143	155	42	99	47	35	17	328	270	111
Washington	31	20	6	5	131	91	45	32	10	18	4	101	123	24	63	30	24	9	232	214	69
Winnipeg	24	17	4	3	123	73	37	24	9	12	3	89	101	21	48	26	16	6	212	174	58
Defunct Clubs	139	79	40	20	408	267	178	140	52	67	21	316	345	125	279	131	107	41	724	612	303
Totals	**2225**	**1117**	**756**	**352**	**7357**	**6084**	**2586**	**2225**	**711**	**1174**	**340**	**6123**	**7635**	**1762**	**4450**	**1828**	**1930**	**692**	**13480**	**13719**	**4348**

Playoffs

	Series	W	L	GP	W	L	T	GF	GA	Last Mtg.	Round	Result
Boston	6	1	5	22	5	16	1	63	97	1978	QF	L 0-4
Buffalo	2	0	2	9	1	8	0	17	36	1980	QF	L 0-4
Calgary	2	0	2	8	1	7	0	17	30	1989	CF	L 1-4
Detroit	13	8	5	64	37	27	0	198	177	1992	DF	W 4-0
Edmonton	4	1	3	20	8	12	0	77	102	1992	CF	W 4-0
Los Angeles	1	1	0	5	4	1	0	10	7	1974	QF	W 4-1
Minnesota	6	4	2	33	19	14	0	119	119	1991	DSF	L 2-4
Montreal	17	5	12	81	29	50	2	185	261	1976	QF	L 0-4
NY Islanders	2	0	2	6	0	6	0	6	21	1979	QF	L 0-4
NY Rangers	5	4	1	24	14	10	0	66	54	1973	SF	W 4-1
Philadelphia	1	1	0	4	4	0	0	20	8	1971	QF	W 4-0
Pittsburgh	2	1	1	8	4	4	0	24	23	1992	F	L 0-4
St. Louis	9	7	2	45	27	18	0	166	129	1993	DSF	L 0-4
Toronto	7	2	5	25	9	15	1	57	76	1986	DSF	L 0-3
Vancouver	1	0	1	5	1	4	0	13	18	1982	CF	L 1-4
Defunct Clubs	4	2	2	9	5	3	1	16	15			
Totals	**82**	**37**	**45**	**368**	**168**	**195**	**5**	**1054**	**1173**			

Playoff Results 1993-89

Year	Round	Opponent	Result	GF	GA
1993	DSF	St. Louis	L 0-4	6	13
1992	F	Pittsburgh	L 0-4	10	15
	CF	Edmonton	W 4-0	21	8
	DF	Detroit	W 4-0	11	6
	DSF	St. Louis	W 4-2	23	19
1991	DSF	Minnesota	L 2-4	16	23
1990	CF	Edmonton	L 2-4	20	25
	DF	St. Louis	W 4-3	28	22
	DSF	Minnesota	W 4-3	21	18
1989	CF	Calgary	L 1-4	8	15
	DF	St. Louis	W 4-1	19	12
	DSF	Detroit	W 4-2	25	18

Abbreviations: Round: F – Final;
CF – conference final; **DF** – division final;
DSF – division semi-final; **SF** – semi-final;
QF – quarter-final; **PR** – preliminary round.
GA – goals against; **GF** – goals for.

1992-93 Results

	Home			Away	
Oct. 11	Tampa Bay	4-4	Oct. 7	Tampa Bay	3-7
15	Edmonton	3-4	10	St. Louis	3-0
18	Vancouver	3-1	17	Toronto	3-4
22	New Jersey	5-6	21	Buffalo	1-4
25	Detroit	8-2	31	Boston	3-2
29	Philadelphia	5-5	Nov. 1	Washington	1-4
Nov. 1	San Jose	4-4	7	Quebec*	7-4
5	Toronto	1-0	14	Minnesota*	0-3
8	Pittsburgh	7-2	17	Detroit	4-5
12	St. Louis	1-0	19	Los Angeles	1-4
15	Minnesota	2-1	21	San Jose	2-1
Dec. 1	Los Angeles	3-6	23	Vancouver	2-5
3	Toronto	4-3	27	Edmonton	8-1
6	Montreal	2-0	28	Calgary	5-2
10	NY Islanders	5-3	Dec. 5	Toronto	2-2
17	Winnipeg	5-1	8	Detroit	3-2
20	Minnesota	4-0	12	Minnesota	3-0
26	St. Louis	2-3	19	Philadelphia*	1-3
27	Detroit	0-4	23	Ottawa	4-2
31	Tampa Bay	5-0	29	Detroit	6-3
Jan. 3	Winnipeg	4-1	Jan. 2	Washington*	2-2
7	Edmonton	3-3	9	St. Louis	1-4
10	Los Angeles	4-5	12	Minnesota	3-1
14	Minnesota	3-1	16	Toronto	5-3
17	Toronto	5-3	19	Winnipeg	2-5
21	Washington	6-2	23	Hartford*	6-2
24	Vancouver	6-2	27	Vancouver	4-4
Feb. 11	Boston	6-3	29	San Jose	4-2
14	Detroit	3-5	30	Los Angeles	2-2
18	Los Angeles	7-2	Feb. 3	Detroit	0-5
21	Calgary*	4-3	13	Pittsburgh*	1-4
28	St. Louis	1-7	25	Tampa Bay	5-1
Mar. 4	Quebec	3-3	27	Detroit*	2-1
7	Ottawa*	4-2	Mar. 5	New Jersey	1-1
11	NY Rangers	1-4	14	Edmonton*	5-4
21	Tampa Bay	3-2	16	Calgary	1-0
25	Buffalo	4-6	20	Montreal	2-6
28	Hartford	3-0	26	NY Rangers	3-1
Apr. 1	Detroit	1-3	Apr. 3	St. Louis	3-3
4	St. Louis	5-4	9	NY Islanders	3-3
11	Tampa Bay*	3-3	10	Tampa Bay*	4-2
15	Toronto	3-2	13	Minnesota	3-2

*Denotes afternoon game

Entry Draft Selections 1993-79

1993
Pick
24	Eric Lecompte
50	Eric Manlow
54	Bogdan Savenko
76	Ryan Huska
90	Eric Daze
102	Patrik Pysz
128	Jonni Vauhkonen
180	Tom White
206	Sergei Petrov
232	Mike Rusk
258	Mike McGhan
284	Tom Noble

1992
Pick
12	Sergei Krivokrasov
36	Jeff Shantz
41	Sergei Klimovich
89	Andy MacIntyre
113	Tim Hogan
137	Gerry Skrypec
161	Mike Prokopec
185	Layne Roland
209	David Hymovitz
233	Richard Raymond

1991
Pick
22	Dean McAmmond
39	Michael Pomichter
44	Jamie Matthews
66	Bobby House
71	Igor Kravchuk
88	Zac Boyer
110	Maco Balkovec
112	Kevin St. Jacques
132	Jacques Auger
154	Scott Kirton
176	Roch Belley
198	Scott MacDonald
220	A. Andriyevsky
242	Mike Larkin
264	Scott Dean

1990
Pick
16	Karl Dykhuis
37	Ivan Droppa
79	Chris Tucker
121	Brett Stickney
124	Derek Edgerly
163	Hugo Belanger
184	Owen Lessard
205	Erik Peterson
226	Steve Dubinsky
247	Dino Grossi

1989
Pick
6	Adam Bennett
27	Michael Speer
48	Bob Kellogg
111	Tommi Pullola
132	Tracy Egeland
153	Milan Tichy
174	Jason Greyerbiehl
195	Matt Saunders
216	Mike Kozak
237	Michael Doneghey

1988
Pick
8	Jeremy Roenick
50	Trevor Dam
71	Stefan Elvenas
92	Joe Cleary
113	Justin Lafayette
134	Craig Woodcroft
155	Jon Pojar
176	Mathew Hentges
197	Daniel Maurice
218	Dirk Tenzer
239	Andreas Lupzig

1987
Pick
8	Jimmy Waite
29	Ryan McGill
50	Cam Russell
60	Mike Dagenais
92	Ulf Sandstrom
113	Mike McCormick
134	Stephen Tepper
155	John Reilly
176	Lance Werness
197	Dale Marquette
218	Bill Lacouture
239	Mike Lappin

1986
Pick
14	Everett Sanipass
35	Mark Kurzawski
77	Frantisek Kucera
98	Lonnie Loach
119	Mario Doyon
140	Mike Hudson
161	Marty Nanne
182	Geoff Benic
203	Glen Lowes
224	Chris Thayer
245	Sean Williams

1985
Pick
11	Dave Manson
53	Andy Helmuth
74	Dan Vincellette
87	Rick Herbert
95	Brad Belland
116	Jonas Heed
137	Victor Posa
158	John Reid
179	Richard LaPlante
200	Brad Hamilton
221	Ian Pound
242	Rick Braccia

1984
Pick
3	Ed Olczyk
45	Trent Yawney
66	Tommy Eriksson
90	Timo Lehkonen
101	Darin Sceviour
111	Chris Clifford
132	Mike Stapleton
153	Glen Greenough
174	Ralph DiFiorie
194	Joakim Persson
215	Bill Brown
224	David Mackey
235	Dan Williams

1983
Pick
18	Bruce Cassidy
39	Wayne Presley
59	Marc Bergevin
79	Tarek Howard
99	Kevin Robinson
115	Jari Torkki
119	Mark Lavarre
139	Scot Birnie
159	Kevin Paynter
179	Brian Noonan
199	Dominik Hasek
219	Steve Pepin

1982
Pick
7	Ken Yaremchuk
28	Rene Badeau
49	Tom McMurchy
70	Bill Watson
91	Brad Beck
112	Mark Hatcher
133	Jay Ness
154	Jeff Smith
175	Phil Patterson
196	Jim Camazzola
217	Mike James
238	Bob Andrea

1981
Pick
12	Tony Tanti
25	Kevin Griffin
54	Darrell Anholt
75	Perry Pelensky
96	Doug Chessell
117	Bill Schafhauser
138	Marc Centrone
159	Johan Mellstrom
180	John Benns
201	Sylvain Roy

1980
Pick
3	Denis Savard
15	Jerome Dupont
28	Steve Ludzik
30	Ken Solheim
36	Len Dawes
57	Troy Murray
58	Marcel Frere
67	Carey Wilson
78	Brian Shaw
99	Kevin Ginnell
120	Steve Larmer
141	Sean Simpson
162	Jim Ralph
183	Don Dietrich
204	Dan Frawley

1979
Pick
7	Keith Brown
28	Tim Trimper
49	Bill Gardner
70	Louis Begin
91	Lowell Loveday
112	Doug Crossman

Club Directory

Chicago Stadium
1800 W. Madison St.
Chicago, IL 60612
Phone **312/733-5300**
FAX 312/733-5356
Capacity: 17,317

President	William W. Wirtz
Executive Vice-President	Arthur Michael Wirtz, Jr.
Vice-President & Assistant to the President	Thomas N. Ivan
Senior Vice-President and General Manager	Robert J. Pulford
Vice President	Jack Davison
Director of Player Personnel	Bob Murray
Head Coach	Darryl Sutter
Assistant Coach	Rich Preston
Assistant Coach	Paul Baxter
Pro Scout	Jim Pappin
Chief Amateur Scout	Michel Dumas
Scouts	Jim Walker, Dave Lucas, Kerry Davison, Steve Lyons, Bruce Franklin
Director of Team Services	Phil Thibodeau
Executive Secretary	Cindy Bodnarchuk
Receptionist/Secretary	Vicki Littleton

Medical Staff
Club Doctors	Louis Kolb, Howard Baim
Club Dentist	Robert Duresa
Head Trainer	Michael Gapski
Equipment Manager/Assistant Trainer	Randy Lacey, Lou Varga
Fitness Consultant	Mark Kling
Massage Therapist	Pawel Prylinski

Finance
Controller	Robert Rinkus
Assistant to the Controller	Penny Swenson
Accounting Secretary	Pat Dema

Public Relations/Marketing
Director of Marketing	Peter Wirtz
Director of Public Relations/Sales	Jim DeMaria
Asst. PR & Director of Community Relations	Tom Finks
Assistant Marketing Director	Karen Lechner
Public Relations Assistant	Barbara Davidson

Ticketing
Ticket Manager	Jim Bare
Switchboard Operators	Esther Cox, Mary Joiner
Team Photographer	Ray Grabowski
Organist	Frank Pellico
Soloist	Wayne Messmer
Public Address Announcer	Harvey Wittenberg
Executive Offices	Chicago Stadium
Home Ice	Chicago Stadium
Seating Capacity	17,317
Largest Hockey Crowd	20,960 on April 10, 1982 vs. Minnesota
Location of Press Box	West end of Stadium
Dimensions of Rink	185 feet by 85 feet
Ends of Rink	Plexi-glass extends above boards all around rink
Club Colors	Red, Black and White
Uniforms	Home - Base color white, trimmed with black and red; Away - Base color red trimmed with black and white
Radio Station	WLUP (AM 1000)
Television Station	SportsChannel
Broadcasters	Pat Foley, Dale Tallon

General Manager

PULFORD, ROBERT JESSE (BOB)
General Manager, Chicago Blackhawks.
Born in Newton Robinson, Ont., March 31, 1936.

A member of the Chicago Blackhawks organization since 1977, Bob Pulford has served as coach, general manager and senior vice president in his 16-year affiliation with the team. In 1992, Pulford resumed the general manager's duties, replacing Mike Keenan, who had served in that capacity since 1990.

A member of the Hockey Hall of Fame as a player and an accomplished hockey executive, Pulford was named as the NHL's Coach of the Year in 1974-75 when he led the Los Angeles Kings to their best record in franchise history. Since joining the Blackhawks family on July 6, 1977, the team has never failed to make the playoffs.

Pulford is also recognized for his outstanding contributions to hockey in the United States, coaching the Team USA entry at the 1976 Canada Cup tournament and serving as the co-General Manager for the 1991 U.S. team at the 1991 Tournament.

NHL Coaching Record

| Season | Team | Regular Season | | | | | Playoffs | | | |
		Games	W	L	T	%	Games	W	L	%
1972-73	Los Angeles	78	31	36	11	.468	....	....	....	....
1973-74	Los Angeles	78	33	33	12	.500	5	1	4	.200
1974-75	Los Angeles	80	42	17	21	.656	3	1	2	.333
1975-76	Los Angeles	80	38	33	9	.531	9	5	4	.556
1976-77	Los Angeles	80	34	31	15	.519	9	4	5	.444
1977-78	Chicago	80	32	29	19	.519	4	0	4	.000
1978-79	Chicago	80	29	36	15	.456	4	0	4	.000
1981-82	Chicago	28	13	13	2	.500	15	8	7	.533
1984-85	Chicago	27	16	7	4	.667	15	9	6	.600
1985-86	Chicago	80	39	33	8	.538	3	0	3	.000
1986-87	Chicago	80	29	37	14	.450	4	0	4	.000
	NHL Totals	771	336	305	130	.520	71	28	43	.394

Coach

SUTTER, DARRYL JOHN
Coach, Chicago Blackhawks. Born in Viking, Alberta, August 19, 1958.

Darryl Sutter was appointed as the 29th coach in Chicago Blackhawks' history on June 11, 1992. Sutter, who spent his entire eight-year playing career with Chicago before injuries forced him to retire in 1987, served as an associate coach to Mike Keenan for the past two seasons. Following his retirement, Sutter spent a year as an assistant coach under Bob Murdoch before taking over the head coaching reins of the Blackhawks' top IHL farm affiliate in Saginaw. In his first season as head coach, Sutter led the squad to 46-26-10 record, the best in the league. When the Saginaw franchise was shifted to Indianapolis for the following season, Sutter guided the team to the IHL's Turner Cup championship, earning IHL coach of the year honors.

Coaching Record

| Season | Team | Regular Season | | | | | Playoffs | | | |
		Games	W	L	T	%	Games	W	L	%
1988-89	Saginaw (IHL)	82	46	26	10	.560	6	2	4	.333
1989-90	Indianapolis (IHL)	82	53	21	8	.646	14	12	2	.857
1992-93	Chicago (NHL)	84	47	25	12	.631	4	0	4	.000
	NHL Totals	84	47	25	12	.631	4	0	4	.000

Dallas Stars

1992-93 Results: 36w-38L-10T 82PTS. Fifth, Norris Division

Year-by-Year Record

		Home			Road			Overall							
Season	GP	W	L	T	W	L	T	W	L	T	GF	GA	Pts.	Finished	Playoff Result
1992-93	84	18	17	7	18	21	3	36	38	10	272	293	82	5th, Norris Div.	Out of Playoffs
1991-92	80	20	16	4	12	26	2	32	42	6	246	278	70	4th, Norris Div.	Lost Div. Semi-Final
1990-91	80	19	15	6	8	24	8	27	39	14	256	266	68	4th, Norris Div.	Lost Final
1989-90	80	26	12	2	10	28	2	36	40	4	284	291	76	4th, Norris Div.	Lost Div. Semi-Final
1988-89	80	17	15	8	10	22	8	27	37	16	258	278	70	3rd, Norris Div.	Lost Div. Semi-Final
1987-88	80	10	24	6	9	24	7	19	48	13	242	349	51	5th, Norris Div.	Out of Playoffs
1986-87	80	17	20	3	13	20	7	30	40	10	296	314	70	5th, Norris Div.	Out of Playoffs
1985-86	80	21	15	4	17	18	5	38	33	9	327	305	85	2nd, Norris Div.	Lost Div. Semi-Final
1984-85	80	14	19	7	11	24	5	25	43	12	268	321	62	4th, Norris Div.	Lost Div. Final
1983-84	80	22	14	4	17	17	6	39	31	10	345	344	88	1st, Norris Div.	Lost Conf. Championship
1982-83	80	23	6	11	17	18	5	40	24	16	321	290	96	2nd, Norris Div.	Lost Div. Final
1981-82	80	21	7	12	16	16	8	37	23	20	346	288	94	1st, Norris Div.	Lost Div. Semi-Final
1980-81	80	23	10	7	12	18	10	35	28	17	291	263	87	3rd, Adams Div.	Lost Final
1979-80	80	25	8	7	11	20	9	36	28	16	311	253	88	3rd, Adams Div.	Lost Semi-Final
1978-79	80	19	15	6	9	25	6	28	40	12	257	289	68	4th, Adams Div.	Out of Playoffs
1977-78	80	12	24	4	6	29	5	18	53	9	218	325	45	5th, Smythe Div.	Out of Playoffs
1976-77	80	17	14	9	6	25	9	23	39	18	240	310	64	2nd, Smythe Div.	Lost Prelim. Round
1975-76	80	15	22	3	5	31	4	20	53	7	195	303	47	4th, Smythe Div.	Out of Playoffs
1974-75	80	17	20	3	6	30	4	23	50	7	221	341	53	4th, Smythe Div.	Out of Playoffs
1973-74	78	18	15	6	5	23	11	23	38	17	235	275	63	7th, West Div.	Out of Playoffs
1972-73	78	26	8	5	11	22	6	37	30	11	254	230	85	3rd, West Div.	Lost Quarter-Final
1971-72	78	22	11	6	15	18	6	37	29	12	212	191	86	2nd, West Div.	Lost Quarter-Final
1970-71	78	16	15	8	12	19	8	28	34	16	191	223	72	4th, West Div.	Lost Semi-Final
1969-70	76	11	16	11	8	19	11	19	35	22	224	257	60	3rd, West Div.	Lost Quarter-Final
1968-69	76	11	21	6	7	22	9	18	43	15	189	270	51	6th, West Div.	Out of Playoffs
1967-68	74	17	12	8	10	20	7	27	32	15	191	226	69	4th, West Div.	Lost Semi-Final

Schedule

	Home			Away
Oct.	Tues. 5 Detroit		**Oct.**	Thur. 7 Toronto
	Sat. 9 Winnipeg			Mon. 18 Chicago
	Tues. 12 Chicago			Wed. 20 Montreal
	Sat. 16 St Louis			Thur. 21 Ottawa
	Wed. 27 Hartford			Sat. 23 Quebec
	Sat. 30 Ottawa			Mon. 25 Detroit
Nov.	Mon. 1 Toronto		**Nov.**	Wed. 3 Anaheim
	Sun. 7 Winnipeg			Fri. 5 San Jose
	Thur. 11 San Jose			Tues. 9 Anaheim
	Wed. 17 Tampa Bay			(at Phoenix)
	Sat. 20 Calgary			Sat. 13 Winnipeg
	Sun. 21 Los Angeles			Sun. 14 Chicago
	Wed. 24 NY Islanders			Sat. 27 Detroit*
Dec.	Sun. 5 Edmonton			Mon. 29 Edmonton
	Wed. 8 Pittsburgh			Tues. 30 Calgary
	Thur. 9 Ottawa		**Dec.**	Sat. 4 St Louis
	(at Minnesota)			Sun. 19 Vancouver*
	Sun. 12 Florida			Wed. 22 Anaheim
	Wed. 15 Chicago			Thur. 23 Los Angeles
	Fri. 17 Anaheim			Fri. 31 Chicago
	Mon. 27 Detroit		**Jan.**	Thur. 13 Toronto
	Wed. 29 Toronto			Fri. 14 Detroit
Jan.	Sun. 2 Quebec			Wed. 26 Calgary
	Tues. 4 Chicago			Thur. 27 Vancouver
	Thur. 6 Philadelphia			Sat. 29 Edmonton
	Sun. 9 St Louis		**Feb.**	Wed. 2 Winnipeg
	Tues. 11 Edmonton			Sat. 12 Pittsburgh*
	Sun. 16 Buffalo			Sun. 13 Buffalo*
	Tues. 18 Los Angeles			Mon. 21 San Jose*
	Mon. 24 New Jersey			Wed. 23 Los Angeles
Feb.	Sun. 6 San Jose		**Mar.**	Wed. 2 Winnipeg
	Wed. 9 Winnipeg			Tues. 8 Philadelphia
	Wed. 16 Boston			Wed. 9 Toronto
	Fri. 18 Calgary			Sat. 12 Hartford*
	Sat. 26 NY Rangers			Sun. 13 New Jersey*
Mar.	Fri. 4 Vancouver			Fri. 25 St Louis
	Sun. 6 Montreal			Sun. 27 Tampa Bay*
	Fri. 18 Washington			Mon. 28 Florida
	Sun. 20 Vancouver			Thur. 31 Boston
	Tues. 22 Anaheim		**Apr.**	Fri. 1 NY Rangers
Apr.	Tues. 5 Toronto			Sun. 3 Washington*
	Tues. 12 St Louis			Fri. 8 NY Islanders
	Thur. 14 Detroit			Sun. 10 St Louis*

* Denotes afternoon game.

Home Starting Times:

Weeknights	7:35 p.m.
Saturdays and Sundays	7:05 p.m.

Franchise date: June 5, 1967. Transferred from Minnesota to Dallas.

CENTRAL DIVISION

27th NHL Season

WESTERN CONFERENCE

Mike Modano led the Stars in points (93), assists (60) and game-winning goals (7) in 1992-93.

1993-94 Player Personnel

FORWARDS

	HT	WT	S	Place of Birth	Date	1992-93 Club
BES, Jeff	6-0	185	L	Tillsonburg, Ont.	7/31/73	Guelph-Kalamazoo
BROTEN, Neal	5-9	170	L	Roseau, MN	11/29/59	Minnesota
BROWN, Rob	5-11	185	L	Kingston, Ont.	4/10/68	Chicago-Indianapolis
BURKETT, Michael	6-3	180	L	Toronto, Ont.	3/15/72	Michigan St.
CHURLA, Shane	6-1	200	R	Fernie, B.C.	6/24/65	Minnesota
COURTNALL, Russ	5-11	183	R	Duncan, B.C.	6/2/65	Minnesota
CRAIG, Mike	6-1	180	R	St. Mary's, Ont.	6/6/71	Minnesota
DAHLEN, Ulf	6-2	195	L	Ostersund, Sweden	1/12/67	Minnesota
EDSTROM, Lars	5-11	185	L	Sweden	7/16/66	Lulea
EVANS, Kevin	5-9	185	L	Peterborough, Ont.	7/10/65	Kalamazoo
EVASON, Dean	5-10	180	R	Flin Flon, Man.	8/22/64	San Jose
GAGNER, Dave	5-10	180	L	Chatham, Ont.	12/11/64	Minnesota
GAVIN, Stewart	6-0	190	L	Ottawa, Ont.	3/15/60	Minnesota
GILCHRIST, Brent	5-11	185	L	Moose Jaw, Sask.	4/3/67	Edmonton-Minnesota
HARVEY, Todd	5-11	190	R	Hamilton, Ont.	2/17/75	Detroit
HEROUX, Yves	5-11	185	R	Terrebonne, Que.	4/27/65	Kalamazoo
JOUBERT, Jacques	6-1	191	L	South Bend, IN	3/23/71	Boston U.
KENNEDY, Mike	5-1	170	R	Vancouver, B.C.	4/13/72	Kalamazoo
KLATT, Trent	6-1	205	R	Robbinsdale, MN	1/30/71	Minnesota-Kalamazoo
KOVACS, Frank	6-2	205	L	Regina, Sask.	6/6/71	Dayton
LANG, Bill	5-10	161	R	Newmarket, Ont.	7/16/73	North Bay
LANGENBRUNNER, J.	5-11	180	R	Duluth, MN	7/24/75	Cloquet HS
LAWRENCE, Mark	6-4	215	R	Burlington, Ont.	1/27/72	Dayton-Kalamazoo
LEHTINEN, Jere	6-0	185	R	Espoo, Finland	6/24/73	Kiekko-Espoo
LIND, Juha	5-11	160	L	Helsinki, Finland	1/2/74	Vantaa HT-Jokerit
LURTSEMA, Bob	6-5	237	L	Burnsville, MN	10/28/74	Burnsville HS
McGOWAN, Cal	6-1	185	L	Sydney, N.S.	6/19/70	Kalamazoo
McPHEE, Mike	6-1	203	L	Sydney, N.S.	7/14/60	Montreal-Minnesota
MODANO, Mike	6-3	190	L	Livonia, MI	6/7/70	Minnesota
PETERSON, Kyle	6-3	195	L	Calgary, Alta.	4/17/74	Thunder Bay
PRATT, Jonathan	6-1	195	L	Danvers, MA	9/25/70	Boston U.
ROMPO, Jeff	6-0	185	L	St. Paul, MN	2/9/74	U. Minn.-Duluth
SIMPSON, Reid	6-1	211	L	Flin Flon, Man.	5/21/69	Kalamazoo-Minnesota
SMITH, Derrick	6-2	215	L	Scarborough, Ont.	1/22/65	Minnesota-Kalamazoo
STASIUK, Jeremy	5-11	189	R	Saskatoon, Sask.	12/26/74	Spokane
SVARTVADET, Per	6-1	180	L	Ornskoldsvik, Sweden	5/17/75	MoDo
VARVIO, Jarkko	5-9	175	R	Tampere, Finland	4/28/72	HPK
WILSON, Ross	6-3	200	R	The Pas, Man.	6/26/69	Kalamazoo

DEFENSEMEN

	HT	WT	S	Place of Birth	Date	1992-93 Club
BAUER, Collin	6-1	185	L	Edmonton, Alta.	9/6/70	Kalamazoo
BERRY, Brad	6-2	190	L	Hibbing, MN	4/1/65	Minnesota-Kalamazoo
CAVALLINI, Paul	6-1	202	L	Toronto, Ont.	10/13/65	St. Louis-Washington
HATCHER, Derian	6-5	205	L	Sterling Hts., MI	6/4/72	Minnesota-Kalamazoo
HERTER, Jason	6-1	190	R	Hafford, Sask.	10/2/70	Hamilton
JERRARD, Paul	5-10	185	R	Winnipeg, Man.	4/20/85	Kalamazoo
JOHNSON, Jim	6-1	190	L	New Hope, MN	8/9/62	Minnesota
JOHNSON, Michael	6-3	175	L	Halifax, N.S.	5/29/74	Ottawa
LEDYARD, Grant	6-2	195	L	Winnipeg, Man.	11/19/61	Buffalo
LUDWIG, Craig	6-3	217	L	Rhinelander, WI	3/15/61	Minnesota
MATVICHUK, Richard	6-2	190	L	Edmonton, Alta.	2/5/73	Minnesota-Kalamazoo
MITCHELL, Roy	6-1	200	R	Edmonton, Alta.	3/14/69	Kalamazoo
MROZIK, Rick	6-2	185	L	Duluth, MN	1/2/75	Cloquet HS
OSIECKI, Mark	6-2	200	L	St. Paul, MN	7/16/71	Ott.-Wpg.-Min.
PETERSON, Cory	6-2	200	L	Minneapolis, MN	6/10/75	Jefferson HS
RICHARDS, Travis	6-1	185	L	Crystal, MN	3/22/70	U. of Minn.
SAVARD, Marc	6-3	205	L	Blainville, Que.	9/19/72	Dayton-Kalamazoo
SJODIN, Tommy	5-11	185	R	Timra, Sweden	8/13/65	Minnesota
STRAUB, Brian	6-2	195	L	Bozeman, MT	7/2/68	Kalamazoo
TINORDI, Mark	6-4	205	L	Red Deer, Alta.	5/9/66	Minnesota

GOALTENDERS

	HT	WT	C	Place of Birth	Date	1992-93 Club
FINCH, Geoff	6-0	180	L	Oshawa, Ont.	4/8/72	Brown
HERLOFSKY, Derek	6-0	160	L	Minneapolis, MN	10/1/71	Boston U.
LANG, Chad	5-10	188	L	Newmarket, Ont.	2/11/75	Peterborough
LEVY, Jeff	5-11	160	L	Salt Lake City, UT	12/9/70	Kalamazoo-Dayton
McKERSIE, John	6-0	210	L	Madison, WI	6/23/72	Boston U.
MOEN, Jeffrey	6-1	170	L	Roseville, MN	2/9/74	U. of Minn.
MOOG, Andy	5-8	170	L	Penticton, B.C.	2/18/60	Boston
STOLP, Jeff	6-0	180	L	Nashwauk, MN	6/20/70	Kalamazoo-Dayton
TORCHIA, Mike	5-11	215	L	Toronto, Ont.	2/23/72	Kalamazoo
TUREK, Roman	6-3	190	L	Pisek, Czech.	5/21/70	Motor C-B
WAKALUK, Darcy	5-11	180	L	Pincher Creek, Alta.	3/14/66	Minnesota
WILLIS, Jordan	5-9	155	L	Kincardine, Ont.	2/28/75	London

1992-93 Scoring

Regular Season

Pos	#	Player	Team	GP	G	A	Pts	+/-	PIM	PP	SH	GW	GT	S	%
C	9	Mike Modano	MIN	82	33	60	93	7–	83	9	0	7	0	307	10.7
R	26	Russ Courtnall	MIN	84	36	43	79	1	49	14	2	3	2	294	12.2
C	15	Dave Gagner	MIN	84	33	43	76	13–	143	17	0	5	1	230	14.3
R	22	Ulf Dahlen	MIN	83	35	39	74	20–	6	13	0	6	0	223	15.7
D	24	Mark Tinordi	MIN	69	15	27	42	1–	157	7	0	2	0	122	12.3
L	17	Mike McPhee	MIN	84	18	22	40	2–	44	1	2	2	0	161	11.2
R	20	Mike Craig	MIN	70	15	23	38	11–	106	7	0	0	0	131	11.5
D	33	Tommy Sjodin	MIN	77	7	29	36	25–	30	5	0	1	0	175	4.0
C	7	Neal Broten	MIN	82	12	21	33	7	22	0	3	3	0	123	9.8
L	10	Gaetan Duchesne	MIN	84	16	13	29	6	30	0	2	3	0	134	11.9
R	29*	Trent Klatt	MIN	47	4	19	23	2	38	1	0	0	0	69	5.8
D	6	Jim Johnson	MIN	79	3	20	23	9	105	1	0	0	0	67	4.5
C	41	Brent Gilchrist	EDM	60	10	10	20	10–	47	2	0	0	0	94	10.6
			MIN	8	0	1	1	2–	2	0	0	0	0	12	.0
			TOTAL	68	10	11	21	12–	49	2	0	0	0	106	9.4
R	27	Shane Churla	MIN	73	5	16	21	8–	286	1	0	1	0	61	8.2
D	2	Derian Hatcher	MIN	67	4	15	19	27–	178	0	0	1	1	73	5.5
R	12	Stewart Gavin	MIN	63	10	8	18	4–	59	0	0	0	0	114	8.8
C	18	Bobby Smith	MIN	45	5	7	12	9–	10	3	0	0	0	53	9.4
D	3	Craig Ludwig	MIN	78	1	10	11	1	153	0	0	0	0	66	1.5
L	16	Brian Propp	MIN	17	3	3	6	10–	0	1	0	1	0	35	8.6
D	4*	Richard Matvichuk	MIN	53	2	3	5	8–	26	1	0	0	0	51	3.9
D	23	Mark Osiecki	OTT	34	0	4	4	21–	12	0	0	0	0	20	.0
			WPG	4	1	0	1	1	2	1	0	0	0	5	20.0
			MIN	5	0	0	0	0	5	0	0	0	0	1	.0
			TOTAL	43	1	4	5	20–	19	1	0	0	0	26	3.8
C	11	Dan Quinn	MIN	11	0	4	4	4–	6	0	0	0	0	20	.0
C	28	James Black	MIN	10	2	1	3	0	4	0	0	0	0	10	20.0
G	35	Darcy Wakaluk	MIN	29	0	3	3	0	20	0	0	0	0	0	.0
G	30	Jon Casey	MIN	60	0	3	3	0	28	0	0	0	0	0	.0
D	5	Brad Berry	MIN	63	0	3	3	2	109	0	0	0	0	49	.0
L	21	Derrick Smith	MIN	9	0	1	1	2–	2	0	0	0	0	3	.0
D	39*	Enrico Ciccone	MIN	31	0	1	1	2–	115	0	0	0	0	13	.0
L	44*	Reid Simpson	MIN	1	0	0	0	0	5	0	0	0	0	0	.0
R	32*	Doug Barrault	MIN	2	0	0	0	1–	2	0	0	0	0	0	.0
D	38*	Roy Mitchell	MIN	3	0	0	0	0	0	0	0	0	0	0	.0

Goaltending

No.	Goaltender	GPI	Mins	Avg	W	L	T	EN	SO	GA	SA	S%
30	Jon Casey	60	3476	3.33	26	26	5	3	3	193	1683	.885
35	Darcy Wakaluk	29	1596	3.65	10	12	5	0	1	97	803	.879
	Totals	84	5090	3.45	36	38	10	3	4	293	2489	.882

Dependable defenceman Jim Johnson led the Stars with a plus/minus rating of +9 during the 1992-93 campaign.

Coaching History

Wren Blair, 1967-68; John Muckler and Wren Blair, 1968-69; Wren Blair and Charlie Bruns, 1969-70; Jackie Gordon, 1970-71 to 1972-73; Jackie Gordon and Parker MacDonald, 1973-74; Jackie Gordon and Charlie Burns, 1974-75; Ted Harris, 1975-76 to 1976-77; Ted Harris, André Beaulieu, Lou Nanne, 1977-78; Harry Howell and Glen Sonmor, 1978-79; Glen Sonmor, 1979-80 to 1981-82; Glen Sonmor and Murray Oliver, 1982-83; Bill Mahoney, 1983-84 to 1984-85; Lorne Henning, 1985-86; Lorne Henning and Glen Sonmor, 1986-87; Herb Brooks, 1987-88; Pierre Page, 1988-89 to 1989-90; Bob Gainey, 1990-91 to date.

Captains' History

Bob Woytowich, 1967-68; Elmer Vasko, 1968-69; Claude Larose, 1969-70; Ted Harris, 1970-71 to 1973-74; Bill Goldsworthy, 1974-75, 1975-76; Bill Hogaboam, 1976-77; Nick Beverly, 1977-78; J.P. Parise, 1978-79; Paul Shmyr, 1979-80, 1980-81; Tim Young, 1981-82; Craig Hartsburg, 1982-83; Brian Bellows, Craig Hartsburg, 1983-84; Craig Hartsburg, 1984-85 to 1987-88; Curt Fraser, Bob Rouse and Curt Giles, 1988-89; Curt Giles, 1989-90 to 1990-91; Mark Tinordi, 1991-92 to date.

General Managers' History

Wren A. Blair, 1967-68 to 1973-74; Jack Gordon, 1974-75 to 1976-77; Lou Nanne, 1977-78 to 1987-88; Jack Ferreira, 1988-89 to 1989-90; Bob Clarke, 1990-91 to 1991-92; Bob Gainey, 1992-93 to date.

Retired Numbers

8	Bill Goldsworthy	1967-1976
19	Bill Masterton	1967-1968

Club Records

Team

(Figures in brackets for season records are games played; records for fewest points, wins, ties, losses, goals, goals against are for 70 or more games)

Most Points	96	1982-83 (80)	
Most Wins	40	1982-83 (80)	
Most Ties	22	1969-70 (76)	
Most Losses	53	1975-76, 1977-78 (80)	
Most Goals	346	1981-82 (80)	
Most Goals Against	349	1987-88 (80)	
Fewest Points	45	1977-78 (80)	
Fewest Wins	18	1968-69 (76)	
		1977-78 (80)	
Fewest Ties	4	1989-90 (80)	
Fewest Losses	23	1981-82 (80)	
Fewest Goals	189	1968-69 (76)	
Fewest Goals Against	191	1971-72 (78)	

Longest Winning Streak
Over-all 7   Mar. 16-28/80
Home 11   Nov. 4-
       Dec. 27/72
Away 7   Nov. 18-
       Dec. 5/92

Longest Undefeated Streak
Over-all 12   Feb. 18-
       Mar. 15/82
       (9 wins, 3 ties)
Home 13   Oct. 28-
       Dec. 27/72
       (12 wins, 1 tie)
       Nov. 21-
       Jan. 9/80
       (10 wins, 3 ties)
       Jan. 17-
       Mar. 17/91
       (11 wins, 2 ties)
Away 7   Nov. 18-
       Dec. 5/92
       (7 wins)

Longest Losing Streak
Over-all 10   Feb. 1-20/76
Home 6   Jan. 17-
       Feb. 4/70
Away 8   Oct. 19-
       Nov. 13/75; Jan. 28-
       Mar. 3/88

Longest Winless Streak
Over-all 20   Jan. 15-
       Feb. 28/70
       (15 losses, 5 ties)
Home 12   Jan. 17-
       Feb. 25/70
       (8 losses, 4 ties)
Away 23   Oct. 25/74-
       Jan. 28/75
       (19 losses, 4 ties)

Most Shutouts, Season 7   1972-73 (78)
Most PIM, Season 2,313   1987-88 (80)
Most Goals, Game 15   Nov. 11/81
       (Wpg. 2 at Minn. 15)

Individual

Most Seasons 13   Neal Broten
Most Games 876   Neal Broten
Most Goals, Career 342   Brian Bellows
Most Assists, Career 547   Neal Broten
Most Points Career 796   Neal Broten
       (249 goals, 547 assists)
Most PIM, Career 1,567   Basil McRae
Most Shutouts, Career 26   Cesare Maniago
Longest Consecutive
   Games Streak 442   Danny Grant
       (Dec. 4/68-Apr. 7/74)
Most Goals, Season 55   Dino Ciccarelli
       (1981-82)
       Brian Bellows
       (1989-90)
Most Assists, Season 76   Neal Broten
       (1985-86)
Most Points, Season 114   Bobby Smith
       (1981-82)
       (43 goals, 71 assists)
Most PIM, Season 382   Basil McRae
       (1987-88)
Most Points, Defenseman
   Season 77   Craig Hartsburg
       (1981-82)
       (17 goals, 60 assists)

Most Points, Center,
   Season 114   Bobby Smith
       (1981-82)
       (43 goals, 71 assists)
Most Points, Right Wing,
   Season 107   Dino Ciccarelli
       (1981-82)
       (55 goals, 52 assists)
Most Point, Left Wing,
   Season 99   Brian Bellows
       (1989-90)
       (55 goals, 44 assists)
Most Points, Rookie,
   Season 98   Neal Broten
       (1981-82)
       (38 goals, 60 assists)
Most Shutouts, Season 6   Cesare Maniago
       (1967-68)
Most Goals, Game 5   Tim Young
       (Jan. 15/79)
Most Assists, Game 5   Murray Oliver
       (Oct. 24/71)
       Larry Murphy
       (Oct. 17/89)
Most Points, Game 7   Bobby Smith
       (Nov. 11/81)

** Records include Minnesota North Stars 1967-68 through 1992-93.

All-time Record vs. Other Clubs

Regular Season

			At Home								On Road								Total				
	GP	W	L	T	GF	GA	PTS	GP	W	L	T	GF	GA	PTS	GP	W	L	T	GF	GA	PTS
Boston	52	13	28	11	145	195	37	52	6	38	8	123	237	20	104	19	66	19	268	432	57
Buffalo	45	20	19	6	142	140	46	44	11	23	10	119	165	32	89	31	42	16	261	305	78
Calgary	40	19	16	5	150	132	43	40	4	26	10	107	169	18	80	23	42	15	257	301	61
Chicago	85	38	36	11	296	284	87	84	18	56	10	217	353	46	169	56	92	21	513	637	133
Detroit	81	43	24	14	310	241	100	79	29	38	12	270	312	70	160	72	62	26	580	553	170
Edmonton	23	6	12	5	82	86	17	22	1	15	6	68	114	8	45	7	27	11	150	200	25
Hartford	21	11	9	1	88	71	23	22	11	9	2	85	82	24	43	22	18	3	173	153	47
Los Angeles	57	33	15	9	231	161	75	56	16	26	14	172	210	46	113	49	41	23	403	371	121
Montreal	51	14	27	10	133	184	38	50	9	34	7	123	225	25	101	23	61	17	256	409	63
New Jersey	36	22	8	6	148	94	50	36	16	17	3	115	119	35	72	38	25	9	263	213	85
NY Islanders	38	14	19	5	112	146	33	38	9	21	8	110	149	26	76	23	40	13	222	295	59
NY Rangers	52	15	29	8	159	204	38	53	11	32	10	148	191	32	105	26	61	18	307	395	70
Ottawa	1	1	0	0	7	2	2	1	1	0	0	3	1	2	2	2	0	0	10	3	4
Philadelphia	58	23	22	13	189	196	59	58	8	40	10	132	232	26	116	31	62	23	321	428	85
Pittsburgh	56	31	20	5	215	190	67	55	16	34	5	149	213	37	111	47	54	10	364	403	104
Quebec	21	13	6	2	84	66	28	22	5	15	2	60	104	12	43	18	21	4	144	170	40
St. Louis	89	39	32	18	306	264	96	92	25	50	17	261	339	67	181	64	82	35	567	603	163
San Jose	3	3	0	0	21	9	6	3	0	3	0	18	7	6	6	3	3	0	39	16	12
Tampa Bay	3	2	1	0	11	9	4	4	3	0	1	11	5	7	7	5	1	1	22	14	11
Toronto	81	41	30	10	316	271	92	83	29	40	14	270	303	72	164	70	70	24	586	574	164
Vancouver	49	29	12	8	204	143	66	49	17	24	8	157	198	42	98	46	36	16	361	341	108
Washington	31	13	10	8	116	92	34	32	12	13	7	99	103	31	63	25	23	15	215	195	65
Winnipeg	25	15	8	2	115	81	32	24	11	12	1	86	90	23	49	26	20	3	201	171	55
Defunct Clubs	33	19	8	6	123	86	44	32	10	16	6	84	105	26	65	29	24	12	207	191	70
Totals	**1031**	**477**	**391**	**163**	**3703**	**3347**	**1117**	**1031**	**281**	**579**	**171**	**2987**	**4026**	**733**	**2062**	**758**	**970**	**334**	**6690**	**7373**	**1850**

Playoffs

	Series	W	L	GP	W	L	T	GF	GA	Last Mtg.	Round	Result
Boston	1	1	0	3	3	0	0	20	13	1981	PR	W 3-0
Buffalo	2	1	1	7	4	3	0	26	28	1981	QF	W 4-1
**Calgary	1	1	0	6	4	2	0	25	18	1981	SF	W 4-2
Chicago	6	2	4	33	14	19	0	119	119	1991	DSF	W 4-2
Detroit	1	0	1	7	3	4	0	19	23	1992	DSF	L 3-4
Edmonton	2	1	1	9	4	5	0	30	36	1991	CF	W 4-1
Los Angeles	1	1	0	7	4	3	0	26	21	1968	QF	W 4-3
Montreal	2	1	1	13	6	7	0	37	48	1980	QF	W 4-3
NY Islanders	1	0	1	5	1	4	0	16	26	1981	F	L 1-4
Philadelphia	2	0	2	11	3	8	0	26	41	1980	SF	L 1-4
Pittsburgh	1	0	1	6	2	4	0	16	28	1991	F	L 2-4
St. Louis	9	4	5	52	26	26	0	158	152	1991	DF	W 4-2
Toronto	2	2	0	7	6	1	0	35	26	1983	DSF	W 3-1
Totals	**31**	**14**	**16**	**166**	**80**	**86**	**0**	**553**	**579**			

Playoff Results 1993-89

Year	Round	Opponent	Result	GF	GA
1992	DSF	Detroit	L 3-4	19	23
1991	F	Pittsburgh	L 2-4	16	28
	CF	Edmonton	W 4-1	20	14
	DF	St. Louis	W 4-2	22	17
	DSF	Chicago	W 4-2	23	16
1990	DSF	Chicago	L 3-4	18	21
1989	DSF	St. Louis	L 1-4	15	23

Abbreviations: Round: F – Final;
CF – conference final; **DF** – division final;
DSF – division semi-final; **SF** – semi-final;
QF – quarter-final; **PR** – preliminary round.
GA – goals against; **GF** – goals for.

1992-93 Results

	Home			Away	
Oct. 8	St. Louis	5-2	Oct. 6	St. Louis	4-6
10	Tampa Bay	2-1	15	St. Louis	5-4
13	Calgary	3-4	17	Montreal	1-8
22	Quebec	5-2	18	Toronto	5-1
24	Los Angeles	5-5	28	Edmonton	2-5
Nov. 5	NY Islanders	3-0	30	Vancouver	3-2
7	Edmonton	2-2	31	Calgary	3-5
10	Pittsburgh	1-4	Nov.15	Chicago	1-2
12	Winnipeg	2-7	18	Winnipeg	5-4
14	Chicago*	3-0	19	Tampa Bay	4-1
25	Vancouver	2-4	21	Buffalo	4-3
27	NY Rangers	4-4	30	NY Rangers	4-2
28	San Jose	10-3	Dec. 1	Ottawa	3-1
Dec.10	Edmonton	2-3	3	Detroit	2-3
12	Chicago	0-3	5	Quebec	7-4
15	Toronto	6-5	20	Chicago	0-4
19	Detroit	3-3	27	Winnipeg	4-7
22	St. Louis	2-2	Jan. 2	NY Islanders	2-3
26	Winnipeg	5-4	3	Hartford	6-6
31	Boston	5-3	6	New Jersey	1-5
Jan. 9	Tampa Bay	6-4	7	Pittsburgh	6-3
12	Chicago	1-3	14	Chicago	1-3
16	Calgary	4-3	19	Tampa Bay	4-2
21	Ottawa	7-2	24	Tampa Bay	2-2
23	Vancouver*	3-3	26	Toronto	2-1
28	New Jersey	4-2	Feb. 1	Vancouver	5-4
30	Tampa Bay	3-4	3	San Jose	7-3
Feb. 9	Washington	2-3	11	Tampa Bay	1-0
14	Toronto	5-6	13	Toronto	1-6
17	Los Angeles	5-10	25	Boston	3-3
20	Philadelphia*	2-3	27	St. Louis	3-3
21	Detroit*	1-4	28	Winnipeg	6-7
Mar. 6	Montreal	4-3	Mar. 3	Toronto	1-3
7	Detroit	1-7	11	Vancouver	4-3
9	San Jose	4-2	13	St. Louis	2-6
14	St. Louis	1-3	16	Philadelphia	3-4
21	Detroit*	2-6	18	Detroit	1-5
25	Toronto	3-3	31	Edmonton	2-5
27	Hartford	1-2	Apr. 1	Calgary	3-5
Apr. 6	Buffalo	3-1	3	Los Angeles	3-0
10	St. Louis	4-3	11	St. Louis	1-5
13	Chicago	2-3	15	Detroit	3-5

*Denotes afternoon game

Entry Draft Selections 1993-79

1993		1989		1985		1981	
Pick		**Pick**		**Pick**		**Pick**	
9	Todd Harvey	7	Doug Zmolek	51	Stephane Roy	13	Ron Meighan
35	Jamie Langenbrunner	28	Mike Craig	69	Mike Berger	27	Dave Donnelly
87	Chad Lang	60	Murray Garbutt	90	Dwight Mullins	31	Mike Sands
136	Rick Mrozik	75	Jean-François Quintin	111	MikeMullowney	33	Tom Hirsch
139	Per Svartvadet	87	Pat MacLeod	132	Mike Kelfer	34	Dave Preuss
165	Jeremy Stasiuk	91	Bryan Schoen	153	Ross Johnson	41	Jali Wahlsten
191	Rob Lurtsema	97	Rhys Hollyman	174	Tim Helmer	69	Terry Tait
243	Jordan Willis	112	Scott Cashman	195	Gordon Ernst	76	Jim Malwitz
249	Bill Lang	154	Jonathan Pratt	216	Ladislav Lubina	97	Kelly Hubbard
269	Cory Peterson	175	Kenneth Blum	237	Tommy Sjodin	118	Paul Guay
		196	Arturs Irbe			139	Jim Archibald
1992		217	Tom Pederson	**1984**		160	Kari Kaervo
Pick		238	Helmut Balderis	**Pick**		181	Scott Bjugstad
34	Jarkko Varvio			13	David Quinn	202	Steve Kudebeh
58	Jeff Bes	**1988**		46	Ken Hodge		
88	Jere Lehtinen	**Pick**		76	Miroslav Maly	**1980**	
130	Michael Johnson	1	Mike Modano	89	Jiri Poner	**Pick**	
154	Kyle Peterson	40	Link Gaetz	97	Kari Takko	16	Brad Palmer
178	Juha Lind	43	Shaun Kane	118	Gary McColgan	37	Don Beaupre
202	Lars Edstrom	64	Jeffrey Stop	139	Vladimir Kyhos	53	Randy Velischek
226	Jeff Romfo	148	Ken MacArthur	160	Darin MacInnis	79	Mark Huglen
250	Jeffrey Moen	169	Travis Richards	181	Duane Wahlin	100	Dave Jensen
		190	Ari Matilainen	201	Mike Orn	121	Dan Zavarise
1991		211	Grant Bischoff	222	Tom Terwilliger	142	Bill Stewart
Pick		232	Trent Andison	242	Mike Nightenale	163	Jeff Walters
8	Richard Matvichuk					184	Bob Lakso
74	Mike Torchia	**1987**		**1983**		205	Dave Richter
97	Mike Kennedy	**Pick**		**Pick**			
118	Mark Lawrence	6	David Archibald	1	Brian Lawton	**1979**	
137	Geoff Finch	35	Scott McCrady	36	Malcolm Parks	**Pick**	
174	MichaelBurkett	48	Kevin Kaminski	38	Frantisek Musil	6	Craig Hartsburg
184	Derek Herlofsky	73	John Weisbrod	56	Mitch Messier	10	Tom McCarthy
206	Tom Nemeth	88	Teppo Kivela	76	Brian Durand	42	Neal Broten
228	Shayne Green	109	Darcy Norton	96	Rich Geist	63	Kevin Maxwell
250	Jukka Suomalainen	130	Timo Kulonen	116	Tom McComb	90	Jim Dobson
		151	Don Schmidt	136	Sean Toomey	111	Brian Gualazzi
1990		172	Jarmo Myllys	156	Don Biggs		
Pick		193	Larry Olimb	176	Paul Pulis		
8	Derian Hatcher	214	Mark Felicio	196	Milos Riha		
50	Laurie Billeck	235	Dave hields	212	Oldrich Valek		
70	Cal McGowan			236	Paul Roff		
71	Frank Kovacs	**1986**					
92	Enrico Ciccone	**Pick**		**1982**			
113	Roman Turek	12	Warren Babe	**Pick**			
134	Jeff Levy	30	Neil Wilkinson	2	Brian Bellows		
155	Doug Barrault	33	Dean Kolstad	59	Wally Chapman		
176	Joe Biondi	54	Eric Bennett	80	Rob Rouse		
197	Troy Binnie	55	Rob Zettler	81	Dusan Pasek		
218	Ole-Eskild Dahlstrom	58	Brad Turner	101	Marty Wiitala		
239	John McKersie	75	Kirk Tomlinson	122	Todd Carlile		
		96	Jari Gronstrand	143	Victor Zhluktov		
		159	Scott Mathias	164	Paul Miller		
		180	Lance Pitlick	185	Pat Micheletti		
		201	Dan Keczmer	206	Arnold Kadlec		
		222	Garth Joy	227	Scott Knutson		
		243	Kurt Stahura				

Coach and General Manager

GAINEY, BOB
Coach and General Manager, Dallas Stars.
Born in Peterborough, Ont., December 13, 1953.

Bob Gainey added the general manager's portfolio to his job description in June, 1992 after Bob Clarke rejoined the Philadelphia Flyers organization.

In his first season as an NHL head coach, Bob Gainey led the Minnesota North Stars through stunning playoff upsets of the League's top two teams and all the way to the Stanley Cup Finals. After surprising the League's top finishing Chicago Blackhawks in the Norris Division Semi-Finals, Gainey's Stars went on to eliminate the League's second place finishers—the St. Louis Blues—in the Norris Division Finals. The North Stars then defeated the defending Stanley Cup Champion Edmonton Oilers before bowing in six games to the Pittsburgh Penguins in the 1991 Stanley Cup Finals.

Gainey, who was appointed head coach of the Stars on June 19, 1990 following a 16-year NHL career and a one-season coaching stint in Epinal, France, was Montreal's first choice (eighth overall) in the 1973 Amateur Draft. During his 16-year career with the Canadiens, Gainey was a member of five Stanley Cup-winning teams and was named the Conn Smythe Trophy winner in 1979. He was a four-time recipient of the Frank Selke Trophy (1978-81), awarded to the League's top defensive forward, and participated in four NHL All-Star Games (1977, 1978, 1980 and 1981). He served as team captain for eight seasons (1981-89). During his career, he played in 1,160 regular-season games, registering 239 goals and 262 assists for 501 points. In addition, he tallied 73 points (25-48-73) in 182 post-season games.

Coaching Record

Season	Team	Regular Season					Playoffs			
		Games	W	L	T	%	Games	W	L	%
1989-90	Epinal	....	....	....	....	....	....	....	....	....
1990-91	Minnesota (NHL)	80	27	39	14	.425	23	14	9	.643
1991-92	Minnesota (NHL)	80	32	42	6	.438	7	3	4	.429
1992-93	Minnesota (NHL)	84	36	38	10	.488	....	....	....	....
	NHL Totals	244	95	119	30	.451	30	17	13	.567

Club Directory

Dallas Stars Hockey Club, Inc.
901 Main Street, Suite 2301
Dallas, TX 75202
Phone **214/712-2890**
FAX 214/712-2800

Reunion Arena　　　　　　　　　　　　　　　　**Capacity:** 16,814

Executive
Owner and Governor . . . . Norman N. Green
President. . . . . James Lites
Vice President of Hockey Operations . . . . Bob Gainey
Vice President of Marketing . . . . William C. Strong
Vice President of Advertising and Promotion. . . . . Jeff Cogen
Vice President of Finance . . . . Rick McLaughlin
Director of Administration . . . . Geoff Moore
Executive Assistant . . . . Sally Turnbull
Executive Assistant . . . . Tracy Schwarzbach

Hockey
General Manager and Head Coach. . . . . Bob Gainey
Assistant General Manager . . . . Les Jackson
Director of Amateur Scouting. . . . . Craig Button
Assistant Coaches . . . . Doug Jarvis, Rick Wilson
Head Trainer . . . . Dave Surprenant
Assistant Trainer. . . . . Dave Smith
Strength Coach . . . . Norm Temnograd
Equipment Manager . . . . Lance Vogt
Assistant to the General Manager . . . . Doug Armstrong
Assistant to the Hockey Department/Team Video . Dan Stuchal
Administrative Assistant . . . . Wendy Flora

Public Relations
Director of Public Relations . . . . Larry Kelly
Assistant Director of Public Relations . . . . Todd Sharrock
Director of Publications . . . . Alicia Braswell
Director of Community Relations . . . . Kristin Laminack

Ticket Sales
Director of Ticket Sales . . . . Murray Cohn
Senior Account Executive . . . . Brian Byrnes
Senior Account Executive . . . . Paul Hart
Manager of Group Sales . . . . Renay Hodgson

Advertising and Promotions
Director of Promotions . . . . Cookie Lehman
Promotions Manager . . . . Jeff Buch
Advertising & Promotions Coordinator . . . . Christy Martinez

Merchandising
Director of Merchandising . . . . Mary Meulman
Merchandising Operations Manager . . . . Jill Warnock
Manager of Retail Merchandising . . . . Pete Waggoner

Corporate Sales
Director of Advertising Sales . . . . Pam Sherrill
Director of Corporate Sales . . . . Jim O'Hickey
Director of Corporate Hospitality . . . . Jill Cogen
Assistant Director of Advertising Sales . . . . Stephen Black

Broadcasting
Director of Broadcasting . . . . Doug Kennedy
Announcers . . . . Mike Fornes, Ralph Strangis
Director of Broadcast and Sales Services . . . . . . Rebecca Whitehead

Finance
Controller . . . . Terry Garcia
Director of Box Office Operations . . . . Augie Manfredo
Staff Accountant . . . . Tim Montrose
Assistant Box Office Manager . . . . Stacey Lesanto
Accounting Assistant . . . . Cliff Johnson
Box Office Assistant . . . . Lori Uselton

Operations
Receptionist . . . . Sonja Mayer-Helmer

Practice Facility . . . . North Dallas Ice Arena
Television . . . . KTXA–21, KTUT–11, HSE (cable)
Radio . . . . KLIF–570 AM
Colors . . . . Black, Green, Gold and White

Detroit Red Wings

1992-93 Results: 47w-28L-9T 103PTS. Second, Norris Division

Dino Ciccarelli, who compiled 97 points in 1992-93, needs just 43 more to reach the 1,000-point career milestone.

Schedule

Home		Away	
Oct. Wed. 13 St Louis		**Oct.** Tues. 5 Dallas	
Sat. 16 Toronto		Fri. 8 Anaheim	
Thur. 21 Winnipeg		Sat. 9 Los Angeles	
Mon. 25 Dallas		Fri. 15 Toronto	
Wed. 27 Los Angeles		Mon. 18 Buffalo	
Nov. Tues. 2 Boston		Sat. 23 Chicago	
Thur. 4 Toronto		Sat. 30 Quebec	
Tues. 9 Edmonton		**Nov.** Sat. 13 Pittsburgh	
Sat. 27 Dallas*		Wed. 17 Winnipeg	
Dec. Fri. 3 Ottawa		Sat. 20 New Jersey*	
Mon. 6 Winnipeg		Sun. 21 St Louis	
Thur. 9 St Louis		Tues. 23 San Jose	
Sat. 11 San Jose*		Wed. 24 Vancouver	
Tues. 14 Anaheim		Sun. 28 NY Islanders*	
Fri. 17 NY Rangers		**Dec.** Wed. 1 Hartford	
Tues. 21 Chicago		Sun. 5 Winnipeg	
Fri. 31 Los Angeles		Sat. 18 Montreal	
Jan. Wed. 12 Tampa Bay		Thur. 23 Philadelphia	
Fri. 14 Dallas		Mon. 27 Dallas	
Wed. 19 Anaheim		**Jan.** Tues. 4 St Louis	
Tues. 25 Chicago		Thur. 6 San Jose	
Sat. 29 Winnipeg*		Sat. 8 Los Angeles	
Feb. Fri. 4 Pittsburgh		Mon. 10 Anaheim	
Tues. 8 Vancouver		Sat. 15 Boston	
Fri. 11 Philadelphia		Mon. 17 Tampa Bay	
Wed. 16 Florida		(at Minnesota)	
Fri. 18 Edmonton		Thur. 27 Chicago	
Wed. 23 New Jersey		Sun. 30 Washington*	
Thur. 24 Hartford		**Feb.** Wed. 2 Tampa Bay	
(at Cleveland)		Sat. 5 Toronto	
Sat. 26 San Jose*		Sat. 12 St Louis	
Mar. Tues. 1 Calgary		Tues. 15 Toronto	
Fri. 4 Toronto		Sun. 20 Florida	
Sun. 6 Buffalo		**Mar.** Mon. 7 NY Rangers	
Tues. 15 Vancouver		Wed. 9 Calgary	
Thur. 17 NY Islanders		Fri. 11 Edmonton	
Tues. 22 Chicago		Sat. 19 Winnipeg	
Fri. 25 Washington		Wed. 23 Ottawa	
Tues. 29 Hartford		Sun. 27 Chicago*	
Thur. 31 Quebec		**Apr.** Tues. 5 Vancouver	
Apr. Sat. 2 Calgary*		Sat. 9 Calgary	
Sun. 3 St Louis*		Sun. 10 Edmonton	
Wed. 13 Montreal		Thur. 14 Dallas	

* Denotes afternoon game.

Home Starting Times:

Weeknights and Saturdays	7:35 p.m.
Sundays	7:05 p.m.
Matinees	1:05 p.m.
Except Sat. Oct. 16	8:05 p.m.

Franchise date: September 25, 1926

CENTRAL DIVISION

WESTERN CONFERENCE

68th NHL Season

Year-by-Year Record

Season	GP	Home W	L	T	Road W	L	T	Overall W	L	T	GF	GA	Pts.	Finished	Playoff Result
1992-93	84	25	14	3	22	14	6	47	28	9	369	280	103	2nd, Norris Div.	Lost Div. Semi-Final
1991-92	80	24	12	4	19	13	8	43	25	12	320	256	98	1st, Norris Div.	Lost Div. Final
1990-91	80	26	14	0	8	24	8	34	38	8	273	298	76	3rd, Norris Div.	Lost Div. Semi-Final
1989-90	80	20	14	6	8	24	8	28	38	14	288	323	70	5th, Norris Div.	Out of Playoffs
1988-89	80	20	14	6	14	20	6	34	34	12	313	316	80	1st, Norris Div.	Lost Div. Semi-Final
1987-88	80	24	10	6	17	18	5	41	28	11	322	269	93	1st, Norris Div.	Lost Conf. Championship
1986-87	80	20	14	6	14	22	4	34	36	10	260	274	78	2nd, Norris Div.	Lost Conf. Championship
1985-86	80	10	26	4	7	31	2	17	57	6	266	415	40	5th, Norris Div.	Out of Playoffs
1984-85	80	19	14	7	8	27	5	27	41	12	313	357	66	3rd, Norris Div.	Lost Div. Semi-Final
1983-84	80	18	20	2	13	22	5	31	42	7	298	323	69	3rd, Norris Div.	Lost Div. Semi-Final
1982-83	80	14	19	7	7	25	8	21	44	15	263	344	57	5th, Norris Div.	Out of Playoffs
1981-82	80	15	19	6	6	28	6	21	47	12	270	351	54	6th, Norris Div.	Out of Playoffs
1980-81	80	16	15	9	3	28	9	19	43	18	252	339	56	5th, Norris Div.	Out of Playoffs
1979-80	80	14	21	5	12	22	6	26	43	11	268	306	63	5th, Norris Div.	Out of Playoffs
1978-79	80	15	17	8	8	24	8	23	41	16	252	295	62	5th, Norris Div.	Out of Playoffs
1977-78	80	22	11	7	10	23	7	32	34	14	252	266	78	2nd, Norris Div.	Lost Quarter-Final
1976-77	80	12	22	6	4	33	3	16	55	9	183	309	41	5th, Norris Div.	Out of Playoffs
1975-76	80	17	15	8	9	29	2	26	44	10	226	300	62	4th, Norris Div.	Out of Playoffs
1974-75	80	17	17	6	6	28	6	23	45	12	259	335	58	4th, Norris Div.	Out of Playoffs
1973-74	78	21	12	6	8	27	4	29	39	10	255	319	68	6th, East Div.	Out of Playoffs
1972-73	78	22	12	5	15	17	7	37	29	12	265	243	86	5th, East Div.	Out of Playoffs
1971-72	78	25	11	3	8	24	7	33	35	10	261	262	76	5th, East Div.	Out of Playoffs
1970-71	78	17	15	7	5	30	4	22	45	11	209	308	55	7th, East Div.	Out of Playoffs
1969-70	76	20	11	7	20	10	8	40	21	15	246	199	95	3rd, East Div.	Lost Quarter-Final
1968-69	76	23	8	7	10	23	5	33	31	12	239	221	78	5th, East Div.	Out of Playoffs
1967-68	74	18	15	4	9	20	8	27	35	12	245	257	66	6th, East Div.	Out of Playoffs
1966-67	70	21	11	3	6	28	1	27	39	4	212	241	58	5th,	Out of Playoffs
1965-66	70	20	8	7	11	19	5	31	27	12	221	194	74	4th,	Lost Final
1964-65	70	25	7	3	15	16	4	40	23	7	224	175	87	1st,	Lost Semi-Final
1963-64	70	23	9	3	7	20	8	30	29	11	191	204	71	4th,	Lost Final
1962-63	70	19	10	6	13	15	7	32	25	13	200	194	77	4th,	Lost Final
1961-62	70	17	11	7	6	22	7	23	33	14	184	219	60	5th,	Out of Playoffs
1960-61	70	15	13	7	10	16	9	25	29	16	195	215	66	4th,	Lost Final
1959-60	70	18	14	3	8	15	12	26	29	15	186	197	67	4th,	Lost Semi-Final
1958-59	70	13	17	5	12	20	3	25	37	8	167	218	58	6th,	Out of Playoffs
1957-58	70	16	11	8	13	18	4	29	29	12	176	207	70	3rd,	Lost Semi-Final
1956-57	70	23	7	5	15	13	7	38	20	12	198	157	88	1st,	Lost Semi-Final
1955-56	70	21	6	8	9	18	8	30	24	16	183	148	76	2nd,	Lost Final
1954-55	**70**	**25**	**5**	**5**	**17**	**12**	**6**	**42**	**17**	**11**	**204**	**134**	**95**	**1st,**	**Won Stanley Cup**
1953-54	**70**	**24**	**4**	**7**	**13**	**15**	**7**	**37**	**19**	**14**	**191**	**132**	**88**	**1st,**	**Won Stanley Cup**
1952-53	70	20	5	10	16	11	8	36	16	18	222	133	90	1st,	Lost Semi-Final
1951-52	**70**	**24**	**7**	**4**	**20**	**7**	**8**	**44**	**14**	**12**	**215**	**133**	**100**	**1st,**	**Won Stanley Cup**
1950-51	70	25	3	7	19	10	6	44	13	13	236	139	101	1st,	Lost Semi-Final
1949-50	**70**	**19**	**9**	**7**	**18**	**10**	**7**	**37**	**19**	**14**	**229**	**164**	**88**	**1st,**	**Won Stanley Cup**
1948-49	60	21	6	3	13	13	4	34	19	7	195	145	75	1st,	Lost Final
1947-48	60	16	9	5	14	9	7	30	18	12	187	148	72	2nd,	Lost Final
1946-47	60	14	10	6	8	17	5	22	27	11	190	193	55	4th,	Lost Semi-Final
1945-46	50	16	5	4	4	15	6	20	20	10	146	159	50	4th,	Lost Semi-Final
1944-45	50	19	5	1	12	9	4	31	14	5	218	161	67	2nd,	Lost Final
1943-44	50	18	5	2	8	13	4	26	18	6	214	177	58	2nd,	Lost Semi-Final
1942-43	**50**	**16**	**4**	**5**	**9**	**10**	**6**	**25**	**14**	**11**	**169**	**124**	**61**	**1st,**	**Won Stanley Cup**
1941-42	48	14	7	3	5	18	1	19	25	4	140	147	42	5th,	Lost Final
1940-41	48	14	5	5	7	11	6	21	16	11	112	102	53	3rd,	Lost Final
1939-40	48	11	10	3	5	16	3	16	26	6	91	126	38	5th,	Lost Semi-Final
1938-39	48	14	8	2	4	16	4	18	24	6	107	128	42	5th,	Lost Semi-Final
1937-38	48	8	10	6	4	15	5	12	25	11	99	133	35	4th, Amn. Div.	Out of Playoffs
1936-37	**48**	**14**	**5**	**5**	**11**	**9**	**4**	**25**	**14**	**9**	**128**	**102**	**59**	**1st, Amn. Div.**	**Won Stanley Cup**
1935-36	**48**	**14**	**5**	**5**	**10**	**11**	**3**	**24**	**16**	**8**	**124**	**103**	**56**	**1st, Amn. Div.**	**Won Stanley Cup**
1934-35	48	11	8	5	8	14	2	19	22	7	127	114	45	4th, Amn. Div.	Out of Playoffs
1933-34*	48	15	5	4	9	9	6	24	14	10	113	98	58	1st, Amn. Div.	Lost Final
1932-33*	48	17	3	4	8	12	4	25	15	8	111	93	58	2nd, Amn. Div.	Lost Semi-Final
1931-32	48	15	3	6	3	17	4	18	20	10	95	108	46	3rd, Amn. Div.	Lost Quarter-Final
1930-31**	44	10	7	5	6	14	2	16	21	7	102	105	39	4th, Amn. Div.	Out of Playoffs
1929-30	44	9	10	3	5	14	3	14	24	6	117	133	34	4th, Amn. Div.	Out of Playoffs
1928-29	44	11	6	5	8	13	1	19	16	9	72	63	47	3rd, Amn. Div.	Lost Quarter-Final
1927-28	44	9	10	3	10	9	3	19	19	6	88	79	44	4th, Amn. Div.	Out of Playoffs
1926-27***	44	6	15	1	6	13	3	12	28	4	76	105	28	5th, Amn. Div.	Out of Playoffs

* Team name changed to Red Wings. ** Team name changed to Falcons. *** Team named Cougars.

1993-94 Player Personnel

FORWARDS	HT	WT	S	Place of Birth	Date	1992-93 Club
AIVAZOFF, Micah	6-0	185	L	Powell River, B.C.	5/4/69	Adirondack
BERMINGHAM, Jim	6-3	201	L	Montreal, Que.	11/12/71	Adirondack
BOWEN, Curtis	6-1	190	L	Kenora, Ont.	3/24/74	Ottawa (OHL)
BURR, Shawn	6-1	195	L	Sarnia, Ont.	7/1/66	Detroit
CASSELMAN, Mike	5-11	180	L	Morrisburg, Ont.	8/23/68	Adirondack
CICCARELLI, Dino	5-10	175	R	Sarnia, Ont.	2/8/60	Detroit
CLOUTIER, Sylvain	6-0	195	L	Mont-Laureir, Que.	2/13/74	Guelph
DRAKE, Dallas	6-0	180	L	Trail, B.C.	2/4/69	Detroit
DRAPER, Kris	5-11	190	L	Toronto, Ont.	5/24/71	Moncton-Winnipeg
FEDOROV, Sergei	6-1	191	L	Pskov, Russia	12/5/69	Detroit
FREDERICK, Joe	6-1	190	R	Madison, WI	8/9/69	North. Mich.-Adirondack
HANAS, Trevor	6-0	175	R	Regina, Sask.	1/20/75	Regina-Adirondack
HARKINS, Brett	6-1	170	L	North Ridgeville, OH	7/2/70	Bowling Green
HENDRY, John	6-1	180	L	Mississauga, Ont.	5/15/70	Lake Superior State
HILLER, Jim	6-2	200	R	Port Alberni, B.C.	5/15/69	Phoe.-L.A.-Detroit
JOHNSON, Greg	5-10	173	R	Thunder Bay, Ont.	3/16/71	North Dakota
KENNEDY, Sheldon	5-10	175	R	Brandon, Man.	6/15/69	Detroit
KOZLOV, Vyacheslav	5-10	172	L	Voskresensk, Russia	5/3/72	Adirondack-Detroit
LAPOINTE, Martin	5-11	200	R	Ville St. Pierre, Que.	9/12/73	Laval-Adirondack
MALTAIS, Steve	6-2	210	L	Arvida, Que.	1/25/69	Tampa Bay-Atlanta
MARTIN, Craig	6-2	219	R	Amherst, N.S.	1/21/71	Moncton
McCARTY, Darren	6-1	214	R	Burnaby, B.C.	4/1/72	Adirondack
McDONALD, Jason	6-0	195	R	Charlottetown, P.E.I.	4/1/74	Owen Sound
PEDERSON, Mark	6-2	196	L	Prelate, Sask.	1/14/68	Philadelphia-San Jose
PRIMEAU, Keith	6-4	220	L	Toronto, Ont.	11/24/71	Detroit
PROBERT, Bob	6-3	215	L	Windsor, Ont.	6/5/65	Detroit
SHEPPARD, Ray	6-1	118	R	Pembroke, Ont.	5/27/66	Detroit
SILLINGER, Mike	5-10	191	R	Regina, Sask.	6/29/71	Adirondack-Detroit
TAYLOR, Tim	6-1	180	L	Stratford, Ont.	2/6/69	Baltimore-Hamilton
YZERMAN, Steve	5-11	185	R	Cranbrook, B.C.	5/9/65	Detroit
DEFENSEMEN						
ANGELHART, Serge	6-2	189	R	Hull, Que.	4/18/70	Adirondack-Ft. Wayne
BARBEAU, Frederic	6-3	198	L	Victoriaville, Que.	4/24/75	St. Jean
BOUGHNER, Bob	5-11	201	R	Windsor, Ont.	3/8/71	Adirondack-Toledo
CHIASSON, Steve	6-1	205	L	Barrie, Ont.	4/14/67	Detroit
COFFEY, Paul	6-1	200	L	Weston, Ont.	6/1/61	Los Angeles-Detroit
HOWE, Mark	5-11	185	L	Detroit, MI	5/28/55	Detroit
KONROYD, Steve	6-1	195	R	Scarborough, Ont.	2/10/61	Hartford-Detroit
KONSTANTINOV, Vlad.	5-11	176	R	Murmansk, Russia	3/19/67	Detroit
KRUPPKE, Gord	6-1	200	R	Slave Lake, Alta.	4/2/69	Adirondack-Detroit
LAROSE, Benoit	6-0	200	L	Ottawa, Ont.	5/31/73	Laval
LIDSTROM, Nicklas	6-2	180	L	Vasteras, Sweden	4/28/70	Detroit
MALGUNAS, Stewart	5-11	190	L	Prince George, B.C.	4/21/70	Adirondack
MALYKHIN, Igor	6-1	176	L	Moscow, Russia	6/6/65	Adirondack
MOTKOV, Dimitri	6-3	190	R	Moscow, Russia	2/23/71	Adirondack
PUSHOR, Jamie	6-3	192	R	Lethbridge, Alta.	2/11/73	Lethbridge
RACINE, Yves	6-0	185	L	Matane, Que.	2/7/69	Detroit
WALKER,Jeff	6-4	190	L	Sudbury, Ont.	2/6/74	Peterborough
WARD, Aaron	6-2	200	R	Windsor, Ont.	1/1/73	Michigan
YORK, Jason	6-1	192	R	Ottawa, Ont.	5/20/70	Adirondack-Detroit
ZYGULSKI, Scott	6-1	190	R	South Bend, IN	4/11/70	Boston College

GOALTENDERS	HT	WT	C	Place of Birth	Date	1992-93 Club
CHEVELDAE, Tim	5-10	I75	L	Melville, Sask.	2/15/68	Detroit
DENOMME, C.J.	5-11	180	L	London, Ont.	4/8/74	Kitchener
GAGNON, Dave	6-0	185	L	Windsor, Ont.	10/31/67	Adirondack-Fort Wayne
HODSON, Kevin	6-0	182	L	Winnipeg, Man.	3/27/72	Sault Ste. Marie
ING, Peter	6-2	170	L	Toronto, Ont.	4/28/69	Det.(Col.)-San Diego
MARACLE, Norm	5-9	175	L	Belleville, Ont.	10/2/74	Saskatoon
OSGOOD, Chris	5-9	156	L	Peace River, Alta.	11/26/72	Adirondack
RIENDEAU, Vincent	5-10	181	L	St. Hyacinthe, Que.	4/20/66	Detroit

Coach

BOWMAN, WILLIAM, SCOTT (SCOTTY)
Coach, Detroit Red Wings. Born in Montreal, Que. September 18, 1933.

The winningest coach in NHL history, Scott Bowman was appointed as the 22nd coach of the Detroit Red Wings on June 15, 1993. Bowman, who ranks first among coaches with an all-time regular season record of 834-380-226 in 1140 games, has also recorded more post-season victories than any other coach, compiling a 137-82 mark in playoff encounters.

One of only two coaches to guide three different teams into the Stanley Cup Finals, Bowman's six Cup victories are second only to Montreal's Toe Blake. After guiding the St. Louis Blues into the championship round in three consecutive seasons from 1968-70, Bowman was appointed head coach of the Montreal Canadiens, who captured five Stanley Cup titles under Bowman's supervision.

Following an eight season term as the general manager of the Buffalo Sabres, and a brief stint as a commentator for CBC Television, Bowman joined the Pittsburgh Penguins as director of player development, eventually returning behind the bench when coach Bob Johnson became ill in September, 1991. Bowman was elected to the Hockey Hall of Fame as a builder in 1991.

NHL Coaching Record

		Regular Season					Playoffs			
Season	Team	Games	W	L	T	%	Games	W	L	%
1967-68	St. Louis	58	23	21	14	.517	18	8	10	.444
1968-69	St. Louis	76	37	25	14	.579	12	8	4	.667
1969-70	St. Louis	76	37	27	12	.566	16	8	8	.500
1970-71	St. Louis	28	13	10	5	.554	6	2	4	.333
1971-72	Montreal	78	46	16	16	.692	6	2	4	.333
1972-73	Montreal	78	52	10	16	.769	17	12	5	.706*
1973-74	Montreal	78	45	24	9	.635	6	2	4	.333
1974-75	Montreal	80	47	14	19	.706	11	6	5	.545
1975-76	Montreal	80	58	11	11	.794	13	12	1	.923*
1976-77	Montreal	80	60	8	12	.825	14	12	2	.857*
1977-78	Montreal	80	59	10	11	.806	15	12	3	.800*
1978-79	Montreal	80	52	17	11	.719	16	12	4	.750*
1979-80	Buffalo	80	47	17	16	.688	14	9	5	.643
1981-82	Buffalo	35	18	10	7	.614	4	1	3	.250

1992-93 Scoring

Regular Season

Pos	#	Player	Team	GP	G	A	Pts	+/-	PIM	PP	SH	GW	GT	S	%
C	19	Steve Yzerman	DET	84	58	79	137	33	44	13	7	6	0	307	18.9
R	22	Dino Ciccarelli	DET	82	41	56	97	12	81	21	0	8	0	200	20.5
C	91	Sergei Fedorov	DET	73	34	53	87	33	72	13	4	3	0	217	15.7
D	77	Paul Coffey	L.A.	50	8	49	57	9	50	2	0	0	0	182	4.4
			DET	30	4	26	30	7	27	3	0	0	0	72	5.6
			TOTAL	80	12	75	87	16	77	5	0	0	0	254	4.7
R	26	Ray Sheppard	DET	70	32	34	66	7	29	10	0	1	0	183	17.5
L	21	Paul Ysebaert	DET	80	34	28	62	19	42	3	3	8	1	186	18.3
D	3	Steve Chiasson	DET	79	12	50	62	14	155	6	0	1	0	227	5.3
C	28*	Dallas Drake	DET	72	18	26	44	15	93	3	2	5	0	89	20.2
R	24	Bob Probert	DET	80	14	29	43	9-	292	6	0	3	0	128	10.9
D	5	Nicklas Lidstrom	DET	84	7	34	41	7	28	3	0	2	0	156	4.5
D	33	Yves Racine	DET	80	9	31	40	10	80	5	0	0	0	163	5.5
L	11	Shawn Burr	DET	80	10	25	35	18	74	1	1	2	0	99	10.1
D	4	Mark Howe	DET	60	3	31	34	22	22	3	0	0	0	72	4.2
L	55	Keith Primeau	DET	73	15	17	32	6-	152	4	1	2	1	75	20.0
R	15	Sheldon Kennedy	DET	68	19	11	30	1-	46	1	0	2	1	110	17.3
L	17	Gerard Gallant	DET	67	10	20	30	20	188	0	0	0	0	81	12.3
D	16	Vlad. Konstantinov	DET	82	5	17	22	22	137	0	0	0	0	85	5.9
C	23*	Mike Sillinger	DET	51	4	17	21	0	16	0	0	0	0	47	8.5
R	14*	Jim Hiller	L.A.	40	6	6	12	0	90	1	0	2	0	59	10.2
			DET	21	2	6	8	7	19	0	0	0	0	24	8.3
			TOTAL	61	8	12	20	7	109	1	0	2	0	83	9.6
D	8	Steve Konroyd	HFD	59	3	11	14	16-	63	0	0	0	0	62	4.8
			DET	6	0	1	1	1	4	0	0	0	0	4	.0
			TOTAL	65	3	12	15	15-	67	0	0	0	0	66	4.5
D	2	Brad McCrimmon	DET	60	1	14	15	21	71	1	0	0	0	53	1.9
L	25	John Ogrodnick	DET	19	6	6	12	2-	2	4	0	0	0	25	24.0
C	13*	Vyacheslav Kozlov	DET	17	4	1	5	1-	14	0	0	0	0	26	15.4
G	32	Tim Cheveldae	DET	67	0	4	4	0	4	0	0	0	0	0	.0
R	27*	Jim Cummins	DET	7	1	1	2	0	58	0	0	0	0	5	20.0
C	18	Chris Tancill	DET	4	1	0	1	2-	2	0	0	0	0	3	33.3
D	29	Dennis Vial	DET	9	0	1	1	1	20	0	0	0	0	5	.0
D	38*	Jason York	DET	2	0	0	0	0	0	0	0	0	0	1	.0
R	20*	Martin Lapointe	DET	3	0	0	0	2-	0	0	0	0	0	2	.0
D	38	Bobby Dollas	DET	6	0	0	0	1-	2	0	0	0	0	5	.0
D	8*	Gord Kruppke	DET	10	0	0	0	1	20	0	0	0	0	7	.0
G	37	Vincent Riendeau	DET	22	0	0	0	0	2	0	0	0	0	0	.0

Goaltending

No.	Goaltender	GPI	Mins	Avg	W	L	T	EN	SO	GA	SA	S%
37	Vincent Riendeau	22	1193	3.22	13	4	2	1	0	64	522	.877
32	Tim Cheveldae	67	3880	3.25	34	24	7	5	4	210	1897	.889
	Totals	**84**	**5088**	**3.30**	**47**	**28**	**9**	**6**	**4**	**280**	**2425**	**.885**

Playoffs

Pos	#	Player	Team	GP	G	A	Pts	+/-	PIM	PP	SH	GW	GT	S	%
D	77	Paul Coffey	DET	7	2	9	11	3-	2	0	0	0	0	24	8.3
C	91	Sergei Fedorov	DET	7	3	6	9	4	23	1	1	0	0	26	11.5
C	19	Steve Yzerman	DET	7	4	3	7	4-	4	1	1	1	0	24	16.7
R	22	Dino Ciccarelli	DET	7	4	2	6	6-	16	3	0	0	0	17	23.5
C	28*	Dallas Drake	DET	7	3	3	6	3	6	1	0	0	0	8	37.5
R	26	Ray Sheppard	DET	7	2	3	5	2	0	2	0	0	0	8	25.0
L	21	Paul Ysebaert	DET	7	3	1	4	2	2	0	1	1	0	11	27.3
D	3	Steve Chiasson	DET	7	2	2	4	3-	19	1	0	1	0	21	9.5
D	4	Mark Howe	DET	7	1	3	4	6	2	0	0	0	0	8	12.5
D	33	Yves Racine	DET	7	1	3	4	4	27	0	0	0	0	6	16.7
L	11	Shawn Burr	DET	7	2	1	3	2-	2	0	1	0	0	8	25.0
L	17	Gerard Gallant	DET	6	1	2	3	4-	4	0	0	0	0	7	14.3
R	24	Bob Probert	DET	7	0	3	3	1-	10	0	0	0	0	14	.0
R	15	Sheldon Kennedy	DET	7	1	1	2	1	2	0	0	0	0	10	10.0
C	13*	Vyacheslav Kozlov	DET	4	0	2	2	1	2	0	0	0	0	5	.0
G	32	Tim Cheveldae	DET	7	0	2	2	0	2	0	0	0	0	0	.0
L	55	Keith Primeau	DET	7	0	2	2	1	26	0	0	0	0	7	.0
D	5	Nicklas Lidstrom	DET	7	1	0	1	2-	0	1	0	0	0	8	12.5
D	16	Vlad. Konstantinov	DET	7	0	1	1	1-	8	0	0	0	0	5	.0
D	8	Steve Konroyd	DET	1	0	0	0	1-	0	0	0	0	0	0	.0
L	25	John Ogrodnick	DET	1	0	0	0	1-	0	0	0	0	0	1	.0
R	14*	Jim Hiller	DET	2	0	0	0	0	4	0	0	0	0	1	.0

Goaltending

No.	Goaltender	GPI	Mins	Avg	W	L	EN	SO	GA	SA	S%
32	Tim Cheveldae	7	423	3.40	3	4	0	0	24	200	.880
	Totals	**7**	**425**	**3.39**	**3**	**4**	**0**	**0**	**24**	**200**	**.880**

NHL Coaching Record – *continued*

		Regular Season					Playoffs			
Season	Team	Games	W	L	T	%	Games	W	L	%
1982-83	Buffalo	80	38	29	13	.556	10	6	4	.600
1983-84	Buffalo	80	48	25	7	.644	3	0	3	.000
1984-85	Buffalo	80	38	28	14	.563	5	2	3	.400
1985-86	Buffalo	37	18	18	1	.500	....	....	....	....
1986-87	Buffalo	12	3	7	2	.333	....	....	....	....
1991-92	Pittsburgh	80	39	32	9	.544	21	16	5	.762*
1992-93	Pittsburgh	84	56	21	7	.708	12	7	5	.583
	NHL Totals	**1440**	**834**	**380**	**226**	**.659**	**219**	**137**	**82**	**.626**

* Won Stanley Cup

Club Records

Team

(Figures in brackets for season records are games played; records for fewest points, wins, ties, losses, goals, goals against are for 70 or more games)

Most Points	103	1992-93 (84)
Most Wins	47	1992-93 (84)
Most Ties	18	1952-53 (70)
		1980-81 (80)
Most Losses	57	1985-86 (80)
Most Goals	369	1992-93 (84)
Most Goals Against	415	1985-86 (80)
Fewest Points	40	1985-86 (80)
Fewest Wins	16	1976-77 (80)
Fewest Ties	4	1966-67 (70)
Fewest Losses	13	1950-51 (70)
Fewest Goals	167	1958-59 (70)
Fewest Goals Against	132	1953-54 (70)

Longest Winning Streak

Over-all	9	Mar. 3-21/51;
		Feb. 27-
		Mar. 20/55
Home	14	Jan. 21-
		Mar. 25/65
Away	5	Five times

Longest Undefeated Streak

Over-all	15	Nov. 27-
		Dec. 28/52
		(8 wins, 7 ties)
Home	18	Dec. 26/54-
		Mar. 20/55
		(13 wins, 5 ties)
Away	15	Oct. 18-
		Dec. 20/51
		(10 wins, 5 ties)

Longest Losing Streak

Over-all	14	Feb. 24-
		Mar. 25/82
Home	7	Feb. 20-
		Mar. 25/82
Away	14	Oct. 19-
		Dec. 21/66

Longest Winless Streak

Over-all	19	Feb. 26-
		Apr. 3/77
		(18 losses, 1 tie)
Home	10	Dec. 11/85-
		Jan. 18/86
		(9 losses, 1 tie)
Away	26	Dec. 15/76-
		Apr. 3/77
		(23 losses, 3 ties)

Most Shutouts, Season	13	1953-54 (70)
Most. PIM, Season	2,393	1985-86 (80)
Most Goals, Game	15	Jan. 23/44
		(NYR 0 at Det. 15)

Individual

Most Seasons	25	Gordie Howe
Most Games	1,687	Gordie Howe
Most Goals, Career	786	Gordie Howe
Most Assists, Career	1,023	Gordie Howe
Most Points, Career	1,809	Gordie Howe
		(786 goals,
		1,023 assists)
Most PIM, Career	1,815	Bob Probert
Most Shutouts, Career	85	Terry Sawchuk

Longest Consecutive

Games Streak	548	Alex Delvecchio
		(Dec. 13/56-
		Nov. 11/64)
Most Goals, Season	65	Steve Yzerman
		(1988-89)
Most Assists, Season	90	Steve Yzerman
		(1988-89)
Most Points, Season	155	Steve Yzerman
		(1988-89)
		(65 goals, 90 assists)
Most PIM, Season	398	Bob Probert
		(1987-88)

Most Points, Defenseman

Season	74	Reed Larson
		(1982-83)
		(22 goals, 52 assists)

Most Points, Center,

Season	155	Steve Yzerman
		(1988-89)
		(65 goals, 90 assists)

Most Points, Right Wing,

Season	103	Gordie Howe
		(1968-69)
		(44 goals, 59 assists)

Most Points, Left Wing,

Season	105	John Ogrodnick
		(1984-85)
		(55 goals, 50 assists)

Most Points, Rookie,

Season	87	Steve Yzerman
		(1983-84)
		(39 goals, 48 assists)
Most Shutouts, Season	12	Terry Sawchuk
		(1951-52; 1953-54;
		1954-55)
		Glenn Hall
		(1955-56)
Most Goals, Game	6	Syd Howe
		(Feb. 3/44)
Most Assists, Game	*7	Billy Taylor
		(Mar. 16/47)
Most Points, Game	7	Carl Liscombe
		(Nov. 5/42)
		Don Grosso
		(Feb. 3/44)
		Billy Taylor
		(Mar. 16/47)

* NHL Record

Retired Numbers

6	Larry Aurie	1927-1939
7	Ted Lindsay	1944-57, 64-65
9	Gordie Howe	1946-1971
10	Alex Delvecchio	1951-1973

All-time Record vs. Other Clubs

Regular Season

		At Home							On Road							Total						
	GP	W	L	T	GF	GA	PTS	GP	W	L	T	GF	GA	PTS	GP	W	L	T	GF	GA	PTS
Boston	277	149	76	52	924	698	350	278	84	151	43	736	984	211	555	233	227	95	1660	1682	561
Buffalo	46	24	17	5	174	142	53	44	6	31	7	118	205	19	90	30	48	12	292	347	72
Calgary	37	19	12	6	145	123	44	38	10	23	5	122	173	25	75	29	35	11	267	296	69
Chicago	306	188	90	28	1054	755	404	306	115	143	48	844	927	278	612	303	233	76	1898	1682	682
Edmonton	22	8	12	2	85	102	18	22	7	11	4	93	112	18	44	15	23	6	178	214	36
Hartford	21	8	7	6	79	66	22	21	7	13	1	57	80	15	42	15	20	7	136	146	37
Los Angeles	57	23	27	7	226	218	53	58	15	32	11	178	247	41	115	38	59	18	404	465	94
Minnesota	79	38	29	12	312	270	88	81	24	43	14	241	310	62	160	62	72	26	553	580	150
Montreal	273	124	96	53	773	703	301	273	62	168	43	607	970	167	546	186	264	96	1380	1673	468
New Jersey	31	18	11	2	136	107	38	32	9	15	8	91	115	26	63	27	26	10	227	222	64
NY Islanders	36	19	15	2	130	120	40	37	13	22	2	105	147	28	73	32	37	4	235	267	68
NY Rangers	277	157	75	45	972	685	359	275	86	131	58	704	849	230	552	243	206	103	1676	1534	589
Ottawa	1	1	0	0	5	4	2	1	1	0	0	3	2	2	2	2	0	0	8	6	4
Philadelphia	50	23	18	9	178	165	55	51	11	29	11	153	209	33	101	34	47	20	331	374	88
Pittsburgh	57	36	10	11	229	158	83	56	13	39	4	162	251	30	113	49	49	15	391	409	113
Quebec	21	12	8	1	86	73	25	22	7	12	3	80	93	17	43	19	20	4	166	166	42
St. Louis	80	34	35	11	296	264	79	80	22	47	11	220	298	55	160	56	82	22	516	562	134
San Jose	3	3	0	0	21	7	6	4	3	0	1	18	11	7	7	6	0	1	39	18	13
Tampa Bay	3	3	0	0	18	9	6	4	3	1	0	30	17	6	7	6	1	0	48	26	12
Toronto	299	157	98	44	891	727	358	298	95	159	44	785	993	234	597	252	257	88	1676	1720	592
Vancouver	44	26	12	6	187	129	58	43	12	24	7	132	179	31	87	38	36	13	319	308	89
Washington	39	16	13	10	140	116	42	37	14	19	4	117	146	32	76	30	32	14	257	262	74
Winnipeg	25	12	10	3	99	96	27	23	7	8	8	71	78	22	48	19	18	11	170	174	49
Defunct Clubs	141	76	40	25	429	307	177	141	49	63	29	363	375	127	282	125	103	54	792	682	304
Totals	2225	1174	711	340	7589	6044	2688	2225	675	1184	366	6030	7771	1716	4450	1849	1895	706	13619	13815	4404

Playoffs

	Series	W	L	GP	W	L	T	GF	GA	Last Mtg.	Round	Result
Boston	7	3	4	33	14	19	0	98	96	1957	SF	L 1-4
**Calgary	1	1	0	2	2	0	0	8	5	1978	PR	W 2-0
Chicago	13	5	8	64	27	37	0	177	198	1992	DF	L 0-4
Edmonton	2	0	2	10	2	8	0	26	39	1988	CF	L 1-4
Minnesota	1	1	0	7	4	3	0	23	19	1992	DSF	W 4-3
Montreal	12	7	5	62	29	33	0	149	161	1978	QF	L 1-4
NY Rangers	5	4	1	23	13	10	0	57	49	1950	F	W 4-3
St. Louis	3	1	2	16	8	8	0	53	51	1991	DSF	L 3-4
Toronto	23	11	12	117	59	58	0	321	311	1993	DSF	L 3-4
Defunct Clubs	4	3	1	10	7	2	1	21	13			
Totals	71	36	35	344	165	178	1	933	942			

Playoff Results 1993-89

Year	Round	Opponent	Result	GF	GA
1993	DSF	Toronto	L 3-4	30	24
1992	DF	Chicago	L 0-4	6	11
	DSF	Minnesota	W 4-3	23	19
1991	DSF	St. Louis	L 3-4	20	24
1989	DSF	Chicago	L 2-4	18	25

Abbreviations: Round: F – Final;
CF – conference final; **DF** – division final;
DSF – division semi-final; **SF** – semi-final;
QF – quarter-final; **PR** – preliminary round.
GA – goals against; **GF** – goals for.

1992-93 Results

	Home				Away	
Oct. 15	Quebec	2-4	Oct. 6	Winnipeg		1-4
17	Edmonton	4-2	8	Los Angeles		5-3
20	Winnipeg	5-3	10	San Jose		6-3
28	San Jose	4-3	22	Pittsburgh		6-9
30	Toronto	7-1	24	St. Louis		6-1
Nov. 4	Montreal	3-4	25	Chicago		2-8
6	Hartford	5-2	31	Toronto		1-3
13	Pittsburgh	8-0	Nov. 7	Montreal		1-5
17	Chicago	5-4	11	Tampa Bay		4-6
19	Winnipeg	3-5	14	Hartford		2-0
23	Tampa Bay	10-5	20	Washington		7-5
25	St. Louis	11-6	28	St. Louis		2-3
27	Los Angeles	3-5	Dec. 2	NY Rangers		3-5
30	Washington	1-4	5	Tampa Bay		9-7
Dec. 3	Minnesota	2-4	9	Toronto		3-5
8	Chicago	2-3	15	Ottawa		3-2
11	Philadelphia	4-2	19	Minnesota		3-3
14	Calgary	0-3	26	Toronto		5-1
18	Boston	6-1	27	Chicago		4-0
22	Toronto	4-4	Jan. 2	Quebec		6-2
29	Chicago	3-6	17	Philadelphia		7-4
31	Ottawa	5-4	23	St. Louis		3-4
Jan. 4	Toronto	2-4	26	Calgary		9-1
8	Vancouver	6-3	27	Edmonton		2-2
11	St. Louis	0-1	30	Vancouver		4-4
13	Tampa Bay	5-3	Feb. 11	Los Angeles		6-6
15	San Jose	6-3	13	St. Louis		3-4
19	NY Rangers	2-2	14	Chicago		5-3
21	St. Louis	5-3	21	Minnesota*		4-1
Feb. 3	Chicago	5-0	22	Philadelphia		5-5
9	New Jersey	8-5	24	Buffalo		7-10
17	Tampa Bay	3-1	28	New Jersey		3-6
19	Calgary	3-3	Mar. 2	NY Islanders		2-3
27	Chicago*	1-2	7	Minnesota		7-1
Mar. 5	Toronto	5-1	10	Edmonton		6-3
16	Washington	2-4	11	Calgary		3-6
18	Minnesota	5-1	14	San Jose*		4-1
23	NY Islanders	3-2	20	Boston*		7-4
29	Los Angeles	3-9	21	Minnesota*		6-2
Apr. 3	Vancouver*	5-1	27	Tampa Bay		8-3
10	Buffalo*	6-5	Apr. 1	Chicago		3-1
15	Minnesota	5-3	8	Tampa Bay		9-1

*Denotes afternoon game

Entry Draft Selections 1993-79

1993 Pick		**1989** Pick		**1986** Pick		**1982** Pick	
22	Anders Eriksson	11	Mike Sillinger	1	Joe Murphy	17	Murray Craven
48	Jonathan Coleman	32	Bob Boughner	22	Adam Graves	23	Yves Courteau
74	Kevin Hilton	53	Nicklas Lidstrom	43	Derek Mayer	44	Carmine Vani
97	John Jakopin	74	Sergei Fedorov	64	Tim Cheveldae	66	Craig Coxe
100	Benoit Larose	95	Shawn McCosh	85	Johan Garpenlov	86	Brad Shaw
126	Norm Maracle	116	Dallas Drake	106	Jay Stark	107	Claude Vilgrain
152	Tim Spitzig	137	Scott Zygulski	127	Per Djoos	128	Greg Hudas
178	Yuri Yeresko	158	Andy Suhy	148	Dean Morton	149	Pat Lahey
204	Vitezslav Skuta	179	Bob Jones	169	Marc Potvin	170	Gary Cullen
230	Ryan Shanahan	200	Greg Bignell	190	Scott King	191	Brent Meckling
256	James Kosecki	204	Rick Judson	211	Tom Bissett	212	Mike Stern
282	Gordon Hunt	221	Vladimir Konstantinov	232	Peter Ekroth	233	Shaun Reagan
		242	Joseph Frederick				
1992 Pick		246	Jason Glickman	**1985** Pick		**1981** Pick	
22	Curtis Bowen	**1988** Pick		8	Brent Fedyk	23	Claude Loiselle
46	Darren McCarty	17	Kory Kocur	29	Jeff Sharples	44	Corrado Micalef
70	Sylvain Cloutier	38	Serge Anglehart	50	Steve Chiasson	86	Larry Trader
118	Mike Sullivan	47	Guy Dupuis	71	Mark Gowans	107	Gerard Gallant
142	Jason MacDonald	59	Petr Hrbek	92	Chris Luongo	128	Greg Stefan
166	Greg Scott	80	Sheldon Kennedy	113	Randy McKay	149	Rick Zombo
183	Justin Krall	143	Kelly Hurd	134	Thomas Bjur	170	Don Leblanc
189	C.J. Denomme	164	Brian McCormack	155	Mike Luckraft	191	Robert Nordmark
214	Jeff Walker	185	Jody Praznik	176	Rob Schenna		
238	Daniel McGillis	206	Glen Goodall	197	Erik Hamalainen	**1980** Pick	
262	Ryan Bach	227	Darren Colbourne	218	Bo Svanberg	11	Mike Blaisdell
		248	Donald Stone	239	Mikael Lindman	46	Mark Osborne
1991 Pick						88	Mike Corrigan
10	Martin Lapointe	**1987** Pick		**1984** Pick		109	Wayne Crawford
32	Jamie Pushor	11	Yves Racine	7	Shawn Burr	130	Mike Braun
54	Chris Osgood	32	Gordon Kruppke	28	Doug Houda	151	John Beukeboom
76	Michael Knuble	41	Bob Wilkie	49	Milan Chalupa	172	Dave Miles
98	Dmitri Motkov	52	Dennis Holland	91	Mats Lundstrom	193	Brian Rorabeck
142	Igor Malykhin	74	Mark Reimer	112	Randy Hansch		
186	Jim Bermingham	95	Radomir Brazda	133	Stefan Larsson	**1979** Pick	
208	Jason Firth	116	Sean Clifford	152	Lars Karlsson	3	Mike Foligno
230	Bart Turner	137	Mike Gober	154	Urban Nordin	45	Jody Gage
252	Andrew Miller	158	Kevin Scott	175	Bill Shibicky	46	Boris Fistric
		179	Mikko Haapakoski	195	Jay Rose	66	John Ogrodnick
1990 Pick		200	Darin Bannister	216	Tim Kaiser	87	Joe Paterson
3	Keith Primeau	221	Craig Quinlan	236	Tom Nickolau	108	Carmine Cirella
45	Vyacheslav Kozlov	242	Tomas Jansson				
66	Stewart Malgunas			**1983** Pick			
87	Tony Burns			4	Steve Yzerman		
108	Claude Barthe			25	Lane Lambert		
129	Jason York			46	Bob Probert		
150	Wes McCauley			68	David Korol		
171	Anthony Gruba			86	Petr Klima		
192	Travis Tucker			88	Joey Kocur		
213	Brett Larson			106	Chris Pusey		
234	John Hendry			126	Bob Pierson		
				146	Craig Butz		
				166	Dave Sikorski		
				186	Stuart Grimson		
				206	Jeff Frank		
				226	Charles Chiatto		

Captains' History

Art Duncan, 1926-27; Reg Noble, 1927-28 to 1929-30; George Hay, 1930-31; Carson Cooper, 1931-32; Larry Aurie, 1932-33; Herbie Lewis, 1933-34; Ebbie Goodfellow, 1934-35; Doug Young, 1935-36 to 1937-38; Ebbie Goodfellow, 1938-39 to 1940-41; Ebbie Goodfellow and Sid Abel, 1941-42; Sid Abel, 1942-43; Mud Bruneteau, Bill Hollett (co-captains), 1943-44; Bill Hollett, 1944-45; Bill Hollett, Sid Abel, 1945-46; Sid Abel, 1946-47 to 1951-52; Ted Lindsay, 1952-53 to 1955-56; Red Kelly, 1956-57, 1957-58; Gordie Howe, 1958-59 to 1961-62; Alex Delvecchio, 1962-63 to 1972-73; Alex Delvecchio, Nick Libett, Red Berenson, Gary Bergman, Ted Harris, Mickey Redmond, Larry Johnston, 1973-74; Marcel Dionne, 1974-75; Danny Grant, Terry Harper, 1975-76; Danny Grant, Dennis Polonich, 1976-77; Dan Maloney, Dennis Hextall, 1977-78; Dennis Hextall, Nick Libett, Paul Woods, 1978-79; Dale McCourt, 1979-80; Errol Thompson, Reed Larson, 1980-81; Reed Larson, 1981-82; Danny Gare, 1982-83 to 1985-86; Steve Yzerman, 1986-87 to date.

General Managers' History

Art Duncan, 1926-27; Jack Adams, 1927-28 to 1962-63; Sid Abel, 1963-64 to 1969-70; Sid Abel and Ned Harkness, 1970-71; Ned Harkness, 1971-72 to 1973-74; Alex Delvecchio, 1974-75 to 1975-76; Alex Delvecchio and Ted Lindsay, 1976-77; Ted Lindsay, 1977-78 to 1979-80; Jimmy Skinner, 1980-81 to 1981-82; Jim Devellano, 1982-83 to 1989-90; Bryan Murray, 1990-91 to date.

Coaching History

Art Duncan, 1926-27; Jack Adams, 1927-28 to 1946-47; Tommy Ivan, 1947-48 to 1953-54; Jimmy Skinner, 1954-55 to 1956-57; Jimmy Skinner and Sid Abel, 1957-58; Sid Abel, 1958-59 to 1967-68; Bill Gadsby, 1968-69; Bill Gadsby and Sid Abel, 1969-70; Ned Harkness and Doug Barkley, 1970-71; Doug Barkley and John Wilson, 1971-72; John Wilson, 1972-73; Ted Garvin and Alex Delvecchio, 1973-74; Alex Delvecchio, 1974-75; Doug Barkley and Alex Delvecchio, 1975-76; Alex Delvecchio and Larry Wilson, 1976-77; Bobby Kromm, 1977-78 to 1978-79; Bobby Kromm and Ted Lindsay, 1979-80; Ted Lindsay and Wayne Maxner, 1980-81; Wayne Maxner and Billy Dea, 1981-82; Nick Polano, 1982-83 to 1984-85; Harry Neale and Brad Park, 1985-86; Jacques Demers, 1986-87 to 1989-90; Bryan Murray, 1990-91 to 1992-93; Scotty Bowman, 1993-94.

Club Directory

Joe Louis Arena
600 Civic Center Drive
Detroit, Michigan 48226
Phone **(313) 396-7544**
FAX PR: (313) 567-0296
Capacity: 19,275

Owner/President	Mike Ilitch
Owner/Secretary-Treasurer	Marian Ilitch
Vice-Presidents	Atanas Ilitch, Christopher Ilitch
Senior Vice-President	Jim Devellano
General Manager	Bryan Murray
Assistant General Manager	Doug MacLean
Head Coach	Scott Bowman
Assistant Coaches	Barry Smith, Dave Lewis
Pro Scouting Director	Dan Belisle
Amateur Scouting Director	Ken Holland
Administrative Assistant/Scouting Coordinator	Michael Abbamont
U.S. Scouting Director	Billy Dea
Western Hockey League Scout	Wayne Meier
Western U.S. Scout	Chris Coury
Eastern U.S. Scout	Mike Addesa
Ontario Scouts	Paul Crowley, Sam McMaster
Eastern Canada Scout	John Stanton
Pro Scout	Jim Clark
European Scouts	Hakan Andersson, Vladimir Havlug, Alexei Khryskov
Controller	Paul MacDonald
Marketing Director	TBA
Public Relations Director	Bill Jamieson
Executive Director/General Sales Manager	Len Perna
Broadcast Sales Director	Amy Goan
Advertising & Sponsorship Sales Director	Terry Murphy
Advertising & Sponsorship Sales Director	Jack Johnson
Advertising & Sponsorship Sales Director	Marty Pawlusiak
Public Relations Coordinator	Howard Berlin
Public Relations Assistants	Kathy Best, Jill Solovich
Box Office Manager	Bob Kerlin
Season Ticket Sales Director	Greg Strausser
Secretary to General Manager	Nancy Beard
Accounting Assistant	Cathy Witzke
Athletic Trainer	John Wharton
Equipment Manager/Trainer	Mark Brennan
Assistant Equipment Manager	Tim Abbott
Team Physicians	Dr. John Finley, D.O., Dr. David Collon, M.D.
Team Dentist	Dr. C.J. Regula, D.M.D.
Team Ophthalmologist	Dr. Charles Slater, M.D.
Home Ice	Joe Louis Arena
Seating Capacity	19,275
Press Box & Radio-TV Booths	Jefferson Avenue side of arena, top of seats
Media Lounge	First-floor hallway near Red Wings' dressing room, river side of arena
Rink Dimensions	200 feet by 85 feet; S.A.R. Plastic above boards
Uniforms	Home: Base color white, trimmed in red
	Road: Base color red, trimmed in white
Radio flagship station	WJR-AM (760)
TV stations	WKBD (Channel 50); PASS Cable; Special Order Sports
Radio announcers	Bruce Martyn, Paul Woods
TV announcers	Dave Strader, Mickey Redmond

General Manager

MURRAY, BRYAN CLARENCE
General Manager, Detroit Red Wings.
Born in Shawville, Que., December 5, 1942.

Appointed coach and G.M. of the Red Wings in the summer of 1990, Bryan Murray guided the Red Wings to the best record in the Norris Division in 1991-92, compiling a 43-25-12 record, Detroit's best finish in 30 years.

A graduate of McGill, his first major coaching experience came in junior hockey when he took over the last-place Regina Pats and carried the team to the WHL championship in 1979-80. His one-year success in Regina translated into a professional coaching job in 1980-81 with the Capitals' AHL farm team, the Hershey Bears, whom he guided to their best season in over 40 years. That first-year effort netted him the Hockey News Minor League Coach-of-the-Year honors. Although he began the 1981-82 campaign in Hershey, Murray was promoted to Washington and the NHL on November 11, 1981.

NHL Coaching Record

		Regular Season					Playoffs			
Season	Team	Games	W	L	T	%	Games	W	L	%
1981-82	Washington (NHL)	76	25	28	13	.477	....	....	....	....
1982-83	Washington (NHL)	80	39	25	16	.588	4	1	3	.250
1983-84	Washington (NHL)	80	48	27	5	.631	8	4	4	.500
1984-85	Washington (NHL)	80	46	25	9	.631	5	2	3	.400
1985-86	Washington (NHL)	80	50	23	7	.669	9	5	4	.556
1986-87	Washington (NHL)	80	38	32	10	.538	7	3	4	.429
1987-88	Washington (NHL)	80	38	33	9	.531	14	7	7	.500
1988-89	Washington (NHL)	80	41	29	10	.575	6	2	4	.333
1989-90	Washington (NHL)	46	18	24	4	.435	....	....	....	....
1990-91	Detroit (NHL)	80	34	38	8	.475	7	3	4	.429
1991-92	Detroit (NHL)	80	43	25	12	.613	11	4	7	.364
1992-93	Detroit (NHL)	84	47	28	9	.613	7	3	4	.429
	NHL Totals	916	467	337	112	.571	78	34	44	.436

Edmonton Oilers
1992-93 Results: 26w-50l-8t 60pts. Fifth, Smythe Division

Schedule

Home

Oct.	Wed.	6	San Jose
	Fri.	8	NY Islanders
	Sat.	16	Vancouver
	Wed.	20	Calgary
	Fri.	22	Boston
	Sun.	24	Washington
	Fri.	29	Buffalo
Nov.	Wed.	3	Ottawa
	Sat.	20	Toronto
	Sun.	21	Anaheim
	Wed.	24	Chicago
	Sat.	27	Vancouver
	Mon.	29	Dallas
Dec.	Wed.	1	Philadelphia
	Wed.	15	Vancouver
	Fri.	17	San Jose
	Sun.	19	St Louis
	Wed.	22	Calgary
	Mon.	27	Winnipeg
	Wed.	29	Montreal
Jan.	Sun.	2	San Jose*
	Fri.	7	Quebec
	Mon.	24	Vancouver
			(at Saskatoon)
	Wed.	26	New Jersey
	Fri.	28	St Louis
	Sat.	29	Dallas
Feb.	Wed.	2	Los Angeles
	Fri.	4	Chicago
	Sun.	6	Winnipeg*
	Wed.	9	Calgary
	Sat.	12	Hartford
	Sun.	13	Anaheim*
	Wed.	23	Toronto
	Fri.	25	Los Angeles
	Sun.	27	Tampa Bay
Mar.	Wed.	9	Florida
	Fri.	11	Detroit
	Wed.	23	NY Rangers
	Fri.	25	Los Angeles
	Sun.	27	Pittsburgh
Apr.	Fri.	8	Anaheim
	Sun.	10	Detroit

Away

Oct.	Mon.	11	Vancouver*
	Wed.	13	Anaheim
	Thur.	14	Los Angeles
	Mon.	18	Winnipeg
	Tues.	26	San Jose
	Sat.	30	Calgary
Nov.	Sat.	6	St Louis
	Sun.	7	Chicago
	Tues.	9	Detroit
	Thur.	11	Boston*
	Sat.	13	Hartford
	Mon.	15	Toronto
	Wed.	17	Montreal
Dec.	Sun.	5	Dallas
	Tues.	7	NY Islanders
	Wed.	8	NY Rangers
	Sat.	11	New Jersey
	Sun.	12	Philadelphia
	Tues.	21	Vancouver
	Thur.	30	Calgary
Jan.	Sun.	9	Chicago
	Tues.	11	Dallas
	Thur.	13	St Louis
	Sat.	15	Pittsburgh*
	Tues.	18	Ottawa
	Wed.	19	Buffalo
Feb.	Mon.	7	Calgary
	Tues.	15	Washington
	Fri.	18	Detroit
	Sat.	19	Toronto
Mar.	Tues.	1	Vancouver
	Thur.	3	San Jose
	Fri.	4	Anaheim
	Wed.	16	Tampa Bay
	Fri.	18	Florida
	Sun.	20	Quebec
	Thur.	31	Anaheim
Apr.	Sat.	2	Los Angeles*
	Sun.	3	Los Angeles*
			(at Sacramento)
	Wed.	6	Winnipeg
	Wed.	13	San Jose
	Thur.	14	Los Angeles

* Denotes afternoon game.

Home Starting Times:

Weeknights	7:35 p.m.
Saturdays and Sundays	6:05 p.m.
Matinees	2:05 p.m.

Franchise date: June 22, 1979

PACIFIC DIVISION

15th NHL Season

WESTERN CONFERENCE

Year-by-Year Record

		Home			Road			Overall							
Season	GP	W	L	T	W	L	T	W	L	T	GF	GA	Pts.	Finished	Playoff Result
1992-93	84	16	21	5	10	29	3	26	50	8	242	337	60	5th, Smythe Div.	Out of Playoffs
1991-92	80	22	13	5	14	21	5	36	34	10	295	297	82	3rd, Smythe Div.	Lost Conf. Championship
1990-91	80	22	15	3	15	22	3	37	37	6	272	272	80	3rd, Smythe Div.	Lost Conf. Championship
1989-90	**80**	**23**	**11**	**6**	**15**	**17**	**8**	**38**	**28**	**14**	**315**	**283**	**90**	**2nd, Smythe Div.**	**Won Stanley Cup**
1988-89	80	21	16	3	17	18	5	38	34	8	325	306	84	3rd, Smythe Div.	Lost Div. Semi-Final
1987-88	**80**	**28**	**8**	**4**	**16**	**17**	**7**	**44**	**25**	**11**	**363**	**288**	**99**	**2nd, Smythe Div.**	**Won Stanley Cup**
1986-87	**80**	**29**	**6**	**5**	**21**	**18**	**1**	**50**	**24**	**6**	**372**	**284**	**106**	**1st, Smythe Div.**	**Won Stanley Cup**
1985-86	80	32	6	2	24	11	5	56	17	7	426	310	119	1st, Smythe Div.	Lost Div. Final
1984-85	**80**	**26**	**7**	**7**	**23**	**13**	**4**	**49**	**20**	**11**	**401**	**298**	**109**	**1st, Smythe Div.**	**Won Stanley Cup**
1983-84	**80**	**31**	**5**	**4**	**26**	**13**	**1**	**57**	**18**	**5**	**446**	**314**	**119**	**1st, Smythe Div.**	**Won Stanley Cup**
1982-83	80	25	9	6	22	12	6	47	21	12	424	315	106	1st, Smythe Div.	Lost Final
1981-82	80	31	5	4.	17	12	11	48	17	15	417	295	111	1st, Smythe Div.	Lost Div. Semi-Final
1980-81	80	17	13	10	12	22	6	29	35	16	328	327	74	4th, Smythe Div.	Lost Quarter-Final
1979-80	80	17	14	9	11	25	4	28	39	13	301	322	69	4th, Smythe Div.	Lost Prelim. Round

Shayne Corson, one of the league's best two-way forwards, was acquired by Edmonton from Montreal on August 27, 1992.

1993-94 Player Personnel

FORWARDS	HT	WT	S	Place of Birth	Date	1992-93 Club
ALLISON, Scott	6-4	194	L	St. Boniface, Man.	4/22/72	Cape Breton-Wheeling
ARNOTT, Jason	6-3	195	R	Collingwood, Ont.	10/11/74	Oshawa
BUCHBERGER, Kelly	6-2	210	L	Langenburg, Sask.	12/2/66	Edmonton
CIERNY, Jozef	6-2	176	L	Zvolen, Czech.	5/13/74	Rochester
CIGER, Zdeno	6-1	190	L	Martin, Slovakia	10/19/69	New Jersey-Edmonton
CORSON, Shayne	6-0	201	L	Barrie, Ont.	8/13/66	Edmonton
DeBRUSK, Louie	6-1	225	L	Cambridge, Ont.	3/19/71	Edmonton
ELIK, Todd	6-2	190	L	Brampton, Ont.	4/15/66	Minnesota-Edmonton
FISHER, Craig	6-3	180	L	Oshawa, Ont.	6/30/70	Cape Breton
HUDSON, Mike	6-1	205	L	Guelph, Ont.	2/6/67	Chicago-Edmonton
INTRANUOVO, Ralph	5-8	180	L	East York, Ont.	12/11/73	Sault Ste. Marie
KERCH, Alexander	5-10	187	R	Riga, Latvia	3/16/67	Pardaugava Riga
MacTAVISH, Craig	6-1	195	L	London, Ont.	8/15/58	Edmonton
MALTBY, Kirk	6-0	180	R	Guelph, Ont.	12/22/72	Cape Breton
MALTSEV, Oleg	6-3	224	L	Chelyabinsk, USSR	4/15/63	Traktor Chelyabinsk
McAMMOND, Dean	5-11	185	L	Grand Cache, Alta.	6/15/73	Pr. Albert-S. Current
OKSIUTA, Roman	6-3	220	L	Murmansk, Russia	8/21/70	Cape Breton-Khimik
PADEN, Kevin	6-3	175	L	Woodhaven, MI	2/12/75	Detroit (OHL)
PEARSON, Scott	6-1	205	L	Cornwall, Ont.	12/19/69	Quebec-Halifax
PODEIN, Shjon	6-2	200	L	Rochester, MN	3/5/68	Edm.-C. Breton
RICE, Steve	6-0	215	R	Kitchener, Ont.	5/26/71	Edmonton
RIIHIJARVI, Juha	6-3	196	R	Salla, Finland	12/15/69	JyP HT
SATAN, Miroslav	6-1	175	L	Topolcany, Slovakia	10/22/74	Dukla Trencin
THORNTON, Scott	6-2	200	L	London, Ont.	1/9/71	Edm.-C. Breton
TODD, Kevin	5-10	180	L	Winnipeg, Man.	5/4/68	N.J.-Edm.-Utica
VUJTEK, Vladimir	6-0	190	L	Ostrava, Czech.	2/17/72	Edm.-C. Breton
VYBORNY, David	5-10	175	L	Jihlava, Czech.	1/22/75	Sparta Praha
WEIGHT, Doug	5-11	191	L	Mt. Clemens, MI	1/21/71	NY Rangers-Edmonton
WHITE, Peter	5-11	200	L	Montreal, Que.	3/15/69	Cape Breton
WRIGHT, Tyler	5-11	170	R	Canora, Sask.	4/6/73	Edmonton-Swift Current
ZAVISHA, Brad	6-2	205	L	Hines Creek, Alta.	1/4/72	Did Not Play-Injured

DEFENSEMEN						
BAKULA, Martin	6-1	190	L	Kladno, Czech.	6/23/70	Alaska-Anchorage
BYAKIN, Ilya	5-9	185	L	Sverdlovsk, USSR	2/2/63	Landshut
GLYNN, Brian	6-4	215	L	Iserlohn, W. Germany	11/23/67	Edmonton
HERBERS, Ian	6-4	225	L	Jasper, Alta.	7/18/67	Cape Breton
JOSEPH, Chris	6-2	210	R	Burnaby, B.C.	10/10/69	Edmonton
KRAVCHUK, Igor	6-1	200	L	Ufa, Russia	9/13/66	Chicago-Edmonton
LAFORGE, Marc	6-2	210	L	Sudbury, Ont.	1/3/68	Cape Breton
LEROUX, Francois	6-6	225	L	Ste-Adele, Que.	4/18/70	Edm.-C. Breton
MANSON, Dave	6-2	202	L	Prince Albert, Sask.	1/27/67	Edmonton
MARK, Gord	6-4	218	R	Edmonton, Alta.	9/10/64	Cape Breton
MARTINI, Darcy	6-4	220	L	Castlegar, B.C.	1/30/69	Cape Breton-Wheeling
POPE, Brent	6-3	214	R	Hamilton, Ont.	2/20/73	Gue.-Ott. (OHL)-Whe.
RICHARDSON, Luke	6-4	210	L	Ottawa, Ont.	3/26/69	Edmonton
SMITH, Geoff	6-3	200	L	Edmonton, Alta.	3/7/69	Edmonton
STAJDUHAR, Nick	6-2	195	L	Kitchener, Ont.	12/6/74	London
WERENKA, Brad	6-2	205	L	Two Hills, Alta.	2/12/69	Edm.-C. Breton-Cdn. Nat.

GOALTENDERS	HT	WT	C	Place of Birth	Date	1992-93 Club
COWLEY, Wayne	6-0	185	L	Scarborough, Ont.	12/4/64	Cape Breton-Wheeling
GAGE, Joaquin	6-0	200	L	Vancouver, B.C.	10/19/73	Portland
RANFORD, Bill	5-10	170	L	Brandon, Man.	12/14/66	Edmonton
VERNER, Andrew	6-0	194	L	Weston, Ont.	11/20/72	Cape Breton

1992-93 Scoring

Regular Season

Pos	#	Player	Team	GP	G	A	Pts	+/-	PIM	PP	SH	GW	GT	S	%
L	85	Petr Klima	EDM	68	32	16	48	15-	100	13	0	2	0	175	18.3
C	39	Doug Weight	NYR	65	15	25	40	4	55	3	0	1	0	90	16.7
			EDM	13	2	6	8	2	10	0	0	0	0	35	5.7
			TOTAL	78	17	31	48	2	65	3	0	1	0	125	13.6
L	9	Shayne Corson	EDM	80	16	31	47	19-	209	9	2	1	0	164	9.8
L	18	Craig Simpson	EDM	60	24	22	46	14-	36	12	0	3	0	91	26.4
D	24	Dave Manson	EDM	83	15	30	45	28-	210	9	1	1	1	244	6.1
C	34	Todd Elik	MIN	46	13	18	31	5-	48	4	0	1	1	76	17.1
			EDM	14	1	9	10	1	8	0	0	0	0	28	3.6
			TOTAL	60	14	27	41	4-	56	4	0	1	1	104	13.5
L	8	Zdeno Ciger	N.J.	27	4	8	12	8-	2	2	0	1	0	39	10.3
			EDM	37	9	15	24	5-	6	0	0	1	0	67	13.4
			TOTAL	64	13	23	36	13-	8	2	0	2	0	106	12.3
D	19	Brian Benning	PHI	37	9	17	26	0	93	6	0	0	0	87	10.3
			EDM	18	1	7	8	1-	59	0	0	0	0	28	3.6
			TOTAL	55	10	24	34	1-	152	6	0	0	0	115	8.7
R	27	Scott Mellanby	EDM	69	15	17	32	4-	147	6	0	3	1	114	13.2
L	16	Kelly Buchberger	EDM	83	12	18	30	27-	133	1	2	3	0	92	13.0
C	14	Craig MacTavish	EDM	82	10	20	30	16-	110	0	3	3	0	101	9.9
D	21	Igor Kravchuk	CHI	38	6	9	15	11	30	3	0	0	0	101	5.9
			EDM	17	4	8	12	8-	2	1	0	0	0	42	9.5
			TOTAL	55	10	17	27	3	32	4	0	0	0	143	7.0
L	7	Martin Gelinas	EDM	65	11	12	23	3	30	0	0	1	0	93	11.8
C	15	Kevin Todd	N.J.	30	5	5	10	4-	16	0	0	2	0	48	10.4
			EDM	25	4	9	13	5-	10	0	0	1	0	39	10.3
			TOTAL	55	9	14	23	9-	26	0	0	3	0	87	10.3
C	26*	Shjon Podein	EDM	40	13	6	19	2-	25	2	1	1	0	64	20.3
D	25	Geoff Smith	EDM	78	4	14	18	11-	30	0	1	0	0	67	6.0
D	6	Brian Glynn	EDM	64	4	12	16	13-	60	2	0	0	0	80	5.0
D	22	Luke Richardson	EDM	82	3	10	13	18-	142	0	2	0	0	78	3.8
D	2	Chris Joseph	EDM	33	2	10	12	9-	48	1	0	0	0	49	4.1
L	23*	Vladimir Vujtek	EDM	30	1	10	11	1-	8	0	0	0	0	49	2.0
L	29	Louie Debrusk	EDM	51	8	2	10	16-	205	0	0	1	0	33	24.2
D	36*	Brad Werenka	EDM	27	5	3	8	1	24	0	1	1	0	38	13.2
C	20	Mike Hudson	CHI	36	1	6	7	6-	44	0	0	0	0	33	3.0
			EDM	5	0	1	1	1-	2	0	0	0	0	2	.0
			TOTAL	41	1	7	8	7-	46	0	0	0	0	35	2.9
R	12*	Steven Rice	EDM	28	2	5	7	4-	28	0	0	1	0	29	6.9
C	20*	Shaun Van Allen	EDM	21	1	4	5	2-	6	0	0	0	0	19	5.3
C	41	Bill McDougall	EDM	4	2	1	3	2	4	0	0	0	0	8	25.0
G	30	Bill Ranford	EDM	67	0	3	3	0	10	0	0	0	0	0	.0
C	19*	Tyler Wright	EDM	7	1	1	2	4-	19	0	0	0	0	7	14.3
C	17	Scott Thornton	EDM	9	0	1	1	4-	0	0	0	0	0	7	.0
D	35*	Francois Leroux	EDM	1	0	0	0	0	4	0	0	0	0	0	.0
L	26*	Dan Currie	EDM	5	0	0	0	4-	4	0	0	0	0	11	.0
G	1	Ron Tugnutt	EDM	26	0	0	0	0	2	0	0	0	0	0	.0

General Managers' History

Glen Sather, 1979-80 to date.

Coaching History

Glen Sather, 1979-80; Bryan Watson and Glen Sather, 1980-81; Glen Sather, 1981-82 to 1988-89; John Muckler, 1989-90 to 1990-91; Ted Green, 1991-92 to date.

Captains' History

Ron Chipperfield, 1979-80; Lee Fogolin, 1980-81 to 1982-83; Wayne Gretzky, 1983-84 to 1987-88; Mark Messier, 1988-89 to 1990-91; Kevin Lowe, 1991-92; Craig MacTavish, 1992-93 to date.

Retired Numbers

3	Al Hamilton	1972-1980

Coach

GREEN, TED
Coach, Edmonton Oilers. Born in Eriksdale, Man., March 23, 1940.

Ted Green, who became the fourth coach of the Edmonton Oilers on June 27, 1991, enters his third season as an NHL coach. He led the Oilers to the conference finals during the 1991-92 season, his first as a head coach. In his playing/coaching career, Green has played a vital role on twelve championship teams. A member of the Memorial Cup-winning Winnipeg Braves in 1959, Green established himself as a steady, "stay-at-home" defenseman in the NHL with the Boston Bruins, earning two All-Star berths and winning the Stanley Cup in 1972.

In 1973, Green joined the WHA, where he added three Avco Cup championship rings to his collection. After retiring as a player, Green coached the Carman Hornets to the Manitoba Intermediate championship. In 1981, Green joined the Oilers' organization as an assistant coach and has been a part of each of the Oilers' Stanley Cup victories. Green also served as an assistant coach for the Team Canada squad that captured the Canada Cup in 1984. Following a one-year sabbatical from the Oilers in 1986, Green rejoined the team in 1987 and was named co-coach in the 1989-90 season.

Coaching Record

		Regular Season					Playoffs			
Season	Team	Games	W	L	T	%	Games	W	L	%
1991-92	Edmonton (NHL)	80	36	34	10	.513	16	8	8	.500
1992-93	Edmonton (NHL)	84	26	50	8	.357	....	....	....	....
	NHL Totals	164	62	84	18	.433	16	8	8	.500

Club Records

Team

(Figures in brackets for season records are games played; records for fewest points, wins, ties, losses, goals, goals against are for 70 or more games)

Most Points	119	1983-84 (80)
		1985-86 (80)
Most Wins	57	1983-84 (80)
Most Ties	16	1980-81 (80)
Most Losses	50	1992-93 (84)
Most Goals	*446	1983-84 (80)
Most Goals Against	327	1980-81 (80)
Fewest Points	60	1992-93 (84)
Fewest Wins	26	1992-93 (84)
Fewest Ties	5	1983-84 (80)
Fewest Losses	17	1981-82 (80)
		1985-86 (80)
Fewest Goals	242	1992-93 (84)
Fewest Goals Against	272	1990-91 (80)

Longest Winning Streak

Over-all	8	Five times
Home	8	Jan. 19/85-
		Feb. 22/85
		Feb. 24-
		Apr. 2/86
Away	8	Dec. 9/86-
		Jan. 17/87

Longest Undefeated Streak

Over-all	15	Oct. 11/84-
		Nov. 9/84
		(12 wins, 3 ties)
Home	14	Nov. 15/89-
		Jan. 6/90
		(11 wins, 3 ties)
Away	9	Jan. 17-
		Mar. 2/82
		(6 wins, 3 ties)
		Nov. 23/82-
		Jan. 18/83
		(7 wins, 2 ties)

Longest Losing Streak

Over-all	9	Oct. 21-
		Nov. 10/90
Home	4	Three times
Away	9	Nov. 25-
		Dec. 30/80

Longest Winless Streak

Over-all	9	Oct. 21-
		Nov. 10/90
Home	7	Oct. 24-
		Nov. 19/80
		(3 losses, 4 ties)
Away	9	Twice
Most Shutouts, Season	4	1987-88 (80)
Most PIM, Season	2,173	1987-88 (80)
Most Goals, Game	13	Nov. 19/83
		(NJ 4 at Edm. 13)
		Nov. 8/85
		(Van. 0 at Edm. 13)

Individual

Most Seasons	13	Kevin Lowe
Most Games	966	Kevin Lowe
Most Goals, Career	583	Wayne Gretzky
Most Assists, Career	1,086	Wayne Gretzky
Most Points, Career	1,669	Wayne Gretzky
		(583 goals, 1,086 assists)
Most PIM, Career	1,278	Kevin McClelland
Most Shutouts, Career	9	Grant Fuhr

Longest Consecutive

Games Streak	521	Craig MacTavish
		(Oct. 11/86-Jan. 2/93)
Most Goals, Season	*92	Wayne Gretzky
		(1981-82)
Most Assists, Season	*163	Wayne Gretzky
		(1985-86)
Most Points, Season	*215	Wayne Gretzky
		(1985-86)
		(52 goals, 163 assists)
Most PIM, Season	286	Steve Smith
		(1987-88)

Most Points, Defenseman,

Season	138	Paul Coffey
		(1985-86)
		(48 goals, 90 assists)

Most Points, Center,

Season	*215	Wayne Gretzky
		(1985-86)
		(52 goals, 163 assists)

Most Points, Right Wing,

Season	135	Jari Kurri
		(1984-85)
		(71 goals, 64 assists)

Most Points, Left Wing,

Season	106	Mark Messier
		(1982-83)
		(48 goals, 58 assists)

Most Points, Rookie,

Season	75	Jari Kurri
		(1980-81)
		(32 goals, 43 assists)
Most Shutouts, Season	4	Grant Fuhr
		(1987-88)
Most Goals, Game	5	Wayne Gretzky
		(Feb. 18/81, Dec. 30/81,
		Dec. 15/84, Dec. 6/87)
		Jari Kurri (Nov. 19/83)
		Pat Hughes (Feb. 3/84)
Most Assists, Game	*7	Wayne Gretzky
		(Feb. 15/80; Dec. 11/85;
		Feb. 14/86)
Most Points, Game	8	Wayne Gretzky
		(Nov. 19/83)
		Paul Coffey
		(Mar. 14/86)
		Wayne Gretzky
		(Jan. 4/84)

* NHL Record.

All-time Record vs. Other Clubs

Regular Season

		At Home						On Road							Total					
	GP	W	L	T	GF	GA	PTS	GP	W	L	T	GF	GA	PTS	GP	W	L	T	GF	GA	PTS
Boston	21	8	10	3	75	73	19	22	4	16	2	62	102	10	43	12	26	5	137	175	29
Buffalo	21	16	3	2	94	53	34	22	9	9	4	89	94	22	43	25	12	6	183	147	56
Calgary	51	27	16	8	220	183	62	51	19	26	6	193	239	44	102	46	42	14	413	422	106
Chicago	23	14	8	1	110	87	29	22	8	11	3	97	96	19	45	22	19	4	207	183	48
Detroit	22	11	7	4	112	93	26	22	12	8	2	102	85	26	44	23	15	6	214	178	52
Hartford	22	17	2	3	100	62	37	21	9	9	3	79	90	21	43	26	11	6	179	152	58
Los Angeles	52	27	13	12	268	197	66	50	21	20	9	230	219	51	102	48	33	21	498	426	117
Minnesota	22	15	1	6	114	68	36	23	12	6	5	86	82	29	45	27	7	11	200	150	65
Montreal	22	12	10	0	76	68	24	21	6	12	3	66	76	15	43	18	22	3	142	144	39
New Jersey	24	13	7	4	121	94	30	24	12	10	2	86	83	26	48	25	17	6	207	177	56
NY Islanders	22	13	5	4	88	69	30	22	5	10	7	88	95	17	44	18	15	11	176	164	47
NY Rangers	21	10	10	1	83	72	21	21	12	6	3	89	86	27	42	22	16	4	172	158	48
Ottawa	1	1	0	0	5	2	2	1	0	1	0	2	3	0	2	1	1	0	7	5	2
Philadelphia	21	12	5	4	80	62	28	22	5	16	1	65	101	11	43	17	21	5	145	163	39
Pittsburgh	22	17	4	1	120	77	35	22	12	9	1	107	86	25	44	29	13	2	227	163	60
Quebec	21	16	5	0	119	62	32	21	12	7	2	102	85	26	42	28	12	2	221	147	58
St. Louis	22	13	6	3	102	86	29	22	10	8	4	95	87	24	44	23	14	7	197	173	53
San Jose	7	6	0	1	36	14	13	7	2	5	0	19	32	4	14	8	5	1	55	46	17
Tampa Bay	2	2	0	0	6	4	4	2	0	2	0	2	9	0	4	2	2	0	8	13	4
Toronto	22	13	4	5	115	75	31	22	12	9	1	111	91	25	44	25	13	6	226	166	56
Vancouver	50	37	9	4	264	157	78	52	27	19	6	224	197	60	102	64	28	10	488	354	138
Washington	21	9	8	4	86	75	22	21	8	12	1	79	94	17	42	17	20	5	165	169	39
Winnipeg	50	31	16	3	231	172	65	49	26	19	4	229	201	56	99	57	35	7	460	373	121
Totals	562	340	149	73	2625	1915	753	562	243	250	69	2302	2333	555	1124	583	399	142	4927	4248	1308

Playoffs

	Series	W	L	GP	W	L	T	GF	GA	Last Mtg.	Round	Result
Boston	2	2	0	9	8	1	0	41	20	1990	F	W 4-1
Calgary	5	4	1	30	19	11	0	132	96	1991	DSF	W 4-3
Chicago	4	3	1	20	12	8	0	102	77	1992	CF	L 0-4
Detroit	2	2	0	10	8	2	0	39	26	1988	CF	W 4-1
Los Angeles	7	5	2	36	24	12	0	154	127	1992	DSF	W 4-2
Minnesota	2	1	1	9	5	4	0	36	30	1991	CF	L 1-4
Montreal	1	1	0	3	3	0	0	15	6	1981	PR	W 3-0
NY Islanders	3	1	2	15	6	9	0	47	58	1984	F	W 4-1
Philadelphia	3	2	1	15	8	7	0	49	44	1987	F	W 4-3
Vancouver	2	2	0	9	7	2	0	35	20	1992	DF	W 4-2
Winnipeg	6	6	0	26	22	4	0	120	75	1990	DSF	W 4-3
Totals	37	29	8	180	120	60	0	770	579			

Playoff Results 1993-89

Year	Round	Opponent	Result	GF	GA
1992	CF	Chicago	L 0-4	8	21
	DF	Vancouver	W 4-2	18	15
	DSF	Los Angeles	W 4-2	23	18
1991	CF	Minnesota	L 1-4	14	20
	DF	Los Angeles	W 4-2	21	20
	DSF	Calgary	W 4-3	22	20
1990	F	**Boston**	**W 4-1**	**20**	**8**
	CF	Chicago	W 4-2	25	20
	DF	Los Angeles	W 4-0	24	10
	DSF	Winnipeg	W 4-3	24	22
1989	DSF	Los Angeles	L 3-4	20	25

Abbreviations: Round: F – Final;
CF – conference final; **DF** – division final;
DSF – division semi-final; **SF** – semi-final;
QF – quarter-final; **PR** – preliminary round.
GA – goals against; **GF** – goals for.

1992-93 Results

	Home				Away	
Oct. 6	Vancouver	4-5	Oct. 8	Calgary	2-7
11	Toronto	3-3	10	Vancouver	2-5
23	Boston	3-6	14	Winnipeg	3-7
25	Calgary	0-4	15	Chicago	4-3
28	Minnesota	5-2	17	Detroit	2-4
31	Washington	4-2	20	Tampa Bay	1-6
Nov. 3	Ottawa	5-2	Nov. 6	Winnipeg	6-1
18	Vancouver	4-2	7	Minnesota	2-2
22	NY Islanders	5-5	10	St. Louis	4-4
25	Los Angeles	1-3	12	San Jose	4-3
27	Chicago	1-8	14	Los Angeles	2-6
28	Tampa Bay	4-3	21	Vancouver	0-9
Dec. 5	St. Louis	1-5	Dec. 1	San Jose	3-1
8	Calgary	3-1	3	Vancouver	1-4
16	Vancouver	4-2	7	Calgary	3-6
18	Los Angeles	5-5	10	Minnesota	3-2
23	San Jose	4-2	12	Tampa Bay	1-3
27	Calgary	3-7	13	NY Islanders	1-4
29	Montreal	3-6	21	Calgary	2-3
Jan. 2	Tampa Bay	2-1	31	Winnipeg*	2-3
3	Philadelphia	2-2	Jan. 5	St. Louis	1-6
13	Winnipeg	1-4	7	Chicago	3-3
15	Hartford	3-1	10	Washington	3-4
17	Buffalo	3-2	10	Philadelphia	0-4
19	Los Angeles	4-5	23	Winnipeg	5-8
22	Pittsburgh	2-1	31	Buffalo*	5-4
27	Detroit	2-2	Feb. 2	Boston	4-3
Feb. 12	San Jose	6-0	3	Ottawa	2-3
14	Quebec*	2-3	9	Los Angeles	6-3
27	NY Rangers	0-1	16	NY Islanders	2-7
28	San Jose	4-1	18	Pittsburgh	5-4
Mar. 4	Winnipeg	3-5	20	Hartford*	3-7
10	Detroit	3-6	21	Montreal	3-4
12	New Jersey	6-4	23	Quebec	3-6
14	Chicago*	4-5	Mar. 6	Los Angeles	1-6
21	Pittsburgh	4-6	7	San Jose	3-6
26	Los Angeles	1-4	17	NY Rangers	4-3
27	Toronto	2-6	18	New Jersey	1-5
31	Minnesota	5-2	20	Toronto	2-4
Apr. 3	Winnipeg	4-6	Apr. 6	San Jose	2-5
11	Winnipeg*	5-7	7	Vancouver	4-5
13	Calgary	2-4	15	Winnipeg	0-3

*Denotes afternoon game

Entry Draft
Selections 1993-79

1993
Pick
7	Jason Arnott
16	Nick Stajduhar
33	David Vyborny
59	Kevin Paden
60	Alexander Kerch
111	Miroslav Satan
163	Alexander Zhurik
189	Martin Bakula
215	Brad Norton
241	Oleg Maltsev
267	Ilja Byakin

1992
Pick
13	Joe Hulbig
37	Martin Reichel
61	Simon Roy
65	Kirk Maltby
96	Ralph Intranuovo
109	Joaquin Gage
157	Steve Gibson
181	Kyuin Shim
190	Colin Schmidt
205	Marko Tuomainen
253	Bryan Rasmussen

1991
Pick
12	Tyler Wright
20	Martin Rucinsky
34	Andrew Verner
56	George Breen
78	Mario Nobili
93	Ryan Haggerty
144	David Oliver
166	Gary Kitching
210	Vegar Barlie
232	Evgeny Belosheikin
254	Juha Riihijarvi

1989
Pick
17	Scott Allison
38	Alexandre Legault
59	Joe Crowley
67	Joel Blain
101	Greg Louder
122	Keijo Sailynoja
143	Mike Power
164	Roman Mejzlik
185	Richard Zemlicka
206	Petr Korinek
227	invalid claim
248	Sami Nuutinen

1989
Pick
15	Jason Soules
36	Richard Borgo
78	Josef Beranek
92	Peter White
120	Anatoli Semenov
140	Davis Payne
141	Sergei Yashin
162	Darcy Martini
225	Roman Bozek

1988
Pick
19	Francois Leroux
39	Petro Koivunen
53	Trevor Sim
61	Collin Bauer
82	Cam Brauer
103	Don Martin
124	Len Barrie
145	Mike Glover
166	Shjon Podein
187	Tom Cole
208	Vladimir Zubkov
229	Darin MacDonald
250	Tim Tisdale

1987
Pick
21	Peter Soberlak
42	Brad Werenka
63	Geoff Smith
64	Peter Eriksson
105	Shaun Van Allen
126	Radek Toupal
147	Tomas Srsen
168	Age Ellingsen
189	Gavin Armstrong
210	Mike Tinkham
231	Jeff Pauletti
241	Jesper Duus
252	Igor Vyazmikin

1986
Pick
21	Kim Issel
42	Jamie Nichols
63	Ron Shudra
84	Dan Currie
105	David Haas
126	Jim Ennis
147	Ivan Matulik
168	Nicolas Beaulieu
189	Mike Greenlay
210	Matt Lanza
231	Mojmir Bozik
252	Tony Hand

1985
Pick
20	Scott Metcalfe
41	Todd Carnelley
62	Mike Ware
104	Tomas Kapusta
125	Brian Tessier
146	Shawn Tyers
167	Tony Fairfield
188	Kelly Buchberger
209	Mario Barbe
230	Peter Headon
251	John Haley

1984
Pick
21	Selmar Odelein
42	Daryl Reaugh
63	Todd Norman
84	Rich Novak
105	Richard Lambert
106	Emanuel Viveiros
126	Ivan Dornic
147	Heikki Riihijarvi
168	Todd Ewen
209	Joel Curtis
229	Simon Wheeldon
250	Darren Gani

1983
Pick
19	Jeff Beukeboom
40	Mike Golden
60	Mike Flanagan
80	Esa Tikkanen
120	Don Barber
140	Dale Derkatch
160	Ralph Vos
180	Dave Roach
200	Warren Yadlowski
220	John Miner
240	Steve Woodburn

1982
Pick
20	Jim Playfair
41	Steve Graves
62	Brent Loney
83	Jaroslav Pouzar
104	Dwayne Boettger
125	Raimo Summanen
146	Brian Small
167	Dean Clark
188	Ian Wood
209	Grant Dion
230	Chris Smith
251	Jeff Crawford

1981
Pick
8	Grant Fuhr
29	Todd Strueby
71	Paul Houck
92	Phil Drouillard
111	Steve Smith
113	Marc Habscheid
155	Mike Sturgeon
176	Miloslav Horava
197	Gord Sherven

1980
Pick
6	Paul Coffey
48	Shawn Babcock
69	Jari Kurri
90	Walt Poddubny
111	Mike Winther
132	Andy Moog
153	Rob PolmanTuin
174	Lars-Gunnar Pettersson

1979
Pick
21	Kevin Lowe
48	Mark Messier
69	Glenn Anderson
84	Maxwell Kostovich
105	Mike Toal
126	Blair Barnes

General Manager

SATHER, GLEN CAMERON
President and General Manager, Edmonton Oilers.
Born in High River, Alta., Sept. 2, 1943.

A journeyman left-winger who played for six different teams during his nine-year NHL career, 50-year-old Glen Sather was one of the League's most successful coaches ever before relinquishing his coaching duties on June 12, 1989. He was the 1985-86 Jack Adams Award winner, led his club to four Stanley Cup championships and had a ten-year winning percentage of .629 (442-241-99). His 442 wins place him sixth on the all-time list in regular season wins. In addition, Sather led his team to 89 play-off victories, fourth on the all-time list. His .706 winning percentage in the playoffs ranks him first.

After closing out his NHL playing career in 1975-76 with an 80-113-193 scoring mark in 660 games, Sather jumped to the Oilers in the World Hockey Association, where he enjoyed his best and last season as a player with totals of 19-34-53 in 81 games. Midway through that 1976-77 campaign, on January 27, 1977, he also assumed the Edmonton coaching duties and led his team to the first of its 11 straight WHA and NHL playoff appearances. Three years later, when the club entered the NHL, Sather took on the added responsibilities of Oilers' president and general manager, which he currently maintains.

NHL Coaching Record

			Regular Season				Playoffs			
Season	Team	Games	W	L	T	%	Games	W	L	%
1979-80	Edmonton (NHL)	80	28	39	13	.431	3	0	3	.000
1980-81	Edmonton (NHL)	62	25	26	11	.492	9	5	4	.555
1981-82	Edmonton (NHL)	80	48	17	15	.694	5	2	3	.400
1982-83	Edmonton (NHL)	80	47	21	12	.663	16	11	5	.687
1983-84	Edmonton (NHL)	80	57	18	5	.744	19	15	4	.789*
1984-85	Edmonton (NHL)	80	49	20	11	.681	18	15	3	.833*
1985-86	Edmonton (NHL)	80	56	17	7	.744	10	6	4	.600
1986-87	Edmonton (NHL)	80	50	24	6	.663	21	16	5	.762*
1987-88	Edmonton (NHL)	80	44	25	11	.619	18	16	2	.889*
1988-89	Edmonton (NHL)	80	38	34	8	.538	7	3	4	.429
	NHL Totals	782	442	241	99	.629	126	89	37	.706

* Stanley Cup win.

Club Directory

Northlands Coliseum
Edmonton, Alberta T5B 4M9
Phone **403/474-8561**
Ticketing 403/471-2191
FAX 403/477-9625
Capacity: 17,313 (standing 190)

Owner/Governor	Peter Pocklington
Alternate Governor	Glen Sather
General Counsel	Lorne Ruzicka
President/General Manager	Glen Sather
Exec. Vice-President/Assistant G.M.	Bruce MacGregor
Coach	Ted Green
Assistant Coaches	Ron Low, Kevin Primeau
Director of Player Personnel/Chief Scout	Barry Fraser
Administrative Assistant Hockey Operations	Kevin Prendergast
Scouting Staff	Ace Bailey, Ed Chadwick, Lorne Davis, Bob Freeman, Harry Howell, Curly Reeves, Jan Slepicka, Brad Smith
Executive Secretary	Betsy Freedman
Receptionist/Secretary	Jody Sarafinchan

Medical and Training Staff
Athletic Trainer/Therapist	Ken Lowe
Athletic Trainer	Barrie Stafford
Assistant Trainer	Lyle Kulchisky
Massage Therapist	Stewart Poirier
Team Medical Chief of Staff / Director of Glen Sather Sports Medicine Clinic	Dr. David C. Reid
Team Physicians	Dr. Don Groot, Dr. Boris Boyko
Team Dentists	Dr. Tony Sneazwell, Dr. Brian Nord
Fitness Consultant	Dr. Art Quinney
Physical Therapist Consultant	Dr. Dave Magee
Sports Psychologist	Dr. Murray Smith

Finance
Vice-President, Finance	Werner Baum
Accountants	Ellie Merrick, Allison Coward, Jill Semple
Executive Secretary	Lisa Colby

Public Relations
Director of Public Relations	Bill Tuele
Coordinator of Publications and Statistics	Steve Knowles
Director of Community Relations/Special Events	Trish Kerr
Public Relations Secretary	Fiona Liew

Marketing
Director of Marketing	Stew MacDonald
Marketing Representative/Properties Mgr.	Darrell Holowaychuk
Marketing Representative	Brad MacGregor
Sales Representative	Dave Semenko
Marketing Secretary	Heather Hansch
Merchandising Clerks	Julia Slade, Kerri Hill
Warehouse Supervisor	Ray MacDonald
Warehouse Assistant	Jim Groff

Ticketing
Director of Ticketing Operations	Sheila Stock
Ticketing Operations	Sheila McCaskill, Marcia Godwin, Marcella Kinsman

Retail Sales
Manager – Champions Retail Store	Skip Krake
Team Administration Offices	Northlands Coliseum, Edmonton, Alta., Canada T5B 4M9
Seating Capacity	17,313 (with standing 17,503)
Location of Press Box	East Side at top (Radio/TV) West Side at top (Media)
Dimensions of Rink	200 feet by 85 feet
Ends of Rink	Herculite extends above boards around rink
Club Colours	Blue, Orange, White
Team Uniforms	Home - Base colour white, trimmed with blue and orange Away - Base colour blue, trimmed with white and orange
Training Camp Site	Northlands Coliseum, Edmonton, Alberta
Television Channel	CFRN (Channel 3, Cable 2) CBXT TV (Channel 5, Cable 4)
Radio Station	CFCW (790 AM)

Florida Panthers
First NHL Season: 1993-94

Scott Mellanby, left, will supply the Panthers with leadership and scoring punch. Mark Fitzpatrick, right, will combine with John Vanbiesbrouck to give Florida an experienced goaltending tandem.

Schedule

Home			Away		
Oct.	Tues. 12	Pittsburgh	**Oct.**	Wed. 6	Chicago
	Thur. 14	Ottawa		Thur. 7	St Louis
	Sun. 17	Tampa Bay		Sat. 9	Tampa Bay
	Tues. 19	Los Angeles		Sat. 23	New Jersey
	Thur. 21	Toronto	**Nov.**	Wed. 3	Toronto
	Tues. 26	Winnipeg		Sun. 7	Quebec*
	Thur. 28	NY Islanders		Wed. 10	Montreal
	Sat. 30	Tampa Bay		Thur. 11	Ottawa
Nov.	Tues. 2	Philadelphia		Fri. 26	Boston*
	Sun. 14	Quebec		Sat. 27	Hartford*
	Tues. 16	NY Rangers	**Dec.**	Sun. 5	San Jose*
	Thur. 18	Chicago		Tues. 7	Anaheim
	Sat. 20	Washington		Wed. 8	Los Angeles
	Tues. 23	Hartford		Fri. 10	Winnipeg
Dec.	Thur. 2	Buffalo		Sun. 12	Dallas
	Wed. 15	Montreal		Sun. 26	Tampa Bay
	Sun. 19	Boston			(at Orlando)
	Wed. 22	NY Rangers		Tues. 28	Washington
Jan.	Sat. 1	Anaheim*		Wed. 29	Hartford
	Wed. 19	Washington	**Jan.**	Mon. 3	NY Rangers
	Mon. 24	Montreal		Fri. 7	New Jersey
	Fri. 28	San Jose		Sat. 8	Boston
Feb.	Fri. 4	Buffalo		Thur. 13	Pittsburgh
	Sun. 6	Boston		Sat. 15	Montreal
	Sun. 13	Vancouver		Mon. 17	NY Islanders*
	Sun. 20	Detroit		Wed. 26	Tampa Bay
	Thur. 24	Washington		Sun. 30	Buffalo*
	Mon. 28	Pittsburgh	**Feb.**	Tues. 1	Pittsburgh
Mar.	Wed. 2	New Jersey		Wed. 2	Ottawa
	Fri. 4	Hartford		Thur. 10	Philadelphia
	Mon. 14	NY Rangers		Sat. 12	NY Islanders
	Wed. 16	Calgary		Wed. 16	Detroit
	Fri. 18	Edmonton		Fri. 18	Buffalo
	Sun. 20	Philadelphia		Tues. 22	Winnipeg
	Mon. 21	New Jersey			(at Hamilton)
	Wed. 23	Toronto		Sat. 26	Washington
		(at Hamilton)	**Mar.**	Mon. 7	Vancouver
	Mon. 28	Dallas		Wed. 9	Edmonton
	Wed. 30	St Louis		Fri. 11	Calgary
Apr.	Sat. 2	Ottawa		Thur. 24	Philadelphia
	Sun. 10	New Jersey		Sat. 26	NY Islanders*
	Tues. 12	Quebec	**Apr.**	Mon. 4	NY Rangers
	Thur. 14	NY Islanders		Tues. 5	Quebec
				Thur. 7	Philadelphia

* Denotes afternoon game.

Home Starting Times:
Weeknights and Saturdays . . . . 7:35 p.m.
Sundays . . . . 6:05 p.m.
Except Sat. Jan. 1 . . . . 12:05 p.m.

Franchise date: June 14, 1993

ATLANTIC DIVISION

NHL

1st NHL Season

EASTERN CONFERENCE

1993-94 Player Personnel

FORWARDS	HT	WT	S	Place of Birth	Date	1992-93 Club
BARRAULT, Doug	6-2	205	R	Golden, B.C.	4/21/70	Minnesota-Kalamazoo
BARRIE, Len	6-0	200	L	Kimberley, B.C.	6/4/69	Philadelphia-Hershey
BELANGER, Jesse	6-0	170	R	St. Georges, Que.	6/15/69	Montreal-Fredericton
CABANA, Chad	6-1	220	L	Bonnyville, Alta.	10/1/74	Tri-City
CIRONE, Jason	5-9	185	L	Toronto, Ont.	2/21/71	Asiago
FITZGERALD, Tom	6-1	195	R	Melrose, MA	8/28/68	NY Islanders
GAUTHIER, Daniel	6-1	190	L	Charlemagne, Que.	5/17/70	Cleveland
GILHEN, Randy	6-0	190	L	Zweibrucken, Ger.	6/13/63	NY Rangers-Tampa Bay
GREENLAW, Jeff	6-1	230	L	Toronto, Ont.	2/28/68	Washington-Baltimore
HOUGH, Mike	6-1	192	L	Montreal, Que.	2/6/63	Quebec
HULL, Jody	6-2	200	R	Cambridge, Ont.	2/2/69	Ottawa
KIMBLE, Darin	6-2	205	R	Lucky Lake, Sask.	11/22/68	Boston-Providence
LABELLE, Marc	6-1	215	L	Maniwaki, Que.	12/20/69	New Haven
LEACH, Jamie	6-1	205	R	Winnipeg, Man.	8/25/69	Pit.-Clev.-Hfd.-Spr.
LEBEAU, Patrick	5-10	172	L	St. Jerome, Que.	3/17/70	Calgary-Salt Lake
LEVINS, Scott	6-4	210	R	Spokane, WA	1/30/70	Winnipeg-Moncton
LINDSAY, Bill	5-11	185	L	Big Fork, MT	5/17/71	Quebec-Halifax
LOMAKIN, Andrei	5-10	175	L	Voskresensk, USSR	4/3/64	Philadelphia
LOWRY, Dave	6-1	195	L	Sudbury, Ont.	2/14/65	St. Louis
McCAULEY, Bill	6-0	173	L	Detroit, MI	4/20/75	Detroit (OHL)
MELLANBY, Scott	6-1	205	R	Montreal, Que.	6/11/66	Edmonton
MONTREUIL, Eric	6-1	170	L	Verdun, Que.	5/18/75	Chicoutimi
NIEDERMAYER, Rob	6-2	200	L	Cassiar, B.C.	12/28/74	Medicine Hat
SKRUDLAND, Brian	6-0	196	L	Peace River, Alta.	7/31/63	Montreal-Calgary
WASHBURN, Steve	6-2	185	L	Ottawa, Ont.	4/10/75	Ottawa (OHL)
YOUNG, C.J.	5-10	180	R	Waban, MA	1/1/68	Calgary-Boston-Providence

DEFENSEMEN						
ARMSTRONG, Chris	6-0	184	L	Regina, Sask.	6/26/75	Moose Jaw
BENNING, Brian	6-0	195	L	Edmonton, Alta.	6/10/66	Philadelphia-Edmonton
CIRELLA, Joe	6-3	210	R	Hamilton, Ont.	5/9/63	NY Rangers
DEMARCO, John	6-4	215	L	Boston, MA	1/27/75	Archbishop Williams
DOYLE, Trevor	6-3	204	R	Ottawa, Ont.	1/1/74	Kingston
EAKINS, Dallas	6-2	195	L	Dade City, FL	2/27/67	Winnipeg-Moncton
GODYNYUK, Alexander	6-0	207	L	Kiev, Ukraine	1/27/70	Calgary
HYNES, Gord	6-1	170	L	Montreal, Que.	7/22/66	Philadelphia-Hershey
IMES, Chris	5-11	195	R	Birchdale, MI	8/27/72	U. of Maine
LAUS, Paul	6-1	212	R	Beamsville, Ont.	9/26/70	Cleveland
MURPHY, Gord	6-2	195	R	Willowdale, Ont.	3/23/67	Boston
NASREDDINE, Alain	6-1	201	L	Montreal, Que.	7/10/75	Drummondville
RICHER, Stephane	5-11	190	R	Hull, Que.	4/28/66	T.B.-Atl.-Bos.-Prov.
SEROWIK, Jeff	6-0	190	R	Manchester, NH	10/1/67	St. John's
SMYTH, Greg	6-3	212	R	Oakville, Ont.	4/23/66	Calgary-Salt Lake
TICHY, Milan	6-3	198	L	Pizen, Czech.	9/22/69	Chicago-Indianapolis
TJALLDEN, Mikael	6-2	194	L	Ornskoldsvik, Swe.	2/16/75	MoDo Hockey
THOMPSON, Briane	6-3	204	L	Peterborough, Ont.	4/17/74	Sault Ste. Marie

GOALTENDERS	HT	WT	C	Place of Birth	Date	1992-93 Club
FITZPATRICK, Mark	6-2	190	L	Toronto, Ont.	11/13/68	NY Islanders
MACDONALD, Todd	6-0	155	L	Charlottetown, P.E.I.	7/5/75	Tacoma
REDDICK, Eldon "Pokey"	5-8	170	L	Halifax, N.S.	10/6/64	Fort Wayne
VANBIESBROUCK, John	5-8	172	L	Detroit, MI	9/4/63	NY Rangers
WEEKES, Kevin	6-0	158	L	Toronto, Ont.	4/4/75	Owen Sound

Entry Draft Selections

1993

Pick	
5	Rob Niedermayer
41	Kevin Weekes
57	Chris Armstrong
67	Mikael Tjallden
78	Steve Washburn
83	Bill McCauley
109	Todd MacDonald
135	Alain Nasreddine
161	Trevor Doyle
187	Briane Thompson
213	Chad Cabana
239	John Demarco
265	Eric Montreuil

Club Directory

Miami Arena

100 North East Third Avenue
Tenth Floor
Fort Lauderdale, FL 33301
Phone **305/768-1900**
FAX 305/768-1920
Capacity: 14,500

Chairman and CEO	H. Wayne Huizenga
President	William A. Torrey
Vice President and General Manager	Bob Clarke
Vice President, Business and Marketing	Dean Jordan
Vice President, Finance and Administration	Jonathan Mariner
Special Counsel	James J. Blosser
Special Consultant	Richard C. Rochon
Consultant	Gary Green
Assistant to the General Manager	Chuck Fletcher
Director of Player Personnel	John Chapman
Head Coach	Roger Neilson
Assistant Coach	Craig Ramsay, Lindy Ruff
Goaltending Coach	Bill Smith
Chief Scout	Dennis Patterson
Eastern Scout	Ron Harris
Director, Public/Media Relations	Greg Bouris
Public/Media Relations Associates	Kevin Dessart, Ron Colangelo
Director, Promotions & Special Projects	Declau J. Bolger
Director, Group/Season Ticket Sales	Bill Beck
Director, Ticket and Game Day Operations	Steve Dangerfield
Director, Corporate Sales and Sponsorship	Kimberly Terranova
Coordinator, Corporate Sales and Sponsorship	Eric Bresler
Director, Merchandise	Ron Dennis
Controller	Larry Cohen
Manager, Ticket Operations	Scott Wampold
Account Executives	Greg Hancssian, Barry Cohen, Jose Velasco
Ticket Operations	Julian Smyle, Matt Coyne
Administrative Assistants	Deanna Cocozzelli, Cathy Stevenson, Laurie Scott, Diana Marchand, Aza Krotz, Susan Gonzalez, Lauren Devine, Janine Amodio, Abby Potts
Intern, Promotions	Alan Keystone
Head Athletic Trainer	David Settlemeyer
Athletic Trainer/Strength Coach	Gordon Hurlbert
Equipment Manager	Tim Leroy
Assistant Equipment Manager	Derek Settlemeyer
Home Ice	Miami Arena
Arena Phone Number	(305) 530-4495
Seating Capacity	14,500
Location of Press Box	Mezzanine, Sec. 211
Dimensions of Rink	200 feet by 85 feet
Team Colors	Red, Navy Blue, Yellow-Gold
Television Station	Sunshine Network & WBFS Channel 33
Television Announcers	TBA
Panthers Radio Network	WQAM, 560 AM
Radio Announcers	TBA

Coach

NEILSON, ROGER PAUL
Coach, Florida Panthers. Born in Toronto, Ont., June 16, 1934.

On June 2, 1993, Roger Neilson became the first coach of the Florida Panthers. Neilson, 59, was most recently the head coach of the New York Rangers from the beginning of the 1989-90 season until being replaced on January 4, 1993. In his three-plus seasons with the Rangers, Neilson led the team to two regular season Patrick Division championships ('90 & '92) and he was twice a finalist for NHL Coach of the Year honors ('90 & '92). In 280 regular season games behind the Rangers bench, Neilson posted a record of 141-104-35 for a winning percentage of .566.

Neilson began his hockey coaching career in 1966-67 when he became the head coach of the Peterborough Petes of the Ontario Hockey Association. Neilson spent 10 seasons with the Petes and during his tenure he captured one OHA championship and his team finished lower than third only twice.

Neilson left the Petes in 1976-77 to take his first professional-level coaching job with the Dallas Blackhawks of the Central Hockey League. After spending only one season in Dallas, Neilson joined the NHL coaching ranks with the Toronto Maple Leafs. Neilson coached the Leafs for two seasons ('77-78 & '78-79) and he led his team to two winning seasons; their last two winning seasons prior to the 1992-93 season. In 1977-78, Neilson led the Leafs to the NHL semi-finals.

Following his two-year stay in Toronto, and prior to joining the Rangers in 1989, Neilson coached with the Buffalo Sabres (1979-81), the Vancouver Canucks (1982-83), the Los Angeles Kings (1983-84), and the Chicago Blackhawks (co-coach 1984-85 through 1986-87).

Coaching Record

Season	Team	Games	Regular Season W	L	T	%	Playoffs Games	W	L	%
1966-67	Peterborough (OHA)					UNAVAILABLE				
1967-68	Peterborough (OHA)	54	13	30	11	.342	....	....	....	....
1968-69	Peterborough (OHA)	54	27	18	9	.583	10	4	6	.400
1969-70	Peterborough (OHA)	54	29	13	12	.648	....	....	....	....
1970-71	Peterborough (OHA)	62	41	13	8	.726	....	....	....	....
1971-72	Peterborough (OHA)	63	34	20	9	.611	....	....	....	....
1972-73	Peterborough (OHA)	63	42	13	8	.730	....	....	....	....
1973-74	Peterborough (OHA)	70	35	21	14	.600	....	....	....	....
1974-75	Peterborough (OHA)	70	37	20	13	.621	....	....	....	....
1975-76	Peterborough (OHA)	66	18	37	11	.356	....	....	....	....
1976-77	Dallas (CHL)	76	35	25	16	.566	....	....	....	....
1977-78	Toronto (NHL)	80	41	29	10	.575	13	6	7	.462
1978-79	Toronto (NHL)	80	34	33	13	.506	6	2	4	.333
1979-80	Buffalo (NHL)	26	14	6	6	.654	....	....	....	....
1980-81	Buffalo (NHL)	80	39	20	21	.619	8	4	4	.500
1981-82	Vancouver (NHL)	5	4	0	1	.900	17	11	6	.647
1982-83	Vancouver (NHL)	80	30	35	15	.469	4	1	3	.250
1983-84	Vancouver (NHL)	48	17	26	5	.406	....	....	....	....
1983-84	Los Angeles (NHL)	28	8	17	3	.339	....	....	....	....
1989-90	NY Rangers (NHL)	80	36	31	13	.531	10	5	5	.500
1990-91	NY Rangers (NHL)	80	36	31	13	.531	6	2	4	.333
1991-92	NY Rangers (NHL)	80	50	25	5	.656	13	6	7	.462
1992-93	NY Rangers (NHL)	40	19	17	4	.525	....	....	....	....
	NHL Totals	707	328	270	109	.541	77	37	40	.481

General Managers' History
Bob Clarke, 1993-94.

Coaching History
Roger Neilson, 1993-94.

General Manager

CLARKE, ROBERT EARLE (BOB)
General Manager, Florida Panthers. Born in Flin Flon, Man., August 13, 1949.

Bob Clarke joins the Panther franchise by way of the Philadelphia Flyers organization, where he served as the Senior Vice President. He previously served as the Minnesota North Stars Vice President and General Manager from 1990-92. Under Clarke's leadership, he helped guide the North Stars to a 59-81-20 record and advance into the 1991 Stanley Cup Finals. Prior to working with the North Stars, Clarke was the Flyers Vice President and General Manager from 1984-90, where the team posted a 256-177-47 record. During his six years as general manager, the Flyers won three divisional titles, two conference championships, reached the Stanley Cup semifinals three times and the Finals twice.

As a player, the former Philadelphia captain led his club to Stanley Cup championships in 1974 and 1975 and captured numerous individual awards, including the Hart Trophy as the League's most valuable player in 1973, 1975 and 1976. The four-time All-Star also received the Masterton Memorial Trophy (perseverance and dedication) in 1972 and the Frank J. Selke Trophy (top defensive forward) in 1983. He appeared in nine All-Star Games and was elected to the Hockey Hall of Fame in 1987. He was awarded the Lester Patrick Trophy in 1979-80 in recognition of his contribution to hockey in the United States. Clarke appeared in 1,144 regular-season games, recording 358 goals and 852 assists for 1,210 points. He also added 119 points in 136 playoff games.

Hartford Whalers

1992-93 Results: 26w-52L-6T 58PTS. Fifth, Adams Division

Schedule

Home		Away	
Oct.	Sat. 9 Philadelphia	**Oct.**	Wed. 6 Montreal
	Wed. 13 Montreal		Sun. 10 Buffalo
	Wed. 20 Quebec		Thur. 14 Chicago
	Sat. 23 Buffalo		Sat. 16 Pittsburgh
	Sat. 30 NY Rangers		Tues. 19 Toronto
Nov.	Mon. 1 St Louis		Wed. 27 Dallas
	Wed. 3 Calgary		Thur. 28 St Louis
	Wed. 10 Ottawa	**Nov.**	Sat. 6 NY Islanders
	Sat. 13 Edmonton		Thur. 18 Philadelphia
	Wed. 17 Boston		Tues. 23 Florida
	Sat. 20 San Jose		Wed. 24 Tampa Bay
	Sat. 27 Florida*		Mon. 29 Ottawa
Dec.	Wed. 1 Detroit	**Dec.**	Tues. 7 Washington
	Sat. 4 Pittsburgh		Sun. 12 Boston
	Wed. 8 Vancouver		Wed. 15 NY Rangers
	Sat. 11 Buffalo		Thur. 23 Ottawa
	Sat. 18 Washington		Tues. 28 New Jersey
	Wed. 22 New Jersey	**Jan.**	Sat. 1 NY Islanders*
	Sun. 26 Ottawa		Wed. 12 Los Angeles
	Wed. 29 Florida		Fri. 14 Anaheim
Jan.	Sun. 2 Pittsburgh		Sat. 15 San Jose
	Wed. 5 Winnipeg		Mon. 17 Boston*
	Thur. 6 St Louis		Thur. 27 Ottawa
	(at Cleveland)	**Feb.**	Tues. 1 Quebec
	Sat. 8 NY Islanders		Wed. 2 Montreal
	Wed. 19 Toronto		Fri. 4 Winnipeg
	Mon. 24 Boston		Sun. 6 Vancouver*
	Wed. 26 Montreal		Fri. 11 Calgary
	Sat. 29 Quebec*		Sat. 12 Edmonton
Feb.	Wed. 16 Buffalo		Thur. 17 Pittsburgh
	Sat. 19 NY Rangers		Thur. 24 Detroit
	Sat. 26 New Jersey*		(at Cleveland)
	Sun. 27 Washington	**Mar.**	Fri. 4 Florida
Mar.	Wed. 2 Los Angeles		Sat. 5 Tampa Bay
	Wed. 9 Tampa Bay		Thur. 10 New Jersey
	Sat. 12 Dallas*		Wed. 16 NY Rangers
	Sun. 13 Pittsburgh*		Thur. 17 Quebec
	Sat. 26 Anaheim		Sat. 19 Philadelphia*
	Wed. 30 Chicago		Tues. 22 Washington
Apr.	Sat. 2 Philadelphia		Fri. 25 Buffalo
	Wed. 6 NY Islanders		Tues. 29 Detroit
	Sun. 10 Tampa Bay*	**Apr.**	Thur. 7 Quebec
	Mon. 11 Montreal		Thur. 14 Boston

* Denotes afternoon game.

Home Starting Times:

Weeknights and Saturdays	. . . .	7:35 p.m.
Sundays	. . . .	6:05 p.m.
Matinees	. . . .	1:35 p.m.

Franchise date: June 22, 1979

NORTHEAST
DIVISION

15th
NHL
Season

EASTERN
CONFERENCE

Andrew Cassels had a career-year in 1992-93, leading the Whalers in assists (64) and shorthanded goals (3).

Year-by-Year Record

		Home			Road			Overall							
Season	GP	W	L	T	W	L	T	W	L	T	GF	GA	Pts.	Finished	Playoff Result
1992-93	84	12	25	5	14	27	1	26	52	6	284	369	58	5th, Adams Div.	Out of Playoffs
1991-92	80	13	17	10	13	24	3	26	41	13	247	283	65	4th, Adams Div.	Lost Div. Semi-Final
1990-91	80	18	16	6	13	22	5	31	38	11	238	276	73	4th, Adams Div.	Lost Div. Semi-Final
1989-90	80	17	18	5	21	15	4	38	33	9	275	268	85	4th, Adams Div.	Lost Div. Semi-Final
1988-89	80	21	17	2	16	21	3	37	38	5	299	290	79	4th, Adams Div.	Lost Div. Semi-Final
1987-88	80	21	14	5	14	24	2	35	38	7	249	267	77	4th, Adams Div.	Lost Div. Semi-Final
1986-87	80	26	9	5	17	21	2	43	30	7	287	270	93	1st, Adams Div.	Lost Div. Semi-Final
1985-86	80	21	17	2	19	19	2	40	36	4	332	302	84	4th, Adams Div.	Lost Div. Final
1984-85	80	17	18	5	13	23	4	30	41	9	268	318	69	5th, Adams Div.	Out of Playoffs
1983-84	80	19	16	5	9	26	5	28	42	10	288	320	66	5th, Adams Div.	Out of Playoffs
1982-83	80	13	22	5	6	32	2	19	54	7	261	403	45	5th, Adams Div.	Out of Playoffs
1981-82	80	13	17	10	8	24	8	21	41	18	264	351	60	5th, Adams Div.	Out of Playoffs
1980-81	80	14	17	9	7	24	9	21	41	18	292	372	60	4th, Norris Div.	Out of Playoffs
1979-80	80	22	12	6	5	22	13	27	34	19	303	312	73	4th, Norris Div.	Lost Prelim. Round

1993-94 Player Personnel

FORWARDS	HT	WT	S	Place of Birth	Date	1992-93 Club
BELANGER, Ken	6-3	190	L	Sault Ste. Marie, Ont.	5/14/74	Ottawa-Guelph
CASSELS, Andrew	6-0	192	L	Bramalea, ONt.	7/23/69	Hartford
CHALIFOUX, Denis	5-8	165	R	Laval, Que.	2/21/71	Springfield
CORRIVEAU, Yvon	6-1	195	L	Welland, Ont.	2/8/67	San Jose-Hartford
CROMBIE, Chris	6-2	195	L	Hamilton, Ont.	4/2/72	Johnstown
CUNNEYWORTH, Randy	6-0	180	L	Etobicoke, Ont.	5/10/61	Hartford
DANIELS, Scott	6-3	200	L	Prince Albert, Sask.	9/19/69	Springfield-Hartford
DUMONT, Louis	5-10	170	R	Calgary, Alta.	1/30/73	Regina
GREIG, Mark	5-11	190	R	High River, Alta.	1/25/70	Springfield-Hartford
GUAY, Paul	5-11	185	R	Providence, RI	9/2/63	Springfield-Brandon
JANSSENS, Mark	6-3	216	L	Surrey, B.C.	5/19/68	Hartford
KRON, Robert	5-10	180	L	Brno, Czech.	2/27/67	Vancouver-Hartford
KYPREOS, Nick	6-0	195	L	Toronto, Ont.	6/4/66	Hartford
McKENZIE, Jim	6-3	210	L	Gull Lake, Sask.	11/3/69	Hartford
MORROW, Scott	6-1	181	L	Chicago, IL	6/18/69	Springfield
NIECKAR, Barry	6-3	200	L	Rama, Sask.	12/16/67	Springfield-Hartford
NYLANDER, Mikael	5-11	176	L	Stockholm, Sweden	10/3/72	Hartford
PETROVICKY, Robert	5-11	172	L	Kosice, Czech.	10/26/73	Springfield-Hartford
POULIN, Patrick	6-1	208	L	Vanier, Que.	4/23/73	Hartford
PROSOFSKY, Jason	6-4	220	R	Medicine Hat, Alta.	4/4/71	Greensboro
REID, Jarrett	5-10	182	R	Sault Ste. Marie, Ont.	3/10/73	Sault Ste. Marie
SANDERSON, Geoff	6-0	185	L	Hay River, N.W.T.	2/1/72	Hartford
SANDLAK, Jim	6-4	219	R	Kitchener, Ont.	12/12/66	Vancouver
SMYTH, Kevin	6-2	217	L	Banff, Alta.	11/22/73	Moose Jaw
STIENBURG, Trevor	6-1	200	R	Kingston, Ont.	5/13/66	Springfield
STORM, Jim	6-2	200	L	Milford, MI	2/5/71	Michigan Tech.
TOMLAK, Mike	6-3	205	L	Thunder Bay, Ont.	10/17/64	Springfield
VERBEEK, Pat	5-9	190	R	Sarnia, Ont.	5/24/64	Hartford

DEFENSEMEN						
AGNEW, Jim	6-1	190	L	Hartney, Man.	3/21/66	Hartford
BEAULIEU, Corey	6-1	210	L	Winnipeg, Man.	9/9/69	Springfield
BLOEMBERG, Jeff	6-2	205	R	Listowel, Ont.	1/31/68	Cape Breton
BURT, Adam	6-0	190	L	Detroit, MI	1/15/69	Hartford
COWIE, Rob	6-0	195	L	Toronto, Ont.	11/3/67	Moncton
DUFFY, Jack	6-1	195	R	Northford, CT	9/25/70	Yale
HAMRLIK, Martin	5-11	176	R	Zlin, Czech.	5/6/73	Springfield-Ottawa
HOUDA, Doug	6-2	200	R	Blairmore, Alta.	6/3/66	Hartford
HUMENJUK, Scott	6-0	190	R	Saskatoon, Sask.	9/10/69	Springfield-Louisville
JOHNSTON, Karl	6-0	190	L	Windsor, Ont.	8/11/67	Springfield-Louisville
JULIEN, Stephane	5-10	188	R	St. Tite, Que.	4/7/74	Sherbrooke
KECZMER, Dan	6-1	190	L	Mt. Clemens, MI	5/25/68	Springfield-Hartford
MALIK, Marek	6-5	207	L	Vitkovice, Czech.	6/24/75	Vitkovice
McBAIN, Jason	6-2	178	R	Ilion, NY	4/12/74	Portland
McCOSH, Shayne	6-0	190	L	Oshawa, Ont.	6/5/69	Windsor
McCRIMMON, Brad	5-11	197	L	Dodsland, Sask.	3/29/59	Detroit
O'SULLIVAN, Kevin	6-0	180	L	Dorchester, MA	11/13/70	Boston U.
PEDERSEN, Allen	6-3	210	L	Ft. Sask., Alta.	1/13/65	Hartford
PRATT, Nolan	6-2	190	L	Fort McMurray, Alta.	8/14/75	Portland
PREMAK, Garth	6-2	205	L	Ituna, Sask.	3/15/68	Cdn. Nat.
PRONGER, Chris	6-5	190	L	Dryden, Ont.	10/10/74	Peterborough
RICHTER, Barry	6-2	205	L	Madison, WI	9/11/70	U. of Wisconsin
ROSENBLATT, Howard	5-10	180	R	Pawtucket, RI	1/3/69	Birmingham-Cincinnati
STEVENS, John	6-1	195	L	Completon, N.B.	5/4/66	Springfield
SUOMALAINEN, Jukka	6-5	198	L	Helsinki, Finland	4/20/66	Springfield
SWINSON, Wes	6-2	183	L	Peterborough, Ont.	5/25/75	Kitchener
WEINRICH, Eric	6-1	205	L	Roanoke, VA	12/19/66	Hartford
YULE, Steve	6-0	210	R	Gleichen, Alta.	5/27/72	Springfield
ZALAPSKI, Zarley	6-1	210	L	Edmonton, Alta.	4/22/68	Hartford

GOALTENDERS	HT	WT	C	Place of Birth	Date	1992-93 Club
BURKE, Sean	6-4	210	L	Windsor, Ont.	1/29/67	Hartford
GOSSELIN, Mario	5-8	160	L	Thetford Mines, Que.	6/15/63	Springfield-Hartford
GRAVISTON, Shaun	5-7	150	L	Calgary, Alta.	11/17/70	Alaska-Anchorage
LEGACE, Manny	5-8	180	L	Toronto, Ont.	2/4/73	Niagara Falls
LENARDUZZI, Mike	6-1	168	L	London, Ont.	9/14/72	Springfield-Hartford
PIETRANGELO, Frank	5-10	185	L	Niagara Falls, Ont.	12/17/64	Hartford

General Managers' History

Jack Kelly, 1979-80 to 1981-82; Emile Francis, 1982-83 to 1988-89; Ed Johnston, 1989-90 to 1991-92; Brian Burke, 1992-93

Coaching History

Don Blackburn, 1979-80; Don Blackburn and Larry Pleau, 1980-81; Larry Pleau, 1981-82; Larry Kish, Larry Pleau and John Cuniff, 1982-83; Jack "Tex" Evans, 1983-84 to 1986-87; Jack "Tex" Evans and Larry Pleau, 1987-88; Larry Pleau, 1988-89; Rick Ley, 1989-90 to 1990-91; Jim Roberts, 1991-92; Paul Holmgren, 1992-93 to date.

Captains' History

Rick Ley, 1979-80; Rick Ley, Mark Howe and Mike Rogers, 1980-81. Dave Keon, 1981-82; Russ Anderson, 1982-83; Mark Johnson, 1983-84; Mark Johnson and Ron Francis, 1984-85; Ron Francis, 1985-86 to 1990-91; Randy Ladouceur, 1991-92. Pat Verbeek, 1992-93 to date.

1992-93 Scoring

Regular Season

Pos	#	Player	Team	GP	G	A	Pts	+/-	PIM	PP	SH	GW	GT	S	%
C	8	Geoff Sanderson	HFD	82	46	43	89	21–	28	21	2	4	0	271	17.0
C	21	Andrew Cassels	HFD	84	21	64	85	11–	62	8	3	1	0	134	15.7
R	16	Pat Verbeek	HFD	84	39	43	82	7–	197	16	0	6	2	235	16.6
D	3	Zarley Zalapski	HFD	83	14	51	65	34–	94	8	1	0	0	192	7.3
C	25	Terry Yake	HFD	66	22	31	53	9	46	4	1	2	0	98	22.4
L	24	* Patrick Poulin	HFD	81	20	31	51	19–	37	4	0	2	0	160	12.5
D	4	Eric Weinrich	HFD	79	7	29	36	11–	76	0	2	2	0	104	6.7
C	36	* Michael Nylander	HFD	59	11	22	33	7–	36	3	0	1	0	85	12.9
C	22	Mark Janssens	HFD	76	12	17	29	15–	237	0	0	1	0	63	19.0
L	20	Nick Kypreos	HFD	75	17	10	27	5–	325	0	1	2	1	81	21.0
C	38	Robert Kron	VAN	32	10	11	21	10	14	2	2	2	1	60	16.7
			HFD	13	4	2	6	5–	4	2	0	0	0	37	10.8
			TOTAL	45	14	13	27	5	18	4	2	2	1	97	14.4
L	11	Yvon Corriveau	S.J.	20	3	7	10	7–	0	1	0	0	0	32	9.4
			HFD	37	5	5	10	13–	14	1	0	1	0	45	11.1
			TOTAL	57	8	12	20	20–	14	2	0	1	0	77	10.4
D	6	Adam Burt	HFD	65	6	14	20	11–	116	0	0	0	0	81	7.4
L	7	Randy Cunneyworth	HFD	39	5	4	9	1–	63	0	0	1	0	47	10.6
C	39	* Robert Petrovicky	HFD	42	3	6	9	10–	45	0	0	0	0	41	7.3
L	33	Jim McKenzie	HFD	64	3	6	9	10–	202	0	0	1	0	36	8.3
D	37	* Dan Keczmer	HFD	23	4	4	8	3–	28	2	0	1	0	38	10.5
D	27	Doug Houda	HFD	60	2	6	8	19–	167	0	0	0	0	43	4.7
R	17	* Mark Greig	HFD	22	1	7	8	11–	27	0	0	0	0	16	6.3
L	15	* Joe Day	HFD	24	1	7	8	8–	47	0	0	0	0	10	10.0
D	29	Randy Ladouceur	HFD	62	2	4	6	18–	109	0	0	0	0	37	5.4
R	12	Tim Kerr	HFD	22	0	6	6	11–	7	0	0	0	0	48	.0
R	34	Jamie Leach	PIT	5	0	0	0	2–	2	0	0	0	0	2	.0
			HFD	19	3	2	5	5–	2	0	0	0	0	17	17.6
			TOTAL	24	3	2	5	7–	4	0	0	0	0	19	15.8
D	41	Allen Pedersen	HFD	59	1	4	5	0	60	0	0	0	0	16	6.3
C	23	Paul Gillis	HFD	21	1	1	2	2–	40	0	0	0	0	8	12.5
G	1	Sean Burke	HFD	50	0	2	2	0	25	0	0	0	0	0	.0
L	14	Chris Govedaris	HFD	7	1	0	1	2–	0	0	0	0	0	6	16.7
G	31	Mario Gosselin	HFD	16	0	1	1	0	2	0	0	0	0	0	.0
G	35	* Corrie D'Alessio	HFD	1	0	0	0	0	0	0	0	0	0	0	.0
L	48	* Scott Daniels	HFD	1	0	0	0	0	19	0	0	0	0	0	.0
L	12	* Barry Nieckar	HFD	2	0	0	0	2–	2	0	0	0	0	1	.0
G	30	* Mike Lenarduzzi	HFD	3	0	0	0	0	0	0	0	0	0	0	.0
D	26	Jim Agnew	HFD	16	0	0	0	3	68	0	0	0	0	3	.0
G	40	Frank Pietrangelo	HFD	30	0	0	0	0	4	0	0	0	0	0	.0

Goaltending

No.	Goaltender	GPI	Mins	Avg	W	L	T	EN	SO	GA	SA	S%
35	* Corrie D'Alessio	1	11	.00	0	0	0	0	0	0	3	1.000
30	* Mike Lenarduzzi	3	168	3.21	1	1	1	0	0	9	87	.897
31	Mario Gosselin	16	867	3.94	5	9	1	1	0	57	499	.886
1	Sean Burke	50	2656	4.16	16	27	3	4	0	184	1485	.876
40	Frank Pietrangelo	30	1373	4.85	4	15	1	3	0	111	783	.858
	Totals	84	5098	4.34	26	52	6	8	0	369	2865	.871

Pat Verbeek, who led the Whalers with six game-winning goals, also collected 16 powerplay goals in 1992-93.

Club Records

Team

(Figures in brackets for season records are games played; records for fewest points, wins, ties, losses, goals, goals against are for 70 or more games)

Most Points	93	1986-87 (80)
Most Wins	43	1986-87 (80)
Most Ties	19	1979-80 (80)
Most Losses	54	1982-83 (80)
Most Goals	332	1985-86 (80)
Most Goals Against	403	1982-83 (80)
Fewest Points	45	1982-83 (80)
Fewest Wins	19	1982-83 (80)
Fewest Ties	4	1985-86 (80)
Fewest Losses	30	1986-87 (80)
Fewest Goals	238	1990-91 (80)
Fewest Goals Against	267	1987-88 (80)

Longest Winning Streak

Over-all	7	Mar. 16-29/85
Home	5	Mar. 17-29/85
Away	6	Nov. 10-Dec. 7/90

Longest Undefeated Streak

Over-all	10	Jan. 20-Feb. 10/82 (6 wins, 4 ties)
Home	7	Mar. 15-Apr. 5/86 (5 wins, 2 ties)
Away	6	Jan. 23-Feb. 10/82 (3 wins, 3 ties) Nov. 30-Dec. 26/89 (5 wins, 1 tie) Nov. 10-Dec. 7/90

Longest Losing Streak

Over-all	9	Feb. 19/83-Mar. 8/83
Home	6	Feb. 19/83-Mar. 12/83 Feb. 10-Mar. 3/85
Away	13	Dec. 18/82-Feb. 5/83

Longest Winless Streak

Over-all	14	Jan. 4/92-Feb. 9/92 (8 losses, 6 ties)
Home	13	Jan. 15-Mar. 10/85 (11 losses, 2 ties)
Away	15	Nov. 11/79-Jan. 9/80 (11 losses, 4 ties)

Most Shutouts, Season	5	1986-87 (80)
Most PIM, Season	2,354	1992-93 (84)
Most Goals, Game	11	Feb. 12/84 (Edm. 0 at Hfd. 11) Oct. 19/85 (Mtl. 6 at Hfd. 11) Jan. 17/86 (Que. 6 at Hfd. 11) Mar. 15/86 (Chi. 4 at Hfd. 11)

Individual

Most Seasons	10	Ron Francis
Most Games	714	Ron Francis
Most Goals, Career	264	Ron Francis
Most Assists, Career	557	Ron Francis
Most Points, Career	821	Ron Francis (264 goals, 557 assists)
Most PIM, Career	1,368	Torrie Robertson
Most Shutouts, Career	13	Mike Liut
Longest Consecutive Games Streak	419	Dave Tippett (Mar. 3/84-Oct. 7/89)
Most Goals, Season	56	Blaine Stoughton (1979-80)
Most Assists, Season	69	Ron Francis (1989-90)
Most Points, Season	105	Mike Rogers (1979-80) (44 goals, 61 assists) (1980-81) (40 goals, 65 assists)
Most PIM, Season	358	Torrie Robertson (1985-86)
Most Points, Defenseman Season	69	Dave Babych (1985-86) (14 goals, 55 assists)

Most Points, Center, Season	105	Mike Rogers (1979-80) (44 goals, 61 assists) Mike Rogers (1980-81) (40 goals, 65 assists)
Most Points, Right Wing, Season	100	Blaine Stoughton (1979-80) (56 goals, 44 assists)
Most Points, Left Wing, Season	89	Geoff Sanderson (1992-93) (46 goals, 43 assists)
Most Points, Rookie, Season	72	Sylvain Turgeon (1983-84) (40 goals, 32 assists)
Most Shutouts, Season	4	Mike Liut (1986-87) Peter Sidorkiewicz (1988-89)
Most Goals, Game	4	Jordy Douglas (Feb. 3/80) Ron Francis (Feb. 12/84)
Most Assists, Game	6	Ron Francis (Mar. 5/87)
Most Points, Game	6	Paul Lawless (Jan. 4/87) Ron Francis (Mar. 5/87, Oct. 8/89)

Retired Numbers

2	Rick Ley	1979-1981
9	Gordie Howe	1979-1980
19	John McKenzie	1976-1979

1992-93 Results

	Home			Away	
Oct. 6	Montreal	1-5	Oct. 8	Boston	2-3
10	Buffalo	2-5	12	NY Rangers	2-6
14	Ottawa	4-1	20	New Jersey	5-4
17	Pittsburgh	3-7	22	Ottawa	5-1
28	New Jersey	3-4	24	NY Islanders	2-4
31	Los Angeles	1-7	Nov. 6	Detroit	2-5
Nov. 3	Quebec	3-3	13	Buffalo	2-8
7	Washington	2-6	19	Ottawa	4-2
11	Calgary	3-4	21	Quebec*	2-8
14	Detroit	0-2	27	Boston*	4-5
18	St. Louis	5-2	Dec. 1	St. Louis	4-8
25	Montreal	1-6	3	San Jose	7-5
28	Boston	4-3	5	Los Angeles	3-7
Dec. 9	Ottawa	6-2	11	Buffalo	3-9
12	Buffalo	1-1	18	Washington	3-4
16	Washington	6-3	21	Montreal	5-2
19	NY Rangers	4-4	27	New Jersey	2-6
23	Tampa Bay	3-1	Jan. 2	Boston	2-3
26	Boston	4-9	13	Montreal	3-7
31	Quebec	2-6	15	Edmonton	1-3
Jan. 3	Minnesota	6-6	16	Vancouver	3-8
6	Buffalo	1-3	18	Winnipeg	7-8
9	Quebec	4-2	24	Philadelphia	4-5
10	Montreal	5-7	27	Montreal	6-5
21	San Jose	3-6	28	Vancouver	2-5
23	Chicago*	2-6	Feb. 3	Buffalo	2-3
30	Winnipeg	3-6	12	Winnipeg	6-2
Feb. 8	St. Louis	1-3	13	Calgary	3-4
17	Quebec	5-3	17	Quebec	5-3
20	Edmonton*	7-3	Mar. 5	Buffalo	4-2
21	Pittsburgh*	3-4	8	Quebec	4-2
24	Philadelphia	2-5	10	Toronto	3-5
28	NY Islanders	6-7	16	Tampa Bay	4-3
Mar. 3	New Jersey	4-7	19	Washington	2-5
6	Vancouver	5-1	22	Boston	4-5
13	Buffalo*	3-3	27	Minnesota	2-1
24	Montreal	5-6	28	Chicago	0-3
30	Boston	1-3	Apr. 1	Pittsburgh	2-10
Apr. 3	Ottawa	7-3	5	NY Rangers	5-4
11	Toronto	2-4	7	Ottawa	6-1
14	NY Islanders	5-4	10	Quebec	3-6
16	Philadelphia	4-5	13	NY Islanders	3-3

*Denotes afternoon game

All-time Record vs. Other Clubs

Regular Season

	GP	W	L	T	At Home GF	GA	PTS	GP	W	On Road L	T	GF	GA	PTS	GP	W	L	Total T	GF	GA	PTS
Boston	51	23	21	7	185	186	53	52	11	37	4	138	217	26	103	34	58	11	323	403	79
Buffalo	53	19	26	8	162	168	46	52	17	28	7	171	221	41	105	36	54	15	333	389	87
Calgary	21	7	11	3	72	84	17	21	4	16	1	74	114	9	42	11	27	4	146	198	26
Chicago	22	9	11	2	77	78	20	21	5	13	3	58	97	13	43	14	24	5	135	175	33
Detroit	21	13	7	1	80	57	27	21	7	8	6	66	79	20	42	20	15	7	146	136	47
Edmonton	21	9	9	3	90	79	21	22	2	17	3	62	100	7	43	11	26	6	152	179	28
Los Angeles	22	12	7	3	89	90	27	21	6	12	3	83	94	15	43	18	19	6	172	184	42
Minnesota	22	9	11	2	82	85	20	21	9	11	1	71	88	19	43	18	22	3	153	173	39
Montreal	52	17	27	8	163	201	42	51	10	35	6	153	235	26	103	27	62	14	316	436	68
New Jersey	22	11	7	4	83	71	26	23	10	11	2	94	90	22	45	21	18	6	177	161	48
NY Islanders	23	9	11	3	81	94	21	22	6	13	3	56	85	15	45	15	24	6	137	179	36
NY Rangers	22	12	7	3	89	80	27	22	7	13	2	69	100	16	44	19	20	5	158	180	43
Ottawa	3	3	0	0	17	6	6	4	3	1	0	17	9	6	7	6	1	0	34	15	12
Philadelphia	22	9	9	4	91	92	22	22	6	15	1	63	92	13	44	15	24	5	154	184	35
Pittsburgh	22	12	9	1	98	89	25	22	9	10	3	93	102	21	44	21	19	4	191	191	46
Quebec	51	22	18	11	181	181	55	52	15	30	7	166	229	37	103	37	48	18	347	410	92
St. Louis	22	9	11	2	71	70	20	22	8	12	2	76	89	18	44	17	23	4	147	159	38
San Jose	3	2	1	0	11	7	4	2	1	1	0	12	11	2	5	3	2	0	23	18	6
Tampa Bay	1	1	0	0	3	1	2	1	1	0	0	4	3	2	2	2	0	0	7	4	4
Toronto	21	12	6	3	99	71	27	21	12	7	2	88	75	26	42	24	13	5	187	146	53
Vancouver	21	9	8	4	72	75	22	22	7	9	6	62	80	20	43	16	17	10	134	155	42
Washington	23	8	12	3	75	92	19	22	8	13	1	66	79	17	45	16	25	4	141	171	36
Winnipeg	21	10	6	5	88	71	25	23	11	12	0	86	84	22	44	21	18	5	174	155	47
Totals	**562**	**247**	**235**	**80**	**2059**	**2028**	**574**	**562**	**175**	**324**	**63**	**1828**	**2373**	**413**	**1124**	**422**	**559**	**143**	**3887**	**4401**	**987**

Playoffs

	Series	W	L	GP	W	L	T	GF	GA	Last Mtg.	Round	Result
Boston	2	0	2	13	5	8	0	38	47	1991	DSF	L 2-4
Montreal	5	0	5	27	8	19	0	70	96	1992	DSF	L 3-4
Quebec	2	1	1	9	5	4	0	35	34	1987	DSF	L 2-4
Totals	**9**	**1**	**8**	**49**	**18**	**31**	**0**	**143**	**177**			

Playoff Results 1993-89

Year	Round	Opponent	Result	GF	GA
1992	DSF	Montreal	L 3-4	18	21
1991	DSF	Boston	L 2-4	17	24
1990	DSF	Boston	L 3-4	21	23
1989	DSF	Montreal	L 0-4	11	18

Abbreviations: Round: F – Final;
CF – conference final; **DF** – division final;
DSF – division semi-final; **SF** – semi-final;
QF – quarter-final; **PR** – preliminary round.
GA – goals against; **GF** – goals for.

Entry Draft
Selections 1993-79

1993
Pick
2	Chris Pronger
72	Marek Malik
84	Trevor Roenick
115	Nolan Pratt
188	Emmanuel Legace
214	Dmitri Gorenko
240	Wes Swinson
266	Igor Chibirev

1992
Pick
9	Robert Petrovicky
47	Andrei Nikolishin
57	Jan Vopat
79	Kevin Smyth
81	Jason McBain
143	Jarret Reid
153	Ken Belanger
177	Konstantin Korotkov
201	Greg Zwakman
225	Steven Halko
249	Joacim Esbjors

1991
Pick
9	Patrick Poulin
31	Martin Hamrlik
53	Todd Hall
59	Mikael Nylander
75	Jim Storm
119	Mike Harding
141	Brian Mueller
163	Steve Yule
185	Chris Belanger
207	Jason Currie
229	Mike Santonelli
251	Rob Peters

1990
Pick
15	Mark Greig
36	Geoff Sanderson
57	Mike Lenarduzzi
78	Chris Bright
120	Cory Keenan
141	Jergus Baca
162	Martin D'Orsonnens
183	Corey Osmak
204	Espen Knutsen
225	Tommie Eriksen
246	Denis Chalifoux

1989
Pick
10	Robert Holik
52	Blair Atcheynum
73	Jim McKenzie
94	James Black
115	Jerome Bechard
136	Scott Daniels
157	Raymond Saumier
178	Michel Picard
199	Trevor Buchanan
220	John Battice
241	Peter Kasowski

1988
Pick
11	Chris Govedaris
32	Barry Richter
74	Dean Dyer
95	Scott Morrow
116	Corey Beaulieu
137	Kerry Russell
158	Jim Burke
179	Mark Hirth
200	Wayde Bucsis
221	Rob White
242	Dan Slatalla

1987
Pick
18	Jody Hull
39	Adam Burt
81	Terry Yake
102	Marc Rousseau
123	Jeff St. Cyr
144	Greg Wolf
165	John Moore
186	Joe Day
228	Kevin Sullivan
249	Steve Laurin

1986
Pick
11	Scott Young
32	Marc Laforge
74	Brian Chapman
95	Bill Horn
116	Joe Quinn
137	Steve Torrel
158	Ron Hoover
179	Robert Glasgow
200	Sean Evoy
221	Cal Brown
242	Brian Verbeek

1985
Pick
5	Dana Murzyn
26	Kay Whitmore
68	Gary Callaghan
110	Shane Churla
131	Chris Brant
152	Brian Puhalsky
173	Greg Dornbach
194	Paul Tory
215	Jerry Pawlowski
236	Bruce Hill

1984
Pick
11	Sylvain Cote
110	Mike Millar
131	Mike Vellucci
173	John Devereaux
193	Brent Regan
214	Jim Culhane
234	Pete Abric

1983
Pick
2	Sylvain Turgeon
20	David Jensen
23	Ville Siren
61	Leif Carlsson
64	Dave MacLean
72	Ron Chyzowski
104	Brian Johnson
124	Joe Reekie
143	Chris Duperron
144	James Falle
164	Bill Fordy
193	Reine Karlsson
204	Allan Acton
224	Darcy Kaminski

1982
Pick
14	Paul Lawless
35	Mark Paterson
56	Kevin Dineen
67	Ulf Samuelsson
88	Ray Ferraro
109	Randy Gilhen
130	Jim Johannson
151	Mickey Kramptoich
172	Kevin Skilliter
214	Martin Linse
235	Randy Cameron

1981
Pick
4	Ron Francis
61	Paul MacDermid
67	Michael Hoffman
93	Bill Maguire
103	Dan Bourbonnais
130	John Mokosak
151	Denis Dore
172	Jeff Poeschl
193	Larry Power

1980
Pick
8	Fred Arthur
29	Michel Galarneau
50	Mickey Volcan
71	Kevin McClelland
92	Darren Jensen
113	Mario Cerri
134	Mike Martin
155	Brent Denat
176	Paul Fricker
197	Lorne Bokshowan

1979
Pick
18	Ray Allison
39	Stuart Smith
60	Don Nachbaur
81	Ray Neufeld
102	Mark Renaud
123	Dave McDonald

Club Directory

Hartford Whalers
242 Trumbull Street
Eighth Floor
Hartford, Connecticut 06103
Phone **203/728-3366**
GM FAX 203/493-2423
FAX 203/522-7707
Capacity: 15,635

Managing General Partner/Governor	Richard Gordon

Hockey Department
General Manager	TBA
Assistant General Manager	Ken Schinkel
Director of Hockey Operations	Tom Rowe
Head Coach	Paul Holmgren
Assistant Coaches	Kevin McCarthy, Pierre Maguire
Strength and Conditioning Coach	Doug McKenney
Director of Pro Scouting	Kevin Maxwell
Pro Scout	Claude Larose
Amateur Scouting Staff	Bruce Haralson, Fred Gore, Willy Lindstrom, Roger Oxborough, Steve Rooney
Executive Secretary	Anne Sullivan
Secretary	Cathy Merrick
Medical Trainer	Frank "Bud" Gouvela
Equipment Manager	Skip Cunningham
Assistant Equipment Manager	TBA
Assistant to Equipment Manager	TBA
Club Doctor	Dr. John Fulkerson
Club Dentist	Dr. Robert Hall

Administration
Vice President of Finance & Administration	Michael J. Amendola
Vice President of Marketing & Sales	Rick Francis
Advertising Sales Manager	Kevin Bauer
Director of Media Relations	John H. Forslund
Director of Public Relations	Mark Mancini
Public Relations Assistant	Mary Lynn Gorman
Chief Statistician/Head Archivist	Frank Polnaszek
Ticket Sales Manager	Jim Baldwin
Ticket Office Supervisors	Mike Barnes, Chris O'Connor

General Information
Radio Play-by-Play	Chuck Kaiton
Radio Color	John Forslund
TV/Cable Play-by-Play	Rick Peckham
TV/Cable Commentator	Gerry Cheevers
Cable TV Outlet	SportsChannel - New England
Radio Network Flagship Station	WTIC-AM (1080)
Home Ice	Hartford Civic Center Veterans Memorial Coliseum
Dimensions of Rink	200 feet by 85 feet

Rookie center Robert Petrovicky was the Whalers' first selection in the 1992 Entry Draft.

Coach

HOLMGREN, PAUL
Coach, Hartford Whalers. Born in St. Paul, MN, December 2, 1955.

Paul Holmgren became the seventh man to be named coach of the Hartford Whalers, succeeding Jimmy Roberts, on June 15, 1992. A sixth round draft selection of the Philadelphia Flyers in 1975, Holmgren spent nine years with the team before finishing his career with the Minnesota North Stars in 1985. The next season, he was named as an assistant to Mike Keenan, spending three years in that role. In 1988, Holmgren became the first former-Flyer to be named as head-coach, serving in that capacity for four seasons. In Philadelphia, Holmgren compiled a 107-126-31 record before being replaced by Bill Dineen on December 4, 1991.

Coaching Record

		Regular Season					Playoffs			
Season	Team	Games	W	L	T	%	Games	W	L	%
1988-89	Philadelphia (NHL)	80	36	36	8	.500	19	10	9	.526
1989-90	Philadelphia (NHL)	80	30	39	11	.444	....	....	....	....
1990-91	Philadelphia (NHL)	80	33	37	10	.475	....	....	....	....
1991-92	Philadelphia (NHL)	24	8	14	2	.375	....	....	....	....
1992-93	Hartford (NHL)	84	26	52	6	.345	....	....	....	....
	NHL Totals	348	133	178	37	.435	19	10	9	.526

Los Angeles Kings

1992-93 Results: 39w-35L-10T 88PTS. Third, Smythe Division

Year-by-Year Record

		Home			Road			Overall							
Season	GP	W	L	T	W	L	T	W	L	T	GF	GA	Pts.	Finished	Playoff Result
1992-93	84	22	15	5	17	20	5	39	35	10	338	340	88	3rd, Smythe Div.	Lost Final
1991-92	80	20	11	9	15	20	5	35	31	14	287	296	84	2nd, Smythe Div.	Lost Div. Semi-Final
1990-91	80	26	9	5	20	15	5	46	24	10	340	254	102	1st, Smythe Div.	Lost Div. Final
1989-90	80	21	16	3	13	23	4	34	39	7	338	337	75	4th, Smythe Div.	Lost Div. Final
1988-89	80	25	12	3	17	19	4	42	31	7	376	335	91	2nd, Smythe Div.	Lost Div. Final
1987-88	80	19	18	3	11	24	5	30	42	8	318	359	68	4th, Smythe Div.	Lost Div. Semi-Final
1986-87	80	20	17	3	11	24	5	31	41	8	318	341	70	4th, Smythe Div.	Out of Playoffs
1985-86	80	9	27	4	14	22	4	23	49	8	284	389	54	5th, Smythe Div.	Lost Div. Semi-Final
1984-85	80	20	14	6	14	18	8	34	32	14	339	326	82	4th, Smythe Div.	Lost Div. Semi-Final
1983-84	80	13	19	8	10	25	5	23	44	13	309	376	59	5th, Smythe Div.	Out of Playoffs
1982-83	80	20	13	7	7	28	5	27	41	12	308	365	66	5th, Smythe Div.	Out of Playoffs
1981-82	80	19	15	6	5	26	9	24	41	15	314	369	63	4th, Smythe Div.	Lost Div. Final
1980-81	80	22	11	7	21	13	6	43	24	13	337	290	99	2nd, Norris Div.	Lost Prelim. Round
1979-80	80	18	13	9	12	23	5	30	36	14	290	313	74	2nd, Norris Div.	Lost Prelim. Round
1978-79	80	20	13	7	14	21	5	34	34	12	292	286	80	3rd, Norris Div.	Lost Prelim. Round
1977-78	80	18	16	6	13	18	9	31	34	15	243	245	77	3rd, Norris Div.	Lost Quarter-Final
1976-77	80	20	13	7	14	18	8	34	31	15	271	241	83	2nd, Norris Div.	Lost Quarter-Final
1975-76	80	22	13	5	16	20	4	38	33	9	263	265	85	2nd, Norris Div.	Lost Quarter-Final
1974-75	80	22	7	11	20	10	10	42	17	21	269	185	105	2nd, Norris Div.	Lost Prelim. Round
1973-74	78	22	13	4	11	20	8	33	33	12	233	231	78	3rd, West Div.	Out of Playoffs
1972-73	78	21	11	7	10	25	4	31	36	11	232	245	73	6th, West Div.	Out of Playoffs
1971-72	78	14	23	2	6	26	7	20	49	9	206	305	49	7th, West Div.	Out of Playoffs
1970-71	78	17	14	8	8	26	5	25	40	13	239	303	63	5th, West Div.	Out of Playoffs
1969-70	76	12	22	4	2	30	6	14	52	10	168	290	38	6th, West Div.	Out of Playoffs
1968-69	76	19	14	5	5	28	5	24	42	10	185	260	58	4th, West Div.	Lost Semi-Final
1967-68	74	20	13	4	11	20	6	31	33	10	200	224	72	2nd, West Div.	Lost Quarter-Final

Schedule

Home

Oct.		
	Wed.	6 Vancouver
	Sat.	9 Detroit
	Sun.	10 San Jose
	Tues.	12 NY Islanders
	Thur.	14 Edmonton
	Sat.	16 Calgary
Nov.	Wed.	3 New Jersey
	Sat.	6 Pittsburgh
	Sat.	13 St Louis
	Thur.	18 Toronto
	Tues.	30 Winnipeg
Dec.	Thur.	2 Anaheim
	Sat.	4 Tampa Bay
	Wed.	8 Florida
	Sat.	11 St Louis
	Thur.	23 Dallas
	Tues.	28 Vancouver
Jan.	Tues.	4 Quebec
	Sat.	8 Detroit
	Wed.	12 Hartford
	Tues.	25 Winnipeg
	Thur.	27 NY Rangers
	Sat.	29 Anaheim
Feb.	Sat.	5 Calgary
	Wed.	9 Chicago
	Sat.	12 Washington
	Mon.	14 Boston
	Fri.	18 Philadelphia
	Mon.	21 Toronto*
	Wed.	23 Dallas
	Mon.	28 Montreal
Mar.	Wed.	9 Chicago
	Sat.	12 Buffalo
	Tues.	15 Ottawa
	Sat.	19 San Jose*
	Wed.	23 Vancouver
	Wed.	30 Anaheim
Apr.	Sat.	2 Edmonton*
	Sun.	3 Edmonton* (at Sacramento)
	Tues.	5 San Jose
	Wed.	13 Calgary
	Thur.	14 Edmonton

Away

Oct.		
	Tues.	19 Florida
	Wed.	20 Tampa Bay
	Fri.	22 Washington
	Sun.	24 NY Rangers
	Tues.	26 NY Islanders
	Wed.	27 Detroit
	Fri.	29 Winnipeg
Nov.	Tues.	9 Calgary
	Wed.	10 Vancouver
	Sat.	20 St Louis
	Sun.	21 Dallas
	Thur.	25 Quebec
	Sat.	27 Montreal
Dec.	Mon.	13 Ottawa
	Tues.	14 Pittsburgh
	Fri.	17 Buffalo
	Sat.	18 Toronto
	Mon.	20 Calgary
	Sun.	26 Anaheim
	Fri.	31 Detroit
Jan.	Sat.	1 Toronto
	Tues.	11 San Jose
	Sat.	15 New Jersey
	Sun.	16 Philadelphia
	Tues.	18 Dallas
	Mon.	24 Calgary (at Phoenix)
	Mon.	31 Vancouver
Feb.	Wed.	2 Edmonton
	Fri.	11 Anaheim
	Sat.	19 San Jose
	Fri.	25 Edmonton
	Sat.	26 Calgary
Mar.	Wed.	2 Hartford
	Thur.	3 Boston
	Sun.	6 Chicago*
	Wed.	16 Anaheim
	Sun.	20 San Jose*
	Fri.	25 Edmonton
	Sun.	27 Vancouver*
Apr.	Thur.	7 St Louis
	Sat.	9 Winnipeg*
	Sun.	10 Chicago*

* Denotes afternoon game.

Home Starting Times:

All Games	7:35 p.m.
Except Fri. Feb. 18	6:05 p.m.
Mon. Feb. 21	4:05 p.m.
Sat. Mar. 19	2:05 p.m.
Sat. Apr. 2	2:05 p.m.

Franchise date: June 5, 1967

PACIFIC
DIVISION

27th
NHL
Season

WESTERN
CONFERENCE

Rob Blake, one of the NHL's finest young rearguards, led all L.A. defensemen with 59 points in 1992-93.

1993-94 Player Personnel

FORWARDS	HT	WT	S	Place of Birth	Date	1992-93 Club
BJUGSTAD, Scott	6-1	185	L	St. Paul, MN	6/2/61	Phoenix
BRESLIN, Tim	6-0	180	L	Downers Grove, IL	12/8/67	Phoenix
BROWN, Kevin	6-1	212	R	Birmingham, England	5/11/74	Detroit
CARSON, Jimmy	6-0	200	R	Southfield, MI	7/20/68	Detroit-Los Angeles
CONACHER, Pat	5-9	190	L	Edmonton, Alta.	5/1/59	Los Angeles
CURRIE, Dan	6-2	195	L	Burlington, Ont.	3/15/68	Cape Breton
DONNELLY, Mike	5-11	185	L	Livonia, MI	10/10/63	Los Angeles
DRUCE, John	6-2	195	R	Peterborough, Ont.	2/23/66	Winnipeg
FORTIER, Marc	6-0	192	R	Windsor, Que.	2/26/66	Phoe-L.A-New Haven-Ott.
GRANATO, Tony	5-10	185	R	Downers Grove, IL	7/25/64	Los Angeles
GRETZKY, Wayne	6-0	170	L	Brantford, Ont.	1/26/61	Los Angeles
HULETT, Dean	6-6	205	R	San Juan, P.R.	7/25/71	Lake Superior
KURRI, Jari	6-1	195	R	Helsinki, Finland	5/18/60	Los Angeles
LANG, Robert	6-2	180	R	Teplice, Czech.	12/19/70	Los Angeles-Phoenix
LEVEQUE, Guy	5-11	166	R	Kingston, Ont.	2/28/72	Los Angeles-Phoenix
McEACHERN, Shawn	6-0	195	L	Waltham, MA	2/28/69	Pittsburgh
McREYNOLDS, Brian	6-1	192	L	Penetanguishene, Ont.	1/5/65	Binghamton
MITCHELL, Jeff	6-1	175	R	Wayne, MI	5/16/75	Detroit OHL
MURPHY, Rob	6-3	205	L	Hull, Que.	4/7/69	Ottawa-New Haven
PICARD, Michel	5-11	190	L	Beauport, Que.	11/7/69	San Jose-Kansas City
POTVIN, Marc	6-1	200	R	Ottawa, Ont.	1/29/67	Adirondack-L.A.
REDMOND, Keith	6-3	208	L	Richmond Hill, Ont.	10/25/72	Phoenix
ROBITAILLE, Luc	6-1	190	L	Montreal, Que.	2/17/66	Los Angeles
RYCHEL, Warren	6-0	190	L	Tecumseh, Ont.	5/12/67	Los Angeles
SANDSTROM, Tomas	6-2	200	L	Jakobstad, Finland	9/4/64	Los Angeles
SEGUIN, Brett	5-9	199	L	Rochester, NY	2/20/72	Phoenix-Muskegon
SEMCHUCK, Brandy	6-1	187	R	Calgary, Alta.	9/22/71	Phoenix-Los Angeles
SHEVALIER, Jeff	5-11	180	L	Mississaugua, Ont.	3/14/74	North Bay
SHUCHUK, Gary	5-10	185	R	Edmonton, Alta.	2/17/67	Adirondack-L.A.
TAYLOR, Dave	6-0	195	R	Levack, Ont.	12/4/55	Los Angeles
THOMLINSON, Dave	6-1	195	L	Edmonton, Alta.	10/22/66	Binghamton
TOPOROWSKI, Shayne	6-2	205	R	Prince Albert, Sask.	8/6/75	Prince Albert
VESEY, Jim	6-1	202	R	Columbus, MA	10/29/65	Providence
VINCELETTE, Daniel	6-2	202	L	Verdun, Que.	8/1/67	Atlanta-San Diego
VUKONICH, Mike	6-1	215	L	Duluth, MN	11/5/68	Phoenix
WILLIAMS, Darryl	5-11	185	L	Mt. Pearl, Nfld.	2/9/68	Los Angeles-Phoenix
WREN, Bob	5-10	175	L	Preston, Ont.	9/16/74	Detroit OHL
DEFENSEMEN						
BLAKE, Rob	6-3	215	R	Simcoe, Ont.	12/10/69	Los Angeles
CHAPMAN, Brian	6-0	195	L	Brockville, Ont.	2/10/66	Springfield
CHYCHRUN, Jeff	6-4	215	R	Lasalle, Que.	3/3/66	Pit.-L.A.-Phoenix
GAUL, Michael	6-1	197	R	Lachine, Que.	4/28/73	Laval
GRANT, Kevin	6-3	210	R	Toronto, Ont.	1/9/69	Salt Lake-Phoenix
HARDY, Mark	5-11	195	L	Semaden, Switz.	2/1/59	Los Angeles-NYR
HOCKING, Justin	6-4	206	R	Coronation, Alta.	1/9/74	Spokane-Med. Hat
HUDDY, Charlie	6-0	210	L	Oshawa, Ont.	6/2/59	Los Angeles
JAY, Bob	5-11	190		Burlington, MS	11/18/65	Fort Wayne
LAVIGNE, Eric	6-3	195	L	Victoriaville, Que.	11/4/72	Hull
LAVOIE, Dominic	6-2	205	R	Montreal, Que.	11/21/67	Providence-New Haven
MAHER, Jim	6-1	205	L	Warren, MI	6/30/70	Phoenix
McSORLEY, Marty	6-1	225	R	Hamilton, Ont.	5/18/63	Los Angeles
OLSSON, Mattias	6-1	183	L	Karlstad, Sweden	4/1/71	Farjestad
STEWART, Dave	5-11	195	R	Norwood, Ont.	1/11/72	Phoenix-Muskegon
SYDOR, Darryl	6-0	205	L	Edmonton, Alta.	5/13/72	Los Angeles
THOMPSON, Brent	6-2	175	L	Calgary, Alta.	1/9/71	Phoenix-Los Angeles
TRETOWICZ, Dave	5-11	195	L	Liverpool, NY	3/15/69	Phoenix
WATTERS, Tim	5-11	185	L	Kamloops, B.C.	7/25/59	Los Angeles-Phoenix
ZHITNIK, Alexei	5-10	180	L	Kiev, Ukraine	10/10/72	Los Angeles

GOALTENDERS	HT	WT	C	Place of Birth	Date	1992-93 Club
ALLAN, Sandy	6-0	175	L	Nassau, Bahamas	1/22/74	North Bay
BEAUBIEN, Frederick	6-1	204	L	Lauzon, Que.	4/1/75	St. Hyacinthe
GOVERDE, David	6-0	210	R	Toronto, Ont.	4/1/75	Phoenix-Los Angeles
HRUDEY, Kelly	5-10	189	L	Edmonton, Alta.	1/13/61	Los Angeles
JAKS, Pauli	6-0	194	L	Schaffhausen, Switz.	1/25/72	Ambri Piotta
KNICKLE, Rick	5-10	175	L	Chatham, N.B.	2/26/60	San Diego-Los Angeles
NEWMAN, Tom	6-1	185	L	Golden Valley, MA	2/23/71	U. Minnesota
SAAL, Jason	5-9	165	L	Detroit, MI	2/1/75	Detroit (OHL)
STAUBER, Robb	5-11	180	L	Duluth, MN	11/25/67	Los Angeles

General Managers' History

Larry Regan, 1967-68 to 1972-73; Larry Regan and Jake Milford, 1973-74; Jake Milford, 1974-75 to 1976-77; George Maguire, 1977-78 to 1982-83; George Maguire and Rogatien Vachon, 1983-84; Rogatien Vachon, 1984-85 to 1991-92; Nick Beverley, 1992-93 to date.

Coaching History

Leonard "Red" Kelly, 1967-68 to 1968-69; Hal Laycoe and John Wilson, 1969-70; Larry Regan, 1970-71; Larry Regan and Fred Glover, 1971-72; Bob Pulford, 1972-73 to 1976-77; Ron Stewart, 1977-78; Bob Berry, 1978-79 to 1980-81; Parker MacDonald and Don Perry, 1981-82; Don Perry, 1982-83; Don Perry, Rogatien Vachon and Roger Neilson, 1983-84; Pat Quinn, 1984-85 to 1985-86; Pat Quinn and Mike Murphy 1986-87; Mike Murphy and Robbie Ftorek, 1987-88; Robbie Ftorek, 1988-89; Tom Webster, 1989-90 to 1991-92; Barry Melrose, 1992-93 to date.

Captains' History

Bob Wall, 1967-68, 1968-69; Larry Cahan, 1969-70, 1970-71; Bob Pulford, 1971-72, 1972-73; Terry Harper, 1973-74, 1974-75; Mike Murphy, 1975-76 to 1980-81; Dave Lewis, 1981-82, 1982-83; Terry Ruskowski, 1983-84, 1984-85; Dave Taylor, 1985-86 to 1988-89; Wayne Gretzky, 1989-90 to date.

1992-93 Scoring

Regular Season

Pos	#	Player	Team	GP	G	A	Pts	+/-	PIM	PP	SH	GW	GT	S	%
L	20	Luc Robitaille	L.A.	84	63	62	125	18	100	24	2	8	1	265	23.8
L	17	Jari Kurri	L.A.	82	27	60	87	19	38	12	2	3	0	210	12.9
L	21	Tony Granato	L.A.	81	37	45	82	1–	171	14	2	6	0	247	15.0
C	12	Jimmy Carson	DET	52	25	26	51	0	18	13	0	4	0	108	23.1
			L.A.	34	12	10	22	2–	14	4	0	1	0	81	14.8
			TOTAL	86	37	36	73	2–	32	17	0	5	0	189	19.6
R	11	Mike Donnelly	L.A.	84	29	40	69	17	45	8	1	2	0	244	11.9
C	99	Wayne Gretzky	L.A.	45	16	49	65	6	6	0	2	1	0	141	11.3
D	4	Rob Blake	L.A.	76	16	43	59	18	152	10	0	4	1	243	6.6
R	7	Tomas Sandstrom	L.A.	39	25	27	52	12	57	8	0	3	1	134	18.7
D	2*	Alexei Zhitnik	L.A.	78	12	36	48	3–	80	5	0	2	0	136	8.8
D	33	Marty McSorley	L.A.	81	15	26	41	1	399	3	3	0	0	197	7.6
C	23	Corey Millen	L.A.	42	23	16	39	16	42	9	2	1	1	100	23.0
D	25*	Darryl Sydor	L.A.	80	6	23	29	2–	63	0	0	1	0	112	5.4
D	22	Charlie Huddy	L.A.	82	2	25	27	16	64	0	0	1	0	106	1.9
L	29*	Lonnie Loach	OTT	3	0	0	0	0	0	0	0	0	0	3	.0
			L.A.	50	10	13	23	3	27	1	0	0	0	55	18.2
			TOTAL	53	10	13	23	3	27	1	0	0	0	58	17.2
L	15	Pat Conacher	L.A.	81	9	8	17	16–	20	0	2	1	0	65	13.8
R	18	Dave Taylor	L.A.	48	6	9	15	1	49	1	0	1	0	53	11.3
D	24	Mark Hardy	NYR	44	1	10	11	2	85	0	0	0	0	28	3.6
			L.A.	11	0	3	3	4–	4	0	0	0	0	20	.0
			TOTAL	55	1	13	14	2–	89	0	0	0	0	48	2.1
L	10	Warren Rychel	L.A.	70	6	7	13	15–	314	0	0	1	0	67	9.0
C	14*	Gary Shuchuk	L.A.	25	2	4	6	0	16	0	0	0	0	24	8.3
C	13*	Robert Lang	L.A.	11	0	5	5	3–	2	0	0	0	0	3	.0
D	3	Brent Thompson	L.A.	30	0	4	4	4–	76	0	0	0	0	18	.0
G	32	Kelly Hrudey	L.A.	50	0	4	4	0	10	0	0	0	0	0	.0
C	28*	Guy Leveque	L.A.	12	2	1	3	4–	19	0	0	0	0	12	16.7
R	9*	Sean Whyte	L.A.	18	0	2	2	1	12	0	0	0	0	7	.0
D	5	Tim Watters	L.A.	22	0	2	2	3–	18	0	0	0	0	8	.0
G	35*	Robb Stauber	L.A.	31	0	2	2	0	4	0	0	0	0	0	.0
C	26	Marc Fortier	OTT	10	0	1	1	7–	6	0	0	0	0	12	.0
			L.A.	6	0	0	0	2–	5	0	0	0	0	2	.0
			TOTAL	16	0	1	1	9–	11	0	0	0	0	14	.0
D	6	Jeff Chychrun	PIT	1	0	0	0	1	2	0	0	0	0	0	.0
			L.A.	17	0	1	1	3–	23	0	0	0	0	3	.0
			TOTAL	18	0	1	1	2–	25	0	0	0	0	3	.0
R	27*	Marc Potvin	L.A.	20	0	1	1	10–	61	0	0	0	0	7	.0
R	19	Jim Thomson	OTT	15	0	1	1	11–	41	0	0	0	0	21	.0
			L.A.	9	0	0	0	1–	56	0	0	0	0	2	.0
			TOTAL	24	0	1	1	12–	97	0	0	0	0	23	.0
R	41*	Brandy Semchuk	L.A.	1	0	0	0	0	2	0	0	0	0	0	.0
G	43*	David Goverde	L.A.	2	0	0	0	0	0	0	0	0	0	0	.0
R	55*	Darryl Williams	L.A.	2	0	0	0	0	10	0	0	0	0	1	.0
R	24	Frank Breault	L.A.	4	0	0	0	1–	6	0	0	0	0	0	.0
G	1	Rick Knickle	L.A.	10	0	0	0	0	2	0	0	0	0	0	.0
D	8*	Rene Chapdelaine	L.A.	13	0	0	0	6–	12	0	0	0	0	5	.0

Goaltending

No.	Goaltender	GPI	Mins	Avg	W	L	T	EN	SO	GA	SA	S%
35	*Robb Stauber	31	1735	3.84	15	8	4	1	0	111	987	.888
32	Kelly Hrudey	50	2718	3.86	18	21	6	4	2	175	1552	.887
1	Rick Knickle	10	532	3.95	6	4	0	0	0	35	292	.880
43	*David Goverde	2	98	7.96	0	2	0	1	0	13	51	.745
	Totals	**84**	**5100**	**4.00**	**39**	**35**	**10**	**6**	**2**	**340**	**2888**	**.882**

Playoffs

Pos	#	Player	Team	GP	G	A	Pts	+/-	PIM	PP	SH	GW	GT	S	%
C	99	Wayne Gretzky	L.A.	24	15	25	40	6	4	4	1	3	1	76	19.7
R	7	Tomas Sandstrom	L.A.	24	8	17	25	2–	12	2	0	2	0	61	13.1
L	20	Luc Robitaille	L.A.	24	9	13	22	13–	28	4	0	2	0	71	12.7
L	17	Jari Kurri	L.A.	24	9	8	17	2	12	2	2	0	0	50	18.0
L	21	Tony Granato	L.A.	24	6	11	17	3	50	1	0	1	0	77	7.8
L	10*	Warren Rychel	L.A.	23	6	7	13	4	39	0	0	2	0	27	22.2
R	11	Mike Donnelly	L.A.	24	6	7	13	3	14	0	0	0	0	43	14.0
D	2*	Alexei Zhitnik	L.A.	24	3	9	12	4–	26	2	0	1	0	42	7.1
D	25*	Darryl Sydor	L.A.	24	3	8	11	4	16	2	0	0	0	29	10.3
L	15	Pat Conacher	L.A.	24	6	4	10	8	6	0	0	0	0	24	25.0
D	4	Rob Blake	L.A.	23	4	6	10	3	46	1	1	0	0	60	6.7
D	33	Marty McSorley	L.A.	24	4	6	10	2–	60	2	0	1	0	42	9.5
C	12	Jimmy Carson	L.A.	18	5	4	9	1	2	2	0	0	0	30	16.7
R	18	Dave Taylor	L.A.	22	3	5	8	7	31	0	2	0	0	32	9.4
C	23	Corey Millen	L.A.	23	2	4	6	1	12	0	0	0	0	33	6.1
D	22	Charlie Huddy	L.A.	23	1	4	5	9	12	0	0	0	0	26	3.8
C	14*	Gary Shuchuk	L.A.	17	2	2	4	6–	12	0	0	1	1	13	15.4
D	24	Mark Hardy	L.A.	15	1	2	3	7	30	0	0	0	0	11	9.1
D	5	Tim Watters	L.A.	22	0	2	2	3–	30	0	0	0	0	9	.0
R	27*	Marc Potvin	L.A.	1	0	0	0	0	0	0	0	0	0	0	.0
R	19	Jim Thomson	L.A.	1	0	0	0	0	0	0	0	0	0	0	.0
L	29*	Lonnie Loach	L.A.	1	0	0	0	0	0	0	0	0	0	0	.0
G	35*	Robb Stauber	L.A.	4	0	0	0	0	0	0	0	0	0	0	.0
G	32	Kelly Hrudey	L.A.	20	0	0	0	0	2	0	0	0	0	0	.0

Goaltending

No.	Goaltender	GPI	Mins	Avg	W	L	EN	SO	GA	SA	S%
32	Kelly Hrudey	20	1261	3.52	10	10	1	0	74	656	.887
35	*Robb Stauber	4	240	4.00	3	1	0	0	16	157	.898
	Totals	**24**	**1504**	**3.63**	**13**	**11**	**1**	**0**	**91**	**814**	**.888**

Club Records

Team

(Figures in brackets for season records are games played; records for fewest points, wins, ties, losses, goals, goals against are for 70 or more games)

Most Points	105	1974-75 (80)
Most Wins	46	1990-91 (80)
Most Ties	21	1974-75 (80)
Most Losses	52	1969-70 (76)
Most Goals	376	1988-89 (80)
Most Goals Against	389	1985-86 (80)
Fewest Points	38	1969-70 (76)
Fewest Wins	14	1969-70 (76)
Fewest Ties	7	1988-89 (80) 1989-90 (80)
Fewest Losses	17	1974-75 (80)
Fewest Goals	168	1969-70 (76)
Fewest Goals Against	185	1974-75 (80)

Longest Winning Streak

Over-all	8	Oct. 21-Nov. 7/72
Home	12	Oct. 10-Dec. 5/92
Away	8	Dec. 18/74-Jan. 16/75

Longest Undefeated Streak

Over-all	11	Feb. 28-Mar. 24/74 (9 wins, 2 ties)
Home	13	Oct. 10-Dec. 8/92 (12 wins, 1 tie)
Away	11	Oct. 10-Dec. 11/74 (6 wins, 5 ties)

Longest Losing Streak

Over-all	10	Feb. 22-Mar. 9/84
Home	9	Feb. 8-Mar. 12/86
Away	12	Jan. 11-Feb. 15/70

Longest Winless Streak

Over-all	17	Jan. 29-Mar. 5/70 (13 losses, 4 ties)
Home	9	Jan. 29-Mar. 5/70 (8 losses, 1 tie) Feb. 8-Mar. 12/86 (9 losses)
Away	21	Jan. 11-Apr. 3/70 (17 losses, 4 ties)

Most Shutouts, Season	9	1974-75 (80)
Most PIM, Season	2,228	1990-91 (80)
Most Goals, Game	12	Nov. 28/84 (Van. 1 at L.A. 12)

Individual

Most Seasons	16	Dave Taylor
Most Games	1,078	Dave Taylor
Most Goals, Career	550	Marcel Dionne
Most Assists, Career	757	Marcel Dionne
Most Points Career	1,307	Marcel Dionne
Most PIM, Career	1,498	Dave Taylor
Most Shutouts, Career	32	Rogie Vachon

Longest Consecutive Games Streak — 324 — Marcel Dionne (Jan. 7/78-Jan. 9/82)

Most Goals, Season — 70 — Bernie Nicholls (1988-89)

Most Assists, Season — 122 — Wayne Gretzky (1990-91)

Most Points, Season — 168 — Wayne Gretzky (1988-89) (54 goals, 114 assists)

Most PIM, Season — 399 — Marty McSorley (1992-93)

Most Points, Defenseman Season — 76 — Larry Murphy (1980-81) (16 goals, 60 assists)

Most Points, Center, Season — 168 — Wayne Gretzky (1988-89) (54 goal, 114 assists)

Most Points, Right Wing, Season — 112 — Dave Taylor (1980-81) (47 goals, 65 assists)

Most Points, Left Wing, Season — *125 — Luc Robitaille (1992-93) (63 goals, 62 assists)

Most Points, Rookie, Season — 84 — Luc Robitaille (1986-87) (45 goals, 39 assists)

Most Shutouts, Season — 8 — Rogie Vachon (1976-77)

Most Goals, Game — 4 — Several players

Most Assists, Game — 6 — Bernie Nicholls (Dec. 1/88)

Most Points, Game — 8 — Bernie Nicholls (Dec. 1/88)

* NHL Record

Retired Numbers

16	Marcel Dionne	1975-1987
30	Rogatien Vachon	1971-1978

All-time Record vs. Other Clubs

Regular Season

		At Home						On Road						Total					
	GP	W	L	T	GF	GA	PTS	GP	W	L	T	GF	GA	PTS	GP	W	L	T	GF	GA	PTS
Boston	52	18	29	5	183	200	41	53	10	40	3	145	255	23	105	28	69	8	328	455	64
Buffalo	45	17	20	8	155	157	42	44	15	21	8	141	181	38	89	32	41	16	296	338	80
Calgary	66	35	25	6	265	245	76	67	17	42	8	227	327	42	133	52	67	14	492	572	118
Chicago	52	23	23	6	181	177	52	53	19	27	7	164	209	45	105	42	50	13	345	386	97
Detroit	58	32	15	11	247	178	75	57	27	23	7	218	226	61	115	59	38	18	465	404	136
Edmonton	50	20	21	9	219	230	49	52	13	27	12	207	268	38	102	33	48	21	426	498	87
Hartford	21	12	6	3	94	83	27	22	7	12	3	90	89	17	43	19	18	6	184	172	44
Minnesota	56	26	16	14	210	172	66	57	15	33	9	161	231	39	113	41	49	23	371	403	105
Montreal	57	15	34	8	175	231	38	56	7	38	11	147	261	25	113	22	72	19	322	492	63
New Jersey	34	25	3	6	186	105	56	34	14	15	5	125	118	33	68	39	18	11	311	223	89
NY Islanders	36	15	14	7	125	120	37	36	13	19	4	108	133	30	72	28	33	11	233	253	67
NY Rangers	51	20	22	9	170	182	49	50	15	30	5	148	204	35	101	35	52	14	318	386	84
Ottawa	1	1	0	0	8	6	2	1	1	0	0	3	2	2	2	2	0	0	11	8	4
Philadelphia	57	17	33	7	168	200	41	55	15	33	7	143	212	37	112	32	66	14	311	412	78
Pittsburgh	61	39	14	8	237	158	86	63	19	36	8	201	239	46	124	58	50	16	438	397	132
Quebec	21	12	8	1	97	76	25	21	9	9	3	85	86	21	42	21	17	4	182	162	46
St. Louis	56	29	19	8	203	163	66	56	14	36	6	150	215	34	112	43	55	14	353	378	100
San Jose	7	6	0	1	33	18	13	7	4	3	0	25	27	8	14	10	3	1	58	45	21
Tampa Bay	2	0	2	0	5	9	0	1	1	0	0	5	2	2	3	1	2	0	10	11	2
Toronto	54	31	16	7	197	152	69	53	14	29	10	176	223	38	107	45	45	17	373	375	107
Vancouver	74	40	24	10	310	237	90	72	25	35	12	250	287	62	146	65	59	22	560	524	152
Washington	38	23	11	4	158	117	50	37	15	16	6	137	160	36	75	38	27	10	295	277	86
Winnipeg	47	18	21	8	197	194	44	50	17	24	9	186	220	43	97	35	45	17	383	414	87
Defunct Clubs	35	27	6	2	141	76	56	34	11	14	9	91	109	31	69	38	20	11	232	185	87
Totals	**1031**	**501**	**382**	**148**	**3964**	**3486**	**1150**	**1031**	**317**	**562**	**152**	**3333**	**4284**	**786**	**2062**	**818**	**944**	**300**	**7297**	**7770**	**1936**

Playoffs

	Series	W	L	GP	W	L	T	GF	GA	Last Mtg.	Round	Result
Boston	2	0	2	13	5	8	0	38	56	1977	QF	L 2-4
**Calgary	6	4	2	26	13	13	0	105	112	1993	DSF	W 4-2
Chicago	1	0	1	5	1	4	0	7	10	1974	QF	L 1-4
Edmonton	7	2	5	36	12	24	0	124	150	1992	DSF	L 2-4
Minnesota	1	0	1	7	3	4	0	21	26	1968	QF	L 3-4
Montreal	1	0	1	5	1	4	0	12	15	1993	F	L 1-4
NY Islanders	1	0	1	4	1	3	0	10	21	1980	PR	L 1-3
NY Rangers	2	0	2	6	1	5	0	14	32	1981	PR	L 1-3
St. Louis	1	0	1	4	0	4	0	5	16	1969	SF	L 0-4
Toronto	3	1	2	12	5	7	0	31	41	1993	CF	W 4-3
Vancouver	3	2	1	17	9	8	0	66	60	1993	DF	W 4-2
Defunct Clubs	1	1	0	7	4	3	0	23	25			
Totals	**29**	**10**	**19**	**142**	**55**	**87**	**0**	**459**	**568**			

Playoff Results 1993-89

Year	Round	Opponent	Result	GF	GA
1993	F	Montreal	L 1-4	12	15
	CF	Toronto	W 4-3	22	23
	DF	Vancouver	W 4-2	26	25
	DSF	Calgary	W 4-2	33	28
1992	DSF	Edmonton	L 2-4	18	23
1991	DF	Edmonton	L 2-4	20	21
	DSF	Vancouver	W 4-2	26	16
1990	DF	Edmonton	L 0-4	10	24
	DSF	Calgary	W 4-2	29	24
1989	DF	Calgary	L 0-4	11	22
	DSF	Edmonton	W 4-3	25	20

Abbreviations: Round: F – Final; **CF** – conference final; **DF** – division final; **DSF** – division semi-final; **SF** – semi-final; **QF** – quarter-final; **PR** – preliminary round. **GA** – goals against; **GF** – goals for.

1992-93 Results

	Home				Away	
Oct. 8	Detroit	3-5	**Oct.** 6	Calgary	5-4
10	Winnipeg	6-3	20	Calgary	2-6
13	San Jose	2-1	23	Winnipeg	2-4
15	Calgary	4-0	24	Minnesota	5-5
17	Boston	8-6	27	NY Islanders	4-3
Nov. 5	New Jersey	5-2	29	Boston	3-8
7	Buffalo	5-2	31	Hartford	7-1
12	Vancouver	7-4	**Nov.** 8	San Jose	11-4
14	Edmonton	6-2	10	Winnipeg	4-4
19	Chicago	4-1	16	Vancouver	3-6
21	Toronto	6-4	17	San Jose	0-6
Dec. 3	Pittsburgh	5-3	25	Edmonton	3-1
5	Hartford	7-3	27	Detroit	5-3
8	Montreal	5-5	28	Toronto	2-3
10	Quebec	4-5	**Dec.** 1	Chicago	6-3
12	St. Louis	6-3	18	Edmonton	5-5
15	Tampa Bay	2-3	19	Calgary	3-5
22	Vancouver	2-6	26	San Jose	2-7
29	Philadelphia	2-10	31	Vancouver	0-4
Jan. 2	Montreal	5-5	**Jan.** 8	Winnipeg	3-6
6	Tampa Bay	3-6	10	Chicago	5-4
16	Winnipeg	2-5	12	Ottawa	3-2
21	Vancouver	4-5	14	New Jersey	1-7
23	NY Rangers	3-8	19	Edmonton	5-4
26	San Jose	7-1	**Feb.** 2	Quebec	2-3
28	Calgary	1-2	3	Montreal	2-7
30	Chicago	2-2	17	Minnesota	10-5
Feb. 9	Edmonton	3-6	18	Chicago	2-7
11	Detroit	6-6	20	Washington*	3-7
13	Washington	3-10	22	Tampa Bay	5-2
15	Vancouver*	3-0	25	St. Louis	0-3
27	Toronto	2-5	**Mar.** 9	NY Rangers	3-4
Mar. 2	Calgary	6-2	11	Pittsburgh	3-4
4	Ottawa	8-6	15	Buffalo	4-2
6	Edmonton	6-1	24	Vancouver	2-6
16	Winnipeg	8-4	26	Edmonton	4-1
18	NY Islanders	7-4	28	Winnipeg*	3-3
20	St. Louis	3-2	29	Detroit	9-3
Apr. 4	Minnesota	0-3	31	Toronto	5-5
6	Calgary	3-3	**Apr.** 1	Philadelphia	3-1
8	San Jose	2-1	10	San Jose	3-2
15	Vancouver	6-8	13	Vancouver	4-7

*Denotes afternoon game

Entry Draft Selections 1993-79

1993
Pick
42	Shayne Toporowski
68	Jeffrey Mitchell
94	Bob Wren
105	Frederick Beaubien
117	Jason Saal
120	Tomas Vlasak
146	Jere Karalahti
172	Justin Martin
198	John-Tra Dillabough
224	Martin Strbak
250	Kimmo Timonen
276	Patrick Howald

1992
Pick
39	Justin Hocking
63	Sandy Allan
87	Kevin Brown
111	Jeff Shevalier
135	Raymond Murray
207	Magnus Wernblom
231	Ryan Pisiak
255	Jukka Tiilikainen

1991
Pick
42	Guy Leveque
79	Keith Redmond
81	Alexei Zhitnik
108	Pauli Jaks
130	Brett Seguin
152	Kelly Fairchild
196	Craig Brown
218	Mattias Olsson
240	Andre Bouliane
262	Michael Gaul

1990
Pick
7	Darryl Sydor
28	Brandy Semchuk
49	Bob Berg
91	David Goverde
112	Erik Andersson
133	Robert Lang
154	Dean Hulett
175	Denis LeBlanc
196	Patrik Ross
217	K.J. (Kevin) White
238	Troy Mohns

1989
Pick
39	Brent Thompson
81	Jim Maher
102	Eric Ricard
103	Thomas Newman
123	Daniel Rydmark
144	Ted Kramer
165	Sean Whyte
182	Jim Giacin
186	Martin Maskarinec
207	Jim Hiller
228	Steve Jaques
249	Kevin Sneddon

1988
Pick
7	Martin Gelinas
28	Paul Holden
49	John Van Kessel
70	Rob Blake
91	Jeff Robison
109	Micah Aivazoff
112	Robert Larsson
133	Jeff Kruesel
154	Timo Peltomaa
175	Jim Larkin
196	Brad Hyatt
217	Doug Laprade
238	Joe Flanagan

1987
Pick
4	Wayne McBean
27	Mark Fitzpatrick
43	Ross Wilson
90	Mike Vukonich
111	Greg Batters
132	Kyosti Karjalainen
174	Jeff Gawlicki
195	John Preston
216	Rostislav Vlach
237	Mikael Lindholm

1986
Pick
2	Jimmy Carson
44	Denis Larocque
65	Sylvain Couturier
86	Dave Guden
107	Robb Stauber
128	Sean Krakiwsky
149	Rene Chapdelaine
170	Trevor Pochipinski
191	Paul Kelly
212	Russ Mann
233	Brian Hayton

1985
Pick
9	Craig Duncanson
10	Dan Gratton
30	Par Edlund
72	Perry Florio
93	Petr Prajsler
135	Tim Flannigan
156	John Hyduke
177	Steve Horner
219	Trent Ciprick
240	Marian Horwath

1984
Pick
6	Craig Redmond
24	Brian Wilks
48	John English
69	Tom Glavine
87	Dave Grannis
108	Greg Strome
129	Tim Hanley
150	Shannon Deegan
171	Luc Robitaille
191	Jeff Crossman
212	Paul Kenny
232	Brian Martin

1983
Pick
47	Bruce Shoebottom
67	Guy Benoit
87	Bob LaForest
100	Garry Galley
107	Dave Lundmark
108	Kevin Stevens
127	Tim Burgess
147	Ken Hammond
167	Bruce Fishback
187	Thomas Ahlen
207	Miroslav Blaha
227	Chad Johnson

1982
Pick
27	Mike Heidt
48	Steve Seguin
64	Dave Gans
82	Dave Ross
90	Darcy Roy
95	Ulf Isaksson
132	Victor Nechaev
153	Peter Helander
174	Dave Chartier
195	John Franzosa
216	Ray Shero
237	Mats Ulander

1981
Pick
2	Doug Smith
39	Dean Kennedy
81	Marty Dallman
123	Brad Thompson
134	Craig Hurley
144	Peter Sawkins
165	Dan Brennan
186	Allan Tuer
207	Jeff Baikie

1980
Pick
4	Larry Murphy
10	Jim Fox
33	Greg Terrion
34	Dave Morrison
52	Steve Bozek
73	Bernie Nicholls
94	Alan Graves
115	Darren Eliot
136	Mike O'Connor
157	Bill O'Dwyer
178	Daryl Evans
199	Kim Collins

1979
Pick
16	Jay Wells
29	Dean Hopkins
30	Mark Hardy
50	John Paul Kelly
71	John Gibson
92	Jim Brown
113	Jay MacFarlane

General Manager

BEVERLEY, NICK
General Manager, Los Angeles Kings. Born in Toronto, Ont., April 21, 1947.
Nick Beverley was appointed as the fifth general manager in Los Angeles' franchise history on June 25, 1992. Following an 11-year NHL playing career that included stops in six cities, including Los Angeles, Beverley joined the Kings' organization in 1980 after accepting the coaching position with the teams minor league affiliate in Houston. Beverley, who also coached the Kings' farm team in New Haven, was named director of player personnel and development in 1988. In 1990, he was named as assistant general manager, and continued in that capacity until being elevated to the G.M.'s office.

Coach

MELROSE, BARRY
Coach, Los Angeles Kings. Born in Kelvington, Sask., July 15, 1956.
Barry Melrose became the 17th head coach of the Los Angeles Kings on June 25, 1992, replacing Tom Webster. In 1993, Melrose guided the Kings to their first-ever Stanley Cup Finals appearance. Melrose, who started his professional playing career at the age of 20 with the Cincinnati Stingers of the WHA, spent eight years in the NHL with Toronto, Winnipeg and Detroit. Following his successful playing career, Melrose turned his attention to coaching and led the WHL's Medicine Hat Tigers to the Memorial Cup title in 1988. For the following three seasons, he was the coach of the AHL's Adirondack Red Wings, Detroit's top farm affiliate. In 1991-92, Melrose guided the Wings to the AHL's Calder Cup championship, the fourth title for the Adirondack franchise since 1981.

Coaching Record

			Regular Season					Playoffs			
Season	Team	Games	W	L	T	%	Games	W	L	%
1987-88	Medicine Hat (WHL)	72	44	22	6	.653	16	12	4	.750
1988-89	Seattle (WHL)	72	33	35	4	.486	....	....	....	....
1989-90	Adirondack (AHL)	80	42	27	11	.594	6	2	4	.333
1990-91	Adirondack (AHL)	80	33	37	10	.475	....	....	....	....
1991-92	Adirondack (AHL)	80	40	36	4	.525	19	14	5	.737
1992-93	**Los Angeles (NHL)**	**84**	**39**	**35**	**10**	**.524**	**24**	**13**	**11**	**.542**
	NHL Totals	**84**	**39**	**35**	**10**	**.524**	**24**	**13**	**11**	**.542**

Club Directory

The Great Western Forum
3900 West Manchester Blvd.
P.O. Box 17013
Inglewood, California 90308
Phone **310/419-3160**
FAX 310/673-8927
Capacity: 16,005

Executive
Chairman of the Board/Governor	Bruce McNall
President/Alternate Governor	Roy A. Mlakar
Special Assistant to Chairman	Rogatien Vachon
Vice-Chairman	Susan A. Waks
Executive Vice-President	Robert Moor
Vice-President	Bruce Bargmann
Vice-President	Nora J. Rothrock
Vice-President, Public Relations	Scott Carmichael
Vice-President, Marketing	Gregory McElroy
Executive Director, Finance	Martin Greenspun
Executive Secretary to President	Kelley Lombardozzi
Secretary	Kay Hylton

Hockey Operations
General Manager	Nick Beverley
Administrative Assistant to General Manager	John Wolf
Executive Secretary to General Manager	Marcia Galloway
Head Coach	Barry Melrose
Assistant Coach	Cap Raeder
Director of Player Personnel and Development	Bob Owen
Director of Pro Scouting	Rick Dudley
Scouting Staff	Jim Anderson, Ron Ansell, Serge Aubry, John Bymark, Gary Harker, Jan Lindegren, Mark Miller, Al Murray, Vaclav Nedomansky, Ted O'Connor, Don Perry, Alex Smart
Video Coordinator	Bill Gurney

Medical Staff
Trainer	Pete Demers
Equipment Manager	Peter Millar
Assistant Equipment Manager	Sal Lombardi
Team Physicians	Kerlan/Jobe Orthopaedic Clinic directed by Dr. Ronald Kvitne
Internist	Dr. Michael Mellman
Team Dentist	Dr. Gordon Knuth

Communications
Director, Media Relations	Rick Minch
Assistant Director, Media Relations	Adam Fell
Director, Publications	Nick Salata
Director, Community and Player Relations	Jim Fox
Communications Coordinator	Angela Ladd
Administrative Assistant	Michelle Guler
Receptionist	Elizabeth Tutt

Finance/Accounting
Director, Human Resources	Barbara Mendez
Accounting Manager	Pete Mazur
Accounts Payable	Emma Harris
Accounts Receivable	Danielle Encheff
Slap Shop Accountant	Carlos Montalvan
Staff Accountant	Marc Esprabens

Marketing/Advertising/Sales
Executive Director, Merchandising	Harvey Boles
Executive Director, Sales	Dennis Metz
Traffic Manager and Event Coordinator	Tricia Webb
Advertising Account Executives	Sergio del Prado, Rory Oldham, Todd Waks, John Covarrubias
Season Seat Account Executives	Keith Jacobson, Andrew Silverman
Office Manager, Sales and Advertising	Susan Long
Executive Assistant, Sales	Shawn Kallan
Sales and Promotions Coordinator	Courtney Ash

Broadcasting
Play-by-Play Announcer, Television	Bob Miller
Color Commentator, Television	Jim Fox
Play-by-Play Announcer, Radio	Nick Nickson
Color Commentator, Radio	Brian Engblom
Television	Prime Ticket Cable Network & KTLA Channel 5
Radio Station	XTRA (690 AM)

Home Ice	The Great Western Forum
Dimensions of Rink	200 feet by 85 feet
Supervisor of Off-Ice Officials	Bill Meuris
Public Address Announcer	David Courtney
Colors	Black, White and Silver
Training Camp	Lake Arrowhead, California
Location of Press Box	West Colonade, Sec. 28, Rows 1-10

Montreal Canadiens
1992-93 Results: 48w-30L-6T 102PTS. Third, Adams Division

The Montreal Canadiens, who captured their 24th Stanley Cup in 1993, established a new NHL record by winning ten consecutive overtime games during the 1993 playoffs.

Schedule

	Home			Away	
Oct.	Wed. 6 Hartford	Oct.	Thur. 7 Pittsburgh		
	Sat. 9 Buffalo		Mon. 11 Boston*		
	Sat. 16 Quebec		Wed. 13 Hartford		
	Wed. 20 Dallas		Mon. 18 Quebec		
	Sat. 23 Anaheim		Tues. 26 New Jersey		
	Sat. 30 Toronto		Thur. 28 NY Rangers		
Nov.	Wed. 3 Tampa Bay	Nov.	Mon. 15 Ottawa		
	Sat. 6 Calgary		Tues. 23 NY Rangers		
	Wed. 10 Florida		Wed. 24 Philadelphia		
	Sat. 13 Ottawa	Dec.	Fri. 3 Washington		
	Wed. 17 Edmonton		Sat. 4 Boston		
	Thur. 18 NY Islanders		Tues. 14 Tampa Bay		
	(at Hamilton)		(at Orlando)		
	Sat. 20 Pittsburgh		Wed. 15 Florida		
	Sat. 27 Los Angeles		Thur. 23 Buffalo		
Dec.	Wed. 1 Ottawa		Mon. 27 St Louis		
	Mon. 6 Vancouver		Wed. 29 Edmonton		
	Wed. 8 New Jersey		Fri. 31 Calgary		
	Sat. 11 Washington	Jan.	Sun. 2 Vancouver*		
	Sat. 18 Detroit		Tues. 4 San Jose		
	Wed. 22 NY Islanders		Wed. 5 Quebec		
Jan.	Sat. 8 NY Rangers		(at Phoenix)		
	Mon. 10 Winnipeg		Fri. 14 NY Islanders		
	Wed. 12 New Jersey		Mon. 24 Florida		
	Sat. 15 Florida		Wed. 26 Hartford		
	Mon. 17 Washington	Feb.	Fri. 4 Washington		
	Wed. 19 Boston		Sat. 5 Ottawa		
	Sat. 29 Buffalo*		Mon. 7 Pittsburgh		
	Sun. 30 Philadelphia*		Fri. 11 Buffalo		
Feb.	Wed. 2 Hartford		Thur. 17 Tampa Bay		
	Wed. 9 NY Rangers		Mon. 21 Philadelphia*		
	Sat. 12 Quebec		Sat. 26 Toronto		
	Sat. 19 Pittsburgh		Mon. 28 Los Angeles		
	Wed. 23 San Jose	Mar.	Wed. 2 Anaheim		
Mar.	Wed. 9 St Louis		Sun. 6 Dallas		
	Sat. 12 Philadelphia		Thur. 10 Quebec		
	Mon. 14 Boston		Wed. 23 Winnipeg		
	Wed. 16 Chicago		Thur. 24 Chicago		
	Sat. 19 Quebec		Sat. 26 Boston*		
	Mon. 28 Ottawa		Tues. 29 New Jersey		
Apr.	Sat. 2 NY Islanders	Apr.	Fri. 1 NY Islanders		
	Wed. 6 Tampa Bay		Fri. 8 Buffalo		
	Sat. 9 Pittsburgh		Mon. 11 Hartford		
			Wed. 13 Detroit		

* Denotes afternoon game.

Home Starting Times:

Weeknights	7:35 p.m.
Saturdays	8:05 p.m.
Except Sat. Jan 29	1:05 p.m.
Sun. Jan. 30	1:35 p.m.

Franchise date: November 22, 1917

NORTHEAST DIVISION

77th NHL Season

EASTERN CONFERENCE

Year-by-Year Record

		Home			Road			Overall							
Season	GP	W	L	T	W	L	T	W	L	T	GF	GA	Pts	Finished	Playoff Result
1992-93	84	27	13	2	21	17	4	48	30	6	326	280	102	3rd, Adams Div.	Won Stanley Cup
1991-92	80	27	8	5	14	20	6	41	28	11	267	207	93	1st, Adams Div.	Lost Div. Final
1990-91	80	23	12	5	16	18	6	39	30	11	273	249	89	2nd, Adams Div.	Lost Div. Final
1989-90	80	26	8	6	15	20	5	41	28	11	288	234	93	3rd, Adams Div.	Lost Div. Final
1988-89	80	30	6	4	23	12	5	53	18	9	315	218	115	1st, Adams Div.	Lost Final
1987-88	80	26	8	6	19	14	7	45	22	13	298	238	103	1st, Adams Div.	Lost Div. Final
1986-87	80	27	9	4	14	20	6	41	29	10	277	241	92	2nd, Adams Div.	Lost Conf. Championship
1985-86	80	25	11	4	15	22	3	40	33	7	330	280	87	2nd, Adams Div.	Won Stanley Cup
1984-85	80	24	10	6	17	17	6	41	27	12	309	262	94	1st, Adams Div.	Lost Div. Final
1983-84	80	19	19	2	16	21	3	35	40	5	286	295	75	4th, Adams Div.	Lost Conf. Championship
1982-83	80	25	6	9	17	18	5	42	24	14	350	286	98	2nd, Adams Div.	Lost Div. Semi-Final
1981-82	80	25	6	9	21	11	8	46	17	17	360	223	109	1st, Adams Div.	Lost Div. Semi-Final
1980-81	80	31	7	2	14	15	11	45	22	13	332	232	103	1st, Norris Div.	Lost Prelim. Round
1979-80	80	30	7	3	17	13	10	47	20	13	328	240	107	1st, Norris Div.	Lost Quarter-Final
1978-79	80	29	6	5	23	11	6	52	17	11	337	204	115	1st, Norris Div.	Won Stanley Cup
1977-78	80	32	4	4	27	6	7	59	10	11	359	183	129	1st, Norris Div.	Won Stanley Cup
1976-77	80	33	1	6	27	7	6	60	8	12	387	171	132	1st, Norris Div.	Won Stanley Cup
1975-76	80	32	3	5	26	8	6	58	11	11	337	174	127	1st, Norris Div.	Won Stanley Cup
1974-75	80	27	8	5	20	6	14	47	14	19	374	225	113	1st, Norris Div.	Lost Semi-Final
1973-74	78	24	12	3	21	12	6	45	24	9	293	240	99	2nd, East Div.	Lost Quarter-inal
1972-73	78	29	4	6	23	6	10	52	10	16	329	184	120	1st, East Div.	Won Stanley Cup
1971-72	78	29	3	7	17	13	9	46	16	16	307	205	108	3rd, East Div.	Lost Quarter-Final
1970-71	78	29	7	3	13	16	10	42	23	13	291	216	97	3rd, East Div.	Won Stanley Cup
1969-70	76	21	9	8	17	13	8	38	22	16	244	201	92	5th, East Div.	Out of Playoffs
1968-69	76	26	7	5	20	12	6	46	19	11	271	202	103	1st, East Div.	Won Stanley Cup
1967-68	74	26	5	6	16	17	4	42	22	10	236	167	94	1st, East Div.	Won Stanley Cup
1966-67	70	19	9	7	13	16	6	32	25	13	202	188	77	2nd,	Lost Final
1965-66	70	23	11	1	18	10	7	41	21	8	239	173	90	1st,	Won Stanley Cup
1964-65	70	20	8	7	16	15	4	36	23	11	211	185	83	2nd,	Won Stanley Cup
1963-64	70	22	7	6	14	14	7	36	21	13	209	167	85	1st,	Lost Semi-Final
1962-63	70	15	10	10	13	9	13	28	19	23	225	183	79	3rd,	Lost Semi-Final
1961-62	70	26	2	7	16	12	7	42	14	14	259	166	98	1st,	Lost Semi-Final
1960-61	70	24	6	5	17	13	5	41	19	10	254	188	92	1st,	Lost Semi-Final
1959-60	70	23	4	8	17	14	4	40	18	12	255	178	92	1st,	Won Stanley Cup
1958-59	70	21	8	6	18	10	7	39	18	13	58	158	91	1st,	Won Stanley Cup
1957-58	70	23	8	4	20	9	6	43	17	10	250	158	96	1st,	Won Stanley Cup
1956-57	70	23	6	6	12	17	6	35	23	12	210	155	82	2nd,	Won Stanley Cup
1955-56	70	29	5	1	16	10	9	45	15	10	222	131	100	1st,	Won Stanley Cup
1954-55	70	26	5	4	15	13	7	41	18	11	228	157	93	2nd,	Lost Final
1953-54	70	27	5	3	8	19	8	35	24	11	195	141	81	2nd,	Lost Final
1952-53	70	18	12	5	10	11	14	28	23	19	155	148	75	2nd,	Won Stanley Cup
1951-52	70	22	8	5	12	18	5	34	26	10	195	164	78	2nd,	Lost Final
1950-51	70	17	10	8	8	20	7	25	30	15	173	184	65	3rd,	Lost Final
1949-50	70	17	8	10	12	14	9	29	22	19	172	150	77	2nd,	Lost Semi-Final
1948-49	60	19	8	3	9	15	6	28	23	9	152	126	65	3rd,	Lost Semi-Final
1947-48	60	13	13	4	7	16	7	20	29	11	147	169	51	5th,	Out of Playoffs
1946-47	60	19	6	5	15	10	5	34	16	10	189	138	78	1st,	Lost Final
1945-46	50	16	6	3	12	11	2	28	17	5	172	134	61	1st,	Won Stanley Cup
1944-45	50	21	2	2	17	6	2	38	8	4	228	121	80	1st,	Lost Semi-Final
1943-44	50	22	0	3	16	5	4	38	5	7	234	109	83	1st,	Won Stanley Cup
1942-43	50	14	4	7	5	15	5	19	19	12	181	191	50	4th,	Lost Semi-Final
1941-42	48	12	10	2	6	17	1	18	27	3	134	173	39	6th,	Lost Quarter-Final
1940-41	48	11	9	4	5	17	2	16	26	6	121	147	38	6th,	Lost Quarter-Final
1939-40	48	5	14	5	5	19	0	10	33	5	90	168	25	7th,	Out of Playoffs
1938-39	48	8	11	5	7	13	4	15	24	9	115	146	39	6th,	Lost Quarter-Final
1937-38	48	13	4	7	5	13	6	18	17	13	123	128	49	3rd, Cdn. Div.	Lost Quarter-Final
1936-37	48	16	8	0	8	10	6	24	18	6	115	111	54	1st, Cdn. Div.	Lost Semi-Final
1935-36	48	5	11	8	6	15	3	11	26	11	82	123	33	4th, Cdn. Div.	Out of Playoffs
1934-35	48	11	11	2	8	12	4	19	23	6	110	145	44	3rd, Cdn. Div.	Lost Quarter-Final
1933-34	48	16	6	2	6	14	4	22	20	6	99	101	50	2nd, Cdn. Div.	Lost Quarter-Final
1932-33	48	15	5	4	3	20	1	18	25	5	92	115	41	3rd, Cdn. Div.	Lost Quarter-Final
1931-32	48	18	3	3	7	13	4	25	16	7	128	111	57	1st, Cdn. Div.	Lost Semi-Final
1930-31	44	15	3	4	11	7	4	26	10	8	129	89	60	1st, Cdn. Div.	Won Stanley Cup
1929-30	44	13	5	4	8	9	5	21	14	9	142	114	51	2nd, Cdn. Div.	Won Stanley Cup
1928-29	44	12	4	6	10	3	9	22	7	15	71	43	59	1st, Cdn. Div.	Lost Semi-Final
1927-28	44	12	7	3	14	4	4	26	11	7	116	48	59	1st, Cdn. Div.	Lost Semi-Final
1926-27	44	15	5	2	13	9	0	28	14	2	99	67	58	2nd, Cdn. Div.	Lost Semi-Final
1925-26	36	5	12	1	6	12	0	11	24	1	79	108	23	7th,	Out of Playoffs
1924-25	30	10	5	0	7	6	2	17	11	2	93	56	36	3rd,	Lost Final
1923-24	24	10	2	0	3	9	0	13	11	0	59	48	26	2nd,	Won Stanley Cup
1922-23	24	10	2	0	3	7	2	13	9	2	73	61	28	2nd,	Lost NHL Final
1921-22	24	8	3	1	4	8	0	12	11	1	88	94	25	3rd,	Out of Playoffs
1920-21	24	16	8	0	8	10	6	13	11	0	112	99	26	3rd and 2nd*	Out of Playoffs
1919-20	24	8	4	0	5	7	0	13	11	0	129	113	26	2nd and 3rd*	Out of Playoffs
1918-19	18	7	2	0	3	6	0	10	8	0	88	78	20	1st and 2nd*	Cup Final but no Decision
1917-18	22	6	7	0	7	6	0	13	13	0	115	84	26	1st and 3rd*	Lost NHL Final

* Season played in two halves with no combined standing at end.
From 1917-18 through 1925-26, NHL champions played against PCHA champions for Stanley Cup.

1993-94 Player Personnel

FORWARDS	HT	WT	S	Place of Birth	Date	1992-93 Club
BELLOWS, Brian	5-11	195	L	St. Catharines, Ont.	9/1/64	Montréal
BRASHEAR, Donald	6-3	206	L	Bedford, IN	1/7/72	Fredericton
BRUNET, Benoit	5-11	184	L	Ste-Anne de Bellevue, Que.	8/24/68	Montréal
CAMPBELL, Jim	6-1	175	R	Worcester, MA	4/3/73	Hull
CARBONNEAU, Guy	5-11	184	R	Sept-Iles, Que.	3/18/60	Montréal
DAMPHOUSSE, Vincent	6-1	185	L	Montréal, Que.	12/17/67	Montréal
DARBY, Craig	6-3	180	R	Oneida, NY	9/26/72	Providence
DIONNE, Gilbert	6-0	194	L	Drummondville, Que.	9/19/70	Montréal-Fredericton
DIPIETRO, Paul	5-9	181	R	Sault Ste-Marie, Ont.	9/8/70	Montréal-Fredericton
FERGUSON, Craig	6-0	185	L	Castro Valley, CA	4/8/70	Fredericton-Wheeling
FORTIER, Sébastien	6-0	198	L	Greenfield Park, Que.	10/12/73	Sherbrooke
GUILLET, Robert	5-11	189	R	Montréal, Que.	2/22/72	Fredericton-Wheeling
KEANE, Mike	5-10	178	R	Winnipeg, Man.	5/29/67	Montréal
KUWABARA, Ryan	6-0	205	R	Hamilton, Ont.	3/23/72	Fredericton-Wheeling
LEBEAU, Stephan	5-10	172	R	St-Jérôme, Que.	2/28/68	Montréal
LeCLAIR, John	6-2	205	L	St. Albans, VT	7/5/69	Montréal-Fredericton
LEEMAN, Gary	5-11	180	R	Toronto, Ont.	2/19/64	Calgary-Montréal
MULLER, Kirk	6-0	205	L	Kingston, Ont.	2/2/66	Montréal
PETROV, Oleg	5-9	161	L	Moscow, Russia	4/18/71	Montréal-Fredericton
POULIN, Charles	6-0	172	L	St-Jean d'Iberville, Que.	7/27/72	Fredericton
PRPIC, Tony	6-4	207	R	Euclid, OH	6/16/73	Tri City
ROBERGE, Mario	5-11	185	L	Quebec, Que.	1/25/64	Montréal
RONAN, Edward	6-0	197	R	Quincy, MA	3/21/68	Montréal-Fredericton
SAVAGE, Brian	6-2	191	L	Sudbury, Ont.	2/24/71	Miami
SARAULT, Yves	6-1	170	L	Valleyfield, Que.	12/23/72	Fredericton-Wheeling
SEVIGNY, Pierre	6-0	189	L	Trois-Rivières, Que.	9/8/71	Fredericton
STEVENSON, Turner	6-3	200	R	Prince George, B.C.	5/18/72	Montréal-Fredericton
WILSON, Ron	5-9	180	L	Toronto, Ont.	5/13/56	St. Louis
DEFENSEMEN						
BILODEAU, Brent	6-4	215	L	Dallas, TX	3/27/73	Swift Current
BRISEBOIS, Patrice	6-2	175	R	Montréal, Que.	1/27/71	Montréal
CHASE, Timothy	6-2	180	R	Gaythersburgh, Man.	3/23/70	Brown-Fredericton
DAIGNEAULT, J.-J.	5-11	185	L	Montréal, Que.	10/12/65	Montréal
DESJARDINS, Eric	6-1	200	R	Rouyn, Que.	6/14/69	Montréal
FLEMING, Gerry	6-5	240	L	Montréal, Que.	10/16/67	Fredericton
HALLER, Kevin	6-2	183	L	Trochu, Alta.	12/5/70	Montréal
LANIEL, Marc	6-1	194	L	Oshawa, Ont.	1/16/68	Fredericton
LAPOINTE, Sylvain	6-0	190	L	Anjou, Que.	3/14/73	Hull
MIURA, Hiroyuki	6-3	170	L	Kushiro City, Japan	12/31/73	Fort Saskatchewan
ODELEIN, Lyle	5-10	206	R	Quill Lake, Sask.	7/21/68	Montréal
PROULX, Christian	6-0	190	L	Sherbrooke, Que.	12/10/73	St-Jean
RAMAGE, Rob	6-2	200	R	Byron, Ont.	1/11/59	Tampa Bay-Montréal
SCHNEIDER, Mathieu	5-11	189	L	New York, NY	6/12/69	Montréal
VALLIS, Lindsay	6-3	207	R	Winnipeg, Man.	1/12/71	Fredericton

GOALTENDERS	HT	WT	C	Place of Birth	Date	1992-93 Club
BROCHU, Martin	5-11	195	L	Anjou, Qué.	3/10/73	Hull
CHABOT, Frédéric	5-11	175	R	Hébertville-Station, Que.	2/12/68	Montréal-Fredericton
KUNTAR, Les	6-2	195	L	Elma, NY	7/28/69	Fredericton
RACICOT, André	5-11	165	L	Rouyn-Noranda, Que.	6/9/69	Montréal
ROY, Patrick	6-0	182	L	Québec, Que.	10/5/65	Montréal

Coach

DEMERS, JACQUES

Coach, Montreal Canadiens. Born in Montreal, Que., August 25, 1944.

Named as the 21st head coach in the history of the Montreal Canadiens in July, 1992, Jacques Demers guided the Habs to their 24th Stanley Cup title in 1992-93, defeating the Los Angeles Kings in five games in the championship finals. Demers, who is the only man in NHL history to win coach of the year honors in back-to-back seasons when he was with Detroit, began his coaching career in the QMJHL before making his professional coaching debut with the WHA's Chicago Cougars in 1972-73. Eventually, Demers joined the Quebec Nordiques' organization and was the teams first coach when the club joined the NHL in 1979-80. In 1981, Demers was appointed as the head of the Nordiques' AHL farm affiliate in Fredericton, where he earned Executive of the Year honors in 1983. The following season, Demers returned to the NHL with the St. Louis Blues, where he spent three seasons as head coach.

Coaching Record

		Regular Season					Playoffs			
Season	Team	Games	W	L	T	%	Games	W	L	%
1975-76	Indianapolis (WHA)	80	35	39	6	.475	7	3	4	.429
1976-77	Indianapolis (WHA)	81	36	37	8	.494	9	5	4	.556
1977-78	Cincinnati (WHA)	80	35	42	3	.456	....	....	....	....
1978-79	Quebec (WHA)	80	41	34	5	.544	4	0	4	.000
1979-80	**Quebec (NHL)**	**80**	**25**	**44**	**11**	**.381**	....	....	....	....
1981-82	Fredericton (AHL)	80	20	55	5	.281	....	....	....	....
1982-83	Fredericton (AHL)	80	45	27	8	.544	12	6	6	.500
1983-84	**St. Louis (NHL)**	**80**	**32**	**41**	**7**	**.444**	**11**	**6**	**5**	**.545**
1984-85	**St. Louis (NHL)**	**80**	**37**	**31**	**12**	**.538**	**3**	**0**	**3**	**.000**
1985-86	**St. Louis (NHL)**	**80**	**37**	**34**	**9**	**.519**	**19**	**10**	**9**	**.526**
1986-87	**Detroit (NHL)**	**80**	**36**	**34**	**10**	**.488**	**16**	**9**	**7**	**.563**
1987-88	**Detroit (NHL)**	**80**	**41**	**28**	**11**	**.581**	**16**	**9**	**7**	**.563**
1988-89	**Detroit (NHL)**	**80**	**34**	**34**	**12**	**.500**	**6**	**2**	**4**	**.333**
1989-90	**Detroit (NHL)**	**80**	**28**	**38**	**14**	**.437**	....	....	....	....
1992-93	**Montreal (NHL)**	**84**	**48**	**30**	**6**	**.607**	**20**	**16**	**4**	**.800***
	NHL Totals	**724**	**316**	**316**	**92**	**.500**	**91**	**52**	**39**	**.571**

* Stanley Cup win.

1992-93 Scoring

Regular Season

Pos	#	Player	Team	GP	G	A	Pts	+/–	PIM	PP	SH	GW	GT	S	%
L	25	Vincent Damphousse	MTL	84	39	58	97	5	98	9	3	8	1	287	13.6
L	11	Kirk Muller	MTL	80	37	57	94	8	77	12	0	4	0	231	16.0
L	23	Brian Bellows	MTL	82	40	48	88	4	44	16	0	5	0	260	15.4
C	47	Stephan Lebeau	MTL	71	31	49	80	23	20	8	0	7	0	150	20.7
R	12	Mike Keane	MTL	77	15	45	60	29	95	0	0	1	0	120	12.5
C	18	Denis Savard	MTL	63	16	34	50	1	90	4	1	2	1	99	16.2
L	45	Gilbert Dionne	MTL	75	20	28	48	5	63	6	1	2	0	145	13.8
D	28	Eric Desjardins	MTL	82	13	32	45	20	98	7	0	1	0	163	8.0
C	17	John LeClair	MTL	72	19	25	44	11	33	2	0	2	0	139	13.7
D	8	Matt Schneider	MTL	60	13	31	44	8	91	3	0	2	0	169	7.7
R	26	Gary Leeman	CGY	30	9	5	14	5	10	0	0	2	0	49	18.4
			MTL	20	6	12	18	9	14	1	0	1	0	36	16.7
			TOTAL	50	15	17	32	14	24	1	0	3	0	85	17.6
D	43	Patrice Brisebois	MTL	70	10	21	31	6	79	4	0	2	0	123	8.1
D	14	Kevin Haller	MTL	73	11	14	25	7	117	6	0	1	0	126	8.7
L	22	Benoit Brunet	MTL	47	10	15	25	13	19	0	0	1	1	71	14.1
D	48	J.J. Daigneault	MTL	66	8	10	18	25	57	0	0	1	0	68	11.8
D	5	Rob Ramage	T.B.	66	5	12	17	21–	138	5	0	0	0	115	4.3
			MTL	8	0	1	1	3–	8	0	0	0	0	16	.0
			TOTAL	74	5	13	18	24–	146	5	0	0	0	131	3.8
C	15	Paul Di Pietro	MTL	29	4	13	17	11	14	0	0	0	0	43	9.3
C	21	Guy Carbonneau	MTL	61	4	13	17	9–	20	0	1	0	0	73	5.5
D	24	Lyle Odelein	MTL	83	2	14	16	35	205	0	0	0	0	79	2.5
R	36	Todd Ewen	MTL	75	5	9	14	6	193	0	0	1	0	59	8.5
R	31*	Ed Ronan	MTL	53	5	7	12	6	20	0	0	1	0	54	9.3
L	32	Mario Roberge	MTL	50	4	4	8	2	142	0	0	3	0	23	17.4
D	38*	Sean Hill	MTL	31	2	6	8	5–	54	1	0	1	0	37	5.4
C	29*	Jesse Belanger	MTL	19	4	2	6	1	4	0	0	0	0	24	16.7
R	6*	Oleg Petrov	MTL	9	2	1	3	2	10	0	0	1	0	20	10.0
D	34	Donald Dufresne	MTL	32	1	2	3	0	32	0	0	0	0	13	7.7
G	33	Patrick Roy	MTL	62	0	2	2	0	16	0	0	0	0	0	.0
G	37	Andre Racicot	MTL	26	0	1	1	0	6	0	0	0	0	0	.0
G	1*	Frederic Chabot	MTL	1	0	0	0	0	0	0	0	0	0	0	.0
R	30*	Turner Stevenson	MTL	1	0	0	0	1–	0	0	0	0	0	1	.0
D	35*	Eric Charron	MTL	3	0	0	0	0	2	0	0	0	0	0	.0
R	20*	Patrik Carnback	MTL	6	0	0	0	4–	2	0	0	0	0	4	.0
R	27*	Patrik Kjellberg	MTL	7	0	0	0	3–	2	0	0	0	0	7	.0

Goaltending

No.	Goaltender	GPI	Mins	Avg	W	L	T	EN	SO	GA	SA	S%
1	*Frederic Chabot	1	40	1.50	0	0	0	0	0	1	19	.947
33	Patrick Roy	62	3595	3.20	31	25	5	5	2	192	1814	.894
37	Andre Racicot	26	1433	3.39	17	5	1	1	1	81	682	.881
	Totals	**84**	**5087**	**3.30**	**48**	**30**	**6**	**6**	**3**	**280**	**2521**	**.889**

Playoffs

Pos	#	Player	Team	GP	G	A	Pts	+/–	PIM	PP	SH	GW	GT	S	%
L	25	Vincent Damphousse	MTL	20	11	12	23	8	16	5	0	3	1	52	21.2
L	11	Kirk Muller	MTL	20	10	7	17	4	18	3	0	3	2	54	18.5
L	23	Brian Bellows	MTL	18	6	9	15	6	18	2	0	0	0	72	8.3
R	12	Mike Keane	MTL	19	2	13	15	10	6	0	0	0	0	27	7.4
D	28	Eric Desjardins	MTL	20	4	10	14	2	23	1	0	1	1	47	8.5
C	15	Paul Di Pietro	MTL	17	8	5	13	2	8	0	0	1	0	38	21.1
L	45	Gilbert Dionne	MTL	20	6	6	12	2–	20	1	0	1	1	42	14.3
C	17	John LeClair	MTL	20	4	6	10	2	14	0	0	3	2	44	9.1
L	22	Benoit Brunet	MTL	20	2	8	10	1	8	1	0	1	0	36	5.6
D	14	Kevin Haller	MTL	17	1	6	7	1–	16	1	0	0	0	24	4.2
C	47	Stephan Lebeau	MTL	13	3	3	6	4	6	1	0	1	1	18	16.7
C	21	Guy Carbonneau	MTL	20	3	3	6	3	10	0	1	2	2	35	8.6
D	24	Lyle Odelein	MTL	20	1	5	6	9	30	0	0	0	0	20	5.0
R	31*	Ed Ronan	MTL	14	2	3	5	5	10	0	0	0	0	9	22.2
C	18	Denis Savard	MTL	14	0	5	5	3–	4	0	0	0	0	15	.0
D	48	J.J. Daigneault	MTL	20	1	3	4	2	22	0	0	0	0	33	3.0
D	43	Patrice Brisebois	MTL	20	0	4	4	5	18	0	0	0	0	35	.0
R	26	Gary Leeman	MTL	11	1	2	3	5–	2	0	0	0	0	11	9.1
D	27	Matt Schneider	MTL	11	1	2	3	10	16	0	0	0	0	24	4.2
C	29*	Jesse Belanger	MTL	9	0	1	1	2–	0	0	0	0	0	6	.0
G	33	Patrick Roy	MTL	20	0	1	1	0	4	0	0	0	0	0	.0
R	36	Todd Ewen	MTL	1	0	0	0	1–	0	0	0	0	0	0	.0
G	37	Andre Racicot	MTL	1	0	0	0	0	0	0	0	0	0	0	.0
R	6*	Oleg Petrov	MTL	1	0	0	0	0	0	0	0	0	0	0	.0
D	34	Donald Dufresne	MTL	2	0	0	0	2	0	0	0	0	0	0	.0
L	32	Mario Roberge	MTL	3	0	0	0	0	0	0	0	0	0	1	.0
D	38*	Sean Hill	MTL	3	0	0	0	1	4	0	0	0	0	2	.0
D	5	Rob Ramage	MTL	7	0	0	0	3–	4	0	0	0	0	8	.0

Goaltending

No.	Goaltender	GPI	Mins	Avg	W	L	EN	SO	GA	SA	S%
33	Patrick Roy	20	1293	2.13	16	4	3	0	46	647	.929
37	Andre Racicot	1	18	6.67	0	0	0	0	2	9	.778
	Totals	**20**	**1313**	**2.33**	**16**	**4**	**3**	**0**	**51**	**659**	**.923**

Captains' History

Newsy Lalonde, 1917-18 to 1920-21; Sprague Cleghorn, 1921-22 to 1924-25; Bill Couture, 1925-26; Sylvio Mantha, 1926-27 to 1931-32; George Hainsworth, 1932-33; Sylvio Mantha, 1933-34 to 1935-36; Babe Seibert, 1936-37 to 1938-39; Walter Buswell, 1939-40; Toe Blake, 1940-41 to 1946-47; Toe Blake, Bill Durnan (co-captains) 1947-48; Emile Bouchard, 1948-49 to 1955-56; Maurice Richard, 1956-57 to 1959-60; Doug Harvey, 1960-61; Jean Beliveau, 1961-62 to 1970-71; Henri Richard, 1971-72 to 1974-75; Yvan Cournoyer, 1975-76 to 1978-79; Serge Savard, 1979-80, 1980-81; Bob Gainey, 1981-82 to 1988-89, Guy Carbonneau and Chris Chelios (co-captains), 1989-90; Guy Carbonneau, 1990-91 to date.

Club Records

Team

(Figures in brackets for season records are games played; records for fewest points, wins, ties, losses, goals, goals against are for 70 or more games)

Most Points	*132	1976-77 (80)
Most Wins	*60	1976-77 (80)
Most Ties	23	1962-63 (70)
Most Losses	40	1983-84 (80)
Most Goals	387	1976-77 (80)
Most Goals Against	295	1983-84 (80)
Fewest Points	65	1950-51 (70)
Fewest Wins	25	1950-51 (70)
Fewest Ties	5	1983-84 (80
Fewest Losses	*8	1976-77 (80)
Fewest Goals	155	1952-53 (70)
Fewest Goals Against ...	*131	1955-56 (70)

Longest Winning Streak
Over-all .... 12 Jan. 6-
Feb. 3/68

Home .... 13 Nov. 2/43-
Jan. 8/44
Jan. 30-
Mar. 26/77

Away .... 8 Dec. 18/77-
Jan. 18/78
Jan. 21-
Feb. 21/82

Longest Undefeated Streak
Over-all .... 28 Dec. 18/77-
Feb. 23/78
(23 wins, 5 ties)

Home .... *34 Nov. 1/76-
Apr. 2/77
(28 wins, 6 ties)

Away .... *23 Nov. 27/74-
Mar. 12/75
(14 wins, 9 ties)

Longest Losing Streak
Over-all .... 12 Feb. 13/26-
Mar. 13/26

Home .... 7 Dec. 16/39-
Jan. 18/40

Away .... 10 Dec. 1/25-
Feb. 2/26

Longest Winless Streak
Over-all .... 12 Feb. 13-
Mar. 13/26
(12 losses)
Nov. 28-
Dec. 29/35
(8 losses, 4 ties)

Home .... *15 Dec. 16/39-
Mar. 7/40
(12 losses, 3 ties)

Away .... 12 Oct. 20-
Dec. 13/51
(8 losses, 4 ties)

Most Shutouts, Season	*22	1928-29 (44)
Most PIM, Season	1,842	1987-88 (80)
Most Goals, Game	*16	Mar. 3/20
		(Mt. 16 at Que. 3)

Individual

Most Seasons	20	Henri Richard, Jean Beliveau
Most Games	1,256	Henri Richard
Most Goals Career	544	Maurice Richard
Most Assists, Career.....	728	Guy Lafleur
Most Points Career	1,246	Guy Lafleur
		(518 goals, 728 assists)
Most PIM, Career	2,248	Chris Nilan
Most Shutouts, Career	75	George Hainsworth

Longest Consecutive
Games Streak .... 560 Doug Jarvis
(Oct. 8/75-Apr. 4/82)

Most Goals, Season ...... 60 Steve Shutt
(1976-77)
Guy Lafleur
(1977-78)

Most Assists, Season ..... 82 Peter Mahovlich
(1974-75)

Most Points, Season ..... 136 Guy Lafleur
(1976-77)
(56 goals, 80 assists)

Most PIM, Season........ 358 Chris Nilan
(1984-85)

Most Points, Defenseman
Season .... 85 Larry Robinson
(1976-77)
(19 goals, 66 assists)

Most Points, Center,
Season .... 117 Peter Mahovlich
(1974-75)
(35 goals, 82 assists)

Most Points, Right Wing,
Season .... 136 Guy Lafleur
(1976-77)
(56 goals, 80 assists)

Most Points, Left Wing,
Season .... 110 Mats Naslund
(1985-86)
(43 goals, 67 assists)

Most Points, Rookie,
Season .... 71 Mats Naslund
(1982-83)
(26 goals, 45 assists)
Kjell Dahlin
(1985-86)
(32 goals, 39 assists)

Most Shutouts, Season ... *22 George Hainsworth
(1928-29)

Most Goals, Game .... 6 Newsy Lalonde
(Jan. 10/20)

Most Assists, Game .... 6 Elmer Lach
(Feb. 6/43)

Most Points, Game .... 8 Maurice Richard
5G-3A
(Dec. 28/44)
Bert Olmstead
4G-4A
(Jan. 9/54)

* NHL Record.

Retired Numbers

2	Doug Harvey	1947-1961
4	Aurèle Joliat	1922-1938
	Jean Béliveau	1950-1971
7	Howie Morenz	1923-1937
9	Maurice Richard	1942-1960
10	Guy Lafleur	1971-1984
16	Elmer Lach	1942-1954
	Henri Richard	1955-1975

All-time Record vs. Other Clubs

Regular Season

	GP	W	L	T	GF	GA	PTS	GP	W	L	T	GF	GA	PTS	GP	W	L	T	GF	GA	PTS
				At Home							On Road							Total			
Boston	306	178	84	44	1044	706	400	306	113	141	52	824	903	278	612	291	225	96	1868	1609	678
Buffalo	75	47	20	8	314	222	102	74	23	33	18	220	233	64	149	70	53	26	534	455	166
Calgary	37	21	10	6	132	90	48	36	20	11	5	130	118	45	73	41	21	11	262	208	93
Chicago	266	167	51	48	1032	626	382	266	121	91	54	742	717	296	532	288	142	102	1774	1343	678
Detroit	273	168	62	43	970	600	379	273	96	124	53	703	773	245	546	264	186	96	1673	1380	624
Edmonton	21	12	6	3	76	66	27	22	10	12	0	68	76	20	43	22	18	3	144	142	47
Hartford	51	35	10	6	235	153	76	52	27	17	8	201	163	62	103	62	27	14	436	316	138
Los Angeles	56	38	7	11	261	147	87	57	34	15	8	231	175	76	113	72	22	19	492	322	163
Minnesota	50	34	9	7	225	123	75	51	27	14	10	184	133	64	101	61	23	17	409	256	139
New Jersey	32	23	5	4	136	82	50	32	23	9	0	155	89	46	64	46	14	4	291	171	96
NY Islanders	37	22	9	6	148	113	50	39	19	16	4	123	129	42	76	41	25	10	271	242	92
NY Rangers	268	179	55	34	1059	618	392	268	109	108	51	782	774	269	536	288	163	85	1841	1392	661
Ottawa	4	4	0	0	17	11	8	3	2	1	0	12	9	4	7	6	1	0	29	20	12
Philadelphia	52	28	14	10	200	151	66	51	21	17	13	153	137	55	103	49	31	23	353	288	121
Pittsburgh	57	47	4	6	292	138	100	57	29	19	9	212	174	67	114	76	23	15	504	312	167
Quebec	51	32	11	8	219	158	72	52	24	26	2	192	181	50	103	56	37	10	411	339	122
St. Louis	51	37	8	6	228	132	80	50	26	10	14	178	127	66	101	63	18	20	406	259	146
San Jose	3	3	0	0	18	6	6	3	2	1	0	6	4	5	6	5	1	0	24	10	11
Tampa Bay	1	1	0	0	4	3	2	1	0	1	0	1	3	0	2	1	1	0	5	6	2
Toronto	313	190	83	40	1114	772	420	314	110	160	44	821	953	264	627	300	243	84	1935	1725	684
Vancouver	44	34	8	2	222	117	70	42	27	7	8	169	105	62	86	61	15	10	391	222	132
Washington	38	26	6	6	175	77	58	38	17	15	6	130	102	40	76	43	21	12	305	179	98
Winnipeg	21	19	2	0	115	49	38	21	9	7	5	83	68	23	42	28	9	5	198	117	61
Defunct Clubs	231	148	58	25	779	469	321	230	98	97	35	586	606	231	461	246	155	60	1365	1075	552
Totals	2338	1493	522	323	9015	5636	3309	2338	987	951	400	6906	6752	2374	4676	2480	1473	723	15921	12388	5683

Playoffs

	Series	W	L	GP	W	L	T	GF	GA	Last Mtg.	Round	Result
Boston	27	21	6	132	84	48	0	410	317	1992	DF	L 0-4
Buffalo	6	4	2	31	18	13	0	114	94	1993	DF	W 4-0
Calgary	2	1	1	11	6	5	0	31	32	1989	F	L 2-4
Chicago	17	12	5	81	50	29	2	261	185	1976	QF	W 4-0
Detroit	12	5	7	62	33	29	0	161	149	1978	QF	W 4-1
Edmonton	1	0	1	3	0	3	0	6	15	1981	PR	L 0-3
Hartford	5	5	0	27	19	8	0	96	70	1992	DSF	W 4-3
Los Angeles	1	1	0	5	4	1	0	15	12	1993	F	W 4-1
Minnesota	2	1	1	13	7	6	0	48	37	1980	QF	L 3-4
NY Islanders	4	3	1	22	14	8	0	64	55	1993	CF	W 4-1
NY Rangers	13	7	6	55	32	21	2	171	139	1986	CF	W 4-1
Philadelphia	4	3	1	21	14	7	0	72	52	1989	CF	W 4-2
Quebec	5	3	2	31	17	14	0	105	85	1993	DSF	W 4-2
St. Louis	3	3	0	12	12	0	0	42	14	1977	QF	W 4-0
Toronto	13	7	6	67	39	28	0	203	148	1979	QF	W 4-0
Vancouver	1	1	0	5	4	1	0	20	9	1975	QF	W 4-1
Defunct Clubs	12	7	5	32	18	10	4	82	83			
Totals	129*	84	44	610	371	231	8	1901	1496			

* 1919 Final incomplete due to influenza epidemic.

Playoff Results 1993-89

Year	Round	Opponent	Result	GF	GA
1993	F	Los Angeles	W 4-1	15	12
	CF	NY Islanders	W 4-1	16	11
	DF	Buffalo	W 4-0	16	12
	DSF	Quebec	W 4-2	19	16
1992	DF	Boston	L 0-4	8	14
	DSF	Hartford	W 4-3	21	18
1991	DF	Boston	L 3-4	18	18
	DSF	Buffalo	W 4-2	29	24
1990	DF	Boston	L 1-4	12	16
	DSF	Buffalo	W 4-2	17	13
1989	F	Calgary	L 2-4	16	19
	CF	Philadelphia	W 4-2	17	8
	DF	Boston	W 4-1	16	13
	DSF	Hartford	W 4-0	18	11

Abbreviations: Round: F — Final;
CF — conference final; DF — division final;
DSF — division semi-final; SF — semi-final;
QF — quarter-final; PR — preliminary round.
GA — goals against; GF — goals for.

1992-93 Results

	Home				Away	
Oct. 10	Pittsburgh	3-3	Oct. 6	Hartford	5-1
17	Minnesota	8-1	8	Ottawa	3-5
19	St. Louis	6-2	11	Buffalo	2-8
21	San Jose	8-4	15	Pittsburgh	2-5
28	Tampa Bay	4-3	23	NY Rangers	3-3
31	NY Rangers	4-3	24	Philadelphia	7-6
Nov. 2	Winnipeg	2-1	Nov. 4	Detroit	4-3
7	Detroit	5-1	11	New Jersey	8-3
9	Calgary	5-2	17	Ottawa	5-3
14	Philadelphia	3-4	19	Quebec	3-4
16	Boston	6-3	25	Hartford	6-1
21	Ottawa	3-1	Dec. 3	Boston	3-4
23	Washington	1-1	5	Winnipeg	3-2
28	Vancouver	5-6	6	Chicago	0-2
30	Buffalo	3-0	8	Los Angeles	5-5
Dec. 12	Boston	5-1	13	NY Rangers	5-10
16	Quebec	1-5	17	Quebec	8-3
19	Buffalo	4-2	27	Vancouver	2-5
21	Hartford	2-5	29	Edmonton	6-3
23	NY Islanders	2-6	31	Calgary	3-5
Jan. 4	San Jose	4-1	Jan. 2	Los Angeles	5-5
9	Toronto	4-5	5	San Jose	2-1
13	Hartford	7-3	10	Hartford	7-5
16	NY Rangers	3-0	14	Quebec	5-3
20	New Jersey	3-2	22	New Jersey	2-6
25	Boston	3-2	23	Toronto	0-4
27	Hartford	5-6	Feb. 9	NY Islanders	5-3
30	Ottawa*	5-3	11	Philadelphia	0-0
31	Philadelphia*	6-4	13	Ottawa	4-1
Feb. 3	Los Angeles	7-2	23	St. Louis	5-1
17	Boston	2-5	26	Buffalo	6-4
20	Ottawa	5-4	Mar. 1	Boston	5-2
21	Edmonton	4-3	3	Tampa Bay	1-3
27	Buffalo	8-4	6	Minnesota	3-4
Mar. 10	NY Islanders	5-1	11	Boston	2-5
13	Quebec	2-5	18	Quebec	5-2
20	Chicago	6-2	24	Hartford	6-5
22	Buffalo	3-8	25	Boston	0-2
27	Ottawa	4-3	Apr. 2	Washington	0-4
31	Quebec	2-6	3	NY Islanders	3-2
Apr. 10	Boston	1-5	7	Pittsburgh	3-4
12	Washington	2-3	13	Buffalo	3-2

*Denotes afternoon game

Entry Draft
Selections 1993-79

1993
Pick
21	Saku Koivu
47	Rory Fitzpatrick
73	Sebastien Bordeleau
85	Adam Wiesel
99	Jean-Francois Houle
113	Jeff Lank
125	Dion Darling
151	Darcy Tucker
177	David Ruhly
203	Alan Letang
229	Alexandre Duchesne
255	Brian Larochelle
281	Russell Guzior

1992
Pick
20	David Wilkie
33	Valeri Bure
44	Keli Corpse
68	Craig Rivet
82	Louis Bernard
92	Marc Lamothe
116	Don Chase
140	Martin Sychra
164	Christian Proulx
188	Michael Burman
212	Earl Cronan
236	Trent Cavicchi
260	Hiroyuki Miura

1991
Pick
17	Brent Bilodeau
28	Jim Campbll
43	Craig Darby
61	Yves Sarault
73	Vladimir Vujtek
83	Sylvain Lapointe
100	Brad Layzell
105	Tony Prpic
127	Oleg Petrov
149	Brady Kramer
171	Brian Savage
193	Scott Fraser
215	Greg MacEachern
237	Paul Lepler
259	Dale Hooper

1990
Pick
12	Turner Stevenson
39	Ryan Kuwabara
58	Charles Poulin
60	Robert Guillet
81	Gilbert Dionne
102	Paul DiPietro
123	Craig Conroy
144	Stephen Rohr
165	Brent Fleetwood
186	Derek Maguire
207	Mark Kettelhut
228	John Uniac
249	Sergei Martynyuk

1989
Pick
13	Lindsay Vallis
30	Patrice Brisebois
41	Steve Larouche
51	Pierre Sevigny
83	Andre Racicot
104	Marc Deschamps
146	Craig Ferguson
167	Patrick Lebeu
188	Roy Mitchell
209	Ed Henrich
230	Justin Duberman
251	Steve Cadieux

1988
Pick
20	Eric Charron
34	Martin St. Amour
46	Neil Carnes
83	Patrik Kjellberg
93	Peter Popovic
104	Jean-Claude Bergeron
125	Patrik Carnback
146	Tim Chase
167	Sean Hill
188	Harijs Vitolinsh
209	Yuri Krivokhizha
230	Kevin Dahl
251	Dave Kunda

1987
Pick
17	Andrew Cassels
33	John LeClair
38	Eric Desjardins
44	Mathieu Schneider
58	Francois Gravel
80	Kris Miller
101	Steve McCool
122	Les Kuntar
143	Rob Kelley
164	Will Geist
185	Eric Tremblay
206	Barry McKinlay
227	Ed Ronan
248	Bryan Herring

1986
Pick
15	Mark Pederson
27	Benoit Brunet
57	Jyrki Lumme
78	Brent Bobyck
94	Eric Aubertin
99	Mario Milani
120	Steve Bisson
141	Lyle Odelein
162	Rick Hayward
183	Antonin Routa
204	Eric Bohemier
225	Charlie Moore
246	Karel Svoboda

1985
Pick
12	Jose Charbonneau
16	Tom Chorske
33	Todd Richards
47	Rocky Dundas
75	Martin Desjardins
79	Brent Gilchrist
96	Tom Sagissor
117	Donald Dufresne
142	Ed Cristofoli
163	Mike Claringbull
184	Roger Beedon
198	Maurice Mansi
205	Chad Arthur
226	Mike Bishop
247	John Ferguson Jr.

1984
Pick
5	Petr Svoboda
8	Shayne Corson
29	Stephane Richer
51	Patrick Roy
54	Graeme Bonar
65	Lee Brodeur
95	Gerald Johannson
116	Jim Nesich
137	Scott MacTavish
158	Brad McCughey
179	Eric Demers
199	Ron Annear
220	Dave Tanner
240	Troy Crosby

1983
Pick
17	Alfie Turcotte
26	Claude Lemieux
27	Sergio Momesso
35	Todd Francis
45	Daniel Letendre
78	John Kordic
98	Dan Wurst
118	Arto Javanainen
138	Vladislav Tretiak
158	Rob Bryden
178	Grant MacKay
198	Thomas Rundqvist
218	Jeff Perpich
238	Jean-Guy Bergeron

1982
Pick
19	Alain Heroux
31	Jocelyn Gauvreau
32	Kent Carlson
33	David Maley
40	Scott Sandelin
61	Scott Harlow
69	John Devoe
103	Kevin Houle
117	Ernie Vargas
124	Michael Dark
145	Hannu Jarvenpaa
150	Steve Smith
166	Tom Kolioupoulos
187	Brian Williams
208	Bob Emery
229	Darren Acheson
250	Bill Brauer

1981
Pick
7	Mark Hunter
18	Gilbert Delorme
19	Jan Ingman
32	Lars Eriksson
40	Chris Chelios
46	Dieter Hegen
82	Kjell Dahlin
88	Steve Rooney
124	Tom Anastos
145	Tom Kurvers
166	Paul Gess
187	Scott Ferguson
208	Danny Burrows

1980
Pick
1	Doug Wickenheiser
27	Ric Nattress
40	John Chabot
45	John Newberry
61	Craig Ludwig
82	Jeff Teal
103	Remi Gagne
124	Mike McPhee
145	Bill Norton
166	Steve Penney
187	John Schmidt
208	Scott Robinson

1979
Pick
27	Gaston Gingras
37	Mats Naslund
43	Craig Levie
44	Guy Carbonneau
58	Rick Wamsley
79	Dave Orleski
100	Yvan Joly
121	Greg Moffett

General Managers' History

Joseph Cattarinich, 1909-1910; George Kennedy, 1910-11 to 1919-20; Leo Dandurand, 1920-21 to 1934-35; Ernest Savard, 1935-36; Cecil Hart, 1936-37 to 1938-39; Jules Dugal, 1939-40; Tom P. Gorman, 1941-42 to 1945-46; Frank J. Selke, 1946-47 to 1963-64; Sam Pollock, 1964-65 to 1977-78; Irving Grundman, 1978-79 to 1982-83; Serge Savard, 1983-84 to date.

Coaching History

George Kennedy, 1917-18 to 1919-20; Léo Dandurand, 1920-21 to 1924-25; Cecil Hart, 1925-26 to 1931-32; Newsy Lalonde, 1932-33 to 1933-34; Newsy Lalonde and Léo Dandurand, 1934-35; Sylvio Mantha, 1935-36; Cecil Hart, 1936-37 to 1937-38; Cecil Hart and Jules Dugal, 1938-39; "Babe" Siebert, 1939*; Pit Lepine, 1939-40; Dick Irvin 1940-41 to 1954-55; Toe Blake, 1955-56 to 1967-68; Claude Ruel, 1968-69 to 1969-70; Claude Ruel and Al MacNeil, 1970-71; Scott Bowman, 1971-72 to 1978-79; Bernie Geoffrion and Claude Ruel, 1979-80; Claude Ruel, 1980-81; Bob Berry, 1981-82 to 1982-83; Bob Berry and Jacques Lemaire, 1983-84; Jacques Lemaire, 1984-85; Jean Perron, 1985-86 to 1987-88; Pat Burns, 1988-89 to 1991-92; Jacques Demers, 1992-93 to date.
* Named coach in summer but died before 1939-40 season began.

Club Directory

Montreal Forum
2313 St. Catherine Street West
Montreal, Quebec H3H 1N2
Phone **514/932-2582**
FAX (Hockey) 514/932-8736
P.R. 514/932-9296
Media 514/932-8285
Capacity: 16,259 (standing 1,700)

Owner: The Molson Companies Limited

Chairman of the Board, President and Governor	Ronald Corey
Vice-President Hockey, Managing Director and Alternate Governor	Serge Savard
Senior Vice-President, Corporate Affairs	Jean Beliveau
Vice-President, Forum Operations	Aldo Giampaolo
Vice-President, Finance and Administration	Fred Steer
Vice-President, Communications and Marketing	Bernard Brisset
Assistant to the Managing Director and Director of Scouting and Managing Director of Les Canadiens de Fredericton	André Boudrias
Director of Team Services	Michele Lapointe
Head Coach	Jacques Demers
Assistant Coaches	Jacques Laperrière, Charles Thiffault, Steve Shutt
Goaltending Instructor	François Allaire
Director of Player Development and Scout	Claude Ruel
Chief Scout	Doug Robinson
Scouting Staff	Neil Armstrong, Scott Baker, Pat Flannery, Pierre Mondou, Gerry O'Flaherty, Richard Scammell, Eric Taylor, Jean-Claude Tremblay, Del Wilson
Farm Team (AHL)	Les Canadiens de Fredericton
Head Coach	Paulin Bordeleau
Assistant Coach	Luc Gauthier
Director of Operations	Wayne Gamble

Medical and Training Staff
Club Physician	Dr. D.G. Kinnear
Athletic Trainer	Gaétan Lefebvre
Assistant to the Athletic Trainer	John Shipman
Equipment Manager	Eddy Palchak
Assistants to the Equipment Manager	Pierre Gervais, Robert Boulanger

Marketing
EFFIX Inc.	François-Xavier Seigneur

Communications
Director of Communications	Donald Beauchamp
Assistant to the Director of Communications	Denis Dessureault

Finance
Controller	Dennis McKinley
Administrative Supervisor	Dave Poulton
Accountants	Françoise Brault, Gilles Viens

Forum
Forum Superintendent	Alain Gauthier
Director of Security	Pierre Sauvé
Director of Events	Louise Laliberté
Director of Computer, Operations	Sylvain Roy
Assistant to the Director of Concessions	André Desforges
Director of Purchasing	Robert Loiseau

Ticketing
Box Office Manager	Richard Primeau
Assistant to the Box Office Manager	Caterina D'Ascoli

Executive Secretaries
President (Lise Beaudry)/Managing Director (Donna Stuart)/Senior V.P., C.A. (Louise Richer)/V.P. Forum Operations (Vicky Mercuri)/V.P. Finance (Susan Cryans)/V.P. Communications and Marketing (Normande Herget)/Press Rel. (Frédérique Cardinal)

Location of Press Box	Suspended above ice — West side
Location of Radio and TV booth	Suspended above ice — East side
Dimensions of rink	200 feet by 85 feet
Ends of rink	Herculite extends above boards all around rink
Club colors	Red, White and Blue
Club trains at	Montreal Forum
Play-by-Play — Radio/TV	Dick Irvin (English) Claude Quenneville, René Pothier, Richard Garneau (French)
TV Channels	CBMT (6), CFTM (10), CBFT (2)
Radio Stations	CBF (690) (French), CJAD (800) (English)

General Manager

SAVARD, SERGE A.
Managing Director, Montreal Canadiens.
Born in Montreal, Que., January 22, 1946.

When Serge Savard was named managing director of the Montreal Canadiens on April 28, 1983, he took over a club that finished in fourth place with 75 points. In 1984-85, the Canadiens were vastly improved, finishing first with 94 points. Evidence of Savard's front office efforts were visible throughout the organization where he spent 14 of his 16 NHL seasons as a standout defenseman and an important part of eight Stanley Cup winning teams. As a player, Savard captured the Conn Smythe Trophy as the most valuable player in the 1969 Stanley Cup playoffs and was recipient of the Bill Masterton Trophy in 1978-79 for his dedication, perseverance and sportsmanship to the game of hockey. He was acquired by the Winnipeg Jets in the 1981 Waiver Draft and closed out his playing career with two seasons as a leader and teacher to the young Jets' team which showed remarkable improvement during Savard's term. In the 1960's, Savard twice suffered multiple leg fractures and most experts doubted he would ever play again. He was named to the NHL's Second All-Star Team in 1978-79.

New Jersey Devils

1992-93 Results: 40w-37L-7T 87PTS. Fourth, Patrick Division

Year-by-Year Record

Season	GP	Home W	L	T	Road W	L	T	Overall W	L	T	GF	GA	Pts.	Finished	Playoff Result
1992-93	84	24	14	4	16	23	3	40	37	7	308	299	87	4th, Patrick Div.	Lost Div. Semi-Final
1991-92	80	24	12	4	14	19	3	38	31	11	289	259	87	4th, Patrick Div.	Lost Div. Semi-Final
1990-91	80	23	10	7	9	23	8	32	33	15	272	264	79	4th, Patrick Div.	Lost Div. Semi-Final
1989-90	80	22	15	3	15	19	6	37	34	9	295	288	83	2nd, Patrick Div.	Lost Div. Semi-Final
1988-89	80	17	18	5	10	23	7	27	41	12	281	325	66	5th, Patrick Div.	Out of Playoffs
1987-88	80	23	16	1	15	20	5	38	36	6	295	296	82	4th, Patrick Div.	Lost Conf. Championship
1986-87	80	20	17	3	9	28	3	29	45	6	293	368	64	6th, Patrick Div.	Out of Playoffs
1985-86	80	17	21	2	11	28	1	28	49	3	300	374	59	6th, Patrick Div.	Out of Playoffs
1984-85	80	13	21	6	9	27	4	22	48	10	264	346	54	5th, Patrick Div.	Out of Playoffs
1983-84	80	10	28	2	7	28	5	17	56	7	231	350	41	5th, Patrick Div.	Out of Playoffs
1982-83	80	11	20	9	6	29	5	17	49	14	230	338	48	5th, Patrick Div.	Out of Playoffs
1981-82	80	14	21	5	4	28	8	18	49	13	241	362	49	5th, Smythe Div.	Out of Playoffs
1980-81	80	15	16	9	7	29	4	22	45	13	258	344	57	5th, Smythe Div.	Out of Playoffs
1979-80	80	12	20	8	7	28	5	19	48	13	234	308	51	6th, Smythe Div.	Out of Playoffs
1978-79	80	8	24	8	7	29	4	15	53	12	210	331	42	4th, Smythe Div.	Out of Playoffs
1977-78	80	17	14	9	2	26	12	19	40	21	257	305	59	2nd, Smythe Div.	Lost Prelim. Round
1976-77	80	12	20	8	8	26	6	20	46	14	226	307	54	5th, Smythe Div.	Out of Playoffs
1975-76	80	8	24	8	4	32	4	12	56	12	190	351	36	5th, Smythe Div.	Out of Playoffs
1974-75	80	12	20	8	3	34	3	15	54	11	184	328	41	5th, Smythe Div.	Out of Playoffs

Schedule

Home			Away		
Oct.	Wed. 6	Tampa Bay	Oct.	Fri. 8	Washington
	Sat. 9	Washington		Sat. 16	NY Islanders
	Tues. 12	Winnipeg		Sun. 31	NY Rangers (at Halifax)
	Wed. 20	Anaheim			
	Sat. 23	Florida	Nov.	Wed. 3	Los Angeles
	Tues. 26	Montreal		Fri. 5	Anaheim
	Sat. 30	Philadelphia*		Sun. 7	San Jose*
Nov.	Wed. 10	NY Islanders		Thur. 11	Philadelphia
	Sat. 13	San Jose*		Thur. 18	Ottawa
	Wed. 17	Buffalo		Tues. 23	Quebec
	Sat. 20	Detroit*		Wed. 24	Buffalo
	Tues. 30	NY Rangers		Fri. 26	St Louis
Dec.	Sat. 4	Chicago	Dec.	Thur. 2	Pittsburgh
	Thur. 9	Quebec		Sun. 5	NY Rangers
	Sat. 11	Edmonton		Wed. 8	Montreal
	Wed. 15	Boston		Tues. 14	NY Islanders
	Sun. 19	Philadelphia		Sat. 18	Quebec*
	Thur. 23	Toronto		Wed. 22	Hartford
	Tues. 28	Hartford		Sun. 26	NY Rangers
Jan.	Tues. 4	NY Islanders	Jan.	Sat. 1	Ottawa
	Fri. 7	Florida		Wed. 12	Montreal
	Sun. 9	Washington		Fri. 14	Washington
	Sat. 15	Los Angeles		Wed. 19	Winnipeg
Feb.	Wed. 2	Buffalo		Mon. 24	Dallas
	Fri. 4	Ottawa		Wed. 26	Edmonton
	Sat. 5	Pittsburgh		Fri. 28	Calgary
	Thur. 10	Vancouver		Sat. 29	Vancouver
	Sat. 19	Tampa Bay*	Feb.	Sat. 12	Boston*
	Thur. 24	NY Rangers		Sun. 13	Tampa Bay
	Mon. 28	St Louis		Thur. 17	Toronto
Mar.	Sat. 5	Calgary*		Sun. 20	Chicago*
	Mon. 7	Quebec		Wed. 23	Detroit
	Thur. 10	Hartford		Sat. 26	Hartford*
	Sat. 12	Boston*	Mar.	Wed. 2	Florida
	Sun. 13	Dallas*		Thur. 3	Tampa Bay
	Thur. 24	Tampa Bay		Tues. 15	NY Islanders
	Sat. 26	Philadelphia*		Thur. 17	Buffalo
	Sun. 27	Quebec (at Minnesota)		Sat. 19	Boston*
	Tues. 29	Montreal		Mon. 21	Florida
Apr.	Sat. 2	NY Rangers	Apr.	Fri. 1	Washington
	Fri. 8	Pittsburgh		Wed. 6	Pittsburgh
	Thur. 14	Ottawa		Sun. 10	Florida
				Tues. 12	Philadelphia

* Denotes afternoon game.

Home Starting Times:
All Games . . . . 7:35 p.m.
Except Matinees . . . . 1:35 p.m.
Sun. Mar. 13 . . . . 5:05 p.m.

Franchise date: June 30, 1982. Transferred from Denver to New Jersey, previously transferred from Kansas City to Denver, Colorado.

ATLANTIC DIVISION

20th NHL Season

EASTERN CONFERENCE

Valeri Zelepukin had an excellent sophomore season for the Devils, collecting 23 goals and 41 assists in 1992-93.

1993-94 Player Personnel

FORWARDS	HT	WT	S	Place of Birth	Date	1992-93 Club
ARMSTRONG, Bill H.	6-2	195	L	London, Ont.	6/25/66	Cincinnati-Utica
BLACK, Ryan	6-1	180	L	Guelph, Ont.	10/25/73	Peterborough
BODNARCHUK, Mike	6-1	175	R	Bramalea, Ont.	3/26/70	Cincinnati-Utica
BRULE, Steve	5-11	185	R	Montreal, Que.	1/15/75	St. Jean
CHRISTIAN, Jeff	6-1	195	L	Burlington, Ont.	7/30/70	Cinn.-Utica-Ham.
CHORSKE, Tom	6-1	205	R	Minneapolis, MN	9/18/66	New Jersey-Utica
DOWD, Jim	6-1	190	R	Brick, NJ	12/25/68	Utica-New Jersey
EMMA, David	5-11	180	L	Cranston, RI	1/14/68	Utica-New Jersey
FRECHETTE, Yanick	6-2	175	R	Ste.-Sophie, Que.	6/20/73	Hull
GUERIN, Bill	6-2	200	R	Wilbraham, MA	11/9/70	Utica-New Jersey
GUIRESTANTE, John	6-2	170	R	Toronto, Ont.	5/11/75	London
HANKINSON, Ben	6-2	210	R	Edina, MN	5/1/69	Utica-New Jersey
HEXTALL, Donevan	6-2	190	L	Wolseley, Sask.	2/24/72	Utica-Canadian Nat'l Jr.
HOLIK, Bobby	6-3	220	R	Jihlava, Czech.	1/1/71	New Jersey-Utica
LEMIEUX, Claude	6-1	215	R	Buckingham, Que.	7/16/65	New Jersey
MacLEAN, John	6-0	200	R	Oshawa, Ont.	11/20/64	New Jersey
McKAY, Randy	6-1	205	R	Montreal, Que.	1/25/67	New Jersey
MILLEN, Corey	5-7	170	R	Cloquet, MN	4/29/64	Los Angeles
MILLER, Jason	6-1	195	L	Edmonton, Alta.	3/1/71	Utica-New Jersey
NICHOLLS, Bernie	6-0	185	R	Haliburton, Ont.	6/24/61	Edmonton-New Jersey
OJANEN, Janne	6-2	200	L	Tampere, Finland	4/9/68	New Jersey-Cincinnati
OLIWA, Krzysztof	6-5	220	R	Tychy, Poland	4/12/73	Welland
PEDERSON, Denis	6-2	190	R	Prince Albert, Sask.	9/10/75	Prince Albert
PELLERIN, Scott	5-11	180	L	Shediac, N.B.	1/9/70	Utica-New Jersey
PELUSO, Mike	6-4	200	L	Pengilly, MN	11/8/65	Ottawa
PROVENCHER, Jimmy	6-3	200	R	Kitchener, Ont.	3/22/75	St. Jean
REGNIER, Curt	6-2	220	L	Prince Albert, Sask.	1/24/72	Utica
RHEAUME, Pascal	6-1	185	L	Quebec, Que.	6/21/73	Sherbrooke
RICHER, Stephane	6-2	215	R	Ripon, Que.	6/7/66	New Jersey
RIEHL, Kevin	5-10	180	L	Leader, Sask.	3/11/71	Birm.-Cinn.-Utica
ROLSTON, Brian	6-2	185	L	Flint, MI	2/21/73	Lake Superior State
SEMAK, Alexander	5-10	180	L	Ufa, USSR	2/11/66	New Jersey
SULLIVAN, Brian	6-4	195	R	S. Windsor, CT	4/23/69	Utica-New Jersey
TOMS, Jeff	6-3	180	L	Swift Current, Sask.	6/4/74	Sault Ste. Marie
YELLE, Stephane	6-1	160	L	Ottawa, Ont.	5/9/74	Oshawa
ZELEPUKIN, Valeri	5-11	190	L	Voskresensk, USSR	9/17/68	New Jersey

DEFENSEMEN	HT	WT	S	Place of Birth	Date	1992-93 Club
ALBELIN, Tommy	6-1	190	L	Stockholm, Sweden	5/21/64	New Jersey
DANEYKO, Ken	6-0	210	L	Windsor, Ont.	4/17/64	New Jersey
DEAN, Kevin	6-2	195	L	Madison, WI	4/1/69	Cincinnati-Utica
DRIVER, Bruce	6-0	185	L	Toronto, Ont.	4/29/62	New Jersey
FETISOV, Viacheslav	6-1	215	L	Moscow, USSR	4/20/58	New Jersey
HULSE, Cale	6-3	210	R	Edmonton, Alta.	11/10/73	Portland
KINNEAR, Geordie	6-1	200	L	Simcoe, Ont.	7/9/73	Peterborough
MALKOC, Dean	6-3	200	L	Vancouver, B.C.	1/26/70	Utica
MODRY, Jaroslav	6-2	195	L	Ceske Budejovice, Czech.	2/27/71	Utica
NELSON, Chris	6-2	190	R	Philadelphia, PA	2/12/69	Utica-Cincinnati
NIEDERMAYER, Scott	6-0	200	L	Edmonton, Alta.	8/31/73	New Jersey
RUCHTY, Matt	6-1	210	L	Kitchener, Ont.	11/27/69	Utica
SEVERYN, Brent	6-2	210	L	Vegreville, Alta.	2/22/66	Utica
SMITH, Jason	6-3	185	R	Calgary, Alta.	11/2/73	Regina
STEVENS, Scott	6-2	210	L	Kitchener, Ont.	4/1/64	New Jersey

GOALTENDERS	HT	WT	C	Place of Birth	Date	1992-93 Club
BRODEUR, Martin	6-1	205	L	Montreal, Que.	5/6/72	Utica
DUNHAM, Mike	6-3	185	L	Johnson City, NY	6/1/72	U. of Maine
ERICKSON, Chad	5-10	180	R	Minneapolis, MN	8/21/70	Utica-Cinn.-Birm.
SCHWAB, Corey	6-0	180	L	N. Battleford, Sask.	11/4/70	Utica-Cincinnati
SIDORKIEWICZ, Peter	5-9	180	L	Dabrowa Bial., Pol.	6/29/63	Ottawa
TERRERI, Chris	5-8	160	L	Providence, RI	11/15/64	New Jersey

1992-93 Scoring

Regular Season

Pos	#	Player	Team	GP	G	A	Pts	+/-	PIM	PP	SH	GW	GT	S	%
R	22	Claude Lemieux	N.J.	77	30	51	81	3	155	13	0	3	2	311	9.6
C	20	Alexander Semak	N.J.	82	37	42	79	24	70	4	1	6	1	217	17.1
R	44	Stephane Richer	N.J.	78	38	35	73	1-	44	7	1	7	1	286	13.3
L	25	Valeri Zelepukin	N.J.	78	23	41	64	19	70	5	1	2	0	174	13.2
C	19	Bernie Nicholls	EDM	46	8	32	40	16-	40	4	0	1	0	86	9.3
			N.J.	23	5	15	20	3	40	1	0	0	0	46	10.9
			TOTAL	69	13	47	60	13-	80	5	0	1	0	132	9.8
D	4	Scott Stevens	N.J.	81	12	45	57	14	120	8	0	1	0	146	8.2
D	23	Bruce Driver	N.J.	83	14	40	54	10-	66	6	0	0	0	177	7.9
R	15	John MacLean	N.J.	80	24	24	48	6-	102	7	1	3	0	195	12.3
C	26	Peter Stastny	N.J.	62	17	23	40	5-	22	7	0	3	0	106	16.0
D	27*	Scott Niedermayer	N.J.	80	11	29	40	8	47	5	0	1	0	131	8.4
L	16	Bobby Holik	N.J.	61	20	19	39	6-	76	7	0	4	0	180	11.1
R	12*	Bill Guerin	N.J.	65	14	20	34	14	63	0	0	2	0	123	11.4
D	2	Viacheslav Fetisov	N.J.	76	4	23	27	7	158	1	1	0	0	63	6.3
R	21	Randy McKay	N.J.	73	11	11	22	0	206	1	0	2	0	94	11.7
R	18*	Scott Pellerin	N.J.	45	10	11	21	1-	41	1	2	0	0	60	16.7
L	9	Tom Chorske	N.J.	50	7	12	19	1-	25	0	1	0	1	63	11.1
D	7	Alexei Kasatonov	N.J.	64	3	14	17	4	57	0	0	0	0	63	4.8
R	11	Dave Barr	N.J.	62	6	8	14	1	61	0	1	1	0	41	14.6
C	34	Janne Ojanen	N.J.	31	4	9	13	2-	14	1	0	1	0	44	9.1
D	3	Ken Daneyko	N.J.	84	2	11	13	4	236	0	0	0	0	71	2.8
L	8	Troy Mallette	N.J.	34	4	3	7	3	56	0	0	0	0	19	21.1
D	6	Tommy Albelin	N.J.	36	1	5	6	0	14	1	0	1	0	33	3.0
R	24	Doug Brown	N.J.	15	0	5	5	3	2	0	0	0	0	17	.0
R	14	Ben Hankinson	N.J.	4	2	1	3	2	9	0	0	0	0	3	66.7
L	28	Claude Vilgrain	N.J.	4	0	2	2	3-	0	0	0	0	0	2	.0
C	10*	Jarrod Skalde	N.J.	11	0	2	2	3-	4	0	0	0	0	11	.0
R	28*	Brian Sullivan	N.J.	2	0	1	1	0	2	0	0	0	0	2	.0
G	1	Craig Billington	N.J.	42	0	1	1	0	8	0	0	0	0	0	.0
C	28*	Jim Dowd	N.J.	1	0	0	0	1-	0	0	0	0	0	1	.0
C	17*	Jason Miller	N.J.	2	0	0	0	1-	0	0	0	0	0	1	.0
R	18*	David Emma	N.J.	2	0	0	0	1-	0	0	0	0	0	2	.0
D	5	Myles O'Connor	N.J.	7	0	0	0	4-	9	0	0	0	0	4	.0
G	31	Chris Terreri	N.J.	48	0	0	0	0	6	0	0	0	0	0	.0

Goaltending

No.	Goaltender	GPI	Mins	Avg	W	L	T	EN	SO	GA	SA	S%
31	Chris Terreri	48	2672	3.39	19	21	3	2	2	151	1324	.886
1	Craig Billington	42	2389	3.67	21	16	4	2	2	146	1178	.876
	Totals	84	5080	3.53	40	37	7	2	4	299	2504	.881

Playoffs

Pos	#	Player	Team	GP	G	A	Pts	+/-	PIM	PP	SH	GW	GT	S	%
R	44	Stephane Richer	N.J.	5	2	2	4	4-	2	1	0	0	0	13	15.4
D	4	Scott Stevens	N.J.	5	2	2	4	2-	10	1	0	0	0	21	9.5
D	23	Bruce Driver	N.J.	5	1	3	4	2-	4	0	1	0	0	19	5.3
D	27*	Scott Niedermayer	N.J.	5	0	3	3	3-	2	0	0	0	0	11	.0
D	6	Tommy Albelin	N.J.	5	2	0	2	1-	0	1	0	1	0	9	22.2
R	22	Claude Lemieux	N.J.	5	2	0	2	3-	19	1	0	0	0	15	13.3
L	16	Bobby Holik	N.J.	5	1	1	2	1-	6	0	0	0	0	10	10.0
R	12*	Bill Guerin	N.J.	5	1	1	2	2-	4	0	0	1	0	3	33.3
C	20	Alexander Semak	N.J.	5	1	1	2	3-	0	0	0	0	0	10	10.0
D	2	Viacheslav Fetisov	N.J.	5	0	2	2	3-	4	0	0	0	0	2	.0
C	26	Peter Stastny	N.J.	5	0	2	2	1-	0	0	0	0	0	5	.0
L	25	Valeri Zelepukin	N.J.	5	0	2	2	1-	0	0	0	0	0	7	.0
R	11	Dave Barr	N.J.	5	1	0	1	2-	6	0	0	0	0	4	25.0
R	15	John MacLean	N.J.	5	0	1	1	5-	10	0	0	0	0	9	.0
L	9	Tom Chorske	N.J.	1	0	0	0	0	0	0	0	0	0	1	.0
G	1	Craig Billington	N.J.	2	0	0	0	0	0	0	0	0	0	0	.0
D	7	Alexei Kasatonov	N.J.	4	0	0	0	0	0	0	0	0	0	7	.0
G	31	Chris Terreri	N.J.	4	0	0	0	0	0	0	0	0	0	0	.0
D	3	Ken Daneyko	N.J.	5	0	0	0	1-	8	0	0	0	0	4	.0
R	21	Randy McKay	N.J.	5	0	0	0	1-	16	0	0	0	0	1	.0
C	19	Bernie Nicholls	N.J.	5	0	0	0	5-	4	0	0	0	0	3	.0

Goaltending

No.	Goaltender	GPI	Mins	Avg	W	L	EN	SO	GA	SA	S%
1	Craig Billington	2	78	3.85	0	1	0	0	5	39	.872
31	Chris Terreri	4	219	4.66	1	3	1	0	17	118	.856
	Totals	5	300	4.60	1	4	1	0	23	158	.854

General Managers' History

(Kansas City) Sidney Abel, 1974-75 to 1975-76; (Colorado) Ray Miron, 1976-77 to 1980-81; Billy MacMillan, 1981-82 to 1982-83; Billy MacMillan and Max McNab, 1983-84; Max McNab 1984-85 to 1986-87; Lou Lamoriello, 1987-88 to date.

Coaching History

(Kansas City) Bep Guidolin, 1974-75; Bep Guidolin, Sid Abel, and Eddie Bush, 1975-76; (Colorado) John Wilson, 1976-77; Pat Kelly, 1977-78; Pat Kelly, Aldo Guidolin, 1978-79; Don Cherry, 1979-80; Bill MacMillan, 1980-81; Bert Marshall and Marshall Johnston, 1981-82; (New Jersey) Bill MacMillan, 1982-83; Bill MacMillan and Tom McVie, 1983-84; Doug Carpenter, 1984-85 to 1986-87; Doug Carpenter and Jim Schoenfeld, 1987-88; Jim Schoenfeld, 1988-89; Jim Schoenfeld and John Cunniff, 1989-90; John Cunniff and Tom McVie, 1990-91; Tom McVie, 1991-92; Herb Brooks, 1992-93; Jacques Lemaire, 1993-94.

Captains' History

Simon Nolet, 1974-75 to 1976-77; Wilf Paiement, 1977-78; Gary Croteau, 1978-79; Mike Christie, Rene Robert, Lanny McDonald, 1979-80; Lanny McDonald, 1980-81, Lanny McDonald, Rob Ramage, 1981-82; Don Lever, 1982-83; Don Lever, Mel Bridgman, 1983-84; Mel Bridgman 1984-85, 1985-86; Kirk Muller, 1987-88 to 1990-91; Bruce Driver, 1991-92; Scott Stevens, 1992-93 to date.

Club Records

Team

(Figures in brackets for season records are games played; records for fewest points, wins, ties, losses, goals, goals against are for 70 or more games)

Most Points	87	1991-92 (80)
		1992-93 (84)
Most Wins	40	1992-93 (84)
Most Ties	21	1977-78 (80)
Most Losses	56	1983-84 (80)
		1975-76 (80)
Most Goals	308	1992-93 (84)
Most Goals Against	374	1985-86 (80)
Fewest Points	*36	1975-76 (80)
	41	1983-84 (80)
Fewest Wins	*12	1975-76 (80)
	17	1982-83 (80)
		1983-84 (80)
Fewest Ties	3	1985-86 (80)
Fewest Losses	31	1991-92 (80)
Fewest Goals	*184	1974-75 (80)
	230	1982-83 (80)
Fewest Goals Against	259	1991-92 (80)

Longest Winning Streak

Over-all	6	Feb. 8-Feb. 18/92
Home	8	Oct. 9-Nov. 7/87
Away	4	Oct. 5-23/89 & Dec. 31/91-Jan. 31/92

Longest Undefeated Streak

Over-all	8	Mar. 20-Apr. 3/88 (7 wins, 1 tie) Dec. 15-30/90 (3 wins, 5 ties)
Home	9	Oct. 9-Nov. 12/87 (8 wins, 1 tie) Nov. 17-Dec. 29/90 (5 wins, 4 ties)
Away	6	Jan. 20-Feb. 9/89 (3 wins, 3 ties) Mar. 12-Apr. 3/88 (5 wins, 1 tie)

Longest Losing Streak

Over-all	*14	Dec. 30/75-Jan. 29/76

	10	Oct. 14-Nov. 4/83
Home	9	Dec. 22/85-Feb. 6/86
Away	12	Oct. 19/83-Dec. 1/83

Longest Winless Streak

Over-all	*27	Feb. 12-Apr. 4/76 (21 losses, 6 ties)
	18	Oct. 20-Nov. 26/82 (14 losses 4 ties)
Home	*14	Feb. 12-Mar. 30/76 (10 losses, 4 ties) Feb. 4-Mar. 31/79 (12 losses, 2 ties)
	9	Dec. 22/85-Feb. 6/86 (9 losses)
Away	*32	Nov. 12/77-Mar. 15/78 (22 losses, 10 ties)
	14	Dec. 26/82-Mar. 5/83 (13 losses, 1 tie)

Most Shutouts, Season	4	1992-93 (84)
Most PIM, Season	2,494	1988-89 (80)
Most Goals, Game	9	Seven times.

Individual

Most Seasons	9	Aaron Broten, Ken Daneyko, John MacLean, Bruce Driver
Most Games	641	Aaron Broten
Most Goals, Career	241	John MacLean
Most Assists, Career	335	Kirk Muller
Most Points, Career	520	Kirk Muller (185 goals, 335 assists)
Most PIM, Career	1,706	Ken Daneyko
Most Shutouts, Career	4	Sean Burke, Chris Terreri, Craig Billington
Longest Consecutive Games Streak	321	Kirk Muller (Apr. 5/87-Mar. 31/91)
Most Goals, Season	46	Pat Verbeek (1987-88)
Most Assists, Season	57	Aaron Broten, Kirk Muller (1987-88)
Most Points, Season	94	Kirk Muller (1987-88) (37 goals, 57 assists)

Most PIM, Season	283	Ken Daneyko (1988-89)
Most Points, Defenseman Season	66	Tom Kurvers (1988-89) (16 goals, 50 assists)
Most Points, Center Season	94	Kirk Muller (1987-88) (37 goals, 57 assists)
Most Points, Right Wing, Season	*87	Wilf Paiement (1977-78) (31 goals, 56 assists)
	87	John MacLean (1988-89) (42 goals, 45 assists)
Most Points, Left Wing, Season	86	Kirk Muller (1989-90) (30 goals, 56 assists)
Most Points, Rookie, Season	63	Kevin Todd (1991-92) (21 goals, 42 assists)
Most Shutouts, Season	3	Sean Burke (1988-89)
Most Goals, Game	4	Bob MacMillan (Jan. 8/82) Pat Verbeek (Feb. 28/88)
Most Assists, Game	5	Kirk Muller (Mar. 25/87) Greg Adams (Oct. 10/86) Tom Kurvers (Feb. 13/89)
Most Points, Game	6	Kirk Muller (Nov. 29/86) (3 goals, 3 assists)

* Records include Kansas City Scouts and Colorado Rockies from 1974-75 through 1981-82

All-time Record vs. Other Clubs

Regular Season

			At Home						On Road						Total					
	GP	W	L	T	GF	GA	PTS	GP	W	L	T	GF	GA	PTS	GP	W	L	T	GF	GA	PTS
Boston	31	5	18	8	84	118	18	34	9	22	3	107	151	21	65	14	40	11	191	269	39
Buffalo	33	7	19	7	104	135	21	32	4	24	4	94	155	12	65	11	43	11	198	290	33
Calgary	36	10	23	3	103	141	23	35	4	27	4	91	170	12	71	14	50	7	194	311	35
Chicago	37	15	14	8	112	113	38	38	9	23	6	111	162	24	75	24	37	14	223	275	62
Detroit	32	15	9	8	115	91	38	31	11	18	2	107	136	24	63	26	27	10	222	227	62
Edmonton	24	10	12	2	83	86	22	24	7	13	4	94	121	18	48	17	25	6	177	207	40
Hartford	23	11	10	2	90	94	24	22	7	11	4	71	83	18	45	18	21	6	161	177	42
Los Angeles	34	15	14	5	118	125	35	34	3	25	6	105	186	12	68	18	39	11	223	311	47
Minnesota	36	17	16	3	119	115	37	36	8	22	6	94	148	22	72	25	38	9	213	263	59
Montreal	32	9	23	0	89	155	18	32	5	23	4	82	136	14	64	14	46	4	171	291	32
NY Islanders	57	17	31	9	183	234	43	56	5	43	8	156	273	18	113	22	74	17	339	507	61
NY Rangers	57	25	28	4	202	223	54	56	15	33	8	180	249	38	113	40	61	12	382	472	92
Ottawa	2	2	0	0	11	6	4	2	0	1	1	4	6	1	4	2	1	1	15	12	5
Philadelphia	55	26	25	4	200	217	56	57	10	40	7	136	248	27	112	36	65	11	336	465	83
Pittsburgh	55	27	19	9	212	193	63	55	19	33	3	200	237	41	110	46	52	12	412	430	104
Quebec	23	11	11	1	100	89	23	22	8	12	2	73	95	18	45	19	23	3	173	184	41
St. Louis	38	16	15	7	123	113	39	37	8	25	4	112	166	20	75	24	40	11	235	279	59
San Jose	3	3	0	0	18	3	6	2	1	1	0	8	4	2	5	4	1	0	26	7	8
Tampa Bay	1	1	0	0	9	3	2	1	1	0	0	2	0	2	2	2	0	0	11	3	4
Toronto	31	12	10	9	117	101	33	32	6	23	3	106	149	15	63	18	33	12	223	250	48
Vancouver	40	17	17	6	123	134	40	40	6	23	11	115	154	23	80	23	40	17	238	288	63
Washington	54	22	26	6	174	174	50	54	12	39	3	161	247	27	108	34	65	9	335	421	77
Winnipeg	20	5	9	6	59	66	16	22	3	16	3	57	92	9	42	8	25	9	116	158	25
Defunct Clubs	8	4	2	2	25	19	10	8	2	3	3	19	27	7	16	6	5	5	44	46	17
Totals	762	302	351	109	2573	2748	713	762	163	500	99	2285	3395	425	1524	465	851	208	4858	6143	1138

Playoffs

	Series	W	L	GP	W	L	T	GF	GA	Last Mtg.	Round	Result
Boston	1	0	1	7	3	4	0	19	30	1988	CF	L 3-4
NY Islanders	1	1	0	6	4	2	0	23	18	1988	DSF	W 4-2
NY Rangers	1	0	1	7	3	4	0	25	28	1992	DSF	L 3-4
Philadelphia	1	0	1	2	0	2	0	3	6	1978	PR	L 0-2
Pittsburgh	2	0	2	12	4	8	0	30	48	1993	DSF	L 1-4
Washington	2	1	1	13	6	7	0	43	44	1990	DSF	L 2-4
Totals	8	2	6	47	20	27	0	143	174			

Playoff Results 1993-89

Year	Round	Opponent	Result	GF	GA
1993	DSF	Pittsburgh	L 1-4	13	23
1992	DSF	NY Rangers	L 3-4	25	28
1991	DSF	Pittsburgh	L 3-4	17	15
1990	DSF	Washington	L 2-4	18	21

Abbreviations: Round: F – Final;
CF – conference final; **DF** – division final;
DSF – division semi-final; **SF** – semi-final;
QF – quarter-final; **PR** – preliminary round.
GA – goals against; **GF** – goals for.

1992-93 Results

		Home				Away	
Oct.	6	NY Islanders	4-3	Oct.	9	Philadelphia	4-6
	10	NY Rangers	4-2		14	NY Rangers	1-6
	12	Washington	4-2		22	Chicago	6-5
	17	Philadelphia	2-0		28	Hartford	4-3
	20	Hartford	4-5		31	NY Islanders	5-3
	24	Pittsburgh	3-4	Nov.	5	Los Angeles	2-5
	30	NY Islanders	1-4		7	San Jose	6-1
Nov.	11	Montreal	3-8		14	Washington	4-3
	13	Washington	3-0		21	Pittsburgh	0-2
	18	Buffalo	3-2		25	Ottawa	1-3
	20	Pittsburgh	1-4		28	Quebec	6-3
Dec.	1	Toronto	8-3	Dec.	3	Ottawa	3-3
	5	Boston*	2-4		6	Buffalo	7-3
	9	Washington	2-6		12	Pittsburgh	5-6
	11	Pittsburgh	2-1		15	Winnipeg	3-4
	21	NY Rangers	0-3		18	Tampa Bay	2-0
	27	Hartford	6-2		23	NY Rangers	5-4
Jan.	2	Winnipeg	2-2		29	Quebec	1-4
	6	Minnesota	5-1	Jan.	1	Washington*	2-9
	8	Ottawa	6-4		4	NY Rangers	3-3
	12	Vancouver	3-2		9	Boston	6-2
	14	Los Angeles	7-1		20	Montreal	2-3
	16	NY Islanders	3-5		23	Boston	5-7
	22	Montreal	6-2		26	NY Islanders	2-8
Feb.	3	Calgary	4-5		28	Minnesota	2-4
	8	NY Rangers	5-4		30	St. Louis	2-2
	13	Philadelphia*	6-4	Feb.	7	Detroit	1-3
	17	St. Louis	4-3		14	Philadelphia*	5-2
	19	Buffalo	3-3		23	Pittsburgh	3-1
	21	Quebec	3-6		25	Philadelphia	2-6
	27	Ottawa*	5-2	Mar.	3	Hartford	7-4
	28	Detroit	6-3		9	Vancouver	2-7
Mar.	5	Chicago	1-1		12	Edmonton	4-6
	7	Philadelphia	7-3		13	Calgary	3-4
	18	Edmonton	5-1		16	Boston	1-3
	20	Quebec*	1-5		21	Philadelphia	3-4
	23	Tampa Bay	9-3		25	Pittsburgh	3-4
	29	San Jose	5-0		27	Washington*	5-2
Apr.	4	Pittsburgh	2-5		31	Buffalo	2-5
	7	NY Rangers	5-2	Apr.	3	Toronto	0-1
	11	NY Islanders	4-5		10	Washington	5-3
	14	Pittsburgh	6-6		16	NY Islanders	4-8

*Denotes afternoon game

Entry Draft
Selections 1993-79

1993
Pick
13 Denis Pederson
32 Jay Pandolfo
39 Brendan Morrison
65 Krzysztof Oliwa
110 John Guirestante
143 Steve Brule
169 Nikolai Zavarukhin
195 Thomas Cullen
221 Judd Lambert
247 Jimmy Provencher
273 Michael Legg

1992
Pick
18 Jason Smith
42 Sergei Brylin
66 Cale Hulse
90 Vitali Tomilin
94 Scott McCabe
114 Ryan Black
138 Daniel Trebil
162 Geordie Kinnear
186 Stephane Yelle
210 Jeff Toms
234 Heath Weenk
258 Vladislav Yakovenko

1991
Pick
3 Scott Niedermayer
11 Brian Rolston
33 Donevan Hextall
55 Fredrik Lindqvist
77 Bradley Willner
121 Curt Regnier
143 David Craievich
165 Paul Wolanski
187 Daniel Reimann
231 Kevin Riehl
253 Jason Hehr

1990
Pick
20 Martin Brodeur
24 David Harlock
29 Chris Gotziaman
53 Michael Dunham
56 Brad Bombardir
64 Mike Bodnarchuk
95 Dean Malkoc
104 Petr Kuchyna
116 Lubomir Kolnik
137 Chris McAlpine
179 Jaroslav Modry
200 Corey Schwab
221 Valeri Zelepukin
242 Todd Reirden

1989
Pick
5 Bill Guerin
18 Jason Miller
26 Jarrod Skalde
47 Scott Pellerin
89 Mike Heinke
110 David Emma
152 Sergei Starikov
173 Andre Faust
215 Jason Simon
236 Peter Larsson

1988
Pick
12 Corey Foster
23 Jeff Christian
54 Zdeno Ciger
65 Matt Ruchty
75 Scott Luik
96 Chris Nelson
117 Chad Johnson
138 Chad Erickson
159 Bryan Lafort
180 Sergei Svetlov
201 Bob Woods
207 Alexander Semak
222 Charles Hughes
243 Michael Pohl

1987
Pick
2 Brendan Shanahan
23 Rickard Persson
65 Brian Sullivan
86 Kevin Dean
107 Ben Hankinson
128 Tom Neziol
149 Jim Dowd
170 John Blessman
191 Peter Fry
212 Alain Charland

1986
Pick
3 Neil Brady
24 Todd Copeland
45 Janne Ojanen
62 Marc Laniel
66 Anders Carlsson
108 Troy Crowder
129 Kevin Todd
150 Ryan Pardoski
171 Scott McCormack
192 Frederic Chabot
213 John Andersen
236 Doug Kirton

1985
Pick
3 Craig Wolanin
24 Sean Burke
32 Eric Weinrich
45 Myles O'Connor
66 Gregg Polak
108 Bill McMillan
129 Kevin Schrader
150 Ed Krayer
171 Jamie Huscroft
192 Terry Shold
213 Jamie McKinley
234 David Williams

1984
Pick
2 Kirk Muller
23 Craig Billington
44 Neil Davey
74 Paul Ysebaert
86 Jon Morris
107 Kirk McLean
128 Ian Ferguson
149 Vladimir Kames
170 Mike Roth
190 Mike Peluso
211 Jarkko Piiparinen
231 Chris Kiene

1983
Pick
6 John MacLean
24 Shawn Evans
85 Chris Terreri
105 Gordon Mark
125 Greg Evtushevski
145 Viacheslav Fetisov
165 Jay Octeau
185 Alexander Chernykh
205 Allan Stewart
225 Alexei Kasatonov

1982
Pick
8 Rocky Trottier
18 Ken Daneyko
43 Pat Verbeek
54 Dave Kasper
5 Scott Brydges
106 Mike Moher
127 Paul Fulcher
148 John Hutchings
169 Alan Hepple
190 Brent Shaw
207 Tony Gilliard
211 Scott Fusco
232 Dan Dorion

1981
Pick
5 Joe Cirella
26 Rich Chernomaz
48 Uli Hiemer
66 Gus Greco
87 Doug Speck
108 Bruce Driver
129 Jeff Larmer
150 Tony Arima
171 Tim Army
192 John Johannson

1980
Pick
19 Paul Gagne
22 Joe Ward
64 Rick LaFerriere
85 Ed Cooper
106 Aaron Broten
127 Dan Fascinato
148 Andre Hidi
169 Shawn MacKenzie
190 Bob Jansch

1979
Pick
1 Rob Ramage
64 Steve Peters
85 Gary Dillon
106 Bob Attwell

Coach

LEMAIRE, JACQUES GERARD
Coach, New Jersey Devils. Born in LaSalle, Quebec, September 7, 1945.

Jacques Lemaire became the eighth coach of the New Jersey Devils on June 28, 1993, returning behind the bench of an NHL team for the first time since the 1984-85 season. Lemaire, who served as the Assistant to the Managing Director of the Montreal Canadiens for seven years, coached the Canadiens from February 24, 1984 to the end of the 1984-85 season. During his successful term as the Habs coach, he led the team to the Conference Finals in 1984 and to a first place finish in the Adams Division in 1984-85.

A member of the Hockey Hall of Fame as a player, Lemaire coached Sierre of the Swiss League and Longueuil of the Quebec Junior League before joining the Canadiens organization in 1983.

Coaching Record

Season	Team	Games	W	L	T	%	Games	W	L	%
			Regular Season					Playoffs		
1979-80	Sierre (SWISS)					UNAVAILABLE				
1980-81	Sierre (SWISS)					UNAVAILABLE				
1982-83	Longueuil (QMJHL)	70	37	29	4	.557	15	9	6	.600
1983-84	Montreal (NHL)	17	7	10	0	.412	45	9	6	.600
1984-85	Montreal (NHL)	80	41	27	12	.588	12	6	6	.500
	NHL Totals	97	48	37	12	.557	27	15	12	.556

Club Directory

Meadowlands Arena
P.O. Box 504
East Rutherford, NJ 07073
Phone **201/935-6050**
GM FAX 201/935-6898
FAX 201/935-2127
Capacity: 19,040

Chairman	John J. McMullen
President & General Manager	Louis A. Lamoriello
Executive Vice President	Max McNab
Senior Vice President, Finance	Chris Modrzynski
Vice President, Merchandising & Licensing	James Bell
Vice President, Community & Corporate Development	Jerry Dailey
Vice President, Marketing & Sales	Mike McCall
Vice President, Operations & Human Resources	Peter McMullen
Vice President, Administration	Mike O'Neil
Administrative Assistants to the President/GM	Marie Carnevale, Charlotte Smaldone

Hockey Club Personnel

Head Coach	Jacques Lemaire
Assistant Coach	Larry Robinson
Goaltending Coach	Jacques Caron
Head Coach, Albany Devils	Robbie Ftorek
Technological Specialist	Dennis Gendron
Strength & Conditioning Coach	
Assistant Director of Scouting	David Conte
Scouting Staff	Claude Carrier, Marcel Pronovost, Milt Fisher, Ed Thomlinson, Dan Labraaten, Glen Dirk, Les Widdifield, Joe Mahoney, Fernie Flaman
Pro Scouting Staff	John Cunniff, Bob Hoffmeyer
Scouting Staff Assistant	Shannon Coiley
Medical Trainer	Ted Schuch
Equipment Manager	Dave Nichols
Assistant Equipment Managers	Paul Boyer, Alex Abasto
Massage Therapist	Bob Huddleston
Team Cardiologist	Dr. Joseph Niznik
Team Dentist	Dr. H. Hugh Gardy
Team Internist	Dr. Richard Commentucci
Team Orthopedists	Dr. Barry Fisher, Dr. Len Jaffe
Exercise Physiologist	Dr. Garret Caffrey
Physical Therapist	David Feniger

Communications Department

Director, Public & Media Relations	David Freed
Senior Director, Broadcast Operations	TBA
Associate Director, Media Relations	Mike Levine
Manager, Community Relations	Michelle Galeano
Receptionist	Jelsa Belotta
Staff Assistant	Richard Kaht

Finance Department

Director of Finance	Scott Struble
Staff Accountants	Richard Rowbotham, Chuck Meyers
Secretary	Eileen Musikant

Marketing Department

Director of Promotions and Sales	Dave Recher
Director, Ticket Sales	Ken Ferriter
Season Sales Managers	Holly Meyer, Dan Sarro, Stan Smith, Frank Tedesco
Group Sales Managers	Neil Desormeaux, John Glynn, Matt Zanelli
Secretary	Karen Lynch

Ticket Department

Senior Director, Ticket Operations	Terry Farmer
Assistant Director, Ticket Operations	Scott Tanfield

Television Outlet	SportsChannel
Broadcasters	Mike Emrick, Play-by-Play; Peter McNab, Color
Radio Outlet	WABC (770 AM)
Broadcasters	TBA, Play-by-Play; Sherry Ross, Color
Team Photographer	Jim Turner
Video Consultant	Mitch Kaufman
Seating Capacity	19,040
Dimensions of Rink	200 feet by 85 feet
Club Colors	Red, Black and White

General Manager

LAMORIELLO, LOU
President and General Manager, New Jersey Devils.
Born in Providence, Rhode Island, October 21, 1942.

Lou Lamoriello's life-long dedication to the game of hockey was rewarded in 1992 when he was named as a recipient of the Lester Patrick Trophy for outstanding service to hockey in the United States. Lamoriello is entering his seventh season as president and general manager of the Devils following a more than 20-year association with Providence College as a player, coach and administrator. A member of the varsity hockey Friars during his undergraduate days, he became an assistant coach with the college club after graduating in 1963. Lamoriello was later named head coach and in the ensuing 15 years, led his teams to a 248-179-13 record, a .578 winning percentage and appearances in 10 post-season tournaments, including the 1983 NCAA Final Four. Lamoriello also served a five-year term as athletic director at Providence and was a co-founder of Hockey East, one of the strongest collegiate hockey conferences in the U.S. He remained as athletic director until he was hired as president of the Devils on April 30, 1987. He assumed the dual responsibility of general manager on September 10, 1987.

New York Islanders

1992-93 Results: 40w-37l-7t 87pts. Third, Patrick Division

Year-by-Year Record

Season	GP	Home W	L	T	Road W	L	T	Overall W	L	T	GF	GA	Pts.	Finished	Playoff Result
1992-93	84	20	19	3	20	18	4	40	37	7	335	297	87	3rd, Patrick Div.	Lost Conf. Championship
1991-92	80	20	15	5	14	20	6	34	35	11	291	299	79	5th, Patrick Div.	Out of Playoffs
1990-91	80	15	19	6	10	26	4	25	45	10	223	290	60	6th, Patrick Div.	Out of Playoffs
1989-90	80	15	17	8	16	21	3	31	38	11	281	288	73	4th, Patrick Div.	Lost Div. Semi-Final
1988-89	80	19	18	3	9	29	2	28	47	5	265	325	61	6th, Patrick Div.	Out of Playoffs
1987-88	80	24	10	6	15	21	4	39	31	10	308	267	88	1st, Patrick Div.	Lost Div. Semi-Final
1986-87	80	20	15	5	15	18	7	35	33	12	279	281	82	3rd, Patrick Div.	Lost Div. Final
1985-86	80	22	11	7	17	18	5	39	29	12	327	284	90	3rd, Patrick Div.	Lost Div. Semi-Final
1984-85	80	26	11	3	14	23	3	40	34	6	345	312	86	3rd, Patrick Div.	Lost Div. Final
1983-84	80	28	11	1	22	15	3	50	26	4	357	269	104	1st, Patrick Div.	Lost Final
1982-83	80	26	11	3	16	15	9	42	26	12	302	226	96	2nd, **Patrick Div.**	**Won Stanley Cup**
1981-82	80	33	3	4	21	13	6	54	16	10	385	250	118	1st, **Patrick Div.**	**Won Stanley Cup**
1980-81	80	23	6	11	25	12	3	48	18	14	355	260	110	1st, **Patrick Div.**	**Won Stanley Cup**
*1979-80	80	26	9	5	13	19	8	39	28	13	281	247	91	2nd, **Patrick Div.**	**Won Stanley Cup**
1978-79	80	31	3	6	20	12	8	51	15	14	358	214	116	1st, Patrick Div.	Lost Semi-Final
1977-78	80	29	3	8	19	14	7	48	17	15	334	210	111	1st, Patrick Div.	Lost Quarter-Final
1976-77	80	24	11	5	23	10	7	47	21	12	288	193	106	2nd, Patrick Div.	Lost Semi-Final
1975-76	80	24	8	8	18	13	9	42	21	17	297	190	101	2nd, Patrick Div.	Lost Semi-Final
1974-75	80	22	6	12	11	19	10	33	25	22	264	221	88	3rd, Patrick Div.	Lost Semi-Final
1973-74	78	13	17	9	6	24	9	19	41	18	182	247	56	8th, East Div.	Out of Playoffs
1972-73	78	10	25	4	2	35	2	12	60	6	170	347	30	8th, East Div.	Out of Playoffs

Schedule

Home			Away		
Oct.	Sat.	16 New Jersey	**Oct.**	Tues.	5 Calgary
	Tues.	19 Pittsburgh		Fri.	8 Edmonton
	Sat.	23 Ottawa		Sun.	10 Anaheim
	Tues.	26 Los Angeles		Tues.	12 Los Angeles
Nov.	Tues.	2 Vancouver		Thur.	21 Philadelphia
	Sat.	6 Hartford		Thur.	28 Florida
	Tues.	9 Winnipeg		Fri.	29 Tampa Bay
	Sat.	13 Boston	**Nov.**	Thur.	4 Chicago
	Sat.	27 NY Rangers*		Wed.	10 New Jersey
	Sun.	28 Detroit*		Wed.	17 Ottawa
	Tues.	30 Washington		Thur.	18 Montreal
Dec.	Fri.	3 Quebec			(at Hamilton)
	Tues.	7 Edmonton		Sun.	21 Philadelphia
	Sat.	11 Philadelphia		Wed.	24 Dallas
	Tues.	14 New Jersey	**Dec.**	Thur.	2 Boston
	Fri.	17 Toronto		Sun.	19 Pittsburgh
	Sun.	26 Buffalo		Wed.	22 Montreal
	Tues.	28 Anaheim		Wed.	29 Quebec
Jan.	Sat.	1 Hartford*	**Jan.**	Tues.	4 New Jersey
	Fri.	7 Calgary		Sat.	8 Hartford
	Fri.	14 Montreal		Mon.	10 Ottawa
	Sat.	15 Chicago		Wed.	19 Tampa Bay
	Mon.	17 Florida*		Wed.	26 Toronto
	Fri.	28 Boston		Sat.	29 Boston
Feb.	Tues.	1 San Jose	**Feb.**	Wed.	2 NY Rangers
	Tues.	8 Buffalo		Sat.	5 Quebec*
	Sat.	12 Florida		Sun.	6 Buffalo
	Tues.	15 Tampa Bay		Thur.	10 Pittsburgh
	Sat.	19 Ottawa		Fri.	18 Washington
	Mon.	21 Washington*		Thur.	24 Philadelphia
	Fri.	25 Philadelphia	**Mar.**	Fri.	4 NY Rangers
	Sun.	27 Quebec		Mon.	7 Winnipeg
Mar.	Tues.	1 St Louis		Wed.	9 Vancouver
	Sat.	5 NY Rangers		Thur.	10 San Jose
	Tues.	15 New Jersey		Sat.	12 St Louis
	Fri.	18 Buffalo		Thur.	17 Detroit
		(at Minnesota)		Sun.	27 Buffalo*
	Sun.	20 Pittsburgh		Tues.	29 Washington
	Tues.	22 Tampa Bay	**Apr.**	Sat.	2 Montreal
	Sat.	26 Florida*		Tues.	5 Washington
Apr.	Fri.	1 Montreal		Wed.	6 Hartford
	Fri.	8 Dallas		Wed.	13 Tampa Bay
	Sun.	10 NY Rangers*		Thur.	14 Florida

* Denotes afternoon game.

Home Starting Times:

Weeknights	7:35 p.m.
Saturdays and Sundays	7:05 p.m.
Matinees	1:05 p.m.

Franchise date: June 6, 1972

ATLANTIC DIVISION

22nd NHL Season

EASTERN CONFERENCE

Ray Ferraro was a post-season hero for the Islanders with 13 goals in 18 playoff games, including a pair of overtime winners.

1993-94 Player Personnel

FORWARDS	HT	WT	S	Place of Birth	Date	1992-93 Club
ARMSTRONG, Derek	5-11	180	R	Ottawa, Ont.	4/2/73	Sudbury
BERTUZZI, Todd	6-3	240	L	Sudbury, Ont.	2/2/75	Guelph
CHYZOWSKI, David	6-1	190	L	Edmonton, Alta.	7/11/71	NYI-Capital District
DALGARNO, Brad	6-3	215	R	Vancouver, B.C.	8/11/67	NYI-Capital District
DAY, Joe	5-11	180	L	Chicago, IL	5/11/68	Hartford-Springfield
DEULING, Jarrett	5-11	195	L	Vernon, B.C.	3/4/74	Kamloops
DOUCET, Wayne	6-2	203	L	Etobicoke, Ont.	6/19/70	Capital District
DUTHIE, Ryan	5-10	180	R	Red Deer, Alta.	9/2/74	Spokane
FERRARO, Ray	5-10	185	L	Trail, B.C.	8/23/64	NY Islanders
FLATLEY, Patrick	6-2	200	R	Toronto, Ont.	10/3/63	NY Islanders
GREEN, Travis	6-2	196	R	Castlegar, B.C.	12/20/70	Capital District-NYI
GRIEVE, Brent	6-1	205	L	Oshawa, Ont.	5/9/69	Capital District
HINKS, Rod	5-10	185	L	Etobicoke, Ont.	4/11/73	Sudbury
HOGUE, Benoit	5-10	190	L	Repentigny, Que.	10/28/66	NY Islanders
JUNKER, Steve	6-0	184	L	Castlegar, B.C.	6/26/72	Capital District-NYI
KING, Derek	6-1	210	L	Hamilton, Ont.	2/11/67	NY Islanders
LACROIX, Martin	5-11	155	R	Rosemere, Que.	1/4/70	Richmond-CDI
LAROCQUE, Stephane	6-1	214	R	Hull, Que.	7/24/74	Sherbrooke
LeBOUTILLIER, Peter	6-1	198	R	Minnedosa, Man.	1/11/75	Red Deer
LOISELLE, Claude	5-11	195	L	Ottawa, Ont.	5/29/63	NY Islanders
McINNIS, Marty	6-0	185	R	Hingham, MA	6/2/70	Capital District-NYI
MULLEN, Brian	5-10	180	L	New York, NY	3/16/62	NY Islanders
O'ROURKE, Steve	6-1	190	R	Calgary, Alta.	9/11/74	Tri-City
PALFFY, Zigmund	5-11	180	L	Skalia, Czech.	5/5/72	Dukla Trencin
PARADIS, Daniel	6-2	185	L	Jonquiere, Que.	11/22/72	Chicoutimi
PLANTE, Dan	5-11	198	R	Hayward, IL	10/5/71	Wisconsin
SCISSONS, Scott	6-1	200	L	Saskatoon, Sask.	10/29/71	Capital District-NYI
TAYLOR, Chris	6-0	190	L	Stratford, Ont.	3/6/72	Capital District
THOMAS, Steve	5-11	185	L	Stockport, U.K.	7/15/63	NY Islanders
TURGEON, Pierre	6-1	203	L	Rouyn, Que.	8/29/69	NY Islanders
VOLEK, David	6-0	190	L	Prague, Czech.	8/16/66	NY Islanders
VUKOTA, Mick	6-2	215	R	Saskatoon, Sask.	9/14/66	NY Islanders

DEFENSEMEN						
CHARLAND, Carl	5-11	180	L	Chicoutimi, Que.	5/13/75	Hull
CHEVELDAYOFF, Kevin	6-0	202	R	Saskatoon, Sask.	2/4/70	Capital District
CHYNOWETH, Dean	6-2	190	R	Calgary, Alta.	10/30/68	Capital District
KASPARAITIS, Darius	5-11	190	L	Elekternai, Latvia	10/16/72	NY Islanders
KRUPP, Uwe	6-6	235	R	Cologne, Germany	6/24/65	NY Islanders
KURVERS, Tom	6-0	205	L	Minneapolis, MN	9/14/62	NYI-Capital District
LACHANCE, Scott	6-2	197	L	Chariottesville, VA	10/22/72	NY Islanders
LEHTO, Joni	6-0	205	L	Turku, Finland	7/15/70	Capital District
LUONGO, Chris	6-0	180	R	Detroit, MI	3/17/67	Ottawa
MALAKHOV, Vladimir	6-5	210	L	Sverdlovsk, USSR	8/30/68	NY Islanders
McBEAN, Wayne	6-2	185	L	Calgary, Alta.	2/21/69	Capital District
McCABE, Bryan	6-1	200	L	St. Catharines, Ont.	6/8/75	Medicine Hat-Spokane
PILON, Richard	6-0	211	L	Saskatoon, Sask.	4/30/68	NY Islanders
VAN IMPE, Darren	6-0	195	L	Saskatoon, Sask.	5/18/73	Red Deer
VASKE, Dennis	6-2	210	L	Rockford, IL	10/11/67	NYI-Capital District
WIDMER, Jason	6-0	205	L	Calgary, Alta.	8/1/73	Lethbridge-CDI

GOALTENDERS	HT	WT	C	Place of Birth	Date	1992-93 Club
HEXTALL, Ron	6-3	192	L	Brandon, Man.	5/3/64	Quebec
HNILICKA, Milan	6-0	180	L	Kladno, Czech.	6/24/73	Swift Current
LORENZ, Danny	5-10	165	L	Murrayville, B.C.	12/12/69	NYI-Capital District
McLENNAN, Jamie	6-0	140	L	Edmonton, Alta.	6/30/71	Capital District

Defenceman Vladimir Malakhov led all Islander rookies in scoring during the 1992-93 campaign, collecting 52 points in 64 games.

1992-93 Scoring

Regular Season

Pos	#	Player	Team	GP	G	A	Pts	+/-	PIM	PP	SH	GW	GT	S	%
C	77	Pierre Turgeon	NYI	83	58	74	132	1-	26	24	0	10	2	301	19.3
L	32	Steve Thomas	NYI	79	37	50	87	3	111	12	0	7	0	264	14.0
L	27	Derek King	NYI	77	38	38	76	4-	47	21	0	7	0	201	18.9
C	33	Benoit Hogue	NYI	70	33	42	75	13	108	5	3	5	0	147	22.4
R	26	Patrick Flatley	NYI	80	13	47	60	5	63	1	2	1	0	139	9.4
D	23*	Vladimir Malakhov	NYI	64	14	38	52	14	59	7	0	0	0	178	7.9
D	8	Jeff Norton	NYI	66	12	38	50	3-	45	5	0	0	0	127	9.4
D	4	Uwe Krupp	NYI	80	9	29	38	6	67	2	0	2	0	116	7.8
D	28	Tom Kurvers	NYI	52	8	30	38	9	38	3	0	1	0	128	6.3
R	16	Brian Mullen	NYI	81	18	14	32	5	28	1	0	1	0	126	14.3
R	15	Brad Dalgarno	NYI	57	15	17	32	17	62	2	0	2	0	62	24.2
C	18*	Marty McInnis	NYI	56	10	20	30	7	24	0	1	0	0	60	16.7
C	20	Ray Ferraro	NYI	46	14	13	27	0	40	3	0	1	0	72	19.4
R	14	Tom Fitzgerald	NYI	77	9	18	27	2-	34	0	3	1	0	83	10.8
C	39*	Travis Green	NYI	61	7	18	25	4	43	1	0	0	0	115	6.1
D	7*	Scott Lachance	NYI	75	7	17	24	1-	67	0	1	2	0	62	11.3
L	25	Dave Volek	NYI	56	8	13	21	1-	34	2	0	1	0	118	6.8
D	11*	Darius Kasparaitis	NYI	79	4	17	21	15	166	0	0	0	0	92	4.3
C	10	Claude Loiselle	NYI	41	5	3	8	5-	90	0	0	0	0	41	12.2
R	17	Dan Marois	NYI	28	2	5	7	3-	35	0	0	0	0	41	4.9
R	12	Mick Vukota	NYI	74	2	5	7	3	216	0	0	0	0	37	5.4
D	37	Dennis Vaske	NYI	27	1	5	6	9	32	0	0	0	0	15	6.7
C	34*	Iain Fraser	NYI	7	2	2	4	1-	2	1	0	0	0	7	28.6
D	47	Richard Pilon	NYI	44	1	3	4	4-	164	0	0	0	0	20	5.0
L	24	Rich Kromm	NYI	1	1	2	3	3	0	0	0	0	0	2	50.0
D	36	Gary Nylund	NYI	22	1	1	2	2-	43	0	0	0	0	19	5.3
G	35	Glenn Healy	NYI	47	0	2	2	0	2	0	0	0	0	0	.0
G	30	Mark Fitzpatrick	NYI	39	0	1	1	0	2	0	0	0	0	0	.0
C	24*	Greg Parks	NYI	2	0	0	0	0	0	0	0	0	0	3	.0
L	38	Graeme Townshend	NYI	2	0	0	0	0	0	0	0	0	0	0	.0
G	1*	Danny Lorenz	NYI	4	0	0	0	0	0	0	0	0	0	0	.0

Goaltending

No.	Goaltender	GPI	Mins	Avg	W	L	T	EN	SO	GA	SA	S%
35	Glenn Healy	47	2655	3.30	22	20	2	6	1	146	1316	.889
30	Mark Fitzpatrick	39	2253	3.46	17	15	5	5	0	130	1066	.878
1	*Danny Lorenz	4	157	3.82	1	2	0	0	0	10	78	.872
	Totals	**84**	**5088**	**3.50**	**40**	**37**	**7**	**11**	**1**	**297**	**2471**	**.880**

Playoffs

Pos	#	Player	Team	GP	G	A	Pts	+/-	PIM	PP	SH	GW	GT	S	%
C	20	Ray Ferraro	NYI	18	13	7	20	5	18	4	1	2	2	47	27.7
L	32	Steve Thomas	NYI	18	9	8	17	1-	37	1	0	1	0	66	13.6
L	27	Derek King	NYI	18	3	11	14	3	14	0	0	1	0	48	6.3
C	77	Pierre Turgeon	NYI	11	6	7	13	2	0	1	0	0	0	45	13.3
C	33	Benoit Hogue	NYI	18	6	6	12	7	31	0	2	1	0	37	16.2
D	23*	Vladimir Malakhov	NYI	17	3	6	9	3-	12	1	0	0	0	53	5.7
R	26	Patrick Flatley	NYI	15	2	7	9	1	12	0	0	1	0	29	6.9
R	16	Brian Mullen	NYI	18	3	4	7	4-	2	0	0	1	1	30	10.0
R	14	Tom Fitzgerald	NYI	18	2	5	7	2	18	0	2	0	0	21	9.5
D	4	Uwe Krupp	NYI	18	1	5	6	2	12	0	0	0	0	28	3.6
D	37	Dennis Vaske	NYI	18	0	6	6	3-	14	0	0	0	0	23	.0
L	25	Dave Volek	NYI	10	4	1	5	1	2	0	0	1	1	21	19.0
D	11*	Darius Kasparaitis	NYI	18	0	5	5	2	31	0	0	0	0	24	.0
C	39*	Travis Green	NYI	12	3	1	4	3-	6	0	0	1	0	27	11.1
R	15	Brad Dalgarno	NYI	18	2	2	4	1	14	0	0	0	0	22	9.1
G	35	Glenn Healy	NYI	18	0	3	3	0	0	0	0	0	0	0	.0
C	10	Claude Loiselle	NYI	18	0	3	3	8-	10	0	0	0	0	19	.0
D	8	Jeff Norton	NYI	10	1	1	2	5-	4	1	0	0	0	19	5.3
D	28	Tom Kurvers	NYI	12	0	2	2	0	6	0	0	0	0	21	.0
C	18*	Marty McInnis	NYI	3	0	1	1	1-	0	0	0	0	0	1	.0
L	17*	Steve Junker	NYI	3	0	1	1	1	0	0	0	0	0	1	.0
C	38*	Scott Scissons	NYI	1	0	1	1	0	0	0	0	0	0	0	.0
C	24*	Greg Parks	NYI	2	0	0	0	0	0	0	0	0	0	1	.0
G	30	Mark Fitzpatrick	NYI	3	0	0	0	0	2	0	0	0	0	0	.0
D	47	Richard Pilon	NYI	15	0	0	0	5	50	0	0	0	0	7	.0
R	12	Mick Vukota	NYI	5	0	0	0	4-	16	0	0	0	0	4	.0

Goaltending

No.	Goaltender	GPI	Mins	Avg	W	L	EN	SO	GA	SA	S%
30	Mark Fitzpatrick	3	77	3.12	0	1	1	0	4	23	.826
35	Glenn Healy	18	1109	3.19	9	8	1	0	59	524	.887
	Totals	**18**	**1189**	**3.28**	**9**	**9**	**2**	**0**	**65**	**549**	**.882**

General Managers' History

William A. Torrey, 1972-73 to 1991-92; Don Maloney, 1992-93 to date.

Coaching History

Phil Goyette and Earl Ingarfield, 1972-73; Al Arbour, 1973-74 to 1985-86; Terry Simpson, 1986-87 to 1987-88; Terry Simpson and Al Arbour, 1988-89; Al Arbour, 1989-90 to date.

Captains' History

Ed Westfall, 1972-73 to 1975-76; Ed Westfall, Clark Gillies, 1976-77; Clark Gillies, 1977-78, 1978-79; Denis Potvin, 1979-80 to 1986-87; Brent Sutter, 1987-88 to 1990-91; Brent Sutter and Patrick Flatley, 1991-92; Patrick Flatley, 1992-93.

Club Records

Team

(Figures in brackets for season records are games played; records for fewest points, wins, ties, losses, goals, goals against are for 70 or more games)

Most Points	118	1981-82 (80)
Most Wins	54	1981-82 (80)
Most Ties	22	1974-75 (80)
Most Losses	60	1972-73 (78)
Most Goals	385	1981-82 (80)
Most Goals Against	347	1972-73 (78)
Fewest Points	30	1972-73 (78)
Fewest Wins	12	1972-73 (78)
Fewest Ties	4	1983-84 (80)
Fewest Losses	15	1978-79 (80)
Fewest Goals	170	1972-73 (78)
Fewest Goals Against	190	1975-76 (80)

Longest Winning Streak

Over-all	15	Jan. 21/82- Feb. 20/82
Home	14	Jan. 2/82- Feb. 27/82
Away	8	Feb. 27/81 Mar. 31/81

Longest Undefeated Streak

Over-all	15	Jan. 21- Feb. 21/82 (15 wins)
		Nov. 4- Dec. 4/80 (13 wins, 2 ties)
Home	23	Oct. 17/78- Jan. 27/79 (19 wins, 4 ties)
		Jan. 2/82- Apr. 3/82 (21 wins, 2 ties)
Away	8	Four times

Longest Losing Streak

Over-all	12	Dec. 27/72- Jan. 18/73
		Nov. 22- Dec. 17/88

Home	5	Jan. 2-23/33 Feb. 28- Mar. 19/74 Nov. 22- Dec. 17/88
Away	15	Jan. 20- Apr. 1/73

Longest Winless Streak

Over-all	15	Nov. 22- Dec. 23/72 (12 losses, 3 ties)
Home	7	Oct. 14- Nov. 21/72 (6 losses, 1 tie)
		Nov. 28- Dec. 23/72 (5 losses, 2 ties)
		Feb. 13- Mar. 13/90 (4 losses, 3 ties)
Away	20	Nov. 3/72- Jan. 13/73 (19 losses, 1 tie)

Most Shutouts, Season	10	1975-76 (80)
Most PIM, Season	1,857	1986-87 (80)
Most Goals, Game	11	Dec. 20/83 (Pit. 3 at NYI 11) Mar. 3/84 (NYI 11 at Tor. 6)

Individual

Most Seasons	17	Billy Smith
Most Games	1,123	Bryan Trottier
Most Goals, Career	573	Mike Bossy
Most Assists, Career	853	Bryan Trottier
Most Points, Career	1,353	Bryan Trottier (500 goals, 853 assists)
Most PIM, Career	1,466	Garry Howatt
Most Shutouts, Career	25	Glenn Resch

Longest Consecutive

Games Streak	576	Bill Harris (Oct. 7/72-Nov. 30/79)
Most Goals, Season	69	Mike Bossy (1978-79)
Most Assists, Season	87	Bryan Trottier (1978-79)
Most Points, Season	147	Mike Bossy (1981-82) (64 goals, 83 assists)

Most PIM, Season	356	Brian Curran (1986-87)
Most Points, Defenseman, Season	101	Denis Potvin (1978-79) (31 goals, 70 assists)
Most Points, Center, Season	134	Bryan Trottier (1978-79) (47 goals, 87 assists)
Most Points, Right Wing, Season	*147	Mike Bossy (1981-82) (64 goals, 83 assists)
Most Points, Left Wing, Season	100	John Tonelli (1984-85) (42 goals, 58 assists)
Most Points, Rookie, Season	95	Bryan Trottier (1975-76) (32 goals, 63 assists)
Most Shutouts, Season	7	Glenn Resch (1975-76)
Most Goals, Game	5	Bryan Trottier (Dec. 23/78; Feb. 13/82) John Tonelli (Jan. 6/81)
Most Assists, Game	6	Mike Bossy (Jan. 6/81)
Most Points, Game	8	Bryan Trottier (Dec. 23/78)

* NHL Record.

Retired Numbers

5	Denis Potvin	1973-1988
22	Mike Bossy	1977-1987
31	Billy Smith	1972-1989

1992-93 Results

	Home				Away	
Oct. 17	NY Rangers	6-3	Oct. 6	New Jersey	3-4
20	Philadelphia	4-3	8	Pittsburgh	3-7
24	Hartford	4-2	10	Boston	3-3
27	Los Angeles	3-4	15	Philadelphia	5-4
31	New Jersey	3-5	18	NY Rangers	3-4
Nov. 7	Tampa Bay	5-6	23	Washington	5-2
14	Buffalo	7-5	30	New Jersey	4-1
28	Philadelphia	9-3	Nov. 3	Pittsburgh	0-2
Dec. 1	Pittsburgh	3-7	5	Minnesota	0-3
5	Washington	3-5	12	Philadelphia	5-8
12	Winnipeg	3-4	19	Boston	2-5
13	Edmonton	4-1	21	Calgary	4-3
17	Ottawa	9-3	22	Edmonton	5-5
26	NY Rangers	6-4	24	Winnipeg	3-3
29	Toronto	2-3	27	Philadelphia*	3-6
Jan. 2	Minnesota	3-2	Dec. 4	Buffalo	5-5
5	Quebec	1-2	7	Tampa Bay	6-1
9	Vancouver	4-5	10	Chicago	3-5
12	Calgary	8-2	15	St. Louis	4-3
14	Washington	0-3	19	Pittsburgh*	4-3
19	Boston	2-2	20	Quebec*	3-5
23	Philadelphia	8-4	23	Montreal	6-2
26	New Jersey	8-2	31	St. Louis	1-5
30	Boston	5-6	Jan. 8	Buffalo	5-6
Feb. 1	NY Rangers	4-4	16	New Jersey	5-3
9	Montreal	3-5	17	Ottawa	7-2
13	NY Rangers	5-2	25	Pittsburgh	5-2
16	Edmonton	7-2	Feb. 3	Toronto	3-2
18	St. Louis	2-4	12	NY Rangers	3-4
20	Pittsburgh*	4-2	25	Quebec	4-6
23	Washington	2-4	27	Philadelphia*	3-2
Mar. 2	Detroit	3-2	28	Hartford	7-6
9	Philadelphia	4-2	Mar. 7	Washington*	3-2
14	Pittsburgh	2-3	10	Montreal	1-5
25	Washington	2-5	16	San Jose	6-0
27	San Jose	7-3	18	Los Angeles	4-7
30	Philadelphia	2-1	20	Vancouver	7-2
Apr. 3	Montreal	2-3	23	Detroit	2-3
8	Chicago	2-3	Apr. 2	NY Rangers	3-2
10	Ottawa	3-5	6	Washington	3-2
13	Hartford	3-3	11	New Jersey	5-4
16	New Jersey	8-4	14	Hartford	4-5

*Denotes afternoon game

All-time Record vs. Other Clubs

Regular Season

			At Home							On Road						Total				
	GP	W	L	T	GF	GA	PTS	GP	W	L	T	GF	GA	PTS	GP	W	L	T	GF	GA	PTS
Boston	38	15	19	4	123	129	34	39	9	21	9	110	153	27	77	24	40	13	233	282	61
Buffalo	39	15	17	7	120	120	37	38	12	21	5	113	137	29	77	27	38	12	233	257	66
Calgary	42	23	10	9	172	112	55	42	13	18	11	135	153	37	84	36	28	20	307	265	92
Chicago	38	16	10	12	136	109	44	40	17	18	5	142	129	39	78	33	28	17	278	238	83
Detroit	37	21	13	3	141	106	45	36	15	19	2	121	131	32	73	36	32	5	262	237	77
Edmonton	22	10	5	7	96	89	27	22	6	11	5	69	82	17	44	16	16	12	165	171	44
Hartford	23	14	6	3	95	58	31	22	11	8	3	90	74	25	45	25	14	6	185	132	56
Los Angeles	37	21	12	4	141	108	46	36	14	15	7	122	125	35	73	35	27	11	263	233	81
Minnesota	38	20	10	8	148	112	48	38	18	15	5	142	112	41	76	38	25	13	290	224	89
Montreal	38	17	17	4	125	116	38	38	10	22	6	117	146	26	76	27	39	10	242	262	64
New Jersey	55	42	6	7	264	154	91	58	30	18	10	236	192	70	113	72	24	17	500	346	161
NY Rangers	67	44	17	6	288	211	94	69	20	44	5	208	276	45	136	64	61	11	496	487	139
Ottawa	2	1	1	0	12	8	2	1	1	0	0	7	2	2	3	2	1	0	19	10	4
Philadelphia	69	38	21	10	276	201	86	68	19	39	10	210	260	48	137	57	60	20	486	461	134
Pittsburgh	62	37	17	8	266	188	82	61	23	28	10	211	234	56	123	60	45	18	477	422	138
Quebec	22	14	7	1	100	78	29	22	10	11	1	76	86	21	44	24	18	2	176	164	50
St. Louis	40	24	7	9	158	88	57	39	17	16	6	128	139	40	79	41	23	15	286	227	97
San Jose	3	3	0	0	20	6	6	2	1	1	0	8	3	2	5	4	1	0	28	9	8
Tampa Bay	1	0	1	0	5	6	0	1	1	0	0	6	1	2	2	1	1	0	11	7	2
Toronto	37	21	13	3	160	115	45	39	18	17	4	144	136	40	76	39	30	7	304	251	85
Vancouver	38	22	8	8	151	102	52	40	19	18	3	133	126	41	78	41	26	11	284	228	93
Washington	58	35	22	1	235	186	71	55	26	22	7	193	171	59	113	61	44	8	428	357	130
Winnipeg	21	10	6	5	79	62	25	21	12	7	2	83	71	26	42	22	13	7	162	133	51
Defunct Clubs	13	11	0	2	75	33	24	13	4	5	4	35	41	12	26	15	5	6	110	74	36
Totals	**840**	**474**	**245**	**121**	**3386**	**2497**	**1069**	**840**	**326**	**394**	**120**	**2839**	**2980**	**772**	**1680**	**800**	**639**	**241**	**6225**	**5477**	**1841**

Playoffs

	Series	W	L	GP	W	L	T	GF	GA	Last Mtg.	Round	Result
Boston	2	2	0	11	8	3	0	49	35	1983	CF	W 4-2
Buffalo	3	3	0	16	12	4	0	59	45	1980	SF	W 4-2
Chicago	2	2	0	6	6	0	0	21	6	1979	QF	W 4-0
Edmonton	3	2	1	15	9	6	0	58	47	1984	F	L 1-4
Los Angeles	1	1	0	4	3	1	0	21	10	1980	PR	W 3-1
Minnesota	1	1	0	5	4	1	0	26	16	1981	F	W 4-1
Montreal	4	1	3	22	8	14	0	55	64	1993	CF	L 1-4
New Jersey	1	0	1	6	2	4	0	18	23	1988	DSF	L 2-4
NY Rangers	7	5	2	35	20	15	0	126	110	1990	DSF	L 1-4
Philadelphia	4	1	3	25	11	14	0	69	83	1987	DF	L 3-4
Pittsburgh	3	3	0	19	11	8	0	67	58	1993	DF	W 4-3
Quebec	1	1	0	4	4	0	0	18	9	1982	CF	W 4-0
Toronto	2	1	1	10	6	4	0	33	20	1981	PR	W 3-0
Vancouver	2	2	0	6	6	0	0	26	14	1982	F	W 4-0
Washington	6	5	1	30	18	12	0	99	88	1993	DSF	W 4-2
Totals	**42**	**30**	**12**	**214**	**128**	**86**	**0**	**745**	**628**			

Playoff Results 1993-89

Year	Round	Opponent	Result	GF	GA
1993	CF	Montreal	L 1-4	11	16
	DF	Pittsburgh	W 4-3	24	27
	DSF	Washington	W 4-2	23	22
1990	DSF	NY Rangers	L 1-4	13	22

Abbreviations: Round: F – Final;
CF – conference final; **DF** – division final;
DSF – division semi-final; **SF** – semi-final;
QF – quarter-final; **PR** – preliminary round.
GA – goals against; **GF** – goals for.

Entry Draft
Selections 1993-79

1993
Pick
23 Todd Bertuzzi
40 Bryan McCabe
66 Vladim Chebaturkin
92 Warren Luhning
118 Tommy Salo
144 Peter Leboutillier
170 Darren Van Impe
196 Rod Hinks
222 Daniel Johansson
248 Stephane Larocque
274 Carl Charland

1992
Pick
5 Darius Kasparaitis
56 Jarrett Deuling
104 Tomas Klimt
105 Ryan Duthie
128 Derek Armstrong
152 Vladimir Grachev
159 Steve O'Rourke
176 Jason Widmer
200 Daniel Paradis
224 David Wainwright
248 Andrei Vasiljev

1991
Pick
4 Scott Lachance
26 Zigmund Palffy
48 Jamie McLennan
70 Milan Hnilicka
92 Steve Junker
114 Robert Valicevic
136 Andreas Johansson
158 Todd Sparks
180 John Johnson
202 Robert Canavan
224 Marcus Thuresson
246 Marty Schriner

1990
Pick
6 Scott Scissons
27 Chris Taylor
48 Dan Plante
90 Chris Marinucci
111 Joni Lehto
132 Michael Guilbert
153 Sylvain Fleury
174 John Joyce
195 Richard Enga
216 Martin Lacroix
237 Andy Shirr

1989
Pick
2 Dave Chyzowski
23 Travis Green
44 Jason Zent
65 Brent Grieve
86 Jace Reed
90 Steve Young
99 Kevin O'Sullivan
128 Jon Larson
133 Brett Harkins
149 Phil Huber
170 Matthew Robbins
191 Vladimir Malakhov
212 Kelly Ens
233 Iain Fraser

1988
Pick
16 Kevin Cheveldayoff
29 Wayne Doucet
37 Sean LeBrun
58 Danny Lorenz
79 Andre Brassard
100 Paul Rutherford
111 Pavel Gross
121 Jason Rathbone
142 Yves Gaucher
163 Marty McInnis
184 Jeff Blumer
205 Jeff Kampersal
226 Phillip Neururer
247 Joe Capprini

1987
Pick
13 Dean Chynoweth
34 Jeff Hackett
55 Dean Ewen
76 George Maneluk
97 Petr Vlk
118 Rob DiMaio
139 Knut Walbye
160 Jeff Saterdalen
181 Shawn Howard
202 John Herlihy
223 Michael Erickson
244 Will Averill

1986
Pick
17 Tom Fitzgerald
38 Dennis Vaske
59 Bill Berg
80 Shawn Byram
101 Dean Sexsmith
104 Todd McLellan
122 Tony Schmalzbauer
138 Will Anderson
143 Richard Pilon
164 Peter Harris
185 Jeff Jablonski
206 Kerry Clark
227 Dan Beaudette
248 Paul Thompson

1985
Pick
6 Brad Dalgarno
13 Derek King
34 Brad Lauer
55 Jeff Finley
76 Kevin Herom
89 Tommy Hedlund
97 Jeff Sveen
118 Rod Dallman
139 Kurt Lackten
160 Hank Lammens
181 Rich Wiest
202 Real Arsenault
223 Mike Volpe
244 Tony Grenier

1984
Pick
20 Duncan MacPherson
41 Bruce Melanson
62 Jeff Norton
70 Doug Wieck
83 Ari Haanpaa
104 Mike Murray
125 Jim Wilharm
146 Kelly Murphy
167 Franco Desantis
187 Tom Warden
208 David Volek
228 Russ Becker
249 Allister Brown

1983
Pick
3 Pat LaFontaine
16 Gerald Diduck
37 Garnet McKechney
57 Mike Neill
65 Mikko Maklla
84 Bob Caulfield
97 Ron Viglasi
117 Darin Illikainen
137 Jim Sprenger
157 Dale Henry
177 Kevin Vescio
197 Dave Shellington
217 John Bjorkman
237 Peter McGeough

1982
Pick
21 Patrick Flatley
42 Vern Smith
63 Garry Lacey
84 Alan Kerr
105 Rene Breton
126 Roger Kortko
147 John Tiano
168 Todd Okerlund
189 Gord Paddock
210 Eric Faust
231 Pat Goff
252 Jim Koudys

1981
Pick
21 Paul Boutilier
42 Gord Dineen
57 Ron Handy
63 Neal Coulter
84 Todd Lumbard
94 Jacques Sylvestre
126 Chuck Brimmer
147 Teppo Virta
168 Bill Dowd
189 Scott MacLellan
210 Dave Randerson

1980
Pick
17 Brent Sutter
38 Kelly Hrudey
59 Dave Simpsn
68 Monty Trottier
80 Greg Gilbert
101 Ken Leiter
122 Dan Revell
143 Mark Hamway
164 Morrison Gare
185 Peter Steblyk
206 Glen Johannesen

1979
Pick
17 Duane Sutter
25 Tomas Jonsson
38 Bill Carroll
59 Roland Melanson
80 Tim Lockridge
101 Glen Duncan
122 John Gibb

General Manager

MALONEY, DON
General Manager, New York Islanders.
Born in Lindsay, Ont., September 5, 1958.

Don Maloney became the second general manager in the NY Islanders' franchise history on August 17, 1992. After a 13-year playing career that included stays with the Rangers, Islanders and Whalers, Maloney joined the Islanders' organization in January, 1991 as a part-time assistant to coach Al Arbour and general manager Bill Torrey. The following season, he became assistant general manager, representing the team in contract discussions and organizing the Islanders' training camp itinerary. In his playing career, Maloney compiled 214 goals and 350 assists in 765 games.

Club Directory

Nassau Veterans'
Memorial Coliseum
Uniondale, NY 11553
Phone **516/794-4100**
GM FAX 516/542-9350
FAX 516/542-9348
Capacity: 16,297

Co-Chairmen	Robert Rosenthal, Stephen Walsh
Chief Operating Officer	Ralph Palleschi
Executive Vice-President	Paul Greenwood
Senior Vice-President & CFO	Arthur J. McCarthy
Consultant	John H. Krumpe
General Counsel	William H. Skehan
Vice-President Hockey Operations/ General Manager	Don Maloney
Assistant General Manager	Darcy Regier
Head Coach	Al Arbour
Assistant Coaches	Lorne Henning, Rick Green
Minor League Coach	Dave Farrish
Minor League Asst. Coach	Chris Pryor
Director of Scouting	Gerry Ehman
Director of Pro Scouting	Ken Morrow
Scouting Staff	Harry Boyd, Earl Ingarfield, Gord Lane, Bert Marshall, Mario Saraceno, Jack Vivian
Vice-President/Communications	Pat Calabria
Director of Media Relations	Ginger Killian
Media Relations Assistant	Eric Mirlis
Director of Publications/ Media Relations Associate	Chris Botta
Director of Community Relations	Maureen Brady
Director of Game Events	Tim Beach
Director of Amateur Hockey Development & Alumni Relations	Bob Nystrom
Director of Ticket Sales	Jim Johnson
Director of Advertising Sales	Glenda Brown
Director of Administration	Joseph Dreyer
Controller	Ralph Sellitti
Administrative Assistants to the General Manager	Joanne Holewa, Tracy Levy, Rosemarie Tully
Athletic Trainer	Ed Tyburski
Equipment Manager	John Doolan
Assistant Trainer	Jerry Iannarelli
Assistant Equipment Manager	Joe McMahon
Team Orthopedists	Jerry Minkoff, M.D., Barry Simonson, M.D.
Team Internists	Gerald Cordani, M.D., Larry Smith, M.D.
Physical Therapist	Steve Wirth
Team Dentists	Bruce Michnick, D.D.S., Jan Sherman, D.D.S.
Photographer	Bruce Bennett
Location of Press Box	East Side of Building
Dimensions of Rink	200 feet by 85 feet
Ends of Rink	Herculite extends above boards around rink
Club Colors	Blue, Orange and White
Television Announcers	Jiggs McDonald, Ed Westfall, Stan Fischler
Television Station	SportsChannel
Radio Announcers	Barry Landers, Bobby Nystrom
Radio Stations	WPAT (930 AM), WGBB (1240 AM), WHRD (1570 AM), WFAS (1230 AM), WBZO (103.1 FM)

Coach

ARBOUR, AL
Coach, New York Islanders. Born in Sudbury, Ont., November 1, 1932.

Al Arbour, who surpassed Dick Irvin's long-standing record for career games coached in 1991-92, guided the NY Islanders to the Conference Finals for the first time in nine seasons in 1992-93. Arbour has been behind the bench for a total of 1,522 regular-season NHL games. He was named head coach of the Islanders' for a second time on June 26, 1989, after serving three years as the club's vice president of player development. Arbour began his coaching career with St. Louis in 1970 before joining the Islanders at the start of the 1973-74 season. He has now won 745 regular-season games and has compiled a career winning percentage of .567.

Coaching Record

		Regular Season					Playoffs			
Season	Team	Games	W	L	T	%	Games	W	L	%
1970-71	St. Louis (NHL)	50	21	15	14	.560	....	....	....	....
1971-72	St. Louis (NHL)	44	19	19	6	.500	11	4	7	.364
1972-73	St. Louis (NHL)	13	2	6	5	.346	....	....	....	....
1973-74	NY Islanders (NHL)	78	19	41	18	.358	....	....	....	....
1974-75	NY Islanders (NHL)	80	33	25	22	.550	....	....	....	....
1975-76	NY Islanders (NHL)	80	42	21	17	.631	13	7	6	.538
1976-77	NY Islanders (NHL)	80	47	21	12	.663	12	8	4	.666
1977-78	NY Islanders (NHL)	80	48	17	15	.694	7	3	4	.429
1978-79	NY Islanders (NHL)	80	51	15	14	.725	10	6	4	.600
1979-80	NY Islanders (NHL)	80	39	28	13	.589	21	15	6	.714*
1980-81	NY Islanders (NHL)	80	48	18	14	.600	18	15	3	.833*
1981-82	NY Islanders (NHL)	80	54	16	10	.738	19	15	4	.789*
1982-83	NY Islanders (NHL)	80	42	26	12	.600	20	15	5	.750*
1983-84	NY Islanders (NHL)	80	50	26	4	.650	21	12	9	.571
1984-85	NY Islanders (NHL)	80	40	34	6	.538	10	4	6	.400
1985-86	NY Islanders (NHL)	80	39	29	12	.563	3	0	3	.000
1988-89	NY Islanders (NHL)	53	21	29	3	.425	....	....	....	....
1989-90	NY Islanders (NHL)	80	31	38	11	.456	5	1	4	.200
1990-91	NY Islanders (NHL)	80	25	45	10	.375	....	....	....	....
1991-92	NY Islanders (NHL)	80	34	35	11	.494	....	....	....	....
1992-93	NY Islanders (NHL)	84	40	37	7	.518	18	9	9	.500
NHL Totals		**1522**	**745**	**541**	**236**	**.567**	**205**	**123**	**82**	**.600**

* Stanley Cup win.

New York Rangers

1992-93 Results: 34w-39l-11t 79pts. Sixth, Patrick Division

Schedule

Home			Away		
Oct.	Tues. 5 Boston	**Oct.**	Sat. 9 Pittsburgh
	Thur. 7 Tampa Bay		Fri. 15 Buffalo
	Mon. 11 Washington		Sat. 16 Philadelphia
	Wed. 13 Quebec		Fri. 22 Tampa Bay
	Tues. 19 Anaheim		Sat. 30 Hartford
	Sun. 24 Los Angeles	**Nov.**	Sat. 6 Quebec*
	Thur. 28 Montreal		Sat. 13 Washington
	Sun. 31 New Jersey		Tues. 16 Florida
	(at Halifax)		Fri. 19 Tampa Bay
Nov.	Wed. 3 Vancouver		Wed. 24 Ottawa
	Mon. 8 Tampa Bay		Sat. 27 NY Islanders*
	Wed. 10 Winnipeg		Tues. 30 New Jersey
	Sun. 14 San Jose	**Dec.**	Sat. 4 Toronto
	Tues. 23 Montreal		Fri. 17 Detroit
	Sun. 28 Washington		Wed. 22 Florida
Dec.	Sun. 5 New Jersey		Thur. 23 Washington
	Wed. 8 Edmonton		Wed. 29 St Louis
	Mon. 13 Buffalo		Fri. 31 Buffalo
	Wed. 15 Hartford	**Jan.**	Sat. 8 Montreal
	Sun. 19 Ottawa		Sun. 16 Chicago
	Sun. 26 New Jersey		Tues. 25 San Jose
Jan.	Mon. 3 Florida		Thur. 27 Los Angeles
	Wed. 5 Calgary		Fri. 28 Anaheim
	Mon. 10 Tampa Bay	**Feb.**	Thur. 3 Boston
	Fri. 14 Philadelphia		Wed. 9 Montreal
	Tues. 18 St Louis		Sat. 12 Ottawa
	Mon. 31 Pittsburgh		Mon. 14 Quebec
Feb.	Wed. 2 NY Islanders		Sat. 19 Hartford
	Mon. 7 Washington		Thur. 24 New Jersey
	Fri. 11 Quebec		Sat. 26 Dallas
	Fri. 18 Ottawa	**Mar.**	Sat. 5 NY Islanders
	Mon. 21 Pittsburgh*		Wed. 9 Washington
	Wed. 23 Boston		(at Halifax)
Mar.	Wed. 2 Philadelphia		Thur. 10 Boston
	Fri. 4 NY Islanders		Sat. 12 Pittsburgh*
	Mon. 7 Detroit		Mon. 14 Florida
	Wed. 16 Hartford		Tues. 22 Calgary
	Fri. 18 Chicago		Wed. 23 Edmonton
Apr.	Fri. 1 Dallas		Fri. 25 Vancouver
	Mon. 4 Florida		Sun. 27 Winnipeg*
	Fri. 8 Toronto		Tues. 29 Philadelphia
	Tues. 12 Buffalo	**Apr.**	Sat. 2 New Jersey
	Thur. 14 Philadelphia		Sun. 10 NY Islanders*

* Denotes afternoon game.

Home Starting Times:
All Games . . . . 7:35 p.m.
Except Matinees . . . . 1:35 p.m.

Franchise date: May 15, 1926

ATLANTIC DIVISION

EASTERN CONFERENCE

68th NHL Season

Tony Amonte, who tied for the club lead with 13 powerplay goals in 1992-93, finished second in team scoring with 76 points.

Year-by-Year Record

Season	GP	Home W	Home L	Home T	Road W	Road L	Road T	Overall W	L	T	GF	GA	Pts.	Finished		Playoff Result
1992-93	84	20	17	5	14	22	6	34	39	11	304	308	79	6th,	Patrick Div.	Out of Playoffs
1991-92	80	28	8	4	22	17	1	50	25	5	321	246	105	1st,	Patrick Div.	Lost Div. Final
1990-91	80	22	11	7	14	20	6	36	31	13	297	265	85	2nd,	Patrick Div.	Lost Div. Semi-Final
1989-90	80	20	11	9	16	20	4	36	31	13	279	267	85	1st,	Patrick Div.	Lost Div. Final
1988-89	80	21	17	2	16	18	6	37	35	8	310	307	82	3rd,	Patrick Div.	Lost Div. Semi-Final
1987-88	80	22	13	5	14	21	5	36	34	10	300	283	82	5th,	Patrick Div.	Out of Playoffs
1986-87	80	18	18	4	16	20	4	34	38	8	307	323	76	4th,	Patrick Div.	Lost Div. Semi-Final
1985-86	80	20	18	2	16	20	4	36	38	6	280	276	78	4th,	Patick Div.	Lost Conf. Championship
1984-85	80	16	18	6	10	26	4	26	44	10	295	345	62	4th,	Patrick Div.	Lost Div. Semi-Final
1983-84	80	27	12	1	15	17	8	42	29	9	314	304	93	4th,	Patrick Div.	Lost Div. Semi-Final
1982-83	80	24	13	3	11	22	7	35	35	10	306	287	80	4th,	Patrick Div.	Lost Div. Final
1981-82	80	19	15	6	20	12	8	39	27	14	316	306	92	2nd,	Patrick Div.	Lost Div. Final
1980-81	80	17	13	10	13	23	4	30	36	14	312	317	74	4th,	Patrick Div.	Lost Semi-Final
1979-80	80	22	10	8	16	22	2	38	32	10	308	284	86	3rd,	Patrick Div.	Lost Quarter-Final
1978-79	80	19	13	8	21	16	3	40	29	11	316	292	91	3rd,	Patrick Div.	Lost Final
1977-78	80	18	15	7	12	22	6	30	37	13	279	280	73	4th,	Patrick Div.	Lost Prelim. Round
1976-77	80	17	18	5	12	19	9	29	37	14	272	310	72	4th,	Patrick Div.	Out of Playoffs
1975-76	80	16	16	8	13	26	1	29	42	9	262	333	67	4th,	Patrick Div.	Out of Playoffs
1974-75	80	21	11	8	16	18	6	37	29	14	319	276	88	2nd,	Patrick Div.	Lost Prelim. Round
1973-74	78	26	7	6	14	17	8	40	24	14	300	251	94	3rd,	East Div.	Lost Semi-Final
1972-73	78	26	8	5	21	15	3	47	23	8	297	208	102	3rd,	East Div.	Lost Semi-Final
1971-72	78	26	6	7	22	11	6	48	17	13	317	192	109	2nd,	East Div.	Lost Final
1970-71	78	30	2	7	19	16	4	49	18	11	259	177	109	2nd,	East Div.	Lost Semi-Final
1969-70	76	22	8	8	16	14	8	38	22	16	246	189	92	4th,	East Div.	Lost Quarter-Final
1968-69	76	27	7	4	14	19	5	41	26	9	231	196	91	3rd,	East Div.	Lost Quarter-Final
1967-68	74	22	8	7	17	15	5	39	23	12	226	183	90	2nd,	East Div.	Lost Quarter-Final
1966-67	70	18	12	5	12	16	7	30	28	12	188	189	72	4th,		Lost Semi-Final
1965-66	70	12	16	7	6	25	4	18	41	11	195	261	47	6th,		Out of Playoffs
1964-65	70	12	19	8	12	19	4	20	38	12	179	246	52	5th,		Out of Playoffs
1963-64	70	14	13	8	8	25	2	22	38	10	186	242	54	5th,		Out of Playoffs
1962-63	70	12	17	6	10	19	6	22	36	12	211	233	56	5th,		Out of Playoffs
1961-62	70	16	11	8	10	21	4	26	32	12	195	207	64	4th,		Lost Semi-Final
1960-61	70	15	15	5	7	23	5	22	38	10	204	248	54	5th,		Out of Playoffs
1959-60	70	10	15	10	7	23	5	17	38	15	187	247	49	6th,		Out of Playoffs
1958-59	70	14	16	5	12	16	7	26	32	12	201	217	64	5th,		Out of Playoffs
1957-58	70	14	15	6	18	10	7	32	25	13	195	188	77	2nd,		Lost Semi-Final
1956-57	70	15	12		11	18	6	26	30	14	184	227	66	4th,		Lost Semi-Final
1955-56	70	20	7	8	12	21	2	32	28	10	204	203	74	3rd,		Lost Semi-Final
1954-55	70	10	12	13	7	23	5	17	35	18	150	210	52	5th,		Out of Playoffs
1953-54	70	18	12	5	11	19	5	29	31	10	161	182	68	5th,		Out of Playoffs
1952-53	70	11	14	10	6	23	6	17	37	16	152	211	50	6th,		Out of Playoffs
1951-52	70	16	13	6	7	21	7	23	34	13	192	219	59	5th,		Out of Playoffs
1950-51	70	14	11	10	6	18	11	20	29	21	169	201	61	5th,		Out of Playoffs
1949-50	70	19	12	4	9	19	7	28	31	11	170	189	67	4th,		Lost Final
1948-49	60	13	12	5	5	19	6	18	31	11	133	172	47	6th,		Out of Playoffs
1947-48	60	11	12	7	10	14	6	21	26	13	176	201	55	4th,		Lost Semi-Final
1946-47	60	11	14	5	11	18	1	22	32	6	167	186	50	5th,		Out of Playoffs
1945-46	50	8	12	5	5	16	4	13	28	9	144	191	35	6th,		Out of Playoffs
1944-45	50	7	11	7	4	18	3	11	29	10	154	247	32	6th,		Out of Playoffs
1943-44	50	4	17	4	2	22	1	6	39	5	162	310	17	6th,		Out of Playoffs
1942-43	50	7	13	5	4	18	3	11	31	8	161	253	30	6th,		Out of Playoffs
1941-42	48	15	8	1	14	9	1	29	17	2	177	143	60	1st,		Lost Semi-Final
1940-41	48	13	4	7	8	12	4	21	19	8	143	125	50	4th,		Lost Quarter-Final
1939-40	**48**	**17**	**4**	**3**	**10**	**7**	**7**	**27**	**11**	**10**	**136**	**77**	**64**	**2nd,**		**Won Stanley Cup**
1938-39	48	13	8	3	13	8	3	26	16	6	149	105	58	2nd,		Lost Semi-Final
1937-38	48	15	5	4	12	10	2	27	15	6	149	96	60	2nd,	Amn. Div.	Lost Quarter-Final
1936-37	48	9	7	8	10	13	1	19	20	9	117	106	47	3rd,	Amn. Div.	Lost Final
1935-36	48	11	6	7	8	11	5	19	17	12	91	96	50	4th,	Amn. Div.	Out of Playoffs
1934-35	48	11	8	5	11	12	1	22	20	6	137	139	50	3rd,	Amn. Div.	Lost Semi-Final
1933-34	48	11	7	6	10	12	2	21	19	8	120	113	50	3rd,	Amn. Div.	Lost Semi-Final
1932-33	**48**	**12**	**7**	**5**	**11**	**10**	**3**	**23**	**17**	**8**	**135**	**107**	**54**	**3rd,**	**Amn. Div.**	**Won Stanley Cup**
1931-32	48	13	4	7	10	10	4	23	17	8	134	112	54	1st,	Amn. Div.	Lost Final
1930-31	44	10	9	3	9	7	6	19	16	9	106	87	47	3rd,	Amn. Div.	Lost Semi-Final
1929-30	44	11	5	6	6	12	4	17	17	10	136	143	44	3rd,	Amn. Div.	Lost Semi-Final
1928-29	44	12	6	4	9	7	6	21	13	10	72	65	52	2nd,	Amn. Div.	Lost Final
1927-28	**44**	**10**	**8**	**4**	**9**	**8**	**5**	**19**	**16**	**9**	**94**	**79**	**47**	**2nd,**	**Amn. Div.**	**Won Stanley Cup**
1926-27	44	13	5	4	12	8	2	25	13	6	95	72	56	1st,	Amn. Div.	Lost Quarter-Final

1993-94 Player Personnel

FORWARDS	HT	WT	S	Place of Birth	Date	1992-93 Club
AMONTE, Tony	6-0	180	L	Hingham, MA	8/2/70	NY Rangers
BOURQUE, Phil	6-1	195	L	Chelmsford, MA	6/8/62	NY Rangers
BROTEN, Paul	5-11	190	R	Roseau, MN	10/27/65	NY Rangers
DUNCANSON, Craig	6-0	190	L	Sudbury, Ont.	3/17/67	NYR-Binghamton
GARTNER, Mike	6-0	190	R	Ottawa, Ont.	10/29/59	NY Rangers
GILBERT, Greg	6-1	191	L	Mississauga, Ont.	12/29/67	Chicago
GRAVES, Adam	6-0	185	L	Toronto, Ont.	4/12/68	NY Rangers
HARTMAN, Mike	6-0	190	L	Detroit, MI	2/7/67	T.B.-NY Rangers
KOCUR, Joe	6-0	210	R	Calgary, Alta.	12/21/64	NY Rangers
KOVALEV, Alexei	6-0	200	L	Togliatti, Russia	2/24/73	NYR-Binghamton
LACROIX, Daniel	6-2	188	L	Montreal, Que.	3/11/69	Binghamton
McCOSH, Shawn	6-0	188	R	Oshawa, Ont.	6/5/69	New Haven-Phoenix
McINTYRE, John	6-1	180	L	Revenswood, Ont.	4/29/69	L.A.-NY Rangers
McLAUGHLIN, Mike	6-1	175	L	Longmeadow, MA	3/29/70	Rochester
MESSIER, Mark	6-1	202	L	Edmonton, Alta.	1/18/61	NY Rangers
MURANO, Eric	6-0	200	R	Montreal, Que.	5/4/67	Hamilton-Baltimore
NEMCHINOV, Sergei	6-0	200	L	Moscow, USSR	1/14/64	NY Rangers
OLCZYK, Eddie	6-1	200	L	Chicago, IL	8/16/66	Wpg.-NY Rangers
ROY, Jean-Yves	5-10	185	L	Rosemere, Que.	2/17/69	Cdn. Nat.-Bing.
TIKKANEN, Esa	6-1	200	L	Helsinki, Finland	1/25/65	Edm.-NY Rangers
TURCOTTE, Darren	6-0	185	L	Boston, MA	3/2/68	NY Rangers

DEFENSEMEN	HT	WT	S	Place of Birth	Date	1992-93 Club
ANDERSSON, Peter	6-0	200	L	Orebro, Sweden	8/29/65	NYR-Binghamton
BEUKEBOOM, Jeff	6-4	223	R	Ajax, Ont.	3/28/65	NY Rangers
FIORENTINO, Peter	6-1	205	R	Niagara Falls, Ont.	12/22/68	Binghamton
HURLBUT, Mike	6-2	200	L	Massena, NY	10/7/66	NYR-Binghamton
KOLSTAD, Dean	6-6	220	L	Edmonton, Alta.	6/16/68	San Jose-Kansas City
LEETCH, Brian	5-11	195	L	Corpus Christi, TX	3/3/68	NY Rangers
LIDSTER, Doug	6-1	200	R	Kamloops, B.C.	10/18/60	Vancouver
LOWE, Kevin	6-2	195	L	Lachute, Que.	4/15/59	NY Rangers
MESSIER, Joby	6-1	207	R	Regina, Sask.	3/2/70	NYR-Binghamton
NORSTROM, Mattias	6-1	196	L	Stockholm, Sweden	1/2/72	AIK
PATRICK, James	6-2	204	R	Winnipeg, Man.	6/14/63	NY Rangers
STEWART, Michael	6-2	205	L	Calgary, Alta.	5/30/72	Binghamton
TILEY, Brad	6-1	185	L	Markdale, Ont.	7/5/71	Binghamton
WELLS, Jay	6-1	210	L	Paris, Ont.	5/18/59	NY Rangers
WERENKA, Darcy	6-1	210	R	Edmonton, Alta.	5/13/73	Lethbridge
ZUBOV, Sergei	6-1	199	R	Moscow, Russia	7/22/70	NYR-Binghamton

GOALTENDERS	HT	WT	C	Place of Birth	Date	1992-93 Club
GILMORE, Mike	5-10	181	L	Detroit, MI	3/11/68	Erie-Binghamton
HEALY, Glenn	5-10	183	L	Pickering, Ont.	8/23/62	NY Islanders
HILLEBRANDT, Jon	5-10	160	L	Cottage Grove, WI	12/18/71	Ill.-Chicago
HIRSCH, Corey	5-9	150	L	Medicine Hat, Alta.	7/1/72	NYR-Binghamton
RICHTER, Mike	5-10	185	L	Abington, PA	9/22/66	NYR-Binghamton
ROUSSON, Boris	6-1	200	R	Valdor, Que.	6/14/70	Binghamton

1992-93 Scoring

Regular Season

Pos	#	Player	Team	GP	G	A	Pts	+/−	PIM	PP	SH	GW	GT	S	%
C	11	Mark Messier	NYR	75	25	66	91	6−	72	7	2	2	0	215	11.6
R	33	Tony Amonte	NYR	83	33	43	76	0	49	13	0	4	1	270	12.2
R	22	Mike Gartner	NYR	84	45	23	68	4−	59	13	0	3	1	323	13.9
L	9	Adam Graves	NYR	84	36	29	65	4−	148	12	1	6	1	275	13.1
C	13	Sergei Nemchinov	NYR	81	23	31	54	15	34	0	1	3	0	144	16.0
C	8	Darren Turcotte	NYR	71	25	28	53	3−	40	7	3	3	1	213	11.7
C	12	Ed Olczyk	WPG	25	8	12	20	11−	26	2	0	0	1	81	9.9
			NYR	46	13	16	29	9	26	0	0	1	0	109	11.9
			TOTAL	71	21	28	49	2−	52	2	0	1	1	190	11.1
L	10	Esa Tikkanen	EDM	66	14	19	33	11−	76	2	4	3	0	162	8.6
			NYR	15	2	5	7	13−	18	0	0	0	0	40	5.0
			TOTAL	81	16	24	40	24−	94	2	4	3	0	202	7.9
R	27 *	Alexei Kovalev	NYR	65	20	18	38	10−	79	3	0	3	1	134	14.9
D	2	Brian Leetch	NYR	36	6	30	36	2	26	2	1	1	0	150	4.0
D	21 *	Sergei Zubov	NYR	49	8	23	31	1−	4	3	0	0	0	93	8.6
D	3	James Patrick	NYR	60	5	21	26	1	61	3	0	0	0	99	5.1
L	29	Phil Bourque	NYR	55	6	14	20	9−	39	0	0	2	0	71	8.5
D	23	Jeff Beukeboom	NYR	82	2	17	19	9	153	0	0	0	0	54	3.7
L	20	Jan Erixon	NYR	45	5	11	16	11	10	0	1	1	0	36	13.9
D	5	Peter Andersson	NYR	31	4	11	15	4	18	3	0	1	0	68	5.9
D	4	Kevin Lowe	NYR	49	3	12	15	2−	58	0	0	0	0	52	5.8
R	37	Paul Broten	NYR	60	5	9	14	6−	48	0	1	0	0	57	8.8
L	25 *	Steven King	NYR	24	7	5	12	4	16	5	0	2	0	42	16.7
D	24	Jay Wells	NYR	53	1	9	10	2−	107	0	0	0	0	32	3.1
D	6	Joe Cirella	NYR	55	3	6	9	1	85	0	1	0	0	37	8.1
R	26	Joey Kocur	NYR	65	3	6	9	9−	131	2	0	0	0	43	7.0
D	32 *	Mike Hurlbut	NYR	23	1	8	9	4	16	1	0	0	0	26	3.8
R	18	Mike Hartman	T.B.	58	4	4	8	7−	154	0	0	0	0	74	5.4
			NYR	3	0	0	0	0	6	0	0	0	0	3	.0
			TOTAL	61	4	4	8	7−	160	0	0	0	0	77	5.2
C	14	John McIntyre	L.A.	49	2	5	7	13−	80	0	0	0	0	31	6.5
			NYR	11	1	0	1	1−	4	0	0	0	0	5	20.0
			TOTAL	60	3	5	8	14−	84	0	0	0	0	36	8.3
G	35	Mike Richter	NYR	38	0	5	5	0	2	0	0	0	0	0	.0
D	44	Per Djoos	NYR	6	1	1	2	0	2	0	0	0	0	4	25.0
R	19	Craig Duncanson	NYR	3	0	1	1	0	0	0	0	0	0	1	.0
G	34	John Vanbiesbrouck	NYR	48	0	1	1	0	18	0	0	0	0	0	.0
D	42 *	Dave Marcinyshyn	NYR	2	0	0	0	1−	2	0	0	0	0	1	.0
G	31 *	Corey Hirsch	NYR	4	0	0	0	0	0	0	0	0	0	0	.0
D	28 *	Joby Messier	NYR	11	0	0	0	0	6	0	0	0	0	11	.0

Goaltending

No.	Goaltender	GPI	Mins	Avg	W	L	T	EN	SO	GA	SA	S%
34	John Vanbiesbrouck	48	2757	3.31	20	18	7	3	4	152	1525	.900
31	* Corey Hirsch	4	224	3.75	1	2	1	1	0	14	116	.879
35	Mike Richter	38	2105	3.82	13	19	3	4	1	134	1180	.886
	Totals	84	5108	3.62	34	39	11	8	5	308	2829	.891

Coaching History

Lester Patrick, 1926-27 to 1938-39; Frank Boucher, 1939-40 to 1947-48; Frank Boucher and Lynn Patrick, 1948-49; Lynn Patrick, 1949-50; Neil Colville, 1950-51; Neil Colville and Bill Cook, 1951-52; Bill Cook, 1952-53; Frank Boucher and Murray Patrick, 1953-54; Murray Patrick, 1954-55; Phil Watson, 1955-56 to 1958-59; Phil Watson and Alf Pike, 1959-60; Alf Pike, 1960-61; Doug Harvey, 1961-62; Murray Patrick and George Sullivan, 1962-63; George Sullivan, 1963-64 to 1964-65; George Sullivan and Emile Francis, 1965-66; Emile Francis, 1966-67 to 1967-68; Bernie Geoffrion and Emile Francis, 1968-69; Emile Francis, 1969-70 to 1972-73; Larry Popein and Emile Francis, 1973-74; Emile Francis, 1974-75; Ron Stewart and John Ferguson, 1975-76; John Ferguson, 1976-77; Jean-Guy Talbot, 1977-78; Fred Shero, 1978-79 to 1979-80; Fred Shero and Craig Patrick, 1980-81; Herb Brooks, 1981-82 to 1983-84; Herb Brooks and Craig Patrick, 1984-85; Ted Sator, 1985-86; Ted Sator, Tom Webster, Phil Esposito 1986-87; Michel Bergeron, 1987-88; Michel Bergeron and Phil Esposito, 1988-89; Roger Neilson, 1989-90 to 1991-92; Roger Neilson and Ron Smith, 1992-93; Mike Keenan, 1993-94.

General Manager

SMITH, NEIL
General Manager, New York Rangers.
Born in Toronto, Ont., January 9, 1954.

The 1993-94 campaign marks Neil Smith's fifth season as general manager of the New York Rangers. Smith, 39-years-old, joined the Rangers on July 17, 1989 after seven seasons with the Detroit Red Wings and two with the New York Islanders. After serving as a scout for the Islanders in 1980-81 and 1981-82, Smith joined the Red Wings. While with the Red Wings, Smith held several positions including director of scouting and player development. He also served as general manager of the Adirondack Red Wings (AHL), leading that club to two Calder Cups (1985-86 and 1988-89).

A former All-American defenseman from Western Michigan University, Smith was drafted in 1974 by the New York Islanders. After receiving his degree in communications and business, Smith played two seasons in the IHL–1978-79 with the Kalamazoo Wings and Saginaw Gears and 1979-80 with the Dayton Gems, Milwaukee Admirals and Muskegon Mohawks.

General Managers' History

Lester Patrick, 1927-28 to 1945-46; Frank Boucher, 1946-47 to 1954-55; Murray ''Muzz'' Patrick, 1955-56 to 1963-64; Emile Francis, 1964-65 to 1974-75; Emile Francis and John Ferguson, 1975-76; John Ferguson, 1976-77 to 1977-78; John Ferguson and Fred Shero, 1978-79; Fred Shero, 1979-80; Fred Shero and Craig Patrick, 1980-81; Craig Patrick, 1981-82 to 1985-86; Phil Esposito, 1986-87 to 1988-89; Neil Smith, 1989-90 to date.

Captains' History

Bill Cook, 1926-27 to 1936-37; Art Coulter, 1937-38 to 1941-42; Ott Heller, 1942-43 to 1944-45; Neil Colville 1945-46 to 1948-49; Buddy O'Connor, 1949-50; Frank Eddolls, 1950-51; Frank Eddolls, Allan Stanley, 1951-52; Allan Stanley, 1952-53; Allan Stanley, Don Raleigh, 1953-54; Don Raleigh, 1954-55; Harry Howell, 1955-56, 1956-57; George Sullivan, 1957-58 to 1960-61; Andy Bathgate, 1961-61, 1962-63; Andy Bathgate, Camille Henry, 1963-64; Camille Henry, Bob Nevin, 1964-65; Bob Nevin 1965-66 to 1970-71; Vic Hadfield, 1971-72 to 1973-74; Brad Park, 1974-75; Brad Park, Phil Esposito, 1975-76; Phil Esposito, 1976-77, 1977-78; Dave Maloney, 1978-79, 1979-80; Dave Maloney, Walt Tkaczuk, Barry Beck, 1980-81; Barry Beck, 1981-82 to 1985-86; Ron Greschner, 1986-87; Ron Greschner and Kelly Kisio, 1987-88; Kelly Kisio, 1988-89 to 1990-91; Mark Messier, 1991-92 to date.

Retired Numbers

1	Eddie Giacomin	1965-1976
7	Rod Gilbert	1960-1978

Club Records

Team

(Figures in brackets for season records are games played; records for fewest points, wins, ties, losses, goals, goals against are for 70 or more games)

Most Points **109** 1970-71 (78)
1971-72 (78)
Most Wins **50** 1991-92 (80)
Most Ties **21** 1950-51 (70)
Most Losses **44** 1984-85 (80)
Most Goals **371** 1991-92 (80)
Most Goals Against **345** 1984-85 (80)
Fewest Points **47** 1965-66 (70)
Fewest Wins **17** 1952-53; 54-55; 59-60 (70)
Fewest Ties **5** 1991-92 (80)
Fewest Losses **17** 1971-72 (78)
Fewest Goals **150** 1954-55 (70)
Fewest Goals Against **177** 1970-71 (78)

Longest Winning Streak
Over-all .... **10** Dec. 19/39-Jan. 13/40
Jan. 19-Feb. 10/73
Home .... **14** Dec. 19/39-Feb. 25/40
Away .... **7** Jan. 12-Feb. 12/35
Oct. 28-Nov. 29/78

Longest Undefeated Streak
Over-all .... **19** Nov. 23/39-Jan. 13/40 (14 wins, 5 ties)
Home .... **26** Mar. 29/70-Feb. 2/71 (19 wins, 7 ties)
Away .... **11** Nov. 5/39-Jan. 13/40 (6 wins, 5 ties)

Longest Losing Streak
Over-all .... **11** Oct. 30-Nov. 27/43
Home .... **7** Oct. 20-Nov. 14/76; Mar. 24-Apr. 14/93
Away .... **10** Oct. 30-Dec. 23/43

Longest Winless Streak
Over-all .... **21** Jan. 23-Mar. 19/44 (17 losses, 4 ties)
Home .... **10** Jan. 30-Mar. 19/44 (7 losses, 3 ties)
Away .... **16** Oct. 9-Dec. 20/52 (12 losses, 4 ties)

Most Shutouts, Season **13** 1928-29 (44)
Most PIM, Season **2,018** 1989-90 (80)
Most Goals, Game .... **12** Nov. 21/71 (Cal. 1 at NYR 12)

Individual

Most Seasons .... **17** Harry Howell
Most Games .... **1,160** Harry Howell
Most Goals, Career .... **406** Rod Gilbert
Most Assists, Career ...... **615** Rod Gilbert
Most Points, Career .... **1,021** Rod Gilbert (406 goals, 615 assists)
Most PIM, Career ...... **1,226** Ron Greschner
Most Shutouts, Career ..... **49** Ed Giacomin
Longest Consecutive Games Streak .... **560** Andy Hebenton (Oct. 7/55-Mar. 24/63)
Most Goals, Season .... **50** Vic Hadfield (1971-72)
Most Assists, Season ...... **80** Brian Leetch (1991-92)
Most Points, Season ...... **109** Jean Ratelle (1971-72) (46 goals, 63 assists)
Most PIM, Season .... **305** Troy Mallette (1989-90)
Most Points, Defenseman Season .... **102** Brian Leetch (1991-92) (22 goals, 80 assists)
Most Points, Center, Season .... **109** Jean Ratelle (1971-72) (46 goals, 63 assists)
Most Points, Right Wing, Season .... **97** Rod Gilbert (1971-72) (43 goals, 54 assists)
Rod Gilbert (1974-75) (36 goals, 61 assists)
Most Points, Left Wing, Season .... **106** Vic Hadfield (1971-72) (50 goals, 56 assists)
Most Points, Rookie, Season .... **76** Mark Pavelich (1981-82) (33 goals, 43 assists)
Most Shutouts, Season .... **13** John Ross Roach (1928-29)
Most Goals, Game .... **5** Don Murdoch (Oct. 12/76)
Mark Pavelich (Feb. 23/83)
Most Assists, Game .... **5** Walt Tkaczuk (Feb. 12/72)
Rod Gilbert (Mar. 2/75; Mar. 30/75; Oct. 8/76)
Don Maloney (Jan. 3/87)
Most Points, Game .... **7** Steve Vickers (Feb. 18/76)

All-time Record vs. Other Clubs

Regular Season

	At Home							On Road							Total						
	GP	W	L	T	GF	GA	PTS	GP	W	L	T	GF	GA	PTS	GP	W	L	T	GF	GA	PTS
Boston	280	122	104	54	851	782	298	276	87	150	39	769	1007	213	556	209	254	93	1620	1789	511
Buffalo	44	19	14	11	159	127	49	46	11	29	6	154	217	28	90	30	43	17	313	344	77
Calgary	43	19	19	5	155	156	43	42	10	24	8	130	192	28	85	29	43	13	285	348	71
Chicago	278	117	107	54	824	783	288	277	110	125	42	772	847	262	555	227	232	96	1596	1630	550
Detroit	275	131	86	58	849	704	320	277	75	157	45	685	972	195	552	206	243	103	1534	1676	515
Edmonton	21	6	12	3	86	89	15	21	10	10	1	72	83	21	42	16	22	4	158	172	36
Hartford	22	13	7	2	100	69	28	22	7	12	3	80	89	17	44	20	19	5	180	158	45
Los Angeles	50	30	15	5	204	148	65	51	22	20	9	182	170	53	101	52	35	14	386	318	118
Minnesota	53	32	11	10	191	148	74	52	29	15	8	204	159	66	105	61	26	18	395	307	140
Montreal	268	108	109	51	774	782	267	268	55	179	34	618	1059	144	536	163	288	85	1392	1841	411
New Jersey	56	33	15	8	249	180	74	57	28	25	4	223	202	60	113	61	40	12	472	382	134
NY Islanders	68	43	19	6	274	204	92	68	16	46	6	207	296	38	136	59	65	12	481	500	130
Ottawa	1	1	0	0	6	2	2	2	2	0	0	8	6	4	3	3	0	0	14	8	6
Philadelphia	82	37	26	19	274	241	93	81	28	40	13	236	284	69	163	65	66	32	510	525	162
Pittsburgh	76	39	30	7	311	267	85	75	36	28	11	285	269	83	151	75	58	18	596	536	168
Quebec	22	14	5	3	92	60	31	23	8	12	3	98	106	19	45	22	17	6	190	166	50
St. Louis	52	41	6	5	224	119	87	54	25	21	8	179	160	58	106	66	27	13	403	279	145
San Jose	2	2	0	0	12	4	4	3	3	0	0	14	6	6	5	5	0	0	26	10	10
Tampa Bay	2	1	1	0	7	10	2	1	1	0	0	5	4	2	3	2	1	0	12	14	4
Toronto	267	110	101	56	816	782	276	266	77	151	38	688	917	192	533	187	252	94	1504	1699	468
Vancouver	46	34	7	5	209	114	73	44	30	11	3	182	142	63	90	64	18	8	391	256	136
Washington	57	28	23	6	237	210	62	58	21	29	8	200	232	50	115	49	52	14	437	442	112
Winnipeg	21	11	8	2	102	88	24	22	12	8	2	86	81	26	43	23	16	4	188	169	50
Defunct Clubs	139	87	30	22	460	290	196	139	82	34	23	441	291	187	278	169	64	45	901	581	383
Totals	**2225**	**1078**	**755**	**392**	**7466**	**6359**	**2548**	**2225**	**785**	**1126**	**314**	**6518**	**7791**	**1884**	**4450**	**1863**	**1881**	**706**	**13984**	**14150**	**4432**

Playoffs

	Series	W	L	GP	W	L	T	GF	GA	Last Mtg.	Round	Result
Boston	9	3	6	42	18	22	2	104	114	1973	QF	W 4-1
Buffalo	1	0	1	3	1	2	0	6	11	1978	PR	L 1-2
**Calgary	1	1	0	4	3	1	0	14	8	1980	PR	W 3-1
Chicago	5	1	4	24	10	14	0	54	66	1973	SF	L 1-4
Detroit	5	1	4	23	10	13	0	49	57	1950	F	L 3-4
Los Angeles	2	2	0	6	5	1	0	32	14	1981	PR	W 3-1
Montreal	13	6	7	55	21	32	2	139	171	1986	CF	L 1-4
New Jersey	1	1	0	7	4	3	0	28	25	1992	DSF	W 4-3
NY Islanders	7	2	5	35	15	20	0	110	126	1990	DSF	W 4-1
Philadelphia	8	4	4	38	19	19	0	130	119	1987	DSF	L 2-4
Pittsburgh	2	0	2	10	2	8	0	30	44	1992	DF	L 2-4
St. Louis	1	1	0	6	4	2	0	29	22	1981	QF	W 4-2
Toronto	8	5	3	35	19	16	0	86	86	1971	QF	W 4-2
Washington	3	1	2	17	7	10	0	51	63	1991	DSF	L 2-4
Defunct	9	6	3	22	11	7	4	43	29			
Totals	**75**	**34**	**41**	**327**	**149**	**170**	**8**	**905**	**954**			

Playoff Results 1993-89

Year	Round	Opponent	Result	GF	GA
1992	DF	Pittsburgh	L 2-4	19	24
	DSF	New Jersey	W 4-3	28	25
1991	DSF	Washington	L 2-4	16	16
1990	DF	Washington	L 1-4	15	22
	DSF	NY Islanders	W 4-1	22	13
1989	DSF	Pittsburgh	L 0-4	11	19

Abbreviations: Round: F – Final; **CF** – conference final; **DF** – division final; **DSF** – division semi-final; **SF** – semi-final; **QF** – quarter-final; **PR** – preliminary round. **GA** – goals against; **GF** – goals for.

1992-93 Results

Home				Away			
Oct.	12	Hartford	6-2	Oct.	9	Washington	4-2
	14	New Jersey	6-1		10	New Jersey	2-4
	18	NY Islanders	4-3		17	NY Islanders	3-6
	21	Washington	2-1		24	Ottawa	3-2
	23	Montreal	3-3		31	Montreal	3-4
	26	Philadelphia	8-4	Nov.	7	Boston	2-2
	29	Quebec	3-6		14	Quebec	3-6
Nov.	2	Buffalo	7-6		19	Philadelphia	3-7
	4	Philadelphia	3-1		21	Winnipeg	5-4
	9	Tampa Bay	1-5		25	Pittsburgh	11-3
	11	Washington	4-7		27	Minnesota	4-4
	23	Pittsburgh	2-5	Dec.	4	Washington	4-8
	30	Minnesota	2-4		11	Tampa Bay	5-4
Dec.	2	Detroit	5-3		17	St. Louis	4-3
	6	Toronto	6-0		19	Hartford	4-4
	9	Tampa Bay	6-5		21	New Jersey	3-0
	13	Montreal	10-5		26	NY Islanders	4-6
	15	Calgary	0-3		29	Washington	3-4
	23	New Jersey	4-5		31	Buffalo	6-11
	27	Boston	6-5	Jan.	2	Pittsburgh	2-5
Jan.	4	New Jersey	3-3		9	Philadelphia*	3-4
	6	Ottawa	6-2		16	Montreal	0-3
	11	Vancouver	3-3		19	Detroit	2-2
	13	Washington	5-4		23	Los Angeles	8-3
	27	Winnipeg	5-2		29	Buffalo	4-6
Feb.	3	Philadelphia	2-2		30	Toronto	1-3
	10	Pittsburgh	0-3	Feb.	1	NY Islanders	4-4
	12	NY Islanders	4-3		8	New Jersey	4-5
	15	St. Louis*	4-1		13	NY Islanders	2-5
Mar.	3	Buffalo	2-2		20	San Jose	6-4
	5	Pittsburgh	3-1		22	San Jose	4-0
	9	Los Angeles	4-3		24	Vancouver	4-5
	15	Boston	1-3		26	Calgary	4-4
	17	Edmonton	3-4		27	Edmonton	1-0
	19	San Jose	8-1	Mar.	6	Quebec	2-10
	24	Philadelphia	4-5		11	Chicago	4-1
	26	Chicago	1-3		22	Ottawa	5-4
	28	Quebec	2-3	Apr.	4	Washington*	4-0
Apr.	2	NY Islanders	2-3		7	New Jersey	2-5
	5	Hartford	4-5		10	Pittsburgh	2-4
	9	Pittsburgh	4-10		12	Philadelphia	0-1
	14	Washington	0-2		16	Washington	2-4

*Denotes afternoon game

Entry Draft
Selections 1993-79

1993
Pick
- 8 Niklas Sundstrom
- 34 Lee Sorochan
- 61 Maxim Galanov
- 86 Sergei Olimpiyev
- 112 Gary Roach
- 138 Dave Trofimenkoff
- 162 Sergei Kondrashkin
- 164 Todd Marchant
- 190 Eddy Campbell
- 216 Ken Shepard
- 242 Andrei Kudinov
- 261 Pavel Komarov
- 268 Maxim Smelnitsky

1992
Pick
- 24 Peter Ferraro
- 48 Mattias Norstrom
- 72 Eric Cairns
- 85 Chris Ferraro
- 120 Dmitri Starostenko
- 144 David Dal Grande
- 168 Matt Oates
- 192 Mickey Elick
- 216 Dan Brierley
- 240 Vladimir Vorobjev

1991
Pick
- 15 Alexei Kovalev
- 37 Darcy Werenka
- 96 Corey Machanic
- 125 Fredrik Jax
- 128 Barry Young
- 147 John Rushin
- 169 Corey Hirsch
- 191 Viacheslav Uvayev
- 213 Jamie Ram
- 235 Vitali Chinakhov
- 257 Brian Wiseman

1990
Pick
- 13 Michael Stewart
- 34 Doug Weight
- 55 John Vary
- 69 Jeff Nielsen
- 76 Rick Willis
- 85 Sergei Zubov
- 99 Lubos Rob
- 118 Jason Weinrich
- 139 Bryan Lonsinger
- 160 Todd Hedlund
- 181 Andrew Silverman
- 202 Jon Hillebrandt
- 223 Brett Lievers
- 244 Sergei Nemchinov

1989
Pick
- 20 Steven Rice
- 40 Jason Prosofsky
- 45 Rob Zamuner
- 49 Louie DeBrusk
- 67 Jim Cummins
- 88 Aaron Miller
- 118 Joby Messier
- 139 Greg Leahy
- 160 Greg Spenrath
- 181 Mark Bavis
- 202 Roman Oksyuta
- 223 Steve Locke
- 244 Ken MacDermid

1988
Pick
- 22 Troy Mallette
- 26 Murray Duval
- 68 Tony Amonte
- 99 Martin Bergeron
- 110 Dennis Vial
- 131 Mike Rosati
- 152 Eric Couvrette
- 173 Shorty Forrest
- 194 Paul Cain
- 202 Eric Fenton
- 215 Peter Fiorentino
- 236 Keith Slifstien

1987
Pick
- 10 Jayson More
- 31 Daniel Lacroix
- 46 Simon Gagne
- 69 Michael Sullivan
- 94 Eric O'Borsky
- 115 Ludek Cajka
- 136 Clint Thomas
- 157 Charles Wiegand
- 178 Eric Burrill
- 199 David Porter
- 205 Brett Barnett
- 220 Lance Marciano

1986
Pick
- 9 Brian Leetch
- 51 Bret Walter
- 53 Shawn Clouston
- 72 Mark Janssens
- 93 Jeff Bloemberg
- 114 Darren Turcotte
- 135 Robb Graham
- 156 Barry Chyzowski
- 177 Pat Scanlon
- 198 Joe Ranger
- 219 Russell Parent
- 240 Soren True

1985
Pick
- 7 Ulf Dahlen
- 28 Mike Richter
- 49 Sam Lindstahl
- 70 Pat Janostin
- 91 Brad Stephan
- 112 Brian McReynolds
- 133 Neil Pilon
- 154 Larry Bernard
- 175 Stephane Brochu
- 196 Steve Nemeth
- 217 Robert Burakowsky
- 238 Rudy Poeschek

1984
Pick
- 14 Terry Carkner
- 35 Raimo Helminen
- 77 Paul Broten
- 98 Clark Donatelli
- 119 Kjell Samuelsson
- 140 Thomas Hussey
- 161 Brian Nelson
- 182 Ville Kentala
- 188 Heinz Ehlers
- 202 Kevin Miller
- 223 Tom Lorentz
- 243 Scott Brower

1983
Pick
- 12 Dave Gagner
- 33 Randy Heath
- 49 Vesa Salo
- 53 Gordie Walker
- 73 Peter Andersson
- 93 Jim Andonoff
- 113 Bob Alexander
- 133 Steve Orth
- 153 Peter Marcov
- 173 Paul Jerrard
- 213 Bryan Walker
- 233 Ulf Nilsson

1982
Pick
- 15 Chris Kontos
- 36 Tomas Sandstrom
- 57 Corey Millen
- 78 Chris Jensen
- 120 Tony Granato
- 141 Sergei Kapustin
- 160 Brian Glynn
- 162 Jan Karlsson
- 183 Kelly Miller
- 193 Simo Saarinen
- 204 Bob Lowes
- 225 Andy Otto
- 246 Dwayne Robinson

1981
Pick
- 9 James Patrick
- 30 Jan Erixon
- 50 Peter Sundstrom
- 51 Mark Morrison
- 72 John Vanbiesbrouck
- 114 Eric Magnuson
- 135 Mike Guentzel
- 156 Ari Lahteenmaki
- 177 Paul Reifenberger
- 198 Mario Proulx

1980
Pick
- 14 Jim Malone
- 35 Mike Allison
- 77 Kurt Kleinendorst
- 98 Scot Kleinendorst
- 119 Reijo Ruotsalainen
- 140 Bob Scurfield
- 161 Bart Wilson
- 182 Chris Wray
- 203 Anders Backstrom

1979
Pick
- 13 Doug Sulliman
- 34 Ed Hospodar
- 76 Pat Conacher
- 97 Dan Makuch
- 118 Stan Adams

Club Directory

Madison Square Garden
4 Pennsylvania Plaza
New York, New York 10001
Phone **212/465-6000**
PR FAX 212/465-6494
Capacity: 18,200

Executive Management
President and General Manager . . . . Neil Smith
Vice-President and General Counsel. . . . . Kenneth W. Munoz
Vice-President, Finance . . . . Jim Abry
Governor. . . . . Stanley R. Jaffe
Alternate Governors . . . . Neil Smith, Bob Gutkowski, Ken Munoz

Hockey Club Personnel
Assistant General Manager/Player Development . Larry Pleau
Head Coach . . . . Mike Keenan
Associate Coach. . . . . Colin Campbell
Assistant Coach . . . . Dick Todd
Development Coach . . . . Al Hill
Scouting Staff . . . . Darwin Bennett, Tony Feltrin, Bob Froese, Herb Hammond, Martin Madden, Christer Rockstrom
Director, Administration . . . . John Gentile
Manager, Team Operations . . . . Matthew Loughran
Manager, Scouting . . . . Bill Short
Executive Administrative Assistant . . . . Barbara Dand
Senior Secretary . . . . Nicole Wetzold
Video Assistant. . . . . Arnie Pappin

Medical/Training Staff
Team Physician and Orthopedic Surgeon . . . . Dr. Barton Nisonson, M.D.
Assistant Team Physician . . . . Dr. Tony Maddalo
Medical Consultants . . . . Dr. Howard Chester, Dr. Frank Gardner, James A. Nicholas, Dr. Ronald Weissman
Team Dentists . . . . Dr. Irwin Miller, Dr. Don Soloman
Sports Psychologist . . . . Dr. Cal Bottevill
Sports Physiologist . . . . Dr. Howie Wenger
Medical Trainer . . . . Dave Smith
Equipment Manager . . . . Mike Folga
Equipment Trainer . . . . Joe Murphy
Lockerroom Assistant . . . . Benny Petrizzi

Communications Department
Director, Communications . . . . Barry Watkins
Manager, Communications . . . . Kevin McDonald
Communications Assistant . . . . John Rosasco
Administrative Assistant . . . . Ann Marie Gilmartin

Marketing Department
Director, Marketing . . . . Kevin Kennedy
Manager, Community Relations. . . . . Rod Gilbert
Manager, Promotions . . . . Caroline Calabrese
Manager, Marketing Operations. . . . . Jim Pfeiffer
Manager, Event Presentation. . . . . Jeannie Baumgartner

Home Ice . . . . Madison Square Garden
Press Facilities . . . . 33rd Street
Television Facilities . . . . 31st Street
Radio Facilities . . . . 33rd Street
Rink Dimensions. . . . . 200 feet by 85 feet
Ends and Sides of Rink . . . . Plexiglass (8 feet)
Club Colors. . . . . Blue, Red and White
Training Camp . . . . Rye, New York
TV Announcers. . . . . Bruce Beck, John Davidson, Sam Rosen, Al Trautwig
Radio Announcers . . . . Marv Albert, Sal Messina, Howie Rose
Television Outlets. Madison Square Garden Cable Network
Radio Outlet . . . . MSG Radio – WFAN (66 AM), WEVD (1050 AM), WXPS (107.1 FM)

The New York Rangers Hockey Club is part of Madison Square Garden

Coach

KEENAN, MICHAEL (MIKE)
Coach, New York Rangers.
Born in Toronto, Ontario, October 21, 1949.

Mike Keenan was introduced as the 26th coach in Rangers history on April 17, 1993. With a career winning percentage of .590, he is fifth on the NHL's all-time list and his 343 career victories rank 13th on the League's all-time win list. Keenan guided the Philadelphia Flyers from 1984-85 to 1987-88, twice taking them to the Stanley Cup Finals. He was behind the bench for the Chicago Blackhawks from 1988-89 through 1991-92, leading them to the Stanley Cup Finals in 1991-92. Keenan also served as the team's General Manager from 1989-90 to November 6, 1992. During his eight-year coaching career, Keenan's teams have finished in first place five times and have won two regular-season championships. He has been behind the bench for three NHL All-Star games, and won two Canada Cup Championships for Team Canada. He received the Jack Adams Trophy as the NHL's Coach of the Year in 1985 and was a finalist for the award in 1991. Keenan's professional coaching career began in 1980-81 with the Rochester Americans of the American Hockey League and in 1982-83 he led the Americans to the Calder Cup Championship. Keenan then moved to the University of Toronto, where he posted a record of 41-5-3 and led the team to the Canadian Collegiate Championship.

Coaching Record

Season	Team	Games	W	L	T	%	Games	W	L	%
			Regular Season					Playoffs		
1979-80	Peterborough (OHL)	68	47	20	1	.699	18	15	3	.833
1980-81	Rochester (AHL)	80	30	42	8	.425	....	....	....	....
1981-82	Rochester (AHL)	80	40	31	9	.556	9	4	5	.444
1982-83	Rochester (AHL)	80	46	25	9	.631	16	12	4	.750
1983-84	U. of Toronto (CIAU)	49	41	5	3	.867	....	....	....	....
1984-85	Philadelphia (NHL)	80	53	20	7	.706	19	12	7	.632
1985-86	Philadelphia (NHL)	80	53	23	4	.688	5	2	3	.400
1986-87	Philadelphia (NHL)	80	46	26	8	.625	26	15	11	.577
1987-88	Philadelphia (NHL)	80	38	33	9	.531	7	3	4	.429
1988-89	Chicago (NHL)	80	27	41	12	.413	16	9	7	.563
1989-90	Chicago (NHL)	80	41	33	6	.550	20	10	10	.500
1990-91	Chicago (NHL)	80	49	23	8	.663	6	2	4	.333
1991-92	Chicago (NHL)	80	36	29	15	.544	18	12	6	.667
	NHL Totals	640	343	228	69	.590	117	65	52	.556

Ottawa Senators

1992-93 Results: 10w-70L-4T 24PTS. Sixth, Adams Division

Year-by-Year Record

Season	GP	Home W	L	T	Road W	L	T	Overall W	L	T	GF	GA	Pts.	Finished	Playoff Result
1992-93	84	9	29	4	1	41	0	10	70	4	202	395	24	6th, Adams Div.	Out of Playoffs

Schedule

Home			Away		
Oct.	Wed. 6	Quebec	**Oct.**	Sat. 9	St Louis
	Thur. 21	Dallas		Thur. 14	Florida
	Mon. 25	Anaheim		Sat. 16	Tampa Bay
	Wed. 27	Philadelphia		Sat. 23	NY Islanders
Nov.	Thur. 11	Florida		Thur. 28	Boston
	Mon. 15	Montreal		Sat. 30	Dallas
	Wed. 17	NY Islanders	**Nov.**	Wed. 3	Edmonton
	Thur. 18	New Jersey		Fri. 5	Winnipeg
	Mon. 22	Buffalo		Wed. 10	Hartford
	Wed. 24	NY Rangers		Sat. 13	Montreal
	Mon. 29	Hartford		Fri. 26	Buffalo
Dec.	Sat. 4	Washington		Sat. 27	Pittsburgh
	Mon. 6	Calgary	**Dec.**	Wed. 1	Montreal
	Wed. 8	Buffalo		Fri. 3	Detroit
	Mon. 13	Los Angeles		Thur. 9	Dallas
	Tues. 21	Quebec			(at Minnesota)
	Thur. 23	Hartford		Sat. 11	Quebec
	Mon. 27	Boston		Wed. 15	Tampa Bay
	Thur. 30	Tampa Bay		Fri. 17	Washington
Jan.	Sat. 1	New Jersey		Sun. 19	NY Rangers
	Mon. 3	Pittsburgh		Sun. 26	Hartford
	Wed. 5	Vancouver	**Jan.**	Thur. 6	Toronto
	Sat. 8	Winnipeg		Tues. 11	Philadelphia
	Mon. 10	NY Islanders		Fri. 14	Vancouver
	Tues. 18	Edmonton		Sat. 15	Calgary
	Thur. 27	Hartford		Tues. 25	Pittsburgh
	Mon. 31	Chicago		Sat. 29	Chicago
Feb.	Wed. 2	Florida	**Feb.**	Fri. 4	New Jersey
	Sat. 5	Montreal		Fri. 18	NY Rangers
	Tues. 8	Philadelphia		Sat. 19	NY Islanders
	Thur. 10	Tampa Bay	**Mar.**	Sat. 5	Boston
	Sat. 12	NY Rangers		Tues. 8	Quebec
	Thur. 24	San Jose		Thur. 10	Philadelphia
	Sat. 26	St Louis		Sun. 13	Anaheim*
	Mon. 28	Toronto		Tues. 15	Los Angeles
Mar.	Wed. 2	Buffalo		Thur. 17	San Jose
	Fri. 4	Winnipeg		Sun. 20	Buffalo*
		(at Minnesota)		Thur. 24	Pittsburgh
	Wed. 23	Detroit		Mon. 28	Montreal
	Wed. 30	Quebec	**Apr.**	Sat. 2	Florida
Apr.	Wed. 6	Washington		Thur. 7	Boston
	Mon. 11	Pittsburgh		Sat. 9	Washington
	Wed. 13	Boston		Thur. 14	New Jersey

* Denotes afternoon game.

Home Starting Times:
Weeknights . . . . 7:35 p.m.
Saturdays . . . . 8:05 p.m.

Franchise date: December 16, 1991

NORTHEAST DIVISION

EASTERN CONFERENCE

2nd NHL Season

Norm Maciver had his finest NHL season in 1992-93, leading the Senators in assists (46) and points (63).

1993-94 Player Personnel

FORWARDS

	HT	WT	S	Place of Birth	Date	1992-93 Club
ARCHIBALD, Dave	6-1	210	L	Chiliwack, B.C.	4/14/69	Ottawa
BODKIN, Rick	6-4	190	L	Hamilton, Ont.	3/30/75	Sudbury
BURAKOWSKI, Robert	5-10	185	R	Malmo, Sweden	11/24/66	Malmo
CIMELLARO, Tony	5-11	179	L	Kingston, Ont.	6/14/71	New Haven
DAIGLE, Alexandre	6-0	175	L	Montreal, Que.	2/7/75	Victoriaville
DEMITRA, Pavol	5-11	178	L	Dubnica, Czech.	11/29/74	Dukla Trencin
DOWNEY, Brian	6-1	188	L	Ottawa, Ont.	6/30/68	Thunder Bay
DUPAUL, Cosmo	6-0	185	L	P.-Claire, Que.	4/11/75	Victoriaville
FAUCHER, Vincent	6-2	195	L	S. Falls, Ont.	10/28/67	New Haven-Thunder Bay
FLINTON, Eric	6-2	195	L	Will. Lake, B.C.	2/2/72	Univ. of New Hampshire
GRIMES, Jake	6-1	196	L	Montreal, Que.	9/13/72	New Haven
GUERARD, Daniel	6-2	211	R	Lasalle, Que.	4/9/74	Victoriaville-Verdun
HUARD, Bill	6-1	215	L	Welland, Ont.	6/10/67	Providence Bruins
JELINEK, Tomas	5-9	182	L	Prague, Czech.	4/29/62	Ottawa
KEKALAINEN, Jarmo	6-0	190	R	Tampere, Finland	7/3/66	Tappara Tampere
KUDELSKI, Bob	6-1	200	R	Springfield, MA	3/3/64	Los Angeles-Ottawa
LAMB, Mark	5-9	180	L	Ponteix, Sask.	8/3/64	Ottawa
LOEWEN, Darcy	5-10	185	L	Calgary, Alta.	2/26/69	Ottawa
MALLETTE, Troy	6-2	210	L	Sudbury, Ont.	2/25/70	New Jersey
McBAIN, Andrew	6-1	205	R	Scarborough, Ont.	1/18/65	Ottawa
MONGEON, Hugues	5-11	180	L	Ottawa, Ont.	3/4/72	New Haven
PANKEWICZ, Greg	6-0	185	R	Dray. Valley, Alta.	10/6/70	New Haven
PENNEY, Chad	6-0	196	L	Labrador City, Nfld.	9/18/73	North Bay-Sault Ste. Marie
ROWLAND, Chris	6-1	188	R	Calgary, Alta.	3/30/71	New Haven-Thunder Bay
RUZICKA, Vladimir	6-3	210	L	Most, Czech.	6/6/63	Boston
ST-AMOUR, Martin	6-3	194	L	Montreal, Que.	1/30/70	New Haven
ST-CYR, Gerry	6-1	188	R	N. Vancouver, B.C.	8/18/71	New Haven
SAVOIE, Claude	5-11	182	R	Montreal, Que.	3/12/73	Victoriaville
SCHNEIDER, Andy	5-9	170	L	Edmonton, Alta.	3/29/72	New Haven-Swift Current
TURGEON, Sylvain	6-0	200	L	Noranda, Que.	1/17/65	Ottawa
YASHIN, Alexei	6-2	196	L	Sverdl., C.I.S.	11/5/73	Dynamo Moscow

DEFENSEMEN

	HT	WT	S	Place of Birth	Date	1992-93 Club
BICANEK, Radek	6-1	178	L	Unh. Hrad. Czech.	1/18/75	Dukla Jihlava
DINEEN, Gord	6-0	195	R	Toronto, Ont.	9/21/62	San Diego-Ottawa
DISHER, Jason	6-0	190	L	Windsor, Ont.	5/28/75	Kingston
FILIMONOV, Dimitri	6-4	207	R	Perm, C.I.S.	10/14/71	Dynamo Moscow
HAMMOND, Ken	6-1	190	R	Port Credit, Ont.	8/22/63	Ottawa
HAMR, Radek	5-11	167	L	Usti-nad-laben, Czech.	6/15/74	New Haven-Ottawa
KENNEY, Jay	6-2	190	L	New York, NY	9/21/73	Providence College
LAMMENS, Hank	6-2	210	L	Brockville, Ont.	2/21/66	Canadian Olympic
MACIVER, Norm	5-11	180	L	Thunder Bay, Ont.	9/8/64	Ottawa
PAYNTER, Kent	6-0	183	L	Summerside, P.E.I.	4/17/65	New Haven
POLISTCHUK, Sergei	6-2	192	L	Moscow, USSR	1/11/75	Dynamo Moscow
RUMBLE, Darren	6-1	200	L	Barrie, Ont.	1/23/69	Ottawa
SCHUWERK, Rick	6-1	212	R	Connecticut	3/22/73	Canterbury Prep. School
SHAW, Brad	6-0	190	R	Cambridge, Ont.	4/28/64	Ottawa
SINCLAIR, Al	6-3	210	R	Mississauga, Ont.	4/3/73	University of Michigan
TRAVERSE, Patrick	6-3	173	L	Montreal, Que.	3/14/74	Shawinigan-St-Jean
VIAL, Dennis	6-2	220	L	Sault Ste. Marie, Ont.	4/10/69	Adirondack-Detroit
WHITE, Scott	6-1	195	L	Ormst., Que.	4/21/68	New Haven

GOALTENDERS

	HT	WT	C	Place of Birth	Date	1992-93 Club
BILLINGTON, Craig	5-10	170	L	London, Ont.	9/11/66	New Jersey
CHARBONNEAU, P.	5-11	217	L	St-J. Ri., Que.	7/22/75	Victoriaville
KVALEVOG, Toby	5-11	170	L	Bemidji, MN	12/22/74	Bemidji High School
MADELEY, Darrin	5-11	170	L	Holland Landing, Ont.	2/25/68	New Haven
MICHAUD, Mark	5-10	175	L	Quebec, Que.	8/15/67	Thunder Bay-New Haven
MIKLENDA, Jaroslav	6-1	176	L	Vesslina Morave, Czech.	3/7/74	Olomouc
RONNQUIST, Petter	5-11	173	L	Stockholm, Sweden	2/7/73	Djurgarden

1992-93 Scoring

Regular Season

Pos	#	Player	Team	GP	G	A	Pts	+/-	PIM	PP	SH	GW	GT	S	%
D	22	Norm Maciver	OTT	80	17	46	63	46-	84	7	1	2	0	184	9.2
C	13	Jamie Baker	OTT	76	19	29	48	20-	54	10	0	2	0	160	11.9
L	61	Sylvain Turgeon	OTT	72	25	18	43	29-	104	8	0	2	1	249	10.0
R	26	Bob Kudelski	L.A.	15	3	3	6	3-	8	0	0	1	0	12	25.0
			OTT	48	21	14	35	22-	22	12	0	2	0	125	16.8
			TOTAL	63	24	17	41	25-	30	12	0	3	0	137	17.5
D	4	Brad Shaw	OTT	81	7	34	41	47-	34	4	0	0	0	166	4.2
R	17	Jody Hull	OTT	69	13	21	34	24-	14	5	1	0	1	134	9.7
C	7	Mark Lamb	OTT	71	7	19	26	40-	64	1	0	0	0	123	5.7
L	44	Mike Peluso	OTT	81	15	10	25	35-	318	2	0	1	0	93	16.1
C	11	Mark Freer	OTT	63	10	14	24	35-	39	3	3	0	0	80	12.5
C	12	Neil Brady	OTT	55	7	17	24	25-	57	5	0	0	0	68	10.3
R	20	Andrew McBain	OTT	59	7	16	23	37-	43	1	0	0	0	71	9.9
C	16	Laurie Boschman	OTT	70	9	7	16	26-	101	0	1	1	1	84	10.7
D	34*	Darren Rumble	OTT	69	3	13	16	24-	61	0	0	0	0	92	3.3
C	15	David Archibald	OTT	44	6	15	16-	32		6	0	0	0	93	9.7
L	9	Doug Smail	OTT	51	4	10	14	34-	51	0	0	1	0	73	5.5
R	25	Tomas Jelinek	OTT	49	7	6	13	21-	52	0	0	0	0	60	11.7
D	23*	Chris Luongo	OTT	76	3	9	12	47-	68	1	0	0	0	76	3.9
L	28	Jeff Lazaro	OTT	26	6	4	10	8-	16	0	1	0	0	38	15.8
C	18	Rob Murphy	OTT	44	3	7	10	23-	30	0	0	0	0	55	5.5
L	10*	Darcy Loewen	OTT	79	4	5	9	26-	145	0	0	0	0	42	9.5
D	5	Ken Hammond	OTT	62	4	4	8	42-	104	0	0	0	0	64	6.3
D	6	Gord Dineen	OTT	32	2	4	6	19-	30	1	0	0	0	36	5.6
D	14	Brad Marsh	OTT	59	0	3	3	29-	30	0	0	0	0	35	.0
D	2	Jim Kyte	OTT	4	0	1	1	0	4	0	0	0	0	1	.0
R	27*	Blair Atcheynum	OTT	4	0	1	1	3-	0	0	0	0	0	5	.0
G	32	Daniel Berthiaume	OTT	25	0	1	1	0	2	0	0	0	0	0	.0
L	21*	Martin St. Amour	OTT	1	0	0	0	0	2	0	0	0	0	2	.0
C	33	Tony Cimellaro	OTT	2	0	0	0	2-	0	0	0	0	0	0	.0
G	30*	Darrin Madeley	OTT	2	0	0	0	0	0	0	0	0	0	0	.0
D	2*	Radek Hamr	OTT	4	0	0	0	4-	0	0	0	0	0	0	.0
D	3	Kent Paynter	OTT	6	0	0	0	7-	20	0	0	0	0	3	.0
G	1	Steve Weeks	OTT	7	0	0	0	0	0	0	0	0	0	0	.0
G	55	Brad Miller	OTT	11	0	0	0	5-	42	0	0	0	0	2	.0
G	31	Peter Sidorkiewicz	OTT	64	0	0	0	0	8	0	0	0	0	0	.0

Goaltending

No.	Goaltender	GPI	Mins	Avg	W	L	T	EN	SO	GA	SA	S%
32	Daniel Berthiaume	25	1326	4.30	2	17	1	3	0	95	739	.871
31	Peter Sidorkiewicz	64	3388	4.43	8	46	3	7	0	250	1737	.856
30	*Darrin Madeley	2	90	6.67	0	2	0	0	0	10	44	.773
1	Steve Weeks	7	249	7.23	0	5	0	0	0	30	144	.792
	Totals	**84**	**5074**	**4.67**	**10**	**70**	**4**	**10**	**0**	**395**	**2674**	**.852**

Sylvain Turgeon led the Senators with 25 goals in 1992-93.

General Manager

SEXTON, RANDY JOHN
General Manager, Ottawa Senators. Born in Brockville, Ont., July 24, 1959.

Randy Sexton was appointed General Manager of the Ottawa Senators on April 15, 1993. Randy began working as the Manager of Operations with Terrace Investments Limited in May 1985. He was promoted to the position of Vice-President in April 1987. Sexton was responsible for the business operations of the team and provides overall direction and management to the club. Prior to the 1992-93 season, Sexton became Chief Executive Officer and Alternate Governor of the Club. On January 26, 1993, Sexton was appointed President and Chief Operating Officer. His post secondary education began at St. Lawrence University where he obtained a Bachelor of Science degree. He played for the St. Lawrence University Varsity Hockey Team from 1979 to 1982, and served as the team Captain for the last two seasons. He acted as Assistant Coach and scout with St. Lawrence from 1983 to 1985. Sexton later received his Master degree in Business Administration from Clarkson University, Potsdam, New York. A driving force in the "Bring Back the Senators" campaign, Sexton ultimately convinced NHL Governors of Ottawa's capacity to support the Senators by implementing strategies such as the season ticket drive, during which over 15,000 Ottawans purchased Priority Registry Numbers guaranteeing a seat to witness the return of NHL hockey to the city.

Club Records

Team

(Figures in brackets for season records are games played; records for fewest points, wins, ties, losses, goals, goals against are for 70 or more games)

Most Points	24	1992-93 (84)
Most Wins	10	1992-93 (84)
Most Ties	4	1992-93 (84)
Most Losses	70	1992-93 (84)
Most Goals	202	1992-93 (84)
Most Goals Against	395	1992-93 (84)
Fewest Points	24	1992-93 (84)
Fewest Wins	10	1992-93 (84)
Fewest Ties	4	1992-93 (84)
Fewest Losses	70	1992-93 (84)
Fewest Goals	202	1992-93 (84)
Fewest Goals Against	395	1992-93 (84)

Longest Winning Streak
Over-all . . . . 2 Feb. 3/93-Feb. 8/93
Home . . . . 2 Feb. 3/93-Feb. 8/93
Away . . . . 1 Apr. 10/93
Longest Undefeated Streak
Over-all . . . . 3 Feb. 1/93-Feb. 8/93 (2-0-1)
Home . . . . 4 Jan. 28/93-Feb. 8/93 (3-0-1)
Away . . . . 1 Apr. 10/93
Longest Losing Streak
Over-all . . . . 14 Mar. 2/93-Apr. 7/93
Home . . . . 7 Mar. 18/93-Apr. 14/93
Away . . . . *39 Oct. 10/92-Apr. 3/93**
Longest Winless Streak
Over-all . . . . 21 Oct. 10/92-Nov. 23/92 (0-20-1)
Home . . . . 9 Oct. 22/92-Nov. 23/92 (0-8-1)
Away . . . . *39 Oct. 10/92-Apr. 3/93 (0-39-0)**

** NHL records do not include neutral site games

General Managers' History

Mel Bridgman, 1992-93; Randy Sexton, 1993-94.

Coaching History

Rick Bowness, 1992-93 to date.

Captains' History

Laurie Boschman, 1992-93.

Most Shutouts, Season	None	
Most PIM, Season	1,716	1992-93 (84)
Most Goals, Game	6	Feb. 28/93 (Que. 4 at Ott. 6) Mar. 4/93 (Ott. 6 at L.A. 8)

Individual

Most Seasons	1	Numerous
Most Games, Career	81	Brad Shaw Mike Peluso
Most Goals, Career	25	Sylvain Turgeon
Most Assists, Career	46	Norm Maciver
Most Points, Career	63	Norm Maciver (17 goals, 46 assits)
Most PIM, Career	318	Mike Peluso
Most Shutouts, Career	None	

Longest Consecutive
Games Streak . . . . 74 Brad Shaw (Oct. 31/92-Apr. 14/93)
Most Games, Season . . . . . 81 Brad Shaw (1992-93)
Most Goals, Season . . . . 25 Sylvain Turgeon (1992-93)
Most Assists, Season . . . . . 46 Norm Maciver (1992-93)
Most Points, Season . . . . 63 Norm Maciver (1992-93) (17 goals, 46 assists)
Most PIM, Season . . . . 318 Mike Peluso (1992-93)
Most Shutouts, Season . . None
Most Points, Defenseman
Season . . . . 63 Norm Maciver (1992-93) (17 goals, 46 assists)
Most Points, Center
Season . . . . 48 Jamie Baker (1992-93) (19 goals, 29 assits)
Most Points, Right Wing
Season . . . . 35 Bob Kudelski (1992-93) (21 goals, 14 assists)
Most Points, Left Wing
Season . . . . 43 Sylvain Turgeon (1992-93) (25 goals, 18 assists)

Most Points, Rookie
Season . . . . 16 Darren Rumble (1992-93) (3 goals, 13 assists)
Most Goals, Game . . . . 3 Bob Kudelski (Jan. 10/93) Laurie Boschman (Apr. 10/93)
Most Assists, Game . . . . 3 Jamie Baker (Mar. 4/93)
Most Points, Game . . . . 3 Bob Kudelski (3-0-3 Jan. 10/93); (2-1-3 Feb. 3/93); (1-2-3 Mar. 4/93); (1-2-3 Apr. 10/93) Jamie Baker (0-3-3 Mar. 4/93) Laurie Boschman (3-0-3 Apr. 10/93) Neil Brady (1-2-3 Oct. 20/92) Mark Freer (1-2-3 Feb. 8/93) Sylvain Turgeon (2-1-3 Dec. 7/92)

* NHL Record.

Retired Numbers

8   Frank Finnigan   1924-1934

All-time Record vs. Other Clubs

Regular Season

	At Home							On Road							Total						
	GP	W	L	T	GF	GA	PTS	GP	W	L	T	GF	GA	PTS	GP	W	L	T	GF	GA	PTS
Boston	3	0	3	0	5	11	0	4	0	4	0	10	20	0	7	0	7	0	15	31	0
Buffalo	4	1	2	1	10	16	3	3	0	3	0	5	19	0	7	1	5	1	15	35	3
Calgary	1	0	0	1	1	1	1	1	0	1	0	4	8	0	2	0	1	1	5	9	1
Chicago	1	0	1	0	2	4	0	1	0	1	0	2	4	0	2	0	2	0	4	8	0
Detroit	1	0	1	0	2	3	0	1	0	1	0	4	5	0	2	0	2	0	6	8	0
Edmonton	1	0	1	0	3	2	0	1	0	1	0	2	5	0	2	1	1	0	5	7	2
Hartford	4	1	3	0	9	17	2	3	0	3	0	6	17	0	6	0	6	0	15	34	2
Los Angeles	1	0	1	0	3	0	0	1	0	1	0	6	8	0	2	0	2	0	8	11	0
Minnesota	1	0	1	0	1	3	0	1	0	1	0	2	7	0	2	0	2	0	3	10	0
Montreal	3	1	2	0	9	12	2	4	0	4	0	11	17	0	7	1	6	0	20	29	2
New Jersey	2	1	0	1	6	4	3	2	0	2	0	6	11	0	4	1	2	1	12	15	3
NY Islanders	1	0	1	0	2	7	0	2	1	1	0	8	12	2	3	1	2	0	10	19	2
NY Rangers	2	0	2	0	6	8	0	1	0	1	0	2	6	0	3	0	3	0	8	14	0
Philadelphia	1	1	0	0	3	2	2	2	0	2	0	3	15	0	3	1	2	0	6	17	2
Pittsburgh	2	1	1	0	4	8	2	2	0	2	0	5	12	0	4	1	3	0	9	20	2
Quebec	5	1	4	0	14	26	2	4	0	4	0	10	25	0	9	1	8	0	24	51	2
St. Louis	1	0	1	0	1	4	0	1	0	1	0	1	5	0	2	0	2	0	2	9	0
San Jose	1	1	0	0	3	2	2	1	0	1	0	2	3	0	2	1	1	0	5	5	2
Tampa Bay	1	0	1	0	2	3	0	1	0	1	0	0	1	0	2	0	2	0	2	4	0
Toronto	1	0	1	0	1	3	0	2	0	2	0	4	10	0	3	0	3	0	5	13	0
Vancouver	1	0	1	0	0	3	0	1	0	1	0	1	4	0	2	0	2	0	1	7	0
Washington	2	0	2	0	8	10	0	2	0	2	0	5	11	0	4	0	4	0	13	21	0
Winnipeg	2	0	1	1	6	12	1	1	1	0	0	3	6	0	3	1	1	1	9	18	1
Totals	**42**	**9**	**29**	**4**	**100**	**164**	**22**	**42**	**1**	**41**	**0**	**102**	**231**	**2**	**84**	**10**	**70**	**4**	**202**	**395**	**24**

1992-93 Results

	Home				Away	
Oct. 8	Montreal	5-3	Oct. 10	Quebec		2-9
22	Hartford	1-5	12	Boston		3-6
24	NY Rangers	2-3	14	Hartford		1-4
27	Pittsburgh	2-7	16	Washington		1-5
31	Buffalo	2-2	20	Toronto		3-5
Nov. 9	Toronto	1-3	30	Buffalo		3-12
11	Quebec	3-7	Nov. 3	Edmonton		2-5
17	Montreal	3-5	5	Calgary		4-8
19	Hartford	2-4	6	Vancouver		1-4
23	Boston	2-3	13	Tampa Bay		0-1
25	New Jersey	3-1	15	Philadelphia		2-7
29	Buffalo	2-5	21	Montreal		1-3
Dec. 1	Minnesota	1-3	27	Buffalo		1-4
3	New Jersey	3-3	Dec. 9	Hartford		2-6
5	Philadelphia	3-2	10	Boston		2-4
7	Washington	5-6	17	NY Islanders		3-9
12	Calgary	1-1	19	Toronto		1-5
15	Detroit	2-3	26	Quebec		2-4
21	Washington	3-4	31	Detroit		4-5
23	Chicago	2-4	Jan. 6	NY Rangers		2-6
27	Quebec	1-6	9	New Jersey		4-6
Jan. 2	Buffalo	2-7	16	Pittsburgh		1-6
10	San Jose*	3-2	21	Minnesota		2-7
12	Los Angeles	2-3	23	Washington		4-6
14	St. Louis	1-4	26	St. Louis		1-5
17	NY Islanders	2-7	30	Montreal*		3-5
19	Quebec	2-5	Feb. 9	Philadelphia		1-8
28	Hartford	5-2	17	Quebec		4-6
Feb. 1	Winnipeg	4-4	20	Montreal		4-5
3	Edmonton	3-2	22	Winnipeg		3-6
8	Buffalo	4-2	27	New Jersey*		2-5
13	Montreal	1-4	Mar. 2	San Jose		2-3
23	Winnipeg	2-8	4	Los Angeles		6-8
25	Pittsburgh	2-1	9	Chicago*		2-4
28	Quebec	6-4	13	Boston*		3-4
Mar. 18	Boston	1-4	27	Montreal		3-4
22	NY Rangers	4-5	28	Buffalo		1-3
25	Tampa Bay	2-3	30	Pittsburgh		4-6
Apr. 1	Quebec	2-4	Apr. 3	Hartford		3-7
4	Vancouver	0-3	10	NY Islanders		5-3
7	Hartford	1-6	11	Boston		2-4
14	Boston	2-4	13	Quebec		2-6

*Denotes afternoon game

Entry Draft Selections 1993-92

1993
Pick
1 Alexandre Daigle
27 Radim Bicanek
53 Patrick Charbonneau
91 Cosmo Dupaul
131 Rick Bodkin
157 Sergei Poleschuk
183 Jason Disher
209 Toby Kvalevog
227 Pavol Demitra
235 Rick Schuwerk

1992
Pick
2 Alexei Yashin
25 Chad Penney
50 Patrick Traverse
73 Radek Hamr
98 Daniel Guerard
121 Al Sinclair
146 Jaroslav Miklenda
169 Jay Kenney
194 Claude Savoie
217 Jake Grimes
242 Tomas Jelinek
264 Petter Ronnqvist

Rick Bowness, who played for Atlanta, Detroit, St. Louis and Winnipeg during his seven-year NHL career, coached the Boston Bruins in 1991-92 before joining the Senators.

Coach

BOWNESS, RICK
Coach, Ottawa Senators. Born in Moncton, N.B., January 25, 1955.

Rick Bowness was appointed the Senator's first Head Coach on June 15, 1992. He coached the Boston Bruins in 1991-92, guiding the team to a 39-32-12 record and a berth in the conference finals. The Moncton native began his coaching career with the AHL's Sherbrooke Jets as a player/coach in 1981, and returned to his hometown in 1987 as the coach and general manager of the Moncton Hawks, the Jets' AHL farm team. In February 1989, Rick took over as interim coach of the Winnipeg Jets (28 games). Bowness then joined the Bruins' organization, coaching the AHL's Maine Mariners for two seasons before assuming head coaching duties for the Bruins for 1991-92. Rick is showing a 54-119-19 coaching record in 192 NHL career games. He collected his 50th NHL win Feb. 3, 1993 vs Edmonton (3-2). In his first season as the Senator's Head Coach, Rick instilled a strong work ethic on the team.

Coaching Record

| Season | Team | Games | Regular Season | | | | Playoffs | | | |
			W	L	T	%	Games	W	L	%
1987-88	Moncton (AHL)	80	27	45	8	.388	....	....	....	....
1988-89	Moncton (AHL)	53	28	20	5	.576	....	....	....	....
	Winnipeg (NHL)	**28**	**8**	**17**	**3**	**.340**	....	....	....	....
1989-90	Maine (AHL)	80	31	38	11	.457	....	....	....	....
1990-91	Maine (AHL)	80	34	34	12	.500	2	0	2	.000
1991-92	Boston (NHL)	80	36	32	12	.525	15	8	7	.533
1992-93	Ottawa (NHL)	84	10	70	4	.143	....	....	....	....
	NHL Totals	**192**	**54**	**119**	**19**	**.331**	**15**	**8**	**7**	**.533**

Club Directory

Ottawa Civic Centre

Ottawa Senators
301 Moodie Drive
Suite 200
Nepean, Ontario
K2H 9C4
Phone **613/721-0115**
FAX 613/726-1419
Capacity: 10,585

Governor, Chairman and CEO	Rod Bryden
President, General Manager and Alternate Governor	Randy J. Sexton
Founder	Bruce M. Firestone
Assistant General Manager	Ray Shero
Director, Player Personnel	John Ferguson
Director, Hockey Operations	Brian McKenna
Head Coach	Rick Bowness
Assistant Coach	E.J. McGuire
Assistant Coach	Alain Vigneault
Goaltender Coach and Scout	Glenn "Chico" Resch
Head Coach & Asst. G.M., Development team	Don MacAdam
Assistant Coach, Development team	Mike Kelly
Professional Scout, Assistant-Director of Player Personnel	Jim Nill
US Eastern Amateur Scout	Paul Castron
Québec Amateur Scout	André Dupont
Ontario Amateur Scout	Tim Higgins
Western Canada Scout	Bruce Southern
Professional Scout	Barry Long
Team Doctor	Jamie Kissick, M.D.
Strength and Conditioning Coach	Mark Slater
Head Equipment Trainer	Ed Georgica
Athletic Trainer	Conrad Lackten
Assistant Trainer	John Gervais
Manager of Team Services	Trevor Timmins
Executive Assistant to the Governor	Sharry Dozois
Executive Assistant to the President	Allison Vaughan
Secretary, Hockey Department	Traudy Tremblay
Secretary, Hockey Department	Erin Galloway
Sr. Vice-President, Commercial Operations	Bernie Ashe
President, Palladium Company	Cyril Leeder
Vice-President, Finance	Jim Ablett
Vice-President, Corporate Communications	John Owens
Executive-Secretary, Commercial Operations	Cheryl Pridmore
Director, Team and Business Development	Brad Marsh
Director, Media Relations	Laurent Benoit
Media Relations Assistant	Dominick Saillant
Public Relations Executive Secretary	Vivianne Dumais
Club Historian	Jim McAuley
Vice-President, Sales	Mark Bonneau
Director, Outaouais Business Development	Enrico Valente
Sales Representative	George Comis
Sales Representative	Brian Jokat
Sales Representative	Chris Knight
Sales Representative	Darren McCartney
Sales Representative	Jamie Simpson
Secretary, Sales	Diane Coughlan
Corporate Sales Coordinator	Kelly MacCallum
Vice-President, Marketing	Jim Steel
Manager, Marketing Services	Mary Dellar
Manager, Marketing Services	Dave Saunders
Secretary, Marketing	Krista Pogue
Publications Manager	Carl Lavigne
Graphic Designer	Kevin Caradonna
Graphic Designer	Jean-Guy Brunet
Vice-President, Guest Services & Tickets	Jeff Kyle
Secretary, Marketing	Paulette Surette
Director of Operations/Guest Services	David Dakers
Guest Services Representative	Cindy Rodrigue
Guest Services Representative	Paul Blinn
Jr. Fan Club Manager	Gilles Mignault
Ticket Coordinator	Tracey Drennan
Ticket Coordinator	Stephanie Jamieson
Director, Promotions	Patti Zebchuck
Director, Special Events	Randy Burgess
Marketing and Events	Mark Seaman
Director, Community Relations	Lisa Brazeau
Community Relations Coordinator	Marie Olney
Community Relations Coordinator	Sylvie Guénette-Craig
Office Coordinator	Renée Keays
Receptionist	Christine Clancy

Philadelphia Flyers

1992-93 Results: 36w-37L-11T 83PTS. Fifth, Patrick Division

Schedule

Home				Away		
Oct.	Tues.	5	Pittsburgh	**Oct.**	Sat.	9 Hartford
	Sun.	10	Toronto		Fri.	15 Washington
	Tues.	12	Buffalo		Tues.	26 Quebec
	Sat.	16	NY Rangers		Wed.	27 Ottawa
	Thur.	21	NY Islanders		Sat.	30 New Jersey*
	Sat.	23	Winnipeg		Sun.	31 Chicago
Nov.	Thur.	4	Quebec	**Nov.**	Tues.	2 Florida
	Sun.	7	Vancouver		Sat.	6 Toronto
	Thur.	11	New Jersey		Wed.	10 Buffalo
	Sat.	13	Buffalo*		Tues.	16 Pittsburgh
	Thur.	18	Hartford		Sat.	20 Boston
	Sun.	21	NY Islanders		Sat.	27 Tampa Bay
	Wed.	24	Montreal	**Dec.**	Wed.	1 Edmonton
	Fri.	26	Tampa Bay*		Thur.	2 Vancouver
Dec.	Thur.	9	Washington		Sat.	4 Calgary
	Sun.	12	Edmonton		Sat.	11 NY Islanders
	Thur.	16	Quebec		Sun.	19 New Jersey
	Sat.	18	Chicago*		Mon.	27 Buffalo
	Tues.	21	Washington		Tues.	28 Pittsburgh
	Thur.	23	Detroit		Fri.	31 Boston
						(at Minnesota)
Jan.	Tues.	11	Ottawa	**Jan.**	Thur.	6 Dallas
	Thur.	13	Boston		Sat.	8 Tampa Bay
	Sun.	16	Los Angeles		Fri.	14 NY Rangers
	Wed.	19	St Louis		Tues.	25 Quebec
	Sat.	29	Washington*		Sun.	30 Montreal*
Feb.	Wed.	2	Washington	**Feb.**	Sat.	5 Boston*
			(at Cleveland)		Tues.	8 Ottawa
	Thur.	3	San Jose		Fri.	11 Detroit
	Thur.	10	Florida		Tues.	15 San Jose
	Sun.	13	Pittsburgh*		Wed.	16 Anaheim
	Mon.	21	Montreal*		Fri.	18 Los Angeles
	Thur.	24	NY Islanders		Fri.	25 NY Islanders
Mar.	Tues.	8	Dallas	**Mar.**	Wed.	2 NY Rangers
	Thur.	10	Ottawa		Fri.	4 Washington
	Sun.	13	Tampa Bay		Sun.	6 Tampa Bay
	Sat.	19	Hartford*		Sat.	12 Montreal
	Thur.	24	Florida		Sun.	20 Florida
	Sun.	27	Anaheim		Tues.	22 St Louis
	Tues.	29	NY Rangers		Sat.	26 New Jersey*
	Thur.	31	Calgary	**Apr.**	Sat.	2 Hartford
Apr.	Thur.	7	Florida		Mon.	4 Winnipeg
	Sun.	10	Boston*		Thur.	14 NY Rangers
	Tues.	12	New Jersey			

* Denotes afternoon game.

Home Starting Times:

Weeknights and Saturdays	7:35 p.m.
Sundays	7:05 p.m.
Matinees	1:05 p.m.

Franchise date: June 5, 1967

ATLANTIC
DIVISION

27th
NHL
Season

EASTERN
CONFERENCE

Despite being slowed by injuries for much of the season, Eric Lindros earned a berth on the NHL/Upper Deck All-Rookie Team after compiling 75 points in 1992-93.

Year-by-Year Record

		Home			Road			Overall							
Season	GP	W	L	T	W	L	T	W	L	T	GF	GA	Pts.	Finished	Playoff Result
1992-93	84	23	14	5	13	23	6	36	37	11	319	319	83	5th, Patrick Div.	Out of Playoffs
1991-92	80	22	11	7	10	26	4	32	37	11	252	273	75	6th, Patrick Div.	Out of Playoffs
1990-91	80	18	16	6	15	21	4	33	37	10	252	267	76	5th, Patrick Div.	Out of Playoffs
1989-90	80	17	19	4	13	20	7	30	39	11	290	297	71	6th, Patrick Div.	Out of Playoffs
1988-89	80	22	15	3	14	21	5	36	36	8	307	285	80	4th, Patrick Div.	Lost Conf. Championship
1987-88	80	20	14	6	18	19	3	38	33	9	292	292	85	3rd, Patrick Div.	Lost Div. Semi-Final
1986-87	80	29	9	2	17	17	6	46	26	8	310	245	100	1st, Patrick Div.	Lost Final
1985-86	80	33	6	1	20	17	3	53	23	4	335	241	110	1st, Patrick Div.	Lost Div. Semi-Final
1984-85	80	32	4	4	21	16	3	53	20	7	348	241	113	1st, Patrick Div.	Lost Final
1983-84	80	25	10	5	19	16	5	44	26	10	350	290	98	3rd, Patrick Div.	Lost Div. Semi-Final
1982-83	80	29	8	3	20	15	5	49	23	8	326	240	106	1st, Patrick Div.	Lost Div. Semi-Final
1981-82	80	25	10	5	13	21	6	38	31	11	325	313	87	3rd, Patrick Div.	Lost Div. Semi-Final
1980-81	80	23	9	8	18	15	7	41	24	15	313	249	97	2nd, Patrick Div.	Lost Quarter-Final
1979-80	80	27	5	8	21	7	12	48	12	20	327	254	116	1st, Patrick Div.	Lost Final
1978-79	80	26	10	4	14	15	11	40	25	15	281	248	95	2nd, Patrick Div.	Lost Quarter-Final
1977-78	80	29	6	5	16	14	10	45	20	15	296	200	105	2nd, Patrick Div.	Lost Semi-Final
1976-77	80	33	6	1	15	10	15	48	16	16	323	213	112	1st, Patrick Div.	Lost Semi-Final
1975-76	80	36	2	2	15	11	14	51	13	16	348	209	118	1st, Patrick Div.	Lost Final
1974-75	**80**	**32**	**6**	**2**	**19**	**12**	**9**	**51**	**18**	**11**	**293**	**181**	**113**	**1st, Patrick Div.**	**Won Stanley Cup**
1973-74	**78**	**28**	**6**	**5**	**22**	**10**	**7**	**50**	**16**	**12**	**273**	**164**	**112**	**1st, West Div.**	**Won Stanley Cup**
1972-73	78	27	8	4	10	22	7	37	30	11	296	256	85	2nd, West Div.	Lost Semi-Final
1971-72	78	19	13	7	7	25	7	26	38	14	200	236	66	5th, West Div.	Out of Playoffs
1970-71	78	20	10	9	8	23	8	28	33	17	207	225	73	3rd, West Div.	Lost Quarter-Final
1969-70	76	11	14	13	6	21	11	17	35	24	197	225	58	5th, West Div.	Out of Playoffs
1968-69	76	14	16	8	6	19	13	20	35	21	174	225	61	3rd, West Div.	Lost Quarter-Final
1967-68	74	17	13	7	14	19	4	31	32	11	173	179	73	1st, West Div.	Lost Quarter-Final

1993-94 Player Personnel

FORWARDS	HT	WT	S	Place of Birth	Date	1992-93 Club
BERANEK, Josef	6-2	190	L	Litvinov, Czech.	10/25/69	Cape Breton-Edm.-Phi.
BOIVIN, Claude	6-2	210	L	Ste. Foy, Que.	3/1/70	Philadelphia
BRIND'AMOUR, Rod	6-1	200	L	Ottawa, Ont.	8/9/70	Philadelphia
BROWN, Dave	6-5	205	R	Saskatoon, Sask.	10/12/62	Philadelphia
BUTSAYEV, Viacheslav	6-2	200	L	Togliatti, USSR	6/13/70	Philadelphia-Hershey
CONROY, Al	5-8	170	R	Calgary, Alta.	1/17/66	Philadelphia-Hershey
COOKE, Jamie	6-2	206	R	Toronto, Ont.	11/05/68	Hershey
CUMMINS, Jim	6-2	203	R	Dearborn, MI	5/17/70	Adirondack-Detroit
DINEEN, Kevin	5-11	190	R	Quebec City, Que.	10/28/63	Philadelphia
DUPRE, Yanick	6-0	189	L	Montreal, Que.	11/20/72	Hershey
EGELAND, Tracy	6-1	180	R	Lethbridge, Alta.	8/20/70	Indianapolis
EKLUND, Pelle	5-10	175	L	Stockholm, Sweden	3/22/63	Philadelphia
FAUST, Andre	6-1	190	L	Joliette, Que.	10/7/69	Philadelphia-Hershey
FEDYK, Brent	6-0	195	R	Yorkton, Sask.	3/8/67	Philadelphia
HEALEY, Paul	6-2	185	R	Edmonton, Alta.	3/20/75	Prince Albert
HERPERGER, Chris	6-0	190	L	Esterhazy, Sask.	2/24/74	Seattle
KRECHIN, Vladimir	5-11	180	L	Chelyabinsk, USSR	3/23/75	Traktor Chelyabinsk
LINDROS, Eric	6-4	235	R	London, Ont.	2/28/73	Philadelphia
METLYUK, Denis	5-10	183	L	Togliatti, Russia	1/30/72	Lada Togliatti
NORRIS, Clayton	6-2	205	R	Edmonton, Alta.	3/8/72	Medicine Hat-Hershey
PAQUIN, Patrice	6-2	192	L	St. Jerome, Que.	6/26/74	Beauport
PROSPAL, Vaclav	6-2	167	L	Ceske-Budejovice, Czech.	2/17/75	Motor Ceske-Budejovice
RECCHI, Mark	5-10	185	L	Kamloops, B.C.	2/1/68	Philadelphia
RENBERG, Mikael	6-2	183	L	Pitea, Sweden	5/5/72	Lulea
TIPPETT, Dave	5-10	180	L	Moosomin, Sask.	8/25/61	Pittsburgh
VILGRAIN, Claude	6-1	205	R	Port-au-Prince, Haiti	3/1/63	Utica-Cincinnati-N.J.
WINNES, Chris	6-0	170	R	Columbus, OH	2/12/68	Providence-Boston

DEFENSEMEN						
BOULIN, Vladislav	6-4	196	L	Penza, USSR	5/18/72	Dynamo Moscow
BOWEN, Jason	6-4	210	L	Port Alice, B.C.	11/11/73	Tri-City-Philadelphia
BRIMANIS, Aris	6-3	195	R	Cleveland, OH	3/14/72	Brandon
CARKNER, Terry	6-3	212	L	Smiths Falls, Ont.	3/7/66	Philadelphia
DANDENAULT, Eric	6-0	193	R	Sherbrooke, Que.	3/10/70	Hershey
FINLEY, Jeff	6-2	204	L	Edmonton, Alta.	4/14/67	Capital District
FOSTER, Corey	6-3	204	L	Ottawa, Ont.	10/27/69	Hershey
GALLEY, Garry	6-0	190	L	Montreal, Que.	4/16/63	Philadelphia
HAWGOOD, Greg	5-10	190	L	Edmonton, Alta.	8/10/68	Edmonton-Philadelphia
HOLAN, Milos	5-11	183	L	Bilovec, Czech.	4/22/71	TJ Vitkovice
KORDIC, Dan	6-5	220	L	Edmonton, Alta.	4/18/71	Hershey
McGILL, Ryan	6-2	195	R	Prince Albert, Sask.	2/28/69	Hershey-Philadelphia
NATTRESS, Ric	6-2	210	R	Hamilton, Ont.	5/25/62	Philadelphia
SANDWITH, Terran	6-4	210	L	Stoney Plain, Alta.	4/17/72	Hershey
SEARS, Sverre	6-1	198	L	Dover, MA	10/17/70	Princeton
STAPLES, Jeff	6-2	207	L	Kitimat, B.C.	3/4/75	Brandon
WILKIE, Bob	6-2	200	R	Calgary, Alta.	2/11/69	Adi.-F. Wayne-Her.
YUSHKEVICH, Dimitri	5-11	187	L	Yaroslavl, USSR	11/19/71	Philadelphia

GOALTENDERS	HT	WT	C	Place of Birth	Date	1992-93 Club
DEGRACE, Yanick	5-11	175	L	Lameque, N.B.	4/16/71	Hershey
FOSTER, Norm	5-9	175	L	Vancouver, B.C.	2/10/65	Kansas City-Cape Breton
LAGRAND, Scott	6-1	170	L	Potsdam, NY	2/11/70	Hershey
ROUSSEL, Dominic	6-1	180	L	Hull, Que.	2/22/70	Hershey-Philadelphia
SODERSTROM, Tommy	5-9	163	L	Stockholm, Sweden	7/17/69	Hershey-Philadelphia

1992-93 Scoring

Regular Season

Pos	#	Player	Team	GP	G	A	Pts	+/-	PIM	PP	SH	GW	GT	S	%
R	8	Mark Recchi	PHI	84	53	70	123	1	95	15	4	6	0	274	19.3
C	17	Rod Brind'Amour	PHI	81	37	49	86	8–	89	13	4	4	1	206	18.0
C	88*	Eric Lindros	PHI	61	41	34	75	28	147	8	1	5	1	180	22.8
R	11	Kevin Dineen	PHI	83	35	28	63	14	201	6	3	7	1	241	14.5
D	3	Garry Galley	PHI	83	13	49	62	18	115	4	1	3	1	231	5.6
R	18	Brent Fedyk	PHI	74	21	38	59	14	48	4	1	2	2	167	12.6
C	9	Pelle Eklund	PHI	55	11	38	49	12	16	4	0	0	0	82	13.4
D	20	Greg Hawgood	EDM	29	5	13	18	1–	35	2	0	0	0	47	10.6
			PHI	40	6	22	28	7–	39	5	0	1	0	91	6.6
			TOTAL	69	11	35	46	8–	74	7	0	1	0	138	8.0
C	42	Josef Beranek	EDM	26	2	6	8	7–	28	0	0	0	0	44	4.5
			PHI	40	13	12	25	1–	50	1	0	0	0	86	15.1
			TOTAL	66	15	18	33	8–	78	1	0	0	0	130	11.5
D	2*	Dimitri Yushkevich	PHI	82	5	27	32	12	71	1	0	1	0	155	3.2
C	25	Keith Acton	PHI	83	8	15	23	10–	51	0	0	0	0	74	10.8
L	15	Doug Evans	PHI	65	8	13	21	9–	70	0	0	1	1	60	13.3
L	23	Andrei Lomakin	PHI	51	8	12	20	15	34	0	0	0	0	64	12.5
D	29	Terry Carkner	PHI	83	3	16	19	18	150	0	0	0	0	45	6.7
D	5	Ric Nattress	PHI	44	7	10	17	1	29	0	0	4	0	57	12.3
C	22*	V. Butsayev	PHI	52	2	14	16	3	61	0	0	0	0	58	3.4
D	27*	Ryan McGill	PHI	72	3	10	13	9	238	0	0	0	0	68	4.4
L	14	Dave Snuggerud	S.J.	25	4	5	9	3–	14	0	1	1	0	51	7.8
			PHI	14	0	2	2	0	0	0	0	0	0	10	.0
			TOTAL	39	4	7	11	3–	14	0	1	1	0	61	6.6
L	10	Claude Boivin	PHI	30	5	4	9	5–	76	0	0	1	0	21	23.8
D	26	Gord Hynes	PHI	37	3	4	7	3–	16	0	0	0	0	39	7.7
C	46	Allan Conroy	PHI	21	3	2	5	1–	17	0	0	1	0	24	12.5
C	34*	Len Barrie	PHI	8	2	2	4	2	9	0	0	0	1	14	14.3
C	36*	Andre Faust	PHI	10	2	2	4	5	4	0	0	0	0	11	18.2
D	44	Shawn Cronin	PHI	35	2	1	3	0	37	0	0	0	0	12	16.7
G	33*	Dominic Roussel	PHI	34	0	2	2	0	11	0	0	0	0	0	.0
G	30*	Tommy Soderstrom	PHI	44	0	2	2	0	4	0	0	0	0	0	.0
R	21	Dave Brown	PHI	70	0	2	2	5–	78	0	0	0	0	19	.0
L	28*	Jason Bowen	PHI	7	1	0	1	1	2	0	0	0	0	3	33.3
G	35	Steph Beauregard	PHI	16	0	1	1	0	0	0	0	0	0	0	.0
C	41*	Glen Mulvenna	PHI	1	0	0	0	0	2	0	0	0	0	1	.0

Goaltending

No.	Goaltender	GPI	Mins	Avg	W	L	T	EN	SO	GA	SA	S%
30	*Tommy Soderstrom	44	2512	3.42	20	17	6	4	5	143	1327	.892
33	*Dominic Roussel	34	1769	3.76	13	11	5	1	1	111	933	.881
35	Steph Beauregard	16	802	4.41	3	9	0	1	0	59	405	.854
	Totals	84	5107	3.75	36	37	11	6	6	319	2671	.881

A potent member of the Flyers "Crazy Eights" Line, Mark Recchi set a franchise record with 123 points during the 1992-93 campaign.

General Managers' History

Bud Poile, 1967-68 to 1968-69; Bud Poile and Keith Allen, 1969-70; Keith Allen, 1970-71 to 1982-83; Bob McCammon, 1983-84; Bobby Clarke, 1984-85 to 1989-90; Russ Farwell, 1990-91 to date.

Captains' History

Lou Angotti, 1967-68; Ed Van Impe, 1968-69 to 1971-72; Ed Van Impe and Bobby Clarke, 1972-73; Bobby Clarke, 1973-74 to 1978-79; Mel Bridgman, 1979-80, 1980-81; Bill Barber, 1981-82; Bill Barber and Bobby Clarke, 1982-83; Bobby Clarke, 1983-84; Dave Poulin, 1984-85 to 1988-89; Dave Poulin and Ron Sutter, 1989-90; Ron Sutter, 1990-91; Rick Tocchet, 1991-92; no captain, 1992-93.

Coaching History

Keith Allen, 1967-68 to 1968-69; Vic Stasiuk, 1969-70 to 1970-71; Fred Shero, 1971-72 to 1977-78; Bob McCammon and Pat Quinn, 1978-79; Pat Quinn, 1979-80 to 1980-81; Pat Quinn and Bob McCammon, 1981-82; Bob McCammon, 1982-83 to 1983-84; Mike Keenan, 1984-85 to 1987-88; Paul Holmgren, 1988-89 to 1990-91; Paul Holmgren and Bill Dineen, 1991-92; Bill Dineen, 1992-93; Terry Simpson, 1993-94.

Retired Numbers

1	Bernie Parent	1967-1971 and 1973-1979
4	Barry Ashbee	1970-1974
7	Bill Barber	1972-1985
16	Bobby Clarke	1969-1984

Club Records

Team

(Figures in brackets for season records are games played; records for fewest points, wins, ties, losses, goals, goals against are for 70 or more games)

Most Points	118	1975-76 (80)
Most Wins	53	1984-85 (80)
		1985-86 (80)
Most Ties	*24	1969-70 (76)
Most Losses	38	1971-72 (78)
Most Goals	350	1983-84 (80)
Most Goals Against	319	1992-93 (84)
Fewest Points	58	1969-70 (76)
Fewest Wins	17	1969-70 (76)
Fewest Ties	4	1985-86 (80)
Fewest Losses	12	1979-80 (80)
Fewest Goals	173	1967-68 (74)
Fewest Goals Against	164	1973-74 (78)

Longest Winning Streak
Over-all	13	Oct. 19-Nov. 17/85
Home	*20	Jan. 4-Apr. 3/76
Away	8	Dec. 22/82-Jan. 16/83

Longest Undefeated Streak
Over-all	*35	Oct. 14/79-Jan. 6/80 (25 wins, 10 ties)
Home	26	Oct. 11/79-Feb. 3/80 (19 wins, 7 ties)
Away	16	Oct. 20/79-Jan. 6/80 (11 wins, 5 ties)

Longest Losing Streak
Over-all	6	Mar. 25-Apr. 4/70; Dec. 5-Dec. 17/92
Home	5	Jan. 30-Feb. 15/69
Away	8	Oct. 25-Nov. 26/72

Longest Winless Streak
Over-all	11	Nov. 21-Dec. 14/69 (9 losses, 2 ties) Dec. 10/70-Jan. 3/71 (9 losses, 2 ties)
Home	8	Dec. 19/68-Jan. 18/69 (4 losses, 4 ties)
Away	19	Oct. 23/71-Jan. 27/72 (15 losses, 4 ties)

Most Shutouts, Season	13	1974-75 (80)
Most PIM, Season	2,621	1980-81 (80)
Most Goals, Game	13	Mar. 22/84 (Pit. 4 at Phi. 13) Oct. 18/84 (Van. 2 at Phil. 13)

Individual

Most Seasons	15	Bobby Clarke
Most Games	1,144	Bobby Clarke
Most Goals, Career	420	Bill Barber
Most Assists, Career	852	Bobby Clarke
Most Points, Career	1,210	Bobby Clarke (358 goals, 852 assists)
Most PIM, Career	1,683	Rick Tocchet
Most Shutouts, Career	50	Bernie Parent
Longest Consecutive Game Streak	287	Rick MacLeish (Oct. 6/72-Feb. 5/76)
Most Goals, Season	61	Reggie Leach (1975-76)
Most Assists, Season	89	Bobby Clarke (1974-75; 1975-76)
Most Points, Season	123	Mark Recchi (1992-93) (53 goals, 70 assists)
Most PIM, Season	*472	Dave Schultz (1974-75)
Most Points, Defenseman, Season	82	Mark Howe (1985-86) (24 goals, 58 assists)
Most Points, Center, Season	119	Bobby Clarke (1975-76) (30 goals, 89 assists)

Most Points, Right Wing, Season	123	Mark Recchi (1992-93) (53 goals, 70 assists)
Most Points, Left Wing, Season	112	Bill Barber (1975-76) (50 goals, 62 assists)
Most Points, Rookie, Season	76	Dave Poulin (1983-84) (31 goals, 45 assists)
Most Shutouts, Season	12	Bernie Parent (1973-74; 1974-75)
Most Goals, Game	4	Rick MacLeish (Feb. 13/73; Mar. 4/73) Tom Bladon (Dec. 11/77) Tim Kerr (Oct. 25/84, Jan. 17/85, Feb. 9/85, Nov. 20/86) Brian Propp (Dec. 2/86) Rick Tocchet (Feb. 27/88; Jan. 25/90)
Most Assists, Game	5	Bobby Clarke (Apr. 1/76)
Most Points, Game	8	Tom Bladon (Dec. 11/77)

* NHL Record.

All-time Record vs. Other Clubs

Regular Season

		At Home							On Road							Total					
	GP	W	L	T	GF	GA	PTS	GP	W	L	T	GF	GA	PTS	GP	W	L	T	GF	GA	PTS
Boston	51	21	24	6	169	158	48	53	12	35	6	156	221	30	104	33	59	12	325	379	78
Buffalo	45	27	10	8	168	118	62	42	15	21	6	129	152	36	87	42	31	14	297	270	98
Calgary	43	30	11	2	179	116	62	44	13	22	9	148	182	35	87	43	33	11	327	298	97
Chicago	53	28	15	10	176	143	66	52	10	24	18	141	185	38	105	38	39	28	317	328	104
Detroit	51	29	11	11	209	153	69	50	18	23	9	165	178	45	101	47	34	20	374	331	114
Edmonton	22	16	5	1	101	65	33	21	5	12	4	62	80	14	43	21	17	5	163	145	47
Hartford	22	15	6	1	92	63	31	22	9	9	4	92	91	22	44	24	15	5	184	154	53
Los Angeles	55	33	15	7	212	143	73	57	33	17	7	200	168	73	112	66	32	14	412	311	146
Minnesota	58	40	8	10	232	132	90	58	22	23	13	196	189	57	116	62	31	23	428	321	147
Montreal	51	17	21	13	137	153	47	52	14	28	10	151	200	38	103	31	49	23	288	353	85
New Jersey	57	40	10	7	248	136	87	55	25	26	4	217	200	54	112	65	36	11	465	336	141
NY Islanders	67	40	19	8	258	203	88	70	21	38	11	209	283	53	137	61	57	19	467	486	141
NY Rangers	81	40	28	13	284	236	93	82	26	37	19	241	274	71	163	66	65	32	525	510	164
Ottawa	2	2	0	0	15	3	4	1	0	1	0	2	3	0	3	2	1	0	17	6	4
Pittsburgh	81	60	14	7	356	208	127	81	31	34	16	259	271	78	162	91	48	23	615	479	205
Quebec	23	18	3	2	96	61	38	22	8	7	7	81	80	23	45	26	10	9	177	141	61
St. Louis	58	39	10	9	229	132	87	58	28	23	7	177	170	63	116	67	33	16	406	302	150
San Jose	2	2	0	0	10	4	4	3	2	1	0	8	5	4	5	4	1	0	18	9	8
Tampa Bay	1	1	0	0	6	2	2	1	0	1	0	1	4	0	2	1	1	0	7	6	2
Toronto	51	33	10	8	207	118	74	51	20	18	13	174	175	53	102	53	28	21	381	293	127
Vancouver	44	30	13	1	200	130	61	44	23	10	11	168	128	57	88	53	23	12	368	258	118
Washington	57	35	18	4	226	160	74	56	25	22	9	204	205	59	113	60	40	13	430	365	133
Winnipeg	22	17	5	0	101	60	34	21	11	9	1	76	70	23	43	28	14	1	177	130	57
Defunct Clubs	34	24	4	6	137	67	54	35	13	14	8	102	89	34	69	37	18	14	239	156	88
Totals	**1031**	**637**	**260**	**134**	**4048**	**2764**	**1408**	**1031**	**384**	**455**	**192**	**3359**	**3603**	**960**	**2062**	**1021**	**715**	**326**	**7407**	**6367**	**2368**

Playoffs

	Series	W	L	GP	W	L	T	GF	GA	Last Mtg.	Round	Result
Boston	4	2	2	20	9	11	0	57	60	1978	QF	L 1-4
Buffalo	2	2	0	11	8	3	0	35	23	1978	QF	W 4-1
**Calgary	2	1	1	11	7	4	0	43	28	1981	QF	L 3-4
Chicago	1	0	1	4	0	4	0	8	20	1971	QF	L 0-4
Edmonton	3	1	2	15	7	8	0	44	49	1987	F	L 3-4
Minnesota	2	2	0	11	8	3	0	41	26	1980	SF	W 4-1
Montreal	4	1	3	21	6	15	0	52	72	1989	CF	L 2-4
*New Jersey	1	1	0	2	2	0	0	6	3	1978	PR	W 2-0
NY Islanders	4	3	1	25	14	11	0	83	69	1987	DF	W 4-3
NY Rangers	8	4	4	38	19	19	0	119	130	1987	DSF	W 4-2
Pittsburgh	1	1	0	7	4	3	0	31	24	1989	DF	W 4-3
Quebec	2	2	0	11	7	4	0	39	29	1985	CF	W 4-2
St. Louis	2	0	2	11	3	8	0	20	34	1969	QF	L 0-4
Toronto	3	3	0	17	12	5	0	67	47	1977	QF	W 4-2
Vancouver	1	1	0	3	2	1	0	15	9	1979	PR	W 2-1
Washington	3	1	2	16	7	9	0	55	65	1989	DSF	W 4-2
Totals	**43**	**25**	**18**	**223**	**116**	**107**	**0**	**715**	**688**			

Playoff Results 1993-89

Year	Round	Opponent	Result	GF	GA
1989	CF	Montreal	L 2-4	8	17
	DF	Pittsburgh	W 4-3	31	24
	DSF	Washington	W 4-2	25	19

Abbreviations: Round: F – Final;
CF – conference final; **DF** – division final;
DSF – division semi-final; **SF** – semi-final;
QF – quarter-final; **PR** – preliminary round.
GA – goals against; **GF** – goals for.

1992-93 Results

	Home				Away	
Oct. 9	New Jersey	6-4	**Oct.** 6	Pittsburgh	3-3	
15	NY Islanders	4-5	10	Washington	4-2	
18	Winnipeg	5-4	13	Quebec	3-6	
22	Vancouver	4-4	17	New Jersey	0-2	
24	Montreal	6-7	20	NY Islanders	3-4	
Nov. 7	St. Louis*	4-2	26	NY Rangers	4-8	
12	NY Islanders	8-5	29	Chicago	5-5	
15	Ottawa	7-2	31	St. Louis	4-6	
19	NY Rangers	7-3	**Nov.** 4	NY Rangers	1-3	
22	Buffalo	4-4	14	Montreal	4-3	
27	NY Islanders*	6-3	21	Boston	3-4	
Dec. 3	Quebec	3-2	28	NY Islanders	3-9	
6	Boston	1-7	**Dec.** 5	Ottawa	2-3	
12	Washington	2-5	11	Detroit	2-4	
17	Pittsburgh	4-5	15	Pittsburgh	2-6	
19	Chicago*	3-1	20	Tampa Bay	1-4	
23	Pittsburgh	0-4	26	Washington	5-5	
Jan. 7	Washington	8-2	29	Los Angeles	10-2	
9	NY Rangers*	4-3	30	San Jose	6-2	
10	Edmonton	4-0	**Jan.** 2	Calgary	3-7	
14	Calgary	4-4	3	Edmonton	2-2	
17	Detroit	4-7	16	Boston	5-4	
21	Boston	4-5	23	NY Islanders	4-8	
24	Hartford	5-4	30	Pittsburgh*	2-4	
26	Buffalo	3-4	31	Montreal*	4-6	
28	Quebec	3-6	**Feb.** 3	NY Rangers	2-3	
Feb. 9	Ottawa	8-1	13	New Jersey*	4-6	
11	Montreal	0-0	16	Calgary	4-4	
14	New Jersey*	2-5	18	Vancouver	3-2	
22	Detroit	5-5	20	Minnesota*	2-5	
25	New Jersey	6-2	24	Hartford	5-2	
27	NY Islanders*	2-3	**Mar.** 5	Washington	3-0	
Mar. 2	Pittsburgh	5-4	7	New Jersey	3-7	
11	Washington	6-4	9	NY Rangers	2-4	
16	Minnesota	4-3	20	Pittsburgh	3-9	
21	New Jersey	2-3	24	NY Rangers	5-4	
25	San Jose	5-2	27	Quebec*	3-8	
Apr. 1	Los Angeles	1-3	30	NY Islanders	1-2	
3	Tampa Bay*	4-2	**Apr.** 4	Winnipeg	4-2	
4	Toronto	4-0	10	Toronto	4-0	
8	Washington	4-3	15	Buffalo	7-4	
12	NY Rangers	1-0	16	Hartford	5-4	

*Denotes afternoon game

Entry Draft Selections 1993-79

1993
Pick
36	Janne Niinimaa
71	Vaclav Prospal
77	Milos Holan
114	Vladimir Krechin
140	Mike Crowley
166	Aaron Israel
192	Paul Healey
218	Tripp Tracy
226	E.J. Bradley
244	Jeffrey Staples
270	Kenneth Hemmenway

1992
Pick
7	Ryan Sittler
15	Jason Bowen
31	Denis Metlyuk
103	Vladislav Buljin
127	Roman Zolotov
151	Kirk Daubenspeck
175	Claude Jutras Jr.
199	Jonas Hakansson
223	Chris Herperger
247	Patrice Paquin

1991
Pick
6	Peter Forsberg
50	Yanick Dupre
86	Aris Brimanis
94	Yanick Degrace
116	Clayton Norris
122	Dmitri Yushkevich
138	Andrei Lomakin
182	James Bode
204	Josh Bartell
226	Neil Little
248	John Porco

1990
Pick
4	Mike Ricci
25	Chris Simon
40	Mikael Renberg
42	Terran Sandwith
44	Kimbi Daniels
46	Bill Armstrong
47	Chris Therien
52	Al Kinisky
88	Dan Kordic
109	Viacheslav Butsayev
151	Patrik Englund
172	Toni Porkka
193	Greg Hanson
214	Tommy Soderstrom
235	William Lund

1989
Pick
33	Greg Johnson
34	Patrik Juhlin
72	Reid Simpson
117	Niklas Eriksson
138	John Callahan Jr.
159	Sverre Sears
180	Glen Wisser
201	Al Kummu
222	Matt Brait
243	James Pollio

1988
Pick
14	Claude Boivin
35	Pat Murray
56	Craig Fisher
63	Dominic Roussel
77	Scott Lagrand
98	Edward O'Brien
119	Gordie Frantti
140	Jamie Cooke
161	Johan Salle
182	Brian Arthur
203	Jeff Dandreta
224	Scott Billey
245	Drahomir Kadlec

1987
Pick
20	Darren Rumble
30	Jeff Harding
62	Martin Hostak
83	Tomaz Eriksson
104	Bill Gall
125	Tony Link
146	Mark Strapon
167	Darryl Ingham
188	Bruce McDonald
209	Steve Morrow
230	Darius Rusnak
251	Dale Roehl

1986
Pick
20	Kerry Huffman
23	Jukka Seppo
28	Kent Hawley
83	Mark Bar
125	Steve Scheifele
146	Sami Wahlsten
167	Murray Baron
188	Blaine Rude
209	Shawn Sabol
230	Brett Lawrence
251	Daniel Stephano

1985
Pick
21	Glen Seabrooke
42	Bruce Rendall
48	Darryl Gilmour
63	Shane Whelan
84	Paul Marshall
105	Daril Holmes
126	Ken Alexander
147	Tony Horacek
168	Mike Cusack
189	Gordon Murphy
231	Rod Williams
252	Paul Maurice

1984
Pick
22	Greg Smyth
27	Scott Mellanby
37	Jeff Chychrun
43	Dave McLay
47	John Stevens
79	Dave Hanson
100	Brian Dobbin
121	John Dzikowski
142	Tom Allen
163	Luke Vitale
184	Bill Powers
204	Daryn Fersovitch
245	Juraj Bakos

1983
Pick
41	Peter Zezel
44	Derrick Smith
81	Alan Bourbeau
101	Jerome Carrier
121	Rick Tocchet
141	Bobby Mormina
161	Per-Erik Eklund
181	Rob Nichols
201	William McCormick
221	Brian Jopling
241	Harold Duvall

1982
Pick
4	Ron Sutter
46	Miroslav Dvorak
47	Bill Campbell
77	Mikael Hjalm
98	Todd Bergen
119	Ron Hextall
140	Dave Brown
161	Alain Lavigne
182	Magnus Roupe
203	Tom Allen
224	Rick Gal
245	Mark Vichorek

1981
Pick
16	Steve Smith
37	Rich Costello
47	Barry Tabobundung
58	Ken Strong
5	David Michayluk
79	Ken Latta
100	Justin Hanley
121	Andre Villeneuve
137	Vladimir Svitek
142	Gil Hudon
163	Steve Taylor
184	Len Hachborn
205	Steve Tsujiura

1980
Pick
21	Mike Stothers
42	Jay Fraser
63	Paul Mercier
84	Taras Zytynsky
105	Daniel Held
126	Brian Tutt
147	Ross Fitzpatrick
168	Mark Botell
189	Peter Dineen
195	Bob O'Brien
210	Andy Brickley

1979
Pick
14	Brian Propp
22	Blake Wesley
35	Pelle Lindbergh
56	Lindsay Carson
77	Don Gillen
98	Thomas Eriksson
119	Gord Williams

Club Directory

The Spectrum
Pattison Place
Philadelphia, PA 19148
Phone **215/465-4500**
PR FAX 215/389-9403
Pres. & GM FAX 215/389-9409
Capacity: 17,380

Board of Directors
Ed Snider, Jay Snider, Joe Scott, Keith Allen, Fred Shabel, Sylvan Tobin, Carl Hirsh, Sanford Lipstein, Ron Ryan

Majority Ownership	Ed Snider and family
Limited Partners	Sylvan and Fran Tobin
President	Jay Snider
Chairman of the Board Emeritus	Joe Scott
Chief Operating Officer	Ron Ryan
Executive Vice-President	Keith Allen
General Manager	Russ Farwell
Head Coach	Terry Simpson
Assistant General Manager	John Blackwell
Assistant Coaches	Craig Hartsburg, Mike Eaves
Goaltending Instructor	Bernie Parent
Physical Conditioning Coach	Pat Croce, LPT, ATC
Director of Pro Scouting	Bill Barber
Chief Scout	Jerry Melnyk
Scouts	Bill Dineen, Inge Hammarstrom, Simon Nolet, Vaclav Slansky, Evgeny Zimin
Athletic Therapist	Gary Smith
Trainers	Jim Evers, Harry Bricker
Manager, Practice Facility	Anthony Tomasco
Medical Staff	Arthur Bartolozzi, M.D., Jeff Hartzell, M.D., Everett Borghesani, D.D.S., Jim Larson, D.D.S.
Director of Team Services	Joe Kadlec
Computer Analyst	David Gelberg
Vice-President, Sales/Marketing	Dick Deleguardia
Vice-President, Finance	Dan Clemmens
Vice-President, Public Relations	Mark Piazza
Vice-President, Sales	Jack Betson
Controller	Jeff Niessen
Manager, Season Ticket Sales	Steve Schiff
Manager, Sponsorships	Karen Buchholz
Assistant Director, Public Relations	Jill Vogel
Public Relations Assistants	Joe Kluge, Jennifer Corey
Director of Community Relations	Linda Panasci
Director of Youth Hockey	Greg Scott
Ticket Manager	Cecilia Baker
Ticket Office Assistant	Rick Ridall
Executive Assistants	Robin Casey, Ileen Forcine, Fran Lucchesi, Peg Manley, Karen Rogan, Dianna Taylor
Receptionist	Aggie Preston
Television Announcers	Gene Hart, Gary Dornhoefer
Radio Announcers	TBD
P.A. Announcer	Lou Nolan
Television Station	WPHL TV (Ch. 17), PRISM, SportsChannel Philadelphia
Radio Station (Flagship)	WIP All SportsRadio (610 AM)

Coach

SIMPSON, TERRY
Coach, Philadelphia Flyers. Born in Brantford, Ont., August 30, 1943.

Terry Simpson was named the ninth head coach in Flyers' history on May 24, 1993. Simpson spent the past three seasons as an assistant coach with the Winnipeg Jets. Prior to joining the Jets, he served as head coach of the New York Islanders for the 1986-87 and 1987-88 seasons and part of the 1988-89 season. In two-plus seasons behind the Islanders' bench he compiled a 81W-82L-24T mark, including a Patrick Division Championship in 1987-88.

Prior to coaching the Islanders, Simpson coached the Prince Albert Raiders of the Saskatchewan Junior League for ten years before the team moved up in rank to the Western Hockey League. In four years of competition in the WHL, Simpson's teams compiled a record of 167W-112L-9T. He coached the 1984-85 Raiders to a Memorial Cup win, symbolic of junior hockey supremacy in Canada. Simpson was also a member of the Canadian National Junior Team coaching staff for three years (1984-86), the last two as head coach. The Canadians won the gold medal in 1985 and won the silver medal in 1986.

Coaching Record

			Regular Season					Playoffs		
Season	Team	Games	W	L	T	%	Games	W	L	%
1982-83	Prince Albert (WHL)	72	16	55	1	.229	....	....	....	....
1983-84	Prince Albert (WHL)	72	41	29	2	.583	5	1	4	.200
1984-85	Prince Albert (WHL)	72	58	11	3	.826	13	12	1	.923
1985-86	Prince Albert (WHL)	72	52	17	3	.743	20	15	5	.750
1986-87	NY Islanders (NHL)	80	35	33	12	.513	14	7	7	.500
1987-88	NY Islanders (NHL)	80	39	31	10	.550	6	2	4	.500
1988-89	NY Islanders (NHL)	27	7	18	2	.296	....	....	....	....
	NHL Totals	187	81	82	24	.497	20	9	11	.450

General Manager

FARWELL, RUSS
General Manager, Philadelphia Flyers.
Born in Peace River, Alta., April 20, 1956.

Before being appointed to his position on June 6, 1990, Russ Farwell, 37, spent eight seasons in the Western Hockey League. He served as general manager of the Seattle Thunderbirds from 1988-90 and was named the WHL and CHL Executive of the Year in 1990. In two seasons under Farwell's leadership, the Thunderbirds were 85-52-7, including a 52-17-3 mark in 1989-90. Prior to his position with Seattle, Farwell spent six seasons as general manager of the Medicine Hat Tigers. During that time, the Tigers were 281-135-16, participated in the WHL's Eastern Division Finals five times and won consecutive Memorial Cup titles in 1986-87 and 1987-88.

Farwell is the first individual to be named an NHL general manager directly from junior hockey since Wren Blair went from Oshawa to Minnesota in 1967-68. The only other man to do so was Leighton "Hap" Emms, who went from Barrie to Boston in 1965-66.

Pittsburgh Penguins

1992-93 Results: 56w-21l-7t 119pts. First, Patrick Division

Year-by-Year Record

Season	GP	Home			Road			Overall						Finished	Playoff Result
		W	L	T	W	L	T	W	L	T	GF	GA	Pts.		
1992-93	84	32	6	4	24	15	3	56	21	7	367	268	119	1st, Patrick Div.	Lost Div. Final
1991-92	**80**	**21**	**13**	**6**	**18**	**19**	**3**	**39**	**32**	**9**	**343**	**308**	**87**	**3rd, Patrick Div.**	**Won Stanley Cup**
1990-91	**80**	**25**	**12**	**3**	**16**	**21**	**3**	**41**	**33**	**6**	**342**	**305**	**88**	**1st, Patrick Div.**	**Won Stanley Cup**
1989-90	80	22	15	3	10	25	5	32	40	8	318	359	72	5th, Patrick Div.	Out of Playoffs
1988-89	80	24	13	3	16	20	4	40	33	7	347	349	87	2nd, Patrick Div.	Lost Div. Final
1987-88	80	22	12	6	14	23	3	36	35	9	319	316	81	6th, Patrick Div.	Out of Playoffs
1986-87	80	19	15	6	11	23	6	30	38	12	297	290	72	5th, Patrick Div.	Out of Playoffs
1985-86	80	20	15	5	14	23	3	34	38	8	313	305	76	5th, Patrick Div.	Out of Playoffs
1984-85	80	17	20	3	7	31	2	24	51	5	276	385	53	6th, Patrick Div.	Out of Playoffs
1983-84	80	7	29	4	9	29	2	16	58	6	254	390	38	6th, Patrick Div.	Out of Playoffs
1982-83	80	14	22	4	4	31	5	18	53	9	257	394	45	6th, Patrick Div.	Out of Playoffs
1981-82	80	21	11	8	10	25	5	31	36	13	310	337	75	4th, Patrick Div.	Lost Div. Semi-Final
1980-81	80	21	16	3	9	21	10	30	37	13	302	345	73	3rd, Norris Div.	Lost Prelim. Round
1979-80	80	20	13	7	10	24	6	30	37	13	251	303	73	3rd, Norris Div.	Lost Prelim. Round
1978-79	80	23	12	5	13	19	8	36	31	13	281	279	85	2nd, Norris Div.	Lost Quarter-Final
1977-78	80	16	15	9	9	22	9	25	37	18	254	321	68	4th, Norris Div.	Out of Playoffs
1976-77	80	22	12	6	12	21	7	34	33	13	240	252	81	3rd, Norris Div.	Lost Prelim. Round
1975-76	80	23	11	6	12	22	6	35	33	12	339	303	82	3rd, Norris Div.	Lost Prelim. Round
1974-75	80	25	5	10	12	23	5	37	28	15	326	289	89	3rd, Norris Div.	Lost Quarter-Final
1973-74	78	15	18	6	13	23	3	28	41	9	242	273	65	5th, West Div.	Out of Playoffs
1972-73	78	24	11	4	8	26	5	32	37	9	257	265	73	5th, West Div.	Out of Playoffs
1971-72	78	18	15	6	8	23	8	26	38	14	220	258	66	4th, West Div.	Lost Quarter-Final
1970-71	78	18	12	9	3	25	11	21	37	20	221	240	62	6th, West Div.	Out of Playoffs
1969-70	76	17	13	8	9	25	4	26	38	12	182	238	64	2nd, West Div.	Lost Semi-Final
1968-69	76	12	20	6	8	25	5	20	45	11	189	252	51	5th, West Div.	Out of Playoffs
1967-68	74	15	12	10	12	22	3	27	34	13	195	216	67	5th, West Div.	Out of Playoffs

---

Schedule

Home			Away		
Oct.	Thur. 7	Montreal	**Oct.**	Tues. 5	Philadelphia
	Sat. 9	NY Rangers		Sun. 10	Quebec
	Sat. 16	Hartford		Tues. 12	Florida
	Sat. 23	St Louis		Thur. 14	Tampa Bay
	Thur. 28	Quebec		Tues. 19	NY Islanders
	Sat. 30	Chicago		Fri. 22	Buffalo
Nov.	Sat. 13	Detroit	**Nov.**	Tues. 2	San Jose
	Tues. 16	Philadelphia		Wed. 3	Buffalo
	Thur. 18	Washington			(at Sacramento)
	Wed. 24	Boston		Sat. 6	Los Angeles
	Sat. 27	Ottawa		Sun. 7	Anaheim
Dec.	Thur. 2	New Jersey		Tues. 9	St Louis
	Tues. 14	Los Angeles		Thur. 11	Chicago
	Thur. 16	Buffalo		Sat. 20	Montreal
	Sun. 19	NY Islanders		Fri. 26	Washington
	Tues. 21	Tampa Bay	**Dec.**	Sat. 4	Hartford
	Tues. 28	Philadelphia		Wed. 8	Dallas
	Fri. 31	Quebec		Sat. 11	Tampa Bay
Jan.	Sat. 8	Calgary		Thur. 23	Boston
	Tues. 11	Boston		Sun. 26	Washington
	Thur. 13	Florida	**Jan.**	Sun. 2	Hartford
	Sat. 15	Edmonton*		Mon. 3	Ottawa
	Tues. 25	Ottawa		Fri. 7	Buffalo
	Thur. 27	Quebec		Tues. 18	Quebec
Feb.	Tues. 1	Florida		Sat. 29	Toronto
	Mon. 7	Montreal		Mon. 31	NY Rangers
	Thur. 10	NY Islanders	**Feb.**	Fri. 4	Detroit
	Sat. 12	Dallas*		Sat. 5	New Jersey
	Tues. 15	Winnipeg		Sun. 13	Philadelphia*
	Thur. 17	Hartford		Sat. 19	Montreal
	Thur. 24	Anaheim		Mon. 21	NY Rangers*
	Sat. 26	Buffalo		Mon. 28	Florida
Mar.	Tues. 8	Boston	**Mar.**	Fri. 4	Buffalo
	Thur. 10	Toronto		Sun. 6	Winnipeg*
	Sat. 12	NY Rangers*		Sun. 13	Hartford*
	Tues. 15	Washington		Thur. 17	Boston
	Sat. 19	Vancouver*		Sun. 20	NY Islanders
	Tues. 22	San Jose		Sat. 26	Calgary
	Thur. 24	Ottawa		Sun. 27	Edmonton
Apr.	Sun. 3	Boston*		Wed. 30	Vancouver
		(at Cleveland)	**Apr.**	Fri. 8	New Jersey
	Mon. 4	Tampa Bay		Sat. 9	Montreal
	Wed. 6	New Jersey		Mon. 11	Ottawa

* Denotes afternoon game.

Home Starting Times:

All Games	7:35 p.m.
Except Matinees	1:35 p.m.
Fri. Dec. 31	6:35 p.m.

Franchise date: June 5, 1967

NORTHEAST
DIVISION

**27th
NHL
Season**

EASTERN
CONFERENCE

*Kevin Stevens compiled his second straight 50-goal, 100-point season
in 1992-93, amassing 55 goals and 56 assists.*

1993-94 Player Personnel

FORWARDS	HT	WT	S	Place of Birth	Date	1992-93 Club
BLACK, Jamie	6-0	185	L	Calgary, Alta.	4/4/72	Tacoma
DANIELS, Jeff	6-1	200	L	Oshawa, Ont.	6/24/68	Pittsburgh
DUBERMAN, Justin	6-1	185	R	New Haven, CT	3/23/70	Cleveland
FRANCIS, Ron	6-2	200	L	Sault Ste. Marie, Ont.	3/1/63	Pittsburgh
HAWKINS, Todd	6-1	195	R	Kingston, Ont.	8/2/66	St. John's
JAGR, Jaromir	6-2	208	L	Kladno, Czech.	2/15/72	Pittsburgh
LEMIEUX, Mario	6-4	210	R	Montreal, Que.	10/5/65	Pittsburgh
McMORRAN, Larry	6-3	193	R	Toronto, Ont.	5/16/75	Seattle
MULLEN, Joe	5-9	180	R	New York, NY	2/25/57	Pittsburgh
NASLUND, Markus	5-11	180	L	Harnosand, Sweden	7/30/73	MoDo
NEEDHAM, Mike	5-10	185	R	Calgary, Alta.	4/4/70	Pittsburgh
PATTERSON, Ed	6-2	210	R	Delta, B.C.	11/14/72	Cleveland
PEACOCK, Shane	5-10	198	R	Winterburn, Alta.	7/7/73	Lethbridge
PITTIS, Domenic	5-11	180	L	Calgary, Alta.	10/1/74	Lethbridge
ROCHE, David	6-4	224	L	Lindsay, Ont.	6/13/75	Peterborough
SELMSER, Sean	6-1	180	L	Calgary, Alta.	11/10/74	Red Deer
SMART, Jason	6-4	212	L	Prince George, B.C.	1/23/70	Cleveland
STAPLETON, Mike	5-10	183	R	Sarnia, Ont.	5/5/66	Pittsburgh
STEVENS, Kevin	6-3	215	L	Brockton, MA	4/15/65	Pittsburgh
STRAKA, Martin	5-10	178	L	Plzen, Czech.	9/3/72	Pittsburgh
TOCCHET, Rick	6-0	205	R	Scarborough, Ont.	4/9/64	Pittsburgh
TOROPCHENKO, Leonid	6-4	220	L	Voskresensk, CIS	8/28/68	Springfield
TROTTIER, Bryan	5-11	195	L	Val Marie, Sask.	7/17/56	Did Not Play
DEFENSEMEN						
ANDRUSAK, Greg	6-1	183	R	Cranbrook, B.C.	11/14/69	Cleveland
BANCROFT, Steve	6-1	214	L	Toronto, Ont.	10/6/70	Indianapolis
DAGENAIS, Mike	6-3	200	L	Gloucester, Ont.	7/22/69	Cincinnati
DYCK, Paul	6-1	192	L	Steinbach, Man.	4/15/71	Cleveland
HEWARD, Jamie	6-2	194	R	Regina, Sask.	3/30/71	Cleveland
HUSSEY, Marc	6-2	182	R	Chatham, N.B.	1/22/74	Moose Jaw
JENNINGS, Grant	6-3	200	L	Hudson Bay, Sask.	5/5/65	Pittsburgh
McSORLEY, Marty	6-1	225	R	Hamilton, Ont.	5/18/63	Los Angeles
MELANSON, Robert	6-1	202	L	Antigonish, N.S.	3/5/71	Cleveland
MURPHY, Larry	6-1	210	R	Scarborough, Ont.	3/8/61	Pittsburgh
PAEK, Jim	6-1	194	L	Seoul, Korea	4/7/67	Pittsburgh
RAMSEY, Mike	6-3	195	L	Minneapolis, MN	12/3/60	Buffalo-Pittsburgh
SAMUELSSON, Kjell	6-6	235	R	Tyngsryd, Sweden	10/18/58	Pittsburgh
SAMUELSSON, Ulf	6-1	195	L	Fagersta, Sweden	3/26/64	Pittsburgh
STANTON, Paul	6-1	193	R	Boston, MA	6/22/67	Pittsburgh
TAGLIANETTI, Peter	6-2	200	L	Framingham, MA	8/15/63	T.B.-Pittsburgh
TAMER, Chris	6-2	185	L	Dearborn, MI	11/17/70	Michigan
THIESSEN, Travis	6-3	203	L	N. Battleford, Sask.	7/11/72	Moose Jaw

GOALTENDERS	HT	WT	C	Place of Birth	Date	1992-93 Club
BARRASSO, Tom	6-3	212	R	Boston, MA	3/31/65	Pittsburgh
DeROUVILLE, Philippe	6-1	183	L	Victoriaville, Que.	8/7/74	Verdun
DOPSON, Rob	6-0	200	L	Smiths Falls, Ont.	8/21/67	Cleveland
LALIME, Patrick	6-2	165	L	St. Bonaventure, Que.	7/7/74	Shawinigan
WREGGET, Ken	6-1	195	L	Brandon, Man.	3/25/64	Pittsburgh

1992-93 Scoring

Regular Season

Pos	#	Player	Team	GP	G	A	Pts	+/-	PIM	PP	SH	GW	GT	S	%
C	66	Mario Lemieux	PIT	60	69	91	160	55	38	16	6	10	0	286	24.1
L	25	Kevin Stevens	PIT	72	55	56	111	17	177	26	0	5	1	326	16.9
R	22	Rick Tocchet	PIT	80	48	61	109	28	252	20	4	5	0	240	20.0
C	10	Ron Francis	PIT	84	24	76	100	6	68	9	2	4	0	215	11.2
R	68	Jaromir Jagr	PIT	81	34	60	94	30	61	10	1	9	0	242	14.0
D	55	Larry Murphy	PIT	83	22	63	85	45	73	6	2	2	0	230	9.6
R	7	Joe Mullen	PIT	72	33	37	70	19	14	9	3	3	2	175	18.9
C	15*	Shawn McEachern	PIT	84	28	33	61	21	46	7	0	6	0	196	14.3
D	5	Ulf Samuelsson	PIT	77	3	26	29	36	249	0	0	1	0	96	3.1
L	14	Dave Tippett	PIT	74	6	19	25	5	56	0	1	1	0	64	9.4
L	24	Troy Loney	PIT	82	5	16	21	1	99	0	0	1	0	83	6.0
D	2	Jim Paek	PIT	77	3	15	18	13	64	0	0	0	0	57	5.3
D	23	Paul Stanton	PIT	77	4	12	16	7	97	2	0	1	0	106	3.8
R	82*	Martin Straka	PIT	42	3	13	16	2	29	0	0	1	0	28	10.7
D	32	Peter Taglianetti	T.B.	61	1	8	9	8	150	0	0	0	0	60	1.7
			PIT	11	1	4	5	4	34	0	0	0	0	18	5.6
			TOTAL	72	2	12	14	12	184	0	0	0	0	78	2.6
R	39*	Mike Needham	PIT	56	8	5	13	1–	14	0	0	2	0	49	16.3
C	26	Mike Stapleton	PIT	78	4	9	13	8–	10	0	1	1	0	78	5.1
D	6	Mike Ramsey	BUF	33	2	8	10	4	20	0	0	0	0	27	7.4
			PIT	12	1	2	3	13	8	0	0	0	0	8	12.5
			TOTAL	45	3	10	13	17	28	0	0	0	0	35	8.6
L	20*	Jeff Daniels	PIT	58	5	4	9	5–	14	0	0	1	0	30	16.7
D	28	Kjell Samuelsson	PIT	63	3	6	9	25	106	0	0	1	0	63	4.8
G	35	Tom Barrasso	PIT	63	0	8	8	0	24	0	0	0	0	0	.0
D	3	Grant Jennings	PIT	58	0	5	5	6	65	0	0	0	0	32	.0
D	33	Bryan Fogarty	PIT	12	0	4	4	3–	4	0	0	0	0	11	.0
G	31	Ken Wregget	PIT	25	0	1	1	0	6	0	0	0	0	0	.0
R	16	Jay Caufield	PIT	26	0	0	0	1–	60	0	0	0	0	6	.0

Goaltending

No.	Goaltender	GPI	Mins	Avg	W	L	T	EN	SO	GA	SA	S%
35	Tom Barrasso	63	3702	3.01	43	14	5	2	4	186	1885	.901
31	Ken Wregget	25	1368	3.42	13	7	2	2	0	78	692	.887
	Totals	**84**	**5083**	**3.16**	**56**	**21**	**7**	**4**	**5**	**268**	**2581**	**.896**

Tom Barrasso and Ken Wregget shared a shutout vs Bos on Feb 8, 1993.

Playoffs

Pos	#	Player	Team	GP	G	A	Pts	+/-	PIM	PP	SH	GW	GT	S	%
C	66	Mario Lemieux	PIT	11	8	10	18	2	10	3	1	1	0	40	20.0
C	10	Ron Francis	PIT	12	6	11	17	5	19	1	0	1	0	26	23.1
L	25	Kevin Stevens	PIT	12	5	11	16	2	22	4	0	0	0	35	14.3
R	22	Rick Tocchet	PIT	12	7	6	13	2	24	1	0	0	0	45	15.6
D	55	Larry Murphy	PIT	12	2	11	13	2	10	2	0	1	0	26	7.7
R	68	Jaromir Jagr	PIT	12	5	4	9	3	23	1	0	1	0	47	10.6
R	7	Joe Mullen	PIT	12	4	2	6	4	6	0	1	1	0	32	12.5
D	5	Ulf Samuelsson	PIT	12	1	5	6	5	24	0	0	0	0	14	7.1
D	6	Mike Ramsey	PIT	12	0	6	6	10	4	0	0	0	0	10	.0
L	20*	Jeff Daniels	PIT	12	3	2	5	1	0	0	0	1	0	16	18.8
C	15*	Shawn McEachern	PIT	12	3	2	5	0	10	0	0	1	0	21	14.3
L	24	Troy Loney	PIT	10	1	4	5	3	0	0	0	0	0	7	14.3
L	14	Dave Tippett	PIT	12	1	4	5	3–	14	0	0	0	0	11	9.1
R	82*	Martin Straka	PIT	11	2	1	3	2	2	0	0	0	0	7	28.6
D	32	Peter Taglianetti	PIT	11	1	2	3	2	16	0	0	0	0	10	10.0
G	35	Tom Barrasso	PIT	12	0	3	3	0	4	0	0	0	0	0	.0
D	28	Kjell Samuelsson	PIT	12	0	3	3	4	2	0	0	0	0	15	.0
R	39*	Mike Needham	PIT	9	1	0	1	1	2	0	0	0	0	1	100.0
D	23	Paul Stanton	PIT	1	0	1	1	0	0	0	0	0	0	1	.0
C	26	Mike Stapleton	PIT	4	0	0	0	1	0	0	0	0	0	1	.0
D	3	Grant Jennings	PIT	12	0	0	0	1	8	0	0	0	0	4	.0

Goaltending

No.	Goaltender	GPI	Mins	Avg	W	L	EN	SO	GA	SA	S%
35	Tom Barrasso	12	722	2.91	7	5	2	2	35	370	.905
	Totals	**12**	**725**	**3.06**	**7**	**5**	**2**	**2**	**37**	**372**	**.901**

Coach

JOHNSTON, ED
Coach, Pittsburgh Penguins. Born in Montreal, Que., November 24, 1935.

Ed Johnston will begin his second stint as coach of the Penguins, having coached the team for three seasons from 1980-81 to 1982-83 compiling a record of 79-126-35. He was named general manager of the team on May 27, 1983, a position he held for five seasons. During the 1988-89 season, his last with the Penguins, Johnston served as the assistant general manager. In 1989, Johnston was named vice president and general manager of the Hartford Whalers, a position he held for three seasons. During Johnston's first season in Hartford (1989-90), the Whalers recorded the second best record (38-33-9) in their NHL history.

Johnston played in the NHL for 16 seasons with Boston, Toronto, St. Louis and Chicago. He was a member of two Stanley Cup Championship teams as a member of the Boston Bruins, and was the last goaltender to play every minute of a season, when he played all 70 games in 1963-64 for the Bruins. Overall, Johnston played in 592 games, recording 236 wins, 32 shutouts and a 3.25 goals against average.

Coaching Record

		Regular Season					Playoffs			
Season	Team	Games	W	L	T	%	Games	W	L	%
1979-80	Chicago (NHL)	80	34	27	19	.544	7	3	4	.429
1980-81	Pittsburgh (NHL)	80	30	37	13	.456	5	2	3	.400
1981-82	Pittsburgh (NHL)	80	31	36	13	.469	5	2	3	.400
1982-83	Pittsburgh (NHL)	80	18	53	9	.281	....	....	....	....
	NHL Totals	320	113	153	54	.438	17	7	10	.412

General Managers' History

Jack Riley, 1967-68 to 1969-70; Leonard "Red" Kelly, 1970-71 to 1971-72; Jack Riley, 1972-73 to 1973-74; Jack Button, 1974-75; Wren A. Blair, 1975-76 to 1976-77; Baz Bastien, 1977-78 to 1982-83; Ed Johnston, 1983-84 to 1987-88; Tony Esposito, 1988-89; Tony Esposito and Craig Patrick, 1989-90; Craig Patrick, 1990-91 to date.

Coaching History

George Sullivan, 1967-68 to 1968-69; Red Kelly, 1969-70 to 1971-72; Red Kelly and Ken Schinkel, 1972-73; Ken Schinkel and Marc Boileau, 1973-74; Marc Boileau, 1974-75; Marc Boileau and Ken Schinkel, 1975-76; Ken Schinkel, 1976-77; John Wilson, 1977-78 to 1979-80; Eddie Johnston, 1980-81 to 1982-83; Lou Angotti, 1983-84; Bob Berry, 1984-85 to 1986-87; Pierre Creamer, 1987-88; Gene Ubriaco, 1988-89; Gene Ubriaco and Craig Patrick, 1989-90; Bob Johnson, 1990-91 to 1991-92; Scotty Bowman, 1991-92 to 1992-93; Eddie Johnston, 1993-94.

Captains' History

Ab McDonald, 1967-68; no captain, 1968-69 to 1972-73; Ron Schock, 1973-74 to 1976-77; Jean Pronovost, 1977-78; Orest Kindrachuk, 1978-79 to 1980-81; Randy Carlyle, 1981-82 to 1983-84; Mike Bullard, 1984-85, 1985-86; Mike Bullard and Terry Ruskowski, 1986-87; Dan Frawley and Mario Lemieux, 1987-88; Mario Lemieux, 1988-89 to date.

Club Records

Team

(Figures in brackets for season records are games played; records for fewest points, wins, ties, losses, goals, goals against are for 70 or more games)

Most Points	119	1992-93 (84)
Most Wins	56	1992-93 (84)
Most Ties	20	1970-71 (78)
Most Losses	58	1983-84 (80)
Most Goals	367	1992-93 (84)
Most Goals Against	394	1982-83 (80)
Fewest Points	38	1983-84 (80)
Fewest Wins	16	1983-84 (80)
Fewest Ties	5	1984-85 (80)
Fewest Losses	28	1974-75 (80)
Fewest Goals	182	1969-70 (76)
Fewest Goals Against	216	1967-68 (74)

Longest Winning Streak
Over-all . . . . *17 Mar. 9-
Apr. 10/93

Home . . . . 11 Jan. 5-
Mar. 7/91

Away . . . . 6 Mar. 14-
Apr. 9/93

Longest Undefeated Streak
Over-all . . . . 18 Mar. 9-
Apr. 14/93
(17 wins, 1 tie)

Home . . . . 20 Nov. 30/74-
Feb. 22/75
(12 wins, 8 ties)

Away . . . . 7 Twice

Longest Losing Streak
Over-all . . . . 11 Jan. 22/83-
Feb. 10/83

Home . . . . 7 Oct. 8-29/83
Away . . . . 18 Dec. 23/82-
Mar. 4/83

Longest Winless Streak
Over-all . . . . 18 Jan. 2-
Feb. 10/83
(17 losses, 1 tie)

Home . . . . 11 Oct. 8-
Nov. 19/83
(9 losses, 2 ties)

Away . . . . 18 Oct. 25/70-
Jan. 14/71
(11 losses, 7 ties)
Dec. 23/82-
Mar. 4/83
(18 losses)

Most Shutouts, Season 6 1967-68 (74)
1976-77 (80)
1988-89 (80)

Most PIM, Season *2,670 1981-82 (80)
Most Goals, Game . . . . 12 Mar. 15/75
(Wash. 1 at Pit. 12)
Dec. 26/91
(Tor. 1 at Pit. 12)

Individual

Most Seasons . . . . 11 Rick Kehoe
Most Games . . . . 753 Jean Pronovost
Most Goals, Career . . . . . . 477 Mario Lemieux
Most Assists, Career . . . . . 697 Mario Lemieux
Most Points, Career . . . . 1,174 Mario Lemieux
(477 goals, 697 assists)

Most PIM, Career . . . . 980 Troy Loney
Most Shutouts, Career . . . . 11 Les Binkley
Longest Consecutive
Games Streak . . . . 320 Ron Schock
(Oct. 24/73-Apr. 3/77)

Most Goals, Season . . . . . . 85 Mario Lemieux
(1988-89)

Most Assists, Season . . . . . 114 Mario Lemieux
(1988-89)

Most Points, Season . . . . . . 199 Mario Lemieux
(1988-89)

Most PIM, Season . . . . 409 Paul Baxter
(1981-82)

Most Points, Defenseman,
Season . . . . 113 Paul Coffey
(1988-89)
(30 goals, 83 assists)

Most Points, Center,
Season . . . . 199 Mario Lemieux
(1988-89)
(85 goals, 114 assists)

Most Points, Right Wing,
Season . . . . 115 Rob Brown
(1988-89)
(49 goals, 66 assists)

Most Points, Left Wing,
Season . . . . 123 Kevin Stevens
(1991-92)
(54 goals, 69 assists)

Most Points, Rookie,
Season . . . . 100 Mario Lemieux
(1984-85)
(43 goals, 57 assists)

Most Shutouts, Season . . . . . 6 Les Binkley
(1967-68)

Most Goals, Game . . . . 5 Mario Lemieux
(Dec. 31/88)

Most Assists, Game . . . . 6 Ron Stackhouse
(Mar. 8/75)
Greg Malone
(Nov. 28/79)
Mario Lemieux
(Oct. 15/88, Dec. 5/92)

Most Points, Game . . . . 8 Mario Lemieux
(Oct. 15/88,
Dec. 31/88)

* NHL Record.

Retired Numbers

21	Michel Briere	1969-1970

All-time Record vs. Other Clubs

Regular Season

	At Home							On Road							Total						
	GP	W	L	T	GF	GA	PTS	GP	W	L	T	GF	GA	PTS	GP	W	L	T	GF	GA	PTS
Boston	54	17	26	11	173	210	45	54	8	40	6	153	254	22	108	25	66	17	326	464	67
Buffalo	46	19	15	12	179	165	50	45	8	23	14	125	205	30	91	27	38	26	304	370	80
Calgary	37	18	10	9	137	123	45	37	9	21	7	111	158	25	74	27	31	16	248	281	70
Chicago	50	23	22	5	177	167	51	51	8	34	9	143	217	25	101	31	56	14	320	384	76
Detroit	56	39	13	4	251	162	82	57	10	36	11	158	229	31	113	49	49	15	409	391	113
Edmonton	22	9	12	1	86	107	19	22	4	17	1	77	120	9	44	13	29	2	163	227	28
Hartford	22	10	9	3	102	93	23	22	9	12	1	89	98	19	44	19	21	4	191	191	42
Los Angeles	63	36	19	8	239	201	80	61	14	39	8	158	237	36	124	50	58	16	397	438	116
Minnesota	55	34	16	5	213	149	73	56	20	31	5	190	215	45	111	54	47	10	403	364	118
Montreal	57	19	29	9	174	212	47	57	4	47	6	138	292	14	114	23	76	15	312	504	61
New Jersey	55	33	19	3	237	200	69	55	19	27	9	193	212	47	110	52	46	12	430	412	116
NY Islanders	62	29	22	11	241	215	69	61	19	34	8	200	262	46	123	48	56	19	441	477	115
NY Rangers	75	28	36	11	269	285	67	76	30	39	7	267	311	67	151	58	75	18	536	596	134
Ottawa	2	2	0	0	12	5	4	2	1	1	0	8	4	2	4	3	1	0	20	9	6
Philadelphia	81	34	31	16	271	259	84	81	14	60	7	208	356	35	162	48	91	23	479	615	119
Quebec	23	13	6	4	106	93	30	21	11	10	0	85	93	22	44	24	16	4	191	186	52
St. Louis	55	25	19	11	206	169	61	56	13	38	5	151	225	31	111	38	57	16	357	394	92
San Jose	2	2	0	0	17	4	4	3	3	0	0	24	7	6	5	5	0	0	41	11	10
Tampa Bay	1	0	0	1	3	3	1	1	1	0	0	5	4	2	2	1	0	1	8	7	3
Toronto	53	28	19	6	221	172	62	52	17	25	10	174	216	44	105	45	44	16	395	388	106
Vancouver	42	27	8	7	189	140	61	42	19	20	3	162	158	41	84	46	28	10	351	298	102
Washington	61	31	24	6	250	213	68	64	24	33	5	245	280	57	125	57	57	11	495	493	125
Winnipeg	22	15	7	0	91	66	30	21	11	9	1	78	80	23	43	26	16	1	169	146	53
Defunct Clubs	35	22	6	7	148	93	51	34	13	10	11	108	101	37	69	35	16	18	256	194	88
Totals	1031	513	368	150	3992	3506	1176	1031	291	606	134	3250	4334	716	2062	804	974	284	7242	7840	1892

Playoffs

	Series	W	L	GP	W	L	T	GF	GA	Last Mtg.	Round	Result
Boston	4	2	2	19	10	9	0	67	62	1992	CF	W 4-0
Buffalo	1	1	0	3	2	1	0	9	9	1979	PR	W 2-1
Chicago	2	1	1	8	4	4	0	23	24	1992	F	W 4-0
Minnesota	1	1	0	6	4	2	0	28	16	1991	F	W 4-2
New Jersey	2	2	0	12	8	4	0	48	30	1993	DSF	W 4-1
NY Islanders	3	0	3	19	8	11	0	58	67	1993	DF	L 3-4
NY Rangers	2	2	0	10	8	2	0	43	30	1992	DF	W 4-2
Philadelphia	1	0	1	7	3	4	0	24	31	1989	DF	L 3-4
St. Louis	3	1	2	13	6	7	0	40	45	1981	PR	L 2-3
Toronto	2	0	2	6	2	4	0	13	21	1977	PR	L 1-2
Washington	2	2	0	12	8	4	0	44	40	1992	DSF	W 4-3
Defunct Clubs	1	1	0	4	4	0	0	13	6			
Totals	24	13	11	119	67	52	0	410	381			

Playoff Results 1993-89

Year	Round	Opponent	Result	GF	GA
1993	DF	NY Islanders	L 3-4	27	24
	DSF	New Jersey	W 4-1	23	13
1992	F	**Chicago**	**W 4-0**	15	10
	CF	Boston	W 4-0	19	7
	DF	NY Rangers	W 4-2	19	14
	DSF	Washington	W 4-3	25	27
1991	F	**Minnesota**	**W 4-2**	28	16
	CF	Boston	W 4-2	27	18
	DF	Washington	W 4-1	19	13
	DSF	New Jersey	W 4-3	25	17
1989	DF	Philadelphia	L 3-4	24	31
	DSF	NY Rangers	W 4-0	19	11

Abbreviations: Round: F – Final;
CF – conference final; **DF** – division final;
DSF – division semi-final; **SF** – semi-final;
QF – quarter-final; **PR** – preliminary round.
GA – goals against; **GF** – goals for.

1992-93 Results

	Home			Away	
Oct. 6	Philadelphia	3-3	Oct. 10 Montreal	3-3
8	NY Islanders	7-3	17 Hartford	7-3
13	Buffalo	6-5	24 New Jersey	4-3
15	Montreal	5-2	27 Ottawa	7-2
20	Vancouver	5-1	29 St. Louis	4-6
22	Detroit	9-6	Nov. 1 Tampa Bay	5-4
Nov. 3	NY Islanders	2-0	7 Toronto	2-4
5	St. Louis	8-4	8 Chicago	2-7
12	Quebec	4-4	10 Minnesota	4-1
17	Buffalo	4-2	13 Detroit	0-8
21	New Jersey	2-0	20 New Jersey	4-1
25	NY Rangers	3-11	23 NY Rangers	5-2
28	Washington	5-3	27 Washington	4-6
Dec. 8	Winnipeg	5-2	Dec. 1 NY Islanders	7-3
12	New Jersey	6-5	3 Los Angeles	3-5
15	Philadelphia	6-2	5 San Jose*	9-4
19	NY Islanders*	3-4	11 New Jersey	1-2
21	Quebec	7-4	17 Philadelphia	5-4
31	Toronto	3-3	23 Philadelphia	4-0
Jan. 2	NY Rangers	5-2	27 Buffalo*	4-2
5	Boston	6-2	Jan. 10 Winnipeg	2-3
7	Minnesota	3-6	14 Boston	0-7
9	Calgary*	3-2	19 Vancouver	5-2
16	Ottawa	6-1	22 Edmonton	1-2
26	Washington	6-3	23 Calgary	4-3
28	NY Islanders	2-5	31 Washington*	2-2
30	Philadelphia*	4-2	Feb. 10 NY Rangers	3-0
Feb. 8	Boston	4-0	14 Buffalo	4-7
13	Chicago*	4-1	20 NY Islanders*	2-4
18	Edmonton	4-5	21 Hartford*	4-2
23	New Jersey	1-3	25 Ottawa	1-2
27	Tampa Bay*	3-3	28 Washington*	4-2
Mar. 9	Boston	3-2	Mar. 2 Philadelphia	4-5
11	Los Angeles	4-3	5 NY Rangers	1-3
18	Washington	7-5	14 NY Islanders	3-2
20	Philadelphia	9-3	21 Edmonton	6-4
23	San Jose	7-2	27 Boston*	5-3
25	New Jersey	4-3	28 Washington	4-1
30	Ottawa	6-4	Apr. 3 Quebec	5-3
Apr. 1	Hartford	10-2	4 New Jersey	5-2
7	Montreal	4-3	9 NY Rangers	10-4
10	NY Rangers	4-2	14 New Jersey	6-6

*Denotes afternoon game

Entry Draft Selections 1993-79

1993
Pick
26 Stefan Bergqvist
52 Domenic Pittis
62 Dave Roche
104 Jonas Andersson-Junkka
130 Chris Kelleher
156 Patrick Lalime
182 Sean Selmser
208 Larry McMorran
234 Timothy Harberts
260 Leonid Toropchenko
286 Hans Jonsson

1992
Pick
19 Martin Straka
43 Marc Hussey
67 Travis Thiessen
91 Todd Klassen
115 Philipp De Rouville
139 Artem Kopot
163 Jan Alinc
187 Fran Bussey
211 Brian Bonin
235 Brian Callahan

1991
Pick
16 Markus Naslund
38 Rusty Fitzgerald
60 Shane Peacock
82 Joe Tamminen
104 Robert Melanson
126 Brian Clifford
148 Ed Patterson
170 Peter McLaughlin
192 Jeff Lembke
214 Chris Tok
236 Paul Dyck
258 Pasi Huura

1990
Pick
5 Jaromir Jagr
61 Joe Dziedzic
68 Chris Tamer
89 Brian Farrell
107 Ian Moran
110 Denis Casey
130 Mika Valila
131 Ken Plaquin
145 Pat Neaton
152 Petteri Koskimaki
173 Ladislav Karabin
194 Timothy Fingerhut
215 Michael Thompson
236 Brian Bruininks

1989
Pick
16 Jamie Heward
37 Paul Laus
58 John Brill
79 Todd Nelson
100 Tom Nevers
121 Mike Markovich
126 Mike Needham
142 Patrick Schafhauser
163 Dave Shute
184 Andrew Wolf
205 Greg Hagen
226 Scott Farrell
247 Jason Smart

1988
Pick
4 Darrin Shannon
25 Mark Major
62 Daniel Gauthier
67 Mark Recchi
88 Greg Andrusak
130 Troy Mick
151 Jeff Blaeser
172 Rob Gaudreau
193 Donald Pancoe
214 Cory Laylin
235 Darren Stolk

1987
Pick
5 Chris Joseph
26 Richard Tabaracci
47 Jamie Leach
68 Risto Kurkinen
89 Jeff Waver
110 Shawn McEachern
131 Jim Bodden
152 Jiri Kucera
173 Jack MacDougall
194 Daryn McBride
215 Mark Carlson
236 Ake Lilljebjorn

1986
Pick
4 Zarley Zalapski
25 Dave Capuano
46 Brad Aitken
67 Rob Brown
88 Sandy Smith
109 Jeff Daniels
130 Doug Hobson
151 Steve Rohlik
172 Dave McLlwain
193 Kelly Cain
214 Stan Drulia
235 Rob Wilson

1985
Pick
2 Craig Simpson
23 Lee Giffin
58 Bruce Racine
86 Steve Gotaas
107 Kevin Clemens
114 Stuart Marston
128 Steve Titus
149 Paul Stanton
170 Jim Paek
191 Steve Shaunessy
212 Doug Greschuk
233 Gregory Choules

1984
Pick
1 Mario Lemieux
9 Doug Bodger
16 Roger Belanger
64 Mark Teevens
85 Arto Javanainen
127 Tom Ryan
169 John Del Col
189 Steve Hurt
210 Jim Steen
230 Mark Ziliotto

1983
Pick
15 Bob Errey
22 Todd Charlesworth
58 Mike Rowe
63 Frank Pietrangelo
103 Patrick Emond
123 Paul Ames
163 Marty Ketola
183 Alec Haidy
203 Garth Hildebrand
223 Dave Goertz

1982
Pick
10 Rich Sutter
38 Tim Hrynewich
52 Troy Loney
94 Grant Sasser
136 Grant Couture
157 Peter Derksen
178 Greg Gravel
199 Stu Wenaas
220 Chris McCauley
241 Stan Bautch

1981
Pick
28 Steve Gatzos
49 Tom Thornbury
70 Norm Schmidt
109 Paul Edwards
112 Rod Buskas
133 Geoff Wilson
154 Mitch Lamoureux
175 Dean Defazio
196 David Hannan

1980
Pick
9 Mike Bullard
51 Randy Boyd
72 Tony Feltrin
93 Doug Shedden
114 Pat Graham
156 Robert Geale
177 Brian Lundberg
198 Steve McKenzie

1979
Pick
31 Paul Marshall
52 Bennett Wolf
73 Brian Cross
94 Nick Ricci
115 Marc Chorney

Club Directory

Civic Arena
Pittsburgh, PA 15219
Phone 412/642-1800
FAX 412/642-1859

Pittsburgh Hockey Associates Directory

Ownership . . . . Howard Baldwin, Morris Belzberg, Thomas Ruta
Chairman of the Board & Governor . . . . Howard Baldwin

Administration
President & Alternate Governor . . . . Jack Kelley
Executive Vice-President & Chief
 Financial Officer . . . . Donn Patton
Senior Vice-President, Marketing &
 Public Relations . . . . Bill Barnes
Executive Vice-President
 PHA Sports Marketing Ltd. & Penvision . . . . . . Richard Chmura
General Counsel . . . . The law firm of Eckert, Seamans, Cherin & Mellott
Executive Assistants . . . . Elaine Heufelder, Paula Nichols

Hockey Operations
Executive Vice-President & General Manager . . . Craig Patrick
Head Coach . . . . Ed Johnston
Assistant Coaches . . . . Rick Kehoe, Bryan Trottier
Goaltending Coach and Scout . . . . Gilles Meloche
Head Scout . . . . Greg Malone
Scouting Staff . . . . Les Binkley, John Gill, Charlie Hodge, Mark Kelley, Ralph Cox
Professional Scout . . . . Phil Russell
Cleveland Lumberjacks Head Coach . . . . Rick Paterson
Strength and Conditioning Coach . . . . John Welday
Equipment Manager . . . . Steve Latin
Trainer . . . . TBA
Assistant Equipment Manager . . . . Kevin Greenway
Team Video Coordinator . . . . Howard Baldwin, Jr.
Executive Assistant . . . . Tracey Botsford
Team Physician . . . . Dr. Charles Burke
Team Dentists . . . . Dr. Raymond Rainka, Dr. Ronald Linaburg, Dr. David Donatelli

Public and Community Relations
Vice-President, Community & Public Relations . . . Phil Langan
Director of Public Relations . . . . Cindy Himes
Director of Media Relations . . . . Harry Sanders
Director of Publications . . . . Emily Nordstrom
Director of Amateur Hockey Development . . . . . . George Kirk
Assistant Media Relations Director . . . . Steve Bovino
Public Relations Secretary . . . . Renee Petrichevich
Director of Special Events . . . . Jamie Belo

Finance
Controller . . . . Kevin Hart
Accounting Staff . . . . Eric Brandenberg, Tracey Clontz, Barb Manion, Rick Patterson

Ticketing
Director of Ticket Sales . . . . Jeff Mercer
General Manager, Choice Seat . . . . Mark Watkins
Box Office Manager . . . . Carol Coulson
Marketing Representatives . . . . Steve Swetcha, Terri Dobos Young
Assistant Box Office Manager . . . . Fred Traynor
Choice Seat Staff . . . . Jim Cuddy, Edna Greeley, Julie Kapples, Tony Miller, Tim Porco

Sales and Communications
Director of Advertising Sales . . . . Taylor Baldwin
Director of Suite Sales and Service . . . . Chuck Saller
Director of Promotions &
 Advertising Sales Coordinator . . . . Amy Novak
Advertising Sales Representative . . . . Chris Clark
Marketing Representatives . . . . Bill Miller, Mark Willand
Secretary . . . . Maryann Dayton

Merchandising
Vice-President, Merchandising . . . . Bill Cox
Director of Memorabilia . . . . Nick Ruta
Director of Merchandising . . . . Tim Carey
Merchandising Manager . . . . Robb Gedrys
Merchandising Representative . . . . Louise Stock
Malls/Office Manager . . . . Jahna Newman
Administrative Assistant . . . . Christine Black

General Information
Home Ice . . . . Civic Arena
Dimensions of Rink . . . . 200 feet by 85 feet
Location of Press Box . . . . West Side of Building
Team Colors . . . . Black, Gold and White
Flagship Radio Station . . . . WTAE (1250 AM)
TV Stations . . . . KBL and KDKA-TV
Announcers . . . . Mike Lange, Paul Steigerwald, Stan Savran, Doug McLeod

General Manager

PATRICK, CRAIG
General Manager, Pittsburgh Penguins. Born in Detroit, MI, May 20, 1946.
Appointed general manager of the Penguins on December 5, 1989, Patrick's teams have since won two Stanley Cups (1991 and 1992), and a Presidents' Trophy (1993). Patrick has laid the groundwork for success through shrewd acquisitions and drafts; his trades for Ulf Samuelsson, Ron Francis, Rick Tocchet and Ken Wregget, and the drafting of Jaromir Jagr are all moves considered crucial to Pittsburgh's recent success.

A 1969 graduate of the University of Denver, Patrick was captain of the Pioneers' NCAA Championship hockey team that year. He returned to his alma mater in 1986 where he served as director of athletics and recreation for two years. Patrick served as administrative assistant to the president of the Amateur Hockey Association of the United States in 1980 and as an assistant coach/assistant general manager for the 1980 gold-medal winning U.S. Olympic hockey team. Before pursuing a coaching career, Patrick played professional hockey with Washington, Kansas City, St. Louis, Minnesota and California from 1971-79. In eight seasons, Patrick tallied 163 points (72-91-163) in 401 games.

NHL Coaching Record

Season	Team	Regular Season					Playoffs			
		Games	W	L	T	%	Games	W	L	%
1980-81	NY Rangers	59	26	23	10	.525	14	7	7	.500
1984-85	NY Rangers	35	11	22	2	.343	3	0	3	.000
1989-90	Pittsburgh	54	22	26	6	.463	....	....	....	....
	NHL Totals	148	59	71	18	.459	17	7	10	.412

Quebec Nordiques

1992-93 Results: 47w-27L-10T 104PTS. Second, Adams Division

Year-by-Year Record

		Home			Road			Overall						
Season	GP	W	L	T	W	L	T	W	L	T	GF	GA	Pts.	Finished	Playoff Result
1992-93	84	23	17	2	24	10	8	47	27	10	351	300	104	2nd, Adams Div.	Lost Div. Semi-Final
1991-92	80	18	19	3	2	29	9	20	48	12	255	318	52	5th, Adams Div.	Out of Playoffs
1990-91	80	9	23	8	7	27	6	16	50	14	236	354	46	5th, Adams Div.	Out of Playoffs
1989-90	80	8	26	6	4	35	1	12	61	7	240	407	31	5th, Adams Div.	Out of Playoffs
1988-89	80	16	20	4	11	26	3	27	46	7	269	342	61	5th, Adams Div.	Out of Playoffs
1987-88	80	15	23	2	17	20	3	32	43	5	271	306	69	5th, Adams Div.	Out of Playoffs
1986-87	80	20	13	7	11	26	3	31	39	10	267	276	72	4th, Adams Div.	Lost Div. Final
1985-86	80	23	13	4	20	18	2	43	31	6	330	289	92	1st, Adams Div.	Lost Div. Semi-Final
1984-85	80	24	12	4	17	18	5	41	30	9	323	275	91	2nd, Adams Div.	Lost Conf. Championship
1983-84	80	24	11	5	18	17	5	42	28	10	360	278	94	3rd, Adams Div.	Lost Div. Final
1982-83	80	23	10	7	11	24	5	34	34	12	343	336	80	4th, Adams Div.	Lost Div. Semi-Final
1981-82	80	24	13	3	9	18	13	33	31	16	356	345	82	4th, Adams Div.	Lost Conf. Championship
1980-81	80	18	11	11	12	21	7	30	32	18	314	318	78	4th, Adams Div.	Lost Prelim. Round
1979-80	80	17	16	7	8	28	4	25	44	11	248	313	61	5th, Adams Div.	Out of Playoffs

Schedule

Home			Away	
Oct.	Sun. 10 Pittsburgh	**Oct.**	Wed. 6 Ottawa
	Mon. 18 Montreal		Sat. 9 Boston
	Sat. 23 Dallas		Wed. 13 NY Rangers
	Tues. 26 Philadelphia		Sat. 16 Montreal
	Sat. 30 Detroit		Wed. 20 Hartford
Nov.	Tues. 2 Tampa Bay		Thur. 21 Chicago
	Sat. 6 NY Rangers*		Thur. 28 Pittsburgh
	Sun. 7 Florida*	**Nov.**	Thur. 4 Philadelphia
	Sat. 20 Winnipeg		Tues. 9 Washington
	Tues. 23 New Jersey		Sat. 13 Tampa Bay
	Thur. 25 Los Angeles		Sun. 14 Florida
	Sat. 27 Buffalo	**Dec.**	Fri. 3 NY Islanders
	Tues. 30 Boston		Thur. 9 New Jersey
Dec.	Sat. 4 Vancouver		Thur. 16 Philadelphia
	Tues. 7 Calgary		Tues. 21 Ottawa
	Sat. 11 Ottawa		Thur. 23 Winnipeg
	Mon. 13 Washington		Fri. 31 Pittsburgh
	Sat. 18 New Jersey*	**Jan.**	Sun. 2 Dallas
	Sun. 19 San Jose*		Tues. 4 Los Angeles
	Tues. 28 Tampa Bay		Fri. 7 Edmonton
	Wed. 29 NY Islanders		Tues. 11 Calgary
Jan.	Wed. 5 Montreal		Wed. 12 Vancouver
	(at Phoenix)		Thur. 27 Pittsburgh
	Sat. 15 Washington		Sat. 29 Hartford*
	Tues. 18 Pittsburgh		Mon. 31 Boston
	Tues. 25 Philadelphia	**Feb.**	Thur. 3 St Louis
Feb.	Tues. 1 Hartford		Fri. 11 NY Rangers
	Sat. 5 NY Islanders*		Sat. 12 Montreal
	Tues. 8 Boston		Thur. 17 San Jose
	Mon. 14 NY Rangers		Fri. 18 Anaheim
	Thur. 24 St Louis		Mon. 21 Buffalo
	Sat. 26 Anaheim		Sun. 27 NY Islanders
Mar.	Tues. 1 Buffalo	**Mar.**	Mon. 7 New Jersey
	Sat. 5 Toronto		Sat. 12 Washington
	Tues. 8 Ottawa		Sat. 19 Montreal
	Thur. 10 Montreal		Sat. 26 Toronto
	Mon. 14 Chicago		Sun. 27 New Jersey
	Thur. 17 Hartford		(at Minnesota)
	Sun. 20 Edmonton		Wed. 30 Ottawa
	Tues. 22 Boston		Thur. 31 Detroit
Apr.	Sat. 2 Buffalo	**Apr.**	Sun. 10 Buffalo*
	Tues. 5 Florida		Tues. 12 Florida
	Thur. 7 Hartford		Thur. 14 Tampa Bay

* Denotes afternoon game.

Home Starting Times:

All Games	7:35 p.m.
Except Matinees	1:35 p.m.
Sat. Mar. 5	8:05 p.m.

Franchise date: June 22, 1979

NORTHEAST
DIVISION

15th NHL Season

EASTERN
CONFERENCE

Joe Sakic, the Quebec Nordiques leader with 20 powerplay goals, tied a career high with 48 goals in 1992-93.

1993-94 Player Personnel

FORWARDS

	HT	WT	S	Place of Birth	Date	1992-93 Club
ANDERSSON, Niclas	5-9	175	L	Kungalv, Sweden	5/20/71	Halifax
BROUSSEAU, Paul	6-2	212	R	Pierrefonds, Qué.	9/18/73	Hull
CHASSÉ, Denis	6-2	190	R	Montréal, Qué.	2/7/70	Halifax
CORBET, René	6-0	176	L	Victoriaville, Qué.	6/25/73	Drummondville
FORSBERG, Peter	5-11	190	L	Ornskoldsvik, Sweden	7/20/73	MoDo
FRASER, Iain	5-10	175	L	Scarborough, Ont.	8/10/69	NY Islanders-Cap. District
GARBUTT, Murray	6-1	205	L	Hanna, Alta.	7/29/71	Did not play
GÉLINAS, Martin	5-11	195	L	Shawinigan, Qué.	6/5/70	Edmonton
HUGHES, Ryan	6-1	180	L	Montréal, Qué.	1/17/72	Cornell University
KAMENSKY, Valeri	6-2	198	R	Voskresensk, CIS	4/18/66	Québec
KLIPPENSTEIN, Wade	6-3	219	L	Boissevain, Man.	5/9/70	Alaska-Fairbanks
KOVALENKO, Andrei	5-10	185	L	Balakovo, CIS	6/7/70	Québec
LAPOINTE, Claude	5-9	173	L	Lachine, Qué.	10/11/68	Québec
MacDERMID, Paul	6-1	205	R	Chesley, Ont.	4/14/63	Washington
McKEE, Mike	6-3	190	L	Toronto, Ont.	6/18/69	Halifax-Greensboro
MONGEAU, Michel	5-9	190	L	Montréal, Qué.	2/9/65	Milwaukee-Halifax
NOLAN, Owen	6-1	194	R	Belfast, Ireland	2/12/72	Québec
NORRIS, Dwayne	5-10	175	R	St. John, Nfld.	1/8/70	Michigan State University
RICCI, Mike	6-0	190	L	Scarborough, Ont.	10/27/71	Québec
RUCINSKY, Martin	5-11	178	L	Most, Czech.	3/11/71	Québec
SAKIC, Joe	5-11	185	L	Burnaby, B.C.	7/7/69	Québec
SAVAGE, Reginald	5-10	187	L	Montréal, Qué.	5/1/70	Baltimore-Washington
SCHULTE, Paxton	6-2	210	L	Ionaway, Alta.	7/16/72	Spokane
SIMARD, Martin	6-1	215	R	Montréal, Qué.	6/25/66	Atl.-T.B.-Hal.
SIMON, Chris	6-3	230	L	Wawa, Ont.	1/30/72	Québec-Halifax
SUNDIN, Mats	6-2	190	R	Bromma, Sweden	2/13/71	Québec
TWIST, Tony	6-1	212	L	Sherwood Park, Sask.	5/9/68	Québec
WARD, Ed	6-3	190	R	Edmonton, Alta.	11/10/69	Halifax
WARRINER, Todd	6-1	172	L	Blenheim, Ont.	1/3/74	Kitchener
WILLETT, Paul	5-9	180	R	New Richmond, Que.	5/10/69	Fort Wayne
YOUNG, Scott	6-0	190	R	Clinton, MA	10/1/67	Québec

DEFENSEMEN

	HT	WT	S	Place of Birth	Date	1992-93 Club
CÔTÉ, Alain	6-0	200	R	Montmagny, Qué.	4/14/67	Fred.-T.B.-Atl.
DUCHESNE, Steve	5-11	195	L	Sept-Iles, Qué.	6/30/65	Québec
FINN, Steven	6-0	198	L	Laval, Qué.	8/20/66	Québec
FOOTE, Adam	6-1	180	R	Toronto, Ont.	7/10/71	Québec
GUSAROV, Alexei	6-2	170	L	Leningrad, CIS	7/8/64	Québec
HUFFMAN, Kerry	6-2	200	L	Peterborough, Ont.	1/3/68	Québec
KARPA, David	6-1	190	R	Regina, Sask.	5/7/71	Québec-Halifax
KARPOTSEV, Alexander	6-2	189	L	Moscow, CIS	4/7/70	Moscow Dynamo
KLEMM, Jon	6-3	200	R	Cranbrook, B.C.	1/8/70	Québec-Halifax
LEPAGE, Martin	6-1	185	L	Longueuil, Qué.	2/26/74	Shawinigan
LESCHYSHYN, Curtis	6-1	205	L	Thompson, Man.	9/21/69	Québec-Halifax
MATIER, Mark	6-1	190	L	St. Catharines, Ont.	12/14/73	Sault Ste. Marie
MILLER, Aaron	6-3	197	R	Buffalo, NY	8/11/71	University of Vermont
PARROTT, Jeff	6-1	195	R	The Pas, Man.	4/6/71	Minnesota-Duluth
SCOTT, Blair	6-0	202	L	Winnipeg, Man.	2/25/72	Detroit Jr.
VELISCHEK, Randy	6-0	200	L	Montréal, Qué.	2/10/62	Halifax
WOLANIN, Craig	6-3	205	L	Grosse Pointe, MI	7/27/67	Québec
ZAYONCE, Dean	6-0	200	R	Kelowna, B.C.	10/28/70	Halifax-Greensboro

GOALTENDERS

	HT	WT	C	Place of Birth	Date	1992-93 Club
CLOUTIER, Jacques	5-7	168	L	Noranda, Qué.	1/3/60	Québec
FISET, Stéphane	6-0	175	L	Montréal, Qué.	6/17/70	Québec-Halifax
KRAKE, Paul	6-0	175	L	Lloydminster, Alta.	3/25/69	Halifax-Oklahoma
LABRECQUE, Patrick	6-0	187	L	Laval, Qué.	3/6/71	Halifax-Greensboro
PASSMORE, Steve	5-9	165	L	Thunder Bay, Ont.	1/29/73	Victoria-Kamloops
SNOW, Garth	6-3	200	L	Wrentham, MA	7/28/69	University of Maine
TANNER, John	6-3	182	L	Cambridge, Ont.	3/17/71	Halifax

1992-93 Scoring

Regular Season

Pos	#	Player	Team	GP	G	A	Pts	+/-	PIM	PP	SH	GW	GT	S	%
R	13	Mats Sundin	QUE	80	47	67	114	21	96	13	4	9	1	215	21.9
C	19	Joe Sakic	QUE	78	48	57	105	3–	40	20	2	4	1	264	18.2
D	28	Steve Duchesne	QUE	82	20	62	82	15	57	8	0	2	1	227	8.8
C	9	Mike Ricci	QUE	77	27	51	78	8	123	12	1	10	1	142	19.0
R	11	Owen Nolan	QUE	73	36	41	77	1–	185	15	0	4	1	241	14.9
R	51 *	Andrei Kovalenko	QUE	81	27	41	68	13	57	8	1	4	0	153	17.6
R	48	Scott Young	QUE	82	30	30	60	5	20	9	6	5	0	225	13.3
L	25 *	Martin Rucinsky	QUE	77	18	30	48	16	51	4	0	1	3	133	13.5
L	31	Valeri Kamensky	QUE	32	15	22	37	13	14	2	3	0	1	94	16.0
C	47	Claude Lapointe	QUE	74	10	26	36	5	98	0	0	1	0	91	11.0
D	7	Curtis Leschyshyn	QUE	82	9	23	32	25	61	4	0	2	0	73	12.3
L	18	Mike Hough	QUE	77	8	22	30	11–	69	2	1	2	0	98	8.2
D	5	Alexei Gusarov	QUE	79	8	22	30	18	57	0	2	1	0	60	13.3
L	44	Gino Cavallini	QUE	67	9	15	24	10	34	0	0	1	0	71	12.7
D	2	Kerry Huffman	QUE	52	4	18	22	0	54	3	0	0	0	86	4.7
D	52	Adam Foote	QUE	81	4	12	16	6	168	0	1	0	0	54	7.4
L	22	Scott Pearson	QUE	41	13	1	14	3	95	0	0	1	0	45	28.9
D	29	Steven Finn	QUE	80	5	9	14	3–	160	0	0	0	0	61	8.2
L	20 *	Bill Lindsay	QUE	44	4	9	13	0	16	0	0	0	0	58	6.9
D	4	Mikhail Tatarinov	QUE	28	2	6	8	6	28	1	0	0	0	46	4.3
D	6	Craig Wolanin	QUE	24	1	6	7	9	49	0	0	0	0	17	5.9
L	12 *	Chris Simon	QUE	16	1	1	2	2–	67	0	0	1	0	15	6.7
L	15	Tony Twist	QUE	34	0	2	2	0	64	0	0	0	0	14	.0
G	35	Stephane Fiset	QUE	37	0	2	2	0	2	0	0	0	0	0	.0
G	27	Ron Hextall	QUE	54	0	2	2	0	56	0	0	0	0	1	.0
R	46 *	Niclas Andersson	QUE	3	0	1	1	0	2	0	0	0	0	4	.0
D	43 *	Leonard Esau	QUE	4	0	1	1	1	2	0	0	0	0	5	.0
D	59 *	Dave Karpa	QUE	12	0	1	1	6–	13	0	0	0	0	2	.0
G	32	Jacques Cloutier	QUE	3	0	0	0	0	0	0	0	0	0	0	.0

Goaltending

No.	Goaltender	GPI	Mins	Avg	W	L	T	EN	SO	GA	SA	S%
35	Stephane Fiset	37	1939	3.40	18	9	4	3	0	110	945	.884
27	Ron Hextall	54	2988	3.45	29	16	5	3	0	172	1529	.888
32	Jacques Cloutier	3	154	3.90	0	2	1	2	0	10	65	.846
	Totals	84	5101	3.53	47	27	10	8	0	300	2547	.882

Playoffs

Pos	#	Player	Team	GP	G	A	Pts	+/-	PIM	PP	SH	GW	GT	S	%
C	19	Joe Sakic	QUE	6	3	3	6	3–	2	1	0	0	0	24	12.5
C	47	Claude Lapointe	QUE	6	2	4	6	4	8	0	0	0	0	9	22.2
C	9	Mike Ricci	QUE	6	0	6	6	5	8	0	0	0	0	7	.0
R	48	Scott Young	QUE	6	4	1	5	5	0	0	0	2	1	23	17.4
D	28	Steve Duchesne	QUE	6	0	5	5	0	6	0	0	0	0	14	.0
D	13	Mats Sundin	QUE	6	3	1	4	4–	6	1	0	0	0	19	15.8
D	7	Curtis Leschyshyn	QUE	6	1	2	3	3	6	1	0	0	0	5	20.0
L	25 *	Martin Rucinsky	QUE	6	1	1	2	3–	4	1	0	0	0	10	10.0
R	51 *	Andrei Kovalenko	QUE	4	1	0	1	5–	2	0	0	0	0	8	12.5
R	11	Owen Nolan	QUE	5	1	0	1	2–	2	0	0	0	0	12	8.3
D	5	Alexei Gusarov	QUE	5	0	1	1	3–	0	0	0	0	0	7	.0
D	29	Steven Finn	QUE	6	0	1	1	3–	8	0	0	0	0	10	.0
L	18	Mike Hough	QUE	6	0	1	1	0	2	0	0	0	0	18	.0
D	52	Adam Foote	QUE	6	0	1	1	3–	2	0	0	0	0	6	.0
L	31	Valeri Kamensky	QUE	6	0	1	1	1–	6	0	0	0	0	21	.0
G	35	Stephane Fiset	QUE	1	0	0	0	0	0	0	0	0	0	0	.0
D	2	Kerry Huffman	QUE	3	0	0	0	2–	0	0	0	0	0	4	.0
L	22	Scott Pearson	QUE	3	0	0	0	0	6	0	0	0	0	3	.0
D	59 *	Dave Karpa	QUE	3	0	0	0	0	2	0	0	0	0	3	.0
L	44	Gino Cavallini	QUE	4	0	0	0	1–	0	0	0	0	0	2	.0
D	6	Craig Wolanin	QUE	4	0	0	0	1–	2	0	0	0	0	2	.0
L	12 *	Chris Simon	QUE	5	0	0	0	2–	26	0	0	0	0	8	.0
G	27	Ron Hextall	QUE	6	0	0	0	0	0	0	0	0	0	0	.0

Goaltending

No.	Goaltender	GPI	Mins	Avg	W	L	EN	SO	GA	SA	S%
35	Stephane Fiset	1	21	2.86	0	0	0	0	1	12	.917
27	Ron Hextall	6	372	2.90	2	4	0	0	18	211	.915
	Totals	6	396	2.88	2	4	0	0	19	223	.915

General Managers' History

Maurice Filion, 1979-80 to 1987-88; Martin Madden 1988-89; Martin Madden and Maurice Filion, 1989-90; Pierre Page, 1990-91 to date.

Coaching History

Jacques Demers, 1979-80; Maurice Filion and Michel Bergeron, 1980-81; Michel Bergeron, 1981-82 to 1986-87; André Savard and Ron Lapointe, 1987-88; Ron Lapointe, and Jean Perron, 1988-89; Michel Bergeron, 1989-90; Dave Chambers, 1990-91; Dave Chambers and Pierre Page, 1991-92; Pierre Page, 1992-93 to date.

Captains' History

Marc Tardif, 1979-80, 1980-81; Robbie Ftorek and Andre Dupont, 1981-82; Mario Marois, 1982-83 to 1984-85; Mario Marois, Peter Stastny, 1985-86; Peter Stastny, 1986-87 to 1989-90; Joe Sakic and Steven Finn, 1990-91; Mike Hough, 1991-92; Joe Sakic, 1992-93.

Retired Numbers

3	J.C. Tremblay	1972-1979
8	Marc Tardif	1979-1983

Club Records

Team

(Figures in brackets for season records are games played; records for fewest points, wins, ties, losses, goals, goals against are for 70 or more games)

Most Points	104	1992-93 (84)
Most Wins	47	1992-93 (84)
Most Ties	18	1980-81 (80)
Most Losses	61	1989-90 (80)
Most Goals	360	1983-84 (80)
Most Goals Against	407	1989-90 (80)
Fewest Points	31	1989-90 (80)
Fewest Wins	12	1989-90 (80)
Fewest Ties	5	1987-88 (80)
Fewest Losses	27	1992-93 (84)
Fewest Goals	236	1990-91 (80)
Fewest Goals Against	275	1984-85 (80)

Longest Winning Streak
Over-all ... 7 Nov. 24-Dec. 10/83
Oct. 10-21/85
Dec. 31/85-Jan. 11/86
Home ... 10 Nov. 26/83-Jan. 10/84
Away ... 5 Feb. 28-Mar. 24, 1986

Longest Undefeated Streak
Over-all ... 11 Mar. 10-31/81 (7 wins, 4 ties)
Home ... 14 Nov. 19/83-Jan. 21/84 (11 wins, 3 ties)
Away ... 8 Feb. 17/81-Mar. 22/81 (6 wins, 2 ties)

Longest Losing Streak
Over-all ... 14 Oct. 21-Nov. 19/90
Home ... 8 Oct. 21-Nov. 24/90
Away ... 18 Jan. 18-Apr. 1/90

Longest Winless Streak
Over-all ... 17 Oct. 21-Nov. 25/90 (15 losses, 2 ties)
Home ... 11 Nov. 14-Dec. 26/89 (7 losses, 4 ties)
Away ... 33 Oct. 8/91-Feb. 27/92 (25 losses, 8 ties)

Most Shutouts, Season ... 6 1985-86 (80)
Most PIM, Season ... 2,104 1989-90 (80)
Most Goals, Game ... 12 Feb. 1/83 (Hfd. 3 at Que. 12) Oct. 20/84 (Que. 12 at Tor. 3)

Individual

Most Seasons ... 11 Michel Goulet
Most Games ... 813 Michel Goulet
Most Goals, Career ... 456 Michel Goulet
Most Assists, Career ... 668 Peter Stastny
Most Points, Career ... 1,048 Peter Stastny (380 goals, 668 assists)
Most PIM, Career ... 1,545 Dale Hunter
Most Shutouts, Career ... 6 Mario Gosselin

Longest Consecutive Games Streak ... 312 Dale Hunter (Oct. 9/80-Mar. 13/84)

Most Goals, Season ... 57 Michel Goulet (1982-83)
Most Assists, Season ... 93 Peter Stastny (1981-82)
Most Points, Season ... 139 Peter Stastny (1981-82) (46 goals, 93 assists)
Most PIM, Season ... 301 Gord Donnelly (1987-88)

Most Points, Defenseman, Season ... 82 Steve Duchesne (1992-93) (20 goals, 62 assists)

Most Points, Center, Season ... 139 Peter Stastny (1981-82) (46 goals, 93 assists)

Most Points, Right Wing, Season ... 103 Jacques Richard (1980-81) (52 goals, 51 assists)

Most Points, Left Wing, Season ... 121 Michel Goulet (1983-84) (56 goals, 65 assists)

Most Points, Rookie, Season ... 109 Peter Stastny (1980-81) (39 goals, 70 assists)

Most Shutouts, Season ... 4 Clint Malarchuk (1985-86)
Most Goals, Game ... 5 Mats Sundin (Mar. 5/92)
Most Assists, Game ... 5 Anton Stastny (Feb. 22/81) Michel Goulet (Jan. 3/84) Owen Nolan (Mar. 5/92) Mike Ricci (Dec. 12/92)
Most Points, Game ... 8 Peter Stastny (Feb. 22/81) Anton Stastny (Feb. 22/81)

1992-93 Results

	Home				Away	
Oct. 10	Ottawa	9-2	Oct. 8	Buffalo	5-4
13	Philadelphia	6-3	15	Detroit	4-2
17	St. Louis	5-6	21	St. Louis	5-5
27	Tampa Bay	4-3	22	Minnesota	2-5
31	Winnipeg	3-2	24	Tampa Bay	2-3
Nov. 7	Chicago*	4-7	29	NY Rangers	6-3
8	Calgary*	5-5	Nov. 3	Hartford	3-3
14	NY Rangers	6-3	5	Boston	4-6
17	Toronto	3-1	11	Ottawa	7-3
19	Montreal	4-3	12	Pittsburgh	4-4
21	Hartford*	8-2	25	Buffalo	1-1
22	Washington*	4-6	26	Toronto	5-4
28	New Jersey	3-6	Dec. 3	Philadelphia	2-3
30	Boston	3-4	10	Los Angeles	5-4
Dec. 5	Minnesota	4-7	12	San Jose	8-7
7	Buffalo	4-3	13	Vancouver	3-3
17	Montreal	3-8	16	Montreal	5-1
20	NY Islanders*	5-3	21	Pittsburgh	4-7
26	Ottawa	4-2	27	Ottawa	6-1
29	New Jersey	4-1	31	Hartford	6-2
Jan. 2	Detroit	2-6	Jan. 5	NY Islanders	2-1
14	Montreal	3-5	7	Boston	3-2
16	San Jose	4-1	9	Hartford	2-4
23	Buffalo	4-3	19	Ottawa	5-2
26	Boston	4-4	22	Buffalo	2-6
Feb. 2	Los Angeles	3-2	28	Philadelphia	6-3
3	Boston	1-4	29	Washington	3-3
9	Vancouver	1-5	Feb. 12	Calgary	4-4
17	Ottawa	6-4	14	Edmonton*	3-2
23	Edmonton	6-3	20	Tampa Bay	5-2
25	NY Islanders	6-4	21	New Jersey	6-3
27	Hartford	3-5	28	Ottawa	4-6
Mar. 6	NY Rangers	10-2	Mar. 2	Winnipeg	7-4
8	Hartford	2-4	4	Chicago	3-3
10	Buffalo	4-7	13	Montreal	4-4
15	Toronto	4-2	20	New Jersey*	5-1
18	Montreal	2-5	23	Washington	1-5
27	Philadelphia*	8-3	28	NY Rangers	3-2
Apr. 3	Pittsburgh	3-5	31	Hartford	6-2
6	Boston	1-7	Apr. 1	Ottawa	4-2
10	Hartford	6-3	8	Boston	2-6
13	Ottawa	6-2	11	Buffalo	3-1

*Denotes afternoon game

All-time Record vs. Other Clubs

Regular Season

		At Home							On Road							Total					
	GP	W	L	T	GF	GA	PTS	GP	W	L	T	GF	GA	PTS	GP	W	L	T	GF	GA	PTS
Boston	52	16	31	5	193	235	37	51	16	27	8	160	209	40	103	32	58	13	353	444	77
Buffalo	51	26	17	8	197	163	60	52	15	29	8	170	212	38	103	41	46	16	367	375	98
Calgary	21	7	9	5	89	86	19	22	4	12	6	72	102	14	43	11	21	11	161	188	33
Chicago	21	8	9	4	89	88	20	22	7	13	2	72	91	16	43	15	22	6	161	179	36
Detroit	22	12	7	3	93	80	27	21	8	12	1	73	86	17	43	20	19	4	166	166	44
Edmonton	21	7	12	2	85	102	16	21	5	16	0	62	119	10	42	12	28	2	147	221	26
Hartford	52	30	15	7	229	166	67	51	18	22	11	181	181	47	103	48	37	18	410	347	114
Los Angeles	21	9	9	3	86	85	21	21	8	12	1	76	97	17	42	17	21	4	162	182	38
Minnesota	22	15	5	2	104	60	32	21	6	13	2	66	84	14	43	21	18	4	170	144	46
Montreal	52	26	24	2	181	192	54	51	11	32	8	158	219	30	103	37	56	10	339	411	84
New Jersey	22	12	8	2	95	73	26	23	11	11	1	89	100	23	45	23	19	3	184	173	49
NY Islanders	23	12	9	2	91	77	26	21	7	13	1	73	94	15	44	19	22	3	164	171	41
NY Rangers	23	12	8	3	106	98	27	22	5	14	3	60	92	13	45	17	22	6	166	190	40
Ottawa	4	4	0	0	25	10	8	5	4	1	0	26	14	8	9	8	1	0	51	24	16
Philadelphia	22	7	8	7	80	81	21	23	3	18	2	61	96	8	45	10	26	9	141	177	29
Pittsburgh	21	10	11	0	93	85	20	23	6	13	4	93	106	16	44	16	24	4	186	191	36
St. Louis	21	9	9	3	76	74	21	21	3	16	2	70	102	8	42	12	25	5	146	176	29
San Jose	2	2	0	0	10	4	4	3	1	2	0	13	18	2	5	3	2	0	23	22	6
Tampa Bay	1	1	0	0	4	3	2	1	1	0	0	7	5	2	2	2	0	0	11	8	4
Toronto	22	12	5	5	90	72	29	22	10	10	2	96	78	22	44	22	15	7	186	150	51
Vancouver	22	8	10	4	64	67	20	21	7	10	4	85	89	18	43	15	20	8	149	156	38
Washington	22	7	11	4	72	91	18	22	8	11	3	75	92	19	44	15	22	7	147	183	37
Winnipeg	22	10	10	2	88	90	22	21	7	9	5	85	89	19	43	17	19	7	173	179	41
Totals	562	262	227	73	2240	2082	597	562	171	317	74	1923	2375	416	1124	433	544	147	4163	4457	1013

Playoffs

	Series	W	L	GP	W	L	T	GF	GA	Last Mtg.	Round	Result
Boston	2	1	1	11	5	6	0	36	37	1983	DSF	L 1-3
Buffalo	2	2	0	8	6	2	0	35	27	1985	DSF	W 3-2
Hartford	2	1	1	9	4	5	0	34	35	1987	DSF	W 4-2
Montreal	5	2	3	31	14	17	0	85	105	1993	DSF	L 2-4
NY Islanders	1	0	1	4	0	4	0	9	18	1982	CF	L 0-4
Philadelphia	2	0	2	11	4	7	0	29	39	1985	CF	L 2-4
Totals	14	6	8	74	33	41	0	228	261			

Playoff Results 1993-89

Year	Round	Opponent	Result	GF	GA
1993	DSF	Montreal	L 2-4	16	19

Abbreviations: Round: F – Final;
CF – conference final; **DF** – division final;
DSF – division semi-final; **SF** – semi-final;
QF – quarter-final; **PR** – preliminary round.
GA – goals against; **GF** – goals for.

Entry Draft
Selections 1993-79

1993 Pick		1989 Pick		1986 Pick		1982 Pick	
10	Jocelyn Thibault	1	Mats Sundin	18	Ken McRae	13	David Shaw
14	Adam Deadmarsh	22	Adam Foote	39	Jean-Marc Routhier	34	Paul Gillis
49	Ashley Buckberger	43	Stephane Morin	41	Stephane Guerard	55	Mario Gosselin
75	Bill Pierce	54	John Tanner	81	Ron Tugnutt	76	Jiri Lala
101	Ryan Tocher	68	Niclas Andersson	102	Gerald Bzdel	97	Phil Stanger
127	Anders Myrvold	76	Eric Dubois	117	Scott White	131	Daniel Poudrier
137	Nicholas Checco	85	Kevin Kaiser	123	Morgan Samuelsson	181	Mike Hough
153	Christian Matte	106	Dan Lambert	134	Mark Vermette	202	Vincent Lukac
179	David Ling	127	Sergei Mylnikov	144	Jean-Francois Nault	223	Andre Martin
205	Petr Franek	148	Paul Krake	165	Keith Miller	244	Jozef Lukac
231	Vincent Auger	169	Viacheslav Bykov	186	Pierre Millier	248	Jan Jasko
257	Mark Pivetz	190	Andrei Khomutov	207	Chris Lappin		
283	John Hillman	211	Byron Witkowski	228	Martin Latreille	**1981 Pick**	
		232	Noel Rahn	249	Sean Boudreault	11	Randy Moller
1992 Pick						53	Jean-Marc Gaulin
4	Todd Warriner	**1988 Pick**		**1985 Pick**		74	Clint Malarchuk
28	Paul Brousseau	3	Curtis Leschyshyn	15	David Latta	95	Ed Lee
29	Tuomas Gronman	5	Daniel Dore	36	Jason Lafreniere	116	Mike Eagles
52	Emmanuel Fernandez	24	Stephane Fiset	57	Max Middendorf	158	Andre Cote
76	Ian McIntyre	45	Petri Aaltonen	65	Peter Massey	179	Marc Brisebois
100	Charlie Wasley	66	Darin Kimble	78	David Espe	200	Kari Takko
124	Paxton Schulte	87	Stephane Venne	99	Bruce Major		
148	Martin LePage	108	Ed Ward	120	Andy Akervik	**1980 Pick**	
172	Mike Jickling	129	Valeri Kamensky	141	Mike Oliverio	24	Normand Rochefort
196	Steve Passmore	150	Sakari Lindfors	162	Mario Brunetta	66	Jay Miller
220	Anson Carter	171	Dan Wiebe	183	Brit Peer	87	Basil McRae
244	Aaron Ellis	213	Alexei Gusarov	204	Tom Sasso	108	Mark Kumpel
		234	Claude Lapointe	225	Gary Murphy	129	Gaston Therrien
1991 Pick				246	Jean Bois	150	Michel Bolduc
1	Eric Lindros	**1987 Pick**				171	Christian Tanguay
24	Rene Corbet	9	Bryan Fogarty	**1984 Pick**		192	William Robinson
46	Richard Brennan	15	Joe Sakic	15	Trevor Stienburg		
68	Dave Karpa	51	Jim Sprott	36	Jeff Brown	**1979 Pick**	
90	Patrick Labrecque	72	Kip Miller	57	Steve Finn	20	Michel Goulet
103	Bill Lindsay	93	Rob Mendel	78	Terry Perkins	41	Dale Hunter
134	Mikael Johansson	114	Garth Snow	120	Darren Cota	62	Lee Norwood
156	Janne Laukkanen	135	Tim Hanus	141	Henrik Cedergren	83	Anton Stastny
157	Aaron Asp	156	Jake Enebak	162	Jyrki Maki	104	Pierre Lacroix
178	Adam Bartell	177	Jaroslav Sevcik	183	Guy Ouellette	125	Scott McGeown
188	Brent Brekke	183	Ladislav Tresl	203	Ken Quinney		
200	Paul Koch	198	Darren Nauss	244	Peter Loob		
222	Doug Friedman	219	Mike Williams				
244	Eric Meloche			**1983 Pick**			
				32	Yves Heroux		
1990 Pick				52	Bruce Bell		
1	Owen Nolan			54	Iiro Jarvi		
22	Ryan Hughes			92	Luc Guenette		
43	Bradley Zavisha			112	Brad Walcott		
106	Jeff Parrott			132	Craig Mack		
127	Dwayne Norris			152	Tommy Albelin		
148	Andrei Kovalenko			172	Wayne Groulx		
158	Alexander Karpovtsev			192	Scott Shaunessy		
169	Pat Mazzoli			232	Bo Berglund		
190	Scott Davis			239	Jindrich Kokrment		
211	Mika Stromberg						
232	Wade Klippenstein						

Coach and General Manager

PAGÉ, PIERRE
Coach and General Manager, Quebec Nordiques.
Born in St. Hermas, Que., April 30, 1948.

Under Pierre Pagé's guidance, the Quebec Nordiques compiled their best record during the 1992-93 season, qualifying for the playoffs for the first time in six seasons. Pagé added the head coaching duties of the Quebec Nordiques to his resume in 1991-92, replacing Dave Chambers 18 games into the season. Under Pagé's direction, the Nordiques compiled a 17-34-9 record. Pagé was named general manager of the Nordiques on May 4, 1990 after two seasons as head coach of the Minnesota North Stars. In his rookie season with Minnesota, the club posted a 27-37-16 record for 70 points, a 19-point improvement over the previous year and earned its first playoff berth since 1985-86. In 1989-90, the North Stars continued improving, finishing the season with 76 points (36-40-4).

Pagé, 45, joined the Calgary Flames in 1980-81 as an assistant coach to Al Mac-Neil. He served in that capacity through the 1981-82 season before accepting a position as coach and general manager of the Flames' top minor league affiliate in Denver (two seasons) and, later, Moncton (one season). In 1985-86, Pagé returned to Calgary as an assistant to head coach Bob Johnson and remained in that capacity through the 1987-88 season under Terry Crisp.

Before joining the Flames, Pagé was head coach of the Dalhousie University Tigers of the CIAU where in 1978-79, he guided his club to a second place finish in the national final. He also served as an assistant coach with the 1980 Canadian Olympic Team and the 1981 Team Canada entry in the Canada Cup.

Club Directory

Colisée de Québec
2205 Ave de Colisée
Québec City, Québec
G1L 4W7
Phone **418/529-8441**
FAX 418/529-1052
Capacity: 15,399

President and Governor . . . . Marcel Aubut
Alternate Governor . . . . Pierre Pagé
Executive Secretaries to the President . . . . Louise Marois, Jeanne Simard
Coordinator – President's Agenda . . . . Sylvie Fiset
Hockey Club Personnel
General Manager and Head Coach . . . . Pierre Pagé
Assistant to the General Manager . . . . Sherwood Bassin
Administrative Assistant to the General Manager . François Giguère
Assistant Coaches . . . . Don Jackson, André Savard, Clément Jodoin
Director of Development . . . . Dave Draper
Professional Scout . . . . Orval Tessier
Scouts . . . . Herb Boxer, Don Boyd, Shannon Currie, Lucien
        Deblois, Roland Duplessis, Yvon Gendron,
        Jan Janda, Frank Jay, Bengt Lundholm, Don
        McKenney, Frank Moberg, Lewis A.
        Mongelluzzo, Don Paarup, Richard Rothermel
Physiotherapist . . . . Jacques Lavergne
Trainers . . . . René Lacasse, René Lavigueur,
        Brian Turpin
Team Physician . . . . Dr. Pierre Beauchemin
Executive Secretary – Hockey Department . . . . . . Martine Bélanger
Secretary – Hockey Department and Travel
  Coordinator . . . . Nathalie Paquet
Administration and Finance
Vice-President/Administration and Finance . . . . . . Jean Laflamme
Controller . . . . François Bilodeau
Assistant to the Controller . . . . Rémi Bolduc
Accountants . . . . Danielle Bhérer, Lucette Lemieux, Manon
        Toutant
Executive Secretary . . . . Huguette Gauthier
Receptionist . . . . Edith Murphy
Sales and Marketing
Vice-President/Sales and Marketing . . . . Roger Doré
Sales Director . . . . André Lestourneau
Sales Director – Promotional Agreements . . . . Bernard Thiboutot
Promotional Agreements Representative . . . . Mark Charest
Sales Representative – Marketing . . . . Simon Dupuy
Supervisor – Promotional Agreements
  Coordination . . . . Jean-François Drolet
Account Assistants – Promotional Agreements
  Coordination . . . . Kevin Donnelly, Chantal Poirier
Supervisor of Nordtel Service . . . . Josée Métivier
Sales Representatives . . . . Christine Côté, Mario Duchesneau, Nicolas
        Labbé, Bernard Nadeau, Reynald Roberge
Supervisor of Novelties & Souvenirs . . . . Anne Latouche
Executive Secretaries – Marketing & Promotions . Marie Godin, Jacinthe Côté, Diane Poulin
Secretaries – Sales . . . . Danielle Tremblay
Communications
Director of Public Relations . . . . TBA
Director of Press Relations . . . . Jean Martineau
Coordinator of Public Relations . . . . Nicole Bouchard
Graphic Communications Coordinator . . . . Pierre Masson
Executive Secretary – Public Relations . . . . Marie Roy
Team Photographer . . . . Jean-Yves Michaud

Location of Press Box . . . . East & West side of building, upper level
Dimensions of Rink . . . . 200 feet by 85 feet
Club Colors . . . . Blue, White and Red
Uniforms . . . . Home – Base color white trimmed
        with blue and red
        Away – Base color blue trimmed
        with white and red
Training Camp Site . . . . Québec City
Radio Station . . . . CJRP 1060
Radio Announcers . . . . Alain Crâte, Jean Perron
TV Station . . . . CFAP (2) Quatre Saisons
TV Announcers . . . . André Côté, Claude Bédard

Coaching Record

			Regular Season					Playoffs			
Season	Team	Games	W	L	T	%	Games	W	L	%
1978-79	Dalhousie (CIAU)	....	....	....	....	....	....	....	....	....
1982-83	Denver (CHL)	80	41	36	3	.531	6	2	4	.333
1983-84	Denver (CHL)	76	48	25	3	.651	6	2	4	.333
1984-85	Moncton (AHL)	80	32	40	8	.450	....	....	....	....
1988-89	Minnesota (NHL)	80	27	37	16	.438	5	1	4	.200
1989-90	Minnesota (NHL)	80	36	40	4	.475	7	3	4	.429
1991-92	Quebec (NHL)	62	17	34	11	.362	....	....	....	....
1992-93	Quebec (NHL)	84	47	27	10	.619	6	2	4	.333
	NHL Totals	**306**	**127**	**138**	**41**	**.482**	**18**	**6**	**12**	**.333**

St. Louis Blues
1992-93 Results: 37w-36L-11T 85PTS. Fourth, Norris Division

Schedule

Home		Away	
Oct. Thur. 7 Florida		**Oct.** Wed. 13 Detroit	
Sat. 9 Ottawa		Sat. 16 Dallas	
Thur. 21 San Jose		Tues. 19 San Jose	
(at Sacramento)		Sat. 23 Pittsburgh	
Thur. 28 Hartford		Tues. 26 Chicago	
Nov. Sat. 6 Edmonton		Sat. 30 Boston	
Tues. 9 Pittsburgh		**Nov.** Mon. 1 Hartford	
Thur. 11 Toronto		Wed. 3 Winnipeg	
Thur. 18 Calgary		Sat. 13 Los Angeles	
Sat. 20 Los Angeles		Tues. 16 Vancouver	
Sun. 21 Detroit		Wed. 24 Washington	
Fri. 26 New Jersey		**Dec.** Wed. 1 Toronto	
Sun. 28 Winnipeg		Thur. 9 Detroit	
Dec. Thur. 2 Toronto		Sat. 11 Los Angeles	
Sat. 4 Dallas		Sun. 12 Anaheim	
Tues. 7 Chicago		Wed. 15 San Jose	
Thur. 23 Tampa Bay		Fri. 17 Calgary	
Sun. 26 Chicago		Sun. 19 Edmonton	
Mon. 27 Montreal		Fri. 31 Winnipeg*	
Wed. 29 NY Rangers		**Jan.** Thur. 6 Hartford	
Jan. Sun. 2 Calgary		(at Cleveland)	
Tues. 4 Detroit		Sun. 9 Dallas	
Sat. 8 Anaheim		Tues. 18 NY Rangers	
Thur. 13 Edmonton		Wed. 19 Philadelphia	
Sat. 15 Buffalo		Mon. 24 Anaheim	
Feb. Tues. 1 Toronto		Tues. 25 Vancouver	
Thur. 3 Quebec		Fri. 28 Edmonton	
Sat. 5 San Jose		Sat. 29 Calgary	
Tues. 8 Winnipeg		**Feb.** Thur. 24 Quebec	
Thur. 10 Washington		Sat. 26 Ottawa	
Sat. 12 Detroit		Mon. 28 New Jersey	
Tues. 15 Vancouver		**Mar.** Tues. 1 NY Islanders	
Fri. 18 Boston		Mon. 7 Toronto	
Sun. 20 Anaheim		Wed. 9 Montreal	
Mar. Thur. 3 Vancouver		Wed. 16 Winnipeg	
Sat. 12 NY Islanders		Fri. 18 Toronto	
Tues. 22 Philadelphia		Sun. 20 Chicago*	
Fri. 25 Dallas		Wed. 23 Buffalo	
Sun. 27 San Jose		Wed. 30 Florida	
Apr. Tues. 5 Chicago		**Apr.** Fri. 1 Tampa Bay	
Thur. 7 Los Angeles		Sun. 3 Detroit*	
Sun. 10 Dallas*		Fri. 8 Chicago	
Thur. 14 Winnipeg		Tues. 12 Dallas	

Denotes afternoon game.

Home Starting Times:
Weeknights and Saturdays .... 7:35 p.m.
Sundays .... 6:05 p.m.
Except Sun. Jan. 2 .... 7:05 p.m.
Sun. Apr. 10 .... 12:05 p.m.

Franchise date: June 5, 1967

CENTRAL DIVISION

27th NHL Season

WESTERN CONFERENCE

Year-by-Year Record

Season	GP	Home W	L	T	Road W	L	T	Overall W	L	T	GF	GA	Pts.	Finished	Playoff Result
1992-93	84	22	13	7	15	23	4	37	36	11	282	278	85	4th, Norris Div.	Lost Div. Final
1991-92	80	25	12	3	11	21	8	36	33	11	279	266	83	3rd, Norris Div.	Lost Div. Semi-Final
1990-91	80	24	9	7	23	13	4	47	22	11	310	250	105	2nd, Norris Div.	Lost Div. Final
1989-90	80	20	15	5	17	19	4	37	34	9	295	279	83	2nd, Norris Div.	Lost Div. Final
1988-89	80	22	11	7	11	24	5	33	35	12	275	285	78	2nd, Norris Div.	Lost Div. Final
1987-88	80	18	17	5	16	21	3	34	38	8	278	294	76	2nd, Norris Div.	Lost Div. Final
1986-87	80	21	12	7	11	21	8	32	33	15	281	293	79	1st, Norris Div.	Lost Div. Semi-Final
1985-86	80	23	11	6	14	23	3	37	34	9	302	291	83	3rd, Norris Div.	Lost Conf. Championship
1984-85	80	21	12	7	16	19	5	37	31	12	299	288	86	1st, Norris Div.	Lost Div. Semi-Final
1983-84	80	23	14	3	9	27	4	32	41	7	293	316	71	2nd, Norris Div.	Lost Div. Final
1982-83	80	16	16	8	9	24	7	25	40	15	285	316	65	4th, Norris Div.	Lost Div. Semi-Final
1981-82	80	22	14	4	10	26	4	32	40	8	315	349	72	3rd Norris Div.	Lost Div. Final
1980-81	80	29	7	4	16	11	13	45	18	17	352	281	107	1st, Smythe Div.	Lost Quarter-Final
1979-80	80	20	13	7	14	21	5	34	34	12	266	278	80	2nd, Smythe Div.	Lost Prelim. Round
1978-79	80	14	20	6	4	30	6	18	50	12	249	348	48	3rd, Smythe Div.	Out of Playoffs
1977-78	80	12	20	8	8	27	5	20	47	13	195	304	53	4th, Smythe Div.	Out of Playoffs
1976-77	80	22	13	5	10	26	4	32	39	9	239	276	73	1st, Smythe Div.	Lost Quarter-Final
1975-76	80	20	12	8	9	25	6	29	37	14	249	290	72	3rd, Smythe Div.	Lost Prelim. Round
1974-75	80	23	13	4	12	18	10	35	31	14	269	267	84	2nd, Smythe Div.	Lost Prelim. Round
1973-74	78	16	16	7	10	24	5	26	40	12	206	248	64	6th, West Div.	Out of Playoffs
1972-73	78	21	11	7	11	23	5	32	34	12	233	251	76	4th, West Div.	Lost Quarter-Final
1971-72	78	17	17	5	11	22	6	28	39	11	208	247	67	3rd, West Div.	Lost Semi-Final
1970-71	78	23	7	9	11	18	10	34	25	19	223	208	87	2nd, West Div.	Lost Quarter-Final
1969-70	76	24	9	5	13	18	7	37	27	12	224	179	86	1st, West Div.	Lost Final
1968-69	76	21	8	9	16	17	5	37	25	14	204	157	88	1st, West Div.	Lost Final
1967-68	74	18	12	7	9	19	9	27	31	16	177	191	70	3rd, West Div.	Lost Final

Brett Hull reached the 50-goal plateau for the fourth consecutive season in 1992-93, scoring 54 times for the Blues.

1993-94 Player Personnel

FORWARDS	HT	WT	S	Place of Birth	Date	1992-93 Club
BASSEN, Bob	5-11	185	L	Calgary, Alta.	5/6/65	St. Louis
BOZON, Philippe	5-10	185	L	Chamonix, France	11/30/66	St. Louis-Peoria
CHASE, Kelly	5-11	195	R	Porcupine Pl., Sask.	10/25/67	St. Louis
EMERSON, Nelson	5-11	180	R	Hamilton, Ont.	8/17/67	St. Louis
FELSNER, Denny	6-0	195	L	Warren, MI	4/29/70	St. Louis-Peoria
FRENETTE, Derek	6-1	210	L	Montreal, Que.	7/13/71	Peoria
HRKAC, Tony	5-11	170	L	Thunder Bay, Ont.	7/7/66	Indianapolis
HULL, Brett	5-10	201	R	Belleville, Ont.	8/9/64	St. Louis
JANNEY, Craig	6-1	190	L	Hartford, CT	9/26/67	St. Louis
KARAMNOV, Vitali	6-2	185	L	Moscow, Soviet Union	7/6/68	St. Louis-Peoria
KOROLEV, Igor	6-1	180	L	Moscow, Soviet Union	9/6/70	St. Louis
LAFAYETTE, Nathan	6-1	195	R	New Westminster, B.C.	2/17/73	Newmarket
LAPERRIERE, Ian	6-1	195	L	Montreal, Que.	1/19/74	Drummondville
MACKEY, Dave	6-4	205	L	Richmond, B.C.	7/24/66	St. Louis-Peoria
McRAE, Basil	6-2	205	L	Beaverton, Ont.	1/5/61	Tampa Bay-St. Louis
MIEHM, Kevin	6-2	200	L	Kitchener, Ont.	6/10/69	St. Louis-Peoria
MILLER, Kevin	5-11	190	R	Lansing, MI	9/9/65	Washington-St. Louis
MONTGOMERY, Jim	5-10	185	R	Montreal, Que.	6/30/69	Maine
PELLERIN, Brian	5-10	185	L	Hinton, Alta.	2/20/70	Peoria
PION, Richard	5-10	180	R	Oxnard, CA	7/20/65	Peoria
PROKHOROV, Vitaly	5-9	185	L	Moscow, USSR	12/25/66	St. Louis
REEVES, Kyle	5-11	190	R	Stonewall, Man.	5/12/71	Peoria
SHANAHAN, Brendan	6-3	215	R	Mimico, Ont.	1/23/69	St. Louis
SUTTER, Rich	5-11	188	R	Viking, Alta.	12/2/63	St. Louis
SUTTER, Ron	6-0	180	R	Viking, Alta.	12/2/63	St. Louis

DEFENSEMEN						
BARON, Murray	6-3	215	L	Prince George, B.C.	6/1/67	St. Louis
BATTERS, Jeff	6-2	215	R	Victoria, B.C.	10/23/70	Peoria
BROWN, Jeff	6-1	204	R	Ottawa, Ont.	4/30/66	St. Louis
BUTCHER, Garth	6-0	205	R	Regina, Sask.	1/8/63	St. Louis
CROSSMAN, Doug	6-2	190	L	Peterborough, Ont.	6/30/60	Tampa Bay-St. Louis
HEDICAN, Bret	6-2	195	L	St. Paul, MN	8/10/70	St. Louis-Peoria
HOLLINGER, Terry	6-1	200	L	Regina, Sask.	2/24/71	Peoria
LAPERRIERE, Daniel	6-1	195	L	Laval, Que.	3/28/69	St. Louis-Peoria
MARSHALL, Jason	6-2	195	R	Cranbrook, B.C.	2/22/71	Peoria
QUINTAL, Stephane	6-3	215	R	Boucherville, Que.	10/22/68	St. Louis
TILLEY, Tom	6-0	190	R	Trenton, Ont.	3/28/65	Milan (Italy)
ZOMBO, Rick	6-1	195	R	Des Plaines, IL	5/8/63	St. Louis

GOALTENDERS	HT	WT	C	Place of Birth	Date	1992-93 Club
DUFFUS, Parris	6-2	193	L	Denver, CO	1/27/70	Peoria-Hampton Rds.
HRIVNAK, Jim	6-2	195	L	Montreal, Que.	5/28/68	Winnipeg-Washington
JOSEPH, Curtis	5-10	182	L	Keswick, Ont.	4/29/67	St. Louis
SARJEANT, Geoff	5-9	180	L	Newmarket, Ont.	11/30/69	Peoria

General Managers' History

Lynn Patrick, 1967-68 to 1968-69; Scotty Bowman, 1969-70 to 1970-71; Lynn Patrick, 1971-72; Sid Abel, 1972-73; Charles Catto, 1973-74; Gerry Ehman, 1974-75; Dennis Ball, 1975-76; Emile Francis, 1976-77 to 1982-83; Ron Caron, 1983-84 to date.

Coaching History

Lynn Patrick and Scott Bowman, 1967-68; Scott Bowman, 1968-69 to 1969-70; Al Arbour and Scott Bowman, 1970-71; Sid Abel, Bill McCreary, Al Arbour, 1971-72; Al Arbour and Jean-Guy Talbot, 1972-73; Jean-Guy Talbot and Lou Angotti, 1973-74; Lou Angotti, Lynn Patrck and Garry Young, 1974-75; Garry Young, Lynn Patrick and Leo Boivin, 1975-76; Emile Francis, 1976-77; Leo Boivin and Barclay Plager, 1977-78; Barclay Plager, 1978-79; Barclay Plager and Red Berenson, 1979-80; Red Berenson, 1980-81; Red Berenson and Emile Francis, 1981-82; Barclay Plager and Emile Francis, 1982-83; Jacques Demers, 1983-84 to 1985-86; Jacques Martin, 1986-87 to 1987-88. Brian Sutter, 1988-89 to 1991-92; Bob Plager and Bob Berry, 1992-93; Bob Berry, 1993-94.

Captains' History

Al Arbour, 1967-68 to 1969-70; Red Berenson, Barclay Plager, 1970-71; Barclay Plager, 1971-72 to 1975-76; no captain, 1976-77; Red Berenson, 1977-78; Barry Gibbs, 1978-79; Brian Sutter, 1979-80 to 1987-88; Bernie Federko, 1988-89; Rick Meagher, 1989-90; Scott Stevens, 1990-91; Garth Butcher, 1991-92; Brett Hull, 1992-93 to date.

Retired Numbers

3	Bob Gassoff	1973-1977
8	Barclay Plager	1967-1977
11	Brian Sutter	1976-1988
24	Bernie Federko	1976-1989

1992-93 Scoring

Regular Season

Pos	#	Player	Team	GP	G	A	Pts	+/-	PIM	PP	SH	GW	GT	S	%
C	15	Craig Janney	STL	84	24	82	106	4-	12	8	0	6	0	137	17.5
R	16	Brett Hull	STL	80	54	47	101	27-	41	29	0	2	1	390	13.8
R	19	Brendan Shanahan	STL	71	51	43	94	10	174	18	0	8	0	232	22.0
D	21	Jeff Brown	STL	71	25	53	78	6-	58	12	2	3	0	220	11.4
C	7	Nelson Emerson	STL	82	22	51	73	2	62	5	2	4	0	196	11.2
R	14	Kevin Miller	WSH	10	0	3	3	4-	35	0	0	0	0	10	.0
			STL	72	24	22	46	6	65	8	3	4	2	153	15.7
			TOTAL	82	24	25	49	2	100	8	3	4	2	163	14.7
D	6	Doug Crossman	T.B.	40	8	21	29	4-	18	2	0	1	0	54	14.8
			STL	19	2	7	9	3-	10	2	0	0	0	24	8.3
			TOTAL	59	10	28	38	7-	28	4	0	1	0	78	12.8
R	23	Rich Sutter	STL	84	13	14	27	4-	100	0	2	1	0	148	8.8
R	22	Ron Sutter	STL	59	12	15	27	11-	99	4	0	3	0	90	13.3
R	38*	Igor Korolev	STL	74	4	23	27	1-	20	2	0	0	0	76	5.3
C	28	Bob Bassen	STL	53	9	10	19	0	63	0	1	0	0	61	14.8
C	18	Ron Wilson	STL	78	8	11	19	8-	44	0	3	1	0	75	10.7
D	5	Garth Butcher	STL	84	5	10	15	0	211	0	0	2	0	83	6.0
D	4	Rick Zombo	STL	71	0	15	15	0	78	0	0	0	0	43	.0
L	10	Dave Lowry	STL	58	5	8	13	18-	101	0	0	0	0	59	8.5
C	36*	Philippe Bozon	STL	54	6	6	12	3-	55	0	0	0	0	90	6.7
D	33	Stephane Quintal	STL	75	1	10	11	6-	100	0	1	0	0	81	1.2
D	20	Lee Norwood	STL	32	3	7	10	5-	63	2	0	0	0	36	8.3
L	17	Basil McRae	T.B.	14	2	3	5	3-	71	1	0	0	0	23	8.7
			STL	33	1	3	4	13-	98	1	0	0	0	22	4.5
			TOTAL	47	3	6	9	16-	169	2	0	0	0	45	6.7
D	44*	Bret Hedican	STL	42	0	8	8	2-	30	0	0	0	0	40	.0
R	39	Kelly Chase	STL	49	2	5	7	9-	204	0	0	0	0	28	7.1
L	25*	Vitali Prokhorov	STL	26	4	1	5	4-	15	0	0	1	0	21	19.0
L	26	Dave Mackey	STL	15	1	4	5	3-	23	0	0	0	0	17	5.9
D	34	Murray Baron	STL	53	2	2	4	5-	59	0	0	1	0	42	4.8
C	37*	Kevin Miehm	STL	8	1	3	4	1	4	0	0	0	0	5	20.0
D	2	Curt Giles	STL	48	0	4	4	2-	40	0	0	0	0	23	.0
R	9*	Denny Felsner	STL	6	0	3	3	4	2	0	0	0	0	4	.0
G	31	Curtis Joseph	STL	68	0	2	2	0	8	0	0	0	0	0	.0
D	41*	Daniel Laperriere	STL	5	0	1	1	3-	0	0	0	0	0	7	.0
L	12*	Vitali Karamnov	STL	7	0	1	1	2-	0	0	0	0	0	7	.0
G	29*	Guy Hebert	STL	24	0	0	0	0	2	0	0	0	0	0	.0

Goaltending

No.	Goaltender	GPI	Mins	Avg	W	L	T	EN	SO	GA	SA	S%
31	Curtis Joseph	68	3890	3.02	29	28	9	7	1	196	2202	.911
29	*Guy Hebert	24	1210	3.67	8	8	2	1	1	74	630	.883
	Totals	**84**	**5110**	**3.26**	**37**	**36**	**11**	**8**	**2**	**278**	**2840**	**.902**

Playoffs

Pos	#	Player	Team	GP	G	A	Pts	+/-	PIM	PP	SH	GW	GT	S	%
R	16	Brett Hull	STL	11	8	5	13	2-	2	5	0	2	0	52	15.4
D	21	Jeff Brown	STL	11	3	8	11	3	6	1	0	2	1	41	7.3
C	15	Craig Janney	STL	11	2	9	11	4	0	1	0	2	1	11	18.2
R	19	Brendan Shanahan	STL	11	4	3	7	0	18	2	0	0	0	36	11.1
C	7	Nelson Emerson	STL	11	1	6	7	3	6	0	0	0	0	43	2.3
R	9*	Denny Felsner	STL	9	2	3	5	4	2	1	0	0	0	7	28.6
R	14	Kevin Miller	STL	10	0	3	3	5-	11	0	0	0	0	21	.0
L	10	Dave Lowry	STL	11	2	0	2	1-	14	0	1	0	0	15	13.3
D	5	Garth Butcher	STL	11	1	1	2	6	20	0	0	0	0	8	12.5
C	36*	Philippe Bozon	STL	9	1	0	1	2	0	0	0	0	0	5	20.0
C	37*	Kevin Miehm	STL	2	0	1	1	0	0	0	0	0	0	2	.0
L	17	Basil McRae	STL	11	0	1	1	0	24	0	0	0	0	4	.0
R	23	Rich Sutter	STL	11	0	1	1	6-	10	0	0	0	0	14	.0
D	4	Rick Zombo	STL	11	0	1	1	9-	12	0	0	0	0	8	.0
G	29*	Guy Hebert	STL	1	0	0	0	0	0	0	0	0	0	0	.0
D	2	Curt Giles	STL	3	0	0	0	1-	2	0	0	0	0	0	.0
R	38*	Igor Korolev	STL	3	0	0	0	1-	0	0	0	0	0	4	.0
D	33	Stephane Quintal	STL	9	0	0	0	0	10	0	0	0	0	10	.0
D	44*	Bret Hedican	STL	10	0	0	0	4-	14	0	0	0	0	5	.0
D	34	Murray Baron	STL	11	0	0	0	5-	12	0	0	0	0	8	.0
C	28	Bob Bassen	STL	11	0	0	0	7-	10	0	0	0	0	4	.0
G	31	Curtis Joseph	STL	11	0	0	0	0	2	0	0	0	0	0	.0
C	18	Ron Wilson	STL	11	0	0	0	7-	12	0	0	0	0	14	.0

Goaltending

No.	Goaltender	GPI	Mins	Avg	W	L	EN	SO	GA	SA	S%
29	*Guy Hebert	1	2	.00	0	0	0	0	0	1	1.000
31	Curtis Joseph	11	715	2.27	7	4	1	2	27	438	.938
	Totals	**11**	**717**	**2.34**	**7**	**4**	**1**	**2**	**28**	**440**	**.936**

Club Records

Team

(Figures in brackets for season records are games played; records for fewest points, wins, ties, losses, goals, goals against are for 70 or more games)

Most Points	107	1980-81 (80)
Most Wins	47	1990-91 (80)
Most Ties	19	1970-71 (78)
Most Losses	50	1978-79 (80)
Most Goals	352	1980-81 (80)
Most Goals Against	349	1981-82 (80)
Fewest Points	48	1978-79 (80)
Fewest Wins	18	1978-79 (80)
Fewest Ties	7	1983-84 (80)
Fewest Losses	18	1980-81 (80)
Fewest Goals	177	1967-68 (74)
Fewest Goals Against	157	1968-69 (76)

Longest Winning Streak

Over-all	7	Jan. 21- Feb. 3/88 Mar. 19-31/91
Home	9	Jan. 26- Feb. 26/91
Away	4	Four times

Longest Undefeated Streak

Over-all	12	Nov. 10- Dec. 8/68 (5 wins, 7 ties)
Home	11	Feb. 12- Mar. 19/69 (5 wins, 6 ties) Feb. 7- Mar. 29/75 (9 wins, 2 ties)
Away	7	Dec. 9-26/87 (4 wins, 3 ties)

Longest Losing Streak

Over-all	7	Nov. 12-26/67; Feb. 12-25/89
Home	5	Nov. 19- Dec. 6/77
Away	10	Jan. 20/82- Mar. 8/82

Longest Winless Streak

Over-all	12	Jan. 17- Feb. 15/78 (10 losses, 2 ties)
Home	7	Dec. 28/82- Jan. 25/83 (5 losses, 2 ties)
Away	17	Jan. 23- Apr. 7/74 (14 losses, 3 ties)

Most Shutouts, Season	13	1968-69 (76)
Most PIM, Season	2,041	1990-91 (80)
Most Goals, Game	10	Feb. 2/82 (Wpg. 6 at St. L. 10) Dec. 1/84 (Det. 5 at St. L. 10) Jan. 15/86 (Tor. 1 at St. L. 10)

Individual

Most Seasons	13	Bernie Federko
Most Games	927	Bernie Federko
Most Goals, Career	352	Bernie Federko
Most Assists, Career	721	Bernie Federko
Most Points, Career	1,073	Bernie Federko
Most PIM, Career	1,786	Brian Sutter
Most Shutouts, Career	16	Glenn Hall
Longest Consecutive Games Streak	662	Garry Unger (Feb. 7/71-Apr. 8/79)
Most Goals, Season	86	Brett Hull (1990-91)
Most Assists, Season	90	Adam Oates (1990-91)
Most Points, Season	131	Brett Hull (1990-91) (86 goals, 45 assists)
Most PIM, Season	306	Bob Gassoff (1975-76)
Most Points, Defenseman Season	78	Jeff Brown (1992-93) (25 goals, 53 assists)
Most Points, Center, Season	115	Adam Oates (1990-91) (25 goals, 90 assists)
Most Points, Right Wing, Season	131	Brett Hull (1990-91) (86 goals, 45 assists)
Most Points, Left Wing, Season	94	Brendan Shanahan (1992-93) (51 goals, 43 assists)
Most Points, Rookie, Season	73	Jorgen Pettersson (1980-81) (37 goals, 36 assists)
Most Shutouts, Season	8	Glenn Hall (1968-69)
Most Goals, Game	6	Red Berenson (Nov. 7/68)
Most Assists, Game	5	Brian Sutter (Nov. 22/88) Bernie Federko (Feb. 27/88) Adam Oates (Jan. 26/91)
Most Points, Game	7	Red Berenson (Nov. 7/68) Garry Unger (Mar. 13/71)

All-time Record vs. Other Clubs

Regular Season

	At Home						On Road						Total					
	GP	W	L	T	GF	GA	PTS	GP	W	L	T	GF	GA	PTS	GP	W	L	T	GF	GA	PTS
Boston	51	20	22	9	160	180	49	50	10	33	7	136	224	27	101	30	55	16	296	404	76
Buffalo	42	25	11	6	163	110	56	43	11	28	4	135	181	26	85	36	39	10	298	291	82
Calgary	41	17	18	6	145	132	40	40	16	21	3	116	145	35	81	33	39	9	261	277	75
Chicago	85	41	28	16	296	266	98	88	24	53	11	273	352	59	173	65	81	27	569	618	157
Detroit	80	47	22	11	298	220	105	80	35	34	11	264	296	81	160	82	56	22	562	516	186
Edmonton	22	8	10	4	87	95	20	22	6	13	3	86	102	15	44	14	23	7	173	197	35
Hartford	22	12	8	2	89	76	26	22	11	9	2	70	71	24	44	23	17	4	159	147	50
Los Angeles	56	36	14	6	215	150	78	56	19	29	8	163	203	46	112	55	43	14	378	353	124
Minnesota	92	50	25	17	339	261	117	89	32	39	18	264	306	82	181	82	64	35	603	567	199
Montreal	50	10	26	14	127	178	34	51	8	37	6	132	228	22	101	18	63	20	259	406	56
New Jersey	37	25	8	4	166	112	54	38	15	16	7	113	123	37	75	40	24	11	279	235	91
NY Islanders	39	16	17	6	141	129	38	40	8	22	10	96	157	26	79	24	39	16	237	286	64
NY Rangers	54	21	25	8	160	179	50	52	6	41	5	119	224	17	106	27	66	13	279	403	67
Ottawa	1	1	0	0	5	1	2	1	1	0	0	4	1	2	2	2	0	0	9	2	4
Philadelphia	58	23	28	7	170	177	53	58	10	39	9	132	229	29	116	33	67	16	302	406	82
Pittsburgh	56	38	13	5	225	151	81	55	19	25	11	169	206	49	111	57	38	16	394	357	130
Quebec	21	16	3	2	102	70	34	21	9	9	3	74	76	21	42	25	12	5	176	146	55
San Jose	4	4	0	0	19	6	8	2	2	0	0	7	4	4	6	6	0	0	26	10	12
Tampa	3	2	1	0	11	9	4	4	2	1	1	15	13	5	7	4	2	1	26	22	9
Toronto	80	47	22	11	282	229	105	80	20	50	10	234	312	50	160	67	72	21	516	541	155
Vancouver	49	28	14	7	195	149	63	50	23	22	5	157	158	51	99	51	36	12	352	307	114
Washington	32	14	10	8	136	107	36	31	12	16	3	96	113	27	63	26	26	11	232	220	63
Winnipeg	24	11	5	8	97	73	30	25	6	13	6	79	91	18	49	17	18	14	176	164	48
Defunct Clubs	32	25	4	3	131	55	53	33	11	10	12	95	100	34	65	36	14	15	226	155	87
Totals	**1031**	**537**	**334**	**160**	**3759**	**3115**	**1234**	**1031**	**316**	**560**	**155**	**3029**	**3915**	**787**	**2062**	**853**	**894**	**315**	**6788**	**7030**	**2021**

Playoffs

	Series	W	L	GP	W	L	T	GF	GA	Last Mtg.	Round	Result
Boston	2	0	2	8	0	8	0	15	48	1972	SF	L 0-4
Buffalo	1	0	1	3	1	2	0	8	7	1976	PR	L 1-2
Calgary	1	0	1	7	3	4	0	22	28	1986	CF	L 3-4
Chicago	9	2	7	45	18	27	0	129	166	1993	DSF	W 4-0
Detroit	3	2	1	16	8	8	0	51	53	1991	DSF	W 4-3
Los Angeles	1	1	0	4	4	0	0	16	5	1969	SF	W 4-0
Minnesota	9	5	4	52	26	26	0	152	158	1991	DF	L 2-4
Montreal	3	0	3	12	0	12	0	14	42	1977	QF	L 0-4
NY Rangers	1	0	1	6	2	4	0	22	29	1981	QF	L 2-4
Philadelphia	2	2	0	11	8	3	0	34	20	1969	QF	W 4-0
Pittsburgh	3	2	1	13	7	6	0	45	40	1981	PR	W 3-2
Toronto	4	2	2	25	13	12	0	67	75	1993	DF	L 3-4
Winnipeg	1	1	0	4	3	1	0	20	13	1982	DSF	W 3-1
Totals	**40**	**17**	**23**	**206**	**93**	**113**	**0**	**595**	**684**			

Playoff Results 1993-89

Year	Round	Opponent	Result	GF	GA
1993	DF	Toronto	L 3-4	11	22
	DSF	Chicago	W 4-0	13	6
1992	DSF	Chicago	L 2-4	19	23
1991	DF	Minnesota	L 2-4	17	22
	DSF	Detroit	W 4-3	24	20
1990	DF	Chicago	L 3-4	22	28
	DSF	Toronto	W 4-1	20	16
1989	DF	Chicago	L 1-4	12	19
	DSF	Minnesota	W 4-1	23	15

Abbreviations: Round: F – Final;
CF – conference final; **DF** – division final;
DSF – division semi-final; **SF** – semi-final;
QF – quarter-final; **PR** – preliminary round.
GA – goals against; **GF** – goals for.

1992-93 Results

	Home				Away	
Oct. 6	Minnesota	6-4	Oct. 8	Minnesota	2-5
10	Chicago	0-3	17	Quebec	6-5
13	Tampa Bay	1-2	19	Montreal	2-6
15	Minnesota	4-5	Nov. 3	Tampa Bay	4-6
21	Quebec	5-5	5	Pittsburgh	4-8
24	Detroit	1-6	7	Philadelphia*	2-4
26	San Jose	4-1	12	Chicago	0-1
29	Pittsburgh	6-4	16	Toronto	2-2
31	Philadelphia	6-4	18	Hartford	2-5
Nov. 10	Edmonton	4-4	25	Detroit	6-11
14	Winnipeg	4-2	Dec. 4	Calgary	3-5
21	Tampa Bay	4-2	5	Edmonton	5-1
26	Vancouver	7-5	7	Vancouver	3-4
28	Detroit	2-2	10	San Jose	3-2
Dec. 1	Hartford	8-4	12	Los Angeles	3-6
15	NY Islanders	3-4	22	Minnesota	2-2
17	NY Rangers	3-4	26	Chicago	3-2
19	Winnipeg	0-1	Jan. 2	Toronto	2-2
27	Toronto	3-6	3	Buffalo	5-6
31	NY Islanders	5-1	11	Detroit	1-0
Jan. 5	Edmonton	6-1	13	Toronto	3-4
7	Calgary	3-2	14	Ottawa	4-1
9	Chicago	4-1	16	Tampa Bay	5-3
19	Toronto	1-5	21	Detroit	3-5
23	Detroit	4-3	28	Tampa Bay	4-2
26	Ottawa	5-1	Feb. 3	Winnipeg	4-2
30	New Jersey	2-2	8	Hartford	3-1
Feb. 1	Toronto	1-1	15	NY Rangers*	1-4
9	Boston	1-6	17	New Jersey	3-4
11	Washington	6-10	18	NY Islanders	4-2
13	Detroit	4-3	21	Washington*	2-5
23	Montreal	1-5	28	Chicago	7-1
25	Los Angeles	3-0	Mar. 6	Boston*	3-4
27	Minnesota	3-2	14	Minnesota	3-1
Mar. 1	Calgary	2-1	20	Los Angeles	2-3
11	San Jose	5-2	22	Vancouver	3-1
13	Minnesota	6-2	24	Calgary	4-2
16	Buffalo	2-2	26	Winnipeg	2-4
30	Vancouver	3-6	Apr. 4	Chicago	4-5
Apr. 3	Chicago	3-3	6	Tampa Bay	2-2
11	Minnesota	5-1	10	Minnesota	3-4
15	Tampa Bay	6-5	13	Toronto	1-2

*Denotes afternoon game

Entry Draft
Selections 1993-79

1993
Pick
37	Maxim Bets
63	Jamie Rivers
89	Jamal Mayers
141	Todd Kelman
167	Mike Buzak
193	Eric Bogniecki
219	Michael Grier
245	Libor Prochazka
271	Alexander Vasilevsky
275	Christer Olsson

1992
Pick
38	Igor Korolev
62	Vitali Karamnov
64	Vitali Prokhorov
86	Lee J. Leslie
134	Bob Lachance
158	Ian LaPerriere
160	Lance Burns
180	Igor Boldin
182	Nicholas Naumenko
206	Todd Harris
230	Yuri Gunko
259	Wade Salzman

1991
Pick
27	Steve Staios
64	Kyle Reeves
65	Nathan Lafayette
87	Grayden Reid
109	Jeff Callinan
131	Bruce Gardiner
153	Terry Hollinger
175	Christopher Kenady
197	Jed Fiebelkorn
219	Chris MacKenzie
241	Kevin Rappana
263	Mike Veisor

1990
Pick
33	Craig Johnson
54	Patrice Tardif
96	Jason Ruff
117	Kurtis Miller
138	Wayne Conlan
180	Parris Duffus
201	Steve Widmeyer
222	Joe Hawley
243	Joe Fleming

1989
Pick
9	Jason Marshall
31	Rick Corriveau
55	Denny Felsner
93	Daniel Laperriere
114	David Roberts
124	Derek Frenette
135	Jeff Batters
156	Kevin Plager
177	John Roderick
198	John Valo
219	Brian Lukowski

1988
Pic
9	Rod Brind' Amour
30	Adrien Plavsic
51	Rob Fournier
72	Jaan Luik
105	Dave Lacouture
114	Dan Fowler
135	Matt Hayes
156	John McCoy
177	Tony Twist
198	Bret Hedican
219	Heath DeBoer
240	Michael Francis

1987
Pick
12	Keith Osborne
54	Kevin Miehm
59	Robert Nordmark
75	Darin Smith
82	Andy Rymsha
117	Rob Robinson
138	Todd Crabtree
159	Guy Hebert
180	Robert Dumas
201	David Marvin
207	Andy Cesarski
222	Dan Rolfe
243	Ray Savard

1986
Pick
10	Jocelyn Lemieux
31	Mike Posma
52	Tony Hejna
73	Glen Featherstone
87	Michael Wolak
115	Mike O'Toole
136	Andy May
157	Randy Skarda
178	Martyn Ball
199	Rod Thacker
220	Terry MacLean
234	Bill Butler
241	David O'Brien

1985
Pick
37	Herb Raglan
44	Nelson Emerson
54	Ned Desmond
100	Dan Brooks
121	Rich Burchill
138	Pat Jablonski
159	Scott Brickey
180	Jeff Urban
201	Vince Guidotti
222	Ron Saatzer
243	Dave Jecha

1984
Pick
26	Brian Benning
32	Tony Hrkac
50	Toby Ducolon
53	Robert Dirk
56	Alan Perry
71	Graham Herring
92	Scott Paluch
113	Steve Tuttle
134	Cliff Ronning
148	Don Porter
155	Jim Vesey
176	Daniel Jomphe
196	Tom Tilley
217	Mark Cupolo
237	Mark Lanigan

1983
DID NOT DRAFT

1982
Pick
50	Mike Posavad
92	Scott Machej
113	Perry Ganchar
134	Doug Gilmour
155	Chris Delaney
176	Matt Christensen
197	John Shumski
218	Brian Ahern
239	Peter Smith

1981
Pick
20	Marty Ruff
36	Hakan Nordin
62	Gordon Donnelly
104	Mike Hickey
125	Peter Aslin
146	Erik Holmberg
167	Alain Vigneault
188	Dan Wood
209	Richard Zemlak

1980
Pick
12	Rik Wilson
54	Jim Pavese
75	Bob Brooke
96	Alain Lemieux
117	Perry Anderson
138	Roger Hagglund
159	Pat Rabbitt
180	Peter Lindgren
201	John Smyth

1979
Pick
2	Perry Turnbull
65	Bob Crawford
86	Mark Reeds
107	Gilles Leduc

Club Directory

St. Louis Arena
5700 Oakland Avenue
St. Louis, MO 63110
Phone **314/781-5300**
FAX 314/645-1340
Capacity: 17,188

Board of Directors
Michael F. Shanahan, Jud Perkins, Andrew Craig,
Edwin Trusheim, John J. Quinn, Horace Wilkins, Alfred Kerth

Chairman of the Board	Michael F. Shanahan
President	John J. Quinn
Vice-President/General Manager	Ronald Caron
Vice-President/Director of Sales	Bruce Affleck
Vice-President/Ass't GM/Director of Player Personnel and Scouting	Ted Hampson
Vice-President/Director of Broadcast Sales	Matt Hyland
Vice-President/Director of Finance and Administration	Jerry Jasiek
Vice-President/Director of Public Relations and Marketing	Susie Mathieu
Vice-President/Director of Player Development	Bob Plager
Head Coach	Bob Berry
Special Counsel	Thomas J. Guilfoil
Assistant Coach	Ted Sator
Head Coach – Peoria Rivermen	Paul MacLean
Assistant Coach – Peoria Rivermen	Mark Reeds
Assistant Director of Scouting	Jack Evans
Western Canada/United States Scout	Pat Ginnell
New England Area Scout	Matt Keator
European Scout	Yuri Karmanov
Director of Promotions/Community Relations	Tracy Lovasz
Assistant Director of Public Relations	Jeff Trammel
Assistant Director of Public Relations	Michael Caruso
Accounting	Marsha McBride, Terri Fischer, Margaret Steinmeyer
Sales	John Casson, Wes Edwards, Tammy Iuli, Jill Mann
Merchandise Manager	George Pavlik
Head Trainer	Tom Nash
Conditioning Consultant	Mackie Shilstone
Equipment Managers	Frank Burns, Terry Roof
Executive Secretary	Lynn Diederichsen
Administrative Assistant Hockey Department	Sue Profeta
Marketing/Public Relations Secretary	Donna Quirk
Receptionist	Pam Barrett
Orthopedic Surgeon	Dr. Jerome Gilden
Internist	Dr. Aaron Birenbaum
Dentist	Dr. Ron Sherstoff
Dentist Emeritus	Dr. Leslie Rich

Coach

BERRY, ROBERT VICTOR (BOB)
Coach, St. Louis Blues. Born in Montreal, Que., November 29, 1943.

Bob Berry became the 17th Head Coach in St. Louis Blues history on October 29, 1992. He replaced Bob Plager after the Blues beat Pittsburgh and ended the Penguins 10-game unbeaten streak. The Blues were 4-6-1 when the change was made and the Blues finished 33-30-10 under Berry, having the second best record in the NHL since January.

Berry is 13th on the National Hockey League coaching list with 776 games coached. He has a career record of 344-322-110. His first NHL coaching job was with the Los Angeles Kings in 1978 after finishing a seven-year playing career with the Kings. He is the third highest scoring left wing in Kings' history and is 9th in games played, 10th in goals, 10th in points and represented the Kings in the 1973 and 1974 NHL All-Star Games. He played in 541 career NHL games and scored 159 goals and 191 assists for 350 points.

He coached the Kings for three seasons and compiled a record of 107-94-39 in 240 games. Berry then moved on to Montreal where his Canadiens finished with 109 and 98 points, respectively, in his first two seasons. He finished there with a career mark of 116-71-36 in 223 games. Berry then coached Pittsburgh for three seasons before being named as assistant coach with the Blues on June 20, 1988.

Coaching Record

			Regular Season				Playoffs			
Season	Team	Games	W	L	T	%	Games	W	L	%
1978-79	Los Angeles (NHL)	80	34	34	12	.500	2	0	2	.000
1979-80	Los Angeles (NHL)	80	30	36	14	.463	4	1	3	.250
1980-81	Los Angeles (NHL)	80	43	24	13	.619	4	1	3	.250
1981-82	Montreal (NHL)	80	46	17	17	.681	5	2	3	.400
1982-83	Montreal (NHL)	80	42	24	14	.613	3	0	3	.000
1983-84	Montreal (NHL)	63	28	30	5	.484	....	....	....	....
1984-85	Pittsburgh (NHL)	80	24	51	5	.331	....	....	....	....
1985-86	Pittsburgh (NHL)	80	34	38	8	.475	....	....	....	....
1986-87	Pittsburgh (NHL)	80	30	38	12	.450	....	....	....	....
1992-93	St. Louis (NHL)	73	33	30	10	.521	11	7	4	.636
	NHL Totals	776	344	322	110	.514	29	11	18	.379

General Manager

CARON, RON
Vice-President General Manager and Alternate Governor, St. Louis Blues. Born in Hull, Que., December 19, 1929.

Ron Caron joined the St. Louis Blues on August 13, 1983 after a 26-year association with the Montreal Canadiens' organization. He joined the Canadiens in 1957 on a part-time scouting basis after coaching in the amateur ranks. In 1966, Caron was promoted to a full-time position as chief scout of the Montreal Junior Canadiens and was instrumental in assembling two Memorial Cup championship teams. In 1968, he was named chief scout of the parent club and served as an assistant to former manager Sam Pollock. In 1969 he added the responsibilities of general manager of the Montreal Voyageurs of the AHL and maintained that role until 1978 when he was named director of scouting and player personnel for the Canadiens. Caron remained with the Montreal organization until the conclusion of the 1982-83 campaign.

San Jose Sharks

1992-93 Results: 11w-71L-2T 24PTS. Sixth, Smythe Division

Year-by-Year Record

		Home			Road			Overall							
Season	GP	W	L	T	W	L	T	W	L	T	GF	GA	Pts.	Finished	Playoff Result
1992-93	84	8	33	1	3	38	1	11	71	2	218	414	24 6th,	Smythe Div.	Out of Playoffs
1991-92	80	14	23	3	3	35	2	17	58	5	219	359	39 6th,	Smythe Div.	Out of Playoffs

Schedule

	Home		Away	
Oct.	Thur. 14 Calgary	**Oct.**	Wed. 6 Edmonton	
	Sat. 16 Boston		Thur. 7 Calgary	
	Tues. 19 St Louis		Sun. 10 Los Angeles	
	Sat. 23 Vancouver		Thur. 21 St Louis	
	Tues. 26 Edmonton		(at Sacramento)	
	Thur. 28 Anaheim		Sun. 24 Vancouver	
	Sat. 30 Washington		Sun. 31 Anaheim	
Nov.	Tues. 2 Pittsburgh	**Nov.**	Thur. 11 Dallas	
	Fri. 5 Dallas		Sat. 13 New Jersey*	
	Sun. 7 New Jersey*		Sun. 14 NY Rangers	
	Tues. 9 Toronto		Tues. 16 Washington	
	Tues. 23 Detroit		Thur. 18 Boston	
	Sat. 27 Anaheim*		Sat. 20 Hartford	
Dec.	Fri. 3 Winnipeg		Sun. 21 Buffalo	
	Sun. 5 Florida*		Fri. 26 Anaheim*	
	Tues. 7 Tampa Bay	**Dec.**	Sat. 11 Detroit*	
	Wed. 15 St Louis		Sun. 12 Chicago	
	Tues. 28 Calgary		Fri. 17 Edmonton	
Jan.	Tues. 4 Montreal		Sun. 19 Quebec*	
	Thur. 6 Detroit		Wed. 22 Toronto	
	Tues. 11 Los Angeles		Thur. 23 Chicago	
	Sat. 15 Hartford		Fri. 31 Vancouver	
	Mon. 17 Calgary*	**Jan.**	Sun. 2 Edmonton*	
	Tues. 25 NY Rangers		Wed. 12 Anaheim	
Feb.	Tues. 8 Chicago		Fri. 28 Florida	
	(at Sacramento)		Sat. 29 Tampa Bay	
	Fri. 11 Chicago	**Feb.**	Tues. 1 NY Islanders	
	Sun. 13 Chicago*		Thur. 3 Philadelphia	
	Tues. 15 Philadelphia		Sat. 5 St Louis	
	Thur. 17 Quebec		Sun. 6 Dallas	
	Sat. 19 Los Angeles		Wed. 23 Montreal	
	Mon. 21 Dallas*		Thur. 24 Ottawa	
Mar.	Thur. 3 Edmonton		Sat. 26 Detroit*	
	Sun. 6 Anaheim*		Mon. 28 Winnipeg	
	Tues. 8 Buffalo	**Mar.**	Sat. 12 Calgary	
	Thur. 10 NY Islanders		Sat. 19 Los Angeles*	
	Thur. 17 Ottawa		Tues. 22 Pittsburgh	
	Sun. 20 Los Angeles*		Thur. 24 Toronto	
	Tues. 29 Winnipeg		Fri. 25 Winnipeg	
	Thur. 31 Toronto		Sun. 27 St Louis	
Apr.	Sat. 2 Vancouver	**Apr.**	Tues. 5 Los Angeles	
	Sun. 10 Vancouver		Thur. 7 Vancouver	
	Wed. 13 Edmonton		Fri. 8 Calgary	

* Denotes afternoon game.

Home Starting Times:
All Games	7:35 p.m.
Except Matinees	2:05 p.m.
Sun. Apr. 10	5:05 p.m.

Franchise date: May 9, 1990

PACIFIC DIVISION

NHL

WESTERN CONFERENCE

3rd NHL Season

Rob Gaudreau, who led all San Jose rookies with 23 goals and 20 assists, registered the first hat-trick in Sharks' history with a trio of goals against Hartford on December 3, 1992.

1993-94 Player Personnel

FORWARDS	HT	WT	S	Place of Birth	Date	1992-93 Club
BAKER, Jamie	6-0	190	L	Ottawa, Ont.	8/31/66	Ottawa
BEAUFAIT, Mark	5-9	165	R	Livonia, MI	5/13/70	San Jose-Kansas City
BRUCE, David	5-11	190	R	Thunder Bay, Ont.	10/7/64	San Jose
CALOUN, Jan	5-10	176	R	Usti-nad-labem, Czech.	12/20/72	Litvinov
CAPUANO, Dave	6-2	190	L	Warwick, RI	7/27/68	Tampa Bay-Atlanta
CHERBAYEV, Alexander	6-1	187	L	Voskresensk, Russia	8/13/73	Khimik
COURTENAY, Ed	6-4	200	R	Verdun, Que.	2/2/68	San Jose-Kansas City
CRAIGWELL, Dale	5-11	180	L	Toronto, Ont.	4/24/71	San Jose-Kansas City
DONOVAN, Shean	6-1	172	R	Timmins, Ont.	1/22/75	Ottawa
DUCHESNE, Gaetan	5-11	200	L	Les Saulles, Que.	7/11/62	Minnesota
ERREY, Bob	5-10	183	L	Montreal, Que.	9/21/64	Pittsburgh-Boston
FALLOON, Pat	5-11	192	R	Foxwarren, Man.	9/22/72	San Jose
FRANTTI, Gord	6-6	228	L	Larium, MI	6/17/70	Kansas City
FREDERICK, Troy	6-5	226	L	Virden, Man.	4/4/69	Kansas City
GARPENLOV, Johan	5-11	183	L	Stockholm, Sweden	3/21/68	San Jose
GAUDREAU, Robert	5-11	185	R	Lincoln, RI	1/20/70	San Jose-Kansas City
HOLT, Todd	5-6	155	R	Estevan, Sask.	1/20/73	Swift Current
KOZLOV, Victor	6-5	209	R	Togliatti, Russia	2/19/75	Moscow Dynamo
KRAVETS, Mikhail	5-10	176	L	St. Petersb'rg, Russia	11/12/63	San Jose-Kansas City
LARIANOV, Igor	5-9	170	L	Voskresensk, Russia	12/3/60	Lugano
LESLIE, Lee J.	6-4	190	L	Prince George, B.C.	8/15/72	Peoria
MAKAROV, Sergei	5-11	185	L	Chelyabinsk, Russia	6/19/58	Calgary
MALEY, David	6-2	195	L	Beaver Dam, WI	4/24/63	Edmonton-San Jose
MATTHEWS, Jamie	6-1	208	R	Amherst, N.S.	5/25/73	Sudbury
McLEAN, Jeff	5-10	186	L	Port Moody, B.C.	9/6/69	Kansas City
MILLER, Kip	5-10	185	L	Lansing, MI	6/11/69	Kalamazoo
MORRIS, Jon	6-0	175	R	Lowell, MA	5/6/66	N.J.-Uti.-Cin.-S.J.
NAZAROV, Andrei	6-4	209	R	Chelyabinsk, Russia	5/22/74	Moscow Dynamo
NILSSON, Fredrick	6-1	198	L	Vasteras, Sweden	4/16/71	Vasteras
ODGERS, Jeff	6-0	195	R	Spy Hill, Sask.	5/31/69	San Jose
OTEVREL, Jaroslav	6-2	185	L	Gottwaldov, Czech.	9/16/68	San Jose-Kansas City
QUINTIN, J.F.	6-0	187	L	St. Jean, Que.	5/28/69	San Jose-Kansas City
SULLIVAN, Mike	6-2	185	L	Marshfield, MA	2/27/68	San Jose
WHITNEY, Ray	5-9	160	R	Ft. Saskatchewan, Alta.	5/8/72	San Jose-Kansas City
WOOD, Dody	5-11	180	L	Chetwynd, B.C.	3/10/72	San Jose-Kansas City
DEFENSEMEN						
BUSCHAN, Andrei	6-2	200	L		8/21/70	Sokol Kiev
COLMAN, Mike	6-3	225	R	Stoneham, MA	8/4/68	Kansas City
CRONIN, Shawn	6-2	210	L	Joliet, IL	8/20/63	Philadelphia-Hershey
GOSSELIN, Guy	5-10	185	L	Rochester, MI	1/6/64	Skelleftea
IGNATJEV, Victor	6-3	198	L	Riga, Latvia	4/26/70	Kansas City
KROUPA, Vlastimil	6-2	176	L	Most, Czech.	4/27/75	Litvinov
LALOR, Mike	6-0	200	L	Buffalo, NY	3/8/63	Winnipeg
MORE, Jayson	6-1	207	R	Souris, Man.	1/12/69	San Jose
NORTON, Jeff	6-2	190	L	Acton, MA	11/25/65	NY Islanders
ODUYA, Fredrik	6-2	185	L	Stockholm, Sweden	5/31/75	Ottawa-Guelph
OSADCHY, Alexander	5-11	191	R	Kharkov, Ukraine	7/19/75	CSKA
OZOLINSH, Sandis	6-1	189	L	Riga, Latvia	3/8/72	San Jose
PEDERSON, Tom	5-9	165	R	Bloomington, MN	1/1/70	San Jose-Kansas City
RATHJE, Mike	6-5	205	L	Mannville, Alta.	5/11/74	Medicine Hat
SMITH, Ryan	6-3	200	L	Tabor, Ont.	6/28/74	Brandon
SYKORA, Michal	6-4	198	L	Pardubice, Czech.	7/5/73	Tacoma
WILSON, Doug	6-1	187	L	Ottawa, Ont.	7/5/57	San Jose
ZETTLER, Rob	6-3	190	L	Sept Iles, Que.	3/8/68	San Jose
ZMOLEK, Doug	6-2	225	L	Rochester, MN	11/3/70	San Jose

GOALTENDERS	HT	WT	C	Place of Birth	Date	1992-93 Club
FLAHERTY, Wade	6-0	170	R	Terrace, B.C.	1/11/68	Kansas City-San Jose
IRBE, Arturs	5-7	180	L	Riga, Latvia	2/2/67	Kansas City-San Jose
ROBINS, Trevor	5-11	180	L	Brandon, Man.	5/31/72	Brandon
RYDER, Dan	6-1	184	L	Kitchener, Ont.	10/24/72	John.-Col.-K.C.
WAITE, Jimmy	6-1	180	L	Sherbrooke, Que.	4/15/69	Chicago

1992-93 Scoring

Regular Season

Pos	#	Player	Team	GP	G	A	Pts	+/-	PIM	PP	SH	GW	GT	S	%
C	11	Kelly Kisio	S.J.	78	26	52	78	15–	90	9	2	2	0	152	17.1
L	10	Johan Garpenlov	S.J.	79	22	44	66	26–	56	14	0	1	0	171	12.9
C	37*	Rob Gaudreau	S.J.	59	23	20	43	18–	18	5	2	1	0	191	12.0
C	12	Dean Evason	S.J.	84	12	19	31	35–	132	3	0	1	1	107	11.2
R	17	Pat Falloon	S.J.	41	14	14	28	25–	12	5	1	1	0	131	10.7
L	36	Jeff Odgers	S.J.	66	12	15	27	26–	253	6	0	0	0	100	12.0
D	6*	Sandis Ozolinsh	S.J.	37	7	16	23	9–	40	2	0	0	0	83	8.4
R	39*	Ed Courtenay	S.J.	39	7	13	20	15–	10	2	0	1	0	56	12.5
D	41*	Tom Pederson	S.J.	44	7	13	20	16–	31	2	0	2	0	102	6.9
D	24	Doug Wilson	S.J.	42	3	17	20	28–	40	1	0	0	0	110	2.7
L	18	Mark Pederson	PHI	14	3	4	7	2–	6	1	0	0	0	21	14.3
			S.J.	27	7	3	10	20–	22	1	0	0	0	42	16.7
			TOTAL	41	10	7	17	22–	28	2	0	0	0	63	15.9
L	20	John Carter	S.J.	55	7	9	16	25–	81	0	1	0	0	110	6.4
D	19*	Doug Zmolek	S.J.	84	5	10	15	50–	229	2	0	0	0	94	5.3
C	47	Mike Sullivan	S.J.	81	6	8	14	42–	30	0	2	0	0	95	6.3
D	3	David Williams	S.J.	40	1	11	12	27–	49	1	0	0	0	60	1.7
D	4	Jay More	S.J.	73	5	6	11	35–	179	0	1	0	0	107	4.7
C	14*	Ray Whitney	S.J.	26	4	6	10	14–	4	1	0	0	0	24	16.7
C	9	Brian Lawton	S.J.	21	2	8	10	9–	12	0	0	0	0	29	6.9
L	25	David Maley	EDM	13	1	1	2	3–	29	0	0	0	0	9	11.1
			S.J.	43	1	6	7	25–	126	1	0	0	0	48	2.1
			TOTAL	56	2	7	9	28–	155	1	0	0	0	57	3.5
C	27	Hubie McDonough	S.J.	30	6	2	8	21–	6	2	0	0	0	41	14.6
D	21	Peter Ahola	L.A.	8	1	1	2	2–	6	0	0	0	0	3	33.3
			PIT	22	0	1	1	2–	14	0	0	0	0	5	.0
			S.J.	20	2	3	5	6–	16	0	0	0	0	32	6.3
			TOTAL	50	3	5	8	10–	36	0	0	0	0	40	7.5
C	8	Larry Depalma	S.J.	20	2	6	8	14–	41	1	0	0	0	29	6.9
D	5	Neil Wilkinson	S.J.	59	1	7	8	50–	96	0	1	0	0	51	2.0
L	26	Petri Skriko	S.J.	17	4	3	7	8–	6	2	1	0	0	35	11.4
C	16	Perry Berezan	S.J.	28	3	4	7	18–	28	1	1	0	0	37	8.1
L	28*	J-Francois Quintin	S.J.	14	2	5	7	4–	4	0	0	0	0	12	16.7
D	2	Rob Zettler	S.J.	80	0	7	7	50–	150	0	0	0	0	60	.0
C	26	Robin Bawa	S.J.	42	5	0	5	25–	47	0	0	1	1	25	20.0
R	22	Lyndon Byers	S.J.	18	4	1	5	2–	122	0	0	0	0	18	22.2
R	15	David Bruce	S.J.	17	2	3	5	14–	33	2	0	0	0	36	5.6
L	44	Michel Picard	S.J.	25	4	0	4	17–	24	2	0	0	0	32	12.5
C	33	Dale Craigwell	S.J.	8	3	1	4	4–	4	0	0	0	0	7	42.9
C	9	Jon Morris	N.J.	2	0	0	0	1–	0	0	0	0	0	1	.0
			S.J.	13	0	3	3	10–	6	0	0	0	0	11	.0
			TOTAL	15	0	3	3	11–	6	0	0	0	0	12	.0
C	45*	Dody Wood	S.J.	13	1	1	2	5–	71	0	0	0	0	10	10.0
C	42*	Jaroslav Otevrel	S.J.	7	0	2	2	6–	0	0	0	0	0	4	.0
D	29	Dean Kolstad	S.J.	10	0	2	2	9–	12	0	0	0	0	22	.0
C	40*	Mark Beaufait	S.J.	5	1	0	1	1–	0	0	0	0	0	3	33.3
D	45*	Claudio Scremin	S.J.	4	0	1	1	1–	4	0	0	0	0	4	.0
D	38	Pat MacLeod	S.J.	13	0	1	1	19–	10	0	0	0	0	20	.0
G	1	Brian Hayward	S.J.	18	0	1	1	0	2	0	0	0	0	0	.0
G	30	Jeff Hackett	S.J.	36	0	1	1	0	4	0	0	0	0	0	.0
G	31*	Wade Flaherty	S.J.	1	0	0	0	0	0	0	0	0	0	0	.0
L	7	Mikhail Kravets	S.J.	1	0	0	0	1–	0	0	0	0	0	0	.0
G	32*	Arturs Irbe	S.J.	36	0	0	0	0	10	0	0	0	0	0	.0

Goaltending

No.	Goaltender	GPI	Mins	Avg	W	L	T	EN	SO	GA	SA	S%
32	*Arturs Irbe	36	2074	4.11	7	26	0	3	1	142	1250	.886
31	*Wade Flaherty	1	60	5.00	0	1	0	0	0	5	46	.891
30	Jeff Hackett	36	2000	5.28	2	30	1	2	0	176	1220	.856
1	Brian Hayward	18	930	5.55	2	14	1	0	0	86	559	.846
	Totals	**84**	**5077**	**4.89**	**11**	**71**	**2**	**5**	**1**	**414**	**3080**	**.866**

Coach

CONSTANTINE, KEVIN
Head Coach, San Jose Sharks.
Born in International Falls, MN, December 27, 1958.

The Sharks' off-season was highlighted by the the hiring of Kevin Constantine as head coach on June 16. Constantine held that position the previous two seasons with the Kansas City Blades, San Jose's development affiliate which won the International Hockey League championship under his leadership in 1991-92.

The International Falls, Minn., native earned his step to the NHL coaching ranks by leading Kansas City to a combined record of 102-48-14 (.659) over the last two regular seasons, including professional hockey's best mark of 56-22-4 in 1991-92, earning him IHL Coach of the Year honors. The Blades eased through that season's IHL playoffs en route to capturing the Turner Cup, symbolic of the league's playoff champion.

Before being hired by the Sharks to coach at Kansas City, Constantine was an assistant coach with the IHL Kalamazoo Wings from 1988-91. His coaching resume also includes experience in international competition. He coached the U.S. National Team to a fourth-place finish and a best-ever record of 4-2-1 at the 1991 World Junior Championships.

Prior to his arrival at Kalamazoo, Constantine guided Rochester (Minn.) to the 1987-88 U.S. Hockey League and national junior "A" titles. He also had coaching experience with Northwood Prep School in Lake Placid, N.Y. and North Iowa of the USHL.

Coaching Record

		Regular Season					Playoffs			
Season	Team	Games	W	L	T	%	Games	W	L	%
1985-86	North Iowa (USHL)	48	17	31	0	.354	....	....	....	....
1987-88	Rochester (USHL)	48	39	7	2	.833	15	9	4	.692 (2 ties)
1991-92	Kansas City (IHL)	82	56	22	4	.707	15	12	3	.800
1992-93	Kansas City (IHL)	82	46	26	10	.622	12	6	6	.500

Arturs Irbe recorded the first shutout in San Jose history, blanking the L.A. Kings 6-0 on November 17, 1992.

Club Records

Team

(Figures in brackets for season records are games played; records for fewest points, wins, ties, losses, goals, goals against are for 70 or more games)

Most Points	39	1991-92 (80)
Most Wins	17	1991-92 (80)
Most Ties	5	1991-92 (80)
Most Losses	*71	1992-93 (84)
Most Goals	219	1991-92 (80)
Most Goals Against	414	1992-93 (84)
Fewest Points	24	1992-93 (84)
Fewest Wins	11	1992-93 (84)
Fewest Ties	2	1992-93 (84)
Fewest Losses	58	1991-92 (80)
Fewest Goals	218	1992-93 (84)
Fewest Goals Against	359	1991-92 (80)

Longest Winning Streak
Overall	2	Four times
Home	2	Five times
Away	1	Six times

Longest Undefeated Streak
Overall	4	Nov. 26/91-Dec. 3/91 (3-0-1)
Home	2	Seven times
Away	2	Three times

Longest Losing Streak
Overall	*17	Jan. 4/93-Feb. 12/93
Home	9	Nov. 19/92-Dec. 19/92
Away	19	Nov. 27/92-Feb. 12/93

Longest Winless Streak
Overall	20	Dec. 29/92-Feb. 12/93 (0-19-1)
Home	9	Nov. 19/92-Dec. 18/92 (0-9-0)
Away	19	Nov. 27/92-Feb. 12/93 (0-19-0)

Most Shutouts, Season	1	1992-93 (84)
Most PIM, Season	2134	1992-93 (84)
Most Goals, Game	7	Four times

General Managers' History

Jack Ferreira, 1991-92.

Coaching History

George Kingston, 1991-92 to 1992-93; Kevin Constantine, 1993-94.

Captains' History

Doug Wilson, 1991-92 to date.

All-time Record vs. Other Clubs

Individual

Most Seasons	2	Numerous
Most Games, Career	158	Dean Evason
Most Goals, Career	39	Pat Falloon
Most Assists, Career	78	Kelly Kisio
Most Points, Career	115	Kelly Kisio (37, 78)
Most PIM, Career	470	Jeff Odgers
Most Shutouts, Career	1	Arturs Irbe

Longest Consecutive
Games Streak	89	Mike Sullivan (Mar. 21/92-Apr. 6/93)
Most Games, Season	84	Doug Zmolek (1992-93)
Most Goals, Season	26	Kelly Kisio (1992-93)
Most Assists, Season	52	Kelly Kisio (1992-93)
Most Points, Season	78	Kelly Kisio (1992-93) (26 goals, 52 assists)
Most PIM, Season	326	Link Gaetz (1991-92)
Most Shutouts, Season	1	Arturs Irbe (Nov. 17/92 L.A. 0 at S.J. 6)
Most Points, Defenseman Season	28	Doug Wilson (9 goals, 19 assists) David Williams (3 goals, 25 assists)
Most Points, Center, Season	78	Kelly Kisio (1992-93) (26 goals, 52 assists)
Most Points, Right Wing, Season	59	Pat Falloon (25 goals, 34 assists)
Most Points, Left Wing, Season	66	John Garpenlov (1992-93) (22 goals, 44 assists)
Most Points, Rookie, Season	59	Pat Falloon (25 goals, 34 assists)

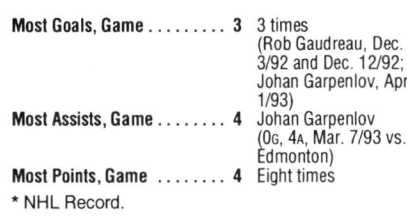

Most Goals, Game	3	3 times (Rob Gaudreau, Dec. 3/92 and Dec. 12/92; Johan Garpenlov, Apr. 1/93)
Most Assists, Game	4	Johan Garpenlov (0G, 4A, Mar. 7/93 vs. Edmonton)
Most Points, Game	4	Eight times

* NHL Record.

1992-93 Results

	Home				**Away**		
Oct.	8	Winnipeg	4-3	Oct.	13	Los Angeles	1-2
	10	Detroit	3-6		21	Montreal	4-8
	15	Boston	2-8		23	Buffalo	4-5
	17	Calgary	2-6		24	Toronto	1-5
Nov.	5	Buffalo	7-5		26	St. Louis	1-4
	7	New Jersey	1-6		28	Detroit	3-4
	8	Los Angeles	4-11		30	Tampa Bay	2-1
	12	Edmonton	3-4	Nov.	1	Chicago	4-4
	14	Vancouver	2-5		10	Vancouver	2-6
	17	Los Angeles	6-0		25	Calgary	4-3
	19	Toronto	0-2		27	Winnipeg	2-3
	21	Chicago	1-2		28	Minnesota	3-10
Dec.	1	Edmonton	1-3	Dec.	9	Vancouver	3-8
	3	Hartford	5-7		18	Vancouver	1-8
	5	Pittsburgh*	4-9		21	Winnipeg	4-5
	10	St. Louis	2-3		23	Edmonton	2-4
	12	Quebec	7-8		29	Vancouver	5-7
	16	Tampa Bay	4-5	Jan.	4	Montreal	1-4
	19	Vancouver	3-6		8	Toronto	1-5
	26	Los Angeles	7-2		10	Ottawa*	2-3
	30	Philadelphia	2-6		12	Winnipeg	1-4
Jan.	2	Vancouver	2-2		15	Detroit	3-6
	5	Montreal	1-2		16	Quebec	1-4
	29	Chicago	2-4		18	Boston*	3-4
	30	Calgary	4-5		21	Hartford	2-4
Feb.	1	Tampa Bay	4-5		23	Tampa Bay	1-5
	3	Minnesota	3-7		26	Los Angeles	1-7
	16	Washington	3-4	Feb.	10	Calgary	1-13
	18	Winnipeg	5-3		12	Edmonton	0-6
	20	NY Rangers	4-6		14	Winnipeg*	3-2
	22	NY Rangers	0-4		27	Calgary	4-5
	23	Calgary	3-6		28	Edmonton	1-4
	25	Toronto	0-5	Mar.	9	Minnesota	2-4
Mar.	2	Ottawa	3-2		11	St. Louis	2-5
	7	Edmonton	6-3		19	NY Rangers	1-8
	14	Detroit*	1-4		21	Washington*	3-5
	16	NY Islanders	0-6		23	Pittsburgh	2-7
Apr.	1	Winnipeg	5-9		25	Philadelphia	2-5
	3	Calgary*	2-3		27	NY Islanders	3-7
	4	Calgary	3-4		29	New Jersey	0-5
	6	Edmonton	5-2	Apr.	8	Los Angeles	1-2
	10	Los Angeles	2-3		15	Calgary	3-7

*Denotes afternoon game.

Regular Season

	At Home						On Road							Total					
	GP	W	L	T	GF	GA	PTS	GP	W	L	T	GF	GA	PTS	GP	W	L	T	GF	GA	PTS
Boston	2	0	2	0	3	12	0	2	0	2	0	9	11	0	4	0	4	0	12	23	0
Buffalo	2	1	1	0	8	12	2	3	0	3	0	11	15	0	5	1	4	0	19	27	2
Calgary	9	1	8	0	25	38	2	7	2	5	0	18	42	4	16	3	13	0	43	80	6
Chicago	3	1	2	0	8	8	2	3	0	2	1	8	16	1	6	1	4	1	16	24	3
Detroit	4	0	3	1	11	18	1	3	0	3	0	7	21	0	7	0	6	1	18	39	1
Edmonton	7	5	2	0	32	19	10	7	0	6	1	14	36	1	14	5	8	1	46	55	11
Hartford	2	1	1	0	11	12	2	3	1	2	0	7	11	2	5	2	3	0	18	23	4
Los Angeles	7	3	4	0	27	25	6	7	0	6	1	18	33	1	14	3	10	1	45	58	7
Minnesota	3	0	3	0	7	18	0	3	0	3	0	9	21	0	6	0	6	0	16	39	0
Montreal	3	0	2	1	4	6	1	3	0	3	0	6	18	0	6	0	5	1	10	24	1
New Jersey	2	1	1	0	4	8	2	3	0	3	0	3	18	0	5	1	4	0	7	26	2
NY Islanders	2	1	1	0	4	9	2	3	0	11	0	22	0	5	1	4	0	15	31	2
NY Rangers	3	0	3	0	6	14	0	2	0	2	0	4	12	0	5	0	5	0	10	26	0
Ottawa	1	1	0	0	3	2	2	1	0	1	0	2	3	0	2	1	1	0	5	5	2
Philadelphia	3	1	2	0	5	8	2	2	0	2	0	4	10	0	5	1	4	0	9	18	2
Pittsburgh	3	0	3	0	7	24	0	2	0	4	0	4	17	0	5	0	5	0	11	41	0
Quebec	3	2	1	0	18	13	4	2	0	2	0	4	10	0	5	2	3	0	22	23	4
St. Louis	2	0	2	0	4	7	0	4	0	4	0	6	19	0	6	0	6	0	10	26	0
Tampa Bay	2	0	2	0	8	10	0	2	1	1	0	3	6	2	4	1	3	0	11	16	2
Toronto	4	1	3	0	5	11	2	3	0	3	0	3	14	0	7	1	6	0	8	25	2
Vancouver	7	1	5	1	18	27	3	7	0	7	0	15	38	0	14	1	12	1	33	65	3
Washington	2	0	2	0	5	8	0	2	0	2	0	5	11	0	4	0	4	0	10	19	0
Winnipeg	6	2	3	1	24	28	5	8	2	6	0	19	32	4	14	4	9	1	43	60	9
Totals	**82**	**22**	**56**	**4**	**247**	**337**	**48**	**82**	**6**	**73**	**3**	**190**	**436**	**15**	**164**	**28**	**129**	**7**	**437**	**773**	**63**

Entry Draft Selections 1993-91

1993 Pick		1992 Pick		1991 Pick	
6	Viktor Kozlov	3	Mike Rathje	2	Pat Falloon
28	Shean Donovan	10	Andrei Nazarov	23	Ray Whitney
45	Vlastimil Kroupa	51	Alexander Cherbajev	30	Sandis Ozolinsh
58	Ville Peltonen	75	Jan Caloun	45	Dody Wood
80	Alexander Osadchy	99	Marcus Ragnarsson	67	Kerry Toporowski
106	Andrei Buschan	123	Michal Sykora	89	Dan Ryder
132	Petri Varis	147	Eric Bellerose	111	Fredrik Nilsson
154	Fredrik Oduya	171	Ryan Smith	133	Jaroslav Otevrel
158	Anatoli Filatov	195	Chris Burns	155	Dean Grillo
184	Todd Holt	219	A. Kholomeyev	177	Corwin Saurdiff
210	Jonas Forsberg	243	Victor Ignatjev	199	Dale Craigdell
236	Jeff Salajko			221	Aaron Kriss
262	Jamie Matthews			243	Mikhail Kravets

Office of the General Manager

LOMBARDI, DEAN
Vice President and Director of Hockey Operations, San Jose Sharks.
Born in Holyoke, Massachusetts, March 5, 1958.

Dean Lombardi enters his sixth year in the National Hockey League, his fourth with the Sharks organization. After two seasons as assistant general manager, he was named to his present position on June 26, 1992. Prior to joining the Sharks, he spent two seasons, 1988-90, as assistant GM with the Minnesota North Stars.

Lombardi, 35, utilizes his skills in contract negotiations and knowledge of the NHL's business and legal workings to benefit the Sharks, as well as working closely with Chuck Grillo in the club's player evaluation process.

He has successfully negotiated contracts which have led the signing of numerous players in the Sharks system, including Entry Draft selections Pat Falloon, Ray Whitney, Sandis Ozolinsh, Dody Wood, Jaroslav Otevrel, Dale Craigwell, Mike Rathje, Alexander Cherbayev and Michal Sykora.

Lombardi's involvement includes an aggressive and innovative approach to negotiating the release of players under contract to European clubs, often traveling overseas to visit players, agents and club officials. He also has contributed significant research and information to assist relations between the NHL and the Russian Ice Hockey Federation.

Raised in Ludlow, Mass., Lombardi sports an impressive resume along with an intense work ethic that has brought him success at all ends of his profession. He graduated third in his class from the University of New Haven and earned a law degree, with honors, from Tulane University where he specialized in labor law. During two years as a player agent, Lombardi represented an impressive list of clients, including five members of the 1988 U.S. Olympic ice hockey squad.

On the ice, Lombardi was captain his final two seasons at the University of New Haven where he received a full athletic scholarship and earned the school's Student/Athlete of the Year Award. He also was named to the Junior All-America team in 1978 while playing for the Springfield (Mass.) Olympics.

GRILLO, CHUCK
Vice President and Director of Player Personnel, San Jose Sharks.
Born in Hibbing, Minnesota, July 24, 1939.

Chuck Grillo fills the role of vice president and director of player personnel for the Sharks, supervising the club's scouting department and player development program. He has held that position since 1990, having the vice president's title, along with some duties of the office of general manager, added on June 26, 1992. Grillo, a native of Hibbing, Minn., served as director of pro scouting from 1988-90 with the Minnesota North Stars, preceded by eight years as a scout for the NY Rangers.

One of only two U.S.-born player personnel directors in the NHL, Grillo is noted for his eye for distinguishing talent and innovative ideas for player development. Since joining the Sharks, Grillo and his scouting staff have seen seven of their 13 selections in the 1991 Entry Draft already see action with the parent club. In addition, many players who contributed to the 1991-92 International Hockey League champion Kansas City Blades (Sharks' development affiliate) were acquired and developed by Grillo and his staff while with Minnesota.

Grillo, 53, also is owner and operator of a successful hockey camp in Minnesota. Many athletes at the camp have gone on to become players, coaches and trainers in the NHL. In addition, many NHL clubs send their players to the camp for off-season development.

Sharks players who have honed their abilities at the camp include Ed Courtenay, Wade Flaherty, Jeff Odgers, Sandis Ozolinsh, Rob Zettler and Doug Zmolek. Most Sharks draft picks, as well as some other players in the system, also spend a portion of their summer at the facility.

Grillo spent 16 years as a high school hockey and baseball coach, taking teams to the Minnesota state tournament 11 times including 1973 when he was named Minnesota State High School League Coach of the Year at Bemidji High School.

Owner of a master's degree in guidance and counseling from Bemidji State University, Grillo is working toward a doctorate in educational administration, also from Bemidji State.

Club Directory

San Jose Arena
525 West Santa Clara Street
P.O. Box 1240
San Jose, California 95113
Phone **408/287-7070**
FAX 408/999-5797
Capacity: 17,310

Executive Staff

Majority Owner & Chairman	George Gund III
Co-Owner & Vice Chairman	Gordon Gund
President & Chief Executive Officer	Arthur L. Savage
Exec. Vice President, Chief Operating Officer	Greg Jamison
Exec. Vice President, Building Operations	Frank Jirik
Exec. Vice President, Chief Financial Officer	Grant Rollin
Exec. Vice President, Development	Matt Levine
Vice-President, Director of Hockey Operations	Dean Lombardi
Vice-President, Director of Player Personnel	Chuck Grillo
Chief of Staff to President & CEO	Karen C. Shiraki
Administrative Assistant to President & CEO	Dawn Beres

Hockey

Head Coach	Kevin Constantine
Assistant Coach & Ass't to the Dir. of Hockey Oper.	Wayne Thomas
Assistant Coach	Vasily Tikhonov
Assistant Coach	Drew Remenda
Assistant Coach	Steve Myrland
Head Coach, Kansas City Blades	Jim Wiley
Scouting Coordinator	Joe Will
Exec. Assistant to V.P., Director of Hockey Operations	Brenda Will
Eastern Scouting Supervisor	Ray Payne
Pro Scouting Supervisor	Tim Burke
European Scouting Supervisor	Sakari Pietila
Regional Scout, Midwest	Rob Grillo
Regional Scouts, West	Pat Funk, Larry Ross
Area Scouts	Joe Bzdel (Saskatchewan); Tim Gorski (Alaska); Ben Hays (New England); Thomas Holm (Sweden); Randy Joevenazzo (Alberta); Konstantin Krylov (Russia); Jack Morganstern (New England); Joe Rowley (Ontario); Dan Summers (Manitoba)
Video Scouting Coordinator	Bob Friedlander
Head Trainer	Tom Woodcock
Equipment Manager	Bob Crocker, Jr.
Assistant Trainer/Massage Therapist	Sergei Tchekmarev
Team Physician	Arthur J. Ting, M.D.
Team Dentist	Robert Bonahoom, D.D.S.
Director of Media Relations	Tim Bryant
Assistant Director of Media Relations	Ken Arnold
Media Relations Assistant	Paul Turner
Administrative Assistant	Steve Perry

Finance

Director of Finance and Accounting	Brent M. Billinger
Manager of Finance	Mike Cain
Accountant	Bonita Tanner
Executive Assistant	Cecilia Briones
Manager, Information Systems	Alex Ignacio
Systems Support Analyst	Wee Yap
Accounts Payable Clerks	Leah Beavers, Julie Burns

Business Operations

Vice President, Broadcast & Media Marketing	David Forier
Director of Broadcasting	Mark Stulberger
Director of Executive Suite Services	Ted Atlee
Director of Ticket Sales	Rich Muschell
Director of Community Development	Alysse Soll
Director of Special Projects	Herb Briggin
Director of San Jose Arena Marketing	Elaine Sullivan-Digre
Arena Marketing Assistant	Beth Brigino
Manager of Event Services	Diane Bloom
Group Account Service Manager	Mary Lewis
Account Service Managers	Wanda Mae Lombardi, Elizabeth Sabatino, Paul Solby, Gene Wiggins
Media Marketing Managers	Jim Josel, Don Olvarado
Executive Assistant	Joyce Coppola
Media Coordinator	Valerie Bigelow
Traffic Coordinator/Sales Assistant	Martha Baumgartner
Ticket Sales Assistants	Annie Chan-Zien, Kris Lyon
Season Ticket Controller	Mary Enriquez
Assistant, Executive Suite Services	Kimberly Brown
Ass't Manager Community Devel./Event Services	Roger Ross
Tour Administrator	Dianna Carthew
Suite Hospitality Managers	Pat Swan, Coleen Zogzas
Mascot	S.J. Sharkie

Building Operations

Vice President, Arena Project Manager	Jim Goddard
Manager of Arena Construction	Tom Hanson
Administrative Ass't & Arena Project Coordinator	Colleen Reilly
Director of Booking & Operations	Jack Larson
Manager of Guest Services	Mike Kolatski
Executive Assistant	Chris Palmer
Mailroom Coordinator	Hunter Van Pelt
Receptionist	Marcia Cady
Manager of Event Conversions/Ice Technician	Bruce Tharaldson
Building Services Manager	John Jordan
Event & Conversion Manager	Blair Engelbrekt
Director of Ticket Operations	Daniel DeBoer
Assistant Ticket Office Manager	Judy Jones

Broadcasters

Play-By-Play (Radio)	Dan Rusanowsky
Play-By-Play (Television)	Randy Hahn
Color Commentator	Pete Stemkowski

Tampa Bay Lightning

1992-93 Results: 23w-54L-7T 53PTS. Sixth, Norris Division

Year-by-Year Record

Season	GP	Home W	L	T	Road W	L	T	Overall W	L	T	GF	GA	Pts.	Finished	Playoff Result
1992-93	84	12	27	3	11	27	4	23	54	7	245	332	53	6th, Norris Div.	Out of Playoffs

Schedule

Home

Oct. Sat. 9 Florida
Thur. 14 Pittsburgh
Sat. 16 Ottawa
Wed. 20 Los Angeles
Fri. 22 NY Rangers
Sat. 23 Toronto
Wed. 27 Winnipeg
Fri. 29 NY Islanders
Nov. Thur. 11 Washington
Sat. 13 Quebec
Fri. 19 NY Rangers
Sat. 20 Chicago
Wed. 24 Hartford
Sat. 27 Philadelphia
Dec. Wed. 1 Buffalo
Sat. 11 Pittsburgh
Tues. 14 Montreal
(at Orlando)
Wed. 15 Ottawa
Sat. 18 Boston
Sun. 26 Florida
(at Orlando)
Jan. Sun. 2 Anaheim
(at Orlando)
Sat. 8 Philadelphia
Mon. 17 Detroit
(at Minnesota)
Wed. 19 NY Islanders
Mon. 24 Buffalo
(at Orlando)
Wed. 26 Florida
Sat. 29 San Jose
Feb. Wed. 2 Detroit
Sat. 12 Vancouver
Sun. 13 New Jersey
Thur. 17 Montreal
Sun. 20 Boston
Mar. Thur. 3 New Jersey
Sat. 5 Hartford
Sun. 6 Philadelphia
Tues. 15 Calgary
Wed. 16 Edmonton
Sun. 20 Washington
(at Orlando)
Sun. 27 Dallas*
Apr. Fri. 1 St Louis
Wed. 13 NY Islanders
Thur. 14 Quebec

Away

Oct. Wed. 6 New Jersey
Thur. 7 NY Rangers
Sun. 17 Florida
Sat. 30 Florida
Nov. Tues. 2 Quebec
Wed. 3 Montreal
Sat. 6 Boston
Mon. 8 NY Rangers
Wed. 17 Dallas
Fri. 26 Philadelphia*
Dec. Sat. 4 Los Angeles
Sun. 5 Anaheim
Tues. 7 San Jose
Sun. 19 Buffalo
Tues. 21 Pittsburgh
Thur. 23 St Louis
Tues. 28 Quebec
Thur. 30 Ottawa
Jan. Sat. 1 Washington*
Tues. 4 Toronto
(at Hamilton)
Mon. 10 NY Rangers
Wed. 12 Detroit
Thur. 13 Chicago
Sun. 16 Winnipeg
Feb. Sat. 5 Washington
Mon. 7 Toronto
Thur. 10 Ottawa
Tues. 15 NY Islanders
Sat. 19 New Jersey*
Thur. 24 Calgary
Sat. 26 Vancouver
Sun. 27 Edmonton
Mar. Tues. 1 Washington
Wed. 9 Hartford
Sun. 13 Philadelphia
Tues. 22 NY Islanders
Thur. 24 New Jersey
Wed. 30 Buffalo
Apr. Mon. 4 Pittsburgh
Wed. 6 Montreal
Sat. 9 Boston*
Sun. 10 Hartford*

* Denotes afternoon game.

Home Starting Times:

Weeknights and Saturdays	7:35 p.m.
Sundays	6:05 p.m.
Matinees	1:35 p.m.
Except Sat. Oct. 23	8:05 p.m.
Sun. Dec. 26, Sun. Jan. 2	7:35 p.m.

Franchise date: December 16, 1991

ATLANTIC DIVISION

EASTERN CONFERENCE

2nd NHL Season

Shawn Chambers led all Tampa Bay defenders in scoring with ten goals and 29 assists.

1993-94 Player Personnel

FORWARDS

	HT	WT	S	Place of Birth	Date	1992-93 Club
ANDERSSON, Mikael	5-11	185	L	Malmo, Sweden	5/10/66	Tampa Bay
BERGLAND, Tim	6-3	194	R	Crookston, MI	1/11/65	Tampa Bay-Atlanta
BLOUIN, Jean	6-0	195	L	Montreal, Que.	2/26/71	Atlanta
BRADLEY, Brian	5-10	177	R	Kitchener, Ont.	1/21/65	Tampa Bay
BUREAU, Marc	6-1	198	R	Trois-Rivieres, Que.	5/19/66	Tampa Bay
CAMPEAU, Christian	5-10	180	L	Verdun, Que.	6/2/71	Atlanta
COLE, Danton	5-11	185	R	Pontiac, MI	1/10/67	Tampa Bay-Atlanta
CREIGHTON, Adam	6-5	210	L	Burlington, Ont.	6/2/65	Tampa Bay
DiMAIO, Rob	5-10	190	R	Calgary, Alta.	2/19/68	Tampa Bay
DRULIA, Stan	5-11	190	R	Elmira, NY	1/5/68	Tampa Bay-Atlanta
EGELAND, Allan	6-0	184	L	Lethbridge, Alta.	1/31/73	Indianapolis
GALLANT, Gerard	5-10	190	L	Summerside, P.E.I.	9/2/63	Detroit
GAVEY, Aaron	6-1	169	L	Sudbury, Ont.	2/22/74	Sault Ste. Marie
GRATTON, Chris	6-3	202	L	Brantford, Ont.	7/5/75	Kingston
GRETZKY, Brent	5-10	160	L	Brantford, Ont.	2/20/72	Atlanta
HILL, Kiley	6-3	205	L	Sudbury, Ont.	1/2/75	Sault Ste. Marie
KACIR, Marian	6-1	183	R	Hodonin, Czech.	9/29/74	Owen Sound
KLIMA, Petr	6-0	190	R	Chaomutov, Czech.	12/23/63	Edmonton
KONTOS, Chris	6-1	195	L	Toronto, Ont.	12/10/63	Tampa Bay
LAFRENIERE, Jason	5-11	185	R	St. Catharines, Ont.	12/6/66	Tampa Bay-Atlanta
MacDONALD, Tom	5-11	190	L	Toronto, Ont.	4/14/74	Sault Ste. Marie
MAXWELL, Dennis	6-0	188	L	Dauphin, Man.	6/4/74	Niagara Falls-Sudbury
McDOUGALL, Bill	6-0	185	R	New Waterford, N.S.	8/10/66	Edm.-Cape Breton
MILLER, Colin	6-0	188	R	Grimsby, Ont.	8/21/71	Atlanta
MYHRES, Brantt	6-3	195	R	Edmonton, Alta.	3/18/74	Lethbridge
NAUSS, Ryan	6-5	196	L	Toronto, Ont.	1/19/75	Peterborough
PETERSON, Brent	6-4	200	L	Calgary, Alta.	7/20/72	Michigan Tech
RUFF, Jason	6-2	192	L	Kelowna, B.C.	1/27/70	St. L.-Peo.-T.B.-Atl.
SAVARD, Denis	5-10	175	R	Pointe Gatineau, Que.	2/4/61	Montreal
SZOKE, Mark	5-9	176	L	High Level, Alta.	8/12/74	Lethbridge
TANGUAY, Martin	5-11	185	L	Ste. Julie, Que.	1/12/73	St-Jean
TARDIF, Marc	6-1	199	L	Montreal, Que.	1/6/73	Sherbrooke
TUCKER, John	6-0	200	R	Windsor, Ont.	9/29/64	Tampa Bay
ZAMUNER, Rob	6-2	202	L	Oakville, Ont.	9/17/69	Tampa Bay

DEFENSEMEN

	HT	WT	S	Place of Birth	Date	1992-93 Club
AHOLA, Peter	6-3	205	L	Espoo, Finland	5/14/68	L.A.-Pit.-Cle.-S.J.
BANNISTER, Drew	6-1	193	R	Belleville, Ont.	4/9/74	Sault Ste. Marie
BEERS, Bob	6-2	200	R	Pittsburgh, PA	5/20/67	Prov.-T.B.-Atl.
BERGEVIN, Marc	6-1	197	L	Montreal, Que.	8/11/65	Tampa Bay
BOSTON, Scott	6-2	180	R	Ottawa, Ont.	7/13/71	Atlanta
BROWN, Ryan	6-3	215	R	Boyle, Alta.	9/19/74	Swift Current
BUCHANAN, Jeff	5-10	165	R	Swift Current, Sask.	5/23/71	Atlanta
CHAMBERS, Shawn	6-2	200	L	Sterling Heights, MI	10/11/66	Tampa Bay-Atlanta
CHARRON, Eric	6-3	192	L	Verdun, Que.	1/14/70	Mtl.-Fred.-Atl.
CROSS, Cory	6-5	212	L	Lloydminster, Alta.	1/3/71	U. of Alberta-Atlanta
DUBOIS, Eric	6-0	195	R	Montreal, Que.	5/9/70	Oklahoma City-Atlanta
DUFRESNE, Donald	6-1	206	R	Quebec City, Que.	4/10/67	Montreal
DUNCAN, Brett	6-0	208	R	Kitchener, Ont.	2/15/73	Seattle
HAMRLIK, Roman	6-2	189	L	Gottwaldov, Czech.	4/12/74	Tampa Bay-Atlanta
KEMPER, Andrew	6-2	186	R	Montreal, Que.	4/7/74	Saskatoon
LAPORTE, Alexandre	6-3	210	R	Cowansville, Que.	5/1/75	Victoriaville
LIPUMA, Chris	6-0	183	L	Chicago, IL	3/23/71	Tampa Bay-Atlanta
POESCHEK, Rudy	6-2	210	R	Kamloops, B.C.	9/29/66	St. John's
RABY, Mathieu	6-2	204	L	Hull, Que.	1/19/75	Victoriaville
REEKIE, Joe	6-3	215	L	Victoria, B.C.	2/22/65	Tampa Bay
RIVERS, Shawn	5-10	185	L	Ottawa, Ont.	1/30/71	Tampa Bay-Atlanta
ROBINSON, Rob	6-1	214	L	St. Catharines, Ont.	4/19/67	Peoria

GOALTENDERS

	HT	WT	C	Place of Birth	Date	1992-93 Club
BERGERON, J.C.	6-2	192	L	Hauterive, Que.	10/14/68	Tampa Bay-Atlanta
GREENLAY, Mike	6-3	200	L	Vitoria, Brazil	9/15/68	Louisville-Atlanta
JABLONSKI, Pat	6-0	178	R	Toledo, OH	6/20/67	Tampa Bay
MOSS, Tyler	6-0	168	R	Ottawa, Ont.	6/29/75	Kingston
PUPPA, Daren	6-3	205	R	Kirkland Lake, Ont.	3/23/65	Buffalo-Toronto
RHEAUME, Manon	5-6	136	L	Lac Beauport, Que.	2/24/72	Atlanta
WILKINSON, Derek	6-0	160	L	LaSalle, Que.	7/29/74	Det. (OHL)-Belleville
YOUNG, Wendell	5-9	181	L	Halifax, N.S.	8/1/63	Tampa Bay-Atlanta

General Manager

ESPOSITO, PHIL
General Manager, Tampa Bay Lightning.
Born in Sault Ste. Marie, Ont., February 20, 1942.

Phil Esposito, who headed up Tampa Bay's successful campaign to obtain an NHL franchise, was rewarded for his hard work when the Lightning were granted a berth in the NHL, beginning in the 1992-93 season. After an 18-year Hall-of-Fame career that included eight All-Star selections as well as winning the Hart Trophy twice, the Art Ross Trophy five times, Esposito was named vice president and general manager of the NY Rangers in 1986, remaining in that role until the start of the 1989-90 season. He also doubled as coach during the 1986-87 campaign and took over the bench duties again at the conclusion of 1988-89. Esposito, who began his career with Chicago and finished his playing days with the NY Rangers, had his most productive days with the Boston Bruins, winning a pair of Stanley Cup titles while establishing numerous team records, including most goals (76) and points (152) in a single season. In 1968-69, he became the first NHL player to record 100 points in a season.

NHL Coaching Record

			Regular Season				Playoffs			
Season	Team	Games	W	L	T	%	Games	W	L	%
1986-87	NY Rangers (NHL)	43	24	19	0	.558	6	2	4	.333
1988-89	NY Rangers (NHL)	2	0	2	0	.000	4	0	4	.000
	NHL Totals	45	24	21	0	.533	10	2	8	.200

1992-93 Scoring

Regular Season

Pos	#	Player	Team	GP	G	A	Pts	+/-	PIM	PP	SH	GW	GT	S	%
C	19	Brian Bradley	T.B.	80	42	44	86	24-	92	16	0	6	1	205	20.5
C	14	John Tucker	T.B.	78	17	39	56	12-	69	5	1	1	0	179	9.5
C	16	Chris Kontos	T.B.	66	27	24	51	7-	12	12	1	3	0	136	19.9
C	7*	Rob Zamuner	T.B.	84	15	28	43	25-	74	1	0	0	2	183	8.2
C	10	Adam Creighton	T.B.	83	19	20	39	19-	110	7	1	0	0	168	11.3
D	22	Shawn Chambers	T.B.	55	10	29	39	21-	36	5	0	1	0	152	6.6
D	2	Bob Beers	T.B.	64	12	24	36	25-	70	7	0	0	0	138	8.7
C	28	Marc Bureau	T.B.	63	10	21	31	12-	111	1	2	1	0	132	7.6
L	34	Mikael Andersson	T.B.	77	16	11	27	14-	14	3	2	4	0	169	9.5
R	24	Danton Cole	T.B.	67	12	15	27	2-	23	0	1	1	0	100	12.0
C	18	Rob Dimaio	T.B.	54	9	15	24	0	62	2	0	0	0	75	12.0
D	44*	Roman Hamrlik	T.B.	67	6	15	21	21-	71	1	0	1	0	113	5.3
L	37	Steve Maltais	T.B.	63	7	13	20	20-	35	4	0	1	0	96	7.3
D	25	Marc Bergevin	T.B.	78	2	12	14	16-	66	0	0	0	0	69	2.9
D	29	Joe Reekie	T.B.	42	2	11	13	2	69	0	0	0	0	53	3.8
C	11	Steve Kasper	PHI	21	1	3	4	4-	2	0	1	0	0	9	11.1
			T.B.	47	3	4	7	13-	18	0	0	0	0	23	13.0
			TOTAL	68	4	7	11	17-	20	0	1	0	0	32	12.5
C	8	Ken Hodge	T.B.	25	2	7	9	6-	2	0	1	0	0	32	6.3
C	20	Randy Gilhen	NYR	33	3	2	5	8-	8	0	1	0	0	34	8.8
			T.B.	11	0	2	2	6-	6	0	0	0	0	11	.0
			TOTAL	44	3	4	7	14-	14	0	1	0	0	45	6.7
C	17	Jason Lafreniere	T.B.	11	3	3	6	6-	4	1	0	1	0	17	17.6
R	21	Tim Bergland	T.B.	27	3	3	6	5-	11	0	0	0	0	44	6.8
D	40*	Chris Lipuma	T.B.	15	0	5	5	1	34	0	0	0	0	17	.0
D	26	Matt Hervey	T.B.	17	0	4	4	6-	38	0	0	0	0	18	.0
L	20*	Jason Ruff	STL	7	2	1	3	1-	8	1	0	1	0	7	28.6
			T.B.	1	0	0	0	0	0	0	0	0	0	1	.0
			TOTAL	8	2	1	3	1-	8	1	0	1	0	8	25.0
R	27*	Stan Drulia	T.B.	24	2	1	3	1	10	0	0	1	0	22	9.1
C	20	Michel Mongeau	T.B.	4	1	1	2	2-	2	0	0	0	0	2	50.0
L	9	Dave Capuano	T.B.	6	1	1	2	4-	2	1	0	0	0	10	10.0
R	12	Jock Callander	T.B.	8	1	1	2	5-	2	0	0	0	0	12	8.3
R	15*	Keith Osborne	T.B.	11	1	1	2	1-	2	0	0	0	0	11	9.1
D	3	Shawn Rivers	T.B.	4	0	2	2	2-	2	0	0	0	0	3	.0
G	1	Wendell Young	T.B.	31	0	2	2	0	2	0	0	0	0	0	.0
G	35	Pat Jablonski	T.B.	43	0	2	2	0	7	0	0	0	0	0	.0
R	9*	Shayne Stevenson	T.B.	8	0	1	1	5-	7	0	0	0	0	4	.0
G	30*	J.C. Bergeron	T.B.	21	0	1	1	0	0	0	0	0	0	0	.0
G	31*	Dave Littman	T.B.	1	0	0	0	0	0	0	0	0	0	0	.0
D	6	Alain Cote	T.B.	2	0	0	0	1-	0	0	0	0	0	1	.0
R	8	Herb Raglan	T.B.	2	0	0	0	0	2	0	0	0	0	0	.0
R	13	Martin Simard	T.B.	7	0	0	0	1-	11	0	0	0	0	1	.0

Goaltending

No.	Goaltender	GPI	Mins	Avg	W	L	T	EN	SO	GA	SA	S%
30	*J.C. Bergeron	21	1163	3.66	8	10	1	3	0	71	574	.876
1	Wendell Young	31	1591	3.66	7	19	2	2	0	97	758	.872
35	Pat Jablonski	43	2268	3.97	8	24	4	2	1	150	1194	.874
31	*Dave Littman	1	45	9.33	0	1	0	0	0	7	21	.667
	Totals	84	5088	3.92	23	54	7	7	1	332	2554	.870

Wendell Young appeared in 31 games for Tampa Bay, recording a goals-against average of 3.66.

Club Records

Team

(Figures in brackets for season records are games played; records for fewest points, wins, ties, losses, goals, goals against are for 70 or more games)

Most Points	53	1992-93 (84)
Most Wins	23	1992-93 (84)
Most Ties	7	1992-93 (84)
Most Losses	54	1992-93 (84)
Most Goals	245	1992-93 (84)
Most Goals Against	332	1992-93 (84)
Fewest Points	53	1992-93 (84)
Fewest Wins	23	1992-93 (84)
Fewest Ties	7	1992-93 (84)
Fewest Losses	54	1992-93 (84)
Fewest Goals	245	1992-93 (84)
Fewest Goals Against	332	1992-93 (84)

Longest Winning Streak
Overall	4	Nov. 7-13/92
Home	3	Nov. 3-13/92
Away	2	Three times

Longest Undefeated Streak
Overall	6	Nov. 3-13/92 (5 wins, 1 tie)
Home	3	Nov. 3-13/92 (3 wins)
Away	3	Nov. 6-9/92 (2 wins, 1 tie)

Longest Losing Streak
Overall	8	Mar. 9-28/93
Home	6	Mar. 9-Apr. 11/93
Away	5	Dec. 22/92-Jan. 4/93

Longest Winless Streak
Overall	8	Mar. 9-28/93 (8 losses)
Home	9	Mar. 9-Apr. 10/93 (8 losses, 1 tie)
Away	8	Feb. 3-Mar. 23/93
Most Shutouts, Season	1	1992-93 (84)
Most PIM, Season	1,625	1992-93 (84)
Most Goals, Game	7	Three times

Individual

Most Seasons	1	Several players
Most Games, Career	84	Rob Zamuner
Most Goals, Career	42	Brian Bradley
Most Assists, Career	44	Brian Bradley
Most Points, Career	86	Brian Bradley
Most PIM, Career	111	Marc Bureau
Most Shutouts, Career	1	Pat Jablonski
Longest Consecutive Games Streak	84	Rob Zamuner
Most Goals, Season	42	Brian Bradley (1992-93)
Most Assists, Season	44	Brian Bradley (1992-93)
Most Points, Season	86	Brian Bradley (1992-93)
Most PIM, Season	154	Mike Hartman (1992-93)
Most Shutouts, Season	1	Pat Jablonski (1992-93)
Most Points, Defenseman Season	39	Shawn Chambers (1992-93)
Most Points, Center, Season	86	Brian Bradley (1992-93)
Most Points, Right Wing, Season	56	John Tucker (1992-93)
Most Points, Left Wing, Season	51	Chris Kontos (1992-93)
Most Points, Rookie, Season	43	Rob Zamuner (1992-93)
Most Goals, Game	4	Chris Kontos (Oct. 7/92)
Most Assists, Game	4	Joe Reekie (Oct. 7/92) Marc Bureau (Dec. 16/92)
Most Points, Game	6	Doug Crossman (Nov. 11/92)

Rightwinger Danton Cole was a valuable member of the Lightning's penalty-killing unit.

General Managers' History
Phil Esposito, 1992-93 to date.

Coaching History
Terry Crisp, 1992-93 to date.

Captains' History
No captain, 1992-93.

All-time Record vs. Other Clubs

Regular Season

	At Home							On Road							Total					
	GP	W	L	T	GF	GA	PTS	GP	W	L	T	GF	GA	PTS	GP	W	L	T	GF	GA	PTS
Boston	1	0	0	1	3	3	1	1	0	1	0	3	5	0	2	0	1	1	6	8	1
Buffalo	1	0	1	0	1	3	0	1	0	1	0	4	5	0	2	0	2	0	5	8	0
Calgary	2	1	1	0	10	9	2	1	0	1	0	2	3	0	3	1	2	0	12	12	2
Chicago	3	1	2	0	10	12	2	4	0	2	2	9	15	2	7	1	4	2	19	27	4
Detroit	4	1	3	0	17	30	2	3	0	3	0	9	18	0	7	1	6	0	26	48	2
Edmonton	2	2	0	0	9	2	4	2	0	2	0	4	6	0	4	2	2	0	13	8	4
Hartford	1	0	1	0	3	4	0	1	0	1	0	3	0	2	2	0	2	0	4	7	0
Los Angeles	1	0	1	0	2	5	0	2	2	0	0	9	5	4	3	2	1	0	11	10	4
Minnesota	4	0	3	1	5	11	1	3	1	2	0	9	11	2	7	1	5	1	14	22	3
Montreal	1	1	0	0	3	1	2	1	0	1	0	3	4	0	2	1	1	0	6	5	2
New Jersey	1	0	1	0	0	2	0	1	0	1	0	3	9	0	2	0	2	0	3	11	0
NY Islanders	1	0	1	0	1	6	0	1	1	0	0	6	5	2	2	1	1	0	7	11	2
NY Rangers	1	0	1	0	4	5	0	2	1	1	0	10	7	2	3	1	2	0	14	12	2
Ottawa	1	1	0	0	1	0	2	1	1	0	0	3	2	2	2	2	0	0	4	2	4
Philadelphia	1	1	0	0	4	1	2	1	0	1	0	2	6	0	2	1	1	0	6	7	2
Pittsburgh	1	0	1	0	4	5	0	1	0	1	1	3	3	1	2	0	2	1	7	8	1
Quebec	2	1	1	0	5	7	2	1	0	1	0	3	4	0	3	1	2	0	8	11	2
St. Louis	4	1	2	1	13	15	3	3	1	2	0	9	11	2	7	2	4	1	22	26	5
San Jose	2	1	1	0	6	3	2	2	0	0	10	8	4	4	3	1	0	16	11	6
Toronto	4	1	3	0	8	16	2	5	1	4	0	11	23	2	9	2	7	0	19	39	4
Vancouver	1	0	1	0	3	5	0	2	0	2	0	11	0	3	0	3	0	5	16	0
Washington	1	0	1	0	3	5	0	1	0	0	1	2	2	1	2	0	1	1	5	7	1
Winnipeg	2	0	2	0	7	10	0	2	0	1	1	6	6	2	4	1	3	0	13	16	2
Totals	**42**	**12**	**27**	**3**	**122**	**160**	**27**	**42**	**11**	**27**	**4**	**123**	**172**	**26**	**84**	**23**	**54**	**7**	**245**	**332**	**53**

1992-93 Results

	Home				Away	
Oct. 7	Chicago	7-3	Oct. 10	Minnesota	1-2
20	Edmonton	6-1	11	Chicago	4-4
22	Toronto	2-5	13	St. Louis	2-1
24	Quebec	3-2	15	Toronto	3-5
30	San Jose	1-2	16	Buffalo	4-5
Nov. 1	Pittsburgh	4-5	27	Quebec	3-4
3	St. Louis	6-4	28	Montreal	3-4
11	Detroit	6-4	Nov. 6	Washington	2-2
13	Ottawa	1-0	9	NY Islanders	6-5
14	Calgary	3-5	9	NY Rangers	5-1
17	Winnipeg	5-6	21	St. Louis	2-4
19	Minnesota	1-4	23	Detroit	5-10
Dec. 5	Detroit	7-9	24	Toronto	3-2
7	NY Islanders	1-6	27	Calgary	2-3
11	NY Rangers	4-5	28	Edmonton	3-4
12	Edmonton	3-1	Dec. 9	NY Rangers	5-6
18	New Jersey	0-2	15	Los Angeles	3-2
20	Philadelphia	4-1	16	San Jose	5-4
Jan. 16	St. Louis	3-5	22	Boston	3-5
17	Washington	3-5	23	Hartford	1-3
19	Minnesota	2-4	31	Chicago	0-5
21	Toronto	1-6	Jan. 2	Edmonton	1-2
23	San Jose	5-1	4	Vancouver	0-7
24	Minnesota	2-2	6	Los Angeles	6-3
28	St. Louis	2-4	9	Minnesota	4-6
Feb. 9	Toronto	3-1	11	Toronto	2-4
11	Minnesota	0-1	13	Detroit	3-5
14	Boston	3-3	30	Minnesota	4-3
20	Quebec	2-5	Feb. 1	San Jose	5-4
22	Los Angeles	2-5	3	Vancouver	2-4
25	Chicago	1-5	17	Detroit	1-3
Mar. 3	Montreal	3-1	19	Toronto	1-4
6	Calgary	7-4	27	Pittsburgh*	3-3
9	Winnipeg	2-4	Mar.12	Toronto	2-8
16	Hartford	3-4	14	Winnipeg*	1-3
18	Toronto	2-4	21	Chicago	2-3
20	Buffalo*	1-3	23	New Jersey	3-9
27	Detroit	3-8	25	Ottawa	3-2
Apr. 1	Vancouver	3-5	Apr. 11	Philadelphia*	2-6
6	St. Louis	2-2	11	Chicago*	3-3
8	Detroit	1-9	13	Winnipeg	5-3
10	Chicago*	2-4	15	St. Louis	5-6

*Denotes afternoon game

Entry Draft
Selections 1993-92

1993
Pick

3 Chris Gratton
29 Tyler Moss
55 Allan Egeland
81 Marian Kacir
107 Ryan Brown
133 Kiley Hill
159 Mathieu Raby
185 Ryan Nauss
211 Alexandre Laporte
237 Brett Duncan
263 Mark Szoke

1992
Pick

1 Roman Hamrlik
26 Drew Bannister
49 Brent Gretzky
74 Aaron Gavey
97 Brantt Myhres
122 Martin Tanguay
145 Derek Wilkinson
170 Dennis Maxwell
193 Andrew Kemper
218 Marc Tardif
241 Tom MacDonald

Brian Bradley holds the Lightning's career and single-season scoring records after an 86-point effort in the franchise's debut season.

Coach

CRISP, TERRY
Coach, Tampa Bay Lightning. Born in Parry Sound, Ont., May 28, 1943.

After a two-year absence, Terry Crisp returned to the NHL's coaching ranks to become the first coach of the Tampa Bay Lightning. Crisp, who won two Stanley Cups as a member of the Philadelphia Flyers, played 11 years in the NHL for the Bruins, Blues, Islanders and Flyers. After retiring in 1976, he joined the Flyers' organization as an assistant coach, serving two terms before leaving to coach the OHL's Sault Ste. Marie Greyhounds. With the Greyhounds, Crisp won three regular-season crowns and twice earned the nod as the league's coach of the year. In 1985, Crisp accepted a coaching position with the Calgary Flames' top AHL affiliate in Moncton and spent two seasons with the Golden Flames before being elevated to the head coaching position with their parent club. Crisp led Calgary to their best-ever finish in 1988-89, winning 54 games and capturing the franchise's first Stanley Cup championship after a six-game final series win over the Montreal Canadiens. After being released by the Flames, Crisp joined the Canadian National Team program as an assistant coach and was with the club when Team Canada won the silver medal at the 1992 Olympics.

Coaching Record

Season	Team	Games	Regular Season				Playoffs				
			W	L	T	%	Games	W	L	T	%
1979-80	S.S. Marie (OHL)	68	22	45	1	.331	....	....	....	....	....
1980-81	S.S. Marie (OHL)	68	47	19	2	.706	19	8	7	4	.526
1981-82	S.S. Marie (OHL)	68	40	25	3	.610	13	4	6	3	.423
1982-83	S.S. Marie (OHL)	70	48	21	1	.693	16	7	6	3	.531
1983-84	S.S. Marie (OHL)	70	38	28	4	.571	16	8	4	4	.625
1984-85	S.S. Marie (OHL)	66	54	11	1	.826	16	12	2	2	.813
1985-86	Moncton (AHL)	80	34	34	12	.500	10	5	5	0	.500
1986-87	Moncton (AHL)	80	43	31	6	.575	6	2	4	0	.333
1987-88	**Calgary (NHL)**	**80**	**48**	**23**	**9**	**.656**	**9**	**4**	**5**	**0**	**.444**
1988-89	Calgary (NHL)	80	54	17	9	.731	22	16	6	0	.727*
1989-90	Calgary (NHL)	80	42	23	15	.619	6	2	4	0	.333
1992-93	Tampa Bay (NHL)	84	23	54	7	.315	....	....	....	....	....
	NHL Totals	**324**	**167**	**117**	**40**	**.577**	**37**	**22**	**15**	**0**	**.595**

* Stanley Cup win.

Club Directory

ThunderDome

501 East Kennedy Boulevard
Suite 175
Tampa, FL 33602
Phone **813/229-2658**
FAX 813/229-3350

Capacity: 28,000

Lightning Partners, Ltd

General Partner	Lightning Partners, Inc.
Limited Partners	Lightning International, Inc.
	Tokyo Tower Development Co., Ltd
	Nippon Meat Packers, Inc.
	John Chase
	Equity Resources Group of Indian River County, Inc.
	James Murphy
	Tampa Bay Hockey Group Partners, Ltd.
Board of Directors	Yoshio Nakamura, Chairman, Phil Esposito, David LeFevre, Fukusaboro Maeda, Dr. Fujio Matsuda, Mushao Miyake, Chris Phillips, Reece Smith, Jr.

Executive Staff

President	Yoshio Nakamura
Governor	David LeFevre
General Manager and Alternate Governor	Phil Esposito
Executive Vice President and Alternate Governor	Chris Phillips
Executive Vice President and Alternate Governor	Mel Lowell

Hockey Operations

President, Tampa Bay Lightning Hockey Club	Phil Esposito
Director of Hockey Operations	Tony Esposito
Counsel	Henry Lee Paul – Lazzara, Laskey, Polli & Paul, D.A.
Head Coach	Terry Crisp
Assistant Coach	Wayne Cashman, Danny Gare
Special Assignment Scout	Don Murdoch
Scouting Staff	Angelo Bumbacco, Jacques Campeau, Jake Goertzen, Doug Macauley, Richard Rose, Jonathan Sparrow, Luke Williams
Head Trainer	Larry Ness
Equipment Manager	Jocko Cayer
Assistant Trainer	John Forristall
Strength and Conditioning	Chris Reichert
Director of Team Services	Carrie Esposito
Administrative Assistant	Teresa P. Huffam
Administrative Assistant	Stacey Fricker
Ice System Supervisors	Michael Wall, Tim Friedenberger

Finance

Chief Financial Officer	Mark Anderson
Accounting Manager	Vincent Ascanio
Accounting Assistant	Irene Canino
Administrative Assistant	Evelyn Hicks

Communications

Vice President/Communications	Gerry Helper
Media Relations Manager	Barry Hanrahan
Publications Manager	Becky Cashman
Communications Assistant	Carrie Schuldt
Receptionist	Cheryll Pricher, Tracy Wolfe

Marketing and Sales

Vice President/Sales and Marketing	Steve Donner
Director of Sales	Paul D'Aiuto
Senior Account Executive	Jon Swensson
Marketing Assistant	Marlene Eskine
Director of Fan Services	Steve Woznick
Director of Merchandising	Kevin L. Murphy
Manager/Lightning Locker	Dan Cohen
Assistant Manager/Lightning Locker	Gene Canon

Ticket Operations

Director of Ticket Operations	Jeff Morander
Box Office Manager	Karen MacKenzie
Ticket Office Representatives	James Ward
Season Ticket Service Manager	Steve Ross
Group Sales Manager	Bill Makris, Ray Mihara
Senior Sales Representative	Mike Eagan, Don Gore
Sales Representatives	Keith Brennan, Missy Davis, Nigel Kirwan

Medical Staff

Team Physician	Dr. David Leffers
Team Dentist	Dr. Joseph Spoto

Television and Radio

Television Stations	Sunshine Network, WTOG-TV 44 & Lightning Television Network
Broadcasters	John Kelly and Bobby Taylor
Radio Station	WFNS 910 AM
Broadcasters	John Kelly and Larry Hirsch

Team Information

Home Arena	Thunder Dome
Seating Capacity	28,000
Rink Dimensions	200 feet by 85 feet
Team Colors	Black, Blue, Silver and White
Training Camp Site	Lakeland Civic Center, Lakeland, Florida

Game Night Staff

Team Photographer	Jonathan Hayt
Off-ice Officials	Jim Galluzzi, Ron Brace, Gerry Dollmont, Ralph Emery, Rich Galipault, Mark Losier, Tony Mancuso, Mike Rees, Bill Shapiro, Dave Walkowiak, Rich Wasilewski, Dan Zabel

Toronto Maple Leafs

1992-93 Results: 44w-29L-11T 99PTS. Third, Norris Division

Selke Trophy recipient Doug Gilmour set Maple Leaf franchise records for assists (95) and points (127) during the 1992-93 season.

Schedule

Home

Oct.
Thur. 7 Dallas
Sat. 9 Chicago
Wed. 13 Washington
Fri. 15 Detroit
Tues. 19 Hartford

Nov. Wed. 3 Florida
Sat. 6 Philadelphia
Sat. 13 Chicago
Mon. 15 Edmonton
Sat. 27 Boston
Mon. 29 Buffalo

Dec. Wed. 1 St Louis
Sat. 4 NY Rangers
Wed. 8 Winnipeg
Sat. 11 Calgary
Wed. 15 Anaheim
Sat. 18 Los Angeles
Wed. 22 San Jose

Jan. Sat. 1 Los Angeles
Tues. 4 Tampa Bay
(at Hamilton)
Thur. 6 Ottawa
Sat. 8 Vancouver
Thur. 13 Dallas
Tues. 18 Anaheim
Wed. 26 NY Islanders
Sat. 29 Pittsburgh

Feb. Sat. 5 Detroit
Mon. 7 Tampa Bay
Tues. 15 Detroit
Thur. 17 New Jersey
Sat. 19 Edmonton
Sat. 26 Montreal

Mar. Mon. 7 St Louis
Wed. 9 Dallas
Sat. 12 Winnipeg
Wed. 16 Vancouver
Fri. 18 St Louis
Sun. 20 Calgary*
Thur. 24 San Jose
Sat. 26 Quebec

Apr. Sun. 10 Winnipeg
Tues. 12 Chicago

Away

Oct.
Sun. 10 Philadelphia
Sat. 16 Detroit
Thur. 21 Florida
Sat. 23 Tampa Bay
Thur. 28 Chicago
Sat. 30 Montreal

Nov. Mon. 1 Dallas
Thur. 4 Detroit
Tues. 9 San Jose
Thur. 11 St Louis
Wed. 17 Anaheim
Thur. 18 Los Angeles
Sat. 20 Edmonton
Mon. 22 Vancouver
Wed. 24 Calgary

Dec. Thur. 2 St Louis
Sun. 12 Winnipeg
Fri. 17 NY Islanders
Thur. 23 New Jersey
Mon. 27 Chicago
Wed. 29 Dallas

Jan. Sun. 2 Buffalo
Mon. 10 Boston
Tues. 11 Washington
Sat. 15 Winnipeg
Wed. 19 Hartford

Feb. Tues. 1 St Louis
Fri. 11 Winnipeg
Sat. 12 Calgary
Mon. 21 Los Angeles*
Wed. 23 Edmonton
Mon. 28 Ottawa

Mar. Fri. 4 Detroit
Sat. 5 Quebec
Thur. 10 Pittsburgh
Wed. 23 Florida
(at Hamilton)
Mon. 28 Vancouver
Thur. 31 San Jose

Apr. Sat. 2 Anaheim
Tues. 5 Dallas
Fri. 8 NY Rangers
Thur. 14 Chicago

* Denotes afternoon game.

Home Starting Times:
Weeknights . . . . 7:35 p.m.
Saturdays . . . . 8:05 p.m.
Sundays . . . . 7:05 p.m.
Except Sun. Mar. 20 . . . . 1:35 p.m.
Sun. Apr. 10 . . . . 8:05 p.m.

Franchise date: November 22, 1917

CENTRAL DIVISION

77th NHL Season

WESTERN CONFERENCE

Year-by-Year Record

Season	GP	Home W	Home L	Home T	Road W	Road L	Road T	Overall W	Overall L	Overall T	GF	GA	Pts.	Finished	Playoff Result
1992-93	84	25	11	6	19	18	5	44	29	11	288	241	99	3rd, Norris Div.	Lost Conf. Championship
1991-92	80	21	16	3	9	27	4	30	43	7	234	294	67	5th, Norris Div.	Out of Playoffs
1990-91	80	15	21	4	8	25	7	23	46	11	241	318	57	5th, Norris Div.	Out of Playoffs
1989-90	80	24	14	2	14	24	2	38	38	4	337	358	80	3rd, Norris Div.	Lost Div. Semi-Final
1988-89	80	15	20	5	13	26	1	28	46	6	259	342	62	5th, Norris Div.	Out of Playoffs
1987-88	80	14	20	6	7	29	4	21	49	10	273	345	52	4th, Norris Div.	Lost Div. Semi-Final
1986-87	80	22	14	4	10	28	2	32	42	6	286	319	70	4th, Norris Div.	Lost Div. Final
1985-86	80	16	21	3	9	27	4	25	48	7	311	386	57	4th, Norris Div.	Lost Div. Final
1984-85	80	10	28	2	10	24	6	20	52	8	253	358	48	5th, Norris Div.	Out of Playoffs
1983-84	80	17	16	7	9	29	2	26	45	9	303	387	61	5th, Norris Div.	Out of Playoffs
1982-83	80	20	15	5	8	25	7	28	40	12	293	330	68	3rd, Norris Div.	Lost Div. Semi-Final
1981-82	80	12	20	8	8	24	8	20	44	16	298	380	56	5th, Norris Div.	Out of Playoffs
1980-81	80	14	21	5	14	16	10	28	37	15	322	367	71	5th, Adams Div.	Lost Prelim. Round
1979-80	80	17	19	4	18	21	1	35	40	5	304	327	75	4th, Adams Div.	Lost Prelim. Round
1978-79	80	20	12	8	14	21	5	34	33	13	267	252	81	3rd, Adams Div.	Lost Quarter-Final
1977-78	80	21	13	6	20	16	4	41	29	10	271	237	92	3rd, Adams Div.	Lost Semi-Final
1976-77	80	18	13	9	15	19	6	33	32	15	301	285	81	3rd, Adams Div.	Lost Quarter-Final
1975-76	80	23	12	5	11	19	10	34	31	15	294	276	83	3rd, Adams Div.	Lost Quarter-Final
1974-75	80	19	12	9	12	21	7	31	33	16	280	309	78	3rd, Adams Div.	Lost Quarter-Final
1973-74	78	21	11	7	14	16	9	35	27	16	274	230	86	4th, East Div.	Lost Quarter-Final
1972-73	78	20	12	7	7	29	3	27	41	10	247	279	64	6th, East Div.	Out of Playoffs
1971-72	78	21	11	7	12	20	7	33	31	14	209	208	80	4th, East Div.	Lost Quarter-Final
1970-71	78	24	9	6	13	24	2	37	33	8	248	211	82	4th, East Div.	Lost Quarter-Final
1969-70	76	18	13	7	11	21	6	29	34	13	222	242	71	6th, East Div.	Out of Playoffs
1968-69	76	20	8	10	15	18	5	35	26	15	234	217	85	4th, East Div.	Lost Quarter-Final
1967-68	74	24	9	4	9	22	6	33	31	10	209	176	76	5th, East Div.	Out of Playoffs
1966-67	70	21	8	6	11	19	5	**32**	**27**	**11**	**204**	**211**	**75**	**3rd,**	**Won Stanley Cup**
1965-66	70	22	9	4	12	16	7	34	25	11	208	187	79	4th,	Lost Semi-Final
1964-65	70	17	15	3	13	11	11	30	26	14	204	173	74	4th,	Lost Semi-Final
1963-64	70	22	7	6	11	18	6	**33**	**25**	**12**	**192**	**172**	**78**	**3rd,**	**Won Stanley Cup**
1962-63	70	21	8	6	14	15	6	**35**	**23**	**12**	**221**	**180**	**82**	**1st,**	**Won Stanley Cup**
1961-62	70	25	5	5	12	17	6	**37**	**22**	**11**	**232**	**180**	**85**	**2nd,**	**Won Stanley Cup**
1960-61	70	21	6	8	18	13	4	39	19	12	234	176	90	2nd,	Lost Semi-Final
1959-60	70	20	9	6	15	17	3	35	26	9	199	195	79	2nd,	Lost Final
1958-59	70	17	13	5	10	19	6	27	32	11	189	201	65	4th,	Lost Final
1957-58	70	12	16	7	9	22	4	21	38	11	192	226	53	6th,	Out of Playoffs
1956-57	70	12	16	7	9	18	8	21	34	15	174	192	57	5th,	Out of Playoffs
1955-56	70	19	10	6	5	23	7	24	33	13	153	181	61	4th,	Lost Semi-Final
1954-55	70	14	10	11	10	14	11	24	24	22	147	135	70	3rd,	Lost Semi-Final
1953-54	70	22	6	7	10	18	7	32	24	14	152	131	78	3rd,	Lost Semi-Final
1952-53	70	17	12	6	10	18	7	27	30	13	156	167	67	5th,	Out of Playoffs
1951-52	70	17	10	8	12	15	8	29	25	16	168	157	74	3rd,	Lost Semi-Final
1950-51	70	22	8	5	19	8	8	**41**	**16**	**13**	**212**	**138**	**95**	**2nd,**	**Won Stanley Cup**
1949-50	70	18	9	8	13	18	4	31	27	12	176	173	74	3rd,	Lost Semi-Final
1948-49	60	12	8	10	10	17	3	**22**	**25**	**13**	**147**	**161**	**57**	**4th,**	**Won Stanley Cup**
1947-48	60	22	3	5	10	12	8	**32**	**15**	**13**	**182**	**143**	**77**	**1st,**	**Won Stanley Cup**
1946-47	60	20	8	2	11	11	8	**31**	**19**	**10**	**209**	**172**	**72**	**2nd,**	**Won Stanley Cup**
1945-46	50	10	13	2	9	11	5	19	24	7	174	185	45	5th,	Out of Playoffs
1944-45	50	13	9	3	11	13	1	**24**	**22**	**4**	**183**	**161**	**52**	**3rd,**	**Won Stanley Cup**
1943-44	50	13	11	1	10	12	3	23	23	4	214	174	50	3rd,	Lost Semi-Final
1942-43	50	17	6	2	5	13	7	22	19	9	198	159	53	3rd,	Lost Semi-Final
1941-42	48	18	6	0	9	12	3	**27**	**18**	**3**	**158**	**136**	**57**	**2nd,**	**Won Stanley Cup**
1940-41	48	16	5	3	12	9	3	28	14	6	145	99	62	2nd,	Lost Semi-Final
1939-40	48	13	8	3	12	9	3	25	17	6	134	110	56	3rd,	Lost Final
1938-39	48	13	8	3	6	12	6	19	20	9	114	107	47	3rd,	Lost Final
1937-38	48	13	6	5	11	9	4	24	15	9	151	127	57	1st, Cdn. Div.	Lost Final
1936-37	48	14	9	1	8	12	4	22	21	5	119	115	49	3rd, Cdn. Div.	Lost Quarter-Final
1935-36	48	15	4	5	8	15	1	23	19	6	126	106	52	2nd, Cdn. Div.	Lost Final
1934-35	48	16	6	2	14	8	2	30	14	4	157	111	64	1st, Cdn. Div.	Lost Final
1933-34	48	19	2	3	7	11	6	26	13	9	174	119	61	1st, Cdn. Div.	Lost Semi-Final
1932-33	48	16	4	4	8	14	2	24	18	6	119	111	54	1st, Cdn. Div.	Lost Final
1931-32	48	17	4	3	6	14	4	**23**	**18**	**7**	**155**	**127**	**53**	**2nd, Cdn. Div.**	**Won Stanley Cup**
1930-31	44	15	4	3	7	9	6	22	13	9	118	99	53	2nd, Cdn. Div.	Lost Quarter-Final
1929-30	44	10	8	4	7	13	2	17	21	6	116	124	40	4th, Cdn. Div.	Out of Playoffs
1928-29	44	15	5	2	6	13	3	21	18	5	85	69	47	3rd, Cdn. Div.	Lost Semi-Final
1927-28	44	9	8	5	9	10	3	18	18	8	89	88	44	4th, Cdn. Div.	Out of Playoffs
1926-27*	44	10	10	2	5	14	3	15	24	5	79	94	35	5th, Cdn. Div.	Out of Playoffs
1925-26	36	11	5	2	1	16	1	12	21	3	92	114	27	6th,	Out of Playoffs
1924-25	30	10	5	0	9	6	0	19	11	0	90	84	38	2nd,	Lost NHL S-Final
1923-24	24	7	5	0	3	9	0	10	14	0	59	85	20	3rd,	Out of Playoffs
1922-23	24	10	1	1	3	9	0	13	10	1	82	88	27	3rd,	Out of Playoffs
1921-22	24	8	4	0	5	6	1	**13**	**10**	**1**	**98**	**97**	**27**	**2nd,**	**Won Stanley Cup**
1920-21	24	9	3	0	6	6	0	15	9	0	105	100	30	2nd and 1st***	Lost NHL Final
1919-20**	24	8	4	0	4	8	0	12	12	0	119	106	24	3rd and 2nd***	Lost NHL Final
1918-19	18	5	4	0	0	9	0	5	13	0	64	92	10	3rd and 3rd***	Out of Playoffs
1917-18	22	10	1	0	3	8	0	**13**	**9**	**0**	**108**	**109**	**26**	**2nd and 1st*****	**Won Stanley Cup**

* Name changed from St. Patricks to Maple Leafs.   ** Name changed from Arenas to St. Patricks.
*** Season played in two halves with no combined standing at end.

1993-94 Player Personnel

FORWARDS	HT	WT	S	Place of Birth	Date	1992-93 Club
ANDERSON, Glenn	6-1	190	L	Vancouver, B.C.	10/2/60	Toronto
ANDREWS, Jeff	6-4	196	L	Lindsay, Ont.	5/10/75	North Bay
ANDREYCHUK, Dave	6-3	225	R	Hamilton, Ont.	9/29/63	Buffalo-Toronto
AUGUSTA, Patrik	5-10	169	L	Jihlava, Czech.	11/13/69	St. John's
BAUMGARTNER, Ken	6-1	200	L	Flin Flon, Man.	3/11/66	Toronto
BERG, Bill	6-1	198	L	St. Catharines, Ont.	10/21/67	NY Islanders-Toronto
BORSCHEVSKY, Nikolai	5-9	180	L	Tomsk, USSR	1/12/65	Toronto
CHEBATOR, Rob	6-0	170	L	Arlington, MA	12/1/70	U. of New Hampshire
CHERNOMAZ, Rich	5-8	185	R	Selkirk, Man.	9/1/63	Salt Lake
CHITARONI, Terry	5-11	200	R	Haileybury, Ont.	9/12/72	St. John's-Baltimore
CLARK, Wendel	5-11	194	L	Kelvington, Sask.	10/25/66	Toronto
CONVERY, Brandon	6-0	180	R	Kingston, Ont.	2/4/74	Sud.-N. Falls-St. John's
CULLEN, John	5-10	187	R	Puslinch, Ont.	8/2/64	Hartford-Toronto
EASTWOOD, Michael	6-2	190	R	Ottawa, Ont.	7/1/67	St. John's-Toronto
FERGUSON, Kyle	6-3	215	R	Toronto, Ont.	8/12/73	Michigan Tech U.
FOLIGNO, Mike	6-2	195	L	Sudbury, Ont.	1/29/59	Toronto
GILMOUR, Doug	5-11	165	L	Kingston, Ont.	6/25/63	Toronto
HAKANSSON, Mikael	6-1	176	L	Stockholm, Sweden	3/31/74	Djurgarden
HENDRICKSON, Darby	6-0	175	L	Richfield, MA	8/28/72	U. of Minnesota
KELLEY, Jonathan	6-1	180	R	Brighton, MA	6/25/73	Princeton U.
KRUSHELNYSKI, Mike	6-2	200	L	Montreal, Que.	4/27/60	Toronto
KUCHARCIK, Tomas	6-2	200	L	Mlada Boleslav, Czech.	10/5/70	Dukla Jihlava
KUDASHOV, Alexei	6-0	180	R	Elektrostal, USSR	7/21/71	Soviet Wings
KUZMINSKY, Alex.	5-11	175	L	Kiev, Ukraine	12/7/72	Brantford
LACROIX, Eric	6-1	200	L	Montreal, Que.	7/15/71	St. John's
LAROSE, Guy	5-9	175	L	Hull, Que.	8/31/67	Toronto-St. John's
MALLGRAVE, Matt	6-0	180	R	Washington, DC	5/3/70	Harvard U.
MANDERVILLE, Kent	6-3	200	L	Edmonton, Alta.	4/12/71	St. John's-Toronto
MARSHALL, Grant	6-1	185	R	Mississauga, Ont.	6/9/73	Ott.(OHL)-Nmkt.-St. John's
McCARTHY, Joe	6-3	190	L	Bangor, ME	11/17/70	U. of Vermont
McINTYRE, Robb	6-0	180	L	Royal Oak, MI	4/27/72	Ferris St.
McLLWAIN, Dave	6-0	190	L	Seaforth, Ont.	6/9/67	Toronto
McRAE, Ken	6-1	195	R	Winchester, Ont.	4/23/68	Toronto-St. John's
NEDVED, Zdenek	5-11	179	L	Pzkladno, Czech.	3/5/75	Sudbury
OSBORNE, Mark	6-2	205	L	Toronto, Ont.	8/13/61	Toronto
PEARSON, Rob	6-1	180	R	Oshawa, Ont.	3/8/71	Toronto
PERREAULT, Yanic	5-11	182	L	Sherbrooke, Que.	4/4/71	St. John's
PERRY, Jeff	6-0	192	L	Sarnia, Ont.	4/12/71	St. John's-Brantford
PROCHAZKA, Martin	5-11	176	R	Slany, Czech.	3/3/72	Poldi Kladno
SACCO, David	6-1	190	R	Malden, MA	7/31/70	Boston U.
STIVER, Dan	6-0	185	R	Chicoutimi, Que.	9/14/71	U. of Michigan
TOMBERLIN, Justin	6-0	191	L	Grand Rapids, MN	11/15/70	U. of Maine
VANDENBUSSCHE, R.	5-11	184	R	Simcoe, Ont.	2/28/73	Nmkt.-Guelph-St. John's
VINCENT, Paul	6-4	200	L	Utica, NY	1/4/75	Cushing Academy
WILSON, Landon	6-2	202	R	St. Louis, MO	3/13/75	Dubuque Jr. A
ZEZEL, Peter	5-9	200	L	Toronto, Ont.	4/22/65	Toronto
DEFENSEMEN						
BEREHOWSKY, Drake	6-1	211	R	Toronto, Ont.	1/3/72	Toronto-St. John's
CROWLEY, Ted	6-2	190	R	Concord, MA	5/3/70	St. John's
DEMPSEY, Nathan	6-0	160	R	Spruce Grove, Alta.	7/14/74	Regina
ELLETT, Dave	6-1	200	L	Cleveland, OH	3/30/64	Toronto
GILL, Todd	6-1	185	L	Brockville, Ont.	11/9/65	Toronto
GRONVALL, Janne	6-3	187	L	Rauma, Finland	7/17/73	Tappara
HUNT, Curtis	6-0	195	L	N. Battleford, Sask.	1/28/67	St. John's
JONSSON, Kenny	6-3	187	L	Angelholm, Sweden	10/6/74	Rogle
LAPIN, Mikhail	6-2	190	L	Moscow, Russia	5/12/75	U. of Western Michigan
LEFEBVRE, Sylvain	6-2	204	L	Richmond, Que.	10/14/67	Toronto
LEHOUX, Guy	5-11	205	L	Disraeli, Que.	10/19/71	St. John's-Brantford
MACOUN, Jamie	6-2	197	L	Newmarket, Ont.	8/17/61	Toronto
MALONE, Scott	6-0	180	L	Boston, MA	1/16/71	U. of New Hampshire
MARTIN, Matt	6-3	190	L	Hamden, CT	4/30/71	U. of Maine-St. John's
McMURTRY, Chris	6-4	185	L	Stoney Creek, Ont.	7/13/74	Guelph
MILLER, Brad	6-4	220	L	Edmonton, Alta.	7/23/69	New Haven-St. John's
MIRONOV, Dmitri	6-2	195	R	Moscow, Russia	12/25/65	Toronto
RAITER, Mark	6-4	220	R	Calgary, Alta.	1/27/73	Saskatoon
ROUSE, Bob	6-1	210	R	Surrey, B.C.	6/18/64	Toronto
SIMONOV, Sergei	6-1	183	L	Saratov, USSR	5/20/74	Saratov
SNELL, Chris	5-11	200	L	Regina, Sask.	5/12/71	Rochester

GOALTENDERS	HT	WT	C	Place of Birth	Date	1992-93 Club
BRUMBY, David	6-0	170	L	Victoria, B.C.	5/21/75	Tri-City
POTVIN, Felix	6-0	185	L	Montreal, Que.	6/23/71	Toronto-St. John's
RACINE, Bruce	6-0	178	L	Cornwall, Ont.	8/9/66	Muskegon
RHODES, Damian	6-0	170	L	St. Paul, MN	5/28/69	St. John's

General Managers' History

Conn Smythe, 1927-28 to 1956-57; Hap Day, 1957-58; George "Punch" Imlach, 1958-59 to 1968-69; Jim Gregory, 1969-70 to 1978-79; Punch Imlach, 1979-80 to 1980-81; Punch Imlach and Gerry McNamara, 1981-82; Gerry McNamara, 1982-83 to 1987-88; Gord Stellick, 1988-89; Floyd Smith, 1989-90 to 1990-91; Cliff Fletcher, 1991-92 to date.

Coaching History

Conn Smythe, 1927-28 to 1929-30; Conn Smythe and Art Duncan, 1930-31; Art Duncan and Dick Irvin, 1931-32; Dick Irvin, 1932-33 to 1939-40; Hap Day, 1940-41 to 1949-50; Joe Primeau, 1950-51 to 1952-53; "King" Clancy, 1953-54 to 1955-56; Howie Meeker, 1956-57; Billy Reay, 1957-58; Billy Reay and "Punch" Imlach, 1958-59; "Punch" Imlach, 1959-60 to 1968-69; John McLellan, 1969-70 to 1970-71; John McLellan and "King" Clancy, 1971-72; John McLellan, 1972-73; Red Kelly, 1973-74 to 1976-77; Roger Neilson, 1977-78 to 1978-79; Floyd Smith, Dick Duff and "Punch" Imlach, 1979-80; "Punch" Imlach, Joe Crozier and Mike Nykoluk, 1980-81; Mike Nykoluk, 1981-82 to 1983-84; Dan Maloney, 1984-85 to 1985-86; John Brophy, 1986-87 to 1987-88; John Brophy and George Armstrong, 1988-89; Doug Carpenter, 1989-90; Doug Carpenter and Tom Watt, 1990-91; Tom Watt, 1991-92; Pat Burns, 1992-93 to date.

1992-93 Scoring

Regular Season

Pos	#	Player	Team	GP	G	A	Pts	+/-	PIM	PP	SH	GW	GT	S	%
C	93	Doug Gilmour	TOR	83	32	95	127	32	100	15	3	2	2	211	15.2
L	14	Dave Andreychuk	BUF	52	29	32	61	8-	48	20	0	2	0	171	17.0
			TOR	31	25	13	38	12	8	12	0	2	1	139	18.0
			TOTAL	83	54	45	99	4	56	32	0	4	1	310	17.4
R	16	Nikolai Borschevsky	TOR	78	34	40	74	33	28	12	0	4	2	204	16.7
R	9	Glenn Anderson	TOR	76	22	43	65	19	117	11	0	3	0	161	13.7
C	19	John Cullen	HFD	19	5	4	9	15-	58	3	0	0	0	38	13.2
			TOR	47	13	28	41	8-	53	10	0	1	0	86	15.1
			TOTAL	66	18	32	50	23-	111	13	0	1	0	124	14.5
D	23	Todd Gill	TOR	69	11	32	43	4	66	5	0	2	0	113	9.7
D	4	Dave Ellett	TOR	70	6	34	40	19	46	4	0	1	0	186	3.2
C	26	Mike Krushelnyski	TOR	84	19	20	39	3	62	6	2	3	0	130	14.6
L	17	Wendel Clark	TOR	66	17	22	39	2	193	2	0	5	1	146	11.6
R	12	Rob Pearson	TOR	78	23	14	37	2-	211	8	0	3	0	164	14.0
C	25	Peter Zezel	TOR	70	12	23	35	0	24	0	0	4	0	102	11.8
D	15	Dimitri Mironov	TOR	59	7	24	31	1-	40	4	0	1	1	105	6.7
L	21	Mark Osborne	TOR	76	12	14	26	7-	89	0	2	2	0	110	10.9
L	10	Bill Berg	NYI	22	6	3	9	4	49	0	2	0	0	30	20.0
			TOR	58	7	8	15	1-	54	0	1	2	0	83	8.4
			TOTAL	80	13	11	24	3	103	0	3	2	0	113	11.5
D	55*	Drake Berehowsky	TOR	41	4	15	19	1	61	1	0	1	0	41	9.8
D	34	Jamie Macoun	TOR	77	4	15	19	3	55	2	0	1	0	114	3.5
C	7	Dave McLlwain	TOR	66	14	4	18	18-	30	1	1	3	0	85	16.5
R	71	Mike Foligno	TOR	55	13	5	18	2	84	5	0	2	1	95	13.7
D	3	Bob Rouse	TOR	82	3	11	14	7	130	0	1	1	0	78	3.8
D	2	Sylvain Lefebvre	TOR	81	2	12	14	8	90	0	0	0	0	81	2.5
L	24	Joe Sacco	TOR	23	4	4	8	4-	8	0	0	0	0	38	10.5
C	32*	Mike Eastwood	TOR	12	1	6	7	2-	21	0	0	0	0	11	9.1
L	18*	Kent Manderville	TOR	18	1	1	2	9-	17	0	0	1	0	15	6.7
D	8	Bob McGill	TOR	19	1	0	1	5	34	0	0	0	0	8	12.5
D	22	Ken Baumgartner	TOR	63	1	0	1	11-	155	0	0	0	0	23	4.3
G	1	Daren Puppa	BUF	24	0	1	1	0	0	0	0	0	0	0	.0
			TOR	8	0	0	0	0	0	0	0	0	0	0	.0
			TOTAL	32	0	1	1	0	0	0	0	0	0	0	.0
G	29*	Felix Potvin	TOR	48	0	1	1	0	4	0	0	0	0	0	.0
C	36	Ken McRae	TOR	2	0	0	0	1-	2	0	0	0	0	3	.0
G	30	Rick Wamsley	TOR	3	0	0	0	0	0	0	0	0	0	0	.0
C	37*	Dave Tomlinson	TOR	3	0	0	0	0	2	0	0	0	0	1	.0
C	11	Guy Larose	TOR	9	0	0	0	3-	8	0	0	0	0	8	.0
D	28	Darryl Shannon	TOR	16	0	0	0	5-	11	0	0	0	0	10	.0

Goaltending

No.	Goaltender	GPI	Mins	Avg	W	L	T	EN	SO	GA	SA	S%
1	Daren Puppa	8	479	2.25	6	2	0	1	2	18	232	.922
29	*Felix Potvin	48	2781	2.50	25	15	7	3	2	116	1286	.910
31	Grant Fuhr	29	1665	3.14	13	9	4	1	1	87	826	.895
30	Rick Wamsley	3	160	5.63	0	3	0	0	0	15	91	.835
	Totals	**84**	**5097**	**2.84**	**44**	**29**	**11**	**5**	**5**	**241**	**2440**	**.901**

Playoffs

Pos	#	Player	Team	GP	G	A	Pts	+/-	PIM	PP	SH	GW	GT	S	%
C	93	Doug Gilmour	TOR	21	10	25	35	16	30	4	0	1	1	51	19.6
L	17	Wendel Clark	TOR	21	10	10	20	15	51	2	0	1	0	71	14.1
L	14	Dave Andreychuk	TOR	21	12	7	19	6	35	4	0	3	0	72	16.7
R	9	Glenn Anderson	TOR	21	7	11	18	7	31	0	0	2	1	46	15.2
D	4	Dave Ellett	TOR	21	4	8	12	4	8	2	0	0	0	62	6.5
D	3	Bob Rouse	TOR	21	3	8	11	3	29	1	0	1	0	33	9.1
D	23	Todd Gill	TOR	21	1	10	11	1	26	0	0	0	0	41	2.4
C	26	Mike Krushelnyski	TOR	16	3	7	10	4	8	1	0	0	0	29	10.3
R	16	Nikolai Borschevsky	TOR	16	2	7	9	2	0	0	0	1	1	30	6.7
R	71	Mike Foligno	TOR	18	2	6	8	9	42	1	0	2	1	36	5.6
D	2	Sylvain Lefebvre	TOR	21	3	3	6	9	20	0	0	0	0	27	11.1
D	34	Jamie Macoun	TOR	21	0	6	6	7	36	0	0	0	0	43	.0
C	19	John Cullen	TOR	12	2	3	5	1-	0	1	0	0	0	10	20.0
R	12	Rob Pearson	TOR	14	2	2	4	9-	31	0	0	0	0	24	8.3
C	25	Peter Zezel	TOR	20	2	1	3	6-	6	0	0	0	0	40	5.0
C	32*	Mike Eastwood	TOR	10	1	2	3	1-	8	0	0	0	0	6	16.7
D	15	Dimitri Mironov	TOR	14	1	2	3	4-	2	1	0	0	0	11	9.1
L	21	Mark Osborne	TOR	19	1	1	2	6-	16	0	0	0	0	34	2.9
L	10	Bill Berg	TOR	21	1	1	2	1	18	0	0	0	0	30	3.3
L	22	Ken Baumgartner	TOR	7	1	0	1	1	0	0	0	0	0	2	50.0
L	18*	Kent Manderville	TOR	18	1	0	1	1-	8	0	0	0	0	17	5.9
G	1	Daren Puppa	TOR	1	0	0	0	0	2	0	0	0	0	0	.0
C	7	Dave McLlwain	TOR	4	0	0	0	4-	0	0	0	0	0	3	.0
G	29*	Felix Potvin	TOR	21	0	0	0	0	6	0	0	0	0	0	.0

Goaltending

No.	Goaltender	GPI	Mins	Avg	W	L	EN	SO	GA	SA	S%
29	*Felix Potvin	21	1308	2.84	11	10	0	1	62	636	.903
1	Daren Puppa	1	20	3.00	0	0	0	0	1	7	.857
	Totals	**21**	**1332**	**2.84**	**11**	**10**	**0**	**1**	**63**	**643**	**.902**

Club Records

Team

(Figures in brackets for season records are games played; records for fewest points, wins, ties, losses, goals, goals against are for 70 or more games)

Most Points	99	1992-93 (84)
Most Wins	44	1992-93 (84)
Most Ties	22	1954-55 (70)
Most Losses	52	1984-85 (80)
Most Goals	337	1989-90 (80)
Most Goals Against	387	1983-84 (80)
Fewest Points	48	1984-85 (80)
Fewest Wins	20	1981-82, 1984-85 (80)
Fewest Ties	4	1989-90 (80)
Fewest Losses	16	1950-51 (70)
Fewest Goals	147	1954-55 (70)
Fewest Goals Against	*131	1953-54 (70)
Longest Winning Streak		
Over-all	9	Jan. 30-Feb. 28/25
Home	9	Nov. 11-Dec. 26/53
Away	7	Nov. 14-Dec. 15/40; Dec. 4/60-Jan. 5/61
Longest Undefeated Streak		
Over-all	11	Oct. 15-Nov. 8/50 (8 wins, 3 ties)
Home	18	Nov. 28/33-Mar. 10/34 (15 wins, 3 ties); Oct. 31/53-Jan. 23/54 (16 wins, 2 ties)
Away	9	Nov. 30/47-Jan. 11/48 (4 wins, 5 ties)
Longest Losing Streak		
Over-all	10	Jan. 15-Feb. 8/67
Home	7	Nov. 10-Dec. 5/84; Jan. 26-Feb. 25/85
Away	11	Feb. 20/-Apr. 1/88
Longest Winless Streak		
Over-all	15	Dec. 26/87-Jan. 25/88 (11 losses, 4 ties)
Home	11	Dec. 19/87-Jan. 25/88 (7 losses, 4 ties)
Away	18	Oct. 6/82-Jan. 5/83 (13 losses, 5 ties)
Most Shutouts, Season	13	1953-54 (70)
Most PIM, Season	2,419	1989-90 (80)
Most Goals, Game	14	Mar. 16/57 (NYR 1 at Tor. 14)

Individual

Most Seasons	21	George Armstrong
Most Games	1,187	George Armstrong
Most Goals, Career	389	Darryl Sittler
Most Assists, Career	620	Borje Salming
Most Points, Career	916	Darryl Sittler (389 goals, 527 assists)
Most PIM, Career	1,670	Dave Williams
Most Shutouts, Career	62	Turk Broda
Longest Consecutive Games Streak	486	Tim Horton (Feb. 11/61-Feb. 4/68)
Most Goals, Season	54	Rick Vaive (1981-82)
Most Assists, Season	95	Doug Gilmour (1992-93)
Most Points, Season	127	Doug Gilmour (1992-93) (32 goals, 95 assists)
Most PIM, Season	351	Dave Williams (1977-78)
Most Points, Defenseman Season	79	Ian Turnbull (1976-77) (22 goals, 57 assists)
Most Points, Center Season	127	Doug Gilmour (1992-93) (32 goals, 95 assists)
Most Points, Right Wing, Season	97	Wilf Paiement (1980-81) (40 goals, 57 assists)
Most Points, Left Wing, Season	94	Vince Damphousse (1989-90) (33 goals, 61 assists)
Most Points, Rookie, Season	66	Peter Ihnacak (1982-83) (28 goals, 38 assists)
Most Shutouts, Season	13	Harry Lumley (1953-54)
Most Goals, Game	6	Corb Denneny (Jan. 26/21); Darryl Sittler (Feb. 7/76)
Most Assists,Game	6	Babe Pratt (Jan. 8/44); Doug Gilmour (Feb. 13/93)
Most Points, Game	*10	Darryl Sittler (Feb. 7/76)

* NHL Record.

Captains' History

Hap Day, 1927-28 to 1936-37; Charlie Conacher, 1937-38; Red Horner, 1938-39, 1939-40; Syl Apps, 1940-41 to 1942-43; Bob Davidson, 1943-44, 1944-45; Syl Apps, 1945-46 to 1947-48; Ted Kennedy, 1948-49 to 1954-55; Sid Smith, 1955-56; Ted Kennedy, Jim Thomson, 1956-57; George Armstrong, 1957-58 to 1968-69; Dave Keon, 1969-70 to 1974-75; Darryl Sittler, 1975-76 to 1980-81; Rick Vaive, 1981-82 to 1985-86; no captain, 1986-87 to 1988-89; Rob Ramage, 1989-90 to 1990-91; Wendel Clark, 1991-92 to date.

Retired Numbers

5	Bill Barilko	1946-1951
6	Irvin "Ace" Bailey	1927-1934

1992-93 Results

Home			Away		
Oct. 7	Washington	5-6	Oct. 10	Calgary	2-3
15	Tampa Bay	5-3	11	Edmonton	3-3
17	Chicago	4-3	22	Tampa Bay	5-2
18	Minnesota	1-5	30	Detroit	1-7
20	Ottawa	5-3	Nov. 5	Chicago	0-1
24	San Jose	5-1	9	Ottawa	3-1
28	Buffalo	4-4	14	Boston	4-1
31	Detroit	3-1	17	Quebec	1-3
Nov. 7	Pittsburgh	4-2	19	San Jose	2-0
16	St. Louis	2-2	21	Los Angeles	4-6
24	Tampa Bay	2-3	Dec. 1	New Jersey	3-8
26	Quebec	4-5	3	Chicago	3-4
28	Los Angeles	3-2	6	NY Rangers	0-6
Dec. 5	Chicago	2-2	15	Minnesota	5-6
9	Detroit	5-3	20	Buffalo	4-5
11	Calgary	3-6	22	Detroit	4-4
19	Ottawa	5-1	27	St. Louis	6-3
26	Detroit	1-5	29	NY Islanders	3-2
Jan. 2	St. Louis	2-2	31	Pittsburgh	3-3
6	Vancouver	2-5	Jan. 4	Detroit	4-2
8	San Jose	5-1	9	Montreal	5-4
11	Tampa Bay	4-2	17	Chicago	3-5
13	St. Louis	4-3	19	St. Louis	5-1
16	Chicago	3-5	21	Tampa Bay	6-1
23	Montreal	4-0	Feb. 1	St. Louis	1-1
26	Minnesota	1-2	9	Tampa Bay	1-3
30	NY Rangers	3-1	14	Minnesota	6-5
Feb. 3	NY Islanders	2-3	22	Vancouver	8-1
11	Vancouver	5-2	25	San Jose	5-0
13	Minnesota	6-1	27	Los Angeles	5-2
17	Calgary	4-2	Mar. 5	Detroit	1-5
19	Tampa Bay	4-1	9	Washington	1-3
20	Boston	4-4	15	Quebec	2-4
Mar. 3	Minnesota	3-1	18	Tampa Bay	4-2
6	Winnipeg	4-2	23	Winnipeg	5-4
10	Hartford	5-3	25	Minnesota	3-3
12	Tampa Bay	8-2	27	Edmonton	6-2
20	Edmonton	4-2	28	Calgary	4-0
31	Los Angeles	5-5	Apr. 4	Philadelphia	0-4
Apr. 3	New Jersey	1-0	8	Winnipeg	3-5
10	Philadelphia	0-4	11	Hartford	4-2
13	St. Louis	2-1	15	Chicago	2-3

*Denotes afternoon game

All-time Record vs. Other Clubs

Regular Season

	At Home							On Road							Total						
	GP	W	L	T	GF	GA	PTS	GP	W	L	T	GF	GA	PTS	GP	W	L	T	GF	GA	PTS
Boston	279	146	86	47	949	726	339	279	81	151	47	746	924	209	558	227	237	94	1695	1650	548
Buffalo	48	18	22	8	152	180	44	49	16	31	2	142	209	34	97	34	53	10	294	389	78
Calgary	38	15	16	7	151	153	37	40	12	24	4	135	181	28	78	27	40	11	286	334	65
Chicago	296	158	87	51	1021	761	367	296	106	151	39	767	916	251	592	264	238	90	1788	1677	618
Detroit	298	159	95	44	993	785	362	299	98	157	44	727	891	240	597	257	252	88	1720	1676	602
Edmonton	22	9	12	1	91	111	19	22	4	13	5	75	115	13	44	13	25	6	166	226	32
Hartford	21	7	12	2	75	88	16	21	6	12	3	71	99	15	42	13	24	5	146	187	31
Los Angeles	53	29	14	10	223	176	68	54	16	31	7	152	197	39	107	45	45	17	375	373	107
Minnesota	83	40	29	14	303	270	94	81	30	41	10	271	316	70	164	70	70	24	574	586	164
Montreal	314	160	110	44	953	821	364	313	83	190	40	772	1114	206	627	243	300	84	1725	1935	570
New Jersey	32	23	6	3	149	106	49	31	10	12	9	101	117	29	63	33	18	12	250	223	78
NY Islanders	39	16	20	3	131	146	35	37	13	21	3	115	160	29	76	29	41	6	246	306	64
NY Rangers	266	151	77	38	917	688	340	267	101	110	56	782	816	258	533	252	187	94	1699	1504	598
Ottawa	2	2	0	0	10	4	4	1	1	0	0	3	1	2	3	3	0	0	13	5	6
Philadelphia	51	18	20	13	175	174	49	51	10	33	8	118	207	28	102	28	53	21	293	381	77
Pittsburgh	52	25	17	10	216	174	60	53	19	28	6	172	221	44	105	44	45	16	388	395	104
Quebec	22	10	10	2	78	96	22	22	5	12	5	72	90	15	44	15	22	7	150	186	37
St. Louis	80	50	20	10	312	234	110	80	22	47	11	229	282	55	160	72	67	21	541	516	165
San Jose	3	3	0	0	14	3	6	4	3	1	0	11	5	6	7	6	1	0	25	8	12
Tampa Bay	5	4	1	0	23	11	8	4	3	1	0	16	8	6	9	7	2	0	39	19	14
Vancouver	45	19	17	9	171	158	47	43	13	23	7	140	149	33	88	32	40	16	311	307	80
Washington	33	18	11	4	157	121	40	34	11	21	2	94	131	24	67	29	32	6	251	252	64
Winnipeg	24	8	15	1	90	109	17	24	8	13	3	102	117	19	48	16	28	4	192	226	36
Defunct Clubs	232	158	53	21	860	515	337	233	84	120	29	607	745	197	465	242	173	50	1467	1260	534
Totals	**2338**	**1246**	**750**	**342**	**8214**	**6610**	**2834**	**2338**	**755**	**1243**	**340**	**6420**	**8011**	**1850**	**4676**	**2001**	**1993**	**682**	**14634**	**14621**	**4684**

Playoffs

	Series	W	L	GP	W	L	T	GF	GA	Last Mtg.	Round	Result
Boston	13	8	5	62	31	30	1	150	153	1974	QF	L 0-4
**Calgary	1	1	0	2	2	0	0	9	5	1979	PR	W 2-0
Chicago	7	5	2	25	15	9	1	76	57	1986	DSF	W 3-0
Detroit	23	12	11	117	58	59	0	311	321	1993	DSF	W 4-3
Los Angeles	3	2	1	12	7	5	0	41	31	1993	CF	L 3-4
Minnesota	2	0	2	7	1	6	0	26	35	1983	DSF	L 1-3
Montreal	13	6	7	67	28	39	0	148	203	1979	QF	L 0-4
NY Islanders	2	1	1	10	4	6	0	20	33	1981	PR	L 0-3
NY Rangers	8	3	5	35	16	19	0	86	86	1971	QF	L 2-4
Philadelphia	3	0	3	17	5	12	0	47	67	1977	QF	L 2-4
Pittsburgh	2	2	0	6	4	2	0	21	13	1977	PR	W 2-1
St. Louis	4	2	2	25	12	13	0	75	67	1993	DF	W 4-3
Defunct	4	3	1	10	5	4	1	20	16			
Totals	**85**	**45**	**40**	**395**	**188**	**204**	**3**	**1030**	**1087**			

Playoff Results 1993-89

Year	Round	Opponent	Result	GF	GA
1993	CF	Los Angeles	L 3-4	23	22
	DF	St. Louis	W 4-3	22	11
	DSF	Detroit	W 4-3	24	30
1990	DSF	St. Louis	L 1-4	16	20
1988	DSF	Detroit	L 2-4	20	32

Abbreviations: Round: F – Final; **CF** – conference final; **DF** – division final; **DSF** – division semi-final; **SF** – semi-final; **QF** – quarter-final; **PR** – preliminary round. **GA** – goals against; **GF** – goals for.

Entry Draft Selections 1993-79

1993
Pick
12 Kenny Jonsson
19 Landon Wilson
123 Zdenek Nedved
149 Paul Vincent
175 Jeff Andrews
201 David Brumby
253 Kyle Ferguson
279 Mikhail Lapin

1992
Pick
8 Brandon Convery
23 Grant Marshall
77 Nikolai Borschevsky
95 Mark Raiter
101 Janne Gronvall
106 Chris Deruiter
125 Mikael Hakansson
149 Patrik Augusta
173 Ryan Vandenbussche
197 Wayne Clarke
221 Sergei Simonov
245 Nathan Dempsey

1991
Pick
47 Yanic Perreault
69 Terry Chitaroni
102 Alexei Kudashov
113 Jeff Perry
120 Alexander Kuzminsky
135 Martin Prochazka
160 Dmitri Mironov
164 Robb McIntyre
167 Tomas Kucharcik
179 Guy Lehoux
201 Gary Miller
223 Jonathan Kelley
245 Chris O'Rourke

1990
Pick
10 Drake Berehowsky
31 Felix Potvin
73 Darby Hendrickson
80 Greg Walters
115 Alexander Godynyuk
136 Eric Lacroix
157 Dan Stiver
178 Robert Horyna
199 Rob Chebator
220 Scott Malone
241 Nick Vachon

1989
Pick
3 Scott Thornton
12 Rob Pearson
21 Steve Bancroft
66 Matt Martin
96 Keith Carney
108 David Burke
125 Michael Doers
129 Keith Merkler
150 Derek Langille
171 Jeffrey St. Laurent
192 Justin Tomberlin
213 Mike Jackson
234 Steve Chartrand

1988
Pick
6 Scott Pearson
27 Tie Domi
48 Peter Ing
69 Ted Crowley
88 Leonard Esau
132 Matt Mallgrave
153 Roger Elvenas
174 Mike Delay
195 David Sacco
216 Mike Gregorio
237 Peter DeBoer

1987
Pick
7 Luke Richardson
28 Daniel Marois
49 John McIntyre
71 Joe Sacco
91 Mike Eastwood
112 Damian Rhodes
133 Trevor Jobe
154 Chris Jensen
175 Brian Blad
196 Ron Bernacci
217 Ken Alexander
238 Alex Weinrich

1986
Pick
6 Vincent Damphousse
36 Darryl Shannon
48 Sean Boland
69 Kent Hulst
90 Scott Taylor
111 Stephane Giguere
132 Danny Hie
153 Stephen Brennan
174 Brian Bellefeuille
195 Sean Davidson
216 Mark Holick
237 Brian Hoard

1985
Pick
1 Wendel Clark
22 Ken Spangler
43 Dave Thomlinson
64 Greg Vey
85 Jeff Serowik
106 Jiri Latal
127 Tim Bean
148 Andy Donahue
169 Todd Whittemore
190 Bob Reynolds
211 Tim Armstrong
232 Mitch Murphy

1984
Pick
4 Al Iafrate
25 Todd Gill
67 Jeff Reese
88 Jack Capuano
109 Joseph Fabian
130 Joe McInnis
151 Derek Laxdal
172 Dan Turner
192 David Buckley
213 Mikael Wurst
233 Peter Slanina

1983
Pick
7 Russ Courtnall
28 Jeff Jackson
48 Allan Bester
83 Dan Hodgson
128 Cam Plante
148 Paul Bifano
168 Cliff Albrecht
184 Greg Rolston
188 Brian Ross
208 Mike Tomlak
228 Ron Choules

1982
Pick
3 Gary Nylund
24 Gary Leeman
25 Peter Ihnacak
45 Ken Wregget
73 Vladimir Ruzicka
87 Eduard Uvira
99 Sylvain Charland
108 Ron Dreger
115 Craig Kales
129 Dom Campedelli
139 Jeff Triano
171 Miroslav Ihnacak
192 Leigh Verstraete
213 Tim Loven
234 Jim Appleby

1981
Pick
6 Jim Benning
24 Gary Yaremchuk
55 Ernie Godden
90 Normand LeFrancois
102 Barry Brigley
132 Andrew Wright
153 Richard Turmel
174 Greg Barber
195 Marc Magnan

1980
Pick
25 Craig Muni
26 Bob McGill
43 Fred Boimistruck
74 Stewart Gavin
95 Hugh Larkin
116 Ron Dennis
137 Russ Adam
158 Fred Perlini
179 Darwin McCutcheon
200 Paul Higgins

1979
Pick
9 Laurie Boschman
51 Normand Aubin
72 Vincent Tremblay
93 Frank Nigro
114 Bill McCreary

Club Directory

Maple Leaf Gardens
60 Carlton Street
Toronto, Ontario M5B 1L1
Phone 416/977-1641
FAX 416/977-5364
Capacity: 15,642 (standing 200)

Board of Directors
Brian P. Bellmore, J. Donald Crump, Terence V. Kelly, Q.C., Ted Nikolaou,
W. Ron Pringle, Steve A. Stavro, George E. Whyte, Q.C.

Chairman of the Board and CEO	Steve A. Stavro
President, Chief Operating Officer and General Manager	Cliff Fletcher
Secretary-Treasurer	J. Donald Crump
Alternate Governors	Cliff Fletcher, Brian P. Bellmore
Assistant General Manager	Bill Watters
Special Consultant to the President	Darryl Sittler
Director of Business Operations and Communications	Bob Stellick
Head Coach	Pat Burns
Assistant Coach	Mike Kitchen
Assistant Coach	Mike Murphy
Goaltending Consultant	Rick Wamsley
Director of Scouting	Pierre Dorion
Director of Professional Development	Floyd Smith
Director of Pro Scouting	Tom Watt
Pro Scout	Dick Duff
Scouts	George Armstrong, Anders Hedberg, Peter Johnson, Garth Malarchuk, Dan Marr, Dick Bouchard, Jack Gardiner, Bob Johnson, Ernie Gare, Doug Woods
Public Relations Coordinator	Pat Park
Administrative Assistants	Mary Speck, Kristy Fletcher
Community Relations	Ellen Salnek
Executive Secretary to the President and G.M.	Shelley Usher
Public Relations Assistant	Casey VandenHeuvel
Head Athletic Therapist	Chris Broadhurst
Athletic Therapist	Brent Smith
Trainers	Brian Papineau, Jim Carey
Vice President of Building Operations	Brian Conacher
Director of Marketing	Bill Cluff
Controller	Ian Clarke
Assistant Controller	Paul Franck
Marketing Representatives	Denis Cordick, Chris Reed
Marketing Coordinator	Nancy McIlveen
Retail Operations Manager	Jeff Newman
Box Office Manager	Donna Henderson
Building Superintendent	Wayne Gillespie
Team Doctors	Dr. Michael Clarfield, Dr. Darrell Ogilvie-Harris, Dr. Leith Douglas, Dr. Michael Easterbrook, Dr. Simon McGrail
Team Dentist	Dr. Ernie Lewis
Team Psychologist	Robert Offenberger, Ph.D.
Head Off Ice Official	Joe Lamantia
AHL Affiliate	St. John's Maple Leafs

Coach

BURNS, PAT
Coach, Toronto Maple Leafs. Born in St-Henri, Que., April 4, 1952.

Pat Burns' opening season as coach of the Maple Leafs was a record-setting run by the franchise. Under Burns' guidance, Toronto established club records for most wins (44), points (99), home ice wins in one season (25), playoff victories in one season (11), and playoff games in one season (21). The Maple Leafs dramatic improvement of 32 points from the previous season was the highest single season turnaround in the club's 76 year history. For his efforts, he captured the Jack Adams Award as Coach of the Year for the second time after completing only his fifth NHL season. He becomes just the third multiple Jack Adams winner, joining Pat Quinn of the Canucks and Jacques Demers of the Canadiens. Burns also joins Quinn as the only two coaches to win the award with two different teams. Burns' efforts last season resulted in his third nomination for NHL Coach of the Year honours and he was also recognized by readers of the Hockey News as their choice for "Hockey News 1992-93 NHL Coach of the Year".

After for seasons behind the bench of the Montreal Canadiens, Pat Burns accepted a new challenge by assuming the head coaching duties of the Toronto Maple Leafs. A native of St-Henri, Que., Burns was the recipient of the Jack Adams Award in 1989, after taking the Canadiens to the Stanley Cup finals in his rookie season as an NHL coach. Burns had been coach of the QMJHL's Olympiques when he joined the Canadiens' organization as the head coach of the Sherbrooke Canadiens, the Habs' top farm team in the AHL. In addition to his other coaching responsibilities, Burns served as an assistant coach for the Canadian National Junior Team at the 1986 World Junior Championships.

Coaching Record

		Regular Season					Playoffs			
Season	Team	Games	W	L	T	%	Games	W	L	%
1983-84	Hull (QMJHL)	70	25	45	0	.357	....	....	....	....
1984-85	Hull (QMJHL)	68	33	34	1	.493	5	1	4	.200
1985-86	Hull (QMJHL)	72	54	18	0	.750	15	15	0	1.000
1986-87	Hull (QMJHL)	70	26	39	5	.407	8	4	4	.500
1987-88	Sherbrooke (AHL)	80	42	34	4	.550	6	2	4	.333
1988-89	Montreal (NHL)	80	53	18	9	.719	21	14	7	.667
1989-90	Montreal (NHL)	80	41	28	11	.581	11	5	6	.455
1990-91	Montreal (NHL)	80	39	30	11	.556	13	7	6	.538
1991-92	Montreal (NHL)	80	41	28	11	.581	11	4	7	.364
1992-93	Toronto (NHL)	84	44	29	11	.589	21	11	10	.524
	NHL Totals	404	218	133	53	.605	77	41	36	.532

General Manager

FLETCHER, CLIFF
President, General Manager and Chief Operating Officer, Toronto Maple Leafs. Born in Montreal, Que., August 16, 1935.

Cliff Fletcher joined the Maple Leafs on July 1, 1991 after 19 years with the Flames franchise. Fletcher's tenure with the Flames was highlighted by the club's 1989 Stanley Cup Championship, but their success was not limited to that championship. In the Flames' eleven seasons under Fletcher after the move from Atlanta to Calgary, the club won one Stanley Cup, two Presidents' Trophies (for top overall finish), two Campbell Conference Championships and three division titles.

A native of Montreal, Fletcher joined the Flames franchise in Atlanta in September, 1972. In the summer of 1980 he organized the successful transfer of the franchise to Calgary. He began his hockey career with the Montreal Junior Canadiens, where he served for 10 years as a scout for Sam Pollock. In 1967 he became the eastern Canada scout for the St. Louis Blues, and two seasons later was promoted to assistant general manager.

Vancouver Canucks

1992-93 Results: 46w-29L-9T 101PTS. First, Smythe Division

Year-by-Year Record

		Home			Road			Overall							
Season	GP	W	L	T	W	L	T	W	L	T	GF	GA	Pts.	Finished	Playoff Result
1992-93	84	27	11	4	19	18	5	46	29	9	346	278	101	1st, Smythe Div.	Lost Div. Final
1991-92	80	23	10	7	19	16	5	42	26	12	285	250	96	1st, Smythe Div.	Lost Div. Final
1990-91	80	18	17	5	10	26	4	28	43	9	243	315	65	4th, Smythe Div.	Lost Div. Semi-Final
1989-90	80	13	16	11	12	25	3	25	41	14	245	306	64	5th, Smythe Div.	Out of Playoffs
1988-89	80	19	15	6	14	24	2	33	39	8	251	253	74	4th, Smythe Div.	Lost Div. Semi-Final
1987-88	80	15	20	5	10	26	4	25	46	9	272	320	59	5th, Smythe Div.	Out of Playoffs
1986-87	80	17	19	4	12	24	4	29	43	8	282	314	66	5th, Smythe Div.	Out of Playoffs
1985-86	80	17	18	5	6	26	8	23	44	13	282	333	59	4th, Smythe Div.	Lost Div. Semi-Final
1984-85	80	15	21	4	10	25	5	25	46	9	284	401	59	5th, Smythe Div.	Out of Playoffs
1983-84	80	20	16	4	12	23	5	32	39	9	306	328	73	3rd, Smythe Div.	Lost Div. Semi-Final
1982-83	80	20	12	8	10	23	7	30	35	15	303	309	75	3rd, Smythe Div.	Lost Div. Semi-Final
1981-82	80	20	8	12	10	25	5	30	33	17	290	286	77	2nd, Smythe Div.	Lost Final
1980-81	80	17	12	11	11	20	9	28	32	20	289	301	76	3rd, Smythe Div.	Lost Prelim. Round
1979-80	80	14	17	9	13	20	7	27	37	16	256	281	70	3rd, Smythe Div.	Lost Prelim. Round
1978-79	80	15	18	7	10	24	6	25	42	13	217	291	63	2nd, Smythe Div.	Lost Prelim. Round
1977-78	80	13	15	12	7	28	5	20	43	17	239	320	57	3rd, Smythe Div.	Out of Playoffs
1976-77	80	13	21	6	12	21	7	25	42	13	235	294	63	4th, Smythe Div.	Out of Playoffs
1975-76	80	22	11	7	11	21	8	33	32	15	271	272	81	2nd, Smythe Div.	Lost Prelim. Round
1974-75	80	23	12	5	15	20	5	38	32	10	271	254	86	1st, Smythe Div.	Lost Quarter-Final
1973-74	78	14	18	7	10	25	4	24	43	11	224	296	59	7th, East Div.	Out of Playoffs
1972-73	78	17	18	4	5	29	5	22	47	9	233	339	53	7th, East Div.	Out of Playoffs
1971-72	78	14	20	5	6	30	3	20	50	8	203	297	48	7th, East Div.	Out of Playoffs
1970-71	78	17	18	4	7	28	4	24	46	8	229	296	56	6th, East Div.	Out of Playoffs

Schedule

Home	Away
Oct. Sat. 9 Calgary	**Oct.** Wed. 6 Los Angeles
Mon. 11 Edmonton*	Sat. 16 Edmonton
Tues. 19 Boston	Thur. 21 Calgary
Sun. 24 San Jose	Sat. 23 San Jose
Wed. 27 Washington	**Nov.** Tues. 2 NY Islanders
Sat. 30 Buffalo	Wed. 3 NY Rangers
Nov. Wed. 10 Los Angeles	Fri. 5 Washington
Sun. 14 Anaheim	Sun. 7 Philadelphia
Tues. 16 St Louis	Sat. 13 Calgary
Fri. 19 Anaheim	Fri. 26 Winnipeg
Mon. 22 Toronto	Sat. 27 Edmonton
Wed. 24 Detroit	**Dec.** Sat. 4 Quebec
Mon. 29 Chicago	Mon. 6 Montreal
Dec. Thur. 2 Philadelphia	Wed. 8 Hartford
Fri. 17 Winnipeg	Thur. 9 Boston
Sun. 19 Dallas*	Tues. 14 Calgary
Tues. 21 Edmonton	Wed. 15 Edmonton
Thur. 23 Calgary	Tues. 28 Los Angeles
(at Saskatoon)	**Jan.** Wed. 5 Ottawa
Fri. 31 San Jose	Sat. 8 Toronto
Jan. Sun. 2 Montreal*	Sun. 9 Buffalo
Wed. 12 Quebec	Sun. 16 Anaheim
Fri. 14 Ottawa	Mon. 24 Edmonton
Wed. 19 Calgary	(at Saskatoon)
Tues. 25 St Louis	**Feb.** Fri. 4 Anaheim
Thur. 27 Dallas	Tues. 8 Detroit
Sat. 29 New Jersey	Thur. 10 New Jersey
Mon. 31 Los Angeles	Sat. 12 Tampa Bay
Feb. Wed. 2 Chicago	Sun. 13 Florida
Sun. 6 Hartford*	Tues. 15 St Louis
Tues. 22 Calgary	Thur. 17 Chicago
Sat. 26 Tampa Bay	**Mar.** Thur. 3 St Louis
Mar. Tues. 1 Edmonton	Fri. 4 Dallas
Mon. 7 Florida	Fri. 11 Winnipeg
Wed. 9 NY Islanders	Sun. 13 Chicago*
Fri. 25 NY Rangers	Tues. 15 Detroit
Sun. 27 Los Angeles*	Wed. 16 Toronto
Mon. 28 Toronto	Sat. 19 Pittsburgh*
Wed. 30 Pittsburgh	Sun. 20 Dallas
Apr. Fri. 1 Winnipeg*	Wed. 23 Los Angeles
Tues. 5 Detroit	**Apr.** Sat. 2 San Jose
Thur. 7 San Jose	Sun. 10 San Jose
Sat. 9 Anaheim	Wed. 13 Anaheim

* Denotes afternoon game.

Home Starting Times:
Weeknights	7:35 p.m.
Saturdays	5:05 p.m.
Sundays and Holidays	7:05 p.m.
Matinees	2:05 p.m.
Except Fri. Apr. 1	5:05 p.m.

Franchise date: May 22, 1970

PACIFIC DIVISION

24th NHL Season

WESTERN CONFERENCE

Dana Murzyn was one of the Vancouver Canucks steadiest rearguards in 1992-93, compiling a plus/minus rating of +34.

1993-94 Player Personnel

FORWARDS	HT	WT	S	Place of Birth	Date	1992-93 Club
ADAMS, Greg	6-3	195	L	Nelson, B.C.	8/1/63	Vancouver
ANTOSKI, Shawn	6-4	240	L	Brantford, Ont.	3/25/70	Vancouver-Hamilton
BURE, Pavel	5-10	189	L	Moscow, USSR	3/31/71	Vancouver
COURTNALL, Geoff	6-1	195	L	Duncan, B.C.	8/18/62	Vancouver
CRAVEN, Murray	6-2	185	L	Medicine Hat, Alta.	7/20/64	Vancouver-Hartford
EISENHUT, Neil	6-1	190	R	Osoyoos, B.C.	2/9/67	Hamilton
HUNTER, Tim	6-2	202	R	Calgary, Alta.	9/10/60	Vancouver-Quebec
JACKSON, Dane	6-1	200	R	Castlegar, B.C.	5/17/70	Hamilton
KESA, Dan	6-0	208	R	Vancouver, B.C.	11/23/71	Hamilton
LINDEN, Trevor	6-4	205	R	Medicine Hat, Alta.	4/11/70	Vancouver
LONEY, Brian	6-2	190	R	Winnipeg, Man.	8/9/72	Red Deer-Hamilton
MAZUR, Jay	6-2	205	R	Hamilton, Ont.	1/22/65	Hamilton
MOGER, Sandy	6-3	210	R	Vernon, B.C.	3/21/69	Hamilton
MOMESSO, Sergio	6-3	215	L	Montreal, Que.	9/4/65	Vancouver
MORIN, Stephane	6-0	174	L	Montreal, Que.	3/27/69	Vancouver-Hamilton
NEDVED, Petr	6-3	185	L	Liberec, Czech.	12/9/71	Vancouver
ODJICK, Gino	6-3	210	L	Maniwaki, Que.	9/7/70	Vancouver
PECA, Mike	5-11	180	R	Toronto, Ont.	3/26/74	Ottawa-Hamilton
POLASEK, Libor	6-3	225	R	Vitkovice, Czech.	4/22/74	Hamilton
RONNING, Cliff	5-8	170	L	Burnaby, B.C.	10/1/65	Vancouver
STOJANOV, Alek	6-4	230	L	Windsor, Ont.	4/25/73	Newmarket-Hamilton
TORREL, Doug	6-2	200	R	Hibbing, MN	4/29/69	Hamilton
VALK, Garry	6-1	195	L	Edmonton, Alta.	11/27/67	Vancouver-Hamilton
WALTER, Ryan	6-0	200	L	Burnaby, B.C.	4/23/58	Vancouver
WARD, Dixon	6-0	192	R	Leduc, Alta.	9/23/68	Vancouver
WOODWARD, Rob	6-4	225	L	Evanston, IL	1/15/71	Michigan State

DEFENSEMEN	HT	WT	S	Place of Birth	Date	1992-93 Club
AUCOIN, Adrian	6-1	194	R	London, Ont.	7/3/73	Cdn. National
BABYCH, Dave	6-2	215	L	Edmonton, Alta.	5/23/61	Vancouver
CULLIMORE, Jassen	6-5	220	L	Simcoe, Ont.	12/4/72	Hamilton
DIDUCK, Gerald	6-2	207	R	Edmonton, Alta.	4/6/65	Vancouver
DIRK, Robert	6-4	210	L	Regina, Sask.	8/20/66	Vancouver
FILIPEK, Daryl	6-1	185	L	Acton, Ont.	11/13/70	Ferris State
LUMME, Jyrki	6-1	207	L	Tampere, Finland	7/16/66	Vancouver
MURZYN, Dana	6-2	200	L	Calgary, Alta.	12/9/66	Vancouver
NEUMEIER, Troy	6-2	195	L	Langenburg, Sask.	9/3/70	Hamilton
PLAVSIC, Adrien	6-1	200	L	Montreal, Que.	1/13/70	Vancouver
RATUSHNY, Dan	6-1	210	R	Nepean, Ont.	10/29/70	Fort Wayne-Vancouver
SLEGR, Jiri	6-1	205	L	Litvinov, Czech.	5/30/71	Vancouver-Hamilton
TULLY, Brent	6-3	190	R	Peterborough, Ont.	3/26/74	Peterborough
VONSTEFENELLI, Philip	6-1	198	L	Vancouver, B.C.	4/10/69	Hamilton
WILSON, Mike	6-4	180	L	Brampton, Ont.	2/26/75	Sudbury

GOALTENDERS	HT	WT	C	Place of Birth	Date	1992-93 Club
FITZSIMMONS, Jason	5-11	180	L	Regina, Sask.	6/3/71	Hamilton-Columbus
FOUNTAIN, Mike	6-1	176	L	North York, Ont.	1/26/72	Cdn. National
McLEAN, Kirk	6-0	180	L	Willowdale, Ont.	6/26/66	Vancouver
TKACHENKO, Serge	6-2	198	L	Kiev, Ukraine	6/6/71	Hamilton
WHITMORE, Kay	5-11	175	L	Sudbury, Ont.	4/10/67	Vancouver

General Managers' History

Normand Robert Poile, 1970-71 to 1972-73; Hal Laycoe, 1973-74; Phil Maloney, 1974-75 to 1976-77; Jake Milford, 1977-78 to 1981-82; Harry Neale, 1982-83 to 1984-85; Jack Gordon, 1985-86 to 1986-87; Pat Quinn, 1987-88 to date.

Coaching History

Hal Laycoe, 1970-71 to 1971-72; Vic Stasiuk, 1972-73; Bill McCreary and Phil Maloney, 1973-74; Phil Maloney, 1974-75 to 1975-76; Phil Maloney and Orland Kurtenbach, 1976-77; Orland Kurtenbach, 1977-78; Harry Neale, 1978-79 to 1980-81; Harry Neale and Roger Neilson, 1981-82; Roger Neilson 1982-83; Roger Neilson and Harry Neale, 1983-84; Harry Neale and Bill Laforge, 1984-85; Tom Watt, 1985-86, 1986-87; Bob McCammon, 1987-88 to 1989-90. Bob McCammon and Pat Quinn, 1990-91; Pat Quinn, 1991-92 to date.

Captains' History

Orland Kurtenbach, 1970-71 to 1973-74; no captain, 1974-75; Andre Boudrias, 1975-76; Chris Oddleifson, 1976-77; Don Lever, 1977-78; Don Lever, Kevin McCarthy, 1978-79; Kevin McCarthy, 1979-80 to 1981-82; Stan Smyl, 1982-83 to 1989-90; Dan Quinn, Doug Lidster and Trevor Linden, 1990-91; Trevor Linden, 1991-92 to date.

Retired Numbers

12	Stan Smyl	1978-1991

1992-93 Scoring

Regular Season

Pos	#	Player	Team	GP	G	A	Pts	+/-	PIM	PP	SH	GW	GT	S	%
L	10	Pavel Bure	VAN	83	60	50	110	35	69	13	7	9	0	407	14.7
C	7	Cliff Ronning	VAN	79	29	56	85	19	30	10	0	2	0	209	13.9
L	14	Geoff Courtnall	VAN	84	31	46	77	27	167	9	0	11	0	214	14.5
L	32	Murray Craven	HFD	67	25	42	67	4–	20	6	3	2	0	139	18.0
			VAN	10	0	10	10	3	12	0	0	0	0	12	.0
			TOTAL	77	25	52	77	1–	32	6	3	2	0	151	16.6
R	16	Trevor Linden	VAN	84	33	39	72	19	64	8	0	3	0	209	15.8
C	19	Petr Nedved	VAN	84	38	33	71	20	96	2	1	3	0	149	25.5
L	8	Greg Adams	VAN	53	25	31	56	31	14	6	1	3	0	124	20.2
R	17*	Dixon Ward	VAN	70	22	30	52	34	82	4	1	0	1	111	19.8
C	20	Anatoli Semenov	T.B.	13	2	3	5	5–	4	0	0	0	0	14	14.3
			VAN	62	10	34	44	21	28	3	2	1	0	88	11.4
			TOTAL	75	12	37	49	16	32	3	2	1	0	102	11.8
D	21	Jyrki Lumme	VAN	74	8	36	44	30	55	3	2	1	0	123	6.5
L	27	Sergio Momesso	VAN	84	18	20	38	11	200	4	0	1	0	146	12.3
R	25	Jim Sandlak	VAN	59	10	18	28	2	122	1	0	1	0	104	9.6
D	6	Adrien Plavsic	VAN	57	6	21	27	28	53	5	0	2	0	62	9.7
D	24*	Jiri Slegr	VAN	41	4	22	26	16	109	2	0	0	0	89	4.5
D	3	Doug Lidster	VAN	71	6	19	25	9	36	3	0	0	0	76	7.9
D	4	Gerald Diduck	VAN	80	6	14	20	32	171	0	1	0	0	92	6.5
D	44	Dave Babych	VAN	43	3	16	19	6	44	0	0	0	0	78	3.8
L	29	Gino Odjick	VAN	75	4	13	17	3	370	0	0	1	0	79	5.1
D	5	Dana Murzyn	VAN	79	5	11	16	34	196	0	0	2	0	82	6.1
C	15	Tom Fergus	VAN	36	5	9	14	1	20	1	1	0	1	29	17.2
L	23	Garry Valk	VAN	48	6	7	13	6	77	0	0	2	1	46	13.0
R	26	Tim Hunter	QUE	48	5	3	8	4–	94	0	0	0	0	28	17.9
			VAN	26	0	4	4	1	99	0	0	0	0	12	.0
			TOTAL	74	5	7	12	3–	193	0	0	0	0	40	12.5
D	22	Robert Dirk	VAN	69	4	8	12	25	150	0	0	2	0	41	9.8
C	9	Ryan Walter	VAN	25	3	0	3	2–	10	0	0	0	0	15	20.0
G	35	Kay Whitmore	VAN	31	0	3	3	0	0	0	0	0	0	0	.0
C	26	Stephane Morin	VAN	1	0	1	1	1–	0	0	0	0	0	3	.0
D	28*	Dan Ratushny	VAN	1	0	1	1	0	2	0	0	0	0	2	.0
G	1	Kirk McLean	VAN	54	0	1	1	0	16	0	0	0	0	0	.0
L	31*	Shawn Antoski	VAN	2	0	0	0	0	0	0	0	0	0	0	.0

Goaltending

No.	Goaltender	GPI	Mins	Avg	W	L	T	EN	SO	GA	SA	S%
35	Kay Whitmore	31	1817	3.10	18	8	4	0	1	94	858	.890
1	Kirk McLean	54	3261	3.39	28	21	5	0	3	184	1615	.886
	Totals	84	5087	3.28	46	29	9	0	4	278	2473	.888

Playoffs

Pos	#	Player	Team	GP	G	A	Pts	+/-	PIM	PP	SH	GW	GT	S	%
L	14	Geoff Courtnall	VAN	12	4	10	14	7	12	1	0	1	0	43	9.3
L	8	Greg Adams	VAN	12	7	6	13	1–	6	5	0	1	1	42	16.7
R	16	Trevor Linden	VAN	12	5	8	13	4	16	2	0	1	0	22	22.7
L	10	Pavel Bure	VAN	12	5	7	12	0	8	0	0	1	0	47	10.6
C	7	Cliff Ronning	VAN	12	2	9	11	8	6	0	0	0	0	35	5.7
L	32	Murray Craven	VAN	12	4	6	10	0	4	1	0	1	0	27	14.8
D	44	Dave Babych	VAN	12	2	5	7	2–	6	1	0	0	0	25	8.0
D	4	Gerald Diduck	VAN	12	2	4	6	1	12	0	0	0	0	17	23.5
D	5	Dana Murzyn	VAN	12	3	2	5	4	18	0	0	0	0	16	18.8
R	17*	Dixon Ward	VAN	9	2	3	5	1	0	0	0	0	0	12	16.7
C	19	Petr Nedved	VAN	12	3	2	5	2–	2	1	0	0	0	14	14.3
D	21	Jyrki Lumme	VAN	12	0	5	5	4	4	0	0	0	0	25	.0
R	25	Jim Sandlak	VAN	6	2	2	4	2–	4	0	0	0	0	11	18.2
C	20	Anatoli Semenov	VAN	12	1	3	4	1–	0	1	0	0	0	12	8.3
L	27	Sergio Momesso	VAN	12	3	0	3	1	30	0	0	1	0	13	23.1
D	24*	Jiri Slegr	VAN	5	0	3	3	0	4	0	0	0	0	6	.0
D	3	Doug Lidster	VAN	12	0	3	3	3	8	0	0	0	0	8	.0
G	1	Kirk McLean	VAN	12	0	3	3	0	2	0	0	0	0	0	.0
L	23	Garry Valk	VAN	7	0	1	1	3–	12	0	0	0	0	6	.0
L	29	Gino Odjick	VAN	1	0	0	0	0	0	0	0	0	0	0	.0
D	22	Robert Dirk	VAN	9	0	0	0	2–	6	0	0	0	0	8	.0
R	26	Tim Hunter	VAN	11	0	0	0	5–	26	0	0	0	0	8	.0

Goaltending

No.	Goaltender	GPI	Mins	Avg	W	L	EN	SO	GA	SA	S%
1	Kirk McLean	12	754	3.34	6	6	1	0	42	369	.886
	Totals	12	757	3.41	6	6	1	0	43	370	.884

Club Records

Team

(Figures in brackets for season records are games played; records for fewest points, wins, ties, losses, goals, goals against are for 70 or more games)

Most Points	101	1992-93 (84)
Most Wins	46	1992-93 (84)
Most Ties	20	1980-81 (80)
Most Losses	50	1971-72 (78)
Most Goals	346	1992-93 (84)
Most Goals Against	401	1984-85 (80)
Fewest Points	48	1971-72 (78)
Fewest Wins	20	1971-72 (78)
		1977-78 (80)
Fewest Ties	8	1970-71 (78)
		1971-72 (78)
		1986-87 (80)
		1988-89 (80)
Fewest Losses	26	1991-92 (80)
Fewest Goals	203	1971-72 (78)
Fewest Goals Against	250	1991-92 (80)

Longest Winning Streak

Over-all	7	Feb. 10-23/89
Home	9	Nov. 6-Dec. 9/92
Away	5	Jan. 14-25/92

Longest Undefeated Streak

Over-all	10	Mar. 5-25/77 (5 wins, 5 ties)
Home	18	Oct. 30/92-Jan. 18/93 (16 wins, 2 ties)
Away	5	Four times

Longest Losing Streak

Over-all	9	Four times
Home	6	Dec. 18/70-Jan. 20/71
		Nov. 3-18/78
Away	12	Nov. 28/81-Feb. 6/82

Longest Winless Streak

Over-all	13	Nov. 9-Dec. 7/73 (10 losses, 3 ties)
Home	11	Dec. 18/70-Feb. 6/71 (10 losses, 1 tie)
Away	20	Jan. 2/86-Apr. 2/86 (14 losses, 6 ties)

Most Shutouts, Season	8	1974-75 (80)
Most PIM, Season	2,326	1992-93 (84)
Most Goals, Game	11	Mar. 28/71 (Cal. 5 at Van. 11)
		Nov. 25/86 (L.A. 5 at Van. 11)
		Mar. 1/92 (Cal. 0 at Van. 11)

Individual

Most Seasons	13	Stan Smyl
Most Games	896	Stan Smyl
Most Goals, Career	262	Stan Smyl
Most Assists, Career	411	Stan Smyl
Most Points, Career	673	Stan Smyl (262 goals, 411 assists)
Most PIM, Career	1,668	Garth Butcher
Most Shutouts, Career	13	Kirk McLean
Longest Consecutive Games Streak	437	Don Lever (Oct. 7/72-Jan. 14/78)
Most Goals, Season	60	Pavel Bure (1992-93)
Most Assists, Season	62	André Boudrias (1974-75)
Most Points, Season	110	Pavel Bure (1992-93) (60 goals, 50 assists)
Most PIM, Season	370	Gino Odjick (1992-93)
Most Points, Defenseman, Season	63	Doug Lidster (1986-87) (12 goals, 51 assists)
Most Points, Center, Season	91	Patrik Sundstrom (1983-84) (38 goals, 53 assists)

Most Points, Right Wing, Season	110	Pavel Bure (1992-93) (60 goals, 50 assists)
Most Points, Left Wing, Season	81	Darcy Rota (1982-83) (42 goals, 39 assists)
Most Points, Rookie, Season	60	Ivan Hlinka (1981-82) (23 goals, 37 assists) Pavel Bure (1991-92) (34 goals, 26 assists)
Most Shutouts, Season	6	Gary Smith (1974-75)
Most Goals, Game	4	Several players
Most Assists, Game	6	Patrik Sundstrom (Feb. 29/84)
Most Points, Game	7	Patrik Sundstrom (Feb. 29/84)

All-time Record vs. Other Clubs

Regular Season

	At Home							On Road							Total						
	GP	W	L	T	GF	GA	PTS	GP	W	L	T	GF	GA	PTS	GP	W	L	T	GF	GA	PTS
Boston	43	13	22	8	144	183	34	42	3	35	4	93	192	10	85	16	57	12	237	375	44
Buffalo	43	21	12	10	165	140	52	44	14	22	8	127	159	36	87	35	34	18	292	299	88
Calgary	68	25	29	14	247	231	64	68	11	48	9	188	309	31	136	36	77	23	435	540	95
Chicago	50	23	15	12	155	143	58	49	12	32	5	115	185	29	99	35	47	17	270	328	87
Detroit	43	24	12	7	179	132	55	44	12	26	6	129	187	30	87	36	38	13	308	319	85
Edmonton	52	19	27	6	197	224	44	50	9	37	4	157	264	22	102	28	64	10	354	488	66
Hartford	22	9	7	6	80	62	24	21	8	9	4	75	72	20	43	17	16	10	155	134	44
Los Angeles	72	35	25	12	287	250	82	74	24	40	10	237	310	58	146	59	65	22	524	560	140
Minnesota	49	24	17	8	198	157	56	49	12	29	8	143	204	32	98	36	46	16	341	361	88
Montreal	42	7	27	8	105	169	22	44	8	34	2	117	222	18	86	15	61	10	222	391	40
New Jersey	40	23	6	11	154	115	57	40	17	17	6	134	123	40	80	40	23	17	288	238	97
NY Islanders	40	17	20	3	130	134	37	38	8	22	8	100	149	24	78	25	42	11	230	283	61
NY Rangers	44	11	30	3	142	182	25	46	7	34	5	114	209	19	90	18	64	8	256	391	44
Ottawa	1	1	0	0	4	1	2	1	1	0	0	3	0	2	2	2	0	0	7	1	4
Philadelphia	44	10	23	11	128	168	31	44	13	30	1	130	200	27	88	23	53	12	258	368	58
Pittsburgh	42	20	19	3	158	162	43	42	8	27	7	140	189	23	84	28	46	10	298	351	66
Quebec	21	10	7	4	89	85	24	22	10	8	4	67	64	24	43	20	15	8	156	149	48
St. Louis	50	22	23	5	158	157	49	49	14	28	7	149	195	35	99	36	51	12	307	352	84
San Jose	7	7	0	0	38	15	14	7	5	1	1	27	18	11	14	12	1	1	65	33	25
Tampa Bay	2	2	0	0	11	2	4	1	1	0	0	5	3	2	3	3	0	0	16	5	6
Toronto	43	23	13	7	149	140	53	45	17	19	9	158	171	43	88	40	32	16	307	311	96
Washington	31	15	12	4	107	99	34	32	11	17	4	101	108	26	63	26	29	8	208	207	60
Winnipeg	50	28	14	8	194	149	64	47	16	24	7	175	185	39	97	44	38	15	369	334	103
Defunct Clubs	19	14	3	2	82	48	30	19	10	8	1	71	68	21	38	24	11	3	153	116	51
Totals	**918**	**403**	**363**	**152**	**3301**	**3148**	**958**	**918**	**251**	**547**	**120**	**2755**	**3786**	**622**	**1836**	**654**	**910**	**272**	**6056**	**6934**	**1580**

Playoffs

	Series	W	L	GP	W	L	T	GF	GA	Last Mtg.	Round	Result
Buffalo	2	0	2	7	1	6	0	14	28	1981	PR	L 0-3
Calgary	4	1	3	18	8	10	0	57	62	1989	DSF	L 3-4
Chicago	1	1	0	5	4	1	0	18	13	1982	CF	W 4-1
Edmonton	2	0	2	9	2	7	0	20	35	1992	DF	L 2-4
Los Angeles	3	1	2	17	10	7	0	60	66	1993	DF	L 2-4
Montreal	1	0	1	5	1	4	0	9	20	1975	QF	L 1-4
NY Islanders	2	0	2	6	0	6	0	14	26	1982	F	L 0-4
Philadelphia	1	0	1	3	1	2	0	9	15	1979	PR	L 1-2
Winnipeg	2	2	0	13	8	5	0	50	34	1993	DSF	W 4-2
Totals	**18**	**5**	**13**	**83**	**33**	**50**	**0**	**251**	**299**			

Playoff Results 1993-89

Year	Round	Opponent	Result	GF	GA
1993	DF	Los Angeles	L 2-4	25	26
	DSF	Winnipeg	W 4-2	21	17
1992	DF	Edmonton	L 2-4	15	18
	DSF	Winnipeg	W 4-3	29	17
1991	DSF	Los Angeles	L 2-4	16	26
1989	DSF	Calgary	L 3-4	20	26

Abbreviations: Round: F – Final;
CF – conference final; **DF** – division final;
DSF – division semi-final; **SF** – semi-final;
QF – quarter-final; **PR** – preliminary round.
GA – goals against; **GF** – goals for.

1992-93 Results

	Home				Away	
Oct. 10	Edmonton	5-2	**Oct.** 6	Edmonton	5-4
12	Winnipeg	8-1	16	Winnipeg	6-2
25	Boston*	3-5	18	Chicago	1-3
28	Washington	4-3	20	Pittsburgh	1-5
30	Minnesota	2-3	22	Philadelphia	4-4
Nov. 4	Calgary	5-5	**Nov.** 2	Calgary	3-5
6	Ottawa	4-1	12	Los Angeles	4-7
8	Winnipeg*	6-1	14	San Jose	5-2
10	San Jose	6-2	18	Edmonton	2-4
16	Los Angeles	6-3	19	Calgary	3-4
21	Edmonton	9-0	25	Minnesota	4-2
23	Chicago	5-2	26	St. Louis	5-7
Dec. 3	Edmonton	4-1	28	Montreal	6-5
7	St. Louis	4-3	**Dec.** 16	Edmonton	2-4
9	San Jose	8-3	19	San Jose	6-3
13	Quebec	3-3	22	Los Angeles	6-2
18	San Jose	8-1	**Jan.** 2	San Jose	2-2
27	Montreal	5-2	6	Toronto	5-2
29	San Jose	7-5	8	Detroit	3-6
31	Los Angeles	4-0	9	NY Islanders	5-4
Jan. 4	Tampa Bay	7-0	11	NY Rangers	3-3
15	Buffalo	4-1	12	New Jersey	2-3
16	Hartford	8-3	21	Los Angeles	3-3
19	Pittsburgh	2-5	23	Minnesota*	3-3
27	Chicago	4-4	24	Chicago	2-6
30	Detroit	4-4	**Feb.** 9	Quebec	5-1
Feb. 1	Minnesota	4-5	11	Toronto	2-5
3	Tampa Bay	4-2	12	Buffalo	3-1
18	Philadelphia	2-3	15	Los Angeles*	0-3
20	Winnipeg	4-2	26	Winnipeg	7-4
22	Toronto	1-8	**Mar.** 1	Buffalo	5-2
24	NY Rangers	5-4	2	Washington	3-3
Mar. 9	New Jersey	7-2	4	Boston	3-4
11	Minnesota	3-4	6	Hartford	1-5
18	Winnipeg	2-5	12	Winnipeg	3-2
20	NY Islanders	2-7	14	Calgary	2-3
22	St. Louis	1-3	30	St. Louis	6-3
24	Los Angeles	6-2	**Apr.** 1	Tampa Bay	5-3
26	Calgary	1-3	3	Detroit*	1-5
Apr. 7	Edmonton	5-4	4	Ottawa	3-0
11	Calgary*	6-3	9	Calgary	1-8
13	Los Angeles	7-4	15	Los Angeles	8-6

*Denotes afternoon game

Entry Draft
Selections 1993-79

1993
Pick
20 Mike Wilson
46 Rick Girard
98 Dieter Kochan
124 Scott Walker
150 Troy Creurer
176 Yevgeny Babariko
202 Sean Tallaire
254 Bert Robertsson
280 Sergei Tkachenko

1992
Pick
21 Libor Polasek
40 Mike Peca
45 Michael Fountain
69 Jeff Connolly
93 Brent Tully
110 Brian Loney
117 Adrian Aucoin
141 Jason Clark
165 Scott Hollis
213 Sonny Mignacca
237 Mark Wotton
261 Aaron Boh

1991
Pick
7 Alex Stojanov
29 Jassen Cullimore
51 Sean Pronger
95 Danny Kesa
117 Evgeny Namestnikov
139 Brent Thurston
161 Eric Johnson
183 David Neilson
205 Brad Barton
227 Jason Fitzsimmons
249 Xavier Majic

1990
Pick
2 Petr Nedved
18 Shawn Antoski
23 Jiri Slegr
65 Darin Bader
86 Gino Odjick
128 Daryl Filipek
149 Paul O'Hagan
170 Mark Cipriano
191 Troy Neumier
212 Tyler Ertel
233 Karri Kivi

1989
Pick
8 Jason Herter
29 Robert Woodward
71 Brett Hauer
113 Pavel Bure
134 James Revenberg
155 Rob Sangster
176 Sandy Moger
197 Gus Morschauser
218 Hayden O'Rear
239 Darcy Cahill
248 Jan Bergman

1988
Pick
2 Trevor Linden
33 Leif Rohlin
44 Dane Jackson
107 Corrie D'Alessio
122 Phil Von Stefenelli
128 Dixon Ward
149 Greg Geldart
170 Roger Akerstrom
191 Paul Constantin
212 Chris Wolanin
233 Stefan Nilsson

1987
Pick
24 Rob Murphy
45 Steve Veilleux
66 Doug Torrel
87 Sean Fabian
108 Garry Valk
129 Todd Fanning
150 Viktor Tumenev
171 Craig Daly
192 John Fletcher
213 Roger Hansson
233 Neil Eisenhut
234 Matt Evo

1986
Pick
7 Dan Woodley
49 Don Gibson
70 Ronnie Stern
91 Eric Murano
112 Steve Herniman
133 Jon Helgeson
154 Jeff Noble
175 Matt Merton
196 Marc Lyons
217 Todd Hawkins
238 Vladimir Krutov

1985
Pick
4 Jim Sandlak
25 Troy Gamble
46 Shane Doyle
67 Randy Siska
88 Robert Kron
109 Martin Hrstka
130 Brian McFarlane
151 Hakan Ahlund
172 Curtis Hunt
193 Carl Valimont
214 Igor Larionov
235 Darren Taylor

1984
Pick
10 J.J. Daigneault
31 Jeff Rohlicek
52 Dave Saunders
55 Landis Chaulk
58 Mike Stevens
73 Brian Bertuzzi
94 Brett MacDonald
115 Jeff Korchinski
136 Blaine Chrest
157 Jim Agnew
178 Rex Grant
198 Ed Lowney
219 Doug Clarke
239 Ed Kister

1983
Pick
9 Cam Neely
30 Dave Bruce
50 Scott Tottle
70 Tim Lorentz
90 Doug Quinn
110 Dave Lowry
130 Terry Maki
150 John Labatt
170 Allan Measures
190 Roger Grillo
210 Steve Kayser
230 Jay Mazur

1982
Pick
11 Michel Petit
53 Yves Lapointe
71 Shawn Kilroy
116 Taylor Hall
137 Parie Proft
158 Newell Brown
179 Don McLaren
200 Al Raymond
221 Steve Driscoll
242 Shawn Green

1981
Pick
10 Garth Butcher
52 Jean-Marc Lanthier
73 Wendell Young
105 Moe Lemay
115 Stu Kulak
136 Bruce Holloway
157 Petri Skriko
178 Frank Caprice
199 Rejean Vignola

1980
Pick
7 Rick Lanz
49 Andy Schliebener
70 Marc Crawford
91 Darrell May
112 Ken Berry
133 Doug Lidster
154 John O'Connor
175 Patrik Sundstrom
196 Grant Martin

1979
Pick
5 Rick Vaive
26 Brent Ashton
47 Ken Ellacott
68 Art Rutland
89 Dirk Graham
110 Shane Swan

Club Directory

Pacific Coliseum
100 North Renfrew Street
Vancouver, B.C. V5K 3N7
Phone **604/254-5141**
FAX 604/251-5123
GM FAX 604/251-5514
Capacity: 16,150

Chairman .... Frank A. Griffiths, C.A.
Vice-Chairman and Governor .... Arthur R. Griffiths
Hockey Department
President, General Manager, Head Coach ...... Pat Quinn
Director of Hockey Operations .... George McPhee
Director of Player Development/Scouting ...... Mike Penny
Assistant Coaches .... Rick Ley, Stan Smyl, Ron Smith
Goaltending Coach .... Glen Hanlon
General Manager, Hamilton Canucks .... Pat Hickey
Head Coach, Hamilton Canucks .... Jack McIlhargey
Assistant Coach, Hamilton Canucks .... Mario Marois
Strength and Conditioning Coach .... Peter Twist
Director of Pro Scouting .... Murray Oliver
Full-time Scouting Staff .... Jack Birch, Ron Delorme, Thomas Gradin, Jack McCartan, Noel Price, Ken Slater
Part-time Scouting Staff .... Mats Dahlberg, Ross Mahoney, Ed McColgan, Al McDonald, Ray Miron, Jim Pavlenko, Jim Eagle

Administration
V.P., Director of Marketing and Communications . Glen Ringdal
Vice President, Finance and Administration ..... Carlos Mascarenhas
Controller .... Dave Cobb
Director of Publishing .... Norm Jewison
Director of Special Events .... Suzanne Campbell-Clement
Director of Retail Operations .... Larry Donen
Director of Sales and Corporate Programs ..... Dave Nonis
General Manager Food and Beverage Operations . Brian Ensor
Sales Manager .... Eric Thomsen
Corporate Sales/Promotions .... Jane Bremner
Ticket Manager .... Denise McDonald
Accounting, Winning Spirit .... TBA
Accounting Services .... Kathy Bianchi, Mindy Chochan, Sharon Mey
Executive Secretaries .... Melodi Kitagawa, Carla Radiuk, Patti Timms
Centre Ice Club .... Silveria Roselli, Giselle Wagner
Winning Spirit, Pacific Coliseum .... Scott Reed, Rob Guzzo
Receptionist .... Brenda Baldwin, Lisa Ryan (Evening)

Medical/Training Staff
Medical Trainer .... Larry Ashley
Equipment Trainers .... Pat O'Neill, Darren Granger
Massage Therapist .... Dave Schima
Sport Psychologist .... Dr. Wayne Halliwell
Doctors .... Dr. Ross Davidson, Dr. Doug Clement
Dentist .... Dr. David Lawson

Media and Public Relations
Director of Media and Public Relations .... Steve Tambellini
Director of Hockey Information............... Steve Frost
Public Relations Assistant .... Veronica Bateman

Miscellaneous Information
Pacific Coliseum seating capacity 16,150
Television .... BCTV (8), CHEK (6), CBC (3)
Radio .... CKNW (980 AM) and Western Information Network
Broadcasters .... Jim Robson, Tom Larscheid (Radio and TV)
Canucks' Booster Club .... Box 4183, Vancouver, BC V6B 3Z6; Tel: (604) 524-1593
Dimensions of Rink........................ 200 feet by 85 feet
Club trains at............................. Kamloops, B.C.

Coach and General Manager

QUINN, PAT
President and General Manager/Head Coach, Vancouver Canucks.
Born in Hamilton, Ont., January 29, 1943.

For the second consecutive year coach and general manager Pat Quinn led the Vancouver Canucks to a record-breaking season and the team's second straight Smythe Division regular season championship. Under Quinn, Vancouver established franchise records for points (101), wins (46) and goals scored (346) in 1992-93. A charter member of the inaugural Vancouver Canucks team, Quinn re-joined the organization as President and General Manager in 1987-88 and three years later, on January 31, 1991, added the coaching responsibilities to his portfolio. In 1991-92 Quinn won the Jack Adams Trophy as NHL Coach-of-the-Year for the second time in his career, and is one of only two coaches to win the award with two different teams. Quinn previously coached Los Angeles from 1984 to 1987 and in Philadelphia from 1978 to 1982. In 1979-80, his first full season behind the Flyers' bench, Quinn guided the team to a Campbell Conference title and the best record in the NHL at 48-12-20. That season he authored an NHL record 35-game undefeated streak and was named Coach-of-the-Year. After leaving the Flyers organization, Quinn remained out of hockey for two years, earning a Law Degree from Delaware Law School. An NHL defenseman himself, Quinn played in more than 600 games over nine years.

NHL Coaching Record

Season	Team	Regular Season					Playoffs			
		Games	W	L	T	%	Games	W	L	%
1978-79	Philadelphia	30	18	8	4	.667	8	3	5	.375
1979-80	Philadelphia	80	48	12	20	.725	19	13	6	.684
1980-81	Philadelphia	80	41	24	15	.606	12	6	6	.500
1981-82	Philadelphia	72	34	29	9	.535	....	....	....	....
1984-85	Los Angeles	80	34	32	14	.513	3	0	3	.000
1985-86	Los Angeles	80	23	49	8	.338	....	....	....	....
1986-87	Los Angeles	42	18	20	4	.476	....	....	....	....
1990-91	Vancouver	26	9	13	4	.423	6	2	4	.333
1991-92	Vancouver	80	42	26	12	.600	13	6	7	.462
1992-93	Vancouver	84	46	29	9	.601	12	6	6	.500
	NHL Totals	654	313	242	99	.554	73	36	37	.493

Washington Capitals

1992-93 Results: 43w-34L-7T 93PTS. Second, Patrick Division

Schedule

	Home			Away	
Oct.	Fri.	8 New Jersey	**Oct.**	Wed.	6 Winnipeg
	Fri.	15 Philadelphia		Sat.	9 New Jersey
	Sat.	16 Buffalo		Mon.	11 NY Rangers
	Fri.	22 Los Angeles		Wed.	13 Toronto
Nov.	Fri.	5 Vancouver		Sun.	24 Edmonton
	Tues.	9 Quebec		Mon.	25 Calgary
	Sat.	13 NY Rangers		Wed.	27 Vancouver
	Tues.	16 San Jose		Fri.	29 Anaheim
	Wed.	24 St Louis		Sat.	30 San Jose
	Fri.	26 Pittsburgh	**Nov.**	Thur.	11 Tampa Bay
Dec.	Fri.	3 Montreal		Thur.	18 Pittsburgh
	Tues.	7 Hartford		Sat.	20 Florida
	Fri.	17 Ottawa		Sun.	28 NY Rangers
	Thur.	23 NY Rangers		Tues.	30 NY Islanders
	Sun.	26 Pittsburgh	**Dec.**	Sat.	4 Ottawa
	Tues.	28 Florida		Thur.	9 Philadelphia
	Thur.	30 Anaheim		Sat.	11 Montreal
Jan.	Sat.	1 Tampa Bay*		Mon.	13 Quebec
	Sat.	8 Chicago*		Sat.	18 Hartford
	Tues.	11 Toronto		Tues.	21 Philadelphia
	Fri.	14 New Jersey	**Jan.**	Sun.	2 Boston*
	Tues.	25 Boston		Sun.	9 New Jersey
	Sun.	30 Detroit*		Sat.	15 Quebec
Feb.	Fri.	4 Montreal		Mon.	17 Montreal
	Sat.	5 Tampa Bay		Wed.	19 Florida
	Tues.	15 Edmonton		Thur.	27 Buffalo
	Fri.	18 NY Islanders		Sat.	29 Philadelphia*
	Sun.	20 Buffalo*	**Feb.**	Wed.	2 Philadelphia
	Sat.	26 Florida			(at Cleveland)
Mar.	Tues.	1 Tampa Bay		Mon.	7 NY Rangers
	Fri.	4 Philadelphia		Thur.	10 St Louis
	Sun.	6 Calgary*		Sat.	12 Los Angeles
	Wed.	9 NY Rangers		Mon.	21 NY Islanders*
		(at Halifax)		Thur.	24 Florida
	Sat.	12 Quebec		Sun.	27 Hartford
	Tues.	22 Hartford	**Mar.**	Mon.	7 Boston
	Sun.	27 Boston*		Tues.	15 Pittsburgh
	Tues.	29 NY Islanders		Fri.	18 Dallas
Apr.	Fri.	1 New Jersey		Sun.	20 Tampa Bay
	Sun.	3 Dallas*			(at Orlando)
	Tues.	5 NY Islanders		Fri.	25 Detroit
	Sat.	9 Ottawa		Thur.	31 Chicago
	Tues.	12 Winnipeg	**Apr.**	Wed.	6 Ottawa
				Thur.	14 Buffalo

* Denotes afternoon game.

Home Starting Times:

Mondays through Thursday	7:35 p.m.
Saturdays and Sundays	7:35 p.m.
Fridays	8:05 p.m.
Matinees	1:35 p.m.
Except Wed. Nov. 24	8:05 p.m.
Sun. Jan. 30	12:05 p.m.

Franchise date: June 11, 1974

ATLANTIC DIVISION

NHL

EASTERN CONFERENCE

20th NHL Season

Kevin Hatcher, who led all NHL defencemen with 34 goals in 1992-93, finished the season with a career-high 79 points.

Year-by-Year Record

		Home			Road			Overall							
Season	GP	W	L	T	W	L	T	W	L	T	GF	GA	Pts.	Finished	Playoff Result
1992-93	84	21	15	6	22	19	1	43	34	7	325	286	93	2nd, Patrick Div.	Lost Div. Semi-Final
1991-92	80	25	12	3	20	15	5	45	27	8	330	275	98	2nd, Patrick Div.	Lost Div. Semi-Final
1990-91	80	21	14	5	16	22	2	37	36	7	258	258	81	3rd, Patrick Div.	Lost Div. Final
1989-90	80	19	18	3	17	20	3	36	38	6	284	275	78	3rd, Patrick Div.	Lost Conf. Championship
1988-89	80	25	12	3	16	17	7	41	29	10	305	259	92	1st, Patrick Div.	Lost Div. Semi-Final
1987-88	80	22	14	4	16	19	5	38	33	9	281	249	85	2nd, Patrick Div.	Lost Div. Final
1986-87	80	22	15	3	16	17	7	38	32	10	285	278	86	2nd, Patrick Div.	Lost Div. Semi-Final
1985-86	80	30	8	2	20	15	5	50	23	7	315	272	107	2nd, Patrick Div.	Lost Div. Final
1984-85	80	27	11	2	19	14	7	46	25	9	322	240	101	2nd, Patrick Div.	Lost Div. Semi-Final
1983-84	80	26	11	3	22	16	2	48	27	5	308	226	101	2nd, Patrick Div.	Lost Div. Final
1982-83	80	22	12	6	17	13	10	39	25	16	306	283	94	3rd, Patrick Div.	Lost Div. Semi-Final
1981-82	80	16	16	8	10	25	5	26	41	13	319	338	65	5th, Patrick Div.	Out of Playoffs
1980-81	80	16	17	7	10	19	11	26	36	18	286	317	70	5th, Patrick Div.	Out of Playoffs
1979-80	80	20	14	6	7	26	7	27	40	13	261	293	67	5th, Patrick Div.	Out of Playoffs
1978-79	80	15	19	6	9	22	9	24	41	15	273	338	63	4th, Norris Div.	Out of Playoffs
1977-78	80	10	23	7	7	26	7	17	49	14	195	321	48	5th, Norris Div.	Out of Playoffs
1976-77	80	17	15	8	7	27	6	24	42	14	221	307	62	4th, Norris Div.	Out of Playoffs
1975-76	80	6	26	8	5	33	2	11	59	10	224	394	32	5th, Norris Div.	Out of Playoffs
1974-75	80	7	28	5	1	39	0	8	67	5	181	446	21	5th, Norris Div.	Out of Playoffs

1993-94 Player Personnel

FORWARDS

	HT	WT	S	Place of Birth	Date	1992-93 Club
ACTON, Keith	5-8	170	L	Stouffville, Ont.	4/15/58	Philadelphia
ALLISON, Jason	6-3	192	R	North York, Ont.	4/29/75	London
BANHAM, Frank	5-11	175	R	Calahoo, Alta.	4/14/75	Saskatoon
BERUBE, Craig	6-1	205	L	Calahoo, Alta.	12/17/65	Calgary
BOBACK, Michael	5-11	180	R	Mt. Clemens, MI	8/13/70	Baltimore
BONDRA, Peter	6-0	200	L	Luck, Ukraine	2/7/68	Washington
BRUNETTE, Andrew	6-0	212	L	Sudbury, Ont.	8/21/73	Owen Sound
BURRIDGE, Randy	5-9	185	L	Ft. Erie, Ont.	1/7/66	Washington-Baltimore
ELYNUIK, Pat	6-0	185	R	Foam Lake, Sask.	10/30/67	Washington
GENDRON, Martin	5-8	182	R	Valleyfield, Que.	2/15/74	Baltimore-St. Hyacinthe
HUNTER, Dale	5-10	198	L	Petrolia, Ont.	7/31/60	Washington
JIRANEK, Martin	5-11	170	L	Bashaw, Alta.	10/3/69	Baltimore
JONES, Keith	6-2	190	R	Brantford, Ont.	11/8/68	Washington-Baltimore
KAMINSKI, Kevin	5-9	170	L	Churchbridge, Sask.	3/13/69	Halifax
KHRISTICH, Dimitri	6-2	195	R	Kiev, Ukraine	6/23/69	Washington
KONOWALCHUK, Steve	6-0	180	L	Salt Lake City, UT	11/11/72	Washington-Baltimore
KONTSEK, Roman	5-11	183	R	Prague, Czech Rep.	6/11/60	Dukla Trencin
KRYGIER, Todd	5-11	180	L	Chicago Heights, IL	10/12/69	Washington
LONGO, Chris	5-10	180	R	Belleville, Ont.	1/5/72	Baltimore
LORENTZ, Dave	5-9	182	L	Kitchener, Ont.	3/13/69	Odenski (Den.)
MACPHERSON, Billy Jo	6-1	200	L	Toronto, Ont.	9/23/73	Oshawa
MATHERS, Mike	5-10	189	L	High Prairie, Alta.	6/20/72	Kamloops
MAY, Alan	6-1	200	R	Swan Hills, Alta.	1/14/65	Washington
McAUSLAND, Darren	5-11	181	L	Grovedale, Alta.	3/3/72	Baltimore
MILLER, Kelly	5-11	197	L	Lansing, MI	3/3/63	Washington
NELSON, Jeff	6-0	180	L	Prince Albert, Sask.	12/18/72	Baltimore
PEAKE, Pat	6-0	195	R	Rochester, MI	5/28/73	Detroit (OHL)
PEARCE, Randy	5-11	203	L	Kitchener, Ont.	2/23/70	Baltimore-Hampton Rds.
PIVONKA, Michael	6-2	198	L	Kladno, Czech Rep.	1/28/66	Washington
POIRIER, Joel	6-1	190	L	Richmond Hill, Ont.	1/15/75	Sudbury
POULIN, Dave	5-11	190	L	Timmins, Ont.	12/17/58	Boston
RIDLEY, Mike	6-0	195	L	Winnipeg, Man.	7/8/63	Washington
STAGG, Brian	6-2	177	R	North Bay, Ont.	5/23/74	Belv'le-Kingston-N. Bay
VARGA, John	5-9	172	L	Chicago, IL	1/31/74	Tacoma

DEFENSEMEN

	HT	WT	S	Place of Birth	Date	1992-93 Club
ANDERSON, Shawn	6-1	200	L	Montreal, Que.	2/7/68	Washington-Baltimore
BOILEAU, Patrick	6-0	185	R	Montreal, Que.	2/22/75	Laval
CICCONE, Enrico	6-4	200	L	Montreal, Que.	4/10/70	Minnesota-Kalamazoo
COTE, Sylvain	5-11	185	R	Quebec City, Que.	1/19/66	Washington
GLADNEY, Jason	5-11	198	L	Toronto, Ont.	1/26/74	Kitchener
HATCHER, Kevin	6-4	225	R	Detroit, MI	9/9/66	Washington
IAFRATE, Al	6-3	220	L	Dearborn, MI	3/21/66	Washington
JOHANSSON, Calle	5-11	205	L	Goteborg, Sweden	2/14/67	Washington
KLEE, Ken	6-1	200	R	Indianapolis, IN	4/24/71	Baltimore
MATHIESON, Jim	6-1	209	L	Kindersley, Sask.	1/24/70	Baltimore
NELSON, Todd	6-0	201	L	Prince Albert, Sask.	5/11/69	Cleveland
PASCUCCI, Ron	6-1	180	L	North Andover, MA	6/9/70	Boston College
SLANEY, John	6-0	185	L	St. John's, Nfld.	2/7/72	Baltimore
WITT, Brendan	6-1	205	L	Humboldt, Sask.	2/20/75	Seattle
WOOLLEY, Jason	6-0	185	L	Toronto, Ont.	7/27/69	Washington-Baltimore

GOALTENDERS

	HT	WT	C	Place of Birth	Date	1992-93 Club
BEAUPRE, Don	5-10	172	L	Waterloo, Ont.	9/19/61	Washington-Baltimore
DAFOE, Brian	5-11	175	L	Sussex, England	2/25/71	Washington-Baltimore
DERKSEN, Duane	6-1	180	L	St. Boniface, Man.	7/7/68	Baltimore-Hampton Rds.
KOLZIG, Olaf	6-3	205	L	Johannesburg, S.A.	4/9/70	Washington-Rochester
TABARACCI, Rick	5-11	180	L	Toronto, Ont.	2/2/69	Wpg.-Moncton-Wsh.

1992-93 Scoring

Regular Season

Pos	#	Player	Team	GP	G	A	Pts	+/-	PIM	PP	SH	GW	GT	S	%
R	12	Peter Bondra	WSH	83	37	48	85	8	70	10	0	7	0	239	15.5
C	17	Mike Ridley	WSH	84	26	56	82	5	44	6	2	3	0	148	17.6
D	4	Kevin Hatcher	WSH	83	34	45	79	7–	114	13	1	6	0	329	10.3
C	32	Dale Hunter	WSH	84	20	59	79	3	198	10	0	2	0	120	16.7
C	20	Michal Pivonka	WSH	69	21	53	74	14	66	6	1	5	0	147	14.3
C	8	Dimitri Khristich	WSH	64	31	35	66	29	28	9	1	1	1	127	24.4
D	34	Al Iafrate	WSH	81	25	41	66	15	169	11	1	4	0	289	8.7
R	19	Pat Elynuik	WSH	80	22	35	57	3	66	8	0	1	0	121	18.2
D	3	Sylvain Cote	WSH	77	21	29	50	28	34	8	2	3	0	206	10.2
L	10	Kelly Miller	WSH	84	18	27	45	2–	32	3	0	3	0	144	12.5
D	6	Calle Johansson	WSH	77	7	38	45	3	56	6	0	0	1	133	5.3
L	11	Bob Carpenter	WSH	68	11	17	28	16–	65	2	0	0	0	141	7.8
R	26	* Keith Jones	WSH	71	12	14	26	18	124	0	0	3	0	73	16.4
L	21	Todd Krygier	WSH	77	11	12	23	13–	60	0	2	0	1	133	8.3
D	14	Paul Cavallini	STL	11	1	4	5	3	10	1	0	0	0	22	4.5
			WSH	71	5	8	13	3	46	0	0	0	0	77	6.5
			TOTAL	82	6	12	18	6	56	1	0	0	0	99	6.1
R	23	Paul MacDermid	WSH	72	9	8	17	13–	80	1	0	3	0	45	20.0
L	16	Alan May	WSH	83	6	10	16	1	268	0	0	1	0	75	8.0
C	22	* Steve Konowalchuk	WSH	36	4	7	11	4	16	1	0	1	0	34	11.8
D	36	Shawn Anderson	WSH	60	2	6	8	2–	18	1	0	0	0	42	4.8
C	15	* Reggie Savage	WSH	16	2	3	5	4–	12	2	0	0	0	20	10.0
L	24	Jeff Greenlaw	WSH	16	1	1	2	3–	18	0	0	0	0	15	6.7
D	25	* Jason Woolley	WSH	26	0	2	2	3	10	0	0	0	0	11	.0
D	28	* Brad Schlegel	WSH	7	0	1	1	1	6	0	0	0	0	8	.0
G	33	Don Beaupre	WSH	58	0	1	1	0	20	0	0	0	0	0	.0
G	29	* Bob Babcock	WSH	1	0	0	0	0	2	0	0	0	0	0	.0
G	31	* Olaf Kolzig	WSH	1	0	0	0	0	0	0	0	0	0	0	.0
G	35	* Byron Dafoe	WSH	1	0	0	0	0	0	0	0	0	0	0	.0
L	18	Randy Burridge	WSH	4	0	0	0	1	0	0	0	0	0	7	.0
R	27	Mark Hunter	WSH	7	0	0	0	1	14	0	0	0	0	5	.0
D	5	Rod Langway	WSH	21	0	0	0	13–	20	0	0	0	0	6	.0
			WPG	19	0	0	0	0	10	0	0	0	0	0	.0
			WSH	6	0	0	0	0	4	0	0	0	0	0	.0
			TOTAL	25	0	0	0	0	14	0	0	0	0	0	.0

Goaltending

No.	Goaltender	GPI	Mins	Avg	W	L	T	EN	SO	GA	SA	S%
35	* Byron Dafoe	1	1	.00	0	0	0	0	0	0	0	.000
31	Rick Tabaracci	6	343	1.75	3	2	0	1	2	10	162	.938
33	Don Beaupre	58	3282	3.31	27	23	5	7	1	181	1530	.882
30	Jim Hrivnak	27	1421	3.50	13	9	2	2	0	83	677	.877
31	* Olaf Kolzig	1	20	6.00	0	0	0	0	0	2	7	.714
	Totals	**84**	**5085**	**3.37**	**43**	**34**	**7**	**10**	**3**	**286**	**2386**	**.880**

Playoffs

Pos	#	Player	Team	GP	G	A	Pts	+/-	PIM	PP	SH	GW	GT	S	%
C	32	Dale Hunter	WSH	6	7	1	8	7–	35	4	0	1	0	18	38.9
C	8	Dimitri Khristich	WSH	6	2	5	7	2–	2	1	0	0	0	15	13.3
D	34	Al Iafrate	WSH	6	6	0	6	3–	4	3	0	1	0	30	20.0
C	17	Mike Ridley	WSH	6	1	5	6	4–	0	1	0	0	0	7	14.3
R	12	Peter Bondra	WSH	6	0	6	6	0	0	0	0	0	0	16	.0
R	19	Pat Elynuik	WSH	6	2	3	5	2–	19	0	0	0	0	7	28.6
L	11	Bob Carpenter	WSH	6	1	4	5	2	6	0	0	0	0	13	7.7
D	6	Calle Johansson	WSH	6	0	5	5	4–	4	0	0	0	0	4	.0
L	10	Kelly Miller	WSH	6	0	3	3	7–	2	0	0	0	0	11	.0
D	3	Sylvain Cote	WSH	6	1	1	2	3–	4	0	0	0	0	8	12.5
L	21	Todd Krygier	WSH	6	1	1	2	1–	4	0	1	0	0	16	6.3
D	14	Paul Cavallini	WSH	6	0	2	2	1–	18	0	0	0	0	5	.0
C	20	Michal Pivonka	WSH	6	0	2	2	3–	0	0	0	0	0	12	.0
L	18	Randy Burridge	WSH	6	1	0	1	0	0	0	0	0	0	2	50.0
C	22	* Steve Konowalchuk	WSH	2	0	1	1	1–	0	0	0	0	0	3	.0
D	4	Kevin Hatcher	WSH	6	0	1	1	5–	14	0	0	0	0	18	.0
L	16	Alan May	WSH	6	0	1	1	2	6	0	0	0	0	4	.0
G	33	Don Beaupre	WSH	2	0	0	0	0	4	0	0	0	0	0	.0
G	31	Rick Tabaracci	WSH	4	0	0	0	0	4	0	0	0	0	0	.0
D	36	Shawn Anderson	WSH	6	0	0	0	3–	0	0	0	0	0	1	.0
R	26	* Keith Jones	WSH	6	0	0	0	3–	10	0	0	0	0	2	.0

Goaltending

No.	Goaltender	GPI	Mins	Avg	W	L	EN	SO	GA	SA	S%
31	Rick Tabaracci	4	304	2.76	1	3	0	0	14	160	.913
33	Don Beaupre	2	119	4.54	1	1	0	0	9	65	.862
	Totals	**6**	**425**	**3.25**	**2**	**4**	**0**	**0**	**23**	**225**	**.898**

General Managers' History

Milt Schmidt, 1974-75 to 1975-76; Max McNab, 1976-77 to 1980-81; Roger Crozier, 1981-82; David Poile, 1982-83 to date.

Coaching History

Jim Anderson, George Sullivan and Milt Schmidt, 1974-75; Milt Schmidt and Tom McVie, 1975-76; Tom McVie, 1976-77 to 1977-78; Danny Belisle, 1978-79; Danny Belisle and Gary Green, 1979-80; Gary Green, 1980-81; Gary Green and Bryan Murray, 1981-82; Bryan Murray, 1982-83 to 1988-89; Bryan Murray and Terry Murray, 1989-90; Terry Murray, 1990-91 to date.

Captains' History

Doug Mohns, 1974-75; Bill Clement and Yvon Labre, 1975-76; Yvon Labre, 1976-77, 1977-78; Guy Charron, 1978-79; Ryan Walter, 1979-80 to 1981-82; Rod Langway, 1982-83 to 1991-92; Rod Langway and Kevin Hatcher, 1992-93; Kevin Hatcher, 1993-94.

Retired Numbers

| 7 | Yvon Labre | 1973-1981 |

Club Records

Team

(Figures in brackets for season records are games played; records for fewest points, wins, ties, losses, goals, goals against are for 70 or more games)

Most Points	107	1985-86 (80)	
Most Wins	50	1985-86 (80)	
Most Ties	18	1980-81 (80)	
Most Losses	67	1974-75 (80)	
Most Goals	330	1991-92 (80)	
Most Goals Against	*446	1974-75 (80)	
Fewest Points	*21	1974-75 (80)	
Fewest Wins	*8	1974-75 (80)	
Fewest Ties	5	1974-75 (80)	
		1983-84 (80)	
Fewest Losses	23	1985-86 (80)	
Fewest Goals	181	1974-75 (80)	
Fewest Goals Against	226	1983-84 (80)	

Longest Winning Streak

Over-all .... 10 Jan. 27-
Feb. 18/84

Home .... 8 Feb. 1-
Mar. 11/86
Mar. 3-
April 1/89

Away .... 6 Feb. 26-
Apr. 1/84

Longest Undefeated Streak

Over-all .... 14 Nov. 24-
Dec. 23/82
(9 wins, 5 ties)

Home .... 13 Nov. 25/92-
Feb. 2/93
(9 wins, 4 ties)

Away .... 10 Nov. 24/82-
Jan. 8/83
(6 wins, 4 ties)

Longest Losing Streak

Over-all .... *17 Feb. 18-
Mar. 26/75

Home .... *11 Feb. 18-
Mar. 30/75

Away .... 37 Oct. 9/74-
Mar. 26/75

Longest Winless Streak

Over-all .... 25 Nov. 29/75-
Jan. 21/76
(22 losses, 3 ties)

Home .... 14 Dec. 3/75-
Jan. 21/76
(11 losses, 3 ties)

Away .... 37 Oct. 9/74-
Mar. 26/75
(37 losses)

Most Shutouts, Season 8 1983-84 (80)
Most PIM, Season 2,204 1989-90 (80)
Most Goals, Game .... 12 Feb. 6/90
(Que. 2 at Wash. 12)

Individual

Most Seasons	11	Rod Langway
Most Games	758	Mike Gartner
Most Goals, Career	397	Mike Gartner
Most Assists, Career	392	Mike Gartner
Most Points, Career	789	Mike Gartner
		(397 goals, 392 assists)
Most PIM, Career	1,630	Scott Stevens
Most Shutouts, Career	10	Don Beaupre

Longest Consecutive

Games Streak .... 422 Bob Carpenter

Most Goals, Season ...... 60 Dennis Maruk
(1981-82)

Most Assists, Season ...... 76 Dennis Maruk
(1981-82)

Most Points, Season ...... 136 Dennis Maruk
(1981-82)
(60 goals, 76 assists)

Most PIM, Season .... 339 Alan May
(1989-90)

Most Points, Defenseman,
Season .... 81 Larry Murphy
(1986-87)
(23 goals, 58 assists)

Most Points, Center,
Season .... 136 Dennis Maruk
(1981-82)
(60 goals, 76 assists)

Most Points, Right Wing,
Season .... 102 Mike Gartner
(1984-85)
(50 goals, 52 assists)

Most Points, Left Wing,
Season .... 87 Ryan Walter
(1981-82)
(38 goals, 49 assists)

Most Points, Rookie,
Season .... 67 Bobby Carpenter
(1981-82)
(32 goals, 35 assists)
Chris Valentine
(1981-82)
(30 goals, 37 assists)

Most Shutouts, Season ..... 5 Don Beaupre
(1990-91)

Most Goals, Game .... 5 Bengt Gustafsson
(Jan. 8/84)

Most Assists, Game .... 6 Mike Ridley
(Jan. 7/89)

Most Points, Game .... 7 Dino Ciccarelli
(Mar. 18/89)

* NHL Record.

All-time Record vs. Other Clubs

Regular Season

		At Home							On Road							Total				
	GP	W	L	T	GF	GA	PTS	GP	W	L	T	GF	GA	PTS	GP	W	L	T	GF	GA	PTS
Boston	34	9	17	8	105	131	26	34	9	21	4	98	142	22	68	18	38	12	203	273	48
Buffalo	34	7	21	6	95	140	20	35	5	26	4	93	156	14	69	12	47	10	188	296	34
Calgary	32	15	13	4	123	117	34	31	6	21	4	75	137	16	63	21	34	8	198	254	50
Chicago	32	18	10	4	123	101	40	31	6	20	5	91	131	17	63	24	30	9	214	232	57
Detroit	37	19	14	4	146	117	42	39	13	16	10	116	140	36	76	32	30	14	262	257	78
Edmonton	21	12	8	1	94	79	25	21	8	9	4	75	86	20	42	20	17	5	169	165	45
Hartford	22	13	8	1	79	66	27	23	12	8	3	92	75	27	45	25	16	4	171	141	54
Los Angeles	37	16	15	6	160	137	38	38	11	23	4	117	158	26	75	27	38	10	277	295	64
Minnesota	32	13	12	7	103	99	33	31	10	13	8	92	116	28	63	23	25	15	195	215	61
Montreal	38	15	17	6	102	130	36	38	6	26	6	77	175	18	76	21	43	12	179	305	54
New Jersey	54	39	12	3	247	161	81	54	26	22	6	174	174	58	108	65	34	9	421	335	139
NY Islanders	56	22	26	8	176	192	52	57	21	35	1	180	235	43	113	43	61	9	356	427	95
NY Rangers	58	29	21	8	232	200	66	57	23	28	6	210	237	52	115	52	49	14	442	437	118
Ottawa	2	2	0	0	11	5	4	2	2	0	0	10	8	4	4	4	0	0	21	13	8
Philadelphia	56	22	25	9	205	204	53	57	18	35	4	160	226	40	113	40	60	13	365	430	93
Pittsburgh	64	33	26	5	280	245	71	61	24	31	6	213	250	54	125	57	57	11	493	495	125
Quebec	22	11	8	3	92	75	25	22	11	7	4	91	72	26	44	22	15	7	183	147	51
St. Louis	31	16	12	3	113	96	35	32	10	14	8	107	136	28	63	26	26	11	220	232	63
San Jose	2	2	0	0	11	5	4	2	2	0	0	8	5	4	4	4	0	0	19	10	8
Tampa Bay	1	0	0	1	2	2	1	1	1	0	0	5	3	2	2	1	0	1	7	5	3
Toronto	34	21	11	2	131	94	44	33	11	18	4	121	157	26	67	32	29	6	252	251	70
Vancouver	32	17	11	4	108	101	38	31	12	15	4	99	107	28	63	29	26	8	207	208	66
Winnipeg	21	14	5	2	100	67	30	22	6	11	5	79	84	17	43	20	16	7	179	151	47
Defunct Clubs	10	2	8	0	28	42	4	10	4	5	1	30	39	9	20	6	13	1	58	81	13
Totals	**762**	**367**	**300**	**95**	**2866**	**2606**	**829**	**762**	**257**	**404**	**101**	**2413**	**3049**	**615**	**1524**	**624**	**704**	**196**	**5279**	**5655**	**1444**

Playoffs

	Series	W	L	GP	W	L	T	GF	GA	Last Mtg.	Round	Result
Boston	1	0	1	4	0	4	0	6	15	1990	CF	L 0-4
New Jersey	2	1	1	13	7	6	0	44	43	1990	DSF	W 4-2
NY Islanders	6	1	5	30	12	18	0	88	89	1993	DSF	L 2-4
NY Rangers	3	2	1	17	10	7	0	63	51	1991	DSF	W 4-2
Philadelphia	3	2	1	16	9	7	0	65	55	1989	DSF	L 2-4
Pittsburgh	2	0	2	12	4	8	0	40	44	1992	DSF	L 3-4
Totals	**17**	**6**	**11**	**92**	**42**	**50**	**0**	**306**	**307**			

Playoff Results 1993-89

Year	Round	Opponent	Result	GF	GA
1993	DSF	NY Islanders	L 2-4	22	23
1992	DSF	Pittsburgh	L 3-4	27	25
1991	DF	Pittsburgh	L 1-4	13	19
	DSF	NY Rangers	W 4-2	16	16
1990	CF	Boston	L 0-4	6	15
	DF	NY Rangers	W 4-1	22	15
	DSF	New Jersey	W 4-2	21	18
1989	DSF	Philadelphia	L 2-4	19	25

Abbreviations: Round: F – Final;
CF – conference final; **DF** – division final;
DSF – division semi-final; **SF** – semi-final;
QF – quarter-final; **PR** – preliminary round.
GA – goals against; **GF** – goals for.

1992-93 Results

Home				Away		
Oct. 9	NY Rangers	2-4	Oct. 7	Toronto	6-5
10	Philadelphia	2-4	12	New Jersey	2-4
16	Ottawa	5-1	21	NY Rangers	1-2
17	Buffalo	6-4	26	Winnipeg	2-6
23	NY Islanders	2-5	28	Vancouver	3-4
Nov. 3	Chicago	4-1	30	Calgary	3-1
6	Tampa Bay	2-2	31	Edmonton	2-4
14	New Jersey	3-4	Nov. 7	Hartford	6-2
18	Minnesota	4-5	11	NY Rangers	7-4
20	Detroit	5-7	13	New Jersey	0-3
25	Boston	6-2	22	Quebec*	6-4
27	Pittsburgh	6-4	23	Montreal	1-1
Dec. 4	NY Rangers	8-4	28	Pittsburgh	3-5
11	Winnipeg	8-6	30	Detroit	4-1
18	Hartford	4-3	Dec. 5	NY Islanders	5-3
26	Philadelphia	5-5	7	Ottawa	6-5
29	NY Rangers	4-3	9	New Jersey	6-2
Jan. 1	New Jersey*	9-2	12	Philadelphia	5-2
2	Chicago*	2-2	16	Hartford	3-6
9	Edmonton	4-3	19	Boston	3-4
23	Ottawa	6-4	21	Ottawa	4-3
29	Quebec	3-3	23	Chicago	2-6
31	Pittsburgh*	2-2	Jan. 7	Philadelphia	2-8
Feb. 2	Calgary	4-6	13	NY Rangers	4-5
20	Los Angeles*	7-3	14	NY Islanders	3-0
21	St. Louis*	5-2	17	Tampa Bay	5-3
28	Pittsburgh*	2-4	21	Chicago	2-6
Mar. 2	Vancouver	3-3	26	Pittsburgh	3-6
5	Philadelphia	0-3	27	Buffalo	3-4
7	NY Islanders*	2-3	Feb. 9	Minnesota	3-2
9	Toronto	3-1	11	St. Louis	10-6
19	Hartford	5-2	13	Los Angeles	10-3
21	San Jose*	5-3	16	San Jose	4-3
23	Quebec	5-1	23	NY Islanders	4-2
27	New Jersey*	2-5	27	Boston*	4-5
28	Pittsburgh*	1-4	Mar.11	Philadelphia	4-6
30	Buffalo	4-1	16	Detroit	4-2
Apr. 2	Montreal	4-0	18	Pittsburgh	5-7
4	NY Rangers*	0-4	25	NY Islanders	5-2
6	NY Islanders	2-3	Apr. 8	Philadelphia	3-4
10	New Jersey	3-5	12	Montreal	3-2
16	NY Rangers	4-2	14	NY Rangers	2-0

*Denotes afternoon game

Entry Draft Selections 1993-79

1993	1989	1986	1982
Pick	**Pick**	**Pick**	**Pick**
11 Brendan Witt	19 Olaf Kolzig	19 Jeff Greenlaw	5 Scott Stevens
17 Jason Allison	35 Byron Dafoe	40 Steve Seftel	58 Milan Novy
69 Patrick Boileau	59 Jim Mathieson	60 Shawn Simpson	89 Dean Evason
147 Frank Banham	81 Jason Woolley	61 Jimmy Hrivnak	110 Ed Kastelic
173 Daniel Hendrickson	82 Trent Klatt	82 Erin Ginnell	152 Wally Schreiber
174 Andrew Brunette	145 Dave Lorentz	103 John Purves	173 Jamie Reeve
199 Joel Poirier	166 Dean Holoien	124 Stefan Nilsson	194 Juha Nurmi
225 Jason Gladney	187 Victor Gervais	145 Peter Choma	215 Wayne Prestage
251 Mark Seliger	208 Jiri Vykoukal	166 Lee Davidson	236 Jon Holden
277 Dany Bousquet	229 Andrei Sidorov	187 Tero Toivola	247 Marco Kallas
	250 Ken House	208 Bobby Bobcock	
1992		229 John Schratz	**1981**
Pick	**1988**	250 Scott McCrory	**Pick**
14 Sergei Gonchar	**Pick**		3 Bob Carpenter
32 Jim Carey	15 Reginald Savage	**1985**	45 Eric Calder
53 Stefan Ustorf	36 Tim Taylor	**Pick**	68 Tony Kellin
71 Martin Gendron	41 Wade Bartley	19 Yvon Corriveau	89 Mike Siltala
119 John Varga	57 Duane Derksen	40 John Druce	91 Peter Sidorkiewicz
167 Mark Matier	78 Rob Krauss	61 Rob Murray	110 Jim McGeough
191 Mike Mathers	120 Dmitri Khristich	82 Bill Houlder	131 Risto Jalo
215 Brian Stagg	141 Keith Jones	83 Larry Shaw	152 Gaetan Duchesne
239 Gregory Callahan	144 Brad Schlegel	103 Claude Dumas	173 George White
263 Billy Jo MacPherson	162 Todd Hilditch	124 Doug Stromback	194 Chris Valentine
	183 Petr Pavlas	145 Jamie Nadjiwan	
1991	192 Mark Sorensen	166 Mark Haarmann	**1980**
Pick	204 Claudio Scremin	187 Steve Hollett	**Pick**
14 Pat Peake	225 Chris Venkus	208 Dallas Eakins	5 Darren Veitch
21 Trevor Halverson	246 Ron Pascucci	229 Steve Hrynewich	47 Dan Miele
25 Eric Lavigne		250 Frank DiMuzio	55 Torrie Robertson
36 Jeff Nelson	**1987**		89 Timo Blomqvist
58 Steve Konowalchuk	**Pick**	**1984**	110 Todd Bidner
80 Justin Morrison	36 Jeff Ballantyne	**Pick**	131 Frank Perkins
146 Dave Morissette	57 Steve Maltais	17 Kevin Hatcher	152 Bruce Raboin
168 Rick Corriveau	78 Tyler Larter	34 Steve Leach	173 Peter Andersson
190 Trevor Duhaime	99 Pat Beauchesne	59 Michal Pivonka	194 Tony Camazzola
209 Rob Leask	120 Rich Defreitas	80 Kris King	
212 Carl LeBlanc	141 Devon Oleniuk	122 Vito Cramarossa	**1979**
234 Rob Puchniak	162 Thomas Sjogren	143 Timo Iljina	**Pick**
256 Bill Kovacs	204 Chris Clarke	164 Frank Joo	4 Mike Gartner
	225 Milos Vanik	185 Jim Thomson	24 Errol Rausse
1990	240 Dan Brettschneider	205 Paul Cavallini	67 Harvie Pocza
Pick	246 Ryan Kummu	225 Mikhail Tatarinov	88 Tim Tookey
9 John Slaney		246 Per Schedrin	109 Greg Theberge
30 Rod Pasma			
51 Chris Longo		**1983**	
72 Randy Pearce		**Pick**	
93 Brian Sakic		75 Tim Bergland	
94 Mark Ouimet		95 Martin Bouliane	
114 Andrei Kovalev		135 Dwaine Hutton	
135 Roman Kontsek		155 Marty Abrams	
156 Peter Bondra		175 David Cowan	
159 Steve Martell		195 Yves Beaudoin	
177 Ken Klee		215 Alain Raymond	
198 Michael Boback		216 Anders Huss	
219 Alan Brown			
240 Todd Hlushko			

Club Directory

U.S. Air Arena
1 Harry S Truman Drive
Landover, Maryland 20785
Phone **301/386-7000**
PR FAX 301/386-7012
GM FAX 301/386-7082
Capacity: 18,130

Board of Directors
David P. Bindeman, Stuart L. Bindeman, James A. Cafritz, A. James Clark, Albert Cohen, J. Martin Irving, R. Robert Linowes, Arthur K. Mason, Dr. Jack Meshel, David M. Osnos, Richard M. Patrick

Management
Chairman and Governor	Abe Pollin
President and Alternate Governor	Richard M. Patrick
Legal Counsel and Alternate Governors	David M. Osnos, Peter O'Malley
Vice-President of Finance	Edmund Stelzer

Hockey Department
Vice-President and General Manager	David Poile
Director of Player Personnel	Jack Button
Head Coach	Terry Murray
Assistant Coach	John Perpich, Keith Allain
Head Coach, Portland Pirates	Barry Trotz
Assistant Coach, Portland Pirates	Paul Gardner
Director of Team Services/Video Coordinator	Tod Button
Administrative Assistant to the General Manager	Pat Young
Assistant to the Hockey Department	Todd Warren
Chief Eastern Scout	Hugh Rogers
Chief Western Scout	Craig Channell
Chief U.S. Scout	TBA
Chief Quebec Scout	Gilles Cote
Scouts	Fred Devereaux, Bud Quinn, Bob Schmidt, Shawn Simpson, Dan Sylvester, Niklas Wikegard, Darryl Young

Front Office Staff
Vice-President of Marketing	Lew Strudler
Assistant Director of Marketing	Debi Angus
Director of Promotions and Advertising	Charles Copeland
Director of Sales	Jerry Murphy
Director of Season Subscriptions	Joanne Kowalski
Corporate Sales Manager	Kerry Gregg
Administrative Assistant to V.P. Marketing	Janice Toepper
Souvenir Coordinator	Kim Moyer
Assistant Souvenir Coordinator	Amy Hobbs
Regional Sales Managers	Bryan Maust, John Oakes, Darren Bruening, Ron Potter
Corporate Sales Manager	David Abrutyn
Sales Representatives	Tim Bronaugh, Bill O'Brien, Brian Rupp
Administrative Assistant to Marketing	Paula Argent
Secretary to the Sales Department	Shelly Finkel
Receptionist	Nancy Woodall
Vice President of Communications	Ed Quinlan
Director of Community Relations	Yvon Labre
Public Relations Assistant	Dan Kaufman
Publications Assistant	Rick Braunstein
Administrative Assistant to the Public Relations Department	Julie Hensley
Controller	Aggie Ballard
Accounting Assistants	Kathleen Brady, Crystal Coffren, Deborah Kostakos, Melanie Loveless

Medical and Training Staff
Head Trainer	Stan Wong
Assistant Trainer/Head Equipment Manager	Doug Shearer
Assistant Equipment Manager	Craig Leydig
Assistant to the Equipment Manager	Rick Harper
Strength and Conditioning Coach	Frank Costello
Team Nutritionist	Pat Mann
Massage Therapist	Curt Millar
Team Physicians	Dr. Richard Grossman, Dr. Stephen Haas, Dr. Carl MacCartee, Dr. Frank Melograna
Team Dentist	Dr. Howard Salob

Coach

MURRAY, TERRY RODNEY
Coach, Washington Capitals. Born in Shawville, Que., July 20, 1950.

Terry Murray was named Capitals' head coach on January 15, 1990, and now is the second longest serving head coach in the NHL. Murray led the Capitals to their second consecutive second place finish in 1992-93, after the club recorded 98 points, 4th best in franchise history, in 1991-92. Murray spent six seasons as a Capitals assistant coach, and served as Head Coach of the Baltimore Skipjacks from 1988 until being named to the Capitals' top job.

Murray was selected 88th overall by California in the 1970 Amateur Draft. He enjoyed a successful playing career in both the NHL and American Hockey League. He led the Maine Mariners to two Calder Cup championships in 1977-78 and 1978-79, and was awarded the AHL's Eddie Shore Trophy as the outstanding defenseman in both seasons. He was an AHL First Team All-Star in three seasons, 1975-76, 1977-78 and 1978-79. Terry played in 302 NHL games over 8 seasons, concluding his career with the Capitals in 1981-82. He is the first ex-Capital to coach the club.

Coaching Record

			Regular Season					Playoffs			
Season	Team	Games	W	L	T	%	Games	W	L	%
1988-89	Baltimore (AHL)	80	30	46	4	.400	....	....	....	....
1989-90	Baltimore (AHL)	44	26	17	1	.603	....	....	....	....
1989-90	Washington (NHL)	34	18	14	2	.559	15	8	7	.533
1990-91	Washington (NHL)	80	37	36	7	.506	11	5	6	.455
1991-92	Washington (NHL)	80	45	27	8	.613	7	3	4	.429
1992-93	Washington (NHL)	84	43	34	7	.554	6	2	4	.333
	NHL Totals	278	143	111	24	.558	39	18	21	.462

General Manager

POILE, DAVID
Vice-President and General Manager, Washington Capitals.
Born in Toronto, Ont., February 14, 1949.

David Poile became the Capitals General Manager on August 30, 1982, and immediately turned the team into a perennial contender. In his initial season, the Capitals made the playoffs for the first time in Club history, and their first winning season. He was named The Sporting News Executive of the Year following that season, and again after the 1984-85 season. He was named Inside Hockey Man of the Year in 1992 after leading the team to a 45-27-8 mark, and championing the instant replay rule. Poile, a graduate of Northeastern University, began his professional hockey management career as an Administrative Assistant with the Atlanta Flames organization, where he served until joining the Washington franchise.

Winnipeg Jets

1992-93 Results: 40W-37L-7T 87PTS. Fourth, Smythe Division

Year-by-Year Record

Season	GP	Home W	L	T	Road W	L	T	Overall W	L	T	GF	GA	Pts.	Finished	Playoff Result
1992-93	84	23	16	3	17	21	4	40	37	7	322	320	87	4th, Smythe Div.	Lost Div. Semi-Final
1991-92	80	20	14	6	13	18	9	33	32	15	251	244	81	4th, Smythe Div.	Lost Div. Semi-Final
1990-91	80	17	18	5	9	25	6	26	43	11	260	288	63	5th, Smythe Div.	Out of Playoffs
1989-90	80	22	13	5	15	19	6	37	32	11	298	290	85	3rd, Smythe Div.	Lost Div. Semi-Final
1988-89	80	17	18	5	9	24	7	26	42	12	300	355	64	5th, Smythe Div.	Out of Playoffs
1987-88	80	20	14	6	13	22	5	33	36	11	292	310	77	3rd, Smythe Div.	Lost Div. Semi-Final
1986-87	80	25	12	3	15	20	5	40	32	8	279	271	88	3rd, Smythe Div.	Lost Div. Final
1985-86	80	18	19	3	8	28	4	26	47	7	295	372	59	3rd, Smythe Div.	Lost Div. Semi-Final
1984-85	80	21	13	6	22	14	4	43	27	10	358	332	96	2nd, Smythe Div.	Lost Div. Final
1983-84	80	17	15	8	14	23	3	31	38	11	340	374	73	4th, Smythe Div.	Lost Div. Semi-Final
1982-83	80	22	16	2	11	23	6	33	39	8	311	333	74	4th, Smythe Div.	Lost Div. Semi-Final
1981-82	80	18	13	9	15	20	5	33	33	14	319	332	80	2nd, Norris Div.	Lost Div. Semi-Final
1980-81	80	7	25	8	2	32	6	9	57	14	246	400	32	6th, Smythe Div.	Out of Playoffs
1979-80	80	13	19	8	7	30	3	20	49	11	214	314	51	5th, Smythe Div.	Out of Playoffs

Schedule

	Home			Away
Oct.	Wed. 6 Washington		Oct.	Sat. 9 Dallas
	Sat. 16 Chicago			Sun. 10 Chicago
	Mon. 18 Edmonton			Tues. 12 New Jersey
	Fri. 29 Los Angeles			Thur. 21 Detroit
	Sun. 31 Calgary			Sat. 23 Philadelphia
Nov.	Wed. 3 St Louis			Tues. 26 Florida
	Fri. 5 Ottawa			Wed. 27 Tampa Bay
	Sat. 13 Dallas		Nov.	Sun. 7 Dallas
	Wed. 17 Detroit			Tues. 9 NY Islanders
	Wed. 24 Anaheim			Wed. 10 NY Rangers
	Fri. 26 Vancouver			Mon. 15 Calgary
Dec.	Sun. 5 Detroit			Fri. 19 Buffalo
	Fri. 10 Florida			Sat. 20 Quebec
	Sun. 12 Toronto			Sun. 28 St Louis
	Mon. 20 Anaheim			Tues. 30 Los Angeles
	Thur. 23 Quebec		Dec.	Wed. 1 Anaheim
	Wed. 29 Chicago			Fri. 3 San Jose
	Fri. 31 St Louis*			Mon. 6 Detroit
Jan.	Wed. 12 Buffalo			Wed. 8 Toronto
	Sat. 15 Toronto			Fri. 17 Vancouver
	Sun. 16 Tampa Bay			Sat. 18 Calgary
	Wed. 19 New Jersey			Mon. 27 Edmonton
Feb.	Wed. 2 Dallas		Jan.	Sun. 2 Chicago
	Fri. 4 Hartford			Wed. 5 Hartford
	Fri. 11 Toronto			Thur. 6 Boston
	Fri. 18 Chicago			Sat. 8 Ottawa
	Sun. 20 Calgary*			Mon. 10 Montreal
	Tues. 22 Florida			Tues. 25 Los Angeles
	(at Hamilton)			Wed. 26 Anaheim
	Fri. 25 Boston			Sat. 29 Detroit*
	Mon. 28 San Jose		Feb.	Sun. 6 Edmonton*
Mar.	Wed. 2 Dallas			Tues. 8 St Louis
	Sun. 6 Pittsburgh*			Wed. 9 Dallas
	Mon. 7 NY Islanders			Tues. 15 Pittsburgh
	Fri. 11 Vancouver			Thur. 24 Chicago
	Wed. 16 St Louis		Mar.	Fri. 4 Ottawa
	Sat. 19 Detroit			(at Minnesota)
	Wed. 23 Montreal			Sat. 12 Toronto
	Fri. 25 San Jose			Tues. 29 San Jose
	Sun. 27 NY Rangers*		Apr.	Fri. 1 Vancouver*
Apr.	Mon. 4 Philadelphia			Sun. 10 Toronto
	Wed. 6 Edmonton			Tues. 12 Washington
	Sat. 9 Los Angeles*			Thur. 14 St Louis

* Denotes afternoon game.

Home Starting Times:

Weeknights	7:35 p.m.
Saturdays and Sundays	7:05 p.m.
Matinees	2:05 p.m.
Except Fri. Dec. 31	4:35 p.m.
Sun. Mar. 6	1:05 p.m.
Fri. Mar. 11	6:35 p.m.

Franchise date: June 22, 1979

CENTRAL DIVISION

NHL

WESTERN CONFERENCE

15th NHL Season

Defenseman Teppo Numminen recorded seven goals and 30 assists in 1992-93, his fifth season with the Winnipeg Jets.

1993-94 Player Personnel

FORWARDS	HT	WT	S	Place of Birth	Date	1992-93 Club
ALATALO, Mika	5-11	185	L	Oulu, Finland	8/11/71	Lukko
BARNES, Stu	5-11	180	R	Edmonton, Alta.	12/25/70	Moncton-Winnipeg
BORSATO, Luciano	5-11	190	R	Richmond Hill, Ont.	1/7/66	Winnipeg
DAVYDOV, Evgeny	6-0	195	R	Chelyabinsk, USSR	5/27/67	Winnipeg
DOMI, Tie	5-10	200	R	Windsor, Ont.	11/1/69	NY Rangers-Winnipeg
EAGLES, Mike	5-10	190	L	Sussex, N.B.	3/7/63	Winnipeg
ERICKSON, Bryan	5-9	175	R	Roseau, MN	3/7/60	Moncton-Winnipeg
FRITSCHE, John	5-9	196	R	Cleveland, OH	3/5/66	Lugano
GERNANDER, Ken	5-10	175	L	Coleraine, MN	6/30/69	Moncton
GROSEK, Michal	6-1	183	R	Vyskov, Czech.	6/1/75	ZPS Zlin
KAMINSKY, Yan	6-1	176	L	Penza, USSR	7/28/71	Dynamo Moscow
KING, Kris	5-11	210	L	Bracebridge, Ont.	2/18/66	NY Rangers-Winnipeg
LeBLANC, John	6-1	190	L	Campbellton, N.B.	1/21/64	Moncton-Winnipeg
McCLELLAND, Kevin	6-2	205	R	Oshawa, Ont.	7/4/62	St. John's
MURRAY, Rob	6-1	180	R	Toronto, Ont.	4/4/67	Moncton-Winnipeg
NUMMINEN, Teemu	6-3	194	L	Tampere, Finland	12/23/73	Tappara
RAISKY, Andrei	6-2	194	L	Ust-Kamenogorsk, USSR	3/30/70	Moncton-Dayton
RAITANEN, Rauli	6-2	183	L	Pori, Finland	1/14/70	Assat
ROMANIUK, Russ	6-0	195	L	Winnipeg, Man.	6/9/70	Wpg.-Ft. Wayne-Monc.
SELANNE, Teemu	6-0	181	R	Helsinki, Finland	7/3/70	Winnipeg
SHANNON, Darrin	6-2	200	L	Barrie, Ont.	12/8/69	Winnipeg
STEEN, Thomas	5-11	185	L	Grums, Sweden	6/8/60	Winnipeg
STEVENSON, Jeremy	6-1	208	L	San Bernadino, CA	7/28/74	Newmarket
TKACHUK, Keith	6-2	215	L	Melrose, MA	3/28/72	Winnipeg
TOMLINSON, Dave	5-11	177	L	North Vancouver, B.C.	5/8/69	Toronto-St. John's
VITOLINSH, Harijs	6-3	205	L	Riga, USSR	4/30/68	N. Haven-T. Bay-Chur
VOLOGZHANINOV, Ivan	6-0	180	L	Kiev, USSR	7/4/74	Lethbridge
YLONEN, Yuha	6-1	178	L	Helsinki, Finland	2/13/72	HPK Hameenlinna
YSEBAERT, Paul	6-1	190	L	Sarnia, Ont.	5/15/66	Detroit
ZHAMNOV, Alexei	6-1	187	L	Moscow, USSR	10/1/70	Winnipeg

DEFENSEMEN						
ALEXEYEV, Alexander	6-0	216	L	Kiev, USSR	3/21/74	Tacoma
BAUTIN, Sergei	6-3	185	L	Rogachev, USSR	3/11/67	Winnipeg
BLOMSTEN, Arto	6-3	198	L	Vaasa, Finland	3/16/65	Djurgarden
HOUSLEY, Phil	5-10	184	L	St.Paul, MN	3/9/64	Winnipeg
KENNEDY, Dean	6-2	212	R	Redvers, Sask.	1/18/63	Winnipeg
MIKULCHIK, Oleg	6-2	200	R	Minsk, USSR	6/27/64	Moncton
MIRONOV, Boris	6-3	196	R	Moscow, USSR	3/21/72	CSKA Moscow
MULLER, Mike	6-2	205	L	Fairview, MN	9/18/71	Dynamo Moscow
NUMMINEN, Teppo	6-1	190	L	Tampere, Finland	7/3/68	Winnipeg
OLAUSSON, Fredrik	6-2	195	L	Dadesjo, Sweden	10/5/66	Winnipeg
SHANNON, Darryl	6-2	195	L	Barrie, Ont.	6/21/68	Toronto-St. John's
SOROKIN, Sergei	5-11	187	L	Gorky, USSR	10/2/69	Dynamo Moscow
ULANOV, Igor	6-2	202	L	Krasnokamsk, USSR	10/1/69	Monc.-Ft. Wayne-Wpg.
VISHEAU, Mark	6-5	201	R	Burlington, Ont.	6/27/73	London
WOODS, Martin	5-10	196	R	Hull, Que.	5/14/75	Victoriaville

GOALTENDERS	HT	WT	C	Place of Birth	Date	1992-93 Club
BEAUREGARD, Stephane	5-11	182	R	Cowansville, Que.	1/10/68	Philadelphia-Hershey
ESSENSA, Bob	6-0	180	L	Toronto, Ont.	1/14/65	Winnipeg
GAUTHIER, Sean	5-11	202	L	Sudbury, Ont.	3/28/71	Moncton
LANGKOW, Scott	5-11	180	L	Edmonton, Alta.	4/21/75	Portland
O'NEILL, Mike	5-7	160	L	LaSalle, Que.	11/3/67	Moncton-Winnipeg
RICHARDS, Mark	5-8	179	L	Jamison, PA	7/24/69	Ft. Wayne-Tol.-Monc.
ROY, Allain	5-10	170	L	Campbellton, N.B.	2/6/70	Team Canada

General Managers' History

John Ferguson, 1979-80 to 1987-88; John Ferguson and Mike Smith, 1988-89; Mike Smith, 1989-90 to date.

Coaching History

Tom McVie, 1979-80; Tom McVie and Bill Sutherland, 1980-81; Tom Watt, 1981-82 to 1982-83; Tom Watt, John Ferguson and Barry Long, 1983-84; Barry Long, 1984-85; Barry Long and John Ferguson, 1985-86. Dan Maloney, 1986-87 to 1987-88, Dan Maloney and Rick Bowness 1988-89; Bob Murdoch, 1989-90 to 1990-91; John Paddock, 1991-92 to date.

Captains' History

Lars-Erik Sjoberg, 1979-80; Morris Lukowich, 1980-81; Dave Christian, 1981-82; Dave Christian and Lucien DeBlois, 1982-83; Lucien DeBlois, 1983-84; Dale Hawerchuk, 1984-85 to 1988-89; Randy Carlyle, Dale Hawerchuk and Thomas Steen, 1989-90; Randy Carlyle and Thomas Steen, 1990-91; Troy Murray, 1991-92; Troy Murray and Dean Kennedy, 1992-93; Dean Kennedy, 1993-94.

Retired Numbers

9	Bobby Hull	1972-1980

1992-93 Scoring

Regular Season

Pos	#	Player	Team	GP	G	A	Pts	+/-	PIM	PP	SH	GW	GT	S	%
R	13*	Teemu Selanne	WPG	84	76	56	132	8	45	24	0	7	0	387	19.6
D	6	Phil Housley	WPG	80	18	79	97	14-	52	6	0	2	0	249	7.2
C	10*	Alexei Zhamnov	WPG	68	25	47	72	7	58	6	1	4	1	163	15.3
C	25	Thomas Steen	WPG	80	22	50	72	8-	75	6	0	6	0	150	14.7
L	34	Darrin Shannon	WPG	84	20	40	60	4-	91	12	0	2	0	116	17.2
D	4	Fredrik Olausson	WPG	68	16	41	57	4-	22	11	0	3	0	165	9.7
R	7*	Keith Tkachuk	WPG	83	28	23	51	13-	201	12	0	2	1	199	14.1
R	11*	Evgeny Davydov	WPG	79	28	21	49	2-	66	7	0	2	0	176	15.9
D	27	Teppo Numminen	WPG	66	7	30	37	4	33	3	1	0	0	103	6.8
C	38	Luciano Borsato	WPG	67	15	20	35	1-	38	1	1	3	0	101	14.9
C	36	Mike Eagles	WPG	84	8	18	26	1-	131	0	1	0	1	67	11.9
D	3*	Sergei Bautin	WPG	71	5	18	23	2-	96	0	0	0	0	82	6.1
C	14	Stu Barnes	WPG	38	12	10	22	3-	10	3	0	3	0	73	16.4
R	15	John Druce	WPG	50	6	14	20	4-	37	0	0	1	0	60	10.0
L	17	Kris King	NYR	30	3	3	6	1-	67	0	0	0	0	23	.0
			WPG	48	8	8	16	5	136	0	0	1	0	51	15.7
			TOTAL	78	8	11	19	4	203	0	0	1	0	74	10.8
C	18	Bryan Erickson	WPG	41	4	12	16	2	14	2	0	1	0	45	8.9
D	5	Igor Ulanov	WPG	56	2	14	16	6	124	0	0	0	0	26	7.7
R	20	Tie Domi	NYR	12	2	0	2	1-	95	0	0	0	0	11	18.2
			WPG	49	3	10	13	2	249	0	0	0	0	29	10.3
			TOTAL	61	5	10	15	1	344	0	0	0	0	40	12.5
D	22	Mike Lalor	WPG	64	1	8	9	10-	76	0	0	0	0	75	1.3
D	26	Dean Kennedy	WPG	78	1	7	8	3-	105	0	0	1	0	50	2.0
G	35	Bob Essensa	WPG	67	0	5	5	0	2	0	0	0	0	0	.0
L	21	Russ Romaniuk	WPG	21	2	2	4	0	22	0	0	1	0	20	15.0
G	30	Jim Hrivnak	WSH	27	0	3	3	0	0	0	0	0	0	0	.0
			WPG	3	0	0	0	0	0	0	0	0	0	0	.0
			TOTAL	30	0	3	3	0	0	0	0	0	0	0	.0
D	8	Randy Carlyle	WPG	22	1	1	2	6-	14	0	0	0	0	21	4.8
D	45	Anatoli Fedotov	WPG	2	1	1	2	1	0	0	0	0	0	1	.0
L	23	Andy Brickley	WPG	12	0	2	2	1	0	0	0	0	0	9	.0
D	52*	Dallas Eakins	WPG	14	0	2	2	2	38	0	0	0	0	9	.0
C	50	Rob Murray	WPG	10	1	0	1	0	8	0	0	0	0	4	25.0
R	12	Alan Kerr	WPG	7	0	1	1	4-	2	0	0	0	0	0	.0
C	24*	Scott Levins	WPG	9	0	1	1	2-	18	0	0	0	0	8	.0
L	28	Bob Joyce	WPG	1	0	0	0	0	0	0	0	0	0	0	.0
G	1*	Michael O'Neill	WPG	2	0	0	0	0	2	0	0	0	0	0	.0
R	37	John LeBlanc	WPG	3	0	0	0	2	0	0	0	0	0	5	.0
C	91*	Kris Draper	WPG	7	0	0	0	6-	2	0	0	0	0	5	.0

Goaltending

No.	Goaltender	GPI	Mins	Avg	W	L	T	EN	SO	GA	SA	S%
35	Bob Essensa	67	3855	3.53	33	26	6	4	2	227	2119	.893
30	Jim Hrivnak	3	180	4.33	2	1	0	0	0	13	96	.865
31	Rick Tabaracci	19	959	4.38	5	10	0	0	0	70	496	.859
1	*Michael O'Neill	2	73	4.93	0	0	1	0	0	6	34	.824
	Totals	84	5084	3.78	40	37	7	4	2	320	2749	.884

Playoffs

Pos	#	Player	Team	GP	G	A	Pts	+/-	PIM	PP	SH	GW	GT	S	%
D	6	Phil Housley	WPG	6	0	7	7	3-	2	0	0	0	0	10	.0
R	13*	Teemu Selanne	WPG	6	4	2	6	3-	2	2	0	1	1	27	14.8
L	34	Darrin Shannon	WPG	6	2	4	6	3-	6	1	0	0	0	13	15.4
R	7*	Keith Tkachuk	WPG	6	4	0	4	5-	14	1	0	0	0	17	23.5
C	25	Thomas Steen	WPG	6	1	3	4	4-	2	1	0	0	0	7	14.3
C	14	Stu Barnes	WPG	6	1	3	4	1	2	0	0	0	0	3	33.3
L	23	Andy Brickley	WPG	1	1	1	2	2	0	0	0	0	1	1	100.0
L	17	Kris King	WPG	6	1	1	2	1-	4	0	0	0	0	12	8.3
D	27	Teppo Numminen	WPG	6	1	1	2	4-	2	1	0	0	0	9	11.1
D	22	Mike Lalor	WPG	4	0	2	2	4	0	0	0	0	0	7	.0
D	4	Fredrik Olausson	WPG	6	0	2	2	0	2	0	0	0	0	5	.0
C	10*	Alexei Zhamnov	WPG	6	0	2	2	4-	2	0	0	0	0	13	.0
R	20	Tie Domi	WPG	6	1	0	1	1	23	0	0	0	0	5	20.0
C	38	Luciano Borsato	WPG	6	1	0	1	2-	4	0	1	0	0	7	14.3
C	36	Mike Eagles	WPG	5	0	1	1	2-	6	0	0	0	0	6	.0
L	21	Russ Romaniuk	WPG	1	0	0	0	1-	0	0	0	0	0	1	.0
R	15	John Druce	WPG	2	0	0	0	0	0	0	0	0	0	1	.0
C	18	Bryan Erickson	WPG	2	0	0	0	3-	0	0	0	0	0	2	.0
R	11*	Evgeny Davydov	WPG	4	0	0	0	1-	0	0	0	0	0	3	.0
D	5	Igor Ulanov	WPG	6	0	0	0	1-	4	0	0	0	0	1	.0
G	35	Bob Essensa	WPG	6	0	0	0	0	2	0	0	0	0	0	.0
D	26	Dean Kennedy	WPG	6	0	0	0	2	2	0	0	0	0	2	.0
D	3*	Sergei Bautin	WPG	6	0	0	0	2-	2	0	0	0	0	5	.0

Goaltending

No.	Goaltender	GPI	Mins	Avg	W	L	EN	SO	GA	SA	S%
35	Bob Essensa	6	367	3.27	2	4	1	0	20	183	.891
	Totals	6	371	3.40	2	4	1	0	21	184	.886

Club Records

Team

(Figures in brackets for season records are games played; records for fewest points, wins, ties, losses, goals, goals against are for 70 or more games)

Most Points	96	1984-85 (80)
Most Wins	43	1984-85 (80)
Most Ties	15	1991-92 (80)
Most Losses	57	1980-81 (80)
Most Goals	358	1984-85 (80)
Most Goals Against	400	1980-81 (80)
Fewest Points	32	1980-81 (80)
Fewest Wins	9	1980-81 (80)
Fewest Ties	7	1985-86 (80)
Fewest Losses	27	1984-85 (80)
Fewest Goals	214	1979-80 (80)
Fewest Goals Against	244	1991-92 (80)

Longest Winning Streak
- Over-all............. 9 Mar. 8-27/85
- Home .... 9 Dec. 27/92-Jan. 23/93
- Away............... 8 Feb. 25-Apr. 6/85

Longest Undefeated Streak
- Over-all............. 13 Mar. 8-Apr. 7/85 (10 wins, 3 ties)
- Home .... 11 Dec. 23/83 Feb. 5/84 (6 wins, 5 ties)
- Away............... 9 Feb. 25-Apr. 7/85 (8 wins, 1 tie)

Longest Losing Streak
- Over-all............. 10 Nov. 30-Dec. 20/80
- Home .... 4 Five times
- Away............... 9 Dec. 26/79-Jan. 22/80

Longest Winless Streak
- Over-all............. *30 Oct. 19-Dec. 20/80 (23 losses, 7 ties)
- Home .... 14 Oct. 19-Dec. 14/80 (9 losses, 5 ties)

Away	18	Oct. 10-Dec. 20/80 (16 losses, 2 ties)
Most Shutouts, Season	7	1991-92 (80)
Most PIM, Season	2,278	1987-88 (80)
Most Goals, Game	12	Feb. 25/85 (Wpg. 12 at NYR. 5)

Individual

Most Seasons	12	Thomas Steen
Most Games	843	Thomas Steen
Most Goals, Career	379	Dale Hawerchuk
Most Assists, Career	550	Dale Hawerchuk
Most Points, Career	929	Dale Hawerchuk (379 goals, 550 assists)
Most PIM, Career	1,338	Laurie Boschman
Most Shutouts, Career	13	Bob Essensa

Longest Consecutive Games Streak .... 475 Dale Hawerchuk (Dec. 19/82-Dec. 10/88)

Most Goals, Season	76	Teemu Selanne (1992-93)
Most Assists, Season	79	Phil Housley (1992-93)
Most Points, Season	132	Teemu Selanne (1992-93) (76 goals, 56 assists)
Most PIM, Season	287	Jimmy Mann (1979-80)

Most Points, Defenseman Season .... 97 Phil Housley (1992-93) (18 goals, 79 assists)

Most Points, Center, Season .... 130 Dale Hawerchuk (1984-85) (53 goals, 77 assists)

Most Points, Right Wing, Season .... 132 Teemu Selanne (1992-93) (76 goals, 56 assists)

Most Points, Left Wing, Season .... 92 Morris Lukowich (1981-82) (43 goals, 49 assists)

Most Points, Rookie, Season .... *132 Teemu Selanne (1992-93) (76 goals, 56 assists)

Most Shutouts, Season	5	Bob Essensa (1991-92)
Most Goals, Game	5	Willy Lindstrom (Mar. 2/82)
Most Assists, Game	5	Dale Hawerchuk (Mar. 6/84, Mar. 18/89, Mar. 4/90) Phil Housley (Jan. 18/93)
Most Points, Game	6	Willy Lindstrom (Mar. 2/82) Dale Hawerchuk (Dec. 14/83, Mar. 18/89) Thomas Steen (Oct. 24/84) Eddie Olczyk (Dec. 21/91)

* NHL Record.

1992-93 Results

	Home			Away	
Oct. 6	Detroit	4-1	**Oct.** 8	San Jose	3-4
14	Edmonton	7-3	10	Los Angeles	3-6
16	Vancouver	2-6	12	Vancouver	1-8
23	Los Angeles	4-2	18	Philadelphia	4-5
26	Washington	6-2	20	Detroit	3-5
28	Calgary	5-7	31	Quebec	2-3
Nov. 6	Edmonton	1-6	**Nov.** 2	Montreal	1-2
10	Los Angeles	4-4	8	Vancouver*	1-6
21	NY Rangers	4-5	12	Minnesota	7-2
24	NY Islanders	3-3	14	St. Louis	2-4
27	San Jose	3-2	17	Tampa Bay	6-5
Dec. 5	Montreal	2-3	19	Detroit	5-3
15	New Jersey	4-3	**Dec.** 2	Calgary	3-3
21	San Jose	5-4	8	Pittsburgh	2-5
23	Calgary	3-4	11	Washington	6-8
27	Minnesota	7-4	12	NY Islanders	4-3
29	Boston	5-4	17	Chicago	1-5
31	Edmonton*	3-2	19	St. Louis	1-0
Jan. 8	Los Angeles	6-3	20	Minnesota	4-5
10	Pittsburgh	3-2	**Jan.** 2	New Jersey	2-2
12	San Jose	4-1	3	Chicago	1-4
18	Hartford	8-7	5	Calgary	4-2
19	Chicago	5-2	13	Edmonton	4-1
23	Edmonton	8-5	16	Los Angeles	5-2
Feb. 3	St. Louis	2-4	22	Calgary	4-4
10	Buffalo	2-6	27	NY Rangers	2-5
12	Hartford	2-6	28	Boston	2-6
14	San Jose*	2-3	30	Hartford	6-3
22	Ottawa	6-3	**Feb.** 1	Ottawa	4-4
26	Vancouver	4-7	18	San Jose	3-5
28	Minnesota	7-6	20	Vancouver	2-4
Mar. 2	Quebec	4-7	23	Ottawa	8-2
12	Vancouver	2-3	**Mar.** 4	Edmonton	5-3
14	Tampa Bay*	3-1	6	Toronto	2-4
21	Calgary*	4-2	7	Buffalo	1-2
23	Toronto	4-5	9	Tampa Bay	4-2
26	St. Louis	4-2	16	Los Angeles	4-8
28	Los Angeles*	3-3	18	Vancouver	5-2
Apr. 6	Philadelphia	2-4	30	Calgary	5-4
8	Toronto	5-3	**Apr.** 1	San Jose	9-5
13	Tampa Bay	3-5	3	Edmonton	6-4
15	Edmonton	3-0	11	Edmonton*	7-5

*Denotes afternoon game

All-time Record vs. Other Clubs

Regular Season

		At Home								On Road								Total					
	GP	W	L	T	GF	GA	PTS	GP	W	L	T	GF	GA	PTS	GP	W	L	T	GF	GA	PTS
Boston	22	9	11	2	77	79	20	21	3	15	3	66	100	9	43	12	26	5	143	179	29
Buffalo	21	8	11	2	68	80	18	21	1	18	2	53	98	4	42	9	29	4	121	178	22
Calgary	48	22	18	8	202	176	52	49	10	32	7	156	235	27	97	32	50	15	358	411	79
Chicago	24	12	9	3	101	89	27	24	4	17	3	73	123	11	48	16	26	6	174	212	38
Detroit	23	8	7	8	78	71	24	25	10	12	3	96	99	23	48	18	19	11	174	170	47
Edmonton	49	19	26	4	201	229	42	50	16	31	3	172	231	35	99	35	57	7	373	460	77
Hartford	23	12	11	0	84	86	24	21	6	10	5	71	88	17	44	18	21	5	155	174	41
Los Angeles	50	24	17	9	220	186	57	47	21	18	8	194	197	50	97	45	35	17	414	383	107
Minnesota	24	12	11	1	90	86	25	25	8	15	2	81	115	18	49	20	26	3	171	201	43
Montreal	21	7	9	5	68	83	19	21	2	19	0	49	115	4	42	9	28	5	117	198	23
New Jersey	22	16	3	3	92	57	35	20	9	5	6	66	59	24	42	25	8	9	158	116	59
NY Islanders	21	7	12	2	68	80	16	22	5	11	6	66	85	16	43	12	23	8	134	165	32
NY Rangers	22	8	12	2	81	86	18	21	8	11	2	88	102	18	43	16	23	4	169	188	36
Ottawa	1	1	0	0	6	3	2	2	1	0	1	12	6	3	3	2	0	1	18	9	5
Philadelphia	21	9	11	1	70	76	19	22	5	17	0	60	101	10	43	14	28	1	130	177	29
Pittsburgh	21	9	11	1	80	78	19	22	7	15	0	66	91	14	43	16	26	1	146	169	33
Quebec	21	9	7	5	89	85	23	22	10	10	2	90	88	22	43	19	17	7	179	173	45
St. Louis	25	13	6	6	91	79	32	24	5	11	8	73	97	18	49	18	17	14	164	176	50
San Jose	8	6	2	0	32	19	12	6	3	2	1	28	24	7	14	9	4	1	60	43	19
Tampa Bay	2	1	1	0	6	6	2	2	2	0	0	10	7	4	4	3	1	0	16	13	6
Toronto	24	13	8	3	117	102	29	24	15	8	1	109	90	31	48	28	16	4	226	192	60
Vancouver	47	24	16	7	185	175	55	50	14	28	8	149	194	36	97	38	44	15	334	369	91
Washington	22	11	6	5	84	79	27	21	5	14	2	67	100	12	43	16	20	7	151	179	39
Totals	562	260	225	77	2190	2090	597	562	170	319	73	1895	2445	413	1124	430	544	150	4085	4535	1010

Playoffs

	Series	W	L	GP	W	L	T	GF	GA	Last Mtg.	Round	Result
Calgary	3	2	1	13	7	6	0	45	43	1987	DSF	W 4-2
Edmonton	6	0	6	26	4	22	0	75	120	1990	DSF	L 3-4
St. Louis	1	0	1	4	1	3	0	13	20	1982	DSF	L 1-3
Vancouver	2	0	2	13	5	8	0	34	50	1993	DSF	L 2-4
Totals	12	2	10	56	17	39	0	167	233			

Playoff Results 1993-89

Year	Round	Opponent	Result	GF	GA
1993	DSF	Vancouver	L 2-4	17	21
1992	DSF	Vancouver	L 3-4	17	29
1990	DSF	Edmonton	L 3-4	22	24

Abbreviations: Round: F – Final;
CF – conference final; DF – division final;
DSF – division semi-final; SF – semi-final;
QF – quarter-final; PR – preliminary round.
GA – goals against; GF – goals for.

Entry Draft Selections 1993-79

1993
Pick
15 Mats Lindgren
31 Scott Langkow
43 Alexei Budayev
79 Ruslan Batyrshin
93 Ravil Gusmanov
119 Larry Courville
145 Michal Grosek
171 Martin Woods
197 Adrian Murray
217 Vladimir Potapov
223 Ilja Stashenkov
228 Harijs Vitolinsh
285 Russell Hewson

1992
Pick
17 Sergei Bautin
27 Boris Mironov
60 Jeremy Stevenson
84 Mark Visheau
132 Alexander Alexeyev
155 Artur Oktyabrev
156 Andrei Raisky
204 Nikolai Khaibulin
228 Yevgeny Garanin
229 Teemu Numminen
252 Andrei Karpovtsev
254 Ivan Vologzhaninov

1991
Pick
5 Aaron Ward
49 Dmitri Filimonov
91 Juha Ylonen
99 Yan Kaminsky
115 Jeff Sebastian
159 Jeff Ricciardi
181 Sean Gauthier
203 Igor Ulanov
225 Jason Jennings
247 Sergei Sorokin

1990
Pick
19 Keith Tkachuk
35 Mike Muller
74 Roman Meluzin
75 Scott Levins
77 Alexei Zhamnov
98 Craig Martin
119 Daniel Jardemyr
140 John Lilley
161 Henrik Andersson
182 Rauli Raitanen
203 Mika Alatalo
224 Sergei Selyanin
245 Keith Morris

1989
Pick
4 Stu Barnes
25 Dan Ratushny
46 Jason Cirone
62 Kris Draper
64 Mark Brownschidle
69 Alain Roy
109 Dan Bylsma
130 Pekka Peltola
131 Doug Evans
151 Jim Solly
172 Stephane Gauvin
193 Joe Larson
214 Bradley Podiak
235 Evgeny Davydov
240 Sergei Kharin

1988
Pick
10 Teemu Selanne
31 Russell Romaniuk
52 Stephane Beauregard
73 Brian Hunt
94 Anthony Joseph
115 Benoit Lebeau
115 Ronald Jones
127 Markus Akerblom
136 Jukka Marttila
157 Mark Smith
178 Mike Helber
199 Pavel Kostichkin
220 Kevin Heise
241 Kyle Galloway

1987
Pick
16 Bryan Marchment
37 Patrik Erickson
79 Don McLennan
96 Ken Gernander
100 Darrin Amundson
121 Joe Harwell
142 Tod Hartje
163 Markku Kyllonen
184 Jim Fernholz
226 Roger Rougelot
247 Hans Goran Elo

1986
Pick
8 Pat Elynuik
29 Teppo Numminen
50 Esa Palosaari
71 Hannu Jarvenpaa
92 Craig Endean
113 Robertson Bateman
155 Frank Furlan
176 Mark Green
197 John Blue
218 Matt Cote
239 Arto Blomsten

1985
Pick
18 Ryan Stewart
39 Roger Ohman
60 Daniel Berthiaume
81 Fredrik Olausson
102 John Borrell
123 Danton Cole
144 Brent Mowery
165 Tom Draper
186 Nevin Kardum
207 Dave Quigley
228 Chris Norton
249 Anssi Melametsa

1984
Pick
30 Peter Douris
68 Chris Mills
72 Sean Clement
93 Scott Schneider
99 Brent Severyn
114 Gary Lorden
135 Luciano Borsato
156 Brad Jones
177 Gord Whitaker
197 Rick Forst
218 Mike Warus
238 Jim Edmonds

1983
Pick
8 Andrew McBain
14 Bobby Dollas
29 Brad Berry
43 Peter Taglianetti
69 Bob Essensa
89 Harry Armstrong
109 Joel Baillargeon
129 Iain Duncan
149 Ron Pessetti
169 Todd Flichel
189 Cory Wright
209 Eric Cormier
229 Jamie Husgen

1982
Pick
12 Jim Kyte
74 Tom Martin
75 Dave Ellett
96 Tim Mishler
138 Derek Ray
159 Guy Gosselin
180 Tom Ward
201 Mike Savage
222 Bob Shaw
243 Jan Urban Ericson

1981
Pick
1 Dale Hawerchuk
22 Scott Arniel
43 Jyrki Seppa
64 Kirk McCaskill
85 Marc Behrend
106 Bob O'Connor
127 Peter Nilsson
148 Dan McFaul
169 Greg Dick
190 Vladimir Kadlec
211 Dave Kirwin

1980
Pick
2 David Babych
23 Moe Mantha
44 Murray Eaves
65 Guy Fournier
86 Glen Ostir
107 Ron Loustel
128 Brian Mullen
135 Mike Lauen
149 Sandy Beadle
170 Ed Christian
191 Dave Chartier

1979
Pick
19 Jimmy Mann
40 Dave Christian
61 Bill Whelton
82 Pat Daley
103 Thomas Steen
124 Tim Watters

Coach

PADDOCK, JOHN
Coach, Winnipeg Jets. Born in Brandon, Man., June 9, 1954.

John Paddock, who was named as the 10th head coach of the Winnipeg Jets on June 17, 1991, led the club to a fourth-place finish in the Smythe Division in 1992-93 with a 40-37-7 record. Paddock joined the Jets after serving one season as head coach of the Binghamton Rangers of the American Hockey League, the league where he got his coaching start in 1983. Paddock, then playing for the Maine Mariners, succeeded Tom McVie behind the Mariners bench when McVie was summoned to New Jersey; the Mariners won the AHL Calder Cup Championship that season. Paddock later joined the Hershey Bears, where he won another Calder Cup and two Coach of the Year awards. Paddock served one season as assistant general manager for the Philadelphia Flyers before joining the New York Rangers organization in 1990.

Paddock played 87 NHL games as a right wing, drafted by the Washington Capitals, and recorded eight goals and 14 assists during his career.

Coaching Record

Season	Team	Games	Regular Season W	L	T	%	Playoffs Games	W	L	%
1983-84	Maine (AHL)	80	33	36	11	.481	17	12	5	.706
1984-85	Maine (AHL)	80	38	32	10	.538	11	5	6	.454
1985-86	Hershey (AHL)	80	48	29	3	.619	18	10	8	.555
1986-87	Hershey (AHL)	80	43	36	1	.544	5	1	4	.200
1987-88	Hershey (AHL)	80	50	27	3	.644	12	12	0	1.000
1988-89	Hershey (AHL)	80	40	30	10	.563	12	7	5	.583
1990-91	Binghamton (AHL)	80	44	30	6	.588	10	4	6	.400
1991-92	Winnipeg (NHL)	80	33	32	15	.506	7	3	4	.429
1992-93	Winnipeg (NHL)	84	40	37	7	.518	6	2	4	.333
	NHL Totals	164	73	69	22	.512	13	5	8	.384

Club Directory

Winnipeg Arena
15-1430 Maroons Road
Winnipeg, Manitoba R3G 0L5
Phone **204/982-5387**
FAX 204/788-4668
Capacity: 15,393

Board of Directors
Barry L. Shenkarow, Bill Davis, Marvin Shenkarow, Harvey Secter, Steve Bannatyne, Dick Archer, Bob Chipman

President & Governor . . . . Barry L. Shenkarow
Alternate Governors . . . . Michael A. Smith, Bill Davis

Hockey Operations
Vice-President & General Manager . . . . Michael A. Smith
Assistant General Manager-Director of Hockey Operations . . . . Dennis McDonald
Head Coach . . . . John Paddock
Assistant Coaches . . . . Andy Murray, Zinetula Bilyaletdinov
Coordinator of Coaching Services . . . . Glen Williamson
Moncton Head Coach . . . . Rob Laird
Director of Scouting . . . . Bill Lesuk
Assistant Director of Scouting . . . . Joe Yannetti
Scouts . . . . Tom Savage, Connie Broden, Sean Coady, Charlie Burroughs, Boris Yemeljanov
Executive Ass't to Vice-President & G.M. . . . . . . Pat MacDonald
Administrative Assistant-Hockey Operations . . . . . Brenda Thompson

Communications
Vice President of Broadcasting & Communications Mike O'Hearn
Communications Assistant . . . . Igor Kuperman
Statistician/Communications . . . . Bruce Barton
Director of Community Relations/
Winnipeg Jets Goals For Kids . . . . Lori Summers
Administrative Assistant-Goals For Kids . . . . Michelle McCrea
Administrative Assistant-Community Relations . . . Heather Reynolds

Finance and Administration
Vice-President, Finance & Administration . . . . Don Binda
Director of Administrative Services . . . . Glenda Leiske
Director of Team Services . . . . Murray Harding
Director of Ticket Operations . . . . Dianne Gabbs
Accounting Supervisor . . . . Joe Leibfried
Accounting/Ticketing Assistant . . . . Sacha Rusaw
Accounting Assistants . . . . Bryan Braun, Doug Bergman
Administrative Assistant-Team Services/
Communications . . . . Roberta Rackal
Administrative Assistant-Novelty Operations . . . . Lynda Sweetland
Jets' All Sports Store Managers . . . . Jennifer Zalnasky, Dave Blackmore
Receptionist . . . . Mary Anne Mazepa
Ticket Assistant . . . . Georgie Jorowski

Marketing
Vice-President of Marketing . . . . Madeline Hanson
Manager of Retail Operations . . . . Val Kuhn
Marketing Assistant . . . . Sherri Wilson
Manager of Ticket Sales . . . . Hartley Miller
Director of Corporate Sales . . . . Dave Baker
National Accounts Manager . . . . Gord Dmytriw
Sales/Licensing Manager . . . . Marlene Benoit
Sales/Licensing Secretary . . . . Teresa Bastian

Dressing Room
Athletic Therapist . . . . Jim Ramsay
Athletic Trainer . . . . Phil Walker
Equipment Managers . . . . Craig Heisinger, Stan Wilson
Team Physician . . . . Dr. Brian Lukie
Team Dentist . . . . Dr. Gene Solmundson

Team Information
Team Colors . . . . Blue, Red and White
Dimensions of Rink . . . . 200 feet by 85 feet
Training Camp . . . . Winnipeg
Press Box Location . . . . East Side
TV Channel . . . . CKND TV (Channel 9 – Cable 12)
Radio Station . . . . CJOB AM 680
Play-by-Play (Radio) . . . . Curt Keilback

General Manager

MIKE SMITH
General Manager, Winnipeg Jets.
Born in Potsdam, New York, August 31, 1945.

Mike Smith was appointed general manager of the club on December 3, 1988 after ten years of service within the Jets organization. He had held the position of assistant general manager and director of scouting since 1984.

Smith began his NHL career in 1976-77 when he was an assistant coach with the New York Rangers under John Ferguson. After two seasons in New York, he assumed the same coaching duties with the Colorado Rockies. When the Jets entered the League in 1979-80, Smith was hired as general manager of their CHL franchise in Tulsa. In 1980-81, midway through the season, Smith was asked to come to Winnipeg to be head coach. In 1981-82 he became the team's director of recruiting.

1992-93 Final Statistics

Standings

Abbreviations: GA – goals against; **GF** – goals for; **GP** – games played; **L** – losses;
PTS – points; **T** – ties; **W** – wins; **%** – percentage of games won.

CLARENCE CAMPBELL CONFERENCE

Norris Division

	GP	W	L	T	GF	GA	PTS	%
Chicago	84	47	25	12	279	230	106	.631
Detroit	84	47	28	9	369	280	103	.613
Toronto	84	44	29	11	288	241	99	.589
St. Louis	84	37	36	11	282	278	85	.506
Minnesota	84	36	38	10	272	293	82	.488
Tampa Bay	84	23	54	7	245	332	53	.315

Smythe Division

	GP	W	L	T	GF	GA	PTS	%
Vancouver	84	46	29	9	346	278	101	.601
Calgary	84	43	30	11	322	282	97	.577
Los Angeles	84	39	35	10	338	340	88	.524
Winnipeg	84	40	37	7	322	320	87	.518
Edmonton	84	26	50	8	242	337	60	.357
San Jose	84	11	71	2	218	414	24	.143

PRINCE OF WALES CONFERENCE

Adams Division

	GP	W	L	T	GF	GA	PTS	%
Boston	84	51	26	7	332	268	109	.649
Quebec	84	47	27	10	351	300	104	.619
Montreal	84	48	30	6	326	280	102	.607
Buffalo	84	38	36	10	335	297	86	.512
Hartford	84	26	52	6	284	369	58	.345
Ottawa	84	10	70	4	202	395	24	.143

Patrick Division

	GP	W	L	T	GF	GA	PTS	%
Pittsburgh	84	56	21	7	367	268	119	.708
Washington	84	43	34	7	325	286	93	.554
NY Islanders	84	40	37	7	335	297	87	.518
New Jersey	84	40	37	7	308	299	87	.518
Philadelphia	84	36	37	11	319	319	83	.494
NY Rangers	84	34	39	11	304	308	79	.470

The "Finnish Flash," Teemu Selanne, set six NHL rookie records including most goals (76), points (132), powerplay goals (24) and game-winning goals (7).

INDIVIDUAL LEADERS

Goal Scoring

Player	Team	GP	G
Alexander Mogilny	Buf.	77	76
*Teemu Selanne	Wpg.	84	76
Mario Lemieux	Pit.	60	69
Luc Robitaille	L.A.	84	63
Pavel Bure	Van.	83	60
Pierre Turgeon	NYI	83	58
Steve Yzerman	Det.	84	58
Kevin Stevens	Pit.	72	55
Brett Hull	St. L.	80	54
Dave Andreychuk	Buf.-Tor.	83	54

Assists

Player	Team	GP	A
Adam Oates	Bos.	84	97
Doug Gilmour	Tor.	83	95
Pat LaFontaine	Buf.	84	95
Mario Lemieux	Pit.	60	91
Craig Janney	St. L.	84	82
Dale Hawerchuk	Buf.	81	80
Phil Housley	Wpg.	80	79
Steve Yzerman	Det.	84	79
Ron Francis	Pit.	84	76
Paul Coffey	L.A.-Det.	80	75

Power-play Goals

Player	Team	GP	PP
Dave Andreychuk	Buf.-Tor.	83	32
Brett Hull	St. L.	80	29
Alexander Mogilny	Buf.	77	27
Kevin Stevens	Pit.	72	26
Pierre Turgeon	NYI	83	24
Adam Oates	Bos.	84	24
Luc Robitaille	L.A.	84	24
*Teemu Selanne	Wpg.	84	24

Short-handed Goals

Player	Team	GP	SH
Pavel Bure	Van.	83	7
Steve Yzerman	Det.	84	7
Mario Lemieux	Pit.	60	6
Scott Young	Que.	82	6
Dave Reid	Bos.	65	5
Dave Poulin	Bos.	84	5

Game-winning Goals

Player	Team	GP	GW
Alexander Mogilny	Buf.	77	11
Geoff Courtnall	Van.	84	11
Adam Oates	Bos.	84	11
Mario Lemieux	Pit.	60	10
Mike Ricci	Que.	77	10
Pierre Turgeon	NYI	83	10
Mats Sundin	Que.	80	9
Jaromir Jagr	Pit.	81	9
Pavel Bure	Van.	83	9

Game-tying Goals

Player	Team	GP	GT
*Martin Rucinsky	Que.	77	3
Jeremy Roenick	Chi.	84	3

Shots

Player	Team	GP	S
Pavel Bure	Van.	83	407
Brett Hull	St. L.	80	390
*Teemu Selanne	Wpg.	84	387
Alexander Mogilny	Buf.	77	360
Ray Bourque	Bos.	78	330

First Goals

Player	Team	GP	FG
Jeremy Roenick	Chi.	84	12
Mario Lemieux	Pit.	60	11
Mark Recchi	Phi.	84	11
Brendan Shanahan	St. L.	71	10
Brett Hull	St. L.	80	10
Dave Andreychuk	Buf.-Tor.	83	10
*Teemu Selanne	Wpg.	84	10

Shooting Percentage

(minimum 84 shots)

Player	Team	GP	G	S	%
Craig Simpson	Edm.	60	24	91	26.4
Petr Nedved	Van.	84	38	149	25.5
Dimitri Khristich	Wsh.	64	31	127	24.4
Mario Lemieux	Pit.	60	69	286	24.1
Luc Robitaille	L.A.	84	63	265	23.8

Penalty Minutes

Player	Team	GP	PIM
Marty McSorley	L.A.	81	399
Gino Odjick	Van.	75	370
Tie Domi	NYR-Wpg.	61	344
Nick Kypreos	Hfd.	75	325
Mike Peluso	Ott.	81	318

Individual Leaders

Abbreviations: * – rookie eligible for Calder Trophy; **A** – assists; **G** – goals; **GP** – games played; **GT** – game-tying goals; **GW** – game-winning goals; **PIM** – penalties in minutes; **PP** – power play goals; **Pts** – points; **S** – shots on goal; **SH** – short-handed goals; **%** – percentage shots resulting in goals; +/– – difference between Goals For (**GF**) scored when a player is on the ice with his team at even strength or short-handed and Goals Against (**GA**) scored when the same player is on the ice with his team at even strength or on a power play.

Individual Scoring Leaders for Art Ross Trophy

Player	Team	GP	G	A	Pts	+/−	PIM	PP	SH	GW	GT	S	%
Mario Lemieux	Pittsburgh	60	69	91	160	55	38	16	6	10	0	286	24.1
Pat LaFontaine	Buffalo	84	53	95	148	11	63	20	2	7	1	306	17.3
Adam Oates	Boston	84	45	97	142	15	32	24	1	11	0	254	17.7
Steve Yzerman	Detroit	84	58	79	137	33	44	13	7	6	0	307	18.9
*Teemu Selanne	Winnipeg	84	76	56	132	8	45	24	0	7	0	387	19.6
Pierre Turgeon	NY Islanders	83	58	74	132	1 –	26	24	0	10	2	301	19.3
Alexander Mogilny	Buffalo	77	76	51	127	7	40	27	0	11	0	360	21.1
Doug Gilmour	Toronto	83	32	95	127	32	100	15	3	2	2	211	15.2
Luc Robitaille	Los Angeles	84	63	62	125	18	100	24	2	8	1	265	23.8
Mark Recchi	Philadelphia	84	53	70	123	1	95	15	4	6	0	274	19.3
Mats Sundin	Quebec	80	47	67	114	21	96	13	4	9	1	215	21.9
Kevin Stevens	Pittsburgh	72	55	56	111	17	177	26	0	5	1	326	16.9
Pavel Bure	Vancouver	83	60	50	110	35	69	13	7	9	0	407	14.7
Rick Tocchet	Pittsburgh	80	48	61	109	28	252	20	4	5	0	240	20.0
Jeremy Roenick	Chicago	84	50	57	107	15	86	22	3	3	3	255	19.6
Craig Janney	St. Louis	84	24	82	106	4 –	12	8	0	6	0	137	17.5
Joe Sakic	Quebec	78	48	57	105	3 –	40	20	2	4	1	264	18.2
*Joe Juneau	Boston	84	32	70	102	23	33	9	0	3	0	229	14.0
Brett Hull	St. Louis	80	54	47	101	27 –	41	29	0	2	1	390	13.8
Theoren Fleury	Calgary	83	34	66	100	14	88	12	2	4	0	250	13.6
Ron Francis	Pittsburgh	84	24	76	100	6	68	9	2	4	0	215	11.2
Dave Andreychuk	Buf-Tor	83	54	45	99	4	56	32	0	4	1	310	17.4
Dino Ciccarelli	Detroit	82	41	56	97	12	81	21	0	8	0	200	20.5
Vincent Damphousse	Montreal	84	39	58	97	5	98	9	3	8	1	287	13.6
Phil Housley	Winnipeg	80	18	79	97	14 –	52	6	0	2	0	249	7.2
Dale Hawerchuk	Buffalo	81	16	80	96	17 –	52	8	0	2	0	259	6.2

Defensemen Scoring Leaders

Player	Team	GP	G	A	Pts	+/−	PIM	PP	SH	GW	GT	S	%
Phil Housley	Winnipeg	80	18	79	97	14 –	52	6	0	2	0	249	7.2
Paul Coffey	L.A-Det	80	12	75	87	16	77	5	0	0	0	254	4.7
Larry Murphy	Pittsburgh	83	22	63	85	45	73	6	2	2	0	230	9.6
Steve Duchesne	Quebec	82	20	62	82	15	57	8	0	2	1	227	8.8
Ray Bourque	Boston	78	19	63	82	38	40	8	0	7	0	330	5.8
Gary Suter	Calgary	81	23	58	81	1 –	112	10	1	2	1	263	8.7
Kevin Hatcher	Washington	83	34	45	79	7 –	114	13	1	6	0	329	10.3
Jeff Brown	St. Louis	71	25	53	78	6 –	58	12	2	3	0	220	11.4
Chris Chelios	Chicago	84	15	58	73	14	282	8	0	2	0	290	5.2
Al Iafrate	Washington	81	25	41	66	15	169	11	1	4	0	289	8.7
Zarley Zalapski	Hartford	83	14	51	65	34 –	94	8	1	0	0	192	7.3
Norm Maciver	Ottawa	80	17	46	63	46 –	84	7	1	2	0	184	9.2

CONSECUTIVE SCORING STREAKS

Goals

Games	Player	Team	G
12	Mario Lemieux	Pittsburgh	18
11	Mario Lemieux	Pittsburgh	21
10	Luc Robitaille	Los Angeles	15
9	*Teemu Selanne	Winnipeg	14
8	Alexander Mogilny	Buffalo	16
8	Gary Roberts	Calgary	10
8	*Teemu Selanne	Winnipeg	9
8	Brian Bradley	Tampa Bay	8
7	Dave Andreychuk	Buf-Tor	8
7	Dave Gagner	Minnesota	7

Assists

Games	Player	Team	A
18	Adam Oates	Boston	28
14	Phil Housley	Winnipeg	21
11	Dino Ciccarelli	Detroit	12
10	Ray Bourque	Boston	13
10	*Alexei Zhamnov	Winnipeg	12
9	Mario Lemieux	Pittsburgh	19
9	Mario Lemieux	Pittsburgh	18
9	Steve Yzerman	Detroit	17
9	Mario Lemieux	Pittsburgh	16
9	Adam Oates	Boston	15

Points

Games	Player	Team	G	A	PTS
30	Mats Sundin	Quebec	21	25	46
21	Adam Oates	Boston	9	30	39
17	Mark Recchi	Philadelphia	14	23	37
17	*Teemu Selanne	Winnipeg	20	14	34
17	Dave Andreychuk	Buffalo	17	14	31
16	Mario Lemieux	Pittsburgh	27	24	51
15	Petr Nedved	Vancouver	15	9	24
15	Steve Duchesne	Quebec	4	17	21

Pavel Bure became the first Vancouver Canuck to reach the 50-goal plateau, firing home 60 goals in 1992-93.

Paul Coffey, traded to Detroit on January 29, 1993, finished second in scoring among defencemen with 87 points in 80 games.

Left: Eric Lindros – here shadowed by Teppo Numminen – finished second among NHL freshmen with 41 goals. Right: Kings' rookie rearguard Alexei Zhitnik led all Los Angeles newcomers in goals (12), assists (36) and points (48).

Individual Rookie Scoring Leaders

Rookie	Team	GP	G	A	Pts	+/−	PIM	PP	SH	GW	GT	S	%
Teemu Selanne	Winnipeg	84	76	56	132	8	45	24	0	7	0	387	19.6
Joe Juneau	Boston	84	32	70	102	23	33	9	0	3	0	229	14.0
Eric Lindros	Philadelphia	61	41	34	75	28	147	8	1	5	1	180	22.8
Alexei Zhamnov	Winnipeg	68	25	47	72	7	58	6	1	4	1	163	15.3
Andrei Kovalenko	Quebec	81	27	41	68	13	57	8	1	4	0	153	17.6
Shawn McEachern	Pittsburgh	84	28	33	61	21	46	7	0	6	0	196	14.3
Dixon Ward	Vancouver	70	22	30	52	34	82	4	1	0	1	111	19.8
Vladimir Malakhov	NY Islanders	64	14	38	52	14	59	7	0	0	0	178	7.9
Keith Tkachuk	Winnipeg	83	28	23	51	13	−	201	12	0	2	1	199	14.1
Patrick Poulin	Hartford	81	20	31	51	19	−	37	4	0	2	0	160	12.5

Goal Scoring

Name	Team	GP	G
Teemu Selanne	Winnipeg	84	76
Eric Lindros	Philadelphia	61	41
Joe Juneau	Boston	84	32
Evgeny Davydov	Winnipeg	79	28
Keith Tkachuk	Winnipeg	83	28
Shawn McEachern	Pittsburgh	84	28
Andrei Kovalenko	Quebec	81	27
Alexei Zhamnov	Winnipeg	68	25

Assists

Name	Team	GP	A
Joe Juneau	Boston	84	70
Teemu Selanne	Winnipeg	84	56
Alexei Zhamnov	Winnipeg	68	47
Andrei Kovalenko	Quebec	81	41
Vladimir Malakhov	NY Islanders	64	38
Alexei Zhitnik	Los Angeles	78	36
Eric Lindros	Philadelphia	61	34
Shawn McEachern	Pittsburgh	84	33

Power Play Goals

Name	Team	GP	PP
Teemu Selanne	Winnipeg	84	24
Keith Tkachuk	Winnipeg	83	12
Joe Juneau	Boston	84	9
Eric Lindros	Philadelphia	61	8
Andrei Kovalenko	Quebec	81	8
Vladimir Malakhov	NY Islanders	64	7
Evgeny Davydov	Winnipeg	79	7
Shawn McEachern	Pittsburgh	84	7

Short Hand Goals

Name	Team	GP	SH
Scott Pellerin	New Jersey	45	2
Rob Gaudreau	San Jose	59	2
Dallas Drake	Detroit	72	2
Stephen Heinze	Boston	73	2
Ted Donato	Boston	82	2

Game Winning Goals

Name	Team	GP	GW
Teemu Selanne	Winnipeg	84	7
Shawn McEachern	Pittsburgh	84	6
Eric Lindros	Philadelphia	61	5
Dallas Drake	Detroit	72	5
Ted Donato	Boston	82	5
Alexei Zhamnov	Winnipeg	68	4
Stephen Heinze	Boston	73	4
Andrei Kovalenko	Quebec	81	4

Game Tying Goals

Name	Team	GP	GT
Martin Rucinsky	Quebec	77	3
Rob Zamuner	Tampa Bay	84	2

Shots

Name	Team	GP	S
Teemu Selanne	Winnipeg	84	387
Joe Juneau	Boston	84	229
Keith Tkachuk	Winnipeg	83	199
Shawn McEachern	Pittsburgh	84	196
Rob Gaudreau	San Jose	59	191
Rob Zamuner	Tampa Bay	84	183
Eric Lindros	Philadelphia	61	180

First Goals

Name	Team	GP	FG
Teemu Selanne	Winnipeg	84	10
Eric Lindros	Philadelphia	61	5
Bill Guerin	New Jersey	65	4
Martin Rucinsky	Quebec	77	4
Evgeny Davydov	Winnipeg	79	4
Keith Tkachuk	Winnipeg	83	4
Joe Juneau	Boston	84	4

Shooting Percentage

(minimum 84 shots)

Name	Team	GP	G	S	%
Eric Lindros	Philadelphia	61	41	180	22.8
Dallas Drake	Detroit	72	18	89	20.2
Dixon Ward	Vancouver	70	22	111	19.8
Teemu Selanne	Winnipeg	84	76	387	19.6
Andrei Kovalenko	Quebec	81	27	153	17.6
Evgeny Davydov	Winnipeg	79	28	176	15.9
Alexei Zhamnov	Winnipeg	68	25	163	15.3

Plus/Minus

Name	Team	GP	+/−
Dixon Ward	Vancouver	70	34
Eric Lindros	Philadelphia	61	28
Joe Juneau	Boston	84	23
Shawn McEachern	Pittsburgh	84	21
Stephen Heinze	Boston	73	20

Three-or-More-Goal Games

Player	Team	Date	Final Score	G
Mikael Andersson	Tampa Bay	Apr. 13	T.B. 5 Wpg 3	3
Dave Andreychuk	Buffalo	Nov. 13	Hfd 2 Buf 8	4
Brian Bellows	Montreal	Feb. 27	Buf 4 Mtl 8	3
Laurie Boschman	Ottawa	Apr. 10	Ott 5 NYI 3	3
Brian Bradley	Tampa Bay	Dec. 05	Det 9 T.B. 7	3
Rod Brind'amour	Philadelphia	Dec. 29	Phi 10 L.A. 2	3
Kelly Buchberger	Edmonton	Jan. 31	Edm 5 Buf 4	3
Pavel Bure	Vancouver	Oct. 12	Wpg 1 Van 8	4
Pavel Bure	Vancouver	Nov. 02	Van 3 Cgy 5	3
Jimmy Carson	Detroit	Nov. 13	Pit 0 Det 8	3
Russ Courtnall	Minnesota	Jan. 21	Ott 2 Min 7	3
Doug Crossman	Tampa Bay	Nov. 07	T.B. 6 NYI 5	3
Ulf Dahlen	Minnesota	Jan. 07	Min 6 Pit 3	3
Vincent Damphousse	Montreal	Nov. 25	Mtl 6 Hfd 1	3
Vincent Damphousse	Montreal	Dec. 08	Mtl 5 L.A. 5	3
*Evgeny Davydov	Winnipeg	Nov. 17	Wpg 6 T.B. 5	3
Kevin Dineen	Philadelphia	Jan. 07	Min 6 Phi 8	3
Kevin Dineen	Philadelphia	Feb. 09	Ott 1 Phi 8	3
Kevin Dineen	Philadelphia	Apr. 15	Phi 7 Buf 4	3
Mike Donnelly	Los Angeles	Nov. 08	L.A. 11 S.J. 4	3
Theoren Fleury	Calgary	Nov. 04	Cgy 5 Van 5	3
Johan Garpenlov	San Jose	Apr. 01	Wpg 9 S.J. 5	3
*Rob Gaudreau	San Jose	Dec. 03	Hfd 7 S.J. 5	3
*Rob Gaudreau	San Jose	Dec. 12	Que 7 S.J. 7	3
Michel Goulet	Chicago	Nov. 08	Pit 2 Chi 7	3
Michel Goulet	Chicago	Jan. 17	Tor 3 Chi 5	3
Adam Graves	NY Rangers	Nov. 25	NYR 11 Pit 3	3
Kevin Hatcher	Washington	Jan. 13	Wsh 4 NYR 5	3
*Stephen Heinze	Boston	Jan. 14	Pit 0 Bos 7	3
Benoit Hogue	NY Islanders	Oct. 24	Hfd 2 NYI 4	3
Bobby Holik	New Jersey	Oct. 10	NYR 2 N.J. 4	3
Bobby Holik	New Jersey	Jan. 22	Mtl 2 N.J. 5	3
Craig Janney	St Louis	Apr. 04	St. L. 4 Chi 5	3
*Joe Juneau	Boston	Jan. 12	Buf 2 Bos 5	3
Yuri Khmylev	Buffalo	Dec. 31	NYR 6 Buf 11	3
Dimitri Khristich	Washington	Feb. 11	Wsh 10 St. L. 6	3
Dimitri Khristich	Washington	Mar. 19	Hfd 2 Wsh 5	3
Chris Kontos	Tampa Bay	Oct. 07	Chi 3 T.B. 7	4
*Andrei Kovalenko	Quebec	Nov. 11	Que 7 Ott 3	3
*Alexei Kovalev	NY Rangers	Dec. 27	Bos 5 NYR 6	3
Bob Kudelski	Ottawa	Jan. 10	S.J. 2 Ott 3	3
Jari Kurri	Los Angeles	Nov. 08	L.A. 11 S.J. 4	3
Pat LaFontaine	Buffalo	Jan. 10	Cgy 3 Buf 5	3
Steve Larmer	Chicago	Nov. 28	Chi 5 Cgy 2	3
Steve Larmer	Chicago	Dec. 23	Chi 4 Ott 2	3
Gary Leeman	Calgary	Nov. 05	Ott 4 Cgy 8	3
Claude Lemieux	New Jersey	Oct. 22	N.J. 6 Chi 5	3
Mario Lemieux	Pittsburgh	Oct. 22	Det 6 Pit 9	3
Mario Lemieux	Pittsburgh	Mar. 18	Wsh 5 Pit 7	3
Mario Lemieux	Pittsburgh	Mar. 20	Phi 3 Pit 9	4
Mario Lemieux	Pittsburgh	Apr. 09	Pit 10 NYR 4	5
*Eric Lindros	Philadelphia	Nov. 15	Ott 2 Phi 7	3
*Eric Lindros	Philadelphia	Dec. 26	Phi 5 Wsh 5	3
*Eric Lindros	Philadelphia	Mar. 24	Phi 5 NYR 4	3
Sergei Makarov	Calgary	Oct. 31	Min 3 Cgy 5	3
Kevin Miller	St Louis	Dec. 01	Hfd 4 Stl 8	3
Alexander Mogilny	Buffalo	Oct. 08	Que 5 Buf 4	3
Alexander Mogilny	Buffalo	Dec. 09	Bos 2 Buf 5	3
Alexander Mogilny	Buffalo	Dec. 23	Wsh 1 Buf 4	3
Alexander Mogilny	Buffalo	Dec. 31	NYR 6 Buf 11	3
Alexander Mogilny	Buffalo	Jan. 02	Buf 7 Ott 2	3
Alexander Mogilny	Buffalo	Feb. 10	Buf 6 Wpg 2	4
Alexander Mogilny	Buffalo	Feb. 24	Det 7 Buf 10	4
Joe Mullen	Pittsburgh	Apr. 09	Pit 10 NYR 4	3
Sergei Nemchinov	NY Rangers	Jan. 29	NYR 4 Buf 6	3
Joe Nieuwendyk	Calgary	Nov. 02	Van 3 Cgy 5	3
Owen Nolan	Quebec	Oct. 10	Ott 2 Que 9	3
Owen Nolan	Quebec	Nov. 26	Que 5 Tor 4	3
*Michael Nylander	Hartford	Apr. 07	Hfd 6 Ott 1	3
Adam Oates	Boston	Oct. 29	L.A. 3 Bos 8	3
Adam Oates	Boston	Jan. 28	Wpg 2 Bos 6	3
Adam Oates	Boston	Mar. 04	Van 3 Bos 4	3
Ed Olczyk	NY Rangers	Mar. 24	Phi 5 NYR 4	3
Greg Paslawski	Philadelphia	Oct. 24	Mtl 7 Phi 6	3
*Vitali Prokhorov	St Louis	Oct. 31	Phi 4 St. L. 6	3
Robert Reichel	Calgary	Jan. 16	Cgy 3 Min 2	3
Robert Reichel	Calgary	Feb. 10	S.J. 1 Cgy 13	3
Stephane Richer	New Jersey	Mar. 29	S.J. 0 N.J. 5	3
Gary Roberts	Calgary	Dec. 04	St. L. 3 Cgy 5	3
Gary Roberts	Calgary	Dec. 27	Cgy 7 Edm 3	3
Luc Robitaille	Los Angeles	Nov. 08	L.A. 11 S.J. 4	3
Luc Robitaille	Los Angeles	Mar. 02	Cgy 2 L.A. 6	3
Jeremy Roenick	Chicago	Nov. 07	Chi 7 Que 4	3
Cliff Ronning	Vancouver	Apr. 15	Van 8 L.A. 6	3
Vladimir Ruzicka	Boston	Oct. 12	Ott 3 Bos 6	3
Geoff Sanderson	Hartford	Nov. 28	Bos 3 Hfd 4	3
Geoff Sanderson	Hartford	Feb. 21	Pit 4 Hfd 3	3
Tomas Sandstrom	Los Angeles	Jan. 21	Van 5 L.A. 4	3
*Teemu Selanne	Winnipeg	Oct. 14	Edm 3 Wpg 7	3
*Teemu Selanne	Winnipeg	Dec. 11	Wpg 6 Wsh 8	3
*Teemu Selanne	Winnipeg	Feb. 28	Min 6 Wpg 7	4
*Teemu Selanne	Winnipeg	Mar. 02	Que 7 Wpg 4	3
*Teemu Selanne	Winnipeg	Mar. 09	Wpg 4 T.B. 2	3
Brendan Shanahan	St Louis	Dec. 17	NYR 4 St. L 3	3
Thomas Steen	Winnipeg	Feb. 22	Ott 3 Wpg 6	3
Ronnie Stern	Calgary	Jan. 10	S.J. 1 Cgy 13	3
Kevin Stevens	Pittsburgh	Oct. 17	Pit 7 Hfd 3	4
Kevin Stevens	Pittsburgh	Dec. 12	N.J. 5 Pit 6	3
Kevin Stevens	Pittsburgh	Jan. 26	Wsh 3 Pit 6	3
Mats Sundin	Quebec	Dec. 05	Min 7 Que 4	3
Rick Tocchet	Pittsburgh	Apr. 01	Hfd 2 Pit 10	3
Rick Tocchet	Pittsburgh	Apr. 07	Mtl 3 Pit 4	3
Pierre Turgeon	NY Islanders	Nov. 22	NYI 5 Edm 5	3
Pierre Turgeon	NY Islanders	Jan. 16	NYI 5 N.J. 3	3
Pierre Turgeon	NY Islanders	Feb. 20	Pit 2 NYI 4	3
Pierre Turgeon	NY Islanders	Apr. 16	N.J. 4 NYI 8	3
Pat Verbeek	Hartford	Feb. 20	Edm 3 Hfd 7	3
Pat Verbeek	Hartford	Feb. 28	NYI 7 Hfd 6	3
Scott Young	Quebec	Dec. 12	Que 8 S.J. 7	3
Steve Yzerman	Detroit	Oct. 24	Det 8 St. L. 1	3
Steve Yzerman	Detroit	Jan. 26	Det 9 Cgy 1	3
Steve Yzerman	Detroit	Feb. 14	Det 5 Chi 3	3

NOTE: 112 Three-or-more-goal games recorded in 1992-93.

Pierre Turgeon connected for a quartet of hat-tricks for the NY Islanders during the 1992-93 campaign.

Toronto's Felix Potvin led all NHL goaltenders with a goals-against average of 2.50 in 1992-93.

Goaltending Leaders

Minimum 27 games

Goals Against Average

Goaltender	Team	GPI	Mins	Ga	Avg
*Felix Potvin	Toronto	48	2781	116	2.50
Ed Belfour	Chicago	71	4106	177	2.59
Tom Barrasso	Pittsburgh	63	3702	186	3.01
Curtis Joseph	St Louis	68	3890	196	3.02
Kay Whitmore	Vancouver	31	1817	94	3.10

Wins

Goaltender	Team	GPI	MINS	W	L	T
Tom Barrasso	Pittsburgh	63	3702	43	14	5
Ed Belfour	Chicago	71	4106	41	18	11
Andy Moog	Boston	55	3194	37	14	3
Tim Cheveldae	Detroit	67	3880	34	24	7
Bob Essensa	Winnipeg	67	3855	33	26	6

Save Percentage

Goaltender	Team	GPI	MINS	GA	SA	S%	W	L	T
Curtis Joseph	St Louis	68	3890	196	2202	.911	29	28	9
*Felix Potvin	Toronto	48	2781	116	1286	.910	25	15	7
Ed Belfour	Chicago	71	4106	177	1880	.906	41	18	11
Tom Barrasso	Pittsburgh	63	3702	186	1885	.901	43	14	5
John Vanbiesbrouck	NY Rangers	48	2757	152	1525	.900	20	18	7

Shutouts

Goaltender	Team	GPI	MINS	SO	W	L	T
Ed Belfour	Chicago	71	4106	7	41	18	11
*Tommy Soderstrom	Philadelphia	44	2512	5	20	17	6
John Vanbiesbrouck	NY Rangers	48	2757	4	20	18	7
Tom Barrasso	Pittsburgh	63	3702	4	43	14	5
Tim Cheveldae	Detroit	67	3880	4	34	24	7

Team-by-Team Point Totals

1988-89 to 1992-93

(Ranked by five-year average)

	92-93	91-92	90-91	89-90	88-89	Average
Montreal	102	93	89	93	115	98.4
Calgary	97	74	100	99	117	97.4
Boston	109	84	100	101	88	96.4
Chicago	106	87	106	88	66	90.6
Pittsburgh	119	87	88	72	87	90.6
Washington	93	98	81	78	92	88.4
Los Angeles	88	84	102	75	91	88.0
NY Rangers	79	105	85	85	82	87.2
St. Louis	85	83	105	83	78	86.8
Detroit	103	98	76	70	80	85.4
Buffalo	86	74	81	98	83	84.4
New Jersey	87	87	79	83	66	80.4
Vancouver	101	96	65	64	74	80.0
Edmonton	60	82	80	90	84	79.2
Philadelphia	83	75	76	71	80	77.0
Winnipeg	87	81	63	85	64	76.0
Minnesota	82	70	68	76	70	73.2
Toronto	99	67	57	80	62	73.0
NY Islanders	87	79	60	73	61	72.0
Hartford	58	65	73	85	79	72.0
Quebec	104	52	46	31	61	58.8
Tampa Bay	53	–	–	–	–	53.0
San Jose	24	39	–	–	–	31.5
Ottawa	24	–	–	–	–	24.0

Team Record When Scoring First Goal of a Game

Team	GP	FG	W	L	T
Boston	84	50	41	6	3
Buffalo	84	43	27	11	5
Calgary	84	50	32	11	7
Chicago	84	51	35	9	7
Detroit	84	45	34	7	4
Edmonton	84	34	15	15	4
Hartford	84	32	16	11	5
Los Angeles	84	45	31	11	3
Minnesota	84	41	27	8	6
Montreal	84	42	30	9	3
New Jersey	84	39	25	12	2
NY Islanders	84	47	28	15	4
NY Rangers	84	40	25	11	4
Ottawa	84	27	5	21	1
Philadelphia	84	41	24	13	4
Pittsburgh	84	63	44	12	7
Quebec	84	43	34	8	1
San Jose	84	28	7	19	2
St. Louis	84	43	28	11	4
Tampa Bay	84	33	15	15	3
Toronto	84	49	34	8	7
Vancouver	84	43	32	5	6
Washington	84	41	28	11	2
Winnipeg	84	37	20	12	5

Team Plus/Minus Differential

Team	GF	PPGF	Net GF	GA	PPGA	Net GA	Goal Differential
Vancouver	346	79	267	278	97	181	+ 86
Pittsburgh	367	105	262	268	72	196	+ 66
Detroit	369	113	256	280	79	201	+ 55
Montreal	326	79	247	280	77	203	+ 44
Boston	332	91	241	268	70	198	+ 43
Calgary	322	85	237	282	83	199	+ 38
Chicago	279	94	185	230	81	149	+ 36
Quebec	351	101	250	300	85	215	+ 35
NY Islanders	335	90	245	297	77	220	+ 25
Philadelphia	319	72	247	319	95	224	+ 23
Toronto	288	98	190	241	69	172	+ 18
Washington	325	97	228	286	74	212	+ 16
Buffalo	335	95	240	297	72	225	+ 15
New Jersey	308	77	231	299	79	220	+ 11
Los Angeles	338	102	236	340	114	226	+ 10
NY Rangers	304	77	227	308	84	224	+ 3
Winnipeg	322	98	224	320	80	240	– 16
St. Louis	282	93	189	278	70	208	– 19
Minnesota	272	85	187	293	81	212	– 25
Edmonton	242	66	176	337	106	231	– 55
Hartford	284	78	206	369	107	262	– 56
Tampa Bay	245	74	171	332	101	231	– 60
Ottawa	202	66	136	395	115	280	–144
San Jose	218	66	152	414	113	301	–149

Team Record when Leading, Trailing, Tied

Team	Leading after 1 period W	L	T	Leading after 2 periods W	L	T	Trailing after 1 period W	L	T	Trailing after 2 periods W	L	T	Tied after 1 period W	L	T	Tied after 2 periods W	L	T
Boston	34	3	3	44	4	3	6	15	2	3	21	2	11	8	1	4	1	2
Buffalo	21	7	3	28	4	2	7	15	3	5	21	3	10	14	4	5	11	5
Calgary	21	7	7	28	1	4	6	17	2	3	20	2	16	6	2	12	9	5
Chicago	23	4	4	38	3	1	7	17	3	3	21	1	17	4	5	6	1	7
Detroit	33	4	4	37	1	1	9	19	2	3	21	1	5	5	3	7	6	7
Edmonton	11	9	3	16	5	6	6	27	2	6	38	0	9	14	3	4	7	2
Hartford	13	7	4	19	5	2	4	35	2	3	39	0	9	10	0	4	8	4
Los Angeles	28	5	2	29	2	5	3	22	5	2	29	2	8	8	3	8	4	3
Minnesota	23	5	2	29	2	3	8	22	2	2	28	4	5	11	6	6	8	3
Montreal	24	4	3	34	1	0	10	18	1	6	26	3	14	8	2	8	3	3
New Jersey	20	5	1	31	4	2	6	18	3	0	31	3	14	14	3	9	2	2
NY Islanders	26	9	3	32	8	0	6	15	1	0	25	2	8	13	3	8	4	5
NY Rangers	16	7	2	24	5	2	5	20	4	4	28	3	13	12	5	6	6	6
Ottawa	3	9	1	6	2	1	3	45	1	4	59	1	4	16	2	0	9	2
Philadelphia	22	4	0	24	2	2	7	21	6	7	31	4	7	12	5	5	4	5
Pittsburgh	38	5	4	50	1	4	6	8	1	2	13	1	12	8	2	4	7	2
Quebec	23	6	0	36	2	0	8	16	8	6	22	6	16	5	2	5	3	4
San Jose	7	5	2	7	4	1	2	48	0	0	57	0	2	18	0	4	10	1
St. Louis	26	10	3	27	3	2	5	18	2	1	27	1	6	8	6	9	6	8
Tampa Bay	12	8	2	16	6	2	3	29	3	2	38	2	8	17	2	5	10	3
Toronto	26	9	3	36	3	2	5	14	2	4	19	2	13	6	6	4	7	7
Vancouver	30	1	1	38	2	3	5	19	3	2	23	2	11	9	5	6	4	4
Washington	22	9	1	33	4	1	7	17	3	3	24	2	14	8	3	7	6	4
Winnipeg	16	4	5	27	2	6	12	23	2	5	28	3	12	10	0	8	7	0

Team Statistics

TEAMS' HOME-AND-ROAD RECORD

Norris Division

	Home								Road							
	GP	W	L	T	GF	GA	PTS	%	GP	W	L	T	GF	GA	PTS	%
CHI	42	25	11	6	155	115	56	.667	42	22	14	6	124	115	50	.595
DET	42	25	14	3	177	131	53	.631	42	22	14	6	192	149	50	.595
TOR	42	25	11	6	148	111	56	.667	42	19	18	5	140	130	43	.512
STL	42	22	13	7	152	133	51	.607	42	15	23	4	130	145	34	.405
MIN	42	18	17	7	141	140	43	.512	42	18	21	3	131	153	39	.464
T.B.	42	12	27	3	122	160	27	.321	42	11	27	4	123	172	26	.310
Total	252	127	93	32	895	790	286	.567	252	107	117	28	840	864	242	.480

Smythe Division

	GP	W	L	T	GF	GA	PTS	%	GP	W	L	T	GF	GA	PTS	%
VAN	42	27	11	4	195	124	58	.690	42	19	18	5	151	154	43	.512
CGY	42	23	14	5	175	139	51	.607	42	20	16	6	147	143	46	.548
L.A.	42	22	15	5	182	163	49	.583	42	17	20	5	156	177	39	.464
WPG	42	23	16	3	168	155	49	.583	42	17	21	4	154	165	38	.452
EDM	42	16	21	5	132	151	37	.440	42	10	29	3	110	186	23	.274
S.J.	42	8	33	1	128	196	17	.202	42	3	38	1	90	218	7	.083
Total	252	119	110	23	980	928	261	.518	252	86	142	24	808	1043	196	.389

Adams Division

	GP	W	L	T	GF	GA	PTS	%	GP	W	L	T	GF	GA	PTS	%
BOS	42	29	10	3	171	128	61	.726	42	22	16	4	161	140	48	.571
QUE	42	23	17	2	180	163	48	.571	42	24	10	8	171	137	56	.667
MTL	42	27	13	2	171	131	56	.667	42	21	17	4	155	149	46	.548
BUF	42	25	15	2	190	145	52	.619	42	13	21	8	145	152	34	.405
HFD	42	12	25	5	141	176	29	.345	42	14	27	1	143	193	29	.345
OTT	42	9	29	4	100	164	22	.262	42	1	41	0	102	231	2	.024
Total	252	125	109	18	953	907	268	.532	252	95	132	25	877	1002	215	.427

Patrick Division

	GP	W	L	T	GF	GA	PTS	%	GP	W	L	T	GF	GA	PTS	%
PIT	42	32	6	4	202	128	68	.810	42	24	15	3	165	140	51	.607
WSH	42	21	15	6	163	135	48	.571	42	22	19	1	162	151	45	.536
NYI	42	20	19	3	175	143	43	.512	42	20	18	4	160	154	44	.524
N.J.	42	24	14	4	165	131	52	.619	42	16	23	3	143	168	35	.417
PHI	42	24	13	5	174	142	51	.607	42	13	23	6	145	177	32	.381
NYR	42	20	17	5	158	142	45	.536	42	14	22	6	146	166	34	.405
Total	252	140	85	27	1037	821	307	.609	252	109	120	23	921	956	241	.478
Total	1008	511	397	100	3865	3446	1122	.557	1008	397	511	100	3446	3865	894	.443

TEAMS' DIVISIONAL RECORD

Norris Division

	Against Own Division								Against Other Divisions							
	GP	W	L	T	GF	GA	PTS	%	GP	W	L	T	GF	GA	PTS	%
CHI	37	22	11	4	111	95	48	.649	47	25	14	8	168	135	58	.617
DET	37	22	12	3	167	108	47	.635	47	25	16	6	202	172	56	.596
TOR	37	18	13	6	122	105	42	.568	47	26	16	5	166	136	57	.606
STL	37	15	15	7	115	116	37	.500	47	22	21	4	167	162	48	.511
MIN	37	13	20	4	94	123	30	.405	47	23	18	6	178	170	52	.553
T.B.	37	7	26	4	100	162	18	.243	47	16	28	3	145	170	35	.372
Total	222	97	97	28	709	709	222	.500	282	137	113	32	1026	945	306	.543

Smythe Division

	GP	W	L	T	GF	GA	PTS	%	GP	W	L	T	GF	GA	PTS	%
VAN	37	25	10	2	177	116	52	.703	47	21	19	7	169	162	49	.521
CGY	37	24	9	4	163	114	52	.703	47	19	21	7	159	168	45	.479
L.A.	37	17	16	4	142	139	38	.514	47	22	19	6	196	201	50	.532
WPG	37	19	14	4	147	143	42	.568	47	21	23	3	175	177	45	.479
EDM	37	10	26	1	109	158	21	.284	47	16	24	7	133	179	39	.415
S.J.	37	8	28	1	108	176	17	.230	47	3	43	1	110	238	7	.074
Total	222	103	103	16	846	846	222	.500	282	102	149	31	942	1125	235	.417

Adams Division

	GP	W	L	T	GF	GA	PTS	%	GP	W	L	T	GF	GA	PTS	%
BOS	37	27	9	1	143	100	55	.743	47	24	17	6	189	168	54	.574
QUE	37	20	14	3	150	131	43	.581	47	27	13	7	201	169	61	.649
MTL	37	23	14	0	149	131	46	.622	47	25	16	6	177	149	56	.596
BUF	37	18	15	4	146	107	40	.541	47	20	21	6	189	190	46	.489
HFD	37	13	21	3	125	153	29	.392	47	13	31	3	159	216	29	.309
OTT	37	4	32	1	89	180	9	.122	47	6	38	3	113	215	15	.160
Total	222	105	105	12	802	802	222	.500	282	115	136	31	1028	1077	261	.463

Patrick Division

	GP	W	L	T	GF	GA	PTS	%	GP	W	L	T	GF	GA	PTS	%
PIT	37	25	9	3	157	111	53	.716	47	31	12	4	210	157	66	.702
WSH	37	13	22	2	123	135	28	.378	47	30	12	5	202	151	65	.691
NYI	37	22	14	1	148	128	45	.608	47	18	23	6	187	169	43	.447
N.J.	37	18	17	2	125	141	38	.514	47	22	20	5	183	158	49	.521
PHI	37	14	20	3	131	151	31	.419	47	22	17	8	188	168	52	.553
NYR	37	12	22	3	122	140	27	.365	47	22	17	8	182	168	52	.553
Total	222	104	104	14	806	806	222	.500	282	145	101	36	1152	971	326	.578

TEAM STREAKS

Consecutive Wins

Games	Team	From	To
17	Pittsburgh	Mar. 9	Apr. 10
8	Montreal	Oct. 24	Nov. 11
8	Calgary	Dec. 14	Jan. 2
8	Winnipeg	Jan. 5	Jan. 19
8	Boston	Mar. 30	Apr. 14
8	Philadelphia	Apr. 3	Apr. 16
7	Pittsburgh	Oct. 13	Oct. 27
7	Washington	Nov. 30	Dec. 12
7	Washington	Feb. 9	Feb. 23

Consecutive Home Wins

Games	Team	From	To
12	Los Angeles	Oct. 10	Dec. 5
10	Pittsburgh	Mar. 9	Apr. 10
9	Vancouver	Nov. 6	Dec. 9
9	Winnipeg	Dec. 27	Jan. 23
8	Montreal	Oct. 17	Nov. 9
7	Pittsburgh	Oct. 8	Nov. 5
7	Buffalo	Oct. 11	Nov. 13
7	Vancouver	Dec. 18	Jan. 16
7	Buffalo	Dec. 31	Jan. 29

Consecutive Road Wins

Games	Team	From	To
8	Boston	Mar. 15	Apr. 14
7	Minnesota	Nov. 18	Dec. 5
7	Pittsburgh	Mar. 14	Apr. 9
6	Detroit	Mar. 14	Apr. 8
5	Washington	Nov. 30	Dec. 12
5	Washington	Feb. 9	Feb. 23
5	Winnipeg	Mar. 18	Apr. 11

Consecutive Undefeated

Games	Team	W	T	From	To
18	Pittsburgh	17	1	Mar. 9	Apr. 14
12	Montreal	11	1	Oct. 17	Nov. 11
10	Pittsburgh	8	2	Oct. 6	Oct. 27
10	Calgary	9	1	Dec. 11	Jan. 2
10	Winnipeg	9	1	Jan. 5	Jan. 23
10	Toronto	9	1	Feb. 11	Mar. 3
9	Vancouver	8	1	Dec. 18	Jan. 6

Consecutive Home Undefeated

Games	Team	W	T	From	To
18	Vancouver	16	2	Nov. 4	Jan. 16
13	Los Angeles	12	1	Oct. 10	Dec. 8
13	Washington	9	4	Nov. 25	Jan. 31
12	Toronto	10	2	Feb. 11	Apr. 3
11	Pittsburgh	9	2	Oct. 6	Nov. 21
11	Pittsburgh	10	1	Feb. 27	Apr. 10

Consecutive Road Undefeated

Games	Team	W	T	From	To
8	Pittsburgh	7	1	Mar. 14	Apr. 14
8	Boston	8	0	Mar. 15	Apr. 14
7	Minnesota	7	0	Nov. 18	Dec. 5
7	Buffalo	4	3	Mar. 3	Mar. 25
6	Calgary	5	1	Dec. 11	Dec. 27
6	Detroit	5	1	Dec. 15	Jan. 17
6	Toronto	4	2	Dec. 22	Jan. 9
6	Minnesota	5	1	Jan. 19	Feb. 11
6	Quebec	4	2	Jan. 28	Feb. 21
6	Montreal	5	1	Feb. 9	Mar. 1
6	Detroit	6	0	Mar. 14	Apr. 8
6	Los Angeles	4	2	Mar. 26	Apr. 10

TEAM PENALTIES

Abbreviations: GP – games played; **PEN** – total penalty minutes including bench minutes; **BMI** – total bench minor minutes; **AVG** – average penalty minutes/game calculated by dividing total penalty minutes by games played

Team	GP	PEN	BMI	AVG
BOS	84	1552	10	18.5
T.B.	84	1625	6	19.3
NYR	84	1657	10	19.7
NYI	84	1701	4	20.3
WSH	84	1709	14	20.3
OTT	84	1716	26	20.4
PIT	84	1776	14	21.1
MTL	84	1788	8	21.3
N.J.	84	1815	16	21.6
TOR	84	1815	12	21.6
DET	84	1832	18	21.8
QUE	84	1846	14	22.0
WPG	84	1851	12	22.0
BUF	84	1873	16	22.3
MIN	84	1885	14	22.4
PHI	84	1887	14	22.5
ST.L.	84	1889	30	22.5
CGY	84	1951	12	23.2
EDM	84	2027	14	24.1
S.J.	84	2134	10	25.4
L.A.	84	2247	34	26.8
VAN	84	2326	18	27.7
HFD	84	2354	24	28.0
CHI	84	2394	12	28.5
TOTAL	**1008**	**45650**	**362**	**45.3**

Jeff Brown, the St. Louis Blues defensive leader, helped his club record the league's best penalty-killing record, turning back 83.7% of opponents' powerplays.

TEAMS' POWER PLAY RECORD

Abbreviations: ADV – total advantages; **PPGF** – power-play goals for; **%** – calculated by dividing number of power-play goals by total advantages.

		Home					Road					Overall		
	Team	GP	ADV	PPGF	%	Team	GP	ADV	PPGF	%	Team	GP	ADV	PPGF	%
1	NYI	42	201	52	25.9	DET	42	223	57	25.6	DET	84	454	113	24.9
2	BUF	42	246	62	25.2	PIT	42	214	53	24.8	PIT	84	440	105	23.9
3	DET	42	231	56	24.2	QUE	42	219	52	23.7	ST.L.	84	425	93	21.9
4	WSH	42	225	53	23.6	TOR	42	219	49	22.4	WSH	84	445	97	21.8
5	BOS	42	239	56	23.4	ST.L.	42	187	38	20.3	QUE	84	464	101	21.8
6	ST.L.	42	238	55	23.1	WSH	42	220	44	20.0	NYI	84	416	90	21.6
7	PIT	42	226	52	23.0	HFD	42	212	42	19.8	TOR	84	466	98	21.0
8	WPG	42	236	52	22.0	WPG	42	232	46	19.8	WPG	84	468	98	20.9
9	L.A.	42	268	56	20.9	NYR	42	207	41	19.8	BOS	84	435	91	20.9
10	VAN	42	236	49	20.8	N.J.	42	197	39	19.8	BUF	84	467	95	20.3
11	CHI	42	277	57	20.6	T.B.	42	184	36	19.6	L.A.	84	507	102	20.1
12	QUE	42	245	49	20.0	MIN	42	220	43	19.5	N.J.	84	400	77	19.3
13	CGY	42	222	44	19.8	L.A.	42	239	46	19.2	MIN	84	445	85	19.1
14	TOR	42	247	49	19.8	MTL	42	203	37	18.2	CGY	84	447	85	19.0
15	PHI	42	203	39	19.2	CGY	42	225	41	18.2	MTL	84	430	80	18.4
16	N.J.	42	203	38	18.7	BOS	42	196	35	17.9	CHI	84	510	94	18.4
17	MIN	42	225	42	18.7	NYI	42	215	38	17.7	NYR	84	420	77	18.3
18	MTL	42	227	42	18.5	OTT	42	205	35	17.1	PHI	84	399	72	18.0
19	S.J.	42	225	41	18.2	PHI	42	196	33	16.8	HFD	84	444	78	17.6
20	EDM	42	216	37	17.1	CHI	42	233	37	15.9	T.B.	84	424	74	17.5
21	NYR	42	213	36	16.9	BUF	42	221	33	14.9	VAN	84	457	79	17.3
22	T.B.	42	240	38	15.8	EDM	42	200	29	14.5	S.J.	84	409	66	16.1
23	HFD	42	232	36	15.5	VAN	42	221	30	13.6	EDM	84	416	66	15.9
24	OTT	42	243	31	12.8	S.J.	42	184	25	13.6	OTT	84	448	66	14.7
TOTAL		**1008**	**5564**	**1122**	**20.2**		**1008**	**5072**	**959**	**18.9**		**1008**	**10636**	**2081**	**19.6**

TEAMS' PENALTY KILLING RECORD

Abbreviations: TSH – total times short-handed; **PPGA** – power-play goals against; **%** – calculated by dividing times short minus power-play goals against by times short.

		Home					Road					Overall		
	TEAM	GP	TSH	PPGA	%	TEAM	GP	TSH	PPGA	%	TEAM	GP	TSH	PPGA	%
1	BOS	42	188	27	85.6	ST.L.	42	205	32	84.4	ST.L.	84	429	70	83.7
2	WSH	42	214	32	85.0	CGY	42	250	40	84.0	CHI	84	490	81	83.5
3	BUF	42	198	30	84.8	PIT	42	214	35	83.6	BUF	84	437	72	83.5
4	MIN	42	217	35	83.9	CHI	42	261	44	83.1	PIT	84	429	72	83.2
5	CHI	42	229	37	83.8	QUE	42	248	43	82.7	CGY	84	492	83	83.1
6	MTL	42	210	35	83.3	WPG	42	231	40	82.7	BOS	84	413	70	83.1
7	ST.L.	42	224	38	83.0	TOR	42	217	38	82.5	WSH	84	433	74	82.9
8	DET	42	211	36	82.9	BUF	42	239	42	82.4	TOR	84	393	69	82.4
9	PIT	42	215	37	82.8	N.J.	42	212	39	81.6	MIN	84	455	81	82.2
10	NYR	42	213	37	82.6	BOS	42	225	43	80.9	MTL	84	427	77	82.0
11	TOR	42	176	31	82.4	WSH	42	219	42	80.8	WPG	84	437	80	81.7
12	CGY	42	242	43	82.2	MIN	42	238	46	80.7	N.J.	84	425	79	81.4
13	N.J.	42	213	40	81.2	MTL	42	217	42	80.6	DET	84	420	79	81.2
14	NYI	42	169	32	81.1	NYR	42	233	47	79.8	NYR	84	446	84	81.2
15	VAN	42	211	40	81.0	DET	42	209	43	79.4	QUE	84	438	85	80.6
16	WPG	42	206	40	80.6	L.A.	42	285	61	78.6	NYI	84	375	77	79.5
17	HFD	42	233	47	79.8	NYI	42	206	45	78.2	VAN	84	452	97	78.5
18	L.A.	42	244	53	78.3	S.J.	42	252	55	78.2	L.A.	84	529	114	78.4
19	PHI	42	211	46	78.2	EDM	42	243	56	77.0	HFD	84	493	107	78.3
20	QUE	42	190	42	77.9	HFD	42	260	60	76.9	PHI	84	421	95	77.4
21	T.B.	42	221	50	77.4	PHI	42	210	49	76.7	EDM	84	464	106	77.2
22	T.B.	42	184	42	77.2	VAN	42	241	57	76.3	S.J.	84	483	113	76.6
23	OTT	42	222	51	77.0	OTT	42	238	64	73.1	OTT	84	460	115	75.0
24	S.J.	42	231	58	74.9	T.B.	42	211	59	72.0	T.B.	84	395	101	74.4
TOTAL		**1008**	**5072**	**959**	**81.1**		**1008**	**5564**	**1122**	**79.8**		**1008**	**10636**	**2081**	**80.4**

SHORT HAND GOALS FOR

		Home			Road			Overall	
	Team	GP	SHGF	Team	GP	SHGF	Team	GP	SHGF
1	QUE	42	12	DET	42	11	QUE	84	21
2	CHI	42	12	EDM	42	10	PIT	84	20
3	PIT	42	10	BUF	42	10	BOS	84	19
4	VAN	42	10	PIT	42	10	DET	84	18
5	BOS	42	9	BOS	42	10	VAN	84	18
6	L.A.	42	9	PHI	42	9	EDM	84	17
7	ST.L.	42	8	QUE	42	9	L.A.	84	16
8	NYR	42	8	CGY	42	9	PHI	84	15
9	EDM	42	7	VAN	42	8	CGY	84	15
10	TOR	42	7	HFD	42	8	ST.L.	84	14
11	DET	42	7	L.A.	42	7	CHI	84	14
12	CGY	42	6	S.J.	42	7	BUF	84	13
13	MIN	42	6	NYI	42	6	S.J.	84	13
14	S.J.	42	6	ST.L.	42	6	HFD	84	12
15	PHI	42	6	MTL	42	5	NYI	84	12
16	NYI	42	6	WSH	42	5	NYR	84	12
17	WSH	42	5	T.B.	42	5	TOR	84	10
18	HFD	42	4	NYR	42	4	WSH	84	10
19	N.J.	42	4	N.J.	42	4	MIN	84	9
20	T.B.	42	3	OTT	42	4	MTL	84	8
21	BUF	42	3	MIN	42	4	N.J.	84	8
22	OTT	42	3	WPG	42	3	T.B.	84	8
23	MTL	42	3	TOR	42	3	OTT	84	7
24	WPG	42	0	CHI	42	2	WPG	84	3
TOTAL		**1008**	**154**		**1008**	**158**		**1008**	**312**

SHORT HAND GOALS AGAINST

		Home			Road			Overall	
	Team	GP	SHGA	Team	GP	SHGA	Team	GP	SHGA
1	PHI	42	1	CHI	42	2	NYI	84	8
2	NYI	42	2	WSH	42	3	WSH	84	8
3	VAN	42	3	OTT	42	3	BOS	84	8
4	WPG	42	4	BOS	42	3	CGY	84	9
5	CGY	42	4	EDM	42	4	DET	84	10
6	BOS	42	5	TOR	42	4	EDM	84	10
7	WSH	42	5	DET	42	5	CHI	84	10
8	DET	42	5	BUF	42	5	PHI	84	11
9	HFD	42	6	CGY	42	5	VAN	84	11
10	EDM	42	6	MTL	42	6	TOR	84	11
11	T.B.	42	6	NYI	42	6	OTT	84	11
12	ST.L.	42	7	QUE	42	6	T.B.	84	12
13	TOR	42	7	T.B.	42	6	MTL	84	13
14	MIN	42	7	S.J.	42	6	HFD	84	14
15	MTL	42	7	L.A.	42	7	WPG	84	14
16	OTT	42	8	VAN	42	8	ST.L.	84	15
17	L.A.	42	8	HFD	42	8	S.J.	84	15
18	CHI	42	8	ST.L.	42	8	L.A.	84	16
19	N.J.	42	9	NYR	42	9	QUE	84	16
20	S.J.	42	9	PIT	42	9	MIN	84	17
21	NYR	42	9	PHI	42	10	BUF	84	17
22	PIT	42	9	MIN	42	10	NYR	84	18
23	QUE	42	10	WPG	42	10	N.J.	84	19
24	BUF	42	12	N.J.	42	10	PIT	84	19
TOTAL		**1008**	**158**		**1008**	**154**		**1008**	**312**

Overtime Results

1984-85 to 1992-93

Team	1992-93 GP	W	L	T	1991-92 GP	W	L	T	1990-91 GP	W	L	T	1989-90 GP	W	L	T	1988-89 GP	W	L	T	1987-88 GP	W	L	T	1986-87 GP	W	L	T	1985-86 GP	W	L	T	1984-85 GP	W	L	T
BOS	15	5	3	7	9	3	0	6	17	5	0	12	14	3	2	9	19	3	2	14	14	4	4	6	12	2	3	7	17	2	3	12	18	4	4	10
BUF	18	4	4	10	7	1	1	5	24	3	2	19	15	4	3	8	13	2	4	7	12	0	1	11	13	1	4	8	9	1	2	6	17	0	3	14
CGY	19	4	4	11	11	1	3	7	15	3	4	8	21	3	3	15	17	5	3	9	15	2	4	9	4	1	0	3	12	1	2	9	14	1	1	12
CHI	16	1	3	12	8	0	0	8	12	3	1	8	10	2	2	6	17	2	3	12	15	4	2	9	15	1	0	14	12	3	1	8	12	2	3	7
DET	11	2	0	9	5	1	0	4	14	2	4	8	17	2	1	14	16	3	1	12	16	2	3	11	17	2	5	10	13	2	5	6	14	0	2	12
EDM	17	5	4	8	5	0	0	5	15	4	5	6	20	5	1	14	15	4	3	8	16	3	2	11	14	5	3	6	14	5	2	7	12	0	1	11
HFD	18	3	9	6	11	0	1	10	18	2	5	11	9	0	0	9	10	1	4	5	12	3	2	7	9	2	0	7	7	1	2	4	17	4	4	9
L.A.	13	2	1	10	9	0	0	9	16	4	2	10	12	3	2	7	14	6	1	7	12	1	3	8	12	2	2	8	14	3	3	8	19	3	2	14
MIN	10	0	0	10	5	0	1	4	17	0	3	14	11	3	4	4	17	4	2	11	17	0	1	16	16	1	2	13	15	4	2	9	15	1	2	12
MTL	14	5	3	6	10	4	1	5	17	3	3	11	17	4	2	11	11	2	0	9	16	1	2	13	16	2	4	10	14	1	6	7	18	3	3	12
N.J.	11	4	0	7	8	2	2	4	17	1	1	15	16	3	4	9	17	1	4	12	12	4	2	6	13	3	4	6	10	4	3	3	12	0	2	10
NYI	13	3	3	7	8	1	2	5	15	2	3	10	16	3	2	11	11	3	3	5	13	3	0	10	20	5	3	12	17	4	1	12	15	1	8	6
NYR	17	2	4	11	7	0	3	4	16	1	2	13	17	2	2	13	10	1	1	8	11	0	1	10	19	5	6	8	13	0	7	6	17	2	5	10
OTT	10	0	6	4																																
PHI	17	4	2	11	10	2	1	7	11	1	0	10	18	2	5	11	14	1	5	8	13	1	3	9	10	1	1	8	9	4	1	4	9	1	1	7
PIT	10	3	0	7	8	1	1	6	12	4	2	6	14	3	3	8	10	2	1	7	16	5	2	9	21	5	4	12	14	3	3	8	8	3	0	5
QUE	15	4	1	10	6	0	3	3	18	1	3	14	8	0	1	7	10	2	1	7	9	2	2	5	14	0	4	10	11	4	1	6	14	3	2	9
ST.L	17	2	4	11	6	2	1	3	18	3	4	11	15	2	4	9	16	3	1	12	14	2	4	8	21	4	2	15	17	5	3	9	15	2	1	12
S.J.	10	3	5	2	6	1	2	3																												
T.B.	14	3	4	7																																
TOR	13	1	1	11	7	4	0	3	17	4	2	11	11	3	4	4	11	1	4	6	13	1	2	10	13	3	4	6	17	4	6	7	15	5	2	8
VAN	10	1	0	9	10	2	1	7	15	3	3	9	21	2	5	14	14	2	4	8	11	0	2	9	10	2	0	8	16	1	2	13	17	7	1	9
WSH	11	2	2	7	4	1	0	3	14	4	3	7	9	2	1	6	16	2	4	10	15	2	4	9	17	5	2	10	11	4	0	7	12	3	0	9
WPG	11	2	2	7	9	1	2	6	14	1	2	11	19	4	4	11	20	6	2	12	21	8	2	11	11	2	1	8	8	0	1	7	14	3	1	10
Totals	**165**	**65**		**100**	**169**	**30**		**139**	**166**	**54**		**112**	**155**	**55**		**100**	**149**	**52**		**97**	**146**	**49**		**97**	**148**	**55**		**93**	**135**	**56**		**79**	**152**	**48**		**104**

1992-93

Home Team Wins: 29
Visiting Team Wins: 36

1992-93 Penalty Shots

Scored

Pierre Turgeon (NY Islanders) scored against Pat Jablonski (Tampa Bay), November 7. Final score: Tampa Bay 6 at Buffalo 5.

Brad May (Buffalo) scored against Andy Moog (Boston), November 11. Final score: Boston 2 at Buffalo 7.

Mike Donnelly (Los Angeles) scored against Kirk McLean (Vancouver), November 12. Final score: Vancouver 4 at Los Angeles 7.

Reggie Savage (Washington) scored against Jon Casey (Minnesota), November 18. Final score: Minnesota 5 at Washington 4.

Paul Ysebaert (Detroit) scored against Robb Stauber (Los Angeles), November 27. Final score: Los Angeles 5 at Detroit 3.

Pat LaFontaine (Buffalo) scored against Peter Sidorkiewicz (Ottawa), November 29. Final score: Buffalo 5 at Ottawa 2.

Theoren Fleury (Calgary) scored against Rick Wamsley (Toronto), December 11. Final score: Calgary 6 at Toronto 3.

Mikael Andersson (Tampa Bay) scored against Robb Stauber (Los Angeles), December 15. Final score: Tampa Bay 3 at Los Angeles 2.

Eric Lindros (Philadelphia) scored against Don Beaupre (Washington), December 26. Final score: Philadelphia 5 at Washington 5.

Laurie Boschman (Ottawa) scored against Michael O'Neill (Winnipeg), February 1. Final score: Winnipeg 4 at Ottawa 4.

Benoit Hogue (NY Islanders) scored against Ron Tugnutt (Edmonton), February 16. Final score: Edmonton 2 at NY Islanders 7.

Teemu Selanne (Winnipeg) scored against Wendell Young (Tampa Bay), March 9. Final score: Winnipeg 4, Tampa Bay 2.

Alexei Gusarov (Quebec) scored against Grant Fuhr (Buffalo), March 10. Final score: Buffalo 7 at Quebec 4.

Philippe Bozon (St. Louis) scored against Ed Belfour (Chicago), April 3. Final score: Chicago 3 at St. Louis 3.

Stopped

Felix Potvin (Toronto) stopped Brian Bradley (Tampa Bay), October 22. Final score: Toronto 5 at Tampa Bay 2.

Bill Ranford (Edmonton) stopped Dave Gagner (Minnesota), October 28. Final score: Minnesota 2 at Edmonton 5.

Curtis Joseph (St. Louis) stopped Phil Housley (Winnipeg), December 19. Final score: Winnipeg 1 at St. Louis 0.

Grant Fuhr (Toronto) stopped Brendan Shanahan (St. Louis), December 27. Final score: Toronto 6 at St. Louis 3.

Bill Ranford (Edmonton) stopped C.J. Young (Calgary), December 27. Final score: Calgary 7 at Edmonton 3.

Glenn Healy (NY Islanders) stopped Brett Hull (St. Louis), December 31. Final score: NY Islanders 1 at St. Louis 5.

Pat Jablonski (Tampa Bay) stopped Bryan Marchment (Chicago), December 31. Final score: Tampa Bay 0 at Chicago 5.

Ken Wregget (Pittsburgh) stopped Joe Nieuwendyk (Calgary), January 23. Final score: Pittsburgh 4 at Calgary 3.

John Blue (Boston) stopped Denis Savard (Montreal), January 25. Final score: Boston 2 at Montreal 3.

Don Beaupre (Washington) stopped Jaromir Jagr (Pittsburgh), January 26. Final score: Washington 3 at Pittsburgh 6.

Kelly Hrudey (Los Angeles) stopped Mats Sundin (Quebec), February 2. Final score: Los Angeles 2 at Quebec 3.

Peter Sidorkiewicz (Ottawa) stopped Stu Barnes (Winnipeg), February 23. Final score: Winnipeg 8 at Ottawa 2.

Ed Belfour (Chicago) stopped Steve Maltais (Tampa Bay), February 25. Final score: Chicago 5 at Tampa Bay 1.

Darcy Wakaluk (Minnesota) stopped Steve Yzerman (Detroit), March 18. Final score: Minnesota 1 at Detroit 5.

Chicago's Ed Belfour stopped Tampa Bay's Steve Maltais on a penalty shot in Chicago's 5-1 victory over the Lightning on February 25, 1993.

Robb Stauber (Los Angeles) stopped Craig Janney (St. Louis), March 20. Final score: St. Louis 2 at Los Angeles 3.

Jon Casey (Minnesota) stopped Luc Robitaille (Los Angeles), April 3. Final score: Minnesota 3 at Los Angeles 0.

Summary

30 penalty shots resulted in 14 goals.

NHL Record Book

Year-By-Year Final Standings & Leading Scorers

*Stanley Cup winner

All-Time Standings of NHL Teams

(ranked by percentage)

Team	Games	Wins	Losses	Tied	Goals For	Goals Against	Points	%
Montreal	4676	2480	1473	723	15921	12388	5683	.608
Edmonton	1124	583	399	142	4927	4248	1308	.582
Philadelphia	2062	1021	715	322	7407	6367	2364	.573
Boston	4516	2171	1675	670	14936	13442	5012	.555
Buffalo	1836	866	674	296	6708	6055	2028	.552
NY Islanders	1680	800	639	241	6225	5477	1841	.548
**Calgary	1680	793	632	255	6448	5839	1841	.548
Toronto	4676	2001	1993	682	14634	14621	4684	.501
NY Rangers	4450	1863	1881	706	13984	14150	4432	.498
Detroit	4450	1849	1895	706	13619	13815	4404	.495
St. Louis	2062	853	894	315	6788	7030	2021	.490
Chicago	4450	1828	1930	692	13480	13719	4348	.489
Washington	1524	624	704	196	5279	5655	1444	.474
Los Angeles	2062	818	916	300	7297	7770	1936	.469
Pittsburgh	2062	804	974	284	7242	7840	1892	.459
Quebec	1124	433	544	147	4163	4457	1013	.451
Minnesota	2062	758	970	334	6690	7373	1850	.449
Winnipeg	1124	430	544	150	4085	4535	1010	.449
Hartford	1124	422	559	143	3887	4401	987	.439
Vancouver	1836	654	910	272	6056	6934	1580	.430
*New Jersey	1524	465	851	208	4858	6143	1138	.373
Tampa Bay	84	23	54	7	245	332	53	.315
San Jose	164	28	129	7	437	773	63	.192
Ottawa	84	10	70	4	202	345	24	.143

* Totals include those of Kansas City (1974-75, 1975-76) and Colorado (1976-77 through 1981-82)
**Totals include those of Atlanta (1972-73 through 1979-80)

1917-18

Team	GP	W	L	T	GF	GA	PTS
Montreal	22	13	9	0	115	84	26
*Toronto	22	13	9	0	108	109	26
Ottawa	22	9	13	0	102	114	18
**Mtl. Wanderers	6	1	5	0	17	35	2

**Montreal Arena burned down and Wanderers forced to withdraw from League. Canadiens and Toronto each counted a win for defaulted games with Wanderers.

Leading Scorers

Player	Club	GP	G	A	PTS
Malone, Joe	Montreal	20	44	—	44
Denneny, Cy	Ottawa	22	36	—	36
Noble, Reg	Toronto	20	28	—	28
Lalonde, Newsy	Montreal	14	23	—	23
Denneny, Corbett	Toronto	21	20	—	20
Pitre, Didier	Montreal	19	17	—	17
Cameron, Harry	Toronto	20	17	—	17
Darragh, Jack	Ottawa	18	14	—	14
Hyland, Harry	Mtl.W., Ott.	16	14	—	14
Skinner, Alf	Toronto	19	13	—	13
Gerard, Eddie	Ottawa	21	13	—	13

1918-19

Team	GP	W	L	T	GF	GA	PTS
Ottawa	18	12	6	0	71	53	24
Montreal	18	10	8	0	88	78	20
Toronto	18	5	13	0	64	92	10

Leading Scorers

Player	Club	GP	G	A	PTS	PIM
Lalonde, Newsy	Montreal	17	21	9	30	40
Cleghorn, Odie	Montreal	17	23	6	29	33
Denneny, Cy	Ottawa	18	18	4	22	43
Nighbor, Frank	Ottawa	18	18	4	22	27
Pitre, Didier	Montreal	17	14	4	18	9
Skinner, Alf	Toronto	17	12	3	15	26
Cameron, Harry	Tor., Ott.	14	11	3	14	35
Noble, Reg	Toronto	17	11	3	14	35
Darragh, Jack	Ottawa	14	12	1	13	27
Randall, Ken	Toronto	14	7	6	13	27

1919-20

Team	GP	W	L	T	GF	GA	PTS
*Ottawa	24	19	5	0	121	64	38
Montreal	24	13	11	0	129	113	26
Toronto	24	12	12	0	119	106	24
Quebec	24	4	20	0	91	177	8

Leading Scorers

Player	Club	GP	G	A	PTS	PIM
Malone, Joe	Quebec	24	39	9	48	12
Lalonde, Newsy	Montreal	23	36	6	42	33
Denneny, Corbett	Toronto	23	23	12	35	18
Nighbor, Frank	Ottawa	23	26	7	33	18
Noble, Reg	Toronto	24	24	7	31	51
Darragh, Jack	Ottawa	22	22	5	27	22
Arbour, Amos	Montreal	20	22	4	26	10
Wilson, Cully	Toronto	23	21	5	26	79
Broadbent, Punch	Ottawa	20	19	4	23	39
Cleghorn, Odie	Montreal	21	19	3	22	30
Pitre, Didier	Montreal	22	15	7	22	6

1920-21

Team	GP	W	L	T	GF	GA	PTS
Toronto	24	15	9	0	105	100	30
*Ottawa	24	14	10	0	97	75	28
Montreal	24	13	11	0	112	99	26
Hamilton	24	6	18	0	92	132	12

Leading Scorers

Player	Club	GP	G	A	PTS	PIM
Lalonde, Newsy	Montreal	24	33	8	41	36
Denneny, Cy	Ottawa	24	34	5	39	0
Dye, Babe	Ham., Tor.	24	35	2	37	32
Malone, Joe	Hamilton	20	30	4	34	2
Cameron, Harry	Toronto	24	18	9	27	35
Noble, Reg	Toronto	24	20	6	26	54
Prodgers, Goldie	Hamilton	23	18	8	26	8
Denneny, Corbett	Toronto	20	17	6	23	27
Nighbor, Frank	Ottawa	24	18	3	21	10
Berlinquette, Louis	Montreal	24	12	9	21	24

1921-22

Team	GP	W	L	T	GF	GA	PTS
Ottawa	24	14	8	2	106	84	30
*Toronto	24	13	10	1	98	97	27
Montreal	24	12	11	1	88	94	25
Hamilton	24	7	17	0	88	105	14

Leading Scorers

Player	Club	GP	G	A	PTS	PIM
Broadbent, Punch	Ottawa	24	32	14	46	24
Denneny, Cy	Ottawa	22	27	12	39	18
Dye, Babe	Toronto	24	30	7	37	18
Malone, Joe	Hamilton	24	25	7	32	4
Cameron, Harry	Toronto	24	19	8	27	18
Denneny, Corbett	Toronto	24	19	7	26	28
Noble, Reg	Toronto	24	17	8	25	10
Cleghorn, Odie	Montreal	23	21	3	24	26
Cleghorn, Sprague	Montreal	24	17	7	24	63
Reise, Leo	Hamilton	24	9	14	23	8

1922-23

Team	GP	W	L	T	GF	GA	PTS
*Ottawa	24	14	9	1	77	54	29
Montreal	24	13	9	2	73	61	28
Toronto	24	13	10	1	82	88	27
Hamilton	24	6	18	0	81	110	12

Leading Scorers

Player	Club	GP	G	A	PTS	PIM
Dye, Babe	Toronto	22	26	11	37	19
Denneny, Cy	Ottawa	24	21	10	31	20
Adams, Jack	Toronto	23	19	9	28	42
Boucher, Billy	Montreal	24	24	4	27	52
Cleghorn, Odie	Montreal	24	19	7	26	14
Roach, Mickey	Hamilton	23	17	8	25	8
Boucher, George	Ottawa	23	15	9	24	44
Joliat, Aurel	Montreal	24	13	9	22	31
Noble, Reg	Toronto	24	12	10	22	41
Wilson, Cully	Hamilton	23	16	3	19	46

1923-24

Team	GP	W	L	T	GF	GA	PTS
Ottawa	24	16	8	0	74	54	32
*Montreal	24	13	11	0	59	48	26
Toronto	24	10	14	0	59	85	20
Hamilton	24	9	15	0	63	68	18

Leading Scorers

Player	Club	GP	G	A	PTS	PIM
Denneny, Cy	Ottawa	21	22	1	23	10
Boucher, Billy	Montreal	23	16	6	22	33
Joliat, Aurel	Montreal	24	15	5	20	19
Dye, Babe	Toronto	19	17	2	19	23
Boucher, George	Ottawa	21	14	5	19	28
Burch, Billy	Hamilton	24	16	2	18	4
Clancy, King	Ottawa	24	9	8	17	18
Adams, Jack	Toronto	22	13	3	16	49
Morenz, Howie	Montreal	24	13	3	16	20
Noble, Reg	Toronto	23	12	3	15	23

1924-25

Team	GP	W	L	T	GF	GA	PTS
Hamilton	30	19	10	1	90	60	39
Toronto	30	19	11	0	90	84	38
Montreal	30	17	11	2	93	56	36
Ottawa	30	17	12	1	83	66	35
Mtl. Maroons	30	9	19	2	45	65	20
Boston	30	6	24	0	49	119	12

Leading Scorers

Player	Club	GP	G	A	PTS	PIM
Dye, Babe	Toronto	29	38	6	44	41
Denneny, Cy	Ottawa	28	27	15	42	16
Joliat, Aurel	Montreal	24	29	11	40	85
Morenz, Howie	Montreal	30	27	7	34	31
Boucher, Billy	Montreal	30	18	13	31	92
Adams, Jack	Toronto	27	21	8	29	66
Burch, Billy	Hamilton	27	20	4	24	10
Green, Red	Hamilton	30	19	4	23	63
Herberts, Jimmy	Boston	30	17	5	22	50
Day, Hap	Toronto	26	10	12	22	27

1925-26

Team	GP	W	L	T	GF	GA	PTS
Ottawa	36	24	8	4	77	42	52
*Mtl. Maroons	36	20	11	5	91	73	45
Pittsburgh	36	19	16	1	82	70	39
Boston	36	17	15	4	92	85	38
NY Americans	36	12	20	4	68	89	28
Toronto	36	12	21	3	92	114	27
Montreal	36	11	24	1	79	108	23

Leading Scorers

Player	Club	GP	G	A	PTS	PIM
Stewart, Nels	Mtl. Maroons	36	34	8	42	119
Denneny, Cy	Ottawa	36	24	12	36	18
Cooper, Carson	Boston	36	28	3	31	10
Herberts, Jimmy	Boston	36	26	5	31	47
Morenz, Howie	Montreal	31	23	3	26	39
Adams, Jack	Toronto	36	21	5	26	52
Joliat, Aurel	Montreal	35	17	9	26	52
Burch, Billy	NY Americans	36	22	3	25	33
Smith, Hooley	Ottawa	28	16	9	25	53
Nighbor, Frank	Ottawa	35	12	13	25	40

1926-27

Canadian Division

Team	GP	W	L	T	GF	GA	PTS
*Ottawa	44	30	10	4	86	69	64
Montreal	44	28	14	2	99	67	58
Mtl. Maroons	44	20	20	4	71	68	44
NY Americans	44	17	25	2	82	91	36
Toronto	44	15	24	5	79	94	35

American Division

Team	GP	W	L	T	GF	GA	PTS
New York	44	25	13	6	95	72	56
Boston	44	21	20	3	97	89	45
Chicago	44	19	22	3	115	116	41
Pittsburgh	44	15	26	3	79	108	33
Detroit	44	12	28	4	76	105	28

Leading Scorers

Player	Club	GP	G	A	PTS	PIM
Cook, Bill	New York	44	33	4	37	58
Irvin, Dick	Chicago	43	18	18	36	34
Morenz, Howie	Montreal	44	25	7	32	49
Fredrickson, Frank	Det., Bos.	41	18	13	31	46
Dye, Babe	Chicago	41	25	5	30	14
Bailey, Ace	Toronto	42	15	13	28	82
Boucher, Frank	New York	44	13	15	28	17
Burch, Billy	NY Americans	43	19	8	27	40
Oliver, Harry	Boston	42	18	6	24	17
Keats, Gordon	Bos., Det.	42	16	8	24	52

1927-28

Canadian Division

Team	GP	W	L	T	GF	GA	PTS
Montreal	44	26	11	7	116	48	59
Mtl. Maroons	44	24	14	6	96	77	54
Ottawa	44	20	14	10	78	57	50
Toronto	44	18	18	8	89	88	44
NY Americans	44	11	27	6	63	128	28

American Division

Team	GP	W	L	T	GF	GA	PTS
Boston	44	20	13	11	77	70	51
*New York	44	19	16	9	94	79	47
Pittsburgh	44	19	17	8	67	76	46
Detroit	44	19	19	6	88	79	44
Chicago	44	7	34	3	68	134	17

Leading Scorers

Player	Club	GP	G	A	PTS	PIM
Morenz, Howie	Montreal	43	33	18	51	66
Joliat, Aurel	Montreal	44	28	11	39	105
Boucher, Frank	New York	44	23	12	35	15
Hay, George	Detroit	42	22	13	35	20
Stewart, Nels	Mtl. Maroons	41	27	7	34	104
Gagne, Art	Montreal	44	20	10	30	75
Cook, Fred	New York	44	14	14	28	45
Carson, Bill	Toronto	32	20	6	26	36
Finnigan, Frank	Ottawa	38	20	5	25	34
Cook, Bill	New York	43	18	6	24	42
Keats, Gordon	Chi., Det.	38	14	10	24	60

1928-29

Canadian Division

Team	GP	W	L	T	GF	GA	PTS
Montreal	44	22	7	15	71	43	59
NY Americans	44	19	13	12	53	53	50
Toronto	44	21	18	5	85	69	47
Ottawa	44	14	17	13	54	67	41
Mtl. Maroons	44	15	20	9	67	65	39

American Division

Team	GP	W	L	T	GF	GA	PTS
*Boston	44	26	13	5	89	52	57
New York	44	21	13	10	72	65	52
Detroit	44	19	16	9	72	63	47
Pittsburgh	44	9	27	8	46	80	26
Chicago	44	7	29	8	33	85	22

Leading Scorers

Player	Club	GP	G	A	PTS	PIM
Bailey, Ace	Toronto	44	22	10	32	78
Stewart, Nels	Mtl. Maroons	44	21	8	29	74
Cooper, Carson	Detroit	43	18	9	27	14
Morenz, Howie	Montreal	42	17	10	27	47
Blair, Andy	Toronto	44	12	15	27	41
Boucher, Frank	New York	44	10	16	26	8
Oliver, Harry	Boston	43	17	6	23	24
Cook, Bill	New York	43	15	8	23	41
Ward, Jimmy	Mtl. Maroons	43	14	8	22	46

Seven players tied with 19 points

1929-30

Canadian Division

Team	GP	W	L	T	GF	GA	PTS
Mtl. Maroons	44	23	16	5	141	114	51
*Montreal	44	21	14	9	142	114	51
Ottawa	44	21	15	8	138	118	50
Toronto	44	17	21	6	116	124	40
NY Americans	44	14	25	5	113	161	33

American Division

Team	GP	W	L	T	GF	GA	PTS
Boston	44	38	5	1	179	98	77
Chicago	44	21	18	5	117	111	47
New York	44	17	17	10	136	143	44
Detroit	44	14	24	6	117	133	34
Pittsburgh	44	5	36	3	102	185	13

Leading Scorers

Player	Club	GP	G	A	PTS	PIM
Weiland, Cooney	Boston	44	43	30	73	27
Boucher, Frank	New York	42	26	36	62	16
Clapper, Dit	Boston	44	41	20	61	48
Cook, Bill	New York	44	29	30	59	56
Kilrea, Hec	Ottawa	44	36	22	58	72
Stewart, Nels	Mtl. Maroons	44	39	16	55	81
Morenz, Howie	Montreal	44	40	10	50	72
Himes, Norm	NY Americans	44	28	22	50	15
Lamb, Joe	Ottawa	44	29	20	49	119
Gainor, Norm	Boston	42	18	31	49	39

1930-31

Canadian Division

Team	GP	W	L	T	GF	GA	PTS
*Montreal	44	26	10	8	129	89	60
Toronto	44	22	13	9	118	99	53
Mtl. Maroons	44	20	18	6	105	106	46
NY Americans	44	18	16	10	76	74	46
Ottawa	44	10	30	4	91	142	24

American Division

Team	GP	W	L	T	GF	GA	PTS
Boston	44	28	10	6	143	90	62
Chicago	44	24	17	3	108	78	51
New York	44	19	16	9	106	87	47
Detroit	44	16	21	7	102	105	39
Philadelphia	44	4	36	4	76	184	12

Leading Scorers

Player	Club	GP	G	A	PTS	PIM
Morenz, Howie	Montreal	39	28	23	51	49
Goodfellow, Ebbie	Detroit	44	25	23	48	32
Conacher, Charlie	Toronto	37	31	12	43	78
Cook, Bill	New York	43	30	12	42	39
Bailey, Ace	Toronto	40	23	19	42	46
Primeau, Joe	Toronto	38	9	32	41	18
Stewart, Nels	Mtl. Maroons	42	25	14	39	75
Boucher, Frank	New York	44	12	27	39	20
Weiland, Cooney	Boston	44	25	13	38	14
Cook, Fred	New York	44	18	17	35	72
Joliat, Aurel	Montreal	43	13	22	35	73

1931-32

Canadian Division

Team	GP	W	L	T	GF	GA	PTS
Montreal	48	25	16	7	128	111	57
*Toronto	48	23	18	7	155	127	53
Mtl. Maroons	48	19	22	7	142	139	45
NY Americans	48	16	24	8	95	142	40

American Division

Team	GP	W	L	T	GF	GA	PTS
New York	48	23	17	8	134	112	54
Chicago	48	18	19	11	86	101	47
Detroit	48	18	20	10	95	108	46
Boston	48	15	21	12	122	117	42

Leading Scorers

Player	Club	GP	G	A	PTS	PIM
Jackson, Harvey	Toronto	48	28	25	53	63
Primeau, Joe	Toronto	46	13	37	50	25
Morenz, Howie	Montreal	48	24	25	49	46
Conacher, Charlie	Toronto	44	34	14	48	66
Cook, Bill	New York	48	34	14	48	33
Trottier, Dave	Mtl. Maroons	48	26	18	44	94
Smith, Reg	Mtl. Maroons	43	11	33	44	49
Siebert, Albert	Mtl. Maroons	48	21	18	39	64
Clapper, Dit	Boston	48	17	22	39	21
Joliat, Aurel	Montreal	48	15	24	39	46

Cap-wearing Normie Himes, far left, tied for seventh in NHL scoring during the 1929-30 season. He spent his nine-year NHL career with the New York Americans. Fred "Bun" Cook, left, was part of the Rangers' famed "A" Line, and finished among the NHL's top-ten scorers in 1927-28 and 1932-33.

1932-33

Canadian Division

Team	GP	W	L	T	GF	GA	PTS
Toronto	48	24	18	6	119	111	54
Mtl. Maroons	48	22	20	6	135	119	50
Montreal	48	18	25	5	92	115	41
NY Americans	48	15	22	11	91	118	41
Ottawa	48	11	27	10	88	131	32

American Division

Team	GP	W	L	T	GF	GA	PTS
Boston	48	25	15	8	124	88	58
Detroit	48	25	15	8	111	93	58
*New York	48	23	17	8	135	107	54
Chicago	48	16	20	12	88	101	44

Leading Scorers

Player	Club	GP	G	A	PTS	PIM
Cook, Bill	New York	48	28	22	50	51
Jackson, Harvey	Toronto	48	27	17	44	43
Northcott, Lawrence	Mtl. Maroons	48	22	21	43	30
Smith, Reg	Mtl. Maroons	48	20	21	41	66
Haynes, Paul	Mtl. Maroons	48	16	25	41	18
Joliat, Aurel	Montreal	48	18	21	39	53
Barry, Marty	Boston	48	24	13	37	40
Cook, Fred	New York	48	22	15	37	35
Stewart, Nels	Boston	47	18	18	36	62
Morenz, Howie	Montreal	46	14	21	35	32
Gagnon, Johnny	Montreal	48	12	23	35	64
Shore, Eddie	Boston	48	8	27	35	102
Boucher, Frank	New York	47	7	28	35	4

1933-34

Canadian Division

Team	GP	W	L	T	GF	GA	PTS
Toronto	48	26	13	9	174	119	61
Montreal	48	22	20	6	99	101	50
Mtl. Maroons	48	19	18	11	117	122	49
NY Americans	48	15	23	10	104	132	40
Ottawa	48	13	29	6	115	143	32

American Division

Team	GP	W	L	T	GF	GA	PTS
Detroit	48	24	14	10	113	98	58
*Chicago	48	20	17	11	88	83	51
New York	48	21	19	8	120	113	50
Boston	48	18	25	5	111	130	41

Leading Scorers

Player	Club	GP	G	A	PTS	PIM
Conacher, Charlie	Toronto	42	32	20	52	38
Primeau, Joe	Toronto	45	14	32	46	8
Boucher, Frank	New York	48	14	30	44	4
Barry, Marty	Boston	48	27	12	39	12
Dillon, Cecil	New York	48	13	26	39	10
Stewart, Nels	Boston	48	21	17	38	68
Jackson, Harvey	Toronto	38	20	18	38	38
Joliat, Aurel	Montreal	48	22	15	37	27
Smith, Reg	Mtl. Maroons	47	18	19	37	58
Thompson, Paul	Chicago	48	20	16	36	17

1934-35

Canadian Division

Team	GP	W	L	T	GF	GA	PTS
Toronto	48	30	14	4	157	111	64
*Mtl. Maroons	48	24	19	5	123	92	53
Montreal	48	19	23	6	110	145	44
NY Americans	48	12	27	9	100	142	33
St. Louis	48	11	31	6	86	144	28

American Division

Team	GP	W	L	T	GF	GA	PTS
Boston	48	26	16	6	129	112	58
Chicago	48	26	17	5	118	88	57
New York	48	22	20	6	137	139	50
Detroit	48	19	22	7	127	114	45

Leading Scorers

Player	Club	GP	G	A	PTS	PIM
Conacher, Charlie	Toronto	47	36	21	57	24
Howe, Syd	St.L., Det.	50	22	25	47	34
Aurie, Larry	Detroit	48	17	29	46	24
Boucher, Frank	New York	48	13	32	45	2
Jackson, Harvey	Toronto	42	22	22	44	27
Lewis, Herb	Detroit	47	16	27	43	26
Chapman, Art	NY Americans	47	9	34	43	4
Barry, Marty	Boston	48	20	20	40	33
Schriner, Sweeney	NY Americans	48	18	22	40	6
Stewart, Nels	Boston	47	21	18	39	45
Thompson, Paul	Chicago	48	16	23	39	20

1935-36

Canadian Division

Team	GP	W	L	T	GF	GA	PTS
Mtl. Maroons	48	22	16	10	114	106	54
Toronto	48	23	19	6	126	106	52
NY Americans	48	16	25	7	109	122	39
Montreal	48	11	26	11	82	123	33

American Division

Team	GP	W	L	T	GF	GA	PTS
*Detroit	48	24	16	8	124	103	56
Boston	48	22	20	6	92	83	50
Chicago	48	21	19	8	93	92	50
New York	48	19	17	12	91	96	50

Leading Scorers

Player	Club	GP	G	A	PTS	PIM
Schriner, Sweeney	NY Americans	48	19	26	45	8
Barry, Marty	Detroit	48	21	19	40	16
Thompson, Paul	Chicago	45	17	23	40	19
Thoms, Bill	Toronto	48	23	15	38	29
Conacher, Charlie	Toronto	44	23	15	38	74
Smith, Reg	Mtl. Maroons	47	19	19	38	75
Romnes, Doc	Chicago	48	13	25	38	6
Chapman, Art	NY Americans	47	10	28	38	14
Lewis, Herb	Detroit	45	14	23	37	25
Northcott, Lawrence	Mtl. Maroons	48	15	21	36	41

1936-37

Canadian Division

Team	GP	W	L	T	GF	GA	PTS
Montreal	48	24	18	6	115	111	54
Mtl. Maroons	48	22	17	9	126	110	53
Toronto	48	22	21	5	119	115	49
NY Americans	48	15	29	4	122	161	34

American Division

Team	GP	W	L	T	GF	GA	PTS
*Detroit	48	25	14	9	128	102	59
Boston	48	23	18	7	120	110	53
New York	48	19	20	9	117	106	47
Chicago	48	14	27	7	99	131	35

Leading Scorers

Player	Club	GP	G	A	PTS	PIM
Schriner, Sweeney	NY Americans	48	21	25	46	17
Apps, Syl	Toronto	48	16	29	45	10
Barry, Marty	Detroit	48	17	27	44	6
Aurie, Larry	Detroit	45	23	20	43	20
Jackson, Harvey	Toronto	46	21	19	40	12
Gagnon, Johnny	Montreal	48	20	16	36	38
Gracie, Bob	Mtl. Maroons	47	11	25	36	18
Stewart, Nels	Bos., NYA	43	23	12	35	37
Thompson, Paul	Chicago	47	17	18	35	28
Cowley, Bill	Boston	46	13	22	35	4

1937-38

Canadian Division

Team	GP	W	L	T	GF	GA	PTS
Toronto	48	24	15	9	151	127	57
NY Americans	48	19	18	11	110	111	49
Montreal	48	18	17	13	123	128	49
Mtl. Maroons	48	12	30	6	101	149	30

American Division

Team	GP	W	L	T	GF	GA	PTS
Boston	48	30	11	7	142	89	67
New York	48	27	15	6	149	96	60
*Chicago	48	14	25	9	97	139	37
Detroit	48	12	25	11	99	133	35

Leading Scorers

Player	Club	GP	G	A	PTS	PIM
Drillon, Gord	Toronto	48	26	26	52	4
Apps, Syl	Toronto	47	21	29	50	9
Thompson, Paul	Chicago	48	22	22	44	14
Mantha, Georges	Montreal	47	23	19	42	12
Dillon, Cecil	New York	48	21	18	39	6
Cowley, Bill	Boston	48	17	22	39	8
Schriner, Sweeney	NY Americans	49	21	17	38	22
Thoms, Bill	Toronto	48	14	24	38	14
Smith, Clint	New York	48	14	23	37	0
Stewart, Nels	NY Americans	48	19	17	36	29
Colville, Neil	New York	45	17	19	36	11

1938-39

Team	GP	W	L	T	GF	GA	PTS
*Boston	48	36	10	2	156	76	74
New York	48	26	16	6	149	105	58
Toronto	48	19	20	9	114	107	47
NY Americans	48	17	21	10	119	157	44
Detroit	48	18	24	6	107	128	42
Montreal	48	15	24	9	115	146	39
Chicago	48	12	28	8	91	132	32

Leading Scorers

Player	Club	GP	G	A	PTS	PIM
Blake, Hector	Montreal	48	24	23	47	10
Schriner, Sweeney	NY Americans	48	13	31	44	20
Cowley, Bill	Boston	34	8	34	42	2
Smith, Clint	New York	48	21	20	41	2
Barry, Marty	Detroit	48	13	28	41	4
Apps, Syl	Toronto	44	15	25	40	4
Anderson, Tom	NY Americans	48	13	27	40	14
Gottselig, Johnny	Chicago	48	16	23	39	15
Haynes, Paul	Montreal	47	5	33	38	27
Conacher, Roy	Boston	47	26	11	37	12
Carr, Lorne	NY Americans	46	19	18	37	16
Colville, Neil	New York	48	18	19	37	12
Watson, Phil	New York	48	15	22	37	42

1939-40

Team	GP	W	L	T	GF	GA	PTS
Boston	48	31	12	5	170	98	67
*New York	48	27	11	10	136	77	64
Toronto	48	25	17	6	134	110	56
Chicago	48	23	19	6	112	120	52
Detroit	48	16	26	6	91	126	38
NY Americans	48	15	29	4	106	140	34
Montreal	48	10	33	5	90	168	25

Leading Scorers

Player	Club	GP	G	A	PTS	PIM
Schmidt, Milt	Boston	48	22	30	52	37
Dumart, Woody	Boston	48	22	21	43	16
Bauer, Bob	Boston	48	17	26	43	2
Drillon, Gord	Toronto	43	21	19	40	13
Cowley, Bill	Boston	48	13	27	40	24
Hextall, Bryan	New York	48	24	15	39	52
Colville, Neil	New York	48	19	19	38	22
Howe, Syd	Detroit	46	14	23	37	17
Blake, Hector	Montreal	48	17	19	36	48
Armstrong, Murray	NY Americans	48	16	20	36	12

1940-41

Team	GP	W	L	T	GF	GA	PTS
*Boston	48	27	8	13	168	102	67
Toronto	48	28	14	6	145	99	62
Detroit	48	21	16	11	112	102	53
New York	48	21	19	8	143	125	50
Chicago	48	16	25	7	112	139	39
Montreal	48	16	26	6	121	147	38
NY Americans	48	8	29	11	99	186	27

Leading Scorers

Player	Club	GP	G	A	PTS	PIM
Cowley, Bill	Boston	46	17	45	62	16
Hextall, Bryan	New York	48	26	18	44	16
Drillon, Gord	Toronto	42	23	21	44	2
Apps, Syl	Toronto	41	20	24	44	6
Patrick, Lynn	New York	48	20	24	44	12
Howe, Syd	Detroit	48	20	24	44	8
Colville, Neil	New York	48	14	28	42	28
Wiseman, Eddie	Boston	48	16	24	40	10
Bauer, Bobby	Boston	48	17	22	39	2
Schriner, Sweeney	Toronto	48	24	14	38	6
Conacher, Roy	Boston	40	24	14	38	7
Schmidt, Milt	Boston	44	13	25	38	23

1941-42

Team	GP	W	L	T	GF	GA	PTS
New York	48	29	17	2	177	143	60
*Toronto	48	27	18	3	158	136	57
Boston	48	25	17	6	160	118	56
Chicago	48	22	23	3	145	155	47
Detroit	48	19	25	4	140	147	42
Montreal	48	18	27	3	134	173	39
Brooklyn	48	16	29	3	133	175	35

Leading Scorers

Player	Club	GP	G	A	PTS	PIM
Hextall, Bryan	New York	48	24	32	56	30
Patrick, Lynn	New York	47	32	22	54	18
Grosso, Don	Detroit	48	23	30	53	13
Watson, Phil	New York	48	15	37	52	48
Abel, Sid	Detroit	48	18	31	49	45
Blake, Hector	Montreal	47	17	28	45	19
Thoms, Bill	Chicago	47	15	30	45	8
Drillon, Gord	Toronto	48	23	18	41	6
Apps, Syl	Toronto	38	18	23	41	0
Anderson, Tom	Brooklyn	48	12	29	41	54

1942-43

Team	GP	W	L	T	GF	GA	PTS
*Detroit	50	25	14	11	169	124	61
Boston	50	24	17	9	195	176	57
Toronto	50	22	19	9	198	159	53
Montreal	50	19	19	12	181	191	50
Chicago	50	17	18	15	179	180	49
New York	50	11	31	8	161	253	30

Leading Scorers

Player	Club	GP	G	A	PTS	PIM
Bentley, Doug	Chicago	50	33	40	73	18
Cowley, Bill	Boston	48	27	45	72	10
Bentley, Max	Chicago	47	26	44	70	2
Patrick, Lynn	New York	50	22	39	61	28
Carr, Lorne	Toronto	50	27	33	60	15
Taylor, Billy	Toronto	50	18	42	60	2
Hextall, Bryan	New York	50	27	32	59	28
Blake, Hector	Montreal	48	23	36	59	28
Lach, Elmer	Montreal	45	18	40	58	14
O'Connor, Herb	Montreal	50	15	43	58	2

1943-44

Team	GP	W	L	T	GF	GA	PTS
*Montreal	50	38	5	7	234	109	83
Detroit	50	26	18	6	214	177	58
Toronto	50	23	23	4	214	174	50
Chicago	50	22	23	5	178	187	49
Boston	50	19	26	5	223	268	43
New York	50	6	39	5	162	310	17

Leading Scorers

Player	Club	GP	G	A	PTS	PIM
Cain, Herb	Boston	48	36	46	82	4
Bentley, Doug	Chicago	50	38	39	77	22
Carr, Lorne	Toronto	50	36	38	74	9
Liscombe, Carl	Detroit	50	36	37	73	17
Lach, Elmer	Montreal	48	24	48	72	23
Smith, Clint	Chicago	50	23	49	72	4
Cowley, Bill	Boston	36	30	41	71	12
Mosienko, Bill	Chicago	50	32	38	70	10
Jackson, Art	Boston	49	28	41	69	8
Bodnar, Gus	Toronto	50	22	40	62	18

Jack Adams coached the Detroit Red Wings to a first-place finish and a Stanley Cup win in 1942-43.

1944-45

Team	GP	W	L	T	GF	GA	PTS
Montreal	50	38	8	4	228	121	80
Detroit	50	31	14	5	218	161	67
*Toronto	50	24	22	4	183	161	52
Boston	50	16	30	4	179	219	36
Chicago	50	13	30	7	141	194	33
New York	50	11	29	10	154	247	32

Leading Scorers

Player	Club	GP	G	A	PTS	PIM
Lach, Elmer	Montreal	50	26	54	80	37
Richard, Maurice	Montreal	50	50	23	73	36
Blake, Hector	Montreal	49	29	38	67	15
Cowley, Bill	Boston	49	25	40	65	2
Kennedy, Ted	Toronto	49	29	25	54	14
Mosienko, Bill	Chicago	50	28	26	54	0
Carveth, Joe	Detroit	50	26	28	54	6
DeMarco, Albert	New York	50	24	30	54	10
Smith, Clint	Chicago	50	23	31	54	0
Howe, Syd	Detroit	46	17	36	53	6

1945-46

Team	GP	W	L	T	GF	GA	PTS
*Montreal	50	28	17	5	172	134	61
Boston	50	24	18	8	167	156	56
Chicago	50	23	20	7	200	178	53
Detroit	50	20	20	10	146	159	50
Toronto	50	19	24	7	174	185	45
New York	50	13	28	9	144	191	35

Leading Scorers

Player	Club	GP	G	A	PTS	PIM
Bentley, Max	Chicago	47	31	30	61	6
Stewart, Gaye	Toronto	50	37	15	52	8
Blake, Hector	Montreal	50	29	21	50	2
Smith, Clint	Chicago	50	26	24	50	2
Richard, Maurice	Montreal	50	27	21	48	50
Mosienko, Bill	Chicago	40	18	30	48	12
DeMarco, Albert	New York	50	20	27	47	20
Lach, Elmer	Montreal	50	13	34	47	34
Kaleta, Alex	Chicago	49	19	27	46	17
Taylor, Billy	Toronto	48	23	18	41	14
Horeck, Pete	Chicago	50	20	21	41	34

1946-47

Team	GP	W	L	T	GF	GA	PTS
Montreal	60	34	16	10	189	138	78
*Toronto	60	31	19	10	209	172	72
Boston	60	26	23	11	190	175	63
Detroit	60	22	27	11	190	193	55
New York	60	22	32	6	167	186	50
Chicago	60	19	37	4	193	274	42

Leading Scorers

Player	Club	GP	G	A	PTS	PIM
Bentley, Max	Chicago	60	29	43	72	12
Richard, Maurice	Montreal	60	45	26	71	69
Taylor, Billy	Detroit	60	17	46	63	35
Schmidt, Milt	Boston	59	27	35	62	40
Kennedy, Ted	Toronto	60	28	32	60	27
Bentley, Doug	Chicago	52	21	34	55	18
Bauer, Bob	Boston	58	30	24	54	4
Conacher, Roy	Detroit	60	30	24	54	6
Mosienko, Bill	Chicago	59	25	27	52	2
Dumart, Woody	Boston	60	24	28	52	12

1947-48

Team	GP	W	L	T	GF	GA	PTS
*Toronto	60	32	15	13	182	143	77
Detroit	60	30	18	12	187	148	72
Boston	60	23	24	13	167	168	59
New York	60	21	26	13	176	201	55
Montreal	60	20	29	11	147	169	51
Chicago	60	20	34	6	195	225	46

Leading Scorers

Player	Club	GP	G	A	PTS	PIM
Lach, Elmer	Montreal	60	30	31	61	72
O'Connor, Buddy	New York	60	24	36	60	8
Bentley, Doug	Chicago	60	20	37	57	16
Stewart, Gaye	Tor., Chi.	61	27	29	56	83
Bentley, Max	Chi., Tor.	59	26	28	54	14
Poile, Bud	Tor., Chi.	58	25	29	54	17
Richard, Maurice	Montreal	53	28	25	53	89
Apps, Syl	Toronto	55	26	27	53	12
Lindsay, Ted	Detroit	60	33	19	52	95
Conacher, Roy	Chicago	52	22	27	49	4

1948-49

Team	GP	W	L	T	GF	GA	PTS
Detroit	60	34	19	7	195	145	75
Boston	60	29	23	8	178	163	66
Montreal	60	28	23	9	152	126	65
*Toronto	60	22	25	13	147	161	57
Chicago	60	21	31	8	173	211	50
New York	60	18	31	11	133	172	47

Leading Scorers

Player	Club	GP	G	A	PTS	PIM
Conacher, Roy	Chicago	60	26	42	68	8
Bentley, Doug	Chicago	58	23	43	66	38
Abel, Sid	Detroit	60	28	26	54	49
Lindsay, Ted	Detroit	50	26	28	54	97
Conacher, Jim	Det., Chi.	59	26	23	49	43
Ronty, Paul	Boston	60	20	29	49	11
Watson, Harry	Toronto	60	26	19	45	0
Reay, Billy	Montreal	60	22	23	45	33
Bodnar, Gus	Chicago	59	19	26	45	14
Peirson, John	Boston	59	22	21	43	45

1949-50

Team	GP	W	L	T	GF	GA	PTS
*Detroit	70	37	19	14	229	164	88
Montreal	70	29	22	19	172	150	77
Toronto	70	31	27	12	176	173	74
New York	70	28	31	11	170	189	67
Boston	70	22	32	16	198	228	60
Chicago	70	22	38	10	203	244	54

Leading Scorers

Player	Club	GP	G	A	PTS	PIM
Lindsay, Ted	Detroit	69	23	55	78	141
Abel, Sid	Detroit	69	34	35	69	46
Howe, Gordie	Detroit	70	35	33	68	69
Richard, Maurice	Montreal	70	43	22	65	114
Ronty, Paul	Boston	70	23	36	59	8
Conacher, Roy	Chicago	70	25	31	56	16
Bentley, Doug	Chicago	64	20	33	53	28
Peirson, John	Boston	57	27	25	52	49
Prystai, Metro	Chicago	65	29	22	51	31
Guidolin, Bep	Chicago	70	17	34	51	42

*The Toronto Maple Leafs, led by (left to right) Ted Kennedy, Max Bentley and Syl Apps,
won four Stanley Cups in five years from 1947 to 1951.*

1950-51

Team	GP	W	L	T	GF	GA	PTS
Detroit	70	44	13	13	236	139	101
*Toronto	70	41	16	13	212	138	95
Montreal	70	25	30	15	173	184	65
Boston	70	22	30	18	178	197	62
New York	70	20	29	21	169	201	62
Chicago	70	13	47	10	171	280	36

Leading Scorers

Player	Club	GP	G	A	PTS	PIM
Howe, Gordie	Detroit	70	43	43	86	74
Richard, Maurice	Montreal	65	42	24	66	97
Bentley, Max	Toronto	67	21	41	62	34
Abel, Sid	Detroit	69	23	38	61	30
Schmidt, Milt	Boston	62	22	39	61	33
Kennedy, Ted	Toronto	63	18	43	61	32
Lindsay, Ted	Detroit	67	24	35	59	110
Sloan, Tod	Toronto	70	31	25	56	105
Kelly, Red	Detroit	70	17	37	54	24
Smith, Sid	Toronto	70	30	21	51	10
Gardner, Cal	Toronto	66	23	28	51	42

1951-52

Team	GP	W	L	T	GF	GA	PTS
*Detroit	70	44	14	12	215	133	100
Montreal	70	34	26	10	195	164	78
Toronto	70	29	25	16	168	157	74
Boston	70	25	29	16	162	176	66
New York	70	23	34	13	192	219	59
Chicago	70	17	44	9	158	241	43

Leading Scorers

Player	Club	GP	G	A	PTS	PIM
Howe, Gordie	Detroit	70	47	39	86	78
Lindsay, Ted	Detroit	70	30	39	69	123
Lach, Elmer	Montreal	70	15	50	65	36
Raleigh, Don	New York	70	19	42	61	14
Smith, Sid	Toronto	70	27	30	57	6
Geoffrion, Bernie	Montreal	67	30	24	54	66
Mosienko, Bill	Chicago	70	31	22	53	10
Abel, Sid	Detroit	62	17	36	53	32
Kennedy, Ted	Toronto	70	19	33	52	33
Schmidt, Milt	Boston	69	21	29	50	57
Peirson, John	Boston	68	20	30	50	30

1952-53

Team	GP	W	L	T	GF	GA	PTS
Detroit	70	36	16	18	222	133	90
*Montreal	70	28	23	19	155	148	75
Boston	70	28	29	13	152	172	69
Chicago	70	27	28	15	169	175	69
Toronto	70	27	30	13	156	167	67
New York	70	17	37	16	152	211	50

Leading Scorers

Player	Club	GP	G	A	PTS	PIM
Howe, Gordie	Detroit	70	49	46	95	57
Lindsay, Ted	Detroit	70	32	39	71	111
Richard, Maurice	Montreal	70	28	33	61	112
Hergesheimer, Wally	New York	70	30	29	59	10
Delvecchio, Alex	Detroit	70	16	43	59	28
Ronty, Paul	New York	70	16	38	54	20
Prystai, Metro	Detroit	70	16	34	50	12
Kelly, Red	Detroit	70	19	27	46	8
Olmstead, Bert	Montreal	69	17	28	45	83
Mackell, Fleming	Boston	65	27	17	44	63
McFadden, Jim	Chicago	70	23	21	44	29

1953-54

Team	GP	W	L	T	GF	GA	PTS
*Detroit	70	37	19	14	191	132	88
Montreal	70	35	24	11	195	141	81
Toronto	70	32	24	14	152	131	78
Boston	70	32	28	10	177	181	74
New York	70	29	31	10	161	182	68
Chicago	70	12	51	7	133	242	31

Leading Scorers

Player	Club	GP	G	A	PTS	PIM
Howe, Gordie	Detroit	70	33	48	81	109
Richard, Maurice	Montreal	70	37	30	67	112
Lindsay, Ted	Detroit	70	26	36	62	110
Geoffrion, Bernie	Montreal	54	29	25	54	87
Olmstead, Bert	Montreal	70	15	37	52	85
Kelly, Red	Detroit	62	16	33	49	18
Reibel, Earl	Detroit	69	15	33	48	18
Sandford, Ed	Boston	70	16	31	47	42
Mackell, Fleming	Boston	67	15	32	47	60
Mosdell, Ken	Montreal	67	22	24	46	64
Ronty, Paul	New York	70	13	33	46	18

1954-55

Team	GP	W	L	T	GF	GA	PTS
*Detroit	70	42	17	11	204	134	95
Montreal	70	41	18	11	228	157	93
Toronto	70	24	24	22	147	135	70
Boston	70	23	26	21	169	188	67
New York	70	17	35	18	150	210	52
Chicago	70	13	40	17	161	235	43

Leading Scorers

Player	Club	GP	G	A	PTS	PIM
Geoffrion, Bernie	Montreal	70	38	37	75	57
Richard, Maurice	Montreal	67	38	36	74	125
Beliveau, Jean	Montreal	70	37	36	73	58
Reibel, Earl	Detroit	70	25	41	66	15
Howe, Gordie	Detroit	64	29	33	62	68
Sullivan, George	Chicago	69	19	42	61	51
Olmstead, Bert	Montreal	70	10	48	58	103
Smith, Sid	Toronto	70	33	21	54	14
Mosdell, Ken	Montreal	70	22	32	54	82
Lewicki, Danny	New York	70	29	24	53	8

1955-56

Team	GP	W	L	T	GF	GA	PTS
*Montreal	70	45	15	10	222	131	100
Detroit	70	30	24	16	183	148	76
New York	70	32	28	10	204	203	74
Toronto	70	24	33	13	153	181	61
Boston	70	23	34	13	147	185	59
Chicago	70	19	39	12	155	216	50

Leading Scorers

Player	Club	GP	G	A	PTS	PIM
Beliveau, Jean	Montreal	70	47	41	88	143
Howe, Gordie	Detroit	70	38	41	79	100
Richard, Maurice	Montreal	70	38	33	71	89
Olmstead, Bert	Montreal	70	14	56	70	94
Sloan, Tod	Toronto	70	37	29	66	100
Bathgate, Andy	New York	70	19	47	66	59
Geoffrion, Bernie	Montreal	59	29	33	62	66
Reibel, Earl	Detroit	68	17	39	56	10
Delvecchio, Alex	Detroit	70	25	26	51	24
Creighton, Dave	New York	70	20	31	51	43
Gadsby, Bill	New York	70	9	42	51	84

1956-57

Team	GP	W	L	T	GF	GA	PTS
Detroit	70	38	20	12	198	157	88
*Montreal	70	35	23	12	210	155	82
Boston	70	34	24	12	195	174	80
New York	70	26	30	14	184	227	66
Toronto	70	21	34	15	174	192	57
Chicago	70	16	39	15	169	225	47

Leading Scorers

Player	Club	GP	G	A	PTS	PIM
Howe, Gordie	Detroit	70	44	45	89	72
Lindsay, Ted	Detroit	70	30	55	85	103
Beliveau, Jean	Montreal	69	33	51	84	105
Bathgate, Andy	New York	70	27	50	77	60
Litzenberger, Ed	Chicago	70	32	32	64	48
Richard, Maurice	Montreal	63	33	29	62	74
McKenney, Don	Boston	69	21	39	60	31
Moore, Dickie	Montreal	70	29	29	58	56
Richard, Henri	Montreal	63	18	36	54	71
Ullman, Norm	Detroit	64	16	36	52	47

1957-58

Team	GP	W	L	T	GF	GA	PTS
*Montreal	70	43	17	10	250	158	96
New York	70	32	25	13	195	188	77
Detroit	70	29	29	12	176	207	70
Boston	70	27	28	15	199	194	69
Chicago	70	24	39	7	163	202	55
Toronto	70	21	38	11	192	226	53

Leading Scorers

Player	Club	GP	G	A	PTS	PIM
Moore, Dickie	Montreal	70	36	48	84	65
Richard, Henri	Montreal	67	28	52	80	56
Bathgate, Andy	New York	65	30	48	78	42
Howe, Gordie	Detroit	64	33	44	77	40
Horvath, Bronco	Boston	67	30	36	66	71
Litzenberger, Ed	Chicago	70	32	30	62	63
Mackell, Fleming	Boston	70	20	40	60	72
Beliveau, Jean	Montreal	55	27	32	59	93
Delvecchio, Alex	Detroit	70	21	38	59	22
McKenney, Don	Boston	70	28	30	58	22

1958-59

Team	GP	W	L	T	GF	GA	PTS
*Montreal	70	39	18	13	258	158	91
Boston	70	32	29	9	205	215	73
Chicago	70	28	29	13	197	208	69
Toronto	70	27	32	11	189	201	65
New York	70	26	32	12	201	217	64
Detroit	70	25	37	8	167	218	58

Leading Scorers

Player	Club	GP	G	A	PTS	PIM
Moore, Dickie	Montreal	70	41	55	96	61
Beliveau, Jean	Montreal	64	45	46	91	67
Bathgate, Andy	New York	70	40	48	88	48
Howe, Gordie	Detroit	70	32	46	78	57
Litzenberger, Ed	Chicago	70	33	44	77	37
Geoffrion, Bernie	Montreal	59	22	44	66	30
Sullivan, George	New York	70	21	42	63	56
Hebenton, Andy	New York	70	33	29	62	8
McKenney, Don	Boston	70	32	30	62	20
Sloan, Tod	Chicago	59	27	35	62	79

1959-60

Team	GP	W	L	T	GF	GA	PTS
*Montreal	70	40	18	12	255	178	92
Toronto	70	35	26	9	199	195	79
Chicago	70	28	29	13	191	180	69
Detroit	70	26	29	15	186	197	67
Boston	70	28	34	8	220	241	64
New York	70	17	38	15	187	247	49

Leading Scorers

Player	Club	GP	G	A	PTS	PIM
Hull, Bobby	Chicago	70	39	42	81	68
Horvath, Bronco	Boston	68	39	41	80	60
Beliveau, Jean	Montreal	60	34	40	74	57
Bathgate, Andy	New York	70	26	48	74	28
Richard, Henri	Montreal	70	30	43	73	66
Howe, Gordie	Detroit	70	28	45	73	46
Geoffrion, Bernie	Montreal	59	30	41	71	36
McKenney, Don	Boston	70	20	49	69	28
Stasiuk, Vic	Boston	69	29	39	68	121
Prentice, Dean	New York	70	32	34	66	43

1960-61

Team	GP	W	L	T	GF	GA	PTS
Montreal	70	41	19	10	254	188	92
Toronto	70	39	19	12	234	176	90
*Chicago	70	29	24	17	198	180	75
Detroit	70	25	29	16	195	215	66
New York	70	22	38	10	204	248	54
Boston	70	15	42	13	176	254	43

Leading Scorers

Player	Club	GP	G	A	PTS	PIM
Geoffrion, Bernie	Montreal	64	50	45	95	29
Béliveau, Jean	Montreal	69	32	58	90	57
Mahovlich, Frank	Toronto	70	48	36	84	131
Bathgate, Andy	New York	70	29	48	77	22
Howe, Gordie	Detroit	64	23	49	72	30
Ullman, Norm	Detroit	70	28	42	70	34
Kelly, Red	Toronto	64	20	50	70	12
Moore, Dickie	Montreal	57	35	34	69	62
Richard, Henri	Montreal	70	24	44	68	91
Delvecchio, Alex	Detroit	70	27	35	62	26

1961-62

Team	GP	W	L	T	GF	GA	PTS
Montreal	70	42	14	14	259	166	98
*Toronto	70	37	22	11	232	180	85
Chicago	70	31	26	13	217	186	75
New York	70	26	32	12	195	207	64
Detroit	70	23	33	14	184	219	60
Boston	70	15	47	8	177	306	38

Leading Scorers

Player	Club	GP	G	A	PTS	PIM
Hull, Bobby	Chicago	70	50	34	84	35
Bathgate, Andy	New Yrk	70	28	56	84	44
Howe, Gordie	Detroit	70	33	44	77	54
Mikita, Stan	Chicago	70	25	52	77	97
Mahovlich, Frank	Toronto	70	33	38	71	87
Delvecchio, Alex	Detroit	70	26	43	69	18
Backstrom, Ralph	Montreal	66	27	38	65	29
Ullman, Norm	Detroit	70	26	38	64	54
Hay, Bill	Chicago	60	11	52	63	34
Provost, Claude	Montreal	70	33	29	62	22

Henri Richard joined the Montreal Canadiens as the club began its unmatched five-year reign as Stanley Cup champions. The Habs and Richard added four more Cup titles in the 1960s and additional championships in 1971 and 1973. Richard retired in 1975 with a record 11 Cup wins in 20 NHL seasons.

1962-63

Team	GP	W	L	T	GF	GA	PTS
*Toronto	70	35	23	12	221	180	82
Chicago	70	32	21	17	194	178	81
Montreal	70	28	19	23	225	183	79
Detroit	70	32	25	13	200	194	77
New York	70	22	36	12	211	233	56
Boston	70	14	39	17	198	281	45

Leading Scorers

Player	Club	GP	G	A	PTS	PIM
Howe, Gordie	Detroit	70	38	48	86	100
Bathgate, Andy	New York	70	35	46	81	54
Mikita, Stan	Chicago	65	31	45	76	69
Mahovlich, Frank	Toronto	67	36	37	73	56
Richard, Henri	Montreal	67	23	50	73	57
Beliveau, Jean	Montreal	69	18	49	67	68
Bucyk, John	Boston	69	27	39	66	36
Delvecchio, Alex	Detroit	70	20	44	64	8
Hull, Bobby	Chicago	65	31	31	62	27
Oliver, Murray	Boston	65	22	40	62	38

1963-64

Team	GP	W	L	T	GF	GA	PTS
Montreal	70	36	21	13	209	167	85
Chicago	70	36	22	12	218	169	84
*Toronto	70	33	25	12	192	172	78
Detroit	70	30	29	11	191	204	71
New York	70	22	38	10	186	242	54
Boston	70	18	40	12	170	212	48

Leading Scorers

Player	Club	GP	G	A	PTS	PIM
Mikita, Stan	Chicago	70	39	50	89	146
Hull, Bobby	Chicago	70	43	44	87	50
Beliveau, Jean	Montreal	68	28	50	78	42
Bathgate, Andy	NYR, Tor.	71	19	58	77	34
Howe, Gordie	Detroit	69	26	47	73	70
Wharram, Ken	Chicago	70	39	32	71	18
Oliver, Murray	Boston	70	24	44	68	41
Goyette, Phil	New York	67	24	41	65	15
Gilbert, Rod	New York	70	24	40	64	62
Keon, Dave	Toronto	70	23	37	60	6

1964-65

Team	GP	W	L	T	GF	GA	PTS
Detroit	70	40	23	7	224	175	87
*Montreal	70	36	23	11	211	185	83
Chicago	70	34	28	8	224	176	76
Toronto	70	30	26	14	204	173	74
New York	70	20	38	12	179	246	52
Boston	70	21	43	6	166	253	48

Leading Scorers

Player	Club	GP	G	A	PTS	PIM
Mikita, Stan	Chicago	70	28	59	87	154
Ullman, Norm	Detroit	70	42	41	83	70
Howe, Gordie	Detroit	70	29	47	76	104
Hull, Bobby	Chicago	61	39	32	71	32
Delvecchio, Alex	Detroit	68	25	42	67	16
Provost, Claude	Montreal	70	27	37	64	28
Gilbert, Rod	New York	70	25	36	61	52
Pilote, Pierre	Chicago	68	14	45	59	162
Bucyk, John	Boston	68	26	29	55	24
Backstrom, Ralph	Montreal	70	25	30	55	41
Esposito, Phil	Chicago	70	23	32	55	44

1965-66

Team	GP	W	L	T	GF	GA	PTS
*Montreal	70	41	21	8	239	173	90
Chicago	70	37	25	8	240	187	82
Toronto	70	34	25	11	208	187	79
Detroit	70	31	27	12	221	194	74
Boston	70	21	43	6	174	275	48
New York	70	18	41	11	195	261	47

Leading Scorers

Player	Club	GP	G	A	PTS	PIM
Hull, Bobby	Chicago	65	54	43	97	70
Mikita, Stan	Chicago	68	30	48	78	58
Rousseau, Bobby	Montreal	70	30	48	78	20
Beliveau, Jean	Montreal	67	29	48	77	50
Howe, Gordie	Detroit	70	29	46	75	83
Ullman, Norm	Detroit	70	31	41	72	35
Delvecchio, Alex	Detroit	70	31	38	69	16
Nevin, Bob	New York	69	29	33	62	10
Richard, Henri	Montreal	62	22	39	61	47
Oliver, Murray	Boston	70	18	42	60	30

1966-67

Team	GP	W	L	T	GF	GA	PTS
Chicago	70	41	17	12	264	170	94
Montreal	70	32	25	13	202	188	77
*Toronto	70	32	27	11	204	211	75
New York	70	30	28	12	188	189	72
Detroit	70	27	39	4	212	241	58
Boston	70	17	43	10	182	253	44

Leading Scorers

Player	Club	GP	G	A	PTS	PIM
Mikita, Stan	Chicago	70	35	62	97	12
Hull, Bobby	Chicago	66	52	28	80	52
Ullman, Norm	Detroit	68	26	44	70	26
Wharram, Ken	Chicago	70	31	34	65	21
Howe, Gordie	Detroit	69	25	40	65	53
Rousseau, Bobby	Montreal	68	19	44	63	58
Esposito, Phil	Chicago	69	21	40	61	40
Goyette, Phil	New York	70	12	49	61	6
Mohns, Doug	Chicago	61	25	35	60	58
Richard, Henri	Montreal	65	21	34	55	28
Delvecchio, Alex	Detroit	70	17	38	55	10

Norm Ullman (#9) and Jean Ratelle (#19) were NHL stars during the 1960s. Both enjoyed lengthy careers and retired with more than 1,200 scoring points.

1967-68

East Division

Team	GP	W	L	T	GF	GA	PTS
*Montreal	74	42	22	10	236	167	94
New York	74	39	23	12	226	183	90
Boston	74	37	27	10	259	216	84
Chicago	74	32	26	16	212	222	80
Toronto	74	33	31	10	209	176	76
Detroit	74	27	35	12	245	257	66

West Division

Team	GP	W	L	T	GF	GA	PTS
Philadelphia	74	31	32	11	173	179	73
Los Angeles	74	31	33	10	200	224	72
St. Louis	74	27	31	16	177	191	70
Minnesota	74	27	32	15	191	226	69
Pittsburgh	74	27	34	13	195	216	67
Oakland	74	15	42	17	153	219	47

Leading Scorers

Player	Club	GP	G	A	PTS	PIM
Mikita, Stan	Chicago	72	40	47	87	14
Esposito, Phil	Boston	74	35	49	84	21
Howe, Gordie	Detroit	74	39	43	82	53
Ratelle, Jean	New York	74	32	46	78	18
Gilbert, Rod	New York	73	29	48	77	12
Hull, Bobby	Chicago	71	44	31	75	39
Ullman, Norm	Det., Tor.	71	35	37	72	28
Delvecchio, Alex	Detroit	74	22	48	70	14
Bucyk, John	Boston	72	30	39	69	8
Wharram, Ken	Chicago	74	27	42	69	18

1968-69

East Division

Team	GP	W	L	T	GF	GA	PTS
*Montreal	76	46	19	11	271	202	103
Boston	76	42	18	16	303	221	100
New York	76	41	26	9	231	196	91
Toronto	76	35	26	15	234	217	85
Detroit	76	33	31	12	239	221	78
Chicago	76	34	33	9	280	246	77

West Division

Team	GP	W	L	T	GF	GA	PTS
St. Louis	76	37	25	14	204	157	88
Oakland	76	29	36	11	219	251	69
Philadelphia	76	20	35	21	174	225	61
Los Angeles	76	24	42	10	185	260	58
Pittsburgh	76	20	45	11	189	252	51
Minnesota	76	18	43	5	189	270	51

Leading Scorers

Player	Club	GP	G	A	PTS	PIM
Esposito, Phil	Boston	74	49	77	126	79
Hull, Bobby	Chicago	74	58	49	107	48
Howe, Gordie	Detroit	76	44	59	103	58
Mikita, Stan	Chicago	74	30	67	97	52
Hodge, Ken	Boston	75	45	45	90	75
Cournoyer, Yvan	Montreal	76	43	44	87	31
Delvecchio, Alex	Detroit	72	25	58	83	8
Berenson, Red	St. Louis	76	35	47	82	43
Beliveau, Jean	Montreal	69	33	49	82	55
Mahovlich, Frank	Detroit	76	49	29	78	38
Ratelle, Jean	New York	75	32	46	78	26

1969-70

East Division

Team	GP	W	L	T	GF	GA	PTS
Chicago	76	45	22	9	250	170	99
*Boston	76	40	17	19	277	216	99
Detroit	76	40	21	15	246	199	95
New York	76	38	22	16	246	189	92
Montreal	76	38	22	16	244	201	92
Toronto	76	29	34	13	222	242	71

West Division

Team	GP	W	L	T	GF	GA	PTS
St. Louis	76	37	27	12	224	179	86
Pittsburgh	76	26	38	12	182	238	64
Minnesota	76	19	35	22	224	257	60
Oakland	76	22	40	14	169	243	58
Philadelphia	76	17	35	24	197	225	58
Los Angeles	76	14	52	10	168	290	38

Leading Scorers

Player	Club	GP	G	A	PTS	PIM
Orr, Bobby	Boston	76	33	87	120	125
Esposito, Phil	Boston	76	43	56	99	50
Mikita, Stan	Chicago	76	39	47	86	50
Goyette, Phil	St. Louis	72	29	49	78	16
Tkaczuk, Walt	New York	76	27	50	77	38
Ratelle, Jean	New York	75	32	42	74	28
Berenson, Red	St. Louis	67	33	39	72	38
Parise, Jean-Paul	Minnesota	74	24	48	72	72
Howe, Gordie	Detroit	76	31	40	71	58
Mahovlich, Frank	Detroit	74	38	32	70	59
Balon, Dave	New York	76	33	37	70	00
McKenzie, John	Boston	72	29	41	70	114

1970-71

East Division

Team	GP	W	L	T	GF	GA	PTS
Boston	78	57	14	7	399	207	121
New York	78	49	18	11	259	177	109
*Montreal	78	42	23	13	291	216	97
Toronto	78	37	33	8	248	211	82
Buffalo	78	24	39	15	217	291	63
Vancouver	78	24	46	8	229	296	56
Detroit	78	22	45	11	209	308	55

West Division

Team	GP	W	L	T	GF	GA	PTS
Chicago	78	49	20	9	277	184	107
St. Louis	78	34	25	19	223	208	87
Philadelphia	78	28	33	17	207	225	73
Minnesota	78	28	34	16	191	223	72
Los Angeles	78	25	40	13	239	303	63
Pittsburgh	78	21	37	20	221	240	62
California	78	20	53	5	199	320	45

Leading Scorers

Player	Club	GP	G	A	PTS	PIM
Esposito, Phil	Boston	78	76	76	152	71
Orr, Bobby	Boston	78	37	102	139	91
Bucyk, John	Boston	78	51	65	116	8
Hodge, Ken	Boston	78	43	62	105	113
Hull, Bobby	Chicago	78	44	52	96	32
Ullman, Norm	Toronto	73	34	51	85	24
Cashman, Wayne	Boston	77	21	58	79	100
McKenzie, John	Boston	65	31	46	77	120
Keon, Dave	Toronto	76	38	38	76	4
Beliveau, Jean	Montreal	70	25	51	76	40
Stanfield, Fred	Boston	75	24	52	76	12

1971-72

East Division

Team	GP	W	L	T	GF	GA	PTS
*Boston	78	54	13	11	330	204	119
New York	78	48	17	13	317	192	109
Montreal	78	46	16	16	307	205	108
Toronto	78	33	31	14	209	208	80
Detroit	78	33	35	10	261	262	76
Buffalo	78	16	43	19	203	289	51
Vancouver	78	20	50	8	203	297	48

West Division

Team	GP	W	L	T	GF	GA	PTS
Chicago	78	46	17	15	256	166	107
Minnesota	78	37	29	12	212	191	86
St. Louis	78	28	39	11	208	247	67
Pittsburgh	78	26	38	14	220	258	66
Philadelphia	78	26	38	14	200	236	66
California	78	21	39	18	216	288	60
Los Angeles	78	20	49	9	206	305	49

Leading Scorers

Player	Club	GP	G	A	PTS	PIM
Esposito, Phil	Boston	76	66	67	133	76
Orr, Bobby	Boston	76	37	80	117	106
Ratelle, Jean	New York	63	46	63	109	4
Hadfield, Vic	New York	78	50	56	106	142
Gilbert, Rod	New York	73	43	54	97	64
Mahovlich, Frank	Montreal	76	43	53	96	36
Hull, Bobby	Chicago	78	50	43	93	24
Cournoyer, Yvan	Montreal	73	47	36	83	15
Bucyk, John	Boston	78	32	51	83	4
Clarke, Bobby	Philadelphia	78	35	46	81	87
Lemaire, Jacques	Montreal	77	32	49	81	26

1972-73

East Division

Team	GP	W	L	T	GF	GA	PTS
*Montreal	78	52	10	16	329	184	120
Boston	78	51	22	5	330	235	107
NY Rangers	78	47	23	8	297	208	102
Buffalo	78	37	27	14	257	219	88
Detroit	78	37	29	12	265	243	86
Toronto	78	27	41	10	247	279	64
Vancouver	78	22	47	9	233	339	53
NY Islanders	78	12	60	6	170	347	30

West Division

Team	GP	W	L	T	GF	GA	PTS
Chicago	78	42	27	9	284	225	93
Philadelphia	78	37	30	11	296	256	85
Minnesota	78	37	30	11	254	230	85
St. Louis	78	32	34	12	233	251	76
Pittsburgh	78	32	37	9	257	265	73
Los Angeles	78	31	36	11	232	245	73
Atlanta	78	25	38	15	191	239	65
California	78	16	46	16	213	323	48

Leading Scorers

Player	Club	GP	G	A	PTS	PIM
Esposito, Phil	Boston	78	55	75	130	87
Clarke, Bobby	Philadelphia	78	37	67	104	80
Orr, Bobby	Boston	63	29	72	101	99
MacLeish, Rick	Philadelphia	78	50	50	100	69
Lemaire, Jacques	Montreal	77	44	51	95	16
Ratelle, Jean	NY Rangers	78	41	53	94	12
Redmond, Mickey	Detroit	76	52	41	93	24
Bucyk, John	Boston	78	40	53	93	12
Mahovlich, Frank	Montreal	78	38	55	93	51
Pappin, Jim	Chicago	76	41	51	92	82

1973-74

East Division

Team	GP	W	L	T	GF	GA	PTS
Boston	78	52	17	9	349	221	113
Montreal	78	45	24	9	293	240	99
NY Rangers	78	40	24	14	300	251	94
Toronto	78	35	27	16	274	230	86
Buffalo	78	32	34	12	242	250	76
Detroit	78	29	39	10	255	319	68
Vancouver	78	24	43	11	224	296	59
NY Islanders	78	19	41	18	182	247	56

West Division

Team	GP	W	L	T	GF	GA	PTS
*Philadelphia	78	50	16	12	273	164	112
Chicago	78	41	14	23	272	164	105
Los Angeles	78	33	33	12	233	231	78
Atlanta	78	30	34	14	214	238	74
Pittsburgh	78	28	41	9	242	273	65
St. Louis	78	26	40	12	206	248	64
Minnesota	78	23	38	17	235	275	63
California	78	13	55	10	195	342	36

Leading Scorers

Player	Club	GP	G	A	PTS	PIM
Esposito, Phil	Boston	78	68	77	145	58
Orr, Bobby	Boston	74	32	90	122	82
Hodge, Ken	Boston	76	50	55	105	43
Cashman, Wayne	Boston	78	30	59	89	111
Clarke, Bobby	Philadelphia	77	35	52	87	113
Martin, Rick	Buffalo	78	52	34	86	38
Apps, Syl	Pittsburgh	75	24	61	85	37
Sittler, Darryl	Toronto	78	38	46	84	55
MacDonald, Lowell	Pittsburgh	78	43	39	82	14
Park, Brad	NY Rangers	78	25	57	82	148
Hextall, Dennis	Minnesota	78	20	62	82	138

1974-75
PRINCE OF WALES CONFERENCE
Norris Division

Team	GP	W	L	T	GF	GA	PTS
Montreal	80	47	14	19	374	225	113
Los Angeles	80	42	17	21	269	185	105
Pittsburgh	80	37	28	15	326	289	89
Detroit	80	23	45	12	259	335	58
Washington	80	8	67	5	181	446	21

Adams Division

Team	GP	W	L	T	GF	GA	PTS
Buffalo	80	49	16	15	354	240	113
Boston	80	40	26	14	345	245	94
Toronto	80	31	33	16	280	309	78
California	80	19	48	13	212	316	51

CLARENCE CAMPBELL CONFERENCE
Patrick Division

Team	GP	W	L	T	GF	GA	PTS
*Philadelphia	80	51	18	11	293	181	113
NY Rangers	80	37	29	14	319	276	88
NY Islanders	80	33	25	22	264	221	88
Atlanta	80	34	31	15	243	233	83

Smythe Division

Team	GP	W	L	T	GF	GA	PTS
Vancouver	80	38	32	10	271	254	86
St. Louis	80	35	31	14	269	267	84
Chicago	80	37	35	8	268	241	82
Minnesota	80	23	50	7	221	341	53
Kansas City	80	15	54	11	184	328	41

Leading Scorers

Player	Club	GP	G	A	PTS	PIM
Orr, Bobby	Boston	80	46	89	135	101
Esposito, Phil	Boston	79	61	66	127	62
Dionne, Marcel	Detroit	80	47	74	121	14
Lafleur, Guy	Montreal	70	53	66	119	37
Mahovlich, Pete	Montreal	80	35	82	117	64
Clarke, Bobby	Philadelphia	80	27	89	116	125
Robert, Rene	Buffalo	74	40	60	100	75
Gilbert, Rod	NY Rangers	76	36	61	97	22
Perreault, Gilbert	Buffalo	68	39	57	96	36
Martin, Rick	Buffalo	68	52	43	95	72

1975-76
PRINCE OF WALES CONFERENCE
Norris Division

Team	GP	W	L	T	GF	GA	PTS
*Montreal	80	58	11	11	337	174	127
Los Angeles	80	38	33	9	263	265	85
Pittsburgh	80	35	33	12	339	303	82
Detroit	80	26	44	10	226	300	62
Washington	80	11	59	10	224	394	32

Adams Division

Team	GP	W	L	T	GF	GA	PTS
Boston	80	48	15	17	313	237	113
Buffalo	80	46	21	13	339	240	105
Toronto	80	34	31	15	294	276	83
California	80	27	42	11	250	278	65

CLARENCE CAMPBELL CONFERENCE
Patrick Division

Team	GP	W	L	T	GF	GA	PTS
Philadelphia	80	51	13	16	348	209	118
NY Islanders	80	42	21	17	297	190	101
Atlanta	80	35	33	12	262	237	82
NY Rangers	80	29	42	9	262	333	67

Smythe Division

Team	GP	W	L	T	GF	GA	PTS
Chicago	80	32	30	18	254	261	82
Vancouver	80	33	32	15	271	272	81
St. Louis	80	29	37	14	249	290	72
Minnesota	80	20	53	7	195	303	47
Kansas City	80	12	56	12	190	351	36

Leading Scorers

Player	Club	GP	G	A	PTS	PIM
Lafleur, Guy	Montreal	80	56	69	125	36
Clarke, Bobby	Philadelphia	76	30	89	119	13
Perreault, Gilbert	Buffalo	80	44	69	113	36
Barber, Bill	Philadelphia	80	50	62	112	104
Larouche, Pierre	Pittsburgh	76	53	58	111	33
Ratelle, Jean	Bos., NYR	80	36	69	105	18
Mahovlich, Pete	Montreal	80	34	71	105	76
Pronovost, Jean	Pittsburgh	80	52	52	104	24
Sittler, Darryl	Toronto	79	41	59	100	90
Apps, Syl	Pittsburgh	80	32	67	99	24

1976-77
PRINCE OF WALES CONFERENCE
Norris Division

Team	GP	W	L	T	GF	GA	PTS
*Montreal	80	60	8	12	387	171	132
Los Angeles	80	34	31	15	271	241	83
Pittsburgh	80	34	33	13	240	252	81
Washington	80	24	42	14	221	307	62
Detroit	80	16	55	9	183	309	41

Adams Division

Team	GP	W	L	T	GF	GA	PTS
Boston	80	49	23	8	312	240	106
Buffalo	80	48	24	8	301	220	104
Toronto	80	33	32	15	301	285	81
Cleveland	80	25	42	13	240	292	63

CLARENCE CAMPBELL CONFERENCE
Patrick Division

Team	GP	W	L	T	GF	GA	PTS
Philadelphia	80	48	16	16	323	213	112
NY Islanders	80	47	21	12	288	193	106
Atlanta	80	34	34	12	264	265	80
NY Rangers	88	29	37	14	272	310	72

Smythe Division

Team	GP	W	L	T	GF	GA	PTS
St. Louis	80	32	39	9	239	276	73
Minnesota	80	23	39	18	240	310	64
Chicago	80	26	43	11	240	298	63
Vancouver	80	25	42	13	235	294	63
Colorado	80	20	46	14	226	307	54

Leading Scorers

Player	Club	GP	G	A	PTS	PIM
Lafleur, Guy	Montreal	80	56	80	136	20
Dionne, Marcel	Los Angeles	80	53	69	122	12
Shutt, Steve	Montreal	80	60	45	105	28
MacLeish, Rick	Philadelphia	79	49	48	97	42
Perreault, Gilbert	Buffalo	80	39	56	95	30
Young, Tim	Minnesota	80	29	66	95	58
Ratelle, Jean	Boston	78	33	61	94	2
McDonald, Lanny	Toronto	80	46	44	90	77
Sittler, Darryl	Toronto	73	38	52	90	89
Clarke, Bobby	Philadelphia	80	27	63	90	71

1977-78
PRINCE OF WALES CONFERENCE
Norris Division

Team	GP	W	L	T	GF	GA	PTS
*Montreal	80	59	10	11	359	183	129
Detroit	80	32	34	14	252	266	78
Los Angeles	80	31	34	15	243	45	77
Pittsburgh	80	25	37	18	254	321	68
Washington	80	17	49	14	195	321	48

Adams Division

Team	GP	W	L	T	GF	GA	PTS
Boston	80	51	18	11	333	218	113
Buffalo	80	44	19	17	288	215	105
Toronto	80	41	29	10	271	237	92
Cleveland	80	22	45	13	230	325	57

CLARENCE CAMPBELL CONFERENCE
Patrick Division

Team	GP	W	L	T	GF	GA	PTS
NY Islanders	80	48	17	15	334	210	111
Philadelphia	80	45	20	15	296	200	105
Atlanta	80	34	27	19	274	252	87
NY Rangers	80	30	37	13	279	280	73

Smythe Division

Team	GP	W	L	T	GF	GA	PTS
Chicago	80	32	29	19	230	220	83
Colorado	80	19	40	21	257	305	59
Vancouver	80	20	43	17	239	320	57
St. Louis	80	20	47	13	195	304	53
Minnesota	80	18	53	9	218	325	45

Leading Scorers

Player	Club	GP	G	A	PTS	PIM
Lafleur, Guy	Montreal	79	60	72	132	26
Trottier, Bryan	NY Islanders	77	46	77	123	46
Sittler, Darryl	Toronto	80	45	72	117	100
Lemaire, Jacques	Montreal	76	36	61	97	14
Potvin, Denis	NY Islanders	80	30	64	94	81
Bossy, Mike	NY Islanders	73	53	38	91	6
O'Reilly, Terry	Boston	77	29	61	90	211
Perreault, Gilbert	Buffalo	79	41	48	89	20
Clarke, Bobby	Philadelphia	71	21	68	89	83
McDonald, Lanny	Toronto	74	47	40	87	54
Paiement, Wilf	Colorado	80	31	56	87	114

1978-79
PRINCE OF WALES CONFERENCE
Norris Division

Team	GP	W	L	T	GF	GA	PTS
*Montreal	80	52	17	11	337	204	115
Pittsburgh	80	36	31	13	281	279	85
Los Angeles	80	34	34	12	292	286	80
Washington	80	24	41	15	273	338	63
Detroit	80	23	41	16	252	295	62

Adams Division

Team	GP	W	L	T	GF	GA	PTS
Boston	80	43	23	14	316	270	100
Buffalo	80	36	28	16	280	263	88
Toronto	80	34	33	13	267	252	81
Minnesota	80	28	40	12	257	289	68

CLARENCE CAMPBELL CONFERENCE
Patrick Division

Team	GP	W	L	T	GF	GA	PTS
NY Islanders	80	51	15	14	358	214	116
Philadelphia	80	40	25	15	281	248	95
NY Rangers	80	40	29	11	316	292	91
Atlanta	80	41	31	8	327	280	90

Smythe Division

Team	GP	W	L	T	GF	GA	PTS
Chicago	80	29	36	15	244	277	73
Vancouver	80	25	42	13	217	291	63
St. Louis	80	18	50	12	249	348	48
Colorado	80	15	53	12	210	331	42

Leading Scorers

Player	Club	GP	G	A	PTS	PIM
Trottier, Bryan	NY Islanders	76	47	87	134	50
Dionne, Marcel	Los Angeles	80	59	71	130	30
Lafleur, Guy	Montreal	80	52	77	129	28
Bossy, Mike	NY Islanders	80	69	57	126	25
MacMillan, Bob	Atlanta	79	37	71	108	14
Chouinard, Guy	Atlanta	80	50	57	107	14
Potvin, Denis	NY Islanders	73	31	70	101	58
Federko, Bernie	St. Louis	74	31	64	95	14
Taylor, Dave	Los Angeles	78	43	48	91	124
Gillies, Clark	NY Islanders	75	35	56	91	68

Cesare Maniago, who started his career with the Toronto Maple Leafs, spent nine productive seasons with the Minnesota North Stars from 1967-68 to 1975-76.

1979-80
PRINCE OF WALES CONFERENCE
Norris Division

Team	GP	W	L	T	GF	GA	PTS
Montreal	80	47	20	13	328	240	107
Los Angeles	80	30	36	14	290	313	74
Pittsburgh	80	30	37	13	251	303	73
Hartford	80	27	34	19	303	312	73
Detroit	80	26	43	11	268	306	63

Adams Division

Buffalo	80	47	17	16	318	201	110
Boston	80	46	21	13	310	234	105
Minnesota	80	36	28	16	311	253	88
Toronto	80	35	40	5	304	327	75
Quebec	80	25	44	11	248	313	61

CLARENCE CAMPBELL CONFERENCE
Patrick Division

Philadelphia	80	48	12	20	327	254	116
*NY Islanders	80	39	28	13	281	247	91
NY Rangers	80	38	32	10	308	284	86
Atlanta	80	35	32	13	282	269	83
Washington	80	27	40	13	261	293	67

Smythe Division

Chicago	80	34	27	19	241	250	87
St. Louis	80	34	34	12	266	278	80
Vancouver	80	27	37	16	256	281	70
Edmonton	80	28	39	13	301	322	69
Winnipeg	80	20	49	11	214	314	51
Colorado	80	19	48	13	234	308	51

Leading Scorers

Player	Club	GP	G	A	PTS	PIM
Dionne, Marcel	Los Angeles	80	53	84	137	32
Gretzky, Wayne	Edmonton	79	51	86	137	21
Lafleur, Guy	Montreal	74	50	75	125	12
Perreault, Gilbert	Buffalo	80	40	66	106	57
Rogers, Mike	Hartford	80	44	61	105	10
Trottier, Bryan	NY Islanders	78	42	62	104	68
Simmer, Charlie	Los Angeles	64	56	45	101	65
Stoughton, Blaine	Hartford	80	56	44	100	16
Sittler, Darryl	Toronto	73	40	57	97	62
MacDonald, Blair	Edmonton	80	46	48	94	6
Federko, Bernie	St. Louis	79	38	56	94	24

St. Louis goaltender Mike Liut backstopped the Blues to a 107-point season in 1980-81. Liut earned a berth on the NHL's First All-Star Team. He also was named the recipient of the Lester B. Pearson Award, presented annually to the NHL's outstanding player as selected by members of the NHL Players' Association.

1980-81
PRINCE OF WALES CONFERENCE
Norris Division

Team	GP	W	L	T	GF	GA	PTS
Montreal	80	45	22	13	332	232	103
Los Angeles	80	43	24	13	337	290	99
Pittsburgh	80	30	37	13	302	345	73
Hartford	80	21	41	18	292	372	60
Detroit	80	19	43	18	252	339	56

Adams Division

Buffalo	80	39	20	21	327	250	99
Boston	80	37	30	13	316	272	87
Minnesota	80	35	28	17	291	263	87
Quebec	80	30	32	18	314	318	78
Toronto	80	28	37	15	322	367	71

CLARENCE CAMPBELL CONFERENCE
Patrick Division

*NY Islanders	80	48	18	14	355	260	110
Philadelphia	80	41	24	15	313	249	97
Calgary	80	39	27	14	329	298	92
NY Rangers	80	30	36	14	312	317	74
Washington	80	26	36	18	286	317	70

Smythe Division

St. Louis	80	45	18	17	352	281	107
Chicago	80	31	33	16	304	315	78
Vancouver	80	28	32	20	289	301	76
Edmonton	80	29	35	16	328	327	74
Colorado	80	22	45	13	258	344	57
Winnipeg	80	9	57	14	246	400	32

Leading Scorers

Player	Club	GP	G	A	PTS	PIM
Gretzky, Wayne	Edmonton	80	55	109	164	28
Dionne, Marcel	Los Angeles	80	58	77	135	70
Nilsson, Kent	Calgary	80	49	82	131	26
Bossy, Mike	NY Islanders	79	68	51	119	32
Taylor, Dave	Los Angeles	72	47	65	112	130
Stastny, Peter	Quebec	77	39	70	109	37
Simmer, Charlie	Los Angeles	65	56	49	105	62
Rogers, Mike	Hartford	80	40	65	105	32
Federko, Bernie	St. Louis	78	31	73	104	47
Richard, Jacques	Quebec	78	52	51	103	39
Middleton, Rick	Boston	80	44	59	103	16
Trottier, Bryan	NY Islanders	73	31	72	103	74

1981-82
CLARENCE CAMPBELL CONFERENCE
Norris Division

Team	GP	W	L	T	GF	GA	PTS
Minnesota	80	37	23	20	346	288	94
Winnipeg	80	33	33	14	319	332	80
St. Louis	80	32	40	8	315	349	72
Chicago	80	30	38	12	332	363	72
Toronto	80	20	44	16	298	380	56
Detroit	80	21	47	12	270	351	54

Smythe Division

Edmonton	80	48	17	15	417	295	111
Vancouver	80	30	33	17	290	286	77
Calgary	80	29	34	17	334	345	75
Los Angeles	80	24	41	15	314	369	63
Colorado	80	18	49	13	241	362	49

PRINCE OF WALES CONFERENCE
Adams Division

Montreal	80	46	17	17	360	223	109
Boston	80	43	27	10	323	285	96
Buffalo	80	39	26	15	307	273	93
Quebec	80	33	31	16	356	345	82
Hartford	80	21	41	18	264	351	60

Patrick Division

*NY Islanders	80	54	16	10	385	250	118
NY Rangers	80	39	27	14	316	306	92
Philadelphia	80	38	31	11	325	313	87
Pittsburgh	80	31	36	13	310	337	75
Washington	80	26	41	13	319	338	65

Leading Scorers

Player	Club	GP	G	A	PTS	PIM
Gretzky, Wayne	Edmonton	80	92	120	212	26
Bossy, Mike	NY Islanders	80	64	83	147	22
Stastny, Peter	Quebec	80	46	93	139	91
Maruk, Dennis	Washington	80	60	76	136	128
Trottier, Bryan	NY Islanders	80	50	79	129	88
Savard, Denis	Chicago	80	32	87	119	82
Dionne, Marcel	Los Angeles	78	50	67	117	50
Smith, Bobby	Minnesota	80	43	71	114	82
Ciccarelli, Dino	Minnesota	76	55	51	106	138
Taylor, Dave	Los Angeles	78	39	67	106	130

1982-83
CLARENCE CAMPBELL CONFERENCE
Norris Division

Team	GP	W	L	T	GF	GA	PTS
Chicago	80	47	23	10	338	268	104
Minnesota	80	40	24	16	321	290	96
Toronto	80	28	40	12	293	330	68
St. Louis	80	25	40	15	285	316	65
Detroit	80	21	44	15	263	344	57

Smythe Division

Edmonton	80	47	21	12	424	315	106
Calgary	80	32	34	14	321	317	78
Vancouver	80	30	35	15	303	309	75
Winnipeg	80	33	39	8	311	333	74
Los Angeles	80	27	41	12	308	365	66

PRINCE OF WALES CONFERENCE
Adams Division

Boston	80	50	20	10	327	228	110
Montreal	80	42	24	14	350	286	98
Buffalo	80	38	29	13	318	285	89
Quebec	80	34	34	12	343	336	80
Hartford	80	19	54	7	261	403	45

Patrick Division

Philadelphia	80	49	23	8	32	240	106
*NY Islanders	80	42	26	12	302	226	96
Washington	80	39	25	16	306	283	94
NY Rangers	80	35	35	10	306	287	80
New Jersey	80	17	49	14	230	338	48
Pittsburgh	80	18	53	9	257	394	45

Leading Scorers

Player	Club	GP	G	A	PTS	PIM
Gretzky, Wayne	Edmonton	80	71	125	196	59
Stastny, Peter	Quebec	75	47	77	124	78
Savard, Denis	Chicago	78	35	86	121	99
Bossy, Mike	NY Islanders	79	60	58	118	20
Dionne, Marcel	Los Angeles	80	56	51	107	22
Pederson, Barry	Boston	77	46	61	107	47
Messier, Mark	Edmonton	77	48	58	106	72
Goulet, Michel	Quebec	80	57	48	105	51
Anderson, Glenn	Edmonton	72	48	56	104	70
Nilsson, Kent	Calgary	80	46	58	104	10
Kurri, Jari	Edmonton	80	45	59	104	22

Quebec's Peter Stastny recorded seven 100-point seasons for the Quebec Nordiques in the 1980s.

1983-84
CLARENCE CAMPBELL CONFERENCE
Norris Division

Team	GP	W	L	T	GF	GA	PTS
Minnesota	80	39	31	10	345	344	88
St. Louis	80	32	41	7	293	316	71
Detroit	80	31	42	7	298	323	69
Chicago	80	30	42	8	277	311	68
Toronto	80	26	45	9	303	387	61

Smythe Division

Team	GP	W	L	T	GF	GA	PTS
*Edmonton	80	57	18	5	446	314	119
Calgary	80	34	32	14	311	314	82
Vancouver	80	32	39	9	306	328	73
Winnipeg	80	31	38	11	340	374	73
Los Angeles	80	23	44	13	309	376	59

PRINCE OF WALES CONFERENCE
Adams Division

Team	GP	W	L	T	GF	GA	PTS
Boston	80	49	25	6	336	261	104
Buffalo	80	48	25	7	315	257	103
Quebec	80	42	28	10	360	278	94
Montreal	80	35	40	5	286	295	75
Hartford	80	28	42	10	288	320	66

Patrick Division

Team	GP	W	L	T	GF	GA	PTS
NY Islanders	80	50	26	4	357	269	104
Washington	80	48	27	5	308	226	101
Philadelphia	80	44	26	10	350	290	98
NY Rangers	80	42	29	9	314	304	93
New Jersey	80	17	56	7	231	350	41
Pittsburgh	80	16	58	6	254	390	38

Leading Scorers

Player	Club	GP	G	A	PTS	PIM
Gretzky, Wayne	Edmonton	74	87	118	205	39
Coffey, Paul	Edmonton	80	40	86	126	104
Goulet, Michel	Quebec	75	56	65	121	76
Stastny, Peter	Quebec	80	46	73	119	73
Bossy, Mike	NY Islanders	67	51	67	118	8
Pederson, Barry	Boston	80	39	77	116	64
Kurri, Jari	Edmonton	64	52	61	113	14
Trottier, Bryan	NY Islanders	68	40	71	111	59
Federko, Bernie	St. Louis	79	41	66	107	43
Middleton, Rick	Boston	80	47	58	105	14

1984-85
CLARENCE CAMPBELL CONFERENCE
Norris Division

Team	GP	W	L	T	GF	GA	PTS
St. Louis	80	37	31	12	299	288	86
Chicago	80	38	35	7	309	299	83
Detroit	80	27	41	12	313	357	66
Minnesota	80	25	43	12	268	321	62
Toronto	80	20	52	8	253	358	48

Smythe Division

Team	GP	W	L	T	GF	GA	PTS
*Edmonton	80	49	20	11	401	298	109
Winnipeg	80	43	27	10	358	332	96
Calgary	80	41	27	12	363	302	94
Los Angeles	80	34	32	14	339	326	82
Vancouver	80	25	46	9	284	401	59

PRINCE OF WALES CONFERENCE
Adams Division

Team	GP	W	L	T	GF	GA	PTS
Montreal	80	41	27	12	309	262	94
Quebec	80	41	30	9	323	275	91
Buffalo	80	38	28	14	290	237	90
Boston	80	36	34	10	303	287	82
Hartford	80	30	41	9	268	318	69

Patrick Division

Team	GP	W	L	T	GF	GA	PTS
Philadelphia	80	53	20	7	348	241	113
Washington	80	46	25	9	322	240	101
NY Islanders	80	40	34	6	345	312	86
NY Rangers	80	26	44	10	295	345	62
New Jersey	80	22	48	10	264	346	54
Pittsburgh	80	24	51	5	276	385	53

Leading Scorers

Player	Club	GP	G	A	PTS	PIM
Gretzky, Wayne	Edmonton	80	73	135	208	52
Kurri, Jari	Edmonton	73	71	64	135	30
Hawerchuk, Dale	Winnipeg	80	53	77	130	74
Dionne, Marcel	Los Angeles	80	46	80	126	46
Coffey, Paul	Edmonton	80	37	84	121	97
Bossy, Mike	NY Islanders	76	58	59	117	38
Ogrodnick, John	Detroit	79	55	50	105	30
Savard, Denis	Chicago	79	38	67	105	56
Federko, Bernie	St. Louis	76	30	73	103	27
Gartner, Mike	Washington	80	50	52	102	7

1985-86
CLARENCE CAMPBELL CONFERENCE
Norris Division

Team	GP	W	L	T	GF	GA	PTS
Chicago	80	39	33	8	351	349	86
Minnesota	80	38	33	9	327	305	85
St. Louis	80	37	34	9	302	291	83
Toronto	80	25	48	7	311	386	57
Detroit	80	17	57	6	266	415	40

Smythe Division

Team	GP	W	L	T	GF	GA	PTS
Edmonton	80	56	17	7	426	310	119
Calgary	80	40	31	9	354	315	89
Winnipeg	80	26	47	7	295	372	59
Vancouver	80	23	44	13	282	333	59
Los Angeles	80	23	49	8	284	389	54

PRINCE OF WALES CONFERENCE
Adams Division

Team	GP	W	L	T	GF	GA	PTS
Quebec	80	43	31	6	330	289	92
*Montreal	80	40	33	7	330	280	87
Boston	80	37	31	12	311	288	86
Hartford	80	40	36	4	332	302	84
Buffalo	80	37	37	6	296	291	80

Patrick Division

Team	GP	W	L	T	GF	GA	PTS
Philadelphia	80	53	23	4	335	241	110
Washington	80	50	23	7	315	272	107
NY Islanders	80	39	29	12	327	284	90
NY Rangers	80	36	38	6	280	276	78
Pittsburgh	80	34	38	8	313	305	76
New Jersey	80	28	49	3	300	374	59

Leading Scorers

Player	Club	GP	G	A	PTS	PIM
Gretzky, Wayne	Edmonton	80	52	163	215	52
Lemieux, Mario	Pittsburgh	79	48	93	141	43
Coffey, Paul	Edmonton	79	48	90	138	120
Kurri, Jari	Edmonton	78	68	63	131	22
Bossy, Mike	NY Islanders	80	61	62	123	14
Stastny, Peter	Quebec	76	41	81	122	60
Savard, Denis	Chicago	80	47	69	116	111
Naslund, Mats	Montreal	80	43	67	110	16
Hawerchuk, Dale	Winnipeg	80	46	59	105	44
Broten, Neal	Minnesota	80	29	76	105	47

1986-87
CLARENCE CAMPBELL CONFERENCE
Norris Division

Team	GP	W	L	T	GF	GA	PTS
St. Louis	80	32	33	15	281	293	79
Detroit	80	34	36	10	260	274	78
Chicago	80	29	37	14	290	310	72
Toronto	80	32	42	6	286	319	70
Minnesota	80	30	40	10	296	314	70

Smythe Division

Team	GP	W	L	T	GF	GA	PTS
*Edmonton	80	50	24	6	372	284	106
Calgary	80	46	31	3	318	289	95
Winnipeg	80	40	32	8	279	271	88
Los Angeles	80	31	41	8	318	341	70
Vancouver	80	29	43	8	282	314	66

PRINCE OF WALES CONFERENCE
Adams Division

Team	GP	W	L	T	GF	GA	PTS
Hartford	80	43	30	7	287	270	93
Montreal	80	41	29	10	277	241	92
Boston	80	39	34	7	301	276	85
Quebec	80	31	39	10	267	276	72
Buffalo	80	28	44	8	280	308	64

Patrick Division

Team	GP	W	L	T	GF	GA	PTS
Philadelphia	80	46	26	8	310	245	100
Washington	80	38	32	10	285	278	86
NY Islanders	80	35	33	12	279	281	82
NY Rangers	80	34	38	8	307	323	76
Pittsburgh	80	30	38	12	297	290	72
New Jersey	80	29	45	6	293	368	64

Leading Scorers

Player	Club	GP	G	A	PTS	PIM
Gretzky, Wayne	Edmonton	79	62	121	183	28
Kurri, Jari	Edmonton	79	54	54	108	41
Lemieux, Mario	Pittsburgh	63	54	53	107	57
Messier, Mark	Edmonton	77	37	70	107	73
Gilmour, Doug	St. Louis	80	42	63	105	58
Ciccarelli, Dino	Minnesota	80	52	51	103	92
Hawerchuk, Dale	Winnipeg	80	47	53	100	54
Goulet, Michel	Quebec	75	49	47	96	61
Kerr, Tim	Philadelphia	75	58	37	95	57
Bourque, Ray	Boston	78	23	72	95	36

1987-88
CLARENCE CAMPBELL CONFERENCE
Norris Division

Team	GP	W	L	T	GF	GA	PTS
Detroit	80	41	28	11	322	269	93
St. Louis	80	34	38	8	278	294	76
Chicago	80	30	41	9	284	326	69
Toronto	80	21	49	10	273	345	52
Minnesota	80	19	48	13	242	349	51

Smythe Division

Team	GP	W	L	T	GF	GA	PTS
Calgary	80	48	23	9	397	305	105
*Edmonton	80	44	25	11	363	288	99
Winnipeg	80	33	36	11	292	310	77
Los Angeles	80	30	42	8	318	359	68
Vancouver	80	25	46	9	272	320	59

PRINCE OF WALES CONFERENCE
Adams Division

Team	GP	W	L	T	GF	GA	PTS
Montreal	80	45	22	13	298	238	103
Boston	80	44	30	6	300	251	94
Buffalo	80	37	32	11	283	305	85
Hartford	80	35	38	7	249	267	77
Quebec	80	32	43	5	271	306	69

Patrick Division

Team	GP	W	L	T	GF	GA	PTS
NY Islanders	80	39	31	10	308	267	88
Washington	80	38	33	9	281	249	85
Philadelphia	80	38	33	9	292	282	85
New Jersey	80	38	36	6	295	296	82
NY Rangers	80	36	34	10	300	283	82
Pittsburgh	80	36	35	9	319	316	81

Leading Scorers

Player	Club	GP	G	A	PTS	PIM
Lemieux, Mario	Pittsburgh	76	70	98	168	92
Gretzky, Wayne	Edmonton	64	40	109	149	24
Savard, Denis	Chicago	80	44	87	131	95
Hawerchuk, Dale	Winnipeg	80	44	77	121	59
Robitaille, Luc	Los Angeles	80	53	58	111	82
Stastny, Peter	Quebec	76	46	65	111	69
Messier, Mark	Edmonton	77	37	74	111	103
Carson, Jimmy	Los Angeles	80	55	52	107	45
Loob, Hakan	Calgary	80	50	56	106	47
Goulet, Michel	Quebec	80	48	58	106	56

1988-89
CLARENCE CAMPBELL CONFERENCE
Norris Division

Team	GP	W	L	T	GF	GA	PTS
Detroit	80	34	34	12	313	316	80
St. Louis	80	33	35	12	275	285	78
Minnesota	80	27	37	16	258	278	70
Chicago	80	27	41	12	297	335	66
Toronto	80	28	46	6	259	342	62

Smythe Division

Team	GP	W	L	T	GF	GA	PTS
*Calgary	80	54	17	9	354	226	117
Los Angeles	80	42	31	7	376	335	91
Edmonton	80	38	34	8	325	306	84
Vancouver	80	33	39	8	251	253	74
Winnipeg	80	26	42	12	300	355	64

PRINCE OF WALES CONFERENCE
Adams Division

Team	GP	W	L	T	GF	GA	PTS
Montreal	80	53	18	9	315	218	115
Boston	80	37	29	14	289	256	88
Buffalo	80	38	35	7	291	299	83
Hartford	80	37	38	5	299	290	79
Quebec	80	27	46	7	269	342	61

Patrick Division

Team	GP	W	L	T	GF	GA	PTS
Washington	80	41	29	10	305	259	92
Pittsburgh	80	40	33	7	347	349	87
NY Rangers	80	37	35	8	310	307	82
Philadelphia	80	36	36	8	307	285	80
New Jersey	80	27	41	12	281	325	66
NY Islanders	80	28	47	5	265	325	61

Leading Scorers

Player	Club	GP	G	A	PTS	PIM
Lemieux, Mario	Pittsburgh	76	85	114	199	100
Gretzky, Wayne	Los Angeles	78	54	114	168	26
Yzerman, Steve	Detroit	80	65	90	155	61
Nicholls, Bernie	Los Angeles	79	70	80	150	96
Brown, Rob	Pittsburgh	68	49	66	115	118
Coffey, Paul	Pittsburgh	75	30	83	113	193
Mullen, Joe	Calgary	79	51	59	110	16
Kurri, Jari	Edmonton	76	44	58	102	69
Carson, Jimmy	Edmonton	80	49	51	100	36
Robitaille, Luc	Los Angeles	78	46	52	98	65

Minnesota right winger Dino Ciccarelli recorded his second 50-goal and 100-point season in 1986-87.

1989-90
CLARENCE CAMPBELL CONFERENCE
Norris Division

Team	GP	W	L	T	GF	GA	PTS
Chicago	80	41	33	6	316	294	88
St. Louis	80	37	34	9	295	279	83
Toronto	80	38	38	4	337	358	80
Minnesota	80	36	40	4	284	291	76
Detroit	80	28	38	14	288	323	70

Smythe Division

Team	GP	W	L	T	GF	GA	PTS
Calgary	80	42	23	15	348	265	99
*Edmonton	80	38	28	14	315	283	90
Winnipeg	80	37	32	11	298	290	85
Los Angeles	80	34	39	7	338	337	75
Vancouver	80	25	41	14	245	306	64

PRINCE OF WALES CONFERENCE
Adams Division

Team	GP	W	L	T	GF	GA	PTS
Boston	80	46	25	9	289	232	101
Buffalo	80	45	27	8	286	248	98
Montreal	80	41	28	11	288	234	93
Hartford	80	38	33	9	275	268	85
Quebec	80	12	61	7	240	407	31

Patrick Division

Team	GP	W	L	T	GF	GA	PTS
NY Rangers	80	36	31	13	279	267	85
New Jersey	80	37	34	9	295	288	83
Washington	80	36	38	6	284	275	78
NY Islanders	80	31	38	11	281	288	73
Pittsburgh	80	32	40	8	318	359	72
Philadelphia	80	30	39	11	290	297	71

Leading Scorers

Player	Club	GP	G	A	PTS	PIM
Gretzky, Wayne	Los Angeles	73	40	102	142	42
Messier, Mark	Edmonton	79	45	84	129	79
Yzerman, Steve	Detroit	79	62	65	127	79
Lemieux, Mario	Pittsburgh	59	45	78	123	78
Hull, Brett	St. Louis	80	72	41	113	24
Nicholls, Bernie	L.A., NYR	79	39	73	112	86
Turgeon, Pierre	Buffalo	80	40	66	106	29
LaFontaine, Pat	NY Islanders	74	54	51	105	38
Coffey, Paul	Pittsburgh	80	29	74	103	95
Sakic, Joe	Quebec	80	39	63	102	27
Oates, Adam	St. Louis	80	23	79	102	30

1990-91
CLARENCE CAMPBELL CONFERENCE
Norris Division

Team	GP	W	L	T	GF	GA	PTS
Chicago	80	49	23	8	284	211	106
St. Louis	80	47	22	11	310	250	105
Detroit	80	34	38	8	273	298	76
Minnesota	80	27	39	14	256	266	68
Toronto	80	23	46	11	241	318	57

Smythe Division

Team	GP	W	L	T	GF	GA	PTS
Los Angeles	80	46	24	10	340	254	102
Calgary	80	46	26	8	344	263	100
Edmonton	80	37	37	6	272	272	80
Vancouver	80	28	43	9	243	315	65
Winnipeg	80	26	43	11	260	288	63

PRINCE OF WALES CONFERENCE
Adams Division

Team	GP	W	L	T	GF	GA	PTS
Boston	80	44	24	12	299	264	100
Montreal	80	39	30	11	273	249	89
Buffalo	80	31	30	19	292	278	81
Hartford	80	31	38	11	238	276	73
Quebec	80	16	50	14	236	354	46

Patrick Division

Team	GP	W	L	T	GF	GA	PTS
*Pittsburgh	80	41	33	6	342	305	88
NY Rangers	80	36	31	13	297	265	85
Washington	80	37	36	7	258	258	81
New Jersey	80	32	33	15	272	264	79
Philadelphia	80	33	37	10	252	267	76
NY Islanders	80	25	45	10	223	290	60

Leading Scorers

Player	Club	GP	G	A	PTS	PIM
Gretzky, Wayne	Los Angeles	78	41	122	163	16
Hull, Brett	St. Louis	78	86	45	131	22
Oates, Adam	St. Louis	61	25	90	115	29
Recchi, Mark	Pittsburgh	78	40	73	113	48
Cullen, John	Pit., Hfd.	78	39	71	110	101
Sakic, Joe	Quebec	80	48	61	109	24
Yzerman, Steve	Detroit	80	51	57	108	34
Fleury, Theo	Calgary	79	51	53	104	136
MacInnis, Al	Calgary	78	28	75	103	90
Larmer, Steve	Chicago	80	44	57	101	79

1991-92
CLARENCE CAMPBELL CONFERENCE
Norris Division

Team	GP	W	L	T	GF	GA	PTS
Detroit	80	43	25	12	320	256	98
Chicago	80	36	29	15	257	236	87
St. Louis	80	36	33	11	279	266	83
Minnesota	80	32	42	6	246	278	70
Toronto	80	30	43	7	234	294	67

Smythe Division

Team	GP	W	L	T	GF	GA	PTS
Vancouver	80	42	26	12	285	250	96
Los Angeles	80	35	31	14	287	296	84
Edmonton	80	36	34	10	295	297	82
Winnipeg	80	33	32	15	251	244	81
Calgary	80	31	37	12	296	305	74
San Jose	80	17	58	5	219	359	39

PRINCE OF WALES CONFERENCE
Adams Division

Team	GP	W	L	T	GF	GA	PTS
Montreal	80	41	28	11	267	207	93
Boston	80	36	32	12	270	275	84
Buffalo	80	31	37	12	289	299	74
Hartford	80	26	41	13	247	283	65
Quebec	80	20	48	12	255	318	52

Patrick Division

Team	GP	W	L	T	GF	GA	PTS
NY Rangers	80	50	25	5	321	246	105
Washington	80	45	27	8	330	275	98
*Pittsburgh	80	39	32	9	343	308	87
New Jersey	80	38	31	11	289	259	87
NY Islanders	80	34	35	11	291	299	79
Philadelphia	80	32	37	11	252	273	75

Leading Scorers

Player	Club	GP	G	A	PTS	PIM
Lemieux, Mario	Pittsburgh	64	44	87	131	94
Stevens, Kevin	Pittsburgh	80	54	69	123	254
Gretzky, Wayne	Los Angeles	74	31	90	121	34
Hull, Brett	St. Louis	73	70	39	109	48
Robitaille, Luc	Los Angeles	80	44	63	107	95
Messier, Mark	NY Rangers	79	35	72	107	76
Roenick, Jeremy	Chicago	80	53	50	103	23
Yzerman, Steve	Detroit	79	45	58	103	64
Leetch, Brian	NY Rangers	80	22	80	102	26
Oates, Adam	St. L., Bos.	80	20	79	99	22

1992-93
CLARENCE CAMPBELL CONFERENCE
Norris Division

Team	GP	W	L	T	GF	GA	PTS
Chicago	84	47	25	12	279	230	106
Detroit	84	47	28	9	369	280	103
Toronto	84	44	29	11	288	241	99
St. Louis	84	37	36	11	282	278	85
Minnesota	84	36	38	10	272	293	82
Tampa Bay	84	23	54	7	245	332	53

Smythe Division

Team	GP	W	L	T	GF	GA	PTS
Vancouver	84	46	29	9	346	278	101
Calgary	84	43	30	11	322	282	97
Los Angeles	84	39	35	10	338	340	88
Winnipeg	84	40	37	7	322	320	87
Edmonton	84	26	50	8	242	337	60
San Jose	84	11	71	2	218	414	24

PRINCE OF WALES CONFERENCE
Adams Division

Team	GP	W	L	T	GF	GA	PTS
Boston	84	51	26	7	332	268	109
Quebec	84	47	27	10	351	300	104
*Montreal	84	48	30	6	326	280	102
Buffalo	84	38	36	10	335	297	86
Hartford	84	26	52	6	284	369	58
Ottawa	84	10	70	4	202	395	24

Patrick Division

Team	GP	W	L	T	GF	GA	PTS
Pittsburgh	84	56	21	7	367	268	119
Washington	84	43	34	7	325	286	93
NY Islanders	84	40	37	7	335	297	87
New Jersey	84	40	37	7	308	299	87
Philadelphia	84	36	37	11	319	319	83
NY Rangers	84	34	39	11	304	308	79

Leading Scorers

Player	Club	GP	G	A	PTS	PIM
Lemieux, Mario	Pittsburgh	60	69	91	160	38
LaFontaine, Pat	Buffalo	84	53	95	148	63
Oates, Adam	Boston	84	45	97	142	32
Yzerman, Steve	Detroit	84	58	79	137	44
Selanne, Teemu	Winnipeg	84	76	56	132	45
Turgeon, Pierre	NY Islanders	83	58	74	132	26
Mogilny, Alexander	Buffalo	77	76	51	127	40
Gilmour, Doug	Toronto	83	32	95	127	100
Robitaille, Luc	Los Angeles	84	63	62	125	100
Recchi, Mark	Philadelphia	84	53	70	123	95

Note: Detailed statistics for 1992-93 are listed in the Final Statistics, 1992-93 section of the **NHL Guide & Record Book.**

Pittsburgh Penguins' goaltender Tom Barrasso led the NHL with 43 wins in 1992-93.

NHL History

1917 — National Hockey League organized November 22 in Montreal following suspension of operations by the National Hockey Association of Canada Limited (NHA). Montreal Canadiens, Montreal Wanderers, Ottawa Senators and Quebec Bulldogs attended founding meeting. Delegates decided to use NHA rules.

Toronto Arenas were later admitted as fifth team; Quebec decided not to operate during the first season. Quebec players allocated to remaining four teams.

Frank Calder elected president and secretary-treasurer.

First NHL games played December 19, with Toronto only arena with artificial ice. Clubs played 22-game split schedule.

1918 — Emergency meeting held January 3 due to destruction by fire of Montreal Arena which was home ice for both Canadiens and Wanderers.

Wanderers withdrew, reducing the NHL to three teams; Canadiens played remaining home games at 3,250-seat Jubilee rink.

Quebec franchise sold to P.J. Quinn of Toronto on October 18 on the condition that the team operate in Quebec City for 1918-19 season. Quinn did not attend the November League meeting and Quebec did not play in 1918-19.

1919-20 — NHL reactivated Quebec Bulldogs franchise. Former Quebec players returned to the club. New Mount Royal Arena became home of Canadiens. Toronto Arenas changed name to St. Patricks. Clubs played 24-game split schedule.

1920-21 — H.P. Thompson of Hamilton, Ontario made application for the purchase of an NHL franchise. Quebec franchise shifted to Hamilton with other NHL teams providing players to strengthen the club.

1921-22 — Split schedule abandoned. First and second place teams at the end of full schedule to play for championship.

1922-23 — Clubs agreed that players could not be sold or traded to clubs in any other league without first being offered to all other clubs in the NHL. In March, Foster Hewitt broadcast radio's first hockey game.

1923-24 — Ottawa's new 10,000-seat arena opened. First U.S. franchise granted to Boston for following season.

Dr. Cecil Hart Trophy donated to NHL to be awarded to the player judged most useful to his team.

1924-25 — Canadian Arena Company of Montreal granted a franchise to operate Montreal Maroons. NHL now six team league with two clubs in Montreal. Inaugural game in new Montreal Forum played November 29, 1924 as Canadiens defeated Toronto 7-1. Forum was home rink for the Maroons, but no ice was available in the Canadiens arena November 29, resulting in shift to Forum.

Hamilton finished first in the standings, receiving a bye into the finals. But Hamilton players, demanding $200 each for additional games in the playoffs, went on strike. The NHL suspended all players, fining them $200 each. Stanley Cup finalist to be the winner of NHL semi-final between Toronto and Canadiens.

Prince of Wales and Lady Byng trophies donated to NHL.

Clubs played 30-game schedule.

1925-26 — Hamilton club dropped from NHL. Players signed by new New York Americans franchise. Franchise granted to Pittsburgh.

Clubs played 36-game schedule.

1926-27 — New York Rangers granted franchise May 15, 1926. Chicago Black Hawks and Detroit Cougars granted franchises September 25, 1926. NHL now ten-team league with an American and a Canadian Division.

Stanley Cup came under the control of NHL. In previous seasons, winners of the now-defunct Western or Pacific Coast leagues would play NHL champion in Cup finals.

Toronto franchise sold to a new company controlled by Hugh Aird and Conn Smythe. Name changed from St. Patricks to Maple Leafs.

Clubs played 44-game schedule.

The Montreal Canadiens donated the Vezina Trophy to be awarded to the team allowing the fewest goals-against in regular season play. The winning team would, in turn, present the trophy to the goaltender playing in the greatest number of games during the season.

1929-30 — Detroit franchise changed name from Cougars to Falcons.

1930-31 — Pittsburgh transferred to Philadelphia for one season. Pirates changed name to Philadelphia Quakers. Trading deadline for teams set at February 15 of each year. NHL approved operation of farm teams by Rangers, Americans, Falcons and Bruins. Four-sided electric arena clock first demonstrated.

1931-32 — Philadelphia dropped out. Ottawa withdrew for one season. New Maple Leaf Gardens completed.

Clubs played 48-game schedule.

1932-33 — Detroit franchise changed name from Falcons to Red Wings. Franchise application received from St. Louis but refused because of additional travel costs. Ottawa team resumed play.

1933-34 — First All-Star Game played as a benefit for injured player Ace Bailey. Leafs defeated All-Stars 7-3 in Toronto.

1934-35 — Ottawa franchise transferred to St. Louis. Team called St. Louis Eagles and consisted largely of Ottawa's players.

1935-36 — Ottawa-St. Louis franchise terminated. Montreal Canadiens finished season with very poor record. To strengthen the club, NHL gave Canadiens first call on the services of all French-Canadian players for three seasons.

1937-38 — Second benefit all-star game staged November 2 in Montreal in aid of the family of the late Canadiens star Howie Morenz.

Montreal Maroons withdrew from the NHL on June 22, 1938, leaving seven clubs in the League.

1938-39 — Expenses for each club regulated at $5 per man per day for meals and $2.50 per man per day for accommodation.

1939-40 — Benefit All-Star Game played October 29, 1939 in Montreal for the children of the late Albert (Babe) Siebert.

1940-41 — Ross-Tyer puck adopted as the official puck of the NHL. Early in the season it was apparent that this puck was too soft. The Spalding puck was adopted in its place.

After the playoffs, Arthur Ross, NHL governor from Boston, donated a perpetual trophy to be awarded annually to the player voted outstanding in the league.

1941-42 — New York Americans changed name to Brooklyn Americans.

1942-43 — Brooklyn Americans withdrew from NHL, leaving six teams: Boston, Chicago, Detroit, Montreal, New York and Toronto. Playoff format saw first-place team play third-place team and second play fourth.

Clubs played 50-game schedule.

Frank Calder, president of the NHL since its inception, died in Montreal. Meryn "Red" Dutton, former manager of the New York Americans, became president. The NHL commissioned the Calder Memorial Trophy to be awarded to the League's outstanding rookie each year.

1945-46 — Philadelphia, Los Angeles and San Francisco applied for NHL franchises.

The Philadelphia Arena Company of the American Hockey League applied for an injunction to prevent the possible operation of an NHL franchise in that city.

1946-47 — Mervyn Dutton retired as president of the NHL prior to the start of the season. He was succeeded by Clarence S. Campbell.

Individual trophy winners and all-star team members to receive $1,000 awards.

Playoff guarantees for players introduced.

Clubs played 60-game schedule.

1947-48 — The first annual All-Star Game for the benefit of the players' pension fund was played when the All-Stars defeated the Stanley Cup Champion Toronto Maple Leafs 4-3 in Toronto on October 13, 1947.

Ross Trophy, awarded to the NHL's outstanding player since 1941, to be awarded annually to the League's scoring leader.

Philadelphia and Los Angeles franchise applications refused.

National Hockey League Pension Society formed.

1949-50 — Clubs played 70-game schedule.

First intra-league draft held April 30, 1950. Clubs allowed to protect 30 players. Remaining players available for $25,000 each.

1951-52 — Referees included in the League's pension plan.

1952-53 — In May of 1952, City of Cleveland applied for NHL franchise. Application denied. In March of 1953, the Cleveland Barons of the AHL challenged the NHL champions for the Stanley Cup. The NHL governors did not accept this challenge.

1953-54 — The James Norris Memorial Trophy presented to the NHL for annual presentation to the League's best defenseman.

Intra-league draft rules amended to allow teams to protect 18 skaters and two goaltenders, claiming price reduced to $15,000.

1954-55 — Each arena to operate an "out-of-town" scoreboard. Referees and linesmen to wear shirts of black and white vertical stripes. Teams agree to wear white uniforms at home and colored uniforms on the road.

1956-57 — Standardized signals for referees and linesmen introduced.

1960-61 — Canadian National Exhibition, City of Toronto and NHL reach agreement for the construction of a Hockey Hall of Fame on the CNE grounds. Hall opens on August 26, 1961.

Gordie Howe led the league in goals, assists and points in 1952-53, a feat that went unmatched until Wayne Gretzky's record-breaking season in 1981-82.

1963-64 — Player development league established with clubs operated by NHL franchises located in Minneapolis, St. Paul, Indianapolis, Omaha and, beginning in 1964-65, Tulsa. First universal amateur draft took place. All players of qualifying age (17) unaffected by sponsorship of junior teams available to be drafted.

1964-65 — Conn Smythe Trophy presented to the NHL to be awarded annually to the outstanding player in the Stanley Cup playoffs.

Minimum age of players subject to amateur draft changed to 18.

1965-66 — NHL announced expansion plans for a second six-team division to begin play in 1967-68.

1966-67 — Fourteen applications for NHL franchises received.

Lester Patrick Trophy presented to the NHL to be awarded annually for outstanding service to hockey in the United States.

NHL sponsorship of junior teams ceased, making all players of qualifying age not already on NHL-sponsored lists eligible for the amateur draft.

1967-68 — Six new teams added: California Seals, Los Angeles Kings, Minnesota North Stars, Philadelphia Flyers, Pittsburgh Penguins, St. Louis Blues. New teams to play in West Division. Remaining six teams to play in East Division.

Minimum age of players subject to amateur draft changed to 20.

Clubs played 74-game schedule.

Clarence S. Campbell Trophy awarded to team finishing the regular season in first place in West Division.

California Seals changed name to Oakland Seals on December 8, 1967.

1968-69 — Clubs played 76-game schedule.

Amateur draft expanded to cover any amateur player of qualifying age throughout the world.

1970-71 — Two new teams added: Buffalo Sabres and Vancouver Canucks. These teams joined East Division: Chicago switched to West Division.

Clubs played 78-game schedule.

1971-72 — Playoff format amended. In each division, first to play fourth; second to play third.

1972-73 — Soviet Nationals and Canadian NHL stars play eight-game pre-season series. Canadians win 4-3-1.

Two new teams added. Atlanta Flames join West Division; New York Islanders join East Division.

1974-75 — Two new teams added: Kansas City Scouts and Washington Capitals. Teams realigned into two nine-team conferences, the Prince of Wales made up of the Norris and Adams Divisions, and the Clarence Campbell made up of the Smythe and Patrick Divisions.

Clubs played 80-game schedule.

1976-77 — California franchise transferred to Cleveland. Team named Cleveland Barons. Kansas City franchise transferred to Denver. Team named Colorado Rockies.

1977-78 — Clarence S. Campbell retires as NHL president. Succeeded by John A. Ziegler, Jr.

1978-79 — Cleveland and Minnesota franchises merge, leaving NHL with 17 teams. Merged team placed in Adams Division, playing home games in Minnesota.

Minimum age of players subject to amateur draft changed to 19.

1979-80 — Four new teams added: Edmonton Oilers, Hartford Whalers, Quebec Nordiques and Winnipeg Jets.

Minimum age of players subject to entry draft changed to 18.

1980-81 — Atlanta franchise shifted to Calgary, retaining "Flames" name.

1981-82 — Teams realigned within existing divisions. New groupings based on geographical areas. Unbalanced schedule adopted.

1982-83 — Colorado Rockies franchise shifted to East Rutherford, New Jersey. Team named New Jersey Devils. Franchise moved to Patrick Division from Smythe; Winnipeg moved to Smythe Division from Norris.

1991-92 — San Jose Sharks added, making the NHL a 22-team league. NHL celebrates 75th Anniversary Season. The 1991-92 regular season suspended due to a strike by members of the NHL Players' Association on April 1, 1992. Play resumed April 12, 1992.

1992-93 — Gil Stein named NHL president (October, 1992). Gary Bettman named first NHL Commissioner (February, 1993). Ottawa Senators and Tampa Bay Lightning added, making the NHL a 24-team league. NHL celebrates Stanley Cup Centennial. Clubs played 84-game schedule.

1993-94 — Mighty Ducks of Anaheim and Florida Panthers added, making the NHL a 26-team league. Minnesota franchise shifted to Dallas, team named Dallas Stars. Prince of Wales and Clarence Campbell Conferences renamed Eastern and Western. Adams, Patrick, Norris and Smythe Divisions renamed Northeast, Atlantic, Central and Pacific. Winnipeg moved to Central Division from Pacific; Tampa Bay moved to Atlantic Division from Central; Pittsburgh moved to Northeast Division from Atlantic.

Major Rule Changes

1910-11 — Game changed from two 30-minute periods to three 20-minute periods.

1911-12 — National Hockey Association (forerunner of the NHL) originated six-man hockey, replacing seven-man game.

1917-18 — Goalies permitted to fall to the ice to make saves. Previously a goaltender was penalized for dropping to the ice.

1918-19 — Penalty rules amended. For minor fouls, substitutes not allowed until penalized player had served three minutes. For major fouls, no substitutes for five minutes. For match fouls, no substitutes allowed for the remainder of the game.

With the addition of two lines painted on the ice twenty feet from center, three playing zones were created, producing a forty-foot neutral center ice area in which forward passing was permitted. Kicking the puck was permitted in this neutral zone.

Tabulation of assists began.

1921-22 — Goaltenders allowed to pass the puck forward up to their own blue line.

Overtime limited to twenty minutes.

Minor penalties changed from three minutes to two minutes.

1923-24 — Match foul defined as actions deliberately injuring or disabling an opponent. For such actions, a player was fined not less than $50 and ruled off the ice for the balance of the game. A player assessed a match penalty may be replaced by a substitute at the end of 20 minutes. Match penalty recipients must meet with the League president who can assess additional punishment.

1925-26 — Delayed penalty rules introduced. Each team must have a minimum of four players on the ice at all times.

Two rules were amended to encourage offense: No more than two defensemen permitted to remain inside a team's own blue line when the puck has left the defensive zone. A faceoff to be called for ragging the puck unless short-handed.

Team captains only players allowed to talk to referees.

Goaltender's leg pads limited to 12-inch width.

Timekeeper's gong to mark end of periods rather than referee's whistle. Teams to dress a maximum of 12 players for each game from a roster of no more than 14 players.

1926-27 — Blue lines repositioned to sixty feet from each goal-line, thereby enlarging the neutral zone and standardizing distance from blueline to goal.

Uniform goal nets adopted throughout NHL with goal posts securely fastened to the ice.

1927-28 — To further encourage offense, forward passes allowed in defending and neutral zones and goaltender's pads reduced in width from 12 to 10 inches.

Game standardized at three twenty-minute periods of stop-time separated by ten-minute intermissions.

Teams to change ends after each period.

Ten minutes of sudden-death overtime to be played if the score is tied after regulation time.

Minor penalty to be assessed to any player other than a goaltender for deliberately picking up the puck while it is in play. Minor penalty to be assessed for deliberately shooting the puck out of play.

The Art Ross goal net adopted as the official net of the NHL.

Maximum length of hockey sticks limited to 53 inches measured from heel of blade to end of handle. No minimum length stipulated.

Home teams given choice of goals to defend at start of game.

1928-29 — Forward passing permitted in defensive and neutral zones and into attacking zone if pass receiver is in neutral zone when pass is made. No forward passing allowed inside attacking zone.

Minor penalty to be assessed to any player who delays the game by passing the puck back into his defensive zone.

Ten-minute overtime without sudden-death provision to be played in games tied after regulation time. Games tied after this overtime period declared a draw.

Exclusive of goaltenders, team to dress at least 8 and no more than 12 skaters.

Six-time All-Star Borje Salming was the first European-trained player to be accorded superstar status in the NHL.

Major Rule Changes — *continued*

1929-30 — Forward passing permitted inside all three zones but not permitted across either blue line.
Kicking the puck allowed, but a goal cannot be scored by kicking the puck in.
No more than three players including the goaltender may remain in their defensive zone when the puck has gone up ice. Minor penalties to be assessed for the first two violations of this rule in a game; major penalties thereafter.
Goaltenders forbidden to hold the puck. Pucks caught must be cleared immediately. For infringement of this rule, a faceoff to be taken ten feet in front of the goal with no player except the goaltender standing between the faceoff spot and the goal-line.
Highsticking penalties introduced.
Maximum number of players in uniform increased from 12 to 15.

December 21, 1929 — Forward passing rules instituted at the beginning of the 1929-30 season more than doubled number of goals scored. Partway through the season, these rules were further amended to read, "No attacking player allowed to precede the play when entering the opposing defensive zone." This is similar to modern offside rule.

1930-31 — A player without a complete stick ruled out of play and forbidden from taking part in further action until a new stick is obtained. A player who has broken his stick must obtain a replacement at his bench.
A further refinement of the offside rule stated that the puck must first be propelled into the attacking zone before any player of the attacking side can enter that zone; for infringement of this rule a faceoff to take place at the spot where the infraction took place.

1931-32 — Though there is no record of a team attempting to play with two goaltenders on the ice, a rule was instituted which stated that each team was allowed only one goaltender on the ice at one time.
Attacking players forbidden to impede the movement or obstruct the vision of opposing goaltenders.
Defending players with the exception of the goaltender forbidden from falling on the puck within 10 feet of the net.

1932-33 — Each team to have captain on the ice at all times.
If the goaltender is removed from the ice to serve a penalty, the manager of the club to appoint a substitute.
Match penalty with substitution after five minutes instituted for kicking another player.

1933-34 — Number of players permitted to stand in defensive zone restricted to three including goaltender.
Visible time clocks required in each rink.
Two referees replace one referee and one linesman.

1934-35 — Penalty shot awarded when a player is tripped and thus prevented from having a clear shot on goal, having no player to pass to other than the offending player. Shot taken from inside a 10-foot circle located 38 feet from the goal. The goaltender must not advance more than one foot from his goal-line when the shot is taken.

1937-38 — Rules introduced governing icing the puck.
Penalty shot awarded when a player other than a goaltender falls on the puck within 10 feet of the goal.

1938-39 — Penalty shot modified to allow puck carrier to skate in before shooting.
One referee and one linesman replace two referee system.
Blue line widened to 12 inches.
Maximum number of players in uniform increased from 14 to 15.

1939-40 — A substitute replacing a goaltender removed from ice to serve a penalty may use a goaltender's stick and gloves but no other goaltending equipment.

1940-41 — Flooding ice surface between periods made obligatory.

1941-42 — Penalty shots classified as minor and major. Minor shot to be taken from a line 28 feet from the goal. Major shot, awarded when a player is tripped with only the goaltender to beat, permits the player taking the penalty shot to skate right into the goalkeeper and shoot from point-blank range.
One referee and two linesmen employed to officiate games.
For playoffs, standby minor league goaltenders employed by NHL as emergency substitutes.

1942-43 — Because of wartime restrictions on train scheduling, regular-season overtime was discontinued on November 21, 1942.
Player limit reduced from 15 to 14. Minimum of 12 men in uniform abolished.

1943-44 — Red line at center ice introduced to speed up the game and reduce offside calls. This rule is considered to mark the beginning of the modern era in the NHL.
Delayed penalty rules introduced.

1945-46 — Goal indicator lights synchronized with official time clock required at all rinks.

1946-47 — System of signals by officials to indicate infractions introduced.
Linesmen from neutral cities employed for all games.

1947-48 — Goal awarded when a player with the puck has an open net to shoot at and a thrown stick prevents the shot on goal. Major penalty to any player who throws his stick in any zone other than defending zone. If a stick is thrown by a player in his defending zone but the thrown stick is not considered to have prevented a goal, a penalty shot is awarded.
All playoff games played until a winner determined, with 20-minute sudden-death overtime periods separated by 10-minute intermissions.

1949-50 — Ice surface painted white.
Clubs allowed to dress 17 players exclusive of goaltenders.
Major penalties incurred by goaltenders served by a member of the goaltender's team instead of resulting in a penalty shot.

1950-51 — Each team required to provide an emergency goaltender in attendance with full equipment at each game for use by either team in the event of illness or injury to a regular goaltender.

1951-52 — Visiting teams to wear basic white uniforms; home teams basic colored uniforms.
Goal crease enlarged from 3 × 7 feet to 4 × 8 feet.
Number of players in uniform reduced to 15 plus goaltenders.
Faceoff circles enlarged from 10-foot to 15-foot radius.

1952-53 — Teams permitted to dress 15 skaters on the road and 16 at home.

1953-54 — Number of players in uniform set at 16 plus goaltenders.

1954-55 — Number of players in uniform set at 18 plus goaltenders up to December 1 and 16 plus goaltenders thereafter.

Frank "King" Clancy was a player, coach, referee and team executive in his 64-year career in the NHL.

1956-57 — Player serving a minor penalty allowed to return to ice when a goal is scored by opposing team.

1959-60 — Players prevented from leaving their benches to enter into an altercation. Substitutions permitted providing substitutes do not enter into altercation.

1960-61 — Number of players in uniform set at 16 plus goaltenders.

1961-62 — Penalty shots to be taken by the player against whom the foul was committed. In the event of a penalty shot called in a situation where a particular player hasn't been fouled, the penalty shot to be taken by any player on the ice when the foul was committed.

1964-65 — No bodily contact on faceoffs.
In playoff games, each team to have its substitute goaltender dressed in his regular uniform except for leg pads and body protector. All previous rules governing standby goaltenders terminated.

1965-66 — Teams required to dress two goaltenders for each regular-season game.

1966-67 — Substitution allowed on coincidental major penalties.
Between-periods intermissions fixed at 15 minutes.

1967-68 — If a penalty incurred by a goaltender is a co-incident major, the penalty to be served by a player of the goaltender's team on the ice at the time the penalty was called.

1970-71 — Home teams to wear basic white uniforms; visiting teams basic colored uniforms.
Limit of curvature of hockey stick blade set at $1/2$ inch.
Minor penalty for deliberately shooting the puck out of the playing area.

1971-72 — Number of players in uniform set at 17 plus 2 goaltenders.
Third man to enter an altercation assessed an automatic game misconduct penalty.

1972-73 — Minimum width of stick blade reduced to 2 inches from $2-1/2$ inches.

1974-75 — Bench minor penalty imposed if a penalized player does not proceed directly and immediately to the penalty box.

1976-77 — Rule dealing with fighting amended to provide a major and game misconduct penalty for any player who is clearly the instigator of a fight.

1977-78 — Teams requesting a stick measurement to be assessed a minor penalty in the event that the measured stick does not violate the rules.

1981-82 — If both of a team's listed goaltenders are incapacitated, the team can dress and play any eligible goaltender who is available.

1982-83 — Number of players in uniform set at 18 plus 2 goaltenders.

1983-84 — Five-minute sudden-death overtime to be played in regular-season games that are tied at the end of regulation time.

1985-86 — Substitutions allowed in the event of co-incidental minor penalties.

1986-87 — Delayed off-side is no longer in effect once the players of the offending team have cleared the opponents' defensive zone.

1991-92 — Video replays employed to assist referees in goal/no goal situations. Size of goal crease increased. Crease changed to semi-circular configuration. Time clock to record tenths of a second in last minute of each period and overtime. Major and game misconduct penalty for checking from behind into boards. Penalties added for crease infringement and unnecessary contact with goaltender. Goal disallowed if puck enters net while a player of the attacking team is standing on the goal crease line, is in the goal crease or places his stick in the goal crease.

1992-93 — No substitutions allowed in the event of coincidental minor penalties called when both teams are at full strength. Wearing of helmets made optional for forwards and defensemen. Minor penalty for attempting to draw a penalty ("diving"). Major and game misconduct penalty for checking from behind into goal frame. Game misconduct penalty for instigating a fight. Highsticking redefined to include any use of the stick above waist-height. Previous rule stipulated shoulder-height.

1993-94 — High sticking redefined to allow goals scored with a high stick below the height of the crossbar of the goal frame.

Team Records

BEST WINNING PERCENTAGE, ONE SEASON:
.875 — **Boston Bruins,** 1929-30. 38w-5L-1T. 77PTS in 44GP
.830 — Montreal Canadiens, 1943-44. 38w-5L-7T. 83PTS in 50GP
.825 — Montreal Canadiens, 1976-77. 60w-8L-12T. 132PTS in 80GP
.806 — Montreal Canadiens, 1977-78. 59w-10L-11T. 129PTS in 80GP
.800 — Montreal Canadiens, 1944-45. 38w-8L-4T. 80PTS in 50GP

MOST POINTS, ONE SEASON:
132 — **Montreal Canadiens,** 1976-77. 60w-8L-12T. 80GP
129 — Montreal Canadien, 1977-78. 59w-10L-11T. 80GP
127 — Montreal Canadiens, 1975-76. 58w-11L-11T. 80GP

FEWEST POINTS, ONE SEASON:
8 — **Quebec Bulldogs,** 1919-20. 4w-20L-0T. 24GP
10 — Toronto Arenas, 1918-19. 5w-13L-0T. 18GP
12 — Hamilton Tigers, 1920-21. 6w-18L-0T. 24GP
— Hamilton Tigers, 1922-23. 6w-18L-0T. 24GP
— Boston Bruins, 1924-25. 6w-24L-0T. 30GP
— Philadelphia Quakers, 1930-31. 4w-36L-4T. 44GP

FEWEST POINTS, ONE SEASON (MINIMUM 70-GAME SCHEDULE):
21 — **Washington Capitals,** 1974-75. 8w-67L-5T. 80GP
24 — Ottawa Senators, 1992-93. 10w-70L-4T. 84GP
— San Jose Sharks, 1992-93. 11w-71L-2T. 84GP
30 — NY Islanders, 1972-73. 12w-60L-6T. 78GP

WORST WINNING PERCENTAGE, ONE SEASON:
.131 — **Washington Capitals,** 1974-75. 8w-67L-5T. 21PTS in 80GP
.136 — Philadelphia Quakers, 1930-31. 4w-36L-4T. 12PTS in 44GP
.143 — Ottawa Senators, 1992-93. 10w-70L-4T. 24PTS in 84GP
.143 — San Jose Sharks, 1992-93. 11w-71L-2T. 24PTS in 84GP
.148 — Pittsburgh Pirates, 1929-30. 5w-36L-3T. 13PTS in 44GP

MOST WINS, ONE SEASON:
60 — **Montreal Canadiens,** 1976-77. 80GP
59 — Montreal Canadiens, 1977-78. 80GP
58 — Montreal Canadiens, 1975-76. 80GP

FEWEST WINS, ONE SEASON:
4 — **Quebec Bulldogs,** 1919-20. 24GP
— **Philadelphia Quakers,** 1930-31. 44GP
5 — Toronto Arenas, 1918-19. 18GP
— Pittsburgh Pirates, 1929-30. 44GP

FEWEST WINS, ONE SEASON (MINIMUM 70-GAME SCHEDULE):
8 — **Washington Capitals,** 1974-75. 80GP
9 — Winnipeg Jets, 1980-81. 80GP
10 — Ottawa Senators, 1992-93. 84GP

MOST LOSSES, ONE SEASON:
71 — **San Jose Sharks,** 1992-93. 84GP
70 — Ottawa Senators, 1992-93. 84GP
67 — Washington Capitals, 1974-75. 80GP
61 — Quebec Nordiques, 1989-90. 80GP

FEWEST LOSSES, ONE SEASON:
5 — **Ottawa Senators,** 1919-20. 24GP
— **Boston Bruins,** 1929-30. 44GP
— **Montreal Canadiens,** 1943-44. 50GP

FEWEST LOSSES, ONE SEASON (MINIMUM 70-GAME SCHEDULE):
8 — **Montreal Canadiens,** 1976-77. 80GP
10 — Montreal Canadiens, 1972-73. 78GP
— Montreal Canadiens, 1977-78. 80GP
11 — Montreal Canadiens, 1975-76. 80GP

MOST TIES, ONE SEASON:
24 — **Philadelphia Flyers,** 1969-70. 76GP
23 — Montreal Canadiens, 1962-63. 70GP
— Chicago Blackhawks, 1973-74. 78GP

FEWEST TIES, ONE SEASON (Since 1926-27):
1 — **Boston Bruins,** 1929-30. 44GP
2 — NY Americans, 1926-27. 44GP
— Montreal Canadiens, 1926-27. 44GP
— Boston Bruins, 1938-39. 48GP
— NY Rangers, 1941-42. 48GP
— San Jose Sharks, 1992-93. 84GP

FEWEST TIES, ONE SEASON (MINIMUM 70-GAME SCHEDULE):
2 — **San Jose Sharks,** 1992-93. 84GP
3 — New Jersey Devils, 1985-86. 80GP
— Calgary Flames, 1986-87. 80GP

MOST HOME WINS, ONE SEASON:
36 — **Philadelphia Flyers,** 1975-76. 40GP
33 — Boston Bruins, 1970-71. 39GP
— Boston Bruins, 1973-74. 39GP
— Montreal Canadiens, 1976-77. 40GP
— Philadelphia Flyers, 1976-77. 40GP
— NY Islanders, 1981-82. 40GP
— Philadelphia Flyers,1985-86. 40GP

MOST ROAD WINS, ONE SEASON:
27 — **Montreal Canadiens,** 1976-77. 40GP
— **Montreal Canadiens,** 1977-78. 40GP
26 — Boston Bruins, 1971-72. 39GP
— Montreal Canadiens, 1975-76. 40GP
— Edmonton Oilers, 1983-84. 40GP

MOST HOME LOSSES, ONE SEASON:
*32 — **San Jose Sharks,** 1992-93. 41GP
29 — Pittsburgh Penguins, 1983-84. 40GP

MOST ROAD LOSSES, ONE SEASON:
*40 — **Ottawa Senators,** 1992-93. 41GP
39 — Washington Capitals, 1974-75. 40GP
37 — California Seals, 1973-74. 39GP
* — San Jose Sharks, 1992-93. 41GP

MOST HOME TIES, ONE SEASON:
13 — **NY Rangers,** 1954-55. 35GP
— **Philadelphia Flyers,** 1969-70. 38GP
— **California Seals,** 1971-72. 39GP
— **California Seals,** 1972-73. 39GP
— **Chicago Blackhawks,** 1973-74. 39GP

MOST ROAD TIES, ONE SEASON:
15 — **Philadelphia Flyers,** 1976-77. 40GP
14 — Montreal Canadiens, 1952-53. 35GP
— Montreal Canadiens, 1974-75. 40GP
— Philadelphia Flyers, 1975-76. 40GP

FEWEST HOME WINS, ONE SEASON:
2 — **Chicago Blackhawks,** 1927-28. 22GP
3 — Boston Bruins, 1924-25. 15GP
— Chicago Blackhawks, 1928-29. 22GP
— Philadelphia Quakers, 1930-31. 22GP

FEWEST HOME WINS, ONE SEASON (MINIMUM 70-GAME SCHEDULE):
6 — **Chicago Blackhawks,** 1954-55. 35GP
— **Washington Capitals,** 1975-76. 40GP
7 — Boston Bruins, 1962-63. 35GP
— Washington Capitals, 1974-75. 40GP
— Winnipeg Jets, 1980-81. 40GP
— Pittsburgh Penguins, 1983-84. 40GP

FEWEST ROAD WINS, ONE SEASON:
0 — **Toronto Arenas,** 1918-19. 9GP
— **Quebec Bulldogs,** 1919-20. 12GP
— **Pittsburgh Pirates,** 1929-30. 22GP
1 — Hamilton Tigers, 1921-22. 12GP
— Toronto St. Patricks, 1925-26. 18GP
— Philadelphia Quakers, 1930-31. 22GP
— NY Americans, 1940-41. 24GP
— Washington Capitals, 1974-75. 40GP
* — Ottawa Senators, 1992-93. 41GP

FEWEST ROAD WINS, ONE SEASON (MINIMUM 70-GAME SCHEDULE):
1 — **Washington Capitals,** 1974-75. 40GP
* — **Ottawa Senators,** 1992-93. 41GP
2 — Boston Bruins, 1960-61. 35GP
— Los Angeles Kings, 1969-70. 38GP
— NY Islanders, 1972-73. 39GP
— California Seals, 1973-74. 39GP
— Colorado Rockies, 1977-78. 40GP
— Winnipeg Jets, 1980-81. 40GP
— Quebec Nordiques, 1991-92. 40GP

FEWEST HOME LOSSES, ONE SEASON:
0 — **Ottawa Senators,** 1922-23. 12GP
— **Montreal Canadiens,** 1943-44. 25GP
1 — Toronto Arenas, 1917-18. 11GP
— Ottawa Senators, 19. 9GP
— Ottawa Senators, 1919-20. 12GP
— Toronto St. Patricks, 1922-23. 12GP
— Boston Bruins, 1929-30 and 1930-31. 22GP
— Montreal Canadiens, 1976-77. 40GP

FEWEST HOME LOSSES, ONE SEASON (MINIMUM 70-GAME SCHEDULE):
1 — **Montreal Canadiens,** 1976-77. 40GP
2 — Montreal Canadiens, 1961-62. 35GP
— NY Rangers, 1970-71. 39GP
— Philadelphia Flyers, 1975-76. 40GP

* Does not include neutral site games

FEWEST ROAD LOSSES, ONE SEASON:
  3 —**Montreal Canadiens**, 1928-29. 22GP
  4 —Ottawa Senators, 1919-20. 12GP
    —Montreal Canadiens, 1927-28. 22GP
    —Boston Bruins, 1929-30. 20GP
    —Boston Bruins, 1940-41. 24GP

FEWEST ROAD LOSSES, ONE SEASON (MINIMUM 70-GAME SCHEDULE):
  6 —**Montreal Canadiens**, 1972-73. 39GP
    —**Montreal Canadiens**, 1974-75. 40GP
    —**Montreal Canadiens**, 1977-78. 40GP
  7 —Detroit Red Wings, 1951-52. 35GP
    —Montreal Canadiens, 1976-77. 40GP
    —Philadelphia Flyers, 1979-80. 40GP

LONGEST WINNING STREAK:
  17 Games —**Pittsburgh Penguins,** Mar. 9, 1993 - Apr. 10, 1993.
  15 Games —NY Islanders, Jan. 21, 1982 - Feb. 20, 1982.
  14 Games —Boston Bruins, Dec. 3, 1929 - Jan. 9, 1930.
  13 Games —Boston Bruins, Feb. 23, 1971 - Mar. 20, 1971.
    —Philadelphia Flyers, Oct. 19, 1985 - Nov. 17, 1985.

LONGEST WINNING STREAK FROM START OF SEASON:
  8 Games —**Toronto Maple Leafs,** 1934-35.
    —**Buffalo Sabres,** 1975-76.
  7 Games —Edmonton Oilers, 1983-84.
    —Quebec Nordiques, 1985-86.
    —Pittsburgh Penguins, 1986-87.

LONGEST WINNING STREAK, INCLUDING PLAYOFFS:
  15 Games —**Detroit Red Wings,** Feb. 27, 1955 - Apr. 5, 1955. Nine regular-season games, six playoff games.

LONGEST HOME WINNING STREAK FROM START OF SEASON:
  11 Games —**Chicago Blackhawks,** 1963-64
  10 Games —Ottawa Senators, 1925-26
  9 Games —Montreal Canadiens, 1953-54
    —Chicago Blackhawks, 1971-72
  8 Games —Boston Bruins, 1983-84
    —Philadelphia Flyers, 1986-87
    —New Jersey Devils, 1987-88

LONGEST HOME WINNING STREAK (ONE SEASON):
  20 Games —**Boston Bruins,** Dec. 3, 1929 - Mar. 18, 1930.
    —**Philadelphia Flyers,** Jan. 4, 1976 - Apr. 3, 1976.

LONGEST HOME WINNING STREAK, INCLUDING PLAYOFFS:
  24 Games —**Philadelphia Flyers,** Jan. 4, 1976 - Apr. 25, 1976. 20 regular-season games, 4 playoff games.

LONGEST ROAD WINNING STREAK (ONE SEASON):
  10 Games —**Buffalo Sabres,** Dec. 10, 1983 - Jan. 23, 1984.
  8 Games —Boston Bruins, Feb. 17, 1972 - Mar. 8, 1972.
    —Los Angeles Kings, Dec. 18, 1974 - Jan. 16, 1975.
    —Montreal Canadiens, Dec. 18, 1977 - Jan. 18. 1978.
    —NY Islanders, Feb. 27, 1981 - Mar. 29, 1981.
    —Montreal Canadiens, Jan. 21, 1982 - Feb. 21, 1982.
    —Philadelphia Flyers, Dec. 22, 1982 - Jan. 16, 1983.
    —Winnipeg Jets, Feb. 25, 1985 - Apr. 6, 1985.
    —Edmonton Oilers, Dec. 9, 1986 - Jan. 17, 1987.
    —Boston Bruins, Mar. 15, 1993 - Apr. 14, 1993.

LONGEST UNDEFEATED STREAK (ONE SEASON):
  35 Games —**Philadelphia Flyers,** Oct. 14, 1979 - Jan. 6, 1980. 25w-10T.
  28 Games —Montreal Canadiens, Dec. 18, 1977 - Feb. 23, 1978. 23w-5T.
  23 Games —Boston Bruins, Dec. 22, 1940 - Feb. 23, 1941. 15w-8T.
    —Philadelphia Flyers, Jan. 29, 1976 - Mar. 18, 1976. 17w-6T.

LONGEST UNDEFEATED STREAK FROM START OF SEASON:
  15 Games —**Edmonton Oilers,** 1984-85. 12w-3T.
  14 Games —Montreal Canadiens, 1943-44. 11w-3T.
  13 Games —Montreal Canadiens, 1972-73. 9w-4T

LONGEST HOME UNDEFEATED STREAK (ONE SEASON):
  34 Games —**Montreal Canadiens,** Nov. 1, 1976 - Apr. 2, 1977. 28w-6T.
  27 Games —Boston Bruins, Nov. 22, 1970 - Mar. 20, 1971. 26w-1T.

LONGEST HOME UNDEFEATED STREAK, INCLUDING PLAYOFFS:
  38 Games —**Montreal Canadiens,** Nov. 1, 1976 - Apr. 26, 1977. 28w-6T in regular season and 4w in playoffs.

LONGEST ROAD UNDEFEATED STREAK (ONE SEASON):
  23 Games —**Montreal Canadiens,** Nov. 27, 1974 - Mar. 12, 1975. 14w-9T.
  17 Games —Montreal Canadiens, Dec. 18, 1977 - Mar. 1, 1978. 14w-3T.
  16 Games —Philadelphia Flyers, Oct. 20, 1979 - Jan. 6, 1980. 11w-5T.

LONGEST LOSING STREAK (ONE SEASON):
  17 Games —**Washington Capitals,** Feb. 18, 1975 - Mar. 26, 1975.
    —**San Jose Sharks,** Jan. 4, 1993 - Feb. 12, 1993.
  15 Games —Philadelphia Quakers, Nov. 29, 1930 - Jan. 8, 1931.

LONGEST LOSING STREAK FROM START OF SEASON:
  11 Games —**NY Rangers,** 1943-44.
  7 Games —Montreal Canadiens, 1938-39.
    —Chicago Blackhawks, 1947-48.
    —Washington Capitals, 1983-84.

LONGEST HOME LOSING STREAK (ONE SEASON):
  11 Games —**Boston Bruins,** Dec. 8, 1924 - Feb. 17, 1925.
    —**Washington Capitals,** Feb. 18, 1975 - Mar. 30, 1975.

LONGEST ROAD LOSING STREAK (ONE SEASON):
  *38 Games —**Ottawa Senators,** Oct. 10, 1992 - Apr. 3, 1993.
  37 Games —Washington Capitals, Oct. 9, 1974 - Mar. 26, 1975.
  * – Does not include neutral site games.

LONGEST WINLESS STREAK (ONE SEASON):
  30 Games —**Winnipeg Jets,** Oct. 19, 1980 - Dec. 20, 1980. 23L-7T.
  27 Games —Kansas City Scouts, Feb. 12, 1976 - Apr. 4, 1976. 21L-6T.
  25 Games —Washington Capitals, Nov. 29, 1975 - Jan. 21, 1976. 22L-3T.

LONGEST WINLESS STREAK FROM START OF SEASON:
  15 Games —**NY Rangers,** 1943-44. 14L-1T.
  12 Games —Pittsburgh Pirates, 1927-28. 9L-3T.
  11 Games —Minnesota North Stars, 1973-74. 5L-6T.

LONGEST HOME WINLESS STREAK (ONE SEASON):
  15 Games —**Chicago Blackhawks,** Dec. 16, 1928 - Feb. 28, 1929. 11L-4T.
    —**Montreal Canadiens,** Dec. 16, 1939 - Mar. 7, 1940. 12L-3T.

LONGEST ROAD WINLESS STREAK (ONE SEASON):
  *38 Games —**Ottawa Senators,** Oct. 10, 1992 - Apr. 3, 1993. 38L-0T.
  37 Games —Washington Capitals, Oct. 9, 1974 - Mar. 26, 1975. 37L-0T.
  * – Does not include neutral site games.

LONGEST NON-SHUTOUT STREAK:
  264 Games —**Calgary Flames,** Nov. 12, 1981 - Jan. 9, 1985.
  262 Games —Los Angeles Kings, Mar. 15, 1986 - Oct. 25, 1989.
  244 Games —Washington Capitals, Oct. 31, 1989 - Nov. 11, 1993.
  230 Games —Quebec Nordiques, Feb. 10, 1980 - Jan. 13, 1983.
  229 Games —Edmonton Oilers, Mar. 15, 1981 - Feb. 11, 1984.

LONGEST NON-SHUTOUT STREAK INCLUDING PLAYOFFS:
  264 Games —**Los Angeles Kings,** Mar. 15 1986 - Apr. 6, 1989. (5 playoff games in 1987; 5 in 1988; 2 in 1989)
  262 Games —Chicago Blackhawks, Mar. 14, 1970 - Feb. 21, 1973. (8 playoff games in 1970; 18 in 1971; 8 in 1972).
  251 Games —Quebec Nordiques, Feb. 10, 1980 - Jan. 13, 1983. (5 playoff games in 1981; 16 in 1982).
  245 Games —Pittsburgh Penguins, Jan. 7, 1989 - Oct. 26, 1991. (11 playoff games in 1989; 23 in 1991).

MOST CONSECUTIVE GAMES SHUT OUT:
  8 —**Chicago Blackhawks,** 1928-29.

MOST SHUTOUTS, ONE SEASON:
  22 —**Montreal Canadiens,** 1928-29. All by George Hainsworth. 44GP
  16 —NY Americans, 1928-29. Roy Worters had 13; Flat Walsh 3. 44GP
  15 —Ottawa Senators, 1925-26. All by Alex Connell. 36GP
    —Ottawa Senators, 1927-28. All by Alex Connell. 44GP
    —Boston Bruins, 1927-28. All by Hal Winkler. 44GP
    —Chicago Blackhawks, 1969-70. All by Tony Esposito. 76GP

MOST GOALS, ONE SEASON:
  446 —**Edmonton Oilers,** 1983-84. 80GP
  426 —Edmonton Oilers, 1985-86. 80GP
  424 —Edmonton Oilers, 1982-83. 80GP
  417 —Edmonton Oilers, 1981-82. 80GP
  401 —Edmonton Oilers, 1984-85. 80GP

HIGHEST GOALS-PER-GAME AVERAGE, ONE SEASON:
  5.58 —**Edmonton Oilers,** 1983-84. 446G in 80GP.
  5.38 —Montreal Canadiens, 1919-20. 129G in 24GP.
  5.33 —Edmonton Oilers, 1985-86. 426G in 80GP.
  5.30 —Edmonton Oilers, 1982-83. 424G in 80GP.
  5.23 —Montreal Canadiens, 1917-18. 115G in 22GP.

FEWEST GOALS, ONE SEASON:
  33 —**Chicago Blackhawks,** 1928-29. 44GP
  45 —Montreal Maroons, 1924-25. 30GP
  46 —Pittsburgh Pirates, 1928-29. 44GP

FEWEST GOALS, ONE SEASON (MINIMUM 70-GAME SCHEDULE):
  133 —**Chicago Blackhawks,** 1953-54. 70GP
  147 —Toronto Maple Leafs, 1954-55. 70GP
    —Boston Bruins, 1955-56. 70GP
  150 —NY Rangers, 1954-55. 70GP

LOWEST GOALS-PER-GAME AVERAGE, ONE SEASON:
  .75 —**Chicago Blackhawks,** 1928-29, 33G in 44GP.
  1.05 —Pittsburgh Pirates, 1928-29. 46G in 44GP.
  1.20 —NY Americans, 1928-29. 53G in 44GP.

MOST GOALS AGAINST, ONE SEASON:
  446 —**Washington Capitals,** 1974-75. 80GP
  415 —Detroit Red Wings, 1985-86. 80GP
  414 —San Jose Sharks, 1992-93. 84GP
  407 —Quebec Nordiques, 1989-90. 80GP
  403 —Hartford Whalers, 1982-83. 80GP

HIGHEST GOALS-AGAINST-PER-GAME AVERAGE, ONE SEASON:
  7.38 —**Quebec Bulldogs,** 1919-20, 177GA vs. in 24GP.
  6.20 —NY Rangers, 1943-44, 310GA vs. in 50GP.
  5.58 —Washington Capitals, 1974-75, 446GA vs. in 80GP.

FEWEST GOALS AGAINST, ONE SEASON:
42 — **Ottawa Senators,** 1925-26. 36GP
43 — Montreal Canadiens, 1928-29. 44GP
48 — Montreal Canadiens, 1923-24. 24GP
— Montreal Canadiens, 1927-28. 44GP

FEWEST GOALS AGAINST, ONE SEASON (MINIMUM 70-GAME SCHEDULE):
131 — **Toronto Maple Leafs,** 1953-54. 70GP
— **Montreal Canadiens,** 1955-56. 70GP
132 — Detroit Red Wings, 1953-54. 70GP
133 — Detroit Red Wings, 1951-52. 70GP
— Detroit Red Wings, 1952-53. 70GP

LOWEST GOALS-AGAINST-PER-GAME AVERAGE, ONE SEASON:
.98 — **Montreal Canadiens,** 1928-29. 43GA vs. in 44GP.
1.09 — Montreal Canadiens, 1927-28. 48GA vs. in 44GP.
1.17 — Ottawa Senators, 1925-26. 42GA vs. in 36GP.

MOST POWER-PLAY GOALS, ONE SEASON:
119 — **Pittsburgh Penguins,** 1988-89. 80GP
113 — Detroit Red Wings, 1992-93. 84GP
111 — NY Rangers, 1987-88. 80GP
110 — Pittsburgh Penguins, 1987-88. 80GP
— Winnipeg Jets, 1987-88, 80GP

MOST POWER-PLAY GOALS AGAINST, ONE SEASON:
122 — **Chicago Blackhawks,** 1988-89. 80GP
120 — Pittsburgh Penguins, 1987-88. 80GP
115 — New Jersey Devils, 1988-89. 80GP
— Ottawa Senators, 1992-93. 84GP
114 — Los Angeles Kings, 1992-93. 84GP
113 — San Jose Sharks, 1992-93. 80GP

MOST SHORTHAND GOALS, ONE SEASON:
36 — **Edmonton Oilers,** 1983-84. 80GP
28 — Edmonton Oilers, 1986-87. 80GP
27 — Edmonton Oilers, 1985-86. 80GP
— Edmonton Oilers, 1988-89. 80GP

MOST SHORTHAND GOALS AGAINST, ONE SEASON:
22 — **Pittsburgh Penguins,** 1984-85. 80GP
— **Minnesota North Stars,** 1991-92. 80GP
21 — Calgary Flames, 1984-85. 80GP
— Pittsburgh Penguins, 1989-90. 80GP
20 — Minnesota North Stars, 1982-83. 80GP
— Quebec Nordiques, 1985-86. 80GP

MOST ASSISTS, ONE SEASON:
737 — **Edmonton Oilers,** 1985-86. 80GP
736 — Edmonton Oilers, 1983-84. 80GP
706 — Edmonton Oilers, 1981-82. 80GP

FEWEST ASSISTS, ONE SEASON:
45 — **NY Rangers,** 1926-27. 44GP

FEWEST ASSISTS, ONE SEASON (MINIMUM 70-GAME SCHEDULE):
206 — **Chicago Blackhawks,** 1953-54. 70GP

MOST SCORING POINTS, ONE SEASON:
1,182 — **Edmonton Oilers,** 1983-84. 80GP
1,163 — Edmonton Oilers, 1985-86. 80GP
1,123 — Edmonton Oilers, 1981-82. 80GP

MOST 50-OR-MORE-GOAL SCORERS, ONE SEASON:
3 — **Edmonton Oilers,** 1983-84. Wayne Gretzky, 87; Glenn Anderson, 54; Jari Kurri, 52 80GP.
— **Edmonton Oilers,** 1985-86. Jari Kurri, 68; Glenn Anderson, 54; Wayne Gretzky, 52. 80GP.
2 — Boston Bruins, 1970-71. Phil Esposito, 76; John Bucyk, 51. 78GP.
— Boston Bruins, 1973-74. Phil Esposito, 68; Ken Hodge, 50. 78GP
— Philadelphia Flyers, 1975-76. Reggie Leach, 61; Bill Barber, 50. 80GP
— Pittsburgh Penguins, 1975-76. Pierre Larouche, 53; Jean Pronovost, 52. 80GP
— Montreal Canadiens, 1976-77. Steve Shutt, 60; Guy Lafleur, 56. 80GP
— Los Angeles Kings, 1979-80. Charlie Simmer, 56; Marcel Dionne, 53. 80GP
— Montreal Canadiens, 1979-80. Pierre Larouche, 50; Guy Lafleur, 50. 80GP
— Los Angeles Kings, 1980-81. Marcel Dionne, 58; Charlie Simmer, 56. 80GP
— Edmonton Oilers, 1981-82. Wayne Gretzky, 92; Mark Messier, 50. 80GP
— NY Islanders, 1981-82. Mike Bossy, 64; Bryan Trottier, 50. 80GP
— Edmonton Oilers, 1984-85. Wayne Gretzky, 73; Jari Kurri, 71. 80GP
— Washington Capitals, 1984-85. Bob Carpenter, 53; Mike Gartner, 50. 80GP
— Edmonton Oilers, 1986-87. Wayne Gretzky, 62; Jari Kurri, 54. 80GP
— Calgary Flames, 1987-88. Joe Nieuwendyk, 51; Hakan Loob, 50. 80GP
— Los Angeles Kings, 1987-88. Jimmy Carson, 55; Luc Robitaille, 53. 80GP
— Los Angeles Kings, 1988-89. Bernie Nicholls, 70; Wayne Gretzky, 54. 80GP
— Calgary Flames, 1988-89. Joe Nieuwendyk, 51; Joe Mullen, 51. 80GP
— Buffalo Sabres, 1992-93. Alexander Mogilny, 76; Pat Lafontaine, 53. 84GP
— Pittsburgh Penguins, 1992-93. Mario Lemieux, 69; Kevin Stevens, 55. 84GP
— St. Louis Blues, 1992-93. Brett Hull, 54; Brendan Shanahan, 51. 84GP

MOST 40-OR-MORE-GOAL SCORERS, ONE SEASON:
4 — **Edmonton Oilers,** 1982-83. Wayne Gretzky, 71; Glenn Anderson, 48; Mark Messier, 48; Jari Kurri, 45. 80GP
— **Edmonton Oilers,** 1983-84. Wayne Gretzky, 87; Glenn Anderson, 54; Jari Kurri, 52; Paul Coffey, 40. 80GP
— **Edmonton Oilers,** 1984-85. Wayne Gretzky, 73; Jari Kurri, 71; Mike Krushelnyski, 43; Glenn Anderson, 42. 80GP
— **Edmonton Oilers,** 1985-86. Jari Kurri, 68; Glenn Anderson, 54; Wayne Gretzky, 52; Paul Coffey, 48. 80GP
— **Calgary Flames,** 1987-88. Joe Nieuwendyk, 51; Hakan Loob, 50; Mike Bullard, 48; Joe Mullen, 40. 80GP
3 — Boston Bruins, 1970-71. Phil Esposito, 76; John Bucyk, 51; Ken Hodge, 43. 78GP
— NY Rangers, 1971-72. Vic Hadfield, 50; Jean Ratelle, 46; Rod Gilbert, 43. 78GP
— Buffalo Sabres, 1975-76. Danny Gare, 50; Rick Martin, 49; Gilbert Perreault, 44. 80GP
— Montreal Canadiens, 1979-80. Guy Lafleur, 50; Pierre Larouche, 50; Steve Shutt, 47. 80GP
— Buffalo Sabres, 1979-80. Danny Gare, 56; Rick Martin, 45; Gilbert Perreault, 40. 80GP
— Los Angeles Kings, 1980-81. Marcel Dionne, 58; Charlie Simmer, 56; Dave Taylor, 47. 80GP
— Los Angeles Kings, 1984-85. Marcel Dionne, 46; Bernie Nicholls, 46; Dave Taylor, 41. 80GP
— NY Islanders, 1984-85. Mike Bossy, 58; Brent Sutter, 42; John Tonelli, 42. 80GP
— Chicago Blackhawks, 1985-86. Denis Savard, 47; Troy Murray, 45; Al Secord, 40. 80GP
— Chicago Blackhawks, 1987-88. Denis Savard, 44; Rick Vaive, 43; Steve Larmer, 41. 80GP
— Edmonton Oilers, 1987-88. Craig Simpson, 43; Jari Kurri, 43; Wayne Gretzky, 40. 80GP
— Los Angeles Kings, 1988-89. Bernie Nicholls, 70; Wayne Gretzky 54; Luc Robitaille, 46. 80GP
— Los Angeles Kings, 1990-91. Luc Robitaille, 45; Tomas Sandstrom, 45; Wayne Gretzky 41. 80GP
— Pittsburgh Penguins, 1991-92. Kevin Stevens, 54; Mario Lemieux, 44; Joe Mullen, 42. 80GP
— Pittsburgh Penguins, 1992-93. Mario Lemieux, 69; Kevin Stevens, 55; Rick Tocchet, 48. 84GP

The Toronto Maple Leafs of 1953-54 and the Montreal Canadiens of 1955-56 share the NHL record for fewest goals-against in a season of 70-or-more games, allowing just 131. The two clubs met in the Stanley Cup Finals in 1959 and 1960.

MOST 30-OR-MORE GOAL SCORERS, ONE SEASON:

6 —**Buffalo Sabres,** 1974-75. Rick Martin, 52; Rene Robert, 40; Gilbert Perreault, 39; Don Luce, 33; Rick Dudley, Danny Gare, 31 each. 80GP
—**NY Islanders,** 1977-78. Mike Bossy, 53; Bryan Trottier, 46; Clark Gillies, 35; Denis Potvin, Bob Nystrom, Bob Bourne, 30 each. 80GP
—**Winnipeg Jets,** 1984-85. Dale Hawerchuk, 53; Paul MacLean, 41; Laurie Boschmn, 32; Brian Mullen, 32; Doug Smail, 31; Thomas Steen, 30. 80GP
5 —Chicago Blackhawks, 1968-69. 76GP
—Boston Bruins, 1970-71. 78GP
—Montreal Canadiens, 1971-72. 78GP
—Philadelphia Flyers, 1972-73. 78GP
—Boston Bruins, 1973-74. 78GP
—Montreal Canadiens, 1974-75. 80GP
—Montreal Canadiens, 1975-76. 80GP
—Pittsburgh Penguins, 1975-76. 80GP
—NY Islanders, 1978-79. 80GP
—Detroit Red Wings, 1979-80. 80GP
—Philadelphia Flyers, 1979-80. 80GP
—NY Islanders, 1980-81. 80GP
—St. Louis Blues, 1980-81. 80GP
—Chicago Blackhawks, 1981-82. 80GP
—Edmonton Oilers, 1981-82. 80GP
—Montreal Canadiens, 1981-82. 80GP
—Quebec Nordiques, 1981-82. 80GP
—Washington Capitals, 1981-82. 80GP
—Edmonton Oilers, 1982-83. 80GP
—Edmonton Oilers, 1983-84. 80GP
—Edmonton Oilers, 1984-85. 80GP
—Los Angeles Kings, 1984-85. 80GP
—Edmonton Oilers, 1985-86. 80GP
—Edmonton Oilers, 1986-87. 80GP
—Edmonton Oilers, 1987-88. 80GP
—Edmonton Oilers, 1988-89. 80GP
—Detroit Red Wings, 1991-92. 80GP
—NY Rangers, 1991-92. 80GP
—Pittsburgh Penguins, 1991-92. 80GP
—Detroit Red Wings, 1992-93. 84GP
—Pittsburgh Penguins, 1992-93. 84GP

MOST 20-OR-MORE GOAL SCORERS, ONE SEASON:

11 —**Boston Bruins,** 1977-78; Peter McNab, 41; Terry O'Reilly, 29; Bobby Schmautz, Stan Jonathan, 27 each; Jean Ratelle, Rick Middleton, 25 each; Wayne Cashman, 24; Gregg Sheppard, 23; Brad Park, 22; Don Marcotte, Bob Miller, 20 each. 80GP
10 —Boston Bruins, 1970-71. 78GP
—Montreal Canadiens, 1974-75. 80GP
—St. Louis Blues, 1980-81. 80GP

MOST 100 OR-MORE-POINT SCORERS, ONE SEASON:

4 —**Boston Bruins,** 1970-71, Phil Esposito, 76G-76A-152PTS; Bobby Orr, 37G-102A-139PTS; John Bucyk, 51G-65A-116PTS; Ken Hodge, 43G-62A-105PTS. 78GP
—**Edmonton Oilers,** 1982-83, Wayne Gretzky, 71G-125A-196PTS; Mark Messier, 48G-58A-106PTS; Glenn Anderson, 48G-56A-104PTS; Jari Kurri, 45G-59A-104PTS. 80GP.
—**Edmonton Oilers,** 1983-84, Wayne Gretzky, 87G-118A-205PTS; Paul Coffey, 40G-86A-126PTS; Jari Kurri, 52G-61A-113PTS; Mark Messier, 37G-64A-101PTS. 80GP.
—**Edmonton Oilers,** 1985-86, Wayne Gretzky, 52G-163A-215PTS; Paul Coffey, 48G-90A-138PTS; Jari Kurri, 68G-63A-131PTS; Glenn Anderson, 54G-48A-102PTS. 80GP
—**Pittsburgh Penguins,** 1992-93, Mario Lemieux, 69G-91A-160PTS; Kevin Stevens, 55G-56A-111PTS; Rick Tocchet, 48G-61A-109PTS; Ron Francis, 24G-76A-100PTS. 84GP
3 —Boston Bruins, 1973-74, Phil Esposito, 68G-77A-145PTS; Bobby Orr, 32G-90A-122PTS; Ken Hodge, 50G-55A-105PTS. 78GP
—NY Islanders, 1978-79, Bryan Trottier, 47G-87A-134PTS; Mike Bossy, 69G-57A-126PTS; Denis Potvin, 31G-70A-101PTS. 80GP
—Los Angeles Kings, 1980-81, Marcel Dionne, 58G-77A-135PTS; Dave Taylor, 47 G-65A-112PTS; Charlie Simmer, 56G-49A-105PTS. 80GP
—Edmonton Oilers, 1984-85, Wayne Gretzky, 73G-135A-208PTS; Jari Kurri, 71G-64A-135PTS; Paul Coffey, 37G-84A-121PTS. 80GP
—NY Islanders, 1984-85, Mike Bossy, 58G-59A-117PTS; Brent Sutter, 42G-60A-102PTS; John Tonelli, 42G-58A-100PTS. 80GP
—Edmonton Oilers, 1986-87, Wayne Gretzky, 62G-121A-183PTS; Jari Kurri, 54G-54A-108PTS; Mark Messier, 37G-70A-107PTS. 80GP
—Pittsburgh Penguins, 1988-89, Mario Lemieux, 85G-114A-199PTS; Rob Brown, 49G-66A-115PTS; Paul Coffey, 30G-83A-113PTS. 80GP

MOST PENALTY MINUTES, ONE SEASON:

2,713 —**Buffalo Sabres,** 1991-92. 80GP
2,670 —Pittsburgh Penguins, 1988-89. 80GP
2,663 —Chicago Blackhawks, 1991-92. 80GP
2,643 —Calgary Flames, 1991-92. 80GP
2,621 —Philadelphia Flyers, 1980-81. 80GP

MOST GOALS, BOTH TEAMS, ONE GAME:

21 —**Montreal Canadiens, Toronto St. Patricks,** at Montreal, Jan. 10, 1920. Montreal won 14-7.
—**Edmonton Oilers, Chicago Blackhawks,** at Chicago, Dec. 11, 1985. Edmonton won 12-9.
20 —Edmonton Oilers, Minnesota North Stars, at Edmonton, Jan. 4, 1984. Edmonton won 12-8.
—Toronto Maple Leafs, Edmonton Oilers, at Toronto, Jan. 8, 1986. Toronto won 11-9.
19 —Montreal Wanderers, Toronto Arenas, at Montreal, Dec. 19, 1917. Montreal won 10-9.
—Montreal Canadiens, Quebec Bulldogs, at Quebec, Mar. 3, 1920, Montreal won 16-3.
—Montreal Canadiens, Hamilton Tigers, at Montreal, Feb. 26, 1921. Canadiens won 13-6.
—Boston Bruins, NY Rangers, at Boston, Mar. 4, 1944, Boston won 10-9.
—Boston Bruins, Detroit Red Wings, at Detroit, Mar. 16, 1944. Detroit won 10-9.
—Vancouver Canucks, Minnesota North Stars, at Vancouver, Oct. 7, 1983. Vancouver won 10-9.

MOST GOALS, ONE TEAM, ONE GAME:

16 —**Montreal Canadiens,** Mar. 3, 1920, at Quebec. Defeated Quebec Bulldogs 16-3.

MOST CONSECUTIVE GOALS, ONE TEAM, ONE GAME:

15 —**Detroit Red Wings,** Jan. 23, 1944, at Detroit. Defeated NY Rangers 15-0.

MOST POINTS, BOTH TEAMS, ONE GAME:

62 —**Edmonton Oilers, Chicago Blackhawks,** at Chicago, Dec. 11, 1985. Edmonton won 12-9. Edmonton had 24A, Chicago, 17.
53 —Quebec Nordiques, Washington Capitals, at Washington, Feb. 22, 1981. Quebec won 11-7. Quebec had 22A, Washington, 13.
—Edmonton Oilers, Minnesota North Stars, at Edmonton, Jan. 4, 1984. Edmonton won 12-8. Edmonton had 20A, Minnesota 13.
—Minnesota North Stars, St. Louis Blues, at St. Louis, Jan. 27, 1984. Minnesota won 10-8. Minnesota had 19A, St. Louis 16.
—Toronto Maple Leafs, Edmonton Oilers, at Toronto, Jan. 8, 1986. Toronto won 11-9. Toronto had 17A, Edmonton 16.
52 —Mtl. Maroons, NY Americans, at New York, Feb. 18, 1936. 8-8 tie. New York had 20A, Montreal 16. (3A allowed for each goal.)
—Vancouver Canucks, Minnesota North Stars, at Vancouver, Oct. 7, 1983. Vancouver won 10-9. Vancouver had 16A, Minnesota 17.

Ken Hodge was one of four Boston Bruins to score 100-or-more points in 1970-71.

MOST POINTS, ONE TEAM, ONE GAME:
40 —**Buffalo Sabres,** Dec. 21, 1975, at Buffalo. Buffalo defeated Washington 14-2, receiving 26A.
39 —**Minnesota North Stars,** Nov. 11, 1981, at Minnesota. Minnesota defeated Winnipeg 15-2, receiving 24A.
37 —**Detroit Red Wings,** Jan. 23, 1944, at Detroit. Detroit defeated NY Rangers 15-0, receiving 22A.
—**Toronto Maple Leafs,** Mar. 16, 1957, at Toronto. Toronto defeated NY Rangers 14-1, receiving 23A.
—**Buffalo Sabres,** Feb. 25, 1978, at Cleveland. Buffalo defeated Cleveland 13-3, receiving 24A.
—**Calgary Flames,** Feb. 10, 1993, at Calgary. Calgary defeated San Jose 13-1, receiving 24A.

MOST SHOTS, BOTH TEAMS, ONE GAME:
141 —**NY Americans, Pittsburgh Pirates,** Dec. 26, 1925, at New York. NY Americans, who won game 3-1, had 73 shots; Pit. Pirates, 68 shots.

MOST SHOTS, ONE TEAM, ONE GAME:
83 —**Boston Bruins,** March 4, 1941, at Boston. Boston defeated Chicago 3-2.
73 —**NY Americans,** Dec. 26, 1925, at New York. NY Americans defeated Pit. Pirates 3-1.
—**Boston Bruins,** March 21, 1991, at Boston. Boston tied Quebec 3-3.
72 —**Boston Bruins,** Dec. 10, 1970, at Boston. Boston defeated Buffalo 8-2.

MOST PENALTIES, BOTH TEAMS, ONE GAME:
85 Penalties — **Edmonton Oilers (44), Los Angeles Kings (41)** at Los Angeles, Feb. 28, 1990. Edmonton received 26 minors, 7 majors, 6 10-minute misconducts, 4 game misconducts and 1 match penalty; Los Angeles received 26 minors, 9 majors, 3 10-minute misconducts and 3 game misconducts.

MOST PENALTY MINUTES, BOTH TEAMS, ONE GAME:
406 Minutes — **Minnesota North Stars, Boston Bruins** at Boston, Feb. 26, 1981. Minnesota received 18 minors, 13 majors, 4 10-minute misconducts and 7 game misconducts; a total of 211PIM. Boston received 20 minors, 13 majors, 3 10-minute misconducts and six game misconducts; a total of 195PIM.

MOST PENALTIES, ONE TEAM, ONE GAME:
44 —**Edmonton Oilers,** Feb. 28, 1990, at Los Angeles. Edmonton received 26 minors, 7 majors, 6 10-minute misconducts, 4 game misconducts and 1 match penalty.
42 —**Minnesota North Stars,** Feb. 26, 1981, at Boston. Minnesota received 18 minors, 13 majors, 4 10-minute misconducts and 7 game misconducts.
—**Boston Bruins,** Feb. 26, 1981, at Boston vs. Minnesota. Boston received 20 minors, 13 majors, 3 10-minute misconducts and 7 game misconducts.

MOST PENALTY MINUTES, ONE TEAM, ONE GAME:
211 —**Minnesota North Stars,** Feb. 26, 1981, at Boston. Minnesota received 18 minors, 13 majors, 4 10-minute misconducts and 7 game misconducts.

MOST GOALS, BOTH TEAMS, ONE PERIOD:
12 —**Buffalo Sabres, Toronto Maple Leafs,** at Buffalo, March 19, 1981, second period. Buffalo scored 9 goals, Toronto 3. Buffalo won 14-4.
—**Edmonton Oilers, Chicago Blackhawks,** at Chicago, Dec. 11, 1985, second period. Edmonton scored 6 goals, Chicago 6. Edmonton won 12-9.
10 —**NY Rangers, NY Americans,** at NY Americans, March 16, 1939, third period. NY Rangers scored 7 goals, NY Americans 3. NY Rangers won 11-5.
—**Toronto Maple Leafs, Detroit Red Wings,** at Detroit, March 17, 1946, third period. Toronto scored 6 goals, Detroit 4. Toronto won 11-7.
—**Vancouver Canucks, Buffalo Sabres,** at Buffalo, Jan. 8, 1976, third period. Buffalo scored 6 goals, Vancouver 4. Buffalo won 8-5.
—**Buffalo Sabres, Montreal Canadiens,** at Montreal, Oct. 26, 1982, first period. Montreal scored 5 goals, Buffalo 5. 7-7 tie.
—**Boston Bruins, Quebec Nordiques,** at Quebec, Dec. 7, 1982, second period. Quebec scored 6 goals, Boston 4. Quebec won 10-5.
—**Calgary Flames, Vancouver Canucks,** at Vancouver, Jan. 16, 1987, first period. Vancouver scored 6 goals, Calgary 4. Vancouver won 9-5.
—**Winnipeg Jets, Detroit Red Wings,** at Detroit, Nov. 25, 1987, third period. Detroit scored 7 goals, Winnipeg 3. Detroit won 10-8.
—**Chicago Blackhawks, St. Louis Blues,** at St. Louis, March 15, 1988, third period. Chicago scored 5 goals, St. Louis 5. 7-7 tie.

MOST GOALS, ONE TEAM, ONE PERIOD:
9 —**Buffalo Sabres,** March 19, 1981, at Buffalo, second period during 14-4 win over Toronto.
8 —**Detroit Red Wings,** Jan. 23, 1944, at Detroit, third period during 15-0 win over NY Rangers.
—**Boston Bruins,** March 16, 1969, at Boston, second period during 11-3 win over Toronto.
—**NY Rangers,** Nov. 21, 1971, at New York, third period during 12-1 win over California.
—**Philadelphia Flyers,** March 31, 1973, at Philadelphia, second period during 10-2 win over NY Islanders.
—**Buffalo Sabres,** Dec. 21, 1975, at Buffalo, third period during 14-2 win over Washington.
—**Minnesota North Stars,** Nov. 11, 1981, at Minnesota, second period during 15-2 win over Winnipeg.
—**Pittsburgh Penguins,** Dec. 17, 1991, at Pittsburgh, second period during 10-2 win over San Jose.

MOST POINTS, BOTH TEAMS, ONE PERIOD:
35 —**Edmonton, Oilers, Chicago Blackhawks,** at Chicago, Dec. 11, 1985, second period. Edmonton had 6G, 12A; Chicago, 6G, 11A. Edmonton won 12-9.
31 —Buffalo Sabres, Toronto Maple Leafs, at Buffalo, March 19, 1981, second period. Buffalo had 9G, 14A; Toronto, 3G, 5A. Buffalo won 14-4.
29 —Winnipeg Jets, Detroit Red Wings, at Detroit, Nov. 25, 1987, third period. Detroit had 7G, 13A; Winnipeg had 3G, 6A. Detroit won 10-8.
—Chicago Blackhawks, St. Louis Blues, at St. Louis, March 15, 1988, third period. St. Louis had 5G, 10A; Chicago had 5G, 9A. 7-7 tie.

Hall-of-Fame goaltenders George Hainsworth and Roy Worters combined to record 160 shutouts in the NHL.

MOST POINTS, ONE TEAM, ONE PERIOD:
  23 — **NY Rangers,** Nov. 21, 1971, at New York, third period during 12-1 win
        over California. NY Rangers scored 8G and 15A.
      — **Buffalo Sabres,** Dec. 21, 1975, at Buffalo, third period during 14-2 win
        over Washington. Buffalo scored 8G and 15A.
      — **Buffalo Sabres,** March 19, 1981, at Buffalo, second period, during 14-4
        win over Toronto. Buffalo scored 9G and 14A.
  22 — **Detroit Red Wings,** Jan. 23, 1944, at Detroit, third period during 15-0 win
        over NY Rangers. Detroit scored 8G and 14A.
      — **Boston Bruins,** March 16, 1969, at Boston, second period during 11-3 win
        over Toronto Maple Leafs. Boston scored 8G and 14A.
      — **Minnesota North Stars,** Nov. 11, 1981, at Minnesota, second period during
        15-2 win over Winnipeg. Minnesota scored 8G and 14A.
      — **Pittsburgh Penguins,** Dec. 17, 1991, at Pittsburgh, second period during
        10-2 win over San Jose. Pittsburgh scored 8G and 14A.

MOST SHOTS, ONE TEAM, ONE PERIOD:
  33 — **Boston Bruins,** March 4, 1941, at Boston, second period. Boston
        defeated Chicago 3-2.

MOST PENALTIES, BOTH TEAMS, ONE PERIOD:
  67 — **Minnesota North Stars, Boston Bruins,** at Boston, Feb. 26, 1981, first
        period. Minnesota received 15 minors, 8 majors, 4 10-minute misconducts
        and 7 game misconducts, a total of 34 penalties. Boston had 16 minors, 8
        majors, 3 10-minute misconducts and 6 game misconducts, a total of 33
        penalties.

MOST PENALTY MINUTES, BOTH TEAMS, ONE PERIOD:
  372 — **Los Angeles Kings, Philadelphia Flyers** at Philadelphia, March 11,
        1979, first period. Philadelphia received 4 minors, 8 majors, 6 10-minute
        misconducts and 8 game misconducts for 188 minutes. Los Angeles
        received 2 minors, 8 majors, 6 10-minute misconducts and 8 game
        misconducts for 184 minutes.

MOST PENALTIES, ONE TEAM, ONE PERIOD:
  34 — **Minnesota North Stars,** Feb. 26, 1981, at Boston, first period. 15 minors,
        8 majors, 4 10-minute misconducts, 7 game misconducts.

MOST PENALTY MINUTES, ONE TEAM, ONE PERIOD:
  188 — **Philadelphia Flyers,** March 11, 1979, at Philadelphia vs. Los Angeles,
        first period. Flyers received 4 minors, 8 majors, 6 10-minute misconducts
        and 8 game misconducts.

FASTEST SIX GOALS, BOTH TEAMS
3 Minutes, 15 Seconds — Montreal Canadiens, Toronto Maple Leafs, at
        Montreal, Jan. 4, 1944, first period. Montreal scored 4G, Toronto 2. Montreal
        won 6-3.

FASTEST FIVE GOALS, BOTH TEAMS:
1 Minute, 24 Seconds — Chicago Blackhawks, Toronto Maple Leafs, at
        Toronto, Oct. 15, 1983, second period. Scorers were: Gaston Gingras,
        Toronto, 16:49; Denis Savard, Chicago, 17:12; Steve Larmer, Chicago,
        17:27; Savard, 17:42; and John Anderson, Toronto, 18:13. Toronto won 10-8.
1 Minute, 39 Seconds — Detroit Red Wings, Toronto Maple Leafs, at Toronto, Nov.
        15, 1944, third period. Scorers were: Ted Kennedy, Toronto, 10:36 and
        10:55; Hal Jackson, Detroit, 11:48; Steve Wochy, Detroit, 12:02; Don
        Grosso, Detroit, 12:15. Detroit won 8-4.

FASTEST FIVE GOALS, ONE TEAM:
2 Minutes, 7 Seconds — Pittsburgh Penguins, at Pittsburgh, Nov. 22, 1972, third
        period. Scorers: Bryan Hextall, 12:00; Jean Pronovost, 12:18; Al
        McDonough, 13:40; Ken Schinkel, 13:49; Ron Schock, 14:07. Pittsburgh
        defeated St. Louis 10-4.
2 Minutes, 37 seconds — NY Islanders, at New York, Jan. 26, 1982, first period.
        Scorers: Duane Sutter, 1:31; John Tonelli, 2:30; Bryan Trottier, 2:46; Bryan
        Trottier, 3:31; Duane Sutter, 4:08. NY Islanders defeated Pittsburgh 9-2.
2 Minutes, 55 Seconds — Boston Bruins, at Boston, Dec. 19, 1974. Scorers: Bobby
        Schmautz, 19:13 (first period); Ken Hodge, 0:18; Phil Esposito, 0:43; Don
        Marcotte, 0:58; John Bucyk, 2:08 (second period). Boston defeated NY
        Rangers 11-3.

FASTEST FOUR GOALS, BOTH TEAMS:
53 Seconds — Chicago Blackhawks, Toronto Maple Leafs, at Toronto, Oct. 15,
        1983, second period. Scorers were: Gaston Gingras, Toronto, 16:49; Denis
        Savard, Chicago, 17:12; Steve Larmer, Chicago, 17:27; and Savard at
        17:42. Toronto won 10-8.
57 Seconds — Quebec Nordiques, Detroit Red Wings, at Quebec, Jan. 27, 1990,
        first period. Scorers were: Paul Gillis, Quebec, 18:01; Claude Loiselle,
        Quebec, 18:12; Joe Sakic, Quebec, 18:27; and Jimmy Carson, Detroit,
        18:58. Detroit won 8-6.
1 Minute, 1 Second — Colorado Rockies, NY Rangers, at New York, Jan. 15, 1980,
        first period. Scorers were: Doug Sulliman, NY Rangers, 7:52; Ed Johnstone,
        NY Rangers, 7:57; Warren Miller, NY Rangers, 8:20; Rob Ramage,
        Colorado, 8:53. 6-6 tie.
    — Chicago Blackhawks, Toronto Maple Leafs, at Toronto, Oct. 15, 1983, second
        period. Scorers were: Denis Savard, Chicago, 17:12; Steve Larmer,
        Chicago, 17:27; Savard, 17:42; John Anderson, Toronto, 18:13. Toronto won
        10-8.

FASTEST FOUR GOALS, ONE TEAM:
1 Minute, 20 Seconds — Boston Bruins, at Boston, Jan. 21, 1945, second period.
        Scorers were: Bill Thoms at 6:34; Frank Mario at 7:08 and 7:27; and Ken
        Smith at 7:54. Boston defeated NY Rangers 14-3.

FASTEST THREE GOALS, BOTH TEAMS:
15 Seconds — Minnesota North Stars, NY Rangers, at Minnesota, Feb. 10, 1983,
        second period. Scorers were: Mark Pavelich, NY Rangers, 19:18; Ron
        Greschner, NY Rangers, 19:27; Willi Plett, Minnesota, 19:33.
        Minnesota won 7-5.
18 Seconds — Montreal Canadiens, NY Rangers, at Montreal, Dec. 12, 1963, first
        period. Scorers were: Dave Balon, Montreal, 0:58; Gilles Tremblay,
        Montreal, 1:04; Camille Henry, NY Rangers, 1:16. Montreal won 6-4.
18 Seconds — California Golden Seals, Buffalo Sabres, at California, Feb. 1, 1976,
        third period. Scorers were: Jim Moxey, California, 19:38; Wayne Merrick,
        California, 19:45; Danny Gare, Buffalo, 19:56. Buffalo won 9-5.

FASTEST THREE GOALS, ONE TEAM:
20 Seconds — Boston Bruins, at Boston, Feb. 25, 1971, third period. John Bucyk
        scored at 4:50, Ed Westfall at 5:02 and Ted Green at 5:10. Boston defeated
        Vancouver 8-3.
21 Seconds — Chicago Blackhawks, at New York, March 23, 1952, third period.
        Bill Mosienko scored all three goals, at 6:09, 6:20 and 6:30. Chicago
        defeated NY Rangers 7-6.
21 Seconds — Washington Capitals, at Washington, Nov. 23, 1990, first period.
        Michal Pivonka scored at 16:18 and Stephen Leach scored at 16:29 and
        16:39. Washington defeated Pittsburgh 7-3.

FASTEST THREE GOALS FROM START OF PERIOD, BOTH TEAMS:
1 Minute, 5 seconds — Hartford Whalers, Montreal Canadiens, at Montreal,
        March 11, 1989, second period. Scorers were: Kevin Dineen, Hartford, 0:11;
        Guy Carbonneau, Montreal, 0:36; Petr Svoboda, Montreal, 1:05. Montreal
        won 5-3.

FASTEST THREE GOALS FROM START OF PERIOD, ONE TEAM:
53 Seconds — Calgary Flames, at Calgary, Feb. 10, 1993, third period. Scorers
        were: Gary Suter at 0:17, Chris Lindbergh at 0:40, Ron Stern at 0:53.
        Calgary defeated San Jose 13-1.

FASTEST TWO GOALS, BOTH TEAMS:
2 Seconds — St. Louis Blues, Boston Bruins, at Boston, Dec. 19, 1987,
        third period. Scorers were: Ken Linseman, Boston, at 19:50; Doug Gilmour,
        St. Louis, at 19:52. St. Louis won 7-5.
3 Seconds — Chicago Blackhawks, Minnesota North Stars, at Minnesota,
        November 5, 1988, third period. Scorers were: Steve Thomas, Chicago, at
        6:03; Dave Gagner, Minnesota, at 6:06. 5-5 tie.

FASTEST TWO GOALS, ONE TEAM:
4 Seconds — Montreal Maroons, at Montreal, Jan. 3, 1931, third period. Nels
        Stewart scored both goals, at 8:24 and 8:28. Mtl. Maroons defeated Boston
        5-3.
    — **Buffalo Sabres,** at Buffalo, Oct. 17, 1974, third period. Scorers were: Lee Fogolin
        at 14:55 and Don Luce at 14:59. Buffalo defeated California 6-1.
    — **Toronto Maple Leafs,** at Quebec, December 29, 1988, third period. Scorers
        were: Ed Olczyk at 5:24 and Gary Leeman at 5:28. Toronto defeated
        Quebec 6-5.
    — **Calgary Flames,** at Quebec, October 17, 1989, third period. Scorers were: Doug
        Gilmour at 19:45 and Paul Ranheim at 19:49. Calgary and Quebec tied 8-8.

FASTEST TWO GOALS FROM START OF PERIOD, BOTH TEAMS:
14 Seconds — NY Rangers, Quebec Nordiques, at Quebec, Nov. 5, 1983, third
        period. Scorers: Andre Savard, Quebec, 0:08; Pierre Larouche, NY Rangers,
        0:14. 4-4 tie.
26 Seconds — Buffalo Sabres, St. Louis Blues, at Buffalo, Jan. 3, 1993, third period.
        Scorers: Alexander Mogilny, Buffalo, 0:08; Phillippe Bozon, St. Louis, 0:26.
        Buffalo won 6-5.
28 Seconds — Boston Bruins, Montreal Canadiens, at Montreal, Oct. 11, 1989, third
        period. Scorers: Jim Wiemer, Boston 0:10; Tom Chorske, Montreal 0:28.
        Montreal won 4-2.

FASTEST TWO GOALS FROM START OF GAME, ONE TEAM:
24 Seconds — Edmonton Oilers, March 28, 1982, at Los Angeles. Mark Messier,
        at 0:14 and Dave Lumley, at 0:24, scored in first period. Edmonton defeated
        Los Angeles 6-2.
29 Seconds — Pittsburgh Penguins, Dec. 6, 1981, at Pittsburgh. George Ferguson
        at 0:17 and Greg Malone at 0:29, scored in first period. Pittsburgh defeated
        Chicago 6-4.
32 Seconds — Calgary Flames, March 11, 1987, at Hartford. Doug Risebrough at
        0:09 and Colin Patterson, at 0:32, in first period. Calgary defeated Hartford
        6-1.

FASTEST TWO GOALS FROM START OF PERIOD, ONE TEAM:
21 Seconds — Chicago Blackhawks, Nov. 5, 1983, at Minnesota, second period.
        Ken Yaremchuk scored at 0:12 and Darryl Sutter at 0:21. Minnesota
        defeated Chicago 10-5.
30 Seconds — Washington Capitals, Jan. 27, 1980, at Washington, second period.
        Mike Gartner scored at 0:08 and Bengt Gustafsson at 0:30. Washington
        defeated NY Islanders 7-1.
31 Seconds — Buffalo Sabres, Jan. 10, 1974, at Buffalo, third period. Rene Robert
        scored at 0:21 and Rick Martin at 0:30. Buffalo defeated NY Rangers 7-2.
    — NY Islanders, Feb. 22, 1986, at New York, third period. Roger Kortko scored at
        0:10 and Bob Bourne at 0:31. NY Islanders defeated Detroit 5-2.

Individual Records

Career

MOST SEASONS:
26 — **Gordie Howe,** Detroit, 1946-47 – 1970-71; Hartford, 1979-80.
24 — Alex Delvecchio, Detroit, 1950-51 – 1973-74.
— Tim Horton, Toronto, NY Rangers, Pittsburgh, Buffalo, 1949-50, 1951-52 – 1973-74.
23 — John Bucyk, Detroit, Boston, 1955-56 – 1977-78.
22 — Dean Prentice, NY Rangers, Boston, Detroit, Pittsburgh, Minnesota, 1952-53 – 1973-74.
— Doug Mohns, Boston, Chicago, Minnesota, Atlanta, Washington, 1953-54 – 1974-75.
— Stan Mikita, Chicago, 1958-59 – 1979-80.

MOST GAMES:
1,767 — **Gordie Howe,** Detroit, 1946-47 – 1970-71; Hartford, 1979-80.
1,549 — Alex Delvecchio, Detroit, 1950-51 – 1973-74.
1,540 — John Bucyk, Detroit, Boston, 1955-56 – 1977-78.

MOST GOALS:
801 — **Gordie Howe,** Detroit, Hartford, in 26 seasons, 1,767GP.
765 — Wayne Gretzky, Edmonton, Los Angeles, in 14 seasons, 1,044GP.
731 — Marcel Dionne, Detroit, Los Angeles, NY Rangers, in 18 seasons, 1,348GP.
717 — Phil Esposito, Chicago, Boston, NY Rangers, in 18 seasons, 1,282GP.
610 — Bobby Hull, Chicago, Winnipeg, Hartford, in 16 seasons, 1,063GP.

HIGHEST GOALS-PER-GAME AVERAGE, CAREER
(AMONG PLAYERS WITH 200 OR MORE GOALS):
.827 — **Mario Lemieux,** Pittsburgh, 477G, 577GP, from 1984-85 – 1992-93.
.776 — Brett Hull, Calgary, St. Louis, 356G, 459GP, from 1986-87 – 1992-93.
.767 — Cy Denneny, Ottawa, Boston, 250G, 326GP, from 1917-18 – 1928-29.
.762 — Mike Bossy, NY Islanders, 573G, 752GP, from 1977-78 – 1986-87.
.733 — Wayne Gretzky, Edmonton, Los Angeles, 765G, 1,044GP, from 1979-80 – 1992-93.

MOST ASSISTS:
1,563 — **Wayne Gretzky,** Edmonton, Los Angeles, in 14 seasons, 1,044GP.
1,049 — Gordie Howe, Detroit, Hartford in 26 seasons, 1,767GP.
1,040 — Marcel Dionne, Detroit, Los Angeles, NY Rangers in 18 seasons, 1,348GP.
926 — Stan Mikita, Chicago, in 22 seasons, 1,394GP.
890 — Bryan Trottier, NY Islanders, Pittsburgh, in 17 seasons, 1,238GP.

HIGHEST ASSIST-PER-GAME AVERAGE, CAREER
(AMONG PLAYERS WITH 300 OR MORE ASSISTS):
1.497 — **Wayne Gretzky,** Edmonton, Los Angeles, 1,563A, 1,044GP from 1979-80 – 1992-93.
1.208 — Mario Lemieux, Pittsburgh, 697A, 577GP from 1984-85 – 1992-93.
.982 — Bobby Orr, Boston, Chicago, 645A, 657GP from 1966-67 – 1978-79.
.914 — Paul Coffey, Edmonton, Pittsburgh, Los Angeles, 871A, 953GP from 1980-81 – 1992-93.
.889 — Adam Oates, Detroit, St. Louis, Boston, 490A, 551GP from 1984-85 – 1992-93.

MOST POINTS:
2,328 — **Wayne Gretzky,** Edmonton, Los Angeles, in 14 seasons, 1,044GP (765G-1,563A).
1,850 — Gordie Howe, Detroit, Hartford, in 26 seasons, 1,767GP (801G-1049A).
1,771 — Marcel Dionne, Detroit, Los Angeles, NY Rangers, in 18 seasons, 1,348GP (731G-1,040A).
1,590 — Phil Esposito, Chicago, Boston, NY Rangers in 18 seasons, 1,282GP (717G-873A).
1,467 — Stan Mikita, Chicago in 22 seasons, 1,394GP (541G-926A).

HIGHEST POINTS-PER-GAME AVERAGE, CAREER:
(AMONG PLAYERS WITH 500 OR MORE POINTS):
2.230 — **Wayne Gretzky,** Edmonton, Los Angeles, 2,328PTS (765G-1,563A), 1,044GP from 1979-80 – 1992-93.
2.035 — Mario Lemieux, Pittsburgh, 1,174PTS (477G-697A), 577GP from 1984-85 – 1992-93.
1.497 — Mike Bossy, NY Islanders, 1,126PTS (573G-553A), 752GP from 1978-79 – 1986-87.
1.393 — Bobby Orr, Boston, Chicago, 915PTS (270G-645A), 657GP from 1966-67 – 1978-79.
1.374 — Steve Yzerman, Detroit, 1,040PTS (445G-595A), 757GP from 1983-84 – 1992-93.

MOST GOALS BY A CENTER, CAREER
765 — **Wayne Gretzky,** Edmonton, Los Angeles, in 14 seasons.
731 — Marcel Dionne, Detroit, Los Angeles, NY Rangers, in 18 seasons.
717 — Phil Esposito, Chicago, Boston, NY Rangers, in 18 seasons.
541 — Stan Mikita, Chicago, in 22 seasons.
520 — Bryan Trottier, NY Islanders, Pittsburgh, in 17 seasons.

MOST ASSISTS BY A CENTER, CAREER;
1,563 — **Wayne Gretzky,** Edmonton, Los Angeles, in 14 seasons.
1,040 — Marcel Dionne, Detroit, Los Angeles, NY Rangers, in 18 seasons.
926 — Stan Mikita, Chicago, in 22 seasons.
890 — Bryan Trottier, NY Islanders, Pittsburgh, in 17 seasons.
873 — Phil Esposito, Chicago, Boston, NY Rangers, in 18 seasons.

Wayne Gretzky has rewritten the NHL record book during his 14-year career, setting or tying over 60 individual records.

MOST POINTS BY A CENTER, CAREER:
2,328 — **Wayne Gretzky,** Edmonton, Los Angeles, in 14 seasons.
1,771 — Marcel Dionne, Detroit, Los Angeles, NY Rangers, in 18 seasons.
1,590 — Phil Esposito, Chicago, Boston, NY Rangers, in 18 seasons.
1,467 — Stan Mikita, Chicago, in 22 seasons
1,410 — Bryan Trottier, NY Islanders, Pittsburgh, in 17 seasons.

MOST GOALS BY A LEFT WING, CAREER:
610 — **Bobby Hull,** Chicago, Winnipeg, Hartford, in 16 seasons.
556 — John Bucyk, Detroit, Boston, in 23 seasons.
533 — Frank Mahovlich, Toronto, Detroit, Montreal, in 18 seasons.
532 — Michel Goulet, Quebec, Chicago, in 14 seasons.
424 — Steve Shutt, Montreal, Los Angeles, in 13 seasons.

MOST ASSISTS BY A LEFT WING, CAREER:
813 — **John Bucyk,** Detroit, Boston, in 23 seasons.
590 — Michel Goulet, Quebec, Chicago, in 14 seasons.
570 — Frank Mahovlich, Toronto, Detroit, Montreal, in 18 seasons.
561 — Brian Propp, Philadelphia, Boston, Minnesota, in 14 seasons.
560 — Bobby Hull, Chicago, Winnipeg, Hartford, in 16 seasons.

MOST POINTS BY A LEFT WING, CAREER:
1,369 — **John Bucyk,** Detroit, Boston, in 23 seasons.
1,170 — Bobby Hull, Chicago, Winnipeg, Hartford, in 16 seasons.
1,122 — Michel Goulet, Quebec, Chicago, in 14 seasons.
1,103 — Frank Mahovlich, Toronto, Detroit, Montreal, in 18 seasons.
974 — Brian Propp, Philadelphia, Boston, MInnesota, in 14 seasons.

MOST GOALS BY A RIGHT WING, CAREER:
801 — **Gordie Howe,** Detroit, Hartford, in 26 seasons.
583 — Mike Gartner, Washington, Minnesota, NY Rangers, in 14 seasons.
573 — Mike Bossy, NY Islanders, in 10 seasons.
560 — Guy Lafleur, Montreal, NY Rangers, Quebec, in 17 seasons.
544 — Maurice Richard, Montreal, in 18 seasons.

MOST ASSISTS BY A RIGHT WING, CAREER:
1,049 — **Gordie Howe,** Detroit, Hartford, in 26 seasons.
793 — Guy Lafleur, Montreal, NY Rangers, Quebec, in 17 seasons.
666 — Jari Kurri, Edmonton, Los Angeles, in 12 seasons.
635 — Dave Taylor, Los Angeles, in 16 seasons.
624 — Andy Bathgate, NY Rangers, Toronto, Detroit, Pittsburgh in 17 seasons.

MOST POINTS BY A RIGHT WING, CAREER:
1,850 — **Gordie Howe,** Detroit, Hartford, in 26 seasons.
1,353 — Guy Lafleur, Montreal, NY Rangers, Quebec, in 17 seasons.
1,126 — Mike Bossy, NY Islanders, in 10 seasons.
1,190 — Jari Kurri, Edmonton, Los Angeles, in 12 seasons.
1,107 — Mike Gartner, Washington, Minnesota, NY Rangers, in 14 seasons.

Terry Sawchuk, who won rookie-of-the-year honors in the USHL, AHL and NHL, went on to become the NHL's career record holder for games played (971) and shutouts (103).

MOST GOALS BY A DEFENSEMAN, CAREER:
330 — **Paul Coffey,** Edmonton, Pittsburgh, Los Angeles, Detroit, in 13 seasons.
310 — Denis Potvin, NY Islanders, in 15 seasons.
291 — Ray Bourque, Boston, in 14 seasons.
270 — Bobby Orr, Boston, Chicago, in 12 seasons.
248 — Doug Mohns, Boston, Chicago, Minnesota, Atlanta, Washington, in 22 seasons.

MOST ASSISTS BY A DEFENSEMAN, CAREER:
871 — **Paul Coffey,** Edmonton, Pittsburgh, Los Angeles, Detroit, in 13 seasons.
806 — Ray Bourque, Boston, in 14 seasons.
750 — Larry Robinson, Montreal, Los Angeles, in 20 seasons.
742 — Denis Potvin, NY Islanders, in 15 seasons.
683 — Brad Park, NY Rangers, Boston, Detroit, in 17 seasons.

MOST POINTS BY A DEFENSEMAN, CAREER:
1,201 — **Paul Coffey,** Edmonton, Pittsburgh, Los Angeles, Detroit, in 13 seasons.
1,097 — Ray Bourque, Boston, in 14 seasons.
1,052 — Denis Potvin, NY Islanders, in 15 seasons.
958 — Larry Robinson, Montreal, Los Angeles, in 20 seasons.
915 — Bobby Orr, Boston, Chicago, in 12 seasons.

MOST OVERTIME GOALS, CAREER:
7 — **Mario Lemieux,** Pittsburgh.
— **Jari Kurri,** Edmonton.
— **Tomas Sandstrom,** NY Rangers, Los Angeles.
— **Bob Sweeney,** Boston, Buffalo.
6 — Paul MacLean, Winnipeg, Detroit, St. Louis.

MOST OVERTIME ASSISTS, CAREER:
11 — **Wayne Gretzky,** Edmonton, Los Angeles.
10 — Mario Lemieux, Pittsburgh.
9 — Bernie Federko, St. Louis.
— Dale Hawerchuk, Winnipeg, Buffalo.
— Mark Messier, Edmonton, NY Rangers.

MOST OVERTIME POINTS, CAREER:
17 — **Mario Lemieux,** Pittsburgh, 7G-10A
13 — Paul MacLean, Winnipeg, Detroit, St. Louis. 6G-7A
— Dale Hawerchuk, Winnipeg, Buffalo. 4G-9A
— Wayne Gretzky, Edmonton, Los Angeles. 2G-11A
— Mark Messier, Edmonton, NY Rangers. 4G-9A
12 — Jari Kurri, Edmonton, Los Angeles. 7G-5A

MOST PENALTY MINUTES:
3,966 — **Dave Williams,** Toronto, Vancouver, Detroit, Los Angeles, Hartford, in 14 seasons, 962GP.
3,043 — Chris Nilan, Monteal, NY Rangers, Boston, in 13 seasons, 688GP.
2,874 — Dale Hunter, Quebec, Washington, in 13 seasons, 1,002GP.
2,598 — Tim Hunter, Calgary, Quebec, Vancouver, in 12 seasons, 619GP.
2,572 — Willi Plett, Atlanta, Calgary, Minnesota, Boston, in 13 seasons, 834GP.

MOST GAMES, INCLUDING PLAYOFFS:
1,924 — **Gordie Howe,** Detroit, Hartford, 1,767 regular-season and 157 playoff games.
1,670 — Alex Delvecchio, Detroit, 1,549 regular-season and 121 playoff games.
1,664 — John Bucyk, Detroit, Boston, 1,540 regular-season and 124 playoff games.

MOST GOALS, INCLUDING PLAYOFFS:
875 — **Wayne Gretzky,** Edmonton, Los Angeles, 765 regular-season and 110 playoff goals.
869 — Gordie Howe, Detroit, Hartford, 801 regular-season goals and 68 playoff goals.
778 — Phil Esposito, Chicago, Boston, NY Rangers, 717 regular-season and 61 playoff goals.
752 — Marcel Dionne, Detroit, Los Angeles, NY Rangers, 731 regular-season and 21 playoff goals.

MOST ASSISTS, INCLUDING PLAYOFFS:
1,799 — **Wayne Gretzky,** Edmonton, Los Angeles, 1,563 regular-season and 236 playoff assists.
1,141 — Gordie Howe, Detroit, Hartford, 1,049 regular-season and 92 playoff assists.
1,064 — Marcel Dionne, Detroit, Los Angeles, NY Rangers, 1,040 regular-season and 24 playoff assists.
1,017 — Stan Mikita, Chicago, 926 regular-season and 91 playoff assists.
1,003 — Bryan Trottier, NY Islanders, 890 regular-season and 113 playoff assists.

MOST POINTS, INCLUDING PLAYOFFS:
2,674 — **Wayne Gretzky,** Edmonton, Los Angeles, 2,328 regular-season and 346 playoff points.
2,010 — Gordie Howe, Detroit, Hartford, 1,850 regular-season and 160 playoff assists.
1,816 — Marcel Dionne, Detroit, Los Angeles, NY Rangers, 1,771 regular-season and 45 playoff points.
1,727 — Phil Esposito, Chicago, Boston, NY Rangers, 1,590 regular-season and 137 playoff points.
1,617 — Stan Mikita, Chicago, 1,467 regular-season and 150 playoff points.

MOST PENALTY MINUTES, INCLUDING PLAYOFFS:
4,421 — **Dave Williams,** Toronto, Vancouver, Detroit, Los Angeles, Hartford, 3,966 in regular season; 455 in playoffs.
3,584 — Chris Nilan, Montreal, NY Rangers, Boston, 3,043 in regular-season; 541 in playoffs.
3,473 — Dale Hunter, Quebec, Washington, 2,874 in regular-season; 599 in playoffs.
3,038 — Willi Plett, Atlanta, Calgary, Minnesota, Boston, 2,572 in regular-season; 466 in playoffs.
2,976 — Tim Hunter, Calgary, Quebec, Vancouver, 2,598 regular-season; 378 in playoffs.

MOST CONSECUTIVE GAMES:
964 — **Doug Jarvis,** Montreal, Washington, Hartford, from Oct. 8, 1975 – Oct. 10, 1987.
914 — Garry Unger, Toronto, Detroit, St. Louis, Atlanta from Feb. 24, 1968, – Dec. 21, 1979.
884 — Steve Larmer, Chicago, from Oct. 6, 1982 to April 16, 1993.
776 — Craig Ramsay, Buffalo, from March 27, 1973, – Feb. 10, 1983.
630 — Andy Hebenton, NY Rangers, Boston, nine complete 70-game seasons from 1955-56 – 1963-64.

MOST GAMES APPEARED IN BY A GOALTENDER, CAREER:
971 — **Terry Sawchuk,** Detroit, Boston, Toronto, Los Angeles, NY Rangers from 1949-50 – 1969-70.
906 — Glenn Hall, Detroit, Chicago, St. Louis from 1952-53 – 1970-71.
886 — Tony Esposito, Montreal, Chicago from 1968-69 – 1983-84.
860 — Lorne "Gump" Worsley, NY Rangers, Montreal, Minnesota from 1952-53 – 1973-74.

MOST CONSECUTIVE COMPLETE GAMES BY A GOALTENDER:
502 — **Glenn Hall,** Detroit, Chicago. Played 502 games from beginning of 1955-56 season - first 12 games of 1962-63. In his 503rd straight game, Nov. 7, 1962, at Chicago, Hall was removed from the game against Boston with a back injury in the first period.

MOST SHUTOUTS BY A GOALTENDER, CAREER:
103 — **Terry Sawchuk,** Detroit, Boston, Toronto, Los Angeles, NY Rangers in 21 seasons.
94 — George Hainsworth, Montreal Canadiens, Toronto in 10 seasons.
84 — Glenn Hall, Detroit, Chicago, St. Louis in 16 seasons.

MOST THREE-OR-MORE GOAL GAMES, CAREER:
49 — **Wayne Gretzky,** Edmonton, Los Angeles, in 14 seasons, 36 three-goal games, 9 four-goal games, 4 five-goal games.
39 — Mike Bossy, NY Islanders, in 10 seasons, 30 three-goal games, 9 four-goal games.
32 — Phil Esposito, Chicago, Boston, NY Rangers, in 18 seasons, 27 three-goal games, 5 four-goal games.
31 — Mario Lemieux, Pittsburgh, in 9 seasons, 21 three-goal games, 8 four-goal games and 2 five-goal games.
28 — Bobby Hull, Chicago, Winnipeg, Hartford, in 16 seasons, 24 three-goal games, 4 four-goal games.
— Marcel Dionne, Detroit, Los Angeles, NY Rangers, in 18 seasons, 25 three-goal games, 3 four-goal games.
26 — Cy Denneny, Ottawa in 12 seasons. 20 three-goal games, 5 four-goal games, 1 six-goal game.
— Maurice Richard, Montreal, in 18 seasons, 23 three-goal games, 2 four-goal games, 1 five-goal game.

MOST 20-OR-MORE GOAL SEASONS:
22 — **Gordie Howe,** Detroit, Hartford in 26 seasons.
17 — Marcel Dionne, Detroit, Los Angeles, NY Rangers, in 18 seasons.
16 — Phil Esposito, Chicago, Boston, NY Rangers, in 18 seasons.
— Norm Ullman, Detroit, Toronto, in 19 seasons.
— John Bucyk, Detroit, Boston, in 22 seasons.
15 — Frank Mahovlich, Toronto, Detroit, Montreal in 17 seasons.
— Gilbert Perreault, Buffalo, in 17 seasons.

MOST CONSECUTIVE 20-OR-MORE GOAL SEASONS:
22 — **Gordie Howe,** Detroit, 1949-50 – 1970-71.
17 — Marcel Dionne, Detroit, Los Angeles, NY Rangers, 1971-72 – 1987-88.
16 — Phil Esposito, Chicago, Boston, NY Rangers, 1964-65 – 1979-80.
14 — Maurice Richard, Montreal, 1943-44 – 1956-57.
— Stan Mikita, Chicago, 1961-62 – 1974-75.
— Mike Gartner, Washington, Minnesota, NY Rangers, 1979-80 – 1992-93.
— Michel Goulet, Quebec, Chicago, 1979-80 – 1992-93.
13 — Bobby Hull, Chicago, 1959-60 – 1971-72.
— Guy Lafleur, Montreal, 1971-72 – 1983-84.
— Bryan Trottier, NY Islanders, 1975-76 – 1987-88.
— Wayne Gretzky, Edmonton, Los Angeles, 1979-80 – 1991-92.

MOST 30-OR-MORE GOAL SEASONS:
14 — **Gordie Howe,** Detroit, Hartford in 26 seasons.
— **Marcel Dionne,** Detroit, Los Angeles, NY Rangers in 18 seasons.
— **Mike Gartner,** Washington, Minnesota, NY Rangers in 14 seasons.
13 — Bobby Hull, Chicago, Winnipeg, Hartford in 16 seasons.
— Phil Esposito, Chicago, Boston, NY Rangers in 18 seasons.
— Wayne Gretzky, Edmonton, Los Angeles in 14 seasons.

Glenn Hall appeared in an NHL record 502 consecutive complete games for the Detroit Red Wings and Chicago Black Hawks between October 6, 1955 and November 7, 1962.

MOST CONSECUTIVE 30-OR-MORE GOAL SEASONS:
14 — **Mike Gartner,** Washington, Minnesota, NY Rangers, 1979-80 – 1992-93.
13 — Bobby Hull, Chicago, 1959-60 – 1971-72.
— Phil Esposito, Boston, NY Rangers, 1967-68 – 1979-80.
— Wayne Gretzky, Edmonton, Los Angeles, 1979-80 – 1991-92.
12 — Marcel Dionne, Detroit, Los Angeles, 1974-75 – 1985-86.
10 — Darryl Sittler, Toronto, Philadelphia, 1973-74 – 1982-83.
— Mike Bossy, NY Islanders, 1977-78 – 1986-87.
— Jari Kurri, Edmonton, 1980-81 – 1989-90.

MOST 40-OR-MORE GOAL SEASONS:
12 — **Wayne Gretzky,** Edmonton, Los Angeles, in 14 seasons.
10 — Marcel Dionne, Detroit, Los Angeles, NY Rangers, in 18 seasons.
9 — Mike Bossy, NY Islanders, in 10 seasons.
— Mike Gartner, Washington, Minnesota, NY Rangers, in 14 seasons.
8 — Bobby Hull, Chicago, Winnipeg, Hartford, in 16 seasons.
— Phil Esposito, Chicago, Boston, NY Rangers, in 18 seasons.
— Jari Kurri, Edmonton, Los Angeles, in 12 seasons.
— Dale Hawerchuk, Winnipeg, Buffalo, in 10 seasons.

MOST CONSECUTIVE 40-OR-MORE GOAL SEASONS:
12 — **Wayne Gretzky,** Edmonton, Los Angeles, 1979-80 – 1990-91.
9 — Mike Bossy, NY Islanders, 1977-78 – 1985-86.
7 — Phil Esposito, Boston, 1968-69 – 1974-75.
— Michel Goulet, Quebec, 1981-82 – 1987-88.
— Jari Kurri, Edmonton, 1982-83 – 1988-89.
— Luc Robitaille, Los Angeles, 1986-87 – 1992-93.
6 — Guy Lafleur, Montreal, 1974-75 – 1979-80.
— Joe Mullen, St. Louis, Calgary, 1983-84 – 1988-89.
— Mario Lemieux, Pittsburgh, 1984-85 – 1989-90.
— Steve Yzerman, Detroit, 1987-88 – 1992-93.

MOST 50-OR-MORE GOAL SEASONS:
9 — **Mike Bossy,** NY Islanders, in 11 seasons.
— **Wayne Gretzky,** Edmonton, Los Angeles, in 14 seasons.
6 — Guy Lafleur, Montreal, NY Rangers, Quebec, in 17 seasons.
— Marcel Dionne, Detroit, Los Angeles, NY Rangers, in 18 seasons.
5 — Bobby Hull, Chicago, Winnipeg, Hartford, in 16 seasons.
— Phil Esposito, Chicago, Boston, NY Rangers, in 18 seasons.

MOST CONSECUTIVE 50-OR-MORE GOAL SEASONS:
9 — **Mike Bossy,** NY Islanders, 1977-78 – 1985-86.
8 — Wayne Gretzky, Edmonton, 1979-80 – 1986-87.
6 — Guy Lafleur, Montreal, 1974-75 – 1979-80.
5 — Phil Esposito, Boston, 1970-71 – 1974-75.
— Marcel Dionne, Los Angeles, 1978-79 – 1982-83.

MOST 60-OR-MORE GOAL SEASONS:
5 — **Mike Bossy,** NY Islanders, in 10 seasons.
— **Wayne Gretzky,** Edmonton, Los Angeles, in 14 seasons.
4 — Phil Esposito, Chicago, Boston, NY Rangers, in 18 seasons.

MOST CONSECUTIVE 60-OR-MORE GOAL SEASONS:
4 — **Wayne Gretzky,** Edmonton, 1981-82 – 1984-85.
3 — Mike Bossy, NY Islanders, 1980-81 – 1982-83.
— Brett Hull, St. Louis, 1989-90 – 1991-92.
2 — Phil Esposito, Boston, 1970-71 – 1971-72, 1973-74 – 1974-75.
— Jari Kurri, Edmonton, 1984-85 – 1985-86.
— Mario Lemieux, Pittsburgh, 1987-88 – 1988-89.
— Steve Yzerman, Detroit, 1988-89 – 1989-90.

MOST 100-OR-MORE POINT SEASONS:
13 —**Wayne Gretzky,** Edmonton, Los Angeles, 1979-80 – 1991-92.
8 —Marcel Dionne, Detroit, 1974-75; Los Angeles, 1976-77; 1978-79 – 1982-83; 1984-85.
—Mario Lemieux, Pittsburgh, 1984-85 – 1989-90; 1991-92; 1992-93.
7 —Mike Bossy, NY Islanders, 1978-79; 1980-81 – 1985-86.
—Peter Stastny, Quebec, 1980-81 – 1985-86; 1987-88.
6 —Phil Esposito, Boston, 1968-69; 1970-71 – 1974-75.
—Bobby Orr, Boston, 1969-70 – 1974-75.
—Guy Lafleur, Montreal, 1974-75 – 1979-80.
—Bryan Trottier, NY Islanders, 1977-78 – 1981-82; 1983-84.
—Dale Hawerchuk, Winnipeg, 1981-82; 1983-84 – 1987-88.
—Jari Kurri, Edmonton, 1982-83 – 1986-87; 1988-89.
—Mark Messier, Edmonton, 1982-83 – 1983-84; 1986-87 – 1987-88; 1989-90; NY Rangers, 1991-92.

MOST CONSECUTIVE 100-OR-MORE POINT SEASONS:
13 —**Wayne Gretzky,** Edmonton, Los Angeles, 1979-80 – 1991-92.
6 —Bobby Orr, Boston, 1969-70 – 1974-75.
—Guy Lafleur, Montreal, 1974-75 – 1979-80.
—Mike Bossy, NY Islanders, 1980-81 – 1985-86.
—Peter Stastny, Quebec, 1980-81 – 1985-86.
—Mario Lemieux, Pittsburgh, 1984-85 – 1989-90.

MOST 40-OR-MORE WIN SEASONS BY A GOALTENDER:
3 —**Jacques Plante,** Montreal, NY Rangers, St. Louis, Toronto, Boston in 18 seasons.
2 —Terry Sawchuck, Detroit, Boston, Toronto, Los Angeles, NY Rangers in 21 seasons.
—Bernie Parent, Boston, Philadelphia, Toronto in 13 seasons.
—Ken Dryden, Montreal, in 8 seasons.
—Ed Belfour, Chicago, in 5 seasons.

MOST CONSECUTIVE 40-OR-MORE WIN SEASONS BY A GOALTENDER:
2 —**Terry Sawchuk,** Detroit, 1950-51 – 1951-52.
—**Bernie Parent,** Philadelphia, 1973-74 – 1974-75.
—**Ken Dryden,** Montreal, 1975-76 – 1976-77.

MOST 30-OR-MORE WIN SEASONS BY A GOALTENDER:
8 —**Tony Esposito,** Montreal, Chicago in 16 seasons.
7 —Jacques Plante, Montreal, NY Rangers, St. Louis, Toronto, Boston in 18 seasons.
—Ken Dryden, Montreal, in 8 seasons.
6 —Glenn Hall, Detroit, Chicago, St. Louis in 18 seasons.

MOST CONSECUTIVE 30-OR-MORE WIN SEASONS BY A GOALTENDER:
7 —**Tony Esposito,** Chicago, 1969-70 – 1975-76.
6 —Jacques Plante, Montreal, 1954-55 – 1959-60.
5 —Ken Dryden, Montreal, 1974-75 – 1978-79.
4 —Terry Sawchuk, Detroit, 1950-51 – 1953-54.
—Ed Giacomin, NY Rangers, 1966-67 – 1969-70.

Single Season

MOST GOALS, ONE SEASON:
92 —**Wayne Gretzky,** Edmonton, 1981-82. 80 game schedule.
87 —Wayne Gretzky, Edmonton, 1983-84. 80 game schedule.
86 —Brett Hull, St. Louis, 1990-91. 80 game schedule.
85 —Mario Lemieux, Pittsburgh, 1988-89. 80 game schedule.
76 —Phil Esposito, Boston, 1970-71. 78 game schedule.
—Alexander Mogilny, Buffalo, 1992-93. 84 game schedule.
—Teemu Selanne, Winnipeg, 1992-93. 84 game schedule.
73 —Wayne Gretzky, Edmonton, 1984-85. 80 game schedule.
72 —Brett Hull, St. Louis, 1989-90. 80 game schedule.
71 —Jari Kurri, Edmonton, 1984-85 80 game schedule.
—Wayne Gretzky, Edmonton, 1982-83. 80 game schedule.
70 —Mario Lemieux, Pittsburgh, 1987-1988. 80 game schedule.
—Bernie Nicholls, Los Angeles, 1988-89. 80 game schedule.
—Brett Hull, St. Louis, 1991-92. 80 game schedule.

MOST ASSISTS, ONE SEASON:
163 —**Wayne Gretzky,** Edmonton , 1985-86. 80 game schedule.
135 —Wayne Gretzky, Edmonton, 1984-85. 80 game schedule.
125 —Wayne Gretzky, Edmonton, 1982-83. 80 game schedule.
122 —Wayne Gretzky, Los Angeles, 1990-91. 80 game schedule.
121 —Wayne Gretzky, Edmonton, 1986-87. 80 game schedule.
120 —Wayne Gretzky, Edmonton, 1981-82. 80 game schedule.
118 —Wayne Gretzky, Edmonton, 1983-84. 80 game schedule.
114 —Wayne Gretzky, Los Angeles, 1988-89. 80 game schedule.
—Mario Lemieux, Pittsburgh, 1988-89. 80 game schedule.
109 —Wayne Gretzky, Edmonton, 1980-81. 80 game schedule.
—Wayne Gretzky, Edmonton, 1987-88. 80 game schedule.
102 —Bobby Orr, Boston, 1970-71. 78 game schedule.
—Wayne Gretzky, Los Angeles, 1989-90. 80 game schedule.

MOST POINTS, ONE SEASON:
215 —**Wayne Gretzky,** Edmonton, 1985-86. 80 game schedule.
212 —Wayne Gretzky, Edmonton, 1981-82. 80 game schedule.
208 —Wayne Gretzky, Edmonton, 1984-85. 80 game schedule.
205 —Wayne Gretzky, Edmonton, 1983-84. 80 game schedule.
199 —Mario Lemieux, Pittsburgh, 1988-89. 80 game schedule.
196 —Wayne Gretzky, Edmonton, 1982-83. 80 game schedule.
183 —Wayne Gretzky, Edmonton, 1986-87. 80 game schedule.
168 —Mario Lemieux, Pittsburgh, 1987-88, 80 game schedule.
—Wayne Gretzky, Los Angeles, 1988-89. 80 game schedule.
164 —Wayne Gretzky, Edmonton, 1980-81. 80 game schedule.
163 —Wayne Gretzky, Los Angeles, 1990-91. 80 game schedule.
160 —Mario Lemieux, Pittsburgh, 1992-93. 84 game schedule.
155 —Steve Yzerman, Detroit, 1988-89. 80 game schedule.
152 —Phil Esposito, Boston, 1970-71. 78 game schedule.
150 —Bernie Nicholls, Los Angeles, 1988-89. 80 game schedule.

MOST THREE-OR-MORE GOAL GAMES, ONE SEASON:
10 —**Wayne Gretzky,** Edmonton, 1981-82. 6 three-goal games, 3 four-goal games, 1 five-goal game.
—**Wayne Gretzky,** Edmonton, 1983-84. 6 three-goal games, 4 four-goal games.
9 —Mike Bossy, NY Islanders, 1980-81. 6 three-goal games, 3 four-goal games.
—Mario Lemieux, Pittsburgh, 1988-89. 7 three-goal games, 1 four-goal game, 1 five-goal game.
8 —Brett Hull, St. Louis, 1991-92. 8 three-goal games.
7 —Joe Malone, Montreal, 1917-18. 2 three-goal games, 2 four-goal games, 3 five-goal games.
—Phil Esposito, Boston, 1970-71. 7 three-goal games.
—Rick Martin, Buffalo, 1975-76. 6 three-goal games, 1 four-goal game.
—Alexander Mogilny, Buffalo, 1992-93. 5 three-goal games, 2 four-goal games.

HIGHEST GOALS-PER-GAME AVERAGE, ONE SEASON (AMONG PLAYERS WITH 20-OR-MORE GOALS):
2.20 —**Joe Malone,** Montreal, 1917-18, with 44G in 20GP.
1.64 —Cy Denneny, Ottawa, 1917-18, with 36G in 22GP.
—Newsy Lalonde, Montreal, 1917-18, with 23G in 14GP.
1.63 —Joe Malone, Qebec, 1919-20, with 39G in 24GP.
1.57 —Newsy Lalonde, Montreal, 1919-20, with 36G in 23GP.
1.50 —Joe Malone, Hamilton, 1920-21, with 30G in 20GP.

HIGHEST GOALS-PER-GAME AVERAGE, ONE SEASON (AMONG PLAYERS WITH 50-OR-MORE GOALS):
1.18 —**Wayne Gretzky,** Edmonton, 1983-84, with 87G in 74GP.
1.15 —Wayne Gretzky, Edmonton, 1981-82, with 92G in 80GP.
—Mario Lemieux, Pittsburgh, 1992-93, with 69G in 60GP.
1.12 —Mario Lemieux, Pittsburgh, 1988-89, with 85G in 76GP.
1.10 —Brett Hull, St. Louis, 1990-91, with 86G in 78GP.
1.00 —Maurice Richard, Montreal, 1944-45, with 50G in 50GP.
.99 —Alexander Mogilny, Buffalo, 1992-93, with 76G in 77GP.
.97 —Phil Esposito, Boston, 1970-71, with 76G in 78GP.
—Jari Kurri, Edmonton, 1984-85, with 71G in 73GP.
.96 —Brett Hull, St. Louis, 1991-92, with 70G in 73GP.

Mike Bossy (#22) recorded seven 100-point campaigns in ten seasons with the NY Islanders.

HIGHEST ASSISTS-PER-GAME AVERAGE, ONE SEASON (AMONG PLAYERS WITH 35-OR-MORE ASSISTS):

2.04 — **Wayne Gretzky,** Edmonton, 1985-86, with 163A in 80GP.
1.70 — Wayne Grezky, Edmonton, 1987-88, with 109A in 64GP.
1.69 — Wayne Gretzky, Edmonton, 1984-85, with 135A in 80GP.
1.59 — Wayne Gretzky, Edmonton, 1983-84, with 118A in 74GP.
1.56 — Wayne Gretzky, Edmonton, 1982-83, with 125A in 80GP.
1.56 — Wayne Gretzky, Los Angeles, 1990-91, with 122A in 78GP.
1.53 — Wayne Gretzky, Edmonton, 1986-87, with 121A in 79GP.
1.52 — Mario Lemieux, Pittsburgh, 1992-93, with 91A in 60GP.
1.50 — Wayne Gretzky, Edmonton, 1981-82, with 120A in 80GP.
1.50 — Mario Lemieux, Pittsburgh, 1988-89, with 114A in 76GP.

HIGHEST POINTS-PER-GAME AVERAGE, ONE SEASON (AMONG PLAYERS WITH 50-OR-MORE POINTS):

2.77 — **Wayne Gretzky,** Edmonton, 1983-84, with 205PTS in 74GP.
2.69 — Wayne Gretzky, Edmonton, 1985-86, with 215PTS in 80GP.
2.67 — Mario Lemieux, Pittsburgh, 1992-93, with 160PTS in 60GP.
2.65 — Wayne Gretzky, Edmonton, 1981-82, with 212PTS in 80GP.
2.62 — Mario Lemieux, Pittsburgh, 1988-89, with 199PTS in 78GP.
2.60 — Wayne Gretzky, Edmonton, 1984-85, with 208PTS in 80GP.
2.45 — Wayne Gretzky, Edmonton, 1982-83, with 196PTS in 80GP.
2.33 — Wayne Gretzky, Edmonton, 1987-88, with 149PTS in 64GP.
2.32 — Wayne Gretzky, Edmonton, 1986-87, with 183PTS in 79GP.
2.18 — Mario Lemieux, Pittsburgh, 1987-88, with 168PTS in 77GP.
2.15 — Wayne Gretzky, Los Angeles, 1988-89, with 168PTS in 78GP.
2.09 — Wayne Gretzky, Los Angeles, 1990-91, with 163 PTS in 78GP.
2.08 — Mario Lemieux, Pittsburgh, 1989-90, with 123 PTS in 59GP.
2.05 — Wayne Gretzky, Edmonton, 1980-81, with 164PTS in 80GP.

In 1988-89, Bernie Nicholls became the fifth NHL player to score 70 goals in one season.

MOST GOALS, ONE SEASON, INCLUDING PLAYOFFS:

100 — **Wayne Gretzky,** Edmonton, 1983-84, 87G in 74 regular-season games and 13G in 19 playoff games.
97 — Wayne Gretzky, Edmonton, 1981-82, 92G in 80 regular-season games and 5G in 5 playoff games.
— Mario Lemieux, Pittsburgh, 1988-89, 85G in 76 regular-season games and 12G in 11 playoff games.
— Brett Hull, St. Louis, 1990-91, 86G in 78 regular-season games and 11G in 13 playoff games.
90 — Wayne Gretzky, Edmonton, 1984-85, 73G in 80 regular season games and 17G in 18 playoff games.
— Jari Kurri, Edmonton, 1984-85, 71G in 80 regular season games and 19G in 18 playoff games.
85 — Mike Bossy, NY Islanders, 1980-81, 68G in 79 regular-season games and 17G in 18 playoff games.
— Brett Hull, St. Louis, 1989-90, 72G in 80 regular season games and 13G in 12 playoff games.
83 — Wayne Gretzky, Edmonton, 1982-83, 71G in 73 regular-season games and 12G in 16 playoff games.
— Alexander Mogilny, Buffalo, 1992-93, 76G in 77 regular-season games and 7G in 7 playoff games.
81 — Mike Bossy, NY Islanders, 1981-82, 64G in 80 regular-season games and 17G in 19 playoff games.

MOST ASSISTS, ONE SEASON, INCLUDING PLAYOFFS:

174 — **Wayne Gretzky,** Edmonton, 1985-86, 163A in 80 regular-season games and 11A in 10 playoff games.
165 — Wayne Gretzky, Edmonton, 1984-85, 135A in 80 regular-season games and 30A in 18 playoff games.
151 — Wayne Gretzky, Edmonton, 1982-83, 125A in 80 regular-season games and 26A in 16 playoff games.
150 — Wayne Gretzky, Edmonton, 1986-87, 121A in 79 regular-season games and 29A in 21 playoff games.
140 — Wayne Gretzky, Edmonton, 1983-84, 118A in 74 regular-season games and 22A in 19 playoff games.
— Wayne Gretzky, Edmonton, 1987-88, 109A in 64 regular-season games and 31A in 19 playoff games.
133 — Wayne Gretzky, Los Angeles, 1990-91, 122A in 78 regular-season games and 11A in 12 playoff games.
131 — Wayne Gretzky, Los Angeles, 1988-89, 114A in 78 regular-season games and 17A in 11 playoff games.
127 — Wayne Gretzky, Edmonton, 1981-82, 120A in 80 regular-season games and 7A in 5 playoff games.
123 — Wayne Gretzky, Edmonton, 1980-81, 109A in 80 regular-season games and 14A in 9 playoff games.
121 — Mario Lemieux, Pittsburgh, 1988-89, 114A in 76 regular-season games and 7A in 11 playoff games.

MOST POINTS, ONE SEASON, INCLUDING PLAYOFFS:

255 — **Wayne Gretzky,** Edmonton, 1984-85, 208PTS in 80 regular-season games and 47PTS in 18 playoff games.
240 — Wayne Gretzky, Edmonton, 1983-84, 205PTS in 74 regular-season games and 35PTS in 19 playoff games.
234 — Wayne Gretzky, Edmonton, 1982-83, 196PTS in 80 regular-season games and 38PTS in 16 playoff games.
— Wayne Gretzky, Edmonton, 1985-86, 215PTS in 80 regular-season games and 19PTS in 10 playoff games.
224 — Wayne Gretzky, Edmonton, 1981-82, 212PTS in 80 regular-season games and 12PTS in 5 playoff games.
218 — Mario Lemieux, Pittsburgh, 1988-89, 199PTS in 76 regular-season games and 19PTS in 11 playoff games.
217 — Wayne Gretzky, Edmonton, 1986-87, 183PTS in 79 regular-season games and 34PTS in 21 playoff games.
192 — Wayne Gretzky, Edmonton, 1987-88, 149PTS in 64 regular-season games and 43PTS in 19 playoff games.
190 — Wayne Gretzky, Los Angeles, 1988-89, 168PTS in 78 regular-season games and 22PTS in 11 playoff games.
185 — Wayne Gretzky, Edmonton, 1980-81, 164PTS in 80 regular-season games and 21PTS in 9 playoff games.

MOST GOALS, ONE SEASON, BY A DEFENSEMAN:

48 — **Paul Coffey,** Edmonton, 1985-86. 80 game schedule.
46 — Bobby Orr, Boston, 1974-75. 80 game schedule.
40 — Paul Coffey, Edmonton, 1983-84. 80 game schedule.
39 — Doug Wilson, Chicago, 1981-82. 80 game schedule.
37 — Bobby Orr, Boston, 1970-71. 78 game schedule.
— Bobby Orr, Boston, 1971-72. 78 game schedule.
— Paul Coffey, Edmonton, 1984-85 80 game schedule..
34 — Kevin Hatcher, Washington, 1992-93. 84 game schedule.
33 — Bobby Orr, Boston, 1969-70. 76 game schedule.
32 — Bobby Orr, Boston, 1973-74. 78 game schedule.
31 — Denis Potvin, NY Islanders, 1975-76. 80 game schedule.
— Denis Potvin, NY Islanders, 1978-79. 80 game schedule.
— Raymond Bourque, Boston, 1983-84. 80 game schedule.
— Phil Housley, Buffalo, 1983-84. 80 game schedule.

MOST GOALS, ONE SEASON, BY A CENTER:

92 — **Wayne Gretzky,** Edmonton, 1981-82. 80 game schedule.
87 — Wayne Gretzky, Edmonton, 1983-84. 80 game schedule.
85 — Mario Lemieux, Pittsburgh, 1988-89. 80 game schedule.
76 — Phil Esposito, Boston, 1970-71. 78 game schedule.
73 — Wayne Gretzky, Edmonton, 1984-85. 80 game schedule.
71 — Wayne Gretzky, Edmonton, 1982-83. 80 game schedule.
70 — Mario Lemieux, Pittsburgh, 1987-88. 80 game schedule.
— Bernie Nicholls, Los Angeles, 1988-89. 80 game schedule.

MOST GOALS, ONE SEASON, BY A RIGHT WINGER:
- **86 — Brett Hull**, St. Louis, 1990-91. 80 game schedule.
- 76 — Alexander Mogilny, Buffalo, 1992-93. 84 game schedule.
- — Teemu Selanne, Winnipeg, 1992-93. 84 game schedule.
- 72 — Brett Hull, St. Louis, 1989-90. 80 game schedule.
- 71 — Jari Kurri, Edmonton, 1984-85. 80 game schedule.
- 70 — Brett Hull, St. Louis, 1991-92. 80 game schedule.
- 69 — Mike Bossy, NY Islanders, 1978-79. 80 game schedule.
- 68 — Jari Kurri, Edmonton, 1985-86. 80 game schedule..
- — Mike Bossy, NY Islanders, 1980-81. 80 game schedule.
- 66 — Lanny McDonald, Calgary, 1982-83. 80 game schedule.
- 64 — Mike Bossy, NY Islanders, 1981-82. 80 game schedule.
- 61 — Reggie Leach, Philadelphia, 1975-76. 80 game schedule.
- — Mike Bossy, NY Islanders, 1985-86. 80 game schedule.

MOST GOALS, ONE SEASON, BY A LEFT WINGER:
- **63 — Luc Robitaille**, Los Angeles, 1992-93. 84 game schedule.
- 60 — Steve Shutt, Montreal, 1976-77. 80 game schedule.
- 58 — Bobby Hull, Chicago, 1968-69. 76 game schedule.
- 57 — Michel Goulet, Quebec, 1982-83. 80 game schedule.
- 56 — Charlie Simmer, Los Angeles, 1979-80. 80 game schedule.
- — Charlie Simmer, Los Angeles, 1980-81. 80 game schedule.
- — Michel Goulet, Quebec, 1983-84. 80 game schedule.
- 55 — Michel Goulet, Quebec, 1984-85. 80 game schedule.
- — John Ogrodnick, Detroit, 1984-85. 80 game schedule.
- — Kevin Stevens, Pittsburgh, 1992-93. 84 game schedule.

MOST GOALS, ONE SEASON, BY A ROOKIE:
- **76 — Teemu Selanne**, Winnipeg, 1992-93. 84 game schedule.
- 53 — Mike Bossy, NY Islanders, 1977-78. 80 game schedule.
- 51 — Joe Nieuwendyk, Calgary, 1987-88. 80 game schedule.
- 45 — Dale Hawerchuk, Winnipeg, 1981-82. 80 game schedule.
- — Luc Robitaille, Los Angeles, 1986-87. 80 game schedule.
- 44 — Richard Martin, Buffalo, 1971-72. 78 game schedule.
- — Barry Pederson, Boston, 1981-82. 80 game schedule.
- 43 — Steve Larmer, Chicago, 1982-83. 80 game schedule.
- — Mario Lemieux, Pittsburgh, 1984-85. 80 game schedule.

MOST GOALS, ONE SEASON, BY A ROOKIE DEFENSEMAN:
- **23 — Brian Leetch**, NY Rangers, 1988-89. 80 game schedule.
- 22 — Barry Beck, Colorado, 1977-78. 80 game schedule.
- 19 — Reed Larson, Detroit, 1977-78. 80 game schedule.
- — Phil Housley, Buffalo, 1982-83. 80 game schedule.

MOST ASSISTS, ONE SEASON, BY A DEFENSEMAN:
- **102 — Bobby Orr**, Boston, 1970-71. 78 game schedule.
- 90 — Paul Coffey, Edmonton, 1985-86. 80 game schedule.
- 90 — Bobby Orr, Boston, 1973-74. 78 game schedule.
- 89 — Bobby Orr, Boston, 1974-75. 80 game schedule.

MOST ASSISTS, ONE SEASON, BY A CENTER:
- **163 — Wayne Gretzky**, Edmonton, 1985-86. 80 game schedule.
- 135 — Wayne Gretzky, Edmonton, 1984-85. 80 game schedule.
- 125 — Wayne Gretzky, Edmonton, 1982-83. 80 game schedule.
- 122 — Wayne Gretzky, Los Angeles, 1990-91. 80 game schedule.
- 121 — Wayne Gretzky, Edmonton, 1986-87. 80 game schedule.
- 120 — Wayne Gretzky, Edmonton, 1981-82. 80 game schedule.
- 118 — Wayne Gretzky, Edmonton, 1983-84. 80 game schedule.
- 114 — Wayne Gretzky, Edmonton, 1988-89. 80 game schedule.
- — Mario Lemieux, Pittsburgh, 1988-89. 80 game schedule.
- 109 — Wayne Gretzky, Edmonton, 1980-81. 80 game schedule.
- — Wayne Gretzky, Edmonton, 1987-88. 80 game schedule.

MOST ASSISTS, ONE SEASON, BY A RIGHT WINGER:
- **83 — Mike Bossy**, NY Islanders, 1981-82. 80 game schedule.
- 80 — Guy Lafleur, Montreal, 1976-77. 80 game schedule.
- 77 — Guy Lafleur, Montreal, 1978-79. 80 game schedule.

MOST ASSISTS, ONE SEASON, BY A LEFT WINGER:
- **70 — Joe Juneau**, Boston, 1992-93. 84 game schedule.
- 69 — Kevin Stevens, Pittsburgh, 1991-92. 80 game schedule.
- 67 — Mats Naslund, Montreal, 1985-86. 80 game schedule.
- 65 — John Bucyk, Boston, 1970-71. 78 game schedule.
- — Michel Goulet, Quebec, 1983-84. 80 game schedule.
- 64 — Mark Messier, Edmonton, 1983-84. 80 game schedule.
- 63 — Luc Robitaille, Los Angeles, 1991-92. 80 game schedule.

Bobby Hull, shown here with the Art Ross Trophy in 1959-60, ranks third in single-season goal-scoring by a left winger with 58 goals in 1968-69

INDIVIDUAL RECORDS, Single Season • **147**

MOST ASSISTS, ONE SEASON, BY A ROOKIE:
70 — Peter Stastny, Quebec, 1980-81. 80 game schedule.
— **Joe Juneau,** Boston, 1992-93. 84 game schedule.
63 — Bryan Trottier, NY Islanders, 1975-76. 80 game schedule.
62 — Sergei Makarov, Calgary, 1989-90. 80 game schedule.
60 — Larry Murphy, Los Angeles, 1980-81. 80 game schedule.

MOST ASSISTS, ONE SEASON, BY A ROOKIE DEFENSEMAN:
60 — Larry Murphy, Los Angeles, 1980-81. 80 game schedule.
55 — Chris Chelios, Montreal, 1984-85. 80 game schedule.
50 — Stefan Persson, NY Islanders, 1977-78. 80 game schedule.
— Gary Suter, Calgary, 1985-86, 80 game schedule..
49 — Nicklas Lidstrom, Detroit, 1991-92. 80 game schedule.
48 — Raymond Bourque, Boston, 1979-80. 80 game schedule.
— Brian Leetch, NY Rangers, 1988-89. 80 game schedule.

MOST POINTS, ONE SEASON, BY A DEFENSEMAN:
139 — Bobby Orr, Boston, 1970-71. 78 game schedule.
138 — Paul Coffey, Edmonton,1985-86. 80 game schedule.
135 — Bobby Orr, Boston, 1974-75. 80 game schedule.
126 — Paul Coffey, Edmonton, 1983-84. 80 game schedule.
122 — Bobby Orr, Boston, 1973-74. 78 game schedule.

MOST POINTS, ONE SEASON, BY A CENTER:
215 — Wayne Gretzky, Edmonton, 1985-86. 80 game schedule.
212 — Wayne Gretzky, Edmonton, 1981-82. 80 game schedule.
208 — Wayne Gretzky, Edmonton, 1984-85. 80 game schedule.
205 — Wayne Gretzky, Edmonton, 1983-84. 80 game schedule.
199 — Mario Lemieux, Pittsburgh, 1988-89. 80 game schedule.
196 — Wayne Gretzky, Edmonton, 1982-83. 80 game schedule.
183 — Wayne Gretzky, Edmonton, 1986-87. 80 game schedule.
168 — Mario Lemieux, Pittsburgh, 1987-88. 80 game schedule.
— Wayne Gretzky, Los Angeles, 1988-89. 80 game schedule.
164 — Wayne Gretzky, Edmonton, 1980-81. 80 game schedule.
163 — Wayne Gretzky, Los Angeles, 1990-91. 80 game schedule.

MOST POINTS, ONE SEASON, BY A RIGHT WINGER:
147 — Mike Bossy, NY Islanders, 1981-82. 80 game schedule.
136 — Guy Lafleur, Montreal, 1976-77. 80 game schedule.
135 — Jari Kurri, Edmonton, 1984-85. 80 game schedule.
132 — Guy Lafleur, Montreal, 1977-78. 80 game schedule.
— Teemu Selanne, Winnipeg, 1992-93. 84 game schedule.

MOST POINTS, ONE SEASON, BY A LEFT WINGER:
125 — Luc Robitaille, Los Angeles, 1992-93. 84 game schedule.
123 — Kevin Stevens, Pittsburgh, 1991-92. 80 game schedule.
121 — Michel Goulet, Quebec, 1983-84. 80 game schedule.
116 — John Bucyk, Boston, 1970-71. 78 game schedule.
112 — Bill Barber, Philadelphia, 1975-76. 80 game schedule.

MOST POINTS, ONE SEASON, BY A ROOKIE:
132 — Teemu Selanne, Winnipeg, 1992-93, 84 game schedule.
109 — Peter Stastny, Quebec, 1980-81. 80 game schedule.
103 — Dale Hawerchuk, Winnipeg, 1981-82. 80 game schedule.
102 — Joe Juneau, Boston, 1992-93. 84 game schedule.
100 — Mario Lemieux, Pittsburgh, 1984-85. 80 game schedule.

MOST POINTS, ONE SEASON, BY A ROOKIE DEFENSEMAN:
76 — Larry Murphy, Los Angeles, 1980-81. 80 game schedule.
71 — Brian Leetch, NY Rangers, 1988-89. 80 game schedule.
68 — Gary Suter, Calgary, 1985-86. 80 game schedule.
66 — Phil Housley, Buffalo, 1982-83. 80 game schedule.
65 — Raymond Bourque, Boston, 1979-80. 80 game schedule.
64 — Chris Chelios, Montreal, 1984-85. 80 game schedule.

MOST POINTS, ONE SEASON, BY A GOALTENDER:
14 — Grant Fuhr, Edmonton, 1983-84. (14A)
9 — Curtis Joseph, St. Louis, 1991-92. (9A)
8 — Mike Palmateer, Washington, 1980-81. (8A)
— Grant Fuhr, Edmonton, 1987-88. (8A)
— Ron Hextall, Philadelphia, 1988-89. (8A)
— Tom Barrasso, Pittsburgh, 1992-93. (8A)
7 — Ron Hextall, Philadelphia, 1987-88. (1G-6A)
— Mike Vernon, Calgary, 1987-88. (7A)

MOST POWER-PLAY GOALS, ONE SEASON:
34 — Tim Kerr, Philadelphia, 1985-86. 80 game schedule.
32 — Dave Andreychuk, Buffalo, Toronto, 1992-93. 84 game schedule.
31 — Joe Nieuwendyk, Calgary, 1987-88. 80 game schedule.
— Mario Lemieux, Pittsburgh, 1988-89. 80 game schedule.
29 — Michel Goulet, Quebec, 1987-88. 80 game schedule.
— Brett Hull, St. Louis, 1990-91. 80 game schedule.
— Brett Hull, St. Louis, 1992-93. 84 game schedule.

MOST SHORTHAND GOALS, ONE SEASON:
13 — Mario Lemieux, Pittsburgh, 1988-89. 80 game schedule.
12 — Wayne Gretzky, Edmonton, 1983-84. 80 game schedule.
11 — Wayne Gretzky, Edmonton, 1984-85. 80 game schedule.
10 — Marcel Dionne, Detroit, 1974-75. 80 game schedule.
— Mario Lemieux, Pittsburgh, 1987-88. 80 game schedule.
— Dirk Graham, Chicago, 1988-89. 80 game schedule.

Detroit defenseman Nicklas Lidstrom recorded 49 assists in his rookie season with the Red Wings.

MOST SHOTS ON GOAL, ONE SEASON:
550 — Phil Esposito, Boston, 1970-71. 78 game schedule.
426 — Phil Esposito, Boston, 1971-72. 78 game schedule.
414 — Bobby Hull, Chicago, 1968-69. 76 game schedule.

MOST PENALTY MINUTES, ONE SEASON:
472 — Dave Schultz, Philadelphia, 1974-75.
409 — Paul Baxter, Pittsburgh, 1981-82.
408 — Mike Peluso, Chicago, 1991-92.
405 — Dave Schultz, Los Angeles, Pittsburgh, 1977-78.

MOST SHUTOUTS, ONE SEASON:
22 — George Hainsworth, Montreal, 1928-29. 44GP
15 — Alex Connell, Ottawa, 1925-26. 36GP
— Alex Connell, Ottawa, 1927-28. 44GP
— Hal Winkler, Boston, 1927-28. 44GP
— Tony Esposito, Chicago, 1969-70. 63GP
14 — George Hainsworth, Montreal, 1926-27. 44GP

LONGEST WINNING STREAK, ONE SEASON, BY A GOALTENDER:
17 — Gilles Gilbert, Boston, 1975-76.
14 — Don Beaupre, Minnesota, 1985-86.
— Ross Brooks, Boston, 1973-74.
— Tiny Thompson, Boston, 1929-30.
— Tom Barrasso, Pittsburgh, 1992-93.

LONGEST UNDEFEATED STREAK BY A GOALTENDER:
32 Games — Gerry Cheevers, Boston, 1971-72. 24W-8T.
31 Games — Pete Peeters, Boston, 1982-83. 26W-5T.
27 Games — Pete Peeters, Philadelphia, 1979-80. 22W-5T.
23 Games — Frank Brimsek, Boston, 1940-41. 15W-8T.
— Glenn Resch, NY Islanders, 1978-79. 15W-8T.
— Grant Fuhr, Edmonton, 1981-82. 15W-8T.

MOST GAMES, ONE SEASON, BY A GOALTENDER:
75 — Grant Fuhr, Edmonton, 1987-88.
74 — Ed Belfour, Chicago, 1990-91.
73 — Bernie Parent, Philadelphia, 1973-74.
72 — Gary Smith, Vancouver, 1974-75.
— Don Edwards, Buffalo, 1977-78.
— Tim Cheveldae, Detroit, 1991-92.
71 — Gary Smith, California, 1970-71.
— Tony Esposito, Chicago, 1974-75.
— Ed Belfour, Chicago, 1992-93.

Toronto Maple Leafs defenceman Ian Turnbull set an NHL record with five goals in a single game against the Detroit Red Wings on February 2, 1977.

MOST WINS, ONE SEASON, BY A GOALTENDER:
47 — Bernie Parent, Philadelphia, 1973-74.
44 — Bernie Parent, Philadelphia, 1974-75.
— Terry Sawchuk, Detroit, 1950-51.
— Terry Sawchuk, Detroit, 1951-52.

LONGEST SHUTOUT SEQUENCE BY A GOALTENDER:
461 Minutes, 29 Seconds — Alex Connell, Ottawa, 1927-28, six consecutive
shutouts. (Forward passing not permitted in attacking zones in 1927-1928.)
343 Minutes, 5 Seconds — George Hainsworth, Montreal, 1928-29, four consecutive
shutouts.
324 Minutes, 40 Seconds — Roy Worters, NY Americans, 1930-31, four consecutive
shutouts.
309 Minutes, 21 Seconds — Bill Durnan, Montreal, 1948-49, four consecutive
shutouts.

MOST GOALS, 50 GAMES FROM START OF SEASON:
61 — Wayne Gretzky, Edmonton, 1981-82. Oct. 7, 1981 - Jan. 22, 1982.
(80-game schedule)
— **Wayne Gretzky,** Edmonton, 1983-84. Oct. 5, 1983 - Jan. 25, 1984.
(80-game schedule)
54 — Mario Lemieux, Pittsburgh, 1988-89. Oct. 7, 1988 - Jan. 31, 1989.
(80-game schedule)
53 — Wayne Gretzky, Edmonton, 1984-85. Oct. 11, 1984 - Jan. 28, 1985.
(80-game schedule)
52 — Brett Hull, St. Louis, 1990-91. Oct. 4, 1990 - Jan. 26, 1991. (80-game
schedule).
50 — Maurice Richard, Montreal, 1944-45. Oct. 28, 1944 - March 18, 1945.
(50-game schedule)
— Mike Bossy, NY Islanders, 1980-81. Oct. 11, 1980 - Jan. 24, 1981.
(80-game schedule)
— Brett Hull, St. Louis, 1991-92. Oct. 5, 1991 – Jan 28, 1992. (80 game
schedule)

LONGEST CONSECUTIVE POINT-SCORING STREAK FROM START OF SEASON:
51 Games — Wayne Gretzky, Edmonton, 1983-84. 61G-92A-153PTS during
streak which was stopped by goaltender Markus Mattsson and
Los Angeles on Jan. 28, 1984.

LONGEST CONSECUTIVE POINT SCORING STREAK:
51 Games — Wayne Gretzky, Edmonton, 1983-84. 61G-92A-153PTS during
streak.
46 Games — Mario Lemieux, Pittsburgh, 1989-90. 39G-64A-103PTS during streak.
39 Games — Wayne Gretzky, Edmonton, 1985-86. 33G-75A-108PTS during streak.
30 Games — Wayne Gretzky, Edmonton, 1982-83. 24G52A76PTS during streak.
— Mats Sundin, Quebec, 1992-93. 21G-25A-46PTS during streak.
28 Games — Guy Lafleur, Montreal, 1976-77. 19G-42A-61PTS during streak.
— Wayne Gretzky, Edmonton, 1984-85. 20G-43A-63PTS during streak.
— Mario Lemieux, Pittsburgh, 1985-86. 21G-38A-59PTS during streak.
— Paul Coffey, Edmonton, 1985-86. 16G-39A-55PTS during streak.
— Steve Yzerman, Detroit, 1988-89. 29G-36A-65PTS during streak.

LONGEST CONSECUTIVE POINT-SCORING STREAK BY A DEFENSEMAN:
28 Games — Paul Coffey, Edmonton, 1985-86. 16G-39A-55PTS during streak.
19 Games — Ray Bourque, Boston, 1987-88. 6G-21A-27PTS during streak.
17 Games — Ray Bourque, Boston, 1984-85. 4G-24A-28PTS during streak.
— Brian Leetch, NY Rangers, 1991-92. 5G-24A-29PTS during streak.
16 Games — Gary Suter, Calgary, 1987-88. 8G-17A-25PTS during streak.
15 Games — Bobby Orr, Boston, 1970-71. 10G-23A-33PTS during streak.
— Bobby Orr, Boston, 1973-74. 8G-15A-23PTS during streak.
— Steve Duchesne, Quebec, 1992-93. 4G-17A-21PTS during streak.

LONGEST CONSECUTIVE GOAL-SCORING STREAK:
16 Games — Harry (Punch) Broadbent, Ottawa, 1921-22.
25 goals during streak.
14 Games — Joe Malone, Montreal, 1917-18. 35 goals during streak.
13 Games — Newsy Lalonde, Montreal, 1920-21. 24 goals during streak.
— Charlie Simmer, Los Angeles, 1979-80. 17 goals during streak.
12 Games — Cy Denneny, Ottawa, 1917-18. 23 goals during streak.
— Dave Lumley, Edmonton, 1981-82. 15 goals during streak.
— Mario Lemieux, Pittsburgh, 1992-93. 18 goals during streak.

LONGEST CONSECUTIVE ASSIST-SCORING STREAK:
23 Games — Wayne Gretzky, Los Angeles, 1990-91. 48A during streak.
18 Games — Adam Oates, Boston, 1992-93. 28A during streak.
17 Games — Wayne Gretzky, Edmonton, 1983-84. 38A during streak.
— Paul Coffey, Edmonton, 1985-86. 27A during streak.
— Wayne Gretzky, Los Angeles, 1989-90. 35A during streak.
15 Games — Jari Kurri, Edmonton, 1983-84. 21A during streak.
— Brian Leetch, NY Rangers, 1991-92. 23A during streak.

Single Game

MOST GOALS, ONE GAME:
7 — Joe Malone, Quebec Bulldogs, Jan. 31, 1920, at Quebec. Quebec 10,
Toronto 6.
6 — Newsy Lalonde, Montreal, Jan. 10, 1920, at Montreal. Montreal 14,
Toronto 7.
— Joe Malone, Quebec Bulldogs, March 10, 1920, at Quebec. Quebec 10,
Ottawa 4.
— Corb Denneny, Toronto, Jan. 26, 1921, at Toronto. Toronto 10, Hamilton 3.
— Cy Denneny, Ottawa, March 7, 1921, at Ottawa. Ottawa 12, Hamilton 5.
— Syd Howe, Detroit, Feb. 3, 1944, at Detroit. Detroit 12, NY Rangers 2.
— Red Berenson, St. Louis, Nov. 7, 1968, at Philadelphia. St. Louis 8,
Philadelphia 0
— Darryl Sittler, Toronto, Feb. 7, 1976, at Toronto. Toronto 11, Boston 4.

MOST GOALS, ONE ROAD GAME:
  6 — **Red Berenson,** St. Louis, Nov. 7, 1968, at Philadelphia. St. Louis 8, Philadelphia 0.
  5 — Joe Malone, Montreal, Dec. 19, 1917, at Ottawa. Montreal 9, Ottawa 4.
   — Redvers Green, Hamilton, Dec. 5, 1924, at Toronto. Hamilton 10, Toronto 3.
   — Babe Dye, Toronto, Dec. 22, 1924, at Boston. Toronto 10, Boston 2.
   — Harry Broadbent, Mtl. Maroons, Jan. 7, 1925, at Hamilton. Mtl. Maroons 6, Hamilton 2.
   — Don Murdoch, NY Rangers, Oct. 12, 1976, at Minnesota. NY Rangers 10, Minnesota 4.
   — Tim Young, Minnesota, Jan. 15, 1979, at NY Rangers. Minnesota 8, NY Rangers 1.
   — Willy Lindstrom, Winnipeg, March 2, 1982, at Philadelphia. Winnipeg 7, Philadelphia 6.
   — Bengt Gustafsson, Washington, Jan. 8, 1984, at Philadelphia. Washington 7, Philadelphia 1.
   — Wayne Gretzky, Edmonton, Dec. 15, 1984, at St. Louis. Edmonton 8, St. Louis 2.
   — Dave Andreychuk, Buffalo, Feb. 6, 1986, at Boston. Buffalo 8, Boston 6.
   — Mats Sundin, Quebec, Mar. 5, 1992, at Hartford. Quebec 10, Hartford 4.
   — Mario Lemieux, Pittsburgh, Apr. 9, 1993, at New York. Pittsburgh 10, NY Rangers 4.

MOST ASSISTS, ONE GAME:
  7 — **Billy Taylor,** Detroit, March 16, 1947, at Chicago. Detroit 10, Chicago 6.
   — **Wayne Gretzky,** Edmonton, Feb. 15, 1980, at Edmonton. Edmonton 8, Washington 2.
   — **Wayne Gretzky,** Edmonton, Dec. 11, 1985, at Chicago. Edmonton 12, Chicago 9.
   — **Wayne Gretzky,** Edmonton, Feb. 14, 1986, at Edmonton. Edmonton 8, Quebec 2.
  6 — Elmer Lach, Montreal, Feb. 6, 1943.
   — Walter (Babe) Pratt, Toronto, Jan. 8, 1944.
   — Don Grosso, Detroit, Feb. 3, 1944.
   — Pat Stapleton, Chicago, March 30, 1969.
   — Ken Hodge, Boston, Feb. 9, 1971.
   — Bobby Orr, Boston, Jan. 1, 1973.
   — Ron Stackhouse, Pittsburgh, March 8, 1975.
   — Greg Malone, Pittsburgh, Nov. 28, 1979.
   — Mike Bossy, NY Islanders, Jan. 6, 1981.
   — Guy Chouinard, Calgary, Feb. 25, 1981.
   — Mark Messier, Edmonton, Jan. 4, 1984.
   — Patrik Sundstrom, Vancouver, Feb 29, 1984.
   — Wayne Gretzky, Edmonton, Dec. 20, 1985.
   — Paul Coffey, Edmonton, March 14, 1986.
   — Gary Suter, Calgary, Apr. 4, 1986.
   — Ron Francis, Hartford, March 5, 1987.
   — Mario Lemieux, Pittsburgh, Oct. 15, 1988.
   — Bernie Nicholls, Los Angeles, Dec. 1, 1988.
   — Mario Lemieux, Pittsburgh, Dec. 31, 1988.
   — Mario Lemieux, Pittsburgh, Dec. 5, 1992.
   — Doug Gilmour, Toronto, Feb. 13, 1993.

MOST ASSISTS, ONE ROAD GAME:
  7 — **Billy Taylor,** Detroit, March 16, 1947, at Chicago. Detroit 10, Chicago 6.
   — **Wayne Gretzky,** Edmonton, Dec. 11, 1985, at Chicago. Edmonton 12, Chicago 9.
  6 — Bobby Orr, Boston, Jan. 1, 1973, at Vancouver. Boston 8, Vancouver 2.
   — Patrik Sundstrom, Vancouver, Feb. 29, 1984, at Pittsburgh. Vancouver 9, Pittsburgh 5.
   — Mario Lemieux, Pittsburgh, Dec. 5, 1992, at San Jose. Pittsburgh 9, San Jose 4.

MOST POINTS, ONE GAME:
 10 — **Darryl Sittler,** Toronto, Feb. 7, 1976, at Toronto, 6G-4A. Toronto 11, Boston 4.
  8 — Maurice Richard, Montreal, Dec. 28, 1944, at Montreal, 5G-3A. Montreal 9, Detroit 1.
   — Bert Olmstead, Montreal, Jan. 9, 1954, at Montreal, 4G-4A. Montreal 12, Chicago 1.
   — Tom Bladon, Philadelphia, Dec. 11, 1977, at Philadelphia, 4G-4A. Philadelphia 11, Cleveland 1.
   — Bryan Trottier, NY Islanders, Dec. 23, 1978, at New York, 5G-3A. NY Islanders 9, NY Rangers 4.
   — Peter Stastny, Quebec, Feb. 22, 1981, at Washington, 4G-4A. Quebec 11, Washington 7.
   — Anton Stastny, Quebec, Feb. 22, 1981, at Washington, 3G-5A. Quebec 11, Washington 7.
   — Wayne Gretzky, Edmonton, Nov. 19, 1983, at Edmonton, 3G-5A. Edmonton 13, New Jersey 4.
   — Wayne Gretzky, Edmonton, Jan. 4, 1984, at Edmonton, 4G-4A. Edmonton 12 Minnesota 8.
   — Paul Coffey, Edmonton, March 14, 1986, at Edmonton, 2G-6A. Edmonton 12, Detroit 3.
   — Mario Lemieux, Pittsburgh, Oct. 15, 1988, at Pittsburgh, 2G-6A. Pittsburgh 9, St. Louis 2.
   — Mario Lemieux, Pittsburgh, Dec. 31, 1988, at Pittsburgh, 5G-3A. Pittsburgh 8, New Jersey 6.
   — Bernie Nicholls, Los Angeles, Dec. 1, 1988, at Los Angeles, 2G-6A. Los Angeles 9, Toronto 3.
  7 — Seven points have been scored by one player in one game on 36 occasions. Most recently, Mario Lemieux of Pittsburgh (Dec. 5, 1992 vs. San Jose).

MOST POINTS, ONE ROAD GAME:
  8 — **Peter Stastny,** Quebec, Feb. 22, 1981, at Washington, 4G-4A. Quebec 11, Washington 7.
   — **Anton Stastny,** Quebec, Feb. 22, 1981, at Washington, 3G-5A. Quebec 11, Washington 7.
  7 — Billy Taylor, Detroit, March 16, 1947, at Chicago, 7A. Detroit 10, Chicago. 6.
   — Red Berenson, St. Louis, Nov. 7, 1968, at Philadelphia, 6G-1A. St. Louis 8, Philadelphia 0.
   — Gilbert Perreault, Buffalo, Feb. 1, 1976, at California, 2G-5A. Buffalo 9, California 5.
   — Peter Stastny, Quebec, April 1, 1982, at Boston, 3G-4A. Quebec 8, Boston 5.
   — Wayne Gretzky, Edmonton, Nov. 6, 1983, at Winnipeg, 4G-3A. Edmonton 8, Winnipeg 5.
   — Patrik Sundstrom, Vancouver, Feb. 29, 1984, at Pittsburgh, 1G-6A. Vancouver 9, Pittsburgh 5.
   — Wayne Gretzky, Edmonton, Dec. 11, 1985, at Chicago. 7A, Edmonton 12, Chicago 9.
   — Mario Lemieux, Pittsburgh, Jan. 21, 1989, at Edmonton, 2G, 5A. Pittsburgh 7, Edmonton 4.
   — Cam Neely, Boston, Oct. 16, 1988, at Chicago, 3G, 4A. Boston 10, Chicago 3.
   — Dino Ciccarelli, Washington, March 18, 1989, at Hartford, 4G, 3A. Washington 8, Hartford 2.
   — Mats Sundin, Quebec, Mar. 5, 1992, at Hartford, 5G, 2A. Quebec 10, Hartford 4.
   — Mario Lemieux, Pittsburgh, Dec. 5, 1992, at San Jose, 1G, 6A. Pittsburgh 9, San Jose 4.

MOST GOALS, ONE GAME, BY A DEFENSEMAN:
  5 — **Ian Turnbull,** Toronto, Feb. 2, 1977, at Toronto. Toronto 9, Detroit 1.
  4 — Harry Cameron, Toronto, Dec. 26, 1917, at Toronto. Toronto 7, Montreal 5.
   — Harry Cameron, Montreal, March 3, 1920, at Quebec City. Montreal 16, Que. Bulldogs 3.
   — Sprague Cleghorn, Montreal, Jan. 14, 1922, at Montreal. Montreal 10, Hamilton 6.
   — Johnny McKinnon, Pit. Pirates, Nov. 19, 1929, at Pittsburgh. Pit. Pirates 10, Toronto 5.
   — Hap Day, Toronto, Nov. 19, 1929, at Pittsburgh. Pit. Pirates 10, Toronto 5.
   — Tom Bladon, Philadelphia, Dec. 11, 1977, at Philadelphia. Philadelphia 11, Cleveland 1.
   — Ian Turnbull, Los Angeles, Dec. 12, 1981, at Los Angeles. Los Angeles 7, Vancouver 5.
   — Paul Coffey, Edmonton, Oct. 26, 1984, at Calgary. Edmonton 6, Calgary 5.

MOST GOALS BY ONE PLAYER IN HIS FIRST NHL GAME:
  3 — **Alex Smart,** Montreal, Jan. 14, 1943, at Montreal. Montreal 5, Chicago 1.
   — **Real Cloutier,** Quebec, Oct. 10, 1979, at Quebec. Atlanta 5, Quebec 3.

MOST GOALS, ONE GAME, BY A PLAYER IN HIS FIRST NHL SEASON:
  5 — **Howie Meeker,** Toronto, Jan. 8, 1947, at Toronto. Toronto 10, Chicago 4.
   — **Don Murdoch,** NY Rangers, Oct. 12, 1976, at Minnesota. NY Rangers 10, Minnesota 4.

MOST ASSISTS, ONE GAME, BY A DEFENSEMAN:
  6 — **Babe Pratt,** Toronto, Jan. 8, 1944, at Toronto. Toronto 12, Boston 3.
   — **Pat Stapleton,** Chicago, March 30, 1969, at Chicago. Chicago 9, Detroit 5.
   — **Bobby Orr,** Boston, Jan. 1, 1973, at Vancouver, Boston 8, Vancouver 2.
   — **Ron Stackhouse,** Pittsburgh, March 8, 1975, at Pittsburgh. Pittsburgh 8, Philadelphia 2.
   — **Paul Coffey,** Edmonton, Mar. 14, 1986, at Edmonton. Edmonton 12, Detroit 3.
   — **Gary Suter,** Calgary, Apr. 4, 1986, at Calgary. Calgary 9, Edmonton 3.

MOST ASSISTS BY ONE PLAYER IN HIS FIRST NHL GAME:
  4 — **Earl (Dutch) Reibel,** Detroit, Oct. 8, 1953, at Detroit. Detroit 4, NY Rangers 1.
   — **Roland Eriksson,** Minnesota, Oct. 6, 1976, at New York. NY Rangers 6, Minnesota 5.
  3 — Al Hill, Philadelphia, Feb. 14, 1977, at Philadelphia. Philadelphia 6, St. Louis 4.

MOST ASSISTS, ONE GAME, BY A PLAYER IN HIS FIRST NHL SEASON:
  7 — **Wayne Gretzky,** Edmonton, Feb. 15, 1980, at Edmonton. Edmonton 8, Washington 2.
  6 — Gary Suter, Calgary, Apr. 4, 1986, at Calgary. Calgary 9, Edmonton 3.

MOST ASSISTS, ONE GAME, BY A GOALTENDER:
  3 — **Jeff Reese,** Calgary, Feb. 10, 1993, at Calgary. Calgary 13, San Jose 1.

MOST POINTS, ONE GAME, BY A DEFENSEMAN:
  8 — **Tom Bladon,** Philadelphia, Dec. 11, 1977, at Philadelphia. 4G-4A. Philadelphia 11, Cleveland 1.
   — **Paul Coffey,** Edmonton, Mar. 14, 1986, at Edmonton. 2G-6A. Edmonton 12, Detroit 3.
  7 — Bobby Orr, Boston, Nov. 15, 1973, at Boston, 3G-4A. Boston 10, NY Rangers 2.

MOST POINTS BY ONE PLAYER IN HIS FIRST NHL GAME:
  5 — **Al Hill,** Philadelphia, Feb. 14, 1977, at Philadelphia. 2G-3A. Philadelphia 6, St. Louis 4.
  4 — Alex Smart, Montreal, Jan. 14, 1943, at Montreal, 3G-1A. Montreal 5, Chicago 1.
   — Earl (Dutch) Reibel, Detroit, Oct. 8, 1953, at Detroit. 4A. Detroit 4, NY Rangers 1.
   — Roland Eriksson, Minnesota, Oct. 6, 1976 at New York. 4A. NY Rangers 6, Minnesota 5.

MOST POINTS, ONE GAME, BY A PLAYER IN HIS FIRST NHL SEASON:

8 — **Peter Stastny,** Quebec, Feb. 22, 1981, at Washington. 4G-4A. Quebec 11, Washington 7.
— **Anton Stastny,** Quebec, Feb. 22, 1981, at Washington. 3G-5A. Quebec 11, Washington 7.
7 — Wayne Gretzky, Edmonton, Feb. 15, 1980, at Edmonton. 7A. Edmonton 8, Washington 2.
— Sergei Makarov, Calgary, Feb. 25, 1990, at Calgary, 2G-5A. Calgary 10, Edmonton 4.
6 — Wayne Gretzky, Edmonton, March 29, 1980, at Toronto. 2G-4A. Edmonton 8, Toronto 5.
— Gary Suter, Calgary, Apr. 4, 1986, at Calgary. 6A. Calgary 9, Edmonton 3.

MOST PENALTIES, ONE GAME:

10 — **Chris Nilan,** Boston, March 31, 1991, at Boston against Hartford. 6 minors, 2 majors, 1 10-minute misconduct.
9 — Jim Dorey, Toronto, Oct. 16, 1968, at Toronto against Pittsburgh. 4 minors, 2 majors, 2 10-minute misconducts, 1 game misconduct.
— Dave Schultz, Pittsburgh, Apr. 6, 1978, at Detroit. 5 minors, 2 majors, 2 10-minute misconducts.
— Randy Holt, Los Angeles, Mar. 11, 1979, at Philadelphia. 1 minor, 3 majors, 2 10-minute misconducts, 3 game misconducts.
— Russ Anderson, Pittsburgh, Jan. 19, 1980, at Pittsburgh. 3 minors, 3 majors, 3 game misconducts.
— Kim Clackson, Quebec, March 8, 1981, at Quebec. 4 minors, 3 majors, 2 game misconducts.
— Terry O'Reilly, Boston, Dec. 19, 1984 at Hartford. 5 minors, 3 majors, 1 game misconduct.
— Larry Playfair, Los Angeles, Dec. 9, 1986, at NY Islanders. 6 minors, 2 majors, 1 10-minute misconduct.
— Marty McSorley, Los Angeles, Apr. 14, 1992, at Vancouver. 5 minors, 2 majors, 1 10-minute misconduct, 1 game misconduct.

MOST PENALTY MINUTES, ONE GAME:

67 — **Randy Holt,** Los Angeles, Mar. 11, 1979, at Philadelphia. 1 minor, 3 majors, 2 10-minute misconducts, 3 game misconducts.
55 — Frank Bathe, Philadelphia, Mar. 11, 1979, at Philadelphia. 3 majors, 2 10-minute misconducts, 2 game misconducts.
51 — Russ Anderson, Pittsburgh, Jan. 19, 1980, at Pittsburgh. 3 minors, 3 majors, 3 game misconducts.

MOST GOALS, ONE PERIOD:

4 — **Harvey (Busher) Jackson,** Toronto, Nov. 20, 1934, at St. Louis, third period. Toronto 5, St. Louis Eagles 2.
— **Max Bentley,** Chicago, Jan. 28, 1943, at Chicago, third period. Chicago 10, NY Rangers 1.
— **Clint Smith,** Chicago, March 4, 1945, at Chicago, third period. Chicago 6, Montreal 4.
— **Red Berenson,** St. Louis, Nov. 7, 1968, at Philadelphia, second period. St. Louis 8, Philadelphia 0.
— **Wayne Gretzky,** Edmonton, Feb. 18, 1981, at Edmonton, third period. Edmonton 9, St. Louis 2.
— **Grant Mulvey,** Chicago, Feb. 3, 1982, at Chicago, first period. Chicago 9, St. Louis 5.
— **Bryan Trottier,** NY Islanders, Feb. 13, 1982, at New York, second period. NY Islanders 8, Philadelphia 2.
— **Al Secord,** Chicago, Jan. 7, 1987 at Chicago, second period. Chicago 6, Toronto 4.
— **Joe Nieuwendyk,** Calgary, Jan. 11, 1989, at Calgary, second period. Calgary 8, Winnipeg 3.

MOST ASSISTS, ONE PERIOD:

5 — **Dale Hawerchuk,** Winnipeg, Mar. 6, 1984, at Los Angeles, second period. Winnipeg 7, Los Angeles 3.
4 — Four assists have been recorded in one period on 42 occasions since Buddy O'Connor of Montreal first accomplished the feat vs. NY Rangers on Nov. 8, 1942. Most recent player, Owen Nolan of Quebec (Mar. 5, 1992 vs Hartford).

MOST POINTS, ONE PERIOD:

6 — **Bryan Trottier,** NY Islanders, Dec. 23, 1978, at NY Islanders, second period. 3G, 3A. NY Islanders 9, NY Rangers 4.
5 — Les Cunningham, Chicago, Jan. 28, 1940, at Chicago, third period. 2G, 3A. Chicago 8, Montreal 1.
— Max Bentley, Chicago, Jan. 28, 1943, at Chicago, third period. 4G, 1A, Chicago 10, NY Rangers 1.
— Leo Labine, Boston, Nov. 28, 1954, at Boston, second period, 3G, 2A. Boston 6, Detroit 2.
— Darryl Sittler, Toronto, Feb. 7, 1976, at Toronto, second period. 3G, 2A. Toronto 11, Boston 4.
— Dale Hawerchuk, Winnipeg, Mar. 6, 1984, at Los Angeles, second period. 5A. Winnipeg 7, Los Angeles 3.
— Jari Kurri, Edmonton, October 26, 1984 at Edmonton, second period. Edmonton 8, Los Angeles 2.
— Pat Elynuik, Winnipeg, Jan. 20, 1989, at Winnipeg, second period. 2G, 3A. Winnipeg 7, Pittsburgh 3.
— Ray Ferraro, Hartford, Dec. 9, 1989, at Hartford, first period. 3G, 2A. Hartford 7, New Jersey 3.
— Stephane Richer, Montreal, Feb. 14, 1990, at Montreal, first period. 2G, 3A. Montreal 10, Vancouver 1.
— Cliff Ronning, Vancouver, Apr. 15, 1993, at Los Angeles, third period. 3G, 2A. Vancouver 8, Los Angeles 6.

MOST PENALTIES, ONE PERIOD:

9 — **Randy Holt,** Los Angeles, Mar. 11, 1979, at Philadelphia, first period. 1 minor, 3 majors, 2 10-minute misconducts, 3 game misconducts.

MOST PENALTY MINUTES, ONE PERIOD:

67 — **Randy Holt,** Los Angeles, Mar. 11, 1979, at Philadelphia, first period. 1 minor, 3 majors, 2 10-minute misconducts, 3 game misconducts.

FASTEST GOAL BY A ROOKIE IN HIS FIRST NHL GAME:

15 Seconds — **Gus Bodnar,** Toronto, Oct. 30, 1943. Toronto 5, NY Rangers 2.
18 Seconds — Danny Gare, Buffalo, Oct. 10, 1974. Buffalo 9, Boston 5.
20 Seconds — Alexander Mogilny, Buffalo, Oct. 5, 1989. Buffalo 4, Quebec 3.

FASTEST GOAL FROM START OF A GAME:

5 Seconds — **Doug Smail,** Winnipeg, Dec. 20, 1981, at Winnipeg. Winnipeg 5, St. Louis 4.
— **Bryan Trottier,** NY Islanders, Mar. 22, 1984, at Boston. NY Islanders 3, Boston 3.
— **Alexander Mogilny,** Buffalo, Dec. 21, 1991, at Toronto. Buffalo 4, Toronto 1.
6 Seconds — Henry Boucha, Detroit, Jan. 28, 1973, at Montreal. Detroit 4, Montreal 2.
— Jean Pronovost, Pittsburgh, March 25, 1976, at St. Louis. St. Louis 5, Pittsburgh 2.
7 Seconds — Charlie Conacher, Toronto, Feb. 6, 1932, at Toronto. Toronto 6, Boston 0.
— Danny Gare, Buffalo, Dec. 17, 1978, at Buffalo. Buffalo 6, Vancouver 3.
— Dave Williams, Los Angeles, Feb. 14, 1987 at Los Angeles. Los Angeles 5, Harford 2.
8 Seconds — Ron Martin, NY Americans, Dec. 4, 1932, at New York. NY Americans 4, Montreal 2.
— Chuck Arnason, Colorado, Jan. 28, 1977, at Atlanta. Colorado 3, Atlanta 3.
— Wayne Gretzky, Edmonton, Dec. 14, 1983, at New York. Edmonton 9, NY Rangers 4.
— Gaetan Duchesne, Washington, Mar. 14, 1987, at St. Louis. Washington 3, St. Louis 1.
— Tim Kerr, Philadelphia, March 7, 1989, at Philadelphia. Philadelphia 4, Edmonton 4.
— Grant Ledyard, Buffalo, Dec. 4, 1991, at Winnipeg. Buffalo 4, Winnipeg 4.

FASTEST GOAL FROM START OF A PERIOD:

4 Seconds — **Claude Provost,** Montreal, Nov. 9, 1957, at Montreal, second period. Montreal 4, Boston 2.
— **Denis Savard,** Chicago, Jan. 12, 1986, at Chicago, third period. Chicago 4, Hartford 2.

FASTEST TWO GOALS:

4 Seconds — **Nels Stewart,** Mtl. Maroons, Jan. 3, 1931, at Montreal at 8:24 and 8:28, third period. Mtl. Maroons 5, Boston 3.
5 Seconds — Pete Mahovlich, Montreal, Feb. 20, 1971, at Montreal at 12:16 and 12:21, third period. Montreal 7, Chicago 1.
6 Seconds — Jim Pappin, Chicago, Feb. 16, 1972, at Chicago at 2:57 and 3:03, third period. Chicago 3, Philadelphia 3.
— Ralph Backstrom, Los Angeles, Nov. 2, 1972, at Los Angeles at 8:30 and 8:36, third period. Los Angeles 5, Boston 2.
— Lanny McDonald, Calgary, Mar. 22, 1984, at Calgary at 16:23 and 16:29, first period. Detroit 6, Calgary 4.
— Sylvain Turgeon, Hartford, Mar. 28, 1987, at Hartford at 13:59 and 14:05, second period. Hartford 5, Pittsburgh 4.

FASTEST THREE GOALS:

21 Seconds — **Bill Mosienko,** Chicago, March 23, 1952, at New York, against goaltender Lorne Anderson. Mosienko scored at 6:09, 6:20 and 6:30 of third period, all with both teams at full strength. Chicago 7, NY Rangers 6.
44 Seconds — Jean Béliveau, Montreal, Nov. 5, 1955, at Montreal, against goaltender Terry Sawchuk. Béliveau scored at :42, 1:08 and 1:26 of second period, all with Montreal holding a 6-4 man advantage. Montreal 4, Boston 2.

FASTEST THREE ASSISTS:

21 Seconds — **Gus Bodnar,** Chicago, March 23, 1952, at New York, Bodnar assisted on Bill Mosienko's three goals at 6:09, 6:20, 6:30 of third period. Chicago 7, NY Rangers 6.
44 Seconds — Bert Olmstead, Montreal, Nov. 5, 1955, at Montreal against Boston. Olmstead assisted on Jean Béliveau's three goals at :42, 1:08 and 1:26 of second period. Montreal 4, Boston 2.

Top 100 All-Time Goal-Scoring Leaders

* active player

(figures in parentheses indicate ranking of top 10 by goals per game)

	Player	Seasons	Games	Goals	Goals per game
1.	Gordie Howe, Det., Hfd.	26	1767	801	.453
*2.	Wayne Gretzky, Edm., L.A.	14	1044	765	.733 (4)
3.	Marcel Dionne, Det., L.A., NYR	18	1348	731	.542
4.	Phil Esposito, Chi., Bos., NYR	18	1282	717	.559
5.	Bobby Hull, Chi., Wpg., Hfd.	16	1063	610	.574 (9)
*6.	Mike Gartner, Wsh., Min., NYR	14	1089	583	.535
7.	Mike Bossy, NYI	10	752	573	.762 (3)
8.	Guy Lafleur, Mtl., NYR, Que.	17	1126	560	.497
9.	John Bucyk, Det., Bos.	23	1540	556	.361
10.	Maurice Richard, Mtl.	18	978	544	.556
11.	Stan Mikita, Chi.	22	1394	541	.388
12.	Frank Mahovlich, Tor., Det., Mtl.	18	1181	533	.451
*13.	Michel Goulet, Que., Chi.	14	1033	532	.515
*14.	Jari Kurri, Edm., L.A.	12	909	524	.576 (7)
*15.	Bryan Trottier, NYI, Pit.	17	1238	520	.420
16.	Gilbert Perreault, Buf.	17	1191	512	.430
17.	Jean Beliveau, Mtl.	20	1125	507	.451
18.	Lanny McDonald, Tor., Col., Cgy.	16	1111	500	.450
19.	Jean Ratelle, NYR, Bos.	21	1281	491	.383
20.	Norm Ullman, Det., Tor.	20	1410	490	.348
*21.	Dino Ciccarelli, Min., Wsh., Det.	13	907	485	.535
22.	Darryl Sittler, Tor., Phi., Det.	15	1096	484	.442
*23.	Mario Lemieux, Pit.	9	577	477	.827 (1)
*24.	Glenn Anderson, Edm., Tor.	13	976	459	.470
25.	Alex Delvecchio, Det.	24	1549	456	.294
*26.	Mark Messier, Edm., NYR	14	1005	452	.450
*27.	Dale Hawerchuk, Wpg., Buf.	12	951	449	.472
28.	Rick Middleton, NYR, Bos.	14	1005	448	.446
*29.	Steve Yzerman, Det.	10	757	445	.588 (6)
*30.	Peter Stastny, Que., N.J.	13	954	444	.465
31.	Rick Vaive, Van., Tor., Chi., Buf.	13	876	441	.503
*32.	Joey Mullen, St.L., Cgy., Pit.	13	842	433	.514
33.	Yvan Cournoyer, Mtl.	16	968	428	.442
*34.	Dave Taylor, L.A.	16	1078	427	.396
35.	Steve Shutt, Mtl., L.A.	13	930	424	.456
*36.	Denis Savard, Chi., Mtl.	13	946	423	.447
37.	Bill Barber, Phi.	12	903	420	.465
*38.	Brian Propp, Phi., Bos., Min.	14	951	413	.434
39.	Garry Unger, Tor., Det., St.L., Atl., L.A., Edm.	16	1105	413	.374
*40.	Steve Larmer, Chi.	13	891	406	.456
41.	Rod Gilbert, NYR	18	1065	406	.381
*42.	John Ogrodnick, Det., Que., NYR	14	928	402	.433
*43.	Bernie Nicholls, L.A., NYR, Edm., N.J.	12	824	397	.482
44.	Dave Keon, Tor., Hfd.	18	1296	396	.306
45.	Pierre Larouche, Pit., Mtl., Hfd., NYR	14	812	395	.486
46.	Bernie Geoffrion, Mtl., NYR	16	883	393	.445
47.	Jean Pronovost, Pit., Atl., Wsh.	14	998	391	.392
48.	Dean Prentice, NYR, Bos., Det., Pit., Min.	22	1378	391	.284
*49.	Pat LaFontaine, NYI, Buf.	10	671	386	.575 (8)
50.	Richard Martin, Buf., L.A.	11	685	384	.561
*51.	Brian Bellows, Min., Mtl.	11	835	382	.457
52.	Reggie Leach, Bos., Cal., Phi., Det.	13	934	381	.408
53.	Ted Lindsay, Det., Chi.	17	1068	379	.355
54.	Butch Goring, L.A., NYI, Bos.	16	1107	375	.339
*55.	Dave Andreychuk, Buf., Tor.	11	794	373	.470
56.	Rick Kehoe, Tor., Pit.	14	906	371	.409
57.	Tim Kerr, Phi., NYR, Hfd.	13	655	370	.565(10)
58.	Bernie Federko, St.L., Det.	14	1000	369	.369
59.	Jacques Lemaire, Mtl.	12	853	366	.429
60.	Peter McNab, Buf., Bos., Van., N.J.	14	954	363	.381
61.	Ivan Boldirev, Bos., Cal., Chi., Atl., Van., Det.	15	1052	361	.343
62.	Bobby Clarke, Phi.	15	1144	358	.313
63.	Henri Richard, Mtl.	20	1256	358	.285
64.	Bobby Smith, Min., Mtl.	15	1077	357	.331
*65.	Brett Hull, Cgy., St.L.	8	459	356	.776 (2)
66.	Dennis Maruk, Cal., Cle., Wsh., Min.	14	888	356	.401
67.	Wilf Paiement, K.C., Col., Tor., Que., NYR, Buf., Pit.	14	946	356	.376
68.	Danny Gare, Buf., Det., Edm.	13	827	354	.428
*69.	Mike Foligno, Det., Buf., Tor.	14	975	351	.360
70.	Rick MacLeish, Phi., Hfd., Pit., Det.	14	846	349	.413
71.	Andy Bathgate, NYR, Tor., Det., Pit.	17	1069	349	.326
*72.	Luc Robitaille, L.A.	7	557	348	.625 (5)
73.	Charlie Simmer, Cal., Cle., L.A., Bos., Pit.	14	712	342	.480
*74.	Dave Christian, Wpg., Wsh., Bos., St.L., Chi.	14	1000	340	.340
75.	Ron Ellis, Tor.	16	1034	332	.321
*76.	Paul Coffey, Edm., Pit., L.A., Det.	13	953	330	.346

Dave Andreychuk, who, in 1992-93, became the only NHL player to score 25-or-more goals for two teams in one NHL season, ranks 55th on the all-time goals scored list.

	Player	Seasons	Games	Goals	Goals per game
77.	Mike Bullard, Pit., Cgy., St.L., Phi., Tor.	11	727	329	.453
78.	Ken Hodge, Chi., Bos., NYR	13	881	328	.372
*79.	Brent Sutter, NYI, Chi.	13	820	325	.396
80.	John Tonelli, NYI, Cgy., L.A., Chi., Que.	14	1028	325	.316
81.	Nels Stewart, Mtl. M., Bos., NYA	15	654	324	.495
82.	Paul MacLean, St. L., Wpg., Det.	11	719	324	.451
83.	Pit Martin, Det., Bos., Chi., Van.	17	1101	324	.294
84.	Vic Hadfield, NYR, Pit.	16	1002	323	.322
85.	Tony McKegney, Buf., Que., Min., St.L., Det., Chi.	14	912	320	.351
86.	Clark Gillies, NYI, Buf.	14	958	319	.333
*87.	Pat Verbeek, N.J., Hfd.	11	783	318	.406
88.	Don Lever, Van., Atl., Cgy., Col., N.J., Buf.	15	1020	313	.307
*89.	Ron Francis, Hfd., Pit.	12	882	311	.353
90.	Denis Potvin, NYI	15	1060	310	.292
91.	Bob Nevin, Tor., NYR, Min., L.A.	18	1128	307	.272
92.	Brian Sutter, St.L.	12	779	303	.389
93.	Dennis Hull, Chi., Det.	14	959	303	.316
94.	George Armstrong, Tor.	21	1187	296	.249
*95.	Cam Neely, Van., Bos.	10	586	292	.498
96.	Tom Lysiak, Atl., Chi.	13	919	292	.318
*97.	Ray Bourque, Bos.	14	1028	291	.283
98.	Peter Mahovlich, Det., Mtl., Pit.	16	884	288	.326
*99.	Tony Tanti, Chi., Van., Pit., Buf.	11	697	287	.412
*100.	Bob Carpenter, Wsh., NYR, L.A., Bos.	12	825	285	.345

Top 100 All-Time Assist Leaders

*active player

(figures in parentheses indicate ranking of top 10 in order of assists per game)

Player	Seasons	Games	Assists	Assists per game
*1. Wayne Gretzky, Edm., L.A.	14	1044	1563	1.497 (1)
2. Gordie Howe, Det., Hfd.	26	1767	1049	.594
3. Marcel Dionne, Det., L.A., NYR	18	1348	1040	.772
4. Stan Mikita, Chi.	22	1394	926	.664
*5. Bryan Trottier, NYI, Pit.	17	1238	890	.719
6. Phil Esposito, Chi., Bos., NYR	18	1282	873	.681
*7. Paul Coffey, Edm., Pit., L.A., Det.	13	953	871	.914 (4)
8. Bobby Clarke, Phi.	15	1144	852	.745
9. Alex Delvecchio, Det.	24	1549	825	.533
10. Gilbert Perreault, Buf.	17	1191	814	.683
11. John Bucyk, Det., Bos.	23	1540	813	.528
*12. Ray Bourque, Bos.	14	1028	806	.784(10)
13. Guy Lafleur, Mtl., NYR, Que.	17	1126	793	.704
*14. Mark Messier, Edm., NYR	14	1005	780	.776
*15. Peter Stastny, Que., N.J.	13	954	777	.814 (6)
16. Jean Ratelle, NYR, Bos.	21	1281	776	.606
*17. Denis Savard, Chi., Mtl.	13	946	769	.813 (7)
*18. Dale Hawerchuk, Wpg., Buf.	12	951	763	.802 (8)
19. Bernie Federko, St.L., Det.	14	1000	761	.761
20. Larry Robinson, Mtl., L.A.	20	1384	750	.542
21. Denis Potvin, NYI	15	1060	742	.700
22. Norm Ullman, Det., Tor.	20	1410	739	.524
23. Jean Beliveau, Mtl.	20	1125	712	.633
*24. Mario Lemieux, Pit.	9	577	697	1.208 (2)
25. Henri Richard, Mtl.	20	1256	688	.548
26. Brad Park, NYR, Bos., Det.	17	1113	683	.614
27. Bobby Smith, Min., Mtl.	15	1077	679	.630
*28. Ron Francis, Hfd., Pit.	12	882	675	.765
*29. Jari Kurri, Edm., L.A.	12	909	666	.733
30. Bobby Orr, Bos., Chi.	12	657	645	.982 (3)
31. Darryl Sittler, Tor., Phi., Det.	15	1096	637	.581
32. Borje Salming, Tor., Det.	17	1148	637	.555
*33. Dave Taylor, L.A.	16	1078	635	.589
*34. Larry Murphy, L.A., Wsh., Min., Pit.	13	1020	631	.619
35. Andy Bathgate, NYR, Tor., Det., Pit.	17	1069	624	.584
36. Rod Gilbert, NYR	18	1065	615	.577
*37. Steve Yzerman, Det.	10	757	595	.786 (9)
*38. Doug Wilson, Chi., S.J.	16	1024	590	.576
*39. Michel Goulet, Que., Chi.	14	1033	590	.571
40. Dave Keon, Tor., Hfd.	18	1296	590	.455
*41. Bernie Nicholls, L.A., NYR, Edm., N.J.	12	824	580	.704
*42. Phil Housley, Buf., Wpg.	11	840	575	.685
43. Frank Mahovlich, Tor., Det., Mtl.	18	1181	570	.483
*44. Dale Hunter, Que., Wsh.	13	1002	570	.569
*45. Brian Propp, Phi., Bos., Min.	14	951	561	.590
46. Bobby Hull, Chi., Wpg., Hfd.	16	1063	560	.527
*47. Glenn Anderson, Edm., Tor.	13	976	559	.573
*48. Al MacInnis, Cgy.	12	728	555	.762
49. Mike Bossy, NYI	10	752	553	.735
50. Ken Linseman, Phi., Edm., Bos., Tor.	14	860	551	.641
51. Tom Lysiak, Atl., Chi.	13	919	551	.600
*52. Doug Gilmour, St.L., Cgy., Tor.	10	773	548	.709
*53. Neal Broten, Min.	13	876	547	.624
54. Red Kelly, Det., Tor.	20	1316	542	.412
55. Rick Middleton, NYR, Bos.	14	1005	540	.537
*56. Mike Gartner, Wsh., Min., NYR.	14	1089	524	.481
57. Dennis Maruk, Cal., Cle., Wsh., Min.	14	888	522	.588
*58. Mark Howe, Hfd., Phi., Det.	14	867	520	.600
*59. Steve Larmer, Chi.	13	891	517	.580
60. Wayne Cashman, Bos.	17	1027	516	.502
61. Butch Goring, L.A., NYI, Bos.	16	1107	513	.463
*62. Thomas Steen, Wpg.	12	843	511	.606
63. John Tonelli, NYI, Cgy., L.A., Chi., Que.	14	1028	511	.497
64. Lanny McDonald, Tor., Col., Cgy.	16	1111	506	.455
65. Ivan Boldirev, Bos., Cal., Chi., Atl., Van., Det.	15	1052	505	.480
66. Randy Carlyle, Tor., Pit., Wpg.	17	1055	499	.473
*67. Adam Oates, Det., St.L., Bos.	8	551	490	.889 (5)
*68. Joey Mullen, St.L., Cgy., Pit.	13	842	486	.577
69. Peter Mahovlich, Det., Mtl., Pit.	16	884	485	.549
70. Pit Martin, Det., Bos., Chi., Van.	17	1101	485	.441
*71. Dave Babych, Wpg., Hfd., Van.	13	857	484	.565
72. Ken Hodge, Chi., Bos., NYR.	13	881	472	.536
*73. Dino Ciccarelli, Min., Wsh., Det.	13	907	472	.520
74. Ted Lindsay, Det., Chi.	17	1068	472	.442
75. Jacques Lemaire, Mtl.	12	853	469	.550
76. Dean Prentice, NYR, Bos., Det., Pit., Min.	22	1378	469	.340
77. Phil Goyette, Mtl., NYR, St.L., Buf.	16	941	467	.496
78. Bill Barber, Phi.	12	903	463	.513
79. Reed Larson, Det., Bos., Edm., NYI, Min., Buf.	14	904	463	.512
*80. Scott Stevens, Wsh., St.L., N.J.	11	828	462	.558
81. Doug Mohns, Bos., Chi., Min., Atl., Wsh.	22	1390	462	.332
82. Bobby Rousseau, Mtl., Min., NYR	15	942	458	.486
83. Wilf Paiement, K.C., Col., Tor., Que., NYR, Buf., Pit.	14	946	458	.484
84. Murray Oliver, Det., Bos., Tor., Min.	17	1127	454	.403
85. Doug Harvey, Mtl., NYR, Det., St.L.	19	1113	452	.406
86. Guy Lapointe, Mtl., St.L., Bos.	16	884	451	.510
87. Walt Tkaczuk, NYR	14	945	451	.477
88. Peter McNab, Buf., Bos., Van., N.J.	14	954	450	.472
89. Mel Bridgman, Phi., Chi., N.J., Det., Van.	14	977	449	.460
90. Bill Gadsby, Chi., NYR, Det.	20	1248	437	.350
*91. Dave Andreychuk, Buf., Tor.	11	794	436	.549
92. Yvan Cournoyer, Mtl.	16	968	435	.449
*93. Kirk Muller, N.J., Mtl.	9	714	433	.606
94. Ron Greschner, NYR	16	982	431	.439
*95. Dave Christian, Wpg., Wsh., Bos., St.L., Chi.	14	1000	430	.430
96. Bernie Geoffrion, Mtl., NYR	16	883	429	.486
*97. Brian Bellows, Min., Mtl.	11	835	428	.513
98. Pierre Larouche, Pit., Mtl., Hfd., NYR	14	812	427	.526
99. Paul Reinhart, Atl., Cgy., Van.	11	648	426	.657
*100. John Ogrodnick, Det., Que., NYR	14	928	425	.458

Jean Beliveau, who was the second NHL player to score 1,000 points in regular-season play, recorded 712 assists in 20 seasons with the Canadiens.

Top 100 All-Time Point Leaders

* active player

(figures in parentheses indicate ranking of top 10 by points per game)

Player	Seasons	Games	Goals	Assists	Points	Points per game
*1. Wayne Gretzky, Edm., L.A. .	14	1044	765	1563	**2328**	2.230 (1)
2. Gordie Howe, Det., Hfd.	26	1767	801	1049	**1850**	1.047
3. Marcel Dionne, Det., L.A., NYR	18	1348	731	1040	**1771**	1.314 (6)
4. Phil Esposito, Chi., Bos., NYR	18	1282	717	873	**1590**	1.240
5. Stan Mikita, Chi.	22	1394	541	926	**1467**	1.052
*6. Bryan Trottier, NYI, Pit.	17	1238	520	890	**1410**	1.139
7. John Bucyk, Det., Bos. .	23	1540	556	813	**1369**	.889
8. Guy Lafleur, Mtl., NYR, Que.	17	1126	560	793	**1353**	1.202
9. Gilbert Perreault, Buf.	17	1191	512	814	**1326**	1.113
10. Alex Delvecchio, Det.	24	1549	456	825	**1281**	.827
11. Jean Ratelle, NYR, Bos.	21	1281	491	776	**1267**	.989
*12. Mark Messier, Edm., NYR . .	14	1005	452	780	**1232**	1.226
13. Norm Ullman, Det., Tor. . .	20	1410	490	739	**1229**	.872
*14. Peter Stastny, Que., N.J. . . .	13	954	444	777	**1221**	1.280 (9)
15. Jean Beliveau, Mtl.	20	1125	507	712	**1219**	1.084
*16. Dale Hawerchuk, Wpg., Buf. .	12	951	449	763	**1212**	1.274(10)
17. Bobby Clarke, Phi.	15	1144	358	852	**1210**	1.058
*18. Paul Coffey, Edm., Pit., L.A., Det.	13	953	330	871	**1201**	1.260
*19. Denis Savard, Chi., Mtl.	13	946	423	769	**1192**	1.260
*20. Jari Kurri, Edm., L.A.	12	909	524	666	**1190**	1.309 (7)
*21. Mario Lemieux, Pit.	9	577	477	697	**1174**	2.035 (2)
22. Bobby Hull, Chi., Wpg., Hfd.	16	1063	610	560	**1170**	1.101
23. Bernie Federko, St.L., Det. . .	14	1000	369	761	**1130**	1.130
24. Mike Bossy, NYI	10	752	573	553	**1126**	1.497 (3)
*25. Michel Goulet, Que., Chi. . . .	14	1033	532	590	**1122**	1.086
26. Darryl Sittler, Tor., Phi., Det.	15	1096	484	637	**1121**	1.023
*27. Mike Gartner, Wsh., Min., NYR	14	1089	583	524	**1107**	1.017
28. Frank Mahovlich, Tor., Det., Mtl.	18	1181	533	570	**1103**	.934
*29. Ray Bourque, Bos.	14	1028	291	806	**1097**	1.067
*30. Dave Taylor, L.A.	16	1078	427	635	**1062**	.985
31. Denis Potvin, NYI	15	1060	310	742	**1052**	.992
32. Henri Richard, Mtl.	20	1256	358	688	**1046**	.833
*33. Steve Yzerman, Det.	10	757	445	595	**1040**	1.374 (5)
34. Bobby Smith, Min., Mtl.	15	1077	357	679	**1036**	.962
35. Rod Gilbert, NYR	18	1065	406	615	**1021**	.959
*36. Glenn Anderson, Edm., Tor. .	13	976	459	559	**1018**	1.043
37. Lanny McDonald, Tor., Col., Cgy.	16	1111	500	506	**1006**	.905
38. Rick Middleton, NYR, Bos. . .	14	1005	448	540	**988**	.983
*39. Ron Francis, Hfd., Pit.	12	882	311	675	**986**	1.118
40. Dave Keon, Tor., Hfd.	18	1296	396	590	**986**	.761
*41. Bernie Nicholls, L.A., NYR, Edm., N.J.	12	824	397	580	**977**	1.186
*42. Brian Propp, Phi., Bos., Min. .	14	951	413	561	**974**	1.024
43. Andy Bathgate, NYR, Tor., Det., Pit.	17	1069	349	624	**973**	.910
44. Maurice Richard, Mtl.	18	978	544	421	**965**	.987
45. Larry Robinson, Mtl., L.A. . . .	20	1384	208	750	**958**	.692
*46. Dino Ciccarelli, Min., Wsh., Det.	13	907	485	472	**957**	1.055
*47. Steve Larmer, Chi.	13	891	406	517	**923**	1.036
*48. Joey Mullen, St.L., Cgy., Pit. .	13	842	433	486	**919**	1.091
49. Bobby Orr, Bos., Chi.	12	657	270	645	**915**	1.393 (4)
50. Brad Park, NYR, Bos., Det. . .	17	1113	213	683	**896**	.805
51. Butch Goring, L.A., NYI, Bos.	16	1107	375	513	**888**	.802
52. Bill Barber, Phi.	12	903	420	463	**883**	.978
53. Dennis Maruk, Cal., Cle., Wsh., Min.	14	888	356	522	**878**	.989
54. Ivan Boldirev, Bos., Cal., Chi., Atl., Van., Det.	15	1052	361	505	**866**	.823
55. Yvan Cournoyer, Mtl.	16	968	428	435	**863**	.892
56. Dean Prentice, NYR, Bos., Det., Pit., Min.	22	1378	391	469	**860**	.624
57. Ted Lindsay, Det., Chi.	17	1068	379	472	**851**	.797
58. Tom Lysiak, Atl., Chi.	13	919	292	551	**843**	.917
*59. Dale Hunter, Que., Wsh.	13	1002	269	570	**839**	.837
60. John Tonelli, NYI, Cgy., L.A., Chi., Que.	14	1028	325	511	**836**	.813
61. Jacques Lemaire, Mtl.	12	853	366	469	**835**	.979
*62. Larry Murphy, L.A., Wsh., Min., Pit.	13	1020	203	631	**834**	.818
*63. John Ogrodnick, Det., Que., NYR	14	928	402	425	**827**	.891
*64. Doug Wilson, Chi., S.J.	16	1024	237	590	**827**	.808
*65. Doug Gilmour, St.L., Cgy., Tor.	10	773	277	548	**825**	1.067
66. Red Kelly, Det., Tor.	20	1316	281	542	**823**	.625
67. Pierre Larouche, Pit., Mtl., Hfd., NYR	14	812	395	427	**822**	1.012
68. Bernie Geoffrion, Mtl., NYR	16	883	393	429	**822**	.931
*69. Phil Housley, Buf., Wpg.	11	840	242	575	**817**	.973
70. Steve Shutt, Mtl., L.A.	13	930	424	393	**817**	.878
71. Wilf Paiement, K.C., Col., Tor., Que., NYR, Buf., Pit. .	14	946	356	458	**814**	.860
72. Peter McNab, Buf., Bos., Van., N.J.	14	954	363	450	**813**	.852
*73. Brian Bellows, Min., Mtl. . . .	11	835	382	428	**810**	.970
*74. Dave Andreychuk, Buf., Tor.	11	794	373	436	**809**	1.019
75. Pit Martin, Det., Bos., Chi., Van.	17	1101	324	485	**809**	.735
*76. Pat LaFontaine, NYI, Buf. . . .	10	671	386	421	**807**	1.203
77. Ken Linseman, Phi., Edm., Bos., Tor.	14	860	256	551	**807**	.938
78. Garry Unger, Tor., Det., St.L., Atl., L.A., Edm.	16	1105	413	391	**804**	.728
79. Ken Hodge, Chi., Bos., NYR	13	881	328	472	**800**	.908
*80. Neal Broten, Min.	13	876	249	547	**796**	.909
81. Wayne Cashman, Bos.	17	1027	277	516	**793**	.772
82. Rick Vaive, Van., Tor., Chi., Buf.	13	876	441	347	**788**	.900
83. Borje Salming, Tor., Det. . .	17	1148	150	637	**787**	.686
84. Jean Pronovost, Pit., Atl., Wsh.	14	998	391	383	**774**	.776
85. Peter Mahovlich, Det., Mtl., Pit.	16	884	288	485	**773**	.874
*86. Dave Christian, Wpg., Wsh., Bos., St.L., Chi.	14	1000	340	430	**770**	.770
87. Rick Kehoe, Tor., Pit.	14	906	371	396	**767**	.847
88. Rick MacLeish, Phi., Hfd., Pit., Det.	14	846	349	410	**759**	.897
*89. Thomas Steen, Wpg.	12	843	240	511	**751**	.891
*90. Al MacInnis, Cgy.	12	728	185	555	**740**	1.016
91. Murray Oliver, Det., Bos., Tor., Min.	17	1127	274	454	**728**	.646
92. Bob Nevin, Tor., NYR, Min., L.A.	18	1128	307	419	**726**	.644
*93. Mike Foligno, Det., Buf., Tor.	14	975	351	367	**718**	.736
*94. Luc Robitaille, L.A.	7	557	348	369	**717**	1.287 (8)
*95. Brent Sutter, NYI, Chi.	13	820	325	389	**714**	.871
96. George Armstrong, Tor.	21	1187	296	417	**713**	.601
*97. Mark Howe, Hfd., Phi., Det. .	14	867	192	520	**712**	.821
98. Vic Hadfield, NYR, Pit.	16	1002	323	389	**712**	.711
99. Charlie Simmer, Cal., Cle., L.A., Bos., Pit.	14	712	342	369	**711**	.999
100. Doug Mohns, Bos., Chi., Min., Atl., Wsh.	22	1390	248	462	**710**	.511

The "Great One," Wayne Gretzky, remains the most prolific scorer in NHL history, averaging 2.23 points-per-game during his 14-year career.

All-Time Games Played Leaders

Regular Season

* active player

	Player	Team	Seasons	GP
1.	Gordie Howe	Detroit	25	1,687
		Hartford	1	80
		Total	**26**	**1,767**
2.	Alex Delvecchio	Detroit	24	1,549
3.	John Bucyk	Detroit	2	104
		Boston	21	1,436
		Total	**23**	**1,540**
4.	Tim Horton	Toronto	19¾	1,185
		NY Rangers	1¼	93
		Pittsburgh	1	44
		Buffalo	2	124
		Total	**24**	**1,446**
5.	Harry Howell	NY Rangers	17	1,160
		California	1½	83
		Los Angeles	2½	168
		Total	**21**	**1,411**
6.	Norm Ullman	Detroit	12½	875
		Toronto	7½	535
		Total	**20**	**1,410**
7.	Stan Mikita	Chicago	22	1,394
8.	Doug Mohns	Boston	11	710
		Chicago	6½	415
		Minnesota	2½	162
		Atlanta	1	28
		Washington	1	75
		Total	**22**	**1,390**
9.	Larry Robinson	Montreal	17	1,202
		Los Angeles	3	182
		Total	**20**	**1,384**
10.	Dean Prentice	NY Rangers	10½	666
		Boston	3	170
		Detroit	3½	230
		Pittsburgh	2	144
		Minnesota	3	168
		Total	**22**	**1,378**
11.	Ron Stewart	Toronto	13	838
		Boston	2	126
		St. Louis	½	19
		NY Rangers	4	306
		Vancouver	1	42
		NY Islanders	½	22
		Total	**21**	**1,353**
12.	Marcel Dionne	Detroit	4	309
		Los Angeles	11¾	921
		NY Rangers	2¼	118
		Total	**18**	**1,348**
13.	Red Kelly	Detroit	12½	846
		Toronto	7½	470
		Total	**20**	**1,316**
14.	Dave Keon	Toronto	15	1,062
		Hartford	3	234
		Total	**18**	**1,296**
15.	Phil Esposito	Chicago	4	235
		Boston	8¼	625
		NY Rangers	5¾	422
		Total	**18**	**1,282**
16.	Jean Ratelle	NY Rangers	15¼	862
		Boston	5¾	419
		Total	**21**	**1,281**
17.	Henri Richard	Montreal	20	1,256
18.	Bill Gadsby	Chicago	8½	468
		NY Rangers	6½	457
		Detroit	5	323
		Total	**20**	**1,248**
19.	Allan Stanley	NY Rangers	6¼	307
		Chicago	1¾	111
		Boston	2	129
		Toronto	9	633
		Philadelphia	1	64
		Total	**21**	**1,244**
*20.	Bryan Trottier	NY Islanders	15	1,123
		Pittsburgh	2	115
		Total	**17**	**1,238**
21.	Eddie Westfall	Boston	11	734
		NY Islanders	7	493
		Total	**18**	**1,227**
22.	Eric Nesterenko	Toronto	5	206
		Chicago	16	1,013
		Total	**21**	**1,219**
23.	Marcel Pronovost	Detroit	16	983
		Toronto	5	223
		Total	**21**	**1,206**
24.	Gilbert Perreault	Buffalo	17	1,191
25.	George Armstrong	Toronto	21	1,187
26.	Frank Mahovlich	Toronto	11¾	720
		Detroit	2¾	198
		Montreal	3½	263
		Total	**18**	**1,181**
27.	Don Marshall	Montreal	10	585
		NY Rangers	7	479
		Buffalo	1	62
		Toronto	1	50
		Total	**19**	**1,176**
28.	Bob Gainey	Montreal	16	1,160
29.	Leo Boivin	Toronto	3¼	137
		Boston	11½	717
		Detroit	1¼	85
		Pittsburgh	1½	114
		Minnesota	1½	97
		Total	**19**	**1,150**
30.	Borje Salming	Toronto	16	1,099
		Detroit	1	49
		Total	**17**	**1,148**
31.	Bobby Clarke	Philadelphia	15	1,144
32.	Bob Nevin	Toronto	5¾	250
		NY Rangers	7¼	505
		Minnesota	2	138
		Los Angeles	3	235
		Total	**18**	**1,128**
33.	Murray Oliver	Detroit	2½	101
		Boston	6½	429
		Toronto	3	226
		Minnesota	5	371
		Total	**17**	**1,127**
34.	Guy Lafleur	Montreal	14	961
		NY Rangers	1	67
		Quebec	2	98
		Total	**17**	**1,126**
35.	Jean Beliveau	Montreal	20	1,125
36.	Doug Harvey	Montreal	14	890
		NY Rangers	3	151
		Detroit	1	2
		St. Louis	1	70
		Total	**19**	**1,113**
37.	Brad Park	NY Rangers	7½	465
		Boston	7½	501
		Detroit	2	147
		Total	**17**	**1,113**
38.	Lanny McDonald	Toronto	6½	477
		Colorado	1¾	142
		Calgary	7¾	441
		Total	**16**	**1,111**
39.	Butch Goring	Los Angeles	10¾	736
		NY Islanders	4¾	332
		Boston	½	39
		Total	**16**	**1,107**
40.	Garry Unger	Toronto	½	15
		Detroit	3	216
		St. Louis	8½	662
		Atlanta	1	79
		Los Angeles	¾	58
		Edmonton	2¼	75
		Total	**16**	**1,105**
41.	Pit Martin	Detroit	3¼	119
		Boston	1¾	111
		Chicago	10¼	740
		Vancouver	1¾	131
		Total	**17**	**1,101**
42.	Darryl Sittler	Toronto	11½	844
		Philadelphia	2½	191
		Detroit	1	61
		Total	**15**	**1,096**
*43.	Mike Gartner	Washington	9¾	758
		Minnesota	1	80
		NY Rangers	3¼	251
		Total	**14**	**1,089**
44.	Carol Vadnais	Montreal	2	42
		Oakland	2	152
		California	1¾	94
		Boston	3½	263
		NY Rangers	6¾	485
		New Jersey	1	51
		Total	**17**	**1,087**
45.	Brad Marsh	Atlanta	2	160
		Calgary	1¼	97
		Philadelphia	6¾	514
		Toronto	2¾	181
		Detroit	1¼	75
		Ottawa	1	59
		Total	**15**	**1,086**

A 1,000-point and 1,000-game player, Bobby Smith's career began with a Calder Trophy win in 1978-79 with Minnesota. He joined the Canadiens in 1983 and rejoined the North Stars in 1990.

	Player	Team	Seasons	GP
46.	Bob Pulford	Toronto	14	947
		Los Angeles	2	132
		Total	**16**	**1,079**
*47.	Dave Taylor	**Los Angeles**	**16**	**1,078**
48.	Bobby Smith	Minnesota	8¼	572
		Montreal	6¾	505
		Total	**15**	**1,077**
49.	Craig Ramsay	**Buffalo**	**14**	**1,070**
50.	Andy Bathgate	NY Rangers	11¾	719
		Toronto	1¼	70
		Detroit	2	130
		Pittsburgh	2	150
		Total	**17**	**1,069**
51.	Ted Lindsay	Detroit	14	862
		Chicago	3	206
		Total	**17**	**1,068**
52.	Terry Harper	Montreal	10	554
		Los Angeles	3	234
		Detroit	4	252
		St. Louis	1	11
		Colorado	1	15
		Total	**19**	**1,066**
53.	Rod Gilbert	**NY Rangers**	**18**	**1,065**
54.	Bobby Hull	Chicago	15	1,036
		Winnipeg	⅔	18
		Hartford	⅓	9
		Total	**16**	**1,063**
55.	Denis Potvin	**NY Islanders**	**15**	**1,060**
56.	Jean Guy Talbot	Montreal	13	791
		Minnesota	¼	4
		Detroit	½	32
		St. Louis	2½	172
		Buffalo	¾	57
		Total	**17**	**1,056**
57.	Randy Carlyle	Toronto	2	94
		Pittsburgh	5¾	397
		Winnipeg	9¼	564
		Total	**17**	**1,055**

	Player	Team	Seasons	GP
58.	Ivan Boldirev	Boston	1¼	13
		California	2¾	191
		Chicago	4¾	384
		Atlanta	1	65
		Vancouver	2¾	216
		Detroit	2½	183
		Total	**15**	**1,052**
59.	Eddie Shack	NY Rangers	2¼	141
		Toronto	8¾	504
		Boston	2	120
		Los Angeles	1¼	84
		Buffalo	1½	111
		Pittsburgh	1¼	87
		Total	**17**	**1,047**
*60.	Wayne Gretzky	Edmonton	9	696
		Los Angeles	5	348
		Total	**14**	**1,044**
61.	Serge Savard	Montreal	15	917
		Winnipeg	2	123
		Total	**17**	**1,040**
*62.	Gordie Roberts	Hartford	1½	107
		Minnesota	7	555
		Philadelphia	¼	11
		St. Louis	2½	166
		Pittsburgh	1¾	134
		Boston	1	65
		Total	**14**	**1,038**
63.	Ron Ellis	**Toronto**	**16**	**1,034**
64.	Harold Snepsts	Vancouver	11¾	781
		Minnesota	1	71
		Detroit	3	120
		St. Louis	1¼	61
		Total	**17**	**1,033**
*65.	Michel Goulet	Quebec	10¾	813
		Chicago	3¼	220
		Total	**14**	**1,033**
66.	Ralph Backstrom	Montreal	14½	844
		Los Angeles	2¼	172
		Chicago	¼	16
		Total	**17**	**1,032**

	Player	Team	Seasons	GP
67.	Dick Duff	Toronto	9¾	582
		NY Rangers	¾	43
		Montreal	5	305
		Los Angeles	¾	39
		Buffalo	1¾	61
		Total	**18**	**1,030**
*68.	Brad McCrimmon	Boston	3	228
		Philadelphia	5	367
		Calgary	3	231
		Detroit	3	203
		Total	**14**	**1,029**
69.	John Tonelli	NY Islanders	7¾	584
		Calgary	2¼	161
		Los Angeles	3	231
		Chicago	¾	33
		Quebec	¼	19
		Total	**14**	**1,028**
*70.	Ray Bourque	**Boston**	**14**	**1,028**
71.	Wayne Cashman	**Boston**	**17**	**1,027**
*72.	Doug Wilson	Chicago	14	938
		San Jose	2	86
		Total	**16**	**1,024**
73.	Jim Neilson	NY Rangers	12	810
		California	2	98
		Cleveland	2	115
		Total	**16**	**1,023**
*74.	Rob Ramage	Colorado	3	234
		St. Louis	5¾	441
		Calgary	1¼	80
		Toronto	2	160
		Minnesota	1	34
		Tampa Bay	¾	66
		Montreal	¼	8
		Total	**14**	**1,023**
75.	Don Lever	Vancouver	7⅔	593
		Atlanta	⅓	28
		Calgary	1¼	85
		Colorado	¾	59
		New Jersey	3	216
		Buffalo	2	39
		Total	**15**	**1,020**
*76.	Larry Murphy	Los Angeles	3¼	242
		Washington	5½	453
		Minnestoa	1¾	121
		Pittsburgh	2½	204
		Total	**13**	**1,020**
77.	Phil Russell	Chicago	6¾	504
		Atlanta	1¼	93
		Calgary	3	229
		New Jersey	2¾	172
		Buffalo	1¼	18
		Total	**15**	**1,016**
*78.	Kevin Lowe	Edmonton	13	966
		NY Rangers	1	49
		Total	**14**	**1,015**
*79.	Laurie Boschman	Toronto	2¾	187
		Edmonton	1	73
		Winnipeg	7¼	526
		New Jersey	2	153
		Ottawa	1	70
		Total	**14**	**1,009**
80.	Dave Lewis	NY Islanders	6¾	514
		Los Angeles	3¼	221
		New Jersey	3	209
		Detroit	2	64
		Total	**15**	**1,008**
81.	Bob Murray	**Chicago**	**15**	**1,008**
82.	Jim Roberts	Montreal	9⅔	611
		St. Louis	5⅓	395
		Total	**15**	**1,006**
83.	Claude Provost	**Montreal**	**15**	**1,005**
84.	Rick Middleton	NY Rangers	2	124
		Boston	12	881
		Total	**14**	**1,005**
*85.	Mark Messier	Edmonton	12	851
		NY Rangers	2	154
		Total	**14**	**1,005**
*86.	Ryan Walter	Washington	4	307
		Montreal	9	604
		Vancouver	2	92
		Total	**15**	**1,003**
87.	Vic Hadfield	NY Rangers	13	839
		Pittsburgh	3	163
		Total	**16**	**1,002**
*88.	Dale Hunter	Quebec	7	523
		Washington	6	479
		Total	**13**	**1,002**
89.	Bernie Federko	St. Louis	14	927
		Detroit	1	73
		Total	**15**	**1,000**
*90.	Dave Christian	Winnipeg	4	230
		Washington	6½	504
		Boston	1½	128
		St. Louis	1	78
		Chicago	1	60
		Total	**14**	**1,000**

Andy Bathgate played 1,069 games with the NY Rangers, Toronto, Detroit and Pittsburgh in 17 seasons. He ranks fourth among NHL right wingers with 624 career assists.

Goaltending Records

All-Time Shutout Leaders

Goaltender	Team	Seasons	Games	Shutouts
Terry Sawchuk	Detroit	14	734	85
(1949-1970)	Boston	2	102	11
	Toronto	3	91	4
	Los Angeles	1	36	2
	NY Rangers	1	8	1
	Total	21	971	**103**
George Hainsworth	Montreal	7½	318	75
(1926-1937)	Toronto	3½	146	19
	Total	11	464	**94**
Glenn Hall	Detroit	4	148	17
(1952-1971)	Chicago	10	618	51
	St. Louis	4	140	16
	Total	18	906	**84**
Jacques Plante	Montreal	11	556	58
(1952-1973)	NY Rangers	2	98	5
	St. Louis	2	69	10
	Toronto	2¾	106	7
	Boston	¼	8	2
	Total	18	837	**82**
Tiny Thompson	Boston	10¼	468	74
(1928-1940)	Detroit	1¾	85	7
	Total	12	553	**81**
Alex Connell	Ottawa	8	293	64
(1924-1937)	Detroit	1	48	6
	NY Americans	1	1	0
	Mtl. Maroons	2	75	11
	Total	12	417	**81**
Tony Esposito	Montreal	1	13	2
(1968-1984)	Chicago	15	873	74
	Total	16	886	**76**
Lorne Chabot	NY Rangers	2	80	21
(1926-1937)	Toronto	5	214	33
	Montreal	1	47	8
	Chicago	1	48	8
	Mtl. Maroons	1	16	2
	NY Americans	1	6	1
	Total	11	411	**73**
Harry Lumley	Detroit	6½	324	26
(1943-1960)	NY Rangers	½	1	0
	Chicago	2	134	5
	Toronto	4	267	34
	Boston	3	78	6
	Total	16	804	**71**
Roy Worters	Pittsburgh Pirates	3	123	22
(1925-1937)	NY Americans	9	360	44
	*Montreal		1	0
	Total	12	484	**66**
Turk Broda	Toronto	14	629	**62**
(1936-1952)				
John Roach	Toronto	7	223	13
(1921-1935)	NY Rangers	4	89	30
	Detroit	3	180	15
	Total	14	492	**58**
Clint Benedict	Ottawa	7	158	19
(1917-1930)	Mtl. Maroons	6	204	38
	Total	13	362	**57**
Bernie Parent	Boston	2	57	1
(1965-1979)	Philadelphia	9½	486	50
	Toronto	1½	65	4
	Total	13	608	**55**
Ed Giacomin	NY Rangers	10¼	539	49
(1965-1978)	Detroit	2¾	71	5
	Total	13	610	**54**
David Kerr	Mtl. Maroons	3	101	11
(1930-1941)	NY Americans	1	1	0
	NY Rangers	7	324	40
	Total	11	426	**51**
Rogie Vachon	Montreal	5¼	206	13
(1966-1982)	Los Angeles	6¾	389	32
	Detroit	2	109	4
	Boston	2	91	2
	Total	16	795	**51**
Ken Dryden	Montreal	8	397	**46**
(1970-1979)				
Gump Worsley	NY Rangers	10	583	24
(1952-1974)	Montreal	6½	172	16
	Minnesota	4½	107	3
	Total	21	862	**43**
Charlie Gardiner	Chicago	7	316	**42**
(1927-1934)				
Frank Brimsek	Boston	9	444	35
(1938-1950)	Chicago	1	70	5
	Total	10	514	**40**
Johnny Bower	NY Rangers	3	77	5
(1953-1970)	Toronto	12	475	32
	Total	15	552	**37**
Bill Durnan	Montreal	7	383	**34**
(1943-1950)				
Eddie Johnston	Boston	11	444	27
(1962-1978)	Toronto	1	26	1
	St. Louis	3⅔	118	4
	Chicago	⅓	4	0
	Total	16	592	**32**
Roger Crozier	Detroit	7	313	20
(1963-1977)	Buffalo	6	202	10
	Washington	1	3	0
	Total	14	518	**30**
Cesare Maniago	Toronto	1	7	0
(1960-1978)	Montreal	1	14	0
	NY Rangers	2	34	2
	Minnesota	9	420	26
	Vancouver	2	93	2
	Total	15	568	**30**

*Played 1 game for Canadiens in 1929-30.

Ten or More Shutouts, One Season

Number of Shutouts	Goaltender	Team	Season	Length of Schedule
22	George Hainsworth	Montreal	1928-29	44
15	Alex Connell	Ottawa	1925-26	36
	Alex Connell	Ottawa	1927-28	44
	Hal Winkler	Boston	1927-28	44
	Tony Esposito	Chicago	1969-70	76
14	George Hainsworth	Montreal	1926-27	44
13	Clint Benedict	Mtl. Maroons	1926-27	44
	Alex Connell	Ottawa	1926-27	44
	George Hainsworth	Montreal	1927-28	44
	John Roach	NY Rangers	1928-29	44
	Roy Worters	NY Americans	1928-29	44
	Harry Lumley	Toronto	1953-54	70
12	Tiny Thompson	Boston	1928-29	44
	Lorne Chabot	Toronto	1928-29	44
	Chuck Gardiner	Chicago	1930-31	44
	Terry Sawchuk	Detroit	1951-52	70
	Terry Sawchuk	Detroit	1953-54	70
	Terry Sawchuk	Detroit	1954-55	70
	Glenn Hall	Detroit	1955-56	70
	Bernie Parent	Philadelphia	1973-74	78
	Bernie Parent	Philadelphia	1974-75	80
11	Lorne Chabot	NY Rangers	1927-28	44
	Harry Holmes	Detroit	1927-28	44
	Clint Benedict	Mtl. Maroons	1928-29	44
	Joe Miller	Pittsburgh Pirates	1928-29	44
	Tiny Thompson	Boston	1932-33	48
	Terry Sawchuk	Detroit	1950-51	70
10	Lorne Chabot	NY Rangers	1926-27	44
	Roy Worters	Pittsburgh Pirates	1927-28	44
	Clarence Dolson	Detroit	1928-29	44
	John Roach	Detroit	1932-33	48
	Chuck Gardiner	Chicago	1933-34	48
	Tiny Thompson	Boston	1935-36	48
	Frank Brimsek	Boston	1938-39	48
	Bill Durnan	Montreal	1948-49	60
	Gerry McNeil	Montreal	1952-53	70
	Harry Lumley	Toronto	1952-53	70
	Tony Esposito	Chicago	1973-74	78
	Ken Dryden	Montreal	1976-77	80

All-Time Win Leaders

(Minimum 200 Wins)

Wins	Goaltender	GP	Decisions	Mins.	Losses	Ties	%
435	Terry Sawchuk	971	960	57,154	337	188	.551
434	Jacques Plante	837	817	49,553	246	137	.615
423	Tony Esposito	886	881	52,585	307	151	.566
407	Glenn Hall	906	899	53,484	327	165	.544
355	Rogie Vachon	795	761	46,298	291	115	.542
335	Gump Worsley	862	838	50,232	353	150	.489
332	Harry Lumley	804	799	48,097	324	143	.505
305	Billy Smith	680	643	38,431	233	105	.556
302	Turk Broda	629	627	38,173	224	101	.562
293	Mike Liut	663	651	38,155	271	74	.507
289	Ed Giacomin	610	592	35,693	206	97	.570
286	Dan Bouchard	655	631	37,919	232	113	.543
284	Tiny Thompson	553	553	34,174	194	75	.581
279	* Andy Moog	496	464	27,957	128	57	.663
275	* Grant Fuhr	547	514	31,043	174	65	.598
270	Bernie Parent	608	588	35,136	197	121	.562
270	Gilles Meloche	788	752	45,401	351	131	.446
258	Ken Dryden	397	389	23,352	57	74	.758
252	Frank Brimsek	514	514	31,210	182	80	.568
251	Johnny Bower	549	537	32,016	196	90	.551
247	George Hainsworth	464	467	29,415	146	74	.608
246	Pete Peeters	489	461	27,699	155	51	.589
244	* Tom Barrasso	502	480	28,948	181	55	.566
236	* Rejean Lemelin	507	461	28,006	162	63	.580
236	Eddie Johnston	592	579	34,209	256	87	.483
231	Glenn Resch	571	537	32,279	224	82	.507
230	Gerry Cheevers	418	398	24,394	94	74	.671
230	* Don Beaupre	532	499	30,166	205	64	.525
225	* Patrick Roy	418	402	24,225	129	48	.619
222	* Mike Vernon	419	406	23,780	138	46	.603
218	John Roach	491	491	30,423	204	69	.514
215	Greg Millen	604	588	35,377	284	89	.441
208	Bill Durnan	383	382	22,945	112	62	.626
208	* Kelly Hrudey	466	433	26,409	166	59	.548
208	Don Edwards	459	440	26,181	155	77	.560
206	Lorne Chabot	411	411	25,309	140	65	.580
206	Roger Crozier	518	477	28,566	197	74	.509
204	* Rick Wamsley	407	381	23,123	131	46	.596
203	David Kerr	426	426	26,519	148	75	.565
200	* John Vanbiesbrouck	449	424	25,380	177	47	.527

Active Shutout Leaders

Goaltender	Teams	Seasons	Games	Shutouts
Patrick Roy	Montreal	9	418	20
Tom Barrasso	Buffalo, Pittsburgh	10	502	19
Andy Moog	Edmonton, Boston	13	496	17
Ed Belfour	Chicago	5	220	16
John Vanbiesbrouck	NY Rangers	11	449	16
Kelly Hrudey	NY Islanders, Los Angeles	10	466	15
Bob Essensa	Winnipeg	5	225	13
Kirk McLean	New Jersey, Vancouver	8	312	13
Don Beaupre	Minnesota, Washington	13	532	13
Jon Casey	Minnesota	8	325	12
Clint Malarchuk	Que., Wsh., Buf.	10	338	12
Grant Fuhr	Edm., Tor., Buf.	12	547	12
Rick Wamsley	Mtl., St. L., Cgy., Tor.	13	407	12
Rejean Lemelin	Atl., Cgy., Bos.	15	507	12

Active Goaltending Leaders

(Ranked by winning percentage; minimum 250 games played)

Goaltender	Teams	Seasons	GP	Decisions	W	L	T	Winning %
Andy Moog	Edmonton, Boston	13	496	464	279	128	57	.663
Patrick Roy	Montreal	9	418	402	225	129	48	.619
Mike Vernon	Calgary	10	419	406	222	138	46	.603
Grant Fuhr	Edm., Tor., Buf.	12	547	514	275	174	65	.598
Rick Wamsley	Mtl., St. L., Cgy., Tor.	13	407	381	204	131	46	.596
Rejean Lemelin	Atl., Cgy., Bos.	15	507	461	236	162	63	.580
Tom Barrasso	Buffalo, Pittsburgh	10	502	480	244	181	55	.566
Ron Hextall	Philadelphia, Quebec	7	335	321	159	126	36	.551
Kelly Hrudey	NYI, L.A.	10	466	433	208	166	59	.548
J. Vanbiesbrouck	NY Rangers	11	449	424	200	177	47	.527
Don Beaupre	Minnesota, Washington	13	532	499	230	205	64	.525
Clint Malarchuk	Que., Wsh., Buf.	10	338	316	141	130	45	.517
Jon Casey	Minnesota	8	325	296	128	126	42	.503
Bill Ranford	Boston, Edmonton	8	330	302	132	136	34	.493
Kirk McLean	New Jersey, Vancouver	8	312	299	130	136	33	.490
Steve Weeks	NYR, Hfd., Van., NYI, L.A., Ott.	13	290	263	111	119	33	.485
Brian Hayward	Wpg., Mtl., Min., S.J.	11	357	336	143	156	37	.481
Glenn Healy	Los Angeles, NY Islanders	7	259	243	103	116	24	.473
Ken Wreggett	Tor., Phi., Pit.	10	341	312	115	169	28	.413

Goals Against Average Leaders

(minimum 27 games played, 1992-93; 25 games played, 1926–27 to 1991-92; 15 games played, 1917–18 to 1925–26.)

Season	Goaltender and Club	GP	Mins.	GA	SO	AVG.
1992-93	Felix Potvin, Toronto	48	2,781	116	2	2.50
1991-92	Patrick Roy, Montreal	67	3,935	155	5	2.36
1990-91	Ed Belfour, Chicago	74	4,127	170	4	2.47
1989-90	Mike Liut, Hartford, Washington	37	2,161	91	4	2.53
1988-89	Patrick Roy, Montreal	48	2,744	113	4	2.47
1987-88	Pete Peeters, Washington	35	1,896	88	2	2.78
1986-87	Brian Hayward, Montreal	37	2,178	102	1	2.81
1985-86	Bob Froese, Philadelphia	51	2,728	116	2	2.55
1984-85	Tom Barrasso, Buffalo	54	3,248	144	5	2.66
1983-84	Pat Riggin, Washington	41	2,299	102	4	2.66
1982-83	Pete Peeters, Boston	62	3,611	142	8	2.36
1981-82	Denis Herron, Montreal	27	1,547	68	3	2.64
1980-81	Richard Sevigny, Montreal	33	1,777	71	2	2.40
1979-80	Bob Sauve, Buffalo	32	1,880	74	4	2.36
1978-79	Ken Dryden, Montreal	47	2,814	108	5	2.30
1977-78	Ken Dryden, Montreal	52	3,071	105	5	2.05
1976-77	Michel Larocque, Montreal	26	1,525	53	4	2.09
1975-76	Ken Dryden, Montreal	62	3,580	121	8	2.03
1974-75	Bernie Parent, Philadelphia	68	4,041	137	12	2.03
1973-74	Bernie Parent, Philadelphia	73	4,314	136	12	1.89
1972-73	Ken Dryden, Montreal	54	3,165	119	6	2.26
1971-72	Tony Esposito, Chicago	48	2,780	82	9	1.77
1970-71	Jacques Plante, Toronto	40	2,329	73	4	1.88
1969-70	Ernie Wakely, St. Louis	30	1,651	58	4	2.11
1968-69	Jacques Plante, St. Louis	37	2,139	70	5	1.96
1967-68	Gump Worsley, Montreal	40	2,213	73	6	1.98
1966-67	Glenn Hall, Chicago	32	1,664	66	2	2.38
1965-66	Johnny Bower, Toronto	35	1,998	75	3	2.25
1964-65	Johnny Bower, Toronto	34	2,040	81	3	2.38
1963-64	Johnny Bower, Toronto	51	3,009	106	5	2.11
1962-63	Jacques Plante, Montreal	56	3,320	138	5	2.49
1961-62	Jacques Plante, Montreal	70	4,200	166	4	2.37
1960-61	Johnny Bower, Toronto	58	3,480	145	2	2.50
1959-60	Jacques Plante, Montreal	69	4,140	175	3	2.54
1958-59	Jacques Plante, Montreal	67	4,000	144	9	2.16
1957-58	Jacques Plante, Montreal	57	3,386	119	9	2.11
1956-57	Jacques Plante, Montreal	61	3,660	123	9	2.02
1955-56	Jacques Plante, Montreal	64	3,840	119	7	1.86

Season	Goaltender and Club	GP	Mins.	GA	SO	AVG.
1954-55	Terry Sawchuk, Detroit	68	4,080	132	12	1.94
1953-54	Harry Lumley, Toronto	69	4,140	128	13	1.86
1952-53	Terry Sawchuk, Detroit	63	3,780	120	9	1.90
1951-52	Terry Sawchuk, Detroit	70	4,200	133	12	1.90
1950-51	Al Rollins, Toronto	40	2,367	70	5	1.77
1949-50	Bill Durnan, Montreal	64	3,840	141	8	2.20
1948-49	Bill Durnan, Montreal	60	3,600	126	10	2.10
1947-48	Turk Broda, Toronto	60	3,600	143	5	2.38
1946-47	Bill Durnan, Montreal	60	3,600	138	4	2.30
1945-46	Bill Durnan, Montreal	40	2,400	104	4	2.60
1944-45	Bill Durnan, Montreal	50	3,000	121	1	2.42
1943-44	Bill Durnan, Montreal	50	3,000	109	2	2.18
1942-43	Johnny Mowers, Detroit	50	3,010	124	6	2.47
1941-42	Frank Brimsek, Boston	47	2,930	115	3	2.35
1940-41	Turk Broda, Toronto	48	2,970	99	5	2.00
1939-40	Dave Kerr, NY Rangers	48	3,000	77	8	1.54
1938-39	Frank Brimsek, Boston	43	2,610	68	10	1.56
1937-38	Tiny Thompson, Boston	48	2,970	89	7	1.80
1936-37	Normie Smith, Detroit	48	2,980	102	6	2.05
1935-36	Tiny Thompson, Boston	48	2,930	82	10	1.68
1934-35	Lorne Chabot, Chicago	48	2,940	88	8	1.80
1933-34	Wilf Cude, Detroit, Montreal	30	1,920	47	5	1.47
1932-33	Tiny Thompson, Boston	48	3,000	88	11	1.76
1931-32	Chuck Gardiner, Chicago	48	2,989	92	4	1.85
1930-31	Roy Worters, NY Americans	44	2,760	74	8	1.61
1929-30	Tiny Thompson, Boston	44	2,680	98	3	2.19
1928-29	George Hainsworth, Montreal	44	2,800	43	22	0.92
1927-28	George Hainsworth, Montreal	44	2,730	48	13	1.05
1926-27	Clint Benedict, Mtl. Maroons	43	2,748	65	13	1.42
1925-26	Alex Connell, Ottawa	36	2,251	42	15	1.12
1924-25	Georges Vezina, Montreal	30	1,860	56	5	1.81
1923-24	Georges Vezina, Montreal	24	1,459	48	3	1.97
1922-23	Clint Benedict, Ottawa	24	1,478	54	4	2.19
1921-22	Clint Benedict, Ottawa	24	1,508	84	2	3.34
1920-21	Clint Benedict, Ottawa	24	1,457	75	2	3.09
1919-20	Clint Benedict, Ottawa	24	1,444	64	5	2.66
1918-19	Clint Benedict, Ottawa	18	1,113	53	2	2.86
1917-18	Georges Vezina, Montreal	21	1,282	84	1	3.93

Coaching Records

(Minimum 600 regular-season games. Ranked by number of games coached.)

Coach	Team	Seasons	Games	Wins	Losses	Ties	%*
Al Arbour	St. Louis	1970-73	107	42	40	25	.509
	NY Islanders	1973-86; 88-93	1,415	703	501	211	.571
	Total		**1,522**	**745**	**541**	**236**	**.567**
Scott Bowman	St. Louis	1967-71	238	110	83	45	.557
	Montreal	1971-79	634	419	110	105	.744
	Buffalo	1979-87	404	210	134	60	.594
	Pittsburgh	1991-93	164	95	53	16	.628
	Total		**1,440**	**834**	**380**	**226**	**.658**
Dick Irvin	Chicago	1930-31; 55-56	114	43	56	15	.443
	Toronto	1931-40	427	216	152	59	.575
	Montreal	1940-55	896	431	313	152	.566
	Total		**1,437**	**690**	**521**	**226**	**.559**
Billy Reay	Toronto	1957-59	90	26	50	14	.367
	Chicago	1963-77	1,012	516	335	161	.589
	Total		**1,102**	**542**	**385**	**175**	**.571**
Jack Adams	Detroit	1927-44	**964**	**413**	**390**	**161**	**.512**
Sid Abel	Chicago	1952-54	140	39	79	22	.357
	Detroit	1957-68; 69-70	810	340	338	132	.501
	St. Louis	1971-72	10	3	6	1	.350
	Kansas City	1975-76	3	0	3	0	.000
	Total		**963**	**382**	**426**	**155**	**.477**
Punch Imlach	Toronto	1958-69; 79-81	840	391	311	138	.548
	Buffalo	1970-72	119	32	62	25	.374
	Total		**959**	**423**	**373**	**163**	**.526**
Bryan Murray	Washington	1981-90	672	343	246	83	.572
	Detroit	1990-93	244	124	91	32	.574
	Total		**916**	**467**	**337**	**115**	**.573**
Toe Blake	Montreal	1955-68	**914**	**500**	**255**	**159**	**.634**
Michel Bergeron	Quebec	1980-87; 89-90	634	265	283	86	.486
	NY Rangers	1987-89	158	73	67	18	.519
	Total		**792**	**338**	**350**	**104**	**.492**
Glen Sather	Edmonton	1979-89	**782**	**442**	**241**	**99**	**.629**
Emile Francis	NY Rangers	1965-75	654	347	209	98	.606
	St. Louis	1976-77, 81-83	124	46	64	14	.427
	Total		**778**	**393**	**273**	**112**	**.577**
Bob Berry	Los Angeles	1978-81	240	107	94	39	.527
	Montreal	1981-84	223	116	71	36	.601
	Pittsburgh	1984-87	240	88	127	25	.419
	St. Louis	1992-93	73	33	30	10	.521
	Total		**776**	**344**	**322**	**110**	**.514**
Bob Pulford	Los Angeles	1972-77	396	178	150	68	.535
	Chicago	1977-79 1981-82; 84-87	375	158	155	62	.504
	Total		**771**	**336**	**305**	**130**	**.520**
Milt Schmidt	Boston	1954-61; 62-66	726	245	360	121	.421
	Washington	1974-76	43	5	33	5	.174
	Total		**769**	**250**	**393**	**126**	**.407**
Red Kelly	Los Angeles	1967-69	150	55	75	20	.433
	Pittsburgh	1969-73	274	90	132	52	.423
	Toronto	1973-77	318	133	123	62	.516
	Total		**742**	**278**	**330**	**134**	**465**
Fred Shero	Philadelphia	1971-78	554	308	151	95	.642
	NY Rangers	1978-81	180	82	74	24	.522
	Total		**734**	**390**	**225**	**119**	**.612**
Art Ross	Boston	1924-45	**728**	**361**	**277**	**90**	**.558**
Jacques Demers	Quebec	1979-80	80	25	44	11	.381
	St. Louis	1983-86	240	106	106	28	.500
	Detroit	1986-90	320	137	136	47	.502
	Montreal	1992-93	84	48	30	6	.607
	Total		**724**	**316**	**316**	**92**	**.500**
Roger Neilson	Toronto	1977-79	160	75	62	23	.541
	Buffalo	1979-81	106	53	26	27	.627
	Vancouver	1982-84	133	51	61	21	.462
	Los Angeles	1984	28	8	17	3	.339
	NY Rangers	1989-93	280	141	104	35	.559
	Total		**707**	**328**	**270**	**109**	**.541**
Pat Quinn	Philadelphia	1978-82	262	141	73	48	.630
	Los Angeles	1984-87	202	75	101	26	.436
	Vancouver	1991-93	190	97	68	25	.576
	Total		**654**	**313**	**242**	**99**	**.554**
Mike Keenan	Philadelphia	1984-88	320	190	102	28	.638
	Chicago	1988-92	320	153	126	41	.542
	Total		**640**	**343**	**228**	**69**	**.590**
Jack Evans	California	1975-76	80	27	42	11	.406
	Cleveland	1976-78	160	47	87	26	.375
	Hartford	1983-88	374	163	174	37	.485
	Total		**614**	**237**	**303**	**74**	**.446**
Tommy Ivan	Detroit	1947-54	470	262	118	90	.653
	Chicago	1956-58	140	40	78	22	.364
	Total		**610**	**302**	**196**	**112**	**.587**
Lester Patrick	NY Rangers	1926-39	**604**	**281**	**216**	**107**	**.554**

* % arrived at by dividing possible points into actual points.

Al Arbour, who won the Stanley Cup with three different teams as a player, is the NHL's all-time leader in games coached.

All-Time Penalty-Minute Leaders

* active player

(Regular season. Minimum 1,500 minutes)

Player	Teams	Seasons	Games	Penalty Minutes	Mins. per game
Dave Williams,	Tor., Van., Det., L.A., Hfd.	14	962	3,966	4.12
Chris Nilan,	Mtl., NYR, Bos.	13	688	3,043	4.42
*Dale Hunter,	Que., Wsh.	13	1,002	2,874	2.87
*Tim Hunter,	Cgy., Que., Van.	12	619	2,598	4.20
Willi Plett,	Atl., Cgy., Minn., Bos.	13	834	2,572	3.08
*Marty McSorley,	Pit., Edm., L.A.	10	601	2,446	4.07
Dave Schultz,	Phi., L.A., Pit., Buf.	9	535	2,294	4.29
*Laurie Boschman,	Tor., Edm., Wpg., N.J., Ott.	14	1,009	2,265	2.24
*Basil McRae,	Que., Tor., Det., Min., St. L.	12	489	2,230	4.56
Bryan Watson,	Mtl., Det., Cal., Pit., St. L., Wsh.	16	878	2,212	2.52
*Rob Ramage,	Col., St. L., Cgy., Tor., Min., T.B., Mtl.	14	1,023	2,210	2.16
*Jay Wells,	L.A., Phi., Buf., NYR	14	879	2,133	2.43
*Garth Butcher,	Van., St. L.	12	775	2,100	2.71
Terry O'Reilly,	Boston	14	891	2,095	2.35
Al Secord,	Bos., Chi., Tor., Phi.	12	766	2,093	2.73
Phil Russell,	Chi., Atl., Cgy., N.J., Buf.	15	1,016	2,038	2.01
*Scott Stevens,	Wsh. St. L., N.J.	11	828	2,022	2.44
Harold Snepsts,	Van., Min., Det., St. L.	17	1,033	2,009	1.94
*Joey Kocur,	Det., NYR	9	520	2,002	3.85
*Mike Foligno,	Det., Buf., Tor.	14	975	1,996	2.05
*Rick Tocchet,	Phi., Pit.	9	630	1,986	3.15
Andre Dupont,	NYR, St. L., Phi., Que.	13	810	1,986	2.45
*Gord Donnelly,	Que., Wpg., Buf.	10	513	1,920	3.74
*Pat Verbeek,	N.J., Hfd.	11	783	1,857	2.37
Garry Howatt,	NYI, Hfd., N.J.	12	720	1,836	2.55
*Bob Probert,	Detroit	8	408	1,815	4.45
Carol Vadnais,	Mtl., Oak., Cal., Bos., NYR, N.J.	17	1,087	1,813	1.67
Larry Playfair,	Buf., L.A.	11	688	1,812	2.63
Ted Lindsay,	Det., Chi.	17	1,068	1,808	1.69
Jim Korn,	Det., Tor., Buf., N.J., Cgy.	10	597	1,801	3.02
Brian Sutter,	St. Louis	12	779	1,786	2.29
Wilf Paiement,	K.C., Col., Tor., Que., NYR, Buf., Pit.	14	946	1,757	1.86
Torrie Robertson,	Wsh., Hfd., Det.	10	442	1,751	3.96
*Mario Marois,	NYR, Van., Que., Wpg., St. L.	15	955	1,746	1.83
Ken Linseman,	Phi., Edm., Bos., Tor.	14	860	1,727	2.01
Jay Miller,	Bos., L.A.	7	446	1,723	3.86
*Bob McGill,	Tor., Chi., S.J., Det.	12	672	1,720	2.56
*Ken Daneyko,	N.J.	10	613	1,703	2.78
Gordie Howe,	Det., Hfd.	26	1,767	1,685	.95
Paul Holmgren,	Phi., Min.	10	527	1,684	3.20
*Kevin McClelland,	Pit., Edm., Det., Tor.	11	582	1,653	2.84
Jerry Korab,	Chi., Van., Buf., L.A.	15	975	1,629	1.67
Mel Bridgman,	Phi., Cgy., N.J., Det., Van.	14	977	1,625	1.66
Tim Horton,	Tor., NYR, Pit., Buf.	24	1,446	1,611	1.11
*Dave Manson,	Chi., Edm.	7	492	1,605	3.26
*Ulf Samuelsson,	Hfd., Pit.	9	616	1,602	2.60
*Gerard Gallant,	Detroit	9	563	1,600	2.84
*Steve Smith,	Edm., Chi.	9	539	1,598	2.96
Paul Baxter,	Que., Pit., Cgy.	8	472	1,564	3.31
*Dave Taylor,	Los Angeles	16	1,078	1,561	1.45
Glen Cochrane,	Phi., Van., Chi., Edm.	9	411	1,556	3.79
Stan Smyl,	Van.	13	896	1,556	1.74
*Dave Brown,	Phi., Edm.	11	593	1,553	2.62
Mike Milbury,	Boston	12	754	1,552	2.06
Dave Hutchison,	L.A., Tor., Chi., N.J.	10	584	1,550	2.65
Doug Risebrough,	Mtl., Cal.	14	740	1,542	2.08
*Gordie Roberts,	Hfd., Min., Phi., St. L., Pit., Bos.	14	1,038	1,542	1.49
Bill Gadsby,	Chi., NYR, Det.	20	1,248	1,539	1.23
*Randy Moller,	Que., NYR, Buf.	12	720	1,522	2.11
*Chris Chelios,	Mtl., Chi.	10	643	1,502	2.34

One Season Scoring Records

Goals-Per-Game Leaders, One Season

(Among players with 20 goals or more in one season)

Player	Team	Season	Games	Goals	Average
Joe Malone	Montreal	1917-18	20	44	2.20
Cy Denneny	Ottawa	1917-18	22	36	1.64
Newsy Lalonde	Montreal	1917-18	14	23	1.64
Joe Malone	Quebec	1919-20	24	39	1.63
Newsy Lalonde	Montreal	1919-20	23	36	1.57
Joe Malone	Hamilton	1920-21	20	30	1.50
Babe Dye	Ham., Tor.	1920-21	24	35	1.46
Cy Denneny	Ottawa	1920-21	24	34	1.42
Reg Noble	Toronto	1917-18	20	28	1.40
Newsy Lalonde	Montreal	1920-21	24	33	1.38
Odie Cleghorn	Montreal	1918-19	17	23	1.35
Harry Broadbent	Ottawa	1921-22	24	32	1.33
Babe Dye	Toronto	1924-25	29	38	1.31
Babe Dye	Toronto	1921-22	24	30	1.25
Newsy Lalonde	Montreal	1918-19	17	21	1.24
Cy Denneny	Ottawa	1921-22	22	27	1.23
Aurel Joliat	Montreal	1924-25	24	29	1.21
Wayne Gretzky	Edmonton	1983-84	74	87	1.18
Babe Dye	Toronto	1922-23	22	26	1.18
Wayne Gretzky	Edmonton	1981-82	80	92	1.15
Mario Lemieux	Pittsburgh	1992-93	60	69	1.15
Frank Nighbor	Ottawa	1919-20	23	26	1.13
Mario Lemieux	Pittsburgh	1988-89	76	85	1.12
Brett Hull	St. Louis	1990-91	78	86	1.10
Amos Arbour	Montreal	1919-20	20	22	1.10
Cy Denneny	Ottawa	1923-24	21	22	1.05
Joe Malone	Hamilton	1921-22	24	25	1.04
Billy Boucher	Montreal	1922-23	24	25	1.04
Maurice Richard	Montreal	1944-45	50	50	1.00
Howie Morenz	Montreal	1924-25	30	30	1.00
Reg Noble	Toronto	1919-20	24	24	1.00
Corbett Denneny	Toronto	1919-20	23	23	1.00
Jack Darragh	Ottawa	1919-20	22	22	1.00
Alexander Mogilny	Buffalo	1992-93	77	76	.99
Cooney Weiland	Boston	1929-30	44	43	.98
Phil Esposito	Boston	1970-71	78	76	.97
Jari Kurri	Edmonton	1984-85	73	71	.97

Assists-Per-Game Leaders, One Season

(Among players with 35 assists or more in one season)

Player	Team	Season	Games	Assists	Average
Wayne Gretzky	Edmonton	1985-86	80	163	2.04
Wayne Gretzky	Edmonton	1987-88	64	109	1.70
Wayne Gretzky	Edmonton	1984-85	80	135	1.69
Wayne Gretzky	Edmonton	1983-84	74	118	1.59
Wayne Gretzky	Edmonton	1982-83	80	125	1.56
Wayne Gretzky	Los Angeles	1990-91	78	122	1.56
Wayne Gretzky	Edmonton	1986-87	79	121	1.53
Mario Lemieux	Pittsburgh	**1992-93**	60	91	1.52
Wayne Gretzky	Edmonton	1981-82	80	120	1.50
Mario Lemieux	Pittsburgh	1988-89	76	114	1.50
Adam Oates	St. Louis	1990-91	61	90	1.48
Wayne Gretzky	Los Angeles	1988-89	78	114	1.46
Wayne Gretzky	Los Angeles	1989-90	73	102	1.40
Wayne Gretzky	Edmonton	1980-81	80	109	1.36
Mario Lemieux	Pittsburgh	1991-92	64	87	1.36
Mario Lemieux	Pittsburgh	1989-90	59	78	1.32
Bobby Orr	Boston	1970-71	78	102	1.31
Mario Lemieux	Pittsburgh	1987-88	77	98	1.27
Bobby Orr	Boston	1973-74	74	90	1.22
Wayne Gretzky	Los Angeles	1991-92	74	90	1.22
Mario Lemieux	Pittsburgh	1985-86	79	93	1.18
Bobby Clarke	Philadelphia	1975-76	76	89	1.17
Peter Stastny	Quebec	1981-82	80	93	1.16
Adam Oates	Boston	**1992-93**	84	97	1.15
Doug Gilmour	Toronto	**1992-93**	83	95	1.14
Paul Coffey	Edmonton	1985-86	79	90	1.14
Bobby Orr	Boston	1969-70	76	87	1.14
Bryan Trottier	NY Islanders	1978-79	76	87	1.14
Bobby Orr	Boston	1972-73	63	72	1.14
Bill Cowley	Boston	1943-44	36	41	1.14
Pat LaFontaine	Buffalo	**1992-93**	84	95	1.13
Steve Yzerman	Detroit	1988-89	80	90	1.13
Paul Coffey	Pittsburgh	1987-88	46	52	1.13
Bobby Orr	Boston	1974-75	80	89	1.11
Bobby Clarke	Philadelphia	1974-75	80	89	1.11
Paul Coffey	Pittsburgh	1988-89	75	83	1.11
Wayne Gretzky	Los Angeles	**1992-93**	45	49	1.11
Denis Savard	Chicago	1982-83	78	86	1.10
Denis Savard	Chicago	1981-82	80	87	1.09
Denis Savard	Chicago	1987-88	80	87	1.09
Wayne Gretzky	Edmonton	1979-80	79	86	1.09
Paul Coffey	Edmonton	1983-84	80	86	1.08
Elmer Lach	Montreal	1944-45	50	54	1.08
Peter Stastny	Quebec	1985-86	76	81	1.07
Mark Messier	Edmonton	1989-90	79	84	1.06
Paul Coffey	Edmonton	1984-85	80	84	1.05
Marcel Dionne	Los Angeles	1979-80	80	84	1.05
Bobby Orr	Boston	1971-72	76	80	1.05
Mike Bossy	NY Islanders	1981-82	80	83	1.04
Phil Esposito	Boston	1968-69	74	77	1.04
Bryan Trottier	NY Islanders	1983-84	68	71	1.04
Pete Mahovlich	Montreal	1974-75	80	82	1.03
Kent Nilsson	Calgary	1980-81	80	82	1.03
Peter Stastny	Quebec	1982-83	75	77	1.03
Bernie Nicholls	Los Angeles	1988-89	79	80	1.01
Guy Lafleur	Montreal	1979-80	74	75	1.01
Guy Lafleur	Montreal	1976-77	80	80	1.00
Marcel Dionne	Los Angeles	1984-85	80	80	1.00
Brian Leetch	NY Rangers	1991-92	80	80	1.00
Bryan Trottier	NY Islanders	1977-78	77	77	1.00
Mike Bossy	NY Islanders	1983-84	67	67	1.00
Jean Ratelle	NY Rangers	1971-72	63	63	1.00
Ron Francis	Hartford	1985-86	53	53	1.00
Guy Chouinard	Calgary	1980-81	52	52	1.00

Penalty Leaders

* Match Misconduct penalty not included in total penalty minutes.
** Three Match Misconduct penalties not included in total penalty minutes.
1946-47 was the first season that a Match penalty was automatically written into the player's total penalty minutes as 20 minutes. Now all penalties, Match, Game Misconduct, and Misconduct, are written as 10 minutes. Penalty minutes not calculated in 1917-18.

Season	Player and Club	GP	PIM
1992-93	Marty McSorley, Los Angeles	81	399
1991-92	Mike Peluso, Chicago	63	408
1990-91	Rob Ray, Buffalo	66	350
1989-90	Basil McRae, Minnesota	66	351
1988-89	Tim Hunter, Calgary	75	375
1987-88	Bob Probert, Detroit	74	398
1986-87	Tim Hunter, Calgary	73	361
1985-86	Joey Kocur, Detroit	59	377
1984-85	Chris Nilan, Montreal	77	358
1983-84	Chris Nilan, Montreal	76	338
1982-83	Randy Holt, Washington	70	275
1981-82	Paul Baxter, Pittsburgh	76	409
1980-81	Dave Williams, Vancouver	77	343
1979-80	Jimmy Mann, Winnipeg	72	287
1978-79	Dave Williams, Toronto	77	298
1977-78	Dave Schultz, L.A., Pit.	74	405
1976-77	Dave Williams, Toronto	77	338
1975-76	Steve Durbano, Pit., K.C.	69	370
1974-75	Dave Schultz, Philadelphia	76	472
1973-74	Dave Schultz, Philadelphia	73	348
1972-73	Dave Schultz, Philadelphia	76	259
1971-72	Bryan Watson, Pittsburgh	75	212
1970-71	Keith Magnuson, Chicago	76	291
1969-70	Keith Magnuson, Chicago	76	213
1968-69	Forbes Kennedy, Phi., Tor.	77	219

Season	Player and Club	GP	PIM
1967-68	Barclay Plager, St. Louis	49	153
1966-67	John Ferguson, Montreal	67	177
1965-66	Reg Fleming, Bos., NYR	69	166
1964-65	Carl Brewer, Toronto	70	177
1963-64	Vic Hadfield, NY Rangers	69	151
1962-63	Howie Young, Detroit	64	273
1961-62	Lou Fontinato, Montreal	54	167
1960-61	Pierre Pilote, Chicago	70	165
1959-60	Carl Brewer, Toronto	67	150
1958-59	Ted Lindsay, Chicago	70	184
1957-58	Lou Fontinato, NY Rangers	70	152
1956-57	Gus Mortson, Chicago	70	147
1955-56	Lou Fontinato, NY Rangers	70	202
1954-55	Fern Flaman, Boston	70	150
1953-54	Gus Mortson, Chicago	68	132
1952-53	Maurice Richard, Montreal	70	112
1951-52	Gus Kyle, Boston	69	127
1950-51	Gus Mortson, Toronto	60	142
1949-50	Bill Ezinicki, Toronto	67	144
1948-49	Bill Ezinicki, Toronto	52	145
1947-48	Bill Barilko, Toronto	57	147
1946-47	Gus Mortson, Toronto	60	133
1945-46	Jack Stewart, Detroit	47	73
1944-45	Pat Egan, Boston	48	86
1943-44	Mike McMahon, Montreal	42	98

Season	Player and Club	GP	PIM
1942-43	Jimmy Orlando, Detroit	40	89*
1941-42	Jimmy Orlando, Detroit	48	81**
1940-41	Jimmy Orlando, Detroit	48	99
1939-40	Red Horner, Toronto	30	87
1938-39	Red Horner, Toronto	48	85
1937-38	Red Horner, Toronto	47	82*
1936-37	Red Horner, Toronto	48	124
1935-36	Red Horner, Toronto	43	167
1934-35	Red Horner, Toronto	46	125
1933-34	Red Horner, Toronto	42	126*
1932-33	Red Horner, Toronto	48	144
1931-32	Red Dutton, NY Americans	47	107
1930-31	Harvey Rockburn, Detroit	42	118
1929-30	Joe Lamb, Ottawa	44	119
1928-29	Red Dutton, Mtl. Maroons	44	139
1927-28	Eddie Shore, Boston	44	165
1926-27	Nels Stewart, Mtl. Maroons	44	133
1925-26	Bert Corbeau, Toronto	36	121
1924-25	Billy Boucher, Montreal	30	92
1923-24	Bert Corbeau, Toronto	24	55
1922-23	Billy Boucher, Montreal	24	52
1921-22	Sprague Cleghorn, Montreal	24	63
1920-21	Bert Corbeau, Montreal	24	86
1919-20	Cully Wilson, Toronto	23	79
1918-19	Joe Hall, Montreal	17	85

Points-Per-Game Leaders, One Season

(Among players with 50 points or more in one season)

Player	Team	Season	Games	Points	Average
Wayne Gretzky	Edmonton	1983-84	74	205	2.77
Wayne Gretzky	Edmonton	1985-86	80	215	2.69
Mario Lemieux	Pittsburgh	**1992-93**	60	160	2.67
Wayne Gretzky	Edmonton	1981-82	80	212	2.65
Mario Lemieux	Pittsburgh	1988-89	76	199	2.62
Wayne Gretzky	Edmonton	1984-85	80	208	2.60
Wayne Gretzky	Edmonton	1982-83	80	196	2.45
Wayne Gretzky	Edmonton	1987-88	64	149	2.33
Wayne Gretzky	Edmonton	1986-87	79	183	2.32
Mario Lemieux	Pittsburgh	1987-88	77	168	2.18
Wayne Gretzky	Los Angeles	1988-89	78	168	2.15
Wayne Gretzky	Los Angeles	1990-91	78	163	2.09
Mario Lemieux	Pittsburgh	1989-90	59	123	2.08
Wayne Gretzky	Edmonton	1980-81	80	164	2.05
Mario Lemieux	Pittsburgh	1991-92	64	131	2.05
Bill Cowley	Boston	1943-44	36	71	1.97
Phil Esposito	Boston	1970-71	78	152	1.95
Wayne Gretzky	Los Angeles	1989-90	73	142	1.95
Steve Yzerman	Detroit	1988-89	80	155	1.94
Bernie Nicholls	Los Angeles	1988-89	79	150	1.90
Adam Oates	St. Louis	1990-91	61	115	1.89
Phil Esposito	Boston	1973-74	78	145	1.86
Jari Kurri	Edmonton	1984-85	73	135	1.85
Mike Bossy	NY Islanders	1981-82	80	147	1.84
Mario Lemieux	Pittsburgh	1985-86	79	141	1.78
Bobby Orr	Boston	1970-71	78	139	1.78
Jari Kurri	Edmonton	1983-84	64	113	1.77
Pat LaFontaine	Buffalo	**1992-93**	84	148	1.76
Bryan Trottier	NY Islanders	1978-79	76	134	1.76
Mike Bossy	NY Islanders	1983-84	67	118	1.76
Paul Coffey	Edmonton	1985-86	79	138	1.75
Phil Esposito	Boston	1971-72	76	133	1.75
Peter Stastny	Quebec	1981-82	80	139	1.74
Wayne Gretzky	Edmonton	1979-80	79	137	1.73
Jean Ratelle	NY Rangers	1971-72	63	109	1.73
Marcel Dionne	Los Angeles	1979-80	80	137	1.71
Herb Cain	Boston	1943-44	48	82	1.71
Guy Lafleur	Montreal	1976-77	80	136	1.70
Dennis Maruk	Washington	1981-82	80	136	1.70
Phil Esposito	Boston	1968-69	74	126	1.70
Guy Lafleur	Montreal	1974-75	70	119	1.70
Mario Lemieux	Pittsburgh	1986-87	63	107	1.70
Adam Oates	Boston	**1992-93**	84	142	1.69
Bobby Orr	Boston	1974-75	80	135	1.69
Marcel Dionne	Los Angeles	1980-81	80	135	1.69
Guy Lafleur	Montreal	1977-78	78	132	1.69
Guy Lafleur	Montreal	1979-80	74	125	1.69
Rob Brown	Pittsburgh	1988-89	68	115	1.69
Jari Kurri	Edmonton	1985-86	78	131	1.68
Brett Hull	St. Louis	1990-91	78	131	1.68
Phil Esposito	Boston	1972-73	78	130	1.67
Cooney Weiland	Boston	1929-30	44	73	1.66
Alexander Mogilny	Buffalo	**1992-93**	77	127	1.65
Peter Stastny	Quebec	1982-83	75	124	1.65
Bobby Orr	Boston	1973-74	74	122	1.65
Kent Nilsson	Calgary	1980-81	80	131	1.64
Wayne Gretzky	Los Angeles	1991-92	74	121	1.64
Denis Savard	Chicago	1987-88	80	131	1.64
Steve Yzerman	Detroit	**1992-93**	84	137	1.63
Marcel Dionne	Los Angeles	1978-79	80	130	1.63
Dale Hawerchuk	Winnipeg	1984-85	80	130	1.63
Mark Messier	Edmonton	1989-90	79	129	1.63
Bryan Trottier	NY Islanders	1983-84	68	111	1.63
Pat LaFontaine	Buffalo	1991-92	57	93	1.63
Charlie Simmer	Los Angeles	1980-81	65	105	1.62
Guy Lafleur	Montreal	1978-79	80	129	1.61
Bryan Trottier	NY Islanders	1981-82	80	129	1.61
Phil Esposito	Boston	1974-75	79	127	1.61
Steve Yzerman	Detroit	1989-90	79	127	1.61
Peter Stastny	Quebec	1985-86	76	122	1.61
Michel Goulet	Quebec	1983-84	75	121	1.61
Bryan Trottier	NY Islanders	1977-78	77	123	1.60
Bobby Orr	Boston	1972-73	63	101	1.60
Guy Chouinard	Calgary	1980-81	52	83	1.60
Elmer Lach	Montreal	1944-45	50	80	1.60
Pierre Larouche	NY Islanders	**1992-93**	83	132	1.59
Steve Yzerman	Detroit	1987-88	64	102	1.59
Mike Bossy	NY Islanders	1978-79	80	126	1.58
Paul Coffey	Edmonton	1983-84	80	126	1.58
Marcel Dionne	Los Angeles	1984-85	80	126	1.58
Bobby Orr	Boston	1969-70	76	120	1.58
Charlie Simmer	Los Angeles	1979-80	64	101	1.58
Teemu Selanne	Winnipeg	**1992-93**	84	132	1.57
Bobby Clarke	Philadelphia	1975-76	76	119	1.57
Guy Lafleur	Montreal	1975-76	80	125	1.56
Dave Taylor	Los Angeles	1980-81	72	112	1.56
Denis Savard	Chicago	1982-83	78	121	1.55
Mike Bossy	NY Islanders	1985-86	80	123	1.54
Bobby Orr	Boston	1971-72	76	117	1.54
Kevin Stevens	Pittsburgh	1991-92	80	123	1.54
Mike Bossy	NY Islanders	1984-85	76	117	1.54
Kevin Stevens	Pittsburgh	**1992-93**	72	111	1.54
Doug Bentley	Chicago	1943-44	50	77	1.54
Doug Gilmour	Toronto	**1992-93**	83	127	1.53
Marcel Dionne	Los Angeles	1976-77	80	122	1.53
Marcel Dionne	Detroit	1974-75	80	121	1.51
Paul Coffey	Pittsburgh	1988-89	75	113	1.51

Steve Yzerman, left, averaged 1.94 points-per-game for the Detroit Red Wings during the 1988-89 season. Bobby Clarke, right, was the first player from a 1967-expansion club to win the Hart Trophy, averaging 1.57 points-per-game for Philadelphia in 1975-76.

Active NHL Players' Three-or-More-Goal Games

Regular Season

Teams named are the ones the players were with at the time of their multiple-scoring games. Players listed alphabetically.

Player	Team	3-Goals	4-Goals	5-Goals
Acton, Keith	Mtl., Min.	3	—	—
Adams, Greg	Vancouver	1	1	—
Amonte, Tony	NY Rangers	1	—	—
Anderson, Glenn	Edm., Tor.	18	3	—
Anderson, Perry	New Jersey	1	—	—
Andersson, Mikael	Tampa Bay	1	—	—
Andreychuk, Dave	Buffalo	6	2	1
Arniel, Scott	Winnipeg	1	—	—
Ashton, Brent	Que., Wpg.	6	—	—
Babych, Dave	Vancouver	1	—	—
Barnes, Stu	Winnipeg	1	—	—
Barr, Dave	St. L., Det.	2	—	—
Bellows, Brian	Min., Mtl.	5	3	—
Bjugstad, Scott	Minnesota	3	—	—
Bondra, Peter	Washington	1	—	—
Boschman, Laurie	Wpg., Ott.	3	—	—
Bourque, Phil	Pittsburgh	1	—	—
Bourque, Ray	Boston	1	—	—
Bradley, Brian	Tampa Bay	1	—	—
Brickley, Andy	Pit., Bos.	2	—	—
Brind'Amour, Rod	Philadelphia	1	—	—
Broten, Neal	Minnesota	6	—	—
Broten, Paul	NY Rangers	1	—	—
Brown, Rob	Pittsburgh	7	—	—
Buchberger, Kelly	Edmonton	1	—	—
Bullard, Mike	Pit., Tor.	8	—	—
Bure, Pavel	Vancouver	1	1	—
Burr, Shawn	Detroit	2	—	—
Burridge, Randy	Boston	2	—	—
Carbonneau, Guy	Montreal	—	1	—
Carpenter, Bob	Wsh., Bos.	2	1	—
Carson, Jimmy	L.A., Edm., Det.	9	1	—
Cavallini, Gino	St. Louis	1	—	—
Chabot, John	Pittsburgh	1	—	—
Christian, Dave	Wpg., Wsh.	2	—	1
Ciccarelli, Dino	Min., Wsh.	14	3	1
Clark, Wendel	Toronto	4	1	—
Coffey, Paul	Edmonton	4	1	—
Corson, Shayne	Montreal	2	—	—
Courtnall, Geoff	Bos., Wsh.	2	—	—
Courtnall, Russ	Tor., Mtl., Min.	3	—	—
Craven, Murray	Philadelphia	3	—	—
Creighton, Adam	Buf., Chi.	2	—	—
Crossman, Doug	Tampa Bay	1	—	—
Cullen, John	Pit., Hfd.	3	—	—
Cunneyworth, R.	Pittsburgh	1	1	—
Cyr, Paul	Buffalo	1	—	—
Dahlen, Ulf	NYR, Min.	3	—	—
Damphousse, V.	Tor., Edm., Mtl.	5	1	—
Davydov, Evgeny	Winnipeg	1	—	—
Dineen, Kevin	Hfd., Phi.	8	—	—
Dionne, Gilbert	Montreal	1	—	—
Donnelly, Mike	Los Angeles	1	—	—
Druce, John	Washington	1	—	—
Duchesne, Steve	L.A., Phi.	2	—	—
Duncan, Iain	Winnipeg	1	—	—
Eklund, Pelle	Philadelphia	1	—	—
Errey, Bob	Pittsburgh	1	—	—
Evason, Dean	Hartford	1	—	—
Fergus, Tom	Toronto	4	—	—
Ferraro, Ray	Hfd., NYI	6	1	—
Flatley, Patrick	NY Islanders	1	1	—
Fleury, Theo	Calgary	6	—	—
Fogarty, Bryan	Quebec	1	—	—
Foligno, Mike	Det., Buf.	8	—	—
Francis, Ron	Hartford	8	1	—
Gagner, Dave	Minnesota	3	—	—
Gallant, Gerard	Detroit	4	—	—
Garpenlov, Johan	Det., S.J.	1	1	—
Gartner, Mike	Wsh., Min., NYR	13	2	—
Gaudreau, Rob	San Jose	2	—	—
Gelinas, Martin	Edmonton	1	—	—
Gilbert, Greg	NY Islanders	2	—	—
Gilchrist, Brent	Montreal	1	—	—
Gillis, Paul	Quebec	1	—	—
Gilmour, Doug	St. Louis	1	—	—
Goulet, Michel	Que., Chi.	14	2	—
Graham, Dirk	Minnesota	1	—	—
Granato, Tony	NYR, L.A.	3	1	—
Graves, Adam	Edm., NYR	3	—	—
Gretzky, Wayne	Edm., L.A.	36	9	4
Hannan, Dave	Edmonton	1	—	—
Hatcher, Kevin	Washington	1	—	—
Hawerchuk, Dale	Wpg., Buf.	13	—	—
Heinze, Stephen	Boston	1	—	—
Hodge, Ken	Boston	2	—	—
Hogue, Benoit	NY Islanders	1	—	—
Holik, Bobby	New Jersey	2	—	—

Player	Team	3-Goal	4-Goal	5-Goal
Horacek, Tony	Philadelphia	1	—	—
Housley, Phil	Buffalo	2	—	—
Howe, Mark	Hartford	1	—	—
Hull, Brett	Cgy., St. L.	18	—	—
Hull, Jody	Hartford	1	—	—
Hunter, Dale	Que., Wsh.	4	—	—
Hunter, Mark	St. L., Cgy.	5	1	—
Jagr, Jaromir	Pittsburgh	1	—	—
Janney, Craig	Bos., St. L.	3	—	—
Juneau, Joe	Boston	1	—	—
Kasper, Steve	Boston	3	—	—
Kerr, Tim	Philadelphia	13	4	—
Khmylev, Yuri	Buffalo	1	—	—
Khristich, Dimitri	Washington	2	—	—
King, Derek	NY Islanders	3	1	—
Klima, Petr	Det., Edm.	6	—	—
Kontos, Chris	Tampa Bay	—	1	—
Kovalenko, Andrei	Quebec	1	—	—
Kovalev, Alexei	NY Rangers	1	—	—
Krushelnyski, Mike	Edmonton	1	—	—
Kudelski, Robert	L.A., Ott.	3	—	—
Kurri, Jari	Edm., L.A.	20	1	1
LaFontaine, Pat	NYI, Buf.	12	—	—
Larionov, Igor	Vancouver	2	—	—
Larmer, Steve	Chicago	9	—	—
Lawton, Brian	Minnesota	2	—	—
Lebeau, Stephan	Montreal	1	—	—
Leeman, Gary	Tor., Cgy.	5	—	—
Lemieux, Claude	Mtl., N.J.	4	—	—
Lemieux, Jocelyn	Chicago	1	—	—
Lemieux, Mario	Pittsburgh	21	8	2
Linden, Trevor	Vancouver	3	—	—
Lindros, Eric	Philadelphia	3	—	—
MacInnis, Al	Calgary	1	—	—
MacLean, John	New Jersey	6	—	—
MacTavish, Craig	Edmonton	2	—	—
Makarov, Sergei	Calgary	3	—	—
Makela, Mikko	NY Islanders	1	—	—
Maley, David	New Jersey	1	—	—
Marois, Daniel	Toronto	3	—	—
McBain, Andrew	Winnipeg	1	—	—
McPhee, Mike	Montreal	3	—	—
Messier, Mark	Edm., NYR	12	4	—
Miller, Kevin	Det., St.L.	2	—	—
Modano, Mike	Minnesota	1	—	—
Mogilny, Alexander	Buffalo	7	2	—
Momesso, Sergio	Montreal	1	—	—
Mullen, Brian	Wpg., NYR	2	—	—
Mullen, Joe	St. L., Cgy., Pit.	7	4	—
Muller, Kirk	N.J., Mtl.	6	—	—
Murray, Troy	Chicago	4	—	—
Murzyn, Dana	Calgary	1	—	—
Neely, Cam	Boston	8	—	—
Nemchinov, Sergei	NY Rangers	1	—	—
Nicholls, Bernie	Los Angeles	12	2	—
Nieuwendyk, Joe	Calgary	5	2	1
Noonan, Brian	Chicago	2	1	—
Nolan, Owen	Quebec	4	—	—
Nylander, Michael	Hartford	1	—	—
Oates, Adam	Boston	3	—	—
Ogrodnick, John	Detroit	6	—	—
Olczyk, Ed	Tor., NYR	3	—	—
Osborne, Mark	Detroit	1	—	—
Otto, Joel	Calgary	1	—	—

Player	Team	3-Goal	4-Goal	5-Goal
Paslawski, Greg	St.L., Phi.	3	—	—
Pivonka, Michal	Washington	1	—	—
Poulin, Dave	Philadelphia	5	—	—
Presley, Wayne	Chicago	1	—	—
Probert, Bob	Detroit	1	—	—
Prokhorov, Vitali	St. Louis	1	—	—
Propp, Brian	Philadelphia	3	1	—
Quinn, Dan	Pit., Van.	4	—	—
Ranheim, Paul	Calgary	1	—	—
Recchi, Mark	Pittsburgh	1	—	—
Reichel, Robert	Calgary	2	—	—
Richer, Stephane	Mtl., N.J.	7	1	—
Ridley, Mike	NYR, Wsh.	3	1	—
Roberts, Gary	Calgary	5	—	—
Robitaille, Luc	Los Angeles	9	1	—
Roenick, Jeremy	Chicago	4	2	—
Ronning, Cliff	St.L., Van.	2	—	—
Ruff, Lindy	Buffalo	1	1	—
Ruzicka, Vladimir	Boston	3	—	—
Sakic, Joe	Quebec	5	—	—
Sanderson, Geoff	Hartford	2	—	—
Sandlak, Jim	Vancouver	1	—	—
Sandstrom, Tomas	NYR, L.A.	7	1	—
Savard, Denis	Chi., Mtl.	12	—	—
Selanne, Teemu	Winnipeg	4	1	—
Shanahan, Brendan	N.J., St.L.	2	—	—
Sheppard, Ray	Buf., Det.	3	—	—
Sinisalo, Ilkka	Philadelphia	3	—	—
Simpson, Craig	Pit., Edm.	3	—	—
Skriko, Petri	Vancouver	4	1	—
Smail, Doug	Winnipeg	2	—	—
Smith, Derrick	Philadelphia	1	—	—
Smith, Bobby	Minnesota	5	1	—
Stastny, Peter	Que., N.J.	15	2	—
Steen, Thomas	Winnipeg	4	—	—
Stern, Ronnie	Calgary	2	—	—
Stevens, Kevin	Pittsburgh	7	2	—
Sundin, Mats	Quebec	3	—	1
Sutter, Brent	NY Islanders	6	—	—
Sutter, Rich	Vancouver	1	—	—
Sweeney, Bob	Boston	1	—	—
Tanti, Tony	Van., Pit., Buf.	11	1	—
Taylor, Dave	Los Angeles	7	1	—
Thomas, Steve	Chi., NYI	3	2	—
Tikkanen, Esa	Edmonton	3	—	—
Tocchet, Rick	Phi., Pit.	9	2	—
Trottier, Bryan	NY Islanders	13	1	2
Tucker, John	Buffalo	1	—	—
Turcotte, Darren	NY Rangers	4	—	—
Turgeon, Pierre	Buf., NYI	8	—	—
Turgeon, Sylvain	Hfd., N.J.	4	—	—
Verbeek, Pat	N.J., Hfd.	6	1	—
Volek, Dave	NY Islanders	1	—	—
Vukota, Mick	NY Islanders	1	—	—
Walter, Ryan	Montreal	1	—	—
Wilson, Carey	Calgary	2	—	—
Wilson, Doug	Chicago	1	—	—
Wood, Randy	NY Islanders	1	—	—
Young, Scott	Quebec	1	—	—
Yzerman, Steve	Detroit	17	1	—
Ysebaert, Paul	Detroit	1	—	—
Zezel, Peter	Philadelphia	1	—	—

Alexander Mogilny has recorded nine three-or-more goal games for the Buffalo Sabres in his first four NHL seasons.

Denis Savard collected 75 points as a rookie for the Chicago Blackhawks in 1980-81.

Rookie Scoring Records

All-Time Top 50 Goal-Scoring Rookies

	Rookie	Team	Position	Season	GP	G	A	PTS
1.	*Teemu Selanne	Winnipeg	Right wing	1992-93	84	76	56	132
2.	*Mike Bossy	NY Islanders	Right wing	1977-78	73	53	38	91
3.	*Joe Nieuwendyk	Calgary	Center	1987-88	75	51	41	92
4.	*Dale Hawerchuk	Winnipeg	Center	1981-82	80	45	58	103
	*Luc Robitaille	Los Angeles	Left wing	1986-87	79	45	39	84
6.	Rick Martin	Buffalo	Left wing	1971-72	73	44	30	74
	Barry Pederson	Boston	Center	1981-82	80	44	48	92
8.	*Steve Larmer	Chicago	Right wing	1982-83	80	43	47	90
	*Mario Lemieux	Pittsburgh	Center	1984-85	73	43	57	100
10.	Eric Lindros	Philadelphia	Center	1992-93	61	41	34	75
11.	Darryl Sutter	Chicago	Left wing	1980-81	76	40	22	62
	Sylvain Turgeon	Hartford	Left wing	1983-84	76	40	32	72
	Warren Young	Pittsburgh	Left wing	1984-85	80	40	32	72
14.	Eric Vail	Atlanta	Left wing	1974-75	72	39	21	60
	Anton Stastny	Quebec	Left wing	1980-81	80	39	46	85
	*Peter Stastny	Quebec	Center	1980-81	77	39	70	109
	Steve Yzerman	Detroit	Center	1983-84	80	39	48	87
18.	*Gilbert Perreault	Buffalo	Center	1970-71	78	38	34	72
	Neal Broten	Minnesota	Center	1981-82	73	38	60	98
	Ray Sheppard	Buffalo	Right wing	1987-88	74	38	27	65
21.	Jorgen Pettersson	St. Louis	Left wing	1980-81	62	37	36	73
	Jimmy Carson	Los Angeles	Centre	1986-87	80	37	42	79
23.	Mike Foligno	Detroit	Right wing	1979-80	80	36	35	71
	Mike Bullard	Pittsburgh	Center	1981-82	75	36	27	63
	Paul MacLean	Winnipeg	Right wing	1981-82	74	36	25	61
	Tony Granato	NY Rangers	Right wing	1988-89	78	36	27	63
27.	Marian Stastny	Quebec	Right wing	1981-82	74	35	54	89
	Brian Bellows	Minnesota	Right wing	1982-83	78	35	30	65
	Tony Amonte	NY Rangers	Right wing	1991-92	79	35	34	69
30.	Nels Stewart	Mtl. Maroons	Center	1925-26	36	34	8	42
	*Danny Grant	Minnesota	Left wing	1968-69	75	34	31	65
	Norm Ferguson	Oakland	Right wing	1968-69	76	34	20	54
	Brian Propp	Philadelphia	Left wing	1979-80	80	34	41	75
	Wendel Clark	Toronto	Left wing	1985-86	66	34	11	45
	*Pavel Bure	Vancouver	Right wing	1991-92	65	34	26	60
36.	*Willi Plett	Atlanta	Right wing	1976-77	64	33	23	56
	Dale McCourt	Detroit	Center	1977-78	76	33	39	72
	Mark Pavelich	NY Rangers	Center	1981-82	79	33	43	76
	Ron Flockhart	Philadelphia	Center	1981-82	72	33	39	72
	Steve Bozek	Los Angeles	Center	1981-82	71	33	23	56
41.	Bill Mosienko	Chicago	Right wing	1943-44	50	32	38	70
	Michel Bergeron	Detroit	Right wing	1975-76	72	32	27	59
	*Bryan Trottier	NY Islanders	Center	1975-76	80	32	63	95
	Don Murdoch	NY Rangers	Right wing	1976-77	59	32	24	56
	Jari Kurri	Edmonton	Left wing	1980-81	75	32	43	75
	Bobby Carpenter	Washington	Center	1981-82	80	32	35	67
	Kjell Dahlin	Montreal	Right wing	1985-86	77	32	39	71
	Petr Klima	Detroit	Left wing	1985-86	74	32	24	56
	Darren Turcotte	NY Rangers	Right wing	1989-90	76	32	34	66
	Joe Juneau	Boston	Center	1992-93	84	32	70	102

* Calder Trophy Winner

All-Time Top 50 Point-Scoring Rookies

	Rookie	Team	Position	Season	GP	G	A	PTS
1.	*Teemu Selanne	Winnipeg	Right wing	1992-93	84	76	56	132
2.	*Peter Stastny	Quebec	Center	1980-81	77	39	70	109
3.	*Dale Hawerchuk	Winnipeg	Center	1981-82	80	45	58	103
4.	Joe Juneau	Boston	Center	1992-93	84	32	70	102
5.	*Mario Lemieux	Pittsburgh	Center	1984-85	73	43	57	100
6.	Neal Broten	Minnesota	Center	1981-82	73	38	60	98
7.	*Bryan Trottier	NY Islanders	Center	1975-76	80	32	63	95
8.	Barry Pederson	Boston	Center	1981-82	80	44	48	92
	*Joe Nieuwendyk	Calgary	Center	1987-88	75	51	41	92
10.	*Mike Bossy	NY Islanders	Right wing	1977-78	73	53	38	91
11.	*Steve Larmer	Chicago	Right wing	1982-83	80	43	47	90
12.	Marian Stastny	Quebec	Right wing	1981-82	74	35	54	89
13.	Steve Yzerman	Detroit	Center	1983-84	80	39	48	87
14.	*Sergei Makarov	Calgary	Right wing	1989-90	80	24	62	86
15.	Anton Stastny	Quebec	Left wing	1980-81	80	39	46	85
16.	*Luc Robitaille	Los Angeles	Left wing	1986-87	79	45	39	84
17.	Jimmy Carson	Los Angeles	Center	1986-87	80	37	42	79
	Sergei Fedorov	Detroit	Center	1990-91	77	31	48	79
19.	Marcel Dionne	Detroit	Center	1971-72	78	28	49	77
20.	Larry Murphy	Los Angeles	Defense	1980-81	80	16	60	76
	Mark Pavelich	NY Rangers	Center	1981-82	79	33	43	76
	Dave Poulin	Philadelphia	Center	1983-84	73	31	45	76
23.	Brian Propp	Philadelphia	Left wing	1979-80	80	34	41	75
	Jari Kurri	Edmonton	Left wing	1980-81	75	32	43	75
	Denis Savard	Chicago	Center	1980-81	76	28	47	75
	Mike Modano	Minnesota	Center	1989-90	80	29	46	75
	Eric Lindros	Philadelphia	Center	1992-93	61	41	34	75
28.	Rick Martin	Buffalo	Left wing	1971-72	73	44	30	74
	*Bobby Smith	Minnesota	Center	1978-79	80	30	44	74
30.	Jorgen Pettersson	St. Louis	Left wing	1980-81	62	37	36	73
31.	*Gilbert Perreault	Buffalo	Center	1970-71	78	38	34	72
	Dale McCourt	Detroit	Center	1977-78	76	33	39	72
	Ron Flockhart	Philadelphia	Center	1981-82	72	33	39	72
	Sylvain Turgeon	Hartford	Left wing	1983-84	76	40	32	72
	Warren Young	Pittsburgh	Left wing	1984-85	80	40	32	72
	Carey Wilson	Calgary	Center	1984-85	74	24	48	72
	Alexei Zhamnov	Winnipeg	Center	1992-93	68	25	47	72
38.	Mike Foligno	Detroit	Right wing	1979-80	80	36	35	71
	Dave Christian	Winnipeg	Center	1980-81	80	28	43	71
	Mats Naslund	Montreal	Left wing	1982-83	74	26	45	71
	Kjell Dahlin	Montreal	Right wing	1985-86	77	32	39	71
	*Brian Leetch	NY Rangers	Defense	1988-89	68	23	48	71
43.	Bill Mosienko	Chicago	Right wing	1943-44	50	32	38	70
44.	Roland Eriksson	Minnesota	Center	1976-77	80	25	44	69
	Tony Amonte	NY Rangers	Right wing	1991-92	79	35	34	69
46.	Jude Drouin	Minnesota	Center	1970-71	75	16	52	68
	Pierre Larouche	Pittsburgh	Center	1974-75	79	31	37	68
	Ron Francis	Hartford	Center	1981-82	59	25	43	68
	*Gary Suter	Calgary	Defense	1985-86	80	18	50	68
50.	Tom Webster	Detroit	Right wing	1970-71	78	30	37	67
	Bobby Carpenter	Washington	Center	1981-82	80	32	35	67
	Chris Valentine	Washington	Center	1981-82	60	30	37	67
	Mark Osborne	Detroit	Left wing	1981-82	80	26	41	67
	Mark Recchi	Pittsburgh	Right wing	1989-90	74	30	37	67

* Calder Trophy Winner

50-Goal Seasons

Mark Messier

Lanny McDonald

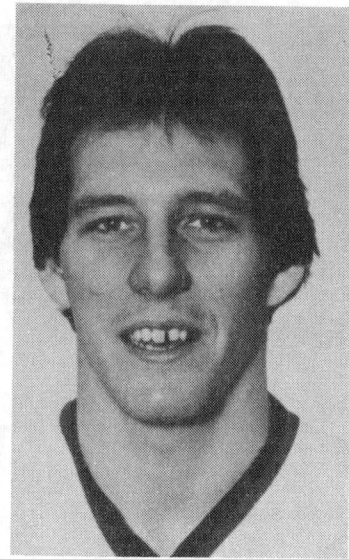

Al Secord

Player	Team	Date of 50th Goal	Score		Goaltender	Player's Game No.	Team Game No.	Total Goals	Total Games	Age When First 50th Scored (Yrs. & Mos.)
Maurice Richard	Mtl.	18-3-45	Mtl. 4	at Bos. 2	Harvey Bennett	50	50	50	50	23.7
Bernie Geoffrion	Mtl.	16-3-61	Tor. 2	at Mtl. 5	Cesare Maniago	62	68	50	64	30.1
Bobby Hull	Chi.	25-3-62	Chi. 1	at NYR 4	Gump Worsley	70	70	50	70	23.2
Bobby Hull	Chi.	2-3-66	Det. 4	at Chi. 5	Hank Bassen	52	57	54	65	
Bobby Hull	Chi.	18-3-67	Chi. 5	at Tor. 9	Bruce Gamble	63	66	52	66	
Bobby Hull	Chi.	5-3-69	NYR 4	at Chi. 4	Ed Giacomin	64	66	58	74	
Phil Esposito	Bos.	20-2-71	Bos. 4	at L.A. 5	Denis DeJordy	58	58	76	78	29.0
John Bucyk	Bos.	16-3-71	Bos. 11	at Det. 4	Roy Edwards	69	69	51	78	35.1
Phil Esposito	Bos.	20-2-72	Bos. 3	at Chi. 1	Tony Esposito	60	60	66	76	
Bobby Hull	Chi.	2-4-72	Det. 1	at Chi. 6	Andy Brown	78	78	50	78	
Vic Hadfield	NYR	2-4-72	Mtl. 6	at NYR 5	Denis DeJordy	78	78	50	78	31.6
Phil Esposito	Bos.	25-3-73	Buf. 1	at Bos. 6	Roger Crozier	75	75	55	78	
Mickey Redmond	Det.	27-3-73	Det. 8	at Tor. 1	Ron Low	73	75	52	76	25.3
Rick MacLeish	Phi.	1-4-73	Phi. 4	at Pit. 5	Cam Newton	78	78	50	78	23.2
Phil Esposito	Bos.	20-2-74	Bos. 5	at Min. 5	Cesare Maniago	56	56	68	78	
Mickey Redmond	Det.	23-3-74	NYR 3	at Det 5	Ed Giacomin	69	71	51	76	
Ken Hodge	Bos.	6-4-74	Bos. 2	at Mtl. 6	Michel Larocque	75	77	50	76	29.10
Rick Martin	Buf.	7-4-74	St. L. 2	at Buf. 5	Wayne Stephenson	78	78	52	78	22.9
Phil Esposito	Bos.	8-2-75	Bos. 8	at Det. 5	Jim Rutherford	54	54	61	79	
Guy Lafleur	Mtl.	29-3-75	K.C. 1	at Mtl. 4	Denis Herron	66	76	53	70	23.6
Danny Grant	Det.	2-4-75	Wsh. 3	at Det. 8	John Adams	78	78	50	80	29.2
Rick Martin	Buf.	3-4-75	Bos. 2	at Buf. 4	Ken Broderick	67	79	52	68	
Reggie Leach	Phi.	14-3-76	Atl. 1	at Phi. 6	Daniel Bouchard	69	69	61	80	25.11
Jean Pronovost	Pit.	24-3-76	Bos. 5	at Pit. 5	Gilles Gilbert	74	74	52	80	31.3
Guy Lafleur	Mtl.	27-3-76	K.C. 2	at Mtl. 8	Denis Herron	76	76	56	80	
Bill Barber	Phi.	3-4-76	Buf. 2	at Phi. 5	Al Smith	79	79	50	80	23.9
Pierre Larouche	Pit.	3-4-76	Wsh. 5	at Pit. 4	Ron Low	75	79	53	76	20.5
Danny Gare	Buf.	4-4-76	Tor. 2	at Buf. 5	Gord McRae	79	80	50	79	21.11
Steve Shutt	Mtl.	1-3-77	Mtl. 5	at NYI 4	Glenn Resch	65	65	60	80	24.8
Guy Lafleur	Mtl.	6-3-77	Mtl. 1	at Buf. 4	Don Edwards	68	68	56	80	
Marcel Dionne	L.A.	2-4-77	Min. 2	at L.A. 7	Pete LoPresti	79	79	53	80	25.8
Guy Lafleur	Mtl.	8-3-78	Wsh. 3	at Mtl. 4	Jim Bedard	63	65	60	78	
Mike Bossy	NYI	1-4-78	Wsh. 2	at NYI 3	Bernie Wolfe	69	76	53	73	21.2
Mike Bossy	NYI	24-2-79	Det. 1	at NYI 3	Rogie Vachon	58	58	69	80	
Marcel Dionne	L.A.	11-3-79	L.A. 3	at Phi. 6	Wayne Stephenson	68	68	59	80	
Guy Lafleur	Mtl.	31-3-79	Pit. 3	at Mtl. 5	Denis Herron	76	76	52	80	
Guy Chouinard	Atl.	6-4-79	NYR 2	at Atl. 9	John Davidson	79	79	50	80	22.5
Marcel Dionne	L.A.	12-3-80	L.A. 2	at Pit. 4	Nick Ricci	70	70	53	80	
Mike Bossy	NYI	16-3-80	NYI 6	at Chi. 1	Tony Esposito	68	71	51	75	
Charlie Simmer	L.A.	19-3-80	Det. 3	at L.A. 4	Jim Rutherford	57	73	56	64	26.0
Pierre Larouche	Mtl.	25-3-80	Chi. 4	at Mtl. 8	Tony Esposito	72	75	50	73	
Danny Gare	Buf.	27-3-80	Det. 1	at Buf. 10	Jim Rutherford	71	75	56	76	
Blaine Stoughton	Hfd.	28-3-80	Hfd. 4	at Van. 4	Glen Hanlon	75	75	56	80	27.0
Guy Lafleur	Mtl.	2-4-80	Mtl. 7	at Det. 2	Rogie Vachon	72	78	50	74	
Wayne Gretzky	Edm.	2-4-80	Min. 1	at Edm. 1	Gary Edwards	78	79	51	79	19.2
Reggie Leach	Phi.	3-4-80	Wsh. 2	at Phi. 4	(empty net)	75	79	50	76	
Mike Bossy	NYI	24-1-81	Que. 3	at NYI 7	Ron Grahame	50	50	68	79	
Charlie Simmer	L.A.	26-1-81	L.A. 7	at Que. 5	Michel Dion	51	51	56	65	
Marcel Dionne	L.A.	8-3-81	L.A. 4	at Wpg. 1	Markus Mattsson	68	68	58	80	
Wayne Babych	St. L.	12-3-81	St. L. 3	at Mtl. 4	Richard Sevigny	70	68	54	78	22.9
Wayne Gretzky	Edm.	15-3-81	Edm. 3	at Cgy. 3	Pat Riggin	69	69	55	80	
Rick Kehoe	Pit.	16-3-81	Pit. 7	at Edm. 6	Eddie Mio	70	70	55	80	29.7
Jacques Richard	Que.	29-3-81	Mtl. 0	at Que. 4	Richard Sevigny	75	75	52	78	28.6
Dennis Maruk	Wsh.	5-4-81	Det. 2	at Wsh. 7	Larry Lozinski	80	80	50	80	25.3
Wayne Gretzky	Edm.	30-12-81	Phi. 5	at Edm. 7	(empty net)	39	39	92	80	
Dennis Maruk	Wsh.	21-2-82	Wpg. 3	at Wsh. 6	Doug Soetaert	61	61	60	80	
Mike Bossy	NYI	4-3-82	Tor. 1	at NYI 10	Michel Larocque	66	66	64	80	
Dino Ciccarelli	Min.	8-3-82	St. L. 1	at Min. 8	Mike Liut	67	68	55	76	21.7
Rick Vaive	Tor.	24-3-82	St. L. 3	at Tor. 4	Mike Liut	72	75	54	77	22.10
Rick Middleton	Bos.	28-3-82	Bos. 5	at Buf. 9	Paul Harrison	72	77	51	75	28.11
Blaine Stoughton	Hfd.	28-3-82	Min. 5	at Hfd. 2	Gilles Meloche	76	76	52	80	28.3
Marcel Dionne	L.A.	30-3-82	Cgy. 7	at L.A. 5	Pat Riggin	75	77	50	78	
Mark Messier	Edm.	31-3-82	L.A. 3	at Edm. 7	Mario Lessard	78	79	50	78	21.3
Bryan Trottier	NYI	3-4-82	Phi. 3	at NYI 6	Pete Peeters	79	79	50	80	25.9
Lanny McDonald	Cgy.	18-2-83	Cgy. 1	at Buf. 5	Bob Sauve	60	60	66	80	30.0
Wayne Gretzky	Edm.	19-2-83	Edm. 10	at Pit. 7	Nick Ricci	60	60	71	80	
Michel Goulet	Que.	5-3-83	Que. 7	at Hfd. 3	Mike Veisor	67	67	57	80	22.11
Mike Bossy	NYI	12-3-83	Wsh. 2	at NYI 6	Al Jensen	70	71	60	79	
Marcel Dionne	L.A.	17-3-83	Que. 3	at L.A. 4	Daniel Bouchard	71	71	56	80	
Al Secord	Chi.	20-3-83	Tor. 3	at Chi. 7	Mike Palmateer	73	73	54	80	25.0
Rick Vaive	Tor.	30-3-83	Tor. 4	at Det. 2	Gilles Gilbert	76	78	51	78	
Wayne Gretzky	Edm.	7-1-84	Hfd. 3	at Edm. 5	Greg Millen	42	42	87	74	
Michel Goulet	Que.	8-3-84	Que. 8	at Pit. 6	Denis Herron	63	69	56	75	
Rick Vaive	Tor.	14-3-84	Min. 3	at Tor. 3	Gilles Meloche	69	72	52	76	
Mike Bullard	Pit.	14-3-84	Pit. 6	at L.A. 7	Markus Mattsson	71	72	51	76	23.0

Player	Team	Date of 50th Goal	Score			Goaltender	Player's Game No.	Team Game No.	Total Goals	Total Games	Age When First 50th Scored (Yrs. & Mos.)
Jari Kurri	Edm.	15-3-84	Edm. 2	at	Mtl. 3	Rick Wamsley	57	73	52	64	23.10
Glenn Anderson	Edm.	21-3-84	Hfd. 3	at	Edm. 5	Greg Millen	76	76	54	80	23.6
Tim Kerr	Phi.	22-3-84	Pit. 4	at	Phi. 13	Denis Herron	74	75	54	79	24.3
Mike Bossy	NYI	31-3-84	NYI 3	at	Wsh. 1	Pat Riggin	67	79	51	67	
Wayne Gretzky	Edm.	26-1-85	Pit. 3	at	Edm. 6	Denis Herron	49	49	73	80	
Jari Kurri	Edm.	3-2-85	Hfd. 3	at	Edm. 6	Greg Millen	50	53	71	73	
Mike Bossy	NYI	5-3-85	Phi. 5	at	NYI 4	Bob Froese	61	65	58	76	
Tim Kerr	Phi.	7-3-85	Wsh. 6	at	Phi. 9	Pat Riggin	63	65	54	74	
John Ogrodnick	Det.	13-3-85	Det. 6	at	Edm. 7	Grant Fuhr	69	69	55	79	25.9
Bob Carpenter	Wsh.	21-3-85	Wsh. 2	at	Mtl. 3	Steve Penney	72	72	53	80	21.9
Michel Goulet	Que.	6-3-85	Buf. 3	at	Que. 4	Tom Barrasso	62	73	55	69	
Dale Hawerchuk	Wpg.	29-4-85	Chi. 5	at	Wpg. 5	W. Skorodenski	77	77	53	80	21.1
Mike Gartner	Wsh.	7-4-85	Pit. 3	at	Wsh. 7	Brian Ford	80	80	50	80	25.5
Jari Kurri	Edm.	4-3-86	Edm. 6	at	Van. 2	Richard Brodeur	63	65	68	78	
Mike Bossy	NYI	11-3-86	Cgy. 4	at	NYI 8	Rejean Lemelin	67	67	61	80	
Glenn Anderson	Edm.	14-3-86	Det. 3	at	Edm. 12	Greg Stefan	63	71	54	72	
Michel Goulet	Que.	17-3-86	Que. 8	at	Mtl. 6	Patrick Roy	67	72	53	75	
Wayne Gretzky	Edm.	18-3-86	Wpg. 2	at	Edm. 6	Brian Hayward	72	72	52	80	
Tim Kerr	Phi.	20-3-86	Pit. 1	at	Phi. 5	Roberto Romano	68	72	58	76	
Wayne Gretzky	Edm.	2-4-87	Edm. 6	at	Min. 5	Don Beaupre	55	55	62	79	
Tim Kerr	Phi.	3-17-87	NYR 1	at	Phi. 4	J. Vanbiesbrouck	67	71	58	75	
Jari Kurri	Edm.	3-17-87	N.J. 4	at	Edm. 7	Craig Billington	69	70	54	79	
Mario Lemieux	Pit.	3-12-87	Que. 3	at	Pit. 6	Mario Gosselin	53	70	54	63	21.5
Dino Ciccarelli	Min.	3-7-87	Pit. 7	at	Min. 3	Gilles Meloche	66	66	52	80	
Mario Lemieux	Pit.	2-2-88	Wsh. 2	at	Pit. 3	Pete Peeters	51	54	70	77	
Steve Yzerman	Det.	1-3-88	Buf. 0	at	Det. 4	Tom Barrasso	64	64	50	64	22.10
Joe Nieuwendyk	Cgy.	12-3-88	Buf. 4	at	Cgy. 10	Tom Barrasso	66	70	51	75	21.5
Craig Simpson	Edm.	15-3-88	Buf. 4	at	Edm. 6	Jacques Cloutier	71	71	56	80	21.1
Jimmy Carson	L.A.	26-3-88	Chi. 5	at	L.A. 9	Darren Pang	77	77	55	88	19.7
Luc Robitaille	L.A.	1-4-88	L.A. 6	at	Cgy. 3	Mike Vernon	79	79	53	80	21.10
Hakan Loob	Cgy.	3-4-88	Min. 1	at	Cgy. 4	Don Beaupre	80	80	50	80	27.9
Stephane Richer	Mtl.	3-4-88	Mtl. 4	at	Buf. 4	Tom Barrasso	72	80	50	72	21.10
Mario Lemieux	Pit.	20-1-89	Pit. 3	at	Wpg. 7	Eldon Reddick	44	46	85	76	
Bernie Nicholls	L.A.	28-1-89	Edm. 7	at	L.A. 6	Grant Fuhr	51	51	70	79	27.7
Steve Yzerman	Det.	5-2-89	Det. 6	at	Wpg. 2	Eldon Reddick	55	55	65	80	
Wayne Gretzky	L.A.	4-3-89	Phi. 2	at	L.A. 6	Ron Hextall	66	67	54	78	
Joe Nieuwendyk	Cgy.	21-3-89	NYI 1	at	Cgy. 4	Mark Fitzpatrick	72	74	51	77	
Joe Mullen	Cgy.	31-3-89	Wpg. 1	at	Cgy. 4	Bob Essensa	78	79	51	79	32.1
Brett Hull	St. L.	6-2-90	Tor. 4	at	St. L. 6	Jeff Reese	54	54	72	80	25.6
Steve Yzerman	Det.	24-2-90	Det. 3	at	NYI 3	Glenn Healy	63	63	62	79	
Cam Neely	Bos.	10-3-90	Bos. 3	at	NYI 3	Mark Fitzpatrick	69	71	55	76	24.9
Brian Bellows	Min.	13-3-90	Min. 5	at	Det. 1	Tim Cheveldae	75	75	55	80	25.
Pat LaFontaine	NYI	24-3-90	NYI 5	at	Edm. 5	Bill Ranford	71	77	54	74	25.1
Luc Robitaille	L.A.	21-3-90	L.A. 3	at	Van. 6	Kirk McLean	79	79	52	80	
Stephane Richer	Mtl.	24-3-90	Mtl. 4	at	Hfd. 7	Peter Sidorkiewicz	75	77	51	75	
Gary Leeman	Tor.	28-3-90	NYI 6	at	Tor. 3	Mark Fitzpatrick	78	78	51	80	26.1
Brett Hull	St. L.	25-1-91	St. L. 9	at	Det. 4	Dave Gagnon	49	49	86	78	
Cam Neely	Bos.	26-3-91	Bos. 7	at	Que. 4	empty net	67	78	51	69	
Theoren Fleury	Cgy.	26-3-91	Van. 2	at	Cgy. 7	Bob Mason	77	77	51	79	22.9
Steve Yzerman	Det.	30-3-91	NYR 5	at	Det. 6	Mike Richter	79	79	51	80	
Brett Hull	St. L.	28-1-92	St. L. 3	at	L.A. 3	Kelly Hrudey	50	50	70	73	
Kevin Stevens	Pit.	24-3-92	Pit. 3	at	Det. 4	Tim Cheveldae	74	74	54	80	26.11
Gary Roberts	Cgy.	31-3-92	Edm. 2	at	Cgy. 5	Bill Ranford	73	77	53	76	25.10
Jeremy Roenick	Chi.	7-3-92	Chi. 2	at	Bos. 1	Daniel Berthiaume	67	67	53	80	22.2
Alexander Mogilny	Buf.	3-2-93	Hfd. 2	at	Buf. 3	Sean Burke	46	53	76	77	23.11
Teemu Selanne	Wpg.	28-2-93	Min. 6	at	Wpg. 7	Darcy Wakaluk	63	63	76	84	22.6
Pavel Bure	Van.	1-3-93	Van. 5	at	Buf. 2*	Grant Fuhr	63	63	60	83	21.11
Steve Yzerman	Det.	10-3-93	Det. 6	at	Edm. 3	Bill Ranford	70	70	58	84	
Luc Robitaille	L.A.	15-3-93	L.A. 4	at	Buf. 2	Grant Fuhr	69	69	63	84	
Brett Hull	St. L.	20-3-93	St. L. 2	at	L.A. 3	Robb Stauber	73	73	54	80	
Mario Lemieux	Pit.	21-3-93	Pit. 6	at	Edm. 4**	Ron Tugnutt	48	72	69	60	
Kevin Stevens	Pit.	21-3-93	Pit. 6	at	Edm. 4**	Ron Tugnutt	62	72	55	72	
Dave Andreychuk	Tor.	23-3-93	Tor. 5	at	Wpg. 4	Bob Essensa	72	73	54	83	29.6
Pat LaFontaine	Buf.	28-3-93	Ott. 1	at	Buf. 3	Peter Sidorkiewicz	75	75	53	84	
Pierre Turgeon	NYI	2-4-93	NYI 3	at	NYR 2	Mike Richter	75	76	58	83	23.8
Mark Recchi	Phi.	4-4-93	T.B. 2	at	Phi. 6	J-C Bergeron	77	77	53	84	25.2
Jeremy Roenick	Chi.	15-4-93	Tor. 2	at	Chi. 3	Felix Potvin	84	84	50	84	
Brendan Shanahan	St. L.	15-4-93	T.B. 5	at	St. L. 6	Pat Jablonski	71	84	51	71	24.3

* neutral site game played at Hamilton; ** neutral site game played at Cleveland

Pierre Turgeon

Kevin Stevens

Brendan Shanahan

100-Point Seasons

Player	Team	Date of 100th Point	G or A		Score		Player's Game No.	Team Game No.	Points G - A PTS	Total Games	Age when first 100th point scored (Yrs. & Mos.)
Phil Esposito	Bos.	2-3-69	(G)	Pit. 0	at	Bos. 4	60	62	49-77 — 126	74	27.1
Bobby Hull	Chi.	20-3-69	(G)	Chi. 5	at	Bos. 5	71	71	58-49 — 107	76	30.2
Gordie Howe	Det.	30-3-69	(G)	Det. 5	at	Chi. 9	76	76	44-59 — 103	76	41.0
Bobby Orr	Bos.	15-3-70	(G)	Det. 5	at	Bos. 5	67	67	33-87 — 120	76	22.11
Phil Esposito	Bos.	6-2-71	(A)	Buf. 3	at	Bos. 4	51	51	76-76 — 152	78	
Bobby Orr	Bos.	22-2-71	(A)	Bos. 4	at	L.A. 5	58	58	37-102 — 139	78	
John Bucyk	Bos.	13-3-71	(A)	Bos. 6	at	Van. 3	68	68	51-65 — 116	78	35.10
Ken Hodge	Bos.	21-3-71	(A)	Buf. 7	at	Bos. 5	72	72	43-62 — 105	78	269
Jean Ratelle	NYR	18-2-72	(A)	NYR 2	at	Cal. 2	58	58	46-63 — 109	63	31.4
Phil Esposito	Bos.	19-2-72	(A)	Bos. 6	at	Min. 4	59	59	66-67 — 133	76	
Bobby Orr	Bos.	2-3-72	(A)	Van. 3	at	Bos. 7	64	64	37-80 — 117	76	
Vic Hadfield	NYR	25-3-72	(A)	NYR 3	at	Mtl. 3	74	74	50-56 — 106	78	31.5
Phil Esposito	Bos.	3-3-73	(A)	Bos. 1	at	Mtl. 5	64	64	55-75 — 130	78	
Bobby Clarke	Phi.	29-3-73	(G)	Atl. 2	at	Phi. 4	76	76	37-67 — 104	78	23.7
Bobby Orr	Bos.	31-3-73	(G)	Bos. 3	at	Tor. 7	62	77	29-72 — 101	63	
Rick MacLeish	Phi.	1-4-73	(G)	Phi. 4	at	Pit. 5	78	78	50-50 — 100	78	23.3
Phil Esposito	Bos.	13-2-74	(A)	Bos. 9	at	Cal. 6	53	53	68-77 — 145	78	
Bobby Orr	Bos.	12-3-74	(A)	Buf. 0	at	Bos. 4	62	66	32-90 — 122	74	
Ken Hodge	Bos.	24-3-74	(A)	Mtl. 3	at	Bos. 6	72	72	50-55 — 105	76	
Phil Esposito	Bos.	8-2-75	(A)	Bos. 8	at	Det. 5	54	54	61-66 — 127	79	
Bobby Orr	Bos.	13-2-75	(A)	Bos. 1	at	Buf. 3	57	57	46-89 — 135	80	
Guy Lafleur	Mtl.	7-3-75	(G)	Wsh. 4	at	Mtl. 8	56	66	53-66 — 119	70	24.6
Pete Mahovlich	Mtl.	9-3-75	(G)	Mtl. 5	at	NYR 3	67	67	35-82 — 117	80	29.5
Marcel Dionne	Det.	9-3-75	(A)	Det. 5	at	Phi. 8	67	67	47-74 — 121	80	23.7
Bobby Clarke	Phi.	22-3-75	(A)	Min. 0	at	Phi. 4	72	72	27-89 — 116	80	
Rene Robert	Buf.	5-4-75	(A)	Buf. 4	at	Tor. 2	74	80	40-60 — 100	74	26.4
Guy Lafleur	Mtl.	10-3-76	(G)	Mtl. 5	at	Chi. 1	69	69	56-69 — 125	80	
Bobby Clarke	Phi.	11-3-76	(A)	Buf. 1	at	Phi. 6	64	68	30-89 — 119	76	
Bill Barber	Phi.	18-3-76	(A)	Van. 2	at	Phi. 3	71	71	50-62 — 112	80	23.8
Gilbert Perreault	Buf.	21-3-76	(A)	K.C. 1	at	Buf. 3	73	73	44-69 — 113	80	25.4
Pierre Larouche	Pit.	24-3-76	(G)	Bos. 5	at	Pit. 5	70	74	53-58 — 111	76	20.4
Pete Mahovlich	Mtl.	28-3-76	(A)	Mtl. 2	at	Bos. 2	77	77	34-71 — 105	80	
Jean Ratelle	Bos.	30-3-76	(A)	Buf. 4	at	Bos. 4	77	77	36-69 — 105	80	
Jean Pronovost	Pit.	3-4-76	(A)	Wsh. 5	at	Pit. 4	79	79	52-52 — 104	80	30.4
Darryl Sittler	Tor.	3-4-76	(A)	Bos. 4	at	Tor. 2	78	79	41-59 — 100	79	26.7
Guy Lafleur	Mtl.	26-2-77	(A)	Clev. 3	at	Mtl. 5	63	63	56-80 — 136	80	
Marcel Dionne	L.A.	5-3-77	(A)	Pit. 3	at	L.A. 3	67	67	53-69 — 122	80	
Steve Shutt	Mtl.	27-3-77	(A)	Mtl. 6	at	Det. 0	77	77	60-45 — 105	80	24.9
Bryan Trottier	NYI	25-2-78	(A)	Chi. 1	at	NYI 7	59	60	46-77 — 123	77	21.7
Guy Lafleur	Mtl.	28-2-78	(G)	Det. 3	at	Mtl. 9	69	61	60-72 — 132	78	
Darryl Sittler	Tor.	12-3-78	(A)	Tor. 7	at	Pit. 1	67	67	45-72 — 117	80	
Guy Lafleur	Mtl.	27-2-79	(A)	Mtl. 3	at	NYI 7	61	61	52-77 — 129	80	
Bryan Trottier	NYI	6-3-79	(A)	Buf. 3	at	NYI 2	59	63	47-87 — 134	76	
Marcel Dionne	L.A.	8-3-79	(A)	L.A. 4	at	Buf. 6	66	66	59-71 — 130	80	
Mike Bossy	NYI	11-3-79	(G)	NYI 4	at	Bos. 4	66	66	69-57 — 126	80	22.2
Bob MacMillan	Atl.	15-3-79	(A)	Atl. 4	at	Phi. 5	68	69	37-71 — 108	79	26.6
Guy Chouinard	Atl.	30-3-79	(A)	L.A. 3	at	Atl. 5	75	75	50-57 — 107	80	22.5
Denis Potvin	NYI	8-4-79	(A)	NYI 5	at	NYR 2	73	80	31-70 — 101	73	25.5
Marcel Dionne	L.A.	6-2-80	(A)	L.A. 3	at	Hfd. 7	53	53	53-84 — 137	80	
Guy Lafleur	Mtl.	10-2-80	(A)	Mtl. 3	at	Bos. 2	55	55	50-75 — 125	74	
Wayne Gretzky	Edm.	24-2-80	(A)	Bos. 4	at	Edm. 2	61	62	51-86 — 137	79	19.2
Bryan Trottier	NYI	30-3-80	(A)	NYI 9	at	Que. 6	75	77	42-62 — 104	78	
Gilbert Perreault	Buf.	1-4-80	(A)	Buf. 5	at	Atl. 2	77	77	40-66 — 106	80	
Mike Rogers	Hfd.	4-4-80	(A)	Que. 2	at	Hfd. 9	79	79	44-61 — 105	80	25.5
Charlie Simmer	L.A.	5-4-80	(G)	Van. 5	at	L.A. 3	64	80	56-45 — 101	64	26.0
Blaine Stoughton	Hfd.	6-4-80	(A)	Det. 3	at	Hfd. 5	80	80	56-44 — 100	80	27.0
Wayne Gretzky	Edm.	6-2-81	(G)	Wpg. 4	at	Edm. 10	53	53	55-109 — 164	80	
Marcel Dionne	L.A.	12-2-81	(A)	L.A. 5	at	Chi. 5	58	58	58-77 — 135	80	
Charlie Simmer	L.A.	14-2-81	(A)	Bos. 5	at	L.A. 4	59	59	56-49 — 105	65	
Kent Nilsson	Cgy.	27-2-81	(G)	Hfd. 1	at	Cgy. 5	64	64	49-82 — 131	80	24.6
Mike Bossy	NYI	3-3-81	(G)	Edm. 8	at	NYI 8	65	66	68-51 — 119	79	
Dave Taylor	L.A.	14-3-81	(G)	Min. 4	at	L.A. 10	63	70	47-65 — 112	72	25.3
Mike Rogers	Hfd.	22-3-81	(G)	Tor. 3	at	Hfd. 3	74	74	40-65 — 105	80	
Bernie Federko	St. L.	28-3-81	(A)	Buf. 4	at	St. L. 7	74	76	31-73 — 104	78	24.10
Rick Middleton	Bos.	28-3-81	(A)	Chi. 2	at	Bos. 5	76	76	44-59 — 103	80	27.4
Jacques Richard	Que.	29-3-81	(G)	Mtl. 0	at	Que. 4	75	76	52-51 — 103	78	28.6
Bryan Trottier	NYI	29-3-81	(G)	NYI 5	at	Wsh. 4	69	76	31-72 — 103	73	
Peter Stastny	Que.	29-3-81	(A)	Mtl. 0	at	Que. 4	73	76	39-70 — 109	77	24.6
Wayne Gretzky	Edm.	27-12-81	(G)	L.A. 3	at	Edm. 10	38	38	92-120 — 212	80	
Mike Bossy	NYI	13-2-82	(A)	Phi. 2	at	NYI 8	55	55	64-83 — 147	80	
Peter Stastny	Que.	16-2-82	(G)	Wpg. 3	at	Que. 7	60	60	46-93 — 139	80	
Dennis Maruk	Wsh.	20-2-82	(G)	Wsh. 3	at	Min. 7	60	60	60-76 — 136	80	26.3
Bryan Trottier	NYI	23-2-82	(G)	Chi. 1	at	NYI 5	61	61	50-79 — 129	80	
Denis Savard	Chi.	27-2-82	(A)	Chi. 5	at	L.A. 3	64	64	32-87 — 119	80	21.1
Bobby Smith	Min.	3-3-82	(A)	Det. 4	at	Min. 6	66	66	43-71 — 114	80	24.1
Marcel Dionne	L.A.	6-3-82	(G)	L.A. 6	at	Hfd. 7	64	66	50-67 — 117	78	
Dave Taylor	L.A.	20-3-82	(A)	Pit. 5	at	L.A. 7	71	72	39-67 — 106	78	
Dale Hawerchuk	Wpg.	24-3-82	(A)	L.A. 3	at	Wpg.	74	74	45-58 — 103	80	18.11
Dino Ciccarelli	Min.	27-3-82	(A)	Min. 6	at	Bos. 5	72	76	55-52 — 107	76	21.8
Glenn Anderson	Edm.	28-3-82	(G)	Edm. 6	at	L.A. 2	78	78	38-67 — 105	80	21.7
Mike Rogers	NYR	2-4-82	(G)	Pit. 7	at	NYR 5	79	79	38-65 — 103	80	

Vic Hadfield

Mike Bossy

Jari Kurri

Player	Team	Date of 100th Point	G or A	Score		Player's Game No.	Team Game No.	Points G - A PTS	Total Games	Age when first 100th point scored (Yrs. & Mos.)
Wayne Gretzky	Edm.	5-1-83	(A)	Edm. 8	at Wpg. 3	42	42	71-125 — 196	80	
Mike Bossy	NYI	3-3-83	(A)	Tor. 1	at NYI. 5	66	67	60-58 — 118	79	
Peter Stastny	Que.	5-3-83	(A)	Hfd. 3	at Que. 10	62	67	47-77 — 124	75	
Denis Savard	Chi.	6-3-83	(A)	Mtl. 4	at Chi. 5	65	67	35-86 — 121	78	
Mark Messier	Edm.	23-3-83	(G)	Edm. 4	at Wpg. 7	73	76	48-58 — 106	77	22.2
Barry Pederson	Bos.	26-3-83	(A)	Hfd. 4	at Bos. 7	73	76	46-61 — 107	77	22.0
Marcel Dionne	L.A.	26-3-83	(A)	Edm. 9	at L.A. 3	75	75	56-51 — 107	80	
Michel Goulet	Que.	27-3-83	(A)	Que. 6	at Buf. 6	77	77	57-48 — 105	80	22.11
Glenn Anderson	Edm.	29-3-83	(A)	Edm. 7	at Van. 4	70	78	48-56 — 104	72	
Jari Kurri	Edm.	29-3-83	(A)	Edm. 7	at Van. 4	78	78	45-59 — 104	80	22.10
Kent Nilsson	Cgy.	29-3-83	(G)	L.A. 3	at Cgy. 5	78	78	46-58 — 104	80	
Wayne Gretzky	Edm.	18-12-83	(G)	Edm. 7	at Wpg. 5	34	34	87-118 — 205	74	
Paul Coffey	Edm.	4-3-84	(A)	Mtl. 1	at Edm. 6	68	68	40-86 — 126	80	22.9
Michel Goulet	Que.	4-3-84	(A)	Que. 1	at Buf. 1	62	67	56-65 — 121	75	
Jari Kurri	Edm.	7-3-84	(A)	Chi. 4	at Edm. 7	53	69	52-61 — 113	64	
Peter Stastny	Que.	8-3-84	(A)	Que. 8	at Pit. 6	69	69	46-73 — 119	80	
Mike Bossy	NYI	8-3-84	(G)	Tor. 5	at NYI 9	56	68	51-67 — 118	67	
Barry Pederson	Bos.	14-3-84	(A)	Bos. 4	at Det. 2	71	71	39-77 — 116	80	
Bryan Trottier	NYI	18-3-84	(G)	NYI 4	at Hfd. 5	62	73	40-71 — 111	68	
Bernie Federko	St. L.	20-3-84	(A)	Wpg. 3	at St. L. 9	75	76	41-66 — 107	79	
Rick Middleton	Bos.	27-3-84	(A)	Bos. 6	at Que. 4	77	77	47-58 — 105	80	
Dale Hawerchuk	Wpg.	27-3-84	(A)	Wpg. 3	at L.A. 3	77	77	37-65 — 102	80	
Mark Messier	Edm.	27-3-84	(G)	Edm. 9	at Cgy. 2	72	79	37-64 — 101	73	
Wayne Gretzky	Edm.	29-12-84	(A)	Det. 3	at Edm. 6	35	35	73-135 — 208	80	
Jari Kurri	Edm.	29-1-85	(G)	Edm. 4	at Cgy. 2	48	51	71-64 — 135	73	
Mike Bossy	NYI	23-2-85	(G)	Bos. 1	at NYI 7	56	60	58-59 — 117	76	
Dale Hawerchuk	Wpg.	25-2-85	(A)	Wpg. 12	at NYR 5	64	64	53-77 — 130	80	
Marcel Dionne	L.A.	5-3-85	(A)	Pit. 0	at L.A. 6	66	66	46-80 — 126	80	22.10
Brent Sutter	NYI	12-3-85	(A)	NYI 6	at St. L. 5	68	68	42-60 — 102	72	22.10
John Ogrodnick	Det.	22-3-85	(A)	NYR 3	at Det. 5	73	73	55-50 — 105	79	25.9
Paul Coffey	Edm.	26-3-85	(G)	Edm. 7	at NYI 5	74	74	37-84 — 121	80	
Denis Savard	Chi.	29-3-8	(A)	Chi. 5	at Wpg. 5	75	76	38-67 — 105	79	
Peter Stastny	Que.	2-4-85	(A)	Bos. 4	at Que. 6	74	77	32-68 — 100	75	
Bernie Federko	St. L.	4-4-85	(A)	NYR 5	at St. L. 4	74	78	30-73 — 103	76	
John Tonelli	NYI	6-4-85	(G)	NJ 5	at NYI 5	80	80	42-58 — 100	80	28.1
Paul MacLean	Wpg.	6-4-85	(A)	Wpg. 6	at Min. 5	78	79	41-60 — 101	79	27.1
Mike Gartner	Wsh.	7-4-85	(G)	Pit. 3	at Wsh. 7	80	80	50-52 — 102	80	25.6
Bernie Nicholls	L.A.	6-4-85	(A)	Van. 4	at L.A. 4	80	80	46-54 — 100	80	22.9
Mario Lemieux	Pit.	7-4-85	(G)	Pit. 3	at Wsh. 7	73	80	43-57 — 100	73	19.6
Wayne Gretzky	Edm.	4-1-86	(A)	Hfd. 3	at Edm. 4	39	39	52-163 — 215	80	
Mario Lemieux	Pit.	15-2-86	(G)	Van. 4	at Pit. 9	55	56	48-93 — 141	79	
Paul Coffey	Edm.	19-2-86	(A)	Tor. 5	at Edm. 9	59	60	48-90 — 138	79	
Jari Kurri	Edm.	2-3-86	(A)	Phi. 1	at Edm. 2	62	64	68-63 — 131	78	
Peter Stastny	Que.	1-3-86	(A)	Buf. 8	at Que. 4	66	68	41-81 — 122	76	
Mike Bossy	NYI	8-3-86	(G)	Wsh. 6	at NYI 2	65	65	61-62 — 123	80	
Denis Savard	Chi.	12-3-86	(A)	Buf. 7	at Chi. 6	69	69	47-69 — 116	80	
Mats Naslund	Mtl.	13-3-86	(A)	Mtl. 2	at Bos. 3	70	70	43-67 — 110	80	26.4
Michel Goulet	Que.	24-3-86	(A)	Que. 1	at Min. 0	70	75	53-50 — 103	75	
Glenn Anderson	Edm.	25-3-86	(A)	Edm. 7	at Det. 2	66	74	54-48 — 102	72	
Neal Broten	Min.	26-3-86	(A)	Min. 6	at Tor. 1	76	76	29-76 — 105	80	26.4
Dale Hawerchuk	Wpg.	31-3-86	(A)	Wpg. 5	at L.A. 2	78	78	46-59 — 105	80	
Bernie Federko	St. L.	5-4-86	(G)	Chi. 5	at St. L. 7	79	79	34-68 — 102	80	
Wayne Gretzky	Edm.	1-11-87	(A)	Cgy. 3	at Edm. 5	42	42	62-121 — 183	79	
Jari Kurri	Edm.	3-14-87	(A)	Buf. 3	at Edm. 5	67	68	54-54 — 108	79	
Mario Lemieux	Pit.	3-18-87	(A)	St. L. 4	at Pit. 5	55	72	54-53 — 107	63	
Mark Messier	Edm.	3-19-87	(A)	Edm. 4	at Cgy. 5	71	71	37-70 — 107	77	
Doug Gilmour	St. L.	4-2-87	(A)	Buf. 3	at St. L. 5	78	78	42-63 — 105	80	23.10
Dino Ciccarelli	Min.	3-30-87	(A)	NYR 6	at Min. 5	78	78	52-51 — 103	80	
Dale Hawerchuk	Wpg.	4-5-87	(A)	Wpg. 3	at Cgy. 1	80	80	47-53 — 100	80	
Mario Lemieux	Pit.	20-1-88	(G)	Plt. 8	at Chi. 3	45	48	70-98 — 168	77	
Wayne Gretzky	Edm.	11-2-88	(A)	Edm. 7	at Van. 2	43	56	40-109 — 149	64	
Denis Savard	Chi.	12-2-88	(A)	St. L. 3	at Chi. 4	57	57	44-87 — 131	80	
Dale Hawerchuk	Wpg.	23-2-88	(G)	Wpg. 4	at Pit. 3	61	61	44-77 — 121	80	
Steve Yzerman	Det.	27-2-88	(A)	Det. 4	at Que. 5	63	63	50-52 — 102	64	22.10
Peter Stastny	Que.	8-3-88	(A)	Hfd. 4	at Que. 6	63	67	46-65 — 111	76	
Mark Messier	Edm.	15-3-88	(A)	Buf. 4	at Edm. 6	68	71	37-74 — 111	77	
Jimmy Carson	L.A.	26-3-88	(A)	Chi. 5	at L.A. 9	77	77	55-52 — 107	80	19.8
Hakan Loob	Cgy.	26-3-88	(A)	Van. 1	at Cgy. 6	76	76	50-56 — 106	80	27.9
Mike Bullard	Cgy.	26-3-88	(A)	Van. 1	at Cgy. 6	76	76	48-55 — 103	79	27.1
Michel Goulet	Que.	27-3-88	(A)	Pit. 6	at Que. 3	76	76	48-58 — 106	80	
Luc Robitaille	L.A.	30-3-88	(G)	Cgy. 7	at L.A. 9	78	78	53-58 — 111	80	22.1
Mario Lemieux	Pit.	31-12-88	(A)	N.J. 6	at Pit. 8	36	38	85-114 — 199	76	
Wayne Gretzky	L.A.	21-1-89	(A)	L.A. 4	at Hfd. 5	47	48	54-114 — 168	78	
Steve Yzerman	Det.	27-1-89	(G)	Tor. 1	at Det. 8	50	50	65-90 — 155	80	
Bernie Nicholls	L.A.	21-1-89	(A)	L.A. 4	at Hfd. 5	48	48	70-80 — 150	79	
Rob Brown	Pit.	16-3-89	(A)	Pit. 2	at N.J. 1	60	72	49-66 — 115	68	20.11
Paul Coffey	Pit.	20-3-89	(A)	Pit. 2	at Min. 7	69	74	30-83 — 113	75	
Joe Mullen	Cgy.	23-3-89	(A)	L.A. 2	at Cgy. 4	74	75	51-59 — 110	79	32.1
Jari Kurri	Edm.	29-3-89	(A)	Edm. 2	at Van. 4	75	79	44-58 — 102	76	
Jimmy Carson	Edm.	2-4-89	(A)	Edm. 2	at Cgy. 4	80	80	49-51 — 100	80	
Mario Lemieux	Pit.	28-1-90	(G)	Pit. 2	at Buf. 7	50	50	45-78 — 123	59	
Wayne Gretzky	L.A.	30-1-90	(A)	N.J. 2	at L.A. 5	51	51	40-102 — 142	73	
Steve Yzerman	Det.	19-2-90	(A)	Mtl. 5	at Det. 5	61	61	62-65 — 127	79	
Mark Messier	Edm.	20-2-90	(A)	Edm. 4	at Van. 2	62	62	45-84 — 129	79	
Brett Hull	St. L.	3-3-90	(A)	NYI 4	at St. L. 5	67	67	72-41 — 113	80	25.7
Bernie Nicholls	NYR	12-3-90	(A)	L.A. 6	at NYR 2	70	71	39-73 — 112	79	
Pierre Turgeon	Buf.	25-3-90	(A)	N.J. 4	at Buf. 3	76	76	40-66 — 106	80	20.7
Paul Coffey	Pit.	25-3-90	(A)	Pit. 2	at Hfd. 4	77	77	29-74 — 103	80	
Pat LaFontaine	NYI	27-3-90	(G)	Cgy. 4	at NYI 2	72	78	54-51 — 105	74	25.1
Adam Oates	St. L.	29-3-90	(A)	Pit 4	at St. L. 5	79	79	23-79 — 102	80	27.7
Joe Sakic	Que.	31-3-90	(G)	Hfd. 3	at Que. 2	79	79	39-63 — 102	80	20.8
Ron Francis	Hfd.	31-3-90	(G)	Hfd. 3	at Que. 2	79	79	32-69 — 101	80	27.0
Luc Robitaille	L.A.	1-4-90	(A)	L.A. 4	at Cgy. 8	80	80	52-49 — 101	80	

Joe Sakic

Adam Oates

Rick Tocchet

Player	Team	Date of 100th Point	G or A	Score	Player's Game No.	Team Game No.	Points G - A — PTS	Total Games	Age when first 100th point scored (Yrs. & Mos.)
Wayne Gretzky	L.A.	30-1-91	(A)	N.J. 4 at L.A. 2	50	51	41-122 — 163	78	
Brett Hull	St. L.	23-2-91	(G)	Bos. 2 at St. L. 9	60	62	86-45 — 131	78	
Mark Recchi	Pit.	5-3-91	(G)	Van. 1 at Pit. 4	66	67	40-73 — 113	78	23.1
Steve Yzerman	Det.	10-3-91	(G)	Det. 4 at St. L. 1	72	72	51-57 — 108	80	
John Cullen	Hfd.	16-3-91	(A)	St. L. 4 at Hfd. 6	71	71	39-71 — 110	78	26.7
Adam Oates	St. L.	17-3-91	(A)	St. L. 4 at Chi. 6	54	73	25-90 — 115	61	
Joe Sakic	Que.	19-3-91	(G)	Edm. 7 at Que. 6	74	74	48-61 — 109	80	
Steve Larmer	Chi.	24-3-91	(A)	Min. 4 at Chi. 5	76	76	44-57 — 101	80	29.9
Theoren Fleury	Cgy.	26-3-91	(G)	Van. 2 at Cgy. 7	77	77	51-53 — 104	79	22.9
Al MacInnis	Cgy.	28-3-91	(A)	Edm. 4 at Cgy. 4	78	78	28-75 — 103	78	27.8
Mario Lemieux	Pit.	10-03-92	(A)	Cgy. 2 at Pit. 5	53	67	44-87 — 131	64	
Kevin Stevens	Pit.	7-3-92	(A)	Pit. 3 at L.A. 5	66	66	54-69 — 123	80	26.11
Wayne Gretzky	L.A.	3-3-92	(A)	Phi. 1 at L.A. 4	60	66	31-90 — 121	74	
Brett Hull	St. L.	2-3-92	(G)	St. L. 5 at Van. 3	66	66	70-39 — 109	80	
Luc Robitaille	L.A.	17-3-92	(A)	Wpg. 4 at L.A. 5	73	73	44-63 — 107	80	
Mark Messier	NYR	22-3-92	(G)	N.J. 3 at NYR 6	74	75	35-72 — 107	79	
Jeremy Roenick	Chi.	29-3-92	(G)	Tor. 1 at Chi. 5	77	77	53-50 — 103	80	22.2
Steve Yzerman	Det.	14-4-92	(G)	Det. 7 at Min. 4	79	80	45-58 — 103	79	
Brian Leetch	NYR	16-4-92	(G)	Pit. 1 at NYR 7	80	80	22-80 — 102	80	24.1
Mario Lemieux	Pit.	31-12-92	(G)	Tor. 3 at Pit. 3	38	39	69-91 — 160	60	
Pat LaFontaine	Buf.	10-2-93	(A)	Buf. 6 at Wpg. 2	55	55	53-95 — 148	84	
Adam Oates	Bos.	14-2-93	(A)	Bos. 3 at T.B. 3	58	58	45-97 — 142	84	
Steve Yzerman	Det.	24-2-93	(A)	Det. 7 at Buf. 10	64	64	58-79 — 137	84	
Pierre Turgeon	NYI	28-2-93	(G)	NYI 7 at Hfd. 6	62	63	58-74 — 132	83	
Doug Gilmour	Tor.	3-3-93	(A)	Min. 1 at Tor. 3	64	64	32-95 — 127	83	
Alexander Mogilny	Buf.	5-3-93	(A)	Hfd. 4 at Buf. 2	58	65	76-51 — 127	77	24.1
Mark Recchi	Phi.	7-3-93	(A)	Phi. 3 at N.J. 7	66	66	53-70 — 123	84	
Teemu Selanne	Wpg.	9-3-93	(G)	Wpg. 4 at T.B. 2	68	68	76-56 — 132	84	22.7
Luc Robitaille	L.A.	15-3-93	(A)	L.A. 4 at Buf. 2	69	69	63-62 — 125	84	
Kevin Stevens	Pit.	23-3-93	(A)	S.J. 2 at Pit. 7	63	73	55-56 — 111	72	
Mats Sundin	Que.	27-3-93	(G)	Phi. 3 at Que. 8	71	75	47-67 — 114	80	22.1
Pavel Bure	Van.	1-4-93	(G)	Van. 5 at T.B. 3	77	77	60-50 — 110	83	22.0
Jeremy Roenick	Chi.	4-4-93	(G)	St. L. 4 at Chi. 5	79	79	50-57 — 107	84	
Craig Janney	St. L.	4-4-93	(G)	St. L. 4 at Chi. 5	79	79	24-82 — 106	84	25.7
Rick Tocchet	Pit.	7-4-93	(G)	Mtl. 3 at Pit. 4	77	81	48-61 — 109	80	28.11
Joe Sakic	Que.	8-4-93	(A)	Que. 2 at Bos. 6	75	81	48-57 — 105	78	
Ron Francis	Pit.	9-4-93	(A)	Pit. 10 at NYR 4	82	82	24-76 — 100	84	
Brett Hull	St. L.	11-4-93	(G)	Min. 1 at St. L. 5	78	82	54-47 — 101	80	
Theoren Fleury	Cgy.	11-4-93	(G)	Cgy. 3 at Van. 6	82	82	34-66 — 100	83	
Joe Juneau	Bos.	14-4-93	(A)	Bos. 4 at Ott. 2	84	84	32-70 — 102	84	25.3

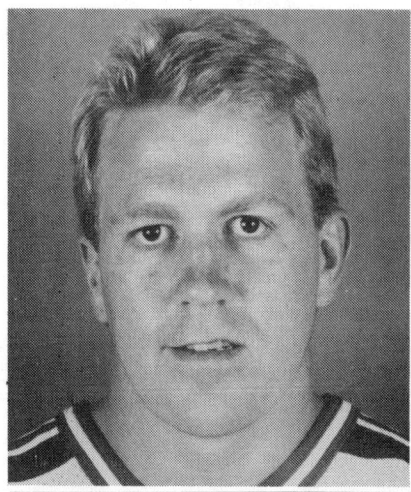

Brian Leetch

Al MacInnis

Five-or-more-Goal Games

Player	Team	Date	Score		Opposing Goaltender
SEVEN GOALS					
Joe Malone	Quebec Bulldogs	Jan. 31/20	Tor. 6	at Que. 10	Ivan Mitchell
SIX GOALS					
Newsy Lalonde	Montreal	Jan. 10/20	Tor. 7	at Mtl. 14	Ivan Mitchell
Joe Malone	Quebec Bulldogs	Mar. 10/20	Ott. 4	at Que. 10	Clint Benedict
Corb Denneny	Toronto St. Pats	Jan. 26/21	Ham. 3	at Tor. 10	Howard Lockhart
Cy Denneny	Ottawa Senators	Mar. 7/21	Ham. 5	at Ott. 12	Howard Lockhart
Syd Howe	Detroit	Feb. 3/44	NYR 2	at Det. 12	Ken McAuley
Red Berenson	St. Louis	Nov. 7/68	St. L. 8	at Phil 0	Doug Favell
Darryl Sittler	Toronto	Feb. 7/76	Bos. 4	at Tor. 11	Dave Reece
FIVE GOALS					
Joe Malone	Montreal	Dec. 19/17	Mtl. 7	at Ott. 4	Clint Benedict
Harry Hyland	Mtl. Wanderers	Dec. 19/17	Tor. 9	at Mtl. W. 10	Arthur Brooks
Joe Malone	Montreal	Jan. 12/18	Ott. 4	at Mtl. 9	Clint Benedict
Joe Malone	Montreal	Feb. 2/18	Tor. 2	at Mtl. 11	Harry Holmes
Mickey Roach	Toronto St. Pats	Mar. 6/20	Que. 2	at Tor. 11	Frank Brophy
Newsy Lalonde	Montreal	Feb. 16/21	Ham. 5	at Mtl. 10	Howard Lockhart
Babe Dye	Toronto St. Pats	Dec. 16/22	Mtl. 2	at Tor. 7	Georges Vezina
Redvers Green	Hamilton Tigers	Dec. 5/24	Ham. 10	at Tor. 3	John Roach
Babe Dye	Toronto St. Pats	Dec. 22/24	Tor. 10	at Bos. 1	Charlie Stewart
Harry Broadbent	Mtl. Maroons	Jan. 7/25	Mtl. 6	at Ham. 2	Vernon Forbes
Pit Lepine	Montreal	Dec. 14/29	Ott. 4	at Mtl. 6	Alex Connell
Howie Morenz	Montreal	Mar. 18/30	NYA 3	at Mtl. 8	Roy Worters
Charlie Conacher	Toronto	Jan. 19/32	NYA 3	at Tor. 11	Roy Worters
Ray Getliffe	Montreal	Feb. 6/43	Bos. 3	at Mtl. 8	Frank Brimsek
Maurice Richard	Montreal	Dec. 28/44	Det. 1	at Mtl. 9	Harry Lumley
Howie Meeker	Toronto	Jan. 8/47	Chi. 4	at Tor. 10	Paul Bibeault
Bernie Geoffrion	Montreal	Feb. 19/55	NYR 2	at Mtl. 10	Gump Worsley
Bobby Rousseau	Montreal	Feb. 1/64	Det. 3	at Mtl. 6	Roger Crozier
Yvan Cournoyer	Montreal	Feb. 15/75	Chi. 3	at Mtl. 12	Mike Veisor
Don Murdoch	NY Rangers	Oct. 12/76	NYR 10	at Min. 4	Gary Smith
Ian Turnbull	Toronto	Feb. 2/77	Det. 1	at Tor. 9	Ed Giacomin (2) / Jim Rutherford (3) / John Davidson (1)
Bryan Trottier	NY Islanders	Dec. 23/78	NYR 4	at NYI 9	Wayne Thomas (4)
Tim Young	Minnesota	Jan. 15/79	Min. 8	at NYR 1	Doug Soetaert (3) / Wayne Thomas (2)
John Tonelli	NY Islanders	Jan. 6/81	Tor. 3	at NYI 6	Jiri Crha (4) / empty net (1)
Wayne Gretzky	Edmonton	Feb. 18/81	St. L. 2	at Edm. 9	Mike Liut (3) / Ed Staniowski (2)
Wayne Gretzky	Edmonton	Dec. 30/81	Phi. 5	at Edm. 7	Pete Peeters (4) / empty net (1)
Grant Mulvey	Chicago	Feb. 3/82	St. L. 5	at Chi. 9	Mike Liut (4) / Gary Edwards (1)
Bryan Trottier	NY Islanders	Feb. 13/82	Phi. 2	at NYI 8	Pete Peeters
Willy Lindstrom	Winnipeg	Mar. 2/82	Wpg. 7	at Phi. 6	Pete Peeters
Mark Pavelich	NY Rangers	Feb. 23/83	Hfd. 3	at NYR 11	Greg Millen
Jari Kurri	Edmonton	Nov. 19/83	N.J. 4	at Edm. 13	Glenn Resch (3) / Ron Low (2)
Bengt Gustafsson	Washington	Jan. 8/84	Wsh. 7	at Phi. 1	Pelle Lindbergh
Pat Hughes	Edmonton	Feb. 3/84	Cgy. 5	at Edm. 10	Don Edwards (3) / Rejean Lemelin (2)
Wayne Gretzky	Edmonton	Dec. 15/84	Edm. 8	at St. L. 2	Rick Wamsley (4) / Mike Liut(1)
Dave Andreychuk	Buffalo	Feb. 6/86	Buf. 8	at Bos. 6	Pat Riggin (1) / Doug Keans (4)
Wayne Gretzky	Edmonton	Dec. 6/87	Min. 4	at Edm. 10	Don Beaupre (4) / Kari Takko (4)
Mario Lemieux	Pittsburgh	Dec. 31/88	N.J. 6	at Pit. 8	Bob Sauve (3) / Chris Terreri (2)
Joe Nieuwendyk	Calgary	Jan. 11/89	Wpg. 3	at Cgy. 8	Daniel Berthiaume (4)
Mats Sundin	Quebec	Mar. 5/92	Que. 10	at Hfd. 4	Peter Sidorkiewicz (3) / Kay Whitmore (2)
Mario Lemieux	Pittsburgh	Apr. 9/93	Pit. 10	at NYR 4	Corey Hirsch (3) / Mike Richter (2)

Players' 500th Goals

Player	Team	Date	Game No.	Score		Opposing Goaltender	Total Goals	Total Games
Maurice Richard	Montreal	Oct. 19/57	863	Chi. 1	at Mtl. 3	Glenn Hall	544	978
Gordie Howe	Detroit	Mar. 14/62	1,045	Det. 2	at NYR 3	Gump Worsley	801	1,767
Bobby Hull	Chicago	Feb. 21/70	861	NYR. 2	at Chi. 4	Ed Giacomin	610	1,063
Jean Béliveau	Montreal	Feb. 11/71	1,101	Min. 2	at Mtl. 6	Gilles Gilbert	507	1,125
Frank Mahovlich	Montreal	Mar. 21/73	1,105	Van. 2	at Mtl. 3	Dunc Wilson	533	1,181
Phil Esposito	Boston	Dec. 22/74	803	Det. 4	at Bos. 5	Jim Rutherford	717	1,282
John Bucyk	Boston	Oct. 30/75	1,370	St. L. 2	at Bos. 3	Yves Bélanger	556	1,540
Stan Mikita	Chicago	Feb. 27/77	1,221	Van. 4	at Chi. 3	Cesare Maniago	541	1,394
Marcel Dionne	Los Angeles	Dec. 14/82	887	L.A. 2	at Wsh. 7	Al Jensen	731	1,348
Guy Lafleur	Montreal	Dec. 20/83	918	Mtl. 6	at N.J. 0	Glenn Resch	560	1,126
Mike Bossy	NYIslanders	Jan. 2/86	647	Bos. 5	at NYI 7	empty net	573	752
Gilbert Perreault	Buffalo	Mar. 9/86	1,159	NJ 3	at Buf. 4	Alain Chevrier	512	1,191
*Wayne Gretzky	Edmonton	Nov. 22/86	575	Van. 2	at Edm. 5	empty net	765	1,044
Lanny McDonald	Calgary	Mar. 21/89	1,107	NYI 1	at Cgy. 4	Mark Fitzpatrick	500	1,111
*Bryan Trottier	NY Islanders	Feb. 13/90	1,104	Cgy. 4	at NYI 2	Rick Wamsley	520	1,238
*Mike Gartner	NY Rangers	Oct. 14/91	936	Wsh. 5	at NYR 3	Mike Liut	583	1,089
*Michel Goulet	Chicago	Feb. 16/92	951	Cgy. 5	at Chi. 5	Jeff Reese	532	1,033
*Jari Kurri	Los Angeles	Oct. 17/92	833	Bos. 6	at L.A. 8	empty net	524	909

*Active

Marcel Dionne

Players' 1,000th Points

Player	Team	Date	Game No.	G or A		Score	G A PTS	Total Games
Gordie Howe	Detroit	Nov. 27/60	938	(A)	Tor. 0	at Det. 2	801-1,049—1,850	1,767
Jean Béliveau	Montreal	Mar. 3/68	911	(G)	Mtl. 2	at Det. 5	507-712—1,219	1,125
Alex Delvecchio	Detroit	Feb. 16/69	1,143	(A)	LA 3	at Det. 6	456-825—1,281	1,549
Bobby Hull	Chicago	Dec. 12/70	909	(A)	Minn. 3	at Chi. 5	610-560—1,170	1,063
Norm Ullman	Toronto	Oct. 16/71	1,113	(A)	NYR 5	at Tor. 3	490-739—1,229	1,410
Stan Mikita	Chicago	Oct. 15/72	924	(A)	St.L. 3	at Chi. 1	541-926—1,467	1,394
John Bucyk	Boston	Nov. 9/72	1,144	(G)	Det. 3	at Bos. 8	556-813—1,369	1,540
Frank Mahovlich	Montreal	Feb. 13/73	1,090	(A)	Phi. 7	at Mtl. 6	533-570—1,103	1,181
Henri Richard	Montreal	Dec. 20/73	1,194	(A)	Mtl. 2	at Buf. 2	358-688—1,046	1,256
Phil Esposito	Boston	Feb. 15/74	745	(A)	Bos. 4	at Van. 2	717-873—1,590	1,282
Rod Gilbert	NY Rangers	Feb. 19/77	1,027	(G)	NYR 2	at NYI 5	406-615—1,021	1,065
Jean Ratelle	Boston	Apr. 3/77	1,007	(A)	Tor. 4	at Bos. 7	491-776—1,267	1,281
Marcel Dionne	Los Angeles	Jan. 7/81	740	(G)	L.A. 5	at Hfd. 3	731-1,040—1,771	1,348
Guy Lafleur	Montreal	Mar. 4/81	720	(G)	Mtl. 9	at Wpg. 3	560-793—1,353	1,126
Bobby Clarke	Philadelphia	Mar. 19/81	922	(G)	Bos. 3	at Phi. 5	358-852—1,210	1,144
Gilbert Perreault	Buffalo	Apr. 3/82	871	(A)	Buf. 5	at Mtl.4	512-814—1,326	1,191
Darryl Sittler	Philadelphia	Jan. 20/83	927	(G)	Cgy 2	at Phi. 5	484-637—1,121	1,096
*Wayne Gretzky	Edmonton	Dec. 19/84	424	(A)	L.A. 3	at Edm. 7	765-1,563—2,328	1,044
*Bryan Trottier	NY Islanders	Jan. 29/85	726	(G)	Min. 4	at NYI 4	520-890—1,410	1,238
Mike Bossy	NY Islanders	Jan. 24/86	656	(A)	NYI 7	at Wsh. 5	573-553—1,126	752
Denis Potvin	NY Islanders	Apr. 4/87	987	(G)	Buf. 6	at NYI 6	310-742—1,052	1,060
Bernie Federko	St. Louis	Mar 19/88	855	(A)	Hfd. 5	at St.L. 3	369-761—1,130	1,000
Lanny McDonald	Calgary	Mar. 7/89	1,101	(G)	Wpg. 5	at Cgy. 9	500-506—1,006	1,111
*Peter Stastny	Quebec	Oct. 19/89	682	(G)	Que. 5	at Chi. 3	444-777—1,221	954
*Jari Kurri	Edmonton	Jan. 2/90	716	(A)	Edm. 6	at St.L. 4	524-666—1,190	909
*Denis Savard	Chicago	Mar. 11/90	727	(A)	St.L. 6	at Chi. 4	423-769—1,192	946
*Paul Coffey	Pittsburgh	Dec. 22/90	770	(A)	Pit. 4	at NYI 3	330-871—1,201	953
*Mark Messier	Edmonton	Jan. 13/91	822	(A)	Edm. 5	at Phi. 3	452-780—1,232	1,005
*Dave Taylor	Los Angeles	Feb. 5/91	930	(A)	L.A. 3	at Phi. 2	427-635—1,062	1,078
*Michel Goulet	Chicago	Feb. 23/91	878	(G)	Chi. 3	at Min. 3	532-590—1,122	1,033
*Dale Hawerchuk	Buffalo	Mar. 8/91	781	(G)	Chi. 5	at Buf. 3	449-763—1,212	951
Bobby Smith	Minnesota	Nov. 30/91	986	(A)	Min. 4	at Tor. 3	357-679—1,036	1,077
*Mike Gartner	NY Rangers	Jan. 4/92	971	(G)	NYR 4	at N.J. 6	583-524—1,107	1,089
*Ray Bourque	Boston	Feb. 29/92	933	(A)	Wsh. 5	at Bos. 5	291-806—1,097	1,028
*Mario Lemieux	Pittsburgh	Mar. 24/92	513	(A)	Pit. 3	at Det. 4	477-697—1,174	577
*Glenn Anderson	Toronto	Feb. 22/93	954	(G)	Tor. 8	at Van. 1	459-559—1,018	976
*Steve Yzerman	Detroit	Feb. 24/93	737	(A)	Det. 7	at Buf. 10	445-595—1,040	757

*Active

Bernie Federko

Mike Gartner

Individual Awards

Hart Memorial Trophy

Art Ross Trophy

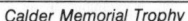

Calder Memorial Trophy

James Norris Memorial Trophy

HART MEMORIAL TROPHY

An annual award "to the player adjudged to be the most valuable to his team". Winner selected in poll by Professional Hockey Writers' Association in the 24 NHL cities at the end of the regular schedule. The winner receives $10,000 and the runners-up $6,000 and $4,000.

History: The Hart Memorial Trophy was presented by the National Hockey League in 1960 after the original Hart Trophy was retired to the Hockey Hall of Fame. The original Hart Trophy was donated to the NHL in 1923 by Dr. David A. Hart, father of Cecil Hart, former manager-coach of the Montreal Canadiens.

1992-93 Winner: Mario Lemieux, Pittsburgh Penguins
Runners-up: Doug Gilmour, Toronto Maple Leafs
Pat LaFontaine, Buffalo Sabres

Pittsburgh Penguins center Mario Lemieux captured the Hart Memorial Trophy, awarded annually "to the player adjudged to be the most valuable to his team".

Lemieux received 49 of 50 first place votes and one second place tally to earn 248 of a possible 250 points. Center Doug Gilmour of the Toronto Maple Leafs placed second in the balloting with 99 points, while Buffalo Sabres' center Pat LaFontaine finished in third place with 52 points.

This season Lemieux captured his fourth Art Ross Trophy as League scoring champion despite missing over a quarter of the season for treatment of Hodgkin's Disease, finishing the regular-season with 160 points (69-91-160) in 60 games. He also led the League in plus-minus with a plus-55 rating. Lemieux led the Penguins to the Presidents' Trophy, awarded to the team earning the most regular-season points, for the first time in team history as they posted a 56-21-7 record for 119 points.

Lemieux captured his second career Hart Trophy in his fourth appearance as a finalist. He previously won the award in 1988 and finished as runner-up in both 1986 and 1989.

ART ROSS TROPHY

An annual award "to the player who leads the league in scoring points at the end of the regular season." The winner receives $10,000 and the runners-up $6,000 and $4,000.

History: Arthur Howie Ross, former manager-coach of Boston Bruins, presented the trophy to the National Hockey League in 1947. If two players finish the schedule with the same number of points, the trophy is awarded in the following manner: 1. Player with most goals. 2. Player with fewer games played. 3. Player scoring first goal of the season.

1992-93 Winner: Mario Lemieux, Pittsburgh Penguins
Runners-up: Pat LaFontaine, Buffalo Sabres
Adam Oates, Boston Bruins

Mario Lemieux of the Pittsburgh Penguins won the fourth Art Ross Trophy of his career in 1992-93, despite missing 24 games after undergoing treatment for Hodgkin's disease. Lemieux recorded 69 goals and 91 assists for 160 points to win his second consecutive scoring title. Pat LaFontaine of the Buffalo Sabres finished second to Lemieux with 53 goals and 95 assists for 148 points. Adam Oates of the Boston Bruins, who led the league with 97 assists, finished third in scoring with 142 points.

CALDER MEMORIAL TROPHY

An annual award "to the player selected as the most proficient in his first year of competition in the National Hockey League". Winner selected in poll by Professional Hockey Writers' Association at the end of the regular schedule. The winner receives $10,000 and the runners-up $6,000 and $4,000.

History: From 1936-37 until his death in 1943, Frank Calder, NHL President, bought a trophy each year to be given permanently to the outstanding rookie. After Calder's death, the NHL presented the Calder Memorial Trophy in his memory and the trophy is to be kept in perpetuity. To be eligible for the award, a player cannot have played more than 25 games in any single preceding season nor in six or more games in each of any two preceding seasons in any major professional league. Beginning in 1990-91, to be eligible for this award a player must not have attained his twenty-sixth birthday by September 15th of the season in which he is eligible.

1992-93 Winner: Teemu Selanne, Winnipeg Jets
Runners-up: Joe Juneau, Boston Bruins
Felix Potvin, Toronto Maple Leafs

Right wing Teemu Selanne of the Winnipeg Jets captured the Calder Memorial Trophy as the "player adjudged to be the most proficient in his first season". To be eligible, a player cannot have played in more than 25 games in any single preceding season nor in six-or-more games in each of any two preceding seasons and must not have attained his 26th birthday by September 15 of the season in which he is eligible.

Selanne was a unanimous selection, receiving all 50 first place ballots for the 250 point maximum. Second place finisher Joe Juneau of the Boston Bruins received 75 points, while Felix Potvin of the Toronto Maple Leafs finished in third place with 63 points.

Selanne led all rookies in scoring in 1992-93 with 132 points. He tallied 76 goals to tie for the overall League lead, added 56 assists and appeared in all 84 games for the Jets. He shattered single-season rookie scoring records, passing Mike Bossy's previous record of 53 goals set in 1977-78 and Peter Stastny's mark of 109 points set in 1980-81. He led all NHL rookies in six offensive categories: goals, assists, points, power-play goals (24), game-winning goals (seven), first goals (10) and shots (387). Selanne joins Dale Hawerchuk as Winnipeg Jets that have won the Calder Trophy since the club joined the NHL in 1979-80. Hawerchuk captured the Calder Trophy in 1982.

JAMES NORRIS MEMORIAL TROPHY

An annual award "to the defense player who demonstrates throughout the season the greatest all-round ability in the position." Winner selected in poll by Professional Hockey Writers' Association at the end of the regular schedule. The winner receives $10,000 and the runners-up $6,000 and $4,000.

History: The James Norris Memorial Trophy was presented in 1953 by the four children of the late James Norris in memory of the former owner-president of the Detroit Red Wings.

1992-93 Winner: Chris Chelios, Chicago Blackhawks
Runners-up: Ray Bourque, Boston Bruins
Larry Murphy, Pittsburgh Penguins

Chris Chelios of the Chicago Blackhawks won his second career Norris Trophy, awarded to the defenseman demonstrating "the greatest all-around ability in the position."

Chelios received 201 of a possible 250 points in the balloting, including 33 first-place votes, to outdistance runners-up Ray Bourque of the Boston Bruins (97 points) and Larry Murphy (93 points).

Chelios equalled his career-high point total in 1992-93, posting 73 points (15-58-73) in 84 games to finish second in Blackhawks' team scoring. His point total placed him among the top 10 defensemen in the NHL and his contributions defensively helped Chicago record the lowest number of goals-against (230) in the League this season.

Chelios previously captured the award with the Montreal Canadiens in 1989. A native of San Diego, Chelios became the first U.S.-born Norris Trophy winner in 1989 and second consecutive Norris winner to hail from the United States. Corpus Christi, Texas native Brian Leetch of the New York Rangers captured the award in 1992. Chelios joins Doug Harvey as the only defenseman to have won the award with multiple clubs. Harvey won nine Norris Trophies with Montreal and one as a New York Ranger.

Vezina Trophy

Lady Byng Memorial Trophy

Frank J. Selke Trophy

Conn Smythe Trophy

VEZINA TROPHY

An annual award "to the goalkeeper adjudged to be the best at his position" as voted by the general managers of each of the 24 clubs. Over-all winner receives $10,000, runners-up $6,000 and $4,000.

History: Leo Dandurand, Louis Letourneau and Joe Cattarinich, former owners of the Montreal Canadiens, presented the trophy to the National Hockey League in 1926-27 in memory of Georges Vezina, outstanding goalkeeper of the Canadiens who collapsed during an NHL game November 28, 1925, and died of tuberculosis a few months later. Until the 1981-82 season, the goalkeeper(s) of the team allowing the fewest number of goals during the regular-season were awarded the Vezina Trophy.

1992-93 Winner: Ed Belfour, Chicago Blackhawks
Runners-up: Tom Barrasso, Pittsburgh Penguins
Curtis Joseph, St. Louis Blues

Ed Belfour of the Chicago Blackhawks captured the Vezina Trophy as the "goalkeeper adjudged to be the best at his position" (Prior to 1981-82, the Vezina was awarded to the goaltender(s) whose team allowed the fewest goals during the regular-season – the current criterion for the William Jennings Trophy).

Belfour received 15 of 24 first-place votes and tallied 94 of a possible 120 points in the balloting to edge second place finisher Tom Barrasso of the Pittsburgh Penguins, who earned 70 points. Curtis Joseph of the St. Louis Blues finished in third place, with 27 points.

In 1992-93, Belfour finished among the top three NHL goaltenders in five categories: shutouts (first place, seven); games played (first, 71); goals-against average (second, 2.59); wins (second, 41) and save percentage (third, .906). He became just the fifth goaltender in NHL history to record two 40-win seasons, following his 43-win season in 1990-91. He joins Hall of Famers Terry Sawchuk, Jacques Plante, Bernie Parent and Ken Dryden in accomplishing this feat.

This represents Belfour's second career Vezina Trophy win, having previously captured the award in his rookie season of 1991. He joins Montreal's Patrick Roy as the only multiple winner of the Vezina Trophy since the criterion was modified in 1981-82.

LADY BYNG MEMORIAL TROPHY

An annual award "to the player adjudged to have exhibited the best type of sportsmanship and gentlemanly conduct combined with a high standard of playing ability." Winner selected in poll by Professional Hockey Writers' Association at the end of the regular schedule. The winner receives $10,000 and the runners-up $6,000 and $4,000.

History: Lady Byng, wife of Canada's Governor-General at the time, presented the Lady Byng Trophy in 1925. After Frank Boucher of New York Rangers won the award seven times in eight seasons, he was given the trophy to keep and Lady Byng donated another trophy in 1936. After Lady Byng's death in 1949, the National Hockey League presented a new trophy, changing the name to Lady Byng Memorial Trophy.

1992-93 Winner: Pierre Turgeon, NY Islanders
Runners-up: Adam Oates, Boston Bruins
Pat LaFontaine, Buffalo Sabres

New York Islanders' center Pierre Turgeon captured the Lady Byng Trophy, awarded annually "to the player adjudged to have exhibited the best type of sportsmanship and gentlemanly conduct combined with a high standard of playing ability".

Turgeon received 25 of 50 first place votes, was named on 38 of 50 ballots and posted 164 total points to win the award in his first appearance as an NHL Trophy finalist. Boston Bruins' center Adam Oates was second in the voting with 104 points, followed by Buffalo Sabres' center Pat LaFontaine with 44 points.

Turgeon enjoyed career-high scoring totals in 1992-93, posting 132 points (58-74-132 in 83 games). His totals included 24 power-play goals and 10 game-winners for the Islanders, who earned a playoff position in the competitive Patrick Division for the first time since 1990. Throughout the regular-season, Turgeon accumulated just 26 minutes in penalties.

Turgeon becomes the second player in the New York Islanders' history to win the Lady Byng Trophy. Mike Bossy captured the award three times, in 1983, 1984 and 1986.

FRANK J. SELKE TROPHY

An annual award "to the forward who best excels in the defensive aspects of the game." Winner selected in poll by Professional Hockey Writers' Association at the end of the regular schedule. The winner receives $10,000 and the runners-up $6,000 and $4,000.

History: Presented to the National Hockey League in 1977 by the Board of Governors of the NHL in honour of Frank J. Selke, one of the great architects of NHL championship teams.

1992-93 Winner: Doug Gilmour, Toronto Maple Leafs
Runners-up: Dave Poulin, Boston Bruins
Joel Otto, Calgary Flames

Center Doug Gilmour of the Toronto Maple Leafs was awarded the Frank J. Selke Trophy in recognition of "the forward who best excels in the defensive aspects of the game" for his first career NHL Trophy win.

Gilmour received 27 of a possible 50 first place votes and was named to 38 of 50 ballots, totalling 160 points. Boston Bruins' center Dave Poulin finished in the runner-up position with 81 points, while center Joel Otto of the Calgary Flames took third place with 63 points.

Gilmour posted an impressive plus-minus rating of plus-32 this season, second best on the club. The Maple Leafs reduced their team goals-against total from 294 in 1991-92 to 241 this season despite playing an increased 84-game schedule (up from 80), finishing with the second best defensive record in the League behind Chicago. Gilmour also set a Maple Leafs' team record for most points in one season, passing Darryl Sittler's mark, by recording totals of 32-95-127 in 83 games.

Gilmour becomes the first member of the Maple Leafs to win a regular-season NHL Trophy since Brit Selby won the Calder Trophy in 1966 and the first Maple Leaf to capture the Selke Trophy since the award was introduced in 1978.

CONN SMYTHE TROPHY

An annual award "to the most valuable player for his team in the playoffs." Winner selected by the Professional Hockey Writers' Association at the conclusion of the final game in the Stanley Cup Finals. The winner receives $10,000.

History: Presented by Maple Leaf Gardens Limited in 1964 to honor Conn Smythe, the former coach, manager, president and owner-governor of the Toronto Maple Leafs.

1992-93 Winner: Patrick Roy, Montreal Canadiens

Patrick Roy of the Montreal Canadiens captured his second Conn Smythe Trophy as playoff MVP, leading the Montreal Canadiens to their 24th Stanley Cup championship. The Canadiens defeated Quebec (4-2), Buffalo (4-0), NY Islanders (4-1) and the Los Angeles Kings (4-1) to win their first Stanley Cup since 1986. Roy led all playoff goaltenders in GAA (2.13) and wins (16), while finishing second in save percentage (.929). Roy, who won his first Conn Smythe Trophy in 1986, was sensational as the Canadiens set an NHL record with ten consecutive overtime victories during the 1992-93 play-offs.

WILLIAM M. JENNINGS TROPHY

An annual award "to the goalkeeper(s) having played a minimum of 25 games for the team having the fewest goals scored against it." Winners selected on regular-season play. Overall winner receives $10,000, runners-up $6,000 and $4,000.

History: The Jennings Trophy was presented in 1981-82 by the National Hockey League's Board of Governors to honor the late William M. Jennings, longtime governor and president of the New York Rangers and one of the great builders of hockey in the United States.

1992-93 Winner: Ed Belfour, Chicago Blackhawks
Runners-up: Felix Potvin, Grant Fuhr, Toronto Maple Leafs
Andy Moog, Boston Bruins

Ed Belfour of the Chicago Blackhawks won his second Jennings Award in three years, helping his team compile a League-leading 2.70 goals-against-average. Belfour, who led the League in shutouts (seven) and games played (71), compiled a goals-against-average of 2.59.

William M. Jennings Trophy	Jack Adams Award	Bill Masterton Trophy	Lester Patrick Trophy	Lester B. Pearson Award

JACK ADAMS AWARD

An annual award presented by the National Hockey League Broadcasters' Association to "the NHL coach adjudged to have contributed the most to his team's success." Winner selected by poll among members of the NHL Broadcasters' Association at the end of the regular season. The winner receives $1,000 from the NHLBA.

History: The award was presented by the NHL Broadcasters' Association in 1974 to commemorate the late Jack Adams, coach and general manager of the Detroit Red Wings, whose lifetime dedication to hockey serves as an inspiration to all who aspire to further the game.

1992-93 Winner: Pat Burns, Toronto Maple Leafs
Runners-up: Brian Sutter, Boston Bruins
Pierre Page, Quebec Nordiques

Toronto Maple Leafs' head coach Pat Burns captured the Jack Adams Award as "the NHL coach adjudged to have contributed the most to his team's success".

Burns received 29 of 52 first place votes, was named on 47 of 52 ballots and totalled 183 points to finish ahead of second place Brian Sutter of the Boston Bruins, who tallied 117 points. Quebec Nordiques' head coach Pierre Page was third, with 82 points.

Burns, in his first season behind the Maple Leafs' bench, guided the club to a team-record 99 point finish in the regular-season, a 32-point improvement for the club over 1991-92. In posting a record of 44-29-11 in 84 games, the Maple Leafs earned a third place finish in the competitive Norris Division, securing a berth in the Stanley Cup playoffs for the first time in three seasons.

Burns, who won the Jack Adams award in 1989 as a rookie head coach with the Montreal Canadiens, becomes the second coach since the award was first presented in 1974 to capture the award with two different clubs. Last year's winner, Vancouver coach Pat Quinn, had previously won the award with Philadelphia in 1980. Burns finished third in the voting for the Adams Award last season.

BILL MASTERTON MEMORIAL TROPHY

An annual award under the trusteeship of the Professional Hockey Writers' Association to "the National Hockey League player who best exemplifies the qualities of perseverance, sportsmanship and dedication to hockey." Winner selected by poll among the 22 chapters of the PHWA at the end of the regular season. A $2,500 grant from the PHWA is awarded annually to the Bill Masterton Scholarship Fund, based in Bloomington, MN, in the name of the Masterton Trophy winner.

History: The trophy was presented by the NHL Writers' Association in 1968 to commemorate the late William Masterton, a player of the Minnesota North Stars, who exhibited to a high degree the qualities of perseverance, sportsmanship and dedication to hockey, and who died January 15, 1968.

1992-93 Winner: Mario Lemieux, Pittsburgh Penguins

Center Mario Lemieux of the Pittsburgh Penguins is the 1992-93 recipient of the Bill Masterton Trophy, presented to "the National Hockey League player who best exemplifies the qualities of perseverance, sportsmanship and dedication to hockey".

Despite a two-month absence during the season for treatment of Hodgkin's Disease, Lemieux returned to capture his fourth career Art Ross Trophy as League scoring champion with 160 points (69-91-160) in 60 games, while being assessed just 38 minutes in penalties. He led the Penguins to the Presidents' Trophy, awarded to the team earning the most regular-season points, for the first time in club history as they posted a 56-21-7 record for 119 points.

Among Lemieux's off-ice contributions are his involvement with the Pittsburgh Cancer Institute and visits to area childrens' and veterans' hospitals.

LESTER PATRICK TROPHY

An annual award "for outstanding service to hockey in the United States." Eligible recipients are players, officials, coaches, executives and referees. Winner selected by an award committee consisting of the President of the NHL, an NHL Governor, a representative of the New York Rangers, a member of the Hockey Hall of Fame Builder's section, a member of the Hockey Hall of Fame Player's section, a member of the U.S. Hockey Hall of Fame, a member of the NHL Broadcasters' Association and a member of the Professional Hockey Writers' Association. Each except the League President is rotated annually. The winner receives a miniature of the trophy.

History: Presented by the New York Rangers in 1966 to honor the late Lester Patrick, longtime general manager and coach of the New York Rangers, whose teams finished out of the playoffs only once in his first 16 years with the club.

1992-93 Winners: Frank Boucher
Mervyn (Red) Dutton
Bruce McNall
Gil Stein

Onetime NY Rangers star Frank Boucher, L.A. Kings owner Bruce McNall and former NHL presidents Mervyn (Red) Dutton and Gil Stein are the 1993 recipients of the Lester Patrick Trophy.

A star with the Vancouver Maroons of the Pacific Coast Hockey Association and the Ottawa Senators of the NHL, Frank Boucher achieved his greatest fame as a member of the NY Rangers. He was a member of the original Rangers in 1926 and stayed with the team for 30 seasons until 1955. Boucher centered one of the greatest lines in hockey history, the "A" Line (or the Cook-Boucher-Cook Line) with brothers Bill and Bun Cook. He played on two Stanley Cup-winning teams and won the Lady Byng Trophy for clean, effective play seven times.

Mervyn (Red) Dutton was a player, coach, manager and owner before being asked to replace Frank Calder as NHL president in 1943. A rugged defenceman who starred with the Montreal Maroons and the NY Americans, Dutton served as NHL president until 1946, when he was succeeded by Clarence Campbell.

Bruce McNall is one of the most visible and progressive owners in the NHL and is currently serving a two-year term as chairman of the NHL's Board of Governors. The sole owner of the Los Angeles Kings since 1986, he was named as the Sporting News and the Hockey News Executive of the Year in 1989.

Gil Stein was named as the League's fifth president on October 1, 1992, serving in that capacity until February 1, 1993. Stein, who served as the NHL's general counsel for 15 years, began his professional hockey career in 1972 when he was named as the general counsel and alternate governor of the Philadelphia Flyers.

LESTER B. PEARSON AWARD

An annual award presented to the NHL's outstanding player as selected by the members of the National Hockey League Players' Association. The winner receives $10,000.

History: The award was presented in 1970-71 by the NHLPA in honor of the late Lester B. Pearson, former Prime Minister of Canada.

1992-93 Winner: Mario Lemieux, Pittsburgh Penguins

King Clancy
Memorial Trophy

Alka-Seltzer
Plus Award

Presidents'
Trophy

KING CLANCY MEMORIAL TROPHY

An annual award "to the player who best exemplifies leadership qualities on and off the ice and has made a noteworthy humanitarian contribution in his community". The winner receives $3,000 and the runner-up $1,000.

History: The King Clancy Memorial Trophy was presented to the National Hockey League by the Board of Governors in 1988 to honor the late Frank "King" Clancy.

1992-93 Winner: Dave Poulin, Boston Bruins
Runner-up: Brad Marsh, Ottawa Senators

Boston Bruins' center Dave Poulin is the 1992-93 recipient of the King Clancy Trophy. The King Clancy Trophy is awarded "to the player who best exemplifies leadership on and off the ice and who has made a noteworthy humanitarian contribution to his community".

Poulin has served as an assistant captain for the Bruins the past two seasons and was captain of the Philadelphia Flyers for five seasons prior to joining Boston. A finalist for the Selke Trophy this year as the League's outstanding defensive player, Poulin appeared in all 84 games, tallying 16 goals and 33 assists for 49 points and a plus-minus rating of +29. He also contributed five shorthanded goals.

Off-ice, Poulin's many contributions to the community include serving on the Board of the American Liver Foundation's annual "Bid for Life" Auction, one of their major fund-raising efforts of the year. He also serves as Co-Chairman of the March of Dimes annual Walk for Life fund-raiser and is the Newton, MA spokesman for the Police DARE program, a drug and alcohol awareness program for local schoolchildren on the dangers of drug and alcohol abuse.

ALKA-SELTZER PLUS AWARD

An annual award "to the player, having played a minimum of 60 games, who leads the League in plus/minus statistics" at the end of the regular season. Miles, Inc. will contribute $5,000 on behalf of the winner to the charity of his choice and $1000 on behalf of each individual team winner.

History: The award was presented to the NHL in 1989-90 by Miles, Inc., to recognize the League leader in plus-minus statistics. Plus-minus statistics are calculated by giving a player a "plus" when on-ice for an even-strength or shorthand goal scored by his team. He receives a "minus" when on-ice for an even-strength or shorthand goal scored by the opposing team. A plus-minus award has been presented since the 1982-83 season.

1992-93 Winner: Mario Lemieux, Pittsburgh Penguins

Pittsburgh center Mario Lemieux was the NHL's leader in +/- ratings in 1992-93 with a total of +55. Lemieux completed the season with a net offensive ranking of 121, having been on the ice for 203 of the Penguins' 367 goals scored, 82 of which came on the powerplay. His net defensive ranking was 66, having been on the ice for 89 of 268 goals-against, 23 of which were scored while Pittsburgh was shorthanded. Team +/- leaders were Boston, Ray Bourque; Buffalo, Doug Bodger; Calgary, Frank Musil; Chicago, Steve Larmer; Detroit, Sergei Fedorov; Edmonton, Martin Gelinas; Hartford, Terry Yake; Los Angeles, Jarri Kurri; Minnesota, Jim Johnson; Montreal, Lyle Odelein; New Jersey, Alexander Semak; NY Islanders, Darius Kasparaitis; NY Rangers, Sergei Nemchinov; Ottawa, Jamie Baker; Philadelphia, Eric Lindros; Pittsburgh, Mario Lemieux; Quebec, Curtis Leschyshyn; San Jose, Kelly Kisio; St. Louis, Brendan Shanahan; Tampa Bay, Danton Cole; Toronto, Nikolai Borschevsky; Vancouver, Pavel Bure; Washington, Dmitri Khristich; Winnipeg, Teemu Selanne.

NHL AWARD MONEY BREAKDOWN

(Players on each club determine how team award money is divided.)

TEAM AWARDS

Stanley Cup Playoffs	Number of Clubs	Share Per Club	Total
Division Semi-Final Losers	8	$ 150,000	$1,200,000
Division Final Losers	4	300,000	1,200,000
Conference Championship Losers	2	450,000	900,000
Stanley Cup Loser	1	625,000	625,000
Stanley Cup Winners	1	1,000,000	1,000,000
TOTAL PLAYOFF AWARD MONEY			**$4,925,000**

Final Standings, Regular Season	Number of Clubs	Share Per Club	Total
Presidents' Trophy			
Club's Share	1	$ 100,000	$ 100,000
Players' Share	1	100,000	100,000
Division Winners	4	375,000	1,500,000
Division Second Place	4	175,000	700,000
TOTAL REGULAR SEASON AWARD MONEY			**$2,400,000**

INDIVIDUAL AWARDS	Winner	First Runner-up	Second Runner-up
Hart, Calder, Norris, Ross, Vezina, Byng, Selke, Jennings Trophies	$10,000	$6,000	$4,000
Conn Smythe Trophy	$10,000		
King Clancy Memorial Award	$ 3,000	$1,000	

	Number of winners	Per Player	Total
First Team All-Stars	6	$10,000	$60,000
Second Team All-Stars	6	5,000	$30,000
TOTAL INDIVIDUAL AWARD MONEY			**$2,400,000**
TOTAL ALL AWARDS			**$7,589,000**

PRESIDENTS' TROPHY

An annual award to the club finishing the regular-season with the best overall record. The winner receives $200,000, to be split evenly between the team and its players.

History: Presented to the National Hockey League in 1985-86 by the NHL Board of Governors to recognize the team compiling the top regular-season record.

1992-93 Winner: Pittsburgh Penguins
Runners-up: Boston Bruins
Chicago Blackhawks

The Pittsburgh Penguins won their first Presidents' Trophy in 1992-93, compiling the NHL's best regular-season record of 56-21-7 for 119 points. The Boston Bruins finished second with a 51-26-7 record while the Chicago Blackhawks had the third best regular season mark with a record of 47-25-12 for 106 points.

1992-93 NHL Player of the Week Award Winners

Player of the Week

Week Ending	Player	Team
Oct. 19	**Mario Lemieux**	Pittsburgh
Oct. 26	**Mario Lemieux**	Pittsburgh
Nov. 2	**Mats Sundin**	Quebec
Nov. 9	**Luc Robitaille**	Los Angeles
Nov. 16	**Mark Recchi**	Philadelphia
Nov. 23	**Tom Barrasso**	Pittsburgh
Nov. 30	**Steve Larmer**	Chicago
Dec. 7	**Adam Oates**	Boston
Dec. 14	**Ed Belfour**	Chicago
Dec. 21	**Mike Vernon**	Calgary
Dec. 28	**Tim Cheveldae**	Detroit
Jan. 4	**Alexander Mogilny**	Buffalo
Jan. 11	**Guy Hebert**	St. Louis
	Tommy Soderstrom	Philadelphia
Jan. 18	**Ed Belfour**	Chicago
Jan. 25	**Felix Potvin**	Toronto
Feb. 1	**Benoit Hogue**	NY Islanders
Feb. 8	**Mike Modano**	Minnesota
Feb. 15	**Steve Yzerman**	Detroit
Feb. 22	**Doug Gilmour**	Toronto
Mar. 1	**Thomas Steen**	Winnipeg
Mar. 8	**Luc Robitaille**	Los Angeles
Mar. 15	**Curtis Joseph**	St. Louis
Mar. 22	**Mario Lemieux**	Pittsburgh
Mar. 29	**Mario Lemieux**	Pittsburgh
Apr. 5	**Andy Moog**	Boston
Apr. 12	**Andy Moog**	Boston

Player of the Month

Month	Player	Team
Oct.	**Mario Lemieux**	Pittsburgh
Nov.	**Jari Kurri**	Los Angeles
Dec.	**Mario Lemieux**	Pittsburgh
	Ed Belfour	Chicago
January	**Alexander Mogilny**	Buffalo
	Teemu Selanne	Winnipeg
February	**Steve Yzerman**	Detroit
March	**Mario Lemieux**	Pittsburgh

1992-93 Upper Deck/NHL Rookie of the Month Award

Month	Player	Team
Oct.	**Teemu Selanne**	Winnipeg
Nov.	**Joe Juneau**	Boston
Dec.	**Rob Gaudreau**	San Jose
Jan.	**Teemu Selanne**	Winnipeg
Feb.	**Felix Potvin**	Toronto
Mar./Apr.	**Teemu Selanne**	Winnipeg

NATIONAL HOCKEY LEAGUE INDIVIDUAL AWARD WINNERS

ART ROSS TROPHY

	Winner	Runner-up
1993	Mario Lemieux, Pit.	Pat LaFontaine, Buf.
1992	Mario Lemieux, Pit.	Kevin Stevens, Pit.
1991	Wayne Gretzky, L.A.	Brett Hull, St.L.
1990	Wayne Gretzky, L.A.	Mark Messier, Edm.
1989	Mario Lemieux, Pit.	Wayne Gretzky, L.A.
1988	Mario Lemieux, Pit.	Wayne Gretzky, Edm.
1987	Wayne Gretzky, Edm.	Jari Kurri, Edm.
1986	Wayne Gretzky, Edm.	Mario Lemieux, Pit.
1985	Wayne Gretzky, Edm.	Jari Kurri, Edm.
1984	Wayne Gretzky, Edm.	Paul Coffey, Edm.
1983	Wayne Gretzky, Edm.	Peter Stastny, Que.
1982	Wayne Gretzky, Edm.	Mike Bossy, NYI
1981	Wayne Gretzky, Edm.	Marcel Dionne, L.A.
1980	Marcel Dionne, L.A.	Wayne Gretzky, Edm.
1979	Bryan Trottier, NYI	Marcel Dionne, L.A.
1978	Guy Lafleur, Mtl.	Bryan Trottier, NYI
1977	Guy Lafleur, Mtl.	Marcel Dionne, L.A.
1976	Guy Lafleur, Mtl.	Bobby Clarke, Phi.
1975	Bobby Orr, Bos.	Phil Esposito, Bos.
1974	Phil Esposito, Bos.	Bobby Orr, Bos.
1973	Phil Esposito, Bos.	Bobby Clarke, Phi.
1972	Phil Esposito, Bos.	Bobby Orr, Bos.
1971	Phil Esposito, Bos.	Bobby Orr, Bos.
1970	Bobby Orr, Bos.	Phil Esposito, Bos.
1969	Phil Esposito, Bos.	Bobby Hull, Chi.
1968	Stan Mikita, Chi.	Phil Esposito, Bos.
1967	Stan Mikita, Chi.	Bobby Hull, Chi.
1966	Bobby Hull, Chi.	Stan Mikita, Chi.
1965	Stan Mikita, Chi.	Norm Ullman, Det.
1964	Stan Mikita, Chi.	Bobby Hull, Chi.
1963	Gordie Howe, Det.	Andy Bathgate, NYR
1962	Bobby Hull, Chi.	Andy Bathgate, NYR
1961	Bernie Geoffrion, Mtl.	Jean Beliveau, Mtl.
1960	Bobby Hull, Chi.	Bronco Horvath, Bos.
1959	Dickie Moore, Mtl.	Jean Beliveau, Mtl.
1958	Dickie Moore, Mtl.	Henri Richard, Mtl.
1957	Gordie Howe, Det.	Ted Lindsay, Det.
1956	Jean Beliveau, Mtl.	Gordie Howe, Det.
1955	Bernie Geoffrion, Mtl.	Maurice Richard, Mtl.
1954	Gordie Howe, Det.	Maurice Richard, Mtl.
1953	Gordie Howe, Det.	Ted Lindsay, Det.
1952	Gordie Howe, Det.	Ted Lindsay, Det.
1951	Gordie Howe, Det.	Maurice Richard, Mtl.
1950	Ted Lindsay, Det.	Sid Abel, Det.
1949	Roy Conacher, Chi.	Doug Bentley, Chi.
1948	Elmer Lach, Mtl.	Buddy O'Connor, NYR
1947 *	Max Bentley, Chi.	Maurice Richard, Mtl.
1946	Max Bentley, Chi.	Gaye Stewart, Tor.
1945	Elmer Lach, Mtl.	Maurice Richard, Mtl.
1944	Herbie Cain, Bos.	Doug Bentley, Chi.
1943	Doug Bentley, Chi.	Bill Cowley, Bos.
1942	Bryan Hextall, NYR	Lynn Patrick, NYR
1941	Bill Cowley, Bos.	Bryan Hextall, NYR
1940	Milt Schmidt, Bos.	Woody Dumart, Bos.
1939	Toe Blake, Mtl.	Dave Schriner, NYA
1938	Gordie Drillon, Tor.	Syl Apps, Tor.
1937	Dave Schriner, NYA	Syl Apps, Tor.
1936	Dave Schriner, NYA	Marty Barry, Det.
1935	Charlie Conacher, Tor.	Syd Howe, St.L-Det.
1934	Charlie Conacher, Tor.	Joe Primeau, Tor.
1933	Bill Cook, NYR	Harvey Jackson, Tor.
1932	Harvey Jackson, Tor.	Joe Primeau, Tor.
1931	Howie Morenz, Mtl.	Ebbie Goodfellow, Det.
1930	Cooney Weiland, Bos.	Frank Boucher, NYR
1929	Ace Bailey, Tor.	Nels Stewart, Mtl.M
1928	Howie Morenz, Mtl.	Aurel Joliat, Mtl.
1927	Bill Cook, NYR	Dick Irvin, Chi.
1926	Nels Stewart, Mtl.M.	Cy Denneny, Ott.
1925	Babe Dye, Tor.	Cy Denneny, Ott.
1924	Cy Denneny, Ott.	Billy Boucher, Mtl.
1923	Babe Dye, Tor.	Cy Denneny, Ott.
1922	Punch Broadbent, Ott.	Cy Denneny, Ott.
1921	Newsy Lalonde, Mtl.	Cy Denneny, Ott.
1920	Joe Malone, Que.	Newsy Lalonde, Mtl.
1919	Newsy Lalonde, Mtl.	Odie Cleghorn, Mtl.
1918	Joe Malone, Mtl.	Cy Denneny, Ott.

* Scoring leader prior to inception of Art Ross Trophy in 1947-48

HART TROPHY

	Winner	Runner-up
1993	Mario Lemieux, Pit.	Doug Gilmour, Tor.
1992	Mark Messier, NYR	Patrick Roy, Mtl.
1991	Brett Hull, St.L.	Wayne Gretzky, L.A.
1990	Mark Messier, Edm.	Ray Bourque, Bos.
1989	Wayne Gretzky, L.A.	Mario Lemieux, Pit.
1988	Mario Lemieux, Pit.	Grant Fuhr, Edm.
1987	Wayne Gretzky, Edm.	Ray Bourque, Bos.
1986	Wayne Gretzky, Edm.	Mario Lemieux, Pit.
1985	Wayne Gretzky, Edm.	Dale Hawerchuk, Wpg.
1984	Wayne Gretzky, Edm.	Rod Langway, Wsh.
1983	Wayne Gretzky, Edm.	Pete Peeters, Bos.
1982	Wayne Gretzky, Edm.	Bryan Trottier, NYI
1981	Wayne Gretzky, Edm.	Mike Liut, St.L.
1980	Wayne Gretzky, Edm.	Marcel Dionne, L.A.
1979	Bryan Trottier, NYI	Guy Lafleur, Mtl
1978	Guy Lafleur, Mtl.	Bryan Trottier, NYI
1977	Guy Lafleur, Mtl.	Bobby Clarke, Phi.
1976	Bobby Clarke, Phi.	Denis Potvin, NYI
1975	Bobby Clarke, Phi.	Rogatien Vachon, L.A.
1974	Phil Esposito, Bos.	Bernie Parent, Phi.
1973	Bobby Clarke, Phi.	Phil Esposito, Bos.
1972	Bobby Orr, Bos.	Ken Dryden, Mtl.
1971	Bobby Orr, Bos.	Phil Esposito, Bos.
1970	Bobby Orr, Bos.	Tony Esposito, Chi.
1969	Phil Esposito, Bos.	Jean Beliveau, Mtl.
1968	Stan Mikita, Chi.	Jean Beliveau, Mtl.
1967	Stan Mikita, Chi.	Ed Giacomin, NYR
1966	Bobby Hull, Chi.	Jean Beliveau, Mtl.
1965	Bobby Hull, Chi.	Norm Ullman, Det.
1964	Jean Beliveau, Mtl.	Bobby Hull, Chi.
1963	Gordie Howe, Det.	Stan Mikita, Chi.
1962	Jacques Plante, Mtl.	Doug Harvey, NYR
1961	Bernie Geoffrion, Mtl.	Johnny Bower, Tor.
1960	Gordie Howe, Det.	Bobby Hull, Chi.
1959	Andy Bathgate, NYR	Gordie Howe, Det.
1958	Gordie Howe, Det.	Andy Bathgate, NYR
1957	Gordie Howe, Det.	Jean Beliveau, Mtl.
1956	Jean Beliveau, Mtl.	Tod Sloan, Tor.
1955	Ted Kennedy, Tor.	Harry Lumley, Tor.
1954	Al Rollins, Chi.	Red Kelly, Det.
1953	Gordie Howe, Det.	Al Rollins, Chi.
1952	Gordie Howe, Det.	Elmer Lach, Mtl.
1951	Milt Schmidt, Bos.	Maurice Richard, Mtl.
1950	Charlie Rayner, NYR	Ted Kennedy, Tor.
1949	Sid Abel, Det.	Bill Durnan, Mtl.
1948	Buddy O'Connor, NYR	Frank Brimsek, Bos.
1947	Maurice Richard, Mtl.	Milt Schmidt, Bos.
1946	Max Bentley, Chi.	Gaye Stewart, Tor.
1945	Elmer Lach, Mtl.	Maurice Richard, Mtl.
1944	Babe Pratt, Tor.	Bill Cowley, Bos.
1943	Bill Cowley, Bos.	Doug Bentley, Chi.
1942	Tom Anderson, Bro.	Syl Apps, Tor.
1941	Bill Cowley, Bos.	Dit Clapper, Bos.
1940	Ebbie Goodfellow, Det.	Syl Apps, Tor.
1939	Toe Blake, Mtl.	Syl Apps, Tor.
1938	Eddie Shore, Bos.	Paul Thompson, Chi.
1937	Babe Siebert, Mtl.	Lionel Conacher, Mtl.M
1936	Eddie Shore, Bos.	Hooley Smith, Mtl.M
1935	Eddie Shore, Bos.	Charlie Conacher, Tor.
1934	Aurel Joliat, Mtl.	Lionel Conacher, Chi.
1933	Eddie Shore, Bos.	Bill Cook, NYR
1932	Howie Morenz, Mtl.	Ching Johnson, NYR
1931	Howie Morenz, Mtl.	Eddie Shore, Bos.
1930	Nels Stewart, Mtl.M.	Lionel Hitchman, Bos.
1929	Roy Worters, NYA	Ace Bailey, Tor.
1928	Howie Morenz, Mtl.	Roy Worters, Pit.
1927	Herb Gardiner, Mtl.	Bill Cook, NYR
1926	Nels Stewart, Mtl.M.	Sprague Cleghorn, Bos.
1925	Billy Burch, Ham.	Howie Morenz, Mtl.
1924	Frank Nighbor, Ott.	Sprague Cleghorn, Mtl.

LESTER B. PEARSON AWARD WINNERS

1993	Mario Lemieux	Pittsburgh
1992	Mark Messier	NY Rangers
1991	Brett Hull	St. Louis
1990	Mark Messier	Edmonton
1989	Steve Yzerman	Detroit
1988	Mario Lemieux	Pittsburgh
1987	Wayne Gretzky	Edmonton
1986	Mario Lemieux	Pittsburgh
1985	Wayne Gretzky	Edmonton
1984	Wayne Gretzky	Edmonton
1983	Wayne Gretzky	Edmonton
1982	Wayne Gretzky	Edmonton
1981	Mike Liut	St. Louis
1980	Marcel Dionne	Los Angeles
1979	Marcel Dionne	Los Angeles
1978	Guy Lafleur	Montreal
1977	Guy Lafleur	Montreal
1976	Guy Lafleur	Montreal
1975	Bobby Orr	Boston
1974	Phil Esposito	Boston
1973	Bobby Clarke	Philadelphia
1972	Jean Ratelle	NY Rangers
1971	Phil Esposito	Boston

LADY BYNG TROPHY

	Winner	Runner-up
1993	Pierre Turgeon, NYI	Adam Oates, Bos.
1992	Wayne Gretzky, L.A.	Joe Sakic, Que.
1991	Wayne Gretzky, L.A.	Brett Hull, St.L.
1990	Brett Hull, St.L.	Wayne Gretzky, L.A.
1989	Joe Mullen, Cgy.	Wayne Gretzky, L.A.
1988	Mats Naslund, Mtl.	Wayne Gretzky, Edm.
1987	Joe Mullen, Cgy.	Wayne Gretzky, Edm.
1986	Mike Bossy, NYI	Jari Kurri, Edm.
1985	Jari Kurri, Edm.	Joe Mullen, St.L.
1984	Mike Bossy, NYI	Rick Middleton, Bos.
1983	Mike Bossy, NYI	Rick Middleton, Bos.
1982	Rick Middleton, Bos.	Mike Bossy, NYI
1981	Rick Kehoe, Pit.	Wayne Gretzky, Edm.
1980	Wayne Gretzky, Edm.	Marcel Dionne, L.A.
1979	Bob MacMillan, Atl.	Marcel Dionne, L.A.
1978	Butch Goring, L.A.	Peter McNab, Bos.
1977	Marcel Dionne, L.A.	Jean Ratelle, Bos.
1976	Jean Ratelle, NYR-Bos.	Jean Pronovost, Pit.
1975	Marcel Dionne, Det.	John Bucyk, Bos.
1974	John Bucyk, Bos.	Lowell MacDonald, Pit.
1973	Gilbert Perreault, Buf.	Jean Ratelle, NYR
1972	Jean Ratelle, NYR	John Bucyk, Bos.
1971	John Bucyk, Bos.	Dave Keon, Tor.
1970	Phil Goyette, St.L.	John Bucyk, Bos.
1969	Alex Delvecchio, Det.	Ted Hampson, Oak.
1968	Stan Mikita, Chi.	John Bucyk, Bos.
1967	Stan Mikita, Chi.	Dave Keon, Tor.
1966	Alex Delvecchio, Det.	Bobby Rousseau, Mtl.
1965	Bobby Hull, Chi.	Alex Delvecchio, Det.
1964	Ken Wharram, Chi.	Dave Keon, Tor.
1963	Dave Keon, Tor.	Camille Henry, NYR
1962	Dave Keon, Tor.	Claude Provost, Mtl.
1961	Red Kelly, Tor.	Norm Ullman, Det.
1960	Don McKenney, Bos.	Andy Hebenton, NYR
1959	Alex Delvecchio, Det.	Andy Hebenton, NYR
1958	Camille Henry, NYR	Don Marshall, Mtl.
1957	Andy Hebenton, NYR	Earl Reibel, Det.
1956	Earl Reibel, Det.	Floyd Curry, Mtl.
1955	Sid Smith, Tor.	Danny Lewicki, NYR
1954	Red Kelly, Det.	Don Raleigh, NYR
1953	Red Kelly, Det.	Wally Hergesheimer, NYR
1952	Sid Smith, Tor.	Red Kelly, Det.
1951	Red Kelly, Det.	Woody Dumart, Bos.
1950	Edgar Laprade, NYR	Red Kelly, Det.
1949	Bill Quackenbush, Det.	Harry Watson, Tor.
1948	Buddy O'Connor, NYR	Syl Apps, Tor.
1947	Bobby Bauer, Bos.	Syl Apps, Tor.
1946	Toe Blake, Mtl.	Clint Smith, Chi.
1945	Bill Mosienko, Chi.	Syd Howe, Det.
1944	Clint Smith, Chi.	Herb Cain, Bos.
1943	Max Bentley, Chi.	Buddy O'Connor, Mtl.
1942	Syl Apps, Tor.	Gordie Drillon, Tor.
1941	Bobby Bauer, Bos.	Gordie Drillon, Tor.
1940	Bobby Bauer, Bos.	Clint Smith, NYR
1939	Clint Smith, NYR	Marty Barry, Det.
1938	Gordie Drillon, Tor.	Clint Smith, NYR
1937	Marty Barry, Det.	Gordie Drillon, Tor.
1936	Doc Romnes, Chi.	Dave Schriner, NYA
1935	Frank Boucher, NYR	Russ Blinco, Mtl.M
1934	Frank Boucher, NYR	Joe Primeau, Tor.
1933	Frank Boucher, NYR	Joe Primeau, Tor.
1932	Joe Primeau, Tor.	Frank Boucher, NYR
1931	Frank Boucher, NYR	Normie Himes, NYA
1930	Frank Boucher, NYR	Normie Himes, NYA
1929	Frank Boucher, NYR	Harry Darragh, Pit.
1928	Frank Boucher, NYR	George Hay, Det.
1927	Billy Burch, NYA	Dick Irvin, Chi.
1926	Frank Nighbor, Ott.	Billy Burch, NYA
1925	Frank Nighbor, Ott.	none

WILLIAM M. JENNINGS TROPHY WINNERS

	Winner	Runner-up
1993	Ed Belfour, Chi.	Felix Potvin, Tor.
		Grant Fuhr
1992	Patrick Roy, Mtl.	Ed Belfour, Chi.
1991	Ed Belfour, Chi.	Patrick Roy, Mtl.
1990	Andy Moog, Bos.	Patrick Roy, Mtl.
	Rejean Lemelin	Brian Hayward
1989	Patrick Roy, Mtl.	Mike Vernon, Cgy.
	Brian Hayward	Rick Wamsley
1988	Patrick Roy, Mtl.	Clint Malarchuk, Wsh.
	Brian Hayward	Pete Peeters
1987	Patrick Roy, Mtl.	Ron Hextall, Phi.
	Brian Hayward	
1986	Bob Froese, Phi.	Al Jensen, Wsh.
	Darren Jensen	Pete Peeters
1985	Tom Barrasso, Buf.	Pat Riggin, Wsh.
	Bob Sauve	
1984	Al Jensen, Wsh.	Tom Barrasso, Buf.
	Pat Riggin	Bob Sauve
1983	Roland Melanson, NYI	Pete Peeters, Bos.
	Bill Smith	
1982	Rick Wamsley, Mtl.	Billy Smith, NYI
	Denis Herron	Roland Melanson

VEZINA TROPHY

	Winner	Runner-up
1993	Ed Belfour, Chi.	Tom Barrasso, Pit.
1992	Patrick Roy, Mtl.	Kirk McLean, Van.
1991	Ed Belfour, Chi.	Patrick Roy, Mtl.
1990	Patrick Roy, Mtl.	Daren Puppa, Buf.
1989	Patrick Roy, Mtl.	Mike Vernon, Cgy.
1988	Grant Fuhr, Edm.	Tom Barrasso, Buf.
1987	Ron Hextall, Phi.	Mike Liut, Hfd.
1986	John Vanbiesbrouck, NYR	Bob Froese, Phi.
1985	Pelle Lindbergh, Phi.	Tom Barrasso, Buf.
1984	Tom Barrasso, Buf.	Rejean Lemelin, Cgy.
1983	Pete Peeters, Bos.	Roland Melanson, NYI
1982	Bill Smith, NYI	Grant Fuhr, Edm.
1981	Richard Sevigny, Mtl.	Pete Peeters, Phi.
	Denis Herron, Mtl.	Rick St. Croix, Phi.
	Michel Larocque, Mtl.	
1980	Bob Sauve, Buf.	Gerry Cheevers, Bos.
	Don Edwards, Buf.	Gilles Gilbert, Bos.
1979	Ken Dryden, Mtl.	Glenn Resch, NYI
	Michel Larocque, Mtl.	Bill Smith, NYI
1978	Ken Dryden, Mtl.	Bernie Parent, Phi.
	Michel Larocque	Wayne Stephenson, Phi.
1977	Ken Dryden, Mtl.	Glenn Resch, NYI
	Michel Larocque, Mtl.	Bill Smith, NYI
1976	Ken Dryden, Mtl.	Glenn Resch, NYI
		Bill Smith, NYI
1975	Bernie Parent, Phi.	Rogie Vachon, L.A.
		Gary Edwards, L.A.
1974	Bernie Parent, Phi. (tie)	Gilles Gilbert, Bos.
	Tony Esposito, Chi. (tie)	
1973	Ken Dryden, Mtl.	Ed Giacomin, NYR
		Gilles Villemure, NYR
1972	Tony Esposito, Chi.	Cesare Maniago, Min.
	Gary Smith, Chi.	Lorne Worsley, Min.
1971	Ed Giacomin, NYR	Tony Esposito, Chi.
	Gilles Villemure, NYR	
1970	Tony Esposito, Chi.	Jacques Plante, St.L.
		Ernie Wakely, St.L.
1969	Jacques Plante, St.L.	Ed Giacomin, NYR
	Glenn Hall, St.L.	
1968	Lorne Worsley, Mtl.	Johnny Bower, Tor.
	Rogatien Vachon, Mtl.	Bruce Gamble, Tor.
1967	Glenn Hall, Chi.	Charlie Hodge, Mtl.
	Denis Dejordy, Chi.	
1966	Lorne Worsley, Mtl.	Glenn Hall, Chi.
	Charlie Hodge, Mtl.	
1965	Terry Sawchuk, Tor.	Roger Crozier, Det.
	Johnny Bower, Tor.	
1964	Charlie Hodge, Mtl.	Glenn Hall, Chi.
1963	Glenn Hall, Chi.	Johnny Bower, Tor.
		Don Simmons, Tor.
1962	Jacques Plante, Mtl.	Johnny Bower, Tor.
1961	Johnny Bower, Tor.	Glenn Hall, Chi.
1960	Jacques Plante, Mtl.	Glenn Hall, Chi.
1959	Jacques Plante, Mtl.	Johnny Bower, Tor.
		Ed Chadwick, Tor.
1958	Jacques Plante, Mtl.	Lorne Worsley, NYR
		Marcel Paille, NYR
1957	Jacques Plante, Mtl.	Glenn Hall, Det.
1956	Jacques Plante, Mtl.	Glenn Hall, Det.
1955	Terry Sawchuk, Det.	Harry Lumley, Tor.
1954	Harry Lumley, Tor.	Terry Sawchuk, Det.
1953	Terry Sawchuk, Det.	Gerry McNeil, Mtl.
1952	Terry Sawchuk, Det.	Al Rollins, Tor.
1951	Al Rollins, Tor.	Terry Sawchuk, Det.
1950	Bill Durnan, Mtl.	Harry Lumley, Det.
1949	Bill Durnan, Mtl.	Harry Lumley, Det.
1948	Turk Broda, Tor.	Harry Lumley, Det.
1947	Bill Durnan, Mtl.	Turk Broda, Tor.
1946	Bill Durnan, Mtl.	Frank Brimsek, Bos.
1945	Bill Durnan, Mtl.	Frank McCool, Tor. (tie)
		Harry Lumley, Det. (tie)
1944	Bill Durnan, Mtl.	Paul Bibeault, Tor.
1943	Johnny Mowers, Det.	Turk Broda, Tor.
1942	Frank Brimsek, Bos.	Turk Broda, Tor.
1941	Turk Broda, Tor.	Frank Brimsek, Bos. (tie)
		Johnny Mowers, Det. (tie)
1940	Dave Kerr, NYR	Frank Brimsek, Bos.
1939	Frank Brimsek, Bos.	Dave Kerr, NYR
1938	Tiny Thompson, Bos.	Dave Kerr, NYR
1937	Normie Smith, Det.	Dave Kerr, NYR
1936	Tiny Thompson, Bos.	Mike Karakas, Chi.
1935	Lorne Chabot, Chi.	Alex Connell, Mtl.M
1934	Charlie Gardiner, Chi.	Wilf Cude, Det.
1933	Tiny Thompson, Bos.	John Roach, Det.
1932	Charlie Gardiner, Chi.	Alex Connell, Det.
1931	Roy Worters, NYA	Charlie Gardiner, Chi.
1930	Tiny Thompson, Bos.	Charlie Gardiner, Chi.
1929	George Hainsworth, Mtl.	Tiny Thompson, Bos.
1928	George Hainsworth, Mtl.	Alex Connell, Ott.
1927	George Hainsworth, Mtl.	Clint Benedict, Mtl.M

KING CLANCY MEMORIAL TROPHY WINNERS

1993	Dave Poulin	Boston
1992	Ray Bourque	Boston
1991	Dave Taylor	Los Angeles
1990	Kevin Lowe	Edmonton
1989	Bryan Trottier	NY Islanders
1988	Lanny McDonald	Calgary

BILL MASTERTON TROPHY WINNERS

1993	Mario Lemieux	Pittsburgh
1992	Mark Fitzpatrick	NY Islanders
1991	Dave Taylor	Los Angeles
1990	Gord Kluzak	Boston
1989	Tim Kerr	Philadelphia
1988	Bob Bourne	Los Angeles
1987	Doug Jarvis	Hartford
1986	Charlie Simmer	Boston
1985	Anders Hedberg	NY Rangers
1984	Brad Park	Detroit
1983	Lanny McDonald	Calgary
1982	Glenn Resch	Colorado
1981	Blake Dunlop	St. Louis
1980	Al MacAdam	Minnesota
1979	Serge Savard	Montreal
1978	Butch Goring	Los Angeles
1977	Ed Westfall	NY Islanders
1976	Rod Gilbert	NY Rangers
1975	Don Luce	Buffalo
1974	Henri Richard	Montreal
1973	Lowell MacDonald	Pittsburgh
1972	Bobby Clarke	Phiiladelphia
1971	Jean Ratelle	NY Rangers
1970	Pit Martin	Chicago
1969	Ted Hampson	Oakland
1968	Claude Provost	Montreal

CALDER MEMORIAL TROPHY WINNERS

	Winner	Runner-up
1993	Teemu Selanne, Wpg.	Joe Juneau, Bos.
1992	Pavel Bure, Van.	Nicklas Lidstrom, Det
1991	Ed Belfour, Chi.	Sergei Fedorov, Det.
1990	Sergei Makarov, Cgy.	Mike Modano, Min.
1989	Brian Leetch, NYR	Trevor Linden, Van.
1988	Joe Nieuwendyk, Cgy.	Ray Sheppard, Buf.
1987	Luc Robitaille, L.A.	Ron Hextall, Phi.
1986	Gary Suter, Cgy.	Wendel Clark, Tor.
1985	Mario Lemieux, Pit.	Chris Chelios, Mtl.
1984	Tom Barrasso, Buf.	Steve Yzerman, Det.
1983	Steve Larmer, Chi.	Phil Housley, Buf.
1982	Dale Hawerchuk, Wpg.	Barry Pederson, Bos.
1981	Peter Stastny, Que.	Larry Murphy, L.A.
1980	Ray Bourque, Bos.	Mike Foligno, Det.
1979	Bobby Smith, Min	Ryan Walter, Wsh.
1978	Mike Bossy, NYI	Barry Beck, Col.
1977	Willi Plett, Atl.	Don Murdoch, NYR
1976	Bryan Trottier, NYI	Glenn Resch, NYI
1975	Eric Vail, Atl.	Pierre Larouche, Pit.
1974	Denis Potvin, NYI	Tom Lysiak, Atl.
1973	Steve Vickers, NYR	Bill Barber, Phi.
1972	Ken Dryden, Mtl.	Rick Martin, Buf.
1971	Gilbert Perreault, Buf.	Jude Drouin, Min.
1970	Tony Esposito, Chi.	Bill Fairbairn, NYR
1969	Danny Grant, Min.	Norm Ferguson, Oak.
1968	Derek Sanderson, Bos.	Jacques Lemaire, Mtl.
1967	Bobby Orr, Bos.	Ed Van Impe, Chi.
1966	Brit Selby, Tor.	Bert Marshall, Det.
1965	Roger Crozier, Det.	Ron Ellis, Tor.
1964	Jacques Laperriere, Mtl.	John Ferguson, Mtl.
1963	Kent Douglas, Tor.	Doug Barkley, Det.
1962	Bobby Rousseu, Mtl.	Cliff Pennington, Bos.
1961	Dave Keon, Tor.	Bob Nevin, Tor.
1960	Bill Hay, Chi.	Murray Oliver, Det.
1959	Ralph Backstrom, Mtl.	Carl Brewer, Tor.
1958	Frank Mahovlich, Tor.	Bobby Hull, Chi.
1957	Larry Regan, Bos.	Ed Chadwick, Tor.
1956	Glenn Hall, Det.	Andy Hebenton, NYR
1955	Ed Litzenberger, Chi.	Don McKenney, Bos.
1954	Camille Henry, NYR	Earl Reibel, Det.
1953	Lorne Worsley, NYR	Gordie Hannigan, Tor.
1952	Bernie Geoffrion, Mtl.	Hy Buller, NYR
1951	Terry Sawchuk, Det.	Al Rollins, Tor.
1950	Jack Gelineau, Bos.	Phil Maloney, Bos.
1949	Pentti Lund, NYR	Allan Stanley, NYR
1948	Jim McFadden, Det.	Pete Babando, Bos.
1947	Howie Meeker, Tor.	Jimmy Conacher, Det.
1946	Edgar Laprade, NYR	George Gee, Chi.
1945	Frank McCool, Tor.	Ken Smith, Bos.
1944	Gus Bodnar, Tor.	Bill Durnan, Mtl.
1943	Gaye Stewart, Tor.	Glen Harmon, Mtl.
1942	Grant Warwick, NYR	Buddy O'Connor, Mtl.
1941	Johnny Quilty, Mtl.	Johnny Mowers, Det.
1940	Kilby MacDonald, NYR	Wally Stanowski, Tor.
1939	Frank Brimsek, Bos.	Roy Conacher, Bos.
1938	Cully Dahlstrom, Chi.	Murph Chamberlain, Tor.
1937	Syl Apps, Tor.	Gordie Drillon, Tor.
1936	Mike Karakas, Chi.	Bucko McDonald, Det.
1935	Dave Schriner, NYA	Bert Connolly, NYR
1934	Russ Blinko, Mtl.M.	
1933	Carl Voss, Det.	

CONN SMYTHE TROPHY WINNERS

1993	Patrick Roy	Montreal
1992	Mario Lemieux	Pittsburgh
1991	Mario Lemieux	Pittsburgh
1990	Bill Ranford	Edmonton
1989	Al MacInnis	Calgary
1988	Wayne Gretzky	Edmonton
1987	Ron Hextall	Philadelphia
1986	Patrick Roy	Montreal
1985	Wayne Gretzky	Edmonton
1984	Mark Messier	Edmonton
1983	Bill Smith	NY Islanders
1982	Mike Bossy	NY Islanders
1981	Butch Goring	NY Islanders
1980	Bryan Trottier	NY Islanders
1979	Bob Gainey	Montreal
1978	Larry Robinson	Montreal
1977	Guy Lafleur	Montreal
1976	Reggie Leach	Philadelphia
1975	Bernie Parent	Philadelphia
1974	Bernie Parent	Philadelphia
1973	Yvan Cournoyer	Montreal
1972	Bobby Orr	Boston
1971	Ken Dryden	Montreal
1970	Bobby Orr	Boston
1969	Serge Savard	Montreal
1968	Glenn Hall	St. Louis
1967	Dave Keon	Toronto
1966	Roger Crozier	Detroit
1965	Jean Béliveau	Montreal

JAMES NORRIS TROPHY WINNERS

	Winner	Runner-up
1993	Chris Chelios, Chi.	Ray Bourque, Bos.
1992	Brian Leetch, NYR	Ray Bourque, Bos.
1991	Ray Bourque, Bos.	Al MacInnis, Cgy.
1990	Ray Bourque, Bos.	Al MacInnis, Cgy.
1989	Chris Chelios, Mtl	Paul Coffey, Pit.
1988	Ray Bourque, Bos.	Scott Stevens, Wsh.
1987	Ray Bourque, Bos.	Mark Howe, Phi.
1986	Paul Coffey, Edm.	Mark Howe, Phi.
1985	Paul Coffey, Edm.	Ray Bourque, Bos.
1984	Rod Langway, Wsh.	Paul Coffey, Edm.
1983	Rod Langway, Wsh.	Mark Howe, Phi.
1982	Doug Wilson, Chi.	Ray Bourque, Bos.
1981	Randy Carlyle, Pit.	Denis Potvin, NYI
1980	Larry Robinson, Mtl.	Borje Salming, Tor.
1979	Denis Potvin, NYI	Larry Robinson, Mtl.
1978	Denis Potvin, NYI	Brad Park, Bos.
1977	Larry Robinson, Mtl.	Borje Salming, Tor.
1976	Denis Potvin, NYI	Brad Park, NYR-Bos.
1975	Bobby Orr, Bos.	Denis Potvin, NYI
1974	Bobby Orr, Bos.	Brad Park, NYR
1973	Bobby Orr, Bos.	Guy Lapointe, Mtl.
1972	Bobby Orr, Bos.	Brad Park, NYR
1971	Bobby Orr, Bos.	Brad Park, NYR
1970	Bobby Orr, Bos.	Brad Park, NYR
1969	Bobby Orr, Bos.	Tim Horton, Tor.
1968	Bobby Orr, Bos.	J.C. Tremblay, Mtl
1967	Harry Howell, NYR	Pierre Pilote, Chi.
1966	Jacques Laperriere, Mtl.	Pierre Pilote, Chi.
1965	Pierre Pilote, Chi.	Jacques Laperriere, Mtl.
1964	Pierre Pilote, Chi.	Tim Horton, Tor.
1963	Pierre Pilote, Chi.	Carl Brewer, Tor.
1962	Doug Harvey, NYR	Pierre Pilote, Chi.
1961	Doug Harvey, Mtl.	Marcel Pronovost, Det.
1960	Doug Harvey, Mtl.	Allan Stanley, Tor.
1959	Tom Johnson, Mtl.	Bill Gadsby, NYR
1958	Doug Harvey, Mtl.	Bill Gadsby, NYR
1957	Doug Harvey, Mtl.	Red Kelly, Det.
1956	Doug Harvey, Mtl.	Bill Gadsby, NYR
1955	Doug Harvey, Mtl.	Red Kelly, Det.
1954	Red Kelly, Det.	Doug Harvey, Mtl.

JACK ADAMS AWARD WINNERS

	Winner	Runner-up
1993	Pat Burns, Tor.	Brian Sutter, Bos.
1992	Pat Quinn, Van.	Roger Neilson, NYR
1991	Brian Sutter, St.L.	Tom Webster, L.A.
1990	Bob Murdoch, Wpg.	Mike Milbury, Bos.
1989	Pat Burns, Mtl.	Bob McCammon, Van.
1988	Jacques Demers, Det.	Terry Crisp, Cgy.
1987	Jacques Demers, Det.	Jack Evans, Hfd.
1986	Glen Sather, Edm.	Jacques Demers, St.L.
1985	Mike Keenan, Phi.	Barry Long, Wpg.
1984	Bryan Murray, Wsh.	Scott Bowman, Buf.
1983	Orval Tessier, Chi.	
1982	Tom Watt, Wpg.	
1981	Red Berenson, St.L.	Bob Berry, L.A.
1980	Pat Quinn, Phi.	
1979	Al Arbour, NYI	Fred Shero, NYR
1978	Bobby Kromm, Det.	Don Cherry, Bos.
1977	Scott Bowman, Mtl.	Tom McVie, Wsh.
1976	Don Cherry, Bos.	
1975	Bob Pulford, L.A.	
1974	Fred Shero, Phi.	

LESTER PATRICK TROPHY WINNERS

1993	Frank Boucher
	Mervyn (Red) Dutton
	Bruce McNall
	Gil Stein
1992	Al Arbour
	Art Berglund
	Lou Lamoriello
1991	Rod Gilbert
	Mike Illitch
1990	Len Ceglarski
1989	Dan Kelly
	Lou Nanne
	*Lynn Patrick
	Bud Poile
1988	Keith Allen
	Fred Cusick
	Bob Johnson
1987	*Hobey Baker
	Frank Mathers
1986	John MacInnes
	Jack Riley
1985	Jack Butterfield
	Arthur M. Wirtz
1984	John A. Ziegler Jr.
	*Arthur Howie Ross
1983	Bill Torrey
1982	Emile P. Francis
1981	Charles M. Schulz
1980	Bobby Clarke
	Edward M. Snider
	Frederick A. Shero
	1980 U.S. Olympic Hockey Team
1979	Bobby Orr
1978	Philip A. Esposito
	Tom Fitzgerald
	William T. Tutt
	William W. Wirtz
1977	John P. Bucyk
	Murray A. Armstrong
	John Mariucci
1976	Stanley Mikita
	George A. Leader
	Bruce A. Norris
1975	Donald M. Clark
	William L. Chadwick
	Thomas N. Ivan
1974	Alex Delvecchio
	Murray Murdoch
	*Weston W. Adams, Sr.
	*Charles L. Crovat
1973	Walter L. Bush, Jr.
1972	Clarence S. Campbell
	John Kelly
	Ralph "Cooney" Weiland
	*James D. Norris
1971	William M. Jennings
	*John B. Sollenberger
	*Terrance G. Sawchuk
1970	Edward W. Shore
	*James C. V. Hendy
1969	Robert M. Hull
	*Edward J. Jeremiah
1968	Thomas F. Lockhart
	*Walter A. Brown
	*Gen. John R. Kilpatrick
1967	Gordon Howe
	*Charles F. Adams
	*James Norris, Sr.
1966	J.J. "Jack" Adams

* awarded posthumously

FRANK J. SELKE TROPHY WINNERS

	Winner	Runner-up
1993	Doug Gilmour, Tor.	Dave Poulin, Bos.
1992	Guy Carbonneau, Mtl.	Sergei Fedorov, Det.
1991	Dirk Graham, Chi.	Esa Tikkanen, Edm.
1990	Rick Meagher, St.L.	Guy Carbonneau, Mtl.
1989	Guy Carbonneau, Mtl.	Esa Tikkanen, Edm.
1988	Guy Carbonneau, Mtl.	Steve Kasper, Bos.
1987	Dave Poulin, Phi.	Guy Carbonneau, Mtl.
1986	Troy Murray, Chi.	Ron Sutter, Phi.
1985	Craig Ramsay, Buf.	Doug Jarvis, Wsh.
1984	Doug Jarvis, Wsh.	Bryan Trottier, NYI
1983	Bobby Clarke, Phi.	Jari Kurri, Edm.
1982	Steve Kasper, Bos.	Bob Gainey, Mtl.
1981	Bob Gainey, Mtl.	Craig Ramsay, Buf.
1980	Bob Gainey, Mtl.	Craig Ramsay, Buf.
1979	Bob Gainey, Mtl.	Don Marcotte, Bos.
1978	Bob Gainey, Mtl.	Craig Ramsay, Buf.

ALKA-SELTZER PLUS AWARD WINNERS

1993	Mario Lemieux	Pittsburgh
1992	Paul Ysebaert	Detroit
1991	Marty McSorley	Los Angeles
	Theoren Fleury	Calgary
1990	Paul Cavallini	St. Louis

Bobby Orr won numerous awards as a member of the Boston Bruins from 1966-67 to 1975-76. Orr won the Calder Trophy in 1967; the Hart Trophy in 1970, 1971 and 1972; the Art Ross Trophy in 1970 and 1975; the Norris Trophy from 1968 to 1975; the Conn Smythe Trophy in 1970 and 1972; and the Lester B. Pearson Award in 1975.

NHL Amateur and Entry Draft

History

Year	Site	Date	Total Players Drafted
1963	Queen Elizabeth Hotel	June 5	21
1964	Queen Elizabeth Hotel	June 11	24
1965	Queen Elizabeth Hotel	April 27	11
1966	Mount Royal Hotel	April 25	24
1967	Queen Elizabeth Hotel	June 7	18
1968	Queen Elizabeth Hotel	June 13	24
1969	Queen Elizabeth Hotel	June 12	84
1970	Queen Elizabeth Hotel	June 11	115
1971	Queen Elizabeth Hotel	June 10	117
1972	Queen Elizabeth Hotel	June 8	152
1973	Mount Royal Hotel	May 15	168
1974	NHL Montreal Office	May 28	247
1975	NHL Montreal Office	June 3	217
1976	NHL Montreal Office	June 1	135
1977	NHL Montreal Office	June 14	185
1978	Queen Elizabeth Hotel	June 15	234
1979	Queen Elizabeth Hotel	August 9	126
1980	Montreal Forum	June 11	210
1981	Montreal Forum	June 10	211
1982	Montreal Forum	June 9	252
1983	Montreal Forum	June 8	242
1984	Montreal Forum	June 9	250
1985	Toronto Convention Centre	June 15	252
1986	Montreal Forum	June 21	252
1987	Joe Louis Sports Arena	June 13	252
1988	Montreal Forum	June 11	252
1989	Metropolitan Sports Center	June 17	252
1990	B. C. Place	June 16	250
1991	Memorial Auditorium	June 9	264
1992	Montreal Forum	June 20	264
1993	Colisée de Québec	June 26	286

* The NHL Amateur Draft became the NHL Entry Draft in 1979

Alexander Daigle was chosen first overall by the Ottawa Senators in the 1993 NHL Entry Draft. In 1992-93, Daigle scored 137 points in 53 games for Victoriaville of the QMJHL. He was also a member of Canada's gold medal winning team at the IIHF World Junior Championships.

First Selections

Year	Player	Pos	Drafted By	Drafted From	Age
1969	Rejean Houle	LW	Montreal	Jr. Canadiens	19.8
1970	Gilbert Perreault	C	Buffalo	Jr. Canadiens	19.7
1971	Guy Lafleur	RW	Montreal	Quebec Remparts	19.9
1972	Billy Harris	RW	NY Islanders	Toronto Marlboros	20.4
1973	Denis Potvin	D	NY Islanders	Ottawa 67's	19.7
1974	Greg Joly	D	Washington	Regina Pats	20.0
1975	Mel Bridgman	C	Philadelphia	Victoria Cougars	20.1
1976	Rick Green	D	Washington	London Knights	20.3
1977	Dale McCourt	C	Detroit	St. Catharines Fincups	20.4
1978	Bobby Smith	C	Minnesota	Ottawa 67's	20.4
1979	Bob Ramage	D	Colorado	London Knights	20.5
1980	Doug Wickenheiser	C	Montreal	Regina Pats	19.2
1981	Dale Hawerchuk	C	Winnipeg	Cornwall Royals	18.2
1982	Gord Kluzak	D	Boston	Nanaimo Islanders	18.3
1983	Brian Lawton	C	Minnesota	Mount St. Charles HS	18.11
1984	Mario Lemieux	C	Pittsburgh	Laval Voisins	18.8
1985	Wendel Clark	LW/D	Toronto	Saskatoon Blades	18.7
1986	Joe Murphy	C	Detroit	Michigan State	18.8
1987	Pierre Turgeon	C	Buffalo	Granby Bisons	17.10
1988	Mike Modano	C	Minnesota	Prince Albert Raiders	18.0
1989	Mats Sundin	RW	Quebec	Nacka (Sweden)	18.4
1990	Owen Nolan	RW	Quebec	Cornwall Royals	18.4
1991	Eric Lindros	C	Quebec	Oshawa Generals	18.3
1992	Roman Hamrlik	D	Tampa Bay	ZPS Zlin (Czech.)	18.2
1993	Alexandre Daigle	C	Ottawa	Victoriaville Tigres	18.5

Draft Summary

Following is a summary of the number of players drafted from the Ontario Hockey League (OHL), Western Hockey League (WHL), Quebec Major Junior Hockey League (QMJHL), United States Colleges, United States High Schools, European Leagues and other Leagues throughout North America since 1969:

	OHL	WHL	QMJHL	US Coll.	US HS	International	Other
1969	36	20	11	7	0	1	9
1970	51	22	13	16	0	0	13
1971	41	28	13	22	0	0	13
1972	46	44	30	21	0	0	11
1973	56	49	24	25	0	0	14
1974	69	66	40	41	0	6	25
1975	55	57	28	59	0	6	12
1976	47	33	18	26	0	8	3
1977	42	44	40	49	0	5	5
1978	59	48	22	73	0	16	16
1979	48	37	19	15	0	6	1
1980	73	41	24	42	7	13	10
1981	59	37	28	21	17	32	17
1982	60	55	17	20	47	35	18
1983	57	41	24	14	35	34	37
1984	55	37	16	22	44	40	36
1985	59	48	15	20	48	31	31
1986	66	32	22	22	40	28	42
1987	32	36	17	40	69	38	20
1988	32	30	22	48	56	39	25
1989	39	44	16	48	47	38	20
1990	39	33	14	38	57	53	16
1991	43	40	25	43	37	55	21
1992	57	45	22	9	25	83	24
1993	60	44	23	17	33	78	31
Total	1281	1011	543	758	562	645	469

Total Drafted, 1969-1993: 5,269

Ontario Hockey League

Club	'69	'70	'71	'72	'73	'74	'75	'76	'77	'78	'79	'80	'81	'82	'83	'84	'85	'86	'87	'88	'89	'90	'91	'92	'93	Total
Peterborough	5	5	4	5	9	4	8	1	4	6	9	10	3	5	7	3	9	2	5	2	2	4	3	4	4	123
Oshawa	5	4	3	5	5	7	6	6	1	3	3	2	9	5	5	6	6	6	3	2	4	2	4	4	4	110
Kitchener	1	6	2	8	4	13	3	1	3	4	4	4	5	5	8	4	6	3	2	1	7	5	3	1	4	107
Ottawa	2	4	3	4	6	5	3	6	5	5	5	3	8	4	9	2	2	3	3	2	1	–	5	5	6	102
London	4	9	1	5	6	6	3	5	4	3	6	2	5	5	3	7	1	3	2	6	3	3	1	3	4	100
Toronto	3	7	6	5	6	8	4	4	7	5	4	10	2	6	4	3	4	1	2	2	–	–	–	–	–	97
Sudbury	–	–	–	–	6	6	4	5	4	4	3	7	2	4	–	2	5	3	1	–	1	2	8	2	10	79
S.S. Marie	–	–	–	–	4	5	2	5	1	5	3	3	8	1	6	4	5	7	1	2	3	1	2	7	3	78
Kingston	–	–	–	–	–	4	4	6	4	9	2	8	5	2	1	3	3	4	1	1	–	2	2	3	5	69
Hamilton	2	3	5	4	6	4	7	3	–	8	1	–	–	–	3	6	4	4	–	–	2	–	–			62
Niagara Falls	4	2	1	4	–	–	–	2	3	5	8	6	6	–	–	–	–	–	4	4	4	4	4			61
St. Catharines	5	5	8	5	4	7	8	4	6	–	–	–	–	–	–	–	–	–	–	–	–	–	–	–	–	52
Windsor	–	–	–	–	–	–	–	2	1	4	2	3	5	3	2	2	3	7	–	5	2	1	–	3	–	45
Cornwall	–	–	–	–	–	–	–	–	–	–	–	7	4	3	2	2	3	3	2	3	3	5	–			37
North Bay	–	–	–	–	–	–	–	–	–	–	–	–	4	4	3	3	3	3	1	4	2	5	2			34
Belleville	–	–	–	–	–	–	–	–	–	–	–	–	3	4	4	5	2	–	4	2	1	4	–			29
Brantford	–	–	–	–	–	–	–	3	8	5	2	7	2	–	–	–	–	–	–	–	–	–	–			27
Guelph	–	–	–	–	–	–	–	–	–	–	–	1	5	3	8	2	–	4	–	–	2	2				27
Montreal	5	6	8	1	–	–	–	–	–	–	–	–	–	–	–	–	–	–	–	–	–	–				20
Detroit	–	–	–	–	–	–	–	–	–	–	–	–	–	–	–	–	–	–	–	–	–	2	2	7		11
Owen Sound	–	–	–	–	–	–	–	–	–	–	–	–	–	–	–	–	–	–	–	1	1	2	4			8
Newmarket	–	–	–	–	–	–	–	–	–	–	–	–	–	–	–	–	–	–	–	–	–	–	3			3

Year	Total Ontario Drafted	Total Players Drafted	Ontario %
1969	36	84	42.9
1970	51	115	44.3
1971	41	117	35.0
1972	46	152	30.3
1973	56	168	33.3
1974	69	247	27.9
1975	55	217	25.3
1976	47	135	34.8
1977	42	185	22.7
1978	59	234	25.2
1979	48	126	38.1
1980	73	210	34.8
1981	59	211	28.0
1982	60	252	23.8
1983	57	242	23.6
1984	55	250	22.0
1985	59	252	23.4
1986	66	252	26.2
1987	32	252	12.7
1988	32	252	12.7
1989	39	252	15.5
1990	39	250	15.6
1991	43	264	16.3
1992	57	264	21.6
1993	60	286	21.0
Total	1281	5269	24.3

Western Hockey League

Club	'69	'70	'71	'72	'73	'74	'75	'76	'77	'78	'79	'80	'81	'82	'83	'84	'85	'86	'87	'88	'89	'90	'91	'92	'93	Total
Regina	–	–	5	5	1	8	5	3	1	4	1	3	5	6	8	4	4	3	2	–	5	1	–	4	–	78
Saskatoon	1	–	1	3	8	4	5	3	4	1	2	2	3	5	5	3	1	5	4	4	3	2	2	3	2	76
Portland	–	–	–	–	–	–	–	–	4	8	7	8	6	7	7	5	2	4	3	1	4	1	1	4	4	76
Victoria	–	–	–	2	2	5	7	4	3	3	1	8	6	2	3	4	2	1	2	4	4	2	–	1	2	68
Medicine Hat	–	–	–	4	6	4	5	3	5	4	–	4	2	1	2	1	6	2	5	1	4	1	3	3	1	67
Calgary	3	5	2	7	4	8	4	4	4	3	–	2	2	4	3	3	3	2	–	–	–	–	–	–	–	66
Brandon	–	3	1	5	2	7	4	–	3	1	10	5	2	2	1	3	2	1	3	3	–	1	1	1	2	63
New Westm'r	–	–	–	6	8	7	9	5	8	6	5	1	–	–	–	2	1	1	2	1	–	–	–	–	–	62
Lethbridge	–	–	–	–	–	3	2	3	5	4	1	4	7	2	1	5	1	–	3	3	4	7	3	4		62
Kamloops	–	–	–	–	4	4	4	4	–	–	–	–	2	4	4	4	3	1	5	4	6	3	2	5		58
Prince Albert	–	–	–	–	–	–	–	–	–	–	–	4	2	2	6	6	1	3	3	4	6	2	5			44
Seattle	–	–	–	–	–	–	–	–	–	4	2	3	–	6	–	1	3	1	2	4	2	6	3	2	4	43
Flin Flon	4	4	5	2	4	7	4	3	1	5	–	–	–	–	–	–	–	–	–	–	–	–	–	–	–	39
Winnipeg	3	2	4	2	5	4	4	–	4	–	–	–	1	4	1	–	–	–	–	–	–	–	–	–	–	34
Edmonton	4	4	5	6	6	2	3	2	–	2	–	–	–	–	–	–	–	–	–	–	–	–	–	–	–	34
Swift Current	1	–	1	–	3	6	–	–	–	–	–	–	–	–	–	5	2	2	2	1	1	5				29
Spokane	–	–	–	–	–	–	–	–	–	–	–	–	–	1	3	2	1	5	7	4						23
Moose Jaw	–	–	–	–	–	–	–	–	–	–	–	4	1	3	–	3	1	2	3	2						19
Tri-Cities	–	–	–	–	–	–	–	–	–	–	–	–	–	–	4	3	3	5	2	–						17
Billings	–	–	–	–	–	4	3	4	2	–	–	–	–	–	–	–	–	–	–	–						13
Estevan	4	4	4	–	–	–	–	–	–	–	–	–	–	–	–	–	–	–	–	–						12
Kelowna	–	–	–	–	–	–	–	–	2	4	5	–														11
Nanaimo	–	–	–	–	–	–	–	5	1	–	–															6
Tacoma	–	–	–	–	–	–	–	–	–	–	–	–	–	–	–	–	–	–	–	–	–	–	3	2		5
Red Deer	–	–	–	–	–	–	–	–	–	–	–	–	–	–	–	–	–	–	–	–	–	–	–	3		3
Vancouver	–	–	–	2	–	–	–	–	–	–	–	–	–	–	–	–	–	–	–	–	–	–	–	–		2

Year	Total Western Drafted	Total Players Drafted	Western %
1969	20	84	23.8
1970	22	115	19.1
1971	28	117	23.9
1972	44	152	28.9
1973	49	168	29.2
1974	66	247	26.7
1975	57	217	26.3
1976	33	135	24.4
1977	44	185	23.8
1978	48	234	20.5
1979	37	126	29.4
1980	41	210	19.5
1981	37	211	17.5
1982	55	252	21.8
1983	41	242	16.9
1984	37	250	14.8
1985	48	252	19.0
1986	32	252	12.7
1987	36	252	14.3
1988	30	252	11.9
1989	44	252	17.5
1990	33	250	13.2
1991	40	264	15.2
1992	45	264	17.0
1993	44	286	15.4
Total	1011	5269	19.2

Quebec Major Junior Hockey League

Club	'69	'70	'71	'72	'73	'74	'75	'76	'77	'78	'79	'80	'81	'82	'83	'84	'85	'86	'87	'88	'89	'90	'91	'92	'93	Total
Shawinigan	3	2	1	6	1	5	3	–	3	–	2	2	5	5	2	–	2	1	–	2	–	2	3	1		51
Quebec	1	1	2	4	6	6	1	3	7	1	3	2	2	1	2	2	3	–	–	–	–	–	–	–	–	47
Trois Rivieres	–	1	2	2	2	2	3	2	6	3	2	2	2	1	3	–	3	–	1	3	3	1	2	1	–	47
Sherbrooke	–	–	2	2	4	3	7	5	6	3	4	1	5	2	–	–	–	–	–	–	–	–	–	–	3	47
Cornwall	2	1	2	6	4	8	1	3	1	6	1	5	5	–	–	–	–	–	–	–	–	–	–	–	–	45
Hull	–	–	–	–	–	3	2	2	3	–	3	1	–	3	1	–	4	3	2	2	3	3	3	3		41
Laval	–	–	–	1	–	2	1	1	4	2	1	–	–	2	1	2	–	5	3	1	3	3	4	1	2	39
Drummondville	2	4	1	4	2	1	–	–	–	–	–	–	1	2	2	2	4	1	–	4	2	2				34
Chicoutimi	–	–	–	–	–	1	–	5	1	1	3	6	1	3	–	3	1	2	2	1	1	–	1	1		33
Montreal	–	–	–	–	4	4	8	1	3	2	4	3	–	3	–	–	–	–	–	–	–	–	–	–		32
Sorel	2	3	1	3	1	8	1	1	3	–	–	5	–	–	–	–	–	–	–	–	–	–	–	–		28
Verdun	–	1	1	2	–	–	–	1	3	3	–	3	3	–	3	0	3	1	–	3	–					27
Granby	–	–	–	–	–	–	–	–	2	1	3	2	2	4	–	2	–	2	–	1						19
St. Jean	–	–	–	–	–	–	–	–	–	2	–	1	1	0	3	1	–	3	1	2						14
Victoriaville	–	–	–	–	–	–	–	–	–	–	–	–	–	4	–	1	–	2	6							13
Longueuil	–	–	–	–	–	–	–	–	1	2	1	2	1	–	2	3	–									12
St. Hyacinthe	–	–	–	–	–	–	–	–	–	–	–	–	3	1	2	1										7
Beauport	–	–	–	–	–	–	–	–	–	–	–	1	3	1												5
St. Jerome	1	–	1	–	–	–	–	–	–	–	–	–	–	–	–	–	–	–	–	–						2

Year	Total Quebec Drafted	Total Players Drafted	Quebec %
1969	11	84	13.1
1970	13	115	11.3
1971	13	117	11.1
1972	30	152	19.7
1973	24	168	14.3
1974	40	247	16.2
1975	28	217	12.9
1976	18	135	13.3
1977	40	185	21.6
1978	22	234	9.4
1979	19	126	15.1
1980	24	210	11.4
1981	28	211	13.3
1982	17	252	6.7
1983	24	242	9.9
1984	16	250	6.4
1985	15	252	5.9
1986	22	252	8.7
1987	17	252	6.7
1988	22	252	8.7
1989	16	252	6.3
1990	14	250	5.6
1991	25	264	9.5
1992	22	264	8.3
1993	23	286	8.0
Total	543	5269	10.3

United States Colleges

Club	'69	'70	'71	'72	'73	'74	'75	'76	'77	'78	'79	'80	'81	'82	'83	'84	'85	'86	'87	'88	'89	'90	'91	'92	'93	Total
Minnesota	1	3	2	–	–	9	4	4	5	5	2	3	1	1	1	–	–	2	1	1	1	–	–	–	–	46
Michigan Tech	–	–	3	1	2	5	4	4	1	2	1	4	–	1	–	2	2	2	1	1	2	1	2	1	–	42
Michigan	1	–	–	2	2	3	3	3	1	6	–	4	–	–	1	1	–	1	2	3	5	4	2	1	–	42
Wisconsin	–	1	2	4	5	4	4	2	3	–	1	–	3	2	–	1	1	–	1	–	1	–	1	–	–	36
Denver	1	3	2	4	2	3	1	2	2	2	1	–	1	–	–	1	2	4	1	1	–	–	–	–	–	35
Boston U.	–	4	–	–	1	1	1	1	4	5	1	–	1	–	1	1	2	2	3	1	2	2	1	1	–	35
Michigan State	–	–	1	–	1	1	1	1	–	–	–	2	–	2	–	2	–	1	1	4	4	5	4	1	1	32
North Dakota	2	3	3	1	4	2	1	–	1	2	3	3	1	–	1	–	–	–	2	1	1	–	–	–	–	31
Providence	–	–	–	–	–	3	2	3	4	–	5	4	1	2	–	1	1	–	–	–	1	–	–	–	–	27
Clarkson	–	–	2	2	1	–	2	–	2	2	1	1	1	1	1	1	–	1	1	1	3	2	1	1	–	27
New Hampshire	–	–	–	1	1	3	6	4	1	1	2	1	1	1	2	–	–	1	–	–	–	–	–	–	–	25
Cornell	–	–	2	1	1	–	1	1	1	–	1	1	1	–	1	2	–	1	2	5	2	–	–	–	1	23
Bowling Green	–	–	–	–	1	3	2	1	1	1	1	–	1	–	–	1	–	–	3	2	1	3	1	–	–	21
Colorado	2	1	–	–	1	3	1	2	2	–	1	–	–	3	–	1	–	1	–	2	–	–	–	–	–	20
W. Michigan	–	–	–	–	–	–	2	–	–	2	–	2	2	–	2	1	1	1	1	4	–	2				20
Lake Superior	–	–	–	1	1	1	1	–	3	–	–	–	–	1	–	3	–	3	2	3	1	–	1			20
Notre Dame	–	–	2	3	–	7	2	–	3	1	1	–	–	–	–	–	–	–	–	–	–	–	–	–	–	19
RPI	–	–	–	1	–	–	1	3	–	1	2	1	1	–	1	–	2	2	–	–	3	1				19
St. Lawrence	–	–	–	–	–	1	–	1	4	–	–	3	–	1	1	1	1	1	1	1	2	–	1			19
Harvard	–	–	2	–	–	2	–	2	2	–	–	1	1	–	2	–	1	1	2	–	–	–	2			18
Boston College	–	1	–	–	1	1	–	5	–	2	1	1	–	–	1	2	–	2	–	–	–	–				17
Northern Mich.	–	–	–	–	–	–	–	4	–	1	2	1	–	–	–	4	1	2	–	1	–					16
Vermont	–	–	–	1	4	–	1	1	–	1	1	–	1	1	2	–	–	1	–	1	–					15
Miami of Ohio	–	–	–	–	–	–	–	–	–	–	–	1	–	2	4	2	–	2	1	1						13
Minn.-Duluth	–	2	1	–	–	–	1	1	–	1	–	–	–	–	2	1	2	1	–							12
Ohio State	–	–	–	–	–	2	1	–	–	1	–	2	2	–	1	1	1	1								12
Brown	–	–	1	2	1	–	3	2	–	1	–	–	–	–	–	–	1									11
Colgate	–	–	1	–	1	–	2	1	–	1	–	1	1	2	2	–	1									10
Yale	–	1	–	1	–	2	–	1	–	1	2	1	–	–	1											10
Maine	–	–	–	–	–	1	1	–	1	1	3	2	1	–	1											10
Northeastern	–	–	1	–	1	–	1	1	1	1	–	1	1													8
Princeton	–	–	–	1	–	1	1	1	–	1	1	1														8
Ferris State	–	–	–	–	–	–	–	2	1	1	1	2														7
St. Louis	–	–	1	2	1	2																				6
U. of Ill.-Chi.	–	–	–	–	1	2	1	2																		6
Pennsylvania	–	1	2	1	–	1																				5
Dartmouth	–	1	–	1	1	1																				5
Union College	–	4																								4
Lowell	1	1	1	1																						4
Merrimack	1	1	1	1																						4
Alaska-Anchorage	2	1	1																							4
Babson College	1	1	1																							3
Alaska-Fairbanks	1	1																								2
Salem State	1																									1
Bemidji State	1																									1
San Diego U.	1																									1
Greenway	1																									1
St. Anselen College	1																									1
Hamilton College	1																									1
St. Thomas	1																									1
St. Cloud State	1																									1
Amer. Int'l College	1																									1

Year	Total College Drafted	Total Players Drafted	College %
1969	7	84	8.3
1970	16	115	13.9
1971	22	117	18.8
1972	21	152	13.8
1973	25	168	14.9
1974	41	247	16.6
1975	59	217	26.7
1976	26	135	19.3
1977	49	185	26.5
1978	73	234	31.2
1979	15	126	11.9
1980	42	210	20.0
1981	21	211	10.0
1982	20	252	7.9
1983	14	242	5.8
1984	22	250	8.8
1985	20	252	7.9
1986	22	252	8.7
1987	40	252	15.9
1988	48	252	19.0
1989	48	252	19.0
1990	38	250	15.2
1991	43	264	16.3
1992	9	264	3.4
1993	17	286	5.9
Total	**758**	**5269**	**14.4**

Neal Broten, left, had already won an Olympic gold medal when he was named the first winner of the Hobey Baker Award as the top U.S. college player in 1981. A student-athlete at the University of Minnesota, he was chosen 42nd overall in the 1979 Entry Draft by the Minnesota North Stars. Another University of Minnesota player, goaltender Robb Stauber, right, was the WCHA's Player of the Year and the Hobey Baker Award winner in 1988. He was selected 107th overall by the Los Angeles Kings in the 1986 Entry Draft.

International

Country	'69	'70	'71	'72	'73	'74	'75	'76	'77	'78	'79	'80	'81	'82	'83	'84	'85	'86	'87	'88	'89	'90	'91	'92	'93	Total
Sweden	–	–	–	–	–	5	2	5	2	8	5	9	14	14	10	14	16	9	15	14	9	7	11	11	18	198
USSR/CIS	–	–	–	–	–	–	1	–	2	–	–	–	3	5	1	2	1	2	11	18	14	25	45	31		161
Czechoslovakia	–	–	–	–	–	–	–	–	2	1	–	4	13	9	13	8	6	11	5	8	21	9	17	15		142
Finland	1	–	–	–	1	3	2	3	2	–	4	12	5	9	10	4	10	6	7	3	9	6	8	9		114
Germany	–	–	–	–	–	–	–	–	2	–	2	–	1	2	1	–	2	–	1	2	–	–	1	1	3	17
Norway	–	–	–	–	–	–	–	–	–	–	–	–	–	–	–	–	–	2	–	2	1	–	–		5
Switzerland	–	–	–	–	–	–	–	1	–	–	–	–	–	–	–	–	–	–	–	–	1	–	2		4
Denmark	–	–	–	–	–	–	–	–	–	–	–	–	–	–	1	1	–	–	–	–	–		2
Scotland	–	–	–	–	–	–	–	–	–	–	–	–	–	–	–	1	–	–	–	–	–	–	–		1
Poland	–	–	–	–	–	–	–	–	–	–	–	–	–	–	–	–	–	–	–	–	1	–		1
Japan	–	–	–	–	–	–	–	–	–	–	–	–	–	–	–	–	–	–	i	–		1

Year	Total International Drafted	Total Players Drafted	International %
1969	1	84	1.2
1970	0	115	0
1971	0	117	0
1972	0	152	0
1973	0	168	0
1974	6	247	2.4
1975	6	217	2.8
1976	8	135	5.9
1977	5	185	2.7
1978	16	234	6.8
1979	6	126	4.8
1980	13	210	6.2
1981	32	211	15.2
1982	35	252	13.9
1983	34	242	14.0
1984	40	250	17.6
1985	31	252	12.3
1986	28	252	11.1
1987	38	252	15.1
1988	39	252	15.5
1989	38	252	15.1
1990	53	250	21.2
1991	55	264	20.8
1992	83	264	31.4
1993	78	286	27.3
Total	**645**	**5269**	**12.2**

Sweden

Club	'74	'75	'76	'77	'78	'79	'80	'81	'82	'83	'84	'85	'86	'87	'88	'89	'90	'91	'92	'93	Total
Djurgarden Stockholm	1	1	1	–	–	1	2	–	1	2	1	–	1	2	–	1	1	2	1	1	19
Farjestad Karlstad	–	–	–	2	2	–	1	2	1	1	2	–	–	1	–	1	2	1		17
AIK Solna	–	–	1	–	1	1	–	2	3	1	–	4	–	–	–	1	1	1		16
Leksand	1	–	–	–	1	–	1	–	2	2	1	1	2	1	–	2	–	2		16
MoDo Hockey Ornskoldsvik	–	1	–	–	1	–	1	–	2	–	–	1	–	–	2	2	5		15
Brynas Gavle	1	–	–	1	1	1	1	–	1	2	–	4	–	–	1	–		13
Sodertalje	–	–	–	1	–	1	1	1	2	2	2	–	2	–	–	1		13
Skelleftea	–	1	1	–	–	1	1	2	1	–	–	1	–	–	1		9
Vasteras	–	–	–	–	–	–	–	–	–	–	–	2	2	1	1	1	7
Vastra Frolunda Goteburg	–	–	–	–	–	–	2	1	–	1	1	1	–	1	–	7
Lulea	–	–	–	–	1	1	–	–	1	1	1	–	1		6
Bjorkloven Umea	–	–	–	–	2	1	–	1	–	1	1	–		5
Orebro	–	1	–	1	–	1	1	1	–		5
Rogle Angelholm	–	–	–	–	–	–	–	–	–	1	2	–	–	2	5
Timra	–	–	–	–	1	2	–	1	1	–		5
HV-71 Jonkoping	–	–	–	–	1	–	–	1	1	1	–		4
Nacka	–	–	–	–	–	–	1	–	1	–	2		4
Falun	–	–	–	–	1	–	–	1	–	1	–		3
Hammarby Stockholm	–	–	–	1	1	–	–	–	–	1	3
Malmo	–	–	–	–	–	–	–	–	–	1	1	3
Team Kiruna	–	1	–	–	1	–	–	–	–	1	3
Boden	1	–	–	–	–	1	–	–		2
Mora	–	–	–	–	1	–	1	–		2
Ostersund	–	–	–	–	–	1	1	–		2
Pitea	–	–	–	1	–	–	1	–		2
Troja	–	–	–	–	1	–	1	–		2
Almtuna	–	–	–	1	–	–		1
Danderyd Hockey	–	–	–	–	–	1	–		1
Fagersta	–	–	–	1	–	–		1
Huddinge	–	–	–	–	–	1	–		1
Karskoga	–	1	–	–	–	–		1
Stocksund	–	–	1	–	–	–		1
S/G Hockey 83 Gavle	–	–	–	1	–	–		1
Talje	–	–	–	–	1	–		1
Tunabro	1	–	–	–	–	–		1
Uppsala	–	–	–	–	–	1		1

Note:
Note: Players drafted in the International category played outside North America in their draft year. European-born players drafted from the OHL, QMJHL, WHL or U.S. Colleges are not counted as International players. See Country of Origin, below.

1993 Entry Draft Analysis

Country of Origin

Country	Players Drafted
Canada	137
USA	56
Russia	34
Sweden	18
Czech Republic	14
Finland	8
Slovakia	4
Ukraine	4
Belarus	3
Latvia	2
Poland	2
Germany	1
Kazahkstan	1
Norway	1
Switzerland	1

Position

Position	Players Drafted
Defense	94
Center	73
Right Wing	37
Left Wing	46
Goaltender	36

Birth Year

Year	Players Drafted
1975	169
1974	67
1973	25
1972	1
1971	6
1970	5
1969	2
1968	4
1967	1
1966	1
1965	2
1963	2

Russia/C.I.S.

Club	'74	'75	'76	'77	'78	'79	'80	'81	'82	'83	'84	'85	'86	'87	'88	'89	'90	'91	'92	'93	Total
CSKA Moscow	–	–	–	1	–	–	1	4	–	1	1	1	5	8	3	4	7	3	39
Dynamo Moscow	–	–	–	–	–	–	–	–	–	–	2	3	4	7	10	2	28
Krylja Sovetov Moscow	–	–	–	–	–	–	–	–	1	1	2	4	3	1	12
Traktor Chelyabinsk	–	–	–	–	–	–	–	–	–	2	–	2	7	11
Pardaugava Riga[1]	–	1	–	–	–	–	–	–	1	2	–	1	4	1	10
Sokol-Eskulap Kiev[2]	–	–	–	–	–	–	1	–	1	–	1	2	3	1	9
Khimik Voskresensk	–	–	–	–	–	–	1	–	–	–	1	3	1	2	–	8
Spartak Moscow	–	–	–	–	–	1	–	1	–	1	–	–	1	4	–	8
SKA St. Peterburg[3]	–	–	1	–	1	–	1	–	–	–	2	1	–	5
Dynamo Minsk	–	–	–	–	–	–	–	1	–	–	–	2	–	3
Dynamo-2 Moscow	–	–	–	–	–	–	–	–	–	2	1	3
Kristall Elektrostal	–	–	–	–	–	–	–	–	–	3	3
Lada Togliatti	–	–	–	–	–	–	–	–	1	2	3
Torpedo Nizhny Novgorod	–	–	–	–	–	–	–	1	2	–	3
Torpedo Yaroslavl	–	–	–	–	–	–	1	2	–	–	3
Metallburg Cherepovets	–	–	–	–	–	–	1	1	2
Salavat Yulayev Ufa	–	–	–	–	–	–	–	2	2
Torpedo Ust Kamenogorsk	–	–	–	–	–	–	1	1	2
Argus Moscow	–	–	–	–	–	–	1	–	1
Dizelist Penza	–	–	–	–	–	–	1	–	1
Dynamo Kharkov	–	–	–	–	–	1	–	–	1
Izhorets St. Peterburg	–	–	–	–	–	1	–	1
Khimik Novopolotsk	–	–	–	–	–	–	1	1
Kristall Saratov	–	–	–	–	–	–	1	1
Krylja Sovetov-2 Moscow	–	–	–	–	–	–	1	1
Avangard Omsk	–	–	–	–	–	–	–	–	0
Itil Kazan	–	–	–	–	–	–	–	–	0

Former club names: [1]–Dynamo Riga, HC Riga, [2]–Sokol Kiev, [3]–SKA Leningrad

Czech Republic and Slovakia

Club	'69	'70	'71	'72	'73	'74	'75	'76	'77	'78	'79	'80	'81	'82	'83	'84	'85	'86	'87	'88	'89	'90	'91	'92	'93	Total
Dukla Jihlava	–	–	–	–	–	–	–	–	–	–	–	–	–	2	4	3	1	–	3	1	1	3	2	1	1	22
Chemopetrol Litvinov[1]	–	–	–	–	–	–	–	–	–	–	–	3	1	2	–	–	–	2	2	1	3	2	–	–	–	16
Sparta Praha	–	–	–	–	–	–	–	–	–	–	–	–	1	–	2	1	1	1	2	1	2	–	1	1	–	13
Dukla Trencin	–	–	–	–	–	–	–	–	–	–	–	–	–	1	–	–	1	1	2	1	2	–	2	2	–	9
Motor Ceske-Budejovice	–	–	–	–	–	–	–	–	–	–	–	2	1	1	–	1	–	1	2	–	–	–	–	1	–	9
Poldi Kladno	–	–	–	–	–	–	–	–	–	2	1	–	1	–	1	–	–	1	2	–	1	–	–	–	–	9
ZPS Zlin[2]	–	–	–	–	–	–	–	–	–	–	–	–	1	–	1	1	1	–	–	2	2	1	–	–	–	9
HC Kosice[3]	–	–	–	–	–	–	–	–	–	1	2	–	2	–	1	–	–	2	–	–	–	–	–	–	–	8
Slovan Bratislava	–	–	–	–	–	–	1	1	–	1	–	2	–	–	1	1	1	–	1	–	–	–	–	–	–	8
TJ Vitkovice	–	–	–	–	–	–	1	–	1	–	–	–	–	–	–	–	1	–	–	–	1	–	–	1	3	7
Zetor Brno	–	–	–	–	–	–	–	–	–	–	–	–	1	–	3	–	2	–	1	–	–	–	–	–	–	7
Skoda Plzen	–	–	–	–	–	–	–	–	–	–	–	–	1	–	1	1	–	3	–	–	–	–	–	–	–	6
HC Pardubice[4]	–	–	–	–	–	–	–	–	–	–	–	–	2	–	2	–	1	–	–	–	–	–	–	–	–	5
AC Nitra	–	–	–	–	–	–	–	–	–	–	–	–	–	–	–	–	–	2	–	1	–	–	–	–	–	3
HC Olomouc[5]	–	–	–	–	–	–	–	–	–	–	–	–	–	–	–	1	–	2	–	–	–	–	–	–	–	3
Slavia Praha	–	–	–	–	–	–	–	–	–	–	–	–	–	1	–	–	–	–	–	–	–	1	–	–	–	2
Ingstavbrno	–	–	–	–	–	–	–	–	–	–	–	–	–	1	–	–	–	–	–	–	–	–	–	–	–	1
Partizan Liptovsky Mikulas	–	–	–	–	–	–	–	–	–	–	–	–	–	–	–	–	–	–	–	–	1	–	–	–	–	1
VTJ Pisek	–	–	–	–	–	–	–	–	–	–	–	–	–	–	–	–	–	–	–	–	1	–	–	–	–	1
ZPA Presov	–	–	–	–	–	–	–	–	–	–	–	–	–	–	–	–	–	–	–	–	–	–	1	–	–	1
ZTK Zvolen	–	–	–	–	–	–	–	–	–	–	–	–	–	–	–	–	–	–	–	–	–	–	1	–	–	1
ZTS Martin	–	–	–	–	–	–	–	–	–	–	–	–	–	–	–	–	–	–	–	–	–	–	1	–	–	1

Former club names: 1–CHZ Litvinov, 2–TJ Gottwaldov, TJ Zlin, 3–VSZ Kosice, 4–Tesla Pardubice, 5–DS Olomouc

Finland

Club	'69	'70	'71	'72	'73	'74	'75	'76	'77	'78	'79	'80	'81	'82	'83	'84	'85	'86	'87	'88	'89	'90	'91	'92	'93	Total
HIFK Helsinki	1	–	–	–	–	1	–	1	–	–	1	1	2	2	1	–	2	1	–	–	2					15
Ilves Tampere	–	–	–	–	–	–	1	2	–	–	2	–	2	2	–	1	–	1	–	1	1	–				13
TPS Turku	–	–	–	–	–	–	–	–	1	6	–	–	1	1	–	–	–	–	–	–	3					12
Jokerit Helsinki	–	–	–	–	–	–	–	2	1	–	–	1	–	–	1	–	1	1	2	–	3	–				11
Assat Pori	–	–	–	–	2	–	–	–	1	–	2	2	–	1	–	1	–	1								10
Karpat Oulu	–	–	–	–	–	–	1	–	1	–	1	–	2	2	–	1	–	1	1							9
Lukko Rauma	–	–	–	2	1	–	–	2	–	1	–	1	–	1	–	1	–	1								9
Tappara Tampere	–	–	1	–	–	–	–	2	–	–	–	–	4	–	1	–	1									9
Reipas Lahti	–	–	–	–	–	–	–	1	1	1	–	–	–	–	–	2	–	1								6
Kiekko-Espoo	–	–	–	–	–	–	–	–	–	–	–	–	1	1	1	2	–									5
HPK Hameenlinna	–	–	–	–	–	–	–	–	–	–	–	1	–	–	2	–	1									3
KalPa Kuopio	–	–	–	–	–	–	–	–	–	1	–	–	–	–	1											2
Saipa Lappeenranta	–	–	–	–	–	–	–	1	–	–	–	–	–	1												2
Sapko Savonlinna	–	–	–	–	–	–	–	–	–	1	1	–														2
Sport Vaasa	–	–	–	–	–	–	–	–	–	1	–	1														2
Grifk Kauniainen	–	–	–	–	–	–	–	–	–	–	–	1														1
JyP HT Jyvaskyla	–	–	–	–	–	–	–	–	–	1																1
Koo Koo Kouvola	–	–	–	–	–	–	–	–	–	–	1															1
S-Kiekko Seinajoki	–	–	–	–	–	–	1																			1

Right winger Jari Kurri, left, became the first European-trained player to record a 50-goal season in the NHL when he scored 52 goals for the Edmonton Oilers in 1983-84. As a member of the Los Angeles Kings, he became the League's 18th career 500-goal scorer on October 17, 1992. He was drafted 69th overall by the Oilers in the 1980 Entry Draft. Kent "Magic" Nilsson, below, became the first European-trained 100-point scorer with a 131-point campaign for the Calgary Flames in 1980-81. Nilsson was selected 64th overall by Atlanta in the 1976 NHL Amateur Draft. The Amateur Draft was renamed the Entry Draft in 1979.

First Round Draft Selections, 1993

1. OTTAWA SENATORS • **ALEXANDRE DAIGLE** • C
An excellent skater and playmaker, Daigle handles the puck well at all speeds and has a great touch around the net. A member of Canada's gold medal-winning team at the '93 World Junior Championships, he was also one of only eight 16-year-olds to score over 100 points in the QMJHL. A tenacious forechecker with a constant desire to excel, Daigle led the Victoriaville Tigres in scoring with 137 points in only 53 games, while being named to the QMJHL's First All-Star Team in '92-93.

2. HARTFORD WHALERS • **CHRIS PRONGER** • D
Pronger was named the OHL's best offensive defenseman in '92-93. Rangy and mobile, he controls the puck well using his long reach. Effective at both ends of the ice, this hard-checking rearguard possesses a very hard slapshot and adept passing skills. Pronger tallied 15 goals and 62 assists for the Peterborough Petes in '92-93 and was named to the OHL First All-Star Team.

3. TAMPA BAY LIGHTNING • **CHRIS GRATTON** • C
A power forward in the style of Mark Messier, Gratton excels at the physical game. An impeccable work ethic and good hockey sense combine to make him a natural leader on the ice. Gratton captained Ontario's under-17 world championship team in '92 and Canada's winning entry at the '92 Pacific Cup. He is a face-off specialist and an excellent open-ice body checker.

4. MIGHTY DUCKS OF ANAHEIM • **PAUL KARIYA** • LW
Kariya is a swift skater and analytical playmaker who can score several ways. As a member of the '92-93 NCAA champion, the U. of Maine Black Bears, Kariya was the first freshman to win the Hobey Baker Award as the outstanding player in U.S. college hockey. A good positional player, he is effective on the power-play and while killing penalties. The Vancouver, B.C., native totalled 24 goals and 69 assists in 36 games for the Black Bears.

5. FLORIDA PANTHERS • **ROB NIEDERMAYER** • C
Aggressive puck control and exceptional stick handling ability characterize the even-tempered Niedermayer. An honors student, he was named rookie of the year and top scholastic player for the Medicine Hat Tigers of the WHL in '90-91. Niedermayer was a gold medal winner with Canada at the '93 World Juniors and was named to the WHL East Division All-Star team in the same season. He is known as a character player.

6. SAN JOSE SHARKS • **VIKTOR KOZLOV** • LW
Kozlov has excellent size, strength and determination. The style of this native of Togliatti, Russia has been compared to that of Mario Lemieux. An accurate passer and shooter, Kozlov is also strong and effective in the corners and along the boards. He played his first game in the senior Russian National League at the age of 16, then joined league champion Moscow Dynamo for the '92-93 season, recording 11 points in 32 games.

7. EDMONTON OILERS • **JASON ARNOTT** • C
A strong, mobile skater, Arnott has good hands and can play in any situation at both ends of the rink. His ability to change speed and see all of the ice allows him to use his wingers effectively. In '92-93, he finished second in scoring on the OHL's Oshawa Generals with 41 goals and 57 assists for 98 points in 56 games. Arnott is a solid team player who will not back down from physical involvement.

8. NEW YORK RANGERS • **NIKLAS SUNDSTROM** • C/LW
Sundstrom is a gifted playmaker who moves the puck quickly and accurately. He plays intelligently around the net with a good selection of shots, which enabled him to score 10 goals on only 18 shots at the '93 World Junior Championships. Sundstrom is a sturdy, powerful player who forechecks tenaciously and makes few mistakes on the ice. He attended a special school for elite student hockey players in Ornskoldsvik, Sweden.

9. DALLAS STARS • **TODD HARVEY** • C
Harvey is a face-off specialist with speed and quickness. He is not afraid of tough action in the slot but is also is a finesse playmaker and superb passer. He makes good use of the boards to bank pucks ahead. Abrasive in a physical game, Harvey anticipates well and checks with authority. In '92-93, with the OHL's Detroit Jr. Red Wings, he tallied 50 goals and 50 assists in 55 games.

10. QUEBEC NORDIQUES • **JOCELYN THIBAULT** • G
Thibault is an excellent butterfly-style goaltender with good positioning, fast leg reflexes and a quick glove hand. He finished '92-93 with 34 wins, 14 losses and 5 ties for the Sherbrooke Faucans of the QMJHL. Thibault earned a number of awards in the QMJHL including: best scholastic player, best goals-against average, best team goals-against, best defensive player, and most valuable player. He also earned a First Team All-Star selection.

11. WASHINGTON CAPITALS • **BRENDAN WITT** • D
A solid checker, Witt clears the front of the net, ties up opponents and blocks shots, leading by example on and off the ice. Scouting reports note that he is a strong backward skater, has good lateral movement and a hard point shot. Witt was named to the WHL West Division First All-Star Team in '92-93. The tough rearguard scored 28 points for the Seattle Thunderbirds while accumulating 239 minutes in penalties.

12. TORONTO MAPLE LEAFS • **KENNY JONSSON** • D
Jonsson became a regular with Rogle Angelholm of the Swedish Elite League in '91-92. A strong, agile skater he has a powerful wrist and slapshot, low and hard from the blueline. Jonsson starred at the '93 World Junior Championships, and was named to the tournament's First All-Star team. Scouts note that he is a good positional player, effective in the corners and in front of the net. He plays aggressive, physical hockey within the rules.

13. NEW JERSEY DEVILS • **DENIS PEDERSON** • C
Pederson is regarded as an excellent team player with an outstanding work effort, strong skating and scoring ability and hockey sense around the net. A relentless forechecker, Pederson netted five short-handed goals as a rookie for the WHL's Prince Albert Raiders in '92-93. He tallied 73 points in 72 games. He is also an award-winning track athlete.

14. QUEBEC NORDIQUES • **ADAM DEADMARSH** • RW
Deadmarsh had a solid season for the '92-93 Portland Winter Hawks of the WHL, finishing with 69 points and a plus-37 in 58 games. A good two-way player, he utilizes his size and strength to best advantage. He handles the puck well in traffic and is a fine passer. Deadmarsh played for Canada on the Under-18 Team at the '92 Pacific Cup and for Team USA at the '93 World Juniors.

15. WINNIPEG JETS • **MATS LINDGREN** • C
Lindgren began playing for Skelleftea of the Swedish Junior League at the age of 15. An explosive skater with a powerful shot, he excels in short-handed or power-play situations. Lindgren played on the Swedish team at the '92 European Junior and the '93 World Junior Championships. He was named an All-Star and best forward team at the Under-18 Four Nation Tournament in '92. Scouts report that he plays an intelligent, unselfish game and is strong in the corners and on face-offs.

16. EDMONTON OILERS • **NICK STAJDUHAR** • D
Stajduhar has impressive speed and jumps quickly into offensive rushes. He is regarded as a prototype NHL defenseman; strong and agile with the ability to handle a hit as well as dispense. Stajduhar was named to the '92-93 OHL Third All-Star team after totalling 60 points in 49 games for the London Knights. The hard shooting blueliner was a member of Canada's silver medal-winning team at the Pacific Cup in '91.

17. WASHINGTON CAPITALS • **JASON ALLISON** • C
A great puckhandler with exceptional hockey sense and moves. Allison led the OHL's London Knights in scoring with 118 points in 66 games during '92-93. An opportunist, 15 of his 42 goals were scored with the man advantage. Scouts note Allison's quick release and shooting accuracy. He is very smart defensively and is willing to use his body along the boards.

18. CALGARY FLAMES • **JESPER MATTSON** • C
Mattson is an excellent skater with speed, balance and agility who can score in a variety of ways. He was the captain of the winning Swedish team at the '92-93 European Junior Championships and recorded 17 points in 40 games with Malmo of the Swedish Senior League in the same season. Mattson plays solid hockey at both ends of the ice.

19. TORONTO MAPLE LEAFS • **LANDON WILSON** • RW
The son of former NHLer Rick Wilson, Landon is a complete player. He can score goals with his heavy shot, make clever passes or deal out punishing body checks. Wilson played for the Dubuque Fighting Saints, champions of the Jr. A USHL in '92-93, scoring 65 points in 43 games while collecting 284 penalty minutes. An all around athlete, Wilson has also won awards in football.

20. VANCOUVER CANUCKS • **MIKE WILSON** • D
Wilson is a steady defender who stays with his man, finishes his check and plays well under pressure. At 6'4" and 180 lbs., he is strong along the boards and in the corners of his own zone. Scouting reports note his strong stride and good low shot from the point. He was named to the OHL First Rookie All-Star Team in '92-93 while scoring 13 points in 53 games for the Sudbury Wolves.

21. MONTREAL CANADIENS • **SAKU KOIVU** • C
Koivu is an exciting player and an excellent competitor who skates with explosive speed and acceleration. Noted for his quick moves, he can weave through traffic and create scoring chances. Koivu played for the '92-93 Finnish Champions, TPS Turku, where he netted three goals and seven points in 46 games. He starred for Finland at the '93 World Juniors and was named to that tournament's Second All-Star team at center.

22. DETROIT RED WINGS • **ANDERS ERIKSSON** • D
The Wings acquired a solid, physical blueliner when they drafted Eriksson. A veteran of international junior tournaments since the age of 15, he played for Sweden's Under-17 team in '91-92 and led all scorers with 10 points in six games. Scouts note that Eriksson seldom turns the puck over, blocks shots and reacts well to game situations as they develop.

23. NEW YORK ISLANDERS • **TODD BERTUZZI** • C/RW
Bertuzzi is a strong forward who can score in traffic from in front of the net. At 6'3" and 227 lbs., he utilizes his size and strength in all facets of the game. A powerful skater with good wrist and slapshots, he will shoot from many positions on the ice. In 59 games for the Guelph Storm of the OHL in '92-93, Bertuzzi tallied 27 goals, 32 assists and 164 penalty minutes.

24. CHICAGO BLACKHAWKS • **ERIC LECOMPTE** • LW
A tall, rangy, power forward who plays in all game situations, Lecompte scored 33 goals and 38 assists for the '92-93 Hull Olympiques of the QMJHL. He had 14 power-play goals, three short-handed goals and a plus/minus rating of +24. He plays well under pressure and is most effective in a fast skating game.

25. BOSTON BRUINS • **KEVYN ADAMS** • C
Adams is a tenacious and determined player who creates scoring chances through hard work and desire. A crafty stickhandler he makes smart plays and finds openings in traffic, Adams earned 32 points in 40 games for the '92-93 University of Miami Redskins of the CCHA and netted his first collegiate hat trick against Lake Superior State. He is personable and a team-oriented forward who plays a sound defensive game.

26. PITTSBURGH PENGUINS • **STEFAN BERGQVIST** • D
At 6'3" and 216 lbs., Bergqvist has the size to play defense in the NHL. He will use his body to move opponents in the corners and along the boards and skates well. He is used on power plays and in penalty killing situations. Bergqvist made his debut in the Swedish Elite League in January '93, after seeing action with the Swedish team at the Under-18 Four Nation Tournament and the '93 European Junior Championships.

1993 Expansion Draft

MIGHTY DUCKS OF ANAHEIM

Player	Pos.	Claimed From
Guy Hebert	G	St. Louis
Glenn Healy	G	NY Islanders
Ron Tugnutt	G	Edmonton
Alexei Kasatonov	D	New Jersey
Sean Hill	D	Montreal
Bill Houlder	D	Buffalo
Bobby Dollas	D	Detroit
Randy Ladouceur	D	Hartford
David Williams	D	San Jose
Dennis Vial	D	Tampa Bay
Mark Ferner	D	Ottawa
Steve King	RW	NY Rangers
Tim Sweeney	LW	Boston
Troy Loney	LW	Pittsburgh
Stu Grimson	LW	Chicago
Terry Yake	C	Hartford
Jarrod Skalde	C	New Jersey
Bob Corkum	C	Buffalo
Anatoli Semenov	C/LW	Vancouver
Joe Sacco	LW	Toronto
Lonnie Loach	LW	Los Angeles
Jim Thomson	RW	Los Angeles
Trevor Halverson	LW	Washington
Robin Bawa	RW	San Jose

1993 EXPANSION DRAFT – Phase II

Player	Pos.	Claimed by	Claimed from
Glenn Healy	G	Tampa Bay	Anaheim
Daren Puppa	G	Tampa Bay	Florida
Dennis Vial	D	Ottawa	Anaheim

FLORIDA PANTHERS

Player	Pos.	Claimed From
John Vanbiesbrouck	G	Vancouver
Mark Fitzpatrick	G	NY Islanders
Daren Puppa	G	Toronto
Milan Tichy	D	Chicago
Paul Laus	D	Pittsburgh
Joe Cirella	D	NY Rangers
Alexander Godynyuk	D	Calgary
Gord Murphy	D	Dallas
Steve Bancroft	D	Winnipeg
Stephane Richer	D	Boston
Gord Hynes	D	Philadelphia
Tom Fitzgerald	RW/C	NY Islanders
Jesse Belanger	C	Montreal
Scott Levins	C	Winnipeg
Scott Mellanby	RW	Edmonton
Brian Skrudland	C	Calgary
Mike Hough	LW	Washington
Dave Lowry	LW	St. Louis
Bill Lindsay	LW	Quebec
Andrei Lomakin	RW	Philadelphia
Randy Gilhen	C	Tampa Bay
Doug Barrault	RW	Dallas
Marc Labelle	LW	Ottawa
Pete Stauber	LW	Detroit

1993 Entry Draft

Transferred draft choice notation:

Example: Tor.-NYI represents a draft choice transferred from Toronto to New York Islanders.

Pick	Player	Claimed By	Amateur Club	Position
ROUND # 1				
1	DAIGLE, Alexandre	Ott.	Victoriaville	C
2	PRONGER, Chris	S.J.-Hfd.	Peterborough	D
3	GRATTON, Chris	T.B.	Kingston	C
4	KARIYA, Paul	Ana.	University of Maine	LW
5	NIEDERMAYER, Rob	Fla.	Medicine Hat	C
6	KOZLOV, Viktor	Hfd.-S.J.	Dynamo Moscow	LW
7	ARNOTT, Jason	Edm.	Oshawa	C
8	SUNDSTROM, Niklas	NYR	MoDo	LW
9	HARVEY, Todd	Dal.	Detroit	C
10	THIBAULT, Jocelyn	Phi.-Que.	Sherbrooke	G
11	WITT, Brendan	St. L.-Wsh.	Seattle	D
12	JONSSON, Kenny	Buf.-Tor.	Rogle Angelholm	D
13	PEDERSON, Denis	N.J.	Prince Albert	C
14	DEADMARSH, Adam	NYI-Que.	Portland	C
15	LINDGREN, Mats	Wpg.	Skelleftea	C
16	STAJDUHAR, Nick	L.A.-Edm.	London	D
17	ALLISON, Jason	Wsh.	London	C
18	MATTSSON, Jesper	Cgy.	Malmo	C
19	WILSON, Landon	Tor.	Dubuque Jr. A	RW
20	WILSON, Mike	Van.	Sudbury	D
21	KOIVU, Saku	Mtl.	TPS Turku	C
22	ERIKSSON, Anders	Det.	MoDo	D
23	BERTUZZI, Todd	Que.-NYI	Guelph	C
24	LECOMPTE, Eric	Chi.	Hull	LW
25	ADAMS, Kevyn	Bos.	Miami-Ohio	C
26	BERGQVIST, Stefan	Pit.	Leksand	D
ROUND # 2				
27	BICANEK, Radim	Ott.	Dukla Jihlava	D
28	DONOVAN, Shean	S.J.	Ottawa	RW
29	MOSS, Tyler	T.B.	Kingston	G
30	TSULYGIN, Nikolai	Ana.	Salavat Yulalev Ufa	D
31	LANGKOW, Scott	Fla.-Wpg.	Portland	G
32	PANDOLFO, Jay	Hfd.-N.J.	Boston University	LW
33	VYBORNY, David	Edm.	Sparta Praha	C
34	SOROCHAN, Lee	NYR	Lethbridge	D
35	LANGENBRUNNER, Jamie	Dal.	Cloquet	C
36	NIINIMAA, Janne	Phi.	Karpat Oulu	D
37	BETS, Maxim	St. L.	Spokane	LW
38	TSYGUROV, Denis	Buf.	Lada Togliatti	D
39	MORRISON, Brendan	N.J.	Penticton T-II Jr. A	C
40	McCABE, Bryan	NYI	Spokane	D
41	WEEKES, Kevin	Wpg.-Fla.	Owen Sound	G
42	TOPOROWSKI, Shayne	L.A.	Prince Albert	RW
43	BUDAYEV, Alexei	Wsh.-Wpg.	Kristall Elektrostal	C
44	ALLISON, Jamie	Cgy.	Detroit	D
45	KROUPA, Vlastimil	Tor.-Hfd.-S.J.	Chemopetrol Litvinov	D
46	GIRARD, Rick	Van.	Swift Current	C
47	FITZPATRICK, Rory	Mtl.	Sudbury	D
48	COLEMAN, Jonathan	Det.	Andover Academy	D
49	BUCKBERGER, Ashley	Que.	Swift Current	RW
50	MANLOW, Eric	Chi.	Kitchener	C
51	ALVEY, Matt	Bos.	Springfield Jr. B	RW
52	PITTIS, Domenic	Pit.	Lethbridge	C
ROUND # 3				
53	CHARBONNEAU, Patrick	Ott.	Victoriaville	G
54	SAVENKO, Bogdan	S.J.-Chi.	Niagara Falls	RW
55	EGELAND, Allan	T.B.	Tacoma	C
56	KARPOV, Valeri	Ana.	Traktor Chelyabinsk	LW
57	ARMSTRONG, Chris	Fla.	Moose Jaw	D
58	PELTONEN, Ville	Hfd.-S.J.	HIFK Helsinki	W
59	PADEN, Kevin	Edm.	Detroit	C
60	KERCH, Alexander	NYR-Edm.	Pardaugava Riga	LW
61	GALANOV, Maxim	Dal.-NYR	Lada Togliatti	D
62	ROCHE, Dave	Phi.-Pit.	Peterborough	LW
63	RIVERS, Jamie	St. L.	Sudbury	D
64	PHILPOTT, Ethan	Buf.	Andover Academy	RW
65	OLIWA, Krzysztof	N.J.	Welland Jr. B	LW
66	CHEBATURKIN, Vladim	NYI	Kristall Elektrostal	D
67	TJALLDEN, Mikael	Wpg.-Fla.	MoDo	D
68	MITCHELL, Jeffrey	L.A.	Detroit	C
69	BOILEAU, Patrick	Wsh.	Laval	D
70	TOMPKINS, Dan	Cgy.	Omaha Jr. A	LW
71	PROSPAL, Vaclav	Tor.-Phi.	Motor-Ceske Bud.	C
72	MALIK, Marek	Van.-Hfd.	TJ Vitkovice	D
73	BORDELEAU, Sebastien	Mtl.	Hull	C
74	HILTON, Kevin	Det.	U. of Michigan	C
75	PIERCE, Bill	Que.	Lawrence Academy	C
76	HUSKA, Ryan	Chi.	Kamloops	LW
77	HOLAN, Milos	Bos.-Phi.	TJ Vitkovice	D
78	WASHBURN, Steve	Pit.-T.B.-Fla.	Ottawa	C

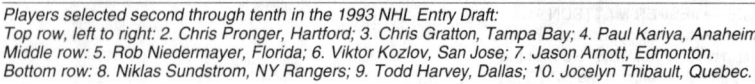

Players selected second through tenth in the 1993 NHL Entry Draft:
Top row, left to right: 2. Chris Pronger, Hartford; 3. Chris Gratton, Tampa Bay; 4. Paul Kariya, Anaheim.
Middle row: 5. Rob Niedermayer, Florida; 6. Viktor Kozlov, San Jose; 7. Jason Arnott, Edmonton.
Bottom row: 8. Niklas Sundstrom, NY Rangers; 9. Todd Harvey, Dallas; 10. Jocelyn Thibault, Quebec.

1993 NHL ENTRY DRAFT

ROUND # 4

#	Name	Team	Club	Pos
79	BATYRSHIN, Ruslan	Ott.-Wpg.	Dynamo-2 Moscow	D
80	OSADCHY, Alexander	S.J.	CSKA Moscow	D
81	KACIR, Marian	T.B.	Owen Sound	RW
82	GAGNON, Joel	Ana.	Oshawa	G
83	McCAULEY, Bill	Fla.	Detroit	C
84	ROENICK, Trevor	Hfd.	Boston Jr. Bruins	RW
85	WIESEL, Adam	Edm.-Mtl.	Springfield Jr. B	D
86	OLIMPIYEV, Sergei	NYR	Dynamo Minsk	LW
87	LANG, Chad	Dal.	Peterborough	G
88	PAQUETTE, Charles	Phi.-Bos.	Sherbrooke	D
89	MAYERS, Jamal	St. L.	Western Michigan	C
90	DAZE, Eric	Buf.-Chi.	Beauport	LW
91	DUPAUL, Cosmo	N.J.-Ott.	Victoriaville	C
92	LUHNING, Warren	NYI	Calgary Royals	RW
93	GUSMANOV, Ravil	Wpg.	Traktor Chelyabinsk	RW
94	WREN, Bob	L.A.	Detroit	LW
95	SMITH, Jason	Wsh.-Hfd.-Cgy.	Princeton University	D
96	MURRAY, Marty	Cgy.	Brandon	C
97	JAKOPIN, John	Tor.-Wsh.-		
		Wpg.-Det.	St. Michael's Jr. A	D
98	KOCHAN, Dieter	Van.	Kelowna T-II Jr. A	G
99	HOULE, Jean-Francois	Mtl.	Northwood Prep	LW
100	LAROSE, Benoit	Det.	Laval	D
101	TOCHER, Ryan	Que.	Niagara Falls	D
102	PYSZ, Patrik	Chi.	Augsburg	C
103	BATES, Shawn	Bos.	Medford	C
104	ANDERSSON-JUNKKA, J.	Pit.	Team Kiruna	D

ROUND # 5

#	Name	Team	Club	Pos
105	BEAUBIEN, Frederick	Ott.-NYR-L.A.	St-Hyacinthe	G
106	BUSCHAN, Andrei	S.J.	Sokol-Eskulap	D
107	BROWN, Ryan	T.B.	Swift Current	D
108	SHTALENKOV, Mikhail	Ana.	Milwaukee	G
109	MacDONALD, Todd	Fla.	Tacoma	G
110	GUIRESTANTE, John	Hfd.-N.J.	London	RW
111	SATAN, Miroslav	Edm.	Dukla Trencin	C
112	ROACH, Gary	NYR	Sault-Ste-Marie	D
113	LANK, Jeff	Dal.-Mtl.	Prince Albert	D
114	KRECHIN, Vladimir	Phi.	Traktor Chelyabinsk	LW
115	PRATT, Nolan	St. L.-Hfd.	Portland	D
116	SAFARIK, Richard	Buf.	AC Nitra	RW
117	SAAL, Jason	N.J.-L.A.	Detroit	G
118	SALO, Tommy	NYI	Vasteras	G
119	COURVILLE, Larry	Wpg.	Newmarket	LW
120	VLASAK, Tomas	L.A.	Slavia Praha	C
121	LAFRANCE, Darryl	Wsh.-Cgy.	Oshawa	C
122	EMMONS, John	Cgy.	Yale University	C
123	NEDVED, Zdenek	Tor.	Sudbury	RW
124	WALKER, Scott	Van.	Owen Sound	D
125	DARLING, Dion	Mtl.	Spokane	D
126	MARACLE, Norm	Det.	Saskatoon	G
127	MYRVOLD, Anders	Que.	Farjestad Karlstad	D
128	VAUHKONEN, Jonni	Chi.	Reipas Lahti	RW
129	SAPOZHNIKOV, Andrei	Bos.	Traktor Chelyabinsk	D
130	KELLEHER, Chris	Pit.	St. Sebastian's	D

ROUND # 6

#	Name	Team	Club	Pos
131	BODKIN, Rick	Ott.	Sudbury	C
132	VARIS, Petri	S.J.	Assat Pori	LW
133	HILL, Kiley	T.B.	Sault-Ste-Marie	LW
134	AALTO, Antti	Ana.	TPS Turku	C
135	NASREDDINE, Alain	Fla.	Drummondville	D
136	MROZIK, Rick	Hfd.-Dal.	Cloquet	D
137	CHECCO, Nicholas	Edm.-Que.	Bloomington-Jeffer.	C
138	TROFIMENKOFF, Dave	NYR	Lethbridge	G
139	SVARTVADET, Per	Dal.	MoDo	D
140	CROWLEY, Mike	Phi.	Bloomington-Jeffer.	D
141	KELMAN, Todd	St. L.	Vernon T-II Jr. A	D
142	POZZO, Kevin	Buf.	Moose Jaw	D
143	BRULE, Steve	N.J.	St-Jean	C
144	LEBOUTILLIER, Peter	NYI	Red Deer	RW
145	GROSEK, Michal	Wpg.	ZPS Zlin	LW
146	KARALAHTI, Jere	L.A.	HIFK Helsinki	D
147	BANHAM, Frank	Wsh.	Saskatoon	RW
148	KARLSSON, Andreas	Cgy.	Leksand	C
149	VINCENT, Paul	Tor.	Cushing Academy	C
150	CREURER, Troy	Van.	Notre Dame T-II Jr. A	D
151	TUCKER, Darcy	Mtl.	Kamloops	C
152	SPITZIG, Tim	Det.	Kitchener	RW
153	MATTE, Christian	Que.	Granby	RW
154	ODUYA, Fredrik	Chi.-S.J.	Ottawa	D
155	MASTAD, Milt	Bos.	Seattle	D
156	LALIME, Patrick	Pit.	Shawinigan	G

ROUND # 7

#	Name	Team	Club	Pos
157	POLESCHUK, Sergei	Ott.	Krylja Sovetov-2	D
158	FILATOV, Anatoli	S.J.	Torpedo Ust-Kamen.	W
159	RABY, Mathieu	T.B.	Victoriaville	D
160	PETERSON, Matt	Ana.	Osseo	D
161	DOYLE, Trevor	Fla.	Kingston	D
162	KONDRASHKIN, Sergei	Hfd.-NYR	Metallurg Cherepovets	RW
163	ZHURIK, Alexander	Edm.	Dynamo Minsk	D
164	MARCHANT, Todd	NYR	Clarkson University	C
165	STASIUK, Jeremy	Dal.	Spokane	RW
166	ISRAEL, Aaron	Phi.	Harvard University	G
167	BUZAK, Mike	St. L.	Michigan State	G
168	PETRENKO, Sergei	Buf.	Dynamo Moscow	LW
169	ZAVARUKHIN, Nikolai	N.J.	Salavat Yulayev Ufa	C
170	VAN IMPE, Darren	NYI	Red Deer	D
171	WOODS, Martin	Wpg.	Victoriaville	D
172	MARTIN, Justin	L.A.	Essex Junction	LW
173	HENDRICKSON, Daniel	Wsh.	St. Paul Jr. A	RW
174	BRUNETTE, Andrew	Cgy.-Wsh.	Owen Sound	LW
175	ANDREWS, Jeff	Tor.	North Bay	LW
176	BABARIKO, Yevgeny	Van.	Torpedo Nizhni Nov.	LW
177	RUHLY, David	Mtl.	Culver Mil. Academy	LW
178	YERESKO, Yuri	Det.	CSKA Moscow	D
179	LING, David	Que.	Kingston	RW
180	WHITE, Tom	Chi.	Westminster	C
181	GOLDEN, Ryan	Bos.	Reading	C
182	SELMSER, Sean	Pit.	Red Deer	LW

ROUND # 8

#	Name	Team	Club	Pos
183	DISHER, Jason	Ott.	Kingston	D
184	HOLT, Todd	S.J.	Swift Current	RW
185	NAUSS, Ryan	T.B.	Peterborough	LW
186	ASKEY, Tom	Ana.	Ohio State	G
187	THOMPSON, Briane	Fla.	Sault-Ste-Marie	D
188	LEGACE, Emmanuel	Hfd.	Niagara Falls	G
189	BAKULA, Martin	Edm.	Alaska-Anchorage	D
190	CAMPBELL, Eddy	NYR	Omaha Jr. A	LW
191	LURTSEMA, Rob	Dal.	Burnsville	LW
192	HEALEY, Paul	Phi.	Prince Albert	RW
193	BOGUNIECKI, Eric	St. L.	Westminster	C
194	BARRIE, Mike	Buf.	Victoria	C
195	CULLEN, Thomas	N.J.	Wexford Jr. A	D
196	HINKS, Rod	NYI	Sudbury	C
197	MURRAY, Adrian	Wpg.	Newmarket	D
198	DILLABOUGH, John-Tra	L.A.	Wexford Jr. A	C
199	POIRIER, Joel	Wsh.	Sudbury	LW
200	SYLVESTER, Derek	Cgy.	Niagara Falls	RW
201	BRUMBY, David	Tor.	Tri-City	G
202	TALLAIRE, Sean	Van.	Lake Superior	RW
203	LETANG, Alan	Mtl.	Newmarket	D
204	SKUTA, Vitezslav	Det.	TJ Vitkovice	D
205	FRANEK, Petr	Que.	Chemopetrol Litvinov	G
206	PETROV, Sergei	Chi.	Cloquet	LW
207	GILL, Hal	Bos.	Nashoba	D
208	McMORRAN, Larry	Pit.	Seattle	C

ROUND # 9

#	Name	Team	Club	Pos
209	KVALEVOG, Toby	Ott.	Bemidji	G
210	FORSBERG, Jonas	S.J.	Djurgarden	G
211	LAPORTE, Alexandre	T.B.	Victoriaville	D
212	KOZEL, Vitaly	Ana.	Khimik Novopolotsk	C
213	CABANA, Chad	Fla.	Tri-City	LW
214	GORENKO, Dmitri	Hfd.	CSKA Moscow	LW
215	NORTON, Brad	Edm.	Cushing Academy	D
216	SHEPARD, Ken	NYR	Oshawa	G
217	POTAPOV, Vladimir	Dal.-Wpg.	Kristall Elektrostal	RW
218	TRACY, Tripp	Phi.	Harvard University	G
219	GRIER, Michael	St. L.	St. Sebastian's	RW
220	MOORE, Barrie	Buf.	Sudbury	LW
221	LAMBERT, Judd	N.J.	Chilliwack T-II Jr. A	G
222	JOHANSSON, Daniel	NYI	Rogle Angelholm	D
223	STASHENKOV, Ilja	Wpg.	Krylja Sovetov	D
224	STRBAK, Martin	L.A.	ZPA Presov	D
225	GLADNEY, Jason	Wsh.	Kitchener	D
226	BRADLEY, E.J.	Cgy.-Phi.	Tabor Academy	C
227	DEMITRA, Pavol	Tor.-Ott.	Dukla Trencin	LW
228	VITOLINSH, Harijs	Van.-Wpg.	Chur	C
229	DUCHESNE, Alexandre	Mtl.	Drummondville	LW
230	SHANAHAN, Ryan	Det.	Sudbury	RW
231	AUGER, Vincent	Que.	Hawkesbury T-II Jr. A	C
232	RUSK, Mike	Chi.	Guelph	D
233	PRPIC, Joel	Bos.	Waterloo Jr. B	C
234	HARBERTS, Timothy	Pit.	Wayzata	C

ROUND # 10

#	Name	Team	Club	Pos
235	SCHUWERK, Rick	Ott.	Canterbury	D
236	SALAJKO, Jeff	S.J.	Ottawa	G
237	DUNCAN, Brett	T.B.	Seattle	D
238	FEDOTOV, Anatoli	Ana.	Moncton	D
239	DEMARCO, John	Fla.	Archbishop Williams	D
240	SWINSON, Wes	Hfd.	Kitchener	D
241	MALTSEV, Oleg	Edm.	Traktor Chelyabinsk	LW
242	KUDINOV, Andrei	NYR	Traktor Chelyabinsk	RW
243	WILLIS, Jordan	Dal.	London	G
244	STAPLES, Jeffrey	Phi.	Brandon	D
245	PROCHAZKA, Libor	St. L.	Poldi Kladno	D
246	DAVIS, Chris	Buf.	Calgary Royals	G
247	PROVENCHER, Jimmy	N.J.	St-Jean	RW
248	LAROCQUE, Stephane	NYI	Sherbrooke	RW
249	LANG, Bill	Wpg.-Dal.	North Bay	C
250	TIMONEN, Kimmo	L.A.	KalPa Kuopio	D
251	SELIGER, Marko	Wsh.	Rosenheim	G
252	TITOV, German	Cgy.	TPS Turku	C
253	FERGUSON, Kyle	Tor.	Michigan Tech U.	RW
254	ROBERTSSON, Bert	Van.	Sodertalje	D
255	LAROCHELLE, Brian	Mtl.	Phillips-Exeter	G
256	KOSECKI, James	Det.	Berkshire	D
257	PIVETZ, Mark	Que.	Saskatoon T-II Jr. A	D
258	McGHAN, Mike	Chi.	Prince Albert	LW
259	PERSSON, Joakim	Bos.	Hammarby Stockholm	G
260	TOROPCHENKO, Leonid	Pit.	Springfield	C

ROUND # 11

#	Name	Team	Club	Pos
261	KOMAROV, Pavel	Ott.-NYR	Torpedo Nizhny Nov.	D
262	MATTHEWS, Jamie	S.J.	Sudbury	C
263	SZOKE, Mark	T.B.	Lethbridge	LW
264	PENNEY, David	Ana.	Worcester Academy	LW
265	MONTREUIL, Eric	Fla.	Chicoutimi	C
266	CHIBIREV, Igor	Hfd.	Fort Wayne	C
267	BYAKIN, Ilja	Edm.	Landshut	D
268	SMELNITSKY, Maxim	NYR	Traktor Chelyabinsk	RW
269	PETERSON, Cory	Dal.	Bloomington-Jeffer.	D
270	HEMMENWAY, Kenneth	Phi.	Alaska All Stars	D
271	VASILEVSKY, Alexander	St. L.	Victoria	LW
272	NICHOL, Scott	Buf.	Portland	C
273	LEGG, Michael	N.J.	London Jr. B	RW
274	CHARLAND, Carl	NYI	Hull	LW
275	OLSSON, Christer	St. L.	Brynas Gavle	D
276	HOWALD, Patrick	L.A.	Lugano	LW
277	BOUSQUET, Dany	Wsh.	Penticton T-II Jr. A	C
278	MURPHY, Burke	Cgy.	St. Lawrence U.	LW
279	LAPIN, Mikhail	Tor.	Western Michigan	D
280	TKACHENKO, Sergei	Van.	Hamilton	G
281	GUZIOR, Russell	Mtl.	Culver Mil. Academy	C
282	HUNT, Gordon	Det.	Detroit Comp. Jr. A	C
283	HILLIMAN, John	Que.	St. Paul Jr. A	C
284	NOBLE, Tom	Chi.	Catholic Memorial	G
285	HEWSON, Russell	Bos.-Chi.-Wpg.	Swift Current	LW
286	JONSSON, Hans	Pit.	MoDo	D

Draft Choices, 1992-69

1992

FIRST ROUND

Selection	Claimed By	Amateur Club
1. HAMRLIK, Roman	T.B.	ZPS Zlin (Czech.)
2. YASHIN, Alexei	Ott.	Dynamo Moscow (CIS)
3. RATHJE, Mike	S.J.	Medicine Hat
4. WARRINER, Todd	Que.	Windsor
5. KASPARAITIS, Darius	NYI	Dynamo Moscow (CIS)
6. STILLMAN, Cory	Cgy.	Windsor
7. SITTLER, Ryan	Phi.	Nichols
8. CONVERY, Brandon	Tor.	Sudbury
9. PETROVICKY, Robert	Hfd.	Dukla Trencin (Czech.)
10. NAZAROV, Andrei	S.J.	Dynamo Moscow (CIS)
11. COOPER, David	Buf.	Medicine Hat
12. KRIVOKRASOV, Sergei	Chi.	CSKA Moscow (CIS)
13. HULBIG, Joe	Edm.	St. Sebastian's
14. GONCHAR, Sergei	Wsh.	Chelybinsk (CIS)
15. BOWEN, Jason	Phi.	Tri-City
16. KVARTALNOV, Dmitri	Bos.	San Diego
17. BAUTIN, Sergei	Wpg.	Dynamo Moscow (CIS)
18. SMITH, Jason	N.J.	Regina
19. STRAKA, Martin	Pit.	Skoda Plzen (Czech.)
20. WILKIE, David	Mtl.	Kamloops
21. POLASEK, Libor	Van.	TJ Vitkovice (Czech.)
22. BOWEN, Curtis	Det.	Ottawa
23. MARSHALL, Grant	Tor.	Ottawa
24. FERRARO, Peter	NYR	Waterloo Jr. A

SECOND ROUND

Selection	Claimed By	Amateur Club
25. PENNEY, Chad	Ott.	North Bay
26. BANNISTER, Drew	T.B.	Sault-Ste-Marie
27. MIRANOV, Boris	Wpg.	CSKA Moscow (CIS)
28. BROUSSEAU, Paul	Que.	Hull
29. GRONMAN, Toumas	Que.	Tacoma
30. O'SULLIVAN, Chris	Cgy.	Catholic Memorial
31. METLYUK, Denis	Phi.	Lada Togliatti (CIS)
32. CAREY, Jim	Wsh.	Catholic Memorial
33. BURE, Valeri	Mtl.	Spokane
34. VARVIO, Jarkko	Min.	HPK (Finland)
35. CIERNY, Jozef	Buf.	ZTK Zvolen (Czech.)
36. SHANTZ, Jeff	Chi.	Regina
37. REICHEL, Martin	Edm.	Freiburg (Germany)
38. KOROLEV, Igor	St. L.	Dynamo Moscow (CIS)
39. HOCKING, Justin	L.A.	Spokane
40. PECA, Mike	Van.	Ottawa
41. KLIMOVICH, Sergei	Chi.	Dynamo Moscow (CIS)
42. BRYLIN, Sergei	N.J.	CSKA Moscow (CIS)
43. HUSSEY, Marc	Pit.	Moose Jaw
44. CORPSE, Keli	Mtl.	Kingston
45. FOUNTAIN, Michael	Van.	Oshawa
46. McCARTY, Darren	Det.	Belleville
47. NIKOLISHIN, Andrei	Hfd.	Dynamo Moscow (CIS)
48. NORSTROM, Mattias	NYR	AIK (Sweden)

1991

FIRST ROUND

Selection	Claimed By	Amateur Club
1. LINDROS, Eric	Que.	Oshawa
2. FALLOON, Pat	S.J.	Spokane
3. NIEDERMAYER, Scott	N.J.	Kamloops
4. LACHANCE, Scott	NYI	Boston University
5. WARD, Aaron	Wpg.	U. of Michigan
6. FORSBERG, Peter	Phi.	MoDo (Sweden)
7. STOJANOV, Alex	Van.	Hamilton
8. MATVICHUK, Richard	Min.	Saskatoon
9. POULIN, Patrick	Hfd.	St.-Hyacinthe
10. LAPOINTE, Martin	Det.	Laval
11. ROLSTON, Brian	N.J.	Detroit Comp. Jr. A
12. WRIGHT, Tyler	Edm.	Swift Current
13. BOUCHER, Phillipe	Buf.	Granby
14. PEAKE, Pat	Wsh.	Detroit
15. KOVALEV, Alexei	NYR	D'amo Moscow (USSR)
16. NASLUND, Markus	Pit.	MoDo
17. BILODEAU, Brent	Mtl.	Seattle
18. MURRAY, Glen	Bos.	Sudbury
19. SUNDBLAD, Niklas	Cgy.	AIK (Sweden)
20. RUCINSKY, Martin	Edm.	CHZ Litvinov (Czech.)
21. HALVERSON, Trevor	Wsh.	North Bay
22. McAMMOND, Dean	Chi.	Prince Albert

SECOND ROUND

Selection	Claimed By	Amateur Club
23. WHITNEY, Ray	S.J.	Spokane
24. CORBET, Rene	Que.	Drummondville
25. LAVIGNE, Eric	Wsh.	Hull
26. PALFFY, Zigmund	NYI	AC Nitra (Czech.)
27. STAIOS, Steve	St. L.	Niagara Falls
28. CAMPBELL, Jim	Mtl.	Northwood Prep
29. CULLIMORE, Jassen	Van.	Peterborough
30. OZOLINSH, Sandis	S.J.	Dynamo Riga (USSR)
31. HAMRLIK, Martin	Hfd.	TJ Zin (Czech.)
32. PUSHOR, Jamie	Det.	Lethbridge
33. HEXTALL, Donevan	N.J.	Prince Albert
34. VERNER, Andrew	Edm.	Peterborough
35. DAWE, Jason	Buf.	Peterborough
36. NELSON, Jeff	Wsh.	Prince Albert
37. WERENKA, Darcy	NYR	Lethbridge
38. FITZGERALD, Rusty	Pit.	Duluth East HS
39. POMICHTER, Michael	Chi.	Springfield Jr. B
40. STUMPEL, Jozef	Bos.	AC Nitra (Czech.)
41. GROLEAU, Francois	Cgy.	Shawinigan
42. LEVEQUE, Guy	L.A.	Cornwall
43. DARBY, Craig	Mtl.	Albany Academy
44. MATTHEWS, Jamie	Chi.	Sudbury

1990

FIRST ROUND

Selection	Claimed By	Amateur Club
1. NOLAN, Owen	Que.	Cornwall
2. NEDVED, Petr	Van.	Seattle
3. PRIMEAU, Keith	Det.	Niagara Falls
4. RICCI, Mike	Phi.	Peterborough
5. JAGR, Jaromir	Pit.	Poldi Kladno (Czech.)
6. SCISSONS, Scott	NYI	Saskatoon
7. SYDOR, Darryl	L.A.	Kamloops
8. HATCHER, Derian	Min.	North Bay
9. SLANEY, John	Wsh.	Cornwall
10. BEREHOWSKY, Drake	Tor.	Kingston
11. KIDD, Trevor	Cgy.	Brandon
12. STEVENSON, Turner	Mtl.	Seattle
13. STEWART, Michael	NYR	Michigan State
14. MAY, Brad	Buf.	Niagara Falls
15. GREIG, Mark	Hfd.	Lethbridge
16. DYKHUIS, Karl	Chi.	Hull
17. ALLISON, Scott	Edm.	Prince Albert
18. ANTOSKI, Shawn	Van.	North Bay
19. TKACHUK, Keith	Wpg.	Malden Catholic
20. BRODEUR, Martin	N.J.	St. Hyacinthe
21. SMOLINSKI, Bryan	Bos.	Michigan State

SECOND ROUND

Selection	Claimed By	Amateur Club
22. HUGHES, Ryan	Que.	Cornell
23. SLEGR, Jiri	Van.	CHZ Litvinov (Czech.)
24. HARLOCK, David	N.J.	U. of Michigan
25. SIMON, Chris	Phi.	Ottawa
26. PERREAULT, Nicolas P.	Cgy.	Hawkesbury Jr. A
27. TAYLOR, Chris	NYI	London
28. SEMCHUK, Brandy	L.A.	Canadian National
29. GOTZIAMAN, Chris	N.J.	Roseau
30. PASMA, Rod	Wsh.	Cornwall
31. POTVIN, Felix	Tor.	Chicoutimi
32. VIITAKOSKI, Vesa	Cgy.	SaiPa (Finland)
33. JOHNSON, Craig	St. L.	Hill-Murray HS
34. WEIGHT, Doug	NYR	Lake Superior
35. MULLER, Mike	Wpg.	Wayzata
36. SANDERSON, Geoff	Hfd.	Swift Current
37. DROPPA, Ivan	Chi.	Partizan (Czech.)
38. LEGAULT, Alexandre	Edm.	Boston University
39. KUWABARA, Ryan	Mtl.	Ottawa
40. RENBERG, Mikael	Phi.	Pitea (Sweden)
41. BELZILE, Etienne	Cgy.	Cornell
42. SANDWITH, Terran	Phi.	Tri-Cities

1989

FIRST ROUND

Selection	Claimed By	Amateur Club
1. SUNDIN, Mats	Que.	Nacka (Sweden)
2. CHYZOWSKI, Dave	NYI	Kamloops
3. THORNTON, Scott	Tor.	Belleville
4. BARNES, Stu	Wpg.	Tri-Cities
5. GUERIN, Bill	N.J.	Springfield Jr. B
6. BENNETT, Adam	Chi.	Sudbury
7. ZMOLEK, Doug	Min.	John Marshall
8. HERTER, Jason	Van.	U. of North Dakota
9. MARSHALL, Jason	St. L.	Vernon Jr. A
10. HOLIK, Robert	Hfd.	Dukla Jihlava (Czech.)
11. SILLINGER, Mike	Det.	Regina
12. PEARSON, Rob	Tor.	Belleville
13. VALLIS, Lindsay	Mtl.	Seattle
14. HALLER, Kevin	Buf.	Regina
15. SOULES, Jason	Edm.	Niagara Falls
16. HEWARD, Jamie	Pit.	Regina
17. STEVENSON, Shayne	Bos.	Kitchener
18. MILLER, Jason	N.J.	Medicine Hat
19. KOLZIG, Olaf	Wsh.	Tri-Cities
20. RICE, Steven	NYR	Kitchener
21. BANCROFT, Steve	Tor.	Belleville

SECOND ROUND

Selection	Claimed By	Amateur Club
22. FOOTE, Adam	Que.	Sault Ste. Marie
23. GREEN, Travis	NYI	Spokane
24. MANDERVILLE, Kent	Cgy.	Notre Dame Jr. A
25. RATUSHNY, Dan	Wpg.	Cornell
26. SKALDE, Jarrod	N.J.	Oshawa
27. SPEER, Michael	Chi.	Guelph
28. CRAIG, Mike	Min.	Oshawa
29. WOODWARD, Robert	Van.	Deerfield
30. BRISEBOIS, Patrice	Mtl.	Laval
31. CORRIVEAU, Rick	St. L.	London
32. BOUGHNER, Bob	Det.	Sault-Ste. Marie
33. JOHNSON, Greg	Phi.	Thunder Bay Jr. A
34. JUHLIN, Patrik	Phi.	Vasteras (Sweden)
35. DAFOE, Byron	Wsh.	Portland
36. BORGO, Richard	Edm.	Kitchener
37. LAUS, Paul	Pit.	Niagara Falls
38. PARSON, Mike	Bos.	Guelph
39. THOMPSON, Brent	L.A.	Medicine Hat
40. PROSOFSKY, Jason	NYR	Medicine Hat
41. LAROUCHE, Steve	Mtl.	Trois-Rivieres
42. DRURY, Ted	Cgy.	Fairfield Prep

1988

FIRST ROUND

Selection	Claimed By	Amateur Club
1. MODANO, Mike	Min.	Prince Albert
2. LINDEN, Trevor	Van.	Medicine Hat
3. LESCHYSHYN, Curtis	Que.	Saskatoon
4. SHANNON, Darrin	Pit.	Windsor
5. DORE, Daniel	Que.	Drummondville
6. PEARSON, Scott	Tor.	Kingston
7. GELINAS, Martin	L.A.	Hull
8. ROENICK, Jeremy	Chi.	Thayer Academy
9. BRIND'AMOUR, Rod	St.L.	Notre Dame Jr. A
10. SELANNE, Teemu	Wpg.	Jokerit (Finland)
11. GOVEDARIS, Chris	Hfd.	Toronto
12. FOSTER, Corey	N.J.	Peterborough
13. SAVAGE, Joel	Buf.	Victoria
14. BOIVIN, Claude	Phi.	Drummondville
15. SAVAGE, Reginald	Wsh.	Victoriaville
16. CHEVELDAYOFF, Kevin	NYI	Brandon
17. KOCUR, Kory	Det.	Saskatoon
18. CIMETTA, Robert	Bos.	Toronto
19. LEROUX, Francois	Edm.	St. Jean
20. CHARRON, Eric	Mtl.	Trois-Rivieres
21. MUZZATTI, Jason	Cgy.	Michigan State

SECOND ROUND

Selection	Claimed By	Amateur Club
22. MALLETTE, Troy	NYR	Sault Ste. Marie
23. CHRISTIAN, Jeff	N.J.	London
24. FISET, Stephane	Que.	Victoriaville
25. MAJOR, Mark	Pit.	North Bay
26. DUVAL, Murray	NYR	Spokane
27. DOMI, Tie	Tor.	Peterborough
28. HOLDEN, Paul	L.A.	London
29. DOUCET, Wayne	NYI	Hamilton
30. PLAVSIC, Adrien	St.L.	U. of New Hampshire
31. ROMANIUK, Russell	Wpg.	St. Boniface Jr. A
32. RICHTER, Barry	Hfd.	Culver Academy
33. ROHLIN, Leif	Van.	Vasteras (Sweden)
34. ST. AMOUR, Martin	Mtl.	Verdun
35. MURRAY, Pat	Phi.	Michigan State
36. TAYLOR, Tim	Wsh.	London
37. LEBRUN, Sean	NYI	New Westminster
38. ANGLEHART, Serge	Det.	Drummondville
39. KOIVUNEN, Petro	Edm.	Espoo (Finland)
40. GAETZ, Link	Min.	Spokane
41. BARTLEY, Wade	Wsh.	Dauphin Jr. A
42. HARKINS, Todd	Cgy.	Miami-Ohio

1987

FIRST ROUND

Selection	Claimed By	Amateur Club
1. TURGEON, Pierre	Buf.	Granby
2. SHANAHAN, Brendan	N.J.	London
3. WESLEY, Glen	Bos.	Portland
4. McBEAN, Wayne	L.A.	Medicine Hat
5. JOSEPH, Chris	Pit.	Seattle
6. ARCHIBALD, David	Min.	Portland
7. RICHARDSON, Luke	Tor.	Peterborough
8. WAITE, Jimmy	Chi.	Chicoutimi
9. FOGARTY, Bryan	Que.	Kingston
10. MORE, Jayson	NYR	New Westminster
11. RACINE, Yves	Det.	Longueuil
12. OSBORNE, Keith	St.L.	North Bay
13. CHYNOWETH, Dean	NYI	Medicine Hat
14. QUINTAL, Stephane	Bos.	Granby
15. SAKIC, Joe	Que.	Swift Current
16. MARCHMENT, Bryan	Wpg.	Belleville
17. CASSELS, Andrew	Mtl.	Ottawa
18. HULL, Jody	Hfd.	Peterborough
19. DEASLEY, Bryan	Cgy.	U. of Michigan
20. RUMBLE, Darren	Phi.	Kitchener
21. SOBERLAK, Peter	Edm.	Swift Current

SECOND ROUND

Selection	Claimed By	Amateur Club
22. MILLER, Brad	Buf.	Regina
23. PERSSON, Rickard	N.J.	Ostersund (Sweden)
24. MURPHY, Rob	Van.	Laval
25. MATTEAU, Stephane	Cgy.	Hull
26. TABARACCI, Richard	Pit.	Cornwall
27. FITZPATRICK, Mark	L.A.	Medicine Hat
28. MAROIS, Daniel	Tor.	Chicoutimi
29. McGILL, Ryan	Chi.	Swift Current
30. HARDING, Jeff	Phi.	St. Michael's Jr. B
31. LACROIX, Daniel	NYR	Granby
32. KRUPPKE, Gordon	Det.	Prince Albert
33. LECLAIR, John	Mtl.	Bellows Academy
34. HACKETT, Jeff	NYI	Oshawa
35. McCRADY, Scott	Min.	Medicine Hat
36. BALLANTYNE, Jeff	Wsh.	Ottawa
37. ERICKSSON, Patrik	Wpg.	Brynas (Sweden)
38. DESJARDINS, Eric	Mtl.	Granby
39. BURT, Adam	Hfd.	North Bay
40. GRANT, Kevin	Cgy.	Kitchener
41. WILKIE, Bob	Det.	Swift Current
42. WERENKA, Brad	Edm.	N. Michigan

1986

FIRST ROUND

Selection	Claimed By	Amateur Club
1. MURPHY, Joe	Det.	Michigan State
2. CARSON, Jimmy	L.A.	Verdun
3. BRADY, Neil	N.J.	Medicine Hat
4. ZALAPSKI, Zarley	Pit.	Canadian National
5. ANDERSON, Shawn	Buf.	Canadian National
6. DAMPHOUSSE, Vincent	Tor.	Laval
7. WOODLEY, Dan	Van.	Portland
8. ELYNUIK, Pat	Wpg.	Prince Albert
9. LEETCH, Brian	NYR	Avon Old Farms HS
10. LEMIEUX, Jocelyn	St.L.	Laval
11. YOUNG, Scott	Hfd.	Boston University
12. BABE, Warren	Min.	Lethbridge
13. JANNEY, Craig	Bos.	Boston College
14. SANIPASS, Everett	Chi.	Verdun
15. PEDERSON, Mark	Mtl.	Medicine Hat
16. PELAWA, George	Cgy.	Bemidji HS
17. FITZGERALD, Tom	NYI	Austin Prep
18. McRAE, Ken	Que.	Sudbury
19. GREENLAW, Jeff	Wsh.	Canadian National
20. HUFFMAN, Kerry	Phi.	Guelph
21. ISSEL, Kim	Edm.	Prince Albert

SECOND ROUND

Selection	Claimed By	Amateur Club
22. GRAVES, Adam	Det.	Windsor
23. SEPPO, Jukka	Phi.	Sport (Finland)
24. COPELAND, Todd	N.J.	Belmont Hill HS
25. CAPUANO, Dave	Pit.	Mt. St. Charles HS
26. BROWN, Greg	Buf.	St. Mark's
27. BRUNET, Benoit	Mtl.	Hull
28. HAWLEY, Kent	Phi.	Ottawa
29. NUMMINEN, Teppo	Wpg.	Tappara (Finland)
30. WILKINSON, Neil	Min.	Selkirk
31. POSMA, Mike	St.L.	Buffalo Jr. A
32. LaFORGE, Marc	Hfd.	Kingston
33. KOLSTAD, Dean	Min.	Prince Albert
34. TIRKKONEN, Pekka	Bos.	SaPKo (Finland)
35. KURZAWSKI, Mark	Chi.	Windsor
36. SHANNON, Darryl	Tor.	Windsor
37. GLYNN, Brian	Cgy.	Saskatoon
38. VASKE, Dennis	NYI	Armstrong HS
39. ROUTHIER, Jean-Marc	Que.	Hull
40. SEFTEL, Steve	Wsh.	Kingston
41. GUERARD, Stephane	Que.	Shawinigan
42. NICHOLS, Jamie	Edm.	Portland

1985

FIRST ROUND

Selection	Claimed By	Amateur Club
1. CLARK, Wendel	Tor.	Saskatoon
2. SIMPSON, Craig	Pit.	Michigan State
3. WOLANIN, Craig	N.J.	Kitchener
4. SANDLAK, Jim	Van.	London
5. MURZYN, Dana	Hfd.	Calgary
6. DALGARNO, Brad	NYI	Hamilton
7. DAHLEN, Ulf	NYR	Ostersund (Sweden)
8. FEDYK, Brent	Det.	Regina
9. DUNCANSON, Craig	L.A.	Sudbury
10. GRATTON, Dan	L.A.	Oshawa
11. MANSON, David	Chi.	Prince Albert
12. CHARBONNEAU, Jose	Mtl.	Drummondville
13. KING, Derek	NYI	Sault Ste. Marie
14. JOHANSSON, Calle	Buf.	V. Frolunda (Sweden)
15. LATTA, Dave	Que.	Kitchener
16. CHORSKE, Tom	Mtl.	Minneapolis SW HS
17. BIOTTI, Chris	Cgy.	Belmont Hill HS
18. STEWART, Ryan	Wpg.	Kamloops
19. CORRIVEAU, Yvon	Wsh.	Toronto
20. METCALFE, Scott	Edm.	Kingston
21. SEABROOKE, Glen	Phi.	Peterborough

SECOND ROUND

Selection	Claimed By	Amateur Club
22. SPANGLER, Ken	Tor.	Calgary
23. GIFFIN, Lee	Pit.	Oshawa
24. BURKE, Sean	N.J.	Toronto
25. GAMBLE, Troy	Van.	Medicine Hat
26. WHITMORE, Kay	Hfd.	Peterborough
27. NIEUWENDYK, Joe	Cgy.	Cornell
28. RICHTER, Mike	NYR	Northwood Prep.
29. SHARPLES, Jeff	Det.	Kelowna
30. EDLUND, Par	L.A.	Bjorkloven (Sweden)
31. COTE, Alain	Bos.	Quebec
32. WEINRICH, Eric	N.J.	North Yarmouth
33. RICHARD, Todd	Mtl.	Armstrong HS
34. LAUER, Brad	NYI	Regina
35. HOGUE, Benoit	Buf.	St-Jean
36. LAFRENIERE, Jason	Que.	Hamilton
37. RAGLAN, Herb	St.L.	Kingston
38. WENAAS, Jeff	Cgy.	Medicine Hat
39. OHMAN, Roger	Wpg.	Leksand (Sweden)
40. DRUCE, John	Wsh.	Peterborough
41. CARNELLEY, Todd	Edm.	Kamloops
42. RENDALL, Bruce	Phi.	Chatham

1984

FIRST ROUND

Selection	Claimed By	Amateur Club
1. LEMIEUX, Mario	Pit.	Laval
2. MULLER, Kirk	N.J.	Cdn-Nat.-Guelph
3. OLCZYK, Ed	Chi.	U.S. National
4. IAFRATE, Al	Tor.	U.S. National-Belleville
5. SVOBODA, Petr	Mtl.	CHZ (Czech.)
6. REDMOND, Craig	L.A.	Canadian National
7. BURR, Shawn	Det.	Kitchener
8. CORSON, Shayne	Mtl.	Brantford
9. BODGER, Doug	Pit.	Kamloops Jr. A
10. DAIGNEAULT, J.J.	Van.	Cdn. Nat.-Longueuil
11. COTE, Sylvain	Hfd.	Quebec
12. ROBERTS, Gary	Cgy.	Ottawa
13. QUINN, David	Min.	Kent HS
14. CARKNER, Terry	NYR	Peterborough
15. STIENBURG, Trevor	Que.	Guelph
16. BELANGER, Roger	Pit.	Kingston
17. HATCHER, Kevin	Wsh.	North Bay
18. ANDERSSON, Mikael	Buf.	V. Frolunda (Sweden)
19. PASIN, Dave	Bos.	Prince Albert
20. MacPHERSON, Duncan	NYI	Saskatoon
21. ODELEIN, Selmar	Edm.	Regina

SECOND ROUND

Selection	Claimed By	Amateur Club
22. SMYTH, Greg	Phi.	London
23. BILLINGTON, Craig	N.J.	Belleville
24. WILKS, Brian	L.A.	Kitchener
25. GILL, Todd	Tor.	Windsor
26. BENNING, Brian	St.L.	Portland
27. MELLANBY, Scott	Phi.	Henry Carr Jr. B
28. HOUDA, Doug	Det.	Calgary
29. RICHER, Stephane	Mtl.	Granby
30. DOURIS, Peter	Wpg.	U. of New Hampshire
31. ROHLICEK, Jeff	Van.	Portland
32. HRKAC, Anthony	St.L.	Orillia Jr. A
33. SABOURIN, Ken	Cgy.	Sault Ste. Marie
34. LEACH, Stephen	Wsh.	Matignon HS
35. HELMINEN, Raimo	NYR	Ilves (Finland)
36. BROWN, Jeff	Que.	Sudbury
37. CHYCHRUN, Jeff	Phi.	Kingston
38. RANHEIM, Paul	Cgy.	Edina Hornets HS
39. TRAPP, Doug	Buf.	Regina
40. PODLOSKI, Ray	Bos.	Portland
41. MELANSON, Bruce	NYI	Oshawa
42. REAUGH, Daryl	Edm.	Kamloops Jr. A

1983

FIRST ROUND

Selection	Claimed By	Amateur Club
1. LAWTON, Brian	Min.	Mount St. Charles HS
2. TURGEON, Sylvain	Hfd.	Hull
3. LaFONTAINE, Pat	NYI	Verdun
4. YZERMAN, Steve	Det.	Peterborough
5. BARRASSO, Tom	Buf.	Acton-Boxboro HS
6. MacLEAN, John	N.J.	Oshawa
7. COURTNALL, Russ	Tor.	Victoria
8. McBAIN, Andrew	Wpg.	North Bay
9. NEELY, Cam	Van.	Portland
10. LACOMBE, Normand	Buf.	U. of New Hampshire
11. CREIGHTON, Adam	Buf.	Ottawa
12. GAGNER, Dave	NYR	Brantford
13. QUINN, Dan	Cgy.	Belleville
14. DOLLAS, Bobby	Wpg.	Laval
15. ERREY, Bob	Pit.	Peterborough
16. DIDUCK, Gerald	NYI	Lethbridge
17. TURCOTTE, Alfie	Mtl.	Portland
18. CASSIDY, Bruce	Chi.	Ottawa
19. BEUKEBOOM, Jeff	Edm.	Sault Ste. Marie
20. JENSEN, David	Hfd.	Lawrence
21. MARKWART, Nevin	Bos.	Regina

SECOND ROUND

Selection	Claimed By	Amateur Club
22. CHARLESWORTH, Todd	Pit.	Oshawa
23. SIREN, Ville	Hfd.	Ilves (Finland)
24. EVANS, Shawn	N.J.	Peterborough
25. LAMBERT, Lane	Det.	Saskatoon
26. LEMIEUX, Claude	Mtl.	Trois-Rivières
27. MOMESSO, Sergio	Mtl.	Shawinigan
28. JACKSON, Jeff	Tor.	Brantford
29. BERRY, Brad	Wpg.	St. Albert
30. BRUCE, Dave	Van.	Kitchener
31. TUCKER, John	Buf.	Kitchener
32. HEROUX, Yves	Que.	Chicoutimi
33. HEATH, Randy	NYR	Portland
34. HAJDU, Richard	Buf.	Kamloops Jr. A
35. FRANCIS, Todd	Mtl.	Brantford
36. PARKS, Malcolm	Min.	St. Albert
37. McKECHNEY, Garnet	NYI	Kitchener
38. MUSIL, Frantisek	Min.	Tesla (Czech.)
39. PRESLEY, Wayne	Chi.	Kitchener
40. GOLDEN, Mike	Edm.	Reading HS
41. ZEZEL, Peter	Phi.	Toronto
42. JOHNSTON, Greg	Bos.	Toronto

1982

FIRST ROUND

Selection	Claimed By	Amateur Club
1. KLUZAK, Gord	Bos.	Nanaimo
2. BELLOWS, Brian	Min.	Kitchener
3. NYLUND, Gary	Tor.	Portland
4. SUTTER, Ron	Phi.	Lethbridge
5. STEVENS, Scott	Wsh.	Kitchener
6. HOUSLEY, Phil	Buf.	S. St. Paul HS
7. YAREMCHUK, Ken	Chi.	Portland
8. TROTTIER, Rocky	N.J.	Nanaimo
9. CYR, Paul	Buf.	Victoria
10. SUTTER, Rich	Pit.	Lethbridge
11. PETIT, Michel	Van.	Sherbrooke
12. KYTE, Jim	Wpg.	Cornwall
13. SHAW, David	Que.	Kitchener
14. LAWLESS, Paul	Hfd.	Windsor
15. KONTOS, Chris	NYR	Toronto
16. ANDREYCHUK, Dave	Buf.	Oshawa
17. CRAVEN, Murray	Det.	Medicine Hat
18. DANEYKO, Ken	N.J.	Seattle
19. HEROUX, Alain	Mtl.	Chicoutimi
20. PLAYFAIR, Jim	Edm.	Portland
21. FLATLEY, Pat	NYI	University of Wisconsin

SECOND ROUND

Selection	Claimed By	Amateur Club
22. CURRAN, Brian	Bos.	Portland
23. COURTEAU, Yves	Det.	Laval
24. LEEMAN, Gary	Tor.	Regina
25. IHNACAK, Peter	Tor.	Sparta (Czech.)
26. ANDERSON, Mike	Buf.	N. St. Paul HS
27. HEIDT, Mike	L.A.	Calgary
28. BADEAU, Rene	Chi.	Quebec
29. REIERSON, Dave	Cgy.	Prince Albert
30. JOHANSSON, Jens	Buf.	Pitea (Sweden)
31. GAUVREAU, Jocelyn	Mtl.	Granby
32. CARLSON, Kent	Mtl.	St. Lawrence University
33. MALEY, David	Mtl.	Edina HS
34. GILLIS, Paul	Que.	Niagara Falls
35. PATERSON, Mark	Hfd.	Ottawa
36. SANDSTROM, Tomas	NYR	Farjestads (Sweden)
37. KROMM, Richard	Cgy.	Portland
38. HRYNEWICH, Tim	Pit.	Sudbury
39. BYERS, Lyndon	Bos.	Regina
40. SANDELIN, Scott	Mtl.	Hibbing HS
41. GRAVES, Steve	Edm.	Sault Ste. Marie
42. SMITH, Vern	NYI	Lethbridge

1981

FIRST ROUND

Selection	Claimed By	Amateur Club
1. HAWERCHUK, Dale	Wpg.	Cornwall
2. SMITH, Doug	L.A.	Ottawa
3. CARPENTER, Bobby	Wsh.	St. John's HS
4. FRANCIS, Ron	Hfd.	Sault Ste. Marie
5. CIRELLA, Joe	Col.	Oshawa
6. BENNING, Jim	Tor.	Portland
7. HUNTER, Mark	Mtl.	Brantford
8. FUHR, Grant	Edm.	Victoria
9. PATRICK, James	NYR	Prince Albert
10. BUTCHER, Garth	Van.	Regina
11. MOLLER, Randy	Que.	Lethbridge
12. TANTI, Tony	Chi.	Oshawa
13. MEIGHAN, Ron	Min.	Niagara Falls
14. LEVEILLE, Normand	Bos.	Chicoutimi
15. MacINNIS, Allan	Cgy.	Kitchener
16. SMITH, Steve	Phi.	Sault Ste. Marie
17. DUDACEK, Jiri	Buf.	Poldi Kladno (Czech.)
18. DELORME, Gilbert	Mtl.	Chicoutimi
19. INGMAN, Jan	Mtl.	Farjestad (Sweden)
20. RUFF, Marty	St.L.	Lethbridge
21. BOUTILIER, Paul	NYI	Sherbrooke

SECOND ROUND

Selection	Claimed By	Amateur Club
22. ARNIEL, Scott	Wpg.	Cornwall
23. LOISELLE, Claude	Det.	Windsor
24. YAREMCHUK, Gary	Tor.	Portland
25. GRIFFIN, Kevin	Chi.	Portland
26. CHERNOMAZ, Rich	Col.	Victoria
27. DONNELLY, Dave	Min.	St. Albert
28. GATZOS, Steve	Pit.	Sault Ste. Marie
29. STRUEBY, Todd	Edm.	Regina
30. ERIXON, Jan	NYR	Skelleftea (Sweden)
31. SANDS, Mike	Min.	Sudbury
32. ERIKSSON, Lars	Mtl.	Brynas (Sweden)
33. HIRSCH, Tom	Min.	Patrick Henry HS
34. PREUSS, Dave	Min.	St. Thomas Academy
35. DUFOUR, Luc	Bos.	Chicoutimi
36. NORDIN, Hakan	St.L.	Farjestad (Sweden)
37. COSTELLO, Rich	Phi.	Natick HS
38. VIRTA, Hannu	Buf.	TPS (Finland)
39. KENNEDY, Dean	L.A.	Brandon
40. CHELIOS, Chris	Mtl.	Moose Jaw
41. WAHLSTEN, Jali	Min.	TPS (Finland)
42. DINEEN, Gord	NYI	Sault Ste. Marie

1980

FIRST ROUND

Selection	Claimed By	Amateur Club
1. WICKENHEISER, Doug	Mtl.	Regina
2. BABYCH, Dave	Wpg.	Portland
3. SAVARD, Denis	Chi.	Montreal
4. MURPHY, Larry	L.A.	Peterborough
5. VEITCH, Darren	Wsh.	Regina
6. COFFEY, Paul	Edm.	Kitchener
7. LANZ, Rick	Van.	Oshawa
8. ARTHUR, Fred	Hfd.	Cornwall
9. BULLARD, Mike	Pit.	Brantford
10. FOX, Jimmy	L.A.	Ottawa
11. BLAISDELL, Mike	Det.	Regina
12. WILSON, Rik	St.L.	Kingston
13. CYR, Denis	Cgy.	Montreal
14. MALONE, Jim	NYR	Toronto
15. DUPONT, Jerome	Chi.	Toronto
16. PALMER, Brad	Min.	Victoria
17. SUTTER, Brent	NYI	Red Deer
18. PEDERSON, Barry	Bos.	Victoria
19. GAGNE, Paul	Col.	Windsor
20. PATRICK, Steve	Buf.	Brandon
21. STOTHERS, Mike	Phi.	Kingston

SECOND ROUND

Selection	Claimed By	Amateur Club
22. WARD, Joe	Col.	Seattle
23. MANTHA, Moe	Wpg.	Toronto
24. ROCHEFORT, Normand	Que.	Quebec
25. MUNI, Craig	Tor.	Kingston
26. McGILL, Bob	Tor.	Victoria
27. NATTRESS, Ric	Mtl.	Brantford
28. LUDZIK, Steve	Chi.	Niagara Falls
29. GALARNEAU, Michel	Hfd.	Hull
30. SOLHEIM, Ken	Chi.	Medicine Hat
31. CURTALE, Tony	Cgy.	Brantford
32. LaVALLEE, Kevin	Cgy.	Brantford
33. TERRION, Greg	L.A.	Brantford
34. MORRISON, Dave	L.A.	Peterborough
35. ALLISON, Mike	NYR	Sudbury
36. DAWES, Len	Chi.	Victoria
37. BEAUPRE, Don	Min.	Sudbury
38. HRUDEY, Kelly	NYI	Medicine Hat
39. KONROYD, Steve	Cgy.	Oshawa
40. CHABOT, John	Mtl.	Hull
41. MOLLER, Mike	Buf.	Lethbridge
42. FRASER, Jay	Phi.	Ottawa

1979

FIRST ROUND

Selection	Claimed By	Amateur Club
1. RAMAGE, Rob	Col.	London
2. TURNBULL, Perry	St.L.	Portland
3. FOLIGNO, Mike	Det.	Sudbury
4. GARTNER, Mike	Wsh.	Niagara Falls
5. VAIVE, Rick	Van.	Sherbrooke
6. HARTSBURG, Craig	Min.	Sault St. Marie
7. BROWN, Keith	Chi.	Portland
8. BOURQUE, Raymond	Bos.	Verdun
9. BOSCHMAN, Laurie	Tor.	Brandon
10. McCARTHY, Tom	Min.	Oshawa
11. RAMSEY, Mike	Buf.	U. of Minnesota
12. REINHART, Paul	Atl.	Kitchener
13. SULLIMAN, Doug	NYR	Kitchener
14. PROPP, Brian	Phi.	Brandon
15. McCRIMMON, Brad	Bos.	Brandon
16. WELLS, Jay	L.A.	Kingston
17. SUTTER, Duane	NYI	Lethbridge
18. ALLISON, Ray	Hfd.	Brandon
19. MANN, Jimmy	Wpg.	Sherbrooke
20. GOULET, Michel	Que.	Quebec
21. LOWE, Kevin	Edm.	Quebec

SECOND ROUND

Selection	Claimed By	Amateur Club
22. WESLEY, Blake	Phi.	Portland
23. PEROVICH, Mike	Atl.	Brandon
24. RAUSSE, Errol	Wsh.	Seattle
25. JONSSON, Tomas	NYI	MoDo AIK (Sweden)
26. ASHTON, Brent	Van.	Saskatoon
27. GINGRAS, Gaston	Mtl.	Hamilton
28. TRIMPER, Tim	Chi.	Peterborough
29. HOPKINS, Dean	L.A.	London
30. HARDY, Mark	L.A.	Montreal
31. MARSHALL, Paul	Pit.	Brantford
32. RUFF, Lindy	Buf.	Lethbridge
33. RIGGIN, Pat	Atl.	London
34. HOSPODAR, Ed	NYR	Ottawa
35. LINDBERGH, Pelle	Phi.	AIK Solna (Sweden)
36. MORRISON, Doug	Bos.	Lethbridge
37. NASLUND, Mats	Mtl.	Brynas IFK (Sweden)
38. CARROLL, Billy	NYI	London
39. SMITH, Stuart	Hfd.	Peterborough
40. CHRISTIAN, Dave	Wpg.	U. of North Dakota
41. HUNTER, Dale	Que.	Sudbury
42. BROTEN, Neal	Min.	U. of Minnesota

1978

FIRST ROUND

Selection	Claimed By	Amateur Club
1. SMITH, Bobby	Min.	Ottawa
2. WALTER, Ryan	Wsh.	Seattle
3. BABYCH, Wayne	St.L.	Portland
4. DERLAGO, Bill	Van.	Brandon
5. GILLIS, Mike	Col.	Kingston
6. WILSON, Behn	Phi.	Kingston
7. LINSEMAN, Ken	Phi.	Kingston
8. GEOFFRION, Danny	Mtl.	Cornwall
9. HUBER, Willie	Det.	Hamilton
10. HIGGINS, Tim	Chi.	Ottawa
11. MARSH, Brad	Atl.	London
12. PETERSON, Brent	Det.	Portland
13. PLAYFAIR, Larry	Buf.	Portland
14. LUCAS, Danny	Phi.	Sault Ste. Marie
15. TAMBELLINI, Steve	NYI	Lethbridge
16. SECORD, Al	Bos.	Hamilton
17. HUNTER, Dave	Mtl.	Sudbury
18. COULIS, Tim	Wsh.	Hamilton

SECOND ROUND

Selection	Claimed By	Amateur Club
19. PAYNE, Steve	Min.	Ottawa
20. MULVEY, Paul	Wsh.	Portland
21. QUENNEVILLE, Joel	Tor.	Windsor
22. FRASER, Curt	Van.	Victoria
23. MacKINNON, Paul	Wsh.	Peterborough
24. CHRISTOFF, Steve	Min.	U. of Minnesota
25. MEEKER, Mike	Pit.	Peterborough
26. MALONEY, Don	NYR	Kitchener
27. MALINOWSKI, Merlin	Col.	Medicine Hat
28. HICKS, Glenn	Det.	Flin Flon
29. LECUYER, Doug	Chi.	Portland
30. YAKIWCHUK, Dale	Mtl.	Portland
31. JENSEN, Al	Det.	Hamilton
32. McKEGNEY, Tony	Buf.	Kingston
33. SIMURDA, Mike	Phi.	Kingston
34. JOHNSTON, Randy	NYI	Peterborough
35. NICOLSON, Graeme	Bos.	Cornwall
36. CARTER, Ron	Mtl.	Sherbrooke

1977

FIRST ROUND

Selection	Claimed By	Amateur Club
1. McCOURT, Dale	Det.	St. Catharines
2. BECK, Barry	Col.	New Westminster
3. PICARD, Robert	Wsh.	Montreal
4. GILLIS, Jere	Van.	Sherbrooke
5. CROMBEEN, Mike	Cle.	Kingston
6. WILSON, Doug	Chi.	Ottawa
7. MAXWELL, Brad	Min.	New Westminster
8. DEBLOIS, Lucien	NYR	Sorel
9. CAMPBELL, Scott	St.L.	London
10. NAPIER, Mark	Mtl.	Toronto
11. ANDERSON, John	Tor.	Toronto
12. JOHANSEN, Trevor	Tor.	Toronto
13. DUGUAY, Ron	NYR	Sudbury
14. SEILING, Ric	Buf.	St. Catharines
15. BOSSY, Mike	NYI	Laval
16. FOSTER, Dwight	Bos.	Kitchener
17. McCARTHY, Kevin	Phi.	Winnipeg
18. DUPONT, Norm	Mtl.	Montreal

SECOND ROUND

Selection	Claimed By	Amateur Club
19. SAVARD, Jean	Chi.	Quebec
20. ZAHARKO, Miles	Atl.	New Westminster
21. LOFTHOUSE, Mark	Wsh.	New Westminster
22. BANDURA, Jeff	Van.	Portland
23. CHICOINE, Daniel	Cle.	Sherbrooke
24. GLADNEY, Bob	Tor.	Oshawa
25. SEMENKO, Dave	Min.	Brandon
26. KEATING, Mike	NYR	St. Catharines
27. LABATTE, Neil	St.L.	Toronto
28. LAURENCE, Don	Atl.	Kitchener
29. SAGANIUK, Rocky	Tor.	Lethbridge
30. HAMILTON, Jim	Pit.	London
31. HILL, Brian	Atl.	Medicine Hat
32. ARESHENKOFF, Ron	Buf.	Medicine Hat
33. TONELLI, John	NYI	Toronto
34. PARRO, Dave	Bos.	Saskatoon
35. GORENCE, Tom	Phi.	U. of Minnesota
36. LANGWAY, Rod	Mtl.	U. of New Hampshire

1976

FIRST ROUND

Selection	Claimed By	Amateur Club
1. GREEN, Rick	Wsh.	London
2. CHAPMAN, Blair	Pit.	Saskatoon
3. SHARPLEY, Glen	Min.	Hull
4. WILLIAMS, Fred	Det.	Saskatoon
5. JOHANSSON, Bjorn	Cal.	Sweden
6. MURDOCH, Don	NYR	Medicine Hat
7. FEDERKO, Bernie	St.L.	Saskatoon
8. SHAND, Dave	Atl.	Peterborough
9. CLOUTIER, Real	Chi.	Quebec
10. PHILLIPOFF, Harold	Atl.	New Westminster
11. GARDNER, Paul	K.C.	Oshawa
12. LEE, Peter	Mtl.	Ottawa
13. SCHUTT, Rod	Mtl.	Sudbury
14. McKENDRY, Alex	NYI	Sudbury
15. CARROLL, Greg	Wsh.	Medicine Hat
16. PACHAL, Clayton	Bos.	New Westminster
17. SUZOR, Mark	Phi.	Kingston
18. BAKER, Bruce	Mtl.	Ottawa

SECOND ROUND

Selection	Claimed By	Amateur Club
19. MALONE, Greg	Pit.	Oshawa
20. SUTTER, Brian	St.L.	Lethbridge
21. CLIPPINGDALE, Steve	L.A.	New Westminster
22. LARSON, Reed	Det.	U. of Minnesota
23. STENLUND, Vern	Cal.	London
24. FARRISH, Dave	NYR	Sudbury
25. SMRKE, John	St.L.	Toronto
26. MANNO, Bob	Van.	St. Catharines
27. McDILL, Jeff	Chi.	Victoria
28. SIMPSON, Bobby	Atl.	Sherbrooke
29. MARSH, Peter	Pit.	Sherbrooke
30. CARLYLE, Randy	Tor.	Sudbury
31. ROBERTS, Jim	Min.	Ottawa
32. KASZYCKI, Mike	NYI	Sault Ste. Marie
33. KOWAL, Joe	Buf.	Hamilton
34. GLOECKNER, Larry	Bos.	Victoria
35. CALLANDER, Drew	Phi.	Regina
36. MELROSE, Barry	Mtl.	Kamloops

1975

FIRST ROUND

Selection	Claimed By	Amateur Club
1. BRIDGMAN, Mel	Phi.	Victoria
2. DEAN, Barry	K.C.	Medicine Hat
3. KLASSEN, Ralph	Cal.	Saskatoon
4. MAXWELL, Brian	Min.	Medicine Hat
5. LAPOINTE, Rick	Det.	Victoria
6. ASHBY, Don	Tor.	Calgary
7. VAYDIK, Greg	Chi.	Medicine Hat
8. MULHERN, Richard	Atl.	Sherbrooke
9. SADLER, Robin	Mtl.	Edmonton
10. BLIGHT, Rick	Van.	Brandon
11. PRICE, Pat	NYI	Saskatoon
12. DILLON, Wayne	NYR	Toronto
13. LAXTON, Gord	Pit.	New Westminster
14. HALWARD, Doug	Bos.	Peterborough
15. MONDOU, Pierre	Mtl.	Montreal
16. YOUNG, Tim	L.A.	Ottawa
17. SAUVE, Bob	Buf.	Laval
18. FORSYTH, Alex	Wsh.	Kingston

SECOND ROUND

Selection	Claimed By	Amateur Club
19. SCAMURRA, Peter	Wsh.	Peterborough
20. CAIRNS, Don	K.C.	Victoria
21. MARUK, Dennis	Cal.	London
22. ENGBLOM, Brian	Mtl.	U. of Wisconsin
23. ROLLINS, Jerry	Det.	Winnipeg
24. JARVIS, Doug	Tor.	Peterborough
25. ARNDT, Daniel	Chi.	Saskatoon
26. BOWNASS, Rick	Atl.	Montreal
27. STANIOWSKI, Ed	St.L.	Regina
28. GASSOFF, Brad	Van.	Kamloops
29. SALVIAN, David	NYI	St. Catharines
30. SOETAERT, Doug	NYR	Edmonton
31. ANDERSON, Russ	Pit.	U. of Minnesota
32. SMITH, Barry	Bos.	New Westminster
33. BUCYK, Terry	L.A.	Lethbridge
34. GREENBANK, Kelvin	Mtl.	Winnipeg
35. BREITENBACH, Ken	Buf.	St. Catharines
36. MASTERS, Jamie	St.L.	Ottawa

1974

FIRST ROUND

Selection	Claimed By	Amateur Club
1. JOLY, Greg	Wsh.	Regina
2. PAIEMENT, Wilfred	K.C.	St. Catharines
3. HAMPTON, Rick	Cal.	St. Catharines
4. GILLIES, Clark	NYI	Regina
5. CONNOR, Cam	Mtl.	Flin Flon
6. HICKS, Doug	Min.	Flin Flon
7. RISEBROUGH, Doug	Mtl.	Kitchener
8. LAROUCHE, Pierre	Pit.	Sorel
9. LOCHEAD, Bill	Det.	Oshawa
10. CHARTRAW, Rick	Mtl.	Kitchener
11. FOGOLIN, Lee	Buf.	Oshawa
12. TREMBLAY, Mario	Mtl.	Montreal
13. VALIQUETTE, Jack	Tor.	Sault Ste. Marie
14. MALONEY, Dave	NYR	Kitchener
15. McTAVISH, Gord	Mtl.	Sudbury
16. MULVEY, Grant	Chi.	Calgary
17. CHIPPERFIELD, Ron	Cal.	Brandon
18. LARWAY, Don	Bos.	Swift Current

SECOND ROUND

Selection	Claimed By	Amateur Club
19. MARSON, Mike	Wsh.	Sudbury
20. BURDON, Glen	K.C.	Regina
21. AFFLECK, Bruce	Cal.	U. of Denver
22. TROTTIER, Bryan	NYI	Swift Current
23. SEDLBAUER, Ron	Van.	Kitchener
24. NANTAIS, Rick	Min.	Quebec
25. HOWE, Mark	Bos.	Toronto
26. HESS, Bob	St.L.	New Westminster
27. COSSETTE, Jacques	Pit.	Sorel
28. CHOUINARD, Guy	Atl.	Quebec
29. GARE, Danny	Buf.	Calgary
30. MacGREGOR, Gary	Mtl.	Cornwall
31. WILLIAMS, Dave	Tor.	Swift Current
32. GRESCHNER, Ron	NYR	New Westminster
33. LUPIEN, Gilles	Mtl.	Montreal
34. DAIGLE, Alain	Chi.	Trois-Rivières
35. McLEAN, Don	Phi.	Sudbury
36. STURGEON, Peter	Bos.	Kitchener

1973

FIRST ROUND

Selection	Claimed By	Amateur Club
1. POTVIN, Denis	NYI	Ottawa
2. LYSIAK, Tom	Atl.	Medicine Hat
3. VERVERGAERT, Dennis	Van.	London
4. McDONALD, Lanny	Tor.	Medicine Hat
5. DAVIDSON, John	St.L.	Calgary
6. SAVARD, Andre	Bos.	Quebec
7. STOUGHTON, Blaine	Pit.	Flin Flon
8. GAINEY, Bob	Mtl.	Peterborough
9. DAILEY, Bob	Van.	Toronto
10. NEELEY, Bob	Tor.	Peterborough
11. RICHARDSON, Terry	Det.	New Westminster
12. TITANIC, Morris	Buf.	Sudbury
13. ROTA, Darcy	Chi.	Edmonton
14. MIDDLETON, Rick	NYR	Oshawa
15. TURNBULL, Ian	Tor.	Ottawa
16. MERCREDI, Vic	Atl.	New Westminster

SECOND ROUND

Selection	Claimed By	Amateur Club
17. GOLDUP, Glen	Mtl.	Toronto
18. DUNLOP, Blake	Min.	Ottawa
19. BORDELEAU, Paulin	Van.	Toronto
20. GOODENOUGH, Larry	Phi.	London
21. VAIL, Eric	Atl.	Sudbury
22. MARRIN, Peter	Mtl.	Toronto
23. BIANCHIN, Wayne	Pit.	Flin Flon
24. PESUT, George	St.L.	Saskatoon
25. ROGERS, John	Min.	Edmonton
26. LEVINS, Brent	Phi.	Swift Current
27. CAMPBELL, Colin	Pit.	Peterborough
28. LANDRY, Jean	Buf.	Quebec
29. THOMAS, Reg	Chi.	London
30. HICKEY, Pat	NYR	Hamilton
31. JONES, Jim	Bos.	Peterborough
32. ANDRUFF, Ron	Mtl.	Flin Flon

1972

FIRST ROUND

Selection	Claimed By	Amateur Club
1. HARRIS, Billy	NYI	Toronto
2. RICHARD, Jacques	Atl.	Quebec
3. LEVER, Don	Van.	Niagara Falls
4. SHUTT, Steve	Mtl.	Toronto
5. SCHOENFELD, Jim	Buf.	Niagara Falls
6. LAROCQUE, Michel	Mtl.	Ottawa
7. BARBER, Bill	Phi.	Kitchener
8. GARDNER, Dave	Mtl.	Toronto
9. MERRICK, Wayne	St.L.	Ottawa
10. BLANCHARD, Albert	NYR	Kitchener
11. FERGUSON, George	Tor.	Toronto
12. BYERS, Jerry	Min.	Kitchener
13. RUSSELL, Phil	Chi.	Edmonton
14. VAN BOXMEER, John	Mtl.	Guelph
15. MacMILLAN, Bobby	NYR	St. Catharines
16. BLOOM, Mike	Bos.	St. Catharines

SECOND ROUND

Selection	Claimed By	Amateur Club
17. HENNING Lorne	NYI	New Westminster
18. BIALOWAS, Dwight	Atl.	Regina
19. McSHEFFREY, Brian	Van.	Ottawa
20. KOZAK, Don	L.A.	Edmonton
21. SACHARUK, Larry	NYR	Saskatoon
22. CASSIDY, Tom	Cal.	Kitchener
23. BLADON, Tom	Phi.	Edmonton
24. LYNCH, Jack	Pit.	Oshawa
25. CARRIERE, Larry	Buf.	Loyola College
26. GUITE, Pierre	Det.	St. Catharines
27. OSBURN, Randy	Tor.	London
28. WEIR, Stan	Cal.	Medicine Hat
29. OGILVIE, Brian	Chi.	Edmonton
30. LUKOWICH, Bernie	Pit.	New Westminster
31. VILLEMURE, Rene	NYR	Shawinigan
32. ELDER, Wayne	Bos.	London

1971

FIRST ROUND

Selection	Claimed By	Amateur Club
1. LAFLEUR, Guy	Mtl.	Quebec
2. DIONNE, Marcel	Det.	St. Catharines
3. GUEVREMONT, Jocelyn	Van.	Montreal
4. CARR, Gene	St.L.	Flin Flon
5. MARTIN, Rick	Buf.	Montreal
6. JONES, Ron	Bos.	Edmonton
7. ARNASON, Chuck	Mtl.	Flin Flon
8. WRIGHT, Larry	Phi.	Regina
9. PLANTE, Pierre	Phi.	Drummondville
10. VICKERS, Steve	NYR	Toronto
11. WILSON, Murray	Mtl.	Ottawa
12. SPRING, Dan	Chi.	Edmonton
13. DURBANO, Steve	NYR	Toronto
14. O'REILLY, Terry	Bos.	Oshawa

SECOND ROUND

Selection	Claimed By	Amateur Club
15. BAIRD, Ken	Cal.	Flin Flon
16. BOUCHA, Henry	Det.	U.S. Nationals
17. LALONDE, Bobby	Van.	Montreal
18. McKENZIE, Brian	Pit.	St. Catharines
19. RAMSAY, Craig	Buf.	Peterborough
20. ROBINSON, Larry	Mtl.	Kitchener
21. NORRISH, Rod	Min.	Regina
22. KEHOE, Rick	Tor.	Hamilton
23. FORTIER, Dave	Tor.	St. Catharines
24. DEGUISE, Michel	Mtl.	Sorel
25. FRENCH, Terry	Mtl.	Ottawa
26. KRYSKOW, Dave	Chi.	Edmonton
27. WILLIAMS, Tom	NYR	Hamilton
28. RIDLEY, Curt	Bos.	Portage

1970

FIRST ROUND

Selection	Claimed By	Amateur Club
1. PERREAULT, Gilbert	Buf.	Montreal
2. TALLON, Dale	Van.	Toronto
3. LEACH, Reg	Bos.	Flin Flon
4. MacLEISH, Rick	Bos.	Peterborough
5. MARTINIUK, Ray	Mtl.	Flin Flon
6. LEFLEY, Chuck	Mtl.	Canadian Nationals
7. POLIS, Greg	Pit.	Estevan
8. SITTLER, Darryl	Tor.	London
9. PLUMB, Ron	Bos.	Peterborough
10. ODDLEIFSON, Chris	Oak.	Winnipeg
11. GRATTON, Norm	NYR	Montreal
12. LAJEUNESSE, Serge	Det.	Montreal
13. STEWART, Bob	Bos.	Oshawa
14. MALONEY, Dan	Chi.	London

SECOND ROUND

Selection	Claimed By	Amateur Club
15. DEADMARSH, Butch	Buf.	Brandon
16. HARGREAVES, Jim	Van.	Winnipeg
17. HARVEY, Fred	Min.	Hamilton
18. CLEMENT, Bill	Phi.	Ottawa
19. LAFRAMBOISE, Pete	Oak.	Ottawa
20. BARRETT, Fred	Min.	Toronto
21. STEWART, John	Pit.	Flin Flon
22. THOMPSON, Errol	Tor.	Charlottetown
23. KEOGAN, Murray	St.L.	U. of Minnesota
24. McDONOUGH, Al	L.A.	St. Catharines
25. MURPHY, Mike	NYR	Toronto
26. GUINDON, Bobby	Det.	Montreal
27. BOUCHARD, Dan	Bos.	London
28. ARCHAMBAULT, Mike	Chi.	Drummondville

1969

FIRST ROUND

Selection	Claimed By	Amateur Club
1. HOULE, Rejean	Mtl.	Montreal
2. TARDIF, Marc	Mtl.	Montreal
3. TANNAHILL, Don	Bos.	Niagara Falls
4. SPRING, Frank	Bos.	Edmonton
5. REDMOND, Dick	Min.	St. Catharines
6. CURRIER, Bob	Phi.	Cornwall
7. FEATHERSTONE, Tony	Oak.	Peterborough
8. DUPONT, Andr;aae	NYR	Montreal
9. MOSER, Ernie	Tor.	Estevan
10. RUTHERFORD, Jim	Det.	Hamilton
11. BOLDIREV, Ivan	Bos.	Oshawa
12. JARRY, Pierre	NYR	Ottawa
13. BORDELEAU, J.-P.	Chi.	Montreal
14. O'BRIEN, Dennis	Min.	St. Catharines

SECOND ROUND

Selection	Claimed By	Amateur Club
15. KESSELL, Rick	Pit.	Oshawa
16. HOGANSON, Dale	L.A.	Estevan
17. CLARKE, Bobby	Phi.	Flin Flon
18. STACKHOUSE, Ron	Oak.	Peterborough
19. LOWE, Mike	St.L.	Loyola College
20. BRINDLEY, Doug	Tor.	Niagara Falls
21. GARWASIUK, Ron	Det.	Regina
22. QUOQUOCHI, Art	Bos.	Montreal
23. WILSON, Bert	NYR	London
24. ROMANCHYCH, Larry	Chi.	Flin Flon
25. GILBERT, Gilles	Min.	London
26. BRIERE, Michel	Pit.	Shawinigan Falls
27. BODDY, Greg	L.A.	Edmonton
28. BROSSART, Bill	Phi.	Estevan

NHL All-Stars

Active Players' All-Star Selection Records

	First Team Selections	Second Team Selections	Total
GOALTENDERS			
Patrick Roy	(3) 1988-89; 1989-90; 1991-92.	(2) 1987-88; 1990-91.	5
Tom Barrasso	(1) 1983-84.	(2) 1984-85; 1992-93.	3
Ed Belfour	(2) 1990-91; 1992-93.	(0)	2
Grant Fuhr	(1) 1987-88.	(1) 1981-82.	2
J.Vanbiesbrouck	(1) 1985-86.	(0)	1
Ron Hextall	(1) 1986-87.	(0)	1
Mike Vernon	(0)	(1) 1988-89.	1
Daren Puppa	(0)	(1) 1989-90.	1
Kirk McLean	(0)	(1) 1991-92.	1
DEFENSEMEN			
Ray Bourque	(10) 1979-80; 1981-82; 1983-84; 1984-85; 1986-87; 1987-88; 1989-90; 1990-91; 1991-92; 1992-93.	(4) 1980-81; 1982-83; 1985-86; 1988-89.	14
Paul Coffey	(3) 1984-85; 1985-86; 1988-89.	(4) 1981-82; 1982-83; 1983-84; 1989-90.	7
Al MacInnis	(2) 1989-90; 1990-91.	(2) 1986-87; 1988-89.	4
Mark Howe	(3) 1982-83; 1985-86; 1986-87.	(0)	3
Rod Langway	(2) 1982-83; 1983-84.	(1) 1984-85.	3
Chris Chelios	(2) 1988-89; 1992-93.	(1) 1990-91.	3
Doug Wilson	(1) 1981-82.	(2) 1984-85; 1989-90.	3
Brian Leetch	(1) 1991-92.	(1) 1990-91.	2
Scott Stevens	(1) 1987-88.	(1) 1991-92	2
Larry Murphy	(0)	(2) 1986-87; 1992-93.	2
Gary Suter	(0)	(1) 1987-88.	1
Brad McCrimmon	(0)	(1) 1987-88.	1
Phil Housley	(0)	(1) 1991-92	1
Al Iafrate	(0)	(1) 1992-93	1
CENTERS			
Wayne Gretzky	(8) 1980-81; 1981-82; 1982-83; 1983-84; 1984-85; 1985-86; 1986-87; 1990-91.	(4) 1979-80; 1987-88; 1988-89; 1989-90.	12
Mario Lemieux	(3) 1987-88; 1988-89; 1992-93.	(3) 1985-86; 1986-87; 1991-92.	6
Bryan Trottier	(2) 1977-78; 1978-79.	(2) 1981-82; 1983-84.	4
Mark Messier	(2) 1989-90; 1991-92.	(0)	2
Denis Savard	(0)	(1) 1982-83.	1
Dale Hawerchuk	(0)	(1) 1984-85.	1
Adam Oates	(0)	(1) 1990-91.	1
Pat LaFontaine	(0)	(1) 1992-93.	1
RIGHT WINGERS			
Jari Kurri	(2) 1984-85; 1986-87.	(3) 1983-84; 1985-86; 1988-89.	5
Brett Hull	(3) 1989-90; 1990-91; 1991-92.	(0)	3
Cam Neely	(0)	(3) 1987-88; 1989-90; 1990-91.	3
Joe Mullen	(1) 1988-89.	(0)	1
Teemu Selanne	(1) 1992-93.	(0)	1
Dave Taylor	(0)	(1) 1980-81.	1
Tim Kerr	(0)	(1) 1986-87.	1
Mark Recchi	(0)	(1) 1991-92.	1
Alexander Mogilny	(0)	(1) 1992-93.	1
LEFT WINGERS			
Luc Robitaille	(5) 1987-88; 1988-89; 1989-90; 1990-91; 1992-93.	(2) 1986-87; 1991-92.	7
Michel Goulet	(3) 1983-84; 1985-86; 1986-87.	(2) 1982-83; 1987-88.	5
Mark Messier	(2) 1981-82; 1982-83.	(1) 1983-84.	3
Kevin Stevens	(1) 1991-92.	(2) 1990-91; 1992-93.	3
John Ogrodnick	(1) 1984-85.	(0)	1
Gerard Gallant	(0)	(1) 1988-89.	1
Brian Bellows	(0)	(1) 1989-90.	1

Leading NHL All-Stars 1930-93

Player	Pos	Team	NHL Seasons	First Team Selections	Second Team Selections	Total Selections
Howe, Gordie	RW	Detroit	26	12	9	21
Richard, Maurice	RW	Montreal	18	8	6	14
* Bourque, Ray	D	Boston	14	10	4	14
Hull, Bobby	LW	Chicago	16	10	2	12
* Gretzky, Wayne	C	Edm., L.A.	14	8	4	12
Harvey, Doug	D	Mtl., NYR	19	10	1	11
Hall, Glenn	G	Chi., St.L.	18	7	4	11
Beliveau, Jean	C	Montreal	20	6	4	10
Seibert, Earl	D	NYR., Chi	15	4	6	10
Orr, Bobby	D	Boston	12	8	1	9
Lindsay, Ted	LW	Detroit	17	8	1	9
Mahovlich, Frank	LW	Tor., Det., Mtl.	18	3	6	9
Shore, Eddie	D	Boston	14	7	1	8
Mikita, Stan	C	Chicago	22	6	2	8
Kelly, Red	D	Detroit	20	6	2	8
Esposito, Phil	C	Boston	18	6	2	8
Pilote, Pierre	D	Chicago	14	5	3	8
Brimsek, Frank	G	Boston	10	2	6	8
Bossy, Mike	RW	NY Islanders	10	5	3	8
* Robitaille, Luc	LW	Los Angeles	7	5	2	7
Potvin, Denis	D	NY Islanders	15	5	2	7
Park, Brad	D	NYR, Bos.	17	5	2	7
* Coffey, Paul	D	Edm., Pit.	13	3	4	7
Plante, Jacques	G	Mtl-Tor	18	3	4	7
Gadsby, Bill	D	Chi., NYR, Det.	20	3	4	7
Sawchuk, Terry	G	Detroit	21	3	4	7
Durnan, Bill	G	Montreal	7	6	0	6
Lafleur, Guy	RW	Montreal	16	6	0	6
Dryden, Ken	G	Montreal	8	5	1	6
* Lemieux, Mario	C	Pittsburgh	9	3	3	6
Robinson, Larry	D	Montreal	20	3	3	6
Horton, Tim	D	Toronto	24	3	3	6
Salming, Borje	D	Toronto	17	1	5	6
Cowley, Bill	C	Boston	13	4	1	5
* Messier, Mark	LW/C	Edm., NYR	14	4	1	5
Jackson, Harvey	LW	Toronto	15	4	1	5
* Goulet, Michel	LW	Quebec	14	3	2	5
Conacher, Charlie	RW	Toronto	12	3	2	5
Stewart, Jack	D	Detroit	12	3	2	5
Lach, Elmer	C	Montreal	14	3	2	5
Quackenbush, Bill	D	Det., Bos.	14	3	2	5
Blake, Toe	LW	Montreal	15	3	2	5
Esposito, Tony	G	Chicago	16	3	2	5
* Roy, Patrick	G	Montreal	9	2	3	5
Reardon, Ken	D	Montreal	7	2	3	5
* Kurri, Jari	RW	Edmonton	12	2	3	5
Apps, Syl	C	Toronto	10	2	3	5
Giacomin, Ed	G	NY Rangers	13	2	3	5

* Active

Position Leaders in All-Star Selections

Position	Player	First Team	Second Team	Total
GOAL	Glenn Hall	7	4	11
	Frank Brimsek	2	6	8
	Jacques Plante	3	4	7
	Terry Sawchuk	3	4	7
	Bill Durnan	6	0	6
	Ken Dryden	5	1	6
DEFENSE	* Ray Bourque	10	4	14
	Doug Harvey	10	1	11
	Earl Seibert	4	6	10
	Bobby Orr	8	1	9
	Eddie Shore	7	1	8
	Red Kelly	6	2	8
	Pierre Pilote	5	3	8

Position	Player	First Team	Second Team	Total
LEFT WING	Bobby Hull	10	2	12
	Ted Lindsay	8	1	9
	Frank Mahovlich	3	6	9
	* Luc Robitaille	5	2	7
	Harvey Jackson	4	1	5
	* Michel Goulet	3	2	5
	Toe Blake	3	2	5
RIGHT WING	Gordie Howe	12	9	21
	Maurice Richard	8	6	14
	Mike Bossy	5	3	8
	Guy Lafleur	6	0	6
	Charlie Conacher	3	2	5
CENTER	* Wayne Gretzky	8	4	12
	Jean Beliveau	6	4	10
	Stan Mikita	6	2	8
	Phil Esposito	6	2	8
	* Mario Lemieux	3	3	6
	Bill Cowley	4	1	5
	Elmer Lach	3	2	5
	Syl Apps	2	3	5

* active player

All-Star Teams

1930-93

Voting for the NHL All-Star Team is conducted among the representatives of the Professional Hockey Writers' Association at the end of the season.

Following is a list of the First and Second All-Star Teams since their inception in 1930-31.

First Team		Second Team
1992-93		
Belfour, Ed, Chi.	G	Barrasso, Tom, Pit.
Chelios, Chris, Chi.	D	Murphy, Larry, Pit.
Bourque, Ray, Bos.	D	Iafrate, Al, Wsh.
Lemieux, Mario, Pit.	C	LaFontaine, Pat, NYI
Selanne, Teemu, Wpg.	RW	Mogilny, Alexander, Buf.
Robitaille, Luc, L.A.	LW	Stevens, Kevin, Pit.
1991-92		
Roy, Patrick, Mtl.	G	Kirk McLean, Van.
Leetch, Brian, NYR	D	Housley, Phil, Wpg.
Bourque, Ray, Bos.	D	Stevens, Scott, N.J.
Messier, Mark, NYR	C	Lemieux, Mario, Pit.
Hull, Brett, St. L.	RW	Recchi, Mark, Pit., Phi.
Stevens, Kevin, Pit.	LW	Robitaille, Luc, L.A.
1990-91		
Belfour, Ed, Chi.	G	Roy, Patrick, Mtl.
Bourque, Ray, Bos.	D	Chelios, Chris, Chi.
MacInnis, Al, Cgy.	D	Leetch, Brian, NYR
Gretzky, Wayne, L.A.	C	Oates, Adam, St. L.
Hull, Brett, St. L.	RW	Neely, Cam, Bos.
Robitaille, Luc, L.A.	LW	Stevens, Kevin, Pit.
1989-90		
Roy, Patrick, Mtl.	G	Puppa, Daren, Buf.
Bourque, Ray, Bos.	D	Coffey, Paul, Pit.
MacInnis, Al, Cgy.	D	Wilson, Doug, Chi.
Messier, Mark, Edm.	C	Gretzky, Wayne, L.A.
Hull, Brett, St. L.	RW	Neely, Cam, Bos.
Robitaille, Luc, L.A.	LW	Bellows, Brian, Min.
1988-89		
Roy, Patrick, Mtl.	G	Vernon, Mike, Cgy.
Chelios, Chris, Mtl.	D	MacInnis, Al, Cgy.
Coffey, Paul, Pit.	D	Bourque, Ray, Bos.
Lemieux, Mario, Pit.	C	Gretzky, Wayne, L.A.
Mullen, Joe, Cgy.	RW	Kurri, Jari, Edm.
Robitaille, Luc, L.A.	LW	Gallant, Gerard, Det.
1987-88		
Fuhr, Grant, Edm.	G	Roy, Patrick, Mtl.
Bourque, Ray, Bos.	D	Suter, Gary, Cgy.
Stevens, Scott, Wsh.	D	McCrimmon, Brad, Cgy.
Lemieux, Mario, Pit.	C	Gretzky, Wayne, Edm.
Loob, Hakan, Cgy.	RW	Neely, Cam, Bos.
Robitaille, Luc, L.A.	LW	Goulet, Michel, Que.
1986-87		
Hextall, Ron, Phi.	G	Liut, Mike, Hfd.
Bourque, Ray, Bos.	D	Murphy, Larry, Wsh.
Howe, Mark, Phi.	D	MacInnis, Al, Cgy.
Gretzky, Wayne, Edm.	C	Lemieux, Mario, Pit.
Kurri, Jari, Edm.	RW	Kerr, Tim, Phi.
Goulet, Michel, Que.	LW	Robitaille, Luc, L.A.
1985-86		
Vanbiesbrouck, J., NYR	G	Froese, Bob, Phi.
Coffey, Paul, Edm.	D	Robinson, Larry, Mtl.
Howe, Mark, Phi.	D	Bourque, Ray, Bos.
Gretzky, Wayne, Edm.	C	Lemieux, Mario, Pit.
Bossy, Mike, NYI	RW	Kurri, Jari, Edm.
Goulet, Michel, Que.	LW	Naslund, Mats, Mtl.

First Team		Second Team
1984-85		
Lindbergh, Pelle, Phi.	G	Barrasso, Tom, Buf.
Coffey, Paul, Edm.	D	Langway, Rod, Wsh.
Bourque, Ray, Bos.	D	Wilson, Doug, Chi.
Gretzky, Wayne, Edm.	C	Hawerchuk, Dale, Wpg.
Kurri, Jari, Edm.	RW	Bossy, Mike, NYI
Ogrodnick, John, Det.	LW	Tonelli, John, NYI
1983-84		
Barrasso, Tom, Buf.	G	Riggin, Pat, Wsh.
Langway, Rod, Wsh.	D	Coffey, Paul, Edm.
Bourque, Ray, Bos.	D	Potvin, Denis, NYI
Gretzky, Wayne, Edm.	C	Trottier, Bryan, NYI
Bossy, Mike, NYI	RW	Kurri, Jari, Edm.
Goulet, Michel, Que.	LW	Messier, Mark, Edm.

First Team		Second Team
1982-83		
Peeters, Pete, Bos.	G	Melanson, Roland, NYI
Howe, Mark, Phi.	D	Bourque, Ray, Bos.
Langway, Rod, Wsh.	D	Coffey, Paul, Edm.
Gretzky, Wayne, Edm.	C	Savard, Denis, Chi.
Bossy, Mike, NYI	RW	McDonald, Lanny, Cgy.
Messier, Mark, Edm.	LW	Goulet, Michel, Que.
1981-82		
Smith, Bill, NYI	G	Fuhr, Grant, Edm.
Wilson, Doug, Chi.	D	Coffey, Paul, Edm.
Bourque, Ray, Bos.	D	Engblom, Brian, Mtl.
Gretzky, Wayne, Edm.	C	Trottier, Bryan, NYI
Bossy, Mike, NYI	RW	Middleton, Rick, Bos.
Messier, Mark, Edm.	LW	Tonelli, John, NYI

Mario Lemieux acknowledges the crowd before leading the Wales Conference to a 12-7 victory over the Campbell Conference in the 1991 All-Star Game.

First Team		Second Team		First Team		Second Team		First Team		Second Team

1980-81

				1972-73				**1964-65**		
Liut, Mike, St.L.	G	Lessard, Mario, L.A.		Dryden, Ken, Mtl.	G	Esposito, Tony, Chi.		Crozier, Roger, Det.	G	Hodge, Charlie, Mtl.
Potvin, Denis, NYI	D	Robinson, Larry, Mtl.		Orr, Bobby, Bos.	D	Park, Brad, NYR		Pilote, Pierre, Chi.	D	Gadsby, Bill, Det.
Carlyle, Randy, Pit.	D	Bourque, Ray, Bos.		Lapointe, Guy, Mtl.	D	White, Bill, Chi.		Laperrière, Jacques, Mtl.	D	Brewer, Carl, Tor.
Gretzky, Wayne, Edm.	C	Dionne, Marcel, L.A.		Esposito, Phil, Bos.	C	Clarke, Bobby, Phi.		Ullman, Norm, Det.	C	Mikita, Stan, Chi.
Bossy, Mike, NYI	RW	Taylor, Dave, L.A.		Redmond, Mickey, Det.	RW	Cournoyer, Yvan, Mtl.		Provost, Claude, Mtl.	RW	Howe, Gordie, Det.
Simmer, Charlie, L.A.	LW	Barber, Bill, Phi.		Mahovlich, Frank, Mtl.	LW	Hull, Dennis, Chi.		Hull, Bobby, Chi.	LW	Mahovlich, Frank, Tor.

1979-80

				1971-72				**1963-64**		
Esposito, Tony, Chi.	G	Edwards, Don, Buf.		Esposito, Tony, Chi.	G	Dryden, Ken, Mtl.		Hall, Glenn, Chi.	G	Hodge, Charlie, Mtl.
Robinson, Larry, Mtl.	D	Salming, Borje, Tor.		Orr, Bobby, Bos.	D	White, Bill, Chi.		Pilote, Pierre, Chi.	D	Vasko, Elmer, Chi.
Bourque, Ray, Bos.	D	Schoenfeld, Jim, Buf.		Park, Brad, NYR	D	Stapleton, Pat, Chi.		Horton, Tim, Tor.	D	Laperrière, Jacques, Mtl.
Dionne, Marcel, L.A.	C	Gretzky, Wayne, Edm.		Esposito, Phil, Bos.	C	Ratelle, Jean, NYR		Mikita, Stan, Chi.	C	Béliveau, Jean, Mtl.
Lafleur, Guy, Mtl.	RW	Gare, Danny, Buf.		Gilbert, Rod, NYR	RW	Cournoyer, Yvan, Mtl.		Wharram, Ken, Chi.	RW	Howe, Gordie, Det.
Simmer, Charlie, L.A.	LW	Shutt, Steve, Mtl.		Hull, Bobby, Chi.	LW	Hadfield, Vic, NYR		Hull, Bobby, Chi.	LW	Mahovlich, Frank, Tor.

1978-79

				1970-71				**1962-63**		
Dryden, Ken, Mtl.	G	Resch, Glenn, NYI		Giacomin, Ed, NYR	G	Plante, Jacques, Tor.		Hall, Glenn, Chi.	G	Sawchuk, Terry, Det.
Potvin, Denis, NYI	D	Salming, Borje, Tor.		Orr, Bobby, Bos.	D	Park, Brad, NYR		Pilote, Pierre, Chi.	D	Horton, Tim, Tor.
Robinson, Larry, Mtl.	D	Savard, Serge, Mtl.		Tremblay, J.C., Mtl.	D	Stapleton, Pat, Chi.		Brewer, Carl, Tor.	D	Vasko, Elmer, Chi.
Trottier, Bryan, NYI	C	Dionne, Marcel, L.A.		Esposito, Phil, Bos.	C	Keon, Dave, Tor.		Mikita, Stan, Chi.	C	Richard, Henri, Mtl.
Lafleur, Guy, Mtl.	RW	Bossy, Mike, NYI		Hodge, Ken, Bos.	RW	Cournoyer, Yvan, Mtl.		Howe, Gordie, Det.	RW	Bathgate, Andy, NYR
Gillies, Clark, NYI	LW	Barber, Bill, Phi.		Bucyk, John, Bos.	LW	Hull, Bobby, Chi.		Mahovlich, Frank, Tor.	LW	Hull, Bobby, Chi.

1977-78

				1969-70				**1961-62**		
Dryden, Ken, Mtl.	G	Edwards, Don, Buf.		Esposito, Tony, Chi.	G	Giacomin, Ed, NYR		Plante, Jacques, Mtl.	G	Hall, Glenn, Chi.
Potvin, Denis, NYI	D	Robinson, Larry, Mtl.		Orr, Bobby, Bos.	D	Brewer, Carl, Det.		Harvey, Doug, NYR	D	Brewer, Carl, Tor.
Park, Brad, Bos.	D	Salming, Borje, Tor.		Park, Brad, NYR	D	Laperrière, Jacques, Mtl.		Talbot, Jean-Guy, Mtl.	D	Pilote, Pierre, Chi.
Trottier, Bryan, NYI	C	Sittler, Darryl, Tor.		Esposito, Phil, Bos.	C	Mikita, Stan, Chi.		Mikita, Stan, Chi.	C	Keon, Dave, Tor.
Lafleur, Guy, Mtl.	RW	Bossy, Mike, NYI		Howe, Gordie, Det.	RW	McKenzie, John, Bos.		Bathgate, Andy, NYR	RW	Howe, Gordie, Det.
Gillies, Clark, NYI	LW	Shutt, Steve, Mtl.		Hull, Bobby, Chi.	LW	Mahovlich, Frank, Det.		Hull, Bobby, Chi.	LW	Mahovlich, Frank, Tor.

1976-77

				1968-69				**1960-61**		
Dryden, Ken, Mtl.	G	Vachon, Rogatien, L.A.		Hall, Glenn, St.L.	G	Giacomin, Ed, NYR		Bower, Johnny, Tor.	G	Hall, Glenn, Chi.
Robinson, Larry, Mtl.	D	Potvin, Denis, NYI		Orr, Bobby, Bos.	D	Green, Ted, Bos.		Harvey, Doug, Mtl.	D	Stanley, Allan, Tor.
Salming, Borje, Tor.	D	Lapointe, Guy, Mtl.		Horton, Tim, Tor.	D	Harris, Ted, Mtl.		Pronovost, Marcel, Det.	D	Pilote, Pierre, Chi.
Dionne, Marcel, L.A.	C	Perreault, Gilbert, Buf.		Esposito, Phil, Bos.	C	Béliveau, Jean, Mtl.		Béliveau, Jean, Mtl.	C	Richard, Henri, Mtl.
Lafleur, Guy, Mtl.	RW	McDonald, Lanny, Tor.		Howe, Gordie, Det.	RW	Cournoyer, Yvan, Mtl.		Geoffrion, Bernie, Mtl.	RW	Howe, Gordie, Det.
Shutt, Steve, Mtl.	LW	Martin, Richard, Buf.		Hull, Bobby, Chi.	LW	Mahovlich, Frank, Det.		Mahovlich, Frank, Tor.	LW	Moore, Dickie, Mtl.

1975-76

				1967-68				**1959-60**		
Dryden, Ken, Mtl.	G	Resch, Glenn, NYI		Worsley, Lorne, Mtl.	G	Giacomin, Ed, NYR		Hall, Glenn, Chi.	G	Plante, Jacques, Mtl.
Potvin, Denis, NYI	D	Salming, Borje, Tor.		Orr, Bobby, Bos.	D	Tremblay, J.C., Mtl.		Harvey, Doug, Mtl.	D	Stanley, Allan, Tor.
Park, Brad, Bos.	D	Lapointe, Guy, Mtl.		Horton, Tim, Tor.	D	Neilson, Jim, NYR		Pronovost, Marcel, Det.	D	Pilote, Pierre, Chi.
Clarke, Bobby, Phi.	C	Perreault, Gilbert, Buf.		Mikita, Stan, Chi.	C	Esposito, Phil, Bos.		Béliveau, Jean, Mtl.	C	Horvath, Bronco, Bos.
Lafleur, Guy, Mtl.	RW	Leach, Reggie, Phi.		Howe, Gordie, Det.	RW	Gilbert, Rod, NYR		Howe, Gordie, Det.	RW	Geoffrion, Bernie, Mtl.
Barber, Bill, Phi.	LW	Martin, Richard, Buf.		Hull, Bobby, Chi.	LW	Bucyk, John, Bos.		Hull, Bobby, Chi.	LW	Prentice, Dean, NYR

1974-75

				1966-67				**1958-59**		
Parent, Bernie, Phi.	G	Vachon, Rogie, L.A.		Giacomin, Ed, NYR	G	Hall, Glenn, Chi.		Plante, Jacques, Mtl.	G	Sawchuk, Terry, Det.
Orr, Bobby, Bos.	D	Lapointe, Guy, Mtl.		Pilote, Pierre, Chi.	D	Horton, Tim, Tor.		Johnson, Tom, Mtl.	D	Pronovost, Marcel, Det.
Potvin, Denis, NYI	D	Salming, Borje, Tor.		Howell, Harry, NYR	D	Orr, Bobby, Bos.		Gadsby, Bill, NYR	D	Harvey, Doug, Mtl.
Clarke, Bobby, Phi.	C	Esposito, Phil, Bos.		Mikita, Stan, Chi.	C	Ullman, Norm, Det.		Béliveau, Jean, Mtl.	C	Richard, Henri, Mtl.
Lafleur, Guy, Mtl.	RW	Robert, René, Buf.		Wharram, Ken, Chi.	RW	Howe, Gordie, Det.		Bathgate, Andy, NYR	RW	Howe, Gordie, Det.
Martin, Richard, Buf.	LW	Vickers, Steve, NYR		Hull, Bobby, Chi.	LW	Marshall, Don, NYR		Moore, Dickie, Mtl.	LW	Delvecchio, Alex, Det.

1973-74

				1965-66				**1957-58**		
Parent, Bernie, Phi.	G	Esposito, Tony, Chi.		Hall, Glenn, Chi.	G	Worsley, Lorne, Mtl.		Hall, Glenn, Chi.	G	Plante, Jacques, Mtl.
Orr, Bobby, Bos.	D	White, Bill, Chi.		Laperrière, Jacques, Mtl.	D	Stanley, Allan, Tor.		Harvey, Doug, Mtl.	D	Flaman, Fern, Bos.
Park, Brad, NYR	D	Ashbee, Barry, Phi.		Pilote, Pierre, Chi.	D	Stapleton, Pat, Chi.		Gadsby, Bill, NYR	D	Pronovost, Marcel, Det.
Esposito, Phil, Bos.	C	Clarke, Bobby, Phi.		Mikita, Stan, Chi.	C	Béliveau, Jean, Mtl.		Richard, Henri, Mtl.	C	Béliveau, Jean, Mtl.
Hodge, Ken, Bos.	RW	Redmond, Mickey, Det.		Howe, Gordie, Det.	RW	Rousseau, Bobby, Mtl.		Howe, Gordie, Det.	RW	Bathgate, Andy, NYR
Martin, Richard, Buf.	LW	Cashman, Wayne, Bos.		Hull, Bobby, Chi.	LW	Mahovlich, Frank, Tor.		Moore, Dickie, Mtl.	LW	Henry, Camille, NYR

1956-57

First Team		Second Team
Hall, Glenn, Det.	G	Plante, Jacques, Mtl.
Harvey, Doug, Mtl.	D	Flaman, Fern, Bos.
Kelly, Red, Det.	D	Gadsby, Bill, NYR
Béliveau, Jean, Mtl.	C	Litzenberger, Eddie, Chi.
Howe, Gordie, Det.	RW	Richard, Maurice, Mtl.
Lindsay, Ted, Det.	LW	Chevrefils, Real, Bos.

1955-56

First Team		Second Team
Plante, Jacques, Mtl.	G	Hall, Glenn, Det.
Harvey, Doug, Mtl.	D	Kelly, Red, Det.
Gadsby, Bill, NYR	D	Johnson, Tom, Mtl.
Béliveau, Jean, Mtl.	C	Sloan, Tod, Tor.
Richard, Maurice, Mtl.	RW	Howe, Gordie, Det.
Lindsay, Ted, Det.	LW	Olmstead, Bert, Mtl.

1954-55

First Team		Second Team
Lumley, Harry, Tor.	G	Sawchuk, Terry, Det.
Harvey, Doug, Mtl.	D	Goldham, Bob, Det.
Kelly, Red, Det.	D	Flaman, Fern, Bos.
Béliveau, Jean, Mtl.	C	Mosdell, Ken, Mtl.
Richard, Maurice, Mtl.	RW	Geoffrion, Bernie, Mtl.
Smith, Sid, Tor.	LW	Lewicki, Danny, NYR

1953-54

First Team		Second Team
Lumley, Harry, Tor.	G	Sawchuk, Terry, Det.
Kelly, Red, Det.	D	Gadsby, Bill, Chi.
Harvey, Doug, Mtl.	D	Horton, Tim, Tor.
Mosdell, Ken, Mtl.	C	Kennedy, Ted, Tor.
Howe, Gordie, Det.	RW	Richard, Maurice, Mtl.
Lindsay, Ted, Det.	LW	Sandford, Ed, Bos.

1952-53

First Team		Second Team
Sawchuk, Terry, Det.	G	McNeil, Gerry, Mtl.
Kelly, Red, Det.	D	Quackenbush, Bill, Bos.
Harvey, Doug, Mtl.	D	Gadsby, Bill, Chi.
Mackell, Fleming, Bos.	C	Delvecchio, Alex, Det.
Howe, Gordie, Det.	RW	Richard, Maurice, Mtl.
Lindsay, Ted, Det.	LW	Olmstead, Bert, Mtl.

1951-52

First Team		Second Team
Sawchuk, Terry, Det.	G	Henry, Jim, Bos.
Kelly, Red, Det.	D	Buller, Hy, NYR
Harvey, Doug, Mtl.	D	Thomson, Jim, Tor.
Lach, Elmer, Mtl.	C	Schmidt, Milt, Bos.
Howe, Gordie, Det.	RW	Richard, Maurice, Mtl.
Lindsay, Ted, Det.	LW	Smith, Sid, Tor.

1950-51

First Team		Second Team
Sawchuk, Terry, Det.	G	Rayner, Chuck, NYR
Kelly, Red, Det.	D	Thomson, Jim, Tor.
Quackenbush, Bill, Bos.	D	Reise, Leo, Det.
Schmidt, Milt, Bos.	C	Abel, Sid, Det.
	(tied)	Kennedy, Ted, Tor.
Howe, Gordie, Det.	RW	Richard, Maurice, Mtl.
Lindsay, Ted, Det.	LW	Smith, Sid, Tor.

1949-50

First Team		Second Team
Durnan, Bill, Mtl.	G	Rayner, Chuck, NYR
Mortson, Gus, Tor.	D	Reise, Leo, Det.
Reardon, Kenny, Mtl.	D	Kelly, Red, Det.
Abel, Sid, Det.	C	Kennedy, Ted, Tor.
Richard, Maurice, Mtl.	RW	Howe, Gordie, Det.
Lindsay, Ted, Det.	LW	Leswick, Tony, NYR

1948-49

First Team		Second Team
Durnan, Bill, Mtl.	G	Rayner, Chuck, NYR
Quackenbush, Bill, Det.	D	Harmon, Glen, Mtl.
Stewart, Jack, Det.	D	Reardon, Kenny, Mtl.
Abel, Sid, Det.	C	Bentley, Doug, Chi.
Richard, Maurice, Mtl.	RW	Howe, Gordie, Det.
Conacher, Roy, Chi.	LW	Lindsay, Ted, Det.

1947-48

First Team		Second Team
Broda, W. "Turk", Tor.	G	Brimsek, Frank, Bos.
Quackenbush, Bill, Det.	D	Reardon, Kenny, Mtl.
Stewart, Jack, Det.	D	Colville, Neil, NYR
Lach, Elmer, Mtl.	C	O'Connor, "Buddy", NYR
Richard, Maurice, Mtl.	RW	Poile, "Bud", Chi.
Lindsay, Ted, Det.	LW	Stewart, Gaye, Chi.

1946-47

First Team		Second Team
Durnan, Bill, Mtl.	G	Brimsek, Frank, Bos.
Reardon, Kenny, Mtl.	D	Stewart, Jack, Det.
Bouchard, Emile, Mtl.	D	Quackenbush, Bill, Det.
Schmidt, Milt, Bos.	C	Bentley, Max, Chi.
Richard, Maurice, Mtl.	RW	Bauer, Bobby, Bos.
Bentley, Doug, Chi.	LW	Dumart, Woody, Bos.

1945-46

First Team		Second Team
Durnan, Bill, Mtl.	G	Brimsek, Frank, Bos.
Crawford, Jack, Bos.	D	Reardon, Kenny, Mtl.
Bouchard, Emile, Mtl.	D	Stewart, Jack, Det.
Bentley, Max, Chi.	C	Lach, Elmer, Mtl.
Richard, Maurice, Mtl.	RW	Mosienko, Bill, Chi.
Stewart, Gaye, Tor.	LW	Blake, "Toe", Mtl.
Irvin, Dick, Mtl.	Coach	Gottselig, John, Chi.

1944-45

First Team		Second Team
Durnan, Bill, Mtl.	G	Karakas, Mike, Chi.
Bouchard, Emile, Mtl.	D	Harmon, Glen, Mtl.
Hollett, Bill, Det.	D	Pratt, "Babe", Tor.
Lach, Elmer, Mtl.	C	Cowley, Bill, Bos.
Richard, Maurice, Mtl.	RW	Mosienko, Bill, Chi.
Blake, "Toe", Mtl.	LW	Howe, Syd, Det.
Irvin, Dick, Mtl.	Coach	Adams, Jack, Det.

1943-44

First Team		Second Team
Durnan, Bill, Mtl.	G	Bibeault, Paul, Tor.
Seibert, Earl, Chi.	D	Bouchard, Emile, Mtl.
Pratt, "Babe", Tor.	D	Clapper, "Dit", Bos.
Cowley, Bill, Bos.	C	Lach, Elmer, Mtl.
Carr, Lorne, Tor.	RW	Richard, Maurice, Mtl.
Bentley, Doug, Chi.	LW	Cain, Herb, Bos.
Irvin, Dick, Mtl.	Coach	Day, "Hap", Tor.

1942-43

First Team		Second Team
Mowers, Johnny, Det.	G	Brimsek, Frank, Bos.
Seibert, Earl, Chi.	D	Crawford, Johnny, Bos.
Stewart, Jack, Det.	D	Hollett, Bill, Bos.
Cowley, Bill, Bos.	C	Apps, Syl, Tor.
Carr, Lorne, Tor.	RW	Hextall, Bryan, NYR
Bentley, Doug, Chi.	LW	Patrick, Lynn, NYR
Adams, Jack, Det.	Coach	Ross, Art, Bos.

1941-42

First Team		Second Team
Brimsek, Frank, Bos.	G	Broda, W. "Turk", Tor.
Seibert, Earl, Chi.	D	Egan, Pat, Bro.
Anderson, Tommy, Bro.	D	McDonald, Bucko, Tor.
Apps, Syl, Tor.	C	Watson, Phil, NYR
Hextall, Bryan, NYR	RW	Drillon, Gord, Tor.
Patrick, Lynn, NYR	LW	Abel, Sid, Det.
Boucher, Frank, NYR	Coach	Thompson, Paul, Chi.

1940-41

First Team		Second Team
Broda, W. "Turk", Tor.	G	Brimsek, Frank, Bos.
Clapper, "Dit", Bos.	D	Seibert, Earl, Chi.
Stanowski, Wally, Tor.	D	Heller, Ott, NYR
Cowley, Bill, Bos.	C	Apps, Syl, Tor.
Hextall, Bryan, NYR	RW	Bauer, Bobby, Bos.
Schriner, Dave, Tor.	LW	Dumart, Woody, Bos.
Weiland, "Cooney", Bos.	Coach	Irvin, Dick, Mtl.

1939-40

First Team		Second Team
Kerr, Dave, NYR	G	Brimsek, Frank, Bos.
Clapper, "Dit", Bos.	D	Coulter, Art, NYR
Goodfellow, Ebbie, Det.	D	Seibert, Earl, Chi.
Schmidt, Milt, Bos.	C	Colville, Neil, NYR
Hextall, Bryan, NYR	RW	Bauer, Bobby, Bos.
Blake, "Toe", Mtl.	LW	Dumart, Woody, Bos.
Thompson, Paul, Chi.	Coach	Boucher, Frank, NYR

1938-39

First Team		Second Team
Brimsek, Frank, Bos.	G	Robertson, Earl, NYA
Shore, Eddie, Bos.	D	Seibert, Earl, Chi.
Clapper, "Dit", Bos.	D	Coulter, Art, NYR
Apps, Syl, Tor.	C	Colville, Neil, NYR
Drillon, Gord, Tor.	RW	Bauer, Bobby, Bos.
Blake, "Toe", Mtl.	LW	Gottselig, Johnny, Chi.
Ross, Art, Bos.	Coach	Dutton, "Red", NYA

1937-38

First Team		Second Team
Thompson, "Tiny", Bos.	G	Kerr, Dave, NYR
Shore, Eddie, Bos.	D	Coulter, Art, NYR
Siebert, "Babe", Mtl.	D	Seibert, Eart, Chi.
Cowley, Bill, Bos.	C	Apps, Syl, Tor.
Dillon, Cecil, NYR	RW	Dillon, Cecil, NYR
Drillon, Gord, Tor.	(tied)	Drillon, Gord, Tor.
Thompson, Paul, Chi.	LW	Blake, Toe, Mtl.
Patrick, Lester, NYR	Coach	Ross, Art, Bos.

1936-37

First Team		Second Team
Smith, Norm, Det.	G	Cude, Wilf, Mtl.
Siebert, "Babe", Mtl.	D	Seibert, Earl, Chi.
Goodfellow, Ebbie, Det.	D	Conacher, Lionel, Mtl. M.
Barry, Marty, Det.	C	Chapman, Art, NYA
Aurie, Larry, Det.	RW	Dillon, Cecil, NYR
Jackson, Harvey, Tor.	LW	Schriner, Dave, NYA
Adams, Jack, Det.	Coach	Hart, Cecil, Mtl.

1935-36

First Team		Second Team
Thompson, "Tiny", Bos.	G	Cude, Wilf, Mtl.
Shore, Eddie, Bos.	D	Seibert, Earl, Chi.
Siebert, "Babe", Bos.	D	Goodfellow, Ebbie, Det.
Smith, "Hooley", Mtl. M.	C	Thoms, Bill, Tor.
Conacher, Charlie, Tor.	RW	Dillon, Cecil, NYR
Schriner, Dave, NYA	LW	Thompson, Paul, Chi.
Patrick, Lester, NYR	Coach	Gorman, T.P., Mtl. M.

1934-35

First Team		Second Team
Chabot, Lorne, Chi.	G	Thompson, "Tiny", Bos.
Shore, Eddie, Bos.	D	Wentworth, Cy, Mtl. M.
Seibert, Earl, NYR	D	Coulter, Art, Chi.
Boucher, Frank, NYR	C	Weiland, "Cooney", Det.
Conacher, Charlie, Tor.	RW	Clapper, "Dit", Bos.
Jackson, Harvey, Tor.	LW	Joliat, Aurel, Mtl.
Patrick, Lester, NYR	Coach	Irvin, Dick, Tor.

1933-34

First Team		Second Team
Gardiner, Charlie, Chi.	G	Worters, Roy, NYA
Clancy, "King", Tor.	D	Shore, Eddie, Bos.
Conacher, Lionel, Chi.	D	Johnson, "Ching", NYR
Boucher, Frank, NYR	C	Primeau, Joe, Tor.
Conacher, Charlie, Tor.	RW	Cook, Bill, NYR
Jackson, Harvey, Tor.	LW	Joliat, Aurel, Mtl.
Patrick, Lester, NYR	Coach	Irvin, Dick, Tor.

1932-33

First Team		Second Team
Roach, John Ross, Det.	G	Gardiner, Charlie, Chi.
Shore, Eddie, Bos.	D	Clancy, "King", Tor.
Johnson, "Ching", NYR	D	Conacher, Lionel, Mtl. M.
Boucher, Frank, NYR	C	Morenz, Howie, Mtl.
Cook, Bill, NYR	RW	Conacher, Charlie, Tor.
Northcott, "Baldy", Mtl M.	LW	Jackson, Harvey, Tor.
Patrick, Lester, NYR	Coach	Irvin, Dick, Tor.

1931-32

First Team		Second Team
Gardiner, Charlie, Chi.	G	Worters, Roy, NYA
Shore, Eddie, Bos.	D	Mantha, Sylvio, Mtl.
Johnson, "Ching", NYR	D	Clancy, "King", Tor.
Morenz, Howie, Mtl.	C	Smith, "Hooley", Mtl. M.
Cook, Bill, NYR	RW	Conacher, Charlie, Tor.
Jackson, Harvey, Tor.	LW	Joliat, Aurel, Mtl.
Patrick, Lester, NYR	Coach	Irvin, Dick, Tor.

1930-31

First Team		Second Team
Gardiner, Charlie, Chi.	G	Thompson, "Tiny", Bos.
Shore, Eddie, Bos.	D	Mantha, Sylvio, Mtl.
Clancy, "King", Tor.	D	Johnson, "Ching", NYR
Morenz, Howie, Mtl.	C	Boucher, Frank, NYR
Cook, Bill, NYR	RW	Clapper, "Dit", Bos.
Joliet, Aurel, Mtl.	LW	Cook, "Bun", NYR
Patrick, Lester, NYR	Coach	Irvin, Dick, Chi.

All-Star Game Results

Year	Venue	Score	Coaches	Attendance
1993	Montreal	Wales 16, Campbell 6	Scotty Bowman, Mike Keenan	17,137
1992	Philadelphia	Campbell 10, Wales 6	Bob Gainey, Scotty Bowman	17,380
1991	Chicago	Campbell 11, Wales 5	John Muckler, Mike Milbury	18,472
1990	Pittsburgh	Wales 12, Campbell 7	Pat Burns, Terry Crisp	16,236
1989	Edmonton	Campbell 9, Wales 5	Glen Sather, Terry O'Reilly	17,503
1988	St. Louis	Wales 6, Campbell 5 OT	Mike Keenan, Glen Sather	17,878
1986	Hartford	Wales 4, Campbell 3 OT	Mike Keenan, Glen Sather	15,100
1985	Calgary	Wales 6, Campbell 4	Al Arbour, Glen Sather	16,825
1984	New Jersey	Wales 7, Campbell 6	Al Arbour, Glen Sather	18,939
1983	NY Islanders	Campbell 9, Wales 3	Roger Neilson, Al Arbour	15,230
1982	Washington	Wales 4, Campbell 2	Al Arbour, Glen Sonmor	18,130
1981	Los Angeles	Campbell 4, Wales 1	Pat Quinn, Scotty Bowman	15,761
1980	Detroit	Wales 6, Campbell 3	Scotty Bowman, Al Arbour	21,002
1978	Buffalo	Wales 3, Campbell 2 OT	Scotty Bowman, Fred Shero	16,433
1977	Vancouver	Wales 4, Campbell 3	Scotty Bowman, Fred Shero	15,607
1976	Philadelphia	Wales 7, Campbell 5	Floyd Smith, Fred Shero	16,436
1975	Montreal	Wales 7, Campbell 1	Bep Guidolin, Fred Shero	16,080
1974	Chicago	West 6, East 4	Billy Reay, Scotty Bowman	16,426
1973	New York	East 5, West 4	Tom Johnson, Billy Reay	16,986
1972	Minnesota	East 3, West 2	Al MacNeil, Billy Reay	15,423
1971	Boston	West 2, East 1	Scotty Bowman, Harry Sinden	14,790
1970	St. Louis	East 4, West 1	Claude Ruel, Scotty Bowman	16,587
1969	Montreal	East 3, West 3	Toe Blake, Scotty Bowman	16,260
1968	Toronto	Toronto 4, All-Stars 3	Punch Imlach, Toe Blake	15,753
1967	Montreal	Montreal 3, All-Stars 0	Toe Blake, Sid Abel	14,284
1965	Montreal	All-Stars 5, Montreal 2	Billy Reay, Toe Blake	13,529
1964	Toronto	All-Stars 3, Toronto 2	Sid Abel, Punch Imlach	14,232
1963	Toronto	All-Stars 3, Toronto 3	Sid Abel, Punch Imlach	14,034
1962	Toronto	Toronto 4, All-Stars 1	Punch Imlach, Rudy Pilous	14,236
1961	Chicago	All-Stars 3, Chicago 1	Sid Abel, Rudy Pilous	14,534
1960	Montreal	All-Stars 2, Montreal 1	Punch Imlach, Toe Blake	13,949
1959	Montreal	Montreal 6, All-Stars 1	Toe Blake, Punch Imlach	13,818
1958	Montreal	Montreal 6, All-Stars 3	Toe Blake, Milt Schmidt	13,989
1957	Montreal	All-Stars 5, Montreal 3	Milt Schmidt, Toe Blake	13,003
1956	Montreal	All-Stars 1, Montreal 1	Jim Skinner, Toe Blake	13,095
1955	Detroit	Detroit 3, All-Stars 1	Jim Skinner, Dick Irvin	10,111
1954	Detroit	All-Stars 2, Detroit 2	King Clancy, Jim Skinner	10,689
1953	Montreal	All-Stars 3, Montreal 1	Lynn Patrick, Dick Irvin	14,153
1952	Detroit	1st team 1, 2nd team 1	Tommy Ivan, Dick Irvin	10,680
1951	Toronto	1st team 2, 2nd team 2	Joe Primeau, Hap Day	11,469
1950	Detroit	Detroit 7, All-Stars 1	Tommy Ivan, Lynn Patrick	9,166
1949	Toronto	All-Stars 3, Toronto 1	Tommy Ivan, Hap Day	13,541
1948	Chicago	All-Stars 3, Toronto 1	Tommy Ivan, Hap Day	12,794
1947	Toronto	All-Stars 4, Toronto 3	Dick Irvin, Hap Day	14,169

There was no All-Star contest during the calendar year of 1966 since the game was moved from the start of season to mid-season. In 1979, the Challenge Cup series between the Soviet Union and Team NHL replaced the All-Star Game. In 1987, Rendez-Vous '87, two games between the Soviet Union and Team NHL replaced the All-Star Game. Rendez-Vous '87 scores: game one, NHL All-Stars 4, Soviet Union 3; game two, Soviet Union 5, NHL All-Stars 3.

1992-93 All-Star Game Summary

February 6, 1993 at Montreal   Wales 16, Campbell 6

PLAYERS ON ICE: **Campbell Conference** — Belfour, Vernon, Casey, Chiasson, Butcher, Housley, Chelios, Carlyle, Manson, Coffey, Modano, Roberts, Kisio, Bure, Selanne, Bradley, Hull, Kurri, Yzerman, Robitaille, Roenick, Gilmour, Gretzky

Wales Conference — Roy, Sidorkiewicz, Billington, Zalapski, Lowe, S. Stevens, Marsh, Duchesne, Iafrate, Bourque, Turgeon, Recchi, Muller, Gartner, Oates, Lafontaine, Bondra, Sakic, Tocchet, K. Stevens, Jagr, Mogilny

GOALTENDERS				
	Campbell:	Belfour	20 minutes	6 goals against
		Vernon	20 minutes	6 goals against
		Casey	20 minutes	4 goals against
	Wales:	Roy	20 minutes	0 goals against
		Sidorkiewicz	20 minutes	2 goals against
		Billington	20 minutes	4 goals against

SUMMARY
First Period

1.	Wales	Gartner	(Lowe, Oates)	3:15
2.	Wales	Gartner	(Oates)	3:37
3.	Wales	Bondra	(Oates, Gartner)	4:23
4.	Wales	Mogilny	(Bourque)	11:40PPG
5.	Wales	Turgeon	(Recchi)	13:05
6.	Wales	Gartner	(Oates, Bondra)	13:22

PENALTIES: Manson (C) 11:12.

Second Period

7.	Wales	Tocchet	(K. Stevens, Recchi)	:19
8.	Wales	Gartner	(Turgeon)	3:33
9.	Wales	Tocchet	(S. Stevens)	4:57
10.	Campbell	Roenick	(Selanne)	5:52
11.	Wales	Recchi	(Marsh)	9:25
12.	Campbell	Kisio	(Roenick, Modano)	10:15
13.	Wales	K. Stevens	(Recchi)	14:50
14.	Wales	Turgeon	(Sakic, Jagr)	17:56

PENALTIES: None.

Third Period

15.	Wales	Lafontaine	(Muller, Mogilny)	8:07
16.	Wales	Jagr	(Sakic, Turgeon)	9:08
17.	Wales	Marsh	(K. Stevens, Recchi)	12:52
18.	Campbell	Gilmour	(Coffey)	13:57
19.	Wales	Turgeon	(Sakic, S. Stevens)	15:51
20.	Campbell	Selanne	(Manson, Kurri)	17:03
21.	Campbell	Bure	(Kisio)	18:44
22.	Campbell	Bure		19:31

PENALTIES: None.

SHOTS ON GOAL BY:

Campbell Conference	11	16	14	**41**
Wales Conference	22	15	12	**49**

Attendance: 17,137

Referee: Dan Marouelli   Linesmen: Kevin Collins, Ryan Bozak

NHL/UPPER DECK ALL-ROOKIE TEAM

Voting for the NHL/Upper Deck All-Rookie Team is conducted among the representatives of the Professional Hockey Writers' Association at the end of the season. The rookie all-star team was first selected for the 1982-83 season.

1992-93

Felix Potvin, Toronto	*Goal*
Vladimir Malakhov, NY Islanders	*Defense*
Scott Niedermayer, New Jersey	*Defense*
Eric Lindros, Philadelphia	*Center*
Teemu Selanne, Winnipeg	*Right Wing*
Joe Juneau, Boston	*Left Wing*

1990-91

Ed Belfour, Chicago	*Goal*
Eric Weinrich, New Jersey	*Defense*
Rob Blake, Los Angeles	*Defense*
Sergei Fedorov, Detroit	*Center*
Ken Hodge, Boston	*Right Wing*
Jaromir Jagr, Pittsburgh	*Left Wing*

1988-89

Peter Sidorkiewicz, Hartford	*Goal*
Brian Leetch, NY Rangers	*Defense*
Zarley Zalapski, Pittsburgh	*Defense*
Trevor Linden, Vancouver	*Center*
Tony Granato, NY Rangers	*Right Wing*
David Volek, NY Islanders	*Left Wing*

1991-92

Dominik Hasek, Chicago	*Goal*
Nicklas Lidstrom, Detroit	*Defense*
Vladimir Konstantinov, Detroit	*Defense*
Kevin Todd, New Jersey	*Center*
Tony Amonte, NY Rangers	*Right Wing*
Gilbert Dionne, Montreal	*Left Wing*

1989-90

Bob Essensa, Winnipeg	*Goal*
Brad Shaw, Hartford	*Defense*
Geoff Smith, Edmonton	*Defense*
Mike Modano, Minnesota	*Center*
Sergei Makarov, Calgary	*Right Wing*
Rod Brind'Amour, St. Louis	*Left Wing*

1987-88

Darren Pang, Chicago	*Goal*
Glen Wesley, Boston	*Defense*
Calle Johansson, Buffalo	*Defense*
Joe Nieuwendyk, Calgary	*Center*
Ray Sheppard, Buffalo	*Right Wing*
Iain Duncan, Winnipeg	*Left Wing*

1986-87

Ron Hextall, Philadelphia	*Goal*
Steve Duchesne, Los Angeles	*Defense*
Brian Benning, St. Louis	*Defense*
Jimmy Carson, Los Angeles	*Center*
Jim Sandlak, Vancouver	*Right Wing*
Luc Robitaille, Los Angeles	*Left Wing*

1984-85

Steve Penney, Montreal	*Goal*
Chris Chelios, Montreal	*Defense*
Bruce Bell, Quebec	*Defense*
Mario Lemieux, Pittsburgh	*Center*
Tomas Sandstrom, NY Rangers	*Right Wing*
Warren Young, Pittsburgh	*Left Wing*

1982-83

Pelle Lindbergh, Philadelphia	*Goal*
Scott Stevens, Washington	*Defense*
Phil Housley, Buffalo	*Defense*
Dan Daoust, Montreal/Toronto	*Center*
Steve Larmer, Chicago	*Right Wing*
Mats Naslund, Montreal	*Left Wing*

1985-86

Patrick Roy, Montreal	*Goal*
Gary Suter, Calgary	*Defense*
Dana Murzyn, Hartford	*Defense*
Mike Ridley, NY Rangers	*Center*
Kjell Dahlin, Montreal	*Right Wing*
Wendel Clark, Toronto	*Left Wing*

1983-84

Tom Barrasso, Buffalo	*Goal*
Thomas Eriksson, Philadelphia	*Defense*
Jamie Macoun, Calgary	*Defense*
Steve Yzerman, Detroit	*Center*
Hakan Loob, Calgary	*Right Wing*
Sylvain Turgeon, Hartford	*Left Wing*

All-Star Game Records 1947 through 1993

TEAM RECORDS

MOST GOALS, BOTH TEAMS, ONE GAME:
22 — Wales 16, Campbell 6, 1993 at Montreal
19 — Wales 12, Campbell 7, 1990 at Pittsburgh
16 — Campbell 11, Wales 5, 1991 at Chicago
— Campbell 10, Wales 6, 1992 at Philadelphia
14 — Campbell 9, Wales 5, 1989 at Edmonton
13 — Wales 7, Campbell 6, 1984 at New Jersey
12 — Campbell 9, Wales 3, 1983 at NY Islanders
— Wales 7, Campbell 5, 1976 at Philadelphia
11 — Wales 6, Campbell 5, 1988 at St. Louis

FEWEST GOALS, BOTH TEAMS, ONE GAME:
2 — NHL All-Stars 1, Montreal Canadiens 1, 1956 at Montreal
— First Team All-Stars 1, Second Team All-Stars 1, 1952 at Detroit
3 — West 2, East 1, 1971 at Boston
— Montreal Canadiens 3, NHL All-Stars 0, 1967 at Montreal
— NHL All-Stars 2, Montreal Canadiens 1, 1960 at Montreal

MOST GOALS, ONE TEAM, ONE GAME:
16 — Wales 16, Campbell 6, 1993 at Montreal
12 — Wales 12, Campbell 7, 1990 at Pittsburgh
11 — Campbell 11, Wales 5, 1991 at Chicago
10 — Campbell 10, Wales 6, 1992 at Philadelphia
9 — Campbell 9, Wales 3, 1983 at NY Islanders
Campbell 9, Wales 5, 1989 at Edmonton
7 — Wales 7, Campbell 5, 1976 at Philadelphia
— Wales 7, Campbell 1, 1975 at Montreal
— Detroit Red Wings 7, NHL All-Stars 1, 1950 at Detroit
— Wales 7, Campbell 6, 1984 at New Jersey
— Campbell 7, Wales 12, 1990 at Pittsburgh

FEWEST GOALS, ONE TEAM, ONE GAME:
0 — NHL All-Stars 0, Montreal Canadiens 3, 1967 at Montreal
1 — 17 times (1981, 1975, 1971, 1970, 1962, 1961, 1960, 1959, both teams 1956, 1955, 1953, both teams 1952, 1950, 1949, 1948)

MOST SHOTS, BOTH TEAMS, ONE GAME (SINCE 1955):
90 — 1993 at Montreal — Wales 16 (49 shots), Campbell 6 (41 shots)
87 — 1990 at Pittsburgh — Wales 12 (45 shots), Campbell 7 (42 shots)
83 — 1992 at Philadelphia — Campbell 10 (42 shots), Wales 6 (41 shots)
82 — 1991 at Chicago — Campbell 11 (41 shots), Wales 5 (41 shots)
81 — 1968 at Toronto — NHL All-Stars 3 (40 shots), Toronto Maple Leafs 4 (41 shots)

FEWEST SHOTS, BOTH TEAMS, ONE GAME (SINCE 1955):
52 — 1978 at Buffalo — Campbell 2 (12 shots) Wales 3 (40 shots)
53 — 1960 at Montreal — NHL All-Stars 2 (27 shots) Montreal Canadiens 1 (26 shots)
55 — 1956 at Montreal — NHL All-Stars 1 (28 shots) Montreal Canadiens 1 (27 shots)
— 1971 at Boston — West 2 (28 shots) East 1 (27 shots)

MOST SHOTS, ONE TEAM, ONE GAME (SINCE 1955):
49 — 1993 at Montreal — Wales (16-6 vs. Campbell)
45 — 1990 at Pittsburgh — Wales (12-7 vs. Campbell)
44 — 1955 at Detroit — Detroit Red Wings (3-1 vs. NHL All-Stars)
— 1970 at St. Louis — East (4-1 vs. West)
43 — 1981 at Los Angeles — Campbell (4-1 vs. Wales)
42 — 1976 at Philadelphia — Wales (7-5 vs. Campbell)
— 1990 at Pittsburgh — Campbell (7-12 vs. Wales)
— 1992 at Philadelphia — Campbell (10-6 vs. Wales)

FEWEST SHOTS, ONE TEAM, ONE GAME (SINCE 1955):
12 — 1978 at Buffalo — Campbell (2-3 vs. Wales)
17 — 1970 at St. Louis — West (1-4 vs. East)
23 — 1961 at Chicago — Chicago Black Hawks (1-3 vs. NHL All-Stars)
24 — 1976 at Philadelphia — Campbell (5-7 vs. Wales)

MOST POWER-PLAY GOALS, BOTH TEAMS, ONE GAME (SINCE 1950):
3 — 1953 at Montreal — NHL All-Stars 3 (2 power-play goals), Montreal Canadiens 1 (1 power-play goal)
— 1954 at Detroit — NHL All-Stars 2 (1 power-play goal) Detroit Red Wings 2 (2 power-play goals)
— 1958 at Montreal — NHL All-Stars 3 (1 power-play goal) Montreal Canadiens 6 (2 power-play goals)

FEWEST POWER-PLAY GOALS, BOTH TEAMS, ONE GAME (SINCE 1950):
0 — 14 times (1952, 1959, 1960, 1967, 1968, 1969, 1972, 1973, 1976, 1980, 1981, 1984, 1985, 1992)

FASTEST TWO GOALS, BOTH TEAMS, FROM START OF GAME:
37 seconds — 1970 at St. Louis — Jacques Laperriere of East scored at 20 seconds and Dean Prentice of West scored at 37 seconds. Final score: East 4, West 1.
3:37 — 1993 at Montreal — Mike Gartner scored at 3:15 and at 3:37 for Wales. Final score: Wales 16, Campbell 6.
4:08 — 1963 at Toronto — Frank Mahovlich scored for Toronto Maple Leafs at 2:22 of first period and Henri Richard scored at 4:08 for NHL All-Stars. Final score: NHL All-Stars 3, Toronto Maple Leafs 3.

FASTEST TWO GOALS, BOTH TEAMS:
10 seconds — 1976 at Philadelphia — Dennis Ververgaert scored at 4:33 and at 4:43 of third period for Campbell. Final score: Wales 7, Campbell 5.
14 seconds — 1989 at Edmonton. Steve Yzerman and Gary Leeman scored at 17:21 and 17:35 of second period for Campbell. Final score: Campbell 9, Wales 5.
16 seconds — 1990 at Pittsburgh. Kirk Muller of Wales scored at 8:47 of second period and Al MacInnis of Campbell scored at 9:03. Final score: Wales 12, Campbell 7.

FASTEST THREE GOALS, BOTH TEAMS:
1:08 — 1993 at Montreal — all by Wales — Mike Gartner scored at 3:15 and at 3:37 of first period; Peter Bondra scored at 4:23. Final score: Wales 16, Campbell 6.
1:25 — 1992 at Philadelphia — Bryan Trottier scored at 4:03 of third period for Wales; Brian Bellows scored at 4:50 for Campbell; Alexander Mogilny scored at 5:28 for Wales. Final score: Campbell 10, Wales 6.
1:32 — 1980 at Detroit — all by Wales — Ron Stackhouse scored at 11:40 of third period, Craig Hartsburg scored at 12:40; and Reed Larson scored at 13:12. Final score: Wales 6, Campbell 3.

FASTEST FOUR GOALS, BOTH TEAMS:
3:40 — 1993 at Montreal — Pierre Turgeon scored at 15:51 of third period for Wales; Teemu Selanne scored at 17:03 for Campbell; Pavel Bure scored at 18:44 and 19:31 for Campbell. Final score: Wales 16, Campbell 6.
4:11 — 1993 at Montreal — Brad Marsh scored at 12:52 of third period for Wales; Doug Gilmour scored at 13:57 for Campbell; Pierre Turgeon scored at 15:51 for Wales; Teemu Selanne scored at 17:03 for Campbell. Final score: Wales 16, Campbell 6.
4:21 — 1990 at Pittsburgh — Steve Yzerman scored at 14:31 of first period for Campbell; Rick Tocchet scored at 16:55 for Wales; Mario Lemieux scored at 17:37 for Wales; Pierre Turgeon scored at 18:52 for Wales. Final score: Wales 12, Campbell 7.

FASTEST TWO GOALS, ONE TEAM, FROM START OF GAME:
3:37 — 1993 at Montreal — Wales — Mike Gartner scored at 3:15 and at 3:37. Final socre: Wales 16, Campbell 6.
4:19 — 1980 at Detroit — Wales — Larry Robinson scored at 3:58 and Steve Payne scored at 4:19. Final score: Wales 6, Campbell 3.
4:38 — 1971 at Boston — West — Chico Maki scored at 36 seconds and Bobby Hull scored at 4:38. Final score: West 2, East 1.

FASTEST TWO GOALS, ONE TEAM:
10 seconds — 1976 at Philadelphia — Campbell — Dennis Ververgaert scored at 4:33 and at 4:43 of third period. Final score: Wales 7, Campbell 5.
14 seconds — 1989 at Edmonton — Campbell — Steve Yzerman and Gary Leeman scored at 17:21 and 17:35 of second period. Final score: Campbell 9, Wales 5.
17 seconds — 1993 at Montreal — Wales — Pierre Turgeon scored at 13:05 of first period and Mike Gartner scored at 13:22. Final score: Wales 16, Campbell 6.

FASTEST THREE GOALS, ONE TEAM:
1:08 — 1993 at Montreal — Wales — Mike Gartner scored at 3:15 and 3:37 of first period; Peter Bondra scored at 4:23. Final socre: Wales 16, Campbell 6.
1:32 — 1980 at Detroit — Wales — Ron Stackhouse scored at 11:40 of third period; Craig Hartsburg scored at 12:40; Reed Larson scored at 13:12. Final score: Wales 6, Campbell 3.
1:42 — 1993 at Montreal — Wales — Alexander Mogilny scored at 11:40 of first period; Pierre Turgeon scored at 13:05; Mike Gartner scored at 13:22. Wales 16, Campbell 6.

FASTEST FOUR GOALS, ONE TEAM:
4:19 — 1992 at Philadelphia — Campbell — Brian Bellows scored at 7:40 of second period, Jeremy Roenick scored at 8:13, Theoren Fleury scored at 11:06, Brett Hull scored at 11:59. Final score: Campbell 10, Wales 6.
4:26 — 1980 at Detroit — Wales — Ron Stackhouse scored at 11:40 of third period; Craig Hartsburg scored at 12:40; Reed Larson scored at 13:12; Real Cloutier scored at 16:06. Final score: Wales 6, Campbell 3.
5:34 — 1993 at Montreal — Campbell — Doug Gilmour scored at 13:57 of third period; Teemu Selanne scored at 17:03; Pavel Bure scored at 18:44 and 19:31. Final score: Wales 16, Campbell 6.

MOST GOALS, BOTH TEAMS, ONE PERIOD:
9 — 1990 at Pittsburgh — First Period — Wales (7), Campbell (2). Final score: Wales 12, Campbell 7.
8 — 1993 at Montreal — Second period — Wales (6), Campbell (2). Final score: Wales 16, Campbell 6.
— 1993 at Montreal — Third period — Wales (4), Campbell (4). Final score: Wales 16, Campbell 6.

MOST GOALS, ONE TEAM, ONE PERIOD:
7 — 1990 at Pittsburgh — First period — Wales. Final score: Wales 12, Campbell 7.
6 — 1983 at NY Islanders — Third period — Campbell.
Final score: Campbell 9, Wales 3.
— 1993 at Montreal — First period — Wales.
Final score: Wales 16, Campbell 6.
— 1993 at Montreal — Second period — Wales.
Final score: Wales 16, Campbell 6.

MOST SHOTS, BOTH TEAMS, ONE PERIOD:
36 — 1990 at Pittsburgh — Third period — Campbell (22), Wales (14). Final score: Wales 12, Campbell 7.
33 — 1992 at Philadelphia — Third period — Wales (18), Campbell (15). Final score: Campbell 10, Wales 6.
— 1993 at Montreal — First period — Wales (22), Campbell (11). Final score: Wales 16, Campbell 6.
31 — 1993 at Montreal — Second period — Campbell (16), Wales (15). Final score: Wales 16, Campbell 6.

MOST SHOTS, ONE TEAM, ONE PERIOD:
22 — 1990 at Pittsburgh — Third period — Campbell. Final score: Wales 12, Campbell 7.
— 1991 at Chicago — Third Period — Wales. Final score: Campbell 11, Wales 5.
— 1993 at Montreal — First period — Wales. Final score: Wales 16, Campbell 6.
20 — 1970 at St. Louis — Third period — East. Final score: East 4, West 1.

FEWEST SHOTS, BOTH TEAMS, ONE PERIOD:
9 — 1971 at Boston — Third period — East (2), West (7). Final score: West 2, East 1.
— 1980 at Detroit — Second period — Campbell (4), Wales (5). Final score: Wales 6, Campbell 3.
13 — 1982 at Washington — Third period — Campbell (6), Wales (7). Final score: Wales 4, Campbell 2.
14 — 1978 at Buffalo — First period — Campbell (7), Wales (7). Final score: Wales 3, Campbell 2.
— 1986 at Hartford — First period — Campbell (6), Wales (8). Final score: Wales 4, Campbell 3.

FEWEST SHOTS, ONE TEAM, ONE PERIOD:
2 — 1971 at Boston   Third period   East
Final score: West 2, East 1
— 1978 at Buffalo   Second period   Campbell
Final score: Wales 3, Campbell 2
3 — 1978 at Buffalo   Third period   Campbell
Final score: Wales 3, Campbell 2
4 — 1955 at Detroit   First period   NHL All-Stars
Final score: Detroit Red Wings 3, NHL All-Stars 1
4 — 1980 at Detroit   Second period   Campbell
Final score: Wales 6, Campbell 3

Boston Bruins defenseman Ray Bourque has recorded a League-leading 10 assists in 12 All-Star Game appearances.

INDIVIDUAL RECORDS

Career

MOST GAMES PLAYED:
23 — **Gordie Howe** from 1948 through 1980
15 — Frank Mahovlich from 1959 through 1974
13 — Jean Beliveau from 1953 through 1969
— Alex Delvecchio from 1953 through 1967
— Doug Harvey from 1951 through 1969
— Maurice Richard from 1947 through 1959
— Wayne Gretzky from 1980 through 1993

MOST GOALS:
12 — **Wayne Gretzky** in 13GP
10 — Gordie Howe in 23GP
9 — Mario Lemieux in 5GP
8 — Frank Mahovlich in 15GP
7 — Maurice Richard in 13GP
6 — Mike Gartner in 6GP

MOST ASSISTS:
10 — **Ray Bourque** in 12GP
9 — Gordie Howe in 23GP
— Larry Robinson in 10GP
— Adam Oates in 3GP
8 — Joe Sakic in 4GP
7 — Doug Harvey in 13GP
— Guy Lafleur in 5GP
— Paul Coffey in 11GP

MOST POINTS:
19 — **Gordie Howe** (10G-9A in 23GP)
17 — Wayne Gretzky (12G-5A in 13GP)
15 — Mario Lemieux (9G-6A in 6GP)
13 — Frank Mahovlich (8G-5A in 15GP)
12 — Ray Bourque (2G-10A in 12GP)
10 — Bobby Hull (5G-5A in 12GP)
— Ted Lindsay (5G-5A in 11GP)
— Luc Robitaille (5G-5A in 6GP)
— Larry Robinson (1G-9A in 10GP)
— Adam Oates (1G-9A in 3GP)

MOST PENALTY MINUTES:
27 — **Gordie Howe** in 23GP
21 — Gus Mortson in 9GP
16 — Harry Howell in 7GP

MOST POWER-PLAY GOALS:
6 — **Gordie Howe** in 23GP
3 — Bobby Hull in 12GP
2 — Maurice Richard in 13GP

Game

MOST GOALS, ONE GAME:
4 — **Wayne Gretzky**, Campbell, 1983
— **Mario Lemieux**, Wales, 1990
— **Vince Damphousse**, Campbell, 1991
— **Mike Gartner**, Wales, 1993
3 — Ted Lindsay, Detroit Red Wings, 1950
— Mario Lemieux, Wales, 1988
— Pierre Turgeon, Wales, 1993
2 — Wally Hergesheimer, NHL All-Stars, 1953
— Earl Reibel, Detroit Red Wings, 1955
— Andy Bathgate, NHL All-Stars, 1958
— Maurice Richard, Montreal Canadiens, 1958
— Frank Mahovlich, Toronto Maple Leafs, 1963
— Gordie Howe, NHL All-Stars, 1965
— John Ferguson, Montreal Canadiens, 1967
— Frank Mahovlich, East All-Stars, 1969
— Greg Polis, West All-Stars, 1973
— Syl Apps, Wales, 1975
— Dennis Ververgaert, Campbell, 1976
— Richard Martin, Wales, 1977
— Lanny McDonald, Wales, 1977
— Mike Bossy, Wales, 1982
— Pierre Larouche, Wales, 1984
— Mario Lemieux, Wales 1985
— Brian Propp, Wales, 1986
— Luc Robitaille, Campbell, 1988
— Joe Mullen, Campbell, 1989
— Pierre Turgeon, Wales, 1990
— Kirk Muller, Wales, 1990
— Luc Robitaille, Campbell, 1990
— Pat LaFontaine, Wales, 1991
— Brett Hull, Campbell, 1992
— Theoren Fleury, Campbell, 1992
— Rick Tocchet, Wales, 1993
— Pavel Bure, Campbell, 1993

MOST ASSISTS, ONE GAME:
5 — **Mats Naslund**, Wales, 1988
4 — Ray Bourque, Wales, 1985
— Adam Oates, Campbell, 1991
— Adam Oates, Wales, 1993
— Mark Recchi, Wales, 1993
3 — Dickie Moore, Montreal Canadiens, 1958
— Doug Harvey, Montreal Canadiens, 1959
— Guy Lafleur, Wales, 1975
— Pete Mahovlich, Wales, 1976
— Mark Messier, Campbell, 1983
— Rick Vaive, Campbell, 1984
— Mark Johnson, Wales, 1984
— Don Maloney, Wales, 1984
— Mike Krushelnyski, Campbell, 1985
— Mario Lemieux, Wales, 1988
— Brett Hull, Campbell, 1990
— Luc Robitaille, Campbell, 1992
— Joe Sakic, Wales, 1993

MOST POINTS, ONE GAME:
6 — **Mario Lemieux**, Wales, 1988 (3G-3A)
5 — Mats Naslund, Wales, 1988 (5A)
— Adam Oates, Campbell, 1991 (1G-4A)
— Mike Gartner, Wales, 1993 (4G-1A)
— Mark Recchi, Wales, 1993 (1G-4A)
— Pierre Turgeon, Wales, 1993 (3G-2A)

MOST GOALS, ONE PERIOD:
4 — **Wayne Gretzky**, Campbell, Third period, 1983
3 — Mario Lemieux, Wales, First period, 1990
— Vince Damphousse, Campbell, Third period, 1991
— Mike Gartner, Wales, First period, 1993
2 — Ted Lindsay, Detroit Red Wings, First period, 1950
— Wally Hergesheimer, NHL All-Stars, First period, 1953
— Andy Bathgate, NHL All-Stars, Third period, 1958
— Frank Mahovlich, Toronto Maple Leafs, First period, 1963
— Dennis Ververgaert, Campbell, Third period, 1976
— Richard Martin, Wales, Third period, 1977
— Pierre Turgeon, Wales, First period, 1990
— Luc Robitaille, Campbell, Third period, 1990
— Theoren Fleury, Campbell, Second period, 1992
— Brett Hull, Campbell, Second period, 1992
— Rick Tocchet, Wales, Second period, 1993
— Pavel Bure, Campbell, Third period, 1993

MOST ASSISTS, ONE PERIOD:
4 — **Adam Oates**, Wales, First period, 1993
3 — Mark Messier, Campbell, Third period, 1983

MOST POINTS, ONE PERIOD:
4 — **Wayne Gretzky**, Campbell, Third period, 1983 (4G)
— Mike Gartner, Wales, First period, 1993 (3G-1A)
— Adam Oates, Wales, First period, 1993 (4A)
3 — Gordie Howe, NHL All-Stars, Second period, 1965 (1G-2A)
— Pete Mahovlich, Wales, First period, 1976 (1G-2A)
— Mark Messier, Campbell, Third period, 1983 (3A)
— Mario Lemieux, Wales, Second period, 1988 (1G-2A)
— Mario Lemieux, Wales, First period, 1990 (3G)
— Vince Damphousse, Campbell, Third period, 1991 (3G)
— Mark Recchi, Wales, Second period, 1993 (1G-2A)

FASTEST GOAL FROM START OF GAME:
19 seconds — Ted Lindsay, Detroit Red Wings, 1950
20 seconds — Jacques Laperriere, East All-Stars, 1970
21 seconds — Mario Lemieux, Wales, 1990
36 seconds — Chico Maki, West All-Stars, 1971
37 seconds — Dean Prentice, West All-Star, 1970

FASTEST GOAL FROM START OF A PERIOD:
19 seconds — Ted Lindsay, Detroit Red Wings, 1950 (first period)
— **Rick Tocchet**, Wales, 1993 (second period)
20 seconds — Jacques Laperriere, East, 1970 (first period)
21 seconds — Mario Lemieux, Wales, 1990 (first period)
26 seconds — Wayne Gretzky, Campbell, 1982 (second period)
28 seconds — Maurice Richard, NHL All-Stars, 1947 (third period)

FASTEST TWO GOALS (ONE PLAYER) FROM START OF GAME:
3:37 — Mike Gartner, Wales, 1993, at 3:15 and 3:37.
5:25 — Wally Hergesheimer, NHL All-Stars, 1953, at 4:06 and 5:25.
12:11 — Frank Mahovlich, Toronto, 1963, at 2:22 and 12:11.

FASTEST TWO GOALS (ONE PLAYER) FROM START OF A PERIOD:
3:37 — Mike Gartner, Wales, 1993, at 3:15 and 3:37 of first period.
4:43 — Dennis Ververgaert, Campbell, 1976, at 4:33 and 4:43 of third period.
4:57 — Rick Tocchet, Wales, 1993, at :19 and 4:57 of second period.

FASTEST TWO GOALS (ONE PLAYER):
10 seconds — Dennis Ververgaert, Campbell, 1976. Scored at 4:33 and 4:43 of third period.
22 seconds — Mike Gartner, Wales, 1993. Scored at 3:15 and 3:37 of first period.
47 seconds — Pavel Bure, Campbell, 1993. Scored at 18:44 and 19:31 of third period.

Goaltenders

MOST GAMES PLAYED:
13 — Glenn Hall from 1955-1969
11 — Terry Sawchuk from 1950-1968
 8 — Jacques Plante from 1956-1970
 6 — Tony Esposito from 1970-1980
— Ed Giacomin from 1967-1973
— Grant Fuhr from 1982-1989

MOST GOALS AGAINST:
22 — Glenn Hall in 13GP
21 — Mike Vernon in 5GP
19 — Terry Sawchuk in 11GP
18 — Jacques Plante in 8GP

BEST GOALS-AGAINST-AVERAGE AMONG THOSE WITH AT LEAST TWO GAMES PLAYED:
0.68 — Gilles Villemure in 3GP
1.02 — Frank Brimsek in 2GP
1.59 — Johnny Bower in 4GP
1.64 — Lorne "Gump" Worsley in 4GP
1.98 — Gerry McNeil in 3GP
2.03 — Don Edwards in 2GP
2.44 — Terry Sawchuk in 11GP

MOST MINUTES PLAYED:
467 — Terry Sawchuk in 11GP
421 — Glenn Hall in 13GP
370 — Jacques Plante in 8GP
209 — Turk Broda in 4GP
182 — Ed Giacomin in 6GP
177 — Grant Fuhr in 6GP
165 — Tony Esposito in 6GP

Walter "Turk" Broda, one of the NHL's leading goaltenders in the 1940s, appeared in the NHL All-Star Game on four occasions.

Hockey Hall of Fame

Location: BCE Place, at the corner of Front and Yonge Streets in the heart of downtown Toronto. Easy access from all major highways running into Toronto. Close to TTC and Union Station.

Telephone: administration (416) 360-7735; information (416) 360-7765.

Hours: Monday, Tuesday, Wednesday 9 a.m. to 6 p.m.
Thursday, Friday 9 a.m. to 9:30 p.m.; Saturday 9 a.m. to 6 p.m.
Sunday 10 a.m. to 6 p.m. Closed Chrismas and New Year's Day

History: The Hockey Hall of Fame was established in 1943. Members were first honored in 1945. On August 26, 1961, the Hockey Hall of Fame opened its doors to the public in a building located on the grounds of the Canadian National Exhibition in Toronto. The Hockey Hall of Fame relocated to its new site at BCE place and welcomed the hockey world on June 18, 1993.

Honor Roll: There are 296 Honored Members in the Hockey Hall of Fame. 203 have been inducted as players, 80 as builders and 13 as Referees/Linesmen. In addition, there are 52 media honorees.

Founding Sponsors: Special thanks to Blockbuster Entertainment, Bell Canada, Coca-Cola Canada, Household Finance, Ford of Canada, Imperial Oil, Molson Breweries, The Sports Network and The Toronto Sun.

(Year of induction to the Hockey Hall of Fame is indicated in brackets after each Member's name.)

Defenseman Guy Lapointe joins Steve Shutt, Billy Smith and Edgar Laprade as the Hockey Hall of Fame's 1993 player inductees. Lapointe played 16 seasons with the Canadiens, Blues and Bruins and was a member of six Stanley Cup-winning teams.

PLAYERS

Abel, Sidney Gerald (1969)
*Adams, John James "Jack" (1959)
Apps, Charles Joseph Sylvanus "Syl" (1961)
Armstrong, George Edward (1975)
*Bailey, Irvine Wallace "Ace" (1975)
*Bain, Donald H. "Dan" (1945)
*Baker, Hobart "Hobey" (1945)
Barber, William Charles "Bill" (1990)
*Barry, Martin J. "Marty" (1965)
Bathgate, Andrew James "Andy" (1978)
Beliveau, Jean Arthur (1972)
*Benedict, Clinton S. (1965)
*Bentley, Douglas Wagner (1964)
*Bentley, Maxwell H. L. (1966)
Blake, Hector "Toe" (1966)
Boivin, Leo Joseph (1986)
*Boon, Richard R. "Dickie" (1952)
Bossy, Michael (1991)
Bouchard, Emile Joseph "Butch" (1966)
*Boucher, Frank (1958)
*Boucher, George "Buck" (1960)
Bower, John William (1976)
*Bowie, Russell (1945)
Brimsek, Francis Charles (1966)
*Broadbent, Harry L. "Punch" (1962)
*Broda, Walter Edward "Turk" (1967)
Bucyk, John Paul (1981)
*Burch, Billy (1974)
*Cameron, Harold Hugh "Harry" (1962)
Cheevers, Gerald Michael "Gerry" (1985)
*Clancy, Francis Michael "King" (1958)
*Clapper, Aubrey "Dit" (1947)
Clarke, Robert "Bobby" (1987)
*Cleghorn, Sprague (1958)
*Colville, Neil MacNeil (1967)
*Conacher, Charles W. (1961)
*Connell, Alex (1958)
*Cook, William Osser (1952)
Coulter, Arthur Edmund (1974)
Cournoyer, Yvan Serge (1982)
Cowley, William Mailes (1968)
*Crawford, Samuel Russell "Rusty" (1962)
*Darragh, John Proctor "Jack" (1962)
*Davidson, Allan M. "Scotty" (1950)
*Day, Clarence Henry "Hap" (1961)
Delvecchio, Alex (1977)
*Denneny, Cyril "Cy" (1959)
Dionne, Marcel (1992)
*Drillon, Gordon Arthur (1975)
*Drinkwater, Charles Graham (1950)
Dryden, Kenneth Wayne (1983)

Dumart, Woodrow "Woody" (1992)
*Dunderdale, Thomas (1974)
*Durnan, William Ronald (1964)
*Dutton, Mervyn A. "Red" (1958)
*Dye, Cecil Henry "Babe" (1970)
Esposito, Anthony James "Tony" (1988)
Esposito, Philip Anthony (1984)
*Farrell, Arthur F. (1965)
Flaman, Ferdinand Charles "Fern" (1990)
*Foyston, Frank (1958)
*Frederickson, Frank (1958)
Gadsby, William Alexander (1970)
Gainey, Bob (1992)
*Gardiner, Charles Robert "Chuck" (1945)
*Gardiner, Herbert Martin "Herb" (1958)
*Gardner, James Henry "Jimmy" (1962)
Geoffrion, Jos. A. Bernard "Boom Boom" (1972)
*Gerard, Eddie (1945)
Giacomin, Edward "Eddie" (1987)
Gilbert, Rodrigue Gabriel "Rod" (1982)
*Gilmour, Hamilton Livingstone "Billy" (1962)
*Goheen, Frank Xavier "Moose" (1952)
*Goodfellow, Ebenezer R. "Ebbie" (1963)
*Grant, Michael "Mike" (1950)
*Green, Wilfred "Shorty" (1962)
*Griffis, Silas Seth "Si" (1950)
*Hainsworth, George (1961)
*Hall, Glenn Henry (1975)
*Hall, Joseph Henry (1961)
*Harvey, Douglas Norman (1973)
*Hay, George (1958)
*Hern, William Milton "Riley" (1962)
*Hextall, Bryan Aldwyn (1969)
*Holmes, Harry "Hap" (1972)
*Hooper, Charles Thomas "Tom" (1962)
Horner, George Reginald "Red" (1965)
*Horton, Miles Gilbert "Tim" (1977)
Howe, Gordon (1972)
*Howe, Sydney Harris (1965)
Howell, Henry Vernon "Harry" (1979)
Hull, Robert Marvin (1983)
*Hutton, John Bower "Bouse" (1962)
*Hyland, Harry M. (1962)
*Irvin, James Dickenson "Dick" (1958)
*Jackson, Harvey "Busher" (1971)
*Johnson, Ernest "Moose" (1952)
*Johnson, Ivan "Ching" (1958)
Johnson, Thomas Christian (1970)
*Joliat, Aurel (1947)
*Keats, Gordon "Duke" (1958)
Kelly, Leonard Patrick "Red" (1969)

Kennedy, Theodore Samuel "Teeder" (1966)
Keon, David Michael (1986)
Lach, Elmer James (1966)
Lafleur, Guy Damien (1988)
*Lalonde, Edouard Charles "Newsy" (1950)
Laperriere, Jacques (1987)
Lapointe, Guy (1993)
Laprade, Edgar (1993)
*Laviolette, Jean Baptiste "Jack" (1962)
*Lehman, Hugh (1958)
Lemaire, Jacques Gerard (1984)
*LeSueur, Percy (1961)
*Lewis, Herbert A. (1989)
Lindsay, Robert Blake Theodore "Ted" (1966)
Lumley, Harry (1980)
*MacKay, Duncan "Mickey" (1952)
Mahovlich, Frank William (1981)
*Malone, Joseph "Joe" (1950)
*Mantha, Sylvio (1960)
*Marshall, John "Jack" (1965)
*Maxwell, Fred G. "Steamer" (1962)
McDonald, Lanny (1992)
*McGee, Frank (1945)
*McGimsie, William George "Billy" (1962)
*McNamara, George (1958)
Mikita, Stanley (1983)
Moore, Richard Winston (1974)
*Moran, Patrick Joseph "Paddy" (1958)
*Morenz, Howie (1945)
Mosienko, William "Billy" (1965)
*Nighbor, Frank (1947)
*Noble, Edward Reginald "Reg" (1962)
*O'Connor, Herbert William "Buddy" (1988)
Oliver, Harry (1967)
Olmstead, Murray Bert "Bert" (1985)
Orr, Robert Gordon (1979)
Parent, Bernard Marcel (1984)
Park, Douglas Bradford "Brad" (1988)
*Patrick, Joseph Lynn (1980)
*Patrick, Lester (1947)
Perreault, Gilbert (1990)
*Phillips, Tommy (1945)
Pilote, Joseph Albert Pierre Paul (1975)
*Pitre, Didier "Pit" (1962)
*Plante, Joseph Jacques Omer (1978)
Potvin, Denis (1991)
*Pratt, Walter "Babe" (1966)
*Primeau, A. Joseph (1963)
Pronovost, Joseph Ren;aae Marcel (1978)
Pulford, Bob (1991)
*Pulford, Harvey (1945)

BUILDERS

*Adams, Charles Francis (1960)
*Adams, Weston W. (1972)
*Ahearn, Thomas Franklin "Frank" (1962)
*Ahearne, John Francis "Bunny" (1977)
*Allan, Sir Montagu (C.V.O.) (1945)
 Allen, Keith (1992)
*Ballard, Harold Edwin (1977)
*Bauer, Father David (1989)
*Bickell, John Paris (1978)
 Bowman, Scott (1991)
*Brown, George V. (1961)
*Brown, Walter A. (1962)
*Buckland, Frank (1975)
 Butterfield, Jack Arlington (1980)
*Calder, Frank (1947)
*Campbell, Angus D. (1964)
*Campbell, Clarence Sutherland (1966)
*Cattarinich, Joseph (1977)
*Dandurand, Joseph Viateur "Leo" (1963)
 Dilio, Francis Paul (1964)
*Dudley, George S. (1958)
*Dunn, James A. (1968)
 Eagleson, Robert Alan (1989)
 Francis, Emile (1982)
*Gibson, Dr. John L. "Jack" (1976)
*Gorman, Thomas Patrick "Tommy" (1963)
 Griffiths, Frank A. (1993)
*Hanley, William (1986)
*Hay, Charles (1974)
*Hendy, James C. (1968)
*Hewitt, Foster (1965)
*Hewitt, William Abraham (1947)
*Hume, Fred J. (1962)
*Imlach, George "Punch" (1984)
 Ivan, Thomas N. (1974)
*Jennings, William M. (1975)
*Johnson, Bob (1992)
 Juckes, Gordon W. (1979)
*Kilpatrick, Gen. John Reed (1960)
 Knox, Seymour H. III (1993)
*Leader, George Alfred (1969)
 LeBel, Robert (1970)
*Lockhart, Thomas F. (1965)
*Loicq, Paul (1961)
*Mariucci, John (1985)
 Mathers, Frank (1992)
*McLaughlin, Major Frederic (1963)
*Milford, John "Jake" (1984)
 Molson, Hon. Hartland de Montarville (1973)
*Nelson, Francis (1947)
*Norris, Bruce A. (1969)
*Norris, Sr., James (1958)
*Norris, James Dougan (1962)
*Northey, William M. (1947)
*O'Brien, John Ambrose (1962)
 Page, Fred (1993)
*Patrick, Frank (1958)
*Pickard, Allan W. (1958)
 Pilous, Rudy (1985)
 Poile, Norman "Bud" (1990)
 Pollock, Samuel Patterson Smyth (1978)
*Raymond, Sen. Donat (1958)
*Robertson, John Ross (1947)
*Robinson, Claude C. (1947)
*Ross, Philip D. (1976)
*Selke, Frank J. (1960)
 Sinden, Harry James (1983)
*Smith, Frank D. (1962)
*Smythe, Conn (1958)
 Snider, Edward M. (1988)
*Stanley of Preston, Lord (G.C.B.) (1945)
*Sutherland, Cap. James T. (1947)
 Tarasov, Anatoli V. (1974)
*Turner, Lloyd (1958)
*Tutt, William Thayer (1978)
 Voss, Carl Potter (1974)
*Waghorn, Fred C. (1961)
*Wirtz, Arthur Michael (1971)
 Wirtz, William W. "Bill" (1976)
 Ziegler, John A. Jr. (1987)

REFEREES/LINESMEN

 Armstrong, Neil (1991)
 Ashley, John George (1981)
 Chadwick, William L. (1964)
 D'Amico, John (1993)
*Elliott, Chaucer (1961)
*Hayes, George William (1988)
*Hewitson, Robert W. (1963)
*Ion, Fred J. "Mickey" (1961)
 Pavelich, Matt (1987)
*Rodden, Michael J. "Mike" (1962)
*Smeaton, J. Cooper (1961)
 Storey, Roy Alvin "Red" (1967)
 Udvari, Frank Joseph (1973)

*Deceased

 Quackenbush, Hubert George "Bill" (1976)
*Rankin, Frank (1961)
 Ratelle, Joseph Gilbert Yvan Jean "Jean" (1985)
 Rayner, Claude Earl "Chuck" (1973)
 Reardon, Kenneth Joseph (1966)
 Richard, Joseph Henri (1979)
 Richard, Joseph Henri Maurice "Rocket" (1961)
*Richardson, George Taylor (1950)
*Roberts, Gordon (1971)
*Ross, Arthur Howie (1945)
*Russel, Blair (1965)
*Russell, Ernest (1965)
*Ruttan, J.D. "Jack" (1962)
 Savard, Serge A. (1986)
*Sawchuk, Terrance Gordon "Terry" (1971)
*Scanlan, Fred (1965)
 Schmidt, Milton Conrad "Milt" (1961)
*Schriner, David "Sweeney" (1962)
*Seibert, Earl Walter (1963)
*Seibert, Oliver Levi (1961)
*Shore, Edward W. "Eddie" (1947)
 Shutt, Stephen (1993)
*Siebert, Albert C. "Babe" (1964)
 Sittler, Darryl Glen (1989)
*Smith, Alfred E. (1962)
 Smith, Clint (1991)
*Smith, Reginald "Hooley" (1972)
*Smith, Thomas James (1973)
 Smith, William John "Billy" (1993)
 Stanley, Allan Herbert (1981)
*Stanley, Russell "Barney" (1962)
*Stewart, John Sherratt "Black Jack" (1964)
*Stewart, Nelson "Nels" (1962)
*Stuart, Bruce (1961)
*Stuart, Hod (1945)
*Taylor, Frederic "Cyclone" (O.B.E.) (1947)
*Thompson, Cecil R. "Tiny" (1959)
 Tretiak, Vladislav (1989)
*Trihey, Col. Harry J. (1950)
 Ullman, Norman Victor Alexander "Norm" (1982)
*Vezina, Georges (1945)
*Walker, John Phillip "Jack" (1960)
*Walsh, Martin "Marty" (1962)
*Watson, Harry E. (1962)
*Weiland, Ralph "Cooney" (1971)
*Westwick, Harry (1962)
*Whitcroft, Fred (1962)
*Wilson, Gordon Allan "Phat" (1962)
 Worsley, Lorne John "Gump" (1980)
*Worters, Roy (1969)

United States Hockey Hall of Fame

The United States Hockey Hall of Fame is located in Eveleth, Minnesota, 60 miles north of Duluth, on Highway 53. The facility is open Monday to Saturday 9 a.m. to 5 p.m. and Sundays 11 a.m to 5 p.m.; Adult $2.50; Seniors $2.00; Juniors 13-17 $1.50; and Children 6-12 $1.25; Children under 6 free. Group rates available.

The Hall was dedicated and opened on June 21, 1973, largely as the result of the work of D. Kelly Campbell, Chairman of the Eveleth Civic Association's Project H Committee. The National Hockey League contributed $100,000 towards the construction of the building. There are now 78 enshrinees consisting of 48 players, 14 coaches, 15 administrators, and one referee. New members are inducted annually in October and must have made a significant contribution toward hockey in the United States through the vehicle of their careers.

PLAYERS

*Abel, Clarence "Taffy"
*Baker, Hobart "Hobey"
Bartholome, Earl
Bessone, Peter
Blake, Robert
Brimsek, Frank
*Chaisson, Ray
Chase, John P.
Christian, Roger
Christian, William "Bill"
Cleary, Robert
Cleary, William
*Conroy, Anthony
Dahlstrom, Carl "Cully"
DesJardins, Victor
Desmond, Richard
*Dill, Robert
Everett, Doug
Ftorek, Robbie
*Garrison, John B.
Garrity, Jack
*Goheen, Frank "Moose"
Harding, Austin "Austie"
Iglehart, Stewart
Johnson, Virgil
Karakas, Mike
Kirrane, Jack
*Lane, Myles J.
Langevin, David R.
*Linder, Joseph
*LoPresti, Sam L.
*Mariucci, John
Matchefts, John
Mayasich, John
McCartan, Jack
Moe, William
*Moseley, Fred
*Murray, Hugh "Muzz" Sr.
*Nelson, Hubert "Hub"
Olson , Eddie
*Owen, Jr., George
*Palmer, Winthrop
Paradise, Robert
Purpur, Clifford "Fido"
Riley, William
*Romnes, Elwin "Doc"
Rondeau, Richard
*Williams, Thomas
*Winters, Frank "Coddy"
*Yackel, Ken

COACHES

*Almquist, Oscar
Bessone, Amo
Brooks, Herbert
Ceglarski, Len
*Fullerton, James
*Gordon, Malcolm K.
Heyliger, Victor
Ikola, Willard
*Jeremiah, Edward J.
*Johnson, Bob
*Kelley, John "Snooks"
Kelley, John H. "Jack"
Pleban, John "Connie"
Riley, Jack
Ross, Larry
*Thompson, Clifford, R.
*Stewart, William
*Winsor, Alfred "Ralph"

ADMINISTRATORS

*Brown, George V.
*Brown, Walter A.
Bush, Walter
Clark, Donald
*Gibson, J.C. "Doc"
*Jennings, William M.
*Kahler, Nick
*Lockhart, Thomas F.
Marvin, Cal
Ridder, Robert
Schulz, Charles M.
Trumble, Harold
*Tutt, William Thayer
Wirtz, William W. "Bill"
*Wright, Lyle Z.

REFEREE

Chadwick, William

*Deceased

© 1958 United Feature Syndicate,Inc.

Charles Schulz, creator of Snoopy and other "Peanuts" characters, was inducted into the U.S. Hockey Hall of Fame in 1993. Schulz is an avid participant and supporter of old-timers hockey and hosts an annual tournament each year at his home rink in Northern California. Snoopy, shown here driving a Zamboni, was the official mascot of the NHL's 75th Anniversary celebrations in 1991-92.

Results

1993 Stanley Cup Playoffs

DIVISION SEMI-FINALS
(Best-of-seven series)

Prince of Wales Conference

Series 'A'
Sun. Apr. 18	Buffalo 5	at	Boston 4
Tue. Apr. 20	Buffalo 4	at	Boston 0
Thu. Apr. 22	Boston 3	at	Buffalo 4
Sat. Apr. 24	Boston 5	at	Buffalo 6

Buffalo won series 4-0

Series 'B'
Sun. Apr. 18	Montreal 2	at	Quebec 3
Tue. Apr. 20	Montreal 1	at	Quebec 4
Thu. Apr. 22	Quebec 1	at	Montreal 2
Sat. Apr. 24	Quebec 2	at	Montreal 3
Mon. Apr. 26	Montreal 5	at	Quebec 4
Wed. Apr. 28	Quebec 2	at	Montreal 6

Montreal won series 4-2

Series 'C'
Sun. Apr. 18	New Jersey 3	at	Pittsburgh 6
Tue. Apr. 20	New Jersey 0	at	Pittsburgh 7
Thu. Apr. 22	Pittsburgh 4	at	New Jersey 3
Sun. Apr. 25	Pittsburgh 1	at	New Jersey 4
Mon. Apr. 26	New Jersey 3	at	Pittsburgh 5

Pittsburgh won series 4-1

Series 'D'
Sun. Apr. 18	NY Islanders 1	at	Washington 3
Tue. Apr. 20	NY Islanders 5	at	Washington 4
Thu. Apr. 22	Washington 3	at	NY Islanders 4
Sat. Apr. 24	Washington 3	at	NY Islanders 4
Mon. Apr. 26	NY Islanders 4	at	Washington 6
Wed. Apr. 28	Washington 3	at	NY Islanders 5

NY Islanders won series 4-2

Clarence Campbell Conference

Series 'E'
Sun. Apr. 18	St Louis 4	at	Chicago 3
Wed. Apr. 21	St Louis 2	at	Chicago 0
Fri. Apr. 23	Chicago 0	at	St Louis 3
Sun. Apr. 25	Chicago 3	at	St Louis 4

St Louis won series 4-0

Series 'F'
Mon. Apr. 19	Toronto 3	at	Detroit 6
Wed. Apr. 21	Toronto 2	at	Detroit 6
Fri. Apr. 23	Detroit 2	at	Toronto 4
Sun. Apr. 25	Detroit 2	at	Toronto 3
Tue. Apr. 27	Toronto 5	at	Detroit 4
Thu. Apr. 29	Detroit 7	at	Toronto 3
Sat. May 1	Toronto 4	at	Detroit 3

Toronto won series 4-3

Series 'G'
Mon. Apr. 19	Winnipeg 2	at	Vancouver 4
Wed. Apr. 21	Winnipeg 2	at	Vancouver 3
Fri. Apr. 23	Vancouver 4	at	Winnipeg 5
Sun. Apr. 25	Vancouver 3	at	Winnipeg 1
Tue. Apr. 27	Winnipeg 4	at	Vancouver 3
Thu. Apr. 29	Vancouver 4	at	Winnipeg 3

Vancouver won series 4-2

Series 'H'
Sun. Apr. 18	Los Angeles 6	at	Calgary 3
Wed. Apr. 21	Los Angeles 4	at	Calgary 9
Fri. Apr. 23	Calgary 5	at	Los Angeles 2
Sun. Apr. 25	Calgary 1	at	Los Angeles 3
Tue. Apr. 27	Los Angeles 9	at	Calgary 4
Thu. Apr. 29	Calgary 6	at	Los Angeles 9

Los Angeles won series 4-2

DIVISION FINALS
(Best-of-seven series)

Prince of Wales Conference

Series 'I'
Sun. May 2	Buffalo 3	at	Montreal 4
Tue. May 4	Buffalo 3	at	Montreal 4
Thu. May 6	Montreal 4	at	Buffalo 3
Sat. May 8	Montreal 4	at	Buffalo 3

Montreal won series 4-0

Series 'J'
Sun. May 2	NY Islanders 3	at	Pittsburgh 2
Tue. May 4	NY Islanders 0	at	Pittsburgh 3
Thu. May 6	Pittsburgh 3	at	NY Islanders 1
Sat. May 8	Pittsburgh 5	at	NY Islanders 6
Mon. May 10	NY Islanders 3	at	Pittsburgh 6
Wed. May 12	Pittsburgh 5	at	NY Islanders 7
Fri. May 14	NY Islanders 4	at	Pittsburgh 3

NY Islanders won series 4-3

Clarence Campbell Conference

Series 'K'
Mon. May 3	St Louis 1	at	Toronto 2
Wed. May 5	St Louis 2	at	Toronto 1
Fri. May 7	Toronto 3	at	St Louis 4
Sun. May 9	Toronto 4	at	St Louis 1
Tue. May 11	St Louis 1	at	Toronto 5
Thu. May 13	Toronto 1	at	St Louis 2
Sat. May 15	St Louis 0	at	Toronto 6

Toronto won series 4-3

Series 'L'
Sun. May 2	Los Angeles 2	at	Vancouver 5
Wed. May 5	Los Angeles 6	at	Vancouver 3
Fri. May 7	Vancouver 4	at	Los Angeles 7
Sun. May 9	Vancouver 7	at	Los Angeles 2
Tue. May 11	Los Angeles 4	at	Vancouver 3
Thu. May 13	Vancouver 3	at	Los Angeles 5

Los Angeles won series 4-2

CONFERENCE CHAMPIONSHIPS
(Best-of-seven series)

Prince of Wales Conference

Series 'M'
Sun. May 16	NY Islanders 1	at	Montreal 4
Tue. May 18	NY Islanders 3	at	Montreal 4
Thu. May 20	Montreal 2	at	NY Islanders 1
Sat. May 22	Montreal 1	at	NY Islanders 4
Mon. May 24	NY Islanders 2	at	Montreal 5

Montreal won series 4-1

Clarence Campbell Conference

Series 'N'
Mon. May 17	Los Angeles 1	at	Toronto 4
Wed. May 19	Los Angeles 3	at	Toronto 2
Fri. May 21	Toronto 2	at	Los Angeles 4
Sun. May 23	Toronto 4	at	Los Angeles 2
Tue. May 25	Los Angeles 2	at	Toronto 3
Thu. May 27	Toronto 4	at	Los Angeles 5
Sat. May 29	Los Angeles 5	at	Toronto 4

Los Angeles won series 4-3

STANLEY CUP CHAMPIONSHIP
(Best-of-seven series)

Series 'O'
Tue. June 1	Los Angeles 4	at	Montreal 1
Thu. June 3	Los Angeles 2	at	Montreal 3
Sat. June 5	Montreal 4	at	Los Angeles 3
Mon. June 7	Montreal 3	at	Los Angeles 2
Wed. June 9	Los Angeles 1	at	Montreal 4

Montreal won series 4-1

Montreal's Guy Carbonneau and Denis Savard accept the Stanley Cup from NHL Commissioner Gary Bettman.

Team Playoff Records

	GP	W	L	GF	GA	%
Montreal	20	16	4	66	51	.800
Los Angeles	24	13	11	93	91	.542
Toronto	21	11	10	69	63	.524
NY Islanders	18	9	9	58	65	.500
St Louis	11	7	4	24	28	.636
Pittsburgh	12	7	5	50	37	.583
Vancouver	12	6	6	46	43	.500
Buffalo	8	4	4	31	28	.500
Detroit	7	3	4	30	24	.429
Calgary	6	2	4	28	33	.333
Washington	6	2	4	22	23	.333
Winnipeg	6	2	4	17	21	.333
Quebec	6	2	4	16	19	.333
New Jersey	5	1	4	13	23	.200
Boston	4	0	4	12	19	.000
Chicago	4	0	4	6	13	.000

Individual Leaders

Abbreviations: * – rookie eligible for Calder Trophy; **A** – assists; **G** – goals; **GP** – Games Played; **OT** – overtime goals; **GW** – game-winning goals; **PIM** – penalties in minutes; **PP** – power play goals; **Pts** – points; **S** – shots on goal; **SH** – short-handed goals; **%** – percentage shots resulting in goals; **+/–** – difference between Goals For (**GF**) scored when a player is on the ice with his team at even strength or short-handed and Goals Against (**GA**) scored when the same player is on the ice with his team at even strength or on a power play.

Playoff Scoring Leaders

Player	Team	GP	G	A	Pts	+/–	PIM	PP	SH	GW	OT	S	%
Wayne Gretzky	Los Angeles	24	15	25	40	6	4	4	1	3	1	76	19.7
Doug Gilmour	Toronto	21	10	25	35	16	30	4	0	1	1	51	19.6
Tomas Sandstrom	Los Angeles	24	8	17	25	2 -	12	2	0	2	0	61	13.1
Vincent Damphousse	Montreal	20	11	12	23	8	16	5	0	3	1	52	21.2
Luc Robitaille	Los Angeles	24	9	13	22	13 -	28	4	0	2	0	71	12.7
Ray Ferraro	NY Islanders	18	13	7	20	5	18	4	1	2	2	47	27.7
Wendel Clark	Toronto	21	10	10	20	15	51	2	0	1	0	71	14.1
Dave Andreychuk	Toronto	21	12	7	19	6	35	4	0	3	0	72	16.7
Mario Lemieux	Pittsburgh	11	8	10	18	2	10	3	1	1	0	40	20.0
Glenn Anderson	Toronto	21	7	11	18	7	31	0	0	2	1	46	15.2
Kirk Muller	Montreal	20	10	7	17	4	18	3	0	3	2	54	18.5
Steve Thomas	NY Islanders	18	9	8	17	1 -	37	1	0	1	0	66	13.6
Jari Kurri	Los Angeles	24	9	8	17	2	12	2	2	0	0	50	18.0
Ron Francis	Pittsburgh	12	6	11	17	5	19	1	0	1	0	26	23.1
Tony Granato	Los Angeles	24	6	11	17	3	50	1	0	1	0	77	7.8
Kevin Stevens	Pittsburgh	12	5	11	16	2	22	4	0	0	0	35	14.3
Brian Bellows	Montreal	18	6	9	15	6	18	2	0	0	0	72	8.3
Mike Keane	Montreal	19	2	13	15	10	6	0	0	0	0	27	7.4
Dale Hawerchuk	Buffalo	8	5	9	14	0	2	3	0	0	0	31	16.1
Geoff Courtnall	Vancouver	12	4	10	14	7	12	1	0	1	0	43	9.3
Eric Desjardins	Montreal	20	4	10	14	2	23	1	0	1	1	47	8.5
Derek King	NY Islanders	18	3	11	14	3	14	0	0	1	0	48	6.3

Playoff Defensemen Scoring Leaders

Player	Team	GP	G	A	Pts	+/–	PIM	PP	SH	GW	OT	S	%
Eric Desjardins	Montreal	20	4	10	14	2	23	1	0	1	1	47	8.5
Larry Murphy	Pittsburgh	12	2	11	13	2	10	2	0	1	0	26	7.7
Dave Ellett	Toronto	21	4	8	12	4	8	2	0	0	0	62	6.5
*Alexei Zhitnik	Los Angeles	24	3	9	12	4 -	26	2	0	1	0	42	7.1
Jeff Brown	St Louis	11	3	8	11	3	6	1	0	2	1	41	7.3
Bob Rouse	Toronto	21	3	8	11	3	29	1	0	1	0	33	9.1
*Darryl Sydor	Los Angeles	24	3	8	11	4	16	2	0	0	0	29	10.3
Paul Coffey	Detroit	7	2	9	11	3 -	2	0	0	0	0	24	8.3
Todd Gill	Toronto	21	1	10	11	1	26	0	0	0	0	41	2.4
Rob Blake	Los Angeles	23	4	6	10	3	46	1	1	0	0	60	6.7
Marty McSorley	Los Angeles	24	4	6	10	2 -	60	2	0	1	0	42	9.5

GOALTENDING LEADERS

Goals Against Average

Goaltender	Team	GPI	Mins.	GA	Avg.
Patrick Roy	Montreal	20	1293	46	2.13
Curtis Joseph	St Louis	11	715	27	2.27
*Felix Potvin	Toronto	21	1308	62	2.84
Tom Barrasso	Pittsburgh	12	722	35	2.91
Glenn Healy	NY Islanders	18	1109	59	3.19

Wins

Goaltender	Team	GPI	Mins.	W	L
Patrick Roy	Montreal	20	1293	16	4
*Felix Potvin	Toronto	21	1308	11	10
Kelly Hrudey	Los Angeles	20	1261	10	10
Glenn Healy	NY Islanders	18	1109	9	8

Save Percentage

Goaltender	Team	GPI	Mins.	GA	SA	S%	W	L
Curtis Joseph	St Louis	11	715	27	438	.938	7	4
Patrick Roy	Montreal	20	1293	46	647	.929	16	4
Tom Barrasso	Pittsburgh	12	722	35	370	.905	7	5
*Felix Potvin	Toronto	21	1308	62	636	.903	11	10
Kelly Hrudey	Los Angeles	20	1261	74	656	.887	10	10
Glenn Healy	NY Islanders	18	1109	59	524	.887	9	8

Shutouts

Goaltender	Team	GPI	Mins.	SO
Curtis Joseph	St Louis	11	715	2
Tom Barrasso	Pittsburgh	12	722	2
Grant Fuhr	Buffalo	8	474	1
*Felix Potvin	Toronto	21	1308	1

First Goals

Name	Team	GP	FG
Dave Andreychuk	Toronto	21	5
Brett Hull	St Louis	11	3
Pierre Turgeon	NY Islanders	11	3
Kirk Muller	Montreal	20	3

Goal Scoring

Name	Team	GP	G
Wayne Gretzky	Los Angeles	24	15
Ray Ferraro	NY Islanders	18	13
Dave Andreychuk	Toronto	21	12
Vincent Damphousse	Montreal	20	11
Kirk Muller	Montreal	20	10
Wendel Clark	Toronto	21	10
Doug Gilmour	Toronto	21	10
Steve Thomas	NY Islanders	18	9
Jari Kurri	Los Angeles	24	9
Luc Robitaille	Los Angeles	24	9
Brett Hull	St Louis	11	8
Mario Lemieux	Pittsburgh	11	8
Paul Di Pietro	Montreal	17	8
Tomas Sandstrom	Los Angeles	24	8

Assists

Name	Team	GP	A
Doug Gilmour	Toronto	21	25
Wayne Gretzky	Los Angeles	24	25
Tomas Sandstrom	Los Angeles	24	17
Mike Keane	Montreal	19	13
Luc Robitaille	Los Angeles	24	13
Vincent Damphousse	Montreal	20	12
Ron Francis	Pittsburgh	12	11
Larry Murphy	Pittsburgh	12	11
Kevin Stevens	Pittsburgh	12	11
Derek King	NY Islanders	18	11
Glenn Anderson	Toronto	21	11
Tony Granato	Los Angeles	24	11

Power-play Goals

Name	Team	GP	PP
Brett Hull	St Louis	11	5
Greg Adams	Vancouver	12	5
Vincent Damphousse	Montreal	20	5

Game-winning Goals

Name	Team	GP	GW
Vincent Damphousse	Montreal	20	3
John LeClair	Montreal	20	3
Kirk Muller	Montreal	20	3
Dave Andreychuk	Toronto	21	3
Wayne Gretzky	Los Angeles	24	3

Short-handed Goals

Name	Team	GP	SH
Benoit Hogue	NY Islanders	18	2
Tom Fitzgerald	NY Islanders	18	2
Dave Taylor	Los Angeles	22	2
Jari Kurri	Los Angeles	24	2

Overtime Goals

Name	Team	GP	OT
Ray Ferraro	NY Islanders	18	2
Guy Carbonneau	Montreal	20	2
John LeClair	Montreal	20	2
Kirk Muller	Montreal	20	2

Shots

Name	Team	GP	S
Tony Granato	Los Angeles	24	77
Wayne Gretzky	Los Angeles	24	76
Brian Bellows	Montreal	18	72
Dave Andreychuk	Toronto	21	72
Wendel Clark	Toronto	21	71
Luc Robitaille	Los Angeles	24	71

Plus/Minus

Name	Team	GP	+/–
Doug Gilmour	Toronto	21	16
Wendel Clark	Toronto	21	15
Matt Schneider	Montreal	11	10
Mike Ramsey	Pittsburgh	12	10
Mike Keane	Montreal	19	10

Team Statistics

TEAMS' HOME-AND-ROAD RECORD

	Home						Road					
	GP	W	L	GF	GA	%	GP	W	L	GF	GA	%
MTL	11	10	1	40	24	.909	9	6	3	26	27	.667
L.A.	11	6	5	44	43	.545	13	7	6	49	48	.538
TOR	11	7	4	37	26	.636	10	4	6	32	37	.400
NYI	8	6	2	32	25	.750	10	3	7	26	40	.300
STL	5	4	1	14	11	.800	6	3	3	10	17	.500
PIT	7	5	2	32	16	.714	5	2	3	18	21	.400
VAN	6	3	3	21	20	.500	6	3	3	25	23	.500
BUF	4	2	2	16	16	.500	4	2	2	15	12	.500
DET	4	2	2	19	14	.500	3	1	2	11	10	.333
CGY	3	1	2	16	19	.333	3	1	2	12	14	.333
WSH	3	2	1	13	10	.667	3	0	3	9	13	.000
WPG	3	1	2	9	11	.333	3	1	2	8	10	.333
QUE	3	2	1	11	8	.667	3	0	3	5	11	.000
N.J.	2	1	1	7	5	.500	3	0	3	6	11	.000
BOS	2	0	2	4	9	.000	2	0	2	8	10	.000
CHI	2	0	2	3	6	.000	2	0	2	3	7	.000
TOTAL	85	52	33	318	263	.612	85	33	52	263	318	.388

TEAMS' POWER-PLAY RECORD

Abbreviations: Adv-total advantages; **PPGF**-power play goals for; **%** arrived by dividing number of power-play goals by total advantages.

	Home						Road						Overall			
	Team	GP	ADV	PPGF	%	Team	GP	ADV	PPGF	%	Team	GP	ADV	PPGF	%	
1	WSH	3	14	6	42.9	DET	3	14	5	35.7	WSH	6	26	9	34.6
2	QUE	3	9	3	33.3	WPG	3	12	4	33.3	DET	7	30	10	33.3
3	DET	4	16	5	31.3	BOS	2	10	3	30.0	WPG	6	23	6	26.1
4	N.J.	2	11	3	27.3	BUF	4	18	5	27.8	BUF	8	39	10	25.6
5	CGY	3	19	5	26.3	WSH	3	12	3	25.0	PIT	12	52	12	23.1
6	VAN	6	31	8	25.8	PIT	5	18	4	22.2	CGY	6	40	9	22.5
7	L.A.	11	62	15	24.2	CGY	3	21	4	19.0	QUE	6	18	4	22.2
8	BUF	4	21	5	23.8	STL	6	21	4	19.0	VAN	12	56	12	21.4
9	PIT	7	34	8	23.5	VAN	6	25	4	16.0	STL	11	51	10	19.6
10	STL	5	30	6	20.0	MTL	9	25	4	16.0	MTL	20	82	15	18.3
11	MTL	11	57	11	19.3	TOR	10	50	8	16.0	BOS	4	22	4	18.2
12	WPG	3	11	2	18.2	QUE	3	9	1	11.1	L.A.	24	133	22	16.5
13	TOR	11	54	9	16.7	L.A.	13	71	7	9.9	TOR	21	104	17	16.3
14	NYI	8	36	5	13.9	NYI	10	49	3	6.1	N.J.	5	28	4	14.3
15	BOS	2	12	1	8.3	N.J.	3	17	1	5.9	NYI	18	85	8	9.4
16	CHI	2	13	1	7.7	CHI	2	11	0	.0	CHI	4	24	1	4.2
	TOTAL	85	430	93	21.6		85	383	60	15.7		85	813	153	18.8

TEAMS' PENALTY KILLING RECORD

Abbreviations: TSH – Total times short-handed; **PPGA** – power-play goals against; **%** arrived by dividing times short minus power-play goals against by times short.

	Home						Road						Overall			
	Team	GP	TSH	PPGA	%	Team	GP	TSH	PPGA	%	Team	GP	TSH	PPGA	%	
1	QUE	3	5	0	100.0	DET	3	17	1	94.1	WSH	6	30	2	93.3
2	PIT	7	37	2	94.6	WSH	3	15	1	93.3	DET	7	34	4	88.2
3	WSH	3	15	1	93.3	CGY	3	20	2	90.0	CGY	6	40	5	87.5
4	N.J.	2	9	1	88.9	WPG	3	14	2	85.7	WPG	6	29	4	86.2
5	STL	5	27	3	88.9	MTL	9	34	6	82.4	PIT	12	61	9	85.2
6	WPG	3	15	2	86.7	NYI	10	48	9	81.3	MTL	20	86	13	84.9
7	MTL	11	52	7	86.5	STL	6	30	6	80.0	STL	11	57	9	84.2
8	CGY	3	20	3	85.0	L.A.	13	71	16	77.5	QUE	6	21	4	81.0
9	TOR	11	43	7	83.7	BOS	2	12	3	75.0	NYI	18	76	15	80.3
10	DET	4	17	3	82.4	CHI	2	16	4	75.0	L.A.	24	126	26	79.4
11	VAN	6	28	5	82.1	QUE	3	16	4	75.0	VAN	12	56	12	78.6
12	L.A.	11	55	10	81.8	BUF	4	20	5	75.0	TOR	21	90	21	76.7
13	NYI	8	28	6	78.6	VAN	6	28	7	75.0	N.J.	5	27	7	74.1
14	BOS	2	7	2	71.4	PIT	5	24	7	70.8	BOS	4	19	5	73.7
15	BUF	4	16	5	68.8	TOR	10	47	14	70.2	BUF	8	36	10	72.2
16	CHI	2	9	3	66.7	N.J.	3	18	6	66.7	CHI	4	25	7	72.0
	TOTAL	85	383	60	84.3		85	430	93	78.4		85	813	153	81.2

SHORT-HANDED GOALS

	For			Against		
Team	Games	Goals	Team	Games	Goals	
L.A.	24	6	STL	11	0
NYI	18	5	DET	7	0
DET	7	4	QUE	6	0
CGY	6	3	WPG	6	0
PIT	12	2	MTL	20	1
BOS	4	1	WSH	6	1
N.J.	5	1	CGY	6	1
WSH	6	1	N.J.	5	1
WPG	6	1	BOS	4	1
BUF	8	1	CHI	4	1
STL	11	1	NYI	18	2
MTL	20	1	VAN	12	2
CHI	4	0	BUF	8	2
QUE	6	0	L.A.	24	3
VAN	12	0	PIT	12	5
TOR	21	0	TOR	21	7
TOTAL	85	27	**TOTAL**	85	27

TEAM PENALTIES

Abbreviations: GP – games played; **PEN** – total penalty minutes, including bench penalties; **BMI** – total bench penalty minutes; **AVG** – average penalty minutes per game.

Team	GP	PEN	BMI	AVG
MTL	20	277	0	13.9
BOS	4	56	0	14.0
WPG	6	85	0	14.2
BUF	8	116	0	14.5
QUE	6	94	2	15.7
VAN	12	188	2	15.7
PIT	12	200	0	16.7
STL	11	185	0	16.8
NYI	18	313	2	17.4
CHI	4	74	2	18.5
L.A.	24	448	4	18.7
TOR	21	413	0	19.7
N.J.	5	99	0	19.8
WSH	6	134	2	22.3
DET	7	163	2	23.3
CGY	6	213	0	35.5
TOTAL	85	3058	16	36.0

Leaf defender Todd Gill, seen here tying up Detroit's Steve Yzerman during the 1993 Norris Division semi-finals, collected ten assists during the 1993 playoffs.

Stanley Cup Record Book

History: The Stanley Cup, the oldest trophy competed for by professional athletes in North America, was donated by Frederick Arthur, Lord Stanley of Preston and son of the Earl of Derby, in 1893. Lord Stanley purchased the trophy for 10 guineas ($50 at that time) for presentation to the amateur hockey champions of Canada. Since 1910, when the National Hockey Association took possession of the Stanley Cup, the trophy has been the symbol of professional hockey supremacy. It has been competed for only by NHL teams since 1926 and has been under the exclusive control of the NHL since 1946.

Stanley Cup Standings

1918-93
(ranked by Cup wins)

Teams	Cup Wins	Yrs.	Series	Wins	Losses	Games Wins	Losses	Ties	Goals For	Goals Against	Winning %
Montreal	23*	68	129**	84	44	610 371	231	8	1901	1496	.615
Toronto	13	55	85	45	40	395 188	204	3	1030	1087	.480
Detroit	7	42	71	36	35	344 165	178	1	933	942	.481
Boston	5	54	94	45	49	453 220	227	6	1345	1344	.492
Edmonton	5	13	37	29	8	180 120	60	0	770	579	.667
NY Islanders	4	16	42	30	12	214 128	86	0	745	628	.598
Chicago	3	48	82	37	45	368 168	195	5	1072	1188	.463
NY Rangers	3	44	75	34	41	327 149	170	8	905	954	.468
Philadelphia	2	20	43	25	18	223 116	107	0	715	688	.520
Pittsburgh	2	13	24	13	11	119 67	52	0	406	385	.563
Calgary***	1	19	29	12	17	138 63	75	0	467	508	.457
St. Louis	0	23	40	17	23	206 93	113	0	595	684	.451
Los Angeles	0	19	29	10	19	142 55	87	0	459	568	.387
Buffalo	0	18	28	10	18	131 58	73	0	421	448	.443
Dallas****	0	17	31	14	17	166 80	86	0	554	579	.482
Vancouver	0	13	18	5	13	83 33	50	0	251	299	.398
Washington	0	11	17	6	11	92 42	50	0	306	307	.457
Winnipeg	0	10	12	2	10	56 17	39	0	167	233	.304
Quebec	0	8	14	6	8	74 33	41	0	228	261	.446
Hartford	0	8	9	1	8	49 18	31	0	143	177	.367
New Jersey*****	0	6	8	2	6	47 20	27	0	147	170	.426

   * Montreal also won the Stanley Cup in 1916.
  ** 1919 final incomplete due to influenza epidemic.
 *** Includes totals of Atlanta 1972-80.
**** Includes totals of Minnesota 1967-93.
***** Includes totals of Colorado 1976-82.

Stanley Cup Winners Prior to Formation of NHL in 1917

Season	Champions	Manager	Coach
1916-17	Seattle Metropolitans	Pete Muldoon	Pete Muldoon
1915-16	Montreal Canadiens	George Kennedy	George Kennedy
1914-15	Vancouver Millionaires	Frank Patrick	Frank Patrick
1913-14	Toronto Blueshirts	Jack Marshall	Scotty Davidson*
1912-13**	Quebec Bulldogs	M.J. Quinn	Joe Malone*
1911-12	Quebec Bulldogs	M.J. Quinn	C. Nolan
1910-11	Ottawa Senators		Bruce Stuart*
1909-10	Montreal Wanderers	R. R. Boon	Pud Glass*
1908-09	Ottawa Senators		Bruce Stuart*
1907-08	Montreal Wanderers	R. R. Boon	Cecil Blachford
1906-07	Montreal Wanderers (March)	R. R. Boon	Cecil Blachford
1906-07	Kenora Thistles (January)	F.A. Hudson	Tommy Phillips*
1905-06	Montreal Wanderers		Cecil Blachford*
1904-05	Ottawa Silver Seven		A. T. Smith
1903-04	Ottawa Silver Seven		A. T. Smith
1902-03	Ottawa Silver Seven		A. T. Smith
1901-02	Montreal A.A.A.		C. McKerrow
1900-01	Winnipeg Victorias		D. H. Bain
1899-1900	Montreal Shamrocks		H.J. Trihey*
1898-99	Montreal Shamrocks		H.J. Trihey*
1897-98	Montreal Victorias		F. Richardson
1896-97	Montreal Victorias		Mike Grant*
1895-96 (December, 1896)	Montreal Victorias		Mike Grant*
1895-96	Winnipeg Victorias (February)		J.C. G. Armytage
1894-95	Montreal Victorias		Mike Grant*
1893-94	Montreal A.A.A.		
1892-93	Montreal A.A.A.		

** Victoria defeated Quebec in challenge series. No official recognition.
 * In the early years the teams were frequently run by the Captain. *Indicates Captain

Stanley Cup Winners

Season	Champions	Manager	Coach
1992-93	Montreal Canadiens	Serge Savard	Jacques Demers
1991-92	Pittsburgh Penguins	Craig Patrick	Scotty Bowman
1990-91	Pittsburgh Penguins	Craig Patrick	Bob Johnson
1989-90	Edmonton Oilers	Glen Sather	John Muckler
1988-89	Calgary Flames	Cliff Fletcher	Terry Crisp
1987-88	Edmonton Oilers	Glen Sather	Glen Sather
1986-87	Edmonton Oilers	Glen Sather	Glen Sather
1985-86	Montreal Canadiens	Serge Savard	Jean Perron
1984-85	Edmonton Oilers	Glen Sather	Glen Sather
1983-84	Edmonton Oilers	Glen Sather	Glen Sather
1982-83	New York Islanders	Bill Torrey	Al Arbour
1981-82	New York Islanders	Bill Torrey	Al Arbour
1980-81	New York Islanders	Bill Torrey	Al Arbour
1979-80	New York Islanders	Bill Torrey	Al Arbour
1978-79	Montreal Canadiens	Irving Grundman	Scotty Bowman
1977-78	Montreal Canadiens	Sam Pollock	Scotty Bowman
1976-77	Montreal Canadiens	Sam Pollock	Scotty Bowman
1975-76	Montreal Canadiens	Sam Pollock	Scotty Bowman
1974-75	Philadelphia Flyers	Keith Allen	Fred Shero
1973-74	Philadelphia Flyers	Keith Allen	Fred Shero
1972-73	Montreal Canadiens	Sam Pollock	Scotty Bowman
1971-72	Boston Bruins	Milt Schmidt	Tom Johnson
1970-71	Montreal Canadiens	Sam Pollock	Al MacNeil
1969-70	Boston Bruins	Milt Schmidt	Harry Sinden
1968-69	Montreal Canadiens	Sam Pollock	Claude Ruel
1967-68	Montreal Canadiens	Sam Pollock	Toe Blake
1966-67	Toronto Maple Leafs	Punch Imach	Punch Imlach
1965-66	Montreal Canadiens	Sam Pollock	Toe Blake
1964-65	Montreal Canadiens	Sam Pollock	Toe Blake
1963-64	Toronto Maple Leafs	Punch Imlach	Punch Imlach
1962-63	Toronto Maple Leafs	Punch Imlach	Punch Imlach
1961-62	Toronto Maple Leafs	Punch Imlach	Punch Imlach
1960-61	Chicago Black Hawks	Tommy Ivan	Rudy Pilous
1959-60	Montreal Canadiens	Frank Selke	Toe Blake
1958-59	Montreal Canadiens	Frank Selke	Toe Blake
1957-58	Montreal Canadiens	Frank Selke	Toe Blake
1956-57	Montreal Canadiens	Frank Selke	Toe Blake
1955-56	Montreal Canadiens	Frank Selke	Toe Blake
1954-55	Detroit Red Wings	Jack Adams	Jimmy Skinner
1953-54	Detroit Red Wings	Jack Adams	Tommy Ivan
1952-53	Montreal Canadiens	Frank Selke	Dick Irvin
1951-52	Detroit Red Wings	Jack Adams	Tommy Ivan
1950-51	Toronto Maple Leafs	Conn Smythe	Joe Primeau
1949-50	Detroit Red Wings	Jack Adams	Tommy Ivan
1948-49	Toronto Maple Leafs	Conn Smythe	Hap Day
1947-48	Toronto Maple Leafs	Conn Smythe	Hap Day
1946-47	Toronto Maple Leafs	Conn Smythe	Hap Day
1945-46	Montreal Canadiens	Tommy Gorman	Dick Irvin
1944-45	Toronto Maple Leafs	Conn Smythe	Hap Day
1943-44	Montreal Canadiens	Tommy Gorman	Dick Irvin
1942-43	Detroit Red Wings	Jack Adams	Jack Adams
1941-42	Toronto Maple Leafs	Conn Smythe	Hap Day
1940-41	Boston Bruins	Art Ross	Cooney Weiland
1939-40	New York Rangers	Lester Patrick	Frank Boucher
1938-39	Boston Bruins	Art Ross	Art Ross
1937-38	Chicago Black Hawks	Bill Stewart	Bill Stewart
1936-37	Detroit Red Wings	Jack Adams	Jack Adams
1935-36	Detroit Red Wings	Jack Adams	Jack Adams
1934-35	Montreal Maroons	Tommy Gorman	Tommy Gorman
1933-34	Chicago Black Hawks	Tommy Gorman	Tommy Gorman
1932-33	New York Rangers	Lester Patrick	Lester Patrick
1931-32	Toronto Maple Leafs	Conn Smythe	Dick Irvin
1930-31	Montreal Canadiens	Cecil Hart	Cecil Hart
1929-30	Montreal Canadiens	Cecil Hart	Cecil Hart
1928-29	Boston Bruins	Art Ross	Cy Denneny
1927-28	New York Rangers	Lester Patrick	Lester Patrick
1926-27	Ottawa Senators	Dave Gill	Dave Gill
1925-26	Montreal Maroons	Eddie Gerard	Eddie Gerard
1924-25	Victoria Cougars	Lester Patrick	Lester Patrick
1923-24	Montreal Canadiens	Leo Dandurand	Leo Dandurand
1922-23	Ottawa Senators	Tommy Gorman	Pete Green
1921-22	Toronto St. Pats	Charlie Querrie	Eddie Powers
1920-21	Ottawa Senators	Tommy Gorman	Pete Green
1919-20	Ottawa Senators	Tommy Gorman	Pete Green
1918-19	No decision*		
1917-18	Toronto Arenas	Charlie Querrie	Dick Carroll

* In the spring of 1919 the Montreal Canadiens travelled to Seattle to meet Seattle, PCHA champions. After five games had been played — teams were tied at 2 wins and 1 tie — the series was called off by the local Department of Health because of an influenza epidemic and the death from influenza of Montreal's Joe Hall.

Championship Trophies

PRINCE OF WALES TROPHY

Beginning with the 1993-94 season, the club which advances to the Stanley Cup Finals as the winner of the Eastern Conference Championship is presented with the Prince of Wales Trophy.

History: His Royal Highness, the Prince of Wales, donated the trophy to the National Hockey League in 1924. From 1927-28 through 1937-38, the award was presented to the team finishing first in the American Division of the NHL. From 1938-39, when the NHL reverted to one section, to 1966-67, it was presented to the team winning the NHL regular season championship. With expansion in 1967-68, it again became a divisional trophy, awarded to the regular season champions of the East Division through to the end of the 1973-74 season. Beginning in 1974-75, it was awarded to the regular-season winner of the conference bearing the name of the trophy. Starting with the 1981-82 season, the trophy was presented to the playoff champion in the Wales Conference. Starting with the 1993-94 season, the trophy will be presented to the playoff champion in the Eastern Conference.

1992-93 Winner: Montreal Canadiens

The Montreal Canadiens won their first Prince of Wales Trophy since the 1988-89 season on May 24, 1993 after defeating the New York Islanders in game five of the Prince of Wales Conference Championship series. Before defeating the Islanders, the Canadiens had series wins over Quebec and Buffalo.

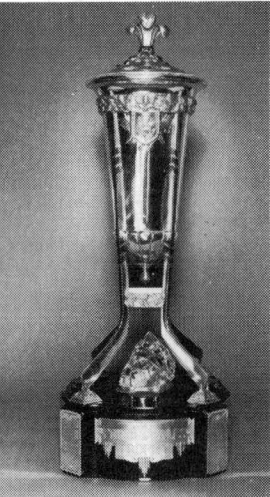

Prince of Wales Trophy

Stanley Cup

PRINCE OF WALES TROPHY WINNERS		
1992-93	**Montreal Canadiens**	1957-58	Montreal Canadiens
1991-92	Pittsburgh Penguins	1956-57	Detroit Red Wings
1990-91	Pittsburgh Penguins	1955-56	Montreal Canadiens
1989-90	Boston Bruins	1954-55	Detroit Red Wings
1988-89	Montreal Canadiens	1953-54	Detroit Red Wings
1987-88	Boston Bruins	1952-53	Detroit Red Wings
1986-87	Philadelphia Flyers	1951-52	Detroit Red Wings
1985-86	Montreal Canadiens	1950-51	Detroit Red Wings
1984-85	Philadelphia Flyers	1949-50	Detroit Red Wings
1983-84	New York Islanders	1948-49	Detroit Red Wings
1982-83	New York Islanders	1947-48	Toronto Maple Leafs
1981-82	New York Islanders	1946-47	Montreal Canadiens
1980-81	Montreal Canadiens	1945-46	Montreal Canadiens
1979-80	Buffalo Sabres	1944-45	Montreal Canadiens
1978-79	Montreal Canadiens	1943-44	Montreal Canadiens
1977-78	Montreal Canadiens	1942-43	Detroit Red Wings
1976-77	Montreal Canadiens	1941-42	New York Rangers
1975-76	Montreal Canadiens	1940-41	Boston Bruins
1974-75	Buffalo Sabres	1939-40	Boston Bruins
1973-74	Boston Bruins	1938-39	Boston Bruins
1972-73	Montreal Canadiens	1937-38	Boston Bruins
1971-72	Boston Bruins	1936-37	Detroit Red Wings
1970-71	Boston Bruins	1935-36	Detroit Red Wings
1969-70	Chicago Blackhawks	1934-35	Boston Bruins
1968-69	Montreal Canadiens	1933-34	Detroit Red Wings
1967-68	Montreal Canadiens	1932-33	Boston Bruins
1966-67	Chicago Blackhawks	1931-32	New York Rangers
1965-66	Montreal Canadiens	1930-31	Boston Bruins
1964-65	Detroit Red Wings	1929-30	Boston Bruins
1963-64	Montreal Canadiens	1928-29	Boston Bruins
1962-63	Toronto Maple Leafs	1927-28	Boston Bruins
1961-62	Montreal Canadiens	1926-27	Ottawa Senators
1960-61	Montreal Canadiens	1925-26	Montreal Maroons
1959-60	Montreal Canadiens	1924-25	Montreal Canadiens
1958-59	Montreal Canadiens	1923-24	Montreal Canadiens

CLARENCE S. CAMPBELL BOWL

Beginning with the 1993-94 season, the club which advances to the Stanley Cup Finals as the winner of the Western Conference Championship is presented with the Clarence S. Campbell Bowl.

History: Presented by the member clubs in 1968 for perpetual competition by the National Hockey League in recognition of the services of Clarence S. Campbell, President of the NHL from 1946 to 1977. From 1967-68 through 1973-74, the trophy was awarded to the regular season champions of the West Division. Beginning in 1974-75, it was awarded to the regular-season winner of the conference bearing the name of the trophy. Starting with the 1981-82 season, the trophy was presented to the playoff champion in the Campbell Conference. Starting with the 1993-94 season, the trophy will be presented to the playoff champion in the Western Conference. The trophy itself is a hallmark piece made of sterling silver and was crafted by a British silversmith in 1878.

1992-93 Winner: Los Angeles Kings

The Los Angeles Kings won their first Clarence S. Campbell Bowl in team history after defeating the Toronto Maple Leafs in game seven of the Clarence S. Campbell Conference Championship series. Prior to facing the Maple Leafs, Los Angeles had series wins over Calgary and Vancouver.

Clarence S. Campbell Bowl

CLARENCE S. CAMPBELL BOWL WINNERS		
		1980-81	New York Islanders
1992-93	**Los Angeles Kings**	1979-80	Philadelphia Flyers
1991-92	Chicago Blackhawks	1978-79	New York Islanders
1990-91	Minnesota North Stars	1977-78	New York Islanders
1989-90	Edmonton Oilers	1976-77	Philadelphia Flyers
1988-89	Calgary Flames	1975-76	Philadelphia Flyers
1987-88	Edmonton Oilers	1974-75	Philadelphia Flyers
1986-87	Edmonton Oilers	1973-74	Philadelphia Flyers
1985-86	Calgary Flames	1972-73	Chicago Blackhawks
1984-85	Edmonton Oilers	1971-72	Chicago Blackhawks
1983-84	Edmonton Oilers	1970-71	Chicago Blackhawks
1982-83	Edmonton Oilers	1969-70	St. Louis Blues
1981-82	Vancouver Canucks	1968-69	St. Louis Blues
		1967-68	Philadelphia Flyers

Stanley Cup Winners:

Rosters and Final Series Scores

1992-93 — Montreal Canadiens — Guy Carbonneau (Captain), Patrick Roy, Mike Keane, Eric Desjardins, Stephan Lebeau, Mathieu Schneider, Jean-Jacques Daigneault, Denis Savard, Lyle Odelein, Todd Ewen, Kirk Muller, John LeClair, Gilbert Dionne, Benoit Brunet, Patrice Brisebois, Paul Di Pietro, Andre Racicot, Donald Dufresne, Mario Roberge, Sean Hill, Ed Ronan, Kevin Haller, Vincent Damphousse, Brian Bellows, Gary Leeman, Rob Ramage, Ronald Corey (President), Serge Savard (Managing Director & Vice-President Hockey), Jacques Demers (Head Coach), Jacques Laperriere (Assistant Coach), Charles Thiffault (Assistant Coach), Francois Allaire (Goaltending Instructor), Jean Béliveau (Senior Vice-President, Corporate Affairs), Fred Steer (Vice-President, Finance & Adminstration), Aldo Giampaolo (Vice-President, Operations), Bernard Brisset (Vice-President, Marketing & Communications), André Boudrias (Assistant to the Managing Director & Director of Scouting), Jacques Lemaire (Assistant to the Managing Director), Gaeten Lefebvre (Athletic Trainer), John Shipman (Assistant to the Athletic Trainer), Eddy Palchak (Equipment Manager), Pierre Gervais (Assistant to the Equipment Manager), Robert Boulanger (Assistant to the Equipment Manager), Pierre Ouellete (Assistant to the Equipment Manager).
Scores: June 1 at Montreal — Los Angeles 4, Montreal 1; June 2 at Montreal — Montreal 3, Los Angeles 2; June 5 at Los Angeles — Montreal 4, Los Angeles 3; June 7 at Los Angeles — Montreal 3, Los Angeles 2; June 9 at Montreal — Montreal 4, Los Angeles 1.

1991-92 — Pittsburgh Penguins — Mario Lemieux (Captain), Ron Francis, Bryan Trottier, Kevin Stevens, Bob Errey, Phil Bourque, Troy Loney, Rick Tocchet, Joe Mullen, Jaromir Jagr, Jiri Hrdina, Shawn McEachern, Ulf Samuelsson, Kjell Samuelsson, Larry Murphy, Gord Roberts, Jim Paek, Paul Stanton, Tom Barrasso, Ken Wregget, Jay Caufield, Jamie Leach, Wendell Young, Grant Jennings, Peter Taglianetti, Jock Callander, Dave Michayluk, Mike Needham, Jeff Chychrun, Ken Priestlay, Jeff Daniels, Howard Baldwin (Owner and President), Morris Belzberg (Owner), Thomas Ruta (Owner), Donn Patton (Executive Vice President and Chief Financial Officer), Paul Martha (Executive Vice President and General Counsel), Craig Patrick (Executive Vice President and General Manager), Bob Johnson (Coach), Scotty Bowman (Director of Player Development and Coach), Barry Smith, Rick Kehoe, Pierre McGuire, Gilles Meloche, Rick Paterson (Assistant Coaches), Steve Latin (Equipment Manager), Skip Thayer (Trainer), John Welday (Strength and Conditioning Coach), Greg Malone, Les Binkley, Charlie Hodge, John Gill, Ralph Cox (Scouts).
Scores: May 26 at Pittsburgh — Pittsburgh 5, Chicago 4; May 28 at Pittsburgh — Pittsburgh 3, Chicago 1; May 30 at Chicago — Pittsburgh 1, Chicago 0; June 1 at Chicago — Pittsburgh 6, Chicago 5.

1990-91 — Pittsburgh Penguins — Mario Lemieux (Captain), Paul Coffey, Randy Hillier, Bob Errey, Tom Barrasso, Phil Bourque, Jay Caufield, Ron Francis, Randy Gilhen, Jiri Hrdina, Jaromir Jagr, Grant Jennings, Troy Loney, Joe Mullen, Larry Murphy, Jim Paek, Frank Pietrangelo, Barry Pederson, Mark Recchi, Gordie Roberts, Ulf Samuelsson, Paul Stanton, Kevin Stevens, Peter Taglianetti, Bryan Trottier, Scott Young, Wendell Young, Edward J. DeBartolo, Sr. (Owner), Marie D. DeBartolo York (President), Paul Martha (Vice-President & General Counsel), Craig Patrick (General Manager), Scotty Bowman (Director of Player Development & Recruitment), Bob Johnson (Coach), Rick Kehoe (Assistant Coach), Gilles Meloche (Goaltending Coach & Scout), Rick Paterson (Assistant Coach), Barry Smith (Assistant Coach), Steve Latin (Equipment Manager), Skip Thayer (Trainer), John Welday (Strength & Conditioning Coach), Greg Malone (Scout).
Scores: May 15 at Pittsburgh — Minnesota 5, Pittsburgh 4; May 17 at Pittsburgh — Pittsburgh 4, Minnesota 1; May 19 at Minnesota — Minnesota 3, Pittsburgh 1; May 21 at Minnesota — Pittsburgh 5, Minnesota 3; May 23 at Pittsburgh — Pittsburgh 6, Minnesota 4; May 25 at Minnesota — Pittsburgh 8, Minnesota 0.

1989-90 — Edmonton Oilers — Kevin Lowe, Steve Smith, Jeff Beukeboom, Mark Lamb, Joe Murphy, Glenn Anderson, Mark Messier, Adam Graves, Craig MacTavish, Kelly Buchberger, Jari Kurri, Craig Simpson, Martin Gelinas, Randy Gregg, Charlie Huddy, Geoff Smith, Reijo Ruotsalainen, Craig Muni, Bill Ranford, Dave Brown, Eldon Reddick, Petr Klima, Esa Tikkanen, Grant Fuhr, Peter Pocklington (Owner), Glen Sather (President/General Manager), John Muckler (Coach), Ted Green (Co-Coach), Ron Low (Ass't Coach), Bruce MacGregor (Ass't General Manager), Barry Fraser (Director of Player Personnel), John Blackwell (Director of Operations, AHL), Ace Bailey, Ed Chadwick, Lorne Davis, Harry Howell, Matti Vaisanen and Albert Reeves (Scouts), Bill Tuele (Director of Public Relations), Werner Baum (Controller), Dr. Gordon Cameron (Medical Chief of Staff), Dr. David Reid (Team Physician), Barrie Stafford (Athletic Trainer), Ken Lowe (Athletic Therapist), Stuart Poirier (Massage Therapist), Lyle Kulchisky (Ass't Trainer).
Scores: May 15 at Boston — Edmonton 3, Boston 2; May 18 at Boston — Edmonton 7, Boston 2; May 20 at Edmonton — Boston 2, Edmonton 1; May 22 at Edmonton — Edmonton 5, Boston 1; May 24 at Boston — Edmonton 4, Boston 1.

1988-89 — Calgary Flames — Mike Vernon, Rick Wamsley, Al MacInnis, Brad McCrimmon, Dana Murzyn, Ric Nattress, Joe Mullen, Lanny McDonald (Co-captain), Gary Roberts, Colin Patterson, Hakan Loob, Theoren Fleury, Jiri Hrdina, Tim Hunter (Ass't. captain), Gary Suter, Mark Hunter, Jim Peplinski (Co-captain), Joe Nieuwendyk, Brian MacLellan, Joel Otto, Jamie Macoun, Doug Gilmour, Rob Ramage. Norman Green, Harley Hotchkiss, Norman Kwong, Sonia Scurfield, B.J. Seaman, D.K. Seaman (Owners), Cliff Fletcher (President and General Manager), Al MacNeil (Ass't General Manager), Al Coates (Ass't to the President), Terry Crisp (Head Coach), Doug Risebrough, Tom Watt (Ass't Coaches), Glenn Hall (Goaltending Consultant), Jim Murray (Trainer), Bob Stewart (Equipment Manager), Al Murray (Ass't Trainer).
Scores: May 14 at Calgary — Calgary 3, Montreal 2; May 17 at Calgary— Montreal 4, Calgary 2; May 19 at Montreal — Montreal 4, Calgary 3; May 21 at Montreal — Calgary 4, Montreal 2; May 23 at Calgary — Calgary 3, Montreal 2; May 25 at Montreal — Calgary 4, Montreal 2.

1987-88 — Edmonton Oilers — Keith Acton, Glenn Anderson, Jeff Beukeboom, Geoff Courtnall, Grant Fuhr, Randy Gregg, Wayne Gretzky, Dave Hannan, Charlie Huddy, Mike Krushelnyski, Jari Kurri, Normand Lacombe, Kevin Lowe, Craig MacTavish, Kevin McClelland, Marty McSorley, Mark Messier, Craig Muni, Bill Ranford, Craig Simpson, Steve Smith, Esa Tikkanen, Peter Pocklington (Owner), Glen Sather (General Manager/Coach), John Muckler (Co-Coach), Ted Green (Ass't Coach), Barry Fraser (Director of Player Personnel), Bill Tuele (Director of Public Relations), Dr. Gordon Cameron (Team Physician), Peter Millar (Athletic Therapist), Barrie Stafford (Trainer), Juergen Mers (Massage Therapist), Lyle Kulchisky (Ass't Trainer).
Scores: May 18 at Edmonton — Edmonton 2, Boston 1; May 20 at Edmonton — Edmonton 4, Boston 2; May 22 at Boston — Edmonton 6, Boston 3; May 24 at Boston — Boston 3, Edmonton 3 (suspended due to power failure); May 26 at Edmonton — Edmonton 6, Boston 3.

1986-87 — Edmonton Oilers — Glenn Anderson, Jeff Beukeboom, Kelly Buchberger, Paul Coffey, Grant Fuhr, Randy Gregg, Wayne Gretzky, Charlie Huddy, Dave Hunter, Mike Krushelnyski, Jari Kurri, Moe Lemay, Kevin Lowe, Craig MacTavish, Kevin McClelland, Marty McSorley, Mark Messier, Andy Moog, Craig Muni, Kent Nilsson, Jaroslav Pouzar, Reijo Ruotsalainen, Steve Smith, Esa Tikkanen, Peter Pocklington (Owner), Glen Sather (General Manager/Coach), John Muckler (Co-Coach), Ted Green (Ass't. Coach), Ron Low (Ass't. Coach), Bruce MacGregor (Ass't General Manager), Barry Fraser (Director of Player Personnel), Peter Millar (Athletic Therapist), Barrie Stafford (Trainer), Lyle Kulchisky (Ass't Trainer).
Scores: May 17 at Edmonton — Edmonton 4, Philadelphia 3; May 20 at Edmonton — Edmonton 3, Philadelphia 2; May 22 at Philadelphia — Philadelphia 5, Edmonton 3; May 24 at Philadelphia — Edmonton 4, Philadelphia 1; May 26 at Edmonton — Philadelphia 4, Edmonton 3; May 28 at Philadelphia — Philadelphia 3, Edmonton 2; May 31 at Edmonton — Edmonton 3, Philadelphia 1.

1985-86 — Montreal Canadiens — Bob Gainey, Doug Soetaert, Patrick Roy, Rick Green, David Maley, Ryan Walter, Serge Boisvert, Mario Tremblay, Bobby Smith, Craig Ludwig, Tom Kurvers, Kjell Dahlin, Larry Robinson, Guy Carbonneau, Chris Chelios, Petr Svoboda, Mats Naslund, Lucien DeBlois, Steve Rooney, Gaston Gingras, Mike Lalor, Chris Nilan, John Kordic, Claude Lemieux, Mike McPhee, Brian Skrudland, Stephane Richer, Ronald Corey (President), Serge Savard (General Manager), Jean Perron (Coach), Jacques Laperrière (Ass't. Coach), Jean Béliveau (Vice President), Francois-Xavier Seigneur (Vice President), Fred Steer (Vice President), Jacques Lemaire (Ass't. General Manager), André Boudrias (Ass't. General Manager), Claude Ruel, Yves Belanger (Athletic Therapist), Gaetan Lefebvre (Ass't. Athletic Therapist), Eddy Palchek (Trainer), Sylvain Toupin (Ass't. Trainer).
Scores: May 16 at Calgary — Calgary 5, Montreal 3; May 18 at Calgary — Montreal 3, Calgary 2; May 20 at Montreal — Montreal 5, Calgary 3; May 22 at Montreal — Montreal 1, Calgary 0; May 24 at Calgary — Montreal 4, Calgary 3.

Calgary's Mike Vernon had three shutouts and 16 wins en route to the Stanley Cup for the Calgary Flames in 1988-89.

1984-85 — Edmonton Oilers — Glenn Anderson, Bill Carroll, Paul Coffey, Lee Fogolin, Grant Fuhr, Randy Gregg, Wayne Gretzky, Charlie Huddy, Pat Hughes, Dave Hunter, Don Jackson, Mike Krushelnyski, Jari Kurri, Willy Lindstrom, Kevin Lowe, Dave Lumley, Kevin McClelland, Larry Melnyk, Mark Messier, Andy Moog, Mark Napier, Jaroslav Pouzar, Dave Semenko, Esa Tikkanen, Peter Pocklington (Owner), Glen Sather (General Manager/Coach), John Muckler (Ass't. Coach), Ted Green (Ass't. Coach), Bruce MacGregor (Ass't. General Manager), Barry Fraser (Director of Player Personnel/Chief Scout), Peter Millar (Athletic Therapist), Barrie Stafford, Lyle Kulchisky (Trainers)
Scores: May 21 at Philadelphia — Philadelphia 4, Edmonton 1; May 23 at Philadelphia — Edmonton 3, Philadelphia 1; May 25 at Edmonton — Edmonton 4, Philadelphia 3; May 28 at Edmonton — Edmonton 5, Philadelphia 3; May 30 at Edmonton — Edmonton 8, Philadelphia 3.

1983-84 — Edmonton Oilers — Glenn Anderson, Paul Coffey, Pat Conacher, Lee Fogolin, Grant Fuhr, Randy Gregg, Wayne Gretzky, Charlie Huddy, Pat Hughes, Dave Hunter, Don Jackson, Jari Kurri, Willy Lindstrom, Ken Linseman, Kevin Lowe, Dave Lumley, Kevin McClelland, Mark Messier, Andy Moog, Jaroslav Pouzar, Dave Semenko, Peter Pocklington (Owner), Glen Sather (General Manager/Coach), John Muckler (Ass't. Coach), Ted Green (Ass't. Coach), Bruce MacGregor (Ass't. General Manager), Barry Fraser (Director of Player Personnel/Chief Scout), Peter Millar (Athletic Therapist), Barrie Stafford (Trainer)
Scores: May 10 at New York — Edmonton 1, NY Islanders 0; May 12 at New York — NY Islanders 6, Edmonton 1; May 15 at Edmonton — Edmonton 7, NY Islanders 2; May 17 at Edmonton — Edmonton 7, NY Islanders 2; May 19 at Edmonton — Edmonton 5, NY Islanders 2.

1982-83 — New York Islanders — Mike Bossy, Bob Bourne, Paul Boutilier, Bill Carroll, Greg Gilbert, Clark Gillies, Butch Goring, Mats Hallin, Tomas Jonsson, Anders Kallur, Gord Lane, Dave Langevin, Mike McEwen, Roland Melanson, Wayne Merrick, Ken Morrow, Bob Nystrom, Stefan Persson, Denis Potvin, Bill Smith, Brent Sutter, Duane Sutter, John Tonelli, Bryan Trottier, Al Arbour (coach), Lorne Henning (ass't coach), Bill Torrey (general manager), Ron Waske, Jim Pickard (trainers)
Scores: May 10 at Edmonton — NY Islanders 2, Edmonton 0; May 12 at Edmonton — NY Islanders 6, Edmonton 3; May 14 at New York — NY Islanders 5, Edmonton 1; May 17 at New York — NY Islanders 4, Edmonton 2

1981-82 — New York Islanders — Mike Bossy, Bob Bourne, Bill Carroll, Butch Goring, Greg Gilbert, Clark Gillies, Tomas Jonsson, Anders Kallur, Gord Lane, Dave Langevin, Hector Marini, Mike McEwen, Roland Melanson, Wayne Merrick, Ken Morrow, Bob Nystrom, Stefan Persson, Denis Potvin, Bill Smith, Brent Sutter, Duane Sutter, John Tonelli, Bryan Trottier, Al Arbour (coach), Lorne Henning (ass't coach), Bill Torrey (general manager), Ron Waske, Jim Pickard (trainers)
Scores: May 8 at New York — NY Islanders 6, Vancouver 5; May 11 at New York — NY Islanders 6, Vancouver 4; May 13 at Vancouver — NY Islanders 3, Vancouver 0; May 16 at Vancouver — NY Islanders 3, Vancouver 1

1980-81 — New York Islanders — Denis Potvin, Mike McEwen, Ken Morrow, Gord Lane, Bob Lorimer, Stefan Persson, Dave Langevin, Mike Bossy, Bryan Trottier, Butch Goring, Wayne Merrick, Clark Gillies, John Tonelli, Bob Nystrom, Bill Carroll, Bob Bourne, Hector Marini, Anders Kallur, Duane Sutter, Garry Howatt, Lorne Henning, Bill Smith, Roland Melanson, Al Arbour (coach), Bill Torrey (general manager), Ron Waske, Jim Pickard (trainers).
Scores: May 12 at New York — NY Islanders 6, Minnesota 3; May 14 at New York — NY Islanders 6, Minnesota 3; May 17 at Minnesota — NY Islanders 7, Minnesota 5; May 19 at Minnesota— Minnesota 4, NY Islanders 2; May 21 at New York — NY Islanders 5, Minnesota 1.

Boston's Bobby Orr begins his in-flight celebration after scoring the Stanley Cup-winning goal against St. Louis in the 1970 Finals.

1979-80 — New York Islanders — Gord Lane, Jean Potvin, Bob Lorimer, Denis Potvin, Stefan Persson, Ken Morrow, Dave Langevin, Duane Sutter, Garry Howatt, Clark Gillies, Lorne Henning, Wayne Merrick, Bob Bourne, Steve Tambellini, Bryan Trottier, Mike Bossy, Bob Nystrom, John Tonelli, Anders Kallur, Butch Goring, Alex McKendry, Glenn Resch, Billy Smith, Al Arbour (coach), Bill Torrey (general manager), Ron Waske, Jim Pickard (trainers).
Scores: May 13 at Philadelphia — NY Islanders 4, Philadelphia 3; May 15 at Philadelphia — Philadelphia 8, NY Islanders 3; May 17 at New York — NY Islanders 6, Philadelphia 2; May 19 at New York — NY Islanders 5, Philadelphia 2; May 22 at Philadelphia — Philadelphia 6, NY Islanders 3; May 24 at New York — NY Islanders 5, Philadelphia 4.

1978-79 — Montreal Canadiens — Ken Dryden, Larry Robinson, Serge Savard, Guy Lapointe, Brian Engblom, Gilles Lupien, Rick Chartraw, Guy Lafleur, Steve Shutt, Jacques Lemaire, Yvan Cournoyer, Réjean Houle, Pierre Mondou, Bob Gainey, Doug Jarvis, Yvon Lambert, Doug Risebrough, Pierre Larouche, Mario Tremblay, Cam Connor, Pat Hughes, Rod Langway, Mark Napier, Michel Larocque, Richard Sévigny, Scotty Bowman (coach), Irving Grundman (managing director), Eddy Palchak, Pierre Meilleur (trainers).
Scores: May 13 at Montreal — NY Rangers 4, Montreal 1; May 15 at Montreal — Montreal 6, NY Rangers 2; May 17 at New York — Montreal 4, NY Rangers 1; May 19 at New York — Montreal 4, NY Rangers 3; May 21 at Montreal — Montreal 4, NY Rangers 1.

1977-78 — Montreal Canadiens — Ken Dryden, Larry Robinson, Serge Savard, Guy Lapointe, Bill Nyrop, Pierre Bouchard, Brian Engblom, Gilles Lupien, Rick Chartraw, Guy Lafleur, Steve Shutt, Jacques Lemaire, Yvon Cournoyer, Réjean Houle, Pierre Mondou, Bob Gainey, Doug Jarvis, Yvon Lambert, Doug Risebrough, Pierre Larouche, Mario Tremblay, Michel Larocque, Murray Wilson, Scotty Bowman (coach), Sam Pollock (general manager), Eddy Palchak, Pierre Meilleur (trainers).
Scores: May 13 at Montreal — Montreal 4, Boston 1; May 16 at Montreal — Montreal 3, Boston 2; May 18 at Boston — Boston 4, Montreal 0; May 21 at Boston — Boston 4, Montreal 3; May 23 at Montreal — Montreal 4, Boston 1; May 25 at Boston — Montreal 4, Boston 1.

1976-77 — Montreal Canadiens — Ken Dryden, Guy Lapointe, Larry Robinson, Serge Savard, Jimmy Roberts, Rick Chartraw, Bill Nyrop, Pierre Bouchard, Brian Engblom, Yvan Cournoyer, Guy Lafleur, Jacques Lemaire, Steve Shutt, Pete Mahovlich, Murray Wilson, Doug Jarvis, Yvon Lambert, Bob Gainey, Doug Risebrough, Mario Tremblay, Rejean Houle, Pierre Mondou, Mike Polich, Michel Larocque, Scotty Bowman (coach), Sam Pollock (general manager), Eddy Palchak, Pierre Meilleur (trainers).
Scores: May 7 at Montreal — Montreal 7, Boston 3; May 10 at Montreal — Montreal 3, Boston 0; May 12 at Boston — Montreal 4, Boston 2; May 14 at Boston — Montreal 2, Boston 1.

1975-76 — Montreal Canadiens — Ken Dryden, Serge Savard, Guy Lapointe, Larry Robinson, Bill Nyrop, Pierre Bouchard, Jim Roberts, Guy Lafleur, Steve Shutt, Pete Mahovlich, Yvan Cournoyer, Jacques Lemaire, Yvon Lambert, Bob Gainey, Doug Jarvis, Doug Risebrough, Murray Wilson, Mario Tremblay, Rick Chartraw, Michel Larocque, Scotty Bowman (coach), Sam Pollock (general manager), Eddy Palchak, Pierre Meilleur (trainers).
Scores: May 9 at Montreal — Montreal 4, Philadelphia 3; May 11 at Montreal — Montreal 2, Philadelphia 1; May 13 at Philadelphia — Montreal 3, Philadelphia 2; May 16 at Philadelphia — Montreal 5, Philadelphia 3.

1974-75 — Philadelphia Flyers — Bernie Parent, Wayne Stephenson, Ed Van Impe, Tom Bladon, André Dupont, Joe Watson, Jim Watson, Ted Harris, Larry Goodenough, Rick MacLeish, Bobby Clarke, Bill Barber, Reggie Leach, Gary Dornhoefer, Ross Lonsberry, Bob Kelly, Terry Crisp, Don Saleski, Dave Schultz, Orest Kindrachuk, Bill Clement, Fred Shero (coach), Keith Allen (general manager), Frank Lewis, Jim McKenzie (trainers).
Scores: May 15 at Philadelphia — Philadelphia 4, Buffalo 1; May 18 at Philadelphia — Philadelphia 2, Buffalo 1; May 20 at Buffalo — Buffalo 5, Philadelphia 4; May 22 at Buffalo — Buffalo 4, Philadelphia 2; May 25 at Philadelphia — Philadelphia 5, Buffalo 1; May 27 at Buffalo — Philadelphia 2, Buffalo 0.

1973-74 — Philadelphia Flyers — Bernie Parent, Ed Van Impe, Tom Bladon, André Dupont, Joe Watson, Jim Watson, Barry Ashbee, Bill Barber, Dave Schultz, Don Saleski, Gary Dornhoefer, Terry Crisp, Bobby Clarke, Simon Nolet, Ross Lonsberry, Rick MacLeish, Bill Flett, Orest Kindrachuk, Bill Clement, Bob Kelly, Bruce Cowick, Al MacAdam, Bobby Taylor, Fred Shero (coach), Keith Allen (general manager), Frank Lewis, Jim McKenzie (trainers).
Scores: May 7 at Boston — Boston 3, Philadelphia 2; May 9 at Boston — Philadelphia 3, Boston 2; May 12 at Philadelphia — Philadelphia 4, Boston 1; May 14 at Philadelphia — Philadelphia 4, Boston 2; May 16 at Boston — Boston 5, Philadelphia 1; May 19 at Philadelphia — Philadelphia 1, Boston 0.

1972-73 — Montreal Canadiens — Ken Dryden, Guy Lapointe, Serge Savard, Larry Robinson, Jacques Laperrière, Bob Murdoch, Pierre Bouchard, Jim Roberts, Yvan Cournoyer, Frank Mahovlich, Jacques Lemaire, Pete Mahovlich, Marc Tardif, Henri Richard, Réjean Houle, Guy Lafleur, Chuck Lefley, Claude Larose, Murray Wilson, Steve Shutt, Michel Plasse, Scotty Bowman (coach), Sam Pollock (general manager), Ed Palchak, Bob Williams (trainers).
Scores: April 29 at Montreal — Montreal 8, Chicago 3; May 1 at Montreal — Montreal 4, Chicago 1; May 3 at Chicago — Chicago 7, Montreal 4; May 6 at Chicago — Montreal 4, Chicago 0; May 8 at Montreal — Chicago 8, Montreal 7; May 10 at Chicago — Montreal 6, Chicago 4.

1971-72 — Boston Bruins — Gerry Cheevers, Ed Johnston, Bobby Orr, Ted Green, Carol Vadnais, Dallas Smith, Don Awrey, Phil Esposito, Ken Hodge, John Bucyk, Mike Walton, Wayne Cashman, Garnet Bailey, Derek Sanderson, Fred Stanfield, Ed Westfall, John McKenzie, Don Marcotte, Garry Peters, Chris Hayes, Tom Johnson (coach), Milt Schmidt (general manager), Dan Canney, John Forristall (trainers).
Scores: April 30 at Boston — Boston 6, NY Rangers 5; May 2 at Boston — Boston 2, NY Rangers 1; May 4 at New York — NY Rangers 5, Boston 2; May 7 at New York — Boston 3, NY Rangers 2; May 9 at Boston — NY Rangers 3, Boston 2; May 11 at New York — Boston 3, NY Rangers 0.

1970-71 — Montreal Canadiens — Ken Dryden, Rogatien Vachon, Jacques Laperrière, Jean-Claude Tremblay, Guy Lapointe, Terry Harper, Pierre Bouchard, Jean Béliveau, Marc Tardif, Yvan Cournoyer, Réjean Houle, Claude Larose, Henri Richard, Phil Roberto, Pete Mahovlich, Leon Rochefort, John Ferguson, Bobby Sheehan, Jacques Lemaire, Frank Mahovlich, Bob Murdoch, Chuck Lefley, Al MacNeil (coach), Sam Pollock (general manager), Yvon Belanger, Ed Palchak (trainers).
Scores: May 4 at Chicago — Chicago 2, Montreal 1; May 6 at Chicago — Chicago 5, Montreal 3; May 9 at Montreal — Montreal 4, Chicago 2; May 11 at Montreal — Montreal 5, Chicago 2; May 13 at Chicago — Chicago 2, Montreal 0; May 16 at Montreal — Montreal 4, Chicago 3; May 18 at Chicago — Montreal 3, Chicago 2.

1969-70 — Boston Bruins — Gerry Cheevers, Ed Johnston, Bobby Orr, Rick Smith, Dallas Smith, Bill Speer, Gary Doak, Don Awrey, Phil Esposito, Ken Hodge, John Bucyk, Wayne Carleton, Wayne Cashman, Derek Sanderson, Fred Stanfield, Ed Westfall, John McKenzie, Jim Lorentz, Don Marcotte, Dan Schock, Harry Sinden (coach), Milt Schmidt (general manager), Dan Canney, John Forristall (trainers).
Scores: May 3 at St. Louis — Boston 6, St. Louis 1; May 5 at St. Louis — Boston 6, St. Louis 2; May 7 at Boston — Boston 4, St. Louis 1; May 10 at Boston — Boston 4, St. Louis 3.

1968-69 — Montreal Canadiens — Lorne Worsley, Rogatien Vachon, Jacques Laperrière, Jean-Claude Tremblay, Ted Harris, Serge Savard, Terry Harper, Larry Hillman, Jean Béliveau, Ralph Backstrom, Dick Duff, Yvan Cournoyer, Claude Provost, Bobby Rousseau, Henri Richard, John Ferguson, Christian Bordeleau, Mickey Redmond, Jacques Lemaire, Lucien Grenier, Tony Esposito, Claude Ruel (coach), Sam Pollock (general manager), Larry Aubut, Eddy Palchak (trainers).
Scores: April 27 at Montreal — Montreal 3, St. Louis 1; April 29 at Montreal — Montreal 3, St. Louis 1; May 1 at St. Louis — Montreal 4, St. Louis 0; May 4 at St. Louis — Montreal 2, St. Louis 1.

1967-68 — Montreal Canadiens — Lorne Worsley, Rogatien Vachon, Jacques Laperrière, Jean-Claude Tremblay, Ted Harris, Serge Savard, Terry Harper, Carol Vadnais, Jean Béliveau, Gilles Tremblay, Ralph Backstrom, Dick Duff, Claude Larose, Yvan Cournoyer, Claude Provost, Bobby Rousseau, Henri Richard, John Ferguson, Danny Grant, Jacques Lemaire, Mickey Redmond, Toe Blake (coach), Sam Pollock (general manager), Larry Aubut, Eddy Palchak (trainers).
Scores: May 5 at St. Louis — Montreal 3, St. Louis 2; May 7 at St. Louis — Montreal 1, St. Louis 0; May 9 at Montreal — Montreal 4, St. Louis 3; May 11 at Montreal — Montreal 3, St. Louis 2.

1966-67 — Toronto Maple Leafs — Johnny Bower, Terry Sawchuk, Larry Hillman, Marcel Pronovost, Tim Horton, Bob Baun, Aut Erickson, Allan Stanley, Red Kelly, Ron Ellis, George Armstrong, Pete Stemkowski, Dave Keon, Mike Walton, Jim Pappin, Bob Pulford, Brian Conacher, Eddie Shack, Frank Mahovlich, Milan Marcetta, Larry Jeffrey, Bruce Gamble, Punch Imlach (manager-coach), Bob Haggart (trainer).
Scores: April 20 at Montreal — Toronto 2, Montreal 6; April 22 at Montreal — Toronto 3, Montreal 0; April 25 at Toronto — Toronto 3, Montreal 2; April 27 at Toronto — Toronto 2, Montreal 6; April 29 at Montreal — Toronto 4, Montreal 1; May 2 at Toronto — Toronto 3, Montreal 1.

1965-66 — Montreal Canadiens — Lorne Worsley, Charlie Hodge, Jean-Claude Tremblay, Ted Harris, Jean-Guy Talbot, Terry Harper, Jacques Laperrière, Noel Price, Jean Béliveau, Ralph Backstrom, Dick Duff, Gilles Tremblay, Claude Larose, Yvan Cournoyer, Claude Provost, Bobby Rousseau, Henri Richard, Dave Balon, John Ferguson, Leon Rochefort, Jim Roberts, Toe Blake (coch), Sam Pollock (general manager), Larry Aubut, Andy Galley (trainers).
Scores: April 24 at Montreal — Detroit 3, Montreal 2; April 26 at Montreal — Detroit 5, Montreal 2; April 28 at Detroit — Montreal 4, Detroit 2; May 1 at Detroit — Montreal 2, Detroit 1; May 3 at Montreal — Montreal 5, Detroit 1; May 5 at Detroit — Montreal 3, Detroit 2.

1964-65 — Montreal Canadiens — Lorne Worsley, Charlie Hodge, Jean-Claude Tremblay, Ted Harris, Jean-Guy Talbot, Terry Harper, Jacques Laperrière, Jean Gauthier, Noel Picard, Jean Béliveau, Ralph Backstrom, Dick Duff, Claude Larose, Yvan Cournoyer, Claude Provost, Bobby Rousseau, Henri Richard, Dave Balon, John Ferguson, Red Berenson, Jim Roberts, Toe Blake (coach), Sam Pollock (general manager), Larry Aubut, Andy Galley (trainers).
Scores: April 17 at Montreal — Montreal 3, Chicago 2; April 20 at Montreal — Montreal 2, Chicago 0; April 22 at Chicago — Montreal 1, Chicago 3; April 25 at Chicago — Montreal 1, Chicago 5; April 7 at Montreal — Montreal 6, Chicago 0; April 29 at Chicago — Montreal 1, Chicago 2; May 1 at Montreal — Montreal 4, Chicago 0.

1963-64 — Toronto Maple Leafs — Johnny Bower, Carl Brewer, Tim Horton, Bob Baun, Allan Stanley, Larry Hillman, Al Arbour, Red Kelly, Gerry Ehman, Andy Bathgate, George Armstrong, Ron Stewart, Dave Keon, Billy Harris, Don McKenney, Jim Pappin, Bob Pulford, Eddie Shack, Frank Mahovlich, Eddie Litzenberger, Punch Imlach (manager-coach), Bob Haggart (trainer).
Scores April 11 at Toronto — Toronto 3, Detroit 2; April 14 at Toronto — Toronto 3, Detroit 4; April 16 at Detroit — Toronto 3, Detroit 4; April 18 at Detroit — Toronto 4, Detroit 2; April 21 at Toronto — Toronto 1, Detroit 2; April 23 at Detroit — Toronto 4, Detroit 3; April 25 at Toronto — Toronto 4, Detroit 0.

1962-63 — Toronto Maple Leafs — Johnny Bower, Don Simmons, Carl Brewer, Tim Horton, Kent Douglas, Allan Stanley, Bob Baun, Larry Hillman, Red Kelly, Dick Duff, George Armstrong, Bob Nevin, Ron Stewart, Dave Keon, Billy Harris, Bob Pulford, Eddie Shack, Ed Litzenberger, Frank Mahovlich, John MacMillan, Punch Imlach (manager-coach), Bob Haggert (trainer).
Scores: April 9 at Toronto — Toronto 4, Detroit 2; April 11 at Toronto — Toronto 4, Detroit 2; April 14 at Detroit — Toronto 3, Detroit 4; April 16 at Detroit — Toronto 4, Detroit 2; April 18 at Toronto — Toronto 3, Detroit 1.

1961-62 — Toronto Maple Leafs — Johnny Bower, Don Simmons, Carl Brewer, Tim Horton, Bob Baun, Allan Stanley, Al Arbour, Larry Hillman, Red Kelly, Dick Duff, George Armstrong, Frank Mahovlich, Bob Nevin, Ron Stewart, Bill Harris, Bert Olmstead, Eddie Litzenberger, John MacMillan, Punch Imlach (manager-coach), Bob Haggert (trainer).
Scores: April 10 at Toronto — Toronto 4, Chicago 1; April 12 at Toronto — Toronto 3, Chicago 2; April 15 at Chicago — Toronto 0, Chicago 3; April 17 at Chicago — Toronto 1, Chicago 4; April 19 at Toronto —Toronto 8, Chicago 4; April 22 at Chicago — Toronto 2, Chicago 1.

1960-61 — Chicago Black Hawks — Glenn Hall, Al Arbour, Pierre Pilote, Elmer Vasko, Jack Evans, Dollard St. Laurent, Reg Fleming, Tod Sloan, Ron Murphy, Eddie Litzenberger, Bill Hay, Bobby Hull, Ab McDonald, Eric Nesterenko, Ken Wharram, Earl Balfour, Stan Mikita, Murray Balfour, Chico Maki, Wayne Hicks, Tommy Ivan (manager), Rudy Pilous (coach), Nick Garen (trainer).
Scores: April 6 at Chicago — Chicago 3, Detroit 2; April 8 at Detroit — Detroit 3, Chicago 1; April 10 at Chicago — Chicago 3, Detroit 1; April 12 at Detroit — Detroit 2, Chicago 1; April 14 at Chicago — Chicago 6, Detroit 3; April 16 at Detroit — Chicago 5, Detroit 1.

1959-60 — Montreal Canadiens — Jacques Plante, Charlie Hodge, Doug Harvey, Tom Johnson, Bob Turner, Jean-Guy Talbot, Albert Langlois, Ralph Backstrom, Jean Béliveau, Marcel Bonin, Bernie Geoffrion, Phil Goyette, Bill Hicke, Don Marshall, Ab McDonald, Dickie Moore, André Pronovost, Claude Provost, Henri Richard, Maurice Richard, Frank Selke (manager), Toe Blake (coach), Hector Dubois, Larry Aubut (trainers).
Scores: April 7 at Montreal — Montreal 4, Toronto 2; April 9 at Montreal — Montreal 2, Toronto 1; April 12 at Toronto — Montreal 5, Toronto 2; April 14 at Toronto — Montreal 4, Toronto 0.

1958-59 — Montreal Canadiens — Jacques Plante, Charlie Hodge, Doug Harvey, Tom Johnson, Bob Turner, Jean-Guy Talbot, Albert Langlois, Bernie Geoffrion, Ralph Backstrom, Bill Hicke, Maurice Richard, Dickie Moore, Claude Provost, Ab McDonald, Henri Richard, Marcel Bonin, Phil Goyette, Don Marshall, André Pronovost, Jean Béliveau, Frank Selke (manager), Toe Blake (coach), Hector Dubois, Larry Aubut (trainers).
Scores: April 9 at Montreal — Montreal 5, Toronto 3; April 11 at Montreal — Montreal 3, Toronto 1; April 14 at Toronto — Toronto 3, Montreal 2; April 16 at Toronto — Montreal 3, Toronto 2; April 18 at Montreal — Montreal 5, Toronto 3.

1957-58 — Montreal Canadiens — Jacques Plante, Gerry McNeil, Doug Harvey, Tom Johnson, Bob Turner, Dollard St-Laurent, Jean-Guy Talbot, Albert Langlois, Jean Béliveau, Bernie Geoffrion, Maurice Richard, Dickie Moore, Claude Provost, Floyd Curry, Bert Olmstead, Henri Richard, Marcel Bonin, Phil Goyette, Don Marshall, André Pronovost, Connie Broden, Frank Selke (manager), Toe Blake (coach), Hector Dubois, Larry Aubut (trainers).
Scores: April 8 at Montreal —Montreal 2, Boston 1; April 10 at Montreal — Boston 5, Montreal 2; April 13 at Boston — Montreal 3, Boston 0; April 15 at Boston — Boston 3, Montreal 1; April 17 at Montreal — Montreal 3, Boston 2; April 20 at Boston — Montreal 5, Boston 3.

Montreal's Doug Harvey wheels away from Toronto's Dick Duff during the 1959 Stanley Cup finals.

1956-57 — Montreal Canadiens — Jacques Plante, Gerry McNeil, Doug Harvey, Tom Johnson, Bob Turner, Dollard St. Laurent, Jean-Guy Talbot, Jean Béliveau, Bernie Geoffrion, Floyd Curry, Dickie Moore, Maurice Richard, Claude Provost, Bert Olmstead, Henri Richard, Phil Goyette, Don Marshall, André Pronovost, Connie Broden, Frank Selke (manager), Toe Blake (coach), Hector Dubois, Larry Aubut (trainers).
Scores: April 6, at Montreal — Montreal 5, Boston 1; April 9, at Montreal — Montreal 1, Boston 0; April 11, at Boston — Montreal 4, Boston 2; April 14, at Boston — Boston 2, Montreal 0; April 16, at Montreal — Montreal 5, Boston 1.

1955-56 — Montreal Canadiens — Jacques Plante, Doug Harvey, Emile Bouchard, Bob Turner, Tom Johnson, Jean-Guy Talbot, Dollard St. Laurent, Jean Béliveau, Bernie Geoffrion, Bert Olmstead, Floyd Curry, Jackie Leclair, Maurice Richard, Dickie Moore, Henri Richard, Ken Mosdell, Don Marshall, Claude Provost, Frank Selke (manager), Toe Blake (coach), Hector Dubois (trainer).
Scores: March 31, at Montreal — Montreal 6, Detroit 4; April 3, at Montreal — Montreal 5, Detroit 1; April 5, at Detroit — Detroit 3, Montreal 1; April 8, at Detroit — Montreal 3, Detroit 0; April 10, at Montreal — Montreal 3, Detroit 1.

1954-55 — Detroit Red Wings — Terry Sawchuk, Red Kelly, Bob Goldham, Marcel Pronovost, Ben Woit, Jim Hay, Larry Hillman, Ted Lindsay, Tony Leswick, Gordie Howe, Alex Delvecchio, Marty Pavelich, Glen Skov, Earl Reibel, John Wilson, Bill Dineen, Vic Stasiuk, Marcel Bonin, Jack Adams (manager), Jimmy Skinner (coach), Carl Mattson (trainer).
Scores: April 3, at Detroit — Detroit 4, Montreal 2; April 5, at Detroit — Detroit 7, Montreal 1, April 7 at Montreal — Montreal 4, Detroit 2; April 9, at Montreal — Montreal 5, Detroit 3; April 10, at Detroit — Detroit 5, Montreal 1; April 12, at Montreal — Montreal 6, Detroit 3; April 14, at Detroit — Detroit 3, Montreal 1

1953-54 — Detroit Red Wings — Terry Sawchuk, Red Kelly, Bob Goldham, Ben Woit, Marcel Pronovost, Al Arbour, Keith Allen, Ted Lindsay, Tony Leswick, Gordie Howe, Marty Pavelich, Alex Delvecchio, Metro Prystai, Glen Skov, John Wilson, Bill Dineen, Jim Peters, Earl Reibel, Vic Stasiuk, Jack Adams (manager), Tommy Ivan (coach), Carl Mattson (trainer).
Scores: April 4, at Detroit — Detroit 3, Montreal 1; April 6, at Detroit — Montreal 3, Detroit 1; April 8, at Montreal — Detroit 5, Montreal 2; April 10, at Montreal — Detroit 2, Montreal 0; April 11, at Detroit — Montreal 1, Detroit 0; April 13, at Montreal — Montreal 4, Detroit 1; April 16, at Detroit — Detroit 2, Montreal 1.

1952-53 — Montreal Canadiens — Gerry McNeil, Jacques Plante, Doug Harvey, Emile Bouchard, Tom Johnson, Dollard St. Laurent, Bud MacPherson, Maurice Richard, Elmer Lach, Bert Olmstead, Bernie Geoffrion, Floyd Curry, Paul Masnick, Billy Reay, Dickie Moore, Ken Mosdell, Dick Gamble, Johnny McCormack, Lorne Davis, Calum McKay, Eddie Mazur, Frank Selke (manager), Dick Irvin (coach), Hector Dubois (trainer).
Scores: April 9, at Montreal — Montreal 4, Boston 2; April 11, at Montreal — Montreal 4, Boston 1; April 12, at Boston — Montreal 3, Boston 0; April 14, at Boston — Montreal 7, Boston 3; April 16, at Montreal — Montreal 1, Boston 0.

1951-52 — Detroit Red Wings — Terry Sawchuk, Bob Goldham, Ben Woit, Red Kelly, Leo Reise, Marcel Pronovost, Ted Lindsay, Tony Leswick, Gordie Howe, Metro Prystai, Marty Pavelich, Sid Abel, Glen Skov, Alex Delvecchio, John Wilson, Vic Stasiuk, Larry Zeidel, Jack Adams (manager) Tommy Ivan (coach), Carl Mattson (trainer).
Scores: April 10, at Montreal — Detroit 3, Montreal 1; April 12 at Montreal — Detroit 2, Montreal 1; April 13, at Detroit — Detroit 3, Montreal 0; April 15, at Detroit — Detroit 3, Montreal 0.

1950-51 — Toronto Maple Leafs — Turk Broda, Al Rollins, Jim Thomson, Gus Mortson, Bill Barilko, Bill Juzda, Fern Flaman, Hugh Bolton, Ted Kennedy, Sid Smith, Tod Sloan, Cal Gardner, Howie Meeker, Harry Watson, Max Bentley, Joe Klukay, Danny Lewicki, Ray Timgren, Fleming Mackell, Johnny McCormack, Bob Hassard, Conn Smythe (manager), Joe Primeau (coach), Tim Daly (trainer).
Scores: April 11, at Toronto — Toronto 3, Montreal 2; April 14, at Toronto — Montreal 3, Toronto 2; April 17, at Montreal — Toronto 2, Montreal 1; April 19, at Montreal — Toronto 3, Montreal 2; April 21, at Toronto — Toronto 3, Montreal 2.

1949-50 — Detroit Red Wings — Harry Lumley, Jack Stewart, Leo Reise, Clare Martin, Al Dewsbury, Lee Fogolin, Marcel Pronovost, Red Kelly, Ted Lindsay, Sid Abel, Gordie Howe, George Gee, Jimmy Peters, Marty Pavelich, Jim McFadden, Pete Babando, Max McNab, Gerry Couture, Joe Carveth, Steve Black, John Wilson, Larry Wilson, Jack Adams (manager), Tommy Ivan (coach), Carl Mattson (trainer).
Scores: April 11, at Detroit — Detroit 4, NY Rangers 1; April 13, at Toronto* — NY Rangers 3, Detroit 1; April 15, at Toronto — Detroit 4, NY Rangers 0; April 18, at Detroit — NY Rangers 4, Detroit 3; April 20, at Detroit — NY Rangers 2, Detroit 1; April 22, at Detroit — Detroit 5, NY Rangers 4; April 23, at Detroit — Detroit 4, NY Rangers 3.
* Ice was unavailable in Madison Square Garden and Rangers elected to play second and third games on Toronto ice.

1948-49 — Toronto Maple Leafs — Turk Broda, Jim Thomson, Gus Mortson, Bill Barilko, Garth Boesch, Bill Juzda, Ted Kennedy, Howie Meeker, Vic Lynn, Harry Watson, Bill Ezinicki, Cal Gardner, Max Bentley, Joe Klukay, Sid Smith, Don Metz, Ray Timgren, Fleming Mackell, Harry Taylor, Bob Dawes, Tod Sloan, Conn Smythe (manager), Hap Day (coach), Tim Daly (trainer).
Scores: April 8, at Detroit — Toronto 3, Detroit 2; April 10, at Detroit — Toronto 3, Detroit 1; April 13, at Toronto — Toronto 3, Detroit 1; April 16, at Toronto — Toronto 3, Detroit 1.

1947-48 — Toronto Maple Leafs — Turk Broda, Jim Thomson, Wally Stanowski, Garth Boesch, Bill Barilko, Gus Mortson, Phil Samis, Syl Apps, Bill Ezinicki, Harry Watson, Ted Kennedy, Howie Meeker, Vic Lynn, Nick Metz, Max Bentley, Joe Klukay, Les Costello, Don Metz, Sid Smith, Conn Smythe (manager), Hap Day (coach), Tim Daly (trainer).
Scores: April 7, at Toronto — Toronto 5, Detroit 3; April 10, at Toronto — Toronto 4, Detroit 2; April 11, at Detroit — Toronto 2, Detroit 0; April 14, at Detroit — Toronto 7, Detroit 2.

The 1951 Stanley Cup champion Toronto Maple Leafs defeated the Montreal Canadiens four games to one to win the Finals. Each game went to overtime. Young defenseman Bill Barilko scored the Cup-winning goal in game five.

The Detroit Red Wings captured their fifth Stanley Cup title in 1952. The Red Wings had become the NHL's first 100-point team in 1950-51, and they again reached the century mark in 1951-52. This powerhouse team was unstoppable in the playoffs, sweeping the Maple Leafs in the Semi-Finals and the Canadiens in the Stanley Cup Finals. The Red Wings' eight-straight playoff wins in 1952 launched the Detroit tradition of throwing octopi onto the ice. The first eight-legged creature made its appearance during the fourth game of the 1952 Finals. Forty-one years later, octopi appeared on the ice surface of the Joe Louis Arena during the 1993 Norris Division Semi-Finals.

1946-47 — Toronto Maple Leafs — Turk Broda, Garth Boesch, Gus Mortson, Jim Thomson, Wally Stanowski, Bill Barilko, Harry Watson, Bud Poile, Ted Kennedy, Syl Apps, Don Metz, Nick Metz, Bill Ezinicki, Vic Lynn, Howie Meeker, Gaye Stewart, Joe Klukay, Gus Bodnar, Bob Goldham, Conn Smythe (manager), Hap Day (coach), Tim Daly (trainer).
Scores: April 8, at Montreal — Montreal 6, Toronto 0; April 10, at Montreal — Toronto 4, Montreal 0; April 12, at Toronto — Toronto 4, Montreal 2; April 15, at Toronto — Toronto 2, Montreal 1; April 17, at Montreal — Montreal 3, Toronto 1; April 19, at Toronto — Toronto 2, Montreal 1.

1945-46 — Montreal Canadiens — Elmer Lach, Toe Blake, Maurice Richard, Bob Fillion, Dutch Hiller, Murph Chamberlain, Ken Mosdell, Buddy O'Connor, Glen Harmon, Jim Peters, Emile Bouchard, Bill Reay, Ken Reardon, Leo Lamoureux, Frank Eddolls, Gerry Plamondon, Bill Durnan, Tommy Gorman (manager), Dick Irvin (coach), Ernie Cook (trainer).
Scores: March 30, at Montreal — Montreal 4, Boston 3; April 2, at Montreal — Montreal 3, Boston 2; April 4, at Boston — Montreal 4, Boston 2; April 7, at Boston — Boston 3, Montreal 2; April 9, at Montreal — Montreal 6, Boston 3.

1944-45 — Toronto Maple Leafs — Don Metz, Frank McCool, Wally Stanowski, Reg Hamilton, Elwyn Morris, Johnny McCreedy, Tommy O'Neill, Ted Kennedy, Babe Pratt, Gus Bodnar, Art Jackson, Jack McLean, Mel Hill, Nick Metz, Bob Davidson, Dave Schriner, Lorne Carr, Conn Smythe (manager), Frank Selke (business manager), Hap Day (coach), Tim Daly (trainer).
Scores: April 6, at Detroit — Toronto 1, Detroit 0; April 8, at Detroit — Toronto 2, Detroit 0; April 12, at Toronto — Toronto 1, Detroit 0; April 14, at Toronto — Detroit 5, Toronto 3; April 19, at Detroit — Detroit 2, Toronto 0; April 21, at Toronto — Detroit 1, Toronto 0; April 22, at Detroit — Toronto 2, Detroit 1.

1943-44 — Montreal Canadiens — Toe Blake, Maurice Richard, Elmer Lach, Ray Getliffe, Murph Chamberlain, Phil Watson, Emile Bouchard, Glen Harmon, Buddy O'Connor, Jerry Heffernan, Mike McMahon, Leo Lamoureux, Fernand Majeau, Bob Fillion, Bill Durnan, Tommy Gorman (manager), Dick Irvin (coach), Ernie Cook (trainer).
Scores: April 4, at Montreal — Montreal 5, Chicago 1; April 6, at Chicago — Montreal 3, Chicago 1; April 9, at Chicago — Montreal 3, Chicago 2; April 13, at Montreal — Montreal 5, Chicago 4.

1942-43 — Detroit Red Wings — Jack Stewart, Jimmy Orlando, Sid Abel, Alex Motter, Harry Watson, Joe Carveth, Mud Bruneteau, Eddie Wares, Johnny Mowers, Cully Simon, Don Grosso, Carl Liscombe, Connie Brown, Syd Howe, Les Douglas, Hal Jackson, Joe Fisher, Jack Adams (manager), Ebbie Goodfellow (playing-coach), Honey Walker (trainer).
Scores: April 1, at Detroit — Detroit 6, Boston 2; April 4, at Detroit — Detroit 4, Boston 3; April 7, at Boston — Detroit 4, Boston 0; April 8, at Boston — Detroit 2, Boston 0.

1941-42 — Toronto Maple Leafs — Wally Stanowski, Syl Apps, Bob Goldham, Gord Drillon, Hank Goldup, Ernie Dickens, Dave Schriner, Bucko McDonald, Bob Davidson, Nick Metz, Bingo Kampman, Don Metz, Gaye Stewart, Turk Broda, Johnny McCreedy, Lorne Carr, Pete Langelle, Billy Taylor, Conn Smythe (manager), Hap Day (coach), Frank Selke (business manager), Tim Daly (trainer).
Scores: April 4, at Toronto — Detroit 3, Toronto 2; April 7, at Toronto — Detroit 4, Toronto 2; April 9, at Detroit — Detroit 5, Toronto 2; April 12, at Detroit — Toronto 4, Detroit 3; April 14, at Toronto — Toronto 9, Detroit 3; April 16, at Detroit — Toronto 3, Detroit 0; April 18, at Toronto — Toronto 3, Detroit 1.

1940-41 — Boston Bruins — Bill Cowley, Des Smith, Dit Clapper, Frank Brimsek, Flash Hollett, John Crawford, Bobby Bauer, Pat McCreavy, Herb Cain, Mel Hill, Milt Schmidt, Woody Dumart, Roy Conacher, Terry Reardon, Art Jackson, Eddie Wiseman, Art Ross (manager), Cooney Weiland (coach), Win Green (trainer).
Scores: April 6, at Boston — Detroit 2, Boston 3; April 8, at Boston — Detroit 1, Boston 2; April 10, at Detroit — Boston 4, Detroit 2; April 12, at Detroit — Boston 3, Detroit 1.

1939-40 — New York Rangers — Dave Kerr, Art Coulter, Ott Heller, Alex Shibicky, Mac Colville, Neil Colville, Phil Watson, Lynn Patrick, Clint Smith, Muzz Patrick, Babe Pratt, Bryan Hextall, Kilby Macdonald, Dutch Hiller, Alf Pike, Sanford Smith, Lester Patrick (manager), Frank Boucher (coach), Harry Westerby (trainer).
Scores: April 2, at New York — NY Rangers 2, Toronto 1; April 3, at New York — NY Rangers 6, Toronto 2; April 6, at Toronto — NY Rangers 1, Toronto 2; April 9, at Toronto — NY Rangers 0, Toronto 3; April 11, at Toronto — NY Rangers 2, Toronto 1; April 13, at Toronto — NY Rangers 3, Toronto 2.

1938-39 — Boston Bruins — Bobby Bauer, Mel Hill, Flash Hollett, Roy Conacher, Gord Pettinger, Milt Schmidt, Woody Dumart, Jack Crawford, Ray Getliffe, Frank Brimsek, Eddie Shore, Dit Clapper, Bill Cowley, Jack Portland, Red Hamill, Cooney Weiland, Art Ross (manager-coach), Win Green (trainer).
Scores: April 6, at Boston — Toronto 1, Boston 2; April 9, at Boston — Toronto 3, Boston 2; April 11, at Toronto — Toronto 1, Boston 3; April 13 at Toronto — Toronto 0, Boston 2; April 16, at Boston — Toronto 1, Boston 3.

1937-38 — Chicago Black Hawks — Art Wiebe, Carl Voss, Hal Jackson, Mike Karakas, Mush March, Jack Shill, Earl Seibert, Cully Dahlstrom, Alex Levinsky, Johnny Gottselig, Lou Trudel, Pete Palangio, Bill MacKenzie, Doc Romnes, Paul Thompson, Roger Jenkins, Alf Moore, Bert Connolly, Virgil Johnson, Paul Goodman, Bill Stewart (manager-coach), Eddie Froelich (trainer).
Scores: April 5, at Toronto — Chicago 3, Toronto 1; April 7, at Toronto — Chicago 1, Toronto 5; April 10 at Chicago — Chicago 2, Toronto 1; April 12, at Chicago — Chicago 4, Toronto 1.

1936-37 — Detroit Red Wings — Normie Smith, Pete Kelly, Larry Aurie, Herbie Lewis, Hec Kilrea, Mud Bruneteau, Syd Howe, Wally Kilrea, Jimmy Franks, Bucko McDonald, Gordon Pettinger, Ebbie Goodfellow, Johnny Gallagher, Scotty Bowman, Johnny Sorrell, Marty Barry, Earl Robertson, Johnny Sherf, Howard Mackie, Jack Adams (manager-coach), Honey Walker (trainer).
Scores: April 6, at New York — Detroit 1, NY Rangers 5; April 8, at Detroit — Detroit 4, NY Rangers 2; April 11, at Detroit — Detroit 0, NY Rangers 1; April 13, at Detroit — Detroit 1, NY Rangers 0; April 15, at Detroit — Detroit 3, NY Rangers 0.

1935-36 — Detroit Red Wings — Johnny Sorrell, Syd Howe, Marty Barry, Herbie Lewis, Mud Bruneteau, Wally Kilrea, Hec Kilrea, Gordon Pettinger, Bucko McDonald, Scotty Bowman, Pete Kelly, Doug Young, Ebbie Goodfellow, Normie Smith, Jack Adams (manager-coach), Honey Walker (trainer).
Scores: April 5, at Detroit — Detroit 3, Toronto 1; April 7, at Detroit — Detroit 9, Toronto 4; April 9, at Toronto — Detroit 3, Toronto 4; April 11, at Toronto — Detroit 3, Toronto 2.

1934-35 — Montreal Maroons — Marvin (Cy) Wentworth, Alex Connell, Toe Blake, Stew Evans, Earl Robinson, Bill Miller, Dave Trottier, Jimmy Ward, Larry Northcott, Hooley Smith, Russ Blinco, Allan Shields, Sammy McManus, Gus Marker, Bob Gracie, Herb Cain, Tommy Gorman (manager), Lionel Conacher (coach), Bill O'Brien (trainer).
Scores: April 4, at Toronto — Mtl. Maroons 3, Toronto 2; April 6, at Toronto — Mtl. Maroons 3, Toronto 1; April 9, at Montreal — Mtl. Maroons 4, Toronto 1.

1933-34 — Chicago Black Hawks — Taffy Abel, Lolo Couture, Lou Trudel, Lionel Conacher, Paul Thompson, Leroy Goldsworthy, Art Coulter, Roger Jenkins, Don McFayden, Tommy Cook, Doc Romnes, Johnny Gottselig, Mush March, Johnny Sheppard, Chuck Gardiner (captain), Bill Kendall, Tommy Gorman (manager-coach), Eddie Froelich (trainer).
Scores: April 3, at Detroit — Chicago 2, Detroit 1; April 5, at Detroit — Chicago 4, Detroit 1; April 8, at Chicago — Detroit 5, Chicago 2; April 10, at Chicago — Chicago 1, Detroit 0.

1932-33 — New York Rangers — Ching Johnson, Butch Keeling, Frank Boucher, Art Somers, Babe Siebert, Bun Cook, Andy Aitkenhead, Ott Heller, Ozzie Asmundson, Gord Pettinger, Doug Brennan, Cecil Dillon, Bill Cook (captain), Murray Murdoch, Earl Seibert, Lester Patrick (manager-coach), Harry Westerby (trainer).
Scores: April 4, at New York — NY Rangers 5, Toronto 1; April 8, at Toronto — NY Rangers 3, Toronto 1; April 11, at Toronto — Toronto 3, NY Rangers 2; April 13, at Toronto — NY Rangers 1, Toronto 0.

1931-32 — Toronto Maple Leafs — Charlie Conacher, Harvey Jackson, King Clancy, Andy Blair, Red Horner, Lorne Chabot, Alex Levinsky, Joe Primeau, Hal Darragh, Hal Cotton, Frank Finnigan, Hap Day, Ace Bailey, Bob Gracie, Fred Robertson, Earl Miller, Conn Smythe (manager), Dick Irvin (coach), Tim Daly (trainer).
Scores: April 5 at New York — Toronto 6, NY Rangers 4; April 7, at Boston* — Toronto 6, NY Rangers 2; April 9, at Toronto — Toronto 6, NY Rangers 4.
* Ice was unavailable in Madison Square Garden and Rangers elected to play the second game on neutral ice.

1930-31 — Montreal Canadiens — George Hainsworth, Wildor Larochelle, Marty Burke, Sylvio Mantha, Howie Morenz, Johnny Gagnon, Aurel Joliat, Armand Mondou, Pit Lepine, Albert Leduc, Georges Mantha, Art Lesieur, Nick Wasnie, Bert McCaffrey, Gus Rivers, Jean Pusie, Léo Dandurand (manager), Cecil Hart (coach), Ed Dufour (trainer).
Scores: April 3, at Chicago — Montreal 2, Chicago 1; April 5, at Chicago — Chicago 2, Montreal 1; April 9, at Montreal — Chicago 3, Montreal 2; April 11, at Montreal — Montreal 4, Chicago 2; April 14, at Montreal — Montreal 2, Chicago 0.

1929-30 — Montreal Canadiens — George Hainsworth, Marty Burke, Sylvio Mantha, Howie Morenz, Bert McCaffrey, Aurel Joliat, Albert Leduc, Pit Lepine, Wildor Larochelle, Nick Wasnie, Gerald Carson, Armand Mondou, Georges Mantha, Gus Rivers, Léo Dandurand (manager), Cecil Hart (coach), Ed Dufour (trainer).
Scores: April 1 at Boston — Montreal 3, Boston 0; April 3 at Montreal — Montreal 4, Boston 3.

1928-29 — Boston Bruins — Cecil (Tiny) Thompson, Eddie Shore, Lionel Hitchman, Perk Galbraith, Eric Pettinger, Frank Fredrickson, Mickey Mackay, Red Green, Dutch Gainor, Harry Oliver, Eddie Rodden, Dit Clapper, Cooney Weiland, Lloyd Klein, Cy Denneny, Bill Carson, George Owen, Myles Lane, Art Ross (manager-coach), Win Green (trainer).
Scores: March 28 at Boston — Boston 2, NY Rangers 0; March 29 at New York — Boston 2, NY Rangers 1.

1927-28 — New York Rangers — Lorne Chabot, Taffy Abel, Leon Bourgault, Ching Johnson, Bill Cook, Bun Cook, Frank Boucher, Billy Boyd, Murray Murdoch, Paul Thompson, Alex Gray, Joe Miller, Patsy Callighen, Lester Patrick (manager-coach), Harry Westerby (trainer).
Scores: April 5 at Montreal — Mtl. Maroons 2, NY Rangers 0; April 7 at Montreal — NY Rangers 2, Mtl. Maroons 1; April 10 at Montreal — Mtl. Maroons 2, NY Rangers 1; April 12 at Montreal — NY Rangers 1, Mtl. Maroons 0; April 14 at Montreal — NY Rangers 2, Mtl. Maroons 1.

1926-27 — Ottawa Senators — Alex Connell, King Clancy, George (Buck) Boucher, Ed Gorman, Frank Finnigan, Alex Smith, Hec Kilrea, Hooley Smith, Cy Denneny, Frank Nighbor, Jack Adams, Milt Halliday, Dave Gill (manager-coach).
Scores: April 7 at Boston — Ottawa 0, Boston 0; April 9 at Boston — Ottawa 3, Boston 1; April 11 at Ottawa — Boston 1, Ottawa 1; April 13 at Ottawa — Ottawa 3, Boston 1.

1925-26 — Montreal Maroons — Clint Benedict, Reg Noble, Frank Carson, Dunc Munro, Nels Stewart, Harry Broadbent, Babe Siebert, Dinny Dinsmore, Bill Phillips, Hobart (Hobie) Kitchen, Sammy Rothschield, Albert (Toots) Holway, Shorty Horne, Bern Brophy, Eddie Gerard (manager-coach), Bill O'Brien (trainer).
Scores: March 30 at Montreal — Mtl. Maroons 3, Victoria 0; April 1 at Montreal — Mtl. Maroons 3, Victoria 0; April 3 at Montreal — Victoria 3, Mtl. Maroons 2; April 6 at Montreal — Mtl. Maroons 2, Victoria 0.

The series in the spring of 1926 ended the annual playoffs between the champions of the East and the champions of the West. Since 1926-27 the annual playoffs in the National Hockey League have decided the Stanley Cup champions.

1924-25 — Victoria Cougars — Harry (Happy) Holmes, Clem Loughlin, Gordie Fraser, Frank Fredrickson, Jack Walker, Harold (Gizzy) Hart, Harold (Slim) Halderson, Frank Foyston, Wally Elmer, Harry Meeking, Jocko Anderson, Lester Patrick (manager-coach).
Scores: March 21 at Victoria — Victoria 5, Montreal 2; March 23 at Vancouver — Victoria 3, Montreal 1; March 27 at Victoria — Montreal 4, Victoria 2; March 30 at Victoria — Victoria 6, Montreal 1.

1923-24 — Montreal Canadiens — Georges Vezina, Sprague Cleghorn, Billy Couture, Howie Morenz, Aurel Joliat, Billy Boucher, Odie Cleghorn, Sylvio Mantha, Bobby Boucher, Billy Bell, Billy Cameron, Joe Malone, Charles Fortier, Leo Dandurand (manager-coach).
Scores: March 18 at Montreal — Montreal 3, Van. Maroons 2; March 20 at Montreal — Montreal 2, Van. Maroons 1. March 22 at Montreal — Montreal 6, Cgy. Tigers 1; March 25 at Ottawa* — Montreal 3, Cgy. Tigers 0.
* Game transferred to Ottawa to benefit from artificial ice surface.

In 1930-31, the Montreal Canadiens won their second consecutive Stanley Cup championship, defeating the Chicago Black Hawks three games to two.

1922-23 — Ottawa Senators — George (Buck) Boucher, Lionel Hitchman, Frank Nighbor, King Clancy, Harry Helman, Clint Benedict, Jack Darragh, Eddie Gerard, Cy Denneny, Harry Broadbent, Tommy Gorman (manager), Pete Green (coach), F. Dolan (trainer).
Scores: March 16 at Vancouver — Ottawa 1, Van. Maroons 0; March 19 at Vancouver — Van. Maroons 4, Ottawa 1; March 23 at Vancouver — Ottawa 3, Van. Maroons 2; March 26 at Vancouver — Ottawa 5, Van. Maroons 1; March 29 at Vancouver — Ottawa 2, Edm. Eskimos 1; March 31 at Vancouver — Ottawa 1, Edm. Eskimos 0.

1921-22 — Toronto St. Pats — Ted Stackhouse, Corb Denneny, Rod Smylie, Lloyd Andrews, John Ross Roach, Harry Cameron, Bill (Red) Stuart, Cecil (Babe) Dye, Ken Randall, Reg Noble, Eddie Gerard (borrowed for one game from Ottawa), Stan Jackson, Nolan Mitchell, Charlie Querrie (manager), Eddie Powers (coach).
Scores: March 17 at Toronto — Toronto 3, Van. Millionaires 2; March 20 at Toronto — Toronto 2, Van. Millionaires 1; March 23 at Toronto — Van. Millionaires 3, Toronto 0; March 25 at Toronto — Toronto 6, Van. Millionaires 0; March 28 at Toronto — Toronto 5, Van. Millionaires 1.

1920-21 — Ottawa Senators — Jack McKell, Jack Darragh, Morley Bruce, George (Buck) Boucher, Eddie Gerard, Clint Benedict, Sprague Cleghorn, Frank Nighbor, Harry Broadbent, Cy Denneny, Leth Graham, Tommy Gorman (manager),Pete Green (coach), F. Dolan (trainer).
Scores: March 21 at Vancouver — Van. Millionaires 2, Ottawa 1; March 24 at Vancouver — Ottawa 4, Van. Millionaires 3; March 28 at Vancouver — Ottawa 3, Van. Millionaires 2; March 31 at Vancouver — Van. Millionaires 3, Ottawa 2; April 4 at Vancouver — Ottawa 2, Van. Millionaires 1

1919-20 — Ottawa Senators — Jack McKell, Jack Darragh, Morley Bruce, Horrace Merrill, George (Buck) Boucher, Eddie Gerard, Clint Benedict, Sprague Cleghorn, Frank Nighbor, Harry Broadbent, Cy Denneny, Price, Tommy Gorman (manager), Pete Green (coach).
Scores: March 22 at Ottawa — Ottawa 3, Seattle 2; March 24 at Ottawa — Ottawa 3, Seattle 0; March 27 at Ottawa — Seattle 3, Ottawa 1; March 30 at Toronto* — Seattle 5, Ottawa 2; April 1 at Toronto* — Ottawa 6, Seattle 1.

* Games transferred to Toronto to benefit from artificial ice surface.

1918-19 — No decision, Series halted by Spanish influenza epidemic, illness of several players and death of Joe Hall of Montreal Canadiens from flu. Five games had been played when the series was halted, each team having won two and tied one. The results are shown:
Scores: March 19 at Seattle — Seattle 7, Montreal 0; March 22 at Seattle — Montreal 4, Seattle 2; March 24 at Seattle — Seattle 7, Montreal 2; March 26 at Seattle — Montreal 0, Seattle 0; March 30 at Seattle — Montreal 4, Seattle 3.

1917-18 — Toronto Arenas — Rusty Crawford, Harry Meeking, Ken Randall, Corb Denneny, Harry Cameron, Jack Adams, Alf Skinner, Harry Mummery, Harry (Happy) Holmes, Reg Noble, Sammy Hebert, Jack Marks, Jack Coughlin, Neville, Charlie Querrie (manager), Dick Carroll (coach), Frank Carroll (trainer).
Scores: March 20 at Toronto — Toronto 5, Van. Millionaires 3; March 23 at Toronto — Van. Millionaires 6, Toronto 4; March 26 at Toronto — Toronto 6, Van. Millionaires 3; March 28 at Toronto — Van. Millionaires 8, Toronto 1; March 30 at Toronto — Toronto 2, Van. Millionaires 1.

1916-17 — Seattle Metropolitans — Harry (Happy) Holmes, Ed Carpenter, Cully Wilson, Jack Walker, Bernie Morris, Frank Foyston, Roy Rickey, Jim Riley, Bobby Rowe (captain), Pete Muldoon (manager).
Scores: March 17 at Seattle — Montreal 8, Seattle 4; March 20 at Seattle — Seattle 6, Montreal 1; March 23 at Seattle — Seattle 4, Montreal 1; March 25 at Seattle — Seattle 9, Montreal 1.

1915-16 — Montreal Canadiens — Georges Vezina, Bert Corbeau, Jack Laviolette, Newsy Lalonde, Louis Berlinguette, Goldie Prodgers, Howard McNamara, Didier Pitre, Skene Ronan, Amos Arbour, Georges Poulin, Jacques Fournier, George Kennedy (manager).
Scores: March 20 at Montreal — Portland 2, Montreal 0; March 22 at Montreal — Montreal 2, Portland 1; March 25 at Montreal — Montreal 6, Portland 3; March 28 at Montreal — Portland 6, Montreal 5; March 30 at Montreal — Montreal 2, Portland 1.

1914-15 — Vancouver Millionaires — Kenny Mallen, Frank Nighbor, Fred (Cyclone) Taylor, Hughie Lehman, Lloyd Cook, Mickey MacKay, Barney Stanley, Jim Seaborn, Si Griffis (captain), Jean Matz, Frank Patrick (playing manager).
Scores: March 22 at Vancouver — Van. Millionaires 6, Ottawa 2; March 24 at Vancouver — Van. Millionaires 8, Ottawa 3; March 26 at Vancouver — Van. Millionaires 12, Ottawa 3.

1913-14 — Toronto Blueshirts — Con Corbeau, F. Roy McGiffen, Jack Walker, George McNamara, Cully Wilson, Frank Foyston, Harry Cameron, Harry (Happy) Holmes, Alan M. Davidson (captain), Harriston, Jack Marshall (playing-manager), Frank and Dick Carroll (trainers).
Scores: March 14 at Toronto — Toronto 5, Victoria 2; March 17 at Toronto — Toronto 6, Victoria 5; March 19 at Toronto — Toronto 2, Victoria 1.

1912-13 — Quebec Bulldogs — Joe Malone, Joe Hall, Paddy Moran, Harry Mummery, Tommy Smith, Jack Marks, Russell Crawford, Billy Creighton, Jeff Malone, Rocket Power, M.J. Quinn (manager), D. Beland (trainer).
Scores: March 8 at Quebec — Que. Bulldogs 14, Sydney 3; March 10 at Quebec — Que. Bulldogs 6, Sydney 2.

Victoria challenged Quebec but the Bulldogs refused to put the Stanley Cup in competition so the two teams played an exhibition series with Victoria winning two games to one by scores of 7-5, 3-6, 6-1. It was the first meeting between the Eastern champions and the Western champions. The following year, and until the Western Hockey League disbanded after the 1926 playoffs, the Cup went to the winner of the series between East and West.

1911-12 — Quebec Bulldogs — Goldie Prodgers, Joe Hall, Walter Rooney, Paddy Moran, Jack Marks, Jack McDonald, Eddie Oatman, George Leonard, Joe Malone (captain), C. Nolan (coach), M.J. Quinn (manager), D. Beland (trainer).
Scores: March 11 at Quebec — Que. Bulldogs 9, Moncton 3; March 13 at Quebec — Que. Bulldogs 8, Moncton 0.

Prior to 1912, teams could challenge the Stanley Cup champions for the title, thus there was more than one Championship Series played in most of the seasons between 1894 and 1911.

1910-11 — Ottawa Senators — Hamby Shore, Percy LeSueur, Jack Darragh, Bruce Stuart, Marty Walsh, Bruce Ridpath, Fred Lake, Albert (Dubby) Kerr, Alex Currie, Horace Gaul.
Scores: March 13 at Ottawa — Ottawa 7, Galt 4; March 16 at Ottawa — Ottawa 13, Port Arthur 4.

1909-10 — Montreal Wanderers — Cecil W. Blachford, Ernie (Moose) Johnson, Ernie Russell, Riley Hern, Harry Hyland, Jack Marshall, Frank (Pud) Glass (captain), Jimmy Gardner, R. R. Boon (manager).
Scores: March 12 at Montreal — Mtl. Wanderers 7, Berlin (Kitchener) 3.

1908-09 — Ottawa Senators — Fred Lake, Percy LeSueur, Fred (Cyclone) Taylor, H.L. (Billy) Gilmour, Albert Kerr, Edgar Dey, Marty Walsh, Bruce Stuart (captain).
Scores: Ottawa, as champions of the Eastern Canada Hockey Association took over the Stanley Cup in 1909 and, although a challenge was accepted by the Cup trustees from Winnipeg Shamrocks, games could not be arranged because of the lateness of the season. No other challenges were made in 1909. The following season — 1909-10 — however, the Senators accepted two challenges as defending Cup Champions. The first was against Galt in a two-game, total-goals series, and the second against Edmonton, also a two-game, total-goals series. Results: January 5 at Ottawa —Ottawa 12, Galt 3; January 7 at Ottawa — Ottawa 3, Galt 1. January 18 at Ottawa — Ottawa 8, Edm. Eskimos 4; January 20 at Ottawa — Ottawa 13, Edm. Eskimos 7.

1907-08 — Montreal Wanderers — Riley Hern, Art Ross, Walter Smaill, Frank (Pud) Glass, Bruce Stuart, Ernie Russell, Ernie (Moose) Johnson, Cecil Blachford (captain), Tom Hooper, Larry Gilmour, Ernie Liffiton, R.R. Boon (manager).
Scores: Wanderers accepted four challenges for the Cup: January 9 at Montreal — Mtl. Wanderers 9, Ott. Victorias 3; January 13 at Montreal — Mtl. Wanderers 13, Ott. Victorias 1; March 10 at Montreal — Mtl. Wanderers 11, Wpg. Maple Leafs 5; March 12 at Montreal — Mtl. Wanderers 9, Wpg. Maple Leafs 3; March 14 at Montreal — Mtl. Wanderers 6, Toronto (OPHL) 4. At start of following season, 1908-09, Wanderers were challenged by Edmonton. Results: December 28 at Montreal — Mtl. Wanderers 7, Edm. Eskimos 3; December 30 at Montreal — Edm. Eskimos 7, Mtl. Wanderers 6. Total goals: Mtl. Wanderers 13, Edm. Eskimos 10.

1906-07 — (March) **— Montreal Wanderers —** W. S. (Billy) Strachan, Riley Hern, Lester Patrick, Hod Stuart, Frank (Pud) Glass, Ernie Russell, Cecil Blachford (captain), Ernie (Moose) Johnson, Rod Kennedy, Jack Marshall, R.R. Boon (manager).
Scores: March 23 at Winnipeg — Mtl. Wanderers 7, Kenora 2; March 25 at Winnipeg — Kenora 6, Mtl. Wanderers 5. Total goals: Mtl. Wanderers 12, Kenora 8.

1906-07 — (January) **— Kenora Thistles —** Eddie Geroux, Art Ross, Si Griffis, Tom Hooper, Billy McGimsie, Roxy Beaudro, Tom Phillips.
Scores: January 17 at Montreal — Kenora 4, Mtl. Wanderers 2; Jan. 21 at Montreal — Kenora 8, Mtl. Wanderers 6.

1905-06 — (March) **— Montreal Wanderers —** Henri Menard, Billy Strachan, Rod Kennedy, Lester Patrick, Frank (Pud) Glass, Ernie Russell, Ernie (Moose) Johnson, Cecil Blachford (captain), Josh Arnold, R.R. Boon (manager).
Scores: March 14 at Montreal — Mtl. Wanderers 9, Ottawa 1; March 17 at Ottawa — Ottawa 9, Mtl. Wanderers 3. Total goals: Mtl. Wanderers 12, Ottawa 10. Wanderers accepted a challenge from New Glasgow, N.S., prior to the start of the 1906-07 season. Results: December 27 at Montreal — Mtl. Wanderers 10, New Glasgow 3; December 29 at Montreal — Mtl. Wanderers 7, New Glasgow 2.

1905-06 — (February) **— Ottawa Silver Seven —** Harvey Pulford (captain), Arthur Moore, Harry Westwick, Frank McGee, Alf Smith (playing coach), Billy Gilmour, Billy Hague, Percy LeSueur, Harry Smith, Tommy Smith, Dion, Ebbs.
Scores: February 27 at Ottawa — Ottawa 16, Queen's University 7; February 28 at Ottawa — Ottawa 12, Queen's University 7; March 6 at Ottawa — Ottawa 6, Smiths Falls 5; March 8 at Ottawa — Ottawa 8, Smiths Falls 2.

1904-05 — Ottawa Silver Seven — Dave Finnie, Harvey Pulford (captain), Arthur Moore, Harry Westwick, Frank McGee, Alf Smith (playing coach), Billy Gilmour, Frank White, Horace Gaul, Hamby Shore, Bones Allen.
Scores: January 13 at Ottawa — Ottawa 9, Dawson City 2; January 16 at Ottawa — Ottawa 23, Dawson City 2; March 7 at Ottawa — Rat Portage 9, Ottawa 3; March 9 at Ottawa — Ottawa 4, Rat Portage 2; March 11 at Ottawa — Ottawa 5, Rat Portage 4.

1903-04 — Ottawa Silver Seven — S.C. (Suddy) Gilmour, Arthur Moore, Frank McGee, J.B. (Bouse) Hutton, H.L. (Billy) Gilmour, Jim McGee, Harry Westwick, E. H. (Harvey) Pulford (captain), Scott, Alf Smith (playing coach).
Scores: December 30 at Ottawa — Ottawa 9, Wpg. Rowing Club 1; January 1 at Ottawa — Wpg. Rowing Club 6, Ottawa 2; January 4 at Ottawa — Ottawa 2, Wpg. Rowing Club 0. February 23 at Ottawa — Ottawa 6, Tor. Marlboros 3; February 25 at Ottawa — Ottawa 11, Tor. Marlboros 2; March 2 at Montreal — Ottawa 5, Mtl. Wanderers 5. Following the tie game, a new two-game series was ordered to be played in Ottawa but the Wanderers refused unless the tie game was replayed in Montreal. When no settlement could be reached, the series was abandoned and Ottawa retained the Cup and accepted a two-game challenge from Brandon. Results: (both games at Ottawa), March 9, Ottawa 6, Brandon 3; March 11, Ottawa 9, Brandon 3.

1902-03 — (March) **— Ottawa Silver Seven —** S.C. (Suddy) Gilmour, P.T. (Percy) Sims, J.B. (Bouse) Hutton, D.J. (Dave) Gilmour, H.L. (Billy) Gilmour, Harry Westwick, Frank McGee, F.H. Wood, A.A. Fraser, Charles D. Spittal, E.H. (Harvey) Pulford (captain), Arthur Moore, Alf Smith (coach.)
Scores: March 7 at Montreal — Ottawa 1, Mtl. Victorias 1; March 10 at Ottawa — Ottawa 8, Mtl. Victorias 0. Total goals: Ottawa 9, Mtl. Victorias 1; March 12 at Ottawa — Ottawa 6, Rat Portage 2; March 14 at Ottawa — Ottawa 4, Rat Portage 2.

1902-03 — (February) **— Montreal AAA —** Tom Hodge, R.R. (Dickie) Boon, W.C. (Billy) Nicholson, Tom Phillips, Art Hooper, W.J. (Billy) Bellingham, Charles A. Liffiton, Jack Marshall, Jim Gardner, Cecil Blachford, George Smith.
Scores: January 29 at Montreal — Mtl. AAA 8, Wpg. Victorias 1; January 31 at Montreal — Wpg. Victorias 2, Mtl. AAA 2; February 2 at Montreal — Wpg. Victorias 4, Mtl. AAA 2; February 4 at Montreal — Mtl. AAA 5, Wpg. Victorias 1.

1901-02 — (March) **— Montreal AAA —** Tom Hodge, R.R. (Dickie) Boon, William C. (Billy) Nicholson, Archie Hooper, W.J. (Billy) Bellingham, Charles A. Liffiton, Jack Marshall, Roland Elliott, Jim Gardner.
Scores: March 13 at Winnipeg — Wpg. Victorias 1, Mtl. AAA 0; March 15 at Winnipeg — Mtl. AAA 5, Wpg. Victorias 0; March 17 at Winnipeg — Mtl. AAA 2, Wpg. Victorias 1.

1901-02 — (January) **— Winnipeg Victorias —** Burke Wood, A.B. (Tony) Gingras, Charles W. Johnstone, R.M. (Rod) Flett, Magnus L. Flett, Dan Bain (captain), Fred Scanlon, F. Cadham, G. Brown.
Scores: January 21 at Winnipeg — Wpg. Victorias 5, Tor Wellingtons 3; January 23 at Winnipeg — Wpg. Victorias 5, Tor. Wellingtons 3.

1900-01 — Winnipeg Victorias — Burke Wood, Jack Marshall, A.B. (Tony) Gingras, Charles W. Johnstone, R.M. (Rod) Flett, Magnus L. Flett, Dan Bain (captain), G. Brown.
Scores: January 29 at Montreal — Wpg. Victorias 4, Mtl. Shamrocks 3; January 31 at Montreal — Wpg. Victorias 2, Mtl. Shamrocks 1.

1899-1900 — Montreal Shamrocks — Joe McKenna, Frank Tansey, Frank Wall, Art Farrell, Fred Scanlon, Harry Trihey (captain), Jack Brannen.
Scores: February 12 at Montreal — Mtl. Shamrocks 4, Wpg. Victorias 3; February 14 at Montreal — Wpg. Victorias 3, Mtl. Shamrocks 2; February 16 at Montreal — Mtl. Shamrocks 5, Wpg. Victorias 4; March 5 at Montreal — Mtl. Shamrocks 10, Halifax 2; March 7 at Montreal — Mtl. Shamrocks 11, Halifax 0.

1898-99 — (March) **— Montreal Shamrocks —** Jim McKenna, Frank Tansey, Frank Wall, Harry Trihey (captain), Art Farrell, Fred Scanlon, Jack Brannen, John Dobby, Charles Hoerner.
Scores: March 14 at Montreal — Mtl. Shamrocks 6, Queen's University 2.

1898-99 — (February) **— Montreal Victorias —** Gordon Lewis, Mike Grant, Graham Drinkwater, Cam Davidson, Bob McDougall, Ernie McLea, Frank Richardson, Jack Ewing, Russell Bowie, Douglas Acer, Fred McRobie.
Scores: February 15 at Montreal — Mtl. Victorias 2, Wpg. Victorias 1; February 18 at Montreal — Mtl. Victorias 3, Wpg. Victorias 2.

1897-98 — Montreal Victorias — Gordon Lewis, Hartland McDougall, Mike Grant, Graham Drinkwater, Cam Davidson, Bob McDougall, Ernie McLea, Frank Richardson (captain), Jack Ewing. The Victorias as champions of the Amateur Hockey Association, retained the Cup and were not called upon to defend it.

1896-97 — Montreal Victorias — Gordon Lewis, Harold Henderson, Mike Grant (captain), Cam Davidson, Graham Drinkwater, Robert McDougall, Ernie McLea, Shirley Davidson, Hartland McDougall, Jack Ewing, Percy Molson, David Gillilan, McLellan.
Scores: December 27 at Montreal — Mtl. Victorias 15, Ott. Capitals 2.

1895-96 — (December) **— Montreal Victorias —** Harold Henderson, Mike Grant (captain), Robert McDougall, Graham Drinkwater, Shirley Davidson, Ernie McLea, Robert Jones, Cam Davidson, David Gillilan, Stanley Willett.
Scores: December 30 at Winnipeg — Mtl. Victorias 6, Wpg. Victorias 5.

1895-96 — (February) **— Winnipeg Victorias —** G.H. Merritt, Rod Flett, Fred Higginbotham, Jack Armitage (captain), C.J. (Tote) Campbell, Dan Bain, Charles Johnstone, H. Howard.
Scores: February 14 at Montreal — Wpg. Victorias 2, Mtl. Victorias 0.

1894-95 — Montreal Victorias — Robert Jones, Harold Henderson, Mike Grant (captain), Shirley Davidson, Bob McDougall, Norman Rankin, Graham Drinkwater, Roland Elliot, William Pullan, Hartland McDougall, Jim Fenwick, A. McDougall. Montreal Victorias as champions of the Amateur Hockey Association were prepared to defend the Stanley Cup. However, the Stanley Cup trustees had already accepted a challenge match between the 1894 champion Montreal AAA and Queen's University. It was declared that if Montreal AAA defeated Queen's University, Montreal Victorias would be declared Stanley Cup champions. If Queen's University won, the Cup would go to the university club. In a game played March 9, 1895, Montreal AAA defeated Queen's University 5-1. As a result, Montreal Victorias were awarded the Stanley Cup.

1893-94 — Montreal AAA — Herbert Collins, Allan Cameron, George James, Billy Barlow, Clare Mussen, Archie Hodgson, Haviland Routh, Alex Irving, James Stewart, A.C. (Toad) Wand, A. Kingan.
Scores: March 17 at Mtl. Victorias — Mtl. AAA 3, Mtl. Victorias 2; March 22 at Montreal — Mtl. AAA 3, Ott. Capitals 1.

1892-93 — Montreal AAA — Tom Paton, James Stewart, Allan Cameron, Haviland Routh, Archie Hodgson, Billy Barlow, A.B. Kingan, G.S. Lowe.
In accordance with the terms governing the presentation of the Stanley Cup, it was awarded for the first time to the Montreal AAA as champions of the Amateur Hockey Association in 1893. Once Montreal AAA had been declared holders of the Stanley Cup, any Canadian hockey team could challenge for the trophy.

All-Time NHL Playoff Formats

1917-18 — The regular-season was split into two halves. The winners of both halves faced each other in a two-game, total-goals series for the NHL championship and the right to meet the PCHA champion in the best-of-five Stanley Cup Finals.

1918-19 — Same as 1917-18, except that the Stanley Cup Finals was extended to a best-of-seven series.

1919-20 — Same as 1917-1918, except that Ottawa won both halves of the split regular-season schedule to earn an automatic berth into the best-of-five Stanley Cup Finals against the PCHA champions.

1921-22 — The top two teams at the conclusion of the regular-season faced each other in a two-game, total-goals series for the NHL championship. The NHL champion then moved on to play the winner of the PCHA-WCHL playoff series in the best-of-five Stanley Cup Finals.

1922-23 — The top two teams at the conclusion of the regular-season faced each other in a two-game, total-goals series for the NHL championship. The NHL champion then moved on to play the PCHA champion in the best-of-three Stanley Cup Semi-Finals, and the winner of the Semi-Finals played the WCHL champion, which had been given a bye, in the best-of-three Stanley Cup Finals.

1923-24 — The top two teams at the conclusion of the regular-season faced each other in a two-game, total-goals series for the NHL championship. The NHL champion then moved on to play the loser of the PCHA-WCHL playoff (the winner of the PCHA-WCHL playoff earned a bye into the Stanley Cup Finals) in the best-of-three Stanley Cup Semi-Finals. The winner of this series met the PCHA-WCHL playoff winner in the best-of-three Stanley Cup Finals.

1924-25 — The first place team (Hamilton) at the conclusion of the regular-season was supposed to play the winner of a two-game, total goals series between the second (Toronto) and third (Montreal) place clubs. However, Hamilton refused to abide by this new format, demanding greater compensation than offered by the League. Thus, Toronto and Montreal played two-game, total-goals series, and the winner (Montreal) earned the NHL title and then played the WCHL champion (Victoria) in the best-of-five Stanley Cup Finals.

1925-26 — The format which was intended for 1924-25 went into effect. The winner of the two-game, total-goals series between the second and third place teams squared off against the first place team in the two-game, total-goals NHL championship series. The NHL champion then moved on to play the WHL champion in the best-of-five Stanley Cup Finals.

After the 1925-26 season, the NHL was the only major professional hockey league still in existence and consequently took over sole control of the Stanley Cup competition.

1926-27 — The 10-team league was divided into two divisions — Canadian and American — of five teams apiece. In each division, the winner of the two-game, total-goals series between the second and third place teams faced the first place team in a two-game, total-goals series for the division title. The two division title winners then met in the best-of-five Stanley Cup Finals.

1928-29 — Both first place teams in the two divisions played each other in a best-of-five series. Both second place teams in the two divisions played each other in a two-game, total-goals series as did the two third place teams. The winners of these latter two series then played each other in a best-of-three series for the right to meet the winner of the series between the two first place clubs. This Stanley Cup Final was a best-of-three.

> Series A: First in Canadian Division versus first in American (best-of-five)
> Series B: Second in Canadian Division versus second in American (two-game, total-goals)
> Series C: Third in Canadian Division versus third in American (two-game, total-goals)
> Series D: Winner of Series B versus winner of Series C (best-of-three)
> Series E: Winner of Series A versus winner of Series D (best of three) for Stanley Cup

1931-32 — Same as 1928-29, except that Series D was changed to a two-game, total-goals format and Series E was changed to best of five.

1936-37 — Same as 1931-32, except that Series B, C, and D were each best-of-three.

1938-39 — With the NHL reduced to seven teams, the two-division system was replaced by one seven-team league. Based on final regular-season standings, the following playoff format was adopted:

> Series A: First versus Second (best-of-seven)
> Series B: Third versus Fourth (best-of-three)
> Series C: Fifth versus Sixth (best-of-three)
> Series D: Winner of Series B versus winner of Series C (best-of-three)
> Series E: Winner of Series A versus winner of Series D (best-of-seven)

1942-43 — With the NHL reduced to six teams (the "original six"), only the top four finishers qualified for playoff action. The best-of-seven Semi-Finals pitted Team #1 vs Team #3 and Team #2 vs Team #4. The winners of each Semi-Final series met in the best-of-seven Stanley Cup Finals.

1967-68 — When it doubled in size from 6 to 12 teams, the NHL once again was divided into two divisions — East and West — of six teams apiece. The top four clubs in each division qualified for the playoffs (all series were best-of-seven):

> Series A; Team #1 (East) vs Team #3 (East)
> Series B: Team #2 (East) vs Team #4 (East)
> Series C: Team #1 (West) vs Team #3 (West)
> Series D: Team #2 (West) vs Team #4 (West)
> Series E: Winner of Series A vs winner of Series B
> Series F: Winner of Series C vs winner of Series D
> Series G: Winner of Series E vs Winner of Series F

1970-71 — Same as 1967-68 except that Series E matched the winners of Series A and D, and Series F matched the winners of Series B and C.

1971-72 — Same as 1970-71, except that Series A and C matched Team #1 vs Team #4, and Series B and D matched Team #2 vs Team #3.

1974-75 — With the League now expanded to 18 teams in four divisions, a completely new playoff format was introduced. First, the #2 and #3 teams in each of the four divisions were pooled together in the Preliminary round. These eight (#2 and #3) clubs were ranked #1 to #8 based on regular-season record:

> Series A: Team #1 vs Team #8 (best-of-three)
> Series B: Team #2 vs Team #7 (best-of-three)
> Series C: Team #3 vs Team #6 (best-of-three)
> Series D: Team #4 vs Team #5 (best-of-three)

The winners of this Preliminary round then pooled together with the four division winners, which had received byes into this Quarter-Final round. These eight teams were again ranked #1 to #8 based on regular-season record:

> Series E: Team #1 vs Team #8 (best-of-seven)
> Series F: Team #2 vs Team #7 (best-of-seven)
> Series G: Team #3 vs Team #6 (best-of-seven)
> Series H: Team #4 vs Team #5 (best-of-seven)

The four Quarter-Finals winners, which moved on to the Semi-Finals, were then ranked #1 to #4 based on regular season record:

> Series I: Team #1 vs Team #4 (best-of-seven)
> Series J: Team #2 vs Team #3 (best-of-seven)
> Series K: Winner of Series I vs winner of Series J (best-of-seven)

1977-78 — Same as 1974-75, except that the Preliminary round consisted of the #2 teams in the four divisions and the next four teams based on regular-season record (not their standings within their divisions).

1979-80 — With the addition of four WHA franchises, the League expanded its playoff structure to include 16 of its 21 teams. The four first place teams in the four divisions automatically earned playoff berths. Among the 17 other clubs, the top 12, according to regular-season record, also earned berths. All 16 teams were then pooled together and ranked #1 to #16 based on regular-season record:

> Series A: Team #1 vs Team #16 (best-of-five)
> Series B: Team #2 vs Team #15 (best-of-five)
> Series C: Team #3 vs Team #14 (best-of-five)
> Series D: Team #4 vs Team #13 (best-of-five)
> Series E: Team #5 vs Team #12 (best-of-five)
> Series F: Team #6 vs Team #11 (best-of-five)
> Series G: Team #7 vs Team #10 (best-of-five)
> Series H: Team #8 vs Team # 9 (best-of-five)

The eight Preliminary round winners, ranked #1 to #8 based on regular-season record, moved on to the Quarter-Finals:

> Series I: Team #1 vs Team #8 (best-of-seven)
> Series J: Team #2 vs Team #7 (best-of-seven)
> Series K: Team #3 vs Team #6 (best-of-seven)
> Series L: Team #4 vs Team #5 (best-of-seven)

The eight Quarter-Finals winners, ranked #1 to #4 based on regular-season record, moved on to the semi-finals:

> Series M: Team #1 vs Team #4 (best-of-seven)
> Series N: Team #2 vs Team #3 (best-of-seven)
> Series O: Winner of Series M vs winner of Series N (best-of-seven)

1981-82 — The first four teams in each division earned playoff berths. In each division, the first-place team opposed the fourth-place team and the second-place team opposed the third-place team in a best-of-five Division Semi-Final series (DSF). In each division, the two winners of the DSF met in a best-of-seven Division Final series (DF). The two winners in each conference met in a best-of-seven Conference Final series (CF). In the Prince of Wales Conference, the Adams Division winner opposed the Patrick Division winner; in the Clarence Campbell Conference, the Smythe Division winner opposed the Norris Division winner. The two CF winners met in a best-of-seven Stanley Cup Final (F) series.

1986-87 — Division Semi-Final series changed from best-of-five to best-of-seven.

1993-94 — The NHL's playoff draw is now conference-based instead of division-based. At the conclusion of the regular season, the top eight teams in each of the Eastern and Western Conferences qualify for the playoffs. The teams that finish in first place in each of the League's divisions will be seeded first and second in each conference's playoff draw and are assured of home ice advantage in the first two playoff rounds. The remaining teams are seeded based on their regular-season point totals. In each conference, the team seeded #1 will play #8; #2 vs. #7; #3 vs. #6; and #4 vs. #5. All series will remain best-of-seven with home ice rotating on a 2-2-1-1-1 basis, with the exception of matchups between Central and Pacific Division teams. These matchups will be played on a 2-3-2 basis to reduce travel. In a 2-3-2 series, the team with the most points will have its choice to start the series at home or on the road. The Eastern Conference champion will face the Western Conference champion in the Stanley Cup Final.

Maurice Richard celebrates his eighth and final Stanley Cup championship after the Canadiens defeated the Toronto Maple Leafs in four straight games in 1960.

Team Records

1918-1993

MOST STANLEY CUP CHAMPIONSHIPS:
23 — **Montreal Canadiens** 1924-30-31-44-46-53-56-57-58-59-60-65-66-68-69-71-73-76-77-78-79-86-93
13 — Toronto Maple Leafs 1918-22-32-42-45-47-48-49-51-62-63-64-67
 7 — Detroit Red Wings 1936-37-43-50-52-54-55

MOST FINAL SERIES APPEARANCES:
33 — **Montreal Canadiens** in 76-year history.
21 — Toronto Maple Leafs in 76-year history.
18 — Detroit Red Wings in 67-year history.

MOST YEARS IN PLAYOFFS:
68 — **Montreal Canadiens** in 76-year history.
55 — Toronto Maple Leafs in 76-year history.
54 — Boston Bruins in 69-year history.

MOST CONSECUTIVE STANLEY CUP CHAMPIONSHIPS:
5 — **Montreal Canadiens** (1956-57-58-59-60)
4 — Montreal Canadiens (1976-77-78-79)
 — NY Islanders (1980-81-82-83)

MOST CONSECUTIVE FINAL SERIES APPEARANCES:
10 — **Montreal Canadiens** (1951-60, inclusive)
5 — Montreal Canadiens, (1965-69, inclusive)
 — NY Islanders, (1980-84, inclusive)

MOST CONSECUTIVE PLAYOFF APPEARANCES:
26 — **Boston Bruins** (1968-93, inclusive)
24 — Chicago Blackhawks (1970-93, inclusive)
23 — Montreal Canadiens (1971-93, inclusive)
21 — Montreal Canadiens (1949-69, inclusive)
20 — Detroit Red Wings (1939-58, inclusive)

MOST GOALS BOTH TEAMS, ONE PLAYOFF SERIES:
69 — **Edmonton Oilers, Chicago Blackhawks** in 1985 CF. Edmonton won best-of-seven series 4-2, outscoring Chicago 44-25.
62 — Chicago Blackhawks, Minnesota North Stars in 1985 DF. Chicago won best-of-seven series 4-2, outscoring Minnesota 33-29.
61 — Los Angeles Kings, Calgary Flames in 1993 DSF. Los Angeles won best-of-seven series 4-2, outscoring Calgary 33-28.

MOST GOALS ONE TEAM, ONE PLAYOFF SERIES:
44 — **Edmonton Oilers** in 1985 CF. Edmonton won best-of-seven series 4-2, outscoring Chicago 44-25.
35 — Edmonton Oilers in 1983 DF. Edmonton won best-of-seven series 4-1, outscoring Calgary 35-13.

MOST GOALS, BOTH TEAMS, TWO-GAME SERIES:
17 — **Toronto St. Patricks, Montreal Canadiens** in 1918 NHL F. Toronto won two-game tota goal series 10-7.
15 — Boston Bruins, Chicago Blackhawks in 1927 QF. Boston won two-game total goal series 10-5.
 — Pittsburgh Penguins, St. Louis Blues in 1975 PR. Pittsburgh won best-of-three series 2-0, outscoring St. Louis 9-6.

MOST GOALS, ONE TEAM, TWO-GAME SERIES:
11 — **Buffalo Sabres** in 1977 PR. Buffalo won best-of-three series 2-0, outscoring Minnesota 11-3.
 — Toronto Maple Leafs in 1978 PR. Toronto won best-of-three series 2-0, outscoring Los Angeles 11-3.
10 — Boston Bruins in 1927 QF. Boston won two-game total goal series 10-5.

MOST GOALS, BOTH TEAMS, THREE-GAME SERIES:
33 — **Minnesota North Stars, Boston Bruins** in 1981 PR. Minnesota won best-of-five series 3-0, outscoring Boston 20-13.
31 — Chicago Blackhawks, Detroit Red Wings in 1985 DSF. Chicago won best-of-five series 3-0, outscoring Detroit 23-8.
28 — Toronto Maple Leafs, NY Rangers in 1932 F. Toronto won best-of-five series 3-0, outscoring New York 18-10.

MOST GOALS, ONE TEAM, THREE-GAME SERIES:
23 — **Chicago Blackhawks** in 1985 DSF. Chicago won best-of-five series 3-0, outscoring Detroit 23-8.
20 — Minnesota North Stars in 1981 PR. Minnesota won best-of-five series 3-0, outscoring Boston 20-13.
 — NY Islanders in 1981 PR. New York won best-of-five series 3-0, outscoring Toronto 20-4.

MOST GOALS, BOTH TEAMS, FOUR-GAME SERIES:
36 — **Boston Bruins, St. Louis Blues** in 1972 SF. Boston won best-of-seven series 4-0, outscoring St. Louis 28-8.
 — **Edmonton Oilers, Chicago Blackhawks** in 1983 CF. Edmonton won best-of-seven series 4-0, outscoring Chicago 25-11.
 — **Minnesota North Stars, Toronto Maple Leafs** in 1983 DSF. Minnesota won best-of-five series 3-1; teams tied in scoring 18-18.
35 — NY Rangers, Los Angeles Kings in 1981 PR. NY Rangers won best-of-five series 3-1, outscoring Los Angeles 23-12.

MOST GOALS, ONE TEAM, FOUR-GAME SERIES:
28 — **Boston Bruins** in 1972 SF. Boston won best-of-seven series 4-0, outscoring St. Louis 28-8.

MOST GOALS, BOTH TEAMS, FIVE-GAME SERIES:
52 — **Edmonton Oilers, Los Angeles Kings** in 1987 DSF. Edmonton won best-of-seven series 4-1, outscoring Los Angeles 32-20.
50 — Los Angeles Kings, Edmonton Oilers in 1982 DSF. Los Angeles won best-of-five series 3-2, outscoring Edmonton 27-23.
48 — Edmonton Oilers, Calgary Flames in 1983 DF. Edmonton won best-of-seven series 4-1, outscoring Calgary 35-13.
— Calgary Flames, Los Angeles Kings in 1988 DSF. Calgary won best-of-seven series 4-1, outscoring Los Angeles 30-18.

MOST GOALS, ONE TEAM, FIVE-GAME SERIES:
35 — **Edmonton Oilers** in 1983 DF. Edmonton won best-of-seven series 4-1, outscoring Calgary 35-13.
32 — Edmonton Oilers in 1987 DSF. Edmonton won best-of-seven series 4-1, outscoring Los Angeles 32-20.
28 — NY Rangers in 1979 QF. NY Rangers won best-of-seven series 4-1, outscoring Philadelphia 28-8.
27 — Philadelphia Flyers in 1980 SF. Philadelphia won best-of-seven series 4-1, outscoring Minnesota 27-14.
— Los Angeles Kings, in 1982 DSF. Los Angeles won best-of-five series 3-2, outscoring Edmonton 27-23.

MOST GOALS, BOTH TEAMS, SIX-GAME SERIES:
69 — **Edmonton Oilers, Chicago Blackhawks** in 1985 CF. Edmonton won best-of-seven series 4-2, outscoring Chicago 44-25.
62 — Chicago Blackhawks, Minnesota North Stars in 1985 DF. Chicago won best-of-seven series 4-2, outscoring Minnesota 33-29.
61 — Los Angeles Kings, Calgary Flames in 1993 DSF. Los Angeles won best-of-seven series 4-2, outscoring Calgary 33-28.

MOST GOALS, ONE TEAM, SIX-GAME SERIES:
44 — **Edmonton Oilers** in 1985 CF. Edmonton won best-of-seven series 4-2, outscoring Chicago 44-25.
33 — Chicago Blackhawks in 1985 DF. Chicago won best-of-seven series 4-2, outscoring Minnesota 33-29.
— Montreal Canadiens in 1973 F. Montreal won best-of-seven series 4-2, outscoring Chicago 33-23.
— Los Angeles Kings in 1993 DSF. Los Angeles won best-of-seven series 4-2, outscoring Calgary 33-28.

MOST GOALS, BOTH TEAMS, SEVEN-GAME SERIES:
60 — **Edmonton Oilers, Calgary Flames** in 1984 DF. Edmonton won best-of-seven series 4-3, outscoring Calgary 33-27.

MOST GOALS, ONE TEAM, SEVEN-GAME SERIES:
33 — **Philadelphia Flyers** in 1976 QF. Philadelphia won best-of-seven series 4-3, outscoring Toronto 33-23.
— **Boston Bruins** in 1983 DF. Boston won best-of-seven series 4-3, outscoring Buffalo 33-23.
— **Edmonton Oilers** in 1984 DF. Edmonton won best-of-seven series 4-3, outscoring Calgary 33-27.

FEWEST GOALS, BOTH TEAMS, TWO-GAME SERIES:
1 — **NY Rangers, NY Americans,** in 1929 SF. NY Rangers defeated NY Americans 1-0 in two-game, total-goal series.
— **Mtl. Maroons, Chicago Blackhawks** in 1935 SF. Mtl. Maroons defeated Chicago 1-0 in two-game, total-goal series.

FEWEST GOALS, ONE TEAM, TWO-GAME SERIES:
0 — **NY Americans** in 1929 SF. Lost two-game total-goal series 1-0 against NY Rangers.
— **Chicago Blackhawks** in 1935 SF. Lost two-game total-goal series 1-0 against Mtl. Maroons.
— **Mtl. Maroons** in 1937 SF. Lost best-of-three series 2-0 to NY Rangers while being outscored 5-0.
— **NY Americans** in 1939 QF. Lost best-of-three series 2-0 to Toronto while being outscored 6-0.

FEWEST GOALS, BOTH TEAMS, THREE-GAME SERIES:
7 — **Boston Bruins, Montreal Canadiens** in 1929 SF. Boston won best-of-five series 3-0, outscoring Montreal 5-2.
— **Detroit Red Wings, Mtl. Maroons** in 1936 SF. Detroit won best-of-five series 3-0, outscoring Mtl. Maroons 6-1.

FEWEST GOALS, ONE TEAM, THREE-GAME SERIES:
1 — **Mtl. Maroons** in 1936 SF. Lost best-of-five series 3-0 to Detroit and were outscored 6-1.

FEWEST GOALS, BOTH TEAMS, FOUR-GAME SERIES:
9 — **Toronto Maple Leafs, Boston Bruins** in 1935 SF. Toronto won best-of-five series 3-1, outscoring Boston 7-2.

FEWEST GOALS, ONE TEAM, FOUR-GAME SERIES:
2 — **Boston Bruins** in 1935 SF. Toronto won best-of-five series 3-1, outscoring Boston 7-2.
— **Montreal Canadiens** in 1952 F. Detroit won best-of-seven series 4-0, outscoring Montreal 11-2.

FEWEST GOALS, BOTH TEAMS, FIVE-GAME SERIES:
11 — **NY Rangers, Mtl. Maroons** in 1928 F. NY Rangers won best-of-five series 3-2 , while outscored by Mtl. Maroons 6-5.

FEWEST GOALS, ONE TEAM, FIVE-GAME SERIES:
5 — **NY Rangers** in 1928 F. NY Rangers won best-of-five series 3-2, while outscored by Mtl. Maroons 6-5.

FEWEST GOALS, BOTH TEAMS, SIX-GAME SERIES:
22 — **Toronto Maple Leafs, Boston Bruins** in 1951 SF. Toronto won best-of-seven series 4-1 with 1 tie, outscoring Boston 17-5.

FEWEST GOALS, ONE TEAM, SIX-GAME SERIES:
5 — **Boston Bruins** in 1951 SF. Toronto won best-of-seven series 4-1 with 1 tie, outscoring Boston 17-5.

FEWEST GOALS, BOTH TEAMS, SEVEN-GAME SERIES:
18 — **Toronto Maple Leafs, Detroit Red Wings** in 1945 F. Toronto won best-of-seven series 4-3; teams tied in scoring 9-9.

FEWEST GOALS, ONE TEAM, SEVEN-GAME SERIES:
9 — **Toronto Maple Leafs,** in 1945 F. Toronto won best-of- seven series 4-3; teams tied in scoring 9-9.
— **Detroit Red Wings,** in 1945 F. Toronto won best-of-seven series 4-3; teams tied in scoring 9-9.

MOST GOALS, BOTH TEAMS, ONE GAME:
18 — **Los Angeles Kings, Edmonton Oilers** at Edmonton, April 7, 1982. Los Angeles 10, Edmonton 8. Los Angeles won best-of-five DSF 3-2.
17 — Pittsburgh Penguins, Philadelphia Flyers at Pittsburgh, April 25, 1989. Pittsburgh 10, Philadelphia 7. Philadelphia won best-of-seven DF 4-3.
16 — Edmonton Oilers, Los Angeles Kings at Edmonton, April 9, 1987. Edmonton 13, Los Angeles 3. Edmonton won best-of-seven DSF 4-1.
— Los Angeles Kings, Calgary Flames at Los Angeles, April 10, 1990. Los Angeles 12, Calgary 4. Los Angeles won best-of-seven DF 4-2.

MOST GOALS, ONE TEAM, ONE GAME:
13 — **Edmonton Oilers** at Edmonton, April 9, 1987. Edmonton 13, Los Angeles 3. Edmonton won best-of-seven DSF 4-1.
12 — Los Angeles Kings at Los Angeles, April 10, 1990. Los Angeles 12, Calgary 4. Los Angeles won best-of-seven DSF 4-2.
11 — Montreal Canadiens at Montreal, March 30, 1944. Montreal 11, Toronto 0. Canadiens won best-of-seven SF 4-1.
— Edmonton Oilers at Edmonton May 4, 1985. Edmonton 11, Chicago 2. Edmonton won best-of-seven CF 4-2.

MOST GOALS, BOTH TEAMS, ONE PERIOD:
9 — **NY Rangers, Philadelphia Flyers,** April 24, 1979, at Philadelphia, third period. NY Rangers won 8-3 scoring six of nine third-period goals.
— **Los Angeles Kings, Calgary Flames** at Los Angeles, April 10, 1990, second period. Los Angeles won game 12-4, scoring five of nine second-period goals.
8 — Chicago Blackhawks, Montreal Canadiens at Montreal, May 8, 1973, in the second period. Chicago won 8-7 scoring five of eight second-period goals.
— Chicago Blackhawks, Edmonton Oilers at Chicago, May 12, 1985 in the first period. Chicago won 8-6, scoring five of eight first-period goals.
— Edmonton Oilers, Winnipeg Jets at Edmonton, April 6, 1988 in the third period. Edmonton won 7-4, scoring six of eight third period goals.
— Hartford Whalers, Montreal Canadiens at Hartford, April 10, 1988 in the third period. Hartford won 7-5, scoring five of eight third period goals.

MOST GOALS, ONE TEAM, ONE PERIOD:
7 — **Montreal Canadiens,** March 30, 1944, at Montreal in third period, during 11-0 win against Toronto.

LONGEST OVERTIME:
116 Minutes, 30 Seconds — **Detroit Red Wings, Mtl. Maroons** at Montreal, March 24, 25, 1936. Detroit 1, Mtl. Maroons 0. Mud Bruneteau scored, assisted by Hec Kilrea, at 16:30 of sixth overtime period, or after 176 minutes, 30 seconds from start of game, which ended at 2:25 a.m. Detroit won best-of-five SF 3-0.

SHORTEST OVERTIME:
9 Seconds — **Montreal Canadiens, Calgary Flames,** at Calgary, May 18, 1986. Montreal won 3-2 on Brian Skrudland's goal and captured the best-of-seven F 4-1.
11 Seconds — NY Islanders, NY Rangers, at NY Rangers, April 11, 1975. NY Islanders won 4-3 on Jean-Paul Parise's goal and captured the best-of-three PR 2-1.

MOST OVERTIME GAMES, ONE PLAYOFF YEAR:
28 — **1993.** Of 85 games played, 28 went into overtime.
16 — 1982. Of 71 games played, 16 went into overtime.

FEWEST OVERTIME GAMES, ONE PLAYOFF YEAR:
0 — **1963.** None of the 16 games went into overtime, the only year since 1926 that no overtime was required in any playoff series.

MOST OVERTIME-GAME VICTORIES, ONE TEAM, ONE PLAYOFF YEAR:
10 — **Montreal Canadiens, 1993.** Two against Quebec in the DSF; three against Buffalo in the DF; two against NY Islanders in the CF; and three against Los Angeles in the F. Montreal played 20 games.
6 — NY Islanders, 1980. One against Los Angeles in the PR; two against Boston in the QF; one against Buffalo in the SF; and two against Philadelphia in the F. Islanders played 21 games.

MOST OVERTIME GAMES, FINAL SERIES:
5 — **Toronto Maple Leafs,, Montreal Canadiens** in 1951. Toronto defeated Montreal 4-1 in best-of-seven series.

MOST OVERTIME GAMES, SEMI-FINAL SERIES:
4 — **Toronto Maple Leafs, Boston Bruins** in 1933. Toronto won best-of-five series 3-2.
— **Boston Bruins, NY Rangers** in 1939. Boston won best-of-seven series 4-3.
— **St. Louis Blues, Minnesota North Stars** in 1968. St. Louis won best-of-seven series 4-3.

MOST GAMES PLAYED BY ALL TEAMS, ONE PLAYOFF YEAR:
92 — **1991.** There were 51 DSF, 24 DF, 11 CF and 6 F games.
87 — 1987. There were 44 DSF, 25 DF, 11 CF and 7 F games.
86 — 1992. There were 54 DSF, 20 DF, 8 CF and 4 F games.
85 — 1990. There were 49 DSF, 21 DF, 10 CF and 5 F games.
— 1993. There were 44 DSF, 24 DF, 12 CF and 5 F games.

MOST GAMES PLAYED, ONE TEAM, ONE PLAYOFF YEAR:
26 — **Philadelphia Flyers,** 1987. Won DSF 4-2 against NY Rangers, DF 4-3 against NY Islanders, CF 4-2 against Montreal, and lost F 4-3 against Edmonton.
24 — Pittsburgh Penguins, 1991. Won DSF 4-3 against New Jersey, DF 4-1 against Washington, CF 4-2 against Boston, and F 4-2 against Minnesota.
— Los Angeles Kings, 1993. Won DSF 4-2 against Calgary, DF 4-2 against Vancouver, CF 4-3 against Toronto, and lost F 4-1 against Montreal.

MOST ROAD VICTORIES, ONE TEAM, ONE PLAYOFF YEAR:
8 — **NY Islanders,** 1980. Won two at Los Angeles in PR; three at Boston in QF; two at Buffalo in SF; and one at Philadelphia in F series.
— **Philadelphia Flyers,** 1987. Won two at NY Rangers in DSF; two at NY Islanders in DF; three at Montreal in CF; and one at Edmonton in F series.
— **Edmonton Oilers,** 1990. Won one at Winnipeg in DSF; two at Los Angeles in DF; two at Chicago in CF and three at Boston in F series.
— **Pittsburgh Penguins,** 1992. Won two at Washington in DSF; two at NY Rangers in DF; two at Boston in CF; and two at Chicago in F series.

MOST HOME VICTORIES, ONE TEAM, ONE PLAYOFF YEAR:
11 — Edmonton Oilers, 1988
10 — Edmonton Oilers, 1985 in 10 home-ice games.
— Montreal Canadiens, 1986
— Montreal Canadiens, 1993
9 — Philadelphia Flyers, 1974
— Philadelphia Flyers, 1980
— NY Islanders, 1981
— NY Islanders, 1983
— Edmonton Oilers, 1984
— Edmonton Oilers, 1987
— Calgary Flames, 1989
— Pittsburgh Penguins, 1991

MOST ROAD VICTORIES, ALL TEAMS, ONE PLAYOFF YEAR:
46 — **1987.** Of 87 games played, road teams won 46 (22 DSF, 14 DF, 8 CF and 2 Stanley Cup).

MOST CONSECUTIVE PLAYOFF GAME VICTORIES:
14 — **Pittsburgh Penguins.** Streak started May 9, 1992, at Pittsburgh with a 5-4 in fourth game of a DF series against NY Rangers, won by Pittsburgh 4-2. Continued with a four-game sweep over Boston in the 1992 CF and a four-game win over Chicago in the 1992 F. Pittsburgh then won the first three games of the 1993 DSF versus New Jersey. New Jersey ended the streak April 25, 1993, at New Jersey with a 4-1 win.
12 — Edmonton Oilers. Streak began May 15, 1984 at Edmonton with a 7-2 win over NY Islanders in third game of F series, and ended May 9, 1985 when Chicago defeated Edmonton 5-2 at Chicago. Included in the streak were three wins over the NY Islanders, in 1984, three over Los Angeles, four over Winnipeg and two over Chicago, all in 1985.
11 — Montreal Canadiens. Streak began April 16, 1959, at Toronto with 3-2 win in fourth game of F series, won by Montreal 4-1, and ended March 23, 1961, when Chicago defeated Montreal 4-3 in second game of SF series. Included in streak were eight straight victories in 1960.
— Montreal Canadiens. Streak began April 28, 1968, at Montreal with 4-3 win in fifth game of SF series, won by Montreal 4-1, and ended April 17, 1969, at Boston when Boston defeated them 5-0 in third game of SF series. Included in the streak were four straight wins over St. Louis in the 1968 F and four straight wins over NY Rangers in a 1969 QF series.
— Boston Bruins. Streak began April 14, 1970, at Boston with 3-2 victory over NY Rangers in fifth game of a QF series, won by Boston 4-2. It continued with a four-game victory over Chicago in the 1970 SF and a four-game win over St. Louis in the 1970 F. Boston then won the first game of a 1971 QF series against Montreal. Montreal ended the streak April 8, 1971, at Boston with a 7-5 victory.
— Montreal Canadiens. Streak started May 6, 1976, at Montreal with 5-2 win in fifth game of a SF series against NY Islanders, won by Montreal 4-1. Continued with a four-game sweep over Philadelphia in the 1976 F and a four-game win against St. Louis in the 1977 QF. Montreal won the first two games of a 1977 SF series against the NY Islanders before NY Islanders ended the streak, April 2, 1977 at New York with a 5-3 victory.
— Chicago Blackhawks. Streak started April 24, 1992, at St. Louis with a 5-3 win in fourth game of a DSF series against St. Louis, won by Chicago 4-2. Continued with a four-game sweep over Detroit in the 1992 DF and a four-game win over Edmonton in the 1992 CF. Pittsburgh ended the streak May 26, 1992, at Pittsburgh with a 5-4 victory.

MOST CONSECUTIVE VICTORIES, ONE PLAYOFF YEAR:
11 — **Chicago Blackhawks** in 1992. Chicago won last three games of best-of-seven DSF against St. Louis to win series 4-2 and then defeated Detroit 4-0 in best-of-seven DF and Edmonton 4-0 in best-of-seven CF.
— **Pittsburgh Penguins** in 1992. Pittsburgh won last three games of best-of-seven DF against NY Rangers to win series 4-2 and then defeated Boston 4-0 in best-of-seven CF and Chicago 4-0 in best-of-seven F.
— **Montreal Canadiens** in 1993. Montreal won last for games of best-of-seven DSF against Quebec to win series 4-2, defeated Buffalo 4-0 in best-of-seven DF and won first three games of CF against NY Islanders.

Grant Fuhr won 66 playoff games for the Edmonton Oilers in the 1980s.

LONGEST PLAYOFF LOSING STREAK:
16 Games — **Chicago Blackhawks.** Streak started in 1975 QF against Buffalo when Chicago lost last two games. Then Chicago lost four games to Montreal in 1976 QF; two games to NY Islanders in 1977 QF; four games to Boston in 1978 QF and four games to NY Islanders in 1979 QF. Streak ended on April 8, 1980 when Chicago defeated St. Louis 3-2 in the opening game of their 1980 PR series.
12 Games — Toronto Maple Leafs. Streak started on April 16, 1979 as Toronto lost four straight games in a QF series against Montreal. Continued with three-game PR defeats versus Philadelphia and NY Islanders in 1980 and 1981 respectively. Toronto failed to qualify for the 1982 playoffs and lost the first two games of a 1983 DSF against Minnesota. Toronto ended the streak with a 6-3 win against the North Stars on April 9, 1983.
10 Games — NY Rangers. Streak started in 1968 QF against Chicago when NY Rangers lost last four games and continued through 1969 (four straight losses to Montreal in QF) and 1970 (two straight losses to Boston in QF) before ending with a 4-3 win against Boston, at New York, April 11, 1970.
— Philadelphia Flyers. Streak started on April 18, 1968, the last game in the 1968 QF series against St. Louis, and continued through 1969 (four straight losses to St. Louis in QF), 1971 (four straight losses to Chicago in QF) and 1973 (opening game loss to Minnesota in QF) before ending with a 4-1 win against Minnesota, at Philadelphia, April 5, 1973.

MOST SHUTOUTS, ONE PLAYOFF YEAR, ALL TEAMS:
12 — **1992.** Of 86 games played, Detroit, Edmonton and Vancouver had 2 each, while Boston, Buffalo, Chicago, Montreal, NY Rangers and Pittsburgh had 1 each.
8 — 1937. Of 17 games played, NY Rangers had 4. Detroit 3, Boston 1.
— 1975. Of 51 games played, Philadelphia had 5, Montreal 2, NY Islanders 1.
— 1980. Of 67 games played, Buffalo had 3, Philadelphia 2, Montreal, NY Islanders and Minnesota 1 each.
— 1984. Of 70 games played, Montreal had 3, Edmonton, Minnesota, NY Rangers, St. Louis and Vancouver 1 each.

FEWEST SHUTOUTS, ONE PLAYOFF YEAR, ALL TEAMS:
0 — 1959. 18 games played.

MOST SHUTOUTS, BOTH TEAMS, ONE SERIES:
5 — **1945 F, Toronto Maple Leafs, Detroit Red Wings.** Toronto had 3 shutouts, Detroit 2. Toronto won best-of-seven series 4-3.
— **1950 SF, Toronto Maple Leafs, Detroit Red Wings.** Toronto had 3 shutouts, Detroit 2. Detroit won best-of-seven series 4-3.

MOST PENALTIES, BOTH TEAMS, ONE SERIES:
219 — New Jersey Devils, Washington Capitals in 1988 DF won by New Jersey 4-3. New Jersey received 98 minors, 11 majors, 9 misconducts and 1 match penalty. Washington received 80 minors, 11 majors, 8 misconducts and 1 match penalty.

MOST PENALTY MINUTES, BOTH TEAMS, ONE SERIES:
656 — New Jersey Devils, Washington Capitals in 1988 DF won by New Jersey 4-3. New Jersey had 351 minutes; Washington 305.

MOST PENALTIES, ONE TEAM, ONE SERIES:
119 — New Jersey Devils in 1988 DF versus Washington. New Jersey received 98 minors, 11 majors, 9 misconducts and 1 match penalty.

MOST PENALTY MINUTES, ONE TEAM, ONE SERIES:
351 — New Jersey Devils in 1988 DF versus Washington. Series won by New Jersey 4-3.

MOST PENALTY MINUTES, BOTH TEAMS, ONE GAME:
298 Minutes — Detroit Red Wings, St. Louis Blues, at St. Louis, April 12, 1991. Detroit received 33 penalties for 152 minutes; St. Louis 33 penalties for 146 minutes. St. Louis won 6-1.
267 Minutes — NY Rangers, Los Angeles Kings, at Los Angeles, April 9, 1981. NY Rangers received 31 penalties for 142 minutes; Los Angeles 28 penalties for 125 minutes. Los Angeles won 5-4.

MOST PENALTIES, BOTH TEAMS, ONE GAME:
66 — Detroit Red Wings, St. Louis Blues, at St. Louis, April 12, 1991. Detroit received 33 penalties; St. Louis 33. St. Louis won 6-1.
62 — New Jersey Devils, Washington Capitals, at New Jersey, April 22, 1988. New Jersey received 32 penalties; Washington 30. New Jersey won 10-4.

MOST PENALTIES, ONE TEAM, ONE GAME:
33 — Detroit Red Wings, at St. Louis, April 12,1991. St. Louis won 6-1.
   — St. Louis Blues, at St. Louis, April 12, 1991. St. Louis won 6-1.
32 — New Jersey Devils, at Washington, April 22,1988. New Jersey won 10-4.
31 — NY Rangers, at Los Angeles, April 9, 1981. Los Angeles won 5-4.
30 — Philadelphia Flyers, at Toronto, April 15, 1976. Toronto won 5-4.

MOST PENALTY MINUTES, ONE TEAM, ONE GAME:
152 — Detroit Red Wings, at St. Louis, April 12, 1991. St. Louis won 6-1.
146 — St. Louis Blues, at St. Louis, April 12, 1991. St. Louis won 6-1.
142 — NY Rangers, at Los Angeles, April 9, 1981. Los Angeles won 5-4.

MOST PENALTIES, BOTH TEAMS, ONE PERIOD:
43 — NY Rangers, Los Angeles Kings, April 9, 1981, at Los Angeles, first period. NY Rangers had 24 penalties; Los Angeles 19. Los Angeles won 5-4.

MOST PENALTY MINUTES, BOTH TEAMS, ONE PERIOD:
248 — NY Islanders, Boston Bruins, April 17, 1980, first period, at Boston. Each team received 124 minutes. Islanders won 5-4.

Murray Balfour slips the puck past Toronto's Don Simmons during the 1962 Finals. The masked goaltender was outstanding as the Leafs captured their first Stanley Cup in 11 years with a six-game victory over the Chicago Black Hawks.

MOST PENALTIES, ONE TEAM, ONE PERIOD: (AND) MOST PENALTY MINUTES, ONE TEAM, ONE PERIOD:
24 Penalties; 125 Minutes — NY Rangers, April 9, 1981, at Los Angeles, first period. Los Angeles won 5-4.

FEWEST PENALTIES, BOTH TEAMS, BEST-OF-SEVEN SERIES:
19 — Detroit Red Wings, Toronto Maple Leafs in 1945 F, won by Toronto 4-3. Detroit received 10 minors. Toronto 9 minors.

FEWEST PENALTIES, ONE TEAM, BEST-OF-SEVEN SERIES:
9 — Toronto Maple Leafs in 1945 F, won by Toronto 4-3 against Detroit.

MOST POWER-PLAY GOALS BY ALL TEAMS, ONE PLAYOFF YEAR:
199 — 1988 in 83 games.

MOST POWER-PLAY GOALS, ONE TEAM, ONE PLAYOFF YEAR:
35 — Minnesota North Stars, 1991 in 23 games.
32 — Edmonton Oilers, 1988 in 18 games.
31 — NY Islanders, 1981, in 18 games.

MOST POWER-PLAY GOALS, BOTH TEAMS, ONE SERIES:
21 — NY Islanders, Philadelphia Flyers in 1980 F, won by NY Islanders 4-2. NY Islanders had 15 and Flyers 6.
   — NY Islanders, Edmonton Oilers in 1981 QF, won by NY Islanders 4-2. NY Islanders had 13 and Edmonton 8.
   — Philadelphia Flyers, Pittsburgh Penguins in 1989 DF, won by Philadelphia 4-3. Philadelphia had 11 and Pittsburgh 10.
   — Minnesota North Stars, Chicago Blackhawks in 1991 DSF, won by Minnesota 4-2. Minnesota had 15 and Chicago 6.
20 — Toronto Maple Leafs, Philadelphia Flyers in 1976 QF series won by Philadelphia 4-3. Toronto had 12 power-pay goals; Philadelphia 8.

MOST POWER-PLAY GOALS, ONE TEAM, ONE SERIES:
15 — NY Islanders in 1980 F against Philadelphia. NY Islanders won series 4-2.
   — Minnesota North Stars in 1991 DSF against Chicago. Minnesota won series 4-2.
13 — NY Islanders in 1981 QF against Edmonton. NY Islanders won series 4-2.
   — Calgary Flames in 1986 CF against St. Louis. Calgary won series 4-3.
12 — Toronto Maple Leafs in 1976 QF series won by Philadelphia 4-3.

MOST POWER-PLAY GOALS, BOTH TEAMS, ONE GAME:
8 — Minnesota North Stars, St. Louis Blues, April 24, 1991 at Minnesota. Minnesota had 4, St. Louis 4. Minnesota won 8-4.
7 — Minnesota North Stars, Edmonton Oilers, April 28, 1984 at Minnesota. Minnesota had 4, Edmonton 3. Edmonton won 8-5.
   — Philadelphia Flyers, NY Rangers, April 13, 1985 at New York. Philadelphia had 4, NY Rangers 3. Philadelphia won 6-5.
   — Edmonton Oilers, Chicago Blackhawks, May 14, 1985 at Edmonton. Chicago had 5, Edmonton 2. Edmonton won 10-5.
   — Edmonton Oilers, Los Angeles Kings, April 9, 1987 at Edmonton. Edmonton had 5, Los Angeles 2. Edmonton won 13-3.
   — Vancouver Canucks, Calgary Flames, April 9, 1989 at Vancouver. Vancouver had 4, Calgary 3. Vancouver won 5-3.

MOST POWER-PLAY GOALS, ONE TEAM, ONE GAME:
6 — Boston Bruins, April 2, 1969, at Boston against Toronto. Boston won 10-0.

MOST POWER-PLAY GOALS, BOTH TEAMS, ONE PERIOD:
5 — Minnesota North Stars, Edmonton Oilers, April 28, 1984, second period, at Minnesota. Minnesota had 4 and Edmonton 1. Edmonton won 8-5.
   — Vancouver Canucks, Calgary Flames, April 9, 1989, third period at Vancouver. Vancouver had 3 and Calgary 2. Vancouver won 5-3.
   — Minnesota North Stars, St. Louis Blues, April 24, 1991, second period, at Minnesota. Minnesota had 4 and St. Louis 1. Minnesota won 8-4.

MOST POWER-PLAY GOALS, ONE TEAM, ONE PERIOD:
4 — Toronto Maple Leafs, March 26, 1936, second period against Boston at Toronto. Toronto won 8-3.
   — Minnesota North Stars, April 28, 1984, second period against Edmonton at Minnesota. Edmonton won 8-5.
   — Boston Bruins, April 11, 1991, third period against Hartford at Boston. Boston won 6-1.
   — Minnesota North Stars, April 24, 1991, second period against St. Louis at Minnesota. Minnesota won 8-4.

MOST SHORTHAND GOALS BY ALL TEAMS, ONE PLAYOFF YEAR:
33 — 1988, in 83 games.

MOST SHORTHAND GOALS, ONE TEAM, ONE PLAYOFF YEAR:
10 — Edmonton Oilers 1983, in 16 games.
 9 — NY Islanders, 1981, in 19 games.
 8 — Philadelphia Flyers, 1989, in 19 games.
 7 — NY Islanders, 1980, in 21 games.
 7 — Chicago Blackhawks, 1989, in 16 games.

MOST SHORTHAND GOALS, BOTH TEAMS, ONE SERIES:
7 — Boston Bruins (4), NY Rangers (3), in 1958 SF, won by Boston 4-2.
   — Edmonton Oilers (5), Calgary Flames (2), in 1983 DF won by Edmonton 4-1.

MOST SHORTHAND GOALS, ONE TEAM, ONE SERIES:

5 — **Edmonton Oilers** in 1983 against Calgary in best-of-seven DF won by Edmonton 4-1.
— **NY Rangers** in 1979 against Philadelphia in best-of-seven QF, won by NY Rangers 4-1.
4 — Boston Bruins in 1958 against NY Rangers in best-of-seven SF series, won by Boston 4-2.
— Minnesota North Stars in 1981 against Calgary in best-of-seven SF, won by Minnesota 4-2.
— Chicago Blackhawks in 1989 against Detroit in best-of-seven DSF won by Chicago 4-2.
— Philadelphia Flyers in 1989 against Pittsburgh in best-of-seven DF won by Philadelphia 4-3.
— NY Rangers in 1992 against New Jersey in best-of-seven DSF won by NY Rangers 4-3.
— Detroit Red Wings in 1993 against Toronto in best-of-seven DSF won by Toronto 4-3.
— NY Islanders in 1993 against Pittsburgh in best-of-seven DF won by NY Islanders 4-3.

MOST SHORTHAND GOALS, BOTH TEAMS, ONE GAME:

4 — **NY Islanders, NY Rangers,** April 17, 1983 at NY Rangers. NY Islanders had 3 shorthand goals, NY Rangers 1. NY Rangers won 7-6.
— **Boston Bruins, Minnesota North Stars,** April 11, 1981, at Minnesota. Boston had 3 shorthand goals, Minnesota 1. Minnesota won 6-3.
3 — Toronto Maple Leafs, Detroit Red Wings, April 5, 1947, at Toronto. Toronto had 2 shorthand goals, Detroit 1. Toronto won 6-1.
— NY Rangers, Boston Bruins, April 1, 1958, at Boston. NY Rangers had 2 shorthand goals, Boston 1. NY Rangers won 5-2.
— Minnesota North Stars, Philadelphia Flyers, May 4, 1980, at Minnesota. Minnesota had 2 shorthand goals, Philadelphia 1. Philadelphia won 5-3.
— Edmonton Oilers, Winnipeg Jets, April 9, 1988 at Winnipeg. Winnipeg had 2 shorthand goals, Edmonton 1. Winnipeg won 6-4.
— New Jersey Devils, NY Islanders, April 14, 1988 at New Jersey. NY Islanders had 2 shorthand goals, New Jersey 1. New Jersey won 6-5.

MOST SHORTHAND GOALS, ONE TEAM, ONE GAME:

3 — **Boston Bruins,** April 11, 1981, at Minnesota. Minnesota won 6-3.
— **NY Islanders,** April 17, 1983, at NY Rangers. NY Rangers won 7-6.

MOST SHORTHAND GOALS, BOTH TEAMS, ONE PERIOD:

3 — **Toronto Maple Leafs, Detroit Red Wings,** April 5, 1947, at Toronto, first period. Toronto had 2 shorthand goals, Detroit 1. Toronto won 6-1.

MOST SHORTHAND GOALS ONE TEAM, ONE PERIOD:

2 — **Toronto Maple Leafs,** April 5, 1947, at Toronto against Detroit, first period. Toronto won 6-1.
— **Toronto Maple Leafs,** April 13, 1965, at Toronto against Montreal, first period. Montreal won 4-3.
— **Boston Bruins,** April 20, 1969, at Boston against Montreal, first period. Boston won 3-2.
— **Boston Bruins,** April 8, 1970, at Boston against NY Rangers, second period. Boston won 8-2.
— **Boston Bruins,** April 30, 1972, at Boston against NY Rangers, first period. Boston won 6-5.
— **Chicago Blackhawks,** May 3, 1973, at Chicago against Montreal, first period. Chicago won 7-4.
— **Montreal Canadiens,** April 23, 1978, at Detroit, first period. Montreal won 8-0.
— **NY Islanders,** April 8, 1980, at New York against Los Angeles, second period. NY Islanders won 8-1.
— **Los Angeles Kings,** April 9, 1980, at NY Islanders, first period. Los Angeles won 6-3.
— **Boston Bruins,** April 13, 1980, at Pittsburgh, second period. Boston won 8-3.
— **Minnesota North Stars,** May 4, 1980, at Minnesota against Philadelphia, second period. Philadelphia won 5-3.
— **Boston Bruins,** April 11, 1981, at Minnesota, third period. Minnesota won 6-3.
— **NY Islanders,** May 12, 1981, at New York against Minnesota, first period. NY Islanders won 6-3.
— **Montreal Canadiens,** April 7, 1982, at Montreal against Quebec, third period. Montreal won 5-1.
— **Edmonton Oilers,** April 24, 1983, at Edmonton against Chicago, third period. Edmonton won 8-4.
— **Winnipeg Jets,** April 14, 1985, at Calgary, second period. Winnipeg won 5-3.
— **Boston Bruins,** April 6, 1988 at Boston against Buffalo, first period. Boston won 7-3.
— **NY Islanders,** April 14, 1988 at New Jersey, third period. New Jersey won 6-5.
— **Detroit Red Wings,** April 29, 1993 at Toronto, second period. Detroit won 7-3.

Two outstanding defensemen in action during the 1981 Stanley Cup playoffs: Larry Robinson of the Montreal Canadiens and Kevin Lowe of the Edmonton Oilers. The Oilers engineered the greatest upset of the 1981 playoffs, eliminating the Canadiens in three straight games in the preliminary round.

Chicago's Dirk Graham combined with Pittsburgh's Kevin Stevens to score three goals in a span of 30 seconds during the 1992 Finals. Graham scored the first and third goal.

FASTEST TWO GOALS, BOTH TEAMS:
5 Seconds — Pittsburgh Penguins, Buffalo Sabres at Buffalo, April 14, 1979. Gilbert Perreault scored for Buffalo at 12:59 and Jim Hamilton for Pittsburgh at 13:04 of first period. Pittsburgh won 4-3 and best-of-three PR 2-1.

8 Seconds — Minnesota North Stars, St. Louis Blues at Minnesota, April 9, 1989. Bernie Federko scored for St. Louis at 2:28 of third period and Perry Berezan at 2:36 for Minnesota. Minnesota won 5-4. St. Louis won best-of-seven DSF 4-1.

9 Seconds — NY Islanders, Washington Capitals at Washington, April 10, 1986. Bryan Trottier scored for New York at 18:26 of second period and Scott Stevens at 18:35 for Washington. Washington won 5-2, and won best-of-five DSF 3-0.

10 Seconds — Washington Capitals, New Jersey Devils at New Jersey, April 5, 1990. Pat Conacher scored for New Jersey at 8:02 of second period and Dale Hunter at 8:12 for Washington. Washington won 5-4, and won best-of-seven DSF 4-2.

— Calgary Flames, Edmonton Oilers at Edmonton, April 8, 1991. Joe Nieuwendyk scored for Calgary at 2:03 of first period and Esa Tikkanen at 2:13 for Edmonton. Edmonton won 4-3, and won best-of-seven DSF 4-3.

FASTEST TWO GOALS, ONE TEAM:
5 Seconds — Detroit Red Wings at Detroit, April 11, 1965, against Chicago. Norm Ullman scored at 17:35 and 17:40, second period. Detroit won 4-2. Chicago won best-of-seven SF 4-3.

FASTEST THREE GOALS, BOTH TEAMS:
21 Seconds — Edmonton Oilers, Chicago Blackhawks at Edmonton, May 7, 1985. Behn Wilson scored for Chicago at 19:22 of third period, Jari Kurri at 19:36 and Glenn Anderson at 19:43 for Edmonton. Edmonton won 7-3 and best-of-seven CF 4-2.

30 Seconds — Chicago Blackhawks, Pittsburgh Penguins at Chicago, June 1, 1992. Dirk Graham scored for Chicago at 6:21 of first period, Kevin Stevens for Pittsburgh at 6:33 and Graham for Chicago at 6:51. Pittsburgh won 6-5 and best-of-seven F 4-0.

31 Seconds — Edmonton Oilers, Philadelphia Flyers at Edmonton, May 25, 1985. Wayne Gretzky scored for Edmonton at 1:10 and 1:25 of first period, Derrick Smith scored for Philadelphia at 1:41. Edmonton won 4-3 and best-of-seven F 4-1.

FASTEST THREE GOALS, ONE TEAM:
23 Seconds — Toronto Maple Leafs at Toronto, April 12, 1979, against Atlanta Flames. Darryl Sittler scored at 4:04 of first period and again at 4:16 and Ron Ellis at 4:27. Leafs won 7-4 and best-of-three PR 2-0.

38 Seconds — NY Rangers at New York, April 12, 1986. Jim Wiemer scored at 12:29 of third period, Bob Brooke at 12:43 and Ron Grescher at 13:07. NY Rangers won 5-2 and best-of-five DSF 3-2.

56 Seconds — Montreal Canadiens at Detroit, April 6, 1954. Dickie Moore scored at 15:03 of first period, Maurice Richard at 15:28 and again at 15:59. Montreal won 3-1. Detroit won best-of-seven F 4-3.

FASTEST FOUR GOALS, BOTH TEAMS:
1 Minute, 33 Seconds — Philadelphia Flyers, Toronto Maple Leafs at Philadelphia, April 20, 1976. Don Saleski of Philadelphia scored at 10:04 of second period; Bob Neely, Toronto, 10:42; Gary Dornhoefer, Philadelphia, 11:24; and Don Saleski, 11:37. Philadelphia won 7-1 and best-of-seven QF series 4-3.

1 minute, 34 seconds — Montreal Canadiens, Calgary Flames at Montreal, May 20, 1986. Joel Otto of Calgary scored at 17:59 of first period; Bobby Smith, Montreal, 18:25; Mats Naslund, Montreal, 19:17; and Bob Gainey, Montreal, 19:33. Montreal won 5-3 and best-of-seven F series 4-1.

1 Minute, 38 Seconds — Boston Bruins, Philadelphia Flyers at Philadelphia, April 26, 1977. Gregg Sheppard of Boston scored at 14:01 of second period; Mike Milbury, Boston, 15:01; Gary Dornhoefer, Philadelphia, 15:16; and Jean Ratelle, Boston, 15:39. Boston won 5-4 and best-of-seven SF series 4-0.

FASTEST FOUR GOALS, ONE TEAM:
2 Minutes, 35 Seconds — Montreal Canadiens at Montreal, March 30, 1944, against Toronto. Toe Blake scored at 7:58 of third period and again at 8:37; Maurice Richard, 9:17; Ray Getliffe, 10:33. Montreal won 11-0 and best-of-seven SF 4-1.

FASTEST FIVE GOALS, BOTH TEAMS:
3 Minutes, 6 Seconds — Chicago Blackhawks, Minnesota North Stars, at Chicago April 21, 1985. Keith Brown scored for Chicago at 1:12, second period; Ken Yaremchuk, Chicago, 1:27; Dino Ciccarelli, Minnesota, 2:48; Tony McKegney, Minnesota, 4:07; and Curt Fraser, Chicago, 4:18. Chicago won 6-2 and best-of-seven DF 4-2.

3 Minutes, 20 Seconds — Minnesota North Stars, Philadelphia Flyers, at Philadelphia, April 29, 1980. Paul Shmyr scored for Minnesota at 13:20, first period; Steve Christoff, Minnesota, 13:59; Ken Linseman, Philadelphia, 14:54; Tom Gorence, Philadelphia, 15:36; and Linseman, 16:40. Minnesota won 6-5. Philadelphia won best-of-seven SF 4-1.

4 Minutes, 19 Seconds — Toronto Maple Leafs, NY Rangers at Toronto, April 9, 1932. Ace Bailey scored for Toronto at 15:07, third period; Fred Cook, NY Rangers, 16:32; Bob Gracie, Toronto, 17:36; Frank Boucher, NY Rangers, 18:26 and again at 19:26. Toronto won 6-4 and best-of-five F 3-0.

FASTEST FIVE GOALS, ONE TEAM:
3 Minutes, 36 Seconds — Montreal Canadiens at Montreal, March 30, 1944, against Toronto. Toe Blake scored at 7:58 of third period and again at 8:37; Maurice Richard, 9:17; Ray Getliffe, 10:33; and Buddy O'Connor, 11:34. Canadiens won 11-0 and best-of-seven SF 4-1.

MOST THREE-OR-MORE GOAL GAMES BY ALL TEAMS, ONE PLAYOFF YEAR:
12 — 1983 in 66 games.
— 1988 in 83 games.
11 — 1985 in 70 games.
— 1992 in 86 games.

MOST THREE-OR-MORE GOAL GAMES, ONE TEAM, ONE PLAYOFF YEAR:
6 — Edmonton Oilers in 16 games, 1983.
— Edmonton Oilers in 18 games, 1985.

Individual Records

Career

MOST YEARS IN PLAYOFFS:
20 — **Gordie Howe, Detroit, Hartford** (1947-58 incl.; 60-61; 63-66 incl.; 70 & 80)
— **Larry Robinson, Montreal, Los Angeles** (1973-92 incl.)
19 — Red Kelly, Detroit, Toronto
18 — Stan Mikita, Chicago
— Henri Richard, Montreal

MOST CONSECUTIVE YEARS IN PLAYOFFS:
20 — **Larry Robinson, Montreal, Los Angeles** (1973-1992, inclusive).
17 — Brad Park, NY Rangers, Boston, Detroit (1969-1985, inclusive).
16 — Jean Beliveau, Montreal (1954-69, inclusive).

MOST PLAYOFF GAMES:
227 — **Larry Robinson, Montreal, Los Angeles**
219 — Bryan Trottier, NY Islanders, Pittsburgh
185 — Denis Potvin, NY Islanders
— Glenn Anderson, Edmonton, Toronto
184 — Bobby Smith, Minnesota, Montreal

MOST POINTS IN PLAYOFFS (CAREER):
346 — **Wayne Gretzky, Edmonton, Los Angeles**, 110G, 236A
229 — Mark Messier, Edmonton, NY Rangers, 87G, 142A
222 — Jari Kurri, Edmonton, Los Angeles, 102G, 120A
201 — Glenn Anderson, Edmonton, Toronto, 88G, 113A
184 — Bryan Trottier, NY Islanders, Pittsburgh 71G, 113A
176 — Jean Beliveau, Montreal, 79G, 97A

MOST GOALS IN PLAYOFFS (CAREER):
110 — **Wayne Gretzky, Edmonton, Los Angeles**
102 — Jari Kurri, Edmonton, Los Angeles
88 — Glenn Anderson, Edmonton, Toronto
87 — Mark Messier, Edmonton, NY Rangers
85 — Mike Bossy, NY Islanders
82 — Maurice Richard, Montreal

MOST ASSISTS IN PLAYOFFS (CAREER):
236 — **Wayne Gretzky, Edmonton, Los Angeles**
142 — Mark Messier, Edmonton, NY Rangers
129 — Jari Kurri, Edmonton, Los Angeles
116 — Larry Robinson, Montreal, Los Angeles
113 — Bryan Trottier, NY Islanders, Pittsburgh
— Glenn Anderson, Edmonton, Toronto
108 — Denis Potvin, NY Islanders

MOST OVERTIME GOALS IN PLAYOFFS (CAREER):
6 — **Maurice Richard, Montreal** (1 in 1946; 3 in 1951; 1 in 1957; 1 in 1958.)
4 — Bob Nystrom, NY Islanders
— Dale Hunter, Quebec, Washington
— Glenn Anderson, Edmonton, Toronto
— Wayne Gretzky, Edmonton, Los Angeles
3 — Mel Hill, Boston
— Rene Robert, Buffalo
— Danny Gare, Buffalo
— Jacques Lemaire, Montreal
— Bobby Clarke, Philadelphia
— Terry O'Reilly, Boston
— Mike Bossy, NY Islanders
— Steve Payne, Minnesota
— Ken Morrow, NY Islanders
— Lanny McDonald, Toronto, Calgary
— Peter Stastny, Quebec
— Dino Ciccarelli, Minnesota, Washington
— Russ Courtnall, Montreal

MOST POWER-PLAY GOALS IN PLAYOFFS (CAREER):
35 — **Mike Bossy, NY Islanders**
30 — Wayne Gretzky, Edmonton, Los Angeles
27 — Denis Potvin, NY Islanders
26 — Jean Beliveau, Montreal
25 — Jari Kurri, Edmonton, Los Angeles
24 — Bobby Smith, Minnesota, Montreal
23 — Glenn Anderson, Edmonton, Toronto
— Brian Propp, Philadelphia, Boston, Minnesota
— Cam Neely, Vancouver, Boston

MOST SHORTHAND GOALS IN PLAYOFFS (CAREER):
13 — **Mark Messier, Edmonton, NY Rangers**
11 — Wayne Gretzky, Edmonton, Los Angeles
9 — Jari Kurri, Edmonton, Los Angeles
8 — Ed Westfall, Boston, NY Islanders
— Hakan Loob, Calgary

MOST GAME-WINNING GOALS IN PLAYOFFS (CAREER):
21 — **Wayne Gretzky, Edmonton, Los Angeles**
18 — Maurice Richard, Montreal
17 — Mike Bossy, NY Islanders
15 — Jean Beliveau, Montreal
— Yvan Cournoyer, Montreal

MOST THREE-OR-MORE-GOAL GAMES IN PLAYOFFS (CAREER):
8 — **Wayne Gretzky, Edmonton.** Six three-goal games; two four-goal games.
7 — Maurice Richard, Montreal. Four three-goal games; two four-goal games; one five-goal game.
— Jari Kurri, Edmonton. Six three-goal games; one four-goal game.
5 — Mike Bossy, NY Islanders. Four three-goal games; one four-goal game.

MOST PENALTY MINUTES IN PLAYOFFS (CAREER):
599 — **Dale Hunter,** Quebec, Washington
541 — Chris Nilan, Montreal, NY Rangers, Boston
466 — Willi Plett, Atlanta, Calgary, Minnesota, Boston
455 — Dave Williams, Toronto, Vancouver, Los Angeles
412 — Dave Schultz, Philadelphia, Los Angeles, Buffalo

MOST SHUTOUTS IN PLAYOFFS (CAREER):
15 — **Clint Benedict,** Ottawa, Mtl. Maroons
14 — Jacques Plante, Montreal, St. Louis
13 — Turk Broda, Toronto
12 — Terry Sawchuk, Detroit, Toronto, Los Angeles

MOST PLAYOFF GAMES APPEARED IN BY A GOALTENDER (CAREER):
132 — **Bill Smith, NY Islanders**
119 — Grant Fuhr, Edmonton, Buffalo
115 — Glenn Hall, Detroit, Chicago, St. Louis
112 — Jacques Plante, Montreal, St. Louis, Toronto, Boston
— Ken Dryden, Montreal
108 — Patrick Roy, Montreal
106 — Terry Sawchuk, Detroit, Toronto, Los Angeles, NY Rangers

MOST MINUTES PLAYED BY A GOALTENDER (CAREER):
7,645 — **Billy Smith, NY Islanders**
7,002 — Grant Fuhr, Edmonton, Buffalo
6,899 — Glenn Hall, Detroit, Chicago, St. Louis
6,846 — Ken Dryden, Montreal
6,651 — Jacques Plante, Montreal, St. Louis, Toronto, Boston

Single Playoff Year

MOST POINTS, ONE PLAYOFF YEAR:
47 — **Wayne Gretzky, Edmonton,** in 1985. 17 goals, 30 assists in 18 games.
44 — Mario Lemieux, Pittsburgh, in 1991. 16 goals, 28 assists in 23 games.
43 — Wayne Gretzky, Edmonton, in 1988. 12 goals, 31 assists in 19 games.
40 — Wayne Gretzky, Los Angeles, in 1993. 15 goals, 25 assists in 24 games.
38 — Wayne Gretzky, Edmonton, in 1983. 12 goals, 26 assists in 16 games.
37 — Paul Coffey, Edmonton, in 1985. 12 goals, 25 assists in 18 games.
35 — Mike Bossy, NY Islanders, in 1981. 17 goals, 18 assists in 18 games.
— Wayne Gretzky, Edmonton, in 1984. 13 goals, 22 assists in 19 games.
— Mark Messier, Edmonton, in 1988. 11 goals, 23 assists in 19 games.
— Doug Gilmour, Toronto, in 1993. 10 goals, 25 assists in 21 games.
34 — Wayne Gretzky, Edmonton, in 1987. 5 goals, 29 assists in 21 games.
— Mark Recchi, Pittsburgh, in 1991. 10 goals, 24 assists in 24 games.
— Mario Lemieux, Pittsburgh, in 1992. 16 goals, 18 assists in 15 games.
33 — Rick Middleton Boston, in 1983. 11 goals, 22 assists in 17 games.
— Kevin Stevens, Pittsburgh, in 1991. 17 goals, 16 assists in 24 games.
32 — Barry Pederson, Boston, in 1983. 14 goals, 18 assists in 17 games.

MOST POINTS BY A DEFENSEMAN, ONE PLAYOFF YEAR:
37 — **Paul Coffey, Edmonton,** in 1985. 12 goals, 25 assists in 18 games.
31 — Al MacInnis, Calgary, in 1989. 7 goals, 24 assists in 18 games.
25 — Denis Potvin, NY Islanders, in 1981. 8 goals, 17 assists in 18 games.
— Ray Bourque, Boston, in 1991. 7 goals, 18 assists in 19 games.
24 — Bobby Orr, Boston, in 1972. 5 goals, 19 assists in 15 games.

MOST POINTS BY A ROOKIE, ONE PLAYOFF YEAR:
21 — **Dino Ciccarelli, Minnesota,** in 1981. 14 goals, 7 assists in 19 games.
20 — Don Maloney, NY Rangers, in 1979. 7 goals, 13 assists in 18 games.

LONGEST CONSECUTIVE POINT-SCORING STREAK, ONE PLAYOFF YEAR:
18 games — **Bryan Trottier, NY Islanders,** 1981. 11 goals, 18 assists, 29 points.
17 games — Wayne Gretzky, Edmonton, 1988. 12 goals, 29 assists, 41 points.
— Al MacInnis, Calgary, 1989. 7 goals, 19 assists, 24 points.

LONGEST CONSECUTIVE POINT-SCORING STREAK, MORE THAN ONE PLAYOFF YEAR:
27 games — **Bryan Trottier, NY Islanders,** 1980, 1981 and 1982. 7 games in 1980 (3 G, 5 A, 8 PTS), 18 games in 1981 (11 G, 18 A, 29 PTS), and two games in 1982 (2 G, 3 A, 5 PTS). Total points, 42.
19 games — Wayne Gretzky, Edmonton, Los Angeles 1988 and 1989. 17 games in 1988 (12 G, 29 A, 41 PTS with Edmonton), 2 games in 1989 (1 G, 2 A, 3 PTS with Los Angeles). Total points, 44.
18 games — Phil Esposito, Boston, 1970 and 1971. 13 G, 20 A, 33 PTS.

MOST GOALS, ONE PLAYOFF YEAR:
19 — **Reggie Leach, Philadelphia,** 1976. 16 games.
— **Jari Kurri, Edmonton,** 1985. 18 games.
17 — Newsy Lalonde, Montreal, 1919. 10 games.
— Mike Bossy, NY Islanders, 1981. 18 games.
— Steve Payne, Minnesota, 1981. 19 games.
— Mike Bossy, NY Islanders, 1982. 19 games.
— Mike Bossy, NY Islanders, 1983. 19 games
— Wayne Gretzky, Edmonton, 1985. 18 games.
— Kevin Stevens, Pittsburgh, 1991. 24 games.

MOST GOALS BY A DEFENSEMAN, ONE PLAYOFF YEAR:
  12 — **Paul Coffey, Edmonton,** 1985. 18 games.
   9 — Bobby Orr, Boston, 1970. 14 games.
    — Brad Park, Boston, 1978. 15 games.
   8 — Denis Potvin, NY Islanders, 1981. 18 games.
    — Raymond Bourque, Boston, 1983. 17 games.
    — Denis Potvin, NY Islanders, 1983. 20 games.
    — Paul Coffey, Edmonton, 1984. 19 games

MOST GOALS BY A ROOKIE, ONE PLAYOFF YEAR:
  14 — **Dino Ciccarelli, Minnesota,** 1981. 19 games.
  11 — Jeremy Roenick, Chicago, 1990. 20 games.
  10 — Claude Lemieux, Montreal, 1986. 20 games.
   9 — Pat Flatley, NY Islanders, 1984. 21 games
   8 — Steve Christoff, Minnesota, 1980. 14 games.
    — Brad Palmer, Minnesota, 1981. 19 games.
    — Mike Krushelnyski, Boston, 1983. 17 games.
    — Bob Joyce, Boston, 1988. 23 games.

MOST GAME-WINNING GOALS, ONE PLAYOFF YEAR:
   5 — **Mike Bossy, NY Islanders,** 1983. 19 games.
    — **Jari Kurri, Edmonton,** 1987. 21 games.
    — **Bobby Smith, Minnesota,** 1991. 23 games.
    — **Mario Lemieux, Pittsburgh,** 1992. 15 games.

MOST OVERTIME GOALS, ONE PLAYOFF YEAR:
   3 — **Mel Hill, Boston,** 1939. All against NY Rangers in best-of-seven SF, won by Boston 4-3.
    — **Maurice Richard, Montreal,** 1951. 2 against Detroit in best-of-seven SF, won by Montreal 4-2; 1 against Toronto best-of-seven F, won by Toronto 4-1.

MOST POWER-PLAY GOALS, ONE PLAYOFF YEAR:
   9 — **Mike Bossy, NY Islanders,** 1981. 18 games against Toronto, Edmonton, NY Rangers and Minnesota.
    — **Cam Neely, Boston,** 1991. 19 games against Hartford, Montreal, Pittsburgh.
   8 — Tim Kerr, Philadelphia, 1989. 19 games.
    — John Druce, Washington, 1990. 15 games
    — Brian Propp, Minnesota, 1991. 23 games.
    — Mario Lemieux, Pittsburgh, 1992. 15 games.
   7 — Michel Goulet, Quebec, 1985. 17 games.
    — Mark Messier, Edmonton, 1988. 19 games.
    — Mario Lemieux, Pittsburgh, 1989. 11 games.
    — Brett Hull, St. Louis, 1990. 12 games.
    — Kevin Stevens, Pittsburgh, 1991. 24 games.

MOST SHORTHAND GOALS, ONE PLAYOFF YEAR:
   3 — **Derek Sanderson, Boston,** 1969. 1 against Toronto in QF, won by Boston 4-0; 2 against Montreal in SF, won by Montreal, 4-2.
    — **Bill Barber, Philadelphia,** 1980. All against Minnesota in SF, won by Philadelphia 4-1.
    — **Lorne Henning, NY Islanders,** 1980. 1 against Boston in QF won by NY Islanders 4-1; 1 against Buffalo in SF, won by NY Islanders 4-2, 1 against Philadelphia in F, won by NY Islanders 4-2.
    — **Wayne Gretzky, Edmonton,** 1983. 2 against Winnipeg in DSF won by Edmonton 3-0; 1 against Calgary in DF, won by Edmonton 4-1.
    — **Wayne Presley, Chicago,** 1989. All against Detroit in DSF won by Chicago 4-2.

MOST THREE-OR-MORE GOAL GAMES, ONE PLAYOFF YEAR:
   4 — **Jari Kurri, Edmonton,** 1985. 1 four-goal game, 3 three-goal games.
   3 — Mark Messier, Edmonton, 1983. 3 three-goal games.
    — Mike Bossy, NY Islanders, 1983. 1 four-goal game, 2 three-goal games
   2 — Newsy Lalonde, Montreal, 1919. 1 five-goal game, 1 four-goal game.
    — Maurice Richard, Montreal, 1944. 1 five-goal game; 1 three-goal game.
    — Doug Bentley, Chicago, 1944. 2 three-goal games.
    — Norm Ullman, Detroit, 1964. 2 three-goal games.
    — Phil Esposito, Boston, 1970. 2 three-goal games.
    — Pit Martin, Chicago, 1973. 2 three-goal games.
    — Rick MacLeish, Philadelphia, 1975. 2 three-goal games.
    — Lanny McDonald, Toronto, 1977. 1 three-goal game; 1 four-goal game.
    — Wayne Gretzky, Edmonton, 1981. 2 three-goal games.
    — Wayne Gretzky, Edmonton, 1983. 2 four-goal games.
    — Wayne Gretzky, Edmonton, 1983. 2 three-goal games.
    — Petr Klima, Detroit, 1988. 2 three-goal games.
    — Cam Neely, Boston, 1991. 2 three-goal games.

LONGEST CONSECUTIVE GOAL-SCORING STREAK, ONE PLAYOFF YEAR:
  9 Games — Reggie Leach, Philadelphia, 1976. Streak started April 17 at Toronto and ended May 9 at Montreal. He scored one goal in each of seven games; two in one game; and five in another; a total of 14 goals.

MOST ASSISTS, ONE PLAYOFF YEAR:
  31 — **Wayne Gretzky, Edmonton,** 1988. 19 games.
  30 — Wayne Gretzky, Edmonton, 1985. 18 games.
  29 — Wayne Gretzky, Edmonton, 1987. 21 games.
  28 — Mario Lemieux, Pittsburgh, 1991. 23 games.
  26 — Wayne Gretzky, Edmonton, 1983. 16 games.
  25 — Paul Coffey, Edmonton, 1985. 18 games.
    — Wayne Gretzky, Los Angeles, 1993. 24 games.
    — Doug Gilmour, Toronto, 1993. 21 games.

MOST ASSISTS BY A DEFENSEMAN, ONE PLAYOFF YEAR:
  25 — **Paul Coffey, Edmonton,** 1985. 18 games.
  24 — Al MacInnis, Calgary, 1989. 22 games.
  19 — Bobby Orr, Boston, 1972. 15 games.
  18 — Ray Bourque, Boston, 1988. 23 games.
    — Ray Bourque, Boston, 1991. 19 games.
    — Larry Murphy, Pittsburgh, 1991. 23 games.
  17 — Larry Robinson, Montreal, 1978. 15 games.
    — Denis Potvin, NY Islanders, 1981. 18 games.
    — Charlie Huddy, Edmonton, 1985. 18 games.
    — Larry Robinson, Montreal, 1987. 17 games.

MOST MINUTES PLAYED BY A GOALTENDER, ONE PLAYOFF YEAR:
  1,540 — **Ron Hextall, Philadelphia,** 1987. 26 games.
  1,401 — Bill Ranford, Edmonton, 1990. 22 games.
  1,381 — Mike Vernon, Calgary, 1989. 22 games.
  1,308 — Felix Potvin, Toronto, 1993. 21 games.
  1,293 — Patrick Roy, Montreal, 1993. 20 games.
  1,261 — Kelly Hrudey, Los Angeles, 1993. 20 games.
  1,233 — Tom Barrasso, Pittsburgh, 1992. 21 games.

MOST WINS BY A GOALTENDER, ONE PLAYOFF YEAR:
  16 — **Grant Fuhr, Edmonton,** 1988. 19 games.
    — **Mike Vernon, Calgary,** 1989. 22 games.
    — **Bill Ranford, Edmonton,** 1990. 22 games.
    — **Tom Barrasso, Pittsburgh,** 1992. 21 games.
    — **Patrick Roy, Montreal,** 1993. 20 games.
  15 — Bill Smith, NY Islanders, 1980. 20 games.
    — Bill Smith, NY Islanders, 1982. 18 games.
    — Grant Fuhr, Edmonton, 1985. 18 games.
    — Patrick Roy, Montreal, 1986. 20 games.
    — Ron Hextall, Philadelphia, 1987. 26 games.
  14 — Bill Smith, NY Islanders, 1981. 17 games.
    — Grant Fuhr, Edmonton, 1987. 19 games.
    — Jon Casey, Minnesota, 1991. 23 games.

MOST CONSECUTIVE WINS BY A GOALTENDER, ONE PLAYOFF YEAR:
  11 — **Ed Belfour, Chicago,** 1992. 3 wins against St. Louis in DSF, won by Chicago 4-2; 4 wins against Detroit in DF, won by Chicago 4-0; and 4 wins against Edmonton in CF, won by Chicago 4-0.
    — **Tom Barrasso, Pittsburgh,** 1992. 3 wins against NY Rangers in DF, won by Pittsburgh 4-2; 4 wins against Boston in CF, won by Pittsburgh 4-0; and 4 wins against Chicago in F, won by Pittsburgh 4-0.
    — **Patrick Roy, Montreal,** 1993. 4 wins against Quebec in DSF, won by Montreal 4-2; 4 wins against Buffalo in DF, won by Montreal 4-0; and 3 wins against NY Islanders in CF, won by Montreal 4-1.

MOST SHUTOUTS, ONE PLAYOFF YEAR:
   4 — **Clint Benedict, Mtl. Maroons,** 1926. 8 games.
    — **Clint Benedict, Mtl. Maroons,** 1928. 9 games.
    — **Dave Kerr, NY Rangers,** 1937. 9 games.
    — **Frank McCool, Toronto,** 1945. 13 games.
    — **Terry Sawchuk, Detroit,** 1952. 8 games.
    — **Bernie Parent, Philadelphia,** 1975. 17 games.
    — **Ken Dryden, Montreal,** 1977. 14 games.

MOST CONSECUTIVE SHUTOUTS:
   3 — **Clint Benedict, Mtl. Maroons,** 1926. Benedict shut out Ottawa 1-0, Mar. 27; he then shut out Victoria twice, 3-0, Mar. 30; 3-0, Apr. 1. Mtl. Maroons won NHL F vs. Ottawa 2 goals to 1 and won the best-of-five F vs. Victoria 3-1.
    — **Frank McCool, Toronto,** 1945. McCool shut out Detroit 1-0, April 6; 2-0, April 8; 1-0, April 12. Toronto won the best-of-seven F 4-3.

LONGEST SHUTOUT SEQUENCE:
248 Minutes, 32 Seconds — **Norm Smith, Detroit,** 1936. In best-of-five SF, Smith shut out Mtl. Maroons 1-0, March 24, in 116:30 overtime; shut out Maroons 3-0 in second game, March 26; and was scored against at 12:02 of first period, March 29, by Gus Marker. Detroit won SF 3-0.

One-Series Records

MOST POINTS IN FINAL SERIES:
  13 — **Wayne Gretzky, Edmonton,** in 1988, 4 games plus suspended game vs. Boston. 3 goals, 10 assists.
  12 — Gordie Howe, Detroit, in 1955, 7 games vs. Montreal. 5 goals, 7 assists.
    — Yvan Cournoyer, Montreal, in 1973, 6 games vs. Chicago. 6 goals, 6 assists.
    — Jacques Lemaire, Montreal, in 1973, 6 games vs. Chicago. 3 goals, 9 assists.
    — Mario Lemieux, Pittsburgh, in 1991, 5 games vs. Minnesota. 5 goals, 7 assists.

MOST GOALS IN FINAL SERIES:
   9 — **Babe Dye, Toronto,** in 1922, 5 games vs. Van. Millionaires.
   8 — Alf Skinner, Toronto, in 1918, 5 games vs. Van. Millionaires.
   7 — Jean Beliveau, Montreal, in 1956, during 5 games vs. Detroit.
    — Mike Bossy, NY Islanders, in 1982, during 4 games vs. Vancouver.
    — Wayne Gretzky, Edmonton, in 1985, during 5 games vs. Philadelphia.

MOST ASSISTS IN FINAL SERIES:
  10 — **Wayne Gretzky, Edmonton,** in 1988, 4 games plus suspended game vs. Boston.
   9 — Jacques Lemaire, Montreal, in 1973, 6 games vs. Chicago.
    — Wayne Gretzky, Edmonton, in 1987, 7 games vs. Philadelphia.
    — Larry Murphy, Pittsburgh, in 1991, 6 games vs. Minnesota.

Philadelphia's Bill Barber, checked here by Montreal's Jimmy Roberts, scored three shorthanded goals against Minnesota in the 1980 Stanley Cup Semi-Finals.

MOST POINTS IN ONE SERIES (OTHER THAN FINAL):
19 — **Rick Middleton, Boston,** in 1983 DF, 7 games vs. Buffalo. 5 goals, 14 assists.
18 — Wayne Gretzky, Edmonton, in 1985 CF, 6 games vs. Chicago. 4 goals, 14 assists.
17 — Mario Lemieux, Pittsburgh, in 1992 DSF, 6 games vs. Washington. 7 goals, 10 assists.
16 — Barry Pederson, Boston, in 1983 DF, 7 games vs. Buffalo. 7 goals, 9 assists.
15 — Jari Kurri, Edmonton, in 1985 CF, 6 games vs. Chicago. 12 goals, 3 assists.
— Wayne Gretzky, Edmonton, in 1987 DSF, 5 games vs. Los Angeles. 2 goals, 13 assists.
— Tim Kerr, Philadelphia, in 1989 DF, 7 games vs. Pittsburgh. 10 goals, 5 assists.
— Mario Lemieux, Pittsburgh, in 1991 CF, 6 games vs. Boston. 6 goals, 9 assists.

MOST GOALS IN ONE SERIES (OTHER THAN FINAL):
12 — **Jari Kurri, Edmonton,** in 1985 CF, 6 games vs. Chicago.
11 — Newsy Lalonde, Montreal, in 1919 NHL F, 5 games vs. Ottawa.
10 — Tim Kerr, Philadelphia, in 1989 DF, 7 games vs. Pittsburgh.
9 — Reggie Leach, Philadelphia, in 1976 SF, 5 games vs. Boston.
— Bill Barber, Philadelphia, in 1980 SF, 5 games vs. Minnesota.
— Mike Bossy, NY Islanders, in 1983 CF, 6 games vs. Boston.
— Mario Lemieux, Pittsburgh, in 1989 DF, 7 games vs. Philadelphia.

MOST ASSISTS IN ONE SERIES (OTHER THAN FINAL):
14 — **Rick Middleton, Boston,** in 1983 DF, 7 games vs. Buffalo.
— **Wayne Gretzky, Edmonton,** in 1985 CF, 6 games vs. Chicago.
13 — Wayne Gretzky, Edmonton, in 1987 DSF, 5 games vs. Los Angeles.
11 — Mark Messier, Edmonton, in 1989 DSF, 7 games vs. Los Angeles.
— Al MacInnis, Calgary, in 1984 DF, 7 games vs. Edmonton.
— Mike Ridley, Washington, in 1992 DSF, 7 games vs. Pittsburgh.
10 — Fleming Mackell, Boston, in 1958 SF, 6 games vs. NY Rangers.
— Stan Mikita, Chicago, in 1962 SF, 6 games vs. Montreal.
— Bob Bourne, NY Islanders, in 1983 DF, 6 games vs. NY Rangers.
— Wayne Gretzky, Edmonton, in 1988 DSF, 5 games vs. Winnipeg.
— Mario Lemieux, Pittsburgh, in 1992 DSF, 6 games vs. Washington.

MOST GAME-WINNING GOALS, ONE PLAYOFF SERIES:
4 — **Mike Bossy, NY Islanders,** 1983, CF vs. Boston, won by NY Islanders 4-2.

MOST OVERTIME GOALS, ONE PLAYOFF SERIES:
3 — **Mel Hill, Boston,** 1939, SF vs. NY Rangers, won by Boston 4-3. Hill scored at 59:25 overtime March 21 for a 2-1 win; at 8:24, March 23 for a 3-2 win; and at 48:00, April 2 for a 2-1 win.

MOST POWER-PLAY GOALS, ONE PLAYOFF SERIES:
6 — **Chris Kontos, Los Angeles,** 1989, DSF vs. Edmonton, won by Los Angeles 4-3.
5 — Andy Bathgate, Detroit, 1966, SF vs. Chicago, won by Detroit 4-2.
— Denis Potvin, NY Islanders, 1981, QF vs. Edmonton, won by NY Islanders 4-2.
— Ken Houston, Calgary, 1981, QF vs. Philadelphia, won by Calgary 4-3.
— Rick Vaive, Chicago, 1988, DSF vs. St. Louis, won by St. Louis 4-1.
— Tim Kerr, Philadelphia, 1989, DF vs. Pittsburgh, won by Philadelphia 4-3.
— Mario Lemieux, Pittsburgh, 1989, DF vs. Philadelphia won by Philadelphia 4-3.
— John Druce, Washington, 1990, DF vs. NY Rangers won by Washington 4-1.
— Pat LaFontaine, Buffalo, 1992, DSF vs. Boston won by Boston 4-3.

MOST SHORTHAND GOALS, ONE PLAYOFF SERIES:
3 — **Bill Barber, Philadelphia,** 1980, SF vs. Minnesota, won by Philadelphia 4-1.
— **Wayne Presley, Chicago,** 1989, DSF vs. Detroit, won by Chicago 4-2.
2 — Mac Colville, NY Rangers, 1940, SF vs. Boston, won by NY Rangers 4-2.
— Jerry Toppazzini, Boston, 1958, SF vs. NY Rangers, won by Boston 4-2.
— Dave Keon, Toronto, 1963, F vs. Detroit, won by Toronto 4-1.
— Bob Pulford, Toronto, 1964, F vs. Detroit, won by Toronto 4-3.
— Serge Savard, Montreal, 1968, F vs. St. Louis, won by Montreal 4-0.
— Derek Sanderson, Boston, 1969, SF vs. Montreal, won by Montreal 4-2.
— Bryan Trottier, NY Islanders, 1980, PR vs. Los Angeles, won by NY Islanders 3-1.
— Bobby Lalonde, Boston, 1981, PR vs. Minnesota, won by Minnesota 3-0.
— Butch Goring, NY Islanders, 1981, SF vs. NY Rangers, won by NY Islanders 4-0.
— Wayne Gretzky, Edmonton, 1983, DSF vs. Winnipeg, won by Edmonton 3-0.
— Mark Messier, Edmonton, 1983, DF vs. Calgary, won by Edmonton 4-1.
— Jari Kurri, Edmonton, 1983, CF vs. Chicago, won by Edmonton 4-0.

— Wayne Gretzky, Edmonton, 1985, DF vs. Winnipeg, won by Edmonton 4-0.
— Kevin Lowe, Edmonton, 1987, F vs. Philadelphia, won by Edmonton 4-3.
— Bob Gould, Washington, 1988, DSF vs. Philadelphia, won by Washington 4-3.
— Dave Poulin, Philadelphia, 1989, DF vs. Pittsburgh, won by Philadelphia 4-3.
— Russ Courtnall, Montreal, 1991, DF vs. Boston, won by Boston 4-3.
— Sergei Fedorov, Detroit, 1992 DSF vs. Minnesota, won by Detroit 4-3.
— Mark Messier, NY Rangers, 1992, DSF vs. New Jersey, won by NY Rangers 4-3.
— Tom Fitzgerald, NY Islanders, 1993, DF vs. Pittsburgh, won by NY Islanders 4-3.

MOST THREE-OR-MORE-GOAL GAMES, ONE PLAYOFF SERIES:
3 — **Jari Kurri, Edmonton** 1985, CF vs. Chicago won by Edmonton 4-2. Kurri scored 3 G May 7 at Edmonton in 7-3 win, 3 G May 14 in 10-5 win and 4 G May 16 at Chicago in 8-2 win.
2 — Doug Bentley, Chicago, 1944, SF vs. Detroit, won by Chicago 4-1. Bentley scored 3 G Mar. 28 at Chicago in 7-1 win and 3 G Mar. 30 at Detroit in 5-2 win.
— Norm Ullman, Detroit, 1964, SF vs. Chicago, won by Detroit 4-3. Ullman scored 3 G Mar. 29 at Chicago in 7-1 win and 3 G April 7 at Detroit in 7-2 win.
— Mark Messier, Edmonton, 1983, DF vs. Calgary won by Edmonton 4-1. Messier scored 4 G April 14 at Edmonton in 6-3 win and 3 G April 17 at Calgary in 10-2 win.
— Mike Bossy, NY Islanders, 1983, CF vs. Boston won by NY Islanders 4-2. Bossy scored 3 G May 3 at New York in 8-3 win and 4 G on May 7 at New York in 8-4 win.

Single Playoff Game Records

MOST POINTS, ONE GAME:
8 — **Patrik Sundstrom, New Jersey,** April 22, 1988 at New Jersey during 10-4 win over Washington. Sundstrom had 3 goals, 5 assists.
— **Mario Lemieux, Pittsburgh,** April 25, 1989 at Pittsburgh during 10-7 win over Philadelphia. Lemieux had 5 goals, 3 assists.
7 — Wayne Gretzky, Edmonton, April 17, 1983 at Calgary during 10-2 win. Gretzky had 4 goals, 3 assists.
— Wayne Gretzky, Edmonton, April 25,1985 at Winnipeg during 8-3 win. Gretzky had 3 goals, 4 assists.
— Wayne Gretzky, Edmonton, April 9, 1987, at Edmonton during 13-3 win over Los Angeles. Gretzky had 1 goal, 6 assists.
6 — Dickie Moore, Montreal, March 25, 1954, at Montreal during 8-1 win over Boston. Moore had 2 goals, 4 assists.
— Phil Esposito, Boston, April 2, 1969, at Boston during 10-0 win over Toronto. Esposito had 4 goals, 2 assists.
— Darryl Sittler, Toronto, April 22, 1976, at Toronto during 8-5 win over Philadelphia. Sittler had 5 goals, 1 assist.
— Guy Lafleur, Montreal, April 11, 1977, at Montreal during 7-2 victory vs. St. Louis. Lafleur had 3 goals, 3 assists.
— Mikko Leinonen, NY Rangers, April 8, 1982, at New York during 7-3 win over Philadelphia. Leinonen had 6 assists.
— Paul Coffey, Edmonton, May 14, 1985 at Edmonton during 10-5 win over Chicago. Coffey had 1 goal, 5 assists.
— John Anderson, Hartford, April 12, 1986 at Hartford during 9-4 win over Quebec. Anderson had 2 goals, 4 assists.
— Mario Lemieux, Pittsburgh, April 23, 1992 at Pittsburgh during 6-4 win over Washington. Lemieux had 3 goals, 3 assists.

MOST POINTS BY A DEFENSEMAN, ONE GAME:
6 — **Paul Coffey, Edmonton,** May 14, 1985 at Edmonton vs. Chicago. 1 goal, 5 assists. Edmonton won 10-5.
5 — Eddie Bush, Detroit, April 9, 1942, at Detroit vs. Toronto. 1 goal, 4 assists. Detroit won 5-2.
— Bob Dailey, Philadelphia, May 1, 1980, at Philadelphia vs. Minnesota. 1 goal, 4 assists. Philadelphia won 7-0.
— Denis Potvin, NY Islanders, April 17, 1981, at New York vs. Edmonton. 3 goals, 2 assists. NY Islanders won 6-3.
— Risto Siltanen, Quebec, April 14, 1987 at Hartford. 5 assists. Quebec won 7-5.

MOST GOALS, ONE GAME:
5 — **Newsy Lalonde, Montreal,** March 1, 1919, at Montreal. Final score: Montreal 6, Ottawa 3.
— **Maurice Richard, Montreal,** March 23, 1944, at Montreal. Final score: Montreal 5, Toronto 1.
— **Darryl Sittler, Toronto,** April 22, 1976, at Toronto. Final score: Toronto 8, Philadelphia 5.
— **Reggie Leach, Philadelphia,** May 6, 1976, at Philadelphia. Final score: Philadelphia 6, Boston 3.
— **Mario Lemieux, Pittsburgh,** April 25, 1989 at Pittsburgh. Final score: Pittsburgh 10, Philadelphia 7.

MOST GOALS BY A DEFENSEMAN, ONE GAME:
3 — **Bobby Orr, Boston,** April 11, 1971 at Montreal. Final score: Boston 5, Montreal 2.
— **Dick Redmond, Chicago,** April 4, 1973 at Chicago. Final score: Chicago 7, St. Louis 1.
— **Denis Potvin, NY Islanders,** April 17, 1981 at New York. Final score: NY Islanders 6, Edmonton 3.
— **Paul Reinhart, Calgary,** April 14, 1983 at Edmonton. Final score: Edmonton 6, Calgary 3.
— **Paul Reinhart, Calgary,** April 8, 1984 at Vancouver. Final score: Calgary 5, Vancouver 1.
— **Doug Halward, Vancouver,** April 7, 1984 at Vancouver. Final score: Vancouver 7, Calgary 0.
— **Al Iafrate, Washington,** April 26, 1993 at Washington. Final score: NY Islanders 4, Washington 6.
— **Eric DesJardins, Montreal,** June 3, 1993 at Montreal. Final score: Los Angeles 3, Montreal 3.

MOST POWER-PLAY GOALS, ONE GAME:
3 — **Syd Howe, Detroit,** March 23, 1939, at Detroit vs. Montreal, Detroit won 7-3.
— Sid Smith, Toronto, April 10, 1949, at Detroit. Toronto won 3-1.
— Phil Esposito, Boston, April 2, 1969, at Boston vs. Toronto. Boston won 10-0.
— John Bucyk, Boston, April 21, 1974, at Boston vs. Chicago. Boston won 8-6.
— Denis Potvin, NY Islanders, April 17, 1981, at New York vs. Edmonton. NY Islanders won 6-3.
— Tim Kerr, Philadelphia, April 13, 1985, at NY Rangers. Philadelphia won 6-5.
— Jari Kurri, Edmonton, April 9, 1987, at Edmonton vs. Los Angeles. Edmonton won 13-3.
— Mark Johnson, New Jersey, April 22, 1988, at New Jersey vs. Washington. New Jersey won 10-4.
— Dino Ciccarelli, Detroit, April 29, 1993, at Toronto, in 7-3 win by Detroit.

MOST SHORTHAND GOALS, ONE GAME:
2 — **Dave Keon, Toronto,** April 18, 1963, at Toronto, in 3-1 win vs. Detroit.
— Bryan Trottier, NY Islanders, April 8, 1980 at New York, in 8-1 win vs. Los Angeles.
— Bobby Lalonde, Boston, April 11, 1981 at Minnesota, in 6-3 win by Minnesota.
— Wayne Gretzky, Edmonton, April 6, 1983 at Edmonton, in 6-3 win vs. Winnipeg.
— Jari Kurri, Edmonton, April 24, 1983, at Edmonton, in 8-3 win vs. Chicago.
— Mark Messier, NY Rangers, April 21, 1992, at New York, in 7-3 loss vs. New Jersey.
— Tom Fitzgerald, NY Islanders, May 8, 1993, at Long Island, in 6-5 win vs. Pittsburgh.

MOST ASSISTS, ONE GAME:
6 — **Mikko Leinonen, NY Rangers,** April 8, 1982, at New York. Final score: NY Rangers 7, Philadelphia 3.
— Wayne Gretzky, Edmonton, April 9, 1987, at Edmonton. Final score: Edmonton 13, Los Angeles 3.
5 — Toe Blake, Montreal, March 23, 1944, at Montreal. Final score: Montreal 5, Toronto 1.
— Maurice Richard, Montreal, March 27, 1956, at Montreal. Final score: Montreal 7, NY Rangers 0.
— Bert Olmstead, Montreal, March 30, 1957, at Montreal. Final score: Montreal 8, NY Rangers 3.
— Don McKenney, Boston, April 5, 1958, at Boston. Final score: Boston 8, NY Rangers 2.
— Stan Mikita, Chicago, April 4, 1973, at Chicago. Final score: Chicago 7, St. Louis 1.
— Wayne Gretzky, Edmonton, April 8, 1981, at Montreal. Final score: Edmonton 6, Montreal 3.
— Paul Coffey, Edmonton, May 14, 1985, at Edmonton. Final score: Edmonton 10, Chicago 5.
— Doug Gilmour, St. Louis, April 15, 1986, at Minnesota. Final score: St. Louis 6, Minnesota 3.
— Risto Siltanen, Quebec, April 14, 1987 at Hartford. Final score: Quebec 7, Hartford 3.
— Patrik Sundstrom, New Jersey, April 22, 1988, at New Jersey. Final score: New Jersey 10, Washington 4.

MOST PENALTY MINUTES, ONE GAME:
42 — **Dave Schultz, Philadelphia,** April 22, 1976, at Toronto. One minor, 2 majors, 1 10-minute misconduct and 2 game-misconducts. Final score: Toronto 8, Philadelphia 5.

MOST PENALTIES, ONE GAME:
8 — **Forbes Kennedy, Toronto,** April 2, 1969, at Boston. Four minors, 2 majors, 1 10-minute misconduct, 1 game misconduct. Final score: Boston 10, Toronto 0.
— Kim Clackson, Pittsburgh, April 14, 1980, at Boston. Five minors, 2 majors, 1 10-minute misconduct. Final score: Boston 6, Pittsburgh 2

MOST POINTS, ONE PERIOD:
4 — **Maurice Richard, Montreal,** March 29, 1945, at Montreal vs. Toronto. Third period, 3 goals, 1 assist. Final score: Montreal 10, Toronto 3.
— Dickie Moore, Montreal, March 25, 1954, at Montreal vs. Boston. First period, 2 goals, 2 assists. Final score: Montreal 8, Boston 1.
— Barry Pederson, Boston, April 8, 1982, at Boston vs. Buffalo. Second period, 3 goals, 1 assist. Final score: Boston 7, Buffalo 3.
— Peter McNab, Boston, April 11, 1982, at Buffalo. Second period, 1 goal, 3 assists. Final score: Boston 5, Buffalo 2.
— Tim Kerr, Philadelphia, April 13, 1985 at New York. Second period, 4 goals. Final score: Philadelphia 6, Rangers 5.
— Ken Linseman, Boston, April 14, 1985 at Boston vs. Montreal. Second period, 2 goals, 2 assists. Final score: Boston 7, Montreal 6.
— Wayne Gretzky, Edmonton, April 12, 1987, at Los Angeles. Third period, 1 goal, 3 assists. Final score: Edmonton 6, Los Angeles 3.
— Glenn Anderson, Edmonton, April 6, 1988, at Edmonton vs. Winnipeg. Third period, 3 goals, 1 assist. Final score: Edmonton 7, Winnipeg 4.
— Mario Lemieux, Pittsburgh, April 25, 1989, at Pittsburgh vs. Philadelphia. First period, 4 goals. Final score: Pittsburgh 10, Philadelphia 7.
— Dave Gagner, Minnesota, April 8, 1991, at Minnesota vs. Chicago. First period, 2 goals, 2 assists. Final score: Chicago 6, Minnesota 5.
— Mario Lemieux, Pittsburgh, April 23, 1992, at Pittsburgh vs. Washington. Second period, 2 goals, 2 assists. Final score: Pittsburgh 6, Washington 4.

MOST GOALS, ONE PERIOD:
4 — **Tim Kerr, Philadelphia,** April 13, 1985, at New York vs. NY Rangers, second period. Final score: Philadelphia 6, NY Rangers 5.
— **Mario Lemieux, Pittsburgh,** April 25, 1989, at Pittsburgh vs. Philadelphia, first period. Final score: Pittsburgh 10, Philadelphia 7.
3 — Harvey (Busher) Jackson, Toronto, April 5, 1932, at New York vs. NY Rangers, second period. Final score: Toronto 6, NY Rangers 4.
— Maurice Richard, Montreal, March 23, 1944, at Montreal vs. Toronto, second period. Final score: Montreal 5, Toronto 1.
— Maurice Richard, Montreal, March 29, 1945, at Montreal vs. Toronto, third period. Final score: Montreal 10, Toronto 3.
— Maurice Richard, Montreal, April 6, 1957 at Montreal vs. Boston, second period. Final score: Montreal 5, Boston 1.
— Ted Lindsay, Detroit, April 5, 1955, at Detroit vs. Montreal, second period. Final score: Detroit 7, Montreal 1.
— Red Berenson, St. Louis, April 15, 1969, at St. Louis vs. Los Angeles, second period. Final score: St. Louis 4, Los Angeles 0.
— Jacques Lemaire, Montreal, April 20, 1971, at Montreal vs. Minnesota, second period. Final score: Montreal 7, Minnesota 2.
— Rick MacLeish, Philadelphia, April 11, 1974, at Philadelphia vs. Atlanta, second period. Final score: Philadelphia 5, Atlanta 1.
— Tom Williams, Los Angeles, April 14, 1974, at Los Angeles vs. Chicago, third period. Final score: Los Angeles 5, Chicago 1.
— Darryl Sittler, Toronto, April 22, 1976, at Toronto vs. Philadelphia, second period. Final score: Toronto 8, Philadelphia 5.
— Reggie Leach, Philadelphia, May 6, 1976, at Philadelphia vs. Boston, second period. Final score: Philadelphia 6, Boston 3.
— Bobby Schmautz, Boston, April 11, 1977, at Boston vs. Los Angeles, first period. Final score: Boston 8, Los Angeles 3.
— George Ferguson, Toronto, April 11, 1978, at Toronto vs. Los Angeles, third period. Final score: Toronto 7, Los Angeles 3.
— Barry Pederson, Boston, April 8, 1982, at Boston vs. Buffalo, second period. Final score: Boston 7, Buffalo 3.
— Peter Stastny, Quebec, April 5, 1983, at Boston, first period. Final score: Boston 4, Quebec 3.
— Wayne Gretzky, Edmonton, April 6, 1983 at Edmonton, second period. Final score: Edmonton 6, Winnipeg 3.
— Mike Bossy, NY Islanders, May 7, 1983 at New York, second period. Final score: NY Islanders 8, Boston 4.
— Dave Andreychuk, Buffalo, April 14, 1985, at Buffalo vs. Quebec, third period. Final score: Buffalo 7, Quebec 4.
— Wayne Gretzky, Edmonton, May 25, 1985, at Edmonton vs. Philadelphia, first period. Final score: Edmonton 4, Philadelphia 3.
— Glenn Anderson, Edmonton, April 6, 1988, at Edmonton vs. Winnipeg, third period. Final score: Edmonton 7, Winnipeg 4.
— Tim Kerr, Philadelphia, April 19, 1989, at Pittsburgh vs. Penguins, first period. Final score: Philadelphia 4, Pittsburgh 2.
— Petr Klima, Edmonton, May 4, 1991, at Edmonton vs. Minnesota, first period. Final score: Edmonton 7, Minnesota 2.
— Dino Ciccarelli, Washington, April 25, 1992, at Pittsburgh, third period. Final score: Washington 7, Pittsburgh 2.
— Kevin Stevens, Pittsburgh, May 17, 1992, at Boston, first period. Final score: Pittsburgh 5, Boston 1.
— Dirk Graham, Chicago, June 1, 1992, at Chicago vs. Pittsburgh, first period. Final score: Pittsburgh 6, Chicago 5.
— Ray Ferraro, NY Islanders, April 26, 1993, at Washington, third period. Final score: Washington 6, NY Islanders 4.

MOST POWER-PLAY GOALS, ONE PERIOD:
3 — **Tim Kerr, Philadelphia,** April 13, 1985 at New York, second period in 6-5 win vs. NY Rangers.
2 — Two power-play goals have been scored by one player in one period on 41 occasions. Charlie Conacher of Toronto was the first to score two power-play goals in one period, setting the mark on Mar. 26, 1936. Dino Ciccarelli of Detroit is the most recent to equal this mark with two power-play goals in the second period at Toronto, April 29, 1993. Final score: Detroit 7, Toronto 3.

MOST SHORTHAND GOALS, ONE PERIOD:
2 — **Bryan Trottier, NY Islanders,** April 8, 1980, second period at New York in 8-1 win vs. Los Angeles.
— **Bobby Lalonde, Boston,** April 11, 1981, third period at Minnesota in 6-3 win by Minnesota.
— **Jari Kurri, Edmonton,** April 24, 1983, third period at Edmonton in 8-4 win vs. Chicago.

MOST ASSISTS, ONE PERIOD:
3 — Three assists by one player in one period of a playoff game has been recorded on 58 occasions. Adam Oates of Boston is the most recent to equal this mark with 3 assists in the first period at Buffalo, April 24, 1993. Final score: Boston 5, Buffalo 6.
Wayne Gretzky has had 3 assists in one period 5 times; Ray Bourque, 3 times; Toe Blake, Jean Beliveau, Doug Harvey and Bobby Orr, twice. Nick Metz of Toronto was the first player to be credited with 3 assists in one period of a playoff game Mar. 21, 1941 at Toronto vs. Boston.

MOST PENALTIES, ONE PERIOD AND MOST PENALTY MINUTES, ONE PERIOD:
6 Penalties; 39 Minutes — **Ed Hospodar, NY Rangers,** April 9, 1981, at Los Angeles, first period. Two minors, 1 major, 1 10-minute misconduct, 2 game misconducts. Final score: Los Angeles 5, NY Rangers 4.

FASTEST TWO GOALS:
5 Seconds — **Norm Ullman, Detroit,** at Detroit, April 11, 1965, vs. Chicago and goaltender Glenn Hall. Ullman scored at 17:35 and 17:40 of second period. Detroit won 4-2.

FASTEST GOAL FROM START OF GAME:
6 Seconds — **Don Kozak, Los Angeles,** April 17, 1977, at Los Angeles vs. Boston and goaltender Gerry Cheevers. Los Angeles won 7-4.
7 Seconds — Bob Gainey, Montreal, May 5, 1977, at New York vs. NY Islanders and goaltender Glenn Resch. Montreal won 2-1.
— Terry Murray, Philadelphia, April 12, 1981, at Quebec vs. goaltender Dan Bouchard. Quebec won 4-3 in overtime.
8 Seconds — Stan Smyl, Vancouver, April 7, 1982, at Vancouver vs. Calgary and goaltender Pat Riggin. Vancouver won 5-3.

FASTEST GOAL FROM START OF PERIOD (OTHER THAN FIRST):
6 Seconds — **Pelle Eklund, Phiadelphia,** April 25, 1989, at Pittsburgh vs. goaltender Tom Barrasso, second period. Pittsburgh won 10-7.
9 Seconds — Bill Collins, Minnesota, April 9, 1968, at Minnesota vs. Los Angeles and goaltender Wayne Rutledge, third period. Minnesota won 7-5.
— Dave Balon, Minnesota, April 25, 1968, at St. Louis vs. goaltender Glenn Hall, third period. Minnesota won 5-1.
— Murray Oliver, Minnesota, April 8, 1971, at St. Louis vs. goaltender Ernie Wakely, third period. St. Louis won 4-2.
— Clark Gillies, NY Islanders, April 15, 1977, at Buffalo vs. goaltender Don Edwards, third period. NY Islanders won 4-3.
— Eric Vail, Atlanta, April 11, 1978, at Atlanta vs. Detroit and goaltender Ron Low, third period. Detroit won 5-3.
— Stan Smyl, Vancouver, April 10, 1979, at Philadelphia vs. goaltender Wayne Stephenson, third period. Vancouver won 3-2.
— Wayne Gretzky, Edmonton, April 6, 1983, at Edmonton vs. Winnipeg and goaltender Brian Hayward, second period. Edmonton won 6-3.
— Mark Messier, Edmonton, April 16, 1984, at Calgary vs. goaltender Don Edwards, third period. Edmonton won 5-3.
— Brian Skrudland, Montreal, May 18, 1986 at Calgary vs. Calgary and goaltender Mike Vernon, overtime. Montreal won 3-2.

FASTEST TWO GOALS FROM START OF GAME:
1 Minute, 8 Seconds — **Dick Duff, Toronto,** April 9, 1963 at Toronto vs. Detroit and goaltender Terry Sawchuk. Duff scored at 49 seconds and 1:08. Final score: Toronto 4, Detroit 2.

FASTEST TWO GOALS FROM START OF PERIOD:
35 Seconds — **Pat LaFontaine, NY Islanders,** May 19, 1984 at Edmonton vs. goaltender Andy Moog. LaFontaine scored at 13 and 35 seconds of third period. Final score: Edmonton 5, NY Islanders 2.

Early Playoff Records

1893-1918
Team Records

MOST GOALS, BOTH TEAMS, ONE GAME:
25 — **Ottawa Silver Seven, Dawson City** at Ottawa, Jan. 16, 1905. Ottawa 23, Dawson City 2. Ottawa won best-of-three series 2-0.

MOST GOALS, ONE TEAM, ONE GAME:
23 — **Ottawa Silver Seven** at Ottawa, Jan. 16, 1905. Ottawa defeated Dawson City 23-2.

MOST GOALS, BOTH TEAMS, BEST-OF-THREE SERIES:
42 — **Ottawa Silver Seven, Queen's University** at Ottawa, 1906. Ottawa defeated Queen's 16-7, Feb. 27, and 12-7, Feb. 28.

MOST GOALS, ONE TEAM, BEST-OF-THREE SERIES:
32 — **Ottawa Silver Seven** in 1905 at Ottawa. Defeated Dawson City 9-2, Jan. 13, and 23-2, Jan. 16.

MOST GOALS, BOTH TEAMS, BEST-OF-FIVE SERIES:
39 — **Toronto Arenas, Vancouver Millionaires** at Toronto, 1918. Toronto won 5-3, Mar. 20; 6-3, Mar. 26; 2-1, Mar. 30. Vancouver won 6-4, Mar. 23, and 8-1, Mar. 28. Toronto scored 18 goals; Vancouver 21.

MOST GOALS, ONE TEAM, BEST-OF-FIVE SERIES:
26 — **Vancouver Millionaires** in 1915 at Vancouver. Defeated Ottawa Senators 6-2, Mar. 22; 8-3, Mar. 24; and 12-3 Mar. 26.

Individual Records

MOST GOALS IN PLAYOFFS:
63 — **Frank McGee, Ottawa Silver Seven,** in 22 playoff games. Seven goals in four games, 1903; 21 goals in eight games, 1904; 18 goals in four games, 1905; 17 goals in six games, 1906.

MOST GOALS, ONE PLAYOFF SERIES:
15 — **Frank McGee, Ottawa Silver Seven,** in two games in 1905 at Ottawa. Scored one goal, Jan. 13, in 9-2 victory over Dawson City and 14 goals, Jan. 16, in 23-2 victory.

MOST GOALS, ONE PLAYOFF GAME:
14 — **Frank McGee, Ottawa Silver Seven,** Jan. 16, 1905 at Ottawa in 23-2 victory over Dawson City.

FASTEST THREE GOALS:
40 Seconds — **Marty Walsh, Ottawa Senators,** at Ottawa, March 16, 1911, at 3:00, 3:10, and 3:40 of third period. Ottawa defeated Port Arthur 13-4.

Doug Gilmour, left, who led all playoff scorers in 1986, has 118 playoff points in his career. Joe Mullen, right, is the NHL's all-time leading scorer among American-born players. He has accumulated 102 playoff points in 12 years of post-season play.

All-Time Playoff
Goal Leaders since 1918
(40 or more goals)

Player	Teams	Yrs.	GP	G
* Wayne Gretzky	Edm., L.A.	14	180	110
* Jari Kurri	Edm., L.A.	12	174	102
* Glenn Anderson	Edm., Tor.	12	185	88
* Mark Messier	Edm., NYR	13	177	87
Mike Bossy	NY Islanders	10	129	85
Maurice Richard	Montreal	15	133	82
Jean Beliveau	Montreal	17	162	79
* Bryan Trottier	NYI, Pit.	16	219	71
Gordie Howe	Det., Hfd.	20	157	68
Yvan Cournoyer	Montreal	12	147	64
* Brian Propp	Phi., Bos., Min.	14	160	64
Bobby Smith	Min., Mtl.	13	184	64
Bobby Hull	Chi., Hfd.	14	119	62
Phil Esposito	Chi., Bos., NYR	15	130	61
Jacques Lemaire	Montreal	11	145	61
* Joe Mullen	St.L., Cgy., Pit.	11	124	59
Stan Mikita	Chicago	18	155	59
Guy Lafleur	Mtl., NYR	14	128	58
Bernie Geoffrion	Mtl., NYR	16	132	58
* Denis Savard	Chi., Mtl.	13	137	58
Denis Potvin	NY Islanders	14	185	56
* Cam Neely	Van., Bos.	7	88	55
Rick MacLeish	Phi., Pit., Det.	11	114	54
* Dino Ciccarelli	Min., Wsh., Det.	11	101	53
Bill Barber	Philadelphia	11	129	53
* Mario Lemieux	Pittsburgh	4	60	52
* Esa Tikkanen	Edm.	8	114	51
Frank Mahovlich	Tor., Det., Mtl.	14	137	51
* Brett Hull	Cgy., St.L.	8	68	50
Steve Shutt	Mtl., L.A.	12	99	50
Henri Richard	Montreal	18	180	49
Reggie Leach	Bos., Phi.	8	94	47
Ted Lindsay	Det., Chi.	16	133	47
Clark Gillies	NYI, Buf.	13	164	47
* Paul Coffey	Edm., Pit., L.A., Det.	11	130	46
Dickie Moore	Mtl., Tor. St.L.	14	135	46
* Steve Larmer	Chicago	11	107	45
Rick Middleton	NYR, Bos.	12	114	45
Lanny McDonald	Tor., Cgy.	13	117	44
Ken Linseman	Phi., Edm., Bos.	11	113	43
* Doug Gilmour	St. L., Cgy., Tor.	9	107	42
Bobby Clarke	Philadelphia	13	136	42
John Bucyk	Det., Bos.	14	124	41
* Tim Kerr	Phi., NYR	10	81	40
* Brian Bellows	Min., Mtl.	9	99	40
Peter McNab	Bos., Van.	10	107	40
Bob Bourne	NYI, L.A.	13	139	40
John Tonelli	NYI, Cgy., L.A.	13	172	40

*— Active player.

All-Time Playoff
Assist Leaders since 1918
(60 or more assists)

Player	Teams	Yrs.	GP	A
* Wayne Gretzky	Edm., L.A.	14	180	236
* Mark Messier	Edm., NYR	13	177	142
* Jari Kurri	Edm., L.A.	12	174	120
Larry Robinson	Mtl., L.A.	20	227	116
* Glenn Anderson	Edm., Tor.	12	185	113
* Bryan Trottier	NYI, Pit.	16	219	113
Denis Potvin	NY Islanders	14	185	108
* Paul Coffey	Edm., Pit., L.A., Det.	11	130	101
Jean Beliveau	Montreal	17	162	97
Bobby Smith	Min., Mtl.	13	184	96
* Ray Bourque	Boston	14	139	95
* Denis Savard	Chi., Mtl.	13	137	94
Gordie Howe	Det., Hfd.	20	157	92
Stan Mikita	Chicago	18	155	91
Brad Park	NYR, Bos., Det.	17	161	90
* Brian Propp	Phi., Bos., Min.	14	160	84
Henri Richard	Montreal	18	180	80
Jacques Lemaire	Montreal	11	145	78
Ken Linseman	Phi., Edm., Bos.	11	113	77
Bobby Clarke	Philadelphia	13	136	77
* Doug Gilmour	St. L., Cgy., Tor.	9	107	76
* Chris Chelios	Mtl., Chi.	10	126	76
Guy Lafleur	Mtl., NYR	14	128	76
Phil Esposito	Chi., Bos., NYR	15	130	76
* Adam Oates	Det., St. L., Bos.	7	82	75
Mike Bossy	NY Islanders	10	129	75
John Tonelli	NYI, Cgy., L.A.	13	172	75
* Peter Stastny	Que., N.J.	11	89	72
* Craig Janney	Bos., St. L.	6	86	71
* Al MacInnis	Calgary	9	88	71
Gilbert Perreault	Buffalo	11	90	70
Alex Delvecchio	Detroit	14	121	69
* Larry Murphy	L.A., Wsh., Min., Pit.	12	124	68
Bobby Hull	Chi., Hfd.	14	119	67
Frank Mahovlich	Tor., Det., Mtl.	14	137	67
Bobby Orr	Boston	8	74	66
Bernie Federko	St. Louis	11	91	66
* Steve Larmer	Chicago	11	107	66
Jean Ratelle	NYR, Bos.	15	123	66
* Charlie Huddy	Edm., L.A.	12	167	66
Dickie Moore	Mtl., Tor., St. L.	14	135	64
Doug Harvey	Mtl., NYR, St. L.	15	137	64
* Mario Lemieux	Pittsburgh	4	60	63
Yvan Cournoyer	Montreal	12	147	63
John Bucyk	Det., Bos.	14	124	62
* Doug Wilson	Chicago	12	95	61

All-Time Playoff
Point Leaders since 1918
(100 or more points)

Player	Teams	Yrs.	GP	G	A	Pts.
* Wayne Gretzky	Edm., L.A.	14	180	110	236	346
* Mark Messier	Edm., NYR	13	177	87	142	229
* Jari Kurri	Edm., L.A.	12	174	102	120	222
* Glenn Anderson	Edm., Tor.	12	185	88	113	201
* Bryan Trottier	NYI, Pit.	16	219	71	113	184
Jean Beliveau	Montreal	17	162	79	97	176
Denis Potvin	NY Islanders	14	185	56	108	164
Mike Bossy	NY Islanders	10	129	85	75	160
Gordie Howe	Det., Hfd.	20	157	68	92	160
Bobby Smith	Min., Mtl.	13	184	64	96	160
* Denis Savard	Chi., Mtl.	13	137	58	94	152
Stan Mikita	Chicago	18	155	59	91	150
* Brian Propp	Phi., Bos., Min.	13	160	64	84	148
* Paul Coffey	Edm., Pit., L.A., Det.	11	130	46	101	147
Larry Robinson	Mtl., L.A.	20	227	28	116	144
Jacques Lemaire	Montreal	11	145	61	78	139
Phil Esposito	Chi., Bos., NYR	15	130	61	76	137
Guy Lafleur	Mtl, NYR	14	128	58	76	134
Bobby Hull	Chi., Hfd.	14	119	62	67	129
Henri Richard	Montreal	18	180	49	80	129
Yvan Cournoyer	Montreal	12	147	64	63	127
Maurice Richard	Montreal	15	133	82	44	126
* Ray Bourque	Boston	14	139	31	95	126
Brad Park	NYR, Bos., Det.	17	161	35	90	125
Ken Linseman	Phi., Edm., Bos.	11	113	43	77	120
Bobby Clarke	Philadelphia	13	136	42	77	119
* Doug Gilmour	St. L.,Cgy., Tor.	9	107	42	76	118
Bernie Geoffrion	Mtl., NYR	16	132	58	60	118
Frank Mahovlich	Tor., Det., Mtl.	14	137	51	67	118
* Mario Lemieux	Pittsburgh	4	60	52	63	115
John Tonelli	NYI, Cgy., L.A.	13	172	40	75	115
* Steve Larmer	Chicago	11	107	45	66	111
Dickie Moore	Mtl., Tor., St. L.	14	135	46	64	110
Bill Barber	Philadelphia	11	129	53	55	108
Rick MacLeish	Phi., Pit., Det.	11	114	54	53	107
* Peter Stastny	Que., N.J.	11	89	33	72	105
Alex Delvecchio	Detroit	14	121	35	69	104
Gilbert Perreault	Buffalo	11	90	33	70	103
John Bucyk	Det., Bos.	14	124	41	62	103
* Joe Mullen	St. L.,Cgy., Pit.	12	124	59	43	102
* Adam Oates	Det., St. L., Bos.	7	82	26	75	101
Bernie Federko	St. Louis	11	91	35	66	101
Rick Middleton	NYR, Bos.	12	114	45	55	100

Three-or-more-Goal Games, Playoffs 1918–1993

Player	Team	Date	City	Total Goals	Opposing Goaltender	Score	
Wayne Gretzky (8)	Edm.	Apr. 11/81	Edm.	3	Richard Sevigny	Edm. 6	Mtl. 2
		Apr. 19/81	Edm.	3	Billy Smith	Edm. 5	NYI 2
		Apr. 6/83	Edm.	4	Brian Hayward	Edm. 6	Wpg. 3
		Apr. 17/83	Cgy.	4	Rejean Lemelin	Edm. 10	Cgy. 2
		Apr. 25/85	Wpg.	3	Bryan Hayward (2) Marc Behrend (1)	Edm. 8	Wpg. 3
		May 25/85	Edm.	3	Pelle Lindbergh	Edm. 4	Phi. 3
		Apr. 24/86	Cgy.	3	Mike Vernon	Edm. 7	Cgy. 4
	L.A.	May 29/93	Tor.	3	Felix Potvin	L.A. 5	Tor. 4
Maurice Richard (7)	Mtl.	Mar.23/44	Mtl.	5	Paul Bibeault	Mtl. 5	Tor. 1
		Apr. 7/44	Chi.	3	Mike Karakas	Mtl. 3	Chi. 1
		Mar.29/45	Mtl.	4	Frank McCool	Mtl. 10	Tor. 3
		Apr. 14/53	Bos.	3	Gord Henry	Mtl. 7	Bos. 3
		Mar.20/56	Mtl.	3	Lorne Worsley	Mtl. 7	NYR 1
		Apr. 6/57	Mtl.	4	Don Simmons	Mtl. 5	Bos. 1
		Apr. 1/58	Det.	3	Terry Sawchuk	Mtl. 4	Det. 3
Jari Kurri (7)	Edm.	Apr. 4/84	Edm.	3	Doug Soetaert (1) Mike Veisor (2)	Edm. 9	Wpg. 2
		Apr. 25/85	Wpg.	3	Bryan Hayward (2) Marc Behrend (1)	Edm. 8	Wpg. 3
		May 7/85	Edm.	3	Murray Bannerman	Edm. 7	Chi. 3
		May 14/85	Edm.	3	Murray Bannerman	Edm. 10	Chi. 5
		May 16/85	Chi.	4	Murray Bannerman	Edm. 8	Chi. 2
		Apr. 9/87	Edm.	4	Roland Melanson (2) Daren Eliot (2)	Edm. 13	L.A. 3
		May 18/90	Bos.	3	Andy Moog (2) Rejean Lemelin (1)	Edm. 7	Bos. 2
Mike Bossy (5)	NYI	Apr. 16/79	NYI	3	Tony Esposito	NYI 6	Chi. 2
		May 8/82	NYI	3	Richard Brodeur	NYI 6	Van. 5
		Apr. 10/83	Wsh.	3	Al Jensen	NYI 6	Wsh. 3
		May 3/83	NYI	3	Pete Peeters	NYI 8	Bos. 3
		May 7/83	NYI	4	Pete Peeters	NYI 8	Bos. 4
Dino Ciccarelli (5)	Min.	May 5/81	Min.	3	Pat Riggin	Min. 7	Cgy. 4
		Apr. 10/82	Min.	3	Murray Bannerman	Min. 7	Chi. 1
	Wsh.	Apr. 5/90	N.J.	3	Sean Burke	Wsh. 5	N.J. 4
		Apr. 25/92	Pit.	4	Tom Barrasso (1) Ken Wregget (3)	Wsh. 7	Pit. 2
	Det.	Apr. 29/93	Tor.	3	Felix Potvin (2) Daren Puppa (1)	Det. 7	Tor. 3
Phil Esposito (4)	Bos.	Apr. 2/69	Bos.	4	Bruce Gamble	Bos. 10	Tor. 0
		Apr. 8/70	Bos.	3	Ed Giacomin	Bos. 8	NYR 2
		Apr. 19/70	Chi.	3	Tony Esposito	Bos. 6	Chi. 3
		Apr. 8/75	Bos.	3	Tony Esposito (2) Michel Dumas (1)	Bos. 8	Chi. 2
Bernie Geoffrion (3)	Mtl.	Mar.27/52	Mtl.	3	Jim Henry	Mtl. 4	Bos. 0
		Apr. 7/55	Mtl.	3	Terry Sawchuk	Mtl. 4	Det. 2
		Mar.30/57	Mtl.	3	Lorne Worsley	Mtl. 8	NYR 3
Norm Ullman (3)	Det.	Mar.29/64	Chi.	3	Glenn Hall	Det. 5	Chi. 4
		Apr. 7/64	Det.	3	Glenn Hall (2) Denis DeJordy (1)	Det. 7	Chi. 2
		Apr. 11/65	Det.	3	Glenn Hall	Det. 4	Chi. 2
John Bucyk (3)	Bos.	May 3/70	St. L.	3	Jacques Plante (1) Ernie Wakely (2)	Bos. 6	St. L. 1
		Apr. 20/72	Bos.	3	Jacques Caron (1) Ernie Wakely (2)	Bos. 10	St. L. 2
		Apr. 21/74	Bos.	3	Tony Esposito	Bos. 8	Chi. 6
Rick MacLeish (3)	Phil	Apr. 11/74	Phil	3	Phil Myre	Phi. 5	Atl. 1
		Apr. 13/75	Phil	3	Gord McRae	Phi. 6	Tor. 3
		May 13/75	Phil	3	Glenn Resch	Phi. 4	NYI 1
Denis Savard (3)	Chi.	Apr. 19/82	Chi.	3	Mike Liut	Chi. 7	StL. 4
		Apr. 10/86	Chi.	4	Ken Wregget	Tor. 6	Chi. 4
		Apr. 9/88	St. L.	3	Greg Millen	Chi. 6	St. L. 3
Mark Messier (3)	Edm.	Apr. 14/83	Edm.	4	Rejean Lemelin	Edm. 6	Cgy. 3
		Apr. 17/83	Cgy.	3	Rejean Lemelin (1) Don Edwards (2)	Edm. 10	Cgy. 2
		Apr. 26/83	Edm.	3	Murray Bannerman	Edm. 8	Chi. 2
Tim Kerr (3)	Phi.	Apr. 13/85	NYR	4	Glen Hanlon	Phi. 6	NYR 5
		Apr. 20/87	Phi.	3	Kelly Hrudey	Phi. 4	NYI 2
		Apr. 19/89	Pit.	3	Tom Barrasso	Phi. 4	Pit. 2
Cam Neely (3)	Bos.	Apr. 9/87	Mtl.	3	Patrick Roy	Mtl. 4	Bos. 3
		Apr. 5/91	Bos.	3	Peter Sidorkiewicz	Bos. 4	Hfd. 3
		Apr. 25/91	Bos.	3	Patrick Roy	Bos. 4	Mtl. 1
Petr Klima (3)	Det.	Apr. 7/88	Tor.	3	Alan Bester (2) Ken Wregett (1)	Det. 6	Tor. 2
		Apr. 21/88	St. L.	3	Greg Millen	Det. 6	St. L. 0
	Edm.	May 4/91	Edm.	3	Jon Casey	Edm. 7	Min. 2
Esa Tikkanen (3)	Edm.	May 22/88	Edm.	3	Rejean Lemelin	Edm. 6	Bos. 3
		Apr. 16/91	Cgy.	3	Mike Vernon	Edm. 5	Cgy. 4
		Apr. 26/92	L.A.	3	Kelly Hrudey	Edm. 5	L.A. 2
Newsy Lalonde (2)	Mtl.	Mar. 1/19	Mtl.	5	Clint Benedict	Mtl. 6	Ott. 3
		Mar.22/19	Sea.	4	Harry Holmes	Mtl. 4	Sea. 2
Howie Morenz (2)	Mtl.	Mar.22/24	Mtl.	3	Charles Reid	Mtl. 6	Cgy.T. 1
		Mar.27/25	Mtl.	3	Harry Holmes	Mtl. 4	Vic. 2
Toe Blake (2)	Mtl.	Mar.22/38	Mtl.	3	Mike Karakas	Mtl. 6	Chi. 4
		Mar.26/46	Chi.	3	Mike Karakas	Mtl. 7	Chi. 2
Doug Bentley (2)	Chi.	Mar.28/44	Chi.	3	Connie Dion	Chi. 7	Det. 1
		Mar.30/44	Det.	3	Connie Dion	Chi. 5	Det. 2
Ted Kennedy (2)	Tor.	Apr. 14/45	Tor.	3	Harry Lumley	Det. 5	Tor. 3
		Mar.27/48	Tor.	4	Frank Brimsek	Tor. 5	Bos. 3
Bobby Hull (2)	Chi.	Apr. 7/63	Det.	3	Terry Sawchuk	Det. 7	Chi. 4
		Apr. 9/72	Pitt	3	Jim Rutherford	Chi. 6	Pit. 5

Player	Team	Date	City	Total Goals	Opposing Goaltender	Score	
F. St. Marseille (2)	St. L.	Apr. 28/70	St. L.	3	Al Smith	St. L. 5	Pit. 0
		Apr. 6/72	Min.	3	Cesare Maniago	Min. 6	St. L. 5
Pit Martin (2)	Chi.	Apr. 4/73	Chi.	3	W. Stephenson	Chi. 7	St. L. 1
		May 10/73	Chi.	3	Ken Dryden	Mtl. 6	Chi. 4
Yvan Cournoyer (2)	Mtl.	Apr. 5/73	Mtl.	3	Dave Dryden	Mtl. 7	Buf. 3
		Apr. 11/74	Mtl.	3	Ed Giacomin	Mtl. 4	NYR 1
Guy Lafleur (2)	Mtl.	May 1/75	Mtl.	3	Roger Crozier (1) Gerry Desjardins (2)	Mtl. 7	Buf. 0
		Apr. 11/77	Mtl.	3	Ed Staniowski	Mtl. 7	St. L. 2
Lanny McDonald (2)	Tor.	Apr. 9/77	Pitt	3	Denis Herron	Tor. 5	Pit. 2
		Apr. 17/77	Tor.	4	W. Stephenson	Phi. 6	Tor. 5
Butch Goring (2)	L.A.	Apr. 9/77	L.A.	3	Phil Myre	L.A. 4	Atl. 2
	NYI	May 17/81	Min.	3	Gilles Meloche	NYI 7	Min. 5
Bryan Trottier (2)	NYI	Apr. 8/80	NYI	3	Doug Keans	NYI 8	L.A. 1
		Apr. 9/81	NYI	3	Michel Larocque	NYI 5	Tor. 1
Bill Barber (2)	Phil	May 4/80	Min.	4	Gilles Meloche	Phi. 5	Min. 3
		Apr. 9/81	Phil	3	Dan Bouchard	Phi. 8	Que. 5
Brian Propp (2)	Phi.	Apr. 22/81	Phi.	3	Pat Riggin	Phi. 9	Cgy. 4
		Apr. 21/85	Phi.	3	Billy Smith	Phi. 5	NYI 2
Paul Reinhart (2)	Cgy	Apr. 14/83	Edm.	3	Andy Moog	Edm. 6	Cgy. 3
		Apr. 8/84	Van	3	Richard Brodeur	Cgy. 5	Van. 1
Peter Stastny (2)	Que.	Apr. 5/83	Bos.	3	Pete Peeters	Bos. 4	Que. 3
		Apr. 11/87	Que.	3	Mike Liut (2) Steve Weeks (1)	Que. 5	Hfd. 1
Glenn Anderson (2)	Edm.	Apr. 26/83	Edm.	4	Murray Bannerman	Edm. 8	Chi. 2
		Apr. 6/88	Wpg.	3	Daniel Berthiaume	Edm. 7	Wpg. 4
Michel Goulet (2)	Que.	Apr. 23/85	Que.	3	Steve Penney	Que. 7	Mtl. 6
		Apr. 12/87	Que.	3	Mike Liut	Que. 4	Hfd. 1
Peter Zezel (2)	Phi.	Apr. 13/86	NYR	3	J. Vanbiesbrouck	Phi. 7	NYR 1
	St. L.	Apr. 11/89	St. L.	3	Jon Casey (2) Kari Takko (1)	St. L. 6	Min. 1
Steve Yzerman (2)	Det.	Apr. 6/89	Det.	3	Alain Chevrier	Chi. 5	Det. 4
		Apr. 4/91	St. L.	3	Vincent Riendeau (2) Pat Jablonski (1)	Det. 6	St. L. 3
Mario Lemieux (2)	Pit.	Apr. 25/89	Pit.	5	Ron Hextall	Pit. 10	Phi. 7
		Apr. 23/92	Pit.	3	Don Beaupre	Pit. 6	Wsh. 4
Mike Gartner (2)	NYR	Apr. 13/90	NYR	3	Mark Fitzpatrick (2) Glenn Healy (1)	NYR 6	NYI 5
		Apr. 27/92	NYR	3	Chris Terreri	NYR 8	N.J. 5
Geoff Courtnall (2)	Van.	Apr. 4/91	L.A.	3	Kelly Hrudey	Van. 6	L.A. 5
		Apr. 30/92	Van.	3	Rick Tabaracci	Van. 5	Win. 5
Harry Meeking	Tor.	Mar.11/18	Tor.	3	Georges Vezina	Tor. 7	Mtl. 3
Alf Skinner	Tor.	Mar.23/18	Tor.	3	Hugh Lehman	Van.M. 6	Tor. 4
Joe Malone	Mtl.	Feb.23/19	Mtl.	3	Clint Benedict	Mtl. 8	Ott. 4
Odie Cleghorn	Mtl.	Feb.27/19	Ott.	3	Clint Benedict	Mtl. 5	Ott. 3
Jack Darragh	Ott.	Apr. 1/20	Tor.	3	Harry Holmes	Ott. 6	Sea. 1
George Boucher	Ott.	Mar.10/21	Ott.	3	Jake Forbes	Ott. 5	Tor. 0
Babe Dye	Tor.	Mar.28/22	Tor.	4	Hugh Lehman	Tor. 5	Van.M. 1
Perk Galbraith	Bos.	Mar.31/27	Bos.	3	Hugh Lehman	Bos. 4	Chi. 4
Busher Jackson	Tor.	Apr. 5/32	NYR	3	John Ross Roach	Tor. 6	NYR 4
Frank Boucher	NYR	Apr. 9/32	Tor.	3	Lorne Chabot	Tor. 6	NYR 4
Charlie Conacher	Tor.	Mar.26/36	Tor.	3	Tiny Thompson	Tor. 8	Bos. 3
Syd Howe	Det.	Mar.23/39	Det.	3	Claude Bourque	Det. 7	Mtl. 3
Bryan Hextall	NYR	Apr. 3/40	NYR	3	Turk Broda	NYR 6	Tor. 2
Joe Benoit	Mtl.	Mar.22/41	Mtl.	3	Sam LoPresti	Mtl. 4	Chi. 3
Syl Apps	Tor.	Mar.25/41	Tor.	3	Frank Brimsek	Tor. 7	Bos. 2
Jack McGill	Bos.	Mar.29/42	Bos.	3	Johnny Mowers	Det. 6	Bos. 4
Don Metz	Tor.	Apr. 14/42	Tor.	3	Johnny Mowers	Tor. 9	Det. 3
Mud Bruneteau	Det.	Apr. 1/43	Det.	3	Frank Brimsek	Det. 6	Bos. 2
Don Grosso	Det.	Apr. 7/43	Bos.	3	Frank Brimsek	Det. 4	Bos. 0
Carl Liscombe	Det.	Apr. 3/45	Bos.	4	Paul Bibeault	Det. 5	Bos. 3
Billy Reay	Mtl.	Apr. 1/47	Bos.	4	Frank Brimsek	Mtl. 5	Bos. 1
Gerry Plamondon	Mtl.	Mar.24/49	Det.	3	Harry Lumley	Mtl. 4	Det. 3
Sid Smith	Tor.	Apr. 10/49	Det.	3	Harry Lumley	Tor. 3	Det. 1
Pentti Lund	NYR	Apr. 2/50	NYR	3	Bill Durnan	NYR 4	Mtl. 1
Ted Lindsay	Det.	Apr. 5/55	Det.	4	Charlie Hodge (1) Jacques Plante (3)	Det. 7	Mtl. 1
Gordie Howe	Det.	Apr. 10/55	Det.	3	Jacques Plante	Det. 5	Mtl. 1
Phil Goyette	Mtl.	Mar.25/58	Mtl.	3	Terry Sawchuk	Mtl. 8	Det. 1
Jerry Toppazzini	Bos.	Apr. 5/58	Bos.	3	Lorne Worsley	Bos. 8	NYR 2
Bob Pulford	Tor.	Apr. 19/62	Tor.	3	Glenn Hall	Tor. 8	Chi. 4
Dave Keon	Tor.	Apr. 9/64	Mtl.	3	Charlie Hodge	Tor. 3	Mtl. 1
Henri Richard	Mtl.	Apr. 20/67	Mtl.	3	Terry Sawchuk (2) Johnny Bower (1)	Mtl. 6	Tor. 2
Rosaire Paiement	Phi.	Apr. 13/68	Phi.	3	Glenn Hall (1) Seth Martin (2)	Phi. 6	St. L. 1
Jean Beliveau	Mtl.	Apr. 20/68	Mtl.	3	Denis DeJordy	Mtl. 4	Chi. 1
Red Berenson	St. L.	Apr. 15/69	St. L.	3	Gerry Desjardins	St. L. 4	L.A. 0
Ken Schinkel	Pit.	Apr. 11/70	Oak.	3	Gary Smith	Pit. 5	Oak. 2
Jim Pappin	Chi.	Apr. 11/71	Phi.	3	Bruce Gamble	Chi. 6	Phi. 2
Bobby Orr	Bos.	Apr. 11/71	Mtl.	3	Ken Dryden	Bos. 5	Mtl. 2
Jacques Lemaire	Mtl.	Apr. 20/71	Mtl.	3	Lorne Worsley	Mtl. 7	Min. 2
Vic Hadfield	NYR	Apr. 22/71	NYR	3	Tony Esposito	NYR 4	Chi. 1
Fred Stanfield	Bos.	Apr. 18/72	Bos.	3	Jacques Caron	Bos. 6	St. L. 1
Ken Hodge	Bos.	Apr. 30/72	Bos.	3	Ed Giacomin	Bos. 6	NYR 5
Steve Vickers	NYR	Apr. 10/73	Bos.	3	Ross Brooks (2) Ed Johnston (1)	NYR 6	Bos. 3
Dick Redmond	Chi.	Apr. 4/73	Chi.	3	Wayne Stephenson	Chi. 7	St. L. 1
Tom Williams	L.A.	Apr. 14/74	L.A.	3	Mike Veisor	L.A. 5	Chi. 1
Marcel Dionne	L.A.	Apr. 15/76	L.A.	3	Gilles Gilbert	L.A. 6	Bos. 4
Don Saleski	Phi.	Apr. 20/76	Phil	3	Wayne Thomas	Phi. 7	Tor. 1
Darryl Sittler	Tor.	Apr. 22/76	Tor.	5	Bernie Parent	Tor. 8	Phi. 5
Reggie Leach	Phi.	May 6/76	Phi.	5	Gilles Gilbert	Phi. 6	Bos. 3

Player	Team	Date	City	Total Goals	Opposing Goaltender	Score	
Jim Lorentz	Buf.	Apr. 7/77	Min.	3	Pete LoPresti (2) Gary Smith (1)	Buf. 7	Min. 1
Bobby Schmautz	Bos.	Apr. 11/77	Bos.	3	Rogatien Vachon	Bos. 8	L.A. 3
Billy Harris	NYI	Apr. 23/77	Mtl.	3	Ken Dryden	Mtl. 4	NYI 3
George Ferguson	Tor.	Apr. 11/78	Tor.	3	Rogatien Vachon	Tor. 7	L.A. 3
Jean Ratelle	Bos.	May 3/79	Bos.	3	Ken Dryden	Bos. 4	Mtl. 3
Stan Jonathan	Bos.	May 8/79	Bos.	3	Ken Dryden	Bos. 5	Mtl. 2
Ron Duguay	NYR	Apr. 20/80	NYR	3	Pete Peeters	NYR 4	Phi. 2
Steve Shutt	Mtl.	Apr. 22/80	Mtl.	3	Gilles Meloche	Mtl. 6	Min. 2
Gilbert Perreault	Buf.	May 6/80	NYI	3	Billy Smith (2) ENG (1)	Buf. 7	NYI 4
Paul Holmgren	Phi.	May 15/80	Phil	3	Billy Smith	Phi. 8	NYI 3
Steve Payne	Min.	Apr. 8/81	Bos.	3	Rogatien Vachon	Min. 5	Bos. 4
Denis Potvin	NYI	Apr. 17/81	NYI	3	Andy Moog	NYI 6	Edm. 3
Barry Pederson	Bos.	Apr. 8/82	Bos.	3	Don Edwards	Bos. 7	Buf. 3
Duane Sutter	NYI	Apr. 15/83	NYI	3	Glen Hanlon	NYI 5	NYR 0
Doug Halward	Van.	Apr. 7/84	Van.	3	Rejean Lemelin (2) Don Edwards (1)	Van. 7	Cgy. 0
Jorgen Pettersson	St. L.	Apr. 8/84	Det.	3	Ed Mio	St. L. 3	Det. 2
Clark Gillies	NYI	May 12/84	NYI	3	Grant Fuhr	NYI 6	Edm. 1
Ken Linseman	Bos.	Apr. 14/85	Bos.	3	Steve Penney	Bos. 7	Mtl. 6
Dave Andreychuk	Buf.	Apr. 14/85	Buf.	3	Dan Bouchard	Que. 4	Buf. 7
Greg Paslawski	StL.	Apr. 15/86	Min.	3	Don Beaupre	St. L. 6	Min. 3
Doug Risebrough	Cgy.	May 4/86	Cgy.	3	Rick Wamsley	Cgy. 8	St. L. 2
Mike McPhee	Mtl.	Apr. 11/87	Bos.	3	Doug Keans	Mtl. 5	Bos. 4
John Ogrodnick	Que.	Apr. 14/87	Hfd.	3	Mike Liut	Que. 7	Hfd. 5
Pelle Eklund	Phi.	May 10/87	Mtl.	3	Patrick Roy (1) Bryan Hayward (2)	Phi. 6	Mtl. 3
John Tucker	Buf.	Apr. 9/88	Bos.	4	Andy Moog	Buf. 6	Bos. 2
Tony Hrkac	St. L.	Apr. 10/88	St. L.	3	Darren Pang	St. L. 6	Chi. 5
Hakan Loob	Cgy.	Apr. 10/88	Cgy.	3	Glenn Healy	Cgy. 7	L.A. 3
Ed Olczyk	Tor.	Apr. 12/88	Tor.	3	Greg Stefan (2) Glen Hanlon (1)	Tor. 6	Det. 5
Aaron Broten	N.J.	Apr. 20/88	N.J.	3	Pete Peeters	N.J. 5	Wsh. 2
Mark Johnson	N.J.	Apr. 22/88	Wsh.	4	Pete Peeters	N.J. 10	Wsh. 4
Patrik Sundstrom	N.J.	Apr. 22/88	Wsh.	3	Pete Peeters (2) Clint Malarchuk (1)	N.J. 10	Wsh. 4
Bob Brooke	Min.	Apr. 5/89	St. L.	3	Greg Millen	St. L. 4	Min. 3
Chris Kontos	L.A.	Apr. 6/89	L.A.	3	Grant Fuhr	L.A. 5	Edm. 2
Wayne Presley	Chi.	Apr. 13/89	Chi.	3	Greg Stefan (1) Glen Hanlon (2)	Chi. 7	Det. 1
Tony Granato	L.A.	Apr. 10/90	L.A.	3	Mike Vernon (1) Rick Wamsley (2)	L.A. 12	Cgy. 4
Tomas Sandstrom	L.A.	Apr. 10/90	L.A.	3	Mike Vernon (1) Rick Wamsley (2)	L.A. 12	Cgy. 4
Dave Taylor	L.A.	Apr. 10/90	L.A.	3	Mike Vernon (1) Rick Wamsley (2)	L.A. 12	Cgy. 4
Bernie Nicholls	NYR	Apr. 19/90	NYR	3	Mike Liut	NYR 7	Wsh. 3
John Druce	Wsh.	Apr. 21/90	NYR	3	John Vanbiesbrouck	Wsh. 6	NYR 3
Adam Oates	St. L.	Apr. 12/91	St. L.	3	Tim Chevaldae	St. L. 6	Det. 1
Luc Robitaille	L.A.	Apr. 26/91	L.A.	3	Grant Fuhr	L.A. 5	Edm. 2
Ron Francis	Pit.	May. 9/92	Pit.	3	Mike Richter (2) John V'brouck (1)	Pit. 5	NYR. 4
Dirk Graham	Chi.	June 1/92	Chi.	3	Tom Barrasso	Pit. 5	Chi. 2
Joe Murphy	Edm.	May 6/92	Edm.	3	Kirk McLean	Edm. 5	Van. 2
Ray Sheppard	Det.	Apr. 24/92	Min.	3	Jon Casey	Min. 5	Det. 2
Kevin Stevens	Pit.	May 21/92	Bos.	4	Andy Moog	Pit. 5	Bos. 2
Pavel Bure	Van.	Apr. 28/92	Wpg.	3	Rick Tabaracci	Van. 8	Wpg. 3
Brian Noonan	Chi.	Apr. 18/93	Chi.	3	Curtis Joseph	St. L. 4	Chi. 3
Dale Hunter	Wsh.	Apr. 20/93	Wsh.	3	Glenn Healy	NYI 5	Wsh. 4
Teemu Selanne	Wpg.	Apr. 23/93	Wpg.	3	Kirk McLean	Wpg. 5	Van. 4
Ray Ferraro	NYI	Apr. 26/93	Wsh.	4	Don Beaupre	Wsh. 6	NYI 4
Al Iafrate	Wsh.	Apr. 26/93	Wsh.	3	Glenn Healy (2) Mark Fitzpatrick (1)	Wsh. 6	NYI 4
Paul Di Pietro	Mtl.	Apr. 28/93	Mtl.	3	Ron Hextall	Mtl. 6	Que. 2
Wendel Clark	Tor.	May 27/93	L.A.	3	Kelly Hrudey	L.A. 5	Tor. 4
Eric Desjardins	Mtl.	Jun. 3/93	Mtl.	3	Kelly Hrudey	Mtl. 3	L.A. 2

Defenseman Eric Desjardins (#28) recorded his first playoff hat-trick during the 1993 Stanley Cup Finals

Leading Playoff Scorers, 1918–1993

Season	Player and Club	Games Played	Goals	Assists	Points
1992-93	Wayne Gretzky, Los Angeles	24	15	25	40
1991-92	Mario Lemieux, Pittsburgh	15	16	18	34
1990-91	Mario Lemieux, Pittsburgh	23	16	28	44
1989-90	Craig Simpson, Edmonton	22	16	15	31
	Mark Messier, Edmonton	22	9	22	31
1988-89	Al MacInnis, Calgary	22	7	24	31
1987-88	Wayne Gretzky, Edmonton	19	12	31	43
1986-87	Wayne Gretzky, Edmonton	21	5	29	34
1985-86	Doug Gilmour, St. Louis	19	9	12	21
	Bernie Federko, St. Louis	19	7	14	21
1984-85	Wayne Gretzky, Edmonton	18	17	30	47
1983-84	Wayne Gretzky, Edmonton	19	13	22	35
1982-83	Wayne Gretzky, Edmonton	16	12	26	38
1981-82	Bryan Trottier, NY Islanders	19	6	23	29
1980-81	Mike Bossy, NY Islanders	18	17	18	35
1979-80	Bryan Trottier, NY Islanders	21	12	17	29
1978-79	Jacques Lemaire, Montreal	16	11	12	23
	Guy Lafleur, Montreal	16	10	13	23
1977-78	Guy Lafleur, Montreal	15	10	11	21
	Larry Robinson, Montreal	15	4	17	21
1976-77	Guy Lafleur, Montreal	14	9	17	26
1975-76	Reggie Leach, Philadelphia	16	19	5	24
1974-75	Rick MacLeish, Philadelphia	17	11	9	20
1973-74	Rick MacLeish, Philadelphia	17	13	9	22
1972-73	Yvan Cournoyer, Montreal	17	15	10	25
1971-72	Phil Esposito, Boston	15	9	15	24
	Bobby Orr, Boston	15	5	19	24
1970-71	Frank Mahovlich, Montreal	20	14	13	27
1969-70	Phil Esposito, Boston	14	13	14	27
1968-69	Phil Esposito, Boston	10	8	10	18
1967-68	Bill Goldsworthy, Minnesota	14	8	7	15
1966-67	Jim Pappin, Toronto	12	7	8	15
1965-66	Norm Ullman, Detroit	12	6	9	15
1964-65	Bobby Hull, Chicago	14	10	7	17
1963-64	Gordie Howe, Detroit	14	9	10	19
1962-63	Gordie Howe, Detroit	11	7	9	16
	Norm Ullman, Detroit	11	4	12	16
1961-62	Stan Mikita, Chicago	12	6	15	21
1960-61	Gordie Howe, Detroit	11	4	11	15
	Pierre Pilote, Chicago	12	3	12	15
1959-60	Henri Richard, Montreal	8	3	9	12
	Bernie Geoffrion, Montreal	8	2	10	12
1958-59	Dickie Moore, Montreal	11	5	12	17
1957-58	Fleming Mackell, Boston	12	5	14	19
1956-57	Bernie Geoffrion, Montreal	11	11	7	18
1955-56	Jean Béliveau, Montreal	10	12	7	19
1954-55	Gordie Howe, Detroit	11	9	11	20
1953-54	Dickie Moore, Montreal	11	5	8	13
1952-53	Ed Sanford, Boston	11	8	3	11
1951-52	Ted Lindsay, Detroit	8	5	2	7
	Floyd Curry, Montreal	11	4	3	7
	Metro Prystai, Detroit	8	2	5	7
	Gordie Howe, Detroit	8	2	5	7
1950-51	Maurice Richard, Montreal	11	9	4	13
	Max Bentley, Toronto	11	2	11	13
1949-50	Pentti Lund, NY Rangers	12	6	5	11
1948-49	Gordie Howe, Detroit	11	8	3	11
1947-48	Ted Kennedy, Toronto	9	8	6	14
1946-47	Maurice Richard, Montreal	10	6	5	11
1945-46	Elmer Lach, Montreal	9	5	12	17
1944-45	Joe Carveth, Detroit	14	5	6	11
1943-44	Toe Blake, Montreal	9	7	11	18
1942-43	Carl Liscombe, Detroit	10	6	8	14
1941-42	Don Grosso, Detroit	12	8	6	14
1940-41	Milt Schmidt, Boston	11	5	6	11
1939-40	Phil Watson, NY Rangers	12	3	6	9
	Neil Colville, NY Rangers	12	2	7	9
1938-39	Bill Cowley, Boston	12	3	11	14
1937-38	Johnny Gottselig, Chicago	10	5	3	8
1936-37	Marty Barry, Detroit	10	4	7	11
1935-36	Buzz Boll, Toronto	9	7	3	10
1934-35	Baldy Northcott, Mtl. Maroons	7	4	1	5
	Harvey Jackson, Toronto	7	3	2	5
	Marvin Wentworth, Mtl. Maroons	7	3	2	5
1933-34	Larry Aurie, Detroit	9	3	7	10
1932-33	Cecil Dillon, NY Rangers	8	8	2	10
1931-32	Frank Boucher, NY Rangers	7	3	6	9
1930-31	Cooney Weiland, Boston	5	6	3	9
1929-30	Marty Barry, Boston	6	3	3	6
	Cooney Weiland, Boston	6	1	5	6
1928-29	Andy Blair, Toronto	4	3	0	3
	Butch Keeling, NY Rangers	6	3	0	3
	Ace Bailey, Toronto	4	1	2	3
1927-28	Frank Boucher, NY Rangers	9	7	3	10
1926-27	Harry Oliver, Boston	8	4	2	6
	Perk Galbraith, Boston	8	3	3	6
	Frank Fredrickson, Boston	8	2	4	6
1925-26	Nels Stewart, Mtl. Maroons	8	6	3	9
1924-25	Howie Morenz, Montreal	6	7	1	8
1923-24	Howie Morenz, Montreal	6	7	2	9
1922-23	Punch Broadbent, Ottawa	8	6	1	7
1921-22	Babe Dye, Toronto	7	11	2	13
1920-21	Cy Denneny, Ottawa	7	4	2	6
1919-20	Frank Nighbor, Ottawa	5	6	1	7
	Jack Darragh, Ottawa	5	5	2	7
1918-19	Newsy Lalonde, Montreal	10	17	1	18
1917-18	Alf Skinner, Toronto	7	8	1	9

Overtime Games since 1918

Abbreviations: Teams/Cities: — **Atl.** - Atlanta; **Bos.** - Boston; **Buf.** - Buffalo; **Cgy.** - Calgary; **Cgy. T.** - Calgary Tigers (Western Canada Hockey League); **Chi.** - Chicago; **Col.** - Colorado; **Det.** - Detroit; **Edm.** - Edmonton; **Edm. E.** - Edmonton Eskimos (WCHL); **Hfd.** - Hartford; **K.C.** - Kansas City; **L.A.** - Los Angeles; **Min.** - Minnesota; **Mtl.** - Montreal; **Mtl.M.** - Montreal Maroons; **N.J.** - New Jersey; **NYA** - NY Americans; **NYI** - New York Islanders; **NYR** - New York Rangers; **Oak.** - Oakland; **Ott.** - Ottawa; **Phi.** - Philadelphia; **Pit.** - Pittsburgh; **Que.** - Quebec; **St. L.** - St. Louis; **Sea.** - Seattle Metropolitans (Pacific Coast Hockey Association); **Tor.** - Toronto; **Van.** - Vancouver; **Van. M** - Vancouver Millionaires (PCHA); **Vic.** - Victoria Cougars (WCHL); **Wpg.** - Winnipeg; **Wsh.** - Washington.
SERIES — **CF** - conference final; **DF** - division final; **DSF** - division semi-final; **F** - final; **PR** - preliminary round; **QF** - quarter final; **SF** - semi-final.

Date	City	Series	Score		Scorer	Overtime	Series Winner
Mar.26/19	Sea.	F	Mtl. 0	Sea. 0	no scorer	20:00	
Mar.29/19	Sea.	F	Mtl. 4	Sea. 3	Odie Cleghorn	15:57	
Mar.21/22	Tor.	F	Tor 2	Van.M. 1	Babe Dye	4:50	Tor.
Mar.29/23	Van.	F	Ott. 2	Edm.E. 1	Cy Denneny	2:08	Ott.
Mar.31/27	Mtl.	QF	Mtl. 1	Mtl. M. 0	Howie Morenz	12:05	Mtl.
Apr. 7/27	Bos.	F	Ott. 0	Bos. 0	no scorer	20:00	Ott.
Apr. 11/27	Ott.	F	Bos. 1	Ott. 1	no scorer	20:00	Ott.
Apr. 3/28	Mtl.	QF	Mtl. M. 1	Mtl. 0	Russ Oatman	8:20	Mtl. M.
Apr. 7/28	Mtl.	F	NYR 2	Mtl. M. 1	Frank Boucher	7:05	NYR
Mar.21/29	NY	QF	NYR 1	NYA 0	Butch Keeling	29:50	NYR
Mar.26/29	Tor.	SF	NYR 2	Tor. 1	Frank Boucher	2:03	NYR
Mar.20/30	Mtl.	SF	Bos. 2	Mtl. M. 1	Harry Oliver	45:35	Bos.
Mar.25/30	Bos.	SF	Mtl. M. 1	Bos. 0	Archie Wilcox	26:27	Bos.
Mar.26/30	Mtl.	QF	Chi. 2	Mtl. 2	Howie Morenz (Mtl.)	51:43	Mtl.
Mar.28/30	Mtl.	SF	Mtl. 2	NYR 1	Gus Rivers	68:52	Mtl.
Mar.24/31	Bos.	SF	Bos. 5	Mtl. 4	Cooney Weiland	18:56	Mtl.
Mar.26/31	Chi.	QF	Chi. 2	Tor. 1	Steward Adams	19:20	Chi.
Mar.28/31	Mtl.	SF	Mtl. 4	Bos. 3	Georges Mantha	5:10	Mtl.
Apr. 1/31	Mtl.	SF	Mtl. 3	Bos. 2	Wildor Larochelle	19:00	Mtl.
Apr. 5/31	Chi.	F	Chi. 2	Mtl. 1	Johnny Gottselig	24:50	Mtl.
Apr. 9/31	Mtl.	F	Chi. 3	Mtl. 2	Cy Wentworth	53:50	Mtl.
Mar.26/32	Mtl.	SF	NYR 4	Mtl. 3	Fred Cook	59:32	NYR
Apr. 2/32	Tor.	SF	Tor. 3	Mtl. M. 2	Bob Gracie	17:59	Tor.
Mar.25/33	Bos.	SF	Bos. 2	Tor. 1	Marty Barry	14:14	Tor.
Mar.28/33	Bos.	SF	Tor. 1	Bos. 0	Busher Jackson	15:03	Tor.
Mar.30/33	Tor.	SF	Bos. 2	Tor. 1	Eddie Shore	4:23	Tor.
Apr. 3/33	Tor.	SF	Tor. 1	Bos. 0	Ken Doraty	104:46	Tor.
Apr. 13/33	Tor.	F	NYR 1	Tor. 0	Bill Cook	7:33	NYR
Mar.22/34	Tor.	SF	Det. 2	Tor. 1	Herbie Lewis	1:33	Det.
Mar.25/34	Chi.	QF	Chi. 1	Mtl. 1	Mush March (Chi)	11:05	Chi.
Apr. 3/34	Det.	F	Chi. 2	Det. 1	Paul Thompson	21:05	Chi.
Apr. 10/34	Chi.	F	Chi. 1	Det. 0	Mush March	30:05	Chi.
Mar.23/35	Bos.	SF	Bos. 1	Tor. 0	Dit Clapper	33:26	Tor.
Mar.26/35	Chi.	QF	Mtl. M. 1	Chi. 0	Baldy Northcott	4:02	Mtl. M.
Mar.30/35	Tor.	SF	Tor. 2	Bos. 1	Pep Kelly	1:36	Tor.
Apr. 4/35	Tor.	F	Mtl. M. 3	Tor. 2	Dave Trottier	5:20	Mtl. M.
Mar.24/36	Mtl.	SF	Det. 1	Mtl. M. 0	Mud Bruneteau	116:30	Det.
Apr. 9/36	Tor.	F	Tor. 4	Det. 3	Buzz Boll	0:31	Det.
Mar.25/37	NY	QF	NYR 2	Tor. 1	Babe Pratt	13:05	NYR
Apr. 1/37	Mtl.	SF	Det. 2	Mtl. 1	Hec Kilrea	51:49	Det.
Mar.22/38	NY	QF	NYA 2	NYR 1	Johnny Sorrell	21:25	NYA
Mar.25/38	Tor.	SF	Tor. 1	Bos. 0	George Parsons	21:31	Tor.
Mar.26/38	Mtl.	QF	Chi. 3	Mtl. 2	Paul Thompson	11:49	Chi.
Mar.27/38	NY	QF	NYA 3	NYR 2	Lorne Carr	60:40	NYA
Mar.29/38	Bos.	SF	Tor. 3	Bos. 2	Gord Drillon	10:04	Tor.
Mar.31/38	Chi.	SF	Chi. 1	NYA 0	Cully Dahlstrom	33:01	Chi.
Mar.21/39	NY	SF	Bos. 2	NYR 1	Mel Hill	59:25	Bos.
Mar.23/39	Bos.	SF	Bos. 3	NYR 2	Mel Hill	8:24	Bos.
Mar.26/39	Det.	QF	Det. 1	Mtl. 0	Marty Barry	7:47	Det.
Mar.30/39	Bos.	SF	NYR 2	Bos. 1	Clint Smith	17:19	Bos.
Apr. 1/39	Tor.	SF	Tor. 5	Det. 4	Gord Drillon	5:42	Tor.
Apr. 2/39	Bos.	SF	Bos. 2	NYR 1	Mel Hill	48:00	Bos.
Apr. 9/39	Bos.	F	Tor. 3	Bos. 2	Doc Romnes	10:38	Bos.
Mar.19/40	Det.	QF	Det. 2	NYA 1	Syd Howe	0:25	Det.
Mar.19/40	Tor.	QF	Tor. 3	Chi. 2	Syl Apps	6:35	Tor.
Apr. 2/40	NY	F	NYR 2	Tor. 1	Alf Pike	15:30	NYR
Apr. 11/40	Tor.	F	NYR 2	Tor. 1	Muzz Patrick	31:43	NYR
Apr. 13/40	Tor.	F	NYR 3	Tor. 2	Bryan Hextall	2:07	NYR
Mar.20/41	Det.	QF	Det. 2	NYR 1	Gus Giesebrecht	12:01	Det.
Mar.22/41	Mtl.	QF	Mtl. 4	Chi. 3	Charlie Sands	34:04	Chi.
Mar.29/41	Bos.	SF	Tor. 2	Bos. 1	Pete Langelle	17:31	Bos.
Mar.30/41	Chi.	SF	Det. 2	Chi. 1	Gus Giesebrecht	9:15	Det.
Mar.22/42	Chi.	QF	Bos. 2	Chi. 1	Des Smith	9:51	Bos.
Mar.21/43	Bos.	SF	Bos. 5	Mtl. 4	Don Gallinger	12:30	Bos.
Mar.23/43	Det.	SF	Tor. 3	Det. 2	Jack McLean	70:18	Det.
Mar.25/43	Mtl.	SF	Bos. 3	Mtl. 2	Harvey Jackson	3:20	Bos.
Mar.30/43	Tor.	SF	Det. 3	Tor. 2	Adam Brown	9:21	Det.
Mar.30/43	Bos.	SF	Bos. 5	Mtl. 4	Ab DeMarco	3:41	Bos.
Apr. 13/44	Mtl.	F	Mtl. 5	Chi. 4	Toe Blake	9:12	Mtl.
Mar.27/45	Tor.	SF	Tor. 4	Mtl. 3	Gus Bodnar	12:36	Tor.
Mar.29/45	Det.	SF	Det. 3	Bos. 2	Mud Bruneteau	17:12	Det.
Apr. 21/45	Tor.	F	Det. 1	Tor. 0	Ed Bruneteau	14:16	Tor.
Mar.28/46	Bos.	SF	Bos. 4	Det. 3	Don Gallinger	9:51	Bos.
Mar.30/46	Mtl.	F	Mtl. 4	Bos. 3	Maurice Richard	9:08	Mtl.
Apr. 2/46	Mtl.	F	Mtl. 3	Bos. 2	Jim Peters	16:55	Mtl.
Apr. 7/46	Bos.	F	Bos. 3	Mtl. 2	Terry Reardon	15:13	Mtl.
Mar.26/47	Tor.	SF	Tor. 3	Det. 2	Howie Meeker	3:05	Tor.
Mar.27/47	Mtl.	SF	Mtl. 2	Bos. 1	Ken Mosdell	5:38	Mtl.
Apr. 3/47	Mtl.	SF	Mtl. 4	Bos. 3	John Quilty	36:40	Mtl.
Apr. 15/47	Tor.	F	Tor. 2	Mtl. 1	Syl Apps	16:36	Tor.
Mar.24/48	Tor.	SF	Tor. 5	Bos. 4	Nick Metz	17:03	Tor.
Mar.22/49	Det.	SF	Det. 2	Mtl. 1	Max McNab	44:52	Det.
Mar.24/49	Det.	SF	Mtl. 4	Det. 3	Gerry Plamondon	2:59	Det.
Mar.26/49	Tor.	SF	Bos. 5	Tor. 4	Woody Dumart	16:14	Tor.
Apr. 8/49	Det.	F	Tor. 3	Det. 2	Joe Klukay	17:31	Tor.
Apr. 4/50	Tor.	SF	Det. 2	Tor. 1	Leo Reise	20:38	Det.
Apr. 4/50	Mtl.	SF	Mtl. 3	NYR 2	Elmer Lach	15:19	Mtl.
Apr. 9/50	Det.	SF	Det. 1	Tor. 0	Leo Reise	8:39	Det.
Apr. 18/50	Det.	F	NYR 4	Det. 3	Don Raleigh	8:34	Det.
Apr. 20/50	Det.	F	NYR 2	Det. 1	Don Raleigh	1:38	Det.
Apr. 23/50	Det.	F	Det. 4	NYR 3	Pete Babando	28:31	Det.
Mar.27/51	Det.	SF	Mtl. 3	Det. 2	Maurice Richard	61:09	Mtl.
Mar.29/51	Det.	SF	Mtl. 1	Det. 0	Maurice Richard	42:20	Mtl.
Mar.31/51	Tor.	SF	Bos. 1	Tor. 1	no scorer	20:00	Tor.
Apr. 11/51	Tor.	F	Tor. 3	Mtl. 2	Sid Smith	5:51	Tor.
Apr. 14/51	Tor.	F	Mtl. 3	Tor. 2	Maurice Richard	2:55	Tor.
Apr. 17/51	Mtl.	F	Tor. 2	Mtl. 1	Ted Kennedy	4:47	Tor.
Apr. 19/51	Mtl.	F	Tor. 3	Mtl. 2	Harry Watson	5:15	Tor.
Apr. 21/51	Tor.	F	Tor. 3	Mtl. 2	Bill Barilko	2:53	Tor.
Apr. 6/52	Bos.	SF	Mtl. 3	Bos. 2	Paul Masnick	27:49	Mtl.
Mar.29/53	Bos.	SF	Bos. 2	Det. 1	Jack McIntyre	12:29	Bos.
Mar.29/53	Chi.	SF	Chi. 2	Mtl. 1	Al Dewsbury	5:18	Mtl.
Apr. 16/53	Mtl.	F	Mtl. 1	Bos. 0	Elmer Lach	1:22	Mtl.
Apr. 1/54	Det.	SF	Det. 4	Tor. 3	Ted Lindsay	21:01	Det.
Apr. 11/54	Det.	F	Mtl. 1	Det. 0	Ken Mosdell	5:45	Det.
Apr. 16/54	Det.	F	Det. 2	Mtl. 1	Tony Leswick	4:29	Det.
Mar.29/55	Bos.	SF	Mtl. 4	Bos. 3	Don Marshall	3:05	Mtl.
Mar.24/56	Tor.	SF	Det. 5	Tor. 4	Ted Lindsay	4:22	Det.
Mar.28/57	NY	SF	NYR 4	Mtl. 3	Andy Hebenton	13:38	Mtl.
Apr. 4/57	Mtl.	SF	Mtl. 4	NYR 3	Maurice Richard	1:11	Mtl.
Mar.27/58	NY	SF	Bos. 4	NYR 3	Jerry Toppazzini	4:46	Bos.
Mar.30/58	Det.	SF	Mtl. 2	Det. 1	André Pronovost	11:52	Mtl.
Apr. 17/58	Mtl.	F	Mtl. 3	Bos. 2	Maurice Richard	5:45	Mtl.
Mar.28/59	Tor.	SF	Tor. 3	Bos. 2	Gerry Ehman	5:02	Tor.
Mar.31/59	Tor.	SF	Tor. 3	Bos. 2	Frank Mahovlich	11:21	Tor.
Apr. 14/59	Tor.	F	Tor. 3	Mtl. 2	Dick Duff	10:06	Mtl.
Mar.26/60	Mtl.	SF	Mtl. 4	Chi. 3	Doug Harvey	8:38	Mtl.
Mar.27/60	Det.	SF	Tor. 5	Det. 4	Frank Mahovlich	43:00	Tor.
Mar.29/60	Det.	SF	Det. 2	Tor. 1	Gerry Melnyk	1:54	Tor.
Mar.22/61	Tor.	SF	Tor. 3	Det. 2	George Armstrong	24:51	Det.
Mar.26/61	Chi.	SF	Chi. 2	Mtl. 1	Murray Balfour	52:12	Chi.
Apr. 5/62	Tor.	SF	Tor. 3	NYR 2	Red Kelly	24:23	Tor.
Apr. 2/64	Det.	SF	Chi. 3	Det. 2	Murray Balfour	8:21	Det.
Apr. 14/64	Tor.	F	Det. 4	Tor. 3	Larry Jeffrey	7:52	Tor.
Apr. 23/64	Det.	F	Tor. 4	Det. 3	Bobby Baun	1:43	Tor.
Apr. 6/65	Tor.	SF	Tor. 3	Mtl. 2	Dave Keon	4:17	Mtl.
Apr. 13/65	Tor.	SF	Mtl. 4	Tor. 3	Claude Provost	16:33	Mtl.
May 5/66	Det.	F	Mtl. 3	Det. 2	Henri Richard	2:20	Mtl.
Apr. 13/67	NY	SF	Mtl. 2	NYR 1	John Ferguson	6:28	Mtl.
Apr. 25/67	Tor.	F	Tor. 3	Mtl. 2	Bob Pulford	28:26	Tor.
Apr. 10/68	St. L.	QF	St. L. 3	Phi. 2	Larry Keenan	24:10	St. L.
Apr. 16/68	St. L.	QF	Phi. 2	St. L. 1	Don Blackburn	31:38	St. L.
Apr. 16/68	Min.	QF	Min. 4	L.A. 3	Milan Marcetta	9:11	Min.
Apr. 22/68	Min.	SF	Min. 3	St. L. 2	Parker MacDonald	3:41	St. L.
Apr. 27/68	St. L.	SF	St. L. 4	Min. 3	Gary Sabourin	1:32	St. L.
Apr. 28/68	Mtl.	SF	Mtl. 4	Chi. 3	Jacques Lemaire	2:14	Mtl.
Apr. 29/68	St. L.	SF	St. L. 3	Min. 2	Bill McCreary	17:27	St. L.
May 3/68	St. L.	SF	St. L. 2	Min. 1	Ron Schock	22:50	St. L.
May 5/68	St. L.	F	Mtl. 3	St. L. 2	Jacques Lemaire	1:41	Mtl.
May 9/68	Mtl.	F	Mtl. 4	St. L. 3	Bobby Rousseau	1:13	Mtl.
Apr. 2/69	Oak.	QF	L.A. 5	Oak. 4	Ted Irvine	0:19	L.A.
Apr. 10/69	Mtl.	SF	Mtl. 3	Bos. 2	Ralph Backstrom	0:42	Mtl.
Apr. 13/69	Mtl.	SF	Mtl. 4	Bos. 3	Mickey Redmond	4:55	Mtl.
Apr. 24/69	Bos.	SF	Mtl. 2	Bos. 1	Jean Béliveau	31:28	Mtl.
Apr. 12/70	Oak.	QF	Pit. 3	Oak. 2	Michel Briere	8:28	Pit.
May10/70	Bos.	F	Bos. 4	St. L. 3	Bobby Orr	0:40	Bos.
Apr. 15/71	Tor.	QF	NYR 2	Tor. 1	Bob Nevin	9:07	NYR
Apr. 18/71	Chi.	SF	NYR 2	Chi. 1	Pete Stemkowski	1:37	Chi.
Apr. 27/71	Chi.	SF	Chi. 3	NYR 2	Bobby Hull	6:35	Chi.
Apr. 29/71	NY	SF	NYR 3	Chi. 2	Pete Stemkowski	41:29	Chi.
May 4/71	Chi.	F	Chi. 2	Mtl. 1	Jim Pappin	21:11	Mtl.
Apr. 6/72	Bos.	QF	Tor. 4	Bos. 3	Jim Harrison	2:58	Bos.
Apr. 6/72	Min.	QF	Min. 6	St. L. 5	Bill Goldsworthy	1:36	St. L.
Apr. 9/72	Pit.	QF	Chi. 6	Pit. 5	Pit Martin	0:12	Chi.
Apr. 16/72	Min.	QF	St. L. 2	Min. 1	Kevin O'Shea	10:07	St. L.
Apr. 1/73	Mtl.	QF	Buf. 3	Mtl. 2	René Robert	9:18	Mtl.
Apr. 10/73	Phi.	QF	Phi. 3	Min. 2	Gary Dornhoefer	8:35	Phi.
Apr. 14/73	Mtl.	SF	Phi. 5	Mtl. 4	Rick MacLeish	2:56	Mtl.
Apr. 17/73	Mtl.	SF	Mtl. 4	Phi. 3	Larry Robinson	6:45	Mtl.
Apr. 14/74	Tor.	QF	Bos. 4	Tor. 3	Ken Hodge	1:27	Bos.
Apr. 14/74	Atl.	QF	Phi. 4	Atl. 3	Dave Schultz	5:40	Phi.
Apr. 16/74	Mtl.	QF	NYR 3	Mtl. 2	Ron Harris	4:07	NYR
Apr. 23/74	Chi.	SF	Chi. 4	Bos. 3	Jim Pappin	3:48	Bos.
Apr. 28/74	NY	SF	NYR 2	Phi. 1	Rod Gilbert	4:20	Phi.
May 9/74	Bos.	F	Phi. 3	Bos. 2	Bobby Clarke	12:01	Phi.
Apr. 8/75	L.A.	PR	L.A. 3	Tor. 2	Mike Murphy	8:53	Tor.
Apr. 10/75	Tor.	PR	Tor. 3	L.A. 2	Blaine Stoughton	10:19	Tor.
Apr. 10/75	Chi.	PR	Chi. 4	Bos. 3	Ivan Boldirev	7:33	Chi.
Apr. 11/75	NY	PR	NYI 4	NYR 3	Jean-Paul Parise	0:11	NYI
Apr. 19/75	Tor.	QF	Phi. 4	Tor. 3	André Dupont	1:45	Phi.
Apr. 17/75	Chi.	QF	Chi. 5	Buf. 4	Stan Mikita	2:31	Buf.
Apr. 22/75	Mtl.	QF	Mtl. 5	Van. 4	Guy Lafleur	17:06	Mtl.
May 1/75	Phi.	SF	Phi. 5	NYI 4	Bobby Clarke	2:56	Phi.
May 7/75	NYI	SF	NYI 4	Phi. 3	Jude Drouin	1:53	Phi.
Apr. 27/75	Buf.	SF	Buf. 6	Mtl. 5	Danny Gare	4:42	Buf.
May 6/75	Buf.	SF	Buf. 5	Mtl. 4	René Robert	5:56	Buf.
May20/75	Buf.	F	Buf. 5	Phi. 4	René Robert	18:29	Phi.
Apr. 8/76	Buf.	PR	Buf. 3	St. L. 2	Danny Gare	11:43	Buf.
Apr. 9/76	Buf.	PR	Buf. 2	St. L. 1	Don Luce	14:27	Buf.
Apr. 13/76	Bos.	QF	L.A. 3	Bos. 2	Butch Goring	0:27	Bos.
Apr. 13/76	Buf.	QF	Buf. 3	NYI 2	Danny Gare	14:04	NYI
Apr. 22/76	L.A.	QF	L.A. 4	Bos. 3	Butch Goring	18:28	Bos.
Apr. 29/76	Phi.	SF	Phi. 2	Bos. 1	Reggie Leach	13:38	Phi.
Apr. 15/77	Tor.	QF	Phi. 4	Tor. 3	Rick MacLeish	2:55	Phi.
Apr. 17/77	Tor.	QF	Phi. 6	Tor. 5	Reggie Leach	19:10	Phi.
Apr. 24/77	Phi.	SF	Bos. 4	Phi. 3	Rick Middleton	2:57	Bos.
Apr. 26/77	Phi.	SF	Bos. 5	Phi. 4	Terry O'Reilly	30:07	Bos.
May 3/77	Mtl.	SF	NYI 4	Mtl. 3	Billy Harris	3:58	Mtl.
May14/77	Bos.	F	Mtl. 2	Bos. 1	Jacques Lemaire	4:32	Mtl.
Apr. 11/78	Phi.	PR	Phi. 3	Col. 2	Mel Bridgman	0:23	Phi.

Date	City	Series	Score		Scorer	Overtime	Series Winner
Apr. 13/78	NY	PR	NYR 4	Buf. 3	Don Murdoch	1:37	Buf.
Apr. 19/78	Bos.	QF	Bos. 4	Chi. 3	Terry O'Reilly	1:50	Bos.
Apr. 19/78	NYI	QF	NYI 3	Tor. 2	Mike Bossy	2:50	Tor.
Apr. 21/78	Chi.	QF	Bos. 4	Chi. 3	Peter McNab	10:17	Bos.
Apr. 25/78	NYI	QF	NYI 2	Tor. 1	Bob Nystrom	8:02	Tor.
Apr. 29/78	NYI	QF	Tor. 2	NYI 1	Lanny McDonald	4:13	Tor.
May 2/78	Bos.	SF	Bos. 3	Phi. 2	Rick Middleton	1:43	Bos.
May 16/78	Mtl.	F	Mtl. 3	Bos. 2	Guy Lafleur1	3:09	Mtl.
May 21/78	Bos.	F	Bos. 4	Mtl. 3	Bobby Schmautz	6:22	Mtl.
Apr. 12/79	L.A.	PR	NYR 2	L.A. 1	Phil Esposito	6:11	NYR
Apr. 14/79	Buf.	PR	Pit. 4	Buf. 3	George Ferguson	0:47	Pit.
Apr. 16/79	Phi.	QF	Phi. 3	NYR 2	Ken Linseman	0:44	NYR
Apr. 18/79	NYI	QF	NYI 1	Chi. 0	Mike Bossy	2:31	NYI
Apr. 21/79	Tor.	QF	Mtl. 4	Tor. 3	Cam Connor	25:25	Mtl.
Apr. 22/79	Tor.	QF	Mtl. 5	Tor. 4	Larry Robinson	4:14	Mtl.
Apr. 28/79	NYI	SF	NYI 4	NYR 3	Denis Potvin	8:02	NYR
May 3/79	NY	SF	NYI 3	NYR 2	Bob Nystrom	3:40	NYR
May 3/79	Bos.	SF	Bos. 4	Mtl. 3	Jean Ratelle	3:46	Mtl.
May 10/79	Mtl.	SF	Mtl. 5	Bos. 4	Yvon Lambert	9:33	Mtl.
May 19/79	NY	F	Mtl. 4	NYR 3	Serge Savard	7:25	Mtl.
Apr. 8/80	NY	PR	NYR 2	Atl. 1	Steve Vickers	0:33	NYR
Apr. 8/80	Phi.	PR	Phi. 4	Edm. 3	Bobby Clarke	8:06	Phi.
Apr. 8/80	Chi.	PR	Chi. 3	St. L. 2	Doug Lecuyer	12:34	Chi.
Apr. 11/80	Hfd.	PR	Mtl. 4	Hfd. 3	Yvon Lambert	0:29	Mtl.
Apr. 11/80	Tor.	PR	Min. 4	Tor. 3	Al MacAdam	0:32	Min.
Apr. 11/80	L.A.	PR	NYI 4	L.A. 3	Ken Morrow	6:55	NYI
Apr. 11/80	Edm.	PR	Phi. 3	Edm. 2	Ken Linseman	23:56	Phi.
Apr. 16/80	Bos.	QF	NYI 2	Bos. 1	Clark Gillies	1:02	NYI
Apr. 17/80	Bos.	QF	NYI 5	Bos. 4	Bob Bourne	1:24	NYI
Apr. 21/80	NYI	QF	Bos. 4	NYI 3	Terry O'Reilly	17:13	NYI
May 1/80	Buf.	SF	NYI 2	Buf. 1	Bob Nystrom	21:20	NYI
May 13/80	Phi.	F	NYI 4	Phi. 3	Denis Potvin	4:07	NYI
May 24/80	NYI	F	NYI 5	Phi. 4	Bob Nystrom	7:11	NYI
Apr. 8/81	Buf.	PR	Buf. 3	Van. 2	Alan Haworth	5:00	Buf.
Apr. 8/81	Bos.	PR	Min. 5	Bos. 4	Steve Payne	3:34	Min.
Apr. 11/81	Chi.	PR	Cgy. 5	Chi. 4	Willi Plett	35:17	Cgy.
Apr. 12/81	Que.	PR	Que. 4	Phi. 3	Dale Hunter	0:37	Phi.
Apr. 14/81	St. L.	PR	St. L. 4	Pit. 3	Mike Crombeen	25:16	St. L.
Apr. 16/81	Buf.	QF	Min. 4	Buf. 3	Steve Payne	0:22	Min.
Apr. 20/81	Min.	QF	Buf. 5	Min. 4	Craig Ramsay	16:32	Min.
Apr. 20/81	Edm.	QF	NYI 5	Edm. 4	Ken Morrow	5:41	NYI
Apr. 7/82	Min.	DSF	Chi. 3	Min. 2	Greg Fox	3:34	Chi.
Apr. 8/82	Edm.	DSF	Edm. 3	L.A. 2	Wayne Gretzky	6:20	L.A.
Apr. 8/82	Van.	DSF	Van. 2	Cgy. 1	Dave Williams	14:20	Van.
Apr. 10/82	Pit.	DSF	Pit. 2	NYI 1	Rick Kehoe	4:14	NYI
Apr. 10/82	L.A.	DSF	L.A. 6	Edm. 5	Daryl Evans	2:35	L.A.
Apr. 13/82	Mtl.	DSF	Que. 3	Mtl. 2	Dale Hunter	0:22	Que.
Apr. 13/82	NY	DSF	NYI 4	Pit. 3	John Tonelli	6:19	NYI
Apr. 16/82	Van.	DF	L.A. 3	Van. 2	Steve Bozek	4:33	Van.
Apr. 18/82	Que.	DF	Que. 3	Bos. 2	Wilf Paiement	11:44	Que.
Apr. 18/82	NY	DF	NYI 4	NYR 3	Bryan Trottier	3:00	NYI
Apr. 18/82	L.A.	DF	Van. 4	L.A. 3	Colin Campbell	1:23	Van.
Apr. 21/82	St. L.	DF	St. L. 3	Chi. 2	Bernie Federko	3:28	Chi.
Apr. 23/82	Que.	DF	Bos. 6	Que. 5	Peter McNab	10:54	Que.
Apr. 27/82	Chi.	CF	Van. 2	Chi. 1	Jim Nill	28:58	Van.
May 1/82	Que.	CF	NYI 5	Que. 4	Wayne Merrick	16:52	NYI
May 8/82	NYI	F	NYI 6	Van. 5	Mike Bossy	19:58	NYI
Apr. 5/83	Bos.	DSF	Bos. 4	Que. 3	Barry Pederson	1:46	Bos.
Apr. 6/83	Cgy.	DSF	Cgy. 4	Van. 3	Eddy Beers	12:27	Cgy.
Apr. 7/83	Min.	DSF	Min. 5	Tor. 4	Bobby Smith	5:03	Min.
Apr. 10/83	Tor.	DSF	Min. 5	Tor. 4	Dino Ciccarelli	8:05	Min.
Apr. 10/83	Van.	DSF	Cgy. 4	Van. 3	Greg Meredith	1:06	Cgy.
Apr. 18/83	Min.	DF	Chi. 4	Min. 3	Rich Preston	10:34	Chi.
Apr. 24/83	Bos.	DF	Bos. 3	Buf. 2	Brad Park	1:52	Bos.
Apr. 5/84	Edm.	DSF	Edm. 5	Wpg. 4	Randy Gregg	0:21	Edm.
Apr. 7/84	Det.	DSF	St. L. 4	Det. 3	Mark Reeds	37:07	St. L.
Apr. 8/84	Det.	DSF	St. L. 3	Det. 2	Jorgen Pettersson	2:42	St. L.
Apr. 10/84	NYI	DSF	NYI 3	NYR 2	Ken Morrow	8:56	NYI
Apr. 13/84	Min.	DF	St. L. 4	Min. 3	Doug Gilmour	16:16	Min.
Apr. 13/84	Edm.	DF	Cgy. 6	Edm. 5	Carey Wilson	3:42	Edm.
Apr. 13/84	NYI	DF	NYI 5	Wsh. 4	Anders Kallur	7:35	NYI
Apr. 16/84	Mtl.	DF	Que. 4	Mtl. 3	Bo Berglund	3:00	Mtl.
Apr. 20/84	Cgy.	DF	Cgy. 5	Edm. 4	Lanny McDonald	1:04	Edm.
Apr. 22/84	Min.	DF	Min. 4	St. L. 3	Steve Payne	6:00	Min.
Apr. 10/85	Phi.	DSF	Phi. 5	NYR 4	Mark Howe	8:01	Phi.
Apr. 10/85	Wsh.	DSF	Wsh. 4	NYI 3	Alan Haworth	2:28	NYI
Apr. 10/85	Edm.	DSF	Edm. 3	L.A. 2	Lee Fogolin	3:01	Edm.
Apr. 10/85	Wpg.	DSF	Wpg. 5	Cgy. 4	Brian Mullen	7:56	Wpg.
Apr. 11/85	Wsh.	DSF	Wsh. 2	NYI 1	Mike Gartner	21:23	NYI
Apr. 13/85	L.A.	DSF	Edm. 4	L.A. 3	Glenn Anderson	0:46	Edm.
Apr. 18/85	Mtl.	DF	Que. 2	Mtl. 1	Mark Kumpel	12:23	Que.
Apr. 23/85	Que.	DF	Que. 7	Mtl. 6	Dale Hunter	18:36	Que.
May 2/85	Mtl.	DF	Que. 3	Mtl. 2	Peter Stastny	2:22	Que.
Apr. 25/85	Min.	DF	Chi. 7	Min. 6	Darryl Sutter	21:57	Chi.
Apr. 28/85	Chi.	DF	Min. 5	Chi. 4	Dennis Maruk	1:14	Chi.
Apr. 30/85	Min.	DF	Chi. 6	Min. 5	Darryl Sutter	15:41	Chi.
May 5/85	Que.	CF	Que. 2	Phi. 1	Peter Stastny	6:20	Phi.
Apr. 9/86	Que.	DSF	Hfd. 3	Que. 2	Sylvain Turgeon	2:36	Hfd.
Apr. 12/86	Wpg.	DSF	Cgy. 4	Wpg. 3	Lanny McDonald	8:25	Cgy.
Apr. 17/86	Wsh.	DF	NYR 4	Wsh. 3	Brian MacLellan	1:16	NYR
Apr. 20/86	Edm.	DF	Edm. 6	Cgy. 5	Glenn Anderson	1:04	Cgy.
Apr. 23/86	Hfd.	DF	Hfd. 2	Mtl. 1	Kevin Dineen	1:07	Mtl.
Apr. 23/86	NYR	DF	NYR 6	Wsh. 5	Bob Brooke	2:40	NYR
Apr. 26/86	St L.	DF	St L. 4	Tor. 3	Mark Reeds	7:11	St L.
Apr. 29/86	Mtl.	DF	Mtl. 2	Hfd. 1	Claude Lemieux	5:55	Mtl.
May 5/86	NYR	CF	Mtl. 4	NYR 3	Claude Lemieux	9:41	Mtl.
May 12/86	St L.	CF	St L. 6	Cgy. 5	Doug Wickenheiser	7:30	Cgy.
May 18/86	Cgy.	F	Mtl. 3	Cgy. 2	Brian Skrudland	0:09	Mtl.
Apr. 8/87	Hfd.	DSF	Hfd. 3	Que. 2	Paul MacDermid	2:20	Que.
Apr. 9/87	Mtl.	DSF	Mtl. 4	Bos. 3	Mats Naslund	2:38	Mtl.
Apr. 9/87	St. L.	DSF	Tor. 3	St. L. 2	Rick Lanz	10:17	Tor.
Apr. 11/87	Wpg.	DSF	Cgy. 3	Wpg. 2	Mike Bullard	3:53	Wpg.
Apr. 11/87	Chi.	DSF	Det. 4	Chi. 3	Shawn Burr	4:51	Det.

Date	City	Series	Score		Scorer	Overtime	Series Winner
Apr. 16/87	Que.	DSF	Que. 5	Hfd. 4	Peter Stastny	6:05	Que.
Apr. 18/87	Wsh.	DSF	NYI 3	Wsh. 2	Pat LaFontaine	68:47	NYI
Apr. 21/87	Edm.	DF	Edm. 3	Wpg. 2	Glenn Anderson	0:36	Edm.
Apr. 26/87	Que.	DF	Mtl. 3	Que. 2	Mats Naslund	5:30	Mtl.
Apr. 27/87	Tor.	DF	Tor. 3	Det. 2	Mike Allison	9:31	Det.
May 4/87	Phi.	CF	Phi. 4	Mtl. 3	Ilkka Sinislao	9:11	Phi.
May 20/87	Edm.	F	Edm. 3	Phi. 2	Jari Kurri	6:50	Edm.
Apr. 6/88	NYI	DSF	NYI 4	N.J. 3	Pat LaFontaine	6:11	N.J.
Apr. 10/88	Phi.	DSF	Phi. 5	Wsh. 4	Murray Craven	1:18	Wsh.
Apr. 10/88	N.J.	DSF	NYI 5	N.J. 4	Brent Sutter	15:07	N.J.
Apr. 10/88	Buf.	DSF	Buf. 6	Bos. 5	John Tucker	5:32	Bos.
Apr. 12/88	Det.	DSF	Tor. 6	Det. 5	Ed Olczyk	0:34	Det.
Apr. 16/88	Wsh.	DSF	Wsh. 5	Phi. 4	Dale Hunter	5:57	Wsh.
Apr. 21/88	Cgy.	DF	Edm. 5	Cgy. 4	Wayne Gretzky	7:54	Edm.
May 4/88	Bos.	CF	N.J. 3	Bos. 2	Doug Brown	17:46	Bos.
May 9/88	Det.	CF	Edm. 4	Det. 3	Jari Kurri	11:02	Edm.
Apr. 5/89	St. L.	DSF	St. L. 4	Min. 3	Brett Hull	11:55	St. L.
Apr. 5/89	Cgy.	DSF	Van. 4	Cgy. 3	Paul Reinhart	2:47	Cgy.
Apr. 6/89	St. L.	DSF	St. L. 4	Min. 3	Rick Meagher	5:30	St. L.
Apr. 6/89	Det.	DSF	Chi. 5	Det. 4	Duane Sutter	14:36	Chi.
Apr. 8/89	Hfd.	DSF	Mtl. 5	Hfd. 4	Stephane Richer	5:01	Mtl.
Apr. 8/89	Phi.	DSF	Wsh. 4	Phi. 3	Kelly Miller	0:51	Phi.
Apr. 9/89	Hfd.	DSF	Mtl. 4	Hfd. 3	Russ Courtnall	15:12	Mtl.
Apr. 15/89	Cgy.	DSF	Cgy. 4	Van. 3	Joel Otto	19:21	Cgy.
Apr. 18/89	Cgy.	DF	Cgy. 4	L.A. 3	Doug Gilmour	7:47	Cgy.
Apr. 19/89	Mtl.	DF	Mtl. 3	Bos. 2	Bobby Smith	12:24	Mtl.
Apr. 20/89	St. L.	DF	St. L. 5	Chi. 4	Tony Hrkac	33:49	Chi.
Apr. 21/89	Phi.	DF	Pit. 4	Phi. 3	Phil Bourque	12:08	Phi.
May 8/89	Chi.	CF	Cgy. 2	Chi. 1	Al MacInnis	15:05	Cgy.
May 9/89	Mtl.	CF	Phi. 2	Mtl. 1	Dave Poulin	5:02	Mtl.
May 19/89	Mtl.	F	Mtl. 4	Cgy. 3	Ryan Walter	38:08	Cgy.
Apr. 5/90	N.J.	DSF	Wsh. 5	N.J. 4	Dino Ciccarelli	5:34	Wsh.
Apr. 6/90	Edm.	DSF	Edm. 3	Wpg. 2	Mark Lamb	4:21	Edm.
Apr. 8/90	Tor.	DSF	St. L. 6	Tor. 5	Sergio Momesso	6:04	St. L.
Apr. 8/90	L.A.	DSF	L.A. 2	Cgy. 1	Tony Granato	8:37	L.A.
Apr. 9/90	Mtl.	DSF	Mtl. 2	Buf. 1	Brian Skrudland	12:35	Mtl.
Apr. 9/90	NYI	DSF	NYI 4	NYR 3	Brent Sutter	20:59	NYR
Apr. 10/90	Wpg.	DSF	Wpg. 4	Edm. 3	Dave Ellett	21:08	Edm.
Apr. 14/90	L.A.	DSF	L.A. 4	Cgy. 3	Mike Krushelnyski	23:14	L.A.
Apr. 15/90	Hfd.	DSF	Hfd. 3	Bos. 2	Kevin Dineen	12:30	Bos.
Apr. 21/90	Bos.	DF	Bos. 5	Mtl. 4	Garry Galley	3:42	Bos.
Apr. 24/90	L.A.	DF	Edm. 6	L.A. 5	Joe Murphy	4:42	Edm.
Apr. 25/90	Wsh.	DF	Wsh. 4	NYR 3	Rod Langway	0:34	Wsh.
Apr. 27/90	NYR	DF	Wsh. 2	NYR 1	John Druce	6:48	Wsh.
May 15/90	Bos.	F	Edm. 3	Bos. 2	Petr Klima	55:13	Edm.
Apr. 4/91	Chi.	DSF	Min. 4	Chi. 3	Brian Propp	4:14	Min.
Apr. 5/91	Pit.	DSF	Pit. 5	N.J. 4	Jaromir Jagr	8:52	Pit.
Apr. 6/91	L.A.	DSF	L.A. 3	Van. 2	Wayne Gretzky	11:08	L.A.
Apr. 8/91	Van.	DSF	Van. 2	L.A. 1	Cliff Ronning	3:12	L.A.
Apr. 11/91	NYR	DSF	Wsh. 5	NYR 4	Dino Ciccarelli	6:44	Wsh.
Apr. 11/91	Mtl.	DSF	Mtl. 4	Buf. 3	Russ Courtnall	5:56	Mtl.
Apr. 14/91	Edm.	DSF	Cgy. 2	Edm. 1	Theo Fleury	4:40	Edm.
Apr. 16/91	Cgy.	DSF	Edm. 5	Cgy. 4	Esa Tikkanen	6:58	Edm.
Apr. 18/91	L.A.	DF	L.A. 4	Edm. 3	Luc Robitaille	2:13	Edm.
Apr. 19/91	Bos.	DF	Mtl. 4	Bos. 3	Stephane Richer	0:27	Bos.
Apr. 19/91	Pit.	DF	Pit. 7	Wsh. 6	Kevin Stevens	8:10	Pit.
Apr. 20/91	L.A.	DF	Edm. 4	L.A. 3	Petr Klima	24:48	Edm.
Apr. 22/91	Edm.	DF	Edm. 4	L.A. 3	Esa Tikkanen	20:48	Edm.
Apr. 27/91	Mtl.	DF	Mtl. 3	Bos. 2	Shayne Corson	17:47	Bos.
Apr. 28/91	Edm.	DF	Edm. 4	L.A. 3	Craig MacTavish	16:57	Edm.
May 3/91	Bos.	CF	Bos. 5	Pit. 4	Vladimir Ruzicka	8:14	Pit.
Apr. 21/92	Bos.	DSF	Bos. 3	Buf. 2	Adam Oates	11:24	Bos.
Apr. 22/92	Min.	DSF	Det. 5	Min. 4	Yves Racine	1:15	Det.
Apr. 22/92	St. L.	DSF	St. L. 5	Chi. 4	Brett Hull	23:33	Chi.
Apr. 25/92	Buf.	DSF	Bos. 5	Buf. 4	Ted Donato	2:08	Bos.
Apr. 28/92	Min.	DSF	Det. 1	Min. 0	Sergei Fedorov	16:13	Det.
Apr. 29/92	Hfd.	DSF	Hfd. 2	Mon. 1	Yvon Corriveau	0:24	Mtl.
May 1/92	Mtl.	DSF	Mtl. 3	Hfd. 2	Russ Courtnall	25:26	Mtl.
May 3/92	Van.	DF	Edm. 4	Van. 3	Joe Murphy	8:36	Edm.
May 5/92	Mtl.	DF	Bos. 3	Mtl. 2	Peter Douris	3:12	Bos.
May 7/92	Pit.	DF	NYR 6	Pit. 5	Kris King	1:29	Pit.
May 9/92	Pit.	DF	Pit. 5	NYR 4	Ron Francis	2:47	Pit.
May 17/92	Pit.	CF	Pit. 4	Bos. 3	Jaromir Jagr	9:44	Pit.
May 20/92	Edm.	CF	Chi. 4	Edm. 3	Jeremy Roenick	2:45	Chi.
Apr. 18/93	Bos.	DSF	Buf. 5	Bos. 4	Bob Sweeney	11:03	Buf.
Apr. 18/93	Que.	DSF	Que. 3	Mtl. 2	Scott Young	16:49	Mtl.
Apr. 20/93	Wsh.	DSF	NYI 5	Wsh. 4	Brian Mullen	34:50	NYI
Apr. 22/93	Mtl.	DSF	Mtl. 2	Que. 1	Vincent Damphousse	10:30	Mtl.
Apr. 22/93	Buf.	DSF	Buf. 4	Bos. 3	Yuri Khmylev	1:05	Buf.
Apr. 22/93	NYI	DSF	NYI 4	Wsh. 3	Ray Ferraro	4:46	NYI
Apr. 24/93	Buf.	DSF	Buf. 6	Bos. 5	Brad May	4:48	Buf.
Apr. 24/93	NYI	DSF	NYI 4	Wsh. 3	Ray Ferraro	25:40	NYI
Apr. 25/93	St. L.	DSF	St. L. 4	Chi. 3	Craig Janney	10:43	St. L.
Apr. 26/93	Que.	DSF	Mtl. 5	Que. 4	Kirk Muller	8:17	Mtl.
Apr. 27/93	Det.	DSF	Tor. 5	Det. 4	Mike Foligno	2:05	Tor.
Apr. 27/93	Van.	DSF	Wpg. 4	Van. 3	Teemu Selanne	6:18	Van.
Apr. 29/93	Wpg.	DSF	Van. 4	Wpg. 3	Greg Adams	4:30	Van.
May 1/93	Det.	DSF	Tor. 4	Det. 3	Nikolai Borschevsky	2:35	Tor.
May 3/93	Tor.	DF	Tor. 2	St. L. 1	Doug Gilmour	23:16	Tor.
May 4/93	Mtl.	DF	Mtl. 4	Buf. 3	Guy Carbonneau	2:50	Mtl.
May 5/93	Tor.	DF	St. L. 2	Tor. 1	Jeff Brown	23:03	Tor.
May 6/93	Buf.	DF	Mtl. 4	Buf. 3	Gilbert Dionne	8:28	Mtl.
May 8/93	Buf.	DF	Mtl. 4	Buf. 3	Kirk Muller	11:37	Mtl.
May 11/93	Van.	DF	L.A. 4	Van. 3	Gary Shuchuk	26:31	L.A.
May 14/93	Pit.	DF	NYI 4	Pit. 3	Dave Volek	5:16	NYI
May 18/93	Mtl.	CF	Mtl. 4	NYI 3	Stephan Lebeau	26:21	Mtl.
May 20/93	NYI	CF	Mtl. 2	NYI 1	Guy Carbonneau	12:34	Mtl.
May 25/93	Tor.	CF	Tor. 3	L.A. 2	Glenn Anderson	19:20	L.A.
May 27/93	L.A.	CF	L.A. 5	Tor. 4	Wayne Gretzky	1:41	L.A.
Jun. 3/93	Mtl.	F	Mtl. 3	L.A. 2	Eric Desjardins	0:51	Mtl.
Jun. 5/93	L.A.	F	Mtl. 4	L.A. 3	John LeClair	0:34	Mtl.
Jun. 7/93	L.A.	F	Mtl. 3	L.A. 2	John LeClair	14:37	Mtl.

Stanley Cup Coaching Records

Coaches listed in order of total games coached in playoffs. Minimum: 65 games.

Coach	Team	Years	Series	W	L	Games G	W	L	T	Cups	%
Bowman, Scott	St. Louis	4	10	6	4	52	26	26	0	0	.500
	Montreal	8	19	16	3	98	70	28	0	5	.714
	Buffalo	5	8	3	5	36	18	18	0	0	.500
	Pittsburgh	2	6	5	1	33	23	10	0	1	.696
	TOTALS	19	43	30	13	219	137	82	0	6	.625
Arbour, Al	St. Louis	1	2	1	1	11	4	7	0	0	.364
	NY Islanders	14	39	29	10	194	119	75	0	4	.613
	TOTALS	15	41	30	11	205	123	82	0	4	.600
Irvin, Dick	Chicago	1	3	2	1	9	5	3	1	0	.611
	Toronto	9	20	12	8	66	33	32	1	1	.508
	Montreal	14	22	11	11	115	62	53	0	3	.539
	TOTALS	24	45	25	20	190	100	88	2	4	.532
Sather, Glen	Edmonton	10	27	21	6	*126	89	37	0	4	.706
Blake, Toe	Montreal	13	23	18	5	119	82	37	0	8	.689
Keenan, Mike	Philadelphia	4	10	6	4	57	32	25	0	0	.561
	Chicago	4	11	7	4	60	33	27	0	0	.550
	TOTALS	8	21	13	8	117	65	52	0	0	.556
Reay, Billy	Chicago	12	22	10	12	117	57	60	0	0	.487
Shero, Fred	Philadelphia	6	16	12	4	83	48	35	0	2	.578
	NY Rangers	2	5	3	2	25	13	12	0	0	.520
	TOTALS	8	21	15	6	108	61	47	0	2	.565
Adams, Jack	Detroit	15	27	15	12	105	52	52	1	3	.500
Francis, Emile	NY Rangers	9	14	5	9	75	34	41	0	0	.453
	St. Louis	3	4	1	3	18	6	12	0	0	.333
	TOTALS	12	18	6	12	93	40	53	0	0	.430
Imlach, Punch	Toronto	11	17	10	7	92	44	48	0	4	.478
Demers, Jacques	St. Louis	3	6	3	3	33	16	17	0	0	.485
	Detroit	3	7	4	3	38	20	18	0	0	.526
	Montreal	1	4	4	0	20	16	4	0	1	.800
	TOTALS	7	17	11	6	91	52	39	0	1	.571
Day, Hap	Toronto	9	14	10	4	80	49	31	0	5	.613
Murray, Bryan	Washington	7	10	3	7	53	24	29	0	0	.452
	Detroit	3	4	1	3	25	10	15	0	0	.400
	TOTALS	10	14	4	10	78	34	44	0	0	.435
Burns, Pat	Montreal	4	10	6	4	56	30	26	0	0	.535
	Toronto	1	3	2	1	21	11	10	0	0	.523
	TOTALS	5	13	8	5	77	41	36	0	0	.532

Coach	Team	Years	Series	W	L	Games G	W	L	T	Cups	%
Johnson, Bob	Calgary	5	10	5	5	52	25	27	0	0	.481
	Pittsburgh	1	4	4	0	24	16	8	0	1	.666
	TOTALS	6	14	9	5	76	41	35	0	1	.539
Abel, Sid	Chicago	1	1	0	1	7	3	4	0	0	.429
	Detroit	8	12	4	8	69	29	40	0	0	.420
	TOTALS	9	13	4	9	76	32	44	0	0	.421
Quinn, Pat	Philadelphia	3	8	5	3	39	22	17	0	0	.564
	Los Angeles	1	1	0	1	3	0	3	0	0	.000
	Vancouver	3	5	2	3	31	14	17	0	0	.451
	TOTALS	7	14	7	7	73	36	37	0	0	.493
Ross, Art	Boston	12	19	9	10	70	32	33	5	2	.493
Bergeron, Michel	Quebec	7	13	6	7	68	31	37	0	0	.456
Ivan, Tommy	Detroit	7	12	8	4	67	36	31	0	3	.537
Neilson, Roger	Toronto	2	5	3	2	19	8	11	0	0	.421
	Buffalo	1	2	1	1	8	4	4	0	0	.500
	Vancouver	2	5	3	2	21	12	9	0	0	.571
	NY Rangers	2	3	1	2	19	8	11	0	0	.421
	TOTALS	7	15	8	7	67	32	35	0	0	.473
Pulford, Bob	Los Angeles	4	6	2	4	26	11	15	0	0	.423
	Chicago	5	9	4	5	41	17	24	0	0	.415
	TOTALS	9	15	6	9	67	28	39	0	0	.418
Patrick, Lester	NY Rangers	12	24	14	10	65	31	26	8	2	.538

* Does not include suspended game, May 24, 1988.

Overtime Record of Current Teams

(Listed by number of OT games played)

Team	Overall GP	W	L	T	Home GP	W	L	T	Last OT Game	Road GP	W	L	T	Last OT Game
Montreal	114	65	47	2	53	35	17	1	Jun. 3/93	61	30	30	1	Jun. 7/93
Boston	89	35	51	3	41	20	20	1	Apr. 18/93	48	15	31	2	Apr. 24/93
Toronto	81	40	40	1	51	24	26	1	May 25/93	30	16	14	0	May 27/93
NY Rangers	52	24	28	0	21	9	12	0	Apr. 11/91	31	15	16	0	May 9/92
Detroit	51	22	29	0	31	10	21	0	May 1/93	20	12	8	0	Apr. 28/92
Chicago	47	22	23	2	23	12	10	1	Apr. 4/91	24	10	13	1	Apr. 25/93
NY Islanders	38	29	9	0	17	14	3	0	May 20/93	21	15	6	0	May 18/93
Philadelphia	34	18	16	0	13	8	5	0	Apr. 21/89	21	10	11	0	May 9/89
St. Louis	31	19	12	0	15	13	2	0	Apr. 25/93	16	6	10	0	May 5/93
Los Angeles	30	12	18	0	16	8	8	0	Jun. 7/93	14	4	10	0	Jun. 3/93
Edmonton	27	17	10	0	14	9	5	0	May 20/92	13	8	5	0	May 3/92
* Dallas	26	11	15	0	14	5	9	0	Apr. 28/92	12	6	6	0	Apr. 4/91
Buffalo	26	13	13	0	16	10	6	0	May 8/93	10	3	7	0	May 4/93
** Calgary	24	11	13	0	9	4	5	0	Apr. 16/91	15	7	8	0	Apr. 14/91
Quebec	18	10	8	0	11	6	5	0	Apr. 26/93	7	4	3	0	Apr. 22/93
Washington	17	8	9	0	7	4	3	0	Apr. 20/93	10	4	6	0	Apr. 24/93
Vancouver	17	6	11	0	7	2	5	0	May 11/93	10	4	6	0	Apr. 29/93
Pittsburgh	14	8	6	0	8	5	3	0	May 14/93	6	3	3	0	May 3/91
Hartford	11	5	6	0	7	4	3	0	Apr. 29/92	4	1	3	0	May 1/92
Winnipeg	9	4	5	0	5	2	3	0	Apr. 29/93	4	2	2	0	Apr. 27/93
*** New Jersey	6	1	5	0	2	0	2	0	Apr. 5/90	4	1	3	0	Apr. 5/91

*Totals include those of Minnesota 1967-93.
**Totals include those of Atlanta 1972-80.
***Totals include those of Kansas City and Colorado 1974-82.

As a player, Toe Blake won Stanley Cup championships with the Montreal Maroons in 1935 and the Montreal Canadiens in 1944 and 1946. He became the Canadiens' coach in 1955-56 and won the Cup eight times before retiring after the conclusion of the 1967-68 playoffs.

Penalty Shots in Stanley Cup Playoff Games

Date	Player	Goaltender	Scored	Final Score		Series
Mar. 25/37	Lionel Conacher, Mtl. Maroons	Tiny Thompson, Boston	No	Mtl. M.	0 at Bos. 4	QF
Apr. 15/37	Alex Shibicky, NY Rangers	Earl Robertson, Detroit	No	NYR	0 at Det. 3	F
Apr. 13/44	Virgil Johnson, Chicago	Bill Durnan, Montreal	No	Chi.	4 at Mtl. 5*	F
Apr. 9/68	Wayne Connelly, Minnesota	Terry Sawchuk, Los Angeles	Yes	L.A.	5 at Min. 7	QF
Apr. 27/68	Jim Roberts, St. Louis	Cesare Maniago, Minnesota	No	St. L.	4 at Min. 3	SF
May 16/71	Frank Mahovlich, Montreal	Tony Esposito, Chicago	No	Chi.	3 at Mtl. 4	F
May 7/75	Bill Barber, Philadelphia	Glenn Resch, NY Islanders	No	Phi.	3 at NYI 4*	SF
Apr. 20/79	Mike Walton, Chicago	Glenn Resch, NY Islanders	No	NYI	4 at Chi. 0	QF
Apr. 9/81	Peter McNab, Boston	Don Beaupre, Minnesota	No	Min.	5 at Bos. 4*	PR
Apr. 17/81	Anders Hedberg, NY Rangers	Mike Liut, St. Louis	Yes	NYR	6 at St. L. 4	QF
Apr. 9/83	Denis Potvin, NY Islanders	Pat Riggin, Washington	No	NYI	6 at Wsh. 2	DSF
Apr. 28/84	Wayne Gretzky, Edmonton	Don Beaupre, Minnesota	Yes	Edm.	8 at Min. 5	CF
May 1/84	Mats Naslund, Montreal	Bill Smith, NY Islanders	No	Mtl.	1 at NYI 3	CF
Apr. 14/85	Bob Carpenter, Washington	Bill Smith, NY Islanders	No	Wsh.	4 at NYI 6	DF
May 28/85	Ron Sutter, Philadelphia	Grant Fuhr, Edmonton	No	Phi.	3 at Edm. 5	F
May 30/85	Dave Poulin, Philadelphia	Grant Fuhr, Edmonton	No	Phi.	3 at Edm. 8	F
Apr. 9/88	John Tucker, Buffalo	Andy Moog, Boston	Yes	Bos.	2 at Buf. 6	DSF
Apr. 9/88	Petr Klima, Detroit	Allan Bester, Toronto	Yes	Det.	6 at Tor. 3	DSF
Apr. 8/89	Neal Broten, Minnesota	Greg Millen, St. Louis	Yes	St. L.	5 at Min. 3	DSF
Apr. 4/90	Al MacInnis, Calgary	Kelly Hrudey, Los Angeles	Yes	L.A.	5 at Cgy. 3	DSF
Apr. 5/90	Randy Wood, NY Islanders	Mike Richter, NY Rangers	No	NYI	1 at NYR 2	DSF
May 3/90	Kelly Miller, Washington	Andy Moog, Boston	No	Wsh.	3 at Bos. 5	CF
May 18/90	Petr Klima, Edmonton	Rejean Lemelin, Boston	No	Edm.	7 at Bos. 2	F
Apr. 6/91	Basil McRae, Minnesota	Ed Belfour, Chicago	Yes	Min.	2 at Chi. 5	DSF
Apr. 10/91	Steve Duchesne, Los Angeles	Kirk McLean, Vancouver	Yes	L.A.	6 at Van. 1	DSF
May 11/92	Jaromir Jagr, Pittsburgh	John Vanbiesbrouck, NYR	Yes	Pit.	3 at NYR 2	DF
May 13/92	Shawn McEachern, Pittsburgh	John Vanbiesbrouck, NYR	No	NYR	1 at Pit. 5	DF

* Game was decided in overtime, but shot taken during regulation time.

Ten Longest Overtime Games

Date	City	Series	Score		Scorer	Overtime	Series Winner
Mar. 24/36	Mtl.	SF	Det. 1	Mtl. M. 0	Mud Bruneteau	116:30	Det.
Apr. 3/33	Tor.	SF	Tor. 1	Bos. 0	Ken Doraty	104:46	Tor.
Mar. 23/43	Det.	SF	Tor. 3	Det. 2	Jack McLean	70:18	Det.
Mar. 28/30	Mtl.	SF	Mtl. 2	NYR 1	Gus Rivers	68:52	Mtl.
Apr. 18/87	Wsh.	DSF	NYI 3	Wsh. 2	Pat LaFontaine	68:47	NYI
Mar. 27/51	Det.	SF	Mtl. 3	Det. 2	Maurice Richard	61:09	Mtl.
Mar. 27/38	NY	QF	NYA 3	NYR 2	Lorne Carr	60:40	NYA
Mar. 26/32	Mtl.	SF	NYR 4	Mtl. 3	Fred Cook	59:32	NYR
Mar. 21/39	NY	SF	Bos. 2	NYR 1	Mel Hill	59:25	Bos.
May 15/90	Bos.	F	Edm. 3	Bos. 2	Petr Klima	55:13	Edm.

Pittsburgh's Jaromir Jagr, left, and Shawn McEachern, right, were awarded penalty shots during the 1992 Patrick Division Final series between Pittsburgh and the New York Rangers. Jagr scored against John Vanbiesbrouck. McEachern was stopped.

Early Stanley Cup champions:
The Winnipeg Victorias, left, were the
first team from the West to win the
Cup, capturing the trophy in 1896.
Winnipeg also lost a controversial Cup
challenge to the Montreal Victorias
in 1899. The Quebec Bulldogs, below,
were led by "Phantom" Joe Malone
(center of photo) and defeated a team
from Sydney, Nova Scotia by scores
of 14-3 and 6-2 to defend their Stanley
Cup title in 1913.

1993-94 Player Register

Note: The 1993-94 Player Register lists forwards and defensemen only. Goaltenders are listed separately. The Player Register lists every skater who appeared in an NHL game in the 1992-93 season, every skater drafted in the first six rounds of the 1992 and 1993 Entry Drafts and other players on NHL Reserve Lists. Trades and roster changes are current as of August 16, 1993.

Abbreviations: A – assists; **G** – goals; **GP** – games played; **Lea** – league; **PIM** – penalties in minutes; **TP** – total points; ***** – league-leading total.

Pronunciations courtesy of the NHL Broadcasters' Association and Igor Kuperman, Winnipeg Jets

Goaltender Register begins on page 409.

LEAGUES:

ACHL	Atlantic Coast Hockey League
AHL	American Hockey League
AJHL	Alberta Junior Hockey League
Alp.	Alpenliga
AUAA	Atlantic Universities Athletic Association
BCJHL	British Columbia Junior Hockey League
CCHA	Central Collegiate Hockey Association
CHL	Central Hockey League
CIAU	Canadian Interuniversity Athletic Union
COJHL	Central Ontario Junior Hockey League
Col.	Colonial Hockey League
CWUAA	Canada West Universities Athletic Association
ECAC	Eastern Collegiate Athletic Association
ECHL	East Coast Hockey League
G.N.	Great Northern
GPAC	Great Plains Athletic Conference
H.E.	Hockey East
HS	High School
IHL	International Hockey League
Jr.	Junior
MJHA	(New York) Metropolitan Junior Hockey Association
MJHL	Manitoba Junior Hockey League
NAHL	North American Hockey League
NCAA	National Collegiate Athletic Association
NHL	**National Hockey League**
OHA	Ontario Hockey Association
OHL	Ontario Hockey League
OMJHL	Ontario Major Junior Hockey League
OPJHL	Ontario Provincial Junior Hockey League
OUAA	Ontario Universities Athletic Association
QJHL	Quebec Junior Hockey League
QMJHL	Quebec Major Junior Hockey League
SJHL	Saskatchewan Junior Hockey League
SOHL	Southern Ontario Hockey League
USHL	United States Hockey League (Junior)
WCHA	Western Collegiate Hockey Association
WHA	World Hockey Association
WHL	Western Hockey League

AALTO, ANTTI

Center. Shoots left. 6'2", 185 lbs.　Born, Lappeenranta, Finland, March 4, 1975.
(Anaheim's 6th choice, 134th overall, in 1993 Entry Draft).

			Regular Season					Playoffs				
Season	Club	Lea	GP	G	A	TP	PIM	GP	G	A	TP	PIM
1991-92	SaiPa	Fin.2	20	6	6	12	20	....	....	....	....	....
1992-93	SaiPa	Fin.2	23	6	8	14	14	....	....	....	....	....
	TPS	Fin.	1	0	0	0	0	....	....	....	....	....

AALTONEN, PETRI　(AL-tuh-nehn)

Center. Shoots left. 5'10", 185 lbs.　Born, Tampere, Finland, May 31, 1970.
(Quebec's 4th choice, 45th overall, in 1988 Entry Draft).

			Regular Season					Playoffs				
Season	Club	Lea	GP	G	A	TP	PIM	GP	G	A	TP	PIM
1986-87	HIFK	Fin. Jr.	30	8	5	13	24	4	0	0	0	0
1987-88	HIFK	Fin. Jr.	34	37	20	57	25	....	....	....	....	....
1988-89	HIFK	Fin.	2	0	0	0	0	....	....	....	....	....
1989-90	HIFK	Fin.	3	0	0	0	0	....	....	....	....	....
1990-91	HIFK	Fin.	43	6	9	15	12	3	1	1	2	0
1991-92	Tappara	Fin.	36	3	4	7	18	....	....	....	....	....
1992-93	Vantaa	Fin. 2	33	15	11	26	50	....	....	....	....	....

ACTON, KEITH EDWARD

Center. Shoots left. 5'8", 170 lbs.　Born, Stouffville, Ont., April 15, 1958.
(Montreal's 8th choice, 103rd overall, in 1978 Amateur Draft).

			Regular Season					Playoffs				
Season	Club	Lea	GP	G	A	TP	PIM	GP	G	A	TP	PIM
1976-77	Peterborough	OHA	65	52	69	121	93	4	1	4	5	6
1977-78	Peterborough	OHA	68	42	86	128	52	21	10	8	18	16
1978-79	Nova Scotia	AHL	79	15	26	41	22	10	4	2	6	4
1979-80	Montreal	NHL	2	0	1	1	0	....	....	....	....	....
a	Nova Scotia	AHL	75	45	53	98	38	6	1	2	3	8
1980-81	Montreal	NHL	61	15	24	39	74	2	0	0	0	6
1981-82	Montreal	NHL	78	36	52	88	88	5	0	4	4	16
1982-83	Montreal	NHL	78	24	26	50	63	3	0	0	0	0
1983-84	Montreal	NHL	9	3	7	10	4	....	....	....	....	....
	Minnesota	NHL	62	17	38	55	60	15	4	7	11	12
1984-85	Minnesota	NHL	78	20	38	58	90	9	4	4	8	6
1985-86	Minnesota	NHL	79	26	32	58	100	5	0	3	3	6
1986-87	Minnesota	NHL	78	16	29	45	56	....	....	....	....	....
1987-88	Minnesota	NHL	46	8	11	19	74	....	....	....	....	....
	Edmonton	NHL	26	3	6	9	21	7	2	0	2	16
1988-89	Edmonton	NHL	46	11	15	26	47	....	....	....	....	....
	Philadelphia	NHL	25	3	10	13	64	16	2	3	5	18
1989-90	Philadelphia	NHL	69	13	14	27	80	....	....	....	....	....
1990-91	Philadelphia	NHL	76	14	23	37	131	....	....	....	....	....
1991-92	Philadelphia	NHL	50	7	10	17	98	....	....	....	....	....
1992-93	Philadelphia	NHL	83	8	15	23	51	....	....	....	....	....
	NHL Totals		**946**	**224**	**351**	**575**	**1101**	**62**	**12**	**21**	**33**	**80**

a　AHL Second All-Star Team (1980)
Played in NHL All-Star Game (1982)
Traded to **Minnesota** by **Montreal** with Mark Napier and Toronto's third round choice (previously acquired by Montreal — Minnesota selected Ken Hodge) in 1984 Entry Draft for Bobby Smith, October 28, 1983. Traded to **Edmonton** by **Minnesota** for Moe Mantha, January 22, 1988. Traded to **Philadelphia** by **Edmonton** with Edmonton's fifth round choice (Dimitri Yushkevich) in 1991 Entry Draft for Dave Brown, February 7, 1989. Traded to **Winnipeg** by **Philadelphia** with Pete Peeters for future considerations, September 28, 1989. Traded to **Philadelphia** by **Winnipeg** with Pete Peeters for Toronto's fifth round choice (previously acquired by Philadelphia — Winnipeg selected Juha Ylonen) in 1991 Entry Draft and the cancellation of future considerations owed Philadelphia from the trade of Shawn Cronin, October 3, 1989. Signed as a free agent by **Washington**, July 28, 1993.

ADAMS, GREG

Left wing. Shoots left. 6'3", 198 lbs.　Born, Nelson, B.C.,, August 1, 1963.

			Regular Season					Playoffs				
Season	Club	Lea	GP	G	A	TP	PIM	GP	G	A	TP	PIM
1982-83	N. Arizona	NCAA	29	14	21	35	19	....	....	....	....	....
1983-84	N. Arizona	NCAA	26	44	29	73	24	....	....	....	....	....
1984-85	**New Jersey**	**NHL**	**36**	**12**	**9**	**21**	**14**	....	....	....	....	....
	Maine	AHL	41	15	20	35	12	11	3	4	7	0
1985-86	**New Jersey**	**NHL**	**78**	**35**	**42**	**77**	**30**	....	....	....	....	....
1986-87	**New Jersey**	**NHL**	**72**	**20**	**27**	**47**	**19**	....	....	....	....	....
1987-88	**Vancouver**	**NHL**	**80**	**36**	**40**	**76**	**30**	....	....	....	....	....
1988-89	**Vancouver**	**NHL**	**61**	**19**	**14**	**33**	**24**	**7**	**2**	**3**	**5**	**2**
1989-90	**Vancouver**	**NHL**	**65**	**30**	**20**	**50**	**18**	....	....	....	....	....
1990-91	**Vancouver**	**NHL**	**55**	**21**	**24**	**45**	**10**	**5**	**0**	**0**	**0**	**2**
1991-92	**Vancouver**	**NHL**	**76**	**30**	**27**	**57**	**26**	**6**	**0**	**2**	**2**	**4**
1992-93	**Vancouver**	**NHL**	**53**	**25**	**31**	**56**	**14**	**12**	**7**	**6**	**13**	**6**
	NHL Totals		**576**	**228**	**234**	**462**	**185**	**30**	**9**	**11**	**20**	**14**

Played in NHL All-Star Game (1988)
Signed as a free agent by **New Jersey**, June 25, 1984. Traded to **Vancouver** by **New Jersey** with Kirk McLean for Patrik Sundstrom and Vancouver's fourth round choice (Matt Ruchty) in 1988 Entry Draft, September 10, 1987.

ADAMS, KEVYN

Center. Shoots right. 6'1", 182 lbs.　Born, Washington, D.C., October 8, 1974.
(Boston's 1st choice, 25th overall, in 1993 Entry Draft).

			Regular Season					Playoffs				
Season	Club	Lea	GP	G	A	TP	PIM	GP	G	A	TP	PIM
1991-92	Niagara	NAJHL	40	25	33	58	51	....	....	....	....	....
1992-93	Miami-Ohio	CCHA	40	17	15	32	18	....	....	....	....	....

AGNEW, JIM

Defense. Shoots left. 6'1", 190 lbs.　Born, Hartney, Man., March 21, 1966.
(Vancouver's 10th choice, 157th overall, in 1984 Entry Draft).

			Regular Season					Playoffs				
Season	Club	Lea	GP	G	A	TP	PIM	GP	G	A	TP	PIM
1982-83	Brandon	WHL	14	1	1	2	9	....	....	....	....	....
1983-84	Brandon	WHL	71	6	17	23	107	12	0	1	1	39
1984-85	Brandon	WHL	19	3	15	18	82	....	....	....	....	....
	Portland	WHL	44	5	24	29	223	6	0	2	2	44
1985-86a	Portland	WHL	70	6	30	36	286	9	0	1	1	48
1986-87	**Vancouver**	**NHL**	**4**	**0**	**0**	**0**	**0**	....	....	....	....	....
	Fredericton	AHL	67	0	5	5	261	....	....	....	....	....
1987-88	**Vancouver**	**NHL**	**10**	**0**	**1**	**1**	**16**	....	....	....	....	....
	Fredericton	AHL	63	2	8	10	188	14	0	2	2	43
1988-89	Milwaukee	IHL	47	2	10	12	181	11	0	2	2	34
1989-90	**Vancouver**	**NHL**	**7**	**0**	**0**	**0**	**36**	....	....	....	....	....
b	Milwaukee	IHL	51	4	10	14	238	....	....	....	....	....
1990-91	**Vancouver**	**NHL**	**20**	**0**	**0**	**0**	**81**	....	....	....	....	....
	Milwaukee	IHL	3	0	0	0	33	....	....	....	....	....
1991-92	**Vancouver**	**NHL**	**24**	**0**	**0**	**0**	**56**	**4**	**0**	**0**	**0**	**6**
1992-93	**Hartford**	**NHL**	**16**	**0**	**0**	**0**	**68**	....	....	....	....	....
	Springfield	AHL	1	0	1	1	2	....	....	....	....	....
	NHL Totals		**81**	**0**	**1**	**1**	**257**	**4**	**0**	**0**	**0**	**6**

a　WHL First All-Star Team, West Division (1986)
b　IHL Second All-Star Team (1990)
Signed as a free agent by **Hartford**, July 8, 1992.

AHLUND, HAKAN

Right wing. Shoots left. 6', 194 lbs. Born, Orebro, Sweden, August 16, 1967.
(Vancouver's 8th choice, 151st overall, in 1985 Entry Draft).

			Regular Season					Playoffs				
Season	Club	Lea	GP	G	A	TP	PIM	GP	G	A	TP	PIM
1983-84	Orebro	Swe. 2	1	0	1	1	0	....	....	....	....	....
1984-85	Orebro	Swe. 2	25	2	6	8	10	....	....	....	....	....
1985-86	Orebro	Swe. 2	20	5	4	9	10	2	0	0	0	0
1986-87	Orebro	Swe. 2	27	16	9	25	6	6	0	3	3	6
1987-88	Orebro	Swe. 2	36	24	23	47	29	6	3	4	7	7
1988-89	Malmo	Swe. 2	35	20	27	47	44	....	....	....	....	....
1989-90	Malmo	Swe. 2	35	12	38	50	30	....	....	....	....	....
1990-91	Malmo	Swe.	39	9	18	27	46	2	0	0	0	0
1991-92	Malmo	Swe.	38	5	12	17	48	10	2	2	4	8
1992-93	Malmo	Swe.	33	5	10	15	30	6	2	1	3	6

AHOLA, PETER

Defense. Shoots left. 6'3", 205 lbs. Born, Espoo, Finland, May 14, 1968.

			Regular Season					Playoffs				
Season	Club	Lea	GP	G	A	TP	PIM	GP	G	A	TP	PIM
1989-90	Boston U.	H.E.	43	3	20	23	65	....	....	....	....	....
1990-91a	Boston U.	H.E.	39	12	24	36	88	....	....	....	....	....
1991-92	**Los Angeles**	**NHL**	71	7	12	19	101	6	0	0	0	2
	Phoenix	IHL	7	3	3	6	34	....	....	....	....	....
1992-93	**Los Angeles**	**NHL**	8	1	1	2	6	....	....	....	....	....
	Pittsburgh	**NHL**	22	0	1	1	14	....	....	....	....	....
	Cleveland	IHL	9	1	0	1	4	....	....	....	....	....
	San Jose	**NHL**	20	2	3	5	16	....	....	....	....	....
	NHL Totals		121	10	17	27	137	6	0	0	0	2

a NCAA East Second All-American Team (1991)

Signed as a free agent by **Los Angeles**, April 5, 1991. Traded to **Pittsburgh** by **Los Angeles** for Jeff Chychrun, November 6, 1992. Traded to **San Jose** by **Pittsburgh** for future considerations, February 26, 1993. Traded to **Tampa Bay** by **San Jose** for Dave Capuano, June 19, 1993.

AIKEN, DAVID
(AY-kin)

Left wing. Shoots left. 6', 200 lbs. Born, St. Stephen, N.B., September 27, 1967.
(Edmonton's 1st choice, 20th overall, in 1989 Supplemental Draft).

			Regular Season					Playoffs				
Season	Club	Lea	GP	G	A	TP	PIM	GP	G	A	TP	PIM
1986-87	N. Hampshire	H.E.	37	19	9	28	10	....	....	....	....	....
1987-88	N. Hampshire	H.E.	29	7	15	22	24	....	....	....	....	....
1988-89	N. Hampshire	H.E.	34	14	17	31	30	....	....	....	....	....
1989-90	N. Hampshire	H.E.	39	12	19	31	37	....	....	....	....	....
1990-91	Richmond	ECHL	64	28	52	80	29	4	1	3	4	0
1991-92	Richmond	ECHL	63	31	36	67	25	7	5	2	7	0
1992-93	Richmond	ECHL	6	1	1	2	0	....	....	....	....	....

AIVAZOFF, MICAH
(AY-va-zoff)

Center. Shoots left. 6', 192 lbs. Born, Powell River, B.C., May 4, 1969.
(Los Angeles' 6th choice, 109th overall, in 1988 Entry Draft).

			Regular Season					Playoffs				
Season	Club	Lea	GP	G	A	TP	PIM	GP	G	A	TP	PIM
1986-87	Victoria	WHL	72	18	39	57	112	5	1	0	1	2
1987-88	Victoria	WHL	69	26	57	83	79	8	3	4	7	14
1988-89	Victoria	WHL	70	35	65	100	136	8	5	7	12	2
1989-90	New Haven	AHL	77	20	39	59	71	....	....	....	....	....
1990-91	New Haven	AHL	79	11	29	40	84	....	....	....	....	....
1991-92	Adirondack	AHL	61	9	20	29	50	19	2	8	10	25
1992-93	Adirondack	AHL	79	32	53	85	100	11	8	6	14	10

AKERBLOM, MARCUS
(OHK-uhr-blum)

Left wing. Shoots left. 6', 189 lbs. Born, Ostersund, Sweden, November 22, 1969.
(Winnipeg's 8th choice, 127th overall, in 1988 Entry Draft).

			Regular Season					Playoffs				
Season	Club	Lea	GP	G	A	TP	PIM	GP	G	A	TP	PIM
1986-87	Ostersund	Swe.2	32	14	18	32	....	....	....	....	....	....
1987-88	Bjorkloven	Swe.	36	6	8	14	22	8	2	0	2	4
1988-89	Bjorkloven	Swe.	21	6	10	16	16	....	....	....	....	....
1989-90	Bjorkloven	Swe.2	15	10	10	20	....	....	....	....	....	....
1990-91	Bjorkloven	Swe.2	22	7	4	11	16	....	....	....	....	....
1991-92	Leksand	Swe.	22	3	5	8	6	....	....	....	....	....
1992-93	Leksand	Swe.	36	4	7	11	14	2	0	1	1	0

AKERSTROM, ROGER
(OHK-uhr-struhm)

Defense. Shoots left. 5'11", 189 lbs. Born, Lulea, Sweden, April 5, 1967.
(Vancouver's 8th choice, 170th overall, in 1988 Entry Draft).

			Regular Season					Playoffs				
Season	Club	Lea	GP	G	A	TP	PIM	GP	G	A	TP	PIM
1987-88	Lulea	Swe.	34	4	3	7	28	....	....	....	....	....
1988-89	Lulea	Swe.	38	6	12	18	32	....	....	....	....	....
1989-90	Lulea	Swe.	36	5	10	15	44	5	3	2	5	2
1990-91	Lulea	Swe.	37	2	10	12	38	5	0	1	1	6
1991-92	Vasteras	Swe.	39	3	9	12	20	....	....	....	....	....
1992-93	Vasteras	Swe.	37	13	13	26	36	3	0	0	0	6

ALATALO, MIKA

Left wing. Shoots left. 5'11", 185 lbs. Born, Oulu, Finland, June 11, 1971.
(Winnipeg's 11th choice, 203rd overall, in 1990 Entry Draft).

			Regular Season					Playoffs				
Season	Club	Lea	GP	G	A	TP	PIM	GP	G	A	TP	PIM
1988-89	KooKoo	Fin.	34	8	6	14	10	....	....	....	....	....
1989-90	KooKoo	Fin.	41	3	5	8	22	....	....	....	....	....
1990-91	Lukko	Fin.	39	10	1	11	10	....	....	....	....	....
1991-92	Lukko	Fin.	43	20	17	37	32	2	0	0	0	0
1992-93	Lukko	Fin.	48	16	19	35	38	3	0	0	0	0

ALBELIN, TOMMY
(AL-buh-LEEN)

Defense. Shoots left. 6'1", 190 lbs. Born, Stockholm, Sweden, May 21, 1964.
(Quebec's 7th choice, 152nd overall, in 1983 Entry Draft).

			Regular Season					Playoffs				
Season	Club	Lea	GP	G	A	TP	PIM	GP	G	A	TP	PIM
1982-83	Djurgarden	Swe.	19	2	5	7	4	6	1	0	1	2
1983-84	Djurgarden	Swe.	30	9	5	14	26	4	0	1	1	2
1984-85	Djurgarden	Swe.	32	9	8	17	22	8	2	1	3	4
1985-86	Djurgarden	Swe.	35	4	8	12	26	....	....	....	....	....
1986-87	Djurgarden	Swe.	33	7	5	12	49	2	0	0	0	0
1987-88	**Quebec**	**NHL**	60	3	23	26	47	....	....	....	....	....
1988-89	**Quebec**	**NHL**	14	2	4	6	27	....	....	....	....	....
	Halifax	AHL	8	2	5	7	4	....	....	....	....	....
	New Jersey	**NHL**	46	7	24	31	40	....	....	....	....	....
1989-90	**New Jersey**	**NHL**	68	6	23	29	63	....	....	....	....	....
1990-91	**New Jersey**	**NHL**	47	2	12	14	44	3	0	1	1	2
	Utica	AHL	14	4	2	6	10	....	....	....	....	....
1991-92	**New Jersey**	**NHL**	19	0	4	4	4	1	1	1	2	0
	Utica	AHL	11	4	6	10	4	....	....	....	....	....
1992-93	**New Jersey**	**NHL**	36	1	5	6	14	5	2	0	2	0
	NHL Totals		290	21	95	116	239	9	3	2	5	2

Traded to **New Jersey** by **Quebec** for New Jersey's fourth round choice (Niclas Andersson) in 1989 Entry Draft, December 12, 1988.

ALEXEYEV, ALEXANDER

Defense. Shoots left. 6', 216 lbs. Born, Kiev, Soviet Union, March 21, 1974.
(Winnipeg's 5th choice, 132nd overall, in 1992 Entry Draft).

			Regular Season					Playoffs				
Season	Club	Lea	GP	G	A	TP	PIM	GP	G	A	TP	PIM
1990-91	Sokol Kiev	USSR	5	0	0	0	2	....	....	....	....	....
1991-92	Sokol Kiev	CIS	25	1	5	6	22	....	....	....	....	....
1992-93	Tacoma	WHL	44	3	33	36	67	7	2	7	9	4

ALINC, JAN

Right wing. Shoots left. 6'1", 180 lbs. Born, Most, Czech., May 27, 1972.
(Pittsburgh's 7th choice, 163rd overall, in 1992 Entry Draft).

			Regular Season					Playoffs				
Season	Club	Lea	GP	G	A	TP	PIM	GP	G	A	TP	PIM
1990-91	Litvinov	Czech.	7	1	1	2	....	....	....	....	....	....
1991-92	Litvinov	Czech.	45	21	16	37	24	....	....	....	....	....
1992-93	Litvinov	Czech.	36	16	13	29	....	....	....	....	....	....

ALLAIN, RICK

Defense. Shoots left. 6', 190 lbs. Born, Guelph, Ont., May 20, 1969.
(Boston's 8th choice, 164th overall, in 1989 Entry Draft).

			Regular Season					Playoffs				
Season	Club	Lea	GP	G	A	TP	PIM	GP	G	A	TP	PIM
1986-87	Kitchener	OHL	18	0	0	0	32	....	....	....	....	....
1987-88	Kitchener	OHL	45	4	9	13	267	....	....	....	....	....
1988-89	Kitchener	OHL	62	2	16	18	245	5	0	0	0	10
1989-90	Kitchener	OHL	55	5	16	21	156	17	0	4	4	46
1990-91	Maine	AHL	13	0	1	1	33	....	....	....	....	....
	Johnstown	ECHL	36	2	12	14	100	10	0	0	0	50
1991-92	Maine	AHL	66	1	11	12	249	....	....	....	....	....
1992-93	Providence	AHL	7	0	0	0	27	6	0	0	0	8

ALLEN, PETER

Defense. Shoots right. 6'2", 185 lbs. Born, Calgary, Alta., March 6, 1970.
(Boston's 1st choice, 24th overall, in 1991 Supplemental Draft).

			Regular Season					Playoffs				
Season	Club	Lea	GP	G	A	TP	PIM	GP	G	A	TP	PIM
1989-90	Yale	ECAC	26	2	4	6	16	....	....	....	....	....
1990-91	Yale	ECAC	17	0	6	6	14	....	....	....	....	....
1991-92	Yale	ECAC	26	5	13	18	26	....	....	....	....	....
1992-93	Yale	ECAC	30	3	15	18	32	....	....	....	....	....

ALLISON, JAMIE

Defense. Shoots left. 6'1", 188 lbs. Born, Lindsay, Ont., May 13, 1975.
(Calgary's 2nd choice, 44th overall, in 1993 Entry Draft).

			Regular Season					Playoffs				
Season	Club	Lea	GP	G	A	TP	PIM	GP	G	A	TP	PIM
1991-92	Windsor	OHL	59	4	8	12	70	4	1	1	2	2
1992-93	Detroit	OHL	61	0	13	13	64	15	2	5	7	23

ALLISON, JASON

Center. Shoots right. 6'2", 192 lbs. Born, North York, Ont., May 29, 1975.
(Washington's 2nd choice, 17th overall, in 1993 Entry Draft).

			Regular Season					Playoffs				
Season	Club	Lea	GP	G	A	TP	PIM	GP	G	A	TP	PIM
1991-92	London	OHL	65	11	19	30	15	7	0	0	0	0
1992-93	London	OHL	66	42	76	118	50	12	7	13	20	8

ALLISON, SCOTT

Center. Shoots left. 6'4", 194 lbs. Born, St. Boniface, Man., April 22, 1972.
(Edmonton's 1st choice, 17th overall, in 1990 Entry Draft).

			Regular Season					Playoffs				
Season	Club	Lea	GP	G	A	TP	PIM	GP	G	A	TP	PIM
1988-89	Prince Albert	WHL	51	6	9	15	37	3	0	0	0	0
1989-90	Prince Albert	WHL	66	22	16	38	73	11	1	4	5	8
1990-91	Prince Albert	WHL	30	5	5	10	57	....	....	....	....	....
	Portland	WHL	44	5	17	22	105	....	....	....	....	....
1991-92	Moose Jaw	WHL	72	37	45	82	238	3	1	1	2	25
1992-93	Cape Breton	AHL	49	3	5	8	34	....	....	....	....	....
	Wheeling	ECHL	6	3	3	6	8	....	....	....	....	....

ALVEY, MATT

Right wing. Shoots right. 6'5", 195 lbs. Born, Troy, NY, May 15, 1975.
(Boston's 2nd choice, 51st overall, in 1993 Entry Draft).

			Regular Season					Playoffs				
Season	Club	Lea	GP	G	A	TP	PIM	GP	G	A	TP	PIM
1991-92	Springfield	NEJHL	32	22	35	57	34	....	....	....	....	....
1992-93	Springfield	NEJHL	38	22	37	59	85	....	....	....	....	....

AMBROZIAK, PETER

Left wing. Shoots left. 6', 206 lbs. Born, Toronto, Ont., September 15, 1971.
(Buffalo's 4th choice, 72nd overall, in 1991 Entry Draft).

			Regular Season					Playoffs				
Season	Club	Lea	GP	G	A	TP	PIM	GP	G	A	TP	PIM
1990-91	Ottawa	OHL	62	30	32	62	56	17	15	9	24	24
1991-92	Ottawa	OHL	49	32	49	81	50	11	3	7	10	33
	Rochester	AHL	2	0	1	1	0	....	....	....	....	....
1992-93	Rochester	AHL	50	8	10	18	37	12	4	3	7	16

AMONTE, TONY

Right wing. Shoots left. 6', 190 lbs. Born, Hingham, MA, August 2, 1970.
(NY Rangers' 3rd choice, 68th overall, in 1988 Entry Draft).

			Regular Season					Playoffs				
Season	Club	Lea	GP	G	A	TP	PIM	GP	G	A	TP	PIM
1989-90	Boston U.	H.E.	41	25	33	58	52	....	....	....	....	....
1990-91ab	Boston U.	H.E.	38	31	37	68	82	....	....	....	....	....
	NY Rangers	**NHL**	....	....	....	....	....	**2**	**0**	**2**	**2**	**2**
1991-92c	**NY Rangers**	**NHL**	**79**	**35**	**34**	**69**	**55**	**13**	**3**	**6**	**9**	**2**
1992-93	**NY Rangers**	**NHL**	**83**	**33**	**43**	**76**	**49**	....	....	....	....	....
	NHL Totals		**162**	**68**	**77**	**145**	**104**	**15**	**3**	**8**	**11**	**4**

a Hockey East Second All-Star Team (1991)
b NCAA Final Four All-Tournament Team (1991)
c NHL/Upper Deck All-Rookie Team (1992)

ANDERSON, GLENN CHRIS

Right wing. Shoots left. 6'1", 190 lbs. Born, Vancouver, B.C., October 2, 1960.
(Edmonton's 3rd choice, 69th overall, in 1979 Entry Draft).

			Regular Season					Playoffs				
Season	Club	Lea	GP	G	A	TP	PIM	GP	G	A	TP	PIM
1978-79	U. of Denver	WCHA	40	26	29	55	58	....	....	....	....	....
1979-80	Seattle	WHL	7	5	5	10	4	....	....	....	....	....
	Cdn. Olympic	....	49	21	21	42	46	....	....	....	....	....
1980-81	**Edmonton**	**NHL**	**58**	**30**	**23**	**53**	**24**	**9**	**5**	**7**	**12**	**12**
1981-82	**Edmonton**	**NHL**	**80**	**38**	**67**	**105**	**71**	**5**	**2**	**5**	**7**	**8**
1982-83	**Edmonton**	**NHL**	**72**	**48**	**56**	**104**	**70**	**16**	**10**	**10**	**20**	**32**
1983-84	**Edmonton**	**NHL**	**80**	**54**	**45**	**99**	**65**	**19**	**6**	**11**	**17**	**33**
1984-85	**Edmonton**	**NHL**	**80**	**42**	**39**	**81**	**69**	**18**	**10**	**16**	**26**	**38**
1985-86	**Edmonton**	**NHL**	**72**	**54**	**48**	**102**	**90**	**10**	**8**	**3**	**11**	**14**
1986-87	**Edmonton**	**NHL**	**80**	**35**	**38**	**73**	**65**	**21**	**14**	**13**	**27**	**59**
1987-88	**Edmonton**	**NHL**	**80**	**38**	**50**	**88**	**58**	**19**	**9**	**16**	**25**	**49**
1988-89	**Edmonton**	**NHL**	**79**	**16**	**48**	**64**	**93**	**7**	**1**	**2**	**3**	**8**
1989-90	**Edmonton**	**NHL**	**73**	**34**	**38**	**72**	**107**	**22**	**10**	**12**	**22**	**20**
1990-91	**Edmonton**	**NHL**	**74**	**24**	**31**	**55**	**59**	**18**	**6**	**7**	**13**	**41**
1991-92	**Toronto**	**NHL**	**72**	**24**	**33**	**57**	**100**	....	....	....	....	....
1992-93	**Toronto**	**NHL**	**76**	**22**	**43**	**65**	**117**	**21**	**7**	**11**	**18**	**31**
	NHL Totals		**976**	**459**	**559**	**1018**	**988**	**185**	**88**	**113**	**201**	**345**

Played in NHL All-Star Game (1984-86, 1988)

Traded to **Toronto** by **Edmonton** with Grant Fuhr and Craig Berube for Vincent Damphousse, Peter Ing, Scott Thornton, Luke Richardson, future considerations and cash, September 19, 1991.

ANDERSON, JOHN MURRAY

Right wing. Shoots left. 5'11", 200 lbs. Born, Toronto, Ont., March 28, 1957.
(Toronto's 1st choice, 11th overall, in 1977 Amateur Draft).

			Regular Season					Playoffs				
Season	Club	Lea	GP	G	A	TP	PIM	GP	G	A	TP	PIM
1973-74	Toronto	OMJHL	38	22	22	44	6	....	....	....	....	....
1974-75	Toronto	OMJHL	70	49	64	113	31	22	16	14	30	14
1975-76	Toronto	OHA	39	26	25	51	19	10	7	4	11	7
1976-77a	Toronto	OHA	64	57	62	119	42	6	3	5	8	0
1977-78	**Toronto**	**NHL**	**17**	**1**	**2**	**3**	**2**	**2**	**0**	**0**	**0**	**0**
	Dallas	CHL	55	22	23	45	6	13	*11	8	*19	2
1978-79	**Toronto**	**NHL**	**71**	**15**	**11**	**26**	**10**	**6**	**0**	**2**	**2**	**0**
1979-80	**Toronto**	**NHL**	**74**	**25**	**28**	**53**	**22**	**3**	**1**	**1**	**2**	**0**
1980-81	**Toronto**	**NHL**	**75**	**17**	**26**	**43**	**31**	**2**	**0**	**0**	**0**	**0**
1981-82	**Toronto**	**NHL**	**69**	**31**	**26**	**57**	**30**	....	....	....	....	....
1982-83	**Toronto**	**NHL**	**80**	**31**	**49**	**80**	**24**	**4**	**2**	**4**	**6**	**0**
1983-84	**Toronto**	**NHL**	**73**	**37**	**31**	**68**	**22**	....	....	....	....	....
1984-85	**Toronto**	**NHL**	**75**	**32**	**31**	**63**	**27**	....	....	....	....	....
1985-86	**Quebec**	**NHL**	**65**	**21**	**28**	**49**	**26**	....	....	....	....	....
	Hartford	**NHL**	**14**	**8**	**17**	**25**	**2**	**10**	**5**	**8**	**13**	**0**
1986-87	**Hartford**	**NHL**	**76**	**31**	**44**	**75**	**19**	**6**	**1**	**2**	**3**	**0**
1987-88	**Hartford**	**NHL**	**63**	**17**	**32**	**49**	**20**	....	....	....	....	....
1988-89	**Hartford**	**NHL**	**62**	**16**	**24**	**40**	**28**	**4**	**0**	**1**	**1**	**2**
1989-90	Binghamton	AHL	3	1	1	2	0	....	....	....	....	....
	Milano	Italy	9	7	9	16	18	....	....	....	....	....
1990-91	Fort Wayne	IHL	63	40	43	83	24	1	3	0	3	0
1991-92bcd	New Haven	AHL	68	41	54	95	24	4	0	4	4	0
1992-93	San Diego	IHL	65	34	46	80	18	11	5	6	11	4
	NHL Totals		**814**	**282**	**349**	**631**	**263**	**37**	**9**	**18**	**27**	**2**

a OHA First All-Star Team (1977)
b Won Fred Hunt Award (Sportsmanship-AHL) (1992)
c AHL First All-Star Team (1992)
d Won Les Cunningham Trophy (MVP-AHL) (1992)

Traded to **Quebec** by **Toronto** for Brad Maxwell, August 21, 1985. Traded to **Hartford** by **Quebec** for Risto Siltanen, March 8, 1986.

ANDERSON, PERRY LYNN

Left wing. Shoots left. 6'1", 225 lbs. Born, Barrie, Ont., October 14, 1961.
(St. Louis' 5th choice, 117th overall, in 1980 Entry Draft).

			Regular Season					Playoffs				
Season	Club	Lea	GP	G	A	TP	PIM	GP	G	A	TP	PIM
1978-79	Kingston	OHA	61	6	13	19	85	5	2	1	3	6
1979-80	Kingston	OHA	63	17	16	33	52	3	0	0	0	6
1980-81	Kingston	OHA	38	9	13	22	118	....	....	....	....	....
	Brantford	OHA	31	8	27	35	43	6	4	2	6	15
1981-82	**St. Louis**	**NHL**	**5**	**1**	**2**	**3**	**0**	**10**	**2**	**0**	**2**	**4**
	Salt Lake	CHL	71	32	32	64	117	2	1	0	1	2
1982-83	**St. Louis**	**NHL**	**18**	**5**	**2**	**7**	**14**	....	....	....	....	....
	Salt Lake	CHL	57	23	19	42	140	....	....	....	....	....
1983-84	**St. Louis**	**NHL**	**50**	**7**	**5**	**12**	**195**	**9**	**0**	**0**	**0**	**27**
	Montana	CHL	8	7	3	10	34	....	....	....	....	....
1984-85	**St. Louis**	**NHL**	**71**	**9**	**9**	**18**	**146**	**3**	**0**	**0**	**0**	**7**
1985-86	**New Jersey**	**NHL**	**51**	**7**	**12**	**19**	**91**	....	....	....	....	....
1986-87	**New Jersey**	**NHL**	**57**	**10**	**9**	**19**	**107**	....	....	....	....	....
	Maine	AHL	9	5	4	9	42	....	....	....	....	....
1987-88	**New Jersey**	**NHL**	**60**	**4**	**6**	**10**	**222**	**10**	**0**	**0**	**0**	**113**
1988-89	**New Jersey**	**NHL**	**39**	**3**	**6**	**9**	**128**	....	....	....	....	....
1989-90	Utica	AHL	71	13	17	30	128	5	0	0	0	24
1990-91	**New Jersey**	**NHL**	**1**	**0**	**0**	**0**	**5**	**4**	**0**	**1**	**1**	**10**
	Utica	AHL	68	19	14	33	245	....	....	....	....	....
1991-92	**San Jose**	**NHL**	**48**	**4**	**8**	**12**	**143**	....	....	....	....	....
1992-93	San Diego	IHL	51	8	13	21	217	5	0	0	0	14
	NHL Totals		**400**	**50**	**59**	**109**	**1051**	**36**	**2**	**1**	**3**	**161**

Traded to **New Jersey** by **St. Louis** for Rick Meagher and New Jersey's twelfth round choice (Bill Butler) in 1986 Entry Draft, August 29, 1985. Signed as a free agent by **San Jose**, July 8, 1991.

ANDERSON, SHAWN

Defense. Shoots left. 6'1", 200 lbs. Born, Montreal, Que., February 7, 1968.
(Buffalo's 1st choice, 5th overall, in 1986 Entry Draft).

			Regular Season					Playoffs				
Season	Club	Lea	GP	G	A	TP	PIM	GP	G	A	TP	PIM
1985-86	Maine	H.E.	16	5	8	13	22	....	....	....	....	....
	Cdn. Olympic	....	49	4	14	18	38	....	....	....	....	....
1986-87	**Buffalo**	**NHL**	**41**	**2**	**11**	**13**	**23**	....	....	....	....	....
	Rochester	AHL	15	2	5	7	11	....	....	....	....	....
1987-88	**Buffalo**	**NHL**	**23**	**1**	**2**	**3**	**17**	....	....	....	....	....
	Rochester	AHL	22	5	16	21	19	6	0	0	0	0
1988-89	**Buffalo**	**NHL**	**33**	**2**	**10**	**12**	**18**	**5**	**0**	**1**	**1**	**4**
	Rochester	AHL	31	5	14	19	24	....	....	....	....	....
1989-90	**Buffalo**	**NHL**	**16**	**1**	**3**	**4**	**8**	....	....	....	....	....
	Rochester	AHL	39	2	16	18	41	9	1	0	1	4
1990-91	**Quebec**	**NHL**	**31**	**3**	**10**	**13**	**21**	....	....	....	....	....
	Halifax	AHL	4	0	1	1	2	....	....	....	....	....
1991-92	Weiswasser	Ger.	38	7	15	22	83	....	....	....	....	....
1992-93	**Washington**	**NHL**	**60**	**2**	**6**	**8**	**18**	**6**	**0**	**0**	**0**	**0**
	Baltimore	AHL	10	1	5	6	8	....	....	....	....	....
	NHL Totals		**204**	**11**	**42**	**53**	**105**	**11**	**0**	**1**	**1**	**4**

Traded to **Washington** by **Buffalo** for Bill Houlder, September 30, 1990. Claimed by **Quebec** in NHL Waiver Draft, October 1, 1990. Traded to **Winnipeg** by **Quebec** for Sergei Kharin, October 22, 1991. Traded to **Washington** by **Winnipeg** for future considerations, October 23, 1991.

ANDERSSON, MIKAEL (AN-duhr-suhn)

Left wing. Shoots left. 5'11", 185 lbs. Born, Malmo, Sweden, May 10, 1966.
(Buffalo's 1st choice, 18th overall, in 1984 Entry Draft).

			Regular Season					Playoffs				
Season	Club	Lea	GP	G	A	TP	PIM	GP	G	A	TP	PIM
1982-83	V. Frolunda	Swe.	1	1	0	1	0	....	....	....	....	....
1983-84	V. Frolunda	Swe.	18	0	3	3	6	....	....	....	....	....
1984-85	V. Frolunda	Swe. 2	30	16	11	27	18	6	3	2	5	2
1985-86	**Buffalo**	**NHL**	**32**	**1**	**9**	**10**	**4**	....	....	....	....	....
	Rochester	AHL	20	10	4	14	6	....	....	....	....	....
1986-87	**Buffalo**	**NHL**	**16**	**0**	**3**	**3**	**0**	....	....	....	....	....
	Rochester	AHL	42	6	20	26	14	9	1	2	3	2
1987-88	**Buffalo**	**NHL**	**37**	**3**	**20**	**23**	**10**	**1**	**1**	**0**	**1**	**0**
	Rochester	AHL	35	12	24	36	16	....	....	....	....	....
1988-89	**Buffalo**	**NHL**	**14**	**0**	**1**	**1**	**4**	....	....	....	....	....
	Rochester	AHL	56	18	33	51	12	....	....	....	....	....
1989-90	**Hartford**	**NHL**	**50**	**13**	**24**	**37**	**6**	**5**	**0**	**3**	**3**	**2**
1990-91	**Hartford**	**NHL**	**41**	**4**	**7**	**11**	**8**	....	....	....	....	....
	Springfield	AHL	26	7	22	29	10	18	*10	8	18	12
1991-92	**Hartford**	**NHL**	**74**	**18**	**29**	**47**	**14**	**7**	**0**	**2**	**2**	**6**
1992-93	**Tampa Bay**	**NHL**	**77**	**16**	**11**	**27**	**14**	....	....	....	....	....
	NHL Totals		**341**	**55**	**104**	**159**	**60**	**13**	**1**	**5**	**6**	**8**

Claimed by **Hartford** in NHL Waiver Draft, October 2, 1989. Signed as a free agent by **Tampa Bay**, June 29, 1992.

ANDERSSON, NICLAS (AN-duhr-suhn)

Left wing. Shoots left. 5'9", 175 lbs. Born, Kungalv, Sweden, May 20, 1971.
(Quebec's 5th choice, 68th overall, in 1989 Entry Draft).

			Regular Season					Playoffs				
Season	Club	Lea	GP	G	A	TP	PIM	GP	G	A	TP	PIM
1987-88	V. Frolunda	Swe. 2	15	5	5	10	6	8	6	4	10	4
1988-89	V. Frolunda	Swe. 2	30	13	24	37	24	....	....	....	....	....
1989-90	V. Frolunda	Swe.	38	10	21	31	14	27	14	18	32	36
1990-91	V. Frolunda	Swe.	22	6	10	16	16	....	....	....	....	....
1991-92	Halifax	AHL	57	8	26	34	41	....	....	....	....	....
1992-93	**Quebec**	**NHL**	**3**	**0**	**1**	**1**	**2**	....	....	....	....	....
	Halifax	AHL	76	32	50	82	42	....	....	....	....	....
	NHL Totals		**3**	**0**	**1**	**1**	**2**	....	....	....	....	....

ANDERSSON, PETER

Defense. Shoots left. 6', 196 lbs. Born, Orebro, Sweden, August 29, 1965.
(NY Rangers' 5th choice, 73rd overall, in 1983 Entry Draft).

			Regular Season					Playoffs				
Season	Club	Lea	GP	G	A	TP	PIM	GP	G	A	TP	PIM
1983-84	Farjestad	Swe.	36	4	7	11	22	....	....	....	....	....
1984-85	Farjestad	Swe.	35	5	12	17	24	....	....	....	....	....
1985-86	Farjestad	Swe.	34	6	10	16	18	....	....	....	....	....
1986-87	Farjestad	Swe.	32	9	8	17	32	....	....	....	....	....
1987-88	Farjestad	Swe.	38	14	20	34	44	....	....	....	....	....
1988-89	Farjestad	Swe.	33	6	17	23	44	....	....	....	....	....
1989-90	Malmo	Swe.	33	15	25	40	32	....	....	....	....	....
1990-91	Malmo	Swe.	34	9	17	26	26	....	....	....	....	....
1991-92	Malmo	Swe.	40	12	20	32	80	....	....	....	....	....
1992-93	**NY Rangers**	**NHL**	**31**	**4**	**11**	**15**	**4**	....	....	....	....	....
	Binghamton	AHL	27	11	22	33	16	....	....	....	....	....
	NHL Totals		**31**	**4**	**11**	**15**	**4**	....	....	....	....	....

ANDERSSON-JUNKKA, JONAS

Defense. Shoots right. 6'2", 165 lbs. Born, Kiruna, Sweden, May 4, 1975.
(Pittsburgh's 4th choice, 104th overall, in 1993 Entry Draft).

			Regular Season					Playoffs				
Season	Club	Lea	GP	G	A	TP	PIM	GP	G	A	TP	PIM
1991-92	Kiruna	Swe.2	1	0	0	0	0	....	....	....	....	....
1992-93	Kiruna	Swe.2	30	3	7	10	32	....	....	....	....	....

ANDREYCHUK, DAVID (DAVE) (an-dray-CHUHK)

Left wing. Shoots right. 6'3", 225 lbs. Born, Hamilton, Ont., September 29, 1963.
(Buffalo's 3rd choice, 16th overall, in 1982 Entry Draft).

			Regular Season					Playoffs				
Season	Club	Lea	GP	G	A	TP	PIM	GP	G	A	TP	PIM
1980-81	Oshawa	OHA	67	22	22	44	80	10	3	2	5	20
1981-82	Oshawa	OHL	67	57	43	100	71	3	1	4	5	16
1982-83	**Buffalo**	**NHL**	**43**	**14**	**23**	**37**	**16**	**4**	**1**	**0**	**1**	**4**
	Oshawa	OHL	14	8	24	32	6	....	....	....	....	....
1983-84	**Buffalo**	**NHL**	**78**	**38**	**42**	**80**	**42**	**2**	**0**	**1**	**1**	**2**
1984-85	**Buffalo**	**NHL**	**64**	**31**	**30**	**61**	**54**	**5**	**4**	**2**	**6**	**4**
1985-86	**Buffalo**	**NHL**	**80**	**36**	**51**	**87**	**61**	....	....	....	....	....
1986-87	**Buffalo**	**NHL**	**77**	**25**	**48**	**73**	**46**	....	....	....	....	....
1987-88	**Buffalo**	**NHL**	**80**	**30**	**48**	**78**	**112**	**6**	**2**	**4**	**6**	**0**
1988-89	**Buffalo**	**NHL**	**56**	**28**	**24**	**52**	**40**	**5**	**0**	**3**	**3**	**0**
1989-90	**Buffalo**	**NHL**	**73**	**40**	**42**	**82**	**42**	**6**	**2**	**5**	**7**	**2**
1990-91	**Buffalo**	**NHL**	**80**	**36**	**33**	**69**	**32**	**6**	**2**	**2**	**4**	**8**
1991-92	**Buffalo**	**NHL**	**80**	**41**	**50**	**91**	**71**	**7**	**1**	**3**	**4**	**12**
1992-93	**Buffalo**	**NHL**	**52**	**29**	**32**	**61**	**48**	....	....	....	....	....
	Toronto	**NHL**	**31**	**25**	**13**	**38**	**8**	**21**	**12**	**7**	**19**	**35**
	NHL Totals		**794**	**373**	**436**	**809**	**572**	**62**	**24**	**27**	**51**	**67**

Played in NHL All-Star Game (1990)

Traded to **Toronto** by **Buffalo** with Daren Puppa and Buffalo's first round choice (Kenny Jonsson) in 1993 Entry Draft for Grant Fuhr and future considerations, February 2, 1993.

ANDRIJEVSKI, ALEXANDER (an-dray-YEHV-skee)

Right wing. Shoots right. 6'5", 211 lbs. Born, Moscow, USSR, August 10, 1968.
(Chicago's 13th choice, 220th overall, in 1991 Entry Draft).

			Regular Season					Playoffs				
Season	Club	Lea	GP	G	A	TP	PIM	GP	G	A	TP	PIM
1990-91	Moscow D'amo	USSR	44	9	8	17	28	....	....	....	....	....
1991-92	Moscow D'amo	CIS	31	9	8	17	14	....	....	....	....	....
1992-93	**Chicago**	**NHL**	**1**	**0**	**0**	**0**	**0**	....	....	....	....	....
	Indianapolis	IHL	66	26	25	51	59	4	2	3	5	10
	NHL Totals		**1**	**0**	**0**	**0**	**0**	....	....	....	....	....

ANDRUSAK, GREG

Defense. Shoots right. 6'1", 183 lbs. Born, Cranbrook, B.C., November 14, 1969.
(Pittsburgh's 5th choice, 88th overall, in 1988 Entry Draft).

			Regular Season					Playoffs				
Season	Club	Lea	GP	G	A	TP	PIM	GP	G	A	TP	PIM
1987-88	Minn.-Duluth	WCHA	37	4	5	9	42	....	....	....	....	....
1988-89	Minn.-Duluth	WCHA	35	4	8	12	74	....	....	....	....	....
	Cdn. Olympic	....	2	0	0	0	0	....	....	....	....	....
1989-90	Minn.-Duluth	WCHA	35	5	29	34	74	....	....	....	....	....
1990-91	Cdn. National	....	53	4	11	15	34	....	....	....	....	....
1991-92a	Minn.-Duluth	WCHA	36	7	27	34	125	....	....	....	....	....
1992-93	Cleveland	IHL	55	3	22	25	78	2	0	0	0	2
	Muskegon	Col.	2	0	3	3	7	....	....	....	....	....

a WCHA First All-Star Team (1992)

ANGLEHART, SERGE

Defense. Shoots right. 6'2", 190 lbs. Born, Hull, Que., April 18, 1970.
(Detroit's 2nd choice, 38th overall, in 1988 Entry Draft).

			Regular Season					Playoffs				
Season	Club	Lea	GP	G	A	TP	PIM	GP	G	A	TP	PIM
1987-88	Drummondville	QMJHL	44	1	8	9	122	17	0	3	3	19
1988-89	Drummondville	QMJHL	39	6	15	21	89	3	0	0	0	37
	Adirondack	AHL	....	....	....	....	....	2	0	0	0	0
1989-90	Laval	QMJHL	48	2	19	21	131	10	1	6	7	69
1990-91	Adirondack	AHL	52	3	8	11	113	....	....	....	....	....
1991-92	Adirondack	AHL	16	0	1	1	43	....	....	....	....	....
1992-93	Adirondack	AHL	3	0	0	0	4	....	....	....	....	....
	Fort Wayne	IHL	2	0	0	0	2	....	....	....	....	....

ANTOS, DEAN

Center. Shoots left. 5'11", 175 lbs. Born, Killam, Alta., May 20, 1967.

			Regular Season					Playoffs				
Season	Club	Lea	GP	G	A	TP	PIM	GP	G	A	TP	PIM
1987-88	N. Michigan	WCHA	35	14	23	37	32	....	....	....	....	....
1988-89	N. Michigan	WCHA	45	25	24	49	28	....	....	....	....	....
1989-90	N. Michigan	WCHA	42	19	22	41	50	....	....	....	....	....
1990-91	N. Michigan	WCHA	40	17	26	43	63	....	....	....	....	....
1991-92	Cape Breton	AHL	15	1	4	5	2	....	....	....	....	....
	Winston-Salem	ECHL	43	9	31	40	56	5	1	6	7	0
1992-93	Cape Breton	AHL	2	0	0	0	0	....	....	....	....	....
	Wheeling	ECHL	61	25	42	67	76	16	2	5	7	30

Signed as a free agent by **Edmonton**, July 17, 1991.

ANTOSKI, SHAWN (an-TAW-skee)

Left wing. Shoots left. 6'4", 235 lbs. Born, Brantford, Ont., March 25, 1970.
(Vancouver's 2nd choice, 18th overall, in 1990 Entry Draft).

			Regular Season					Playoffs				
Season	Club	Lea	GP	G	A	TP	PIM	GP	G	A	TP	PIM
1987-88	North Bay	OHL	52	3	4	7	163	....	....	....	....	....
1988-89	North Bay	OHL	57	6	21	27	201	9	5	3	8	24
1989-90	North Bay	OHL	59	25	31	56	201	5	1	2	3	17
1990-91	**Vancouver**	**NHL**	**2**	**0**	**0**	**0**	**0**	....	....	....	....	....
	Milwaukee	IHL	62	17	7	24	330	5	1	2	3	10
1991-92	**Vancouver**	**NHL**	**4**	**0**	**0**	**0**	**29**	....	....	....	....	....
	Milwaukee	IHL	52	17	16	33	346	5	2	0	2	20
1992-93	**Vancouver**	**NHL**	**2**	**0**	**0**	**0**	**0**	....	....	....	....	....
	Hamilton	AHL	41	3	4	7	172	....	....	....	....	....
	Johnstown	ECHL	8	1	3	4	2	....	....	....	....	....
	NHL Totals		**8**	**0**	**0**	**0**	**29**	....	....	....	....	....

ARCHIBALD, DAVE

Center/Left wing. Shoots left. 6'1", 190 lbs. Born, Chilliwack, B.C., April 14, 1969.
(Minnesota's 1st choice, 6th overall, in 1987 Entry Draft).

			Regular Season					Playoffs				
Season	Club	Lea	GP	G	A	TP	PIM	GP	G	A	TP	PIM
1984-85	Portland	WHL	47	7	11	18	10	3	0	2	2	0
1985-86	Portland	WHL	70	29	35	64	56	15	6	7	13	11
1986-87	Portland	WHL	65	50	57	107	40	20	10	18	28	11
1987-88	**Minnesota**	**NHL**	**78**	**13**	**20**	**33**	**26**	....	....	....	....	....
1988-89	**Minnesota**	**NHL**	**72**	**14**	**19**	**33**	**14**	**5**	**0**	**1**	**1**	**0**
1989-90	**Minnesota**	**NHL**	**12**	**1**	**5**	**6**	**6**	....	....	....	....	....
	NY Rangers	**NHL**	**19**	**2**	**3**	**5**	**6**	....	....	....	....	....
	Flint	IHL	41	14	38	52	16	4	3	2	5	0
1990-91	Cdn. National	....	29	19	12	31	20	....	....	....	....	....
1991-92	Cdn. National	....	58	20	43	63	62	....	....	....	....	....
	Cdn. Olympic	....	8	7	1	8	18	....	....	....	....	....
	Bolzano	....	5	4	3	7	16	7	8	5	13	7
1992-93	Binghamton	AHL	8	6	3	9	10	....	....	....	....	....
	Ottawa	**NHL**	**44**	**9**	**6**	**15**	**32**	....	....	....	....	....
	NHL Totals		**225**	**39**	**53**	**92**	**84**	**5**	**0**	**1**	**1**	**0**

Traded to **NY Rangers** by **Minnesota** for Jayson More, November 1, 1989. Traded to **Ottawa** by **NY Rangers** for Ottawa's fifth round choice (later traded to Los Angeles – Los Angeles selected Frederick Beaubien) in 1993 Entry Draft, November 5, 1992.

ARMSTRONG, BILL

Defense. Shoots left. 6'4", 215 lbs. Born, Richmond Hill, Ont., May 18, 1970.
(Philadelphia's 6th choice, 46th overall, in 1990 Entry Draft).

			Regular Season					Playoffs				
Season	Club	Lea	GP	G	A	TP	PIM	GP	G	A	TP	PIM
1987-88	Toronto	OHL	64	1	10	11	99	....	....	....	....	....
1988-89	Toronto	OHL	64	1	16	17	82	....	....	....	....	....
1989-90	Hamilton	OHL	18	0	2	2	38	....	....	....	....	....
	Niagara Falls	OHL	4	0	1	1	13	....	....	....	....	....
	Oshawa	OHL	41	2	8	10	115	17	0	7	7	39
1990-91	Hershey	AHL	56	1	9	10	117	....	....	....	....	....
1991-92	Hershey	AHL	80	2	14	16	159	3	0	0	0	2
1992-93	Hershey	AHL	80	2	10	12	205	....	....	....	....	....

Signed as a free agent by **Boston**, July 22, 1993.

ARMSTRONG, CHRIS

Defense. Shoots left. 6', 184 lbs. Born, Regina, Sask., June 26, 1975.
(Florida's 3rd choice, 57th overall, in 1993 Entry Draft).

			Regular Season					Playoffs				
Season	Club	Lea	GP	G	A	TP	PIM	GP	G	A	TP	PIM
1991-92	Moose Jaw	WHL	43	2	7	9	19	4	0	0	0	0
1992-93	Moose Jaw	WHL	67	9	35	44	104	....	....	....	....	....

ARMSTRONG, DEREK

Center. Shoots right. 5'11", 180 lbs. Born, Ottawa, Ont., April 23, 1973.
(NY Islanders' 5th choice, 128th overall, in 1992 Entry Draft).

			Regular Season					Playoffs				
Season	Club	Lea	GP	G	A	TP	PIM	GP	G	A	TP	PIM
1991-92	Sudbury	OHL	66	31	54	85	22	9	2	2	4	2
1992-93	Sudbury	OHL	66	44	62	106	56	14	9	10	19	26

ARNIEL, SCOTT (ar-NEEL)

Left wing. Shoots left. 6'1", 188 lbs. Born, Kingston, Ont., September 17, 1962.
(Winnipeg's 2nd choice, 22nd overall, in 1981 Entry Draft).

			Regular Season					Playoffs				
Season	Club	Lea	GP	G	A	TP	PIM	GP	G	A	TP	PIM
1980-81	Cornwall	QJHL	68	52	71	123	102	19	14	19	33	24
1981-82	**Winnipeg**	**NHL**	**17**	**1**	**8**	**9**	**14**	**3**	**0**	**0**	**0**	**0**
	Cornwall	OHL	24	18	26	44	43	....	....	....	....	....
1982-83	**Winnipeg**	**NHL**	**75**	**13**	**5**	**18**	**46**	**2**	**0**	**0**	**0**	**0**
1983-84	**Winnipeg**	**NHL**	**80**	**21**	**35**	**56**	**68**	**2**	**0**	**0**	**0**	**5**
1984-85	**Winnipeg**	**NHL**	**79**	**22**	**22**	**44**	**81**	**8**	**1**	**2**	**3**	**9**
1985-86	**Winnipeg**	**NHL**	**80**	**18**	**25**	**43**	**40**	**3**	**0**	**0**	**0**	**12**
1986-87	**Buffalo**	**NHL**	**63**	**11**	**14**	**25**	**59**	....	....	....	....	....
1987-88	**Buffalo**	**NHL**	**73**	**17**	**23**	**40**	**61**	**6**	**0**	**1**	**1**	**5**
1988-89	**Buffalo**	**NHL**	**80**	**18**	**23**	**41**	**46**	**5**	**1**	**0**	**1**	**4**
1989-90	**Buffalo**	**NHL**	**79**	**18**	**14**	**32**	**77**	**5**	**1**	**0**	**1**	**4**
1990-91	**Winnipeg**	**NHL**	**75**	**5**	**17**	**22**	**87**	....	....	....	....	....
1991-92	**Boston**	**NHL**	**29**	**5**	**3**	**8**	**20**	....	....	....	....	....
	Maine	AHL	14	4	4	8	8	....	....	....	....	....
	New Haven	AHL	11	3	3	6	10	....	....	....	....	....
1992-93	San Diego	IHL	79	35	48	83	116	14	6	5	11	16
	NHL Totals		**730**	**149**	**189**	**338**	**599**	**34**	**3**	**3**	**6**	**39**

Traded to **Buffalo** by **Winnipeg** for Gilles Hamel, June 21, 1986. Traded to **Winnipeg** by **Buffalo** with Phil Housley, Jeff Parker and Buffalo's first round choice (Keith Tkachuk) in 1990 Entry Draft for Dale Hawerchuk, Winnipeg's first round choice (Brad May) in 1990 Entry Draft and future considerations, June 16, 1990. Traded to **Boston** by **Winnipeg** for future considerations, November 22, 1991.

ARNOTT, JASON
Center. Shoots right. 6'3", 193 lbs.   Born, Collingwood, Ont., October 11, 1974.
(Edmonton's 1st choice, 7th overall, in 1993 Entry Draft).

			Regular Season					Playoffs			
Season	Club	Lea	GP	G	A	TP	PIM	GP	G	A	TP	PIM
1991-92	Oshawa	OHL	57	9	15	24	12	....	....	....	....	....
1992-93	Oshawa	OHL	56	41	57	98	74	13	9	9	18	20

ASHTON, BRENT KENNETH
Left wing. Shoots left. 6'1", 210 lbs.   Born, Saskatoon, Sask., May 18, 1960.
(Vancouver's 2nd choice, 26th overall, in 1979 Entry Draft).

			Regular Season					Playoffs			
Season	Club	Lea	GP	G	A	TP	PIM	GP	G	A	TP	PIM
1977-78	Saskatoon	WHL	46	38	26	64	47	....	....	....	....	....
1978-79	Saskatoon	WHL	62	64	55	119	80	11	14	4	18	5
1979-80	Vancouver	NHL	47	5	14	19	11	4	1	0	1	6
1980-81	Vancouver	NHL	77	18	11	29	57	3	0	0	0	0
1981-82	Colorado	NHL	80	24	36	60	26	....	....	....	....	....
1982-83	New Jersey	NHL	76	14	19	33	47	....	....	....	....	....
1983-84	Minnesota	NHL	68	7	10	17	54	12	1	2	3	22
1984-85	Minnesota	NHL	29	4	7	11	15	....	....	....	....	....
	Quebec	NHL	49	27	24	51	38	18	6	4	10	13
1985-86	Quebec	NHL	77	26	32	58	64	3	2	1	3	9
1986-87	Quebec	NHL	46	25	19	44	17	....	....	....	....	....
	Detroit	NHL	35	15	16	31	22	16	4	9	13	6
1987-88	Detroit	NHL	73	26	27	53	50	16	7	5	12	10
1988-89	Winnipeg	NHL	75	31	37	68	36	....	....	....	....	....
1989-90	Winnipeg	NHL	79	22	34	56	37	7	3	1	4	2
1990-91	Winnipeg	NHL	61	12	24	36	58	....	....	....	....	....
1991-92	Winnipeg	NHL	7	1	0	1	4	....	....	....	....	....
	Boston	NHL	61	17	22	39	47	....	....	....	....	....
1992-93	Boston	NHL	26	2	2	4	11	....	....	....	....	....
	Providence	AHL	11	4	8	12	10	....	....	....	....	....
	Calgary	NHL	32	8	11	19	41	6	0	3	3	2
	NHL Totals		**998**	**284**	**345**	**629**	**635**	**85**	**24**	**25**	**49**	**70**

Traded to **Winnipeg** by **Vancouver** with Vancouver's fourth round choice (Tom Martin) in the 1982 Entry Draft as compensation for Vancouver's signing of Ivan Hlinka, July 15, 1981. Traded to **Colorado** by **Winnipeg** with Winnipeg's third round choice (Dave Kasper) in 1982 Entry Draft for Lucien DeBlois, July 15, 1981. Traded to **Minnesota** by **New Jersey** for Dave Lewis, October 3, 1983. Traded to **Quebec** by **Minnesota** with Brad Maxwell for Tony McKegney and Bo Berglund, December 14, 1984. Traded to **Detroit** by **Quebec** with Gilbert Delorme and Mark Kumpel for Basil McRae, John Ogrodnick and Doug Shedden, January 17, 1987. Traded to **Winnipeg** by **Detroit** for Paul MacLean, June 13, 1988. Traded to **Boston** by **Winnipeg** for Petri Skriko, October 29, 1991. Traded to **Calgary** by **Boston** for C.J. Young, February 1, 1993.

ASP, AARON
Center. Shoots right. 6'2", 195 lbs.   Born, Cobble Hill, B.C., February 16, 1971.
(Quebec's 9th choice, 157th overall, in 1991 Entry Draft).

			Regular Season					Playoffs			
Season	Club	Lea	GP	G	A	TP	PIM	GP	G	A	TP	PIM
1989-90	Ferris State	CCHA	10	1	1	2	2	....	....	....	....	....
1990-91	Ferris State	CCHA	37	11	23	34	12	....	....	....	....	....
1991-92	Ferris State	CCHA	33	9	10	19	14	....	....	....	....	....
1992-93	Ferris State	CCHA	14	3	7	10	10	....	....	....	....	....

ASTLEY, MARK
Defense. Shoots left. 5'11", 185 lbs.   Born, Calgary, Alta., March 30, 1969.
(Buffalo's 9th choice, 194th overall, in 1989 Entry Draft).

			Regular Season					Playoffs			
Season	Club	Lea	GP	G	A	TP	PIM	GP	G	A	TP	PIM
1988-89	Lake Superior	CCHA	42	3	12	15	26	....	....	....	....	....
1989-90	Lake Superior	CCHA	43	7	25	32	29	....	....	....	....	....
1990-91a	Lake Superior	CCHA	45	19	27	46	50	....	....	....	....	....
1991-92bcd	Lake Superior	CCHA	39	11	36	47	65	....	....	....	....	....
1992-93	Lugano	Switz.	30	10	12	22	57	....	....	....	....	....
	Cdn. National	....	22	4	14	18	14	....	....	....	....	....

a CCHA Second All-Star Team (1991)
b CCHA First All-Star Team (1992)
c NCAA West First All-American Team (1992)
d NCAA All-Tournament Team (1992)

ATCHEYNUM, BLAIR   (ATCH-uh-num)
Right wing. Shoots right. 6'2", 190 lbs.   Born, Estevan, Sask., April 20, 1969.
(Hartford's 2nd choice, 52nd overall, in 1989 Entry Draft).

			Regular Season					Playoffs			
Season	Club	Lea	GP	G	A	TP	PIM	GP	G	A	TP	PIM
1985-86	Saskatoon	WHL	19	1	4	5	22	....	....	....	....	....
1986-87	Saskatoon	WHL	21	0	4	4	4	....	....	....	....	....
	Swift Current	WHL	5	2	1	3	0	....	....	....	....	....
	Moose Jaw	WHL	12	3	0	3	2	....	....	....	....	....
1987-88	Moose Jaw	WHL	60	32	16	48	52	....	....	....	....	....
1988-89a	Moose Jaw	WHL	71	70	68	138	70	7	2	5	7	13
1989-90	Binghamton	AHL	78	20	21	41	45	....	....	....	....	....
1990-91	Springfield	AHL	72	25	27	52	42	13	0	6	6	6
1991-92	Springfield	AHL	62	16	21	37	64	6	1	1	2	2
1992-93	Ottawa	NHL	4	0	1	1	0	....	....	....	....	....
	New Haven	AHL	51	16	18	34	47	....	....	....	....	....
	NHL Totals		**4**	**0**	**1**	**1**	**0**	....	....	....	....	....

a WHL First All-Star Team (1989)

Claimed by **Ottawa** from **Hartford** in Expansion Draft, June 18, 1992.

AUCOIN, ADRIAN
Defense. Shoots right. 6'1", 194 lbs.   Born, Ottawa, Ont., July 3, 1973.
(Vancouver's 7th choice, 117th overall, in 1992 Entry Draft).

			Regular Season					Playoffs			
Season	Club	Lea	GP	G	A	TP	PIM	GP	G	A	TP	PIM
1991-92	Boston U.	H.E.	32	2	10	12	60	....	....	....	....	....
1992-93	Cdn. National	....	42	8	10	18	71	....	....	....	....	....

AUDETTE, DONALD
Right wing. Shoots right. 5'8", 175 lbs.   Born, Laval, Que., September 23, 1969.
(Buffalo's 8th choice, 183rd overall, in 1989 Entry Draft).

			Regular Season					Playoffs			
Season	Club	Lea	GP	G	A	TP	PIM	GP	G	A	TP	PIM
1986-87	Laval	QMJHL	66	17	22	39	36	14	2	6	8	10
1987-88	Laval	QMJHL	63	48	61	109	56	14	7	12	19	20
1988-89a	Laval	QMJHL	70	76	85	161	123	17	17	12	29	43
1989-90bc	Rochester	AHL	70	42	46	88	78	15	9	8	17	29
	Buffalo	NHL	....	....	....	....	....	2	0	0	0	0
1990-91	Buffalo	NHL	8	4	3	7	4	....	....	....	....	....
	Rochester	AHL	5	4	0	4	2	....	....	....	....	....
1991-92	Buffalo	NHL	63	31	17	48	75	....	....	....	....	....
1992-93	Buffalo	NHL	44	12	7	19	51	8	2	2	4	6
	Rochester	AHL	6	8	4	12	10	....	....	....	....	....
	NHL Totals		**115**	**47**	**27**	**74**	**130**	**10**	**2**	**2**	**4**	**6**

a QMJHL First All-Star Team (1989)
b AHL First All-Star Team (1990)
c Won Dudley "Red" Garret Memorial Trophy (Top Rookie-AHL) (1990)

AUGUSTA, PATRIK
Right wing. Shoots left. 5'10", 169 lbs.   Born, Jihlava, Czech., November 13, 1969.
(Toronto's 8th choice, 149th overall, in 1992 Entry Draft).

			Regular Season					Playoffs			
Season	Club	Lea	GP	G	A	TP	PIM	GP	G	A	TP	PIM
1988-89	Dukla Jihlava	Czech.	15	3	1	4	4	....	....	....	....	....
1989-90	Dukla Jihlava	Czech.	46	12	12	24	....	....	....	....	....	....
1990-91	Dukla Jihlava	Czech.	51	20	23	43	....	....	....	....	....	....
1991-92	Dukla Jihlava	Czech.	42	16	16	32	26	....	....	....	....	....
1992-93	St. John's	AHL	75	32	45	77	74	8	3	3	6	23

AVERILL, WILLIAM
Defense. Shoots right. 5'11", 175 lbs.   Born, Wayland, MA, December 20, 1968.
(NY Islanders' 12th choice, 244th overall, in 1987 Entry Draft).

			Regular Season					Playoffs			
Season	Club	Lea	GP	G	A	TP	PIM	GP	G	A	TP	PIM
1987-88	Northeastern	H.E.	36	2	23	25	36	....	....	....	....	....
1988-89	Northeastern	H.E.	36	4	16	20	40	....	....	....	....	....
1989-90	Northeastern	H.E.	35	6	13	19	41	....	....	....	....	....
1990-91	Northeastern	H.E.	35	6	16	22	40	....	....	....	....	....
1991-92	Capital Dist.	AHL	12	0	0	0	0	....	....	....	....	....
	Richmond	ECHL	33	3	23	26	18	....	....	....	....	....
1992-93	Richmond	ECHL	53	7	29	36	63	1	1	0	1	0

BABCOCK, BOBBY
Defense. Shoots left. 6'1", 222 lbs.   Born, Agincourt, Ont., August 3, 1968.
(Washington's 11th choice, 208th overall, in 1986 Entry Draft).

			Regular Season					Playoffs			
Season	Club	Lea	GP	G	A	TP	PIM	GP	G	A	TP	PIM
1985-86	S.S. Marie	OHL	50	1	7	8	188	....	....	....	....	....
1986-87	S.S. Marie	OHL	62	7	8	15	243	4	0	0	0	11
1987-88	S.S. Marie	OHL	8	0	2	2	30	....	....	....	....	....
	Cornwall	OHL	42	0	16	16	120	....	....	....	....	....
1988-89	Cornwall	OHL	42	0	9	9	163	18	1	3	4	29
1989-90	Baltimore	AHL	67	0	4	4	249	7	0	0	0	23
1990-91	Washington	NHL	1	0	0	0	0	....	....	....	....	....
	Baltimore	AHL	38	0	3	3	112	....	....	....	....	....
1991-92	Baltimore	AHL	26	0	2	2	55	....	....	....	....	....
1992-93	Washington	NHL	1	0	0	0	2	....	....	....	....	....
	Baltimore	AHL	26	0	2	2	93	....	....	....	....	....
	Hampton Rds.	ECHL	26	3	13	16	96	1	0	0	0	10
	NHL Totals		**2**	**0**	**0**	**0**	**2**	....	....	....	....	....

BABYCH, DAVID MICHAEL (DAVE)   (BAB-itch)
Defense. Shoots left. 6'2", 215 lbs.   Born, Edmonton, Alta., May 23, 1961.
(Winnipeg's 1st choice, 2nd overall, in 1980 Entry Draft).

			Regular Season					Playoffs			
Season	Club	Lea	GP	G	A	TP	PIM	GP	G	A	TP	PIM
1978-79	Portland	WHL	67	20	59	79	63	25	7	22	29	22
1979-80ab	Portland	WHL	50	22	60	82	71	8	1	10	11	2
1980-81	Winnipeg	NHL	69	6	38	44	90	....	....	....	....	....
1981-82	Winnipeg	NHL	79	19	49	68	92	4	1	2	3	29
1982-83	Winnipeg	NHL	79	13	61	74	56	3	0	0	0	0
1983-84	Winnipeg	NHL	66	18	39	57	62	3	1	1	2	0
1984-85	Winnipeg	NHL	78	13	49	62	78	8	2	7	9	6
1985-86	Winnipeg	NHL	19	4	12	16	14	....	....	....	....	....
	Hartford	NHL	62	10	43	53	36	8	1	3	4	14
1986-87	Hartford	NHL	66	8	33	41	44	6	1	1	2	14
1987-88	Hartford	NHL	71	14	36	50	54	6	3	2	5	2
1988-89	Hartford	NHL	70	6	41	47	54	4	1	5	6	2
1989-90	Hartford	NHL	72	6	37	43	62	7	1	2	3	0
1990-91	Hartford	NHL	8	0	6	6	4	....	....	....	....	....
1991-92	Vancouver	NHL	75	5	24	29	63	13	2	6	8	10
1992-93	Vancouver	NHL	43	3	16	19	44	12	2	5	7	6
	NHL Totals		**857**	**125**	**484**	**609**	**753**	**74**	**15**	**34**	**49**	**83**

a WHL First All-Star Team (1980)
b Named WHL's Top Defenseman (1980)

Played in NHL All-Star Game (1983, 1984)

Traded to **Hartford** by **Winnipeg** for Ray Neufeld, November 21, 1985. Claimed by **Minnesota** from **Hartford** in Expansion Draft, May 30, 1991. Traded to **Vancouver** by **Minnesota** for Tom Kurvers, June 22, 1991.

BACA, JERGUS

Defense. Shoots left. 6'2", 211 lbs. Born, Liptovsky Mikulas, Czech., January 4, 1965.
(Hartford's 6th choice, 141st overall, in 1990 Entry Draft).

			Regular Season					Playoffs				
Season	Club	Lea	GP	G	A	TP	PIM	GP	G	A	TP	PIM
1987-88	VSZ Kosice	Czech.	40	5	5	10	32	....	....	....	....	....
1988-89a	VSZ Kosice	Czech.	42	3	10	13	46	....	....	....	....	....
1989-90a	VSZ Kosice	Czech.	47	9	16	25	....	....	....	....	....	....
1990-91	**Hartford**	**NHL**	**9**	**0**	**2**	**2**	**14**	....	....	....	....	....
	Springfield	AHL	57	6	23	29	89	18	3	13	16	18
1991-92	**Hartford**	**NHL**	**1**	**0**	**0**	**0**	**0**	....	....	....	....	....
	Springfield	AHL	64	6	20	26	88	11	0	6	6	20
1992-93	Milwaukee	IHL	73	9	29	38	108	6	0	3	3	2
	NHL Totals		**10**	**0**	**2**	**2**	**14**	....	....	....	....	....

a Czechoslovakian National League First Team All-Star (1989, 1990)

BAKER, JAMIE

Center. Shoots left. 6', 190 lbs. Born, Ottawa, Ont., August 31, 1966.
(Quebec's 2nd choice, 8th overall, in 1988 Supplemental Draft).

			Regular Season					Playoffs				
Season	Club	Lea	GP	G	A	TP	PIM	GP	G	A	TP	PIM
1985-86	St. Lawrence	ECAC	31	9	16	25	52	....	....	....	....	....
1986-87	St. Lawrence	ECAC	32	8	24	32	59	....	....	....	....	....
1987-88	St. Lawrence	ECAC	34	26	24	50	38	....	....	....	....	....
1988-89	St. Lawrence	ECAC	13	11	16	27	16	....	....	....	....	....
1989-90	**Quebec**	**NHL**	**1**	**0**	**0**	**0**	**0**	....	....	....	....	....
	Halifax	AHL	74	17	43	60	47	6	0	0	0	7
1990-91	**Quebec**	**NHL**	**18**	**2**	**0**	**2**	**8**	....	....	....	....	....
	Halifax	AHL	50	14	22	36	85	....	....	....	....	....
1991-92	**Quebec**	**NHL**	**52**	**7**	**10**	**17**	**32**	....	....	....	....	....
	Halifax	AHL	9	5	0	5	12	....	....	....	....	....
1992-93	**Ottawa**	**NHL**	**76**	**19**	**29**	**48**	**54**	....	....	....	....	....
	NHL Totals		**147**	**28**	**39**	**67**	**94**	....	....	....	....	....

Signed as a free agent by **Ottawa,** September 2, 1992. Signed as a free agent by **San Jose,** August 18, 1993.

BALKOVEC, MACO

Defense. Shoots left. 6'2", 190 lbs. Born, New Westminster, B.C., January 17, 1971.
(Chicago's 5th choice, 110th overall, in 1991 Entry Draft).

			Regular Season					Playoffs				
Season	Club	Lea	GP	G	A	TP	PIM	GP	G	A	TP	PIM
1991-92	U. Wisconsin	WCHA	35	7	11	18	95	....	....	....	....	....
1992-93	U. Wisconsin	WCHA	16	1	9	10	16	....	....	....	....	....

BANCROFT, STEVE

Defense. Shoots left. 6'1", 214 lbs. Born, Toronto, Ont., October 6, 1970.
(Toronto's 3rd choice, 21st overall, in 1989 Entry Draft).

			Regular Season					Playoffs				
Season	Club	Lea	GP	G	A	TP	PIM	GP	G	A	TP	PIM
1987-88	Belleville	OHL	56	1	8	9	42	....	....	....	....	....
1988-89	Belleville	OHL	66	7	30	37	99	5	0	2	2	10
1989-90	Belleville	OHL	53	10	33	43	135	11	3	9	12	38
1990-91	Newmarket	AHL	9	0	3	3	22	....	....	....	....	....
	Maine	AHL	53	2	12	14	46	2	0	0	0	2
1991-92	Maine	AHL	26	1	3	4	45	....	....	....	....	....
	Indianapolis	IHL	36	8	23	31	49	....	....	....	....	....
1992-93	**Chicago**	**NHL**	**1**	**0**	**0**	**0**	**0**	....	....	....	....	....
	Indianapolis	IHL	53	10	35	45	138	....	....	....	....	....
	Moncton	AHL	21	3	13	16	16	5	0	0	0	16
	NHL Totals		**1**	**0**	**0**	**0**	**0**	....	....	....	....	....

Traded to **Boston** by **Toronto** for Rob Cimetta, November 9, 1990. Traded to **Chicago** by **Boston** with Boston's eleventh round choice (later traded to Winnipeg — Winnipeg selected Russel Hewson) in 1993 Entry Draft for Chicago's eleventh round choice (Eugene Pavlov) in 1992 Entry Draft, January 9, 1992. Traded to **Winnipeg** by **Chicago** with future considerations for Troy Murray, February 21, 1993. Claimed by **Florida** from **Winnipeg** in Expansion Draft, June 24, 1993.

BANHAM, FRANK

Right wing. Shoots right. 5'11", 175 lbs. Born, Calahoo, Alta., April 14, 1975.
(Washington's 4th choice, 147th overall, in 1993 Entry Draft).

			Regular Season					Playoffs				
Season	Club	Lea	GP	G	A	TP	PIM	GP	G	A	TP	PIM
1991-92	Fernie	Midget	47	45	45	90	120	....	....	....	....	....
1992-93	Saskatoon	WHL	71	29	33	62	55	9	2	7	9	8

BANKS, DARREN ALEXANDER

Left wing. Shoots left. 6'2", 215 lbs. Born, Toronto, Ont., March 18, 1966.

			Regular Season					Playoffs				
Season	Club	Lea	GP	G	A	TP	PIM	GP	G	A	TP	PIM
1986-87	Brock	OUAA	24	5	3	8	82	....	....	....	....	....
1987-88	Brock	OUAA	26	10	11	21	110	....	....	....	....	....
1988-89	Brock	OUAA	26	19	14	33	88	....	....	....	....	....
1989-90	Salt Lake	IHL	6	0	0	0	11	1	0	0	0	10
	Fort Wayne	IHL	2	0	1	1	0	....	....	....	....	....
	Knoxville	ECHL	52	25	22	47	258	....	....	....	....	....
1990-91	Salt Lake	IHL	56	9	7	16	286	3	0	1	1	6
1991-92	Salt Lake	IHL	55	5	5	10	303	....	....	....	....	....
1992-93	**Boston**	**NHL**	**16**	**2**	**1**	**3**	**64**	....	....	....	....	....
	Providence	AHL	43	9	5	14	199	1	0	0	0	0
	NHL Totals		**16**	**2**	**1**	**3**	**64**	....	....	....	....	....

Signed as a free agent by **Calgary,** December 12, 1990. Signed as a free agent by **Boston,** July 23, 1992.

BANNISTER, DARIN

Defense. Shoots right. 6', 185 lbs. Born, Calgary, Alta., January 16, 1967.
(Detroit's 11th choice, 200th overall, in 1987 Entry Draft).

			Regular Season					Playoffs				
Season	Club	Lea	GP	G	A	TP	PIM	GP	G	A	TP	PIM
1986-87	Ill.-Chicago	CCHA	38	4	16	20	38	....	....	....	....	....
1987-88	Ill.-Chicago	CCHA	39	2	26	28	96	....	....	....	....	....
1988-89	Ill.-Chicago	CCHA	41	7	26	33	88	....	....	....	....	....
1989-90	Ill.-Chicago	CCHA	37	5	22	27	72	....	....	....	....	....
	Hampton Rds.	ECHL	5	0	2	2	22	4	0	2	2	9
1990-91	San Diego	IHL	81	4	11	15	108	....	....	....	....	....
1991-92	Adirondack	AHL	26	0	3	3	32	....	....	....	....	....
	Toledo	ECHL	27	3	29	32	68	5	1	3	4	14
1992-93	Cdn. National	....	2	0	0	0	0	....	....	....	....	....

BANNISTER, DREW

Defense. Shoots right. 6'1", 195 lbs. Born, Bellevile, Ont., September 4, 1974.
(Tampa Bay's 2nd choice, 26th overall, in 1992 Entry Draft).

			Regular Season					Playoffs				
Season	Club	Lea	GP	G	A	TP	PIM	GP	G	A	TP	PIM
1990-91	S.S. Marie	OHL	41	2	8	10	51	4	0	0	0	0
1991-92	S.S. Marie	OHL	64	4	21	25	122	16	3	10	13	36
1992-93a	S.S. Marie	OHL	59	5	28	33	114	18	2	7	9	12

a Memorial Cup All-Star Team (1993)

BARNABY, MATTHEW

Left wing. Shoots left. 6', 170 lbs. Born, Ottawa, Ont., May 4, 1973.
(Buffalo's 5th choice, 83rd overall, in 1992 Entry Draft).

			Regular Season					Playoffs				
Season	Club	Lea	GP	G	A	TP	PIM	GP	G	A	TP	PIM
1990-91	Beauport	QMJHL	52	9	5	14	262	....	....	....	....	....
1991-92	Beauport	QMJHL	63	29	37	66	*476	....	....	....	....	....
1992-93	**Buffalo**	**NHL**	**2**	**1**	**0**	**1**	**10**	**1**	**0**	**1**	**1**	**4**
	Victoriaville	QMJHL	65	44	67	111	*448	6	2	4	6	44
	NHL Totals		**2**	**1**	**0**	**1**	**10**	**1**	**0**	**1**	**1**	**4**

BARNES, STU

Center. Shoots right. 5'11", 180 lbs. Born, Edmonton, Alta., December 25, 1970.
(Winnipeg's 1st choice, 4th overall, in 1989 Entry Draft).

			Regular Season					Playoffs				
Season	Club	Lea	GP	G	A	TP	PIM	GP	G	A	TP	PIM
1987-88	N. Westminster	WHL	71	37	64	101	88	5	2	3	5	6
1988-89ab	Tri-City	WHL	70	59	82	141	117	7	6	5	11	10
1989-90	Tri-City	WHL	63	52	92	144	165	7	1	5	6	26
1990-91	Cdn. National	....	53	22	27	49	68	....	....	....	....	....
1991-92	**Winnipeg**	**NHL**	**46**	**8**	**9**	**17**	**26**	....	....	....	....	....
	Moncton	AHL	30	13	19	32	10	11	3	9	12	6
1992-93	**Winnipeg**	**NHL**	**38**	**12**	**10**	**22**	**10**	**6**	**1**	**3**	**4**	**2**
	Moncton	AHL	42	23	31	54	58	....	....	....	....	....
	NHL Totals		**84**	**20**	**19**	**39**	**36**	**6**	**1**	**3**	**4**	**2**

a WHL West Second All-Star Team (1989)
b WHL Player of the Year (1989)

BARON, MURRAY

Defense. Shoots left. 6'3", 215 lbs. Born, Prince George, B.C., June 1, 1967.
(Philadelphia's 7th choice, 167th overall, in 1986 Entry Draft).

			Regular Season					Playoffs				
Season	Club	Lea	GP	G	A	TP	PIM	GP	G	A	TP	PIM
1986-87	North Dakota	WCHA	41	4	10	14	62	....	....	....	....	....
1987-88	North Dakota	WCHA	41	1	10	11	95	....	....	....	....	....
1988-89	North Dakota	WCHA	40	2	6	8	92	....	....	....	....	....
	Hershey	AHL	9	0	3	3	8	....	....	....	....	....
1989-90	**Philadelphia**	**NHL**	**16**	**2**	**2**	**4**	**12**	....	....	....	....	....
	Hershey	AHL	50	0	10	10	101	....	....	....	....	....
1990-91	**Philadelphia**	**NHL**	**67**	**8**	**8**	**16**	**74**	....	....	....	....	....
	Hershey	AHL	6	2	3	5	0	....	....	....	....	....
1991-92	**St. Louis**	**NHL**	**67**	**3**	**8**	**11**	**94**	**2**	**0**	**0**	**0**	**2**
1992-93	**St. Louis**	**NHL**	**53**	**2**	**2**	**4**	**59**	**11**	**0**	**0**	**0**	**12**
	NHL Totals		**203**	**15**	**20**	**35**	**239**	**13**	**0**	**0**	**0**	**14**

Traded to **St. Louis** by **Philadelphia** with Ron Sutter for Dan Quinn and Rod Brind'Amour, September 22, 1991.

BARR, DAVID (DAVE)

Right wing. Shoots right. 6'1", 195 lbs. Born, Toronto, Ont., November 30, 1960.

			Regular Season					Playoffs				
Season	Club	Lea	GP	G	A	TP	PIM	GP	G	A	TP	PIM
1979-80	Lethbridge	WHL	60	16	38	54	47	....	....	....	....	....
1980-81	Lethbridge	WHL	72	26	62	88	106	....	....	....	....	....
1981-82	Boston	NHL	2	0	0	0	0	5	1	0	1	0
	Erie	AHL	76	18	48	66	29	....	....	....	....	....
1982-83	Boston	NHL	10	1	1	2	7	10	0	0	0	2
	Baltimore	AHL	72	27	51	78	67	....	....	....	....	....
1983-84	NY Rangers	NHL	6	0	0	0	2	....	....	....	....	....
	Tulsa	CHL	50	28	37	65	24	....	....	....	....	....
	St. Louis	NHL	1	0	0	0	0	....	....	....	....	....
1984-85	St. Louis	NHL	75	16	18	34	32	2	0	0	0	2
1985-86	St. Louis	NHL	72	13	38	51	70	11	1	1	2	14
1986-87	St. Louis	NHL	2	0	0	0	0	....	....	....	....	....
	Hartford	NHL	30	2	4	6	19	....	....	....	....	....
	Detroit	NHL	37	13	13	26	49	13	1	0	1	14
1987-88	Detroit	NHL	51	14	26	40	58	16	5	7	12	22
1988-89	Detroit	NHL	73	27	32	59	69	6	3	1	4	6
1989-90	Detroit	NHL	62	10	25	35	45	....	....	....	....	....
	Adirondack	AHL	9	1	14	15	17	....	....	....	....	....
1990-91	Detroit	NHL	70	18	22	40	55	....	....	....	....	....
1991-92	New Jersey	NHL	41	6	12	18	32	....	....	....	....	....
	Utica	AHL	1	0	0	0	7	....	....	....	....	....
1992-93	New Jersey	NHL	62	6	8	14	61	5	1	0	1	6
	NHL Totals		594	126	199	325	499	68	12	9	21	66

Signed as a free agent by **Boston**, September 28, 1981. Traded to **NY Rangers** by **Boston** for Dave Silk, October 5, 1983. Traded to **St. Louis** by **NY Rangers** with NY Rangers' third round choice (Alan Perry) in the 1984 Entry Draft for Larry Patey and Bob Brooke, March 5, 1984. Traded to **Hartford** by **St. Louis** for Tim Bothwell, October 21, 1986. Traded to **Detroit** by **Hartford** for Randy Ladouceur, January 12, 1987. Acquired by **New Jersey** from **Detroit** with Randy McKay as compensation for Detroit's signing of free agent Troy Crowder, September 9, 1991.

BARRAULT, DOUGLAS

Right wing. Shoots right. 6'2", 205 lbs. Born, Golden, B.C., April 21, 1970.
(Minnesota's 8th choice, 155th overall, in 1990 Entry Draft).

			Regular Season					Playoffs				
Season	Club	Lea	GP	G	A	TP	PIM	GP	G	A	TP	PIM
1988-89	Lethbridge	WHL	57	14	13	27	34	....	....	....	....	....
1989-90	Lethbridge	WHL	54	14	16	30	36	19	7	3	10	0
1990-91a	Lethbridge	WHL	4	2	2	4	16	....	....	....	....	....
	Seattle	WHL	61	42	42	84	69	6	5	3	8	4
1991-92	Kalamazoo	IHL	60	5	14	19	26	....	....	....	....	....
1992-93	Minnesota	NHL	2	0	0	0	2	....	....	....	....	....
	Kalamazoo	IHL	78	32	34	66	74	....	....	....	....	....
	NHL Totals		2	0	0	0	2	....	....	....	....	....

a WHL West Second All-Star Team (1991)

Claimed by **Florida** from **Dallas** in Expansion Draft, June 24, 1993.

BARRIE, LEN

Center. Shoots left. 6', 200 lbs. Born, Kimberley, B.C., June 4, 1969.
(Edmonton's 7th choice, 124th overall, in 1988 Entry Draft).

			Regular Season					Playoffs				
Season	Club	Lea	GP	G	A	TP	PIM	GP	G	A	TP	PIM
1985-86	Calgary	WHL	32	3	0	3	18	....	....	....	....	....
1986-87	Calgary	WHL	34	13	13	26	81	....	....	....	....	....
	Victoria	WHL	34	7	6	13	92	5	0	1	1	15
1987-88	Victoria	WHL	70	37	49	86	192	8	2	0	2	29
1988-89	Victoria	WHL	67	39	48	87	157	7	5	2	7	23
1989-90	Philadelphia	NHL	1	0	0	0	0	....	....	....	....	....
a	Kamloops	WHL	70	*85	*100	*185	108	17	*14	23	*37	24
1990-91	Hershey	AHL	63	26	32	58	60	7	4	0	4	12
1991-92	Hershey	AHL	75	42	43	85	78	3	0	2	2	32
1992-93	Philadelphia	NHL	8	2	2	4	9	....	....	....	....	....
	Hershey	AHL	61	31	45	76	162	....	....	....	....	....
	NHL Totals		9	2	2	4	9	....	....	....	....	....

a WHL West First All-Star Team (1990)

Signed as a free agent by **Philadelphia**, February 28, 1990. Signed as a free agent by **Florida**, July 20, 1993.

BARRIE, MIKE

Center. Shoots right. 6'1", 170 lbs. Born, Kelowna, B.C., March 16, 1974.
(Buffalo's 6th choice, 194th overall, in 1993 Entry Draft).

			Regular Season					Playoffs				
Season	Club	Lea	GP	G	A	TP	PIM	GP	G	A	TP	PIM
1991-92	Victoria	WHL	54	15	15	30	165	....	....	....	....	....
1992-93	Victoria	WHL	70	31	39	70	244	....	....	....	....	....

BARTELL, ADAM

Defense. Shoots right. 6'1", 182 lbs. Born, Buffalo, NY, April 27, 1973.
(Quebec's 10th choice, 178th overall, in 1991 Entry Draft).

			Regular Season					Playoffs				
Season	Club	Lea	GP	G	A	TP	PIM	GP	G	A	TP	PIM
1991-92	RPI	ECAC	31	5	13	18	18	....	....	....	....	....
1992-93	RPI	ECAC	32	2	17	19	46	....	....	....	....	....

BARTELL, JOSH

Defense. Shoots left. 6'3", 205 lbs. Born, Syracuse, NY, April 14, 1973.
(Philadelphia's 9th choice, 204th overall, in 1991 Entry Draft).

			Regular Season					Playoffs				
Season	Club	Lea	GP	G	A	TP	PIM	GP	G	A	TP	PIM
1991-92	Northwood	HS	32	5	15	20	....					
1992-93	Clarkson	ECAC	22	1	0	1	24	....	....	....	....	....

BARTON, BRAD

Defense. Shoots right. 6'2", 192 lbs. Born, Uxbridge, Ont., May 15, 1972.
(Vancouver's 10th choice, 205th overall, in 1991 Entry Draft).

			Regular Season					Playoffs				
Season	Club	Lea	GP	G	A	TP	PIM	GP	G	A	TP	PIM
1990-91	Kitchener	OHL	55	2	18	20	125	6	1	4	5	23
1991-92	Kitchener	OHL	64	9	26	35	160	14	1	2	3	14
1992-93	Kingston	OHL	12	0	1	1	15	....	....	....	....	....

BASSEN, BOB

Center. Shoots left. 5'11", 185 lbs. Born, Calgary, Alta., May 6, 1965.

			Regular Season					Playoffs				
Season	Club	Lea	GP	G	A	TP	PIM	GP	G	A	TP	PIM
1982-83	Medicine Hat	WHL	4	3	2	5	0	3	0	0	0	4
1983-84	Medicine Hat	WHL	72	29	29	58	93	14	5	11	16	12
1984-85a	Medicine Hat	WHL	65	32	50	82	143	10	2	8	10	39
1985-86	NY Islanders	NHL	11	2	1	3	6	3	0	1	1	0
	Springfield	AHL	54	13	21	34	111	....	....	....	....	....
1986-87	NY Islanders	NHL	77	7	10	17	89	14	1	2	3	21
1987-88	NY Islanders	NHL	77	6	16	22	99	6	0	1	1	23
1988-89	NY Islanders	NHL	19	1	4	5	21	....	....	....	....	....
	Chicago	NHL	49	4	12	16	62	10	1	1	2	34
1989-90	Chicago	NHL	6	1	1	2	8	1	0	0	0	2
b	Indianapolis	IHL	73	22	32	54	179	12	3	8	11	33
1990-91	St. Louis	NHL	79	16	18	34	183	13	1	3	4	24
1991-92	St. Louis	NHL	79	7	25	32	167	6	0	2	2	4
1992-93	St. Louis	NHL	53	9	10	19	63	11	0	0	0	10
	NHL Totals		450	53	97	150	698	64	3	10	13	118

a WHL First All-Star Team (1985)
b IHL First All-Star Team (1990)

Signed as a free agent by **NY Islanders**, October 19, 1984. Traded to **Chicago** by **NY Islanders** with Steve Konroyd for Marc Bergevin and Gary Nylund, November 25, 1988. Claimed by **St. Louis** in NHL Waiver Draft, October 1, 1990.

BATES, SHAWN

Center. Shoots right. 5'11", 160 lbs. Born, Melrose, MA, April 3, 1975.
(Boston's 4th choice, 103rd overall, in 1993 Entry Draft).

			Regular Season					Playoffs				
Season	Club	Lea	GP	G	A	TP	PIM	GP	G	A	TP	PIM
1991-92	Medford	HS	23	31	41	72	6	....	....	....	....	....
1992-93	Medford	HS	25	49	46	95	20	....	....	....	....	....

BATTERS, JEFF

Defense. Shoots right. 6'2", 215 lbs. Born, Victoria, B.C., October 23, 1970.
(St. Louis' 7th choice, 135th overall, in 1989 Entry Draft).

			Regular Season					Playoffs				
Season	Club	Lea	GP	G	A	TP	PIM	GP	G	A	TP	PIM
1988-89	Alaska-Anch.	G.N.	33	8	14	22	123	....	....	....	....	....
1989-90	Alaska-Anch.	G.N.	34	6	9	15	102	....	....	....	....	....
1990-91	Alaska-Anch.	G.N.	39	16	14	30	90	....	....	....	....	....
1991-92	Alaska-Anch.	G.N.	33	6	16	22	84	....	....	....	....	....
1992-93	Peoria	IHL	74	5	18	23	113	4	0	0	0	10

BATYRSHIN, RUSLAN (ba-TEER-shihn)

Defense. Shoots left. 6'1", 180 lbs. Born, Moscow, Soviet Union, February 19, 1975.
(Winnipeg's 4th choice, 79th overall, in 1993 Entry Draft).

			Regular Season					Playoffs				
Season	Club	Lea	GP	G	A	TP	PIM	GP	G	A	TP	PIM
1991-92	Mosc.D'amo-2	CIS 3	40	0	2	2	52	....	....	....	....	....
1992-93	Mosc.D'amo-2	CIS 2			UNAVAILABLE							

BAUER, COLLIN

Defense. Shoots left. 6'1", 185 lbs. Born, Edmonton, Alta., September 6, 1970.
(Edmonton's 4th choice, 61st overall, in 1988 Entry Draft).

			Regular Season					Playoffs				
Season	Club	Lea	GP	G	A	TP	PIM	GP	G	A	TP	PIM
1986-87	Saskatoon	WHL	61	1	25	26	37	11	0	6	6	10
1987-88	Saskatoon	WHL	70	9	53	62	66	10	2	5	7	16
1988-89a	Saskatoon	WHL	61	17	62	79	71	8	1	8	9	8
1989-90	Saskatoon	WHL	29	4	25	29	49	10	1	8	9	14
1990-91	Cape Breton	AHL	40	4	14	18	18	4	1	1	2	4
1991-92	Cape Breton	AHL	55	7	15	22	36	3	0	0	0	7
1992-93	Kalamazoo	IHL	32	4	14	18	31	....	....	....	....	....

a WHL East All-Star Team (1989)

Traded to **Minnesota** by **Edmonton** for future considerations, August 4, 1992.

BAUMGARTNER, KEN

Defense/Center. Shoots left. 6'1", 200 lbs. Born, Flin Flon, Man., March 11, 1966.
(Buffalo's 12th choice, 245th overall, in 1985 Entry Draft).

			Regular Season					Playoffs				
Season	Club	Lea	GP	G	A	TP	PIM	GP	G	A	TP	PIM
1984-85	Prince Albert	WHL	60	3	9	12	252	13	1	3	4	89
1985-86	Prince Albert	WHL	70	4	23	27	277	20	3	9	12	112
1986-87	New Haven	AHL	13	0	3	3	99	6	0	0	0	60
1987-88	Los Angeles	NHL	30	2	3	5	189	5	0	1	1	28
	New Haven	AHL	48	1	5	6	181	....	....	....	....	....
1988-89	Los Angeles	NHL	49	1	3	4	288	5	0	0	0	8
	New Haven	AHL	10	1	3	4	26	....	....	....	....	....
1989-90	Los Angeles	NHL	12	1	0	1	28	....	....	....	....	....
	NY Islanders	NHL	53	0	5	5	194	4	0	0	0	27
1990-91	NY Islanders	NHL	78	1	6	7	282	....	....	....	....	....
1991-92	NY Islanders	NHL	44	0	1	1	202	....	....	....	....	....
	Toronto	NHL	11	0	0	0	23	....	....	....	....	....
1992-93	Toronto	NHL	63	1	0	1	155	7	1	0	1	0
	NHL Totals		340	6	18	24	1361	21	1	1	2	63

Traded to **Los Angeles** by **Buffalo** with Sean McKenna and Larry Playfair for Brian Engblom and Doug Smith, January 29, 1986. Traded to **NY Islanders** by **Los Angeles** with Hubie McDonough for Mikko Makela, November 29, 1989. Traded to **Toronto** by **NY Islanders** with Dave McLlwain for Daniel Marois and Claude Loiselle, March 10, 1992.

BAUTIN, SERGEI (BOW-tin)

Defense. Shoots left. 6'3", 185 lbs. Born, Rogachev, Soviet Union, March 11, 1967.
(Winnipeg's 1st choice, 17th overall, in 1992 Entry Draft).

			Regular Season					Playoffs				
Season	Club	Lea	GP	G	A	TP	PIM	GP	G	A	TP	PIM
1990-91	Moscow D'amo	USSR	33	2	0	2	28	....	....	....	....	....
1991-92	Moscow D'amo	CIS	37	1	3	4	88	....	....	....	....	....
1992-93	Winnipeg	NHL	71	5	18	23	96	6	0	0	0	2
	NHL Totals		71	5	18	23	96	6	0	0	0	2

BAVIS, MARK

Center. Shoots left. 6', 175 lbs.   Born, Roslindale, MA, March 13, 1970.
(NY Rangers' 10th choice, 181st overall, in 1989 Entry Draft).

			Regular Season					Playoffs			
Season	Club	Lea	GP	G	A	TP	PIM	GP	G	A	TP	PIM
1989-90	Boston U.	H.E.	44	6	5	11	50	....	....	....	....	....
1990-91	Boston U.	H.E.	33	7	9	16	30	....	....	....	....	....
1991-92	Boston U.	H.E.	34	9	17	26	30	....	....	....	....	....
1992-93	Boston U.	H.E.	40	14	10	24	58	....	....	....	....	....

BAVIS, MICHAEL

Right wing. Shoots right. 6', 180 lbs.   Born, Roslindale, MA, March 13, 1970.
(Buffalo's 12th choice, 245th overall, in 1989 Entry Draft).

			Regular Season					Playoffs			
Season	Club	Lea	GP	G	A	TP	PIM	GP	G	A	TP	PIM
1989-90	Boston U.	H.E.	44	2	11	13	28	....	....	....	....	....
1990-91	Boston U.	H.E.	40	5	18	23	47	....	....	....	....	....
1991-92	Boston U.	H.E.	34	11	13	24	32	....	....	....	....	....
1992-93	Boston U.	H.E.	40	12	11	23	87	....	....	....	....	....

BAWA, ROBIN   (BAH-wuh)

Right wing. Shoots right. 6'2", 214 lbs.   Born, Chemainus, B.C., March 26, 1966.

			Regular Season					Playoffs			
Season	Club	Lea	GP	G	A	TP	PIM	GP	G	A	TP	PIM
1982-83	Kamloops	WHL	66	10	24	34	17	7	1	2	3	0
1983-84	Kamloops	WHL	64	16	28	44	40	13	4	2	6	4
1984-85	Kamloops	WHL	52	6	19	25	45	15	4	9	13	14
1985-86	Kamloops	WHL	63	29	43	72	78	16	5	13	18	4
1986-87a	Kamloops	WHL	62	57	56	113	91	13	6	7	13	22
1987-88	Fort Wayne	IHL	55	12	27	39	239	6	1	3	4	24
1988-89	Baltimore	AHL	75	23	24	47	205	....	....	....	....	....
1989-90	**Washington**	**NHL**	**5**	**1**	**0**	**1**	**6**	....	....	....	....	....
	Baltimore	AHL	61	7	18	25	189	11	1	2	3	49
1990-91	Fort Wayne	IHL	72	21	26	47	381	18	4	4	8	87
1991-92	**Vancouver**	**NHL**	**2**	**0**	**0**	**0**	**0**	**1**	**0**	**0**	**0**	**0**
	Milwaukee	IHL	70	27	14	41	238	5	2	2	4	8
1992-93	Hamilton	AHL	23	3	4	7	58	....	....	....	....	....
	San Jose	**NHL**	**42**	**5**	**0**	**5**	**47**	....	....	....	....	....
	Kansas City	IHL	5	2	0	2	20	....	....	....	....	....
	NHL Totals		**49**	**6**	**0**	**6**	**53**	**1**	**0**	**0**	**0**	**0**

a   WHL West All-Star Team (1987)
Signed as a free agent by **Washington**, May 22, 1987. Traded to **Vancouver** by **Washington** for cash, July 31, 1991. Traded to **San Jose** by **Vancouver** for Rick Lessard, December 15, 1992. Claimed by **Anaheim** from **San Jose** in Expansion Draft, June 24, 1993.

BEAUFAIT, MARK

Center. Shoots right. 5'9", 165 lbs.   Born, Royal Oak, MI, May 13, 1970.
(San Jose's 2nd choice, 7th overall, in 1991 Supplemental Draft).

			Regular Season					Playoffs			
Season	Club	Lea	GP	G	A	TP	PIM	GP	G	A	TP	PIM
1988-89	N. Michigan	WCHA	11	2	1	3	2	....	....	....	....	....
1989-90	N. Michigan	WCHA	34	10	14	24	12	....	....	....	....	....
1990-91	N. Michigan	WCHA	47	19	30	49	18	....	....	....	....	....
1991-92	N. Michigan	WCHA	39	31	44	75	43	....	....	....	....	....
1992-93	**San Jose**	**NHL**	**5**	**1**	**0**	**1**	**0**	....	....	....	....	....
	Kansas City	IHL	66	19	40	59	22	9	1	1	2	8
	NHL Totals		**5**	**1**	**0**	**1**	**0**					

BEAULIEU, COREY

Defense. Shoots left. 6'1", 210 lbs.   Born, Winnipeg, Man., September 10, 1969.
(Hartford's 5th choice, 116th overall, in 1988 Entry Draft).

			Regular Season					Playoffs			
Season	Club	Lea	GP	G	A	TP	PIM	GP	G	A	TP	PIM
1985-86	Moose Jaw	WHL	68	3	1	4	111	13	1	1	2	13
1986-87	Moose Jaw	WHL	63	2	7	9	188	9	0	0	0	17
1987-88	Seattle	WHL	67	2	9	11	225	....	....	....	....	....
1988-89	Seattle	WHL	32	0	3	3	134	....	....	....	....	....
	Moose Jaw	WHL	29	3	17	20	91	7	1	2	3	16
1989-90	Binghamton	AHL	56	0	2	2	191	....	....	....	....	....
1990-91					DID NOT PLAY							
1991-92	Louisville	ECHL	8	1	5	6	60	....	....	....	....	....
	Springfield	AHL	52	0	0	0	157	2	0	0	0	2
1992-93	Springfield	AHL	68	1	5	6	201	4	0	1	1	21

BEERS, BOB

Defense. Shoots right. 6'2", 200 lbs.   Born, Pittsburgh, PA, May 20, 1967.
(Boston's 10th choice, 210th overall, in 1985 Entry Draft).

			Regular Season					Playoffs			
Season	Club	Lea	GP	G	A	TP	PIM	GP	G	A	TP	PIM
1985-86	N. Arizona	NCAA	28	11	39	50	96	....	....	....	....	....
1986-87	U. of Maine	H.E.	38	0	13	13	45	....	....	....	....	....
1987-88	U. of Maine	H.E.	41	3	11	14	72	....	....	....	....	....
1988-89ab	U. of Maine	H.E.	44	10	27	37	53	....	....	....	....	....
1989-90	**Boston**	**NHL**	**3**	**0**	**1**	**1**	**6**	**14**	**1**	**1**	**2**	**18**
	Maine	AHL	74	7	36	43	63	....	....	....	....	....
1990-91	**Boston**	**NHL**	**16**	**0**	**1**	**1**	**10**	**6**	**0**	**0**	**0**	**4**
	Maine	AHL	36	2	16	18	21	....	....	....	....	....
1991-92	**Boston**	**NHL**	**31**	**0**	**5**	**5**	**29**	**1**	**0**	**0**	**0**	**0**
	Maine	AHL	33	6	23	29	24	....	....	....	....	....
1992-93	Providence	AHL	6	1	2	3	10	....	....	....	....	....
	Tampa Bay	**NHL**	**64**	**12**	**24**	**36**	**70**	....	....	....	....	....
	Atlanta	IHL	1	0	0	0	0	....	....	....	....	....
	NHL Totals		**114**	**12**	**31**	**43**	**115**	**21**	**1**	**1**	**2**	**22**

a   Hockey East Second All-Star Team (1989)
b   NCAA East Second All-American Team (1989)
Traded to **Tampa Bay** by **Boston** for Stephane Richer, October 28, 1992.

BELANGER, CHRIS

Defense. Shoots right. 6'2", 185 lbs.   Born, Welland, Ont., April 4, 1972.
(Hartford's 9th choice, 185th overall, in 1991 Entry Draft).

			Regular Season					Playoffs			
Season	Club	Lea	GP	G	A	TP	PIM	GP	G	A	TP	PIM
1990-91	W. Michigan	CCHA	2	0	0	0	2	....	....	....	....	....
1991-92	W. Michigan	CCHA	36	7	24	31	28	....	....	....	....	....
1992-93	W. Michigan	CCHA	27	3	16	19	23	....	....	....	....	....

BELANGER, HUGO

Left wing. Shoots left. 6'1", 190 lbs.   Born, St. Hubert, Que., May 28, 1970.
(Chicago's 6th choice, 163rd overall, in 1990 Entry Draft).

			Regular Season					Playoffs			
Season	Club	Lea	GP	G	A	TP	PIM	GP	G	A	TP	PIM
1989-90	Clarkson	ECAC	36	14	25	39	12	....	....	....	....	....
1990-91	Clarkson	ECAC	40	32	43	75	18	....	....	....	....	....
1991-92a	Clarkson	ECAC	32	18	31	49	26	....	....	....	....	....
1992-93	Clarkson	ECAC	31	17	23	40	36	....	....	....	....	....

a   ECAC Second All-Star Team (1992)

BELANGER, JESSE

Center. Shoots right. 6', 170 lbs.   Born, St. Georges de Beauce, Que., June 15, 1969.

			Regular Season					Playoffs			
Season	Club	Lea	GP	G	A	TP	PIM	GP	G	A	TP	PIM
1987-88	Granby	QMJHL	69	33	43	76	10	5	3	3	6	0
1988-89	Granby	QMJHL	67	40	63	103	26	4	0	5	5	0
1989-90	Granby	QMJHL	67	53	54	107	53	....	....	....	....	....
1990-91	Fredericton	AHL	75	40	58	98	30	6	2	4	6	0
1991-92	**Montreal**	**NHL**	**4**	**0**	**0**	**0**	**0**	....	....	....	....	....
	Fredericton	AHL	65	30	41	71	26	7	3	3	6	2
1992-93	**Montreal**	**NHL**	**19**	**4**	**2**	**6**	**4**	**9**	**0**	**1**	**1**	**0**
	Fredericton	AHL	39	19	32	51	24	....	....	....	....	....
	NHL Totals		**23**	**4**	**2**	**6**	**4**	**9**	**0**	**1**	**1**	**0**

Signed as a free agent by **Montreal**, October 3, 1990. Claimed by **Florida** from **Montreal** in Expansion Draft, June 24, 1993.

BELANGER, KEN

Left wing. Shoots left. 6'3", 189 lbs.   Born, Sault Ste. Marie, Ont., May 14, 1974.
(Hartford's 7th choice, 153rd overall, in 1992 Entry Draft).

			Regular Season					Playoffs			
Season	Club	Lea	GP	G	A	TP	PIM	GP	G	A	TP	PIM
1991-92	Ottawa	OHL	51	4	4	8	174	11	0	0	0	24
1992-93	Ottawa	OHL	34	6	12	18	139	....	....	....	....	....
	Guelph	OHL	29	10	14	24	86	5	2	1	3	14

BELLEROSE, ERIC

Left wing. Shoots left. 6'1", 202 lbs.   Born, Montreal, Que., February 7, 1972.
(San Jose's 7th choice, 147th overall, in 1992 Entry Draft).

			Regular Season					Playoffs			
Season	Club	Lea	GP	G	A	TP	PIM	GP	G	A	TP	PIM
1988-89	Trois-Rivières	QMJHL	10	0	0	0	4	....	....	....	....	....
1989-90	St-Hyacinthe	QMJHL	69	20	57	77	63	12	4	8	12	21
1990-91	St-Hyacinthe	QMJHL	22	5	16	21	12	....	....	....	....	....
	Hull	QMJHL	46	23	35	58	75	6	2	3	5	4
1991-92	Hull	QMJHL	8	7	6	13	35	....	....	....	....	....
	Trois-Rivières	QMJHL	62	36	59	95	98	15	7	*16	23	26
1992-93	Cdn. National	....	62	19	20	39	64	....	....	....	....	....

BELLOWS, BRIAN

Left wing. Shoots right. 5'11", 195 lbs.   Born, St. Catharines, Ont., September 1, 1964.
(Minnesota's 1st choice, 2nd overall, in 1982 Entry Draft).

			Regular Season					Playoffs			
Season	Club	Lea	GP	G	A	TP	PIM	GP	G	A	TP	PIM
1980-81a	Kitchener	OHA	66	49	67	116	23	16	14	13	27	13
1981-82bc	Kitchener	OHL	47	45	52	97	23	15	16	13	29	11
1982-83	**Minnesota**	**NHL**	**78**	**35**	**30**	**65**	**27**	**9**	**5**	**4**	**9**	**18**
1983-84	**Minnesota**	**NHL**	**78**	**41**	**42**	**83**	**66**	**16**	**2**	**12**	**14**	**6**
1984-85	**Minnesota**	**NHL**	**78**	**26**	**36**	**62**	**72**	**9**	**2**	**4**	**6**	**9**
1985-86	**Minnesota**	**NHL**	**77**	**31**	**48**	**79**	**46**	**5**	**5**	**0**	**5**	**16**
1986-87	**Minnesota**	**NHL**	**65**	**26**	**27**	**53**	**34**	....	....	....	....	....
1987-88	**Minnesota**	**NHL**	**77**	**40**	**41**	**81**	**81**	....	....	....	....	....
1988-89	**Minnesota**	**NHL**	**60**	**23**	**27**	**50**	**55**	**5**	**2**	**3**	**5**	**8**
1989-90d	**Minnesota**	**NHL**	**80**	**55**	**44**	**99**	**72**	**7**	**4**	**3**	**7**	**10**
1990-91	**Minnesota**	**NHL**	**80**	**35**	**40**	**75**	**43**	**23**	**10**	**19**	**29**	**30**
1991-92	**Minnesota**	**NHL**	**80**	**30**	**45**	**75**	**41**	**7**	**4**	**4**	**8**	**14**
1992-93	**Montreal**	**NHL**	**82**	**40**	**48**	**88**	**44**	**18**	**6**	**9**	**15**	**18**
	NHL Totals		**835**	**382**	**428**	**810**	**581**	**99**	**40**	**58**	**98**	**129**

a   OHA Third All-Star Team (1981)
b   OHL First All-Star Team (1982)
c   Most Sportsmanlike Player, Memorial Cup Tournament (1982)
d   NHL Second All-Star Team (1990)
Played in NHL All-Star Game (1984, 1988, 1992)
Traded to **Montreal** by **Minnesota** for Russ Courtnall, August 31, 1992.

BELZILE, ETIENNE

Defense. Shoots left. 6'1", 185 lbs.   Born, Quebec City, Que., May 2, 1972.
(Calgary's 4th choice, 41st overall, in 1990 Entry Draft).

			Regular Season					Playoffs			
Season	Club	Lea	GP	G	A	TP	PIM	GP	G	A	TP	PIM
1989-90	Cornell	ECAC	27	1	5	6	22	....	....	....	....	....
1990-91	Cornell	ECAC	32	2	3	5	40	....	....	....	....	....
1991-92	Cornell	ECAC	29	1	1	2	20	....	....	....	....	....
1992-93	Cornell	ECAC	26	2	2	4	24	....	....	....	....	....

BENNETT, ADAM

Defense. Shoots right. 6'4", 206 lbs.   Born, Georgetown, Ont., March 30, 1971.
(Chicago's 1st choice, 6th overall, in 1989 Entry Draft).

			Regular Season					Playoffs			
Season	Club	Lea	GP	G	A	TP	PIM	GP	G	A	TP	PIM
1988-89	Sudbury	OHL	66	7	22	29	133	....	....	....	....	....
1989-90a	Sudbury	OHL	65	18	43	61	116	7	1	2	3	23
1990-91b	Sudbury	OHL	54	21	29	50	123	5	1	2	3	11
	Indianapolis	IHL	3	0	1	1	12	2	0	0	0	0
1991-92	**Chicago**	**NHL**	**5**	**0**	**0**	**0**	**12**	....	....	....	....	....
	Indianapolis	IHL	59	4	10	14	89	....	....	....	....	....
1992-93	**Chicago**	**NHL**	**16**	**0**	**2**	**2**	**8**	....	....	....	....	....
	Indianapolis	IHL	39	8	16	24	69	....	....	....	....	....
	NHL Totals		**21**	**0**	**2**	**2**	**20**					

a   OHL Third All-Star Team (1990)
b   OHL Second All-Star Team (1991)

BENNETT, RICK

Left wing. Shoots left. 6'4", 215 lbs. Born, Springfield, MA, July 24, 1967.
(Minnesota's 4th choice, 54th overall, in 1986 Entry Draft).

			Regular Season					Playoffs				
Season	Club	Lea	GP	G	A	TP	PIM	GP	G	A	TP	PIM
1986-87	Providence	H.E.	32	15	12	27	34	....	....	....	....	....
1987-88	Providence	H.E.	33	9	16	25	70	....	....	....	....	....
1988-89a	Providence	H.E.	32	14	32	46	74	....	....	....	....	....
1989-90b	Providence	H.E.	31	12	24	36	74	....	....	....	....	....
	NY Rangers	**NHL**	**6**	**1**	**0**	**1**	**5**	....	....	....	....	....
1990-91	**NY Rangers**	**NHL**	**6**	**0**	**0**	**0**	**6**	....	....	....	....	....
	Binghamton	AHL	71	27	32	59	206	10	2	1	3	27
1991-92	**NY Rangers**	**NHL**	**3**	**0**	**1**	**1**	**2**	....	....	....	....	....
	Binghamton	AHL	69	19	23	42	112	11	0	1	1	23
1992-93	Binghamton	AHL	76	15	22	37	114	10	0	0	0	30
	NHL Totals		**15**	**1**	**1**	**2**	**13**	....	....	....	....	....

a NCAA East Second All-American Team (1989)
b Hockey East All-Star Team (1990)

Rights traded to **NY Rangers** by **Minnesota** with Brian Lawton and Igor Liba for Paul Jerrard, Mark Tinordi, the rights to Bret Barnett and Mike Sullivan, and Los Angeles' third round choice (previously acquired by NY Rangers — Minnesota selected Murray Garbutt) in 1989 Entry Draft, October 11, 1988.

BENNING, BRIAN

Defense. Shoots left. 6', 195 lbs. Born, Edmonton, Alta., June 10, 1966.
(St. Louis' 1st choice, 26th overall, in 1984 Entry Draft).

			Regular Season					Playoffs				
Season	Club	Lea	GP	G	A	TP	PIM	GP	G	A	TP	PIM
1983-84	Portland	WHL	38	6	41	47	108	....	....	....	....	....
1984-85	**St. Louis**	**NHL**	**4**	**0**	**2**	**2**	**0**	....	....	....	....	....
	Kamloops	WHL	17	3	18	21	26	....	....	....	....	....
1985-86	Cdn. Olympic	....	60	6	13	19	43	....	....	....	....	....
	St. Louis	**NHL**	....	....	....	....	....	**6**	**1**	**2**	**3**	**13**
1986-87a	**St. Louis**	**NHL**	**78**	**13**	**36**	**49**	**110**	**6**	**0**	**4**	**4**	**9**
1987-88	**St. Louis**	**NHL**	**77**	**8**	**29**	**37**	**107**	**10**	**1**	**6**	**7**	**25**
1988-89	**St. Louis**	**NHL**	**66**	**8**	**26**	**34**	**102**	**7**	**1**	**1**	**2**	**11**
1989-90	**St. Louis**	**NHL**	**7**	**1**	**1**	**2**	**2**	....	....	....	....	....
	Los Angeles	**NHL**	**48**	**5**	**18**	**23**	**104**	**7**	**0**	**2**	**2**	**10**
1990-91	**Los Angeles**	**NHL**	**61**	**7**	**24**	**31**	**127**	**12**	**0**	**5**	**5**	**6**
1991-92	**Los Angeles**	**NHL**	**53**	**2**	**30**	**32**	**99**	....	....	....	....	....
	Philadelphia	**NHL**	**22**	**2**	**12**	**14**	**35**	....	....	....	....	....
1992-93	**Philadelphia**	**NHL**	**37**	**9**	**17**	**26**	**93**	....	....	....	....	....
	Edmonton	**NHL**	**18**	**1**	**7**	**8**	**59**	....	....	....	....	....
	NHL Totals		**471**	**56**	**202**	**258**	**838**	**48**	**3**	**20**	**23**	**74**

a NHL All-Rookie Team (1987)

Traded to **Los Angeles** by **St Louis** for Los Angeles' third round choice (Kyle Reeves) in 1991 Entry Draft, November 10, 1989. Traded to **Pittsburgh** by **Los Angeles** with Jeff Chychrun and Los Angeles' first round choice (later traded to Philadelphia — Philadelphia selected Jason Bowen) in 1992 Entry Draft for Paul Coffey, February 19, 1992. Traded to **Philadelphia** by **Pittsburgh** with Mark Recchi and Los Angeles' first choice (previously acquired by Pittsburgh — Philadelphia selected Jason Bowen) in 1992 Entry Draft previously acquired by **Pittsburgh** for Rick Tocchet, Kjell Samuelsson and Ken Wregget, February 19, 1992. Traded to **Edmonton** by **Philadelphia** for Greg Hawgood and Josef Beranek, January 16, 1993.

BERANEK, JOSEF (beh-RAH-nehk)

Left wing. Shoots left. 6'2", 185 lbs. Born, Most, Czechoslovakia, October 25, 1969.
(Edmonton's 3rd choice, 78th overall, in 1989 Entry Draft).

			Regular Season					Playoffs				
Season	Club	Lea	GP	G	A	TP	PIM	GP	G	A	TP	PIM
1987-88	Litvinov	Czech.	14	7	4	11	12	....	....	....	....	....
1988-89	Litvinov	Czech.	32	18	10	28	47	....	....	....	....	....
1989-90	Dukla Trencin	Czech.	49	19	23	42	....	....	....	....	....	....
1990-91	Litvinov	Czech.	58	29	31	60	98	....	....	....	....	....
1991-92	**Edmonton**	**NHL**	**58**	**12**	**16**	**28**	**18**	**12**	**2**	**1**	**3**	**0**
1992-93	**Edmonton**	**NHL**	**26**	**2**	**6**	**8**	**28**	....	....	....	....	....
	Cape Breton	AHL	6	1	2	3	8	....	....	....	....	....
	Philadelphia	**NHL**	**40**	**13**	**12**	**25**	**50**	....	....	....	....	....
	NHL Totals		**124**	**27**	**34**	**61**	**96**	**12**	**2**	**1**	**3**	**0**

Traded to **Philadelphia** by **Edmonton** with Greg Hawgood for Brian Benning, January 16, 1993.

BEREHOWSKY, DRAKE (beh-reh-HOW-skee)

Defense. Shoots right. 6'1", 211 lbs. Born, Toronto, Ont., January 3, 1972.
(Toronto's 1st choice, 10th overall, in 1990 Entry Draft).

			Regular Season					Playoffs				
Season	Club	Lea	GP	G	A	TP	PIM	GP	G	A	TP	PIM
1988-89	Kingston	OHL	63	7	39	46	85	....	....	....	....	....
1989-90	Kingston	OHL	9	3	11	14	28	....	....	....	....	....
1990-91	**Toronto**	**NHL**	**8**	**0**	**1**	**1**	**25**	....	....	....	....	....
	Kingston	OHL	13	5	13	18	38	....	....	....	....	....
	North Bay	OHL	26	7	23	30	51	10	2	7	9	21
1991-92	**Toronto**	**NHL**	**1**	**0**	**0**	**0**	**0**	....	....	....	....	....
abc	North Bay	OHL	62	19	63	82	147	21	7	24	31	22
	St. John's	AHL	....	....	....	....	....	6	0	5	5	21
1992-93	**Toronto**	**NHL**	**41**	**4**	**15**	**19**	**61**	....	....	....	....	....
	St. John's	AHL	28	10	17	27	38	....	....	....	....	....
	NHL Totals		**50**	**4**	**16**	**20**	**86**	....	....	....	....	....

a Canadian Major Junior Defenseman of the Year (1992)
b OHL First All-Star Team (1992)
c OHL's Most Outstanding Defenseman (1992)

BEREZAN, PERRY EDMUND (BAIR-ih-ZAN)

Center. Shoots right. 6'2", 190 lbs. Born, Edmonton, Alta., December 5, 1964.
(Calgary's 3rd choice, 56th overall, in 1983 Entry Draft).

			Regular Season					Playoffs				
Season	Club	Lea	GP	G	A	TP	PIM	GP	G	A	TP	PIM
1983-84	North Dakota	WCHA	44	28	24	52	29	....	....	....	....	....
1984-85a	North Dakota	WCHA	42	23	35	58	32	....	....	....	....	....
	Calgary	**NHL**	**9**	**3**	**2**	**5**	**4**	**2**	**1**	**0**	**1**	**4**
1985-86	**Calgary**	**NHL**	**55**	**12**	**21**	**33**	**39**	**8**	**1**	**1**	**2**	**6**
1986-87	**Calgary**	**NHL**	**24**	**5**	**3**	**8**	**24**	**2**	**0**	**2**	**2**	**7**
1987-88	**Calgary**	**NHL**	**29**	**7**	**12**	**19**	**66**	**8**	**0**	**2**	**2**	**13**
1988-89	**Calgary**	**NHL**	**35**	**4**	**4**	**8**	**23**	....	....	....	....	....
	Minnesota	**NHL**	**16**	**1**	**4**	**5**	**4**	**5**	**1**	**2**	**3**	**4**
1989-90	**Minnesota**	**NHL**	**64**	**3**	**12**	**15**	**31**	**5**	**1**	**0**	**1**	**0**
1990-91	**Minnesota**	**NHL**	**52**	**11**	**6**	**17**	**30**	**1**	**0**	**0**	**0**	**0**
	Kalamazoo	IHL	2	0	0	0	2	....	....	....	....	....
1991-92	**San Jose**	**NHL**	**66**	**12**	**7**	**19**	**30**	....	....	....	....	....
1992-93	**San Jose**	**NHL**	**28**	**3**	**4**	**7**	**28**	....	....	....	....	....
	Kansas City	IHL	9	4	4	8	31	....	....	....	....	....
	NHL Totals		**378**	**61**	**75**	**136**	**279**	**31**	**4**	**7**	**11**	**34**

a WCHA Second All-Star Team (1985)

Traded to **Minnesota** by **Calgary** with Shane Churla for Brian MacLellan and Minnesota's fourth round choice (Robert Reichel) in 1989 Entry Draft, March 4, 1989. Signed as a free agent by **San Jose**, October 10, 1991.

BERG, BILL

Left wing. Shoots left. 6'1", 205 lbs. Born, St. Catharines, Ont., October 21, 1967.
(NY Islanders' 3rd choice, 59th overall, in 1986 Entry Draft).

			Regular Season					Playoffs				
Season	Club	Lea	GP	G	A	TP	PIM	GP	G	A	TP	PIM
1985-86	Toronto	OHL	64	3	35	38	143	4	0	0	0	19
	Springfield	AHL	4	1	1	2	4	....	....	....	....	....
1986-87	Toronto	OHL	57	3	15	18	138	....	....	....	....	....
1987-88	Springfield	AHL	76	6	26	32	148	....	....	....	....	....
	Peoria	IHL	5	0	1	1	8	7	0	3	3	31
1988-89	**NY Islanders**	**NHL**	**7**	**1**	**2**	**3**	**10**	....	....	....	....	....
	Springfield	AHL	69	17	32	49	122	....	....	....	....	....
1989-90	Springfield	AHL	74	12	42	54	74	15	5	12	17	35
1990-91	**NY Islanders**	**NHL**	**78**	**9**	**14**	**23**	**67**	....	....	....	....	....
1991-92	**NY Islanders**	**NHL**	**47**	**5**	**9**	**14**	**28**	....	....	....	....	....
	Capital Dist.	AHL	3	0	2	2	16	....	....	....	....	....
1992-93	**NY Islanders**	**NHL**	**22**	**6**	**3**	**9**	**49**	....	....	....	....	....
	Toronto	**NHL**	**58**	**7**	**8**	**15**	**54**	**21**	**1**	**1**	**2**	**18**
	NHL Totals		**212**	**28**	**36**	**64**	**208**	**21**	**1**	**1**	**2**	**18**

Claimed on waivers by **Toronto** from **NY Islanders**, December 3, 1992.

BERG, BOB

Left wing. Shoots left. 6'2", 190 lbs. Born, Beamsville, Ont., July 2, 1970.
(Los Angeles' 3rd choice, 49th overall, in 1990 Entry Draft).

			Regular Season					Playoffs				
Season	Club	Lea	GP	G	A	TP	PIM	GP	G	A	TP	PIM
1987-88	Belleville	OHL	61	15	27	42	59	....	....	....	....	....
1988-89	Belleville	OHL	66	33	51	84	88	5	1	3	4	8
1989-90a	Belleville	OHL	66	48	49	97	124	8	2	2	4	14
1990-91	New Haven	AHL	19	0	1	1	8	....	....	....	....	....
	Niagara Falls	OHL	12	8	4	12	11	....	....	....	....	....
	Sudbury	OHL	23	12	15	27	34	5	2	1	3	6
1991-92	Phoenix	IHL	24	2	8	10	18	....	....	....	....	....
	Richmond	ECHL	37	19	14	33	65	6	2	1	3	0
1992-93	Phoenix	IHL	1	0	0	0	0	....	....	....	....	....

a OHL First All-Star Team (1990)

BERGEVIN, MARC

Defense. Shoots left. 6', 185 lbs. Born, Montreal, Que., August 11, 1965.
(Chicago's 3rd choice, 59th overall, in 1983 Entry Draft).

			Regular Season					Playoffs				
Season	Club	Lea	GP	G	A	TP	PIM	GP	G	A	TP	PIM
1982-83	Chicoutimi	QMJHL	64	3	27	30	113	....	....	....	....	....
1983-84	Chicoutimi	QMJHL	70	10	35	45	125	....	....	....	....	....
	Springfield	AHL	7	0	1	1	2	....	....	....	....	....
1984-85	**Chicago**	**NHL**	**60**	**0**	**6**	**6**	**54**	**6**	**0**	**3**	**3**	**2**
	Springfield	AHL	....	....	....	....	....	4	0	0	0	0
1985-86	**Chicago**	**NHL**	**71**	**7**	**7**	**14**	**60**	**3**	**0**	**0**	**0**	**0**
1986-87	**Chicago**	**NHL**	**66**	**4**	**10**	**14**	**66**	**3**	**1**	**0**	**1**	**2**
1987-88	**Chicago**	**NHL**	**58**	**1**	**6**	**7**	**85**	....	....	....	....	....
	Saginaw	IHL	10	2	7	9	20	....	....	....	....	....
1988-89	**Chicago**	**NHL**	**11**	**0**	**0**	**0**	**18**	....	....	....	....	....
	NY Islanders	**NHL**	**58**	**2**	**13**	**15**	**62**	....	....	....	....	....
1989-90	**NY Islanders**	**NHL**	**18**	**0**	**4**	**4**	**30**	....	....	....	....	....
	Springfield	AHL	47	7	16	23	66	17	2	11	13	16
1990-91	Capital Dist.	AHL	7	0	5	5	6	....	....	....	....	....
	Hartford	**NHL**	**4**	**0**	**0**	**0**	**4**	....	....	....	....	....
	Springfield	AHL	58	4	23	27	85	18	0	7	7	26
1991-92	**Hartford**	**NHL**	**75**	**7**	**17**	**24**	**64**	**5**	**0**	**0**	**0**	**2**
1992-93	**Tampa Bay**	**NHL**	**78**	**2**	**12**	**14**	**66**	....	....	....	....	....
	NHL Totals		**499**	**23**	**75**	**98**	**509**	**17**	**1**	**3**	**4**	**6**

Traded to **NY Islanders** by **Chicago** with Gary Nylund for Steve Konroyd and Bob Bassen, November 25, 1988. Traded to **Hartford** by **NY Islanders** for future considerations, October 30, 1990. Signed as a free agent by **Tampa Bay**, July 9, 1992.

BERGLAND, TIM

Right wing. Shoots right. 6'3", 194 lbs. Born, Crookston, MN, January 11, 1965.
(Washington's 1st choice, 75th overall, in 1983 Entry Draft).

			Regular Season					Playoffs				
Season	Club	Lea	GP	G	A	TP	PIM	GP	G	A	TP	PIM
1983-84	U. Minnesota	WCHA	24	4	11	15	4	....	....	....	....	....
1984-85	U. Minnesota	WCHA	34	5	9	14	8	....	....	....	....	....
1985-86	U. Minnesota	WCHA	48	11	16	27	26	....	....	....	....	....
1986-87	U. Minnesota	WCHA	49	18	17	35	48	....	....	....	....	....
1987-88	Fort Wayne	IHL	13	2	1	3	9	....	....	....	....	....
	Binghamton	AHL	63	21	26	47	31	4	0	0	0	0
1988-89	Baltimore	AHL	78	24	29	53	39	....	....	....	....	....
1989-90	**Washington**	**NHL**	**32**	**2**	**5**	**7**	**31**	**15**	**1**	**1**	**2**	**10**
	Baltimore	AHL	47	12	19	31	55	....	....	....	....	....
1990-91	**Washington**	**NHL**	**47**	**5**	**9**	**14**	**21**	**11**	**1**	**1**	**2**	**12**
	Baltmore	AHL	15	8	9	17	16	....	....	....	....	....
1991-92	**Washington**	**NHL**	**22**	**1**	**4**	**5**	**2**	....	....	....	....	....
	Baltimore	AHL	11	6	10	16	5	....	....	....	....	....
1992-93	**Tampa Bay**	**NHL**	**27**	**3**	**3**	**6**	**11**	....	....	....	....	....
	Atlanta	IHL	49	18	21	39	26	9	3	3	6	10
	NHL Totals		**128**	**11**	**21**	**32**	**65**	**26**	**2**	**2**	**4**	**22**

Claimed by **Tampa Bay** from **Washington** in Expansion Draft, June 18, 1992.

BERGMAN, JAN (BURG-muhn)

Defense. Shoots left. 5'11", 194 lbs. Born, Sodertalje, Sweden, August 7, 1969.
(Vancouver's 11th choice, 248th overall, in 1989 Entry Draft).

			Regular Season					Playoffs				
Season	Club	Lea	GP	G	A	TP	PIM	GP	G	A	TP	PIM
1988-89	Sodertalje	Swe.	34	2	4	6	14	....	....	....	....	....
1989-90	Sodertalje	Swe.	31	0	4	4	10	2	1	0	1	0
1990-91	Sodertalje	Swe.	40	4	4	8	16	2	0	0	0	0
1991-92	Sodertalje	Swe.	21	1	1	2	8	....	....	....	....	....
1992-93	Sodertalje	Swe. 2	24	6	4	10	8	....	....	....	....	....

BERGQVIST, STEFAN

Defense. Shoots left. 6'3", 216 lbs. Born, Leksand, Sweden, March 10, 1975.
(Pittsburgh's 1st choice, 26th overall, in 1993 Entry Draft).

			Regular Season					Playoffs				
Season	Club	Lea	GP	G	A	TP	PIM	GP	G	A	TP	PIM
1992-93	Leksand	Swe.	15	0	0	0	6	....	....	....	....	....

BERMINGHAM, JIM

Center. Shoots left. 6'3", 201 lbs. Born, Montreal, Que., November 12, 1971.
(Detroit's 7th choice, 186th overall, in 1991 Entry Draft).

			Regular Season					Playoffs				
Season	Club	Lea	GP	G	A	TP	PIM	GP	G	A	TP	PIM
1990-91	Laval	QMJHL	67	21	39	60	109	13	4	8	12	17
1991-92	Laval	QMJHL	65	37	66	103	88	10	3	6	9	28
1992-93	Adirondack	AHL	21	0	2	2	8	....	....	....	....	....
	Toledo	ECHL	18	8	9	17	21	....	....	....	....	....

BERNARD, LOUIS

Defense. Shoots right. 6'1", 198 lbs. Born, Victoriaville, Que., July 10, 1974.
(Montreal's 5th choice, 82nd overall, in 1992 Entry Draft).

			Regular Season					Playoffs				
Season	Club	Lea	GP	G	A	TP	PIM	GP	G	A	TP	PIM
1991-92	Drummondville	QMJHL	70	8	24	32	59	4	0	1	1	4
1992-93	Drummondville	QMJHL	68	8	38	46	78	10	0	4	4	14

BERRY, BRAD

Defense. Shoots left. 6'2", 190 lbs. Born, Bashaw, Alta., April 1, 1965.
(Winnipeg's 3rd choice, 29th overall, in 1983 Entry Draft).

			Regular Season					Playoffs				
Season	Club	Lea	GP	G	A	TP	PIM	GP	G	A	TP	PIM
1983-84	North Dakota	WCHA	32	2	7	9	8	....	....	....	....	....
1984-85	North Dakota	WCHA	40	4	26	30	26	....	....	....	....	....
1985-86	North Dakota	WCHA	40	6	29	35	26	....	....	....	....	....
	Winnipeg	**NHL**	**13**	**1**	**0**	**1**	**10**	**3**	**0**	**0**	**0**	**0**
1986-87	**Winnipeg**	**NHL**	**52**	**2**	**8**	**10**	**60**	**7**	**0**	**1**	**1**	**14**
1987-88	**Winnipeg**	**NHL**	**48**	**0**	**6**	**6**	**75**	....	....	....	....	....
	Moncton	AHL	10	1	3	4	14	....	....	....	....	....
1988-89	**Winnipeg**	**NHL**	**38**	**0**	**9**	**9**	**45**	....	....	....	....	....
	Moncton	AHL	38	3	16	19	39	....	....	....	....	....
1989-90	**Winnipeg**	**NHL**	**12**	**1**	**2**	**3**	**6**	**1**	**0**	**0**	**0**	**0**
	Moncton	AHL	38	1	9	10	58	....	....	....	....	....
1990-91	Brynas	Swe.	38	3	1	4	38	....	....	....	....	....
1991-92	**Minnesota**	**NHL**	**7**	**0**	**0**	**0**	**6**	**2**	**0**	**0**	**0**	**2**
	Kalamazoo	IHL	65	5	18	23	90	5	2	0	2	6
1992-93	**Minnesota**	**NHL**	**63**	**0**	**3**	**3**	**109**	....	....	....	....	....
	NHL Totals		**233**	**4**	**28**	**32**	**311**	**13**	**0**	**1**	**1**	**16**

Signed as a free agent by **Minnesota**, October 4, 1991.

BERTUZZI, TODD

Center. Shoots left. 6'3", 227 lbs. Born, Sudbury, Ont., February 2, 1975.
(NY Islanders' 1st choice, 23rd overall, in 1993 Entry Draft).

			Regular Season					Playoffs				
Season	Club	Lea	GP	G	A	TP	PIM	GP	G	A	TP	PIM
1991-92	Guelph	OHL	47	7	14	21	145	....	....	....	....	....
1992-93	Guelph	OHL	59	27	32	59	164	5	2	2	4	6

BERUBE, CRAIG (buh-ROO-bee)

Left wing. Shoots left. 6'1", 205 lbs. Born, Calahoo, Alta., December 17, 1965.

			Regular Season					Playoffs				
Season	Club	Lea	GP	G	A	TP	PIM	GP	G	A	TP	PIM
1982-83	Kamloops	WHL	4	0	0	0	0	....	....	....	....	....
1983-84	N. Westminster	WHL	70	11	20	31	104	8	1	2	3	5
1984-85	N. Westminster	WHL	70	25	44	69	191	10	3	2	5	4
1985-86	Kamloops	WHL	32	17	14	31	119	....	....	....	....	....
	Medicine Hat	WHL	34	14	16	30	95	25	7	8	15	102
1986-87	**Philadelphia**	**NHL**	**7**	**0**	**0**	**0**	**57**	**5**	**0**	**0**	**0**	**17**
	Hershey	AHL	63	7	17	24	325	....	....	....	....	....
1987-88	**Philadelphia**	**NHL**	**27**	**3**	**2**	**5**	**108**	....	....	....	....	....
	Hershey	AHL	31	5	9	14	119	....	....	....	....	....
1988-89	**Philadelphia**	**NHL**	**53**	**1**	**1**	**2**	**199**	**16**	**0**	**0**	**0**	**56**
	Hershey	AHL	7	0	2	2	19	....	....	....	....	....
1989-90	**Philadelphia**	**NHL**	**74**	**4**	**14**	**18**	**291**	....	....	....	....	....
1990-91	**Philadelphia**	**NHL**	**74**	**8**	**9**	**17**	**293**	....	....	....	....	....
1991-92	**Toronto**	**NHL**	**40**	**5**	**7**	**12**	**109**	....	....	....	....	....
	Calgary	**NHL**	**36**	**1**	**4**	**5**	**155**	....	....	....	....	....
1992-93	**Calgary**	**NHL**	**77**	**4**	**8**	**12**	**209**	**6**	**0**	**1**	**1**	**21**
	NHL Totals		**388**	**26**	**45**	**71**	**1421**	**27**	**0**	**1**	**1**	**94**

Signed as a free agent by **Philadelphia**, March 19, 1986. Traded to **Edmonton** by **Philadelphia** with Craig Fisher and Scott Mellanby for Dave Brown, Corey Foster and Jari Kurri, May 30, 1991. Traded to **Toronto** by **Edmonton** with Grant Fuhr and Glenn Anderson for Vincent Damphousse, Peter Ing, Scott Thornton, Luke Richardson, future considerations and cash, September 19, 1991. Traded to **Calgary** by **Toronto** with Alexander Godynyuk, Gary Leeman, Michel Petit and Jeff Reese for Doug Gilmour, Jamie Macoun, Ric Nattress, Rick Wamsley and Kent Manderville, January 2, 1992. Traded to **Washington** by **Calgary** for Washington's fifth round choice (Darryl Lafrance) in 1993 Entry Draft, June 26, 1993.

BES, JEFF

Center. Shoots left. 6', 186 lbs. Born, Tillsonburg, Ont., July 31, 1973.
(Minnesota's 2nd choice, 58th overall, in 1992 Entry Draft).

			Regular Season					Playoffs				
Season	Club	Lea	GP	G	A	TP	PIM	GP	G	A	TP	PIM
1990-91	Hamilton	OHL	66	23	47	70	53	4	1	4	5	4
1991-92	Guelph	OHL	62	40	62	102	123	....	....	....	....	....
1992-93	Guelph	OHL	59	48	67	115	128	5	3	5	8	4
	Kalamazoo	IHL	3	1	3	4	6	....	....	....	....	....

BETS, MAXIM

Left wing. Shoots left. 6', 192 lbs. Born, Chelyabinsk, Soviet Union, January 31, 1974.
(St. Louis' 1st choice, 37th overall, in 1993 Entry Draft).

			Regular Season					Playoffs				
Season	Club	Lea	GP	G	A	TP	PIM	GP	G	A	TP	PIM
1991-92	Chelyabinsk	CIS	25	1	1	2	8	....	....	....	....	....
1992-93	Spokane	WHL	54	49	67	106	130	9	5	6	11	20

BEUKEBOOM, JEFF (BOO-kuh-BOOM)

Defense. Shoots right. 6'5", 225 lbs. Born, Ajax, Ont., March 28, 1965.
(Edmonton's 1st choice, 19th overall, in 1983 Entry Draft).

			Regular Season					Playoffs				
Season	Club	Lea	GP	G	A	TP	PIM	GP	G	A	TP	PIM
1982-83	S.S. Marie	OHL	70	0	25	25	143	16	1	4	5	46
1983-84	S.S. Marie	OHL	61	6	30	36	178	16	1	7	8	43
1984-85a	S.S. Marie	OHL	37	4	20	24	85	16	4	6	10	47
1985-86	Nova Scotia	AHL	77	9	20	29	175	....	....	....	....	....
	Edmonton	**NHL**	....	....	....	....	....	**1**	**0**	**0**	**0**	**4**
1986-87	**Edmonton**	**NHL**	**44**	**3**	**8**	**11**	**124**	....	....	....	....	....
	Nova Scotia	AHL	14	1	7	8	35	....	....	....	....	....
1987-88	**Edmonton**	**NHL**	**73**	**5**	**20**	**25**	**201**	**7**	**0**	**0**	**0**	**16**
1988-89	**Edmonton**	**NHL**	**36**	**0**	**5**	**5**	**94**	**1**	**0**	**0**	**0**	**2**
	Cape Breton	AHL	8	0	4	4	36	....	....	....	....	....
1989-90	**Edmonton**	**NHL**	**46**	**1**	**12**	**13**	**86**	**2**	**0**	**0**	**0**	**0**
1990-91	**Edmonton**	**NHL**	**67**	**3**	**7**	**10**	**150**	**18**	**1**	**3**	**4**	**28**
1991-92	**Edmonton**	**NHL**	**18**	**0**	**5**	**5**	**78**	....	....	....	....	....
	NY Rangers	**NHL**	**56**	**1**	**10**	**11**	**122**	**13**	**2**	**3**	**5**	**47**
1992-93	**NY Rangers**	**NHL**	**82**	**2**	**17**	**19**	**153**	....	....	....	....	....
	NHL Totals		**422**	**15**	**84**	**99**	**1008**	**42**	**3**	**6**	**9**	**97**

a OHL First All-Star Team (1985)

Traded to **NY Rangers** by **Edmonton** for David Shaw, November 12, 1991.

BICANEK, RADIM (BEE-chah-nehk)

Defense. Shoots left. 6'1", 178 lbs. Born, Uherske Hradiste, Czech., January 18, 1975.
(Ottawa's 2nd choice, 27th overall, in 1993 Entry Draft).

			Regular Season					Playoffs				
Season	Club	Lea	GP	G	A	TP	PIM	GP	G	A	TP	PIM
1992-93	Dukla Jihlava	Czech.	43	2	3	5	....	....	....	....	....	....

BIGGS, DON

Center. Shoots right. 5'8", 185 lbs. Born, Mississauga, Ont., April 7, 1965.
(Minnesota's 9th choice, 156th overall, in 1983 Entry Draft).

			Regular Season					Playoffs				
Season	Club	Lea	GP	G	A	TP	PIM	GP	G	A	TP	PIM
1982-83	Oshawa	OHL	70	22	53	75	145	16	3	6	9	17
1983-84	Oshawa	OHL	58	31	60	91	149	7	4	4	8	18
1984-85	**Minnesota**	**NHL**	**1**	**0**	**0**	**0**	**0**	....	....	....	....	....
	Springfield	AHL	6	0	3	3	0	2	1	0	1	0
	Oshawa	OHL	60	48	69	117	105	5	3	4	7	6
1985-86	Springfield	AHL	28	15	16	31	46	....	....	....	....	....
	Nova Scotia	AHL	47	6	23	29	36	....	....	....	....	....
1986-87	Nova Scotia	AHL	80	22	25	47	165	5	1	2	3	4
1987-88	Hershey	AHL	77	38	41	79	151	12	5	*11	*16	22
1988-89	Hershey	AHL	76	36	67	103	158	11	5	9	14	30
1989-90	**Philadelphia**	**NHL**	**11**	**2**	**0**	**2**	**8**	....	....	....	....	....
	Hershey	AHL	66	39	53	92	125	....	....	....	....	....
1990-91	Rochester	AHL	65	31	57	88	115	15	9	*14	*23	14
1991-92	Binghamton	AHL	74	32	50	82	122	11	3	7	10	8
1992-93abc	Binghamton	AHL	78	54	*84	*138	112	14	3	9	12	32
	NHL Totals		**12**	**2**	**0**	**2**	**8**	....	....	....	....	....

a Won Les Cunningham Plaque (AHL MVP) (1993)
b Won John B. Sollenberger Trophy (AHL Leading Scorer) (1993)
c AHL First All-Star Team (1993)

Traded to **Edmonton** by **Minnesota** with Gord Sherven for Marc Habscheid, Don Barber and Emanuel Viveiros, December 20, 1985. Signed as a free agent by **Philadelphia**, July 17, 1987. Traded to **NY Rangers** by **Philadelphia** for future considerations, August 8, 1991.

BILODEAU, BRENT

Defense. Shoots left. 6'4", 215 lbs. Born, Dallas, TX, March 27, 1973.
(Montreal's 1st choice, 17th overall, in 1991 Entry Draft).

			Regular Season					Playoffs				
Season	Club	Lea	GP	G	A	TP	PIM	GP	G	A	TP	PIM
1989-90	Seattle	WHL	68	14	29	43	170	13	3	5	8	31
1990-91	Seattle	WHL	55	7	18	25	145	6	1	0	1	12
1991-92a	Seattle	WHL	7	1	2	3	43	....	....	....	....	....
	Swift Current	WHL	56	10	47	57	118	8	2	3	5	11
1992-93a	Swift Current	WHL	59	11	57	68	77	17	5	14	19	18

a WHL East Second All-Star Team (1992, 1993)

BIONDI, JOSEPH

Center. Shoots left. 6'1", 175 lbs. Born, Warroad, MN, June 25, 1970.
(Minnesota's 9th choice, 176th overall, in 1990 Entry Draft).

			Regular Season					Playoffs				
Season	Club	Lea	GP	G	A	TP	PIM	GP	G	A	TP	PIM
1989-90	Minn.-Duluth	WCHA	37	10	17	27	8	....	....	....	....	....
1990-91	Minn.-Duluth	WCHA	30	6	8	14	4	....	....	....	....	....
1991-92	Minn.-Duluth	WCHA	34	8	6	14	10	....	....	....	....	....
1992-93	Minn. Duluth	WCHA	40	15	18	33	24	....	....	....	....	....

BJUGSTAD, SCOTT (BYOOG-stad)

Right wing. Shoots left. 6'1", 185 lbs. Born, St. Paul, MN, June 2, 1961.
(Minnesota's 13th choice, 181st overall, in 1981 Entry Draft).

			Regular Season					Playoffs				
Season	Club	Lea	GP	G	A	TP	PIM	GP	G	A	TP	PIM
1979-80	U. Minnesota	WCHA	18	2	2	4	2	....	....	....	....	....
1980-81	U. Minnesota	WCHA	35	12	23	25	34	....	....	....	....	....
1981-82	U. Minnesota	WCHA	36	29	14	43	24	....	....	....	....	....
1982-83a	U. Minnesota	WCHA	26	21	35	56	12	....	....	....	....	....
1983-84	U.S. National	....	54	31	20	51	28	....	....	....	....	....
	U.S. Olympic	....	6	3	2	5	6	....	....	....	....	....
	Minnesota	**NHL**	**5**	**0**	**0**	**0**	**2**	....	....	....	....	....
	Salt Lake	CHL	15	10	8	18	6	5	3	4	7	0
1984-85	**Minnesota**	**NHL**	**72**	**11**	**4**	**15**	**32**	....	....	....	....	....
	Springfield	AHL	5	2	3	5	2	....	....	....	....	....
1985-86	**Minnesota**	**NHL**	**80**	**43**	**33**	**76**	**24**	**5**	**0**	**1**	**1**	**0**
1986-87	**Minnesota**	**NHL**	**39**	**4**	**9**	**13**	**43**	....	....	....	....	....
	Springfield	AHL	11	4	6	10	7	....	....	....	....	....
1987-88	**Minnesota**	**NHL**	**33**	**10**	**12**	**22**	**15**	....	....	....	....	....
1988-89	**Pittsburgh**	**NHL**	**24**	**3**	**0**	**3**	**4**	....	....	....	....	....
	Kalamazoo	IHL	4	5	0	5	4	....	....	....	....	....
1989-90	**Los Angeles**	**NHL**	**11**	**1**	**2**	**3**	**2**	**2**	**0**	**0**	**0**	**2**
	New Haven	AHL	47	45	21	66	40	....	....	....	....	....
1990-91	**Los Angeles**	**NHL**	**31**	**2**	**4**	**6**	**12**	**2**	**0**	**0**	**0**	**0**
	Phoenix	IHL	3	7	2	9	2	....	....	....	....	....
1991-92	**Los Angeles**	**NHL**	**22**	**2**	**4**	**6**	**10**	....	....	....	....	....
	Phoenix	IHL	28	14	14	28	12	....	....	....	....	....
1992-93	Phoenix	IHL	7	5	4	9	4	....	....	....	....	....
	NHL Totals		**317**	**76**	**68**	**144**	**144**	**9**	**0**	**1**	**1**	**2**

a WCHA First All-Star Team (1983)

Traded to **Pittsburgh** by **Minnesota** with Gord Dineen for Ville Siren and Steve Gotaas, December 17, 1988. Signed as a free agent by **Los Angeles**, August 21, 1989.

BLACK, JAMES

Center. Shoots left. 5'11", 185 lbs. Born, Regina, Sask., August 15, 1969.
(Hartford's 4th choice, 94th overall, in 1989 Entry Draft).

			Regular Season					Playoffs				
Season	Club	Lea	GP	G	A	TP	PIM	GP	G	A	TP	PIM
1987-88	Portland	WHL	72	30	50	80	50	....	....	....	....	....
1988-89	Portland	WHL	71	45	51	96	57	19	13	6	19	28
1989-90	**Hartford**	**NHL**	**1**	**0**	**0**	**0**	**0**	....	....	....	....	....
	Binghamton	AHL	80	37	35	72	34	....	....	....	....	....
1990-91	**Hartford**	**NHL**	**1**	**0**	**0**	**0**	**0**	....	....	....	....	....
	Springfield	AHL	79	35	61	96	34	18	9	9	18	6
1991-92	**Hartford**	**NHL**	**30**	**4**	**6**	**10**	**10**	....	....	....	....	....
	Springfield	AHL	47	15	25	40	33	10	3	2	5	18
1992-93	**Minnesota**	**NHL**	**10**	**2**	**1**	**3**	**4**	....	....	....	....	....
	Kalamazoo	IHL	63	25	45	70	40	....	....	....	....	....
	NHL Totals		**42**	**6**	**7**	**13**	**14**	....	....	....	....	....

Traded to **Minnesota** by **Hartford** for Mark Janssens, September 3, 1992.

BLACK, RYAN

Left wing. Shoots left. 6'1", 180 lbs. Born, Guelph, Ont., October 25, 1973.
(New Jersey's 6th choice, 114th overall, in 1992 Entry Draft).

			Regular Season					Playoffs				
Season	Club	Lea	GP	G	A	TP	PIM	GP	G	A	TP	PIM
1990-91	Peterborough	OHL	59	7	16	23	41	4	0	1	1	0
1991-92	Peterborough	OHL	66	18	33	51	57	7	1	1	2	11
1992-93	Peterborough	OHL	66	30	41	71	43	20	7	4	11	28

BLAIN, JOEL

Left wing. Shoots left. 6', 195 lbs. Born, Malartic, Que., October 12, 1971.
(Edmonton's 4th choice, 67th overall, in 1990 Entry Draft).

			Regular Season					Playoffs				
Season	Club	Lea	GP	G	A	TP	PIM	GP	G	A	TP	PIM
1989-90	Hull	QMJHL	65	31	47	78	137	11	6	6	12	16
1990-91	Hull	QMJHL	61	19	31	50	95	6	4	3	7	17
1991-92	Hull	QMJHL	60	24	35	59	146	6	4	2	6	27
1992-93	Wheeling	ECHL	29	5	9	14	29	14	3	2	5	18

BLAKE, ROBERT (ROB)

Defense. Shoots right. 6'3", 215 lbs. Born, Simcoe, Ont., December 10, 1969.
(Los Angeles' 4th choice, 70th overall, in 1988 Entry Draft).

			Regular Season					Playoffs				
Season	Club	Lea	GP	G	A	TP	PIM	GP	G	A	TP	PIM
1987-88	Bowling Green	CCHA	43	5	8	13	88	....	....	....	....	....
1988-89a	Bowling Green	CCHA	46	11	21	32	140	....	....	....	....	....
1989-90bc	Bowling Green	CCHA	42	23	36	59	140	....	....	....	....	....
	Los Angeles	**NHL**	**4**	**0**	**0**	**0**	**4**	**8**	**1**	**3**	**4**	**4**
1990-91d	**Los Angeles**	**NHL**	**75**	**12**	**34**	**46**	**125**	**12**	**1**	**4**	**5**	**26**
1991-92	**Los Angeles**	**NHL**	**57**	**7**	**13**	**20**	**102**	**6**	**2**	**1**	**3**	**12**
1992-93	**Los Angeles**	**NHL**	**76**	**16**	**43**	**59**	**152**	**23**	**4**	**6**	**10**	**46**
	NHL Totals		**212**	**35**	**90**	**125**	**383**	**49**	**8**	**14**	**22**	**88**

a CCHA Second All-Star Team (1989)
b CCHA First All-Star Team (1990)
c NCAA West First All-American Team (1990)
d NHL/Upper Deck All-Rookie Team (1991)

BLOEMBERG, JEFF (BLOOM-buhrg)

Defense. Shoots right. 6'2", 205 lbs. Born, Listowel, Ont., January 31, 1968.
(NY Rangers' 5th choice, 93rd overall, in 1986 Entry Draft).

			Regular Season					Playoffs				
Season	Club	Lea	GP	G	A	TP	PIM	GP	G	A	TP	PIM
1985-86	North Bay	OHL	60	2	11	13	76	8	1	2	3	9
1986-87	North Bay	OHL	60	5	13	18	91	21	1	6	7	13
1987-88	Colorado	IHL	5	0	0	0	0	11	1	0	1	8
	North Bay	OHL	46	9	26	35	60	4	1	4	5	2
1988-89	**NY Rangers**	**NHL**	**9**	**0**	**0**	**0**	**0**	....	....	....	....	....
	Denver	IHL	64	7	22	29	55	1	0	0	0	0
1989-90	**NY Rangers**	**NHL**	**28**	**3**	**3**	**6**	**25**	**7**	**0**	**3**	**3**	**5**
	Flint	IHL	41	7	14	21	24	....	....	....	....	....
1990-91	**NY Rangers**	**NHL**	**3**	**0**	**2**	**2**	**0**	....	....	....	....	....
a	Binghamton	AHL	77	16	46	62	28	10	0	6	6	10
1991-92	**NY Rangers**	**NHL**	**3**	**0**	**1**	**1**	**0**	....	....	....	....	....
	Binghamton	AHL	66	6	41	47	22	11	1	10	11	10
1992-93	Cape Breton	AHL	76	6	45	51	34	16	5	10	15	10
	NHL Totals		**43**	**3**	**6**	**9**	**25**	**7**	**0**	**3**	**3**	**5**

a AHL Second All-Star Team (1991)

Claimed by **Tampa Bay** from **NY Rangers** in Expansion Draft, June 18, 1992. Traded to **Edmonton** by **Tampa Bay** for future considerations, September 25, 1992. Signed as a free agent by **Hartford**, August 9, 1993.

BLOMSTEN, ARTO (BLOOM-stehn)

Defense. Shoots left. 6'3", 198 lbs. Born, Vaasa, Finland, March 16, 1965.
(Winnipeg's 11th choice, 239th overall, in 1986 Entry Draft).

			Regular Season					Playoffs				
Season	Club	Lea	GP	G	A	TP	PIM	GP	G	A	TP	PIM
1983-84	Djurgarden	Swe.	3	0	0	0	4	....	....	....	....	....
1984-85	Djurgarden	Swe.	19	3	1	4	22	8	0	0	0	8
1985-86	Djurgarden	Swe.	8	0	3	3	6	....	....	....	....	....
1986-87	Djurgarden	Swe.	29	2	4	6	28	....	....	....	....	....
1987-88	Djurgarden	Swe.	39	12	6	18	36	2	1	0	1	0
1988-89	Djurgarden	Swe.	40	10	9	19	38	....	....	....	....	....
1989-90	Djurgarden	Swe.	36	5	21	26	28	8	0	1	1	6
1990-91	Djurgarden	Swe.	38	2	9	11	38	7	2	1	3	12
1991-92	Djurgarden	Swe.	39	6	8	14	34	10	2	0	2	8
1992-93	Djurgarden	Swe.	40	4	16	20	52	....	....	....	....	....

BLOUIN, JEAN

Left wing. Shoots left. 6', 195 lbs. Born, Montreal, Que., February 26, 1971.

			Regular Season					Playoffs				
Season	Club	Lea	GP	G	A	TP	PIM	GP	G	A	TP	PIM
1990-91	Laval	QMJHL	43	31	26	57	56	....	....	....	....	....
1991-92	Laval	QMJHL	25	27	21	48	44	10	5	8	13	41
1992-93	Atlanta	IHL	61	11	11	22	69	....	....	....	....	....

Signed as a free agent by **Tampa Bay**, July 10, 1992.

BOBACK, MICHAEL

Center. Shoots right. 5'11", 180 lbs. Born, Mt. Clemens, MI, August 13, 1970.
(Washington's 12th choice, 198th overall, in 1990 Entry Draft).

			Regular Season					Playoffs				
Season	Club	Lea	GP	G	A	TP	PIM	GP	G	A	TP	PIM
1988-89	Providence	H.E.	38	21	27	48	26	....	....	....	....	....
1989-90a	Providence	H.E.	31	13	29	42	28	....	....	....	....	....
1990-91	Providence	H.E.	26	15	24	39	6	....	....	....	....	....
1991-92b	Providence	H.E.	36	24	*48	*72	34	....	....	....	....	....
1992-93	Baltimore	AHL	69	11	68	79	14	5	3	3	6	6

a Hockey East Second All-Star Team (1990)
b Hockey East First All-Star Team (1992)

BODE, JAMES

Right wing. Shoots right. 5'11", 183 lbs. Born, Robbinsdale, MN, July 26, 1973.
(Philadelphia's 9th choice, 182nd overall, in 1991 Entry Draft).

			Regular Season					Playoffs				
Season	Club	Lea	GP	G	A	TP	PIM	GP	G	A	TP	PIM
1991-92	Armstrong	HS	24	19	21	40	....	....	....	....	....	....
1992-93	Des Moines	USHL	26	9	7	16	26	....	....	....	....	....

BODGER, DOUG

Defense. Shoots left. 6'2", 213 lbs. Born, Chemainus, B.C., June 18, 1966.
(Pittsburgh's 2nd choice, 9th overall, in 1984 Entry Draft).

			Regular Season					Playoffs				
Season	Club	Lea	GP	G	A	TP	PIM	GP	G	A	TP	PIM
1982-83a	Kamloops	WHL	72	26	66	92	98	7	0	5	5	2
1983-84	Kamloops	WHL	70	21	77	98	90	17	2	15	17	12
1984-85	**Pittsburgh**	**NHL**	**65**	**5**	**26**	**31**	**67**	....	....	....	....	....
1985-86	**Pittsburgh**	**NHL**	**79**	**4**	**33**	**37**	**63**	....	....	....	....	....
1986-87	**Pittsburgh**	**NHL**	**76**	**11**	**38**	**49**	**52**	....	....	....	....	....
1987-88	**Pittsburgh**	**NHL**	**69**	**14**	**31**	**45**	**103**	....	....	....	....	....
1988-89	**Pittsburgh**	**NHL**	**10**	**1**	**4**	**5**	**7**	....	....	....	....	....
	Buffalo	**NHL**	**61**	**7**	**40**	**47**	**52**	**5**	**1**	**1**	**2**	**11**
1989-90	**Buffalo**	**NHL**	**71**	**12**	**36**	**48**	**64**	**6**	**1**	**5**	**6**	**6**
1990-91	**Buffalo**	**NHL**	**58**	**5**	**23**	**28**	**54**	**4**	**0**	**1**	**1**	**0**
1991-92	**Buffalo**	**NHL**	**73**	**11**	**35**	**46**	**108**	**7**	**2**	**1**	**3**	**2**
1992-93	**Buffalo**	**NHL**	**81**	**9**	**45**	**54**	**87**	**8**	**2**	**3**	**5**	**0**
	NHL Totals		**643**	**79**	**311**	**390**	**657**	**30**	**6**	**11**	**17**	**19**

a WHL Second All-Star Team (1983)

Traded to **Buffalo** by **Pittsburgh** wih Darrin Shannon for Tom Barrasso and Buffalo's third round choice (Joe Dziedzic) in 1990 Entry Draft, November 12, 1988.

BODKIN, RICK

Center. Shoots left. 6'4", 179 lbs. Born, Hamilton, Ont., March 30, 1975.
(Ottawa's 5th choice, 131st overall, in 1993 Entry Draft).

			Regular Season					Playoffs				
Season	Club	Lea	GP	G	A	TP	PIM	GP	G	A	TP	PIM
1991-92	Grimsby	OHA Jr. C	36	11	17	28	44	....	....	....	....	....
1992-93	Sudbury	OHL	50	4	4	8	17	11	0	0	0	0

BODNARCHUK, MICHAEL

Right wing. Shoots right. 6'1", 175 lbs. Born, Bramalea, Ont., March 26, 1970.
(New Jersey's 6th choice, 64th overall, in 1990 Entry Draft).

			Regular Season					Playoffs				
Season	Club	Lea	GP	G	A	TP	PIM	GP	G	A	TP	PIM
1988-89	Kingston	OHL	63	22	38	60	30	....	....	....	....	....
1989-90a	Kingston	OHL	66	41	59	100	31	....	....	....	....	....
1990-91	Utica	AHL	69	23	32	55	28	....	....	....	....	....
1991-92	Utica	AHL	76	21	19	40	36	4	0	2	2	0
1992-93	Cincinnati	IHL	47	15	18	33	65	....	....	....	....	....
	Utica	AHL	21	6	10	16	4	4	2	0	2	4

a OHL Second All-Star Team (1990)

BOH, AARON

Defense. Shoots left. 6'2", 177 lbs. Born, Lethbridge, Alta., April 4, 1974.
(Vancouver's 12th choice, 261st overall, in 1992 Entry Draft).

			Regular Season					Playoffs				
Season	Club	Lea	GP	G	A	TP	PIM	GP	G	A	TP	PIM
1991-92	Spokane	WHL	59	3	19	22	213	8	0	2	2	17
1992-93	Medicine Hat	WHL	73	9	31	40	235	10	0	4	4	27

BOILEAU, PATRICK

Defense. Shoots right. 6', 184 lbs. Born, Montreal, Que., February 22, 1975.
(Washington's 3rd choice, 69th overall, in 1993 Entry Draft).

			Regular Season					Playoffs				
Season	Club	Lea	GP	G	A	TP	PIM	GP	G	A	TP	PIM
1991-92	Laval	Midget	42	9	36	45	94	....	....	....	....	....
1992-93	Laval	QMJHL	69	4	19	23	73	13	1	2	3	10

BOIVIN, CLAUDE

Left wing. Shoots left. 6'2", 200 lbs. Born, Ste. Foy, Que., March 1, 1970.
(Philadelphia's 1st choice, 14th overall, in 1988 Entry Draft).

			Regular Season					Playoffs				
Season	Club	Lea	GP	G	A	TP	PIM	GP	G	A	TP	PIM
1987-88	Drummondville	QMJHL	63	23	26	49	233	17	5	3	8	74
1988-89	Drummondville	QMJHL	63	20	36	56	218	4	0	2	2	27
1989-90	Laval	QMJHL	59	24	51	75	309	13	7	13	20	59
1990-91	Hershey	AHL	65	13	32	45	159	7	1	5	6	28
1991-92	**Philadelphia**	**NHL**	**58**	**5**	**13**	**18**	**187**	....	....	....	....	....
	Hershey	AHL	20	4	5	9	96	....	....	....	....	....
1992-93	**Philadelphia**	**NHL**	**30**	**5**	**4**	**9**	**76**	....	....	....	....	....
	NHL Totals		**88**	**10**	**17**	**27**	**263**	....	....	....	....	....

BOLDIN, IGOR

Center. Shoots left. 5'11", 174 lbs. Born, Moscow, Soviet Union, February 2, 1964.
(St. Louis' 8th choice, 180th overall, in 1992 Entry Draft).

			Regular Season					Playoffs				
Season	Club	Lea	GP	G	A	TP	PIM	GP	G	A	TP	PIM
1981-82	Spartak	USSR	3	1	0	1	0	....	....	....	....	....
1982-83	Spartak	USSR	41	14	8	22	4	....	....	....	....	....
1983-84	Spartak	USSR	40	12	19	31	2	....	....	....	....	....
1984-85	Spartak	USSR	48	10	10	20	12	....	....	....	....	....
1985-86	Spartak	USSR	36	8	6	14	2	....	....	....	....	....
1986-87	Spartak	USSR	40	5	8	13	8	....	....	....	....	....
1987-88	Spartak	USSR	41	20	9	29	4	....	....	....	....	....
1988-89	Spartak	USSR	43	9	7	16	6	....	....	....	....	....
1989-90	Spartak	USSR	45	13	18	31	8	....	....	....	....	....
1990-91	Spartak	USSR	43	8	15	23	8	....	....	....	....	....
1991-92	Spartak	CIS	41	8	25	33	4	....	....	....	....	....
1992-93	Spartak	CIS	DID NOT PLAY									

BOMBARDIR, BRAD

Defense. Shoots left. 6'2", 190 lbs. Born, Powell River, B.C., May 5, 1972.
(New Jersey's 5th choice, 56th overall, in 1990 Entry Draft).

			Regular Season					Playoffs				
Season	Club	Lea	GP	G	A	TP	PIM	GP	G	A	TP	PIM
1990-91	North Dakota	WCHA	33	3	6	9	18	....	....	....	....	....
1991-92	North Dakota	WCHA	35	3	14	17	54	....	....	....	....	....
1992-93	North Dakota	WCHA	38	8	15	23	34	....	....	....	....	....

BONDRA, PETER

Right wing. Shoots left. 6', 200 lbs. Born, Lutsk, Soviet Union, February 7, 1968.
(Washington's 9th choice, 156th overall, in 1990 Entry Draft).

			Regular Season					Playoffs				
Season	Club	Lea	GP	G	A	TP	PIM	GP	G	A	TP	PIM
1986-87	VSZ Kosice	Czech.	32	4	5	9	24	....	....	....	....	....
1987-88	VSZ Kosice	Czech.	45	27	11	38	20	....	....	....	....	....
1988-89	VSZ Kosice	Czech.	40	30	10	40	20	....	....	....	....	....
1989-90	VSZ Kosice	Czech.	49	36	19	55	....	....	....	....	....	....
1990-91	**Washington**	**NHL**	**54**	**12**	**16**	**28**	**47**	**4**	**0**	**1**	**1**	**2**
1991-92	**Washington**	**NHL**	**71**	**28**	**28**	**56**	**42**	**7**	**6**	**2**	**8**	**4**
1992-93	**Washington**	**NHL**	**83**	**37**	**48**	**85**	**70**	**6**	**0**	**6**	**6**	**0**
	NHL Totals		**208**	**77**	**92**	**169**	**159**	**17**	**6**	**9**	**15**	**6**

Played in NHL All-Star Game (1993)

BONIN, BRIAN

Center. Shoots left. 5'9", 165 lbs. Born, White Bear Lake, MN, November 28, 1973.
(Pittsburgh's 9th choice, 211th overall, in 1992 Entry Draft).

			Regular Season					Playoffs				
Season	Club	Lea	GP	G	A	TP	PIM	GP	G	A	TP	PIM
1991-92	White Bear Lake	HS	23	22	35	57	8	....	....	....	....	....
1992-93	U. Minnesota	WCHA	38	10	18	28	10	....	....	....	....	....

BORDELEAU, SEBASTIEN

Center. Shoots right. 5'10", 176 lbs. Born, Vancouver, B.C., February 15, 1975.
(Montreal's 3rd choice, 73rd overall, in 1993 Entry Draft).

			Regular Season					Playoffs				
Season	Club	Lea	GP	G	A	TP	PIM	GP	G	A	TP	PIM
1991-92	Hull	QMJHL	62	26	32	58	91	5	0	3	3	23
1992-93	Hull	QMJHL	60	18	39	57	95	10	3	8	11	20

BORGO, RICHARD

Right wing. Shoots right. 5'11", 190 lbs. Born, Thunder Bay, Ont., September 25, 1970.
(Edmonton's 2nd choice, 36th overall, in 1989 Entry Draft).

			Regular Season					Playoffs				
Season	Club	Lea	GP	G	A	TP	PIM	GP	G	A	TP	PIM
1986-87	Kitchener	OHL	62	5	10	15	29	....	....	....	....	....
1987-88	Kitchener	OHL	64	24	22	46	81	4	0	4	4	0
1988-89	Kitchener	OHL	66	23	23	46	75	5	0	1	1	4
1989-90	Kitchener	OHL	32	13	22	35	43	17	5	5	10	10
1990-91	Kitchener	OHL	60	43	56	99	50	6	1	0	1	12
1991-92	Cape Breton	AHL	52	10	14	24	90	3	0	0	0	6
1992-93	Cape Breton	AHL	45	7	13	20	26	1	0	0	0	2

BORSATO, LUCIANO

Center. Shoots right. 5'11", 190 lbs. Born, Richmond Hill, Ont., January 7, 1966.
(Winnipeg's 7th choice, 135th overall, in 1984 Entry Draft).

			Regular Season					Playoffs				
Season	Club	Lea	GP	G	A	TP	PIM	GP	G	A	TP	PIM
1984-85	Clarkson	ECAC	33	15	17	32	37	....	....	....	....	....
1985-86	Clarkson	ECAC	28	14	17	31	44	....	....	....	....	....
1986-87	Clarkson	ECAC	31	16	41	57	55	....	....	....	....	....
1987-88ab	Clarkson	ECAC	33	15	29	44	38	....	....	....	....	....
	Moncton	AHL	3	1	1	2	0	....	....	....	....	....
1988-89	Moncton	AHL	6	2	5	7	4	....	....	....	....	....
	Tappara	Fin.	44	31	36	67	69	7	0	3	3	4
1989-90	Moncton	AHL	1	1	0	1	0	....	....	....	....	....
1990-91	**Winnipeg**	**NHL**	**1**	**0**	**1**	**1**	**2**	....	....	....	....	....
	Moncton	AHL	41	14	24	38	40	9	3	7	10	22
1991-92	**Winnipeg**	**NHL**	**56**	**15**	**21**	**36**	**45**	**1**	**0**	**0**	**0**	**0**
	Moncton	AHL	14	2	7	9	39	....	....	....	....	....
1992-93	**Winnipeg**	**NHL**	**67**	**15**	**20**	**35**	**38**	**6**	**1**	**0**	**1**	**4**
	NHL Totals		**124**	**30**	**42**	**72**	**85**	**7**	**1**	**0**	**1**	**4**

a ECAC Second All-Star Team (1988)
b NCAA East Second All-American Team (1988)

BORSCHEVSKY, NIKOLAI (bohr-SHEHV-skee)

Right wing. Shoots left. 5'9", 180 lbs. Born, Tomsk, Soviet Union, January 12, 1965.
(Toronto's 3rd choice, 77th overall, in 1992 Entry Draft).

			Regular Season					Playoffs				
Season	Club	Lea	GP	G	A	TP	PIM	GP	G	A	TP	PIM
1983-84	Moscow D'amo	USSR	34	4	5	9	4	....	....	....	....	....
1984-85	Moscow D'amo	USSR	34	5	9	14	6	....	....	....	....	....
1985-86	Moscow D'amo	USSR	31	6	4	10	4	....	....	....	....	....
1986-87	Moscow D'amo	USSR	28	1	4	5	8	....	....	....	....	....
1987-88	Moscow D'amo	USSR	37	11	7	18	6	....	....	....	....	....
1988-89	Moscow D'amo	USSR	43	7	8	15	18	....	....	....	....	....
1989-90	Spartak	USSR	48	17	25	42	8	....	....	....	....	....
1990-91	Spartak	USSR	45	19	16	35	16	....	....	....	....	....
1991-92	Spartak	CIS	40	25	14	39	16	....	....	....	....	....
1992-93	**Toronto**	**NHL**	**78**	**34**	**40**	**74**	**28**	**16**	**2**	**7**	**9**	**0**
	NHL Totals		**78**	**34**	**40**	**74**	**28**	**16**	**2**	**7**	**9**	**0**

BOSCHMAN, LAURIE JOSEPH (BOSH-man)

Center. Shoots left. 6', 185 lbs. Born, Major, Sask., June 4, 1960.
(Toronto's 1st choice, 9th overall, in 1979 Entry Draft).

			Regular Season					Playoffs				
Season	Club	Lea	GP	G	A	TP	PIM	GP	G	A	TP	PIM
1976-77	Brandon	WHL	3	0	1	1	0	12	1	1	2	17
1977-78	Brandon	WHL	72	42	57	99	227	8	2	5	7	45
1978-79a	Brandon	WHL	65	66	83	149	215	22	11	23	34	56
1979-80	Toronto	NHL	80	16	32	48	78	3	1	1	2	18
1980-81	Toronto	NHL	53	14	19	33	178	3	0	0	0	7
	New Brunswick	AHL	4	4	1	5	47	....	....	....	....	....
1981-82	Toronto	NHL	54	9	19	28	150	....	....	....	....	....
	Edmonton	NHL	11	2	3	5	37	3	0	1	1	4
1982-83	Edmonton	NHL	62	8	12	20	183	....	....	....	....	....
	Winnipeg	NHL	12	3	5	8	36	3	0	1	1	12
1983-84	Winnipeg	NHL	61	28	46	74	234	3	0	1	1	5
1984-85	Winnipeg	NHL	80	32	44	76	180	8	2	1	3	21
1985-86	Winnipeg	NHL	77	27	42	69	241	3	0	1	1	6
1986-87	Winnipeg	NHL	80	17	24	41	152	10	2	3	5	32
1987-88	Winnipeg	NHL	80	25	23	48	229	5	1	3	4	9
1988-89	Winnipeg	NHL	70	10	26	36	163	....	....	....	....	....
1989-90	Winnipeg	NHL	66	10	17	27	103	2	0	0	0	2
1990-91	New Jersey	NHL	78	11	9	20	79	7	1	1	2	16
1991-92	New Jersey	NHL	75	8	20	28	121	7	1	0	1	8
1992-93	Ottawa	NHL	70	9	7	16	101	....	....	....	....	....
	NHL Totals		1009	229	348	577	2265	57	8	13	21	140

a WHL First All-Star Team (1979)

Traded to **Edmonton** by **Toronto** for Walt Poddubny and Phil Drouilliard, March 8, 1982. Traded to **Winnipeg** by **Edmonton** for Willy Lindstrom, March 7, 1983. Traded to **New Jersey** by **Winnipeg** for Bob Brooke, September 6, 1990. Claimed by **Ottawa** from **New Jersey** in Expansion Draft, June 18, 1992.

BOSTON, SCOTT

Defense. Shoots right. 6'2", 180 lbs. Born, Ottawa, Ont., July 13, 1971.

			Regular Season					Playoffs				
Season	Club	Lea	GP	G	A	TP	PIM	GP	G	A	TP	PIM
1990-91	Belleville	OHL	66	12	39	51	70	6	1	2	3	6
1991-92a	Belleville	OHL	65	13	71	84	89	5	0	6	6	10
1992-93	Atlanta	IHL	76	2	17	19	75	2	0	0	0	0

a OHL First All-Star Team (1992)

Signed as a free agent by **Tampa Bay**, June 29, 1992.

BOUCHARD, JOEL

Defense. Shoots left. 6', 180 lbs. Born, Montreal, Que., January 23, 1974.
(Calgary's 7th choice, 129th overall, in 1992 Entry Draft).

			Regular Season					Playoffs				
Season	Club	Lea	GP	G	A	TP	PIM	GP	G	A	TP	PIM
1990-91	Longueuil	QMJHL	53	3	19	22	34	8	1	0	1	11
1991-92	Verdun	QMJHL	70	9	20	29	55	19	1	7	8	20
1992-93	Verdun	QMJHL	60	10	49	59	126	4	0	2	2	4

BOUCHER, PHILIPPE

Defense. Shoots right. 6'2", 189 lbs. Born, St. Apollinaire, Que., March 24, 1973.
(Buffalo's 1st choice, 13th overall, in 1991 Entry Draft).

			Regular Season					Playoffs				
Season	Club	Lea	GP	G	A	TP	PIM	GP	G	A	TP	PIM
1990-91ab	Granby	QMJHL	69	21	46	67	92	....	....	....	....	....
1991-92	Granby	QMJHL	49	22	37	59	47	....	....	....	....	....
b	Laval	QMJHL	16	7	11	18	36	10	5	6	11	8
1992-93	Buffalo	NHL	18	0	4	4	14	....	....	....	....	....
	Laval	QMJHL	16	12	15	27	37	13	6	15	21	12
	Rochester	AHL	5	4	3	7	8	3	0	1	1	2
	NHL Totals		18	0	4	4	14	....	....	....	....	....

a Canadian Major Junior Rookie of the Year (1991)
b QMJHL Second All-Star Team (1991, 1992)

BOUGHNER, BOB (BOOG-nuhr)

Defense. Shoots right. 6', 201 lbs. Born, Windsor, Ont., March 8, 1971.
(Detroit's 2nd choice, 32nd overall, in 1989 Entry Draft).

			Regular Season					Playoffs				
Season	Club	Lea	GP	G	A	TP	PIM	GP	G	A	TP	PIM
1988-89	S.S. Marie	OHL	64	6	15	21	182	....	....	....	....	....
1989-90	S.S. Marie	OHL	49	7	23	30	122	....	....	....	....	....
1990-91	S.S. Marie	OHL	64	13	33	46	156	14	2	9	11	35
1991-92	Toledo	ECHL	28	3	10	13	79	5	2	0	2	15
	Adirondack	AHL	1	0	0	0	7	....	....	....	....	....
1992-93	Adirondack	AHL	69	1	16	17	190	....	....	....	....	....

BOURQUE, PHILLIPPE RICHARD (PHIL) (BOHRK)

Left wing. Shoots left. 6'1", 196 lbs. Born, Chelmsford, MA, June 8, 1962.

			Regular Season					Playoffs				
Season	Club	Lea	GP	G	A	TP	PIM	GP	G	A	TP	PIM
1980-81	Kingston	OHL	47	4	4	8	46	6	0	0	0	10
1981-82	Kingston	OHL	67	11	40	51	111	4	0	0	0	0
1982-83	Baltimore	AHL	65	1	15	16	93	....	....	....	....	....
1983-84	Pittsburgh	NHL	5	0	1	1	12	....	....	....	....	....
	Baltimore	AHL	58	5	17	22	96	....	....	....	....	....
1984-85	Baltimore	AHL	79	6	15	21	164	13	2	5	7	23
1985-86	Pittsburgh	NHL	4	0	0	0	2	....	....	....	....	....
	Baltimore	AHL	74	8	18	26	226	....	....	....	....	....
1986-87	Pittsburgh	NHL	22	2	3	5	32	....	....	....	....	....
	Baltimore	AHL	49	15	16	31	183	....	....	....	....	....
1987-88	Pittsburgh	NHL	21	4	12	16	20	....	....	....	....	....
ab	Muskegon	IHL	52	16	36	52	66	6	1	2	3	16
1988-89	Pittsburgh	NHL	80	17	26	43	97	11	4	1	5	66
1989-90	Pittsburgh	NHL	76	22	17	39	108	....	....	....	....	....
1990-91	Pittsburgh	NHL	78	20	14	34	106	24	6	7	13	16
1991-92	Pittsburgh	NHL	58	10	16	26	58	21	3	4	7	25
1992-93	NY Rangers	NHL	55	6	14	20	39	....	....	....	....	....
	NHL Totals		399	81	103	184	474	56	13	12	25	107

a IHL First All-Star Team (1988)
b Won Governor's Trophy (Outstanding Defenseman-IHL) (1988)

Signed as a free agent by **Pittsburgh**, October 4, 1982. Signed as a free agent by **NY Rangers**, August 31, 1992.

BOURQUE, RAYMOND JEAN (BOHRK)

Defense. Shoots left. 5'11", 215 lbs. Born, Montreal, Que., December 28, 1960.
(Boston's 1st choice, 8th overall, in 1979 Entry Draft).

			Regular Season					Playoffs				
Season	Club	Lea	GP	G	A	TP	PIM	GP	G	A	TP	PIM
1976-77	Sorel	QJHL	69	12	36	48	61	....	....	....	....	....
1977-78	Verdun	QJHL	72	22	57	79	90	4	2	1	3	0
1978-79	Verdun	QJHL	63	22	71	93	44	11	3	16	19	18
1979-80ab	Boston	NHL	80	17	48	65	73	10	2	9	11	27
1980-81c	Boston	NHL	67	27	29	56	96	3	0	1	1	2
1981-82b	Boston	NHL	65	17	49	66	51	9	1	5	6	16
1982-83c	Boston	NHL	65	22	51	73	20	17	8	15	23	10
1983-84b	Boston	NHL	78	31	65	96	57	3	0	2	2	0
1984-85b	Boston	NHL	73	20	66	86	53	5	0	3	3	4
1985-86c	Boston	NHL	74	19	58	77	68	3	0	0	0	0
1986-87bd	Boston	NHL	78	23	72	95	36	4	1	2	3	0
1987-88bd	Boston	NHL	78	17	64	81	72	23	3	18	21	26
1988-89c	Boston	NHL	60	18	43	61	52	10	0	4	4	6
1989-90bd	Boston	NHL	76	19	65	84	50	17	5	12	17	16
1990-91bd	Boston	NHL	76	21	73	94	75	19	7	18	25	12
1991-92be	Boston	NHL	80	21	60	81	56	12	3	6	9	12
1992-93b	Boston	NHL	78	19	63	82	40	4	1	0	1	2
	NHL Totals		1028	291	806	1097	799	139	31	95	126	133

a Won Calder Memorial Trophy (1980)
b NHL First All-Star Team (1980, 1982, 1984, 1985, 1987, 1988, 1990, 1991, 1992, 1993)
c NHL Second All-Star Team (1981, 1983, 1986, 1989)
d Won James Norris Memorial Trophy (1987, 1988, 1990, 1991)
e Won King Clancy Memorial Trophy (1992)

Played in NHL All-Star Game (1981-86, 1988-93)

BOWEN, CURTIS

Left wing. Shoots left. 6'1", 189 lbs. Born, Kenora, Ont., March 24, 1974.
(Detroit's 1st choice, 22nd overall, in 1992 Entry Draft).

			Regular Season					Playoffs				
Season	Club	Lea	GP	G	A	TP	PIM	GP	G	A	TP	PIM
1990-91	Ottawa	OHL	42	12	14	26	31	....	....	....	....	....
1991-92	Ottawa	OHL	65	31	45	76	94	11	3	7	10	11
1992-93	Ottawa	OHL	21	9	19	28	51	....	....	....	....	....

BOWEN, JASON

Defense. Shoots left. 6'4", 215 lbs. Born, Port Alice, B.C., November 11, 1973.
(Philadelphia's 2nd choice, 15th overall, in 1992 Entry Draft).

			Regular Season					Playoffs				
Season	Club	Lea	GP	G	A	TP	PIM	GP	G	A	TP	PIM
1989-90	Tri-City	WHL	61	8	5	13	129	7	0	3	3	4
1990-91	Tri-City	WHL	60	7	13	20	252	6	2	2	4	18
1991-92	Tri-City	WHL	19	5	3	8	135	5	0	1	1	42
1992-93	Philadelphia	NHL	7	1	0	1	2	....	....	....	....	....
	Tri-City	WHL	62	10	12	22	219	3	1	1	2	18
	NHL Totals		7	1	0	1	2	....	....	....	....	....

BOYER, ZAC

Right wing. Shoots right. 6'1", 185 lbs. Born, Inuvik, N.W.T., October 25, 1971.
(Chicago's 4th choice, 88th overall, in 1991 Entry Draft).

			Regular Season					Playoffs				
Season	Club	Lea	GP	G	A	TP	PIM	GP	G	A	TP	PIM
1988-89	Kamloops	WHL	42	10	17	27	22	....	....	....	....	....
1989-90	Kamloops	WHL	71	24	47	71	163	17	4	4	8	8
1990-91	Kamloops	WHL	64	45	60	105	58	12	6	10	16	8
1991-92	Kamloops	WHL	70	40	69	109	90	17	9	*20	*29	16
1992-93	Indianapolis	IHL	59	7	14	21	26	....	....	....	....	....

BOZON, PHILIPPE (boh-ZOHN)

Left wing. Shoots left. 5'10", 185 lbs. Born, Chamonix, France, November 30, 1966.

			Regular Season					Playoffs				
Season	Club	Lea	GP	G	A	TP	PIM	GP	G	A	TP	PIM
1984-85	St-Jean	QMJHL	67	32	50	82	82	5	0	5	5	4
1985-86a	St-Jean	QMJHL	65	59	52	111	72	10	10	6	16	16
	Peoria	IHL	....	....	....	....	....	5	1	0	1	0
1986-87	Peoria	IHL	28	4	11	15	17	....	....	....	....	....
	St-Jean	QMJHL	25	20	21	41	75	8	5	5	10	30
1987-88	Mont-Blanc	France	18	11	15	26	34	10	15	6	21	6
1988-89	Mont Blanc	France	18	11	18	29	18	11	11	17	28	38
1989-90	Grenoble	France	36	45	38	83	34	6	4	3	7	2
1990-91	Grenoble	France	26	22	16	38	16	10	7	8	15	8
1991-92	Chamonix	France	10	12	8	20	20	....	....	....	....	....
	St. Louis	NHL	9	1	3	4	4	6	1	0	1	27
1992-93	St. Louis	NHL	54	6	6	12	55	9	1	0	1	0
	Peoria	IHL	4	3	2	5	2	....	....	....	....	....
	NHL Totals		63	7	9	16	59	15	2	0	2	27

a QMJHL Second All-Star Team (1986)

Signed as a free agent by **St. Louis**, September 29, 1985.

BRADLEY, BRIAN WALTER RICHARD

Center. Shoots right. 5'10", 177 lbs. Born, Kitchener, Ont., January 21, 1965.
(Calgary's 2nd choice, 51st overall, in 1983 Entry Draft).

			Regular Season					Playoffs				
Season	Club	Lea	GP	G	A	TP	PIM	GP	G	A	TP	PIM
1982-83	London	OHL	67	37	82	119	37	3	1	0	1	0
1983-84	London	OHL	49	40	60	100	24	4	2	4	6	0
1984-85	London	OHL	32	27	49	76	22	8	5	10	15	4
1985-86	Calgary	NHL	5	0	1	1	0	1	0	0	0	0
	Moncton	AHL	59	23	42	65	40	10	6	9	15	4
1986-87	Calgary	NHL	40	10	18	28	16	....	....	....	....	....
	Moncton	AHL	20	12	16	28	8	....	....	....	....	....
1987-88	Cdn. National	....	47	18	19	37	42	....	....	....	....	....
	Cdn. Olympic	....	7	0	4	4	0	....	....	....	....	....
	Vancouver	NHL	11	3	5	8	6	....	....	....	....	....
1988-89	Vancouver	NHL	71	18	27	45	42	7	3	4	7	10
1989-90	Vancouver	NHL	67	19	29	48	65	....	....	....	....	....
1990-91	Vancouver	NHL	44	11	20	31	42	....	....	....	....	....
	Toronto	NHL	26	0	11	11	20	....	....	....	....	....
1991-92	Toronto	NHL	59	10	21	31	48	....	....	....	....	....
1992-93	Tampa Bay	NHL	80	42	44	86	92	....	....	....	....	....
	NHL Totals		403	113	176	289	331	8	3	4	7	10

Played in NHL All-Star Game (1993)

Traded to **Vancouver** by **Calgary** with Peter Bakovic and Kevin Guy for Craig Coxe, March 6, 1988. Traded to **Toronto** by **Vancouver** for Tom Kurvers, January 12, 1991. Claimed by **Tampa Bay** from **Toronto** in Expansion Draft, June 18, 1992.

BRADY, NEIL

Center. Shoots left. 6'2", 200 lbs. Born, Montreal, Que., April 12, 1968.
(New Jersey's 1st choice, 3rd overall, in 1986 Entry Draft).

			Regular Season					Playoffs				
Season	Club	Lea	GP	G	A	TP	PIM	GP	G	A	TP	PIM
1984-85	Calgary	Midget	37	25	50	75	75	....	....	....	....	....
	Medicine Hat	WHL	....	....	....	....	....	3	0	0	0	2
1985-86a	Medicine Hat	WHL	72	21	60	81	104	21	9	11	20	23
1986-87	Medicine Hat	WHL	57	19	64	83	126	18	1	4	5	25
1987-88	Medicine Hat	WHL	61	16	35	51	110	15	0	3	3	19
1988-89	Utica	AHL	75	16	21	37	56	4	0	3	3	0
1989-90	New Jersey	NHL	19	1	4	5	13	....	....	....	....	....
	Utica	AHL	38	10	13	23	21	5	0	1	1	10
1990-91	New Jersey	NHL	3	0	0	0	0	....	....	....	....	....
	Utica	AHL	77	33	63	96	91	....	....	....	....	....
1991-92	New Jersey	NHL	7	1	0	1	4	....	....	....	....	....
	Utica	AHL	33	12	30	42	28	....	....	....	....	....
1992-93	Ottawa	NHL	55	7	17	24	57	....	....	....	....	....
	New Haven	AHL	8	6	3	9	2	....	....	....	....	....
	NHL Totals		84	9	21	30	74	....	....	....	....	....

a WHL East Rookie of the Year (1986)

Traded to **Ottawa** by **New Jersey** for future considerations, September 3, 1992.

BRASHEAR, DONALD

Left wing. Shoots left. 6'3", 206 lbs. Born, Bedford, IN, January 7, 1972.

			Regular Season					Playoffs				
Season	Club	Lea	GP	G	A	TP	PIM	GP	G	A	TP	PIM
1989-90	Longueuil	QMJHL	64	12	14	26	169	7	0	0	0	11
1990-91	Longueuil	QMJHL	68	12	26	38	195	8	0	3	3	33
1991-92	Verdun	QMJHL	65	18	24	42	283	18	4	2	6	98
1992-93	Fredericton	AHL	76	11	3	14	261	5	0	0	0	8

Signed as a free agent by **Montreal**, July 28, 1992.

BRAZDA, RADOMIR (BRAHZ-duh)

Defense. Shoots right. 6'2", 185 lbs. Born, Pardubice, Czechoslovakia, October 11, 1967.
(Detroit's 6th choice, 95th overall, in 1987 Entry Draft).

			Regular Season					Playoffs				
Season	Club	Lea	GP	G	A	TP	PIM	GP	G	A	TP	PIM
1985-86	Pardubice	Czech.	28	0	0	0	....	....	....	....	....	....
1986-87	Pardubice	Czech.	40	1	1	2	22	....	....	....	....	....
1987-88	Pardubice	Czech.	19	3	2	5	28	....	....	....	....	....
1988-89	Dukla Trencin	Czech.	35	1	1	2	18	....	....	....	....	....
1989-90	Dukla Trencin	Czech.	21	2	1	3	....	....	....	....	....	....
	Pardubice	Czech.	5	0	0	0	....	....	....	....	....	....
1990-91	Pardubice	Czech.	40	5	11	16	24	....	....	....	....	....
1991-92	Pardubice	Czech.	42	4	9	13	70	....	....	....	....	....
1992-93	Hradec Kralove	Czech. 2	36	5	9	14	....	....	....	....	....	....

BREAULT, FRANCOIS

Right wing. Shoots left. 5'11", 185 lbs. Born, Acton Vale, Que., May 11, 1967.

			Regular Season					Playoffs				
Season	Club	Lea	GP	G	A	TP	PIM	GP	G	A	TP	PIM
1986-87	Granby	QMJHL	60	24	33	57	134	....	....	....	....	....
1987-88	Trois-Rivières	QMJHL	28	16	19	35	108	....	....	....	....	....
	Maine	AHL	11	0	1	1	37	....	....	....	....	....
1988-89	New Haven	AHL	68	21	24	45	51	....	....	....	....	....
1989-90	New Haven	AHL	37	17	21	38	33	....	....	....	....	....
1990-91	Los Angeles	NHL	17	1	4	5	6	....	....	....	....	....
1991-92	Los Angeles	NHL	6	1	0	1	30	....	....	....	....	....
	Phoenix	IHL	54	14	19	33	40	....	....	....	....	....
1992-93	Los Angeles	NHL	4	0	0	0	6	....	....	....	....	....
	Phoenix	IHL	31	5	11	16	26	....	....	....	....	....
	Utica	AHL	32	8	20	28	56	4	2	0	2	0
	NHL Totals		27	2	4	6	42	....	....	....	....	....

Signed as a free agent by **Los Angeles**, May 25, 1990.

BREEN, GEORGE

Right wing. Shoots right. 6'2", 200 lbs. Born, Webster, MA, August 3, 1973.
(Edmonton's 4th choice, 56th overall, in 1991 Entry Draft).

			Regular Season					Playoffs				
Season	Club	Lea	GP	G	A	TP	PIM	GP	G	A	TP	PIM
1991-92	Providence	H.E.	36	8	4	12	24	....	....	....	....	....
1992-93	Providence	H.E.	31	11	7	18	45	....	....	....	....	....

BREKKE, BRENT

Defense. Shoots left. 6'1", 175 lbs. Born, Minot, ND, August 16, 1971.
(Quebec's 9th choice, 188th overall, in 1991 Entry Draft).

			Regular Season					Playoffs				
Season	Club	Lea	GP	G	A	TP	PIM	GP	G	A	TP	PIM
1990-91	W. Michigan	CCHA	38	1	8	9	57	....	....	....	....	....
1991-92	W. Michigan	CCHA	36	1	10	11	68	....	....	....	....	....
1992-93	W. Michigan	CCHA	38	3	2	5	42	....	....	....	....	....

BRENNAN, RICHARD

Defense. Shoots right. 6'2", 200 lbs. Born, Schenectady, NY, November 26, 1972.
(Quebec's 3rd choice, 46th overall, in 1991 Entry Draft).

			Regular Season					Playoffs				
Season	Club	Lea	GP	G	A	TP	PIM	GP	G	A	TP	PIM
1991-92	Boston U.	H.E.	30	4	13	17	50	....	....	....	....	....
1992-93	Boston U.	H.E.	40	9	11	20	68	....	....	....	....	....

BRESLIN, TIM

Left wing. Shoots left. 6', 180 lbs. Born, Downers Grove, IL, December 8, 1967.

			Regular Season					Playoffs				
Season	Club	Lea	GP	G	A	TP	PIM	GP	G	A	TP	PIM
1987-88	Lake Superior	CCHA	38	6	13	19	16	....	....	....	....	....
1988-89	Lake Superior	CCHA	42	7	13	20	34	....	....	....	....	....
1989-90	Lake Superior	CCHA	46	8	17	25	20	....	....	....	....	....
1990-91	Lake Superior	CCHA	45	25	37	62	26	....	....	....	....	....
1991-92	Phoenix	IHL	45	8	21	29	12	....	....	....	....	....
1992-93	Phoenix	IHL	79	14	30	44	55	....	....	....	....	....

Signed as a free agent by **Los Angeles**, July 16, 1992.

BREWER, MIKE

Center. Shoots left. 5'10", 175 lbs. Born, Chestwick, Ont., April 13, 1969.
(Washington's 1st choice, 20th overall, in 1991 Supplemental Draft).

			Regular Season					Playoffs				
Season	Club	Lea	GP	G	A	TP	PIM	GP	G	A	TP	PIM
1988-89	Brown	ECAC	23	5	8	13	10	....	....	....	....	....
1989-90a	Brown	ECAC	29	7	24	31	64	....	....	....	....	....
1990-91b	Brown	ECAC	21	4	18	22	44	....	....	....	....	....
1991-92ac	Brown	ECAC	28	13	34	47	62	....	....	....	....	....
1992-93	Cdn. National	....	55	9	24	33	24	....	....	....	....	....

a ECAC First All-Star Team (1990, 1992)
b ECAC Second All-Star Team (1991)
c NCAA East First All-American Team (1992)

BRICKLEY, ANDY

Left wing/Center. Shoots left. 5'11", 200 lbs. Born, Melrose, MA, August 9, 1961.
(Philadelphia's 10th choice, 210th overall, in 1980 Entry Draft).

			Regular Season					Playoffs				
Season	Club	Lea	GP	G	A	TP	PIM	GP	G	A	TP	PIM
1979-80	N. Hampshire	ECAC	27	15	17	32	8	....	....	....	....	....
1980-81	N. Hampshire	ECAC	31	27	25	52	16	....	....	....	....	....
1981-82ab	N. Hampshire	ECAC	35	26	27	53	6	....	....	....	....	....
1982-83	Philadelphia	NHL	3	1	1	2	0	....	....	....	....	....
c	Maine	AHL	76	29	54	83	10	17	9	5	14	0
1983-84	Springfield	AHL	7	1	5	6	2	....	....	....	....	....
	Pittsburgh	NHL	50	18	20	38	9	....	....	....	....	....
	Baltimore	AHL	4	0	5	5	2	....	....	....	....	....
1984-85	Pittsburgh	NHL	45	7	15	22	10	....	....	....	....	....
	Baltimore	AHL	31	13	14	27	8	15	*10	8	18	0
1985-86	Maine	AHL	60	26	34	60	20	5	0	4	4	0
1986-87	New Jersey	NHL	51	11	12	23	8	....	....	....	....	....
1987-88	New Jersey	NHL	45	8	14	22	14	4	0	1	1	4
	Utica	AHL	9	5	8	13	4	....	....	....	....	....
1988-89	Boston	NHL	71	13	22	35	20	10	0	2	2	0
1989-90	Boston	NHL	43	12	28	40	8	2	0	0	0	0
1990-91	Boston	NHL	40	2	9	11	8	....	....	....	....	....
	Maine	AHL	17	8	17	25	2	1	0	0	0	0
1991-92	Boston	NHL	23	10	17	27	2	....	....	....	....	....
	Maine	AHL	14	5	15	20	2	....	....	....	....	....
1992-93	Winnipeg	NHL	12	0	2	2	2	1	1	1	2	0
	Moncton	AHL	38	15	36	51	10	5	4	2	6	0
	NHL Totals		383	82	140	222	81	17	1	4	5	4

a ECAC First All-Star Team (1982)
b NCAA All-American Team (1982)
c AHL Second All-Star Team (1983)

Traded to **Pittsburgh** by **Philadelphia** with Mark Taylor, Ron Flockhart, Philadelphia's first round (Roger Belanger) and third round (later traded to Vancouver — Vancouver selected Mike Stevens) choices in 1984 Entry Draft for Rich Sutter and Pittsburgh's second round (Greg Smyth) and third round (David McLay) choices in 1984 Entry Draft, October 23, 1983. Signed as a free agent by **New Jersey**, July 8, 1986. Claimed by **Boston** in NHL Waiver Draft, October 3, 1988. Signed as a free agent by **Winnipeg**, November 11, 1992.

BRIERLEY, DAN

Defense. Shoots left. 6'2", 185 lbs. Born, Nashua, NH, January 23, 1974.
(NY Rangers' 9th choice, 216th overall, in 1992 Entry Draft).

			Regular Season					Playoffs				
Season	Club	Lea	GP	G	A	TP	PIM	GP	G	A	TP	PIM
1991-92	Choate	HS	22	10	12	22	15	....	....	....	....	....
1992-93	Yale	ECAC	29	0	7	7	32	....	....	....	....	....

BRILL, JOHN

Right wing. Shoots left. 6'3", 180 lbs. Born, St. Paul, MN, December 3, 1970.
(Pittsburgh's 3rd choice, 58th overall, in 1989 Entry Draft).

			Regular Season					Playoffs				
Season	Club	Lea	GP	G	A	TP	PIM	GP	G	A	TP	PIM
1989-90	U. Minnesota	WCHA	34	2	8	10	22	....	....	....	....	....
1990-91	U. Minnesota	WCHA	44	6	13	19	36	....	....	....	....	....
1991-92	U. Minnesota	WCHA	35	7	9	16	46	....	....	....	....	....
1992-93	U. Minnesota	WCHA	41	12	13	25	64	....	....	....	....	....

BRIMANIS, ARIS

Defense. Shoots right. 6'3", 195 lbs. Born, Cleveland, OH, March 14, 1972.
(Philadelphia's 4th choice, 86th overall, in 1991 Entry Draft).

			Regular Season					Playoffs				
Season	Club	Lea	GP	G	A	TP	PIM	GP	G	A	TP	PIM
1990-91	Bowling Green	CCHA	38	3	6	9	42	....	....	....	....	....
1991-92	Bowling Green	CCHA	32	2	9	11	38	....	....	....	....	....
1992-93	Brandon	WHL	71	8	50	58	110	4	2	1	3	7

BRIND'AMOUR, ROD

Center. Shoots left. 6'1", 202 lbs. Born, Ottawa, Ont., August 9, 1970.
(St. Louis' 1st choice, 9th overall, in 1988 Entry Draft).

			Regular Season					Playoffs				
Season	Club	Lea	GP	G	A	TP	PIM	GP	G	A	TP	PIM
1988-89a	Michigan State	CCHA	42	27	32	59	63	....	....	....	....	....
	St. Louis	**NHL**	....	....	....	....	....	5	2	0	2	4
1989-90b	**St. Louis**	**NHL**	79	26	35	61	46	12	5	8	13	6
1990-91	**St. Louis**	**NHL**	78	17	32	49	93	13	2	5	7	10
1991-92	**Philadelphia**	**NHL**	80	33	44	77	100	....	....	....	....	....
1992-93	**Philadelphia**	**NHL**	81	37	49	86	89	....	....	....	....	....
	NHL Totals		**318**	**113**	**160**	**273**	**328**	**30**	**9**	**13**	**22**	**20**

a CCHA Freshman of the Year (1989)
b NHL All-Rookie Team (1990)

Played in NHL All-Star Game (1992)

Traded to **Philadelphia** by **St. Louis** with Dan Quinn for Ron Sutter and Murray Baron, September 22, 1991.

BRISEBOIS, PATRICE

Defense. Shoots right. 6'2", 175 lbs. Born, Montreal, Que., January 27, 1971.
(Montreal's 2nd choice, 30th overall, in 1989 Entry Draft).

			Regular Season					Playoffs				
Season	Club	Lea	GP	G	A	TP	PIM	GP	G	A	TP	PIM
1987-88	Laval	QMJHL	48	10	34	44	95	6	0	2	2	2
1988-89	Laval	QMJHL	50	20	45	65	95	17	8	14	22	45
1989-90a	Laval	QMJHL	56	18	70	88	108	13	7	9	16	26
1990-91	**Montreal**	**NHL**	10	0	2	2	4	....	....	....	....	....
bcd	Drummondville	QMJHL	54	17	44	61	72	14	6	18	24	49
1991-92	**Montreal**	**NHL**	26	2	8	10	20	11	2	4	6	6
	Fredericton	AHL	53	12	27	39	51	....	....	....	....	....
1992-93	**Montreal**	**NHL**	70	10	21	31	79	20	0	4	4	18
	NHL Totals		**106**	**12**	**31**	**43**	**103**	**31**	**2**	**8**	**10**	**24**

a QMJHL Second All-Star Team (1990)
b QMJHL and Canadian Major Junior Defenseman of the Year (1991)
c QMJHL First All-Star Team (1991)
d Memorial Cup All-Star Team (1991)

BROTEN, NEAL (BRAH-tuhn)

Center. Shoots left. 5'9", 170 lbs. Born, Roseau, MN, November 29, 1959.
(Minnesota's 3rd choice, 42nd overall, in 1979 Entry Draft).

			Regular Season					Playoffs				
Season	Club	Lea	GP	G	A	TP	PIM	GP	G	A	TP	PIM
1978-79	U. Minnesota	WCHA	40	21	50	71	18	....	....	....	....	....
1979-80	U.S. National	....	55	25	30	55	20	....	....	....	....	....
	U.S. Olympic	....	7	2	1	3	2	....	....	....	....	....
1980-81ab	U. Minnesota	WCHA	36	17	54	71	56	....	....	....	....	....
	Minnesota	**NHL**	3	2	0	2	12	19	1	7	8	9
1981-82	**Minnesota**	**NHL**	73	38	60	98	42	4	0	2	2	0
1982-83	**Minnesota**	**NHL**	79	32	45	77	43	9	1	6	7	10
1983-84	**Minnesota**	**NHL**	76	28	61	89	43	16	5	5	10	4
1984-85	**Minnesota**	**NHL**	80	19	37	56	39	9	2	5	7	10
1985-86	**Minnesota**	**NHL**	80	29	76	105	47	5	3	2	5	2
1986-87	**Minnesota**	**NHL**	46	18	35	53	33	....	....	....	....	....
1987-88	**Minnesota**	**NHL**	54	9	30	39	32	....	....	....	....	....
1988-89	**Minnesota**	**NHL**	68	18	38	56	57	5	2	2	4	4
1989-90	**Minnesota**	**NHL**	80	23	62	85	45	7	2	2	4	18
1990-91	**Minnesota**	**NHL**	79	13	56	69	26	23	9	13	22	6
1991-92	Preussen	Ger.	8	3	5	8	2	....	....	....	....	....
	Minnesota	**NHL**	76	8	26	34	16	7	1	5	6	2
1992-93	**Minnesota**	**NHL**	82	12	21	33	22	....	....	....	....	....
	NHL Totals		**876**	**249**	**547**	**796**	**457**	**104**	**26**	**49**	**75**	**65**

a WCHA First All-Star Team (1981)
b Won Hobey Baker Memorial Trophy (Top U.S. College Player) (1981)

Played in NHL All-Star Game (1983-86)

BROTEN, PAUL (BRAH-tuhn)

Right wing. Shoots right. 5'11", 188 lbs. Born, Roseau, MN, October 27, 1965.
(NY Rangers' 3rd choice, 77th overall, in 1984 Entry Draft).

			Regular Season					Playoffs				
Season	Club	Lea	GP	G	A	TP	PIM	GP	G	A	TP	PIM
1984-85	U. Minnesota	WCHA	44	8	8	16	26	....	....	....	....	....
1985-86	U. Minnesota	WCHA	38	6	16	22	24	....	....	....	....	....
1986-87	U. Minnesota	WCHA	48	17	22	39	52	....	....	....	....	....
1987-88	U. Minnesota	WCHA	38	18	21	39	42	....	....	....	....	....
1988-89	Denver	IHL	77	28	31	59	133	4	0	2	2	6
1989-90	**NY Rangers**	**NHL**	32	5	3	8	26	6	1	1	2	2
	Flint	IHL	28	17	9	26	55	....	....	....	....	....
1990-91	**NY Rangers**	**NHL**	28	4	6	10	18	5	0	0	0	2
	Binghamton	AHL	8	2	2	4	4	....	....	....	....	....
1991-92	**NY Rangers**	**NHL**	74	13	15	28	102	13	1	2	3	10
1992-93	**NY Rangers**	**NHL**	60	5	9	14	48	....	....	....	....	....
	NHL Totals		**194**	**27**	**33**	**60**	**194**	**24**	**2**	**3**	**5**	**14**

BROUSSEAU, PAUL

Right wing. Shoots right. 6'2", 212 lbs. Born, Pierrefonds, Que., September 18, 1973.
(Quebec's 2nd choice, 28th overall, in 1992 Entry Draft).

			Regular Season					Playoffs				
Season	Club	Lea	GP	G	A	TP	PIM	GP	G	A	TP	PIM
1989-90	Chicoutimi	QMJHL	57	17	24	41	32	7	0	3	3	0
1990-91	Trois-Rivières	QMJHL	67	30	66	96	48	6	3	2	5	2
1991-92	Hull	QMJHL	57	35	61	96	54	6	3	5	8	10
1992-93	Hull	QMJHL	59	27	48	75	49	10	7	8	15	6

BROWN, ALAN

Defense. Shoots left. 6', 180 lbs. Born, Nepean, Ont., January 26, 1971.
(Washington's 13th choice, 219th overall, in 1990 Entry Draft).

			Regular Season					Playoffs				
Season	Club	Lea	GP	G	A	TP	PIM	GP	G	A	TP	PIM
1989-90	Colgate	ECAC	33	2	3	5	22	....	....	....	....	....
1990-91	Colgate	ECAC	32	0	5	5	26	....	....	....	....	....
1991-92	Colgate	ECAC	29	1	10	11	28	....	....	....	....	....
1992-93	Colgate	ECAC	32	4	9	13	38	....	....	....	....	....

BROWN, DAVID

Right wing. Shoots right. 6'5", 205 lbs. Born, Saskatoon, Sask., October 12, 1962.
(Philadelphia's 7th choice, 140th overall, in 1982 Entry Draft).

			Regular Season					Playoffs				
Season	Club	Lea	GP	G	A	TP	PIM	GP	G	A	TP	PIM
1980-81	Spokane	WHL	9	2	2	4	21	....	....	....	....	....
1981-82	Saskatoon	WHL	62	11	33	44	344	5	1	0	1	4
1982-83	**Philadelphia**	**NHL**	2	0	0	0	5	....	....	....	....	....
	Maine	AHL	71	8	6	14	*418	16	0	0	0	*107
1983-84	**Philadelphia**	**NHL**	19	1	5	6	98	2	0	0	0	12
	Springfield	AHL	59	17	14	31	150	....	....	....	....	....
1984-85	**Philadelphia**	**NHL**	57	3	6	9	165	11	0	0	0	59
1985-86	**Philadelphia**	**NHL**	76	10	7	17	277	5	0	0	0	16
1986-87	**Philadelphia**	**NHL**	62	7	3	10	274	26	1	2	3	59
1987-88	**Philadelphia**	**NHL**	47	12	5	17	114	7	1	0	1	27
1988-89	**Philadelphia**	**NHL**	50	0	3	3	100	....	....	....	....	....
	Edmonton	**NHL**	22	0	2	2	56	7	0	0	0	6
1989-90	**Edmonton**	**NHL**	60	0	6	6	145	3	0	0	0	0
1990-91	**Edmonton**	**NHL**	58	3	4	7	160	16	0	1	1	30
1991-92	**Philadelphia**	**NHL**	70	4	2	6	81	....	....	....	....	....
1992-93	**Philadelphia**	**NHL**	70	0	2	2	78	....	....	....	....	....
	NHL Totals		**593**	**40**	**45**	**85**	**1553**	**77**	**2**	**3**	**5**	**209**

Traded to **Edmonton** by **Philadelphia** for Keith Acton and Edmonton's fifth round choice (Dimitri Yushkevich) in 1991 Entry Draft, February 7, 1989. Traded to **Philadelphia** by **Edmonton** with Corey Foster and Jari Kurri for Craig Fisher, Scott Mellanby and Craig Berube, May 30, 1991.

BROWN, DOUG

Right wing. Shoots right. 5'10", 185 lbs. Born, Southborough, MA, June 12, 1964.

			Regular Season					Playoffs				
Season	Club	Lea	GP	G	A	TP	PIM	GP	G	A	TP	PIM
1982-83	Boston College	ECAC	22	9	8	17	0	....	....	....	....	....
1983-84	Boston College	ECAC	38	11	10	21	6	....	....	....	....	....
1984-85a	Boston College	H.E.	45	37	31	68	10	....	....	....	....	....
1985-86a	Boston College	H.E.	38	16	40	56	16	....	....	....	....	....
1986-87	**New Jersey**	**NHL**	4	0	1	1	0	....	....	....	....	....
	Maine	AHL	73	24	34	58	15	....	....	....	....	....
1987-88	**New Jersey**	**NHL**	70	14	11	25	20	19	5	1	6	6
	Utica	AHL	2	0	2	2	2	....	....	....	....	....
1988-89	**New Jersey**	**NHL**	63	15	10	25	15	....	....	....	....	....
	Utica	AHL	4	1	4	5	0	....	....	....	....	....
1989-90	**New Jersey**	**NHL**	69	14	20	34	16	6	0	1	1	2
1990-91	**New Jersey**	**NHL**	58	14	16	30	4	7	2	2	4	2
1991-92	**New Jersey**	**NHL**	71	11	17	28	27	....	....	....	....	....
1992-93	**New Jersey**	**NHL**	15	0	5	5	2	....	....	....	....	....
	Utica	AHL	25	11	17	28	8	....	....	....	....	....
	NHL Totals		**350**	**68**	**80**	**148**	**84**	**32**	**7**	**4**	**11**	**10**

a Hockey East First All-Star Team (1985, 1986)

Signed as a free agent by **New Jersey**, August 6, 1986.

BROWN, GREG

Defense. Shoots right. 6', 185 lbs. Born, Hartford, CT, March 7, 1968. .
(Buffalo's 2nd choice, 26th overall, in 1986 Entry Draft).

			Regular Season					Playoffs				
Season	Club	Lea	GP	G	A	TP	PIM	GP	G	A	TP	PIM
1986-87	Boston College	H.E.	37	10	27	37	22	....	....	....	....	....
1987-88	U.S. National	....	55	6	29	35	22	....	....	....	....	....
	U.S. Olympic	....	6	0	4	4	2	....	....	....	....	....
1988-89abc	Boston College	H.E.	40	9	34	43	24	....	....	....	....	....
1989-90abc	Boston College	H.E.	42	5	35	40	42	....	....	....	....	....
1990-91	**Buffalo**	**NHL**	39	1	2	3	35	....	....	....	....	....
	Rochester	AHL	31	6	17	23	16	14	1	4	5	8
1991-92	Rochester	AHL	56	8	30	38	25	16	1	5	6	4
	U.S. National	....	8	0	0	0	5	....	....	....	....	....
	U.S. Olympic	....	7	0	0	0	2	....	....	....	....	....
1992-93	**Buffalo**	**NHL**	10	0	1	1	6	....	....	....	....	....
	Rochester	AHL	61	11	38	49	46	16	3	8	11	14
	NHL Totals		**49**	**1**	**3**	**4**	**41**	....	....	....	....	....

a Hockey East First All-Star Team (1989, 1990)
b Hockey East Player of the Year (1989, 1990)
c NCAA East First All-American Team (1989, 1990)

BROWN, JEFF

Defense. Shoots right. 6'1", 204 lbs. Born, Ottawa, Ont., April 30, 1966.
(Quebec's 2nd choice, 36th overall, in 1984 Entry Draft).

			Regular Season					Playoffs				
Season	Club	Lea	GP	G	A	TP	PIM	GP	G	A	TP	PIM
1982-83	Sudbury	OHL	65	9	37	46	39	....	....	....	....	....
1983-84	Sudbury	OHL	68	17	60	77	39	....	....	....	....	....
1984-85	Sudbury	OHL	56	16	48	64	26	....	....	....	....	....
1985-86	**Quebec**	**NHL**	8	3	2	5	6	1	0	0	0	0
a	Sudbury	OHL	45	22	28	50	24	4	0	2	2	11
	Fredericton	AHL	....	....	....	....	....	1	0	1	1	0
1986-87	**Quebec**	**NHL**	44	7	22	29	16	13	3	3	6	2
	Fredericton	AHL	26	2	14	16	16	....	....	....	....	....
1987-88	**Quebec**	**NHL**	78	16	36	52	64	....	....	....	....	....
1988-89	**Quebec**	**NHL**	78	21	47	68	62	....	....	....	....	....
1989-90	**Quebec**	**NHL**	29	6	10	16	18	....	....	....	....	....
	St. Louis	**NHL**	48	10	28	38	37	12	2	10	12	4
1990-91	**St. Louis**	**NHL**	67	12	47	59	39	13	3	9	12	6
1991-92	**St. Louis**	**NHL**	80	20	39	59	38	6	2	1	3	2
1992-93	**St. Louis**	**NHL**	71	25	53	78	58	11	3	8	11	6
	NHL Totals		**503**	**120**	**284**	**404**	**338**	**56**	**13**	**31**	**44**	**20**

a OHL First All-Star Team (1986)

Traded to **St Louis** by **Quebec** for Tony Hrkac and Greg Millen, December 13, 1989.

BROWN, KEITH JEFFREY

Defense. Shoots right. 6'1", 192 lbs. Born, Corner Brook, Nfld., May 6, 1960.
(Chicago's 1st choice, 7th overall, in 1979 Entry Draft).

			Regular Season					Playoffs				
Season	Club	Lea	GP	G	A	TP	PIM	GP	G	A	TP	PIM
1977-78a	Portland	WHL	72	11	53	64	51	8	0	3	3	2
1978-79bc	Portland	WHL	70	11	85	96	75	25	3	*30	33	21
1979-80	**Chicago**	**NHL**	**76**	**2**	**18**	**20**	**27**	**6**	**0**	**0**	**0**	**4**
1980-81	**Chicago**	**NHL**	**80**	**9**	**34**	**43**	**80**	**3**	**0**	**2**	**2**	**2**
1981-82	**Chicago**	**NHL**	**33**	**4**	**20**	**24**	**26**	**4**	**0**	**2**	**2**	**5**
1982-83	**Chicago**	**NHL**	**50**	**4**	**27**	**31**	**20**	**7**	**0**	**0**	**0**	**11**
1983-84	**Chicago**	**NHL**	**74**	**10**	**25**	**35**	**94**	**5**	**0**	**1**	**1**	**10**
1984-85	**Chicago**	**NHL**	**56**	**1**	**22**	**23**	**55**	**11**	**2**	**7**	**9**	**31**
1985-86	**Chicago**	**NHL**	**70**	**11**	**29**	**40**	**87**	**3**	**0**	**1**	**1**	**9**
1986-87	**Chicago**	**NHL**	**73**	**4**	**23**	**27**	**86**	**4**	**0**	**1**	**1**	**6**
1987-88	**Chicago**	**NHL**	**24**	**3**	**6**	**9**	**45**	**5**	**0**	**2**	**2**	**10**
1988-89	**Chicago**	**NHL**	**74**	**2**	**16**	**18**	**84**	**13**	**1**	**3**	**4**	**25**
1989-90	**Chicago**	**NHL**	**67**	**5**	**20**	**25**	**87**	**18**	**0**	**4**	**4**	**43**
1990-91	**Chicago**	**NHL**	**45**	**1**	**10**	**11**	**55**	**6**	**1**	**0**	**1**	**8**
1991-92	**Chicago**	**NHL**	**57**	**6**	**10**	**16**	**69**	**14**	**0**	**8**	**8**	**18**
1992-93	**Chicago**	**NHL**	**33**	**2**	**6**	**8**	**39**	**4**	**0**	**1**	**1**	**2**
	NHL Totals		**812**	**64**	**266**	**330**	**854**	**103**	**4**	**32**	**36**	**184**

a Shared WHL's Rookie of the Year with John Ogrodnick (New Westminster) (1978)
b Named WHL's Top Defenseman (1979)
c WHL First All-Star Team (1979)

BROWN, KEVIN

Right wing. Shoots right. 6'1", 212 lbs. Born, Birmingham, England, May 11, 1974.
(Los Angeles' 3rd choice, 87th overall, in 1992 Entry Draft).

			Regular Season					Playoffs				
Season	Club	Lea	GP	G	A	TP	PIM	GP	G	A	TP	PIM
1991-92	Belleville	OHL	66	24	24	48	52	5	1	4	5	8
1992-93a	Belleville	OHL	6	2	5	7	4	....	....	....	....	....
	Detroit	OHL	56	48	86	134	76	15	10	18	28	18

a OHL Second All-Star Team (1993)

BROWN, ROB

Right wing. Shoots left. 5'11", 185 lbs. Born, Kingston, Ont., April 10, 1968.
(Pittsburgh's 4th choice, 67th overall, in 1986 Entry Draft).

			Regular Season					Playoffs				
Season	Club	Lea	GP	G	A	TP	PIM	GP	G	A	TP	PIM
1984-85	Kamloops	WHL	60	29	50	79	95	15	8	8	26	28
1985-86ab	Kamloops	WHL	69	58	*115	*173	171	16	*18	*28	*46	14
1986-87abc	Kamloops	WHL	63	*76	*136	*212	101	5	6	5	11	6
1987-88	**Pittsburgh**	**NHL**	**51**	**24**	**20**	**44**	**56**	....	....	....	....	....
1988-89	**Pittsburgh**	**NHL**	**68**	**49**	**66**	**115**	**118**	**11**	**5**	**3**	**8**	**22**
1989-90	**Pittsburgh**	**NHL**	**80**	**33**	**47**	**80**	**102**	....	....	....	....	....
1990-91	**Pittsburgh**	**NHL**	**25**	**6**	**10**	**16**	**31**	....	....	....	....	....
	Hartford	**NHL**	**44**	**18**	**24**	**42**	**101**	**5**	**1**	**0**	**1**	**7**
1991-92	**Hartford**	**NHL**	**42**	**16**	**15**	**31**	**39**	....	....	....	....	....
	Chicago	**NHL**	**25**	**5**	**11**	**16**	**34**	**8**	**2**	**4**	**6**	**4**
1992-93	**Chicago**	**NHL**	**15**	**1**	**6**	**7**	**33**	....	....	....	....	....
	Indianapolis	IHL	19	14	19	33	32	2	0	1	1	2
	NHL Totals		**350**	**152**	**199**	**351**	**514**	**24**	**8**	**7**	**15**	**33**

a WHL Player of the Year (1986, 1987)
b WHL First All-Star Team (1986, 1987)
c Canadian Major Junior Player of the Year (1987)

Played in NHL All-Star Game (1989)

Traded to **Hartford** by **Pittsburgh** for Scott Young, December 21, 1990. Traded to **Chicago** by **Hartford** for Steve Konroyd, January 24, 1992.

BROWN, RYAN

Defense. Shoots right. 6'3", 215 lbs. Born, Boyle, Alta., September 19, 1974.
(Tampa Bay's 5th choice, 107th overall, in 1993 Entry Draft).

			Regular Season					Playoffs				
Season	Club	Lea	GP	G	A	TP	PIM	GP	G	A	TP	PIM
1991-92	Seattle	WHL	60	1	1	2	230	14	0	2	2	38
1992-93	Swift Current	WHL	66	1	5	6	174	17	0	2	2	18

BRUCE, DAVID

Left wing/Center. Shoots right. 5'11", 190 lbs. Born, Thunder Bay, Ont., October 7, 1964.
(Vancouver's 2nd choice, 30th overall, in 1983 Entry Draft).

			Regular Season					Playoffs				
Season	Club	Lea	GP	G	A	TP	PIM	GP	G	A	TP	PIM
1982-83	Kitchener	OHL	67	36	35	71	199	12	7	9	16	27
1983-84	Kitchener	OHL	62	52	40	92	203	10	5	8	13	20
1984-85	Fredericton	AHL	56	14	11	25	104	5	0	0	0	37
1985-86	**Vancouver**	**NHL**	**12**	**0**	**1**	**1**	**14**	**1**	**0**	**0**	**0**	**0**
	Fredericton	AHL	66	25	16	41	151	2	0	1	1	12
1986-87	**Vancouver**	**NHL**	**50**	**9**	**7**	**16**	**109**	....	....	....	....	....
	Fredericton	AHL	17	7	6	13	73	....	....	....	....	....
1987-88	**Vancouver**	**NHL**	**28**	**7**	**3**	**10**	**57**	....	....	....	....	....
	Fredericton	AHL	30	27	18	45	115	....	....	....	....	....
1988-89	**Vancouver**	**NHL**	**53**	**7**	**7**	**14**	**65**	....	....	....	....	....
1989-90a	Milwaukee	IHL	68	40	35	75	148	6	5	3	8	0
1990-91	**St. Louis**	**NHL**	**12**	**1**	**2**	**3**	**14**	**2**	**0**	**0**	**0**	**2**
ab	Peoria	IHL	60	*64	52	116	78	18	*18	11	*29	40
1991-92	**San Jose**	**NHL**	**60**	**22**	**16**	**38**	**46**	....	....	....	....	....
	Kansas City	IHL	7	5	5	10	6	....	....	....	....	....
1992-93	**San Jose**	**NHL**	**17**	**2**	**3**	**5**	**33**	....	....	....	....	....
	NHL Totals		**232**	**48**	**39**	**87**	**338**	**3**	**0**	**0**	**0**	**2**

a IHL First All-Star Team (1990, 1991)
b Won James Gatschene Memorial Trophy (MVP—IHL) (1991)

Signed as a free agent by **St. Louis**, July 6, 1990. Claimed by **San Jose** from **St. Louis** in Expansion Draft, May 30, 1991.

BRULE, STEVE

Center. Shoots right. 5'11", 184 lbs. Born, Montreal, Que., January 15, 1975.
(New Jersey's 6th choice, 143rd overall, in 1993 Entry Draft).

			Regular Season					Playoffs				
Season	Club	Lea	GP	G	A	TP	PIM	GP	G	A	TP	PIM
1991-92	Bourassa	Midget	38	41	26	67	14	....	....	....	....	....
1992-93	St-Jean	QMJHL	70	33	47	80	46	4	0	0	0	9

BRUNET, BENOIT (broo-NAY)

Left wing. Shoots left. 5'11", 184 lbs. Born, Pointe-Claire, Que., August 24, 1968.
(Montreal's 2nd choice, 27th overall, in 1986 Entry Draft).

			Regular Season					Playoffs				
Season	Club	Lea	GP	G	A	TP	PIM	GP	G	A	TP	PIM
1985-86	Hull	QMJHL	71	33	37	70	81	....	....	....	....	....
1986-87a	Hull	QMJHL	60	43	67	110	105	6	7	5	12	8
1987-88	Hull	QMJHL	62	54	89	143	131	10	3	10	13	11
1988-89	**Montreal**	**NHL**	**2**	**0**	**1**	**1**	**0**	....	....	....	....	....
b	Sherbrooke	AHL	73	41	76	117	95	6	2	0	2	4
1989-90	Sherbrooke	AHL	72	32	35	67	82	12	8	7	15	20
1990-91	**Montreal**	**NHL**	**17**	**1**	**3**	**4**	**0**	....	....	....	....	....
	Fredericton	AHL	24	13	18	31	16	6	5	6	11	2
1991-92	**Montreal**	**NHL**	**18**	**4**	**6**	**10**	**14**	....	....	....	....	....
	Fredericton	AHL	6	7	9	16	27	....	....	....	....	....
1992-93	**Montreal**	**NHL**	**47**	**10**	**15**	**25**	**19**	**20**	**2**	**8**	**10**	**8**
	NHL Totals		**84**	**15**	**25**	**40**	**33**	**20**	**2**	**8**	**10**	**8**

a QMJHL Second All-Star Team (1987)
b AHL First All-Star Team (1989)

BRYLIN, SERGEI (BRIH-lin)

Center. Shoots left. 5'9", 176 lbs. Born, Moscow, Soviet Union, January 13, 1974.
(New Jersey's 2nd choice, 42nd overall, in 1992 Entry Draft).

			Regular Season					Playoffs				
Season	Club	Lea	GP	G	A	TP	PIM	GP	G	A	TP	PIM
1991-92	CSKA	CIS	44	1	6	7	4	....	....	....	....	....
1992-93	CSKA	CIS	42	5	4	9	36	....	....	....	....	....

BUCHANAN, JEFF

Defense. Shoots right. 5'10", 165 lbs. Born, Swift Current, Sask., May 23, 1971.

			Regular Season					Playoffs				
Season	Club	Lea	GP	G	A	TP	PIM	GP	G	A	TP	PIM
1989-90	Saskatoon	WHL	66	7	12	19	96	9	0	2	2	2
1990-91	Saskatoon	WHL	69	10	26	36	123	....	....	....	....	....
1991-92	Saskatoon	WHL	72	17	37	54	145	....	....	....	....	....
1992-93	Atlanta	IHL	68	4	18	22	282	9	0	0	0	26

Signed as a free agent by **Tampa Bay**, July 13, 1992.

BUCHBERGER, KELLY (BUHK-BUHR-GUHR)

Left wing. Shoots left. 6'2", 210 lbs. Born, Langenburg, Sask., December 2, 1966.
(Edmonton's 8th choice, 188th overall, in 1985 Entry Draft).

			Regular Season					Playoffs				
Season	Club	Lea	GP	G	A	TP	PIM	GP	G	A	TP	PIM
1984-85	Moose Jaw	WHL	51	12	17	29	114	....	....	....	....	....
1985-86	Moose Jaw	WHL	72	14	22	36	206	13	11	4	15	37
1986-87	Nova Scotia	AHL	70	12	20	32	257	5	0	1	1	23
	Edmonton	**NHL**	....	....	....	....	....	**3**	**0**	**1**	**1**	**5**
1987-88	**Edmonton**	**NHL**	**19**	**1**	**0**	**1**	**81**	....	....	....	....	....
	Nova Scotia	AHL	49	21	23	44	206	2	0	0	0	11
1988-89	**Edmonton**	**NHL**	**66**	**5**	**9**	**14**	**234**	....	....	....	....	....
1989-90	**Edmonton**	**NHL**	**55**	**2**	**6**	**8**	**168**	**19**	**0**	**5**	**5**	**13**
1990-91	**Edmonton**	**NHL**	**64**	**3**	**1**	**4**	**160**	**12**	**2**	**1**	**3**	**25**
1991-92	**Edmonton**	**NHL**	**79**	**20**	**24**	**44**	**157**	**16**	**1**	**4**	**5**	**32**
1992-93	**Edmonton**	**NHL**	**83**	**12**	**18**	**30**	**133**	....	....	....	....	....
	NHL Totals		**366**	**43**	**58**	**101**	**933**	**50**	**3**	**11**	**14**	**75**

BUCKBERGER, ASHLEY

Right wing. Shoots right. 6'2", 200 lbs. Born, Esterhazy, Sask., February 19, 1975.
(Quebec's 3rd choice, 49th overall, in 1993 Entry Draft).

			Regular Season					Playoffs				
Season	Club	Lea	GP	G	A	TP	PIM	GP	G	A	TP	PIM
1991-92	Swift Current	WHL	67	23	22	45	38	8	2	1	3	2
1992-93	Swift Current	WHL	72	23	44	67	41	17	6	7	13	6

BUCKLEY, JEROME

Right wing. Shoots right. 6'2", 200 lbs. Born, Needham, MA, June 27, 1971.
(Boston's 3rd choice, 84th overall, in 1990 Entry Draft).

			Regular Season					Playoffs				
Season	Club	Lea	GP	G	A	TP	PIM	GP	G	A	TP	PIM
1991-92	Boston College	H.E.	30	2	0	2	46	....	....	....	....	....
1992-93	Boston College	H.E.	31	3	11	14	44	....	....	....	....	....

BUDAYEV, ALEXEI

Center. Shoots right. 6'2", 183 lbs. Born, Elektrostal, Soviet Union, April 24, 1975.
(Winnipeg's 3rd choice, 43rd overall, in 1993 Entry Draft).

			Regular Season					Playoffs				
Season	Club	Lea	GP	G	A	TP	PIM	GP	G	A	TP	PIM
1992-93	Elektrostal	CIS 2				UNAVAILABLE						

BULJIN, VLADISLAV

Defense. Shoots left. 6'2", 196 lbs. Born, Penza, USSR, May 18, 1972.
(Philadelphia's 4th choice, 103rd overall, in 1992 Entry Draft).

			Regular Season					Playoffs				
Season	Club	Lea	GP	G	A	TP	PIM	GP	G	A	TP	PIM
1990-91	Dizelist Penza	CIS				UNAVAILABLE						
1991-92						UNAVAILABLE						
1992-93	Moscow D'amo	CIS	32	2	1	3	55	....	....	....	....	....

BULLARD, MICHAEL BRIAN (MIKE) (BULL-ard)

Center. Shoots left. 6', 195 lbs. Born, Ottawa, Ont., March 10, 1961.
(Pittsburgh's 1st choice, 9th overall, in 1980 Entry Draft).

			Regular Season					Playoffs				
Season	Club	Lea	GP	G	A	TP	PIM	GP	G	A	TP	PIM
1978-79	Brantford	OHA	66	43	56	99	66	....	....	....	....	....
1979-80a	Brantford	OHA	66	66	84	150	86	11	10	6	16	29
1980-81	Pittsburgh	NHL	15	1	2	3	19	4	3	3	6	0
b	Brantford	OHA	42	47	60	107	55	6	4	5	9	10
1981-82	Pittsburgh	NHL	75	36	27	63	91	5	1	1	2	4
1982-83	Pittsburgh	NHL	57	22	22	44	60	....	....	....	....	....
1983-84	Pittsburgh	NHL	76	51	41	92	57	....	....	....	....	....
1984-85	Pittsburgh	NHL	68	32	31	63	75	....	....	....	....	....
1985-86	Pittsburgh	NHL	77	41	42	83	69	....	....	....	....	....
1986-87	Pittsburgh	NHL	14	2	10	12	17	....	....	....	....	....
	Calgary	NHL	57	28	26	54	34	6	4	3	7	2
1987-88	Calgary	NHL	79	48	55	103	68	6	0	2	2	6
1988-89	St. Louis	NHL	20	4	12	16	46	....	....	....	....	....
	Philadelphia	NHL	54	23	26	49	60	19	3	9	12	32
1989-90	Philadelphia	NHL	70	27	37	64	67	....	....	....	....	....
1990-91	Ambri-Piotta	Switz.	36	36	33	69	....	5	6	4	10	....
1991-92	Toronto	NHL	65	14	14	28	40	....	....	....	....	....
1992-93	Rapperswil	Switz.2			UNAVAILABLE							
	NHL Totals		727	329	345	674	703	40	11	18	29	44

a OHA Third All-Star Team (1979)
b OHA Second All-Star Team (1980)

Traded to **Calgary** by **Pittsburgh** for Dan Quinn, November 12, 1986. Traded to **St. Louis** by **Calgary** with Craig Coxe and Tim Corkery for Mark Hunter, Doug Gilmour, Steve Bozek and Michael Dark, September 6, 1988. Traded to **Philadelphia** by **St. Louis** for Peter Zezel, November 29, 1988. Rights traded to **Toronto** by **Philadelphia** for Toronto's third round choice (Vaclav Prospal) in 1993 Entry Draft, July 29, 1991.

BURAKOVSKY, ROBERT (boo-ruh-KAHV-skee)

Right wing. Shoots right. 5'10", 185 lbs. Born, Malmo, Sweden, November 24, 1966.
(NY Rangers' 11th choice, 217th overall, in 1985 Entry Draft).

			Regular Season					Playoffs				
Season	Club	Lea	GP	G	A	TP	PIM	GP	G	A	TP	PIM
1985-86	Leksand	Swe.	19	4	3	7	4	....	....	....	....	....
1986-87	Leksand	Swe.	36	21	15	36	26	....	....	....	....	....
1987-88	Leksand	Swe.	36	10	11	21	10	1	0	0	0	2
1988-89	Leksand	Swe.	40	23	20	43	44	10	6	7	13	4
1989-90	AIK	Swe.	37	27	29	56	32	3	0	2	2	12
1990-91	AIK	Swe.	30	8	15	23	26	....	....	....	....	....
1991-92	Malmo	Swe.	40	19	22	41	42	9	5	0	5	4
1992-93	Malmo	Swe.	32	8	10	18	40	6	4	4	8	9

Traded to **Ottawa** by **NY Rangers** for future considerations, May 7, 1993.

BURE, PAVEL (boo-RAY)

Right wing. Shoots left. 5'10", 189 lbs. Born, Moscow, Soviet Union, March 31, 1971.
(Vancouver's 4th choice, 113th overall, in 1989 Entry Draft).

			Regular Season					Playoffs				
Season	Club	Lea	GP	G	A	TP	PIM	GP	G	A	TP	PIM
1987-88	CSKA	USSR	5	1	1	2	0	....	....	....	....	....
1988-89a	CSKA	USSR	32	17	9	26	8	....	....	....	....	....
1989-90	CSKA	USSR	46	14	10	24	20	....	....	....	....	....
1990-91	CSKA	USSR	44	35	11	46	24	....	....	....	....	....
1991-92b	Vancouver	NHL	65	34	26	60	30	13	6	4	10	14
1992-93	Vancouver	NHL	83	60	50	110	69	12	5	7	12	8
	NHL Totals		148	94	76	170	99	25	11	11	22	22

a Named Soviet National League Rookie-of-the-Year (1989)
b Won Calder Memorial Trophy (1992)

Played in NHL All-Star Game (1993)

BURE, VALERI (boo-RAY)

Right wing. Shoots right. 5'9", 164 lbs. Born, Moscow, Soviet Union, June 13, 1974.
(Montreal's 2nd choice, 33rd overall, in 1992 Entry Draft).

			Regular Season					Playoffs				
Season	Club	Lea	GP	G	A	TP	PIM	GP	G	A	TP	PIM
1990-91	CSKA	USSR	3	0	0	0	0	....	....	....	....	....
1991-92	Spokane	WHL	53	27	22	49	78	10	11	6	17	10
1992-93a	Spokane	WHL	66	68	79	147	49	9	6	11	17	14

a WHL West First All-Star Team (1993)

BUREAU, MARC (BEWR-oh)

Center. Shoots right. 6'1", 198 lbs. Born, Trois-Rivières, Que., May 19, 1966.

			Regular Season					Playoffs				
Season	Club	Lea	GP	G	A	TP	PIM	GP	G	A	TP	PIM
1983-84	Chicoutimi	QMJHL	56	6	16	22	14	....	....	....	....	....
1984-85	Chicoutimi	QMJHL	41	30	25	55	15	....	....	....	....	....
	Granby	QMJHL	27	20	45	65	14	....	....	....	....	....
1985-86	Granby	QMJHL	19	6	17	23	36	....	....	....	....	....
	Chicoutimi	QMJHL	44	30	45	75	33	9	3	7	10	10
1986-87	Longueuil	QMJHL	66	54	58	112	68	20	17	20	37	12
1987-88	Salt Lake	IHL	69	7	20	27	86	7	0	3	3	8
1988-89	Salt Lake	IHL	76	28	36	64	119	14	7	5	12	31
1989-90	Calgary	NHL	5	0	0	0	4	....	....	....	....	....
a	Salt Lake	IHL	67	43	48	91	173	11	4	8	12	0
1990-91	Calgary	NHL	5	0	0	0	2	....	....	....	....	....
a	Salt Lake	IHL	54	40	48	88	101	....	....	....	....	....
	Minnesota	NHL	9	0	6	6	4	23	3	2	5	20
1991-92	Minnesota	NHL	46	6	4	10	50	5	0	0	0	14
	Kalamazoo	IHL	7	2	8	10	2	....	....	....	....	....
1992-93	Tampa Bay	NHL	63	10	21	31	111	....	....	....	....	....
	NHL Totals		128	16	31	47	171	28	3	2	5	34

a IHL Second All-Star Team (1990, 1991)

Signed as a free agent by **Calgary**, May 19, 1987. Traded to **Minnesota** by **Calgary** for Minnesota's third round choice (Sandy McCarthy) in 1991 Entry Draft, March 5, 1991. Claimed on waivers by **Tampa Bay** from **Minnesota**, October 16, 1992.

BURKETT, MICHAEL

Left wing. Shoots left. 6'3", 180 lbs. Born, Toronto, Ont., March 15, 1972.
(Minnesota's 8th choice, 174th overall, in 1991 Entry Draft).

			Regular Season					Playoffs				
Season	Club	Lea	GP	G	A	TP	PIM	GP	G	A	TP	PIM
1990-91	Michigan State	CCHA	35	3	6	9	14	....	....	....	....	....
1991-92	Michigan State	CCHA	33	7	5	12	42	....	....	....	....	....
1992-93	Michigan State	CCHA	39	2	10	12	28	....	....	....	....	....
	Cdn. National	....	2	1	2	3	0	....	....	....	....	....

BURMAN, MICHAEL

Defense. Shoots left. ', lbs. Born, North Bay, Ont., April 1, 1974.
(Montreal's 8th choice, 188th overall, in 1992 Entry Draft).

			Regular Season					Playoffs				
Season	Club	Lea	GP	G	A	TP	PIM	GP	G	A	TP	PIM
1990-91	North Bay	OHL	57	1	18	19	30	10	0	1	1	4
1991-92	North Bay	OHL	63	3	22	25	64	21	3	12	15	21
1992-93	North Bay	OHL	64	10	37	47	59	5	1	3	4	2

BURR, SHAWN

Left wing/Center. Shoots left. 6'1", 200 lbs. Born, Sarnia, Ont., July 1, 1966.
(Detroit's 1st choice, 7th overall, in 1984 Entry Draft).

			Regular Season					Playoffs				
Season	Club	Lea	GP	G	A	TP	PIM	GP	G	A	TP	PIM
1983-84	Kitchener	OHL	68	41	44	85	50	16	5	12	17	22
1984-85	Detroit	NHL	9	0	0	0	2	....	....	....	....	....
	Adirondack	AHL	4	0	0	0	2	....	....	....	....	....
	Kitchener	OHL	48	24	42	66	50	4	3	3	6	2
1985-86	Detroit	NHL	5	1	0	1	4	....	....	....	....	....
	Adirondack	AHL	3	2	2	4	2	17	5	7	12	32
a	Kitchener	OHL	59	60	67	127	104	5	2	3	5	8
1986-87	Detroit	NHL	80	22	25	47	107	16	7	2	9	20
1987-88	Detroit	NHL	78	17	23	40	97	9	3	1	4	14
1988-89	Detroit	NHL	79	19	27	46	78	6	1	2	3	6
1989-90	Detroit	NHL	76	24	32	56	82	....	....	....	....	....
	Adirondack	AHL	3	4	2	6	2	....	....	....	....	....
1990-91	Detroit	NHL	80	20	30	50	112	7	0	4	4	15
1991-92	Detroit	NHL	79	19	32	51	118	11	1	5	6	10
1992-93	Detroit	NHL	80	10	25	35	74	7	2	1	3	2
	NHL Totals		566	132	194	326	674	56	14	15	29	67

a OHL Second All-Star Team (1986)

BURRIDGE, RANDY

Left wing. Shoots left. 5'9", 185 lbs. Born, Fort Erie, Ont., January 7, 1966.
(Boston's 7th choice, 157th overall, in 1985 Entry Draft).

			Regular Season					Playoffs				
Season	Club	Lea	GP	G	A	TP	PIM	GP	G	A	TP	PIM
1983-84	Peterborough	OHL	55	6	7	13	44	8	3	2	5	7
1984-85	Peterborough	OHL	66	49	57	106	88	17	9	16	25	18
1985-86	Boston	NHL	52	17	25	42	28	3	0	4	4	12
	Peterborough	OHL	17	15	11	26	23	3	1	3	4	2
	Moncton	AHL	....	....	....	....	....	3	0	2	2	2
1986-87	Boston	NHL	23	1	4	5	16	2	1	0	1	2
	Moncton	AHL	47	26	41	67	139	3	1	2	3	30
1987-88	Boston	NHL	79	27	28	55	105	23	2	10	12	16
1988-89	Boston	NHL	80	31	30	61	39	10	5	2	7	6
1989-90	Boston	NHL	63	17	15	32	47	21	4	11	15	14
1990-91	Boston	NHL	62	15	13	28	40	19	0	3	3	39
1991-92	Washington	NHL	66	23	44	67	50	2	0	1	1	0
1992-93	Washington	NHL	4	0	0	0	0	4	1	0	1	0
	Baltimore	AHL	2	0	1	1	2	....	....	....	....	....
	NHL Totals		429	131	159	290	325	84	13	31	44	89

Played in NHL All-Star Game (1992)

Traded to **Washington** by **Boston** for Stephen Leach, June 21, 1991.

BURT, ADAM

Defense. Shoots left. 6', 190 lbs. Born, Detroit, MI, January 15, 1969.
(Hartford's 2nd choice, 39th overall, in 1987 Entry Draft).

			Regular Season					Playoffs				
Season	Club	Lea	GP	G	A	TP	PIM	GP	G	A	TP	PIM
1985-86	North Bay	OHL	49	0	11	11	81	10	0	0	0	24
1986-87	North Bay	OHL	57	4	27	31	138	24	1	6	7	68
1987-88	Binghamton	AHL	....	....	....	....	....	2	1	1	2	0
a	North Bay	OHL	66	17	53	70	176	2	0	3	3	6
1988-89	Hartford	NHL	5	0	0	0	6	....	....	....	....	....
	Binghamton	AHL	5	0	2	2	13	....	....	....	....	....
	North Bay	OHL	23	4	11	15	45	12	2	12	14	12
1989-90	Hartford	NHL	63	4	8	12	105	2	0	0	0	0
1990-91	Hartford	NHL	42	2	7	9	63	....	....	....	....	....
	Springfield	AHL	9	1	3	4	22	....	....	....	....	....
1991-92	Hartford	NHL	66	9	15	24	93	2	0	0	0	0
1992-93	Hartford	NHL	65	6	14	20	116	....	....	....	....	....
	NHL Totals		241	21	44	65	383	4	0	0	0	0

a OHL Second All-Star Team (1988)

BUSCHAN, ANDREI

Defense. Shoots left. 6'2", 194 lbs. Born, Kharkov, Soviet Union, August 21, 1970.
(San Jose's 6th choice, 106th overall, in 1993 Entry Draft).

			Regular Season					Playoffs				
Season	Club	Lea	GP	G	A	TP	PIM	GP	G	A	TP	PIM
1988-89	Kharkov	USSR	2	0	0	0	0	....	....	....	....	....
1989-90	Kharkov	USSR	21	0	0	0	10	....	....	....	....	....
1990-91	Kharkov	USSR 2	62	0	3	3	14	....	....	....	....	....
1991-92	Kharkov	CIS 2				UNAVAILABLE						
1992-93	Sokol Kiev	CIS	41	8	5	13	16	3	0	0	0	4

BUSKAS, ROD

Defense. Shoots right. 6'1", 206 lbs. Born, Wetaskiwin, Alta., January 7, 1961.
(Pittsburgh's 5th choice, 112th overall, in 1981 Entry Draft).

			Regular Season					Playoffs				
Season	Club	Lea	GP	G	A	TP	PIM	GP	G	A	TP	PIM
1978-79	Billings	WHL	1	0	0	0	0	....	....	....	....	....
	Medicine Hat	WHL	34	1	12	13	60	....	....	....	....	....
1979-80	Medicine Hat	WHL	72	7	40	47	284	....	....	....	....	....
1980-81	Medicine Hat	WHL	72	14	46	60	164	5	1	1	2	8
1981-82	Erie	AHL	69	1	18	19	78	....	....	....	....	....
1982-83	**Pittsburgh**	**NHL**	**41**	**2**	**2**	**4**	**102**	....	....	....	....	....
	Baltimore	AHL	31	2	8	10	45	....	....	....	....	....
1983-84	**Pittsburgh**	**NHL**	**47**	**2**	**4**	**6**	**60**	....	....	....	....	....
	Baltimore	AHL	33	2	12	14	100	10	1	3	4	22
1984-85	**Pittsburgh**	**NHL**	**69**	**2**	**7**	**9**	**191**	....	....	....	....	....
1985-86	**Pittsburgh**	**NHL**	**72**	**2**	**7**	**9**	**159**	....	....	....	....	....
1986-87	**Pittsburgh**	**NHL**	**68**	**3**	**15**	**18**	**123**	....	....	....	....	....
1987-88	**Pittsburgh**	**NHL**	**76**	**4**	**8**	**12**	**206**	....	....	....	....	....
1988-89	**Pittsburgh**	**NHL**	**52**	**1**	**5**	**6**	**105**	**10**	**0**	**0**	**0**	**23**
1989-90	**Vancouver**	**NHL**	**17**	**0**	**3**	**3**	**36**	....	....	....	....	....
	Pittsburgh	**NHL**	**6**	**0**	**0**	**0**	**13**	....	....	....	....	....
1990-91	**Los Angeles**	**NHL**	**57**	**3**	**8**	**11**	**182**	**2**	**0**	**2**	**2**	**22**
1991-92	**Los Angeles**	**NHL**	**5**	**0**	**0**	**0**	**11**	....	....	....	....	....
	Chicago	**NHL**	**42**	**0**	**4**	**4**	**80**	**6**	**0**	**1**	**1**	**0**
1992-93	**Chicago**	**NHL**	**4**	**0**	**0**	**0**	**26**	....	....	....	....	....
	Indianapolis	IHL	15	0	3	3	40	....	....	....	....	....
	Salt Lake	IHL	31	0	2	2	52	....	....	....	....	....
	NHL Totals		**556**	**19**	**63**	**82**	**1294**	**18**	**0**	**3**	**3**	**45**

Traded to **Vancouver** by **Pittsburgh** for Vancouver's sixth round choice (Ian Moran) in 1990 Entry Draft, October 24, 1989. Traded to **Pittsburgh** by **Vancouver** with Barry Pederson and Tony Tanti for Dave Capuano, Andrew McBain and Dan Quinn, January 8, 1990. Claimed by **Los Angeles** in NHL Waiver Draft, October 1, 1990. Traded to **Chicago** by **Los Angeles** for Chris Norton and future considerations, October 28, 1991.

BUSSEY, FRAN

Center. Shoots left. 6'3", 182 lbs. Born, Duluth, MN, July 9, 1974.
(Pittsburgh's 8th choice, 187th overall, in 1992 Entry Draft).

			Regular Season					Playoffs				
Season	Club	Lea	GP	G	A	TP	PIM	GP	G	A	TP	PIM
1990-91	Duluth East	HS	32	12	13	25	0	....	....	....	....	....
1991-92	Duluth East	HS	23	17	26	43	8	....	....	....	....	....
1992-93	Duluth East	HS	24	18	20	38	14	....	....	....	....	....

BUTCHER, GARTH

Defense. Shoots right. 6', 200 lbs. Born, Regina, Sask., January 8, 1963.
(Vancouver's 1st choice, 10th overall, in 1981 Entry Draft).

			Regular Season					Playoffs				
Season	Club	Lea	GP	G	A	TP	PIM	GP	G	A	TP	PIM
1979-80	Regina	WHL	13	0	4	4	20	....	....	....	....	....
1980-81a	Regina	WHL	69	9	77	86	230	11	5	17	22	60
1981-82	**Vancouver**	**NHL**	**5**	**0**	**0**	**0**	**9**	**1**	**0**	**0**	**0**	**0**
a	Regina	WHL	65	24	68	92	318	19	3	17	20	95
1982-83	**Vancouver**	**NHL**	**55**	**1**	**13**	**14**	**104**	**3**	**1**	**0**	**1**	**2**
1983-84	**Vancouver**	**NHL**	**28**	**2**	**0**	**2**	**34**	....	....	....	....	....
	Fredericton	AHL	25	4	13	17	43	6	0	2	2	19
1984-85	**Vancouver**	**NHL**	**75**	**3**	**9**	**12**	**152**	....	....	....	....	....
	Fredericton	AHL	3	1	0	1	11	....	....	....	....	....
1985-86	**Vancouver**	**NHL**	**70**	**4**	**7**	**11**	**188**	**3**	**0**	**0**	**0**	**0**
1986-87	**Vancouver**	**NHL**	**70**	**5**	**15**	**20**	**207**	....	....	....	....	....
1987-88	**Vancouver**	**NHL**	**80**	**6**	**17**	**23**	**285**	....	....	....	....	....
1988-89	**Vancouver**	**NHL**	**78**	**0**	**20**	**20**	**227**	**7**	**1**	**1**	**2**	**22**
1989-90	**Vancouver**	**NHL**	**80**	**6**	**14**	**20**	**205**	....	....	....	....	....
1990-91	**Vancouver**	**NHL**	**69**	**6**	**12**	**18**	**257**	....	....	....	....	....
	St. Louis	**NHL**	**13**	**0**	**4**	**4**	**32**	**13**	**2**	**1**	**3**	**54**
1991-92	**St. Louis**	**NHL**	**68**	**5**	**15**	**20**	**189**	**5**	**1**	**2**	**3**	**16**
1992-93	**St. Louis**	**NHL**	**84**	**5**	**10**	**15**	**211**	**11**	**1**	**1**	**2**	**20**
	NHL Totals		**775**	**43**	**136**	**179**	**2100**	**43**	**6**	**5**	**11**	**114**

a WHL First All-Star Team (1981, 1982)

Played in NHL All-Star Game (1993)

Traded to **St. Louis** by **Vancouver** with Dan Quinn for Geoff Courtnall, Robert Dirk, Sergio Momesso, Cliff Ronning and future considerations, March 5, 1991.

BUTSAYEV, VYACHESLAV (boot-SIGH-ehv)

Center. Shoots left. 6'2", 200 lbs. Born, Togliatti, Soviet Union, June 13, 1970.
(Philadelphia's 10th choice, 109th overall, in 1990 Entry Draft).

			Regular Season					Playoffs				
Season	Club	Lea	GP	G	A	TP	PIM	GP	G	A	TP	PIM
1989-90	CSKA	USSR	48	14	4	18	30	....	....	....	....	....
1990-91	CSKA	USSR	46	14	9	23	32	....	....	....	....	....
1991-92	CSKA	CIS	36	12	13	25	26	....	....	....	....	....
1992-93	CSKA	CIS	5	3	4	7	6	....	....	....	....	....
	Philadelphia	**NHL**	**52**	**2**	**14**	**16**	**61**	....	....	....	....	....
	Hershey	AHL	24	8	10	18	51	....	....	....	....	....
	NHL Totals		**52**	**2**	**14**	**16**	**61**	....	....	....	....	....

BYCE, JOHN

Center. Shoots left. 6'1", 180 lbs. Born, Madison, WI, August 9, 1967.
(Boston's 11th choice, 220th overall, in 1985 Entry Draft).

			Regular Season					Playoffs				
Season	Club	Lea	GP	G	A	TP	PIM	GP	G	A	TP	PIM
1986-87	U. Wisconsin	WCHA	40	1	4	5	12	....	....	....	....	....
1987-88	U. Wisconsin	WCHA	41	22	12	34	18	....	....	....	....	....
1988-89a	U. Wisconsin	WCHA	42	27	28	55	16	....	....	....	....	....
1989-90ab	U. Wisconsin	WCHA	46	27	44	71	20	....	....	....	....	....
	Boston	**NHL**	....	....	....	....	....	**8**	**2**	**0**	**2**	**2**
1990-91	**Boston**	**NHL**	**18**	**1**	**3**	**4**	**6**	....	....	....	....	....
	Maine	AHL	53	19	29	48	20	....	....	....	....	....
1991-92	**Boston**	**NHL**	**3**	**1**	**0**	**1**	**0**	....	....	....	....	....
	Maine	AHL	55	29	21	50	41	....	....	....	....	....
	Baltimore	AHL	20	9	5	14	4	....	....	....	....	....
1992-93	Baltimore	AHL	62	35	44	79	26	7	4	5	9	4
	NHL Totals		**21**	**2**	**3**	**5**	**6**	**8**	**2**	**0**	**2**	**2**

a WCHA Second All-Star Team (1989, 1990)
b NCAA All-Tournament Team (1990)

Traded to **Washington** by **Boston** with Dennis Smith for Brent Hughes and future considerations, February 24, 1992.

BYERS, LYNDON

Right wing. Shoots right. 6'1", 200 lbs. Born, Nipawin, Sask., February 29, 1964.
(Boston's 3rd choice, 39th overall, in 1982 Entry Draft).

			Regular Season					Playoffs				
Season	Club	Lea	GP	G	A	TP	PIM	GP	G	A	TP	PIM
1981-82	Regina	WHL	57	18	25	43	169	20	5	6	11	48
1982-83	Regina	WHL	70	32	38	70	153	5	1	1	2	16
1983-84	**Boston**	**NHL**	**10**	**2**	**4**	**6**	**32**	....	....	....	....	....
	Regina	WHL	58	32	57	89	154	23	17	18	35	78
1984-85	**Boston**	**NHL**	**33**	**3**	**8**	**11**	**41**	....	....	....	....	....
	Hershey	AHL	27	4	6	10	55	....	....	....	....	....
1985-86	**Boston**	**NHL**	**5**	**0**	**2**	**2**	**9**	....	....	....	....	....
	Moncton	AHL	14	2	4	6	26	....	....	....	....	....
	Milwaukee	IHL	8	0	2	2	22	....	....	....	....	....
1986-87	**Boston**	**NHL**	**18**	**2**	**3**	**5**	**53**	**1**	**0**	**0**	**0**	**0**
	Moncton	AHL	27	5	5	10	63	....	....	....	....	....
1987-88	**Boston**	**NHL**	**53**	**10**	**14**	**24**	**236**	**11**	**1**	**2**	**3**	**62**
	Maine	AHL	2	0	1	1	18	....	....	....	....	....
1988-89	**Boston**	**NHL**	**49**	**0**	**4**	**4**	**218**	**2**	**0**	**0**	**0**	**0**
	Maine	AHL	4	1	3	4	2	....	....	....	....	....
1989-90	**Boston**	**NHL**	**43**	**4**	**4**	**8**	**159**	**17**	**1**	**0**	**1**	**12**
1990-91	**Boston**	**NHL**	**19**	**2**	**2**	**4**	**82**	**1**	**0**	**0**	**0**	**10**
1991-92	**Boston**	**NHL**	**31**	**1**	**1**	**2**	**129**	**5**	**0**	**0**	**0**	**12**
	Maine	AHL	11	5	4	9	47	....	....	....	....	....
1992-93	**San Jose**	**NHL**	**18**	**4**	**1**	**5**	**122**	....	....	....	....	....
	Kansas City	IHL	4	1	1	2	22	....	....	....	....	....
	San Diego	IHL	9	0	3	3	35	....	....	....	....	....
	NHL Totals		**279**	**28**	**43**	**71**	**1081**	**37**	**2**	**2**	**4**	**96**

Signed as a free agent by **San Jose**, November 7, 1992.

BYKOV, VIACHESLAV (BIH-kahf)

Center. Shoots left. 5'8", 175 lbs. Born, Chelyabinsk, Soviet Union, July 24, 1960.
(Quebec's 11th choice, 169th overall, in 1989 Entry Draft).

			Regular Season					Playoffs				
Season	Club	Lea	GP	G	A	TP	PIM	GP	G	A	TP	PIM
1979-80	Chelyabinsk	USSR	3	2	0	2	0	....	....	....	....	....
1980-81	Chelyabinsk	USSR	48	26	16	42	4	....	....	....	....	....
1981-82	Chelyabinsk	USSR	44	20	16	36	14	....	....	....	....	....
1982-83	CSKA	USSR	44	22	22	44	10	....	....	....	....	....
1983-84	CSKA	USSR	44	22	11	33	12	....	....	....	....	....
1984-85	CSKA	USSR	36	21	14	35	4	....	....	....	....	....
1985-86	CSKA	USSR	36	10	10	20	6	....	....	....	....	....
1986-87	CSKA	USSR	40	18	15	33	10	....	....	....	....	....
1987-88	CSKA	USSR	47	17	30	47	26	....	....	....	....	....
1988-89	CSKA	USSR	40	16	20	36	10	....	....	....	....	....
1989-90	CSKA	USSR	48	21	16	37	12	....	....	....	....	....
1990-91	Fribourg	Switz.	36	35	49	84	....	8	8	14	22	....
1991-92	Fribourg	Switz.	34	38	47	85	24	14	4	14	18	10
1992-93	Fribourg	Switz.	35	25	50	75	14	....	....	....	....	....

CAIRNS, ERIC

Defense. Shoots left. 6'5", 217 lbs. Born, Oakville, Ont., June 27, 1974.
(NY Rangers' 3rd choice, 72nd overall, in 1992 Entry Draft).

			Regular Season					Playoffs				
Season	Club	Lea	GP	G	A	TP	PIM	GP	G	A	TP	PIM
1991-92	Detroit	OHL	64	1	11	12	232	7	0	0	0	31
1992-93	Detroit	OHL	64	3	13	16	194	15	0	3	3	24

CALLAHAN, BRIAN

Center. Shoots left. 6'1", 180 lbs. Born, Boston, MA, July 13, 1974.
(Pittsburgh's 10th choice, 235th overall, in 1992 Entry Draft).

			Regular Season					Playoffs				
Season	Club	Lea	GP	G	A	TP	PIM	GP	G	A	TP	PIM
1990-91	Belmont Hill	HS	32	30	40	70	30	....	....	....	....	....
1991-92	Belmont Hill	HS	25	20	18	38	....	....	....	....	....	....
1992-93	Belmont Hill	HS	15	19	16	35	16	....	....	....	....	....

CALLAHAN, GREGORY

Defense. Shoots left. 6'3", 200 lbs. Born, Chesnut Hill, MA, April 25, 1973.
(Washington's 9th choice, 239th overall, in 1992 Entry Draft).

			Regular Season					Playoffs				
Season	Club	Lea	GP	G	A	TP	PIM	GP	G	A	TP	PIM
1991-92	Belmont Hill	HS	25	15	29	44	62	....	....	....	....	....
1992-93	Boston College	H.E.	38	1	4	5	49	....	....	....	....	....

CALLANDER, JOHN (JOCK)

Right wing. Shoots right. 6'1", 188 lbs. Born, Regina, Sask., April 23, 1961.

			Regular Season					Playoffs				
Season	Club	Lea	GP	G	A	TP	PIM	GP	G	A	TP	PIM
1979-80	Regina	WHL	39	9	11	20	25	18	8	5	13	0
1980-81	Regina	WHL	72	67	86	153	37	11	6	7	13	14
1981-82	Regina	WHL	71	79	111	*190	59	20	13	*26	39	37
1982-83	Salt Lake	CHL	68	20	27	47	26	6	0	1	1	9
1983-84	Montana	CHL	72	27	32	59	69	....	....	....	....	....
	Toledo	IHL	2	0	0	0	0	....	....	....	....	....
1984-85	Muskegon	IHL	82	39	68	107	86	17	13	*21	*34	33
1985-86a	Muskegon	IHL	82	39	72	111	121	14	*12	11	*23	12
1986-87bcd	Muskegon	IHL	82	54	82	*136	110	15	13	7	20	23
1987-88	**Pittsburgh**	**NHL**	**41**	**11**	**16**	**27**	**45**	....	....	....	....	....
	Muskegon	IHL	31	20	36	56	49	6	2	3	5	25
1988-89	**Pittsburgh**	**NHL**	**30**	**6**	**5**	**11**	**20**	**10**	**2**	**5**	**7**	**10**
	Muskegon	IHL	48	25	39	64	40	7	5	5	10	30
1989-90	**Pittsburgh**	**NHL**	**30**	**4**	**7**	**11**	**49**	....	....	....	....	....
	Muskegon	IHL	46	29	49	78	118	15	6	*14	20	54
1990-91	Muskegon	IHL	30	14	20	34	102	....	....	....	....	....
1991-92b	Muskegon	IHL	81	42	70	112	160	10	4	10	14	13
	Pittsburgh	**NHL**	....	....	....	....	....	**12**	**1**	**3**	**4**	**2**
1992-93	**Tampa Bay**	**NHL**	**8**	**1**	**1**	**2**	**2**	....	....	....	....	....
	Atlanta	IHL	69	34	50	84	172	9	*7	5	12	25
	NHL Totals		**109**	**22**	**29**	**51**	**116**	**22**	**3**	**8**	**11**	**12**

a IHL Playoff MVP (1986)
b IHL First All-Star Team (1987, 1992)
c Shared James Gatschene Memorial Trophy (MVP-IHL) with Jeff Pyle (1987)
d Shared Leo P. Lamoureux Memorial Trophy (Top Scorer-IHL) with Jeff Pyle (1987)

Signed as a free agent by **St. Louis**, September 28, 1981. Signed as a free agent by **Pittsburgh**, July 31, 1987. Signed as a free agent by **Tampa Bay**, July 29, 1992.

CALOUN, JAN (CHAH-lohn)

Right wing. Shoots right. 5'10", 176 lbs. Born, Usti-Nad-Labem, Czech., December 20, 1972.
(San Jose's 4th choice, 75th overall, in 1992 Entry Draft).

			Regular Season					Playoffs				
Season	Club	Lea	GP	G	A	TP	PIM	GP	G	A	TP	PIM
1990-91	Litvinov	Czech.	50	28	19	47	12	....	....	....	....	....
1991-92	Litvinov	Czech.	46	39	13	52	24	....	....	....	....	....
1992-93	Litvinov	Czech.	47	45	22	67	....	....	....	....	....	....

CAMPBELL, JIM

Center. Shoots right. 6'1", 175 lbs. Born, Worcester, MA, April 3, 1973.
(Montreal's 2nd choice, 28th overall, in 1991 Entry Draft).

			Regular Season					Playoffs				
Season	Club	Lea	GP	G	A	TP	PIM	GP	G	A	TP	PIM
1991-92	Hull	QMJHL	64	41	44	85	51	6	7	3	10	8
1992-93	Hull	QMJHL	50	42	29	71	66	8	11	4	15	43

CAMPEAU, CHRISTIAN

Right wing. Shoots right. 5'10", 178 lbs. Born, Verdun, Que., June 2, 1971.

			Regular Season					Playoffs				
Season	Club	Lea	GP	G	A	TP	PIM	GP	G	A	TP	PIM
1990-91	Granby	QMJHL	69	16	27	43	128	....	....	....	....	....
1991-92	Rouen	France	16	3	5	8	12	....	....	....	....	....
1992-93	Atlanta	IHL	66	3	5	8	40	3	0	0	0	2

Signed as a free agent by **Tampa Bay**, July 10, 1992.

CANAVAN, ROBERT

Left wing. Shoots left. 5'11", 180 lbs. Born, Boston, MA, February 4, 1973.
(NY Islanders' 10th choice, 202nd overall, in 1991 Entry Draft).

			Regular Season					Playoffs				
Season	Club	Lea	GP	G	A	TP	PIM	GP	G	A	TP	PIM
1991-92	Boston College	H.E.	30	7	4	11	28	....	....	....	....	....
1992-93	Boston College	H.E.	30	8	8	16	30	....	....	....	....	....

CAPUANO, DAVE (KAP-yew-AN-oh)

Left wing. Shoots left. 6'2", 190 lbs. Born, Warwick, RI, July 27, 1968.
(Pittsburgh's 2nd choice, 25th overall, in 1986 Entry Draft).

			Regular Season					Playoffs				
Season	Club	Lea	GP	G	A	TP	PIM	GP	G	A	TP	PIM
1986-87	U. of Maine	H.E.	38	18	41	59	14	....	....	....	....	....
1987-88abc	U. of Maine	H.E.	42	*34	*51	*85	51	....	....	....	....	....
1988-89ac	U. of Maine	H.E.	41	37	30	67	38	....	....	....	....	....
1989-90	**Pittsburgh**	**NHL**	**6**	**0**	**0**	**0**	**2**	....	....	....	....	....
	Muskegon	IHL	27	15	15	30	22	....	....	....	....	....
	Vancouver	**NHL**	**27**	**3**	**5**	**8**	**10**	....	....	....	....	....
	Milwaukee	IHL	2	0	4	4	0	6	1	5	6	0
1990-91	**Vancouver**	**NHL**	**61**	**13**	**31**	**44**	**42**	**6**	**1**	**1**	**2**	**5**
1991-92	Milwaukee	IHL	9	2	6	8	8	....	....	....	....	....
1992-93	Hamilton	AHL	4	0	1	1	0	....	....	....	....	....
	Tampa Bay	**NHL**	**6**	**1**	**1**	**2**	**2**	....	....	....	....	....
	Atlanta	IHL	58	19	40	59	50	8	2	2	4	9
	NHL Totals		**100**	**17**	**37**	**54**	**56**	**6**	**1**	**1**	**2**	**5**

a NCAA East First All-American Team (1988, 1989)
b NCAA All-Tournament Team (1988)
c Hockey East First All-Star Team (1988, 1989)

Traded to **Vancouver** by **Pittsburgh** with Andrew McBain and Dan Quinn for Rod Buskas, Barry Pederson and Tony Tanti, January 8, 1990. Traded to **Tampa Bay** by **Vancouver** with Vancouver's fourth round choice in 1994 Entry Draft for Anatoli Semenov, November 3, 1992. Traded to **San Jose** by **Tampa Bay** for Peter Ahola, June 19, 1993.

CAPUANO, DEAN

Defense. Shoots right. 6'1", 175 lbs. Born, Providence, RI, November 3, 1971.
(Boston's 10th choice, 210th overall, in 1990 Entry Draft).

			Regular Season					Playoffs				
Season	Club	Lea	GP	G	A	TP	PIM	GP	G	A	TP	PIM
1990-91	Providence	H.E.	19	3	5	8	6	....	....	....	....	....
1991-92	Providence	H.E.	3	0	0	0	0	....	....	....	....	....
1992-93	Merrimac	H.E.				DID NOT PLAY						

CARBONNEAU, GUY (KAR-buhn-oh, GEE)

Center. Shoots right. 5'11", 184 lbs. Born, Sept-Iles, Que., March 18, 1960.
(Montreal's 4th choice, 44th overall, in 1979 Entry Draft).

			Regular Season					Playoffs				
Season	Club	Lea	GP	G	A	TP	PIM	GP	G	A	TP	PIM
1976-77	Chicoutimi	QJHL	59	9	20	29	8	4	1	0	1	0
1977-78	Chicoutimi	QJHL	70	28	55	83	60	....	....	....	....	....
1978-79	Chicoutimi	QJHL	72	62	79	141	47	4	2	1	3	4
1979-80	Chicoutimi	QJHL	72	72	110	182	66	12	9	15	24	28
	Nova Scotia	AHL	....	....	....	....	....	2	1	1	2	2
1980-81	**Montreal**	**NHL**	**2**	**0**	**1**	**1**	**0**	....	....	....	....	....
	Nova Scotia	AHL	78	35	53	88	87	6	1	3	4	9
1981-82	Nova Scotia	AHL	77	27	67	94	124	9	2	7	9	8
1982-83	**Montreal**	**NHL**	**77**	**18**	**29**	**47**	**68**	**3**	**0**	**0**	**0**	**2**
1983-84	**Montreal**	**NHL**	**78**	**24**	**30**	**54**	**75**	**15**	**4**	**3**	**7**	**12**
1984-85	**Montreal**	**NHL**	**79**	**23**	**34**	**57**	**43**	**12**	**4**	**3**	**7**	**8**
1985-86	**Montreal**	**NHL**	**80**	**20**	**36**	**56**	**57**	**20**	**7**	**5**	**12**	**35**
1986-87	**Montreal**	**NHL**	**79**	**18**	**27**	**45**	**68**	**17**	**3**	**8**	**11**	**20**
1987-88a	**Montreal**	**NHL**	**80**	**17**	**21**	**38**	**61**	**11**	**0**	**4**	**4**	**2**
1988-89a	**Montreal**	**NHL**	**79**	**26**	**30**	**56**	**44**	**21**	**4**	**5**	**9**	**10**
1989-90	**Montreal**	**NHL**	**68**	**19**	**36**	**55**	**37**	**11**	**2**	**3**	**5**	**6**
1990-91	**Montreal**	**NHL**	**78**	**20**	**24**	**44**	**63**	**13**	**1**	**5**	**6**	**10**
1991-92a	**Montreal**	**NHL**	**72**	**18**	**21**	**39**	**39**	**11**	**1**	**1**	**2**	**6**
1992-93	**Montreal**	**NHL**	**61**	**4**	**13**	**17**	**20**	**20**	**3**	**3**	**6**	**10**
	NHL Totals		**833**	**207**	**302**	**509**	**575**	**154**	**29**	**40**	**69**	**121**

a Won Frank J. Selke Trophy (1988, 1989, 1992)

CARKNER, TERRY

Defense. Shoots left. 6'3", 212 lbs. Born, Smiths Falls, Ont., March 7, 1966.
(NY Rangers' 1st choice, 14th overall, in 1984 Entry Draft).

			Regular Season					Playoffs				
Season	Club	Lea	GP	G	A	TP	PIM	GP	G	A	TP	PIM
1983-84	Peterborough	OHL	58	4	19	23	77	8	0	6	6	13
1984-85a	Peterborough	OHL	64	14	47	61	125	17	2	10	12	11
1985-86b	Peterborough	OHL	54	12	32	44	106	16	1	7	8	17
1986-87	**NY Rangers**	**NHL**	**52**	**2**	**13**	**15**	**118**	**1**	**0**	**0**	**0**	**0**
	New Haven	AHL	12	2	6	8	56	3	1	0	1	0
1987-88	**Quebec**	**NHL**	**63**	**3**	**24**	**27**	**159**	....	....	....	....	....
1988-89	**Philadelphia**	**NHL**	**78**	**11**	**32**	**43**	**149**	**19**	**1**	**5**	**6**	**28**
1989-90	**Philadelphia**	**NHL**	**63**	**4**	**18**	**22**	**169**	....	....	....	....	....
1990-91	**Philadelphia**	**NHL**	**79**	**7**	**25**	**32**	**204**	....	....	....	....	....
1991-92	**Philadelphia**	**NHL**	**73**	**4**	**12**	**16**	**195**	....	....	....	....	....
1992-93	**Philadelphia**	**NHL**	**83**	**3**	**16**	**19**	**150**	....	....	....	....	....
	NHL Totals		**491**	**34**	**140**	**174**	**1144**	**20**	**1**	**5**	**6**	**28**

a OHL Second All-Star Team (1985)
b OHL First All-Star Team (1986)

Traded to **Quebec** by **NY Rangers** with Jeff Jackson for John Ogrodnick and David Shaw, September 30, 1987. Traded to **Philadelphia** by **Quebec** for Greg Smyth and Philadelphia's third round choice (John Tanner) in the 1989 Entry Draft, July 25, 1988.

CARLSON, MARK

Left wing. Shoots left. 6', 193 lbs. Born, Danbury, CT, February 5, 1969.
(Pittsburgh's 11th choice, 215th overall, in 1987 Entry Draft).

			Regular Season					Playoffs				
Season	Club	Lea	GP	G	A	TP	PIM	GP	G	A	TP	PIM
1990-91	Lowell	H.E.	11	0	1	1	20	....	....	....	....	....
1991-92	Lowell	H.E.	23	3	1	4	20	....	....	....	....	....
1992-93	Lowell	H.E.	30	3	1	4	12	....	....	....	....	....

CARLYLE, RANDY ROBERT

Defense. Shoots left. 5'10", 200 lbs. Born, Sudbury, Ont., April 19, 1956.
(Toronto's 1st choice, 30th overall, in 1976 Amateur Draft).

			Regular Season					Playoffs				
Season	Club	Lea	GP	G	A	TP	PIM	GP	G	A	TP	PIM
1974-75	Sudbury	OMJHL	67	17	47	64	118	15	3	6	9	21
1975-76a	Sudbury	OHA	60	15	64	79	126	17	6	13	19	50
1976-77	**Toronto**	**NHL**	**45**	**0**	**5**	**5**	**51**	**9**	**0**	**1**	**1**	**20**
	Dallas	CHL	26	2	7	9	63	....	....	....	....	....
1977-78	**Toronto**	**NHL**	**49**	**2**	**11**	**13**	**31**	**7**	**0**	**1**	**1**	**8**
	Dallas	CHL	21	3	14	17	31					
1978-79	**Pittsburgh**	**NHL**	**70**	**13**	**34**	**47**	**78**	**7**	**0**	**0**	**0**	**12**
1979-80	**Pittsburgh**	**NHL**	**67**	**8**	**28**	**36**	**45**	**5**	**1**	**0**	**1**	**4**
1980-81bc	**Pittsburgh**	**NHL**	**76**	**16**	**67**	**83**	**136**	**5**	**4**	**5**	**9**	**9**
1981-82	**Pittsburgh**	**NHL**	**73**	**11**	**64**	**75**	**131**	**5**	**1**	**3**	**4**	**16**
1982-83	**Pittsburgh**	**NHL**	**61**	**15**	**41**	**56**	**110**	....	....	....	....	....
1983-84	**Pittsburgh**	**NHL**	**50**	**3**	**23**	**26**	**82**	....	....	....	....	....
	Winnipeg	**NHL**	**5**	**0**	**3**	**3**	**2**	**3**	**0**	**2**	**2**	**4**
1984-85	**Winnipeg**	**NHL**	**71**	**13**	**38**	**51**	**98**	**8**	**1**	**5**	**6**	**13**
1985-86	**Winnipeg**	**NHL**	**68**	**16**	**33**	**49**	**93**	....	....	....	....	....
1986-87	**Winnipeg**	**NHL**	**71**	**16**	**26**	**42**	**93**	**10**	**1**	**5**	**6**	**18**
1987-88	**Winnipeg**	**NHL**	**78**	**15**	**44**	**59**	**210**	**5**	**0**	**2**	**2**	**10**
1988-89	**Winnipeg**	**NHL**	**78**	**6**	**38**	**44**	**78**	....	....	....	....	....
1989-90	**Winnipeg**	**NHL**	**53**	**3**	**15**	**18**	**50**	....	....	....	....	....
1990-91	**Winnipeg**	**NHL**	**52**	**9**	**19**	**28**	**44**	....	....	....	....	....
1991-92	**Winnipeg**	**NHL**	**66**	**1**	**9**	**10**	**54**	**5**	**1**	**0**	**1**	**6**
1992-93	**Winnipeg**	**NHL**	**22**	**1**	**1**	**2**	**14**	....	....	....	....	....
	NHL Totals		**1055**	**148**	**499**	**647**	**1400**	**69**	**9**	**24**	**33**	**120**

a OHA Second All-Star Team (1976)
b Won James Norris Memorial Trophy (1981)
c NHL First All-Star Team (1981)

Played in NHL All-Star Game (1981-83, 1985, 1993)

Traded to **Pittsburgh** by **Toronto** with George Ferguson for Dave Burrows, June 14, 1978. Traded to **Winnipeg** by **Pittsburgh** for Winnipeg's first round choice (Doug Bodger) in 1984 Entry Draft and future considerations (Moe Mantha, May 1, 1984), March 5, 1984.

CARNBACK, PATRIK (KAHRN-buhk)

Left wing. Shoots left. 6', 189 lbs. Born, Goteborg, Sweden, February 1, 1968.
(Montreal's 7th choice, 125th overall, in 1988 Entry Draft).

			Regular Season					Playoffs				
Season	Club	Lea	GP	G	A	TP	PIM	GP	G	A	TP	PIM
1986-87	V. Frolunda	Swe.2	28	3	1	4	4	....	....	....	....	....
1987-88	V. Frolunda	Swe.2	33	16	19	35	24	11	4	5	9	8
1988-89	V. Frolunda	Swe.2	53	39	36	75	52	....	....	....	....	....
1989-90	V. Frolunda	Swe.	40	26	27	53	34	....	....	....	....	....
1990-91	V. Frolunda	Swe.	22	10	9	19	46	28	15	24	39	24
1991-92	V. Frolunda	Swe.	33	17	22	39	32	3	1	5	6	20
1992-93	**Montreal**	**NHL**	**6**	**0**	**0**	**0**	**2**	....	....	....	....	....
	Fredericton	AHL	45	20	37	57	45	5	0	3	3	14
	NHL Totals		**6**	**0**	**0**	**0**	**2**	....	....	....	....	....

Traded to **Anaheim** by **Montreal** with Todd Ewen for Anaheim's third round choice in 1994 Entry Draft, August 10, 1993.

CARNEY, KEITH

Defense. Shoots left. 6'1", 180 lbs. Born, Cumberland, RI, February 7, 1971.
(Toronto's 5th choice, 96th overall, in 1989 Entry Draft).

			Regular Season					Playoffs				
Season	Club	Lea	GP	G	A	TP	PIM	GP	G	A	TP	PIM
1989-90	Lowell	H.E.	8	0	2	2	2	....	....	....	....	....
1990-91	Lowell	H.E.	11	0	2	2	8	....	....	....	....	....
1991-92	Lowell	H.E.	22	1	6	7	24	....	....	....	....	....
1992-93	Lowell	H.E.	30	2	10	12	28	....	....	....	....	....

CARNEY, KEITH E.

Defense. Shoots left. 6'2", 205 lbs. Born, Providence, RI, February 3, 1970.
(Buffalo's 3rd choice, 76th overall, in 1988 Entry Draft).

			Regular Season					Playoffs				
Season	Club	Lea	GP	G	A	TP	PIM	GP	G	A	TP	PIM
1988-89	U. of Maine	H.E.	40	4	22	26	24	....	....	....	....	....
1989-90ab	U. of Maine	H.E.	41	3	41	44	43	....	....	....	....	....
1990-91cd	U. of Maine	H.E.	40	7	49	56	38	....	....	....	....	....
1991-92	U.S. National	....	49	2	17	19	16	....	....	....	....	....
	Buffalo	**NHL**	**14**	**1**	**2**	**3**	**18**	**7**	**0**	**3**	**3**	**0**
	Rochester	AHL	24	1	10	11	2	2	0	2	2	0
1992-93	**Buffalo**	**NHL**	**30**	**2**	**4**	**6**	**55**	**8**	**0**	**3**	**3**	**6**
	Rochester	AHL	41	5	21	26	32	....	....	....	....	....
	NHL Totals		**44**	**3**	**6**	**9**	**73**	**15**	**0**	**6**	**6**	**6**

a Hockey East Second All-Star Team (1990)
b NCAA East Second All-American Team (1990)
c Hockey East First All-Star Team (1991)
d NCAA East First All-American Team (1991)

CARPENTER, ROBERT (BOB)

Center/Left wing. Shoots left. 6', 190 lbs. Born, Beverly, MA, July 13, 1963.
(Washington's 1st choice, 3rd overall, in 1981 Entry Draft).

			Regular Season					Playoffs				
Season	Club	Lea	GP	G	A	TP	PIM	GP	G	A	TP	PIM
1980-81	St. John's	HS	18	14	24	38	....	....	....	....	....	....
1981-82	**Washington**	**NHL**	**80**	**32**	**35**	**67**	**69**	....	....	....	....	....
1982-83	**Washington**	**NHL**	**80**	**32**	**37**	**69**	**64**	**4**	**1**	**0**	**1**	**2**
1983-84	**Washington**	**NHL**	**80**	**28**	**40**	**68**	**51**	**8**	**2**	**1**	**3**	**25**
1984-85	**Washington**	**NHL**	**80**	**53**	**42**	**95**	**87**	**5**	**1**	**4**	**5**	**8**
1985-86	**Washington**	**NHL**	**80**	**27**	**29**	**56**	**105**	**9**	**5**	**4**	**9**	**12**
1986-87	**Washington**	**NHL**	**22**	**5**	**7**	**12**	**21**	....	....	....	....	....
	NY Rangers	**NHL**	**28**	**2**	**8**	**10**	**20**	....	....	....	....	....
	Los Angeles	**NHL**	**10**	**2**	**3**	**5**	**6**	**5**	**1**	**2**	**3**	**2**
1987-88	**Los Angeles**	**NHL**	**71**	**19**	**33**	**52**	**84**	**5**	**1**	**1**	**2**	**0**
1988-89	**Los Angeles**	**NHL**	**39**	**11**	**15**	**26**	**16**	....	....	....	....	....
	Boston	**NHL**	**18**	**5**	**9**	**14**	**10**	**8**	**1**	**1**	**2**	**4**
1989-90	**Boston**	**NHL**	**80**	**25**	**31**	**56**	**97**	**21**	**4**	**6**	**10**	**39**
1990-91	**Boston**	**NHL**	**29**	**8**	**8**	**16**	**22**	**1**	**0**	**1**	**1**	**2**
1991-92	**Boston**	**NHL**	**60**	**25**	**23**	**48**	**46**	**8**	**0**	**1**	**1**	**6**
1992-93	**Washington**	**NHL**	**68**	**11**	**17**	**28**	**65**	**6**	**1**	**4**	**5**	**6**
	NHL Totals		**825**	**285**	**337**	**622**	**763**	**80**	**17**	**25**	**42**	**106**

Played in NHL All-Star Game (1985)

Traded to **NY Rangers** by **Washington** with Washington's second round choice (Jason Prosofsky) in 1989 Entry Draft for Bob Crawford, Kelly Miller and Mike Ridley, January 1, 1987. Traded to **Los Angeles** by **NY Rangers** with Tom Laidlaw for Jeff Crossman, Marcel Dionne and Los Angeles' third round choice (later traded to Minnesota — Minnesota selected Murray Garbutt) in 1989 Entry Draft. Traded to **Boston** by **Los Angeles** for Steve Kasper, January 23, 1989. Signed as a free agent by **Washington**, June 30, 1992.

CARPER, BRANDON

Defense. Shoots left. 6'2", 190 lbs. Born, Highland Park, IL, April 2, 1972.
(Calgary's 9th choice, 198th overall, in 1992 Entry Draft).

			Regular Season					Playoffs				
Season	Club	Lea	GP	G	A	TP	PIM	GP	G	A	TP	PIM
1991-92	Bowling Green	CCHA	34	2	16	18	44	....	....	....	....	....
1992-93	Bowling Green	CCHA	41	7	20	27	72	....	....	....	....	....

CARSON, JIMMY

Center. Shoots right. 6', 200 lbs. Born, Southfield, MI, July 20, 1968.
(Los Angeles' 1st choice, 2nd overall, in 1986 Entry Draft).

			Regular Season					Playoffs				
Season	Club	Lea	GP	G	A	TP	PIM	GP	G	A	TP	PIM
1984-85	Verdun	QMJHL	68	44	72	116	12	14	9	17	26	12
1985-86a	Verdun	QMJHL	69	70	83	153	46	5	2	6	8	0
1986-87b	**Los Angeles**	**NHL**	**80**	**37**	**42**	**79**	**22**	**5**	**1**	**2**	**3**	**6**
1987-88	**Los Angeles**	**NHL**	**80**	**55**	**52**	**107**	**45**	**5**	**5**	**3**	**8**	**4**
1988-89	**Edmonton**	**NHL**	**80**	**49**	**51**	**100**	**36**	**7**	**2**	**1**	**3**	**6**
1989-90	**Edmonton**	**NHL**	**4**	**1**	**2**	**3**	**0**	....	....	....	....	....
	Detroit	**NHL**	**44**	**20**	**16**	**36**	**8**	....	....	....	....	....
1990-91	**Detroit**	**NHL**	**64**	**21**	**25**	**46**	**28**	**7**	**2**	**1**	**3**	**4**
1991-92	**Detroit**	**NHL**	**80**	**34**	**35**	**69**	**30**	**11**	**2**	**3**	**5**	**0**
1992-93	**Detroit**	**NHL**	**52**	**25**	**26**	**51**	**18**	....	....	....	....	....
	Los Angeles	**NHL**	**34**	**12**	**10**	**22**	**14**	**18**	**5**	**4**	**9**	**2**
	NHL Totals		**518**	**254**	**259**	**513**	**201**	**53**	**17**	**14**	**31**	**22**

a QMJHL Second All-Star Team (1986)
b Named to NHL All-Rookie Team (1987)

Played in NHL All-Star Game (1989)

Traded to **Edmonton** by **Los Angeles** with Martin Gelinas, Los Angeles' first round choices in 1989 (later traded to New Jersey — New Jersey selected Jason Miller), 1991 (Martin Rucinsky) and 1993(Nick Stajduhar) Entry Drafts and cash for Wayne Gretzky, Mike Krushelnyski and Marty McSorley, August 9, 1988. Traded to **Detroit** by **Edmonton** with Kevin McClelland and Edmonton's fifth round choice (later traded to Montreal — Montreal selected Brad Layzell) in 1991 Entry Draft for Petr Klima, Joe Murphy, Adam Graves and Jeff Sharples, November 2, 1989. Traded to **Los Angeles** by **Detroit** with Marc Potvin and Gary Shuchuk for Paul Coffey, Sylvain Couturier and Jim Hiller, January 29, 1993.

CARTER, ANSON

Center. Shoots right. 6'1", 175 lbs. Born, Toronto, Ont., June 6, 1974.
(Quebec's 10th choice, 220th overall, in 1992 Entry Draft).

			Regular Season					Playoffs				
Season	Club	Lea	GP	G	A	TP	PIM	GP	G	A	TP	PIM
1991-92	Wexford	OHA Jr. A	42	18	22	40	24	....	....	....	....	....
1992-93	Michigan State	CCHA	34	15	7	22	20	....	....	....	....	....

CARTER, JOHN

Left wing. Shoots left. 5'10", 181 lbs. Born, Winchester, MA, May 3, 1963.

			Regular Season					Playoffs				
Season	Club	Lea	GP	G	A	TP	PIM	GP	G	A	TP	PIM
1982-83	RPI	ECAC	29	16	22	38	33	....	....	....	....	....
1983-84	RPI	ECAC	38	35	39	74	52	....	....	....	....	....
1984-85	RPI	ECAC	37	43	29	72	52	....	....	....	....	....
1985-86	RPI	ECAC	27	23	18	41	68	....	....	....	....	....
	Boston	**NHL**	**3**	**0**	**0**	**0**	**0**	....	....	....	....	....
1986-87	**Boston**	**NHL**	**8**	**0**	**1**	**1**	**0**	....	....	....	....	....
	Moncton	AHL	58	25	30	55	60	6	2	3	5	5
1987-88	**Boston**	**NHL**	**4**	**0**	**1**	**1**	**2**	....	....	....	....	....
	Maine	AHL	76	38	38	76	145	10	4	4	8	44
1988-89	**Boston**	**NHL**	**44**	**12**	**10**	**22**	**24**	**10**	**1**	**2**	**3**	**6**
	Maine	AHL	24	13	6	19	12	....	....	....	....	....
1989-90	**Boston**	**NHL**	**76**	**17**	**22**	**39**	**26**	**21**	**6**	**3**	**9**	**45**
	Maine	AHL	2	2	2	4	2	....	....	....	....	....
1990-91	**Boston**	**NHL**	**50**	**4**	**7**	**11**	**68**	....	....	....	....	....
	Maine	AHL	16	5	9	14	16	1	0	0	0	10
1991-92	**San Jose**	**NHL**	**4**	**0**	**0**	**0**	**0**	....	....	....	....	....
	Kansas City	IHL	42	11	15	26	116	15	6	9	15	18
1992-93	**San Jose**	**NHL**	**55**	**7**	**9**	**16**	**81**	....	....	....	....	....
	Kansas City	IHL	9	4	2	6	14	....	....	....	....	....
	NHL Totals		**244**	**40**	**50**	**90**	**201**	**31**	**7**	**5**	**12**	**51**

Signed as a free agent by **Boston**, May 3, 1986. Signed as a free agent by **San Jose**, August 22, 1991.

CARUSO, BRIAN

Left wing. Shoots left. 6'2", 225 lbs. Born, Thunder Bay, Ont., September 20, 1972.
(Calgary's 4th choice, 63rd overall, in 1991 Entry Draft).

			Regular Season					Playoffs				
Season	Club	Lea	GP	G	A	TP	PIM	GP	G	A	TP	PIM
1990-91	Minn.-Duluth	WCHA	31	5	6	11	24	....	....	....	....	....
1991-92	Minn.-Duluth	WCHA	29	2	3	5	34	....	....	....	....	....
1992-93	Minn. Duluth	WCHA	40	12	13	25	24	....	....	....	....	....
	Cdn. National	....	2	0	0	0	2	....	....	....	....	....

CARVEL, GREG

Center. Shoots left. 5'11", 185 lbs. Born, Canton, NY, August 17, 1970.
(Pittsburgh's 1st choice, 22nd overall, in 1991 Supplemental Draft).

			Regular Season					Playoffs				
Season	Club	Lea	GP	G	A	TP	PIM	GP	G	A	TP	PIM
1989-90	St. Lawrence	ECAC	30	5	16	21	18	....	....	....	....	....
1990-91	St. Lawrence	ECAC	34	7	15	22	18	....	....	....	....	....
1991-92	St. Lawrence	ECAC	34	12	20	32	23	....	....	....	....	....
1992-93	St. Lawrence	ECAC	32	14	34	48	30	....	....	....	....	....

CASSELMAN, MIKE

Center. Shoots left. 5'11", 180 lbs. Born, Morrisburg, Ont., August 23, 1968.
(Detroit's 1st choice, 3rd overall, in 1990 Supplemental Draft).

			Regular Season					Playoffs				
Season	Club	Lea	GP	G	A	TP	PIM	GP	G	A	TP	PIM
1987-88	Clarkson	ECAC	24	4	1	5	....	....	....	....	....	....
1988-89	Clarkson	ECAC	31	3	14	17	....	....	....	....	....	....
1989-90	Clarkson	ECAC	34	22	21	43	69	....	....	....	....	....
1990-91	Clarkson	ECAC	40	19	35	54	44	....	....	....	....	....
1991-92a	Toledo	ECHL	61	39	60	99	83	5	0	1	1	6
	Adirondack	AHL	1	0	0	0	0	....	....	....	....	....
1992-93	Adirondack	AHL	60	12	19	31	27	8	3	3	6	0
	Toledo	ECHL	3	0	1	1	2	....	....	....	....	....

a ECHL Second All-Star Team (1992)

CASSELS, ANDREW (CASTLES)

Center. Shoots left. 6', 192 lbs. Born, Bramalea, Ont., July 23, 1969.
(Montreal's 1st choice, 17th overall, in 1987 Entry Draft).

			Regular Season					Playoffs				
Season	Club	Lea	GP	G	A	TP	PIM	GP	G	A	TP	PIM
1986-87a	Ottawa	OHL	66	26	66	92	28	11	5	9	14	7
1987-88bc	Ottawa	OHL	61	48	*103	*151	39	16	8	*24	*32	13
1988-89c	Ottawa	OHL	56	37	97	134	66	12	5	10	15	10
1989-90	**Montreal**	**NHL**	**6**	**2**	**0**	**2**	**2**	....	....	....	....	....
	Sherbrooke	AHL	55	22	45	67	25	12	2	11	13	6
1990-91	**Montreal**	**NHL**	**54**	**6**	**19**	**25**	**20**	**8**	**0**	**2**	**2**	**2**
1991-92	**Hartford**	**NHL**	**67**	**11**	**30**	**41**	**18**	**7**	**2**	**4**	**6**	**6**
1992-93	**Hartford**	**NHL**	**84**	**21**	**64**	**85**	**62**	....	....	....	....	....
	NHL Totals		**211**	**40**	**113**	**153**	**102**	**15**	**2**	**6**	**8**	**8**

a OHL Rookie of the Year (1987)
b OHL Player of the Year (1988)
c OHL First All-Star Team (1988,1989)

Traded to **Hartford** by **Montreal** for Hartford's second round choice (Valeri Bure) in 1992 Entry Draft, September 17, 1991.

CAUFIELD, JAY

Right wing. Shoots right. 6'4", 237 lbs. Born, Philadelphia, PA, July 17, 1960.

			Regular Season					Playoffs				
Season	Club	Lea	GP	G	A	TP	PIM	GP	G	A	TP	PIM
1984-85	North Dakota	WCHA	1	0	0	0	0	....	....	....	....	....
1985-86	Toledo	IHL	30	5	4	9	54	....	....	....	....	....
	New Haven	AHL	40	2	3	5	40	1	0	0	0	0
1986-87	**NY Rangers**	**NHL**	**13**	**2**	**1**	**3**	**45**	**3**	**0**	**0**	**0**	**12**
	Flint	IHL	12	4	3	7	59	....	....	....	....	....
	New Haven	AHL	13	0	0	0	43	....	....	....	....	....
1987-88	**Minnesota**	**NHL**	**1**	**0**	**0**	**0**	**0**	....	....	....	....	....
	Kalamazoo	IHL	65	5	10	15	273	6	0	1	1	47
1988-89	**Pittsburgh**	**NHL**	**58**	**1**	**4**	**5**	**285**	**9**	**0**	**0**	**0**	**28**
1989-90	**Pittsburgh**	**NHL**	**37**	**1**	**2**	**3**	**123**	....	....	....	....	....
1990-91	**Pittsburgh**	**NHL**	**23**	**1**	**1**	**2**	**71**	....	....	....	....	....
	Muskegon	IHL	3	1	0	1	18	....	....	....	....	....
1991-92	**Pittsburgh**	**NHL**	**50**	**0**	**0**	**0**	**175**	**5**	**0**	**0**	**0**	**2**
1992-93	**Pittsburgh**	**NHL**	**26**	**0**	**0**	**0**	**60**	....	....	....	....	....
	NHL Totals		**208**	**5**	**8**	**13**	**759**	**17**	**0**	**0**	**0**	**42**

Signed as a free agent by **NY Rangers**, October 8, 1985. Traded to **Minnesota** by **NY Rangers** with Dave Gagne for Jari Gronstrand and Paul Boutilier, October 8, 1987. Claimed by **Pittsburgh** in NHL Waiver Draft, October 3, 1988.

CAVALLINI, GINO JOHN

Left wing. Shoots left. 6'1", 215 lbs. Born, Toronto, Ont., November 24, 1962.

			Regular Season					Playoffs				
Season	Club	Lea	GP	G	A	TP	PIM	GP	G	A	TP	PIM
1982-83	Bowling Green	CCHA	40	8	16	24	52	....	....	....	....	....
1983-84	Bowling Green	CCHA	43	25	23	48	16	....	....	....	....	....
1984-85	**Calgary**	**NHL**	**27**	**6**	**10**	**16**	**14**	**3**	**0**	**0**	**0**	**4**
	Moncton	AHL	51	29	19	48	28	....	....	....	....	....
1985-86	**Calgary**	**NHL**	**27**	**7**	**7**	**14**	**26**	....	....	....	....	....
	Moncton	AHL	4	3	2	5	7	....	....	....	....	....
	St. Louis	**NHL**	**30**	**6**	**5**	**11**	**36**	**17**	**4**	**5**	**9**	**10**
1986-87	**St. Louis**	**NHL**	**80**	**18**	**26**	**44**	**54**	**6**	**3**	**1**	**4**	**2**
1987-88	**St. Louis**	**NHL**	**64**	**15**	**17**	**32**	**62**	**10**	**5**	**5**	**10**	**19**
1988-89	**St. Louis**	**NHL**	**74**	**20**	**23**	**43**	**79**	**9**	**0**	**2**	**2**	**17**
1989-90	**St. Louis**	**NHL**	**80**	**15**	**15**	**30**	**77**	**12**	**1**	**3**	**4**	**12**
1990-91	**St. Louis**	**NHL**	**78**	**8**	**27**	**35**	**81**	**13**	**1**	**3**	**4**	**2**
1991-92	**St. Louis**	**NHL**	**48**	**9**	**7**	**16**	**40**	....	....	....	....	....
	Quebec	**NHL**	**18**	**1**	**7**	**8**	**4**	....	....	....	....	....
1992-93	**Quebec**	**NHL**	**67**	**9**	**15**	**24**	**34**	**4**	**0**	**0**	**0**	**0**
	NHL Totals		**593**	**114**	**159**	**273**	**507**	**74**	**14**	**19**	**33**	**66**

Signed as a free agent by **Calgary**, May 16, 1984. Traded to **St. Louis** by **Calgary** with Eddy Beers and Charles Bourgeois for Joe Mullen, Terry Johnson and Rik Wilson, February 1, 1986. Claimed on waivers by **Quebec** from **St. Louis**, February 27, 1992.

CAVALLINI, PAUL

Defense. Shoots left. 6'1", 210 lbs. Born, Toronto, Ont., October 13, 1965.
(Washington's 9th choice, 205th overall, in 1984 Entry Draft).

			Regular Season					Playoffs				
Season	Club	Lea	GP	G	A	TP	PIM	GP	G	A	TP	PIM
1984-85	Providence	H.E.	37	4	10	14	52	....	....	....	....	....
1985-86	Cdn. Olympic	....	52	1	11	12	95	....	....	....	....	....
	Binghamton	AHL	15	3	4	7	20	6	0	2	2	56
1986-87	**Washington**	**NHL**	**6**	**0**	**2**	**2**	**8**	....	....	....	....	....
	Binghamton	AHL	66	12	24	36	188	13	2	7	9	35
1987-88	**Washington**	**NHL**	**24**	**2**	**3**	**5**	**66**	....	....	....	....	....
	St. Louis	**NHL**	**48**	**4**	**7**	**11**	**86**	**10**	**1**	**6**	**7**	**26**
1988-89	**St. Louis**	**NHL**	**65**	**4**	**20**	**24**	**128**	**10**	**2**	**2**	**4**	**14**
1989-90a	**St. Louis**	**NHL**	**80**	**8**	**39**	**47**	**106**	**12**	**2**	**3**	**5**	**20**
1990-91	**St. Louis**	**NHL**	**67**	**10**	**25**	**35**	**89**	**13**	**2**	**3**	**5**	**20**
1991-92	**St. Louis**	**NHL**	**66**	**10**	**25**	**35**	**95**	**4**	**0**	**1**	**1**	**6**
1992-93	**St. Louis**	**NHL**	**11**	**1**	**4**	**5**	**10**	....	....	....	....	....
	Washington	**NHL**	**71**	**5**	**8**	**13**	**46**	**6**	**0**	**2**	**2**	**18**
	NHL Totals		**438**	**44**	**133**	**177**	**634**	**55**	**7**	**17**	**24**	**104**

a Won Alka-Seltzer Plus Award (NHL plus/minus leader) (1990)

Played in NHL All-Star Game (1990)

Traded to **St. Louis** by **Washington** for Montreal's second round choice (previously acquired by St. Louis — Washington selected Wade Bartley) in 1988 Entry Draft, December 11, 1987. Traded to **Washington** by **St. Louis** for Kevin Miller, November 2, 1992. Traded to **Dallas** by **Washington** for future considerations (Enrico Ciccone, June 25, 1993), June 20, 1993.

CERNICH, KORD

Defense. Shoots left. 5'11", 195 lbs. Born, Ketchikan, AK, October 20, 1966.

			Regular Season					Playoffs				
Season	Club	Lea	GP	G	A	TP	PIM	GP	G	A	TP	PIM
1986-87	Lake Superior	CCHA	39	4	18	22	32	....	....	....	....	....
1987-88a	Lake Superior	CCHA	46	17	22	39	78	....	....	....	....	....
1988-89b	Lake Superior	CCHA	46	7	31	38	74	....	....	....	....	....
1989-90bc	Lake Superior	CCHA	46	11	25	36	59	....	....	....	....	....
1990-91	Binghamton	AHL	52	5	10	15	36	....	....	....	....	....
1991-92	Binghamton	AHL	5	1	3	4	6	....	....	....	....	....
	San Diego	IHL	64	5	18	23	53	3	1	0	1	0
1992-93	Rochester	AHL	4	0	0	0	2	....	....	....	....	....
	Capital Dist.	AHL	6	0	0	0	4	....	....	....	....	....
	San Diego	IHL	17	1	5	6	4	3	0	0	0	2
	Detroit	Col.	31	5	12	17	18	....	....	....	....	....

a CCHA Second All-Star Team (1988)
b CCHA First All-Star Team (1989, 1990)
c NCAA West Second All-American Team (1990)

Signed as a free agent by **NY Rangers**, July 19, 1990.

CHABOT, JOHN DAVID (shah-BAHT)

Center. Shoots left. 6'2", 200 lbs. Born, Summerside, P.E.I., May 18, 1962.
(Montreal's 3rd choice, 40th overall, in 1980 Entry Draft).

			Regular Season					Playoffs				
Season	Club	Lea	GP	G	A	TP	PIM	GP	G	A	TP	PIM
1979-80	Hull	QMJHL	68	26	57	83	28	4	1	2	3	0
1980-81	Hull	QMJHL	70	27	62	89	24	....	....	....	....	....
	Nova Scotia	AHL	1	0	0	0	0	2	0	0	0	0
1981-82ab	Sherbrooke	QMJHL	62	34	*109	143	42	19	6	26	32	6
1982-83	Nova Scotia	AHL	76	16	73	89	19	7	1	3	4	0
1983-84	**Montreal**	**NHL**	**56**	**18**	**25**	**43**	**13**	**11**	**1**	**4**	**5**	**0**
1984-85	**Montreal**	**NHL**	**10**	**1**	**6**	**7**	**2**	....	....	....	....	....
	Pittsburgh	**NHL**	**67**	**8**	**45**	**53**	**12**	....	....	....	....	....
1985-86	**Pittsburgh**	**NHL**	**77**	**14**	**31**	**45**	**6**	....	....	....	....	....
1986-87	**Pittsburgh**	**NHL**	**72**	**14**	**22**	**36**	**8**	....	....	....	....	....
1987-88	**Detroit**	**NHL**	**78**	**13**	**44**	**57**	**10**	**16**	**4**	**15**	**19**	**2**
1988-89	**Detroit**	**NHL**	**52**	**2**	**10**	**12**	**6**	**6**	**1**	**1**	**2**	**0**
	Adirondack	AHL	8	3	12	15	0	....	....	....	....	....
1989-90	**Detroit**	**NHL**	**69**	**9**	**40**	**49**	**24**	....	....	....	....	....
1990-91	**Detroit**	**NHL**	**27**	**5**	**5**	**10**	**4**	....	....	....	....	....
	Adirondack	AHL	27	11	30	41	4	2	0	1	1	0
1991-92	Milano	Italy	18	10	36	46	4	12	3	13	16	2
1992-93	Preussen Berlin	Ger.	20	10	17	27	14	....	....	....	....	....
	NHL Totals		**508**	**84**	**228**	**312**	**85**	**33**	**6**	**20**	**26**	**2**

a QMJHL First All-Star Team (1982)
b QMJHL Most Valuable Player (1982)

Traded to **Pittsburgh** by **Montreal** for Ron Flockhart, November 9, 1984. Signed as a free agent by **Detroit**, June 25, 1987.

CHALIFOUX, DENIS

Center. Shoots right. 5'8", 165 lbs. Born, Laval, Que., February 28, 1971.
(Hartford's 11th choice, 246th overall, in 1990 Entry Draft).

			Regular Season					Playoffs				
Season	Club	Lea	GP	G	A	TP	PIM	GP	G	A	TP	PIM
1989-90	Laval	QMJHL	70	41	68	109	32	14	*14	14	*28	14
1990-91a	Laval	QMJHL	67	38	79	117	77	4	1	1	2	4
1991-92	Springfield	AHL	66	17	20	37	26	4	1	0	1	4
1992-93	Springfield	AHL	64	17	27	44	22	15	5	8	13	14

a QMJHL Second All-Star Team (1991)

CHAMBERS, SHAWN

Defense. Shoots left. 6'2", 200 lbs. Born, Royal Oaks, MI, October 11, 1966.
(Minnesota's 1st choice, 4th overall, in 1987 Supplemental Draft).

			Regular Season					Playoffs				
Season	Club	Lea	GP	G	A	TP	PIM	GP	G	A	TP	PIM
1985-86	Alaska-Fair.	G.N.	25	15	21	36	34	....	....	....	....	....
1986-87	Alaska-Fair.	G.N.	28	8	29	37	84	....	....	....	....	....
	Seattle	WHL	28	8	25	33	58	....	....	....	....	....
	Fort Wayne	IHL	12	2	6	8	0	10	1	4	5	5
1987-88	**Minnesota**	**NHL**	**19**	**1**	**7**	**8**	**21**	....	....	....	....	....
	Kalamazoo	IHL	19	1	6	7	22	....	....	....	....	....
1988-89	**Minnesota**	**NHL**	**72**	**5**	**19**	**24**	**80**	**3**	**0**	**2**	**2**	**0**
1989-90	**Minnesota**	**NHL**	**78**	**8**	**18**	**26**	**81**	**7**	**2**	**1**	**3**	**10**
1990-91	**Minnesota**	**NHL**	**29**	**1**	**3**	**4**	**24**	**23**	**0**	**7**	**7**	**16**
	Kalamazoo	IHL	3	1	1	2	0	....	....	....	....	....
1991-92	**Washington**	**NHL**	**2**	**0**	**0**	**0**	**2**	....	....	....	....	....
	Baltimore	AHL	5	2	3	5	9	....	....	....	....	....
1992-93	**Tampa Bay**	**NHL**	**55**	**10**	**29**	**39**	**36**	....	....	....	....	....
	Atlanta	IHL	6	0	2	2	18	....	....	....	....	....
	NHL Totals		**255**	**25**	**76**	**101**	**244**	**33**	**2**	**10**	**12**	**26**

Traded to **Washington** by **Minnesota** for Steve Maltais and Trent Klatt, June 21, 1991. Claimed by **Tampa Bay** from **Washington** in Expansion Draft, June 18, 1992.

CHAPDELAINE, RENE (SHAP-duh-LAYN)

Defense. Shoots right. 6'1", 195 lbs. Born, Weyburn, Sask., September 27, 1966.
(Los Angeles' 7th choice, 149th overall, in 1986 Entry Draft).

			Regular Season					Playoffs				
Season	Club	Lea	GP	G	A	TP	PIM	GP	G	A	TP	PIM
1985-86	Lake Superior	CCHA	32	1	4	5	47	....	....	....	....	....
1986-87	Lake Superior	CCHA	28	1	5	6	51	....	....	....	....	....
1987-88	Lake Superior	CCHA	35	1	9	10	44	....	....	....	....	....
1988-89	Lake Superior	CCHA	46	4	9	13	62	....	....	....	....	....
1989-90	New Haven	AHL	41	0	1	1	35	....	....	....	....	....
1990-91	**Los Angeles**	**NHL**	**3**	**0**	**1**	**1**	**10**	....	....	....	....	....
	New Haven	AHL	65	3	11	14	49	....	....	....	....	....
	Phoenix	IHL	17	0	2	2	10	11	0	0	0	8
1991-92	**Los Angeles**	**NHL**	**16**	**0**	**1**	**1**	**10**	....	....	....	....	....
	Phoenix	IHL	62	4	22	26	87	....	....	....	....	....
	New Haven	AHL	....	....	....	....	....	4	0	2	2	0
1992-93	**Los Angeles**	**NHL**	**13**	**0**	**0**	**0**	**12**	....	....	....	....	....
	Phoenix	IHL	44	1	17	18	54	....	....	....	....	....
	San Diego	IHL	9	1	1	2	8	14	0	1	1	27
	NHL Totals		**32**	**0**	**2**	**2**	**32**	....	....	....	....	....

CHAPMAN, BRIAN

Defense. Shoots left. 6', 195 lbs. Born, Brockville, Ont., February 10, 1968.
(Hartford's 3rd choice, 74th overall, in 1986 Entry Draft).

			Regular Season					Playoffs				
Season	Club	Lea	GP	G	A	TP	PIM	GP	G	A	TP	PIM
1985-86	Belleville	OHL	66	6	31	37	168	24	2	6	8	54
1986-87	Belleville	OHL	54	4	32	36	142	6	1	1	2	10
1987-88	Belleville	OHL	63	11	57	68	180	6	1	4	5	13
1988-89	Binghamton	AHL	71	5	25	30	216	....	....	....	....	....
1989-90	Binghamton	AHL	68	2	15	17	180	....	....	....	....	....
1990-91	**Hartford**	**NHL**	**3**	**0**	**0**	**0**	**29**	....	....	....	....	....
	Springfield	AHL	60	4	23	27	200	18	1	4	5	62
1991-92	Springfield	AHL	73	3	26	29	245	10	2	2	4	25
1992-93	Springfield	AHL	72	17	34	51	212	15	2	5	7	43
	NHL Totals		**3**	**0**	**0**	**0**	**29**	....	....	....	....	....

CHARBONNEAU, STEPHANE (SHAHR-buh-NOH)

Right wing. Shoots right. 6'2", 195 lbs. Born, Ste-Adele, Que., June 27, 1970.

			Regular Season					Playoffs				
Season	Club	Lea	GP	G	A	TP	PIM	GP	G	A	TP	PIM
1989-90	Shawinigan	QMJHL	62	37	58	95	154	....	....	....	....	....
1990-91	Shawinigan	QMJHL	6	4	3	7	2	....	....	....	....	....
	Chicoutimi	QMJHL	55	37	30	67	109	17	*13	9	22	43
1991-92	**Quebec**	**NHL**	**2**	**0**	**0**	**0**	**0**	....	....	....	....	....
	Halifax	AHL	64	22	25	47	183	....	....	....	....	....
1992-93	Halifax	AHL	56	18	20	38	125	....	....	....	....	....
	NHL Totals		**2**	**0**	**0**	**0**	**0**	....	....	....	....	....

Signed as a free agent by **Quebec**, April 25, 1991.

CHARRON, ERIC

Defense. Shoots left. 6'3", 192 lbs. Born, Verdun, Que., January 14, 1970.
(Montreal's 1st choice, 20th overall, in 1988 Entry Draft).

			Regular Season					Playoffs				
Season	Club	Lea	GP	G	A	TP	PIM	GP	G	A	TP	PIM
1987-88	Trois-Rivières	QMJHL	67	3	13	16	135	....	....	....	....	....
1988-89	Trois-Rivières	QMJHL	38	2	16	18	111	....	....	....	....	....
	Verdun	QMJHL	28	2	15	17	66	....	....	....	....	....
	Sherbrooke	AHL	1	0	0	0	0	....	....	....	....	....
1989-90	St-Hyacinthe	QMJHL	68	13	38	51	152	11	3	4	7	67
	Sherbrooke	AHL	....	....	....	....	....	2	0	0	0	0
1990-91	Fredericton	AHL	71	1	11	12	108	2	1	0	1	29
1991-92	Fredericton	AHL	59	2	11	13	98	6	1	0	1	4
1992-93	**Montreal**	**NHL**	**3**	**0**	**0**	**0**	**2**	....	....	....	....	....
	Fredericton	AHL	54	3	13	16	93	....	....	....	....	....
	Atlanta	IHL	11	0	2	2	12	3	0	1	1	6
	NHL Totals		**3**	**0**	**0**	**0**	**2**	....	....	....	....	....

Traded to **Tampa Bay** by **Montreal** with Alain Cote and future considerations (Donald Dufresne, June 18, 1993) for Rob Ramage, March 20, 1993.

CHASE, DON

Center. Shoots right. 5'11", 190 lbs. Born, Springfield, MA, March 17, 1974.
(Montreal's 7th choice, 116th overall, in 1992 Entry Draft).

			Regular Season					Playoffs				
Season	Club	Lea	GP	G	A	TP	PIM	GP	G	A	TP	PIM
1991-92	Springfield	US Jr.	49	69	75	144	80	....	....	....	....	....
1992-93	Boston College	H.E.	38	7	5	12	48	....	....	....	....	....

CHASE, KELLY WAYNE

Right wing. Shoots right. 5'11", 195 lbs. Born, Porcupine Plain, Sask., October 25, 1967.

			Regular Season					Playoffs				
Season	Club	Lea	GP	G	A	TP	PIM	GP	G	A	TP	PIM
1985-86	Saskatoon	WHL	57	7	18	25	172	10	3	4	7	37
1986-87	Saskatoon	WHL	68	17	29	46	285	11	2	8	10	37
1987-88	Saskatoon	WHL	70	21	34	55	*343	9	3	5	8	32
1988-89	Peoria	IHL	38	14	7	21	278	....	....	....	....	....
1989-90	**St. Louis**	**NHL**	**43**	**1**	**3**	**4**	**244**	**9**	**1**	**0**	**1**	**46**
	Peoria	IHL	10	1	2	3	76	....	....	....	....	....
1990-91	**St. Louis**	**NHL**	**2**	**1**	**0**	**1**	**15**	**6**	**0**	**0**	**0**	**18**
	Peoria	IHL	61	20	34	54	406	10	4	3	7	61
1991-92	**St. Louis**	**NHL**	**46**	**1**	**2**	**3**	**264**	**1**	**0**	**0**	**0**	**7**
1992-93	**St. Louis**	**NHL**	**49**	**2**	**5**	**7**	**204**	....	....	....	....	....
	NHL Totals		**140**	**5**	**10**	**15**	**727**	**16**	**1**	**0**	**1**	**71**

Signed as a free agent by **St. Louis**, February 23, 1988.

CHASE, TIMOTHY

Center. Shoots left. 6'2", 180 lbs. Born, Gaithersburg, MD, March 23, 1970.
(Montreal's 8th choice, 146th overall, in 1988 Entry Draft).

			Regular Season					Playoffs				
Season	Club	Lea	GP	G	A	TP	PIM	GP	G	A	TP	PIM
1989-90	Brown	ECAC	8	0	0	0	0	....	....	....	....	....
1990-91	Brown	ECAC	19	5	8	13	18	....	....	....	....	....
1991-92	Brown	ECAC	29	19	10	29	25	....	....	....	....	....
1992-93	Brown	ECAC	13	3	4	7	12	....	....	....	....	....
	Fredericton	AHL	25	4	8	12	16	3	0	0	0	0

CHEBATOR, ROB

Defense. Shoots left. 6', 170 lbs. Born, Arlington, MA, December 1, 1970.
(Toronto's 9th choice, 199th overall, in 1990 Entry Draft).

			Regular Season					Playoffs				
Season	Club	Lea	GP	G	A	TP	PIM	GP	G	A	TP	PIM
1990-91	N. Hampshire	H.E.	33	4	2	6	14	....	....	....	....	....
1991-92	N. Hampshire	H.E.	36	5	6	11	24	....	....	....	....	....
1992-93	N. Hampshire	HE	38	3	10	13	68	....	....	....	....	....

CHEBATURKIN, VLADIMIR

Defense. Shoots left. 6'2", 189 lbs. Born, Tyumen, Soviet Union, April 23, 1975.
(NY Islanders' 3rd choice, 66th overall, in 1993 Entry Draft).

			Regular Season					Playoffs				
Season	Club	Lea	GP	G	A	TP	PIM	GP	G	A	TP	PIM
1992-93	Elektrostal	CIS 2			UNAVAILABLE							

CHECCO, NICHOLAS

Center. Shoots left. 5'11", 185 lbs. Born, Minneapolis, MN, November 18, 1974.
(Quebec's 7th choice, 137th overall, in 1993 Entry Draft).

			Regular Season					Playoffs				
Season	Club	Lea	GP	G	A	TP	PIM	GP	G	A	TP	PIM
1991-92	Bloom'ton-Jeff.	HS	28	17	17	34	22	....	....	....	....	....
1992-93	Bloom'ton-Jeff.	HS	26	22	23	45	18	....	....	....	....	....

CHELIOS, CHRIS (CHELL-EE-ohs)

Defense. Shoots right. 6'1", 186 lbs. Born, Chicago, IL, January 25, 1962.
(Montreal's 5th choice, 40th overall, in 1981 Entry Draft).

			Regular Season					Playoffs				
Season	Club	Lea	GP	G	A	TP	PIM	GP	G	A	TP	PIM
1981-82	U. Wisconsin	WCHA	43	6	43	49	50	....	....	....	....	....
1982-83ab	U. Wisconsin	WCHA	26	9	17	26	50	....	....	....	....	....
1983-84	U.S. National	....	60	14	35	49	58	....	....	....	....	....
	U.S. Olympic	....	6	0	4	4	8	....	....	....	....	....
	Montreal	**NHL**	**12**	**0**	**2**	**2**	**12**	**15**	**1**	**9**	**10**	**17**
1984-85c	**Montreal**	**NHL**	**74**	**9**	**55**	**64**	**87**	**9**	**2**	**8**	**10**	**17**
1985-86	**Montreal**	**NHL**	**41**	**8**	**26**	**34**	**67**	**20**	**2**	**9**	**11**	**49**
1986-87	**Montreal**	**NHL**	**71**	**11**	**33**	**44**	**124**	**17**	**4**	**9**	**13**	**38**
1987-88	**Montreal**	**NHL**	**71**	**20**	**41**	**61**	**172**	**11**	**3**	**1**	**4**	**29**
1988-89de	**Montreal**	**NHL**	**80**	**15**	**58**	**73**	**185**	**21**	**4**	**15**	**19**	**28**
1989-90	**Montreal**	**NHL**	**53**	**9**	**22**	**31**	**136**	**5**	**0**	**1**	**1**	**8**
1990-91f	**Chicago**	**NHL**	**77**	**12**	**52**	**64**	**192**	**6**	**1**	**7**	**8**	**46**
1991-92	**Chicago**	**NHL**	**80**	**9**	**47**	**56**	**245**	**18**	**6**	**15**	**21**	**37**
1992-93de	**Chicago**	**NHL**	**84**	**15**	**58**	**73**	**282**	**4**	**0**	**2**	**2**	**14**
	NHL Totals		**643**	**108**	**394**	**502**	**1502**	**126**	**23**	**76**	**99**	**283**

a WCHA Second All-Star Team (1983)
b NCAA All-Tournament Team (1983)
c NHL All-Rookie Team (1985)
d NHL First All-Star Team (1989, 1993)
e Won Norris Trophy (1989, 1993)
f NHL Second All-Star Team (1991)

Played in NHL All-Star Game (1985, 1990-93)

Traded to **Chicago** by **Montreal** with Montreal's second round choice (Michael Pomichter) in 1991 Entry Draft for Denis Savard, June 29, 1990.

CHERBAYEV, ALEXANDER (cher-BIGH-ev)

Left wing. Shoots left. 6'1", 187 lbs. Born, Voskresensk, Soviet Union, August 13, 1973.
(San Jose's 3rd choice, 51st overall, in 1992 Entry Draft).

			Regular Season					Playoffs				
Season	Club	Lea	GP	G	A	TP	PIM	GP	G	A	TP	PIM
1990-91	Khimik	USSR	16	2	2	4	0	....	....	....	....	....
1991-92	Khimik	CIS	38	3	3	6	14	....	....	....	....	....
1992-93	Khimik	CIS	33	18	9	27	74	2	1	0	1	0

CHERNOMAZ, RICHARD (RICH) (CHUR-noh-maz)

Right wing. Shoots right. 5'8", 185 lbs. Born, Selkirk, Man., September 1, 1963.
(Colorado's 2nd choice, 26th overall, in 1981 Entry Draft).

			Regular Season					Playoffs				
Season	Club	Lea	GP	G	A	TP	PIM	GP	G	A	TP	PIM
1980-81	Victoria	WHL	72	49	64	113	92	15	11	15	26	38
1981-82	**Colorado**	**NHL**	**2**	**0**	**0**	**0**	**0**	....	....	....	....	....
	Victoria	WHL	49	36	62	98	69	4	1	2	3	13
1982-83a	Victoria	WHL	64	71	53	124	113	12	10	5	15	18
1983-84	**New Jersey**	**NHL**	**7**	**2**	**1**	**3**	**2**	....	....	....	....	....
	Maine	AHL	69	17	29	46	39	2	0	1	1	0
1984-85	**New Jersey**	**NHL**	**3**	**0**	**2**	**2**	**2**	....	....	....	....	....
	Maine	AHL	64	17	34	51	64	10	2	2	4	4
1985-86	Maine	AHL	78	21	28	49	82	5	0	0	0	2
1986-87	**New Jersey**	**NHL**	**25**	**6**	**4**	**10**	**8**	....	....	....	....	....
	Maine	AHL	58	35	27	62	65	....	....	....	....	....
1987-88	**Calgary**	**NHL**	**2**	**1**	**0**	**1**	**0**	....	....	....	....	....
b	Salt Lake	IHL	73	48	47	95	122	18	4	14	18	30
1988-89	**Calgary**	**NHL**	**1**	**0**	**0**	**0**	**0**	....	....	....	....	....
	Salt Lake	IHL	81	33	68	101	122	14	7	5	12	47
1989-90	Salt Lake	IHL	65	39	35	74	170	11	6	6	12	32
1990-91b	Salt Lake	IHL	81	39	58	97	213	4	3	1	4	8
1991-92	**Calgary**	**NHL**	**11**	**0**	**0**	**0**	**6**	....	....	....	....	....
	Salt Lake	IHL	66	20	40	60	201	5	1	2	3	10
1992-93	Salt Lake	IHL	76	26	48	74	172	....	....	....	....	....
	NHL Totals		**51**	**9**	**7**	**16**	**18**	....	....	....	....	....

a WHL First All-Star Team (1983)
b IHL Second All-Star Team (1988, 1991)

Signed as a free agent by **Calgary**, August 4, 1987. Signed as a free agent by **Toronto**, August 3, 1993.

CHERVYAKOV, DENIS (chair-vigh-KAWV)

Defense. Shoots left. 6', 185 lbs. Born, Leningrad, Soviet Union, April 20, 1970.
(Boston's 9th choice, 256th overall, in 1992 Entry Draft).

			Regular Season					Playoffs				
Season	Club	Lea	GP	G	A	TP	PIM	GP	G	A	TP	PIM
1990-91	Leningrad	USSR	28	2	1	3	40	....	....	....	....	....
1991-92	Riga	CIS	14	0	1	1	12	....	....	....	....	....
1992-93	**Boston**	**NHL**	**2**	**0**	**0**	**0**	**2**	....	....	....	....	....
	Providence	AHL	48	4	12	16	99	....	....	....	....	....
	NHL Totals		**2**	**0**	**0**	**0**	**2**	....	....	....	....	....

CHEVELDAYOFF, KEVIN (sheh-vehl-DAY-ahf)

Defense. Shoots right. 6', 202 lbs. Born, Saskatoon, Sask., February 4, 1970.
(NY Islanders' 1st choice, 16th overall, in 1988 Entry Draft).

			Regular Season					Playoffs				
Season	Club	Lea	GP	G	A	TP	PIM	GP	G	A	TP	PIM
1986-87	Brandon	WHL	70	0	16	16	259	....	....	....	....	....
1987-88	Brandon	WHL	71	3	29	32	265	4	0	2	2	20
1988-89	Brandon	WHL	40	4	12	16	135	....	....	....	....	....
1989-90	Brandon	WHL	33	5	12	17	56	....	....	....	....	....
	Springfield	AHL	4	0	0	0	0	....	....	....	....	....
1990-91	Capital Dist.	AHL	76	0	14	14	203	....	....	....	....	....
1991-92	Capital Dist.	AHL	44	0	4	4	110	7	0	0	0	22
1992-93	Capital Dist.	AHL	79	3	8	11	113	4	0	1	1	8

CHIASSON, STEVE (CHAY-sahn)

Defense. Shoots left. 6'1", 205 lbs. Born, Barrie, Ont., April 14, 1967.
(Detroit's 3rd choice, 50th overall, in 1985 Entry Draft).

			Regular Season					Playoffs				
Season	Club	Lea	GP	G	A	TP	PIM	GP	G	A	TP	PIM
1984-85	Guelph	OHL	61	8	22	30	139	....	....	....	....	....
1985-86	Guelph	OHL	54	12	30	42	126	18	10	10	20	37
1986-87	**Detroit**	**NHL**	**45**	**1**	**4**	**5**	**73**	**2**	**0**	**0**	**0**	**19**
1987-88	**Detroit**	**NHL**	**29**	**2**	**9**	**11**	**57**	**9**	**2**	**2**	**4**	**31**
	Adirondack	AHL	23	6	11	17	58	....	....	....	....	....
1988-89	**Detroit**	**NHL**	**65**	**12**	**35**	**47**	**149**	**5**	**2**	**1**	**3**	**6**
1989-90	**Detroit**	**NHL**	**67**	**14**	**28**	**42**	**114**	....	....	....	....	....
1990-91	**Detroit**	**NHL**	**42**	**3**	**17**	**20**	**80**	**5**	**3**	**1**	**4**	**19**
1991-92	**Detroit**	**NHL**	**62**	**10**	**24**	**34**	**136**	**11**	**1**	**5**	**6**	**12**
1992-93	**Detroit**	**NHL**	**79**	**12**	**50**	**62**	**155**	**7**	**2**	**2**	**4**	**19**
	NHL Totals		**389**	**54**	**167**	**221**	**764**	**39**	**10**	**11**	**21**	**106**

Played in NHL All-Star Game (1993)

CHINAKHOV, VITALI (chih-NAH-khov)

Center. Shoots left. 5'11", 183 lbs. Born, Perm, Soviet Union, January 15, 1972.
(NY Rangers' 10th choice, 235th overall, in 1991 Entry Draft).

			Regular Season					Playoffs				
Season	Club	Lea	GP	G	A	TP	PIM	GP	G	A	TP	PIM
1990-91	Torpedo Yaro.	USSR	21	1	2	3	10	....	....	....	....	....
1991-92	Torpedo Yaro.	CIS	18	4	1	5	4	....	....	....	....	....
1992-93	Torpedo Yaro.	CIS	3	0	0	0	0	....	....	....	....	....
	Perm	CIS	20	2	4	6	12	....	....	....	....	....

CHITARONI, TERRY

Center. Shoots right. 5'11", 200 lbs. Born, Haileybury, Ont., December 9, 1972.
(Toronto's 2nd choice, 69th overall, in 1991 Entry Draft).

			Regular Season					Playoffs				
Season	Club	Lea	GP	G	A	TP	PIM	GP	G	A	TP	PIM
1988-89	Sudbury	OHL	58	17	23	40	103	....	....	....	....	....
1989-90	Sudbury	OHL	65	21	47	68	173	7	4	1	5	15
1990-91	Sudbury	OHL	61	28	43	71	162	5	1	1	2	18
1991-92	Sudbury	OHL	51	31	47	78	119	11	7	5	12	39
	St. John's	AHL	....	....	....	....	....	2	0	1	1	5
1992-93	St. John's	AHL	30	4	7	11	107	....	....	....	....	....
	Baltimore	AHL	16	2	1	3	14	....	....	....	....	....

CHORSKE, TOM

Right/Left wing. Shoots right. 6'1", 204 lbs. Born, Minneapolis, MN, September 18, 1966.
(Montreal's 2nd choice, 16th overall, in 1985 Entry Draft).

			Regular Season					Playoffs				
Season	Club	Lea	GP	G	A	TP	PIM	GP	G	A	TP	PIM
1985-86	U. Minnesota	WCHA	39	6	4	10	16	....	....	....	....	....
1986-87	U. Minnesota	WCHA	47	20	22	42	20	....	....	....	....	....
1987-88	U.S. National	....	36	9	16	25	24	....	....	....	....	....
1988-89a	U. Minnesota	WCHA	37	25	24	49	28	....	....	....	....	....
1989-90	**Montreal**	**NHL**	**14**	**3**	**1**	**4**	**2**	....	....	....	....	....
	Sherbrooke	AHL	59	22	24	46	54	12	4	4	8	8
1990-91	**Montreal**	**NHL**	**57**	**9**	**11**	**20**	**32**	....	....	....	....	....
1991-92	**New Jersey**	**NHL**	**76**	**19**	**17**	**36**	**32**	**7**	**0**	**3**	**3**	**4**
1992-93	**New Jersey**	**NHL**	**50**	**7**	**12**	**19**	**25**	**1**	**0**	**0**	**0**	**0**
	Utica	AHL	6	1	4	5	2	....	....	....	....	....
	NHL Totals		**197**	**38**	**41**	**79**	**91**	**8**	**0**	**3**	**3**	**4**

a WCHA First All-Star Team (1989)

Traded to **New Jersey** by **Montreal** with Stephane Richer for Kirk Muller and Roland Melanson, September 20, 1991.

CHRISTIAN, DAVID (DAVE)

Right wing. Shoots right. 5'11", 175 lbs. Born, Warroad, MN, May 12, 1959.
(Winnipeg's 2nd choice, 40th overall, in 1979 Entry Draft).

			Regular Season					Playoffs				
Season	Club	Lea	GP	G	A	TP	PIM	GP	G	A	TP	PIM
1977-78	North Dakota	WCHA	38	8	16	24	14	....	....	....	....	....
1978-79	North Dakota	WCHA	40	22	24	46	22	....	....	....	....	....
1979-80	U.S. National	....	59	10	20	30	26	....	....	....	....	....
	U.S. Olympic	....	7	0	8	8	6	....	....	....	....	....
	Winnipeg	**NHL**	**15**	**8**	**10**	**18**	**2**	....	....	....	....	....
1980-81	**Winnipeg**	**NHL**	**80**	**28**	**43**	**71**	**22**	....	....	....	....	....
1981-82	**Winnipeg**	**NHL**	**80**	**25**	**51**	**76**	**28**	**4**	**0**	**1**	**1**	**2**
1982-83	**Winnipeg**	**NHL**	**55**	**18**	**26**	**44**	**23**	**3**	**0**	**0**	**0**	**0**
1983-84	**Washington**	**NHL**	**80**	**29**	**52**	**81**	**28**	**8**	**5**	**4**	**9**	**5**
1984-85	**Washington**	**NHL**	**80**	**26**	**43**	**69**	**14**	**5**	**1**	**1**	**2**	**0**
1985-86	**Washington**	**NHL**	**80**	**41**	**42**	**83**	**15**	**9**	**4**	**4**	**8**	**0**
1986-87	**Washington**	**NHL**	**76**	**23**	**27**	**50**	**8**	**7**	**1**	**3**	**4**	**6**
1987-88	**Washington**	**NHL**	**80**	**37**	**21**	**58**	**26**	**14**	**5**	**6**	**11**	**6**
1988-89	**Washington**	**NHL**	**80**	**34**	**31**	**65**	**12**	**6**	**1**	**1**	**2**	**0**
1989-90	**Washington**	**NHL**	**28**	**3**	**8**	**11**	**4**	....	....	....	....	....
	Boston	**NHL**	**50**	**12**	**17**	**29**	**8**	**21**	**4**	**1**	**5**	**4**
1990-91	**Boston**	**NHL**	**78**	**32**	**21**	**53**	**41**	**19**	**8**	**4**	**12**	**4**
1991-92	**St. Louis**	**NHL**	**78**	**20**	**24**	**44**	**41**	**4**	**3**	**0**	**3**	**0**
1992-93	**Chicago**	**NHL**	**60**	**4**	**14**	**18**	**12**	**1**	**0**	**0**	**0**	**0**
	NHL Totals		**1000**	**340**	**430**	**770**	**284**	**101**	**32**	**25**	**57**	**27**

Played in NHL All-Star Game (1991)

Traded to **Washington** by **Winnipeg** for Washington's first round choice (Bob Dollas) in the 1983 Entry Draft, June 8, 1983. Traded to **Boston** by **Washington** for Bob Joyce, December 13, 1989. Acquired by **St. Louis** from **Boston** with Boston's third round choice (Vitali Prokhorov) in 1992 Entry Draft and Boston's seventh round choice (Lance Burns) in 1992 Entry Draft as compensation for Boston's free agent signings of Glen Featherstone and Dave Thomlinson, July 30, 1991. Claimed by **Chicago** from **St. Louis** in NHL Waiver Draft, October 4, 1992.

CHRISTIAN, JEFF

Left wing. Shoots left. 6'1", 195 lbs. Born, Burlington, Ont., July 30, 1970.
(New Jersey's 2nd choice, 23rd overall, in 1988 Entry Draft).

			Regular Season					Playoffs				
Season	Club	Lea	GP	G	A	TP	PIM	GP	G	A	TP	PIM
1987-88	London	OHL	64	15	29	44	154	9	1	5	6	27
1988-89	London	OHL	64	27	30	57	221	20	3	4	7	56
1989-90	London	OHL	18	14	7	21	64	....	....	....	....	....
	Owen Sound	OHL	37	19	26	45	145	10	6	7	13	43
1990-91	Utica	AHL	80	24	42	66	165	....	....	....	....	....
1991-92	**New Jersey**	**NHL**	**2**	**0**	**0**	**0**	**2**	....	....	....	....	....
	Utica	AHL	76	27	24	51	198	4	0	0	0	16
1992-93	Utica	AHL	22	4	6	10	39	....	....	....	....	....
	Hamilton	AHL	11	2	5	7	35	....	....	....	....	....
	Cincinnati	IHL	36	5	12	17	113	....	....	....	....	....
	NHL Totals		**2**	**0**	**0**	**0**	**2**	....	....	....	....	....

CHURLA, SHANE

Right wing. Shoots right. 6'1", 200 lbs. Born, Fernie, B.C., June 24, 1965.
(Hartford's 4th choice, 110th overall, in 1985 Entry Draft).

			Regular Season					Playoffs				
Season	Club	Lea	GP	G	A	TP	PIM	GP	G	A	TP	PIM
1983-84	Medicine Hat	WHL	48	3	7	10	115	14	1	5	6	41
1984-85	Medicine Hat	WHL	70	14	20	34	370	9	1	0	1	55
1985-86	Binghamton	AHL	52	4	10	14	306	3	0	0	0	22
1986-87	**Hartford**	**NHL**	**20**	**0**	**1**	**1**	**78**	**2**	**0**	**0**	**0**	**42**
	Binghamton	AHL	24	1	5	6	249	....	....	....	....	....
1987-88	**Hartford**	**NHL**	**2**	**0**	**0**	**0**	**14**	....	....	....	....	....
	Binghamton	AHL	25	5	8	13	168	....	....	....	....	....
	Calgary	**NHL**	**29**	**1**	**5**	**6**	**132**	**7**	**0**	**1**	**1**	**17**
1988-89	**Calgary**	**NHL**	**5**	**0**	**0**	**0**	**25**	....	....	....	....	....
	Salt Lake	IHL	32	3	13	16	278	....	....	....	....	....
	Minnesota	**NHL**	**13**	**1**	**0**	**1**	**54**	....	....	....	....	....
1989-90	**Minnesota**	**NHL**	**53**	**2**	**3**	**5**	**292**	**7**	**0**	**0**	**0**	**44**
1990-91	**Minnesota**	**NHL**	**40**	**2**	**2**	**4**	**286**	**22**	**2**	**1**	**3**	**90**
1991-92	**Minnesota**	**NHL**	**57**	**4**	**1**	**5**	**278**	....	....	....	....	....
1992-93	**Minnesota**	**NHL**	**73**	**5**	**16**	**21**	**286**	....	....	....	....	....
	NHL Totals		**292**	**15**	**28**	**43**	**1445**	**38**	**2**	**2**	**4**	**193**

Traded to **Calgary** by **Hartford** with Dana Murzyn for Neil Sheehy, Carey Wilson, and the rights to Lane MacDonald, January 3, 1988. Traded to **Minnesota** by **Calgary** with Perry Berezan for Brian MacLellan and Minnesota's fourth round choice (Robert Reichel) in 1989 Entry Draft, March 4, 1989. Claimed by **San Jose** from **Minnesota** in Dispersal Draft, May 30, 1991. Traded to **Minnesota** by **San Jose** for Kelly Kisio, June 3, 1991.

CHYCHRUN, JEFF (CHIHK-rihn)

Defense. Shoots right. 6'4", 215 lbs. Born, LaSalle, Que., May 3, 1966.
(Philadelphia's 3rd choice, 37th overall, in 1984 Entry Draft).

			Regular Season					Playoffs				
Season	Club	Lea	GP	G	A	TP	PIM	GP	G	A	TP	PIM
1983-84	Kingston	OHL	63	1	13	14	137	....	....	....	....	....
1984-85	Kingston	OHL	58	4	10	14	206	....	....	....	....	....
1985-86	Kingston	OHL	61	4	21	25	127	10	2	1	3	17
	Hershey	AHL	....	....	....	....	....	4	0	1	1	9
	Kalamazoo	IHL	....	....	....	....	....	3	1	0	1	0
1986-87	**Philadelphia**	**NHL**	**1**	**0**	**0**	**0**	**4**	....	....	....	....	....
	Hershey	AHL	74	1	17	18	239	4	0	0	0	10
1987-88	**Philadelphia**	**NHL**	**3**	**0**	**0**	**0**	**4**	....	....	....	....	....
	Hershey	AHL	55	0	5	5	210	12	0	2	2	44
1988-89	**Philadelphia**	**NHL**	**80**	**1**	**4**	**5**	**245**	**19**	**0**	**2**	**2**	**65**
1989-90	**Philadelphia**	**NHL**	**79**	**2**	**7**	**9**	**250**	....	....	....	....	....
1990-91	**Philadelphia**	**NHL**	**36**	**0**	**6**	**6**	**105**	....	....	....	....	....
1991-92	**Los Angeles**	**NHL**	**26**	**0**	**3**	**3**	**76**	....	....	....	....	....
	Phoenix	IHL	3	0	0	0	6	....	....	....	....	....
	Pittsburgh	**NHL**	**17**	**0**	**1**	**1**	**35**	....	....	....	....	....
1992-93	**Pittsburgh**	**NHL**	**1**	**0**	**0**	**0**	**2**	....	....	....	....	....
	Los Angeles	**NHL**	**17**	**0**	**1**	**1**	**23**	....	....	....	....	....
	Phoenix	IHL	11	2	0	2	44	....	....	....	....	....
	NHL Totals		**260**	**3**	**22**	**25**	**744**	**19**	**0**	**2**	**2**	**65**

Traded to **Los Angeles** by **Philadelphia** with Jari Kurri for Steve Duchesne, Steve Kasper and Los Angeles' fourth round choice (Aris Brimanis) in 1991 Entry Draft, May 30, 1991. Traded to **Pittsburgh** by **Los Angeles** with Brian Benning and Los Angeles' first round choice (later traded to Philadelphia — Philadelphia selected Jason Bowen) in 1992 Entry Draft, for Paul Coffey, February 19, 1992. Traded to **Los Angeles** by **Pittsburgh** for Peter Ahola, November 6, 1992.

CHYNOWETH, DEAN (shih-NOWTH)

Defense. Shoots right. 6'2", 190 lbs. Born, Calgary, Alta., October 30, 1968.
(NY Islanders' 1st choice, 13th overall, in 1987 Entry Draft).

			Regular Season					Playoffs				
Season	Club	Lea	GP	G	A	TP	PIM	GP	G	A	TP	PIM
1985-86	Medicine Hat	WHL	69	3	12	15	208	17	3	2	5	52
1986-87	Medicine Hat	WHL	67	3	18	21	285	13	4	2	6	28
1987-88	Medicine Hat	WHL	64	1	21	22	274	16	0	6	6	*87
1988-89	**NY Islanders**	**NHL**	**6**	**0**	**0**	**0**	**48**	....	....	....	....	....
1989-90	**NY Islanders**	**NHL**	**20**	**0**	**2**	**2**	**39**	....	....	....	....	....
	Springfield	AHL	40	0	7	7	98	17	0	4	4	36
1990-91	**NY Islanders**	**NHL**	**25**	**1**	**1**	**2**	**59**	....	....	....	....	....
	Capital Dist.	AHL	44	1	5	6	176	....	....	....	....	....
1991-92	**NY Islanders**	**NHL**	**11**	**1**	**0**	**1**	**23**	....	....	....	....	....
	Capital Dist.	AHL	43	4	6	10	164	6	1	1	2	39
1992-93	Capital Dist.	AHL	52	3	10	13	197	4	0	1	1	9
	NHL Totals		**62**	**2**	**3**	**5**	**169**	....	....	....	....	....

CHYZOWSKI, DAVID   (chih-ZOW-skee)

Left wing. Shoots left. 6'1", 190 lbs.   Born, Edmonton, Alta., July 11, 1971.
(NY Islanders' 1st choice, 2nd overall, in 1989 Entry Draft).

				Regul	ar Se	ason				Play	offs	
Season	Club	Lea	GP	G	A	TP	PIM	GP	G	A	TP	PIM
1987-88	Kamloops	WHL	66	16	17	33	117	18	2	4	6	26
1988-89a	Kamloops	WHL	68	56	48	104	139	16	15	13	28	32
1989-90	**NY Islanders**	**NHL**	34	8	6	14	45	....	....	....	....	....
	Springfield	AHL	4	0	0	0	7	....	....	....	....	....
	Kamloops	WHL	4	5	2	7	17	17	11	6	17	46
1990-91	**NY Islanders**	**NHL**	56	5	9	14	61	....	....	....	....	....
	Capital Dist.	AHL	7	3	6	9	22	....	....	....	....	....
1991-92	**NY Islanders**	**NHL**	12	1	1	2	17	....	....	....	....	....
	Capital Dist.	AHL	55	15	18	33	121	6	1	1	2	23
1992-93	Capital Dist.	AHL	66	15	21	36	177	3	2	0	2	0
	NHL Totals		102	14	16	30	123	....	....	....	....	....

a WHL West All-Star Team (1989)

CIAVAGLIA, PETER

Center. Shoots left. 5'10", 173 lbs.   Born, Albany, NY, July 15, 1969.
(Calgary's 8th choice, 145th overall, in 1987 Entry Draft).

				Regul	ar Se	ason				Play	offs	
Season	Club	Lea	GP	G	A	TP	PIM	GP	G	A	TP	PIM
1987-88	Harvard	ECAC	30	10	23	33	16	....	....	....	....	....
1988-89a	Harvard	ECAC	34	15	48	63	36	....	....	....	....	....
1989-90	Harvard	ECAC	28	17	18	35	22	....	....	....	....	....
1990-91abc	Harvard	ECAC	27	24	*38	*62	2	....	....	....	....	....
1991-92	**Buffalo**	**NHL**	2	0	0	0	0	....	....	....	....	....
	Rochester	AHL	77	37	61	98	16	6	2	5	7	6
1992-93	**Buffalo**	**NHL**	3	0	0	0	0	....	....	....	....	....
	Rochester	AHL	64	35	67	102	32	17	9	16	25	12
	NHL Totals		5	0	0	0	0	....	....	....	....	....

a ECAC Second All-Star Team (1989, 1991)
b ECAC Player of the Year (1991)
c NCAA East Second All-American Team (1991)
Signed as a free agent by **Buffalo**, August 30, 1991.

CICCARELLI, DINO   (sih-sih-REHL-ee)

Right wing. Shoots right. 5'10", 175 lbs.   Born, Sarnia, Ont., February 8, 1960.

				Regul	ar Se	ason				Play	offs	
Season	Club	Lea	GP	G	A	TP	PIM	GP	G	A	TP	PIM
1977-78a	London	OHA	68	72	70	142	49	9	6	10	16	6
1978-79	London	OHA	30	8	11	19	35	7	3	5	8	0
1979-80	London	OHA	62	50	53	103	72	5	2	6	8	15
1980-81	**Minnesota**	**NHL**	32	18	12	30	29	19	14	7	21	25
	Oklahoma City	CHL	48	32	25	57	45	....	....	....	....	....
1981-82	**Minnesota**	**NHL**	76	55	51	106	138	4	3	1	4	2
1982-83	**Minnesota**	**NHL**	77	37	38	75	94	9	4	6	10	11
1983-84	**Minnesota**	**NHL**	79	38	33	71	58	16	4	5	9	27
1984-85	**Minnesota**	**NHL**	51	15	17	32	41	9	3	3	6	8
1985-86	**Minnesota**	**NHL**	75	44	45	89	51	5	0	1	1	6
1986-87	**Minnesota**	**NHL**	80	52	51	103	88	....	....	....	....	....
1987-88	**Minnesota**	**NHL**	67	41	45	86	79	....	....	....	....	....
1988-89	**Minnesota**	**NHL**	65	32	27	59	64	....	....	....	....	....
	Washington	**NHL**	11	12	3	15	12	6	3	3	6	12
1989-90	**Washington**	**NHL**	80	41	38	79	122	8	8	3	11	6
1990-91	**Washington**	**NHL**	54	21	18	39	66	11	5	4	9	22
1991-92	**Washington**	**NHL**	78	38	38	76	78	7	5	4	9	14
1992-93	**Detroit**	**NHL**	82	41	56	97	81	7	4	2	6	16
	NHL Totals		907	485	472	957	1001	101	53	39	92	149

a OHA Second All-Star Team (1978)
Played in NHL All-Star Game (1982, 1983,1989)
Signed as a free agent by **Minnesota**, September 28, 1979. Traded to **Washington** by **Minnesota** with Bob Rouse for Mike Gartner and Larry Murphy, March 7, 1989. Traded to **Detroit** by **Washington** for Kevin Miller, June 20, 1992.

CICCONE, ENRICO

Defense. Shoots left. 6'4", 200 lbs.   Born, Montreal, Que., April 10, 1970.
(Minnesota's 5th choice, 92nd overall, in 1990 Entry Draft).

				Regul	ar Se	ason				Play	offs	
Season	Club	Lea	GP	G	A	TP	PIM	GP	G	A	TP	PIM
1987-88	Shawinigan	QMJHL	61	2	12	14	324	....	....	....	....	....
1988-89	Shawinigan	QMJHL	34	7	11	18	132	....	....	....	....	....
	Trois-Rivières	QMJHL	24	0	7	7	153	....	....	....	....	....
1989-90	Trois-Rivières	QMJHL	40	4	24	28	227	3	0	0	0	15
1990-91	Kalamazoo	IHL	57	4	9	13	384	4	0	1	1	32
1991-92	**Minnesota**	**NHL**	11	0	0	0	48	....	....	....	....	....
	Kalamazoo	IHL	53	4	16	20	406	10	0	1	1	58
1992-93	**Minnesota**	**NHL**	31	0	1	1	115	....	....	....	....	....
	Kalamazoo	IHL	13	1	3	4	50	....	....	....	....	....
	Hamilton	AHL	6	1	3	4	44	....	....	....	....	....
	NHL Totals		42	0	1	1	163	....	....	....	....	....

Traded to **Washington** by **Dallas** to complete June 20, 1993 trade which sent Paul Cavallini to Dallas for future considerations, June 25, 1993.

CICHOCKI, CHRIS   (chih-HAH-kee)

Right wing. Shoots right. 5'11", 185 lbs.   Born, Detroit, MI, September 17, 1963.

				Regul	ar Se	ason				Play	offs	
Season	Club	Lea	GP	G	A	TP	PIM	GP	G	A	TP	PIM
1982-83	Michigan Tech	CCHA	36	12	10	22	10	....	....	....	....	....
1983-84	Michigan Tech	CCHA	40	25	20	45	36	....	....	....	....	....
1984-85	Michigan Tech	CCHA	40	30	24	54	14	....	....	....	....	....
1985-86	**Detroit**	**NHL**	59	10	11	21	21	....	....	....	....	....
	Adirondack	AHL	9	4	4	8	6	....	....	....	....	....
1986-87	**Detroit**	**NHL**	2	0	0	0	2	....	....	....	....	....
	Adirondack	AHL	55	31	34	65	27	....	....	....	....	....
	Maine	AHL	7	2	2	4	0	....	....	....	....	....
1987-88	**New Jersey**	**NHL**	5	1	0	1	2	....	....	....	....	....
	Utica	AHL	69	36	30	66	66	....	....	....	....	....
1988-89	**New Jersey**	**NHL**	2	0	1	1	2	....	....	....	....	....
	Utica	AHL	59	32	31	63	50	5	0	1	1	2
1989-90	Utica	AHL	11	3	1	4	10	....	....	....	....	....
	Binghamton	AHL	60	21	26	47	22	....	....	....	....	....
1990-91	Binghamton	AHL	80	35	30	65	70	9	0	4	4	2
1991-92	Binghamton	AHL	75	28	29	57	132	6	5	4	9	4
1992-93	Binghamton	AHL	65	23	29	52	78	9	3	2	5	25
	NHL Totals		68	11	12	23	27	....	....	....	....	....

Signed as a free agent by **Detroit**, June 28, 1985. Traded to **New Jersey** by **Detroit** with Detroit's third round choice (later traded to Buffalo – Buffalo selected Andrew MacVicar) in 1987 Entry Draft for Mel Bridgman, March 9, 1987. Traded to **Hartford** by **New Jersey** for Jim Thomson, October 31, 1989. Signed as a free agent by **NY Rangers**, September 6, 1990.

CIERNY, JOZEF   (chee-ER-nee)

Left wing. Shoots left. 6'2", 183 lbs.   Born, Zvolen, Czech., May 13, 1974.
(Buffalo's 2nd choice, 35th overall, in 1992 Entry Draft).

				Regul	ar Se	ason				Play	offs	
Season	Club	Lea	GP	G	A	TP	PIM	GP	G	A	TP	PIM
1991-92	ZTK Zvolen	Czech.2	26	10	3	13	8	....	....	....	....	....
1992-93	Rochester	AHL	54	27	27	54	36	....	....	....	....	....

CIGER, ZDENO   (SEE-gur)

Left wing. Shoots left. 6'1", 190 lbs.   Born, Martin, Czech., October 19, 1969.
(New Jersey's 3rd choice, 54th overall, in 1988 Entry Draft).

				Regul	ar Se	ason				Play	offs	
Season	Club	Lea	GP	G	A	TP	PIM	GP	G	A	TP	PIM
1987-88	Dukla Trencin	Czech.	8	3	4	7	2	....	....	....	....	....
1988-89	Dukla Trencin	Czech.	43	18	13	31	18	....	....	....	....	....
1989-90	Dukla Trencin	Czech.	53	18	28	46	....	....	....	....	....	....
1990-91	**New Jersey**	**NHL**	45	8	17	25	8	6	0	2	2	4
	Utica	AHL	8	5	4	9	2	....	....	....	....	....
1991-92	**New Jersey**	**NHL**	20	6	5	11	10	7	2	4	6	0
1992-93	**New Jersey**	**NHL**	27	4	8	12	2	....	....	....	....	....
	Edmonton	**NHL**	37	9	15	24	6	....	....	....	....	....
	NHL Totals		129	27	45	72	26	13	2	6	8	4

Traded to **Edmonton** by **New Jersey** with Kevin Todd for Bernie Nicholls, January 13, 1993.

CIMELLARO, TONY

Center. Shoots left. 5'11", 180 lbs.   Born, Kingston, Ont., June 14, 1971.

				Regul	ar Se	ason				Play	offs	
Season	Club	Lea	GP	G	A	TP	PIM	GP	G	A	TP	PIM
1990-91	Kingston	OHL	64	26	25	51	42	....	....	....	....	....
1991-92	Belleville	OHL	48	39	44	83	51	5	6	4	10	10
1992-93	**Ottawa**	**NHL**	2	0	0	0	0	....	....	....	....	....
	New Haven	AHL	76	18	16	34	73	....	....	....	....	....
	NHL Totals		2	0	0	0	0	....	....	....	....	....

Signed as a free agent by **Ottawa**, July 30, 1992.

CIMETTA, ROBERT

Left/Right wing. Shoots left. 6', 190 lbs.   Born, Toronto, Ont., February 15, 1970.
(Boston's 1st choice, 18th overall, in 1988 Entry Draft).

				Regul	ar Se	ason				Play	offs	
Season	Club	Lea	GP	G	A	TP	PIM	GP	G	A	TP	PIM
1986-87	Toronto	OHL	66	21	35	56	65	....	....	....	....	....
1987-88	Toronto	OHL	64	34	42	76	90	4	2	2	4	7
1988-89	**Boston**	**NHL**	7	2	0	2	0	1	0	0	0	15
a	Toronto	OHL	58	*55	47	102	89	6	3	3	6	0
1989-90	**Boston**	**NHL**	47	8	9	17	33	....	....	....	....	....
	Maine	AHL	9	3	2	5	13	....	....	....	....	....
1990-91	**Toronto**	**NHL**	25	2	4	6	21	....	....	....	....	....
	Newmarket	AHL	29	16	18	34	24	....	....	....	....	....
1991-92	**Toronto**	**NHL**	24	4	3	7	12	....	....	....	....	....
	St. John's	AHL	19	4	13	17	23	10	3	7	10	24
1992-93	St. John's	AHL	76	28	57	85	125	9	2	10	12	32
	NHL Totals		103	16	16	32	66	1	0	0	0	15

a OHL First All-Star Team (1989)
Traded to **Toronto** by **Boston** for Steve Bancroft, November 9, 1990.

CIRELLA, JOE

(suh-REHL-uh)

Defense. Shoots right. 6'3", 210 lbs.   Born, Hamilton, Ont., May 9, 1963.
(Colorado's 1st choice, 5th overall, in 1981 Entry Draft).

			Regular Season					Playoffs				
Season	Club	Lea	GP	G	A	TP	PIM	GP	G	A	TP	PIM
1980-81	Oshawa	OHA	56	5	31	36	220	11	0	2	2	41
1981-82	Colorado	NHL	65	7	12	19	52	....	....	....	....	....
	Oshawa	OHL	3	0	1	1	0	11	7	10	17	32
1982-83	New Jersey	NHL	2	0	1	1	4	....	....	....	....	....
a	Oshawa	OHL	56	13	55	68	110	17	4	16	20	37
1983-84	New Jersey	NHL	79	11	33	44	137	....	....	....	....	....
1984-85	New Jersey	NHL	66	6	18	24	141	....	....	....	....	....
1985-86	New Jersey	NHL	66	6	23	29	147	....	....	....	....	....
1986-87	New Jersey	NHL	65	9	22	31	111	....	....	....	....	....
1987-88	New Jersey	NHL	80	8	31	39	191	19	0	7	7	49
1988-89	New Jersey	NHL	80	3	19	22	155	....	....	....	....	....
1989-90	Quebec	NHL	56	4	14	18	67	....	....	....	....	....
1990-91	Quebec	NHL	39	2	10	12	59	....	....	....	....	....
	NY Rangers	NHL	19	1	0	1	52	6	0	2	2	26
1991-92	NY Rangers	NHL	67	3	12	15	121	13	0	4	4	23
1992-93	NY Rangers	NHL	55	3	6	9	85	....	....	....	....	....
	NHL Totals		**739**	**63**	**201**	**264**	**1322**	**38**	**0**	**13**	**13**	**98**

a   OHL First All-Star Team (1983)
Played in NHL All-Star Game (1984)

Traded to **Quebec** by **New Jersey** with Claude Loiselle and New Jersey's eighth round choice (Alexander Karpovtsev) in 1990 Entry Draft for Walt Poddubny and Quebec's fourth round choice (Mike Bodnarchuk) in 1990 Entry Draft, June 17, 1989. Traded to **NY Rangers** by **Quebec** for Aaron Miller and NY Rangers' fifth round choice (Bill Lindsay) in 1991 Entry Draft, January 17, 1991. Claimed by **Florida** from **NY Rangers** in Expansion Draft, June 24, 1993.

CIRONE, JASON

(sih-ROHN)

Center. Shoots left. 5'9", 185 lbs.   Born, Toronto, Ont., February 21, 1971.
(Winnipeg's 3rd choice, 46th overall, in 1989 Entry Draft).

			Regular Season					Playoffs				
Season	Club	Lea	GP	G	A	TP	PIM	GP	G	A	TP	PIM
1987-88	Cornwall	OHL	53	12	11	23	41	11	1	2	3	4
1988-89	Cornwall	OHL	64	39	44	83	67	17	19	8	27	14
1989-90	Cornwall	OHL	32	22	41	63	56	6	4	2	6	14
1990-91	Cornwall	OHL	40	31	29	60	66	....	....	....	....	....
a	Windsor	OHL	23	27	23	50	31	11	9	8	17	14
1991-92	**Winnipeg**	**NHL**	**3**	**0**	**0**	**0**	**2**	....	....	....	....	....
	Moncton	AHL	64	32	27	59	124	10	1	1	2	8
1992-93	Asiago	Alp.	25	24	14	38	36	....	....	....	....	....
	Asiago	Italy	16	6	5	11	18	2	1	5	6	18
	NHL Totals		**3**	**0**	**0**	**0**	**2**	....	....	....	....	....

a   OHL Third All-Star Team (1991)
Traded to **Florida** by **Winnipeg** for Dave Tomlinson, August 3, 1993.

CLANCY, CHRIS

Left wing. Shoots left. 6'2", 198 lbs.   Born, Kitchener, Ont., November 28, 1972.
(Buffalo's 11th choice, 251st overall, in 1992 Entry Draft).

			Regular Season					Playoffs				
Season	Club	Lea	GP	G	A	TP	PIM	GP	G	A	TP	PIM
1990-91	Cornwall	OHL	64	10	22	32	107	....	....	....	....	....
1991-92	Cornwall	OHL	66	28	38	66	117	6	1	2	3	4
1992-93	Belleville	OHL	62	10	21	31	76	7	0	3	3	20

CLARK, JASON

Center. Shoots left. 6', 180 lbs.   Born, London, Ont., May 6, 1972.
(Vancouver's 8th choice, 141st overall, in 1992 Entry Draft).

			Regular Season					Playoffs				
Season	Club	Lea	GP	G	A	TP	PIM	GP	G	A	TP	PIM
1991-92	St. Thomas	Jr. B	47	25	52	77	66	....	....	....	....	....
1992-93	Bowling Green	CCHA	40	10	17	27	42	....	....	....	....	....

CLARK, KERRY

Right wing. Shoots right. 6'1", 190 lbs.   Born, Kelvington, Sask., August 21, 1968.
(NY Islanders' 12th choice, 206th overall, in 1986 Entry Draft).

			Regular Season					Playoffs				
Season	Club	Lea	GP	G	A	TP	PIM	GP	G	A	TP	PIM
1985-86	Regina	WHL	23	4	4	8	58	....	....	....	....	....
	Saskatoon	WHL	39	5	8	13	104	13	2	2	4	33
1986-87	Saskatoon	WHL	54	12	10	22	229	8	0	1	1	23
1987-88	Saskatoon	WHL	67	15	11	26	241	10	2	2	4	16
1988-89	Springfield	AHL	63	7	7	14	264	....	....	....	....	....
	Indianapolis	IHL	3	0	1	1	12	....	....	....	....	....
1989-90	Springfield	AHL	21	0	1	1	73	....	....	....	....	....
	Phoenix	IHL	38	4	8	12	262	....	....	....	....	....
1990-91	Salt Lake	IHL	62	14	14	28	372	4	1	1	2	12
1991-92	Salt Lake	IHL	74	12	14	26	266	5	1	0	1	34
1992-93	Salt Lake	IHL	64	14	15	29	255	....	....	....	....	....

Signed as a free agent by **Calgary**, July 23, 1990.

CLARK, WENDEL

Left wing. Shoots left. 5'11", 194 lbs.   Born, Kelvington, Sask., October 25, 1966.
(Toronto's 1st choice, 1st overall, in 1985 Entry Draft).

			Regular Season					Playoffs				
Season	Club	Lea	GP	G	A	TP	PIM	GP	G	A	TP	PIM
1983-84	Saskatoon	WHL	72	23	45	68	225	....	....	....	....	....
1984-85ab	Saskatoon	WHL	64	32	55	87	253	3	2	3	6	7
1985-86c	Toronto	NHL	66	34	11	45	227	10	5	1	6	47
1986-87	Toronto	NHL	80	37	23	60	271	13	6	5	11	38
1987-88	Toronto	NHL	28	12	11	23	80	....	....	....	....	....
1988-89	Toronto	NHL	15	7	4	11	66	....	....	....	....	....
1989-90	Toronto	NHL	38	18	8	26	116	5	1	1	2	19
1990-91	Toronto	NHL	63	18	16	34	152	....	....	....	....	....
1991-92	Toronto	NHL	43	19	21	40	123	....	....	....	....	....
1992-93	Toronto	NHL	66	17	22	39	193	21	10	10	20	51
	NHL Totals		**399**	**162**	**116**	**278**	**1228**	**49**	**22**	**17**	**39**	**155**

a   WHL First All-Star Team, East Division (1985)
b   Named WHL's Top Defenceman (1985)
c   NHL All-Rookie Team (1986)
Played in NHL All-Star Game (1986)

CLARKE, WAYNE

Right wing. Shoots right. 6'2", 175 lbs.   Born, Sterling, Ont., August 30, 1972.
(Toronto's 9th choice, 197th overall, in 1992 Entry Draft).

			Regular Season					Playoffs				
Season	Club	Lea	GP	G	A	TP	PIM	GP	G	A	TP	PIM
1991-92	RPI	ECAC	33	12	17	29	28	....	....	....	....	....
1992-93	RPI	ECAC	32	13	16	29	23	....	....	....	....	....

CLEARY, JOSEPH

Defense. Shoots right. 5'11", 186 lbs.   Born, Buffalo, NY, January 17, 1970.
(Chicago's 4th choice, 92nd overall, in 1988 Entry Draft).

			Regular Season					Playoffs				
Season	Club	Lea	GP	G	A	TP	PIM	GP	G	A	TP	PIM
1988-89	Boston College	H.E.	38	5	7	12	36	....	....	....	....	....
1989-90	Boston College	H.E.	42	5	21	26	56	....	....	....	....	....
1990-91	Boston College	H.E.	36	4	19	23	34	....	....	....	....	....
1991-92	Boston College	H.E.	29	5	20	25	66	....	....	....	....	....
1992-93	Indianapolis	IHL	63	10	17	27	110	3	1	0	1	4

CLIFFORD, BRIAN

Center. Shoots right. 6', 180 lbs.   Born, Buffalo, NY, June 18, 1973.
(Pittsburgh's 6th choice, 126th overall, in 1991 Entry Draft).

			Regular Season					Playoffs				
Season	Club	Lea	GP	G	A	TP	PIM	GP	G	A	TP	PIM
1991-92	Nichols	HS	29	27	31	58	46	....	....	....	....	....
1992-93	Michigan State	CCHA	34	15	7	22	20	....	....	....	....	....

CLOUSTON, SHAUN

Left wing. Shoots left. 6'1", 205 lbs.   Born, Viking, Alta., February 21, 1968.
(NY Rangers' 3rd choice, 53rd overall, in 1986 Entry Draft).

			Regular Season					Playoffs				
Season	Club	Lea	GP	G	A	TP	PIM	GP	G	A	TP	PIM
1985-86	U. of Alberta	CWUAA	53	18	21	39	75	....	....	....	....	....
1986-87	Portland	WHL	70	6	25	31	93	19	0	5	5	45
1987-88	Portland	WHL	68	29	50	79	144	....	....	....	....	....
1988-89	Portland	WHL	72	45	47	92	150	19	7	10	17	28
1989-90	Milwaukee	IHL	54	6	16	22	61	....	....	....	....	....
	Virginia	ECHL	5	3	2	5	14	2	0	0	0	2
1990-91	Milwaukee	IHL	78	13	27	40	93	6	2	0	2	8
1991-92	Cincinnati	ECHL	33	16	27	43	42	9	6	5	11	8
1992-93	Tulsa	CHL	44	23	25	48	43	12	8	6	14	4
	Cincinnati	IHL	2	0	0	0	2	....	....	....	....	....

Signed as a free agent by **Vancouver**, May 27, 1989.

CLOUTIER, SYLVAIN

(kloo-CHAY)

Center. Shoots left. 6', 195 lbs.   Born, Mont-Laurier, Que., February 13, 1974.
(Detroit's 3rd choice, 70th overall, in 1992 Entry Draft).

			Regular Season					Playoffs				
Season	Club	Lea	GP	G	A	TP	PIM	GP	G	A	TP	PIM
1991-92	Guelph	OHL	62	35	31	66	74	....	....	....	....	....
1992-93	Guelph	OHL	44	26	29	55	78	5	0	5	5	14

COFFEY, PAUL DOUGLAS

Defense. Shoots left. 6', 195 lbs.   Born, Weston, Ont., June 1, 1961.
(Edmonton's 1st choice, 6th overall, in the 1980 Entry Draft).

			Regular Season					Playoffs				
Season	Club	Lea	GP	G	A	TP	PIM	GP	G	A	TP	PIM
1978-79a	S.S. Marie	OHA	68	17	72	89	103	....	....	....	....	....
1979-80b	S.S. Marie	OHA	23	10	21	31	63	....	....	....	....	....
	Kitchener	OHA	52	19	52	71	130	....	....	....	....	....
1980-81	Edmonton	NHL	74	9	23	32	130	9	4	3	7	22
1981-82c	Edmonton	NHL	80	29	60	89	106	5	1	1	2	6
1982-83c	Edmonton	NHL	80	29	67	96	87	16	7	7	14	14
1983-84c	Edmonton	NHL	80	40	86	126	104	19	8	14	22	21
1984-85de	Edmonton	NHL	80	37	84	121	97	18	12	25	37	44
1985-86de	Edmonton	NHL	79	48	90	138	120	10	1	9	10	30
1986-87	Edmonton	NHL	59	17	50	67	49	17	3	8	11	30
1987-88	Pittsburgh	NHL	46	15	52	67	93	....	....	....	....	....
1988-89e	Pittsburgh	NHL	75	30	83	113	195	11	2	13	15	31
1989-90c	Pittsburgh	NHL	80	29	74	103	95	....	....	....	....	....
1990-91	Pittsburgh	NHL	76	24	69	93	128	12	2	9	11	6
1991-92	Pittsburgh	NHL	54	10	54	64	62	....	....	....	....	....
	Los Angeles	NHL	10	1	4	5	25	6	4	3	7	2
1992-93	Los Angeles	NHL	50	8	49	57	50	....	....	....	....	....
	Detroit	NHL	30	4	26	30	27	7	2	9	11	2
	NHL Totals		**953**	**330**	**871**	**1201**	**1368**	**130**	**46**	**101**	**147**	**208**

a   OHA Third All-Star Team (1979)
b   OHA Second All-Star Team (1980)
c   NHL Second All-Star Team (1982, 1983, 1984, 1990)
d   Won James Norris Memorial Trophy (1985, 1986)
e   NHL First All-Star Team (1985, 1986, 1989)
Played in NHL All-Star Game (1982-86, 1988-93)

Traded to **Pittsburgh** by **Edmonton** with Dave Hunter and Wayne Van Dorp for Craig Simpson, Dave Hannan, Moe Mantha and Chris Joseph, November 24, 1987. Traded to **Los Angeles** by **Pittsburgh** for Brian Benning, Jeff Chychrun and Los Angeles' first round choice (later traded to Philadelphia — Philadelphia selected Jason Bowen) in 1992 Entry Draft, February 19, 1992. Traded to **Detroit** by **Los Angeles** with Sylvain Couturier and Jim Hiller for Jimmy Carson, Marc Potvin and Gary Shuchuk, January 29, 1993.

COLE, DANTON

Center/Right wing. Shoots right. 5'11", 185 lbs. Born, Pontiac, MI, January 10, 1967.
(Winnipeg's 6th choice, 123rd overall, in 1985 Entry Draft).

			Regular Season					Playoffs				
Season	Club	Lea	GP	G	A	TP	PIM	GP	G	A	TP	PIM
1985-86	Michigan State	CCHA	43	11	10	21	22	....	....	....	....	....
1986-87	Michigan State	CCHA	44	9	15	24	16	....	....	....	....	....
1987-88	Michigan State	CCHA	46	20	36	56	38	....	....	....	....	....
1988-89	Michigan State	CCHA	47	29	33	62	46	....	....	....	....	....
1989-90	**Winnipeg**	**NHL**	**2**	**1**	**1**	**2**	**0**	....	....	....	....	....
	Moncton	AHL	80	31	42	73	18	....	....	....	....	....
1990-91	**Winnipeg**	**NHL**	**66**	**13**	**11**	**24**	**24**	....	....	....	....	....
	Moncton	AHL	3	1	1	2	0	....	....	....	....	....
1991-92	**Winnipeg**	**NHL**	**52**	**7**	**5**	**12**	**32**	....	....	....	....	....
1992-93	**Tampa Bay**	**NHL**	**67**	**12**	**15**	**27**	**23**	....	....	....	....	....
	Atlanta	IHL	1	1	0	1	2	....	....	....	....	....
	NHL Totals		**187**	**33**	**32**	**65**	**79**	....	....	....	....	....

Traded to **Tampa Bay** by **Winnipeg** for future considerations, June 19, 1992.

COLEMAN, JONATHAN

Defense. Shoots right. 6'1", 190 lbs. Born, Boston, MA, March 9, 1975.
(Detroit's 2nd choice, 48th overall, in 1993 Entry Draft).

			Regular Season					Playoffs				
Season	Club	Lea	GP	G	A	TP	PIM	GP	G	A	TP	PIM
1991-92	Andover	HS	23	14	20	34	10	....	....	....	....	....
1992-93	Andover	HS	23	14	33	47	0	....	....	....	....	....

COLMAN, MICHAEL

Defense. Shoots right. 6'3", 225 lbs. Born, Stoneham, MA, August 4, 1968.

			Regular Season					Playoffs				
Season	Club	Lea	GP	G	A	TP	PIM	GP	G	A	TP	PIM
1989-90	Ferris State	CCHA	23	0	4	4	62	....	....	....	....	....
1990-91	Kansas City	IHL	66	1	6	7	115	....	....	....	....	....
1991-92	**San Jose**	**NHL**	**15**	**0**	**1**	**1**	**32**	....	....	....	....	....
	Kansas City	IHL	59	0	4	4	130	3	0	0	0	4
1992-93	Kansas City	IHL	80	1	5	6	191	12	1	0	1	34
	NHL Totals		**15**	**0**	**1**	**1**	**32**	....	....	....	....	....

Signed as a free agent by **San Jose**, September 3, 1991.

CONACHER, PATRICK JOHN (PAT) (KAH-nuh-kuhr)

Left wing. Shoots left. 5'8", 190 lbs. Born, Edmonton, Alta., May 1, 1959.
(NY Rangers' 3rd choice, 76th overall, in 1979 Entry Draft).

			Regular Season					Playoffs				
Season	Club	Lea	GP	G	A	TP	PIM	GP	G	A	TP	PIM
1977-78	Billings	WHL	72	31	44	75	105	20	15	14	29	22
1978-79	Billings	WHL	39	25	37	62	50	....	....	....	....	....
	Saskatoon	WHL	33	15	32	47	37	....	....	....	....	....
1979-80	**NY Rangers**	**NHL**	**17**	**0**	**5**	**5**	**4**	**3**	**0**	**1**	**1**	**2**
	New Haven	AHL	53	11	14	25	43	7	1	1	2	4
1980-81			DID NOT PLAY									
1981-82	Springfield	AHL	77	23	22	45	38	....	....	....	....	....
1982-83	**NY Rangers**	**NHL**	**5**	**0**	**1**	**1**	**4**	....	....	....	....	....
	Tulsa	CHL	63	29	28	57	44	....	....	....	....	....
1983-84	**Edmonton**	**NHL**	**45**	**2**	**8**	**10**	**31**	**3**	**1**	**0**	**1**	**2**
	Moncton	AHL	28	7	16	23	30	....	....	....	....	....
1984-85	Nova Scotia	AHL	68	20	45	65	44	6	3	2	5	0
1985-86	**New Jersey**	**NHL**	**2**	**0**	**2**	**2**	**2**	....	....	....	....	....
	Maine	AHL	69	15	30	45	83	5	1	1	2	11
1986-87	Maine	AHL	56	12	14	26	47	....	....	....	....	....
1987-88	**New Jersey**	**NHL**	**24**	**2**	**5**	**7**	**12**	**17**	**2**	**2**	**4**	**14**
	Utica	AHL	47	14	33	47	32	....	....	....	....	....
1988-89	**New Jersey**	**NHL**	**55**	**7**	**5**	**12**	**14**	....	....	....	....	....
1989-90	**New Jersey**	**NHL**	**19**	**3**	**3**	**6**	**4**	**5**	**1**	**0**	**1**	**10**
	Utica	AHL	57	13	36	49	53	....	....	....	....	....
1990-91	**New Jersey**	**NHL**	**49**	**5**	**11**	**16**	**27**	**7**	**0**	**2**	**2**	**2**
	Utica	AHL	4	0	1	1	6	....	....	....	....	....
1991-92	**New Jersey**	**NHL**	**44**	**7**	**3**	**10**	**16**	**7**	**1**	**1**	**2**	**4**
1992-93	**Los Angeles**	**NHL**	**81**	**9**	**8**	**17**	**20**	**24**	**6**	**4**	**10**	**6**
	NHL Totals		**341**	**35**	**51**	**86**	**134**	**66**	**11**	**10**	**21**	**40**

Signed as a free agent by **Edmonton**, October 4, 1983. Signed as a free agent by **New Jersey**, August 14, 1985. Traded to **Los Angeles** by **New Jersey** for future considerations, September 3, 1992.

CONLAN, WAYNE

Center. Shoots right. 5'10", 180 lbs. Born, New Haven, CT, January 9, 1972.
(St. Louis' 5th choice, 138th overall, in 1990 Entry Draft).

			Regular Season					Playoffs				
Season	Club	Lea	GP	G	A	TP	PIM	GP	G	A	TP	PIM
1991-92	U. of Maine	H.E.	22	8	1	9	10	....	....	....	....	....
1992-93	U. of Maine	H.E.	3	0	3	3	0	....	....	....	....	....

CONN, ROB

Left/Right wing. Shoots right. 6'2", 200 lbs. Born, Calgary, Alta., September 3, 1968.

			Regular Season					Playoffs				
Season	Club	Lea	GP	G	A	TP	PIM	GP	G	A	TP	PIM
1988-89	Alaska-Anch.	G.N.	33	21	17	38	46	....	....	....	....	....
1989-90	Alaska-Anch.	G.N.	34	27	21	48	46	....	....	....	....	....
1990-91	Alaska-Anch.	G.N.	43	28	32	60	53	....	....	....	....	....
1991-92	**Chicago**	**NHL**	**2**	**0**	**0**	**0**	**2**	....	....	....	....	....
	Indianapolis	IHL	72	19	16	35	100	....	....	....	....	....
1992-93	Indianapolis	IHL	75	13	14	27	81	5	0	1	1	6
	NHL Totals		**2**	**0**	**0**	**0**	**2**	....	....	....	....	....

Signed as a free agent by **Chicago**, July 31, 1991.

CONNOLLY, JEFF

Center. Shoots right. 6', 185 lbs. Born, Worcester, MA, February 1, 1974.
(Vancouver's 4th choice, 69th overall, in 1992 Entry Draft).

			Regular Season					Playoffs				
Season	Club	Lea	GP	G	A	TP	PIM	GP	G	A	TP	PIM
1991-92	St. Sebastien's	HS	28	31	35	66	....	....	....	....	....	....
1992-93	St. Sebastien's	HS	24	17	34	51	....	....	....	....	....	....

CONROY, CRAIG

Center. Shoots right. 6'2", 190 lbs. Born, Potsdam, NY, September 4, 1971.
(Montreal's 7th choice, 123rd overall, in 1990 Entry Draft).

			Regular Season					Playoffs				
Season	Club	Lea	GP	G	A	TP	PIM	GP	G	A	TP	PIM
1990-91	Clarkson	ECAC	40	8	21	29	24	....	....	....	....	....
1991-92	Clarkson	ECAC	31	19	17	36	36	....	....	....	....	....
1992-93	Clarkson	ECAC	35	10	23	33	26	....	....	....	....	....

CONROY, JOHN (AL)

Center. Shoots right. 5'8", 170 lbs. Born, Calgary, Alta., January 17, 1966.

			Regular Season					Playoffs				
Season	Club	Lea	GP	G	A	TP	PIM	GP	G	A	TP	PIM
1989-90	Adirondack	AHL	77	23	33	56	147	....	....	....	....	....
1990-91	Adirondack	AHL	80	26	39	65	172	....	....	....	....	....
1991-92	**Philadelphia**	**NHL**	**31**	**2**	**9**	**11**	**74**	....	....	....	....	....
	Hershey	AHL	47	17	28	45	90	6	4	2	6	12
1992-93	**Philadelphia**	**NHL**	**21**	**3**	**2**	**5**	**17**	....	....	....	....	....
	Hershey	AHL	60	28	32	60	130	....	....	....	....	....
	NHL Totals		**52**	**5**	**11**	**16**	**91**	....	....	....	....	....

Signed as a free agent by **Detroit**, August 16, 1989. Signed as a free agent by **Philadelphia**, August 21, 1991.

CONVERY, BRANDON

Center. Shoots right. 6', 180 lbs. Born, Kingston, Ont., February 4, 1974.
(Toronto's 1st choice, 8th overall, in 1992 Entry Draft).

			Regular Season					Playoffs				
Season	Club	Lea	GP	G	A	TP	PIM	GP	G	A	TP	PIM
1990-91	Sudbury	OHL	56	26	22	48	18	5	1	1	2	2
1991-92	Sudbury	OHL	44	40	26	66	44	5	3	2	5	4
1992-93	Sudbury	OHL	7	7	9	16	6	....	....	....	....	....
	Niagara Falls	OHL	51	38	39	77	24	4	1	3	4	4
	St. John's	AHL	3	0	0	0	0	5	0	1	1	0

COOKE, JAMES (JAMIE)

Right wing. Shoots right. 6'2", 206 lbs. Born, Bramalea, Ont., November 5, 1968.
(Philadelphia's 8th choice, 140th overall, in 1988 Entry Draft).

			Regular Season					Playoffs				
Season	Club	Lea	GP	G	A	TP	PIM	GP	G	A	TP	PIM
1988-89	Colgate	ECAC	28	13	11	24	26	....	....	....	....	....
1989-90	Colgate	ECAC	38	16	20	36	24	....	....	....	....	....
1990-91	Colgate	ECAC	32	29	26	55	22	....	....	....	....	....
1991-92	Hershey	AHL	66	15	26	41	49	....	....	....	....	....
1992-93	Hershey	AHL	36	11	7	18	12	....	....	....	....	....

COOPER, DAVID

Defense. Shoots left. 6'2", 204 lbs. Born, Ottawa, Ont., November 2, 1973.
(Buffalo's 1st choice, 11th overall, in 1992 Entry Draft).

			Regular Season					Playoffs				
Season	Club	Lea	GP	G	A	TP	PIM	GP	G	A	TP	PIM
1989-90	Medicine Hat	WHL	61	4	11	15	65	3	0	2	2	2
1990-91	Medicine Hat	WHL	64	12	31	43	66	11	1	3	4	23
1991-92a	Medicine Hat	WHL	72	17	47	64	176	4	1	4	5	8
1992-93	Medicine Hat	WHL	63	15	50	65	88	10	2	2	4	32

a WHL East First All-Star Team (1992)

CORBET, RENE

Left wing. Shoots left. 6', 176 lbs. Born, Victoriaville, Que., June 25, 1973.
(Quebec's 2nd choice, 24th overall, in 1991 Entry Draft).

			Regular Season					Playoffs				
Season	Club	Lea	GP	G	A	TP	PIM	GP	G	A	TP	PIM
1990-91	Drummondville	QMJHL	45	25	40	65	34	14	11	6	17	15
1991-92	Drummondville	QMJHL	56	46	50	96	90	4	1	2	3	17
1992-93ab	Drummondville	QMJHL	63	*79	69	*148	143	10	7	13	20	16

a QMJHL First All-Star Team (1993)
b Canadian Major Junior First All-Star Team (1993)

CORKUM, BOB

Center. Shoots right. 6'2", 212 lbs. Born, Salisbury, MA, December 18, 1967.
(Buffalo's 3rd choice, 47th overall, in 1986 Entry Draft).

			Regular Season					Playoffs				
Season	Club	Lea	GP	G	A	TP	PIM	GP	G	A	TP	PIM
1985-86	U. of Maine	H.E.	39	7	26	33	53	....	....	....	....	....
1986-87	U. of Maine	H.E.	35	18	11	29	24	....	....	....	....	....
1987-88	U. of Maine	H.E.	40	14	18	32	64	....	....	....	....	....
1988-89	U. of Maine	H.E.	45	17	31	48	64	....	....	....	....	....
1989-90	**Buffalo**	**NHL**	**8**	**2**	**0**	**2**	**4**	**5**	**1**	**0**	**1**	**4**
	Rochester	AHL	43	8	11	19	45	12	2	5	7	16
1990-91	Rochester	AHL	69	13	21	34	77	15	4	4	8	4
1991-92	**Buffalo**	**NHL**	**20**	**2**	**4**	**6**	**21**	**4**	**1**	**0**	**1**	**0**
	Rochester	AHL	52	16	12	28	47	8	0	6	6	8
1992-93	**Buffalo**	**NHL**	**68**	**6**	**4**	**10**	**38**	**5**	**0**	**0**	**0**	**2**
	NHL Totals		**96**	**10**	**8**	**18**	**63**	**14**	**2**	**0**	**2**	**6**

Claimed by **Anaheim** from **Buffalo** in Expansion Draft, June 24, 1993.

CORPSE, KELI

Center. Shoots left. 5'11", 176 lbs. Born, London, Ont., May 14, 1974.
(Montreal's 3rd choice, 44th overall, in 1992 Entry Draft).

			Regular Season					Playoffs				
Season	Club	Lea	GP	G	A	TP	PIM	GP	G	A	TP	PIM
1990-91	Kingston	OHL	58	18	33	51	34	....	....	....	....	....
1991-92	Kingston	OHL	65	31	52	83	20	....	....	....	....	....
1992-93	Kingston	OHL	54	32	75	107	45	16	9	*20	29	10

CORRIVEAU, YVON (koh-RIV-oh)

Left wing. Shoots left. 6'1", 195 lbs. Born, Welland, Ont., February 8, 1967.
(Washington's 1st choice, 19th overall, in 1985 Entry Draft).

			Regular Season					Playoffs				
Season	Club	Lea	GP	G	A	TP	PIM	GP	G	A	TP	PIM
1984-85	Toronto	OHL	59	23	28	51	65	3	0	0	0	5
1985-86	**Washington**	**NHL**	**2**	**0**	**0**	**0**	**0**	**4**	**0**	**3**	**3**	**2**
	Toronto	OHL	59	54	36	90	75	4	1	1	2	0
1986-87	**Washington**	**NHL**	**17**	**1**	**1**	**2**	**24**	....	....	....	....	....
	Toronto	OHL	23	14	19	33	23	....	....	....	....	....
	Binghamton	AHL	7	0	0	0	2	8	0	1	1	0
1987-88	**Washington**	**NHL**	**44**	**10**	**9**	**19**	**84**	**13**	**1**	**2**	**3**	**30**
	Binghamton	AHL	35	15	14	29	64	....	....	....	....	....
1988-89	**Washington**	**NHL**	**33**	**3**	**2**	**5**	**62**	**1**	**0**	**0**	**0**	**0**
	Baltimore	AHL	33	16	23	39	65	....	....	....	....	....
1989-90	**Washington**	**NHL**	**50**	**9**	**6**	**15**	**50**	....	....	....	....	....
	Hartford	**NHL**	**13**	**4**	**1**	**5**	**22**	**4**	**1**	**0**	**1**	**0**
1990-91	**Hartford**	**NHL**	**23**	**1**	**1**	**2**	**18**	....	....	....	....	....
	Springfield	AHL	44	17	25	42	10	18	*10	6	16	31
1991-92	**Hartford**	**NHL**	**38**	**12**	**8**	**20**	**36**	**7**	**3**	**2**	**5**	**18**
	Springfield	AHL	39	26	15	41	40	....	....	....	....	....
1992-93	**San Jose**	**NHL**	**20**	**3**	**7**	**10**	**0**	....	....	....	....	....
	Hartford	**NHL**	**37**	**5**	**5**	**10**	**14**	....	....	....	....	....
	NHL Totals		**277**	**48**	**40**	**88**	**310**	**29**	**5**	**7**	**12**	**50**

Traded to **Hartford** by **Washington** for Mike Liut, March 6, 1990. Traded to **Washington** by **Hartford** to complete June 15, 1992 deal in which Mark Hunter and future considerations were traded to Washington for Nick Kypreos, August 20, 1992. Claimed on waivers by **San Jose** from **Washington**, October 4, 1992. Traded to **Hartford** by **San Jose** to complete October 9, 1992 trade in which Michel Picard was traded to San Jose for future considerations, January 21, 1993.

CORSON, SHAYNE

Left wing. Shoots left. 6'1", 201 lbs. Born, Barrie, Ont., August 13, 1966.
(Montreal's 2nd choice, 8th overall, in 1984 Entry Draft).

			Regular Season					Playoffs				
Season	Club	Lea	GP	G	A	TP	PIM	GP	G	A	TP	PIM
1983-84	Brantford	OHL	66	25	46	71	165	6	4	1	5	26
1984-85	Hamilton	OHL	54	27	63	90	154	11	3	7	10	19
1985-86	**Montreal**	**NHL**	**3**	**0**	**0**	**0**	**2**	....	....	....	....	....
	Hamilton	OHL	47	41	57	98	153	....	....	....	....	....
1986-87	**Montreal**	**NHL**	**55**	**12**	**11**	**23**	**144**	**17**	**6**	**5**	**11**	**30**
1987-88	**Montreal**	**NHL**	**71**	**12**	**27**	**39**	**152**	**3**	**1**	**0**	**1**	**12**
1988-89	**Montreal**	**NHL**	**80**	**26**	**24**	**50**	**193**	**21**	**4**	**5**	**9**	**65**
1989-90	**Montreal**	**NHL**	**76**	**31**	**44**	**75**	**144**	**11**	**2**	**8**	**10**	**20**
1990-91	**Montreal**	**NHL**	**71**	**23**	**24**	**47**	**138**	**13**	**9**	**6**	**15**	**36**
1991-92	**Montreal**	**NHL**	**64**	**17**	**36**	**53**	**118**	**10**	**2**	**5**	**7**	**15**
1992-93	**Edmonton**	**NHL**	**80**	**16**	**31**	**47**	**209**	....	....	....	....	....
	NHL Totals		**500**	**137**	**197**	**334**	**1100**	**75**	**24**	**29**	**53**	**178**

Played in NHL All-Star Game (1990)

Traded to **Edmonton** by **Montreal** with Brent Gilchrist and Vladimir Vujtek for Vincent Damphousse and Edmonton's fourth round choice (Adam Wiesel) in 1993 Entry Draft, August 27, 1992.

COTE, ALAIN GABRIEL (koh-TAY)

Defense. Shoots right. 6', 200 lbs. Born, Montmagny, Que., April 14, 1967.
(Boston's 1st choice, 31st overall, in 1985 Entry Draft).

			Regular Season					Playoffs				
Season	Club	Lea	GP	G	A	TP	PIM	GP	G	A	TP	PIM
1983-84	Quebec	QMJHL	60	3	17	20	40	5	1	3	4	8
1984-85	Quebec	QMJHL	68	9	25	34	173	4	0	1	1	12
1985-86	**Boston**	**NHL**	**32**	**0**	**6**	**6**	**14**	....	....	....	....	....
	Granby	QMJHL	22	4	12	16	48	....	....	....	....	....
1986-87	**Boston**	**NHL**	**3**	**0**	**0**	**0**	**0**	....	....	....	....	....
	Granby	QMJHL	43	7	24	31	185	4	0	3	3	2
1987-88	**Boston**	**NHL**	**2**	**0**	**0**	**0**	**0**	....	....	....	....	....
	Maine	AHL	69	9	34	43	108	9	2	4	6	19
1988-89	**Boston**	**NHL**	**31**	**2**	**3**	**5**	**51**	....	....	....	....	....
	Maine	AHL	37	5	16	21	111	....	....	....	....	....
1989-90	**Washington**	**NHL**	**2**	**0**	**0**	**0**	**7**	....	....	....	....	....
	Baltimore	AHL	57	5	19	24	161	3	0	0	0	9
1990-91	**Montreal**	**NHL**	**28**	**0**	**6**	**6**	**26**	**11**	**0**	**2**	**2**	**26**
	Fredericton	AHL	49	8	19	27	110	....	....	....	....	....
1991-92	**Montreal**	**NHL**	**13**	**0**	**3**	**3**	**22**	....	....	....	....	....
	Fredericton	AHL	20	1	10	11	24	7	0	1	1	4
1992-93	Fredericton	AHL	61	10	17	27	83	....	....	....	....	....
	Tampa Bay	**NHL**	**2**	**0**	**0**	**0**	**0**	....	....	....	....	....
	Atlanta	IHL	8	1	0	1	0	1	0	0	0	0
	NHL Totals		**113**	**2**	**18**	**20**	**120**	**11**	**0**	**2**	**2**	**26**

Traded to **Washington** by **Boston** for Bob Gould, September 28, 1989. Traded to **Montreal** by **Washington** for Marc Deschamps, June 22, 1990. Traded to **Tampa Bay** by **Montreal** with Eric Charron and future considerations (Donald Dufresne, June 18, 1993) for Rob Ramage, March 20, 1993. Signed as a free agent by **Quebec**, July 2, 1993.

COTE, SYLVAIN (COH-tay)

Defense. Shoots right. 5'11", 185 lbs. Born, Quebec City, Que., January 19, 1966.
(Hartford's 1st choice, 11th overall, in 1984 Entry Draft).

			Regular Season					Playoffs				
Season	Club	Lea	GP	G	A	TP	PIM	GP	G	A	TP	PIM
1982-83	Quebec	QMJHL	66	10	24	34	50	....	....	....	....	....
1983-84	Quebec	QMJHL	66	15	50	65	89	5	1	1	2	0
1984-85	**Hartford**	**NHL**	**67**	**3**	**9**	**12**	**17**	....	....	....	....	....
1985-86	**Hartford**	**NHL**	**2**	**0**	**0**	**0**	**0**	....	....	....	....	....
a	Hull	QMJHL	26	10	33	43	14	13	6	*28	34	22
	Binghamton	AHL	12	2	4	6	0	....	....	....	....	....
1986-87	**Hartford**	**NHL**	**67**	**2**	**8**	**10**	**20**	**2**	**0**	**2**	**2**	**2**
1987-88	**Hartford**	**NHL**	**67**	**7**	**21**	**28**	**30**	**6**	**1**	**1**	**2**	**4**
1988-89	**Hartford**	**NHL**	**78**	**8**	**9**	**17**	**49**	**3**	**0**	**1**	**1**	**4**
1989-90	**Hartford**	**NHL**	**28**	**4**	**2**	**6**	**14**	....	....	....	....	....
1990-91	**Hartford**	**NHL**	**73**	**7**	**12**	**19**	**17**	**6**	**0**	**2**	**2**	**2**
1991-92	**Washington**	**NHL**	**78**	**11**	**29**	**40**	**31**	**7**	**1**	**2**	**3**	**4**
1992-93	**Washington**	**NHL**	**77**	**21**	**29**	**50**	**34**	**6**	**1**	**1**	**2**	**4**
	NHL Totals		**537**	**63**	**119**	**182**	**212**	**30**	**3**	**9**	**12**	**20**

a QMJHL First All-Star Team (1986).

Traded to **Washington** by **Hartford** for Washington's second round choice (Andrei Nikolishin) in 1992 Entry Draft, September 8, 1991.

COURTENAY, EDWARD

Right wing. Shoots right. 6'4", 216 lbs. Born, Verdun, Que., February 2, 1968.

			Regular Season					Playoffs				
Season	Club	Lea	GP	G	A	TP	PIM	GP	G	A	TP	PIM
1987-88	Granby	QMJHL	54	37	34	71	19	5	1	1	2	2
1988-89	Granby	QMJHL	68	59	55	114	68	4	1	1	2	22
	Kalamazoo	IHL	1	0	0	0	0	1	0	0	0	2
1989-90	Kalamazoo	IHL	57	25	28	53	16	3	0	0	0	0
1990-91	Kalamazoo	IHL	76	35	36	71	37	8	2	3	5	12
1991-92	**San Jose**	**NHL**	**5**	**0**	**0**	**0**	**0**	....	....	....	....	....
	Kansas City	IHL	36	14	12	26	46	15	8	9	17	15
1992-93	**San Jose**	**NHL**	**39**	**7**	**13**	**20**	**10**	....	....	....	....	....
	Kansas City	IHL	32	15	12	27	25	....	....	....	....	....
	NHL Totals		**44**	**7**	**13**	**20**	**10**	....	....	....	....	....

Signed as a free agent by **Minnesota**, October 1, 1989. Claimed by **San Jose** from **Minnesota** in Dispersal Draft, May 30, 1991.

COURTNALL, GEOFF

Left wing. Shoots left. 6'1", 195 lbs. Born, Victoria, B.C., August 18, 1962.

			Regular Season					Playoffs				
Season	Club	Lea	GP	G	A	TP	PIM	GP	G	A	TP	PIM
1980-81	Victoria	WHL	11	3	4	7	6	15	2	1	3	7
1981-82	Victoria	WHL	72	35	57	90	100	4	1	0	1	2
1982-83	Victoria	WHL	71	41	73	114	186	12	6	7	13	42
1983-84	**Boston**	**NHL**	**4**	**0**	**0**	**0**	**0**	....	....	....	....	....
	Hershey	AHL	74	14	12	26	51	....	....	....	....	....
1984-85	**Boston**	**NHL**	**64**	**12**	**16**	**28**	**82**	**5**	**0**	**2**	**2**	**7**
	Hershey	AHL	9	8	4	12	4	....	....	....	....	....
1985-86	**Boston**	**NHL**	**64**	**21**	**16**	**37**	**61**	**3**	**0**	**0**	**0**	**2**
	Moncton	AHL	12	8	8	16	6	....	....	....	....	....
1986-87	**Boston**	**NHL**	**65**	**13**	**23**	**36**	**117**	**1**	**0**	**0**	**0**	**0**
1987-88	**Boston**	**NHL**	**62**	**32**	**26**	**58**	**108**	....	....	....	....	....
	Edmonton	**NHL**	**12**	**4**	**4**	**8**	**15**	**19**	**0**	**3**	**3**	**23**
1988-89	**Washington**	**NHL**	**79**	**42**	**38**	**80**	**112**	**6**	**2**	**5**	**7**	**12**
1989-90	**Washington**	**NHL**	**80**	**35**	**39**	**74**	**104**	**15**	**4**	**9**	**13**	**32**
1990-91	**St. Louis**	**NHL**	**66**	**27**	**30**	**57**	**56**	....	....	....	....	....
	Vancouver	**NHL**	**11**	**6**	**2**	**8**	**8**	**6**	**3**	**5**	**8**	**4**
1991-92	**Vancouver**	**NHL**	**70**	**23**	**34**	**57**	**116**	**12**	**6**	**8**	**14**	**20**
1992-93	**Vancouver**	**NHL**	**84**	**31**	**46**	**77**	**167**	**12**	**4**	**10**	**14**	**12**
	NHL Totals		**661**	**246**	**274**	**520**	**946**	**79**	**19**	**42**	**61**	**112**

Signed as a free agent by **Boston**, July 6, 1983. Traded to **Edmonton** by **Boston** with Bill Ranford and future considerations for Andy Moog, March 8, 1988. Rights traded to **Washington** by **Edmonton** for Greg C. Adams, July 22, 1988. Traded to **St. Louis** by **Washington** for Peter Zezel and Mike Lalor, July 13, 1990. Traded to **Vancouver** by **St. Louis** with Robert Dirk, Sergio Momesso, Cliff Ronning and future considerations for Dan Quinn and Garth Butcher, March 5, 1991.

COURTNALL, RUSSELL (RUSS)

Right wing. Shoots right. 5'11", 185 lbs. Born, Duncan, B.C., June 2, 1965.
(Toronto's 1st choice, 7th overall, in 1983 Entry Draft).

			Regular Season					Playoffs				
Season	Club	Lea	GP	G	A	TP	PIM	GP	G	A	TP	PIM
1982-83	Victoria	WHL	60	36	61	97	33	12	11	7	18	6
1983-84	Victoria	WHL	32	29	37	66	63	....	....	....	....	....
	Cdn. Olympic	....	16	4	7	11	10	....	....	....	....	....
	Toronto	**NHL**	**14**	**3**	**9**	**12**	**6**	....	....	....	....	....
1984-85	**Toronto**	**NHL**	**69**	**12**	**10**	**22**	**44**	....	....	....	....	....
1985-86	**Toronto**	**NHL**	**73**	**22**	**38**	**60**	**52**	**10**	**3**	**6**	**9**	**8**
1986-87	**Toronto**	**NHL**	**79**	**29**	**44**	**73**	**90**	**13**	**3**	**4**	**7**	**11**
1987-88	**Toronto**	**NHL**	**65**	**23**	**26**	**49**	**47**	**6**	**2**	**1**	**3**	**0**
1988-89	**Toronto**	**NHL**	**9**	**1**	**1**	**2**	**4**	....	....	....	....	....
	Montreal	**NHL**	**64**	**22**	**17**	**39**	**15**	**21**	**8**	**5**	**13**	**18**
1989-90	**Montreal**	**NHL**	**80**	**27**	**32**	**59**	**27**	**11**	**5**	**1**	**6**	**10**
1990-91	**Montreal**	**NHL**	**79**	**26**	**50**	**76**	**29**	**13**	**8**	**3**	**11**	**7**
1991-92	**Montreal**	**NHL**	**27**	**7**	**14**	**21**	**6**	**10**	**1**	**1**	**2**	**4**
1992-93	**Minnesota**	**NHL**	**84**	**36**	**43**	**79**	**49**	....	....	....	....	....
	NHL Totals		**643**	**208**	**284**	**492**	**369**	**84**	**30**	**21**	**51**	**58**

Traded to **Montreal** by **Toronto** for John Kordic and Montreal's sixth round choice (Michael Doers) in 1989 Entry Draft, November 7, 1988. Traded to **Minnesota** by **Montreal** for Brian Bellows, August 31, 1992.

COURVILLE, LARRY

Left wing. Shoots left. 6'1", 180 lbs. Born, Timmins, Ont., April 2, 1974.
(Winnipeg's 6th choice, 119th overall, in 1993 Entry Draft).

			Regular Season					Playoffs				
Season	Club	Lea	GP	G	A	TP	PIM	GP	G	A	TP	PIM
1991-92	Cornwall	OHL	60	8	12	20	80	6	0	0	0	8
1992-93	Newmarket	OHL	64	21	18	39	181	7	0	6	6	14

COUTURIER, SYLVAIN (koo-TOOR-ee-yah, SIHL-vay)

Center. Shoots left. 6'2", 205 lbs. Born, Greenfield Park, Que., April 23, 1968.
(Los Angeles' 3rd choice, 65th overall, in 1986 Entry Draft).

			Regular Season					Playoffs				
Season	Club	Lea	GP	G	A	TP	PIM	GP	G	A	TP	PIM
1985-86	Laval	QMJHL	68	21	37	58	64	14	1	7	8	28
1986-87	Laval	QMJHL	67	39	51	90	77	13	12	14	26	19
1987-88a	Laval	QMJHL	67	70	67	137	115	....	....	....	....	....
1988-89	**Los Angeles**	**NHL**	**16**	**1**	**3**	**4**	**2**	....	....	....	....	....
	New Haven	AHL	44	18	20	38	33	10	2	2	4	11
1989-90	New Haven	AHL	50	9	8	17	47	....	....	....	....	....
1990-91	**Los Angeles**	**NHL**	**3**	**0**	**1**	**1**	**0**	....	....	....	....	....
	Phoenix	IHL	66	50	37	87	49	10	8	2	10	10
1991-92	**Los Angeles**	**NHL**	**14**	**3**	**1**	**4**	**2**	....	....	....	....	....
	Phoenix	IHL	39	19	20	39	68	....	....	....	....	....
1992-93	Phoenix	IHL	38	23	16	39	63	....	....	....	....	....
	Adirondack	AHL	29	17	17	34	12	11	3	5	8	10
	Fort Wayne	IHL	....	....	....	....	....	4	2	3	5	2
	NHL Totals		**33**	**4**	**5**	**9**	**4**	....	....	....	....	....

a QMJHL Third All-Star Team (1988)

Traded to **Detroit** by **Los Angeles** with Paul Coffey and Jim Hiller for Jimmy Carson, Marc Potvin and Gary Shuchuk, January 29, 1993.

COWIE, ROB

Defense. Shoots left. 6', 195 lbs. Born, Toronto, Ont., November 3, 1967.

			Regular Season					Playoffs				
Season	Club	Lea	GP	G	A	TP	PIM	GP	G	A	TP	PIM
1987-88	Northeastern	H.E.	36	7	8	15	38	....	....	....	....	....
1988-89a	Northeastern	H.E.	36	7	34	41	60	....	....	....	....	....
1989-90bc	Northeastern	H.E.	34	14	31	45	54	....	....	....	....	....
1990-91a	Northeastern	H.E.	33	18	23	41	56	....	....	....	....	....
1991-92	Moncton	AHL	64	11	30	41	89	5	1	1	2	0
1992-93	Moncton	AHL	67	12	20	32	91	5	3	5	8	2

a Hockey East Second All-Star Team (1989,1991)
b Hockey East First All-Star Team (1990)
c NCAA East First All-American Team (1990)

Signed as a free agent by **Winnipeg**, July 4, 1991. Signed as a free agent by **Hartford**, August 9, 1993.

COXE, CRAIG

Left wing. Shoots left. 6'4", 210 lbs. Born, Chula Vista, CA, January 21, 1964.
(Detroit's 4th choice, 66th overall, in 1982 Entry Draft).

			Regular Season					Playoffs				
Season	Club	Lea	GP	G	A	TP	PIM	GP	G	A	TP	PIM
1982-83	Belleville	OHL	64	14	27	41	102	4	1	2	3	2
1983-84	Belleville	OHL	45	17	28	45	90	3	2	0	2	4
1984-85	Vancouver	NHL	9	0	0	0	49	....	....	....	....	....
	Fredericton	AHL	62	8	7	15	242	4	2	1	3	16
1985-86	Vancouver	NHL	57	3	5	8	176	3	0	0	0	2
1986-87	Vancouver	NHL	15	1	0	1	31	....	....	....	....	....
	Fredericton	AHL	46	1	12	13	168	....	....	....	....	....
1987-88	Vancouver	NHL	64	5	12	17	186	....	....	....	....	....
	Calgary	NHL	7	2	3	5	32	2	1	0	1	16
1988-89	St. Louis	NHL	41	0	7	7	127	....	....	....	....	....
	Peoria	IHL	8	2	7	9	38	....	....	....	....	....
1989-90	Vancouver	NHL	25	1	4	5	66	....	....	....	....	....
	Milwaukee	IHL	5	0	5	5	4	....	....	....	....	....
1990-91	Vancouver	NHL	7	0	0	0	27	....	....	....	....	....
	Milwaukee	IHL	36	9	21	30	116	6	3	2	5	22
1991-92	San Jose	NHL	10	2	0	2	19	....	....	....	....	....
	Kansas City	IHL	51	17	21	38	106	....	....	....	....	....
	Kalamazoo	IHL	6	4	5	9	13	10	2	4	6	37
1992-93	Cincinnati	IHL	20	5	3	8	34	....	....	....	....	....
	Kalamazoo	IHL	12	1	1	2	8	....	....	....	....	....
	NHL Totals		235	14	31	45	713	5	1	0	1	18

Signed as a free agent by **Vancouver**, June 26, 1984. Traded to **Calgary** by **Vancouver** for Brian Bradley and Peter Bakovic, March 6, 1988. Traded to **St. Louis** by **Calgary** with Mike Bullard and Tim Corkery for Mark Hunter, Doug Gilmour, Steve Bozek and Michael Dark, September 6, 1988. Traded to **Chicago** by **St. Louis** for Rik Wilson, September 27, 1989. Claimed by **Vancouver** in NHL Waiver Draft, October 2, 1989. Claimed by **San Jose** from **Vancouver** in Expansion Draft, May 30, 1991.

CRAIEVICH, DAVID

Defense. Shoots right. 6'1", 209 lbs. Born, Chatham, Ont., May 3, 1971.
(New Jersey's 7th choice, 143rd overall, in 1991 Entry Draft).

			Regular Season					Playoffs				
Season	Club	Lea	GP	G	A	TP	PIM	GP	G	A	TP	PIM
1990-91	Oshawa	OHL	66	12	30	42	118	16	4	5	9	21
1991-92	Utica	AHL	9	0	0	0	4	1	0	0	0	4
	Cincinnati	ECHL	50	11	29	40	166	8	1	8	9	15
1992-93	Birmingham	ECHL	56	10	35	45	139	....	....	....	....	....
	Cincinnati	IHL	21	0	3	3	33	....	....	....	....	....

CRAIG, MIKE

Right wing. Shoots right. 6'1", 185 lbs. Born, St. Mary, Ont., June 6, 1971.
(Minnesota's 2nd choice, 28th overall, in 1989 Entry Draft).

			Regular Season					Playoffs				
Season	Club	Lea	GP	G	A	TP	PIM	GP	G	A	TP	PIM
1987-88	Oshawa	OHL	61	6	10	16	39	7	7	0	1	11
1988-89	Oshawa	OHL	63	36	36	72	34	6	3	1	4	6
1989-90	Oshawa	OHL	43	36	40	76	85	17	10	16	26	46
1990-91	Minnesota	NHL	39	8	4	12	32	10	1	1	2	20
1991-92	Minnesota	NHL	67	15	16	31	155	4	1	0	1	7
1992-93	Minnesota	NHL	70	15	23	38	106	....	....	....	....	....
	NHL Totals		176	38	43	81	293	14	2	1	3	27

CRAIGWELL, DALE

Center. Shoots left. 5'11", 180 lbs. Born, Toronto, Ont., April 24, 1971.
(San Jose's 11th choice, 199th overall, in 1991 Entry Draft).

			Regular Season					Playoffs				
Season	Club	Lea	GP	G	A	TP	PIM	GP	G	A	TP	PIM
1988-89	Oshawa	OHL	55	9	14	23	15	....	....	....	....	....
1989-90	Oshawa	OHL	64	22	41	63	39	17	7	7	14	11
1990-91	Oshawa	OHL	56	27	68	95	34	16	7	16	23	9
1991-92	San Jose	NHL	32	5	11	16	8	....	....	....	....	....
	Kansas City	IHL	48	6	19	25	29	12	4	7	11	4
1992-93	San Jose	NHL	8	3	1	4	4	....	....	....	....	....
	Kansas City	IHL	60	15	38	53	24	12	*7	5	12	2
	NHL Totals		40	8	12	20	12	....	....	....	....	....

CRAVEN, MURRAY

Left wing. Shoots left. 6'2", 185 lbs. Born, Medicine Hat, Alta., July 20, 1964.
(Detroit's 1st choice, 17th overall, in 1982 Entry Draft).

			Regular Season					Playoffs				
Season	Club	Lea	GP	G	A	TP	PIM	GP	G	A	TP	PIM
1980-81	Medicine Hat	WHL	69	5	10	15	18	5	0	0	0	2
1981-82	Medicine Hat	WHL	72	35	46	81	49	....	....	....	....	....
1982-83	Detroit	NHL	31	4	7	11	6	....	....	....	....	....
	Medicine Hat	WHL	28	17	29	46	35	....	....	....	....	....
1983-84	Detroit	NHL	15	0	4	4	6	....	....	....	....	....
	Medicine Hat	WHL	48	38	56	94	53	4	5	3	8	4
1984-85	Philadelphia	NHL	80	26	35	61	30	19	4	6	10	11
1985-86	Philadelphia	NHL	78	21	33	54	34	5	0	3	3	4
1986-87	Philadelphia	NHL	77	19	30	49	38	12	3	1	4	9
1987-88	Philadelphia	NHL	72	30	46	76	58	7	2	5	7	4
1988-89	Philadelphia	NHL	51	9	28	37	52	1	0	0	0	0
1989-90	Philadelphia	NHL	76	25	50	75	42	....	....	....	....	....
1990-91	Philadelphia	NHL	77	19	47	66	53	....	....	....	....	....
1991-92	Philadelphia	NHL	12	3	3	6	8	....	....	....	....	....
	Hartford	NHL	61	24	30	54	38	7	3	3	6	6
1992-93	Hartford	NHL	67	25	42	67	20	....	....	....	....	....
	Vancouver	NHL	10	0	10	10	12	12	4	6	10	4
	NHL Totals		707	205	365	570	397	63	16	24	40	38

Traded to **Philadelphia** by **Detroit** with Joe Paterson for Darryl Sittler, October 10, 1984. Traded to **Hartford** by **Philadelphia** with future considerations for Kevin Dineen, November 13, 1991. Traded to **Vancouver** by **Hartford** with Vancouver's fifth round choice (previously acquired by Hartford — Vancouver selected Scott Walker) in 1993 Entry Draft for Robert Kron, Vancouver's third round choice (Marek Malik) in 1993 Entry Draft and future considerations (Jim Sandlak, May 17, 1993), March 22, 1993.

CREAGH, BRENDAN

Defense. Shoots left. 6', 195 lbs. Born, Hartford, CT, February 1, 1970.
(Los Angeles' 1st choice, 26th overall, in 1991 Supplemental Draft).

			Regular Season					Playoffs				
Season	Club	Lea	GP	G	A	TP	PIM	GP	G	A	TP	PIM
1989-90	U. of Vermont	ECAC	30	4	7	11	12	....	....	....	....	....
1990-91	U. of Vermont	ECAC	31	3	7	10	26	....	....	....	....	....
1991-92	U. of Vermont	ECAC	21	6	7	13	10	....	....	....	....	....
1992-93	U. of Vermont	ECAC	30	3	15	18	24	....	....	....	....	....

CREIGHTON, ADAM (KRAY-ton)

Center. Shoots left. 6'5", 210 lbs. Born, Burlington, Ont., June 2, 1965.
(Buffalo's 3rd choice, 11th overall, in 1983 Entry Draft).

			Regular Season					Playoffs				
Season	Club	Lea	GP	G	A	TP	PIM	GP	G	A	TP	PIM
1981-82	Ottawa	OHL	60	15	27	42	73	17	7	1	8	40
1982-83	Ottawa	OHL	68	44	46	90	88	9	0	2	2	12
1983-84	Buffalo	NHL	7	2	2	4	4	....	....	....	....	....
	Ottawa	OHL	56	42	49	91	79	13	16	11	27	28
1984-85	Buffalo	NHL	30	2	8	10	33	....	....	....	....	....
	Rochester	AHL	6	5	3	8	2	5	2	1	3	20
	Ottawa	OHL	10	4	14	18	23	5	6	2	8	11
1985-86	Buffalo	NHL	19	1	1	2	2	....	....	....	....	....
	Rochester	AHL	32	17	21	38	27	....	....	....	....	....
1986-87	Buffalo	NHL	56	18	22	40	26	....	....	....	....	....
1987-88	Buffalo	NHL	36	10	17	27	87	....	....	....	....	....
1988-89	Buffalo	NHL	24	7	10	17	44	....	....	....	....	....
	Chicago	NHL	43	15	14	29	92	15	5	6	11	44
1989-90	Chicago	NHL	80	34	36	70	224	20	3	6	9	59
1990-91	Chicago	NHL	72	22	29	51	135	6	0	1	1	10
1991-92	Chicago	NHL	11	6	6	12	16	....	....	....	....	....
	NY Islanders	NHL	66	15	9	24	102	....	....	....	....	....
1992-93	Tampa Bay	NHL	83	19	20	39	110	....	....	....	....	....
	NHL Totals		527	151	174	325	875	41	8	13	21	113

Traded to **Chicago** by **Buffalo** for Rick Vaive, December 26, 1988. Traded to **NY Islanders** by **Chicago** with Steve Thomas for Brent Sutter and Brad Lauer, October 25, 1991. Claimed by **Tampa Bay** from **NY Islanders** in NHL Waiver Draft, October 4, 1992.

CREURER, TROY

Defense. Shoots left. 6'1", 180 lbs. Born, Regina, Sask., May 2, 1975.
(Vancouver's 5th choice, 158th overall, in 1993 Entry Draft).

			Regular Season					Playoffs				
Season	Club	Lea	GP	G	A	TP	PIM	GP	G	A	TP	PIM
1992-93	Notre Dame	SJHL	62	6	21	27	71	....	....	....	....	....

CRONAN, EARL

Left wing. Shoots left. 6'1", 195 lbs. Born, Warwick, RI, January 2, 1973.
(Montreal's 9th choice, 212th overall, in 1992 Entry Draft).

			Regular Season					Playoffs				
Season	Club	Lea	GP	G	A	TP	PIM	GP	G	A	TP	PIM
1991-92	St. Mark's	HS	....	....	....	....	....	....	....	....	....	....
1992-93	Colgate	ECAC	33	8	9	17	40	....	....	....	....	....

CRONIN, SHAWN

Defense. Shoots left. 6'2", 210 lbs. Born, Joliet, IL, August 20, 1963.

			Regular Season					Playoffs				
Season	Club	Lea	GP	G	A	TP	PIM	GP	G	A	TP	PIM
1983-84	Ill.-Chicago	CCHA	32	0	4	4	41	....	....	....	....	....
1984-85	Ill.-Chicago	CCHA	31	2	6	8	52	....	....	....	....	....
1985-86	Ill.-Chicago	CCHA	35	3	8	11	70	....	....	....	....	....
1986-87	Salt Lake	IHL	53	8	16	24	118	....	....	....	....	....
	Binghamton	AHL	12	0	1	1	60	10	0	0	0	41
1987-88	Binghamton	AHL	65	3	8	11	212	4	0	0	0	15
1988-89	**Washington**	**NHL**	**1**	**0**	**0**	**0**	**0**	....	....	....	....	....
	Baltimore	AHL	75	3	9	12	267	....	....	....	....	....
1989-90	**Winnipeg**	**NHL**	**61**	**0**	**4**	**4**	**243**	**5**	**0**	**0**	**0**	**7**
1990-91	**Winnipeg**	**NHL**	**67**	**1**	**5**	**6**	**189**	....	....	....	....	....
1991-92	**Winnipeg**	**NHL**	**65**	**0**	**4**	**4**	**271**	**4**	**0**	**0**	**0**	**6**
1992-93	**Philadelphia**	**NHL**	**35**	**2**	**1**	**3**	**37**	....	....	....	....	....
	Hershey	AHL	7	0	1	1	12	....	....	....	....	....
	NHL Totals		**229**	**3**	**14**	**17**	**740**	**9**	**0**	**0**	**0**	**13**

Signed as a free agent by **Hartford**, March, 1986. Signed as a free agent by **Washington**, June 6, 1988. Signed as a free agent by **Philadelphia**, June 12, 1989. Traded to **Winnipeg** by **Philadelphia** for future considerations (Keith Acton and Pete Peeters were traded to Philadelphia for Toronto's fifth round choice (previously acquired by Philadelphia — Winnipeg selected Juha Ylonen), October 3, 1989), July 21, 1989. Traded to **Quebec** by **Winnipeg** for Dan Lambert, August 25, 1992. Claimed by **Philadelphia** from **Quebec** in NHL Waiver Draft, October 4, 1992. Traded to **San Jose** by **Philadelphia** for cash, August 5, 1993.

CROSS, CORY

Defense. Shoots left. 6'5", 212 lbs. Born, Lloydminster, Alta., January 3, 1971.
(Tampa Bay's 1st choice, 1st overall, in 1992 Supplemental Draft).

			Regular Season					Playoffs				
Season	Club	Lea	GP	G	A	TP	PIM	GP	G	A	TP	PIM
1989-90	U. of Alberta	CWUAA				UNAVAILABLE						
1990-91	U. of Alberta	CWUAA				UNAVAILABLE						
1991-92	U. of Alberta	CWUAA	41	4	11	15	82	....	....	....	....	....
1992-93	U. of Alberta	CWUAA	43	11	28	39	105	....	....	....	....	....
	Atlanta	IHL	7	0	1	1	2	4	0	0	0	6

CROSSMAN, DOUGLAS (DOUG)

Defense. Shoots left. 6'2", 190 lbs. Born, Peterborough, Ont., June 30, 1960.
(Chicago's 6th choice, 112th overall, in 1979 Entry Draft).

			Regular Season					Playoffs				
Season	Club	Lea	GP	G	A	TP	PIM	GP	G	A	TP	PIM
1977-78	Ottawa	OHA	65	4	17	21	17	....	....	....	....	....
1978-79	Ottawa	OHA	67	12	51	63	65	4	1	3	4	0
1979-80	Ottawa	OHA	66	20	96	116	48	11	7	6	13	19
1980-81	**Chicago**	**NHL**	**9**	**0**	**2**	**2**	**2**	....	....	....	....	....
	New Brunswick	AHL	70	13	43	56	90	13	5	6	11	36
1981-82	**Chicago**	**NHL**	**70**	**12**	**28**	**40**	**24**	**11**	**0**	**3**	**3**	**4**
1982-83	**Chicago**	**NHL**	**80**	**13**	**40**	**53**	**46**	**13**	**3**	**7**	**10**	**6**
1983-84	**Philadelphia**	**NHL**	**78**	**7**	**28**	**35**	**63**	**3**	**0**	**0**	**0**	**0**
1984-85	**Philadelphia**	**NHL**	**80**	**4**	**33**	**37**	**65**	**19**	**4**	**6**	**10**	**38**
1985-86	**Philadelphia**	**NHL**	**80**	**6**	**37**	**43**	**55**	**5**	**0**	**1**	**1**	**4**
1986-87	**Philadelphia**	**NHL**	**78**	**9**	**31**	**40**	**29**	**26**	**4**	**14**	**18**	**31**
1987-88	**Philadelphia**	**NHL**	**76**	**9**	**29**	**38**	**43**	**7**	**1**	**1**	**2**	**8**
1988-89	**Los Angeles**	**NHL**	**74**	**10**	**15**	**25**	**53**	**2**	**0**	**1**	**1**	**2**
	New Haven	AHL	3	0	0	0	0	....	....	....	....	....
1989-90	**NY Islanders**	**NHL**	**80**	**15**	**44**	**59**	**54**	**5**	**0**	**1**	**1**	**6**
1990-91	**NY Islanders**	**NHL**	**16**	**1**	**6**	**7**	**12**	....	....	....	....	....
	Hartford	**NHL**	**41**	**4**	**19**	**23**	**19**	....	....	....	....	....
	Detroit	**NHL**	**17**	**3**	**4**	**7**	**17**	**6**	**0**	**5**	**5**	**6**
1991-92	**Detroit**	**NHL**	**26**	**0**	**8**	**8**	**14**	....	....	....	....	....
1992-93	**Tampa Bay**	**NHL**	**40**	**8**	**21**	**29**	**18**	....	....	....	....	....
	St. Louis	**NHL**	**19**	**2**	**7**	**9**	**10**	....	....	....	....	....
	NHL Totals		**864**	**103**	**352**	**455**	**524**	**97**	**12**	**39**	**51**	**105**

Traded to **Philadelphia** by **Chicago** with Chicago's second round choice (Scott Mellanby) in 1984 Entry Draft for Behn Wilson, June 8, 1983. Traded to **Los Angeles** by **Philadelphia** for Jay Wells, September 29, 1988. Traded to **NY Islanders** by **Los Angeles** to complete February 22, 1989, transaction in which Mark Fitzpatrick, Wayne McBean and future considerations were traded to **NY Islanders** by **Los Angeles** for Kelly Hrudey, May 23, 1989. Traded to **Hartford** by **NY Islanders** for Ray Ferraro, November 13, 1990. Traded to **Detroit** by **Hartford** for Doug Houda, February 20, 1991. Traded to **Quebec** by **Detroit** with Dennis Vial for cash, June 15, 1992. Claimed by **Tampa Bay** from **Quebec** in Expansion Draft, June 18, 1992. Traded to **St. Louis** by **Tampa Bay** with Basil McRae and Tampa Bay's fourth round choice in 1996 Entry Draft for Jason Ruff and future considerations, January 28, 1993.

CROWDER, TROY

Right wing. Shoots right. 6'4", 220 lbs. Born, Sudbury, Ont., May 3, 1968.
(New Jersey's 6th choice, 108th overall, in 1986 Entry Draft).

			Regular Season					Playoffs				
Season	Club	Lea	GP	G	A	TP	PIM	GP	G	A	TP	PIM
1985-86	Hamilton	OHL	56	4	4	8	178	....	....	....	....	....
1986-87	Belleville	OHL	21	5	5	10	52	....	....	....	....	....
	North Bay	OHL	35	6	11	17	90	23	3	9	12	99
1987-88	North Bay	OHL	9	1	2	3	44	....	....	....	....	....
	Belleville	OHL	46	12	27	39	103	6	2	3	5	24
	Utica	AHL	3	0	0	0	36	....	....	....	....	....
	New Jersey	**NHL**	....	....	....	....	....	**1**	**0**	**0**	**0**	**12**
1988-89	Utica	AHL	62	6	4	10	152	2	0	0	0	25
1989-90	**New Jersey**	**NHL**	**10**	**0**	**0**	**0**	**23**	**2**	**0**	**0**	**0**	**10**
	Nashville	ECHL	3	0	0	0	15	....	....	....	....	....
1990-91	**New Jersey**	**NHL**	**59**	**6**	**3**	**9**	**182**	....	....	....	....	....
1991-92	**Detroit**	**NHL**	**7**	**0**	**0**	**0**	**35**	**1**	**0**	**0**	**0**	**0**
1992-93					DID NOT PLAY – INJURED							
	NHL Totals		**76**	**6**	**3**	**9**	**240**	**4**	**0**	**0**	**0**	**22**

Signed as a free agent by **Detroit**, August 27, 1991.

CROWLEY, EDWARD (TED)

Defense. Shoots right. 6'2", 188 lbs. Born, Concord, MA, May 3, 1970.
(Toronto's 4th choice, 69th overall, in 1988 Entry Draft).

			Regular Season					Playoffs				
Season	Club	Lea	GP	G	A	TP	PIM	GP	G	A	TP	PIM
1989-90	Boston College	H.E.	39	7	24	31	34	....	....	....	....	....
1990-91ab	Boston College	H.E.	39	12	24	36	61	....	....	....	....	....
1991-92	U.S. National	....	42	6	7	13	65	....	....	....	....	....
	St. John's	AHL	29	5	4	9	33	10	3	1	4	11
1992-93	St. John's	AHL	79	19	38	57	41	9	2	2	4	4

a Hockey East First All-Star Team (1991)
b NCAA East Second All-American Team (1991)

CROWLEY, JOE

Left wing. Shoots left. 6'2", 195 lbs. Born, Concord, MA, February 29, 1972.
(Edmonton's 3rd choice, 59th overall, in 1990 Entry Draft).

			Regular Season					Playoffs				
Season	Club	Lea	GP	G	A	TP	PIM	GP	G	A	TP	PIM
1990-91	Boston College	H.E.	17	3	0	3	14	....	....	....	....	....
1991-92	Hull	QMJHL	37	10	9	19	120	....	....	....	....	....
	Trois-Rivières	QMJHL	4	1	3	4	4	....	....	....	....	....
	Winston-Salem	ECHL	6	0	0	0	0	....	....	....	....	....
1992-93	Indianapolis	IHL	55	2	3	5	111	....	....	....	....	....

Traded to **Chicago** by **Edmonton** for Justin Lafayette, October 22, 1992.

CROWLEY, MIKE

Defense. Shoots left. 5'11", 165 lbs. Born, Minnesota, MN, July 4, 1975.
(Philadelphia's 5th choice, 140th overall, in 1993 Entry Draft).

			Regular Season					Playoffs				
Season	Club	Lea	GP	G	A	TP	PIM	GP	G	A	TP	PIM
1992-93	Bloom'ton-Jeff.	HS	22	10	32	42	18	....	....	....	....	....

CULLEN, JOHN

Center. Shoots right. 5'10", 180 lbs. Born, Puslinch, Ont., August 2, 1964.
(Buffalo's 2nd choice, 10th overall, in 1986 Supplemental Draft).

			Regular Season					Playoffs				
Season	Club	Lea	GP	G	A	TP	PIM	GP	G	A	TP	PIM
1983-84a	Boston U.	ECAC	40	23	33	56	28	....	....	....	....	....
1984-85b	Boston U.	H.E.	41	27	32	59	46	....	....	....	....	....
1985-86bc	Boston U.	H.E.	43	25	49	74	54	....	....	....	....	....
1986-87d	Boston U.	H.E.	36	23	29	52	35	....	....	....	....	....
1987-88efgh	Flint	IHL	81	48	*109	*157	113	16	11	*15	26	16
1988-89	**Pittsburgh**	**NHL**	**79**	**12**	**37**	**49**	**112**	**11**	**3**	**6**	**9**	**28**
1989-90	**Pittsburgh**	**NHL**	**72**	**32**	**60**	**92**	**138**	....	....	....	....	....
1990-91	**Pittsburgh**	**NHL**	**65**	**31**	**63**	**94**	**83**	....	....	....	....	....
	Hartford	**NHL**	**13**	**8**	**8**	**16**	**18**	**6**	**2**	**7**	**9**	**10**
1991-92	**Hartford**	**NHL**	**77**	**26**	**51**	**77**	**141**	**7**	**2**	**1**	**3**	**12**
1992-93	**Hartford**	**NHL**	**19**	**5**	**4**	**9**	**58**	....	....	....	....	....
	Toronto	**NHL**	**47**	**13**	**28**	**41**	**53**	**12**	**2**	**3**	**5**	**0**
	NHL Totals		**372**	**127**	**251**	**378**	**603**	**36**	**9**	**17**	**26**	**50**

a ECAC Rookie of the Year (1984)
b Hockey East First All-Star Team (1985, 1986)
c NCAA East Second All-American Team (1986)
d Hockey East Second All-Star Team (1987)
e IHL First All-Star Team (1988)
f Won James Gatschene Memorial Trophy (MVP-IHL) (1988)
g Shared Garry F. Longman Memorial Trophy (Top Rookie-IHL) with Ed Belfour (1988)
h Won Leo P. Lamoureux Memorial Trophy (Top Scorer-IHL) (1988)

Played in NHL All-Star Game (1991, 1992)

Signed as a free agent by **Pittsburgh**, June 21, 1988. Traded to **Hartford** by **Pittsburgh** with Jeff Parker and Zarley Zalapski for Ron Francis, Grant Jennings and Ulf Samuelsson, March 4, 1991. Traded to **Toronto** by **Hartford** for future considerations, November 24, 1992.

CULLIMORE, JASSEN

Defense. Shoots left. 6'5", 225 lbs. Born, Simcoe, Ont., December 4, 1972.
(Vancouver's 2nd choice, 29th overall, in 1991 Entry Draft).

			Regular Season					Playoffs				
Season	Club	Lea	GP	G	A	TP	PIM	GP	G	A	TP	PIM
1989-90	Peterborough	OHL	59	2	6	8	61	11	0	2	2	8
1990-91	Peterborough	OHL	62	8	16	24	74	4	1	0	1	7
1991-92a	Peterborough	OHL	54	9	37	46	65	10	3	6	9	8
1992-93	Hamilton	AHL	56	5	7	12	60	....	....	....	....	....

a OHL Second All-Star Team (1992)

CUMMINS, JIM

Right wing. Shoots right. 6'2", 203 lbs. Born, Dearborn, MI, May 17, 1970.
(NY Rangers' 5th choice, 67th overall, in 1989 Entry Draft).

			Regular Season					Playoffs				
Season	Club	Lea	GP	G	A	TP	PIM	GP	G	A	TP	PIM
1988-89	Michigan State	CCHA	30	3	8	11	98	....	....	....	....	....
1989-90	Michigan State	CCHA	41	8	7	15	94	....	....	....	....	....
1990-91	Michigan State	CCHA	34	9	6	15	110	....	....	....	....	....
1991-92	**Detroit**	**NHL**	**1**	**0**	**0**	**0**	**7**	....	....	....	....	....
	Adirondack	AHL	65	7	13	20	338	5	0	0	0	19
1992-93	**Detroit**	**NHL**	**7**	**1**	**1**	**2**	**58**	....	....	....	....	....
	Adirondack	AHL	43	16	4	20	179	9	3	1	4	4
	NHL Totals		**8**	**1**	**1**	**2**	**65**	....	....	....	....	....

Traded to **Detroit** by **NY Rangers** with Kevin Miller and Dennis Vial for Joey Kocur and Per Djoos, March 5, 1991. Traded to **Philadelphia** by **Detroit** with Philadelphia's fourth round choice (previously acquired by Detroit — later traded to Boston — Boston selected Charles Paquette) in 1993 Entry Draft for Greg Johnson and future considerations, June 20, 1993.

CUNNEYWORTH, RANDY WILLIAM

Left wing. Shoots left. 6', 180 lbs. Born, Etobicoke, Ont., May 10, 1961.
(Buffalo's 9th choice, 167th overall, in 1980 Entry Draft).

			Regular Season					Playoffs				
Season	Club	Lea	GP	G	A	TP	PIM	GP	G	A	TP	PIM
1979-80	Ottawa	OHA	63	16	25	41	145	11	0	1	1	13
1980-81	Buffalo	NHL	1	0	0	0	2	....	....	....	....	....
	Rochester	AHL	1	0	1	1	2	....	....	....	....	....
	Ottawa	OHA	67	54	74	128	240	15	5	8	13	35
1981-82	Buffalo	NHL	20	2	4	6	47	....	....	....	....	....
	Rochester	AHL	57	12	15	27	86	9	4	0	4	30
1982-83	Rochester	AHL	78	23	33	56	111	16	4	4	8	35
1983-84	Rochester	AHL	54	18	17	35	85	17	5	5	10	55
1984-85	Rochester	AHL	72	30	38	68	148	5	2	1	3	16
1985-86	Pittsburgh	NHL	75	15	30	45	74	....	....	....	....	....
1986-87	Pittsburgh	NHL	79	26	27	53	142	....	....	....	....	....
1987-88	Pittsburgh	NHL	71	35	39	74	141	....	....	....	....	....
1988-89	Pittsburgh	NHL	70	25	19	44	156	11	3	5	8	26
1989-90	Winnipeg	NHL	28	5	6	11	34	....	....	....	....	....
	Hartford	NHL	43	9	9	18	41	4	0	0	0	2
1990-91	Hartford	NHL	32	9	5	14	49	1	0	0	0	0
	Springfield	AHL	2	0	0	0	5	....	....	....	....	....
1991-92	Hartford	NHL	39	7	10	17	71	7	3	0	3	9
1992-93	Hartford	NHL	39	5	4	9	63	....	....	....	....	....
	NHL Totals		497	138	153	291	820	23	6	5	11	37

Traded to **Pittsburgh** by **Buffalo** with Mike Moller for Pat Hughes, October 4, 1985. Traded to **Winnipeg** by **Pittsburgh** with Rick Tabaracci and Dave McLlwain for Jim Kyte, Andrew McBain and Randy Gilhen, June 17, 1989. Traded to **Hartford** by **Winnipeg** for Paul MacDermid, December 13, 1989.

CURRAN, BRIAN

Defense. Shoots left. 6'5", 220 lbs. Born, Toronto, Ont., November 5, 1963.
(Boston's 2nd choice, 22nd overall, in 1982 Entry Draft).

			Regular Season					Playoffs				
Season	Club	Lea	GP	G	A	TP	PIM	GP	G	A	TP	PIM
1980-81	Portland	WHL	59	2	28	30	275	7	0	1	1	13
1981-82	Portland	WHL	51	2	16	18	132	14	1	7	8	63
1982-83	Portland	WHL	56	1	30	31	187	14	1	3	4	57
1983-84	Boston	NHL	16	1	1	2	57	3	0	0	0	7
	Hershey	AHL	23	0	2	2	94	....	....	....	....	....
1984-85	Boston	NHL	56	0	1	1	158	....	....	....	....	....
	Hershey	AHL	4	0	0	0	19	....	....	....	....	....
1985-86	Boston	NHL	43	2	5	7	192	2	0	0	0	4
1986-87	NY Islanders	NHL	68	0	10	10	356	8	0	0	0	51
1987-88	NY Islanders	NHL	22	0	1	1	68	....	....	....	....	....
	Springfield	AHL	8	1	0	1	43	....	....	....	....	....
	Toronto	NHL	7	0	1	1	19	6	0	0	0	41
1988-89	Toronto	NHL	47	1	4	5	185	....	....	....	....	....
1989-90	Toronto	NHL	72	2	9	11	301	5	0	1	1	19
1990-91	Toronto	NHL	4	0	0	0	7	....	....	....	....	....
	Newmarket	AHL	6	0	1	1	32	....	....	....	....	....
	Buffalo	NHL	17	0	1	1	43	....	....	....	....	....
	Rochester	AHL	10	0	0	0	36	....	....	....	....	....
1991-92	Buffalo	NHL	3	0	0	0	14	....	....	....	....	....
	Rochester	AHL	36	0	3	3	122	....	....	....	....	....
1992-93	Cape Breton	AHL	61	2	24	26	223	12	0	3	3	12
	NHL Totals		355	6	33	39	1400	24	0	1	1	122

Signed as a free agent by **NY Islanders**, August 29, 1987. Traded to **Toronto** by **NY Islanders** for Toronto's sixth round choice (Pavel Gross) in 1988 Entry Draft, March 8, 1988. Traded to **Buffalo** by **Toronto** with Lou Franceschetti for Mike Foligno and Buffalo's eighth round choice (Thomas Kucharcik) in 1991 Entry Draft, December 17, 1990. Signed as a free agent by **Edmonton**, October 27, 1992.

CURRIE, DAN

Left wing. Shoots left. 6'2", 195 lbs. Born, Burlington, Ont., March 15, 1968.
(Edmonton's 4th choice, 84th overall, in 1986 Entry Draft).

			Regular Season					Playoffs				
Season	Club	Lea	GP	G	A	TP	PIM	GP	G	A	TP	PIM
1985-86	S.S. Marie	OHL	66	21	24	45	37	....	....	....	....	....
1986-87	S.S. Marie	OHL	66	31	52	83	53	4	2	1	3	2
1987-88	Nova Scotia	AHL	3	4	2	6	0	5	4	3	7	0
	S.S. Marie	OHL	57	50	59	109	53	6	3	9	12	4
1988-89	Cape Breton	AHL	77	29	36	65	29	....	....	....	....	....
1989-90	Cape Breton	AHL	77	36	40	76	28	6	4	4	8	0
1990-91	Edmonton	NHL	5	0	0	0	0	....	....	....	....	....
	Cape Breton	AHL	71	47	45	92	51	4	3	1	4	8
1991-92	Edmonton	NHL	7	1	0	1	0	....	....	....	....	....
a	Cape Breton	AHL	66	*50	42	92	39	5	4	5	9	4
1992-93	Edmonton	NHL	5	0	0	0	4	....	....	....	....	....
	Cape Breton	AHL	75	57	41	98	73	16	7	4	11	29
	NHL Totals		17	1	0	1	4	....	....	....	....	....

a AHL Second All-Star Team (1992)
b AHL First All-Star Team (1993)

CYR, PAUL

Left wing. Shoots left. 5'10", 180 lbs. Born, Port Alberni, B.C., October 31, 1963.
(Buffalo's 2nd choice, 9th overall, in 1982 Entry Draft).

			Regular Season					Playoffs				
Season	Club	Lea	GP	G	A	TP	PIM	GP	G	A	TP	PIM
1980-81	Victoria	WHL	64	36	22	58	85	14	6	5	11	46
1981-82a	Victoria	WHL	58	52	56	108	167	4	3	2	5	12
1982-83	Victoria	WHL	20	21	22	43	61	....	....	....	....	....
	Buffalo	NHL	36	15	12	27	59	10	1	3	4	6
1983-84	Buffalo	NHL	71	16	27	43	52	3	0	1	1	0
1984-85	Buffalo	NHL	71	22	24	46	63	5	2	2	4	15
1985-86	Buffalo	NHL	71	20	31	51	120	....	....	....	....	....
1986-87	Buffalo	NHL	73	11	16	27	122	....	....	....	....	....
1987-88	Buffalo	NHL	20	1	1	2	38	....	....	....	....	....
	NY Rangers	NHL	40	4	13	17	41	....	....	....	....	....
1988-89	NY Rangers	NHL	1	0	0	0	2	....	....	....	....	....
1989-90			DID NOT PLAY – INJURED									
1990-91	Hartford	NHL	70	12	13	25	107	6	1	0	1	10
1991-92	Hartford	NHL	17	0	3	3	19	....	....	....	....	....
	Springfield	AHL	43	11	18	29	30	11	0	3	3	12
1992-93	Springfield	AHL	41	7	14	21	44	15	3	2	5	12
	NHL Totals		470	101	140	241	623	24	4	6	10	31

a WHL Second All-Star Team (1982)

Traded to **NY Rangers** by **Buffalo** with Buffalo's tenth round choice (Eric Fenton) in 1988 Entry Draft for Mike Donnelly and NY Rangers' fifth round choice (Alexander Mogilny) in 1988 Entry Draft, December 31, 1987. Signed as a free agent by **Hartford**, September 30, 1990.

CZERKAWSKI, MARIUSZ (chehr-KAWV-skee)

Right wing. Shoots right. 5'11", 185 lbs. Born, Radomsko, Poland, April 13, 1972.
(Boston's 5th choice, 106th overall, in 1991 Entry Draft).

			Regular Season					Playoffs				
Season	Club	Lea	GP	G	A	TP	PIM	GP	G	A	TP	PIM
1990-91	GKS Tychy	Poland	24	25	15	40	....	....	....	....	....	....
1991-92	Djurgarden	Swe.	39	8	5	13	4	3	0	0	0	2
1992-93	Hammarby	Swe.2	32	39	30	69	74	....	....	....	....	....

DAHL, KEVIN

Defense. Shoots right. 5'11", 190 lbs. Born, Regina, Sask., December 30, 1968.
(Montreal's 12th choice, 230th overall, in 1988 Entry Draft).

			Regular Season					Playoffs				
Season	Club	Lea	GP	G	A	TP	PIM	GP	G	A	TP	PIM
1986-87	Bowling Green	CCHA	32	2	6	8	54	....	....	....	....	....
1987-88	Bowling Green	CCHA	44	2	23	25	78	....	....	....	....	....
1988-89	Bowling Green	CCHA	46	9	26	35	51	....	....	....	....	....
1989-90	Bowling Green	CCHA	43	8	22	30	74	....	....	....	....	....
1990-91	Fredericton	AHL	32	1	15	16	45	9	0	1	1	11
	Winston-Salem	ECHL	36	7	17	24	58	....	....	....	....	....
1991-92	Cdn. National	....	45	2	15	17	44	....	....	....	....	....
	Cdn. Olympic	....	8	2	0	2	6	....	....	....	....	....
	Salt Lake	IHL	13	0	2	2	12	5	0	0	0	13
1992-93	Calgary	NHL	61	2	9	11	56	6	0	2	2	8
	NHL Totals		61	2	9	11	56	6	0	2	2	8

Signed as a free agent by **Calgary**, July 27, 1991.

DAHLEN, ULF (DAH-lehn)

Right wing. Shoots left. 6'2", 195 lbs. Born, Ostersund, Sweden, January 12, 1967.
(NY Rangers' 1st choice, 7th overall, in 1985 Entry Draft).

			Regular Season					Playoffs				
Season	Club	Lea	GP	G	A	TP	PIM	GP	G	A	TP	PIM
1983-84	Ostersund	Swe.2	36	15	11	26	10	....	....	....	....	....
1984-85	Ostersund	Swe.2	36	33	26	59	20	....	....	....	....	....
1985-86	Bjorkloven	Swe.	22	4	3	7	8	....	....	....	....	....
1986-87	Bjorkloven	Swe.	31	9	12	21	20	6	6	2	8	4
1987-88	NY Rangers	NHL	70	29	23	52	26	....	....	....	....	....
	Colorado	IHL	2	2	2	4	0	....	....	....	....	....
1988-89	NY Rangers	NHL	56	24	19	43	50	4	0	0	0	0
1989-90	NY Rangers	NHL	63	18	18	36	30	....	....	....	....	....
	Minnesota	NHL	13	2	4	6	0	7	1	4	5	2
1990-91	Minnesota	NHL	66	21	18	39	6	15	2	6	8	4
1991-92	Minnesota	NHL	79	36	30	66	10	7	0	3	3	2
1992-93	Minnesota	NHL	83	35	39	74	6	....	....	....	....	....
	NHL Totals		430	165	151	316	128	33	3	13	16	8

Traded to **Minnesota** by **NY Rangers** with Los Angeles' fourth round choice (previously acquired by NY Rangers — Minnesota selected Cal McGowan) in 1990 Entry Draft and future considerations for Mike Gartner, March 6, 1990.

DAHLQUIST, CHRIS (DAHL-kwist)

Defense. Shoots left. 6'1", 195 lbs. Born, Fridley, MN, December 14, 1962.

			Regular Season					Playoffs				
Season	Club	Lea	GP	G	A	TP	PIM	GP	G	A	TP	PIM
1981-82	Lake Superior	CCHA	39	4	10	14	62	....	....	....	....	....
1982-83	Lake Superior	CCHA	35	0	12	12	63	....	....	....	....	....
1983-84	Lake Superior	CCHA	40	4	19	23	76	....	....	....	....	....
1984-85	Lake Superior	CCHA	32	4	10	14	18	....	....	....	....	....
1985-86	Pittsburgh	NHL	5	1	2	3	2	....	....	....	....	....
	Baltimore	AHL	65	4	21	25	64	....	....	....	....	....
1986-87	Pittsburgh	NHL	19	0	1	1	20	....	....	....	....	....
	Baltimore	AHL	51	1	16	17	50	....	....	....	....	....
1987-88	Pittsburgh	NHL	44	3	6	9	69	....	....	....	....	....
1988-89	Pittsburgh	NHL	43	1	5	6	42	2	0	0	0	0
	Muskegon	IHL	10	3	6	9	14	....	....	....	....	....
1989-90	Pittsburgh	NHL	62	4	10	14	56	....	....	....	....	....
	Muskegon	IHL	6	1	1	2	8	....	....	....	....	....
1990-91	Pittsburgh	NHL	22	1	2	3	30	....	....	....	....	....
	Minnesota	NHL	42	2	6	8	33	23	1	6	7	20
1991-92	Minnesota	NHL	74	1	13	14	68	7	0	0	0	6
1992-93	Calgary	NHL	74	3	7	10	66	6	3	1	4	4
	NHL Totals		385	16	52	68	386	38	4	7	11	30

Signed as a free agent by **Pittsburgh**, May 7, 1985. Traded to **Minnesota** by **Pittsburgh** with Jim Johnson for Larry Murphy and Peter Taglianetti, December 11, 1990. Claimed by **Calgary** from **Minnesota** in NHL Waiver Draft, October 4, 1992.

DAIGLE, ALEXANDRE (DAYG-leh)

Center. Shoots left. 6', 170 lbs. Born, Montreal, Que., February 7, 1975.
(Ottawa's 1st choice, 1st overall, in 1993 Entry Draft).

			Regular Season					Playoffs				
Season	Club	Lea	GP	G	A	TP	PIM	GP	G	A	TP	PIM
1991-92ab	Victoriaville	QMJHL	66	35	75	110	63	.....	....	....	....	.....
1992-93c	Victoriaville	QMJHL	53	45	92	137	85	6	5	6	11	4

a QMJHL Second All-Star Team (1992)
b Canadian Major Junior Rookie of the Year (1992)
c QMJHL First All-Star Team (1993)

DAIGNEAULT, JEAN-JACQUES (DAYN-yoh)

Defense. Shoots left. 5'11", 185 lbs. Born, Montreal, Que., October 12, 1965.
(Vancouver's 1st choice, 10th overall, in 1984 Entry Draft).

			Regular Season					Playoffs				
Season	Club	Lea	GP	G	A	TP	PIM	GP	G	A	TP	PIM
1981-82	Laval	QMJHL	64	4	25	29	41	18	1	3	4	2
1982-83ab	Longueuil	QMJHL	70	26	58	84	58	15	4	11	15	35
1983-84	Cdn. Olympic	....	62	6	15	21	40	....	....	....	....	....
	Longueuil	QMJHL	10	2	11	13	6	14	3	13	16	30
1984-85	Vancouver	NHL	67	4	23	27	69	....	....	....	....	....
1985-86	Vancouver	NHL	64	5	23	28	45	3	0	2	2	0
1986-87	Philadelphia	NHL	77	6	16	22	56	9	1	0	1	0
1987-88	Philadelphia	NHL	28	2	2	4	12	....	....	....	....	....
	Hershey	AHL	10	1	5	6	8	....	....	....	....	....
1988-89	Hershey	AHL	12	0	10	10	13	....	....	....	....	....
	Sherbrooke	AHL	63	10	33	43	48	6	1	3	4	2
1989-90	Montreal	NHL	36	2	10	12	14	9	0	0	0	2
	Sherbrooke	AHL	28	8	19	27	18	....	....	....	....	....
1990-91	Montreal	NHL	51	3	16	19	31	5	0	1	1	0
1991-92	Montreal	NHL	79	4	14	18	36	11	0	3	3	4
1992-93	Montreal	NHL	66	8	10	18	25	20	1	3	4	2
	NHL Totals		468	34	114	148	288	57	2	9	11	8

a QMJHL First All-Star Team (1983)
b Named QMJHL's Top Defenseman (1983)

Traded to **Philadelphia** by **Vancouver** with Vancouver's second round choice (Kent Hawley) in 1986 Entry Draft for Dave Richter, Rich Sutter and Vancouver's third round choice (previously acquired by Philadelphia — Vancouver selected Don Gibson) in 1986 Entry Draft, June 6, 1986. Traded to **Montreal** by **Philadelphia** for Scott Sandelin, November 7, 1988.

DALGARNO, BRAD

Right wing. Shoots right. 6'3", 215 lbs. Born, Vancouver, B.C., August 11, 1967.
(NY Islanders' 1st choice, 6th overall, in 1985 Entry Draft).

			Regular Season					Playoffs				
Season	Club	Lea	GP	G	A	TP	PIM	GP	G	A	TP	PIM
1984-85	Hamilton	OHA	66	23	30	53	86	....	....	....	....	....
1985-86	**NY Islanders**	**NHL**	2	1	0	1	0	....	....	....	....	....
	Hamilton	OHL	54	22	43	65	79	....	....	....	....	....
1986-87	Hamilton	OHL	60	27	32	59	100	....	....	....	....	....
1987-88	**NY Islanders**	**NHL**	38	2	8	10	58	....	....	....	....	....
	Springfield	AHL	39	13	11	24	76	....	....	....	....	....
1988-89	**NY Islanders**	**NHL**	55	11	10	21	86	....	....	....	....	....
1989-90							DID NOT PLAY					
1990-91	**NY Islanders**	**NHL**	41	3	12	15	24	....	....	....	....	....
	Capital Dist.	AHL	27	6	14	20	26	....	....	....	....	....
1991-92	**NY Islanders**	**NHL**	15	2	1	3	12	....	....	....	....	....
	Capital Dist.	AHL	14	7	8	15	34	....	....	....	....	....
1992-93	**NY Islanders**	**NHL**	57	15	17	32	62	18	2	2	4	14
	Capital Dist.	AHL	19	10	4	14	16	....	....	....	....	....
	NHL Totals		208	34	48	82	242	18	2	2	4	14

DAL GRANDE, DAVID

Defense. Shoots left. 6'5", 195 lbs. Born, Ottawa, Ont., July 8, 1974.
(NY Rangers' 6th choice, 144th overall, in 1992 Entry Draft).

			Regular Season					Playoffs				
Season	Club	Lea	GP	G	A	TP	PIM	GP	G	A	TP	PIM
1991-92	Ottawa	COJHL	53	7	28	35	54	....	....	....	....	....
1992-93	Notre Dame	CCHA	22	1	1	2	10	....	....	....	....	....

DAMPHOUSSE, VINCENT (DAM-fooz)

Left wing. Shoots left. 6'1", 190 lbs. Born, Montreal, Que., December 17, 1967.
(Toronto's 1st choice, 6th overall, in 1986 Entry Draft).

			Regular Season					Playoffs				
Season	Club	Lea	GP	G	A	TP	PIM	GP	G	A	TP	PIM
1983-84	Laval	QMJHL	66	29	36	65	25	....	....	....	....	....
1984-85	Laval	QMJHL	68	35	68	103	62	....	....	....	....	....
1985-86a	Laval	QMJHL	69	45	110	155	70	14	9	27	36	12
1986-87	Toronto	NHL	80	21	25	46	26	12	1	5	6	8
1987-88	Toronto	NHL	75	12	36	48	40	6	0	1	1	10
1988-89	Toronto	NHL	80	26	42	68	75	....	....	....	....	....
1989-90	Toronto	NHL	80	33	61	94	56	5	0	2	2	2
1990-91	Toronto	NHL	79	26	47	73	65	....	....	....	....	....
1991-92	Edmonton	NHL	80	38	51	89	53	16	6	8	14	8
1992-93	Montreal	NHL	84	39	58	97	98	20	11	12	23	16
	NHL Totals		558	195	320	515	413	59	18	28	46	44

a QMJHL Second All-Star Team (1986)

Played in NHL All-Star Game (1991, 1992)

Traded to **Edmonton** by **Toronto** with Peter Ing, Scott Thornton, Luke Richardson, future considerations and cash for Grant Fuhr, Glenn Anderson and Craig Berube, September 19, 1991. Traded to **Montreal** by **Edmonton** with Edmonton's fourth round choice (Adam Wiesel) in 1993 Entry Draft for Shayne Corson, Brent Gilchrist and Vladimir Vujtek, August 27, 1992.

DANDENAULT, ERIC

Left wing. Shoots right. 6', 193 lbs. Born, Sherbrooke, Que., March 10, 1970.

			Regular Season					Playoffs				
Season	Club	Lea	GP	G	A	TP	PIM	GP	G	A	TP	PIM
1990-91	Drummondville	QMJHL	67	14	33	47	215	14	5	6	11	84
1991-92	Hershey	AHL	69	6	13	19	149	3	0	0	0	4
1992-93	Hershey	AHL	72	20	19	39	118	....	....	....	....	....

Signed as a free agent by **Philadelphia**, December 4, 1991.

DANEYKO, KENNETH (KEN) (DAN-ee-koh)

Defense. Shoots left. 6'1", 210 lbs. Born, Windsor, Ont., April 17, 1964.
(New Jersey's 2nd choice, 18th overall, in 1982 Entry Draft).

			Regular Season					Playoffs				
Season	Club	Lea	GP	G	A	TP	PIM	GP	G	A	TP	PIM
1980-81	Spokane	WHL	62	6	13	19	40	4	0	0	0	6
1981-82	Spokane	WHL	26	1	11	12	147	....	....	....	....	....
	Seattle	WHL	38	1	22	23	151	14	1	9	10	49
1982-83	Seattle	WHL	69	17	43	60	150	4	1	3	4	14
1983-84	New Jersey	NHL	11	1	4	5	17	....	....	....	....	....
	Kamloops	WH	19	6	28	34	52	17	4	9	13	28
1984-85	New Jersey	NHL	1	0	0	0	10	....	....	....	....	....
	Maine	AHL	80	4	9	13	206	11	1	3	4	36
1985-86	New Jersey	NHL	44	0	10	10	100	....	....	....	....	....
	Maine	AHL	21	3	2	5	75	....	....	....	....	....
1986-87	New Jersey	NHL	79	2	12	14	183	....	....	....	....	....
1987-88	New Jersey	NHL	80	5	7	12	239	20	1	6	7	83
1988-89	New Jersey	NHL	80	5	5	10	283	....	....	....	....	....
1989-90	New Jersey	NHL	74	6	15	21	216	6	2	0	2	21
1990-91	New Jersey	NHL	80	4	16	20	249	7	0	1	1	10
1991-92	New Jersey	NHL	80	1	7	8	170	7	0	3	3	16
1992-93	New Jersey	NHL	84	2	11	13	236	5	0	0	0	8
	NHL Totals		613	26	87	113	1703	45	3	10	13	138

DANIELS, JEFF

Left wing. Shoots left. 6'1", 200 lbs. Born, Oshawa, Ont., June 24, 1968.
(Pittsburgh's 6th choice, 109th overall, in 1986 Entry Draft).

			Regular Season					Playoffs				
Season	Club	Lea	GP	G	A	TP	PIM	GP	G	A	TP	PIM
1984-85	Oshawa	OHL	59	7	11	18	16	....	....	....	....	....
1985-86	Oshawa	OHL	62	13	19	32	23	6	0	1	1	0
1986-87	Oshawa	OHL	54	14	9	23	22	15	3	2	5	5
1987-88	Oshawa	OHL	64	29	39	68	59	4	2	3	5	0
1988-89	Muskegon	IHL	58	21	21	42	58	11	3	5	8	11
1989-90	Muskegon	IHL	80	30	47	77	39	6	1	1	2	7
1990-91	Pittsburgh	NHL	11	0	2	2	2	....	....	....	....	....
	Muskegon	IHL	62	23	29	52	18	5	1	3	4	2
1991-92	Pittsburgh	NHL	2	0	0	0	0	....	....	....	....	....
	Muskegon	IHL	44	19	16	35	38	10	5	4	9	9
1992-93	Pittsburgh	NHL	58	5	4	9	14	12	3	2	5	0
	Cleveland	IHL	3	2	1	3	0	....	....	....	....	....
	NHL Totals		71	5	6	11	16	12	3	2	5	0

DANIELS, KIMBI

Center. Shoots right. 5'10", 175 lbs. Born, Brandon, Man., January 19, 1972.
(Philadelphia's 5th choice, 44th overall, in 1990 Entry Draft).

			Regular Season					Playoffs				
Season	Club	Lea	GP	G	A	TP	PIM	GP	G	A	TP	PIM
1988-89	Swift Current	WHL	68	30	31	61	48	12	6	6	12	12
1989-90	Swift Current	WHL	69	43	51	94	84	4	1	3	4	10
1990-91	Philadelphia	NHL	2	0	1	1	0	....	....	....	....	....
	Swift Current	WHL	69	54	64	118	68	3	4	2	6	6
1991-92	Philadelphia	NHL	25	1	1	2	4	....	....	....	....	....
	Seattle	WHL	19	7	14	21	133	15	5	10	15	27
1992-93	Tri-City	WHL	9	9	12	21	12	3	0	1	1	8
	NHL Totals		27	1	2	3	4	....	....	....	....	....

DANIELS, SCOTT

Left wing. Shoots left. 6'3", 200 lbs. Born, Prince Albert, Sask., September 19, 1969.
(Hartford's 6th choice, 136th overall, in 1989 Entry Draft).

			Regular Season					Playoffs				
Season	Club	Lea	GP	G	A	TP	PIM	GP	G	A	TP	PIM
1986-87	Kamloops	WHL	43	6	4	10	68	....	....	....	....	....
	N. Westminster	WHL	19	4	7	11	30	....	....	....	....	....
1987-88	N. Westminster	WHL	37	6	11	17	157	....	....	....	....	....
	Regina	WHL	19	2	3	5	83	....	....	....	....	....
1988-89	Regina	WHL	64	21	26	47	241	....	....	....	....	....
1989-90	Regina	WHL	52	28	31	59	171	....	....	....	....	....
1990-91	Springfield	AHL	40	2	6	8	121	....	....	....	....	....
	Louisville	ECHL	9	5	3	8	34	1	0	2	2	0
1991-92	Springfield	AHL	54	7	15	22	213	10	0	0	0	32
1992-93	Hartford	NHL	1	0	0	0	19	....	....	....	....	....
	Springfield	AHL	60	11	12	23	181	12	2	7	9	12
	NHL Totals		1	0	0	0	19	....	....	....	....	....

DANYLUK, CAM

Left wing. Shoots left. 6'4", 215 lbs. Born, Andrew, Alta., September 6, 1972.

			Regular Season					Playoffs				
Season	Club	Lea	GP	G	A	TP	PIM	GP	G	A	TP	PIM
1991-92	Medicine Hat	WHL	63	30	30	60	211	4	0	2	2	2
1992-93	Medicine Hat	WHL	57	29	19	48	214	10	9	5	14	29

Signed as a free agent by **Vancouver**, April 21, 1993.

DARBY, CRAIG

Center. Shoots right. 6'3", 180 lbs. Born, Oneida, NY, September 26, 1972.
(Montreal's 3rd choice, 43rd overall, in 1991 Entry Draft).

			Regular Season					Playoffs				
Season	Club	Lea	GP	G	A	TP	PIM	GP	G	A	TP	PIM
1991-92	Providence	H.E.	35	17	24	41	47	....	....	....	....	....
1992-93	Providence	H.E.	35	11	21	32	62	....	....	....	....	....

DARLING, DION

Defense. Shoots left. 6'3", 205 lbs. Born, Edmonton, Alta., October 22, 1974.
(Montreal's 7th choice, 125th overall, in 1993 Entry Draft).

			Regular Season					Playoffs				
Season	Club	Lea	GP	G	A	TP	PIM	GP	G	A	TP	PIM
1991-92	St. Albert	AJHL	29	5	15	20	101	....	....	....	....	....
1992-93	Spokane	WHL	69	1	4	5	168	9	0	1	1	14

DAVYDOV, EVGENY (dah-VEE-dohv, yev-GEHN-ee)

Left wing. Shoots right. 6', 195 lbs. Born, Chelyabinsk, Soviet Union, May 27, 1967.
(Winnipeg's 14th choice, 235th overall, in 1989 Entry Draft).

			Regular Season					Playoffs				
Season	Club	Lea	GP	G	A	TP	PIM	GP	G	A	TP	PIM
1984-85	Chelyabinsk	USSR	5	1	0	1	2	....	....	....	....	....
1985-86	Chelyabinsk	USSR	39	11	5	16	22	....	....	....	....	....
1986-87	CSKA	USSR	32	11	2	13	8	....	....	....	....	....
1987-88	CSKA	USSR	44	16	7	23	18	....	....	....	....	....
1988-89	CSKA	USSR	35	9	7	16	4	....	....	....	....	....
1989-90	CSKA	USSR	44	17	6	23	16	....	....	....	....	....
1990-91	CSKA	USSR	44	10	10	20	26	....	....	....	....	....
1991-92	CSKA	CIS	27	13	12	25	14	....	....	....	....	....
	Winnipeg	**NHL**	**12**	**4**	**3**	**7**	**8**	**7**	**2**	**2**	**4**	**2**
1992-93	**Winnipeg**	**NHL**	**79**	**28**	**21**	**49**	**66**	**4**	**0**	**0**	**0**	**0**
	NHL Totals		**91**	**32**	**24**	**56**	**74**	**11**	**2**	**2**	**4**	**2**

DAWE, JASON

Left wing. Shoots left. 5'10", 195 lbs. Born, Scarborough, Ont., May 29, 1973.
(Buffalo's 2nd choice, 35th overall, in 1991 Entry Draft).

			Regular Season					Playoffs				
Season	Club	Lea	GP	G	A	TP	PIM	GP	G	A	TP	PIM
1989-90	Peterborough	OHL	50	15	18	33	19	12	4	7	11	4
1990-91	Peterborough	OHL	66	43	27	70	43	4	3	1	4	0
1991-92a	Peterborough	OHL	66	53	55	108	55	4	5	0	5	0
1992-93bc	Peterborough	OHL	59	58	68	126	80	21	18	33	51	18
	Rochester	AHL	....	....	....	....	....	3	1	0	1	0

a OHL Third All-Star Team (1992)
b OHL First All-Star Team (1993)
c Canadian Major Junior Second All-Star Team (1993)

DAY, JOSEPH (JOE)

Left wing. Shoots left. 5'11", 180 lbs. Born, Chicago, IL, May 11, 1968.
(Hartford's 8th choice, 186th overall, in 1987 Entry Draft).

			Regular Season					Playoffs				
Season	Club	Lea	GP	G	A	TP	PIM	GP	G	A	TP	PIM
1986-87	St. Lawrence	ECAC	33	9	11	20	25	....	....	....	....	....
1987-88	St. Lawrence	ECAC	30	21	16	37	36	....	....	....	....	....
1988-89	St. Lawrence	ECAC	36	21	27	48	44	....	....	....	....	....
1989-90a	St. Lawrence	ECAC	32	19	26	45	30	....	....	....	....	....
1990-91	Springfield	AHL	75	24	29	53	82	18	5	5	10	27
1991-92	**Hartford**	**NHL**	**24**	**0**	**3**	**3**	**10**	....	....	....	....	....
	Springfield	AHL	50	33	25	58	92	....	....	....	....	....
1992-93	**Hartford**	**NHL**	**24**	**1**	**7**	**8**	**47**	....	....	....	....	....
	Springfield	AHL	33	15	20	35	118	15	0	8	8	40
	NHL Totals		**48**	**1**	**10**	**11**	**57**	....	....	....	....	....

a ECAC Second All-Star Team (1990)

DAZE, ERIC

Left wing. Shoots left. 6'4", 202 lbs. Born, Montreal, Que., July 2, 1975.
(Chicago's 5th choice, 90th overall, in 1993 Entry Draft).

			Regular Season					Playoffs				
Season	Club	Lea	GP	G	A	TP	PIM	GP	G	A	TP	PIM
1991-92	Laval	Midget	35	30	29	59	40	....	....	....	....	....
1992-93	Beauport	QMJHL	68	19	36	55	24	....	....	....	....	....

DEADMARSH, ADAM

Center. Shoots right. 6', 195 lbs. Born, Trail, B.C., May 10, 1975.
(Quebec's 2nd choice, 14th overall, in 1993 Entry Draft).

			Regular Season					Playoffs				
Season	Club	Lea	GP	G	A	TP	PIM	GP	G	A	TP	PIM
1991-92	Portland	WHL	68	30	30	60	81	6	3	3	6	13
1992-93	Portland	WHL	58	33	36	69	126	16	7	8	15	29

DEAN, KEVIN

Defense. Shoots left. 6'2", 195 lbs. Born, Madison, WI, April 1, 1969.
(New Jersey's 4th choice, 86th overall, in 1987 Entry Draft).

			Regular Season					Playoffs				
Season	Club	Lea	GP	G	A	TP	PIM	GP	G	A	TP	PIM
1987-88	N. Hampshire	H.E.	27	1	6	7	34	....	....	....	....	....
1988-89	N. Hampshire	H.E.	34	1	12	13	28	....	....	....	....	....
1989-90	N. Hampshire	H.E.	39	2	6	8	42	....	....	....	....	....
1990-91	N. Hampshire	H.E.	31	10	12	22	22	....	....	....	....	....
	Utica	AHL	7	0	1	1	2	....	....	....	....	....
1991-92	Utica	AHL	23	0	3	3	6	....	....	....	....	....
	Cincinnati	ECHL	30	3	22	25	43	9	1	6	7	8
1992-93	Utica	AHL	57	2	16	18	76	5	1	0	1	8
	Cincinnati	IHL	13	2	1	3	15	....	....	....	....	....

DEAN, SCOTT

Defense. Shoots left. 5'11", 200 lbs. Born, Lake Forest, IL, June 12, 1972.
(Chicago's 12th choice, 264th overall, in 1991 Entry Draft).

			Regular Season					Playoffs				
Season	Club	Lea	GP	G	A	TP	PIM	GP	G	A	TP	PIM
1991-92	Michigan State	CCHA	18	1	2	3	26	....	....	....	....	....
1992-93	Michigan State	CCHA	10	1	1	2	22	....	....	....	....	....

DEASLEY, BRYAN

Left wing. Shoots left. 6'3", 205 lbs. Born, Toronto, Ont., November 26, 1968.
(Calgary's 1st choice, 19th overall, in 1987 Entry Draft).

			Regular Season					Playoffs				
Season	Club	Lea	GP	G	A	TP	PIM	GP	G	A	TP	PIM
1986-87	U. of Michigan	CCHA	38	13	11	24	74	....	....	....	....	....
1987-88	U. of Michigan	CCHA	27	18	4	22	38	....	....	....	....	....
1988-89	Cdn. National	....	54	19	19	38	32	....	....	....	....	....
	Salt Lake	IHL	....	....	....	....	....	7	3	3	6	25
1989-90	Salt Lake	IHL	71	16	11	27	46	11	4	0	4	8
1990-91	Salt Lake	IHL	75	24	21	45	63	....	....	....	....	....
1991-92	Salt Lake	IHL	65	12	23	35	67	2	0	0	0	4
1992-93	Halifax	AHL	37	9	11	20	46	....	....	....	....	....

Traded to **Quebec** by **Calgary** for future considerations, October 27, 1992.

DEBRUSK, LOUIE (dah-BRUHSK)

Left wing. Shoots left. 6'2", 215 lbs. Born, Cambridge, Ont., March 19, 1971.
(NY Rangers' 4th choice, 49th overall, in 1989 Entry Draft).

			Regular Season					Playoffs				
Season	Club	Lea	GP	G	A	TP	PIM	GP	G	A	TP	PIM
1988-89	London	OHL	59	11	11	22	149	19	1	1	2	43
1989-90	London	OHL	61	21	19	40	198	6	2	2	4	24
1990-91	London	OHL	61	31	33	64	*223	7	2	2	4	14
	Binghamton	AHL	2	0	0	0	7	2	0	0	0	9
1991-92	**Edmonton**	**NHL**	**25**	**2**	**1**	**3**	**124**	....	....	....	....	....
	Cape Breton	AHL	28	2	2	4	73	....	....	....	....	....
1992-93	**Edmonton**	**NHL**	**51**	**8**	**2**	**10**	**205**	....	....	....	....	....
	NHL Totals		**76**	**10**	**3**	**13**	**329**	....	....	....	....	....

Traded to **Edmonton** by **NY Rangers** with Bernie Nicholls and Steven Rice for Mark Messier and future considerations, October 4, 1991.

DEMPSEY, NATHAN

Defense. Shoots left. 6', 160 lbs. Born, Spruce Grove, Alta., July 14, 1974.
(Toronto's 11th choice, 148th overall, in 1992 Entry Draft).

			Regular Season					Playoffs				
Season	Club	Lea	GP	G	A	TP	PIM	GP	G	A	TP	PIM
1991-92	Regina	WHL	70	4	22	26	72	....	....	....	....	....
1992-93	Regina	WHL	72	12	29	41	95	13	3	8	11	14

DEPALMA, LARRY

Left wing. Shoots left. 6', 195 lbs. Born, Trenton, MI, October 27, 1965.

			Regular Season					Playoffs				
Season	Club	Lea	GP	G	A	TP	PIM	GP	G	A	TP	PIM
1984-85	N. Westminster	WHL	65	14	16	30	87	10	1	1	2	25
1985-86	Saskatoon	WHL	65	61	51	112	232	13	7	9	16	58
	Minnesota	**NHL**	**1**	**0**	**0**	**0**	**0**	....	....	....	....	....
1986-87	**Minnesota**	**NHL**	**56**	**9**	**6**	**15**	**219**	....	....	....	....	....
	Springfield	AHL	9	2	2	4	82	....	....	....	....	....
1987-88	**Minnesota**	**NHL**	**7**	**1**	**1**	**2**	**15**	....	....	....	....	....
	Baltimore	AHL	16	8	10	18	121	....	....	....	....	....
	Kalamazoo	IHL	22	6	11	17	215	....	....	....	....	....
1988-89	**Minnesota**	**NHL**	**43**	**5**	**7**	**12**	**102**	**2**	**0**	**0**	**0**	**6**
1989-90	Kalamazoo	IHL	36	7	14	21	218	4	1	1	2	32
1990-91	**Minnesota**	**NHL**	**14**	**3**	**0**	**3**	**26**	....	....	....	....	....
	Kalamazoo	IHL	55	27	32	59	160	11	5	4	9	25
1991-92	Kansas City	IHL	62	28	29	57	188	15	7	*13	20	34
1992-93	**San Jose**	**NHL**	**20**	**2**	**6**	**8**	**41**	....	....	....	....	....
	Kansas City	IHL	30	11	11	22	83	10	1	4	5	20
	NHL Totals		**141**	**20**	**20**	**40**	**403**	**2**	**0**	**0**	**0**	**6**

Signed as a free agent by **San Jose**, August 30, 1991.

DE RUITER, CHRIS

Right wing. Shoots right. 6'2", 190 lbs. Born, Kingston, Ont., February 27, 1974.
(Toronto's 6th choice, 106th overall, in 1992 Entry Draft).

			Regular Season					Playoffs				
Season	Club	Lea	GP	G	A	TP	PIM	GP	G	A	TP	PIM
1991-92	Kingston	OHAJrA	29	27	24	51	52	....	....	....	....	....
1992-93	Clarkson	ECAC	32	2	5	7	40	....	....	....	....	....

DESJARDINS, ERIC (day-jar-DAN)

Defense. Shoots right. 6'1", 200 lbs. Born, Rouyn, Que., June 14, 1969.
(Montreal's 3rd choice, 38th overall, in 1987 Entry Draft).

			Regular Season					Playoffs				
Season	Club	Lea	GP	G	A	TP	PIM	GP	G	A	TP	PIM
1986-87a	Granby	QMJHL	66	14	24	38	178	8	3	2	5	10
1987-88	Sherbrooke	AHL	3	0	0	0	6	4	0	2	2	2
bc	Granby	QMJHL	62	18	49	67	138	5	0	3	3	10
1988-89	**Montreal**	**NHL**	**36**	**2**	**12**	**14**	**26**	**14**	**1**	**1**	**2**	**6**
1989-90	**Montreal**	**NHL**	**55**	**3**	**13**	**16**	**51**	**6**	**0**	**0**	**0**	**10**
1990-91	**Montreal**	**NHL**	**62**	**7**	**18**	**25**	**27**	**13**	**1**	**4**	**5**	**8**
1991-92	**Montreal**	**NHL**	**77**	**6**	**32**	**38**	**50**	**11**	**3**	**3**	**6**	**4**
1992-93	**Montreal**	**NHL**	**82**	**13**	**32**	**45**	**98**	**20**	**4**	**10**	**14**	**23**
	NHL Totals		**312**	**31**	**107**	**138**	**252**	**64**	**9**	**18**	**27**	**51**

a QMJHL Second All-Star Team (1987)
b QMJHL First All-Star Team (1988)
c QMJHL Top Defenseman (1988)

Played in NHL All-Star Game (1992)

DEULING, JARRETT

Left wing. Shoots left. 5'11", 194 lbs. Born, Vernon, B.C., March 4, 1974.
(NY Islanders' 2nd choice, 56th overall, in 1992 Entry Draft).

			Regular Season					Playoffs				
Season	Club	Lea	GP	G	A	TP	PIM	GP	G	A	TP	PIM
1990-91	Kamloops	WHL	48	4	12	16	43	12	5	2	7	7
1991-92	Kamloops	WHL	68	28	26	54	79	17	10	6	16	18
1992-93	Kamloops	WHL	68	31	32	63	93	13	6	7	13	14

DIDUCK, GERALD   (DID-uck)

Defense. Shoots right. 6'2", 207 lbs.   Born, Edmonton, Alta., April 6, 1965.
(NY Islanders' 2nd choice, 16th overall, in 1983 Entry Draft).

			Regular Season					Playoffs				
Season	Club	Lea	GP	G	A	TP	PIM	GP	G	A	TP	PIM
1981-82	Lethbridge	WHL	71	1	15	16	81	12	0	3	3	27
1982-83	Lethbridge	WHL	67	8	16	24	151	20	3	12	15	49
1983-84	Lethbridge	WHL	65	10	24	34	133	5	1	4	5	27
	Indianapolis	IHL	....	....	....	....	....	10	1	6	7	19
1984-85	**NY Islanders**	**NHL**	65	2	8	10	80	....	....	....	....	....
1985-86	**NY Islanders**	**NHL**	10	1	2	3	2	....	....	....	....	....
	Springfield	AHL	61	6	14	20	173	....	....	....	....	....
1986-87	**NY Islanders**	**NHL**	30	2	3	5	67	14	0	1	1	35
	Springfield	AHL	45	6	8	14	120	....	....	....	....	....
1987-88	**NY Islanders**	**NHL**	68	7	12	19	113	6	1	0	1	42
1988-89	**NY Islanders**	**NHL**	65	11	21	32	155	....	....	....	....	....
1989-90	**NY Islanders**	**NHL**	76	3	17	20	163	5	0	0	0	12
1990-91	**Montreal**	**NHL**	32	1	2	3	39	....	....	....	....	....
	Vancouver	**NHL**	31	3	7	10	66	6	1	0	1	11
1991-92	**Vancouver**	**NHL**	77	6	21	27	229	5	0	0	0	10
1992-93	**Vancouver**	**NHL**	80	6	14	20	171	12	4	2	6	12
	NHL Totals		**534**	**42**	**107**	**149**	**1085**	**48**	**6**	**3**	**9**	**122**

Traded to **Montreal** by **NY Islanders** for Craig Ludwig, September 4, 1990. Traded to **Vancouver** by **Montreal** for Vancouver's fourth round choice (Vladimir Vujtek) in 1991 Entry Draft, January 12, 1991.

DIMAIO, ROBERT (ROB)   (duh-MIGH-oh)

Center. Shoots right. 5'10", 190 lbs.   Born, Calgary, Alta., February 19, 1968.
(NY Islanders' 6th choice, 118th overall, in 1987 Entry Draft).

			Regular Season					Playoffs				
Season	Club	Lea	GP	G	A	TP	PIM	GP	G	A	TP	PIM
1986-87	Medicine Hat	WHL	70	27	43	70	130	20	7	11	18	46
1987-88	Medicine Hat	WHL	54	47	43	90	120	14	12	19	*31	59
1988-89	**NY Islanders**	**NHL**	16	1	0	1	30	....	....	....	....	....
	Springfield	AHL	40	13	18	31	67	....	....	....	....	....
1989-90	**NY Islanders**	**NHL**	7	0	0	0	2	1	1	0	1	4
	Springfield	AHL	54	25	27	52	69	16	4	7	11	45
1990-91	**NY Islanders**	**NHL**	1	0	0	0	0	....	....	....	....	....
	Capital Dist.	AHL	12	3	4	7	22	....	....	....	....	....
1991-92	**NY Islanders**	**NHL**	50	5	2	7	43	....	....	....	....	....
1992-93	**Tampa Bay**	**NHL**	54	9	15	24	62	....	....	....	....	....
	NHL Totals		**128**	**15**	**17**	**32**	**137**	**1**	**1**	**0**	**1**	**4**

Claimed by **Tampa Bay** from **NY Islanders** in Expansion Draft, June 18, 1992.

DINEEN, GORDON (GORD)

Defense. Shoots right. 6', 195 lbs.   Born, Quebec City, Que., September 21, 1962.
(NY Islanders' 2nd choice, 42nd overall, in 1981 Entry Draft).

			Regular Season					Playoffs				
Season	Club	Lea	GP	G	A	TP	PIM	GP	G	A	TP	PIM
1980-81	S.S. Marie	OHA	68	4	26	30	158	19	1	7	8	58
1981-82	S.S. Marie	OHL	68	9	45	54	185	13	1	2	3	52
1982-83	**NY Islanders**	**NHL**	2	0	0	0	4	....	....	....	....	....
abc	Indianapolis	CHL	73	10	47	57	78	13	2	10	12	29
1983-84	**NY Islanders**	**NHL**	43	1	11	12	32	9	1	1	2	28
	Indianapolis	CHL	26	4	13	17	63	....	....	....	....	....
1984-85	**NY Islanders**	**NHL**	48	1	12	13	89	10	0	0	0	26
	Springfield	AHL	25	1	8	9	46	....	....	....	....	....
1985-86	**NY Islanders**	**NHL**	57	1	8	9	81	3	0	0	0	2
	Springfield	AHL	11	2	3	5	20	....	....	....	....	....
1986-87	**NY Islanders**	**NHL**	71	4	10	14	110	7	0	4	4	4
1987-88	**NY Islanders**	**NHL**	57	4	12	16	62	....	....	....	....	....
	Minnesota	**NHL**	13	1	1	2	21	....	....	....	....	....
1988-89	**Minnesota**	**NHL**	2	0	1	1	2	....	....	....	....	....
	Kalamazoo	IHL	25	2	6	8	49	....	....	....	....	....
	Pittsburgh	**NHL**	38	1	2	3	42	11	0	2	2	8
1989-90	**Pittsburgh**	**NHL**	69	1	8	9	125	....	....	....	....	....
1990-91	**Pittsburgh**	**NHL**	9	0	0	0	4	....	....	....	....	....
	Muskegon	IHL	40	1	14	15	57	5	0	2	2	0
1991-92	**Pittsburgh**	**NHL**	1	0	0	0	0	....	....	....	....	....
d	Muskegon	IHL	79	8	37	45	83	14	2	4	6	33
1992-93	**Ottawa**	**NHL**	32	2	4	6	30	....	....	....	....	....
	San Diego	IHL	41	6	23	29	36	....	....	....	....	....
	NHL Totals		**442**	**16**	**69**	**85**	**602**	**40**	**1**	**7**	**8**	**68**

a CHL First All-Star Team (1983)
b Won Bob Gassoff Trophy (CHL's Most Improved Defenseman) (1983)
c Won Bobby Orr Trophy (CHL's Top Defenseman) (1983)
d IHL First All-Star Team (1992)

Traded to **Minnesota** by **NY Islanders** for Chris Pryor and future considerations, March 8, 1988. Traded to **Pittsburgh** by **Minnesota** with Scott Bjugstad for Ville Siren and Steve Gotaas, December 17, 1988. Signed as a free agent by **Ottawa**, August 31, 1992.

DINEEN, KEVIN

Right wing. Shoots right. 5'11", 190 lbs.   Born, Quebec City, Que., October 28, 1963.
(Hartford's 3rd choice, 56th overall, in 1982 Entry Draft).

			Regular Season					Playoffs				
Season	Club	Lea	GP	G	A	TP	PIM	GP	G	A	TP	PIM
1981-82	U. of Denver	WCHA	26	10	10	20	70	....	....	....	....	....
1982-83	U. of Denver	WCHA	36	16	13	29	108	....	....	....	....	....
1983-84	Cdn. Olympic	....	52	5	11	16	2	....	....	....	....	....
1984-85	**Hartford**	**NHL**	57	25	16	41	120	....	....	....	....	....
	Binghamton	AHL	25	15	8	23	41	....	....	....	....	....
1985-86	**Hartford**	**NHL**	57	33	35	68	124	10	6	7	13	18
1986-87	**Hartford**	**NHL**	78	40	39	79	110	6	2	1	3	31
1987-88	**Hartford**	**NHL**	74	25	25	50	217	6	4	4	8	8
1988-89	**Hartford**	**NHL**	79	45	44	89	167	4	1	0	1	10
1989-90	**Hartford**	**NHL**	67	25	41	66	164	6	3	2	5	18
1990-91a	**Hartford**	**NHL**	61	17	30	47	104	6	1	0	1	16
1991-92	**Hartford**	**NHL**	16	4	2	6	23	....	....	....	....	....
	Philadelphia	**NHL**	64	26	30	56	130	....	....	....	....	....
1992-93	**Philadelphia**	**NHL**	83	35	28	63	201	....	....	....	....	....
	NHL Totals		**636**	**275**	**290**	**565**	**1360**	**38**	**17**	**14**	**31**	**101**

a Won Bud Light/NHL Man of the Year Award (1991)
Played in NHL All-Star Game (1988, 1989)

Traded to **Philadelphia** by **Hartford** for Murray Craven and future considerations, November 13, 1991.

DIONNE, GILBERT

Left wing. Shoots left. 6', 194 lbs.   Born, Drummondville, Que., September 19, 1970.
(Montreal's 5th choice, 81st overall, in 1990 Entry Draft).

			Regular Season					Playoffs				
Season	Club	Lea	GP	G	A	TP	PIM	GP	G	A	TP	PIM
1988-89	Kitchener	OHL	66	11	33	44	13	5	1	1	2	4
1989-90a	Kitchener	OHL	64	48	57	105	85	17	13	10	23	22
1990-91	**Montreal**	**NHL**	2	0	0	0	0	....	....	....	....	....
	Fredericton	AHL	77	40	47	87	62	9	6	5	11	8
1991-92b	**Montreal**	**NHL**	39	21	13	34	10	11	3	4	7	10
	Fredericton	AHL	29	19	27	46	20	....	....	....	....	....
1992-93	**Montreal**	**NHL**	75	20	28	48	63	20	6	6	12	20
	Fredericton	AHL	3	4	3	7	0	....	....	....	....	....
	NHL Totals		**116**	**41**	**41**	**82**	**73**	**31**	**9**	**10**	**19**	**30**

a OHL Third All-Star Team (1990)
b NHL/Upper Deck All-Rookie Team (1992)

DI PIETRO, PAUL

Center. Shoots right. 5'9", 181 lbs.   Born, Sault Ste. Marie, Ont., September 8, 1970.
(Montreal's 6th choice, 102nd overall, in 1990 Entry Draft).

			Regular Season					Playoffs				
Season	Club	Lea	GP	G	A	TP	PIM	GP	G	A	TP	PIM
1986-87	Sudbury	OHL	49	5	11	16	13	....	....	....	....	....
1987-88	Sudbury	OHL	63	25	42	67	27	....	....	....	....	....
1988-89	Sudbury	OHL	57	31	48	79	27	....	....	....	....	....
1989-90a	Sudbury	OHL	66	56	63	119	57	7	3	6	9	7
1990-91	Fredericton	AHL	78	39	31	70	38	9	5	6	11	2
1991-92	**Montreal**	**NHL**	33	4	6	10	25	....	....	....	....	....
	Fredericton	AHL	43	26	31	57	52	7	3	4	7	8
1992-93	**Montreal**	**NHL**	29	4	13	17	14	17	8	5	13	8
	Fredericton	AHL	26	8	16	24	16	....	....	....	....	....
	NHL Totals		**62**	**8**	**19**	**27**	**39**	**17**	**8**	**5**	**13**	**8**

a OHL Third All-Star Team (1990)

DIRK, ROBERT

Defense. Shoots left. 6'4", 218 lbs.   Born, Regina, Sask., August 20, 1966.
(St. Louis' 4th choice, 53rd overall, in 1984 Entry Draft).

			Regular Season					Playoffs				
Season	Club	Lea	GP	G	A	TP	PIM	GP	G	A	TP	PIM
1982-83	Regina	WHL	1	0	0	0	0	....	....	....	....	....
1983-84	Regina	WHL	62	2	10	12	64	23	1	12	13	24
1984-85	Regina	WHL	69	10	34	44	97	8	0	0	0	4
1985-86	Regina	WHL	72	19	60	79	140	10	3	5	8	8
1986-87	Peoria	IHL	76	5	17	22	155	....	....	....	....	....
1987-88	**St. Louis**	**NHL**	7	0	1	1	16	6	0	1	1	2
	Peoria	IHL	54	4	21	25	126	....	....	....	....	....
1988-89	**St. Louis**	**NHL**	9	0	1	1	11	....	....	....	....	....
	Peoria	IHL	22	0	2	2	54	....	....	....	....	....
1989-90	**St. Louis**	**NHL**	37	1	1	2	128	3	0	0	0	0
	Peoria	IHL	24	1	2	3	79	....	....	....	....	....
1990-91	**St. Louis**	**NHL**	41	1	3	4	100	....	....	....	....	....
	Peoria	IHL	3	0	0	0	2	....	....	....	....	....
	Vancouver	**NHL**	11	1	0	1	20	6	0	0	0	13
1991-92	**Vancouver**	**NHL**	72	2	7	9	126	13	0	0	0	20
1992-93	**Vancouver**	**NHL**	69	4	8	12	150	9	0	0	0	6
	NHL Totals		**246**	**9**	**21**	**30**	**551**	**37**	**0**	**1**	**1**	**41**

Traded to **Vancouver** by **St. Louis** with Geoff Courtnall, Sergio Momesso, Cliff Ronning and future considerations for Dan Quinn and Garth Butcher, March 5, 1991.

DJOOS, PER   (JUICE)

Defense. Shoots right. 5'11", 176 lbs.   Born, Mora, Sweden, May 11, 1968.
(Detroit's 7th choice, 127th overall, in 1986 Entry Draft).

			Regular Season					Playoffs				
Season	Club	Lea	GP	G	A	TP	PIM	GP	G	A	TP	PIM
1984-85	Mora	Swe.2	20	2	3	5	2	....	....	....	....	....
1985-86	Mora	Swe.2	30	9	5	14	14	....	....	....	....	....
1986-87	Brynas	Swe.	23	1	2	3	16	....	....	....	....	....
1987-88	Brynas	Swe.	34	4	11	15	18	....	....	....	....	....
1988-89	Brynas	Swe.	40	1	17	18	44	....	....	....	....	....
1989-90	Brynas	Swe.	37	5	13	18	34	5	1	3	4	6
1990-91	**Detroit**	**NHL**	26	0	12	12	16	....	....	....	....	....
	Adirondack	AHL	20	2	9	11	6	....	....	....	....	....
	Binghamton	AHL	14	1	8	9	10	9	2	2	4	4
1991-92	**NY Rangers**	**NHL**	50	1	18	19	40	....	....	....	....	....
1992-93	**NY Rangers**	**NHL**	6	1	1	2	2	....	....	....	....	....
a	Binghamton	AHL	70	16	53	69	75	14	2	8	10	8
	NHL Totals		**82**	**2**	**31**	**33**	**58**					

a AHL Second All-Star Team (1993)

Traded to **NY Rangers** by **Detroit** with Joey Kocur for Kevin Miller, Jim Cummins and Dennis Vial, March 5, 1991.

DOBBIN, BRIAN

Right wing. Shoots right. 5'11", 205 lbs. Born, Petrolia, Ont., August 18, 1966.
(Philadelphia's 7th choice, 100th overall, in 1984 Entry Draft).

			Regular Season					Playoffs				
Season	Club	Lea	GP	G	A	TP	PIM	GP	G	A	TP	PIM
1982-83	Kingston	OHL	69	16	39	55	35	....	....	....	....	....
1983-84	London	OHL	70	30	40	70	70	....	....	....	....	....
1984-85	London	OHL	53	42	57	99	63	8	7	4	11	2
1985-86	London	OHL	59	38	55	93	113	5	2	1	3	9
	Hershey	AHL	2	1	0	1	0	18	5	5	10	21
1986-87	**Philadelphia**	**NHL**	**12**	**2**	**1**	**3**	**14**	....	....	....	....	....
	Hershey	AHL	52	26	35	61	66	5	4	2	6	15
1987-88	**Philadelphia**	**NHL**	**21**	**3**	**5**	**8**	**6**	....	....	....	....	....
	Hershey	AHL	54	36	47	83	58	12	7	8	15	15
1988-89	**Philadelphia**	**NHL**	**14**	**0**	**1**	**1**	**8**	**2**	**0**	**0**	**0**	**17**
a	Hershey	AHL	59	43	48	91	61	11	7	6	13	12
1989-90	**Philadelphia**	**NHL**	**9**	**1**	**1**	**2**	**11**	....	....	....	....	....
b	Hershey	AHL	68	38	47	85	58	....	....	....	....	....
1990-91	Hershey	AHL	80	35	43	78	82	7	1	2	3	7
1991-92	New Haven	AHL	33	16	21	37	20	....	....	....	....	....
	Boston	**NHL**	**7**	**1**	**0**	**1**	**22**	....	....	....	....	....
	Maine	AHL	33	21	15	36	14	....	....	....	....	....
1992-93	Milwaukee	IHL	80	39	45	84	50	6	4	3	7	6
	NHL Totals		**63**	**7**	**8**	**15**	**61**	**2**	**0**	**0**	**0**	**17**

a AHL First All-Star Team (1989)
b AHL Second All-Star Team (1990)

Traded to **Boston** by **Philadelphia** with Gord Murphy and Philadelphia's third round choice (Sergei Zholtok) in 1992 Entry Draft for Garry Galley, Wes Walz and future considerations, January 2, 1992.

DOERS, MICHAEL

Right wing. Shoots right. 6', 175 lbs. Born, Madison, WI, June 17, 1971.
(Toronto's 7th choice, 125th overall, in 1989 Entry Draft).

			Regular Season					Playoffs				
Season	Club	Lea	GP	G	A	TP	PIM	GP	G	A	TP	PIM
1991-92	U. Wisconsin	WCHA	37	3	3	6	18	....	....	....	....	....
1992-93	U. Wisconsin	WCHA	40	4	5	9	30	....	....	....	....	....

DOLLAS, BOBBY

Defense. Shoots left. 6'2", 212 lbs. Born, Montreal, Que., January 31, 1965.
(Winnipeg's 2nd choice, 14th overall, in 1983 Entry Draft).

			Regular Season					Playoffs				
Season	Club	Lea	GP	G	A	TP	PIM	GP	G	A	TP	PIM
1982-83a	Laval	QMJHL	63	16	45	61	144	11	5	5	10	23
1983-84	**Winnipeg**	**NHL**	**1**	**0**	**0**	**0**	**0**	....	....	....	....	....
	Laval	QMJHL	54	12	33	45	80	14	1	8	9	23
1984-85	**Winnipeg**	**NHL**	**9**	**0**	**0**	**0**	**0**	....	....	....	....	....
	Sherbrooke	AHL	8	1	3	4	4	17	3	6	9	17
1985-86	**Winnipeg**	**NHL**	**46**	**0**	**5**	**5**	**66**	**3**	**0**	**0**	**0**	**2**
	Sherbrooke	AHL	25	4	7	11	29	....	....	....	....	....
1986-87	Sherbrooke	AHL	75	6	18	24	87	16	2	4	6	13
1987-88	**Quebec**	**NHL**	**9**	**0**	**0**	**0**	**2**	....	....	....	....	....
	Moncton	AHL	26	4	10	14	20	....	....	....	....	....
	Fredericton	AHL	33	4	8	12	27	15	2	2	4	24
1988-89	**Quebec**	**NHL**	**16**	**0**	**3**	**3**	**16**	....	....	....	....	....
	Halifax	AHL	57	5	19	24	65	4	1	0	1	14
1989-90	Cdn. National	....	68	8	29	37	60	....	....	....	....	....
1990-91	**Detroit**	**NHL**	**56**	**3**	**5**	**8**	**20**	**7**	**1**	**0**	**1**	**13**
1991-92	**Detroit**	**NHL**	**27**	**3**	**1**	**4**	**20**	**2**	**0**	**1**	**1**	**0**
	Adirondack	AHL	19	1	6	7	33	18	7	4	11	22
1992-93	**Detroit**	**NHL**	**6**	**0**	**0**	**0**	**2**	....	....	....	....	....
c	Adirondack	AHL	64	7	36	43	54	11	3	8	11	8
	NHL Totals		**170**	**6**	**14**	**20**	**126**	**12**	**1**	**1**	**2**	**15**

a QMJHL Second All-Star Team (1983)
b Won Eddie Shore Plaque (AHL's Outstanding Defenseman) (1993)
c AHL First All-Star Team (1993)

Traded to **Quebec** by **Winnipeg** for Stu Kulak, December 17, 1987. Signed as a free agent by **Detroit**, October 18, 1990. Claimed by **Anaheim** from **Detroit** in Expansion Draft, June 24, 1993.

DOMI, TIE (DOH-mee)

Right wing. Shoots right. 5'10", 200 lbs. Born, Windsor, Ont., November 1, 1969.
(Toronto's 2nd choice, 27th overall, in 1988 Entry Draft).

			Regular Season					Playoffs				
Season	Club	Lea	GP	G	A	TP	PIM	GP	G	A	TP	PIM
1986-87	Peterborough	OHL	18	1	1	2	79	....	....	....	....	....
1987-88	Peterborough	OHL	60	22	21	43	292	12	3	9	12	24
1988-89	Peterborough	OHL	43	14	16	30	175	17	10	9	19	70
1989-90	**Toronto**	**NHL**	**2**	**0**	**0**	**0**	**42**	....	....	....	....	....
	Newmarket	AHL	57	14	11	25	285	....	....	....	....	....
1990-91	**NY Rangers**	**NHL**	**28**	**1**	**0**	**1**	**185**	....	....	....	....	....
	Binghamton	AHL	25	11	6	17	219	7	3	2	5	16
1991-92	**NY Rangers**	**NHL**	**42**	**2**	**4**	**6**	**246**	**6**	**1**	**1**	**2**	**32**
1992-93	**NY Rangers**	**NHL**	**12**	**2**	**0**	**2**	**95**	....	....	....	....	....
	Winnipeg	**NHL**	**49**	**3**	**10**	**13**	**249**	**6**	**1**	**0**	**1**	**23**
	NHL Totals		**133**	**8**	**14**	**22**	**817**	**12**	**2**	**1**	**3**	**55**

Traded to **NY Rangers** by **Toronto** with Mark LaForest for Greg Johnston, June 28, 1990. Traded to **Winnipeg** by **NY Rangers** with Kris King for Ed Olczyk, December 28, 1992.

DONATELLI, CLARK

Left wing. Shoots left. 5'10", 180 lbs. Born, Providence, RI, November 22, 1967.
(NY Rangers' 4th choice, 98th overall, in 1984 Entry Draft).

			Regular Season					Playoffs				
Season	Club	Lea	GP	G	A	TP	PIM	GP	G	A	TP	PIM
1984-85	Boston U.	H.E.	40	17	18	35	46	....	....	....	....	....
1985-86ab	Boston U.	H.E.	43	28	34	62	30	....	....	....	....	....
1986-87	Boston U.	H.E.	37	15	23	38	46	....	....	....	....	....
1987-88	U.S. National	....	50	11	27	38	26	....	....	....	....	....
	U.S. Olympic	....	6	2	1	3	5	....	....	....	....	....
1988-89						DID NOT PLAY						
1989-90	**Minnesota**	**NHL**	**25**	**3**	**3**	**6**	**17**	....	....	....	....	....
	Kalamazoo	IHL	27	8	9	17	47	4	0	2	2	12
1990-91	San Diego	IHL	46	17	10	27	45	....	....	....	....	....
1991-92	U.S. National	....	42	13	25	38	50	....	....	....	....	....
	U.S. Olympic	....	8	2	1	3	6	....	....	....	....	....
	Boston	**NHL**	**10**	**0**	**1**	**1**	**22**	**2**	**0**	**0**	**0**	**0**
1992-93	Providence	AHL	57	12	14	26	40	4	2	1	3	2
	NHL Totals		**35**	**3**	**4**	**7**	**39**	**2**	**0**	**0**	**0**	**0**

a NCAA East Second All-American Team (1986)
b Hockey East Second All-Star Team (1986)

Traded to **Edmonton** by **NY Rangers** with Ville Kentala, Reijo Ruotsalainen and Jim Wiemer for Mike Golden, Don Jackson and Miloslav Horava, October 2, 1986. Signed as a free agent by **Minnesota**, June 20, 1989. Signed as a free agent by **Boston**, March 10, 1992.

DONATO, EDWARD (TED)

Center. Shoots left. 5'10", 180 lbs. Born, Dedham, MA, April 28, 1969.
(Boston's 6th choice, 98th overall, in 1987 Entry Draft).

			Regular Season					Playoffs				
Season	Club	Lea	GP	G	A	TP	PIM	GP	G	A	TP	PIM
1987-88	Harvard	ECAC	28	12	14	26	24	....	....	....	....	....
1988-89	Harvard	ECAC	34	14	37	51	30	....	....	....	....	....
1989-90	Harvard	ECAC	16	5	6	11	34	....	....	....	....	....
1990-91a	Harvard	ECAC	27	19	*37	56	26	....	....	....	....	....
1991-92	U.S. National	....	52	11	22	33	24	....	....	....	....	....
	U.S. Olympic	....	8	4	3	7	8	....	....	....	....	....
	Boston	**NHL**	**10**	**1**	**2**	**3**	**8**	**15**	**3**	**4**	**7**	**4**
1992-93	**Boston**	**NHL**	**82**	**15**	**20**	**35**	**61**	**4**	**0**	**1**	**1**	....
	NHL Totals		**92**	**16**	**22**	**38**	**69**	**19**	**3**	**5**	**8**	**4**

a ECAC First All-Star Team (1991)

DONNELLY, GORDON (GORD)

Right wing. Shoots right. 6'1", 202 lbs. Born, Montreal, Que., April 5, 1962.
(St. Louis' 3rd choice, 62nd overall, in 1981 Entry Draft).

			Regular Season					Playoffs				
Season	Club	Lea	GP	G	A	TP	PIM	GP	G	A	TP	PIM
1980-81	Sherbrooke	QMJHL	67	15	23	38	252	14	1	2	3	35
1981-82	Sherbrooke	QMJHL	60	8	41	49	250	22	2	7	9	106
1982-83	Salt Lake	CHL	67	3	12	15	222	6	1	1	2	8
1983-84	**Quebec**	**NHL**	**38**	**0**	**5**	**5**	**60**	....	....	....	....	....
	Fredericton	AHL	30	2	3	5	146	7	1	1	2	43
1984-85	**Quebec**	**NHL**	**22**	**0**	**0**	**0**	**33**	....	....	....	....	....
	Fredericton	AHL	42	1	5	6	134	6	0	1	1	25
1985-86	**Quebec**	**NHL**	**36**	**2**	**2**	**4**	**85**	**1**	**0**	**0**	**0**	**0**
	Fredericton	AHL	38	3	5	8	103	5	0	0	0	33
1986-87	**Quebec**	**NHL**	**38**	**0**	**2**	**2**	**143**	**13**	**0**	**0**	**0**	**53**
1987-88	**Quebec**	**NHL**	**63**	**4**	**3**	**7**	**301**	....	....	....	....	....
1988-89	**Quebec**	**NHL**	**16**	**4**	**0**	**4**	**46**	....	....	....	....	....
	Winnipeg	**NHL**	**57**	**6**	**10**	**16**	**228**	....	....	....	....	....
1989-90	**Winnipeg**	**NHL**	**55**	**3**	**3**	**6**	**222**	**6**	**0**	**1**	**1**	**8**
1990-91	**Winnipeg**	**NHL**	**57**	**3**	**4**	**7**	**265**	....	....	....	....	....
1991-92	**Winnipeg**	**NHL**	**4**	**0**	**0**	**0**	**11**	....	....	....	....	....
	Buffalo	**NHL**	**67**	**2**	**3**	**5**	**305**	**6**	**0**	**1**	**1**	**0**
1992-93	**Buffalo**	**NHL**	**60**	**3**	**8**	**11**	**221**	....	....	....	....	....
	NHL Totals		**513**	**27**	**40**	**67**	**1920**	**26**	**0**	**2**	**2**	**61**

Rights transferred to **Quebec** by **St. Louis** with rights to Claude Julien when St. Louis signed Jacques Demers as coach, August 19, 1983. Traded to **Winnipeg** by **Quebec** for Mario Marois, December 6, 1988. Traded to **Buffalo** by **Winnipeg** with Dave McLlwain, Winnipeg's fifth round choice (Yuri Khmylev) in 1992 Entry Draft and future considerations for Darrin Shannon, Mike Hartman and Dean Kennedy, October 11, 1991.

DONNELLY, MIKE

Left wing. Shoots left. 5'11", 185 lbs. Born, Detroit, MI, October 10, 1963.

			Regular Season					Playoffs				
Season	Club	Lea	GP	G	A	TP	PIM	GP	G	A	TP	PIM
1982-83	Michigan State	CCHA	24	7	13	20	8	....	....	....	....	....
1983-84	Michigan State	CCHA	44	18	14	32	40	....	....	....	....	....
1984-85	Michigan State	CCHA	44	26	21	47	48	....	....	....	....	....
1985-86ab	Michigan State	CCHA	44	*59	38	97	65	....	....	....	....	....
1986-87	**NY Rangers**	**NHL**	**5**	**1**	**1**	**2**	**0**	....	....	....	....	....
	New Haven	AHL	58	27	34	61	52	7	2	0	2	9
1987-88	**NY Rangers**	**NHL**	**17**	**2**	**2**	**4**	**8**	....	....	....	....	....
	Colorado	IHL	8	7	11	18	15	....	....	....	....	....
	Buffalo	**NHL**	**40**	**6**	**8**	**14**	**44**	....	....	....	....	....
1988-89	**Buffalo**	**NHL**	**22**	**4**	**6**	**10**	**10**	....	....	....	....	....
	Rochester	AHL	53	32	37	69	53	....	....	....	....	....
1989-90	**Buffalo**	**NHL**	**12**	**1**	**2**	**3**	**8**	....	....	....	....	....
	Rochester	AHL	68	43	55	98	71	16	*12	7	19	9
1990-91	**Los Angeles**	**NHL**	**53**	**7**	**5**	**12**	**41**	**12**	**5**	**4**	**9**	**6**
	New Haven	AHL	18	10	6	16	2	....	....	....	....	....
1991-92	**Los Angeles**	**NHL**	**80**	**29**	**16**	**45**	**20**	**6**	**1**	**0**	**1**	**4**
1992-93	**Los Angeles**	**NHL**	**84**	**29**	**40**	**69**	**45**	**24**	**6**	**7**	**13**	**14**
	NHL Totals		**313**	**79**	**80**	**159**	**176**	**42**	**12**	**11**	**23**	**24**

a CCHA First All-Star Team (1986)
b NCAA West First All-American Team (1986)

Signed as a free agent by **NY Rangers**, August 15, 1986. Traded to **Buffalo** by **NY Rangers** with Rangers' fifth round choice (Alexander Mogilny) in 1988 Entry Draft for Paul Cyr and Buffalo's tenth round choice (Eric Fenton) in 1988 Entry Draft, December 31, 1987. Traded to **Los Angeles** by **Buffalo** for Mikko Makela, September 30, 1990.

DONOVAN, SHEAN

Right wing. Shoots right. 6'1", 178 lbs. Born, Timmins, Ont., January 22, 1975.
(San Jose's 2nd choice, 28th overall, in 1993 Entry Draft).

			Regular Season					Playoffs				
Season	Club	Lea	GP	G	A	TP	PIM	GP	G	A	TP	PIM
1991-92	Ottawa	OHL	58	11	8	19	14	11	1	0	1	5
1992-93	Ottawa	OHL	66	29	23	52	33	....	....	....	....	....

DOPITA, JIRI

Center. Shoots left. 6'3", 202 lbs. Born, Sumperk, Czech., December 2, 1968.
(Boston's 4th choice, 133rd overall, in 1992 Entry Draft).

			Regular Season					Playoffs				
Season	Club	Lea	GP	G	A	TP	PIM	GP	G	A	TP	PIM
1989-90	Dukla Jihlava	Czech.	5	1	2	3	....	....	....	....	....	....
1990-91	Olomouc	Czech.	42	11	13	24	26	....	....	....	....	....
1991-92	Olomouc	Czech.	41	25	24	49	28	....	....	....	....	....
1992-93	Olomouc	Czech.	28	12	17	29	....	....	....	....	....	....
	Eisbaren Berlin	Ger.	11	7	8	15	49	....	....	....	....	....

DORE, DANIEL

Right wing. Shoots right. 6'3", 202 lbs. Born, Ferme-Neuve, Que., April 9, 1970.
(Quebec's 2nd choice, 5th overall, in 1988 Entry Draft).

			Regular Season					Playoffs				
Season	Club	Lea	GP	G	A	TP	PIM	GP	G	A	TP	PIM
1986-87	Drummondville	QMJHL	68	23	41	64	229	8	0	1	1	18
1987-88	Drummondville	QMJHL	64	24	39	63	218	17	7	11	18	42
1988-89	Drummondville	QMJHL	62	33	58	91	236	4	2	3	5	14
1989-90	**Quebec**	**NHL**	**16**	**2**	**3**	**5**	**59**	....	....	....	....	....
	Chicoutimi	QMJHL	24	6	23	29	112	6	0	3	3	27
1990-91	**Quebec**	**NHL**	**1**	**0**	**0**	**0**	**0**	....	....	....	....	....
	Halifax	AHL	50	7	10	17	139	....	....	....	....	....
1991-92	Halifax	AHL	29	4	1	5	45	....	....	....	....	....
	Greensboro	ECHL	6	1	0	1	34	....	....	....	....	....
1992-93	Hershey	AHL	65	12	10	22	192	....	....	....	....	....
	NHL Totals		**17**	**2**	**3**	**5**	**59**	....	....	....	....	....

Signed as a free agent by **Philadelphia**, December 14, 1992.

D'ORSONNENS, MARTIN

Defense. Shoots left. 5'11", 185 lbs. Born, Repentigny, Que., February 11, 1972.
(Hartford's 7th choice, 162nd overall, in 1990 Entry Draft).

			Regular Season					Playoffs				
Season	Club	Lea	GP	G	A	TP	PIM	GP	G	A	TP	PIM
1989-90	Clarkson	ECAC	35	5	8	13	81	....	....	....	....	....
1990-91	Clarkson	ECAC	39	2	8	10	84	....	....	....	....	....
1991-92	Clarkson	ECAC	31	2	10	12	49	....	....	....	....	....
1992-93	Clarkson	ECAC	35	2	12	14	76	....	....	....	....	....

DOUCET, WAYNE

Left wing. Shoots left. 6'2", 203 lbs. Born, Etobicoke, Ont., June 19, 1970.
(NY Islanders' 2nd choice, 29th overall, in 1988 Entry Draft).

			Regular Season					Playoffs				
Season	Club	Lea	GP	G	A	TP	PIM	GP	G	A	TP	PIM
1986-87	Sudbury	OHL	64	20	28	48	85	....	....	....	....	....
1987-88	Sudbury	OHL	23	9	4	13	53	....	....	....	....	....
	Hamilton	OHL	37	11	14	25	7	1	0	0	0	8
1988-89	Springfield	AHL	6	2	2	4	4	....	....	....	....	....
	Niagara Falls	OHL	11	3	2	5	58	....	....	....	....	....
	Kingston	OHL	53	22	29	51	193	....	....	....	....	....
1989-90	Kingston	OHL	66	32	47	79	127	7	2	5	7	18
1990-91	Capital Dist.	AHL	21	11	6	17	93	....	....	....	....	....
1991-92	Capital Dist.	AHL	60	11	7	18	116	7	1	1	2	6
1992-93	Capital Dist.	AHL	72	11	16	27	155	3	0	0	0	2

DOURIS, PETER

Right wing. Shoots right. 6'1", 202 lbs. Born, Toronto, Ont., February 19, 1966.
(Winnipeg's 1st choice, 30th overall, in 1984 Entry Draft).

			Regular Season					Playoffs				
Season	Club	Lea	GP	G	A	TP	PIM	GP	G	A	TP	PIM
1983-84	N. Hampshire	ECAC	37	19	15	34	14	....	....	....	....	....
1984-85	N. Hampshire	H.E.	42	27	24	51	34	....	....	....	....	....
1985-86	**Winnipeg**	**NHL**	**11**	**0**	**0**	**0**	**0**	....	....	....	....	....
	Cdn. Olympic	....	33	16	7	23	18	....	....	....	....	....
1986-87	**Winnipeg**	**NHL**	**6**	**0**	**0**	**0**	**0**	....	....	....	....	....
	Sherbrooke	AHL	62	14	28	42	24	17	7	*15	*22	16
1987-88	**Winnipeg**	**NHL**	**4**	**0**	**2**	**2**	**0**	**1**	**0**	**0**	**0**	**0**
	Moncton	AHL	73	42	37	79	53	....	....	....	....	....
1988-89	Peoria	IHL	81	28	41	69	32	4	1	2	3	0
1989-90	**Boston**	**NHL**	**36**	**5**	**6**	**11**	**15**	**8**	**0**	**1**	**1**	**8**
	Maine	AHL	38	17	20	37	14	....	....	....	....	....
1990-91	**Boston**	**NHL**	**39**	**5**	**2**	**7**	**9**	**7**	**0**	**1**	**1**	**6**
	Maine	AHL	35	16	15	31	9	2	3	0	3	2
1991-92	**Boston**	**NHL**	**54**	**10**	**13**	**23**	**10**	**7**	**2**	**3**	**5**	**0**
	Maine	AHL	12	4	3	7	2	....	....	....	....	....
1992-93	**Boston**	**NHL**	**19**	**4**	**4**	**8**	**4**	**4**	**1**	**0**	**1**	**0**
	Providence	AHL	50	29	26	55	12	....	....	....	....	....
	NHL Totals		**169**	**24**	**27**	**51**	**38**	**27**	**3**	**5**	**8**	**14**

Traded to **St. Louis** by **Winnipeg** for Kent Carlson and St. Louis' twelfth round choice (Sergei Kharin) in 1989 Entry Draft and St. Louis' fourth round choice (Scott Levins) in 1990 Entry Draft, September 29, 1988. Signed as a free agent by **Boston**, June 27, 1989. Signed as a free agent by **Anaheim**, July 22, 1993.

DOWD, JAMES (JIM)

Center. Shoots right. 6'1", 185 lbs. Born, Brick, NJ, December 25, 1968.
(New Jersey's 7th choice, 149th overall, in 1987 Entry Draft).

			Regular Season					Playoffs				
Season	Club	Lea	GP	G	A	TP	PIM	GP	G	A	TP	PIM
1987-88	Lake Superior	CCHA	45	18	27	45	16	....	....	....	....	....
1988-89	Lake Superior	CCHA	46	24	35	59	40	....	....	....	....	....
1989-90ab	Lake Superior	CCHA	46	25	*67	92	30	....	....	....	....	....
1990-91cde	Lake Superior	CCHA	44	24	*54	*78	53	....	....	....	....	....
1991-92	**New Jersey**	**NHL**	**1**	**0**	**0**	**0**	**0**	....	....	....	....	....
	Utica	AHL	78	17	42	59	47	4	2	2	4	4
1992-93	**New Jersey**	**NHL**	**1**	**0**	**0**	**0**	**0**	....	....	....	....	....
	Utica	AHL	78	27	45	72	62	5	1	7	8	10
	NHL Totals		**2**	**0**	**0**	**0**	**0**	....	....	....	....	....

a CCHA Second All-Star Team (1990)
b NCAA West Second All-American Team (1990)
c CCHA Player of the Year (1991)
d CCHA First All-Star Team (1991)
e NCAA West First All-American Team (1991)

DOWNEY, BRIAN

Left wing. Shoots left. 6'1", 190 lbs. Born, Manotick Station, Ont., June 30, 1968.

			Regular Season					Playoffs				
Season	Club	Lea	GP	G	A	TP	PIM	GP	G	A	TP	PIM
1989-90	U. of Maine	H.E.	32	11	15	26	8	....	....	....	....	....
1990-91	U. of Maine	H.E.	43	29	34	63	20	....	....	....	....	....
1991-92	U. of Maine	H.E.	37	19	32	51	29	....	....	....	....	....
1992-93	New Haven	AHL	6	0	2	2	0	....	....	....	....	....

Signed as a free agent by **Ottawa**, July 30, 1992.

DOYON, MARIO (doh-YAWN)

Defense. Shoots right. 6', 174 lbs. Born, Quebec City, Que., August 27, 1968.
(Chicago's 5th choice, 119th overall, in 1986 Entry Draft).

			Regular Season					Playoffs				
Season	Club	Lea	GP	G	A	TP	PIM	GP	G	A	TP	PIM
1985-86	Drummondville	QMJHL	71	5	14	19	129	23	5	4	9	32
1986-87	Drummondville	QMJHL	65	18	47	65	150	8	1	3	4	30
1987-88	Drummondville	QMJHL	68	23	54	77	233	17	3	14	17	46
1988-89	**Chicago**	**NHL**	**7**	**1**	**1**	**2**	**6**	....	....	....	....	....
	Saginaw	IHL	71	16	32	48	69	6	0	0	0	8
1989-90	Indianapolis	IHL	66	9	25	34	50	....	....	....	....	....
	Quebec	**NHL**	**9**	**2**	**3**	**5**	**6**	....	....	....	....	....
	Halifax	AHL	5	1	2	3	0	6	1	3	4	2
1990-91	**Quebec**	**NHL**	**12**	**0**	**0**	**0**	**4**	....	....	....	....	....
	Halifax	AHL	59	14	23	37	58	....	....	....	....	....
1991-92	Halifax	AHL	9	0	0	0	22	....	....	....	....	....
	New Haven	AHL	64	11	29	40	44	5	1	1	2	2
1992-93	Halifax	AHL	79	5	31	36	73	....	....	....	....	....
	NHL Totals		**28**	**3**	**4**	**7**	**16**	....	....	....	....	....

Traded to **Quebec** by **Chicago** with Everett Sanipass and Dan Vincelette for Greg Millen, Michel Goulet and Quebec's sixth round choice (Kevin St. Jacques) in 1991 Entry Draft, March 5, 1990.

DRAKE, DALLAS

Center. Shoots left. 6', 180 lbs. Born, Trail, B.C., February 4, 1969.
(Detroit's 6th choice, 116th overall, in 1989 Entry Draft).

			Regular Season					Playoffs				
Season	Club	Lea	GP	G	A	TP	PIM	GP	G	A	TP	PIM
1988-89	N. Michigan	WCHA	38	17	22	39	22	....	....	....	....	....
1989-90	N. Michigan	WCHA	46	13	24	37	42	....	....	....	....	....
1990-91	N. Michigan	WCHA	44	22	36	58	89	....	....	....	....	....
1991-92ab	N. Michigan	WCHA	38	*39	41	*80	46	....	....	....	....	....
1992-93	**Detroit**	**NHL**	**72**	**18**	**26**	**44**	**93**	**7**	**3**	**3**	**6**	**6**
	NHL Totals		**72**	**18**	**26**	**44**	**93**	**7**	**3**	**3**	**6**	**6**

a WCHA First All-Star Team (1992)
b NCAA West First All-American Team (1992)

DRAPER, KRIS

Center. Shoots left. 5'11", 190 lbs. Born, Toronto, Ont., May 24, 1971.
(Winnipeg's 4th choice, 62nd overall, in 1989 Entry Draft).

			Regular Season					Playoffs				
Season	Club	Lea	GP	G	A	TP	PIM	GP	G	A	TP	PIM
1988-89	Cdn. National	....	60	11	15	26	16	....	....	....	....	....
1989-90	Cdn. National	....	61	12	22	34	44	....	....	....	....	....
1990-91	**Winnipeg**	**NHL**	**3**	**1**	**0**	**1**	**5**	....	....	....	....	....
	Ottawa	OHL	39	19	42	61	35	17	8	11	19	20
	Moncton	AHL	7	2	1	3	2	....	....	....	....	....
1991-92	**Winnipeg**	**NHL**	**10**	**2**	**0**	**2**	**2**	**2**	**0**	**0**	**0**	**0**
	Moncton	AHL	61	11	18	29	113	4	0	1	1	6
1992-93	**Winnipeg**	**NHL**	**7**	**0**	**0**	**0**	**2**	....	....	....	....	....
	Moncton	AHL	67	12	23	35	40	5	2	2	4	18
	NHL Totals		**20**	**3**	**0**	**3**	**9**	**2**	**0**	**0**	**0**	**0**

Traded to **Detroit** by **Winnipeg** for future considerations, June 30, 1993.

DRIVER, BRUCE

Defense. Shoots left. 6', 185 lbs. Born, Toronto, Ont., April 29, 1962.
(Colorado's 6th choice, 108th overall, in 1981 Entry Draft).

				Regular Season					Playoffs			
Season	Club	Lea	GP	G	A	TP	PIM	GP	G	A	TP	PIM
1980-81	U. Wisconsin	WCHA	42	5	15	20	42	....	....	....	....	....
1981-82ab	U. Wisconsin	WCHA	46	7	37	44	84	....	....	....	....	....
1982-83c	U. Wisconsin	WCHA	49	19	42	61	100	....	....	....	....	....
1983-84	Cdn. Olympic	....	61	11	17	28	44	....	....	....	....	....
	New Jersey	**NHL**	**4**	**0**	**2**	**2**	**0**	....	....	....	....	....
	Maine	AHL	12	2	6	8	15	16	0	10	10	8
1984-85	**New Jersey**	**NHL**	**67**	**9**	**23**	**32**	**36**	....	....	....	....	....
1985-86	**New Jersey**	**NHL**	**40**	**3**	**15**	**18**	**32**	....	....	....	....	....
	Maine	AHL	15	4	7	11	16	....	....	....	....	....
1986-87	**New Jersey**	**NHL**	**74**	**6**	**28**	**34**	**36**	....	....	....	....	....
1987-88	**New Jersey**	**NHL**	**74**	**15**	**40**	**55**	**68**	**20**	**3**	**7**	**10**	**14**
1988-89	**New Jersey**	**NHL**	**27**	**1**	**15**	**16**	**24**	....	....	....	....	....
1989-90	**New Jersey**	**NHL**	**75**	**7**	**46**	**53**	**63**	**6**	**1**	**5**	**6**	**6**
1990-91	**New Jersey**	**NHL**	**73**	**9**	**36**	**45**	**62**	**7**	**1**	**2**	**3**	**12**
1991-92	**New Jersey**	**NHL**	**78**	**7**	**35**	**42**	**66**	**7**	**0**	**4**	**4**	**2**
1992-93	**New Jersey**	**NHL**	**83**	**14**	**40**	**54**	**66**	**5**	**1**	**3**	**4**	**4**
	NHL Totals		**595**	**71**	**280**	**351**	**453**	**45**	**6**	**21**	**27**	**38**

a WCHA First All-Star Team (1982)
b NCAA All-Tournament Team (1982)
c WCHA Second All-Star Team (1983)

DROPPA, IVAN

Defense. Shoots left. 6'2", 209 lbs. Born, Liptovsky Mikulas, Czech., February 1, 1972.
(Chicago's 2nd choice, 37th overall, in 1990 Entry Draft).

				Regular Season					Playoffs			
Season	Club	Lea	GP	G	A	TP	PIM	GP	G	A	TP	PIM
1990-91	VSZ Kosice	Czech.	54	1	7	8	12	....	....	....	....	....
1991-92	VSZ Kosice	Czech.	43	4	9	13	24	....	....	....	....	....
1992-93	Indianapolis	IHL	77	14	29	43	92	5	0	1	1	2

DRUCE, JOHN

Right wing. Shoots right. 6'2", 195 lbs. Born, Peterborough, Ont., February 23, 1966.
(Washington's 2nd choice, 40th overall, in 1985 Entry Draft).

				Regular Season					Playoffs			
Season	Club	Lea	GP	G	A	TP	PIM	GP	G	A	TP	PIM
1984-85	Peterborough	OHL	54	12	14	26	90	17	6	2	8	21
1985-86	Peterborough	OHL	49	22	24	46	84	16	0	5	5	34
1986-87	Binghamton	AHL	77	13	9	22	131	12	0	3	3	28
1987-88	Binghamton	AHL	68	32	29	61	82	1	0	0	0	0
1988-89	**Washington**	**NHL**	**48**	**8**	**7**	**15**	**62**	**1**	**0**	**0**	**0**	**0**
	Baltimore	AHL	16	2	11	13	10	....	....	....	....	....
1989-90	**Washington**	**NHL**	**45**	**8**	**3**	**11**	**52**	**15**	**14**	**3**	**17**	**23**
	Baltimore	AHL	26	15	16	31	38	....	....	....	....	....
1990-91	**Washington**	**NHL**	**80**	**22**	**36**	**58**	**46**	**11**	**1**	**1**	**2**	**7**
1991-92	**Washington**	**NHL**	**67**	**19**	**18**	**37**	**39**	**7**	**1**	**0**	**1**	**2**
1992-93	**Winnipeg**	**NHL**	**50**	**6**	**14**	**20**	**37**	**2**	**0**	**0**	**0**	**0**
	NHL Totals		**290**	**63**	**78**	**141**	**236**	**36**	**16**	**4**	**20**	**32**

Traded to **Winnipeg** by **Washington** with future considerations for Pat Elynuik, October 1, 1992. Signed as a free agent by Los Angeles, August 2, 1993.

DRULIA, STAN

Right wing. Shoots right. 5'11", 190 lbs. Born, Elmira, NY, January 5, 1968.
(Pittsburgh's 11th choice, 214th overall, in 1986 Entry Draft).

				Regular Season					Playoffs			
Season	Club	Lea	GP	G	A	TP	PIM	GP	G	A	TP	PIM
1985-86	Belleville	OHL	66	43	36	79	73	....	....	....	....	....
1986-87	Hamilton	OHL	55	27	51	78	26	....	....	....	....	....
1987-88a	Hamilton	OHL	65	52	69	121	44	14	8	16	24	12
1988-89	Maine	AHL	3	1	1	2	0	....	....	....	....	....
b	Niagara Falls	OHL	47	52	93	145	59	17	11	*26	37	18
1989-90	Phoenix	IHL	16	6	3	9	2	....	....	....	....	....
	Cape Breton	AHL	31	5	7	12	2	....	....	....	....	....
1990-91cd	Knoxville	ECHL	64	*63	77	*140	39	3	3	2	5	4
1991-92e	New Haven	AHL	77	49	53	102	46	5	2	4	6	4
1992-93	**Tampa Bay**	**NHL**	**24**	**2**	**1**	**3**	**10**	....	....	....	....	....
	Atlanta	IHL	47	28	26	54	38	3	2	3	5	4
	NHL Totals		**24**	**2**	**1**	**3**	**10**	....	....	....	....	....

a OHL Third All-Star Team (1988)
b OHL First All-Star Team (1989)
c MVP — ECHL (1991)
d ECHL First All-Star Team (1991)
e AHL Second All-Star Team (1992)

Signed as a free agent by **Edmonton**, February 24, 1989. Signed as a free agent by **Tampa Bay**, September 1, 1992.

DRURY, TED

Center. Shoots left. 6', 190 lbs. Born, Boston, MA, September 13, 1971.
(Calgary's 2nd choice, 42nd overall, in 1989 Entry Draft).

				Regular Season					Playoffs			
Season	Club	Lea	GP	G	A	TP	PIM	GP	G	A	TP	PIM
1989-90	Harvard	ECAC	17	9	13	22	10	....	....	....	....	....
1990-91	Harvard	ECAC	25	18	18	36	22	....	....	....	....	....
1991-92	U.S. National	....	53	11	23	34	30	....	....	....	....	....
	U.S. Olympic	....	7	1	1	2	0	....	....	....	....	....
1992-93ab	Harvard	ECAC	31	22	*41	*63	28	....	....	....	....	....

a ECAC First All-Star Team (1993)
b NCAA East First All-America Team (1993)

DUBERMAN, JUSTIN

Right wing. Shoots right. 6'1", 185 lbs. Born, New Haven, CT, March 23, 1970.
(Montreal's 11th choice, 230th overall, in 1989 Entry Draft).

				Regular Season					Playoffs			
Season	Club	Lea	GP	G	A	TP	PIM	GP	G	A	TP	PIM
1988-89	North Dakota	WCHA	33	3	1	4	30	....	....	....	....	....
1989-90	North Dakota	WCHA	42	10	9	19	50	....	....	....	....	....
1990-91	North Dakota	WCHA	42	19	18	37	68	....	....	....	....	....
1991-92	North Dakota	WCHA	39	17	27	44	90	....	....	....	....	....
1992-93	Cleveland	IHL	77	29	42	71	69	4	0	0	0	12

DUBINSKY, STEVE

Center. Shoots left. 6', 190 lbs. Born, Montreal, Que., July 9, 1970.
(Chicago's 9th choice, 226th overall, in 1990 Entry Draft).

				Regular Season					Playoffs			
Season	Club	Lea	GP	G	A	TP	PIM	GP	G	A	TP	PIM
1989-90	Clarkson	ECAC	35	7	10	17	24	....	....	....	....	....
1990-91	Clarkson	ECAC	39	13	23	36	26	....	....	....	....	....
1991-92	Clarkson	ECAC	32	20	31	51	40	....	....	....	....	....
1992-93	Clarkson	ECAC	35	18	26	44	58	....	....	....	....	....

DUBOIS, ERIC

Defense. Shoots right. 6', 195 lbs. Born, Montreal, Que., May 9, 1970.
(Quebec's 6th choice, 76th overall, in 1989 Entry Draft).

				Regular Season					Playoffs			
Season	Club	Lea	GP	G	A	TP	PIM	GP	G	A	TP	PIM
1986-87	Laval	QMJHL	61	1	17	18	29	....	....	....	....	....
1987-88	Laval	QMJHL	69	8	32	40	132	14	1	7	8	12
1988-89	Laval	QMJHL	68	15	44	59	126	17	1	11	12	55
1989-90	Laval	QMJHL	66	9	36	45	153	13	3	8	11	29
1990-91	Laval	QMJHL	57	15	45	60	122	13	3	5	8	29
1991-92	Halifax	AHL	14	0	0	0	8	....	....	....	....	....
	New Haven	AHL	1	0	0	0	2	....	....	....	....	....
	Greensboro	ECHL	36	7	17	24	62	11	4	4	8	40
1992-93	Oklahoma City	CHL	25	5	20	25	70	....	....	....	....	....
	Atlanta	IHL	43	3	9	12	44	9	0	0	0	10

DUCHESNE, GAETAN (doo-SHAYN)

Left wing. Shoots left. 5'11", 200 lbs. Born, Les Saulles, Que., July 11, 1962.
(Washington's 8th choice, 152nd overall, in 1981 Entry Draft).

				Regular Season					Playoffs			
Season	Club	Lea	GP	G	A	TP	PIM	GP	G	A	TP	PIM
1979-80	Quebec	QJHL	46	9	28	37	22	5	0	2	2	9
1980-81	Quebec	QJHL	72	27	45	72	63	7	1	4	5	6
1981-82	**Washington**	**NHL**	**74**	**9**	**14**	**23**	**46**	....	....	....	....	....
1982-83	**Washington**	**NHL**	**77**	**18**	**19**	**37**	**52**	**4**	**1**	**1**	**2**	**4**
	Hershey	AHL	1	1	0	1	0	....	....	....	....	....
1983-84	**Washington**	**NHL**	**79**	**17**	**19**	**36**	**29**	**8**	**2**	**1**	**3**	**2**
1984-85	**Washington**	**NHL**	**67**	**15**	**23**	**38**	**32**	**5**	**0**	**1**	**1**	**7**
1985-86	**Washington**	**NHL**	**80**	**11**	**28**	**39**	**39**	**9**	**4**	**3**	**7**	**12**
1986-87	**Washington**	**NHL**	**74**	**17**	**35**	**52**	**53**	**7**	**3**	**0**	**3**	**14**
1987-88	**Quebec**	**NHL**	**80**	**24**	**23**	**47**	**83**	....	....	....	....	....
1988-89	**Quebec**	**NHL**	**70**	**8**	**21**	**29**	**56**	....	....	....	....	....
1989-90	**Minnesota**	**NHL**	**72**	**12**	**8**	**20**	**33**	**7**	**0**	**0**	**0**	**6**
1990-91	**Minnesota**	**NHL**	**68**	**9**	**9**	**18**	**18**	**23**	**2**	**3**	**5**	**34**
1991-92	**Minnesota**	**NHL**	**73**	**8**	**15**	**23**	**102**	**7**	**1**	**0**	**1**	**6**
1992-93	**Minnesota**	**NHL**	**84**	**16**	**13**	**29**	**30**	....	....	....	....	....
	NHL Totals		**898**	**164**	**227**	**391**	**573**	**70**	**13**	**9**	**22**	**85**

Traded to **Quebec** by **Washington** with Alan Haworth and Washington's first round choice (Joe Sakic) in 1987 Entry Draft for Clint Malarchuk and Dale Hunter, June 13, 1987. Traded to **Minnesota** by **Quebec** for Kevin Kaminski, June 19, 1989. Traded to **San Jose** by **Dallas** for San Jose's sixth round choice (later traded back to San Jose — San Jose selected Petri Varis) in 1993 Entry Draft, June 20, 1993.

DUCHESNE, STEVE (doo-SHAYN)

Defense. Shoots left. 5'11", 195 lbs. Born, Sept-Iles, Que., June 30, 1965.

				Regular Season					Playoffs			
Season	Club	Lea	GP	G	A	TP	PIM	GP	G	A	TP	PIM
1983-84	Drummondville	QMJHL	67	1	34	35	79	....	....	....	....	....
1984-85a	Drummondville	QMJHL	65	22	54	76	94	5	4	7	11	8
1985-86	New Haven	AHL	75	14	35	49	76	5	0	2	2	9
1986-87b	**Los Angeles**	**NHL**	**75**	**13**	**25**	**38**	**74**	**5**	**2**	**2**	**4**	**4**
1987-88	**Los Angeles**	**NHL**	**71**	**16**	**39**	**55**	**109**	**5**	**1**	**3**	**4**	**14**
1988-89	**Los Angeles**	**NHL**	**79**	**25**	**50**	**75**	**92**	**11**	**4**	**4**	**8**	**12**
1989-90	**Los Angeles**	**NHL**	**79**	**20**	**42**	**62**	**36**	**10**	**2**	**9**	**11**	**6**
1990-91	**Los Angeles**	**NHL**	**78**	**21**	**41**	**62**	**66**	**12**	**4**	**8**	**12**	**8**
1991-92	**Philadelphia**	**NHL**	**78**	**18**	**38**	**56**	**86**	....	....	....	....	....
1992-93	**Quebec**	**NHL**	**82**	**20**	**62**	**82**	**57**	**6**	**0**	**5**	**5**	**6**
	NHL Totals		**542**	**133**	**297**	**430**	**520**	**49**	**13**	**31**	**44**	**50**

a QMJHL First All-Star Team (1985)
b NHL All-Rookie Team (1987)

Played in NHL All-Star Game (1989, 1990, 1993)

Signed as a free agent by **Los Angeles,** October 1, 1984. Traded to **Philadelphia** by **Los Angeles** with Steve Kasper and Los Angeles' fourth round choice (Aris Brimanis) in 1991 Entry Draft for Jari Kurri and Jeff Chychrun, May 30, 1991. Traded to **Quebec** by **Philadelphia** with Peter Forsberg, Kerry Huffman, Mike Ricci, Ron Hextall, Chris Simon, Philadelphia's first choice in the 1993 (Jocelyn Thibault) and 1994 Entry Drafts and cash for Eric Lindros, June 30, 1992.

DUFFY, JACK

Defense. Shoots right. 6'1", 195 lbs. Born, Northford, CT, September 25, 1970.
(NY Islanders' 2nd choice, 10th overall, in 1991 Supplemental Draft).

				Regular Season					Playoffs			
Season	Club	Lea	GP	G	A	TP	PIM	GP	G	A	TP	PIM
1989-90	Yale	ECAC	26	1	6	7	48	....	....	....	....	....
1990-91	Yale	ECAC	29	4	8	12	48	....	....	....	....	....
1991-92a	Yale	ECAC	27	3	24	27	78	....	....	....	....	....
1992-93bc	Yale	ECAC	31	8	17	25	60	....	....	....	....	....

a ECAC Second All-Star Team (1992)
b ECAC First All-Star Team (1993)
c NCAA Second All-American team (1993)

DUFRESNE, DONALD (DOO-FRAYN)

Defense. Shoots right. 6'1", 206 lbs. Born, Quebec City, Que., April 10, 1967.
(Montreal's 8th choice, 117th overall, in 1985 Entry Draft).

			Regular Season					Playoffs				
Season	Club	Lea	GP	G	A	TP	PIM	GP	G	A	TP	PIM
1983-84	Trois-Rivières	QMJHL	67	7	12	19	97	....	....	....	....	....
1984-85	Trois-Rivières	QMJHL	65	5	30	35	112	7	1	3	4	12
1985-86a	Trois-Rivières	QMJHL	63	8	32	40	160	1	0	0	0	0
1986-87a	Trois-Rivières	QMJHL	51	5	21	26	79	....	....	....	....	....
	Longueuil	QMJHL	16	0	8	8	18	20	1	8	9	38
1987-88	Sherbrooke	AHL	47	1	8	9	107	6	1	0	1	34
1988-89	**Montreal**	**NHL**	**13**	**0**	**1**	**1**	**43**	6	1	1	2	4
	Sherbrooke	AHL	47	0	12	12	170	....	....	....	....	....
1989-90	**Montreal**	**NHL**	**18**	**0**	**4**	**4**	**23**	10	0	1	1	18
	Sherbrooke	AHL	38	2	11	13	104	....	....	....	....	....
1990-91	**Montreal**	**NHL**	**53**	**2**	**13**	**15**	**55**	10	0	1	1	21
	Fredericton	AHL	10	1	4	5	35	1	0	0	0	0
1991-92	**Montreal**	**NHL**	**3**	**0**	**0**	**0**	**2**	....	....	....	....	....
	Fredericton	AHL	31	8	12	20	60	7	0	0	0	10
1992-93	**Montreal**	**NHL**	**32**	**1**	**2**	**3**	**32**	2	0	0	0	0
	NHL Totals		**119**	**3**	**20**	**23**	**155**	**28**	**1**	**3**	**4**	**43**

a QMJHL Second All-Star Team (1986, 1987)
Traded to **Tampa Bay** by **Montreal** to complete March 20, 1993 trade in which Rob Ramage was traded to Montreal for Eric Charron, Alain Cote and future considerations, June 20, 1993.

DUNCAN, IAIN

Left wing. Shoots left. 6'1", 200 lbs. Born, Weston, Ont., August 4, 1963.
(Winnipeg's 8th choice, 129th overall, in 1983 Entry Draft).

			Regular Season					Playoffs				
Season	Club	Lea	GP	G	A	TP	PIM	GP	G	A	TP	PIM
1983-84	Bowling Green	CCHA	44	11	20	31	65	....	....	....	....	....
1984-85	Bowling Green	CCHA	37	9	21	30	105	....	....	....	....	....
1985-86	Bowling Green	CCHA	41	26	26	52	124	....	....	....	....	....
1986-87a	Bowling Green	CCHA	39	28	40	68	141	....	....	....	....	....
	Winnipeg	**NHL**	**6**	**1**	**2**	**3**	**0**	7	0	2	2	6
1987-88b	**Winnipeg**	**NHL**	**62**	**19**	**23**	**42**	**73**	4	0	1	1	0
	Moncton	AHL	8	1	3	4	26	....	....	....	....	....
1988-89	**Winnipeg**	**NHL**	**57**	**14**	**30**	**44**	**74**	....	....	....	....	....
1989-90	Moncton	AHL	49	16	25	41	81	....	....	....	....	....
1990-91	**Winnipeg**	**NHL**	**2**	**0**	**0**	**0**	**2**	....	....	....	....	....
	Moncton	AHL	66	19	45	64	105	8	3	4	7	40
1991-92	Phoenix	IHL	46	12	24	36	103	....	....	....	....	....
1992-93	Adirondack	AHL	1	0	0	0	2	....	....	....	....	....
c	Toledo	ECHL	50	40	50	90	190	16	9	*19	28	55
	NHL Totals		**127**	**34**	**55**	**89**	**149**	**11**	**0**	**3**	**3**	**6**

a CCHA First All-Star Team (1987)
b NHL All-Rookie Team (1988)
c ECHL Second All-Star Team (1993)

DUNCANSON, CRAIG

Left wing. Shoots left. 6', 190 lbs. Born, Sudbury, Ont., March 17, 1967.
(Los Angeles' 1st choice, 9th overall, in 1985 Entry Draft).

			Regular Season					Playoffs				
Season	Club	Lea	GP	G	A	TP	PIM	GP	G	A	TP	PIM
1983-84	Sudbury	OHL	62	38	38	76	176	....	....	....	....	....
1984-85a	Sudbury	OHL	53	35	28	63	129	....	....	....	....	....
1985-86	**Los Angeles**	**NHL**	**2**	**0**	**1**	**1**	**0**	....	....	....	....	....
	Sudbury	OHL	21	12	17	29	55	....	....	....	....	....
	Cornwall	OHL	40	31	50	81	135	6	4	7	11	2
	New Haven	AHL	....	....	....	....	....	2	0	0	0	5
1986-87	**Los Angeles**	**NHL**	**2**	**0**	**0**	**0**	**24**	....	....	....	....	....
	Cornwall	OHL	52	22	45	67	88	5	4	3	7	20
1987-88	**Los Angeles**	**NHL**	**9**	**0**	**0**	**0**	**12**	....	....	....	....	....
	New Haven	AHL	57	15	25	40	170	....	....	....	....	....
1988-89	**Los Angeles**	**NHL**	**5**	**0**	**0**	**0**	**0**	....	....	....	....	....
	New Haven	AHL	69	25	39	64	200	17	4	8	12	60
1989-90	**Los Angeles**	**NHL**	**10**	**3**	**2**	**5**	**9**	....	....	....	....	....
	New Haven	AHL	51	17	30	47	152	....	....	....	....	....
1990-91	**Winnipeg**	**NHL**	**7**	**2**	**0**	**2**	**16**	....	....	....	....	....
	Moncton	AHL	58	16	34	50	107	9	3	11	14	31
1991-92	Baltimore	AHL	46	20	26	46	98	....	....	....	....	....
	Moncton	AHL	19	12	9	21	6	11	6	4	10	10
1992-93	**NY Rangers**	**NHL**	**3**	**0**	**1**	**1**	**0**	....	....	....	....	....
	Binghamton	AHL	69	35	59	94	126	14	7	5	12	9
	NHL Totals		**38**	**5**	**4**	**9**	**61**					

a OHL Third All-Star Team (1985)
Traded to **Minnesota** by **Los Angeles** for Daniel Berthiaume, September 6, 1990. Traded to **Washington** by **Winnipeg** with Brent Hughes and Simon Wheeldon for Bob Joyce, Tyler Larter and Kent Paynter, May 21, 1991. Traded to **Winnipeg** by **Minnesota** for Brian Hunt, September 6, 1990. Signed as a free agent by **NY Rangers**, September 4, 1992.

DUPAUL, COSMO

Center. Shoots left. 6', 186 lbs. Born, Pointe-Claire, Que., April 11, 1975.
(Ottawa's 4th choice, 91st overall, in 1993 Entry Draft).

			Regular Season					Playoffs				
Season	Club	Lea	GP	G	A	TP	PIM	GP	G	A	TP	PIM
1991-92	Lac St. Louis	Midget	38	41	26	67	14	....	....	....	....	....
1992-93	Victoriaville	QMJHL	67	23	35	58	16	6	1	3	4	2

DUPRE, YANICK (dew-PRAY)

Left wing. Shoots left. 6', 189 lbs. Born, Montreal, Que., November 20, 1972.
(Philadelphia's 2nd choice, 50th overall, in 1991 Entry Draft).

			Regular Season					Playoffs				
Season	Club	Lea	GP	G	A	TP	PIM	GP	G	A	TP	PIM
1989-90	Chicoutimi	QMJHL	24	5	9	14	27	....	....	....	....	....
	Drummondville	QMJHL	30	10	10	20	27	....	....	....	....	....
1990-91	Drummondville	QMJHL	58	29	38	67	87	11	8	5	13	33
1991-92	**Philadelphia**	**NHL**	**1**	**0**	**0**	**0**	**0**	....	....	....	....	....
	Drummondville	QMJHL	28	19	17	36	48	....	....	....	....	....
	Verdun	QMJHL	12	7	14	21	21	19	9	9	18	20
1992-93	Hershey	AHL	63	13	24	37	22	....	....	....	....	....
	NHL Totals		**1**	**0**	**0**	**0**	**0**					

DUTHIE, RYAN

Center. Shoots right. 5'10", 180 lbs. Born, Red Deer, Alta., September 2, 1974.
(NY Islanders' 4th choice, 105th overall, in 1992 Entry Draft).

			Regular Season					Playoffs				
Season	Club	Lea	GP	G	A	TP	PIM	GP	G	A	TP	PIM
1991-92	Spokane	WHL	67	23	37	60	119	10	5	10	15	18
1992-93	Spokane	WHL	60	26	58	84	122	9	7	2	9	8

DYCK, PAUL

Defense. Shoots left. 6'1", 192 lbs. Born, Steinbach, Man., April 20, 1971.
(Pittsburgh's 11th choice, 236th overall, in 1991 Entry Draft).

			Regular Season					Playoffs				
Season	Club	Lea	GP	G	A	TP	PIM	GP	G	A	TP	PIM
1990-91	Moose Jaw	WHL	72	12	41	53	63	8	0	7	7	17
1991-92	Muskegon	IHL	73	6	21	27	40	14	1	3	4	4
1992-93	Cleveland	IHL	69	6	21	27	69	1	0	0	0	0

DYKHUIS, KARL (DIGHK-HOWS)

Defense. Shoots left. 6'3", 195 lbs. Born, Sept-Iles, Que., July 8, 1972.
(Chicago's 1st choice, 16th overall, in 1990 Entry Draft).

			Regular Season					Playoffs				
Season	Club	Lea	GP	G	A	TP	PIM	GP	G	A	TP	PIM
1988-89	Hull	QMJHL	63	2	29	31	59	9	1	9	10	6
1989-90a	Hull	QMJHL	69	10	46	56	119	11	2	5	7	2
1990-91	Cdn. National	....	37	2	9	11	16	....	....	....	....	....
	Longueuil	QMJHL	3	1	4	4	6	8	2	5	7	6
1991-92	**Chicago**	**NHL**	**6**	**1**	**3**	**4**	**4**	....	....	....	....	....
	Verdun	QMJHL	29	5	19	24	55	17	0	12	12	14
1992-93	**Chicago**	**NHL**	**12**	**0**	**5**	**5**	**0**	....	....	....	....	....
	Indianapolis	IHL	59	5	18	23	76	5	1	1	2	8
	NHL Totals		**18**	**1**	**8**	**9**	**4**					

a QMJHL First All-Star Team (1990)

DZIEDZIC, JOE

Left wing. Shoots left. 6'3", 200 lbs. Born, Minneapolis, MN, December 18, 1971.
(Pittsburgh's 2nd choice, 61st overall, in 1990 Entry Draft).

			Regular Season					Playoffs				
Season	Club	Lea	GP	G	A	TP	PIM	GP	G	A	TP	PIM
1990-91	U. Minnesota	WCHA	20	6	4	10	26	....	....	....	....	....
1991-92	U. Minnesota	WCHA	34	8	9	17	68	....	....	....	....	....
1992-93	U. Minnesota	WCHA	41	11	14	25	62	....	....	....	....	....

EAGLES, MICHAEL (MIKE)

Center/Left wing. Shoots left. 5'10", 190 lbs. Born, Sussex, N.B., March 7, 1963.
(Quebec's 5th choice, 116th overall, in 1981 Entry Draft).

			Regular Season					Playoffs				
Season	Club	Lea	GP	G	A	TP	PIM	GP	G	A	TP	PIM
1980-81	Kitchener	OHA	56	11	27	38	64	18	4	2	6	36
1981-82	Kitchener	OHL	62	26	40	66	148	15	3	11	14	27
1982-83	**Quebec**	**NHL**	**2**	**0**	**0**	**0**	**2**	....	....	....	....	....
	Kitchener	OHL	58	26	36	62	133	12	5	7	12	27
1983-84	Fredericton	AHL	68	13	29	42	85	4	0	0	0	5
1984-85	Fredericton	AHL	36	4	20	24	80	3	0	0	0	2
1985-86	**Quebec**	**NHL**	**73**	**11**	**12**	**23**	**49**	3	0	0	0	2
1986-87	**Quebec**	**NHL**	**73**	**13**	**19**	**32**	**55**	4	1	0	1	10
1987-88	**Quebec**	**NHL**	**76**	**10**	**10**	**20**	**74**	....	....	....	....	....
1988-89	**Chicago**	**NHL**	**47**	**5**	**11**	**16**	**44**	....	....	....	....	....
1989-90	**Chicago**	**NHL**	**23**	**1**	**2**	**3**	**34**	....	....	....	....	....
	Indianapolis	IHL	24	11	13	24	47	13	*10	10	20	34
1990-91	**Winnipeg**	**NHL**	**44**	**0**	**9**	**9**	**79**	....	....	....	....	....
	Indianapolis	IHL	25	15	14	29	47	....	....	....	....	....
1991-92	**Winnipeg**	**NHL**	**65**	**7**	**10**	**17**	**118**	7	0	0	0	8
1992-93	**Winnipeg**	**NHL**	**84**	**8**	**18**	**26**	**131**	5	0	1	1	6
	NHL Totals		**487**	**55**	**91**	**146**	**586**	**19**	**1**	**1**	**2**	**26**

Traded to **Chicago** by **Quebec** for Bob Mason, July 5, 1988. Traded to **Winnipeg** by **Chicago** for Winnipeg's fourth round choice (Igor Kravchuk) in 1991 Entry Draft, December 14, 1990.

EAKINS, DALLAS

Defense. Shoots left. 6'2", 195 lbs. Born, Dade City, FL, February 27, 1967.
(Washington's 11th choice, 208th overall, in 1985 Entry Draft).

			Regular Season					Playoffs				
Season	Club	Lea	GP	G	A	TP	PIM	GP	G	A	TP	PIM
1984-85	Peterborough	OHL	48	0	8	8	96	7	0	0	0	18
1985-86	Peterborough	OHL	60	6	16	22	134	16	0	1	1	30
1986-87	Peterborough	OHL	54	3	11	14	145	12	1	4	5	37
1987-88	Peterborough	OHL	64	11	27	38	129	12	3	12	15	16
1988-89	Baltimore	AHL	62	0	10	10	139	....	....	....	....	....
1989-90	Moncton	AHL	75	2	11	13	189	....	....	....	....	....
1990-91	Moncton	AHL	75	1	12	13	132	9	0	1	1	44
1991-92	Moncton	AHL	67	3	13	16	136	11	2	1	3	16
1992-93	**Winnipeg**	**NHL**	**14**	**0**	**2**	**2**	**38**	....	....	....	....	....
	Moncton	AHL	55	4	6	10	132	....	....	....	....	....
	NHL Totals		**14**	**0**	**2**	**2**	**38**					

Signed as a free agent by **Winnipeg**, October 17, 1989.

EASTWOOD, MICHAEL

Center. Shoots right. 6'2", 190 lbs. Born, Ottawa, Ont., July 1, 1967.
(Toronto's 5th choice, 91st overall, in 1987 Entry Draft).

			Regular Season					Playoffs				
Season	Club	Lea	GP	G	A	TP	PIM	GP	G	A	TP	PIM
1987-88	W. Michigan	CCHA	42	5	8	13	14	....	....	....	....	....
1988-89	W. Michigan	CCHA	40	10	13	23	87	....	....	....	....	....
1989-90	W. Michigan	CCHA	40	25	27	52	36	....	....	....	....	....
1990-91a	W. Michigan	CCHA	42	29	32	61	84	....	....	....	....	....
1991-92	**Toronto**	**NHL**	**9**	**0**	**2**	**2**	**4**	....	....	....	....	....
	St. John's	AHL	61	18	25	43	28	16	9	10	19	16
1992-93	**Toronto**	**NHL**	**12**	**1**	**6**	**7**	**21**	10	1	2	3	8
	St. John's	AHL	60	24	35	59	32	....	....	....	....	....
	NHL Totals		**21**	**1**	**8**	**9**	**25**	**10**	**1**	**2**	**3**	**8**

a CCHA Second All-Star Team (1991)

EDLUND, PAR

(EHD-luhnd, PEHR)

Left wing. Shoots right. 5'11", 196 lbs.   Born, Nynoshamn, Sweden, April 9, 1967.
(Los Angeles' 3rd choice, 30th overall, in 1985 Entry Draft).

				Regular Season						Playoffs		
Season	Club	Lea	GP	G	A	TP	PIM	GP	G	A	TP	PIM
1985-86	Bjorkloven	Swe.	6	0	1	1	2	....	....	....	....	....
1986-87	Bjorkloven	Swe.	4	0	0	0	0	....	....	....	....	....
1987-88	Bjorkloven	Swe.	37	6	4	10	14	7	1	0	1	2
1988-89	Bjorkloven	Swe.	22	10	3	13	26	....	....	....	....	....
1989-90	Bjorkloven	Swe.2	18	14	9	23	26	....	....	....	....	....
1990-91	V. Frolunda	Swe.	15	5	4	9	10	....	....	....	....	....
1991-92	V. Frolunda	Swe.	35	13	9	22	46	2	0	0	0	4
1992-93	V. Frolunda	Swe.	22	7	3	10	28	....	....	....	....	....

EDSTROM, LARS

Left wing. Shoots left. 5'11", 185 lbs.   Born, Glommetrask, Sweden, July 16, 1966.
(Minnesota's 7th choice, 202nd overall, in 1992 Entry Draft).

				Regular Season						Playoffs		
Season	Club	Lea	GP	G	A	TP	PIM	GP	G	A	TP	PIM
1987-88	Lulea	Swe.	6	0	1	1	2	....	....	....	....	....
1988-89	Lulea	Swe.	13	5	6	11	6	3	0	0	0	0
1989-90	Lulea	Swe.	32	11	15	26	16	4	0	2	2	0
1990-91	Lulea	Swe.	37	8	19	27	41	5	4	1	5	0
1991-92	Lulea	Swe.	35	17	19	36	20	1	0	0	0	0
1992-93	Lulea	Swe.	38	12	21	33	14	11	2	1	3	20

EGELAND, ALLAN

Center. Shoots left. 6', 184 lbs.   Born, Lethbridge, Alta., January 31, 1973.
(Tampa Bay's 3rd choice, 55th overall, in 1993 Entry Draft).

				Regular Season						Playoffs		
Season	Club	Lea	GP	G	A	TP	PIM	GP	G	A	TP	PIM
1990-91	Lethbridge	WHL	67	2	16	18	57	9	0	0	0	0
1991-92	Tacoma	WHL	72	35	39	74	135	4	0	1	1	18
1992-93a	Tacoma	WHL	71	56	57	113	119	20	9	7	16	18

a   WHL West First All-Star Team (1993)

EGELAND, TRACY

Left wing. Shoots right. 6'1", 180 lbs.   Born, Lethbridge, Alta., August 20, 1970.
(Chicago's 5th choice, 132nd overall, in 1989 Entry Draft).

				Regular Season						Playoffs		
Season	Club	Lea	GP	G	A	TP	PIM	GP	G	A	TP	PIM
1986-87	Swift Current	WHL	48	3	2	5	20	....	....	....	....	....
1987-88	Swift Current	WHL	63	10	22	32	34	....	....	....	....	....
1988-89	Medicine Hat	WHL	42	11	12	23	64	....	....	....	....	....
	Prince Albert	WHL	24	17	10	27	24	4	0	1	1	13
1989-90	Prince Albert	WHL	61	39	26	65	160	13	7	10	17	26
1990-91	Indianapolis	IHL	79	17	22	39	205	7	2	1	3	21
1991-92	Indianapolis	IHL	66	20	11	31	214	....	....	....	....	....
1992-93	Indianapolis	IHL	43	11	14	25	122	....	....	....	....	....

Signed as a free agent by **Philadelphia**, August 4, 1993.

EHLERS, HEINZ

Center. Shoots . 5'11", 177 lbs.   Born, Aalborg, Denmark, January 25, 1966.
(NY Rangers' 9th choice, 188th overall, in 1984 Entry Draft).

				Regular Season						Playoffs		
Season	Club	Lea	GP	G	A	TP	PIM	GP	G	A	TP	PIM
1992-93	Rogle	Swe.	38	7	26	33	97	....	....	....	....	....

EISENHUT, NEIL

Center. Shoots left. 6'1", 190 lbs.   Born, Osoyoos, B.C., February 9, 1967.
(Vancouver's 11th choice, 238th overall, in 1987 Entry Draft).

				Regular Season						Playoffs		
Season	Club	Lea	GP	G	A	TP	PIM	GP	G	A	TP	PIM
1987-88	North Dakota	WCHA	42	12	20	32	14	....	....	....	....	....
1988-89	North Dakota	WCHA	41	22	16	38	20	....	....	....	....	....
1989-90	North Dakota	WCHA	45	22	32	54	46	....	....	....	....	....
1990-91	North Dakota	WCHA	20	9	15	24	10	....	....	....	....	....
1991-92	Milwaukee	IHL	76	13	23	36	26	2	1	2	3	0
1992-93	Hamilton	AHL	72	22	40	62	41	....	....	....	....	....

EKLUND, PER-ERIK (PELLE)

(EHK-luhnd)

Center. Shoots left. 5'10", 175 lbs.   Born, Stockholm, Sweden, March 22, 1963.
(Philadelphia's 7th choice, 167th overall, in 1983 Entry Draft).

				Regular Season						Playoffs		
Season	Club	Lea	GP	G	A	TP	PIM	GP	G	A	TP	PIM
1981-82	AIK	Swe.	23	2	3	5	2	....	....	....	....	....
1982-83	AIK	Swe.	34	13	17	30	14	3	1	4	5	2
1983-84	AIK	Swe.	35	9	18	27	24	6	6	7	13	2
1984-85	AIK	Swe.	35	16	33	49	10	....	....	....	....	....
1985-86	Philadelphia	NHL	70	15	51	66	12	5	0	2	2	0
1986-87	Philadelphia	NHL	72	14	41	55	2	26	7	20	27	2
1987-88	Philadelphia	NHL	71	10	32	42	12	7	0	3	3	0
1988-89	Philadelphia	NHL	79	18	51	69	23	19	3	8	11	2
1989-90	Philadelphia	NHL	70	23	39	62	16	....	....	....	....	....
1990-91	Philadelphia	NHL	73	19	50	69	14	....	....	....	....	....
1991-92	Philadelphia	NHL	51	7	16	23	4	....	....	....	....	....
1992-93	Philadelphia	NHL	55	11	38	49	16	....	....	....	....	....
	NHL Totals		**541**	**117**	**318**	**435**	**99**	**57**	**10**	**33**	**43**	**4**

ELICK, MICKEY

Defense. Shoots left. 6'1", 180 lbs.   Born, Calgary, Alta., March 17, 1974.
(NY Rangers' 8th choice, 192nd overall, in 1992 Entry Draft).

				Regular Season						Playoffs		
Season	Club	Lea	GP	G	A	TP	PIM	GP	G	A	TP	PIM
1991-92	Calgary	AJHL	41	18	32	50	54	....	....	....	....	....
1992-93	U. Wisconsin	WCHA	33	1	6	7	24	....	....	....	....	....

ELIK, TODD

(EL-ik)

Center. Shoots left. 6'2", 190 lbs.   Born, Brampton, Ont., April 15, 1966.

				Regular Season						Playoffs		
Season	Club	Lea	GP	G	A	TP	PIM	GP	G	A	TP	PIM
1984-85	Kingston	OHL	34	14	11	25	6	....	....	....	....	....
	North Bay	OHL	23	4	6	10	2	4	2	0	2	0
1985-86	North Bay	OHL	40	12	34	46	20	10	7	6	13	0
1986-87	U. of Regina	CWUAA	27	26	34	60	137	....	....	....	....	....
1987-88	Colorado	IHL	81	44	56	100	83	12	8	12	20	9
1988-89	Denver	IHL	28	20	15	35	22	....	....	....	....	....
	New Haven	AHL	43	11	25	36	31	17	10	12	22	44
1989-90	Los Angeles	NHL	48	10	23	33	41	10	3	9	12	10
	New Haven	AHL	32	20	23	43	42	....	....	....	....	....
1990-91	Los Angeles	NHL	74	21	37	58	58	12	2	7	9	6
1991-92	Minnesota	NHL	62	14	32	46	125	5	1	1	2	2
1992-93	Minnesota	NHL	46	13	18	31	48	....	....	....	....	....
	Edmonton	NHL	14	1	9	10	8	....	....	....	....	....
	NHL Totals		**244**	**59**	**119**	**178**	**280**	**27**	**6**	**17**	**23**	**18**

Signed as a free agent by **NY Rangers**, February 26, 1988. Traded to **Los Angeles** by **NY Rangers** with Igor Liba, Michael Boyce and future considerations for Dean Kennedy and Denis Larocque, December 12, 1988. Traded to **Minnesota** by **Los Angeles** for Randy Gilhen, Charlie Huddy, Jim Thomson and NY Rangers' fourth round choice (previously acquired by Minnesota — Los Angeles selected Alexei Zhitnik) in 1991 Entry Draft, June 22, 1991. Traded to **Edmonton** by **Minnesota** for Brent Gilchrist, March 5, 1993.

ELLETT, DAVID

Defense. Shoots left. 6'2", 200 lbs.   Born, Cleveland, OH, March 30, 1964.
(Winnipeg's 3rd choice, 75th overall, in 1982 Entry Draft).

				Regular Season						Playoffs		
Season	Club	Lea	GP	G	A	TP	PIM	GP	G	A	TP	PIM
1982-83	Bowling Green	CCHA	40	4	13	17	34	....	....	....	....	....
1983-84ab	Bowling Green	CCHA	43	15	39	54	96	....	....	....	....	....
1984-85	Winnipeg	NHL	80	11	27	38	85	8	1	5	6	4
1985-86	Winnipeg	NHL	80	15	31	46	96	3	0	1	1	0
1986-87	Winnipeg	NHL	78	13	31	44	53	10	0	8	8	2
1987-88	Winnipeg	NHL	68	13	45	58	106	5	1	2	3	10
1988-89	Winnipeg	NHL	75	22	34	56	62	....	....	....	....	....
1989-90	Winnipeg	NHL	77	17	29	46	96	7	2	0	2	6
1990-91	Winnipeg	NHL	17	4	7	11	6	....	....	....	....	....
	Toronto	NHL	60	8	30	38	69	....	....	....	....	....
1991-92	Toronto	NHL	79	18	33	51	95	....	....	....	....	....
1992-93	Toronto	NHL	70	6	34	40	46	21	4	8	12	8
	NHL Totals		**684**	**127**	**301**	**428**	**714**	**54**	**8**	**24**	**32**	**30**

a   CCHA Second All-Star Team (1984)
b   Named to NCAA All-Tournament Team (1984)
Played in NHL All-Star Game (1989, 1992)

Traded to **Toronto** by **Winnipeg** with Paul Fenton for Ed Olczyk and Mark Osborne, November 10, 1990.

ELVENAS, ROGER

Center. Shoots left. 6'1", 187 lbs.   Born, Lund, Sweden, April 29, 1968.
(Toronto's 7th choice, 153rd overall, in 1988 Entry Draft).

				Regular Season						Playoffs		
Season	Club	Lea	GP	G	A	TP	PIM	GP	G	A	TP	PIM
1987-88	Rogle	Swe.2	35	21	18	39	10	2	0	0	0	2
1988-89	Rogle	Swe.2	36	24	40	64	....	....	....	....	....	....
1989-90	Rogle	Swe.2	35	16	25	41	24	....	....	....	....	....
1990-91	Rogle	Swe.2	32	17	26	43	12	....	....	....	....	....
1991-92	Rogle	Swe.2	36	13	21	34	10	....	....	....	....	....
1992-93	Rogle	Swe.	40	8	10	18	18	....	....	....	....	....

ELVENAS, STEFAN

Right wing. Shoots left. 6'1", 183 lbs.   Born, Lund, Sweden, March 30, 1970.
(Chicago's 3rd choice, 71st overall, in 1988 Entry Draft).

				Regular Season						Playoffs		
Season	Club	Lea	GP	G	A	TP	PIM	GP	G	A	TP	PIM
1987-88	Rogle	Swe.2	36	21	17	38	30	2	0	0	0	2
1988-89	Rogle	Swe.2				UNAVAILABLE						
1989-90	Rogle	Swe.2	35	18	25	43	56	....	....	....	....	....
1990-91	Rogle	Swe.2	18	14	6	20	10	....	....	....	....	....
1991-92	Rogle	Swe.2	35	31	19	50	10	....	....	....	....	....
1992-93	Rogle	Swe.	40	18	14	32	18	....	....	....	....	....

ELYNUIK, PAT

(EL-ih-NYUK)

Right wing. Shoots right. 6', 185 lbs.   Born, Foam Lake, Sask., October 30, 1967.
(Winnipeg's 1st choice, 8th overall, in 1986 Entry Draft).

				Regular Season						Playoffs		
Season	Club	Lea	GP	G	A	TP	PIM	GP	G	A	TP	PIM
1984-85	Prince Albert	WHL	70	23	20	43	54	13	9	3	12	7
1985-86a	Prince Albert	WHL	68	53	53	106	62	20	7	9	16	17
1986-87a	Prince Albert	WHL	64	51	62	113	40	8	5	5	10	12
1987-88	Winnipeg	NHL	13	1	3	4	12	....	....	....	....	....
	Moncton	AHL	30	11	18	29	35	....	....	....	....	....
1988-89	Winnipeg	NHL	56	26	25	51	29	....	....	....	....	....
	Moncton	AHL	7	8	2	10	2	....	....	....	....	....
1989-90	Winnipeg	NHL	80	32	42	74	83	7	2	4	6	2
1990-91	Winnipeg	NHL	80	31	34	65	73	....	....	....	....	....
1991-92	Winnipeg	NHL	60	25	25	50	65	7	2	2	4	4
1992-93	Washington	NHL	80	22	35	57	66	6	2	3	5	19
	NHL Totals		**369**	**137**	**164**	**301**	**328**	**20**	**6**	**9**	**15**	**25**

a   WHL East All-Star Team (1986, 1987)
Traded to **Washington** by **Winnipeg** for John Druce and future considerations, October 1, 1992.

EMERSON, NELSON

Center. Shoots right. 5'11", 180 lbs. Born, Hamilton, Ont., August 17, 1967.
(St. Louis' 2nd choice, 44th overall, in 1985 Entry Draft).

			Regular Season					Playoffs				
Season	Club	Lea	GP	G	A	TP	PIM	GP	G	A	TP	PIM
1986-87a	Bowling Green	CCHA	45	26	35	61	28	....	....	....	....	....
1987-88bc	Bowling Green	CCHA	45	34	49	83	54	....	....	....	....	....
1988-89d	Bowling Green	CCHA	44	22	46	68	46	....	....	....	....	....
1989-90ce	Bowling Green	CCHA	44	30	52	82	42	....	....	....	....	....
	Peoria	IHL	3	1	1	2	0	....	....	....	....	....
1990-91	**St. Louis**	**NHL**	**4**	**0**	**3**	**3**	**2**	....	....	....	....	....
fg	Peoria	IHL	73	36	79	115	91	17	9	12	21	16
1991-92	**St. Louis**	**NHL**	**79**	**23**	**36**	**59**	**66**	**6**	**3**	**3**	**6**	**21**
1992-93	**St. Louis**	**NHL**	**82**	**22**	**51**	**73**	**62**	**11**	**1**	**6**	**7**	**6**
	NHL Totals		**165**	**45**	**90**	**135**	**130**	**17**	**4**	**9**	**13**	**27**

a CCHA Freshman of the Year (1987)
b NCAA West Second All-American Team (1988)
c CCHA First All-Star Team (1988, 1990)
d CCHA Second All-Star Team (1989)
e NCAA West First All-American Team (1990)
f IHL First All-Star Team (1991)
g Won Garry F. Longman Memorial Trophy (Top Rookie — IHL) (1991)

EMMA, DAVID

Center. Shoots left. 5'11", 180 lbs. Born, Cranston, RI, January 14, 1968.
(New Jersey's 6th choice, 110th overall, in 1989 Entry Draft).

			Regular Season					Playoffs				
Season	Club	Lea	GP	G	A	TP	PIM	GP	G	A	TP	PIM
1987-88	Boston College	H.E.	30	19	16	35	30	....	....	....	....	....
1988-89	Boston College	H.E.	36	20	31	51	36	....	....	....	....	....
1989-90ab	Boston College	H.E.	42	38	34	*72	46	....	....	....	....	....
1990-91abcd	Boston College	H.E.	39	*35	46	*81	44	....	....	....	....	....
1991-92	U.S. National	....	55	15	16	31	32	....	....	....	....	....
	U.S. Olympic	....	6	0	1	1	6	....	....	....	....	....
	Utica	AHL	15	4	7	11	12	4	1	1	2	2
1992-93	**New Jersey**	**NHL**	**2**	**0**	**0**	**0**	**0**	....	....	....	....	....
	Utica	AHL	61	21	40	61	47	5	2	1	3	6
	NHL Totals		**2**	**0**	**0**	**0**	**0**	....	....	....	....	....

a Hockey East First All-Star Team (1990, 1991)
b NCAA East First All-American Team (1990, 1991)
c Hockey East Player of the Year (1991)
d Won Hobey Baker Award (Top U.S. Collegiate Player) (1991)

ENGA, RICHARD

Center. Shoots right. 5'10", 156 lbs. Born, Bitburg, Germany, February 15, 1972.
(NY Islanders' 9th choice, 195th overall, in 1990 Entry Draft).

			Regular Season					Playoffs				
Season	Club	Lea	GP	G	A	TP	PIM	GP	G	A	TP	PIM
1991-92	Colorado	WCHA	40	11	16	27	18	....	....	....	....	....
1992-93	Colorado	WCHA	36	12	19	31	16	....	....	....	....	....

ENGLUND, PATRIK

Left wing. Shoots left. 6', 185 lbs. Born, Stockholm, Sweden, June 3, 1970.
(Philadelphia's 11th choice, 151st overall, in 1990 Entry Draft).

			Regular Season					Playoffs				
Season	Club	Lea	GP	G	A	TP	PIM	GP	G	A	TP	PIM
1988-89	AIK	Swe.	19	2	3	5	6	....	....	....	....	....
1989-90	AIK	Swe.	31	11	7	18	2	3	0	0	0	12
1990-91	AIK	Swe.	40	9	6	15	6	....	....	....	....	....
1991-92	AIK	Swe.	39	8	5	13	8	3	0	0	0	0
1992-93	AIK	Swe.	22	3	1	4	8	....	....	....	....	....

ERICKSON, BRYAN

Right wing. Shoots right. 5'9", 175 lbs. Born, Roseau, MN, March 7, 1960.

			Regular Season					Playoffs				
Season	Club	Lea	GP	G	A	TP	PIM	GP	G	A	TP	PIM
1981-82	U. Minnesota	WCHA	35	25	20	45	20	....	....	....	....	....
1982-83	U. Minnesota	WCHA	42	35	47	82	34	....	....	....	....	....
	Hershey	AHL	1	0	1	1	0	3	3	0	3	0
1983-84	**Washington**	**NHL**	**45**	**12**	**17**	**29**	**16**	**8**	**2**	**3**	**5**	**7**
	Hershey	AHL	31	16	12	28	11	....	....	....	....	....
1984-85	**Washington**	**NHL**	**57**	**15**	**13**	**28**	**23**	....	....	....	....	....
	Binghamton	AHL	13	6	11	17	8	....	....	....	....	....
1985-86	**Los Angeles**	**NHL**	**55**	**20**	**23**	**43**	**36**	....	....	....	....	....
	Binghamton	AHL	7	5	3	8	2	....	....	....	....	....
	New Haven	AHL	14	8	3	11	11	....	....	....	....	....
1986-87	**Los Angeles**	**NHL**	**68**	**20**	**30**	**50**	**26**	**3**	**1**	**1**	**2**	**0**
1987-88	**Los Angeles**	**NHL**	**42**	**6**	**15**	**21**	**20**	....	....	....	....	....
	New Haven	AHL	3	0	0	0	0	....	....	....	....	....
	Pittsburgh	**NHL**	**11**	**1**	**4**	**5**	**0**	....	....	....	....	....
1988-89					DID NOT PLAY							
1989-90	Moncton	AHL	13	4	7	11	4	....	....	....	....	....
1990-91	**Winnipeg**	**NHL**	**6**	**0**	**7**	**7**	**0**	....	....	....	....	....
	Moncton	AHL	36	18	14	32	16	9	9	2	11	6
1991-92	**Winnipeg**	**NHL**	**10**	**2**	**4**	**6**	**0**	....	....	....	....	....
1992-93	**Winnipeg**	**NHL**	**41**	**4**	**12**	**16**	**14**	**3**	**0**	**0**	**0**	**0**
	Moncton	AHL	2	1	1	2	4	....	....	....	....	....
	NHL Totals		**335**	**80**	**125**	**205**	**135**	**14**	**3**	**4**	**7**	**7**

Signed as a free agent by **Washington**, April 5, 1983. Traded to **Los Angeles** by **Washington** for Bruce Shoebottom, October 31, 1985. Traded to **Pittsburgh** by **Los Angeles** for Chris Kontos and Pittsburgh's sixth round draft choice (Micah Aivazoff) in 1988 Entry Draft, February 5, 1988. Signed as a free agent by **Winnipeg**, March 2, 1990.

ERICKSON, PATRIK (AIR-ihk-suhn)

Right wing. Shoots left. 5'11", 183 lbs. Born, Gavle, Sweden, March 13, 1969.
(Winnipeg's 2nd choice, 37th overall, in 1987 Entry Draft).

			Regular Season					Playoffs				
Season	Club	Lea	GP	G	A	TP	PIM	GP	G	A	TP	PIM
1986-87	Brynas	Swe.	25	10	5	15	8	....	....	....	....	....
1987-88	Brynas	Swe.	35	14	9	23	6	....	....	....	....	....
1988-89	Brynas	Swe.	33	6	10	16	14	....	....	....	....	....
1989-90	Brynas	Swe.	40	16	17	33	18	5	3	2	3	4
1990-91	Brynas	Swe.	33	9	14	23	36	2	1	1	2	4
1991-92	AIK	Swe.	37	7	19	26	34	3	1	0	1	0
1992-93	AIK	Swe.	22	7	7	14	14	....	....	....	....	....

ERIKSSON, ANDERS

Defense. Shoots left. 6'3", 218 lbs. Born, Bollnas, Sweden, January 9, 1975.
(Detroit's 1st choice, 22nd overall, in 1993 Entry Draft).

			Regular Season					Playoffs				
Season	Club	Lea	GP	G	A	TP	PIM	GP	G	A	TP	PIM
1992-93	MoDo	Swe.	20	0	2	2	2	1	0	0	0	0

ERIKSSON, NIKLAS (AIR-ihk-suhn)

Center. Shoots left. 5'10", 183 lbs. Born, Vastervik, Sweden, February 17, 1969.
(Philadelphia's 4th choice, 117th overall, in 1989 Entry Draft).

			Regular Season					Playoffs				
Season	Club	Lea	GP	G	A	TP	PIM	GP	G	A	TP	PIM
1987-88	Leksand	Swe.	16	1	8	9	4	2	0	0	0	0
1988-89	Leksand	Swe.	33	18	12	30	22	....	....	....	....	....
1989-90	Leksand	Swe.	40	18	16	34	16	3	0	2	2	2
1990-91	Leksand	Swe.	8	2	2	4	2	....	....	....	....	....
1991-92	Leksand	Swe.	22	10	7	17	16	....	....	....	....	....
1992-93	Leksand	Swe.	37	6	19	25	28	2	0	1	1	2

ERIKSSON, TOMAZ (AIR-ihk-suhn)

Left wing. Shoots left. 6', 194 lbs. Born, Stockholm, Sweden, March 23, 1967.
(Philadelphia's 4th choice, 83rd overall, in 1987 Entry Draft).

			Regular Season					Playoffs				
Season	Club	Lea	GP	G	A	TP	PIM	GP	G	A	TP	PIM
1986-87	Djurgarden	Swe.	20	7	4	11	14	2	2	0	2	0
1987-88	Djurgarden	Swe.	26	4	5	9	16	....	....	....	....	....
1988-89	Djurgarden	Swe.	4	0	0	0	0	....	....	....	....	....
1989-90	Sodertalje	Swe.	39	14	10	24	26	2	1	1	2	2
1990-91	Sodertalje	Swe.	26	12	14	26	26	2	0	0	0	2
1991-92	Sodertalje	Swe.	22	3	6	9	14	....	....	....	....	....
1992-93	Sodertalje	Swe. 2	27	16	18	34	66	....	....	....	....	....

ERIXON, JAN (AIR-ihk-suhn)

Left wing. Shoots left. 6', 196 lbs. Born, Skelleftea, Sweden, July 8, 1962.
(NY Rangers' 2nd choice, 30th overall, in 1981 Entry Draft).

			Regular Season					Playoffs				
Season	Club	Lea	GP	G	A	TP	PIM	GP	G	A	TP	PIM
1979-80	Skelleftea	Swe.	15	1	0	1	2	....	....	....	....	....
1980-81	Skelleftea	Swe.	32	6	6	12	4	3	1	0	1	0
1981-82	Skelleftea	Swe.	30	7	7	14	26	....	....	....	....	....
1982-83	Skelleftea	Swe.	36	10	19	29	32	....	....	....	....	....
1983-84	**NY Rangers**	**NHL**	**75**	**5**	**25**	**30**	**16**	**5**	**2**	**0**	**2**	**4**
1984-85	**NY Rangers**	**NHL**	**66**	**7**	**22**	**29**	**33**	**2**	**0**	**0**	**0**	**2**
1985-86	**NY Rangers**	**NHL**	**31**	**2**	**17**	**19**	**4**	**12**	**0**	**1**	**1**	**4**
1986-87	**NY Rangers**	**NHL**	**68**	**8**	**18**	**26**	**24**	**6**	**1**	**0**	**1**	**0**
1987-88	**NY Rangers**	**NHL**	**70**	**7**	**19**	**26**	**33**	....	....	....	....	....
1988-89	**NY Rangers**	**NHL**	**44**	**4**	**11**	**15**	**27**	**4**	**0**	**1**	**1**	**2**
1989-90	**NY Rangers**	**NHL**	**58**	**4**	**9**	**13**	**8**	**10**	**1**	**0**	**1**	**2**
1990-91	**NY Rangers**	**NHL**	**53**	**7**	**18**	**25**	**8**	**6**	**1**	**2**	**3**	**0**
1991-92	**NY Rangers**	**NHL**	**46**	**8**	**9**	**17**	**4**	**13**	**2**	**3**	**5**	**2**
1992-93	**NY Rangers**	**NHL**	**45**	**5**	**11**	**16**	**10**	....	....	....	....	....
	NHL Totals		**556**	**57**	**159**	**216**	**167**	**58**	**7**	**7**	**14**	**16**

ERREY, BOB (AIRY)

Left wing. Shoots left. 5'10", 183 lbs. Born, Montreal, Que., September 21, 1964.
(Pittsburgh's 1st choice, 15th overall, in 1983 Entry Draft).

			Regular Season					Playoffs				
Season	Club	Lea	GP	G	A	TP	PIM	GP	G	A	TP	PIM
1981-82	Peterborough	OHL	68	29	31	60	39	9	3	1	4	9
1982-83a	Peterborough	OHL	67	53	47	100	74	4	1	3	4	7
1983-84	**Pittsburgh**	**NHL**	**65**	**9**	**13**	**22**	**29**	....	....	....	....	....
1984-85	**Pittsburgh**	**NHL**	**16**	**0**	**2**	**2**	**7**	....	....	....	....	....
	Baltimore	AHL	59	17	24	41	14	8	3	4	7	11
1985-86	**Pittsburgh**	**NHL**	**37**	**11**	**6**	**17**	**8**	....	....	....	....	....
	Baltimore	AHL	18	8	7	15	28	....	....	....	....	....
1986-87	**Pittsburgh**	**NHL**	**72**	**16**	**18**	**34**	**46**	....	....	....	....	....
1987-88	**Pittsburgh**	**NHL**	**17**	**3**	**6**	**9**	**18**	....	....	....	....	....
1988-89	**Pittsburgh**	**NHL**	**76**	**26**	**32**	**58**	**124**	**11**	**1**	**2**	**3**	**12**
1989-90	**Pittsburgh**	**NHL**	**78**	**20**	**19**	**39**	**109**	....	....	....	....	....
1990-91	**Pittsburgh**	**NHL**	**79**	**20**	**22**	**42**	**115**	**24**	**5**	**2**	**7**	**29**
1991-92	**Pittsburgh**	**NHL**	**78**	**19**	**16**	**35**	**119**	**14**	**3**	**0**	**3**	**10**
1992-93	**Pittsburgh**	**NHL**	**54**	**8**	**6**	**14**	**76**	....	....	....	....	....
	Buffalo	**NHL**	**8**	**1**	**3**	**4**	**4**	**4**	**0**	**1**	**1**	**10**
	NHL Totals		**580**	**133**	**143**	**276**	**655**	**53**	**9**	**5**	**14**	**61**

a OHL First All-Star Team (1983)

Traded to **Buffalo** by **Pittsburgh** for Mike Ramsey, March 22, 1993. Signed as a free agent by **San Jose,** August 17, 1993.

ESAU, LEONARD

Defense. Shoots right. 6'3", 195 lbs. Born, Meadow Lake, Sask., March 16, 1968.
(Toronto's 5th choice, 86th overall, in 1988 Entry Draft).

			Regular Season					Playoffs				
Season	Club	Lea	GP	G	A	TP	PIM	GP	G	A	TP	PIM
1988-89	St. Cloud	NCAA	35	12	27	39	69	....	....	....	....	....
1989-90	St. Cloud	NCAA	29	8	11	19	83	....	....	....	....	....
1990-91	Newmarket	AHL	76	4	14	18	28	....	....	....	....	....
1991-92	**Toronto**	**NHL**	**2**	**0**	**0**	**0**	**0**	....	....	....	....	....
	St. John's	AHL	78	9	29	38	68	13	0	2	2	14
1992-93	**Quebec**	**NHL**	**4**	**0**	**1**	**1**	**2**	....	....	....	....	....
	Halifax	AHL	75	11	31	42	79	....	....	....	....	....
	NHL Totals		**6**	**0**	**1**	**1**	**2**	....	....	....	....	....

Traded to **Quebec** by **Toronto** for Ken McRae, July 21, 1992.

ESBJORS, JOACIM

Defense. Shoots left. 6'1", 194 lbs. Born, Goteborg, Sweden, July 4, 1970.
(Hartford's 11th choice, 249th overall, in 1992 Entry Draft).

			Regular Season					Playoffs				
Season	Club	Lea	GP	G	A	TP	PIM	GP	G	A	TP	PIM
1989-90	V. Frolunda	Swe.	24	0	4	4	23	....	....	....	....	....
1990-91	V. Frolunda	Swe.	22	1	5	6	16	....	....	....	....	....
1991-92	V. Frolunda	Swe.	40	9	9	18	22	3	1	0	1	2
1992-93	V. Frolunda	Swe.	20	1	6	7	26	....	....	....	....	....

EVANS, DOUG

Left wing. Shoots left. 5'9", 185 lbs. Born, Peterborough, Ont., June 2, 1963.

			Regular Season					Playoffs				
Season	**Club**	**Lea**	**GP**	**G**	**A**	**TP**	**PIM**	**GP**	**G**	**A**	**TP**	**PIM**
1981-82	Peterborough	OHL	56	17	49	66	176	9	0	2	2	41
1982-83	Peterborough	OHL	65	31	55	86	165	4	0	3	3	23
1983-84	Peterborough	OHL	61	45	79	124	98	8	4	12	16	26
1984-85	Peoria	IHL	81	36	61	97	189	20	18	14	32	*88
1985-86	**St. Louis**	**NHL**	**13**	**1**	**0**	**1**	**2**	....	....	....	....	....
a	Peoria	IHL	60	46	51	97	179	10	4	6	10	32
1986-87	**St. Louis**	**NHL**	**53**	**3**	**13**	**16**	**91**	**5**	**0**	**0**	**0**	**10**
	Peoria	IHL	18	10	15	25	39	....	....	....	....	....
1987-88	**St. Louis**	**NHL**	**41**	**5**	**7**	**12**	**49**	**2**	**0**	**0**	**0**	**0**
	Peoria	IHL	11	4	16	20	64	....	....	....	....	....
1988-89	**St. Louis**	**NHL**	**53**	**7**	**12**	**19**	**81**	**7**	**1**	**2**	**3**	**16**
1989-90	**St. Louis**	**NHL**	**3**	**0**	**0**	**0**	**0**	....	....	....	....	....
	Peoria	IHL	42	19	28	47	128	....	....	....	....	....
	Winnipeg	**NHL**	**27**	**10**	**8**	**18**	**33**	**7**	**2**	**2**	**4**	**10**
1990-91	**Winnipeg**	**NHL**	**70**	**7**	**27**	**34**	**108**	....	....	....	....	....
1991-92	Peoria	IHL	16	5	14	19	38	....	....	....	....	....
	Winnipeg	**NHL**	**30**	**7**	**7**	**14**	**68**	**1**	**0**	**0**	**0**	**2**
	Moncton	AHL	10	7	8	15	10	....	....	....	....	....
1992-93	**Philadelphia**	**NHL**	**65**	**8**	**13**	**21**	**70**	....	....	....	....	....
	NHL Totals		**355**	**48**	**87**	**135**	**502**	**22**	**3**	**4**	**7**	**38**

a IHL First All-Star Team (1986)

Signed as a free agent by **St. Louis**, June 10, 1985. Traded to **Winnipeg** by **St. Louis** for Ron Wilson, January 22, 1990. Traded to **Boston** by **Winnipeg** for Daniel Berthiaume, June 10, 1992. Claimed by **Philadelphia** from **Boston** in NHL Waiver Draft, October 4, 1992.

EVANS, KEVIN ROBERT

Left wing. Shoots left. 5'9", 185 lbs. Born, Peterborough, Ont., July 10, 1965.

			Regular Season					Playoffs				
Season	**Club**	**Lea**	**GP**	**G**	**A**	**TP**	**PIM**	**GP**	**G**	**A**	**TP**	**PIM**
1984-85	London	OHL	52	3	7	10	148	....	....	....	....	....
1985-86	Victoria	WHL	66	16	39	55	441	....	....	....	....	....
	Kalamazoo	IHL	11	3	5	8	97	6	3	0	3	56
1986-87	Kalamazoo	IHL	73	19	31	50	*648	3	1	0	1	24
1987-88	Kalamazoo	IHL	54	9	28	37	404	5	1	1	2	46
1988-89	Kalamazoo	IHL	50	22	34	56	326	....	....	....	....	....
1989-90	Kalamazoo	IHL	76	30	54	84	346	10	8	4	12	86
1990-91	**Minnesota**	**NHL**	**4**	**0**	**0**	**0**	**19**	....	....	....	....	....
	Kalamazoo	IHL	16	10	12	22	70	....	....	....	....	....
1991-92	**San Jose**	**NHL**	**5**	**0**	**1**	**1**	**25**	....	....	....	....	....
	Kansas City	IHL	66	10	39	49	342	14	2	*13	15	70
1992-93	Kalamazoo	IHL	49	7	24	31	283	....	....	....	....	....
	NHL Totals		**9**	**0**	**1**	**1**	**44**	....	....	....	....	....

Signed as a free agent by **Minnesota**, August 8, 1988. Claimed by **San Jose** from **Minnesota** in Dispersal Draft, May 30, 1991. Signed as a free agent by **Minnesota**, July 20, 1992.

EVASON, DEAN (EH-vuh-suhn)

Center. Shoots right. 5'10", 180 lbs. Born, Flin Flon, Man., August 22, 1964.
(Washington's 3rd choice, 89th overall, in 1982 Entry Draft).

			Regular Season					Playoffs				
Season	**Club**	**Lea**	**GP**	**G**	**A**	**TP**	**PIM**	**GP**	**G**	**A**	**TP**	**PIM**
1980-81	Spokane	WHL	3	1	1	2	0	....	....	....	....	....
1981-82	Spokane	WHL	26	8	14	22	65	....	....	....	....	....
	Kamloops	WHL	44	21	55	76	47	4	2	1	3	0
1982-83	Kamloops	WHL	70	71	93	164	102	7	5	7	12	18
1983-84	**Washington**	**NHL**	**2**	**0**	**0**	**0**	**2**	....	....	....	....	....
a	Kamloops	WHL	57	49	88	137	89	17	*21	20	41	33
1984-85	**Washington**	**NHL**	**15**	**3**	**4**	**7**	**2**	....	....	....	....	....
	Hartford	**NHL**	**2**	**0**	**0**	**0**	**0**	....	....	....	....	....
	Binghamton	AHL	65	27	49	76	38	8	3	5	8	9
1985-86	**Hartford**	**NHL**	**55**	**20**	**28**	**48**	**65**	**10**	**1**	**4**	**5**	**10**
	Binghamton	AHL	26	9	17	26	29	....	....	....	....	....
1986-87	**Hartford**	**NHL**	**80**	**22**	**37**	**59**	**67**	**5**	**3**	**2**	**5**	**35**
1987-88	**Hartford**	**NHL**	**77**	**10**	**18**	**28**	**115**	**6**	**1**	**1**	**2**	**2**
1988-89	**Hartford**	**NHL**	**67**	**11**	**17**	**28**	**60**	**4**	**1**	**2**	**3**	**10**
1989-90	**Hartford**	**NHL**	**78**	**18**	**25**	**43**	**138**	**7**	**2**	**2**	**4**	**22**
1990-91	**Hartford**	**NHL**	**75**	**6**	**23**	**29**	**170**	**6**	**0**	**4**	**4**	**29**
1991-92	**San Jose**	**NHL**	**74**	**11**	**15**	**26**	**99**	....	....	....	....	....
1992-93	**San Jose**	**NHL**	**84**	**12**	**19**	**31**	**132**	....	....	....	....	....
	NHL Totals		**609**	**113**	**186**	**299**	**850**	**38**	**8**	**15**	**23**	**108**

a WHL First All-Star Team, West Division (1984)

Traded to **Hartford** by **Washington** with Peter Sidorkiewicz for David Jensen, March 12, 1985. Traded to **San Jose** by **Hartford** for Dan Keczmer, October 2, 1991. Traded to **Dallas** by **San Jose** for San Jose's sixth round choice (previously acquired by Dallas — San Jose selected Petri Varis) in 1993 Entry Draft, June 26, 1993.

EWEN, TODD

Right wing. Shoots right. 6'2", 220 lbs. Born, Saskatoon, Sask., March 22, 1966.
(Edmonton's 9th choice, 168th overall, in 1984 Entry Draft).

			Regular Season					Playoffs				
Season	**Club**	**Lea**	**GP**	**G**	**A**	**TP**	**PIM**	**GP**	**G**	**A**	**TP**	**PIM**
1982-83	Kamloops	WHL	3	0	0	0	2	2	0	0	0	0
1983-84	N. Westminster	WHL	68	11	13	24	176	7	2	1	3	15
1984-85	N. Westminster	WHL	56	11	20	31	304	10	1	8	9	60
1985-86	N. Westminster	WHL	60	28	24	52	289	....	....	....	....	....
	Maine	AHL	....	....	....	....	....	3	0	0	0	7
1986-87	**St. Louis**	**NHL**	**23**	**2**	**0**	**2**	**84**	**4**	**0**	**0**	**0**	**23**
	Peoria	IHL	16	3	3	6	110	....	....	....	....	....
1987-88	**St. Louis**	**NHL**	**64**	**4**	**2**	**6**	**227**	**6**	**0**	**0**	**0**	**21**
1988-89	**St. Louis**	**NHL**	**34**	**4**	**5**	**9**	**171**	**2**	**0**	**0**	**0**	**21**
1989-90	**St. Louis**	**NHL**	**3**	**0**	**0**	**0**	**11**	....	....	....	....	....
	Peoria	IHL	2	0	0	0	12	....	....	....	....	....
	Montreal	**NHL**	**41**	**4**	**6**	**10**	**158**	**10**	**0**	**0**	**0**	**4**
1990-91	**Montreal**	**NHL**	**28**	**3**	**2**	**5**	**128**	....	....	....	....	....
1991-92	**Montreal**	**NHL**	**46**	**1**	**2**	**3**	**130**	**3**	**0**	**0**	**0**	**18**
1992-93	**Montreal**	**NHL**	**75**	**5**	**9**	**14**	**193**	**1**	**0**	**0**	**0**	**0**
	NHL Totals		**314**	**23**	**26**	**49**	**1102**	**26**	**0**	**0**	**0**	**87**

Traded to **St. Louis** by **Edmonton** for Shawn Evans, October 15, 1986. Traded to **Montreal** by **St. Louis** for future considerations, December 12, 1989. Traded to **Anaheim** by **Montreal** with Patrik Carnback for Anaheim's third round choice in 1994 Entry Draft, August 10, 1993.

FAIRCHILD, KELLY

Defense. Shoots left. 5'11", 180 lbs. Born, Hibbing, MN, April 9, 1973.
(Los Angeles' 7th choice, 152nd overall, in 1991 Entry Draft).

			Regular Season					Playoffs				
Season	**Club**	**Lea**	**GP**	**G**	**A**	**TP**	**PIM**	**GP**	**G**	**A**	**TP**	**PIM**
1991-92	U. Wisconsin	WCHA	37	11	10	21	45	....	....	....	....	....
1992-93	U. Wisconsin	WCHA	42	25	29	54	54	....	....	....	....	....

FALLOON, PAT

Right wing. Shoots right. 5'11", 192 lbs. Born, Foxwarren, Man., September 22, 1972.
(San Jose's 1st choice, 2nd overall, in 1991 Entry Draft).

			Regular Season					Playoffs				
Season	**Club**	**Lea**	**GP**	**G**	**A**	**TP**	**PIM**	**GP**	**G**	**A**	**TP**	**PIM**
1988-89	Spokane	WHL	72	22	56	78	41	....	....	....	....	....
1989-90	Spokane	WHL	71	60	64	124	48	6	5	8	13	4
1990-91abcd	Spokane	WHL	61	64	74	138	33	15	10	14	24	10
1991-92	**San Jose**	**NHL**	**79**	**25**	**34**	**59**	**16**	....	....	....	....	....
1992-93	**San Jose**	**NHL**	**41**	**14**	**14**	**28**	**12**	....	....	....	....	....
	NHL Totals		**120**	**39**	**48**	**87**	**28**	....	....	....	....	....

a WHL West First All-Star Team (1991)
b Canadian Major Junior Most Sportsmanlike Player of the Year (1991)
c Memorial Cup All-Star Team (1991)
d Won Stafford Smythe Memorial Trophy (Memorial Cup MVP) (1991)

FARRELL, BRIAN

Center. Shoots left. 5'11", 182 lbs. Born, West Hartford, CT, April 16, 1972.
(Pittsburgh's 4th choice, 89th overall, in 1990 Entry Draft).

			Regular Season					Playoffs				
Season	**Club**	**Lea**	**GP**	**G**	**A**	**TP**	**PIM**	**GP**	**G**	**A**	**TP**	**PIM**
1990-91	Harvard	ECAC	28	3	8	11	16	....	....	....	....	....
1991-92	Harvard	ECAC	9	5	3	8	6	....	....	....	....	....
1992-93	Harvard	ECAC	31	10	23	33	33	....	....	....	....	....

FAUCHER, VINCENT

Left wing. Shoots left. 6'2", 195 lbs. Born, Dorion, Que., October 28, 1967.

			Regular Season					Playoffs				
Season	**Club**	**Lea**	**GP**	**G**	**A**	**TP**	**PIM**	**GP**	**G**	**A**	**TP**	**PIM**
1988-89	Lake Superior	CCHA	27	2	3	5	18	....	....	....	....	....
1989-90	Lake Superior	CCHA	16	5	3	8	12	....	....	....	....	....
1990-91	Lake Superior	CCHA	40	6	20	26	68	....	....	....	....	....
1991-92	Lake Superior	CCHA	38	21	22	43	86	....	....	....	....	....
1992-93	New Haven	AHL	36	7	8	15	22	....	....	....	....	....
	Thunder Bay	Col.	30	20	26	46	8	....	....	....	....	....

Signed as a free agent by **Ottawa**, July 16, 1992.

FAUST, ANDRE

Center. Shoots left. 6'1", 180 lbs. Born, Joliette, Que., October 7, 1969.
(New Jersey's 8th choice, 173rd overall, in 1989 Entry Draft).

			Regular Season					Playoffs				
Season	**Club**	**Lea**	**GP**	**G**	**A**	**TP**	**PIM**	**GP**	**G**	**A**	**TP**	**PIM**
1988-89	Princeton	ECAC	27	15	24	39	28	....	....	....	....	....
1989-90a	Princeton	ECAC	22	9	28	37	20	....	....	....	....	....
1990-91	Princeton	ECAC	26	15	22	37	51	....	....	....	....	....
1991-92a	Princeton	ECAC	27	14	21	35	38	....	....	....	....	....
1992-93	**Philadelphia**	**NHL**	**10**	**2**	**2**	**4**	**4**	....	....	....	....	....
	Hershey	AHL	62	26	25	51	71	....	....	....	....	....
	NHL Totals		**10**	**2**	**2**	**4**	**4**	....	....	....	....	....

a ECAC Second All-Star Team (1990, 1992)

Signed as a free agent by **Philadelphia**, October 5, 1992.

FEARNS, KENT

Defense. Shoots left. 6', 180 lbs. Born, Langley, B.C., September 13, 1972.
(Hartford's 1st choice, 6th overall, in 1993 Supplemental Draft).

			Regular Season					Playoffs				
Season	**Club**	**Lea**	**GP**	**G**	**A**	**TP**	**PIM**	**GP**	**G**	**A**	**TP**	**PIM**
1991-92	Colorado	WCHA	41	10	27	37	48	....	....	....	....	....
1992-93	Colorado	WCHA	33	7	15	22	76	....	....	....	....	....

FEATHERSTONE, GLEN

Defense. Shoots left. 6'4", 215 lbs. Born, Toronto, Ont., July 8, 1968.
(St. Louis' 4th choice, 73rd overall, in 1986 Entry Draft).

			Regular Season					Playoffs				
Season	**Club**	**Lea**	**GP**	**G**	**A**	**TP**	**PIM**	**GP**	**G**	**A**	**TP**	**PIM**
1985-86	Windsor	OHL	49	0	6	6	135	14	1	1	2	23
1986-87	Windsor	OHL	47	6	11	17	154	14	2	6	8	19
1987-88	Windsor	OHL	53	7	27	34	201	12	6	9	15	47
1988-89	**St. Louis**	**NHL**	**18**	**0**	**2**	**2**	**22**	**6**	**0**	**0**	**0**	**0**
	Peoria	IHL	37	5	19	24	97	....	....	....	....	....
1989-90	**St. Louis**	**NHL**	**58**	**0**	**12**	**12**	**145**	**12**	**0**	**2**	**2**	**47**
	Peoria	IHL	15	1	4	5	43	....	....	....	....	....
1990-91	**St. Louis**	**NHL**	**68**	**5**	**15**	**20**	**204**	**9**	**0**	**0**	**0**	**31**
1991-92	**Boston**	**NHL**	**7**	**1**	**0**	**1**	**20**	....	....	....	....	....
1992-93	**Boston**	**NHL**	**34**	**5**	**5**	**10**	**102**	....	....	....	....	....
	Providence	AHL	8	3	4	7	60	....	....	....	....	....
	NHL Totals		**185**	**11**	**34**	**45**	**493**	**27**	**0**	**2**	**2**	**78**

Signed as a free agent by **Boston**, July 25, 1991.

FEDOROV, SERGEI (FE-duh-rahf)

Center. Shoots left. 6'1", 200 lbs. Born, Pskov, Soviet Union, December 13, 1969.
(Detroit's 4th choice, 74th overall, in 1989 Entry Draft).

			Regular Season					Playoffs				
Season	**Club**	**Lea**	**GP**	**G**	**A**	**TP**	**PIM**	**GP**	**G**	**A**	**TP**	**PIM**
1986-87	CSKA	USSR	29	6	6	12	12	....	....	....	....	....
1987-88	CSKA	USSR	48	7	9	16	20	....	....	....	....	....
1988-89	CSKA	USSR	44	9	8	17	35	....	....	....	....	....
1989-90	CSKA	USSR	48	19	10	29	22	....	....	....	....	....
1990-91a	**Detroit**	**NHL**	**77**	**31**	**48**	**79**	**66**	**7**	**1**	**5**	**6**	**4**
1991-92	**Detroit**	**NHL**	**80**	**32**	**54**	**86**	**72**	**11**	**5**	**5**	**10**	**8**
1992-93	**Detroit**	**NHL**	**73**	**34**	**53**	**87**	**72**	**7**	**3**	**6**	**9**	**23**
	NHL Totals		**230**	**97**	**155**	**252**	**210**	**25**	**9**	**16**	**25**	**35**

a NHL/Upper Deck All-Rookie Team (1991)

Played in NHL All-Star Game (1992)

FEDOTOV, ANATOLI

Defense. Shoots left. 5'11", 178 lbs. Born, Saratov, Soviet Union, May 11, 1966.
(Anaheim's 10th choice, 238th overall, in 1993 Entry Draft).

			Regular Season					Playoffs				
Season	Club	Lea	GP	G	A	TP	PIM	GP	G	A	TP	PIM
1985-86	Moscow D'amo	USSR	35	0	2	2	10	....	....	....	....	....
1986-87	Moscow D'amo	USSR	18	3	2	5	12	....	....	....	....	....
1987-88	Moscow D'amo	USSR	48	2	3	5	38	....	....	....	....	....
1988-89	Moscow D'amo	USSR	40	2	1	3	24	....	....	....	....	....
1989-90	Moscow D'amo	USSR	41	2	4	6	22	....	....	....	....	....
1990-91			DID NOT PLAY									
1991-92	Moscow D'amo	CIS	11	1	0	1	8	....	....	....	....	....
1992-93	**Winnipeg**	**NHL**	**1**	**0**	**2**	**2**	**0**	....	....	....	....	....
	Moncton	AHL	76	10	37	47	99	2	0	0	0	0
	NHL Totals		**1**	**0**	**2**	**2**	**0**	....	....	....	....	....

FEDYK, BRENT (FEH-dihk)

Left wing. Shoots right. 6', 195 lbs. Born, Yorkton, Sask., March 8, 1967.
(Detroit's 1st choice, 8th overall, in 1985 Entry Draft).

			Regular Season					Playoffs				
Season	Club	Lea	GP	G	A	TP	PIM	GP	G	A	TP	PIM
1983-84	Regina	WHL	63	15	28	43	30	23	8	7	15	6
1984-85	Regina	WHL	66	35	35	70	48	8	5	4	9	0
1985-86	Regina	WHL	50	43	34	77	47	5	0	1	1	0
1986-87	Regina	WHL	12	9	6	15	9	....	....	....	....	....
	Seattle	WHL	13	5	11	16	9	....	....	....	....	....
	Portland	WHL	11	5	4	9	6	14	5	6	11	0
1987-88	**Detroit**	**NHL**	**2**	**0**	**1**	**1**	**2**	....	....	....	....	....
	Adirondack	AHL	34	9	11	20	22	5	0	2	2	6
1988-89	**Detroit**	**NHL**	**5**	**2**	**0**	**2**	**0**	....	....	....	....	....
	Adirondack	AHL	66	40	28	68	33	15	7	8	15	23
1989-90	**Detroit**	**NHL**	**27**	**1**	**4**	**5**	**6**	....	....	....	....	....
	Adirondack	AHL	33	14	15	29	24	6	2	1	3	4
1990-91	**Detroit**	**NHL**	**67**	**16**	**19**	**35**	**38**	**6**	**1**	**0**	**1**	**2**
1991-92	**Detroit**	**NHL**	**61**	**5**	**8**	**13**	**42**	**1**	**0**	**0**	**0**	**2**
	Adirondack	AHL	1	0	2	2	0	....	....	....	....	....
1992-93	**Philadelphia**	**NHL**	**74**	**21**	**38**	**59**	**48**	....	....	....	....	....
	NHL Totals		**236**	**45**	**70**	**115**	**136**	**7**	**1**	**0**	**1**	**4**

Traded to **Philadelphia** by **Detroit** for Philadelphia's fourth round choice (later traded to Boston — Boston selected Charles Paquette) in 1993 Entry Draft, October 1, 1992.

FELSNER, DENNY

Left wing. Shoots left. 6', 195 lbs. Born, Warren, MI, April 29, 1970.
(St. Louis' 3rd choice, 55th overall, in 1989 Entry Draft).

			Regular Season					Playoffs				
Season	Club	Lea	GP	G	A	TP	PIM	GP	G	A	TP	PIM
1988-89	U. of Michigan	CCHA	39	30	19	49	22	....	....	....	....	....
1989-90	U. of Michigan	CCHA	33	27	16	43	24	....	....	....	....	....
1990-91ab	U. of Michigan	CCHA	46	*40	35	75	58	....	....	....	....	....
1991-92ac	U. of Michigan	CCHA	44	42	52	94	46	....	....	....	....	....
	St. Louis	**NHL**	**3**	**0**	**1**	**1**	**0**	**1**	**0**	**0**	**0**	**0**
1992-93	**St. Louis**	**NHL**	**6**	**0**	**3**	**3**	**2**	**9**	**2**	**3**	**5**	**2**
	Peoria	IHL	29	14	21	35	8	....	....	....	....	....
	NHL Totals		**9**	**0**	**4**	**4**	**2**	**10**	**2**	**3**	**5**	**2**

a CCHA First All-Star Team (1991, 1992)
b NCAA West Second All-American Team (1991)
c NCAA West First All-American Team (1992)

FENTON, ERIC

Center. Shoots right. 6'2", 190 lbs. Born, Troy, NY, July 17, 1969.
(NY Rangers' 10th choice, 202nd overall, in 1988 Entry Draft).

			Regular Season					Playoffs				
Season	Club	Lea	GP	G	A	TP	PIM	GP	G	A	TP	PIM
1989-90	U. of Maine	H.E.	7	2	2	4	2	....	....	....	....	....
1990-91	U. of Maine	H.E.	10	0	1	1	16	....	....	....	....	....
1992-93	U. of Maine	H.E.	31	21	15	36	76	....	....	....	....	....

FENYVES, DAVID (FEHN-vehs)

Defense. Shoots left. 6', 192 lbs. Born, Dunnville, Ont., April 29, 1960.

			Regular Season					Playoffs				
Season	Club	Lea	GP	G	A	TP	PIM	GP	G	A	TP	PIM
1978-79	Peterborough	OHA	66	2	23	25	122	19	0	5	5	18
1979-80a	Peterborough	OHA	66	9	36	45	92	14	0	3	3	14
1980-81	Rochester	AHL	77	6	16	22	146	....	....	....	....	....
1981-82	Rochester	AHL	73	3	14	17	68	5	0	1	1	4
1982-83	**Buffalo**	**NHL**	**24**	**0**	**8**	**8**	**14**	**4**	**0**	**0**	**0**	**0**
	Rochester	AHL	51	2	19	21	45	....	....	....	....	....
1983-84	**Buffalo**	**NHL**	**10**	**0**	**4**	**4**	**9**	**2**	**0**	**0**	**0**	**7**
	Rochester	AHL	70	3	16	19	55	16	1	4	5	22
1984-85	**Buffalo**	**NHL**	**60**	**1**	**8**	**9**	**27**	**5**	**0**	**0**	**0**	**2**
	Rochester	AHL	9	0	3	3	8	....	....	....	....	....
1985-86	**Buffalo**	**NHL**	**47**	**0**	**7**	**7**	**37**	....	....	....	....	....
1986-87	**Buffalo**	**NHL**	**7**	**1**	**0**	**1**	**0**	....	....	....	....	....
bc	Rochester	AHL	71	6	16	22	57	18	3	12	15	10
1987-88	**Philadelphia**	**NHL**	**5**	**0**	**0**	**0**	**0**	....	....	....	....	....
de	Hershey	AHL	75	11	40	51	47	12	1	8	9	10
1988-89	**Philadelphia**	**NHL**	**1**	**0**	**1**	**1**	**0**	....	....	....	....	....
de	Hershey	AHL	79	15	51	66	41	12	2	6	8	6
1989-90	**Philadelphia**	**NHL**	**12**	**0**	**0**	**0**	**4**	....	....	....	....	....
	Hershey	AHL	66	6	37	43	57	....	....	....	....	....
1990-91	**Philadelphia**	**NHL**	**40**	**1**	**4**	**5**	**28**	....	....	....	....	....
	Hershey	AHL	29	4	11	15	13	7	0	3	3	6
1991-92	Hershey	AHL	68	4	24	28	29	6	1	1	2	10
1992-93	Hershey	AHL	42	3	11	14	14	....	....	....	....	....
	NHL Totals		**206**	**3**	**32**	**35**	**119**	**11**	**0**	**0**	**0**	**9**

a OHA Second All-Star Team (1980)
b AHL Second All-Star Team (1987)
c Named AHL Playoff MVP (1987)
d AHL First All-Star Team (1988, 1989)
e Won Eddie Shore Plaque (Outstanding Defenseman-AHL) (1988, 1989)

Signed as a free agent by **Buffalo**, October 31, 1979. Claimed by **Philadelphia** in NHL Waiver Draft, October 5, 1987.

FERGUS, THOMAS JOSEPH (TOM)

Center. Shoots left. 6'3", 210 lbs. Born, Chicago, IL, June 16, 1962.
(Boston's 2nd choice, 60th overall, in 1980 Entry Draft).

			Regular Season					Playoffs				
Season	Club	Lea	GP	G	A	TP	PIM	GP	G	A	TP	PIM
1979-80	Peterborough	OHA	63	8	6	14	14	14	1	5	6	6
1980-81	Peterborough	OHA	63	43	45	88	33	5	1	4	5	2
1981-82	**Boston**	**NHL**	**61**	**15**	**24**	**39**	**12**	**6**	**3**	**0**	**3**	**0**
1982-83	**Boston**	**NHL**	**80**	**28**	**35**	**63**	**39**	**15**	**2**	**2**	**4**	**15**
1983-84	**Boston**	**NHL**	**69**	**25**	**36**	**61**	**12**	**3**	**2**	**0**	**2**	**9**
1984-85	**Boston**	**NHL**	**79**	**30**	**43**	**73**	**75**	**5**	**0**	**0**	**0**	**4**
1985-86	**Toronto**	**NHL**	**78**	**31**	**42**	**73**	**64**	**10**	**5**	**7**	**12**	**6**
1986-87	**Toronto**	**NHL**	**57**	**21**	**28**	**49**	**57**	**2**	**0**	**1**	**1**	**2**
	Newmarket	AHL	1	0	1	1	0	....	....	....	....	....
1987-88	**Toronto**	**NHL**	**63**	**19**	**31**	**50**	**81**	**6**	**2**	**3**	**5**	**2**
1988-89	**Toronto**	**NHL**	**80**	**22**	**45**	**67**	**48**	....	....	....	....	....
1989-90	**Toronto**	**NHL**	**54**	**19**	**26**	**45**	**62**	**5**	**2**	**1**	**3**	**4**
1990-91	**Toronto**	**NHL**	**14**	**5**	**4**	**9**	**8**	....	....	....	....	....
1991-92	**Toronto**	**NHL**	**11**	**1**	**3**	**4**	**4**	....	....	....	....	....
	Vancouver	**NHL**	**44**	**14**	**20**	**34**	**17**	**13**	**5**	**3**	**8**	**6**
1992-93	**Vancouver**	**NHL**	**36**	**5**	**9**	**14**	**20**	....	....	....	....	....
	NHL Totals		**726**	**235**	**346**	**581**	**499**	**65**	**21**	**17**	**38**	**48**

Traded to **Toronto** by **Boston** for Bill Derlago, October 11, 1985. Traded to **Vancouver** by **Toronto** for cash, December 18, 1991.

FERGUSON, CRAIG

Right wing. Shoots left. 6', 185 lbs. Born, Castro Valley, CA, April 8, 1970.
(Montreal's 7th choice, 146th overall, in 1989 Entry Draft).

			Regular Season					Playoffs				
Season	Club	Lea	GP	G	A	TP	PIM	GP	G	A	TP	PIM
1988-89	Yale	ECAC	24	11	6	17	20	....	....	....	....	....
1989-90	Yale	ECAC	28	6	13	19	36	....	....	....	....	....
1990-91	Yale	ECAC	29	11	10	21	34	....	....	....	....	....
1991-92	Yale	ECAC	27	9	16	25	26	....	....	....	....	....
1992-93	Fredericton	AHL	55	15	13	28	20	5	0	1	1	2
	Wheeling	ECHL	9	6	5	11	24	....	....	....	....	....

FERNER, MARK

Defense. Shoots left. 6', 193 lbs. Born, Regina, Sask., September 5, 1965.
(Buffalo's 12th choice, 194th overall, in 1983 Entry Draft).

			Regular Season					Playoffs				
Season	Club	Lea	GP	G	A	TP	PIM	GP	G	A	TP	PIM
1982-83	Kamloops	WHL	69	6	15	21	81	7	0	0	0	7
1983-84	Kamloops	WHL	72	9	30	39	169	14	1	8	9	20
1984-85a	Kamloops	WHL	69	15	39	54	91	15	4	9	13	21
1985-86	Rochester	AHL	63	3	14	17	87	....	....	....	....	....
1986-87	**Buffalo**	**NHL**	**13**	**0**	**3**	**3**	**9**	....	....	....	....	....
	Rochester	AHL	54	0	12	12	157	....	....	....	....	....
1987-88	Rochester	AHL	69	1	25	26	165	7	1	4	5	31
1988-89	**Buffalo**	**NHL**	**2**	**0**	**0**	**0**	**2**	....	....	....	....	....
	Rochester	AHL	55	0	18	18	97	....	....	....	....	....
1989-90	**Washington**	**NHL**	**2**	**0**	**0**	**0**	**0**	....	....	....	....	....
	Baltimore	AHL	74	7	28	35	76	11	1	2	3	21
1990-91	**Washington**	**NHL**	**7**	**0**	**1**	**1**	**4**	....	....	....	....	....
b	Baltimore	AHL	61	14	40	54	38	6	1	4	5	24
1991-92	Baltimore	AHL	57	7	38	45	67	....	....	....	....	....
	St. John's	AHL	15	1	8	9	6	14	2	14	16	38
1992-93	New Haven	AHL	34	5	7	12	69	....	....	....	....	....
	San Diego	IHL	26	0	15	15	34	11	1	2	3	8
	NHL Totals		**24**	**0**	**4**	**4**	**15**	....	....	....	....	....

a WHL First All-Star Team, West Division (1985)
b AHL Second All-Star Team (1991)

Traded to **Washington** by **Buffalo** for Scott McCrory, June 1, 1989. Traded to **Toronto** by **Washington** for future considerations, February 27, 1992. Claimed by **Anaheim** from **Ottawa** in Expansion Draft, June 24, 1993.

FERRARO, CHRIS

Right wing. Shoots right. 5'10", 175 lbs. Born, Port Jefferson, NY, January 24, 1973.
(NY Rangers' 4th choice, 85th overall, in 1992 Entry Draft).

			Regular Season					Playoffs				
Season	Club	Lea	GP	G	A	TP	PIM	GP	G	A	TP	PIM
1991-92	Dubuque	USHL	20	30	19	49	52	....	....	....	....	....
	Waterloo	USHL	18	19	31	50	54	....	....	....	....	....
1992-93	U. of Maine	H.E.	39	25	26	51	46	....	....	....	....	....

FERRARO, PETER

Center. Shoots right. 5'10", 175 lbs. Born, Port Jefferson, NY, January 24, 1973.
(NY Rangers' 1st choice, 24th overall, in 1992 Entry Draft).

			Regular Season					Playoffs				
Season	Club	Lea	GP	G	A	TP	PIM	GP	G	A	TP	PIM
1991-92	Dubuque	USHL	21	25	25	50	92	....	....	....	....	....
	Waterloo	USHL	21	23	28	51	76	....	....	....	....	....
1992-93	U. of Maine	H.E.	36	18	32	50	106	....	....	....	....	....

FERRARO, RAY

Center. Shoots left. 5'10", 185 lbs. Born, Trail, B.C., August 23, 1964.
(Hartford's 5th choice, 88th overall, in 1982 Entry Draft).

			Regular Season					Playoffs				
Season	Club	Lea	GP	G	A	TP	PIM	GP	G	A	TP	PIM
1982-83	Portland	WHL	50	41	49	90	39	14	14	10	24	13
1983-84ab	Brandon	WHL	72	*108	84	*192	84	11	13	15	28	20
1984-85	**Hartford**	**NHL**	**44**	**11**	**17**	**28**	**40**	....	....	....	....	....
	Binghamton	AHL	37	20	13	33	29	....	....	....	....	....
1985-86	**Hartford**	**NHL**	**76**	**30**	**47**	**77**	**57**	**10**	**3**	**6**	**9**	**4**
1986-87	**Hartford**	**NHL**	**80**	**27**	**32**	**59**	**42**	**6**	**1**	**1**	**2**	**8**
1987-88	**Hartford**	**NHL**	**68**	**21**	**29**	**50**	**81**	**6**	**1**	**1**	**2**	**6**
1988-89	**Hartford**	**NHL**	**80**	**41**	**35**	**76**	**86**	**4**	**2**	**0**	**2**	**4**
1989-90	**Hartford**	**NHL**	**79**	**25**	**29**	**54**	**109**	**7**	**0**	**3**	**3**	**2**
1990-91	**Hartford**	**NHL**	**15**	**2**	**5**	**7**	**18**	....	....	....	....	....
	NY Islanders	**NHL**	**61**	**19**	**16**	**35**	**52**	....	....	....	....	....
1991-92	**NY Islanders**	**NHL**	**80**	**40**	**40**	**80**	**92**	....	....	....	....	....
1992-93	**NY Islanders**	**NHL**	**46**	**14**	**13**	**27**	**40**	**18**	**13**	**7**	**20**	**18**
	Capital Dist.	AHL	1	0	2	2	2	....	....	....	....	....
	NHL Totals		**629**	**230**	**263**	**493**	**617**	**51**	**20**	**18**	**38**	**42**

a WHL First All-Star Team (1984)
b WHL Most Valuable Player (1984)

Played in NHL All-Star Game (1992)

Traded to **NY Islanders** by **Hartford** for Doug Crossman, November 13, 1990.

FETISOV, VIACHESLAV (SLAVA) (feh-TEE-sahf)

Defense. Shoots left. 6'1", 220 lbs. Born, Moscow, Soviet Union, April 20, 1958.
(New Jersey's 6th choice, 150th overall, in 1983 Entry Draft).

			Regular Season					Playoffs				
Season	Club	Lea	GP	G	A	TP	PIM	GP	G	A	TP	PIM
1974-75	CSKA	USSR	1	0	0	0	0	....	....	....	....	....
1976-77	CSKA	USSR	27	3	4	7	14	....	....	....	....	....
1977-78a	CSKA	USSR	35	9	18	27	46	....	....	....	....	....
1978-79	CSKA	USSR	29	10	19	29	40	....	....	....	....	....
1979-80	CSKA	USSR	37	10	14	24	46	....	....	....	....	....
1980-81	CSKA	USSR	48	13	16	29	44	....	....	....	....	....
1981-82ac	CSKA	USSR	46	15	26	41	20	....	....	....	....	....
1982-83a	CSKA	USSR	43	6	17	23	46	....	....	....	....	....
1983-84ab	CSKA	USSR	44	19	30	49	38	....	....	....	....	....
1984-85a	CSKA	USSR	20	13	12	25	6	....	....	....	....	....
1985-86abc	CSKA	USSR	40	15	19	34	12	....	....	....	....	....
1986-87ab	CSKA	USSR	39	13	20	33	18	....	....	....	....	....
1987-88ab	CSKA	USSR	46	18	17	35	26	....	....	....	....	....
1988-89	CSKA	USSR	23	9	9	18	18	....	....	....	....	....
1989-90	**New Jersey**	**NHL**	**72**	**8**	**34**	**42**	**52**	**6**	**0**	**2**	**2**	**10**
1990-91	**New Jersey**	**NHL**	**67**	**3**	**16**	**19**	**62**	**7**	**0**	**0**	**0**	**17**
	Utica	AHL	1	1	1	2	0	....	....	....	....	....
1991-92	**New Jersey**	**NHL**	**70**	**3**	**23**	**26**	**108**	**6**	**0**	**3**	**3**	**8**
1992-93	**New Jersey**	**NHL**	**76**	**4**	**23**	**27**	**158**	**5**	**0**	**2**	**2**	**4**
	NHL Totals		**285**	**18**	**96**	**114**	**380**	**24**	**0**	**7**	**7**	**39**

a Soviet National League All-Star Team (1979, 1980, 1982-88)
b Leningradskaya-Pravda Trophy-Top Scoring Defenseman (1984, 1986-88)
c Soviet Player of the Year (1982, 1986, 1988)

FIEBELKORN, JED

Right wing. Shoots right. 6'3", 220 lbs. Born, Minneapolis, MN, September 1, 1972.
(St. Louis' 9th choice, 197th overall, in 1991 Entry Draft).

			Regular Season					Playoffs				
Season	Club	Lea	GP	G	A	TP	PIM	GP	G	A	TP	PIM
1991-92	U. Minnesota	WCHA	7	0	0	0	10	....	....	....	....	....
1992-93	Minnesota	WCHA	34	8	5	13	42	....	....	....	....	....

FILIMONOV, DMITRI

Defense. Shoots left. 6'4", 207 lbs. Born, Perm, Soviet Union, October 14, 1971.
(Winnipeg's 2nd choice, 49th overall, in 1991 Entry Draft).

			Regular Season					Playoffs				
Season	Club	Lea	GP	G	A	TP	PIM	GP	G	A	TP	PIM
1990-91	Moscow D'amo	USSR	45	4	6	10	12	....	....	....	....	....
1991-92	Moscow D'amo	CIS	38	3	2	5	12	....	....	....	....	....
1992-93	Moscow D'amo	CIS	42	2	3	5	30	10	1	2	3	2

Rights traded to **Ottawa** by **Winnipeg** for Ottawa's fourth round choice (Ruslam Batyrshin) in 1993 Entry Draft, March 14, 1993.

FILIPEK, DARYL

Defense. Shoots left. 6'1", 185 lbs. Born, Acton, Ont., November 13, 1970.
(Vancouver's 6th choice, 128th overall, in 1990 Entry Draft).

			Regular Season					Playoffs				
Season	Club	Lea	GP	G	A	TP	PIM	GP	G	A	TP	PIM
1989-90	Ferris State	CCHA	38	4	20	24	44	....	....	....	....	....
1990-91	Ferris State	CCHA	39	6	11	17	68	....	....	....	....	....
1991-92	Ferris State	CCHA	30	4	6	10	28	....	....	....	....	....
1992-93	Ferris State	CCHA	41	12	12	24	62	....	....	....	....	....

FINLEY, JEFF

Defense. Shoots left. 6'2", 204 lbs. Born, Edmonton, Alta., April 14, 1967.
(NY Islanders' 4th choice, 55th overall, in 1985 Entry Draft).

			Regular Season					Playoffs				
Season	Club	Lea	GP	G	A	TP	PIM	GP	G	A	TP	PIM
1983-84	Portland	WHL	5	0	0	0	5	5	0	1	1	4
1984-85	Portland	WHL	69	6	44	50	57	6	1	2	3	2
1985-86	Portland	WHL	70	11	59	70	83	15	1	7	8	16
1986-87	Portland	WHL	72	13	53	66	113	20	1	*21	22	27
1987-88	**NY Islanders**	**NHL**	**10**	**0**	**5**	**5**	**15**	**1**	**0**	**0**	**0**	**2**
	Springfield	AHL	52	5	18	23	50	....	....	....	....	....
1988-89	**NY Islanders**	**NHL**	**4**	**0**	**0**	**0**	**6**	....	....	....	....	....
	Springfield	AHL	65	3	16	19	55	....	....	....	....	....
1989-90	**NY Islanders**	**NHL**	**11**	**0**	**1**	**1**	**0**	**5**	**0**	**2**	**2**	**2**
	Springfield	AHL	57	1	15	16	41	13	1	4	5	23
1990-91	**NY Islanders**	**NHL**	**11**	**0**	**0**	**0**	**4**	....	....	....	....	....
	Capital Dist.	AHL	67	10	34	44	34	....	....	....	....	....
1991-92	**NY Islanders**	**NHL**	**51**	**1**	**10**	**11**	**26**	....	....	....	....	....
	Capital Dist.	AHL	20	1	9	10	6	....	....	....	....	....
1992-93	Capital Dist.	AHL	61	6	29	35	34	4	0	1	1	0
	NHL Totals		**87**	**1**	**16**	**17**	**51**	**6**	**0**	**2**	**2**	**4**

Traded to **Ottawa** by **NY Islanders** for Chris Luongo, June 30, 1993. Signed as a free agent by **Philadelphia**, July 30, 1993.

FINN, SHANNON

Defense. Shoots left. 6'2", 190 lbs. Born, Brampton, Ont., January 25, 1972.
(Philadelphia's 1st choice, 10th overall, in 1993 Supplemental Draft).

			Regular Season					Playoffs				
Season	Club	Lea	GP	G	A	TP	PIM	GP	G	A	TP	PIM
1991-92	Ill.-Chicago	CCHA	36	6	14	20	80	....	....	....	....	....
1992-93	Ill.-Chicago	CCHA	36	6	13	19	48	....	....	....	....	....

FINN, STEVEN

Defense. Shoots left. 6', 198 lbs. Born, Laval, Que., August 20, 1966.
(Quebec's 3rd choice, 57th overall, in 1984 Entry Draft).

			Regular Season					Playoffs				
Season	Club	Lea	GP	G	A	TP	PIM	GP	G	A	TP	PIM
1982-83	Laval	QMJHL	69	7	30	37	108	6	0	2	2	6
1983-84	Laval	QMJHL	68	7	39	46	159	14	1	6	7	27
1984-85a	Laval	QMJHL	61	20	33	53	169	....	....	....	....	....
	Fredericton	AHL	4	0	0	0	14	6	1	1	2	4
1985-86	**Quebec**	**NHL**	**17**	**0**	**1**	**1**	**28**	....	....	....	....	....
	Laval	QMJHL	29	4	15	19	111	14	6	16	22	57
1986-87	**Quebec**	**NHL**	**36**	**2**	**5**	**7**	**40**	**13**	**0**	**2**	**2**	**29**
	Fredericton	AHL	38	7	19	26	73	....	....	....	....	....
1987-88	**Quebec**	**NHL**	**75**	**3**	**7**	**10**	**198**	....	....	....	....	....
1988-89	**Quebec**	**NHL**	**77**	**2**	**6**	**8**	**235**	....	....	....	....	....
1989-90	**Quebec**	**NHL**	**64**	**3**	**9**	**12**	**208**	....	....	....	....	....
1990-91	**Quebec**	**NHL**	**71**	**6**	**13**	**19**	**228**	....	....	....	....	....
1991-92	**Quebec**	**NHL**	**65**	**4**	**7**	**11**	**194**	....	....	....	....	....
1992-93	**Quebec**	**NHL**	**80**	**5**	**9**	**14**	**160**	**6**	**0**	**1**	**1**	**8**
	NHL Totals		**485**	**25**	**57**	**82**	**1291**	**19**	**0**	**3**	**3**	**37**

a QMJHL Second All-Star Team (1985)

FIORENTINO, PETER

Defense. Shoots right. 6'1", 205 lbs. Born, Niagara Falls, Ont., December 22, 1968.
(NY Rangers' 11th choice, 215th overall, in 1988 Entry Draft).

			Regular Season					Playoffs				
Season	Club	Lea	GP	G	A	TP	PIM	GP	G	A	TP	PIM
1985-86	S.S. Marie	OHL	58	1	6	7	87	....	....	....	....	....
1986-87	S.S. Marie	OHL	64	1	12	13	187	....	....	....	....	....
1987-88	S.S. Marie	OHL	65	5	27	32	252	6	2	2	4	21
1988-89	S.S. Marie	OHL	55	5	24	29	220	....	....	....	....	....
	Denver	IHL	10	0	0	0	39	4	0	0	0	24
1989-90	Flint	IHL	64	2	7	9	302	....	....	....	....	....
1990-91	Binghamton	AHL	55	2	11	13	361	1	0	0	0	0
1991-92	**NY Rangers**	**NHL**	**1**	**0**	**0**	**0**	**0**	....	....	....	....	....
	Binghamton	AHL	70	2	11	13	340	5	0	1	1	24
1992-93	Binghamton	AHL	64	9	5	14	286	13	0	3	3	22
	NHL Totals		**1**	**0**	**0**	**0**	**0**	....	....	....	....	....

FISHER, CRAIG

Center. Shoots left. 6'3", 180 lbs. Born, Oshawa, Ont., June 30, 1970.
(Philadelphia's 3rd choice, 56th overall, in 1988 Entry Draft).

			Regular Season					Playoffs				
Season	Club	Lea	GP	G	A	TP	PIM	GP	G	A	TP	PIM
1988-89	Miami-Ohio	CCHA	37	22	20	42	37	....	....	....	....	....
1989-90a	Miami-Ohio	CCHA	39	37	29	66	38	....	....	....	....	....
	Philadelphia	**NHL**	**2**	**0**	**0**	**0**	**0**	....	....	....	....	....
1990-91	**Philadelphia**	**NHL**	**2**	**0**	**0**	**0**	**0**	....	....	....	....	....
	Hershey	AHL	77	43	36	79	46	7	5	3	8	2
1991-92	Cape Breton	AHL	60	20	25	45	28	1	0	0	0	0
1992-93	Cape Breton	AHL	75	32	29	61	74	1	0	0	0	2
	NHL Totals		**4**	**0**	**0**	**0**	**0**	....	....	....	....	....

a CCHA First All-Star Team (1990)

Traded to **Edmonton** by **Philadelphia** with Scott Mellanby and Craig Berube for Dave Brown, Corey Foster and Jari Kurri, May 30, 1991.

FITZGERALD, RUSTY

Center. Shoots left. 6'1", 186 lbs. Born, Minneapolis, MN, October 4, 1972.
(Pittsburgh's 2nd choice, 38th overall, in 1991 Entry Draft).

			Regular Season					Playoffs				
Season	Club	Lea	GP	G	A	TP	PIM	GP	G	A	TP	PIM
1991-92	Minn.-Duluth	WCHA	37	9	11	20	40	....	....	....	....	....
1992-93	Minn.-Duluth	WCHA	39	24	23	47	48	....	....	....	....	....

FITZGERALD, TOM

Right wing/Center. Shoots right. 6'1", 195 lbs. Born, Melrose, MA, August 28, 1968.
(NY Islanders' 1st choice, 17th overall, in 1986 Entry Draft).

			Regular Season					Playoffs				
Season	Club	Lea	GP	G	A	TP	PIM	GP	G	A	TP	PIM
1986-87	Providence	H.E.	27	8	14	22	22	....	....	....	....	....
1987-88	Providence	H.E.	36	19	15	34	50	....	....	....	....	....
1988-89	**NY Islanders**	**NHL**	**23**	**3**	**5**	**8**	**10**	....	....	....	....	....
	Springfield	AHL	61	24	18	42	43	....	....	....	....	....
1989-90	**NY Islanders**	**NHL**	**19**	**2**	**5**	**7**	**4**	**4**	**1**	**0**	**1**	**4**
	Springfield	AHL	53	30	23	53	32	14	2	9	11	13
1990-91	**NY Islanders**	**NHL**	**41**	**5**	**5**	**10**	**24**	....	....	....	....	....
	Capital Dist.	AHL	27	7	7	14	50	....	....	....	....	....
1991-92	**NY Islanders**	**NHL**	**45**	**6**	**11**	**17**	**28**	....	....	....	....	....
	Capital Dist.	AHL	4	1	1	2	4	....	....	....	....	....
1992-93	**NY Islanders**	**NHL**	**77**	**9**	**18**	**27**	**34**	**18**	**2**	**5**	**7**	**18**
	NHL Totals		**205**	**25**	**44**	**69**	**100**	**22**	**3**	**5**	**8**	**22**

Claimed by **Florida** from **NY Islanders** in Expansion Draft, June 24, 1993.

FITZPATRICK, RORY

Defense. Shoots right. 6'1", 190 lbs. Born, Rochester, NY, January 11, 1975.
(Montreal's 2nd choice, 47th overall, in 1993 Entry Draft).

			Regular Season					Playoffs				
Season	Club	Lea	GP	G	A	TP	PIM	GP	G	A	TP	PIM
1991-92	Rochester	NEJHL	20	8	28	36	141	....	....	....	....	....
1992-93	Sudbury	OHL	58	4	20	24	68	14	0	0	0	17

FLATLEY, PATRICK (FLAT-lee)

Right wing. Shoots right. 6'2", 197 lbs. Born, Toronto, Ont., October 3, 1963.
(NY Islanders' 1st choice, 21st overall, in 1982 Entry Draft).

			Regular Season					Playoffs				
Season	Club	Lea	GP	G	A	TP	PIM	GP	G	A	TP	PIM
1981-82	U. Wisconsin	WCHA	17	10	9	19	40	....	....	....	....	....
1982-83ab	U. Wisconsin	WCHA	26	17	24	41	48	....	....	....	....	....
1983-84	Cdn. Olympic	....	57	33	17	50	136	....	....	....	....	....
	NY Islanders	**NHL**	**16**	**2**	**7**	**9**	**6**	**21**	**9**	**6**	**15**	**14**
1984-85	**NY Islanders**	**NHL**	**78**	**20**	**31**	**51**	**106**	**4**	**1**	**0**	**1**	**6**
1985-86	**NY Islanders**	**NHL**	**73**	**18**	**34**	**52**	**66**	**3**	**0**	**0**	**0**	**21**
1986-87	**NY Islanders**	**NHL**	**63**	**16**	**35**	**51**	**81**	**11**	**3**	**2**	**5**	**6**
1987-88	**NY Islanders**	**NHL**	**40**	**9**	**15**	**24**	**28**	....	....	....	....	....
1988-89	**NY Islanders**	**NHL**	**41**	**10**	**15**	**25**	**31**	....	....	....	....	....
	Springfield	AHL	2	1	1	2	2	....	....	....	....	....
1989-90	**NY Islanders**	**NHL**	**62**	**17**	**32**	**49**	**101**	**5**	**3**	**0**	**3**	**2**
1990-91	**NY Islanders**	**NHL**	**56**	**20**	**25**	**45**	**74**	....	....	....	....	....
1991-92	**NY Islanders**	**NHL**	**38**	**8**	**28**	**36**	**31**	....	....	....	....	....
1992-93	**NY Islanders**	**NHL**	**80**	**13**	**47**	**60**	**63**	**15**	**2**	**7**	**9**	**12**
	NHL Totals		**547**	**133**	**269**	**402**	**587**	**59**	**18**	**15**	**33**	**61**

a WCHA First All-Star Team (1983)
b Named to NCAA All-Tournament Team (1983)

FLEMING, GERRY

Defense. Shoots left. 6'5", 240 lbs. Born, Montreal, Que., October 16, 1967.

			Regular Season					Playoffs				
Season	Club	Lea	GP	G	A	TP	PIM	GP	G	A	TP	PIM
1990-91	U.P.E.I.	AUAA				UNAVAILABLE						
1991-92	Charlottetown	Sr.				UNAVAILABLE						
	Fredericton	AHL	37	4	6	10	133	1	0	0	0	7
1992-93	Fredericton	AHL	64	9	17	26	262	5	1	2	3	14

Signed as a free agent by **Montreal**, February 17, 1992.

FLEURY, THEOREN

Right wing. Shoots right. 5'6", 160 lbs. Born, Oxbow, Sask., June 29, 1968.
(Calgary's 9th choice, 166th overall, in 1987 Entry Draft).

			Regular Season					Playoffs				
Season	Club	Lea	GP	G	A	TP	PIM	GP	G	A	TP	PIM
1984-85	Moose Jaw	WHL	71	29	46	75	82	....	....	....	....	....
1985-86	Moose Jaw	WHL	72	43	65	108	124	....	....	....	....	....
1986-87	Moose Jaw	WHL	66	61	68	129	110	9	7	9	16	34
1987-88	Moose Jaw	WHL	65	68	92	*160	235	....	....	....	....	....
	Salt Lake	IHL	2	3	4	7	7	8	11	5	16	16
1988-89	**Calgary**	**NHL**	**36**	**14**	**20**	**34**	**46**	**22**	**5**	**6**	**11**	**24**
	Salt Lake	IHL	40	37	37	74	81	....	....	....	....	....
1989-90	**Calgary**	**NHL**	**80**	**31**	**35**	**66**	**157**	**6**	**2**	**3**	**5**	**10**
1990-91a	**Calgary**	**NHL**	**79**	**51**	**53**	**104**	**136**	**7**	**2**	**5**	**7**	**14**
1991-92	**Calgary**	**NHL**	**80**	**33**	**40**	**73**	**133**	....	....	....	....	....
1992-93	**Calgary**	**NHL**	**83**	**34**	**66**	**100**	**88**	**6**	**5**	**7**	**12**	**27**
	NHL Totals		**358**	**163**	**214**	**377**	**560**	**41**	**14**	**21**	**35**	**75**

a Co-winner of Alka-Seltzer Plus Award with Marty McSorley (1991)
Played in NHL All-Star Game (1991, 1992)

FLINTON, ERIC

Left wing. Shoots left. 6'2", 200 lbs. Born, William Lake, B.C., February 2, 1972.
(Ottawa's 1st choice, 1st overall, in 1993 Supplemental Draft).

			Regular Season					Playoffs				
Season	Club	Lea	GP	G	A	TP	PIM	GP	G	A	TP	PIM
1991-92	N. Hampshire	H.E.	36	6	4	10	10	....	....	....	....	....
1992-93	N. Hampshire	H.E.	37	18	18	36	14	....	....	....	....	....

FLOMENHOFT, STEVE

Center. Shoots right. 6', 215 lbs. Born, Riverwoods, IL, May 4, 1971.
(Ottawa's 1st choice, 2nd overall, in 1992 Supplemental Draft).

			Regular Season					Playoffs				
Season	Club	Lea	GP	G	A	TP	PIM	GP	G	A	TP	PIM
1989-90	Harvard	ECAC	28	5	5	10	22	....	....	....	....	....
1990-91	Harvard	ECAC	29	12	14	26	48	....	....	....	....	....
1991-92	Harvard	ECAC	27	14	17	31	30	....	....	....	....	....
1992-93	Harvard	ECAC	31	11	25	36	60	....	....	....	....	....
	New Haven	AHL	2	0	1	1	0	....	....	....	....	....

FOGARTY, BRYAN

Defense. Shoots left. 6'2", 198 lbs. Born, Brantford, Ont., June 11, 1969.
(Quebec's 1st choice, 9th overall, in 1987 Entry Draft).

			Regular Season					Playoffs				
Season	Club	Lea	GP	G	A	TP	PIM	GP	G	A	TP	PIM
1985-86	Kingston	OHL	47	2	19	21	14	10	1	3	4	4
1986-87a	Kingston	OHL	56	20	50	70	46	12	2	3	5	5
1987-88	Kingston	OHL	48	11	36	47	50	....	....	....	....	....
1988-89abc	Niagara Falls	OHL	60	47	*108	*155	88	17	10	22	32	36
1989-90	**Quebec**	**NHL**	**45**	**4**	**10**	**14**	**31**	....	....	....	....	....
	Halifax	AHL	22	5	14	19	6	6	2	4	6	0
1990-91	**Quebec**	**NHL**	**45**	**9**	**22**	**31**	**24**	....	....	....	....	....
	Halifax	AHL	5	0	2	2	0	....	....	....	....	....
1991-92	**Quebec**	**NHL**	**20**	**3**	**12**	**15**	**16**	....	....	....	....	....
	Halifax	AHL	2	0	0	0	2	....	....	....	....	....
	New Haven	AHL	4	0	1	1	6	....	....	....	....	....
	Muskegon	IHL	8	2	4	6	30	....	....	....	....	....
1992-93	**Pittsburgh**	**NHL**	**12**	**0**	**4**	**4**	**4**	....	....	....	....	....
	Cleveland	IHL	15	2	5	7	8	3	0	1	1	17
	NHL Totals		**122**	**16**	**48**	**64**	**75**	....	....	....	....	....

a OHL First All-Star Team (1987, 1989)
b OHL Player of the Year (1989)
c Canadian Major Junior Player of the Year (1989)
Traded to **Pittsburgh** by **Quebec** for Scott Young, March 10, 1992.

FOLIGNO, MIKE ANTHONY (foh-LEE-noh)

Right wing. Shoots right. 6'2", 195 lbs. Born, Sudbury, Ont., January 29, 1959.
(Detroit's 1st choice, 3rd overall, in 1979 Entry Draft).

			Regular Season					Playoffs				
Season	Club	Lea	GP	G	A	TP	PIM	GP	G	A	TP	PIM
1975-76	Sudbury	OHA	57	22	14	36	45	....	....	....	....	....
1976-77	Sudbury	OHA	66	31	44	75	62	....	....	....	....	....
1977-78	Sudbury	OHA	67	47	39	86	112	....	....	....	....	....
1978-79a	Sudbury	OHA	68	65	85	*150	98	10	5	5	10	14
1979-80	**Detroit**	**NHL**	**80**	**36**	**35**	**71**	**109**	....	....	....	....	....
1980-81	**Detroit**	**NHL**	**80**	**28**	**35**	**63**	**210**	....	....	....	....	....
1981-82	**Detroit**	**NHL**	**26**	**13**	**13**	**26**	**28**	....	....	....	....	....
	Buffalo	**NHL**	**56**	**20**	**31**	**51**	**149**	**4**	**2**	**0**	**2**	**9**
1982-83	**Buffalo**	**NHL**	**66**	**22**	**25**	**47**	**135**	**10**	**2**	**3**	**5**	**39**
1983-84	**Buffalo**	**NHL**	**70**	**32**	**31**	**63**	**151**	**3**	**2**	**1**	**3**	**19**
1984-85	**Buffalo**	**NHL**	**77**	**27**	**29**	**56**	**154**	**5**	**1**	**3**	**4**	**12**
1985-86	**Buffalo**	**NHL**	**79**	**41**	**39**	**80**	**168**	....	....	....	....	....
1986-87	**Buffalo**	**NHL**	**75**	**30**	**29**	**59**	**176**	....	....	....	....	....
1987-88	**Buffalo**	**NHL**	**74**	**29**	**28**	**57**	**220**	**6**	**3**	**2**	**5**	**31**
1988-89	**Buffalo**	**NHL**	**75**	**27**	**22**	**49**	**156**	**5**	**3**	**1**	**4**	**21**
1989-90	**Buffalo**	**NHL**	**61**	**15**	**25**	**40**	**99**	**6**	**0**	**1**	**1**	**12**
1990-91	**Buffalo**	**NHL**	**31**	**4**	**5**	**9**	**42**	....	....	....	....	....
	Toronto	**NHL**	**37**	**8**	**7**	**15**	**65**	....	....	....	....	....
1991-92	**Toronto**	**NHL**	**33**	**6**	**8**	**14**	**50**	....	....	....	....	....
1992-93	**Toronto**	**NHL**	**55**	**13**	**5**	**18**	**84**	**18**	**2**	**6**	**8**	**42**
	NHL Totals		**975**	**351**	**367**	**718**	**1996**	**57**	**15**	**17**	**32**	**185**

a OHL First All-Star Team (1979)
Traded to **Buffalo** by **Detroit** with Dale McCourt and Brent Peterson for Danny Gare, Jim Schoenfeld and Derek Smith, December 2, 1981. Traded to **Toronto** by **Buffalo** with Buffalo's eighth round choice (Thomas Kucharcik) in 1991 Entry Draft for Brian Curran and Lou Franceschetti, December 17, 1990.

FOOTE, ADAM

Defense. Shoots right. 6'1", 180 lbs. Born, Toronto, Ont., July 10, 1971.
(Quebec's 2nd choice, 22nd overall, in 1989 Entry Draft).

			Regular Season					Playoffs				
Season	Club	Lea	GP	G	A	TP	PIM	GP	G	A	TP	PIM
1988-89	S.S. Marie	OHL	66	7	32	39	120	....	....	....	....	....
1989-90	S.S. Marie	OHL	61	12	43	55	199	....	....	....	....	....
1990-91a	S.S. Marie	OHL	59	18	51	69	93	14	5	12	17	28
1991-92	**Quebec**	**NHL**	**46**	**2**	**5**	**7**	**44**	....	....	....	....	....
	Halifax	AHL	6	0	1	1	2	....	....	....	....	....
1992-93	**Quebec**	**NHL**	**81**	**4**	**12**	**16**	**168**	**6**	**0**	**1**	**1**	**2**
	NHL Totals		**127**	**6**	**17**	**23**	**212**	**6**	**0**	**1**	**1**	**2**

a OHL First All-Star Team (1991)

FORSBERG, PETER (FOHRS-buhrg)

Center. Shoots left. 6', 190 lbs. Born, Ornskoldsvik, Sweden, July 20, 1973.
(Philadelphia's 1st choice, 6th overall, in 1991 Entry Draft).

			Regular Season					Playoffs				
Season	Club	Lea	GP	G	A	TP	PIM	GP	G	A	TP	PIM
1990-91	MoDo	Swe.	23	7	10	17	22	....	....	....	....	....
1991-92	MoDo	Swe.	39	9	18	27	78	....	....	....	....	....
1992-93	MoDo	Swe.	39	23	24	47	92	3	4	1	5	0

Traded to **Quebec** by **Philadelphia** with Steve Duchesne, Kerry Huffman, Mike Ricci, Ron Hextall, Chris Simon, Philadelphia's first choice in the 1993 (Jocelyn Thibault) and 1994 Entry Drafts and cash for Eric Lindros, June 30, 1992.

FORSLUND, TOMAS (FOHRS-luhnd)

Right wing. Shoots left. 5'11", 200 lbs. Born, Falun, Sweden, November 24, 1968.
(Calgary's 4th choice, 85th overall, in 1988 Entry Draft).

			Regular Season					Playoffs				
Season	Club	Lea	GP	G	A	TP	PIM	GP	G	A	TP	PIM
1986-87	Leksand	Swe.	23	3	5	8	4	....	....	....	....	....
1987-88	Leksand	Swe.	36	9	10	19	22	3	1	1	2	2
1988-89	Leksand	Swe.	39	14	16	30	58	10	2	4	6	6
1989-90	Leksand	Swe.	38	14	21	35	48	3	0	1	1	2
1990-91	Leksand	Swe.	22	5	10	15	10	....	....	....	....	....
1991-92	**Calgary**	**NHL**	**38**	**5**	**9**	**14**	**12**	....	....	....	....	....
	Salt Lake	IHL	22	10	6	16	25	5	2	2	4	2
1992-93	**Calgary**	**NHL**	**6**	**0**	**2**	**2**	**0**	....	....	....	....	....
	Salt Lake	IHL	63	31	23	54	68	....	....	....	....	....
	NHL Totals		**44**	**5**	**11**	**16**	**12**	....	....	....	....	....

FORTIER, MARC
Center. Shoots right. 6', 192 lbs.   Born, Windsor, Que., February 26, 1966.

			Regular Season					Playoffs				
Season	Club	Lea	GP	G	A	TP	PIM	GP	G	A	TP	PIM
1983-84	Chicoutimi	QMJHL	67	16	30	46	51	....	....	....	....	....
1984-85	Chicoutimi	QMJHL	68	35	63	98	114	14	8	4	12	16
1985-86	Chicoutimi	QMJHL	71	47	86	133	49	9	2	14	16	12
1986-87	Chicoutimi	QMJHL	65	66	135	201	39	19	11	40	51	20
1987-88	**Quebec**	**NHL**	27	4	10	14	12	....	....	....	....	....
	Fredericton	AHL	50	26	36	62	48	....	....	....	....	....
1988-89	**Quebec**	**NHL**	57	20	19	39	45	....	....	....	....	....
	Halifax	AHL	16	11	11	22	14	....	....	....	....	....
1989-90	**Quebec**	**NHL**	59	13	17	30	28	....	....	....	....	....
	Halifax	AHL	15	5	6	11	6	....	....	....	....	....
1990-91	**Quebec**	**NHL**	14	0	4	4	6	....	....	....	....	....
	Halifax	AHL	58	24	32	56	85	....	....	....	....	....
1991-92	**Quebec**	**NHL**	39	5	9	14	33	....	....	....	....	....
	Halifax	AHL	16	9	16	25	44	....	....	....	....	....
1992-93	**Ottawa**	**NHL**	10	0	1	1	6	....	....	....	....	....
	New Haven	AHL	16	9	15	24	42	....	....	....	....	....
	Los Angeles	**NHL**	6	0	0	0	5	....	....	....	....	....
	Phoenix	IHL	17	4	9	13	34	....	....	....	....	....
	NHL Totals		212	42	60	102	135					

Signed as a free agent by **Quebec**, February 3, 1987. Signed as a free agent by **Ottawa**, October 1, 1992. Traded to **Los Angeles** by **Ottawa** with Jim Thomson for Bob Kudelski and Shawn McCosh, December 19, 1992.

FORTIER, SEBASTIEN
Left wing. Shoots left. 6', 198 lbs.   Born, Greenfield Park, Que., October 12, 1973.

			Regular Season					Playoffs				
Season	Club	Lea	GP	G	A	TP	PIM	GP	G	A	TP	PIM
1991-92	Granby	QMJHL	62	14	31	45	65	....	....	....	....	....
1992-93	Sherbrooke	QMJHL	38	10	20	30	33	14	1	6	7	21

Signed as a free agent by **Montreal**, September 18, 1992.

FOSTER, COREY
Defense. Shoots left. 6'3", 204 lbs.   Born, Ottawa, Ont., October 27, 1969.
(New Jersey's 1st choice, 12th overall, in 1988 Entry Draft).

			Regular Season					Playoffs				
Season	Club	Lea	GP	G	A	TP	PIM	GP	G	A	TP	PIM
1986-87	Peterborough	OHL	30	3	4	7	4	1	0	0	0	0
1987-88	Peterborough	OHL	66	13	31	44	58	11	5	9	14	13
1988-89	**New Jersey**	**NHL**	2	0	0	0	0	....	....	....	....	....
a	Peterborough	OHL	55	14	42	56	42	17	1	17	18	12
1989-90	Cape Breton	AHL	54	7	17	24	32	1	0	0	0	0
1990-91	Cape Breton	AHL	67	14	11	25	51	4	2	4	6	4
1991-92	**Philadelphia**	**NHL**	25	3	4	7	20	....	....	....	....	....
	Hershey	AHL	19	5	9	14	26	6	1	1	2	5
1992-93	Hershey	AHL	80	9	25	34	102	....	....	....	....	....
	NHL Totals		27	3	4	7	20					

a OHL Third All-Star Team (1989)

Traded to **Edmonton** by **New Jersey** for Edmonton's first round choice (Jason Miller) in 1989 Entry Draft, June 17, 1989. Traded to **Philadelphia** by **Edmonton** with Dave Brown and Jari Kurri for Craig Fisher, Scott Mellanby and Craig Berube, May 30, 1991.

FOSTER, STEPHEN
Defense. Shoots right. 6'3", 210 lbs.   Born, Brockton, MA, March 21, 1971.
(Boston's 6th choice, 122nd overall, in 1989 Entry Draft).

			Regular Season					Playoffs				
Season	Club	Lea	GP	G	A	TP	PIM	GP	G	A	TP	PIM
1989-90	Boston U.	H.E.	28	0	8	8	26	....	....	....	....	....
1990-91	Boston U.	H.E.			DID NOT PLAY							
1991-92	Boston U.	H.E.	12	0	4	4	12	....	....	....	....	....
1992-93	Boston U.	H.E.	34	2	6	8	42	....	....	....	....	....

FOY, CHRIS
Defense. Shoots left. 6', 190 lbs.   Born, Toronto, Ont., September 16, 1970.
(NY Islanders' 1st choice, 8th overall, in 1992 Supplemental Draft).

			Regular Season					Playoffs				
Season	Club	Lea	GP	G	A	TP	PIM	GP	G	A	TP	PIM
1989-90	Northeastern	H.E.	37	0	5	5	48	....	....	....	....	....
1990-91	Northeastern	H.E.	33	0	3	3	20	....	....	....	....	....
1991-92	Northeastern	H.E.	33	8	11	19	45	....	....	....	....	....
1992-93	Northeastern	H.E.	22	7	8	15	34	....	....	....	....	....

FRANCIS, RONALD (RON)
Center. Shoots left. 6'2", 200 lbs.   Born, Sault Ste. Marie, Ont., March 1, 1963.
(Hartford's 1st choice, 4th overall, in 1981 Entry Draft).

			Regular Season					Playoffs				
Season	Club	Lea	GP	G	A	TP	PIM	GP	G	A	TP	PIM
1980-81	S.S. Marie	OHA	64	26	43	69	33	19	7	8	15	34
1981-82	**Hartford**	**NHL**	59	25	43	68	51	....	....	....	....	....
	S.S. Marie	OHL	25	18	30	48	46	....	....	....	....	....
1982-83	**Hartford**	**NHL**	79	31	59	90	60	....	....	....	....	....
1983-84	**Hartford**	**NHL**	72	23	60	83	45	....	....	....	....	....
1984-85	**Hartford**	**NHL**	80	24	57	81	66	....	....	....	....	....
1985-86	**Hartford**	**NHL**	53	24	53	77	24	10	1	2	3	4
1986-87	**Hartford**	**NHL**	75	30	63	93	45	6	2	2	4	6
1987-88	**Hartford**	**NHL**	80	25	50	75	87	6	2	5	7	2
1988-89	**Hartford**	**NHL**	69	29	48	77	36	4	0	2	2	0
1989-90	**Hartford**	**NHL**	80	32	69	101	73	7	3	3	6	8
1990-91	**Hartford**	**NHL**	67	21	55	76	51	....	....	....	....	....
	Pittsburgh	**NHL**	14	2	9	11	21	24	7	10	17	24
1991-92	**Pittsburgh**	**NHL**	70	21	33	54	30	21	8	*19	27	6
1992-93	**Pittsburgh**	**NHL**	84	24	76	100	68	12	6	11	17	19
	NHL Totals		882	311	675	986	657	90	29	54	83	69

Played in NHL All-Star Game (1983, 1985, 1990)

Traded to **Pittsburgh** by **Hartford** with Grant Jennings and Ulf Samuelsson for John Cullen, Jeff Parker and Zarley Zalapski, March 4, 1991.

FRANTTI, GORDON
Left wing. Shoots left. 6'6", 240 lbs.   Born, Laurium, MI, July 17, 1970.
(Philadelphia's 7th choice, 119th overall, in 1988 Entry Draft).

			Regular Season					Playoffs				
Season	Club	Lea	GP	G	A	TP	PIM	GP	G	A	TP	PIM
1989-90	W. Michigan	CCHA	30	7	4	11	16	....	....	....	....	....
1990-91	W. Michigan	CCHA	3	0	1	1	7	....	....	....	....	....
	Tri-Cities	WHL	48	20	21	41	86	7	3	2	5	8
1991-92	Kansas City	IHL	55	17	15	32	40	2	0	0	0	0
1992-93	Kansas City	IHL	21	3	6	9	47	....	....	....	....	....

Signed as a free agent by **San Jose**, September 9, 1991.

FRASER, IAIN
Center. Shoots left. 5'10", 175 lbs.   Born, Scarborough, Ont., August 10, 1969.
(NY Islanders' 12th choice, 233rd overall, in 1989 Entry Draft).

			Regular Season					Playoffs				
Season	Club	Lea	GP	G	A	TP	PIM	GP	G	A	TP	PIM
1986-87	Oshawa	OHL	5	1	2	3	0	....	....	....	....	....
1987-88	Oshawa	OHL	16	4	4	8	22	6	2	3	5	2
1988-89	Oshawa	OHL	62	33	57	90	87	6	2	8	10	12
1989-90a	Oshawa	OHL	56	40	65	105	75	17	10	*22	32	8
1990-91	Capital Dist.	AHL	32	5	13	18	16	....	....	....	....	....
	Richmond	ECHL	3	1	1	2	0	....	....	....	....	....
1991-92	Capital Dist.	AHL	45	9	11	20	24	....	....	....	....	....
1992-93	**NY Islanders**	**NHL**	7	2	2	4	2	....	....	....	....	....
b	Capital Dist.	AHL	74	41	69	110	16	4	0	1	1	0
	NHL Totals		7	2	2	4	2					

a Memorial Cup All-Star Team, Tournament MVP (1990)
b AHL Second All-Star Team (1993)

Signed as a free agent by **Quebec**, August 3, 1993.

FRASER, SCOTT
Center. Shoots right. 6'1", 178 lbs.   Born, Moncton, N.B., May 3, 1972.
(Montreal's 9th choice, 193rd overall, in 1991 Entry Draft).

			Regular Season					Playoffs				
Season	Club	Lea	GP	G	A	TP	PIM	GP	G	A	TP	PIM
1990-91	Dartmouth	ECAC	24	10	10	20	30	....	....	....	....	....
1991-92	Dartmouth	ECAC	24	11	7	18	60	....	....	....	....	....
1992-93	Cdn. National	.....	5	1	0	1	0	....	....	....	....	....
a	Dartmouth	ECAC	26	21	23	44	13	....	....	....	....	....

a ECAC Second All-Star Team (1993)

FRECHETTE, YANNICK
Left wing. Shoots left. 6'1", 172 lbs.   Born, Ste-Sophie, Que., June 20, 1973.

			Regular Season					Playoffs				
Season	Club	Lea	GP	G	A	TP	PIM	GP	G	A	TP	PIM
1990-91	Laval	QMJHL	67	10	18	28	83	13	0	3	3	20
1991-92	Laval	QMJHL	47	10	23	33	80	....	....	....	....	....
	Granby	QMJHL	7	0	1	1	16	....	....	....	....	....
1992-93	Hull	QMJHL	45	18	21	39	128	....	....	....	....	....

Signed as a free agent by **New Jersey**, October 1, 1992.

FREDERICK, JOSEPH
Right wing. Shoots right. 6'1", 190 lbs.   Born, St. Hubert, Que., August 6, 1969.
(Detroit's 13th choice, 242nd overall, in 1989 Entry Draft).

			Regular Season					Playoffs				
Season	Club	Lea	GP	G	A	TP	PIM	GP	G	A	TP	PIM
1990-91	N. Michigan	WCHA	40	9	11	20	77	....	....	....	....	....
1991-92	N. Michigan	WCHA	36	23	8	31	100	....	....	....	....	....
1992-93a	N. Michigan	WCHA	29	28	20	48	100	....	....	....	....	....
	Adirondack	AHL	5	0	1	1	2	8	0	0	0	6

a WCHA Second All-Star Team (1993)

FREDERICK, TROY
Center. Shoots left. 6'5", 226 lbs.   Born, Virden, Man., April 4, 1969.

			Regular Season					Playoffs				
Season	Club	Lea	GP	G	A	TP	PIM	GP	G	A	TP	PIM
1987-88	Brandon	WHL	66	15	13	28	17	4	3	1	4	6
1988-89	Brandon	WHL	72	26	30	56	72	....	....	....	....	....
1989-90	Brandon	WHL	70	27	29	56	133	....	....	....	....	....
1990-91	Kansas City	IHL	39	2	3	5	79	....	....	....	....	....
	Knoxville	ECHL	4	0	3	3	71	....	....	....	....	....
1991-92	Kansas City	IHL	13	0	3	3	29	....	....	....	....	....
1992-93	Kansas City	IHL	16	0	1	1	27	....	....	....	....	....

Signed as a free agent by **San Jose**, September 3, 1991.

FREER, MARK   (FRIHR)
Center. Shoots left. 5'10", 180 lbs.   Born, Peterborough, Ont., July 14, 1968.

			Regular Season					Playoffs				
Season	Club	Lea	GP	G	A	TP	PIM	GP	G	A	TP	PIM
1985-86	Peterborough	OHL	65	16	28	44	24	14	3	4	7	13
1986-87	**Philadelphia**	**NHL**	1	0	1	1	0	....	....	....	....	....
	Peterborough	OHL	65	39	43	82	44	12	2	6	8	5
1987-88	**Philadelphia**	**NHL**	1	0	0	0	0	....	....	....	....	....
	Peterborough	OHL	63	38	70	108	63	12	5	12	17	4
1988-89	**Philadelphia**	**NHL**	5	0	1	1	0	....	....	....	....	....
	Hershey	AHL	75	30	49	79	77	12	4	6	10	2
1989-90	**Philadelphia**	**NHL**	2	0	0	0	0	....	....	....	....	....
	Hershey	AHL	65	28	36	64	31	....	....	....	....	....
1990-91	Hershey	AHL	77	18	44	62	45	7	1	3	4	17
1991-92	**Philadelphia**	**NHL**	50	6	7	13	18	....	....	....	....	....
	Hershey	AHL	31	13	11	24	38	6	0	3	3	2
1992-93	**Ottawa**	**NHL**	63	10	14	24	39	....	....	....	....	....
	NHL Totals		122	16	23	39	57					

Signed as a free agent by **Philadelphia**, October 7, 1986. Claimed by **Ottawa** from **Philadelphia** in Expansion Draft, June 18, 1992.

FRENETTE, DEREK

Left wing. Shoots left. 6'1", 205 lbs. Born, Montreal, Que., July 13, 1971.
(St. Louis' 6th choice, 124th overall, in 1989 Entry Draft).

			Regular Season					Playoffs				
Season	Club	Lea	GP	G	A	TP	PIM	GP	G	A	TP	PIM
1988-89	Ferris State	CCHA	25	3	4	7	17	....	....	....	....	....
1989-90	Ferris State	CCHA	28	1	4	5	48	....	....	....	....	....
1990-91	Hull	QMJHL	66	27	42	69	72	6	4	3	7	12
	Peoria	IHL	....	....	....	....	....	6	0	0	0	0
1991-92	Peoria	IHL	46	2	11	13	51	10	0	3	3	4
1992-93	Peoria	IHL	73	18	19	37	44	4	1	2	3	2

FRIEDMAN, DOUG

Left wing. Shoots left. 6'1", 189 lbs. Born, Cape Elizabeth, ME, September 1, 1971.
(Quebec's 11th choice, 222nd overall, in 1991 Entry Draft).

			Regular Season					Playoffs				
Season	Club	Lea	GP	G	A	TP	PIM	GP	G	A	TP	PIM
1990-91	Boston U.	H.E.	36	6	6	12	37	....	....	....	....	....
1991-92	Boston U.	H.E.	34	11	8	19	42	....	....	....	....	....
1992-93	Boston U.	H.E.	38	17	24	41	62	....	....	....	....	....

GAETZ, LINK (GAYTZ)

Defense. Shoots left. 6'3", 215 lbs. Born, Vancouver, B.C., October 2, 1968.
(Minnesota's 2nd choice, 40th overall, in 1988 Entry Draft).

			Regular Season					Playoffs				
Season	Club	Lea	GP	G	A	TP	PIM	GP	G	A	TP	PIM
1986-87	N. Westminster	WHL	44	2	7	9	52	....	....	....	....	....
1987-88	Spokane	WHL	59	9	20	29	313	10	2	2	4	70
1988-89	**Minnesota**	**NHL**	**12**	**0**	**2**	**2**	**53**	....	....	....	....	....
	Kalamazoo	IHL	37	3	4	7	192	5	0	0	0	56
1989-90	**Minnesota**	**NHL**	**5**	**0**	**0**	**0**	**33**	....	....	....	....	....
	Kalamazoo	IHL	61	5	16	21	318	9	2	2	4	59
1990-91	Kalamazoo	IHL	9	0	1	1	44	....	....	....	....	....
	Kansas City	IHL	18	1	10	11	178	....	....	....	....	....
1991-92	**San Jose**	**NHL**	**48**	**6**	**6**	**12**	**326**	....	....	....	....	....
1992-93	Nashville	ECHL	3	1	0	1	10	....	....	....	....	....
	Kansas City	IHL	2	0	0	0	14	....	....	....	....	....
	NHL Totals		**65**	**6**	**8**	**14**	**412**	....	....	....	....	....

Claimed by **San Jose** from **Minnesota** in Dispersal Draft, May 30, 1991.

GAGE, JOSEPH WILLIAM (JODY)

Right wing. Shoots right. 6', 190 lbs. Born, Toronto, Ont., November 29, 1959.
(Detroit's 2nd choice, 45th overall, in 1979 Entry Draft).

			Regular Season					Playoffs				
Season	Club	Lea	GP	G	A	TP	PIM	GP	G	A	TP	PIM
1977-78	Hamilton	OHA	32	15	18	33	19	....	....	....	....	....
	Kitchener	OHA	36	17	27	44	21	9	4	3	7	4
1978-79	Kitchener	OHA	58	46	43	89	40	10	1	2	3	6
1979-80	Adirondack	AHL	63	25	21	46	15	5	2	1	3	0
1980-81	**Detroit**	**NHL**	**16**	**2**	**2**	**4**	**22**	....	....	....	....	....
	Adirondack	AHL	59	17	31	48	44	17	9	6	15	12
1981-82	**Detroit**	**NHL**	**31**	**9**	**10**	**19**	**2**	....	....	....	....	....
	Adirondack	AHL	47	21	20	41	21	....	....	....	....	....
1982-83	Adirondack	AHL	65	23	30	53	33	6	1	5	6	8
1983-84	**Detroit**	**NHL**	**3**	**0**	**0**	**0**	**0**	....	....	....	....	....
	Adirondack	AHL	73	40	32	72	32	6	3	4	7	2
1984-85	Adirondack	AHL	78	27	33	60	55	....	....	....	....	....
1985-86	**Buffalo**	**NHL**	**7**	**3**	**2**	**5**	**0**	....	....	....	....	....
a	Rochester	AHL	73	42	57	99	56	....	....	....	....	....
1986-87	Rochester	AHL	70	26	39	65	60	17	*14	5	19	24
1987-88	**Buffalo**	**NHL**	**2**	**0**	**0**	**0**	**0**	....	....	....	....	....
ab	Rochester	AHL	76	*60	44	104	46	5	2	5	7	10
1988-89	Rochester	AHL	65	31	38	69	60	....	....	....	....	....
1989-90	Rochester	AHL	75	45	38	83	42	17	4	6	10	12
1990-91a	Rochester	AHL	73	42	43	85	34	15	6	10	16	14
1991-92	**Buffalo**	**NHL**	**9**	**0**	**1**	**1**	**2**	....	....	....	....	....
	Rochester	AHL	67	40	40	80	54	16	5	9	14	10
1992-93	Rochester	AHL	71	40	40	80	76	9	5	8	13	2
	NHL Totals		**68**	**14**	**15**	**29**	**26**	....	....	....	....	....

a AHL First All-Star Team (1986, 1988, 1991)
b Won Les Cunningham Trophy (MVP-AHL) (1988)

Signed as a free agent by **Buffalo**, July 31, 1985.

GAGNER, DAVE (GAH-nyay)

Center. Shoots left. 5'10", 180 lbs. Born, Chatham, Ont., December 11, 1964.
(NY Rangers' 1st choice, 12th overall, in 1983 Entry Draft).

			Regular Season					Playoffs				
Season	Club	Lea	GP	G	A	TP	PIM	GP	G	A	TP	PIM
1981-82	Brantford	OHL	68	30	46	76	31	11	3	6	9	6
1982-83a	Brantford	OHL	70	55	66	121	57	8	5	5	10	4
1983-84	Cdn. Olympic	....	50	19	18	37	26	....	....	....	....	....
	Brantford	OHL	12	7	13	20	4	6	0	4	4	6
1984-85	**NY Rangers**	**NHL**	**38**	**6**	**6**	**12**	**16**	....	....	....	....	....
	New Haven	AHL	38	13	20	33	23	....	....	....	....	....
1985-86	**NY Rangers**	**NHL**	**32**	**4**	**6**	**10**	**19**	....	....	....	....	....
	New Haven	AHL	16	10	11	21	11	4	1	2	3	2
1986-87	**NY Rangers**	**NHL**	**10**	**1**	**4**	**5**	**12**	....	....	....	....	....
	New Haven	AHL	56	22	41	63	50	7	1	5	6	18
1987-88	**Minnesota**	**NHL**	**51**	**8**	**11**	**19**	**55**	....	....	....	....	....
	Kalamazoo	IHL	14	16	10	26	26	....	....	....	....	....
1988-89	**Minnesota**	**NHL**	**75**	**35**	**43**	**78**	**104**	....	....	....	....	....
	Kalamazoo	IHL	1	0	1	1	4	....	....	....	....	....
1989-90	**Minnesota**	**NHL**	**79**	**40**	**38**	**78**	**54**	**7**	**2**	**3**	**5**	**16**
1990-91	**Minnesota**	**NHL**	**73**	**40**	**42**	**82**	**114**	**23**	**12**	**15**	**27**	**28**
1991-92	**Minnesota**	**NHL**	**78**	**31**	**40**	**71**	**107**	**7**	**2**	**4**	**6**	**8**
1992-93	**Minnesota**	**NHL**	**84**	**33**	**43**	**76**	**143**	....	....	....	....	....
	NHL Totals		**520**	**198**	**233**	**431**	**624**	**37**	**16**	**22**	**38**	**52**

a OHL Second All-Star Team (1983)

Played in NHL All-Star Game (1991)

Traded to **Minnesota** by **NY Rangers** with Jay Caulfield for Jari Gronstrand and Paul Boutilier, October 8, 1987.

GALANOV, MAXIM

Defense. Shoots left. 6'1", 167 lbs. Born, Krasnoyarsk, Soviet Union, March 13, 1974.
(NY Rangers' 3rd choice, 61st overall, in 1993 Entry Draft).

			Regular Season					Playoffs				
Season	Club	Lea	GP	G	A	TP	PIM	GP	G	A	TP	PIM
1992-93	Togliatti	CIS	41	4	2	6	12	10	1	1	2	12

GALLANT, GERARD (guh-LAHNT)

Left wing. Shoots left. 5'10", 190 lbs. Born, Summerside, P.E.I., September 2, 1963.
(Detroit's 4th choice, 107th overall, in 1981 Entry Draft).

			Regular Season					Playoffs				
Season	Club	Lea	GP	G	A	TP	PIM	GP	G	A	TP	PIM
1980-81	Sherbrooke	QMJHL	68	41	59	100	265	14	6	13	19	46
1981-82	Sherbrooke	QMJHL	58	34	58	92	260	22	14	24	38	84
1982-83	St-Jean	QMJHL	33	28	25	53	139	....	....	....	....	....
	Verdun	QMJHL	29	26	49	75	105	15	14	19	33	84
1983-84	Adirondack	AHL	77	31	33	64	195	7	1	3	4	34
1984-85	**Detroit**	**NHL**	**32**	**6**	**12**	**18**	**66**	**3**	**0**	**0**	**0**	**11**
	Adirondack	AHL	46	18	29	47	131	....	....	....	....	....
1985-86	**Detroit**	**NHL**	**52**	**20**	**19**	**39**	**106**	....	....	....	....	....
1986-87	**Detroit**	**NHL**	**80**	**38**	**34**	**72**	**216**	**16**	**8**	**6**	**14**	**43**
1987-88	**Detroit**	**NHL**	**73**	**34**	**39**	**73**	**242**	**16**	**6**	**9**	**15**	**55**
1988-89a	**Detroit**	**NHL**	**76**	**39**	**54**	**93**	**230**	**6**	**1**	**2**	**3**	**40**
1989-90	**Detroit**	**NHL**	**69**	**36**	**44**	**80**	**254**	....	....	....	....	....
1990-91	**Detroit**	**NHL**	**45**	**10**	**16**	**26**	**111**	....	....	....	....	....
1991-92	**Detroit**	**NHL**	**69**	**14**	**22**	**36**	**187**	**11**	**2**	**2**	**4**	**25**
1992-93	**Detroit**	**NHL**	**67**	**10**	**20**	**30**	**188**	**6**	**1**	**2**	**3**	**4**
	NHL Totals		**563**	**207**	**260**	**467**	**1600**	**58**	**18**	**21**	**39**	**178**

a NHL Second All-Star Team (1989).

Signed as a free agent by **Tampa Bay**, July 21, 1993.

GALLEY, GARRY

Defense. Shoots left. 6', 190 lbs. Born, Montreal, Que., April 16, 1963.
(Los Angeles' 4th choice, 100th overall, in 1983 Entry Draft).

			Regular Season					Playoffs				
Season	Club	Lea	GP	G	A	TP	PIM	GP	G	A	TP	PIM
1981-82	Bowling Green	CCHA	42	3	36	39	48	....	....	....	....	....
1982-83	Bowling Green	CCHA	40	17	29	46	40	....	....	....	....	....
1983-84ab	Bowling Green	CCHA	44	15	52	67	61	....	....	....	....	....
1984-85	**Los Angeles**	**NHL**	**78**	**8**	**30**	**38**	**82**	**3**	**1**	**0**	**1**	**2**
1985-86	**Los Angeles**	**NHL**	**49**	**9**	**13**	**22**	**46**	....	....	....	....	....
	New Haven	AHL	4	2	6	8	6	....	....	....	....	....
1986-87	**Los Angeles**	**NHL**	**30**	**5**	**11**	**16**	**57**	....	....	....	....	....
	Washington	**NHL**	**18**	**1**	**10**	**11**	**10**	**2**	**0**	**0**	**0**	**0**
1987-88	**Washington**	**NHL**	**58**	**7**	**23**	**30**	**44**	**13**	**2**	**4**	**6**	**13**
1988-89	**Boston**	**NHL**	**78**	**8**	**21**	**29**	**80**	**9**	**0**	**1**	**1**	**33**
1989-90	**Boston**	**NHL**	**71**	**8**	**27**	**35**	**75**	**21**	**3**	**3**	**6**	**34**
1990-91	**Boston**	**NHL**	**70**	**6**	**21**	**27**	**84**	**16**	**1**	**5**	**6**	**17**
1991-92	**Boston**	**NHL**	**38**	**2**	**12**	**14**	**83**	....	....	....	....	....
	Philadelphia	**NHL**	**39**	**3**	**15**	**18**	**34**	....	....	....	....	....
1992-93	**Philadelphia**	**NHL**	**83**	**13**	**49**	**62**	**115**	....	....	....	....	....
	NHL Totals		**612**	**70**	**232**	**302**	**710**	**64**	**7**	**13**	**20**	**99**

a CCHA First All-Star Team (1984)
b NCAA All-American (1984)

Played in NHL All-Star Game (1991)

Traded to **Washington** by **Los Angeles** for Al Jensen, February 14, 1987. Signed as a free agent by **Boston**, July 8, 1988. Traded to **Philadelphia** by **Boston** with Wes Walz and future considerations for Gord Murphy, Brian Dobbin and Philadelphia's third round choice (Sergei Zholtok) in 1992 Entry Draft, January 2, 1992.

GARANIN, YEVGENY

Center. Shoots left. 6'4", 191 lbs. Born, Voskresensk, Soviet Union, August 3, 1973.
(Winnipeg's 9th choice, 228th overall, in 1992 Entry Draft).

			Regular Season					Playoffs				
Season	Club	Lea	GP	G	A	TP	PIM	GP	G	A	TP	PIM
1991-92	Khimik	CIS	1	1	0	1	0	....	....	....	....	....
1992-93	Khimik	CIS	34	5	4	9	10	1	0	0	0	2

GARBUTT, MURRAY

Center. Shoots left. 6'1", 205 lbs. Born, Hanna, Alta., July 29, 1971.
(Minnesota's 3rd choice, 60th overall, in 1989 Entry Draft).

			Regular Season					Playoffs				
Season	Club	Lea	GP	G	A	TP	PIM	GP	G	A	TP	PIM
1987-88	Medicine Hat	WHL	9	2	1	3	15	16	0	1	1	15
1988-89	Medicine Hat	WHL	64	14	24	38	145	3	1	0	1	6
1989-90	Medicine Hat	WHL	72	38	27	65	221	3	1	0	1	21
1990-91	Medicine Hat	WHL	30	15	26	41	97	....	....	....	....	....
	Spokane	WHL	31	17	19	36	90	15	4	8	12	44
1991-92	Kansas City	IHL	25	2	6	8	19	....	....	....	....	....
1992-93			DID NOT PLAY									

Claimed by **San Jose** from **Minnesota** in Dispersal Draft, May 30, 1991. Traded to **Quebec** by **San Jose** for Don Barber, March 7, 1992.

GARDINER, BRUCE

Center. Shoots right. 6'1", 185 lbs. Born, Barrie, Ont., February 11, 1971.
(St. Louis' 6th choice, 131st overall, in 1991 Entry Draft).

			Regular Season					Playoffs				
Season	Club	Lea	GP	G	A	TP	PIM	GP	G	A	TP	PIM
1990-91	Colgate	ECAC	27	4	9	13	72	....	....	....	....	....
1991-92	Colgate	ECAC	23	7	8	15	77	....	....	....	....	....
1992-93	Colgate	ECAC	33	17	12	29	64	....	....	....	....	....

GARPENLOV, JOHAN (GAHR-puhn-luhv)

Left wing. Shoots left. 5'11", 183 lbs. Born, Stockholm, Sweden, March 21, 1968.
(Detroit's 5th choice, 85th overall, in 1986 Entry Draft).

			Regular Season					Playoffs				
Season	Club	Lea	GP	G	A	TP	PIM	GP	G	A	TP	PIM
1986-87	Djurgarden	Swe.	29	5	8	13	22	2	0	0	0	0
1987-88	Djurgarden	Swe.	30	7	10	17	12	3	1	3	4	4
1988-89	Djurgarden	Swe.	36	12	19	31	20	8	3	4	7	10
1989-90	Djurgarden	Swe.	39	20	13	33	35	8	2	4	6	4
1990-91	**Detroit**	**NHL**	**71**	**18**	**22**	**40**	**18**	**6**	**0**	**1**	**1**	**4**
1991-92	**Detroit**	**NHL**	**16**	**1**	**1**	**2**	**4**	....	....	....	....	....
	Adirondack	AHL	9	3	3	6	6	....	....	....	....	....
	San Jose	**NHL**	**12**	**5**	**6**	**11**	**4**	....	....	....	....	....
1992-93	**San Jose**	**NHL**	**79**	**22**	**44**	**66**	**56**	....	....	....	....	....
	NHL Totals		**178**	**46**	**73**	**119**	**82**	**6**	**0**	**1**	**1**	**4**

Traded to **San Jose** by **Detroit** for Bob McGill and Vancouver's eighth round choice (previously acquired by Detroit — San Jose selected C.J. Denomme) in 1992 Entry Draft, March 9, 1992.

GARTNER, MICHAEL ALFRED (MIKE)

Right wing. Shoots right. 6', 190 lbs. Born, Ottawa, Ont., October 29, 1959.
(Washington's 1st choice, 4th overall, in 1979 Entry Draft).

			Regular Season					Playoffs				
Season	Club	Lea	GP	G	A	TP	PIM	GP	G	A	TP	PIM
1976-77	Niagara Falls	OHA	62	33	42	75	125	....	....	....	....	....
1977-78a	Niagara Falls	OHA	64	41	49	90	56	....	....	....	....	....
1978-79	Cincinnati	WHA	78	27	25	52	123	3	0	2	2	2
1979-80	**Washington**	**NHL**	**77**	**36**	**32**	**68**	**66**	....	....	....	....	....
1980-81	**Washington**	**NHL**	**80**	**48**	**46**	**94**	**100**	....	....	....	....	....
1981-82	**Washington**	**NHL**	**80**	**35**	**45**	**80**	**121**	....	....	....	....	....
1982-83	**Washington**	**NHL**	**73**	**38**	**38**	**76**	**54**	**4**	**0**	**0**	**0**	**4**
1983-84	**Washington**	**NHL**	**80**	**40**	**45**	**85**	**90**	**8**	**3**	**7**	**10**	**16**
1984-85	**Washington**	**NHL**	**80**	**50**	**52**	**102**	**71**	**5**	**4**	**3**	**7**	**9**
1985-86	**Washington**	**NHL**	**74**	**35**	**40**	**75**	**63**	**9**	**2**	**10**	**12**	**4**
1986-87	**Washington**	**NHL**	**78**	**41**	**32**	**73**	**61**	**7**	**4**	**3**	**7**	**14**
1987-88	**Washington**	**NHL**	**80**	**48**	**33**	**81**	**73**	**14**	**3**	**4**	**7**	**14**
1988-89	**Washington**	**NHL**	**56**	**26**	**29**	**55**	**71**	....	....	....	....	....
	Minnesota	**NHL**	**13**	**7**	**7**	**14**	**2**	**5**	**0**	**0**	**0**	**6**
1989-90	**Minnesota**	**NHL**	**67**	**34**	**36**	**70**	**32**	....	....	....	....	....
	NY Rangers	**NHL**	**12**	**11**	**5**	**16**	**6**	**10**	**5**	**3**	**8**	**12**
1990-91	**NY Rangers**	**NHL**	**79**	**49**	**20**	**69**	**53**	**6**	**1**	**1**	**2**	**0**
1991-92	**NY Rangers**	**NHL**	**76**	**40**	**41**	**81**	**55**	**13**	**8**	**8**	**16**	**4**
1992-93	**NY Rangers**	**NHL**	**84**	**45**	**23**	**68**	**59**	....	....	....	....	....
	NHL Totals		**1089**	**583**	**524**	**1107**	**977**	**81**	**30**	**39**	**69**	**83**

a OHA First All-Star Team (1978)

Played in NHL All-Star Game (1980, 1985, 1986, 1988, 1990, 1993)

Traded to **Minnesota** by **Washington** with Larry Murphy for Dino Ciccarelli and Bob Rouse, March 7, 1989. Traded to **NY Rangers** by **Minnesota** for Ulf Dahlen, Los Angeles' fourth round choice (previously acquired by NY Rangers — Minnesota selected Cal McGowan) in 1990 Entry Draft and future considerations, March 6, 1990.

GAUDREAU, ROBERT (ROB)

Right wing. Shoots right. 5'11", 185 lbs. Born, Lincoln, RI, January 20, 1970.
(Pittsburgh's 8th choice, 172nd overall, in 1988 Entry Draft).

			Regular Season					Playoffs				
Season	Club	Lea	GP	G	A	TP	PIM	GP	G	A	TP	PIM
1988-89a	Providence	H.E.	42	28	29	57	32	....	....	....	....	....
1989-90	Providence	H.E.	32	20	18	38	12	....	....	....	....	....
1990-91b	Providence	H.E.	36	34	27	61	20	....	....	....	....	....
1991-92cd	Providence	H.E.	36	21	34	55	22	....	....	....	....	....
1992-93	**San Jose**	**NHL**	**59**	**23**	**20**	**43**	**18**	....	....	....	....	....
	Kansas City	IHL	19	8	6	14	6	....	....	....	....	....
	NHL Totals		**59**	**23**	**20**	**43**	**18**	....	....	....	....	....

a Co-winner Hockey East Rookie of the Year (1989)
b Hockey East Second All-Star Team (1991)
c NCAA East Second All-American Team (1992)
d Hockey East First All-Star Team (1992)

Rights traded to **Minnesota** by **Pittsburgh** for Richard Zemlak, November 1, 1988. Claimed by **San Jose** from **Minnesota** in Dispersal Draft, May 30, 1991.

GAUL, MICHAEL

Defense. Shoots right. 6'1", 197 lbs. Born, Dorval, Que., April 22, 1973.
(Los Angeles' 12th choice, 262nd overall, in 1991 Entry Draft).

			Regular Season					Playoffs				
Season	Club	Lea	GP	G	A	TP	PIM	GP	G	A	TP	PIM
1990-91	St. Lawrence	ECAC	31	1	3	4	46	....	....	....	....	....
1991-92	Laval	QMJHL	50	6	38	44	44	10	0	2	2	20
1992-93a	Laval	QMJHL	57	16	57	73	66	13	3	10	13	10

a Memorial Cup All-Star Team (1993)

GAUTHIER, DANIEL

Left wing. Shoots left. 6'1", 190 lbs. Born, Charlemagne, Que., May 17, 1970.
(Pittsburgh's 3rd choice, 62nd overall, in 1988 Entry Draft).

			Regular Season					Playoffs				
Season	Club	Lea	GP	G	A	TP	PIM	GP	G	A	TP	PIM
1986-87	Longueuil	QMJHL	64	23	22	45	23	18	4	5	9	15
1987-88	Victoriaville	QMJHL	66	43	47	90	53	5	2	1	3	0
1988-89	Victoriaville	QMJHL	64	41	75	116	84	16	12	17	29	30
1989-90	Victoriaville	QMJHL	62	45	69	114	32	16	8	*19	27	16
1990-91	Albany	IHL	1	1	0	1	0	....	....	....	....	....
ab	Knoxville	ECHL	61	41	*93	134	40	2	0	4	4	4
1991-92	Muskegon	IHL	68	19	18	37	28	9	3	6	9	8
1992-93	Cleveland	IHL	80	40	66	106	88	4	2	2	4	14

a ECHL First All-Star Team (1991)
b Top Rookie — ECHL (1991)

Signed as a free agent by **Florida**, July 14, 1993.

GAUTHIER, LUC (GOH-chay)

Defense. Shoots right. 5'9", 195 lbs. Born, Longueuil, Que., April 19, 1964.

			Regular Season					Playoffs				
Season	Club	Lea	GP	G	A	TP	PIM	GP	G	A	TP	PIM
1983-84	Longueuil	QMJHL	70	8	54	62	207	....	....	....	....	....
1984-85	Longueuil	QMJHL	60	13	47	60	111	....	....	....	....	....
1985-86	Saginaw	IHL	66	9	29	38	160	....	....	....	....	....
1986-87	Sherbrooke	AHL	78	5	17	22	8	17	2	4	6	31
1987-88	Sherbrooke	AHL	61	4	10	14	105	6	0	0	0	18
1988-89	Sherbrooke	AHL	77	8	20	28	178	6	0	0	0	10
1989-90	Sherbrooke	AHL	79	3	23	26	139	12	0	4	4	35
1990-91	**Montreal**	**NHL**	**3**	**0**	**0**	**0**	**2**	....	....	....	....	....
	Fredericton	AHL	69	7	20	27	238	9	1	1	2	10
1991-92	Fredericton	AHL	80	4	14	18	252	7	1	1	2	26
1992-93	Fredericton	AHL	78	9	33	42	167	5	2	1	3	20
	NHL Totals		**3**	**0**	**0**	**0**	**2**	....	....	....	....	....

Signed as a free agent by **Montreal**, October 7, 1986.

GAVEY, AARON

Center. Shoots left. 6'1", 170 lbs. Born, Sudbury, Ont., February 22, 1974.
(Tampa Bay's 4th choice, 74th overall, in 1992 Entry Draft).

			Regular Season					Playoffs				
Season	Club	Lea	GP	G	A	TP	PIM	GP	G	A	TP	PIM
1991-92	S.S. Marie	OHL	48	7	11	18	27	19	5	1	6	10
1992-93	S.S. Marie	OHL	62	45	39	84	116	18	5	9	14	36

GAVIN, ROBERT (STEWART)

Left wing. Shoots left. 6', 190 lbs. Born, Ottawa, Ont., March 15, 1960.
(Toronto's 4th choice, 74th overall, in 1980 Entry Draft).

			Regular Season					Playoffs				
Season	Club	Lea	GP	G	A	TP	PIM	GP	G	A	TP	PIM
1978-79	Toronto	OHA	61	24	25	49	83	3	1	0	1	0
1979-80	Toronto	OHA	68	27	30	57	52	4	1	1	2	2
1980-81	**Toronto**	**NHL**	**14**	**1**	**2**	**3**	**13**	....	....	....	....	....
	New Brunswick	AHL	46	7	12	19	42	13	1	0	1	2
1981-82	**Toronto**	**NHL**	**38**	**5**	**6**	**11**	**29**	....	....	....	....	....
1982-83	**Toronto**	**NHL**	**63**	**6**	**5**	**11**	**44**	**4**	**0**	**0**	**0**	**0**
	St. Catharines	AHL	6	2	4	6	17	....	....	....	....	....
1983-84	**Toronto**	**NHL**	**80**	**10**	**22**	**32**	**90**	....	....	....	....	....
1984-85	**Toronto**	**NHL**	**73**	**12**	**13**	**25**	**38**	....	....	....	....	....
1985-86	**Hartford**	**NHL**	**76**	**26**	**29**	**55**	**51**	**10**	**4**	**1**	**5**	**13**
1986-87	**Hartford**	**NHL**	**79**	**20**	**21**	**41**	**28**	**6**	**2**	**4**	**6**	**10**
1987-88	**Hartford**	**NHL**	**56**	**11**	**10**	**21**	**59**	**6**	**2**	**2**	**4**	**4**
1988-89	**Minnesota**	**NHL**	**73**	**8**	**18**	**26**	**34**	**5**	**3**	**1**	**4**	**10**
1989-90	**Minnesota**	**NHL**	**80**	**12**	**13**	**25**	**76**	**7**	**0**	**2**	**2**	**12**
1990-91	**Minnesota**	**NHL**	**38**	**4**	**4**	**8**	**36**	**21**	**3**	**10**	**13**	**20**
1991-92	**Minnesota**	**NHL**	**35**	**5**	**4**	**9**	**27**	**7**	**0**	**0**	**0**	**6**
1992-93	**Minnesota**	**NHL**	**63**	**10**	**8**	**18**	**59**	....	....	....	....	....
	NHL Totals		**768**	**130**	**155**	**285**	**584**	**66**	**14**	**20**	**34**	**75**

Traded to **Hartford** by **Toronto** for Chris Kotsopoulos, October 7, 1985. Claimed by **Minnesota** in NHL Waiver Draft, October 3, 1988.

GEARY, DEREK

Right wing. Shoots right. 6'3", 180 lbs. Born, Gloucester, MA, February 18, 1970.
(Boston's 5th choice, 123rd overall, in 1988 Entry Draft).

			Regular Season					Playoffs				
Season	Club	Lea	GP	G	A	TP	PIM	GP	G	A	TP	PIM
1990-91	Boston U.	H.E.				DID NOT PLAY						
1991-92	Dartmouth	ECAC	26	7	6	13	30	....	....	....	....	....
1992-93	Dartmouth	ECAC	27	7	8	15	4	....	....	....	....	....

GELINAS, MARTIN (JEL-in-uh)

Left wing. Shoots left. 5'11", 195 lbs. Born, Shawinigan, Que., June 5, 1970.
(Los Angeles' 1st choice, 7th overall, in 1988 Entry Draft).

			Regular Season					Playoffs				
Season	Club	Lea	GP	G	A	TP	PIM	GP	G	A	TP	PIM
1987-88	Hull	QMJHL	65	63	68	131	74	17	15	18	33	32
1988-89	**Edmonton**	**NHL**	**6**	**1**	**2**	**3**	**0**	....	....	....	....	....
	Hull	QMJHL	41	38	39	77	31	9	5	4	9	14
1989-90	**Edmonton**	**NHL**	**46**	**17**	**8**	**25**	**30**	**20**	**2**	**3**	**5**	**6**
1990-91	**Edmonton**	**NHL**	**73**	**20**	**20**	**40**	**34**	**18**	**3**	**6**	**9**	**25**
1991-92	**Edmonton**	**NHL**	**68**	**11**	**18**	**29**	**62**	**15**	**1**	**3**	**4**	**10**
1992-93	**Edmonton**	**NHL**	**65**	**11**	**12**	**23**	**30**	....	....	....	....	....
	NHL Totals		**258**	**60**	**60**	**120**	**156**	**53**	**6**	**12**	**18**	**41**

Traded to **Edmonton** by **Los Angeles** with Jimmy Carson and Los Angeles' first round choices in 1989, (acquired by New Jersey — New Jersey selected Jason Miller), 1991 (Martin Rucinsky) and 1993 (Nick Stajduhar) Entry Drafts and cash for Wayne Gretzky, Mike Krushelnyski and Marty McSorley, August 9, 1988. Traded to **Quebec** by **Edmonton** with Edmonton's sixth round choice (Nicholas Checco) in 1993 Entry Draft for Scott Pearson, June 20, 1993.

GENDRON, MARTIN

Right wing. Shoots right. 5'8", 182 lbs. Born, Valleyfield, Que., February 15, 1974.
(Washington's 4th choice, 71st overall, in 1992 Entry Draft).

			Regular Season					Playoffs				
Season	Club	Lea	GP	G	A	TP	PIM	GP	G	A	TP	PIM
1990-91	St-Hyacinthe	QMJHL	55	34	23	57	33	4	1	2	3	0
1991-92a	St-Hyacinthe	QMJHL	69	*71	66	137	45	6	7	4	11	14
1992-93bc	St-Hyacinthe	QMJHL	63	73	61	134	44	....	....	....	....	....
	Baltimore	AHL	10	1	2	3	2	3	0	0	0	0

a QMJHL First All-Star Team (1992)
b QMJHL Second All-Star Team (1993)
c Canadian Major Junior First All-Star Team (1993)

GERNANDER, KEN

Center. Shoots left. 5'10", 175 lbs. Born, Coleraine, MN, June 30, 1969.
(Winnipeg's 4th choice, 96th overall, in 1987 Entry Draft).

			Regular Season					Playoffs				
Season	Club	Lea	GP	G	A	TP	PIM	GP	G	A	TP	PIM
1987-88	U. Minnesota	WCHA	44	14	14	28	14	....	....	....	....	....
1988-89	U. Minnesota	WCHA	44	9	11	20	2	....	....	....	....	....
1989-90	U. Minnesota	WCHA	44	32	17	49	24	....	....	....	....	....
1990-91	U. Minnesota	WCHA	44	23	20	43	24	....	....	....	....	....
1991-92	Fort Wayne	IHL	13	7	6	13	2	....	....	....	....	....
	Moncton	AHL	43	8	18	26	9	8	1	1	2	2
1992-93	Moncton	AHL	71	18	29	47	20	5	1	4	5	0

GIACIN, JIM

Left wing. Shoots left. 6'1", 200 lbs. Born, St. Louis, MO, January 6, 1971.
(Los Angeles' 8th choice, 182nd overall, in 1989 Entry Draft).

			Regular Season					Playoffs				
Season	Club	Lea	GP	G	A	TP	PIM	GP	G	A	TP	PIM
1989-90	St. Lawrence	ECAC	28	4	2	6	32	....	....	....	....	....
1990-91	St. Lawrence	ECAC	35	3	5	8	22	....	....	....	....	....
1991-92	St. Lawrence	ECAC	DID NOT PLAY – INJURED									
1992-93	St. Lawrence	ECAC	19	1	1	2	14	....	....	....	....	....

GIBSON, STEVE

Left wing. Shoots left. 6', 204 lbs. Born, Listowel, Ont., October 10, 1972.
(Edmonton's 7th choice, 157th overall, in 1992 Entry Draft).

			Regular Season					Playoffs				
Season	Club	Lea	GP	G	A	TP	PIM	GP	G	A	TP	PIM
1990-91	Windsor	OHL	62	15	18	33	37	11	1	3	4	6
1991-92	Windsor	OHL	63	49	40	89	41	7	4	1	5	6
1992-93	Windsor	OHL	60	48	52	100	49	....	....	....	....	....

GILBERT, GREGORY SCOTT (GREG)

Left wing. Shoots left. 6'1", 191 lbs. Born, Mississauga, Ont., January 22, 1962.
(NY Islanders' 5th choice, 80th overall, in 1980 Entry Draft).

			Regular Season					Playoffs				
Season	Club	Lea	GP	G	A	TP	PIM	GP	G	A	TP	PIM
1979-80	Toronto	OHA	68	10	11	21	35	....	....	....	....	....
1980-81	Toronto	OHA	64	30	37	67	73	5	2	6	8	16
1981-82	**NY Islanders**	**NHL**	**1**	**1**	**0**	**1**	**0**	**4**	**1**	**1**	**2**	**2**
a	Toronto	OHL	65	41	67	108	119	10	4	12	16	23
1982-83	**NY Islanders**	**NHL**	**45**	**8**	**11**	**19**	**30**	**10**	**1**	**0**	**1**	**14**
	Indianapolis	CHL	24	11	16	27	23	....	....	....	....	....
1983-84	**NY Islanders**	**NHL**	**79**	**31**	**35**	**66**	**59**	**21**	**5**	**7**	**12**	**39**
1984-85	**NY Islanders**	**NHL**	**58**	**13**	**25**	**38**	**36**	....	....	....	....	....
1985-86	**NY Islanders**	**NHL**	**60**	**9**	**19**	**28**	**82**	**2**	**0**	**0**	**0**	**9**
	Springfield	AHL	2	0	0	0	2	....	....	....	....	....
1986-87	**NY Islanders**	**NHL**	**51**	**6**	**7**	**13**	**26**	**10**	**2**	**2**	**4**	**6**
1987-88	**NY Islanders**	**NHL**	**76**	**17**	**28**	**45**	**46**	**4**	**0**	**0**	**0**	**6**
1988-89	**NY Islanders**	**NHL**	**55**	**8**	**13**	**21**	**45**	....	....	....	....	....
	Chicago	**NHL**	**4**	**0**	**0**	**0**	**0**	**15**	**1**	**5**	**6**	**20**
1989-90	**Chicago**	**NHL**	**70**	**12**	**25**	**37**	**54**	**19**	**5**	**8**	**13**	**34**
1990-91	**Chicago**	**NHL**	**72**	**10**	**15**	**25**	**58**	**5**	**0**	**1**	**1**	**2**
1991-92	**Chicago**	**NHL**	**50**	**7**	**5**	**12**	**35**	**10**	**1**	**3**	**4**	**16**
1992-93	**Chicago**	**NHL**	**77**	**13**	**19**	**32**	**57**	**3**	**0**	**0**	**0**	**0**
	NHL Totals		**698**	**135**	**202**	**337**	**528**	**103**	**16**	**27**	**43**	**148**

a OHL Third All-Star Team (1982)

Traded to **Chicago** by **NY Islanders** for Chicago's fifth round choice (Steve Young) in 1989 Entry Draft, March 7, 1989. Signed as a free agent by **NY Rangers**, July 29, 1993.

GILCHRIST, BRENT

Left wing. Shoots left. 5'11", 181 lbs. Born, Moose Jaw, Sask., April 3, 1967.
(Montreal's 6th choice, 79th overall, in 1985 Entry Draft).

			Regular Season					Playoffs				
Season	Club	Lea	GP	G	A	TP	PIM	GP	G	A	TP	PIM
1983-84	Kelowna	WHL	69	16	11	27	16	....	....	....	....	....
1984-85	Kelowna	WHL	51	35	38	73	58	6	5	2	7	8
1985-86	Spokane	WHL	52	45	45	90	57	9	6	7	13	19
1986-87	Spokane	WHL	46	45	55	100	71	5	2	7	9	6
	Sherbrooke	AHL	....	....	....	....	....	10	2	7	9	2
1987-88	Sherbrooke	AHL	77	26	48	74	83	6	1	3	4	6
1988-89	**Montreal**	**NHL**	**49**	**8**	**16**	**24**	**16**	**9**	**1**	**1**	**2**	**10**
	Sherbrooke	AHL	7	6	5	11	7	....	....	....	....	....
1989-90	**Montreal**	**NHL**	**57**	**9**	**15**	**24**	**28**	**8**	**2**	**0**	**2**	**2**
1990-91	**Montreal**	**NHL**	**51**	**6**	**9**	**15**	**10**	**13**	**5**	**3**	**8**	**6**
1991-92	**Montreal**	**NHL**	**79**	**23**	**27**	**50**	**57**	**11**	**2**	**4**	**6**	**6**
1992-93	**Edmonton**	**NHL**	**60**	**10**	**10**	**20**	**47**	....	....	....	....	....
	Minnesota	**NHL**	**8**	**0**	**1**	**1**	**2**	....	....	....	....	....
	NHL Totals		**304**	**56**	**78**	**134**	**160**	**41**	**10**	**8**	**18**	**24**

Traded to **Edmonton** by **Montreal** with Shayne Corson and Vladimir Vujtek for Vincent Damphousse and Edmonton's fourth round choice (Adam Wiesel) in 1993 Entry Draft, August 27, 1992. Traded to **Minnesota** by **Edmonton** for Todd Elik, March 5, 1993.

GILES, CURT (JIGHLS)

Defense. Shoots left. 5'8", 175 lbs. Born, The Pas, Man., November 30, 1958.
(Minnesota's 4th choice, 54th overall, in 1978 Amateur Draft).

			Regular Season					Playoffs				
Season	Club	Lea	GP	G	A	TP	PIM	GP	G	A	TP	PIM
1977-78	Minn.-Duluth	WCHA	34	11	36	47	62	....	....	....	....	....
1978-79	Minn.-Duluth	WCHA	30	3	38	41	38	....	....	....	....	....
1979-80	**Minnesota**	**NHL**	**37**	**2**	**7**	**9**	**31**	**12**	**2**	**4**	**6**	**10**
	Oklahoma City	CHL	42	4	24	28	35	....	....	....	....	....
1980-81	**Minnesota**	**NHL**	**67**	**5**	**22**	**27**	**56**	**19**	**1**	**4**	**5**	**14**
1981-82	**Minnesota**	**NHL**	**74**	**3**	**12**	**15**	**87**	**4**	**0**	**0**	**0**	**2**
1982-83	**Minnesota**	**NHL**	**76**	**2**	**21**	**23**	**70**	**5**	**0**	**2**	**2**	**6**
1983-84	**Minnesota**	**NHL**	**70**	**6**	**22**	**28**	**59**	**16**	**1**	**3**	**4**	**25**
1984-85	**Minnesota**	**NHL**	**77**	**5**	**25**	**30**	**49**	**9**	**0**	**0**	**0**	**17**
1985-86	**Minnesota**	**NHL**	**69**	**6**	**21**	**27**	**30**	**5**	**0**	**1**	**1**	**10**
1986-87	**Minnesota**	**NHL**	**11**	**0**	**3**	**3**	**4**	....	....	....	....	....
	NY Rangers	**NHL**	**61**	**2**	**17**	**19**	**50**	**5**	**0**	**0**	**0**	**6**
1987-88	**NY Rangers**	**NHL**	**13**	**0**	**0**	**0**	**10**	....	....	....	....	....
	Minnesota	**NHL**	**59**	**1**	**12**	**13**	**66**	....	....	....	....	....
1988-89	**Minnesota**	**NHL**	**76**	**5**	**10**	**15**	**77**	**5**	**0**	**0**	**0**	**4**
1989-90	**Minnesota**	**NHL**	**74**	**1**	**12**	**13**	**48**	**7**	**0**	**1**	**1**	**6**
1990-91	**Minnesota**	**NHL**	**70**	**4**	**10**	**14**	**48**	**10**	**1**	**0**	**1**	**16**
1991-92	Cdn. National	....	31	3	6	9	37	....	....	....	....	....
	Cdn. Olympic	....	8	1	0	1	6	....	....	....	....	....
	St. Louis	**NHL**	**13**	**1**	**1**	**2**	**8**	**3**	**1**	**1**	**2**	**0**
1992-93	**St. Louis**	**NHL**	**48**	**0**	**4**	**4**	**40**	**3**	**0**	**0**	**0**	**2**
	NHL Totals		**895**	**43**	**199**	**242**	**733**	**103**	**6**	**16**	**22**	**118**

Traded to **NY Rangers** by **Minnesota** with Tony McKegney and Minnesota's second round choice (Troy Mallette) in 1988 Entry Draft for Bob Brooke and Minnesota's fourth round choice (previously acquired by NY Rangers — Minnesota selected Jeffery Stolp) in 1988 Entry Draft, November 13, 1986. Traded to **Minnesota** by **NY Rangers** for Byron Lomow and future considerations, November 20, 1987. Signed as a free agent by **St. Louis**, February 29, 1992.

GILHEN, RANDY (GIHL-uhn)

Center. Shoots left. 6', 190 lbs. Born, Zweibrucken, West Germany, June 13, 1963.
(Hartford's 6th choice, 109th overall, in 1982 Entry Draft).

			Regular Season					Playoffs				
Season	Club	Lea	GP	G	A	TP	PIM	GP	G	A	TP	PIM
1980-81	Saskatoon	WHL	68	10	5	15	154	....	....	....	....	....
1981-82	Saskatoon	WHL	25	15	9	24	45	....	....	....	....	....
	Winnipeg	WHL	36	26	28	54	42	....	....	....	....	....
1982-83	**Hartford**	**NHL**	**2**	**0**	**1**	**1**	**0**	....	....	....	....	....
	Winnipeg	WHL	71	57	44	101	84	3	2	2	4	0
1983-84	Binghamton	AHL	73	8	12	20	72	....	....	....	....	....
1984-85	Salt Lake	IHL	57	20	20	40	28	....	....	....	....	....
	Binghamton	AHL	18	3	3	6	9	8	4	1	5	16
1985-86	Fort Wayne	IHL	82	44	40	84	48	15	10	8	18	6
1986-87	**Winnipeg**	**NHL**	**2**	**0**	**0**	**0**	**0**	....	....	....	....	....
	Sherbrooke	AHL	75	36	29	65	44	17	7	13	20	10
1987-88	**Winnipeg**	**NHL**	**13**	**3**	**2**	**5**	**15**	**4**	**1**	**0**	**1**	**10**
	Moncton	AHL	68	40	47	87	51	....	....	....	....	....
1988-89	**Winnipeg**	**NHL**	**64**	**5**	**3**	**8**	**38**	....	....	....	....	....
1989-90	**Pittsburgh**	**NHL**	**61**	**5**	**11**	**16**	**54**	....	....	....	....	....
1990-91	**Pittsburgh**	**NHL**	**72**	**15**	**10**	**25**	**51**	**16**	**1**	**0**	**1**	**14**
1991-92	**Los Angeles**	**NHL**	**33**	**3**	**6**	**9**	**14**	....	....	....	....	....
	NY Rangers	**NHL**	**40**	**7**	**7**	**14**	**14**	**13**	**1**	**2**	**3**	**2**
1992-93	**NY Rangers**	**NHL**	**33**	**3**	**2**	**5**	**8**	....	....	....	....	....
	Tampa Bay	**NHL**	**11**	**0**	**2**	**2**	**6**	....	....	....	....	....
	NHL Totals		**331**	**41**	**44**	**85**	**200**	**33**	**3**	**2**	**5**	**26**

Signed as a free agent by **Winnipeg**, November 8, 1985. Traded to **Pittsburgh** by **Winnipeg** with Jim Kyte and Andrew McBain for Randy Cunneyworth, Rick Tabaracci and Dave McLlwain, June 17, 1989. Claimed by **Minnesota** from **Pittsburgh** in Expansion Draft, May 30, 1991. Traded to **Los Angeles** by **Minnesota** with Charlie Huddy, Jim Thomson and NY Rangers' fourth round choice (previously acquired by Minnesota — Los Angeles selected Alexei Zhitnik) in 1991 Entry Draft for Todd Elik, June 22, 1991. Traded to **NY Rangers** by **Los Angeles** for Corey Millen, December 23, 1991. Traded to **Tampa Bay** by **NY Rangers** for Mike Hartman, March 22, 1993. Claimed by **Florida** from **Tampa Bay** in Expansion Draft, June 24, 1993.

GILL, TODD

Defense. Shoots left. 6', 185 lbs. Born, Brockville, Ont., November 9, 1965.
(Toronto's 2nd choice, 25th overall, in 1984 Entry Draft).

			Regular Season					Playoffs				
Season	Club	Lea	GP	G	A	TP	PIM	GP	G	A	TP	PIM
1982-83	Windsor	OHL	70	12	24	36	108	3	0	0	0	11
1983-84	Windsor	OHL	68	9	48	57	184	3	1	1	2	10
1984-85	**Toronto**	**NHL**	**10**	**1**	**0**	**1**	**13**	....	....	....	....	....
a	Windsor	OHL	53	17	40	57	148	4	0	1	1	14
1985-86	**Toronto**	**NHL**	**15**	**1**	**2**	**3**	**28**	**1**	**0**	**0**	**0**	**0**
	St. Catharines	AHL	58	8	25	33	90	10	1	6	7	17
1986-87	**Toronto**	**NHL**	**61**	**4**	**27**	**31**	**92**	**13**	**2**	**2**	**4**	**42**
	Newmarket	AHL	11	1	8	9	33	....	....	....	....	....
1987-88	**Toronto**	**NHL**	**65**	**8**	**17**	**25**	**131**	**6**	**1**	**3**	**4**	**20**
	Newmarket	AHL	2	0	1	1	2	....	....	....	....	....
1988-89	**Toronto**	**NHL**	**59**	**11**	**14**	**25**	**72**	....	....	....	....	....
1989-90	**Toronto**	**NHL**	**48**	**1**	**14**	**15**	**92**	**5**	**0**	**3**	**3**	**16**
1990-91	**Toronto**	**NHL**	**72**	**2**	**22**	**24**	**113**	....	....	....	....	....
1991-92	**Toronto**	**NHL**	**74**	**2**	**15**	**17**	**91**	....	....	....	....	....
1992-93	**Toronto**	**NHL**	**69**	**11**	**32**	**43**	**66**	**21**	**1**	**10**	**11**	**26**
	NHL Totals		**473**	**41**	**143**	**184**	**698**	**46**	**4**	**18**	**22**	**104**

a OHL Third All-Star Team (1985)

GILLINGHAM, TODD

Left wing. Shoots left. 6'2", 200 lbs. Born, Labrador City, Nfld., January 31, 1970.

			Regular Season					Playoffs				
Season	Club	Lea	GP	G	A	TP	PIM	GP	G	A	TP	PIM
1988-89	Verdun	QMJHL	67	16	25	41	253	....	....	....	....	....
1989-90	Trois-Rivières	QMJHL	62	22	36	58	349	6	3	1	4	72
1990-91a	Trois-Rivières	QMJHL	66	46	102	148	353	6	2	4	6	40
1991-92	St. John's	AHL	66	12	35	47	306	16	4	7	11	80
	Salt Lake	IHL	1	0	0	0	2	....	....	....	....	....
1992-93	Salt Lake	IHL	75	12	21	33	267	....	....	....	....	....

a QMJHL First All-Star Team (1991)

Signed as a free agent by **Calgary**, May 1, 1991. Traded to **Toronto** by **Calgary** for cash, January 15, 1992. Traded to **Calgary** by **Toronto** for cash, June 2, 1992.

GILLIS, PAUL

Center. Shoots left. 5'11", 198 lbs. Born, Toronto, Ont., December 31, 1963.
(Quebec's 2nd choice, 34th overall, in 1982 Entry Draft).

			Regular Season					Playoffs				
Season	Club	Lea	GP	G	A	TP	PIM	GP	G	A	TP	PIM
1980-81	Niagara Falls	OHA	59	14	19	33	165	....	....	....	....	....
1981-82	Niagara Falls	OHL	65	27	62	89	247	5	1	5	6	26
1982-83	**Quebec**	**NHL**	**7**	**0**	**2**	**2**	**2**	....	....	....	....	....
	North Bay	OHL	61	34	52	86	151	6	1	3	4	26
1983-84	**Quebec**	**NHL**	**57**	**8**	**9**	**17**	**59**	**1**	**0**	**0**	**0**	**2**
	Fredericton	AHL	18	7	8	15	47	....	....	....	....	....
1984-85	**Quebec**	**NHL**	**77**	**14**	**28**	**42**	**168**	**18**	**1**	**7**	**8**	**73**
1985-86	**Quebec**	**NHL**	**80**	**19**	**24**	**43**	**203**	**3**	**0**	**2**	**2**	**14**
1986-87	**Quebec**	**NHL**	**76**	**13**	**26**	**39**	**267**	**13**	**2**	**4**	**6**	**65**
1987-88	**Quebec**	**NHL**	**80**	**7**	**10**	**17**	**164**	....	....	....	....	....
1988-89	**Quebec**	**NHL**	**79**	**15**	**25**	**40**	**163**	....	....	....	....	....
1989-90	**Quebec**	**NHL**	**71**	**8**	**14**	**22**	**234**	....	....	....	....	....
1990-91	**Quebec**	**NHL**	**49**	**3**	**8**	**11**	**91**	....	....	....	....	....
	Chicago	**NHL**	**13**	**0**	**5**	**5**	**53**	**2**	**0**	**0**	**0**	**2**
1991-92	**Chicago**	**NHL**	**2**	**0**	**0**	**0**	**6**	....	....	....	....	....
	Indianapolis	IHL	42	10	15	25	170	....	....	....	....	....
	Hartford	**NHL**	**12**	**0**	**2**	**2**	**48**	**5**	**0**	**1**	**1**	**0**
1992-93	**Hartford**	**NHL**	**21**	**1**	**1**	**2**	**40**	....	....	....	....	....
	NHL Totals		**624**	**88**	**154**	**242**	**1498**	**42**	**3**	**14**	**17**	**156**

Traded to **Chicago** by **Quebec** with Dan Vincelette for Ryan McGill and Mike McNeil, March 5, 1991. Traded to **Hartford** by **Chicago** for future considerations, January 27, 1992.

GILMOUR, DOUG

Center. Shoots left. 5'11", 165 lbs. Born, Kingston, Ont., June 25, 1963.
(St. Louis' 4th choice, 134th overall, in 1982 Entry Draft).

			Regular Season					Playoffs				
Season	Club	Lea	GP	G	A	TP	PIM	GP	G	A	TP	PIM
1981	Cornwall	OHL	67	46	73	119	42	5	6	9	15	2
1982-83ab	Cornwall	OHL	68	70	*107	*177	62	8	8	10	18	16
1983-84	St. Louis	NHL	80	25	28	53	57	11	2	9	11	10
1984-85	St. Louis	NHL	78	21	36	57	49	3	1	1	2	2
1985-86	St. Louis	NHL	74	25	28	53	41	19	9	12	*21	25
1986-87	St. Louis	NHL	80	42	63	105	58	6	2	2	4	16
1987-88	St. Louis	NHL	72	36	50	86	59	10	3	14	17	18
1988-89	Calgary	NHL	72	26	59	85	44	22	11	11	22	20
1989-90	Calgary	NHL	78	24	67	91	54	6	3	1	4	8
1990-91	Calgary	NHL	78	20	61	81	144	7	1	1	2	0
1991-92	Calgary	NHL	38	11	27	38	46	....	....	....	....	....
	Toronto	NHL	40	15	34	49	32	....	....	....	....	....
1992-93c	Toronto	NHL	83	32	95	127	100	21	10	*25	35	30
	NHL Totals		773	277	548	825	684	105	42	76	118	129

a OHL First All-Star Team (1983)
b Named OHL's Most Outstanding Player (1983)
c Won Frank J. Selke Trophy (1993)

Played in NHL All-Star Game (1993)

Traded to **Calgary** by **St. Louis** with Mark Hunter, Steve Bozek and Michael Dark for Mike Bullard, Craig Coxe and Tim Corkery, September 6, 1988. Traded to **Toronto** by **Calgary** with Jamie Macoun, Ric Nattress, Kent Manderville and Rick Wamsley for Gary Leeman, Alexander Godynyuk, Jeff Reese, Michel Petit and Craig Berube, January 2, 1992.

GIRARD, RICK

Center. Shoots left. 5'11", 180 lbs. Born, Edmonton, Alta., May 1, 1974.
(Vancouver's 2nd choice, 46th overall, in 1993 Entry Draft).

			Regular Season					Playoffs				
Season	Club	Lea	GP	G	A	TP	PIM	GP	G	A	TP	PIM
1991-92	Swift Current	WHL	45	14	17	31	6	8	2	0	2	2
1992-93ab	Swift Current	WHL	72	71	70	141	25	17	9	17	26	10

a WHL East First All-Star Team (1993)
b Canadian Major Junior Sportsmanlike Player of the Year (1993)

GLYNN, BRIAN

Defense. Shoots left. 6'4", 220 lbs. Born, Iserlohn, West Germany, November 23, 1967.
(Calgary's 2nd choice, 37th overall, in 1986 Entry Draft).

			Regular Season					Playoffs				
Season	Club	Lea	GP	G	A	TP	PIM	GP	G	A	TP	PIM
1984-85	Saskatoon	WHL	12	1	0	1	2	3	0	0	0	0
1985-86	Saskatoon	WHL	66	7	25	32	131	13	0	3	3	30
1986-87	Saskatoon	WHL	44	2	26	28	163	11	1	3	4	19
1987-88	Calgary	NHL	67	5	14	19	87	1	0	0	0	0
1988-89	Calgary	NHL	9	0	1	1	19	....	....	....	....	....
	Salt Lake	IHL	31	3	10	13	105	14	3	7	10	31
1989-90	Calgary	NHL	1	0	0	0	0	....	....	....	....	....
ab	Salt Lake	IHL	80	17	44	61	164	....	....	....	....	....
1990-91	Salt Lake	IHL	8	1	3	4	18	....	....	....	....	....
	Minnesota	NHL	66	8	11	19	83	23	2	6	8	18
1991-92	Minnesota	NHL	37	2	12	14	24	....	....	....	....	....
	Edmonton	NHL	25	2	6	8	6	16	4	1	5	12
1992-93	Edmonton	NHL	64	4	12	16	60	....	....	....	....	....
	NHL Totals		269	21	56	77	279	40	6	7	13	30

a IHL First All-Star Team (1990)
b Won Governors' Trophy (Outstanding Defenseman-IHL) (1990)

Traded to **Minnesota** by **Calgary** for Frantisek Musil, October 26, 1990. Traded to **Edmonton** by **Minnesota** for David Shaw, January 21, 1992.

GODYNYUK, ALEXANDER (goh-dih-NYOOK)

Defense. Shoots left. 6', 207 lbs. Born, Kiev, Soviet Union, January 27, 1970.
(Toronto's 5th choice, 115th overall, in 1990 Entry Draft).

			Regular Season					Playoffs				
Season	Club	Lea	GP	G	A	TP	PIM	GP	G	A	TP	PIM
1986-87	Sokol Kiev	USSR	9	0	1	1	2	....	....	....	....	....
1987-88	Sokol Kiev	USSR	2	0	0	0	2	....	....	....	....	....
1988-89	Sokol Kiev	USSR	30	3	3	6	12	....	....	....	....	....
1989-90	Sokol Kiev	USSR	37	3	2	5	31	....	....	....	....	....
1990-91	Sokol Kiev	USSR	19	3	1	4	20	....	....	....	....	....
	Toronto	NHL	18	0	3	3	16	....	....	....	....	....
	Newmarket	AHL	11	0	1	1	29	....	....	....	....	....
1991-92	Toronto	NHL	31	3	6	9	59	....	....	....	....	....
	Calgary	NHL	6	0	1	1	4	....	....	....	....	....
	Salt Lake	IHL	17	2	1	3	24	....	....	....	....	....
1992-93	Calgary	NHL	27	3	4	7	19	....	....	....	....	....
	NHL Totals		82	6	14	20	98	....	....	....	....	....

Traded to **Calgary** by **Toronto** with Craig Berube, Gary Leeman, Michel Petit and Jeff Reese for Doug Gilmour, Jamie Macoun, Ric Nattress, Rick Wamsley and Kent Manderville, January 2, 1992. Claimed by **Florida** from **Calgary** in Expansion Draft, June 24, 1993.

GOMOLYAKO, SERGI (goh-mohl-YAW-khav)

Center. Shoots . 6'1", 207 lbs. Born, Chelyabinsk, Soviet Union, January 19, 1970.
(Calgary's 10th choice, 189th overall, in 1989 Entry Draft).

			Regular Season					Playoffs				
Season	Club	Lea	GP	G	A	TP	PIM	GP	G	A	TP	PIM
1991-92	Chelyabinsk	CIS	30	5	10	15	18	....	....	....	....	....
1992-93	Chelyabinsk	CIS	39	13	19	32	48	....	....	....	....	....

GONCHAR, SERGEI (gohn-CHAR)

Defense. Shoots left. 6', 190 lbs. Born, Chelyabinsk, Soviet Union, April 13, 1974.
(Washington's 1st choice, 14th overall, in 1992 Entry Draft).

			Regular Season					Playoffs				
Season	Club	Lea	GP	G	A	TP	PIM	GP	G	A	TP	PIM
1991-92	Chelyabinsk	CIS	31	1	0	1	6	....	....	....	....	....
1992-93	Moscow D'amo	CIS	31	1	3	4	70	10	0	0	0	12

GORDIOUK, VIKTOR (gohr-dee-YOOK)

Left wing. Shoots right. 5'10", 176 lbs. Born, Odintsovo, Soviet Union, April 11, 1970.
(Buffalo's 6th choice, 142nd overall, in 1990 Entry Draft).

			Regular Season					Playoffs				
Season	Club	Lea	GP	G	A	TP	PIM	GP	G	A	TP	PIM
1986-87	Soviet Wings	USSR	2	0	0	0	0	....	....	....	....	....
1987-88	Soviet Wings	USSR	26	2	2	4	6	....	....	....	....	....
1988-89	Soviet Wings	USSR	41	5	1	6	10	....	....	....	....	....
1989-90	Soviet Wings	USSR	48	11	4	15	24	....	....	....	....	....
1990-91	Soviet Wings	USSR	46	12	10	22	22	....	....	....	....	....
1991-92	Soviet Wings	CIS	42	16	7	23	24	....	....	....	....	....
1992-93	Buffalo	NHL	16	3	6	9	0	....	....	....	....	....
	Rochester	AHL	35	11	14	25	8	17	9	9	18	4
	NHL Totals		16	3	6	9	0	....	....	....	....	....

GOTZIAMAN, CHRIS

Right wing. Shoots right. 6'3", 200 lbs. Born, Roseau, MN, November 29, 1971.
(New Jersey's 3rd choice, 29th overall, in 1990 Entry Draft).

			Regular Season					Playoffs				
Season	Club	Lea	GP	G	A	TP	PIM	GP	G	A	TP	PIM
1990-91	North Dakota	WCHA	40	11	8	19	26	....	....	....	....	....
1991-92	North Dakota	WCHA	38	9	6	15	47	....	....	....	....	....
1992-93	North Dakota	WCHA	35	10	10	20	50	....	....	....	....	....

GOULET, MICHEL (goo-LAY)

Left wing. Shoots left. 6'1", 195 lbs. Born, Peribonka, Que., April 21, 1960.
(Quebec's 1st choice, 20th overall, in 1979 Entry Draft).

			Regular Season					Playoffs				
Season	Club	Lea	GP	G	A	TP	PIM	GP	G	A	TP	PIM
1976-77	Quebec	QJHL	37	17	18	35	9	14	3	8	11	19
1977-78	Quebec	QJHL	72	73	62	135	109	1	0	1	1	0
1978-79	Birmingham	WHA	78	28	30	58	65	....	....	....	....	....
1979-80	Quebec	NHL	77	22	32	54	48	....	....	....	....	....
1980-81	Quebec	NHL	76	32	39	71	45	4	3	4	7	7
1981-82	Quebec	NHL	80	42	42	84	48	16	8	5	13	6
1982-83a	Quebec	NHL	80	57	48	105	51	4	0	0	0	6
1983-84b	Quebec	NHL	75	56	65	121	76	9	2	4	6	17
1984-85	Quebec	NHL	69	55	40	95	55	17	11	10	21	17
1985-86b	Quebec	NHL	75	53	51	104	64	3	1	2	3	10
1986-87b	Quebec	NHL	75	49	47	96	61	13	9	5	14	35
1987-88a	Quebec	NHL	80	48	58	106	56	....	....	....	....	....
1988-89	Quebec	NHL	69	26	38	64	67	....	....	....	....	....
1989-90	Quebec	NHL	57	16	29	45	42	....	....	....	....	....
	Chicago	NHL	8	4	1	5	9	14	2	4	6	6
1990-91	Chicago	NHL	74	27	38	65	65	....	....	....	....	....
1991-92	Chicago	NHL	75	22	41	63	69	9	3	4	7	6
1992-93	Chicago	NHL	63	23	21	44	43	3	0	1	1	0
	NHL Totals		1033	532	590	1122	799	92	39	39	78	110

a NHL Second All-Star Team (1983, 1988)
b NHL First All-Star Team (1984, 1986, 1987)

Played in NHL All-Star Game (1983-86, 1988)

Traded to **Chicago** by **Quebec** with Greg Millen and Quebec's sixth round choice (Kevin St. Jacques) in 1991 Entry Draft for Mario Doyon, Everett Sanipass and Dan Vincelette, March 5, 1990.

GOVEDARIS, CHRIS (goh-va-DAIR-us)

Left wing. Shoots left. 6', 200 lbs. Born, Toronto, Ont., February 2, 1970.
(Hartford's 1st choice, 11th overall, in 1988 Entry Draft).

			Regular Season					Playoffs				
Season	Club	Lea	GP	G	A	TP	PIM	GP	G	A	TP	PIM
1986-87	Toronto	OHL	64	36	28	64	148	....	....	....	....	....
1987-88	Toronto	OHL	62	42	38	80	118	4	2	1	3	10
1988-89	Toronto	OHL	49	41	38	79	117	6	2	3	5	0
1989-90	Hartford	NHL	12	0	1	1	6	2	0	0	0	2
	Binghamton	AHL	14	3	3	6	4	....	....	....	....	....
	Hamilton	OHL	23	11	21	32	53	....	....	....	....	....
1990-91	Hartford	NHL	14	1	3	4	4	....	....	....	....	....
	Springfield	AHL	56	26	36	62	133	9	2	5	7	36
1991-92	Springfield	AHL	43	14	25	39	55	11	3	2	5	25
1992-93	Hartford	NHL	7	1	0	1	0	....	....	....	....	....
	Springfield	AHL	65	31	24	55	58	15	7	4	11	18
	NHL Totals		33	2	4	6	10	2	0	0	0	2

GRACHEV, VLADIMIR

Left wing. Shoots left. 6', 178 lbs. Born, Moscow, Soviet Union, January 28, 1973.
(NY Islanders' 6th choice, 152nd overall, in 1992 Entry Draft).

			Regular Season					Playoffs				
Season	Club	Lea	GP	G	A	TP	PIM	GP	G	A	TP	PIM
1991-92	Moscow D'amo	CIS 3	62	13	3	16	26	....	....	....	....	....
1992-93	Moscow D'amo	CIS	33	2	1	3	26	7	0	0	0	2

GRAHAM, DIRK MILTON

Left/Right wing. Shoots right. 5'11", 198 lbs. Born, Regina, Sask., July 29, 1959.
(Vancouver's 5th choice, 89th overall, in 1979 Entry Draft).

			Regular Season					Playoffs				
Season	Club	Lea	GP	G	A	TP	PIM	GP	G	A	TP	PIM
1975-76	Regina	WCHL	2	0	0	0	0	6	1	1	2	5
1976-77	Regina	WCHL	65	37	28	65	66	....	....	....	....	....
1977-78	Regina	WCHL	72	49	61	110	87	13	15	19	34	37
1978-79	Regina	WHL	71	48	60	108	252	....	....	....	....	....
1979-80	Dallas	CHL	62	17	15	32	96	....	....	....	....	....
1980-81	Fort Wayne	IHL	6	1	2	3	12	....	....	....	....	....
a	Toledo	IHL	61	40	45	85	88	....	....	....	....	....
1981-82	Toledo	IHL	72	49	56	105	68	13	10	11	*21	8
1982-83b	Toledo	IHL	78	70	55	125	88	11	13	7	*20	30
1983-84	**Minnesota**	**NHL**	**6**	**1**	**1**	**2**	**0**	**1**	**0**	**0**	**0**	**2**
c	Salt Lake	CHL	57	37	57	94	72	5	3	8	11	2
1984-85	**Minnesota**	**NHL**	**36**	**12**	**11**	**23**	**23**	**9**	**0**	**4**	**4**	**7**
	Springfield	AHL	37	20	28	48	41	....	....	....	....	....
1985-86	**Minnesota**	**NHL**	**80**	**22**	**33**	**55**	**87**	**5**	**3**	**1**	**4**	**2**
1986-87	**Minnesota**	**NHL**	**76**	**25**	**29**	**54**	**142**	....	....	....	....	....
1987-88	**Minnesota**	**NHL**	**28**	**7**	**5**	**12**	**39**	....	....	....	....	....
	Chicago	**NHL**	**42**	**17**	**19**	**36**	**32**	**4**	**1**	**2**	**3**	**4**
1988-89	**Chicago**	**NHL**	**80**	**33**	**45**	**78**	**89**	**16**	**2**	**4**	**6**	**38**
1989-90	**Chicago**	**NHL**	**73**	**22**	**32**	**54**	**102**	**5**	**1**	**5**	**6**	**2**
1990-91d	**Chicago**	**NHL**	**80**	**24**	**21**	**45**	**88**	**6**	**1**	**2**	**3**	**17**
1991-92	**Chicago**	**NHL**	**80**	**17**	**30**	**47**	**89**	**18**	**7**	**5**	**12**	**8**
1992-93	**Chicago**	**NHL**	**84**	**20**	**17**	**37**	**139**	**4**	**0**	**0**	**0**	**0**
	NHL Totals		**665**	**200**	**243**	**443**	**830**	**68**	**15**	**23**	**38**	**80**

a IHL Second All-Star Team (1981)
b IHL First All-Star Team (1983)
c CHL First All-Star Team (1984)
d Won Frank J. Selke Trophy (1991)

Signed as a free agent by **Minnesota**, August 17, 1983. Traded to **Chicago** by **Minnesota** for Curt Fraser, January 4, 1988.

GRANATO, TONY

Left wing. Shoots right. 5'10", 185 lbs. Born, Downers Grove, IL, July 25, 1964.
(NY Rangers' 5th choice, 120th overall, in 1982 Entry Draft).

			Regular Season					Playoffs				
Season	Club	Lea	GP	G	A	TP	PIM	GP	G	A	TP	PIM
1983-84	U. Wisconsin	WCHA	35	14	17	31	48	....	....	....	....	....
1984-85	U. Wisconsin	WCHA	42	33	34	67	94	....	....	....	....	....
1985-86	U. Wisconsin	WCHA	33	25	24	49	36	....	....	....	....	....
1986-87ab	U. Wisconsin	WCHA	42	28	45	73	64	....	....	....	....	....
1987-88	U.S. National	....	49	40	31	71	55	....	....	....	....	....
	U.S. Olympic	....	6	1	7	8	4	....	....	....	....	....
	Colorado	IHL	22	13	14	27	36	8	9	4	13	16
1988-89c	**NY Rangers**	**NHL**	**78**	**36**	**27**	**63**	**140**	**4**	**1**	**1**	**2**	**21**
1989-90	**NY Rangers**	**NHL**	**37**	**7**	**18**	**25**	**77**	....	....	....	....	....
	Los Angeles	**NHL**	**19**	**5**	**6**	**11**	**45**	**10**	**5**	**4**	**9**	**12**
1990-91	**Los Angeles**	**NHL**	**68**	**30**	**34**	**64**	**154**	**12**	**1**	**4**	**5**	**28**
1991-92	**Los Angeles**	**NHL**	**80**	**39**	**29**	**68**	**187**	**6**	**1**	**5**	**6**	**10**
1992-93	**Los Angeles**	**NHL**	**81**	**37**	**45**	**82**	**171**	**24**	**6**	**11**	**17**	**50**
	NHL Totals		**363**	**154**	**159**	**313**	**774**	**56**	**14**	**25**	**39**	**121**

a WCHA Second All-Star Team (1987)
b NCAA West Second All-American Team (1987)
c NHL All-Rookie Team (1989)

Traded to **Los Angeles** by **NY Rangers** with Tomas Sandstrom for Bernie Nicholls, January 20, 1990.

GRANT, KEVIN

Defense. Shoots right. 6'3", 210 lbs. Born, Toronto, Ont., January 9, 1969.
(Calgary's 3rd choice, 40th overall, in 1987 Entry Draft).

			Regular Season					Playoffs				
Season	Club	Lea	GP	G	A	TP	PIM	GP	G	A	TP	PIM
1985-86	Kitchener	OHL	63	2	15	17	204	5	0	1	1	11
1986-87	Kitchener	OHL	52	5	18	23	125	4	0	1	1	16
1987-88	Kitchener	OHL	48	3	20	23	138	4	0	1	1	4
1988-89	Salt Lake	IHL	3	0	1	1	5	3	0	0	0	12
	Sudbury	OHL	60	9	41	50	186	....	....	....	....	....
1989-90	Salt Lake	IHL	78	7	17	24	117	11	0	2	2	22
1990-91	Salt Lake	IHL	63	6	19	25	200	3	0	0	0	8
1991-92	Salt Lake	IHL	73	7	16	23	181	....	....	....	....	....
1992-93	Salt Lake	IHL	1	0	0	0	2	....	....	....	....	....
	Phoenix	IHL	49	4	17	21	119	....	....	....	....	....

Traded to **Los Angeles** by **Calgary** for Paul Holden, October 16, 1992.

GRATTON, CHRIS

Center. Shoots left. 6'3", 202 lbs. Born, Brantford, Ont., July 5, 1975.
(Tampa Bay's 1st choice, 3rd overall, in 1993 Entry Draft).

			Regular Season					Playoffs				
Season	Club	Lea	GP	G	A	TP	PIM	GP	G	A	TP	PIM
1991-92	Kingston	OHL	62	27	29	66	37	....	....	....	....	....
1992-93	Kingston	OHL	58	55	54	109	125	16	11	18	29	42

GRAVELLE, DAN

Center. Shoots left. 5'11", 190 lbs. Born, Montreal, Que., March 10, 1970.
(Chicago's 1st choice, 28th overall, in 1991 Supplemental Draft).

			Regular Season					Playoffs				
Season	Club	Lea	GP	G	A	TP	PIM	GP	G	A	TP	PIM
1989-90	Merrimack	H.E.	10	2	1	3	13	....	....	....	....	....
1990-91	Merrimack	H.E.	32	18	21	39	22	....	....	....	....	....
1991-92	Merrimack	H.E.	34	23	28	51	40	....	....	....	....	....
1992-93	Merrimack	H.E.	36	18	24	42	59	....	....	....	....	....

GRAVES, ADAM

Center. Shoots left. 6', 207 lbs. Born, Toronto, Ont., April 12, 1968.
(Detroit's 2nd choice, 22nd overall, in 1986 Entry Draft).

			Regular Season					Playoffs				
Season	Club	Lea	GP	G	A	TP	PIM	GP	G	A	TP	PIM
1985-86	Windsor	OHL	62	27	37	64	35	16	5	11	16	10
1986-87	Windsor	OHL	66	45	55	100	70	14	9	8	17	32
	Adirondack	AHL	....	....	....	....	....	5	0	1	1	0
1987-88	**Detroit**	**NHL**	**9**	**0**	**1**	**1**	**8**	....	....	....	....	....
	Windsor	OHL	37	28	32	60	107	12	14	18	*32	16
1988-89	**Detroit**	**NHL**	**56**	**7**	**5**	**12**	**60**	**5**	**0**	**0**	**0**	**4**
	Adirondack	AHL	14	10	11	21	28	14	11	7	18	17
1989-90	**Detroit**	**NHL**	**13**	**0**	**1**	**1**	**13**	....	....	....	....	....
	Edmonton	**NHL**	**63**	**9**	**12**	**21**	**123**	**22**	**5**	**6**	**11**	**17**
1990-91	**Edmonton**	**NHL**	**76**	**7**	**18**	**25**	**127**	**18**	**2**	**4**	**6**	**22**
1991-92	**NY Rangers**	**NHL**	**80**	**26**	**33**	**59**	**139**	**10**	**5**	**3**	**8**	**22**
1992-93	**NY Rangers**	**NHL**	**84**	**36**	**29**	**65**	**148**	....	....	....	....	....
	NHL Totals		**381**	**85**	**99**	**184**	**618**	**55**	**12**	**13**	**25**	**65**

Traded to **Edmonton** by **Detroit** with Petr Klima, Joe Murphy and Jeff Sharples for Jimmy Carson, Kevin McClelland and Edmonton's fifth round choice (later traded to Montreal — Montreal selected Brad Layzell) in 1991 Entry Draft, November 2, 1989. Signed as a free agent by **NY Rangers**, September 3, 1991.

GREEN, MARK

Center. Shoots right. 6'4", 200 lbs. Born, Watertown, NY, December 26, 1967.
(Winnipeg's 8th choice, 176th overall, in 1986 Entry Draft).

			Regular Season					Playoffs				
Season	Club	Lea	GP	G	A	TP	PIM	GP	G	A	TP	PIM
1987-88	Clarkson	ECAC	18	3	6	9	18	....	....	....	....	....
1988-89	Clarkson	ECAC	30	16	11	27	42	....	....	....	....	....
1989-90	Clarkson	ECAC	32	18	17	35	4	....	....	....	....	....
1990-91	Clarkson	ECAC	38	21	24	45	32	....	....	....	....	....
1991-92a	Johnstown	ECHL	64	68	49	117	44	6	2	3	5	4
1992-93	Louisville	ECHL	61	48	29	77	57	....	....	....	....	....
	Atlanta	IHL	5	0	1	1	0	....	....	....	....	....

a ECHL First All-Star Team (1992)

Signed as a free agent by **Tampa Bay**, August 18, 1992.

GREEN, SHAYNE

Right wing. Shoots right. 6', 193 lbs. Born, Quesnel, B.C., August 13, 1971.
(Minnesota's 11th choice, 228th overall, in 1991 Entry Draft).

			Regular Season					Playoffs				
Season	Club	Lea	GP	G	A	TP	PIM	GP	G	A	TP	PIM
1988-89	Victoria	WHL	13	3	3	6	0	....	....	....	....	....
1989-90	Victoria	WHL	43	16	14	30	26	....	....	....	....	....
1990-91	Victoria	WHL	16	5	7	12	4	....	....	....	....	....
	Portland	WHL	22	6	14	20	12	....	....	....	....	....
	Kamloops	WHL	32	15	15	30	43	12	4	8	12	14
1991-92	Kamloops	WHL	71	43	55	98	167	17	10	11	21	32
1992-93	Dayton	ECHL	55	17	24	41	117	3	0	1	1	0
	Kalamazoo	IHL	1	0	0	0	0	....	....	....	....	....

GREEN, TRAVIS

Center. Shoots right. 6'2", 200 lbs. Born, Castlegar, B.C., December 20, 1970.
(NY Islanders' 2nd choice, 23rd overall, in 1989 Entry Draft).

			Regular Season					Playoffs				
Season	Club	Lea	GP	G	A	TP	PIM	GP	G	A	TP	PIM
1986-87	Spokane	WHL	64	8	17	25	27	3	0	0	0	0
1987-88	Spokane	WHL	72	33	54	87	42	15	10	10	20	13
1988-89	Spokane	WHL	75	51	51	102	79	....	....	....	....	....
1989-90	Spokane	WHL	50	45	44	89	80	....	....	....	....	....
	Medicine Hat	WHL	25	15	24	39	19	3	0	0	0	2
1990-91	Capital Dist.	AHL	73	21	34	55	26	....	....	....	....	....
1991-92	Capital Dist.	AHL	71	23	27	50	10	7	0	4	4	21
1992-93	**NY Islanders**	**NHL**	**61**	**7**	**18**	**25**	**43**	**12**	**3**	**1**	**4**	**6**
	Capital Dist.	AHL	20	12	11	23	39	....	....	....	....	....
	NHL Totals		**61**	**7**	**18**	**25**	**43**	**12**	**3**	**1**	**4**	**6**

GREENLAW, JEFF

Left wing. Shoots left. 6'1", 230 lbs. Born, Toronto, Ont., February 28, 1968.
(Washington's 1st choice, 19th overall, in 1986 Entry Draft).

			Regular Season					Playoffs				
Season	Club	Lea	GP	G	A	TP	PIM	GP	G	A	TP	PIM
1985-86	Cdn. Olympic	....	57	3	16	19	81	....	....	....	....	....
1986-87	**Washington**	**NHL**	**22**	**0**	**3**	**3**	**44**	....	....	....	....	....
	Binghamton	AHL	4	0	2	2	0	....	....	....	....	....
1987-88	Binghamton	AHL	56	8	7	15	142	1	0	0	0	2
	Washington	**NHL**	....	....	....	....	....	**1**	**0**	**0**	**0**	**19**
1988-89	Baltimore	AHL	55	12	15	27	115	....	....	....	....	....
1989-90	Baltimore	AHL	10	3	2	5	26	7	1	0	1	13
1990-91	**Washington**	**NHL**	**10**	**2**	**0**	**2**	**10**	**1**	**0**	**0**	**0**	**2**
	Baltimore	AHL	50	17	17	34	93	3	1	1	2	2
1991-92	**Washington**	**NHL**	**5**	**0**	**1**	**1**	**34**	....	....	....	....	....
	Baltimore	AHL	37	6	8	14	57	....	....	....	....	....
1992-93	**Washington**	**NHL**	**16**	**1**	**1**	**2**	**18**	....	....	....	....	....
	Baltimore	AHL	49	12	14	26	66	7	3	1	4	0
	NHL Totals		**53**	**3**	**5**	**8**	**106**	**2**	**0**	**0**	**0**	**21**

GREIG, MARK (GREG)

Right wing. Shoots right. 5'11", 190 lbs. Born, High River, Alta., January 25, 1970.
(Hartford's 1st choice, 15th overall, in 1990 Entry Draft).

			Regular Season					Playoffs				
Season	Club	Lea	GP	G	A	TP	PIM	GP	G	A	TP	PIM
1987-88	Lethbridge	WHL	65	9	18	27	38	....	....	....	....	....
1988-89	Lethbridge	WHL	71	36	72	108	113	8	5	5	10	16
1989-90a	Lethbridge	WHL	65	55	80	135	149	18	11	21	32	35
1990-91	**Hartford**	**NHL**	**4**	**0**	**0**	**0**	**0**	....	....	....	....	....
	Springfield	AHL	73	32	55	87	73	17	2	6	8	22
1991-92	**Hartford**	**NHL**	**17**	**0**	**5**	**5**	**6**	....	....	....	....	....
	Springfield	AHL	50	20	27	47	38	9	1	1	2	20
1992-93	**Hartford**	**NHL**	**22**	**1**	**7**	**8**	**27**	....	....	....	....	....
	Springfield	AHL	55	20	38	58	86	....	....	....	....	....
	NHL Totals		**43**	**1**	**12**	**13**	**33**	....	....	....	....	....

a WHL East First All-Star Team (1990)

GRETZKY, BRENT (GRETZ-kee)
Center. Shoots left. 5'10", 160 lbs.   Born, Brantford, Ont., February 20, 1972.
(Tampa Bay's 3rd choice, 49th overall, in 1992 Entry Draft).

			Regular Season					Playoffs			
Season	Club	Lea	GP	G	A	TP	PIM	GP	G	A	TP	PIM
1989-90	Belleville	OHL	66	15	32	47	30	11	0	0	0	0
1990-91	Belleville	OHL	66	26	56	82	25	6	3	3	6	2
1991-92	Belleville	OHL	62	43	78	121	37	....	....	....	....	....
1992-93	Atlanta	IHL	77	20	34	54	84	9	3	2	5	8

GRETZKY, WAYNE (GRETZ-kee)
Center. Shoots left. 6', 170 lbs.   Born, Brantford, Ont., January 26, 1961.

			Regular Season					Playoffs			
Season	Club	Lea	GP	G	A	TP	PIM	GP	G	A	TP	PIM
1976-77	Peterborough	OHA	3	0	3	3	0	....	....	....	....	....
1977-78ab	S.S. Marie	OHA	64	70	112	182	14	13	6	20	26	0
1978-79	Indianapolis	WHA	8	3	3	6	0	....	....	....	....	....
cd	Edmonton	WHA	72	43	61	104	19	13	*10	10	*20	2
1979-80efg	Edmonton	NHL	79	51	*86	*137	21	3	2	1	3	0
1980-81 ehijk	Edmonton	NHL	80	55	*109	*164	28	9	7	14	21	4
1981-82 ehijklmq	Edmonton	NHL	80	*92	*120	*212	26	5	5	7	12	8
1982-83 ehijmno	Edmonton	NHL	80	*71	*125	*196	59	16	12	*26	*38	4
1983-84 ehimq	Edmonton	NHL	74	*87	*118	*205	39	19	13	*22	*35	12
1984-85 ehijmnopqr	Edmonton	NHL	80	*73	*135	*208	52	18	17	*30	*47	4
1985-86 ehijkr	Edmonton	NHL	80	52	*163	*215	46	10	8	11	19	2
1986-87 ehimqr	Edmonton	NHL	79	*62	*121	*183	28	21	5	*29	*34	6
1987-88gnp	Edmonton	NHL	64	40	*109	149	24	19	12	*31	*43	16
1988-89egs	Los Angeles	NHL	78	54	*114	168	26	11	5	17	22	0
1989-90gi	Los Angeles	NHL	73	40	*102	*142	42	7	3	7	10	0
1990-91fhi	Los Angeles	NHL	78	41	*122	*163	16	12	4	11	15	2
1991-92f	Los Angeles	NHL	74	31	*90	121	34	6	2	5	7	2
1992-93	Los Angeles	NHL	45	16	49	65	6	24	*15	*25	*40	4
	NHL Totals		**1044**	**765**	**1563**	**2328**	**447**	**180**	**110**	**236**	**346**	**64**

a OHA Second All-Star Team (1978)
b Named OHA's Rookie of the Year (1978)
c WHA Second All-Star Team (1979)
d Named WHA's Rookie of the Year (1979)
e Won Hart Trophy (1980, 1981, 1982, 1983, 1984, 1985, 1986, 1987, 1989)
f Won Lady Byng Trophy (1980, 1991, 1992)
g NHL Second All-Star Team (1980, 1988, 1989, 1990)
h NHL First All-Star Team (1981, 1982, 1983, 1984, 1985, 1986, 1987, 1991)
i Won Art Ross Trophy (1981, 1982, 1983, 1984, 1985, 1986, 1987, 1990, 1991)
j NHL record for assists in regular season (1981, 1982, 1983, 1985, 1986)
k NHL record for points in regular season (1981, 1982, 1986)
l NHL record for goals in regular season (1982)
m Won Lester B. Pearson Award (1982, 1983, 1984, 1985, 1987)
n NHL record for assists in one playoff year (1983, 1985, 1988)
o NHL record for points in one playoff year (1983, 1985)
p Won Conn Smythe Trophy (1985, 1988)
q NHL Plus/Minus Leader (1982, 1984, 1985, 1987)
r Selected Chrysler-Dodge/NHL Performer of the Year (1985, 1986, 1987)
s Won Dodge Performance of the Year Award (1989)
Played in NHL All-Star Game (1980-1986, 1988-93)

Reclaimed by **Edmonton** as an under-age junior prior to Expansion Draft, June 9, 1979. Claimed as priority selection by **Edmonton**, June 9, 1979. Traded to **Los Angeles** by **Edmonton** with Mike Krushelnyski and Marty McSorley for Jimmy Carson, Martin Gelinas, Los Angeles' first round choices in 1989 (acquired by New Jersey — New Jersey selected Jason Miller), 1991 (Martin Rucinsky) and 1993 (Nick Stajduhar) Entry Drafts and cash, August 9, 1988.

GRIEVE, BRENT
Left wing. Shoots left. 6'1", 202 lbs.   Born, Oshawa, Ont., May 9, 1969.
(NY Islanders' 4th choice, 65th overall, in 1989 Entry Draft).

			Regular Season					Playoffs			
Season	Club	Lea	GP	G	A	TP	PIM	GP	G	A	TP	PIM
1986-87	Oshawa	OHL	60	9	19	28	102	24	3	8	11	22
1987-88	Oshawa	OHL	55	19	20	39	122	7	0	1	1	8
1988-89	Oshawa	OHL	49	34	33	67	105	6	4	3	7	4
1989-90	Oshawa	OHL	62	46	47	93	125	17	10	10	20	26
1990-91	Capital Dist.	AHL	61	14	13	27	80	....	....	....	....	....
	Kansas City	IHL	5	2	2	4	2	....	....	....	....	....
1991-92	Capital Dist.	AHL	74	34	32	66	84	7	3	1	4	16
1992-93	Capital Dist.	AHL	79	34	28	62	122	4	1	1	2	10

GRILLO, DEAN
Right wing. Shoots right. 6'2", 210 lbs.   Born, Bemidji, MN, December 8, 1972.
(San Jose's 9th choice, 155th overall, in 1991 Entry Draft).

			Regular Season					Playoffs			
Season	Club	Lea	GP	G	A	TP	PIM	GP	G	A	TP	PIM
1991-92	Waterloo	USHL	48	27	38	65	42	....	....	....	....	....
1992-93	North Dakota	WCHA	29	7	4	11	14	....	....	....	....	....

GRIMES, JAKE
Center. Shoots left. 6'1", 196 lbs.   Born, Montreal, Que., September 13, 1972.
(Ottawa's 10th choice, 217th overall, in 1992 Entry Draft).

			Regular Season					Playoffs			
Season	Club	Lea	GP	G	A	TP	PIM	GP	G	A	TP	PIM
1990-91	Belleville	OHL	66	31	41	72	16	6	2	0	2	0
1991-92	Belleville	OHL	66	44	69	113	18	5	4	0	4	0
1992-93	New Haven	AHL	76	18	20	38	30	....	....	....	....	....

GRIMSON, STU
Left wing. Shoots left. 6'5", 227 lbs.   Born, Kamloops, B.C., May 20, 1965.
(Calgary's 8th choice, 143rd overall, in 1985 Entry Draft).

			Regular Season					Playoffs			
Season	Club	Lea	GP	G	A	TP	PIM	GP	G	A	TP	PIM
1982-83	Regina	WHL	48	0	1	1	105	5	0	0	0	14
1983-84	Regina	WHL	63	8	8	16	131	21	0	1	1	29
1984-85	Regina	WHL	71	24	32	56	248	8	1	2	3	14
1985-86	U. Manitoba	CWUAA	12	7	4	11	113	3	1	1	2	20
1986-87	U. Manitoba	CWUAA	29	8	8	16	67	14	4	2	6	28
1987-88	Salt Lake	IHL	38	9	5	14	268	....	....	....	....	....
1988-89	Calgary	NHL	1	0	0	0	5	....	....	....	....	....
	Salt Lake	IHL	72	9	18	27	397	14	2	3	5	86
1989-90	Calgary	NHL	3	0	0	0	17	....	....	....	....	....
	Salt Lake	IHL	62	8	8	16	319	4	0	0	0	8
1990-91	Chicago	NHL	35	0	1	1	183	5	0	0	0	46
1991-92	Chicago	NHL	54	2	2	4	234	14	0	1	1	10
	Indianapolis	IHL	5	1	1	2	17	....	....	....	....	....
1992-93	Chicago	NHL	78	1	1	2	193	2	0	0	0	4
	NHL Totals		**171**	**3**	**4**	**7**	**632**	**21**	**0**	**1**	**1**	**60**

Claimed by **Chicago** on conditional waivers, October 1, 1990. Claimed by **Anaheim** from **Chicago** in Expansion Draft, June 24, 1993.

GROLEAU, FRANCOIS
Defense. Shoots left. 6', 200 lbs.   Born, Longueuil, Que., January 23, 1973.
(Calgary's 2nd choice, 41st overall, in 1991 Entry Draft).

			Regular Season					Playoffs			
Season	Club	Lea	GP	G	A	TP	PIM	GP	G	A	TP	PIM
1989-90ab	Shawinigan	QMJHL	65	11	54	65	80	6	0	1	1	12
1990-91	Shawinigan	QMJHL	70	9	60	69	70	6	0	3	3	2
1991-92c	Shawinigan	QMJHL	65	8	70	78	74	10	5	15	20	8
1992-93	St-Jean	QMJHL	48	7	38	45	66	4	0	1	1	14

a QMJHL Defensive Rookie of the Year (1990)
b QMJHL Second All-Star Team (1990)
c QMJHL First All-Star Team (1992)

GRONMAN, TUOMAS (GROHN-mahn)
Defense. Shoots right. 6'3", 198 lbs.   Born, Viitasaari, Finland, March 22, 1974.
(Quebec's 3rd choice, 29th overall, in 1992 Entry Draft).

			Regular Season					Playoffs			
Season	Club	Lea	GP	G	A	TP	PIM	GP	G	A	TP	PIM
1991-92	Tacoma	WHL	61	5	18	23	102	4	0	1	1	2
1992-93	Lukko	Fin.	45	2	11	13	46	3	1	0	1	2

GRONVALL, JANNE (GROHN-vahl, YAH-neh)
Defense. Shoots left. 6'3", 194 lbs.   Born, Rauma, Finland, July 17, 1973.
(Toronto's 5th choice, 101st overall, in 1992 Entry Draft).

			Regular Season					Playoffs			
Season	Club	Lea	GP	G	A	TP	PIM	GP	G	A	TP	PIM
1989-90	Lukko	Fin.	5	0	0	0	0	....	....	....	....	....
1990-91	Lukko	Fin.	40	2	8	10	30	....	....	....	....	....
1991-92	Lukko	Fin.	42	2	6	8	40	2	0	0	0	2
1992-93	Tappara	Fin.	46	1	7	8	54	....	....	....	....	....

GROSEK, MICHAL
Left wing. Shoots right. 6'1", 183 lbs.   Born, Vyskov, Czech., June 1, 1975.
(Winnipeg's 7th choice, 145th overall, in 1993 Entry Draft).

			Regular Season					Playoffs			
Season	Club	Lea	GP	G	A	TP	PIM	GP	G	A	TP	PIM
1992-93	ZPS Zlin	Czech.	17	1	3	4						

GROSS, PAVEL (GROHSS)
Right wing. Shoots right. 6'3", 195 lbs.   Born, Ustin Ogroh, Czechoslovakia, May 11, 1968.
(NY Islanders' 7th choice, 111th overall, in 1988 Entry Draft).

			Regular Season					Playoffs			
Season	Club	Lea	GP	G	A	TP	PIM	GP	G	A	TP	PIM
1987-88	Sparta Praha	Czech.	29	4	6	10	10	....	....	....	....	....
1988-89	Sparta Praha	Czech.	39	13	9	22	22	....	....	....	....	....
1989-90	Sparta Praha	Czech.	36	10	9	19		....	....	....	....	....
1990-91	Freiburg	Ger.	32	11	24	35	66	....	....	....	....	....
1991-92	Freiburg	Ger.	43	15	22	37	59	....	....	....	....	....
1992-93	Freiburg	Ger.	41	11	20	31	62	8	5	5	10	6

GROSSI, DINO
Right wing. Shoots right. 6', 195 lbs.   Born, Toronto, Ont., June 25, 1970.
(Chicago's 10th choice, 247th overall, in 1990 Entry Draft).

			Regular Season					Playoffs			
Season	Club	Lea	GP	G	A	TP	PIM	GP	G	A	TP	PIM
1989-90	Northeastern	H.E.	31	6	9	15	43	....	....	....	....	....
1990-91	Northeastern	H.E.	34	11	11	22	70	....	....	....	....	....
1991-92	Northeastern	H.E.	31	15	11	26	50	....	....	....	....	....
1992-93	Northeastern	H.E.	35	18	16	34	69	....	....	....	....	....

GRUBA, ANTHONY
Right wing. Shoots right. 6', 205 lbs.   Born, St. Paul, MN, August 23, 1972.
(Detroit's 8th choice, 171st overall, in 1990 Entry Draft).

			Regular Season					Playoffs			
Season	Club	Lea	GP	G	A	TP	PIM	GP	G	A	TP	PIM
1990-91	St. Cloud	WCHA	29	1	5	6	34	....	....	....	....	....
1991-92	St. Cloud	WCHA	37	14	22	36	76	....	....	....	....	....
1992-93	St. Cloud	WCHA	35	15	27	42	79	....	....	....	....	....

GRUDEN, JOHN
Defense. Shoots left. 6', 180 lbs.   Born, Hastings, MN, April 6, 1970.
(Boston's 7th choice, 168th overall, in 1990 Entry Draft).

			Regular Season					Playoffs			
Season	Club	Lea	GP	G	A	TP	PIM	GP	G	A	TP	PIM
1990-91	Ferris State	CCHA	37	4	11	15	27	....	....	....	....	....
1991-92	Ferris State	CCHA	37	9	14	23	24	....	....	....	....	....
1992-93	Ferris State	CCHA	41	16	14	30	58	....	....	....	....	....

GRUHL, SCOTT KENNETH (GROOL)

Left wing. Shoots left. 5'11", 185 lbs. Born, Port Colborne, Ont., September 13, 1959.

			Regular Season					Playoffs				
Season	Club	Lea	GP	G	A	TP	PIM	GP	G	A	TP	PIM
1978-79	Sudbury	OHA	68	35	49	94	78	10	5	7	12	15
1979-80	Binghamton	AHL	4	1	0	1	0	....	....	....	....	....
a	Saginaw	IHL	75	53	40	93	100	7	2	6	8	16
1980-81	Houston	CHL	4	0	0	0	0	....	....	....	....	....
	Saginaw	IHL	77	56	34	90	87	13	*11	8	*19	12
1981-82	**Los Angeles**	**NHL**	**7**	**2**	**1**	**3**	**2**	....	....	....	....	....
	New Haven	AHL	73	28	41	69	107	4	0	4	4	2
1982-83	**Los Angeles**	**NHL**	**7**	**0**	**2**	**2**	**4**	....	....	....	....	....
	New Haven	AHL	68	25	38	63	114	12	3	3	6	22
1983-84b	Muskegon	IHL	56	40	56	96	46	....	....	....	....	....
1984-85bc	Muskegon	IHL	82	62	64	126	102	17	7	16	23	25
1985-86a	Muskegon	IHL	82	*59	50	109	178	14	7	*13	20	22
1986-87	Muskegon	IHL	67	34	39	73	157	15	5	7	12	54
1987-88	**Pittsburgh**	**NHL**	**6**	**1**	**0**	**1**	**0**	....	....	....	....	....
	Muskegon	IHL	55	28	47	75	115	6	5	1	6	12
1988-89	Muskegon	IHL	79	37	55	92	163	14	8	11	19	37
1989-90	Muskegon	IHL	80	41	51	92	206	15	8	6	14	26
1990-91	Fort Wayne	IHL	59	23	47	70	109	19	4	6	10	39
1991-92a	Fort Wayne	IHL	78	44	61	105	196	6	2	2	4	48
1992-93	Fort Wayne	IHL	73	34	47	81	290	12	4	11	15	14
	NHL Totals		**20**	**3**	**3**	**6**	**6**	....	....	....	....	....

a IHL Second All-Star Team (1980, 1986, 1992)
b IHL First All-Star Team (1984, 1985)
c Won James Gatschene Memorial Trophy (MVP-IHL) (1985)

Signed as a free agent by **Los Angeles**, October 11, 1979. Signed as a free agent by **Pittsburgh**, December 14, 1987.

GUAY, PAUL (GAY)

Right wing. Shoots right. 5'11", 185 lbs. Born, Providence, RI, September 2, 1963.
(Minnesota's 10th choice, 118th overall, in 1981 Entry Draft).

			Regular Season					Playoffs				
Season	Club	Lea	GP	G	A	TP	PIM	GP	G	A	TP	PIM
1981-82	Providence	ECAC	33	23	17	40	38	....	....	....	....	....
1982-83a	Providence	ECAC	42	34	31	65	83	....	....	....	....	....
1983-84	U.S. National	....	62	20	18	38	44	....	....	....	....	....
	U.S. Olympic	....	6	1	0	1	8	....	....	....	....	....
	Philadelphia	**NHL**	**14**	**2**	**6**	**8**	**14**	**3**	**0**	**0**	**0**	**4**
1984-85	**Philadelphia**	**NHL**	**2**	**0**	**1**	**1**	**0**	....	....	....	....	....
	Hershey	AHL	74	23	30	53	123	....	....	....	....	....
1985-86	**Los Angeles**	**NHL**	**23**	**3**	**3**	**6**	**18**	....	....	....	....	....
	New Haven	AHL	57	15	36	51	101	5	3	0	3	11
1986-87	**Los Angeles**	**NHL**	**35**	**2**	**5**	**7**	**16**	**2**	**0**	**0**	**0**	**0**
	New Haven	AHL	6	1	3	4	11	....	....	....	....	....
1987-88	**Los Angeles**	**NHL**	**33**	**4**	**4**	**8**	**40**	**4**	**0**	**1**	**1**	**8**
	New Haven	AHL	42	21	26	47	53	....	....	....	....	....
1988-89	**Los Angeles**	**NHL**	**2**	**0**	**0**	**0**	**2**	....	....	....	....	....
	New Haven	AHL	4	4	6	10	20	....	....	....	....	....
	Boston	**NHL**	**5**	**0**	**2**	**2**	**0**	....	....	....	....	....
	Maine	AHL	61	15	29	44	77	....	....	....	....	....
1989-90	Utica	AHL	75	25	30	55	103	5	2	2	4	13
1990-91	**NY Islanders**	**NHL**	**3**	**0**	**2**	**2**	**2**	....	....	....	....	....
	Capital Dist.	AHL	74	26	35	61	81	....	....	....	....	....
1991-92	Milwaukee	IHL	81	24	33	57	93	3	2	1	3	7
1992-93	Springfield	AHL	65	10	32	42	90	11	1	2	3	6
	NHL Totals		**117**	**11**	**23**	**34**	**92**	**9**	**0**	**1**	**1**	**12**

a ECAC Second All-Star Team (1983)

Rights traded to **Philadelphia** by **Minnesota** with Minnesota's third round choice (Darryl Gilmour) in 1985 Entry Draft for Paul Holmgren, February 23, 1984. Traded to **Los Angeles** by **Philadelphia** with Philadelphia's fourth round choice (Sylvain Couturier) in 1986 Entry Draft for Steve Seguin and Los Angeles' second round choice (Jukka Seppo) in 1986 Entry Draft, October 11, 1985. Traded to **Boston** by **Los Angeles** for the rights to Dave Pasin, November 3, 1988. Signed as a free agent by **New Jersey**, August 14, 1989. Signed as a free agent by **NY Islanders**, August 13, 1990. Signed as a free agent by **Vancouver**, August 22, 1991.

GUERARD, DANIEL

Right wing. Shoots right. 6'4", 211 lbs. Born, LaSalle, Que., April 9, 1974.
(Ottawa's 5th choice, 98th overall, in 1992 Entry Draft).

			Regular Season					Playoffs				
Season	Club	Lea	GP	G	A	TP	PIM	GP	G	A	TP	PIM
1991-92	Victoriaville	QMJHL	31	5	16	21	66	....	....	....	....	....
1992-93	Verdun	QMJHL	58	31	26	57	131	4	1	1	2	17
	New Haven	AHL	2	2	1	3	0	....	....	....	....	....

GUERIN, BILL (GAIR-ihn)

Center/Right wing. Shoots right. 6'2", 190 lbs. Born, Wilbraham, MA, November 9, 1970.
(New Jersey's 1st choice, 5th overall, in 1989 Entry Draft).

			Regular Season					Playoffs				
Season	Club	Lea	GP	G	A	TP	PIM	GP	G	A	TP	PIM
1989-90	Boston College	H.E.	39	14	11	25	54	....	....	....	....	....
1990-91	U.S. National	....	46	12	15	27	67	....	....	....	....	....
	Boston College	H.E.	38	26	19	45	102	....	....	....	....	....
1991-92	**New Jersey**	**NHL**	**5**	**0**	**1**	**1**	**9**	**6**	**3**	**0**	**3**	**4**
	Utica	AHL	22	13	10	23	6	4	1	3	4	14
1992-93	**New Jersey**	**NHL**	**65**	**14**	**20**	**34**	**63**	**5**	**1**	**1**	**2**	**4**
	Utica	AHL	18	10	7	17	47	....	....	....	....	....
	NHL Totals		**70**	**14**	**21**	**35**	**72**	**11**	**4**	**1**	**5**	**8**

GUILBERT, MICHAEL

Defense. Shoots left. 6'2", 195 lbs. Born, Manchester, NH, December 11, 1971.
(NY Islanders' 6th choice, 132nd overall, in 1990 Entry Draft).

			Regular Season					Playoffs				
Season	Club	Lea	GP	G	A	TP	PIM	GP	G	A	TP	PIM
1991-92	N. Hampshire	H.E.	3	2	0	2	0	....	....	....	....	....
1992-93	N. Hampshire	H.E.	5	0	0	0	4	....	....	....	....	....

GUILLET, ROBERT

Right wing. Shoots right. 5'11", 189 lbs. Born, Montreal, Que., February 22, 1972.
(Montreal's 4th choice, 60th overall, in 1990 Entry Draft).

			Regular Season					Playoffs				
Season	Club	Lea	GP	G	A	TP	PIM	GP	G	A	TP	PIM
1989-90	Longueuil	QMJHL	69	32	40	72	132	7	2	1	3	15
1990-91a	Longueuil	QMJHL	69	55	32	87	96	8	4	7	11	27
1991-92b	Verdun	QMJHL	67	56	62	118	104	19	*14	11	*25	26
1992-93	Fredericton	AHL	42	16	15	31	38	1	0	0	0	0
	Wheeling	ECHL	15	16	14	30	8	....	....	....	....	....

a QMJHL First All-Star Team (1991)
b QMJHL Second All-Star Team (1992)

GUIRESTANTE, JOHN

Right wing. Shoots right. 6'2", 172 lbs. Born, Toronto, Ont., May 11, 1975.
(New Jersey's 5th choice, 110th overall, in 1993 Entry Draft).

			Regular Season					Playoffs				
Season	Club	Lea	GP	G	A	TP	PIM	GP	G	A	TP	PIM
1991-92	Mississauga	Midget	24	11	21	32	50	....	....	....	....	....
1992-93	London	OHL	32	7	12	19	13	4	0	0	0	0

GUNKO, YURI

Defense. Shoots left. 6'1", 187 lbs. Born, Kiev, Soviet Union, February 28, 1972.
(St. Louis' 11th choice, 230th overall, in 1992 Entry Draft).

			Regular Season					Playoffs				
Season	Club	Lea	GP	G	A	TP	PIM	GP	G	A	TP	PIM
1990-91	Sokol Kiev	USSR	14	0	0	0	8	....	....	....	....	....
1991-92	Sokol Kiev	CIS	22	1	0	1	16	....	....	....	....	....
1992-93	Sokol Kiev	CIS	40	2	3	5	28	....	....	....	....	....

GUSAROV, ALEXEI (goo-SAH-rahf)

Defense. Shoots left. 6'2", 170 lbs. Born, Leningrad, Soviet Union, July 8, 1964.
(Quebec's 11th choice, 213th overall, in 1988 Entry Draft).

			Regular Season					Playoffs				
Season	Club	Lea	GP	G	A	TP	PIM	GP	G	A	TP	PIM
1981-82	SKA Leningrad	USSR	20	1	2	3	16	....	....	....	....	....
1982-83	SKA Leningrad	USSR	42	2	1	3	32	....	....	....	....	....
1983-84	SKA Leningrad	USSR	43	2	3	5	32	....	....	....	....	....
1984-85	CSKA	USSR	36	3	2	5	26	....	....	....	....	....
1985-86	CSKA	USSR	40	3	5	8	30	....	....	....	....	....
1986-87	CSKA	USSR	38	4	7	11	24	....	....	....	....	....
1987-88	CSKA	USSR	39	3	2	5	28	....	....	....	....	....
1988-89	CSKA	USSR	42	5	4	9	37	....	....	....	....	....
1989-90	CSKA	USSR	42	4	7	11	42	....	....	....	....	....
1990-91	CSKA	USSR	15	0	0	0	12	....	....	....	....	....
	Quebec	**NHL**	**36**	**3**	**9**	**12**	**12**	....	....	....	....	....
	Halifax	AHL	2	0	3	3	2	....	....	....	....	....
1991-92	**Quebec**	**NHL**	**68**	**5**	**18**	**23**	**22**	....	....	....	....	....
	Halifax	AHL	3	0	0	0	0	....	....	....	....	....
1992-93	**Quebec**	**NHL**	**79**	**8**	**22**	**30**	**57**	**5**	**0**	**1**	**1**	**0**
	NHL Totals		**183**	**16**	**49**	**65**	**91**	**5**	**0**	**1**	**1**	**0**

GUSMANOV, RAVIL

Right wing. Shoots left. 6'3", 185 lbs. Born, Naberezhnye Chelny, Soviet Uni, July 25, 1972.
(Winnipeg's 5th choice, 93rd overall, in 1993 Entry Draft).

			Regular Season					Playoffs				
Season	Club	Lea	GP	G	A	TP	PIM	GP	G	A	TP	PIM
1990-91	Chelyabinsk	USSR	15	0	0	0	10	....	....	....	....	....
1991-92	Chelyabinsk	CIS	38	4	4	8	20	....	....	....	....	....
1992-93	Chelyabinsk	CIS	39	15	8	23	30	....	....	....	....	....

GUY, KEVAN (GIGH)

Defense. Shoots right. 6'3", 202 lbs. Born, Edmonton, Alta., July 16, 1965.
(Calgary's 5th choice, 71st overall, in 1983 Entry Draft).

			Regular Season					Playoffs				
Season	Club	Lea	GP	G	A	TP	PIM	GP	G	A	TP	PIM
1982-83	Medicine Hat	WHL	69	7	20	27	89	5	0	3	3	16
1983-84	Medicine Hat	WHL	72	15	42	57	117	14	3	4	7	14
1984-85	Medicine Hat	WHL	31	7	17	24	46	10	1	2	3	2
1985-86	Moncton	AHL	73	4	20	24	56	10	0	2	2	6
1986-87	**Calgary**	**NHL**	**24**	**0**	**4**	**4**	**19**	**4**	**0**	**1**	**1**	**23**
	Moncton	AHL	46	2	10	12	38	....	....	....	....	....
1987-88	**Calgary**	**NHL**	**11**	**0**	**3**	**3**	**8**	....	....	....	....	....
	Salt Lake	IHL	61	6	30	36	51	19	1	6	7	26
1988-89	**Vancouver**	**NHL**	**45**	**2**	**2**	**4**	**34**	**1**	**0**	**0**	**0**	**0**
1989-90	**Vancouver**	**NHL**	**30**	**2**	**5**	**7**	**32**	....	....	....	....	....
	Milwaukee	IHL	29	2	11	13	33	....	....	....	....	....
1990-91	**Vancouver**	**NHL**	**39**	**1**	**6**	**7**	**39**	....	....	....	....	....
	Calgary	**NHL**	**4**	**0**	**0**	**0**	**4**	....	....	....	....	....
1991-92	**Calgary**	**NHL**	**3**	**0**	**0**	**0**	**2**	....	....	....	....	....
	Salt Lake	IHL	60	3	14	17	89	5	0	1	1	4
1992-93	Salt Lake	IHL	33	1	9	10	50	....	....	....	....	....
	NHL Totals		**156**	**5**	**20**	**25**	**138**	**5**	**0**	**1**	**1**	**23**

Traded to **Vancouver** by **Calgary** with Brian Bradley and Peter Bakovic for Craig Coxe, March 6, 1988. Traded to **Calgary** by **Vancouver** with Ron Stern and future considerations, March 5, 1991.

HAAPAKOSKI, MIKKO (HAH-puh-koh-skee)

Defense. Shoots left. 5'10", 174 lbs. Born, Oulu, Finland, January 19, 1967.
(Detroit's 10th choice, 179th overall, in 1987 Entry Draft).

			Regular Season					Playoffs				
Season	Club	Lea	GP	G	A	TP	PIM	GP	G	A	TP	PIM
1985-86	Karpat	Fin.	17	0	4	4	0	5	1	0	1	6
1986-87	Karpat	Fin.	41	13	15	28	18	9	1	1	2	4
1987-88	Karpat	Fin.	43	7	7	14	40	....	....	....	....	....
1988-89	Karpat	Fin.	40	7	18	25	20	5	1	1	2	2
1989-90	TPS	Fin.	44	4	10	14	14	9	0	1	1	16
1990-91	TPS	Fin.	40	9	12	21	10	9	1	4	5	4
1991-92	TPS	Fin.	43	11	13	24	18	1	0	0	0	0
1992-93	TPS	Fin.	38	3	10	13	20	12	2	5	7	12

HAAS, DAVID

Left wing. Shoots left. 6'2", 196 lbs. Born, Toronto, Ont., June 23, 1968.
(Edmonton's 5th choice, 105th overall, in 1986 Entry Draft).

			Regular Season					Playoffs				
Season	Club	Lea	GP	G	A	TP	PIM	GP	G	A	TP	PIM
1985-86	London	OHL	62	4	13	17	91	5	0	1	1	0
1986-87	London	OHL	5	1	0	1	5	....	....	....	....	....
	Kitchener	OHL	4	0	1	1	4	....	....	....	....	....
	Belleville	OHL	55	10	13	23	86	6	3	0	3	13
1987-88a	Windsor	OHL	63	60	47	107	246	11	9	11	20	50
1988-89	Cape Breton	AHL	61	9	9	18	325	....	....	....	....	....
1989-90	Cape Breton	AHL	53	6	12	18	230	4	2	2	4	15
1990-91	**Edmonton**	**NHL**	**5**	**1**	**0**	**1**	**0**	....	....	....	....	....
	Cape Breton	AHL	60	24	23	47	137	3	0	2	2	12
1991-92	Cape Breton	AHL	16	3	7	10	32	....	....	....	....	....
	New Haven	AHL	50	13	23	36	97	5	3	0	3	13
1992-93	Cape Breton	AHL	73	22	56	78	121	16	11	13	24	36
	NHL Totals		**5**	**1**	**0**	**1**	**0**	....	....	....	....	....

a OHL Second All-Star Team (1988)

HAGEN, GREG

Right wing. Shoots right. 5'11", 175 lbs. Born, St. Paul, MN, July 10, 1971.
(Pittsburgh's 11th choice, 205th overall, in 1989 Entry Draft).

			Regular Season					Playoffs				
Season	Club	Lea	GP	G	A	TP	PIM	GP	G	A	TP	PIM
1990-91	St. Cloud	WCHA	23	4	4	8	2	....	....	....	....	....
1991-92	St. Cloud	WCHA	34	10	8	18	28	....	....	....	....	....
1992-93	St. Cloud	WCHA	36	21	15	36	34	....	....	....	....	....

HAGGERTY, RYAN

Center. Shoots left. 6'1", 185 lbs. Born, Rye, NY, May 2, 1973.
(Edmonton's 6th choice, 93rd overall, in 1991 Entry Draft).

			Regular Season					Playoffs				
Season	Club	Lea	GP	G	A	TP	PIM	GP	G	A	TP	PIM
1991-92	Boston College	H.E.	34	12	5	17	16	....	....	....	....	....
1992-93	Boston College	H.E.	32	6	5	11	12	....	....	....	....	....

HAKANSSON, JONAS

Left wing. Shoots right. 6'1", 202 lbs. Born, Malmo, Sweden, January 4, 1974.
(Philadelphia's 8th choice, 199th overall, in 1992 Entry Draft).

			Regular Season					Playoffs				
Season	Club	Lea	GP	G	A	TP	PIM	GP	G	A	TP	PIM
1990-91	Malmo	Swe.	8	0	0	0	0	1	0	0	0	0
1991-92	Malmo Jrs.	Swe.				UNAVAILABLE						
1992-93	Malmo	Swe.	11	0	0	0	0	....	....	....	....	....

HAKANSSON, MIKAEL

Center. Shoots left. 6'1", 180 lbs. Born, Stockholm, Sweden, May 31, 1974.
(Toronto's 7th choice, 125th overall, in 1992 Entry Draft).

			Regular Season					Playoffs				
Season	Club	Lea	GP	G	A	TP	PIM	GP	G	A	TP	PIM
1990-91	Nacka	Swe.2	27	2	5	7	6	....	....	....	....	....
1991-92	Nacka	Swe.2	29	3	15	18	24	....	....	....	....	....
1992-93	Djurgarden	Swe.	40	0	1	1	6	3	0	0	0	0

HALKIDIS, BOB (hal-KEE-dihs)

Defense. Shoots left. 5'11", 200 lbs. Born, Toronto, Ont., March 5, 1966.
(Buffalo's 4th choice, 81st overall, in 1984 Entry Draft).

			Regular Season					Playoffs				
Season	Club	Lea	GP	G	A	TP	PIM	GP	G	A	TP	PIM
1983-84	London	OHL	51	9	22	31	123	8	0	2	2	27
1984-85ab	London	OHL	62	14	50	64	154	8	3	6	9	22
	Buffalo	**NHL**	....	....	....	....	....	**4**	**0**	**0**	**0**	**19**
1985-86	**Buffalo**	**NHL**	**37**	**1**	**9**	**10**	**115**	....	....	....	....	....
1986-87	**Buffalo**	**NHL**	**6**	**1**	**1**	**2**	**19**	....	....	....	....	....
	Rochester	AHL	59	1	8	9	144	8	0	0	0	43
1987-88	**Buffalo**	**NHL**	**30**	**0**	**3**	**3**	**115**	**4**	**0**	**0**	**0**	**22**
	Rochester	AHL	15	2	5	7	50	....	....	....	....	....
1988-89	**Buffalo**	**NHL**	**16**	**0**	**1**	**1**	**66**	....	....	....	....	....
	Rochester	AHL	16	0	6	6	64	....	....	....	....	....
1989-90	Rochester	AHL	18	1	13	14	70	....	....	....	....	....
	Los Angeles	**NHL**	**20**	**0**	**4**	**4**	**56**	....	....	....	....	....
	New Haven	AHL	30	3	17	20	67	....	....	....	....	....
1990-91	**Los Angeles**	**NHL**	**34**	**1**	**3**	**4**	**133**	**3**	**0**	**0**	**0**	**0**
	New Haven	AHL	7	1	3	4	10	....	....	....	....	....
	Phoenix	IHL	4	1	5	6	6	....	....	....	....	....
1991-92	**Toronto**	**NHL**	**46**	**3**	**3**	**6**	**145**	....	....	....	....	....
1992-93	St. John's	AHL	29	2	13	15	61	....	....	....	....	....
	Milwaukee	IHL	26	0	9	9	79	5	0	1	1	27
	NHL Totals		**189**	**6**	**24**	**30**	**649**	**11**	**0**	**0**	**0**	**41**

a Named Outstanding Defenseman in OHL (1985)
b OHL First All-Star Team (1985)

Traded to **Los Angeles** by **Buffalo** with future considerations for Dale DeGray and future considerations, November 24, 1989. Signed as a free agent by **Toronto**, July 24, 1991.

HALKO, STEVEN

Defense. Shoots right. 6'1", 183 lbs. Born, Etobicoke, Ont., March 8, 1974.
(Hartford's 10th choice, 225th overall, in 1992 Entry Draft).

			Regular Season					Playoffs				
Season	Club	Lea	GP	G	A	TP	PIM	GP	G	A	TP	PIM
1991-92	Thornhill	OHA Jr. A	44	15	46	61	43	....	....	....	....	....
1992-93	U. of Michigan	CCHA	39	1	12	13	12	....	....	....	....	....

HALL, TODD

Defense. Shoots left. 6'1", 212 lbs. Born, Hamden, CT, January 22, 1973.
(Hartford's 3rd choice, 53rd overall, in 1991 Entry Draft).

			Regular Season					Playoffs				
Season	Club	Lea	GP	G	A	TP	PIM	GP	G	A	TP	PIM
1991-92	Boston College	H.E.	33	2	10	12	14	....	....	....	....	....
1992-93	Boston College	H.E.	34	2	10	12	22	....	....	....	....	....

HALLER, KEVIN

Defense. Shoots left. 6'2", 183 lbs. Born, Trochu, Alta., December 5, 1970.
(Buffalo's 1st choice, 14th overall, in 1989 Entry Draft).

			Regular Season					Playoffs				
Season	Club	Lea	GP	G	A	TP	PIM	GP	G	A	TP	PIM
1988-89	Regina	WHL	72	10	31	41	99	....	....	....	....	....
1989-90	**Buffalo**	**NHL**	**2**	**0**	**0**	**0**	**0**	....	....	....	....	....
a	Regina	WHL	58	16	37	53	93	11	2	9	11	16
1990-91	**Buffalo**	**NHL**	**21**	**1**	**8**	**9**	**20**	**6**	**1**	**4**	**5**	**10**
	Rochester	AHL	52	2	8	10	53	10	2	1	3	6
1991-92	**Buffalo**	**NHL**	**58**	**6**	**15**	**21**	**75**	....	....	....	....	....
	Rochester	AHL	4	0	0	0	18	....	....	....	....	....
	Montreal	**NHL**	**8**	**2**	**2**	**4**	**17**	**9**	**0**	**0**	**0**	**6**
1992-93	**Montreal**	**NHL**	**73**	**11**	**14**	**25**	**117**	**17**	**1**	**6**	**7**	**16**
	NHL Totals		**162**	**20**	**39**	**59**	**229**	**32**	**2**	**10**	**12**	**32**

a WHL East First All-Star Team (1990)

Traded to **Montreal** by **Buffalo** for Petr Svoboda, March 10, 1992.

HALVERSON, TREVOR

Left wing. Shoots left. 6'1", 195 lbs. Born, White River, Ont., April 6, 1971.
(Washington's 2nd choice, 21st overall, in 1991 Entry Draft).

			Regular Season					Playoffs				
Season	Club	Lea	GP	G	A	TP	PIM	GP	G	A	TP	PIM
1989-90	North Bay	OHL	54	22	20	42	172	2	2	1	3	2
1990-91a	North Bay	OHL	64	59	36	95	128	10	3	6	9	4
1991-92	Baltimore	AHL	74	10	11	21	181	....	....	....	....	....
1992-93	Baltimore	AHL	67	19	21	40	170	2	1	0	1	0
	Hampton Rds.	ECHL	9	7	5	12	6	....	....	....	....	....

a OHL First All-Star Team (1991)

Claimed by **Anaheim** from **Washington** in Expansion Draft, June 24, 1993.

HAMALAINEN, ERIK (HAH-muhl-ahy-nehn)

Defense. Shoots left. 6'2", 198 lbs. Born, Rauma, Finland, April 20, 1965.
(Detroit's 10th choice, 197th overall, in 1985 Entry Draft).

			Regular Season					Playoffs				
Season	Club	Lea	GP	G	A	TP	PIM	GP	G	A	TP	PIM
1982-83	Lukko	Fin.	35	2	1	3	48	....	....	....	....	....
1983-84	Lukko	Fin.2	36	8	2	10	16	5	1	3	4	10
1984-85	Lukko	Fin.	36	4	3	7	25	....	....	....	....	....
1985-86	Lukko	Fin.	31	13	6	19	32	....	....	....	....	....
1986-87	Lukko	Fin.	44	8	8	16	49	....	....	....	....	....
1987-88	Lukko	Fin.	44	8	4	12	52	8	0	3	3	2
1988-89	KalPa	Fin.	43	7	4	11	14	2	0	0	0	2
1989-90	KalPa	Fin.	44	9	20	29	32	....	....	....	....	....
1990-91	KalPa	Fin.	44	14	14	28	34	8	3	4	7	4
1991-92	KalPa	Fin.	44	12	21	33	22	....	....	....	....	....
1992-93	Jokerit	Fin.	48	16	21	37	30	3	3	0	3	4

HAMMOND, KEN

Defense. Shoots left. 6'1", 190 lbs. Born, Port Credit, Ont., August 22, 1963.
(Los Angeles' 8th choice, 152nd overall, in 1983 Entry Draft).

			Regular Season					Playoffs				
Season	Club	Lea	GP	G	A	TP	PIM	GP	G	A	TP	PIM
1982-83	RPI	ECAC	28	17	26	43	8	....	....	....	....	....
1983-84	RPI	ECAC	34	5	11	16	72	....	....	....	....	....
1984-85	**Los Angeles**	**NHL**	**3**	**1**	**0**	**1**	**0**	**3**	**0**	**0**	**0**	**4**
ab	RPI	ECAC	38	11	28	39	90	....	....	....	....	....
1985-86	**Los Angeles**	**NHL**	**3**	**0**	**1**	**1**	**2**	....	....	....	....	....
	New Haven	AHL	67	4	12	16	96	4	0	0	0	7
1986-87	**Los Angeles**	**NHL**	**10**	**0**	**2**	**2**	**11**	....	....	....	....	....
	New Haven	AHL	66	1	15	16	76	6	0	1	1	21
1987-88	**Los Angeles**	**NHL**	**46**	**7**	**9**	**16**	**69**	**2**	**0**	**0**	**0**	**4**
	New Haven	AHL	26	3	8	11	27	....	....	....	....	....
1988-89	**Edmonton**	**NHL**	**5**	**0**	**1**	**1**	**8**	....	....	....	....	....
	NY Rangers	**NHL**	**3**	**0**	**0**	**0**	**0**	....	....	....	....	....
	Denver	IHL	38	5	18	23	24	....	....	....	....	....
	Toronto	**NHL**	**14**	**0**	**2**	**2**	**12**	....	....	....	....	....
1989-90	Newmarket	AHL	75	9	45	54	106	....	....	....	....	....
1990-91	**Boston**	**NHL**	**1**	**1**	**0**	**1**	**2**	**8**	**0**	**0**	**0**	**10**
	Maine	AHL	80	10	41	51	159	2	0	1	1	16
1991-92	**San Jose**	**NHL**	**46**	**5**	**10**	**15**	**82**	....	....	....	....	....
	Vancouver	**NHL**	....	....	....	....	....	**2**	**0**	**0**	**0**	**6**
1992-93	**Ottawa**	**NHL**	**62**	**4**	**4**	**8**	**104**	....	....	....	....	....
	New Haven	AHL	4	0	1	1	4	....	....	....	....	....
	NHL Totals		**193**	**18**	**29**	**47**	**290**	**15**	**0**	**0**	**0**	**24**

a ECAC First All-Star Team (1985)
b Named to NCAA All-American Team (1985)

Claimed by **Edmonton** in NHL Waiver Draft, October 3, 1988. Claimed on waivers by **NY Rangers** from **Edmonton**, November 1, 1988. Traded to **Toronto** by **NY Rangers** for Chris McRae, February 21, 1989. Traded to **Boston** by **Toronto** for cash, August 20, 1990. Signed as a free agent by **San Jose**, August 9, 1991. Traded to **Vancouver** by **San Jose** for Vancouver's eighth round choice (later traded to Detroit — Detroit selected C.J. Denomme) in 1992 Entry Draft, March 9, 1992. Claimed by **Ottawa** from **Vancouver** in Expansion Draft, June 18, 1992.

HAMR, RADEK (HAHM-er)

Defense. Shoots left. 5'11", 167 lbs. Born, Prague, Czech., June 15, 1974.
(Ottawa's 4th choice, 73rd overall, in 1992 Entry Draft).

			Regular Season					Playoffs				
Season	Club	Lea	GP	G	A	TP	PIM	GP	G	A	TP	PIM
1991-92	Sparta Praha	Czech.	3	0	0	0	....	....	....	....	....	....
1992-93	**Ottawa**	**NHL**	**4**	**0**	**0**	**0**	**0**	....	....	....	....	....
	New Haven	AHL	59	4	21	25	18	....	....	....	....	....
	NHL Totals		**4**	**0**	**0**	**0**	**0**	....	....	....	....	....

HAMRLIK, MARTIN (HAHM-reh-lik)

Defense. Shoots right. 5'11", 185 lbs. Born, Gottwaldov, Czechoslovakia, May 6, 1973.
(Hartford's 2nd choice, 31st overall, in 1991 Entry Draft).

			Regular Season					Playoffs				
Season	Club	Lea	GP	G	A	TP	PIM	GP	G	A	TP	PIM
1989-90	TJ Zlin	Czech.	11	2	0	2	....	....	....	....	....	....
1990-91	TJ Zlin	Czech.	50	8	14	22	44	....	....	....	....	....
1991-92	ZPS Zlin	Czech.	4	0	2	2	23	....	....	....	....	....
1992-93	Ottawa	OHL	26	4	11	15	41	....	....	....	....	....
	Springfield	AHL	8	1	3	4	16	....	....	....	....	....

HAMRLIK, ROMAN (HAHM-reh-lik)

Defense. Shoots left. 6'2", 189 lbs. Born, Gottwaldov, Czech., April 12, 1974.
(Tampa Bay's 1st choice, 1st overall, in 1992 Entry Draft).

			Regular Season					Playoffs				
Season	Club	Lea	GP	G	A	TP	PIM	GP	G	A	TP	PIM
1990-91	TJ Zlin	Czech.	14	2	2	4	18	....	....	....	....	....
1991-92	ZPS Zlin	Czech.	34	5	5	10	50	....	....	....	....	....
1992-93	**Tampa Bay**	**NHL**	**67**	**6**	**15**	**21**	**71**	....	....	....	....	....
	Atlanta	IHL	2	1	1	2	2	....	....	....	....	....
	NHL Totals		**67**	**6**	**15**	**21**	**71**	....	....	....	....	....

HANKINSON, BEN

Right wing. Shoots right. 6'2", 180 lbs. Born, Edina, MN, May 1, 1969.
(New Jersey's 5th choice, 107th overall, in 1987 Entry Draft).

			Regular Season					Playoffs				
Season	Club	Lea	GP	G	A	TP	PIM	GP	G	A	TP	PIM
1987-88	U. Minnesota	WCHA	24	4	7	11	36	....	....	....	....	....
1988-89	U. Minnesota	WCHA	43	7	11	18	115	....	....	....	....	....
1989-90a	U. Minnesota	WCHA	46	25	41	66	34	....	....	....	....	....
1990-91	U. Minnesota	WCHA	43	19	21	40	133	....	....	....	....	....
1991-92	Utica	AHL	77	17	16	33	186	4	3	1	4	2
1992-93	**New Jersey**	**NHL**	**4**	**2**	**1**	**3**	**9**	....	....	....	....	....
	Utica	AHL	75	35	27	62	145	5	2	2	4	6
	NHL Totals		**4**	**2**	**1**	**3**	**9**	....	....	....	....	....

a WCHA First All-Star Team (1990)

HANNAN, DAVID (DAVE)

Center. Shoots left. 5'10", 185 lbs. Born, Sudbury, Ont., November 26, 1961.
(Pittsburgh's 9th choice, 196th overall, in 1981 Entry Draft).

			Regular Season					Playoffs				
Season	Club	Lea	GP	G	A	TP	PIM	GP	G	A	TP	PIM
1979-80	S.S. Marie	OHA	28	11	10	21	31	....	....	....	....	....
	Brantford	OHA	25	5	10	15	26	....	....	....	....	....
1980-81	Brantford	OHA	56	46	35	81	155	6	2	4	6	20
1981-82	**Pittsburgh**	**NHL**	**1**	**0**	**0**	**0**	**0**	....	....	....	....	....
	Erie	AHL	76	33	37	70	129	....	....	....	....	....
1982-83	**Pittsburgh**	**NHL**	**74**	**11**	**22**	**33**	**127**	....	....	....	....	....
	Baltimore	AHL	5	2	2	4	13	....	....	....	....	....
1983-84	**Pittsburgh**	**NHL**	**24**	**2**	**3**	**5**	**33**	....	....	....	....	....
	Baltimore	AHL	47	18	24	42	98	10	2	6	8	27
1984-85	**Pittsburgh**	**NHL**	**30**	**6**	**7**	**13**	**43**	....	....	....	....	....
	Baltimore	AHL	49	20	25	45	91	....	....	....	....	....
1985-86	**Pittsburgh**	**NHL**	**75**	**17**	**18**	**35**	**91**	....	....	....	....	....
1986-87	**Pittsburgh**	**NHL**	**58**	**10**	**15**	**25**	**56**	....	....	....	....	....
1987-88	**Pittsburgh**	**NHL**	**21**	**4**	**3**	**7**	**23**	....	....	....	....	....
	Edmonton	**NHL**	**51**	**9**	**11**	**20**	**43**	**12**	**1**	**1**	**2**	**8**
1988-89	**Pittsburgh**	**NHL**	**72**	**10**	**20**	**30**	**157**	**8**	**0**	**1**	**1**	**4**
1989-90	**Toronto**	**NHL**	**39**	**6**	**9**	**15**	**55**	**3**	**1**	**0**	**1**	**4**
1990-91	**Toronto**	**NHL**	**74**	**11**	**23**	**34**	**82**	....	....	....	....	....
1991-92	**Toronto**	**NHL**	**35**	**2**	**2**	**4**	**16**	....	....	....	....	....
	Cdn. National	....	3	0	0	0	2	....	....	....	....	....
	Cdn. Olympic	....	8	3	5	8	8	....	....	....	....	....
	Buffalo	**NHL**	**12**	**2**	**4**	**6**	**48**	**7**	**2**	**0**	**2**	**2**
1992-93	**Buffalo**	**NHL**	**55**	**5**	**15**	**20**	**43**	**8**	**1**	**1**	**2**	**18**
	NHL Totals		**621**	**95**	**152**	**247**	**817**	**38**	**5**	**3**	**8**	**36**

Traded to **Edmonton** by **Pittsburgh** with Craig Simpson, Moe Mantha and Chris Joseph for Paul Coffey, Dave Hunter and Wayne Van Dorp, November 24, 1987. Claimed by **Pittsburgh** in NHL Waiver Draft, October 3, 1988. Claimed by **Toronto** in NHL Waiver Draft, October 2, 1989. Traded to **Buffalo** by **Toronto** for future considerations, March 10, 1992.

HANSON, GREG

Defense. Shoots left. 6'3", 215 lbs. Born, Bloomington, MN, September 4, 1971.
(Philadelphia's 13th choice, 193rd overall, in 1990 Entry Draft).

			Regular Season					Playoffs				
Season	Club	Lea	GP	G	A	TP	PIM	GP	G	A	TP	PIM
1991-92	Dubuque	USHL	39	4	21	25	69	....	....	....	....	....
1992-93	Minn. Duluth	WCHA	15	0	2	2	12	....	....	....	....	....

HANUS, TIM

Left wing. Shoots left. 6'1", 185 lbs. Born, Minneapolis, MN, May 12, 1969.
(Quebec's 7th choice, 135th overall, in 1987 Entry Draft).

			Regular Season					Playoffs				
Season	Club	Lea	GP	G	A	TP	PIM	GP	G	A	TP	PIM
1988-89	St. Cloud	NCAA	33	13	22	35	31	....	....	....	....	....
1989-90	St. Cloud	NCAA	34	22	24	46	54	....	....	....	....	....
1990-91	St. Cloud	WCHA	40	21	26	47	26	....	....	....	....	....
1991-92	St. Cloud	WCHA	37	17	27	44	36	....	....	....	....	....
1992-93	Johnstown	ECHL	47	26	34	60	77	....	....	....	....	....
	Kansas City	IHL	7	2	1	3	2	....	....	....	....	....

HARDING, MIKE

Right wing. Shoots right. 6'4", 221 lbs. Born, Edsow, Alta., February 24, 1971.
(Hartford's 6th choice, 119th overall, in 1991 Entry Draft).

			Regular Season					Playoffs				
Season	Club	Lea	GP	G	A	TP	PIM	GP	G	A	TP	PIM
1990-91	N. Michigan	WCHA			UNAVAILABLE							
1991-92	N. Michigan	WCHA	28	6	8	14	46	....	....	....	....	....
1992-93	N. Michigan	WCHA	39	17	18	35	66	....	....	....	....	....

HARDY, MARK LEA

Defense. Shoots left. 5'11", 195 lbs. Born, Semaden, Switzerland, February 1, 1959.
(Los Angeles' 3rd choice, 30th overall, in 1979 Entry Draft).

			Regular Season					Playoffs				
Season	Club	Lea	GP	G	A	TP	PIM	GP	G	A	TP	PIM
1977-78	Montreal	QJHL	72	25	57	82	150	13	3	10	13	22
1978-79	Montreal	QJHL	67	18	52	70	117	11	5	8	13	40
1979-80	Binghamton	AHL	56	3	13	16	32	....	....	....	....	....
	Los Angeles	**NHL**	**15**	**0**	**1**	**1**	**10**	**4**	**1**	**1**	**2**	**9**
1980-81	**Los Angeles**	**NHL**	**77**	**5**	**20**	**25**	**77**	**4**	**1**	**2**	**3**	**4**
1981-82	**Los Angeles**	**NHL**	**77**	**6**	**39**	**45**	**130**	**10**	**1**	**2**	**3**	**9**
1982-83	**Los Angeles**	**NHL**	**74**	**5**	**34**	**39**	**101**	....	....	....	....	....
1983-84	**Los Angeles**	**NHL**	**79**	**8**	**41**	**49**	**122**	....	....	....	....	....
1984-85	**Los Angeles**	**NHL**	**78**	**14**	**39**	**53**	**97**	**3**	**0**	**1**	**1**	**2**
1985-86	**Los Angeles**	**NHL**	**55**	**6**	**21**	**27**	**71**	....	....	....	....	....
1986-87	**Los Angeles**	**NHL**	**73**	**3**	**27**	**30**	**120**	**5**	**1**	**2**	**3**	**10**
1987-88	**Los Angeles**	**NHL**	**61**	**6**	**22**	**28**	**99**	....	....	....	....	....
	NY Rangers	**NHL**	**19**	**2**	**2**	**4**	**31**	....	....	....	....	....
1988-89	**Minnesota**	**NHL**	**15**	**2**	**4**	**6**	**26**	....	....	....	....	....
	NY Rangers	**NHL**	**45**	**2**	**12**	**14**	**45**	**4**	**0**	**1**	**1**	**31**
1989-90	**NY Rangers**	**NHL**	**54**	**0**	**15**	**15**	**94**	**3**	**0**	**1**	**1**	**2**
1990-91	**NY Rangers**	**NHL**	**70**	**1**	**5**	**6**	**89**	**6**	**0**	**1**	**1**	**30**
1991-92	**NY Rangers**	**NHL**	**52**	**1**	**8**	**9**	**65**	**13**	**0**	**3**	**3**	**31**
1992-93	**NY Rangers**	**NHL**	**44**	**1**	**10**	**11**	**85**	....	....	....	....	....
	Los Angeles	**NHL**	**11**	**0**	**3**	**3**	**4**	**15**	**1**	**2**	**3**	**30**
	NHL Totals		**899**	**62**	**303**	**365**	**1266**	**67**	**5**	**16**	**21**	**158**

Traded to **NY Rangers** by **Los Angeles** for Ron Duguay, February 23, 1988. Traded to **Minnesota** by **NY Rangers** for future considerations (Louie Debrusk) June 13, 1988. Traded to **NY Rangers** by **Minnesota** for Larry Bernard and NY Rangers' fifth round choice (Rhys Hollyman) in 1989 Entry Draft, December 9, 1988. Traded to **Los Angeles** by **NY Rangers** with Ottawa's fifth round choice (previously acquired by NY Rangers — Los Angeles selected Frederick Beaubien) in 1993 Entry Draft for John McIntyre, March 22, 1993.

HARKINS, BRETT

Left wing. Shoots left. 6'1", 170 lbs. Born, North Ridgeville, OH, July 2, 1970.
(NY Islanders' 9th choice, 133rd overall, in 1989 Entry Draft).

			Regular Season					Playoffs				
Season	Club	Lea	GP	G	A	TP	PIM	GP	G	A	TP	PIM
1989-90	Bowling Green	CCHA	41	11	43	54	45	....	....	....	....	....
1990-91	Bowling Green	CCHA	40	22	38	60	30	....	....	....	....	....
1991-92	Bowling Green	CCHA	34	8	39	47	32	....	....	....	....	....
1992-93	Bowling Green	CCHA	35	19	28	47	28	....	....	....	....	....

HARKINS, TODD

Center. Shoots right. 6'3", 210 lbs. Born, Cleveland, OH, October 8, 1968.
(Calgary's 2nd choice, 42nd overall, in 1988 Entry Draft).

			Regular Season					Playoffs				
Season	Club	Lea	GP	G	A	TP	PIM	GP	G	A	TP	PIM
1987-88	Miami-Ohio	CCHA	34	9	7	16	133	....	....	....	....	....
1988-89	Miami-Ohio	CCHA	36	8	7	15	77	....	....	....	....	....
1989-90	Miami-Ohio	CCHA	40	27	17	44	78	....	....	....	....	....
1990-91	Salt Lake	IHL	79	15	27	42	113	3	0	0	0	0
1991-92	**Calgary**	**NHL**	**5**	**0**	**0**	**0**	**7**	....	....	....	....	....
	Salt Lake	IHL	72	32	30	62	67	5	1	1	2	6
1992-93	**Calgary**	**NHL**	**15**	**2**	**3**	**5**	**22**	....	....	....	....	....
	Salt Lake	IHL	53	13	21	34	90	....	....	....	....	....
	NHL Totals		**20**	**2**	**3**	**5**	**29**	....	....	....	....	....

HARLOCK, DAVID

Defense. Shoots left. 6'2", 195 lbs. Born, Toronto, Ont., March 16, 1971.
(New Jersey's 2nd choice, 24th overall, in 1990 Entry Draft).

			Regular Season					Playoffs				
Season	Club	Lea	GP	G	A	TP	PIM	GP	G	A	TP	PIM
1989-90	U. of Michigan	CCHA	42	2	13	15	44	....	....	....	....	....
1990-91	U. of Michigan	CCHA	39	2	8	10	70	....	....	....	....	....
1991-92	U. of Michigan	CCHA	44	1	6	7	80	....	....	....	....	....
1992-93	Cdn. National	....	4	0	0	0	2	....	....	....	....	....
	U. of Michigan	CCHA	38	3	9	12	58	....	....	....	....	....

HARPER, KELLY

Center. Shoots right. 6'2", 180 lbs. Born, Sudbury, Ont., May 9, 1972.
(Calgary's 8th choice, 151st overall, in 1991 Entry Draft).

			Regular Season					Playoffs				
Season	Club	Lea	GP	G	A	TP	PIM	GP	G	A	TP	PIM
1990-91	Michigan State	CCHA	34	1	8	9	21	....	....	....	....	....
1991-92	Michigan State	CCHA	33	4	4	8	2	....	....	....	....	....
1992-93	Michigan State	CCHA	39	11	20	31	20	....	....	....	....	....

HARRIS, TIM

Right wing. Shoots right. 6'2", 190 lbs. Born, Uxbridge, Ont., October 16, 1967.
(Calgary's 5th choice, 70th overall, in 1987 Entry Draft).

			Regular Season					Playoffs				
Season	Club	Lea	GP	G	A	TP	PIM	GP	G	A	TP	PIM
1987-88	Lake Superior	CCHA	43	8	10	18	79	....	....	....	....	....
1988-89	Lake Superior	CCHA	29	1	5	6	78	....	....	....	....	....
1989-90	Lake Superior	CCHA	39	6	17	23	71	....	....	....	....	....
1990-91	Lake Superior	CCHA	45	17	22	39	122	....	....	....	....	....
1991-92	Salt Lake	IHL	71	11	21	32	91	3	0	1	1	4
1992-93	Salt Lake	IHL	52	5	10	15	48	....	....	....	....	....

HARTJE, TODD (HAHRT-jee)

Center. Shoots left. 6'1", 190 lbs. Born, Anoka, MN, February 27, 1968.
(Winnipeg's 7th choice, 142nd overall, in 1987 Entry Draft).

			Regular Season					Playoffs				
Season	Club	Lea	GP	G	A	TP	PIM	GP	G	A	TP	PIM
1986-87	Harvard	ECAC	32	3	9	12	36	....	....	....	....	....
1987-88	Harvard	ECAC	32	5	17	22	40	....	....	....	....	....
1988-89	Harvard	ECAC	33	4	17	21	40	....	....	....	....	....
1989-90	Harvard	ECAC	28	6	10	16	29	....	....	....	....	....
1990-91	Sokol Kiev	USSR	32	2	4	6	18	....	....	....	....	....
	Fort Wayne	IHL	1	1	0	1	2	....	....	....	....	....
1991-92	Moncton	AHL	38	9	9	18	35	....	....	....	....	....
1992-93	Moncton	AHL	29	3	7	10	2	....	....	....	....	....
	Fort Wayne	IHL	5	1	2	3	6	....	....	....	....	....
	Providence	AHL	29	2	14	16	32	4	1	0	1	20

HARTMAN, MIKE

Left wing. Shoots left. 6', 190 lbs. Born, Detroit, MI, February 7, 1967.
(Buffalo's 8th choice, 131st overall, in 1986 Entry Draft).

			Regular Season					Playoffs				
Season	Club	Lea	GP	G	A	TP	PIM	GP	G	A	TP	PIM
1984-85	Belleville	OHL	49	13	12	25	119	....	....	....	....	....
1985-86	Belleville	OHL	4	2	1	3	5	....	....	....	....	....
	North Bay	OHL	53	19	16	35	205	10	2	4	6	34
1986-87	**Buffalo**	**NHL**	**17**	**3**	**3**	**6**	**69**	....	....	....	....	....
	North Bay	OHL	32	15	24	39	144	19	7	8	15	88
1987-88	**Buffalo**	**NHL**	**18**	**3**	**1**	**4**	**90**	**6**	**0**	**0**	**0**	**35**
	Rochester	AHL	57	13	14	27	283	4	1	0	1	22
1988-89	**Buffalo**	**NHL**	**70**	**8**	**9**	**17**	**316**	**5**	**0**	**0**	**0**	**34**
1989-90	**Buffalo**	**NHL**	**60**	**11**	**10**	**21**	**211**	**6**	**0**	**0**	**0**	**18**
1990-91	**Buffalo**	**NHL**	**60**	**9**	**3**	**12**	**204**	**2**	**0**	**0**	**0**	**17**
1991-92	**Winnipeg**	**NHL**	**75**	**4**	**4**	**8**	**264**	**2**	**0**	**0**	**0**	**2**
1992-93	**Tampa Bay**	**NHL**	**58**	**4**	**4**	**8**	**154**	....	....	....	....	....
	NY Rangers	**NHL**	**3**	**0**	**0**	**0**	**6**	....	....	....	....	....
	NHL Totals		**361**	**42**	**34**	**76**	**1314**	**21**	**0**	**0**	**0**	**106**

Traded to **Winnipeg** by **Buffalo** with Darrin Shannon and Dean Kennedy for Dave McLlwain, Gord Donnelly, Winnipeg's fifth round choice (Yuri Khmylev) in 1992 Entry Draft and future considerations, October 11, 1991. Claimed by **Tampa Bay** from **Winnipeg** in Expansion Draft, June 18, 1992. Traded to **NY Rangers** by **Tampa Bay** for Randy Gilhen, March 22, 1993.

HARVEY, TODD

Center. Shoots right. 5'11", 190 lbs. Born, Hamilton, Ont., February 17, 1975.
(Dallas' 1st choice, 9th overall, in 1993 Entry Draft).

			Regular Season					Playoffs				
Season	Club	Lea	GP	G	A	TP	PIM	GP	G	A	TP	PIM
1991-92	Detroit	OHL	50	21	43	64	141	7	3	5	8	30
1992-93	Detroit	OHL	55	50	50	100	83	15	9	12	21	39

HASSELBLAD, PETER

Defense. Shoots left. 6'5", 216 lbs. Born, Orebro, Sweden, April 20, 1966.
(Calgary's 12th choice, 229th overall, in 1987 Entry Draft).

			Regular Season					Playoffs				
Season	Club	Lea	GP	G	A	TP	PIM	GP	G	A	TP	PIM
1989-90	Farjestad	Swe.	36	3	6	9	51	10	1	2	3	12
1990-91	Farjestad	Swe.	40	0	7	7	56	8	0	0	0	16
1991-92	Team Boro	Swe.2	27	2	12	14	52	....	....	....	....	....
1992-93	Malmo	Swe.	39	4	9	13	52	6	0	0	0	6

HATCHER, DERIAN

Defense. Shoots left. 6'5", 205 lbs. Born, Sterling Heights, MI, June 4, 1972.
(Minnesota's 1st choice, 8th overall, in 1990 Entry Draft).

			Regular Season					Playoffs				
Season	Club	Lea	GP	G	A	TP	PIM	GP	G	A	TP	PIM
1989-90	North Bay	OHL	64	14	38	52	81	5	2	3	5	8
1990-91a	North Bay	OHL	64	13	49	62	163	10	2	10	12	28
1991-92	**Minnesota**	**NHL**	**43**	**8**	**4**	**12**	**88**	**5**	**0**	**2**	**2**	**8**
1992-93	**Minnesota**	**NHL**	**67**	**4**	**15**	**19**	**178**	....	....	....	....	....
	Kalamazoo	IHL	2	1	2	3	21	....	....	....	....	....
	NHL Totals		**110**	**12**	**19**	**31**	**266**	**5**	**0**	**2**	**2**	**8**

a OHL Third All-Star Team (1991)

HATCHER, KEVIN

Defense. Shoots right. 6'4", 225 lbs. Born, Detroit, MI, September 9, 1966.
(Washington's 1st choice, 17th overall, in 1984 Entry Draft).

			Regular Season					Playoffs				
Season	Club	Lea	GP	G	A	TP	PIM	GP	G	A	TP	PIM
1983-84	North Bay	OHL	67	10	39	49	61	4	2	2	4	11
1984-85	**Washington**	**NHL**	**2**	**1**	**0**	**1**	**0**	**1**	**0**	**0**	**0**	**0**
a	North Bay	OHL	58	26	37	63	75	8	3	8	11	9
1985-86	**Washington**	**NHL**	**79**	**9**	**10**	**19**	**119**	**9**	**1**	**1**	**2**	**19**
1986-87	**Washington**	**NHL**	**78**	**8**	**16**	**24**	**144**	**7**	**1**	**0**	**1**	**20**
1987-88	**Washington**	**NHL**	**71**	**14**	**27**	**41**	**137**	**14**	**5**	**7**	**12**	**55**
1988-89	**Washington**	**NHL**	**62**	**13**	**27**	**40**	**101**	**6**	**1**	**4**	**5**	**20**
1989-90	**Washington**	**NHL**	**80**	**13**	**41**	**54**	**102**	**11**	**0**	**8**	**8**	**32**
1990-91	**Washington**	**NHL**	**79**	**24**	**50**	**74**	**69**	**11**	**3**	**3**	**6**	**8**
1991-92	**Washington**	**NHL**	**79**	**17**	**37**	**54**	**105**	**7**	**2**	**4**	**6**	**19**
1992-93	**Washington**	**NHL**	**83**	**34**	**45**	**79**	**114**	**6**	**0**	**1**	**1**	**14**
	NHL Totals		**613**	**133**	**253**	**386**	**891**	**72**	**13**	**28**	**41**	**187**

a OHL Second All-Star Team (1985)

Played in NHL All-Star Game (1990, 1991, 1992)

HAUER, BRETT

Defense. Shoots right. 6'2", 190 lbs. Born, Edina, MN, July 11, 1971.
(Vancouver's 3rd choice, 71st overall, in 1989 Entry Draft).

			Regular Season					Playoffs				
Season	Club	Lea	GP	G	A	TP	PIM	GP	G	A	TP	PIM
1989-90	Minn.-Duluth	WCHA	37	2	6	8	44	....	....	....	....	....
1990-91	Minn.-Duluth	WCHA	30	1	7	8	54	....	....	....	....	....
1991-92	Minn.-Duluth	WCHA	33	8	14	22	40	....	....	....	....	....
1992-93ab	Minn. Duluth	WCHA	40	10	46	56	52	....	....	....	....	....

a WCHA First All-Star Team (1993)
b NCAA West First All-American Team (1993)

HAWERCHUK, DALE (HOW-uhr-CHUHK)

Center. Shoots left. 5'11", 190 lbs. Born, Toronto, Ont., April 4, 1963.
(Winnipeg's 1st choice, 1st overall, in 1981 Entry Draft).

			Regular Season					Playoffs				
Season	Club	Lea	GP	G	A	TP	PIM	GP	G	A	TP	PIM
1979-80	Cornwall	QJHL	72	37	66	103	21	18	20	25	45	0
1980-81abc	Cornwall	QJHL	72	81	102	183	69	19	15	20	35	8
1981-82d	**Winnipeg**	**NHL**	**80**	**45**	**58**	**103**	**47**	**4**	**1**	**7**	**8**	**5**
1982-83	**Winnipeg**	**NHL**	**79**	**40**	**51**	**91**	**31**	**3**	**1**	**4**	**5**	**8**
1983-84	**Winnipeg**	**NHL**	**80**	**37**	**65**	**102**	**73**	**3**	**1**	**1**	**2**	**0**
1984-85e	**Winnipeg**	**NHL**	**80**	**53**	**77**	**130**	**74**	**3**	**2**	**1**	**3**	**4**
1985-86	**Winnipeg**	**NHL**	**80**	**46**	**59**	**105**	**44**	**3**	**0**	**3**	**3**	**0**
1986-87	**Winnipeg**	**NHL**	**80**	**47**	**53**	**100**	**52**	**10**	**5**	**8**	**13**	**4**
1987-88	**Winnipeg**	**NHL**	**80**	**44**	**77**	**121**	**59**	**5**	**3**	**4**	**7**	**16**
1988-89	**Winnipeg**	**NHL**	**75**	**41**	**55**	**96**	**28**	....	....	....	....	....
1989-90	**Winnipeg**	**NHL**	**79**	**26**	**55**	**81**	**60**	**7**	**3**	**5**	**8**	**2**
1990-91	**Buffalo**	**NHL**	**80**	**31**	**58**	**89**	**32**	**6**	**2**	**4**	**6**	**10**
1991-92	**Buffalo**	**NHL**	**77**	**23**	**75**	**98**	**27**	**7**	**2**	**5**	**7**	**0**
1992-93	**Buffalo**	**NHL**	**81**	**16**	**80**	**96**	**52**	**8**	**5**	**9**	**14**	**2**
	NHL Totals		**951**	**449**	**763**	**1212**	**579**	**59**	**25**	**51**	**76**	**51**

a QMJHL First All-Star Team (1981)
b QMJHL Player of the Year (1981)
c Canadian Major Junior Player of the Year (1981)
d Won Calder Memorial Trophy (1982)
e NHL Second All-Star Team (1985)

Played in NHL All-Star Game (1982, 1985, 1986, 1988)

Traded to **Buffalo** by **Winnipg** with Winnipeg's first round choice (Brad May) in 1990 Entry Draft and future considerations for Phil Housley, Scott Arniel, Jeff Parker and Buffalo's first round choice (Keith Tkachuk) in 1990 Entry Draft, June 16, 1990.

HAWGOOD, GREG

Defense. Shoots left. 5'10", 190 lbs. Born, Edmonton, Alta., August 10, 1968.
(Boston's 9th choice, 202nd overall, in 1986 Entry Draft).

			Regular Season					Playoffs				
Season	Club	Lea	GP	G	A	TP	PIM	GP	G	A	TP	PIM
1983-84	Kamloops	WHL	49	10	23	33	39	....	....	....	....	....
1984-85	Kamloops	WHL	66	25	40	65	72	....	....	....	....	....
1985-86a	Kamloops	WHL	71	34	85	119	86	16	9	22	31	16
1986-87a	Kamloops	WHL	61	30	93	123	139	....	....	....	....	....
1987-88	**Boston**	**NHL**	**1**	**0**	**0**	**0**	**0**	**3**	**1**	**0**	**1**	**0**
ab	Kamloops	WHL	63	48	85	133	142	16	10	16	26	33
1988-89	**Boston**	**NHL**	**56**	**16**	**24**	**40**	**84**	**10**	**0**	**2**	**2**	**2**
	Maine	AHL	21	2	9	11	41	....	....	....	....	....
1989-90	**Boston**	**NHL**	**77**	**11**	**27**	**38**	**76**	**15**	**1**	**3**	**4**	**12**
1990-91	Asiago	Italy	2	3	0	3	9	....	....	....	....	....
	Edmonton	**NHL**	**6**	**0**	**1**	**1**	**6**	....	....	....	....	....
	Maine	AHL	5	0	1	1	13	....	....	....	....	....
	Cape Breton	AHL	55	10	32	42	73	4	0	3	3	23
1991-92	**Edmonton**	**NHL**	**20**	**2**	**11**	**13**	**22**	**13**	**0**	**3**	**3**	**23**
cd	Cape Breton	AHL	56	20	55	75	26	3	2	2	4	0
1992-93	**Edmonton**	**NHL**	**29**	**5**	**13**	**18**	**35**	....	....	....	....	....
	Philadelphia	**NHL**	**40**	**6**	**22**	**28**	**39**	....	....	....	....	....
	NHL Totals		**229**	**40**	**98**	**138**	**262**	**41**	**2**	**8**	**10**	**37**

a WHL West All-Star Team (1986, 1987, 1988)
b WHL and Canadian Major Junior Defenseman of the Year (1988)
c AHL First All-Star Team (1992)
d Won Eddie Shore Plaque (Top Defenseman-AHL) (1992)

Traded to **Edmonton** by **Boston** for Vladimir Ruzicka, October 22, 1990. Traded to **Philadelphia** by **Edmonton** with Josef Beranek for Brian Benning, January 16, 1993.

HAWKINS, TODD

Left/Right wing. Shoots right. 6'1", 195 lbs. Born, Kingston, Ont., August 2, 1966.
(Vancouver's 10th choice, 217th overall, in 1986 Entry Draft).

			Regular Season					Playoffs				
Season	Club	Lea	GP	G	A	TP	PIM	GP	G	A	TP	PIM
1984-85	Belleville	OHL	58	7	16	23	117	12	1	0	1	10
1985-86	Belleville	OHL	60	14	13	27	172	24	9	7	16	60
1986-87	Belleville	OHL	60	47	40	87	187	6	3	5	8	16
1987-88	Flint	IHL	50	13	13	26	337	16	3	5	8	*174
	Fredericton	AHL	2	0	4	4	11	....	....	....	....	....
1988-89	**Vancouver**	**NHL**	**4**	**0**	**0**	**0**	**9**	....	....	....	....	....
	Milwaukee	IHL	63	12	14	26	307	9	1	0	1	33
1989-90	**Vancouver**	**NHL**	**4**	**0**	**0**	**0**	**6**	....	....	....	....	....
	Milwaukee	IHL	61	23	17	40	273	5	4	1	5	19
1990-91	Newmarket	AHL	22	2	5	7	66	....	....	....	....	....
	Milwaukee	IHL	39	9	11	20	134	....	....	....	....	....
1991-92	**Toronto**	**NHL**	**2**	**0**	**0**	**0**	**0**	....	....	....	....	....
	St. John's	AHL	66	30	27	57	139	7	1	0	1	10
1992-93	St. John's	AHL	72	21	41	62	103	9	1	3	4	10
	NHL Totals		**10**	**0**	**0**	**0**	**15**	....	....	....	....	....

Traded to **Toronto** by **Vancouver** for Brian Blad, January 22, 1991.

HAWLEY, JOE

Right wing. Shoots right. 5'10", 186 lbs. Born, Peterborough, Ont., March 13, 1971.
(St. Louis' 8th choice, 222nd overall, in 1990 Entry Draft).

			Regular Season					Playoffs				
Season	Club	Lea	GP	G	A	TP	PIM	GP	G	A	TP	PIM
1989-90	Peterborough	OHL	66	8	40	48	59	12	2	3	5	26
1990-91	Peterborough	OHL	63	17	47	64	70	4	2	3	5	11
	Peoria	IHL	5	0	0	0	0	10	1	1	2	8
1991-92	Peoria	IHL	40	6	7	13	42	....	....	....	....	....
	Dayton	ECHL	7	3	6	9	12	....	....	....	....	....
1992-93	Peoria	IHL	50	12	11	23	52	....	....	....	....	....

HEAPHY, SHAWN

Center. Shoots left. 5'8", 180 lbs. Born, Sudbury, Ont., November 27, 1968.
(Calgary's 1st choice, 26th overall, in 1989 Supplemental Draft).

			Regular Season					Playoffs				
Season	**Club**	**Lea**	**GP**	**G**	**A**	**TP**	**PIM**	**GP**	**G**	**A**	**TP**	**PIM**
1987-88	Michigan State	CCHA	44	19	24	43	48	....	....	....	....	....
1988-89	Michigan State	CCHA	47	26	17	43	80	....	....	....	....	....
1989-90	Michigan State	CCHA	45	28	31	59	54	....	....	....	....	....
1990-91	Michigan State	CCHA	39	30	19	49	57	....	....	....	....	....
	Salt Lake	IHL	....	....	....	....	....	1	0	0	0	0
1991-92	Salt Lake	IHL	76	41	36	77	85	5	2	2	4	2
1992-93	**Calgary**	**NHL**	**1**	**0**	**0**	**0**	**0**	....	....	....	....	....
	Salt Lake	IHL	78	29	36	65	63	....	....	....	....	....
	NHL Totals		**1**	**0**	**0**	**0**	**0**	....	....	....	....	....

HEDICAN, BRET

Defense. Shoots left. 6'2", 195 lbs. Born, St. Paul, MN, August 10, 1970.
(St. Louis' 10th choice, 198th overall, in 1988 Entry Draft).

			Regular Season					Playoffs				
Season	**Club**	**Lea**	**GP**	**G**	**A**	**TP**	**PIM**	**GP**	**G**	**A**	**TP**	**PIM**
1988-89	St. Cloud	NCAA	28	5	3	8	28	....	....	....	....	....
1989-90	St. Cloud	NCAA	36	4	17	21	37	....	....	....	....	....
1990-91a	St. Cloud	WCHA	41	21	26	47	26	....	....	....	....	....
1991-92	U.S. National	....	54	1	8	9	59	....	....	....	....	....
	U.S. Olympic	....	8	0	0	0	4	....	....	....	....	....
	St. Louis	**NHL**	**4**	**1**	**0**	**1**	**0**	**5**	**0**	**0**	**0**	**0**
1992-93	**St. Louis**	**NHL**	**42**	**0**	**8**	**8**	**30**	**10**	**0**	**0**	**0**	**14**
	Peoria	IHL	19	0	8	8	10	....	....	....	....	....
	NHL Totals		**46**	**1**	**8**	**9**	**30**	**15**	**0**	**0**	**0**	**14**

a WCHA First All-Star Team (1991)

HEDLUND, TODD

Right wing. Shoots right. 6'1", 177 lbs. Born, Roseau, MN, August 20, 1971.
(NY Rangers' 10th choice, 160th overall, in 1990 Entry Draft).

			Regular Season					Playoffs				
Season	**Club**	**Lea**	**GP**	**G**	**A**	**TP**	**PIM**	**GP**	**G**	**A**	**TP**	**PIM**
1990-91	U. Wisconsin	WCHA				DID NOT PLAY						
1991-92	U. Wisconsin	WCHA	5	0	1	1	2	....	....	....	....	....
1992-93	U. Wisconsin	WCHA	8	0	0	0	0	....	....	....	....	....

HEED, JONAS (HAD)

Defense. Shoots left. 6'1", 202 lbs. Born, Sodertalje, Sweden, January 3, 1967.
(Chicago's 6th choice, 116th overall, in 1985 Entry Draft).

			Regular Season					Playoffs				
Season	**Club**	**Lea**	**GP**	**G**	**A**	**TP**	**PIM**	**GP**	**G**	**A**	**TP**	**PIM**
1984-85	Sodertalje	Swe.	8	0	0	0	0	....	....	....	....	....
1985-86	Sodertalje	Swe.	17	3	2	5	6	....	....	....	....	....
1986-87	Sodertalje	Swe.	24	0	3	3	12	....	....	....	....	....
1987-88	Sodertalje	Swe.	26	1	4	5	12	2	0	0	0	4
1988-89	Sodertalje	Swe.	38	4	9	13	22	....	....	....	....	....
1989-90	Sodertalje	Swe.	36	7	4	11	28	2	0	0	0	0
1990-91	V. Frolunda	Swe.	21	1	1	2	14	....	....	....	....	....
1991-92	V. Frolunda	Swe.	33	2	1	3	34	3	0	0	0	0
1992-93	V. Frolunda	Swe.	21	2	2	4	34	....	....	....	....	....

HEHR, JASON

Defense. Shoots left. 6'1", 193 lbs. Born, Medicine Hat, Alta., February 8, 1971.
(New Jersey's 12th choice, 253rd overall, in 1991 Entry Draft).

			Regular Season					Playoffs				
Season	**Club**	**Lea**	**GP**	**G**	**A**	**TP**	**PIM**	**GP**	**G**	**A**	**TP**	**PIM**
1991-92	N. Michigan	WCHA	40	8	17	25	38	....	....	....	....	....
1992-93	N. Michigan	WCHA	43	8	27	35	40	....	....	....	....	....

HEINZE, STEPHEN

Right wing. Shoots right. 5'11", 192 lbs. Born, Lawrence, MA, January 30, 1970.
(Boston's 2nd choice, 60th overall, in 1988 Entry Draft).

			Regular Season					Playoffs				
Season	**Club**	**Lea**	**GP**	**G**	**A**	**TP**	**PIM**	**GP**	**G**	**A**	**TP**	**PIM**
1988-89	Boston College	H.E.	36	26	23	49	26	....	....	....	....	....
1989-90ab	Boston College	H.E.	40	27	36	63	41	....	....	....	....	....
1990-91	Boston College	H.E.	35	21	26	47	35	....	....	....	....	....
1991-92	U.S. National	....	49	18	15	33	38	....	....	....	....	....
	U.S. Olympic	....	8	1	3	4	8	....	....	....	....	....
	Boston	**NHL**	**14**	**3**	**4**	**7**	**6**	**7**	**0**	**3**	**3**	**17**
1992-93	**Boston**	**NHL**	**73**	**18**	**13**	**31**	**24**	**4**	**1**	**1**	**2**	**2**
	NHL Totals		**87**	**21**	**17**	**38**	**30**	**11**	**1**	**4**	**5**	**19**

a Hockey East First All-Star Team (1990)
b NCAA East First All-American Team (1990)

HELENIUS, SAMI

Defense. Shoots left. 6'5", 200 lbs. Born, Finland, January 22, 1974.
(Calgary's 5th choice, 102nd overall, in 1992 Entry Draft).

			Regular Season					Playoffs				
Season	**Club**	**Lea**	**GP**	**G**	**A**	**TP**	**PIM**	**GP**	**G**	**A**	**TP**	**PIM**
1992-93	Jokerit	Fin.	1	0	0	0	0	....	....	....	....	....

HENDRICKSON, DARBY

Center. Shoots left. 6', 175 lbs. Born, Richfield, MN, August 28, 1972.
(Toronto's 3rd choice, 73rd overall, in 1990 Entry Draft).

			Regular Season					Playoffs				
Season	**Club**	**Lea**	**GP**	**G**	**A**	**TP**	**PIM**	**GP**	**G**	**A**	**TP**	**PIM**
1991-92	U. Minnesota	WCHA	41	25	28	53	61	....	....	....	....	....
1992-93	U. Minnesota	WCHA	31	12	15	27	35	....	....	....	....	....

HENDRY, JOHN

Left wing. Shoots left. 6'1", 180 lbs. Born, Mississauga, Ont., May 15, 1970.
(Detroit's 11th choice, 234th overall, in 1990 Entry Draft).

			Regular Season					Playoffs				
Season	**Club**	**Lea**	**GP**	**G**	**A**	**TP**	**PIM**	**GP**	**G**	**A**	**TP**	**PIM**
1989-90	Lake Superior	CCHA	41	4	7	11	30	....	....	....	....	....
1990-91	Lake Superior	CCHA	44	7	10	17	42	....	....	....	....	....
1991-92	Lake Superior	CCHA	39	12	8	20	53	....	....	....	....	....
1992-93	Lake Superior	CCHA	37	13	20	33	46	....	....	....	....	....

HENRICH, ED

Defense. Shoots left. 6'2", 185 lbs. Born, Buffalo, NY, February 2, 1971.
(Montreal's 10th choice, 209th overall, in 1989 Entry Draft).

			Regular Season					Playoffs				
Season	**Club**	**Lea**	**GP**	**G**	**A**	**TP**	**PIM**	**GP**	**G**	**A**	**TP**	**PIM**
1990-91	Clarkson	ECAC	37	4	23	27	22	....	....	....	....	....
1991-92	Clarkson	ECAC	28	2	11	13	22	....	....	....	....	....
1992-93	Clarkson	ECAC	35	0	11	11	30	....	....	....	....	....

HERBERS, IAN

Defense. Shoots left. 6'4", 225 lbs. Born, Jasper, Alta., July 18, 1967.
(Buffalo's 11th choice, 190th overall, in 1987 Entry Draft).

			Regular Season					Playoffs				
Season	**Club**	**Lea**	**GP**	**G**	**A**	**TP**	**PIM**	**GP**	**G**	**A**	**TP**	**PIM**
1984-85	Kelowna	WHL	68	3	14	17	120	6	0	1	1	9
1985-86	Spokane	WHL	29	1	6	7	85	....	....	....	....	....
	Lethbridge	WHL	32	1	4	5	109	10	1	0	1	37
1986-87	Swift Current	WHL	72	5	8	13	230	4	1	1	2	12
1987-88	Swift Current	WHL	56	5	14	19	238	4	0	2	2	4
1988-89	U. of Alberta	CWUAA	47	4	22	26	137	....	....	....	....	....
1989-90a	U. of Alberta	CWUAA	45	5	31	36	83	....	....	....	....	....
1990-91bc	U. of Alberta	CWUAA	45	6	24	30	87	....	....	....	....	....
1991-92bcde	U. of Alberta	CWUAA	43	14	34	48	86	....	....	....	....	....
1992-93	Cape Breton	AHL	77	7	15	22	129	10	0	1	1	16

a CWUAA Second All-Star Team (1990)
b CWUAA First All-Star Team (1991, 1992)
c CIAU All-Canadian Team (1991, 1992)
d Mervyn "Red" Dutton Trophy (CWUAA Outstanding Defenseman) (1992)
e CWUAA Student-Athlete-of-the-Year (1992)

Signed as a free agent by **Edmonton**, September 9, 1992.

HEROUX, YVES (ay-ROO, EEV)

Right wing. Shoots right. 5'11", 185 lbs. Born, Terrebonne, Que., April 27, 1965.
(Quebec's 1st choice, 32nd overall, in 1983 Entry Draft).

			Regular Season					Playoffs				
Season	**Club**	**Lea**	**GP**	**G**	**A**	**TP**	**PIM**	**GP**	**G**	**A**	**TP**	**PIM**
1982-83	Chicoutimi	QMJHL	70	41	40	81	44	5	0	4	4	8
1983-84	Chicoutimi	QMJHL	56	28	25	53	67	....	....	....	....	....
	Fredericton	AHL	4	0	0	0	0	....	....	....	....	....
1984-85	Chicoutimi	QMJHL	66	42	54	96	123	14	5	8	13	16
1985-86	Fredericton	AHL	31	12	10	22	42	2	0	1	1	7
	Muskegon	IHL	42	14	8	22	41	....	....	....	....	....
1986-87	**Quebec**	**NHL**	**1**	**0**	**0**	**0**	**0**	....	....	....	....	....
	Fredericton	AHL	37	8	6	14	13	....	....	....	....	....
	Muskegon	IHL	25	6	8	14	31	2	0	0	0	0
1987-88	Baltimore	AHL	5	0	2	2	2	....	....	....	....	....
1988-89	Flint	IHL	82	43	42	85	98	....	....	....	....	....
1989-90	Peoria	IHL	14	3	2	5	42	5	2	2	4	0
1990-91	Albany	IHL	45	22	18	40	46	....	....	....	....	....
	Peoria	IHL	33	16	8	24	26	17	4	4	8	16
1991-92	Peoria	IHL	80	41	36	77	72	8	5	1	6	6
1992-93	Kalamazoo	IHL	80	38	30	68	86	....	....	....	....	....
	NHL Totals		**1**	**0**	**0**	**0**	**0**	....	....	....	....	....

Signed as a free agent by **St. Louis**, March 13, 1990. Signed as a free agent by **Minnesota**, August 10, 1992.

HERPERGER, CHRIS

Left wing. Shoots left. 6', 190 lbs. Born, Esterhazy, Sask., February 24, 1974.
(Philadelphia's 10th choice, 223rd overall, in 1992 Entry Draft).

			Regular Season					Playoffs				
Season	**Club**	**Lea**	**GP**	**G**	**A**	**TP**	**PIM**	**GP**	**G**	**A**	**TP**	**PIM**
1990-91	Swift Current	WHL	10	0	1	1	5	....	....	....	....	....
1991-92	Swift Current	WHL	72	14	19	33	44	8	0	1	1	9
1992-93	Seattle	WHL	66	29	18	47	61	5	1	1	2	6

HERTER, JASON

Defense. Shoots right. 6'1", 190 lbs. Born, Hafford, Sask., October 2, 1970.
(Vancouver's 1st choice, 8th overall, in 1989 Entry Draft).

			Regular Season					Playoffs				
Season	**Club**	**Lea**	**GP**	**G**	**A**	**TP**	**PIM**	**GP**	**G**	**A**	**TP**	**PIM**
1988-89	North Dakota	WCHA	41	8	24	32	62	....	....	....	....	....
1989-90a	North Dakota	WCHA	38	11	39	50	40	....	....	....	....	....
1990-91a	North Dakota	WCHA	39	11	26	37	52	....	....	....	....	....
1991-92	Milwaukee	IHL	56	7	18	25	34	1	0	0	0	2
1992-93	Hamilton	AHL	70	7	16	23	68	....	....	....	....	....

a WCHA Second All-Star Team (1990, 1991)

HERVEY, MATT

Defense. Shoots right. 5'11", 205 lbs. Born, Whittier, CA, May 16, 1968.

			Regular Season					Playoffs				
Season	**Club**	**Lea**	**GP**	**G**	**A**	**TP**	**PIM**	**GP**	**G**	**A**	**TP**	**PIM**
1983-84	Victoria	WHL	67	4	19	23	89	....	....	....	....	....
1984-85	Victoria	WHL	14	1	3	4	17	....	....	....	....	....
	Lethbridge	WHL	54	3	9	12	88	....	....	....	....	....
1985-86	Lethbridge	WHL	60	9	17	26	110	....	....	....	....	....
1986-87	Seattle	WHL	66	4	5	9	59	....	....	....	....	....
1987-88	Moncton	AHL	69	9	20	29	265	....	....	....	....	....
1988-89	**Winnipeg**	**NHL**	**2**	**0**	**0**	**0**	**4**	....	....	....	....	....
	Moncton	AHL	73	8	28	36	295	10	1	2	3	42
1989-90	Moncton	AHL	47	3	13	16	168	....	....	....	....	....
1990-91	Moncton	AHL	71	4	28	32	132	7	0	1	1	23
1991-92	**Boston**	**NHL**	**16**	**0**	**1**	**1**	**55**	**5**	**0**	**0**	**0**	**6**
	Maine	AHL	36	1	7	8	47	....	....	....	....	....
1992-93	**Tampa Bay**	**NHL**	**17**	**0**	**4**	**4**	**38**	....	....	....	....	....
	Atlanta	IHL	49	12	19	31	122	9	0	3	3	19
	NHL Totals		**35**	**0**	**5**	**5**	**97**	**5**	**0**	**0**	**0**	**6**

Signed as a free agent by **Winnipeg**, September 27, 1988. Signed as a free agent by **Boston**, August 15, 1991. Traded to **Tampa Bay** by **Boston** with Ken Hodge for Darin Kimble and future considerations, September 4, 1992.

HEWARD, JAMIE

Right wing. Shoots right. 6'2", 183 lbs. Born, Regina, Sask., March 30, 1971.
(Pittsburgh's 1st choice, 16th overall, in 1989 Entry Draft).

			Regular Season					Playoffs				
Season	Club	Lea	GP	G	A	TP	PIM	GP	G	A	TP	PIM
1987-88	Regina	WHL	68	10	17	27	17	4	1	1	2	2
1988-89	Regina	WHL	52	31	28	59	29	....	....	....	....	....
1989-90	Regina	WHL	72	14	44	58	42	11	2	2	4	10
1990-91a	Regina	WHL	71	23	61	84	41	8	2	9	11	6
1991-92	Muskegon	IHL	54	6	21	27	37	14	1	4	5	4
1992-93	Cleveland	IHL	58	9	18	27	64	....	....	....	....	....

a WHL East First All-Star Team (1991)

HEXTALL, DONEVAN

Left wing. Shoots left. 6'2", 192 lbs. Born, Wolseley, Sask., February 24, 1972.
(New Jersey's 3rd choice, 33rd overall, in 1991 Entry Draft).

			Regular Season					Playoffs				
Season	Club	Lea	GP	G	A	TP	PIM	GP	G	A	TP	PIM
1989-90	Weyburn	SJHL	63	23	45	68	127	....	....	....	....	....
	Prince Albert	WHL	7	1	2	3	4	....	....	....	....	....
1990-91	Prince Albert	WHL	70	30	59	89	55	3	1	3	4	0
1991-92a	Prince Albert	WHL	71	33	71	104	105	10	3	6	9	10
1992-93	Cdn. National	....	6	0	1	1	4	....	....	....	....	....
	Utica	AHL	51	11	11	22	12	2	1	0	1	0

a WHL East Second All-Star Team (1992)

HILL, KILEY

Left wing. Shoots left. 6'3", 205 lbs. Born, Sudbury, Ont., January 2, 1975.
(Tampa Bay's 6th choice, 133rd overall, in 1993 Entry Draft).

			Regular Season					Playoffs				
Season	Club	Lea	GP	G	A	TP	PIM	GP	G	A	TP	PIM
1991-92	S.S. Marie	OHL	32	4	3	7	28	5	1	0	1	0
1992-93	S.S. Marie	OHL	49	6	8	14	76	1	0	0	0	2

HILL, SEAN

Defense. Shoots right. 6', 195 lbs. Born, Duluth, MN, February 14, 1970.
(Montreal's 9th choice, 167th overall, in 1988 Entry Draft).

			Regular Season					Playoffs				
Season	Club	Lea	GP	G	A	TP	PIM	GP	G	A	TP	PIM
1988-89	U. Wisconsin	WCHA	45	2	23	25	69	....	....	....	....	....
1989-90a	U. Wisconsin	WCHA	42	14	39	53	78	....	....	....	....	....
1990-91ab	U. Wisconsin	WCHA	37	19	32	51	122	....	....	....	....	....
	Montreal	**NHL**	....	....	....	....	....	**1**	**0**	**0**	**0**	**0**
	Fredericton	AHL	....	....	....	....	....	3	0	2	2	2
1991-92	Fredericton	AHL	42	7	20	27	65	7	1	3	4	6
	U.S. National	....	12	4	3	7	16	....	....	....	....	....
	U.S. Olympic	....	8	2	0	2	6	....	....	....	....	....
	Montreal	**NHL**	....	....	....	....	....	**4**	**1**	**0**	**1**	**2**
1992-93	**Montreal**	**NHL**	**31**	**2**	**6**	**8**	**54**	**3**	**0**	**0**	**0**	**4**
	Fredericton	AHL	6	1	3	4	10	....	....	....	....	....
	NHL Totals		**31**	**2**	**6**	**8**	**54**	**8**	**1**	**0**	**1**	**6**

a WCHA Second All-Star Team (1990, 1991)
b NCAA West Second All-American Team (1991)

Claimed by **Anaheim** from **Montreal** in Expansion Draft, June 24, 1993.

HILLER, JIM

Right wing. Shoots right. 6', 190 lbs. Born, Port Alberni, B.C., May 15, 1969.
(Los Angeles' 10th choice, 207th overall, in 1989 Entry Draft).

			Regular Season					Playoffs				
Season	Club	Lea	GP	G	A	TP	PIM	GP	G	A	TP	PIM
1989-90	N. Michigan	WCHA	39	23	33	56	52	....	....	....	....	....
1990-91	N. Michigan	WCHA	43	22	41	63	59	....	....	....	....	....
1991-92ab	N. Michigan	WCHA	39	28	52	80	115	....	....	....	....	....
1992-93	**Los Angeles**	**NHL**	**40**	**6**	**6**	**12**	**90**	....	....	....	....	....
	Phoenix	IHL	3	0	2	2	2	....	....	....	....	....
	Detroit	**NHL**	**21**	**2**	**6**	**8**	**19**	**2**	**0**	**0**	**0**	**4**
	NHL Totals		**61**	**8**	**12**	**20**	**109**	**2**	**0**	**0**	**0**	**4**

a NCAA West Second All-American Team (1992)
b WCHA Second All-Star Team (1992)

Traded to **Detroit** by **Los Angeles** with Paul Coffey and Sylvain Couturier for Jimmy Carson, Marc Potvin and Gary Shuchuk, January 29, 1993.

HILTON, KEVIN

Center. Shoots left. 5'11", 170 lbs. Born, Trenton, MI, January 5, 1975.
(Detroit's 3rd choice, 74th overall, in 1993 Entry Draft).

			Regular Season					Playoffs				
Season	Club	Lea	GP	G	A	TP	PIM	GP	G	A	TP	PIM
1991-92	Det. Compuware	NAJHL	39	35	42	77	42	....	....	....	....	....
1992-93	U. of Michigan	CCHA	36	16	15	31	8	....	....	....	....	....

HOCKING, JUSTIN

Defense. Shoots right. 6'4", 205 lbs. Born, Stettler, Alta., January 9, 1974.
(Los Angeles' 1st choice, 39th overall, in 1992 Entry Draft).

			Regular Season					Playoffs				
Season	Club	Lea	GP	G	A	TP	PIM	GP	G	A	TP	PIM
1991-92	Spokane	WHL	71	4	6	10	309	10	0	3	3	28
1992-93	Medicine Hat	WHL	70	1	10	11	194	10	0	1	1	13

HODGE, DAN

Defense. Shoots right. 6'3", 205 lbs. Born, Melrose, MA, September 18, 1971.
(Boston's 8th choice, 194th overall, in 1991 Entry Draft).

			Regular Season					Playoffs				
Season	Club	Lea	GP	G	A	TP	PIM	GP	G	A	TP	PIM
1990-91	Merrimack	H.E.	11	2	3	5	4	....	....	....	....	....
1991-92	Omaha	USHL	45	5	18	23	89	....	....	....	....	....
1992-93	Merrimack	H.E.	36	3	17	20	30	....	....	....	....	....

HODGE, KENNETH DAVID (KEN)

Center/Right wing. Shoots left. 6'1", 200 lbs. Born, Windsor, Ont., April 13, 1966.
(Minnesota's 2nd choice, 46th overall, in 1984 Entry Draft).

			Regular Season					Playoffs				
Season	Club	Lea	GP	G	A	TP	PIM	GP	G	A	TP	PIM
1984-85	Boston College	H.E.	41	20	44	64	28	....	....	....	....	....
1985-86	Boston College	H.E.	21	11	17	28	16	....	....	....	....	....
1986-87	Boston College	H.E.	37	29	33	62	30	....	....	....	....	....
1987-88	Kalamazoo	IHL	70	15	35	50	24	....	....	....	....	....
1988-89	**Minnesota**	**NHL**	**5**	**1**	**1**	**2**	**0**	....	....	....	....	....
	Kalamazoo	IHL	72	26	45	71	34	6	1	5	6	16
1989-90	Kalamazoo	IHL	68	33	53	86	19	10	5	13	18	2
1990-91a	**Boston**	**NHL**	**70**	**30**	**29**	**59**	**20**	**15**	**4**	**6**	**10**	**6**
	Maine	AHL	8	7	10	17	2	....	....	....	....	....
1991-92	**Boston**	**NHL**	**42**	**6**	**11**	**17**	**10**	....	....	....	....	....
	Maine	AHL	19	6	11	17	4	....	....	....	....	....
1992-93	**Tampa Bay**	**NHL**	**25**	**2**	**7**	**9**	**2**	....	....	....	....	....
	Atlanta	IHL	16	10	17	27	0	....	....	....	....	....
	San Diego	IHL	30	11	24	35	16	14	4	6	10	6
	NHL Totals		**142**	**39**	**48**	**87**	**32**	**15**	**4**	**6**	**10**	**6**

a NHL/Upper Deck All-Rookie Team (1991)

Traded to **Boston** by **Minnesota** for future considerations, August 21, 1990. Traded to **Tampa Bay** by **Boston** with Matt Hervey for Darin Kimble and future considerations, September 4, 1992.

HOGAN, TIM

Defense. Shoots right. 6'2", 180 lbs. Born, Oshawa, Ont., January 7, 1974.
(Chicago's 5th choice, 113th overall, in 1992 Entry Draft).

			Regular Season					Playoffs				
Season	Club	Lea	GP	G	A	TP	PIM	GP	G	A	TP	PIM
1991-92	U. of Michigan	CCHA	34	2	8	10	34	....	....	....	....	....
1992-93	U. of Michigan	CCHA	22	4	1	5	24	....	....	....	....	....

HOGLUND, JONAS

Right wing. Shoots right. 6'3", 200 lbs. Born, Hammaro, Sweden, August 29, 1972.
(Calgary's 11th choice, 222nd overall, in 1992 Entry Draft).

			Regular Season					Playoffs				
Season	Club	Lea	GP	G	A	TP	PIM	GP	G	A	TP	PIM
1988-89	Farjestad	Swe.	1	0	0	0	0	....	....	....	....	....
1989-90	Farjestad	Swe.	1	0	0	0	0	....	....	....	....	....
1990-91	Farjestad	Swe.	40	5	5	10	4	8	1	0	1	0
1991-92	Farjestad	Swe.	40	14	11	25	6	6	2	4	6	2
1992-93	Farjestad	Swe.	40	13	13	26	14	3	1	0	1	0

HOGUE, BENOIT (HOHG)

Center. Shoots left. 5'10", 190 lbs. Born, Repentigny, Que., October 28, 1966.
(Buffalo's 2nd choice, 35th overall, in 1985 Entry Draft).

			Regular Season					Playoffs				
Season	Club	Lea	GP	G	A	TP	PIM	GP	G	A	TP	PIM
1983-84	St-Jean	QMJHL	59	14	11	25	42	....	....	....	....	....
1984-85	St-Jean	QMJHL	63	46	44	90	92	....	....	....	....	....
1985-86	St-Jean	QMJHL	65	54	54	108	115	9	6	4	10	26
1986-87	Rochester	AHL	52	14	20	34	52	12	5	4	9	8
1987-88	**Buffalo**	**NHL**	**3**	**1**	**1**	**2**	**0**	....	....	....	....	....
	Rochester	AHL	62	24	31	55	141	7	6	1	7	46
1988-89	**Buffalo**	**NHL**	**69**	**14**	**30**	**44**	**120**	**5**	**0**	**0**	**0**	**17**
1989-90	**Buffalo**	**NHL**	**45**	**11**	**7**	**18**	**79**	**3**	**0**	**0**	**0**	**10**
1990-91	**Buffalo**	**NHL**	**76**	**19**	**28**	**47**	**76**	**5**	**3**	**1**	**4**	**10**
1991-92	**Buffalo**	**NHL**	**3**	**0**	**1**	**1**	**0**	....	....	....	....	....
	NY Islanders	**NHL**	**72**	**30**	**45**	**75**	**67**	....	....	....	....	....
1992-93	**NY Islanders**	**NHL**	**70**	**33**	**42**	**75**	**108**	**18**	**6**	**6**	**12**	**31**
	NHL Totals		**338**	**108**	**154**	**262**	**450**	**31**	**9**	**7**	**16**	**68**

Traded to **NY Islanders** by **Buffalo** with Pierre Turgeon, Uwe Krupp and Dave McLlwain for Pat Lafontaine, Randy Hillier, Randy Wood and future considerations, October 25, 1991.

HOLAN, MILOS

Defense. Shoots left. 5'11", 183 lbs. Born, Bilovec, Czech., April 22, 1971.
(Philadelphia's 3rd choice, 77th overall, in 1993 Entry Draft).

			Regular Season					Playoffs				
Season	Club	Lea	GP	G	A	TP	PIM	GP	G	A	TP	PIM
1988-89	TJ Vitkovice	Czech.	7	0	0	0	0	....	....	....	....	....
1989-90	TJ Vitkovice	Czech.	50	8	8	16	....	....	....	....	....	....
1990-91	Dukla Trencin	Czech.	53	6	13	19	....	....	....	....	....	....
1991-92	Dukla Trencin	Czech.	51	13	22	35	32	....	....	....	....	....
1992-93a	TJ Vitkovice	Czech.	53	35	33	68	....	....	....	....	....	....

a Czechoslovakian Player of the Year (1993)

HOLDEMAN, TOM

Right wing. Shoots right. 6'2", 205 lbs. Born, Columbus, IN, November 8, 1970.
(Edmonton's 1st choice, 18th overall, in 1991 Supplemental Draft).

			Regular Season					Playoffs				
Season	Club	Lea	GP	G	A	TP	PIM	GP	G	A	TP	PIM
1989-90	Miami-Ohio	CCHA	28	3	1	4	8	....	....	....	....	....
1990-91	Miami-Ohio	CCHA	28	2	2	4	42	....	....	....	....	....
1991-92	W. Michigan	CCHA				DID NOT PLAY						
1992-93	Wheeling	ECHL	2	0	1	1	2	....	....	....	....	....

HOLDEN, PAUL

Defense. Shoots left. 6'3", 210 lbs. Born, Kitchener, Ont., March 15, 1970.
(Los Angeles' 2nd choice, 28th overall, in 1988 Entry Draft).

			Regular Season					Playoffs				
Season	Club	Lea	GP	G	A	TP	PIM	GP	G	A	TP	PIM
1987-88	London	OHL	65	8	12	20	87	12	1	1	2	10
1988-89	London	OHL	54	11	21	32	90	20	1	3	4	17
1989-90a	London	OHL	61	11	31	42	78	6	1	1	2	7
	New Haven	AHL	2	1	1	2	2	....	....	....	....	....
1990-91	New Haven	AHL	59	2	8	10	23	....	....	....	....	....
1991-92	Phoenix	IHL	47	3	3	6	63	....	....	....	....	....
1992-93	Phoenix	IHL	3	0	0	0	6	....	....	....	....	....
	Salt Lake	IHL	63	5	8	13	86	....	....	....	....	....

a OHL Second All-Star Team (1990)

Traded to **Calgary** by **Los Angeles** for Kevin Grant, October 16, 1992.

HOLIK, BOBBY (HOH-leek)

Left/Right wing. Shoots right. 6'3", 210 lbs. Born, Jihlava, Czechoslovakia, January 1, 1971.
(Hartford's 1st choice, 10th overall, in 1989 Entry Draft).

			Regular Season					Playoffs				
Season	Club	Lea	GP	G	A	TP	PIM	GP	G	A	TP	PIM
1987-88	Dukla Jihlava	Czech.	31	7	11	18	16	....	....	....	....	....
1988-89	Dukla Jihlava	Czech.	36	15	10	25	32	....	....	....	....	....
1989-90	Dukla Jihlava	Czech.	42	15	26	41	....	....	....	....	....	....
1990-91	**Hartford**	**NHL**	**78**	**21**	**22**	**43**	**113**	**6**	**0**	**0**	**0**	**7**
1991-92	**Hartford**	**NHL**	**76**	**21**	**24**	**45**	**44**	**7**	**0**	**1**	**1**	**6**
1992-93	**New Jersey**	**NHL**	**61**	**20**	**19**	**39**	**76**	**5**	**1**	**1**	**2**	**6**
	Utica	AHL	1	0	0	0	2	....	....	....	....	....
	NHL Totals		**215**	**62**	**65**	**127**	**233**	**18**	**1**	**2**	**3**	**19**

Traded to **New Jersey** by **Hartford** with Hartford's second round choice (Jay Pandolfo) in 1993 Entry Draft and future considerations for Sean Burke and Eric Weinrich, August 28, 1992.

HOLLINGER, TERRY

Defense. Shoots left. 6'1", 200 lbs. Born, Regina, Sask., February 24, 1971.
(St. Louis' 7th choice, 153rd overall, in 1991 Entry Draft).

			Regular Season					Playoffs				
Season	Club	Lea	GP	G	A	TP	PIM	GP	G	A	TP	PIM
1990-91	Regina	WHL	8	1	6	7	6	....	....	....	....	....
	Lethbridge	WHL	62	9	32	41	113	16	3	14	17	22
1991-92	Lethbridge	WHL	65	23	62	85	155	5	1	2	3	13
	Peoria	IHL	1	0	2	2	0	5	0	1	1	0
1992-93	Peoria	IHL	72	2	28	30	67	4	1	1	2	0

HOLLIS, SCOTT

Right wing. Shoots right. 5'11", 183 lbs. Born, Kingston, Ont., September 18, 1972.
(Vancouver's 7th choice, 165th overall, in 1992 Entry Draft).

			Regular Season					Playoffs				
Season	Club	Lea	GP	G	A	TP	PIM	GP	G	A	TP	PIM
1990-91	Oshawa	OHL	66	24	33	57	91	16	5	3	8	20
1991-92a	Oshawa	OHL	66	47	54	101	183	7	7	3	10	8
1992-93	Oshawa	OHL	62	49	53	102	148	13	8	15	23	22

a OHL Second All-Star Team (1992)

HOLZINGER, BRIAN

Center. Shoots right. 5'11", 180 lbs. Born, Parma, OH, October 10, 1972.
(Buffalo's 7th choice, 124th overall, in 1991 Entry Draft).

			Regular Season					Playoffs				
Season	Club	Lea	GP	G	A	TP	PIM	GP	G	A	TP	PIM
1991-92	Bowling Green	CCHA	30	14	8	22	36	....	....	....	....	....
1992-93a	Bowling Green	CCHA	41	31	26	57	44	....	....	....	....	....

a CCHA Second All-Star Team (1993)

HOOVER, RON

Center. Shoots left. 6'1", 185 lbs. Born, Oakville, Ont., October 28, 1966.
(Hartford's 7th choice, 158th overall, in 1986 Entry Draft).

			Regular Season					Playoffs				
Season	Club	Lea	GP	G	A	TP	PIM	GP	G	A	TP	PIM
1985-86	W. Michigan	CCHA	43	10	23	33	36	....	....	....	....	....
1986-87	W. Michigan	CCHA	34	7	10	17	22	....	....	....	....	....
1987-88a	W. Michigan	CCHA	42	39	23	62	40	....	....	....	....	....
1988-89	W. Michigan	CCHA	42	32	27	59	66	....	....	....	....	....
1989-90	**Boston**	**NHL**	**2**	**0**	**0**	**0**	**0**	....	....	....	....	....
	Maine	AHL	75	28	26	54	57	....	....	....	....	....
1990-91	**Boston**	**NHL**	**15**	**4**	**0**	**4**	**31**	**8**	**0**	**0**	**0**	**18**
	Maine	AHL	62	28	16	44	40	....	....	....	....	....
1991-92	**St. Louis**	**NHL**	**1**	**0**	**0**	**0**	**0**	....	....	....	....	....
	Peoria	IHL	71	27	34	61	30	10	4	4	8	4
1992-93	Peoria	IHL	58	17	13	30	28	4	1	1	2	2
	NHL Totals		**18**	**4**	**0**	**4**	**31**	**8**	**0**	**0**	**0**	**18**

a CCHA Second All-Star Team (1988)

Signed as a free agent by **Boston**, September 1, 1989. Signed as a free agent by **St. Louis**, July 23, 1991.

HORACEK, TONY (HOHR-uh-chehk)

Left wing. Shoots left. 6'4", 210 lbs. Born, Vancouver, B.C., February 3, 1967.
(Philadelphia's 8th choice, 147th overall, in 1985 Entry Draft).

			Regular Season					Playoffs				
Season	Club	Lea	GP	G	A	TP	PIM	GP	G	A	TP	PIM
1984-85	Kelowna	WHL	67	9	18	27	114	6	0	1	1	11
1985-86	Spokane	WHL	64	19	28	47	129	9	4	5	9	29
1986-87	Spokane	WHL	64	23	37	60	177	5	1	3	4	18
	Hershey	AHL	....	....	....	....	....	1	0	0	0	0
1987-88	Hershey	AHL	1	0	0	0	0	....	....	....	....	....
	Spokane	WHL	24	17	23	40	63	....	....	....	....	....
	Kamloops	WHL	26	14	17	31	51	18	6	4	10	73
1988-89	Hershey	AHL	10	0	0	0	38	....	....	....	....	....
	Indianapolis	IHL	43	11	13	24	138	....	....	....	....	....
1989-90	**Philadelphia**	**NHL**	**48**	**5**	**5**	**10**	**117**	....	....	....	....	....
	Hershey	AHL	12	0	5	5	25	....	....	....	....	....
1990-91	**Philadelphia**	**NHL**	**34**	**3**	**6**	**9**	**49**	....	....	....	....	....
	Hershey	AHL	19	5	3	8	35	4	2	0	2	14
1991-92	**Philadelphia**	**NHL**	**34**	**1**	**3**	**4**	**51**	....	....	....	....	....
	Chicago	**NHL**	**12**	**1**	**4**	**5**	**21**	**2**	**1**	**0**	**1**	**2**
1992-93	Indianapolis	IHL	6	1	1	2	28	5	3	2	5	18
	NHL Totals		**128**	**10**	**18**	**28**	**238**	**2**	**1**	**0**	**1**	**2**

Traded to **Chicago** by **Philadelphia** for Ryan McGill, February 7, 1992.

HOSTAK, MARTIN (HOHS-tahk)

Center. Shoots left. 6'3", 198 lbs. Born, Hradec Kralove, Czech., November 11, 1967.
(Philadelphia's 3rd choice, 62nd overall, in 1987 Entry Draft).

			Regular Season					Playoffs				
Season	Club	Lea	GP	G	A	TP	PIM	GP	G	A	TP	PIM
1986-87	Sparta Praha	Czech.	40	7	2	9	2	....	....	....	....	....
1987-88	Sparta Praha	Czech.	26	8	9	17	4	....	....	....	....	....
1988-89	Sparta Praha	Czech.	35	11	15	26	10	....	....	....	....	....
1989-90	Sparta Praha	Czech.	55	30	33	63	....	....	....	....	....	....
1990-91	**Philadelphia**	**NHL**	**50**	**3**	**10**	**13**	**22**	....	....	....	....	....
	Hershey	AHL	11	6	2	8	2	3	1	0	1	0
1991-92	**Philadelphia**	**NHL**	**5**	**0**	**1**	**1**	**2**	....	....	....	....	....
	Hershey	AHL	63	27	36	63	77	6	1	2	3	2
1992-93	MoDo	Swe.	40	15	19	34	42	3	2	1	3	4
	NHL Totals		**55**	**3**	**11**	**14**	**24**	....	....	....	....	....

HOUDA, DOUG (HOO-duh)

Defense. Shoots right. 6'2", 190 lbs. Born, Blairmore, Alta., June 3, 1966.
(Detroit's 2nd choice, 28th overall, in 1984 Entry Draft).

			Regular Season					Playoffs				
Season	Club	Lea	GP	G	A	TP	PIM	GP	G	A	TP	PIM
1982-83	Calgary	WHL	71	5	23	28	99	16	1	3	4	44
1983-84	Calgary	WHL	69	6	30	36	195	4	0	0	0	7
1984-85a	Calgary	WHL	65	20	54	74	182	8	3	4	7	29
1985-86	**Detroit**	**NHL**	**6**	**0**	**0**	**0**	**4**	....	....	....	....	....
	Calgary	WHL	16	4	10	14	60	....	....	....	....	....
	Medicine Hat	WHL	35	9	23	32	80	25	4	19	23	64
1986-87	Adirondack	AHL	77	6	23	29	142	11	1	8	9	50
1987-88	**Detroit**	**NHL**	**11**	**1**	**1**	**2**	**10**	....	....	....	....	....
b	Adirondack	AHL	71	10	32	42	169	11	0	3	3	44
1988-89	**Detroit**	**NHL**	**57**	**2**	**11**	**13**	**67**	**6**	**0**	**1**	**1**	**0**
	Adirondack	AHL	7	0	3	3	8	....	....	....	....	....
1989-90	**Detroit**	**NHL**	**73**	**2**	**9**	**11**	**127**	....	....	....	....	....
1990-91	**Detroit**	**NHL**	**22**	**0**	**4**	**4**	**43**	....	....	....	....	....
	Adirondack	AHL	38	9	17	26	67	....	....	....	....	....
	Hartford	**NHL**	**19**	**1**	**2**	**3**	**41**	**6**	**0**	**0**	**0**	**8**
1991-92	**Hartford**	**NHL**	**56**	**3**	**6**	**9**	**125**	**6**	**0**	**2**	**2**	**13**
1992-93	**Hartford**	**NHL**	**60**	**2**	**6**	**8**	**167**	....	....	....	....	....
	NHL Totals		**304**	**11**	**39**	**50**	**584**	**18**	**0**	**3**	**3**	**21**

a WHL Second All-Star Team, East Division (1985)
b AHL First All-Star Team (1988)

Traded to **Hartford** by **Detroit** for Doug Crossman, February 20, 1991.

HOUGH, MIKE (HUHF)

Left wing. Shoots left. 6'1", 192 lbs. Born, Montreal, Que., February 6, 1963.
(Quebec's 7th choice, 181st overall, in 1982 Entry Draft).

			Regular Season					Playoffs				
Season	Club	Lea	GP	G	A	TP	PIM	GP	G	A	TP	PIM
1981-82	Kitchener	OHL	58	14	24	38	172	14	4	1	5	16
1982-83	Kitchener	OHL	61	17	27	44	156	12	5	4	9	30
1983-84	Fredericton	AHL	69	11	16	27	142	1	0	0	0	7
1984-85	Fredericton	AHL	76	21	27	48	49	6	1	1	2	2
1985-86	Fredericton	AHL	74	21	33	54	68	6	0	3	3	8
1986-87	**Quebec**	**NHL**	**56**	**6**	**8**	**14**	**79**	**9**	**0**	**3**	**3**	**26**
	Fredericton	AHL	10	1	3	4	20	....	....	....	....	....
1987-88	**Quebec**	**NHL**	**17**	**3**	**2**	**5**	**2**	....	....	....	....	....
	Fredericton	AHL	46	16	25	41	133	15	4	8	12	55
1988-89	**Quebec**	**NHL**	**46**	**9**	**10**	**19**	**39**	....	....	....	....	....
	Halifax	AHL	22	11	10	21	87	....	....	....	....	....
1989-90	**Quebec**	**NHL**	**43**	**13**	**13**	**26**	**84**	....	....	....	....	....
1990-91	**Quebec**	**NHL**	**63**	**13**	**20**	**33**	**111**	....	....	....	....	....
1991-92	**Quebec**	**NHL**	**61**	**16**	**22**	**38**	**77**	....	....	....	....	....
1992-93	**Quebec**	**NHL**	**77**	**8**	**22**	**30**	**69**	**6**	**0**	**1**	**1**	**2**
	NHL Totals		**363**	**68**	**97**	**165**	**461**	**15**	**0**	**4**	**4**	**28**

Traded to **Washington** by **Quebec** for Reggie Savage and Paul MacDermid, June 20, 1993. Claimed by **Florida** from **Washington** in Expansion Draft, June 24, 1993.

HOULDER, BILL

Defense. Shoots left. 6'3", 218 lbs. Born, Thunder Bay, Ont., March 11, 1967.
(Washington's 4th choice, 82nd overall, in 1985 Entry Draft).

			Regular Season					Playoffs				
Season	Club	Lea	GP	G	A	TP	PIM	GP	G	A	TP	PIM
1984-85	North Bay	OHL	66	4	20	24	37	8	0	0	0	2
1985-86	North Bay	OHL	59	5	30	35	97	10	1	6	7	12
1986-87a	North Bay	OHL	62	17	51	68	68	22	4	19	23	20
1987-88	**Washington**	**NHL**	**30**	**1**	**2**	**3**	**10**	....	....	....	....	....
	Fort Wayne	IHL	43	10	14	24	32	....	....	....	....	....
1988-89	**Washington**	**NHL**	**8**	**0**	**3**	**3**	**4**	....	....	....	....	....
	Baltimore	AHL	65	10	36	46	50	....	....	....	....	....
1989-90	**Washington**	**NHL**	**41**	**1**	**11**	**12**	**28**	....	....	....	....	....
	Baltimore	AHL	26	3	7	10	12	7	0	2	2	2
1990-91	**Buffalo**	**NHL**	**7**	**0**	**2**	**2**	**4**	....	....	....	....	....
b	Rochester	AHL	69	13	53	66	28	15	5	13	18	4
1991-92	**Buffalo**	**NHL**	**10**	**1**	**0**	**1**	**8**	....	....	....	....	....
	Rochester	AHL	42	8	26	34	16	16	5	6	11	4
1992-93	**Buffalo**	**NHL**	**15**	**3**	**5**	**8**	**6**	**8**	**0**	**2**	**2**	**4**
	San Diego	IHL	64	24	48	72	39	....	....	....	....	....
	NHL Totals		**111**	**6**	**23**	**29**	**60**	**8**	**0**	**2**	**2**	**4**

a OHL Third All-Star Team (1987)
b AHL First All-Star Team (1991)
c Won Governor's Trophy (IHL's Outstanding Defenseman) (1993)
d IHL First All-Star Team (1993)

Traded to **Buffalo** by **Washington** for Shawn Anderson, September 30, 1990. Claimed by **Anaheim** from **Buffalo** in Expansion Draft, June 24, 1993.

HOULE, JEAN-FRANCOIS

Left wing. Shoots left. 5'8", 145 lbs. Born, LaSalle, Que., January 14, 1975.
(Montreal's 5th choice, 99th overall, in 1993 Entry Draft).

			Regular Season					Playoffs				
Season	Club	Lea	GP	G	A	TP	PIM	GP	G	A	TP	PIM
1992-93	Northwood	HS	28	37	45	82	0	....	....	....	....	....

HOUSE, BOBBY

Right wing. Shoots right. 6'1", 200 lbs.   Born, Whitehorse, Yukon, January 7, 1973.
(Chicago's 4th choice, 66th overall, in 1991 Entry Draft).

			Regular Season					Playoffs				
Season	Club	Lea	GP	G	A	TP	PIM	GP	G	A	TP	PIM
1989-90	Spokane	WHL	64	18	16	34	74	5	0	0	0	6
1990-91	Spokane	WHL	38	11	19	30	63	....	....	....	....	....
	Brandon	WHL	23	18	7	25	14	....	....	....	....	....
1991-92	Brandon	WHL	71	35	42	77	133	....	....	....	....	....
1992-93a	Brandon	WHL	61	57	39	96	87	4	2	2	4	0

a WHL East Second All-Star Team (1993)

HOUSLEY, PHIL   (HOWZ-lee)

Defense. Shoots left. 5'10", 184 lbs.   Born, St. Paul, MN, March 9, 1964.
(Buffalo's 1st choice, 6th overall, in 1982 Entry Draft).

			Regular Season					Playoffs				
Season	Club	Lea	GP	G	A	TP	PIM	GP	G	A	TP	PIM
1981-82	South St. Paul	HS	22	31	34	65	18	....	....	....	....	....
1982-83a	Buffalo	NHL	77	19	47	66	39	10	3	4	7	2
1983-84	Buffalo	NHL	75	31	46	77	33	3	0	0	0	6
1984-85	Buffalo	NHL	73	16	53	69	28	5	3	2	5	2
1985-86	Buffalo	NHL	79	15	47	62	54	....	....	....	....	....
1986-87	Buffalo	NHL	78	21	46	67	57	....	....	....	....	....
1987-88	Buffalo	NHL	74	29	37	66	96	6	2	4	6	6
1988-89	Buffalo	NHL	72	26	44	70	47	5	1	3	4	2
1989-90	Buffalo	NHL	80	21	60	81	32	6	1	4	5	4
1990-91	Winnipeg	NHL	78	23	53	76	24	....	....	....	....	....
1991-92b	Winnipeg	NHL	74	23	63	86	92	7	1	4	5	0
1992-93	Winnipeg	NHL	80	18	79	97	52	6	0	7	7	2
	NHL Totals		**840**	**242**	**575**	**817**	**554**	**48**	**11**	**28**	**39**	**24**

a NHL All-Rookie Team (1983)
b NHL Second All-Star Team (1992)

Played in NHL All-Star Game (1984, 1989-93)

Traded to **Winnipeg** by **Buffalo** with Scott Arniel, Jeff Parker and Buffalo's first round choice (Keith Tkachuk) in 1990 Entry Draft for Dale Hawerchuk, Winnipeg's first round choice (Brad May) in 1990 Entry Draft and future considerations, June 16, 1990.

HOWE, MARK STEVEN

Defense. Shoots left. 5'11", 185 lbs.   Born, Detroit, MI, May 28, 1955.
(Boston's 2nd choice, 25th overall, in 1974 Amateur Draft).

			Regular Season					Playoffs				
Season	Club	Lea	GP	G	A	TP	PIM	GP	G	A	TP	PIM
1972-73	Toronto	OMJHL	60	38	66	104	27	....	....	....	....	....
1973-74ab	Houston	WHA	76	38	41	79	20	14	9	10	19	4
1974-75	Houston	WHA	74	36	40	76	30	13	*10	12	*22	0
1975-76	Houston	WHA	72	39	37	76	38	17	6	10	16	18
1976-77a	Houston	WHA	57	23	52	75	46	10	4	10	14	2
1977-78	New England	WHA	70	30	61	91	32	14	8	7	15	18
1978-79c	New England	WHA	77	42	65	107	32	6	4	2	6	6
1979-80	Hartford	NHL	74	24	56	80	20	3	1	2	3	2
1980-81	Hartford	NHL	63	19	46	65	54	....	....	....	....	....
1981-82	Hartford	NHL	76	8	45	53	18	....	....	....	....	....
1982-83d	Philadelphia	NHL	76	20	47	67	18	3	0	2	2	4
1983-84	Philadelphia	NHL	71	19	34	53	44	3	0	0	0	2
1984-85	Philadelphia	NHL	73	18	39	57	31	19	3	8	11	6
1985-86de	Philadelphia	NHL	77	24	58	82	36	5	0	4	4	0
1986-87d	Philadelphia	NHL	69	15	43	58	37	26	2	10	12	4
1987-88	Philadelphia	NHL	75	19	43	62	62	7	3	6	9	4
1988-89	Philadelphia	NHL	52	9	29	38	45	19	0	15	15	10
1989-90	Philadelphia	NHL	40	7	21	28	24	....	....	....	....	....
1990-91	Philadelphia	NHL	19	0	10	10	8	....	....	....	....	....
1991-92	Philadelphia	NHL	42	7	18	25	18	....	....	....	....	....
1992-93	Detroit	NHL	60	3	31	34	22	7	1	3	4	2
	NHL Totals		**867**	**192**	**520**	**712**	**437**	**92**	**10**	**50**	**60**	**34**

a WHA Second All-Star Team (1974, 1977)
b Named WHA's Rookie of the Year (1974)
c WHA First All-Star Team (1979)
d NHL First All-Star Team (1983, 1986, 1987)
e NHL Plus/Minus Leader (1986)

Played in NHL All-Star Game (1981, 1983, 1986, 1988)

Reclaimed by **Boston** from **Hartford** prior to Expansion Draft, June 9, 1979. Claimed as priority selection by **Hartford**, June 9, 1979. Traded to **Philadelphia** by **Hartford** with Hartford's third round choice (Derrick Smith) in 1983 Entry Draft for Ken Linseman, Greg Adams and Philadelphia's first (David Jensen) and third round choices (Leif Karlsson) in the 1983 Entry Draft, August 19, 1982. Signed as a free agent by **Detroit**, July 7, 1992.

HRBEK, PETR   (huhr-BEHK)

Right wing. Shoots right. 5'11", 180 lbs.   Born, Prague, Czechoslovakia, April 3, 1969.
(Detroit's 4th choice, 59th overall, in 1988 Entry Draft).

			Regular Season					Playoffs				
Season	Club	Lea	GP	G	A	TP	PIM	GP	G	A	TP	PIM
1985-86	Sparta-Praha	Czech.	1	0	1	1	0	....	....	....	....	....
1986-87	Sparta Praha	Czech.	11	2	0	2	0	....	....	....	....	....
1987-88	Sparta Praha	Czech.	44	14	7	21	4	....	....	....	....	....
1988-89	Sparta Praha	Czech.	41	10	13	23	4	....	....	....	....	....
1989-90	Dukla Jihlava	Czech.	32	12	7	19	....	....	....	....	....	....
1990-91	Sparta Praha	Czech.	39	20	17	37	14	....	....	....	....	....
1991-92	Sparta Praha	Czech.	46	33	20	53	35	....	....	....	....	....
1992-93	Adirondack	AHL	37	10	12	22	6	....	....	....	....	....
	Sparta Praha	Czech.	18	17	10	27	....	....	....	....	....	....

HRKAC, ANTHONY (TONY)   (HUHR-kuhz)

Center. Shoots left. 5'11", 170 lbs.   Born, Thunder Bay, Ont., July 7, 1966.
(St. Louis' 2nd choice, 32nd overall, in 1984 Entry Draft).

			Regular Season					Playoffs				
Season	Club	Lea	GP	G	A	TP	PIM	GP	G	A	TP	PIM
1984-85	North Dakota	WCHA	36	18	36	54	16	....	....	....	....	....
1985-86	Cdn. Olympic	....	62	19	30	49	36	....	....	....	....	....
1986-87abcd	North Dakota	WCHA	48	46	79	125	48	....	....	....	....	....
	St. Louis	NHL	....	....	....	....	....	3	0	0	0	0
1987-88	St. Louis	NHL	67	11	37	48	22	10	6	1	7	4
1988-89	St. Louis	NHL	70	17	28	45	8	4	1	1	2	0
1989-90	St. Louis	NHL	28	5	12	17	8	....	....	....	....	....
	Quebec	NHL	22	4	8	12	2	....	....	....	....	....
	Halifax	AHL	20	12	21	33	4	6	5	9	14	4
1990-91	Quebec	NHL	70	16	32	48	16	....	....	....	....	....
	Halifax	AHL	3	4	1	5	2	....	....	....	....	....
1991-92	San Jose	NHL	22	2	10	12	4	....	....	....	....	....
	Chicago	NHL	18	1	2	3	6	3	0	0	0	2
1992-93efg	Indianapolis	IHL	80	45	*87	*132	70	5	0	2	2	2
	NHL Totals		**297**	**56**	**129**	**185**	**66**	**20**	**7**	**2**	**9**	**6**

a WCHA First All-Star Team, Player of the Year (1987)
b NCAA West First All-American Team (1987)
c NCAA All-Tournament Team, Tournament MVP (1987)
d Winner of the 1987 Hobey Baker Memorial Trophy (Top U.S. Collegiate Player) (1987)
e Won James Gatschene Memorial Trophy (IHL MVP) (1993)
f Won Leo P. Lamoureux Trophy (IHL Leading Scorer) (1993)
g IHL First All-Star Team (1993)

Traded to **Quebec** by **St. Louis** with Greg Millen for Jeff Brown, December 13, 1989. Traded to **San Jose** by **Quebec** for Greg Paslawski, May 31, 1991. Traded to **Chicago** by **San Jose** for future considerations, February 7, 1992. Signed as a free agent by **St. Louis**, July 30, 1993.

HUARD, BILL

Left wing. Shoots left. 6'1", 200 lbs.   Born, Welland, Ont., June 24, 1967.

			Regular Season					Playoffs				
Season	Club	Lea	GP	G	A	TP	PIM	GP	G	A	TP	PIM
1986-87	Peterborough	OHL	61	14	11	25	61	12	5	2	7	19
1987-88	Peterborough	OHL	66	28	33	61	132	12	7	8	15	33
1988-89	Carolina	ECHL	40	27	21	48	177	10	7	2	9	70
1989-90	Utica	AHL	27	1	7	8	67	5	0	1	1	33
	Nashville	ECHL	34	24	27	51	212	....	....	....	....	....
1990-91	Utica	AHL	72	11	16	27	359	....	....	....	....	....
1991-92	Utica	AHL	62	9	11	20	233	4	1	1	2	4
1992-93	Boston	NHL	2	0	0	0	0	....	....	....	....	....
	Providence	AHL	72	18	19	37	302	6	3	0	3	9
	NHL Totals		**2**	**0**	**0**	**0**	**0**	....	....	....	....	....

Signed as a free agent by **New Jersey**, October 1, 1989. Signed as a free agent by **Boston**, December 4, 1992. Signed as a free agent by **Ottawa**, June 30, 1993.

HUDDY, CHARLES WILLIAM (CHARLIE)

Defense. Shoots left. 6', 210 lbs.   Born, Oshawa, Ont., June 2, 1959.

			Regular Season					Playoffs				
Season	Club	Lea	GP	G	A	TP	PIM	GP	G	A	TP	PIM
1977-78	Oshawa	OHA	59	17	18	35	81	6	2	1	3	10
1978-79	Oshawa	OHA	64	20	38	58	108	5	3	4	7	12
1979-80	Houston	CHL	79	14	34	48	46	6	1	0	1	2
1980-81	Edmonton	NHL	12	2	5	7	6	....	....	....	....	....
	Wichita	CHL	47	8	36	44	71	17	3	11	14	10
1981-82	Edmonton	NHL	41	4	11	15	46	5	1	2	3	14
	Wichita	CHL	32	7	19	26	51	....	....	....	....	....
1982-83a	Edmonton	NHL	76	20	37	57	58	15	1	6	7	10
1983-84	Edmonton	NHL	75	8	34	42	43	12	1	9	10	8
1984-85	Edmonton	NHL	80	7	44	51	46	18	3	17	20	17
1985-86	Edmonton	NHL	76	6	35	41	55	7	0	2	2	0
1986-87	Edmonton	NHL	58	4	15	19	35	21	1	7	8	21
1987-88	Edmonton	NHL	77	13	28	41	71	13	4	5	9	10
1988-89	Edmonton	NHL	76	11	33	44	52	7	2	0	2	4
1989-90	Edmonton	NHL	70	1	23	24	56	22	0	6	6	11
1990-91	Edmonton	NHL	53	5	22	27	32	18	3	7	10	10
1991-92	Los Angeles	NHL	56	4	19	23	43	6	1	1	2	10
1992-93	Los Angeles	NHL	82	2	25	27	64	23	1	4	5	12
	NHL Totals		**832**	**87**	**331**	**418**	**607**	**167**	**18**	**66**	**84**	**127**

a NHL Plus/Minus Leader (1983)

Signed as a free agent by **Edmonton**, September 14, 1979. Claimed by **Minnesota** from **Edmonton** in Expansion Draft, May 30, 1991. Traded to **Los Angeles** by **Minnesota** with Randy Gilhen, Jim Thomson and NY Rangers' fourth round choice (previously acquired by Minnesota — Los Angeles selected Alexei Zhitnik) in 1991 Entry Draft for Todd Elik, June 22, 1991.

HUDSON, MIKE

Center/Left wing. Shoots left. 6'1", 205 lbs.   Born, Guelph, Ont., February 6, 1967.
(Chicago's 6th choice, 140th overall, in 1986 Entry Draft).

			Regular Season					Playoffs				
Season	Club	Lea	GP	G	A	TP	PIM	GP	G	A	TP	PIM
1984-85	Hamilton	OHL	50	10	12	22	13	....	....	....	....	....
1985-86	Hamilton	OHL	7	3	2	5	4	....	....	....	....	....
	Sudbury	OHL	59	35	42	77	20	4	2	5	7	7
1986-87	Sudbury	OHL	63	40	57	97	18	....	....	....	....	....
1987-88	Saginaw	IHL	75	18	30	48	44	10	2	3	5	20
1988-89	Chicago	NHL	41	7	16	23	20	10	1	2	3	18
	Saginaw	IHL	30	15	17	32	10	....	....	....	....	....
1989-90	Chicago	NHL	49	9	12	21	56	4	0	0	0	2
1990-91	Chicago	NHL	55	7	9	16	62	6	0	2	2	8
	Indianapolis	IHL	3	1	2	3	0	....	....	....	....	....
1991-92	Chicago	NHL	76	14	15	29	92	16	3	5	8	26
1992-93	Chicago	NHL	36	1	6	7	44	....	....	....	....	....
	Edmonton	NHL	5	0	1	1	2	....	....	....	....	....
	NHL Totals		**262**	**38**	**59**	**97**	**276**	**36**	**4**	**9**	**13**	**54**

Traded to **Edmonton** by **Chicago** for Craig Muni, March 22, 1993.

HUFFMAN, KERRY

Defense. Shoots left. 6'2", 200 lbs.   Born, Peterborough, Ont., January 3, 1968.
(Philadelphia's 1st choice, 20th overall, in 1986 Entry Draft).

			Regular Season					Playoffs				
Season	Club	Lea	GP	G	A	TP	PIM	GP	G	A	TP	PIM
1985-86	Guelph	OHL	56	3	24	27	35	20	1	10	11	10
1986-87	**Philadelphia**	**NHL**	9	0	0	0	2	....	....	....	....	....
	Hershey	AHL	3	0	1	1	0	4	0	0	0	0
a	Guelph	OHL	44	4	31	35	20	5	0	2	2	8
1987-88	**Philadelphia**	**NHL**	52	6	17	23	34	2	0	0	0	0
1988-89	**Philadelphia**	**NHL**	29	0	11	11	31	....	....	....	....	....
	Hershey	AHL	29	2	13	15	16	....	....	....	....	....
1989-90	**Philadelphia**	**NHL**	43	1	12	13	34	....	....	....	....	....
1990-91	**Philadelphia**	**NHL**	10	1	2	3	10	....	....	....	....	....
	Hershey	AHL	45	5	29	34	20	7	1	2	3	0
1991-92	**Philadelphia**	**NHL**	60	14	18	32	41	....	....	....	....	....
1992-93	**Quebec**	**NHL**	52	4	18	22	54	3	0	0	0	0
	NHL Totals		**255**	**26**	**78**	**104**	**206**	**5**	**0**	**0**	**0**	**0**

a OHL First All-Star Team (1987)

Traded to **Quebec** by **Philadelphia** with Peter Forsberg, Steve Duchesne, Mike Ricci, Ron Hextall, Chris Simon, Philadelphia's first choice in the 1993 (Jocelyn Thibault) and 1994 Entry Drafts and cash for Eric Lindros, June 30, 1992.

HUGHES, BRENT ALLEN

Left wing. Shoots left. 5'11", 194 lbs.   Born, New Westminster, B.C., April 5, 1966.

			Regular Season					Playoffs				
Season	Club	Lea	GP	G	A	TP	PIM	GP	G	A	TP	PIM
1983-84	N. Westminster	WHL	67	21	18	39	133	9	2	2	4	27
1984-85	N. Westminster	WHL	64	25	32	57	135	11	2	1	3	37
1985-86	N. Westminster	WHL	71	28	52	80	180	....	....	....	....	....
1986-87	N. Westminster	WHL	8	5	4	9	22	....	....	....	....	....
	Victoria	WHL	61	38	61	99	146	5	4	1	5	8
1987-88	Moncton	AHL	73	13	19	32	206	....	....	....	....	....
1988-89	**Winnipeg**	**NHL**	28	3	2	5	82	....	....	....	....	....
	Moncton	AHL	54	34	34	68	286	10	9	4	13	40
1989-90	**Winnipeg**	**NHL**	11	1	2	3	33	....	....	....	....	....
	Moncton	AHL	65	31	29	60	277	....	....	....	....	....
1990-91	Moncton	AHL	63	21	22	43	144	3	0	0	0	7
1991-92	Baltimore	AHL	55	25	29	54	190	....	....	....	....	....
	Boston	**NHL**	8	1	1	2	38	10	2	0	2	20
	Maine	AHL	12	6	4	10	34	....	....	....	....	....
1992-93	**Boston**	**NHL**	62	5	4	9	191	1	0	0	0	2
	NHL Totals		**109**	**10**	**9**	**19**	**344**	**11**	**2**	**0**	**2**	**22**

Signed as a free agent by **Winnipeg**, June 13, 1988. Traded to **Washington** by **Winnipeg** with Craig Duncanson and Simon Wheeldon for Bob Joyce, Tyler Larter and Kent Paynter, May 21, 1991. Traded to **Boston** by **Washington** with future considerations for John Byce and Dennis Smith, February 24, 1992.

HUGHES, RYAN

Center. Shoots left. 6'1", 180 lbs.   Born, Montreal, Que., January 17, 1972.
(Quebec's 2nd choice, 22nd overall, in 1990 Entry Draft).

			Regular Season					Playoffs				
Season	Club	Lea	GP	G	A	TP	PIM	GP	G	A	TP	PIM
1989-90	Cornell	ECAC	27	7	16	23	35	....	....	....	....	....
1990-91	Cornell	ECAC	32	18	34	52	28	....	....	....	....	....
1991-92	Cornell	ECAC	27	8	13	21	36	....	....	....	....	....
1992-93	Cornell	ECAC	26	8	14	22	30	....	....	....	....	....

HULBIG, JOE

Left wing. Shoots left. 6'3", 212 lbs.   Born, Norwood, MA, September 29, 1973.
(Edmonton's 1st choice, 13th overall, in 1992 Entry Draft).

			Regular Season					Playoffs				
Season	Club	Lea	GP	G	A	TP	PIM	GP	G	A	TP	PIM
1991-92	St. Sebastian's	HS	17	19	24	43	30	....	....	....	....	....
1992-93	Providence	H.E.	26	3	13	16	22	....	....	....	....	....

HULETT, DEAN

Right wing. Shoots right. 6'6", 210 lbs.   Born, San Juan, Puerto Rico, July 25, 1971.
(Los Angeles' 7th choice, 154th overall, in 1990 Entry Draft).

			Regular Season					Playoffs				
Season	Club	Lea	GP	G	A	TP	PIM	GP	G	A	TP	PIM
1989-90	Lake Superior	CCHA	13	1	4	5	18	....	....	....	....	....
1990-91	Lake Superior	CCHA	36	5	8	13	52	....	....	....	....	....
1991-92	Lake Superior	CCHA	33	10	12	22	56	....	....	....	....	....
1992-93	Lake Superior	CCHA	42	12	27	39	71	....	....	....	....	....

HULL, BRETT

Right wing. Shoots right. 5'10", 201 lbs.   Born, Belleville, Ont., August 9, 1964.
(Calgary's 6th choice, 117th overall, in 1984 Entry Draft).

			Regular Season					Playoffs				
Season	Club	Lea	GP	G	A	TP	PIM	GP	G	A	TP	PIM
1984-85	Minn.-Duluth	WCHA	48	32	28	60	24	....	....	....	....	....
1985-86a	Minn.-Duluth	WCHA	42	52	32	84	46	....	....	....	....	....
	Calgary	**NHL**	....	....	....	....	....	2	0	0	0	0
1986-87	**Calgary**	**NHL**	5	1	0	1	0	4	2	1	3	0
bc	Moncton	AHL	67	50	42	92	16	3	2	2	4	2
1987-88	**Calgary**	**NHL**	52	26	24	50	12	....	....	....	....	....
	St. Louis	**NHL**	13	6	8	14	4	10	7	2	9	4
1988-89	**St. Louis**	**NHL**	78	41	43	84	33	10	5	5	10	6
1989-90def	**St. Louis**	**NHL**	80	*72	41	113	24	12	13	8	21	17
1990-91 dfghi	**St. Louis**	**NHL**	78	*86	45	131	22	13	11	8	19	4
1991-92d	**St. Louis**	**NHL**	73	*70	39	109	48	6	4	4	8	4
1992-93	**St. Louis**	**NHL**	80	54	47	101	41	11	8	5	13	2
	NHL Totals		**459**	**356**	**247**	**603**	**184**	**68**	**50**	**33**	**83**	**37**

a WCHA First All-Star Team (1986)
b AHL First All-Star Team (1987)
c Won Dudley "Red" Garrett Memorial Trophy (AHL's Top Rookie) (1987)
d NHL First All-Star Team (1990, 1991, 1992)
e Won Lady Byng Trophy (1990)
f Won Dodge Ram Tough Award (1990, 1991)
g Won Hart Memorial Trophy (1991)
h Won Lester B. Pearson Award (1991)
i Won ProSet/NHL Player of the Year Award (1991)
Played in NHL All-Star Game (1989, 1990, 1992, 1993)

Traded to **St. Louis** by **Calgary** with Steve Bozek for Rob Ramage and Rick Wamsley, March 7, 1988.

HULL, JODY

Right wing. Shoots right. 6'2", 200 lbs.   Born, Cambridge, Ont., February 2, 1969.
(Hartford's 1st choice, 18th overall, in 1987 Entry Draft).

			Regular Season					Playoffs				
Season	Club	Lea	GP	G	A	TP	PIM	GP	G	A	TP	PIM
1985-86	Peterborough	OHL	61	20	22	42	29	16	1	5	6	4
1986-87	Peterborough	OHL	49	18	34	52	22	12	4	9	13	14
1987-88a	Peterborough	OHL	60	50	44	94	33	12	10	8	18	8
1988-89	**Hartford**	**NHL**	60	16	18	34	10	1	0	0	0	2
1989-90	**Hartford**	**NHL**	38	7	10	17	21	5	0	1	1	2
	Binghamton	AHL	21	7	10	17	6	....	....	....	....	....
1990-91	**NY Rangers**	**NHL**	47	5	8	13	10	....	....	....	....	....
1991-92	**NY Rangers**	**NHL**	3	0	0	0	2	....	....	....	....	....
	Binghamton	AHL	69	34	31	65	28	11	5	2	7	4
1992-93	**Ottawa**	**NHL**	69	13	21	34	14	....	....	....	....	....
	NHL Totals		**217**	**41**	**57**	**98**	**57**	**6**	**0**	**1**	**1**	**4**

a OHL Second All-Star Team (1988)

Traded to **NY Rangers** by **Hartford** for Carey Wilson and NY Rangers' third round choice (Mikael Nylander) in the 1991 Entry Draft, July 9, 1990. Traded to **Ottawa** by **NY Rangers** for future considerations, July 28, 1992.

HULSE, CALE

Defense. Shoots right. 6'3", 205 lbs.   Born, Edmonton, Alta., November 10, 1973.
(New Jersey's 3rd choice, 66th overall, in 1992 Entry Draft).

			Regular Season					Playoffs				
Season	Club	Lea	GP	G	A	TP	PIM	GP	G	A	TP	PIM
1991-92	Portland	WHL	70	4	18	22	250	6	0	2	2	27
1992-93	Portland	WHL	72	10	26	36	284	16	4	4	8	65

HUMENIUK, SCOTT

Defense. Shoots right. 6', 190 lbs.   Born, Saskatoon, Sask., September 10, 1969.

			Regular Season					Playoffs				
Season	Club	Lea	GP	G	A	TP	PIM	GP	G	A	TP	PIM
1986-87	Spokane	WHL	10	0	2	2	2	1	0	0	0	0
1987-88	Spokane	WHL	58	6	20	26	154	8	1	0	1	19
1988-89	Moose Jaw	WHL	56	18	39	57	159	7	5	0	5	32
1989-90a	Moose Jaw	WHL	71	23	47	70	141	....	....	....	....	....
	Binghamton	AHL	4	0	1	1	11	....	....	....	....	....
1990-91	Springfield	AHL	57	6	17	23	69	14	2	2	4	18
1991-92	Springfield	AHL	28	2	3	5	27	....	....	....	....	....
	Louisville	ECHL	26	7	21	28	93	13	1	11	12	33
1992-93	Springfield	AHL	16	0	3	3	28	14	1	3	4	8
	Louisville	ECHL	36	14	31	45	117	....	....	....	....	....

a WHL East Second All-Star Team (1990)

Signed as a free agent by **Hartford**, March 23, 1990.

HUNT, CURTIS

Defense. Shoots left. 6', 195 lbs.   Born, North Battleford, Sask., January 28, 1967.
(Vancouver's 9th choice, 172nd overall, in 1985 Entry Draft).

			Regular Season					Playoffs				
Season	Club	Lea	GP	G	A	TP	PIM	GP	G	A	TP	PIM
1984-85	Prince Albert	WHL	64	2	13	15	61	13	0	3	3	24
1985-86	Prince Albert	WHL	72	5	29	34	108	18	2	8	10	28
1986-87	Prince Albert	WHL	47	6	31	37	101	8	1	3	4	4
1987-88	Flint	IHL	76	4	17	21	181	2	0	0	0	16
	Fredericton	AHL	1	0	0	0	2	....	....	....	....	....
1988-89	Milwaukee	IHL	65	3	17	20	226	11	1	2	3	43
1989-90	Milwaukee	IHL	69	8	25	33	237	3	0	1	1	4
1990-91	Albany	IHL	45	2	12	14	122	....	....	....	....	....
	Milwaukee	IHL	27	1	5	6	85	6	0	1	1	10
1991-92	St. John's	AHL	52	5	18	23	106	12	1	5	6	36
1992-93	St. John's	AHL	48	4	19	23	148	7	0	3	3	6

Signed as a free agent by **Toronto**, July 19, 1991.

HUNTER, DALE ROBERT

Center. Shoots left. 5'10", 198 lbs. Born, Petrolia, Ont., July 31, 1960.
(Quebec's 2nd choice, 41st overall, in 1979 Entry Draft).

			Regular Season					Playoffs				
Season	Club	Lea	GP	G	A	TP	PIM	GP	G	A	TP	PIM
1977-78	Kitchener	OHA	68	22	42	64	115	....	....	....	....	....
1978-79	Sudbury	OHA	59	42	68	110	188	10	4	12	16	47
1979-80	Sudbury	OHA	61	34	51	85	189	9	6	9	15	45
1980-81	**Quebec**	**NHL**	**80**	**19**	**44**	**63**	**226**	**5**	**4**	**2**	**6**	**34**
1981-82	**Quebec**	**NHL**	**80**	**22**	**50**	**72**	**272**	**16**	**3**	**7**	**10**	**52**
1982-83	**Quebec**	**NHL**	**80**	**17**	**46**	**63**	**206**	**4**	**2**	**1**	**3**	**24**
1983-84	**Quebec**	**NHL**	**77**	**24**	**55**	**79**	**232**	**9**	**2**	**3**	**5**	**41**
1984-85	**Quebec**	**NHL**	**80**	**20**	**52**	**72**	**209**	**17**	**4**	**6**	**10**	***97**
1985-86	**Quebec**	**NHL**	**80**	**28**	**42**	**70**	**265**	**3**	**0**	**0**	**0**	**15**
1986-87	**Quebec**	**NHL**	**46**	**10**	**29**	**39**	**135**	**13**	**1**	**7**	**8**	**56**
1987-88	**Washington**	**NHL**	**79**	**22**	**37**	**59**	**240**	**14**	**7**	**5**	**12**	**98**
1988-89	**Washington**	**NHL**	**80**	**20**	**37**	**57**	**219**	**6**	**0**	**4**	**4**	**29**
1989-90	**Washington**	**NHL**	**80**	**23**	**39**	**62**	**233**	**15**	**4**	**8**	**12**	**61**
1990-91	**Washington**	**NHL**	**76**	**16**	**30**	**46**	**234**	**11**	**1**	**9**	**10**	**41**
1991-92	**Washington**	**NHL**	**80**	**28**	**50**	**78**	**205**	**7**	**1**	**4**	**5**	**16**
1992-93	**Washington**	**NHL**	**84**	**20**	**59**	**79**	**198**	**6**	**7**	**1**	**8**	**35**
	NHL Totals		**1002**	**269**	**570**	**839**	**2874**	**126**	**36**	**57**	**93**	**599**

Traded to **Washington** by **Quebec** with Clint Malarchuk for Gaetan Duchesne, Alan Haworth, and Washington's first round choice (Joe Sakic) in 1987 Entry Draft, June 13, 1987.

HUNTER, MARK

Right wing. Shoots right. 6', 200 lbs. Born, Petrolia, Ont., November 12, 1962.
(Montreal's 1st choice, 7th overall, in 1981 Entry Draft).

			Regular Season					Playoffs				
Season	Club	Lea	GP	G	A	TP	PIM	GP	G	A	TP	PIM
1979-80	Brantford	OHA	66	34	56	90	171	11	2	8	10	27
1980-81	Brantford	OHA	53	39	40	79	157	6	3	3	6	27
1981-82	**Montreal**	**NHL**	**71**	**18**	**11**	**29**	**143**	**5**	**0**	**0**	**0**	**20**
1982-83	**Montreal**	**NHL**	**31**	**8**	**8**	**16**	**73**	....	....	....	....	....
1983-84	**Montreal**	**NHL**	**22**	**6**	**4**	**10**	**42**	**14**	**2**	**1**	**3**	**69**
1984-85	**Montreal**	**NHL**	**72**	**21**	**12**	**33**	**123**	**11**	**0**	**3**	**3**	**13**
1985-86	**St. Louis**	**NHL**	**78**	**44**	**30**	**74**	**171**	**19**	**7**	**7**	**14**	**48**
1986-87	**St. Louis**	**NHL**	**74**	**36**	**33**	**69**	**167**	**5**	**0**	**3**	**3**	**10**
1987-88	**St. Louis**	**NHL**	**66**	**32**	**31**	**63**	**136**	**5**	**2**	**3**	**5**	**24**
1988-89	**Calgary**	**NHL**	**66**	**22**	**8**	**30**	**194**	**10**	**2**	**2**	**4**	**23**
1989-90	**Calgary**	**NHL**	**10**	**2**	**3**	**5**	**39**	....	....	....	....	....
1990-91	**Calgary**	**NHL**	**57**	**10**	**15**	**25**	**125**	....	....	....	....	....
	Hartford	**NHL**	**11**	**4**	**3**	**7**	**40**	**6**	**5**	**1**	**6**	**17**
1991-92	**Hartford**	**NHL**	**63**	**10**	**13**	**23**	**159**	**4**	**0**	**0**	**0**	**6**
1992-93	**Washington**	**NHL**	**7**	**0**	**0**	**0**	**14**	....	....	....	....	....
	Baltimore	AHL	28	13	18	31	66	7	3	1	4	12
	NHL Totals		**628**	**213**	**171**	**384**	**1426**	**79**	**18**	**20**	**38**	**230**

Played in NHL All-Star Game (1986)

Traded to **St. Louis** by **Montreal** with Michael Dark and Montreal's second (Herb Raglan), third (Nelson Emerson), fifth (Dan Brooks), and sixth (Rick Burchill) round choices in 1985 Entry Draft for St. Louis' first (Jose Charbonneau), second (Todd Richard), fourth (Martin Desjardins), fifth (Tom Sagissor), and sixth (Don Dufresne) round choices in 1985 Entry Draft, June 15, 1985. Traded to **Calgary** by **St. Louis** with Doug Gilmour, Steve Bozek and Michael Dark for Mike Bullard, Craig Coxe and Tim Corkery, September 6, 1988. Traded to **Hartford** by **Calgary** for Carey Wilson, March 5, 1991. Traded to **Washington** by **Hartford** with future considerations (Yvon Corriveau, August 20, 1992) for Nick Kypreos, June 15, 1992.

HUNTER, TIMOTHY ROBERT (TIM)

Right wing. Shoots right. 6'2", 202 lbs. Born, Calgary, Alta., September 10, 1960.
(Atlanta's 4th choice, 54th overall, in 1979 Entry Draft).

			Regular Season					Playoffs				
Season	Club	Lea	GP	G	A	TP	PIM	GP	G	A	TP	PIM
1979-80	Seattle	WHL	72	14	53	67	311	12	1	2	3	41
1980-81	Birmingham	CHL	58	3	5	8	*236	....	....	....	....	....
	Nova Scotia	AHL	17	0	0	0	62	6	0	1	1	45
1981-82	**Calgary**	**NHL**	**2**	**0**	**0**	**0**	**9**	....	....	....	....	....
	Oklahoma City	CHL	55	4	12	16	222	....	....	....	....	....
1982-83	**Calgary**	**NHL**	**16**	**1**	**0**	**1**	**54**	**9**	**1**	**0**	**1**	***70**
	Colorado	CHL	46	5	12	17	225	....	....	....	....	....
1983-84	**Calgary**	**NHL**	**43**	**4**	**4**	**8**	**130**	**7**	**0**	**0**	**0**	**21**
1984-85	**Calgary**	**NHL**	**71**	**11**	**11**	**22**	**259**	**4**	**0**	**0**	**0**	**24**
1985-86	**Calgary**	**NHL**	**66**	**8**	**7**	**15**	**291**	**19**	**0**	**3**	**3**	**108**
1986-87	**Calgary**	**NHL**	**73**	**6**	**15**	**21**	***361**	**6**	**0**	**0**	**0**	**51**
1987-88	**Calgary**	**NHL**	**68**	**8**	**5**	**13**	**337**	**9**	**4**	**0**	**4**	**32**
1988-89	**Calgary**	**NHL**	**75**	**3**	**9**	**12**	***375**	**19**	**0**	**4**	**4**	**32**
1989-90	**Calgary**	**NHL**	**67**	**2**	**3**	**5**	**279**	**6**	**0**	**0**	**0**	**4**
1990-91	**Calgary**	**NHL**	**34**	**5**	**2**	**7**	**143**	**7**	**0**	**0**	**0**	**10**
1991-92	**Calgary**	**NHL**	**30**	**1**	**3**	**4**	**167**	....	....	....	....	....
1992-93	**Quebec**	**NHL**	**48**	**5**	**3**	**8**	**94**	....	....	....	....	....
	Vancouver	**NHL**	**26**	**0**	**4**	**4**	**99**	**11**	**0**	**0**	**0**	**26**
	NHL Totals		**619**	**54**	**66**	**120**	**2598**	**97**	**5**	**7**	**12**	**378**

Claimed by **Tampa Bay** from **Calgary** in Expansion Draft, June 18, 1992. Traded to **Quebec** by **Tampa Bay** for future considerations (Martin Simard, September 14, 1992), June 19, 1992. Claimed on waivers by **Vancouver** from **Quebec**, February 12, 1993.

HURD, KELLY

Right wing. Shoots right. 5'11", 170 lbs. Born, Castlegar, B.C., May 13, 1968.
(Detroit's 6th choice, 143rd overall, in 1988 Entry Draft).

			Regular Season					Playoffs				
Season	Club	Lea	GP	G	A	TP	PIM	GP	G	A	TP	PIM
1987-88	Michigan Tech	WCHA	41	18	22	40	34	....	....	....	....	....
1988-89	Michigan Tech	WCHA	42	18	14	32	36	....	....	....	....	....
1989-90	Michigan Tech	WCHA	37	12	13	25	50	....	....	....	....	....
1990-91a	Michigan Tech	WCHA	35	29	22	51	44	....	....	....	....	....
1991-92	Adirondack	AHL	36	9	7	16	16	8	1	4	5	2
	Fort Wayne	IHL	30	13	9	22	12	....	....	....	....	....
1992-93	Fort Wayne	IHL	71	23	31	54	81	10	4	5	9	12

a WCHA Second All-Star Team (1991)

HURLBUT, MICHAEL (MIKE)

Defense. Shoots left. 6'2", 195 lbs. Born, Massena, NY, October 7, 1966.
(NY Rangers' 1st choice, 5th overall, in 1988 Supplemental Draft).

			Regular Season					Playoffs				
Season	Club	Lea	GP	G	A	TP	PIM	GP	G	A	TP	PIM
1985-86	St. Lawrence	ECAC	25	2	10	12	40	....	....	....	....	....
1986-87	St. Lawrence	ECAC	35	8	15	23	44	....	....	....	....	....
1987-88	St. Lawrence	ECAC	38	6	12	18	18	....	....	....	....	....
1988-89a	St. Lawrence	ECAC	36	8	25	33	30	....	....	....	....	....
	Denver	IHL	8	0	2	2	13	4	1	2	3	2
1989-90	Flint	IHL	74	3	34	37	38	3	0	1	1	2
1990-91	San Diego	IHL	2	1	0	1	0	....	....	....	....	....
	Binghamton	AHL	33	2	11	13	27	3	0	1	1	0
1991-92	Binghamton	AHL	79	16	39	55	64	11	2	7	9	8
1992-93	**NY Rangers**	**NHL**	**23**	**1**	**8**	**9**	**16**	....	....	....	....	....
	Binghamton	AHL	45	11	25	36	46	14	2	5	7	12
	NHL Totals		**23**	**1**	**8**	**9**	**16**	....	....	....	....	....

a ECAC First All-Star Team (1989)

HUSCROFT, JAMIE

Defense. Shoots right. 6'2", 200 lbs. Born, Creston, B.C., January 9, 1967.
(New Jersey's 9th choice, 171st overall, in 1985 Entry Draft).

			Regular Season					Playoffs				
Season	Club	Lea	GP	G	A	TP	PIM	GP	G	A	TP	PIM
1983-84	Seattle	WHL	63	0	12	12	77	5	0	0	0	15
1984-85	Seattle	WHL	69	3	13	16	273	....	....	....	....	....
1985-86	Seattle	WHL	66	6	20	26	394	5	0	1	1	18
1986-87	Seattle	WHL	21	1	18	19	99	....	....	....	....	....
	Medicine Hat	WHL	35	4	21	25	170	20	0	3	3	*125
1987-88	Utica	AHL	71	5	7	12	316	....	....	....	....	....
	Flint	IHL	3	1	0	1	2	16	0	1	1	110
1988-89	**New Jersey**	**NHL**	**15**	**0**	**2**	**2**	**51**	....	....	....	....	....
	Utica	AHL	41	2	10	12	215	5	0	0	0	40
1989-90	**New Jersey**	**NHL**	**42**	**2**	**3**	**5**	**149**	**5**	**0**	**0**	**0**	**16**
	Utica	AHL	22	3	6	9	122	....	....	....	....	....
1990-91	**New Jersey**	**NHL**	**8**	**0**	**1**	**1**	**27**	**3**	**0**	**0**	**0**	**6**
	Utica	AHL	59	3	15	18	339	....	....	....	....	....
1991-92	Utica	AHL	50	4	7	11	224	....	....	....	....	....
1992-93	Providence	AHL	69	2	15	17	257	2	0	1	1	6
	NHL Totals		**65**	**2**	**6**	**8**	**227**	**8**	**0**	**0**	**0**	**22**

Signed as a free agent by **Boston**, July 23, 1992.

HUSKA, RYAN

Left wing. Shoots left. 6'2", 194 lbs. Born, Cranbrook, B.C., July 2, 1975.
(Chicago's 4th choice, 76th overall, in 1993 Entry Draft).

			Regular Season					Playoffs				
Season	Club	Lea	GP	G	A	TP	PIM	GP	G	A	TP	PIM
1991-92	Kamloops	WHL	44	4	5	9	23	6	0	1	1	0
1992-93	Kamloops	WHL	68	17	15	32	50	13	2	6	8	4

HUSS, ANDERS (HUHS)

Center. Shoots right. 5'10", 183 lbs. Born, Solleftea, Sweden, April 6, 1964.
(Washington's 8th choice, 225th overall, in 1983 Entry Draft).

			Regular Season					Playoffs				
Season	Club	Lea	GP	G	A	TP	PIM	GP	G	A	TP	PIM
1983-84	Brynas	Swe.	35	13	6	19	18	....	....	....	....	....
1984-85	Brynas	Swe.	35	11	8	19	22	....	....	....	....	....
1985-86	Brynas	Swe.	36	20	7	27	36	3	0	0	0	0
1986-87	Brynas	Swe.	33	12	13	25	40	....	....	....	....	....
1987-88	Brynas	Swe.	40	14	12	26	28	....	....	....	....	....
1988-89	Brynas	Swe.	40	22	17	39	26	....	....	....	....	....
1989-90	Brynas	Swe.	36	19	18	37	32	5	3	1	4	0
1990-91	Brynas	Swe.	35	9	5	14	30	2	0	1	1	2
1991-92	Brynas	Swe.	39	14	29	43	26	5	1	1	2	0
1992-93	Brynas	Swe.	39	8	16	24	38	10	2	5	7	2

HUSSEY, MARC

Defense. Shoots right. 6'4", 182 lbs. Born, Chatam, N.B., January 22, 1974.
(Pittsburgh's 2nd choice, 43rd overall, in 1992 Entry Draft).

			Regular Season					Playoffs				
Season	Club	Lea	GP	G	A	TP	PIM	GP	G	A	TP	PIM
1990-91	Moose Jaw	WHL	68	5	8	13	67	8	2	2	4	7
1991-92	Moose Jaw	WHL	72	7	27	34	203	4	1	1	2	0
1992-93	Moose Jaw	WHL	68	12	28	40	121	....	....	....	....	....

HUURA, PASI (HOO-rah)

Defense. Shoots left. 6'4", 220 lbs. Born, Tampere, Finland, March 23, 1966.
(Pittsburgh's 12th choice, 258th overall, in 1991 Entry Draft).

			Regular Season					Playoffs				
Season	Club	Lea	GP	G	A	TP	PIM	GP	G	A	TP	PIM
1987-88	Ilves	Fin.	8	1	0	1	2	....	....	....	....	....
1988-89	Ilves	Fin.	35	3	5	8	22	....	....	....	....	....
1989-90	Ilves	Fin.	41	1	4	5	48	9	1	0	1	17
1990-91	Ilves	Fin.	39	2	6	8	50	....	....	....	....	....
1991-92	Lukko	Fin.	44	1	5	6	40	2	0	0	0	2
1992-93	Lukko	Fin.	48	6	6	12	38	3	0	0	0	4

HYMOVITZ, DAVID

Left wing. Shoots left. 5'11", 170 lbs. Born, Boston, MA, May 30, 1974.
(Chicago's 9th choice, 209th overall, in 1992 Entry Draft).

			Regular Season					Playoffs				
Season	Club	Lea	GP	G	A	TP	PIM	GP	G	A	TP	PIM
1991-92	Thayer	HS	26	28	21	49	22	....	....	....	....	....
1992-93	Boston College	H.E.	37	7	6	13	6	....	....	....	....	....

HYNES, GORD

Defense. Shoots left. 6'1", 170 lbs. Born, Montreal, Que., July 22, 1966.
(Boston's 5th choice, 115th overall, in 1985 Entry Draft).

			Regular Season					Playoffs				
Season	Club	Lea	GP	G	A	TP	PIM	GP	G	A	TP	PIM
1983-84	Medicine Hat	WHL	72	5	14	19	39	14	0	0	0	0
1984-85	Medicine Hat	WHL	70	18	45	63	61	10	6	9	15	17
1985-86	Medicine Hat	WHL	58	22	39	61	45	25	8	15	23	32
1986-87	Moncton	AHL	69	2	19	21	21	4	0	0	0	2
1987-88	Maine	AHL	69	5	30	35	65	7	1	3	4	4
1988-89	Cdn. National	....	61	8	38	46	44	....	....	....	....	....
1989-90	Cdn. National	....	12	3	1	4	4	....	....	....	....	....
	Varese	Italy	29	13	36	49	16	3	3	3	6	0
1990-91	Cdn. National	....	57	12	30	42	62	....	....	....	....	....
1991-92	Cdn. National	....	48	12	22	34	50	....	....	....	....	....
	Cdn. Olympic	....	8	3	3	6	6	....	....	....	....	....
	Boston	NHL	15	0	5	5	6	12	1	2	3	6
1992-93	Philadelphia	NHL	37	3	4	7	16	....	....	....	....	....
	Hershey	AHL	9	1	3	4	4	....	....	....	....	....
	NHL Totals		52	3	9	12	22	12	1	2	3	6

Signed as a free agent by **Philadelphia**, August 25, 1992. Claimed by **Florida** from **Philadelphia** in Expansion Draft, June 24, 1993.

HYNNES, CHRIS

Defense. Shoots left. 6', 185 lbs. Born, Thunder Bay, Ont., December 8, 1970.
(Quebec's 2nd choice, 8th overall, in 1991 Supplemental Draft).

			Regular Season					Playoffs				
Season	Club	Lea	GP	G	A	TP	PIM	GP	G	A	TP	PIM
1989-90	Colorado	WCHA	17	0	3	3	10	....	....	....	....	....
1990-91	Colorado	WCHA	40	8	18	26	64	....	....	....	....	....
1991-92ab	Colorado	WCHA	40	12	31	43	59	....	....	....	....	....
1992-93	Colorado	WCHA	36	8	18	26	68	....	....	....	....	....

a NCAA West Second All-American Team (1992)
b WCHA First All-Star Team (1992)

IAFRATE, AL (IGH-uh-FRAY-tee)

Defense. Shoots left. 6'3", 220 lbs. Born, Dearborn, MI, March 21, 1966.
(Toronto's 1st choice, 4th overall, in 1984 Entry Draft).

			Regular Season					Playoffs				
Season	Club	Lea	GP	G	A	TP	PIM	GP	G	A	TP	PIM
1983-84a	U.S. National	....	55	4	17	21	26	....	....	....	....	....
	U.S. Olympic	....	6	0	0	0	2	....	....	....	....	....
	Belleville	OHL	10	2	4	6	2	3	0	1	1	5
1984-85	Toronto	NHL	68	5	16	21	51	....	....	....	....	....
1985-86	Toronto	NHL	65	8	25	33	40	10	0	3	3	4
1986-87	Toronto	NHL	80	9	21	30	55	13	1	3	4	11
1987-88	Toronto	NHL	77	22	30	52	80	6	3	4	7	6
1988-89	Toronto	NHL	65	13	20	33	72	....	....	....	....	....
1989-90	Toronto	NHL	75	21	42	63	135	....	....	....	....	....
1990-91	Toronto	NHL	42	3	15	18	113	....	....	....	....	....
	Washington	NHL	30	6	8	14	124	10	1	3	4	22
1991-92	Washington	NHL	78	17	34	51	180	7	4	2	6	14
1992-93a	Washington	NHL	81	25	41	66	169	6	6	0	6	4
	NHL Totals		661	129	252	381	1019	52	15	15	30	61

a NHL Second All-Star Team (1993)
Played in NHL All-Star Game (1988, 1990, 1993)
Traded to **Washington** by **Toronto** for Peter Zezel and Bob Rouse, January 16, 1991.

IGNATJEV, VIKTOR

Defense. Shoots left. 6'3", 198 lbs. Born, Riga, Soviet Union, April 26, 1970.
(San Jose's 11th choice, 243rd overall, in 1992 Entry Draft).

			Regular Season					Playoffs				
Season	Club	Lea	GP	G	A	TP	PIM	GP	G	A	TP	PIM
1989-90	Riga	USSR	40	0	0	0	26	....	....	....	....	....
1990-91	Riga	USSR	10	0	0	0	2	....	....	....	....	....
1991-92	Riga	CIS	22	4	5	9	22	....	....	....	....	....
1992-93	Kansas City	IHL	64	5	16	21	68	4	1	2	3	24

IMES, CHRIS

Defense. Shoots right. 5'11", 195 lbs. Born, South Paris, ME, August 27, 1972.
(Florida's 1st choice, 4th overall, in 1993 Supplemental Draft).

			Regular Season					Playoffs				
Season	Club	Lea	GP	G	A	TP	PIM	GP	G	A	TP	PIM
1990-91	U. of Maine	H.E.	37	6	8	14	16	....	....	....	....	....
1991-92	U. of Maine	H.E.	31	4	19	23	22	....	....	....	....	....
1992-93abc	U. of Maine	H.E.	45	12	23	35	24	....	....	....	....	....

a Hockey East First All-Star Team (1993)
b NCAA East First All-American Team (1993)
c NCAA Final Four All-Tournament Team (1993)

INTRANUOVO, RALPH

Center. Shoots left. 5'8", 185 lbs. Born, East York, Ont., December 11, 1973.
(Edmonton's 5th choice, 96th overall, in 1992 Entry Draft).

			Regular Season					Playoffs				
Season	Club	Lea	GP	G	A	TP	PIM	GP	G	A	TP	PIM
1990-91	S.S. Marie	OHL	63	25	42	67	22	14	7	13	20	17
1991-92	S.S. Marie	OHL	65	50	63	113	44	18	10	14	24	12
1992-93ab	S.S. Marie	OHL	54	31	47	78	61	18	10	16	26	30

a Memorial Cup Tournament MVP (1993)
b Memorial Cup All-Star Team (1993)

IOB, TONY

Left wing. Shoots left. 5'11", 206 lbs. Born, Renfrew, Ont., January 2, 1971.
(Buffalo's 10th choice, 189th overall, in 1991 Entry Draft).

			Regular Season					Playoffs				
Season	Club	Lea	GP	G	A	TP	PIM	GP	G	A	TP	PIM
1990-91	S.S. Marie	OHL	57	38	35	73	185	14	14	7	21	44
1991-92	S.S. Marie	OHL	42	28	34	62	157	19	17	17	34	45
	Rochester	AHL	1	0	0	0	0	....	....	....	....	....
1992-93	Rochester	AHL	20	12	8	20	70	7	1	1	2	14
	Erie	ECHL	25	14	13	27	194	5	2	2	4	45

JACKSON, DANE

Right wing. Shoots right. 6'1", 200 lbs. Born, Castlegar, B.C., May 17, 1970.
(Vancouver's 3rd choice, 44th overall, in 1988 Entry Draft).

			Regular Season					Playoffs				
Season	Club	Lea	GP	G	A	TP	PIM	GP	G	A	TP	PIM
1988-89	North Dakota	WCHA	30	4	5	9	33	....	....	....	....	....
1989-90	North Dakota	WCHA	44	15	11	26	56	....	....	....	....	....
1990-91	North Dakota	WCHA	37	17	9	26	79	....	....	....	....	....
1991-92	North Dakota	WCHA	39	23	19	42	81	....	....	....	....	....
1992-93	Hamilton	AHL	68	23	20	43	59	....	....	....	....	....

JAGR, JAROMIR (YAH-guhr)

Right wing. Shoots left. 6'2", 208 lbs. Born, Kladno, Czechoslovakia, February 15, 1972.
(Pittsburgh's 1st choice, 5th overall, in 1990 Entry Draft).

			Regular Season					Playoffs				
Season	Club	Lea	GP	G	A	TP	PIM	GP	G	A	TP	PIM
1988-89	Kladno	Czech.	39	8	10	18	4	....	....	....	....	....
1989-90	Kladno	Czech.	51	30	29	59	....	....	....	....	....	....
1990-91a	Pittsburgh	NHL	80	27	30	57	42	24	3	10	13	6
1991-92	Pittsburgh	NHL	70	32	37	69	34	21	11	13	24	6
1992-93	Pittsburgh	NHL	81	34	60	94	61	12	5	4	9	23
	NHL Totals		231	93	127	220	137	57	19	27	46	35

a NHL/Upper Deck All-Rookie Team (1991)
Played in NHL All-Star Game (1992, 1993)

JAKOPIN, JOHN

Defense. Shoots right. 6'5", 220 lbs. Born, Toronto, Ont., May 16, 1975.
(Detroit's 4th choice, 97th overall, in 1993 Entry Draft).

			Regular Season					Playoffs				
Season	Club	Lea	GP	G	A	TP	PIM	GP	G	A	TP	PIM
1992-93	St. Michael's	OHA Jr. A	45	9	21	30	42	....	....	....	....	....

JANNEY, CRAIG

Center. Shoots left. 6'1", 190 lbs. Born, Hartford, CT, September 26, 1967.
(Boston's 1st choice, 13th overall, in 1986 Entry Draft).

			Regular Season					Playoffs				
Season	Club	Lea	GP	G	A	TP	PIM	GP	G	A	TP	PIM
1985-86	Boston College	H.E.	34	13	14	27	8	....	....	....	....	....
1986-87ab	Boston College	H.E.	37	26	55	81	6	....	....	....	....	....
1987-88	U.S. National	....	52	26	44	70	6	....	....	....	....	....
	U.S. Olympic	....	5	3	1	4	2	....	....	....	....	....
	Boston	NHL	15	7	9	16	0	23	6	10	16	11
1988-89	Boston	NHL	62	16	46	62	12	10	4	9	13	21
1989-90	Boston	NHL	55	24	38	62	4	18	3	19	22	2
1990-91	Boston	NHL	77	26	66	92	8	18	4	18	22	11
1991-92	Boston	NHL	53	12	39	51	20	....	....	....	....	....
	St. Louis	NHL	25	6	30	36	2	6	0	6	6	0
1992-93	St. Louis	NHL	84	24	82	106	12	11	2	9	11	0
	NHL Totals		371	115	310	425	58	86	19	71	90	45

a Hockey East First All-Star Team (1987)
b NCAA East First All-American Team (1987)
Traded to **St. Louis** by **Boston** with Stephane Quintal for Adam Oates, February 7, 1992.

JANSSENS, MARK

Center. Shoots left. 6'3", 216 lbs. Born, Surrey, B.C., May 19, 1968.
(NY Rangers' 4th choice, 72nd overall, in 1986 Entry Draft).

			Regular Season					Playoffs				
Season	Club	Lea	GP	G	A	TP	PIM	GP	G	A	TP	PIM
1984-85	Regina	WHL	70	8	22	30	51	....	....	....	....	....
1985-86	Regina	WHL	71	25	38	63	146	9	0	2	2	17
1986-87	Regina	WHL	68	24	38	62	209	3	0	1	1	14
1987-88	NY Rangers	NHL	1	0	0	0	0	....	....	....	....	....
	Colorado	IHL	6	2	2	4	24	12	3	2	5	20
	Regina	WHL	71	39	51	90	202	4	3	4	7	6
1988-89	NY Rangers	NHL	5	0	0	0	0	....	....	....	....	....
	Denver	IHL	38	19	19	38	104	4	3	0	3	18
1989-90	NY Rangers	NHL	80	5	8	13	161	9	2	1	3	10
1990-91	NY Rangers	NHL	67	9	7	16	172	6	3	0	3	6
1991-92	NY Rangers	NHL	4	0	0	0	5	....	....	....	....	....
	Binghamton	AHL	55	10	23	33	109	....	....	....	....	....
	Minnesota	NHL	3	0	0	0	0	....	....	....	....	....
	Kalamazoo	IHL	2	0	0	0	2	11	1	2	3	22
1992-93	Hartford	NHL	76	12	17	29	237	....	....	....	....	....
	NHL Totals		236	26	32	58	575	15	5	1	6	16

Traded to **Minnesota** by **NY Rangers** for Mario Thyer and Minnesota's third round choice (Maxim Galanov) in 1993 Entry Draft, March 10, 1992. Traded to **Hartford** by **Minnesota** for James Black, September 3, 1992.

JANTUNEN, MARKO (YAHN-tuh-nen)

Center. Shoots left. 5'10", 180 lbs. Born, Lahti, Finland, February 14, 1971.
(Calgary's 12th choice, 239th overall, in 1991 Entry Draft).

			Regular Season					Playoffs				
Season	Club	Lea	GP	G	A	TP	PIM	GP	G	A	TP	PIM
1990-91	Reipas	Fin.	39	9	20	29	20	....	....	....	....	....
1991-92	Reipas	Fin.	42	10	14	24	46	....	....	....	....	....
1992-93	KalPa	Fin.	48	21	27	48	63	....	....	....	....	....

JARDEMYR, DANIEL

Defense. Shoots left. 6'2", 216 lbs. Born, Almtuna, Sweden, May 28, 1971.
(Winnipeg's 7th choice, 119th overall, in 1990 Entry Draft).

			Regular Season					Playoffs				
Season	Club	Lea	GP	G	A	TP	PIM	GP	G	A	TP	PIM
1989-90	Uppsala	Swe.2	27	5	9	14	32	....	....	....	....	....
1990-91	AIK	Swe.	27	1	2	3	32	....	....	....	....	....
1991-92	AIK	Swe.	25	2	1	3	12	....	....	....	....	....
1992-93	AIK	Swe.	14	1	0	1	12	....	....	....	....	....

JAX, FREDRIK

Right wing. Shoots left. 5'11", 183 lbs.   Born, Leksand, Sweden, February 6, 1972.
(NY Rangers' 5th choice, 125th overall, in 1991 Entry Draft).

			Regular Season					Playoffs				
Season	Club	Lea	GP	G	A	TP	PIM	GP	G	A	TP	PIM
1990-91	Leksand	Swe.	8	0	0	0	4	15	2	1	3	0
1991-92	Leksand	Swe.	22	2	3	5	8	....	....	....	....	....
1992-93	Binghamton	AHL	20	3	2	5	4	....	....	....	....	....
	Erie	ECHL	38	21	23	44	21	5	1	1	2	6

JELINEK, TOMAS

Right wing. Shoots left. 5'9", 189 lbs.   Born, Prague, Czech., April 29, 1962.
(Ottawa's 11th choice, 242nd overall, in 1992 Entry Draft).

			Regular Season					Playoffs				
Season	Club	Lea	GP	G	A	TP	PIM	GP	G	A	TP	PIM
1979-80	Sparta Praha	Czech.	7	0	1	1		....	....	....	....	....
1980-81	Dukla Trencin	Czech.	34	5	6	11		....	....	....	....	....
1981-82	Dukla Trencin	Czech.	36	9	3	12	46	....	....	....	....	....
1982-83	Sparta Praha	Czech.	40	20	25	45		....	....	....	....	....
1983-84	Sparta Praha	Czech.	43	13	5	18	48	....	....	....	....	....
1984-85	Sparta Praha	Czech.	44	15	4	19	70	....	....	....	....	....
1985-86	Sparta Praha	Czech.	40	7	2	9		....	....	....	....	....
1986-87	Sparta Praha	Czech.	36	7	5	12	58	....	....	....	....	....
1987-88	Sparta Praha	Czech.	45	14	11	25	45	....	....	....	....	....
1988-89	Sparta Praha	Czech.	45	15	17	32	87	....	....	....	....	....
1989-90	Budejovice	Czech.	48	23	20	43		....	....	....	....	....
1990-91	Budejovice	Czech.	51	24	23	47	102	....	....	....	....	....
1991-92	HPK	Fin.	41	24	23	47	98	....	....	....	....	....
1992-93	**Ottawa**	**NHL**	49	7	6	13	52	....	....	....	....	....
	NHL Totals		**49**	**7**	**6**	**13**	**52**	....	....	....	....	....

JENNINGS, GRANT

Defense. Shoots left. 6'3", 210 lbs.   Born, Hudson Bay, Sask., May 5, 1965.

			Regular Season					Playoffs				
Season	Club	Lea	GP	G	A	TP	PIM	GP	G	A	TP	PIM
1983-84	Saskatoon	WHL	64	5	13	18	102	....	....	....	....	....
1984-85	Saskatoon	WHL	47	10	24	34	134	2	1	0	1	2
1985-86	Binghamton	AHL	51	0	4	4	109	....	....	....	....	....
1986-87	Fort Wayne	IHL	3	0	0	0	0	....	....	....	....	....
	Binghamton	AHL	47	1	5	6	125	13	0	2	2	17
1987-88	**Washington**	**NHL**	....	....	....	....	....	1	0	0	0	0
	Binghamton	AHL	56	2	12	14	195	3	1	0	1	15
1988-89	**Hartford**	**NHL**	55	3	10	13	159	4	1	0	1	17
	Binghamton	AHL	2	0	0	0	2	....	....	....	....	....
1989-90	**Hartford**	**NHL**	64	3	6	9	171	7	0	0	0	13
1990-91	**Hartford**	**NHL**	44	1	4	5	82	....	....	....	....	....
	Pittsburgh	**NHL**	13	1	3	4	26	13	1	1	2	16
1991-92	**Pittsburgh**	**NHL**	53	4	5	9	104	10	0	0	0	12
1992-93	**Pittsburgh**	**NHL**	58	0	5	5	65	12	0	0	0	8
	NHL Totals		**287**	**12**	**33**	**45**	**607**	**47**	**2**	**1**	**3**	**66**

Signed as a free agent by **Washington**, June 25, 1985. Traded to **Hartford** by **Washington** with Ed Kastelic for Mike Millar and Neil Sheehy, July 6, 1988. Traded to **Pittsburgh** by **Hartford** with Ron Francis and Ulf Samuelsson for John Cullen, Jeff Parker and Zarley Zalapski, March 4, 1991.

JENNINGS, JASON

Right wing. Shoots right. 5'11", 185 lbs.   Born, Vancouver, B.C., March 16, 1971.
(Winnipeg's 9th choice, 225th overall, in 1991 Entry Draft).

			Regular Season					Playoffs				
Season	Club	Lea	GP	G	A	TP	PIM	GP	G	A	TP	PIM
1989-90	W. Michigan	CCHA	28	3	1	4	50	....	....	....	....	....
1990-91	W. Michigan	CCHA	42	10	19	29	50	....	....	....	....	....
1991-92	W. Michigan	CCHA	35	8	9	17	52	....	....	....	....	....
1992-93	W. Michigan	CCHA	37	11	9	20	36	....	....	....	....	....

JENSEN, CHRIS

Right wing. Shoots right. 5'11", 180 lbs.   Born, Fort St. John, B.C., October 28, 1963.
(NY Rangers' 4th choice, 78th overall, in 1982 Entry Draft).

			Regular Season					Playoffs				
Season	Club	Lea	GP	G	A	TP	PIM	GP	G	A	TP	PIM
1982-83	North Dakota	WCHA	13	3	3	6	28	....	....	....	....	....
1983-84	North Dakota	WCHA	44	24	25	49	100	....	....	....	....	....
1984-85	North Dakota	WCHA	40	25	27	52	80	....	....	....	....	....
1985-86	North Dakota	WCHA	34	25	40	65	53	....	....	....	....	....
	NY Rangers	**NHL**	9	1	3	4	0	....	....	....	....	....
1986-87	**NY Rangers**	**NHL**	37	6	7	13	21	....	....	....	....	....
	New Haven	AHL	14	4	9	13	41	....	....	....	....	....
1987-88	**NY Rangers**	**NHL**	7	0	1	1	2	....	....	....	....	....
	Colorado	IHL	43	10	23	33	68	10	3	7	10	8
1988-89	Hershey	AHL	45	27	31	58	66	10	4	5	9	29
1989-90	**Philadelphia**	**NHL**	1	0	0	0	2	....	....	....	....	....
	Hershey	AHL	43	16	26	42	101	....	....	....	....	....
1990-91	**Philadelphia**	**NHL**	18	2	1	3	2	....	....	....	....	....
	Hershey	AHL	50	26	20	46	83	6	2	2	4	10
1991-92	**Philadelphia**	**NHL**	2	0	0	0	0	....	....	....	....	....
	Hershey	AHL	71	38	33	71	134	6	0	1	1	2
1992-93	Hershey	AHL	74	33	47	80	95	....	....	....	....	....
	NHL Totals		**74**	**9**	**12**	**21**	**27**	....	....	....	....	....

Traded to **Philadelphia** by **NY Rangers** for Michael Boyce, September 28, 1988.

JERRARD, PAUL

Defense. Shoots right. 5'10", 185 lbs.   Born, Winnipeg, Man., April 20, 1965.
(NY Rangers' 10th choice, 173rd overall, in 1983 Entry Draft).

			Regular Season					Playoffs				
Season	Club	Lea	GP	G	A	TP	PIM	GP	G	A	TP	PIM
1983-84	Lake Superior	CCHA	40	8	18	26	48	....	....	....	....	....
1984-85	Lake Superior	CCHA	43	9	25	34	61	....	....	....	....	....
1985-86	Lake Superior	CCHA	40	13	11	24	34	....	....	....	....	....
1986-87	Lake Superior	CCHA	35	10	19	29	56	....	....	....	....	....
1987-88	Colorado	IHL	77	20	28	48	182	11	2	4	6	40
1988-89	Denver	IHL	2	1	1	2	21	....	....	....	....	....
	Minnesota	**NHL**	5	0	0	0	4	....	....	....	....	....
	Kalamazoo	IHL	68	15	25	40	195	6	2	1	3	37
1989-90	Kalamazoo	IHL	60	9	18	27	134	7	1	1	2	11
1990-91	Albany	IHL	7	0	3	3	30	....	....	....	....	....
	Kalamazoo	IHL	62	10	23	33	111	7	0	0	0	13
1991-92	Kalamazoo	IHL	76	4	24	28	123	12	1	7	8	31
1992-93	Kalamazoo	IHL	80	8	11	19	187	....	....	....	....	....
	NHL Totals		**5**	**0**	**0**	**0**	**4**	....	....	....	....	....

Traded to **Minnesota** by **NY Rangers** with Mark Tinordi, the rights to Bret Barnett and Mike Sullivan, and Los Angeles' third round choice (previously acquired by NY Rangers — Minnesota selected Murray Garbutt) in 1989 Entry Draft for Brian Lawton, Igor Liba and the rights to Eric Bennett, October 11, 1988.

JESTADT, JEFF

Left wing. Shoots left. 6'1", 195 lbs.   Born, Hinsdale, IL, September 6, 1970.
(Winnipeg's 2nd choice, 11th overall, in 1991 Supplemental Draft).

			Regular Season					Playoffs				
Season	Club	Lea	GP	G	A	TP	PIM	GP	G	A	TP	PIM
1989-90	Ferris State	CCHA	35	7	2	9	52	....	....	....	....	....
1990-91	Ferris State	CCHA	33	8	8	16	31	....	....	....	....	....
1991-92	Ferris State	CCHA	34	12	7	19	21	....	....	....	....	....
1992-93	Ferris State	CCHA	40	19	9	28	55	....	....	....	....	....
	Toledo	ECHL	....	....	....	....	....	2	0	0	0	0

JICKLING, MIKE

Center. Shoots right. 5'11", 191 lbs.   Born, Eckville, Alta., January 5, 1973.
(Quebec's 8th choice, 172nd overall, in 1992 Entry Draft).

			Regular Season					Playoffs				
Season	Club	Lea	GP	G	A	TP	PIM	GP	G	A	TP	PIM
1990-91	Spokane	WHL	71	10	27	37	67	15	5	1	6	6
1991-92	Spokane	WHL	69	30	44	74	92	10	7	6	13	20
1992-93	Medicine Hat	WHL	62	22	39	61	97	10	3	3	6	6

JIRANEK, MARTIN

Center. Shoots left. 5'11", 170 lbs.   Born, Bashaw, Alta., October 3, 1969.
(Washington's 1st choice, 14th overall, in 1990 Supplemental Draft).

			Regular Season					Playoffs				
Season	Club	Lea	GP	G	A	TP	PIM	GP	G	A	TP	PIM
1988-89	Bowling Green	CCHA	41	9	18	27	36	....	....	....	....	....
1989-90	Bowling Green	CCHA	41	13	21	34	38	....	....	....	....	....
1990-91	Bowling Green	CCHA	39	31	23	54	33	....	....	....	....	....
1991-92a	Bowling Green	CCHA	34	25	28	53	46	....	....	....	....	....
	Baltimore	AHL	8	2	8	10	0	....	....	....	....	....
1992-93	Baltimore	AHL	64	18	26	44	39	7	1	2	3	23

a   CCHA Second All-Star Team (1992)

JOHANSSON, ANDREAS

Center. Shoots left. 5'10", 198 lbs.   Born, Hofors, Sweden, May 19, 1973.
(NY Islanders' 7th choice, 136th overall, in 1991 Entry Draft).

			Regular Season					Playoffs				
Season	Club	Lea	GP	G	A	TP	PIM	GP	G	A	TP	PIM
1990-91	Falun	Swe.2	31	12	10	22	38	....	....	....	....	....
1991-92	Farjestad	Swe.	30	3	1	4	10	6	0	0	0	4
1992-93	Farjestad	Swe.	38	4	7	11	38	2	0	0	0	0

JOHANSSON, CALLE   (yo-HAHN-suhn)

Defense. Shoots left. 5'11", 205 lbs.   Born, Goteborg, Sweden, February 14, 1967.
(Buffalo's 1st choice, 14th overall, in 1985 Entry Draft).

			Regular Season					Playoffs				
Season	Club	Lea	GP	G	A	TP	PIM	GP	G	A	TP	PIM
1983-84	V. Frolunda	Swe.	28	4	4	8	10	....	....	....	....	....
1984-85	V. Frolunda	Swe.2	25	8	13	21	16	6	1	2	3	4
1985-86	Bjorkloven	Swe.	17	1	2	3	4	....	....	....	....	....
1986-87	Bjorkloven	Swe.	30	2	13	15	20	6	1	3	4	6
1987-88a	**Buffalo**	**NHL**	71	4	38	42	37	6	0	1	1	0
1988-89	**Buffalo**	**NHL**	47	2	11	13	33	....	....	....	....	....
	Washington	**NHL**	12	1	7	8	4	6	1	2	3	0
1989-90	**Washington**	**NHL**	70	8	31	39	25	15	1	6	7	4
1990-91	**Washington**	**NHL**	80	11	41	52	23	10	2	7	9	8
1991-92	**Washington**	**NHL**	80	14	42	56	49	7	0	5	5	4
1992-93	**Washington**	**NHL**	77	7	38	45	56	6	0	5	5	4
	NHL Totals		**437**	**47**	**208**	**255**	**227**	**50**	**4**	**26**	**30**	**20**

a   Named to NHL All-Rookie Team (1988)

Traded to **Washington** by **Buffalo** with Buffalo's second round choice (Byron Dafoe) in 1989 Entry Draft for Clint Malarchuk, Grant Ledyard and Washington's sixth round choice (Brian Holzinger) in 1991 Entry Draft, March 7, 1989.

JOHANSSON, MATHIAS

Center. Shoots left. 6'2", 190 lbs.   Born, Oskarshamn, Sweden, February 22, 1974.
(Calgary's 3rd choice, 54th overall, in 1992 Entry Draft).

			Regular Season					Playoffs				
Season	Club	Lea	GP	G	A	TP	PIM	GP	G	A	TP	PIM
1990-91	Farjestad	Swe.	3	0	0	0	0	....	....	....	....	....
1991-92	Farjestad	Swe.	16	0	0	0	2	1	0	0	0	0
1992-93	Farjestad	Swe.	11	2	1	3	4	3	0	0	0	0

JOHANSSON, MIKAEL

Center. Shoots left. 5'10", 183 lbs. Born, Stockholm, Sweden, June 12, 1966.
(Quebec's 7th choice, 134th overall, in 1991 Entry Draft).

			Regular Season					Playoffs				
Season	Club	Lea	GP	G	A	TP	PIM	GP	G	A	TP	PIM
1986-87	Djurgarden	Swe.	32	9	16	25	8	....	....	....	....	....
1987-88	Djurgarden	Swe.	38	11	22	33	10	3	1	1	2	0
1988-89	Djurgarden	Swe.	29	6	15	21	10	....	....	....	....	....
1989-90	Djurgarden	Swe.	37	14	20	34	12	8	5	4	9	0
1990-91	Djurgarden	Swe.	39	13	27	40	21	7	2	7	9	0
1991-92	Djurgarden	Swe.	30	15	21	36	12	9	1	5	6	4
1992-93	Kloten	Switz.	36	18	30	48	2	....	....	....	....	....

JOHANSSON, ROGER (yo-HAHN-suhn)

Defense. Shoots left. 6'1", 190 lbs. Born, Ljungby, Sweden, April 17, 1967.
(Calgary's 5th choice, 80th overall, in 1985 Entry Draft).

			Regular Season					Playoffs				
Season	Club	Lea	GP	G	A	TP	PIM	GP	G	A	TP	PIM
1983-84	Troja	Swe.2	11	2	2	4	12	....	....	....	....	....
1984-85	Troja	Swe.2	30	1	6	7	20	9	0	4	4	8
1985-86	Troja	Swe.2	32	5	16	21	42	....	....	....	....	....
1986-87	Farjestad	Swe.	31	6	11	17	20	7	1	1	2	8
1987-88	Farjestad	Swe.	24	3	11	14	20	9	1	6	7	12
1988-89	Farjestad	Swe.	40	5	15	20	38	....	....	....	....	....
1989-90	**Calgary**	**NHL**	**35**	**0**	**5**	**5**	**48**	....	....	....	....	....
1990-91	**Calgary**	**NHL**	**38**	**4**	**13**	**17**	**47**	....	....	....	....	....
1991-92	Leksand	Swe.	22	3	9	12	42	....	....	....	....	....
1992-93	**Calgary**	**NHL**	**77**	**4**	**16**	**20**	**62**	**5**	**0**	**1**	**1**	**2**
	NHL Totals		**150**	**8**	**34**	**42**	**157**	**5**	**0**	**1**	**1**	**2**

JOHNSON, CHAD

Center. Shoots left. 6', 175 lbs. Born, Grand Forks, ND, January 10, 1970.
(New Jersey's 7th choice, 117th overall, in 1988 Entry Draft).

			Regular Season					Playoffs				
Season	Club	Lea	GP	G	A	TP	PIM	GP	G	A	TP	PIM
1990-91	North Dakota	WCHA	37	2	5	7	30	....	....	....	....	....
1991-92	North Dakota	WCHA	32	0	6	6	41	....	....	....	....	....
1992-93	North Dakota	WCHA	26	4	5	9	45	....	....	....	....	....

JOHNSON, CRAIG

Left wing/Center. Shoots left. 6'2", 197 lbs. Born, St. Paul, MN, March 18, 1972.
(St. Louis' 1st choice, 33rd overall, in 1990 Entry Draft).

			Regular Season					Playoffs				
Season	Club	Lea	GP	G	A	TP	PIM	GP	G	A	TP	PIM
1990-91	U. Minnesota	WCHA	33	13	18	31	34	....	....	....	....	....
1991-92	U. Minnesota	WCHA	41	17	38	55	66	....	....	....	....	....
1992-93	U. Minnesota	WCHA	42	22	24	46	70	....	....	....	....	....

JOHNSON, ERIC

Right wing. Shoots right. 6'1", 196 lbs. Born, Minneapolis, MN, December 31, 1972.
(Vancouver's 8th choice, 161st overall, in 1991 Entry Draft).

			Regular Season					Playoffs				
Season	Club	Lea	GP	G	A	TP	PIM	GP	G	A	TP	PIM
1991-92	St. Cloud	WCHA	20	0	2	2	8	....	....	....	....	....
1992-93	St. Cloud	WCHA	33	3	7	10	6	....	....	....	....	....

JOHNSON, GREG

Center. Shoots left. 5'10", 173 lbs. Born, Thunder Bay, Ont., March 16, 1971.
(Philadelphia's 1st choice, 33rd overall, in 1989 Entry Draft).

			Regular Season					Playoffs				
Season	Club	Lea	GP	G	A	TP	PIM	GP	G	A	TP	PIM
1989-90	North Dakota	WCHA	44	17	38	55	11	....	....	....	....	....
1990-91ab	North Dakota	WCHA	38	18	*61	79	6	....	....	....	....	....
1991-92ac	North Dakota	WCHA	39	20	*54	74	8	....	....	....	....	....
1992-93ab	North Dakota	WCHA	34	19	45	64	18	....	....	....	....	....
	Cdn. National	....	23	6	14	20	2	....	....	....	....	....

a WCHA First All-Star Team (1991, 1993)
b NCAA West First All-American Team (1991, 1993)
c NCAA West Second All-American Team (1992)

Traded to **Detroit** by **Philadelphia** with future considerations for Jim Cummins and Philadelphia's fourth round choice in (previously acquired by Detroit — later traded to Boston — Boston selected Charles Paquette) 1993 Entry Draft, June 20, 1993.

JOHNSON, JIM

Defense. Shoots left. 6'1", 190 lbs. Born, New Hope, MN, August 9, 1962.

			Regular Season					Playoffs				
Season	Club	Lea	GP	G	A	TP	PIM	GP	G	A	TP	PIM
1981-82	Minn.-Duluth	WCHA	40	0	10	10	62	....	....	....	....	....
1982-83	Minn.-Duluth	WCHA	44	3	18	21	118	....	....	....	....	....
1983-84	Minn.-Duluth	WCHA	43	3	13	16	116	....	....	....	....	....
1984-85	Minn.-Duluth	WCHA	47	7	29	36	49	....	....	....	....	....
1985-86	**Pittsburgh**	**NHL**	**80**	**3**	**26**	**29**	**115**	....	....	....	....	....
1986-87	**Pittsburgh**	**NHL**	**80**	**5**	**25**	**30**	**116**	....	....	....	....	....
1987-88	**Pittsburgh**	**NHL**	**55**	**1**	**12**	**13**	**87**	....	....	....	....	....
1988-89	**Pittsburgh**	**NHL**	**76**	**2**	**14**	**16**	**163**	**11**	**0**	**5**	**5**	**44**
1989-90	**Pittsburgh**	**NHL**	**75**	**3**	**13**	**16**	**154**	....	....	....	....	....
1990-91	**Pittsburgh**	**NHL**	**24**	**0**	**5**	**5**	**23**	....	....	....	....	....
	Minnesota	**NHL**	**44**	**1**	**9**	**10**	**100**	**14**	**0**	**1**	**1**	**52**
1991-92	**Minnesota**	**NHL**	**71**	**4**	**10**	**14**	**102**	**7**	**1**	**3**	**4**	**18**
1992-93	**Minnesota**	**NHL**	**79**	**3**	**20**	**23**	**105**	....	....	....	....	....
	NHL Totals		**584**	**22**	**134**	**156**	**965**	**32**	**1**	**9**	**10**	**114**

Signed as a free agent by **Pittsburgh**, June 9, 1985. Traded to **Minnesota** by **Pittsburgh** with Chris Dahlquist for Larry Murphy and Peter Taglianetti, December 11, 1990.

JOHNSON, MICHAEL

Defense. Shoots left. 6'3", 175 lbs. Born, Halifax, N.S., May 29, 1974.
(Minnesota's 4th choice, 130th overall, in 1992 Entry Draft).

			Regular Season					Playoffs				
Season	Club	Lea	GP	G	A	TP	PIM	GP	G	A	TP	PIM
1991-92	Ottawa	OHL	63	1	8	9	49	11	1	0	1	14
1992-93	Ottawa	OHL	66	7	10	17	139	....	....	....	....	....

JOHNSTON, KARL

Defense. Shoots left. 6', 190 lbs. Born, Windsor, Ont., August 11, 1967.

			Regular Season					Playoffs				
Season	Club	Lea	GP	G	A	TP	PIM	GP	G	A	TP	PIM
1987-88	Lake Superior	CCHA	42	7	13	20	38	....	....	....	....	....
1988-89	Lake Superior	CCHA	43	7	19	26	38	....	....	....	....	....
1989-90	Lake Superior	CCHA	43	12	28	40	32	....	....	....	....	....
1990-91ab	Lake Superior	CCHA	45	14	36	50	86	....	....	....	....	....
1991-92	Springfield	AHL	34	1	11	12	17	....	....	....	....	....
1992-93	Springfield	AHL	24	3	4	7	12	....	....	....	....	....
	Louisville	ECHL	28	5	20	25	29	....	....	....	....	....

a CCHA First All-Star Team (1991)
b NCAA West Second All-American Team (1991)

Signed as a free agent by **Hartford**, August 14, 1991.

JONES, BRAD

Left wing. Shoots left. 6', 195 lbs. Born, Sterling Heights, MI, June 26, 1965.
(Winnipeg's 8th choice, 156th overall, in 1984 Entry Draft).

			Regular Season					Playoffs				
Season	Club	Lea	GP	G	A	TP	PIM	GP	G	A	TP	PIM
1983-84	U. of Michigan	CCHA	37	8	26	34	32	....	....	....	....	....
1984-85	U. of Michigan	CCHA	34	21	27	48	66	....	....	....	....	....
1985-86a	U. of Michigan	CCHA	36	28	39	67	40	....	....	....	....	....
1986-87bc	U. of Michigan	CCHA	40	32	46	78	64	....	....	....	....	....
	Winnipeg	**NHL**	**4**	**1**	**0**	**1**	**0**	....	....	....	....	....
1987-88	**Winnipeg**	**NHL**	**19**	**2**	**5**	**7**	**15**	**1**	**0**	**0**	**0**	**0**
	U.S. National	....	50	27	23	50	59	....	....	....	....	....
1988-89	**Winnipeg**	**NHL**	**22**	**6**	**5**	**11**	**6**	....	....	....	....	....
	Moncton	AHL	44	20	19	39	62	7	0	1	1	22
1989-90	**Winnipeg**	**NHL**	**2**	**0**	**0**	**0**	**0**	....	....	....	....	....
	Moncton	AHL	15	5	6	11	47	....	....	....	....	....
	New Haven	AHL	36	8	11	19	71	....	....	....	....	....
1990-91	**Los Angeles**	**NHL**	**53**	**9**	**11**	**20**	**57**	**8**	**1**	**1**	**2**	**2**
1991-92	**Philadelphia**	**NHL**	**48**	**7**	**10**	**17**	**44**	....	....	....	....	....
1992-93	Ilves	Fin.	26	10	7	17	62	....	....	....	....	....
	New Haven	AHL	4	2	1	3	6	....	....	....	....	....
	NHL Totals		**148**	**25**	**31**	**56**	**122**	**9**	**1**	**1**	**2**	**2**

a CCHA Second All-Star Team (1986)
b CCHA First All-Star Team (1987)
c NCAA West Second All-American Team (1987)

Traded to **Los Angeles** by **Winnipeg** for Phil Sykes, December 1, 1989. Signed as a free agent by **Philadelphia**, August 6, 1991.

JONES, KEITH

Right wing. Shoots left. 6'2", 190 lbs. Born, Brantford, Ont., November 8, 1968.
(Washington's 7th choice, 141st overall, in 1988 Entry Draft).

			Regular Season					Playoffs				
Season	Club	Lea	GP	G	A	TP	PIM	GP	G	A	TP	PIM
1988-89	W. Michigan	CCHA	37	9	12	21	51	....	....	....	....	....
1989-90	W. Michigan	CCHA	40	19	18	37	82	....	....	....	....	....
1990-91	W. Michigan	CCHA	41	30	19	49	106	....	....	....	....	....
1991-92a	W. Michigan	CCHA	35	25	31	56	77	....	....	....	....	....
	Baltimore	AHL	6	2	4	6	0	....	....	....	....	....
1992-93	**Washington**	**NHL**	**71**	**12**	**14**	**26**	**124**	**6**	**0**	**0**	**0**	**10**
	Baltimore	AHL	8	7	3	10	4	....	....	....	....	....
	NHL Totals		**71**	**12**	**14**	**26**	**124**	**6**	**0**	**0**	**0**	**10**

a CCHA First All-Star Team (1992)

JONSSON, KENNY (YAHN-suhn)

Defense. Shoots left. 6'3", 189 lbs. Born, Angelholm, Sweden, October 6, 1974.
(Toronto's 1st choice, 12th overall, in 1993 Entry Draft).

			Regular Season					Playoffs				
Season	Club	Lea	GP	G	A	TP	PIM	GP	G	A	TP	PIM
1991-92	Rogle	Swe.2	30	4	11	15	24	....	....	....	....	....
1992-93a	Rogle	Swe.	39	3	10	13	42	....	....	....	....	....

a Swedish Rookie of the Year (1993)

JONSSON, STEFAN (YAHN-suhn)

Defense. Shoots left. 6'1", 194 lbs. Born, Sodertalje, Sweden, June 13, 1965.
(Calgary's 11th choice, 221st overall, in 1984 Entry Draft).

			Regular Season					Playoffs				
Season	Club	Lea	GP	G	A	TP	PIM	GP	G	A	TP	PIM
1983-84	Sodertalje	Swe.	11	1	0	1	6	....	....	....	....	....
1984-85	Sodertalje	Swe.	33	3	4	7	24	7	2	3	5	2
1985-86	Sodertalje	Swe.	33	4	1	5	16	7	0	0	0	4
1986-87	Sodertalje	Swe.	35	2	1	3	16	....	....	....	....	....
1987-88	Sodertalje	Swe.	36	4	6	10	24	2	0	0	0	8
1988-89	Sodertalje	Swe.	37	4	2	6	44	....	....	....	....	....
1989-90	Sodertalje	Swe.	37	5	10	15	62	2	0	1	1	0
1990-91	Sodertalje	Swe.	37	5	6	11	42	2	0	0	0	2
1991-92	Sodertalje	Swe.	22	2	3	5	20	....	....	....	....	....
1992-93	Lulea	Swe.	38	4	5	9	75	11	2	5	7	16

JOSEPH, CHRIS

Defense. Shoots right. 6'2", 210 lbs. Born, Burnaby, B.C., September 10, 1969.
(Pittsburgh's 1st choice, 5th overall, in 1987 Entry Draft).

			Regular Season					Playoffs				
Season	Club	Lea	GP	G	A	TP	PIM	GP	G	A	TP	PIM
1985-86	Seattle	WHL	72	4	8	12	50	5	0	3	3	12
1986-87	Seattle	WHL	67	13	45	58	155	....	....	....	....	....
1987-88	**Pittsburgh**	**NHL**	**17**	**0**	**4**	**4**	**12**	....	....	....	....	....
	Seattle	WHL	23	5	14	19	49	....	....	....	....	....
	Edmonton	**NHL**	**7**	**0**	**4**	**4**	**6**	....	....	....	....	....
	Nova Scotia	AHL	8	0	2	2	8	4	0	0	0	9
1988-89	**Edmonton**	**NHL**	**44**	**4**	**5**	**9**	**54**	....	....	....	....	....
	Cape Breton	AHL	5	1	1	2	18	....	....	....	....	....
1989-90	**Edmonton**	**NHL**	**4**	**0**	**2**	**2**	**2**	....	....	....	....	....
	Cape Breton	AHL	61	10	20	30	69	6	2	1	3	4
1990-91	**Edmonton**	**NHL**	**49**	**5**	**17**	**22**	**59**	....	....	....	....	....
1991-92	**Edmonton**	**NHL**	**7**	**0**	**0**	**0**	**8**	**5**	**1**	**3**	**4**	**2**
	Cape Breton	AHL	63	14	29	43	72	5	0	2	2	8
1992-93	**Edmonton**	**NHL**	**33**	**2**	**10**	**12**	**48**	....	....	....	....	....
	NHL Totals		**161**	**11**	**42**	**53**	**189**	**5**	**1**	**3**	**4**	**2**

Traded to **Edmonton** by **Pittsburgh** with Craig Simpson, Dave Hannan and Moe Mantha for Paul Coffey, Dave Hunter and Wayne Van Dorp, November 24, 1987.

JOUBERT, JACQUES

Forward. Shoots . 6'1", 191 lbs. Born, South Bend, IN, March 23, 1971.
(Dallas' 1st choice, 9th overall, in 1993 Supplemental Draft).

			Regular Season					Playoffs				
Season	Club	Lea	GP	G	A	TP	PIM	GP	G	A	TP	PIM
1992-93	Boston U.	H.E.	40	17	18	35	54	....	....	....	....	....

JOYCE, DUANE

Defense. Shoots right. 6'2", 203 lbs. Born, Pembroke, MA, May 5, 1965.

			Regular Season					Playoffs				
Season	Club	Lea	GP	G	A	TP	PIM	GP	G	A	TP	PIM
1989-90	Kalamazoo	IHL	2	0	0	0	2	....	....	....	....	....
	Fort Wayne	IHL	66	10	26	36	53	....	....	....	....	....
	Muskegon	IHL	13	3	10	13	8	12	3	7	10	13
1990-91	Kalamazoo	IHL	80	12	32	44	53	11	0	3	3	6
1991-92	Kansas City	IHL	80	12	32	44	62	15	6	11	17	8
1992-93	Kansas City	IHL	75	15	25	40	30	12	1	2	3	6

Signed as a free agent by **San Jose**, August 13, 1991.

JOYCE, JOHN

Center. Shoots right. 6'3", 185 lbs. Born, Wilbraham, MA, November 23, 1970.
(NY Islanders' 8th choice, 174th overall, in 1990 Entry Draft).

			Regular Season					Playoffs				
Season	Club	Lea	GP	G	A	TP	PIM	GP	G	A	TP	PIM
1990-91	Boston College	H.E.	18	1	4	5	6	....	....	....	....	....
1991-92	Boston College	H.E.	35	9	13	22	32	....	....	....	....	....
1992-93	Boston College	H.E.	38	12	31	43	50	....	....	....	....	....

JOYCE, ROBERT THOMAS (BOB)

Left wing. Shoots left. 6', 195 lbs. Born, St. John, N.B., July 11, 1966.
(Boston's 4th choice, 82nd overall, in 1984 Entry Draft).

			Regular Season					Playoffs				
Season	Club	Lea	GP	G	A	TP	PIM	GP	G	A	TP	PIM
1984-85	North Dakota	WCHA	41	18	16	34	10	....	....	....	....	....
1985-86	North Dakota	WCHA	38	31	28	59	40	....	....	....	....	....
1986-87abc	North Dakota	WCHA	48	52	37	89	42	....	....	....	....	....
1987-88	Cdn. National	....	46	12	10	22	28	....	....	....	....	....
	Cdn. Olympic	....	4	1	0	1	0	....	....	....	....	....
	Boston	**NHL**	**15**	**7**	**5**	**12**	**10**	**23**	**8**	**6**	**14**	**18**
1988-89	**Boston**	**NHL**	**77**	**18**	**31**	**49**	**46**	**9**	**5**	**2**	**7**	**2**
1989-90	**Boston**	**NHL**	**23**	**1**	**2**	**3**	**22**	....	....	....	....	....
	Washington	**NHL**	**24**	**5**	**8**	**13**	**4**	**14**	**2**	**1**	**3**	**9**
1990-91	**Washington**	**NHL**	**17**	**3**	**3**	**6**	**8**	....	....	....	....	....
	Baltimore	AHL	36	10	8	18	14	6	1	0	1	4
1991-92	**Winnipeg**	**NHL**	**1**	**0**	**0**	**0**	**0**	....	....	....	....	....
	Moncton	AHL	66	19	29	48	51	10	0	5	5	9
1992-93	**Winnipeg**	**NHL**	**1**	**0**	**0**	**0**	**0**	....	....	....	....	....
	Moncton	AHL	75	25	32	57	52	5	0	0	0	2
	NHL Totals		**158**	**34**	**49**	**83**	**90**	**46**	**15**	**9**	**24**	**29**

a WCHA First All-Star Team (1987)
b NCAA West First All-American Team (1987)
c Named to NCAA All-Tournament Team (1987)

Traded to **Washington** by **Boston** for Dave Christian, December 13, 1989. Traded to **Winnipeg** by **Washington** with Tyler Larter and Kent Paynter for Craig Duncanson, Brent Hughes and Simon Wheeldon, May 21, 1991.

JUDSON, RICK

Left wing. Shoots left. 5'11", 180 lbs. Born, Toledo, OH, August 13, 1969.
(Detroit's 11th choice, 204th overall, in 1989 Entry Draft).

			Regular Season					Playoffs				
Season	Club	Lea	GP	G	A	TP	PIM	GP	G	A	TP	PIM
1988-89	Ill.-Chicago	CCHA	42	14	20	34	20	....	....	....	....	....
1989-90	Ill.-Chicago	CCHA	38	19	22	41	18	....	....	....	....	....
1990-91	Ill.-Chicago	CCHA	38	24	26	50	12	....	....	....	....	....
1991-92	Ill.-Chicago	CCHA	35	17	19	36	26	....	....	....	....	....
	Toledo	ECHL	2	1	0	1	2	....	....	....	....	....
1992-93	Adirondack	AHL	7	3	0	3	0	....	....	....	....	....
	Toledo	ECHL	56	23	28	51	39	16	7	16	23	10

JUHLIN, PATRIK (ew-LEEN)

Left wing. Shoots left. 6', 194 lbs. Born, Vasteras, Sweden, April 24, 1970.
(Philadelphia's 2nd choice, 34th overall, in 1989 Entry Draft).

			Regular Season					Playoffs				
Season	Club	Lea	GP	G	A	TP	PIM	GP	G	A	TP	PIM
1987-88	Vasteras	Swe.2	2	0	0	0	0	....	....	....	....	....
1988-89	Vasteras	Swe.	5	0	0	0	0	....	....	....	....	....
1989-90	Vasteras	Swe.	35	10	13	23	18	2	0	0	0	0
1990-91	Vasteras	Swe.	40	13	9	22	24	4	3	1	4	0
1991-92	Vasteras	Swe.	39	15	12	27	40	....	....	....	....	....
1992-93	Vasteras	Swe.	34	14	12	26	22	3	0	1	1	2

JUNEAU, JOE

Center/Left Wing. Shoots right. 6', 195 lbs. Born, Pont-Rouge, Que., January 5, 1968.
(Boston's 3rd choice, 81st overall, in 1988 Entry Draft).

			Regular Season					Playoffs				
Season	Club	Lea	GP	G	A	TP	PIM	GP	G	A	TP	PIM
1987-88	RPI	ECAC	31	16	29	45	18	....	....	....	....	....
1988-89	RPI	ECAC	30	12	23	35	40	....	....	....	....	....
1989-90a	RPI	ECAC	34	18	*52	*70	31	....	....	....	....	....
1990-91bc	RPI	ECAC	29	23	40	63	68	....	....	....	....	....
	Cdn. National	....	7	2	3	5	0	....	....	....	....	....
1991-92	Cdn. National	....	60	20	49	69	35	....	....	....	....	....
	Cdn. Olympic	....	8	6	9	15	4	....	....	....	....	....
	Boston	**NHL**	**14**	**5**	**14**	**19**	**4**	**15**	**4**	**8**	**12**	**21**
1992-93d	**Boston**	**NHL**	**84**	**32**	**70**	**102**	**33**	**4**	**2**	**4**	**6**	**6**
	NHL Totals		**98**	**37**	**84**	**121**	**37**	**19**	**6**	**12**	**18**	**27**

a NCAA East First All-American Team (1990)
b ECAC Second All-Star Team (1991)
c NCAA East Second All-American Team (1991)
d NHL/Upper Deck All-Rookie Team (1993)

JUNKER, STEVE

Left wing. Shoots left. 6', 184 lbs. Born, Castlegar, B.C., June 26, 1972.
(NY Islanders' 5th choice, 92nd overall, in 1991 Entry Draft).

			Regular Season					Playoffs				
Season	Club	Lea	GP	G	A	TP	PIM	GP	G	A	TP	PIM
1990-91	Spokane	WHL	71	39	38	77	86	15	5	13	18	6
1991-92	Spokane	WHL	58	28	32	60	110	10	6	7	13	18
1992-93	Capital Dist.	AHL	79	16	31	47	20	4	0	0	0	0
	NY Islanders	**NHL**	....	....	....	....	....	**3**	**0**	**1**	**1**	**0**
	NHL Totals		**0**	**0**	**0**	**0**	**0**	**3**	**0**	**1**	**1**	**0**

KACIR, MARIAN

Right wing. Shoots left. 6'1", 183 lbs. Born, Hodonin, Czech., September 29, 1974.
(Tampa Bay's 4th choice, 81st overall, in 1993 Entry Draft).

			Regular Season					Playoffs				
Season	Club	Lea	GP	G	A	TP	PIM	GP	G	A	TP	PIM
1992-93	Owen Sound	OHL	56	20	36	56	8	8	3	5	8	4

KAMENSKY, VALERI (kah-MEHN-skee)

Left wing. Shoots right. 6'2", 198 lbs. Born, Voskresensk, Soviet Union, April 18, 1966.
(Quebec's 8th choice, 129th overall, in 1988 Entry Draft).

			Regular Season					Playoffs				
Season	Club	Lea	GP	G	A	TP	PIM	GP	G	A	TP	PIM
1982-83	Khimik	USSR	5	0	0	0	0	....	....	....	....	....
1983-84	Khimik	USSR	20	2	2	4	6	....	....	....	....	....
1984-85	Khimik	USSR	45	9	3	12	24	....	....	....	....	....
1985-86	CSKA	USSR	40	15	9	24	8	....	....	....	....	....
1986-87	CSKA	USSR	37	13	8	21	16	....	....	....	....	....
1987-88	CSKA	USSR	51	26	20	46	40	....	....	....	....	....
1988-89	CSKA	USSR	40	18	10	28	30	....	....	....	....	....
1989-90	CSKA	USSR	45	19	18	37	40	....	....	....	....	....
1990-91	CSKA	USSR	46	20	26	46	66	....	....	....	....	....
1991-92	**Quebec**	**NHL**	**23**	**7**	**14**	**21**	**14**	....	....	....	....	....
1992-93	**Quebec**	**NHL**	**32**	**15**	**22**	**37**	**14**	**6**	**0**	**1**	**1**	**6**
	NHL Totals		**55**	**22**	**36**	**58**	**28**	**6**	**0**	**1**	**1**	**6**

KAMINSKI, KEVIN (kah-MIN-skee)

Center. Shoots left. 5'9", 170 lbs. Born, Churchbridge, Sask., March 13, 1969.
(Minnesota's 3rd choice, 48th overall, in 1987 Entry Draft).

			Regular Season					Playoffs				
Season	Club	Lea	GP	G	A	TP	PIM	GP	G	A	TP	PIM
1986-87	Saskatoon	WHL	67	26	44	70	325	11	5	6	11	45
1987-88	Saskatoon	WHL	55	38	61	99	247	10	5	7	12	37
1988-89	**Minnesota**	**NHL**	**1**	**0**	**0**	**0**	**0**	....	....	....	....	....
	Saskatoon	WHL	52	25	43	68	199	8	4	9	13	25
1989-90	**Quebec**	**NHL**	**1**	**0**	**0**	**0**	**0**	....	....	....	....	....
	Halifax	AHL	19	3	4	7	128	2	0	0	0	5
1990-91	Halifax	AHL	7	1	0	1	44	....	....	....	....	....
	Fort Wayne	IHL	56	9	15	24	*455	19	4	2	6	*169
1991-92	**Quebec**	**NHL**	**5**	**0**	**0**	**0**	**45**	....	....	....	....	....
	Halifax	AHL	63	18	27	45	329	....	....	....	....	....
1992-93	Halifax	AHL	79	27	37	64	*345	....	....	....	....	....
	NHL Totals		**7**	**0**	**0**	**0**	**45**	....	....	....	....	....

Traded to **Quebec** by **Minnesota** for Gaetan Duchesne, June 19, 1989. Traded to **Washington** by **Quebec** for Mark Matier, June 15, 1993.

KAMINSKY, YAN (kah-MEHN-skee)

Right wing. Shoots left. 6'1", 176 lbs. Born, Penza, Soviet Union, July 28, 1971.
(Winnipeg's 4th choice, 99th overall, in 1991 Entry Draft).

			Regular Season					Playoffs				
Season	Club	Lea	GP	G	A	TP	PIM	GP	G	A	TP	PIM
1989-90	Moscow D'amo	USSR	6	1	0	1	4	....	....	....	....	....
1990-91	Moscow D'amo	USSR	25	10	5	15	2	....	....	....	....	....
1991-92	Moscow D'amo	CIS	42	9	7	16	22	....	....	....	....	....
1992-93	Moscow D'amo	CIS	39	15	14	29	12	10	2	5	7	8

KAMPERSAL, JEFFREY

Defense. Shoots right. 6'2", 190 lbs. Born, Beverly, MA, January 27, 1970.
(NY Islanders' 12th choice, 205th overall, in 1988 Entry Draft).

			Regular Season					Playoffs				
Season	Club	Lea	GP	G	A	TP	PIM	GP	G	A	TP	PIM
1988-89	Princeton	ECAC	26	0	3	3	32	....	....	....	....	....
1989-90	Princeton	ECAC	27	3	7	10	26	....	....	....	....	....
1990-91	Princeton	ECAC	27	5	7	12	14	....	....	....	....	....
1991-92	Princeton	ECAC	27	7	10	17	36	....	....	....	....	....
1992-93	Capital Dist.	AHL	8	1	3	4	0	....	....	....	....	....
	Richmond	ECHL	56	6	18	24	45	1	0	0	0	0

KANE, SHAUN

Defense. Shoots left. 6'3", 195 lbs. Born, Holyoke, MA, February 24, 1970.
(Minnesota's 3rd choice, 43rd overall, in 1988 Entry Draft).

			Regular Season					Playoffs				
Season	Club	Lea	GP	G	A	TP	PIM	GP	G	A	TP	PIM
1988-89	Providence	H.E.	37	2	9	11	54	....	....	....	....	....
1989-90	Providence	H.E.	31	9	8	17	46	....	....	....	....	....
1990-91a	Providence	H.E.	36	5	20	25	86	....	....	....	....	....
1991-92	Providence	H.E.	36	11	11	22	59	....	....	....	....	....
1992-93	Columbus	ECHL	41	7	25	32	68	....	....	....	....	....
	Kalamazoo	IHL	4	0	2	2	0	....	....	....	....	....
	Kansas City	IHL	2	0	0	0	2	....	....	....	....	....
	Milwaukee	IHL	4	0	0	0	0	....	....	....	....	....
	Cincinnati	IHL	22	0	3	3	10	....	....	....	....	....

a Hockey East Second All-Star Team (1991)

Claimed by **San Jose** from **Minnesota** in Dispersal Draft, May 30, 1991.

KAPUSTA, TOMAS (ka-POOS-tah)

Center. Shoots left. 6', 187 lbs.   Born, Zlin, Czechoslovakia, February 23, 1967.
(Edmonton's 4th choice, 104th overall, in 1985 Entry Draft).

			Regular Season					Playoffs			
Season	Club	Lea	GP	G	A	TP	PIM	GP	G	A	TP	PIM
1986-87	TJ Gottwaldov	Czech.	32	6	4	10	18	....				....
1987-88	Dukla Jihlava	Czech.	15	0	2	2	6	....				....
1988-89	Dukla Trencin	Czech.	45	8	14	22	36	....				....
1989-90	TJ Zlin	Czech.	16	9	6	15		....				....
	Cape Breton	AHL	55	12	37	49	56	6	2	7	9	4
1990-91	Cape Breton	AHL	73	21	46	67	47	4	0	2	2	21
1991-92	Cape Breton	AHL	67	18	33	51	55	5	1	2	3	2
1992-93	HPK	Fin.	48	30	17	47	40	12	4	2	6	12

KARABIN, LADISLAV (kar-ah-BIN)

Left wing. Shoots left. 6'1", 189 lbs.   Born, Spisska Nova Ves, Czech., February 16, 1970.
(Pittsburgh's 11th choice, 173rd overall, in 1990 Entry Draft).

			Regular Season					Playoffs			
Season	Club	Lea	GP	G	A	TP	PIM	GP	G	A	TP	PIM
1988-89	Bratislava	Czech.	31	7	2	9	10	....				....
1989-90	Bratislava	Czech.2				UNAVAILABLE						
1990-91	Bratislava	Czech.	49	21	7	28	57	....				....
1991-92	Bratislava	Czech.	27	4	8	12	10	....				....
1992-93	Bratislava	Czech.	39	21	23	44		....				....

KARALAHTI, JERE

Defense. Shoots right. 6'1", 180 lbs.   Born, Helsinki, Finland, March 25, 1975.
(Los Angeles' 7th choice, 146th overall, in 1993 Entry Draft).

			Regular Season					Playoffs			
Season	Club	Lea	GP	G	A	TP	PIM	GP	G	A	TP	PIM
1992-93	HIFK Jrs.	Fin.	30	2	13	15	49	....				....

KARAMNOV, VITALI (kuh-RAHM-nov)

Left wing. Shoots left. 6'2", 185 lbs.   Born, Moscow, Soviet Union, July 6, 1968.
(St. Louis' 2nd choice, 62nd overall, in 1992 Entry Draft).

			Regular Season					Playoffs			
Season	Club	Lea	GP	G	A	TP	PIM	GP	G	A	TP	PIM
1986-87	Moscow D'amo	USSR	4	0	0	0	0	....				....
1987-88	Moscow D'amo	USSR	2	0	1	1	0	....				....
1988-89	D'amo Kharkov	USSR	23	4	1	5	19	....				....
1989-90	Torpedo Yaro.	USSR	47	6	7	13	32	....				....
1990-91	Torpedo Yaro.	USSR	45	14	7	21	30	....				....
1991-92	Moscow D'amo	CIS	40	13	19	32	25	....				....
1992-93	**St. Louis**	**NHL**	**7**	**0**	**1**	**1**	**0**	....				....
	Peoria	IHL	23	8	12	20	47	....				....
	NHL Totals		**7**	**0**	**1**	**1**	**0**	....				....

KARIYA, PAUL

Left wing. Shoots left. 5'10", 157 lbs.   Born, Vancouver, B.C., October 16, 1974.
(Anaheim's 1st choice, 4th overall, in 1993 Entry Draft).

			Regular Season					Playoffs			
Season	Club	Lea	GP	G	A	TP	PIM	GP	G	A	TP	PIM
1991-92	Penticton	BCJHL	41	45	87	132	16	....				....
1992-93												
abcdef	U. of Maine	H.E.	36	24	*69	*93	12	....				....

a   Hockey East First All-Star Team (1993)
b   Hockey East Rookie of the Year (1993)
c   Hockey East Most Valuable Player (1993)
d   NCAA East First All-American Team (1993)
e   NCAA Final Four All-Tournament Team (1993)
f   Won Hobey Baker Memorial Award (Top U.S. Collegiate Player) (1993)

KARJALAINEN, KYOSTI (kahr-ya-LAY-nehn)

Right wing. Shoots right. 6'2", 190 lbs.   Born, Gavle, Sweden, June 19, 1967.
(Los Angeles' 6th choice, 132nd overall, in 1987 Entry Draft).

			Regular Season					Playoffs			
Season	Club	Lea	GP	G	A	TP	PIM	GP	G	A	TP	PIM
1986-87	Brynas	Swe.	11	3	2	5	0	....				....
1987-88	Brynas	Swe.	20	2	1	3	10	....				....
1988-89	Brynas	Swe.	39	20	17	37	16	....				....
1989-90	Brynas	Swe.	38	17	15	32	16	5	0	3	3	0
1990-91	Phoenix	IHL	70	14	35	49	10	6	2	3	5	6
1991-92	**Los Angeles**	**NHL**	**28**	**1**	**8**	**9**	**12**	**3**	**0**	**1**	**1**	**2**
	Phoenix	IHL	43	14	22	36	30	....				....
1992-93	Lulea	Swe.	39	7	5	12	44	11	0	1	1	0
	NHL Totals		**28**	**1**	**8**	**9**	**12**	**3**	**0**	**1**	**1**	**2**

KARLSSON, ANDREAS

Center. Shoots left. 6'2", 180 lbs.   Born, Leksand, Sweden, August 19, 1975.
(Calgary's 8th choice, 148th overall, in 1993 Entry Draft).

			Regular Season					Playoffs			
Season	Club	Lea	GP	G	A	TP	PIM	GP	G	A	TP	PIM
1992-93	Leksand	Swe.	13	0	0	0	6	....				....

KARLSSON, LARS (KAHRL-suhn)

Left wing. Shoots left. 6'3", 205 lbs.   Born, Karlstad, Sweden, August 18, 1966.
(Detroit's 7th choice, 152nd overall, in 1984 Entry Draft).

			Regular Season					Playoffs			
Season	Club	Lea	GP	G	A	TP	PIM	GP	G	A	TP	PIM
1987-88	Farjestad	Swe.	39	6	12	18	42	9	1	0	1	20
1988-89	Farjestad	Swe.	40	9	9	18	32	2	0	1	1	6
1989-90	Farjestad	Swe.	27	8	5	13	12	10	3	2	5	8
1990-91	Farjestad	Swe.	36	10	6	16	46	8	0	3	3	6
1991-92	Farjestad	Swe.	39	16	17	33	36	6	2	3	5	6
1992-93	Farjestad	Swe.	39	5	12	17	54	3	1	1	2	4

KARPA, DAVE

Defense. Shoots right. 6'1", 190 lbs.   Born, Regina, Sask., May 7, 1971.
(Quebec's 4th choice, 68th overall, in 1991 Entry Draft).

			Regular Season					Playoffs			
Season	Club	Lea	GP	G	A	TP	PIM	GP	G	A	TP	PIM
1990-91	Ferris State	CCHA	41	6	19	25	109	....				....
1991-92	Ferris State	CCHA	34	7	12	19	124	....				....
	Quebec	**NHL**	**4**	**0**	**0**	**0**	**14**	....				....
	Halifax	AHL	2	0	0	0	4	....				....
1992-93	**Quebec**	**NHL**	**12**	**0**	**1**	**1**	**13**	**3**	**0**	**0**	**0**	**0**
	Halifax	AHL	71	4	27	31	167	....				....
	NHL Totals		**16**	**0**	**1**	**1**	**27**	**3**	**0**	**0**	**0**	**0**

KARPOV, VALERI

Left wing. Shoots left. 5'10", 176 lbs.   Born, Chelyabinsk, Soviet Union, August 5, 1971.
(Anaheim's 3rd choice, 56th overall, in 1993 Entry Draft).

			Regular Season					Playoffs			
Season	Club	Lea	GP	G	A	TP	PIM	GP	G	A	TP	PIM
1988-89	Chelyabinsk	USSR	5	0	0	0	0	....				....
1989-90	Chelyabinsk	USSR	24	1	2	3	6	....				....
1990-91	Chelyabinsk	USSR	25	8	4	12	15	....				....
1991-92	Chelyabinsk	CIS	44	16	10	26	34	....				....
1992-93	CSKA	CIS	9	2	6	8	0	....				....
a	Chelyabinsk	CIS	29	10	15	25	6	8	0	1	1	10

a   CIS All-Star Team (1993)

KARPOVTSEV, ALEXANDER (kar-POV-tzev)

Defense. Shoots right. 6'2", 189 lbs.   Born, Moscow, Soviet Union, April 7, 1970.
(Quebec's 7th choice, 158th overall, in 1990 Entry Draft).

			Regular Season					Playoffs			
Season	Club	Lea	GP	G	A	TP	PIM	GP	G	A	TP	PIM
1987-88	Moscow D'amo	USSR	2	0	1	1	10	....				....
1989-90	Moscow D'amo	USSR	35	1	1	2	27	....				....
1990-91	Moscow D'amo	USSR	40	0	5	5	15	....				....
1991-92	Moscow D'amo	CIS	35	4	2	6	26	....				....
1992-93	Moscow D'amo	CIS	36	3	11	14	100	7	2	1	3	0

KARPOVTSEV, ANDREI (kar-POV-tzev)

Left wing. Shoots left. 6'2", 211 lbs.   Born, Moscow, Soviet Union, February 25, 1974.
(Winnipeg's 11th choice, 252nd overall, in 1992 Entry Draft).

			Regular Season					Playoffs			
Season	Club	Lea	GP	G	A	TP	PIM	GP	G	A	TP	PIM
1991-92	Mosc.D'amo-2	CIS 3	33	4	0	4	39	....				....
1992-93	Mosc.D'amo-2	CIS 2				UNAVAILABLE						

KASATONOV, ALEXEI (kah-sah-TOH-nahf)

Defense. Shoots left. 6'1", 215 lbs.   Born, Leningrad, Soviet Union, October 14, 1959.
(New Jersey's 10th choice, 225th overall, in 1983 Entry Draft).

			Regular Season					Playoffs			
Season	Club	Lea	GP	G	A	TP	PIM	GP	G	A	TP	PIM
1976-77	SKA Leningrad	USSR	7	0	0	0	0	....				....
1977-78	SKA Leningrad	USSR	35	4	7	11	15	....				....
1978-79	CSKA	USSR	40	5	14	19	30	....				....
1979-80a	CSKA	USSR	37	5	8	13	26	....				....
1980-81a	CSKA	USSR	47	10	12	22	38	....				....
1981-82a	CSKA	USSR	46	12	27	39	45	....				....
1982-83a	CSKA	USSR	44	12	19	31	37	....				....
1983-84a	CSKA	USSR	39	12	24	36	20	....				....
1984-85a	CSKA	USSR	40	18	18	36	26	....				....
1985-86a	CSKA	USSR	40	6	17	23	27	....				....
1986-87a	CSKA	USSR	40	13	17	30	16	....				....
1987-88a	CSKA	USSR	43	8	12	20	8	....				....
1988-89	CSKA	USSR	41	8	14	22	8	....				....
1989-90	CSKA	USSR	30	6	7	13	16	....				....
	New Jersey	**NHL**	**39**	**6**	**15**	**21**	**16**	**6**	**0**	**3**	**3**	**14**
	Utica	AHL	3	0	2	2	7	....				....
1990-91	**New Jersey**	**NHL**	**78**	**10**	**31**	**41**	**76**	**7**	**1**	**3**	**4**	**10**
1991-92	**New Jersey**	**NHL**	**76**	**12**	**28**	**40**	**70**	**7**	**1**	**1**	**2**	**12**
1992-93	**New Jersey**	**NHL**	**64**	**3**	**14**	**17**	**57**	**4**	**0**	**0**	**0**	**0**
	NHL Totals		**257**	**31**	**88**	**119**	**219**	**24**	**2**	**7**	**9**	**36**

a   Soviet National League All-Star Team (1980-88)

Claimed by **Anaheim** from **New Jersey** in Expansion Draft, June 24, 1993.

KASPARAITIS, DARIUS (kahs-pah-RIGH-tis, DAH-roos)

Defense. Shoots left. 5'11", 187 lbs.   Born, Elektrenai, Soviet Union, October 16, 1972.
(NY Islanders' 1st choice, 5th overall, in 1992 Entry Draft).

			Regular Season					Playoffs			
Season	Club	Lea	GP	G	A	TP	PIM	GP	G	A	TP	PIM
1988-89	Moscow D'amo	USSR	3	0	0	0	0	....				....
1989-90	Moscow D'amo	USSR	1	0	0	0	0	....				....
1990-91	Moscow D'amo	USSR	17	0	1	1	10	....				....
1991-92	Moscow D'amo	CIS	31	2	10	12	14	....				....
1992-93	Moscow D'amo	CIS	7	1	3	4	8	....				....
	NY Islanders	**NHL**	**79**	**4**	**17**	**21**	**166**	**18**	**0**	**5**	**5**	**31**
	NHL Totals		**79**	**4**	**17**	**21**	**166**	**18**	**0**	**5**	**5**	**31**

KASPER, STEPHEN NEIL (STEVE)

Center. Shoots left. 5'8", 175 lbs. Born, Montreal, Que., September 28, 1961.
(Boston's 3rd choice, 81st overall, in 1980 Entry Draft).

			Regular Season					Playoffs				
Season	Club	Lea	GP	G	A	TP	PIM	GP	G	A	TP	PIM
1978-79	Verdun	QJHL	67	37	67	104	53	11	7	6	13	22
1979-80	Sorel	QJHL	70	57	65	122	117	....	....	....	....	....
1980-81	**Boston**	**NHL**	**76**	**21**	**35**	**56**	**94**	**3**	**0**	**1**	**1**	**0**
1981-82a	**Boston**	**NHL**	**73**	**20**	**31**	**51**	**72**	**11**	**3**	**6**	**9**	**22**
1982-83	**Boston**	**NHL**	**24**	**2**	**6**	**8**	**24**	**12**	**2**	**1**	**3**	**10**
1983-84	**Boston**	**NHL**	**27**	**3**	**11**	**14**	**19**	**3**	**0**	**0**	**0**	**7**
1984-85	**Boston**	**NHL**	**77**	**16**	**24**	**40**	**33**	**5**	**1**	**0**	**1**	**9**
1985-86	**Boston**	**NHL**	**80**	**17**	**23**	**40**	**73**	**3**	**1**	**0**	**1**	**4**
1986-87	**Boston**	**NHL**	**79**	**20**	**30**	**50**	**51**	**3**	**0**	**2**	**2**	**0**
1987-88	**Boston**	**NHL**	**79**	**26**	**44**	**70**	**35**	**23**	**7**	**6**	**13**	**10**
1988-89	**Boston**	**NHL**	**49**	**10**	**16**	**26**	**49**	....	....	....	....	....
	Los Angeles	**NHL**	**29**	**9**	**15**	**24**	**14**	**11**	**1**	**5**	**6**	**10**
1989-90	**Los Angeles**	**NHL**	**77**	**17**	**28**	**45**	**27**	**10**	**1**	**1**	**2**	**2**
1990-91	**Los Angeles**	**NHL**	**67**	**9**	**19**	**28**	**33**	**10**	**4**	**6**	**10**	**8**
1991-92	**Philadelphia**	**NHL**	**16**	**3**	**2**	**5**	**10**	....	....	....	....	....
1992-93	**Philadelphia**	**NHL**	**21**	**1**	**3**	**4**	**2**	....	....	....	....	....
	Tampa Bay	**NHL**	**47**	**3**	**4**	**7**	**18**	....	....	....	....	....
	NHL Totals		**821**	**177**	**291**	**468**	**554**	**94**	**20**	**28**	**48**	**82**

a Won Frank J. Selke Trophy (1982)

Traded to **Los Angeles** by **Boston** for Bobby Carpenter, January 23, 1989. Traded to **Philadelphia** by **Los Angeles** with Steve Duchesne and Los Angeles' fourth round choice (Aris Brimanis) in 1991 Entry Draft for Jari Kurri and Jeff Chychrun, May 30, 1991. Traded to **Tampa Bay** by **Philadelphia** for Dan Vincelette, December 8, 1992.

KASTELIC, EDWARD (ED) (KAS-tuh-lihk)

Right/Left wing. Shoots right. 6'4", 215 lbs. Born, Toronto, Ont., January 29, 1964.
(Washington's 4th choice, 110th overall, in 1982 Entry Draft).

			Regular Season					Playoffs				
Season	Club	Lea	GP	G	A	TP	PIM	GP	G	A	TP	PIM
1981-82	London	OHL	68	5	18	23	63	4	0	1	1	4
1982-83	London	OHL	68	12	11	23	96	3	0	0	0	5
1983-84	London	OHL	68	17	16	33	218	8	0	2	2	41
1984-85	Moncton	AHL	62	5	11	16	187	....	....	....	....	....
	Binghamton	AHL	4	0	0	0	7	....	....	....	....	....
	Fort Wayne	IHL	5	1	0	1	37	....	....	....	....	....
1985-86	**Washington**	**NHL**	**15**	**0**	**0**	**0**	**73**	....	....	....	....	....
	Binghamton	AHL	23	7	9	16	76	....	....	....	....	....
1986-87	**Washington**	**NHL**	**23**	**1**	**1**	**2**	**83**	**5**	**1**	**0**	**1**	**13**
	Binghamton	AHL	48	17	11	28	124	....	....	....	....	....
1987-88	**Washington**	**NHL**	**35**	**1**	**0**	**1**	**78**	**1**	**0**	**0**	**0**	**19**
	Binghamton	AHL	6	4	1	5	6	....	....	....	....	....
1988-89	**Hartford**	**NHL**	**10**	**0**	**2**	**2**	**15**	....	....	....	....	....
	Binghamton	AHL	35	9	6	15	124	....	....	....	....	....
1989-90	**Hartford**	**NHL**	**67**	**6**	**2**	**8**	**198**	**2**	**0**	**0**	**0**	**0**
1990-91	**Hartford**	**NHL**	**45**	**2**	**2**	**4**	**211**	....	....	....	....	....
1991-92	**Hartford**	**NHL**	**25**	**1**	**3**	**4**	**61**	....	....	....	....	....
1992-93	Phoenix	IHL	57	11	7	18	158	....	....	....	....	....
	NHL Totals		**220**	**11**	**10**	**21**	**719**	**8**	**1**	**0**	**1**	**32**

Traded to **Hartford** by **Washington** with Grant Jennings for Mike Millar and Neil Sheehy, July 6, 1988.

KAUTONEN, VELI-PEKKA (KAH-uh-toh-nehn)

Defense. Shoots right. 6'2", 205 lbs. Born, Helsinki, Finland, May 9, 1970.
(Calgary's 3rd choice, 50th overall, in 1989 Entry Draft).

			Regular Season					Playoffs				
Season	Club	Lea	GP	G	A	TP	PIM	GP	G	A	TP	PIM
1988-89	HIFK	Fin.	36	4	5	9	6	2	....	....	....	....
1989-90	HIFK	Fin.	36	2	1	3	10	2	0	0	0	0
1990-91	SaiPa	Fin.	43	12	19	31	36	....	....	....	....	....
1991-92	Tappara	Fin.	44	6	12	18	30	....	....	....	....	....
1992-93	Tappara	Fin.	42	4	3	7	22	....	....	....	....	....

KEANE, MIKE

Right wing. Shoots right. 5'10", 178 lbs. Born, Winnipeg, Man., May 29, 1967.

			Regular Season					Playoffs				
Season	Club	Lea	GP	G	A	TP	PIM	GP	G	A	TP	PIM
1984-85	Moose Jaw	WHL	65	17	26	43	141	....	....	....	....	....
1985-86	Moose Jaw	WHL	67	34	49	83	162	13	6	8	14	9
1986-87	Moose Jaw	WHL	53	25	45	70	107	9	3	9	12	11
	Sherbrooke	AHL	....	....	....	....	....	9	2	2	4	16
1987-88	Sherbrooke	AHL	78	25	43	68	70	6	1	1	2	18
1988-89	**Montreal**	**NHL**	**69**	**16**	**19**	**35**	**69**	**21**	**4**	**3**	**7**	**17**
1989-90	**Montreal**	**NHL**	**74**	**9**	**15**	**24**	**78**	**11**	**0**	**1**	**1**	**8**
1990-91	**Montreal**	**NHL**	**73**	**13**	**23**	**36**	**50**	**12**	**3**	**2**	**5**	**6**
1991-92	**Montreal**	**NHL**	**67**	**11**	**30**	**41**	**64**	**8**	**1**	**1**	**2**	**16**
1992-93	**Montreal**	**NHL**	**77**	**15**	**45**	**60**	**95**	**19**	**2**	**13**	**15**	**6**
	NHL Totals		**360**	**64**	**132**	**196**	**356**	**71**	**10**	**20**	**30**	**53**

Signed as a free agent by **Montreal**, September 25, 1985.

KEARNEY, FRANCIS (TOBY)

Left wing. Shoots left. 6'2", 185 lbs. Born, Newburyport, MA, September 2, 1970.
(Calgary's 7th choice, 105th overall, in 1989 Entry Draft).

			Regular Season					Playoffs				
Season	Club	Lea	GP	G	A	TP	PIM	GP	G	A	TP	PIM
1989-90	U. of Vermont	ECAC	25	2	3	5	24	....	....	....	....	....
1990-91	U. of Vermont	ECAC	33	8	11	19	16	....	....	....	....	....
1991-92	U. of Vermont	ECAC	31	6	11	17	56	....	....	....	....	....
1992-93	U. of Vermont	ECAC	29	6	10	16	42	....	....	....	....	....

KECZMER, DAN

Defense. Shoots left. 6'1", 190 lbs. Born, Mt. Clemens, MI, May 25, 1968.
(Minnesota's 11th choice, 201st overall, in 1986 Entry Draft).

			Regular Season					Playoffs				
Season	Club	Lea	GP	G	A	TP	PIM	GP	G	A	TP	PIM
1986-87	Lake Superior	CCHA	38	3	5	8	26	....	....	....	....	....
1987-88	Lake Superior	CCHA	41	2	15	17	34	....	....	....	....	....
1988-89	Lake Superior	CCHA	46	3	26	29	68	....	....	....	....	....
1989-90a	Lake Superior	CCHA	43	13	23	36	48	....	....	....	....	....
1990-91	**Minnesota**	**NHL**	**9**	**0**	**1**	**1**	**6**	....	....	....	....	....
	Kalamazoo	IHL	60	4	20	24	60	9	1	2	3	10
1991-92	U.S. National	....	51	3	11	14	56	....	....	....	....	....
	Hartford	**NHL**	**1**	**0**	**0**	**0**	**0**	....	....	....	....	....
	Springfield	AHL	18	3	4	7	10	4	0	0	0	6
1992-93	**Hartford**	**NHL**	**23**	**4**	**4**	**8**	**28**	....	....	....	....	....
	Springfield	AHL	37	1	13	14	38	12	0	4	4	14
	NHL Totals		**33**	**4**	**5**	**9**	**34**	....	....	....	....	....

a CCHA Second All-Star Team (1990)

Claimed by **San Jose** from **Minnesota** in Dispersal Draft, May 30, 1991. Traded to **Hartford** by **San Jose** for Dean Evason, October 2, 1991.

KEKALAINEN, JARMO (kee-kuh-LAY-nehn, YAHR-moh)

Left wing. Shoots left. 6', 190 lbs. Born, Tampere, Finland, July 3, 1966.

			Regular Season					Playoffs				
Season	Club	Lea	GP	G	A	TP	PIM	GP	G	A	TP	PIM
1985-86	Ilves	Fin.	29	6	6	12	8	....	....	....	....	....
1986-87	Ilves	Fin.	42	3	4	7	4	....	....	....	....	....
1987-88	Clarkson	ECAC	32	7	11	18	38	....	....	....	....	....
1988-89	Clarkson	ECAC	31	19	25	44	47	....	....	....	....	....
1989-90	**Boston**	**NHL**	**11**	**2**	**2**	**4**	**8**	....	....	....	....	....
	Maine	AHL	18	5	11	16	6	....	....	....	....	....
1990-91	**Boston**	**NHL**	**16**	**2**	**1**	**3**	**6**	....	....	....	....	....
	Maine	AHL	11	2	4	6	4	1	0	1	1	0
1991-92	KalPa	Fin.	24	2	8	10	24	....	....	....	....	....
1992-93	Tappara	Fin.	47	15	12	27	34	....	....	....	....	....
	NHL Totals		**27**	**4**	**3**	**7**	**14**	....	....	....	....	....

Signed as a free agent by **Boston**, May 3, 1989.

KELLEHER, CHRIS

Defense. Shoots left. 6'1", 215 lbs. Born, Cambridge, MA, March 23, 1975.
(Pittsburgh's 5th choice, 130th overall, in 1993 Entry Draft).

			Regular Season					Playoffs				
Season	Club	Lea	GP	G	A	TP	PIM	GP	G	A	TP	PIM
1991-92	St. Sebastien's	HS	28	7	27	34	12	....	....	....	....	....
1992-93	St. Sebastien's	HS	25	8	30	38	16	....	....	....	....	....

KELLEY, JONATHAN

Center. Shoots right. 6'1", 180 lbs. Born, Brighton, MA, June 25, 1973.
(Toronto's 12th choice, 223rd overall, in 1991 Entry Draft).

			Regular Season					Playoffs				
Season	Club	Lea	GP	G	A	TP	PIM	GP	G	A	TP	PIM
1990-91	Arlington	HS	21	42	28	70	0	....	....	....	....	....
1992-93	Princeton	ECAC	23	4	3	7	34	....	....	....	....	....

KELLOGG, BOB

Defense. Shoots left. 6'4", 210 lbs. Born, Springfield, MA, February 16, 1971.
(Chicago's 3rd choice, 48th overall, in 1989 Entry Draft).

			Regular Season					Playoffs				
Season	Club	Lea	GP	G	A	TP	PIM	GP	G	A	TP	PIM
1989-90	Northeastern	H.E.	36	3	12	15	30	....	....	....	....	....
1990-91	Northeastern	H.E.	2	0	0	0	6	....	....	....	....	....
1991-92	Northeastern	H.E.	27	2	3	5	34	....	....	....	....	....
1992-93	Northeastern	H.E.	35	5	15	20	44	....	....	....	....	....

KELMAN, TODD

Defense. Shoots left. 6'1", 190 lbs. Born, Calgary, Alta., January 5, 1975.
(St. Louis' 4th choice, 141st overall, in 1993 Entry Draft).

			Regular Season					Playoffs				
Season	Club	Lea	GP	G	A	TP	PIM	GP	G	A	TP	PIM
1992-93	Vernon	BCJHL	48	16	30	46	54	....	....	....	....	....

KEMPER, ANDREW

Defense. Shoots right. 6'2", 186 lbs. Born, Montreal, Que., April 7, 1974.
(Tampa Bay's 9th choice, 193rd overall, in 1992 Entry Draft).

			Regular Season					Playoffs				
Season	Club	Lea	GP	G	A	TP	PIM	GP	G	A	TP	PIM
1991-92	Seattle	WHL	68	2	9	11	90	1	0	0	0	0
1992-93	Saskatoon	WHL	54	1	6	7	75	9	1	1	2	27

KENADY, CHRISTOPHER

Right wing. Shoots right. 6'2", 195 lbs. Born, Mound, MN, April 10, 1973.
(St. Louis' 8th choice, 175th overall, in 1991 Entry Draft).

			Regular Season					Playoffs				
Season	Club	Lea	GP	G	A	TP	PIM	GP	G	A	TP	PIM
1991-92	U. of Denver	WCHA	36	8	5	13	56	....	....	....	....	....
1992-93	U. of Denver	WCHA	38	8	16	24	95	....	....	....	....	....

KENNEDY, DEAN

Defense. Shoots right. 6'2", 212 lbs. Born, Redvers, Sask., January 18, 1963.
(Los Angeles' 2nd choice, 39th overall, in 1981 Entry Draft).

			Regular Season					Playoffs				
Season	Club	Lea	GP	G	A	TP	PIM	GP	G	A	TP	PIM
1980-81	Brandon	WHL	71	3	29	32	157	5	0	2	2	7
1981-82	Brandon	WHL	49	5	38	43	103	....	....	....	....	....
1982-83	**Los Angeles**	**NHL**	**55**	**0**	**12**	**12**	**97**	....	....	....	....	....
	Brandon	WHL	14	2	15	17	22	....	....	....	....	....
	Saskatoon	WHL	....	....	....	....	....	4	0	3	3	0
1983-84	**Los Angeles**	**NHL**	**37**	**1**	**5**	**6**	**50**	....	....	....	....	....
	New Haven	AHL	26	1	7	8	23	....	....	....	....	....
1984-85	New Haven	AHL	76	3	14	17	104	....	....	....	....	....
1985-86	**Los Angeles**	**NHL**	**78**	**2**	**10**	**12**	**132**	....	....	....	....	....
1986-87	**Los Angeles**	**NHL**	**66**	**6**	**14**	**20**	**91**	**5**	**0**	**2**	**2**	**10**
1987-88	**Los Angeles**	**NHL**	**58**	**1**	**11**	**12**	**158**	**4**	**0**	**1**	**1**	**10**
1988-89	**NY Rangers**	**NHL**	**16**	**0**	**1**	**1**	**40**	....	....	....	....	....
	Los Angeles	**NHL**	**51**	**3**	**10**	**13**	**63**	**11**	**0**	**2**	**2**	**8**
1989-90	**Buffalo**	**NHL**	**80**	**2**	**12**	**14**	**53**	**6**	**1**	**1**	**2**	**12**
1990-91	**Buffalo**	**NHL**	**64**	**4**	**8**	**12**	**119**	**2**	**0**	**1**	**1**	**17**
1991-92	**Winnipeg**	**NHL**	**18**	**2**	**4**	**6**	**21**	**2**	**0**	**0**	**0**	**0**
1992-93	**Winnipeg**	**NHL**	**78**	**1**	**7**	**8**	**105**	**6**	**0**	**0**	**0**	**2**
	NHL Totals		**601**	**22**	**94**	**116**	**929**	**36**	**1**	**7**	**8**	**59**

Traded to **NY Rangers** by **Los Angeles** with Denis Larocque for Igor Liba, Michael Boyce, Todd Elik and future considerations, December 12, 1988. Traded to **Los Angeles** by **NY Rangers** for Los Angeles' fourth round choice – later traded to Minnesota (Cal McGowan) – in 1990 Entry Draft, February 3, 1989. Traded to **Buffalo** by **Los Angeles** for Buffalo's fourth round choice (Keith Redmond) in 1991 Entry Draft, October 4, 1989. Traded to **Winnipeg** by **Buffalo** with Darrin Shannon and Mike Hartman for Dave McLlwain, Gord Donnelly, Winnipeg's fifth round choice (Yuri Khmylev) in 1992 Entry Draft and future considerations, October 11, 1991.

KENNEDY, MIKE

Center. Shoots right. 6'1", 170 lbs. Born, Vancouver, B.C., April 13, 1972.
(Minnesota's 5th choice, 97th overall, in 1991 Entry Draft).

			Regular Season					Playoffs				
Season	Club	Lea	GP	G	A	TP	PIM	GP	G	A	TP	PIM
1989-90	U.B.C.	CIAU	9	5	7	12	0	....	....	....	....	....
1990-91	U.B.C.	CIAU	28	17	17	34	18	....	....	....	....	....
1991-92a	Seattle	WHL	71	42	47	89	134	15	11	6	17	20
1992-93	Kalamazoo	IHL	77	21	30	51	39	....	....	....	....	....

a WHL West Second All-Star Team (1992)

KENNEDY, SHELDON

Right wing. Shoots right. 5'11", 175 lbs. Born, Brandon, Man., June 15, 1969.
(Detroit's 5th choice, 80th overall, in 1988 Entry Draft).

			Regular Season					Playoffs				
Season	Club	Lea	GP	G	A	TP	PIM	GP	G	A	TP	PIM
1986-87	Swift Current	WHL	49	23	41	64	43	4	0	3	3	4
1987-88	Swift Current	WHL	59	53	64	117	45	10	8	9	17	12
1988-89	Swift Current	WHL	51	58	48	106	92	12	9	15	24	22
1989-90	**Detroit**	**NHL**	**20**	**2**	**7**	**9**	**10**	....	....	....	....	....
	Adirondack	AHL	26	11	15	26	35	....	....	....	....	....
1990-91	**Detroit**	**NHL**	**7**	**1**	**0**	**1**	**12**	....	....	....	....	....
	Adirondack	AHL	11	1	3	4	8	....	....	....	....	....
1991-92	**Detroit**	**NHL**	**27**	**3**	**8**	**11**	**24**	....	....	....	....	....
	Adirondack	AHL	46	25	24	49	56	16	5	9	14	12
1992-93	**Detroit**	**NHL**	**68**	**19**	**11**	**30**	**46**	**7**	**1**	**1**	**2**	**2**
	NHL Totals		**122**	**25**	**26**	**51**	**92**	**7**	**1**	**1**	**2**	**2**

KENNEY, JAY

Defense. Shoots left. 6'2", 190 lbs. Born, New York, NY, September 21, 1973.
(Ottawa's 8th choice, 169th overall, in 1992 Entry Draft).

			Regular Season					Playoffs				
Season	Club	Lea	GP	G	A	TP	PIM	GP	G	A	TP	PIM
1991-92	Canterbury	HS	35	7	36	43	0	....	....	....	....	....
1992-93	Providence	H.E.	24	1	8	9	10	....	....	....	....	....

KENNHOLT, KENNETH

Defense. Shoots right. 6'3", 198 lbs. Born, Stockholm, Sweden, January 13, 1965.
(Calgary's 13th choice, 252nd overall, in 1989 Entry Draft).

			Regular Season					Playoffs				
Season	Club	Lea	GP	G	A	TP	PIM	GP	G	A	TP	PIM
1987-88	Nacka	Swe.2	31	11	11	22	38	3	1	0	1	4
1988-89	Djurgarden	Swe.	34	6	10	16	30	....	....	....	....	....
1989-90	Djurgarden	Swe.	38	7	10	17	30	8	0	1	1	6
1990-91	Djurgarden	Swe.	39	9	13	22	30	7	2	0	2	4
1991-92	Djurgarden	Swe.	33	4	6	10	22	10	2	4	6	10
1992-93	Djurgarden	Swe.	35	4	8	12	30	6	4	3	7	6

KENNY, ROB

Left wing. Shoots left. 6'1", 205 lbs. Born, New York. NY, September 19, 1968.

			Regular Season					Playoffs				
Season	Club	Lea	GP	G	A	TP	PIM	GP	G	A	TP	PIM
1989-90	Northeastern	H.E.	32	2	7	9	29	....	....	....	....	....
1990-91	Northeastern	H.E.	29	6	11	17	40	....	....	....	....	....
1991-92	Northeastern	H.E.	34	19	14	33	44	....	....	....	....	....
1992-93	Binghamton	AHL	66	12	11	23	56	8	2	4	6	8

Signed as a free agent by **NY Rangers**, August 24, 1992.

KERCH, ALEXANDER

Left wing. Shoots right. 5'10", 187 lbs. Born, Arkhangelsk, Soviet Union, March 16, 1967.
(Edmonton's 5th choice, 60th overall, in 1993 Entry Draft).

			Regular Season					Playoffs				
Season	Club	Lea	GP	G	A	TP	PIM	GP	G	A	TP	PIM
1984-85	Riga	USSR	8	0	0	0	6	....	....	....	....	....
1985-86	Riga	USSR	23	5	2	7	16	....	....	....	....	....
1986-87	Riga	USSR	26	5	4	9	10	....	....	....	....	....
1987-88	Riga	USSR	50	14	4	18	28	....	....	....	....	....
1988-89	Riga	USSR	39	6	7	13	41	....	....	....	....	....
1989-90	Riga	USSR	46	9	11	20	22	....	....	....	....	....
1990-91	Riga	USSR	46	16	17	33	46	....	....	....	....	....
1991-92	Riga	CIS	27	7	9	16	20	....	....	....	....	....
1992-93	Riga	CIS	42	23	14	37	28	2	1	2	3	2

KERR, ALAN

Right wing. Shoots right. 5'11", 195 lbs. Born, Hazelton, B.C., March 28, 1964.
(NY Islanders' 4th choice, 84th overall, in 1982 Entry Draft).

			Regular Season					Playoffs				
Season	Club	Lea	GP	G	A	TP	PIM	GP	G	A	TP	PIM
1981-82	Seattle	WHL	68	15	18	33	107	10	6	6	12	32
1982-83	Seattle	WHL	71	38	53	91	183	4	2	3	5	0
1983-84a	Seattle	WHL	66	46	66	112	141	5	1	4	5	12
1984-85	**NY Islanders**	**NHL**	**19**	**3**	**1**	**4**	**24**	**4**	**1**	**0**	**1**	**4**
	Springfield	AHL	62	32	27	59	140	4	1	2	3	2
1985-86	**NY Islanders**	**NHL**	**7**	**0**	**1**	**1**	**16**	**1**	**0**	**0**	**0**	**0**
	Springfield	AHL	71	35	36	71	127	....	....	....	....	....
1986-87	**NY Islanders**	**NHL**	**72**	**7**	**10**	**17**	**175**	**14**	**1**	**4**	**5**	**25**
1987-88	**NY Islanders**	**NHL**	**80**	**24**	**34**	**58**	**198**	**6**	**1**	**0**	**1**	**14**
1988-89	**NY Islanders**	**NHL**	**71**	**20**	**18**	**38**	**144**	....	....	....	....	....
1989-90	**NY Islanders**	**NHL**	**75**	**15**	**21**	**36**	**129**	**4**	**0**	**0**	**0**	**10**
1990-91	**NY Islanders**	**NHL**	**2**	**0**	**0**	**0**	**5**	....	....	....	....	....
	Capital Dist.	AHL	43	11	21	32	131	....	....	....	....	....
1991-92	**Detroit**	**NHL**	**58**	**3**	**8**	**11**	**133**	**9**	**2**	**0**	**2**	**17**
1992-93	**Winnipeg**	**NHL**	**7**	**0**	**1**	**1**	**2**	....	....	....	....	....
	Moncton	AHL	36	6	10	16	85	5	0	2	2	11
	NHL Totals		**391**	**72**	**94**	**166**	**826**	**38**	**5**	**4**	**9**	**70**

a WHL First All-Star Team, West Division (1984)

Traded to **Detroit** by **NY Islanders** with future considerations for Rick Green, May 26, 1991. Traded to **Winnipeg** by **Detroit** to complete June 11, 1993 trade in which Paul Ysebaert was traded to Winnipeg with future considerations for Aaron Ward and Toronto's fourth round choice (previously acquired by Winnipeg — Detroit selected John Jakopin) in 1993 Entry Draft, June 18, 1993.

KERR, TIM

Center/Right wing. Shoots right. 6'3", 230 lbs. Born, Windsor, Ont., January 5, 1960.

			Regular Season					Playoffs				
Season	Club	Lea	GP	G	A	TP	PIM	GP	G	A	TP	PIM
1978-79	Kingston	OHA	57	17	25	42	27	6	1	1	2	2
1979-80	Kingston	OHA	63	40	33	73	39	3	0	1	1	16
	Maine	AHL	7	2	4	6	2	....	....	....	....	....
1980-81	**Philadelphia**	**NHL**	**68**	**22**	**23**	**45**	**84**	**10**	**1**	**3**	**4**	**2**
1981-82	**Philadelphia**	**NHL**	**61**	**21**	**30**	**51**	**138**	**4**	**0**	**2**	**2**	**2**
1982-83	**Philadelphia**	**NHL**	**24**	**11**	**8**	**19**	**6**	**2**	**2**	**0**	**2**	**0**
1983-84	**Philadelphia**	**NHL**	**79**	**54**	**39**	**93**	**29**	**3**	**0**	**0**	**0**	**0**
1984-85	**Philadelphia**	**NHL**	**74**	**54**	**44**	**98**	**57**	**12**	**10**	**4**	**14**	**13**
1985-86	**Philadelphia**	**NHL**	**76**	**58**	**26**	**84**	**79**	**5**	**3**	**3**	**6**	**8**
1986-87a	**Philadelphia**	**NHL**	**75**	**58**	**37**	**95**	**57**	**12**	**8**	**5**	**13**	**2**
1987-88	**Philadelphia**	**NHL**	**8**	**3**	**2**	**5**	**12**	**6**	**1**	**3**	**4**	**4**
1988-89b	**Philadelphia**	**NHL**	**69**	**48**	**40**	**88**	**73**	**19**	**14**	**11**	**25**	**27**
1989-90	**Philadelphia**	**NHL**	**40**	**24**	**24**	**48**	**34**	....	....	....	....	....
1990-91	**Philadelphia**	**NHL**	**27**	**10**	**14**	**24**	**8**	....	....	....	....	....
1991-92	**NY Rangers**	**NHL**	**32**	**7**	**11**	**18**	**12**	**8**	**1**	**0**	**1**	**0**
1992-93	**Hartford**	**NHL**	**22**	**0**	**6**	**6**	**7**	....	....	....	....	....
	NHL Totals		**655**	**370**	**304**	**674**	**596**	**81**	**40**	**31**	**71**	**58**

a NHL Second All-Star Team (1987)
b Won Bill Masterton Award (1989)

Played in NHL All-Star Game (1984-86)

Signed as a free agent by **Philadelphia**, October 25, 1979. Claimed by **San Jose** from **Philadelphia** in Expansion Draft, May 30, 1991. Traded to **NY Rangers** by **San Jose** for Brian Mullen and future considerations, May 30, 1991. Traded to **Hartford** by **NY Rangers** for future considerations, July 9, 1992.

KESA, DANNY

Right wing. Shoots right. 6', 208 lbs. Born, Vancouver, B.C., November 23, 1971.
(Vancouver's 5th choice, 95th overall, in 1991 Entry Draft).

			Regular Season					Playoffs				
Season	Club	Lea	GP	G	A	TP	PIM	GP	G	A	TP	PIM
1990-91	Prince Albert	WHL	69	30	23	53	116	3	1	1	2	0
1991-92	Prince Albert	WHL	62	46	51	97	201	10	9	10	19	27
1992-93	Hamilton	AHL	62	16	24	40	76	....	....	....	....	....

KESKINEN, ESA (KEHS-kee-nehn)

Center. Shoots right. 5'9", 198 lbs. Born, Ylojarvi, Finland, February 3, 1965.
(Calgary's 6th choice, 101st overall, in 1985 Entry Draft).

			Regular Season					Playoffs				
Season	Club	Lea	GP	G	A	TP	PIM	GP	G	A	TP	PIM
1982-83	FoPS	Fin.2	15	5	14	19	8	4	4	6	10	0
1983-84	TPS	Fin.	31	10	25	35	0	6	0	0	0	0
1984-85	TPS	Fin.	35	11	22	33	66	10	2	3	5	0
1985-86	TPS	Fin.	36	18	28	46	4	7	2	0	2	0
1986-87	TPS	Fin.	46	25	36	61	4	5	1	1	2	0
1987-88	TPS	Fin.	44	14	55	69	14	....	....	....	....	....
1988-89	Lukko	Fin.	41	24	46	70	12	....	....	....	....	....
1989-90	Lukko	Fin.	44	25	26	51	16	....	....	....	....	....
1990-91	Lukko	Fin.	44	17	51	68	14	....	....	....	....	....
1991-92	TPS	Fin.	44	24	45	69	12	3	1	1	2	0
1992-93	TPS	Fin.	46	16	43	59	12	12	1	6	7	4

KHMYLEV, YURI (kheh-meh-LUHV)

Left wing. Shoots right. 6'1", 189 lbs. Born, Moscow, Soviet Union, August 9, 1964.
(Buffalo's 7th choice, 108th overall, in 1992 Entry Draft).

			Regular Season					Playoffs				
Season	Club	Lea	GP	G	A	TP	PIM	GP	G	A	TP	PIM
1981-82	Soviet Wings	USSR	8	2	2	4	2	....	....	....	....	....
1982-83	Soviet Wings	USSR	51	9	7	16	14	....	....	....	....	....
1983-84	Soviet Wings	USSR	43	7	8	15	10	....	....	....	....	....
1984-85	Soviet Wings	USSR	30	11	4	15	24	....	....	....	....	....
1985-86	Soviet Wings	USSR	40	24	9	33	22	....	....	....	....	....
1986-87	Soviet Wings	USSR	40	15	15	30	48	....	....	....	....	....
1987-88	Soviet Wings	USSR	48	21	8	29	46	....	....	....	....	....
1988-89	Soviet Wings	USSR	44	16	18	34	38	....	....	....	....	....
1989-90	Soviet Wings	USSR	44	14	13	27	30	....	....	....	....	....
1990-91	Soviet Wings	USSR	45	25	14	39	26	....	....	....	....	....
1991-92	Soviet Wings	CIS	42	19	17	36	20	....	....	....	....	....
1992-93	**Buffalo**	**NHL**	**68**	**20**	**19**	**39**	**28**	**8**	**4**	**3**	**7**	**4**
	NHL Totals		**68**	**20**	**19**	**39**	**28**	**8**	**4**	**3**	**7**	**4**

KHOLOMEYEV, ALEXANDER (khoh-MAY-ehv)

Left wing. Shoots left. 6'1", 194 lbs. Born, Leningrad, Soviet Union, March 23, 1969.
(San Jose's 10th choice, 219th overall, in 1992 Entry Draft).

			Regular Season					Playoffs				
Season	Club	Lea	GP	G	A	TP	PIM	GP	G	A	TP	PIM
1988-89	Zvezda	USSR 3	5	2	1	3	2					
1989-90	Izhorets	USSR 2	63	16	8	24	36					
1990-91	Izhorets	USSR 2	64	35	30	65	88					
1991-92	Izhorets	CIS 3	61	41	24	65	154					
1992-93	Fort Worth	CHL	42	23	22	45	124					

KHOMUTOV, ANDREI (hoh-moo-TAHF)

Right wing. Shoots left. 5'10", 176 lbs. Born, Yaroslavl, Soviet Union, April 21, 1961.
(Quebec's 12th choice, 190th overall, in 1989 Entry Draft).

			Regular Season					Playoffs				
Season	Club	Lea	GP	G	A	TP	PIM	GP	G	A	TP	PIM
1979-80	CSKA	USSR	4	0	0	0	0					
1980-81	CSKA	USSR	43	23	18	41	4					
1981-82	CSKA	USSR	44	17	13	30	12					
1982-83	CSKA	USSR	44	21	17	38	6					
1983-84	CSKA	USSR	39	17	9	26	14					
1984-85	CSKA	USSR	37	21	13	34	18					
1985-86	CSKA	USSR	38	14	15	29	10					
1986-87	CSKA	USSR	33	15	18	33	22					
1987-88	CSKA	USSR	48	29	14	43	22					
1988-89	CSKA	USSR	44	19	16	35	14					
1989-90a	CSKA	USSR	47	21	14	35	16					
1990-91	Fribourg	Switz.	36	39	43	82	....	8	13	12	25	....
1991-92	Fribourg	Switz.	35	31	43	74	34	14	10	12	22	6
1992-93	Fribourg	Switz.	27	23	36	59	14					

a Soviet Player of the Year (1990)

KHRISTICH, DIMITRI (kris-tich)

Left wing/Center. Shoots right. 6'2", 195 lbs. Born, Kiev, Soviet Union, July 23, 1969.
(Washington's 6th choice, 120th overall, in 1988 Entry Draft).

			Regular Season					Playoffs				
Season	Club	Lea	GP	G	A	TP	PIM	GP	G	A	TP	PIM
1985-86	Sokol Kiev	USSR	4	0	0	0	0					
1986-87	Sokol Kiev	USSR	20	3	0	3	4					
1987-88	Sokol Kiev	USSR	37	9	1	10	18					
1988-89	Sokol Kiev	USSR	42	17	10	27	15					
1989-90	Sokol Kiev	USSR	47	14	22	36	32					
1990-91	Sokol Kiev	USSR	28	10	12	22	20					
	Washington	**NHL**	**40**	**13**	**14**	**27**	**21**	**11**	**1**	**3**	**4**	**6**
	Baltimore	AHL	3	0	0	0	0					
1991-92	**Washington**	**NHL**	**80**	**36**	**37**	**73**	**35**	**7**	**3**	**2**	**5**	**15**
1992-93	**Washington**	**NHL**	**64**	**31**	**35**	**66**	**28**	**6**	**2**	**5**	**7**	**2**
	NHL Totals		**184**	**80**	**86**	**166**	**84**	**24**	**6**	**10**	**16**	**23**

KIENASS, TORSTEN

Defense. Shoots left. 5'11", 180 lbs. Born, Berlin, East Germany, February 23, 1971.
(Boston's 11th choice, 260th overall, in 1991 Entry Draft).

			Regular Season					Playoffs				
Season	Club	Lea	GP	G	A	TP	PIM	GP	G	A	TP	PIM
1990-91	Dynamo Berlin	Ger.	27	1	1	2	19	7	1	0	1	4
1991-92	Dynamo Berlin	Ger.2	45	8	6	14	33					
1992-93	Ratingen	Ger.	44	3	12	15	16	3	0	0	0	2

KIMBLE, DARIN

Right wing. Shoots right. 6'2", 210 lbs. Born, Lucky Lake, Sask., November 22, 1968.
(Quebec's 5th choice, 66th overall, in 1988 Entry Draft).

			Regular Season					Playoffs				
Season	Club	Lea	GP	G	A	TP	PIM	GP	G	A	TP	PIM
1985-86	Calgary	WHL	37	14	8	22	93					
	N. Westminster	WHL	11	1	1	2	22					
	Brandon	WHL	15	1	6	7	39					
1986-87	Prince Albert	WHL	68	17	13	30	190					
1987-88	Prince Albert	WHL	67	35	36	71	307	10	3	2	5	4
1988-89	**Quebec**	**NHL**	**26**	**3**	**1**	**4**	**154**					
	Halifax	AHL	39	8	6	14	188					
1989-90	**Quebec**	**NHL**	**44**	**5**	**5**	**10**	**185**					
	Halifax	AHL	18	6	6	12	37	6	1	1	2	61
1990-91	**Quebec**	**NHL**	**35**	**2**	**5**	**7**	**114**					
	Halifax	AHL	7	1	4	5	20					
	St. Louis	**NHL**	**26**	**1**	**1**	**2**	**128**	**13**	**0**	**0**	**0**	**38**
1991-92	**St. Louis**	**NHL**	**46**	**1**	**3**	**4**	**166**	**5**	**0**	**0**	**0**	**7**
1992-93	**Boston**	**NHL**	**55**	**7**	**3**	**10**	**177**	**4**	**0**	**0**	**0**	**2**
	Providence	AHL	12	1	4	5	34					
	NHL Totals		**232**	**19**	**18**	**37**	**924**	**22**	**0**	**0**	**0**	**47**

Traded to **St. Louis** by **Quebec** for Herb Raglan, Tony Twist and Andy Rymsha, February 4, 1991. Traded to **Tampa Bay** by **St. Louis** with Pat Jablonski and Steve Tuttle for future considerations, June 19, 1992. Traded to **Boston** by **Tampa Bay** with future considerations for Ken Hodge and Matt Hervey, September 4, 1992.

KING, DEREK

Left wing. Shoots left. 6'1", 203 lbs. Born, Hamilton, Ont., February 11, 1967.
(NY Islanders' 2nd choice, 13th overall, in 1985 Entry Draft).

			Regular Season					Playoffs				
Season	Club	Lea	GP	G	A	TP	PIM	GP	G	A	TP	PIM
1984-85a	S.S. Marie	OHL	63	35	38	73	106	16	3	13	16	11
1985-86	S.S. Marie	OHL	25	12	17	29	33					
	Oshawa	OHL	19	8	13	21	15	6	3	2	5	13
1986-87	**NY Islanders**	**NHL**	**2**	**0**	**0**	**0**	**0**					
b	Oshawa	OHL	57	53	53	106	74	17	14	10	24	40
1987-88	**NY Islanders**	**NHL**	**55**	**12**	**24**	**36**	**30**	**5**	**0**	**2**	**2**	**2**
	Springfield	AHL	10	7	6	13	6					
1988-89	**NY Islanders**	**NHL**	**60**	**14**	**29**	**43**	**14**					
	Springfield	AHL	4	4	0	4	0					
1989-90	**NY Islanders**	**NHL**	**46**	**13**	**27**	**40**	**20**	**4**	**0**	**0**	**0**	**4**
	Springfield	AHL	21	11	12	23	33					
1990-91	**NY Islanders**	**NHL**	**66**	**19**	**26**	**45**	**44**					
1991-92	**NY Islanders**	**NHL**	**80**	**40**	**38**	**78**	**46**					
1992-93	**NY Islanders**	**NHL**	**77**	**38**	**38**	**76**	**47**	**18**	**3**	**11**	**14**	**14**
	NHL Totals		**386**	**136**	**182**	**318**	**201**	**27**	**3**	**13**	**16**	**20**

a OHL Rookie of the Year (1985)
b OHL First All-Star Team (1987)

KING, KRIS

Left wing. Shoots left. 5'11", 210 lbs. Born, Bracebridge, Ont., February 18, 1966.
(Washington's 4th choice, 80th overall, in 1984 Entry Draft).

			Regular Season					Playoffs				
Season	Club	Lea	GP	G	A	TP	PIM	GP	G	A	TP	PIM
1983-84	Peterborough	OHL	62	13	18	31	168	8	3	3	6	14
1984-85	Peterborough	OHL	61	18	35	53	222	16	2	8	10	28
1985-86	Peterborough	OHL	58	19	40	59	254	8	4	0	4	21
1986-87	Binghamton	AHL	7	0	0	0	18					
	Peterborough	OHL	46	23	33	56	160	12	5	8	13	41
1987-88	**Detroit**	**NHL**	**3**	**1**	**0**	**1**	**2**					
	Adirondack	AHL	76	21	32	53	337	10	4	4	8	53
1988-89	**Detroit**	**NHL**	**55**	**2**	**3**	**5**	**168**	**2**	**0**	**0**	**0**	**2**
1989-90	**NY Rangers**	**NHL**	**68**	**6**	**7**	**13**	**286**	**10**	**0**	**1**	**1**	**38**
1990-91	**NY Rangers**	**NHL**	**72**	**11**	**14**	**25**	**154**	**6**	**2**	**0**	**2**	**36**
1991-92	**NY Rangers**	**NHL**	**79**	**10**	**9**	**19**	**224**	**13**	**4**	**1**	**5**	**14**
1992-93	**NY Rangers**	**NHL**	**30**	**0**	**3**	**3**	**67**					
	Winnipeg	**NHL**	**48**	**8**	**8**	**16**	**136**	**6**	**1**	**1**	**2**	**4**
	NHL Totals		**355**	**38**	**44**	**82**	**1037**	**37**	**7**	**3**	**10**	**94**

Signed as a free agent by **Detroit**, March 23, 1987. Traded to **NY Rangers** by **Detroit** for Chris McRae and Detroit's fifth round choice (previously acquired by NY Rangers — Detroit selected Tony Burns) in 1990 Entry Draft, September 7, 1989. Traded to **Winnipeg** by **NY Rangers** with Tie Domi for Ed Olczyk, December 28, 1992.

KING, STEVE

Right wing. Shoots right. 6', 190 lbs. Born, Greenwich, RI, July 22, 1969.
(NY Rangers' 1st choice, 21st overall, in 1991 Supplemental Draft).

			Regular Season					Playoffs				
Season	Club	Lea	GP	G	A	TP	PIM	GP	G	A	TP	PIM
1989-90	Brown	ECAC	27	19	8	27	53					
1990-91	Brown	ECAC	27	19	15	34	76					
1991-92	Binghamton	AHL	66	27	15	42	56	10	2	0	2	14
1992-93	**NY Rangers**	**NHL**	**24**	**7**	**5**	**12**	**16**					
	Binghamton	AHL	53	35	33	68	100	14	7	9	16	26
	NHL Totals		**24**	**7**	**5**	**12**	**16**					

Claimed by **Anaheim** from **NY Rangers** in Expansion Draft, June 24, 1993.

KINNEAR, GEORDIE

Defense. Shoots left. 6'1", 200 lbs. Born, Simcoe, Ont., July 9, 1973.
(New Jersey's 7th choice, 162nd overall, in 1992 Entry Draft).

			Regular Season					Playoffs				
Season	Club	Lea	GP	G	A	TP	PIM	GP	G	A	TP	PIM
1990-91	Peterborough	OHL	37	1	0	1	76	2	0	0	0	10
1991-92	Peterborough	OHL	63	5	16	21	195	10	0	2	2	36
1992-93	Peterborough	OHL	58	6	22	28	161	19	1	5	6	43

KIRTON, SCOTT

Right wing. Shoots right. 6'4", 215 lbs. Born, Penetanguishene, Ont., October 4, 1971.
(Chicago's 7th choice, 154th overall, in 1991 Entry Draft).

			Regular Season					Playoffs				
Season	Club	Lea	GP	G	A	TP	PIM	GP	G	A	TP	PIM
1991-92	North Dakota	WCHA	37	5	6	11	68					
1992-93	North Dakota	WCHA	30	4	16	20	100					

KISIO, KELLY

Center. Shoots right. 5'10", 185 lbs. Born, Peace River, Alta., September 18, 1959.

			Regular Season					Playoffs				
Season	Club	Lea	GP	G	A	TP	PIM	GP	G	A	TP	PIM
1978-79a	Calgary	WHL	70	60	61	121	73					
1979-80	Calgary	WHL	71	65	73	138	64					
1980-81	Adirondack	AHL	41	10	14	24	43					
	Kalamazoo	IHL	31	27	16	43	48	8	7	7	14	13
1981-82	Dallas	CHL	78	*62	39	101	59	16	*12	*17	*29	38
1982-83	Davos	Switz.	40	49	38	87						
	Detroit	**NHL**	**15**	**4**	**3**	**7**	**0**					
1983-84	**Detroit**	**NHL**	**70**	**23**	**37**	**60**	**34**	**4**	**1**	**0**	**1**	**4**
1984-85	**Detroit**	**NHL**	**75**	**20**	**41**	**61**	**56**	**3**	**0**	**2**	**2**	**2**
1985-86	**Detroit**	**NHL**	**76**	**21**	**48**	**69**	**85**					
1986-87	**NY Rangers**	**NHL**	**70**	**24**	**40**	**64**	**73**	**4**	**0**	**1**	**1**	**2**
1987-88	**NY Rangers**	**NHL**	**77**	**23**	**55**	**78**	**88**					
1988-89	**NY Rangers**	**NHL**	**70**	**26**	**36**	**62**	**91**	**4**	**0**	**0**	**0**	**9**
1989-90	**NY Rangers**	**NHL**	**68**	**22**	**44**	**66**	**105**	**10**	**2**	**8**	**10**	**8**
1990-91	**NY Rangers**	**NHL**	**51**	**15**	**20**	**35**	**58**					
1991-92	**San Jose**	**NHL**	**48**	**11**	**26**	**37**	**54**					
1992-93	**San Jose**	**NHL**	**78**	**26**	**52**	**78**	**90**					
	NHL Totals		**698**	**215**	**402**	**617**	**734**	**25**	**3**	**11**	**14**	**25**

a WHL Rookie of the Year (1979)
Played in NHL All-Star Game (1993)

Signed as a free agent by **Detroit**, May 2, 1983. Traded to **NY Rangers** by **Detroit** with Lane Lambert and Jim Leavins for Glen Hanlon and New York's third round choices in 1987 (Dennis Holland) and 1988 (Guy Dupuis) Entry Drafts, July 29, 1986. Claimed by **Minnesota** from **NY Rangers** in Expansion Draft, May 30, 1991. Traded to **San Jose** by **Minnesota** for Shane Churla, June 3, 1991. Signed as a free agent by **Calgary**, August 18, 1993.

KITCHING, GARY

Center. Shoots left. 6'2", 190 lbs. Born, Thunder Bay, Ont., January 9, 1971.
(Edmonton's 8th choice, 166th overall, in 1991 Entry Draft).

			Regular Season					Playoffs				
Season	Club	Lea	GP	G	A	TP	PIM	GP	G	A	TP	PIM
1991-92	Ferris State	CCHA	36	7	9	16	52					
1992-93	Ferris State	CCHA	28	8	19	27	62					

KIVI, KARRI

Defense. Shoots left. 6', 180 lbs. Born, Turku, Finland, January 31, 1970.
(Vancouver's 11th choice, 233rd overall, in 1990 Entry Draft).

			Regular Season					Playoffs				
Season	Club	Lea	GP	G	A	TP	PIM	GP	G	A	TP	PIM
1988-89	Ilves	Fin.	39	5	7	12	10	5	0	0	0	0
1989-90	Ilves	Fin.	43	6	15	21	14	8	1	4	5	2
1990-91	Ilves	Fin.	43	2	9	11	18					
1991-92	TPS	Fin.	33	3	1	4	14	3	0	0	0	0
1992-93	Kiekko-67	Fin. 2	11	2	7	9	4					
	Assat	Fin.	34	2	11	13	16	8	1	2	3	0

KJELLBERG, PATRIK (CHEHL-buhrg)

Left wing. Shoots left. 6'2", 196 lbs. Born, Falun, Sweden, June 17, 1969.
(Montreal's 4th choice, 83rd overall, in 1988 Entry Draft).

			Regular Season					Playoffs				
Season	Club	Lea	GP	G	A	TP	PIM	GP	G	A	TP	PIM
1986-87	Falun	Swe.2	27	11	13	24	14	....	....	....	....	....
1987-88	Falun	Swe.2	29	15	10	25	6	....	....	....	....	....
1988-89	AIK	Swe.	25	7	9	16	8	....	....	....	....	....
1989-90	AIK	Swe.	33	8	16	24	6	3	1	0	1	0
1990-91	AIK	Swe.	38	4	11	15	18	....	....	....	....	....
1991-92	AIK	Swe.	40	20	13	33	14	3	1	0	1	2
1992-93	**Montreal**	**NHL**	**7**	**0**	**0**	**0**	**2**	....	....	....	....	....
	Fredericton	AHL	41	10	27	37	14	5	2	2	4	0
	NHL Totals		**7**	**0**	**0**	**0**	**2**	....	....	....	....	....

KLASSEN, TODD

Defense. Shoots right. 6', 204 lbs. Born, Saskatoon, Sask., April 17, 1974.
(Pittsburgh's 4th choice, 91st overall, in 1992 Entry Draft).

			Regular Season					Playoffs				
Season	Club	Lea	GP	G	A	TP	PIM	GP	G	A	TP	PIM
1990-91	Tri-City	WHL	67	6	27	33	72	7	0	1	1	2
1991-92a	Tri-City	WHL	69	23	42	65	60	5	0	0	0	2
1992-93	Tri-City	WHL	72	12	35	47	51	4	1	2	3	8

a WHL West Second All-Star Team (1992)

KLATT, TRENT

Right wing. Shoots right. 6'1", 205 lbs. Born, Robbinsdale, MN, January 30, 1971.
(Washington's 5th choice, 82nd overall, in 1989 Entry Draft).

			Regular Season					Playoffs				
Season	Club	Lea	GP	G	A	TP	PIM	GP	G	A	TP	PIM
1989-90	U. Minnesota	WCHA	38	22	14	36	16	....	....	....	....	....
1990-91	U. Minnesota	WCHA	39	16	28	44	58	....	....	....	....	....
1991-92	U. Minnesota	WCHA	41	27	36	63	76	....	....	....	....	....
	Minnesota	**NHL**	**1**	**0**	**0**	**0**	**0**	**6**	**0**	**0**	**0**	**2**
1992-93	**Minnesota**	**NHL**	**47**	**4**	**19**	**23**	**38**	....	....	....	....	....
	Kalamazoo	IHL	31	8	11	19	18	....	....	....	....	....
	NHL Totals		**48**	**4**	**19**	**23**	**38**	**6**	**0**	**0**	**0**	**2**

Traded to **Minnesota** by **Washington** with Steve Maltais for Shawn Chambers, June 21, 1991.

KLEE, KEN

Defense. Shoots right. 6'1", 200 lbs. Born, Indianapolis, IN, April 24, 1971.
(Washington's 11th choice, 177th overall, in 1990 Entry Draft).

			Regular Season					Playoffs				
Season	Club	Lea	GP	G	A	TP	PIM	GP	G	A	TP	PIM
1989-90	Bowling Green	CCHA	39	0	5	5	52	....	....	....	....	....
1990-91	Bowling Green	CCHA	37	7	28	35	50	....	....	....	....	....
1991-92	Bowling Green	CCHA	10	0	1	1	14	....	....	....	....	....
1992-93	Baltimore	AHL	77	4	14	18	93	7	0	1	1	15

KLEMM, JON

Defense. Shoots right. 6'3", 200 lbs. Born, Cranbrook, B.C., January 8, 1970.

			Regular Season					Playoffs				
Season	Club	Lea	GP	G	A	TP	PIM	GP	G	A	TP	PIM
1988-89	Seattle	WHL	2	1	1	2	0	....	....	....	....	....
	Spokane	WHL	66	6	34	40	42	....	....	....	....	....
1989-90	Spokane	WHL	66	3	28	31	100	6	1	1	2	5
1990-91	Spokane	WHL	72	7	58	65	65	15	3	6	9	8
1991-92	**Quebec**	**NHL**	**4**	**0**	**1**	**1**	**0**	....	....	....	....	....
	Halifax	AHL	70	6	13	19	40	....	....	....	....	....
1992-93	Halifax	AHL	80	3	20	23	32	....	....	....	....	....
	NHL Totals		**4**	**0**	**1**	**1**	**0**	....	....	....	....	....

Signed as a free agent by **Quebec**, May 14, 1991.

KLIMA, PETR (KLEE-muh)

Right/Left wing. Shoots right. 6', 190 lbs. Born, Chomutov, Czech., December 23, 1964.
(Detroit's 5th choice, 86th overall, in 1983 Entry Draft).

			Regular Season					Playoffs				
Season	Club	Lea	GP	G	A	TP	PIM	GP	G	A	TP	PIM
1981-82	Litvinov	Czech.	18	7	3	10	8	....	....	....	....	....
1982-83	Litvinov	Czech.	44	19	17	36	74	....	....	....	....	....
1983-84	Dukla Jihlava	Czech.	41	20	16	36	46	....	....	....	....	....
1984-85	Dukla Jihlava	Czech.	35	23	22	45	76	....	....	....	....	....
1985-86	**Detroit**	**NHL**	**74**	**32**	**24**	**56**	**16**	....	....	....	....	....
1986-87	**Detroit**	**NHL**	**77**	**30**	**23**	**53**	**42**	**13**	**1**	**2**	**3**	**4**
1987-88	**Detroit**	**NHL**	**78**	**37**	**25**	**62**	**46**	**12**	**10**	**8**	**18**	**10**
1988-89	**Detroit**	**NHL**	**51**	**25**	**16**	**41**	**44**	**6**	**2**	**4**	**6**	**19**
	Adirondack	AHL	5	5	1	6	4	....	....	....	....	....
1989-90	**Detroit**	**NHL**	**13**	**5**	**5**	**10**	**6**	....	....	....	....	....
	Edmonton	**NHL**	**63**	**25**	**28**	**53**	**66**	**21**	**5**	**0**	**5**	**8**
1990-91	**Edmonton**	**NHL**	**70**	**40**	**28**	**68**	**113**	**18**	**7**	**6**	**13**	**16**
1991-92	**Edmonton**	**NHL**	**57**	**21**	**13**	**34**	**52**	**15**	**1**	**4**	**5**	**8**
1992-93	**Edmonton**	**NHL**	**68**	**32**	**16**	**48**	**100**	....	....	....	....	....
	NHL Totals		**551**	**247**	**178**	**425**	**485**	**85**	**26**	**24**	**50**	**65**

Traded to **Edmonton** by **Detroit** with Joe Murphy, Adam Graves and Jeff Sharples for Jimmy Carson, Kevin McClelland and Edmonton's fifth round choice (later traded to Montreal — Montreal selected Brad Layzell) in 1991 Entry Draft, November 2, 1989. Traded to **Tampa Bay** by **Edmonton** for future considerations, June 16, 1993.

KLIMOVICH, SERGEI (klee-MOH-vich)

Center. Shoots right. 6'3", 189 lbs. Born, Novosibirsk, Soviet Union, March 8, 1974.
(Chicago's 3rd choice, 41st overall, in 1992 Entry Draft).

			Regular Season					Playoffs				
Season	Club	Lea	GP	G	A	TP	PIM	GP	G	A	TP	PIM
1991-92	Moscow D'amo	CIS	3	0	0	0	0	....	....	....	....	....
1992-93	Moscow D'amo	CIS	30	4	1	5	14	10	1	0	1	2

KLIMT, TOMAS

Center. Shoots left. 6'1", 183 lbs. Born, Plzen, Czech., December 26, 1973.
(NY Islanders' 3rd choice, 104th overall, in 1992 Entry Draft).

			Regular Season					Playoffs				
Season	Club	Lea	GP	G	A	TP	PIM	GP	G	A	TP	PIM
1991-92	Skoda Plzen	Czech.	40	3	6	9	4	....	....	....	....	....
1992-93	Skoda Plzen	Czech.	34	3	8	11	....	....	....	....	....	....

KLIPPENSTEIN, WADE

Left wing. Shoots left. 6'3", 219 lbs. Born, Boissevain, Man., May 9, 1970.
(Quebec's 11th choice, 232nd overall, in 1990 Entry Draft).

			Regular Season					Playoffs				
Season	Club	Lea	GP	G	A	TP	PIM	GP	G	A	TP	PIM
1989-90	Alaska-Fair.	G.N.	37	17	14	31	....	....	....	....	....	....
1990-91	Alaska-Fair.	G.N.	35	22	11	33	32	....	....	....	....	....
1991-92	Alaska-Fair.	G.N.	33	12	13	25	108	....	....	....	....	....
1992-93	Alaska-Fair.	CCHA	36	29	22	51	48	....	....	....	....	....

KNUBLE, MICHAEL

Right wing. Shoots right. 6'3", 208 lbs. Born, Toronto, Ont., July 4, 1972.
(Detroit's 4th choice, 76th overall, in 1991 Entry Draft).

			Regular Season					Playoffs				
Season	Club	Lea	GP	G	A	TP	PIM	GP	G	A	TP	PIM
1991-92	U. of Michigan	CCHA	43	7	8	15	48	....	....	....	....	....
1992-93	U. of Michigan	CCHA	39	26	16	42	57	....	....	....	....	....

KNUTSEN, ESPEN

Center. Shoots left. 5'11", 172 lbs. Born, Oslo, Norway, January 12, 1972.
(Hartford's 9th choice, 204th overall, in 1990 Entry Draft).

			Regular Season					Playoffs				
Season	Club	Lea	GP	G	A	TP	PIM	GP	G	A	TP	PIM
1989-90	Valerengen	Nor.	34	22	26	48	....	....	....	....	....	....
1990-91	Valerengen	Nor.	31	30	24	54	42	5	3	4	7	....
1991-92	Valerengen	Nor.	30	28	26	54	37	8	7	8	15	....
1992-93	Valerengen	Nor.	13	11	13	24	4	....	....	....	....	....

KOCH, PAUL

Defense. Shoots left. 6'3", 205 lbs. Born, St. Paul, MN, June 30, 1971.
(Quebec's 12th choice, 200th overall, in 1991 Entry Draft).

			Regular Season					Playoffs				
Season	Club	Lea	GP	G	A	TP	PIM	GP	G	A	TP	PIM
1991-92	U. of Denver	WCHA	36	4	13	17	48	....	....	....	....	....
1992-93	U. of Denver	WCHA	37	0	9	9	111	....	....	....	....	....

KOCUR, JOEY (KOH-suhr)

Right wing. Shoots right. 6', 201 lbs. Born, Calgary, Alta., December 21, 1964.
(Detroit's 6th choice, 88th overall, in 1983 Entry Draft).

			Regular Season					Playoffs				
Season	Club	Lea	GP	G	A	TP	PIM	GP	G	A	TP	PIM
1982-83	Saskatoon	WHL	62	23	17	40	289	6	2	3	5	25
1983-84	Saskatoon	WHL	69	40	41	81	258	....	....	....	....	....
	Adirondack	AHL	....	....	....	....	....	5	0	0	0	20
1984-85	**Detroit**	**NHL**	**17**	**1**	**0**	**1**	**64**	**3**	**1**	**0**	**1**	**5**
	Adirondack	AHL	47	12	7	19	171	....	....	....	....	....
1985-86	**Detroit**	**NHL**	**59**	**9**	**6**	**15**	***377**	....	....	....	....	....
	Adirondack	AHL	9	6	2	8	34	....	....	....	....	....
1986-87	**Detroit**	**NHL**	**77**	**9**	**9**	**18**	**276**	**16**	**2**	**3**	**5**	**71**
1987-88	**Detroit**	**NHL**	**63**	**7**	**7**	**14**	**263**	**10**	**0**	**1**	**1**	**13**
1988-89	**Detroit**	**NHL**	**60**	**9**	**9**	**18**	**213**	**3**	**0**	**1**	**1**	**6**
1989-90	**Detroit**	**NHL**	**71**	**16**	**20**	**36**	**268**	....	....	....	....	....
1990-91	**Detroit**	**NHL**	**52**	**5**	**4**	**9**	**253**	....	....	....	....	....
	NY Rangers	**NHL**	**5**	**0**	**0**	**0**	**36**	**6**	**0**	**2**	**2**	**21**
1991-92	**NY Rangers**	**NHL**	**51**	**7**	**4**	**11**	**121**	**12**	**1**	**1**	**2**	**38**
1992-93	**NY Rangers**	**NHL**	**65**	**3**	**6**	**9**	**131**	....	....	....	....	....
	NHL Totals		**520**	**66**	**65**	**131**	**2002**	**50**	**4**	**8**	**12**	**154**

Traded to **NY Rangers** by **Detroit** with Per Djoos for Kevin Miller, Jim Cummins and Dennis Vial, March 5, 1991.

KOCUR, KORY

Right wing. Shoots right. 5'11", 188 lbs. Born, Kelvington, Sask., March 6, 1969.
(Detroit's 1st choice, 17th overall, in 1988 Entry Draft).

			Regular Season					Playoffs				
Season	Club	Lea	GP	G	A	TP	PIM	GP	G	A	TP	PIM
1986-87	Saskatoon	WHL	62	13	17	30	98	4	0	0	0	7
1987-88	Saskatoon	WHL	69	34	37	71	95	10	5	4	9	18
1988-89	Saskatoon	WHL	66	45	57	102	111	8	7	11	18	15
1989-90	Adirondack	AHL	79	18	37	55	36	6	1	2	3	2
1990-91	Adirondack	AHL	65	8	13	21	83	2	0	0	0	12
1991-92	Fort Wayne	IHL	69	25	40	65	68	7	3	3	6	49
1992-93	Adirondack	AHL	2	0	0	0	0	....	....	....	....	....
	Fort Wayne	IHL	66	21	36	57	77	4	1	1	2	6

KOIVU, SAKU (KOY-VOO, SA-KOO)

Center. Shoots left. 5'9", 165 lbs. Born, Turku, Finland, November 23, 1974.
(Montreal's 1st choice, 21st overall, in 1993 Entry Draft).

			Regular Season					Playoffs				
Season	Club	Lea	GP	G	A	TP	PIM	GP	G	A	TP	PIM
1992-93	TPS	Fin.	46	3	7	10	28	11	3	2	5	2

KOIVUNEN, PETRO

Right wing. Shoots right. 6', 183 lbs. Born, Espoo, Finland, May 30, 1970.
(Edmonton's 2nd choice, 39th overall, in 1988 Entry Draft).

			Regular Season					Playoffs				
Season	Club	Lea	GP	G	A	TP	PIM	GP	G	A	TP	PIM
1988-89	Espoo	Fin.2	39	32	37	69	42	....	....	....	....	....
1989-90	Espoo	Fin.2	39	24	35	59	28	....	....	....	....	....
1990-91	HIFK	Fin.	39	8	15	23	20	3	0	1	1	4
1991-92	HIFK	Fin.	41	11	3	14	0	8	0	0	0	2
1992-93	Kiekko-Espoo	Fin.	47	12	13	25	24	....	....	....	....	....

KOLNIK, LUBOMIR (KOHL-neek)

Right wing. Shoots left. 5'11", 178 lbs. Born, Nitra, Czechoslovakia, January 23, 1968.
(New Jersey's 9th choice, 116th overall, in 1990 Entry Draft).

			Regular Season					Playoffs				
Season	Club	Lea	GP	G	A	TP	PIM	GP	G	A	TP	PIM
1987-88	Dukla Trencin	Czech.	42	14	8	22	12	....	....	....	....	....
1988-89	Dukla Trencin	Czech.	36	10	7	17	8	....	....	....	....	....
1989-90	Dukla Trencin	Czech.	53	37	25	62	....	....	....	....	....	....
1990-91	Dukla Trencin	Czech.	58	39	40	79	12	....	....	....	....	....
1991-92	Dukla Trencin	Czech.	49	26	23	49	26	....	....	....	....	....
1992-93	JoKP	Fin. 2	44	46	38	84	26	6	1	2	3	10

KOLSTAD, DEAN

Defense. Shoots left. 6'6", 220 lbs.   Born, Edmonton, Alta., June 16, 1968.
(Minnesota's 3rd choice, 33rd overall, in 1986 Entry Draft).

				Regular Season					Playoffs			
Season	Club	Lea	GP	G	A	TP	PIM	GP	G	A	TP	PIM
1985-86	N. Westminster	WHL	13	0	0	0	16	....	....	....	....	....
	Prince Albert	WHL	54	2	15	17	80	20	5	3	8	26
1986-87	Prince Albert	WHL	72	17	37	54	112	8	1	5	6	8
1987-88	Prince Albert	WHL	72	14	37	51	121	10	0	9	9	20
1988-89	**Minnesota**	**NHL**	25	1	5	6	42	....	....	....	....	....
	Kalamazoo	IHL	51	10	23	33	91	6	1	0	1	23
1989-90a	Kalamazoo	IHL	77	10	40	50	172	10	3	4	7	14
1990-91	**Minnesota**	**NHL**	5	0	0	0	15	....	....	....	....	....
	Kalamazoo	IHL	33	4	8	12	50	9	1	6	7	4
1991-92	Kansas City	IHL	74	9	20	29	83	15	3	6	9	8
1992-93	**San Jose**	**NHL**	10	0	2	2	12	....	....	....	....	....
	Kansas City	IHL	63	9	21	30	79	3	0	0	0	2
	NHL Totals		40	1	7	8	69					

a IHL Second All-Star Team (1990)

Claimed by **San Jose** from **Minnesota** in Dispersal Draft, May 30, 1991.

KONOWALCHUK, BRIAN

Center. Shoots left. 5'11", 180 lbs.   Born, Prince Albert, Sask., October 14, 1971.
(San Jose's 1st choice, 3rd overall, in 1992 Supplemental Draft).

				Regular Season					Playoffs			
Season	Club	Lea	GP	G	A	TP	PIM	GP	G	A	TP	PIM
1990-91	U. of Denver	WCHA	38	8	19	27	40	....	....	....	....	....
1991-92	U. of Denver	WCHA	33	8	17	25	53	....	....	....	....	....
1992-93	U. of Denver	WCHA	37	12	20	32	59	....	....	....	....	....

KONOWALCHUK, STEVE

Center. Shoots left. 6', 180 lbs.   Born, Salt Lake City, UT, November 11, 1972.
(Washington's 5th choice, 58th overall, in 1991 Entry Draft).

				Regular Season					Playoffs			
Season	Club	Lea	GP	G	A	TP	PIM	GP	G	A	TP	PIM
1990-91	Portland	WHL	72	43	49	92	78	....	....	....	....	....
1991-92	**Washington**	**NHL**	1	0	0	0	0	....	....	....	....	....
	Baltimore	AHL	3	1	1	2	0	....	....	....	....	....
a	Portland	WHL	64	51	53	104	95	6	3	6	9	12
1992-93	**Washington**	**NHL**	36	4	7	11	16	2	0	1	1	0
	Baltimore	AHL	37	18	28	46	74	....	....	....	....	....
	NHL Totals		37	4	7	11	16	2	0	1	1	0

a WHL West First All-Star Team (1992)

KONROYD, STEPHEN MARK (STEVE)   (KON-royd)

Defense. Shoots left. 6'1", 195 lbs.   Born, Scarborough, Ont., February 10, 1961.
(Atlanta's 4th choice, 39th overall, in 1980 Entry Draft).

				Regular Season					Playoffs			
Season	Club	Lea	GP	G	A	TP	PIM	GP	G	A	TP	PIM
1979-80	Oshawa	OHA	62	11	23	34	133	7	0	2	2	14
1980-81	**Calgary**	**NHL**	4	0	0	0	4	....	....	....	....	....
a	Oshawa	OHA	59	19	47	68	232	11	3	11	14	35
1981-82	**Calgary**	**NHL**	63	3	14	17	78	3	0	0	0	12
	Oklahoma City	CHL	14	2	3	5	15	....	....	....	....	....
1982-83	**Calgary**	**NHL**	79	4	13	17	73	9	2	1	3	18
1983-84	**Calgary**	**NHL**	80	1	13	14	94	8	1	2	3	8
1984-85	**Calgary**	**NHL**	64	3	23	26	73	4	1	4	5	2
1985-86	**Calgary**	**NHL**	59	7	20	27	64	....	....	....	....	....
	NY Islanders	**NHL**	14	0	5	5	16	3	0	0	0	6
1986-87	**NY Islanders**	**NHL**	72	5	16	21	70	14	1	4	5	10
1987-88	**NY Islanders**	**NHL**	62	2	15	17	99	6	1	0	1	4
1988-89	**NY Islanders**	**NHL**	21	1	5	6	2	....	....	....	....	....
	Chicago	**NHL**	57	5	7	12	40	16	2	0	2	10
1989-90	**Chicago**	**NHL**	75	3	14	17	34	20	1	3	4	19
1990-91	**Chicago**	**NHL**	70	0	12	12	40	6	1	0	1	8
1991-92	**Chicago**	**NHL**	49	2	14	16	65	....	....	....	....	....
	Hartford	**NHL**	33	2	10	12	32	7	0	1	1	2
1992-93	**Hartford**	**NHL**	59	3	11	14	63	....	....	....	....	....
	Detroit	**NHL**	6	0	1	1	4	1	0	0	0	0
	NHL Totals		867	41	193	234	851	97	10	15	25	99

a OHA Second All-Star Team (1981)

Traded to **NY Islanders** by **Calgary** with Richard Kromm for John Tonelli, March 11, 1986. Traded to **Chicago** by **NY Islanders** with Bob Bassen for Marc Bergevin and Gary Nylund, November 25, 1988. Traded to **Hartford** by **Chicago** for Rob Brown, January 24, 1992. Traded to **Detroit** by **Hartford** for Detroit's sixth round choice (later traded back to Detroit — Detroit selected Tim Spitzig) in 1993 Entry Draft, March 22, 1993.

KONSTANTINOV, VLADIMIR   (kohn-stahn-TEE-nahf)

Defense. Shoots right. 5'11", 176 lbs.   Born, Murmansk, Soviet Union, March 19, 1967.
(Detroit's 12th choice, 221st overall, in 1989 Entry Draft).

				Regular Season					Playoffs			
Season	Club	Lea	GP	G	A	TP	PIM	GP	G	A	TP	PIM
1984-85	CSKA	USSR	40	1	4	5	10	....	....	....	....	....
1985-86	CSKA	USSR	26	4	3	7	12	....	....	....	....	....
1986-87	CSKA	USSR	35	2	2	4	19	....	....	....	....	....
1987-88	CSKA	USSR	50	3	6	9	32	....	....	....	....	....
1988-89	CSKA	USSR	37	7	8	15	20	....	....	....	....	....
1989-90	CSKA	USSR	47	14	14	28	44	....	....	....	....	....
1990-91	CSKA	USSR	45	5	12	17	42	....	....	....	....	....
1991-92a	**Detroit**	**NHL**	79	8	26	34	172	11	0	1	1	16
1992-93	**Detroit**	**NHL**	82	5	17	22	137	7	0	1	1	8
	NHL Totals		161	13	43	56	309	18	0	2	2	24

a NHL/Upper Deck All-Rookie Team (1992)

KONTOS, CHRISTOPHER (CHRIS)   (KONN-tohs)

Left wing/Center. Shoots left. 6'1", 195 lbs.   Born, Toronto, Ont., December 10, 1963.
(NY Rangers' 1st choice, 15th overall, in 1982 Entry Draft).

				Regular Season					Playoffs			
Season	Club	Lea	GP	G	A	TP	PIM	GP	G	A	TP	PIM
1980-81	Sudbury	OHA	57	17	27	44	36	....	....	....	....	....
1981-82	Sudbury	OHL	12	6	6	12	18	....	....	....	....	....
	Toronto	OHL	59	36	56	92	68	10	7	9	16	2
1982-83	**NY Rangers**	**NHL**	44	8	7	15	33	....	....	....	....	....
	Toronto	OHL	28	21	33	54	23	....	....	....	....	....
1983-84	**NY Rangers**	**NHL**	6	0	1	1	8	....	....	....	....	....
	Tulsa	CHL	21	5	13	18	8	....	....	....	....	....
1984-85	**NY Rangers**	**NHL**	28	4	8	12	24	....	....	....	....	....
	New Haven	AHL	48	19	24	43	30	....	....	....	....	....
1985-86	Ilves	Fin.	36	16	15	31	30	....	....	....	....	....
	New Haven	AHL	21	8	15	23	12	5	4	2	6	4
1986-87	**Pittsburgh**	**NHL**	31	8	9	17	6	....	....	....	....	....
	New Haven	AHL	36	14	17	31	29	....	....	....	....	....
1987-88	**Pittsburgh**	**NHL**	36	1	7	8	12	....	....	....	....	....
	Muskegon	IHL	10	3	6	9	8	....	....	....	....	....
	Los Angeles	**NHL**	6	2	10	12	2	4	1	0	1	4
	New Haven	AHL	16	8	16	24	4	....	....	....	....	....
1988-89	EHC Kloten	Swiss	36	33	22	55	....	6	6	2	8	....
	Los Angeles	**NHL**	7	2	1	3	2	11	9	0	9	8
1989-90	**Los Angeles**	**NHL**	6	2	2	4	4	5	1	0	1	0
	New Haven	AHL	42	10	20	30	25	....	....	....	....	....
1990-91	Phoenix	IHL	69	26	36	62	19	11	9	12	21	0
1991-92	Cdn. National	....	25	10	10	20	16	....	....	....	....	....
1992-93	**Tampa Bay**	**NHL**	66	27	24	51	12	....	....	....	....	....
	NHL Totals		230	54	69	123	103	20	11	0	11	12

Traded to **Pittsburgh** by **NY Rangers** for Ron Duguay, January 21, 1987. Traded to **Los Angeles** by **Pittsburgh** with Pittsburgh's sixth round choice (Micah Aivazoff) in 1988 Entry Draft for Bryan Erickson, February 5, 1988. Signed as a free agent by **Tampa Bay**, July 21, 1992.

KONTSEK, ROMAN   (KON-chek)

Right wing. Shoots left. 5'11", 183 lbs.   Born, Zilina, Czechoslovakia, June 11, 1970.
(Washington's 8th choice, 135th overall, in 1990 Entry Draft).

				Regular Season					Playoffs			
Season	Club	Lea	GP	G	A	TP	PIM	GP	G	A	TP	PIM
1988-89	Dukla Trencin	Czech.	21	4	8	12	12	....	....	....	....	....
1989-90	Dukla Trencin	Czech.	21	8	7	15	....	....	....	....	....	....
1990-91	Dukla Trencin	Czech.	54	15	23	38	24	....	....	....	....	....
1991-92	Dukla Trencin	Czech.	35	5	6	11	12	....	....	....	....	....
1992-93	Dukla Trencin	Czech.	49	12	23	35	....	....	....	....	....	....

KORDIC, DAN

Defense. Shoots left. 6'5", 220 lbs.   Born, Edmonton, Alta., April 18, 1971.
(Philadelphia's 9th choice, 88th overall, in 1990 Entry Draft).

				Regular Season					Playoffs			
Season	Club	Lea	GP	G	A	TP	PIM	GP	G	A	TP	PIM
1987-88	Medicine Hat	WHL	63	1	5	6	75	....	....	....	....	....
1988-89	Medicine Hat	WHL	70	1	13	14	190	....	....	....	....	....
1989-90	Medicine Hat	WHL	59	4	12	16	182	3	0	0	0	9
1990-91	Medicine Hat	WHL	67	8	15	23	150	12	2	6	8	42
1991-92	**Philadelphia**	**NHL**	46	1	3	4	126	....	....	....	....	....
1992-93	Hershey	AHL	14	0	2	2	17	....	....	....	....	....
	NHL Totals		46	1	3	4	126	....	....	....	....	....

KOROLEV, IGOR   (koh-roh-LEV)

Right wing. Shoots left. 6'1", 187 lbs.   Born, Moscow, Soviet Union, September 6, 1970.
(St. Louis' 1st choice, 38th overall, in 1992 Entry Draft).

				Regular Season					Playoffs			
Season	Club	Lea	GP	G	A	TP	PIM	GP	G	A	TP	PIM
1988-89	Moscow D'amo	USSR	1	0	0	0	2	....	....	....	....	....
1989-90	Moscow D'amo	USSR	17	3	2	5	2	....	....	....	....	....
1990-91	Moscow D'amo	USSR	38	12	4	16	12	....	....	....	....	....
1991-92	Moscow D'amo	CIS	39	15	12	27	16	....	....	....	....	....
1992-93	Moscow D'amo	CIS	5	1	2	3	4	....	....	....	....	....
	St. Louis	**NHL**	74	4	23	27	20	3	0	0	0	0
	NHL Totals		74	4	23	27	20	3	0	0	0	0

KOROTKOV, KONSTANTIN   (KOH-raht-kohv)

Center. Shoots left. 5'9", 174 lbs.   Born, Moscow, Soviet Union, January 25, 1972.
(Hartford's 8th choice, 177th overall, in 1992 Entry Draft).

				Regular Season					Playoffs			
Season	Club	Lea	GP	G	A	TP	PIM	GP	G	A	TP	PIM
1987-88	Spartak	USSR	1	0	0	0	0	....	....	....	....	....
1988-89	Spartak	USSR	3	0	0	0	0	....	....	....	....	....
1989-90	Spartak	USSR	31	2	3	5	2	....	....	....	....	....
1990-91	Spartak	USSR	34	3	3	6	11	....	....	....	....	....
1991-92	Spartak	CIS	35	4	1	5	46	....	....	....	....	....
1992-93	Spartak	CIS	39	5	6	11	32	3	0	2	2	4

KOSKIMAKI, PETTERI   (koz-kih-MAH-kee, PEH-ter-ee)

Center. Shoots left. 6'1", 180 lbs.   Born, Helsinki, Finland, May 5, 1971.
(Pittsburgh's 10th choice, 152nd overall, in 1990 Entry Draft).

				Regular Season					Playoffs			
Season	Club	Lea	GP	G	A	TP	PIM	GP	G	A	TP	PIM
1989-90	Boston U.	H.E.	44	12	12	24	15	....	....	....	....	....
1990-91	Boston U.	H.E.	37	16	22	38	12	....	....	....	....	....
1991-92	Boston U.	H.E.	32	19	18	37	12	....	....	....	....	....
1992-93	Boston U.	H.E.	27	2	9	11	10	....	....	....	....	....

KOSTICHKIN, PAVEL   (kohs-TEECH-keen)

Right wing. Shoots left. 6'1", 190 lbs.   Born, Moscow, Soviet Union, November 9, 1968.
(Winnipeg's 12th choice, 199th overall, in 1988 Entry Draft).

				Regular Season					Playoffs			
Season	Club	Lea	GP	G	A	TP	PIM	GP	G	A	TP	PIM
1985-86	CSKA	USSR	16	5	4	9	12	....	....	....	....	....
1986-87	CSKA	USSR	13	0	3	3	4	....	....	....	....	....
1987-88	CSKA	USSR	40	8	0	8	20	....	....	....	....	....
1988-89	CSKA	USSR	31	4	2	6	16	....	....	....	....	....
1989-90	CSKA	USSR	25	3	4	7	14	....	....	....	....	....
1990-91	CSKA	USSR	26	4	4	8	10	....	....	....	....	....
1991-92	CSKA	CIS	11	1	2	3	10	....	....	....	....	....
1992-93	Moncton	AHL	65	16	18	34	51	....	....	....	....	....

KOVACS, BILL

Left wing. Shoots left. 6'3", 224 lbs. Born, Hamilton, Ont., May 11, 1971.
(Washington's 12th choice, 256th overall, in 1991 Entry Draft).

			Regular Season					Playoffs				
Season	Club	Lea	GP	G	A	TP	PIM	GP	G	A	TP	PIM
1989-90	Hamilton	OHL	13	4	4	8	30	....	....	....	....	....
	Sudbury	OHL	47	4	14	18	63	....	....	....	....	....
1990-91	Sudbury	OHL	66	26	25	51	86	5	1	2	3	10
1991-92	Sudbury	OHL	5	3	4	7	8	....	....	....	....	....
	Guelph	OHL	55	35	38	73	61	....	....	....	....	....
	Baltimore	AHL	4	0	0	0	0	....	....	....	....	....
1992-93	Raleigh	ECHL	19	4	6	10	32	....	....	....	....	....
	Birmingham	ECHL	36	16	13	29	40	....	....	....	....	....

KOVACS, FRANK

Left wing. Shoots left. 6'2", 205 lbs. Born, Regina, Sask., June 6, 1971.
(Minnesota's 4th choice, 71st overall, in 1990 Entry Draft).

			Regular Season					Playoffs				
Season	Club	Lea	GP	G	A	TP	PIM	GP	G	A	TP	PIM
1987-88	Regina	WHL	70	10	8	18	48	4	0	1	1	4
1988-89	Regina	WHL	70	16	27	43	90	....	....	....	....	....
1989-90	Regina	WHL	70	26	32	58	165	11	4	4	8	10
1990-91	Regina	WHL	72	50	51	101	148	8	10	3	13	15
1991-92a	Regina	WHL	69	46	45	91	274	....	....	....	....	....
1992-93	Kalamazoo	IHL	1	0	0	0	2	....	....	....	....	....
	Dayton	ECHL	61	31	36	67	177	3	3	1	4	2

a WHL East Second All-Star Team (1992)

KOVALENKO, ANDREI

Right wing. Shoots left. 5'10", 185 lbs. Born, Balakovo, Soviet Union, June 7, 1970.
(Quebec's 6th choice, 148th overall, in 1990 Entry Draft).

			Regular Season					Playoffs				
Season	Club	Lea	GP	G	A	TP	PIM	GP	G	A	TP	PIM
1988-89	CSKA	USSR	10	1	0	1	0	....	....	....	....	....
1989-90	CSKA	USSR	48	8	5	13	20	....	....	....	....	....
1990-91	CSKA	USSR	45	13	8	21	26	....	....	....	....	....
1991-92	CSKA	CIS	44	19	13	32	32	....	....	....	....	....
1992-93	CSKA	CIS	3	3	1	4	4	....	....	....	....	....
	Quebec	**NHL**	**81**	**27**	**41**	**68**	**57**	**4**	**1**	**0**	**1**	**2**
	NHL Totals		**81**	**27**	**41**	**68**	**57**	**4**	**1**	**0**	**1**	**2**

KOVALEV, ALEXEI

Right wing. Shoots left. 6', 200 lbs. Born, Togliatti, Soviet Union, February 24, 1973.
(NY Rangers' 1st choice, 15th overall, in 1991 Entry Draft).

			Regular Season					Playoffs				
Season	Club	Lea	GP	G	A	TP	PIM	GP	G	A	TP	PIM
1989-90	Moscow D'amo	USSR	1	0	0	0	0	....	....	....	....	....
1990-91	Moscow D'amo	USSR	18	1	2	3	4	....	....	....	....	....
1991-92	Moscow D'amo	CIS	33	16	9	25	20	....	....	....	....	....
1992-93	**NY Rangers**	**NHL**	**65**	**20**	**18**	**38**	**79**	....	....	....	....	....
	Binghamton	AHL	13	13	11	24	35	9	3	5	8	14
	NHL Totals		**65**	**20**	**18**	**38**	**79**	....	....	....	....	....

KOWALSKY, RICK

Right wing. Shoots right. 6', 184 lbs. Born, Simcoe, Ont., March 20, 1972.
(Buffalo's 10th choice, 227th overall, in 1992 Entry Draft).

			Regular Season					Playoffs				
Season	Club	Lea	GP	G	A	TP	PIM	GP	G	A	TP	PIM
1990-91	S.S. Marie	OHL	46	5	9	14	59	13	4	4	8	17
1991-92	S.S. Marie	OHL	66	25	44	39	119	19	6	10	16	39
1992-93	S.S. Marie	OHL	54	23	47	70	58	10	7	6	13	30

KOZLOV, VIKTOR (KOHZ-LOHV)

Left wing. Shoots right. 6'5", 209 lbs. Born, Togliatti, Soviet Union, February 14, 1975.
(San Jose's 1st choice, 6th overall, in 1993 Entry Draft).

			Regular Season					Playoffs				
Season	Club	Lea	GP	G	A	TP	PIM	GP	G	A	TP	PIM
1990-91	Togliatti	USSR 2	2	2	0	2	0	....	....	....	....	....
1991-92	Togliatti	CIS	3	0	0	0	0	....	....	....	....	....
1992-93	Moscow D'amo	CIS	30	6	5	11	4	10	3	0	3	0

KOZLOV, VYACHESLAV (KOHZ-LOHV)

Center. Shoots left. 5'10", 172 lbs. Born, Voskresensk, Soviet Union, May 3, 1972.
(Detroit's 2nd choice, 45th overall, in 1990 Entry Draft).

			Regular Season					Playoffs				
Season	Club	Lea	GP	G	A	TP	PIM	GP	G	A	TP	PIM
1987-88	Khimik	USSR	2	0	0	0	0	....	....	....	....	....
1988-89	Khimik	USSR	14	0	1	1	2	....	....	....	....	....
1989-90	Khimik	USSR	45	14	12	26	38	....	....	....	....	....
1990-91	Khimik	USSR	45	11	13	24	46	....	....	....	....	....
1991-92	CSKA	CIS	11	6	5	11	12	....	....	....	....	....
	Detroit	**NHL**	**7**	**0**	**2**	**2**	**2**	....	....	....	....	....
1992-93	**Detroit**	**NHL**	**17**	**4**	**1**	**5**	**14**	**4**	**0**	**2**	**2**	**2**
	Adirondack	AHL	45	23	36	59	54	4	1	1	2	4
	NHL Totals		**24**	**4**	**3**	**7**	**16**	**4**	**0**	**2**	**2**	**2**

KRALL, JUSTIN

Defense. Shoots left. 6'2", 170 lbs. Born, Toledo, OH, February 20, 1974.
(Detroit's 8th choice, 183rd overall, in 1992 Entry Draft).

			Regular Season					Playoffs				
Season	Club	Lea	GP	G	A	TP	PIM	GP	G	A	TP	PIM
1991-92	Omaha	USJHL	43	1	4	5	10	....	....	....	....	....
1992-93	Miami-Ohio	CCHA	39	5	6	11	26	....	....	....	....	....

KRAMER, BRADY

Center. Shoots left. 6'2", 170 lbs. Born, Philadelphia, PA, June 13, 1973.
(Montreal's 7th choice, 149th overall, in 1991 Entry Draft).

			Regular Season					Playoffs				
Season	Club	Lea	GP	G	A	TP	PIM	GP	G	A	TP	PIM
1991-92	Providence	H.E.	36	11	10	21	47	....	....	....	....	....
1992-93	Providence	H.E.	32	14	14	28	52	....	....	....	....	....

KRAMER, TED

Right wing. Shoots right. 6', 190 lbs. Born, Findlay, OH, October 29, 1969.
(Los Angeles' 6th choice, 144th overall, in 1989 Entry Draft).

			Regular Season					Playoffs				
Season	Club	Lea	GP	G	A	TP	PIM	GP	G	A	TP	PIM
1988-89	U. of Michigan	CCHA	37	16	14	30	70	....	....	....	....	....
1989-90	U. of Michigan	CCHA	42	21	24	45	111	....	....	....	....	....
1990-91	U. of Michigan	CCHA	47	15	17	32	107	....	....	....	....	....
1991-92	U. of Michigan	CCHA	44	17	14	31	52	....	....	....	....	....
1992-93	Phoenix	IHL	31	3	4	7	4	....	....	....	....	....

KRAVCHUK, IGOR (krahv-CHOOK)

Defense. Shoots left. 6'1", 200 lbs. Born, Ufa, Soviet Union, September 13, 1966.
(Chicago's 5th choice, 71st overall, in 1991 Entry Draft).

			Regular Season					Playoffs				
Season	Club	Lea	GP	G	A	TP	PIM	GP	G	A	TP	PIM
1982-83	Yulayev	USSR	10	0	0	0	0	....	....	....	....	....
	Yulayev	USSR 2	....	....	....	....	....	....	....	....	....	....
1984-85	Yulayev	USSR 2	50	3	2	5	22	....	....	....	....	....
1985-86	Yulayev	USSR	21	2	2	4	6	....	....	....	....	....
1986-87	Yulayev	USSR	22	0	1	1	8	....	....	....	....	....
1987-88	CSKA	USSR	48	1	8	9	12	....	....	....	....	....
1988-89	CSKA	USSR	22	3	3	6	2	....	....	....	....	....
1989-90	CSKA	USSR	48	1	3	4	16	....	....	....	....	....
1990-91	CSKA	USSR	41	6	5	11	16	....	....	....	....	....
1991-92	CSKA	CIS	30	3	8	11	6	....	....	....	....	....
	Chicago	**NHL**	**18**	**1**	**8**	**9**	**4**	**18**	**2**	**6**	**8**	**8**
1992-93	**Chicago**	**NHL**	**38**	**6**	**9**	**15**	**30**	....	....	....	....	....
	Edmonton	**NHL**	**17**	**4**	**8**	**12**	**2**	....	....	....	....	....
	NHL Totals		**73**	**11**	**25**	**36**	**36**	**18**	**2**	**6**	**8**	**8**

Traded to **Edmonton** by **Chicago** with Dean McAmmond for Joe Murphy, February 24, 1993.

KRAVETS, MIKHAIL

Right wing. Shoots left. 5'10", 190 lbs. Born, Leningrad, Soviet Union, November 12, 1963.
(San Jose's 13th choice, 243rd overall, in 1991 Entry Draft).

			Regular Season					Playoffs				
Season	Club	Lea	GP	G	A	TP	PIM	GP	G	A	TP	PIM
1985-86	SKA Leningrad	USSR	38	14	7	21	20	....	....	....	....	....
1986-87	SKA Leningrad	USSR	36	16	11	27	37	....	....	....	....	....
1987-88	SKA Leningrad	USSR	44	9	5	14	36	....	....	....	....	....
1988-89	SKA Leningrad	USSR	43	8	18	26	20	....	....	....	....	....
1989-90	SKA Leningrad	USSR	30	10	14	24	36	....	....	....	....	....
1990-91	SKA Leningrad	USSR	25	8	8	16	28	....	....	....	....	....
1991-92	**San Jose**	**NHL**	**1**	**0**	**0**	**0**	**0**	....	....	....	....	....
	Kansas City	IHL	74	10	32	42	172	15	6	8	14	12
1992-93	**San Jose**	**NHL**	**1**	**0**	**0**	**0**	**0**	....	....	....	....	....
	Kansas City	IHL	71	19	49	68	153	10	2	5	7	55
	NHL Totals		**2**	**0**	**0**	**0**	**0**	....	....	....	....	....

KRECHIN, VLADIMIR

Left wing. Shoots left. 5'11", 180 lbs. Born, Chelyabinsk, Soviet Union, March 23, 1975.
(Philadelphia's 4th choice, 114th overall, in 1993 Entry Draft).

			Regular Season					Playoffs				
Season	Club	Lea	GP	G	A	TP	PIM	GP	G	A	TP	PIM
1992-93	Chelyabinsk	CIS	1	0	0	0	0	....	....	....	....	....

KRISS, AARON

Defense. Shoots left. 6'2", 185 lbs. Born, Parma, OH, September 17, 1972.
(San Jose's 11th choice, 221st overall, in 1991 Entry Draft).

			Regular Season					Playoffs				
Season	Club	Lea	GP	G	A	TP	PIM	GP	G	A	TP	PIM
1991-92	Lowell	H.E.	29	1	4	5	22	....	....	....	....	....
1992-93	Lowell	H.E.	25	3	5	8	10	....	....	....	....	....

KRIVOKRASOV, SERGEI (kree-voh-KRAS-ohv)

Right wing. Shoots left. 5'10", 174 lbs. Born, Angarsk, Soviet Union, April 15, 1974.
(Chicago's 1st choice, 12th overall, in 1992 Entry Draft).

			Regular Season					Playoffs				
Season	Club	Lea	GP	G	A	TP	PIM	GP	G	A	TP	PIM
1990-91	CSKA	USSR	41	4	0	4	8	....	....	....	....	....
1991-92	CSKA	CIS	42	10	8	18	35	....	....	....	....	....
1992-93	**Chicago**	**NHL**	**4**	**0**	**0**	**0**	**2**	....	....	....	....	....
	Indianapolis	IHL	78	36	33	69	157	5	3	1	4	2
	NHL Totals		**4**	**0**	**0**	**0**	**2**	....	....	....	....	....

KROMM, RICHARD GORDON (RICH)

Left wing. Shoots left. 5'11", 180 lbs. Born, Trail, B.C., March 29, 1964.
(Calgary's 2nd choice, 37th overall, in 1982 Entry Draft).

			Regular Season					Playoffs				
Season	Club	Lea	GP	G	A	TP	PIM	GP	G	A	TP	PIM
1981-82	Portland	WHL	60	16	38	54	30	14	0	3	3	17
1982-83	Portland	WHL	72	35	68	103	64	14	7	13	20	12
1983-84	**Calgary**	**NHL**	**53**	**11**	**12**	**23**	**27**	**11**	**1**	**1**	**2**	**9**
	Portland	WHL	10	10	4	14	13	....	....	....	....	....
1984-85	**Calgary**	**NHL**	**73**	**20**	**32**	**52**	**32**	**3**	**0**	**1**	**1**	**4**
1985-86	**Calgary**	**NHL**	**63**	**12**	**17**	**29**	**31**	....	....	....	....	....
	NY Islanders	**NHL**	**14**	**7**	**7**	**14**	**4**	**3**	**0**	**1**	**1**	**0**
1986-87	**NY Islanders**	**NHL**	**70**	**12**	**17**	**29**	**20**	**14**	**1**	**3**	**4**	**4**
1987-88	**NY Islanders**	**NHL**	**71**	**5**	**10**	**15**	**20**	**5**	**0**	**0**	**0**	**5**
1988-89	**NY Islanders**	**NHL**	**20**	**1**	**6**	**7**	**4**	....	....	....	....	....
	Springfield	AHL	48	21	26	47	15	....	....	....	....	....
1989-90	Leksand	Swe.	40	8	16	24	28	3	3	1	4	0
	Springfield	AHL	9	3	4	7	4	16	1	5	6	4
1990-91	**NY Islanders**	**NHL**	**6**	**1**	**0**	**1**	**0**	....	....	....	....	....
	Capital Dist.	AHL	76	19	36	55	18	....	....	....	....	....
1991-92	**NY Islanders**	**NHL**	**1**	**0**	**0**	**0**	**0**	....	....	....	....	....
	Capital Dist.	AHL	76	16	39	55	36	7	2	3	5	6
1992-93	**NY Islanders**	**NHL**	**1**	**1**	**2**	**3**	**0**	....	....	....	....	....
	Capital Dist.	AHL	79	20	34	54	28	3	0	0	0	0
	NHL Totals		**372**	**70**	**103**	**173**	**138**	**36**	**2**	**6**	**8**	**22**

Traded to **NY Islanders** by **Calgary** with Steve Konroyd for John Tonelli, March 11, 1986.

KRON, ROBERT (KROHN)

Left wing. Shoots left. 5'10", 180 lbs. Born, Brno, Czech., February 27, 1967.
(Vancouver's 5th choice, 88th overall, in 1985 Entry Draft).

			Regular Season					Playoffs				
Season	Club	Lea	GP	G	A	TP	PIM	GP	G	A	TP	PIM
1983-84	Ingstav Brno	Czech.2	3	0	1	1	0	....	....	....	....	....
1984-85	Zetor Brno	Czech.	40	6	8	14	6	....	....	....	....	....
1985-86	Zetor Brno	Czech.	44	5	6	11	....	....	....	....	....	....
1986-87	Zetor Brno	Czech.	34	18	11	29	10	....	....	....	....	....
1987-88	Zetor Brno	Czech.	44	14	7	21	30	....	....	....	....	....
1988-89	Dukla Trencin	Czech.	43	28	19	47	26	....	....	....	....	....
1989-90	Dukla Trencin	Czech.	39	22	22	44	....	....	....	....	....	....
1990-91	**Vancouver**	**NHL**	**76**	**12**	**20**	**32**	**21**	....	....	....	....	....
1991-92	**Vancouver**	**NHL**	**36**	**2**	**2**	**4**	**2**	**11**	**1**	**2**	**3**	**2**
1992-93	**Vancouver**	**NHL**	**32**	**10**	**11**	**21**	**14**	....	....	....	....	....
	Hartford	**NHL**	**13**	**4**	**2**	**6**	**4**	....	....	....	....	....
	NHL Totals		**157**	**28**	**35**	**63**	**41**	**11**	**1**	**2**	**3**	**2**

Traded to **Hartford** by **Vancouver** with Vancouver's third round choice (Marek Malik) in 1993 Entry Draft and future considerations (Jim Sandlak, May 17, 1993) for Murray Craven and Vancouver's fifth round choice (previously acquired by Hartford — Vancouver selected Scott Walker) in 1993 Entry Draft, March 22, 1993.

KROUPA, VLASTIMIL

Defense. Shoots left. 6'3", 176 lbs. Born, Most, Czech., April 27, 1975.
(San Jose's 3rd choice, 45th overall, in 1993 Entry Draft).

			Regular Season					Playoffs				
Season	Club	Lea	GP	G	A	TP	PIM	GP	G	A	TP	PIM
1992-93	Litvinov	Czech.	9	0	1	1	....	....	....	....	....	....

KRUPP, UWE (KROOP, OO-VAY)

Defense. Shoots right. 6'6", 235 lbs. Born, Cologne, West Germany, June 24, 1965.
(Buffalo's 13th choice, 214th overall, in 1983 Entry Draft).

			Regular Season					Playoffs				
Season	Club	Lea	GP	G	A	TP	PIM	GP	G	A	TP	PIM
1982-83	Koln	W.Ger.	11	0	0	0	0	....	....	....	....	....
1983-84	Koln	W.Ger.	26	0	4	4	22	....	....	....	....	....
1984-85	Koln	W.Ger.	39	11	8	19	36	....	....	....	....	....
1985-86	Koln	W.Ger.	45	10	21	31	83	....	....	....	....	....
1986-87	**Buffalo**	**NHL**	**26**	**1**	**4**	**5**	**23**	....	....	....	....	....
	Rochester	AHL	42	3	19	22	50	17	1	11	12	16
1987-88	**Buffalo**	**NHL**	**75**	**2**	**9**	**11**	**151**	**6**	**0**	**0**	**0**	**15**
1988-89	**Buffalo**	**NHL**	**70**	**5**	**13**	**18**	**55**	**5**	**0**	**1**	**1**	**4**
1989-90	**Buffalo**	**NHL**	**74**	**3**	**20**	**23**	**85**	**6**	**0**	**0**	**0**	**4**
1990-91	**Buffalo**	**NHL**	**74**	**12**	**32**	**44**	**66**	**6**	**1**	**1**	**2**	**6**
1991-92	**Buffalo**	**NHL**	**8**	**2**	**0**	**2**	**6**	....	....	....	....	....
	NY Islanders	**NHL**	**59**	**6**	**29**	**35**	**43**	....	....	....	....	....
1992-93	**NY Islanders**	**NHL**	**80**	**9**	**29**	**38**	**67**	**18**	**1**	**5**	**6**	**12**
	NHL Totals		**466**	**40**	**136**	**176**	**496**	**41**	**2**	**7**	**9**	**41**

Played in NHL All-Star Game (1991)

Traded to **NY Islanders** by **Buffalo** with Pierre Turgeon, Benoit Hogue and Dave McLlwain for Pat Lafontaine, Randy Hillier, Randy Wood and future considerations, October 25, 1991.

KRUPPKE, GORD (KRUP-kee)

Defense. Shoots right. 6'1", 200 lbs. Born, Slave Lake, Alta., April 2, 1969.
(Detroit's 2nd choice, 32nd overall, in 1987 Entry Draft).

			Regular Season					Playoffs				
Season	Club	Lea	GP	G	A	TP	PIM	GP	G	A	TP	PIM
1985-86	Prince Albert	WHL	62	1	8	9	81	20	4	4	8	22
1986-87	Prince Albert	WHL	49	2	10	12	129	8	0	0	0	9
1987-88	Prince Albert	WHL	54	8	8	16	113	10	0	0	0	46
1988-89	Prince Albert	WHL	62	6	26	32	254	3	0	0	0	11
1989-90	Adirondack	AHL	59	2	12	14	103	....	....	....	....	....
1990-91	**Detroit**	**NHL**	**4**	**0**	**0**	**0**	**0**	....	....	....	....	....
	Adirondack	AHL	45	1	8	9	153	....	....	....	....	....
1991-92	Adirondack	AHL	65	3	9	12	208	16	0	1	1	52
1992-93	**Detroit**	**NHL**	**10**	**0**	**0**	**0**	**20**	....	....	....	....	....
	Adirondack	AHL	41	2	12	14	197	9	1	2	3	20
	NHL Totals		**14**	**0**	**0**	**0**	**20**	....	....	....	....	....

KRUSE, PAUL

Left wing. Shoots left. 6', 202 lbs. Born, Merritt, B.C., March 15, 1970.
(Calgary's 6th choice, 83rd overall, in 1990 Entry Draft).

			Regular Season					Playoffs				
Season	Club	Lea	GP	G	A	TP	PIM	GP	G	A	TP	PIM
1988-89	Kamloops	WHL	68	8	15	23	209	....	....	....	....	....
1989-90	Kamloops	WHL	67	22	23	45	291	17	3	5	8	79
1990-91	**Calgary**	**NHL**	**1**	**0**	**0**	**0**	**7**	....	....	....	....	....
	Salt Lake	IHL	83	24	20	44	313	4	1	1	2	4
1991-92	**Calgary**	**NHL**	**16**	**3**	**1**	**4**	**65**	....	....	....	....	....
	Salt Lake	IHL	57	14	15	29	267	5	1	2	3	19
1992-93	**Calgary**	**NHL**	**27**	**2**	**3**	**5**	**41**	....	....	....	....	....
	Salt Lake	IHL	35	1	4	5	206	....	....	....	....	....
	NHL Totals		**44**	**5**	**4**	**9**	**113**	....	....	....	....	....

KRUSHELNYSKI, MICHAEL (MIKE) (KROO-shuhl-NIH-skee)

Left wing/Center. Shoots left. 6'2", 200 lbs. Born, Montreal, Que., April 27, 1960.
(Boston's 7th choice, 120th overall, in 1979 Entry Draft).

			Regular Season					Playoffs				
Season	Club	Lea	GP	G	A	TP	PIM	GP	G	A	TP	PIM
1978-79	Montreal	QJHL	46	15	29	44	42	11	3	4	7	8
1979-80	Montreal	QJHL	72	39	60	99	78	6	2	3	5	2
1980-81	Springfield	AHL	80	25	28	53	47	7	1	1	2	29
1981-82	**Boston**	**NHL**	**17**	**3**	**3**	**6**	**2**	**1**	**0**	**0**	**0**	**2**
	Erie	AHL	62	31	52	83	44	....	....	....	....	....
1982-83	**Boston**	**NHL**	**79**	**23**	**42**	**65**	**43**	**17**	**8**	**6**	**14**	**12**
1983-84	**Boston**	**NHL**	**66**	**25**	**20**	**45**	**55**	**2**	**0**	**0**	**0**	**0**
1984-85	**Edmonton**	**NHL**	**80**	**43**	**45**	**88**	**60**	**18**	**5**	**8**	**13**	**22**
1985-86	**Edmonton**	**NHL**	**54**	**16**	**24**	**40**	**22**	**10**	**4**	**5**	**9**	**16**
1986-87	**Edmonton**	**NHL**	**80**	**16**	**35**	**51**	**67**	**21**	**3**	**4**	**7**	**18**
1987-88	**Edmonton**	**NHL**	**76**	**20**	**27**	**47**	**64**	**19**	**4**	**6**	**10**	**12**
1988-89	**Los Angeles**	**NHL**	**78**	**26**	**36**	**62**	**110**	**11**	**1**	**4**	**5**	**4**
1989-90	**Los Angeles**	**NHL**	**63**	**16**	**25**	**41**	**50**	**10**	**1**	**3**	**4**	**12**
1990-91	**Los Angeles**	**NHL**	**15**	**1**	**5**	**6**	**10**	....	....	....	....	....
	Toronto	**NHL**	**59**	**17**	**22**	**39**	**48**	....	....	....	....	....
1991-92	**Toronto**	**NHL**	**72**	**9**	**15**	**24**	**72**	....	....	....	....	....
1992-93	**Toronto**	**NHL**	**84**	**19**	**20**	**39**	**62**	**16**	**3**	**7**	**10**	**8**
	NHL Totals		**823**	**234**	**319**	**553**	**665**	**125**	**29**	**43**	**72**	**106**

Played in NHL All-Star Game (1985)

Traded to **Edmonton** by **Boston** for Ken Linseman, June 21, 1984. Traded to **Los Angeles** by **Edmonton** with Wayne Gretzky and Marty McSorley for Jimmy Carson, Martin Gelinas, Los Angeles' first round choices in 1989 (acquired by New Jersey — New Jersey selected Jason Miller), 1991 (Martin Rucinsky) and 1993 (Nick Stajduhar) Entry Drafts and cash, August 9, 1988. Traded to **Toronto** by **Los Angeles** for John McIntyre, November 9, 1990.

KRYGIER, TODD (KREE-guhr)

Left wing. Shoots left. 5'11", 180 lbs. Born, Chicago Heights, MI, October 12, 1965.
(Hartford's 1st choice, 16th overall, in 1988 Supplemental Draft).

			Regular Season					Playoffs				
Season	Club	Lea	GP	G	A	TP	PIM	GP	G	A	TP	PIM
1984-85	U. Connecticut	NCAA	14	14	11	25	12	....	....	....	....	....
1985-86	U. Connecticut	NCAA	32	29	27	56	46	....	....	....	....	....
1986-87	U. Connecticut	NCAA	28	24	24	48	44	....	....	....	....	....
1987-88	U. Connecticut	NCAA	27	32	39	71	28	....	....	....	....	....
	New Haven	AHL	13	1	5	6	34	....	....	....	....	....
1988-89	Binghamton	AHL	76	26	42	68	77	....	....	....	....	....
1989-90	**Hartford**	**NHL**	**58**	**18**	**12**	**30**	**52**	**7**	**2**	**1**	**3**	**4**
	Binghamton	AHL	12	1	9	10	16	....	....	....	....	....
1990-91	**Hartford**	**NHL**	**72**	**13**	**17**	**30**	**95**	**6**	**0**	**2**	**2**	**0**
1991-92	**Washington**	**NHL**	**67**	**13**	**17**	**30**	**107**	**5**	**2**	**1**	**3**	**4**
1992-93	**Washington**	**NHL**	**77**	**11**	**12**	**23**	**60**	**6**	**1**	**1**	**2**	**4**
	NHL Totals		**274**	**55**	**58**	**113**	**314**	**24**	**5**	**5**	**10**	**12**

Traded to **Washington** by **Hartford** for future considerations (Washington's fourth round choice (later traded to Calgary—Calgary selected Jason Smith) in 1993 Entry Draft, October 3, 1991.

KRYS, MARK

Defense. Shoots right. 6', 185 lbs. Born, Timmins, Ont., May 29, 1969.
(Boston's 6th choice, 165th overall, in 1988 Entry Draft).

			Regular Season					Playoffs				
Season	Club	Lea	GP	G	A	TP	PIM	GP	G	A	TP	PIM
1987-88	Boston U.	H.E.	34	0	6	6	40	....	....	....	....	....
1988-89	Boston U.	H.E.	35	0	7	7	54	....	....	....	....	....
1989-90	Boston U.	H.E.	30	0	4	4	34	....	....	....	....	....
1990-91	Boston U.	H.E.	36	1	9	10	18	....	....	....	....	....
1991-92	Maine	AHL	28	1	2	3	18	....	....	....	....	....
	Johnstown	ECHL	43	8	12	20	73	....	....	....	....	....
1992-93	Providence	AHL	34	1	10	11	36	6	0	0	0	2
	Johnstown	ECHL	25	4	14	18	18	....	....	....	....	....
	Cincinnati	IHL	3	0	1	1	2	....	....	....	....	....

KUCERA, FRANTISEK (kuh-CHEH-rah)

Defense. Shoots right. 6'2", 205 lbs. Born, Prague, Czechoslovakia, February 3, 1968.
(Chicago's 3rd choice, 77th overall, in 1986 Entry Draft).

			Regular Season					Playoffs				
Season	Club	Lea	GP	G	A	TP	PIM	GP	G	A	TP	PIM
1985-86	Sparta Praha	Czech.	15	0	0	0	....	....	....	....	....	....
1986-87	Sparta Praha	Czech.	40	5	2	7	14	....	....	....	....	....
1987-88	Sparta Praha	Czech.	46	7	2	9	30	....	....	....	....	....
1988-89	Dukla Jihlava	Czech.	45	10	9	19	28	....	....	....	....	....
1989-90	Dukla Jihlava	Czech.	43	9	10	19	....	....	....	....	....	....
1990-91	**Chicago**	**NHL**	**40**	**2**	**12**	**14**	**32**	....	....	....	....	....
	Indianapolis	IHL	35	8	19	27	23	7	0	1	1	15
1991-92	**Chicago**	**NHL**	**61**	**3**	**10**	**13**	**36**	**6**	**0**	**0**	**0**	**0**
	Indianapolis	IHL	7	1	2	3	4	....	....	....	....	....
1992-93	**Chicago**	**NHL**	**71**	**5**	**14**	**19**	**59**	....	....	....	....	....
	NHL Totals		**172**	**10**	**36**	**46**	**127**	**6**	**0**	**0**	**0**	**0**

KUCERA, JIRI (kuh-CHEH-rah)

Center. Shoots left. 5'11", 180 lbs. Born, Plzen, Czechoslovakia, March 28, 1966.
(Pittsburgh's 8th choice, 152nd overall, in 1987 Entry Draft).

			Regular Season					Playoffs				
Season	Club	Lea	GP	G	A	TP	PIM	GP	G	A	TP	PIM
1986-87	Dukla Jihlava	Czech.	43	13	12	25	18	....	....	....	....	....
1987-88	Skoda Plzen	Czech.	41	21	24	45	22	....	....	....	....	....
1988-89	Skoda Plzen	Czech.	40	20	15	35	22	....	....	....	....	....
1989-90	Skoda Plzen	Czech.	47	13	24	37	....	....	....	....	....	....
1990-91	Tappara	Fin.	44	23	34	57	26	3	0	2	2	4
1991-92	Tappara	Fin.	44	22	20	42	8	....	....	....	....	....
1992-93	Tappara	Fin.	48	22	32	54	20	....	....	....	....	....

KUCHARCIK, TOMAS (koo-HAHR-chihk)

Center. Shoots left. 6'2", 189 lbs. Born, Vlasim, Czechoslovakia, May 10, 1970.
(Toronto's 11th choice, 167th overall, in 1991 Entry Draft).

			Regular Season					Playoffs				
Season	Club	Lea	GP	G	A	TP	PIM	GP	G	A	TP	PIM
1990-91	Dukla Jihlava	Czech.	30	10	6	16	6	....	....	....	....	....
1991-92	Dukla Jihlava	Czech.	45	16	23	39	24	....	....	....	....	....
1992-93	Dukla Jihlava	Czech.	39	17	20	37	....	....	....	....	....	....

KUCHYNA, PETR (kuh-HEE-nah)

Defense. Shoots right. 6'3", 180 lbs. Born, Jihlava, Czechoslovakia, January 14, 1970.
(New Jersey's 8th choice, 104th overall, in 1990 Entry Draft).

			Regular Season					Playoffs				
Season	Club	Lea	GP	G	A	TP	PIM	GP	G	A	TP	PIM
1989-90	Dukla Jihlava	Czech.	32	2	2	4	....	....	....	....	....	....
1990-91	Dukla Jihlava	Czech.	54	4	6	10	35	....	....	....	....	....
1991-92	Dukla Jihlava	Czech.	18	5	4	9	8	....	....	....	....	....
	Utica	AHL	53	3	6	9	22	4	0	0	0	2
1992-93	Utica	AHL	76	3	24	27	56	4	0	0	0	4

KUDASHOV, ALEXEI (koo-dah-SHOV)

Center. Shoots right. 6', 183 lbs. Born, Elektrostal, Soviet Union, July 21, 1971.
(Toronto's 3rd choice, 102nd overall, in 1991 Entry Draft).

			Regular Season					Playoffs				
Season	Club	Lea	GP	G	A	TP	PIM	GP	G	A	TP	PIM
1989-90	Soviet Wings	USSR	45	0	5	5	14	....	....	....	....	....
1990-91	Soviet Wings	USSR	45	9	5	14	10	....	....	....	....	....
1991-92	Soviet Wings	CIS	42	9	16	25	14	....	....	....	....	....
1992-93	Soviet Wings	CIS	41	8	20	28	24	7	1	3	4	4

KUDELSKI, BOB

Right wing. Shoots right. 6'1", 200 lbs. Born, Springfield, MA, March 3, 1964.
(Los Angeles' 1st choice, 2nd overall, in 1986 Supplemental Draft).

			Regular Season					Playoffs				
Season	Club	Lea	GP	G	A	TP	PIM	GP	G	A	TP	PIM
1983-84	Yale	ECAC	21	14	12	26	12	....	....	....	....	....
1984-85	Yale	ECAC	32	21	23	44	38	....	....	....	....	....
1985-86	Yale	ECAC	31	18	23	41	48	....	....	....	....	....
1986-87a	Yale	ECAC	30	25	22	47	34	....	....	....	....	....
1987-88	**Los Angeles**	**NHL**	**26**	**0**	**1**	**1**	**8**	....	....	....	....	....
	New Haven	AHL	50	15	19	34	41	....	....	....	....	....
1988-89	**Los Angeles**	**NHL**	**14**	**1**	**3**	**4**	**17**	....	....	....	....	....
	New Haven	AHL	60	32	19	51	43	17	8	5	13	12
1989-90	**Los Angeles**	**NHL**	**62**	**23**	**13**	**36**	**49**	**8**	**1**	**2**	**3**	**2**
1990-91	**Los Angeles**	**NHL**	**72**	**23**	**13**	**36**	**46**	**8**	**3**	**2**	**5**	**2**
1991-92	**Los Angeles**	**NHL**	**80**	**22**	**21**	**43**	**42**	**6**	**0**	**0**	**0**	**0**
1992-93	**Los Angeles**	**NHL**	**15**	**3**	**3**	**6**	**8**	....	....	....	....	....
	Ottawa	**NHL**	**48**	**21**	**14**	**35**	**22**	....	....	....	....	....
	NHL Totals		**317**	**93**	**68**	**161**	**192**	**22**	**4**	**4**	**8**	**4**

a ECAC First All-Star Team (1987)

Traded to **Ottawa** by **Los Angeles** wish Shawn McCosh for Marc Fortier and Jim Thompson, December 19, 1992.

KULONEN, TIMO (KOO-loh-nehn)

Defense. Shoots right. 6'5", 220 lbs. Born, Forssa, Finland, November 1, 1967.
(Minnesota's 7th choice, 130th overall, in 1987 Entry Draft).

			Regular Season					Playoffs				
Season	Club	Lea	GP	G	A	TP	PIM	GP	G	A	TP	PIM
1983-84	FoPS	Fin.2	17	1	0	1	14	....	....	....	....	....
1984-85	FoPS	Fin.2	42	11	18	29	60	....	....	....	....	....
1985-86	FoPS	Fin.2	40	14	25	39	48	....	....	....	....	....
1986-87	KalPa	Fin.	39	2	8	10	20	....	....	....	....	....
1987-88	KalPa	Fin.	44	7	15	22	32	....	....	....	....	....
1988-89	KalPa	Fin.	40	9	16	25	18	2	0	1	1	0
1989-90	KalPa	Fin.	44	5	20	25	34	6	0	0	0	2
1990-91	HPK	Fin.	42	1	10	11	16	8	0	2	2	4
1991-92	Lukko	Fin.	44	8	17	25	14	2	0	0	0	0
1992-93	Lukko	Fin.	48	8	10	18	48	3	0	0	0	2

KUMMU, AL

Defense. Shoots right. 6'4", 195 lbs. Born, Kitchener, Ont., January 21, 1969.
(Philadelphia's 8th choice, 201st overall, in 1989 Entry Draft).

			Regular Season					Playoffs				
Season	Club	Lea	GP	G	A	TP	PIM	GP	G	A	TP	PIM
1989-90	RPI	ECAC	33	9	13	22	50	....	....	....	....	....
1990-91	RPI	ECAC	29	6	8	14	86	....	....	....	....	....
1991-92	RPI	ECAC	31	6	14	20	54	....	....	....	....	....
1992-93	RPI	ECAC	35	4	8	12	72	....	....	....	....	....

KUNTOS, JIRI (KOON-tohsh)

Defense. Shoots left. 5'11", 207 lbs. Born, Vlasim, Czech., December 11, 1971.
(Buffalo's 9th choice, 162nd overall, in 1991 Entry Draft).

			Regular Season					Playoffs				
Season	Club	Lea	GP	G	A	TP	PIM	GP	G	A	TP	PIM
1990-91	Dukla Jihlava	Czech.	15	3	1	4	....	....	....	....	....	....
1991-92	Dukla Jihlava	Czech.	45	2	8	10	49	....	....	....	....	....
1992-93	Dukla Jihlava	Czech.	35	4	2	6	....	....	....	....	....	....

KURRI, JARI (KUHR-ree, YAH-ree)

Right wing. Shoots right. 6'1", 195 lbs. Born, Helsinki, Finland, May 18, 1960.
(Edmonton's 3rd choice, 69th overall, in 1980 Entry Draft).

			Regular Season					Playoffs				
Season	Club	Lea	GP	G	A	TP	PIM	GP	G	A	TP	PIM
1977-78	Jokerit	Fin.	29	2	9	11	12	....	....	....	....	....
1978-79	Jokerit	Fin.	33	16	14	30	12	....	....	....	....	....
1979-80	Jokerit	Fin.	33	23	16	39	22	6	7	2	9	13
1980-81	**Edmonton**	**NHL**	**75**	**32**	**43**	**75**	**40**	**9**	**5**	**7**	**12**	**4**
1981-82	**Edmonton**	**NHL**	**71**	**32**	**54**	**86**	**32**	**5**	**2**	**5**	**7**	**10**
1982-83	**Edmonton**	**NHL**	**80**	**45**	**59**	**104**	**22**	**16**	**8**	**15**	**23**	**8**
1983-84a	**Edmonton**	**NHL**	**64**	**52**	**61**	**113**	**14**	**19**	***14**	**14**	**28**	**13**
1984-85bc	**Edmonton**	**NHL**	**73**	**71**	**64**	**135**	**30**	**18**	***19**	**12**	**31**	**6**
1985-86a	**Edmonton**	**NHL**	**78**	***68**	**63**	**131**	**22**	**10**	**2**	**10**	**12**	**4**
1986-87c	**Edmonton**	**NHL**	**79**	**54**	**54**	**108**	**41**	**21**	***15**	**10**	**25**	**20**
1987-88	**Edmonton**	**NHL**	**80**	**43**	**53**	**96**	**30**	**19**	***14**	**17**	**31**	**12**
1988-89a	**Edmonton**	**NHL**	**76**	**44**	**58**	**102**	**69**	**7**	**3**	**5**	**8**	**6**
1989-90	**Edmonton**	**NHL**	**78**	**33**	**60**	**93**	**48**	**22**	**10**	**15**	**25**	**18**
1990-91	Milan Devils	Italy	30	27	48	75	6	10	10	12	22	2
1991-92	**Los Angeles**	**NHL**	**73**	**23**	**37**	**60**	**24**	**4**	**1**	**2**	**3**	**4**
1992-93	**Los Angeles**	**NHL**	**82**	**27**	**60**	**87**	**38**	**24**	**9**	**8**	**17**	**12**
	NHL Totals		**909**	**524**	**666**	**1190**	**410**	**174**	**102**	**120**	**222**	**117**

a NHL Second All-Star Team (1984, 1986, 1989)
b Won Lady Byng Memorial Trophy (1985)
c NHL First All-Star Team (1985, 1987)

Played in NHL All-Star Game (1983, 1985, 1986, 1988-90, 1993)

Traded to **Philadelphia** by **Edmonton** with Dave Brown and Corey Foster for Craig Fisher, Scott Mellanby and Craig Berube, May 30, 1991. Traded to **Los Angeles** by **Philadelphia** with Jeff Chychrun for Steve Duchesne, Steve Kasper and Los Angeles' fourth round choice (Aris Brimanis) in 1991 Entry Draft, May 30, 1991.

KURVERS, TOM

Defense. Shoots left. 6'2", 195 lbs. Born, Minneapolis, MN, September 14, 1962.
(Montreal's 10th choice, 145th overall, in 1981 Entry Draft).

			Regular Season					Playoffs				
Season	Club	Lea	GP	G	A	TP	PIM	GP	G	A	TP	PIM
1980-81	Minn.-Duluth	WCHA	39	6	24	30	48	....	....	....	....	....
1981-82	Minn.-Duluth	WCHA	37	11	31	42	18	....	....	....	....	....
1982-83	Minn.-Duluth	WCHA	26	4	23	27	24	....	....	....	....	....
1983-84ab	Minn.-Duluth	WCHA	43	18	58	76	46	....	....	....	....	....
1984-85	**Montreal**	**NHL**	**75**	**10**	**35**	**45**	**30**	**12**	**0**	**6**	**6**	**6**
1985-86	**Montreal**	**NHL**	**62**	**7**	**23**	**30**	**36**	....	....	....	....	....
1986-87	**Montreal**	**NHL**	**1**	**0**	**0**	**0**	**0**	....	....	....	....	....
	Buffalo	**NHL**	**55**	**6**	**17**	**23**	**22**	....	....	....	....	....
1987-88	**New Jersey**	**NHL**	**56**	**5**	**29**	**34**	**46**	**19**	**6**	**9**	**15**	**38**
1988-89	**New Jersey**	**NHL**	**74**	**16**	**50**	**66**	**38**	....	....	....	....	....
1989-90	**New Jersey**	**NHL**	**1**	**0**	**0**	**0**	**0**	....	....	....	....	....
	Toronto	**NHL**	**70**	**15**	**37**	**52**	**29**	**5**	**0**	**3**	**3**	**4**
1990-91	**Toronto**	**NHL**	**19**	**0**	**3**	**3**	**8**	....	....	....	....	....
	Vancouver	**NHL**	**32**	**4**	**23**	**27**	**20**	**6**	**2**	**2**	**4**	**12**
1991-92	**NY Islanders**	**NHL**	**74**	**9**	**47**	**56**	**30**	....	....	....	....	....
1992-93	**NY Islanders**	**NHL**	**52**	**8**	**30**	**38**	**38**	**12**	**0**	**2**	**2**	**6**
	Capital Dist.	AHL	7	3	4	7	8	....	....	....	....	....
	NHL Totals		**571**	**80**	**294**	**374**	**297**	**54**	**8**	**22**	**30**	**66**

a WCHA First All-Star Team (1984)
b Won Hobey Baker Memorial Trophy (1984)

Traded to **Buffalo** by **Montreal** for Buffalo's second round choice (Martin St. Amour) in 1988 Entry Draft, November 18, 1986. Traded to **New Jersey** by **Buffalo** for Detroit's third round choice (previously acquired by New Jersey — Buffalo selected Andrew MacVicar) in 1987 Entry Draft, June 13, 1987. Traded to **Toronto** by **New Jersey** for Toronto's first round choice (Scott Niedermayer) in 1991 Entry Draft, October 16, 1989. Traded to **Vancouver** by **Toronto** for Brian Bradley, January 12, 1991. Traded to **Minnesota** by **Vancouver** for Dave Babych, June 22, 1991. Traded to **NY Islanders** by **Minnesota** for Craig Ludwig, June 22, 1991.

KUSHNER, DALE

Right wing. Shoots left. 6'1", 195 lbs. Born, Terrace, B.C., June 13, 1966.

			Regular Season					Playoffs				
Season	Club	Lea	GP	G	A	TP	PIM	GP	G	A	TP	PIM
1983-84	Prince Albert	WHL	1	2	0	2	5	....	....	....	....	....
1984-85	Prince Albert	WHL	2	0	0	0	2	....	....	....	....	....
	Moose Jaw	WHL	17	5	2	7	23	....	....	....	....	....
	Medicine Hat	WHL	48	23	17	40	173	10	3	3	6	18
1985-86	Medicine Hat	WHL	66	25	19	44	218	25	0	5	5	114
1986-87	Medicine Hat	WHL	63	34	34	68	250	20	8	13	21	57
1987-88	Springfield	AHL	68	13	23	36	201	....	....	....	....	....
1988-89	Springfield	AHL	45	5	8	13	132	....	....	....	....	....
1989-90	**NY Islanders**	**NHL**	**2**	**0**	**0**	**0**	**2**	....	....	....	....	....
	Springfield	AHL	45	14	11	25	163	7	2	3	5	61
1990-91	**Philadelphia**	**NHL**	**63**	**7**	**11**	**18**	**195**	....	....	....	....	....
	Hershey	AHL	5	3	4	7	14	....	....	....	....	....
1991-92	**Philadelphia**	**NHL**	**19**	**3**	**2**	**5**	**18**	....	....	....	....	....
	Hershey	AHL	46	9	7	16	98	6	0	2	2	23
1992-93	Hershey	AHL	26	1	7	8	98	....	....	....	....	....
	Capital Dist.	AHL	7	0	1	1	29	2	1	0	1	29
	NHL Totals		**84**	**10**	**13**	**23**	**215**	....	....	....	....	....

Signed as a free agent by **NY Islanders**, April 7, 1987. Signed as a free agent by **Philadelphia**, July 31, 1990.

KUWABARA, RYAN

Right wing. Shoots right. 6', 205 lbs. Born, Hamilton, Ont., March 23, 1972.
(Montreal's 2nd choice, 39th overall, in 1990 Entry Draft).

			Regular Season					Playoffs				
Season	Club	Lea	GP	G	A	TP	PIM	GP	G	A	TP	PIM
1989-90	Ottawa	OHL	66	30	38	68	62	4	0	0	0	0
1990-91	Ottawa	OHL	64	34	38	72	67	17	12	15	27	25
1991-92	Ottawa	OHL	66	43	57	100	84	10	6	5	11	9
1992-93	Fredericton	AHL	10	0	2	2	4	....	....	....	....	....
	Wheeling	ECHL	18	7	13	20	22	16	5	8	13	40

KVARTALNOV, DMITRI (kvahr-TAHL-nov)

Left wing. Shoots left. 5'11", 180 lbs. Born, Voskresensk, Soviet Union, March 25, 1966.
(Boston's 1st choice, 16th overall, in 1992 Entry Draft).

			Regular Season					Playoffs				
Season	Club	Lea	GP	G	A	TP	PIM	GP	G	A	TP	PIM
1982-83	Khimik	USSR	7	0	0	0	0	....	....	....	....	....
1983-84	Khimik	USSR	2	0	0	0	0	....	....	....	....	....
1984-85	SKA Kalinen	USSR 2	UNAVAILABLE									
1985-86	SKA Kalinin	USSR 2	UNAVAILABLE									
1986-87	Khimik	USSR	40	11	6	17	28	....	....	....	....	....
1987-88	Khimik	USSR	43	16	11	27	16	....	....	....	....	....
1988-89	Khimik	USSR	44	20	12	32	18	....	....	....	....	....
1989-90	Khimik	USSR	46	25	28	53	33	....	....	....	....	....
1990-91	Khimik	USSR	42	12	10	22	18	....	....	....	....	....
1991-92abcd	San Diego	IHL	77	*60	58	*118	16	4	2	0	2	2
1992-93	Khimik	CIS	3	0	0	0	0	....	....	....	....	....
	Boston	**NHL**	**73**	**30**	**42**	**72**	**16**	**4**	**0**	**0**	**0**	**0**
	NHL Totals		**73**	**30**	**42**	**72**	**16**	**4**	**0**	**0**	**0**	**0**

a Won James Gatschene Memorial Trophy (MVP–IHL) 1992
b Won Leo P. Lamoureaux Memorial Trophy (Top Scorer–IHL) 1992
c Won Garry F. Longman Memorial Trophy (Top Rookie–IHL) 1992
d IHL First All-Star Team (1992)

KYPREOS, NICHOLAS (NICK) (KIH-pree-ohz)

Left wing. Shoots left. 6', 195 lbs. Born, Toronto, Ont., June 4, 1966.

			Regular Season					Playoffs				
Season	Club	Lea	GP	G	A	TP	PIM	GP	G	A	TP	PIM
1983-84	North Bay	OHL	51	12	11	23	36	4	3	2	5	9
1984-85	North Bay	OHL	64	41	36	77	71	8	2	2	4	15
1985-86a	North Bay	OHL	64	62	35	97	112	....	....	....	....	....
1986-87	Hershey	AHL	10	0	1	1	4	....	....	....	....	....
b	North Bay	OHL	46	49	41	90	54	24	11	5	16	78
1987-88	Hershey	AHL	71	24	20	44	101	12	0	2	2	17
1988-89	Hershey	AHL	28	12	15	27	19	12	4	5	9	11
1989-90	**Washington**	**NHL**	**31**	**5**	**4**	**9**	**82**	**7**	**1**	**0**	**1**	**15**
	Baltimore	AHL	14	6	5	11	6	7	4	1	5	17
1990-91	**Washington**	**NHL**	**79**	**9**	**9**	**18**	**196**	**9**	**0**	**1**	**1**	**38**
1991-92	**Washington**	**NHL**	**65**	**4**	**6**	**10**	**206**	....	....	....	....	....
1992-93	**Hartford**	**NHL**	**75**	**17**	**10**	**27**	**325**	....	....	....	....	....
	NHL Totals		**250**	**35**	**29**	**64**	**809**	**16**	**1**	**1**	**2**	**53**

a OHL First All-Star Team (1986)
b OHL Second All-Star Team (1987)

Signed as a free agent by **Philadelphia**, September 30, 1984. Claimed by **Washington** in NHL Waiver Draft, October 2, 1989. Traded to **Hartford** by **Washington** for Mark Hunter and future considerations (Yvon Corriveau, August 20, 1992), June 15, 1992.

KYTE, JAMES (JIM) (KITE)

Defense. Shoots left. 6'5", 210 lbs. Born, Ottawa, Ont., March 21, 1964.
(Winnipeg's 1st choice, 12th overall, in 1982 Entry Draft).

			Regular Season					Playoffs				
Season	Club	Lea	GP	G	A	TP	PIM	GP	G	A	TP	PIM
1981-82	Cornwall	OHL	52	4	13	17	148	5	0	0	0	10
1982-83	**Winnipeg**	**NHL**	**2**	**0**	**0**	**0**	**0**	....	....	....	....	....
	Cornwall	OHL	65	6	30	36	195	8	0	2	2	24
1983-84	**Winnipeg**	**NHL**	**58**	**1**	**2**	**3**	**55**	**3**	**0**	**0**	**0**	**11**
1984-85	**Winnipeg**	**NHL**	**71**	**0**	**3**	**3**	**111**	**8**	**0**	**0**	**0**	**14**
1985-86	**Winnipeg**	**NHL**	**71**	**1**	**3**	**4**	**126**	**3**	**0**	**0**	**0**	**12**
1986-87	**Winnipeg**	**NHL**	**72**	**5**	**5**	**10**	**162**	**10**	**0**	**4**	**4**	**36**
1987-88	**Winnipeg**	**NHL**	**51**	**1**	**3**	**4**	**128**	....	....	....	....	....
1988-89	**Winnipeg**	**NHL**	**74**	**3**	**9**	**12**	**190**	....	....	....	....	....
1989-90	**Pittsburgh**	**NHL**	**56**	**3**	**1**	**4**	**125**	....	....	....	....	....
1990-91	**Pittsburgh**	**NHL**	**1**	**0**	**0**	**0**	**2**	....	....	....	....	....
	Muskegon	IHL	25	2	5	7	157	....	....	....	....	....
	Calgary	**NHL**	**42**	**0**	**9**	**9**	**153**	**7**	**0**	**0**	**0**	**7**
1991-92	**Calgary**	**NHL**	**21**	**0**	**1**	**1**	**107**	....	....	....	....	....
	Salt Lake	IHL	6	0	1	1	9	....	....	....	....	....
1992-93	**Ottawa**	**NHL**	**4**	**0**	**1**	**1**	**4**	....	....	....	....	....
	New Haven	AHL	63	6	18	24	163	....	....	....	....	....
	NHL Totals		**523**	**14**	**37**	**51**	**1163**	**31**	**0**	**4**	**4**	**80**

Traded to **Pittsburgh** by **Winnipeg** with Andrew McBain and Randy Gilhen for Randy Cunneyworth, Rick Tabaracci and Dave McLlwain, June 17, 1989. Traded to **Calgary** by **Pittsburgh** for Jiri Hrdina, December 13, 1990. Signed as a free agent by **Ottawa**, September 10, 1992.

LABELLE, MARC

Left wing. Shoots left. 6'1", 215 lbs. Born, Maniwaki, Que., December 20, 1969.

			Regular Season					Playoffs				
Season	Club	Lea	GP	G	A	TP	PIM	GP	G	A	TP	PIM
1987-88	Victoriaville	QMJHL	63	11	14	25	236	5	2	4	6	20
1988-89	Victoriaville	QMJHL	62	9	26	35	202	15	6	3	9	30
1989-90	Victoriaville	QMJHL	56	18	21	39	192	16	4	8	12	42
1990-91	Fredericton	AHL	25	1	4	5	95	4	0	2	2	25
	Richmond	ECHL	5	1	1	2	37	....	....	....	....	....
1991-92	Fredericton	AHL	62	7	10	17	238	3	0	0	0	6
1992-93	San Diego	IHL	5	0	2	2	5	....	....	....	....	....
	New Haven	AHL	31	5	4	9	124	....	....	....	....	....

a ECAC First All-Star Team (1987)

Traded to **Ottawa** by **Los Angeles** with Shawn McCosh for Marc Fortier and Jim Thomson, December 19, 1992. Claimed by **Florida** from **Ottawa** in Expansion Draft, June 24, 1993.

LACHANCE, BOB

Right wing. Shoots right. 5'11", 180 lbs. Born, Northampton, MA, February 1, 1974.
(St. Louis' 5th choice, 134th overall, in 1992 Entry Draft).

			Regular Season					Playoffs				
Season	Club	Lea	GP	G	A	TP	PIM	GP	G	A	TP	PIM
1991-92	Springfield	US Jr.	46	40	98	138	87	....	....	....	....	....
1992-93	Boston U.	H.E.	33	4	10	14	24	....	....	....	....	....

LACHANCE, SCOTT

Defense. Shoots left. 6'1", 197 lbs. Born, Charlottesville, VA, October 22, 1972.
(NY Islanders' 1st choice, 4th overall, in 1991 Entry Draft).

			Regular Season					Playoffs				
Season	Club	Lea	GP	G	A	TP	PIM	GP	G	A	TP	PIM
1990-91	Boston U.	H.E.	31	5	19	24	48	....	....	....	....	....
1991-92	U.S. National	....	36	1	10	11	34	....	....	....	....	....
	U.S. Olympic	....	8	0	1	1	6	....	....	....	....	....
	NY Islanders	**NHL**	**17**	**1**	**4**	**5**	**9**	....	....	....	....	....
1992-93	**NY Islanders**	**NHL**	**75**	**7**	**17**	**24**	**67**	....	....	....	....	....
	NHL Totals		**92**	**8**	**21**	**29**	**76**	....	....	....	....	....

LACOUTURE, DAVID

Right wing. Shoots right. 6'3", 210 lbs. Born, Framingham, MA, December 30, 1969.
(St. Louis' 5th choice, 105th overall, in 1988 Entry Draft).

			Regular Season					Playoffs				
Season	Club	Lea	GP	G	A	TP	PIM	GP	G	A	TP	PIM
1989-90	U. of Maine	H.E.	9	0	2	2	6	....	....	....	....	....
1990-91	U. of Maine	H.E.	40	7	9	16	33	....	....	....	....	....
1991-92	U. of Maine	H.E.	28	5	4	9	30	....	....	....	....	....
1992-93	U. of Maine	H.E.	43	8	6	14	78	....	....	....	....	....

LACROIX, DANIEL (la-QUAH)

Left wing. Shoots left. 6'2", 188 lbs. Born, Montreal, Que., March 11, 1969.
(NY Rangers' 2nd choice, 31st overall, in 1987 Entry Draft).

			Regular Season					Playoffs				
Season	Club	Lea	GP	G	A	TP	PIM	GP	G	A	TP	PIM
1986-87	Granby	QMJHL	54	9	16	25	311	8	1	2	3	22
1987-88	Granby	QMJHL	58	24	50	74	468	5	0	4	4	12
1988-89	Granby	QMJHL	70	45	49	94	320	4	1	1	2	57
	Denver	IHL	2	0	1	1	0	2	0	1	1	0
1989-90	Flint	IHL	61	12	16	28	128	4	2	0	2	24
1990-91	Binghamton	AHL	54	7	12	19	237	5	1	0	4	24
1991-92	Binghamton	AHL	52	12	20	32	149	11	2	4	6	28
1992-93	Binghamton	AHL	73	21	22	43	255	....	....	....	....	....

LACROIX, ERIC

Left wing. Shoots left. 6'1", 200 lbs. Born, Montreal, Que., July 15, 1971.
(Toronto's 6th choice, 136th overall, in 1990 Entry Draft).

			Regular Season					Playoffs				
Season	Club	Lea	GP	G	A	TP	PIM	GP	G	A	TP	PIM
1990-91	St. Lawrence	ECAC	35	13	11	24	35	....	....	....	....	....
1991-92	St. Lawrence	ECAC	34	11	20	31	40	....	....	....	....	....
1992-93	St. John's	AHL	76	15	19	34	59	9	5	3	8	4

LACROIX, MARTIN

Right wing. Shoots right. 5'11", 155 lbs. Born, Rosemere, Que., January 4, 1970.
(NY Islanders' 10th choice, 216th overall, in 1990 Entry Draft).

			Regular Season					Playoffs				
Season	Club	Lea	GP	G	A	TP	PIM	GP	G	A	TP	PIM
1988-89	St. Lawrence	ECAC	19	1	5	6	23	....	....	....	....	....
1989-90	St. Lawrence	ECAC	32	11	8	19	14	....	....	....	....	....
1990-91	St. Lawrence	ECAC	35	16	26	42	46	....	....	....	....	....
1991-92	St. Lawrence	ECAC	22	17	17	34	24	....	....	....	....	....
1992-93	Capital Dist.	AHL	20	1	4	5	21	....	....	....	....	....
	Richmond	ECHL	17	5	13	18	40	....	....	....	....	....

LADOUCEUR, RANDY (LAD-uh-SOOR)

Defense. Shoots left. 6'2", 220 lbs. Born, Brockville, Ont., June 30, 1960.

			Regular Season					Playoffs				
Season	Club	Lea	GP	G	A	TP	PIM	GP	G	A	TP	PIM
1978-79	Brantford	OHA	64	3	17	20	141	....	....	....	....	....
1979-80	Brantford	OHA	37	6	15	21	125	8	0	5	5	18
1980-81	Kalamazoo	IHL	80	7	30	37	52	8	1	3	4	10
1981-82	Adirondack	AHL	78	4	28	32	78	5	1	1	2	6
1982-83	**Detroit**	**NHL**	**27**	**0**	**4**	**4**	**16**	....	....	....	....	....
	Adirondack	AHL	48	11	21	32	54	....	....	....	....	....
1983-84	**Detroit**	**NHL**	**71**	**3**	**17**	**20**	**58**	**4**	**1**	**0**	**1**	**6**
	Adirondack	AHL	11	3	5	8	12	....	....	....	....	....
1984-85	**Detroit**	**NHL**	**80**	**3**	**27**	**30**	**108**	**3**	**1**	**0**	**1**	**0**
1985-86	**Detroit**	**NHL**	**78**	**5**	**13**	**18**	**196**	....	....	....	....	....
1986-87	**Detroit**	**NHL**	**34**	**3**	**6**	**9**	**70**	....	....	....	....	....
	Hartford	**NHL**	**36**	**2**	**3**	**5**	**51**	**6**	**0**	**2**	**2**	**12**
1987-88	**Hartford**	**NHL**	**67**	**1**	**7**	**8**	**91**	**6**	**1**	**1**	**2**	**4**
1988-89	**Hartford**	**NHL**	**75**	**2**	**5**	**7**	**95**	**1**	**0**	**0**	**0**	**10**
1989-90	**Hartford**	**NHL**	**71**	**3**	**12**	**15**	**126**	**7**	**1**	**0**	**1**	**10**
1990-91	**Hartford**	**NHL**	**67**	**1**	**3**	**4**	**118**	**6**	**1**	**4**	**5**	**6**
1991-92	**Hartford**	**NHL**	**74**	**1**	**9**	**10**	**127**	**7**	**0**	**1**	**1**	**11**
1992-93	**Hartford**	**NHL**	**62**	**2**	**4**	**6**	**109**	....	....	....	....	....
	NHL Totals		**742**	**26**	**110**	**136**	**1165**	**40**	**5**	**8**	**13**	**59**

Signed as a free agent by **Detroit**, November 1, 1979. Traded to **Hartford** by **Detroit** for Dave Barr, January 12, 1987. Claimed by **Anaheim** from **Hartford** in Expansion Draft, June 24, 1993.

LAFAYETTE, NATHAN

Center. Shoots right. 6'1", 194 lbs. Born, New Westminster, B.C., February 17, 1973.
(St. Louis' 3rd choice, 65th overall, in 1991 Entry Draft).

			Regular Season					Playoffs				
Season	Club	Lea	GP	G	A	TP	PIM	GP	G	A	TP	PIM
1989-90	Kingston	OHL	53	6	8	14	14	7	0	1	1	0
1990-91	Kingston	OHL	35	13	13	26	10	....	....	....	....	....
	Cornwall	OHL	28	16	22	38	25	....	....	....	....	....
1991-92a	Cornwall	OHL	66	28	45	73	26	6	2	5	7	15
1992-93	Newmarket	OHL	58	49	38	87	26	7	4	5	9	19

a Canadian Major Junior Scholastic Player of the Year (1992)

LaFONTAINE, PAT

Center. Shoots right. 5'10", 177 lbs. Born, St. Louis, MO, February 22, 1965.
(NY Islanders' 1st choice, 3rd overall, in 1983 Entry Draft).

			Regular Season					Playoffs				
Season	Club	Lea	GP	G	A	TP	PIM	GP	G	A	TP	PIM
1982-83abcd	Verdun	QMJHL	70	*104	*130	*234	10	15	11	*24	*35	4
1983-84	U.S. National	....	58	56	55	111	22	....	....	....	....	....
	U.S. Olympic	....	6	5	5	10	0	....	....	....	....	....
	NY Islanders	NHL	15	13	6	19	6	16	3	6	9	8
1984-85	NY Islanders	NHL	67	19	35	54	32	9	1	2	3	4
1985-86	NY Islanders	NHL	65	30	23	53	43	3	1	0	1	0
1986-87	NY Islanders	NHL	80	38	32	70	70	14	5	7	12	10
1987-88	NY Islanders	NHL	75	47	45	92	52	6	4	5	9	8
1988-89	NY Islanders	NHL	79	45	43	88	26	....	....	....	....	....
1989-90e	NY Islanders	NHL	74	54	51	105	38	2	0	1	1	0
1990-91	NY Islanders	NHL	75	41	44	85	42	....	....	....	....	....
1991-92	Buffalo	NHL	57	46	47	93	98	7	8	3	11	4
1992-93f	Buffalo	NHL	84	53	95	148	63	7	2	10	12	0
	NHL Totals		671	386	421	807	470	64	24	34	58	34

a QMJHL First All-Star Team (1983)
b QMJHL Most Valuable Player (1983)
c QMJHL Most Valuable Player in Playoffs (1983)
d Canadian Major Junior Player of the Year (1983)
e Won Dodge Performer of the Year Award (1990)
f NHL Second All-Star Team (1993)

Played in NHL All-Star Game (1988-91, 1993)

Traded to **Buffalo** by **NY Islanders** with Randy Hillier, Randy Wood and future considerations for Pierre Turgeon, Uwe Krupp, Benoit Hogue and Dave McLlwain, October 25, 1991.

LAFORGE, MARC

Left wing. Shoots left. 6'2", 210 lbs. Born, Sudbury, Ont., January 3, 1968.
(Hartford's 2nd choice, 32nd overall, in 1986 Entry Draft).

			Regular Season					Playoffs				
Season	Club	Lea	GP	G	A	TP	PIM	GP	G	A	TP	PIM
1984-85	Kingston	OHL	57	1	5	6	214	....	....	....	....	....
1985-86	Kingston	OHL	60	1	13	14	248	10	0	1	1	30
1986-87	Binghamton	AHL	....	....	....	....	....	4	0	0	0	7
	Kingston	OHL	53	2	10	12	224	12	1	0	1	79
1987-88	Sudbury	OHL	14	0	2	2	68	....	....	....	....	....
1988-89	Binghamton	AHL	38	2	2	4	179	....	....	....	....	....
	Indianapolis	IHL	14	0	2	2	138	....	....	....	....	....
1989-90	Hartford	NHL	9	0	0	0	43	....	....	....	....	....
	Binghamton	AHL	25	2	6	8	111	....	....	....	....	....
	Cape Breton	AHL	3	0	1	1	24	3	0	0	0	27
1990-91	Cape Breton	AHL	49	1	7	8	217	....	....	....	....	....
1991-92	Cape Breton	AHL	59	0	14	14	341	4	0	0	0	24
1992-93	Cape Breton	AHL	77	1	12	13	208	15	1	2	3	*78
	NHL Totals		9	0	0	0	43	....	....	....	....	....

Traded to **Edmonton** by **Hartford** for the rights to Cam Brauer, March 6, 1990.

LAFRANCE, DARRYL

Center. Shoots right. 5'11", 175 lbs. Born, Sudbury, Ont., March 20, 1974.
(Calgary's 6th choice, 121st overall, in 1993 Entry Draft).

			Regular Season					Playoffs				
Season	Club	Lea	GP	G	A	TP	PIM	GP	G	A	TP	PIM
1991-92	Oshawa	OHL	48	12	20	32	24	7	0	1	1	2
1992-93	Oshawa	OHL	66	35	51	86	24	13	8	8	16	0

LAFRENIERE, JASON (LAH-frehn-YAIR)

Center. Shoots right. 5'11", 185 lbs. Born, St. Catharines, Ont., December 6, 1966.
(Quebec's 2nd choice, 36th overall, in 1985 Entry Draft).

			Regular Season					Playoffs				
Season	Club	Lea	GP	G	A	TP	PIM	GP	G	A	TP	PIM
1983-84	Brantford	OHL	70	24	57	81	4	6	2	4	6	2
1984-85	Hamilton	OHL	59	26	69	95	10	17	12	16	28	0
1985-86a	Hamilton	OHL	14	12	10	22	2	....	....	....	....	....
a	Belleville	OHL	48	37	73	110	2	23	10	*22	*32	6
1986-87	Quebec	NHL	56	13	15	28	8	12	1	5	6	2
	Fredericton	AHL	11	3	11	14	0	....	....	....	....	....
1987-88	Quebec	NHL	40	10	19	29	4	....	....	....	....	....
	Fredericton	AHL	32	12	19	31	38	....	....	....	....	....
1988-89	NY Rangers	NHL	38	8	16	24	6	3	0	0	0	17
	Denver	IHL	24	10	19	29	17	....	....	....	....	....
1989-90	Flint	IHL	41	9	25	34	34	....	....	....	....	....
	Phoenix	IHL	14	4	9	13	0	....	....	....	....	....
1990-91	Cdn. National	....	59	26	33	59	50	....	....	....	....	....
1991-92	Landshut	Ger.	23	7	22	29	16	....	....	....	....	....
	San Diego	IHL	5	1	2	3	2	....	....	....	....	....
1992-93	Tampa Bay	NHL	11	3	3	6	4	....	....	....	....	....
	Atlanta	IHL	63	23	47	70	34	9	3	4	7	22
	NHL Totals		145	34	53	87	22	15	1	5	6	19

a OHL First All-Star Team (1986)

Traded to **NY Rangers** by **Quebec** with Normand Rochefort for Bruce Bell, Jari Gronstrand, Walt Poddubny and NY Rangers' fourth round choice (Eric Dubois) in 1989 Entry Draft, August 1, 1988. Signed as a free agent by **Tampa Bay**, July 29, 1992.

LALOR, MIKE

Defense. Shoots left. 6', 200 lbs. Born, Buffalo, NY, March 8, 1963.

			Regular Season					Playoffs				
Season	Club	Lea	GP	G	A	TP	PIM	GP	G	A	TP	PIM
1981-82	Brantford	OHL	64	3	13	16	114	11	0	6	6	11
1982-83	Brantford	OHL	65	10	30	40	113	8	1	3	4	20
1983-84	Nova Scotia	AHL	67	5	11	16	80	12	0	2	2	13
1984-85	Sherbrooke	AHL	79	9	23	32	114	17	3	5	8	36
1985-86	Montreal	NHL	62	3	5	8	56	17	1	2	3	29
1986-87	Montreal	NHL	57	0	10	10	47	13	2	1	3	29
1987-88	Montreal	NHL	66	1	10	11	113	11	0	0	0	11
1988-89	Montreal	NHL	12	1	4	5	15	....	....	....	....	....
	St. Louis	NHL	36	1	14	15	54	10	1	1	2	14
1989-90	St. Louis	NHL	78	0	16	16	81	12	0	2	2	31
1990-91	Washington	NHL	68	1	5	6	61	10	1	2	3	22
1991-92	Washington	NHL	64	5	7	12	64	....	....	....	....	....
	Winnipeg	NHL	15	2	3	5	14	7	0	0	0	19
1992-93	Winnipeg	NHL	64	1	8	9	76	4	0	2	2	4
	NHL Totals		522	15	82	97	581	84	5	10	15	159

Signed as a free agent by **Montreal**, September, 1983. Traded to **St. Louis** by **Montreal** for the option (exercised by Montreal) to switch first round choices in 1990 Entry Draft and St. Louis' third round choices in the 1991 Entry Draft, January 16, 1989. Traded to **Washington** by **St. Louis** with Peter Zezel for Geoff Courtnall, July 13, 1990. Traded to **Winnipeg** by **Washington** for Paul MacDermid, March 2, 1992. Signed as a free agent by **San Jose**, August 13, 1993.

LAMB, MARK

Center. Shoots left. 5'9", 180 lbs. Born, Ponteix, Sask., August 3, 1964.
(Calgary's 5th choice, 72nd overall, in 1982 Entry Draft).

			Regular Season					Playoffs				
Season	Club	Lea	GP	G	A	TP	PIM	GP	G	A	TP	PIM
1981-82	Billings	WHL	72	45	56	101	46	5	4	6	10	4
1982-83	Nanaimo	WHL	30	14	37	51	16	....	....	....	....	....
	Medicine Hat	WHL	46	22	43	65	33	5	3	2	5	4
	Colorado	CHL	....	....	....	....	....	6	0	2	2	0
1983-84a	Medicine Hat	WHL	72	59	77	136	30	14	12	11	23	6
1984-85	Moncton	AHL	80	23	49	72	53	....	....	....	....	....
1985-86	Calgary	NHL	1	0	0	0	0	....	....	....	....	....
	Moncton	AHL	79	26	50	76	51	10	2	6	8	17
1986-87	Detroit	NHL	22	2	1	3	8	11	0	0	0	11
	Adirondack	AHL	49	14	36	50	45	....	....	....	....	....
1987-88	Edmonton	NHL	2	0	0	0	0	....	....	....	....	....
	Nova Scotia	AHL	69	27	61	88	45	5	0	5	5	6
1988-89	Edmonton	NHL	20	2	8	10	14	6	0	2	2	8
	Cape Breton	AHL	54	33	49	82	29	....	....	....	....	....
1989-90	Edmonton	NHL	58	12	16	28	42	22	6	11	17	2
1990-91	Edmonton	NHL	37	4	8	12	25	15	0	5	5	20
1991-92	Edmonton	NHL	59	6	22	28	46	16	1	1	2	10
1992-93	Ottawa	NHL	71	7	19	26	64	....	....	....	....	....
	NHL Totals		270	33	74	107	199	70	7	19	26	51

a WHL First All-Star Team, East Division (1984)

Signed as a free agent by **Detroit**, July 28, 1986. Claimed by **Edmonton** in NHL Waiver Draft, October 5, 1987. Claimed by **Ottawa** from **Edmonton** in Expansion Draft, June 18, 1992.

LAMBERT, DAN

Defense. Shoots left. 5'8", 177 lbs. Born, St. Boniface, Man., January 12, 1970.
(Quebec's 8th choice, 106th overall, in 1989 Entry Draft).

			Regular Season					Playoffs				
Season	Club	Lea	GP	G	A	TP	PIM	GP	G	A	TP	PIM
1986-87	Swift Current	WHL	68	13	53	66	95	4	1	1	2	9
1987-88	Swift Current	WHL	69	20	63	83	120	10	2	10	12	45
1988-89ab	Swift Current	WHL	57	25	77	102	158	12	9	19	28	12
1989-90a	Swift Current	WHL	50	17	51	68	119	4	2	3	5	12
1990-91	Quebec	NHL	1	0	0	0	0	....	....	....	....	....
	Halifax	AHL	30	7	13	20	20	....	....	....	....	....
	Fort Wayne	IHL	49	10	27	37	65	19	4	10	14	20
1991-92	Quebec	NHL	28	6	9	15	22	....	....	....	....	....
	Halifax	AHL	47	3	28	31	33	....	....	....	....	....
1992-93	Moncton	AHL	73	11	30	41	100	5	1	2	3	2
	NHL Totals		29	6	9	15	22	....	....	....	....	....

a WHL East First All-Star Team (1989, 1990)
b WHL Best Defenseman (1989)

Traded to **Winnipeg** by **Quebec** for Shawn Cronin, August 25, 1992.

LAMMENS, HANK

Defense. Shoots left. 6'2", 210 lbs. Born, Brockville, Ont., February 21, 1966.
(NY Islanders' 10th choice, 160th overall, in 1985 Entry Draft).

			Regular Season					Playoffs				
Season	Club	Lea	GP	G	A	TP	PIM	GP	G	A	TP	PIM
1984-85	St. Lawrence	ECAC	21	17	9	26	16	....	....	....	....	....
1985-86	St. Lawrence	ECAC	30	3	14	17	60	....	....	....	....	....
1986-87ab	St. Lawrence	ECAC	35	6	13	19	92	....	....	....	....	....
1987-88a	St. Lawrence	ECAC	32	3	6	9	64	....	....	....	....	....
1988-89	Springfield	AHL	69	1	13	14	55	....	....	....	....	....
1989-90	Springfield	AHL	43	0	6	6	27	....	....	....	....	....
1990-91	Capital Dist.	AHL	32	0	5	5	14	....	....	....	....	....
	Kansas City	IHL	17	0	1	1	27	....	....	....	....	....
1992-93	Cdn. Olympic	....	75	8	22	30	75	....	....	....	....	....

a ECAC Second All-Star Team (1987, 1988)
b NCAA East Second All-American Team (1987)

Signed as a free agent by **Ottawa**, June 25, 1993.

LANG, ROBERT

Center. Shoots right. 6'2", 189 lbs. Born, Most, Czechoslovakia, December 19, 1970.
(Los Angeles' 6th choice, 133rd overall, in 1990 Entry Draft).

			Regular Season					Playoffs				
Season	Club	Lea	GP	G	A	TP	PIM	GP	G	A	TP	PIM
1988-89	Litvinov	Czech.	7	3	2	5	0	....	....	....	....	....
1989-90	Litvinov	Czech.	39	11	10	21	....	....	....	....	....	....
1990-91	Litvinov	Czech.	56	26	26	52	38	....	....	....	....	....
1991-92	Litvinov	Czech.	43	12	31	43	34	....	....	....	....	....
1992-93	Los Angeles	NHL	11	0	5	5	2	....	....	....	....	....
	Phoenix	IHL	38	9	21	30	20	....	....	....	....	....
	NHL Totals		11	0	5	5	2	....	....	....	....	....

LANGENBRUNNER, JAMIE

Center. Shoots right. 5'11", 180 lbs. Born, Duluth, MN, July 24, 1975.
(Dallas' 2nd choice, 35th overall, in 1993 Entry Draft).

			Regular Season					Playoffs				
Season	Club	Lea	GP	G	A	TP	PIM	GP	G	A	TP	PIM
1991-92	Cloquet	HS	23	16	23	39	24	....	....	....	....	....
1992-93	Cloquet	HS	27	27	62	89	18	....	....	....	....	....

LANGWAY, ROD CORRY

Defense. Shoots left. 6'3", 218 lbs. Born, Maag, Formosa, May 3, 1957.
(Montreal's 3rd choice, 36th overall, in 1977 Amateur Draft).

			Regular Season					Playoffs				
Season	Club	Lea	GP	G	A	TP	PIM	GP	G	A	TP	PIM
1976-77	N. Hampshire	ECAC	34	10	43	53	52	....	....	....	....	....
1977-78	Hampton	AHL	30	6	16	22	50	....	....	....	....	....
	Birmingham	WHA	52	3	18	21	52	4	0	0	0	9
1978-79	**Montreal**	**NHL**	**45**	**3**	**4**	**7**	**30**	**8**	**0**	**0**	**0**	**16**
	Nova Scotia	AHL	18	6	13	19	29	....	....	....	....	....
1979-80	**Montreal**	**NHL**	**77**	**7**	**29**	**36**	**81**	**10**	**3**	**3**	**6**	**2**
1980-81	**Montreal**	**NHL**	**80**	**11**	**34**	**45**	**120**	**3**	**0**	**0**	**0**	**6**
1981-82	**Montreal**	**NHL**	**66**	**5**	**34**	**39**	**116**	**5**	**0**	**3**	**3**	**18**
1982-83ab	**Washington**	**NHL**	**80**	**3**	**29**	**32**	**75**	**4**	**0**	**0**	**0**	**0**
1983-84ab	**Washington**	**NHL**	**80**	**9**	**24**	**33**	**61**	**8**	**0**	**5**	**5**	**7**
1984-85c	**Washington**	**NHL**	**79**	**4**	**22**	**26**	**54**	**5**	**0**	**1**	**1**	**6**
1985-86	**Washington**	**NHL**	**71**	**1**	**17**	**18**	**61**	**9**	**1**	**2**	**3**	**6**
1986-87	**Washington**	**NHL**	**78**	**2**	**25**	**27**	**53**	**7**	**0**	**1**	**1**	**2**
1987-88	**Washington**	**NHL**	**63**	**3**	**13**	**16**	**28**	**6**	**0**	**0**	**0**	**8**
1988-89	**Washington**	**NHL**	**76**	**2**	**19**	**21**	**65**	**6**	**0**	**0**	**0**	**6**
1989-90	**Washington**	**NHL**	**58**	**0**	**8**	**8**	**39**	**15**	**1**	**4**	**5**	**12**
1990-91	**Washington**	**NHL**	**56**	**1**	**7**	**8**	**24**	**11**	**0**	**2**	**2**	**6**
1991-92	**Washington**	**NHL**	**64**	**0**	**13**	**13**	**22**	**7**	**0**	**1**	**1**	**2**
1992-93	**Washington**	**NHL**	**21**	**0**	**0**	**0**	**20**	....	....	....	....	....
	NHL Totals		**994**	**51**	**278**	**329**	**849**	**104**	**5**	**22**	**27**	**97**

a Won James Norris Memorial Trophy (1983, 1984)
b NHL First All-Star Team (1983, 1984)
c NHL Second All-Star Team (1985)

Played in NHL All-Star Game (1981-86)

Claimed by **Montreal** as fill in Expansion Draft, June 13, 1979. Traded to **Washington** by **Montreal** with Doug Jarvis, Craig Laughlin and Brian Engblom for Ryan Walter and Rick Green, September 9, 1982.

LANIEL, MARC

Defense. Shoots left. 6'1", 194 lbs. Born, Oshawa, Ont., January 16, 1968.
(New Jersey's 4th choice, 62nd overall, in 1986 Entry Draft).

			Regular Season					Playoffs				
Season	Club	Lea	GP	G	A	TP	PIM	GP	G	A	TP	PIM
1985-86	Oshawa	OHL	66	9	25	34	27	6	2	3	5	6
1986-87	Oshawa	OHL	63	14	31	45	42	26	3	13	16	20
1987-88	Oshawa	OHL	41	8	32	40	56	7	2	2	4	4
	Utica	AHL	2	0	0	0	....	....	....	....	....	....
1988-89	Utica	AHL	80	6	28	34	43	5	0	1	1	2
1989-90	Utica	AHL	20	0	0	0	25	....	....	....	....	....
	Phoenix	IHL	26	3	15	18	10	....	....	....	....	....
1990-91	Utica	AHL	57	6	9	15	45	....	....	....	....	....
1991-92	San Diego	AHL	10	0	2	2	16	....	....	....	....	....
	Winston-Salem	ECHL	57	15	36	51	90	....	....	....	....	....
1992-93	Cincinnati	IHL	13	1	9	10	2	....	....	....	....	....
	Birmingham	ECHL	21	5	9	14	26	....	....	....	....	....
	Fredericton	AHL	7	0	1	1	6	5	0	2	2	23

Signed as a free agent by **Montreal**, May 3, 1993.

LANK, JEFF

Defense. Shoots left. 6'3", 185 lbs. Born, Indian Head, Sask., January -27, 0.
(Montreal's 6th choice, 113th overall, in 1993 Entry Draft).

			Regular Season					Playoffs				
Season	Club	Lea	GP	G	A	TP	PIM	GP	G	A	TP	PIM
1991-92	Prince Albert	WHL	56	2	8	10	26	9	0	0	0	2
1992-93	Prince Albert	WHL	63	1	11	12	60	....	....	....	....	....

LANZ, RICK ROMAN

Defense. Shoots right. 6'2", 203 lbs. Born, Karlouy Vary, Czech., September 16, 1961.
(Vancouver's 1st choice, 7th overall, in 1980 Entry Draft).

			Regular Season					Playoffs				
Season	Club	Lea	GP	G	A	TP	PIM	GP	G	A	TP	PIM
1978-79	Oshawa	OHA	65	12	47	59	88	5	1	3	4	14
1979-80a	Oshawa	OHA	52	18	38	56	51	7	2	3	5	6
1980-81	**Vancouver**	**NHL**	**76**	**7**	**22**	**29**	**40**	**3**	**0**	**0**	**0**	**4**
1981-82	**Vancouver**	**NHL**	**39**	**3**	**11**	**14**	**48**	....	....	....	....	....
1982-83	**Vancouver**	**NHL**	**74**	**10**	**38**	**48**	**46**	**4**	**2**	**1**	**3**	**0**
1983-84	**Vancouver**	**NHL**	**79**	**18**	**39**	**57**	**45**	**4**	**0**	**4**	**4**	**2**
1984-85	**Vancouver**	**NHL**	**57**	**2**	**17**	**19**	**69**	....	....	....	....	....
1985-86	**Vancouver**	**NHL**	**75**	**15**	**38**	**53**	**73**	**3**	**0**	**0**	**0**	**0**
1986-87	**Vancouver**	**NHL**	**17**	**1**	**6**	**7**	**10**	....	....	....	....	....
	Toronto	**NHL**	**44**	**2**	**19**	**21**	**32**	**13**	**1**	**3**	**4**	**27**
1987-88	**Toronto**	**NHL**	**75**	**6**	**22**	**28**	**65**	**1**	**0**	**0**	**0**	**2**
1988-89	**Toronto**	**NHL**	**32**	**1**	**9**	**10**	**18**	....	....	....	....	....
1989-90	Ambri-Piotta	Switz.	36	4	14	18	....	....	....	....	....	....
1990-91	Indianapolis	IHL	8	0	5	5	18	....	....	....	....	....
1991-92	**Chicago**	**NHL**	**1**	**0**	**0**	**0**	**2**	....	....	....	....	....
	Phoenix	IHL	38	7	14	21	21	....	....	....	....	....
1992-93	Atlanta	IHL	25	6	12	18	30	....	....	....	....	....
	NHL Totals		**569**	**65**	**221**	**286**	**448**	**28**	**3**	**8**	**11**	**35**

a OHA Third All-Star Team (1980)

Traded to **Toronto** by **Vancouver** for Jim Benning and Dan Hodgson, December 2, 1986. Signed as a free agent by **Chicago**, August 13, 1990. Traded to **Los Angeles** by **Chicago** for cash, November 29, 1991. Signed as a free agent by **Tampa Bay**, September 1, 1992.

LAPERRIERE, DANIEL

Defense. Shoots left. 6'1", 195 lbs. Born, Laval, Que., March 28, 1969.
(St. Louis' 4th choice, 93rd overall, in 1989 Entry Draft).

			Regular Season					Playoffs				
Season	Club	Lea	GP	G	A	TP	PIM	GP	G	A	TP	PIM
1988-89	St. Lawrence	ECAC	28	0	7	7	10	....	....	....	....	....
1989-90	St. Lawrence	ECAC	31	6	19	25	16	....	....	....	....	....
1990-91a	St. Lawrence	ECAC	34	7	31	38	18	....	....	....	....	....
1991-92bc	St. Lawrence	ECAC	32	8	*45	53	36	....	....	....	....	....
1992-93	**St. Louis**	**NHL**	**5**	**0**	**1**	**1**	**0**	....	....	....	....	....
	Peoria	IHL	54	4	20	24	28	....	....	....	....	....
	NHL Totals		**5**	**0**	**1**	**1**	**0**	....	....	....	....	....

a ECAC Second All-Star Team (1991)
b ECAC First All-Star Team (1992)
c NCAA East First All-American Team (1992)

LAPERRIERE, IAN

Center. Shoots right. 6', 191 lbs. Born, Montreal, Que., January 19, 1974.
(St. Louis' 6th choice, 158th overall, in 1992 Entry Draft).

			Regular Season					Playoffs				
Season	Club	Lea	GP	G	A	TP	PIM	GP	G	A	TP	PIM
1990-91	Drummondville	QMJHL	65	19	29	48	117	14	2	9	11	48
1991-92	Drummondville	QMJHL	70	28	49	77	160	4	2	2	4	9
1992-93a	Drummondville	QMJHL	60	44	*96	140	188	10	6	13	19	20

a QMJHL Second All-Star Team (1993)

LAPOINTE, CLAUDE

Center. Shoots left. 5'9", 173 lbs. Born, Lachine, Que., October 11, 1968.
(Quebec's 12th choice, 234th overall, in 1988 Entry Draft).

			Regular Season					Playoffs				
Season	Club	Lea	GP	G	A	TP	PIM	GP	G	A	TP	PIM
1986-87	Trois-Rivières	QMJHL	70	47	57	104	123	....	....	....	....	....
1987-88	Laval	QMJHL	69	37	83	120	143	13	2	17	19	53
1988-89	Laval	QMJHL	63	32	72	104	158	17	5	14	19	66
1989-90	Halifax	AHL	63	18	19	37	51	6	1	1	2	34
1990-91	**Quebec**	**NHL**	**13**	**2**	**2**	**4**	**4**	....	....	....	....	....
	Halifax	AHL	43	17	17	34	46	....	....	....	....	....
1991-92	**Quebec**	**NHL**	**78**	**13**	**20**	**33**	**86**	....	....	....	....	....
1992-93	**Quebec**	**NHL**	**74**	**10**	**26**	**36**	**98**	**6**	**2**	**4**	**6**	**8**
	NHL Totals		**165**	**25**	**48**	**73**	**188**	**6**	**2**	**4**	**6**	**8**

LAPOINTE, MARTIN

Right wing. Shoots right. 5'11", 200 lbs. Born, Lachine, Que., September 12, 1973.
(Detroit's 1st choice, 10th overall, in 1991 Entry Draft).

			Regular Season					Playoffs				
Season	Club	Lea	GP	G	A	TP	PIM	GP	G	A	TP	PIM
1989-90ab	Laval	QMJHL	65	42	54	96	77	14	8	17	25	54
1990-91c	Laval	QMJHL	64	44	54	98	66	13	7	14	21	26
1991-92	**Detroit**	**NHL**	**4**	**0**	**1**	**1**	**5**	**3**	**0**	**1**	**1**	**4**
	Laval	QMJHL	31	25	30	55	84	10	4	10	14	32
	Adirondack	AHL	....	....	....	....	....	8	2	2	4	4
1992-93	**Detroit**	**NHL**	**3**	**0**	**0**	**0**	**0**	....	....	....	....	....
de	Laval	QMJHL	35	38	51	89	41	13	*13	*17	*30	22
	Adirondack	AHL	8	1	2	3	9	....	....	....	....	....
	NHL Totals		**7**	**0**	**1**	**1**	**5**	**3**	**0**	**1**	**1**	**4**

a QMJHL First All-Star Team (1990)
b QMJHL Offensive Rookie of the Year (1990)
c QMJHL Second All-Star Team (1991)
d QMJHL First All-Star Team (1993)
e Memorial Cup All-Star Team (1993)

LAPOINTE, SYLVAIN

Defense. Shoots left. 6', 190 lbs. Born, Anjou, Que., March 14, 1973.
(Montreal's 4th choice, 83rd overall, in 1991 Entry Draft).

			Regular Season					Playoffs				
Season	Club	Lea	GP	G	A	TP	PIM	GP	G	A	TP	PIM
1990-91	Clarkson	ECAC	40	2	12	14	30	....	....	....	....	....
1991-92	Hull	QMJHL	67	0	11	11	65	6	1	1	2	10
1992-93	Hull	QMJHL	70	5	19	24	64	10	1	0	1	2

LARIONOV, IGOR (LAIR-ee-AH-nohv)

Center. Shoots left. 5'9", 165 lbs. Born, Voskresensk, Soviet Union, December 3, 1960.
(Vancouver's 11th choice, 214th overall, in 1985 Entry Draft).

			Regular Season					Playoffs				
Season	Club	Lea	GP	G	A	TP	PIM	GP	G	A	TP	PIM
1977-78	Khimik	USSR	6	3	0	3	4	....	....	....	....	....
1978-79	Khimik	USSR	32	3	4	7	12	....	....	....	....	....
1979-80	Khimik	USSR	42	11	7	18	24	....	....	....	....	....
1980-81	Khimik	USSR	43	22	23	45	36	....	....	....	....	....
1981-82	CSKA	USSR	46	31	22	53	6	....	....	....	....	....
1982-83a	CSKA	USSR	44	20	19	39	20	....	....	....	....	....
1983-84	CSKA	USSR	43	15	26	41	30	....	....	....	....	....
1984-85	CSKA	USSR	40	18	28	46	20	....	....	....	....	....
1985-86a	CSKA	USSR	40	21	31	52	33	....	....	....	....	....
1986-87a	CSKA	USSR	39	20	26	46	34	....	....	....	....	....
1987-88ab	CSKA	USSR	51	25	32	57	54	....	....	....	....	....
1988-89	CSKA	USSR	31	15	12	27	22	....	....	....	....	....
1989-90	**Vancouver**	**NHL**	**74**	**17**	**27**	**44**	**20**	....	....	....	....	....
1990-91	**Vancouver**	**NHL**	**64**	**13**	**21**	**34**	**14**	**6**	**1**	**0**	**1**	**6**
1991-92	**Vancouver**	**NHL**	**72**	**21**	**44**	**65**	**54**	**13**	**3**	**7**	**10**	**4**
1992-93	Lugano	Switz.	24	10	19	29	44	....	....	....	....	....
	NHL Totals		**210**	**51**	**92**	**143**	**88**	**19**	**4**	**7**	**11**	**10**

a Soviet National League All-Star (1983, 1985-88)
b Soviet Player of the Year (1988)

Claimed by **San Jose** from **Vancouver** in NHL Waiver Draft, October 4, 1992.

LARKIN, MIKE

Defense. Shoots right. 6'1", 180 lbs. Born, Boston, MA, March 15, 1973.
(Chicago's 11th choice, 242nd overall, in 1991 Entry Draft).

			Regular Season					Playoffs				
Season	Club	Lea	GP	G	A	TP	PIM	GP	G	A	TP	PIM
1991-92	U. of Vermont	ECAC	14	2	2	4	14	....	....	....	....	....
1992-93	U. of Vermont	ECAC	28	0	2	2	66	....	....	....	....	....

LARMER, STEVE DONALD

Right wing. Shoots left. 5'11", 189 lbs. Born, Peterborough, Ont., June 16, 1961.
(Chicago's 11th choice, 120th overall, in 1980 Entry Draft).

			Regular Season					Playoffs				
Season	Club	Lea	GP	G	A	TP	PIM	GP	G	A	TP	PIM
1977-78	Peterborough	OHA	62	24	17	41	51	18	5	7	12	27
1978-79	Niagara Falls	OHA	66	37	47	84	108	....	....	....	....	....
1979-80	Niagara Falls	OHA	67	45	69	114	71	10	5	9	14	15
1980-81	**Chicago**	**NHL**	**4**	**0**	**1**	**1**	**0**	....	....	....	....	....
a	Niagara Falls	OHA	61	55	78	133	73	12	13	8	21	24
1981-82	**Chicago**	**NHL**	**3**	**0**	**0**	**0**	**0**	....	....	....	....	....
b	New Brunswick	AHL	74	38	44	82	46	15	6	6	12	0
1982-83cd	**Chicago**	**NHL**	**80**	**43**	**47**	**90**	**28**	**11**	**5**	**7**	**12**	**8**
1983-84	**Chicago**	**NHL**	**80**	**35**	**40**	**75**	**34**	**5**	**2**	**2**	**4**	**7**
1984-85	**Chicago**	**NHL**	**80**	**46**	**40**	**86**	**16**	**15**	**9**	**13**	**22**	**14**
1985-86	**Chicago**	**NHL**	**80**	**31**	**45**	**76**	**47**	**3**	**0**	**3**	**3**	**4**
1986-87	**Chicago**	**NHL**	**80**	**28**	**56**	**84**	**22**	**4**	**0**	**0**	**0**	**2**
1987-88	**Chicago**	**NHL**	**80**	**41**	**48**	**89**	**42**	**5**	**1**	**6**	**7**	**0**
1988-89	**Chicago**	**NHL**	**80**	**43**	**44**	**87**	**54**	**16**	**8**	**9**	**17**	**22**
1989-90	**Chicago**	**NHL**	**80**	**31**	**59**	**90**	**40**	**20**	**7**	**15**	**22**	**2**
1990-91	**Chicago**	**NHL**	**80**	**44**	**57**	**101**	**79**	**6**	**5**	**1**	**6**	**4**
1991-92	**Chicago**	**NHL**	**80**	**29**	**45**	**74**	**65**	**18**	**8**	**7**	**15**	**6**
1992-93	**Chicago**	**NHL**	**84**	**35**	**35**	**70**	**48**	**4**	**0**	**3**	**3**	**0**
	NHL Totals		**891**	**406**	**517**	**923**	**475**	**107**	**45**	**66**	**111**	**69**

a OHA Second All-Star Team (1981)
b AHL Second All-Star Team (1982)
c Won Calder Trophy (1983)
d NHL All-Rookie Team (1983)

Played in NHL All-Star Game (1990, 1991)

LAROSE, BENOIT

Defense. Shoots left. 6', 200 lbs. Born, Ottawa, Ont., May 31, 1973.
(Detroit's 5th choice, 100th overall, in 1993 Entry Draft).

			Regular Season					Playoffs				
Season	Club	Lea	GP	G	A	TP	PIM	GP	G	A	TP	PIM
1991-92a	Laval	QMJHL	70	11	53	64	171	10	5	6	11	20
1992-93b	Laval	QMJHL	63	16	62	78	218	8	1	6	7	10

a QMJHL Second All-Star Team (1992)
b QMJHL First All-Star Team (1993)

LAROSE, GUY

Center. Shoots left. 5'9", 175 lbs. Born, Hull, Que., August 31, 1967.
(Buffalo's 11th choice, 224th overall, in 1985 Entry Draft).

			Regular Season					Playoffs				
Season	Club	Lea	GP	G	A	TP	PIM	GP	G	A	TP	PIM
1984-85	Guelph	OHL	58	30	30	60	63	....	....	....	....	....
1985-86	Guelph	OHL	37	12	36	48	55	....	....	....	....	....
	Ottawa	OHL	28	19	25	44	63	....	....	....	....	....
1986-87	Ottawa	OHL	66	28	49	77	77	11	2	8	10	27
1987-88	Moncton	AHL	77	22	31	53	127	....	....	....	....	....
1988-89	**Winnipeg**	**NHL**	**3**	**0**	**1**	**1**	**6**	....	....	....	....	....
	Moncton	AHL	72	32	27	59	176	10	4	4	8	37
1989-90	Moncton	AHL	79	44	26	70	232	....	....	....	....	....
1990-91	**Winnipeg**	**NHL**	**7**	**0**	**0**	**0**	**8**	....	....	....	....	....
	Moncton	AHL	35	14	10	24	60	....	....	....	....	....
	Binghamton	AHL	34	21	15	36	48	10	8	5	13	37
1991-92	Binghamton	AHL	30	10	11	21	36	....	....	....	....	....
	Toronto	**NHL**	**34**	**9**	**5**	**14**	**27**	....	....	....	....	....
	St. John's	AHL	15	7	7	14	26	....	....	....	....	....
1992-93	**Toronto**	**NHL**	**9**	**0**	**0**	**0**	**8**	....	....	....	....	....
	St. John's	AHL	5	0	1	1	8	9	5	2	7	6
	NHL Totals		**53**	**9**	**6**	**15**	**49**	....	....	....	....	....

Signed as a free agent by **Winnipeg**, July 16, 1987. Traded to **NY Rangers** by **Winnipeg** for Rudy Poeschek, January 22, 1991. Traded to **Toronto** by **NY Rangers** for Mike Stevens, December 26, 1991.

LAROUCHE, STEVE

Center. Shoots right. 6', 180 lbs. Born, Rouyn, Que., April 14, 1971.
(Montreal's 3rd choice, 41st overall, in 1989 Entry Draft).

			Regular Season					Playoffs				
Season	Club	Lea	GP	G	A	TP	PIM	GP	G	A	TP	PIM
1987-88	Trois-Rivières	QMJHL	66	11	29	40	25	....	....	....	....	....
1988-89	Trois-Rivières	QMJHL	70	51	102	153	53	4	4	2	6	6
1989-90a	Trois-Rivières	QMJHL	60	55	90	145	40	7	3	5	8	8
1990-91	Chicoutimi	QMJHL	45	35	41	76	64	17	*13	*20	*33	20
1991-92	Fredericton	AHL	74	21	35	56	41	7	1	0	1	0
1992-93	Fredericton	AHL	77	27	65	92	52	5	2	5	7	6

a QMJHL Second All-Star Team (1990)

LARSON, BRETT

Defense. Shoots right. 6', 175 lbs. Born, Duluth, MN, August 20, 1972.
(Detroit's 10th choice, 213th overall, in 1990 Entry Draft).

			Regular Season					Playoffs				
Season	Club	Lea	GP	G	A	TP	PIM	GP	G	A	TP	PIM
1991-92	Minn.-Duluth	WCHA	26	2	1	3	20	....	....	....	....	....
1992-93	Minn.-Duluth	WCHA	32	2	3	5	8	....	....	....	....	....

LARSON, JON

Defense. Shoots left. 6'1", 190 lbs. Born, Roseau, MN, April 12, 1971.
(NY Islanders' 7th choice, 128th overall, in 1989 Entry Draft).

			Regular Season					Playoffs				
Season	Club	Lea	GP	G	A	TP	PIM	GP	G	A	TP	PIM
1989-90	North Dakota	WCHA	18	0	1	1	10	....	....	....	....	....
1990-91	North Dakota	WCHA	13	0	0	0	4	....	....	....	....	....
1991-92	North Dakota	WCHA	33	1	3	4	16	....	....	....	....	....
1992-93	North Dakota	WCHA	30	2	6	8	28	....	....	....	....	....

LARSSON, PETER (LAHR-suhn)

Center. Shoots left. 5'8", 176 lbs. Born, Sodertalje, Sweden, April 9, 1968.
(New Jersey's 10th choice, 236th overall, in 1989 Entry Draft).

			Regular Season					Playoffs				
Season	Club	Lea	GP	G	A	TP	PIM	GP	G	A	TP	PIM
1985-86	Sodertalje	Swe.	10	0	1	1	2	....	....	....	....	....
1986-87	Sodertalje	Swe.	26	3	4	7	8	....	....	....	....	....
1987-88	Sodertalje	Swe.	34	14	15	29	20	2	1	0	1	0
1988-89	Sodertalje	Swe.	40	20	17	37	26	....	....	....	....	....
1989-90	Sodertalje	Swe.	33	13	14	27	28	2	2	0	2	2
1990-91	Brynas	Swe.	40	13	12	25	12	1	0	2	2	0
1991-92	Brynas	Swe.	40	17	21	38	10	5	1	3	4	2
1992-93	Brynas	Swe.	34	7	23	30	12	10	2	8	10	4

LAUER, BRAD (LAU-er)

Left wing. Shoots left. 6', 195 lbs. Born, Humboldt, Sask., October 27, 1966.
(NY Islanders' 3rd choice, 34th overall, in 1985 Entry Draft).

			Regular Season					Playoffs				
Season	Club	Lea	GP	G	A	TP	PIM	GP	G	A	TP	PIM
1983-84	Regina	WHL	60	5	7	12	51	16	0	1	1	24
1984-85	Regina	WHL	72	33	46	79	57	8	6	6	12	9
1985-86	Regina	WHL	57	36	38	74	69	10	4	5	9	2
1986-87	**NY Islanders**	**NHL**	**61**	**7**	**14**	**21**	**65**	**6**	**2**	**0**	**2**	**4**
1987-88	**NY Islanders**	**NHL**	**69**	**17**	**18**	**35**	**67**	**5**	**3**	**1**	**4**	**4**
1988-89	**NY Islanders**	**NHL**	**14**	**3**	**2**	**5**	**2**	....	....	....	....	....
	Springfield	AHL	8	1	5	6	0	....	....	....	....	....
1989-90	**NY Islanders**	**NHL**	**63**	**6**	**18**	**24**	**19**	**4**	**0**	**2**	**2**	**10**
	Springfield	AHL	7	4	2	6	0	....	....	....	....	....
1990-91	**NY Islanders**	**NHL**	**44**	**4**	**8**	**12**	**45**	....	....	....	....	....
	Capital Dist.	AHL	11	5	11	16	14	....	....	....	....	....
1991-92	**NY Islanders**	**NHL**	**8**	**1**	**0**	**1**	**2**	....	....	....	....	....
	Chicago	**NHL**	**6**	**0**	**0**	**0**	**4**	**7**	**1**	**1**	**2**	**2**
	Indianapolis	IHL	57	24	30	54	46	....	....	....	....	....
1992-93	**Chicago**	**NHL**	**7**	**0**	**1**	**1**	**2**	....	....	....	....	....
	Indianapolis	IHL	62	*50	41	91	80	5	3	1	4	6
	NHL Totals		**272**	**38**	**61**	**99**	**206**	**22**	**6**	**4**	**10**	**20**

a IHL First All-Star Team (1993)

Traded to **Chicago** by **NY Islanders** with Brent Sutter for Adam Creighton and Steve Thomas, October 25, 1991.

LAUKKANEN, JANNE (LOW-kah-nehn)

Defense. Shoots left. 6', 180 lbs. Born, Lahti, Finland, March 19, 1970.
(Quebec's 8th choice, 156th overall, in 1991 Entry Draft).

			Regular Season					Playoffs				
Season	Club	Lea	GP	G	A	TP	PIM	GP	G	A	TP	PIM
1990-91	Reipas	Fin.	44	8	14	22	56	....	....	....	....	....
1991-92	HPK	Fin.	43	5	14	19	62	....	....	....	....	....
1992-93	HPK	Fin.	47	8	21	29	76	12	1	4	5	10

LAUS, PAUL

Defense. Shoots right. 6'1", 212 lbs. Born, Beamsville, Ont., September 26, 1970.
(Pittsburgh's 2nd choice, 37th overall, in 1989 Entry Draft).

			Regular Season					Playoffs				
Season	Club	Lea	GP	G	A	TP	PIM	GP	G	A	TP	PIM
1987-88	Hamilton	OHL	56	1	9	10	171	14	0	0	0	28
1988-89	Niagara Falls	OHL	49	1	10	11	225	15	0	5	5	56
1989-90	Niagara Falls	OHL	60	13	35	48	231	16	6	16	22	71
1990-91	Albany	IHL	7	0	0	0	7	....	....	....	....	....
	Knoxville	ECHL	20	6	12	18	83	....	....	....	....	....
	Muskegon	IHL	35	3	4	7	103	4	0	0	0	13
1991-92	Muskegon	IHL	75	0	21	21	248	14	2	5	7	70
1992-93	Cleveland	IHL	76	8	18	26	427	4	1	0	1	27

Claimed by **Florida** from **Pittsburgh** in Expansion Draft, June 24, 1993.

LAVIGNE, ERIC

Defense. Shoots left. 6'3", 195 lbs. Born, Victoriaville, Que., November 4, 1972.
(Washington's 3rd choice, 25th overall, in 1991 Entry Draft).

			Regular Season					Playoffs				
Season	Club	Lea	GP	G	A	TP	PIM	GP	G	A	TP	PIM
1989-90	Hull	QMJHL	69	7	11	18	203	11	0	0	0	32
1990-91	Hull	QMJHL	66	11	11	22	153	4	0	1	1	16
1991-92	Hull	QMJHL	46	4	17	21	101	6	0	0	0	32
1992-93	Hull	QMJHL	59	7	20	27	221	10	2	4	6	47

LAVIOLETTE, PETER (LAH-vee-oh-LEHT)

Defense. Shoots left. 6'2", 200 lbs. Born, Norwood, MA, December 7, 1964.

			Regular Season					Playoffs				
Season	Club	Lea	GP	G	A	TP	PIM	GP	G	A	TP	PIM
1985-86	Westfield State	NCAA	19	12	8	20	44	....	....	....	....	....
1986-87	Indianapolis	IHL	72	10	20	30	146	....	....	....	....	....
1987-88	U.S. National	....	54	4	20	24	82	....	....	....	....	....
	U.S. Olympic	....	5	0	2	2	4	....	....	....	....	....
	Colorado	IHL	19	2	5	7	27	9	3	5	8	7
1988-89	**NY Rangers**	**NHL**	**12**	**0**	**0**	**0**	**6**	....	....	....	....	....
	Denver	IHL	57	6	19	25	120	3	0	0	0	4
1989-90	Flint	IHL	62	6	18	24	82	4	0	0	0	4
1990-91	Binghamton	AHL	65	12	24	36	72	10	2	7	9	30
1991-92	Binghamton	AHL	50	4	10	14	50	11	2	7	9	9
1992-93	Providence	AHL	74	13	42	55	64	6	0	4	4	10
	NHL Totals		**12**	**0**	**0**	**0**	**6**	....	....	....	....	....

Signed as a free agent by **NY Rangers**, August 12, 1987.

LAVISH, JAMES

Right wing. Shoots right. 5'11", 175 lbs. Born, Albany, NY, October 13, 1970.
(Boston's 9th choice, 185th overall, in 1989 Entry Draft).

			Regular Season					Playoffs				
Season	Club	Lea	GP	G	A	TP	PIM	GP	G	A	TP	PIM
1989-90	Yale	ECAC	27	6	11	17	40	....	....	....	....	....
1990-91	Yale	ECAC	29	13	7	20	42	....	....	....	....	....
1991-92	Yale	ECAC	26	16	14	30	44	....	....	....	....	....
1992-93	Yale	ECAC	29	17	19	36	36	....	....	....	....	....

LAVOIE, DOMINIC

Defense. Shoots right. 6'2", 205 lbs. Born, Montreal, Que., November 21, 1967.

			Regular Season					Playoffs				
Season	Club	Lea	GP	G	A	TP	PIM	GP	G	A	TP	PIM
1985-86	St-Jean	QMJHL	70	12	37	49	99	10	2	3	5	20
1986-87	St-Jean	QMJHL	64	12	42	54	97	8	2	7	9	2
1987-88	Peoria	IHL	65	7	26	33	54	7	2	2	4	8
1988-89	**St. Louis**	**NHL**	**1**	**0**	**0**	**0**	**0**	....	....	....	....	....
	Peoria	IHL	69	11	31	42	98	4	0	0	0	4
1989-90	**St. Louis**	**NHL**	**13**	**1**	**1**	**2**	**16**	....	....	....	....	....
	Peoria	IHL	58	19	23	42	32	5	2	2	4	16
1990-91	**St. Louis**	**NHL**	**6**	**1**	**2**	**3**	**2**	....	....	....	....	....
a	Peoria	IHL	46	15	25	40	72	16	5	7	12	22
1991-92	**St. Louis**	**NHL**	**6**	**0**	**1**	**1**	**10**	....	....	....	....	....
b	Peoria	IHL	58	20	32	52	87	10	3	4	7	12
1992-93	**Ottawa**	**NHL**	**2**	**0**	**1**	**1**	**0**	....	....	....	....	....
	New Haven	AHL	14	2	7	9	14	....	....	....	....	....
	Boston	**NHL**	**2**	**0**	**0**	**0**	**2**	....	....	....	....	....
	Providence	AHL	53	16	27	43	62	6	1	2	3	24
	NHL Totals		**30**	**2**	**5**	**7**	**30**	....	....	....	....	....

a IHL First All-Star Team (1991)
b IHL Second All-Star Team (1992)

Signed as a free agent by **St. Louis**, September 22, 1986. Claimed by **Ottawa** from **St. Louis** in Expansion Draft, June 18, 1992. Claimed on waivers by **Boston** from **Ottawa**, November 20, 1992.

LAWRENCE, MARK

Right wing. Shoots right. 6'4", 212 lbs. Born, Burlington, Ont., January 27, 1972.
(Minnesota's 6th choice, 118th overall, in 1991 Entry Draft).

			Regular Season					Playoffs				
Season	Club	Lea	GP	G	A	TP	PIM	GP	G	A	TP	PIM
1988-89	Niagara Falls	OHL	63	9	27	36	142	....	....	....	....	....
1989-90	Niagara Falls	OHL	54	15	18	33	123	16	2	5	7	42
1990-91	Detroit	OHL	66	27	38	65	53	....	....	....	....	....
1991-92	Detroit	OHL	28	19	26	45	54	....	....	....	....	....
	North Bay	OHL	24	13	14	27	21	21	*23	12	35	36
1992-93	Dayton	ECHL	20	8	14	22	46	....	....	....	....	....
	Kalamazoo	IHL	57	22	13	35	47	....	....	....	....	....

LAWTON, BRIAN

Left wing. Shoots left. 6', 180 lbs. Born, New Brunswick, NJ, June 29, 1965.
(Minnesota's 1st choice, 1st overall, in 1983 Entry Draft).

			Regular Season					Playoffs				
Season	Club	Lea	GP	G	A	TP	PIM	GP	G	A	TP	PIM
1982-83	Mt. St. Charles	HS	23	40	43	83	....	....	....	....	....	....
1983-84	**Minnesota**	**NHL**	**58**	**10**	**21**	**31**	**33**	**5**	**0**	**0**	**0**	**10**
1984-85	**Minnesota**	**NHL**	**40**	**5**	**6**	**11**	**24**	....	....	....	....	....
	Springfield	AHL	42	14	28	42	37	4	1	1	2	2
1985-86	**Minnesota**	**NHL**	**65**	**18**	**17**	**35**	**36**	**3**	**0**	**1**	**1**	**2**
1986-87	**Minnesota**	**NHL**	**66**	**21**	**23**	**44**	**86**	....	....	....	....	....
1987-88	**Minnesota**	**NHL**	**74**	**17**	**24**	**41**	**71**	....	....	....	....	....
1988-89	**NY Rangers**	**NHL**	**30**	**7**	**10**	**17**	**39**	....	....	....	....	....
	Hartford	**NHL**	**35**	**10**	**16**	**26**	**28**	**3**	**1**	**0**	**1**	**0**
1989-90	**Hartford**	**NHL**	**13**	**2**	**1**	**3**	**6**	....	....	....	....	....
	Quebec	**NHL**	**14**	**5**	**6**	**11**	**10**	....	....	....	....	....
	Boston	**NHL**	**8**	**0**	**0**	**0**	**14**	....	....	....	....	....
	Maine	AHL	5	0	0	0	14	....	....	....	....	....
1990-91	Phoenix	IHL	63	26	40	66	108	11	4	9	13	40
1991-92	**San Jose**	**NHL**	**59**	**15**	**22**	**37**	**42**	....	....	....	....	....
1992-93	**San Jose**	**NHL**	**21**	**2**	**8**	**10**	**12**	....	....	....	....	....
	Kansas City	IHL	9	6	4	10	10	....	....	....	....	....
	Cincinnati	IHL	17	5	11	16	30	....	....	....	....	....
	NHL Totals		**483**	**112**	**154**	**266**	**401**	**11**	**1**	**1**	**2**	**12**

Traded to **NY Rangers** by **Minnesota** with Igor Liba, and the rights to Eric Bennett for Paul Jerrard and Mark Tinordi, the rights to Bret Barnett and Mike Sullivan, and Los Angeles' third round choice (previously acquired by NY Rangers — Minnesota selected Murray Garbutt) in 1989 Entry Draft October 11, 1988. Traded to **Hartford** by **NY Rangers** with Norm MacIver and Don Maloney for Carey Wilson and Hartford's fifth round choice (Lubos Rob) in 1990 Entry Draft, December 26, 1988. Claimed on waivers by **Quebec** from **Hartford**, December 1, 1989. Signed as a free agent by **Boston**, February 7, 1990. Signed as a free agent by **Los Angeles**, July 27, 1990. Signed as a free agent by **San Jose**, August 9, 1991. Traded to **New Jersey** by **San Jose** for future considerations, January 22, 1993.

LAYZELL, BRAD

Defense. Shoots left. 6'3", 200 lbs. Born, Beaconsfield, Que., March 15, 1972.
(Montreal's 5th choice, 100th overall, in 1991 Entry Draft).

			Regular Season					Playoffs				
Season	Club	Lea	GP	G	A	TP	PIM	GP	G	A	TP	PIM
1990-91	RPI	ECAC	24	1	2	3	28	....	....	....	....	....
1991-92	RPI	ECAC	31	1	8	9	46	....	....	....	....	....
1992-93a	RPI	ECAC	35	5	24	29	40	....	....	....	....	....

a ECAC Second All-Star Team (1993)

LAZARO, JEFF

Left wing. Shoots left. 5'10", 180 lbs. Born, Waltham, MA, March 21, 1968.

			Regular Season					Playoffs				
Season	Club	Lea	GP	G	A	TP	PIM	GP	G	A	TP	PIM
1986-87	N. Hampshire	H.E.	38	7	14	21	38	....	....	....	....	....
1987-88	N. Hampshire	H.E.	30	4	13	17	48	....	....	....	....	....
1988-89	N. Hampshire	H.E.	31	8	14	22	38	....	....	....	....	....
1989-90	N. Hampshire	H.E.	39	16	19	35	34	....	....	....	....	....
1990-91	**Boston**	**NHL**	**49**	**5**	**13**	**18**	**67**	**19**	**3**	**2**	**5**	**30**
	Maine	AHL	26	8	11	19	18	....	....	....	....	....
1991-92	**Boston**	**NHL**	**27**	**3**	**6**	**9**	**31**	**9**	**0**	**1**	**1**	**2**
	Maine	AHL	21	8	4	12	32	....	....	....	....	....
1992-93	**Ottawa**	**NHL**	**26**	**6**	**4**	**10**	**16**	....	....	....	....	....
	New Haven	AHL	27	12	13	25	49	....	....	....	....	....
	NHL Totals		**102**	**14**	**23**	**37**	**114**	**28**	**3**	**3**	**6**	**32**

Signed as a free agent by **Boston**, September 26, 1990. Claimed by **Ottawa** from **Boston** in Expansion Draft, June 18, 1992.

LEACH, JAMIE

Right wing. Shoots right. 6'1", 205 lbs. Born, Winnipeg, Man., August 25, 1969.
(Pittsburgh's 3rd choice, 47th overall, in 1987 Entry Draft).

			Regular Season					Playoffs				
Season	Club	Lea	GP	G	A	TP	PIM	GP	G	A	TP	PIM
1985-86	N. Westminster	WHL	58	8	7	15	20	....	....	....	....	....
1986-87	Hamilton	OHL	64	12	19	31	67	....	....	....	....	....
1987-88	Hamilton	OHL	64	24	19	43	79	14	6	7	13	12
1988-89a	Niagara Falls	OHL	58	45	62	107	47	17	9	11	20	25
1989-90	**Pittsburgh**	**NHL**	**10**	**0**	**3**	**3**	**0**	....	....	....	....	....
	Muskegon	IHL	72	22	36	58	39	15	9	4	13	14
1990-91	**Pittsburgh**	**NHL**	**7**	**2**	**0**	**2**	**0**	....	....	....	....	....
	Muskegon	IHL	43	33	22	55	26	....	....	....	....	....
1991-92	**Pittsburgh**	**NHL**	**38**	**5**	**4**	**9**	**8**	....	....	....	....	....
	Muskegon	IHL	3	1	1	2	2	....	....	....	....	....
1992-93	**Pittsburgh**	**NHL**	**5**	**0**	**0**	**0**	**2**	....	....	....	....	....
	Cleveland	IHL	9	5	3	8	2	4	1	2	3	0
	Hartford	**NHL**	**19**	**3**	**2**	**5**	**2**	....	....	....	....	....
	Springfield	AHL	29	13	15	28	33	....	....	....	....	....
	NHL Totals		**79**	**10**	**9**	**19**	**12**	....	....	....	....	....

a OHL Third All-Star Team (1989)

Claimed on waivers by **Hartford** from **Pittsburgh**, November 21, 1992.

LEACH, STEPHEN

Right wing. Shoots right. 5'11", 195 lbs. Born, Cambridge, MA, January 16, 1966.
(Washington's 2nd choice, 34th overall, in 1984 Entry Draft).

			Regular Season					Playoffs				
Season	Club	Lea	GP	G	A	TP	PIM	GP	G	A	TP	PIM
1984-85	N. Hampshire	H.E.	41	12	25	37	53	....	....	....	....	....
1985-86	**Washington**	**NHL**	**11**	**1**	**1**	**2**	**2**	**6**	**0**	**1**	**1**	**0**
	N. Hampshire	H.E.	25	22	6	28	30	....	....	....	....	....
1986-87	**Washington**	**NHL**	**15**	**1**	**0**	**1**	**6**	....	....	....	....	....
	Binghamton	AHL	54	18	21	39	39	13	3	1	4	6
1987-88	**Washington**	**NHL**	**8**	**1**	**1**	**2**	**17**	**9**	**2**	**1**	**3**	**0**
	U.S. National	....	49	26	20	46	30	....	....	....	....	....
	U.S. Olympic	....	6	1	2	3	0	....	....	....	....	....
1988-89	**Washington**	**NHL**	**74**	**11**	**19**	**30**	**94**	**6**	**1**	**0**	**1**	**12**
1989-90	**Washington**	**NHL**	**70**	**18**	**14**	**32**	**104**	**14**	**2**	**2**	**4**	**8**
1990-91	**Washington**	**NHL**	**68**	**11**	**19**	**30**	**99**	**9**	**1**	**2**	**3**	**8**
1991-92	**Boston**	**NHL**	**78**	**31**	**29**	**60**	**147**	**15**	**4**	**0**	**4**	**10**
1992-93	**Boston**	**NHL**	**79**	**26**	**25**	**51**	**126**	**4**	**1**	**1**	**2**	**2**
	NHL Totals		**403**	**100**	**108**	**208**	**595**	**63**	**11**	**7**	**18**	**40**

Traded to **Boston** by **Washington** for Randy Burridge, June 21, 1991.

LEASK, ROB

Defense. Shoots left. 6'2", 211 lbs. Born, Toronto, Ont., June 9, 1971.
(Washington's 10th choice, 209th overall, in 1991 Entry Draft).

			Regular Season					Playoffs				
Season	Club	Lea	GP	G	A	TP	PIM	GP	G	A	TP	PIM
1989-90	Hamilton	OHL	43	6	18	24	50	....	....	....	....	....
1990-91	Hamilton	OHL	62	11	27	38	85	4	1	2	3	2
1991-92	Guelph	OHL	7	0	1	1	15	....	....	....	....	....
	Oshawa	OHL	49	13	27	40	90	7	1	4	5	4
	Baltimore	AHL	4	0	0	0	0	....	....	....	....	....
1992-93	Baltimore	AHL	68	4	8	12	76	7	0	1	1	14

LEBEAU, PATRICK

Left wing. Shoots left. 5'10", 172 lbs. Born, St. Jerome, Que., March 17, 1970.
(Montreal's 8th choice, 167th overall, in 1989 Entry Draft).

			Regular Season					Playoffs				
Season	Club	Lea	GP	G	A	TP	PIM	GP	G	A	TP	PIM
1986-87	Shawinigan	QMJHL	66	26	52	78	90	13	2	6	8	17
1987-88	Shawinigan	QMJHL	53	43	56	99	116	11	3	9	12	16
1988-89	Shawinigan	QMJHL	17	19	17	36	18	....	....	....	....	....
	St-Jean	QMJHL	66	62	87	149	89	4	4	3	7	6
1989-90a	Victoriaville	QMJHL	72	68	*106	*174	109	16	7	15	22	12
1990-91	**Montreal**	**NHL**	**2**	**1**	**1**	**2**	**0**	....	....	....	....	....
bc	Fredericton	AHL	69	50	51	101	32	9	4	7	11	8
1991-92	Fredericton	AHL	55	33	38	71	48	7	4	5	9	10
	Cdn. National	....	7	4	1	5	6	....	....	....	....	....
	Cdn. Olympic	....	8	1	3	4	4	....	....	....	....	....
1992-93	**Calgary**	**NHL**	**1**	**0**	**0**	**0**	**0**	....	....	....	....	....
	Salt Lake	IHL	75	40	60	100	65	....	....	....	....	....
	NHL Totals		**3**	**1**	**1**	**2**	**0**	....	....	....	....	....

a QMJHL First All-Star Team (1990)
b AHL Second All-Star Team (1991)
c Won Dudley "Red" Garrett Memorial Trophy (Top Rookie – AHL) (1991)

Traded to **Calgary** by **Montreal** for future considerations, October 5, 1992.

LEBEAU, STEPHAN (leh-BOH)

Center. Shoots right. 5'10", 172 lbs. Born, St. Jerome, Que., February 28, 1968.

			Regular Season					Playoffs				
Season	Club	Lea	GP	G	A	TP	PIM	GP	G	A	TP	PIM
1984-85	Shawinigan	QMJHL	66	41	38	79	18	9	4	5	9	4
1985-86	Shawinigan	QMJHL	72	69	77	146	22	5	4	2	6	4
1986-87a	Shawinigan	QMJHL	65	77	90	167	60	14	9	20	29	20
1987-88a	Shawinigan	QMJHL	67	*94	94	188	66	11	17	9	26	10
	Sherbrooke	AHL	....	....	....	....	....	1	0	1	1	0
1988-89	**Montreal**	**NHL**	**1**	**0**	**1**	**1**	**2**	....	....	....	....	....
bcde	Sherbrooke	AHL	78	*70	64	*134	47	6	1	4	5	8
1989-90	**Montreal**	**NHL**	**57**	**15**	**20**	**35**	**11**	**2**	**3**	**0**	**3**	**0**
1990-91	**Montreal**	**NHL**	**73**	**22**	**31**	**53**	**24**	**7**	**2**	**1**	**3**	**2**
1991-92	**Montreal**	**NHL**	**77**	**27**	**31**	**58**	**14**	**8**	**1**	**3**	**4**	**4**
1992-93	**Montreal**	**NHL**	**71**	**31**	**49**	**80**	**20**	**13**	**3**	**3**	**6**	**6**
	NHL Totals		**279**	**95**	**132**	**227**	**71**	**30**	**9**	**7**	**16**	**12**

a QMJHL Second All-Star Team (1987, 1988)
b AHL First All-Star Team (1989)
c Won Dudley "Red" Garrett Memorial Trophy (Top Rookie-AHL) (1989)
d Won John B. Sollenberger Trophy (Top Scorer-AHL) (1989)
e Won Les Cunningham Trophy (MVP-AHL) (1989)

Signed as a free agent by **Montreal**, September 27, 1986.

LEBLANC, JOHN GLENN

Left wing. Shoots left. 6'1", 190 lbs. Born, Campbellton, N.B., January 21, 1964.

			Regular Season					Playoffs				
Season	Club	Lea	GP	G	A	TP	PIM	GP	G	A	TP	PIM
1983-84	Hull	QMJHL	69	39	35	74	32	....	....	....	....	....
1984-85	New Brunswick	AUAA	24	25	34	59	32	....	....	....	....	....
1985-86a	New Brunswick	AUAA	24	38	28	66	35	....	....	....	....	....
1986-87	**Vancouver**	**NHL**	**2**	**1**	**0**	**1**	**0**	....	....	....	....	....
	Fredericton	AHL	75	40	30	70	27	....	....	....	....	....
1987-88	**Vancouver**	**NHL**	**41**	**12**	**10**	**22**	**18**	....	....	....	....	....
	Fredericton	AHL	35	26	25	51	54	15	6	7	13	34
1988-89	Milwaukee	IHL	61	39	31	70	42	....	....	....	....	....
	Edmonton	**NHL**	**2**	**1**	**0**	**1**	**0**	**1**	**0**	**0**	**0**	**0**
	Cape Breton	AHL	3	4	0	4	0	....	....	....	....	....
1989-90	Cape Breton	AHL	77	*54	34	88	50	6	4	0	4	4
1990-91						DID NOT PLAY						
1991-92	**Winnipeg**	**NHL**	**16**	**6**	**1**	**7**	**6**	....	....	....	....	....
	Moncton	AHL	56	31	22	53	24	10	3	2	5	8
1992-93	**Winnipeg**	**NHL**	**3**	**0**	**0**	**0**	**2**	....	....	....	....	....
	Moncton	AHL	77	48	40	88	29	5	2	1	3	6
	NHL Totals		**64**	**20**	**11**	**31**	**26**	**1**	**0**	**0**	**0**	**0**

a Canadian University Player of the Year (1986)

Signed as a free agent by **Vancouver**, April 12, 1986. Traded to **Edmonton** by **Vancouver** with Vancouver's fifth round choice (Peter White) in 1989 Entry Draft for Doug Smith and Gregory C. Adams, March 7, 1989. Traded to **Winnipeg** by **Edmonton** with Edmonton's tenth round choice (Teemu Numminen) in 1992 Entry Draft for Winnipeg's fifth round choice (Ryan Haggerty) in 1991 Entry Draft, June 12, 1991.

LEBOUTILLIER, PETER

Right wing. Shoots right. 6'1", 198 lbs. Born, Neepawa, Man., January 11, 1975.
(NY Islanders' 6th choice, 144th overall, in 1993 Entry Draft).

			Regular Season					Playoffs				
Season	Club	Lea	GP	G	A	TP	PIM	GP	G	A	TP	PIM
1991-92	Neepawa	MJHL	35	11	14	25	99	....	....	....	....	....
1992-93	Red Deer	WHL	67	8	26	34	284	2	0	1	1	5

LEBRUN, SEAN (luh-BRUN)

Left wing. Shoots left. 6'2", 200 lbs. Born, Prince George, B.C., May 2, 1969.
(NY Islanders' 3rd choice, 37th overall, in 1988 Entry Draft).

			Regular Season					Playoffs				
Season	Club	Lea	GP	G	A	TP	PIM	GP	G	A	TP	PIM
1985-86	Spokane	WHL	70	6	11	17	41	....	....	....	....	....
1986-87	Spokane	WHL	6	2	5	7	9	....	....	....	....	....
	N. Westminster	WHL	55	21	32	53	47	....	....	....	....	....
1987-88a	N. Westminster	WHL	72	36	53	89	59	5	1	3	4	2
1988-89	Tri-Cities	WHL	71	52	73	125	92	5	0	4	4	13
1989-90	Springfield	AHL	63	9	33	42	20	....	....	....	....	....
1990-91	Capital Dist.	AHL	56	14	26	40	35	....	....	....	....	....
1991-92	Richmond	ECHL	2	0	0	0	2	....	....	....	....	....
	Capital Dist.	AHL	14	0	2	2	15	....	....	....	....	....
1992-93	Capital Dist.	AHL	39	11	20	31	25	1	0	0	0	0
	Richmond	ECHL	22	18	26	44	17	....	....	....	....	....

a WHL West Division Second All-Star Team (1988)

LECLAIR, JOHN

Left wing. Shoots left. 6'2", 205 lbs. Born, St. Albans, VT, July 5, 1969.
(Montreal's 2nd choice, 33rd overall, in 1987 Entry Draft).

			Regular Season					Playoffs				
Season	Club	Lea	GP	G	A	TP	PIM	GP	G	A	TP	PIM
1987-88	U. of Vermont	ECAC	31	12	22	34	62	....	....	....	....	....
1988-89	U. of Vermont	ECAC	18	9	12	21	40	....	....	....	....	....
1989-90	U. of Vermont	ECAC	10	10	6	16	38	....	....	....	....	....
1990-91a	U. of Vermont	ECAC	33	25	20	45	58	....	....	....	....	....
	Montreal	**NHL**	**10**	**2**	**5**	**7**	**2**	**3**	**0**	**0**	**0**	**0**
1991-92	**Montreal**	**NHL**	**59**	**8**	**11**	**19**	**14**	**8**	**1**	**1**	**2**	**4**
	Fredericton	AHL	8	7	7	14	10	2	0	0	0	4
1992-93	**Montreal**	**NHL**	**72**	**19**	**25**	**44**	**33**	**20**	**4**	**6**	**10**	**14**
	NHL Totals		**141**	**29**	**41**	**70**	**49**	**31**	**5**	**7**	**12**	**18**

a ECAC Second All-Star Team (1991)

LECOMPTE, ERIC

Left wing. Shoots left. 6'4", 190 lbs. Born, Montreal, Que., April 4, 1975.
(Chicago's 1st choice, 24th overall, in 1993 Entry Draft).

			Regular Season					Playoffs				
Season	Club	Lea	GP	G	A	TP	PIM	GP	G	A	TP	PIM
1991-92	Hull	QMJHL	60	16	17	33	138	6	1	0	1	4
1992-93	Hull	QMJHL	66	33	38	71	149	10	4	4	8	52

LEDYARD, GRANT

Defense. Shoots left. 6'2", 195 lbs. Born, Winnipeg, Man., November 19, 1961.

			Regular Season					Playoffs				
Season	Club	Lea	GP	G	A	TP	PIM	GP	G	A	TP	PIM
1980-81	Saskatoon	WHL	71	9	28	37	148	....	....	....	....	....
1981-82	Fort Garry	MJHL	63	25	45	70	150	....	....	....	....	....
1982-83	Tulsa	CHL	80	13	29	42	115	....	....	....	....	....
1983-84a	Tulsa	CHL	58	9	17	26	71	9	5	4	9	10
1984-85	**NY Rangers**	**NHL**	**42**	**8**	**12**	**20**	**53**	**3**	**0**	**2**	**2**	**4**
	New Haven	AHL	36	6	20	26	18	....	....	....	....	....
1985-86	**NY Rangers**	**NHL**	**27**	**2**	**9**	**11**	**20**	....	....	....	....	....
	Los Angeles	**NHL**	**52**	**7**	**18**	**25**	**78**	....	....	....	....	....
1986-87	**Los Angeles**	**NHL**	**67**	**14**	**23**	**37**	**93**	**5**	**0**	**0**	**0**	**10**
1987-88	**Los Angeles**	**NHL**	**23**	**1**	**7**	**8**	**52**	....	....	....	....	....
	New Haven	AHL	3	2	1	3	4	....	....	....	....	....
	Washington	**NHL**	**21**	**4**	**3**	**7**	**14**	**14**	**1**	**0**	**1**	**30**
1988-89	**Washington**	**NHL**	**61**	**3**	**11**	**14**	**43**	....	....	....	....	....
	Buffalo	**NHL**	**13**	**1**	**5**	**6**	**8**	**5**	**1**	**2**	**3**	**2**
1989-90	**Buffalo**	**NHL**	**67**	**2**	**13**	**15**	**37**	....	....	....	....	....
1990-91	**Buffalo**	**NHL**	**60**	**8**	**23**	**31**	**46**	**6**	**3**	**3**	**6**	**10**
1991-92	**Buffalo**	**NHL**	**50**	**5**	**16**	**21**	**45**	....	....	....	....	....
1992-93	**Buffalo**	**NHL**	**50**	**2**	**14**	**16**	**45**	**8**	**0**	**0**	**0**	**8**
	Rochester	AHL	5	0	2	2	8	....	....	....	....	....
	NHL Totals		**533**	**57**	**154**	**211**	**534**	**41**	**5**	**7**	**12**	**64**

a Won Bob Gassoff Trophy (CHL's Most Improved Defenseman) (1984)

Signed as a free agent by **NY Rangers**, July 7, 1982. Traded to **Los Angeles** by **NY Rangers** with Roland Melanson for Los Angeles' fourth round choice (Mike Sullivan) in 1987 Entry Draft and Brian MacLellan, December 7, 1985. Traded to **Washington** by **Los Angeles** for Craig Laughlin, February 9, 1988. Traded to **Buffalo** by **Washington** with Clint Malarchuk and Washington's sixth round choice (Brian Holzinger) in 1991 Entry Draft for Calle Johansson and Buffalo's second round choice (Byron Dafoe) in 1989 Entry Draft, March 7, 1989.

LEEMAN, GARY

Right wing. Shoots right. 5'11", 175 lbs. Born, Toronto, Ont., February 19, 1964.
(Toronto's 2nd choice, 24th overall, in 1982 Entry Draft).

			Regular Season					Playoffs				
Season	Club	Lea	GP	G	A	TP	PIM	GP	G	A	TP	PIM
1981-82	Regina	WHL	72	19	41	60	112	3	2	2	4	0
1982-83ab	Regina	WHL	63	24	62	86	88	5	1	5	6	4
	Toronto	**NHL**	....	....	....	....	....	**2**	**0**	**0**	**0**	**0**
1983-84	**Toronto**	**NHL**	**52**	**4**	**8**	**12**	**31**	....	....	....	....	....
1984-85	**Toronto**	**NHL**	**53**	**5**	**26**	**31**	**72**	....	....	....	....	....
	St. Catharines	AHL	7	2	2	4	11	....	....	....	....	....
1985-86	**Toronto**	**NHL**	**53**	**9**	**23**	**32**	**20**	**10**	**2**	**10**	**12**	**2**
	St. Catharines	AHL	25	15	13	28	6	....	....	....	....	....
1986-87	**Toronto**	**NHL**	**80**	**21**	**31**	**52**	**66**	**5**	**0**	**1**	**1**	**14**
1987-88	**Toronto**	**NHL**	**80**	**30**	**31**	**61**	**62**	**2**	**2**	**0**	**2**	**2**
1988-89	**Toronto**	**NHL**	**61**	**32**	**43**	**75**	**66**	....	....	....	....	....
1989-90	**Toronto**	**NHL**	**80**	**51**	**44**	**95**	**63**	**5**	**3**	**3**	**6**	**16**
1990-91	**Toronto**	**NHL**	**52**	**17**	**12**	**29**	**39**	....	....	....	....	....
1991-92	**Toronto**	**NHL**	**34**	**7**	**13**	**20**	**44**	....	....	....	....	....
	Calgary	**NHL**	**29**	**2**	**7**	**9**	**27**	....	....	....	....	....
1992-93	**Calgary**	**NHL**	**30**	**9**	**5**	**14**	**10**	....	....	....	....	....
	Montreal	**NHL**	**20**	**6**	**12**	**18**	**14**	**11**	**1**	**2**	**3**	**2**
	NHL Totals		**624**	**193**	**255**	**448**	**514**	**35**	**8**	**16**	**24**	**36**

a WHL First All-Star Team (1983)
b Named WHL's Top Defenseman (1983)

Played in NHL All-Star Game (1989)

Traded to **Calgary** by **Toronto** with Craig Berube, Alexander Godynyuk, Michel Petit and Jeff Reese for Doug Gilmour, Jamie Macoun, Ric Nattress, Rick Wamsley and Kent Manderville, January 2, 1992. Traded to **Montreal** by **Calgary** for Brian Skrudland, January 28, 1993.

LEETCH, BRIAN

Defense. Shoots left. 5'11", 195 lbs. Born, Corpus Christi, TX, March 3, 1968.
(NY Rangers' 1st choice, 9th overall, in 1986 Entry Draft).

			Regular Season					Playoffs				
Season	Club	Lea	GP	G	A	TP	PIM	GP	G	A	TP	PIM
1986-87abcd	Boston College	H.E.	37	9	38	47	10	....	....	....	....	....
1987-88	U.S. National	....	50	13	61	74	38	....	....	....	....	....
	U.S. Olympic	....	6	1	5	6	4	....	....	....	....	....
	NY Rangers	**NHL**	**17**	**2**	**12**	**14**	**0**	....	....	....	....	....
1988-89ef	**NY Rangers**	**NHL**	**68**	**23**	**48**	**71**	**50**	**4**	**3**	**2**	**5**	**2**
1989-90	**NY Rangers**	**NHL**	**72**	**11**	**45**	**56**	**26**	....	....	....	....	....
1990-91g	**NY Rangers**	**NHL**	**80**	**16**	**72**	**88**	**42**	**6**	**1**	**3**	**4**	**0**
1991-92ij	**NY Rangers**	**NHL**	**80**	**22**	**80**	**102**	**26**	**13**	**4**	**11**	**15**	**4**
1992-93	**NY Rangers**	**NHL**	**36**	**6**	**30**	**36**	**26**	....	....	....	....	....
	NHL Totals		**353**	**80**	**287**	**367**	**170**	**23**	**8**	**16**	**24**	**6**

a Hockey East Player of the Year (1987)
b Hockey East Rookie of the Year (1987)
c Hockey East First All-Star Team (1987)
d NCAA East First All-American Team (1987)
e NHL All-Rookie Team (1989)
f Won Calder Memorial Trophy (1989)
g NHL Second All-Star Team (1991)
i Won James Norris Memorial Trophy (1992)
j NHL First All-Star Team (1992)

Played in NHL All-Star Game (1990-92)

LEFEBVRE, SYLVAIN

Defense. Shoots left. 6'2", 204 lbs. Born, Richmond, Que., October 14, 1967.

			Regular Season					Playoffs				
Season	Club	Lea	GP	G	A	TP	PIM	GP	G	A	TP	PIM
1984-85	Laval	QMJHL	66	7	5	12	31	....	....	....	....	....
1985-86	Laval	QMJHL	71	8	17	25	48	14	1	0	1	25
1986-87	Laval	QMJHL	70	10	36	46	44	15	1	6	7	12
1987-88	Sherbrooke	AHL	79	3	24	27	73	6	2	3	5	4
1988-89a	Sherbrooke	AHL	77	15	32	47	119	6	1	3	4	4
1989-90	**Montreal**	**NHL**	**68**	**3**	**10**	**13**	**61**	**6**	**0**	**0**	**0**	**2**
1990-91	**Montreal**	**NHL**	**63**	**5**	**18**	**23**	**30**	**11**	**1**	**0**	**1**	**6**
1991-92	**Montreal**	**NHL**	**69**	**3**	**14**	**17**	**91**	**2**	**0**	**0**	**0**	**2**
1992-93	**Toronto**	**NHL**	**81**	**2**	**12**	**14**	**90**	**21**	**3**	**3**	**6**	**20**
	NHL Totals		**281**	**13**	**54**	**67**	**272**	**40**	**4**	**3**	**7**	**30**

a AHL Second All-Star Team (1989)

Signed as a free agent by **Montreal**, September 24, 1986. Traded to **Toronto** by **Montreal** for Toronto's third round choice in 1994 Entry Draft, August 20, 1992.

LEHOUX, GUY

Defense. Shoots left. 5'11", 205 lbs.   Born, Disraeli, Que., October 19, 1971.
(Toronto's 9th choice, 179th overall, in 1991 Entry Draft).

			Regular Season					Playoffs				
Season	Club	Lea	GP	G	A	TP	PIM	GP	G	A	TP	PIM
1989-90	Drummondville	QMJHL	66	4	17	21	178	....	....	....	....	....
1990-91	Drummondville	QMJHL	63	8	26	34	107	14	1	7	8	24
1991-92	St. John's	AHL	67	1	7	8	134	....	....	....	....	....
1992-93	St. John's	AHL	42	3	2	5	89	....	....	....	....	....
	Brantford	Col.	13	0	5	5	28	....	....	....	....	....

LEHTINEN, JERE   (lehkh-TIH-nehn)

Right wing. Shoots right. 6', 185 lbs.   Born, Espoo, Finland, June 24, 1973.
(Minnesota's 3rd choice, 88th overall, in 1992 Entry Draft).

			Regular Season					Playoffs				
Season	Club	Lea	GP	G	A	TP	PIM	GP	G	A	TP	PIM
1990-91	Espoo	Fin.2	32	15	9	24	12	....	....	....	....	....
1991-92	Espoo	Fin.2	43	32	17	49	6	....	....	....	....	....
1992-93	Kiekko-Espoo	Fin.	45	13	14	27	6	....	....	....	....	....

LEHTO, JONI   (lehkh-TOH)

Defense. Shoots left. 6', 175 lbs.   Born, Turku, Finland, July 15, 1970.
(NY Islanders' 5th choice, 111th overall, in 1990 Entry Draft).

			Regular Season					Playoffs				
Season	Club	Lea	GP	G	A	TP	PIM	GP	G	A	TP	PIM
1988-89	Ottawa	OHL	63	9	25	34	26	....	....	....	....	....
1989-90a	Ottawa	OHL	60	17	55	72	58	....	....	....	....	....
1990-91	Ottawa	OHL	8	2	10	12	8	....	....	....	....	....
1991-92	Capital Dist.	AHL	26	2	5	7	6	....	....	....	....	....
	Richmond	ECHL	18	2	9	11	10	....	....	....	....	....
1992-93	Capital Dist.	AHL	57	4	13	17	33	3	1	1	2	2

a   OHL Second All-Star Team (1990)

LEMIEUX, CLAUDE   (lehm-YOO)

Right wing. Shoots right. 6'1", 215 lbs.   Born, Buckingham, Que., July 16, 1965.
(Montreal's 2nd choice, 26th overall, in 1983 Entry Draft).

			Regular Season					Playoffs				
Season	Club	Lea	GP	G	A	TP	PIM	GP	G	A	TP	PIM
1982-83	Trois-Rivières	QMJHL	62	28	38	66	187	4	1	0	1	30
1983-84	**Montreal**	**NHL**	**8**	**1**	**1**	**2**	**12**	....	....	....	....	....
	Verdun	QMJHL	51	41	45	86	225	9	8	12	20	63
	Nova Scotia	AHL	....	....	....	....	....	2	1	0	1	0
1984-85	**Montreal**	**NHL**	**1**	**0**	**1**	**1**	**7**	....	....	....	....	....
ab	Verdun	QMJHL	52	58	66	124	152	14	23	17	40	38
1985-86	**Montreal**	**NHL**	**10**	**1**	**2**	**3**	**22**	**20**	**10**	**6**	**16**	**68**
	Sherbrooke	AHL	58	21	32	53	145	....	....	....	....	....
1986-87	**Montreal**	**NHL**	**76**	**27**	**26**	**53**	**156**	**17**	**4**	**9**	**13**	**41**
1987-88	**Montreal**	**NHL**	**78**	**31**	**30**	**61**	**137**	**11**	**3**	**2**	**5**	**20**
1988-89	**Montreal**	**NHL**	**69**	**29**	**22**	**51**	**136**	**18**	**4**	**3**	**7**	**58**
1989-90	**Montreal**	**NHL**	**39**	**8**	**10**	**18**	**106**	**11**	**1**	**3**	**4**	**38**
1990-91	**New Jersey**	**NHL**	**78**	**30**	**17**	**47**	**105**	**7**	**4**	**0**	**4**	**34**
1991-92	**New Jersey**	**NHL**	**74**	**41**	**27**	**68**	**109**	**7**	**4**	**3**	**7**	**26**
1992-93	**New Jersey**	**NHL**	**77**	**30**	**51**	**81**	**155**	**5**	**2**	**0**	**2**	**19**
	NHL Totals		**510**	**198**	**187**	**385**	**945**	**96**	**32**	**26**	**58**	**304**

a   Named Most Valuable Player in QMJHL Playoffs (1985)
b   QMJHL First All-Star Team (1985)
Traded to **New Jersey** by **Montreal** for Sylvain Turgeon, September 4, 1990.

LEMIEUX, JOCELYN   (lehm-YOO)

Right wing. Shoots left. 5'10", 200 lbs.   Born, Mont-Laurier, Que., November 18, 1967.
(St. Louis' 1st choice, 10th overall, in 1986 Entry Draft).

			Regular Season					Playoffs				
Season	Club	Lea	GP	G	A	TP	PIM	GP	G	A	TP	PIM
1984-85	Laval	QMJHL	68	13	19	32	92	....	....	....	....	....
1985-86a	Laval	QMJHL	71	57	68	125	131	14	9	15	24	37
1986-87	**St. Louis**	**NHL**	**53**	**10**	**8**	**18**	**94**	**5**	**0**	**1**	**1**	**6**
1987-88	**St. Louis**	**NHL**	**23**	**1**	**0**	**1**	**42**	**5**	**0**	**0**	**0**	**15**
	Peoria	IHL	8	0	5	5	35	....	....	....	....	....
1988-89	**Montreal**	**NHL**	**1**	**0**	**1**	**1**	**0**	....	....	....	....	....
	Sherbrooke	AHL	73	25	28	53	134	4	3	1	4	6
1989-90	**Montreal**	**NHL**	**34**	**4**	**2**	**6**	**61**	....	....	....	....	....
	Chicago	**NHL**	**39**	**10**	**11**	**21**	**47**	**18**	**1**	**8**	**9**	**28**
1990-91	**Chicago**	**NHL**	**67**	**6**	**7**	**13**	**119**	**4**	**0**	**0**	**0**	**0**
1991-92	**Chicago**	**NHL**	**78**	**6**	**10**	**16**	**80**	**18**	**3**	**1**	**4**	**33**
1992-93	**Chicago**	**NHL**	**81**	**10**	**21**	**31**	**111**	**4**	**1**	**0**	**1**	**2**
	NHL Totals		**376**	**47**	**60**	**107**	**554**	**54**	**5**	**10**	**15**	**84**

a   QMJHL First All-Star Team (1986)
Traded to **Montreal** by **St. Louis** with Darrell May and St. Louis' second round choice (Patrice Brisebois) in the 1989 Entry Draft for Sergio Momesso and Vincent Riendeau, August 9, 1988. Traded to **Chicago** by **Montreal** for Chicago's third round choice (Charles Poulin) in 1990 Entry Draft, January 5, 1990.

LEMIEUX, MARIO   (lehm-YOO)

Center. Shoots right. 6'4", 210 lbs.   Born, Montreal, Que., October 5, 1965.
(Pittsburgh's 1st choice, 1st overall, in 1984 Entry Draft).

			Regular Season					Playoffs				
Season	Club	Lea	GP	G	A	TP	PIM	GP	G	A	TP	PIM
1981-82	Laval	QMJHL	64	30	66	96	22	18	5	9	14	31
1982-83a	Laval	QMJHL	66	84	100	184	76	12	14	18	32	18
1983-84bcd	Laval	QMJHL	70	*133	*149	*282	92	14	*29	*23	*52	29
1984-85ef	**Pittsburgh**	**NHL**	**73**	**43**	**57**	**100**	**54**	....	....	....	....	....
1985-86gh	**Pittsburgh**	**NHL**	**79**	**48**	**93**	**141**	**43**	....	....	....	....	....
1986-87g	**Pittsburgh**	**NHL**	**63**	**54**	**53**	**107**	**57**	....	....	....	....	....
1987-88												
hijklm	Pittsburgh	NHL	77	*70	98	*168	92	....	....	....	....	....
1988-89jkmn	**Pittsburgh**	**NHL**	**76**	***85**	***114**	***199**	**100**	**11**	**12**	**7**	**19**	**16**
1989-90	**Pittsburgh**	**NHL**	**59**	**45**	**78**	**123**	**78**	....	....	....	....	....
1990-91o	**Pittsburgh**	**NHL**	**26**	**19**	**26**	**45**	**30**	**23**	**16**	***28**	***44**	**16**
1991-92gjop	**Pittsburgh**	**NHL**	**64**	**44**	**87**	***131**	**94**	**15**	***16**	**18**	***34**	**2**
1992-93												
hijkq	Pittsburgh	NHL	60	69	91	*160	38	11	8	10	18	10
	NHL Totals		**577**	**477**	**697**	**1174**	**586**	**60**	**52**	**63**	**115**	**44**

a   QMJHL Second All-Star Team (1983)
b   QMJHL First All-Star Team (1984)
c   QMJHL Most Valuable Player (1984)
d   Canadian Major Junior Player of the Year (1984)
e   Won Calder Memorial Trophy (1985)
f   NHL All-Rookie Team (1985)
g   NHL Second All-Star Team (1986, 1987, 1992)
h   Won Lester B. Pearson Award (1986, 1988, 1993)
i   Won Hart Trophy (1988, 1993)
j   Won Art Ross Trophy (1988, 1989, 1992, 1993)
k   NHL First All-Star Team (1988, 1989, 1993)
l   Won Dodge Performance of the Year Award (1988)
m   Won Dodge Ram Tough Award (1989)
n   Won Dodge Performer of the Year Award (1988, 1989)
o   Won Conn Smythe Trophy (1991, 1992)
p   Won ProSet/NHL Player of the Year Award (1992)
q   Won Bill Masterton Memorial Trophy (1993)
Played in NHL All-Star Game (1985, 1986, 1988-90, 1992)

LEPAGE, MARTIN

Defense. Shoots left. 6'1", 185 lbs.   Born, Longueuil, Que., February 26, 1974.
(Quebec's 7th choice, 148th overall, in 1992 Entry Draft).

			Regular Season					Playoffs				
Season	Club	Lea	GP	G	A	TP	PIM	GP	G	A	TP	PIM
1990-91	Hull	QMJHL	60	0	8	8	48	6	0	1	1	6
1991-92	Hull	QMJHL	69	2	10	12	71	6	0	0	0	4
1992-93	Shawinigan	QMJHL	61	7	26	33	133	....	....	....	....	....

LEPLER, PAUL

Defense. Shoots left. 6'3", 185 lbs.   Born, Granite Falls, MN, November 26, 1972.
(Montreal's 14th choice, 237th overall, in 1991 Entry Draft).

			Regular Season					Playoffs				
Season	Club	Lea	GP	G	A	TP	PIM	GP	G	A	TP	PIM
1990-91	Rochester	NEJHL	48	2	11	13	46	....	....	....	....	....
1991-92					UNAVAILABLE							
1992-93	St. Cloud	WCHA	26	2	4	6	16	....	....	....	....	....

LEROUX, FRANCOIS

Defense. Shoots left. 6'6", 225 lbs.   Born, Ste.-Adele, Que., April 18, 1970.
(Edmonton's 1st choice, 19th overall, in 1988 Entry Draft).

			Regular Season					Playoffs				
Season	Club	Lea	GP	G	A	TP	PIM	GP	G	A	TP	PIM
1987-88	St-Jean	QMJHL	58	3	8	11	143	7	2	0	2	21
1988-89	**Edmonton**	**NHL**	**2**	**0**	**0**	**0**	**0**	....	....	....	....	....
	St-Jean	QMJHL	57	8	34	42	185	....	....	....	....	....
1989-90	**Edmonton**	**NHL**	**3**	**0**	**1**	**1**	**0**	....	....	....	....	....
	Victoriaville	QMJHL	54	4	33	37	169	....	....	....	....	....
1990-91	**Edmonton**	**NHL**	**1**	**0**	**2**	**2**	**0**	....	....	....	....	....
	Cape Breton	AHL	71	2	7	9	124	4	0	1	1	19
1991-92	**Edmonton**	**NHL**	**4**	**0**	**0**	**0**	**7**	....	....	....	....	....
	Cape Breton	AHL	61	7	22	29	114	5	0	0	0	8
1992-93	**Edmonton**	**NHL**	**1**	**0**	**0**	**0**	**4**	....	....	....	....	....
	Cape Breton	AHL	55	10	24	34	139	16	0	5	5	29
	NHL Totals		**11**	**0**	**3**	**3**	**11**	....	....	....	....	....

LESCHYSHYN, CURTIS   (lez-CHIH-shihn)

Defense. Shoots left. 6'1", 205 lbs.   Born, Thompson, Man., September 21, 1969.
(Quebec's 1st choice, 3rd overall, in 1988 Entry Draft).

			Regular Season					Playoffs				
Season	Club	Lea	GP	G	A	TP	PIM	GP	G	A	TP	PIM
1986-87	Saskatoon	WHL	70	14	26	40	107	11	1	5	6	14
1987-88	Saskatoon	WHL	56	14	41	55	86	10	2	5	7	16
1988-89	**Quebec**	**NHL**	**71**	**4**	**9**	**13**	**71**	....	....	....	....	....
1989-90	**Quebec**	**NHL**	**68**	**2**	**6**	**8**	**44**	....	....	....	....	....
1990-91	**Quebec**	**NHL**	**55**	**3**	**7**	**10**	**49**	....	....	....	....	....
1991-92	**Quebec**	**NHL**	**42**	**5**	**12**	**17**	**42**	....	....	....	....	....
	Halifax	AHL	6	0	2	2	4	....	....	....	....	....
1992-93	**Quebec**	**NHL**	**82**	**9**	**23**	**32**	**61**	**6**	**1**	**1**	**2**	**6**
	NHL Totals		**318**	**23**	**57**	**80**	**267**	**6**	**1**	**1**	**2**	**6**

LESLIE, LEE J.

Left wing. Shoots left. 6'4", 191 lbs.   Born, Prince George, B.C., August 15, 1972.
(St. Louis' 4th choice, 86th overall, in 1992 Entry Draft).

			Regular Season					Playoffs				
Season	Club	Lea	GP	G	A	TP	PIM	GP	G	A	TP	PIM
1989-90	Prince Albert	WHL	62	14	16	30	13	14	2	3	5	4
1990-91	Prince Albert	WHL	72	29	42	71	68	3	0	0	0	5
1991-92	Prince Albert	WHL	72	52	48	100	70	10	6	6	12	12
1992-93	Peoria	IHL	72	22	24	46	46	4	0	3	3	2

Signed as a free agent by **San Jose**, June 21, 1993.

LESSARD, RICK

Defense. Shoots left. 6'2", 206 lbs. Born, Timmins, Ont., January 9, 1968.
(Calgary's 6th choice, 142nd overall, in 1986 Entry Draft).

			Regular Season					Playoffs				
Season	Club	Lea	GP	G	A	TP	PIM	GP	G	A	TP	PIM
1985-86	Ottawa	OHL	64	1	20	21	231	....	....	....	....	....
1986-87	Ottawa	OHL	66	5	36	41	188	11	1	7	8	30
1987-88	Ottawa	OHL	58	5	34	39	210	16	1	0	1	31
1988-89	**Calgary**	**NHL**	**6**	**0**	**1**	**1**	**2**	....	....	....	....	....
a	Salt Lake	IHL	76	10	42	52	239	14	1	6	7	35
1989-90	Salt Lake	IHL	66	3	18	21	169	10	1	2	3	64
1990-91	**Calgary**	**NHL**	**1**	**0**	**1**	**1**	**0**	....	....	....	....	....
	Salt Lake	IHL	80	8	27	35	272	4	0	1	1	12
1991-92	**San Jose**	**NHL**	**8**	**0**	**2**	**2**	**16**	....	....	....	....	....
	Kansas City	IHL	46	3	16	19	117	3	0	0	0	2
1992-93	Kansas City	IHL	1	0	0	0	0	....	....	....	....	....
	Providence	AHL	6	0	0	0	6	....	....	....	....	....
	Hamilton	AHL	52	0	17	17	151	....	....	....	....	....
	NHL Totals		**15**	**0**	**4**	**4**	**18**	....	....	....	....	....

a IHL First All-Star Team (1989)

Claimed by **San Jose** from **Calgary** in Expansion Draft, May 30, 1991. Traded to **Vancouver** by **San Jose** for Robin Bawa, December 15, 1992.

LEVEQUE, GUY

Center. Shoots right. 5'11", 166 lbs. Born, Kingston, Ont., December 28, 1972.
(Los Angeles' 1st choice, 42nd overall, in 1991 Entry Draft).

			Regular Season					Playoffs				
Season	Club	Lea	GP	G	A	TP	PIM	GP	G	A	TP	PIM
1989-90	Cornwall	OHL	62	10	15	25	30	3	0	0	0	4
1990-91	Cornwall	OHL	66	41	56	97	34	....	....	....	....	....
1991-92	Cornwall	OHL	37	23	36	59	40	6	3	5	8	2
1992-93	**Los Angeles**	**NHL**	**12**	**2**	**1**	**3**	**19**	....	....	....	....	....
	Phoenix	IHL	56	27	30	57	71	....	....	....	....	....
	NHL Totals		**12**	**2**	**1**	**3**	**19**	....	....	....	....	....

LEVINS, SCOTT

Center. Shoots right. 6'4", 210 lbs. Born, Spokane, WA, January 30, 1970.
(Winnipeg's 4th choice, 75th overall, in 1990 Entry Draft).

			Regular Season					Playoffs				
Season	Club	Lea	GP	G	A	TP	PIM	GP	G	A	TP	PIM
1989-90a	Tri-Cities	WHL	71	25	37	62	132	6	2	3	5	18
1990-91	Moncton	AHL	74	12	26	38	133	4	0	0	0	4
1991-92	Moncton	AHL	69	15	18	33	271	11	3	4	7	30
1992-93	**Winnipeg**	**NHL**	**9**	**0**	**1**	**1**	**18**	....	....	....	....	....
	Moncton	AHL	54	22	26	48	158	5	1	3	4	14
	NHL Totals		**9**	**0**	**1**	**1**	**18**	....	....	....	....	....

a WHL West Second All-Star Team (1990)

Claimed by **Florida** from **Winnipeg** in Expansion Draft, June 24, 1993.

LIDSTER, DOUG

Defense. Shoots right. 6'1", 200 lbs. Born, Kamloops, B.C., October 18, 1960.
(Vancouver's 6th choice, 133rd overall, in 1980 Entry Draft).

			Regular Season					Playoffs				
Season	Club	Lea	GP	G	A	TP	PIM	GP	G	A	TP	PIM
1977-78	Seattle	WHL	2	0	0	0	0	....	....	....	....	....
1978-79	Kamloops	BCJHL	59	36	47	83	50	....	....	....	....	....
1979-80	Colorado	WCHA	39	18	25	43	52	....	....	....	....	....
1980-81	Colorado	WCHA	36	10	30	40	54	....	....	....	....	....
1981-82	Colorado	WCHA	36	13	22	35	32	....	....	....	....	....
1982-83	Colorado	WCHA	34	15	41	56	30	....	....	....	....	....
1983-84	Cdn. Olympic	....	59	6	20	26	28	....	....	....	....	....
	Vancouver	**NHL**	**8**	**0**	**0**	**0**	**4**	**2**	**0**	**1**	**1**	**0**
1984-85	**Vancouver**	**NHL**	**78**	**6**	**24**	**30**	**55**	....	....	....	....	....
1985-86	**Vancouver**	**NHL**	**78**	**12**	**16**	**28**	**56**	**3**	**0**	**1**	**1**	**2**
1986-87	**Vancouver**	**NHL**	**80**	**12**	**51**	**63**	**40**	....	....	....	....	....
1987-88	**Vancouver**	**NHL**	**64**	**4**	**32**	**36**	**105**	....	....	....	....	....
1988-89	**Vancouver**	**NHL**	**63**	**5**	**17**	**22**	**78**	**7**	**1**	**1**	**2**	**9**
1989-90	**Vancouver**	**NHL**	**80**	**8**	**28**	**36**	**36**	....	....	....	....	....
1990-91	**Vancouver**	**NHL**	**78**	**6**	**32**	**38**	**77**	**6**	**0**	**2**	**2**	**6**
1991-92	**Vancouver**	**NHL**	**66**	**6**	**23**	**29**	**39**	**11**	**1**	**2**	**3**	**11**
1992-93	**Vancouver**	**NHL**	**71**	**6**	**19**	**25**	**36**	**12**	**0**	**3**	**3**	**8**
	NHL Totals		**666**	**65**	**242**	**307**	**526**	**41**	**2**	**10**	**12**	**36**

Traded to **NY Rangers** by **Vancouver** to complete June 20, 1993 trade which sent John Vanbiesbrouck to Vancouver for future considerations, June 25, 1993.

LIDSTROM, NICKLAS (LID-struhm)

Defense. Shoots left. 6'2", 180 lbs. Born, Vasteras, Sweden, April 28, 1970.
(Detroit's 3rd choice, 53rd overall, in 1989 Entry Draft).

			Regular Season					Playoffs				
Season	Club	Lea	GP	G	A	TP	PIM	GP	G	A	TP	PIM
1987-88	Vasteras	Swe.2	3	0	0	0	....	....	....	....	....	....
1988-89	Vasteras	Swe.	19	0	2	2	4	....	....	....	....	....
1989-90	Vasteras	Swe.	39	8	8	16	14	2	0	1	1	2
1990-91	Vasteras	Swe.	38	4	19	23	2	4	0	0	0	4
1991-92a	**Detroit**	**NHL**	**80**	**11**	**49**	**60**	**22**	**11**	**1**	**2**	**3**	**0**
1992-93	**Detroit**	**NHL**	**84**	**7**	**34**	**41**	**28**	**7**	**1**	**0**	**1**	**0**
	NHL Totals		**164**	**18**	**83**	**101**	**50**	**18**	**2**	**2**	**4**	**0**

a NHL/Upper Deck All-Rookie Team (1992)

LIEVERS, BRETT

Center. Shoots right. 6', 170 lbs. Born, Syracuse, NY, June 18, 1971.
(NY Rangers' 13th choice, 223rd overall, in 1990 Entry Draft).

			Regular Season					Playoffs				
Season	Club	Lea	GP	G	A	TP	PIM	GP	G	A	TP	PIM
1990-91	St. Cloud	WCHA	40	14	18	32	4	....	....	....	....	....
1991-92	St. Cloud	WCHA	16	2	10	12	2	....	....	....	....	....
1992-93	St. Cloud	WCHA			DID NOT PLAY							

LILLEY, JOHN

Center. Shoots right. 5'8", 178 lbs. Born, Wakefield, MA, August 3, 1972.
(Winnipeg's 8th choice, 140th overall, in 1990 Entry Draft).

			Regular Season					Playoffs				
Season	Club	Lea	GP	G	A	TP	PIM	GP	G	A	TP	PIM
1991-92	Boston U.	H.E.	23	9	9	18	43	....	....	....	....	....
1992-93	Boston U.	H.E.	4	0	1	1	13	....	....	....	....	....
	Seattle	WHL	45	22	28	50	55	5	1	3	4	9

LIND, JUHA

Center. Shoots left. 5'11", 172 lbs. Born, Helsinki, Finland, January 2, 1974.
(Minnesota's 6th choice, 178th overall, in 1992 Entry Draft).

			Regular Season					Playoffs				
Season	Club	Lea	GP	G	A	TP	PIM	GP	G	A	TP	PIM
1991-92	Jokerit Jrs.	Fin.	28	16	24	40	10	....	....	....	....	....
1992-93	Vantaa	Fin.2	25	8	12	20	8	....	....	....	....	....
	Jokerit	Fin.	6	0	0	0	2	1	0	0	0	0

LINDBERG, CHRIS

Left wing. Shoots left. 6'1", 190 lbs. Born, Fort Frances, Ont., April 16, 1967.

			Regular Season					Playoffs				
Season	Club	Lea	GP	G	A	TP	PIM	GP	G	A	TP	PIM
1987-88	Minn.-Duluth	WCHA	35	12	10	22	36	....	....	....	....	....
1988-89	Minn.-Duluth	WCHA	36	15	18	33	51	....	....	....	....	....
1989-90	Binghamton	AHL	32	4	4	8	36	....	....	....	....	....
	Virginia	ECHL	26	11	23	34	27	4	0	3	3	2
1990-91	Cdn. National	....	55	25	31	56	53	....	....	....	....	....
	Springfield	AHL	1	0	0	0	2	1	0	0	0	0
1991-92	Cdn. National	....	56	33	35	68	63	....	....	....	....	....
	Cdn. Olympic	....	8	1	4	5	4	....	....	....	....	....
	Calgary	**NHL**	**17**	**2**	**5**	**7**	**17**	....	....	....	....	....
1992-93	**Calgary**	**NHL**	**62**	**9**	**12**	**21**	**18**	**2**	**0**	**1**	**1**	**2**
	NHL Totals		**79**	**11**	**17**	**28**	**35**	**2**	**0**	**1**	**1**	**2**

Signed as a free agent by **Hartford**, March 17, 1989. Signed as a free agent by **Calgary**, August 2, 1991. Claimed by **Ottawa** from **Calgary** in Expansion Draft, June 18, 1992. Traded to **Calgary** by **Ottawa** for Mark Osiecki, June 22, 1992.

LINDEN, TREVOR

Center/Right wing. Shoots right. 6'4", 205 lbs. Born, Medicine Hat, Alta., April 11, 1970.
(Vancouver's 1st choice, 2nd overall, in 1988 Entry Draft).

			Regular Season					Playoffs				
Season	Club	Lea	GP	G	A	TP	PIM	GP	G	A	TP	PIM
1986-87	Medicine Hat	WHL	72	14	22	36	59	20	5	4	9	17
1987-88	Medicine Hat	WHL	67	46	64	110	76	16	*13	12	25	19
1988-89a	**Vancouver**	**NHL**	**80**	**30**	**29**	**59**	**41**	**7**	**3**	**4**	**7**	**8**
1989-90	**Vancouver**	**NHL**	**73**	**21**	**30**	**51**	**43**	....	....	....	....	....
1990-91	**Vancouver**	**NHL**	**80**	**33**	**37**	**70**	**65**	**6**	**0**	**7**	**7**	**2**
1991-92	**Vancouver**	**NHL**	**80**	**31**	**44**	**75**	**101**	**13**	**4**	**8**	**12**	**6**
1992-93	**Vancouver**	**NHL**	**84**	**33**	**39**	**72**	**64**	**12**	**5**	**8**	**13**	**16**
	NHL Totals		**397**	**148**	**179**	**327**	**314**	**38**	**12**	**27**	**39**	**32**

a NHL All-Rookie Team (1989)

Played in NHL All-Star Game (1991, 1992)

LINDGREN, MATS

Center. Shoots left. 6'1", 187 lbs. Born, Skelleftea, Sweden, October 1, 1974.
(Winnipeg's 1st choice, 15th overall, in 1993 Entry Draft).

			Regular Season					Playoffs				
Season	Club	Lea	GP	G	A	TP	PIM	GP	G	A	TP	PIM
1991-92	Skelleftea	Swe.2	29	14	8	22	14	....	....	....	....	....
1992-93	Skelleftea	Swe.2	32	20	14	34	18	....	....	....	....	....

LINDQUIST, FREDRIK

Center. Shoots left. 5'11", 176 lbs. Born, Sodertalje, Sweden, June 21, 1973.
(New Jersey's 4th choice, 55th overall, in 1991 Entry Draft).

			Regular Season					Playoffs				
Season	Club	Lea	GP	G	A	TP	PIM	GP	G	A	TP	PIM
1989-90	Huddinge	Swe.2	2	0	0	0	0	....	....	....	....	....
1990-91	Djurgarden	Swe.	28	6	4	10	0	7	1	0	1	2
1991-92	Djurgarden	Swe.	39	9	6	15	14	10	1	1	2	2
1992-93	Djurgarden	Swe.	39	9	11	20	8	4	1	2	3	2

LINDROS, ERIC (LIHND-RAHZ)

Center. Shoots right. 6'4", 235 lbs. Born, London, Ont., February 28, 1973.
(Quebec's 1st choice, 1st overall, in 1991 Entry Draft).

			Regular Season					Playoffs				
Season	Club	Lea	GP	G	A	TP	PIM	GP	G	A	TP	PIM
1989-90	Det. Compuware	USHL	14	23	29	52	123	....	....	....	....	....
a	Oshawa	OHL	25	17	19	36	61	17	18	18	36	76
1990-91bc	Oshawa	OHL	57	*71	78	*149	189	16	*18	20	*38	*93
1991-92	Oshawa	OHL	13	9	22	31	54	....	....	....	....	....
	Cdn. National	....	24	19	16	35	34	....	....	....	....	....
	Cdn. Olympic	....	8	5	6	11	6	....	....	....	....	....
1992-93d	**Philadelphia**	**NHL**	**61**	**41**	**34**	**75**	**147**	....	....	....	....	....
	NHL Totals		**61**	**41**	**34**	**75**	**147**	....	....	....	....	....

a Memorial Cup All-Star Team (1990)
b OHL First All-Star Team (1991)
c Canadian Major Junior Player of the Year (1991)
d NHL/Upper Deck All-Rookie Team (1993)

Traded to **Philadelphia** by **Quebec** for Peter Forsberg, Steve Duchesne, Kerry Huffman, Mike Ricci, Ron Hextall, Chris Simon, Philadelphia's first choice in the 1993 (Jocelyn Thibault) and 1994 Entry Drafts and cash, June 30, 1992.

LINDSAY, BILL

Left wing. Shoots left. 5'11", 185 lbs. Born, Big Fork, MT, May 17, 1971.
(Quebec's 6th choice, 103rd overall, in 1991 Entry Draft).

			Regular Season					Playoffs				
Season	Club	Lea	GP	G	A	TP	PIM	GP	G	A	TP	PIM
1990-91	Tri-Cities	WHL	63	46	47	93	151	5	3	6	9	10
1991-92	**Quebec**	**NHL**	**23**	**2**	**4**	**6**	**14**	....	....	....	....	....
a	Tri-Cities	WHL	42	34	59	93	111	3	2	3	5	16
1992-93	**Quebec**	**NHL**	**44**	**4**	**9**	**13**	**16**	....	....	....	....	....
	Halifax	AHL	20	11	13	24	18	....	....	....	....	....
	NHL Totals		**67**	**6**	**13**	**19**	**30**	....	....	....	....	....

a WHL West Second All-Star Team (1992)

Claimed by **Florida** from **Quebec** in Expansion Draft, June 24, 1993.

LIPUMA, CHRIS

Defense. Shoots left. 6', 183 lbs. Born, Bridgeview, IL, March 23, 1971.

			Regular Season					Playoffs				
Season	Club	Lea	GP	G	A	TP	PIM	GP	G	A	TP	PIM
1990-91	Kitchener	OHL	61	6	30	36	145	4	0	1	1	4
1991-92	Kitchener	OHL	61	13	59	72	115	14	4	9	13	34
1992-93	**Tampa Bay**	**NHL**	**15**	**0**	**5**	**5**	**34**	....	....	....	....	....
	Atlanta	IHL	66	4	14	18	379	9	1	1	2	35
	NHL Totals		**15**	**0**	**5**	**5**	**34**	....	....	....	....	....

Signed as a free agent by **Tampa Bay**, June 29, 1992.

LOACH, LONNIE

Left wing. Shoots left. 5'10", 181 lbs. Born, New Liskeard, Ont., April 14, 1968.
(Chicago's 4th choice, 98th overall, in 1986 Entry Draft).

			Regular Season					Playoffs				
Season	Club	Lea	GP	G	A	TP	PIM	GP	G	A	TP	PIM
1985-86a	Guelph	OHL	65	41	42	83	63	20	7	8	15	16
1986-87	Guelph	OHL	56	31	24	55	42	5	2	1	3	2
1987-88	Guelph	OHL	66	43	49	92	75	....	....	....	....	....
1988-89	Flint	IHL	41	22	26	48	30	....	....	....	....	....
	Saginaw	IHL	32	7	6	13	27	....	....	....	....	....
1989-90	Indianapolis	IHL	3	0	0	0	0	....	....	....	....	....
	Fort Wayne	IHL	54	15	33	48	40	5	4	2	6	15
1990-91bc	Fort Wayne	IHL	81	55	76	*131	45	19	5	11	16	13
1991-92	Adirondack	AHL	67	37	49	86	69	19	*13	4	17	10
1992-93	**Ottawa**	**NHL**	**3**	**0**	**0**	**0**	**0**	....	....	....	....	....
	Los Angeles	**NHL**	**50**	**10**	**13**	**23**	**27**	**1**	**0**	**0**	**0**	**0**
	Phoenix	IHL	4	2	3	5	10	....	....	....	....	....
	NHL Totals		**53**	**10**	**13**	**23**	**27**	**1**	**0**	**0**	**0**	**0**

a OHL Rookie of the Year (1986)
b IHL Second All-Star Team (1991)
c Won Leo P. Lamoureux Trophy (Leading Scorer – IHL) (1991)

Signed as a free agent by **Detroit**, June 7, 1991. Claimed by **Ottawa** from **Detroit** in Expansion Draft, June 18, 1992. Claimed on waivers by **Los Angeles** from **Ottawa**, October 21, 1992. Claimed by **Anaheim** from **Los Angeles** in Expansion Draft, June 24, 1993.

LOEWEN, DARCY

Left wing. Shoots left. 5'10", 185 lbs. Born, Calgary, Alta., February 26, 1969.
(Buffalo's 2nd choice, 55th overall, in 1988 Entry Draft).

			Regular Season					Playoffs				
Season	Club	Lea	GP	G	A	TP	PIM	GP	G	A	TP	PIM
1986-87	Spokane	WHL	68	15	25	40	129	5	0	0	0	16
1987-88	Spokane	WHL	72	30	44	74	231	15	7	5	12	54
1988-89	Spokane	WHL	60	31	27	58	194	....	....	....	....	....
	Cdn. National	....	2	0	0	0	0	....	....	....	....	....
1989-90	**Buffalo**	**NHL**	**4**	**0**	**0**	**0**	**4**	....	....	....	....	....
	Rochester	AHL	50	7	11	18	193	5	1	0	1	6
1990-91	**Buffalo**	**NHL**	**6**	**0**	**0**	**0**	**8**	....	....	....	....	....
	Rochester	AHL	71	13	15	28	130	15	1	5	6	14
1991-92	**Buffalo**	**NHL**	**2**	**0**	**0**	**0**	**2**	....	....	....	....	....
	Rochester	AHL	73	11	20	31	193	4	0	1	1	8
1992-93	**Ottawa**	**NHL**	**79**	**4**	**5**	**9**	**145**	....	....	....	....	....
	NHL Totals		**91**	**4**	**5**	**9**	**159**	....	....	....	....	....

Claimed by **Ottawa** from **Buffalo** in Expansion Draft, June 18, 1992.

LOISELLE, CLAUDE (LWAH-ZEHL)

Center. Shoots left. 5'11", 195 lbs. Born, Ottawa, Ont., May 29, 1963.
(Detroit's 1st choice, 23rd overall, in 1981 Entry Draft).

			Regular Season					Playoffs				
Season	Club	Lea	GP	G	A	TP	PIM	GP	G	A	TP	PIM
1980-81	Windsor	OHA	68	38	56	94	103	11	3	3	6	40
1981-82	**Detroit**	**NHL**	**4**	**1**	**0**	**1**	**2**	....	....	....	....	....
	Windsor	OHL	68	36	73	109	192	9	2	10	12	42
1982-83	**Detroit**	**NHL**	**18**	**2**	**0**	**2**	**15**	....	....	....	....	....
	Adirondack	AHL	6	1	7	8	0	6	2	4	6	0
1983-84	**Detroit**	**NHL**	**28**	**4**	**6**	**10**	**32**	....	....	....	....	....
	Adirondack	AHL	29	13	16	29	59	....	....	....	....	....
1984-85	**Detroit**	**NHL**	**30**	**8**	**1**	**9**	**45**	**3**	**0**	**2**	**2**	**0**
	Adirondack	AHL	47	22	29	51	24	....	....	....	....	....
1985-86	**Detroit**	**NHL**	**48**	**7**	**15**	**22**	**142**	....	....	....	....	....
	Adirondack	AHL	21	15	11	26	32	16	5	10	15	38
1986-87	**New Jersey**	**NHL**	**75**	**16**	**24**	**40**	**137**	....	....	....	....	....
1987-88	**New Jersey**	**NHL**	**68**	**17**	**18**	**35**	**121**	**20**	**4**	**6**	**10**	**50**
1988-89	**New Jersey**	**NHL**	**74**	**7**	**14**	**21**	**209**	....	....	....	....	....
1989-90	**Quebec**	**NHL**	**72**	**11**	**14**	**25**	**104**	....	....	....	....	....
1990-91	**Quebec**	**NHL**	**59**	**5**	**10**	**15**	**86**	....	....	....	....	....
	Toronto	**NHL**	**7**	**1**	**1**	**2**	**2**	....	....	....	....	....
1991-92	**Toronto**	**NHL**	**64**	**6**	**9**	**15**	**102**	....	....	....	....	....
	NY Islanders	**NHL**	**11**	**1**	**1**	**2**	**13**	....	....	....	....	....
1992-93	**NY Islanders**	**NHL**	**41**	**5**	**3**	**8**	**90**	**18**	**0**	**3**	**3**	**10**
	NHL Totals		**599**	**91**	**116**	**207**	**1100**	**41**	**4**	**11**	**15**	**60**

Traded to **New Jersey** by **Detroit** for Tim Higgins, June 25, 1986. Traded to **Quebec** by **New Jersey** with Joe Cirella and New Jersey's eighth round choice (Alexander Karpovtsev) in 1990 Entry Draft for Walt Poddubny and Quebec's fourth round choice (Mike Bodnarchuk) in 1990 Entry Draft, June 17, 1989. Claimed on waivers by **Toronto**, March 5, 1991. Traded to **NY Islanders** by **Toronto** with Daniel Marois for Ken Baumgartner and Dave McLlwain, March 10, 1992.

LOMAKIN, ANDREI

Right wing. Shoots left. 5'10", 175 lbs. Born, Voskresensk, Soviet Union, April 3, 1964.
(Philadelphia's 7th choice, 138th overall, in 1991 Entry Draft).

			Regular Season					Playoffs				
Season	Club	Lea	GP	G	A	TP	PIM	GP	G	A	TP	PIM
1981-82	Khimik	USSR	8	1	1	2	2	....	....	....	....	....
1982-83	Khimik	USSR	56	15	8	23	32	....	....	....	....	....
1983-84	Khimik	USSR	44	10	8	18	26	....	....	....	....	....
1984-85	Khimik	USSR	52	13	10	23	24	....	....	....	....	....
1985-86					DID NOT PLAY							
1986-87	Moscow D'amo	USSR	40	15	14	29	30	....	....	....	....	....
1987-88	Moscow D'amo	USSR	45	10	15	25	24	....	....	....	....	....
1988-89	Moscow D'amo	USSR	44	9	16	25	22	....	....	....	....	....
1989-90	Moscow D'amo	USSR	48	11	15	26	36	....	....	....	....	....
1990-91	Moscow D'amo	USSR	45	16	17	33	22	....	....	....	....	....
1991-92	Moscow D'amo	CIS	2	1	3	4	2	....	....	....	....	....
	Philadelphia	**NHL**	**57**	**14**	**16**	**30**	**26**	....	....	....	....	....
1992-93	**Philadelphia**	**NHL**	**51**	**8**	**12**	**20**	**34**	....	....	....	....	....
	NHL Totals		**108**	**22**	**28**	**50**	**60**	....	....	....	....	....

Claimed by **Florida** from **Philadelphia** in Expansion Draft, June 24, 1993.

LOMBARDI, STEPHEN

Left wing. Shoots left. 6'1", 180 lbs. Born, South Easton, MA, April 14, 1973.
(Boston's 10th choice, 238th overall, in 1991 Entry Draft).

			Regular Season					Playoffs				
Season	Club	Lea	GP	G	A	TP	PIM	GP	G	A	TP	PIM
1991-92	Yale	ECAC	14	2	3	5	2	....	....	....	....	....
1992-93	Yale	ECAC	27	1	6	7	14	....	....	....	....	....

LONEY, BRIAN

Right wing. Shoots right. 6'1", 195 lbs. Born, Winnipeg, Man., August 9, 1972.
(Vancouver's 6th choice, 110th overall, in 1992 Entry Draft).

			Regular Season					Playoffs				
Season	Club	Lea	GP	G	A	TP	PIM	GP	G	A	TP	PIM
1991-92	Ohio State	CCHA	37	21	34	55	109	....	....	....	....	....
1992-93	Red Deer	WHL	66	39	36	75	147	4	1	1	2	19
	Cdn. National	....	1	0	1	1	0	....	....	....	....	....
	Hamilton	AHL	3	0	2	2	0	....	....	....	....	....

LONEY, TROY

Left wing. Shoots left. 6'3", 209 lbs. Born, Bow Island, Alta., September 21, 1963.
(Pittsburgh's 3rd choice, 52nd overall, in 1982 Entry Draft).

			Regular Season					Playoffs				
Season	Club	Lea	GP	G	A	TP	PIM	GP	G	A	TP	PIM
1980-81	Lethbridge	WHL	71	18	13	31	100	9	2	2	5	14
1981-82	Lethbridge	WHL	71	26	33	59	152	12	3	3	6	10
1982-83	Lethbridge	WHL	72	33	34	67	156	20	10	7	17	43
1983-84	**Pittsburgh**	**NHL**	**13**	**0**	**0**	**0**	**9**	....	....	....	....	....
	Baltimore	AHL	63	18	13	31	147	10	0	2	2	19
1984-85	**Pittsburgh**	**NHL**	**46**	**10**	**8**	**18**	**59**	....	....	....	....	....
	Baltimore	AHL	15	4	2	6	25	....	....	....	....	....
1985-86	**Pittsburgh**	**NHL**	**47**	**3**	**9**	**12**	**95**	....	....	....	....	....
	Baltimore	AHL	33	12	11	23	84	....	....	....	....	....
1986-87	**Pittsburgh**	**NHL**	**23**	**8**	**7**	**15**	**22**	....	....	....	....	....
	Baltimore	AHL	40	13	14	27	134	....	....	....	....	....
1987-88	**Pittsburgh**	**NHL**	**65**	**5**	**13**	**18**	**151**	....	....	....	....	....
1988-89	**Pittsburgh**	**NHL**	**69**	**10**	**6**	**16**	**165**	**11**	**1**	**3**	**4**	**24**
1989-90	**Pittsburgh**	**NHL**	**67**	**11**	**16**	**27**	**168**	....	....	....	....	....
1990-91	**Pittsburgh**	**NHL**	**44**	**7**	**9**	**16**	**85**	**24**	**2**	**2**	**4**	**41**
	Muskegon	IHL	2	0	0	0	5	....	....	....	....	....
1991-92	**Pittsburgh**	**NHL**	**76**	**10**	**16**	**26**	**127**	**21**	**4**	**5**	**9**	**32**
1992-93	**Pittsburgh**	**NHL**	**82**	**5**	**16**	**21**	**99**	**10**	**1**	**4**	**5**	**0**
	NHL Totals		**532**	**69**	**100**	**169**	**980**	**66**	**8**	**14**	**22**	**97**

Claimed by **Anaheim** from **Pittsburgh** in Expansion Draft, June 24, 1993.

LONGO, CHRIS

Right wing. Shoots right. 5'10", 180 lbs. Born, Belleville, Ont., January 5, 1972.
(Washington's 3rd choice, 51st overall, in 1990 Entry Draft).

			Regular Season					Playoffs				
Season	Club	Lea	GP	G	A	TP	PIM	GP	G	A	TP	PIM
1989-90a	Peterborough	OHL	66	33	41	74	48	11	2	3	5	14
1990-91	Peterborough	OHL	64	30	38	68	68	4	1	0	1	0
1991-92	Peterborough	OHL	25	5	14	19	16	10	5	6	11	16
1992-93	Baltimore	AHL	74	7	18	25	52	7	0	1	1	0

a OHL Rookie of the Year (1990)

LOSINGER, BRYAN

Defense. Shoots right. 6'2", 210 lbs. Born, Caldwell, NY, July 21, 1972.
(NY Rangers' 9th choice, 139th overall, in 1990 Entry Draft).

			Regular Season					Playoffs				
Season	Club	Lea	GP	G	A	TP	PIM	GP	G	A	TP	PIM
1991-92	Harvard	ECAC	19	1	5	6	4	....	....	....	....	....
1992-93	Harvard	ECAC	31	2	9	11	6	....	....	....	....	....

LOWE, KEVIN HUGH
(LOH)

Defense. Shoots left. 6'2", 195 lbs. Born, Lachute, Que., April 15, 1959.
(Edmonton's 1st choice, 21st overall, in 1979 Entry Draft).

			Regular Season					Playoffs				
Season	Club	Lea	GP	G	A	TP	PIM	GP	G	A	TP	PIM
1977-78	Quebec	QJHL	64	13	52	65	86	4	1	2	3	6
1978-79a	Quebec	QJHL	68	26	60	86	120	6	1	7	8	36
1979-80	Edmonton	NHL	64	2	19	21	70	3	0	1	1	0
1980-81	Edmonton	NHL	79	10	24	34	94	9	0	2	2	11
1981-82	Edmonton	NHL	80	9	31	40	63	5	0	3	3	0
1982-83	Edmonton	NHL	80	6	34	40	43	16	1	8	9	10
1983-84	Edmonton	NHL	80	4	42	46	59	19	3	7	10	16
1984-85	Edmonton	NHL	80	4	21	25	104	16	0	5	5	8
1985-86	Edmonton	NHL	74	2	16	18	90	10	1	3	4	15
1986-87	Edmonton	NHL	77	8	29	37	94	21	2	4	6	22
1987-88	Edmonton	NHL	70	9	15	24	89	19	0	2	2	26
1988-89	Edmonton	NHL	76	7	18	25	98	7	1	2	3	4
1989-90bc	Edmonton	NHL	78	7	26	33	140	20	0	2	2	10
1990-91	Edmonton	NHL	73	3	13	16	113	14	1	1	2	14
1991-92	Edmonton	NHL	55	2	8	10	107	11	0	3	3	16
1992-93	NY Rangers	NHL	49	3	12	15	58	....	....	....	....	....
	NHL Totals		1015	76	308	384	1222	170	9	43	52	152

a QMJHL Second All-Star Team (1979)
b Won Bud Man of the Year Award (1990)
c Won King Clancy Memorial Trophy (1990)

Played in NHL All-Star Game (1984-86, 1988-90, 1993)

Traded to **NY Rangers** by **Edmonton** for Roman Oksyuta and NY Rangers' third round choice (Alexander Kerch) in 1993 Entry Draft, December 11, 1992.

LOWRY, DAVE

Left wing. Shoots left. 6'1", 195 lbs. Born, Sudbury, Ont., February 14, 1965.
(Vancouver's 6th choice, 110th overall, in 1983 Entry Draft).

			Regular Season					Playoffs				
Season	Club	Lea	GP	G	A	TP	PIM	GP	G	A	TP	PIM
1982-83	London	OHL	42	11	16	27	48	3	0	0	0	14
1983-84	London	OHL	66	29	47	76	125	8	6	6	12	41
1984-85a	London	OHL	61	60	60	120	94	8	6	5	11	10
1985-86	Vancouver	NHL	73	10	8	18	143	3	0	0	0	0
1986-87	Vancouver	NHL	70	8	10	18	176	....	....	....	....	....
1987-88	Vancouver	NHL	22	1	3	4	38	....	....	....	....	....
	Fredericton	AHL	46	18	27	45	59	14	7	3	10	72
1988-89	St. Louis	NHL	21	3	3	6	11	10	0	5	5	4
	Peoria	IHL	58	31	35	66	45	....	....	....	....	....
1989-90	St. Louis	NHL	78	19	6	25	75	12	2	1	3	39
1990-91	St. Louis	NHL	79	19	21	40	168	13	1	4	5	35
1991-92	St. Louis	NHL	75	7	13	20	77	6	0	1	1	20
1992-93	St. Louis	NHL	58	5	8	13	101	11	2	0	2	14
	NHL Totals		476	72	72	144	789	55	5	11	16	112

a OHL First All-Star Team (1985)

Traded to **St. Louis** by **Vancouver** for Ernie Vargas, September 29, 1988. Claimed by **Florida** from **St. Louis** in Expansion Draft, June 24, 1993.

LUDWIG, CRAIG LEE

Defense. Shoots left. 6'3", 222 lbs. Born, Rhinelander, WI, March 15, 1961.
(Montreal's 5th choice, 61st overall, in 1980 Entry Draft).

			Regular Season					Playoffs				
Season	Club	Lea	GP	G	A	TP	PIM	GP	G	A	TP	PIM
1979-80	North Dakota	WCHA	33	1	8	9	32	....	....	....	....	....
1980-81	North Dakota	WCHA	34	4	8	12	48	....	....	....	....	....
1981-82	North Dakota	WCHA	37	4	17	21	42	....	....	....	....	....
1982-83	Montreal	NHL	80	0	25	25	59	3	0	0	0	2
1983-84	Montreal	NHL	80	7	18	25	52	15	0	3	3	23
1984-85	Montreal	NHL	72	5	14	19	90	12	0	2	2	6
1985-86	Montreal	NHL	69	2	4	6	63	20	0	1	1	48
1986-87	Montreal	NHL	75	4	12	16	105	17	2	3	5	30
1987-88	Montreal	NHL	74	4	10	14	69	11	1	1	2	6
1988-89	Montreal	NHL	74	3	13	16	73	21	0	2	2	24
1989-90	Montreal	NHL	73	1	15	16	108	11	0	1	1	16
1990-91	NY Islanders	NHL	75	1	8	9	77	....	....	....	....	....
1991-92	Minnesota	NHL	73	2	9	11	54	7	0	1	1	19
1992-93	Minnesota	NHL	78	1	10	11	153	....	....	....	....	....
	NHL Totals		823	30	138	168	903	117	3	14	17	174

Traded to **NY Islanders** by **Montreal** for Gerald Diduck, September 4, 1990. Traded to **Minnesota** by **NY Islanders** for Tom Kurvers, June 22, 1991.

LUHNING, WARREN

Right wing. Shoots right. 6'2", 185 lbs. Born, Edmonton, Alta., July 3, 1975.
(NY Islanders' 4th choice, 92nd overall, in 1993 Entry Draft).

			Regular Season					Playoffs				
Season	Club	Lea	GP	G	A	TP	PIM	GP	G	A	TP	PIM
1991-92	Cgy. Royals	Midget	21	14	18	32	65	....	....	....	....	....
1992-93	Cgy. Royals	AJHL	46	18	25	43	287	....	....	....	....	....

LUMME, JYRKI
(LOOM-meh)

Defense. Shoots left. 6'1", 205 lbs. Born, Tampere, Finland, July 16, 1966.
(Montreal's 3rd choice, 57th overall, in 1986 Entry Draft).

			Regular Season					Playoffs				
Season	Club	Lea	GP	G	A	TP	PIM	GP	G	A	TP	PIM
1984-85	KooVee	Fin.3	30	6	4	10	44	....	....	....	....	....
1985-86	Ilves	Fin.	31	1	4	5	4	....	....	....	....	....
1986-87	Ilves	Fin.	43	12	12	24	52	4	0	1	1	2
1987-88	Ilves	Fin.	43	8	22	30	75	....	....	....	....	....
1988-89	Montreal	NHL	21	1	3	4	10	....	....	....	....	....
	Sherbrooke	AHL	26	4	11	15	10	6	1	3	4	4
1989-90	Montreal	NHL	54	1	19	20	41	....	....	....	....	....
	Vancouver	NHL	11	3	7	10	8	....	....	....	....	....
1990-91	Vancouver	NHL	80	5	27	32	59	6	2	3	5	0
1991-92	Vancouver	NHL	75	12	32	44	65	13	2	3	5	4
1992-93	Vancouver	NHL	74	8	36	44	55	12	0	5	5	6
	NHL Totals		315	30	124	154	238	31	4	11	15	10

Traded to **Vancouver** by **Montreal** for St. Louis' second round choice (previously acquired by Vancouver — Montreal selected Craig Darby) in 1991 Entry Draft, March 6, 1990.

LUONGO, CHRISTOPHER (CHRIS)
(loo-ON-go)

Defense. Shoots right. 6', 180 lbs. Born, Detroit, MI, March 17, 1967.
(Detroit's 5th choice, 92nd overall, in 1985 Entry Draft).

			Regular Season					Playoffs				
Season	Club	Lea	GP	G	A	TP	PIM	GP	G	A	TP	PIM
1985-86	Michigan State	CCHA	38	1	5	6	29	....	....	....	....	....
1986-87a	Michigan State	CCHA	27	4	16	20	38	....	....	....	....	....
1987-88	Michigan State	CCHA	45	3	15	18	49	....	....	....	....	....
1988-89b	Michigan State	CCHA	47	4	21	25	42	....	....	....	....	....
1989-90	Adirondack	AHL	53	9	14	23	37	3	0	0	0	0
	Phoenix	IHL	23	5	9	14	41	....	....	....	....	....
1990-91	Detroit	NHL	4	0	1	1	4	....	....	....	....	....
	Adirondack	AHL	76	14	25	39	71	2	0	0	0	7
1991-92	Adirondack	AHL	80	6	20	26	60	19	3	5	8	10
1992-93	Ottawa	NHL	76	3	9	12	68	....	....	....	....	....
	New Haven	AHL	7	0	2	2	2	....	....	....	....	....
	NHL Totals		80	3	10	13	72					

a Named to NCAA All-Tournament Team (1987)
b CCHA Second All-Star Team (1989)

Signed as a free agent by **Ottawa**, September 9, 1992. Traded to **NY Islanders** by Ottawa for Jeff Finley, June 30, 1993.

MacARTHUR, KENNETH

Defense. Shoots left. 6'2", 185 lbs. Born, Rossland, B.C., March 15, 1968.
(Minnesota's 5th choice, 148th overall, in 1988 Entry Draft).

			Regular Season					Playoffs				
Season	Club	Lea	GP	G	A	TP	PIM	GP	G	A	TP	PIM
1987-88	U. of Denver	WCHA	38	6	16	22	69	....	....	....	....	....
1988-89	U. of Denver	WCHA	42	11	19	30	77	....	....	....	....	....
1989-90	U. of Denver	WCHA	38	12	29	41	96	....	....	....	....	....
	Cdn. National	....	13	2	1	3	14	....	....	....	....	....
1990-91	Cdn. National	....	59	4	11	15	34	....	....	....	....	....
1991-92	U. of Denver	WCHA	3	2	1	3	20	....	....	....	....	....
1992-93	U. of Denver	WCHA	35	5	16	21	70	....	....	....	....	....

MacDERMID, PAUL

Right wing. Shoots right. 6'1", 205 lbs. Born, Chesley, Ont., April 14, 1963.
(Hartford's 2nd choice, 61st overall, in 1981 Entry Draft).

			Regular Season					Playoffs				
Season	Club	Lea	GP	G	A	TP	PIM	GP	G	A	TP	PIM
1980-81	Windsor	OHA	68	15	17	32	106	....	....	....	....	....
1981-82	Hartford	NHL	3	1	0	1	2	....	....	....	....	....
	Windsor	OHL	65	26	45	71	179	9	6	4	10	17
1982-83	Hartford	NHL	7	0	0	0	2	....	....	....	....	....
	Windsor	OHL	42	35	45	80	9	....	....	....	....	....
1983-84	Hartford	NHL	3	0	1	1	0	....	....	....	....	....
	Binghamton	AHL	70	31	30	61	130	....	....	....	....	....
1984-85	Hartford	NHL	31	4	7	11	29	....	....	....	....	....
	Binghamton	AHL	48	9	31	40	87	....	....	....	....	....
1985-86	Hartford	NHL	74	13	10	23	160	10	2	1	3	20
1986-87	Hartford	NHL	72	7	11	18	202	6	2	1	3	34
1987-88	Hartford	NHL	80	20	15	35	139	6	0	5	5	14
1988-89	Hartford	NHL	74	17	27	44	141	4	1	1	2	16
1989-90	Hartford	NHL	29	6	12	18	69	....	....	....	....	....
	Winnipeg	NHL	44	7	10	17	100	7	0	2	2	8
1990-91	Winnipeg	NHL	69	15	21	36	128	....	....	....	....	....
1991-92	Winnipeg	NHL	59	10	11	21	151	....	....	....	....	....
	Washington	NHL	15	2	5	7	43	7	0	1	1	22
1992-93	Washington	NHL	72	9	8	17	80	....	....	....	....	....
	NHL Totals		632	111	138	249	1246	40	5	11	16	114

Traded to **Winnipeg** by **Hartford** for Randy Cunneyworth, December 13, 1989. Traded to **Washington** by **Winnipeg** for Mike Lalor, March 2, 1992. Traded to **Quebec** by **Washington** with Reggie Savage for Mike Hough, June 20, 1993.

MacDONALD, BRUCE

Defense. Shoots left. 6'1", 195 lbs. Born, Plaistow, NH, December 16, 1967.
(Philadelphia's 9th choice, 188th overall, in 1987 Entry Draft).

			Regular Season					Playoffs				
Season	Club	Lea	GP	G	A	TP	PIM	GP	G	A	TP	PIM
1987-88	N. Hampshire	H.E.	12	0	1	1	8	....	....	....	....	....
1988-89	N. Hampshire	H.E.	21	1	3	4	8	....	....	....	....	....
1989-90	N. Hampshire	H.E.	35	2	3	5	16	....	....	....	....	....
1990-91	N. Hampshire	H.E.	25	2	4	6	14	....	....	....	....	....
	Moncton	AHL	2	0	0	0	0	7	1	3	4	4
1991-92	Toledo	ECHL	42	29	26	55	32	5	0	4	4	22
1992-93	Toledo	ECHL	55	20	27	47	80	14	5	3	8	16

MacDONALD, DOUG

Left wing. Shoots left. 6', 192 lbs. Born, Port Moody, B.C., February 8, 1969.
(Buffalo's 3rd choice, 77th overall, in 1989 Entry Draft).

			Regular Season					Playoffs				
Season	Club	Lea	GP	G	A	TP	PIM	GP	G	A	TP	PIM
1988-89	U. Wisconsin	WCHA	44	23	25	48	50	....	....	....	....	....
1989-90	U. Wisconsin	WCHA	44	16	35	51	52	....	....	....	....	....
1990-91	U. Wisconsin	WCHA	31	20	26	46	50	....	....	....	....	....
1991-92	U. Wisconsin	WCHA	29	14	25	39	58	....	....	....	....	....
1992-93	Buffalo	NHL	5	1	0	1	2	....	....	....	....	....
	Rochester	AHL	64	25	33	58	58	7	0	2	2	4
	NHL Totals		5	1	0	1	2					

MacDONALD, GARRETT

Defense. Shoots left. 6', 183 lbs. Born, Burnaby, B.C., January 12, 1971.
(Philadelphia's 1st choice, 7th overall, in 1992 Supplemental Draft).

			Regular Season					Playoffs				
Season	Club	Lea	GP	G	A	TP	PIM	GP	G	A	TP	PIM
1990-91	N. Michigan	WCHA	41	2	8	10	56	....	....	....	....	....
1991-92	N. Michigan	WCHA	34	0	5	5	39	....	....	....	....	....
1992-93	N. Michigan	WCHA	39	4	12	16	68	....	....	....	....	....

MacDONALD, JASON

Right wing. Shoots right. 6', 195 lbs. Born, Charlottetown, P.E.I., April 1, 1974.
(Detroit's 5th choice, 142nd overall, in 1992 Entry Draft).

			Regular Season					Playoffs				
Season	Club	Lea	GP	G	A	TP	PIM	GP	G	A	TP	PIM
1990-91	North Bay	OHL	57	12	15	27	126	10	3	3	6	15
1991-92	North Bay	OHL	17	5	8	13	50	....	....	....	....	....
	Owen Sound	OHL	42	17	19	36	129	5	0	3	3	16
1992-93	Owen Sound	OHL	56	46	43	89	197	8	6	5	11	28

MacDONALD, SCOTT

Defense. Shoots right. 6'3", 202 lbs. Born, Brockton, MA, September 13, 1972.
(Chicago's 9th choice, 198th overall, in 1991 Entry Draft).

			Regular Season					Playoffs				
Season	Club	Lea	GP	G	A	TP	PIM	GP	G	A	TP	PIM
1991-92	U. of Vermont	ECAC	28	0	6	6	18	....	....	....	....	....
1992-93	U. of Vermont	ECAC	1	0	0	0	0	....	....	....	....	....

MacDONALD, TOM

Center. Shoots left. 5'11", 190 lbs. Born, Toronto, Ont., April 14, 1974.
(Tampa Bay's 11th choice, 241st overall, in 1992 Entry Draft).

			Regular Season					Playoffs				
Season	Club	Lea	GP	G	A	TP	PIM	GP	G	A	TP	PIM
1990-91	S.S. Marie	OHL	41	3	6	9	71	6	0	1	1	19
1991-92	S.S. Marie	OHL	52	11	15	26	139	19	3	7	10	31
1992-93	S.S. Marie	OHL	50	13	24	37	134	18	5	9	14	62

MACHANIC, COREY

Defense. Shoots right. 6'3", 197 lbs. Born, Rome, NY, September 26, 1972.
(NY Rangers' 5th choice, 96th overall, in 1991 Entry Draft).

			Regular Season					Playoffs				
Season	Club	Lea	GP	G	A	TP	PIM	GP	G	A	TP	PIM
1990-91	U. of Vermont	ECAC	31	0	8	8	30	....	....	....	....	....
1991-92	U. of Vermont	ECAC	30	3	8	11	24	....	....	....	....	....
1992-93	U. of Vermont	ECAC	31	1	4	5	16	....	....	....	....	....

MacINNIS, ALLAN (AL)

Defense. Shoots right. 6'2", 196 lbs. Born, Inverness, N.S., July 11, 1963.
(Calgary's 1st choice, 15th overall, in 1981 Entry Draft).

			Regular Season					Playoffs				
Season	Club	Lea	GP	G	A	TP	PIM	GP	G	A	TP	PIM
1980-81	Kitchener	OHA	47	11	28	39	59	18	4	12	16	20
1981-82	Calgary	NHL	2	0	0	0	0	....	....	....	....	....
a	Kitchener	OHL	59	25	50	75	145	15	5	10	15	44
1982-83	Calgary	NHL	14	1	3	4	9	....	....	....	....	....
a	Kitchener	OHL	51	38	46	84	67	8	3	8	11	9
1983-84	Calgary	NHL	51	11	34	45	42	11	2	12	14	13
	Colorado	CHL	19	5	14	19	22	....	....	....	....	....
1984-85	Calgary	NHL	67	14	52	66	75	4	1	2	3	8
1985-86	Calgary	NHL	77	11	57	68	76	21	4	*15	19	30
1986-87b	Calgary	NHL	79	20	56	76	97	4	1	0	1	0
1987-88	Calgary	NHL	80	25	58	83	114	7	3	6	9	18
1988-89bc	Calgary	NHL	79	16	58	74	126	22	7	*24	*31	46
1989-90d	Calgary	NHL	79	28	62	90	82	6	2	3	5	8
1990-91d	Calgary	NHL	78	28	75	103	90	7	2	3	5	8
1991-92	Calgary	NHL	72	20	57	77	83	....	....	....	....	....
1992-93	Calgary	NHL	50	11	43	54	61	6	1	6	7	10
	NHL Totals		728	185	555	740	855	88	23	71	94	141

a OHL First All-Star Team (1982, 1983)
b NHL Second All-Star Team (1987, 1989)
c Won Conn Smythe Trophy (1989)
d NHL First All-Star Team (1990, 1991)

Played in NHL All-Star Game (1985, 1988, 1990, 1991, 1992)

MacINTYRE, ANDY

Left wing. Shoots left. 6'1", 190 lbs. Born, Thunder Bay, Ont., April 16, 1974.
(Chicago's 4th choice, 89th overall, in 1992 Entry Draft).

			Regular Season					Playoffs				
Season	Club	Lea	GP	G	A	TP	PIM	GP	G	A	TP	PIM
1990-91	Seattle	WHL	71	16	13	29	52	4	0	0	0	2
1991-92	Seattle	WHL	12	6	2	8	18	....	....	....	....	....
	Saskatoon	WHL	55	22	13	35	66	....	....	....	....	....
1992-93	Saskatoon	WHL	72	35	29	64	82	9	3	2	5	2

MACIVER, NORM (mac-IGH-ver)

Defense. Shoots left. 5'11", 180 lbs. Born, Thunder Bay, Ont., September 8, 1964.

			Regular Season					Playoffs				
Season	Club	Lea	GP	G	A	TP	PIM	GP	G	A	TP	PIM
1982-83	Minn.-Duluth	WCHA	45	1	26	27	40	6	0	2	2	2
1983-84a	Minn.-Duluth	WCHA	31	13	28	41	28	8	1	10	11	8
1984-85bc	Minn.-Duluth	WCHA	47	14	47	61	63	10	3	3	6	6
1985-86bc	Minn.-Duluth	WCHA	42	11	51	62	36	4	2	3	5	2
1986-87	NY Rangers	NHL	3	0	1	1	0	....	....	....	....	....
	New Haven	AHL	71	6	30	36	73	7	0	0	0	9
1987-88	NY Rangers	NHL	37	9	15	24	14	....	....	....	....	....
	Colorado	IHL	27	6	20	26	22	....	....	....	....	....
1988-89	NY Rangers	NHL	26	0	10	10	14	....	....	....	....	....
	Hartford	NHL	37	1	22	23	24	1	0	0	0	2
1989-90	Binghamton	AHL	2	0	0	0	0	....	....	....	....	....
	Edmonton	NHL	1	0	0	0	0	....	....	....	....	....
	Cape Breton	AHL	68	13	37	50	55	6	0	7	7	10
1990-91	Edmonton	NHL	21	2	5	7	14	18	0	4	4	8
de	Cape Breton	AHL	56	13	46	59	60	....	....	....	....	....
1991-92	Edmonton	NHL	57	6	34	40	38	13	1	2	3	10
1992-93	Ottawa	NHL	80	17	46	63	84	....	....	....	....	....
	NHL Totals		262	35	133	168	188	32	1	6	7	20

a WCHA Second All-Star Team (1984)
b WCHA First All-Star Team (1985, 1986)
c NCAA West First All-Star Team (1985, 1986)
d AHL First All-Star Team (1991)
e Won Eddie Shore Plaque (Top Defenseman – AHL) (1991)

Signed as a free agent by **NY Rangers**, September 8, 1986. Traded to **Hartford** by **NY Rangers** with Brian Lawton and Don Maloney for Carey Wilson and Hartford's fifth round choice (Lubos Rob) in 1990 Entry Draft, December 26, 1988. Traded to **Edmonton** by **Hartford** for Jim Ennis, October 10, 1989. Claimed by **Ottawa** from **Edmonton** in NHL Waiver Draft, October 4, 1992.

MACKEY, DAVID

Left wing. Shoots left. 6'4", 205 lbs. Born, Richmond, B.C., July 24, 1966.
(Chicago's 12th choice, 224th overall, in 1984 Entry Draft).

			Regular Season					Playoffs				
Season	Club	Lea	GP	G	A	TP	PIM	GP	G	A	TP	PIM
1982-83	Victoria	WHL	69	16	16	32	53	12	11	1	2	4
1983-84	Victoria	WHL	69	15	15	30	97	....	....	....	....	....
1984-85	Victoria	WHL	16	5	6	11	45	....	....	....	....	....
	Portland	WHL	56	28	32	60	122	6	2	1	3	13
1985-86	Kamloops	WHL	9	3	4	7	13	....	....	....	....	....
	Medicine Hat	WHL	60	25	32	57	167	25	6	3	9	72
1986-87	Saginaw	IHL	81	26	49	75	173	10	5	6	11	22
1987-88	Chicago	NHL	23	1	3	4	71	....	....	....	....	....
	Saginaw	IHL	62	29	22	51	211	10	3	7	10	44
1988-89	Chicago	NHL	23	1	2	3	78	....	....	....	....	....
	Saginaw	IHL	57	22	23	45	223	....	....	....	....	....
1989-90	Minnesota	NHL	16	2	0	2	28	....	....	....	....	....
1990-91	Milwaukee	IHL	82	28	30	58	226	6	7	2	9	6
1991-92	St. Louis	NHL	19	1	0	1	49	1	0	0	0	0
	Peoria	IHL	35	20	17	37	90	....	....	....	....	....
1992-93	St. Louis	NHL	15	1	4	5	23	....	....	....	....	....
	Peoria	IHL	42	24	22	46	112	4	1	0	1	22
	NHL Totals		96	6	9	15	249	1	0	0	0	0

Claimed by **Minnesota** in NHL Waiver Draft, October 2, 1989. Traded to **Vancouver** by **Minnesota** for future considerations, September 7, 1990. Signed as a free agent by **St. Louis**, August 7, 1991.

MACKEY, JAMES

Defense. Shoots right. 6'4", 225 lbs. Born, Saratoga Springs, NY, January 20, 1972.
(Boston's 6th choice, 147th overall, in 1990 Entry Draft).

			Regular Season					Playoffs				
Season	Club	Lea	GP	G	A	TP	PIM	GP	G	A	TP	PIM
1990-91	Yale	ECAC	18	0	1	1	12	....	....	....	....	....
1991-92	Yale	ECAC	27	1	7	8	44	....	....	....	....	....
1992-93	Yale	ECAC	31	1	4	5	52	....	....	....	....	....

MacLEAN, JOHN

Right wing. Shoots right. 6', 200 lbs. Born, Oshawa, Ont., November 20, 1964.
(New Jersey's 1st choice, 6th overall, in 1983 Entry Draft).

			Regular Season					Playoffs				
Season	Club	Lea	GP	G	A	TP	PIM	GP	G	A	TP	PIM
1981-82	Oshawa	OHL	67	17	22	39	197	12	3	6	9	63
1982-83	Oshawa	OHL	66	47	51	98	138	17	*18	20	*38	35
1983-84	New Jersey	NHL	23	1	0	1	10	....	....	....	....	....
	Oshawa	OHL	30	23	36	59	58	7	2	5	7	18
1984-85	New Jersey	NHL	61	13	20	33	44	....	....	....	....	....
1985-86	New Jersey	NHL	74	21	36	57	112	....	....	....	....	....
1986-87	New Jersey	NHL	80	31	36	67	120	....	....	....	....	....
1987-88	New Jersey	NHL	76	23	16	39	147	20	7	11	18	60
1988-89	New Jersey	NHL	74	42	45	87	122	....	....	....	....	....
1989-90	New Jersey	NHL	80	41	38	79	80	6	4	1	5	12
1990-91	New Jersey	NHL	78	45	33	78	150	7	5	3	8	20
1991-92			DID NOT PLAY – INJURED									
1992-93	New Jersey	NHL	80	24	24	48	102	5	0	1	1	10
	NHL Totals		626	241	248	489	887	38	16	16	32	102

Played in NHL All-Star Game (1989, 1991)

MacLEOD, PAT

Defense. Shoots left. 5'11", 190 lbs. Born, Melfort, Sask., June 15, 1969.
(Minnesota's 5th choice, 87th overall, in 1989 Entry Draft).

			Regular Season					Playoffs				
Season	Club	Lea	GP	G	A	TP	PIM	GP	G	A	TP	PIM
1987-88	Kamloops	WHL	50	13	33	46	27	18	2	7	9	6
1988-89	Kamloops	WHL	37	11	34	45	14	15	7	18	25	24
1989-90	Kalamazoo	IHL	82	9	38	47	27	10	1	6	7	2
1990-91	Minnesota	NHL	1	0	1	1	0	....	....	....	....	....
	Kalamazoo	IHL	59	10	30	40	16	11	1	2	3	5
1991-92	San Jose	NHL	37	5	11	16	4	....	....	....	....	....
	Kansas City	IHL	45	9	21	30	19	11	1	4	5	4
1992-93	San Jose	NHL	13	0	1	1	10	....	....	....	....	....
	Kansas City	IHL	18	8	8	16	14	10	2	4	6	7
	NHL Totals		51	5	13	18	14	....	....	....	....	....

Claimed by **San Jose** from **Minnesota** in Dispersal Draft, May 30, 1991.

MACOUN, JAMIE (muh-KOW-uhn)

Defense. Shoots left. 6'2", 197 lbs. Born, Newmarket, Ont., August 17, 1961.

			Regular Season					Playoffs				
Season	Club	Lea	GP	G	A	TP	PIM	GP	G	A	TP	PIM
1980-81	Ohio State	CCHA	38	9	20	29	83	....	....	....	....	....
1981-82	Ohio State	CCHA	25	2	18	20	89	....	....	....	....	....
1982-83	Ohio State	CCHA	19	6	21	27	54	....	....	....	....	....
	Calgary	NHL	22	1	4	5	25	9	0	2	2	8
1983-84a	Calgary	NHL	72	9	23	32	97	11	1	0	1	0
1984-85	Calgary	NHL	70	9	30	39	67	4	1	0	1	4
1985-86	Calgary	NHL	77	11	21	32	81	22	1	6	7	23
1986-87	Calgary	NHL	79	7	33	40	111	3	0	1	1	8
1987-88			DID NOT PLAY – INJURED									
1988-89	Calgary	NHL	72	8	19	27	76	22	3	6	9	30
1989-90	Calgary	NHL	78	8	27	35	70	6	0	3	3	10
1990-91	Calgary	NHL	79	7	15	22	84	7	0	1	1	4
1991-92	Calgary	NHL	37	2	12	14	53	....	....	....	....	....
	Toronto	NHL	39	3	13	16	18	....	....	....	....	....
1992-93	Toronto	NHL	77	4	15	19	55	21	0	6	6	36
	NHL Totals		702	69	212	281	737	105	6	25	31	123

a NHL All-Rookie Team (1984)

Signed as a free agent by **Calgary**, January 30, 1983. Traded to **Toronto** by **Calgary** with Doug Gilmour, Ric Natress, Kent Manderville and Rick Wamsley for Gary Leeman, Alexander Godynyuk, Jeff Reese, Michel Petit and Craig Berube, January 2, 1992.

MACPHERSON, BILLY JO

Left wing. Shoots left. 6'1", 200 lbs. Born, Toronto, Ont., September 23, 1973.
(Washington's 10th choice, 263rd overall, in 1992 Entry Draft).

			Regular Season					Playoffs				
Season	Club	Lea	GP	G	A	TP	PIM	GP	G	A	TP	PIM
1990-91	Oshawa	OHL	57	8	16	24	77	16	3	1	4	25
1991-92	Oshawa	OHL	60	20	32	52	108	7	2	5	7	27
1992-93	Oshawa	OHL	57	42	55	97	112	13	7	14	21	30

MacTAVISH, CRAIG

Center. Shoots left. 6'1", 195 lbs. Born, London, Ont., August 15, 1958.
(Boston's 9th choice, 153rd overall, in 1978 Amateur Draft).

			Regular Season					Playoffs				
Season	Club	Lea	GP	G	A	TP	PIM	GP	G	A	TP	PIM
1978-79	Lowell	ECAC	....	....	....	....	....	....	....	....	....	....
1979-80	**Boston**	**NHL**	**46**	**11**	**17**	**28**	**8**	**10**	**2**	**3**	**5**	**7**
	Binghamton	AHL	34	17	15	32	29	....	....	....	....	....
1980-81	**Boston**	**NHL**	**24**	**3**	**5**	**8**	**13**	....	....	....	....	....
	Springfield	AHL	53	19	24	43	81	7	5	4	9	8
1981-82	**Boston**	**NHL**	**2**	**0**	**1**	**1**	**0**	....	....	....	....	....
	Erie	AHL	72	23	32	55	37	....	....	....	....	....
1982-83	**Boston**	**NHL**	**75**	**10**	**20**	**30**	**18**	**17**	**3**	**1**	**4**	**18**
1983-84	**Boston**	**NHL**	**70**	**20**	**23**	**43**	**35**	**1**	**0**	**0**	**0**	**0**
1984-85					DID NOT PLAY							
1985-86	**Edmonton**	**NHL**	**74**	**23**	**24**	**47**	**70**	**10**	**4**	**4**	**8**	**11**
1986-87	**Edmonton**	**NHL**	**79**	**20**	**19**	**39**	**55**	**21**	**1**	**9**	**10**	**16**
1987-88	**Edmonton**	**NHL**	**80**	**15**	**17**	**32**	**47**	**19**	**0**	**1**	**1**	**31**
1988-89	**Edmonton**	**NHL**	**80**	**21**	**31**	**52**	**55**	**7**	**0**	**1**	**1**	**8**
1989-90	**Edmonton**	**NHL**	**80**	**21**	**22**	**43**	**89**	**22**	**2**	**6**	**8**	**29**
1990-91	**Edmonton**	**NHL**	**80**	**17**	**15**	**32**	**76**	**18**	**3**	**3**	**6**	**20**
1991-92	**Edmonton**	**NHL**	**80**	**12**	**18**	**30**	**98**	**16**	**3**	**0**	**3**	**28**
1992-93	**Edmonton**	**NHL**	**82**	**10**	**20**	**30**	**110**	....	....	....	....	....
	NHL Totals		**852**	**183**	**232**	**415**	**674**	**141**	**18**	**28**	**46**	**168**

Signed as a free agent by **Edmonton,** February 1, 1985.

MADILL, JEFF (muh-DILL)

Right wing. Shoots left. 5'11", 195 lbs. Born, Oshawa, Ont., June 21, 1965.
(New Jersey's 2nd choice, 7th overall, in 1987 Supplemental Draft).

			Regular Season					Playoffs				
Season	Club	Lea	GP	G	A	TP	PIM	GP	G	A	TP	PIM
1984-85	Ohio State	CCHA	12	5	6	11	18	....	....	....	....	....
1985-86	Ohio State	CCHA	41	32	25	57	65	....	....	....	....	....
1986-87	Ohio State	CCHA	43	38	32	70	139	....	....	....	....	....
1987-88	Utica	AHL	58	18	15	33	127	....	....	....	....	....
1988-89	Utica	AHL	69	23	25	48	225	4	1	0	1	35
1989-90	Utica	AHL	74	43	26	69	233	4	1	2	3	33
1990-91	**New Jersey**	**NHL**	**14**	**4**	**0**	**4**	**46**	**7**	**0**	**2**	**2**	**8**
a	Utica	AHL	54	42	35	77	151	....	....	....	....	....
1991-92	Kansas City	IHL	62	32	20	52	167	6	2	2	4	30
1992-93	Cincinnati	IHL	58	36	17	53	175	....	....	....	....	....
	Milwaukee	IHL	23	13	6	19	53	4	3	0	3	9
	NHL Totals		**14**	**4**	**0**	**4**	**46**	**7**	**0**	**2**	**2**	**8**

a AHL Second All-Star Team (1991)
b IHL Second All-Star Team (1993)

Claimed by **San Jose** from **New Jersey** in Expansion Draft, May 30, 1991.

MAGNUSSON, STEVEN

Center. Shoots left. 5'11", 180 lbs. Born, Coon Rapids, MN, November 15, 1972.
(Calgary's 5th choice, 85th overall, in 1991 Entry Draft).

			Regular Season					Playoffs				
Season	Club	Lea	GP	G	A	TP	PIM	GP	G	A	TP	PIM
1991-92	U. Minnesota	WCHA	38	9	21	30	54	....	....	....	....	....
1992-93	U. Minnesota	WCHA	21	1	10	11	22	....	....	....	....	....

MAGUIRE, DEREK

Defense. Shoots right. 6', 185 lbs. Born, Delbarton, NJ, December 9, 1971.
(Montreal's 10th choice, 186th overall, in 1990 Entry Draft).

			Regular Season					Playoffs				
Season	Club	Lea	GP	G	A	TP	PIM	GP	G	A	TP	PIM
1990-91	Harvard	ECAC	25	3	14	17	12	....	....	....	....	....
1991-92	Harvard	ECAC	25	1	16	17	16	....	....	....	....	....
1992-93	Harvard	ECAC	16	3	9	12	10	....	....	....	....	....

MAHER, JIM

Defense. Shoots left. 6'1", 210 lbs. Born, Warren, MI, June 30, 1970.
(Los Angeles' 2nd choice, 81st overall, in 1989 Entry Draft).

			Regular Season					Playoffs				
Season	Club	Lea	GP	G	A	TP	PIM	GP	G	A	TP	PIM
1988-89	Ill.-Chicago	CCHA	31	1	5	6	40	....	....	....	....	....
1989-90	Ill.-Chicago	CCHA	38	4	12	16	64	....	....	....	....	....
1990-91	Ill.-Chicago	CCHA	37	6	8	14	49	....	....	....	....	....
1991-92	Ill.-Chicago	CCHA	34	5	9	14	52	....	....	....	....	....
	Phoenix	IHL	9	0	3	3	21	....	....	....	....	....
1992-93	Phoenix	IHL	47	5	13	18	72	....	....	....	....	....

MAJIC, XAVIER

Center. Shoots left. 6', 190 lbs. Born, Fernie, B.C., March 10, 1973.
(Vancouver's 12th choice, 249th overall, in 1991 Entry Draft).

			Regular Season					Playoffs				
Season	Club	Lea	GP	G	A	TP	PIM	GP	G	A	TP	PIM
1990-91	RPI	ECAC	31	4	10	14	26	....	....	....	....	....
1991-92	RPI	ECAC	32	13	19	32	48	....	....	....	....	....
1992-93	RPI	ECAC	35	16	26	42	18	....	....	....	....	....

MAKAROV, SERGEI (mah-KAH-rahf)

Right wing. Shoots left. 5'11", 185 lbs. Born, Chelyabinsk, Soviet Union, June 19, 1958.
(Calgary's 14th choice, 231st overall, in 1983 Entry Draft).

			Regular Season					Playoffs				
Season	Club	Lea	GP	G	A	TP	PIM	GP	G	A	TP	PIM
1976-77	Chelyabinsk	USSR	11	1	0	1	4	....	....	....	....	....
1977-78	Chelyabinsk	USSR	36	18	13	31	10	....	....	....	....	....
1978-79a	CSKA	USSR	44	18	21	39	12	....	....	....	....	....
1979-80bc	CSKA	USSR	44	29	39	68	16	....	....	....	....	....
1980-81ab	CSKA	USSR	49	42	37	79	22	....	....	....	....	....
1981-82ab	CSKA	USSR	46	32	43	75	18	....	....	....	....	....
1982-83a	CSKA	USSR	30	25	17	42	6	....	....	....	....	....
1983-84ab	CSKA	USSR	44	36	37	73	28	....	....	....	....	....
1984-85abc	CSKA	USSR	40	26	39	65	28	....	....	....	....	....
1985-86ab	CSKA	USSR	40	30	32	62	28	....	....	....	....	....
1986-87ab	CSKA	USSR	40	21	32	53	26	....	....	....	....	....
1987-88ab	CSKA	USSR	51	23	45	68	50	....	....	....	....	....
1988-89bc	CSKA	USSR	44	21	33	54	42	....	....	....	....	....
1989-90de	**Calgary**	**NHL**	**80**	**24**	**62**	**86**	**55**	**6**	**0**	**6**	**6**	**0**
1990-91	**Calgary**	**NHL**	**78**	**30**	**49**	**79**	**44**	**3**	**1**	**0**	**1**	**0**
1991-92	**Calgary**	**NHL**	**68**	**22**	**48**	**70**	**60**	....	....	....	....	....
1992-93	**Calgary**	**NHL**	**71**	**18**	**39**	**57**	**40**	....	....	....	....	....
	NHL Totals		**297**	**94**	**198**	**292**	**199**	**9**	**1**	**6**	**7**	**0**

a Soviet National League All-Star (1981-88)
b Izvestia Trophy - leading scorer (1980-82, 1984-89)
c Soviet Player of the Year (1980, 1985, 1989)
d NHL All-Rookie Team (1990)
e Won Calder Memorial Trophy (1990)

Traded to **Hartford** by **Calgary** for future considerations (Washington's fourth round choice (previously acquired by Hartford — Calgary selected Jason Smith) in 1993 Entry Draft, June 26, 1993), June 20, 1993. Traded to **San Jose** by **Hartford** with Hartford's first (Viktor Kozlov) and third (Ville Peltonen) round choices in 1993 Entry Draft and Toronto's second round choice (previously acquired by Hartford — San Jose selected Vlastimil Kroupa) in 1993 Entry Draft for San Jose's first round choice (Chris Pronger) in 1993 Entry Draft, June 26, 1993.

MAKELA, MIKKO (MAK-uh-luh, MEE-koh)

Left wing. Shoots left. 6'1", 194 lbs. Born, Tampere, Finland, February 28, 1965.
(NY Islanders' 5th choice, 65th overall, in 1983 Entry Draft).

			Regular Season					Playoffs				
Season	Club	Lea	GP	G	A	TP	PIM	GP	G	A	TP	PIM
1983-84	Ilves	Fin.	35	17	11	28	26	2	0	1	1	0
1984-85a	Ilves	Fin.	36	34	25	59	24	9	4	7	11	10
1985-86	**NY Islanders**	**NHL**	**58**	**16**	**20**	**36**	**28**	....	....	....	....	....
	Springfield	AHL	2	1	1	2	0	....	....	....	....	....
1986-87	**NY Islanders**	**NHL**	**80**	**24**	**33**	**57**	**24**	**11**	**2**	**4**	**6**	**8**
1987-88	**NY Islanders**	**NHL**	**73**	**36**	**40**	**76**	**22**	**6**	**1**	**4**	**5**	**6**
1988-89	**NY Islanders**	**NHL**	**76**	**17**	**28**	**45**	**22**	....	....	....	....	....
1989-90	**NY Islanders**	**NHL**	**20**	**2**	**3**	**5**	**2**	....	....	....	....	....
	Los Angeles	**NHL**	**45**	**7**	**14**	**21**	**16**	**1**	**0**	**0**	**0**	**0**
1990-91	**Buffalo**	**NHL**	**60**	**15**	**7**	**22**	**25**	....	....	....	....	....
1991-92	TPS	Fin.	44	25	45	*70	38	3	2	3	5	0
1992-93	TPS	Fin.	38	17	27	44	22	11	4	8	12	0
	NHL Totals		**412**	**117**	**145**	**262**	**139**	**18**	**3**	**8**	**11**	**14**

a Finnish League First All-Star Team (1985)

Traded to **Los Angeles** by **NY Islanders** for Ken Baumgartner and Hubie McDonough, November 29, 1989. Traded to **Buffalo** by **Los Angeles** for Mike Donnelly, September 30, 1990.

MALAKHOV, VLADIMIR (mah-LAH-kahf)

Defense. Shoots left. 6'2", 207 lbs. Born, Sverdlovsk, Soviet Union, August 30, 1968.
(NY Islanders' 12th choice, 191st overall, in 1989 Entry Draft).

			Regular Season					Playoffs				
Season	Club	Lea	GP	G	A	TP	PIM	GP	G	A	TP	PIM
1986-87	Spartak	USSR	22	0	1	1	12	....	....	....	....	....
1987-88	Spartak	USSR	28	2	2	4	26	....	....	....	....	....
1988-89	CSKA	USSR	34	6	2	8	16	....	....	....	....	....
1989-90	CSKA	USSR	48	2	10	12	34	....	....	....	....	....
1990-91	CSKA	USSR	46	5	13	18	22	....	....	....	....	....
1991-92	CSKA	CIS	40	1	9	10	12	....	....	....	....	....
1992-93a	**NY Islanders**	**NHL**	**64**	**14**	**38**	**52**	**59**	**17**	**3**	**6**	**9**	**12**
	Capital Dist.	AHL	3	2	1	3	11	....	....	....	....	....
	NHL Totals		**64**	**14**	**38**	**52**	**59**	**17**	**3**	**6**	**9**	**12**

a NHL/Upper Deck All-Rookie Team (1993)

MALEY, DAVID

Left wing. Shoots left. 6'2", 195 lbs. Born, Beaver Dam, WI, April 24, 1963.
(Montreal's 4th choice, 33rd overall, in 1982 Entry Draft).

			Regular Season					Playoffs				
Season	Club	Lea	GP	G	A	TP	PIM	GP	G	A	TP	PIM
1982-83	U. Wisconsin	WCHA	47	17	23	40	24	....	....	....	....	....
1983-84	U. Wisconsin	WCHA	38	10	28	38	56	....	....	....	....	....
1984-85	U. Wisconsin	WCHA	38	19	9	28	86	....	....	....	....	....
1985-86	U. Wisconsin	WCHA	42	20	40	60	135	....	....	....	....	....
	Montreal	**NHL**	**3**	**0**	**0**	**0**	**0**	**7**	**1**	**3**	**4**	**2**
1986-87	**Montreal**	**NHL**	**48**	**6**	**12**	**18**	**55**	....	....	....	....	....
	Sherbrooke	AHL	11	1	5	6	25	12	7	7	14	10
1987-88	**New Jersey**	**NHL**	**44**	**4**	**2**	**6**	**65**	**20**	**3**	**1**	**4**	**80**
	Utica	AHL	9	5	3	8	40	....	....	....	....	....
1988-89	**New Jersey**	**NHL**	**68**	**5**	**6**	**11**	**249**	....	....	....	....	....
1989-90	**New Jersey**	**NHL**	**67**	**8**	**17**	**25**	**160**	**6**	**0**	**0**	**0**	**25**
1990-91	**New Jersey**	**NHL**	**64**	**8**	**14**	**22**	**151**	....	....	....	....	....
1991-92	**New Jersey**	**NHL**	**37**	**7**	**11**	**18**	**58**	....	....	....	....	....
	Edmonton	**NHL**	**23**	**3**	**6**	**9**	**46**	**10**	**1**	**1**	**2**	**4**
1992-93	**Edmonton**	**NHL**	**13**	**1**	**1**	**2**	**29**	....	....	....	....	....
	San Jose	**NHL**	**43**	**1**	**6**	**7**	**126**	....	....	....	....	....
	NHL Totals		**410**	**43**	**75**	**118**	**939**	**43**	**5**	**5**	**10**	**111**

Traded to **New Jersey** by **Montreal** for New Jersey's third round choice (Mathieu Schneider) in 1987 Entry Draft, June 13, 1987. Traded to **Edmonton** by **New Jersey** for Troy Mallette, January 12, 1992. Claimed on waivers by **San Jose** from **Edmonton**, January 1, 1993.

MALIK, MAREK (MAW-leck)

Defense. Shoots left. 6'5", 185 lbs. Born, Ostrava, Czech., June 24, 1975.
(Hartford's 2nd choice, 72nd overall, in 1993 Entry Draft).

			Regular Season					Playoffs				
Season	Club	Lea	GP	G	A	TP	PIM	GP	G	A	TP	PIM
1992-93	TJ Vitkovice Jr.	Czech.	20	5	10	15	16	....	....	....	....	....

MALKOC, DEAN

Defense. Shoots left. 6'3", 200 lbs.   Born, Vancouver, B.C., January 26, 1970.
(New Jersey's 7th choice, 95th overall, in 1990 Entry Draft).

			Regular Season					Playoffs				
Season	Club	Lea	GP	G	A	TP	PIM	GP	G	A	TP	PIM
1989-90	Kamloops	WHL	48	3	18	21	209	17	0	3	3	56
1990-91	Kamloops	WHL	8	1	4	5	47					
	Swift Current	WHL	56	10	23	33	248	3	0	2	2	5
	Utica	AHL	1	0	0	0	0					
1991-92	Utica	AHL	66	1	11	12	274	4	0	2	2	6
1992-93	Utica	AHL	73	5	19	24	255	5	0	1	1	8

MALLETTE, TROY

Left wing. Shoots left. 6'2", 210 lbs.   Born, Sudbury, Ont., February 25, 1970.
(NY Rangers' 1st choice, 22nd overall, in 1988 Entry Draft).

			Regular Season					Playoffs				
Season	Club	Lea	GP	G	A	TP	PIM	GP	G	A	TP	PIM
1986-87	S.S. Marie	OHL	65	20	25	45	157	4	0	2	2	12
1987-88	S.S. Marie	OHL	62	18	30	48	186	6	1	3	4	12
1988-89	S.S. Marie	OHL	64	39	37	76	172					
1989-90	**NY Rangers**	**NHL**	79	13	16	29	305	10	2	2	4	81
1990-91	**NY Rangers**	**NHL**	71	12	10	22	252	5	0	0	0	18
1991-92	**Edmonton**	**NHL**	15	1	3	4	36					
	New Jersey	**NHL**	17	3	4	7	43					
1992-93	**New Jersey**	**NHL**	34	4	3	7	56					
	Utica	AHL	5	3	3	6	17					
	NHL Totals		**216**	**33**	**36**	**69**	**692**	**15**	**2**	**2**	**4**	**99**

Acquired by **Edmonton** from **NY Rangers** as compensation for NY Rangers' signing of free agent Adam Graves, September 12, 1991. Traded to **New Jersey** by **Edmonton** for David Maley, January 12, 1992. Traded to **Ottawa** by **New Jersey** with Craig Billington and New Jersey's fourth round choice (Cosmo Dupaul) in 1993 Entry Draft for Peter Sidorkiewicz and future considerations (Mike Peluso, June 26, 1993), June 20, 1993.

MALLGRAVE, MATTHEW

Right wing. Shoots right. 6', 180 lbs.   Born, Washington, D.C., May 3, 1970.
(Toronto's 6th choice, 132nd overall, in 1988 Entry Draft).

			Regular Season					Playoffs				
Season	Club	Lea	GP	G	A	TP	PIM	GP	G	A	TP	PIM
1989-90	Harvard	ECAC	26	3	3	6	33					
1990-91	Harvard	ECAC	25	5	14	19	14					
1991-92	Harvard	ECAC	27	12	15	27	20					
1992-93	Harvard	ECAC	31	*27	13	40	36					

MALONE, SCOTT

Defense. Shoots left. 6', 180 lbs.   Born, Boston, MA, January 16, 1971.
(Toronto's 10th choice, 220th overall, in 1990 Entry Draft).

			Regular Season					Playoffs				
Season	Club	Lea	GP	G	A	TP	PIM	GP	G	A	TP	PIM
1991-92	N. Hampshire	H.E.	27	0	4	4	52					
1992-93	N. Hampshire	H.E.	36	5	6	11	96					

MALTAIS, STEVE   (MAHL-tayz)

Left wing. Shoots left. 6'2", 210 lbs.   Born, Arvida, Que., January 25, 1969.
(Washington's 2nd choice, 57th overall, in 1987 Entry Draft).

			Regular Season					Playoffs				
Season	Club	Lea	GP	G	A	TP	PIM	GP	G	A	TP	PIM
1986-87	Cornwall	OHL	65	32	12	44	29	5	0	0	0	2
1987-88	Cornwall	OHL	59	39	46	85	30	11	9	6	15	33
1988-89	Cornwall	OHL	58	53	70	123	67	18	14	16	30	16
	Fort Wayne	IHL						4	2	1	3	0
1989-90	**Washington**	**NHL**	8	0	0	0	2	1	0	0	0	0
	Baltimore	AHL	67	29	37	66	54	12	6	10	16	6
1990-91	**Washington**	**NHL**	7	0	0	0	2					
	Baltimore	AHL	73	36	43	79	97	6	1	4	5	10
1991-92	**Minnesota**	**NHL**	12	2	1	3	2					
	Kalamazoo	IHL	48	25	31	56	51					
	Halifax	AHL	10	3	3	6	0					
1992-93	**Tampa Bay**	**NHL**	63	7	13	20	35					
	Atlanta	IHL	16	14	10	24	22					
	NHL Totals		**90**	**9**	**14**	**23**	**41**	**1**	**0**	**0**	**0**	**0**

Traded to **Minnesota** by **Washington** with Trent Klatt for Shawn Chambers, June 21, 1991. Traded to **Quebec** by **Minnesota** for Kip Miller, March 8, 1992. Claimed by **Tampa Bay** from **Quebec** in Expansion Draft, June 18, 1992. Traded to **Detroit** by **Tampa Bay** for Dennis Vial, June 8, 1993.

MALTBY, KIRK

Right wing. Shoots right. 6', 180 lbs.   Born, Guelph, Ont., December 22, 1972.
(Edmonton's 4th choice, 65th overall, in 1992 Entry Draft).

			Regular Season					Playoffs				
Season	Club	Lea	GP	G	A	TP	PIM	GP	G	A	TP	PIM
1989-90	Owen Sound	OHL	61	12	15	27	90	12	1	6	7	15
1990-91	Owen Sound	OHL	66	34	32	66	100					
1991-92	Owen Sound	OHL	66	50	41	91	99	5	3	3	6	18
1992-93	Cape Breton	AHL	73	22	23	45	130	16	3	3	6	45

MALYKHIN, IGOR   (mahl-EE-khihn)

Defense. Shoots left. 6'1", 189 lbs.   Born, Kharkov, Soviet Union, June 6, 1969.
(Detroit's 6th choice, 142nd overall, in 1991 Entry Draft).

			Regular Season					Playoffs				
Season	Club	Lea	GP	G	A	TP	PIM	GP	G	A	TP	PIM
1987-88	CSKA	USSR	44	0	1	1	28					
1988-89	CSKA	USSR	36	0	3	3	18					
1989-90	CSKA	USSR	39	1	4	5	28					
1990-91	CSKA	USSR	38	2	2	4	10					
1991-92	CSKA	CIS	42	1	5	6	20					
1992-93	Adirondack	AHL	78	6	22	28	95	6	0	0	0	4

MANDERVILLE, KENT

Left wing. Shoots left. 6'3", 207 lbs.   Born, Edmonton, Alta., April 12, 1971.
(Calgary's 1st choice, 24th overall, in 1989 Entry Draft).

			Regular Season					Playoffs				
Season	Club	Lea	GP	G	A	TP	PIM	GP	G	A	TP	PIM
1989-90a	Cornell	ECAC	26	11	15	26	28					
1990-91	Cornell	ECAC	28	17	14	31	60					
	Cdn. National	.....	3	1	2	3	0					
1991-92	Cdn. National	.....	63	16	23	39	75					
	Cdn. Olympic	.....	8	1	2	3	0					
	Toronto	**NHL**	15	0	4	4	0					
	St. John's	AHL						12	5	9	14	14
1992-93	**Toronto**	**NHL**	18	1	1	2	17	18	1	0	1	8
	St. John's	AHL	56	19	28	47	86	2	0	2	2	0
	NHL Totals		**33**	**1**	**5**	**6**	**17**	**18**	**1**	**0**	**1**	**8**

a ECAC Rookie of the Year (1990)

Traded to **Toronto** by **Calgary** with Doug Gilmour, Jamie Macoun, Rick Wamsley and Ric Nattress for Gary Leeman, Alexander Godynyuk, Jeff Reese, Michel Petit and Craig Berube, January 2, 1992.

MANLOW, ERIC

Center. Shoots left. 6', 190 lbs.   Born, Belleville, Ont., April 7, 1975.
(Chicago's 2nd choice, 50th overall, in 1993 Entry Draft).

			Regular Season					Playoffs				
Season	Club	Lea	GP	G	A	TP	PIM	GP	G	A	TP	PIM
1991-92	Kitchener	OHL	59	26	21	47	31	14	2	5	7	10
1992-93	Kitchener	OHL	53	12	20	32	17	4	0	1	1	2

MANSON, DAVE

Defense. Shoots left. 6'2", 210 lbs.   Born, Prince Albert, Sask., January 27, 1967.
(Chicago's 1st choice, 11th overall, in 1985 Entry Draft).

			Regular Season					Playoffs				
Season	Club	Lea	GP	G	A	TP	PIM	GP	G	A	TP	PIM
1983-84	Prince Albert	WHL	70	2	7	9	233	5	0	0	0	4
1984-85	Prince Albert	WHL	72	8	30	38	247	13	1	0	1	34
1985-86	Prince Albert	WHL	70	14	34	48	177	20	1	8	9	63
1986-87	**Chicago**	**NHL**	63	1	8	9	146	3	0	0	0	10
1987-88	**Chicago**	**NHL**	54	1	6	7	185	5	0	0	0	27
	Saginaw	IHL	6	0	3	3	37					
1988-89	**Chicago**	**NHL**	79	18	36	54	352	16	0	8	8	84
1989-90	**Chicago**	**NHL**	59	5	23	28	301	20	2	4	6	46
1990-91	**Chicago**	**NHL**	75	14	15	29	191	6	0	1	1	36
1991-92	**Edmonton**	**NHL**	79	15	32	47	220	16	3	9	12	44
1992-93	**Edmonton**	**NHL**	83	15	30	45	210					
	NHL Totals		**492**	**69**	**150**	**219**	**1605**	**66**	**5**	**22**	**27**	**247**

Played in NHL All-Star Game (1989, 1993)

Traded to **Edmonton** by **Chicago** with future considerations for Steve Smith, October 2, 1991.

MARCHMENT, BRYAN

Defense. Shoots left. 6'1", 198 lbs.   Born, Scarborough, Ont., May 1, 1969.
(Winnipeg's 1st choice, 16th overall, in 1987 Entry Draft).

			Regular Season					Playoffs				
Season	Club	Lea	GP	G	A	TP	PIM	GP	G	A	TP	PIM
1985-86	Belleville	OHL	57	5	15	20	225	21	0	7	7	83
1986-87	Belleville	OHL	52	6	38	44	238	6	0	4	4	17
1987-88	Belleville	OHL	56	7	51	58	200	6	1	3	4	19
1988-89	**Winnipeg**	**NHL**	2	0	0	0	2					
a	Belleville	OHL	43	14	36	50	118	5	0	1	1	12
1989-90	**Winnipeg**	**NHL**	7	0	2	2	28					
	Moncton	AHL	56	4	19	23	217					
1990-91	**Winnipeg**	**NHL**	28	2	2	4	91					
	Moncton	AHL	33	2	11	13	101					
1991-92	**Chicago**	**NHL**	58	5	10	15	168	16	1	0	1	36
1992-93	**Chicago**	**NHL**	78	5	15	20	313	4	0	0	0	12
	NHL Totals		**173**	**12**	**29**	**41**	**602**	**20**	**1**	**0**	**1**	**48**

a OHL Second All-Star Team (1989)

Traded to **Chicago** by **Winnipeg** with Chris Norton for Troy Murray and Warren Rychel, July 22, 1991.

MARCINYSHYN, DAVID   (MAIR-sih-NIH-shuhn)

Defense. Shoots left. 6'3", 210 lbs.   Born, Edmonton, Alta., February 4, 1967.

			Regular Season					Playoffs				
Season	Club	Lea	GP	G	A	TP	PIM	GP	G	A	TP	PIM
1985-86	Kamloops	WHL	57	2	7	9	111	16	1	3	4	12
1986-87	Kamloops	WHL	68	5	27	32	106	13	0	3	3	35
1987-88	Utica	AHL	73	2	7	9	179					
	Flint	IHL	3	0	0	0	4	16	0	2	2	31
1988-89	Utica	AHL	74	4	14	18	101	5	0	0	0	13
1989-90	Utica	AHL	74	6	18	24	164	5	0	2	2	21
1990-91	**New Jersey**	**NHL**	9	0	1	1	21					
	Utica	AHL	52	4	9	13	81					
1991-92	**Quebec**	**NHL**	5	0	0	0	26					
	Halifax	AHL	74	10	42	52	138					
1992-93	**NY Rangers**	**NHL**	2	0	0	0	2					
	Binghamton	AHL	67	5	25	30	184	6	0	3	3	14
	NHL Totals		**16**	**0**	**1**	**1**	**49**					

Signed as a free agent by **New Jersey**, September 26, 1986. Traded to **Quebec** by **New Jersey** for Brent Severyn, June 3, 1991. Signed as a free agent by **NY Rangers**, August 5, 1992.

MARINUCCI, CHRIS

Center. Shoots left. 6', 175 lbs.   Born, Grand Rapids, MN, December 29, 1971.
(NY Islanders' 4th choice, 90th overall, in 1990 Entry Draft).

			Regular Season					Playoffs				
Season	Club	Lea	GP	G	A	TP	PIM	GP	G	A	TP	PIM
1990-91	Minn.-Duluth	WCHA	36	6	10	16	20					
1991-92	Minn.-Duluth	WCHA	37	6	13	19	41					
1992-93a	Minn. Duluth	WCHA	40	35	42	77	52					

a WCHA Second All-Star Team (1993)

MAROIS, DANIEL

Right wing. Shoots right. 6', 190 lbs. Born, Montreal, Que., October 3, 1968.
(Toronto's 2nd choice, 28th overall, in 1987 Entry Draft).

			Regular Season					Playoffs				
Season	Club	Lea	GP	G	A	TP	PIM	GP	G	A	TP	PIM
1985-86	Verdun	QMJHL	58	42	35	77	110	5	4	2	6	6
1986-87	Chicoutimi	QMJHL	40	22	26	48	143	16	7	14	21	25
1987-88	Verdun	QMJHL	67	52	36	88	153	....	....	....	....	....
	Newmarket	AHL	8	4	4	8	4	....	....	....	....	....
	Toronto	**NHL**	....	....	....	....	....	**3**	**1**	**0**	**1**	**0**
1988-89	**Toronto**	**NHL**	**76**	**31**	**23**	**54**	**76**	....	....	....	....	....
1989-90	**Toronto**	**NHL**	**68**	**39**	**37**	**76**	**82**	**5**	**2**	**2**	**4**	**12**
1990-91	**Toronto**	**NHL**	**78**	**21**	**9**	**30**	**112**	....	....	....	....	....
1991-92	**Toronto**	**NHL**	**63**	**15**	**11**	**26**	**76**	....	....	....	....	....
	NY Islanders	**NHL**	**12**	**2**	**5**	**7**	**18**	....	....	....	....	....
1992-93	**NY Islanders**	**NHL**	**28**	**2**	**5**	**7**	**35**	....	....	....	....	....
	Capital Dist.	AHL	4	2	0	2	0	....	....	....	....	....
	NHL Totals		**325**	**110**	**90**	**200**	**399**	**8**	**3**	**2**	**5**	**12**

Traded to **NY Islanders** by **Toronto** with Claude Loiselle for Ken Baumgartner and Dave McLlwain, March 10, 1992. Traded to **Boston** by **NY Islanders** for future considerations, March 18, 1993.

MAROIS, MARIO (MAIR-wah)

Defense. Shoots right. 5'11", 190 lbs. Born, Quebec City, Que., December 15, 1957.
(NY Rangers' 5th choice, 62nd overall, in 1977 Amateur Draft).

			Regular Season					Playoffs				
Season	Club	Lea	GP	G	A	TP	PIM	GP	G	A	TP	PIM
1975-76	Quebec	QJHL	67	11	42	53	270	15	2	3	5	86
1976-77	Quebec	QJHL	72	17	67	84	239	14	1	17	18	75
1977-78	**NY Rangers**	**NHL**	**8**	**1**	**1**	**2**	**15**	**1**	**0**	**0**	**0**	**5**
	New Haven	AHL	52	8	23	31	147	12	5	3	8	31
1978-79	**NY Rangers**	**NHL**	**71**	**5**	**26**	**31**	**153**	**18**	**0**	**6**	**6**	**29**
1979-80	**NY Rangers**	**NHL**	**79**	**8**	**23**	**31**	**142**	**9**	**0**	**2**	**2**	**8**
1980-81	**NY Rangers**	**NHL**	**8**	**1**	**2**	**3**	**46**	....	....	....	....	....
	Vancouver	**NHL**	**50**	**4**	**12**	**16**	**115**	....	....	....	....	....
	Quebec	**NHL**	**11**	**0**	**7**	**7**	**20**	**5**	**0**	**1**	**1**	**6**
1981-82	**Quebec**	**NHL**	**71**	**11**	**32**	**43**	**161**	**13**	**1**	**2**	**3**	**44**
1982-83	**Quebec**	**NHL**	**36**	**2**	**12**	**14**	**108**	....	....	....	....	....
1983-84	**Quebec**	**NHL**	**80**	**13**	**36**	**49**	**151**	**9**	**1**	**4**	**5**	**6**
1984-85	**Quebec**	**NHL**	**76**	**6**	**37**	**43**	**91**	**18**	**0**	**8**	**8**	**12**
1985-86	**Quebec**	**NHL**	**20**	**1**	**12**	**13**	**42**	....	....	....	....	....
	Winnipeg	**NHL**	**56**	**4**	**28**	**32**	**110**	**3**	**1**	**4**	**5**	**6**
1986-87	**Winnipeg**	**NHL**	**79**	**4**	**40**	**44**	**106**	**10**	**1**	**3**	**4**	**23**
1987-88	**Winnipeg**	**NHL**	**79**	**7**	**44**	**51**	**111**	**5**	**0**	**4**	**4**	**6**
1988-89	**Winnipeg**	**NHL**	**7**	**1**	**1**	**2**	**17**	....	....	....	....	....
	Quebec	**NHL**	**42**	**2**	**11**	**13**	**101**	....	....	....	....	....
1989-90	**Quebec**	**NHL**	**67**	**3**	**15**	**18**	**104**	....	....	....	....	....
1990-91	**St. Louis**	**NHL**	**64**	**2**	**14**	**16**	**81**	**9**	**0**	**0**	**0**	**37**
1991-92	**St. Louis**	**NHL**	**17**	**0**	**1**	**1**	**38**	....	....	....	....	....
	Winnipeg	**NHL**	**34**	**1**	**3**	**4**	**34**	....	....	....	....	....
1992-93	Hamilton	AHL	68	5	27	32	86	....	....	....	....	....
	NHL Totals		**955**	**76**	**357**	**433**	**1746**	**100**	**4**	**34**	**38**	**182**

Traded to **Vancouver** by **NY Rangers** with Jim Mayer for Jere Gillis and Jeff Bandura, November 11, 1980. Traded to **Quebec** by **Vancouver** for Garry Lariviere, March 10, 1981. Traded to **Winnipeg** by **Quebec** for Robert Picard, November 27, 1985. Traded to **Quebec** by **Winnipeg** for Gord Donnelly, December 6, 1988. Claimed by **St. Louis** in NHL Waiver Draft, October 1, 1990. Traded to **Winnipeg** by **St. Louis** for future considerations, November 26, 1991.

MARSH, CHARLES BRADLEY (BRAD)

Defense. Shoots left. 6'3", 220 lbs. Born, London, Ont., March 31, 1958.
(Atlanta's 1st choice, 11th overall, in 1978 Amateur Draft).

			Regular Season					Playoffs				
Season	Club	Lea	GP	G	A	TP	PIM	GP	G	A	TP	PIM
1976-77a	London	OHA	63	7	33	40	121	20	3	5	8	47
1977-78b	London	OHA	62	8	55	63	192	11	2	10	12	21
1978-79	**Atlanta**	**NHL**	**80**	**0**	**19**	**19**	**101**	**2**	**0**	**0**	**0**	**17**
1979-80	**Atlanta**	**NHL**	**80**	**2**	**9**	**11**	**119**	**4**	**0**	**1**	**1**	**2**
1980-81	**Calgary**	**NHL**	**80**	**1**	**12**	**13**	**87**	**16**	**0**	**5**	**5**	**8**
1981-82	**Calgary**	**NHL**	**17**	**0**	**1**	**1**	**10**	....	....	....	....	....
	Philadelphia	**NHL**	**66**	**2**	**22**	**24**	**106**	**4**	**0**	**0**	**0**	**2**
1982-83	**Philadelphia**	**NHL**	**68**	**2**	**11**	**13**	**52**	**2**	**0**	**1**	**1**	**0**
1983-84	**Philadelphia**	**NHL**	**77**	**3**	**14**	**17**	**83**	**3**	**1**	**1**	**2**	**2**
1984-85	**Philadelphia**	**NHL**	**77**	**2**	**18**	**20**	**91**	**19**	**0**	**6**	**6**	**65**
1985-86	**Philadelphia**	**NHL**	**79**	**0**	**13**	**13**	**123**	**5**	**0**	**0**	**0**	**2**
1986-87	**Philadelphia**	**NHL**	**77**	**2**	**9**	**11**	**124**	**26**	**3**	**4**	**7**	**16**
1987-88	**Philadelphia**	**NHL**	**70**	**3**	**9**	**12**	**57**	**7**	**1**	**0**	**1**	**8**
1988-89	**Toronto**	**NHL**	**80**	**1**	**15**	**16**	**79**	....	....	....	....	....
1989-90	**Toronto**	**NHL**	**79**	**1**	**13**	**14**	**95**	**5**	**1**	**0**	**1**	**2**
1990-91	**Toronto**	**NHL**	**22**	**0**	**0**	**0**	**15**	....	....	....	....	....
	Detroit	**NHL**	**20**	**1**	**3**	**4**	**16**	**1**	**0**	**0**	**0**	**0**
1991-92	**Detroit**	**NHL**	**55**	**3**	**4**	**7**	**53**	**3**	**0**	**0**	**0**	**0**
1992-93	**Ottawa**	**NHL**	**59**	**0**	**3**	**3**	**30**	....	....	....	....	....
	NHL Totals		**1086**	**23**	**175**	**198**	**1241**	**97**	**6**	**18**	**24**	**124**

a OHA Third All-Star Team (1977)
b OHA First All-Star Team (1978)

Played in NHL All-Star Game (1993)

Claimed by **Atlanta** as fill in Expansion Draft, June 13, 1979. Traded to **Philadelphia** by **Calgary** for Mel Bridgman, November 11, 1981. Claimed by **Toronto** in NHL Waiver Draft, October 3, 1988. Traded to **Detroit** by **Toronto** for Detroit's eighth round choice (Robb McIntyre) in 1991 Entry Draft, February 4, 1991. Traded to **Toronto** by **Detroit** for cash, June 10, 1992. Traded to **Ottawa** by **Toronto** for future considerations, July 20, 1992.

MARSHALL, BOBBY

Defense. Shoots left. 6'1", 190 lbs. Born, North York, Ont., April 11, 1972.
(Calgary's 6th choice, 129th overall, in 1991 Entry Draft).

			Regular Season					Playoffs				
Season	Club	Lea	GP	G	A	TP	PIM	GP	G	A	TP	PIM
1990-91	Miami-Ohio	CCHA	37	3	15	18	44	....	....	....	....	....
1991-92	Miami-Ohio	CCHA	40	5	20	25	48	....	....	....	....	....
1992-93ab	Miami-Ohio	CCHA	40	2	43	45	40	....	....	....	....	....

a CCHA Second All-Star Team (1993)
b NCAA West Second All-American Team (1993)

MARSHALL, GRANT

Right wing. Shoots right. 6'1", 185 lbs. Born, Mississauga, Ont., June 9, 1973.
(Toronto's 2nd choice, 23rd overall, in 1992 Entry Draft).

			Regular Season					Playoffs				
Season	Club	Lea	GP	G	A	TP	PIM	GP	G	A	TP	PIM
1990-91	Ottawa	OHL	26	6	11	17	25	1	0	0	0	0
1991-92	Ottawa	OHL	64	34	100	134	70	11	6	11	17	11
1992-93	Ottawa	OHL	30	14	29	43	83	....	....	....	....	....
	Newmarket	OHL	31	11	25	36	89	7	4	7	11	20
	St. John's	AHL	2	0	0	0	0	2	0	0	0	2

MARSHALL, JASON

Defense. Shoots right. 6'2", 195 lbs. Born, Cranbrook, B.C., February 22, 1971.
(St. Louis' 1st choice, 9th overall, in 1989 Entry Draft).

			Regular Season					Playoffs				
Season	Club	Lea	GP	G	A	TP	PIM	GP	G	A	TP	PIM
1989-90	Cdn. National	....	72	1	11	12	57	....	....	....	....	....
1990-91	Tri-Cities	WHL	59	10	34	44	236	7	1	2	3	20
	Peoria	IHL	....	....	....	....	....	18	0	1	1	48
1991-92	**St. Louis**	**NHL**	**2**	**1**	**0**	**1**	**4**	....	....	....	....	....
	Peoria	IHL	78	4	18	22	178	10	0	1	1	16
1992-93	Peoria	IHL	77	4	16	20	229	4	0	0	0	20
	NHL Totals		**2**	**1**	**0**	**1**	**4**	....	....	....	....	....

MARTELL, STEVE

Right wing. Shoots right. 5'10", 185 lbs. Born, Sydney, N.S., March 3, 1970.
(Washington's 10th choice, 159th overall, in 1990 Entry Draft).

			Regular Season					Playoffs				
Season	Club	Lea	GP	G	A	TP	PIM	GP	G	A	TP	PIM
1988-89	London	OHL	65	9	17	26	59	21	2	5	7	18
1989-90	London	OHL	63	19	24	43	91	6	1	1	2	10
1990-91a	London	OHL	63	32	40	72	105	7	3	1	4	8
1991-92	Baltimore	AHL	42	5	7	12	120	....	....	....	....	....
	Hampton Rds.	ECHL	20	9	25	34	34	11	4	5	9	47
1992-93	Baltimore	AHL	5	3	2	5	0	....	....	....	....	....
	Hampton Rds.	ECHL	57	17	43	60	161	4	0	2	2	26

a OHL Third All-Star Team (1991)

MARTIN, CRAIG

Right wing. Shoots right. 6'2", 219 lbs. Born, Amherst, N.S., January 21, 1971.
(Winnipeg's 6th choice, 98th overall, in 1990 Entry Draft).

			Regular Season					Playoffs				
Season	Club	Lea	GP	G	A	TP	PIM	GP	G	A	TP	PIM
1989-90	Hull	QMJHL	66	14	31	45	299	11	2	1	3	65
1990-91	Hull	QMJHL	18	5	6	11	87	....	....	....	....	....
	St-Hyacinthe	QMJHL	36	8	9	17	166	....	....	....	....	....
1991-92	Moncton	AHL	11	1	1	2	70	....	....	....	....	....
	Fort Wayne	IHL	24	0	0	0	115	....	....	....	....	....
1992-93	Moncton	AHL	64	5	13	18	198	5	0	1	1	22

MARTIN, MATT

Defense. Shoots left. 6'3", 190 lbs. Born, Hamden, CT, April 30, 1971.
(Toronto's 4th choice, 66th overall, in 1989 Entry Draft).

			Regular Season					Playoffs				
Season	Club	Lea	GP	G	A	TP	PIM	GP	G	A	TP	PIM
1990-91	U. of Maine	H.E.	35	3	12	15	48	....	....	....	....	....
1991-92	U. of Maine	H.E.	30	4	14	18	46	....	....	....	....	....
1992-93	U. of Maine	H.E.	44	6	26	32	88	....	....	....	....	....
	St. John's	AHL	2	0	0	0	2	9	1	5	6	4

MARTINI, DARCY

Defense. Shoots left. 6'4", 220 lbs. Born, Castlegar, B.C., January 30, 1969.
(Edmonton's 8th choice, 162nd overall, in 1989 Entry Draft).

			Regular Season					Playoffs				
Season	Club	Lea	GP	G	A	TP	PIM	GP	G	A	TP	PIM
1988-89	Michigan Tech	WCHA	35	1	2	3	103	....	....	....	....	....
1989-90	Michigan Tech	WCHA	36	3	6	9	151	....	....	....	....	....
1990-91	Michigan Tech	WCHA	34	10	13	23	*184	....	....	....	....	....
1991-92	Michigan Tech	WCHA	17	5	13	18	58	....	....	....	....	....
1992-93	Cape Breton	AHL	47	1	6	7	36	2	0	1	1	0
	Wheeling	ECHL	6	0	2	2	2	....	....	....	....	....

MARTTILA, JUKKA (MAHR-tee-lah)

Defense. Shoots left. 6'1", 187 lbs. Born, Tampere, Finland, April 15, 1968.
(Winnipeg's 9th choice, 136th overall, in 1988 Entry Draft).

			Regular Season					Playoffs				
Season	Club	Lea	GP	G	A	TP	PIM	GP	G	A	TP	PIM
1986-87	Tappara	Fin.	39	5	7	12	16	9	1	....	1	2
1987-88	Tappara	Fin.	33	4	1	5	18	10	2	1	3	2
1988-89	Tappara	Fin.	43	11	20	31	32	8	2	4	6	4
1989-90	Tappara	Fin.	44	12	14	26	14	7	2	2	4	4
1990-91	Tappara	Fin.	42	10	21	31	32	3	0	0	0	0
1991-92	Tappara	Fin.	17	2	4	6	14	....	....	....	....	....
1992-93	Tappara	Fin.	32	1	3	4	36	....	....	....	....	....

MARTYNYUK, SERGEI (mar-tih-NYOOK)

Center. Shoots left. 6', 183 lbs. Born, Rybinsk, Soviet Union, January 30, 1971.
(Montreal's 13th choice, 249th overall, in 1990 Entry Draft).

			Regular Season					Playoffs				
Season	Club	Lea	GP	G	A	TP	PIM	GP	G	A	TP	PIM
1987-88	Torpedo Yaro.	USSR	1	0	0	0	0	....	....	....	....	....
1988-89	Torpedo Yaro.	USSR	18	0	1	1	4	....	....	....	....	....
1989-90	Torpedo Yaro.	USSR	40	5	1	6	8	....	....	....	....	....
1990-91	Torpedo Yaro.	USSR	39	7	14	21	52	....	....	....	....	....
1991-92	Torpedo Yaro.	CIS	29	12	5	17	32	....	....	....	....	....
1992-93	Torpedo Yaro	CIS	27	5	2	7	8	....	....	....	....	....

MASTAD, MILT

Defense. Shoots left. 6'3", 205 lbs. Born, Regina, Sask., March 5, 1975.
(Boston's 6th choice, 155th overall, in 1993 Entry Draft).

			Regular Season					Playoffs				
Season	Club	Lea	GP	G	A	TP	PIM	GP	G	A	TP	PIM
1991-92	Surrey	BCJHL	55	1	13	14	122	....	....	....	....	....
1992-93	Seattle	WHL	60	1	1	2	123	5	0	1	1	14

MATHERS, MIKE

Left wing. Shoots left. 5'10", 188 lbs. Born, High Prairie, Alta., June 20, 1972.
(Washington's 7th choice, 191st overall, in 1992 Entry Draft).

			Regular Season					Playoffs				
Season	Club	Lea	GP	G	A	TP	PIM	GP	G	A	TP	PIM
1990-91	Kamloops	WHL	54	14	22	36	50	12	3	2	5	6
1991-92a	Kamloops	WHL	70	30	40	70	39	16	10	7	17	17
1992-93b	Kamloops	WHL	69	52	56	108	63	13	5	12	17	15

a Memorial Cup All-Star Team (1992)
b WHL West First All-Star Team (1993)

MATHIESON, JIM

Defense. Shoots left. 6'1", 209 lbs. Born, Kindersley, Sask., January 24, 1970.
(Washington's 3rd choice, 59th overall, in 1989 Entry Draft).

			Regular Season					Playoffs				
Season	Club	Lea	GP	G	A	TP	PIM	GP	G	A	TP	PIM
1986-87	Regina	WHL	40	0	9	9	40	3	0	1	1	2
1987-88	Regina	WHL	72	3	12	15	115	4	0	2	2	4
1988-89	Regina	WHL	62	5	22	27	151	....	....	....	....	....
1989-90	**Washington**	**NHL**	**2**	**0**	**0**	**0**	**4**	....	....	....	....	....
	Regina	WHL	67	1	26	27	158	11	0	7	7	16
	Baltimore	AHL	....	....	....	....	....	3	0	0	0	4
1990-91	Baltimore	AHL	65	3	5	8	168	4	1	0	1	6
1991-92	Baltimore	AHL	74	2	9	11	206	....	....	....	....	....
1992-93	Baltimore	AHL	46	3	5	8	88	3	0	1	1	23
	NHL Totals		**2**	**0**	**0**	**0**	**4**	....	....	....	....	....

MATIER, MARK

Defense. Shoots left. 6'1", 190 lbs. Born, St. Catharines, Ont., December 14, 1973.
(Washington's 6th choice, 167th overall, in 1992 Entry Draft).

			Regular Season					Playoffs				
Season	Club	Lea	GP	G	A	TP	PIM	GP	G	A	TP	PIM
1991-92	S.S. Marie	OHL	46	0	5	5	15	19	3	5	8	14
1992-93	S.S. Marie	OHL	64	7	27	34	89	18	1	4	5	13

Traded to **Quebec** by **Washington** for Kevin Kaminski, June 15, 1993.

MATIKAINEN, PETRI (mah-tee-KAY-nehn)

Defense. Shoots left. 6', 189 lbs. Born, Savonlinna, Finland, January 7, 1967.
(Buffalo's 7th choice, 140th overall, in 1985 Entry Draft).

			Regular Season					Playoffs				
Season	Club	Lea	GP	G	A	TP	PIM	GP	G	A	TP	PIM
1984-85	SapKo	Fin.2	24	0	4	4	34	....	....	....	....	....
1985-86	Oshawa	OHL	53	14	42	56	27	....	....	....	....	....
1986-87	Oshawa	OHL	50	8	34	42	53	21	2	12	14	36
1987-88	Tappara	Fin.	41	5	1	6	58	10	0	2	2	4
1988-89	Tappara	Fin.	44	4	13	17	32	8	0	0	0	10
1989-90	JoKP	Fin.	44	6	8	14	34	....	....	....	....	....
1990-91	JoKP	Fin.2	43	16	25	41	35	....	....	....	....	....
1991-92	JoKP	Fin.	42	4	8	12	38	....	....	....	....	....
1992-93	JoKP	Fin.2	42	20	21	41	51	6	3	2	5	2

MATTE, CHRISTIAN

Right wing. Shoots right. 5'11", 164 lbs. Born, Hull, Que., January 20, 1975.
(Quebec's 8th choice, 153rd overall, in 1993 Entry Draft).

			Regular Season					Playoffs				
Season	Club	Lea	GP	G	A	TP	PIM	GP	G	A	TP	PIM
1992-93	Granby	QMJHL	68	17	36	53	59	....	....	....	....	....

MATTEAU, STEPHANE (mah-TOH)

Left wing. Shoots left. 6'3", 195 lbs. Born, Rouyn-Noranda, Que., September 2, 1969.
(Calgary's 2nd choice, 25th overall, in 1987 Entry Draft).

			Regular Season					Playoffs				
Season	Club	Lea	GP	G	A	TP	PIM	GP	G	A	TP	PIM
1985-86	Hull	QMJHL	60	6	8	14	19	4	0	0	0	0
1986-87	Hull	QMJHL	69	27	48	75	113	8	3	7	10	8
1987-88	Hull	QMJHL	57	17	40	57	179	18	5	14	19	94
1988-89	Hull	QMJHL	59	44	45	89	202	9	8	6	14	30
	Salt Lake	IHL	....	....	....	....	....	9	0	4	4	13
1989-90	Salt Lake	IHL	81	23	35	58	130	10	6	3	9	38
1990-91	**Calgary**	**NHL**	**78**	**15**	**19**	**34**	**93**	**5**	**0**	**1**	**1**	**0**
1991-92	**Calgary**	**NHL**	**4**	**1**	**0**	**1**	**19**	....	....	....	....	....
	Chicago	**NHL**	**20**	**5**	**8**	**13**	**45**	**18**	**4**	**6**	**10**	**24**
1992-93	**Chicago**	**NHL**	**79**	**15**	**18**	**33**	**98**	**3**	**0**	**1**	**1**	**2**
	NHL Totals		**181**	**36**	**45**	**81**	**255**	**26**	**4**	**8**	**12**	**26**

Traded to **Chicago** by **Calgary** for Trent Yawney, December 16, 1991.

MATTHEWS, JAMIE

Center. Shoots right. 6'1", 190 lbs. Born, Amherst, N.S., May 25, 1973.
(Chicago's 3rd choice, 44th overall, in 1991 Entry Draft).

			Regular Season					Playoffs				
Season	Club	Lea	GP	G	A	TP	PIM	GP	G	A	TP	PIM
1989-90	Sudbury	OHL	60	16	17	33	25	7	1	0	1	4
1990-91	Sudbury	OHL	66	14	38	52	41	5	3	5	8	8
1991-92	Sudbury	OHL	64	26	69	95	30	11	2	11	13	4
1992-93	Sudbury	OHL	65	30	62	92	65	14	7	17	24	22

MATTSSON, JESPER

Center. Shoots right. 6', 176 lbs. Born, Malmo, Sweden, May 13, 1975.
(Calgary's 1st choice, 18th overall, in 1993 Entry Draft).

			Regular Season					Playoffs				
Season	Club	Lea	GP	G	A	TP	PIM	GP	G	A	TP	PIM
1991-92	Malmo	Swe.	24	0	1	1	2	....	....	....	....	....
1992-93	Malmo	Swe.	40	9	8	17	14	5	0	0	0	0

MATVICHUK, RICHARD (MAT-vih-chuhk)

Defense. Shoots left. 6'2", 190 lbs. Born, Edmonton, Alta., February 5, 1973.
(Minnesota's 1st choice, 8th overall, in 1991 Entry Draft).

			Regular Season					Playoffs				
Season	Club	Lea	GP	G	A	TP	PIM	GP	G	A	TP	PIM
1989-90	Saskatoon	WHL	56	8	24	32	126	10	2	8	10	16
1990-91	Saskatoon	WHL	68	13	36	49	117	....	....	....	....	....
1991-92a	Saskatoon	WHL	58	14	40	54	126	....	....	....	....	....
1992-93	**Minnesota**	**NHL**	**53**	**2**	**3**	**5**	**26**	....	....	....	....	....
	Kalamazoo	IHL	3	0	1	1	6	....	....	....	....	....
	NHL Totals		**53**	**2**	**3**	**5**	**26**	....	....	....	....	....

a WHL East First All-Star Team (1992)

MAXWELL, DENNIS

Center. Shoots left. 6', 188 lbs. Born, Dauphin, Man., June 4, 1974.
(Tampa Bay's 8th choice, 170th overall, in 1992 Entry Draft).

			Regular Season					Playoffs				
Season	Club	Lea	GP	G	A	TP	PIM	GP	G	A	TP	PIM
1991-92	Niagara Falls	OHL	66	19	26	45	139	17	4	9	13	32
1992-93	Niagara Falls	OHL	12	5	9	14	21	....	....	....	....	....
	Sudbury	OHL	52	15	24	39	116	14	3	4	7	42

MAY, ALAN

Right wing. Shoots right. 6'1", 200 lbs. Born, Swan Hills, Alta., January 14, 1965.

			Regular Season					Playoffs				
Season	Club	Lea	GP	G	A	TP	PIM	GP	G	A	TP	PIM
1985-86	Medicine Hat	WHL	6	1	0	1	25	....	....	....	....	....
	N. Westminster	WHL	32	8	9	17	81	....	....	....	....	....
1986-87	Springfield	AHL	4	0	2	2	11	....	....	....	....	....
	Carolina	ACHL	42	23	14	37	310	5	2	2	4	57
1987-88	**Boston**	**NHL**	**3**	**0**	**0**	**0**	**15**	....	....	....	....	....
	Maine	AHL	61	14	11	25	257	....	....	....	....	....
	Nova Scotia	AHL	13	4	1	5	54	4	0	0	0	51
1988-89	**Edmonton**	**NHL**	**3**	**1**	**0**	**1**	**7**	....	....	....	....	....
	Cape Breton	AHL	50	12	13	25	214	....	....	....	....	....
	New Haven	AHL	12	2	8	10	99	16	6	3	9	*105
1989-90	**Washington**	**NHL**	**77**	**7**	**10**	**17**	**339**	**15**	**0**	**0**	**0**	**37**
1990-91	**Washington**	**NHL**	**67**	**4**	**6**	**10**	**264**	**11**	**1**	**1**	**2**	**37**
1991-92	**Washington**	**NHL**	**75**	**6**	**9**	**15**	**221**	**7**	**0**	**0**	**0**	**0**
1992-93	**Washington**	**NHL**	**83**	**6**	**10**	**16**	**268**	**6**	**0**	**1**	**1**	**6**
	NHL Totals		**308**	**24**	**35**	**59**	**1114**	**39**	**1**	**2**	**3**	**80**

Signed as a free agent by **Boston**, October 30, 1987. Traded to **Edmonton** by **Boston** for Moe Lemay, March 8, 1988. Traded to **Los Angeles** by **Edmonton** with Jim Wiemer for Brian Wilks and John English, March 7, 1989. Traded to **Washington** by **Los Angeles** for Washington's fifth round choice (Thomas Newman) in 1989 Entry Draft, June 17, 1989.

MAY, BRAD

Left wing. Shoots left. 6', 200 lbs. Born, Toronto, Ont., November 29, 1971.
(Buffalo's 1st choice, 14th overall, in 1990 Entry Draft).

			Regular Season					Playoffs				
Season	Club	Lea	GP	G	A	TP	PIM	GP	G	A	TP	PIM
1988-89	Niagara Falls	OHL	65	8	14	22	304	17	0	1	1	55
1989-90a	Niagara Falls	OHL	61	32	58	90	223	16	9	13	22	64
1990-91a	Niagara Falls	OHL	34	37	32	69	93	14	11	14	25	53
1991-92	**Buffalo**	**NHL**	**69**	**11**	**6**	**17**	**309**	**7**	**1**	**4**	**5**	**2**
1992-93	**Buffalo**	**NHL**	**82**	**13**	**13**	**26**	**242**	**8**	**1**	**1**	**2**	**14**
	NHL Totals		**151**	**24**	**19**	**43**	**551**	**15**	**2**	**5**	**7**	**16**

a OHL Second All-Star Team (1990, 1991)

MAYERS, JAMAL

Center. Shoots right. 6', 190 lbs. Born, Toronto, Ont., October 24, 1974.
(St. Louis' 3rd choice, 89th overall, in 1993 Entry Draft).

			Regular Season					Playoffs				
Season	Club	Lea	GP	G	A	TP	PIM	GP	G	A	TP	PIM
1991-92	Thornhill	OHA Jr. A	56	38	69	107	36	....	....	....	....	....
1992-93	W. Michigan	CCHA	38	8	17	25	26	....	....	....	....	....

MAZUR, JAY

Center/Right wing. Shoots right. 6'2", 205 lbs. Born, Hamilton, Ont., January 22, 1965.
(Vancouver's 12th choice, 230th overall, in 1983 Entry Draft).

			Regular Season					Playoffs				
Season	Club	Lea	GP	G	A	TP	PIM	GP	G	A	TP	PIM
1983-84	Maine	H.E.	34	14	9	23	14	....	....	....	....	....
1984-85	Maine	H.E.	31	0	6	6	20	....	....	....	....	....
1985-86	Maine	H.E.	34	5	7	12	18	....	....	....	....	....
1986-87	Maine	H.E.	39	16	10	26	61	....	....	....	....	....
1987-88	Flint	IHL	39	17	11	28	28	....	....	....	....	....
	Fredericton	AHL	31	14	6	20	28	15	4	2	6	38
1988-89	**Vancouver**	**NHL**	**1**	**0**	**0**	**0**	**0**	....	....	....	....	....
	Milwaukee	IHL	73	33	31	64	86	11	6	5	11	2
1989-90	**Vancouver**	**NHL**	**5**	**0**	**0**	**0**	**4**	....	....	....	....	....
	Milwaukee	IHL	70	20	27	47	63	6	3	0	3	6
1990-91	**Vancouver**	**NHL**	**36**	**11**	**7**	**18**	**14**	**6**	**0**	**1**	**1**	**8**
	Milwaukee	IHL	7	2	3	5	21	....	....	....	....	....
1991-92	**Vancouver**	**NHL**	**5**	**0**	**0**	**0**	**2**	....	....	....	....	....
	Milwaukee	IHL	56	17	20	37	49	5	2	3	5	0
1992-93	Hamilton	AHL	59	21	17	38	30	....	....	....	....	....
	NHL Totals		**47**	**11**	**7**	**18**	**20**	**6**	**0**	**1**	**1**	**8**

McALPINE, CHRIS

Defense. Shoots right. 6', 190 lbs. Born, Roseville, MN, December 1, 1971.
(New Jersey's 10th choice, 137th overall, in 1990 Entry Draft).

			Regular Season					Playoffs				
Season	Club	Lea	GP	G	A	TP	PIM	GP	G	A	TP	PIM
1990-91	U. Minnesota	WCHA	38	7	9	16	112	....	....	....	....	....
1991-92	U. Minnesota	WCHA	39	3	9	12	126	....	....	....	....	....
1992-93	U. Minnesota	WCHA	41	14	9	23	82	....	....	....	....	....

McAMMOND, DEAN

Center. Shoots left. 5'11", 185 lbs. Born, Grand Cache, Alta., June 15, 1973.
(Chicago's 1st choice, 22nd overall, in 1991 Entry Draft).

			Regular Season					Playoffs				
Season	Club	Lea	GP	G	A	TP	PIM	GP	G	A	TP	PIM
1989-90	Prince Albert	WHL	53	11	11	22	49	14	2	3	5	18
1990-91	Prince Albert	WHL	71	33	35	68	108	2	0	1	1	6
1991-92	**Chicago**	**NHL**	**5**	**0**	**2**	**2**	**0**	**3**	**0**	**0**	**0**	**2**
	Prince Albert	WHL	63	37	54	91	189	10	12	11	23	26
1992-93	Swift Current	WHL	48	29	42	71	73	17	*16	19	35	20
	NHL Totals		**5**	**0**	**2**	**2**	**0**	**3**	**0**	**0**	**0**	**2**

Traded to **Edmonton** by **Chicago** with Igor Kravchuk for Joe Murphy, February 24, 1993.

McBAIN, ANDREW

Right wing. Shoots right. 6'1", 205 lbs. Born, Scarborough, Ont., January 18, 1965.
(Winnipeg's 1st choice, 8th overall, in 1983 Entry Draft).

			Regular Season					Playoffs				
Season	Club	Lea	GP	G	A	TP	PIM	GP	G	A	TP	PIM
1981-82	Niagara Falls	OHL	68	19	25	44	35	5	0	3	3	4
1982-83a	North Bay	OHL	67	33	87	120	61	8	2	6	8	17
1983-84	**Winnipeg**	**NHL**	**78**	**11**	**19**	**30**	**37**	**3**	**2**	**0**	**2**	**0**
1984-85	**Winnipeg**	**NHL**	**77**	**7**	**15**	**22**	**45**	**7**	**1**	**0**	**1**	**0**
1985-86	**Winnipeg**	**NHL**	**28**	**3**	**3**	**6**	**17**	....	....	....	....	....
1986-87	**Winnipeg**	**NHL**	**71**	**11**	**21**	**32**	**106**	**9**	**0**	**2**	**2**	**10**
1987-88	**Winnipeg**	**NHL**	**74**	**32**	**31**	**63**	**145**	**5**	**2**	**5**	**7**	**29**
1988-89	**Winnipeg**	**NHL**	**80**	**37**	**40**	**77**	**71**	....	....	....	....	....
1989-90	**Pittsburgh**	**NHL**	**41**	**5**	**9**	**14**	**51**	....	....	....	....	....
	Vancouver	**NHL**	**26**	**4**	**5**	**9**	**22**	....	....	....	....	....
1990-91	**Vancouver**	**NHL**	**13**	**0**	**5**	**5**	**32**	....	....	....	....	....
	Milwaukee	IHL	47	27	24	51	69	6	2	5	7	12
1991-92	**Vancouver**	**NHL**	**6**	**1**	**0**	**1**	**0**	....	....	....	....	....
	Milwaukee	IHL	65	24	54	78	132	5	1	2	3	10
1992-93	**Ottawa**	**NHL**	**59**	**7**	**16**	**23**	**43**	....	....	....	....	....
	New Haven	AHL	1	0	1	1	4	....	....	....	....	....
	NHL Totals		**553**	**118**	**164**	**282**	**569**	**24**	**5**	**7**	**12**	**39**

a OHL Second All-Star Team (1983)

Traded to **Pittsburgh** by **Winnipeg** with Jim Kyte and Randy Gilhen for Randy Cunneyworth, Rick Tabaracci and Dave McLlwain, June 17, 1989. Traded to **Vancouver** by **Pittsburgh** with Dave Capuano and Dan Quinn for Rod Buskas, Barry Pederson and Tony Tanti, January 8, 1990. Signed as a free agent by **Ottawa**, July 30, 1992.

McBAIN, JASON

Defense. Shoots right. 6'2", 178 lbs. Born, Ilion, NY, April 12, 1974.
(Hartford's 5th choice, 81st overall, in 1992 Entry Draft).

			Regular Season					Playoffs				
Season	Club	Lea	GP	G	A	TP	PIM	GP	G	A	TP	PIM
1990-91	Lethbridge	WHL	52	2	7	9	39	1	0	0	0	0
1991-92	Lethbridge	WHL	13	0	1	1	12	....	....	....	....	....
	Portland	WHL	54	9	23	32	95	6	1	0	1	13
1992-93	Portland	WHL	71	9	35	44	76	16	2	12	14	14

McBEAN, WAYNE

Defense. Shoots left. 6'2", 190 lbs. Born, Calgary, Alta., February 21, 1969.
(Los Angeles' 1st choice, 4th overall, in 1987 Entry Draft).

			Regular Season					Playoffs				
Season	Club	Lea	GP	G	A	TP	PIM	GP	G	A	TP	PIM
1985-86	Medicine Hat	WHL	67	1	14	15	73	25	1	5	6	36
1986-87a	Medicine Hat	WHL	71	12	41	53	163	20	2	8	10	40
1987-88	**Los Angeles**	**NHL**	**27**	**0**	**1**	**1**	**26**	....	....	....	....	....
	Medicine Hat	WHL	30	15	30	45	48	16	6	17	23	50
1988-89	**Los Angeles**	**NHL**	**33**	**0**	**5**	**5**	**23**	....	....	....	....	....
	New Haven	AHL	7	1	1	2	2	....	....	....	....	....
	NY Islanders	**NHL**	**19**	**0**	**1**	**1**	**12**	....	....	....	....	....
1989-90	**NY Islanders**	**NHL**	**5**	**0**	**1**	**1**	**2**	**2**	**1**	**1**	**2**	**0**
	Springfield	AHL	58	6	33	39	48	17	4	11	15	31
1990-91	**NY Islanders**	**NHL**	**52**	**5**	**14**	**19**	**47**	....	....	....	....	....
	Capital Dist.	AHL	22	9	9	18	19	....	....	....	....	....
1991-92	**NY Islanders**	**NHL**	**25**	**2**	**4**	**6**	**18**	....	....	....	....	....
1992-93	Capital Dist.	AHL	20	1	9	10	35	3	0	1	1	9
	NHL Totals		**161**	**7**	**26**	**33**	**128**	**2**	**1**	**1**	**2**	**0**

a WHL East All-Star Team (1987)

Traded to **NY Islanders** by **Los Angeles** with Mark Fitzpatrick and future considerations (Doug Crossman, May 23, 1989) for Kelly Hrudey, February 22, 1989.

McCABE, BRYAN

Defense. Shoots left. 6'1", 200 lbs. Born, St. Catharines, Ont., June 8, 1975.
(NY Islanders' 2nd choice, 40th overall, in 1993 Entry Draft).

			Regular Season					Playoffs				
Season	Club	Lea	GP	G	A	TP	PIM	GP	G	A	TP	PIM
1991-92	Medicine Hat	WHL	68	6	24	30	157	....	....	....	....	....
1992-93a	Spokane	WHL	60	3	57	60	217	6	1	5	6	28

a WHL West Second All-Star Team (1993)

McCABE, SCOTT

Defense. Shoots left. 6'4", 189 lbs. Born, St. Clair Shores, MI, May 28, 1974.
(New Jersey's 4th choice, 94th overall, in 1992 Entry Draft).

			Regular Season					Playoffs				
Season	Club	Lea	GP	G	A	TP	PIM	GP	G	A	TP	PIM
1991-92	GPD	Midget	57	35	36	71	....	....	....	....	....	....
1992-93	Lake Superior	CCHA				DID NOT PLAY						

McCARTHY, BRIAN

Center. Shoots left. 6'2", 190 lbs. Born, Salem, MA, December 6, 1971.
(Buffalo's 2nd choice, 82nd overall, in 1990 Entry Draft).

			Regular Season					Playoffs				
Season	Club	Lea	GP	G	A	TP	PIM	GP	G	A	TP	PIM
1990-91	Providence	H.E.	33	7	6	13	33	....	....	....	....	....
1991-92						DID NOT PLAY						
1992-93	St. Lawrence	ECAC	18	7	5	12	44	....	....	....	....	....

McCARTHY, JOE

Defense. Shoots left. 6'1", 200 lbs. Born, Bangor, ME, November 17, 1970.
(Toronto's 2nd choice, 9th overall, in 1991 Supplemental Draft).

			Regular Season					Playoffs				
Season	Club	Lea	GP	G	A	TP	PIM	GP	G	A	TP	PIM
1989-90	U. of Vermont	ECAC	31	2	1	3	21	....	....	....	....	....
1990-91	U. of Vermont	ECAC	33	3	7	10	16	....	....	....	....	....
1991-92	U. of Vermont	ECAC	26	2	7	9	21	....	....	....	....	....
1992-93	U. of Vermont	ECAC	17	1	2	3	31	....	....	....	....	....

McCARTHY, SANDY

Right wing. Shoots right. 6'3", 224 lbs. Born, Toronto, Ont., June 15, 1972.
(Calgary's 3rd choice, 52nd overall, in 1991 Entry Draft).

			Regular Season					Playoffs				
Season	Club	Lea	GP	G	A	TP	PIM	GP	G	A	TP	PIM
1989-90	Laval	QMJHL	65	10	11	21	269	14	3	3	6	60
1990-91	Laval	QMJHL	68	21	19	40	297	13	6	5	11	67
1991-92	Laval	QMJHL	62	39	51	90	326	8	4	5	9	81
1992-93	Salt Lake	IHL	77	18	20	38	220	....	....	....	....	....

McCARTY, DARREN

Right wing. Shoots right. 6'1", 214 lbs. Born, Burnaby, B.C., April 1, 1972.
(Detroit's 2nd choice, 46th overall, in 1992 Entry Draft).

			Regular Season					Playoffs				
Season	Club	Lea	GP	G	A	TP	PIM	GP	G	A	TP	PIM
1990-91	Belleville	OHL	60	30	37	67	151	6	2	2	4	13
1991-92a	Belleville	OHL	65	*55	72	127	177	5	1	4	5	13
1992-93	Adirondack	AHL	73	17	19	36	278	11	0	1	1	33

a OHL First All-Star Team (1992)

McCAULEY, BILL

Center. Shoots left. 6', 173 lbs. Born, Detroit, MI, April 20, 1975.
(Florida's 6th choice, 83rd overall, in 1993 Entry Draft).

			Regular Season					Playoffs				
Season	Club	Lea	GP	G	A	TP	PIM	GP	G	A	TP	PIM
1991-92	Detroit	USJr.A	38	25	35	60	64	....	....	....	....	....
1992-93	Detroit	OHL	65	13	37	50	24	15	1	4	5	6

McCAULEY, WES

Defense. Shoots left. 6', 175 lbs. Born, Toronto, Ont., January 11, 1972.
(Detroit's 7th choice, 150th overall, in 1990 Entry Draft).

			Regular Season					Playoffs				
Season	Club	Lea	GP	G	A	TP	PIM	GP	G	A	TP	PIM
1989-90	Michigan State	CCHA	42	2	7	9	15	....	....	....	....	....
1990-91	Michigan State	CCHA	28	1	2	3	9	....	....	....	....	....
1991-92	Michigan State	CCHA	39	2	10	12	42	....	....	....	....	....
1992-93	Michigan State	CCHA	33	3	6	9	34	....	....	....	....	....

McCLELLAND, KEVIN WILLIAM

Right wing. Shoots right. 6'2", 205 lbs. Born, Oshawa, Ont., July 4, 1962.
(Hartford's 4th choice, 71st overall, in 1980 Entry Draft).

			Regular Season					Playoffs				
Season	Club	Lea	GP	G	A	TP	PIM	GP	G	A	TP	PIM
1980-81	Niagara Falls	OHA	68	36	72	108	186	12	8	13	21	42
1981-82	**Pittsburgh**	**NHL**	**10**	**1**	**4**	**5**	**4**	**5**	**1**	**1**	**2**	**5**
	Niagara Falls	OHL	46	36	47	83	184	....	....	....	....	....
1982-83	**Pittsburgh**	**NHL**	**38**	**5**	**4**	**9**	**73**	....	....	....	....	....
1983-84	**Pittsburgh**	**NHL**	**24**	**2**	**4**	**6**	**62**	....	....	....	....	....
	Baltimore	AHL	3	1	1	2	0	....	....	....	....	....
	Edmonton	**NHL**	**52**	**8**	**20**	**28**	**127**	**18**	**4**	**6**	**10**	**42**
1984-85	**Edmonton**	**NHL**	**62**	**8**	**15**	**23**	**205**	**18**	**1**	**3**	**4**	**75**
1985-86	**Edmonton**	**NHL**	**79**	**11**	**25**	**36**	**266**	**10**	**1**	**0**	**1**	**32**
1986-87	**Edmonton**	**NHL**	**72**	**12**	**13**	**25**	**238**	**21**	**2**	**3**	**5**	**43**
1987-88	**Edmonton**	**NHL**	**74**	**10**	**6**	**16**	**281**	**19**	**2**	**3**	**5**	**68**
1988-89	**Edmonton**	**NHL**	**79**	**6**	**14**	**20**	**161**	**7**	**0**	**2**	**2**	**16**
1989-90	**Edmonton**	**NHL**	**10**	**1**	**1**	**2**	**13**	....	....	....	....	....
	Detroit	**NHL**	**61**	**4**	**5**	**9**	**183**	....	....	....	....	....
1990-91	**Detroit**	**NHL**	**3**	**0**	**0**	**0**	**7**	....	....	....	....	....
	Adirondack	AHL	27	5	14	19	125	....	....	....	....	....
1991-92	**Toronto**	**NHL**	**18**	**0**	**1**	**1**	**33**	....	....	....	....	....
	St. John's	AHL	34	7	15	22	199	5	0	1	1	9
1992-93	St. John's	AHL	55	7	20	27	221	1	0	0	0	7
	NHL Totals		**582**	**68**	**112**	**180**	**1653**	**98**	**11**	**18**	**29**	**281**

Traded to **Pittsburgh** by **Hartford** with Pat Boutette as compensation for Hartford's signing of free agent goaltender Greg Millen, June 29, 1981. Traded to **Edmonton** by **Pittsburgh** with Pittsburgh's sixth round choice (Emanuel Viveiros) in 1984 Entry Draft for Tom Roulston, December 5, 1983. Traded to **Detroit** by **Edmonton** with Jimmy Carson and Edmonton's fifth round choice (later traded to Montreal — Montreal selected Brad Layzell) in 1991 Entry Draft for Petr Klima, Joe Murphy, Adam Graves and Jeff Sharples, November 2, 1989. Signed as a free agent by **Toronto**, September 2, 1991. Traded to **Winnipeg** by **Toronto** for cash, August 12, 1993.

McCOSH, SHAWN

Center. Shoots right. 6', 188 lbs. Born, Oshawa, Ont., June 5, 1969.
(Detroit's 5th choice, 95th overall, in 1989 Entry Draft).

			Regular Season					Playoffs				
Season	Club	Lea	GP	G	A	TP	PIM	GP	G	A	TP	PIM
1986-87	Hamilton	OHL	50	11	17	28	49	6	1	0	1	2
1987-88	Hamilton	OHL	64	17	36	53	96	14	6	8	14	14
1988-89	Niagara Falls	OHL	56	41	62	103	75	14	4	13	17	23
1989-90	Niagara Falls	OHL	9	6	10	16	24	....	....	....	....	....
	Hamilton	OHL	39	24	28	52	65	....	....	....	....	....
1990-91	New Haven	AHL	66	16	21	37	104	....	....	....	....	....
1991-92	**Los Angeles**	**NHL**	**4**	**0**	**0**	**0**	**4**	....	....	....	....	....
	Phoenix	IHL	71	21	32	53	118	....	....	....	....	....
	New Haven	AHL	....	....	....	....	....	5	0	1	1	0
1992-93	New Haven	AHL	46	22	32	54	54	....	....	....	....	....
	Phoenix	IHL	22	9	8	17	36	....	....	....	....	....
	NHL Totals		**4**	**0**	**0**	**0**	**4**					

Traded to **Los Angeles** by **Detroit** for future considerations, August 15, 1990. Traded to **Ottawa** by **Los Angeles** with Bob Kudelski for Marc Fortier and Jim Thomson, December 19, 1992. Signed as a free agent by **NY Rangers**, August 17, 1993.

McCOSH, SHAYNE

Defense. Shoots left. 6', 183 lbs. Born, Oshawa, Ont., January 27, 1974.

			Regular Season					Playoffs				
Season	Club	Lea	GP	G	A	TP	PIM	GP	G	A	TP	PIM
1990-91	Kitchener	OHL	62	3	22	25	26	6	0	1	1	4
1991-92	Kitchener	OHL	62	7	36	43	46	14	1	2	3	28
1992-93	Windsor	OHL	68	12	60	72	81	....	....	....	....	....

Signed as a free agent by **Hartford**, October 5, 1992.

McCRIMMON, BYRON (BRAD)

Defense. Shoots left. 5'11", 197 lbs. Born, Dodsland, Sask., March 29, 1959.
(Boston's 2nd choice, 15th overall, in 1979 Entry Draft).

			Regular Season					Playoffs				
Season	Club	Lea	GP	G	A	TP	PIM	GP	G	A	TP	PIM
1977-78ab	Brandon	WHL	65	19	78	97	245	8	2	11	13	20
1978-79a	Brandon	WHL	66	24	74	98	139	22	9	19	28	34
1979-80	Boston	NHL	72	5	11	16	94	10	1	1	2	28
1980-81	Boston	NHL	78	11	18	29	148	3	0	1	1	2
1981-82	Boston	NHL	78	1	8	9	83	2	0	0	0	2
1982-83	Philadelphia	NHL	79	4	21	25	61	3	0	0	0	4
1983-84	Philadelphia	NHL	71	0	24	24	76	1	0	0	0	4
1984-85	Philadelphia	NHL	66	8	35	43	81	11	2	1	3	15
1985-86	Philadelphia	NHL	80	13	43	56	85	5	2	0	2	2
1986-87	Philadelphia	NHL	71	10	29	39	52	26	3	5	8	30
1987-88cd	Calgary	NHL	80	7	35	42	98	9	2	3	5	22
1988-89	Calgary	NHL	72	5	17	22	96	22	0	3	3	30
1989-90	Calgary	NHL	79	4	15	19	78	6	0	2	2	8
1990-91	Detroit	NHL	64	0	13	13	81	7	1	1	2	21
1991-92	Detroit	NHL	79	7	22	29	118	11	0	1	1	8
1992-93	Detroit	NHL	60	1	14	15	71	....	....	....	....	....
	NHL Totals		1029	76	305	381	1222	116	11	18	29	176

a WHL First All-Star Team (1978, 1979)
b Named WHL's Top Defenseman (1978)
c NHL Second All-Star Team (1988)
d NHL Plus/Minus Leader (1988)

Played in NHL All-Star Game (1988)

Traded to **Philadelphia** by **Boston** for Pete Peeters, June 9, 1982. Traded to **Calgary** by **Philadelphia** for Calgary's third round choice (Dominic Roussel) in 1988 Entry Draft and first round choice (later traded to Toronto — Toronto selected Steve Bancroft) in 1989 Entry Draft, August 26, 1987. Traded to **Detroit** by **Calgary** for Detroit's second round choice (later traded to New Jersey — New Jersey selected David Harlock) in 1990 Entry Draft, June 15, 1990. Traded to **Hartford** by **Detroit** for Detroit's sixth round choice (previously acquired by Hartford — Detroit selected Tim Spitzig) in 1993 Entry Draft, June 1, 1993.

McDONOUGH, HUBIE

Center. Shoots left. 5'9", 180 lbs. Born, Manchester, NH, July 8, 1963.

			Regular Season					Playoffs				
Season	Club	Lea	GP	G	A	TP	PIM	GP	G	A	TP	PIM
1986-87	Flint	IHL	82	27	52	79	59	6	3	2	5	0
1987-88	New Haven	AHL	78	30	29	59	43	....	....	....	....	....
1988-89	Los Angeles	NHL	4	0	1	1	0	....	....	....	....	....
	New Haven	AHL	74	37	55	92	41	17	10	*21	*31	6
1989-90	Los Angeles	NHL	22	3	4	7	10	....	....	....	....	....
	NY Islanders	NHL	54	18	11	29	26	5	1	0	1	4
1990-91	NY Islanders	NHL	52	6	6	12	10	....	....	....	....	....
	Capital Dist.	AHL	17	9	9	18	4	....	....	....	....	....
1991-92	NY Islanders	NHL	33	7	2	9	15	....	....	....	....	....
	Capital Dist.	AHL	21	11	18	29	14	....	....	....	....	....
1992-93	San Jose	NHL	30	6	2	8	6	....	....	....	....	....
	San Diego	IHL	48	26	49	75	26	14	4	7	11	6
	NHL Totals		195	40	26	66	67	5	1	0	1	4

a IHL Second All-Star Team (1993)

Signed as a free agent by **Los Angeles**, April 18, 1988. Traded to **NY Islanders** by **Los Angeles** with Ken Baumgartner for Mikko Makela, November 29, 1989. Traded to **San Jose** by **NY Islanders** for cash, August 28, 1992.

McDOUGALL, WILLIAM HENRY

Center. Shoots right. 6', 185 lbs. Born, Mississauga, Ont., August 10, 1966.

			Regular Season					Playoffs				
Season	Club	Lea	GP	G	A	TP	PIM	GP	G	A	TP	PIM
1988-89	Pt. Basques	Sr.	26	20	41	61	129	....	....	....	....	....
1989-90abc	Erie	ECHL	57	80	68	148	226	7	5	5	10	20
	Adirondack	AHL	11	10	7	17	4	2	1	1	2	2
1990-91	Detroit	NHL	2	0	1	1	0	1	0	0	0	0
	Adirondack	AHL	71	47	52	99	192	2	1	2	3	2
1991-92	Adirondack	AHL	45	28	24	52	112	....	....	....	....	....
	Cape Breton	AHL	22	8	18	26	36	4	0	1	1	8
1992-93	Edmonton	NHL	4	2	1	3	4	....	....	....	....	....
d	Cape Breton	AHL	71	42	46	88	16	16	*26	*26	*52	30
	NHL Totals		6	2	2	4	4	1	0	0	0	0

a Named ECHL Most Valuable Player (1990)
b Named ECHL Rookie of the Year (1990)
c ECHL First Team All-Star (1990)
d Won Jack A. Butterfield Trophy (AHL Playoff MVP) (1993)

Signed as a free agent by **Detroit**, January 9, 1990. Traded to **Edmonton** by **Detroit** for Max Middendorf, February 22, 1992.

McEACHERN, SHAWN

Center. Shoots left. 5'11", 195 lbs. Born, Waltham, MA, February 28, 1969.
(Pittsburgh's 6th choice, 110th overall, in 1987 Entry Draft).

			Regular Season					Playoffs				
Season	Club	Lea	GP	G	A	TP	PIM	GP	G	A	TP	PIM
1988-89	Boston U.	H.E.	36	20	28	48	32	....	....	....	....	....
1989-90a	Boston U.	H.E.	43	25	31	56	78	....	....	....	....	....
1990-91bc	Boston U.	H.E.	41	34	48	82	43	....	....	....	....	....
1991-92	U.S. National	....	57	26	23	49	38	....	....	....	....	....
	U.S. Olympic	....	8	1	0	1	10	....	....	....	....	....
	Pittsburgh	NHL	15	0	4	4	0	19	2	7	9	4
1992-93	Pittsburgh	NHL	84	28	33	61	46	12	3	2	5	10
	NHL Totals		99	28	37	65	46	31	5	9	14	14

a Hockey East Second All-Star Team (1990)
b Hockey East First All-Star Team (1991)
c NCAA East First All-American Team (1991)

Traded to **Los Angeles** by **Pittsburgh** for Marty McSorley, August 27, 1993.

McGILL, BOB

Defense. Shoots right. 6'1", 193 lbs. Born, Edmonton, Alta., April 27, 1962.
(Toronto's 2nd choice, 26th overall, in 1980 Entry Draft).

			Regular Season					Playoffs				
Season	Club	Lea	GP	G	A	TP	PIM	GP	G	A	TP	PIM
1979-80	Victoria	WHL	70	3	18	21	230	15	0	5	5	64
1980-81	Victoria	WHL	66	5	36	41	295	11	1	5	6	67
1981-82	Toronto	NHL	68	1	10	11	263	....	....	....	....	....
1982-83	Toronto	NHL	30	0	0	0	146	....	....	....	....	....
	St. Catharines	AHL	32	2	5	7	95	....	....	....	....	....
1983-84	Toronto	NHL	11	0	2	2	51	....	....	....	....	....
	St. Catharines	AHL	55	1	15	16	217	6	0	0	0	26
1984-85	Toronto	NHL	72	0	5	5	250	....	....	....	....	....
1985-86	Toronto	NHL	61	1	4	5	141	9	0	0	0	35
1986-87	Toronto	NHL	56	1	4	5	103	3	0	0	0	0
1987-88	Chicago	NHL	67	4	7	11	131	3	0	0	0	2
1988-89	Chicago	NHL	68	0	4	4	155	16	0	0	0	33
1989-90	Chicago	NHL	69	2	10	12	204	5	0	0	0	2
1990-91	Chicago	NHL	77	4	5	9	151	5	0	0	0	2
1991-92	San Jose	NHL	62	3	1	4	70	....	....	....	....	....
	Detroit	NHL	12	0	0	0	21	8	0	0	0	14
1992-93	Toronto	NHL	19	1	0	1	34	....	....	....	....	....
	NHL Totals		672	17	52	69	1720	49	0	0	0	88

Traded to **Chicago** by **Toronto** with Steve Thomas and Rick Vaive for Al Secord and Ed Olczyk, September 3, 1987. Claimed by **San Jose** from **Chicago** in Expansion Draft, May 30, 1991. Traded to **Detroit** by **San Jose** with Vancouver's eighth round choice (previously acquired by San Jose — Detroit selected C.J. Denomme) in 1992 Entry Draft, March 10, 1992. Claimed by **Tampa Bay** from **Detroit** in Expansion Draft, June 18, 1992. Claimed on waivers by **Toronto** from **Tampa Bay**, September 9, 1992.

McGILL, RYAN

Defense. Shoots right. 6'2", 195 lbs. Born, Prince Albert, Sask., February 28, 1969.
(Chicago's 2nd choice, 29th overall, in 1987 Entry Draft).

			Regular Season					Playoffs				
Season	Club	Lea	GP	G	A	TP	PIM	GP	G	A	TP	PIM
1985-86	Lethbridge	WHL	64	5	10	15	171	10	0	1	1	9
1986-87	Swift Current	WHL	72	12	36	48	226	4	1	0	1	9
1987-88	Medicine Hat	WHL	67	5	30	35	224	15	7	3	10	47
1988-89	Medicine Hat	WHL	57	26	45	71	172	3	0	2	2	15
	Saginaw	IHL	8	2	0	2	12	6	0	0	0	42
1989-90	Indianapolis	IHL	77	11	17	28	215	14	2	2	4	29
1990-91	Halifax	AHL	7	0	4	4	6	....	....	....	....	....
a	Indianapolis	IHL	63	11	40	51	200	....	....	....	....	....
1991-92	Chicago	NHL	9	0	2	2	20	....	....	....	....	....
	Indianapolis	IHL	40	7	19	26	170	....	....	....	....	....
	Hershey	AHL	17	3	5	8	67	6	1	1	2	4
1992-93	Philadelphia	NHL	72	3	10	13	238	....	....	....	....	....
	Hershey	AHL	4	0	2	2	26	....	....	....	....	....
	NHL Totals		81	3	12	15	258	....	....	....	....	....

a IHL Second All-Star Team (1991)

Traded to **Quebec** by **Chicago** with Mike McNeil for Paul Gillis and Dan Vincelette, March 5, 1991. Traded to **Chicago** by **Quebec** for Mike Dagenais, September 27, 1991. Traded to **Philadelphia** by **Chicago** for Tony Horacek, February 7, 1992.

McGILLIS, DANIEL

Defense. Shoots left. 6'2", 220 lbs. Born, Hawkesbury, Ont., July 1, 1972.
(Detroit's 10th choice, 238th overall, in 1992 Entry Draft).

			Regular Season					Playoffs				
Season	Club	Lea	GP	G	A	TP	PIM	GP	G	A	TP	PIM
1991-92	Hawkesbury	COJHL	36	5	19	24	106	....	....	....	....	....
1992-93	Northeastern	H.E.	35	5	12	17	42	....	....	....	....	....

McGOWAN, CAL

Center. Shoots left. 6'1", 185 lbs. Born, Sydney, N.S., June 19, 1970.
(Minnesota's 3rd choice, 70th overall, in 1990 Entry Draft).

			Regular Season					Playoffs				
Season	Club	Lea	GP	G	A	TP	PIM	GP	G	A	TP	PIM
1988-89	Kamloops	WHL	72	21	31	52	44	....	....	....	....	....
1989-90	Kamloops	WHL	71	33	45	78	76	17	4	5	9	42
1990-91a	Kamloops	WHL	71	58	81	139	147	12	7	7	14	24
1991-92	Kalamazoo	IHL	77	13	30	43	62	1	0	0	0	2
1992-93	Kalamazoo	IHL	78	18	42	60	62	....	....	....	....	....

a WHL West First All-Star Team (1991)

McHUGH, MICHAEL (MIKE)

Left wing. Shoots left. 5'10", 190 lbs. Born, Bowdoin, MA, August 16, 1965.
(Minnesota's 1st choice, 1st overall, in 1988 Supplemental Draft).

			Regular Season					Playoffs				
Season	Club	Lea	GP	G	A	TP	PIM	GP	G	A	TP	PIM
1984-85	U. of Maine	H.E.	25	9	8	17	9	....	....	....	....	....
1985-86	U. of Maine	H.E.	38	9	10	19	24	....	....	....	....	....
1986-87	U. of Maine	H.E.	42	21	29	50	40	....	....	....	....	....
1987-88	U. of Maine	H.E.	44	29	37	66	90	....	....	....	....	....
1988-89	Minnesota	NHL	3	0	0	0	2	....	....	....	....	....
	Kalamazoo	IHL	70	17	29	46	89	6	3	1	4	17
1989-90	Minnesota	NHL	3	0	0	0	0	....	....	....	....	....
	Kalamazoo	IHL	73	14	17	31	96	10	0	6	6	16
1990-91	Minnesota	NHL	6	0	0	0	0	....	....	....	....	....
	Kalamazoo	IHL	69	27	38	65	82	11	3	8	11	6
1991-92	San Jose	NHL	8	1	0	1	14	....	....	....	....	....
	Springfield	AHL	70	23	31	54	51	11	4	7	11	25
1992-93	Springfield	AHL	67	19	27	46	111	11	5	2	7	12
	NHL Totals		20	1	0	1	16	....	....	....	....	....

Claimed by **San Jose** from **Minnesota** in Dispersal Draft, May 30, 1991. Traded to **Hartford** by **San Jose** for Paul Fenton, October 18, 1991.

McINNIS, MARTY

Center. Shoots right. 6', 185 lbs. Born, Hingham, MA., June 2, 1970.
(NY Islanders' 10th choice, 163rd overall, in 1988 Entry Draft).

			Regular Season					Playoffs				
Season	Club	Lea	GP	G	A	TP	PIM	GP	G	A	TP	PIM
1988-89	Boston College	H.E.	39	13	19	32	8	....	....	....	....	....
1989-90	Boston College	H.E.	41	24	29	53	43	....	....	....	....	....
1990-91	Boston College	H.E.	38	21	36	57	40	....	....	....	....	....
1991-92	U.S. National	....	54	15	19	34	20	....	....	....	....	....
	U.S. Olympic	....	8	6	2	8	4	....	....	....	....	....
	NY Islanders	**NHL**	**15**	**3**	**5**	**8**	**0**	....	....	....	....	....
1992-93	**NY Islanders**	**NHL**	**56**	**10**	**20**	**30**	**24**	**3**	**0**	**1**	**1**	**0**
	Capital Dist.	AHL	10	4	12	16	2	....	....	....	....	....
	NHL Totals		**71**	**13**	**25**	**38**	**24**	**3**	**0**	**1**	**1**	**0**

McINTYRE, IAN

Defense. Shoots left. 6', 187 lbs. Born, Montreal, Que., February 12, 1974.
(Quebec's 5th choice, 76th overall, in 1992 Entry Draft).

			Regular Season					Playoffs				
Season	Club	Lea	GP	G	A	TP	PIM	GP	G	A	TP	PIM
1991-92	Beauport	QMJHL	63	29	32	61	250	....	....	....	....	....
1992-93	Beauport	QMJHL	44	14	18	32	115	....	....	....	....	....

McINTYRE, JOHN

Center. Shoots left. 6'1", 180 lbs. Born, Ravenswood, Ont., April 29, 1969.
(Toronto's 3rd choice, 49th overall, in 1987 Entry Draft).

			Regular Season					Playoffs				
Season	Club	Lea	GP	G	A	TP	PIM	GP	G	A	TP	PIM
1985-86	Guelph	OHL	30	4	6	10	25	20	1	5	6	31
1986-87	Guelph	OHL	47	8	22	30	95	....	....	....	....	....
1987-88	Guelph	OHL	39	24	18	42	109	....	....	....	....	....
1988-89	Guelph	OHL	52	30	26	56	129	7	5	4	9	25
	Newmarket	AHL	3	0	2	2	7	5	1	1	2	20
1989-90	**Toronto**	**NHL**	**59**	**5**	**12**	**17**	**117**	**2**	**0**	**0**	**0**	**2**
	Newmarket	AHL	6	2	2	4	12	....	....	....	....	....
1990-91	**Toronto**	**NHL**	**13**	**0**	**3**	**3**	**25**	....	....	....	....	....
	Los Angeles	**NHL**	**56**	**8**	**5**	**13**	**115**	**12**	**0**	**1**	**1**	**24**
1991-92	**Los Angeles**	**NHL**	**73**	**5**	**19**	**24**	**100**	**6**	**0**	**4**	**4**	**12**
1992-93	**Los Angeles**	**NHL**	**49**	**2**	**5**	**7**	**80**	....	....	....	....	....
	NY Rangers	**NHL**	**11**	**1**	**0**	**1**	**4**	....	....	....	....	....
	NHL Totals		**261**	**21**	**44**	**65**	**441**	**20**	**0**	**5**	**5**	**38**

Traded to **Los Angeles** by **Toronto** for Mike Krushelnyski, November 9, 1990. Traded to **NY Rangers** by **Los Angeles** for Mark Hardy and Ottawa's fifth round choice (previously acquired by NY Rangers — Los Angeles selected Frederick Beaubien) in 1993 Entry Draft, March 22, 1993.

McINTYRE, ROBB

Left wing. Shoots left. 6', 180 lbs. Born, Royal Oak, MI, April 27, 1972.
(Toronto's 10th choice, 164th overall, in 1991 Entry Draft).

			Regular Season					Playoffs				
Season	Club	Lea	GP	G	A	TP	PIM	GP	G	A	TP	PIM
1991-92	Ferris State	CCHA	32	4	3	7	48	....	....	....	....	....
1992-93	Ferris State	CCHA	32	10	9	19	76	....	....	....	....	....

McKAY, RANDY

Right wing. Shoots right. 6'1", 205 lbs. Born, Montreal, Que., January 25, 1967.
(Detroit's 6th choice, 113th overall, in 1985 Entry Draft).

			Regular Season					Playoffs				
Season	Club	Lea	GP	G	A	TP	PIM	GP	G	A	TP	PIM
1984-85	Michigan Tech	WCHA	25	4	5	9	32	....	....	....	....	....
1985-86	Michigan Tech	WCHA	40	12	22	34	46	....	....	....	....	....
1986-87	Michigan Tech	WCHA	39	5	11	16	46	....	....	....	....	....
1987-88	Michigan Tech	WCHA	41	17	24	41	70	....	....	....	....	....
	Adirondack	AHL	10	0	3	3	12	6	0	4	4	0
1988-89	**Detroit**	**NHL**	**3**	**0**	**0**	**0**	**0**	**2**	**0**	**0**	**0**	**2**
	Adirondack	AHL	58	29	34	63	170	14	4	7	11	60
1989-90	**Detroit**	**NHL**	**33**	**3**	**6**	**9**	**51**	....	....	....	....	....
	Adirondack	AHL	36	16	23	39	99	6	3	0	3	35
1990-91	**Detroit**	**NHL**	**47**	**1**	**7**	**8**	**183**	**5**	**0**	**1**	**1**	**41**
1991-92	**New Jersey**	**NHL**	**80**	**17**	**16**	**33**	**246**	**7**	**1**	**3**	**4**	**10**
1992-93	**New Jersey**	**NHL**	**73**	**11**	**11**	**22**	**206**	**5**	**0**	**0**	**0**	**16**
	NHL Totals		**236**	**32**	**40**	**72**	**686**	**19**	**1**	**4**	**5**	**69**

Acquired by **New Jersey** from **Detroit** with Dave Barr as compensation for Detroit's signing of free agent Troy Crowder, September 9, 1991.

McKEE, MIKE

Left wing. Shoots right. 6'3", 190 lbs. Born, Toronto, Ont., June 18, 1969.
(Quebec's 1st choice, 1st overall, in 1990 Supplemental Draft).

			Regular Season					Playoffs				
Season	Club	Lea	GP	G	A	TP	PIM	GP	G	A	TP	PIM
1988-89	Princeton	ECAC	16	2	1	3	14	....	....	....	....	....
1989-90a	Princeton	ECAC	26	7	18	25	18	....	....	....	....	....
1990-91	Princeton	ECAC	15	1	4	5	16	....	....	....	....	....
1991-92	Princeton	ECAC	27	12	17	29	34	....	....	....	....	....
1992-93	Halifax	AHL	32	6	7	13	25	....	....	....	....	....
	Greensboro	ECHL	7	1	3	4	6	....	....	....	....	....

a ECAC Second All-Star Team (1990)

McKENZIE, JIM

Left wing/Defense. Shoots left. 6'3", 205 lbs. Born, Gull Lake, Sask., November 3, 1969.
(Hartford's 3rd choice, 73rd overall, in 1989 Entry Draft).

			Regular Season					Playoffs				
Season	Club	Lea	GP	G	A	TP	PIM	GP	G	A	TP	PIM
1985-86	Moose Jaw	WHL	3	0	2	2	0	....	....	....	....	....
1986-87	Moose Jaw	WHL	65	5	3	8	125	9	0	0	0	7
1987-88	Moose Jaw	WHL	62	1	17	18	134	....	....	....	....	....
1988-89	Victoria	WHL	67	15	27	42	176	8	1	4	5	30
1989-90	**Hartford**	**NHL**	**5**	**0**	**0**	**0**	**4**	....	....	....	....	....
	Binghamton	AHL	56	4	12	16	149	....	....	....	....	....
1990-91	**Hartford**	**NHL**	**41**	**4**	**3**	**7**	**108**	**6**	**0**	**0**	**0**	**8**
	Springfield	AHL	24	3	4	7	102	....	....	....	....	....
1991-92	**Hartford**	**NHL**	**67**	**5**	**1**	**6**	**87**	....	....	....	....	....
1992-93	**Hartford**	**NHL**	**64**	**3**	**6**	**9**	**202**	....	....	....	....	....
	NHL Totals		**177**	**12**	**10**	**22**	**401**	**6**	**0**	**0**	**0**	**8**

McKIM, ANDREW HARRY

Center. Shoots right. 5'8", 175 lbs. Born, St. John, N.B., July 6, 1970.

			Regular Season					Playoffs				
Season	Club	Lea	GP	G	A	TP	PIM	GP	G	A	TP	PIM
1988-89	Verdun	QMJHL	68	50	56	106	36	....	....	....	....	....
1989-90ab	Hull	QMJHL	70	66	84	130	44	11	8	10	18	8
1990-91	Salt Lake	IHL	74	30	30	60	48	4	0	2	2	6
1991-92	St. John's	AHL	79	43	50	93	79	16	11	12	23	4
1992-93	**Boston**	**NHL**	**7**	**1**	**3**	**4**	**0**	....	....	....	....	....
	Providence	AHL	61	23	46	69	64	6	2	2	4	0
	NHL Totals		**7**	**1**	**3**	**4**	**0**	....	....	....	....	....

a QMJHL First All-Star Team (1990)
b QMJHL Player of the Year (1990)

Signed as a free agent by **Calgary**, October 5, 1990. Signed as a free agent by **Boston**, July 23, 1992.

McLAUGHLIN, MICHAEL

Left wing. Shoots left. 6'1", 175 lbs. Born, Longmeadow, MA, March 29, 1970.
(Buffalo's 7th choice, 118th overall, in 1988 Entry Draft).

			Regular Season					Playoffs				
Season	Club	Lea	GP	G	A	TP	PIM	GP	G	A	TP	PIM
1988-89	U. of Vermont	ECAC	32	5	6	11	12	....	....	....	....	....
1989-90	U. of Vermont	ECAC	29	11	12	23	37	....	....	....	....	....
1990-91	U. of Vermont	ECAC	32	12	14	26	34	....	....	....	....	....
1991-92	U. of Vermont	ECAC	30	9	9	18	34	....	....	....	....	....
1992-93	Rochester	AHL	71	19	35	54	27	16	4	2	6	8

Signed as a free agent by **NY Rangers**, August 17, 1993.

McLAUGHLIN, PETER

Defense. Shoots left. 6'3", 190 lbs. Born, Norwood, MA, June 29, 1973.
(Pittsburgh's 8th choice, 170th overall, in 1991 Entry Draft).

			Regular Season					Playoffs				
Season	Club	Lea	GP	G	A	TP	PIM	GP	G	A	TP	PIM
1991-92	Belmont Hills	HS	22	22	18	40	24	....	....	....	....	....
1992-93	Harvard	ECAC	31	2	6	8	28	....	....	....	....	....

McLEAN, JEFF

Center. Shoots left. 5'10", 185 lbs. Born, Port Moody, B.C., October 6, 1969.
(San Jose's 1st choice, 1st overall, in 1991 Supplemental Draft).

			Regular Season					Playoffs				
Season	Club	Lea	GP	G	A	TP	PIM	GP	G	A	TP	PIM
1989-90	North Dakota	WCHA	45	10	16	26	42	....	....	....	....	....
1990-91	North Dakota	WCHA	42	19	26	45	22	....	....	....	....	....
1991-92	North Dakota	WCHA	38	27	43	70	40	....	....	....	....	....
1992-93	Kansas City	IHL	60	21	23	44	45	10	3	1	4	2

McLLWAIN, DAVE (MA-kuhl-WAYN)

Center/Right wing. Shoots left. 6', 185 lbs. Born, Seaforth, Ont., January 9, 1967.
(Pittsburgh's 9th choice, 172nd overall, in 1986 Entry Draft).

			Regular Season					Playoffs				
Season	Club	Lea	GP	G	A	TP	PIM	GP	G	A	TP	PIM
1984-85	Kitchener	OHL	61	13	21	34	29	....	....	....	....	....
1985-86	Kitchener	OHL	13	7	7	14	12	....	....	....	....	....
	North Bay	OHL	51	30	28	58	25	10	4	4	8	2
1986-87a	North Bay	OHL	60	46	73	119	35	24	7	18	25	40
1987-88	**Pittsburgh**	**NHL**	**66**	**11**	**8**	**19**	**40**	....	....	....	....	....
	Muskegon	IHL	9	4	6	10	23	6	2	3	5	8
1988-89	**Pittsburgh**	**NHL**	**24**	**1**	**2**	**3**	**4**	**3**	**0**	**1**	**1**	**0**
	Muskegon	IHL	46	37	35	72	51	7	8	2	10	6
1989-90	**Winnipeg**	**NHL**	**80**	**25**	**26**	**51**	**60**	**7**	**0**	**1**	**1**	**2**
1990-91	**Winnipeg**	**NHL**	**60**	**14**	**11**	**25**	**46**	....	....	....	....	....
1991-92	**Winnipeg**	**NHL**	**3**	**1**	**1**	**2**	**2**	....	....	....	....	....
	Buffalo	**NHL**	**5**	**0**	**0**	**0**	**2**	....	....	....	....	....
	NY Islanders	**NHL**	**54**	**8**	**15**	**23**	**28**	....	....	....	....	....
	Toronto	**NHL**	**11**	**1**	**2**	**3**	**4**	....	....	....	....	....
1992-93	**Toronto**	**NHL**	**66**	**14**	**4**	**18**	**30**	**4**	**0**	**0**	**0**	**0**
	NHL Totals		**369**	**75**	**69**	**144**	**216**	**14**	**0**	**2**	**2**	**2**

a OHL Second All-Star Team (1987)

Traded to **Winnipeg** by **Pittsburgh** with Randy Cunneyworth and Rick Tabaracci for Jim Kyte, Andrew McBain and Randy Gilhen, June 17, 1989. Traded to **Buffalo** by **Winnipeg** with Gord Donnelly, Winnipeg's fifth round choice (Yuri Khmylev) in 1992 Entry Draft and future considerations for Darrin Shannon, Mike Hartman and Dean Kennedy, October 11, 1991. Traded to **NY Islanders** by **Buffalo** with Pierre Turgeon, Uwe Krupp and Benoit Hogue for Pat Lafontaine, Randy Hillier, Randy Wood and future considerations, October 25, 1991. Traded to **Toronto** by **NY Islanders** with Ken Baumgartner for Daniel Marois and Claude Loiselle, March 10, 1992.

McMURTRY, CHRIS

Defense. Shoots left. 6'4", 190 lbs. Born, Hamilton, Ont., July 13, 1974.

			Regular Season					Playoffs				
Season	Club	Lea	GP	G	A	TP	PIM	GP	G	A	TP	PIM
1991-92	Guelph	OHL	55	2	9	11	56	....	....	....	....	....
1992-93	Guelph	OHL	57	1	10	11	38	....	....	....	....	....

Signed as a free agent by **Toronto**, October 5, 1992.

McNEILL, MICHAEL

Right wing. Shoots left. 6'1", 195 lbs. Born, Winona, MN, July 22, 1966.
(St. Louis' 1st choice, 14th overall, in 1988 Supplemental Draft).

			Regular Season					Playoffs				
Season	Club	Lea	GP	G	A	TP	PIM	GP	G	A	TP	PIM
1984-85	Notre Dame	NCAA	28	16	26	42	12	....	....	....	....	....
1985-86	Notre Dame	NCAA	34	18	29	47	32	....	....	....	....	....
1986-87	Notre Dame	NCAA	30	21	16	37	24	....	....	....	....	....
1987-88	Notre Dame	NCAA	32	28	44	72	12	....	....	....	....	....
1988-89	Moncton	AHL	1	0	0	0	0	....	....	....	....	....
	Fort Wayne	IHL	75	27	35	62	12	11	1	5	6	2
1989-90a	Indianapolis	IHL	74	17	24	41	10	14	6	4	10	21
1990-91	**Chicago**	**NHL**	**23**	**2**	**2**	**4**	**6**	....	....	....	....	....
	Indianapolis	IHL	33	16	9	25	19	....	....	....	....	....
	Quebec	**NHL**	**14**	**2**	**5**	**7**	**4**	....	....	....	....	....
1991-92	**Quebec**	**NHL**	**26**	**1**	**4**	**5**	**8**	....	....	....	....	....
	Halifax	AHL	30	10	8	18	20	....	....	....	....	....
1992-93	Milwaukee	IHL	75	17	17	34	34	6	2	0	2	0
	NHL Totals		**63**	**5**	**11**	**16**	**18**	....	....	....	....	....

a Won N.R. Poile Trophy (Playoff MVP–IHL) (1990)

Signed as a free agent by **Chicago**, September, 1989. Traded to **Quebec** by **Chicago** with Ryan McGill for Paul Gillis and Dan Vincelette, March 5, 1991.

McPHEE, MICHAEL JOSEPH (MIKE)

Left wing. Shoots left. 6'1", 203 lbs. Born, Sydney, N.S., July 14, 1960.
(Montreal's 8th choice, 124th overall, in 1980 Entry Draft).

			Regular Season					Playoffs				
Season	Club	Lea	GP	G	A	TP	PIM	GP	G	A	TP	PIM
1980-81	RPI	ECAC	29	28	18	46	22	....	....	....	....	....
1981-82	RPI	ECAC	6	0	3	3	4	....	....	....	....	....
1982-83	Nova Scotia	AHL	42	10	15	25	29	7	1	1	2	14
1983-84	**Montreal**	**NHL**	**14**	**5**	**2**	**7**	**41**	**15**	**1**	**0**	**1**	**31**
	Nova Scotia	AHL	67	22	33	55	101	....	....	....	....	....
1984-85	**Montreal**	**NHL**	**70**	**17**	**22**	**39**	**120**	**12**	**4**	**1**	**5**	**32**
1985-86	**Montreal**	**NHL**	**70**	**19**	**21**	**40**	**69**	**20**	**3**	**4**	**7**	**45**
1986-87	**Montreal**	**NHL**	**79**	**18**	**21**	**39**	**58**	**17**	**7**	**2**	**9**	**13**
1987-88	**Montreal**	**NHL**	**77**	**23**	**20**	**43**	**53**	**11**	**4**	**3**	**7**	**8**
1988-89	**Montreal**	**NHL**	**73**	**19**	**22**	**41**	**74**	**20**	**4**	**7**	**11**	**30**
1989-90	**Montreal**	**NHL**	**56**	**23**	**18**	**41**	**47**	**9**	**1**	**1**	**2**	**16**
1990-91	**Montreal**	**NHL**	**64**	**22**	**21**	**43**	**56**	**13**	**1**	**7**	**8**	**12**
1991-92	**Montreal**	**NHL**	**78**	**16**	**15**	**31**	**63**	**8**	**1**	**1**	**2**	**4**
1992-93	**Minnesota**	**NHL**	**84**	**18**	**22**	**40**	**44**	....	....	....	....	....
	NHL Totals		**665**	**180**	**184**	**364**	**625**	**125**	**26**	**26**	**52**	**191**

Played in NHL All-Star Game (1989)

Traded to **Minnesota** by **Montreal** for Minnesota's fifth round choice (Jeff Lank) in 1993 Entry Draft, August 14, 1992.

McRAE, BASIL PAUL

Left wing. Shoots left. 6'2", 205 lbs. Born, Beaverton, Ont., January 5, 1961.
(Quebec's 3rd choice, 87th overall, in 1980 Entry Draft).

			Regular Season					Playoffs				
Season	Club	Lea	GP	G	A	TP	PIM	GP	G	A	TP	PIM
1979-80	London	OHA	67	24	36	60	116	5	0	0	0	18
1980-81	London	OHA	65	29	23	52	266	....	....	....	....	....
1981-82	**Quebec**	**NHL**	**20**	**4**	**3**	**7**	**69**	**9**	**1**	**0**	**1**	**34**
	Fredericton	AHL	47	11	15	26	175	....	....	....	....	....
1982-83	**Quebec**	**NHL**	**22**	**1**	**1**	**2**	**59**	....	....	....	....	....
	Fredericton	AHL	53	22	19	41	146	12	1	5	6	75
1983-84	**Toronto**	**NHL**	**3**	**0**	**0**	**0**	**19**	....	....	....	....	....
	St. Catharines	AHL	78	14	25	39	187	6	0	0	0	40
1984-85	**Toronto**	**NHL**	**1**	**0**	**0**	**0**	**0**	....	....	....	....	....
	St. Catharines	AHL	72	30	25	55	186	....	....	....	....	....
1985-86	**Detroit**	**NHL**	**4**	**0**	**0**	**0**	**5**	....	....	....	....	....
	Adirondack	AHL	69	22	30	52	259	17	5	4	9	101
1986-87	**Detroit**	**NHL**	**36**	**2**	**2**	**4**	**193**	....	....	....	....	....
	Quebec	**NHL**	**33**	**9**	**5**	**14**	**149**	**13**	**3**	**1**	**4**	***99**
1987-88	**Minnesota**	**NHL**	**80**	**5**	**11**	**16**	**382**	....	....	....	....	....
1988-89	**Minnesota**	**NHL**	**78**	**12**	**19**	**31**	**365**	**5**	**0**	**0**	**0**	**58**
1989-90	**Minnesota**	**NHL**	**66**	**9**	**17**	**26**	***351**	**7**	**1**	**0**	**1**	**24**
1990-91	**Minnesota**	**NHL**	**40**	**1**	**3**	**4**	**224**	**22**	**1**	**1**	**2**	***94**
1991-92	**Minnesota**	**NHL**	**59**	**5**	**8**	**13**	**245**	....	....	....	....	....
1992-93	**Tampa Bay**	**NHL**	**14**	**2**	**3**	**5**	**71**	....	....	....	....	....
	St. Louis	**NHL**	**33**	**1**	**3**	**4**	**98**	**11**	**0**	**1**	**1**	**24**
	NHL Totals		**489**	**51**	**75**	**126**	**2230**	**67**	**6**	**3**	**9**	**333**

Traded to **Toronto** by **Quebec** for Richard Turmel, August 12, 1983. Signed as a free agent by **Detroit**, July 17, 1985. Traded to **Quebec** by **Detroit** with John Ogrodnick and Doug Shedden for Brent Ashton, Gilbert Delorme and Mark Kumpel, January 17, 1987. Signed as a free agent by **Minnesota**, June 29, 1987. Claimed by **Tampa Bay** from **Minnesota** in Expansion Draft, June 18, 1992. Traded to **St. Louis** by **Tampa Bay** with Doug Crossman and Tampa Bay's fourth round choice in 1996 Entry Draft for Jason Ruff and future considerations, January 28, 1993.

McRAE, KEN

Center. Shoots right. 6'1", 195 lbs. Born, Winchester, Ont., April 23, 1968.
(Quebec's 1st choice, 18th overall, in 1986 Entry Draft).

			Regular Season					Playoffs				
Season	Club	Lea	GP	G	A	TP	PIM	GP	G	A	TP	PIM
1985-86	Sudbury	OHL	66	25	49	74	127	4	2	1	3	12
1986-87	Sudbury	OHL	21	12	15	27	40	....	....	....	....	....
	Hamilton	OHL	20	7	12	19	25	7	1	1	2	12
1987-88	**Quebec**	**NHL**	**1**	**0**	**0**	**0**	**0**	....	....	....	....	....
	Hamilton	OHL	62	30	55	85	158	14	13	9	22	35
	Fredericton	AHL	....	....	....	....	....	3	0	0	0	8
1988-89	**Quebec**	**NHL**	**37**	**6**	**11**	**17**	**68**	....	....	....	....	....
	Halifax	AHL	41	20	21	41	87	....	....	....	....	....
1989-90	**Quebec**	**NHL**	**66**	**7**	**8**	**15**	**191**	....	....	....	....	....
1990-91	**Quebec**	**NHL**	**12**	**0**	**0**	**0**	**36**	....	....	....	....	....
	Halifax	AHL	60	10	36	46	193	....	....	....	....	....
1991-92	**Quebec**	**NHL**	**10**	**0**	**1**	**1**	**31**	....	....	....	....	....
	Halifax	AHL	52	30	41	71	184	....	....	....	....	....
1992-93	**Toronto**	**NHL**	**2**	**0**	**0**	**0**	**2**	....	....	....	....	....
	St. John's	AHL	64	30	44	74	135	9	6	6	12	27
	NHL Totals		**128**	**13**	**20**	**33**	**328**	....	....	....	....	....

Traded to **Toronto** by **Quebec** for Len Esau, July 21, 1992.

McREYNOLDS, BRIAN

Center. Shoots left. 6'1", 192 lbs. Born, Penetanguishene, Ont., January 5, 1965.
(NY Rangers' 6th choice, 112th overall, in 1985 Entry Draft).

			Regular Season					Playoffs				
Season	Club	Lea	GP	G	A	TP	PIM	GP	G	A	TP	PIM
1985-86	Michigan State	CCHA	45	14	24	38	78	....	....	....	....	....
1986-87	Michigan State	CCHA	45	16	24	40	68	....	....	....	....	....
1987-88	Michigan State	CCHA	43	10	24	34	50	....	....	....	....	....
1988-89	Cdn. National	....	58	5	25	30	59	....	....	....	....	....
1989-90	**Winnipeg**	**NHL**	**9**	**0**	**2**	**2**	**4**	....	....	....	....	....
	Moncton	AHL	72	18	41	59	87	....	....	....	....	....
1990-91	**NY Rangers**	**NHL**	**1**	**0**	**0**	**0**	**0**	....	....	....	....	....
	Binghamton	AHL	77	30	42	72	74	10	0	4	4	6
1991-92	Binghamton	AHL	48	19	28	47	22	7	2	2	4	12
1992-93	Binghamton	AHL	79	30	70	100	88	14	3	10	13	18
	NHL Totals		**10**	**0**	**2**	**2**	**4**	....	....	....	....	....

Signed as a free agent by **Winnipeg**, June 20, 1989. Traded to **NY Rangers** by **Winnipeg** for Simon Wheeldon, July 10, 1990.

McSORLEY, MARTIN J. (MARTY)

Defense. Shoots right. 6'1", 235 lbs. Born, Hamilton, Ont., May 18, 1963.

			Regular Season					Playoffs				
Season	Club	Lea	GP	G	A	TP	PIM	GP	G	A	TP	PIM
1981-82	Belleville	OHL	58	6	13	19	234	....	....	....	....	....
1982-83	Belleville	OHL	70	10	41	51	183	4	0	0	0	7
	Baltimore	AHL	2	0	0	0	22	....	....	....	....	....
1983-84	**Pittsburgh**	**NHL**	**72**	**2**	**7**	**9**	**224**	....	....	....	....	....
1984-85	**Pittsburgh**	**NHL**	**15**	**0**	**0**	**0**	**15**	....	....	....	....	....
	Baltimore	AHL	58	6	24	30	154	14	0	7	7	47
1985-86	**Edmonton**	**NHL**	**59**	**11**	**12**	**23**	**265**	**8**	**0**	**2**	**2**	**50**
	Nova Scotia	AHL	9	2	4	6	34	....	....	....	....	....
1986-87	**Edmonton**	**NHL**	**41**	**2**	**4**	**6**	**159**	**21**	**4**	**3**	**7**	**65**
	Nova Scotia	AHL	7	2	2	4	48	....	....	....	....	....
1987-88	**Edmonton**	**NHL**	**60**	**9**	**17**	**26**	**223**	**16**	**0**	**3**	**3**	**67**
1988-89	**Los Angeles**	**NHL**	**66**	**10**	**17**	**27**	**350**	**11**	**0**	**2**	**2**	**33**
1989-90	**Los Angeles**	**NHL**	**75**	**15**	**21**	**36**	**322**	**10**	**1**	**3**	**4**	**18**
1990-91a	**Los Angeles**	**NHL**	**61**	**7**	**32**	**39**	**221**	**12**	**0**	**0**	**0**	**58**
1991-92	**Los Angeles**	**NHL**	**71**	**7**	**22**	**29**	**268**	**6**	**1**	**0**	**1**	**21**
1992-93	**Los Angeles**	**NHL**	**81**	**15**	**26**	**41**	***399**	**24**	**4**	**6**	**10**	***60**
	NHL Totals		**601**	**78**	**158**	**236**	**2446**	**108**	**10**	**19**	**29**	**372**

a Co-winner of Alka-Seltzer Plus Award with Theoren Fleury (1991)

Signed as a free agent by **Pittsburgh**, July 30, 1982. Traded to **Edmonton** by **Pittsburgh** with Tim Hrynewich and future considerations (Craig Muni, October 6, 1986) for Gilles Meloche, September 12, 1985. Traded to **Los Angeles** by **Edmonton** with Wayne Gretzky and Mike Krushelnyski for Jimmy Carson, Martin Gelinas, Los Angeles' first round choices in 1989 (acquired by New Jersey — New Jersey selected Jason Miller), 1991 (Martin Rucinsky) and 1993 (Nick Stajduhar) Entry Drafts and cash, August 9, 1988. Traded to **Pittsburgh** by **Los Angeles**, for Shawn McEachern, August 27, 1993.

McSWEEN, DON

Defense. Shoots left. 5'11", 197 lbs. Born, Detroit, MI, June 9, 1964.
(Buffalo's 10th choice, 154th overall, in 1983 Entry Draft).

			Regular Season					Playoffs				
Season	Club	Lea	GP	G	A	TP	PIM	GP	G	A	TP	PIM
1983-84	Michigan State	CCHA	46	10	26	36	30	....	....	....	....	....
1984-85	Michigan State	CCHA	44	2	23	25	52	....	....	....	....	....
1985-86a	Michigan State	CCHA	45	9	29	38	18	....	....	....	....	....
1986-87abc	Michigan State	CCHA	45	7	23	30	34	....	....	....	....	....
1987-88	**Buffalo**	**NHL**	**5**	**0**	**1**	**1**	**6**	....	....	....	....	....
	Rochester	AHL	63	9	29	38	108	6	0	1	1	15
1988-89	Rochester	AHL	66	7	22	29	45	....	....	....	....	....
1989-90	**Buffalo**	**NHL**	**4**	**0**	**0**	**0**	**6**	....	....	....	....	....
d	Rochester	AHL	70	16	43	59	43	17	3	10	13	12
1990-91	Rochester	AHL	74	7	44	51	57	15	2	5	7	8
1991-92	Rochester	AHL	75	6	32	38	60	16	5	6	11	18
1992-93	San Diego	IHL	80	15	40	55	85	14	1	2	3	10
	NHL Totals		**9**	**0**	**1**	**1**	**12**	....	....	....	....	....

a CCHA First All-Star Team (1986, 1987)
b NCAA West Second All-American Team (1987)
c Named to NCAA All-Tournament Team (1987)
d AHL First All-Star Team (1990)

MEANY, SPENCER

Right wing. Shoots right. 6', 205 lbs. Born, Atikokan, Ont., April 8, 1971.
(Buffalo's 11th choice, 211th overall, in 1991 Entry Draft).

			Regular Season					Playoffs				
Season	Club	Lea	GP	G	A	TP	PIM	GP	G	A	TP	PIM
1990-91	St. Lawrence	ECAC	31	6	11	17	92	....	....	....	....	....
1991-92	St. Lawrence	ECAC	30	12	8	20	123	....	....	....	....	....
1992-93	St. Lawrence	ECAC	28	8	15	23	97	....	....	....	....	....

MEARS, GLEN

Defense. Shoots right. 6'3", 215 lbs. Born, Anchorage, AK, July 14, 1972.
(Calgary's 5th choice, 62nd overall, in 1990 Entry Draft).

			Regular Season					Playoffs				
Season	Club	Lea	GP	G	A	TP	PIM	GP	G	A	TP	PIM
1990-91	Bowling Green	CCHA	40	0	7	7	54	....	....	....	....	....
1991-92	Bowling Green	CCHA	32	1	2	3	38	....	....	....	....	....
1992-93	Bowling Green	CCHA	39	0	7	7	22	....	....	....	....	....

MEEHAN, SCOTT

Defense. Shoots left. 6'1", 185 lbs. Born, Walpole, MA, November 27, 1970.
(Vancouver's 1st choice, 13th overall, in 1991 Supplemental Draft).

			Regular Season					Playoffs				
Season	Club	Lea	GP	G	A	TP	PIM	GP	G	A	TP	PIM
1989-90	Lowell	H.E.	24	0	0	0	16	....	....	....	....	....
1990-91	Lowell	H.E.	27	1	2	3	20	....	....	....	....	....
1991-92	Lowell	H.E.	34	0	2	2	28	....	....	....	....	....
1992-93	Lowell	H.E.	39	3	5	8	46	....	....	....	....	....

MELANSON, DEAN

Defense. Shoots right. 5'11", 211 lbs. Born, Antigonish, N.S., November 19, 1973.
(Buffalo's 4th choice, 80th overall, in 1992 Entry Draft).

			Regular Season					Playoffs				
Season	Club	Lea	GP	G	A	TP	PIM	GP	G	A	TP	PIM
1990-91	St-Hyacinthe	QMJHL	69	10	17	27	110	4	0	1	1	2
1991-92	St-Hyacinthe	QMJHL	42	8	19	27	158	6	1	2	3	25
1992-93	Rochester	AHL	8	0	1	1	6	14	1	6	7	18
	St. Hyacinthe	QMJHL	57	13	29	42	253	....	....	....	....	....

MELANSON, ROBERT

Defense. Shoots left. 6'1", 202 lbs. Born, Antigonish, N.S., March 5, 1971.
(Pittsburgh's 5th choice, 104th overall, in 1991 Entry Draft).

			Regular Season					Playoffs				
Season	Club	Lea	GP	G	A	TP	PIM	GP	G	A	TP	PIM
1990-91	Hull	QMJHL	66	1	8	9	210	6	0	1	1	34
1991-92	Knoxville	ECHL	49	0	11	11	186	....	....	....	....	....
	Muskegon	IHL	7	0	2	2	2	1	0	0	0	0
1992-93	Cleveland	IHL	27	0	5	5	123	1	0	0	0	0

MELLANBY, SCOTT

Right wing. Shoots right. 6'1", 205 lbs. Born, Montreal, Que., June 11, 1966.
(Philadelphia's 2nd choice, 27th overall, in 1984 Entry Draft).

			Regular Season					Playoffs				
Season	Club	Lea	GP	G	A	TP	PIM	GP	G	A	TP	PIM
1984-85	U. Wisconsin	WCHA	40	14	24	38	60	....	....	....	....	....
1985-86	U. Wisconsin	WCHA	32	21	23	44	89	....	....	....	....	....
	Philadelphia	**NHL**	**2**	**0**	**0**	**0**	**0**	....	....	....	....	....
1986-87	**Philadelphia**	**NHL**	**71**	**11**	**21**	**32**	**94**	**24**	**5**	**5**	**10**	**46**
1987-88	**Philadelphia**	**NHL**	**75**	**25**	**26**	**51**	**185**	**7**	**0**	**1**	**1**	**16**
1988-89	**Philadelphia**	**NHL**	**76**	**21**	**29**	**50**	**183**	**19**	**4**	**5**	**9**	**28**
1989-90	**Philadelphia**	**NHL**	**57**	**6**	**17**	**23**	**77**	....	....	....	....	....
1990-91	**Philadelphia**	**NHL**	**74**	**20**	**21**	**41**	**155**	....	....	....	....	....
1991-92	**Edmonton**	**NHL**	**80**	**23**	**27**	**50**	**197**	**16**	**2**	**1**	**3**	**29**
1992-93	**Edmonton**	**NHL**	**69**	**15**	**17**	**32**	**147**	....	....	....	....	....
	NHL Totals		**504**	**121**	**158**	**279**	**1038**	**66**	**11**	**12**	**23**	**119**

Traded to **Edmonton** by **Philadelphia** with Craig Fisher and Craig Berube for Dave Brown, Corey Foster and Jari Kurri, May 30, 1991. Claimed by **Florida** from **Edmonton** in Expansion Draft, June 24, 1993.

MELROSE, KEVAN

Defense. Shoots left. 5'10", 185 lbs. Born, Calgary, Alta., March 28, 1966.
(Calgary's 7th choice, 138th overall, in 1984 Entry Draft).

			Regular Season					Playoffs				
Season	Club	Lea	GP	G	A	TP	PIM	GP	G	A	TP	PIM
1986-87	Cdn. National	....	8	1	0	1	4	....	....	....	....	....
	Red Deer	AJHL	29	15	15	30	171	19	8	16	24	60
1987-88	Harvard	ECAC	31	4	6	10	50	....	....	....	....	....
1988-89	Harvard	ECAC	32	2	13	15	126	....	....	....	....	....
1989-90	Harvard	ECAC	16	1	6	7	124	....	....	....	....	....
1990-91	Salt Lake	IHL	60	6	14	20	82	4	1	2	3	10
1991-92	Salt Lake	IHL	82	5	14	19	187	5	0	0	0	4
1992-93	Salt Lake	IHL	33	3	6	9	74	....	....	....	....	....
	Kalamazoo	IHL	40	3	8	11	48	....	....	....	....	....

MELUZIN, ROMAN (MEH-loo-zin)

Right wing. Shoots right. 6', 176 lbs. Born, Blanska, Czechoslovakia, June 17, 1972.
(Winnipeg's 3rd choice, 74th overall, in 1990 Entry Draft).

			Regular Season					Playoffs				
Season	Club	Lea	GP	G	A	TP	PIM	GP	G	A	TP	PIM
1989-90	Zetor Brno	Czech.	34	4	6	10	....	....	....	....	....	....
1990-91	Zetor Brno	Czech.2	30	14	8	22	8	....	....	....	....	....
1991-92	Zetor Brno	Czech.	37	13	13	26	....	....	....	....	....	....
1992-93	ZPS Zlin	Czech.	46	10	21	31	....	....	....	....	....	....

MESSIER, JOBY

Defense. Shoots right. 6', 193 lbs. Born, Regina, Sask., March 2, 1970.
(NY Rangers' 7th choice, 118th overall, in 1989 Entry Draft).

			Regular Season					Playoffs				
Season	Club	Lea	GP	G	A	TP	PIM	GP	G	A	TP	PIM
1988-89	Michigan State	CCHA	39	2	10	12	66	....	....	....	....	....
1989-90	Michigan State	CCHA	42	1	11	12	58	....	....	....	....	....
1990-91	Michigan State	CCHA	39	5	11	16	71	....	....	....	....	....
1991-92ab	Michigan State	CCHA	41	13	15	28	81	....	....	....	....	....
1992-93	**NY Rangers**	**NHL**	**11**	**0**	**0**	**0**	**6**	....	....	....	....	....
	Binghamton	AHL	60	5	16	21	63	14	1	1	2	6
	NHL Totals		**11**	**0**	**0**	**0**	**6**	....	....	....	....	....

a CCHA First All-Star Team (1992)
b NCAA West First All-American Team (1992)

MESSIER, MARK DOUGLAS (MEHZ-yay)

Center. Shoots left. 6'1", 210 lbs. Born, Edmonton, Alta., January 18, 1961.
(Edmonton's 2nd choice, 48th overall, in 1979 Entry Draft).

			Regular Season					Playoffs				
Season	Club	Lea	GP	G	A	TP	PIM	GP	G	A	TP	PIM
1977-78	Portland	WHL	....	....	....	....	....	7	4	1	5	2
1978-79	Indianapolis	WHA	5	0	0	0	0	....	....	....	....	....
	Cincinnati	WHA	47	1	10	11	58	....	....	....	....	....
1979-80	**Edmonton**	**NHL**	**75**	**12**	**21**	**33**	**120**	**3**	**1**	**2**	**3**	**2**
	Houston	CHL	4	0	3	3	4	....	....	....	....	....
1980-81	**Edmonton**	**NHL**	**72**	**23**	**40**	**63**	**102**	**9**	**2**	**5**	**7**	**13**
1981-82a	**Edmonton**	**NHL**	**78**	**50**	**38**	**88**	**119**	**5**	**1**	**2**	**3**	**8**
1982-83a	**Edmonton**	**NHL**	**77**	**48**	**58**	**106**	**72**	**15**	**15**	**6**	**21**	**14**
1983-84bc	**Edmonton**	**NHL**	**73**	**37**	**64**	**101**	**165**	**19**	**8**	**18**	**26**	**19**
1984-85	**Edmonton**	**NHL**	**55**	**23**	**31**	**54**	**57**	**18**	**12**	**13**	**25**	**12**
1985-86	**Edmonton**	**NHL**	**63**	**35**	**49**	**84**	**68**	**10**	**4**	**6**	**10**	**18**
1986-87	**Edmonton**	**NHL**	**77**	**37**	**70**	**107**	**73**	**21**	**12**	**16**	**28**	**16**
1987-88	**Edmonton**	**NHL**	**77**	**37**	**74**	**111**	**103**	**19**	**11**	**23**	**34**	**29**
1988-89	**Edmonton**	**NHL**	**72**	**33**	**61**	**94**	**130**	**7**	**1**	**11**	**12**	**8**
1989-90ade	**Edmonton**	**NHL**	**79**	**45**	**84**	**129**	**79**	**22**	**9**	***22**	**31**	**20**
1990-91	**Edmonton**	**NHL**	**53**	**12**	**52**	**64**	**34**	**18**	**4**	**11**	**15**	**16**
1991-92ade	**NY Rangers**	**NHL**	**79**	**35**	**72**	**107**	**76**	**11**	**7**	**7**	**14**	**6**
1992-93	**NY Rangers**	**NHL**	**75**	**25**	**66**	**91**	**72**	....	....	....	....	....
	NHL Totals		**1005**	**452**	**780**	**1232**	**1270**	**177**	**87**	**142**	**229**	**181**

a NHL First All-Star Team (1982, 1983, 1990, 1992)
b NHL Second All-Star Team (1984)
c Won Conn Smythe Trophy (1984)
d Won Hart Trophy (1990, 1992)
e Won Lester B. Pearson Award (1990, 1992)

Played in NHL All-Star Game (1982-86, 1988-92)

Traded to **NY Rangers** by **Edmonton** with future considerations for Bernie Nicholls, Steven Rice and Louie DeBrusk, October 4, 1991.

MESSIER, MITCH

Center. Shoots right. 6'2", 200 lbs. Born, Regina, Sask., August 21, 1965.
(Minnesota's 4th choice, 56th overall, in 1983 Entry Draft).

			Regular Season					Playoffs				
Season	Club	Lea	GP	G	A	TP	PIM	GP	G	A	TP	PIM
1983-84	Michigan State	CCHA	37	6	15	21	22	....	....	....	....	....
1984-85	Michigan State	CCHA	42	12	21	33	46	....	....	....	....	....
1985-86	Michigan State	CCHA	38	24	40	64	36	....	....	....	....	....
1986-87ab	Michigan State	CCHA	45	44	48	92	89	....	....	....	....	....
1987-88	**Minnesota**	**NHL**	**13**	**0**	**1**	**1**	**11**	....	....	....	....	....
	Kalamazoo	IHL	69	29	37	66	42	4	2	1	3	0
1988-89	**Minnesota**	**NHL**	**3**	**0**	**1**	**1**	**0**	....	....	....	....	....
	Kalamazoo	IHL	67	34	46	80	71	6	4	3	7	0
1989-90	**Minnesota**	**NHL**	**2**	**0**	**0**	**0**	**0**	....	....	....	....	....
	Kalamazoo	IHL	65	26	58	84	56	8	4	3	7	25
1990-91	**Minnesota**	**NHL**	**2**	**0**	**0**	**0**	**0**	....	....	....	....	....
	Kalamazoo	IHL	73	30	46	76	34	11	4	8	12	2
1991-92	Kalamazoo	IHL	77	43	33	76	42	12	3	3	6	25
1992-93	Milwaukee	IHL	62	18	23	41	84	6	0	1	1	0
	NHL Totals		**20**	**0**	**2**	**2**	**11**	....	....	....	....	....

a CCHA First All-Star Team (1987)
b NCAA West First All-American Team (1987)

METLYUK, DENIS (met-lee-OOK)

Center. Shoots left. 5'10", 183 lbs. Born, Togliatti, Soviet Union, January 30, 1972.
(Philadelphia's 3rd choice, 31st overall, in 1992 Entry Draft).

			Regular Season					Playoffs				
Season	Club	Lea	GP	G	A	TP	PIM	GP	G	A	TP	PIM
1990-91	Togliatti	USSR 2	25	5	6	11	8	....	....	....	....	....
1991-92	Togliatti	CIS	26	0	1	1	6	....	....	....	....	....
1992-93	Togliatti	CIS	39	7	12	19	20	10	0	1	1	2

MICHAYLUK, DAVID (DAVE) (muh-KIGH-luhk)

Left wing. Shoots left. 5'10", 189 lbs. Born, Wakaw, Sask., May 18, 1962.
(Philadelphia's 5th choice, 65th overall, in 1981 Entry Draft).

			Regular Season					Playoffs				
Season	Club	Lea	GP	G	A	TP	PIM	GP	G	A	TP	PIM
1980-81a	Regina	WHL	72	62	71	133	39	11	5	12	17	8
1981-82	**Philadelphia**	**NHL**	**1**	**0**	**0**	**0**	**0**	....	....	....	....	....
b	Regina	WHL	72	62	111	172	128	12	16	24	*40	23
1982-83	**Philadelphia**	**NHL**	**13**	**2**	**6**	**8**	**8**	....	....	....	....	....
	Maine	AHL	69	32	40	72	16	8	0	2	2	0
1983-84	Springfield	AHL	79	18	44	62	37	4	0	0	0	2
1984-85	Hershey	AHL	3	0	2	2	2	....	....	....	....	....
c	Kalamazoo	IHL	82	*66	33	99	49	11	7	7	14	0
1985-86	Nova Scotia	AHL	3	0	1	1	0	....	....	....	....	....
	Muskegon	IHL	77	52	52	104	73	14	6	9	15	12
1986-87d	Muskegon	IHL	82	47	53	100	29	15	2	14	16	8
1987-88d	Muskegon	IHL	81	*56	81	137	46	6	2	0	2	18
1988-89defg	Muskegon	IHL	80	50	72	*122	84	13	*9	12	*21	24
1989-90d	Muskegon	IHL	79	*51	51	102	80	15	8	*14	22	10
1990-91	Muskegon	IHL	83	40	62	102	16	5	2	2	4	4
1991-92c	Muskegon	IHL	82	39	63	102	154	13	9	8	17	4
	Pittsburgh	**NHL**	....	....	....	....	....	**7**	**1**	**1**	**2**	**0**
1992-93d	Cleveland	IHL	82	47	65	112	104	4	1	2	3	4
	NHL Totals		**14**	**2**	**6**	**8**	**8**	**7**	**1**	**1**	**2**	**0**

a WHL Rookie of the Year (1981)
b WHL Second All-Star Team (1982)
c IHL Second All-Star Team (1985, 1992)
d IHL First All-Star Team (1987, 1988, 1989, 1990, 1993)
e IHL Playoff MVP (1989)
f Won James Gatschene Memorial Trophy (MVP-IHL) (1989)
g Won Leo P. Lamoureux Memorial Trophy (Top Scorer-IHL) (1989)

Signed as a free agent by **Pittsburgh**, May 24, 1989.

MIDDENDORF, MAX

Right wing. Shoots right. 6'4", 210 lbs. Born, Syracuse, NY, August 18, 1967.
(Quebec's 3rd choice, 57th overall, in 1985 Entry Draft).

			Regular Season					Playoffs				
Season	Club	Lea	GP	G	A	TP	PIM	GP	G	A	TP	PIM
1984-85	Sudbury	OHL	63	16	28	44	106	....	....	....	....	....
1985-86	Sudbury	OHL	61	40	42	82	71	4	4	2	6	11
1986-87	**Quebec**	**NHL**	**6**	**1**	**4**	**5**	**4**	....	....	....	....	....
	Sudbury	OHL	31	31	29	60	7	....	....	....	....	....
	Kitchener	OHL	17	7	15	22	6	4	2	5	7	5
1987-88	**Quebec**	**NHL**	**1**	**0**	**0**	**0**	**0**	....	....	....	....	....
	Fredericton	AHL	38	11	13	24	57	12	4	4	8	18
1988-89	Halifax	AHL	72	41	39	80	85	4	1	2	3	6
1989-90	**Quebec**	**NHL**	**3**	**0**	**0**	**0**	**0**	....	....	....	....	....
	Halifax	AHL	48	20	17	37	60	....	....	....	....	....
1990-91	**Edmonton**	**NHL**	**3**	**1**	**0**	**1**	**2**	....	....	....	....	....
	Fort Wayne	IHL	15	9	11	20	12	....	....	....	....	....
	Cape Breton	AHL	44	14	21	35	82	4	0	1	1	6
1991-92	Cape Breton	AHL	51	20	19	39	108	....	....	....	....	....
	Adirondack	AHL	6	3	5	8	12	5	0	1	1	16
1992-93	Fort Wayne	IHL	24	9	13	22	58	....	....	....	....	....
	San Diego	IHL	30	15	11	26	25	8	1	2	3	8
	NHL Totals		**13**	**2**	**4**	**6**	**6**	....	....	....	....	....

Traded to **Edmonton** by **Quebec** for Edmonton's ninth round choice (Brent Brekke) in 1991 Entry Draft, November 10, 1990. Traded to **Detroit** by **Edmonton** for Bill McDougall, February 22, 1992.

MIEHM, KEVIN (MEE-yuhm)

Centre. Shoots left. 6'2", 200 lbs. Born, Kitchener, Ont., September 10, 1969.
(St. Louis' 2nd choice, 54th overall, in 1987 Entry Draft).

			Regular Season					Playoffs				
Season	Club	Lea	GP	G	A	TP	PIM	GP	G	A	TP	PIM
1986-87	Oshawa	OHL	61	12	27	39	19	26	1	8	9	12
1987-88	Oshawa	OHL	52	16	36	52	30	7	2	5	7	0
1988-89a	Oshawa	OHL	63	43	79	122	19	6	6	6	12	0
	Peoria	IHL	3	1	1	2	0	4	0	2	2	0
1989-90	Peoria	IHL	76	23	38	61	20	3	0	0	0	4
1990-91	Peoria	IHL	73	25	39	64	14	16	5	7	12	2
1991-92	Peoria	IHL	66	21	53	74	22	10	3	4	7	2
1992-93	**St. Louis**	**NHL**	**8**	**1**	**3**	**4**	**4**	**2**	**0**	**1**	**1**	**0**
	Peoria	IHL	30	12	33	45	13	4	0	1	1	2
	NHL Totals		**8**	**1**	**3**	**4**	**4**	**2**	**0**	**1**	**1**	**0**

a OHL Third All-Star Team (1989)

MILLEN, COREY

Center. Shoots right. 5'7", 168 lbs. Born, Cloquet, MN, April 29, 1964.
(NY Rangers' 3rd choice, 57th overall, in 1982 Entry Draft).

			Regular Season					Playoffs				
Season	Club	Lea	GP	G	A	TP	PIM	GP	G	A	TP	PIM
1982-83	U. Minnesota	WCHA	21	14	15	29	18	....	....	....	....	....
1983-84	U.S. Olympic	....	45	15	11	26	10	....	....	....	....	....
1984-85	U. Minnesota	WCHA	38	28	36	64	60	....	....	....	....	....
1985-86ab	U. Minnesota	WCHA	48	41	42	83	64	....	....	....	....	....
1986-87bc	U. Minnesota	WCHA	42	36	29	65	62	....	....	....	....	....
1987-88	U.S. National	....	47	41	43	84	26	....	....	....	....	....
	U.S. Olympic	....	6	6	5	11	4	....	....	....	....	....
1988-89	Ambri	Switz.	36	32	22	54	18	6	4	3	7	0
1989-90	**NY Rangers**	**NHL**	**4**	**0**	**0**	**0**	**2**	....	....	....	....	....
	Flint	IHL	11	4	5	9	2	....	....	....	....	....
1990-91	**NY Rangers**	**NHL**	**4**	**3**	**1**	**4**	**0**	**6**	**1**	**2**	**3**	**0**
	Binghamton	AHL	40	19	37	56	68	6	0	7	7	6
1991-92	**NY Rangers**	**NHL**	**11**	**1**	**4**	**5**	**10**	....	....	....	....	....
	Binghamton	AHL	15	8	7	15	44	....	....	....	....	....
	Los Angeles	**NHL**	**46**	**20**	**21**	**41**	**44**	**6**	**0**	**1**	**1**	**6**
1992-93	**Los Angeles**	**NHL**	**42**	**23**	**16**	**39**	**42**	**23**	**2**	**4**	**6**	**12**
	NHL Totals		**107**	**47**	**42**	**89**	**98**	**35**	**3**	**7**	**10**	**18**

a NCAA West Second All-American Team (1986)
b WCHA Second All-Star Team (1986, 1987)
c Named to NCAA All-Tournament Team (1987)

Traded to **Los Angeles** by **NY Rangers** for Randy Gilhen, December 23, 1991. Traded to **New Jersey** by **Los Angeles** for New Jersey's fifth round choice (Jason Saal) in 1993 Entry Draft, June 26, 1993.

MILLER, AARON

Defense. Shoots right. 6'3", 197 lbs. Born, Buffalo, NY, August 11, 1971.
(NY Rangers' 6th choice, 88th overall, in 1989 Entry Draft).

			Regular Season					Playoffs				
Season	Club	Lea	GP	G	A	TP	PIM	GP	G	A	TP	PIM
1989-90	U. of Vermont	ECAC	31	1	15	16	24	....	....	....	....	....
1990-91	U. of Vermont	ECAC	30	3	7	10	22	....	....	....	....	....
1991-92	U. of Vermont	ECAC	31	3	16	19	28	....	....	....	....	....
1992-93ab	U. of Vermont	ECAC	30	4	13	17	16	....	....	....	....	....

a ECAC First All-Star Team (1993)
b NCAA East Second All-American Team (1993)

Traded to **Quebec** by **NY Rangers** with NY Rangers' fifth round choice (Bill Lindsay) in 1991 Entry Draft for Joe Cirella, January 17, 1991.

MILLER, ANDREW

Right wing. Shoots right. 5'11", 200 lbs. Born, North York, Ont., January 20, 1971.
(Detroit's 10th choice, 252nd overall, in 1991 Entry Draft).

			Regular Season					Playoffs				
Season	Club	Lea	GP	G	A	TP	PIM	GP	G	A	TP	PIM
1991-92	Miami-Ohio	CCHA	40	9	16	25	34	....	....	....	....	....
1992-93	Miami-Ohio	CCHA	25	5	5	10	8	....	....	....	....	....

MILLER, BRAD

Defense. Shoots left. 6'4", 220 lbs. Born, Edmonton, Alta., July 23, 1969.
(Buffalo's 2nd choice, 22nd overall, in 1987 Entry Draft).

			Regular Season					Playoffs				
Season	Club	Lea	GP	G	A	TP	PIM	GP	G	A	TP	PIM
1985-86	Regina	WHL	71	2	14	16	99	10	1	1	2	4
1986-87	Regina	WHL	67	10	38	48	154	3	0	0	0	6
1987-88	Rochester	AHL	3	0	0	0	4	2	0	0	0	2
	Regina	WHL	61	9	34	43	148	4	1	1	2	12
1988-89	**Buffalo**	**NHL**	**7**	**0**	**0**	**0**	**6**	....	....	....	....	....
	Regina	WHL	34	8	18	26	95	....	....	....	....	....
	Rochester	AHL	3	0	0	0	4	....	....	....	....	....
1989-90	**Buffalo**	**NHL**	**1**	**0**	**0**	**0**	**0**	....	....	....	....	....
	Rochester	AHL	60	2	10	12	273	8	1	0	1	52
1990-91	**Buffalo**	**NHL**	**13**	**0**	**0**	**0**	**67**	....	....	....	....	....
	Rochester	AHL	49	0	9	9	248	12	0	4	4	67
1991-92	**Buffalo**	**NHL**	**42**	**1**	**4**	**5**	**192**	....	....	....	....	....
	Rochester	AHL	27	0	4	4	113	11	0	0	0	61
1992-93	**Ottawa**	**NHL**	**11**	**0**	**0**	**0**	**42**	....	....	....	....	....
	New Haven	AHL	41	1	9	10	138	....	....	....	....	....
	St. John's	AHL	20	0	3	3	61	8	0	2	2	10
	NHL Totals		**74**	**1**	**4**	**5**	**307**	....	....	....	....	....

Claimed by **Ottawa** from **Buffalo** in Expansion Draft, June 18, 1992. Traded to **Toronto** by **Ottawa** for Toronto's ninth round choice (Pavol Demitra) in 1993 Entry Draft, February 25, 1993.

MILLER, COLIN

Center. Shoots right. 6', 188 lbs. Born, Grimsby, Ont., August 21, 1971.

			Regular Season					Playoffs				
Season	Club	Lea	GP	G	A	TP	PIM	GP	G	A	TP	PIM
1990-91	S.S. Marie	OHL	62	26	60	86	35	14	4	18	22	17
1991-92ab	S.S. Marie	OHL	66	37	73	110	52	19	10	23	33	18
1992-93	Atlanta	IHL	76	20	39	59	52	9	2	4	6	22

a Memorial Cup All-Star Team (1992)
b Memorial Cup Most Sportsmanlike Player (1992)

Signed as a free agent by **Tampa Bay**, June 29, 1992.

MILLER, JASON

Center. Shoots left. 6'1", 190 lbs. Born, Edmonton, Alta., March 1, 1971.
(New Jersey's 2nd choice, 18th overall, in 1989 Entry Draft).

			Regular Season					Playoffs				
Season	Club	Lea	GP	G	A	TP	PIM	GP	G	A	TP	PIM
1987-88	Medicine Hat	WHL	71	11	18	29	28	15	0	1	1	2
1988-89	Medicine Hat	WHL	72	51	55	106	44	3	1	2	3	2
1989-90	Medicine Hat	WHL	66	43	56	99	40	3	3	2	5	0
1990-91	**New Jersey**	**NHL**	**1**	**0**	**0**	**0**	**0**	....	....	....	....	....
a	Medicine Hat	WHL	66	60	76	136	31	12	9	10	19	8
1991-92	**New Jersey**	**NHL**	**3**	**0**	**0**	**0**	**0**	....	....	....	....	....
	Utica	AHL	71	23	32	55	31	4	1	3	4	0
1992-93	**New Jersey**	**NHL**	**2**	**0**	**0**	**0**	**0**	....	....	....	....	....
	Utica	AHL	72	28	42	70	43	5	4	4	8	2
	NHL Totals		**6**	**0**	**0**	**0**	**0**	....	....	....	....	....

a WHL East Second All-Star Team (1991)

MILLER, KELLY

Left wing. Shoots left. 5'11", 197 lbs. Born, Lansing, MI, March 3, 1963.
(NY Rangers' 9th choice, 183rd overall, in 1982 Entry Draft).

			Regular Season					Playoffs				
Season	Club	Lea	GP	G	A	TP	PIM	GP	G	A	TP	PIM
1981-82	Michigan State	CCHA	38	11	18	29	17	....	....	....	....	....
1982-83	Michigan State	CCHA	36	16	19	35	12	....	....	....	....	....
1983-84	Michigan State	CCHA	46	28	21	49	12	....	....	....	....	....
1984-85ab	Michigan State	CCHA	43	27	23	50	21	....	....	....	....	....
	NY Rangers	**NHL**	**5**	**0**	**2**	**2**	**2**	**3**	**0**	**0**	**0**	**2**
1985-86	**NY Rangers**	**NHL**	**74**	**13**	**20**	**33**	**52**	**16**	**3**	**4**	**7**	**4**
1986-87	**NY Rangers**	**NHL**	**38**	**6**	**14**	**20**	**22**	....	....	....	....	....
	Washington	**NHL**	**39**	**10**	**12**	**22**	**26**	**7**	**2**	**2**	**4**	**0**
1987-88	**Washington**	**NHL**	**80**	**9**	**23**	**32**	**35**	**14**	**4**	**4**	**8**	**10**
1988-89	**Washington**	**NHL**	**78**	**19**	**21**	**40**	**45**	**6**	**1**	**0**	**1**	**2**
1989-90	**Washington**	**NHL**	**80**	**18**	**22**	**40**	**49**	**15**	**3**	**5**	**8**	**23**
1990-91	**Washington**	**NHL**	**80**	**24**	**26**	**50**	**29**	**11**	**4**	**2**	**6**	**6**
1991-92	**Washington**	**NHL**	**78**	**14**	**38**	**52**	**49**	**7**	**1**	**2**	**3**	**4**
1992-93	**Washington**	**NHL**	**84**	**18**	**27**	**45**	**32**	**6**	**0**	**3**	**3**	**2**
	NHL Totals		**636**	**131**	**205**	**336**	**341**	**85**	**18**	**22**	**40**	**53**

a CCHA First All-Star Team (1985)
b Named to NCAA All-American Team (1985)

Traded to **Washington** by **NY Rangers** with Bob Crawford and Mike Ridley for Bob Carpenter and Washington's second round choice (Jason Prosofsky) in 1989 Entry Draft, January 1, 1987.

MILLER, KEVIN

Center. Shoots right. 5'11", 190 lbs. Born, Lansing, MI, September 9, 1965.
(NY Rangers' 10th choice, 202nd overall, in 1984 Entry Draft).

			Regular Season					Playoffs				
Season	Club	Lea	GP	G	A	TP	PIM	GP	G	A	TP	PIM
1984-85	Michigan State	CCHA	44	11	29	40	84	....	....	....	....	....
1985-86	Michigan State	CCHA	45	19	52	71	112	....	....	....	....	....
1986-87	Michigan State	CCHA	42	25	56	81	63	....	....	....	....	....
1987-88	U.S. National	....	48	31	32	63	33	....	....	....	....	....
	U.S. Olympic	....	5	1	3	4	4	....	....	....	....	....
	Michigan State	CCHA	9	6	3	9	18	....	....	....	....	....
1988-89	**NY Rangers**	**NHL**	**24**	**3**	**5**	**8**	**2**	....	....	....	....	....
	Denver	IHL	55	29	47	76	19	4	2	1	3	2
1989-90	**NY Rangers**	**NHL**	**16**	**0**	**5**	**5**	**2**	**1**	**0**	**0**	**0**	**0**
	Flint	IHL	48	19	23	42	41	....	....	....	....	....
1990-91	**NY Rangers**	**NHL**	**63**	**17**	**27**	**44**	**63**	....	....	....	....	....
	Detroit	**NHL**	**11**	**5**	**2**	**7**	**4**	**7**	**3**	**2**	**5**	**20**
1991-92	**Detroit**	**NHL**	**80**	**20**	**26**	**46**	**53**	**9**	**0**	**2**	**2**	**4**
1992-93	**Washington**	**NHL**	**10**	**0**	**3**	**3**	**35**	....	....	....	....	....
	St. Louis	**NHL**	**72**	**24**	**22**	**46**	**65**	**10**	**0**	**3**	**3**	**11**
	NHL Totals		**276**	**69**	**90**	**159**	**224**	**27**	**3**	**7**	**10**	**35**

Traded to **Detroit** by **NY Rangers** with Jim Cummins and Dennis Vial for Joey Kocur and Per Djoos, March 5, 1991. Traded to **Washington** by **Detroit** for Dino Ciccarelli, June 20, 1992. Traded to **St. Louis** by **Washington** for Paul Cavallini, November 2, 1992.

MILLER, KIP

Center. Shoots left. 5'10", 185 lbs.   Born, Lansing, MI, June 11, 1969.
(Quebec's 4th choice, 72nd overall, in 1987 Entry Draft).

			Regular Season					Playoffs				
Season	Club	Lea	GP	G	A	TP	PIM	GP	G	A	TP	PIM
1986-87	Michigan State	CCHA	41	20	19	39	92	....	....	....	....	....
1987-88	Michigan State	CCHA	39	16	25	41	51	....	....	....	....	....
1988-89ab	Michigan State	CCHA	47	32	45	77	94	....	....	....	....	....
1989-90abcd	Michigan State	CCHA	45	*48	53	*101	60	....	....	....	....	....
1990-91	**Quebec**	**NHL**	**13**	**4**	**3**	**7**	**7**	....	....	....	....	....
	Halifax	AHL	66	36	33	69	40	....	....	....	....	....
1991-92	**Quebec**	**NHL**	**36**	**5**	**10**	**15**	**12**	....	....	....	....	....
	Halifax	AHL	24	9	17	26	8	....	....	....	....	....
	Minnesota	**NHL**	**3**	**1**	**2**	**3**	**2**	....	....	....	....	....
	Kalamazoo	IHL	6	1	8	9	4	12	3	9	12	12
1992-93	Kalamazoo	IHL	61	17	39	56	59	....	....	....	....	....
	NHL Totals		**52**	**10**	**15**	**25**	**21**					

a CCHA First All-Star Team (1989, 1990)
b NCAA West First All-American Team (1989, 1990)
c CCHA Player of the Year (1990)
d Won Hobey Baker Memorial Award (Top U.S. Collegiate Player) (1990)
Traded to **Minnesota** by **Quebec** for Steve Maltais, March 8, 1992. Signed as a free agent by **San Jose**, August 10, 1993.

MILLER, KRIS

Defense. Shoots left. 6', 200 lbs.   Born, Bemidji, MN, March 30, 1969.
(Montreal's 6th choice, 80th overall, in 1987 Entry Draft).

			Regular Season					Playoffs				
Season	Club	Lea	GP	G	A	TP	PIM	GP	G	A	TP	PIM
1987-88	Minn.-Duluth	WCHA	32	1	6	7	30	....	....	....	....	....
1988-89	Minn.-Duluth	WCHA	39	2	10	12	37	....	....	....	....	....
1989-90	Minn.-Duluth	WCHA	39	2	11	13	59	....	....	....	....	....
1990-91	Minn.-Duluth	WCHA	40	6	22	28	24	....	....	....	....	....
1991-92	Phoenix	IHL	16	1	2	3	17	....	....	....	....	....
	Utica	AHL	1	0	0	0	0	....	....	....	....	....
	Raleigh	ECHL	42	12	27	39	78	4	2	3	5	8
1992-93	Raleigh	ECHL	30	8	24	32	62	....	....	....	....	....
	Salt Lake	IHL	45	4	21	25	45	....	....	....	....	....

MILLER, KURTIS

Left wing. Shoots left. 5'11", 190 lbs.   Born, Bemidji, MN, June 1, 1970.
(St. Louis' 4th choice, 117th overall, in 1990 Entry Draft).

			Regular Season					Playoffs				
Season	Club	Lea	GP	G	A	TP	PIM	GP	G	A	TP	PIM
1990-91	Lake Superior	CCHA	45	10	12	22	48	....	....	....	....	....
1991-92	Lake Superior	CCHA	15	6	7	13	32	....	....	....	....	....
1992-93	Lake Superior	CCHA	26	9	14	23	24	....	....	....	....	....

MIRONOV, BORIS   (mih-RAWN-ohv)

Defense. Shoots right. 6'3", 196 lbs.   Born, Moscow, Soviet Union, March 21, 1972.
(Winnipeg's 2nd choice, 27th overall, in 1992 Entry Draft).

			Regular Season					Playoffs				
Season	Club	Lea	GP	G	A	TP	PIM	GP	G	A	TP	PIM
1988-89	CSKA	USSR	1	0	0	0	0	....	....	....	....	....
1989-90	CSKA	USSR	7	0	0	0	0	....	....	....	....	....
1990-91	CSKA	USSR	36	1	5	6	16	....	....	....	....	....
1991-92	CSKA	CIS	36	2	1	3	22	....	....	....	....	....
1992-93	CSKA	CIS	19	0	5	5	20	....	....	....	....	....

MIRONOV, DMITRI   (mih-RAWN-ohv)

Defense. Shoots right. 6'2", 192 lbs.   Born, Moscow, Soviet Union, December 25, 1965.
(Toronto's 9th choice, 160th overall, in 1991 Entry Draft).

			Regular Season					Playoffs				
Season	Club	Lea	GP	G	A	TP	PIM	GP	G	A	TP	PIM
1985-86	CSKA	USSR	9	0	1	1	8	....	....	....	....	....
1986-87	CSKA	USSR	20	1	3	4	10	....	....	....	....	....
1987-88	Soviet Wings	USSR	44	12	6	18	30	....	....	....	....	....
1988-89	Soviet Wings	USSR	44	5	6	11	44	....	....	....	....	....
1989-90	Soviet Wings	USSR	45	4	11	15	34	....	....	....	....	....
1990-91	Soviet Wings	USSR	45	16	12	28	22	....	....	....	....	....
1991-92	Soviet Wings	CIS	35	15	16	31	62	....	....	....	....	....
	Toronto	**NHL**	**7**	**1**	**0**	**1**	**0**	....	....	....	....	....
1992-93	**Toronto**	**NHL**	**59**	**7**	**24**	**31**	**40**	**14**	**1**	**2**	**3**	**2**
	NHL Totals		**66**	**8**	**24**	**32**	**40**	**14**	**1**	**2**	**3**	**2**

MITCHELL, JEFF

Center/Right wing. Shoots right. 6'1", 175 lbs.   Born, Wayne, MI, May 16, 1975.
(Los Angeles' 2nd choice, 68th overall, in 1993 Entry Draft).

			Regular Season					Playoffs				
Season	Club	Lea	GP	G	A	TP	PIM	GP	G	A	TP	PIM
1991-92	Fraser	Midget	65	65	52	117	114	....	....	....	....	....
1992-93	Detroit	OHL	62	10	15	25	100	15	3	3	6	16

MITCHELL, ROY

Defense. Shoots right. 6'1", 199 lbs.   Born, Edmonton, Alta., March 14, 1969.
(Montreal's 9th choice, 188th overall, in 1989 Entry Draft).

			Regular Season					Playoffs				
Season	Club	Lea	GP	G	A	TP	PIM	GP	G	A	TP	PIM
1986-87	Portland	WHL	68	7	32	39	103	20	0	3	3	23
1987-88	Portland	WHL	72	5	42	47	219	....	....	....	....	....
1988-89	Portland	WHL	72	9	34	43	177	19	1	8	9	38
1989-90	Sherbrooke	AHL	77	5	12	17	98	12	0	2	2	31
1990-91	Fredericton	AHL	71	2	15	17	137	9	0	1	1	11
1991-92	Kalamazoo	IHL	69	3	26	29	102	11	1	4	5	18
1992-93	**Minnesota**	**NHL**	**3**	**0**	**0**	**0**	**0**	....	....	....	....	....
	Kalamazoo	IHL	79	7	25	32	119	....	....	....	....	....
	NHL Totals		**3**	**0**	**0**	**0**	**0**					

Signed as a free agent by **Minnesota**, July 25, 1991.

MIURA, HIROYUKI

Defense. Shoots left. 6'3", 187 lbs.   Born, Kushiro, Japan, December 31, 1973.
(Montreal's 13th choice, 260th overall, in 1992 Entry Draft).

			Regular Season					Playoffs				
Season	Club	Lea	GP	G	A	TP	PIM	GP	G	A	TP	PIM
1991-92	Kushiro H.S.	Jap.2			UNAVAILABLE			....	....	....	....	....
1992-93	Ft. Sask.	AJHL	57	7	24	31	89	....	....	....	....	....

MODANO, MICHAEL (MIKE)

Center. Shoots left. 6'3", 190 lbs.   Born, Livonia, MI, June 7, 1970.
(Minnesota's 1st choice, 1st overall, in 1988 Entry Draft).

			Regular Season					Playoffs				
Season	Club	Lea	GP	G	A	TP	PIM	GP	G	A	TP	PIM
1986-87	Prince Albert	WHL	70	32	30	62	96	8	1	4	5	4
1987-88	Prince Albert	WHL	65	47	80	127	80	9	7	11	18	18
1988-89a	Prince Albert	WHL	41	39	66	105	74					
	Minnesota	**NHL**	....	....	....	....	....	2	0	0	0	0
1989-90b	Minnesota	NHL	80	29	46	75	63	7	1	1	2	12
1990-91	Minnesota	NHL	79	28	36	64	65	23	8	12	20	16
1991-92	Minnesota	NHL	76	33	44	77	46	7	3	2	5	4
1992-93	Minnesota	NHL	82	33	60	93	83	....	....	....	....	....
	NHL Totals		**317**	**123**	**186**	**309**	**257**	**39**	**12**	**15**	**27**	**32**

a WHL East All-Star Team (1989)
b NHL All-Rookie Team (1990)
Played in NHL All-Star Game (1993)

MODRY, JAROSLAV   (MOHD-ree)

Defense. Shoots left. 6'2", 195 lbs.   Born, Ceske-Budejovice, Czech., February 27, 1971.
(New Jersey's 11th choice, 179th overall, in 1990 Entry Draft).

			Regular Season					Playoffs				
Season	Club	Lea	GP	G	A	TP	PIM	GP	G	A	TP	PIM
1987-88	Budejovice	Czech.	3	0	0	0	0	....	....	....	....	....
1988-89	Budejovice	Czech.	28	0	1	1	8	....	....	....	....	....
1989-90	Budejovice	Czech.	41	2	2	4	....	....	....	....	....	....
1990-91	Dukla Trencin	Czech.	37	1	11	12	6	....	....	....	....	....
1991-92	Dukla Trencin	Czech.	18	0	4	4	6	....	....	....	....	....
	Budejovice	Czech.2	14	4	10	14	....	....	....	....	....	....
1992-93	Utica	AHL	80	7	35	42	62	5	0	2	2	2

MOGER, SANDY

Right wing. Shoots right. 6'3", 200 lbs.   Born, Vernon, B.C., March 21, 1969.
(Vancouver's 7th choice, 176th overall, in 1989 Entry Draft).

			Regular Season					Playoffs				
Season	Club	Lea	GP	G	A	TP	PIM	GP	G	A	TP	PIM
1988-89	Lake Superior	CCHA	21	3	5	8	26	....	....	....	....	....
1989-90	Lake Superior	CCHA	46	17	15	32	76	....	....	....	....	....
1990-91	Lake Superior	CCHA	45	27	21	48	*172	....	....	....	....	....
1991-92a	Lake Superior	CCHA	38	24	24	48	93	....	....	....	....	....
1992-93	Hamilton	AHL	78	23	26	49	57	....	....	....	....	....

a CCHA Second All-Star Team (1992)

MOGILNY, ALEXANDER   (moh-GIHL-nee)

Right wing. Shoots left. 5'11", 187 lbs.   Born, Khabarovsk, Soviet Union, February 18, 1969.
(Buffalo's 4th choice, 89th overall, in 1988 Entry Draft).

			Regular Season					Playoffs				
Season	Club	Lea	GP	G	A	TP	PIM	GP	G	A	TP	PIM
1986-87	CSKA	USSR	28	15	1	16	4	....	....	....	....	....
1987-88	CSKA	USSR	39	12	8	20	14	....	....	....	....	....
1988-89	CSKA	USSR	31	11	11	22	24	....	....	....	....	....
1989-90	**Buffalo**	**NHL**	**65**	**15**	**28**	**43**	**16**	**4**	**0**	**1**	**1**	**2**
1990-91	**Buffalo**	**NHL**	**62**	**30**	**34**	**64**	**16**	**6**	**0**	**6**	**6**	**2**
1991-92	**Buffalo**	**NHL**	**67**	**39**	**45**	**84**	**73**	**2**	**0**	**2**	**2**	**0**
1992-93a	**Buffalo**	**NHL**	**77**	***76**	**51**	**127**	**40**	**7**	**7**	**3**	**10**	**6**
	NHL Totals		**271**	**160**	**158**	**318**	**145**	**19**	**7**	**12**	**19**	**10**

a NHL Second All-Star Team (1993)
Played in NHL All-Star Game (1992, 1993)

MOHNS, TROY

Defense. Shoots right. 6', 185 lbs.   Born, Pembroke, Ont., April 20, 1971.
(Los Angeles' 11th choice, 238th overall, in 1990 Entry Draft).

			Regular Season					Playoffs				
Season	Club	Lea	GP	G	A	TP	PIM	GP	G	A	TP	PIM
1989-90	Colgate	ECAC	34	2	11	13	36	....	....	....	....	....
1990-91	Colgate	ECAC	21	0	0	0	10	....	....	....	....	....
1991-92	Colgate	ECAC	20	1	6	7	16	....	....	....	....	....
1992-93	Colgate	ECAC	32	1	8	9	50	....	....	....	....	....

MOLLER, RANDY

Defense. Shoots right. 6'2", 207 lbs.   Born, Red Deer, Alta., August 23, 1963.
(Quebec's 1st choice, 11th overall, in 1981 Entry Draft).

			Regular Season					Playoffs				
Season	Club	Lea	GP	G	A	TP	PIM	GP	G	A	TP	PIM
1980-81	Lethbridge	WHL	46	4	21	25	176	9	0	4	4	24
1981-82a	Lethbridge	WHL	60	20	55	75	249	12	4	6	10	65
	Quebec	**NHL**	....	....	....	....	....	1	0	0	0	0
1982-83	**Quebec**	**NHL**	**75**	**2**	**12**	**14**	**145**	**4**	**1**	**0**	**1**	**4**
1983-84	**Quebec**	**NHL**	**74**	**4**	**14**	**18**	**147**	**9**	**1**	**0**	**1**	**45**
1984-85	**Quebec**	**NHL**	**79**	**7**	**22**	**29**	**120**	**18**	**2**	**2**	**4**	**40**
1985-86	**Quebec**	**NHL**	**69**	**5**	**18**	**23**	**141**	**3**	**0**	**0**	**0**	**26**
1986-87	**Quebec**	**NHL**	**71**	**5**	**9**	**14**	**144**	**13**	**1**	**4**	**5**	**23**
1987-88	**Quebec**	**NHL**	**66**	**3**	**22**	**25**	**169**	....	....	....	....	....
1988-89	**Quebec**	**NHL**	**74**	**7**	**22**	**29**	**136**	....	....	....	....	....
1989-90	**NY Rangers**	**NHL**	**60**	**1**	**12**	**13**	**139**	**10**	**1**	**6**	**7**	**32**
1990-91	**NY Rangers**	**NHL**	**61**	**4**	**19**	**23**	**161**	**6**	**0**	**2**	**2**	**11**
1991-92	**NY Rangers**	**NHL**	**43**	**2**	**7**	**9**	**78**	....	....	....	....	....
	Binghamton	AHL	3	0	1	1	0	....	....	....	....	....
	Buffalo	**NHL**	**13**	**1**	**2**	**3**	**59**	**7**	**0**	**0**	**0**	**8**
1992-93	**Buffalo**	**NHL**	**35**	**2**	**7**	**9**	**83**	....	....	....	....	....
	Rochester	AHL	3	1	0	1	10	....	....	....	....	....
	NHL Totals		**720**	**43**	**166**	**209**	**1522**	**71**	**6**	**14**	**20**	**189**

a WHL Second All-Star Team (1982)
Traded to **NY Rangers** by **Quebec** for Michel Petit, October 5, 1989. Traded to **Buffalo** by **NY Rangers** for Jay Wells, March 9, 1992.

MOMESSO, SERGIO (moh-MESS-oh)

Left wing. Shoots left. 6'3", 215 lbs. Born, Montreal, Que., September 4, 1965.
(Montreal's 3rd choice, 27th overall, in 1983 Entry Draft).

			Regular Season					Playoffs				
Season	Club	Lea	GP	G	A	TP	PIM	GP	G	A	TP	PIM
1982-83	Shawinigan	QMJHL	70	27	42	69	93	10	5	4	9	55
1983-84	Montreal	NHL	1	0	0	0	0	....	....	....	....	....
	Shawinigan	QMJHL	68	42	88	130	235	6	4	4	8	13
	Nova Scotia	AHL	....	....	....	....	....	8	0	2	2	4
1984-85a	Shawinigan	QMJHL	64	56	90	146	216	8	7	8	15	17
1985-86	Montreal	NHL	24	8	7	15	46	....	....	....	....	....
1986-87	Montreal	NHL	59	14	17	31	96	11	1	3	4	31
	Sherbrooke	AHL	6	1	6	7	10	....	....	....	....	....
1987-88	Montreal	NHL	53	7	14	21	101	6	0	2	2	16
1988-89	St. Louis	NHL	53	9	17	26	139	10	2	5	7	24
1989-90	St. Louis	NHL	79	24	32	56	199	12	3	2	5	63
1990-91	St. Louis	NHL	59	10	18	28	131	....	....	....	....	....
	Vancouver	NHL	11	6	2	8	43	6	0	3	3	25
1991-92	Vancouver	NHL	58	20	23	43	198	13	0	5	5	30
1992-93	Vancouver	NHL	84	18	20	38	200	12	3	0	3	30
	NHL Totals		481	116	150	266	1153	70	9	20	29	219

a QMJHL First All-Star Team (1985)

Traded to **St. Louis** by **Montreal** with Vincent Riendeau for Jocelyn Lemieux, Darrell May and St. Louis' second round choice (Patrice Brisebois) in the 1989 Entry Draft, August 9, 1988. Traded to **Vancouver** by **St. Louis** with Geoff Courtnall, Robert Dirk, Cliff Ronning and future considerations for Dan Quinn and Garth Butcher, March 5, 1991.

MONGEAU, MICHEL

Center. Shoots left. 5'9", 190 lbs. Born, Montreal, Que., February 9, 1965.

			Regular Season					Playoffs				
Season	Club	Lea	GP	G	A	TP	PIM	GP	G	A	TP	PIM
1983-84	Laval	QMJHL	60	45	49	94	30	....	....	....	....	....
1984-85	Laval	QMJHL	67	60	84	144	56	....	....	....	....	....
1985-86	Laval	QMJHL	72	71	109	180	45	....	....	....	....	....
1986-87	Saginaw	IHL	76	42	53	95	34	10	3	6	9	6
1987-88	France	....	30	31	21	52	....	....	....	....	....	....
1988-89	Flint	IHL	82	41	76	117	57	....	....	....	....	....
1989-90	St. Louis	NHL	7	1	5	6	2	2	0	1	1	0
abc	Peoria	IHL	73	39	*78	*117	53	5	3	4	7	6
1990-91	St. Louis	NHL	7	1	1	2	0	....	....	....	....	....
de	Peoria	IHL	73	41	65	106	114	19	10	*16	26	32
1991-92	St. Louis	NHL	36	3	12	15	6	....	....	....	....	....
	Peoria	IHL	32	21	34	55	77	10	5	14	19	8
1992-93	Tampa Bay	NHL	4	1	1	2	2	....	....	....	....	....
	Milwaukee	IHL	45	24	41	65	69	4	1	4	5	4
	Halifax	AHL	22	13	18	31	10	....	....	....	....	....
	NHL Totals		54	6	19	25	10	2	0	1	1	0

a IHL First All-Star Team (1990)
b Won James Gatschene Memorial Trophy (MVP-IHL) (1990)
c Won Leo P. Lamoureux Memorial Trophy (Top Scorer-IHL) (1990)
d IHL Second All-Star Team (1991)
e Won N.R. Poile Trophy (MVP in Playoffs–IHL) (1991)

Signed as a free agent by **St. Louis**, August 21, 1989. Claimed by **Tampa Bay** from **St. Louis** in Expansion Draft, June 18, 1992. Traded to **Quebec** by **Tampa Bay** with Martin Simard and Steve Tuttle for Herb Raglan, February 12, 1993.

MONGEON, HUGHES

Center. Shoots left. 5'11", 180 lbs. Born, Ottawa, Ont., March 4, 1972.

			Regular Season					Playoffs				
Season	Club	Lea	GP	G	A	TP	PIM	GP	G	A	TP	PIM
1990-91	Shawinigan	QMJHL	69	37	37	74	24	6	3	2	5	2
1991-92	Granby	QMJHL	51	48	67	115	24	....	....	....	....	....
	Laval	QMJHL	11	5	10	15	11	10	2	4	6	8
1992-93	New Haven	AHL	73	14	27	41	26	....	....	....	....	....

Signed as a free agent by **Ottawa**, October 9, 1992.

MONTGOMERY, JIM

Center. Shoots right. 5'10", 180 lbs. Born, Montreal, Que., June 30, 1969.

			Regular Season					Playoffs				
Season	Club	Lea	GP	G	A	TP	PIM	GP	G	A	TP	PIM
1989-90	U. of Maine	H.E.	45	26	34	60	35	....	....	....	....	....
1990-91	U. of Maine	H.E.	43	24	*57	81	44	....	....	....	....	....
1991-92a	U. of Maine	H.E.	37	21	44	65	46	....	....	....	....	....
1992-93bcde	U. of Maine	H.E.	45	32	63	95	40	....	....	....	....	....

a Hockey East Second All-Star Team (1992)
b Hockey East First All-Star Team (1993)
c NCAA East Second All-American Team (1993)
d NCAA Final Four All-Tournament Team (1993)
e NCAA Final Four Tournament Most Valuable Player (1993)

Signed as a free agent by **St. Louis**, June 2, 1993.

MORAN, IAN

Defense. Shoots right. 5'11", 175 lbs. Born, Cleveland, OH, August 24, 1972.
(Pittsburgh's 6th choice, 107th overall, in 1990 Entry Draft).

			Regular Season					Playoffs				
Season	Club	Lea	GP	G	A	TP	PIM	GP	G	A	TP	PIM
1991-92	Boston College	H.E.	30	2	16	18	44	....	....	....	....	....
1992-93	Boston College	H.E.	31	8	12	20	32	....	....	....	....	....

MORE, JAYSON

Defense. Shoots right. 6'1", 202 lbs. Born, Souris, Man., January 12, 1969.
(NY Rangers' 1st choice, 10th overall, in 1987 Entry Draft).

			Regular Season					Playoffs				
Season	Club	Lea	GP	G	A	TP	PIM	GP	G	A	TP	PIM
1984-85	Lethbridge	WHL	71	3	9	12	101	4	1	0	1	7
1985-86	Lethbridge	WHL	61	7	18	25	155	9	0	2	2	36
1986-87	Brandon	WHL	21	4	6	10	62	....	....	....	....	....
	N. Westminster	WHL	43	4	23	27	155	....	....	....	....	....
1987-88a	N. Westminster	WHL	70	13	47	60	270	5	0	2	2	26
1988-89	NY Rangers	NHL	1	0	0	0	0	....	....	....	....	....
	Denver	IHL	62	7	15	22	138	3	0	1	1	26
1989-90	Flint	IHL	9	1	5	6	41	....	....	....	....	....
	Minnesota	NHL	5	0	0	0	16	....	....	....	....	....
	Kalamazoo	IHL	64	9	25	34	316	10	0	3	3	13
1990-91	Kalamazoo	IHL	10	0	5	5	46	....	....	....	....	....
	Fredericton	AHL	57	7	17	24	152	9	1	1	2	34
1991-92	San Jose	NHL	46	4	13	17	85	....	....	....	....	....
	Kansas City	IHL	2	0	2	2	4	....	....	....	....	....
1992-93	San Jose	NHL	73	5	6	11	179	....	....	....	....	....
	NHL Totals		125	9	19	28	280	....	....	....	....	....

a WHL All-Star Team (1988)

Traded to **Minnesota** by **NY Rangers** for Dave Archibald, November 1, 1989. Traded to **Montreal** by **Minnesota** for Brian Hayward, November 7, 1990. Claimed by **San Jose** from **Montreal** in Expansion Draft, May 30, 1991.

MORIN, STEPHANE (mohr-AN)

Center. Shoots left. 6', 174 lbs. Born, Montreal, Que., March 27, 1969.
(Quebec's 3rd choice, 43rd overall, in 1989 Entry Draft).

			Regular Season					Playoffs				
Season	Club	Lea	GP	G	A	TP	PIM	GP	G	A	TP	PIM
1986-87	Shawinigan	QMJHL	65	9	14	23	28	....	....	....	....	....
1987-88	Chicoutimi	QMJHL	68	38	45	83	18	6	3	8	11	2
1988-89ab	Chicoutimi	QMJHL	70	77	*109	*186	71	....	....	....	....	....
1989-90	Quebec	NHL	6	0	2	2	2	....	....	....	....	....
	Halifax	AHL	65	28	32	60	60	6	3	4	7	6
1990-91	Quebec	NHL	48	13	27	40	30	....	....	....	....	....
	Halifax	AHL	17	8	14	22	18	....	....	....	....	....
1991-92	Quebec	NHL	30	2	8	10	14	....	....	....	....	....
	Halifax	AHL	30	17	13	30	29	....	....	....	....	....
1992-93	Vancouver	NHL	1	0	1	1	0	....	....	....	....	....
	Hamilton	AHL	70	31	54	85	49	....	....	....	....	....
	NHL Totals		85	15	38	53	46	....	....	....	....	....

a QMJHL First All-Star Team (1989)
b QMJHL Player of the Year (1989)

Signed as a free agent by **Vancouver**, October 5, 1992.

MORRIS, JON

Center. Shoots right. 6', 175 lbs. Born, Lowell, MA, May 6, 1966.
(New Jersey's 5th choice, 86th overall, in 1984 Entry Draft).

			Regular Season					Playoffs				
Season	Club	Lea	GP	G	A	TP	PIM	GP	G	A	TP	PIM
1984-85	Lowell	H.E.	42	29	31	60	16	....	....	....	....	....
1985-86	Lowell	H.E.	39	25	31	56	52	....	....	....	....	....
1986-87ab	Lowell	H.E.	35	28	33	61	48	....	....	....	....	....
1987-88	Lowell	H.E.	37	15	39	54	39	....	....	....	....	....
1988-89	New Jersey	NHL	4	0	2	2	0	....	....	....	....	....
1989-90	New Jersey	NHL	20	6	7	13	8	6	1	3	4	23
	Utica	AHL	49	27	37	64	6	....	....	....	....	....
1990-91	New Jersey	NHL	53	9	19	28	27	5	0	4	4	2
	Utica	AHL	6	4	2	6	5	....	....	....	....	....
1991-92	New Jersey	NHL	7	1	2	3	6	....	....	....	....	....
	Utica	AHL	7	1	4	5	0	....	....	....	....	....
1992-93	New Jersey	NHL	2	0	0	0	0	....	....	....	....	....
	Utica	AHL	31	16	24	40	28	....	....	....	....	....
	Cincinnati	IHL	18	7	19	26	24	....	....	....	....	....
	San Jose	NHL	13	0	3	3	6	....	....	....	....	....
	NHL Totals		99	16	33	49	47	11	1	7	8	25

a Hockey East First All-Star Team (1987)
b NCAA East Second All-American Team (1987)

Claimed on waivers by **San Jose** from **New Jersey**, March 13, 1993.

MORRIS, KEITH

Center. Shoots left. 6'1", 185 lbs. Born, Winnipeg, Man., April 24, 1971.
(Winnipeg's 13th choice, 245th overall, in 1990 Entry Draft).

			Regular Season					Playoffs				
Season	Club	Lea	GP	G	A	TP	PIM	GP	G	A	TP	PIM
1989-90	Alaska-Anch.	G.N.	28	10	18	28	14	....	....	....	....	....
1990-91	Alaska-Anch.	G.N.	25	11	11	22	36	....	....	....	....	....
1991-92	Alaska-Anch.	G.N.	35	24	26	50	18	....	....	....	....	....
1992-93	Cdn. National	....	53	7	16	23	27	....	....	....	....	....

MORRISON, BRENDAN

Center. Shoots left. 5'11", 170 lbs. Born, N. Vancouver, B.C., August 12, 1975.
(New Jersey's 3rd choice, 39th overall, in 1993 Entry Draft).

			Regular Season					Playoffs				
Season	Club	Lea	GP	G	A	TP	PIM	GP	G	A	TP	PIM
1991-92	Ridge Meadows	Midget	55	56	111	167	56	....	....	....	....	....
1992-93	Penticton	BCJHL	56	35	59	94	45	....	....	....	....	....

MORRISON, JUSTIN

Center. Shoots right. 5'10", 185 lbs. Born, Newmarket, Ont., February 9, 1972.
(Washington's 4th choice, 80th overall, in 1991 Entry Draft).

			Regular Season					Playoffs				
Season	Club	Lea	GP	G	A	TP	PIM	GP	G	A	TP	PIM
1989-90	Kingston	OHL	65	27	40	67	201	....	....	....	....	....
1990-91	Kingston	OHL	61	44	57	101	222	....	....	....	....	....
1991-92	Kingston	OHL	23	18	21	39	63	....	....	....	....	....
	Owen Sound	OHL	36	9	43	52	106	5	3	2	5	11
1992-93	Belleville	OHL	37	25	48	73	65	7	3	11	14	11
	Toledo	ECHL	13	6	8	14	47	....	....	....	....	....

MORROW, SCOTT

Left wing. Shoots left. 6'1", 181 lbs. Born, Chicago, IL, June 18, 1969.
(Hartford's 4th choice, 95th overall, in 1988 Entry Draft).

			Regular Season					Playoffs				
Season	Club	Lea	GP	G	A	TP	PIM	GP	G	A	TP	PIM
1988-89	N. Hampshire	H.E.	19	6	7	13	14	....	....	....	....	....
1989-90	N. Hampshire	H.E.	29	10	11	21	35	....	....	....	....	....
1990-91	N. Hampshire	H.E.	31	11	11	22	52	....	....	....	....	....
1991-92a	N. Hampshire	H.E.	35	30	23	53	65	....	....	....	....	....
	Springfield	AHL	2	0	1	1	0	5	0	0	0	9
1992-93	Springfield	AHL	70	22	29	51	80	15	6	9	15	21

a Hockey East Second All-Star Team (1992)

MORROW, STEVEN

Defense. Shoots left. 6'2", 220 lbs. Born, Evanston, IL, April 3, 1968.
(Philadelphia's 10th choice, 209th overall, in 1987 Entry Draft).

			Regular Season					Playoffs				
Season	Club	Lea	GP	G	A	TP	PIM	GP	G	A	TP	PIM
1988-89	N. Hampshire	H.E.	30	0	0	0	28	....	....	....	....	....
1989-90	N. Hampshire	H.E.	35	2	7	9	40	....	....	....	....	....
1990-91	N. Hampshire	H.E.	33	2	14	16	58	....	....	....	....	....
1991-92	Hershey	AHL	31	1	2	3	6	....	....	....	....	....
1992-93	Fort Worth	CHL	10	1	4	5	6	....	....	....	....	....
	Hershey	AHL	38	0	4	4	59	....	....	....	....	....

MOSER, JOHN (JAY)

Defense. Shoots left. 6'2", 170 lbs. Born, Cottage Grove, MN, December 26, 1972.
(Boston's 7th choice, 172nd overall, in 1991 Entry Draft).

			Regular Season					Playoffs				
Season	Club	Lea	GP	G	A	TP	PIM	GP	G	A	TP	PIM
1991-92	St. Cloud	WCHA	35	3	9	12	40	....	....	....	....	....
1992-93	St. Cloud	WCHA	33	2	9	11	77	....	....	....	....	....

MOTKOV, DMITRI (moht-KOHV)

Defense. Shoots left. 6'3", 191 lbs. Born, Moscow, Soviet Union, February 23, 1971.
(Detroit's 5th choice, 98th overall, in 1991 Entry Draft).

			Regular Season					Playoffs				
Season	Club	Lea	GP	G	A	TP	PIM	GP	G	A	TP	PIM
1989-90	CSKA	USSR	30	0	1	1	20	....	....	....	....	....
1990-91	CSKA	USSR	32	0	2	2	14	....	....	....	....	....
1991-92	CSKA	CIS	44	1	3	4	59	....	....	....	....	....
1992-93	Adirondack	AHL	41	3	7	10	30	....	....	....	....	....

MROZIK, RICK

Defense. Shoots left. 6'2", 185 lbs. Born, Duluth, MN, January 2, 1975.
(Dallas' 4th choice, 136th overall, in 1993 Entry Draft).

			Regular Season					Playoffs				
Season	Club	Lea	GP	G	A	TP	PIM	GP	G	A	TP	PIM
1992-93	Cloquet	HS	28	9	38	47	12	....	....	....	....	....

MUELLER, BRIAN

Defense. Shoots left. 5'11", 200 lbs. Born, Liverpool, NY, June 2, 1972.
(Hartford's 7th choice, 141st overall, in 1991 Entry Draft).

			Regular Season					Playoffs				
Season	Club	Lea	GP	G	A	TP	PIM	GP	G	A	TP	PIM
1991-92	Clarkson	ECAC	28	4	13	17	30	....	....	....	....	....
1992-93	Clarkson	ECAC	32	6	23	29	12	....	....	....	....	....

MULHERN, RYAN

Center. Shoots right. 6'1", 180 lbs. Born, Philadelphia, PA, January 11, 1973.
(Calgary's 8th choice, 174th overall, in 1992 Entry Draft).

			Regular Season					Playoffs				
Season	Club	Lea	GP	G	A	TP	PIM	GP	G	A	TP	PIM
1991-92	Canterbury	HS	37	51	27	78	50	....	....	....	....	....
1992-93	Brown	ECAC	31	15	9	24	46	....	....	....	....	....

MULLEN, BRIAN

Right wing. Shoots left. 5'10", 180 lbs. Born, New York, NY, March 16, 1962.
(Winnipeg's 7th choice, 128th overall, in 1980 Entry Draft).

			Regular Season					Playoffs				
Season	Club	Lea	GP	G	A	TP	PIM	GP	G	A	TP	PIM
1980-81	U. Wisconsin	WCHA	38	11	13	24	28	....	....	....	....	....
1981-82	U. Wisconsin	WCHA	33	20	17	37	10	....	....	....	....	....
1982-83	**Winnipeg**	**NHL**	**80**	**24**	**26**	**50**	**14**	**3**	**1**	**0**	**1**	**0**
1983-84	**Winnipeg**	**NHL**	**75**	**21**	**41**	**62**	**28**	**3**	**0**	**3**	**3**	**6**
1984-85	**Winnipeg**	**NHL**	**69**	**32**	**39**	**71**	**32**	**8**	**1**	**2**	**3**	**4**
1985-86	**Winnipeg**	**NHL**	**79**	**28**	**34**	**62**	**38**	**3**	**1**	**2**	**3**	**6**
1986-87	**Winnipeg**	**NHL**	**69**	**19**	**32**	**51**	**20**	**9**	**4**	**2**	**6**	**0**
1987-88	**NY Rangers**	**NHL**	**74**	**25**	**29**	**54**	**42**	....	....	....	....	....
1988-89	**NY Rangers**	**NHL**	**78**	**29**	**35**	**64**	**60**	**3**	**0**	**1**	**1**	**4**
1989-90	**NY Rangers**	**NHL**	**76**	**27**	**41**	**68**	**42**	**10**	**2**	**2**	**4**	**8**
1990-91	**NY Rangers**	**NHL**	**79**	**19**	**43**	**62**	**44**	**5**	**0**	**2**	**2**	**0**
1991-92	**San Jose**	**NHL**	**72**	**18**	**28**	**46**	**66**	....	....	....	....	....
1992-93	**NY Islanders**	**NHL**	**81**	**18**	**14**	**32**	**28**	**18**	**3**	**4**	**7**	**2**
	NHL Totals		**832**	**260**	**362**	**622**	**414**	**62**	**12**	**18**	**30**	**30**

Played in NHL All-Star Game (1989)

Traded to **NY Rangers** by **Winnipeg** with Winnipeg's tenth round choice (Brett Barnett) in 1987 Entry Draft for NY Rangers' fifth round choice (Benoit Lebeau) in 1988 Entry Draft and NY Rangers' third round choice (later traded to St. Louis — St. Louis selected Denny Felsner) in 1989 Entry Draft, June 8, 1987. Traded to **San Jose** by **NY Rangers** with future considerations for Tim Kerr, May 30, 1991. Traded to **NY Islanders** by **San Jose** for the rights to Marcus Thuresson, August 24, 1992.

MULLEN, JOE

Right wing. Shoots right. 5'9", 180 lbs. Born, New York, NY, February 26, 1957.

			Regular Season					Playoffs				
Season	Club	Lea	GP	G	A	TP	PIM	GP	G	A	TP	PIM
1977-78a	Boston College	ECAC	34	34	34	68	12	....	....	....	....	....
1978-79a	Boston College	ECAC	25	32	24	56	8	....	....	....	....	....
1979-80bc	Salt Lake	CHL	75	40	32	72	21	13	*9	11	20	0
	St. Louis	**NHL**	....	....	....	....	....	**1**	**0**	**0**	**0**	**0**
1980-81de	Salt Lake	CHL	80	59	58	*117	8	17	11	9	20	0
1981-82	**St. Louis**	**NHL**	**45**	**25**	**34**	**59**	**4**	**10**	**7**	**11**	**18**	**4**
	Salt Lake	CHL	27	21	27	48	12	....	....	....	....	....
1982-83	**St. Louis**	**NHL**	**49**	**17**	**30**	**47**	**6**	....	....	....	....	....
1983-84	**St. Louis**	**NHL**	**80**	**41**	**44**	**85**	**19**	**6**	**2**	**0**	**2**	**0**
1984-85	**St. Louis**	**NHL**	**79**	**40**	**52**	**92**	**6**	**3**	**0**	**0**	**0**	**0**
1985-86	**St. Louis**	**NHL**	**48**	**28**	**24**	**52**	**10**	....	....	....	....	....
	Calgary	**NHL**	**29**	**16**	**22**	**38**	**11**	**21**	***12**	**7**	**19**	**4**
1986-87f	**Calgary**	**NHL**	**79**	**47**	**40**	**87**	**14**	**6**	**2**	**1**	**3**	**0**
1987-88	**Calgary**	**NHL**	**80**	**40**	**44**	**84**	**30**	**7**	**2**	**4**	**6**	**10**
1988-89fgh	**Calgary**	**NHL**	**79**	**51**	**59**	**110**	**16**	**21**	***16**	**8**	**24**	**4**
1989-90	**Calgary**	**NHL**	**78**	**36**	**33**	**69**	**24**	**6**	**3**	**0**	**3**	**0**
1990-91	**Pittsburgh**	**NHL**	**47**	**17**	**22**	**39**	**6**	**22**	**8**	**9**	**17**	**4**
1991-92	**Pittsburgh**	**NHL**	**77**	**42**	**45**	**87**	**30**	**9**	**3**	**1**	**4**	**4**
1992-93	**Pittsburgh**	**NHL**	**72**	**33**	**37**	**70**	**14**	**12**	**4**	**2**	**6**	**6**
	NHL Totals		**842**	**433**	**486**	**919**	**190**	**124**	**59**	**43**	**102**	**36**

a ECAC First All-Star Team (1978, 1979)
b CHL Second All-Star Team (1980)
c Won Ken McKenzie Trophy (CHL's Top Rookie) (1980)
d CHL First All-Star Team (1981)
e Won Tommy Ivan Trophy (CHL's Most Valuable Player) (1981)
f Won Lady Byng Trophy (1987, 1989)
g NHL First All-Star Team (1989)
h NHL Plus/Minus Leader (1989)

Played in NHL All-Star Game (1989, 1990)

Signed as a free agent by **St. Louis,** August 16, 1979. Traded to **Calgary** by **St. Louis** with Terry Johnson and Rik Wilson for Ed Beers, Charles Bourgeois and Gino Cavallini, February 1, 1986. Traded to **Pittsburgh** by **Calgary** for Pittsburgh's second round choice (Nicolas Perreault) in 1990 Entry Draft, June 16, 1990.

MULLER, KIRK

Left wing. Shoots left. 6', 205 lbs. Born, Kingston, Ont., February 8, 1966.
(New Jersey's 1st choice, 2nd overall, in 1984 Entry Draft).

			Regular Season					Playoffs				
Season	Club	Lea	GP	G	A	TP	PIM	GP	G	A	TP	PIM
1981-82	Kingston	OHL	67	12	39	51	27	4	5	1	6	4
1982-83ab	Guelph	OHL	66	52	60	112	41	....	....	....	....	....
1983-84b	Cdn. Olympic	....	21	4	3	7	6	....	....	....	....	....
	Guelph	OHL	49	31	63	94	27	....	....	....	....	....
1984-85	**New Jersey**	**NHL**	**80**	**17**	**37**	**54**	**69**	....	....	....	....	....
1985-86	**New Jersey**	**NHL**	**77**	**25**	**41**	**66**	**45**	....	....	....	....	....
1986-87	**New Jersey**	**NHL**	**79**	**26**	**50**	**76**	**75**	....	....	....	....	....
1987-88	**New Jersey**	**NHL**	**80**	**37**	**57**	**94**	**114**	**20**	**4**	**8**	**12**	**37**
1988-89	**New Jersey**	**NHL**	**80**	**31**	**43**	**74**	**119**	....	....	....	....	....
1989-90	**New Jersey**	**NHL**	**80**	**30**	**56**	**86**	**74**	**6**	**1**	**3**	**4**	**11**
1990-91	**New Jersey**	**NHL**	**80**	**19**	**51**	**70**	**76**	**7**	**0**	**2**	**2**	**10**
1991-92	**Montreal**	**NHL**	**78**	**36**	**41**	**77**	**86**	**11**	**4**	**3**	**7**	**31**
1992-93	**Montreal**	**NHL**	**80**	**37**	**57**	**94**	**77**	**20**	**10**	**7**	**17**	**18**
	NHL Totals		**714**	**258**	**433**	**691**	**735**	**64**	**19**	**23**	**42**	**107**

a OHL's Most Gentlemanly Player (1983)
b OHL Third All-Star Team (1983, 1984)

Played in NHL All-Star Game (1985, 1986, 1988, 1990, 1992, 1993)

Traded to **Montreal** by **New Jersey** with Roland Melanson for Stephane Richer and Tom Chorske, September 20, 1991.

MULLER, MIKE

Defense. Shoots left. 6'2", 205 lbs. Born, Fairview, MN, September 18, 1971.
(Winnipeg's 2nd choice, 35th overall, in 1990 Entry Draft).

			Regular Season					Playoffs				
Season	Club	Lea	GP	G	A	TP	PIM	GP	G	A	TP	PIM
1990-91	U. Minnesota	WCHA	33	4	4	8	44	....	....	....	....	....
1991-92	U. Minnesota	WCHA	41	4	12	16	52	....	....	....	....	....
1992-93	Moscow D'amo	CIS	11	1	0	1	8	....	....	....	....	....

MULVENNA, GLENN

Center. Shoots left. 5'11", 187 lbs. Born, Calgary, Alta., February 18, 1967.

			Regular Season					Playoffs				
Season	Club	Lea	GP	G	A	TP	PIM	GP	G	A	TP	PIM
1986-87	N. Westminster	WHL	53	24	44	68	43	....	....	....	....	....
	Kamloops	WHL	18	13	8	21	18	13	4	6	10	10
1987-88	Kamloops	WHL	38	21	38	59	35	....	....	....	....	....
1988-89	Flint	IHL	32	9	14	23	12	....	....	....	....	....
	Muskegon	IHL	11	3	2	5	0	....	....	....	....	....
1989-90	Muskegon	IHL	52	14	21	35	17	11	2	3	5	0
	Fort Wayne	IHL	6	2	5	7	2	....	....	....	....	....
1990-91	Muskegon	IHL	48	9	27	36	25	5	1	1	2	0
1991-92	**Pittsburgh**	**NHL**	**1**	**0**	**0**	**0**	**2**	....	....	....	....	....
	Muskegon	IHL	70	15	27	42	24	14	5	6	11	11
1992-93	**Philadelphia**	**NHL**	**1**	**0**	**0**	**0**	**2**	....	....	....	....	....
	Hershey	AHL	35	5	17	22	8	....	....	....	....	....
	NHL Totals		**2**	**0**	**0**	**0**	**4**	....	....	....	....	....

Signed as a free agent by **Pittsburgh**, December 3, 1987. Signed as a free agent by **Philadelphia**, July 11, 1992.

MUNI, CRAIG DOUGLAS (MYEW-nee)

Defense. Shoots left. 6'3", 200 lbs. Born, Toronto, Ont., July 19, 1962.
(Toronto's 1st choice, 25th overall, in 1980 Entry Draft).

			Regular Season					Playoffs				
Season	Club	Lea	GP	G	A	TP	PIM	GP	G	A	TP	PIM
1980-81	Kingston	OHA	38	2	14	16	65	....	....	....	....	....
	Windsor	OHA	25	5	11	16	41	11	1	4	5	14
	New Brunswick	AHL	....	....	....	....	....	2	0	1	1	10
1981-82	**Toronto**	**NHL**	**3**	**0**	**0**	**0**	**2**	....	....	....	....	....
	Windsor	OHL	49	5	32	37	92	9	2	3	5	16
	Cincinnati	CHL	....	....	....	....	....	3	0	2	2	2
1982-83	**Toronto**	**NHL**	**2**	**0**	**1**	**1**	**0**	....	....	....	....	....
	St. Catharines	AHL	64	6	32	38	52	....	....	....	....	....
1983-84	St. Catharines	AHL	64	4	16	20	79	7	0	1	1	0
1984-85	**Toronto**	**NHL**	**8**	**0**	**0**	**0**	**0**	....	....	....	....	....
	St. Catharines	AHL	68	7	17	24	54	....	....	....	....	....
1985-86	**Toronto**	**NHL**	**6**	**0**	**1**	**1**	**4**	....	....	....	....	....
	St. Catharines	AHL	73	3	34	37	91	13	0	5	5	16
1986-87	**Edmonton**	**NHL**	**79**	**7**	**22**	**29**	**85**	**14**	**0**	**2**	**2**	**17**
1987-88	**Edmonton**	**NHL**	**72**	**4**	**15**	**19**	**77**	**19**	**0**	**4**	**4**	**31**
1988-89	**Edmonton**	**NHL**	**69**	**5**	**13**	**18**	**71**	**7**	**0**	**3**	**3**	**8**
1989-90	**Edmonton**	**NHL**	**71**	**5**	**12**	**17**	**81**	**22**	**0**	**3**	**3**	**16**
1990-91	**Edmonton**	**NHL**	**76**	**1**	**9**	**10**	**77**	**18**	**0**	**3**	**3**	**20**
1991-92	**Edmonton**	**NHL**	**54**	**2**	**5**	**7**	**34**	**3**	**0**	**0**	**0**	**2**
1992-93	**Edmonton**	**NHL**	**72**	**0**	**11**	**11**	**67**	....	....	....	....	....
	Chicago	**NHL**	**9**	**0**	**0**	**0**	**8**	**4**	**0**	**0**	**0**	**2**
	NHL Totals		**521**	**24**	**89**	**113**	**506**	**87**	**0**	**15**	**15**	**96**

Signed as a free agent by **Edmonton,** August 18, 1986. Sold to **Buffalo** by **Edmonton,** October 2, 1986. Traded to **Pittsburgh** by **Buffalo** for future considerations, October 3, 1986. Traded to **Edmonton** by **Pittsburgh** to complete September 11, 1985 trade which sent Gilles Meloche to Pittsburgh for Tim Hrynewich, Marty McSorley and future considerations, October 6, 1986. Traded to **Chicago** by **Edmonton** for Mike Hudson, March 22, 1993.

MURANO, ERIC

Center. Shoots right. 6', 200 lbs. Born, Montreal, Que., May 4, 1967.
(Vancouver's 4th choice, 91st overall, in 1986 Entry Draft).

			Regular Season					Playoffs				
Season	Club	Lea	GP	G	A	TP	PIM	GP	G	A	TP	PIM
1986-87	U. of Denver	WCHA	31	5	7	12	12	....	....	....	....	....
1987-88	U. of Denver	WCHA	37	8	13	21	26	....	....	....	....	....
1988-89	U. of Denver	WCHA	42	13	16	29	52	....	....	....	....	....
1989-90a	U. of Denver	WCHA	42	33	35	68	52	....	....	....	....	....
	Cdn. Olympic	....	6	1	0	1	4	....	....	....	....	....
1990-91	Milwaukee	IHL	63	32	35	67	63	3	0	1	1	4
1991-92	Milwaukee	IHL	80	35	48	83	61	5	3	4	7	0
1992-93	Hamilton	AHL	42	25	24	49	10	....	....	....	....	....
	Baltimore	AHL	32	16	14	30	10	7	7	5	12	6

a WCHA Second All-Star Team (1990)

Traded to **Washington** by **Vancouver** for Tim Taylor, January 29, 1993.

MURPHY, DANIEL

Defense. Shoots left. 6'1", 185 lbs. Born, Needham, MA, May 13, 1970.
(Boston's 5th choice, 102nd overall, in 1988 Entry Draft).

			Regular Season					Playoffs				
Season	Club	Lea	GP	G	A	TP	PIM	GP	G	A	TP	PIM
1989-90	U. of Maine	H.E.	42	1	9	10	26	....	....	....	....	....
1990-91	U. of Maine	H.E.	42	1	5	6	26	....	....	....	....	....
1991-92	U. of Maine	H.E.	36	0	6	6	44	....	....	....	....	....
1992-93	U. of Maine	H.E.	44	0	11	11	56	....	....	....	....	....

MURPHY, GORDON (GORD)

Defense. Shoots right. 6'2", 195 lbs. Born, Willowdale, Ont., March 23, 1967.
(Philadelphia's 10th choice, 189th overall, in 1985 Entry Draft).

			Regular Season					Playoffs				
Season	Club	Lea	GP	G	A	TP	PIM	GP	G	A	TP	PIM
1984-85	Oshawa	OHL	59	3	12	15	25	....	....	....	....	....
1985-86	Oshawa	OHL	64	7	15	22	56	6	1	1	2	6
1986-87	Oshawa	OHL	56	7	30	37	95	24	6	16	22	22
1987-88	Hershey	AHL	62	8	20	28	44	12	0	8	8	12
1988-89	**Philadelphia**	**NHL**	**75**	**4**	**31**	**35**	**68**	**19**	**2**	**7**	**9**	**13**
1989-90	**Philadelphia**	**NHL**	**75**	**14**	**27**	**41**	**95**	....	....	....	....	....
1990-91	**Philadelphia**	**NHL**	**80**	**11**	**31**	**42**	**58**	....	....	....	....	....
1991-92	**Philadelphia**	**NHL**	**31**	**2**	**8**	**10**	**33**	....	....	....	....	....
	Boston	**NHL**	**42**	**3**	**6**	**9**	**51**	**15**	**1**	**0**	**1**	**12**
1992-93	**Boston**	**NHL**	**49**	**5**	**12**	**17**	**62**	....	....	....	....	....
	Providence	AHL	2	1	3	4	2	....	....	....	....	....
	NHL Totals		**352**	**39**	**115**	**154**	**367**	**34**	**3**	**7**	**10**	**25**

Traded to **Boston** by **Philadelphia** with Brian Dobbin and Philadelphia's third round choice (Sergei Zholtok) in 1992 Entry Draft for Garry Galley, Wes Walz and future considerations, January 2, 1992. Traded to **Dallas** by **Boston** for future considerations (John Casey traded to Boston for Andy Moog, June 25, 1993), June 20, 1993. Claimed by **Florida** from **Dallas** in Expansion Draft, June 24, 1993.

MURPHY, JOE

Right wing. Shoots left. 6'1", 190 lbs. Born, London, Ont., October 16, 1967.
(Detroit's 1st choice, 1st overall, in 1986 Entry Draft).

			Regular Season					Playoffs				
Season	Club	Lea	GP	G	A	TP	PIM	GP	G	A	TP	PIM
1985-86	Cdn. Olympic	....	8	3	3	6	2	....	....	....	....	....
a	Michigan State	CCHA	35	24	37	61	50	....	....	....	....	....
1986-87	**Detroit**	**NHL**	**5**	**0**	**1**	**1**	**2**	....	....	....	....	....
	Adirondack	AHL	71	21	38	59	61	10	2	1	3	33
1987-88	**Detroit**	**NHL**	**50**	**10**	**9**	**19**	**37**	**8**	**0**	**1**	**1**	**6**
	Adirondack	AHL	6	5	6	11	4	....	....	....	....	....
1988-89	**Detroit**	**NHL**	**26**	**1**	**7**	**8**	**28**	....	....	....	....	....
	Adirondack	AHL	47	31	35	66	66	16	6	11	17	17
1989-90	**Detroit**	**NHL**	**9**	**3**	**1**	**4**	**4**	....	....	....	....	....
	Edmonton	**NHL**	**62**	**7**	**18**	**25**	**56**	**22**	**6**	**8**	**14**	**16**
1990-91	**Edmonton**	**NHL**	**80**	**27**	**35**	**62**	**35**	**15**	**2**	**5**	**7**	**14**
1991-92	**Edmonton**	**NHL**	**80**	**35**	**47**	**82**	**52**	**16**	**8**	**16**	**24**	**12**
1992-93	**Chicago**	**NHL**	**19**	**7**	**10**	**17**	**18**	**4**	**0**	**0**	**0**	**8**
	NHL Totals		**331**	**90**	**128**	**218**	**232**	**65**	**16**	**30**	**46**	**56**

a CCHA Rookie of the Year (1986)

Traded to **Edmonton** by **Detroit** with Petr Klima, Adam Graves and Jeff Sharples for Jimmy Carson, Kevin McClelland and Edmonton's fifth round choice (later traded to Montreal — Montreal selected Brad Layzell) in 1991 Entry Draft, November 2, 1989. Traded to **Chicago** by **Edmonton** for Igor Kravchuk and Dean McAmmond, February 24, 1993.

MURPHY, LAWRENCE THOMAS (LARRY)

Defense. Shoots right. 6'2", 210 lbs. Born, Scarborough, Ont., March 8, 1961.
(Los Angeles' 1st choice, 4th overall, in 1980 Entry Draft).

			Regular Season					Playoffs				
Season	Club	Lea	GP	G	A	TP	PIM	GP	G	A	TP	PIM
1978-79	Peterborough	OHA	66	6	21	27	82	19	1	9	10	42
1979-80a	Peterborough	OHA	68	21	68	89	88	14	4	13	17	20
1980-81	**Los Angeles**	**NHL**	**80**	**16**	**60**	**76**	**79**	**4**	**3**	**0**	**3**	**2**
1981-82	**Los Angeles**	**NHL**	**79**	**22**	**44**	**66**	**95**	**10**	**2**	**8**	**10**	**12**
1982-83	**Los Angeles**	**NHL**	**77**	**14**	**48**	**62**	**81**	....	....	....	....	....
1983-84	**Los Angeles**	**NHL**	**6**	**0**	**3**	**3**	**0**	....	....	....	....	....
	Washington	**NHL**	**72**	**13**	**33**	**46**	**50**	**8**	**0**	**3**	**3**	**6**
1984-85	**Washington**	**NHL**	**79**	**13**	**42**	**55**	**51**	**5**	**2**	**3**	**5**	**0**
1985-86	**Washington**	**NHL**	**78**	**21**	**44**	**65**	**50**	**9**	**1**	**5**	**6**	**6**
1986-87b	**Washington**	**NHL**	**80**	**23**	**58**	**81**	**39**	**7**	**2**	**2**	**4**	**6**
1987-88	**Washington**	**NHL**	**79**	**8**	**53**	**61**	**72**	**13**	**4**	**4**	**8**	**33**
1988-89	**Washington**	**NHL**	**65**	**7**	**29**	**36**	**70**	....	....	....	....	....
	Minnesota	**NHL**	**13**	**4**	**6**	**10**	**12**	**5**	**0**	**2**	**2**	**8**
1989-90	**Minnesota**	**NHL**	**77**	**10**	**58**	**68**	**44**	**7**	**1**	**2**	**3**	**31**
1990-91	**Minnesota**	**NHL**	**31**	**4**	**11**	**15**	**38**	....	....	....	....	....
	Pittsburgh	**NHL**	**44**	**5**	**23**	**28**	**30**	**23**	**5**	**18**	**23**	**44**
1991-92	**Pittsburgh**	**NHL**	**77**	**21**	**56**	**77**	**48**	**21**	**6**	**10**	**16**	**19**
1992-93b	**Pittsburgh**	**NHL**	**83**	**22**	**63**	**85**	**73**	**12**	**2**	**11**	**13**	**10**
	NHL Totals		**1020**	**203**	**631**	**834**	**832**	**124**	**28**	**68**	**96**	**177**

a OHA First All-Star Team (1980)
b NHL Second All-Star Team (1987, 1993)

Traded to **Washington** by **Los Angeles** for Ken Houston and Brian Engblom, October 18, 1983. Traded to **Minnesota** by **Washington** with Mike Gartner for Dino Ciccarelli and Bob Rouse, March 7, 1989. Traded to **Pittsburgh** by **Minnesota** with Peter Taglianetti for Chris Dahlquist and Jim Johnson, December 11, 1990.

MURPHY, ROB

Center. Shoots left. 6'3", 205 lbs. Born, Hull, Que., April 7, 1969.
(Vancouver's 1st choice, 24th overall, in 1987 Entry Draft).

			Regular Season					Playoffs				
Season	Club	Lea	GP	G	A	TP	PIM	GP	G	A	TP	PIM
1986-87	Laval	QMJHL	70	35	54	89	86	14	3	4	7	15
1987-88	**Vancouver**	**NHL**	**5**	**0**	**0**	**0**	**2**	....	....	....	....	....
	Laval	QMJHL	26	11	25	36	82	....	....	....	....	....
	Drummondville	QMJHL	33	16	28	44	41	17	4	15	19	45
1988-89	**Vancouver**	**NHL**	**8**	**0**	**1**	**1**	**2**	....	....	....	....	....
	Milwaukee	IHL	8	4	2	6	4	11	3	5	8	34
	Drummondville	QMJHL	26	13	25	38	16	4	1	3	4	20
1989-90	**Vancouver**	**NHL**	**12**	**1**	**1**	**2**	**0**	....	....	....	....	....
a	Milwaukee	IHL	64	24	47	71	87	6	2	6	8	12
1990-91	**Vancouver**	**NHL**	**42**	**5**	**1**	**6**	**90**	**4**	**0**	**0**	**0**	**2**
	Milwaukee	IHL	23	1	7	8	48	....	....	....	....	....
1991-92	**Vancouver**	**NHL**	**6**	**0**	**1**	**1**	**6**	....	....	....	....	....
	Milwaukee	IHL	73	26	38	64	141	5	0	3	3	2
1992-93	**Ottawa**	**NHL**	**44**	**3**	**7**	**10**	**30**	....	....	....	....	....
	New Haven	AHL	26	8	12	20	28	....	....	....	....	....
	NHL Totals		**117**	**9**	**11**	**20**	**130**	**4**	**0**	**0**	**0**	**2**

a Won Garry F. Longman Memorial Trophy (Top Rookie-IHL) (1990)

Claimed by **Ottawa** from **Vancouver** in Expansion Draft, June 18, 1992. Signed as a free agent by **Los Angeles**, August 2, 1993.

MURRAY, GLEN

Right wing. Shoots right. 6'2", 210 lbs. Born, Halifax, N.S., November 1, 1972.
(Boston's 1st choice, 18th overall, in 1991 Entry Draft).

			Regular Season					Playoffs				
Season	Club	Lea	GP	G	A	TP	PIM	GP	G	A	TP	PIM
1989-90	Sudbury	OHL	62	8	28	36	17	7	0	0	0	4
1990-91	Sudbury	OHL	66	27	38	65	82	5	8	4	12	10
1991-92	**Boston**	**NHL**	**5**	**3**	**1**	**4**	**0**	**15**	**4**	**2**	**6**	**10**
	Sudbury	OHL	54	37	47	84	93	11	7	4	11	18
1992-93	**Boston**	**NHL**	**27**	**3**	**4**	**7**	**8**	....	....	....	....	....
	Providence	AHL	48	30	26	56	42	6	1	4	5	4
	NHL Totals		**32**	**6**	**5**	**11**	**8**	**15**	**4**	**2**	**6**	**10**

MURRAY, MARTY

Center. Shoots left. 5'8", 164 lbs. Born, Deloraine, Man., February 16, 1975.
(Calgary's 5th choice, 96th overall, in 1993 Entry Draft).

			Regular Season					Playoffs				
Season	Club	Lea	GP	G	A	TP	PIM	GP	G	A	TP	PIM
1991-92	Brandon	WHL	68	20	36	56	22	....	....	....	....	....
1992-93	Brandon	WHL	67	29	15	94	50	4	1	3	4	0

MURRAY, MICHAEL

Right wing. Shoots right. 6'1", 185 lbs. Born, Cumberland, RI, April 18, 1971.
(Calgary's 10th choice, 188th overall, in 1990 Entry Draft).

			Regular Season					Playoffs				
Season	Club	Lea	GP	G	A	TP	PIM	GP	G	A	TP	PIM
1990-91	Lowell	H.E.	30	5	8	13	18	....	....	....	....	....
1991-92	Lowell	H.E.	31	22	15	37	40	....	....	....	....	....
1992-93a	Lowell	H.E.	39	23	33	56	78	....	....	....	....	....

a Hockey East Second All-Star Team (1993)

MURRAY, PAT

Left wing. Shoots left. 6'2", 185 lbs. Born, Stratford, Ont., August 20, 1969.
(Philadelphia's 2nd choice, 35th overall, in 1988 Entry Draft).

			Regular Season					Playoffs				
Season	Club	Lea	GP	G	A	TP	PIM	GP	G	A	TP	PIM
1987-88	Michigan State	CCHA	42	14	21	35	26	....	....	....	....	....
1988-89	Michigan State	CCHA	46	21	41	62	65	....	....	....	....	....
1989-90a	Michigan State	CCHA	45	24	60	84	36	....	....	....	....	....
1990-91	Philadelphia	NHL	16	2	1	3	15	....	....	....	....	....
	Hershey	AHL	57	15	38	53	8	7	5	2	7	0
1991-92	Philadelphia	NHL	9	1	0	1	0	....	....	....	....	....
	Hershey	AHL	69	19	43	62	25	6	1	2	3	0
1992-93	Hershey	AHL	69	21	32	53	63	....	....	....	....	....
	NHL Totals		25	3	1	4	15	....	....	....	....	....

a CCHA Second All-Star Team (1990)

MURRAY, RAYMOND (REM)

Left wing. Shoots left. 6'1", 178 lbs. Born, Stratford, Ont., October 9, 1972.
(Los Angeles' 5th choice, 135th overall, in 1992 Entry Draft).

			Regular Season					Playoffs				
Season	Club	Lea	GP	G	A	TP	PIM	GP	G	A	TP	PIM
1991-92	Michigan State	CCHA	41	12	36	48	16	....	....	....	....	....
1992-93	Michigan State	CCHA	40	22	35	57	24	....	....	....	....	....

MURRAY, ROB

Center. Shoots right. 6'1", 180 lbs. Born, Toronto, Ont., April 4, 1967.
(Washington's 3rd choice, 61st overall, in 1985 Entry Draft).

			Regular Season					Playoffs				
Season	Club	Lea	GP	G	A	TP	PIM	GP	G	A	TP	PIM
1984-85	Peterborough	OHL	63	12	9	21	155	17	2	7	9	45
1985-86	Peterborough	OHL	52	14	18	32	125	16	1	2	3	50
1986-87	Peterborough	OHL	62	17	37	54	204	3	1	4	5	8
1987-88	Fort Wayne	IHL	80	12	21	33	139	6	0	2	2	16
1988-89	Baltimore	AHL	80	11	23	34	235	....	....	....	....	....
1989-90	Washington	NHL	41	2	7	9	58	9	0	0	0	18
	Baltimore	AHL	23	5	4	9	63	....	....	....	....	....
1990-91	Washington	NHL	17	0	3	3	19	....	....	....	....	....
	Baltimore	AHL	48	6	20	26	177	4	0	0	0	12
1991-92	Winnipeg	NHL	9	0	1	1	18	....	....	....	....	....
	Moncton	AHL	60	16	15	31	247	8	0	1	1	56
1992-93	Winnipeg	NHL	10	1	0	1	6	....	....	....	....	....
	Moncton	AHL	56	16	21	37	147	3	0	0	0	6
	NHL Totals		77	3	11	14	101	9	0	0	0	18

Claimed by **Minnesota** from **Washington** in Expansion Draft, May 30, 1991. Traded to **Winnipeg** by **Minnesota** with future considerations for Winnipeg's seventh round choice (Geoff Finch) in 1991 Entry Draft and future considerations, May 31, 1991.

MURRAY, TROY NORMAN

Center. Shoots right. 6'1", 195 lbs. Born, Calgary, Alta., July 31, 1962.
(Chicago's 6th choice, 57th overall, in 1980 Entry Draft).

			Regular Season					Playoffs				
Season	Club	Lea	GP	G	A	TP	PIM	GP	G	A	TP	PIM
1980-81ab	North Dakota	WCHA	38	33	45	78	28	....	....	....	....	....
1981-82b	North Dakota	WCHA	26	13	17	30	62	....	....	....	....	....
	Chicago	NHL	1	0	0	0	0	7	1	0	1	5
1982-83	Chicago	NHL	54	8	8	16	27	2	0	0	0	0
1983-84	Chicago	NHL	61	15	15	30	45	5	1	0	1	7
1984-85	Chicago	NHL	80	26	40	66	82	15	5	14	19	24
1985-86c	Chicago	NHL	80	45	54	99	94	2	0	0	0	2
1986-87	Chicago	NHL	77	28	43	71	59	4	0	0	0	5
1987-88	Chicago	NHL	79	22	36	58	96	5	1	0	1	8
1988-89	Chicago	NHL	79	21	30	51	113	16	3	6	9	25
1989-90	Chicago	NHL	68	17	38	55	86	20	4	4	8	2
1990-91	Chicago	NHL	75	14	23	37	74	6	0	1	1	12
1991-92	Winnipeg	NHL	74	17	30	47	69	7	0	0	0	2
1992-93	Winnipeg	NHL	29	3	4	7	34	....	....	....	....	....
	Chicago	NHL	22	1	3	4	25	4	0	0	0	2
	NHL Totals		779	217	324	541	804	93	15	25	40	94

a WCHA Rookie of the Year (1981)
b WCHA Second All-Star Team (1981, 1982)
c Won Frank J. Selke Memorial Trophy (1986)

Traded to **Winnipeg** by **Chicago** with Warren Rychel for Bryan Marchment and Chris Norton, July 22, 1991. Traded to **Chicago** by **Winnipeg** for Steve Bancroft and future considerations, February 21, 1993.

MURZYN, DANA (MUR-zihn)

Defense. Shoots left. 6'2", 200 lbs. Born, Calgary, Alta., December 9, 1966.
(Hartford's 1st choice, 5th overall, in 1985 Entry Draft).

			Regular Season					Playoffs				
Season	Club	Lea	GP	G	A	TP	PIM	GP	G	A	TP	PIM
1983-84	Calgary	WHL	65	11	20	31	135	2	0	0	0	10
1984-85a	Calgary	WHL	72	32	60	92	233	8	1	11	12	16
1985-86b	Hartford	NHL	78	3	23	26	125	4	0	0	0	10
1986-87	Hartford	NHL	74	9	19	28	95	6	2	1	3	29
1987-88	Hartford	NHL	33	1	6	7	45	....	....	....	....	....
	Calgary	NHL	41	6	5	11	94	5	2	0	2	13
1988-89	Calgary	NHL	63	3	19	22	142	21	0	3	3	20
1989-90	Calgary	NHL	78	7	13	20	140	6	2	2	4	2
1990-91	Calgary	NHL	19	0	2	2	30	....	....	....	....	....
	Vancouver	NHL	10	1	0	1	8	6	0	1	1	8
1991-92	Vancouver	NHL	70	3	11	14	147	1	0	0	0	15
1992-93	Vancouver	NHL	79	5	11	16	196	12	3	2	5	18
	NHL Totals		545	38	109	147	1022	61	9	9	18	115

a WHL First All-Star Team, East Division (1985)
b NHL All-Rookie Team (1986)

Traded to **Calgary** by **Hartford** with Shane Churla for Neil Sheehy, Carey Wilson and the rights to Lane MacDonald, January 3, 1988. Traded to **Vancouver** by **Calgary** for Ron Stern, Kevan Guy and future considerations, March 5, 1991.

MUSIL, FRANTISEK (moo-SIHL)

Defense. Shoots left. 6'3", 205 lbs. Born, Vysoke Myto, Czech., December 17, 1964.
(Minnesota's 3rd choice, 38th overall, in 1983 Entry Draft).

			Regular Season					Playoffs				
Season	Club	Lea	GP	G	A	TP	PIM	GP	G	A	TP	PIM
1980-81	Pardubice	Czech.	2	0	0	0	0	....	....	....	....	....
1981-82	Pardubice	Czech.	35	1	3	4	34	....	....	....	....	....
1982-83	Pardubice	Czech.	33	1	2	3	44	....	....	....	....	....
1983-84	Pardubice	Czech.	37	4	8	12	72	....	....	....	....	....
1984-85	Dukla Jihlava	Czech.	44	4	6	10	76	....	....	....	....	....
1985-86	Dukla Jihlava	Czech.	34	4	7	11	42	....	....	....	....	....
1986-87	Minnesota	NHL	72	2	9	11	148	....	....	....	....	....
1987-88	Minnesota	NHL	80	9	8	17	213	....	....	....	....	....
1988-89	Minnesota	NHL	55	1	19	20	54	5	1	1	2	4
1989-90	Minnesota	NHL	56	2	8	10	109	4	0	0	0	14
1990-91	Minnesota	NHL	8	0	2	2	23	....	....	....	....	....
	Calgary	NHL	67	7	14	21	160	7	0	0	0	10
1991-92	Calgary	NHL	78	4	8	12	103	....	....	....	....	....
1992-93	Calgary	NHL	80	6	10	16	131	6	1	1	2	7
	NHL Totals		496	31	78	109	941	22	2	2	4	35

Traded to **Calgary** by **Minnesota** for Brian Glynn, October 26, 1990.

MYHRES, BRANTT

Left wing. Shoots right. 6'3", 200 lbs. Born, Edmonton, Alta., March 18, 1974.
(Tampa Bay's 6th choice, 122nd overall, in 1992 Entry Draft).

			Regular Season					Playoffs				
Season	Club	Lea	GP	G	A	TP	PIM	GP	G	A	TP	PIM
1990-91	Portland	WHL	59	2	7	9	125	....	....	....	....	....
1991-92	Portland	WHL	4	0	2	2	22	....	....	....	....	....
	Lethbridge	WHL	53	4	11	15	359	5	0	0	0	36
1992-93	Lethbridge	WHL	64	13	35	48	277	3	0	0	0	11

MYRVOLD, ANDERS

Defense. Shoots left. 6'1", 178 lbs. Born, Lorenskog, Norway, August 12, 1975.
(Quebec's 6th choice, 127th overall, in 1993 Entry Draft).

			Regular Season					Playoffs				
Season	Club	Lea	GP	G	A	TP	PIM	GP	G	A	TP	PIM
1992-93	Farjestad	Swe.	2	0	0	0	0	....	....	....	....	....

NAMESTNIKOV, YEVGENY (nah-MEST-nih-kov, yev-GAIN-ee)

Defense. Shoots right. 5'11", 176 lbs. Born, Arzamis-lg, Soviet Union, October 9, 1971.
(Vancouver's 6th choice, 117th overall, in 1991 Entry Draft).

			Regular Season					Playoffs				
Season	Club	Lea	GP	G	A	TP	PIM	GP	G	A	TP	PIM
1988-89	Torpedo Gorky	USSR	2	0	0	0	2	....	....	....	....	....
1989-90	Torpedo Gorky	USSR	23	0	0	0	25	....	....	....	....	....
1990-91	Torpedo Niz.	USSR	42	1	2	3	49	....	....	....	....	....
1991-92	CSKA	CIS	42	1	1	2	47	....	....	....	....	....
1992-93	CSKA	CIS	42	5	5	10	68	....	....	....	....	....

NASLUND, MARKUS (NAZ-luhnd)

Right wing. Shoots left. 6', 186 lbs. Born, Ornskoldsvik, Sweden, July 30, 1973.
(Pittsburgh's 1st choice, 16th overall, in 1991 Entry Draft).

			Regular Season					Playoffs				
Season	Club	Lea	GP	G	A	TP	PIM	GP	G	A	TP	PIM
1990-91	MoDo	Swe.	32	10	9	19	14	....	....	....	....	....
1991-92	MoDo	Swe.	39	22	18	40	54	....	....	....	....	....
1992-93	MoDo	Swe.	39	22	17	39	67	3	3	2	5	0

NASREDDINE, ALAIN

Defense. Shoots left. 6'1", 201 lbs. Born, Montreal, Que., July 10, 1975.
(Florida's 8th choice, 135th overall, in 1993 Entry Draft).

			Regular Season					Playoffs				
Season	Club	Lea	GP	G	A	TP	PIM	GP	G	A	TP	PIM
1991-92	Drummondville	QMJHL	61	1	9	10	78	4	0	0	0	17
1992-93	Drummondville	QMJHL	64	0	14	14	137	10	0	1	1	36

NATTRESS, ERIC (RIC)

Defense. Shoots right. 6'2", 210 lbs. Born, Hamilton, Ont., May 25, 1962.
(Montreal's 2nd choice, 27th overall, in 1980 Entry Draft).

			Regular Season					Playoffs				
Season	Club	Lea	GP	G	A	TP	PIM	GP	G	A	TP	PIM
1979-80	Brantford	OHA	65	3	21	24	94	11	1	6	7	38
1980-81	Brantford	OHA	51	8	34	42	106	6	1	4	5	19
1981-82	Brantford	OHL	59	11	50	61	126	11	3	7	10	17
	Nova Scotia	AHL	....	....	....	....	....	5	0	1	1	7
1982-83	Montreal	NHL	40	1	3	4	19	3	0	0	0	10
	Nova Scotia	AHL	9	0	4	4	16	....	....	....	....	....
1983-84	Montreal	NHL	34	0	12	12	15	....	....	....	....	....
1984-85	Montreal	NHL	5	0	1	1	2	2	0	0	0	2
	Sherbrooke	AHL	72	8	40	48	37	16	4	13	17	20
1985-86	St. Louis	NHL	78	4	20	24	52	18	1	4	5	24
1986-87	St. Louis	NHL	73	6	22	28	24	6	0	0	0	2
1987-88	Calgary	NHL	63	2	13	15	37	6	1	3	4	0
1988-89	Calgary	NHL	38	1	8	9	47	19	0	3	3	20
1989-90	Calgary	NHL	49	1	14	15	26	6	2	0	2	0
1990-91	Calgary	NHL	58	5	13	18	63	7	1	0	1	2
1991-92	Calgary	NHL	18	0	5	5	31	....	....	....	....	....
	Toronto	NHL	36	2	14	16	32	....	....	....	....	....
1992-93	Philadelphia	NHL	44	7	10	17	29	....	....	....	....	....
	NHL Totals		536	29	135	164	377	67	5	10	15	60

Rights sold to **St. Louis** by **Montreal**, October 7, 1985. Traded to **Calgary** by **St. Louis** for Calgary's fourth round choice (Andy Rymsha) in 1987 Entry Draft and fifth round choice (Dave Lacouture) in 1988 Entry Draft, June 13, 1987. Traded to **Toronto** by **Calgary** with Doug Gilmour, Jamie Macoun, Kent Manderville and Rick Wamsley for Gary Leeman, Alexander Godynyuk, Jeff Reese, Michel Petit and Craig Berube, January 2, 1992. Signed as a free agent by **Philadelphia**, August 21, 1992.

NAUMENKO, NICHOLAS

Defense. Shoots right. 5'11", 180 lbs. Born, Chicago, IL, July 7, 1974.
(St. Louis' 9th choice, 182nd overall, in 1992 Entry Draft).

			Regular Season					Playoffs				
Season	Club	Lea	GP	G	A	TP	PIM	GP	G	A	TP	PIM
1991-92	Dubuque	USHL	24	6	19	25	4	....	....	....	....	....
1992-93	North Dakota	WCHA	38	10	24	34	26	....	....	....	....	....

NAZAROV, ANDREI (nah-ZAH-rohv)

Left wing. Shoots right. 6'5", 220 lbs. Born, Chelyabinsk, Soviet Union, May 22, 1974.
(San Jose's 2nd choice, 10th overall, in 1992 Entry Draft).

			Regular Season					Playoffs				
Season	Club	Lea	GP	G	A	TP	PIM	GP	G	A	TP	PIM
1991-92	Moscow D'amo	CIS	2	1	0	1	2	....	....	....	....	....
1992-93	Moscow D'amo	CIS	42	8	2	10	79	10	1	1	2	8

NEATON, PAT

Defense. Shoots left. 6', 180 lbs. Born, Redford, MI, May 21, 1971.
(Pittsburgh's 9th choice, 145th overall, in 1990 Entry Draft).

			Regular Season					Playoffs				
Season	Club	Lea	GP	G	A	TP	PIM	GP	G	A	TP	PIM
1989-90	U. of Michigan	CCHA	42	3	23	26	36	....	....	....	....	....
1990-91a	U. of Michigan	CCHA	44	15	28	43	78	....	....	....	....	....
1991-92	U. of Michigan	CCHA	43	10	20	30	62	....	....	....	....	....
1992-93b	U. of Michigan	CCHA	38	10	18	28	37	....	....	....	....	....

a CCHA Second All-Star Team (1991)
b CCHA First All-Star Team (1993)

NEDOMA, MILAN (neh-DOH-mah)

Defense. Shoots left. 5'10", 180 lbs. Born, Brno, Czech., March 29, 1972.
(Buffalo's 7th choice, 166th overall, in 1990 Entry Draft).

			Regular Season					Playoffs				
Season	Club	Lea	GP	G	A	TP	PIM	GP	G	A	TP	PIM
1989-90	Zetor Brno	Czech.	35	1	4	5	....	....	....	....	....	....
1990-91	Zetor Brno	Czech.2			UNAVAILABLE							
1991-92	Dukla Trencin	Czech.	47	4	5	9	22	....	....	....	....	....
1992-93	Dukla Trencin	Czech.	43	10	16	26	....	....	....	....	....	....

NEDVED, PETR (NEHD-VEHD)

Center. Shoots left. 6'3", 185 lbs. Born, Liberec, Czechoslovakia, December 9, 1971.
(Vancouver's 1st choice, 2nd overall, in 1990 Entry Draft).

			Regular Season					Playoffs				
Season	Club	Lea	GP	G	A	TP	PIM	GP	G	A	TP	PIM
1988-89	Litvinov	Czech.Jrs.	20	32	19	51	12	....	....	....	....	....
1989-90a	Seattle	WHL	71	65	80	145	80	11	4	9	13	2
1990-91	Vancouver	NHL	61	10	6	16	20	6	0	1	1	0
1991-92	Vancouver	NHL	77	15	22	37	36	10	1	4	5	16
1992-93	Vancouver	NHL	84	38	33	71	96	12	2	3	5	2
	NHL Totals		222	63	61	124	152	28	3	8	11	18

a WHL and CHL Rookie of the Year (1990)

NEDVED, ZDENEK

Right wing. Shoots left. 6', 179 lbs. Born, Lany, Czech., March 3, 1975.
(Toronto's 3rd choice, 123rd overall, in 1993 Entry Draft).

			Regular Season					Playoffs				
Season	Club	Lea	GP	G	A	TP	PIM	GP	G	A	TP	PIM
1991-92	Kladno	Czech.	19	15	12	27	22	....	....	....	....	....
1992-93	Sudbury	OHL	18	3	9	12	6	....	....	....	....	....

NEEDHAM, MICHAEL

Right wing. Shoots right. 5'10", 185 lbs. Born, Calgary, Alta., April 4, 1970.
(Pittsburgh's 7th choice, 126th overall, in 1989 Entry Draft).

			Regular Season					Playoffs				
Season	Club	Lea	GP	G	A	TP	PIM	GP	G	A	TP	PIM
1986-87	Kamloops	WHL	3	1	2	3	0	11	2	1	3	5
1987-88	Kamloops	WHL	64	31	33	64	93	5	0	1	1	5
1988-89	Kamloops	WHL	49	24	27	51	55	16	2	9	11	13
1989-90a	Kamloops	WHL	60	59	66	125	75	17	11	13	24	10
1990-91	Muskegon	IHL	65	14	31	45	17	5	2	2	4	5
1991-92	Muskegon	IHL	80	41	37	78	83	8	4	4	8	6
	Pittsburgh	NHL	....	....	....	....	....	5	1	0	1	2
1992-93	Pittsburgh	NHL	56	8	5	13	14	9	1	0	1	2
	Cleveland	IHL	1	2	0	2	0	....	....	....	....	....
	NHL Totals		56	8	5	13	14	14	2	0	2	4

a WHL West First All-Star Team (1990)

NEELY, CAMERON MICHAEL (CAM)

Right wing. Shoots right. 6'1", 217 lbs. Born, Comox, B.C., June 6, 1965.
(Vancouver's 1st choice, 9th overall, in 1983 Entry Draft).

			Regular Season					Playoffs				
Season	Club	Lea	GP	G	A	TP	PIM	GP	G	A	TP	PIM
1982-83	Portland	WHL	72	56	64	120	130	14	9	11	20	17
1983-84	Vancouver	NHL	56	16	15	31	57	4	2	0	2	2
	Portland	WHL	19	8	18	26	29	....	....	....	....	....
1984-85	Vancouver	NHL	72	21	18	39	137	....	....	....	....	....
1985-86	Vancouver	NHL	73	14	20	34	126	3	0	0	0	6
1986-87	Boston	NHL	75	36	36	72	143	4	5	1	6	8
1987-88a	Boston	NHL	69	42	27	69	175	23	9	8	17	51
1988-89	Boston	NHL	74	37	38	75	190	10	7	2	9	8
1989-90a	Boston	NHL	76	55	37	92	117	21	12	16	28	51
1990-91a	Boston	NHL	69	51	40	91	98	19	16	4	20	36
1991-92	Boston	NHL	9	9	3	12	16	....	....	....	....	....
1992-93	Boston	NHL	13	11	7	18	25	4	4	1	5	4
	NHL Totals		586	292	241	533	1084	88	55	32	87	166

a NHL Second All-Star Team (1988, 1990, 1991)

Played in NHL All-Star Game (1988-91)

Traded to **Boston** by **Vancouver** with Vancouver's first round choice (Glen Wesley) in 1987 Entry Draft for Barry Pederson, June 6, 1986.

NELSON, CHRISTOPHER

Defense. Shoots right. 6'2", 190 lbs. Born, Philadelphia, PA, February 12, 1969.
(New Jersey's 6th choice, 96th overall, in 1988 Entry Draft).

			Regular Season					Playoffs				
Season	Club	Lea	GP	G	A	TP	PIM	GP	G	A	TP	PIM
1988-89	U. Wisconsin	WCHA	21	1	4	5	24	....	....	....	....	....
1989-90	U. Wisconsin	WCHA	34	1	3	4	38	....	....	....	....	....
1990-91	U. Wisconsin	WCHA	42	5	12	17	48	....	....	....	....	....
1991-92	U. Wisconsin	WCHA	39	4	12	16	84	....	....	....	....	....
1992-93	Utica	AHL	21	1	1	2	20	1	0	0	0	2
	Cincinnati	IHL	58	4	26	30	69	....	....	....	....	....

NELSON, JEFF

Center. Shoots left. 6', 180 lbs. Born, Prince Albert, Sask., December 18, 1972.
(Washington's 4th choice, 36th overall, in 1991 Entry Draft).

			Regular Season					Playoffs				
Season	Club	Lea	GP	G	A	TP	PIM	GP	G	A	TP	PIM
1989-90	Prince Albert	WHL	72	28	69	97	79	14	2	11	13	10
1990-91a	Prince Albert	WHL	72	46	74	120	58	3	1	1	2	4
1991-92a	Prince Albert	WHL	64	48	65	113	84	9	7	14	21	18
1992-93	Baltimore	AHL	72	14	38	52	12	7	1	3	4	2

a WHL East Second All-Star Team (1991, 1992)

NELSON, TODD

Defense. Shoots left. 6', 201 lbs. Born, Prince Albert, Sask., May 11, 1969.
(Pittsburgh's 4th choice, 79th overall, in 1989 Entry Draft).

			Regular Season					Playoffs				
Season	Club	Lea	GP	G	A	TP	PIM	GP	G	A	TP	PIM
1985-86	Prince Albert	WHL	4	0	0	0	0	....	....	....	....	....
1986-87	Prince Albert	WHL	35	1	6	7	10	4	0	0	0	0
1987-88	Prince Albert	WHL	72	3	21	24	59	10	3	2	5	4
1988-89a	Prince Albert	WHL	72	14	45	59	72	4	1	3	4	4
1989-90a	Prince Albert	WHL	69	13	42	55	88	14	3	12	15	12
1990-91	Muskegon	IHL	79	4	20	24	32	3	0	0	0	4
1991-92	Pittsburgh	NHL	1	0	0	0	0	....	....	....	....	....
	Muskegon	IHL	80	6	35	41	46	14	1	11	12	4
1992-93	Cleveland	IHL	76	7	35	42	115	4	0	2	2	4
	NHL Totals		1	0	0	0	0	....	....	....	....	....

a WHL East Second All-Star Team (1989, 1990)

NEMCHINOV, SERGEI (nehm-CHEE-nawv)

Center. Shoots left. 6', 201 lbs. Born, Moscow, Soviet Union, January 14, 1964.
(NY Rangers' 14th choice, 244th overall, in 1990 Entry Draft).

			Regular Season					Playoffs				
Season	Club	Lea	GP	G	A	TP	PIM	GP	G	A	TP	PIM
1981-82	Soviet Wings	USSR	15	1	0	1	0	....	....	....	....	....
1982-83	CSKA	USSR	11	0	0	0	2	....	....	....	....	....
1983-84	CSKA	USSR	20	6	5	11	4	....	....	....	....	....
1984-85	CSKA	USSR	31	2	4	6	4	....	....	....	....	....
1985-86	Soviet Wings	USSR	39	7	12	19	28	....	....	....	....	....
1986-87	Soviet Wings	USSR	40	13	9	22	24	....	....	....	....	....
1987-88	Soviet Wings	USSR	48	17	11	28	26	....	....	....	....	....
1988-89	Soviet Wings	USSR	43	15	14	29	28	....	....	....	....	....
1989-90	Soviet Wings	USSR	48	17	16	33	34	....	....	....	....	....
1990-91	Soviet Wings	USSR	46	21	24	45	30	....	....	....	....	....
1991-92	NY Rangers	NHL	73	30	28	58	15	13	1	4	5	8
1992-93	NY Rangers	NHL	81	23	31	54	34	....	....	....	....	....
	NHL Totals		154	53	59	112	49	13	1	4	5	8

NEMETH, TOM

Defense. Shoots left. 6'2", 180 lbs. Born, St. Catharines, Ont., January 16, 1971.
(Minnesota's 10th choice, 206th overall, in 1991 Entry Draft).

			Regular Season					Playoffs				
Season	Club	Lea	GP	G	A	TP	PIM	GP	G	A	TP	PIM
1988-89	Cornwall	OHL	51	4	23	27	25	....	....	....	....	....
1989-90	Cornwall	OHL	41	12	15	27	14	6	0	2	2	0
1990-91	Cornwall	OHL	65	17	43	60	46	....	....	....	....	....
1991-92	Cornwall	OHL	66	25	49	74	33	6	3	2	5	4
1992-93	Dayton	ECHL	26	9	28	37	14	....	....	....	....	....
	Kalamazoo	IHL	48	6	13	19	24	....	....	....	....	....

NEUMEIER, TROY

Defense. Shoots left. 6'2", 195 lbs. Born, Langenburg, Sask., September 3, 1970.
(Vancouver's 9th choice, 191st overall, in 1990 Entry Draft).

			Regular Season					Playoffs				
Season	Club	Lea	GP	G	A	TP	PIM	GP	G	A	TP	PIM
1989-90	Prince Albert	WHL	72	8	26	34	73	14	3	5	8	12
1990-91a	Prince Albert	WHL	72	6	27	33	56	3	0	0	0	0
	Milwaukee	IHL	6	0	0	0	2	....	....	....	....	....
1991-92	Milwaukee	IHL	72	1	9	10	55	3	0	0	0	0
1992-93	Hamilton	AHL	79	3	11	14	73	....	....	....	....	....

a WHL East First All-Star Team (1991)

NICHOLLS, BERNIE IRVINE (NICK-els)

Center. Shoots right. 6'1", 185 lbs. Born, Haliburton, Ont., June 24, 1961.
(Los Angeles' 6th choice, 73rd overall, in 1980 Entry Draft).

			Regular Season					Playoffs				
Season	Club	Lea	GP	G	A	TP	PIM	GP	G	A	TP	PIM
1979-80	Kingston	OHA	68	36	43	79	85	3	1	0	1	10
1980-81	Kingston	OHA	65	63	89	152	109	14	8	10	18	17
1981-82	Los Angeles	NHL	22	14	18	32	27	10	4	0	4	23
	New Haven	AHL	55	41	30	71	31	....	....	....	....	....
1982-83	Los Angeles	NHL	71	28	22	50	124	....	....	....	....	....
1983-84	Los Angeles	NHL	78	41	54	95	83	....	....	....	....	....
1984-85	Los Angeles	NHL	80	46	54	100	76	3	1	1	2	9
1985-86	Los Angeles	NHL	80	36	61	97	78	....	....	....	....	....
1986-87	Los Angeles	NHL	80	33	48	81	101	5	2	5	7	6
1987-88	Los Angeles	NHL	65	32	46	78	114	5	2	6	8	11
1988-89a	Los Angeles	NHL	79	70	80	150	96	11	7	9	16	12
1989-90	Los Angeles	NHL	47	27	48	75	66	....	....	....	....	....
	NY Rangers	NHL	32	12	25	37	20	10	7	5	12	16
1990-91	NY Rangers	NHL	71	25	48	73	96	5	4	3	7	8
1991-92	NY Rangers	NHL	1	0	0	0	0	....	....	....	....	....
	Edmonton	NHL	49	20	29	49	60	16	8	11	19	25
1992-93	Edmonton	NHL	46	8	32	40	40	....	....	....	....	....
	New Jersey	NHL	23	5	15	20	40	5	0	0	0	6
	NHL Totals		824	397	580	977	1021	70	35	40	75	116

a NHL Second All-Star Team (1989)

Played in NHL All-Star Game (1984, 1989, 1990)

Traded to **NY Rangers** by **Los Angeles** for Tomas Sandstrom and Tony Granato, January 20, 1990. Traded to **Edmonton** by **NY Rangers** with Steven Rice and Louie DeBrusk for Mark Messier and future considerations, October 4, 1991. Traded to **New Jersey** by **Edmonton** for Zdeno Ciger and Kevin Todd, January 13, 1993.

NIECKAR, BARRY

Left wing. Shoots left. 6'3", 200 lbs. Born, Rama, Sask., December 16, 1967.

			Regular Season					Playoffs				
Season	Club	Lea	GP	G	A	TP	PIM	GP	G	A	TP	PIM
1991-92	Phoenix	IHL	5	0	0	0	9	....	....	....	....	....
	Raleigh	ECHL	46	10	18	28	229	4	4	0	4	22
1992-93	Hartford	NHL	2	0	0	0	2	....	....	....	....	....
	Springfield	AHL	21	2	4	6	65	6	1	0	1	14
	NHL Totals		2	0	0	0	2	....	....	....	....	....

Signed as a free agent by **Hartford**, September 25, 1992.

NIEDERMAYER, ROB

Center. Shoots left. 6'2", 200 lbs. Born, Cassiar, B.C., December 28, 1974.
(Florida's 1st choice, 5th overall, in 1993 Entry Draft).

			Regular Season					Playoffs				
Season	Club	Lea	GP	G	A	TP	PIM	GP	G	A	TP	PIM
1990-91	Medicine Hat	WHL	71	24	26	50	8	12	3	7	10	2
1991-92	Medicine Hat	WHL	71	32	46	78	77	4	2	3	5	2
1992-93a	Medicine Hat	WHL	52	43	34	77	67	....	....	....	....	....

a WHL East First All-Star Team (1993)

NIEDERMAYER, SCOTT

Defense. Shoots left. 6', 200 lbs. Born, Edmonton, Alta., August 31, 1973.
(New Jersey's 1st choice, 3rd overall, in 1991 Entry Draft).

			Regular Season					Playoffs				
Season	Club	Lea	GP	G	A	TP	PIM	GP	G	A	TP	PIM
1989-90	Kamloops	WHL	64	14	55	69	64	17	2	14	16	35
1990-91ab	Kamloops	WHL	57	26	56	82	52	....	....	....	....	....
1991-92	New Jersey	NHL	4	0	1	1	2	....	....	....	....	....
acd	Kamloops	WHL	35	7	32	39	61	17	9	14	23	28
1992-93e	New Jersey	NHL	80	11	29	40	47	5	0	3	3	2
	NHL Totals		84	11	30	41	49	5	0	3	3	2

a WHL West First All-Star Team (1991, 1992)
b Canadian Major Junior Scholastic Player of the Year (1991)
c Memorial Cup All-Star Team (1992)
d Won Stafford Smythe Memorial Trophy (Memorial Cup MVP) (1992)
e NHL/Upper Deck All-Rookie Team (1993)

NIELSON, JEFF

Right wing. Shoots right. 6', 170 lbs. Born, Grand Rapids, MN, September 20, 1971.
(NY Rangers' 4th choice, 69th overall, in 1990 Entry Draft).

			Regular Season					Playoffs				
Season	Club	Lea	GP	G	A	TP	PIM	GP	G	A	TP	PIM
1990-91	U. Minnesota	WCHA	45	11	14	25	50	....	....	....	....	....
1991-92	U. Minnesota	WCHA	41	14	14	28	70	....	....	....	....	....
1992-93	U. Minnesota	WCHA	42	21	20	41	80	....	....	....	....	....

NIEUWENDYK, JOE (NOO-ihn-DIGHK)

Center. Shoots left. 6'1", 195 lbs. Born, Oshawa, Ont., September 10, 1966.
(Calgary's 2nd choice, 27th overall, in 1985 Entry Draft).

			Regular Season					Playoffs				
Season	Club	Lea	GP	G	A	TP	PIM	GP	G	A	TP	PIM
1984-85a	Cornell	ECAC	23	18	21	39	20	....	....	....	....	....
1985-86bc	Cornell	ECAC	21	21	21	42	45	....	....	....	....	....
1986-87bcd	Cornell	ECAC	23	26	26	52	26	....	....	....	....	....
	Calgary	NHL	9	5	1	6	0	6	2	2	4	0
1987-88efg	Calgary	NHL	75	51	41	92	23	8	3	4	7	2
1988-89	Calgary	NHL	77	51	31	82	40	22	10	4	14	10
1989-90	Calgary	NHL	79	45	50	95	40	6	4	6	10	4
1990-91	Calgary	NHL	79	45	40	85	36	7	4	1	5	10
1991-92	Calgary	NHL	69	22	34	56	55	....	....	....	....	....
1992-93	Calgary	NHL	79	38	37	75	52	6	3	6	9	10
	NHL Totals		467	257	234	491	246	55	26	23	49	36

a ECAC Rookie of the Year (1985)
b NCAA East First All-American Team (1986, 1987)
c ECAC First All-Star Team (1986, 1987)
d ECAC Player of the Year (1987)
e Won Calder Memorial Trophy (1988)
f NHL All-Rookie Team (1988)
g Won Dodge Ram Tough Award (1988)

Played in NHL All-Star Game (1988-90)

NIINIMAA, JANNE

Defense. Shoots left. 6'1", 196 lbs. Born, Raahe, Finland, May 22, 1975.
(Philadelphia's 1st choice, 36th overall, in 1993 Entry Draft).

			Regular Season					Playoffs				
Season	Club	Lea	GP	G	A	TP	PIM	GP	G	A	TP	PIM
1991-92	Karpat	Fin.2	41	2	11	13	49	....	....	....	....	....
1992-93	Karpat	Fin.2	29	2	3	5	14	....	....	....	....	....

NIKOLIC, ALEX

Left wing. Shoots left. 6'1", 200 lbs. Born, Sudbury, Ont., March 1, 1970.
(Calgary's 8th choice, 147th overall, in 1989 Entry Draft).

			Regular Season					Playoffs				
Season	Club	Lea	GP	G	A	TP	PIM	GP	G	A	TP	PIM
1988-89	Cornell	ECAC	13	0	3	3	31	....	....	....	....	....
1989-90	Cornell	ECAC	28	6	9	15	54	....	....	....	....	....
1990-91	Cornell	ECAC	15	4	3	7	16	....	....	....	....	....
1991-92	Cornell	ECAC	26	5	9	14	60	....	....	....	....	....
1992-93	Salt Lake	IHL	37	4	4	8	133	....	....	....	....	....

NIKOLISHIN, ANDREI (nee-koh-LEE-shin)

Left wing. Shoots left. 5'11", 180 lbs. Born, Vorkuta, Soviet Union, March 25, 1973.
(Hartford's 2nd choice, 47th overall, in 1992 Entry Draft).

			Regular Season					Playoffs				
Season	Club	Lea	GP	G	A	TP	PIM	GP	G	A	TP	PIM
1990-91	Moscow D'amo	USSR	2	0	0	0	0	....	....	....	....	....
1991-92	Moscow D'amo	CIS	18	1	0	1	4	....	....	....	....	....
1992-93	Moscow D'amo	CIS	42	5	7	12	30	10	2	1	3	8

NILSSON, FREDRIK (NEEL-suhn)

Center. Shoots left. 6'1", 198 lbs. Born, Stockholm, Sweden, April 16, 1971.
(San Jose's 7th choice, 111th overall, in 1991 Entry Draft).

			Regular Season					Playoffs				
Season	Club	Lea	GP	G	A	TP	PIM	GP	G	A	TP	PIM
1988-89	Vasteras	Swe.	1	0	0	0	0	....	....	....	....	....
1989-90	Vasteras	Swe.	23	1	1	2	4	1	0	0	0	0
1990-91	Vasteras	Swe.	35	13	7	20	20	4	0	1	1	2
1991-92	Vasteras	Swe.	40	5	14	19	40	....	....	....	....	....
1992-93	Vasteras	Swe.	40	14	15	29	69	1	1	1	2	0

NILSSON, STEFAN (NEEL-suhn)

Center. Shoots right. 5'11", 185 lbs. Born, Lulea, Sweden, April 5, 1968.
(Washington's 7th choice, 124th overall, in 1986 Entry Draft).

			Regular Season					Playoffs				
Season	Club	Lea	GP	G	A	TP	PIM	GP	G	A	TP	PIM
1985-86	Lulea	Swe.	4	0	0	0	0	....	....	....	....	....
1986-87	Lulea	Swe.	23	3	9	12	14	....	....	....	....	....
1987-88	Lulea	Swe.	31	10	10	20	24	....	....	....	....	....
1988-89	Lulea	Swe.	40	9	22	31	24	3	0	1	1	0
1989-90	Lulea	Swe.	38	11	26	37	32	5	0	0	0	4
1990-91	Lulea	Swe.	38	7	39	46	64	5	0	3	3	2
1991-92	Lulea	Swe.	37	7	*40	47	42	2	1	1	2	8
1992-93	Lulea	Swe.	40	7	32	39	26	11	4	6	10	22

NOLAN, OWEN

Right wing. Shoots right. 6'1", 194 lbs. Born, Belfast, Northern Ireland, September 22, 1971.
(Quebec's 1st choice, 1st overall, in 1990 Entry Draft).

			Regular Season					Playoffs				
Season	Club	Lea	GP	G	A	TP	PIM	GP	G	A	TP	PIM
1988-89a	Cornwall	OHL	62	34	25	59	213	18	5	11	16	41
1989-90b	Cornwall	OHL	58	51	59	110	240	6	7	5	12	26
1990-91	Quebec	NHL	59	3	10	13	109	....	....	....	....	....
	Halifax	AHL	6	4	4	8	11	....	....	....	....	....
1991-92	Quebec	NHL	75	42	31	73	183	....	....	....	....	....
1992-93	Quebec	NHL	73	36	41	77	185	5	1	0	1	2
	NHL Totals		207	81	82	163	477	5	1	0	1	2

a OHL Rookie of the Year (1989)
b OHL First All-Star Team (1990)

Played in NHL All-Star Game (1992)

NOONAN, BRIAN

Right wing. Shoots right. 6'1", 180 lbs. Born, Boston, MA, May 29, 1965.
(Chicago's 10th choice, 179th overall, in 1983 Entry Draft).

			Regular Season					Playoffs				
Season	Club	Lea	GP	G	A	TP	PIM	GP	G	A	TP	PIM
1984-85	N. Westminster	WHL	72	50	66	116	76	11	8	7	15	4
1985-86	Nova Scotia	AHL	2	0	0	0	0	....	....	....	....	....
	Saginaw	IHL	76	39	39	78	69	11	6	3	9	6
1986-87	Nova Scotia	AHL	70	25	26	51	30	5	3	1	4	4
1987-88	**Chicago**	**NHL**	**77**	**10**	**20**	**30**	**44**	**3**	**0**	**0**	**0**	**4**
1988-89	**Chicago**	**NHL**	**45**	**4**	**12**	**16**	**28**	**1**	**0**	**0**	**0**	**0**
	Saginaw	IHL	19	18	13	31	36	1	0	0	0	0
1989-90	**Chicago**	**NHL**	**8**	**0**	**2**	**2**	**6**	....	....	....	....	....
a	Indianapolis	IHL	56	40	36	76	85	14	6	9	15	20
1990-91	**Chicago**	**NHL**	**7**	**0**	**4**	**4**	**2**	....	....	....	....	....
b	Indianapolis	IHL	59	38	53	91	67	7	6	4	10	18
1991-92	**Chicago**	**NHL**	**65**	**19**	**12**	**31**	**81**	**18**	**6**	**9**	**15**	**30**
1992-93	**Chicago**	**NHL**	**63**	**16**	**14**	**30**	**82**	**4**	**3**	**0**	**3**	**4**
	NHL Totals		**265**	**49**	**64**	**113**	**243**	**26**	**9**	**9**	**18**	**38**

a IHL Second All-Star Team (1990)
b IHL First All-Star Team (1991)

NORRIS, CLAYTON

Right wing. Shoots right. 6'2", 205 lbs. Born, Edmonton, Alta., March 8, 1972.
(Philadelphia's 6th choice, 116th overall, in 1991 Entry Draft).

			Regular Season					Playoffs				
Season	Club	Lea	GP	G	A	TP	PIM	GP	G	A	TP	PIM
1990-91	Medicine Hat	WHL	71	26	27	53	165	12	5	4	9	41
1991-92a	Medicine Hat	WHL	69	26	39	65	300	2	0	0	0	9
1992-93	Medicine Hat	WHL	41	21	16	37	128	10	3	2	5	14
	Hershey	AHL	4	0	0	0	5	....	....	....	....	....
	Roanoke	ECHL	4	0	0	0	0	....	....	....	....	....

a WHL East Second All-Star Team (1992)

NORRIS, DWAYNE

Right wing. Shoots right. 5'10", 175 lbs. Born, St. John's, Nfld., January 8, 1970.
(Quebec's 5th choice, 127th overall, in 1990 Entry Draft).

			Regular Season					Playoffs				
Season	Club	Lea	GP	G	A	TP	PIM	GP	G	A	TP	PIM
1988-89	Michigan State	CCHA	40	16	21	37	32	....	....	....	....	....
1989-90	Michigan State	CCHA	33	18	25	43	30	....	....	....	....	....
1990-91	Michigan State	CCHA	40	26	25	51	60	....	....	....	....	....
1991-92ab	Michigan State	CCHA	41	40	38	78	58	....	....	....	....	....
1992-93	Halifax	AHL	50	25	28	53	62	....	....	....	....	....

a CCHA First All-Star Team (1992)
b NCAA West First All-American Team (1992)

NORSTROM, MATTIAS

Defense. Shoots left. 6'1", 200 lbs. Born, Mora, Sweden, January 2, 1972.
(NY Rangers' 2nd choice, 48th overall, in 1992 Entry Draft).

			Regular Season					Playoffs				
Season	Club	Lea	GP	G	A	TP	PIM	GP	G	A	TP	PIM
1991-92	AIK	Swe.	39	4	3	7	28	3	0	2	2	2
1992-93	AIK	Swe.	22	0	1	1	16	....	....	....	....	....

NORTON, JEFF

Defense. Shoots left. 6'2", 195 lbs. Born, Acton, MA, November 25, 1965.
(NY Islanders' 3rd choice, 62nd overall, in 1984 Entry Draft).

			Regular Season					Playoffs				
Season	Club	Lea	GP	G	A	TP	PIM	GP	G	A	TP	PIM
1984-85	U. of Michigan	CCHA	37	8	16	24	103	....	....	....	....	....
1985-86	U. of Michigan	CCHA	37	15	30	45	99	....	....	....	....	....
1986-87a	U. of Michigan	CCHA	39	12	36	48	92	....	....	....	....	....
1987-88	U.S. National	....	54	7	22	29	52	....	....	....	....	....
	U.S. Olympic	....	6	0	4	4	4	....	....	....	....	....
	NY Islanders	**NHL**	**15**	**1**	**6**	**7**	**14**	**3**	**0**	**2**	**2**	**13**
1988-89	**NY Islanders**	**NHL**	**69**	**1**	**30**	**31**	**74**	....	....	....	....	....
1989-90	**NY Islanders**	**NHL**	**60**	**4**	**49**	**53**	**65**	**4**	**1**	**3**	**4**	**17**
1990-91	**NY Islanders**	**NHL**	**44**	**3**	**25**	**28**	**16**	....	....	....	....	....
1991-92	**NY Islanders**	**NHL**	**28**	**1**	**18**	**19**	**18**	....	....	....	....	....
1992-93	**NY Islanders**	**NHL**	**66**	**12**	**38**	**50**	**45**	**10**	**1**	**1**	**2**	**4**
	NHL Totals		**282**	**22**	**166**	**188**	**232**	**17**	**2**	**6**	**8**	**34**

a CCHA Second All-Star Team (1987)

Traded to **San Jose** by **NY Islanders** for San Jose's third round choice in 1994 Entry Draft and future considerations, June 20, 1993.

NORTON, STEVE

Defense. Shoots left. 6'3", 210 lbs. Born, Mississauga, Ont., February 29, 1972.
(Boston's 9th choice, 216th overall, in 1991 Entry Draft).

			Regular Season					Playoffs				
Season	Club	Lea	GP	G	A	TP	PIM	GP	G	A	TP	PIM
1990-91	Michigan State	CCHA	39	1	4	5	42	....	....	....	....	....
1991-92	Michigan State	CCHA	41	0	6	6	36	....	....	....	....	....
1992-93	Michigan State	CCHA	40	2	9	11	58	....	....	....	....	....

NORWOOD, LEE CHARLES

Defense. Shoots left. 6'1", 198 lbs. Born, Oakland, CA, February 2, 1960.
(Quebec's 3rd choice, 62nd overall, in 1979 Entry Draft).

			Regular Season					Playoffs				
Season	Club	Lea	GP	G	A	TP	PIM	GP	G	A	TP	PIM
1978-79	Oshawa	OHA	61	23	38	61	171	5	2	2	4	17
1979-80	Oshawa	OHA	60	13	39	52	143	6	2	7	9	15
1980-81	**Quebec**	**NHL**	**11**	**1**	**1**	**2**	**9**	**3**	**0**	**0**	**0**	**2**
	Hershey	AHL	52	11	32	43	78	8	0	4	4	14
1981-82	**Quebec**	**NHL**	**2**	**0**	**0**	**0**	**2**	....	....	....	....	....
	Fredericton	AHL	29	6	13	19	74	....	....	....	....	....
	Washington	**NHL**	**26**	**7**	**10**	**17**	**125**	....	....	....	....	....
1982-83	**Washington**	**NHL**	**8**	**0**	**1**	**1**	**14**	....	....	....	....	....
	Hershey	AHL	67	12	36	48	90	5	0	1	1	2
1983-84	St. Catharines	AHL	75	13	46	59	91	7	0	5	5	31
1984-85ab	Peoria	IHL	80	17	60	77	229	18	1	11	12	62
1985-86	**St. Louis**	**NHL**	**71**	**5**	**24**	**29**	**134**	**19**	**2**	**7**	**9**	**64**
1986-87	**Detroit**	**NHL**	**57**	**6**	**21**	**27**	**163**	**16**	**1**	**6**	**7**	**31**
	Adirondack	AHL	3	0	3	3	0	....	....	....	....	....
1987-88	**Detroit**	**NHL**	**51**	**9**	**22**	**31**	**131**	**16**	**2**	**6**	**8**	**40**
1988-89	**Detroit**	**NHL**	**66**	**10**	**32**	**42**	**100**	**6**	**1**	**2**	**3**	**16**
1989-90	**Detroit**	**NHL**	**64**	**8**	**14**	**22**	**95**	....	....	....	....	....
1990-91	**Detroit**	**NHL**	**21**	**3**	**7**	**10**	**50**	....	....	....	....	....
	New Jersey	**NHL**	**28**	**3**	**2**	**5**	**87**	**4**	**0**	**0**	**0**	**18**
1991-92	**Hartford**	**NHL**	**6**	**0**	**0**	**0**	**16**	....	....	....	....	....
	St. Louis	**NHL**	**44**	**3**	**11**	**14**	**94**	**1**	**0**	**1**	**1**	**0**
1992-93	**St. Louis**	**NHL**	**32**	**3**	**7**	**10**	**63**	....	....	....	....	....
	NHL Totals		**487**	**58**	**152**	**210**	**1083**	**65**	**6**	**22**	**28**	**171**

a Won Governors' Trophy (IHL's Top Defenseman) (1985)
b IHL First All-Star Team (1985)

Traded to **Washington** by **Quebec** for Tim Tookey and Washington's seventh round choice (Daniel Poudrier) in 1982 Entry Draft, February 1, 1982. Traded to **Toronto** by **Washington** for Dave Shand, October 6, 1983. Signed as a free agent by **St. Louis**, August 13, 1985. Traded to **Detroit** by **St. Louis** for Larry Trader, August 7, 1986. Traded to **New Jersey** by **Detroit** with future considerations for Paul Ysebaert, November 27, 1990. Traded to **Hartford** by **New Jersey** for future considerations, October 3, 1991. Traded to **St. Louis** by **Hartford** for future considerations, November 13, 1991.

NUMMINEN, TEEMU

Center. Shoots left. 6'3", 194 lbs. Born, Tampere, Finland, December 23, 1973.
(Winnipeg's 10th choice, 229th overall, in 1992 Entry Draft).

			Regular Season					Playoffs				
Season	Club	Lea	GP	G	A	TP	PIM	GP	G	A	TP	PIM
1991-92	Stoneham	HS				UNAVAILABLE						
1992-93	Tappara	Fin.	7	0	0	0	0	....	....	....	....	....

NUMMINEN, TEPPO (NOO-mih-nehn)

Defense. Shoots right. 6'1", 190 lbs. Born, Tampere, Finland, July 3, 1968.
(Winnipeg's 2nd choice, 29th overall, in 1986 Entry Draft).

			Regular Season					Playoffs				
Season	Club	Lea	GP	G	A	TP	PIM	GP	G	A	TP	PIM
1985-86	Tappara	Fin.	31	2	4	6	6	8	0	0	0	0
1986-87	Tappara	Fin.	44	9	9	18	16	9	4	1	5	4
1987-88	Tappara	Fin.	40	10	10	20	29	10	6	6	12	6
1988-89	**Winnipeg**	**NHL**	**69**	**1**	**14**	**15**	**36**	....	....	....	....	....
1989-90	**Winnipeg**	**NHL**	**79**	**11**	**32**	**43**	**20**	**7**	**1**	**2**	**3**	**10**
1990-91	**Winnipeg**	**NHL**	**80**	**8**	**25**	**33**	**28**	....	....	....	....	....
1991-92	**Winnipeg**	**NHL**	**80**	**5**	**34**	**39**	**32**	**7**	**0**	**0**	**0**	**0**
1992-93	**Winnipeg**	**NHL**	**66**	**7**	**30**	**37**	**33**	**6**	**1**	**1**	**2**	**2**
	NHL Totals		**374**	**32**	**135**	**167**	**149**	**20**	**2**	**3**	**5**	**12**

NUUTINEN, SAMI

Defense. Shoots left. 6'1", 189 lbs. Born, Espoo, Finland, June 11, 1971.
(Edmonton's 11th choice, 248th overall, in 1990 Entry Draft).

			Regular Season					Playoffs				
Season	Club	Lea	GP	G	A	TP	PIM	GP	G	A	TP	PIM
1988-89	Espoo	Fin.2	39	18	10	28	46	....	....	....	....	....
1989-90	Espoo	Fin.2	40	8	15	23	....	....	....	....	....	....
1990-91	K-Kissat	Fin.2	3	1	0	1	0	....	....	....	....	....
	HIFK	Fin.	27	1	3	4	6	3	0	0	0	0
1991-92	HIFK	Fin.	44	5	6	11	10	9	0	1	1	4
1992-93	Kiekko-Espoo	Fin.	48	7	11	18	59	....	....	....	....	....

NYLANDER, MIKAEL (nigh-LAHN-der, mi-KIH-ehl)

Center. Shoots left. 5'11", 187 lbs. Born, Stockholm, Sweden, October 3, 1972.
(Hartford's 4th choice, 59th overall, in 1991 Entry Draft).

			Regular Season					Playoffs				
Season	Club	Lea	GP	G	A	TP	PIM	GP	G	A	TP	PIM
1989-90	Huddinge	Swe.2	31	7	15	22	4	....	....	....	....	....
1990-91	Huddinge	Swe.2	33	14	20	34	10	....	....	....	....	....
1991-92	AIK	Swe.	40	11	17	28	30	3	1	4	5	4
1992-93	**Hartford**	**NHL**	**59**	**11**	**22**	**33**	**36**	....	....	....	....	....
	Springfield	AHL	....	....	....	....	....	3	3	3	6	2
	NHL Totals		**59**	**11**	**22**	**33**	**36**	....	....	....	....	....

NYLUND, GARY   (NIGH-lund)

Defense. Shoots left. 6'4", 210 lbs. Born, Surrey, B.C., October 28, 1963.
(Toronto's 1st choice, 3rd overall, in 1982 Entry Draft).

				Regular Season					Playoffs			
Season	Club	Lea	GP	G	A	TP	PIM	GP	G	A	TP	PIM
1979-80	Portland	WHL	72	5	21	26	59	8	0	1	1	2
1980-81a	Portland	WHL	70	6	40	46	186	9	1	7	8	17
1981-82bc	Portland	WHL	65	7	59	66	267	15	3	16	19	74
1982-83	Toronto	NHL	16	0	3	3	16	....	....	....	....	....
1983-84	Toronto	NHL	47	2	14	16	103	....	....	....	....	....
1984-85	Toronto	NHL	76	3	17	20	99	....	....	....	....	....
1985-86	Toronto	NHL	79	2	16	18	180	10	0	2	2	25
1986-87	Chicago	NHL	80	7	20	27	190	4	0	2	2	11
1987-88	Chicago	NHL	76	4	15	19	208	5	0	0	0	10
1988-89	Chicago	NHL	23	3	2	5	63	....	....	....	....	....
	NY Islanders	NHL	46	4	8	12	74	....	....	....	....	....
1989-90	NY Islanders	NHL	64	4	21	25	144	5	0	2	2	17
1990-91	NY Islanders	NHL	72	2	21	23	105	....	....	....	....	....
1991-92	NY Islanders	NHL	7	0	1	1	10	....	....	....	....	....
	Capital Dist.	AHL	4	0	0	0	0	....	....	....	....	....
1992-93	NY Islanders	NHL	22	1	1	2	43	....	....	....	....	....
	Capital Dist.	AHL	2	0	0	0	0	....	....	....	....	....
	NHL Totals		**608**	**32**	**139**	**171**	**1235**	**24**	**0**	**6**	**6**	**63**

a WHL Second All-Star Team (1981)
b WHL First All-Star Team (1982)
c Named WHL's Top Defenseman (1982)
Signed as a free agent by **Chicago**, August 27, 1986. Traded to **NY Islanders** by Chicago with Marc Bergevin for Steve Konroyd and Bob Bassen, November 25, 1988.

OATES, ADAM

Center. Shoots right. 5'11", 190 lbs. Born, Weston, Ont., August 27, 1962.

				Regular Season					Playoffs			
Season	Club	Lea	GP	G	A	TP	PIM	GP	G	A	TP	PIM
1982-83	RPI	ECAC	22	9	33	42	8	....	....	....	....	....
1983-84	RPI	ECAC	38	26	57	83	15	....	....	....	....	....
1984-85ab	RPI	ECAC	38	31	60	91	29	....	....	....	....	....
1985-86	Detroit	NHL	38	9	11	20	10	....	....	....	....	....
	Adirondack	AHL	34	18	28	46	4	17	7	14	21	4
1986-87	Detroit	NHL	76	15	32	47	21	16	4	7	11	6
1987-88	Detroit	NHL	63	14	40	54	20	16	8	12	20	6
1988-89	Detroit	NHL	69	16	62	78	14	6	0	8	8	2
1989-90	St. Louis	NHL	80	23	79	102	30	12	2	12	14	4
1990-91c	St. Louis	NHL	61	25	90	115	29	13	7	13	20	10
1991-92	St. Louis	NHL	54	10	59	69	12	....	....	....	....	....
	Boston	NHL	26	10	20	30	10	15	5	14	19	4
1992-93	Boston	NHL	84	45	*97	142	32	4	0	9	9	4
	NHL Totals		**551**	**167**	**490**	**657**	**178**	**82**	**26**	**75**	**101**	**36**

a ECAC First All-Star Team (1985)
b Named to NCAA All-American Team (1985)
c NHL Second All-Star Team (1991)
Played in NHL All-Star Game (1991-93)
Signed as a free agent by **Detroit**, June 28, 1985. Traded to **St. Louis** by Detroit with Paul MacLean for Bernie Federko and Tony McKegney, June 15, 1989. Traded to **Boston** by St. Louis for Craig Janney and Stephane Quintal, February 7, 1992.

OATES, MATT

Left wing. Shoots left. 6'3", 204 lbs. Born, Evanston, IL, December 20, 1972.
(NY Rangers' 7th choice, 168th overall, in 1992 Entry Draft).

				Regular Season					Playoffs			
Season	Club	Lea	GP	G	A	TP	PIM	GP	G	A	TP	PIM
1991-92	Miami-Ohio	CCHA	40	8	13	21	23	....	....	....	....	....
1992-93	Miami-Ohio	CCHA	38	11	14	25	82	....	....	....	....	....

O'BRIEN, JAMES

Defense. Shoots left. 6', 190 lbs. Born, Stoney Creek, Ont., May 8, 1970.
(Calgary's 1st choice, 6th overall, in 1992 Supplemental Draft).

				Regular Season					Playoffs			
Season	Club	Lea	GP	G	A	TP	PIM	GP	G	A	TP	PIM
1989-90	Brown	ECAC	29	3	12	15	78	....	....	....	....	....
1990-91	Brown	ECAC	25	3	8	11	50	....	....	....	....	....
1991-92	Brown	ECAC	28	3	11	14	61	....	....	....	....	....
1992-93	Brown	ECAC	26	5	10	15	60	....	....	....	....	....

O'CONNOR, MYLES

Defense. Shoots left. 5'11", 165 lbs. Born, Calgary, Alta., April 2, 1967.
(New Jersey's 4th choice, 45th overall, in 1985 Entry Draft).

				Regular Season					Playoffs			
Season	Club	Lea	GP	G	A	TP	PIM	GP	G	A	TP	PIM
1985-86	U. of Michigan	CCHA	37	6	19	25	73	....	....	....	....	....
	Cdn. National	....	8	0	0	0	0	....	....	....	....	....
1986-87	U. of Michigan	CCHA	39	15	39	54	111	....	....	....	....	....
1987-88	U. of Michigan	CCHA	40	9	25	34	78	....	....	....	....	....
1988-89ab	U. of Michigan	CCHA	40	3	31	34	91	....	....	....	....	....
	Utica	AHL	1	0	0	0	0	....	....	....	....	....
1989-90	Utica	AHL	76	14	33	47	124	5	1	2	3	26
1990-91	New Jersey	NHL	22	3	1	4	41	....	....	....	....	....
	Utica	AHL	33	6	17	23	62	....	....	....	....	....
1991-92	New Jersey	NHL	9	0	2	2	13	....	....	....	....	....
	Utica	AHL	66	9	39	48	184	....	....	....	....	....
1992-93	New Jersey	NHL	7	0	0	0	9	....	....	....	....	....
	Utica	AHL	9	1	5	6	10	....	....	....	....	....
	NHL Totals		**38**	**3**	**3**	**6**	**63**	....	....	....	....	....

a CCHA First All-Star Team (1989)
b NCAA West First All-American Team (1989)
Signed as a free agent by **Anaheim**, July 22, 1993.

ODELEIN, LYLE   (ah-duh-LEEN)

Defense. Shoots right. 5'10", 206 lbs. Born, Quill Lake, Sask., July 21, 1968.
(Montreal's 8th choice, 141st overall, in 1986 Entry Draft).

				Regular Season					Playoffs			
Season	Club	Lea	GP	G	A	TP	PIM	GP	G	A	TP	PIM
1985-86	Moose Jaw	WHL	67	9	37	46	117	13	1	6	7	34
1986-87	Moose Jaw	WHL	59	9	50	59	70	9	2	5	7	26
1987-88	Moose Jaw	WHL	63	15	43	58	166	....	....	....	....	....
1988-89	Sherbrooke	AHL	33	3	4	7	120	3	0	2	2	5
	Peoria	IHL	36	2	8	10	116	....	....	....	....	....
1989-90	Montreal	NHL	8	0	2	2	33	....	....	....	....	....
	Sherbrooke	AHL	68	7	24	31	265	12	6	5	11	79
1990-91	Montreal	NHL	52	0	2	2	259	12	0	0	0	54
1991-92	Montreal	NHL	71	1	7	8	212	7	0	0	0	11
1992-93	Montreal	NHL	83	2	14	16	205	20	1	5	6	30
	NHL Totals		**214**	**3**	**25**	**28**	**709**	**39**	**1**	**5**	**6**	**95**

ODGERS, JEFF

Right wing. Shoots right. 6', 195 lbs. Born, Spy Hill, Sask., May 31, 1969.

				Regular Season					Playoffs			
Season	Club	Lea	GP	G	A	TP	PIM	GP	G	A	TP	PIM
1988-89	Brandon	WHL	71	31	29	60	277	....	....	....	....	....
1989-90	Brandon	WHL	64	37	28	65	209	....	....	....	....	....
1990-91	Kansas City	IHL	77	12	19	31	318	....	....	....	....	....
1991-92	San Jose	NHL	61	7	4	11	217	....	....	....	....	....
	Kansas City	IHL	12	2	2	4	56	4	2	1	3	0
1992-93	San Jose	NHL	66	12	15	27	253	....	....	....	....	....
	NHL Totals		**127**	**19**	**19**	**38**	**470**	....	....	....	....	....

Signed as a free agent by **San Jose**, September 3, 1991.

ODJICK, GINO

Left wing. Shoots left. 6'3", 220 lbs. Born, Maniwaki, Que., September 7, 1970.
(Vancouver's 5th choice, 86th overall, in 1990 Entry Draft).

				Regular Season					Playoffs			
Season	Club	Lea	GP	G	A	TP	PIM	GP	G	A	TP	PIM
1988-89	Laval	QMJHL	50	9	15	24	278	16	0	9	9	129
1989-90	Laval	QMJHL	51	12	26	38	280	....	....	....	....	....
1990-91	Vancouver	NHL	45	7	1	8	296	6	0	0	0	18
	Milwaukee	IHL	17	7	3	10	102	....	....	....	....	....
1991-92	Vancouver	NHL	65	4	6	10	348	4	0	0	0	6
1992-93	Vancouver	NHL	75	4	13	17	370	1	0	0	0	0
	NHL Totals		**185**	**15**	**20**	**35**	**1014**	**11**	**0**	**0**	**0**	**24**

O'DONNELL, SEAN

Defense. Shoots left. 6'2", 224 lbs. Born, Ottawa, Ont., October 13, 1971.
(Buffalo's 6th choice, 123rd overall, in 1991 Entry Draft).

				Regular Season					Playoffs			
Season	Club	Lea	GP	G	A	TP	PIM	GP	G	A	TP	PIM
1990-91	Sudbury	OHL	66	8	23	31	114	5	1	4	5	10
1991-92	Rochester	AHL	73	4	9	13	193	16	1	2	3	21
1992-93	Rochester	AHL	74	3	18	21	203	17	1	6	7	38

ODUYA, FREDRIK

Defense. Shoots left. 6'2", 184 lbs. Born, Stockholm, Sweden, May 31, 1975.
(San Jose's 8th choice, 154th overall, in 1993 Entry Draft).

				Regular Season					Playoffs			
Season	Club	Lea	GP	G	A	TP	PIM	GP	G	A	TP	PIM
1991-92	Windsor	Jr. B	43	2	8	10	24	....	....	....	....	....
1992-93	Guelph	OHL	23	2	4	6	29	....	....	....	....	....
	Ottawa	OHL	17	0	3	3	70	....	....	....	....	....

OGRODNICK, JOHN ALEXANDER   (oh-GRAHD-nik)

Left wing. Shoots left. 6', 204 lbs. Born, Ottawa, Ont., June 20, 1959.
(Detroit's 4th choice, 66th overall, in 1979 Entry Draft).

				Regular Season					Playoffs			
Season	Club	Lea	GP	G	A	TP	PIM	GP	G	A	TP	PIM
1977-78a	N. Westminster	WHL	72	59	29	88	47	21	14	7	21	14
1978-79	N. Westminster	WHL	72	48	36	84	38	6	2	0	2	4
1979-80	Detroit	NHL	41	8	24	32	8	....	....	....	....	....
	Adirondack	AHL	39	13	20	33	21	....	....	....	....	....
1980-81	Detroit	NHL	80	35	35	70	14	....	....	....	....	....
1981-82	Detroit	NHL	80	28	26	54	28	....	....	....	....	....
1982-83	Detroit	NHL	80	41	44	85	30	....	....	....	....	....
1983-84	Detroit	NHL	64	42	36	78	14	4	0	0	0	0
1984-85b	Detroit	NHL	79	55	50	105	30	3	1	1	2	0
1985-86	Detroit	NHL	76	38	32	70	18	....	....	....	....	....
1986-87	Detroit	NHL	39	12	28	40	6	....	....	....	....	....
	Quebec	NHL	32	11	16	27	4	13	9	4	13	6
1987-88	NY Rangers	NHL	64	22	32	54	16	....	....	....	....	....
1988-89	NY Rangers	NHL	60	13	29	42	14	3	2	0	2	0
	Denver	IHL	3	2	0	2	0	....	....	....	....	....
1989-90	NY Rangers	NHL	80	43	31	74	44	10	6	3	9	0
1990-91	NY Rangers	NHL	79	31	23	54	10	4	0	0	0	0
1991-92	NY Rangers	NHL	55	17	13	30	22	3	0	0	0	0
1992-93	Detroit	NHL	19	6	6	12	2	1	0	0	0	0
	Adirondack	AHL	4	2	2	4	0	....	....	....	....	....
	NHL Totals		**928**	**402**	**425**	**827**	**260**	**41**	**18**	**8**	**26**	**6**

a Shared WHL Rookie of the Year Award with Keith Brown (Portland) (1978)
b NHL First All-Star Team (1985)
Played in NHL All-Star Game (1981, 1982, 1984-86)
Traded to **Quebec** by Detroit with Basil McRae and Doug Shedden for Brent Ashton, Gilbert Delorme and Mark Kumpel, January 17, 1987. Traded to **NY Rangers** by Quebec with David Shaw for Jeff Jackson and Terry Carkner, September 30, 1987.

OHMAN, PAUL

Defense. Shoots left. 6'1", 185 lbs. Born, Worcester, MA, July 30, 1969.
(Boston's 9th choice, 182nd overall, in 1987 Entry Draft).

				Regular Season					Playoffs			
Season	Club	Lea	GP	G	A	TP	PIM	GP	G	A	TP	PIM
1989-90	Brown	ECAC	23	1	4	5	14	....	....	....	....	....
1990-91	Brown	ECAC	13	0	0	0	6	....	....	....	....	....
1991-92	Brown	ECAC	16	0	0	0	14	....	....	....	....	....
1992-93	Providence	AHL	2	0	0	0	2	....	....	....	....	....
	Johnstown	ECHL	52	3	10	13	31	5	0	0	0	14

OJANEN, JANNE (OY-uh-nehn, YAHN-ee)

Center. Shoots left. 6'2", 200 lbs. Born, Tampere, Finland, April 9, 1968.
(New Jersey's 3rd choice, 45th overall, in 1986 Entry Draft).

			Regular Season					Playoffs				
Season	Club	Lea	GP	G	A	TP	PIM	GP	G	A	TP	PIM
1985-86	Tappara	Fin. Jr.	14	5	17	22	14	5	2	3	5	8
	Tappara	Fin.	3	0	0	0	2	....	....	....	....	....
1986-87	Tappara	Fin.	40	18	13	31	16	9	4	6	10	2
1987-88	Tappara	Fin.	44	21	31	52	30	10	4	4	8	12
1988-89	**New Jersey**	**NHL**	**3**	**0**	**1**	**1**	**2**	....	....	....	....	....
	Utica	AHL	72	23	37	60	10	5	0	3	3	0
1989-90	**New Jersey**	**NHL**	**64**	**17**	**13**	**30**	**12**	....	....	....	....	....
1990-91	Tappara	Fin.	44	15	33	48	36	3	1	2	3	6
1991-92	Tappara	Fin.	44	21	27	48	24	....	....	....	....	....
	New Jersey	**NHL**	....	....	....	....	....	**3**	**0**	**2**	**2**	**0**
1992-93	**New Jersey**	**NHL**	**31**	**4**	**9**	**13**	**14**	....	....	....	....	....
	Cincinnati	IHL	7	1	8	9	0	....	....	....	....	....
	NHL Totals		**98**	**21**	**23**	**44**	**28**	**3**	**0**	**2**	**2**	**0**

OKSYUTA, ROMAN (ohk-SEW-tah)

Right wing. Shoots left. 6'3", 207 lbs. Born, Murmansk, Soviet Union, August 21, 1970.
(NY Rangers' 11th choice, 202nd overall, in 1989 Entry Draft).

			Regular Season					Playoffs				
Season	Club	Lea	GP	G	A	TP	PIM	GP	G	A	TP	PIM
1987-88	Khimik	USSR	11	1	0	1	4	....	....	....	....	....
1988-89	Khimik	USSR	34	13	3	16	14	....	....	....	....	....
1989-90	Khimik	USSR	37	13	6	19	16	....	....	....	....	....
1990-91	Khimik	USSR	41	12	8	20	24	....	....	....	....	....
1991-92	Khimik	CIS	42	24	20	44	28	....	....	....	....	....
1992-93	Khimik	CIS	20	11	2	13	42	....	....	....	....	....
	Cape Breton	AHL	43	26	25	51	22	16	9	19	28	12

Traded to **Edmonton** by **NY Rangers** with NY Rangers' third round choice (Alexander Kerch) in 1993 Entry Draft for Kevin Lowe, December 11, 1992.

OKTYABREV, ARTUR

Defense. Shoots left. 5'11", 183 lbs. Born, Irkutsk, Soviet Union, November 26, 1973.
(Winnipeg's 6th choice, 155th overall, in 1992 Entry Draft).

			Regular Season					Playoffs				
Season	Club	Lea	GP	G	A	TP	PIM	GP	G	A	TP	PIM
1991-92	CSKA	CIS	38	1	2	3	19	....	....	....	....	....
1992-93	CSKA	CIS	41	0	5	5	44	....	....	....	....	....

OLAUSSON, FREDRIK (OHL-AH-SUHN)

Defense. Shoots right. 6'2", 195 lbs. Born, Dadesjo, Sweden, October 5, 1966.
(Winnipeg's 4th choice, 81st overall, in 1985 Entry Draft).

			Regular Season					Playoffs				
Season	Club	Lea	GP	G	A	TP	PIM	GP	G	A	TP	PIM
1982-83	Nybro	Swe.2	31	4	4	8	12	....	....	....	....	....
1983-84	Nybro	Swe.2	28	8	14	22	32	....	....	....	....	....
1984-85	Farjestad	Swe.	29	5	12	17	22	3	1	0	1	0
1985-86	Farjestad	Swe.	33	4	12	16	22	8	3	2	5	6
1986-87	**Winnipeg**	**NHL**	**72**	**7**	**29**	**36**	**24**	**10**	**2**	**3**	**5**	**4**
1987-88	**Winnipeg**	**NHL**	**38**	**5**	**10**	**15**	**18**	**5**	**1**	**1**	**2**	**0**
1988-89	**Winnipeg**	**NHL**	**75**	**15**	**47**	**62**	**32**	....	....	....	....	....
1989-90	**Winnipeg**	**NHL**	**77**	**9**	**46**	**55**	**32**	**7**	**0**	**2**	**2**	**2**
1990-91	**Winnipeg**	**NHL**	**71**	**12**	**29**	**41**	**24**	....	....	....	....	....
1991-92	**Winnipeg**	**NHL**	**77**	**20**	**42**	**62**	**34**	**7**	**1**	**5**	**6**	**4**
1992-93	**Winnipeg**	**NHL**	**68**	**16**	**41**	**57**	**22**	**6**	**0**	**2**	**2**	**2**
	NHL Totals		**478**	**84**	**244**	**328**	**186**	**35**	**4**	**13**	**17**	**12**

OLCZYK, ED (OHL-chehk)

Center. Shoots left. 6'1", 200 lbs. Born, Chicago, IL, August 16, 1966.
(Chicago's 1st choice, 3rd overall, in 1984 Entry Draft).

			Regular Season					Playoffs				
Season	Club	Lea	GP	G	A	TP	PIM	GP	G	A	TP	PIM
1983-84	U.S. Olympic	....	62	21	47	68	36	....	....	....	....	....
1984-85	**Chicago**	**NHL**	**70**	**20**	**30**	**50**	**67**	**15**	**6**	**5**	**11**	**11**
1985-86	**Chicago**	**NHL**	**79**	**29**	**50**	**79**	**47**	**3**	**0**	**0**	**0**	**0**
1986-87	**Chicago**	**NHL**	**79**	**16**	**35**	**51**	**119**	**4**	**1**	**1**	**2**	**4**
1987-88	**Toronto**	**NHL**	**80**	**42**	**33**	**75**	**55**	**6**	**5**	**4**	**9**	**2**
1988-89	**Toronto**	**NHL**	**80**	**38**	**52**	**90**	**75**	....	....	....	....	....
1989-90	**Toronto**	**NHL**	**79**	**32**	**56**	**88**	**78**	**5**	**1**	**2**	**3**	**14**
1990-91	**Toronto**	**NHL**	**18**	**4**	**10**	**14**	**13**	....	....	....	....	....
	Winnipeg	**NHL**	**61**	**26**	**31**	**57**	**69**	....	....	....	....	....
1991-92	**Winnipeg**	**NHL**	**64**	**32**	**33**	**65**	**67**	**6**	**2**	**1**	**3**	**4**
1992-93	**Winnipeg**	**NHL**	**25**	**8**	**12**	**20**	**26**	....	....	....	....	....
	NY Rangers	**NHL**	**46**	**13**	**16**	**29**	**26**	....	....	....	....	....
	NHL Totals		**681**	**260**	**358**	**618**	**642**	**39**	**15**	**13**	**28**	**35**

Traded to **Toronto** by **Chicago** with Al Secord for Rick Vaive, Steve Thomas and Bob McGill, September 3, 1987. Traded to **Winnipeg** by **Toronto** with Mark Osborne for Dave Ellett and Paul Fenton, November 10, 1990. Traded to **NY Rangers** by **Winnipeg** for Kris King and Tie Domi, December 28, 1992.

O'LEARY, RYAN

Center. Shoots left. 6'1", 205 lbs. Born, Duluth, MN, June 8, 1971.
(Calgary's 6th choice, 84th overall, in 1989 Entry Draft).

			Regular Season					Playoffs				
Season	Club	Lea	GP	G	A	TP	PIM	GP	G	A	TP	PIM
1989-90	U. of Denver	WCHA	39	4	6	10	30	....	....	....	....	....
1990-91	U. of Denver	WCHA	38	3	6	9	40	....	....	....	....	....
1991-92	U. of Denver	WCHA	17	5	4	9	22	....	....	....	....	....
1992-93	U. of Denver	WCHA	37	5	7	12	37	....	....	....	....	....

OLIMPIYEV, SERGEI

Left wing. Shoots left. 6'1", 189 lbs. Born, Minsk, Soviet Union, January 12, 1975.
(NY Rangers' 4th choice, 86th overall, in 1993 Entry Draft).

			Regular Season					Playoffs				
Season	Club	Lea	GP	G	A	TP	PIM	GP	G	A	TP	PIM
1991-92	Lipetsk	CIS 3	20	0	0	0	2	....	....	....	....	....
1992-93	Minsk Dynamo	CIS	6	1	0	1	2	....	....	....	....	....

OLIVER, DAVID

Right wing. Shoots right. 5'11", 185 lbs. Born, Sechelt, B.C., April 17, 1971.
(Edmonton's 7th choice, 144th overall, in 1991 Entry Draft).

			Regular Season					Playoffs				
Season	Club	Lea	GP	G	A	TP	PIM	GP	G	A	TP	PIM
1990-91	U. of Michigan	CCHA	27	13	11	24	34	....	....	....	....	....
1991-92	U. of Michigan	CCHA	44	31	27	58	32	....	....	....	....	....
1992-93a	U. of Michigan	CCHA	40	35	20	55	18	....	....	....	....	....

a CCHA Second All-Star Team (1993)

OLIWA, KRZYSZTOF

Left wing. Shoots left. 6'5", 220 lbs. Born, Tychy, Poland, April 12, 1973.
(New Jersey's 4th choice, 65th overall, in 1993 Entry Draft).

			Regular Season					Playoffs				
Season	Club	Lea	GP	G	A	TP	PIM	GP	G	A	TP	PIM
1991-92	GKS Tychy	Poland	10	3	7	10	6	....	....	....	....	....
1992-93	Welland	OHAJr.B	30	13	21	34	127	....	....	....	....	....

OLSEN, DARRYL

Defense. Shoots left. 6', 180 lbs. Born, Calgary, Alta., October 7, 1966.
(Calgary's 10th choice, 185th overall, in 1985 Entry Draft).

			Regular Season					Playoffs				
Season	Club	Lea	GP	G	A	TP	PIM	GP	G	A	TP	PIM
1985-86	N. Michigan	WCHA	37	5	20	25	46	....	....	....	....	....
1986-87	N. Michigan	WCHA	37	5	20	25	96	....	....	....	....	....
1987-88	N. Michigan	WCHA	35	11	20	31	59	....	....	....	....	....
1988-89	Cdn. National	....	3	1	0	1	4	....	....	....	....	....
ab	N. Michigan	WCHA	45	16	26	42	88	....	....	....	....	....
1989-90	Salt Lake	IHL	72	16	50	66	90	11	3	6	9	2
1990-91	Salt Lake	IHL	76	15	40	55	89	4	1	5	6	2
1991-92	**Calgary**	**NHL**	**1**	**0**	**0**	**0**	**0**	....	....	....	....	....
	Salt Lake	IHL	59	7	33	40	80	5	2	1	3	4
1992-93	Providence	AHL	50	7	27	34	38	....	....	....	....	....
	San Diego	IHL	21	2	8	10	26	10	1	3	4	30
	NHL Totals		**1**	**0**	**0**	**0**	**0**	....	....	....	....	....

a NCAA West Second All-American Team (1989)
b WCHA First All-Star Team (1989)

Signed as a free agent by **Boston**, July 23, 1992.

OLSSON, MATTIAS

Defense. Shoots right. 6'1", 191 lbs. Born, Karlstad, Sweden, April 1, 1971.
(Los Angeles' 10th choice, 218th overall, in 1991 Entry Draft).

			Regular Season					Playoffs				
Season	Club	Lea	GP	G	A	TP	PIM	GP	G	A	TP	PIM
1988-89	Farjestad	Swe.	4	1	1	2	2	....	....	....	....	....
1989-90	Farjestad	Swe.	33	2	8	10	18	10	0	2	2	2
1990-91	Farjestad	Swe.	36	3	7	10	22	8	0	0	0	8
1991-92	Farjestad	Swe.	40	5	11	16	28	6	0	0	0	4
1992-93	Farjestad	Swe.	35	6	6	12	26	3	0	1	1	0

O'ROURKE, STEVE

Right wing. Shoots right. 6', 190 lbs. Born, Calgary, Alta., September 11, 1974.
(NY Islanders' 7th choice, 159th overall, in 1992 Entry Draft).

			Regular Season					Playoffs				
Season	Club	Lea	GP	G	A	TP	PIM	GP	G	A	TP	PIM
1991-92	Tri-City	WHL	42	3	9	12	45	2	0	1	1	2
1992-93	Tri-City	WHL	61	3	17	20	104	3	0	2	2	2

OSADCHY, ALEXANDER (oh-SAHD-chee)

Defense. Shoots right. 5'11", 191 lbs. Born, Kharkov, Soviet Union, July 19, 1975.
(San Jose's 5th choice, 80th overall, in 1993 Entry Draft).

			Regular Season					Playoffs				
Season	Club	Lea	GP	G	A	TP	PIM	GP	G	A	TP	PIM
1992-93	CSKA	CIS	37	0	1	1	60	....	....	....	....	....

OSBORNE, KEITH

Right wing. Shoots right. 6'1", 180 lbs. Born, Toronto, Ont., April 2, 1969.
(St. Louis' 1st choice, 12th overall, in 1987 Entry Draft).

			Regular Season					Playoffs				
Season	Club	Lea	GP	G	A	TP	PIM	GP	G	A	TP	PIM
1986-87	North Bay	OHL	61	34	55	89	31	24	11	11	22	25
1987-88	North Bay	OHL	30	14	22	36	20	4	1	5	6	8
1988-89	North Bay	OHL	15	11	15	26	12	....	....	....	....	....
	Niagara Falls	OHL	50	34	49	83	45	17	12	12	24	36
1989-90	**St. Louis**	**NHL**	**5**	**0**	**2**	**2**	**8**	....	....	....	....	....
	Peoria	IHL	56	23	24	47	58	5	1	1	2	4
1990-91	Peoria	IHL	54	10	20	30	79	....	....	....	....	....
	Newmarket	AHL	12	0	3	3	6	....	....	....	....	....
1991-92	St. John's	AHL	53	11	16	27	21	4	0	1	1	2
1992-93	**Tampa Bay**	**NHL**	**11**	**1**	**1**	**2**	**8**	....	....	....	....	....
	Atlanta	IHL	72	40	49	89	91	8	1	5	6	2
	NHL Totals		**16**	**1**	**3**	**4**	**16**	....	....	....	....	....

Traded to **Toronto** by **St. Louis** for Darren Veitch and future considerations, March 5, 1991. Claimed by **Tampa Bay** from **Toronto** in Expansion Draft, June 18, 1992.

OSBORNE, MARK ANATOLE (AWS-born)

Left wing. Shoots left. 6'2", 205 lbs. Born, Toronto, Ont., August 13, 1961.
(Detroit's 2nd choice, 46th overall, in 1980 Entry Draft).

			Regular Season					Playoffs				
Season	Club	Lea	GP	G	A	TP	PIM	GP	G	A	TP	PIM
1979-80	Niagara Falls	OHA	52	10	33	43	104	10	2	1	3	23
1980-81	Niagara Falls	OHA	54	39	41	80	140	12	11	10	21	20
	Adirondack	AHL	....	....	....	....	....	13	2	3	5	2
1981-82	**Detroit**	**NHL**	**80**	**26**	**41**	**67**	**61**	....	....	....	....	....
1982-83	**Detroit**	**NHL**	**80**	**19**	**24**	**43**	**83**	....	....	....	....	....
1983-84	**NY Rangers**	**NHL**	**73**	**23**	**28**	**51**	**88**	**5**	**0**	**1**	**1**	**7**
1984-85	**NY Rangers**	**NHL**	**23**	**4**	**4**	**8**	**33**	**3**	**0**	**0**	**0**	**4**
1985-86	**NY Rangers**	**NHL**	**62**	**16**	**24**	**40**	**80**	**15**	**2**	**3**	**5**	**26**
1986-87	**NY Rangers**	**NHL**	**58**	**17**	**15**	**32**	**101**	....	....	....	....	....
	Toronto	**NHL**	**16**	**5**	**10**	**15**	**12**	**9**	**1**	**3**	**4**	**6**
1987-88	**Toronto**	**NHL**	**79**	**23**	**37**	**60**	**102**	**6**	**1**	**3**	**4**	**16**
1988-89	**Toronto**	**NHL**	**75**	**16**	**30**	**46**	**112**	....	....	....	....	....
1989-90	**Toronto**	**NHL**	**78**	**23**	**50**	**73**	**91**	**5**	**2**	**3**	**5**	**12**
1990-91	**Toronto**	**NHL**	**18**	**3**	**3**	**6**	**4**	....	....	....	....	....
	Winnipeg	**NHL**	**37**	**8**	**8**	**16**	**59**	....	....	....	....	....
1991-92	**Winnipeg**	**NHL**	**43**	**4**	**12**	**16**	**65**	....	....	....	....	....
	Toronto	**NHL**	**11**	**3**	**1**	**4**	**8**	....	....	....	....	....
1992-93	**Toronto**	**NHL**	**76**	**12**	**14**	**26**	**89**	**19**	**1**	**1**	**2**	**16**
	NHL Totals		**809**	**202**	**301**	**503**	**988**	**62**	**7**	**14**	**21**	**87**

Traded to **NY Rangers** by **Detroit** with Willie Huber and Mike Blaisdell for Ron Duguay, Eddie Mio and Eddie Johnstone, June 13, 1983. Traded to **Toronto** by **NY Rangers** for Jeff Jackson and Toronto's third round choice (Rod Zamuner) in 1989 Entry Draft, March 5, 1987. Traded to **Winnipeg** by **Toronto** with Ed Olcyk for Dave Ellett and Paul Fenton, November 10, 1990. Traded to **Toronto** by **Winnipeg** for Lucien Deblois, March 10, 1992.

O'SHEA, DAN

Right wing. Shoots right. 6'1", 180 lbs. Born, St. Cloud, MN, September 4, 1970.
(Minnesota's 1st choice, 14th overall, in 1991 Supplemental Draft).

			Regular Season					Playoffs				
Season	Club	Lea	GP	G	A	TP	PIM	GP	G	A	TP	PIM
1990-91	St. Cloud	WCHA	31	4	9	13	60	....	....	....	....	....
1991-92	St. Cloud	WCHA	35	10	14	24	65	....	....	....	....	....
1992-93	St. Cloud	WCHA	33	11	11	22	48	....	....	....	....	....

OSIECKI, MARK

Defense. Shoots right. 6'2", 200 lbs. Born, St. Paul, MN, July 23, 1968.
(Calgary's 10th choice, 187th overall, in 1987 Entry Draft).

			Regular Season					Playoffs				
Season	Club	Lea	GP	G	A	TP	PIM	GP	G	A	TP	PIM
1986-87	U. Wisconsin	WCHA	8	0	1	1	4	....	....	....	....	....
1987-88	U. Wisconsin	WCHA	18	0	1	1	22	....	....	....	....	....
1988-89	U. Wisconsin	WCHA	44	1	3	4	56	....	....	....	....	....
1989-90a	U. Wisconsin	WCHA	46	5	38	43	78	....	....	....	....	....
1990-91	Salt Lake	IHL	75	1	24	25	36	4	2	0	2	2
1991-92	**Calgary**	**NHL**	**50**	**2**	**7**	**9**	**24**	....	....	....	....	....
	Salt Lake	IHL	1	0	0	0	0	....	....	....	....	....
1992-93	**Ottawa**	**NHL**	**34**	**0**	**4**	**4**	**12**	....	....	....	....	....
	New Haven	AHL	4	0	1	1	0	....	....	....	....	....
	Winnipeg	**NHL**	**4**	**1**	**0**	**1**	**2**	....	....	....	....	....
	Minnesota	**NHL**	**5**	**0**	**0**	**0**	**5**	....	....	....	....	....
	NHL Totals		**93**	**3**	**11**	**14**	**43**	....	....	....	....	....

a NCAA All-Tournament Team (1990)

Traded to **Ottawa** by **Calgary** for Chris Lindberg, June 22, 1992. Claimed on waivers by **Winnipeg** from **Ottawa**, February 20, 1993. Traded to **Minnesota** by **Winnipeg** with Winnipeg's tenth round choice (Bill Lang) in 1993 Entry Draft for Minnesota's ninth round choice (Vladimir Potatov) in 1993 Entry Draft, March 20, 1993.

OSMAK, COREY

Center. Shoots left. 6'1", 180 lbs. Born, Edmonton, Alta., August 20, 1970.
(Hartford's 8th choice, 183rd overall, in 1990 Entry Draft).

			Regular Season					Playoffs				
Season	Club	Lea	GP	G	A	TP	PIM	GP	G	A	TP	PIM
1990-91	Minn.-Duluth	WCHA	22	3	0	3	34	....	....	....	....	....
1991-92	Minn.-Duluth	WCHA	26	1	4	5	58	....	....	....	....	....
1992-93	Minn. Duluth	WCHA	39	11	15	26	86	....	....	....	....	....

O'SULLIVAN, CHRIS

Defense. Shoots left. 6'2", 185 lbs. Born, Dorchester, MA, May 15, 1974.
(Calgary's 2nd choice, 30th overall, in 1992 Entry Draft).

			Regular Season					Playoffs				
Season	Club	Lea	GP	G	A	TP	PIM	GP	G	A	TP	PIM
1991-92	Catholic Mem.	HS	26	26	23	49	65	....	....	....	....	....
1992-93	Boston U.	H.E.	5	0	2	2	4	....	....	....	....	....

O'SULLIVAN, KEVIN

Defense. Shoots left. 6', 180 lbs. Born, Dorchester, MA, November 13, 1970.
(NY Islanders' 7th choice, 99th overall, in 1989 Entry Draft).

			Regular Season					Playoffs				
Season	Club	Lea	GP	G	A	TP	PIM	GP	G	A	TP	PIM
1989-90	Boston U.	H.E.	43	0	6	6	42	....	....	....	....	....
1990-91	Boston U.	H.E.	37	4	7	11	50	....	....	....	....	....
1991-92a	Boston U.	H.E.	32	3	18	21	62	....	....	....	....	....
1992-93b	Boston U.	H.E.	40	5	20	25	78	....	....	....	....	....

a Hockey East Second All-Star Team (1992)
b Hockey East First All-Star Team (1993)

OTEVREL, JAROSLAV (oh-TEHV-rehl)

Left wing. Shoots left. 6'3", 200 lbs. Born, Gottwaldov, Czech., September 16, 1968.
(San Jose's 8th choice, 133rd overall, in 1991 Entry Draft).

			Regular Season					Playoffs				
Season	Club	Lea	GP	G	A	TP	PIM	GP	G	A	TP	PIM
1987-88	TJ Gottwaldov	Czech.	32	4	7	11	18	....	....	....	....	....
1988-89	TJ Gottwaldov	Czech.	40	14	6	20	37	....	....	....	....	....
1989-90	Dukla Trencin	Czech.	43	7	10	17	20	....	....	....	....	....
1990-91	TJ Zlin	Czech.	49	24	26	50	105	....	....	....	....	....
1991-92	ZPS Zlin	Czech.	40	14	15	29	44	....	....	....	....	....
1992-93	**San Jose**	**NHL**	**7**	**0**	**2**	**2**	**0**	....	....	....	....	....
	Kansas City	IHL	62	17	27	44	58	6	1	4	5	4
	NHL Totals		**7**	**0**	**2**	**2**	**0**	....	....	....	....	....

OTTO, JOEL STUART

Center. Shoots right. 6'4", 220 lbs. Born, Elk River, MN, October 29, 1961.

			Regular Season					Playoffs				
Season	Club	Lea	GP	G	A	TP	PIM	GP	G	A	TP	PIM
1980-81	Bemidji State	NCAA	23	5	11	16	10	....	....	....	....	....
1981-82	Bemidji State	NCAA	31	19	33	52	24	....	....	....	....	....
1982-83	Bemidji State	NCAA	37	33	28	61	68	....	....	....	....	....
1983-84	Bemidji State	NCAA	31	32	43	75	32	....	....	....	....	....
1984-85	**Calgary**	**NHL**	**17**	**4**	**8**	**12**	**30**	**3**	**2**	**1**	**3**	**10**
	Moncton	AHL	56	27	36	63	89	....	....	....	....	....
1985-86	**Calgary**	**NHL**	**79**	**25**	**34**	**59**	**188**	**22**	**5**	**10**	**15**	**80**
1986-87	**Calgary**	**NHL**	**68**	**19**	**31**	**50**	**185**	**2**	**0**	**2**	**2**	**6**
1987-88	**Calgary**	**NHL**	**62**	**13**	**39**	**52**	**194**	**9**	**3**	**2**	**5**	**26**
1988-89	**Calgary**	**NHL**	**72**	**23**	**30**	**53**	**213**	**22**	**6**	**13**	**19**	**46**
1989-90	**Calgary**	**NHL**	**75**	**13**	**20**	**33**	**116**	**6**	**2**	**2**	**4**	**2**
1990-91	**Calgary**	**NHL**	**76**	**19**	**20**	**39**	**183**	**7**	**1**	**2**	**3**	**8**
1991-92	**Calgary**	**NHL**	**78**	**13**	**21**	**34**	**161**	....	....	....	....	....
1992-93	**Calgary**	**NHL**	**75**	**19**	**33**	**52**	**150**	**6**	**4**	**2**	**6**	**4**
	NHL Totals		**602**	**148**	**236**	**384**	**1420**	**77**	**23**	**34**	**57**	**182**

Signed as a free agent by **Calgary**, September 11, 1984.

OUIMET, MARK

Center. Shoots left. 5'10", 165 lbs. Born, Poplar Hill, Ont., October 2, 1971.
(Washington's 6th choice, 94th overall, in 1990 Entry Draft).

			Regular Season					Playoffs				
Season	Club	Lea	GP	G	A	TP	PIM	GP	G	A	TP	PIM
1989-90	U. of Michigan	CCHA	38	15	32	47	14	....	....	....	....	....
1990-91	U. of Michigan	CCHA	46	18	32	50	22	....	....	....	....	....
1991-92	U. of Michigan	CCHA	40	10	19	29	30	....	....	....	....	....
1992-93	U. of Michigan	CCHA	39	15	*45	60	23	....	....	....	....	....
	Baltimore	AHL	1	0	1	1	0	....	....	....	....	....

OZOLINSH, SANDIS (oh-zohl-INSH)

Defense. Shoots left. 6'1", 195 lbs. Born, Riga, Soviet Union, August 3, 1972.
(San Jose's 3rd choice, 30th overall, in 1991 Entry Draft).

			Regular Season					Playoffs				
Season	Club	Lea	GP	G	A	TP	PIM	GP	G	A	TP	PIM
1990-91	Riga	USSR	44	0	3	3	51	....	....	....	....	....
1991-92	Riga	CIS	30	6	0	6	42	....	....	....	....	....
	Kansas City	IHL	34	6	9	15	20	15	2	5	7	22
1992-93	**San Jose**	**NHL**	**37**	**7**	**16**	**23**	**40**	....	....	....	....	....
	NHL Totals		**37**	**7**	**16**	**23**	**40**	....	....	....	....	....

PADEN, KEVIN

Center/Left wing. Shoots left. 6'3", 175 lbs. Born, Woodhaven, MI, February 12, 1975.
(Edmonton's 4th choice, 59th overall, in 1993 Entry Draft).

			Regular Season					Playoffs				
Season	Club	Lea	GP	G	A	TP	PIM	GP	G	A	TP	PIM
1991-92	Detroit L.C.	Midget	29	21	26	47	77	....	....	....	....	....
1992-93	Detroit	OHL	54	14	9	23	41	15	1	1	2	2

PAEK, JIM (PAYK)

Defense. Shoots left. 6'1", 195 lbs. Born, Seoul, South Korea, April 7, 1967.
(Pittsburgh's 9th choice, 170th overall, in 1985 Entry Draft).

			Regular Season					Playoffs				
Season	Club	Lea	GP	G	A	TP	PIM	GP	G	A	TP	PIM
1984-85	Oshawa	OHL	54	2	13	15	57	5	1	0	1	9
1985-86	Oshawa	OHL	64	5	21	26	122	6	0	1	1	9
1986-87	Oshawa	OHL	57	5	17	22	75	26	1	14	15	43
1987-88	Muskegon	IHL	82	7	52	59	141	6	0	0	0	29
1988-89	Muskegon	IHL	80	3	54	57	96	14	1	10	11	24
1989-90	Muskegon	IHL	81	9	41	50	115	15	1	10	11	41
1990-91	Cdn. National	....	48	2	12	14	24	....	....	....	....	....
	Pittsburgh	**NHL**	**3**	**0**	**0**	**0**	**9**	**8**	**1**	**0**	**1**	**2**
1991-92	**Pittsburgh**	**NHL**	**49**	**1**	**7**	**8**	**36**	**19**	**0**	**4**	**4**	**6**
1992-93	**Pittsburgh**	**NHL**	**77**	**3**	**15**	**18**	**64**	....	....	....	....	....
	NHL Totals		**129**	**4**	**22**	**26**	**109**	**27**	**1**	**4**	**5**	**8**

PALFFY, ZIGMUND (PAWL-FEE)

Left wing. Shoots left. 5'10", 169 lbs. Born, Skalica, Czechoslovakia, May 5, 1972.
(NY Islanders' 2nd choice, 26th overall, in 1991 Entry Draft).

			Regular Season					Playoffs				
Season	Club	Lea	GP	G	A	TP	PIM	GP	G	A	TP	PIM
1990-91	Nitra	Czech.	50	34	16	50	18	....	....	....	....	....
1991-92	Dukla Trencin	Czech.	45	41	33	74	36	....	....	....	....	....
1992-93	Dukla Trencin	Czech.	43	38	41	79	....	....	....	....	....	....

PANDOLFO, JAY

Left wing. Shoots left. 6'1", 195 lbs. Born, Winchester, MA, December 27, 1974.
(New Jersey's 2nd choice, 32nd overall, in 1993 Entry Draft).

			Regular Season					Playoffs				
Season	Club	Lea	GP	G	A	TP	PIM	GP	G	A	TP	PIM
1991-92	Burlington	HS	20	35	34	69	20	....	....	....	....	....
1992-93	Boston U.	H.E.	37	16	22	38	16	....	....	....	....	....

PANKEWICZ, GREG

Right wing. Shoots right. 6', 185 lbs. Born, Dray Valley, Alta., October 6, 1970.

			Regular Season					Playoffs				
Season	Club	Lea	GP	G	A	TP	PIM	GP	G	A	TP	PIM
1989-90	Regina	WHL	63	14	24	38	136	10	1	3	4	19
1990-91	Regina	WHL	72	39	41	80	134	8	4	7	11	12
1991-92	Knoxville	ECHL	59	41	39	80	214	....	....	....	....	....
1992-93	New Haven	AHL	62	23	20	43	163	....	....	....	....	....

Signed as a free agent by **Ottawa**, May 27, 1993.

PANTELEEV, GRIGORY (pan-teh-LAY-ehv)

Left wing. Shoots left. 5'9", 185 lbs. Born, Gastello, Soviet Union, November 13, 1972.
(Boston's 5th choice, 136th overall, in 1992 Entry Draft).

			Regular Season					Playoffs				
Season	Club	Lea	GP	G	A	TP	PIM	GP	G	A	TP	PIM
1990-91	Riga	USSR	23	4	1	5	4	....	....	....	....	....
1991-92	Riga	CIS	26	4	8	12	4	....	....	....	....	....
1992-93	**Boston**	**NHL**	**39**	**8**	**6**	**14**	**12**	....	....	....	....	....
	Providence	AHL	39	17	30	47	22	3	0	0	0	10
	NHL Totals		**39**	**8**	**6**	**14**	**12**	....	....	....	....	....

PAQUETTE, CHARLES

Defense. Shoots left. 6'1", 193 lbs. Born, Lachute, Que., June 17, 1975.
(Boston's 3rd choice, 88th overall, in 1993 Entry Draft).

			Regular Season					Playoffs				
Season	Club	Lea	GP	G	A	TP	PIM	GP	G	A	TP	PIM
1991-92	Trois-Rivieres	QMJHL	60	1	7	8	101	6	0	0	0	2
1992-93	Sherbrooke	QMJHL	54	2	5	7	104	15	0	0	0	33

PAQUIN, PATRICE

Left wing. Shoots left. 6'2", 192 lbs. Born, St. Jerome, Que., June 26, 1974.
(Philadelphia's 11th choice, 247th overall, in 1992 Entry Draft).

			Regular Season					Playoffs				
Season	Club	Lea	GP	G	A	TP	PIM	GP	G	A	TP	PIM
1991-92	Beauport	QMJHL	60	10	15	25	169	....	....	....	....	....
1992-93	Beauport	QMJHL	59	17	23	40	271	....	....	....	....	....

PARADIS, DANIEL

Center. Shoots left. 6'2", 185 lbs. Born, Jonquiere, Que., November 22, 1972.
(NY Islanders' 9th choice, 200th overall, in 1992 Entry Draft).

			Regular Season					Playoffs				
Season	Club	Lea	GP	G	A	TP	PIM	GP	G	A	TP	PIM
1990-91	Chicoutimi	QMJHL	62	14	30	44	69	12	1	2	3	11
1991-92	Chicoutimi	QMJHL	70	42	47	89	97	4	4	3	7	8
1992-93	Chicoutimi	QMJHL	69	43	59	102	176	4	3	2	5	15

PARKS, GREG

Center. Shoots right. 5'9", 180 lbs. Born, Edmonton, Alta., March 25, 1967.

			Regular Season					Playoffs				
Season	Club	Lea	GP	G	A	TP	PIM	GP	G	A	TP	PIM
1985-86	Bowling Green	CCHA	41	16	26	42	43	....	....	....	....	....
1986-87	Bowling Green	CCHA	45	23	27	50	52	....	....	....	....	....
1987-88	Bowling Green	CCHA	45	30	44	74	84	....	....	....	....	....
1988-89a	Bowling Green	CCHA	47	32	42	74	98	....	....	....	....	....
1989-90	Springfield	AHL	49	22	32	54	30	18	9	*13	*22	22
	Johnstown	ECHL	8	5	9	14	7	....	....	....	....	....
1990-91	**NY Islanders**	**NHL**	**20**	**1**	**2**	**3**	**4**	....	....	....	....	....
	Capital Dist.	AHL	48	32	43	75	67	....	....	....	....	....
1991-92	**NY Islanders**	**NHL**	**1**	**0**	**0**	**0**	**2**	....	....	....	....	....
	Capital Dist.	AHL	70	36	57	93	84	7	5	8	13	4
1992-93	Leksand	Swe.	39	21	19	40	66	1	0	0	0	4
	Cdn. National	....	9	2	2	4	4	....	....	....	....	....
	NY Islanders	**NHL**	**2**	**0**	**0**	**0**	**0**	**2**	**0**	**0**	**0**	**0**
	NHL Totals		**23**	**1**	**2**	**3**	**6**	**2**	**0**	**0**	**0**	**0**

a NCAA West First All-Star Team (1989)

Signed as a free agent by **NY Islanders**, August 13, 1990.

PARROTT, JEFF

Defense. Shoots right. 6'1", 195 lbs. Born, The Pas, Man., April 6, 1971.
(Quebec's 4th choice, 106th overall, in 1990 Entry Draft).

			Regular Season					Playoffs				
Season	Club	Lea	GP	G	A	TP	PIM	GP	G	A	TP	PIM
1989-90	Minn.-Duluth	WCHA	35	1	5	6	60	....	....	....	....	....
1990-91	Minn.-Duluth	WCHA	39	2	8	10	65	....	....	....	....	....
1991-92	Minn.-Duluth	WCHA	33	1	8	9	78	....	....	....	....	....
1992-93	Minn. Duluth	WCHA	39	4	13	17	116	....	....	....	....	....

PASCALL, BRAD

Defense. Shoots left. 6'2", 192 lbs. Born, Coquitlam, B.C., July 29, 1970.
(Buffalo's 5th choice, 103rd overall, in 1990 Entry Draft).

			Regular Season					Playoffs				
Season	Club	Lea	GP	G	A	TP	PIM	GP	G	A	TP	PIM
1989-90	North Dakota	WCHA	45	1	9	10	98	....	....	....	....	....
1990-91	North Dakota	WCHA	38	1	4	5	81	....	....	....	....	....
1991-92	North Dakota	WCHA	28	0	7	7	85	....	....	....	....	....
1992-93	Rochester	AHL	18	0	1	1	38	....	....	....	....	....
	Erie	ECHL	24	0	6	6	26	5	0	1	1	18

PASCUCCI, RONALD

Defense. Shoots left. 6'1", 180 lbs. Born, North Andover, MA, June 9, 1970.
(Washington's 14th choice, 246th overall, in 1988 Entry Draft).

			Regular Season					Playoffs				
Season	Club	Lea	GP	G	A	TP	PIM	GP	G	A	TP	PIM
1989-90	Boston College	H.E.	37	0	6	6	12	....	....	....	....	....
1990-91	Boston College	H.E.	37	1	13	14	30	....	....	....	....	....
1991-92	Boston College	H.E.	35	2	6	8	30	....	....	....	....	....
1992-93	Boston College	H.E.	38	3	7	10	58	....	....	....	....	....

PASLAWSKI, GREGORY STEPHEN (GREG) (pas-LAW-skee)

Right wing. Shoots right. 5'11", 190 lbs. Born, Kindersley, Sask., August 25, 1961.

			Regular Season					Playoffs				
Season	Club	Lea	GP	G	A	TP	PIM	GP	G	A	TP	PIM
1980-81	Prince Albert	SJHL	59	55	60	115	106	....	....	....	....	....
1981-82	Nova Scotia	AHL	43	15	11	26	31	....	....	....	....	....
1982-83	Nova Scotia	AHL	75	46	42	88	32	6	1	3	4	8
1983-84	**Montreal**	**NHL**	**26**	**1**	**4**	**5**	**4**	....	....	....	....	....
	St. Louis	**NHL**	**34**	**8**	**6**	**14**	**17**	**9**	**1**	**0**	**1**	**2**
1984-85	**St. Louis**	**NHL**	**72**	**22**	**20**	**42**	**21**	**3**	**0**	**0**	**0**	**2**
1985-86	**St. Louis**	**NHL**	**56**	**22**	**11**	**33**	**18**	**17**	**10**	**7**	**17**	**13**
1986-87	**St. Louis**	**NHL**	**76**	**29**	**35**	**64**	**27**	**6**	**1**	**1**	**2**	**4**
1987-88	**St. Louis**	**NHL**	**17**	**2**	**1**	**3**	**4**	**3**	**1**	**1**	**2**	**2**
1988-89	**St. Louis**	**NHL**	**75**	**26**	**26**	**52**	**18**	**9**	**2**	**1**	**3**	**2**
1989-90	**Winnipeg**	**NHL**	**71**	**18**	**30**	**48**	**14**	**7**	**1**	**3**	**4**	**0**
1990-91	**Winnipeg**	**NHL**	**43**	**9**	**10**	**19**	**10**	....	....	....	....	....
	Buffalo	**NHL**	**12**	**2**	**1**	**3**	**4**	....	....	....	....	....
1991-92	**Quebec**	**NHL**	**80**	**28**	**17**	**45**	**18**	....	....	....	....	....
1992-93	**Philadelphia**	**NHL**	**60**	**14**	**19**	**33**	**12**	....	....	....	....	....
	Calgary	**NHL**	**13**	**4**	**5**	**9**	**0**	**6**	**3**	**0**	**3**	**0**
	NHL Totals		**635**	**185**	**185**	**370**	**167**	**60**	**19**	**13**	**32**	**25**

Signed as a free agent by **Montreal**, October 5, 1981. Traded to **St. Louis** by **Montreal** with Gilbert Delorme and Doug Wickenheiser for Perry Turnbull, December 21, 1983. Traded to **Winnipeg** by **St. Louis** with St. Louis' third round choice (Kris Draper) in 1989 Entry Draft for Winnipeg's third round choice (Denny Felsner) in 1989 Entry Draft and second round choice (Steve Staios) in 1991 Entry Draft, June 17, 1989. Traded to **Buffalo** by **Winnipeg** for future considerations, February 4, 1991. Claimed by **San Jose** from **Buffalo** in Expansion Draft, May 30, 1991. Traded to **Quebec** by **San Jose** for Tony Hrkac, May 31, 1991. Signed as a free agent by **Philadelphia**, August 25, 1992. Traded to **Calgary** by **Philadelphia** for Calgary's ninth round choice (E.J. Bradley) in 1993 Entry Draft, March 18, 1993.

PATRICK, JAMES

Defense. Shoots right. 6'2", 198 lbs. Born, Winnipeg, Man., June 14, 1963.
(NY Rangers' 1st choice, 9th overall, in 1981 Entry Draft).

			Regular Season					Playoffs				
Season	Club	Lea	GP	G	A	TP	PIM	GP	G	A	TP	PIM
1981-82abc	North Dakota	WCHA	42	5	24	29	26	....	....	....	....	....
1982-83de	North Dakota	WCHA	36	12	36	48	29	....	....	....	....	....
1983-84	Cdn. Olympic	....	63	7	24	31	52	....	....	....	....	....
	NY Rangers	**NHL**	**12**	**1**	**7**	**8**	**2**	**5**	**0**	**3**	**3**	**2**
1984-85	**NY Rangers**	**NHL**	**75**	**8**	**28**	**36**	**71**	**3**	**0**	**0**	**0**	**4**
1985-86	**NY Rangers**	**NHL**	**75**	**14**	**29**	**43**	**88**	**16**	**1**	**5**	**6**	**34**
1986-87	**NY Rangers**	**NHL**	**78**	**10**	**45**	**55**	**62**	**6**	**1**	**2**	**3**	**2**
1987-88	**NY Rangers**	**NHL**	**70**	**17**	**45**	**62**	**52**	....	....	....	....	....
1988-89	**NY Rangers**	**NHL**	**68**	**11**	**36**	**47**	**41**	**4**	**0**	**1**	**1**	**2**
1989-90	**NY Rangers**	**NHL**	**73**	**14**	**43**	**57**	**50**	**10**	**3**	**8**	**11**	**0**
1990-91	**NY Rangers**	**NHL**	**74**	**10**	**49**	**59**	**58**	**6**	**0**	**0**	**0**	**6**
1991-92	**NY Rangers**	**NHL**	**80**	**14**	**57**	**71**	**54**	**13**	**0**	**7**	**7**	**12**
1992-93	**NY Rangers**	**NHL**	**60**	**5**	**21**	**26**	**61**	....	....	....	....	....
	NHL Totals		**665**	**104**	**360**	**464**	**539**	**63**	**5**	**26**	**31**	**62**

a WCHA Rookie of the Year (1982)
b WCHA Second All-Star Team (1982)
c Named to NCAA All-Tournament Team (1982)
d WCHA First All-Star Team (1983)
e NCAA All American (West) (1983)

PATTERSON, COLIN

Right/Left wing. Shoots right. 6'2", 195 lbs. Born, Rexdale, Ont., May 11, 1960.

			Regular Season					Playoffs				
Season	Club	Lea	GP	G	A	TP	PIM	GP	G	A	TP	PIM
1980-81	Clarkson	ECAC	34	20	31	51	8	....	....	....	....	....
1981-82	Clarkson	ECAC	34	21	31	52	32	....	....	....	....	....
1982-83	Clarkson	ECAC	31	23	29	52	30	....	....	....	....	....
	Colorado	CHL	7	1	1	2	0	3	0	0	0	15
1983-84	**Calgary**	**NHL**	**56**	**13**	**14**	**27**	**15**	**11**	**1**	**1**	**2**	**6**
	Colorado	CHL	6	2	3	5	9	....	....	....	....	....
1984-85	**Calgary**	**NHL**	**57**	**22**	**21**	**43**	**5**	**4**	**0**	**0**	**0**	**5**
1985-86	**Calgary**	**NHL**	**61**	**14**	**13**	**27**	**22**	**19**	**6**	**3**	**9**	**10**
1986-87	**Calgary**	**NHL**	**68**	**13**	**13**	**26**	**41**	**6**	**0**	**2**	**2**	**2**
1987-88	**Calgary**	**NHL**	**39**	**7**	**11**	**18**	**28**	**9**	**1**	**0**	**1**	**8**
1988-89	**Calgary**	**NHL**	**74**	**14**	**24**	**38**	**56**	**22**	**3**	**10**	**13**	**24**
1989-90	**Calgary**	**NHL**	**61**	**5**	**3**	**8**	**20**	....	....	....	....	....
1990-91	**Calgary**	**NHL**	....	....	....	....	....	**1**	**0**	**0**	**0**	**0**
1991-92	**Buffalo**	**NHL**	**52**	**4**	**8**	**12**	**30**	**5**	**1**	**0**	**1**	**0**
1992-93	**Buffalo**	**NHL**	**36**	**4**	**2**	**6**	**22**	**8**	**0**	**1**	**1**	**2**
	NHL Totals		**504**	**96**	**109**	**205**	**239**	**85**	**12**	**17**	**29**	**57**

Signed as a free agent by **Calgary**, March 24, 1983. Traded to **Buffalo** by **Calgary** for future considerations, October 24, 1991.

PATTERSON, ED

Right wing. Shoots right. 6'2", 213 lbs. Born, Delta, B.C., November 14, 1972.
(Pittsburgh's 7th choice, 148th overall, in 1991 Entry Draft).

			Regular Season					Playoffs				
Season	Club	Lea	GP	G	A	TP	PIM	GP	G	A	TP	PIM
1990-91	Swift Current	WHL	7	2	7	9	0	....	....	....	....	....
	Kamloops	WHL	55	14	33	47	134	5	0	0	0	7
1991-92	Kamloops	WHL	38	19	25	44	120	1	0	0	0	0
1992-93	Cleveland	IHL	63	4	16	20	131	3	1	1	2	2

PAVLOV, YEVGENY

Right wing. Shoots right. 6'2", 195 lbs. Born, Leningrad, Soviet Union, January 22, 1971.
(Boston's 10th choice, 257th overall, in 1992 Entry Draft).

			Regular Season					Playoffs				
Season	Club	Lea	GP	G	A	TP	PIM	GP	G	A	TP	PIM
1987-88	Leningrad	USSR	1	0	0	0	0	....	....	....	....	....
1988-89	Leningrad-2	USSR 3	44	5	3	8	14	....	....	....	....	....
1989-90	Leningrad-2	USSR 3	15	7	3	10	10	....	....	....	....	....
1990-91	Leningrad	USSR	18	0	0	0	8	....	....	....	....	....
1991-92	Leningrad	CIS 2	36	20	7	27	24	....	....	....	....	....
1992-93	Providence	AHL	9	2	1	3	8	....	....	....	....	....
	Johnstown	ECHL	24	8	9	17	40	....	....	....	....	....

PAYNE, DAVIS

Left wing. Shoots left. 6'1", 190 lbs.   Born, King City, Ont., October 24, 1970.
(Edmonton's 6th choice, 140th overall, in 1989 Entry Draft).

			Regular Season					Playoffs				
Season	Club	Lea	GP	G	A	TP	PIM	GP	G	A	TP	PIM
1988-89	Michigan Tech	WCHA	33	5	3	8	39	....	....	....	....	....
1989-90	Michigan Tech	WCHA	36	11	10	21	81	....	....	....	....	....
1990-91	Michigan Tech	WCHA	41	15	20	35	82	....	....	....	....	....
1991-92	Michigan Tech	WCHA	24	6	1	7	71	....	....	....	....	....
1992-93	Greensboro	ECHL	57	15	20	35	178	1	0	0	0	4

PAYNTER, KENT

Defense. Shoots left. 6', 183 lbs.   Born, Summerside, P.E.I., April 17, 1965.
(Chicago's 9th choice, 159th overall, in 1983 Entry Draft).

			Regular Season					Playoffs				
Season	Club	Lea	GP	G	A	TP	PIM	GP	G	A	TP	PIM
1982-83	Kitchener	OHL	65	4	11	15	97	12	1	0	1	20
1983-84	Kitchener	OHL	65	9	27	36	94	16	4	9	13	18
1984-85	Kitchener	OHL	58	7	28	35	93	4	2	1	3	4
1985-86	Nova Scotia	AHL	23	1	2	3	36	....	....	....	....	....
	Saginaw	IHL	4	0	1	1	2	....	....	....	....	....
1986-87	Nova Scotia	AHL	66	2	6	8	57	2	0	0	0	0
1987-88	**Chicago**	**NHL**	**2**	**0**	**0**	**0**	**2**	....	....	....	....	....
	Saginaw	IHL	74	8	20	28	141	10	0	1	1	30
1988-89	**Chicago**	**NHL**	**1**	**0**	**0**	**0**	**2**	....	....	....	....	....
	Saginaw	IHL	69	12	14	26	148	6	2	2	4	17
1989-90	**Washington**	**NHL**	**13**	**1**	**2**	**3**	**18**	**3**	**0**	**0**	**0**	**10**
	Baltimore	AHL	60	7	20	27	110	11	5	6	1	34
1990-91	**Washington**	**NHL**	**1**	**0**	**0**	**0**	**15**	**1**	**0**	**0**	**0**	**0**
	Baltimore	AHL	43	10	17	27	64	6	2	1	3	8
1991-92	**Winnipeg**	**NHL**	**5**	**0**	**0**	**0**	**4**	....	....	....	....	....
	Moncton	AHL	62	3	30	33	71	11	2	6	8	25
1992-93	**Ottawa**	**NHL**	**6**	**0**	**0**	**0**	**20**	....	....	....	....	....
	New Haven	AHL	48	7	17	24	81	....	....	....	....	....
	NHL Totals		**28**	**1**	**2**	**3**	**61**	**4**	**0**	**0**	**0**	**10**

Signed as a free agent by **Washington**, August 21, 1989. Traded to **Winnipeg** by **Washington** with Tyler Larter and Bob Joyce for Craig Duncanson, Brent Hughes and Simon Wheeldon, May 21, 1991. Claimed by **Ottawa** from **Winnipeg** in Expansion Draft, June 18, 1992.

PEACOCK, SHANE

Defense. Shoots right. 5'10", 198 lbs.   Born, Winterburn, Alta., July 7, 1973.
(Pittsburgh's 3rd choice, 60th overall, in 1991 Entry Draft).

			Regular Season					Playoffs				
Season	Club	Lea	GP	G	A	TP	PIM	GP	G	A	TP	PIM
1989-90	Lethbridge	WHL	65	7	23	30	60	19	2	8	10	42
1990-91	Lethbridge	WHL	69	12	50	62	102	16	1	14	15	26
1991-92	Lethbridge	WHL	67	35	45	80	217	5	2	5	7	2
1992-93	Lethbridge	WHL	65	27	75	102	100	4	4	3	7	2

PEAKE, PAT

Centre. Shoots right. 6', 200 lbs.   Born, Rochester, MI, May 28, 1973.
(Washington's 1st choice, 14th overall, in 1991 Entry Draft).

			Regular Season					Playoffs				
Season	Club	Lea	GP	G	A	TP	PIM	GP	G	A	TP	PIM
1990-91	Detroit	OHL	63	39	51	90	54	....	....	....	....	....
1991-92	Detroit	OHL	53	41	52	93	44	7	8	9	17	10
	Baltimore	AHL	3	1	0	1	4	....	....	....	....	....
1992-93abcd	Detroit	OHL	46	58	78	136	64	2	1	3	4	2

a OHL's Most Outstanding Player (1993)
b Canadian Major Junior Player of the Year (1993)
c Canadian Major Junior First All-Star Team (1993)
d OHL First All-Star Team (1993)

PEARCE, RANDY

Left wing. Shoots left. 5'11", 203 lbs.   Born, Kitchener, Ont., February 23, 1970.
(Washington's 4th choice, 72nd overall, in 1990 Entry Draft).

			Regular Season					Playoffs				
Season	Club	Lea	GP	G	A	TP	PIM	GP	G	A	TP	PIM
1988-89	Kitchener	OHL	64	23	21	44	87	5	0	1	1	6
1989-90	Kitchener	OHL	62	31	34	65	139	17	8	15	23	42
1990-91			DID NOT PLAY – INJURED									
1991-92	Hampton Rds.	ECHL	55	32	46	78	134	11	5	9	14	56
	Baltimore	AHL	12	2	2	4	8	....	....	....	....	....
1992-93	Baltimore	AHL	42	12	5	17	46	....	....	....	....	....
	Hampton Rds.	ECHL	16	10	14	24	53	....	....	....	....	....

PEARSON, ROB

Right wing. Shoots right. 6'3", 198 lbs.   Born, Oshawa, Ont., March 8, 1971.
(Toronto's 2nd choice, 12th overall, in 1989 Entry Draft).

			Regular Season					Playoffs				
Season	Club	Lea	GP	G	A	TP	PIM	GP	G	A	TP	PIM
1988-89	Belleville	OHL	26	8	12	20	51	....	....	....	....	....
1989-90	Belleville	OHL	58	48	40	88	174	11	5	5	10	26
1990-91	Belleville	OHL	10	6	3	9	27	....	....	....	....	....
a	Oshawa	OHL	41	57	52	109	76	16	16	17	33	39
	Newmarket	AHL	3	0	0	0	29	....	....	....	....	....
1991-92	**Toronto**	**NHL**	**47**	**14**	**10**	**24**	**58**	....	....	....	....	....
	St. John's	AHL	27	15	14	29	107	13	5	4	9	40
1992-93	**Toronto**	**NHL**	**78**	**23**	**14**	**37**	**211**	**14**	**2**	**2**	**4**	**31**
	NHL Totals		**125**	**37**	**24**	**61**	**269**	**14**	**2**	**2**	**4**	**31**

a OHL First All-Star Team (1991)

PEARSON, SCOTT

Left wing. Shoots left. 6'1", 205 lbs.   Born, Cornwall, Ont., December 19, 1969.
(Toronto's 1st choice, 6th overall, in 1988 Entry Draft).

			Regular Season					Playoffs				
Season	Club	Lea	GP	G	A	TP	PIM	GP	G	A	TP	PIM
1986-87	Kingston	OHL	62	30	24	54	101	9	3	3	6	42
1987-88	Kingston	OHL	46	26	32	58	117	....	....	....	....	....
1988-89	**Toronto**	**NHL**	**9**	**0**	**1**	**1**	**2**	....	....	....	....	....
	Kingston	OHL	13	9	8	17	34	....	....	....	....	....
	Niagara Falls	OHL	32	26	34	60	90	17	14	10	24	53
1989-90	**Toronto**	**NHL**	**41**	**5**	**10**	**15**	**90**	**2**	**2**	**0**	**2**	**10**
	Newmarket	AHL	18	12	11	23	64	....	....	....	....	....
1990-91	**Toronto**	**NHL**	**12**	**0**	**0**	**0**	**20**	....	....	....	....	....
	Quebec	**NHL**	**35**	**11**	**4**	**15**	**86**	....	....	....	....	....
	Halifax	AHL	24	12	15	27	44	....	....	....	....	....
1991-92	**Quebec**	**NHL**	**10**	**1**	**2**	**3**	**14**	....	....	....	....	....
	Halifax	AHL	5	2	1	3	4	....	....	....	....	....
1992-93	**Quebec**	**NHL**	**41**	**13**	**1**	**14**	**95**	**3**	**0**	**0**	**0**	**0**
	Halifax	AHL	5	3	1	4	25	....	....	....	....	....
	NHL Totals		**148**	**30**	**18**	**48**	**307**	**5**	**2**	**0**	**2**	**10**

Traded to **Quebec** by **Toronto** with Toronto's second round choices in 1991 (later traded to Washington — Washington selected Eric Lavigne) and 1992 (Tuomas Gronman) Entry Drafts for Aaron Broten, Lucien Deblois and Michel Petit, November 17, 1990. Traded to **Edmonton** by **Quebec** for Martin Gelinas and Edmonton's sixth round choice (Nicholas Checco) in 1993 Entry Draft, June 20, 1993.

PECA, MICHAEL

Right wing. Shoots right. 5'11", 180 lbs.   Born, Toronto, Ont., March 26, 1974.
(Vancouver's 2nd choice, 40th overall, in 1992 Entry Draft).

			Regular Season					Playoffs				
Season	Club	Lea	GP	G	A	TP	PIM	GP	G	A	TP	PIM
1990-91	Sudbury	OHL	62	14	27	41	24	5	1	0	1	7
1991-92	Sudbury	OHL	39	16	34	50	61	....	....	....	....	....
	Ottawa	OHL	27	8	17	25	32	11	6	10	16	6
1992-93	Ottawa	OHL	55	38	64	102	80	....	....	....	....	....
	Hamilton	AHL	9	6	3	9	11	....	....	....	....	....

PEDERSEN, ALLEN

Defense. Shoots left. 6'3", 210 lbs.   Born, Fort Saskatchewan, Alta., January 13, 1965.
(Boston's 5th choice, 105th overall, in 1983 Entry Draft).

			Regular Season					Playoffs				
Season	Club	Lea	GP	G	A	TP	PIM	GP	G	A	TP	PIM
1982-83	Medicine Hat	WHL	63	3	10	13	49	5	0	0	0	7
1983-84	Medicine Hat	WHL	44	0	11	11	47	14	0	2	2	24
1984-85	Medicine Hat	WHL	72	6	16	22	66	10	0	0	0	9
1985-86	Moncton	AHL	59	1	8	9	39	3	0	0	0	0
1986-87	**Boston**	**NHL**	**79**	**1**	**11**	**12**	**71**	**4**	**0**	**0**	**0**	**4**
1987-88	**Boston**	**NHL**	**78**	**0**	**6**	**6**	**90**	**21**	**0**	**0**	**0**	**34**
1988-89	**Boston**	**NHL**	**51**	**0**	**6**	**6**	**69**	**10**	**0**	**0**	**0**	**2**
1989-90	**Boston**	**NHL**	**68**	**1**	**2**	**3**	**71**	**21**	**0**	**0**	**0**	**41**
1990-91	**Boston**	**NHL**	**57**	**2**	**6**	**8**	**107**	**8**	**0**	**0**	**0**	**10**
	Maine	AHL	15	0	6	6	18	2	0	1	1	2
1991-92	**Minnesota**	**NHL**	**29**	**0**	**1**	**1**	**10**	....	....	....	....	....
1992-93	**Hartford**	**NHL**	**59**	**1**	**4**	**5**	**60**	....	....	....	....	....
	NHL Totals		**421**	**5**	**36**	**41**	**478**	**64**	**0**	**0**	**0**	**91**

Claimed by **Minnesota** from **Boston** in Expansion Draft, May 30, 1991. Traded to **Hartford** by **Minnesota** for future considerations, June 15, 1992.

PEDERSON, DENIS

Center. Shoots right. 6'2", 189 lbs.   Born, Prince Albert, Sask., September 10, 1975.
(New Jersey's 1st choice, 13th overall, in 1993 Entry Draft).

			Regular Season					Playoffs				
Season	Club	Lea	GP	G	A	TP	PIM	GP	G	A	TP	PIM
1991-92	Prince Albert	Midget	21	33	25	58	40	7	0	1	1	13
1992-93	Prince Albert	WHL	72	33	40	73	134	....	....	....	....	....

PEDERSON, MARK

Left wing. Shoots left. 6'2", 196 lbs.   Born, Prelate, Sask., January 14, 1968.
(Montreal's 1st choice, 15th overall, in 1986 Entry Draft).

			Regular Season					Playoffs				
Season	Club	Lea	GP	G	A	TP	PIM	GP	G	A	TP	PIM
1984-85	Medicine Hat	WHL	71	42	40	82	63	10	3	2	5	0
1985-86	Medicine Hat	WHL	72	46	60	106	46	25	12	6	18	25
1986-87a	Medicine Hat	WHL	69	56	46	102	58	20	*19	7	26	14
1987-88	Medicine Hat	WHL	62	53	58	111	55	16	*13	6	19	16
1988-89	Sherbrooke	AHL	75	43	38	81	53	6	7	5	12	4
1989-90	**Montreal**	**NHL**	**9**	**0**	**2**	**2**	**2**	**2**	**0**	**0**	**0**	**0**
b	Sherbrooke	AHL	72	53	42	95	60	11	10	8	18	19
1990-91	**Montreal**	**NHL**	**47**	**8**	**15**	**23**	**18**	....	....	....	....	....
	Philadelphia	**NHL**	**12**	**2**	**1**	**3**	**5**	....	....	....	....	....
1991-92	**Philadelphia**	**NHL**	**58**	**15**	**25**	**40**	**22**	....	....	....	....	....
1992-93	**Philadelphia**	**NHL**	**14**	**3**	**4**	**7**	**6**	....	....	....	....	....
	San Jose	**NHL**	**27**	**7**	**3**	**10**	**22**	....	....	....	....	....
	NHL Totals		**167**	**35**	**50**	**85**	**75**	**2**	**0**	**0**	**0**	**0**

a WHL East All-Star Team (1987)
b AHL First All-Star Team (1990)

Traded to **Philadelphia** by **Montreal** for Philadelphia's second round choice (Jim Campbell) in 1991 Entry Draft, March 5, 1991. Traded to **San Jose** by **Philadelphia** with future considerations for Dave Snuggerud, December 19, 1992.

PEDERSON, THOMAS

Defense. Shoots right. 5'9", 175 lbs.   Born, Bloomington, MN, January 14, 1970.
(Minnesota's 12th choice, 217th overall, in 1989 Entry Draft).

			Regular Season					Playoffs				
Season	Club	Lea	GP	G	A	TP	PIM	GP	G	A	TP	PIM
1988-89	U. Minnesota	WCHA	36	4	20	24	40	....	....	....	....	....
1989-90	U. Minnesota	WCHA	43	8	30	38	58	....	....	....	....	....
1990-91	U. Minnesota	WCHA	36	12	20	32	46	....	....	....	....	....
1991-92	U.S. National	....	44	3	11	14	41	....	....	....	....	....
	Kansas City	IHL	20	6	9	15	16	13	1	6	7	14
1992-93	**San Jose**	**NHL**	**44**	**7**	**13**	**20**	**31**	....	....	....	....	....
	Kansas City	IHL	26	6	15	21	10	12	1	6	7	2
	NHL Totals		**44**	**7**	**13**	**20**	**31**	....	....	....	....	....

Claimed by **San Jose** from **Minnesota** in Dispersal Draft, May 30, 1991.

PELLERIN, BRIAN

Right wing. Shoots right. 5'10", 185 lbs. Born, Hinton, Alta., February 20, 1970.

			Regular Season					Playoffs				
Season	Club	Lea	GP	G	A	TP	PIM	GP	G	A	TP	PIM
1987-88	Prince Albert	WHL	62	6	2	8	113	10	0	0	0	17
1988-89	Prince Albert	WHL	60	17	16	33	216	3	0	1	1	27
1989-90	Prince Albert	WHL	53	6	15	21	175	10	1	3	4	26
1990-91a	Prince Albert	WHL	68	46	42	88	223	3	0	0	0	12
1991-92	Peoria	IHL	70	7	16	23	231	10	1	2	3	49
1992-93	Peoria	IHL	78	15	25	40	204	4	1	1	2	8

a WHL East First All-Star Team (1991)

Signed as a free agent by **St. Louis**, May 31, 1991.

PELLERIN, SCOTT

Left wing. Shoots left. 5'11", 180 lbs. Born, Shediac, N.B., January 9, 1970.
(New Jersey's 4th choice, 47th overall, in 1989 Entry Draft).

			Regular Season					Playoffs				
Season	Club	Lea	GP	G	A	TP	PIM	GP	G	A	TP	PIM
1988-89a	U. of Maine	H.E.	45	29	33	62	92	....	....	....	....	....
1989-90	U. of Maine	H.E.	42	22	34	56	68	....	....	....	....	....
1990-91	U. of Maine	H.E.	43	23	25	48	60	....	....	....	....	....
1991-92bcd	U. of Maine	H.E.	37	*32	25	57	54	....	....	....	....	....
	Utica	AHL	....	....	....	....	....	3	1	0	1	0
1992-93	**New Jersey**	**NHL**	**45**	**10**	**11**	**21**	**41**	....	....	....	....	....
	Utica	AHL	27	15	18	33	33	2	0	1	1	0
	NHL Totals		**45**	**10**	**11**	**21**	**41**	....	....	....	....	....

a Co-winner Hockey East Rookie of the Year (1989)
b Won Hobey Baker Memorial Award (Top U.S. Collegiate Player) (1992)
c Hockey East First All-Star Team (1992)
d NCAA East First All-American Team (1992)

PELTOLA, PEKKA (PEHL-TUH-lah)

Right wing. Shoots left. 6'2", 194 lbs. Born, Helsinki, Finland, April 24, 1965.
(Winnipeg's 8th choice, 130th overall, in 1989 Entry Draft).

			Regular Season					Playoffs				
Season	Club	Lea	GP	G	A	TP	PIM	GP	G	A	TP	PIM
1988-89	HPK	Fin.	43	28	30	58	62	....	....	....	....	....
1989-90	HPK	Fin.	44	25	24	49	42	....	....	....	....	....
1990-91	HPK	Fin.	41	23	18	41	66	8	3	2	5	10
1991-92	HPK	Fin.	37	22	20	42	91	....	....	....	....	....
1992-93	Lukko	Fin.	48	26	24	50	42	3	0	0	0	4

PELTONEN, VILLE (PEHL-TOH-ner)

Left wing. Shoots left. 5'11", 172 lbs. Born, Vantaa, Finland, May 24, 1973.
(San Jose's 4th choice, 58th overall, in 1993 Entry Draft).

			Regular Season					Playoffs				
Season	Club	Lea	GP	G	A	TP	PIM	GP	G	A	TP	PIM
1991-92	HIFK	Fin.	6	0	0	0	0	....	....	....	....	....
1992-93	HIFK	Fin.	46	13	24	37	16	4	0	2	2	2

PELUSO, MIKE

Left wing/Defense. Shoots left. 6'4", 200 lbs. Born, Pengilly, MN, November 8, 1965.
(New Jersey's 10th choice, 190th overall, in 1984 Entry Draft).

			Regular Season					Playoffs				
Season	Club	Lea	GP	G	A	TP	PIM	GP	G	A	TP	PIM
1985-86	Alaska-Anch.	G.N.	32	2	11	13	59	....	....	....	....	....
1986-87	Alaska-Anch.	G.N.	30	5	21	26	68	....	....	....	....	....
1987-88	Alaska-Anch.	G.N.	35	4	33	37	76	....	....	....	....	....
1988-89	Alaska-Anch.	G.N.	33	10	27	37	75	....	....	....	....	....
1989-90	**Chicago**	**NHL**	**2**	**0**	**0**	**0**	**15**	....	....	....	....	....
	Indianapolis	IHL	75	7	10	17	279	14	0	1	1	58
1990-91	**Chicago**	**NHL**	**53**	**6**	**1**	**7**	**320**	**3**	**0**	**0**	**0**	**2**
	Indianapolis	IHL	6	2	1	3	21	5	0	2	2	40
1991-92	**Chicago**	**NHL**	**63**	**6**	**3**	**9**	***408**	**17**	**1**	**2**	**3**	**8**
	Indianapolis	IHL	4	0	1	1	15	....	....	....	....	....
1992-93	**Ottawa**	**NHL**	**81**	**15**	**10**	**25**	**318**	....	....	....	....	....
	NHL Totals		**199**	**27**	**14**	**41**	**1061**	**20**	**1**	**2**	**3**	**10**

Signed as a free agent by **Chicago**, September 7, 1989. Claimed by **Ottawa** from **Chicago** in Expansion Draft, June 18, 1992. Traded to **New Jersey** by **Ottawa** to complete June 20, 1993 trade which sent Craig Billington, Troy Mallette and New Jersey's fourth round choice (Cosmo Dupaul) in 1993 Entry Draft to Ottawa for Peter Sidorkiewicz and future considerations, June 26, 1993.

PENNEY, CHAD

Left wing. Shoots left. 6', 196 lbs. Born, Labrador City, Nfld., September 18, 1973.
(Ottawa's 2nd choice, 25th overall, in 1992 Entry Draft).

			Regular Season					Playoffs				
Season	Club	Lea	GP	G	A	TP	PIM	GP	G	A	TP	PIM
1990-91	North Bay	OHL	66	33	34	67	56	10	2	6	8	12
1991-92	North Bay	OHL	57	25	27	52	90	21	13	17	30	9
1992-93	North Bay	OHL	18	8	7	15	19	....	....	....	....	....
a	S.S. Marie	OHL	48	29	44	73	67	18	7	10	17	18

a Memorial Cup All-Star Team (1993)

PERREAULT, NICOLAS P.

Defense. Shoots left. 6'3", 200 lbs. Born, Loretteville, Que., April 24, 1972.
(Calgary's 2nd choice, 26th overall, in 1990 Entry Draft).

			Regular Season					Playoffs				
Season	Club	Lea	GP	G	A	TP	PIM	GP	G	A	TP	PIM
1990-91	Michigan State	CCHA	34	1	7	8	32	....	....	....	....	....
1991-92	Michigan State	CCHA	41	11	11	22	75	....	....	....	....	....
1992-93	Michigan State	CCHA	38	7	6	13	90	....	....	....	....	....

PERREAULT, YANIC

Center. Shoots left. 5'11", 182 lbs. Born, Sherbrooke, Que., April 4, 1971.
(Toronto's 1st choice, 47th overall, in 1991 Entry Draft).

			Regular Season					Playoffs				
Season	Club	Lea	GP	G	A	TP	PIM	GP	G	A	TP	PIM
1988-89	Trois-Rivières	QMJHL	70	53	55	108	48	....	....	....	....	....
1989-90	Trois-Rivières	QMJHL	63	51	63	114	75	7	6	5	11	19
1990-91a	Trois-Rivières	QMJHL	67	*87	98	*185	103	6	4	7	11	6
1991-92	St. John's	AHL	62	38	38	76	19	16	7	8	15	4
1992-93	St. John's	AHL	79	49	46	95	56	9	4	5	9	2

a QMJHL First All-Star Team (1991)

PERRY, JEFF

Left wing. Shoots left. 6', 192 lbs. Born, Sarnia, Ont., April 12, 1971.
(Toronto's 6th choice, 113th overall, in 1991 Entry Draft).

			Regular Season					Playoffs				
Season	Club	Lea	GP	G	A	TP	PIM	GP	G	A	TP	PIM
1990-91	Owen Sound	OHL	60	31	49	80	83	....	....	....	....	....
1991-92	Owen Sound	OHL	7	0	5	5	8	....	....	....	....	....
	St. John's	AHL	6	0	1	1	4	....	....	....	....	....
	Raleigh	ECHL	8	2	2	4	18	4	0	1	1	11
1992-93	St. John's	AHL	13	1	1	2	22	....	....	....	....	....
	Brantford	Col.	23	1	13	24	36	....	....	....	....	....

PERSSON, RICKARD

Defense. Shoots left. 6'1", 205 lbs. Born, Ostersund, Sweden, August 24, 1969.
(New Jersey's 2nd choice, 23rd overall, in 1987 Entry Draft).

			Regular Season					Playoffs				
Season	Club	Lea	GP	G	A	TP	PIM	GP	G	A	TP	PIM
1985-86	Ostersund	Swe.2	24	2	2	4	16	....	....	....	....	....
1986-87	Ostersund	Swe.2	31	10	11	21	28	....	....	....	....	....
1987-88	Leksand	Swe.	21	2	0	2	8	2	0	1	1	2
1988-89	Leksand	Swe.	33	2	4	6	28	9	0	1	1	6
1989-90	Leksand	Swe.	40	9	10	19	56	3	0	0	0	6
1990-91	Leksand	Swe.	19	3	4	7	22	....	....	....	....	....
1991-92	Leksand	Swe.	21	0	7	7	28	....	....	....	....	....
1992-93	Leksand	Swe.	36	7	15	22	63	2	0	2	2	0

PETERS, ROB

Defense. Shoots left. 6'6", 205 lbs. Born, North Tonowanda, NY, May 15, 1972.
(Hartford's 12th choice, 251st overall, in 1991 Entry Draft).

			Regular Season					Playoffs				
Season	Club	Lea	GP	G	A	TP	PIM	GP	G	A	TP	PIM
1990-91	Ohio State	CCHA	33	0	1	1	65	....	....	....	....	....
1991-92	Ohio State	CCHA	28	3	7	10	53	....	....	....	....	....
1992-93	Ohio State	CCHA	35	2	9	11	72	....	....	....	....	....

PETERSON, BRENT

Left wing. Shoots left. 6'3", 195 lbs. Born, Calgary, Alta., July 20, 1972.
(Tampa Bay's 1st choice, 3rd overall, in 1993 Supplemental Draft).

			Regular Season					Playoffs				
Season	Club	Lea	GP	G	A	TP	PIM	GP	G	A	TP	PIM
1991-92	Michigan Tech	WCHA	39	11	9	20	18	....	....	....	....	....
1992-93	Michigan Tech	WCHA	37	24	18	42	32	....	....	....	....	....

PETERSON, ERIK

Center. Shoots left. 6', 185 lbs. Born, Boston, MA, March 31, 1972.
(Chicago's 8th choice, 205th overall, in 1990 Entry Draft).

			Regular Season					Playoffs				
Season	Club	Lea	GP	G	A	TP	PIM	GP	G	A	TP	PIM
1990-91	Providence	H.E.	34	8	4	12	12	....	....	....	....	....
1991-92	Providence	H.E.	32	9	5	14	26	....	....	....	....	....
1992-93	Providence	H.E.	34	7	14	21	28	....	....	....	....	....

PETERSON, KYLE

Center. Shoots left. 6'3", 195 lbs. Born, Calgary, Alta., April 17, 1974.
(Minnesota's 5th choice, 154th overall, in 1992 Entry Draft).

			Regular Season					Playoffs				
Season	Club	Lea	GP	G	A	TP	PIM	GP	G	A	TP	PIM
1991-92	Thunder Bay	USHL	23	5	7	12	18	....	....	....	....	....
1992-93	Thunder Bay	USHL	24	8	23	31	22	....	....	....	....	....

PETIT, MICHEL (puh-TEE)

Defense. Shoots right. 6'1", 205 lbs. Born, St. Malo, Que., February 12, 1964.
(Vancouver's 1st choice, 11th overall, in 1982 Entry Draft).

			Regular Season					Playoffs				
Season	Club	Lea	GP	G	A	TP	PIM	GP	G	A	TP	PIM
1981-82a	Sherbrooke	QMJHL	63	10	39	49	106	22	5	20	25	24
1982-83	**Vancouver**	**NHL**	**2**	**0**	**0**	**0**	**0**	....	....	....	....	....
a	St-Jean	QMJHL	62	19	67	86	196	3	0	0	0	35
1983-84	Cdn. Olympic	....	19	3	10	13	58	....	....	....	....	....
	Vancouver	**NHL**	**44**	**6**	**9**	**15**	**53**	**1**	**0**	**0**	**0**	**0**
1984-85	**Vancouver**	**NHL**	**69**	**5**	**26**	**31**	**127**	....	....	....	....	....
1985-86	**Vancouver**	**NHL**	**32**	**1**	**6**	**7**	**27**	....	....	....	....	....
	Fredericton	AHL	25	0	13	13	79	....	....	....	....	....
1986-87	**Vancouver**	**NHL**	**69**	**12**	**13**	**25**	**131**	....	....	....	....	....
1987-88	**Vancouver**	**NHL**	**10**	**0**	**3**	**3**	**35**	....	....	....	....	....
	NY Rangers	**NHL**	**64**	**9**	**24**	**33**	**223**	....	....	....	....	....
1988-89	**NY Rangers**	**NHL**	**69**	**8**	**25**	**33**	**154**	**4**	**0**	**2**	**2**	**27**
1989-90	**Quebec**	**NHL**	**63**	**12**	**24**	**36**	**215**	....	....	....	....	....
1990-91	**Quebec**	**NHL**	**19**	**4**	**7**	**11**	**47**	....	....	....	....	....
	Toronto	**NHL**	**54**	**9**	**19**	**28**	**132**	....	....	....	....	....
1991-92	**Toronto**	**NHL**	**34**	**1**	**13**	**14**	**85**	....	....	....	....	....
	Calgary	**NHL**	**36**	**3**	**10**	**13**	**79**	....	....	....	....	....
1992-93	**Calgary**	**NHL**	**35**	**3**	**9**	**12**	**54**	....	....	....	....	....
	NHL Totals		**600**	**73**	**188**	**261**	**1362**	**5**	**0**	**2**	**2**	**27**

a QMJHL First All-Star Team (1982, 1983)

Traded to **NY Rangers** by **Vancouver** for Willie Huber and Larry Melnyk, November 4, 1987. Traded to **Quebec** by **NY Rangers** for Randy Moller, October 5, 1989. Traded to **Toronto** by **Quebec** with Aaron Broten and Lucien Deblois for Scott Pearson and Toronto's second round choices in 1991 (later traded to Washington — Washington selected Eric Lavigne) and 1992 (Tuomas Gronman) Entry Drafts, November 17, 1990. Traded to **Calgary** by **Toronto** with Craig Berube, Alexander Godynyuk, Gary Leeman and Jeff Reese for Doug Gilmour, Jamie Macoun, Ric Nattress, Rick Wamsley and Kent Manderville, January 2, 1992.

PETROV, OLEG

Right wing. Shoots left. 5'9", 161 lbs. Born, Moscow, Soviet Union, April 18, 1971.
(Montreal's 6th choice, 127th overall, in 1991 Entry Draft).

			Regular Season					Playoffs				
Season	Club	Lea	GP	G	A	TP	PIM	GP	G	A	TP	PIM
1989-90	CSKA	USSR	30	4	7	11	4	....	....	....	....	....
1990-91	CSKA	USSR	43	7	4	11	8	....	....	....	....	....
1991-92	CSKA	CIS	42	10	16	26	8	....	....	....	....	....
1992-93	**Montreal**	**NHL**	**9**	**2**	**1**	**3**	**10**	**1**	**0**	**0**	**0**	**0**
	Fredericton	AHL	55	26	29	55	36	5	4	1	5	0
	NHL Totals		**9**	**2**	**1**	**3**	**10**	**1**	**0**	**0**	**0**	**0**

PETROVICKY, ROBERT   (peh-troh-VIHT-skee)

Center. Shoots left. 5'11", 172 lbs.   Born, Kosice, Czech., October 26, 1973.
(Hartford's 1st choice, 9th overall, in 1992 Entry Draft).

			Regular Season					Playoffs			
Season	Club	Lea	GP	G	A	TP	PIM	GP	G	A	TP	PIM
1990-91	Dukla Trencin	Czech.	33	9	14	23	12	.....	.....	.....	.....	.....
1991-92	Dukla Trencin	Czech.	46	25	36	61	28	.....	.....	.....	.....	.....
1992-93	**Hartford**	**NHL**	**42**	**3**	**6**	**9**	**45**	.....	.....	.....	.....	.....
	Springfield	AHL	16	5	3	8	39	15	5	6	11	14
	NHL Totals		**42**	**3**	**6**	**9**	**45**					

PHILPOTT, ETHAN

Right wing. Shoots right. 6'4", 230 lbs.   Born, Rochester, MN, February 11, 1975.
(Buffalo's 2nd choice, 64th overall, in 1993 Entry Draft).

			Regular Season					Playoffs			
Season	Club	Lea	GP	G	A	TP	PIM	GP	G	A	TP	PIM
1991-92	Andover	HS	22	7	20	27	16	.....	.....	.....	.....	.....
1992-93	Andover	HS	18	17	19	36	22	.....	.....	.....	.....	.....

PICARD, MICHEL

Left wing. Shoots left. 5'11", 190 lbs.   Born, Beauport, Que., November 7, 1969.
(Hartford's 8th choice, 178th overall, in 1989 Entry Draft).

			Regular Season					Playoffs			
Season	Club	Lea	GP	G	A	TP	PIM	GP	G	A	TP	PIM
1986-87	Trois-Rivières	QMJHL	66	33	35	68	53	.....	.....	.....	.....	.....
1987-88	Trois-Rivières	QMJHL	69	40	55	95	71	.....	.....	.....	.....	.....
1988-89	Trois-Rivières	QMJHL	66	59	81	140	170	4	1	3	4	2
1989-90	Binghamton	AHL	67	16	24	40	98	.....	.....	.....	.....	.....
1990-91	**Hartford**	**NHL**	**5**	**1**	**0**	**1**	**2**	.....	.....	.....	.....	.....
a	Springfield	AHL	77	*56	40	96	61	18	8	13	21	18
1991-92	**Hartford**	**NHL**	**25**	**3**	**5**	**8**	**6**	.....	.....	.....	.....	.....
	Springfield	AHL	40	21	17	38	44	11	2	0	2	34
1992-93	**San Jose**	**NHL**	**25**	**4**	**0**	**4**	**24**	.....	.....	.....	.....	.....
	Kansas City	IHL	33	7	10	17	51	12	3	2	5	20
	NHL Totals		**55**	**8**	**5**	**13**	**32**					

a AHL First All-Star Team (1991)

Traded to **San Jose** by **Hartford** for future considerations (Yvon Corriveau, January 21, 1993), October 9, 1992.

PIERCE, WILLIAM

Center. Shoots left. 6'1", 190 lbs.   Born, Woburn, MA, October 6, 1974.
(Quebec's 4th choice, 75th overall, in 1993 Entry Draft).

			Regular Season					Playoffs			
Season	Club	Lea	GP	G	A	TP	PIM	GP	G	A	TP	PIM
1991-92	Lawrence	HS	20	20	26	46	26	.....	.....	.....	.....	.....
1992-93	Lawrence	HS	20	12	26	38	22	.....	.....	.....	.....	.....

PILON, RICHARD

Defense. Shoots left. 6', 202 lbs.   Born, Saskatoon, Sask., April 30, 1968.
(NY Islanders' 9th choice, 143rd overall, in 1986 Entry Draft).

			Regular Season					Playoffs			
Season	Club	Lea	GP	G	A	TP	PIM	GP	G	A	TP	PIM
1986-87	Prince Albert	WHL	68	4	21	25	192	7	1	6	7	17
1987-88	Prince Albert	WHL	65	13	34	47	177	9	0	6	6	38
1988-89	**NY Islanders**	**NHL**	**62**	**0**	**14**	**14**	**242**	.....	.....	.....	.....	.....
1989-90	**NY Islanders**	**NHL**	**14**	**0**	**2**	**2**	**31**	.....	.....	.....	.....	.....
1990-91	**NY Islanders**	**NHL**	**60**	**1**	**4**	**5**	**126**	.....	.....	.....	.....	.....
1991-92	**NY Islanders**	**NHL**	**65**	**1**	**6**	**7**	**183**	.....	.....	.....	.....	.....
1992-93	**NY Islanders**	**NHL**	**44**	**1**	**3**	**4**	**164**	15	0	0	0	50
	Capital Dist.	AHL	6	0	1	1	8	.....	.....	.....	.....	.....
	NHL Totals		**245**	**3**	**29**	**32**	**746**	**15**	**0**	**0**	**0**	**50**

PION, RICHARD

Right wing. Shoots right. 5'10", 180 lbs.   Born, Oxnard, CA, July 20, 1965.

			Regular Season					Playoffs			
Season	Club	Lea	GP	G	A	TP	PIM	GP	G	A	TP	PIM
1985-86	Merrimack	NCAA	14	9	13	22	10	.....	.....	.....	.....	.....
1986-87	Merrimack	NCAA	37	31	33	64	46	.....	.....	.....	.....	.....
1987-88	Merrimack	NCAA	40	35	40	75	58	4	3	3	6	
1988-89	Merrimack	NCAA	34	28	42	70	34	.....	.....	.....	.....	.....
1989-90	Peoria	IHL	69	10	21	31	58	5	0	0	0	0
1990-91	Peoria	IHL	76	14	24	38	113	17	3	5	8	36
1991-92	Peoria	IHL	82	21	50	71	173	9	3	1	4	30
1992-93	Peoria	IHL	74	20	35	55	119	3	2	1	3	8

Signed as a free agent by **St. Louis**, August 21, 1989.

PITLICK, LANCE

Defense. Shoots right. 6', 190 lbs.   Born, Minneapolis, MN, November 5, 1967.
(Minnesota's 10th choice, 108th overall, in 1986 Entry Draft).

			Regular Season					Playoffs			
Season	Club	Lea	GP	G	A	TP	PIM	GP	G	A	TP	PIM
1986-87	U. Minnesota	WCHA	45	0	9	9	88	.....	.....	.....	.....	.....
1987-88	U. Minnesota	WCHA	38	3	9	12	76	.....	.....	.....	.....	.....
1988-89	U. Minnesota	WCHA	47	4	9	13	95	.....	.....	.....	.....	.....
1989-90	U. Minnestoa	WCHA	14	3	2	5	26	.....	.....	.....	.....	.....
1990-91	Hershey	AHL	64	6	15	21	75	3	0	0	0	9
1991-92	U.S. National	.....	19	0	1	1	38	.....	.....	.....	.....	.....
	Hershey	AHL	4	0	0	0	6	3	0	0	0	4
1992-93	Hershey	AHL	53	5	10	15	77	.....	.....	.....	.....	.....

Signed as a free agent by **Philadelphia**, September 5, 1990.

PITTIS, DOMENIC

Center. Shoots left. 5'11", 180 lbs.   Born, Calgary, Alta., October 1, 1974.
(Pittsburgh's 2nd choice, 52nd overall, in 1993 Entry Draft).

			Regular Season					Playoffs			
Season	Club	Lea	GP	G	A	TP	PIM	GP	G	A	TP	PIM
1991-92	Lethbridge	WHL	65	6	17	23	48	5	0	2	2	4
1992-93	Lethbridge	WHL	66	46	73	119	69	4	3	3	6	8

PIVONKA, MICHAL   (pih-VAHN-kuh)

Center. Shoots left. 6'2", 198 lbs.   Born, Kladno, Czechoslovakia, January 28, 1966.
(Washington's 3rd choice, 59th overall, in 1984 Entry Draft).

			Regular Season					Playoffs			
Season	Club	Lea	GP	G	A	TP	PIM	GP	G	A	TP	PIM
1984-85	Dukla Jihlava	Czech.	33	8	11	19	18	.....	.....	.....	.....	.....
1985-86	Dukla Jihlava	Czech.	42	5	13	18	18	.....	.....	.....	.....	.....
1986-87	**Washington**	**NHL**	**73**	**18**	**25**	**43**	**41**	7	1	1	2	2
1987-88	**Washington**	**NHL**	**71**	**11**	**23**	**34**	**28**	14	4	9	13	4
1988-89	**Washington**	**NHL**	**52**	**8**	**19**	**27**	**30**	6	3	1	4	10
	Baltimore	AHL	31	12	24	36	19	.....	.....	.....	.....	.....
1989-90	**Washington**	**NHL**	**77**	**25**	**39**	**64**	**54**	11	0	2	2	6
1990-91	**Washington**	**NHL**	**79**	**20**	**50**	**70**	**34**	11	2	3	5	8
1991-92	**Washington**	**NHL**	**80**	**23**	**57**	**80**	**47**	7	1	5	6	13
1992-93	**Washington**	**NHL**	**69**	**21**	**53**	**74**	**66**	6	0	2	2	0
	NHL Totals		**501**	**126**	**266**	**392**	**300**	**62**	**11**	**23**	**34**	**43**

PLAGER, KEVIN

Right wing. Shoots right. 6'1", 205 lbs.   Born, St. Louis, MO, April 25, 1971.
(St. Louis' 8th choice, 156th overall, in 1989 Entry Draft).

			Regular Season					Playoffs			
Season	Club	Lea	GP	G	A	TP	PIM	GP	G	A	TP	PIM
1990-91	Kalamazoo	USHL	45	10	12	22	20	.....	.....	.....	.....	.....
1991-92	U. Wisc.-St. Pt.	NCAA		DID NOT PLAY								
1992-93	U. Wisc.-St. Pt.	NCAA	15	3	3	6	63	.....	.....	.....	.....	.....

PLANTE, DAN

Right wing. Shoots right. 5'11", 198 lbs.   Born, St. Louis, MO, October 5, 1971.
(NY Islanders' 3rd choice, 48th overall, in 1990 Entry Draft).

			Regular Season					Playoffs			
Season	Club	Lea	GP	G	A	TP	PIM	GP	G	A	TP	PIM
1990-91	U. Wisconsin	WCHA	33	1	2	3	54	.....	.....	.....	.....	.....
1991-92	U. Wisconsin	WCHA	36	13	13	26	107	.....	.....	.....	.....	.....
1992-93	U. Wisconsin	WCHA	42	26	31	57	142	.....	.....	.....	.....	.....

PLANTE, DEREK

Center. Shoots left. 5'11", 160 lbs.   Born, Duluth, MN, January 17, 1971.
(Buffalo's 7th choice, 161st overall, in 1989 Entry Draft).

			Regular Season					Playoffs			
Season	Club	Lea	GP	G	A	TP	PIM	GP	G	A	TP	PIM
1989-90	Minn.-Duluth	WCHA	28	10	11	21	12	.....	.....	.....	.....	.....
1990-91	Minn.-Duluth	WCHA	36	23	20	43	6	.....	.....	.....	.....	.....
1991-92a	Minn.-Duluth	WCHA	37	27	36	63	28	.....	.....	.....	.....	.....
1992-93bc	Minn.-Duluth	WCHA	37	*36	*56	*92	30	.....	.....	.....	.....	.....

a WCHA Second All-Star Team (1992)
b WCHA First All-Star Team (1993)
c NCAA West First All-American Team (1993)

PLAQUIN, KEN

Defense. Shoots left. 6'2", 190 lbs.   Born, Calgary, Alta., February 22, 1970.
(Pittsburgh's 8th choice, 131st overall, in 1990 Entry Draft).

			Regular Season					Playoffs			
Season	Club	Lea	GP	G	A	TP	PIM	GP	G	A	TP	PIM
1989-90	Michigan Tech	WCHA	33	2	13	15	20	.....	.....	.....	.....	.....
1990-91	Michigan Tech	WCHA	37	3	6	9	8	.....	.....	.....	.....	.....
1991-92	Michigan Tech	WCHA	32	3	7	10	10	.....	.....	.....	.....	.....
1992-93	Michigan Tech	WCHA	26	1	4	5	10	.....	.....	.....	.....	.....

PLAVSIC, ADRIEN

Defense. Shoots left. 6'1", 200 lbs.   Born, Montreal, Que., January 13, 1970.
(St. Louis' 2nd choice, 30th overall, in 1988 Entry Draft).

			Regular Season					Playoffs			
Season	Club	Lea	GP	G	A	TP	PIM	GP	G	A	TP	PIM
1987-88	N. Hampshire	H.E.	30	5	6	11	45	.....	.....	.....	.....	.....
1988-89	Cdn. National	.....	62	5	10	15	25	.....	.....	.....	.....	.....
1989-90	**St. Louis**	**NHL**	**4**	**0**	**1**	**1**	**2**	.....	.....	.....	.....	.....
	Peoria	IHL	51	7	14	21	87	.....	.....	.....	.....	.....
	Vancouver	**NHL**	**11**	**3**	**2**	**5**	**8**	.....	.....	.....	.....	.....
	Milwaukee	IHL	3	1	2	3	14	6	1	3	4	6
1990-91	**Vancouver**	**NHL**	**48**	**2**	**10**	**12**	**62**	.....	.....	.....	.....	.....
1991-92	Cdn. National	.....	38	6	8	14	29	.....	.....	.....	.....	.....
	Cdn. Olympic	.....	8	0	2	2	0	.....	.....	.....	.....	.....
	Vancouver	**NHL**	**16**	**1**	**9**	**10**	**14**	13	1	7	8	4
1992-93	**Vancouver**	**NHL**	**57**	**6**	**21**	**27**	**53**	.....	.....	.....	.....	.....
	NHL Totals		**136**	**12**	**43**	**55**	**139**	**13**	**1**	**7**	**8**	**4**

Traded to **Vancouver** by **St. Louis** with Montreal's first round choice (previously acquired by St. Louis — Vancouver selected Shawn Antoski) in 1990 Entry Draft and St. Louis' second round choice (later traded to Montreal — Montreal selected Craig Darby) in 1991 Entry Draft for Rich Sutter, Harold Snepsts and St. Louis' second round choice (previously acquired by Vancouver — St. Louis selected Craig Johnson) in 1990 Entry Draft, March 6, 1990.

PODEIN, SHJON

Center. Shoots left. 6'2", 200 lbs.   Born, Rochester, MN, March 5, 1968.
(Edmonton's 9th choice, 166th overall, in 1988 Entry Draft).

			Regular Season					Playoffs			
Season	Club	Lea	GP	G	A	TP	PIM	GP	G	A	TP	PIM
1987-88	Minn.-Duluth	WCHA	30	4	4	8	48	.....	.....	.....	.....	.....
1988-89	Minn.-Duluth	WCHA	36	7	5	12	46	.....	.....	.....	.....	.....
1989-90	Minn.-Duluth	WCHA	35	21	18	39	36	.....	.....	.....	.....	.....
1990-91	Cape Breton	AHL	63	14	15	29	65	4	0	0	0	5
1991-92	Cape Breton	AHL	80	30	24	54	46	5	3	1	4	2
1992-93	**Edmonton**	**NHL**	**40**	**13**	**6**	**19**	**25**	.....	.....	.....	.....	.....
	Cape Breton	AHL	38	18	21	39	32	9	2	2	4	29
	NHL Totals		**40**	**13**	**6**	**19**	**25**					

POESCHEK, RUDY (POH-shehk)

Right wing/Defense. Shoots right. 6'2", 210 lbs. Born, Kamloops, B.C., September 29, 1966.
(NY Rangers' 12th choice, 238th overall, in 1985 Entry Draft).

			Regular Season					Playoffs				
Season	Club	Lea	GP	G	A	TP	PIM	GP	G	A	TP	PIM
1983-84	Kamloops	WHL	47	3	9	12	93	8	0	2	2	7
1984-85	Kamloops	WHL	34	6	7	13	100	15	0	3	3	56
1985-86	Kamloops	WHL	32	3	13	16	92	16	3	7	10	40
1986-87	Kamloops	WHL	54	13	18	31	153	15	2	4	6	37
1987-88	**NY Rangers**	**NHL**	**1**	**0**	**0**	**0**	**2**	....	....	....	....	....
	Colorado	IHL	82	7	31	38	210	12	2	2	4	31
1988-89	**NY Rangers**	**NHL**	**52**	**0**	**2**	**2**	**199**	....	....	....	....	....
	Colorado	IHL	2	0	0	0	6	....	....	....	....	....
1989-90	**NY Rangers**	**NHL**	**15**	**0**	**0**	**0**	**55**	....	....	....	....	....
	Flint	IHL	38	8	13	21	109	4	0	0	0	16
1990-91	Binghamton	AHL	38	1	3	4	162	....	....	....	....	....
	Winnipeg	**NHL**	**1**	**0**	**0**	**0**	**5**	....	....	....	....	....
	Moncton	AHL	23	2	4	6	67	9	1	1	2	41
1991-92	**Winnipeg**	**NHL**	**4**	**0**	**0**	**0**	**17**	....	....	....	....	....
	Moncton	AHL	63	4	18	22	170	11	0	2	2	48
1992-93	St. John's	AHL	78	7	24	31	189	9	0	4	4	13
	NHL Totals		**73**	**0**	**2**	**2**	**278**	....	....	....	....	....

Traded to **Winnipeg** by **NY Rangers** for Guy Larose, January 22, 1991. Signed as a free agent by **Toronto**, July 8, 1992.

POHL, MICHAEL (POHL)

Center. Shoots left. 6'1", 163 lbs. Born, Rosenheim, West Germany, January 25, 1968.
(New Jersey's 14th choice, 243rd overall, in 1988 Entry Draft).

			Regular Season					Playoffs				
Season	Club	Lea	GP	G	A	TP	PIM	GP	G	A	TP	PIM
1986-87	Rosenheim	W.Ger.	32	7	10	17	21	....	....	....	....	....
1987-88	Rosenheim	W.Ger.	44	7	9	16	22	....	....	....	....	....
1988-89	Rosenheim	W.Ger.	33	8	9	17	30	11	0	5	5	8
1989-90	Rosenheim	W.Ger.	33	9	9	18	18	11	1	2	3	12
1990-91	Rosenheim	Ger.	41	10	7	17	34	10	1	3	4	2
1991-92	Rosenheim	Ger.	49	3	8	11	30	....	....	....	....	....
1992-93	Kaufbeuren	Ger.	38	9	9	18	20	3	0	1	1	6

POLASEK, LIBOR (poh-LAH-shehk)

Center. Shoots right. 6'3", 198 lbs. Born, Vitkovice, Czech., April 22, 1974.
(Vancouver's 1st choice, 21st overall, in 1992 Entry Draft).

			Regular Season					Playoffs				
Season	Club	Lea	GP	G	A	TP	PIM	GP	G	A	TP	PIM
1991-92	TJ Vitkovice	Czech.	17	2	2	4	4	....	....	....	....	....
1992-93	Hamilton	AHL	60	7	12	19	34	....	....	....	....	....

POMICHTER, MICHAEL

Center. Shoots left. 6'1", 200 lbs. Born, New Haven, CT, September 10, 1973.
(Chicago's 2nd choice, 39th overall, in 1991 Entry Draft).

			Regular Season					Playoffs				
Season	Club	Lea	GP	G	A	TP	PIM	GP	G	A	TP	PIM
1991-92	Boston U.	H.E.	34	11	27	38	14	....	....	....	....	....
1992-93	Boston U.	H.E.	30	16	14	30	23	....	....	....	....	....

POPOVIC, PETER

Defense. Shoots right. 6'5", 224 lbs. Born, Koping, Sweden, February 10, 1968.
(Montreal's 5th choice, 93rd overall, in 1988 Entry Draft).

			Regular Season					Playoffs				
Season	Club	Lea	GP	G	A	TP	PIM	GP	G	A	TP	PIM
1986-87	Vasteras	Swe.2	24	1	2	3	10	....	....	....	....	....
1987-88	Vasteras	Swe.2	28	3	17	20	16	....	....	....	....	....
1988-89	Vasteras	Swe.	22	1	4	5	32	....	....	....	....	....
1989-90	Vasteras	Swe.	30	2	10	12	24	2	0	1	1	2
1990-91	Vasteras	Swe.	40	3	2	5	62	4	0	0	0	4
1991-92	Vasteras	Swe.	34	7	10	17	30	....	....	....	....	....
1992-93	Vasteras	Swe.	39	6	12	18	46	3	0	1	1	2

PORCO, JOHN

Center. Shoots left. 5'11", 181 lbs. Born, Sault Ste. Marie, Ont., August 25, 1971.
(Philadelphia's 11th choice, 248th overall, in 1991 Entry Draft).

			Regular Season					Playoffs				
Season	Club	Lea	GP	G	A	TP	PIM	GP	G	A	TP	PIM
1990-91	Belleville	OHL	63	40	54	94	41	....	....	....	....	....
1991-92		Italy				UNAVAILABLE						
1992-93	Asiago	Italy	16	10	16	26	15	9	5	7	12	6

PORKKA, TONI

Defense. Shoots right. 6'2", 190 lbs. Born, Rauma, Finland, February 4, 1970.
(Philadelphia's 12th choice, 172nd overall, in 1990 Entry Draft).

			Regular Season					Playoffs				
Season	Club	Lea	GP	G	A	TP	PIM	GP	G	A	TP	PIM
1988-89	Lukko	Fin.	44	2	2	4	18	....	....	....	....	....
1989-90	Lukko	Fin.	41	0	3	3	18	....	....	....	....	....
1990-91	Lukko	Fin.	34	2	2	4	8	....	....	....	....	....
1991-92	Hershey	AHL	64	3	5	8	34	....	....	....	....	....
1992-93	Hershey	AHL	49	6	13	19	22	....	....	....	....	....

POTAICHUK, ANDREI

Right wing. Shoots left. 5'10", 198 lbs. Born, Temirtau, Soviet Union, August 18, 1970.
(Calgary's 12th choice, 246th overall, in 1992 Entry Draft).

			Regular Season					Playoffs				
Season	Club	Lea	GP	G	A	TP	PIM	GP	G	A	TP	PIM
1987-88	Soviet Wings	USSR	11	1	0	1	0	....	....	....	....	....
1988-89	Soviet Wings	USSR	22	2	1	3	6	....	....	....	....	....
1989-90	Soviet Wings	USSR	46	8	8	16	22	....	....	....	....	....
1990-91	Soviet Wings	USSR	34	8	6	14	12	....	....	....	....	....
1991-92	Soviet Wings	CIS	41	16	7	23	34	....	....	....	....	....
1992-93	Soviet Wings	CIS	42	17	12	29	54	7	4	2	6	4

POTVIN, MARC (POT-vahn)

Right wing. Shoots right. 6'1", 200 lbs. Born, Ottawa, Ont., January 29, 1967.
(Detroit's 9th choice, 169th overall, in 1986 Entry Draft).

			Regular Season					Playoffs				
Season	Club	Lea	GP	G	A	TP	PIM	GP	G	A	TP	PIM
1986-87	Bowling Green	CCHA	43	5	15	20	74	....	....	....	....	....
1987-88	Bowling Green	CCHA	45	15	21	36	80	....	....	....	....	....
1988-89	Bowling Green	CCHA	46	23	12	35	63	....	....	....	....	....
1989-90	Bowling Green	CCHA	40	19	17	36	72	....	....	....	....	....
	Adirondack	AHL	5	2	1	3	9	4	0	1	1	23
1990-91	**Detroit**	**NHL**	**9**	**0**	**0**	**0**	**55**	**6**	**0**	**0**	**0**	**32**
	Adirondack	AHL	63	9	13	22	*365	....	....	....	....	....
1991-92	**Detroit**	**NHL**	**5**	**1**	**0**	**1**	**52**	**1**	**0**	**0**	**0**	**0**
	Adirondack	AHL	51	13	16	29	314	19	5	4	9	57
1992-93	Adirondack	AHL	37	8	12	20	109	....	....	....	....	....
	Los Angeles	**NHL**	**20**	**0**	**1**	**1**	**61**	**1**	**0**	**0**	**0**	**0**
	NHL Totals		**34**	**1**	**1**	**2**	**168**	**8**	**0**	**0**	**0**	**32**

Traded to **Los Angeles** by **Detroit** with Jimmy Carson and Gary Shuchuk for Paul Coffey, Sylvain Couturier and Jim Hiller, January 29, 1993.

POULIN, CHARLES

Center. Shoots left. 6', 172 lbs. Born, St. Jean d'Iberville, Que., July 27, 1972.
(Montreal's 3rd choice, 58th overall, in 1990 Entry Draft).

			Regular Season					Playoffs				
Season	Club	Lea	GP	G	A	TP	PIM	GP	G	A	TP	PIM
1989-90	St-Hyacinthe	QMJHL	65	39	45	84	132	11	5	8	13	47
1990-91	St-Hyacinthe	QMJHL	64	25	46	71	166	4	1	1	2	6
1991-92ab	St-Hyacinthe	QMJHL	68	38	*97	135	113	6	2	2	4	20
1992-93	Fredericton	AHL	58	12	19	31	99	1	0	0	0	0

a QMJHL First All-Star Team (1992)
b Canadian Major Junior Player of the Year (1992)

POULIN, DAVID JAMES (DAVE) (POO-lihn)

Center. Shoots left. 5'11", 190 lbs. Born, Timmins, Ont., December 17, 1958.

			Regular Season					Playoffs				
Season	Club	Lea	GP	G	A	TP	PIM	GP	G	A	TP	PIM
1978-79	Notre Dame	WCHA	37	28	31	59	32	....	....	....	....	....
1979-80	Notre Dame	WCHA	24	19	24	43	46	....	....	....	....	....
1980-81	Notre Dame	WCHA	35	13	22	35	53	....	....	....	....	....
1981-82a	Notre Dame	CCHA	39	29	30	59	44	....	....	....	....	....
1982-83	Rogle	Swe.	32	35	27	62	64	....	....	....	....	....
	Philadelphia	**NHL**	**2**	**2**	**0**	**2**	**2**	**3**	**1**	**3**	**4**	**9**
	Maine	AHL	16	7	9	16	2	....	....	....	....	....
1983-84	**Philadelphia**	**NHL**	**73**	**31**	**45**	**76**	**47**	**3**	**0**	**0**	**0**	**2**
1984-85	**Philadelphia**	**NHL**	**73**	**30**	**44**	**74**	**59**	**11**	**3**	**5**	**8**	**6**
1985-86	**Philadelphia**	**NHL**	**79**	**27**	**42**	**69**	**49**	**5**	**2**	**0**	**2**	**2**
1986-87b	**Philadelphia**	**NHL**	**75**	**25**	**45**	**70**	**53**	**15**	**3**	**3**	**6**	**14**
1987-88	**Philadelphia**	**NHL**	**68**	**19**	**32**	**51**	**32**	**7**	**2**	**6**	**8**	**4**
1988-89	**Philadelphia**	**NHL**	**69**	**18**	**17**	**35**	**49**	**19**	**6**	**5**	**11**	**16**
1989-90	**Philadelphia**	**NHL**	**28**	**9**	**8**	**17**	**12**	....	....	....	....	....
	Boston	**NHL**	**32**	**6**	**19**	**25**	**12**	**18**	**8**	**5**	**13**	**8**
1990-91	**Boston**	**NHL**	**31**	**8**	**12**	**20**	**25**	**16**	**0**	**9**	**9**	**20**
1991-92	**Boston**	**NHL**	**18**	**4**	**4**	**8**	**18**	**15**	**3**	**3**	**6**	**22**
1992-93c	**Boston**	**NHL**	**84**	**16**	**33**	**49**	**62**	**4**	**1**	**1**	**2**	**10**
	NHL Totals		**632**	**195**	**301**	**496**	**420**	**116**	**29**	**40**	**69**	**113**

a CCHA Second All-Star Team (1982)
b Won Frank J. Selke Trophy (1987)
c Won King Clancy Memorial Trophy (1993)

Played in NHL All-Star Game (1986, 1988)

Signed as a free agent by **Philadelphia**, March 8, 1983. Traded to **Boston** by **Philadelphia** for Ken Linseman, January 16, 1990. Signed as a free agent by **Washington**, August 3, 1993.

POULIN, PATRICK (poo-LIHN)

Left wing. Shoots left. 6'1", 208 lbs. Born, Vanier, Que., April 23, 1973.
(Hartford's 1st choice, 9th overall, in 1991 Entry Draft).

			Regular Season					Playoffs				
Season	Club	Lea	GP	G	A	TP	PIM	GP	G	A	TP	PIM
1989-90	St-Hyacinthe	QMJHL	60	25	26	51	55	12	1	9	10	5
1990-91	St-Hyacinthe	QMJHL	56	32	38	70	82	4	0	2	2	23
1991-92	**Hartford**	**NHL**	**1**	**0**	**0**	**0**	**2**	**7**	**2**	**1**	**3**	**0**
a	St-Hyacinthe	QMJHL	56	52	86	*138	58	5	2	2	4	4
	Springfield	AHL	....	....	....	....	....	1	0	0	0	0
1992-93	**Hartford**	**NHL**	**81**	**20**	**31**	**51**	**37**	....	....	....	....	....
	NHL Totals		**82**	**20**	**31**	**51**	**39**	**7**	**2**	**1**	**3**	**0**

a QMJHL First All-Star Team (1992)

POZZO, KEVIN

Defense. Shoots right. 6'1", 176 lbs. Born, Calgary, Alta., October 11, 1974.
(Buffalo's 4th choice, 142nd overall, in 1993 Entry Draft).

			Regular Season					Playoffs				
Season	Club	Lea	GP	G	A	TP	PIM	GP	G	A	TP	PIM
1991-92	Cgy. Buffaloes	Midget	32	3	21	24	85	....	....	....	....	....
1992-93	Moose Jaw	WHL	72	10	29	39	95	....	....	....	....	....

PRATT, JONATHAN

Center. Shoots left. 6'1", 195 lbs. Born, Danvers, MA, September 25, 1970.
(Minnesota's 9th choice, 154th overall, in 1989 Entry Draft).

			Regular Season					Playoffs				
Season	Club	Lea	GP	G	A	TP	PIM	GP	G	A	TP	PIM
1990-91	Boston U.	H.E.	16	3	1	4	26	....	....	....	....	....
1991-92	Boston U.	H.E.	29	8	4	12	42	....	....	....	....	....
1992-93	Boston U.	H.E.	31	9	8	17	70	....	....	....	....	....

PRATT, NOLAN

Defense. Shoots left. 6'2", 190 lbs. Born, Fort McMurray, Alta., August 14, 1975.
(Hartford's 4th choice, 115th overall, in 1993 Entry Draft).

			Regular Season					Playoffs				
Season	Club	Lea	GP	G	A	TP	PIM	GP	G	A	TP	PIM
1991-92	Portland	WHL	72	2	9	11	13	6	1	3	4	12
1992-93	Portland	WHL	70	4	19	23	97	16	2	7	9	31

PRESLEY, WAYNE

Right wing. Shoots right. 5'11", 180 lbs. Born, Detroit, MI, March 23, 1965.
(Chicago's 2nd choice, 39th overall, in 1983 Entry Draft).

			Regular Season					Playoffs				
Season	Club	Lea	GP	G	A	TP	PIM	GP	G	A	TP	PIM
1982-83	Kitchener	OHL	70	39	48	87	99	12	1	4	5	9
1983-84a	Kitchener	OHL	70	63	76	139	156	16	12	16	28	38
1984-85	**Chicago**	**NHL**	**3**	**0**	**1**	**1**	**0**	....	....	....	....	....
	Kitchener	OHL	31	25	21	46	77	....	....	....	....	....
	S.S. Marie	OHL	11	5	9	14	14	16	13	9	22	13
1985-86	**Chicago**	**NHL**	**38**	**7**	**8**	**15**	**38**	**3**	**0**	**0**	**0**	**0**
	Nova Scotia	AHL	29	6	9	15	22	....	....	....	....	....
1986-87	**Chicago**	**NHL**	**80**	**32**	**29**	**61**	**114**	**4**	**1**	**0**	**1**	**9**
1987-88	**Chicago**	**NHL**	**42**	**12**	**10**	**22**	**52**	**5**	**0**	**0**	**0**	**4**
1988-89	**Chicago**	**NHL**	**72**	**21**	**19**	**40**	**100**	**14**	**7**	**5**	**12**	**18**
1989-90	**Chicago**	**NHL**	**49**	**6**	**7**	**13**	**69**	**19**	**9**	**6**	**15**	**29**
1990-91	**Chicago**	**NHL**	**71**	**15**	**19**	**34**	**122**	**6**	**0**	**1**	**1**	**38**
1991-92	**San Jose**	**NHL**	**47**	**8**	**14**	**22**	**76**	....	....	....	....	....
	Buffalo	**NHL**	**12**	**2**	**2**	**4**	**57**	**7**	**3**	**3**	**6**	**14**
1992-93	**Buffalo**	**NHL**	**79**	**15**	**17**	**32**	**96**	**8**	**1**	**0**	**1**	**6**
	NHL Totals		**493**	**118**	**126**	**244**	**724**	**66**	**21**	**15**	**36**	**118**

a OHL First All-Star Team (1984)

Traded to **San Jose** by **Chicago** for San Jose's third round choice (Bogdan Savenko) in 1993 Entry Draft, September 20, 1991. Traded to **Buffalo** by **San Jose** for Dave Snuggerud, March 9, 1992.

PRIESTLAY, KEN

Center. Shoots left. 5'10", 190 lbs. Born, Richmond, B.C., August 24, 1967.
(Buffalo's 5th choice, 98th overall, in 1985 Entry Draft).

			Regular Season					Playoffs				
Season	Club	Lea	GP	G	A	TP	PIM	GP	G	A	TP	PIM
1983-84	Victoria	WHL	55	10	18	28	31	....	....	....	....	....
1984-85	Victoria	WHL	50	25	37	62	48	....	....	....	....	....
1985-86	Victoria	WHL	72	73	72	145	45	....	....	....	....	....
	Rochester	AHL	4	0	2	2	0	....	....	....	....	....
1986-87	**Buffalo**	**NHL**	**34**	**11**	**6**	**17**	**8**	....	....	....	....	....
	Victoria	WHL	33	43	39	82	37	....	....	....	....	....
	Rochester	AHL	....	....	....	....	....	8	3	2	5	4
1987-88	**Buffalo**	**NHL**	**33**	**5**	**12**	**17**	**35**	**6**	**0**	**0**	**0**	**11**
	Rochester	AHL	43	27	24	51	47	....	....	....	....	....
1988-89	**Buffalo**	**NHL**	**15**	**2**	**0**	**2**	**2**	**3**	**0**	**0**	**0**	**2**
	Rochester	AHL	64	56	37	93	60	....	....	....	....	....
1989-90	**Buffalo**	**NHL**	**35**	**7**	**7**	**14**	**14**	**5**	**0**	**0**	**0**	**8**
	Rochester	AHL	40	19	39	58	46	....	....	....	....	....
1990-91	Cdn. National	....	40	20	26	46	34	....	....	....	....	....
	Pittsburgh	**NHL**	**2**	**0**	**1**	**1**	**0**	....	....	....	....	....
1991-92	**Pittsburgh**	**NHL**	**49**	**2**	**8**	**10**	**4**	....	....	....	....	....
	Muskegon	IHL	13	4	11	15	6	13	5	11	16	10
1992-93	Cleveland	IHL	66	33	36	69	72	4	2	1	3	4
	NHL Totals		**168**	**27**	**34**	**61**	**63**	**14**	**0**	**0**	**0**	**21**

Traded to **Pittsburgh** by **Buffalo** for Tony Tanti, March 5, 1991.

PRIMEAU, KEITH

Center. Shoots left. 6'4", 220 lbs. Born, Toronto, Ont., November 24, 1971.
(Detroit's 1st choice, 3rd overall, in 1990 Entry Draft).

			Regular Season					Playoffs				
Season	Club	Lea	GP	G	A	TP	PIM	GP	G	A	TP	PIM
1987-88	Hamilton	OHL	47	6	6	12	69	....	....	....	....	....
1988-89	Niagara Falls	OHL	48	20	35	55	56	17	9	16	25	12
1989-90a	Niagara Falls	OHL	65	*57	70	*127	97	16	*16	17	*33	49
1990-91	**Detroit**	**NHL**	**58**	**3**	**12**	**15**	**106**	**5**	**1**	**1**	**2**	**25**
	Adirondack	AHL	6	3	5	8	8	....	....	....	....	....
1991-92	**Detroit**	**NHL**	**35**	**6**	**10**	**16**	**83**	**11**	**0**	**0**	**0**	**14**
	Adirondack	AHL	42	21	24	45	89	9	1	7	8	27
1992-93	**Detroit**	**NHL**	**73**	**15**	**17**	**32**	**152**	**7**	**0**	**2**	**2**	**26**
	NHL Totals		**166**	**24**	**39**	**63**	**341**	**23**	**1**	**3**	**4**	**65**

a OHL Second All-Star Team (1990)

PROBERT, BOB (PROH-buhrt)

Right wing. Shoots left. 6'3", 225 lbs. Born, Windsor, Ont., June 5, 1965.
(Detroit's 3rd choice, 46th overall, in 1983 Entry Draft).

			Regular Season					Playoffs				
Season	Club	Lea	GP	G	A	TP	PIM	GP	G	A	TP	PIM
1982-83	Brantford	OHL	51	12	16	28	133	8	2	2	4	23
1983-84	Brantford	OHL	65	35	38	73	189	6	0	3	3	16
1984-85	S.S. Marie	OHL	44	20	52	72	172	....	....	....	....	....
	Hamilton	OHL	4	0	1	1	21	....	....	....	....	....
1985-86	**Detroit**	**NHL**	**44**	**8**	**13**	**21**	**186**	....	....	....	....	....
	Adirondack	AHL	32	12	15	27	152	10	2	3	5	68
1986-87	**Detroit**	**NHL**	**63**	**13**	**11**	**24**	**221**	**16**	**3**	**4**	**7**	**63**
	Adirondack	AHL	7	1	4	5	15	....	....	....	....	....
1987-88	**Detroit**	**NHL**	**74**	**29**	**33**	**62**	***398**	**16**	**8**	**13**	**21**	**51**
1988-89	**Detroit**	**NHL**	**25**	**4**	**2**	**6**	**106**	....	....	....	....	....
1989-90	**Detroit**	**NHL**	**4**	**3**	**0**	**3**	**21**	....	....	....	....	....
1990-91	**Detroit**	**NHL**	**55**	**16**	**23**	**39**	**315**	**6**	**1**	**2**	**3**	**50**
1991-92	**Detroit**	**NHL**	**63**	**20**	**24**	**44**	**276**	**11**	**1**	**6**	**7**	**28**
1992-93	**Detroit**	**NHL**	**80**	**14**	**29**	**43**	**292**	**7**	**0**	**3**	**3**	**10**
	NHL Totals		**408**	**107**	**135**	**242**	**1815**	**56**	**13**	**28**	**41**	**202**

Played in NHL All-Star Game (1988)

PROCHAZKA, MARTIN (pro-HAHS-kah)

Center. Shoots right. 5'11", 180 lbs. Born, Slany, Czech., March 3, 1972.
(Toronto's 8th choice, 135th overall, in 1991 Entry Draft).

			Regular Season					Playoffs				
Season	Club	Lea	GP	G	A	TP	PIM	GP	G	A	TP	PIM
1989-90	Kladno	Czech.	49	18	12	30	....	....	....	....	....	....
1990-91	Kladno	Czech.	50	19	10	29	21	....	....	....	....	....
1991-92	Dukla Jihlava	Czech.	44	18	11	29	2	....	....	....	....	....
1992-93	Kladno	Czech.	46	26	12	38	....	....	....	....	....	....

PROKHOROV, VITALI (PROH-kohr-ohv)

Left wing. Shoots left. 5'9", 185 lbs. Born, Moscow, Soviet Union, December 25, 1966.
(St. Louis' 3rd choice, 64th overall, in 1992 Entry Draft).

			Regular Season					Playoffs				
Season	Club	Lea	GP	G	A	TP	PIM	GP	G	A	TP	PIM
1983-84	Spartak	USSR	5	0	0	0	0	....	....	....	....	....
1984-85	Spartak	USSR	31	1	1	2	10	....	....	....	....	....
1985-86	Spartak	USSR	29	3	9	12	4	....	....	....	....	....
1986-87	Spartak	USSR	27	1	6	7	2	....	....	....	....	....
1987-88	Spartak	USSR	19	5	0	5	4	....	....	....	....	....
1988-89	Spartak	USSR	37	11	5	16	10	....	....	....	....	....
1989-90	Spartak	USSR	43	13	8	21	35	....	....	....	....	....
1990-91	Spartak	USSR	43	21	10	31	29	....	....	....	....	....
1991-92	Spartak	CIS	38	13	19	32	68	....	....	....	....	....
1992-93	**St. Louis**	**NHL**	**26**	**4**	**1**	**5**	**15**	....	....	....	....	....
	NHL Totals		**26**	**4**	**1**	**5**	**15**	....	....	....	....	....

PROKOPEC, MIKE

Right wing. Shoots right. 6'1", 175 lbs. Born, Toronto, Ont., May 17, 1974.
(Chicago's 7th choice, 161st overall, in 1992 Entry Draft).

			Regular Season					Playoffs				
Season	Club	Lea	GP	G	A	TP	PIM	GP	G	A	TP	PIM
1991-92	Cornwall	OHL	59	12	15	27	75	6	0	0	0	0
1992-93	Newmarket	OHL	40	6	14	20	70	....	....	....	....	....
	Guelph	OHL	28	10	14	24	27	5	1	0	1	14

PRONGER, CHRIS

Defense. Shoots left. 6'5", 190 lbs. Born, Dryden, Ont., October 10, 1974.
(Hartford's 1st choice, 2nd overall, in 1993 Entry Draft).

			Regular Season					Playoffs				
Season	Club	Lea	GP	G	A	TP	PIM	GP	G	A	TP	PIM
1991-92	Peterborough	OHL	63	17	45	62	90	10	1	8	9	28
1992-93ab	Peterborough	OHL	61	15	62	77	108	21	15	25	40	51

a OHL First All-Star Team (1993)
b Canadian Major Junior First All-Star Team (1993)

PRONGER, SEAN

Center. Shoots left. 6'2", 195 lbs. Born, Dryden, Ont., November 30, 1972.
(Vancouver's 3rd choice, 51st overall, in 1991 Entry Draft).

			Regular Season					Playoffs				
Season	Club	Lea	GP	G	A	TP	PIM	GP	G	A	TP	PIM
1990-91	Bowling Green	CCHA	40	3	7	10	30	....	....	....	....	....
1991-92	Bowling Green	CCHA	34	9	7	16	28	....	....	....	....	....
1992-93	Bowling Green	CCHA	39	23	23	46	35	....	....	....	....	....

PROPP, BRIAN PHILIP

Left wing. Shoots left. 5'10", 195 lbs. Born, Lanigan, Sask., February 15, 1959.
(Philadelphia's 1st choice, 14th overall, in 1979 Entry Draft).

			Regular Season					Playoffs				
Season	Club	Lea	GP	G	A	TP	PIM	GP	G	A	TP	PIM
1976-77a	Brandon	WHL	72	55	80	135	47	16	*14	12	26	5
1977-78b	Brandon	WHL	70	70	*112	*182	200	8	7	6	13	12
1978-79bc	Brandon	WHL	71	*94	*100	*194	127	22	15	23	*38	40
1979-80	**Philadelphia**	**NHL**	**80**	**34**	**41**	**75**	**54**	**19**	**5**	**10**	**15**	**29**
1980-81	**Philadelphia**	**NHL**	**79**	**26**	**40**	**66**	**110**	**12**	**6**	**6**	**12**	**32**
1981-82	**Philadelphia**	**NHL**	**80**	**44**	**47**	**91**	**117**	**4**	**2**	**2**	**4**	**4**
1982-83	**Philadelphia**	**NHL**	**80**	**40**	**42**	**82**	**72**	**3**	**1**	**2**	**3**	**8**
1983-84	**Philadelphia**	**NHL**	**79**	**39**	**53**	**92**	**37**	**3**	**0**	**1**	**1**	**6**
1984-85	**Philadelphia**	**NHL**	**76**	**43**	**53**	**96**	**43**	**19**	**8**	**10**	**18**	**6**
1985-86	**Philadelphia**	**NHL**	**72**	**40**	**57**	**97**	**47**	**5**	**0**	**2**	**2**	**4**
1986-87	**Philadelphia**	**NHL**	**53**	**31**	**36**	**67**	**45**	**26**	**12**	**16**	**28**	**10**
1987-88	**Philadelphia**	**NHL**	**74**	**27**	**49**	**76**	**76**	**7**	**4**	**2**	**6**	**8**
1988-89	**Philadelphia**	**NHL**	**77**	**32**	**46**	**78**	**37**	**18**	**14**	**9**	**23**	**14**
1989-90	**Philadelphia**	**NHL**	**40**	**13**	**15**	**28**	**31**	....	....	....	....	....
	Boston	**NHL**	**14**	**3**	**9**	**12**	**10**	**20**	**4**	**9**	**13**	**2**
1990-91	**Minnesota**	**NHL**	**79**	**26**	**47**	**73**	**58**	**23**	**8**	**15**	**23**	**28**
1991-92	**Minnesota**	**NHL**	**51**	**12**	**23**	**35**	**49**	**1**	**0**	**0**	**0**	**0**
1992-93	**Minnesota**	**NHL**	**17**	**3**	**3**	**6**	**0**	....	....	....	....	....
	Lugano	Switz.	24	21	6	27	32	....	....	....	....	....
	Cdn. National	....	3	3	1	4	2	....	....	....	....	....
	NHL Totals		**951**	**413**	**561**	**974**	**786**	**160**	**64**	**84**	**148**	**151**

a WHL Rookie of the Year (1977)
b WHL First All-Star Team (1978, 1979)
c WHL Player of the Year (1979)

Played in NHL All-Star Game (1980, 1982, 1984, 1986, 1990)

Traded to **Boston** by **Philadelphia** for Boston's second round choice (Terran Sandwith) in 1990 Entry Draft, March 2, 1990. Signed as a free agent by **Minnesota**, July 25, 1990.

PROSPAL, VACLAV

Center. Shoots left. 6'2", 167 lbs. Born, Ceske-Budejovice, Czech., February 17, 1975.
(Philadelphia's 2nd choice, 71st overall, in 1993 Entry Draft).

			Regular Season					Playoffs				
Season	Club	Lea	GP	G	A	TP	PIM	GP	G	A	TP	PIM
1992-93	Budejovice Jrs.	Czech.	32	26	31	57	24	....	....	....	....	....

PROULX, CHRISTIAN

Defense. Shoots left. 5'11", 188 lbs. Born, Coaticook, Que., December 10, 1973.
(Montreal's 7th choice, 164th overall, in 1992 Entry Draft).

			Regular Season					Playoffs				
Season	Club	Lea	GP	G	A	TP	PIM	GP	G	A	TP	PIM
1990-91	St-Jean	QMJHL	67	1	8	9	73	....	....	....	....	....
1991-92	St-Jean	QMJHL	68	1	17	18	180	....	....	....	....	....
1992-93	St-Jean	QMJHL	70	3	34	37	147	4	0	0	0	12

PRPIC, TONY

Right wing. Shoots right. 6'4", 207 lbs. Born, Euclid, OH, June 16, 1973.
(Montreal's 5th choice, 105th overall, in 1991 Entry Draft).

			Regular Season					Playoffs				
Season	Club	Lea	GP	G	A	TP	PIM	GP	G	A	TP	PIM
1991-92	Sioux City	USHL	38	20	24	44	51	....	....	....	....	....
1992-93	Tri-City	WHL	63	16	17	33	119	1	....	1	1	....

PULLOLA, TOMMI (PUHL-loh-lah)

Center. Shoots left. 6'5", 207 lbs. Born, Vaasa, Finland, May 18, 1971.
(Chicago's 4th choice, 111th overall, in 1989 Entry Draft).

			Regular Season					Playoffs				
Season	Club	Lea	GP	G	A	TP	PIM	GP	G	A	TP	PIM
1988-89	Sport	Fin.2	40	11	13	24	....	....	....	....	....	....
1989-90	Lukko	Fin.	40	7	9	16	8	....	....	....	....	....
1990-91	Lukko	Fin.	42	17	17	34	40	....	....	....	....	....
1991-92	Lukko	Fin.	44	15	9	24	36	2	1	0	1	2
1992-93	Lukko	Fin.	25	3	7	10	14	....	....	....	....	....

PURVES, JOHN (PUR-vihs)

Right wing. Shoots right. 6'1", 201 lbs. Born, Toronto, Ont., February 12, 1968.
(Washington's 6th choice, 103rd overall, in 1986 Entry Draft).

			Regular Season					Playoffs				
Season	Club	Lea	GP	G	A	TP	PIM	GP	G	A	TP	PIM
1985-86	Belleville	OHL	16	3	9	12	6	....	....	....	....	....
	Hamilton	OHL	36	13	28	41	36	....	....	....	....	....
1986-87	Hamilton	OHL	28	12	11	23	37	9	2	0	2	12
1987-88	Hamilton	OHL	64	39	44	83	65	14	7	18	25	4
1988-89a	Niagara Falls	OHL	5	5	11	16	2	....	....	....	....	....
	North Bay	OHL	42	34	52	86	38	12	14	12	26	16
1989-90	Baltimore	AHL	75	29	35	64	12	9	5	7	12	4
1990-91	**Washington**	**NHL**	**7**	**1**	**0**	**1**	**0**	....	....	....	....	....
	Baltimore	AHL	53	22	29	51	27	6	2	3	5	0
1991-92	Baltimore	AHL	78	43	46	89	47	....	....	....	....	....
1992-93	Kaufbeuren	Ger.	43	15	17	32	34	....	....	....	....	....
	NHL Totals		**7**	**1**	**0**	**1**	**0**	....	....	....	....	....

a OHL Second All-Star Team (1989)

PUSHOR, JAMIE

Defense. Shoots right. 6'3", 192 lbs. Born, Lethbridge, Alta., February 11, 1973.
(Detroit's 2nd choice, 32nd overall, in 1991 Entry Draft).

			Regular Season					Playoffs				
Season	Club	Lea	GP	G	A	TP	PIM	GP	G	A	TP	PIM
1989-90	Lethbridge	WHL	10	0	2	2	2	....	....	....	....	....
1990-91	Lethbridge	WHL	71	1	13	14	193	....	....	....	....	....
1991-92	Lethbridge	WHL	49	2	15	17	232	5	0	0	0	33
1992-93	Lethbridge	WHL	72	6	22	28	200	4	0	1	1	9

PYSZ, PATRIK

Center. Shoots left. 5'11", 187 lbs. Born, Zakopane, Poland, January 15, 1975.
(Chicago's 6th choice, 102nd overall, in 1993 Entry Draft).

			Regular Season					Playoffs				
Season	Club	Lea	GP	G	A	TP	PIM	GP	G	A	TP	PIM
1991-92	Nowy Targ	Poland				UNAVAILABLE						
1992-93	Augsburg	Ger.2	36	7	5	12	12	8	2	1	3	0

QUINN, DAN

Center. Shoots left. 5'11", 182 lbs. Born, Ottawa, Ont., June 1, 1965.
(Calgary's 1st choice, 13th overall, in 1983 Entry Draft).

			Regular Season					Playoffs				
Season	Club	Lea	GP	G	A	TP	PIM	GP	G	A	TP	PIM
1981-82	Belleville	OHL	67	19	32	51	41	....	....	....	....	....
1982-83	Belleville	OHL	70	59	88	147	27	4	2	6	8	2
1983-84	**Calgary**	**NHL**	**54**	**19**	**33**	**52**	**20**	**8**	**3**	**5**	**8**	**4**
	Belleville	OHL	24	23	36	59	12	....	....	....	....	....
1984-85	**Calgary**	**NHL**	**74**	**20**	**38**	**58**	**22**	**3**	**0**	**0**	**0**	**0**
1985-86	**Calgary**	**NHL**	**78**	**30**	**42**	**72**	**44**	**18**	**8**	**7**	**15**	**10**
1986-87	**Calgary**	**NHL**	**16**	**3**	**6**	**9**	**14**	....	....	....	....	....
	Pittsburgh	**NHL**	**64**	**28**	**43**	**71**	**40**	....	....	....	....	....
1987-88	**Pittsburgh**	**NHL**	**70**	**40**	**39**	**79**	**50**	....	....	....	....	....
1988-89	**Pittsburgh**	**NHL**	**79**	**34**	**60**	**94**	**102**	**11**	**6**	**3**	**9**	**10**
1989-90	**Pittsburgh**	**NHL**	**41**	**9**	**20**	**29**	**22**	....	....	....	....	....
	Vancouver	**NHL**	**37**	**16**	**18**	**34**	**27**	....	....	....	....	....
1990-91	**Vancouver**	**NHL**	**64**	**18**	**31**	**49**	**46**	....	....	....	....	....
	St. Louis	**NHL**	**14**	**4**	**7**	**11**	**20**	**13**	**4**	**7**	**11**	**32**
1991-92	**Philadelphia**	**NHL**	**67**	**11**	**26**	**37**	**26**	....	....	....	....	....
1992-93	**Minnesota**	**NHL**	**11**	**0**	**4**	**4**	**6**	....	....	....	....	....
	NHL Totals		**669**	**232**	**367**	**599**	**439**	**53**	**21**	**22**	**43**	**56**

Traded to **Pittsburgh** by **Calgary** for Mike Bullard, November 12, 1986. Traded to **Vancouver** by **Pittsburgh** with Dave Capuano and Andrew McBain for Rod Buskas, Barry Pederson and Tony Tanti, January 8, 1990. Traded to **St. Louis** by **Vancouver** with Garth Butcher for Geoff Courtnall, Robert Dirk, Sergio Momesso, Cliff Ronning and future considerations, March 5, 1991. Traded to **Philadelphia** by **St. Louis** with Rod Brind'Amour for Ron Sutter and Murray Baron, September 22, 1991. Signed as a free agent by **Minnesota**, October 4, 1992.

QUINNEY, KEN (KWIH-nee)

Right wing. Shoots right. 5'10", 186 lbs. Born, New Westminster, B.C., May 23, 1965.
(Quebec's 9th choice, 203rd overall, in 1984 Entry Draft).

			Regular Season					Playoffs				
Season	Club	Lea	GP	G	A	TP	PIM	GP	G	A	TP	PIM
1981-82	Calgary	WHL	63	11	17	28	55	2	0	0	0	15
1982-83	Calgary	WHL	71	26	25	51	71	16	6	1	7	46
1983-84	Calgary	WHL	71	64	54	118	38	4	5	2	7	0
1984-85a	Calgary	WHL	56	47	67	114	65	7	6	4	10	15
1985-86	Fredericton	AHL	61	11	26	37	34	6	2	2	4	9
1986-87	**Quebec**	**NHL**	**25**	**2**	**7**	**9**	**16**	....	....	....	....	....
	Fredericton	AHL	48	14	27	41	20	....	....	....	....	....
1987-88	**Quebec**	**NHL**	**15**	**2**	**2**	**4**	**5**	....	....	....	....	....
	Fredericton	AHL	58	37	39	76	39	13	3	5	8	35
1988-89	Halifax	AHL	72	41	49	90	65	4	3	0	3	0
1989-90	Halifax	AHL	44	9	16	25	63	2	0	0	0	2
1990-91	**Quebec**	**NHL**	**19**	**3**	**4**	**7**	**2**	....	....	....	....	....
	Halifax	AHL	44	20	20	40	76	....	....	....	....	....
1991-92	Adirondack	AHL	63	31	29	60	33	19	7	12	19	9
1992-93	Adirondack	AHL	63	32	34	66	15	10	2	9	11	9
	NHL Totals		**59**	**7**	**13**	**20**	**23**	....	....	....	....	....

a WHL First All-Star Team, East Division (1985)

Signed as a free agent by **Detroit**, August 12, 1991.

QUINTAL, STEPHANE (kihn-TAHL)

Defense. Shoots right. 6'3", 220 lbs. Born, Boucherville, Que., October 22, 1968.
(Boston's 2nd choice, 14th overall, in 1987 Entry Draft).

			Regular Season					Playoffs				
Season	Club	Lea	GP	G	A	TP	PIM	GP	G	A	TP	PIM
1985-86	Granby	QMJHL	67	2	17	19	144	....	....	....	....	....
1986-87a	Granby	QMJHL	67	13	41	54	178	8	0	9	9	10
1987-88	Hull	QMJHL	38	13	23	36	138	19	7	12	19	30
1988-89	**Boston**	**NHL**	**26**	**0**	**1**	**1**	**29**	....	....	....	....	....
	Maine	AHL	16	4	10	14	28	....	....	....	....	....
1989-90	**Boston**	**NHL**	**38**	**2**	**2**	**4**	**22**	....	....	....	....	....
	Maine	AHL	37	4	16	20	27	....	....	....	....	....
1990-91	**Boston**	**NHL**	**45**	**2**	**6**	**8**	**89**	**3**	**0**	**1**	**1**	**7**
	Maine	AHL	23	1	5	6	30	....	....	....	....	....
1991-92	**Boston**	**NHL**	**49**	**4**	**10**	**14**	**77**	....	....	....	....	....
	St. Louis	**NHL**	**26**	**0**	**6**	**6**	**32**	**4**	**1**	**2**	**3**	**6**
1992-93	**St. Louis**	**NHL**	**75**	**1**	**10**	**11**	**100**	**9**	**0**	**0**	**0**	**8**
	NHL Totals		**259**	**9**	**35**	**44**	**349**	**16**	**1**	**3**	**4**	**21**

a QMJHL First All-Star Team (1987)

Traded to **St. Louis** by **Boston** with Craig Janney for Adam Oates, February 7, 1992.

QUINTIN, JEAN-FRANCOIS

Left wing. Shoots left. 6', 187 lbs. Born, St. Jean, Que., May 28, 1969.
(Minnesota's 4th choice, 75th overall, in 1989 Entry Draft).

			Regular Season					Playoffs				
Season	Club	Lea	GP	G	A	TP	PIM	GP	G	A	TP	PIM
1987-88	Shawinigan	QMJHL	70	28	70	98	143	11	5	8	13	26
1988-89	Shawinigan	QMJHL	69	52	100	152	105	10	9	15	24	16
1989-90	Kalamazoo	IHL	68	20	18	38	38	10	8	4	12	14
1990-91	Kalamazoo	IHL	78	31	43	74	64	9	1	5	6	11
1991-92	**San Jose**	**NHL**	**8**	**3**	**0**	**3**	**0**	....	....	....	....	....
	Kansas City	IHL	21	4	6	10	29	13	2	10	12	29
1992-93	**San Jose**	**NHL**	**14**	**2**	**5**	**7**	**4**	....	....	....	....	....
	Kansas City	IHL	64	20	29	49	169	11	2	1	3	16
	NHL Totals		**22**	**5**	**5**	**10**	**4**	....	....	....	....	....

Claimed by **San Jose** from **Minnesota** in Dispersal Draft, May 30, 1991.

RACINE, YVES

Defense. Shoots left. 6', 200 lbs. Born, Matane, Que., February 7, 1969.
(Detroit's 1st choice, 11th overall, in 1987 Entry Draft).

			Regular Season					Playoffs				
Season	Club	Lea	GP	G	A	TP	PIM	GP	G	A	TP	PIM
1986-87	Longueuil	QMJHL	70	7	43	50	50	20	3	11	14	14
1987-88	Adirondack	AHL	....	....	....	....	....	9	4	2	6	2
a	Victoriaville	QMJHL	69	10	84	94	150	5	0	0	0	13
1988-89a	Victoriaville	QMJHL	63	23	85	108	95	16	3	*30	*33	41
	Adirondack	AHL	....	....	....	....	....	2	1	1	2	0
1989-90	**Detroit**	**NHL**	**28**	**4**	**9**	**13**	**23**	....	....	....	....	....
	Adirondack	AHL	46	8	27	35	31	....	....	....	....	....
1990-91	**Detroit**	**NHL**	**62**	**7**	**40**	**47**	**33**	**7**	**2**	**0**	**2**	**0**
	Adirondack	AHL	16	3	9	12	10	....	....	....	....	....
1991-92	**Detroit**	**NHL**	**61**	**2**	**22**	**24**	**94**	**11**	**2**	**1**	**3**	**10**
1992-93	**Detroit**	**NHL**	**80**	**9**	**31**	**40**	**80**	**7**	**1**	**3**	**4**	**27**
	NHL Totals		**231**	**22**	**102**	**124**	**230**	**25**	**5**	**4**	**9**	**37**

a QMJHL First-All Star Team (1988, 1989)

RAGLAN, HERB

Right wing. Shoots right. 6', 205 lbs. Born, Peterborough, Ont., August 5, 1967.
(St. Louis' 1st choice, 37th overall, in 1985 Entry Draft).

			Regular Season					Playoffs				
Season	Club	Lea	GP	G	A	TP	PIM	GP	G	A	TP	PIM
1984-85	Peterborough	OHL	58	20	22	42	166	....	....	....	....	....
1985-86	**St. Louis**	**NHL**	**7**	**0**	**0**	**0**	**5**	**10**	**1**	**1**	**2**	**24**
	Kingston	OHL	28	10	9	19	88	10	5	2	7	30
1986-87	**St. Louis**	**NHL**	**62**	**6**	**10**	**16**	**159**	**4**	**0**	**0**	**0**	**2**
1987-88	**St. Louis**	**NHL**	**73**	**10**	**15**	**25**	**190**	**10**	**1**	**3**	**4**	**11**
1988-89	**St. Louis**	**NHL**	**50**	**7**	**10**	**17**	**144**	**8**	**1**	**2**	**3**	**13**
1989-90	**St. Louis**	**NHL**	**11**	**0**	**1**	**1**	**21**	....	....	....	....	....
1990-91	**St. Louis**	**NHL**	**32**	**3**	**3**	**6**	**52**	....	....	....	....	....
	Quebec	**NHL**	**15**	**1**	**3**	**4**	**30**	....	....	....	....	....
1991-92	**Quebec**	**NHL**	**62**	**6**	**14**	**20**	**120**	....	....	....	....	....
1992-93	Halifax	AHL	28	3	9	12	83	....	....	....	....	....
	Tampa Bay	**NHL**	**2**	**0**	**0**	**0**	**2**	....	....	....	....	....
	Atlanta	IHL	24	4	10	14	139	9	3	3	6	32
	NHL Totals		**314**	**33**	**56**	**89**	**723**	**32**	**3**	**6**	**9**	**50**

Traded to **Quebec** by **St. Louis** with Tony Twist and Andy Rymsha for Darin Kimble, February 4, 1991. Traded to **Tampa Bay** by **Quebec** for Martin Simard, Steve Tuttle and Michel Mongeau, February 12, 1993.

RAGNARSSON, MARCUS

Defense. Shoots left. 6'1", 200 lbs. Born, Ostervala, Sweden, August 13, 1971.
(San Jose's 5th choice, 99th overall, in 1992 Entry Draft).

			Regular Season					Playoffs				
Season	Club	Lea	GP	G	A	TP	PIM	GP	G	A	TP	PIM
1989-90	Djurgarden	Swe.	13	0	2	2	0	1	0	0	0	0
1990-91	Djurgarden	Swe.	35	4	1	5	12	7	0	0	0	6
1991-92	Djurgarden	Swe.	40	8	5	13	14	10	0	1	1	4
1992-93	Djurgarden	Swe.	35	3	3	6	53	6	0	3	3	8

RAHN, NOEL

Center. Shoots left. 6', 155 lbs. Born, Edina, MN, February 6, 1971.
(Quebec's 14th choice, 232nd overall, in 1989 Entry Draft).

			Regular Season					Playoffs				
Season	Club	Lea	GP	G	A	TP	PIM	GP	G	A	TP	PIM
1989-90	U. Wisconsin	WCHA	4	0	0	0	0	....	....	....	....	....
1990-91	U. Wisconsin	WCHA				DID NOT PLAY						
1991-92	St. Cloud	WCHA	23	8	1	9	23	....	....	....	....	....
1992-93	St. Cloud	WCHA	32	1	5	6	18	....	....	....	....	....

RAISKY, ANDREI

Center. Shoots left. 6'2", 194 lbs.   Born, Ust-Kamenogorsk, Soviet Union, March 30, 1970.
(Winnipeg's 7th choice, 156th overall, in 1992 Entry Draft).

			Regular Season					Playoffs				
Season	Club	Lea	GP	G	A	TP	PIM	GP	G	A	TP	PIM
1987-88	Torpedo Ust	USSR	2	0	1	1	0	....	....	....	....	....
1988-89	SKA Sverdlovsk	USSR 2				UNAVAILABLE						
1989-90	Torpedo Ust	USSR	18	4	2	6	18	....	....	....	....	....
1990-91	Torpedo Ust	USSR	41	6	5	11	46	....	....	....	....	....
1991-92	Torpedo Ust	CIS	40	16	14	30	53	....	....	....	....	....
1992-93	Dayton	ECHL	11	6	7	13	6	....	....	....	....	....
	Moncton	AHL	35	7	10	17	14	1	0	0	0	10

RAITANEN, RAULI

Center. Shoots left. 6'2", 187 lbs.   Born, Pori, Finland, January 14, 1970.
(Winnipeg's 10th choice, 182nd overall, in 1990 Entry Draft).

			Regular Season					Playoffs				
Season	Club	Lea	GP	G	A	TP	PIM	GP	G	A	TP	PIM
1987-88	Assat	Fin.	18	1	5	6	2	....	....	....	....	....
1988-89	Assat	Fin.	40	21	17	38	18	....	....	....	....	....
1989-90	Assat	Fin.2	41	17	44	61	20	....	....	....	....	....
1990-91	Assat	Fin.	43	6	16	22	14	....	....	....	....	....
1991-92	Assat	Fin.	41	12	22	34	34	8	1	5	6	2
1992-93	Assat	Fin.	43	15	20	35	28	8	0	4	4	6

RAITER, MARK

Defense. Shoots right. 6'4", 220 lbs.   Born, Calgary, Alta., January 27, 1973.
(Toronto's 4th choice, 95th overall, in 1992 Entry Draft).

			Regular Season					Playoffs				
Season	Club	Lea	GP	G	A	TP	PIM	GP	G	A	TP	PIM
1990-91	Saskatoon	WHL	35	2	3	5	73	....	....	....	....	....
1991-92	Saskatoon	WHL	72	2	12	14	354	....	....	....	....	....
1992-93	Saskatoon	WHL	57	3	11	14	173	9	1	1	2	19

RAJNOHA, PAVEL

Defense. Shoots left. 6', 185 lbs.   Born, Gottwaldov, Czech., February 23, 1974.
(Calgary's 8th choice, 150th overall, in 1992 Entry Draft).

			Regular Season					Playoffs				
Season	Club	Lea	GP	G	A	TP	PIM	GP	G	A	TP	PIM
1990-91	TJ Zlin	Czech.	6	0	0	0	4	....	....	....	....	....
1991-92	ZPS Zlin	Czech.	24	0	1	1	4	....	....	....	....	....
1992-93	ZPS Zlin	Czech.	26	2	1	3	....	....	....	....	....	....

RAMAGE, GEORGE (ROB)   (RAM-ihj)

Defense. Shoots right. 6'2", 200 lbs.   Born, Byron, Ont., January 11, 1959.
(Colorado's 1st choice, 1st overall, in 1979 Entry Draft).

			Regular Season					Playoffs				
Season	Club	Lea	GP	G	A	TP	PIM	GP	G	A	TP	PIM
1975-76	London	OHA	65	12	31	43	113	5	0	1	1	11
1976-77a	London	OHA	65	15	58	73	177	20	3	11	14	55
1977-78b	London	OHA	59	17	48	65	162	11	4	5	9	29
1978-79	Birmingham	WHA	80	12	36	48	165	....	....	....	....	....
1979-80	**Colorado**	**NHL**	75	8	20	28	135	....	....	....	....	....
1980-81	**Colorado**	**NHL**	79	20	42	62	193	....	....	....	....	....
1981-82	**Colorado**	**NHL**	80	13	29	42	201	....	....	....	....	....
1982-83	**St. Louis**	**NHL**	78	16	35	51	193	4	0	3	3	22
1983-84	**St. Louis**	**NHL**	80	15	45	60	121	11	1	8	9	32
1984-85	**St. Louis**	**NHL**	80	7	31	38	178	3	1	3	4	6
1985-86	**St. Louis**	**NHL**	77	10	56	66	171	19	1	10	11	66
1986-87	**St. Louis**	**NHL**	59	11	28	39	108	6	2	2	4	21
1987-88	**St. Louis**	**NHL**	67	8	34	42	127	....	....	....	....	....
	Calgary	**NHL**	12	1	6	7	37	9	1	3	4	21
1988-89	**Calgary**	**NHL**	68	3	13	16	156	20	1	11	12	26
1989-90	**Toronto**	**NHL**	80	8	41	49	202	5	1	2	3	20
1990-91	**Toronto**	**NHL**	80	10	25	35	173	....	....	....	....	....
1991-92	**Minnesota**	**NHL**	34	4	5	9	69	....	....	....	....	....
1992-93	**Tampa Bay**	**NHL**	66	5	12	17	138	....	....	....	....	....
	Montreal	**NHL**	8	0	1	1	8	7	0	0	0	4
	NHL Totals		1023	139	423	562	2210	84	8	42	50	218

a OHA Third All-Star Team (1977)
b OHA First All-Star Team (1978)
Played in NHL All-Star Game (1981, 1984, 1986, 1988)
Traded to **St. Louis** by **New Jersey** for St. Louis' first round choice (Rocky Trottier) in 1982 Entry Draft and first round choice (John MacLean) in 1983 Entry Draft, June 9, 1982. Traded to **Calgary** by **St. Louis** with Rick Wamsley for Brett Hull and Steve Bozek, March 7, 1988. Traded to **Toronto** by **Calgary** for Toronto's second round choice (Kent Manderville) in 1989 Entry Draft, June 16, 1989. Claimed by **Minnesota** from **Toronto** in Expansion Draft, May 30, 1991. Claimed by **Tampa Bay** from **Minnesota** in Expansion Draft, June 18, 1992. Traded to **Montreal** by **Tampa Bay** for Eric Charron, Alain Cote and future considerations (Donald Dufresne, June 18, 1993), March 20, 1993.

RAMSEY, MICHAEL ALLEN (MIKE)

Defense. Shoots left. 6'3", 195 lbs.   Born, Minneapolis, MN, December 3, 1960.
(Buffalo's 1st choice, 11th overall, in 1979 Entry Draft).

			Regular Season					Playoffs				
Season	Club	Lea	GP	G	A	TP	PIM	GP	G	A	TP	PIM
1978-79	U. Minnesota	WCHA	26	6	11	17	30	....	....	....	....	....
1979-80	U.S. National	....	56	11	22	33	55	....	....	....	....	....
	U.S. Olympic	....	7	0	2	2	8	....	....	....	....	....
	Buffalo	**NHL**	13	1	6	7	6	13	1	2	3	12
1980-81	**Buffalo**	**NHL**	72	3	14	17	56	8	0	3	3	20
1981-82	**Buffalo**	**NHL**	80	7	23	30	56	4	1	1	2	14
1982-83	**Buffalo**	**NHL**	77	8	30	38	55	10	4	4	8	15
1983-84	**Buffalo**	**NHL**	72	9	22	31	82	3	0	1	1	6
1984-85	**Buffalo**	**NHL**	79	8	22	30	102	5	0	1	1	23
1985-86	**Buffalo**	**NHL**	76	7	21	28	117	....	....	....	....	....
1986-87	**Buffalo**	**NHL**	80	8	31	39	109	....	....	....	....	....
1987-88	**Buffalo**	**NHL**	63	5	16	21	77	6	0	3	3	29
1988-89	**Buffalo**	**NHL**	56	2	14	16	84	5	1	0	1	11
1989-90	**Buffalo**	**NHL**	73	4	21	25	47	6	0	1	1	8
1990-91	**Buffalo**	**NHL**	71	6	14	20	46	5	1	0	1	12
1991-92	**Buffalo**	**NHL**	66	3	14	17	67	7	0	2	2	8
1992-93	**Buffalo**	**NHL**	33	2	8	10	20	....	....	....	....	....
	Pittsburgh	**NHL**	12	1	2	3	8	12	0	6	6	4
	NHL Totals		923	74	258	332	932	84	8	24	32	162

Played in NHL All-Star Game (1982, 1983, 1985, 1986)
Traded to **Pittsburgh** by **Buffalo** for Bob Errey, March 22, 1993.

RANHEIM, PAUL

Left wing. Shoots right. 6', 195 lbs.   Born, St. Louis, MO, January 25, 1966.
(Calgary's 3rd choice, 38th overall, in 1984 Entry Draft).

			Regular Season					Playoffs				
Season	Club	Lea	GP	G	A	TP	PIM	GP	G	A	TP	PIM
1984-85	U. Wisconsin	WCHA	42	11	11	22	40	....	....	....	....	....
1985-86	U. Wisconsin	WCHA	33	17	17	34	34	....	....	....	....	....
1986-87a	U. Wisconsin	WCHA	42	24	35	59	54	....	....	....	....	....
1987-88bc	U. Wisconsin	WCHA	44	36	26	62	63	....	....	....	....	....
1988-89	**Calgary**	**NHL**	5	0	0	0	0	....	....	....	....	....
def	Salt Lake	IHL	75	*68	29	97	16	14	5	5	10	8
1989-90	**Calgary**	**NHL**	80	26	28	54	23	6	1	3	4	2
1990-91	**Calgary**	**NHL**	39	14	16	30	4	7	2	2	4	0
1991-92	**Calgary**	**NHL**	80	23	20	43	32	....	....	....	....	....
1992-93	**Calgary**	**NHL**	83	21	22	43	26	6	0	1	1	0
	NHL Totals		287	84	86	170	85	19	3	6	9	2

a WCHA Second All-Star Team (1987)
b NCAA West First All-American Team (1988)
c WCHA First All-Star Team (1988)
d IHL Second All-Star Team (1989)
e Won Garry F. Longman Memorial Trophy (Top Rookie-IHL) (1989)
f Won Ken McKenzie Trophy (Outstanding U.S.-born Rookie-IHL) (1989)

RAPPANA, KEVIN

Defense. Shoots right. 6'2", 182 lbs.   Born, Duluth, MN, January 24, 1973.
(St. Louis' 11th choice, 241st overall, in 1991 Entry Draft).

			Regular Season					Playoffs				
Season	Club	Lea	GP	G	A	TP	PIM	GP	G	A	TP	PIM
1992-93	North Dakota	WCHA	12	0	0	0	0	....	....	....	....	....

RATHJE, MIKE   (RATH-gee)

Defense. Shoots left. 6'5", 205 lbs.   Born, Mannville, Alta., May 11, 1974.
(San Jose's 1st choice, 3rd overall, in 1992 Entry Draft).

			Regular Season					Playoffs				
Season	Club	Lea	GP	G	A	TP	PIM	GP	G	A	TP	PIM
1990-91	Medicine Hat	WHL	64	1	16	17	28	12	0	4	4	2
1991-92a	Medicine Hat	WHL	67	11	23	34	109	4	0	1	1	2
1992-93a	Medicine Hat	WHL	57	12	37	49	103	10	3	3	6	12
	Kansas City	IHL	5	0	0	0	12	....	....	....	....	....

a WHL East Second All-Star Team (1992, 1993)

RATUSHNY, DAN

Defense. Shoots right. 6'1", 210 lbs.   Born, Nepean, Ont., October 29, 1970.
(Winnipeg's 2nd choice, 25th overall, in 1989 Entry Draft).

			Regular Season					Playoffs				
Season	Club	Lea	GP	G	A	TP	PIM	GP	G	A	TP	PIM
1988-89	Cornell	ECAC	28	2	13	15	50	....	....	....	....	....
1989-90ab	Cornell	ECAC	26	5	14	19	54	....	....	....	....	....
1990-91ac	Cornell	ECAC	26	7	24	31	52	....	....	....	....	....
	Cdn. National	....	12	0	1	1	6	....	....	....	....	....
1991-92	Cdn. National	....	58	5	13	18	50	....	....	....	....	....
	Cdn. Olympic	....	8	0	0	0	4	....	....	....	....	....
1992-93	Fort Wayne	IHL	63	6	19	25	48	....	....	....	....	....
	Vancouver	**NHL**	1	0	1	1	2	....	....	....	....	....
	NHL Totals		1	0	1	1	2	....	....	....	....	....

a ECAC First All-Star Team (1990, 1991)
b NCAA East Second All-American Team (1990)
c NCAA East First All-American Team (1991)
Traded to **Vancouver** by **Winnipeg** for Vancouver's ninth round choice (Harijs Vitolinsh) in 1993 Entry Draft, March 22, 1993.

RAY, ROBERT

Left wing. Shoots left. 6', 203 lbs.   Born, Belleville, Ont., June 8, 1968.
(Buffalo's 5th choice, 97th overall, in 1988 Entry Draft).

			Regular Season					Playoffs				
Season	Club	Lea	GP	G	A	TP	PIM	GP	G	A	TP	PIM
1985-86	Cornwall	OHL	53	6	13	19	253	6	0	0	0	26
1986-87	Cornwall	OHL	46	17	20	37	158	5	1	1	2	16
1987-88	Cornwall	OHL	61	11	41	52	179	11	2	3	5	33
1988-89	Rochester	AHL	74	11	18	29	*446	....	....	....	....	....
1989-90	**Buffalo**	**NHL**	27	2	1	3	99	....	....	....	....	....
	Rochester	AHL	43	2	13	15	335	17	1	3	4	115
1990-91	**Buffalo**	**NHL**	66	8	8	16	*350	6	1	1	2	56
	Rochester	AHL	8	1	1	2	15	....	....	....	....	....
1991-92	**Buffalo**	**NHL**	63	5	3	8	354	7	0	0	0	2
1992-93	**Buffalo**	**NHL**	68	3	2	5	211	....	....	....	....	....
	NHL Totals		224	18	14	32	1014	13	1	1	2	58

RAYMOND, RICHARD
Defense. Shoots right. 6'1", 187 lbs.   Born, Sudbury, Ont., April 4, 1974.
(Chicago's 10th choice, 233rd overall, in 1992 Entry Draft).

			Regular Season					Playoffs				
Season	Club	Lea	GP	G	A	TP	PIM	GP	G	A	TP	PIM
1990-91	Cornwall	OHL	48	1	14	15	18	....	....	....	....	....
1991-92	Cornwall	OHL	60	6	15	21	55	....	....	....	....	....
1992-93	Newmarket	OHL	9	1	15	21	55	....	....	....	....	....
	Kingston	OHL	43	7	26	33	39	8	0	4	4	0

RECCHI, MARK
Right wing. Shoots left. 5'10", 185 lbs.   Born, Kamloops, B.C., February 1, 1968.
(Pittsburgh's 4th choice, 67th overall, in 1988 Entry Draft).

			Regular Season					Playoffs				
Season	Club	Lea	GP	G	A	TP	PIM	GP	G	A	TP	PIM
1985-86	N. Westminster	WHL	72	21	40	61	55	....	....	....	....	....
1986-87	Kamloops	WHL	40	26	50	76	63	13	3	16	19	17
1987-88a	Kamloops	WHL	62	61	*93	154	75	17	10	*21	*31	18
1988-89	**Pittsburgh**	**NHL**	**15**	**1**	**1**	**2**	**0**	....	....	....	....	....
b	Muskegon	IHL	63	50	49	99	86	14	7	*14	*21	28
1989-90	**Pittsburgh**	**NHL**	**74**	**30**	**37**	**67**	**44**	....	....	....	....	....
	Muskegon	IHL	4	7	4	11	2	....	....	....	....	....
1990-91	**Pittsburgh**	**NHL**	**78**	**40**	**73**	**113**	**48**	**24**	**10**	**24**	**34**	**33**
1991-92c	**Pittsburgh**	**NHL**	**58**	**33**	**37**	**70**	**78**	....	....	....	....	....
c	**Philadelphia**	**NHL**	**22**	**10**	**17**	**27**	**18**	....	....	....	....	....
1992-93	**Philadelphia**	**NHL**	**84**	**53**	**70**	**123**	**95**	....	....	....	....	....
	NHL Totals		**331**	**167**	**235**	**402**	**283**	**24**	**10**	**24**	**34**	**33**

a   WHL West All-Star Team (1988)
b   IHL Second All-Star Team (1989)
c   NHL Second All-Star Team (1992)
Played in NHL All-Star Game (1991, 1993)

Traded to **Philadelphia** by **Pittsburgh** with Brian Benning and Los Angeles' first round choice (previously acquired by Pittsburgh — Philadelphia selected Jason Bowen) in 1992 Entry Draft for Rick Tocchet, Kjell Samuelsson and Ken Wregget, February 19, 1992.

REDMOND, KEITH
Left wing. Shoots left. 6'3", 205 lbs.   Born, Richmond Hill, Ont., October 25, 1972.
(Los Angeles' 4th choice, 79th overall, in 1991 Entry Draft).

			Regular Season					Playoffs				
Season	Club	Lea	GP	G	A	TP	PIM	GP	G	A	TP	PIM
1990-91	Bowling Green	CCHA	35	1	3	4	72	....	....	....	....	....
1991-92	Bowling Green	CCHA	8	0	0	0	14	....	....	....	....	....
	Belleville	OHL	16	1	7	8	52	....	....	....	....	....
	Detroit	OHL	25	6	12	18	61	7	1	3	4	49
1992-93	Phoenix	IHL	53	6	10	16	285	....	....	....	....	....

REEKIE, JOE
Defense. Shoots left. 6'3", 215 lbs.   Born, Victoria, B.C., February 22, 1965.
(Buffalo's 6th choice, 119th overall, in 1985 Entry Draft).

			Regular Season					Playoffs				
Season	Club	Lea	GP	G	A	TP	PIM	GP	G	A	TP	PIM
1982-83	North Bay	OHL	59	2	9	11	49	8	0	1	1	11
1983-84	North Bay	OHL	9	1	0	1	18	....	....	....	....	....
	Cornwall	OHL	53	6	27	33	166	3	0	0	0	4
1984-85	Cornwall	OHL	65	19	63	82	134	9	4	13	17	18
1985-86	**Buffalo**	**NHL**	**3**	**0**	**0**	**0**	**14**	....	....	....	....	....
	Rochester	AHL	77	3	25	28	178	....	....	....	....	....
1986-87	**Buffalo**	**NHL**	**56**	**1**	**8**	**9**	**82**	....	....	....	....	....
	Rochester	AHL	22	0	6	6	52	....	....	....	....	....
1987-88	**Buffalo**	**NHL**	**30**	**1**	**4**	**5**	**68**	**2**	**0**	**0**	**0**	**4**
1988-89	**Buffalo**	**NHL**	**15**	**1**	**3**	**4**	**26**	....	....	....	....	....
	Rochester	AHL	21	1	2	3	56	....	....	....	....	....
1989-90	**NY Islanders**	**NHL**	**31**	**1**	**8**	**9**	**43**	....	....	....	....	....
	Springfield	AHL	15	1	4	5	24	....	....	....	....	....
1990-91	**NY Islanders**	**NHL**	**66**	**3**	**16**	**19**	**96**	....	....	....	....	....
	Capital Dist.	AHL	2	1	0	1	0	....	....	....	....	....
1991-92	**NY Islanders**	**NHL**	**54**	**4**	**12**	**16**	**85**	....	....	....	....	....
	Capital Dist.	AHL	3	2	2	4	2	....	....	....	....	....
1992-93	**Tampa Bay**	**NHL**	**42**	**2**	**11**	**13**	**69**	....	....	....	....	....
	NHL Totals		**297**	**13**	**62**	**75**	**483**	**2**	**0**	**0**	**0**	**4**

Traded to **NY Islanders** by **Buffalo** for NY Islanders' sixth round choice (Bill Pye) in 1989 Entry Draft, June 17, 1989. Claimed by **Tampa Bay** from **NY Islanders** in Expansion Draft, June 18, 1992.

REEVES, KYLE
Right wing. Shoots right. 5'11", 190 lbs.   Born, Stonewall, Man., May 12, 1971.
(St. Louis' 2nd choice, 64th overall, in 1991 Entry Draft).

			Regular Season					Playoffs				
Season	Club	Lea	GP	G	A	TP	PIM	GP	G	A	TP	PIM
1988-89	Swift Current	WHL	2	1	1	2	2	....	....	....	....	....
1989-90	Tri-City	WHL	67	67	36	103	94	7	2	1	3	8
1990-91a	Tri-City	WHL	63	*89	40	129	146	3	1	3	4	10
1991-92	Peoria	IHL	60	12	7	19	92	....	....	....	....	....
1992-93	Peoria	IHL	50	17	14	31	83	3	0	2	2	2

a   WHL West Second All-Star Team (1991)

REGNIER, CURT
Right wing. Shoots left. 6'2", 218 lbs.   Born, Prince Albert, Sask., January 24, 1972.
(New Jersey's 6th choice, 121st overall, in 1991 Entry Draft).

			Regular Season					Playoffs				
Season	Club	Lea	GP	G	A	TP	PIM	GP	G	A	TP	PIM
1990-91	Prince Albert	WHL	69	20	39	59	40	3	2	2	4	6
1991-92	Prince Albert	WHL	58	30	42	72	98	10	1	9	10	2
1992-93	Utica	AHL	37	6	4	10	21	2	0	1	1	0

REICHEL, MARTIN   (RIGH-khul)
Right wing. Shoots left. 6'1", 183 lbs.   Born, Most, Czech., November 7, 1973.
(Edmonton's 2nd choice, 37th overall, in 1992 Entry Draft).

			Regular Season					Playoffs				
Season	Club	Lea	GP	G	A	TP	PIM	GP	G	A	TP	PIM
1990-91	Freiburg	Ger.	23	7	8	15	19	....	....	....	....	....
1991-92	Freiburg	Ger.	27	15	16	31	8	4	1	1	2	4
1992-93	Freiburg	Ger.	37	13	9	22	27	9	4	4	8	11

REICHEL, ROBERT   (RIGH-khul)
Center. Shoots left. 5'11", 185 lbs.   Born, Most, Czechoslovakia, June 25, 1971.
(Calgary's 5th choice, 70th overall, in 1989 Entry Draft).

			Regular Season					Playoffs				
Season	Club	Lea	GP	G	A	TP	PIM	GP	G	A	TP	PIM
1987-88	Litvinov	Czech.	36	17	10	27	8	....	....	....	....	....
1988-89	Litvinov	Czech.	44	23	25	48	32	....	....	....	....	....
1989-90	Litvinov	Czech.	52	*49	34	*83		....	....	....	....	....
1990-91	**Calgary**	**NHL**	**66**	**19**	**22**	**41**	**22**	**6**	**1**	**1**	**2**	**0**
1991-92	**Calgary**	**NHL**	**77**	**20**	**34**	**54**	**32**	....	....	....	....	....
1992-93	**Calgary**	**NHL**	**80**	**40**	**48**	**88**	**54**	**6**	**2**	**4**	**6**	**2**
	NHL Totals		**223**	**79**	**104**	**183**	**108**	**12**	**3**	**5**	**8**	**2**

REID, DAVID
Left wing. Shoots left. 6'1", 215 lbs.   Born, Toronto, Ont., May 15, 1964.
(Boston's 4th choice, 60th overall, in 1982 Entry Draft).

			Regular Season					Playoffs				
Season	Club	Lea	GP	G	A	TP	PIM	GP	G	A	TP	PIM
1981-82	Peterborough	OHL	68	10	32	42	41	9	2	3	5	11
1982-83	Peterborough	OHL	70	23	34	57	33	4	3	1	4	0
1983-84	**Boston**	**NHL**	**8**	**1**	**0**	**1**	**2**	....	....	....	....	....
	Peterborough	OHL	60	33	64	97	12	....	....	....	....	....
1984-85	**Boston**	**NHL**	**35**	**14**	**13**	**27**	**27**	**5**	**1**	**0**	**1**	**0**
	Hershey	AHL	43	10	14	24	6	....	....	....	....	....
1985-86	**Boston**	**NHL**	**37**	**10**	**10**	**20**	**10**	....	....	....	....	....
	Moncton	AHL	26	14	18	32	4	....	....	....	....	....
1986-87	**Boston**	**NHL**	**12**	**3**	**3**	**6**	**0**	**2**	**0**	**0**	**0**	**0**
	Moncton	AHL	40	12	22	34	23	5	0	1	1	0
1987-88	**Boston**	**NHL**	**3**	**0**	**0**	**0**	**0**	....	....	....	....	....
	Maine	AHL	63	21	37	58	40	10	6	7	13	0
1988-89	**Toronto**	**NHL**	**77**	**9**	**21**	**30**	**22**	....	....	....	....	....
1989-90	**Toronto**	**NHL**	**70**	**9**	**19**	**28**	**9**	**3**	**0**	**0**	**0**	**0**
1990-91	**Toronto**	**NHL**	**69**	**15**	**13**	**28**	**18**	....	....	....	....	....
1991-92	**Boston**	**NHL**	**43**	**7**	**7**	**14**	**27**	**15**	**2**	**5**	**7**	**4**
	Maine	AHL	12	1	5	6	4	....	....	....	....	....
1992-93	**Boston**	**NHL**	**65**	**20**	**16**	**36**	**10**	....	....	....	....	....
	NHL Totals		**419**	**88**	**102**	**190**	**125**	**25**	**3**	**5**	**8**	**4**

Signed as a free agent by **Toronto**, June 23, 1988. Signed as a free agent by **Boston**, December 1, 1991.

REID, GRAYDEN
Center. Shoots left. 6', 185 lbs.   Born, Mississauga, Ont., January 7, 1972.
(St. Louis' 4th choice, 87th overall, in 1991 Entry Draft).

			Regular Season					Playoffs				
Season	Club	Lea	GP	G	A	TP	PIM	GP	G	A	TP	PIM
1990-91	Owen Sound	OHL	66	23	74	97	58	....	....	....	....	....
1991-92	Owen Sound	OHL	8	2	10	12	4	....	....	....	....	....
	Ottawa	OHL	54	10	26	36	18	11	0	2	2	2
1992-93	Kitchener	OHL	8	4	5	9	4	....	....	....	....	....
	Regina	WHL	52	5	24	29	22	13	3	4	7	4

REID, JARRETT
Center. Shoots right. 5'10", 180 lbs.   Born, Sault Ste. Marie, Ont., March 10, 1973.
(Hartford's 6th choice, 143rd overall, in 1992 Entry Draft).

			Regular Season					Playoffs				
Season	Club	Lea	GP	G	A	TP	PIM	GP	G	A	TP	PIM
1990-91	S.S. Marie	OHL	63	37	29	66	18	14	5	12	17	14
1991-92	S.S. Marie	OHL	61	53	40	93	67	19	5	13	18	17
1992-93	S.S. Marie	OHL	64	36	60	96	28	18	*19	16	*35	20

REIMANN, DANIEL
Defense. Shoots left. 6'1", 190 lbs.   Born, Fridley, MN, December 17, 1972.
(New Jersey's 9th choice, 187th overall, in 1991 Entry Draft).

			Regular Season					Playoffs				
Season	Club	Lea	GP	G	A	TP	PIM	GP	G	A	TP	PIM
1991-92	Des Moines	USHL	47	6	14	20	78	....	....	....	....	....
1992-93	St. Cloud	WCHA	36	5	2	7	58	....	....	....	....	....

REIRDEN, TODD
Defense. Shoots left. 6'4", 175 lbs.   Born, Arlington Heights, IL, June 25, 1971.
(New Jersey's 14th choice, 242nd overall, in 1990 Entry Draft).

			Regular Season					Playoffs				
Season	Club	Lea	GP	G	A	TP	PIM	GP	G	A	TP	PIM
1990-91	Bowling Green	CCHA	28	1	5	6	22	....	....	....	....	....
1991-92	Bowling Green	CCHA	33	8	7	15	34	....	....	....	....	....
1992-93	Bowling Green	CCHA	41	8	17	25	48	....	....	....	....	....

RENBERG, MIKAEL   (REHN-buhrg)
Right wing. Shoots left. 6'1", 205 lbs.   Born, Pitea, Sweden, May 5, 1972.
(Philadelphia's 3rd choice, 40th overall, in 1990 Entry Draft).

			Regular Season					Playoffs				
Season	Club	Lea	GP	G	A	TP	PIM	GP	G	A	TP	PIM
1988-89	Pitea	Swe.2	12	6	3	9		....	....	....	....	....
1989-90	Pitea	Swe.2	29	15	19	34		....	....	....	....	....
1990-91	Lulea	Swe.	29	11	6	17	12	5	1	1	2	4
1991-92	Lulea	Swe.	38	8	14	22	18	2	0	0	0	0
1992-93	Lulea	Swe.	39	19	13	32	61	11	4	4	8	4

RHEAUME, PASCAL
Center. Shoots left. 6', 185 lbs.   Born, Quebec, Que., June 21, 1973.

			Regular Season					Playoffs				
Season	Club	Lea	GP	G	A	TP	PIM	GP	G	A	TP	PIM
1991-92	Trois Rivières	QMJHL	65	17	20	37	84	14	5	4	9	23
1992-93	Sherbrooke	QMJHL	65	28	34	62	88	14	6	5	11	31

Signed as a free agent by **New Jersey**, October 1, 1992.

RICCI, MIKE (REECH-ee)

Center. Shoots left. 6', 190 lbs. Born, Scarborough, Ont., October 27, 1971.
(Philadelphia's 1st choice, 4th overall, in 1990 Entry Draft).

			Regular Season					Playoffs				
Season	Club	Lea	GP	G	A	TP	PIM	GP	G	A	TP	PIM
1987-88	Peterborough	OHL	41	24	37	61	20	....	....	....	....	....
1988-89a	Peterborough	OHL	60	54	52	106	43	17	19	16	35	18
1989-90bcd	Peterborough	OHL	60	52	64	116	39	12	5	7	12	26
1990-91	**Philadelphia**	**NHL**	**68**	**21**	**20**	**41**	**64**	....	....	....	....	....
1991-92	**Philadelphia**	**NHL**	**78**	**20**	**36**	**56**	**93**	....	....	....	....	....
1992-93	**Quebec**	**NHL**	**77**	**27**	**51**	**78**	**123**	**6**	**0**	**6**	**6**	**8**
	NHL Totals		**223**	**68**	**107**	**175**	**280**	**6**	**0**	**6**	**6**	**8**

a OHL Second All-Star Team (1989)
b Canadian Major Junior Player of the Year (1990)
c OHL First All-Star Team (1990)
d OHL Player of the Year (1990)

Traded to **Quebec** by **Philadelphia** with Peter Forsberg, Steve Duchesne, Kerry Huffman, Ron Hextall, Chris Simon, Philadelphia's first choice in the 1993 (Jocelyn Thibault) and 1994 Entry Drafts and cash for Eric Lindros, June 30, 1992.

RICCIARDI, JEFF

Defense. Shoots left. 5'10", 203 lbs. Born, Thunder Bay, Ont., June 22, 1971.
(Winnipeg's 8th choice, 159th overall, in 1991 Entry Draft).

			Regular Season					Playoffs				
Season	Club	Lea	GP	G	A	TP	PIM	GP	G	A	TP	PIM
1990-91	Ottawa	OHL	54	12	40	52	172	17	1	11	12	61
1991-92a	Ottawa	OHL	61	15	41	56	220	11	3	8	11	45
1992-93	Providence	AHL	3	0	0	0	0	....	....	....	....	....
	Johnstown	ECHL	61	7	29	36	248	5	2	2	4	6

a OHL Second All-Star Team (1992)

Traded to **Boston** by **Winnipeg** for future considerations, September 8, 1992.

RICE, STEVEN

Right wing. Shoots right. 6', 215 lbs. Born, Kitchener, Ont., May 26, 1971.
(NY Rangers' 1st choice, 20th overall, in 1989 Entry Draft).

			Regular Season					Playoffs				
Season	Club	Lea	GP	G	A	TP	PIM	GP	G	A	TP	PIM
1987-88	Kitchener	OHL	59	11	14	25	43	4	0	1	1	0
1988-89	Kitchener	OHL	64	36	30	66	42	5	2	1	3	8
1989-90ab	Kitchener	OHL	58	39	37	76	102	16	4	8	12	24
1990-91	**NY Rangers**	**NHL**	**11**	**1**	**1**	**2**	**4**	**2**	**2**	**1**	**3**	**6**
	Binghamton	AHL	8	4	1	5	12	5	2	0	2	2
c	Kitchener	OHL	29	30	30	60	43	6	5	6	11	2
1991-92	**Edmonton**	**NHL**	**3**	**0**	**0**	**0**	**2**	....	....	....	....	....
	Cape Breton	AHL	45	32	20	52	38	5	4	4	8	10
1992-93	**Edmonton**	**NHL**	**28**	**2**	**5**	**7**	**28**	....	....	....	....	....
	Cape Breton	AHL	51	34	28	62	63	14	4	6	10	22
	NHL Totals		**42**	**3**	**6**	**9**	**34**	**2**	**2**	**1**	**3**	**6**

a OHL Third All-Star Team (1990)
b Memorial Cup All-Star Team (1990)
c OHL Second All-Star Team (1991)
d AHL Second All-Star Team (1993)

Traded to **Edmonton** by **NY Rangers** with Bernie Nicholls and Louie DeBrusk for Mark Messier and future considerations, October 4, 1991.

RICHARD, JEAN-MARC

Defense. Shoots left. 5'11", 178 lbs. Born, St.-Raymond, Que., October 8, 1966.

			Regular Season					Playoffs				
Season	Club	Lea	GP	G	A	TP	PIM	GP	G	A	TP	PIM
1985-86a	Chicoutimi	QMJHL	72	20	87	107	111	9	3	5	8	14
1986-87a	Chicoutimi	QMJHL	67	21	81	102	105	16	6	25	31	28
1987-88	**Quebec**	**NHL**	**4**	**2**	**1**	**3**	**2**	....	....	....	....	....
	Fredericton	AHL	68	14	42	56	52	7	2	1	3	4
1988-89	Halifax	AHL	57	8	25	33	38	4	1	0	1	4
1989-90	**Quebec**	**NHL**	**1**	**0**	**0**	**0**	**0**	....	....	....	....	....
	Halifax	AHL	40	1	24	25	38	....	....	....	....	....
1990-91	Halifax	AHL	80	7	41	48	76	....	....	....	....	....
	Fort Wayne	IHL	1	0	0	0	0	19	3	9	12	8
1991-92bc	Fort Wayne	IHL	82	18	68	86	109	7	0	5	5	20
1992-93	San Diego	IHL	6	1	0	1	4	....	....	....	....	....
	Fort Wayne	IHL	52	10	33	43	48	12	6	11	17	6
	NHL Totals		**5**	**2**	**1**	**3**	**2**	....	....	....	....	....

a QMJHL First All-Star Team (1986, 1987)
b Won Governors' Trophy (Top Defenseman-IHL) (1992)
c IHL First All-Star Team (1992)

Signed as a free agent by **Quebec**, April 13, 1987.

RICHARDS, TODD

Defense. Shoots right. 6', 194 lbs. Born, Robindale, MN, October 20, 1966.
(Montreal's 3rd choice, 33rd overall, in 1985 Entry Draft).

			Regular Season					Playoffs				
Season	Club	Lea	GP	G	A	TP	PIM	GP	G	A	TP	PIM
1985-86	U. Minnesota	WCHA	38	6	23	29	38	....	....	....	....	....
1986-87	U. Minnesota	WCHA	49	8	43	51	70	....	....	....	....	....
1987-88a	U. Minnesota	WCHA	34	10	30	40	26	....	....	....	....	....
1988-89abc	U. Minnesota	WCHA	46	6	32	38	60	....	....	....	....	....
1989-90	Sherbrooke	AHL	71	6	18	24	73	5	1	2	3	6
1990-91	Fredericton	AHL	3	0	1	1	2	....	....	....	....	....
	Hartford	**NHL**	**2**	**0**	**4**	**4**	**2**	**6**	**0**	**0**	**0**	**2**
	Springfield	AHL	71	10	41	51	62	14	2	8	10	2
1991-92	**Hartford**	**NHL**	**6**	**0**	**0**	**0**	**2**	**5**	**0**	**3**	**3**	**4**
	Springfield	AHL	43	6	23	29	33	11	0	3	3	2
1992-93	Springfield	AHL	78	13	42	55	53	9	1	5	6	2
	NHL Totals		**8**	**0**	**4**	**4**	**4**	**11**	**0**	**3**	**3**	**6**

a WCHA Second All-Star Team (1988, 1989)
b NCAA West Second All-American Team (1989)
c NCAA All-Tournament Team (1989)

Traded to **Hartford** by **Montreal** for future considerations, October 11, 1990.

RICHARDS, TRAVIS

Defense. Shoots left. 6'1", 185 lbs. Born, Crystal, MN, March 22, 1970.
(Minnesota's 6th choice, 169th overall, in 1988 Entry Draft).

			Regular Season					Playoffs				
Season	Club	Lea	GP	G	A	TP	PIM	GP	G	A	TP	PIM
1988-89	U. Minnesota	WCHA			DID NOT PLAY							
1989-90	U. Minnesota	WCHA	45	4	24	28	38	....	....	....	....	....
1990-91	U. Minnesota	WCHA	45	9	25	34	28	....	....	....	....	....
1991-92a	U. Minnesota	WCHA	41	10	22	32	65	....	....	....	....	....
1992-93a	U. Minnesota	WCHA	42	12	26	38	52	....	....	....	....	....

a WCHA Second All-Star Team (1992, 1993)

RICHARDSON, LUKE

Defense. Shoots left. 6'4", 210 lbs. Born, Ottawa, Ont., March 26, 1969.
(Toronto's 1st choice, 7th overall, in 1987 Entry Draft).

			Regular Season					Playoffs				
Season	Club	Lea	GP	G	A	TP	PIM	GP	G	A	TP	PIM
1985-86	Peterborough	OHL	63	6	18	24	57	16	2	1	3	50
1986-87	Peterborough	OHL	59	13	32	45	70	12	0	5	5	24
1987-88	**Toronto**	**NHL**	**78**	**4**	**6**	**10**	**90**	**2**	**0**	**0**	**0**	**0**
1988-89	**Toronto**	**NHL**	**55**	**2**	**7**	**9**	**106**	....	....	....	....	....
1989-90	**Toronto**	**NHL**	**67**	**4**	**14**	**18**	**122**	**5**	**0**	**0**	**0**	**22**
1990-91	**Toronto**	**NHL**	**78**	**1**	**9**	**10**	**238**	....	....	....	....	....
1991-92	**Edmonton**	**NHL**	**75**	**2**	**19**	**21**	**118**	**16**	**0**	**5**	**5**	**45**
1992-93	**Edmonton**	**NHL**	**82**	**3**	**10**	**13**	**142**	....	....	....	....	....
	NHL Totals		**435**	**16**	**65**	**81**	**816**	**23**	**0**	**5**	**5**	**67**

Traded to **Edmonton** by **Toronto** with Vincent Damphousse, Peter Ing, Scott Thornton, future considerations and cash for Grant Fuhr, Glenn Anderson and Craig Berube, September 19, 1991.

RICHER, STEPHANE J. G. (REE-shay)

Defense. Shoots right. 5'11", 190 lbs. Born, Hull, Que., April 28, 1966.

			Regular Season					Playoffs				
Season	Club	Lea	GP	G	A	TP	PIM	GP	G	A	TP	PIM
1986-87	Hull	QMJHL	33	6	22	28	74	8	3	4	7	17
1987-88	Baltimore	AHL	22	0	3	3	6	....	....	....	....	....
	Sherbrooke	AHL	41	4	7	11	46	5	1	0	1	10
1988-89	Sherbrooke	AHL	70	7	26	33	158	6	1	2	3	18
1989-90	Sherbrooke	AHL	60	10	12	22	85	12	4	9	13	16
1990-91	New Haven	AHL	3	0	1	1	0	....	....	....	....	....
	Phoenix	IHL	67	11	38	49	48	11	4	6	10	6
1991-92a	Fredericton	AHL	80	17	47	64	74	7	0	5	5	18
1992-93	**Tampa Bay**	**NHL**	**3**	**0**	**0**	**0**	**0**	....	....	....	....	....
	Atlanta	IHL	3	0	4	4	4	....	....	....	....	....
	Boston	**NHL**	**21**	**1**	**4**	**5**	**18**	**3**	**0**	**0**	**0**	**0**
	NHL Totals		**24**	**1**	**4**	**5**	**18**	**3**	**0**	**0**	**0**	**0**

a AHL Second All-Star Team (1992)

Signed as a free agent by **Montreal**, January 9, 1988. Signed as a free agent by **Los Angeles**, July 11, 1990. Signed as a free agent by **Tampa Bay**, July 29, 1992. Traded to **Boston** by **Tampa Bay** for Bob Beers, October 28, 1992. Claimed by **Florida** from **Boston** in Expansion Draft, June 24, 1993.

RICHER, STEPHANE J. J. (REE-shay)

Right wing. Shoots right. 6'2", 215 lbs. Born, Ripon, Que., June 7, 1966.
(Montreal's 3rd choice, 29th overall, in 1984 Entry Draft).

			Regular Season					Playoffs				
Season	Club	Lea	GP	G	A	TP	PIM	GP	G	A	TP	PIM
1983-84a	Granby	QMJHL	67	39	37	76	58	3	1	1	2	4
1984-85	Granby	QMJHL	30	30	27	57	31	....	....	....	....	....
b	Chicoutimi	QMJHL	27	31	32	63	40	12	13	13	26	25
	Montreal	**NHL**	**1**	**0**	**0**	**0**	**0**	....	....	....	....	....
	Sherbrooke	AHL	....	....	....	....	....	9	6	3	9	10
1985-86	**Montreal**	**NHL**	**65**	**21**	**16**	**37**	**50**	**16**	**4**	**1**	**5**	**23**
1986-87	**Montreal**	**NHL**	**57**	**20**	**19**	**39**	**80**	**5**	**3**	**2**	**5**	**0**
	Sherbrooke	AHL	12	10	4	14	11	....	....	....	....	....
1987-88	**Montreal**	**NHL**	**72**	**50**	**28**	**78**	**72**	**8**	**7**	**5**	**12**	**6**
1988-89	**Montreal**	**NHL**	**68**	**25**	**35**	**60**	**61**	**21**	**6**	**5**	**11**	**14**
1989-90	**Montreal**	**NHL**	**75**	**51**	**40**	**91**	**46**	**9**	**7**	**3**	**10**	**2**
1990-91	**Montreal**	**NHL**	**75**	**31**	**30**	**61**	**53**	**13**	**9**	**5**	**14**	**6**
1991-92	**New Jersey**	**NHL**	**74**	**29**	**35**	**64**	**25**	**7**	**1**	**2**	**3**	**0**
1992-93	**New Jersey**	**NHL**	**78**	**38**	**35**	**73**	**44**	**5**	**2**	**2**	**4**	**4**
	NHL Totals		**565**	**265**	**238**	**503**	**431**	**84**	**39**	**25**	**64**	**55**

a QMJHL Rookie of the Year (1984)
b QMJHL Second All-Star Team (1985)

Played in NHL All-Star Game (1990)

Traded to **New Jersey** by **Montreal** with Tom Chorske for Kirk Muller and Roland Melanson, September 20, 1991.

RICHTER, BARRY

Defense. Shoots left. 6'2", 185 lbs. Born, Madison, WI, September 11, 1970.
(Hartford's 2nd choice, 32nd overall, in 1988 Entry Draft).

			Regular Season					Playoffs				
Season	Club	Lea	GP	G	A	TP	PIM	GP	G	A	TP	PIM
1989-90	U. Wisconsin	WCHA	42	13	23	36	36	....	....	....	....	....
1990-91	U. Wisconsin	WCHA	43	15	20	35	42	....	....	....	....	....
1991-92a	U. Wisconsin	WCHA	39	10	25	35	62	....	....	....	....	....
1992-93bc	U. Wisconsin	WCHA	42	14	32	46	74	....	....	....	....	....

a NCAA All-Tournament Team (1992)
b WCHA First All-Star Team (1993)
c NCAA West First All-American Team (1993)

RIDLEY, MIKE

Center. Shoots left. 6', 195 lbs. Born, Winnipeg, Man., July 8, 1963.

			Regular Season					Playoffs				
Season	Club	Lea	GP	G	A	TP	PIM	GP	G	A	TP	PIM
1983-84a	U. of Manitoba	GPAC	46	39	41	80	....	....	....	....	....	....
1984-85b	U. of Manitoba	GPAC	30	29	38	67	48	....	....	....	....	....
1985-86c	**NY Rangers**	**NHL**	**80**	**22**	**43**	**65**	**69**	**16**	**6**	**8**	**14**	**26**
1986-87	**NY Rangers**	**NHL**	**38**	**16**	**20**	**36**	**20**	....	....	....	....	....
	Washington	**NHL**	**40**	**15**	**19**	**34**	**20**	**7**	**2**	**1**	**3**	**6**
1987-88	**Washington**	**NHL**	**70**	**28**	**31**	**59**	**22**	**14**	**6**	**5**	**11**	**10**
1988-89	**Washington**	**NHL**	**80**	**41**	**48**	**89**	**49**	**6**	**0**	**5**	**5**	**2**
1989-90	**Washington**	**NHL**	**74**	**30**	**43**	**73**	**27**	**14**	**3**	**4**	**7**	**8**
1990-91	**Washington**	**NHL**	**79**	**23**	**48**	**71**	**26**	**11**	**3**	**4**	**7**	**8**
1991-92	**Washington**	**NHL**	**80**	**29**	**40**	**69**	**38**	**7**	**0**	**11**	**11**	**0**
1992-93	**Washington**	**NHL**	**84**	**26**	**56**	**82**	**44**	**6**	**1**	**5**	**6**	**0**
	NHL Totals		**625**	**230**	**348**	**578**	**315**	**81**	**21**	**43**	**64**	**60**

a Canadian University Player of the Year; CIAU All-Canadian, GPAC MVP and First All-Star Team (1984)
b CIAU All-Canadian, GPAC First All-Star Team (1985)
c NHL All-Rookie Team (1986)

Played in NHL All-Star Game (1989)

Signed as a free agent by **NY Rangers**, September 26, 1985. Traded to **Washington** by **NY Rangers** with Bob Crawford and Kelly Miller for Bob Carpenter and Washington's second round choice (Jason Prosofsky) in 1989 Entry Draft, January 1, 1987.

RIEHL, KEVIN

Center. Shoots left. 5'10", 180 lbs. Born, Leader, Sask., March 11, 1971.
(New Jersey's 11th choice, 231st overall, in 1991 Entry Draft).

			Regular Season					Playoffs				
Season	Club	Lea	GP	G	A	TP	PIM	GP	G	A	TP	PIM
1990-91	Medicine Hat	WHL	72	66	50	116	43	....	....	....	....	....
1991-92	Medicine Hat	WHL	69	*65	50	115	125	4	2	2	4	4
1992-93	Utica	AHL	3	0	0	0	2	....	....	....	....	....
	Cincinnati	IHL	3	0	2	2	0	....	....	....	....	....
	Birmingham	ECHL	34	23	18	41	36	....	....	....	....	....

RIIHIJARVI, HEIKKI (ree-hee-YAHR-vee)

Defense. Shoots left. 6'5", 222 lbs. Born, Salla, Finland, June 4, 1966.
(Edmonton's 8th choice, 147th overall, in 1984 Entry Draft).

			Regular Season					Playoffs				
Season	Club	Lea	GP	G	A	TP	PIM	GP	G	A	TP	PIM
1983-84	S-Kiekko	Fin.3	23	14	11	25	6	....	....	....	....	....
1984-85	TPS	Fin.	4	0	0	0	2	....	....	....	....	....
1986-87	Karpat	Fin.	36	4	4	8	10	9	1	0	1	2
1987-88	Karpat	Fin.	21	0	5	5	0	....	....	....	....	....
1988-89	Karpat	Fin.	43	8	11	19	14	5	0	2	2	4
1989-90	Jokerit	Fin.	44	3	10	13	16	....	....	....	....	....
1990-91	Jokerit	Fin.	36	4	4	8	12	....	....	....	....	....
1991-92	Jokerit	Fin.	43	3	8	11	10	10	2	2	4	8
1992-93	Jokerit	Fin.	43	7	5	12	14	3	0	0	0	0

RIIHIJARVI, JUHA (ree-hee-YAHR-vee)

Right wing. Shoots left. 6'2", 207 lbs. Born, Kemin Mlk, Finland, December 15, 1969.
(Edmonton's 11th choice, 254th overall, in 1991 Entry Draft).

			Regular Season					Playoffs				
Season	Club	Lea	GP	G	A	TP	PIM	GP	G	A	TP	PIM
1987-88	Karpat	Fin.	1	0	0	0	0	....	....	....	....	....
1988-89	Karpat	Fin.	44	11	23	34	22	....	....	....	....	....
1989-90	Karpat	Fin.2				UNAVAILABLE						
1990-91	Karpat	Fin.2	42	29	41	70	34	....	....	....	....	....
1991-92	JyP HT	Fin.	38	29	33	62	37	10	4	4	8	10
1992-93	JyP HT	Fin.	41	25	31	56	38	9	4	2	6	2

RIVERS, JAMIE

Defense. Shoots left. 6', 180 lbs. Born, Ottawa, Ont., March 16, 1975.
(St. Louis' 2nd choice, 63rd overall, in 1993 Entry Draft).

			Regular Season					Playoffs				
Season	Club	Lea	GP	G	A	TP	PIM	GP	G	A	TP	PIM
1991-92	Sudbury	OHL	55	3	13	16	20	8	0	0	0	0
1992-93	Sudbury	OHL	62	12	43	55	20	14	7	19	26	4

RIVERS, SHAWN

Defense. Shoots left. 5'10", 185 lbs. Born, Ottawa, Ont., January 30, 1971.

			Regular Season					Playoffs				
Season	Club	Lea	GP	G	A	TP	PIM	GP	G	A	TP	PIM
1988-89	St. Lawrence	ECAC	36	3	23	26	20	....	....	....	....	....
1989-90	St. Lawrence	ECAC	26	3	14	17	29	....	....	....	....	....
1990-91	Sudbury	OHL	66	18	33	51	43	5	2	7	9	0
1991-92	Sudbury	OHL	64	26	54	80	34	11	0	4	4	10
1992-93	**Tampa Bay**	**NHL**	**4**	**0**	**2**	**2**	**2**	....	....	....	....	....
	Atlanta	IHL	78	9	34	43	101	9	1	3	4	8
	NHL Totals		**4**	**0**	**2**	**2**	**2**	....	....	....	....	....

Signed as a free agent by **Tampa Bay**, June 29, 1992.

RIVET, CRAIG

Defense. Shoots right. 6'2", 178 lbs. Born, North Bay, Ont., September 13, 1974.
(Montreal's 4th choice, 68th overall, in 1992 Entry Draft).

			Regular Season					Playoffs				
Season	Club	Lea	GP	G	A	TP	PIM	GP	G	A	TP	PIM
1991-92	Kingston	OHL	66	5	21	26	97	....	....	....	....	....
1992-93	Kingston	OHL	64	19	55	74	117	16	5	7	12	39

ROACH, GARY

Defense. Shoots left. 6'1", 180 lbs. Born, Sault Ste. Marie, Ont., February 4, 1975.
(NY Rangers' 5th choice, 112th overall, in 1993 Entry Draft).

			Regular Season					Playoffs				
Season	Club	Lea	GP	G	A	TP	PIM	GP	G	A	TP	PIM
1991-92	S.S. Marie	OHL	41	2	9	11	6	9	0	0	0	0
1992-93	S.S. Marie	OHL	65	4	27	31	31	18	0	8	8	4

ROB, LUBOS

Center. Shoots left. 5'11", 183 lbs. Born, Budejovice, Czech., August 5, 1970.
(NY Rangers' 7th choice, 99th overall, in 1990 Entry Draft).

			Regular Season					Playoffs				
Season	Club	Lea	GP	G	A	TP	PIM	GP	G	A	TP	PIM
1989-90	Budejovice	Czech.	42	16	24	40	....	....	....	....	....	....
1990-91						UNAVAILABLE						
1991-92						UNAVAILABLE						
1992-93	Budejovice	Czech.	40	23	21	44	....	....	....	....	....	....

ROBERGE, MARIO (ro-BAIRZH)

Left wing. Shoots left. 5'11", 185 lbs. Born, Quebec City, Que., January 25, 1964.

			Regular Season					Playoffs				
Season	Club	Lea	GP	G	A	TP	PIM	GP	G	A	TP	PIM
1987-88	Pt. Basques	Sr.	35	25	64	89	152	....	....	....	....	....
1988-89	Sherbrooke	AHL	58	4	9	13	249	6	0	2	2	8
1989-90	Sherbrooke	AHL	73	13	27	40	247	12	5	2	7	53
1990-91	**Montreal**	**NHL**	**5**	**0**	**0**	**0**	**21**	**12**	**0**	**0**	**0**	**24**
	Fredericton	AHL	68	12	27	39	*365	2	0	2	2	5
1991-92	**Montreal**	**NHL**	**20**	**2**	**1**	**3**	**62**	....	....	....	....	....
	Fredericton	AHL	6	1	2	3	20	7	0	2	2	20
1992-93	**Montreal**	**NHL**	**50**	**4**	**4**	**8**	**142**	**3**	**0**	**0**	**0**	**0**
	NHL Totals		**75**	**6**	**5**	**11**	**225**	**15**	**0**	**0**	**0**	**24**

Signed as a free agent by **Montreal**, October 5, 1988.

ROBERGE, SERGE (ro-BAIRZH)

Right wing. Shoots right. 6'1", 195 lbs. Born, Quebec City, Que., March 31, 1965.

			Regular Season					Playoffs				
Season	Club	Lea	GP	G	A	TP	PIM	GP	G	A	TP	PIM
1984-85	Drummondville	QMJHL	45	8	19	27	299	....	....	....	....	....
1985-86						DID NOT PLAY						
1986-87	Virginia	ACHL	47	9	15	24	346	....	....	....	....	....
1987-88	Sherbrooke	AHL	30	0	1	1	130	5	0	0	0	21
1988-89	Sherbrooke	AHL	65	5	7	12	352	6	0	1	1	10
1989-90	Sherbrooke	AHL	66	8	5	13	343	12	2	0	2	44
1990-91	**Quebec**	**NHL**	**9**	**0**	**0**	**0**	**24**	....	....	....	....	....
	Halifax	AHL	52	0	5	5	152	....	....	....	....	....
1991-92	Halifax	AHL	66	2	8	10	319	....	....	....	....	....
1992-93	Halifax	AHL	16	2	2	4	34	....	....	....	....	....
	Utica	AHL	28	0	3	3	85	1	0	0	0	0
	NHL Totals		**9**	**0**	**0**	**0**	**24**	....	....	....	....	....

Signed as a free agent by **Montreal**, January 25, 1988. Signed as a free agent by **Quebec**, December 28, 1990.

ROBERTS, DAVID

Left wing. Shoots left. 6', 185 lbs. Born, Alameda, CA, May 28, 1970.
(St. Louis' 5th choice, 114th overall, in 1989 Entry Draft).

			Regular Season					Playoffs				
Season	Club	Lea	GP	G	A	TP	PIM	GP	G	A	TP	PIM
1989-90a	U. of Michigan	CCHA	42	21	32	53	46	....	....	....	....	....
1990-91bc	U. of Michigan	CCHA	43	40	35	75	58	....	....	....	....	....
1991-92	U. of Michigan	CCHA	44	16	42	58	68	....	....	....	....	....
1992-93b	U. of Michigan	CCHA	40	27	38	65	40	....	....	....	....	....

a CCHA Rookie of the Year (1990)
b CCHA Second All-Star Team (1991, 1993)
c NCAA West Second All-American Team (1991)

ROBERTS, GARY

Left wing. Shoots left. 6'1", 190 lbs. Born, North York, Ont., May 23, 1966.
(Calgary's 1st choice, 12th overall, in 1984 Entry Draft).

			Regular Season					Playoffs				
Season	Club	Lea	GP	G	A	TP	PIM	GP	G	A	TP	PIM
1982-83	Ottawa	OHL	53	12	8	20	83	5	1	0	1	19
1983-84	Ottawa	OHL	48	27	30	57	144	13	10	7	17	62
1984-85	Moncton	AHL	7	4	2	6	7	....	....	....	....	....
a	Ottawa	OHL	59	44	62	106	186	5	2	8	10	10
1985-86a	Ottawa	OHL	24	26	25	51	83	....	....	....	....	....
a	Guelph	OHL	23	18	15	33	65	20	18	13	31	43
1986-87	**Calgary**	**NHL**	**32**	**5**	**10**	**15**	**85**	**2**	**0**	**0**	**0**	**4**
	Moncton	AHL	38	20	18	38	72	....	....	....	....	....
1987-88	**Calgary**	**NHL**	**74**	**13**	**15**	**28**	**282**	**9**	**2**	**3**	**5**	**29**
1988-89	**Calgary**	**NHL**	**71**	**22**	**16**	**38**	**250**	**22**	**5**	**7**	**12**	**57**
1989-90	**Calgary**	**NHL**	**78**	**39**	**33**	**72**	**222**	**6**	**2**	**5**	**7**	**41**
1990-91	**Calgary**	**NHL**	**80**	**22**	**31**	**53**	**252**	**7**	**1**	**3**	**4**	**18**
1991-92	**Calgary**	**NHL**	**76**	**53**	**37**	**90**	**207**	....	....	....	....	....
1992-93	**Calgary**	**NHL**	**58**	**38**	**41**	**79**	**172**	**5**	**1**	**6**	**7**	**43**
	NHL Totals		**469**	**192**	**183**	**375**	**1470**	**51**	**11**	**24**	**35**	**192**

a OHL Second All-Star Team (1985, 1986)

Played in NHL All-Star Game (1992, 1993)

ROBERTS, GORDON (GORDIE)

Defense. Shoots left. 6'1", 195 lbs. Born, Detroit, MI, October 2, 1957.
(Montreal's 7th choice, 54th overall, in 1977 Amateur Draft).

			Regular Season					Playoffs				
Season	Club	Lea	GP	G	A	TP	PIM	GP	G	A	TP	PIM
1974-75	Victoria	WHL	53	19	45	64	145	12	1	9	10	42
1975-76	New England	WHA	77	3	19	22	102	17	2	9	11	36
1976-77	New England	WHA	77	13	33	46	169	5	2	2	4	6
1977-78	New England	WHA	78	15	46	61	118	14	0	5	5	29
1978-79	New England	WHA	79	11	46	57	113	10	0	4	4	10
1979-80	Hartford	NHL	80	8	28	36	89	3	1	1	2	2
1980-81	Hartford	NHL	27	2	11	13	81	....	....	....	....	....
	Minnesota	NHL	50	6	31	37	94	19	1	5	6	17
1981-82	Minnesota	NHL	79	4	30	34	119	4	0	3	3	27
1982-83	Minnesota	NHL	80	3	41	44	103	9	1	5	6	14
1983-84	Minnesota	NHL	77	8	45	53	132	15	3	7	10	23
1984-85	Minnesota	NHL	78	6	36	42	112	9	1	6	7	6
1985-86	Minnesota	NHL	76	2	21	23	101	5	0	4	4	8
1986-87	Minnesota	NHL	67	3	10	13	68	....	....	....	....	....
1987-88	Minnesota	NHL	48	1	10	11	103	....	....	....	....	....
	Philadelphia	NHL	11	1	2	3	15	....	....	....	....	....
	St. Louis	NHL	11	1	3	4	25	10	1	2	3	33
1988-89	St. Louis	NHL	77	2	24	26	90	10	1	7	8	8
1989-90	St. Louis	NHL	75	3	14	17	140	10	0	2	2	26
1990-91	St. Louis	NHL	3	0	1	1	8	....	....	....	....	....
	Peoria	IHL	6	0	8	8	4	....	....	....	....	....
	Pittsburgh	NHL	61	3	12	15	70	24	1	2	3	63
1991-92	Pittsburgh	NHL	73	2	22	24	87	19	0	2	2	32
1992-93	Boston	NHL	65	5	12	17	105	4	0	0	0	6
	NHL Totals		1038	60	353	413	1542	141	10	46	56	265

Claimed by **Hartford** from **Montreal** in 1979 Expansion Draft, June 22, 1979. Traded to **Minnesota** by **Hartford** for Mike Fidler, December 16, 1980. Traded to **Philadelphia** by **Minnesota** for future considerations, February 8, 1988. Traded to **St. Louis** by **Philadelphia** for future considerations, March 8, 1988. Traded to **Pittsburgh** by **St. Louis** for future considerations, October 27, 1990. Signed as a free agent by **Boston**, July 23, 1992.

ROBINSON, ROBERT (ROB)

Defense. Shoots left. 6'1", 214 lbs. Born, St. Catharines, Ont., April 19, 1967.
(St. Louis' 6th choice, 117th overall, in 1987 Entry Draft).

			Regular Season					Playoffs				
Season	Club	Lea	GP	G	A	TP	PIM	GP	G	A	TP	PIM
1985-86	Miami-Ohio	CCHA	38	1	9	10	24	....	....	....	....	....
1986-87	Miami-Ohio	CCHA	33	3	5	8	32	....	....	....	....	....
1987-88	Miami-Ohio	CCHA	35	1	3	4	56	....	....	....	....	....
1988-89	Miami-Ohio	CCHA	30	3	4	7	42	....	....	....	....	....
	Peoria	IHL	11	2	0	2	6	....	....	....	....	....
1989-90	Peoria	IHL	60	2	11	13	72	5	0	1	1	10
1990-91a	Peoria	IHL	79	2	21	23	42	19	0	6	6	8
1991-92	St. Louis	NHL	22	0	1	1	8	....	....	....	....	....
	Peoria	IHL	35	1	10	11	29	10	0	2	2	12
1992-93	Peoria	IHL	34	0	4	4	38	....	....	....	....	....
	NHL Totals		22	0	1	1	8	....	....	....	....	....

a IHL Second All-Star Team (1991)

Traded to **Tampa Bay** by **St. Louis** for future considerations, June 19, 1992.

ROBITAILLE, LUC (ROH-buh-tigh)

Left wing. Shoots left. 6'1", 190 lbs. Born, Montreal, Que., February 17, 1966.
(Los Angeles' 9th choice, 171st overall, in 1984 Entry Draft).

			Regular Season					Playoffs				
Season	Club	Lea	GP	G	A	TP	PIM	GP	G	A	TP	PIM
1983-84	Hull	QMJHL	70	32	53	85	48	....	....	....	....	....
1984-85a	Hull	QMJHL	64	55	94	149	115	5	4	2	6	27
1985-86bcd	Hull	QMJHL	63	68	123	191	91	15	17	27	44	28
1986-87ef	Los Angeles	NHL	79	45	39	84	28	5	1	4	5	2
1987-88g	Los Angeles	NHL	80	53	58	111	82	5	2	5	7	18
1988-89g	Los Angeles	NHL	78	46	52	98	65	11	2	6	8	10
1989-90g	Los Angeles	NHL	80	52	49	101	38	10	5	5	10	10
1990-91g	Los Angeles	NHL	76	45	46	91	68	12	12	4	16	22
1991-92f	Los Angeles	NHL	80	44	63	107	95	6	3	4	7	12
1992-93g	Los Angeles	NHL	84	63	62	125	100	24	9	13	22	28
	NHL Totals		557	348	369	717	476	73	34	41	75	102

a QMJHL Second All-Star Team (1985)
b QMJHL First All-Star Team (1986)
c QMJHL Player of the Year (1986)
d Canadian Major Junior Player of the Year (1986)
e Won Calder Memorial Trophy (1987)
f NHL Second All-Star Team (1987, 1992)
g NHL First All-Star Team (1988, 1989, 1990, 1991, 1993)

Played in NHL All-Star Game (1988-93)

ROCHE, DAVE

Center. Shoots left. 6'4", 224 lbs. Born, Lindsay, Ont., June 13, 1975.
(Pittsburgh's 3rd choice, 62nd overall, in 1993 Entry Draft).

			Regular Season					Playoffs				
Season	Club	Lea	GP	G	A	TP	PIM	GP	G	A	TP	PIM
1991-92	Peterborough	OHL	62	10	17	27	134	10	0	0	0	34
1992-93	Peterborough	OHL	56	40	60	100	105	21	14	15	29	42

RODERICK, JOHN

Defense. Shoots left. 6'2", 195 lbs. Born, Cambridge, MA, February 25, 1971.
(St. Louis' 9th choice, 177th overall, in 1989 Entry Draft).

			Regular Season					Playoffs				
Season	Club	Lea	GP	G	A	TP	PIM	GP	G	A	TP	PIM
1989-90	St. Lawrence	ECAC	16	0	1	1	20	....	....	....	....	....
1990-91	St. Lawrence	ECAC	21	0	2	2	20	....	....	....	....	....
1991-92	St. Lawrence	ECAC	28	1	1	2	40	....	....	....	....	....
1992-93	St. Lawrence	ECAC	27	2	2	4	40	....	....	....	....	....

ROENICK, JEREMY (ROH-nihk)

Center. Shoots right. 6', 170 lbs. Born, Boston, MA, January 17, 1970.
(Chicago's 1st choice, 8th overall, in 1988 Entry Draft).

			Regular Season					Playoffs				
Season	Club	Lea	GP	G	A	TP	PIM	GP	G	A	TP	PIM
1988-89a	Hull	QMJHL	28	34	36	70	14	....	....	....	....	....
	U.S. Jr. Nat'l.	....	11	8	8	16	0	....	....	....	....	....
	Chicago	NHL	20	9	9	18	4	10	1	3	4	7
1989-90	Chicago	NHL	78	26	40	66	54	20	11	7	18	8
1990-91	Chicago	NHL	79	41	53	94	80	6	3	5	8	4
1991-92	Chicago	NHL	80	53	50	103	98	18	12	10	22	12
1992-93	Chicago	NHL	84	50	57	107	86	4	1	2	3	2
	NHL Totals		341	179	209	388	322	58	28	27	55	33

a QMJHL Second All-Star Team (1989)

Played in NHL All-Star Game (1991-93)

ROENICK, TREVOR

Right wing. Shoots right. 6'1", 200 lbs. Born, Derby, CT, October 7, 1974.
(Hartford's 3rd choice, 84th overall, in 1993 Entry Draft).

			Regular Season					Playoffs				
Season	Club	Lea	GP	G	A	TP	PIM	GP	G	A	TP	PIM
1991-92	Thayer	HS	26	16	16	32	8	....	....	....	....	....
1992-93	Jr. Bruins	NEJHL	58	61	48	109	94	....	....	....	....	....

ROHLIN, LEIF (roh-LEEN)

Defense. Shoots left. 6'1", 198 lbs. Born, Vasteras, Sweden, February 26, 1968.
(Vancouver's 2nd choice, 33rd overall, in 1988 Entry Draft).

			Regular Season					Playoffs				
Season	Club	Lea	GP	G	A	TP	PIM	GP	G	A	TP	PIM
1986-87	Vasteras	Swe.2	27	2	5	7	12	12	0	2	2	8
1987-88	Vasteras	Swe.2	30	2	15	17	46	7	0	4	4	8
1988-89	Vasteras	Swe.	22	3	7	10	18	....	....	....	....	....
1989-90	Vasteras	Swe.	32	3	6	9	40	2	0	0	0	2
1990-91	Vasteras	Swe.	40	4	10	14	46	4	0	1	1	8
1991-92	Vasteras	Swe.	39	4	6	10	52	....	....	....	....	....
1992-93	Vasteras	Swe.	37	5	7	12	24	2	0	0	0	0

ROHLOFF, JON

Defense. Shoots right. 5'11", 200 lbs. Born, Mankato, MN, October 3, 1969.
(Boston's 7th choice, 186th overall, in 1988 Entry Draft).

			Regular Season					Playoffs				
Season	Club	Lea	GP	G	A	TP	PIM	GP	G	A	TP	PIM
1988-89	Minn.-Duluth	WCHA	39	1	2	3	44	....	....	....	....	....
1989-90	Minn.-Duluth	WCHA	5	0	1	1	6	....	....	....	....	....
1990-91	Minn.-Duluth	WCHA	32	6	11	17	38	....	....	....	....	....
1991-92	Minn.-Duluth	WCHA	27	9	9	18	48	....	....	....	....	....
1992-93a	Minn.-Duluth	WCHA	36	15	20	35	87	....	....	....	....	....

a WCHA Second All-Star Team (1993)

ROHR, STEPHEN

Center. Shoots right. 6'3", 200 lbs. Born, Flint, MI, March 22, 1972.
(Montreal's 8th choice, 144th overall, in 1990 Entry Draft).

			Regular Season					Playoffs				
Season	Club	Lea	GP	G	A	TP	PIM	GP	G	A	TP	PIM
1990-91	Miami-Ohio	CCHA	26	6	6	12	8	....	....	....	....	....
1991-92	Miami-Ohio	CCHA	21	1	3	4	26	....	....	....	....	....
1992-93	Miami-Ohio	CCHA	27	9	8	17	20	....	....	....	....	....

ROLAND, LAYNE

Right wing. Shoots right. 6'1", 215 lbs. Born, Vernon, B.C., February 6, 1974.
(Chicago's 8th choice, 185th overall, in 1992 Entry Draft).

			Regular Season					Playoffs				
Season	Club	Lea	GP	G	A	TP	PIM	GP	G	A	TP	PIM
1990-91	Portland	WHL	60	10	12	22	56	....	....	....	....	....
1991-92	Portland	WHL	67	28	31	59	80	6	3	2	5	10
1992-93	Portland	WHL	69	41	36	77	99	15	6	9	15	16

ROLSTON, BRIAN

Center. Shoots left. 6'1", 175 lbs. Born, Flint, MI, February 21, 1973.
(New Jersey's 2nd choice, 11th overall, in 1991 Entry Draft).

			Regular Season					Playoffs				
Season	Club	Lea	GP	G	A	TP	PIM	GP	G	A	TP	PIM
1991-92a	Lake Superior	CCHA	37	14	23	37	14	....	....	....	....	....
1992-93abc	Lake Superior	CCHA	39	33	31	64	20	....	....	....	....	....

a NCAA Final Four All-Tournament Team (1992, 1993)
b CCHA First All-Star Team (1993)
c NCAA West Second All-American Team (1993)

ROMANIUK, RUSSELL

Left wing. Shoots left. 6', 195 lbs. Born, Winnipeg, Man., June 9, 1970.
(Winnipeg's 2nd choice, 31st overall, in 1988 Entry Draft).

			Regular Season					Playoffs				
Season	Club	Lea	GP	G	A	TP	PIM	GP	G	A	TP	PIM
1988-89	North Dakota	WCHA	39	17	14	31	32	....	....	....	....	....
	Cdn. National	....	3	1	0	1	0	....	....	....	....	....
1989-90	North Dakota	WCHA	45	36	15	51	54	....	....	....	....	....
1990-91a	North Dakota	WCHA	39	40	28	68	30	....	....	....	....	....
1991-92	Winnipeg	NHL	27	3	5	8	18	....	....	....	....	....
	Moncton	AHL	45	16	15	31	25	10	5	4	9	19
1992-93	Winnipeg	NHL	28	3	1	4	22	1	0	0	0	0
	Moncton	AHL	28	18	8	26	40	5	0	4	4	2
	Fort Wayne	IHL	4	2	0	2	7	....	....	....	....	....
	NHL Totals		55	6	6	12	40	1	0	0	0	0

a WCHA First All-Star Team (1991)

ROMFO, JEFF

Center. Shoots left. 6', 185 lbs. Born, St. Paul, MN, February 9, 1974.
(Minnesota's 10th choice, 226th overall, in 1992 Entry Draft).

			Regular Season					Playoffs				
Season	Club	Lea	GP	G	A	TP	PIM	GP	G	A	TP	PIM
1991-92	Blaine	HS	22	18	17	35	6	....	....	....	....	....
1992-93	Minn.-Duluth	WCHA	38	4	4	8	8	....	....	....	....	....

RONAN, EDWARD (ED)

Right wing. Shoots right. 6', 197 lbs. Born, Quincy, MA, March 21, 1968.
(Montreal's 13th choice, 227th overall, in 1987 Entry Draft).

			Regular Season					Playoffs				
Season	Club	Lea	GP	G	A	TP	PIM	GP	G	A	TP	PIM
1987-88	Boston U.	H.E.	31	2	5	7	20	....	....	....	....	....
1988-89	Boston U.	H.E.	36	4	11	15	34	....	....	....	....	....
1989-90	Boston U.	H.E.	44	17	23	40	50	....	....	....	....	....
1990-91	Boston U.	H.E.	41	16	19	35	38	....	....	....	....	....
1991-92	**Montreal**	**NHL**	**3**	**0**	**0**	**0**	**0**	....	....	....	....	....
	Fredericton	AHL	78	25	34	59	82	7	5	1	6	6
1992-93	**Montreal**	**NHL**	**53**	**5**	**7**	**12**	**20**	**14**	**2**	**3**	**5**	**10**
	Fredericton	AHL	16	10	5	15	15	5	2	4	6	6
	NHL Totals		**56**	**5**	**7**	**12**	**20**	**14**	**2**	**3**	**5**	**10**

RONNING, CLIFF

Center. Shoots left. 5'8", 170 lbs. Born, Burnaby, B.C., October 1, 1965.
(St. Louis' 9th choice, 134th overall, in 1984 Entry Draft).

			Regular Season					Playoffs				
Season	Club	Lea	GP	G	A	TP	PIM	GP	G	A	TP	PIM
1983-84a	N. Westminster	WHL	71	69	67	136	10	9	8	13	21	10
1984-85bc	N. Westminster	WHL	70	*89	108	*197	20	11	10	14	24	4
1985-86	Cdn. Olympic	....	71	55	63	118	53	....	....	....	....	....
	St. Louis	**NHL**	....	....	....	....	....	**5**	**1**	**1**	**2**	**2**
1986-87	**St. Louis**	**NHL**	**42**	**11**	**14**	**25**	**6**	**4**	**0**	**1**	**1**	**0**
	Cdn. Olympic	....	26	16	16	32	12	....	....	....	....	....
1987-88	**St. Louis**	**NHL**	**26**	**5**	**8**	**13**	**12**	....	....	....	....	....
1988-89	**St. Louis**	**NHL**	**64**	**24**	**31**	**55**	**18**	**7**	**1**	**3**	**4**	**0**
	Peoria	IHL	12	11	20	31	8	....	....	....	....	....
1989-90	Asiago	Italy	36	67	49	116	25	6	7	12	19	4
1990-91	**St. Louis**	**NHL**	**48**	**14**	**18**	**32**	**10**	....	....	....	....	....
	Vancouver	**NHL**	**11**	**6**	**6**	**12**	**0**	**6**	**6**	**3**	**9**	**12**
1991-92	**Vancouver**	**NHL**	**80**	**24**	**47**	**71**	**42**	**13**	**8**	**5**	**13**	**6**
1992-93	**Vancouver**	**NHL**	**79**	**29**	**56**	**85**	**30**	**12**	**2**	**9**	**11**	**6**
	NHL Totals		**350**	**113**	**180**	**293**	**118**	**47**	**18**	**22**	**40**	**26**

a WHL Rookie of the Year (1984)
b WHL First All-Star Team (1985)
c WHL Most Valuable Player (1985)

Traded to **Vancouver** by **St. Louis** with Geoff Courtnall, Robert Dirk, Sergio Momesso and future considerations for Dan Quinn and Garth Butcher, March 5, 1991.

ROSS, PATRIK

Right wing. Shoots left. 6'2", 198 lbs. Born, Jonkoping, Sweden, February 27, 1970.
(Los Angeles' 9th choice, 196th overall, in 1990 Entry Draft).

			Regular Season					Playoffs				
Season	Club	Lea	GP	G	A	TP	PIM	GP	G	A	TP	PIM
1988-89	HV-71	Swe.	28	3	1	4	8	....	....	....	....	....
1989-90	HV-71	Swe.	37	14	7	21	16	....	....	....	....	....
1990-91	HV-71	Swe.	21	4	1	5	0	2	0	0	0	4
1991-92	HV-71	Swe.	37	8	5	13	8	3	0	0	0	4
1992-93	HV-71	Swe.	40	9	7	16	18	....	....	....	....	....

ROUSE, ROBERT (BOB)

Defense. Shoots right. 6'1", 210 lbs. Born, Surrey, B.C., June 18, 1964.
(Minnesota's 3rd choice, 80th overall, in 1982 Entry Draft).

			Regular Season					Playoffs				
Season	Club	Lea	GP	G	A	TP	PIM	GP	G	A	TP	PIM
1980-81	Billings	WHL	70	0	13	13	116	5	0	0	0	2
1981-82	Billings	WHL	71	7	22	29	209	5	0	2	2	10
1982-83	Nanaimo	WHL	29	7	20	27	86	....	....	....	....	....
	Lethbridge	WHL	42	8	30	38	82	20	2	13	15	55
1983-84	**Minnesota**	**NHL**	**1**	**0**	**0**	**0**	**0**	....	....	....	....	....
ab	Lethbridge	WHL	71	18	42	60	101	5	0	1	1	28
1984-85	**Minnesota**	**NHL**	**63**	**2**	**9**	**11**	**113**	....	....	....	....	....
	Springfield	AHL	8	0	3	3	6	....	....	....	....	....
1985-86	**Minnesota**	**NHL**	**75**	**1**	**14**	**15**	**151**	**3**	**0**	**0**	**0**	**0**
1986-87	**Minnesota**	**NHL**	**72**	**2**	**10**	**12**	**179**	....	....	....	....	....
1987-88	**Minnesota**	**NHL**	**74**	**0**	**12**	**12**	**168**	....	....	....	....	....
1988-89	**Minnesota**	**NHL**	**66**	**4**	**13**	**17**	**124**	....	....	....	....	....
	Washington	**NHL**	**13**	**0**	**2**	**2**	**36**	**6**	**2**	**0**	**2**	**4**
1989-90	**Washington**	**NHL**	**70**	**4**	**16**	**20**	**123**	**15**	**2**	**3**	**5**	**47**
1990-91	**Washington**	**NHL**	**47**	**5**	**15**	**20**	**65**	....	....	....	....	....
	Toronto	**NHL**	**13**	**2**	**4**	**6**	**10**	....	....	....	....	....
1991-92	**Toronto**	**NHL**	**79**	**3**	**19**	**22**	**97**	....	....	....	....	....
1992-93	**Toronto**	**NHL**	**82**	**3**	**11**	**14**	**130**	**21**	**3**	**8**	**11**	**29**
	NHL Totals		**655**	**26**	**125**	**151**	**1196**	**45**	**7**	**11**	**18**	**80**

a WHL First All-Star Team, East Division (1984)
b Named WHL's Top Defenceman (1984)

Traded to **Washington** by **Minnesota** with Dino Ciccarelli for Mike Gartner and Larry Murphy, March 7, 1989. Traded to **Toronto** by **Washington** with Peter Zezel for Al Iafrate, January 16, 1991.

ROWLUND, CHRIS

Right wing. Shoots right. 6'1", 188 lbs. Born, Calgary, Alta., March 30, 1971.

			Regular Season					Playoffs				
Season	Club	Lea	GP	G	A	TP	PIM	GP	G	A	TP	PIM
1990-91	Portland	WHL	67	15	24	39	163	....	....	....	....	....
1991-92	Portland	WHL	70	34	31	65	246	6	2	4	6	28
1992-93	New Haven	AHL	34	4	4	8	65	....	....	....	....	....
	Thunder Bay	Col.	22	5	3	8	65	....	....	....	....	....

Signed as a free agent by **Ottawa**, July 30, 1992.

ROY, JEAN-YVES

Right wing. Shoots left. 5'10", 185 lbs. Born, Rosemere, Que., February 17, 1969.

			Regular Season					Playoffs				
Season	Club	Lea	GP	G	A	TP	PIM	GP	G	A	TP	PIM
1989-90a	U. of Maine	H.E.	46	*39	26	65	52	....	....	....	....	....
1990-91bcd	U. of Maine	H.E.	43	37	45	82	62	....	....	....	....	....
1991-92ce	U. of Maine	H.E.	35	32	24	56	62	....	....	....	....	....
1992-93	Binghamton	AHL	49	13	15	28	21	14	5	2	7	4

a NCAA East Second All-American Team (1990)
b Hockey East First All-Star Team (1991)
c NCAA East First All-American Team (1991, 1992)
d NCAA Final Four All-Tournament Team (1991)
e Hockey East Second All-Star Team (1992)

Signed as a free agent by **NY Rangers**, July 20, 1992.

ROY, SIMON

Defense. Shoots left. 6'1", 177 lbs. Born, Montreal, Que., June 14, 1974.
(Edmonton's 3rd choice, 61st overall, in 1992 Entry Draft).

			Regular Season					Playoffs				
Season	Club	Lea	GP	G	A	TP	PIM	GP	G	A	TP	PIM
1991-92	Shawinigan	QMJHL	63	3	24	27	24	10	1	4	5	9
1992-93	Shawinigan	QMJHL	68	5	34	39	56	....	....	....	....	....

RUBACHUK, BRAD

Center. Shoots left. 5'11", 185 lbs. Born, Winnipeg, Man., June 11, 1970.
(Buffalo's 11th choice, 250th overall, in 1990 Entry Draft).

			Regular Season					Playoffs				
Season	Club	Lea	GP	G	A	TP	PIM	GP	G	A	TP	PIM
1988-89	Lethbridge	WHL	66	19	13	32	161	6	3	1	4	25
1989-90	Lethbridge	WHL	67	37	36	73	179	16	3	7	10	51
1990-91	Lethbridge	WHL	70	64	68	132	237	16	*14	14	28	55
1991-92	Rochester	AHL	70	18	16	34	201	13	4	0	4	19
1992-93	Rochester	AHL	61	10	15	25	218	12	3	1	4	63

RUCHTY, MATTHEW

Defense. Shoots left. 6'1", 210 lbs. Born, Kitchener, Ont., November 27, 1969.
(New Jersey's 4th choice, 65th overall, in 1988 Entry Draft).

			Regular Season					Playoffs				
Season	Club	Lea	GP	G	A	TP	PIM	GP	G	A	TP	PIM
1987-88	Bowling Green	CCHA	41	6	15	21	78	....	....	....	....	....
1988-89	Bowling Green	CCHA	43	11	21	32	110	....	....	....	....	....
1989-90	Bowling Green	CCHA	42	28	21	49	135	....	....	....	....	....
1990-91	Bowling Green	CCHA	38	13	18	31	147	....	....	....	....	....
1991-92	Utica	AHL	73	9	14	23	250	4	0	0	0	25
1992-93	Utica	AHL	74	4	14	18	253	4	0	2	2	15

RUCINSKY, MARTIN (roo-CHIHN-skee)

Left wing. Shoots left. 6', 178 lbs. Born, Most, Czechoslovakia, March 11, 1971.
(Edmonton's 2nd choice, 20th overall, in 1991 Entry Draft).

			Regular Season					Playoffs				
Season	Club	Lea	GP	G	A	TP	PIM	GP	G	A	TP	PIM
1988-89	Litvinov	Czech.	3	1	0	1	2	....	....	....	....	....
1989-90	Litvinov	Czech.	47	17	9	26	....	....	....	....	....	....
1990-91	Litvinov	Czech.	56	24	20	44	69	....	....	....	....	....
1991-92	**Edmonton**	**NHL**	**2**	**0**	**0**	**0**	**0**	....	....	....	....	....
	Cape Breton	AHL	35	11	12	23	34	....	....	....	....	....
	Quebec	**NHL**	**4**	**1**	**1**	**2**	**2**	....	....	....	....	....
	Halifax	AHL	7	1	1	2	6	....	....	....	....	....
1992-93	**Quebec**	**NHL**	**77**	**18**	**30**	**48**	**51**	**6**	**1**	**1**	**2**	**4**
	NHL Totals		**83**	**19**	**31**	**50**	**53**	**6**	**1**	**1**	**2**	**4**

Traded to **Quebec** by **Edmonton** for Ron Tugnutt and Brad Zavisha, March 10, 1992.

RUFF, JASON

Left wing. Shoots left. 6'2", 192 lbs. Born, Kelowna, B.C., January 27, 1970.
(St Louis' 3rd choice, 96th overall, in 1990 Entry Draft).

			Regular Season					Playoffs				
Season	Club	Lea	GP	G	A	TP	PIM	GP	G	A	TP	PIM
1989-90	Lethbridge	WHL	72	55	64	119	114	19	9	10	19	18
1990-91a	Lethbridge	WHL	66	61	75	136	154	16	12	17	29	18
	Peoria	IHL	....	....	....	....	....	5	0	0	0	2
1991-92	Peoria	IHL	67	27	45	72	148	10	7	7	14	19
1992-93	**St. Louis**	**NHL**	**7**	**2**	**1**	**3**	**8**	....	....	....	....	....
	Peoria	IHL	40	22	21	43	81	....	....	....	....	....
	Tampa Bay	**NHL**	**1**	**0**	**0**	**0**	**0**	....	....	....	....	....
	Atlanta	IHL	26	11	14	25	90	7	2	1	3	26
	NHL Totals		**8**	**2**	**1**	**3**	**8**	....	....	....	....	....

a WHL East First All-Star Team (1991)

Traded to **Tampa Bay** by **St. Louis** with future considerations for Doug Crossman, Basil McRae and Tampa Bay's fourth round choice in 1996 Entry Draft, January 28, 1993.

RUFF, LINDY CAMERON

Defense/Left wing. Shoots left. 6'2", 201 lbs. Born, Warburg, Alta., February 17, 1960.
(Buffalo's 2nd choice, 32nd overall, in 1979 Entry Draft).

			Regular Season					Playoffs				
Season	Club	Lea	GP	G	A	TP	PIM	GP	G	A	TP	PIM
1977-78	Lethbridge	WHL	66	9	24	33	219	8	2	8	10	4
1978-79	Lethbridge	WHL	24	9	18	27	108	6	0	1	1	0
1979-80	**Buffalo**	**NHL**	**63**	**5**	**14**	**19**	**38**	**8**	**1**	**1**	**2**	**19**
1980-81	**Buffalo**	**NHL**	**65**	**8**	**18**	**26**	**121**	**6**	**3**	**1**	**4**	**23**
1981-82	**Buffalo**	**NHL**	**79**	**16**	**32**	**48**	**194**	**4**	**0**	**0**	**0**	**28**
1982-83	**Buffalo**	**NHL**	**60**	**12**	**17**	**29**	**130**	**10**	**4**	**2**	**6**	**47**
1983-84	**Buffalo**	**NHL**	**58**	**14**	**31**	**45**	**101**	**3**	**1**	**0**	**1**	**9**
1984-85	**Buffalo**	**NHL**	**39**	**13**	**11**	**24**	**45**	**5**	**2**	**4**	**6**	**15**
1985-86	**Buffalo**	**NHL**	**54**	**20**	**12**	**32**	**158**	....	....	....	....	....
1986-87	**Buffalo**	**NHL**	**50**	**6**	**14**	**20**	**74**	....	....	....	....	....
1987-88	**Buffalo**	**NHL**	**77**	**2**	**23**	**25**	**179**	**6**	**0**	**2**	**2**	**23**
1988-89	**Buffalo**	**NHL**	**63**	**6**	**11**	**17**	**86**	....	....	....	....	....
	NY Rangers	**NHL**	**13**	**0**	**5**	**5**	**31**	**2**	**0**	**0**	**0**	**17**
1989-90	**NY Rangers**	**NHL**	**56**	**3**	**6**	**9**	**80**	**8**	**0**	**3**	**3**	**12**
1990-91	**NY Rangers**	**NHL**	**14**	**0**	**1**	**1**	**27**	....	....	....	....	....
1991-92	Rochester	AHL	62	10	24	34	110	13	0	4	4	18
1992-93	San Diego	IHL	81	10	32	42	100	14	1	6	7	26
	NHL Totals		**691**	**105**	**195**	**300**	**1264**	**52**	**11**	**13**	**24**	**193**

Traded to **NY Rangers** by **Buffalo** for NY Rangers' fifth round choice (Richard Smehlik) in 1990 Entry Draft, March 7, 1989.

RUMBLE, DARREN

Defense. Shoots left. 6'1", 200 lbs.   Born, Barrie, Ont., January 23, 1969.
(Philadelphia's 1st choice, 20th overall, in 1987 Entry Draft).

			Regular Season					Playoffs				
Season	Club	Lea	GP	G	A	TP	PIM	GP	G	A	TP	PIM
1986-87	Kitchener	OHL	64	11	32	43	44	4	0	1	1	9
1987-88	Kitchener	OHL	55	15	50	65	64	....	....	....	....	....
1988-89	Kitchener	OHL	46	11	28	39	25	5	1	0	1	2
1989-90	Hershey	AHL	57	2	13	15	31	....	....	....	....	....
1990-91	**Philadelphia**	**NHL**	**3**	**1**	**0**	**1**	**0**	....	....	....	....	....
	Hershey	AHL	73	6	35	41	48	3	0	5	5	2
1991-92	Hershey	AHL	79	12	54	66	118	6	0	3	3	2
1992-93	**Ottawa**	**NHL**	**69**	**3**	**13**	**16**	**61**	....	....	....	....	....
	New Haven	AHL	2	1	0	1	0	....	....	....	....	....
	NHL Totals		**72**	**4**	**13**	**17**	**61**					

Claimed by **Ottawa** from **Philadelphia** in Expansion Draft, June 18, 1992.

RUOHO, DANIEL

Defense. Shoots left. 6'3", 220 lbs.   Born, Madison, WI, June 22, 1970.
(Buffalo's 9th choice, 160th overall, in 1988 Entry Draft).

			Regular Season					Playoffs				
Season	Club	Lea	GP	G	A	TP	PIM	GP	G	A	TP	PIM
1989-90	N. Michigan	WCHA	18	2	4	6	26	....	....	....	....	....
1990-91	N. Michigan	WCHA	6	0	1	1	9	....	....	....	....	....
1991-92	N. Michigan	WCHA	10	2	2	4	26	....	....	....	....	....
1992-93	N. Michigan	WCHA	37	8	8	16	53	....	....	....	....	....

RUSHFORTH, PAUL

Center. Shoots right. 6', 189 lbs.   Born, Prince George, B.C., April 22, 1974.
(Buffalo's 8th choice, 131st overall, in 1992 Entry Draft).

			Regular Season					Playoffs				
Season	Club	Lea	GP	G	A	TP	PIM	GP	G	A	TP	PIM
1991-92	North Bay	OHL	65	8	11	19	24	19	0	2	2	6
1992-93	North Bay	OHL	21	4	10	14	24	....	....	....	....	....
	Belleville	OHL	36	21	19	40	38	7	7	2	9	4

RUSHIN, JOHN

Center. Shoots right. 6'5", 201 lbs.   Born, Edina, MN, September 12, 1972.
(NY Rangers' 7th choice, 147th overall, in 1991 Entry Draft).

			Regular Season					Playoffs				
Season	Club	Lea	GP	G	A	TP	PIM	GP	G	A	TP	PIM
1991-92	Notre Dame	NCAA	17	8	2	10	30	....	....	....	....	....
1992-93	Notre Dame	CCHA	36	1	4	5	46	....	....	....	....	....

RUSSELL, CAM

Defense. Shoots left. 6'4", 174 lbs.   Born, Halifax, N.S., January 12, 1969.
(Chicago's 3rd choice, 50th overall, in 1987 Entry Draft).

			Regular Season					Playoffs				
Season	Club	Lea	GP	G	A	TP	PIM	GP	G	A	TP	PIM
1985-86	Hull	QMJHL	56	3	4	7	24	15	0	2	2	4
1986-87	Hull	QMJHL	66	3	16	19	119	8	0	1	1	16
1987-88a	Hull	QMJHL	53	9	18	27	141	19	2	5	7	39
1988-89	Hull	QMJHL	66	8	32	40	109	9	2	6	8	6
1989-90	**Chicago**	**NHL**	**19**	**0**	**1**	**1**	**27**	**1**	**0**	**0**	**0**	**0**
	Indianapolis	IHL	46	3	15	18	114	9	0	1	1	24
1990-91	**Chicago**	**NHL**	**3**	**0**	**0**	**0**	**5**	**1**	**0**	**0**	**0**	**0**
	Indianapolis	IHL	53	5	9	14	125	6	0	2	2	30
1991-92	**Chicago**	**NHL**	**19**	**0**	**0**	**0**	**34**	**12**	**0**	**2**	**2**	**2**
	Indianapolis	IHL	41	4	9	13	78	....	....	....	....	....
1992-93	**Chicago**	**NHL**	**67**	**2**	**4**	**6**	**151**	**4**	**0**	**0**	**0**	**0**
	NHL Totals		**108**	**2**	**5**	**7**	**217**	**18**	**0**	**2**	**2**	**2**

a QMJHL Third All-Star Team (1988)

RUUTTU, CHRISTIAN   (ROO-TOO)

Center. Shoots left. 5'11", 194 lbs.   Born, Lappeenranta, Finland, February 20, 1964.
(Buffalo's 9th choice, 134th overall, in 1983 Entry Draft).

			Regular Season					Playoffs				
Season	Club	Lea	GP	G	A	TP	PIM	GP	G	A	TP	PIM
1982-83	Assat	Fin.	36	15	18	33	34	....	....	....	....	....
1983-84	Assat	Fin.	37	18	42	60	72	9	2	5	7	12
1984-85	Assat	Fin.	32	14	32	46	34	8	1	6	7	8
1985-86	HIFK	Fin.	36	16	38	54	47	10	3	6	9	8
1986-87	**Buffalo**	**NHL**	**76**	**22**	**43**	**65**	**62**	....	....	....	....	....
1987-88	**Buffalo**	**NHL**	**73**	**26**	**45**	**71**	**85**	**6**	**2**	**5**	**7**	**4**
1988-89	**Buffalo**	**NHL**	**67**	**14**	**46**	**60**	**98**	**2**	**0**	**0**	**0**	**2**
1989-90	**Buffalo**	**NHL**	**75**	**19**	**41**	**60**	**66**	**6**	**0**	**0**	**0**	**4**
1990-91	**Buffalo**	**NHL**	**77**	**16**	**34**	**50**	**96**	**6**	**1**	**3**	**4**	**29**
1991-92	**Buffalo**	**NHL**	**70**	**4**	**21**	**25**	**76**	**3**	**0**	**0**	**0**	**6**
1992-93	**Chicago**	**NHL**	**84**	**17**	**37**	**54**	**134**	**4**	**0**	**0**	**0**	**2**
	NHL Totals		**522**	**118**	**267**	**385**	**617**	**27**	**3**	**8**	**11**	**47**

Played in NHL All-Star Game (1988)

Traded to **Winnipeg** by **Buffalo** with future considerations for Stephane Beauregard, June 15, 1992. Traded to **Chicago** by **Winnipeg** for Stephane Beauregard, August 10, 1992.

RUZICKA, VLADIMIR   (ROO-zheech-kah)

Center. Shoots left. 6'3", 215 lbs.   Born, Most, Czechoslovakia, June 6, 1963.
(Toronto's 5th choice, 73rd overall, in 1982 Entry Draft).

			Regular Season					Playoffs				
Season	Club	Lea	GP	G	A	TP	PIM	GP	G	A	TP	PIM
1979-80	Litvinov	Czech.	9	1	1	2	0	....	....	....	....	....
1980-81	Litvinov	Czech.	41	12	13	25	10	....	....	....	....	....
1981-82	Litvinov	Czech.	44	27	22	49	50	....	....	....	....	....
1982-83	Litvinov	Czech.	43	22	24	46	40	....	....	....	....	....
1983-84	Litvinov	Czech.	44	31	23	54	50	....	....	....	....	....
1984-85	Litvinov	Czech.	41	38	22	60	29	....	....	....	....	....
1985-86	Litvinov	Czech.	43	41	32	73		....	....	....	....	....
1986-87	Litvinov	Czech.	39	29	21	50	46	....	....	....	....	....
1987-88	Dukla Trencin	Czech.	44	38	27	65	70	....	....	....	....	....
1988-89	Dukla Trencin	Czech.	45	46	38	84	42	....	....	....	....	....
1989-90	Litvinov	Czech.	32	21	23	44		....	....	....	....	....
	Edmonton	**NHL**	**25**	**11**	**6**	**17**	**10**	....	....	....	....	....
1990-91	**Boston**	**NHL**	**29**	**8**	**8**	**16**	**19**	**17**	**2**	**11**	**13**	**0**
1991-92	**Boston**	**NHL**	**77**	**39**	**36**	**75**	**48**	**13**	**2**	**3**	**5**	**2**
1992-93	**Boston**	**NHL**	**60**	**19**	**22**	**41**	**38**	....	....	....	....	....
	NHL Totals		**191**	**77**	**72**	**149**	**115**	**30**	**4**	**14**	**18**	**2**

Traded to **Edmonton** by **Toronto** for Edmonton's fourth round choice (Greg Walters) in 1990 Entry Draft, December 21, 1989. Traded to **Boston** by **Edmonton** for Greg Hawgood, October 22, 1990. Signed as a free agent by **Ottawa**, August 12, 1993.

RYCHEL, WARREN   (RIGH-kuhl)

Left wing. Shoots left. 6', 190 lbs.   Born, Tecumseh, Ont., May 12, 1967.

			Regular Season					Playoffs				
Season	Club	Lea	GP	G	A	TP	PIM	GP	G	A	TP	PIM
1984-85	Sudbury	OHL	35	5	8	13	74	....	....	....	....	....
	Guelph	OHL	29	1	3	4	48	....	....	....	....	....
1985-86	Guelph	OHL	38	14	5	19	119	....	....	....	....	....
	Ottawa	OHL	29	11	18	29	54	....	....	....	....	....
1986-87	Ottawa	OHL	28	11	7	18	57	....	....	....	....	....
	Kitchener	OHL	21	5	5	10	39	4	0	0	0	9
1987-88	Peoria	IHL	7	2	1	3	7	....	....	....	....	....
	Saginaw	IHL	51	2	7	9	113	1	0	0	0	0
1988-89	**Chicago**	**NHL**	**2**	**0**	**0**	**0**	**17**	....	....	....	....	....
	Saginaw	IHL	50	15	14	29	226	6	0	0	0	51
1989-90	Indianapolis	IHL	77	23	16	39	374	14	1	3	4	64
1990-91	Indianapolis	IHL	68	33	30	63	338	5	2	1	3	30
	Chicago	**NHL**	....	....	....	....	....	**3**	**1**	**3**	**4**	**2**
1991-92	Moncton	AHL	36	14	15	29	211	....	....	....	....	....
	Kalamazoo	IHL	45	15	20	35	165	8	0	3	3	51
1992-93	**Los Angeles**	**NHL**	**70**	**6**	**7**	**13**	**314**	**23**	**6**	**7**	**13**	**39**
	NHL Totals		**72**	**6**	**7**	**13**	**331**	**26**	**7**	**10**	**17**	**41**

Signed as a free agent by **Chicago**, September 19, 1986. Traded to **Winnipeg** by **Chicago** with Troy Murray for Bryan Marchment and Chris Norton, July 22, 1991. Traded to **Minnesota** by **Winnipeg** for Tony Joseph, December 30, 1991. Signed as a free agent by **Los Angeles**, October 1, 1992.

RYDMARK, DANIEL   (REWD-mahrk)

Center. Shoots left. 5'10", 180 lbs.   Born, Surahammar, Sweden, February 23, 1970.
(Los Angeles' 5th choice, 123rd overall, in 1989 Entry Draft).

			Regular Season					Playoffs				
Season	Club	Lea	GP	G	A	TP	PIM	GP	G	A	TP	PIM
1986-87	Farjestad	Swe.	4	0	1	1	0	....	....	....	....	....
1987-88	Farjestad	Swe.	28	2	1	3	10	5	0	0	0	2
1988-89	Farjestad	Swe.	35	9	9	18	24	....	....	....	....	....
1989-90	Farjestad	Swe.	35	9	12	21	20	5	0	0	0	4
1990-91	Malmo	Swe.	39	14	13	27	34	1	0	0	0	0
1991-92	Malmo	Swe.	30	17	15	32	56	7	0	3	3	6
1992-93	Malmo	Swe.	39	18	13	31	70	6	5	4	9	8

RYMSHA, ANDREW (ANDY)

Defense. Shoots left. 6'3", 210 lbs.   Born, St. Catharines, Ont., December 10, 1968.
(St. Louis' 5th choice, 82nd overall, in 1987 Entry Draft).

			Regular Season					Playoffs				
Season	Club	Lea	GP	G	A	TP	PIM	GP	G	A	TP	PIM
1986-87	W. Michigan	CCHA	41	7	12	19	60	....	....	....	....	....
1987-88	W. Michigan	CCHA	42	5	6	11	114	....	....	....	....	....
1988-89	W. Michigan	CCHA	35	3	4	7	139	....	....	....	....	....
1989-90	W. Michigan	CCHA	37	1	10	11	108	....	....	....	....	....
1990-91	Halifax	AHL	12	1	2	3	22	....	....	....	....	....
	Peoria	IHL	45	2	9	11	64	....	....	....	....	....
1991-92	**Quebec**	**NHL**	**6**	**0**	**0**	**0**	**23**	....	....	....	....	....
	Halifax	AHL	44	4	7	11	54	....	....	....	....	....
	New Haven	AHL	16	0	5	5	20	....	....	....	....	....
1992-93	Cdn. National	....	6	8	2	10	16	....	....	....	....	....
	Halifax	AHL	43	4	6	10	62	....	....	....	....	....
	NHL Totals		**6**	**0**	**0**	**0**	**23**					

Traded to **Quebec** by **St. Louis** with Herb Raglan and Tony Twist for Darin Kimble, February 4, 1991.

SABOURIN, KEN

Defense. Shoots left. 6'3", 205 lbs. Born, Scarborough, Ont., April 28, 1966.
(Calgary's 2nd choice, 33rd overall, in 1984 Entry Draft).

			Regular Season					Playoffs				
Season	Club	Lea	GP	G	A	TP	PIM	GP	G	A	TP	PIM
1982-83	S.S. Marie	OHL	58	0	8	8	90	10	0	0	0	14
1983-84	S.S. Marie	OHL	63	7	14	21	157	9	0	1	1	25
1984-85	S.S. Marie	OHL	63	5	19	24	139	16	1	4	5	10
1985-86	Moncton	AHL	3	0	0	0	0	6	0	1	1	2
	S.S. Marie	OHL	25	1	5	6	77	....	....	....	....	....
	Cornwall	OHL	37	3	12	15	94	6	1	2	3	6
1986-87	Moncton	AHL	75	1	10	11	166	6	0	1	1	27
1987-88	Salt Lake	IHL	71	2	8	10	186	16	1	6	7	57
1988-89	**Calgary**	**NHL**	**6**	**0**	**1**	**1**	**26**	**1**	**0**	**0**	**0**	**0**
	Salt Lake	IHL	74	2	18	20	197	11	0	1	1	26
1989-90	**Calgary**	**NHL**	**5**	**0**	**0**	**0**	**10**	....	....	....	....	....
	Salt Lake	IHL	76	5	19	24	336	11	0	2	2	40
1990-91	**Calgary**	**NHL**	**16**	**1**	**3**	**4**	**36**	....	....	....	....	....
	Salt Lake	IHL	28	2	15	17	77	....	....	....	....	....
	Washington	**NHL**	**28**	**1**	**4**	**5**	**81**	**11**	**0**	**0**	**0**	**34**
1991-92	**Washington**	**NHL**	**19**	**0**	**0**	**0**	**48**	....	....	....	....	....
	Baltimore	AHL	30	3	8	11	106	....	....	....	....	....
1992-93	Baltimore	AHL	30	5	14	19	68	....	....	....	....	....
	Salt Lake	IHL	52	2	11	13	140	....	....	....	....	....
	NHL Totals		**74**	**2**	**8**	**10**	**201**	**12**	**0**	**0**	**0**	**34**

Traded to **Washington** by **Calgary** for Paul Fenton, January 24, 1991. Traded to **Calgary** by **Washington** for future considerations, December 16, 1992.

SACCO, DAVID (SA-KOH)

Right wing. Shoots right. 6'1", 190 lbs. Born, Malden, MA, July 31, 1970.
(Toronto's 9th choice, 195th overall, in 1988 Entry Draft).

			Regular Season					Playoffs				
Season	Club	Lea	GP	G	A	TP	PIM	GP	G	A	TP	PIM
1988-89	Boston U.	H.E.	35	14	29	43	40	....	....	....	....	....
1989-90	Boston U.	H.E.	3	0	4	4	2	....	....	....	....	....
1990-91	Boston U.	H.E.	40	21	40	61	24	....	....	....	....	....
1991-92ab	Boston U.	H.E.	34	13	32	45	30	....	....	....	....	....
1992-93ab	Boston U.	H.E.	40	25	37	62	86	....	....	....	....	....

a NCAA East First All-American Team (1992, 1993)
b Hockey East First All-Star Team (1992, 1993)

SACCO, JOSEPH (JOE) (SA-KOH)

Left wing. Shoots right. 6'1", 195 lbs. Born, Medford, MA, February 4, 1969.
(Toronto's 4th choice, 71st overall, in 1987 Entry Draft).

			Regular Season					Playoffs				
Season	Club	Lea	GP	G	A	TP	PIM	GP	G	A	TP	PIM
1987-88	Boston U.	H.E.	34	16	20	36	40	....	....	....	....	....
1988-89	Boston U.	H.E.	33	21	19	40	66	....	....	....	....	....
1989-90	Boston U.	H.E.	44	28	24	52	70	....	....	....	....	....
1990-91	**Toronto**	**NHL**	**20**	**0**	**5**	**5**	**2**	....	....	....	....	....
	Newmarket	AHL	49	18	17	35	24	....	....	....	....	....
1991-92	U.S. National	....	50	11	26	37	61	....	....	....	....	....
	U.S. Olympic	....	8	0	2	2	0	....	....	....	....	....
	Toronto	**NHL**	**17**	**7**	**4**	**11**	**4**	....	....	....	....	....
	St. John's	AHL	....	....	....	....	....	1	1	1	2	0
1992-93	**Toronto**	**NHL**	**23**	**4**	**4**	**8**	**8**	....	....	....	....	....
	St. John's	AHL	37	14	16	30	45	7	6	4	10	2
	NHL Totals		**60**	**11**	**13**	**24**	**14**	....	....	....	....	....

Claimed by **Anaheim** from **Toronto** in Expansion Draft, June 24, 1993.

SAFARIK, RICHARD

Right wing. Shoots left. 6'3", 194 lbs. Born, Nova Zamky, Czech., February 26, 1975.
(Buffalo's 3rd choice, 116th overall, in 1993 Entry Draft).

			Regular Season					Playoffs				
Season	Club	Lea	GP	G	A	TP	PIM	GP	G	A	TP	PIM
1991-92	Nitra	Czech.2	2	0	0	0	0	....	....	....	....	....
1992-93	Nitra	Czech.2	16	0	0	0	2	....	....	....	....	....

SAILYNOJA, KEIJO (sayl-yeh-NOY-ah)

Left wing. Shoots left. 6'2", 187 lbs. Born, Vantaa, Finland, February 17, 1970.
(Edmonton's 6th choice, 122nd overall, in 1990 Entry Draft).

			Regular Season					Playoffs				
Season	Club	Lea	GP	G	A	TP	PIM	GP	G	A	TP	PIM
1989-90	Jokerit	Fin.	41	15	13	28	14	....	....	....	....	....
1990-91	Jokerit	Fin.	44	21	25	46	14	....	....	....	....	....
1991-92	Jokerit	Fin.	42	21	25	46	14	10	5	6	11	2
1992-93	Jokerit	Fin.	47	29	13	42	14	3	1	1	2	0

ST. AMOUR, MARTIN

Left wing. Shoots left. 6'3", 194 lbs. Born, Montreal, Que., January 30, 1970.
(Montreal's 2nd choice, 34th overall, in 1988 Entry Draft).

			Regular Season					Playoffs				
Season	Club	Lea	GP	G	A	TP	PIM	GP	G	A	TP	PIM
1987-88	Verdun	QMJHL	61	20	50	70	111	....	....	....	....	....
1988-89	Verdun	QMJHL	28	19	17	36	87	....	....	....	....	....
	Trois-Rivières	QMJHL	26	8	21	29	69	4	1	2	3	0
1989-90	Trois-Rivières	QMJHL	60	57	79	136	162	7	7	9	16	19
	Sherbrooke	AHL	....	....	....	....	....	1	0	0	0	0
1990-91	Fredericton	AHL	45	13	16	29	51	1	0	0	0	0
1991-92	Cincinnati	ECHL	60	44	44	88	183	9	4	9	13	18
1992-93	**Ottawa**	**NHL**	**1**	**0**	**0**	**0**	**2**	....	....	....	....	....
	New Haven	AHL	71	21	39	60	78	....	....	....	....	....
	NHL Totals		**1**	**0**	**0**	**0**	**2**	....	....	....	....	....

Signed as a free agent by **Ottawa**, July 16, 1992.

ST. CYR, GERRY

Left wing. Shoots right. 6'1", 188 lbs. Born, North Vancouver, B.C., August 18, 1971.

			Regular Season					Playoffs				
Season	Club	Lea	GP	G	A	TP	PIM	GP	G	A	TP	PIM
1991-92	Victoria	WHL	70	38	55	93	407	....	....	....	....	....
1992-93	New Haven	AHL	40	5	5	10	195	....	....	....	....	....

Signed as a free agent by **Ottawa**, July 30, 1992.

ST. JACQUES, KEVIN

Left wing. Shoots right. 5'11", 190 lbs. Born, Edmonton, Alta., February 25, 1971.
(Chicago's 6th choice, 112th overall, in 1991 Entry Draft).

			Regular Season					Playoffs				
Season	Club	Lea	GP	G	A	TP	PIM	GP	G	A	TP	PIM
1990-91a	Lethbridge	WHL	72	45	63	108	64	16	13	10	23	20
1991-92b	Lethbridge	WHL	71	*65	75	140	159	3	2	2	4	2
1992-93	Indianapolis	IHL	71	10	21	31	93	4	0	0	0	0

a WHL East Second All-Star Team (1991)
b WHL East First All-Star Team (1992)

ST. PIERRE, DAVID

Center. Shoots right. 6', 180 lbs. Born, Montreal, Que., March 22, 1972.
(Calgary's 9th choice, 173rd overall, in 1991 Entry Draft).

			Regular Season					Playoffs				
Season	Club	Lea	GP	G	A	TP	PIM	GP	G	A	TP	PIM
1990-91	Longueuil	QMJHL	66	34	45	79	51	8	4	4	8	8
1991-92	Verdun	QMJHL	69	40	55	95	98	15	3	6	9	15
1992-93	Salt Lake	IHL	35	7	8	15	18	....	....	....	....	....

SAKIC, BRIAN (SA-kik)

Center. Shoots left. 5'10", 156 lbs. Born, Burnaby, B.C., September 4, 1971.
(Washington's 5th choice, 93rd overall, in 1990 Entry Draft).

			Regular Season					Playoffs				
Season	Club	Lea	GP	G	A	TP	PIM	GP	G	A	TP	PIM
1987-88	Swift Current	WHL	65	12	37	49	12	9	3	8	11	0
1988-89	Swift Current	WHL	71	36	64	100	28	12	9	9	18	8
1989-90a	Swift Current	WHL	8	6	7	13	4	....	....	....	....	....
a	Tri-City	WHL	58	47	92	139	8	....	....	....	....	....
1990-91	Tri-City	WHL	69	40	*122	162	19	5	2	3	5	4
1991-92	Tri-City	WHL	72	45	*83	128	35	5	4	4	8	14
1992-93	Erie	ECHL	51	18	33	51	22	....	....	....	....	....

a WHL West Second All-Star Team (1990)

Signed as a free agent by **NY Rangers**, August 13, 1992.

SAKIC, JOE (SA-kik)

Center. Shoots left. 5'11", 185 lbs. Born, Burnaby, B.C., July 7, 1969.
(Quebec's 2nd choice, 15th overall, in 1987 Entry Draft).

			Regular Season					Playoffs				
Season	Club	Lea	GP	G	A	TP	PIM	GP	G	A	TP	PIM
1986-87ab	Swift Current	WHL	72	60	73	133	31	4	0	1	1	0
1987-88acd	Swift Current	WHL	64	*78	82	*160	64	10	11	13	24	12
1988-89	**Quebec**	**NHL**	**70**	**23**	**39**	**62**	**24**	....	....	....	....	....
1989-90	**Quebec**	**NHL**	**80**	**39**	**63**	**102**	**27**	....	....	....	....	....
1990-91	**Quebec**	**NHL**	**80**	**48**	**61**	**109**	**24**	....	....	....	....	....
1991-92	**Quebec**	**NHL**	**69**	**29**	**65**	**94**	**20**	....	....	....	....	....
1992-93	**Quebec**	**NHL**	**78**	**48**	**57**	**105**	**40**	**6**	**3**	**3**	**6**	**2**
	NHL Totals		**377**	**187**	**285**	**472**	**135**	**6**	**3**	**3**	**6**	**2**

a WHL Player of the Year (1987, 1988)
b WHL Rookie of the Year (1987)
c Canadian Major Junior Player of the Year (1988)
d WHL East All-Star Team (1988)

Played in NHL All-Star Game (1990-93)

SALLE, JOHAN

Defense. Shoots left. 6'1", 200 lbs. Born, Lindloven, Sweden, February 21, 1967.
(Philadelphia's 9th choice, 161st overall, in 1988 Entry Draft).

			Regular Season					Playoffs				
Season	Club	Lea	GP	G	A	TP	PIM	GP	G	A	TP	PIM
1987-88	Orebro	Swe.2	36	9	4	13	48	8	1	1	2	14
1988-89	Malmo	Swe.2	32	10	15	25	60	....	....	....	....	....
1989-90	Malmo	Swe.2	32	12	16	28	98	....	....	....	....	....
1990-91	Malmo	Swe.	38	4	5	9	34	2	0	0	0	12
1991-92	Malmo	Swe.	29	2	5	7	62	10	2	0	2	12
1992-93	Malmo	Swe.	30	3	2	5	38	6	0	0	0	8

SALMING, ANDERS BORJE (SAHL-mihng, BOHR-yuh)

Defense. Shoots left. 6'1", 193 lbs. Born, Kiruna, Sweden, April 17, 1951.

			Regular Season					Playoffs				
Season	Club	Lea	GP	G	A	TP	PIM	GP	G	A	TP	PIM
1970-71	Brynas	Swe.	27	2	6	8	22	....	....	....	....	....
1971-72	Brynas	Swe.	28	1	5	6	50	....	....	....	....	....
1972-73	Brynas	Swe.	26	5	4	9	34	....	....	....	....	....
1973-74	**Toronto**	**NHL**	**76**	**5**	**34**	**39**	**48**	**4**	**0**	**1**	**1**	**4**
1974-75a	**Toronto**	**NHL**	**60**	**12**	**25**	**37**	**34**	**7**	**0**	**4**	**4**	**6**
1975-76a	**Toronto**	**NHL**	**78**	**16**	**41**	**57**	**70**	**10**	**3**	**4**	**7**	**9**
1976-77b	**Toronto**	**NHL**	**76**	**12**	**66**	**78**	**46**	**9**	**3**	**6**	**9**	**6**
1977-78a	**Toronto**	**NHL**	**80**	**16**	**60**	**76**	**70**	**6**	**2**	**2**	**4**	**6**
1978-79a	**Toronto**	**NHL**	**78**	**17**	**56**	**73**	**76**	**6**	**0**	**1**	**1**	**8**
1979-80a	**Toronto**	**NHL**	**74**	**19**	**52**	**71**	**94**	**3**	**1**	**1**	**2**	**2**
1980-81	**Toronto**	**NHL**	**72**	**5**	**61**	**66**	**154**	**3**	**0**	**2**	**2**	**4**
1981-82	**Toronto**	**NHL**	**69**	**12**	**44**	**56**	**170**	....	....	....	....	....
1982-83	**Toronto**	**NHL**	**69**	**7**	**38**	**45**	**104**	**4**	**1**	**4**	**5**	**10**
1983-84	**Toronto**	**NHL**	**68**	**5**	**38**	**43**	**92**	....	....	....	....	....
1984-85	**Toronto**	**NHL**	**73**	**6**	**33**	**39**	**76**	....	....	....	....	....
1985-86	**Toronto**	**NHL**	**41**	**7**	**15**	**22**	**48**	**10**	**1**	**6**	**7**	**14**
1986-87	**Toronto**	**NHL**	**56**	**4**	**16**	**20**	**42**	**13**	**0**	**3**	**3**	**14**
1987-88	**Toronto**	**NHL**	**66**	**2**	**24**	**26**	**82**	**6**	**1**	**3**	**4**	**8**
1988-89	**Toronto**	**NHL**	**63**	**3**	**17**	**20**	**86**	....	....	....	....	....
1989-90	**Detroit**	**NHL**	**49**	**2**	**17**	**19**	**52**	....	....	....	....	....
1990-91	AIK	Swe.	36	4	9	13	46	....	....	....	....	....
1991-92	AIK	Swe.	38	6	14	20	98	3	0	2	2	6
1992-93	AIK	Swe.	6	1	0	1	10	....	....	....	....	....
	NHL Totals		**1148**	**150**	**637**	**787**	**1344**	**81**	**12**	**37**	**49**	**91**

a NHL Second All-Star Team (1975, 1976, 1978, 1979, 1980)
b NHL First All-Star Team (1977)

Played in NHL All-Star Game (1976-78)

Signed as a free agent by **Toronto**, May 12, 1973. Signed as a free agent by **Detroit**, June 12, 1989.

SAMUELSSON, KJELL (suh-MOO-ehl-suhn, SHELL)

Defense. Shoots right. 6'6", 235 lbs. Born, Tingsryd, Sweden, October 18, 1958.
(NY Rangers' 5th choice, 119th overall, in 1984 Entry Draft).

			Regular Season					Playoffs				
Season	Club	Lea	GP	G	A	TP	PIM	GP	G	A	TP	PIM
1977-78	Tingsryd	Swe.2	20	3	0	3	41	....	....	....	....	....
1978-79	Tingsryd	Swe.2	24	3	4	7	67	....	....	....	....	....
1979-80	Tingsryd	Swe.2	26	5	4	9	45	....	....	....	....	....
1980-81	Tingsryd	Swe.2	35	6	7	13	61	2	0	1	1	14
1981-82	Tingsryd	Swe.2	33	11	14	25	68	3	0	2	2	2
1982-83	Tingsryd	Swe.2	32	11	6	17	57	....	....	....	....	....
1983-84	Leksand	Swe.	36	6	6	12	59	....	....	....	....	....
1984-85	Leksand	Swe.	35	9	5	14	34	....	....	....	....	....
1985-86	**NY Rangers**	**NHL**	**9**	**0**	**0**	**0**	**10**	**9**	**0**	**1**	**1**	**8**
	New Haven	AHL	56	6	21	27	87	3	0	0	0	10
1986-87	**NY Rangers**	**NHL**	**30**	**2**	**6**	**8**	**50**	....	....	....	....	....
	Philadelphia	**NHL**	**46**	**1**	**6**	**7**	**86**	**26**	**0**	**4**	**4**	**25**
1987-88	**Philadelphia**	**NHL**	**74**	**6**	**24**	**30**	**184**	**7**	**2**	**5**	**7**	**23**
1988-89	**Philadelphia**	**NHL**	**69**	**3**	**14**	**17**	**140**	**19**	**1**	**3**	**4**	**24**
1989-90	**Philadelphia**	**NHL**	**66**	**5**	**17**	**22**	**91**	....	....	....	....	....
1990-91	**Philadelphia**	**NHL**	**78**	**9**	**19**	**28**	**82**	....	....	....	....	....
1991-92	**Philadelphia**	**NHL**	**54**	**4**	**9**	**13**	**76**	....	....	....	....	....
	Pittsburgh	**NHL**	**20**	**1**	**2**	**3**	**34**	**15**	**0**	**3**	**3**	**12**
1992-93	**Pittsburgh**	**NHL**	**63**	**3**	**6**	**9**	**106**	**12**	**0**	**3**	**3**	**2**
	NHL Totals		**509**	**34**	**103**	**137**	**859**	**88**	**3**	**19**	**22**	**94**

Played in NHL All-Star Game (1988)

Traded to **Philadelphia** by **NY Rangers** with NY Rangers' second round choice (Patrik Juhlin) in 1989 Entry Draft for Bob Froese, December 18, 1986. Traded to **Pittsburgh** by **Philadelphia** with Rick Tocchet and Ken Wregget for Mark Recchi, Brian Benning and Los Angeles' first round choice (previously acquired by Pittsburgh — Philadelphia selected Jason Bowen) in 1992 Entry Draft, February 19, 1992.

SAMUELSSON, ULF (suh-MOO-ehl-suhn)

Defense. Shoots left. 6'1", 195 lbs. Born, Fagersta, Sweden, March 26, 1964.
(Hartford's 4th choice, 67th overall, in 1982 Entry Draft).

			Regular Season					Playoffs				
Season	Club	Lea	GP	G	A	TP	PIM	GP	G	A	TP	PIM
1981-82	Leksand	Swe.	31	3	1	4	40	....	....	....	....	....
1982-83	Leksand	Swe.	33	9	6	15	72	....	....	....	....	....
1983-84	Leksand	Swe.	36	5	11	16	53	....	....	....	....	....
1984-85	**Hartford**	**NHL**	**41**	**2**	**6**	**8**	**83**	....	....	....	....	....
	Binghamton	AHL	36	5	11	16	92	....	....	....	....	....
1985-86	**Hartford**	**NHL**	**80**	**5**	**19**	**24**	**174**	**10**	**1**	**2**	**3**	**38**
1986-87	**Hartford**	**NHL**	**78**	**2**	**31**	**33**	**162**	**5**	**0**	**1**	**1**	**41**
1987-88	**Hartford**	**NHL**	**76**	**8**	**33**	**41**	**159**	**5**	**0**	**0**	**0**	**8**
1988-89	**Hartford**	**NHL**	**71**	**9**	**26**	**35**	**181**	**4**	**0**	**2**	**2**	**4**
1989-90	**Hartford**	**NHL**	**55**	**2**	**11**	**13**	**177**	**7**	**1**	**0**	**1**	**2**
1990-91	**Hartford**	**NHL**	**62**	**3**	**18**	**21**	**174**	....	....	....	....	....
	Pittsburgh	**NHL**	**14**	**1**	**4**	**5**	**37**	**20**	**3**	**2**	**5**	**34**
1991-92	**Pittsburgh**	**NHL**	**62**	**1**	**14**	**15**	**206**	**21**	**0**	**2**	**2**	**39**
1992-93	**Pittsburgh**	**NHL**	**77**	**3**	**26**	**29**	**249**	**12**	**1**	**5**	**6**	**24**
	NHL Totals		**616**	**36**	**188**	**224**	**1602**	**84**	**6**	**14**	**20**	**190**

Traded to **Pittsburgh** by **Hartford** with Ron Francis and Grant Jennings for John Cullen, Jeff Parker and Zarley Zalapski, March 4, 1991.

SANDERSON, GEOFF

Center. Shoots left. 6', 185 lbs. Born, Hay River, N.W.T., February 1, 1972.
(Hartford's 2nd choice, 36th overall, in 1990 Entry Draft).

			Regular Season					Playoffs				
Season	Club	Lea	GP	G	A	TP	PIM	GP	G	A	TP	PIM
1988-89	Swift Current	WHL	58	17	11	28	16	12	3	5	8	6
1989-90	Swift Current	WHL	70	32	62	94	56	4	1	4	5	8
1990-91	**Hartford**	**NHL**	**2**	**1**	**0**	**1**	**0**	**3**	**0**	**0**	**0**	**0**
	Swift Current	WHL	70	62	50	112	57	3	1	2	3	4
	Springfield	AHL	....	....	....	....	....	1	0	0	0	2
1991-92	**Hartford**	**NHL**	**64**	**13**	**18**	**31**	**18**	**7**	**0**	**1**	**1**	**2**
1992-93	**Hartford**	**NHL**	**82**	**46**	**43**	**89**	**28**	....	....	....	....	....
	NHL Totals		**148**	**60**	**61**	**121**	**46**	**10**	**0**	**1**	**1**	**2**

SANDLAK, JIM

Right wing. Shoots right. 6'4", 219 lbs. Born, Kitchener, Ont., December 12, 1966.
(Vancouver's 1st choice, 4th overall, in 1985 Entry Draft).

			Regular Season					Playoffs				
Season	Club	Lea	GP	G	A	TP	PIM	GP	G	A	TP	PIM
1983-84	London	OHL	68	23	18	41	143	8	1	11	12	13
1984-85a	London	OHL	58	40	24	64	128	8	3	2	5	14
1985-86	**Vancouver**	**NHL**	**23**	**1**	**3**	**4**	**10**	**3**	**0**	**1**	**1**	**0**
	London	OHL	16	8	14	22	38	5	2	3	5	24
1986-87b	**Vancouver**	**NHL**	**78**	**15**	**21**	**36**	**66**	....	....	....	....	....
1987-88	**Vancouver**	**NHL**	**49**	**16**	**15**	**31**	**81**	....	....	....	....	....
	Fredericton	AHL	24	10	15	25	47	....	....	....	....	....
1988-89	**Vancouver**	**NHL**	**72**	**20**	**20**	**40**	**99**	**6**	**1**	**1**	**2**	**2**
1989-90	**Vancouver**	**NHL**	**70**	**15**	**8**	**23**	**104**	....	....	....	....	....
1990-91	**Vancouver**	**NHL**	**59**	**7**	**6**	**13**	**125**	....	....	....	....	....
1991-92	**Vancouver**	**NHL**	**66**	**16**	**24**	**40**	**176**	**13**	**4**	**6**	**10**	**22**
1992-93	**Vancouver**	**NHL**	**59**	**10**	**18**	**28**	**122**	**6**	**2**	**2**	**4**	**4**
	NHL Totals		**476**	**100**	**115**	**215**	**783**	**28**	**7**	**10**	**17**	**28**

a OHL Third All-Star Team (1985)
b NHL All-Rookie Team (1987)

Traded to **Hartford** by **Vancouver** to complete March 22, 1993 deal which sent Murray Craven to Vancouver by Hartford with Vancouver's fifth round choice (previously acquired by Hartford — Vancouver selected Scott Walker) in 1993 Entry Draft for Robert Kron, Vancouver's third round choice (Marek Malik) in 1993 Entry Draft and future considerations, May 17, 1993.

SANDSTROM, TOMAS (SAND-struhm)

Right wing. Shoots left. 6'2", 200 lbs. Born, Jakobstad, Finland, September 4, 1964.
(NY Rangers' 2nd choice, 36th overall, in 1982 Entry Draft).

			Regular Season					Playoffs				
Season	Club	Lea	GP	G	A	TP	PIM	GP	G	A	TP	PIM
1981-82	Fagersta	Swe.2	32	28	11	39	74	....	....	....	....	....
1982-83	Brynas	Swe.	36	23	14	37	50	....	....	....	....	....
1983-84	Brynas	Swe.	34	19	10	29	81	....	....	....	....	....
1984-85a	**NY Rangers**	**NHL**	**74**	**29**	**29**	**58**	**51**	**3**	**0**	**2**	**2**	**0**
1985-86	**NY Rangers**	**NHL**	**73**	**25**	**29**	**54**	**109**	**16**	**4**	**6**	**10**	**20**
1986-87	**NY Rangers**	**NHL**	**64**	**40**	**34**	**74**	**60**	**6**	**1**	**2**	**3**	**20**
1987-88	**NY Rangers**	**NHL**	**69**	**28**	**40**	**68**	**95**	....	....	....	....	....
1988-89	**NY Rangers**	**NHL**	**79**	**32**	**56**	**88**	**148**	**4**	**3**	**2**	**5**	**12**
1989-90	**NY Rangers**	**NHL**	**48**	**19**	**19**	**38**	**100**	....	....	....	....	....
	Los Angeles	**NHL**	**28**	**13**	**20**	**33**	**28**	**10**	**5**	**4**	**9**	**19**
1990-91	**Los Angeles**	**NHL**	**68**	**45**	**44**	**89**	**106**	**10**	**4**	**4**	**8**	**14**
1991-92	**Los Angeles**	**NHL**	**49**	**17**	**22**	**39**	**70**	**6**	**0**	**3**	**3**	**8**
1992-93	**Los Angeles**	**NHL**	**39**	**25**	**27**	**52**	**57**	**24**	**8**	**17**	**25**	**12**
	NHL Totals		**591**	**273**	**320**	**593**	**824**	**79**	**25**	**40**	**65**	**105**

a NHL All-Rookie Team (1985)
Played in NHL All-Star Game (1988, 1991)

Traded to **Los Angeles** by **NY Rangers** with Tony Granato for Bernie Nicholls, January 20, 1990.

SANDWITH, TERRAN

Defense. Shoots left. 6'4", 210 lbs. Born, Stoney Plain, Alta., April 17, 1972.
(Philadelphia's 4th choice, 42nd overall, in 1990 Entry Draft).

			Regular Season					Playoffs				
Season	Club	Lea	GP	G	A	TP	PIM	GP	G	A	TP	PIM
1988-89	Tri-City	WHL	31	0	0	0	29	6	0	0	0	4
1989-90	Tri-City	WHL	70	4	14	18	92	7	0	2	2	14
1990-91	Tri-City	WHL	46	5	17	22	132	7	1	0	1	14
1991-92	Brandon	WHL	41	6	14	20	145	....	....	....	....	....
	Saskatoon	WHL	18	2	5	7	53	....	....	....	....	....
1992-93	Hershey	AHL	61	1	12	13	140	....	....	....	....	....

SANTONELLI, MIKE

Center. Shoots left. 6', 165 lbs. Born, Arlington, MA, April 12, 1973.
(Hartford's 11th choice, 229th overall, in 1991 Entry Draft).

			Regular Season					Playoffs				
Season	Club	Lea	GP	G	A	TP	PIM	GP	G	A	TP	PIM
1991-92	Matignon	HS	24	35	34	69	....	....	....	....	....	....
1992-93	U. of Maine	H.E.	DID NOT PLAY									

SAPOZHNIKOV, ANDREI (sa-PAWZH-nik-kawv)

Defense. Shoots left. 6'1", 185 lbs. Born, Chelyabinsk, Soviet Union, June 15, 1971.
(Boston's 5th choice, 129th overall, in 1993 Entry Draft).

			Regular Season					Playoffs				
Season	Club	Lea	GP	G	A	TP	PIM	GP	G	A	TP	PIM
1990-91	Chelyabinsk	USSR	28	0	0	0	14	....	....	....	....	....
1991-92	Chelyabinsk	CIS	43	3	4	7	22	....	....	....	....	....
1992-93	Chelyabinsk	CIS	40	2	7	9	30	8	0	1	1	6

SARAULT, YVES

Left wing. Shoots left. 6'1", 170 lbs. Born, Valleyfield, Que., December 23, 1972.
(Montreal's 3rd choice, 61st overall, in 1991 Entry Draft).

			Regular Season					Playoffs				
Season	Club	Lea	GP	G	A	TP	PIM	GP	G	A	TP	PIM
1989-90	Victoriaville	QMJHL	70	12	28	40	140	16	0	3	3	26
1990-91	St-Jean	QMJHL	56	22	24	46	113	....	....	....	....	....
1991-92a	St-Jean	QMJHL	50	28	38	66	96	....	....	....	....	....
a	Trois-Rivières	QMJHL	18	15	14	29	12	15	10	10	20	18
1992-93	Fredericton	AHL	59	14	17	31	41	3	0	1	1	2
	Wheeling	ECHL	2	1	3	4	0	....	....	....	....	....

a QMJHL Second All-Star Team (1992)

SATAN, MIROSLAV

Center. Shoots left. 6'1", 176 lbs. Born, Topolcany, Czech., October 22, 1974.
(Edmonton's 6th choice, 111th overall, in 1993 Entry Draft).

			Regular Season					Playoffs				
Season	Club	Lea	GP	G	A	TP	PIM	GP	G	A	TP	PIM
1991-92	Topocalny	Czech.2	9	2	1	3	6	....	....	....	....	....
1992-93	Dukla Trencin	Czech.	38	11	6	17	....	....	....	....	....	....

SAVAGE, BRIAN

Center. Shoots left. 6'2", 191 lbs. Born, Sudbury, Ont., February 24, 1971.
(Montreal's 8th choice, 171st overall, in 1991 Entry Draft).

			Regular Season					Playoffs				
Season	Club	Lea	GP	G	A	TP	PIM	GP	G	A	TP	PIM
1990-91	Miami-Ohio	CCHA	28	5	6	11	26	....	....	....	....	....
1991-92	Miami-Ohio	CCHA	40	24	16	40	43	....	....	....	....	....
1992-93ab	Miami-Ohio	CCHA	38	*37	21	58	44	....	....	....	....	....
	Cdn. National	....	9	3	0	3	12	....	....	....	....	....

a CCHA First All-Star Team (1993)
b NCAA West Second All-American Team (1993)

SAVAGE, JOEL

Right wing. Shoots right. 5'11", 205 lbs. Born, Surrey, B.C., December 25, 1969.
(Buffalo's 1st choice, 13th overall, in 1988 Entry Draft).

			Regular Season					Playoffs				
Season	Club	Lea	GP	G	A	TP	PIM	GP	G	A	TP	PIM
1986-87	Victoria	WHL	68	14	13	27	48	5	2	0	2	0
1987-88	Victoria	WHL	69	37	32	69	73	....	....	....	....	....
1988-89	Victoria	WHL	60	17	30	47	95	6	1	1	2	8
1989-90	Rochester	AHL	43	6	7	13	39	5	0	1	1	4
1990-91	**Buffalo**	**NHL**	**3**	**0**	**1**	**1**	**0**	....	....	....	....	....
	Rochester	AHL	61	25	19	44	45	15	3	3	6	8
1991-92	Rochester	AHL	59	8	14	22	39	9	2	0	2	8
1992-93	Rochester	AHL	6	1	1	2	6	3	0	0	0	12
	Fort Wayne	IHL	46	21	16	37	60	10	3	5	8	22
	NHL Totals		**3**	**0**	**1**	**1**	**0**	....	....	....	....	....

SAVAGE, REGINALD (REGGIE)

Center. Shoots left. 5'10", 187 lbs. Born, Montreal, Que., May 1, 1970.
(Washington's 1st choice, 15th overall, in 1988 Entry Draft).

			Regular Season					Playoffs				
Season	Club	Lea	GP	G	A	TP	PIM	GP	G	A	TP	PIM
1987-88	Victoriaville	QMJHL	68	68	54	122	77	5	2	3	5	8
1988-89	Victoriaville	QMJHL	54	58	55	113	178	16	15	13	28	52
1989-90	Victoriaville	QMJHL	63	51	43	94	79	16	13	10	23	40
1990-91	**Washington**	**NHL**	**1**	**0**	**0**	**0**	**0**	....	....	....	....	....
	Baltimore	AHL	62	32	29	61	10	6	1	1	2	6
1991-92	Baltimore	AHL	77	42	28	70	51	....	....	....	....	....
1992-93	**Washington**	**NHL**	**16**	**2**	**3**	**5**	**12**	....	....	....	....	....
	Baltimore	AHL	40	37	18	55	28	....	....	....	....	....
	NHL Totals		**17**	**2**	**3**	**5**	**12**	....	....	....	....	....

Traded to **Quebec** by **Washington** with Paul MacDermid for Mike Hough, June 20, 1993.

SAVARD, DENIS JOSEPH (sa-VARH, den-NY)

Center. Shoots right. 5'10", 175 lbs. Born, Pointe Gatineau, Que., February 4, 1961.
(Chicago's 1st choice, 3rd overall, in 1980 Entry Draft).

			Regular Season					Playoffs				
Season	Club	Lea	GP	G	A	TP	PIM	GP	G	A	TP	PIM
1978-79	Montreal	QJHL	70	46	*112	158	88	11	5	6	11	46
1979-80ab	Montreal	QJHL	72	63	118	181	93	10	7	16	23	8
1980-81	**Chicago**	**NHL**	**76**	**28**	**47**	**75**	**47**	**3**	**0**	**0**	**0**	**0**
1981-82	**Chicago**	**NHL**	**80**	**32**	**87**	**119**	**82**	**15**	**11**	**7**	**18**	**52**
1982-83c	**Chicago**	**NHL**	**78**	**35**	**86**	**121**	**99**	**13**	**8**	**9**	**17**	**22**
1983-84	**Chicago**	**NHL**	**75**	**37**	**57**	**94**	**71**	**5**	**1**	**3**	**4**	**9**
1984-85	**Chicago**	**NHL**	**79**	**38**	**67**	**105**	**56**	**15**	**9**	**20**	**29**	**20**
1985-86	**Chicago**	**NHL**	**80**	**47**	**69**	**116**	**111**	**3**	**4**	**1**	**5**	**6**
1986-87	**Chicago**	**NHL**	**70**	**40**	**50**	**90**	**108**	**4**	**1**	**0**	**1**	**12**
1987-88	**Chicago**	**NHL**	**80**	**44**	**87**	**131**	**95**	**5**	**4**	**3**	**7**	**17**
1988-89	**Chicago**	**NHL**	**58**	**23**	**59**	**82**	**110**	**16**	**8**	**11**	**19**	**10**
1989-90	**Chicago**	**NHL**	**60**	**27**	**53**	**80**	**56**	**20**	**7**	**15**	**22**	**41**
1990-91	**Montreal**	**NHL**	**70**	**28**	**31**	**59**	**52**	**13**	**2**	**11**	**13**	**35**
1991-92	**Montreal**	**NHL**	**77**	**28**	**42**	**70**	**73**	**11**	**3**	**9**	**12**	**8**
1992-93	**Montreal**	**NHL**	**63**	**16**	**34**	**50**	**90**	**14**	**0**	**5**	**5**	**4**
	NHL Totals		**946**	**423**	**769**	**1192**	**1050**	**137**	**58**	**94**	**152**	**236**

a QMJHL First All-Star Team (1980)
b Named QMJHL's Most Valuable Player (1980)
c NHL Second All-Star Team (1983)

Played in NHL All-Star Game (1982-84, 1986, 1988, 1991)

Traded to **Montreal** by **Chicago** for Chris Chelios and Montreal's second round choice (Michael Pomichter) in 1991 Entry Draft, June 29, 1990. Signed as a free agent by **Tampa Bay**, July 29, 1993.

SAVARD, MARC

Forward. Shoots left. 6'2", 200 lbs. Born, Blainville, Que., September 19, 1972.

			Regular Season					Playoffs				
Season	Club	Lea	GP	G	A	TP	PIM	GP	G	A	TP	PIM
1990-91	Drummondville	QMJHL	66	6	28	34	42	14	0	2	2	2
1991-92	Shawinigan	QMJHL	71	8	23	31	78	10	1	3	4	20
1992-93	Kalamazoo	IHL	20	1	1	2	24	....	....	....	....	....

Signed as a free agent by **Minnesota**, August 28, 1992.

SAVENKO, BOGDAN

Right wing. Shoots right. 6'1", 192 lbs. Born, Kiev, Soviet Union, November 20, 1974.
(Chicago's 3rd choice, 54th overall, in 1993 Entry Draft).

			Regular Season					Playoffs				
Season	Club	Lea	GP	G	A	TP	PIM	GP	G	A	TP	PIM
1990-91	SVSM Kiev	USSR 2	40	30	18	48	24	....	....	....	....	....
1991-92	Sokol Kiev	CIS	25	3	1	4	4	....	....	....	....	....
1992-93	Niagara Falls	OHL	51	29	19	48	15	2	1	0	1	2

SAVOIE, CLAUDE

Right wing. Shoots right. 5'11", 182 lbs. Born, Montreal, Que., March 12, 1973.
(Ottawa's 9th choice, 194th overall, in 1992 Entry Draft).

			Regular Season					Playoffs				
Season	Club	Lea	GP	G	A	TP	PIM	GP	G	A	TP	PIM
1990-91	Victoriaville	QMJHL	61	20	22	42	101	....	....	....	....	....
1991-92	Victoriaville	QMJHL	69	39	40	79	140	....	....	....	....	....
1992-93	Victoriaville	QMJHL	67	70	61	131	113	6	4	5	9	6

SCHLEGEL, BRAD (shlay-GUHL)

Defense. Shoots right. 5'10", 188 lbs. Born, Kitchener, Ont., July 22, 1968.
(Washington's 8th choice, 144th overall, in 1988 Entry Draft).

			Regular Season					Playoffs				
Season	Club	Lea	GP	G	A	TP	PIM	GP	G	A	TP	PIM
1986-87	London	OHL	65	4	23	27	24	....	....	....	....	....
1987-88a	London	OHL	66	13	63	76	49	12	8	17	25	6
1988-89	Cdn. National	....	60	2	22	24	30	....	....	....	....	....
1989-90	Cdn. National	....	72	7	25	32	44	....	....	....	....	....
1990-91	Cdn. National	....	59	8	20	28	64	....	....	....	....	....
1991-92	Cdn. National	....	61	3	18	21	84	....	....	....	....	....
	Cdn. Olympic	....	8	1	2	3	4	....	....	....	....	....
	Washington	**NHL**	**15**	**0**	**1**	**1**	**0**	**7**	**0**	**1**	**1**	**2**
	Baltimore	AHL	2	0	1	1	0	....	....	....	....	....
1992-93	**Washington**	**NHL**	**7**	**0**	**1**	**1**	**6**	....	....	....	....	....
	Baltimore	AHL	61	3	20	23	40	7	0	5	5	6
	NHL Totals		**22**	**0**	**2**	**2**	**6**	**7**	**0**	**1**	**1**	**2**

a OHL Second All-Star Team (1988)

Traded to **Calgary** by **Washington** for Calgary's seventh round choice (Andrew Brunette) in 1993 Entry Draft, June 26, 1993.

SCHMIDT, COLIN

Center. Shoots left. 5'11", 185 lbs. Born, Regina, Sask., February 3, 1974.
(Edmonton's 9th choice, 190th overall, in 1992 Entry Draft).

			Regular Season					Playoffs				
Season	Club	Lea	GP	G	A	TP	PIM	GP	G	A	TP	PIM
1991-92	Regina	Midget			UNAVAILABLE							
1992-93	Colorado	WCHA	27	8	13	21	26	....	....	....	....	....

SCHNEIDER, ANDY

Left wing. Shoots left. 5'9", 170 lbs. Born, Edmonton, Alta., March 29, 1972.

			Regular Season					Playoffs				
Season	Club	Lea	GP	G	A	TP	PIM	GP	G	A	TP	PIM
1990-91	Swift Current	WHL	69	12	74	86	103	3	0	0	0	2
1991-92	Swift Current	WHL	63	44	60	104	120	8	4	9	13	8
1992-93ab	Swift Current	WHL	38	19	66	85	78	17	13	*26	*39	40
	New Haven	AHL	19	2	2	4	13	....	....	....	....	....

a WHL East Second All-Star Team (1993)
b WHL Playoff MVP (1993)

Signed as a free agent by **Ottawa**, October 9, 1992.

SCHNEIDER, MATHIEU

Defense. Shoots left. 5'11", 189 lbs. Born, New York, NY, June 12, 1969.
(Montreal's 4th choice, 44th overall, in 1987 Entry Draft).

			Regular Season					Playoffs				
Season	Club	Lea	GP	G	A	TP	PIM	GP	G	A	TP	PIM
1986-87	Cornwall	OHL	63	7	29	36	75	5	0	0	0	22
1987-88	**Montreal**	**NHL**	**4**	**0**	**0**	**0**	**2**	....	....	....	....	....
a	Cornwall	OHL	48	21	40	61	83	11	2	6	8	14
	Sherbrooke	AHL	....	....	....	....	....	3	0	3	3	12
1988-89	Cornwall	OHL	59	16	57	73	96	18	7	20	27	30
1989-90	**Montreal**	**NHL**	**44**	**7**	**14**	**21**	**25**	**9**	**1**	**3**	**4**	**31**
	Sherbrooke	AHL	28	6	13	19	20	....	....	....	....	....
1990-91	**Montreal**	**NHL**	**69**	**10**	**20**	**30**	**63**	**13**	**2**	**7**	**9**	**18**
1991-92	**Montreal**	**NHL**	**78**	**8**	**24**	**32**	**72**	**10**	**1**	**4**	**5**	**6**
1992-93	**Montreal**	**NHL**	**60**	**13**	**31**	**44**	**91**	**11**	**1**	**2**	**3**	**16**
	NHL Totals		**255**	**38**	**89**	**127**	**253**	**43**	**5**	**16**	**21**	**71**

a OHL First All-Star Team (1988)

SCHRINER, MARTY

Center. Shoots left. 5'11", 175 lbs. Born, Port Huron, MI, May 20, 1972.
(NY Islanders' 12th choice, 246th overall, in 1991 Entry Draft).

			Regular Season					Playoffs				
Season	Club	Lea	GP	G	A	TP	PIM	GP	G	A	TP	PIM
1990-91	North Dakota	WCHA	40	6	11	17	90	....	....	....	....	....
1991-92	North Dakota	WCHA	32	10	12	22	112	....	....	....	....	....
1992-93	North Dakota	WCHA	36	8	19	27	*156	....	....	....	....	....

SCHULTE, PAXTON

Left wing. Shoots left. 6'2", 210 lbs. Born, Ionaway, Alta., July 16, 1972.
(Quebec's 7th choice, 124th overall, in 1992 Entry Draft).

			Regular Season					Playoffs				
Season	Club	Lea	GP	G	A	TP	PIM	GP	G	A	TP	PIM
1990-91	North Dakota	WCHA	38	2	4	6	32	....	....	....	....	....
1991-92	Spokane	WHL	70	42	42	84	222	10	2	8	10	48
1992-93	Spokane	WHL	45	38	35	73	142	10	5	6	11	12

SCISSONS, SCOTT (SIHS-UHNS)

Center. Shoots left. 6'1", 201 lbs. Born, Saskatoon, Sask., October 29, 1971.
(NY Islanders' 1st choice, 6th overall, in 1990 Entry Draft).

			Regular Season					Playoffs				
Season	Club	Lea	GP	G	A	TP	PIM	GP	G	A	TP	PIM
1988-89	Saskatoon	WHL	71	30	56	86	65	7	0	4	4	16
1989-90	Saskatoon	WHL	61	40	47	87	81	10	3	8	11	6
1990-91	**NY Islanders**	**NHL**	**1**	**0**	**0**	**0**	**0**	....	....	....	....	....
	Saskatoon	WHL	57	24	53	77	61	....	....	....	....	....
1991-92					DID NOT PLAY – INJURED							
1992-93	Capital Dist.	AHL	43	14	30	44	33	4	0	0	0	0
	NY Islanders	**NHL**	....	....	....	....	....	**1**	**0**	**0**	**0**	**0**
	NHL Totals		**1**	**0**	**0**	**0**	**0**	**1**	**0**	**0**	**0**	**0**

SCREMIN, CLAUDIO

Defense. Shoots right. 6'2", 205 lbs. Born, Burnaby, B.C., May 28, 1968.
(Washington's 12th choice, 204th overall, in 1988 Entry Draft).

			Regular Season					Playoffs				
Season	Club	Lea	GP	G	A	TP	PIM	GP	G	A	TP	PIM
1986-87	U. of Maine	H.E.	15	0	1	1	2	....	....	....	....	....
1987-88	U. of Maine	H.E.	44	6	18	24	22	....	....	....	....	....
1988-89	U. of Maine	H.E.	45	5	24	29	42	....	....	....	....	....
1989-90	U. of Maine	H.E.	45	4	26	30	14	....	....	....	....	....
1990-91	Kansas City	IHL	77	7	14	21	60	....	....	....	....	....
1991-92	**San Jose**	**NHL**	**13**	**0**	**0**	**0**	**25**	....	....	....	....	....
	Kansas City	IHL	70	5	23	28	44	15	1	6	7	14
1992-93	**San Jose**	**NHL**	**4**	**0**	**1**	**1**	**4**	....	....	....	....	....
	Kansas City	IHL	75	10	22	32	93	12	0	5	5	18
	NHL Totals		**17**	**0**	**1**	**1**	**29**	....	....	....	....	....

Traded to **Minnesota** by **Washington** for Don Beaupre, November 1, 1988. Signed as a free agent by **San Jose**, September 3, 1991.

SEARS, SVERRE

Defense. Shoots left. 6'2", 185 lbs. Born, Boston, MA, October 17, 1970.
(Philadelphia's 6th choice, 159th overall, in 1989 Entry Draft).

			Regular Season					Playoffs				
Season	Club	Lea	GP	G	A	TP	PIM	GP	G	A	TP	PIM
1989-90	Princeton	ECAC	3	0	1	1	14	....	....	....	....	....
1990-91	Princeton	ECAC	27	2	9	11	56	....	....	....	....	....
1991-92	Princeton	ECAC	25	3	9	12	62	....	....	....	....	....
1992-93	Princeton	ECAC	23	3	9	12	96	....	....	....	....	....

SEGUIN, BRETT

Center. Shoots left. 5'9", 199 lbs. Born, Rochester, NY, February 20, 1972.
(Los Angeles' 6th choice, 130th overall, in 1991 Entry Draft).

			Regular Season					Playoffs				
Season	Club	Lea	GP	G	A	TP	PIM	GP	G	A	TP	PIM
1989-90	Ottawa	OHL	63	28	*80	108	30	....	....	....	....	....
1990-91	Ottawa	OHL	63	24	*87	111	85	17	10	*25	35	21
1991-92	Ottawa	OHL	64	34	*100	134	70	11	8	10	18	16
1992-93	Phoenix	IHL	16	2	7	9	8	....	....	....	....	....
	Muskegon	Col.	49	24	40	64	48	....	....	....	....	....

SEHER, KURT

Defense. Shoots left. 6'1", 180 lbs. Born, Lethbridge, Alta., April 15, 1973.
(Boston's 8th choice, 184th overall, in 1992 Entry Draft).

			Regular Season					Playoffs				
Season	Club	Lea	GP	G	A	TP	PIM	GP	G	A	TP	PIM
1990-91	Swift Current	WHL	59	4	26	30	63	2	0	0	0	0
1991-92	Seattle	WHL	60	15	23	38	128	15	3	12	15	32
1992-93	Seattle	WHL	69	9	20	29	125	5	0	3	3	10

SELANNE, TEEMU (SEH-lahn-nay, TEE-moo)

Right wing. Shoots right. 6', 191 lbs. Born, Helsinki, Finland, July 3, 1970.
(Winnipeg's 1st choice, 10th overall, in 1988 Entry Draft).

			Regular Season					Playoffs				
Season	Club	Lea	GP	G	A	TP	PIM	GP	G	A	TP	PIM
1987-88	Jokerit	Fin. Jr.	33	43	23	66	18	5	4	3	7	2
	Jokerit	Fin.2	5	1	1	2	0	....	....	....	....	....
1988-89	Jokerit	Fin.2	34	35	33	68	12	5	7	3	10	4
1989-90	Jokerit	Fin.	11	4	8	12	0	....	....	....	....	....
1990-91	Jokerit	Fin.	42	33	25	58	12	....	....	....	....	....
1991-92	Jokerit	Fin.	44	*39	23	62	20	10	10	7	17	18
1992-93abc	**Winnipeg**	**NHL**	**84**	***76**	**56**	**132**	**45**	**6**	**4**	**2**	**6**	**2**
	NHL Totals		**84**	**76**	**56**	**132**	**45**	**6**	**4**	**2**	**6**	**2**

a Won Calder Memorial Trophy (1993)
b NHL First All-Star Team (1993)
c NHL/Upper Deck All-Rookie Team (1993)

Played in NHL All-Star Game (1993)

SELYANIN, SERGEI (sel-AN-in)

Defense. Shoots left. 5'11", 198 lbs. Born, Novosibirsk, Soviet Union, September 20, 1966.
(Winnipeg's 12th choice, 224th overall, in 1990 Entry Draft).

			Regular Season					Playoffs				
Season	Club	Lea	GP	G	A	TP	PIM	GP	G	A	TP	PIM
1982-83	Sibir	USSR 2	4	0	0	0	4	....	....	....	....	....
1983-84	Sibir	USSR	30	0	1	1	20	....	....	....	....	....
1984-85	Sibir	USSR 2				UNAVAILABLE						
1985-86	CSKA	USSR	8	0	0	0	6	....	....	....	....	....
1986-87	CSKA	USSR	34	0	0	0	28	....	....	....	....	....
1987-88	CSKA	USSR	21	2	0	2	16	....	....	....	....	....
	Khimik	USSR	11	2	2	4	8	....	....	....	....	....
1988-89	Khimik	USSR	44	6	4	10	42	....	....	....	....	....
1989-90	Khimik	USSR	33	2	4	6	63	....	....	....	....	....
1990-91	Khimik	USSR	43	4	7	11	56	....	....	....	....	....
1991-92	Khimik	CIS	41	3	13	16	42	....	....	....	....	....
1992-93	Khimik	CIS	27	1	2	3	72	1	0	0	0	2

SEMAK, ALEXANDER (seh-MAHK)

Center. Shoots right. 5'10", 185 lbs. Born, Ufa, Soviet Union, February 11, 1966.
(New Jersey's 12th choice, 207th overall, in 1988 Entry Draft).

			Regular Season					Playoffs				
Season	Club	Lea	GP	G	A	TP	PIM	GP	G	A	TP	PIM
1982-83	Yulayev	USSR	13	2	1	3	4	....	....	....	....	....
1983-84	Yulayev	USSR 2				UNAVAILABLE						
1984-85	Yulayev	USSR 2	47	19	17	36	64	....	....	....	....	....
1985-86	Yulayev	USSR	22	9	7	16	22	....	....	....	....	....
1986-87	Moscow D'amo	USSR	40	20	8	28	32	....	....	....	....	....
1987-88	Moscow D'amo	USSR	47	21	14	35	40	....	....	....	....	....
1988-89	Moscow D'amo	USSR	44	18	10	28	22	....	....	....	....	....
1989-90	Moscow D'amo	USSR	43	23	11	34	33	....	....	....	....	....
1990-91	Moscow D'amo	USSR	46	17	21	38	48	....	....	....	....	....
1991-92	Moscow D'amo	CIS	26	10	13	23	26	....	....	....	....	....
	New Jersey	**NHL**	**25**	**5**	**6**	**11**	**0**	**1**	**0**	**0**	**0**	**0**
	Utica	AHL	7	3	2	5	0	....	....	....	....	....
1992-93	**New Jersey**	**NHL**	**82**	**37**	**42**	**79**	**70**	**5**	**1**	**1**	**2**	**0**
	NHL Totals		**107**	**42**	**48**	**90**	**70**	**6**	**1**	**1**	**2**	**0**

SEMCHUK, THOMAS (BRANDY)

Right wing. Shoots right. 6'1", 185 lbs. Born, Calgary, Alta., September 22, 1971.
(Los Angeles' 2nd choice, 28th overall, in 1990 Entry Draft).

			Regular Season					Playoffs				
Season	Club	Lea	GP	G	A	TP	PIM	GP	G	A	TP	PIM
1988-89	Cdn. National	....	42	11	11	22	60	....	....	....	....	....
1989-90	Cdn. National	....	55	10	15	25	40	....	....	....	....	....
1990-91	Lethbridge	WHL	14	9	8	17	10	15	8	5	13	18
	New Haven	AHL	21	1	4	5	6	....	....	....	....	....
1991-92	Phoenix	IHL	15	1	5	6	6	....	....	....	....	....
	Raleigh	ECHL	5	1	2	3	16	2	1	0	1	4
1992-93	**Los Angeles**	**NHL**	**1**	**0**	**0**	**0**	**2**	....	....	....	....	....
	Phoenix	IHL	56	13	12	25	58	....	....	....	....	....
	NHL Totals		**1**	**0**	**0**	**0**	**2**	....	....	....	....	....

SEMENOV, ANATOLI (seh-MEH-nahf)

Center/Left wing. Shoots left. 6'2", 190 lbs. Born, Moscow, Soviet Union, March 5, 1962.
(Edmonton's 5th choice, 120th overall, in 1989 Entry Draft).

			Regular Season					Playoffs				
Season	Club	Lea	GP	G	A	TP	PIM	GP	G	A	TP	PIM
1979-80	Moscow D'amo	USSR	8	3	0	3	2	....	....	....	....	....
1980-81	Moscow D'amo	USSR	47	18	14	32	18	....	....	....	....	....
1981-82	Moscow D'amo	USSR	44	12	14	26	28	....	....	....	....	....
1982-83	Moscow D'amo	USSR	44	22	18	40	26	....	....	....	....	....
1983-84	Moscow D'amo	USSR	19	10	5	15	14	....	....	....	....	....
1984-85	Moscow D'amo	USSR	30	17	12	29	32	....	....	....	....	....
1985-86	Moscow D'amo	USSR	32	18	17	35	19	....	....	....	....	....
1986-87	Moscow D'amo	USSR	40	15	29	44	32	....	....	....	....	....
1987-88	Moscow D'amo	USSR	32	17	8	25	22	....	....	....	....	....
1988-89	Moscow D'amo	USSR	31	9	12	21	24	....	....	....	....	....
1989-90	Moscow D'amo	USSR	48	13	20	33	16	....	....	....	....	....
	Edmonton	**NHL**	....	....	....	....	....	**2**	**0**	**0**	**0**	**0**
1990-91	**Edmonton**	**NHL**	**57**	**15**	**16**	**31**	**26**	**12**	**5**	**5**	**10**	**6**
1991-92	**Edmonton**	**NHL**	**59**	**20**	**22**	**42**	**16**	**8**	**1**	**1**	**2**	**6**
1992-93	**Tampa Bay**	**NHL**	**13**	**2**	**3**	**5**	**4**	....	....	....	....	....
	Vancouver	**NHL**	**62**	**10**	**34**	**44**	**28**	**12**	**1**	**3**	**4**	**0**
	NHL Totals		**191**	**47**	**75**	**122**	**74**	**34**	**7**	**9**	**16**	**12**

Claimed by **Tampa Bay** from **Edmonton** in Expansion Draft, June 18, 1992. Traded to **Vancouver** by **Tampa Bay** for Dave Capuano and Vancouver's fourth round choice in 1994 Entry Draft, November 3, 1992. Claimed by **Anaheim** from **Vancouver** in Expansion Draft, June 24, 1993.

SEPPO, JUKKA (SEHP-poh)

Center. Shoots left. 6'2", 198 lbs. Born, Vaasa, Finland, January 22, 1968.
(Philadelphia's 2nd choice, 23rd overall, in 1986 Entry Draft).

			Regular Season					Playoffs				
Season	Club	Lea	GP	G	A	TP	PIM	GP	G	A	TP	PIM
1986-87	Tappara	Fin.	39	11	16	27	50	9	1	4	5	14
1987-88	Sport	Fin.2	42	28	37	65	78	....	....	....	....	....
1988-89	HIFK	Fin.	35	7	13	20	28	2	2	1	3	2
1989-90	HIFK	Fin.	39	15	27	42	50	....	....	....	....	....
1990-91	HIFK	Fin.	35	17	22	39	81	1	1	0	1	0
1991-92	HIFK	Fin.	43	16	31	47	53	7	2	4	6	33
1992-93	HIFK	Fin.	45	16	17	33	52	4	0	1	1	2

SEROWIK, JEFF (sir-OH-ik)

Defense. Shoots right. 6', 190 lbs. Born, Manchester, NH, October 1, 1967.
(Toronto's 5th choice, 85th overall, in 1985 Entry Draft).

			Regular Season					Playoffs				
Season	Club	Lea	GP	G	A	TP	PIM	GP	G	A	TP	PIM
1986-87	Providence	H.E.	33	3	8	11	22	....	....	....	....	....
1987-88	Providence	H.E.	33	3	9	12	44	....	....	....	....	....
1988-89	Providence	H.E.	35	3	14	17	48	....	....	....	....	....
1989-90a	Providence	H.E.	35	6	19	25	34	....	....	....	....	....
1990-91	**Toronto**	**NHL**	**1**	**0**	**0**	**0**	**0**	....	....	....	....	....
	Newmarket	AHL	60	8	15	23	45	....	....	....	....	....
1991-92	St. John's	AHL	78	11	34	45	60	16	4	9	13	22
1992-93b	St. John's	AHL	77	19	35	54	92	9	1	5	6	8
	NHL Totals		**1**	**0**	**0**	**0**	**0**	....	....	....	....	....

a Hockey East Second All-Star Team (1990)
b AHL Second All-Star Team (1993)

Signed as a free agent by **Florida**, July 20, 1993.

SEVERYN, BRENT

Defense. Shoots left. 6'2", 210 lbs. Born, Vegreville, Alta., February 22, 1966.

			Regular Season					Playoffs				
Season	Club	Lea	GP	G	A	TP	PIM	GP	G	A	TP	PIM
1983-84	Seattle	WHL	72	14	22	36	49	....	....	....	....	....
1984-85	Seattle	WHL	38	8	32	40	54	....	....	....	....	....
	Brandon	WHL	26	7	16	23	57	....	....	....	....	....
1985-86	Seattle	WHL	33	11	20	31	164	....	....	....	....	....
	Saskatoon	WHL	9	1	4	5	38	....	....	....	....	....
1986-87	U. of Alberta	CWUAA	....	....	....	....	....	....	....	....	....	....
1987-88	U. of Alberta	CWUAA	46	21	29	50	178	....	....	....	....	....
1988-89	Halifax	AHL	47	2	12	14	141	....	....	....	....	....
1989-90	**Quebec**	**NHL**	**35**	**0**	**2**	**2**	**42**	....	....	....	....	....
	Halifax	AHL	43	6	9	15	105	6	1	2	3	49
1990-91	Halifax	AHL	50	7	26	33	202	....	....	....	....	....
1991-92	Utica	AHL	80	11	33	44	211	4	0	1	1	4
1992-93a	Utica	AHL	77	20	32	52	240	5	0	0	0	35
	NHL Totals		**35**	**0**	**2**	**2**	**42**	....	....	....	....	....

a AHL First All-Star Team (1993)

Signed as a free agent by **Quebec**, July 15, 1988. Traded to **New Jersey** by **Quebec** for Dave Marcinyshyn, June 3, 1991.

SEVIGNY, PIERRE (seh-VIH-nee)

Left wing. Shoots left. 6', 189 lbs. Born, Trois-Rivières, Que., September 8, 1971.
(Montreal's 4th choice, 51st overall, in 1989 Entry Draft).

			Regular Season					Playoffs				
Season	Club	Lea	GP	G	A	TP	PIM	GP	G	A	TP	PIM
1988-89	Verdun	QMJHL	67	27	43	70	88	....	....	....	....	....
1989-90a	St-Hyacinthe	QMJHL	67	47	72	119	205	12	8	8	16	42
1990-91a	St-Hyacinthe	QMJHL	60	36	46	82	203	....	....	....	....	....
1991-92	Fredericton	AHL	74	22	37	59	145	7	1	1	2	26
1992-93	Fredericton	AHL	80	36	40	76	113	5	1	1	2	2

a QMJHL Second All-Star Team (1990, 1991)

SHANAHAN, BRENDAN

Left wing. Shoots right. 6'3", 215 lbs. Born, Mimico, Ont., January 23, 1969.
(New Jersey's 1st choice, 2nd overall, in 1987 Entry Draft).

			Regular Season					Playoffs				
Season	Club	Lea	GP	G	A	TP	PIM	GP	G	A	TP	PIM
1985-86	London	OHL	59	28	34	62	70	5	5	5	10	5
1986-87	London	OHL	56	39	53	92	92	....	....	....	....	....
1987-88	**New Jersey**	**NHL**	**65**	**7**	**19**	**26**	**131**	**12**	**2**	**1**	**3**	**44**
1988-89	**New Jersey**	**NHL**	**68**	**22**	**28**	**50**	**115**	....	....	....	....	....
1989-90	**New Jersey**	**NHL**	**73**	**30**	**42**	**72**	**137**	**6**	**3**	**3**	**6**	**20**
1990-91	**New Jersey**	**NHL**	**75**	**29**	**37**	**66**	**141**	**7**	**3**	**5**	**8**	**12**
1991-92	**St. Louis**	**NHL**	**80**	**33**	**36**	**69**	**171**	**6**	**2**	**3**	**5**	**14**
1992-93	**St. Louis**	**NHL**	**71**	**51**	**43**	**94**	**174**	**11**	**4**	**3**	**7**	**18**
	NHL Totals		**432**	**172**	**205**	**377**	**869**	**42**	**14**	**15**	**29**	**108**

Signed as a free agent by **St. Louis**, July 25, 1991.

SHANK, DANIEL

Right wing. Shoots right. 5'10", 190 lbs. Born, Montreal, Que., May 12, 1967.

			Regular Season					Playoffs				
Season	Club	Lea	GP	G	A	TP	PIM	GP	G	A	TP	PIM
1985-86	Shawinigan	QMJHL	51	34	38	72	184	....	....	....	....	....
1986-87	Hull	QMJHL	46	26	43	69	325	....	....	....	....	....
1987-88	Hull	QMJHL	42	23	34	57	274	5	3	2	5	16
1988-89	Adirondack	AHL	42	5	20	25	113	17	11	8	19	102
1989-90	**Detroit**	**NHL**	**57**	**11**	**13**	**24**	**143**	....	....	....	....	....
	Adirondack	AHL	14	8	8	16	36	....	....	....	....	....
1990-91	**Detroit**	**NHL**	**7**	**0**	**1**	**1**	**14**	....	....	....	....	....
	Adirondack	AHL	60	26	49	75	278	....	....	....	....	....
1991-92	Adirondack	AHL	27	13	21	34	112	....	....	....	....	....
	Hartford	**NHL**	**13**	**2**	**0**	**2**	**18**	**5**	**0**	**0**	**0**	**22**
	Springfield	AHL	31	9	19	28	83	8	8	0	8	48
1992-93a	San Diego	IHL	77	39	53	92	*495	14	5	10	15	*131
	NHL Totals		**77**	**13**	**14**	**27**	**175**	**5**	**0**	**0**	**0**	**22**

a IHL First All-Star Team (1993)

Signed as a free agent by **Detroit**, May 26, 1989. Traded to **Hartford** by **Detroit** for Chris Tancill, December 18, 1991.

SHANNON, DARRIN

Left wing. Shoots left. 6'2", 200 lbs. Born, Barrie, Ont., December 8, 1969.
(Pittsburgh's 1st choice, 4th overall, in 1988 Entry Draft).

			Regular Season					Playoffs				
Season	Club	Lea	GP	G	A	TP	PIM	GP	G	A	TP	PIM
1986-87	Windsor	OHL	60	16	67	83	116	14	4	6	10	8
1987-88	Windsor	OHL	43	33	41	74	49	12	6	12	18	9
1988-89	**Buffalo**	**NHL**	**3**	**0**	**0**	**0**	**0**	**2**	**0**	**0**	**0**	**0**
	Windsor	OHL	54	33	48	81	47	4	1	6	7	2
1989-90	**Buffalo**	**NHL**	**17**	**2**	**7**	**9**	**4**	**6**	**0**	**1**	**1**	**4**
	Rochester	AHL	50	20	23	43	25	9	4	1	5	2
1990-91	**Buffalo**	**NHL**	**34**	**8**	**6**	**14**	**12**	**6**	**1**	**2**	**3**	**4**
	Rochester	AHL	49	26	34	60	56	10	3	5	8	22
1991-92	**Buffalo**	**NHL**	**1**	**0**	**1**	**1**	**0**	....	....	....	....	....
	Winnipeg	**NHL**	**68**	**13**	**26**	**39**	**41**	**7**	**0**	**1**	**1**	**10**
1992-93	**Winnipeg**	**NHL**	**84**	**20**	**40**	**60**	**91**	**6**	**2**	**4**	**6**	**6**
	NHL Totals		**207**	**43**	**80**	**123**	**148**	**27**	**3**	**8**	**11**	**24**

Traded to **Buffalo** by **Pittsburgh** with Doug Bodger for Tom Barrasso and Buffalo's third round choice (Joe Dziedzic) in 1990 Entry Draft, November 12, 1988. Traded to **Winnipeg** by **Buffalo** with Mike Hartman and Dean Kennedy for Dave McLlwain, Gord Donnelly, Winnipeg's fifth round choice (Yuri Khmylev) in 1992 Entry Draft and future considerations, October 11, 1991.

SHANNON, DARRYL

Defense. Shoots left. 6'2", 195 lbs. Born, Barrie, Ont., June 21, 1968.
(Toronto's 2nd choice, 36th overall, in 1986 Entry Draft).

			Regular Season					Playoffs				
Season	Club	Lea	GP	G	A	TP	PIM	GP	G	A	TP	PIM
1985-86	Windsor	OHL	57	6	21	27	52	16	5	6	11	22
1986-87a	Windsor	OHL	64	23	27	50	83	14	4	8	12	18
1987-88b	Windsor	OHL	60	16	67	83	116	12	3	8	11	17
1988-89	**Toronto**	**NHL**	**14**	**1**	**3**	**4**	**6**	....	....	....	....	....
	Newmarket	AHL	61	5	24	29	37	5	0	3	3	10
1989-90	**Toronto**	**NHL**	**10**	**0**	**1**	**1**	**12**	....	....	....	....	....
	Newmarket	AHL	47	4	15	19	58	....	....	....	....	....
1990-91	**Toronto**	**NHL**	**10**	**0**	**1**	**1**	**0**	....	....	....	....	....
	Newmarket	AHL	47	2	14	16	51	....	....	....	....	....
1991-92	**Toronto**	**NHL**	**48**	**2**	**8**	**10**	**23**	....	....	....	....	....
1992-93	**Toronto**	**NHL**	**16**	**0**	**0**	**0**	**11**	....	....	....	....	....
	St. John's	AHL	7	1	1	2	4	....	....	....	....	....
	NHL Totals		**98**	**3**	**13**	**16**	**52**	....	....	....	....	....

a OHL Second All-Star Team (1987)
b OHL First All-Star Team, Defenseman of the Year (1988)

Signed as a free agent by **Winnipeg**, June 30, 1993.

SHANTZ, JEFF

Center. Shoots right. 6', 184 lbs. Born, Duchess, Alta., October 10, 1973.
(Chicago's 2nd choice, 36th overall, in 1992 Entry Draft).

			Regular Season					Playoffs				
Season	Club	Lea	GP	G	A	TP	PIM	GP	G	A	TP	PIM
1990-91	Regina	WHL	69	16	21	37	22	8	2	2	4	2
1991-92	Regina	WHL	72	39	50	89	75	....	....	....	....	....
1992-93a	Regina	WHL	64	29	54	83	75	13	2	12	14	14

a WHL East First All-Star Team (1993)

SHARPLES, JEFF

Defense. Shoots left. 6'1", 195 lbs. Born, Terrace, B.C., July 28, 1967.
(Detroit's 2nd choice, 29th overall, in 1985 Entry Draft).

			Regular Season					Playoffs				
Season	Club	Lea	GP	G	A	TP	PIM	GP	G	A	TP	PIM
1983-84	Kelowna	WHL	72	9	24	33	51	....	....	....	....	....
1984-85a	Kelowna	WHL	72	12	41	53	90	6	0	1	1	6
1985-86	Spokane	WHL	3	0	0	0	4	....	....	....	....	....
	Portland	WHL	19	2	6	8	44	15	2	6	8	6
1986-87	**Detroit**	**NHL**	**3**	**0**	**1**	**1**	**2**	**2**	**0**	**0**	**0**	**2**
	Portland	WHL	44	25	35	60	92	20	7	15	22	23
1987-88	**Detroit**	**NHL**	**56**	**10**	**25**	**35**	**42**	**4**	**0**	**3**	**3**	**4**
	Adirondack	AHL	4	2	1	3	4	....	....	....	....	....
1988-89	**Detroit**	**NHL**	**46**	**4**	**9**	**13**	**26**	**1**	**0**	**0**	**0**	**0**
	Adirondack	AHL	10	0	4	4	8	....	....	....	....	....
1989-90	Adirondack	AHL	9	2	5	7	6	....	....	....	....	....
	Cape Breton	AHL	38	4	13	17	28	....	....	....	....	....
	Utica	AHL	13	2	5	7	19	5	1	2	3	15
1990-91	Utica	AHL	64	16	29	45	42	....	....	....	....	....
1991-92	Capital Dist.	AHL	31	3	12	15	18	7	6	5	11	4
1992-93	Kansas City	IHL	39	5	21	26	43	8	0	0	0	6
	NHL Totals		**105**	**14**	**35**	**49**	**70**	**7**	**0**	**3**	**3**	**6**

a WHL West Second All-Star Team (1985)

Traded to **Edmonton** by **Detroit** with Petr Klima, Joe Murphy and Adam Graves for Jimmy Carson, Kevin McClelland and Edmonton's fifth round choice (later traded to Montreal — Montreal selected Brad Layzell) in 1991 Entry Draft, November 2, 1989. Traded to **New Jersey** by **Edmonton** for Reijo Ruotsalainen, March 6, 1990.

SHAW, BRAD

Defense. Shoots right. 6', 190 lbs. Born, Cambridge, Ont., April 28, 1964.
(Detroit's 5th choice, 86th overall, in 1982 Entry Draft).

			Regular Season					Playoffs				
Season	Club	Lea	GP	G	A	TP	PIM	GP	G	A	TP	PIM
1981-82	Ottawa	OHL	68	13	59	72	24	15	1	13	14	4
1982-83	Ottawa	OHL	63	12	66	78	24	9	2	9	11	4
1983-84a	Ottawa	OHL	68	11	71	82	75	13	2	*27	29	9
1984-85	Binghamton	AHL	24	1	10	11	4	8	1	8	9	6
	Salt Lake	IHL	44	3	29	32	25	....	....	....	....	....
1985-86	**Hartford**	**NHL**	**8**	**0**	**2**	**2**	**4**	....	....	....	....	....
	Binghamton	AHL	64	10	44	54	33	5	0	2	2	6
1986-87	**Hartford**	**NHL**	**2**	**0**	**0**	**0**	**0**	....	....	....	....	....
bc	Binghamton	AHL	77	9	30	39	43	12	1	8	9	2
1987-88	**Hartford**	**NHL**	**1**	**0**	**0**	**0**	**0**	....	....	....	....	....
b	Binghamton	AHL	73	12	50	62	50	4	0	5	5	4
1988-89	Verese	Italy	35	10	30	40	44	11	4	8	12	13
	Cdn. National	....	4	1	0	1	2	....	....	....	....	....
	Hartford	**NHL**	**3**	**1**	**0**	**1**	**0**	**3**	**1**	**0**	**1**	**0**
1989-90d	**Hartford**	**NHL**	**64**	**3**	**32**	**35**	**30**	**7**	**2**	**5**	**7**	**0**
1990-91	**Hartford**	**NHL**	**72**	**4**	**28**	**32**	**29**	**6**	**1**	**2**	**3**	**2**
1991-92	**Hartford**	**NHL**	**62**	**3**	**22**	**25**	**44**	**3**	**0**	**1**	**1**	**4**
1992-93	**Ottawa**	**NHL**	**81**	**7**	**34**	**41**	**34**	....	....	....	....	....
	NHL Totals		**293**	**18**	**118**	**136**	**141**	**19**	**4**	**8**	**12**	**6**

a OHL First All-Star Team (1984)
b AHL First All-Star Team (1987, 1988)
c Won Eddie Shore Plaque (AHL Outstanding Defenseman) (1987)
d NHL All-Rookie Team (1990)

Rights traded to **Hartford** by **Detroit** for Hartford's eighth round choice (Urban Nordin) in 1984 Entry Draft, May 29, 1984. Traded to **New Jersey** by **Hartford** for cash, June 13, 1992. Claimed by **Ottawa** from **New Jersey** in Expansion Draft, June 18, 1992.

SHAW, DAVID

Defense. Shoots right. 6'2", 205 lbs. Born, St. Thomas, Ont., May 25, 1964.
(Quebec's 1st choice, 13th overall, in 1982 Entry Draft).

			Regular Season					Playoffs				
Season	Club	Lea	GP	G	A	TP	PIM	GP	G	A	TP	PIM
1981-82	Kitchener	OHL	68	6	25	31	94	15	2	2	4	51
1982-83	**Quebec**	**NHL**	**2**	**0**	**0**	**0**	**0**	....	....	....	....	....
	Kitchener	OHL	57	18	56	74	78	12	2	10	12	18
1983-84	**Quebec**	**NHL**	**3**	**0**	**0**	**0**	**0**	....	....	....	....	....
a	Kitchener	OHL	58	14	34	48	73	16	4	9	13	12
1984-85	**Quebec**	**NHL**	**14**	**0**	**0**	**0**	**11**	....	....	....	....	....
	Fredericton	AHL	48	7	6	13	73	2	0	0	0	7
1985-86	**Quebec**	**NHL**	**73**	**7**	**19**	**26**	**78**	....	....	....	....	....
1986-87	**Quebec**	**NHL**	**75**	**0**	**19**	**19**	**69**	....	....	....	....	....
1987-88	**NY Rangers**	**NHL**	**68**	**7**	**25**	**32**	**100**	....	....	....	....	....
1988-89	**NY Rangers**	**NHL**	**63**	**6**	**11**	**17**	**88**	**4**	**0**	**2**	**2**	**30**
1989-90	**NY Rangers**	**NHL**	**22**	**2**	**10**	**12**	**22**	....	....	....	....	....
1990-91	**NY Rangers**	**NHL**	**77**	**2**	**10**	**12**	**89**	**6**	**0**	**0**	**0**	**11**
1991-92	**NY Rangers**	**NHL**	**10**	**0**	**1**	**1**	**15**	....	....	....	....	....
	Edmonton	**NHL**	**12**	**1**	**1**	**2**	**8**	....	....	....	....	....
	Minnesota	**NHL**	**37**	**0**	**7**	**7**	**49**	**7**	**2**	**2**	**4**	**10**
1992-93	**Boston**	**NHL**	**77**	**10**	**14**	**24**	**108**	**4**	**0**	**1**	**1**	**6**
	NHL Totals		**533**	**35**	**117**	**152**	**637**	**21**	**2**	**5**	**7**	**57**

a OHL First All-Star Team (1984)

Traded to **NY Rangers** by **Quebec** with John Ogrodnick for Jeff Jackson and Terry Carkner, September 30, 1987. Traded to **Edmonton** by **NY Rangers** for Jeff Beukeboom, November 12, 1991. Traded to **Minnesota** by **Edmonton** for Brian Glynn, January 21, 1992. Traded to **Boston** by **Minnesota** for future considerations, September 2, 1992.

SHEPPARD, RAY

Right wing. Shoots right. 6'1", 195 lbs. Born, Pembroke, Ont., May 27, 1966.
(Buffalo's 3rd choice, 60th overall, in 1984 Entry Draft).

			Regular Season					Playoffs				
Season	Club	Lea	GP	G	A	TP	PIM	GP	G	A	TP	PIM
1983-84	Cornwall	OHL	68	44	36	80	69	....	....	....	....	....
1984-85	Cornwall	OHL	49	25	33	58	51	9	2	12	14	4
1985-86ab	Cornwall	OHL	63	*81	61	*142	25	6	7	4	11	0
1986-87	Rochester	AHL	55	18	13	31	11	15	12	3	15	2
1987-88c	**Buffalo**	**NHL**	**74**	**38**	**27**	**65**	**14**	**6**	**1**	**1**	**2**	**2**
1988-89	**Buffalo**	**NHL**	**67**	**22**	**21**	**43**	**15**	**1**	**0**	**1**	**1**	**0**
1989-90	**Buffalo**	**NHL**	**18**	**4**	**2**	**6**	**0**	....	....	....	....	....
	Rochester	AHL	5	3	5	8	2	17	8	7	15	9
1990-91	**NY Rangers**	**NHL**	**59**	**24**	**23**	**47**	**21**	....	....	....	....	....
1991-92	**Detroit**	**NHL**	**74**	**36**	**26**	**62**	**27**	**11**	**6**	**2**	**8**	**4**
1992-93	**Detroit**	**NHL**	**70**	**32**	**34**	**66**	**29**	**7**	**2**	**3**	**5**	**0**
	NHL Totals		**362**	**156**	**133**	**289**	**106**	**25**	**9**	**7**	**16**	**6**

a OHL Player of the Year (1986)
b OHL First All-Star Team (1986)
c NHL All-Rookie Team (1988)

Traded to **NY Rangers** by **Buffalo** for cash and future considerations, July 9, 1990. Signed as a free agent by **Detroit**, August 5, 1991.

SHEVALIER, JEFF

Left wing. Shoots left. 5'11", 178 lbs. Born, Mississauga, Ont., March 14, 1974.
(Los Angeles' 4th choice, 111th overall, in 1992 Entry Draft).

			Regular Season					Playoffs				
Season	Club	Lea	GP	G	A	TP	PIM	GP	G	A	TP	PIM
1991-92	North Bay	OHL	64	28	29	57	26	21	5	11	16	25
1992-93	North Bay	OHL	62	59	54	113	46	2	1	2	3	4

SHIER, ANDREW

Center. Shoots right. 5'11", 165 lbs. Born, Lansing, MI, August 15, 1971.
(NY Islanders' 11th choice, 237th overall, in 1990 Entry Draft).

			Regular Season					Playoffs				
Season	Club	Lea	GP	G	A	TP	PIM	GP	G	A	TP	PIM
1990-91	U. Wisconsin	WCHA	20	4	9	13	28	....	....	....	....	....
1991-92	U. Wisconsin	WCHA	39	10	25	35	60	....	....	....	....	....
1992-93	U. Wisconsin	WCHA	41	22	36	58	87	....	....	....	....	....

SHIM, KYUIN

Right wing. Shoots right. 6'2", 190 lbs. Born, Edmonton, Alta., April 5, 1974.
(Edmonton's 8th choice, 181st overall, in 1992 Entry Draft).

			Regular Season					Playoffs				
Season	Club	Lea	GP	G	A	TP	PIM	GP	G	A	TP	PIM
1991-92	Sherwood Park	AJHL	55	38	38	76	97	....	....	....	....	....
1992-93	N. Michigan	WCHA	20	4	2	6	6	....	....	....	....	....
	Tri-City	WHL	2	0	1	1	6	....	....	....	....	....

SHUCHUK, GARY (SHOO-chuk)

Right wing. Shoots right. 5'10", 185 lbs. Born, Edmonton, Alta., February 17, 1967.
(Detroit's 1st choice, 22nd overall, in 1988 Supplemental Draft).

			Regular Season					Playoffs				
Season	Club	Lea	GP	G	A	TP	PIM	GP	G	A	TP	PIM
1986-87	U. Wisconsin	WCHA	42	19	11	30	72	....	....	....	....	....
1987-88	U. Wisconsin	WCHA	44	7	22	29	70	....	....	....	....	....
1988-89	U. Wisconsin	WCHA	46	18	19	37	102	....	....	....	....	....
1989-90abc	U. Wisconsin	WCHA	45	*41	39	*80	70	....	....	....	....	....
1990-91	**Detroit**	**NHL**	**6**	**1**	**2**	**3**	**6**	**3**	**0**	**0**	**0**	**0**
	Adirondack	AHL	59	23	24	47	32	....	....	....	....	....
1991-92	Adirondack	AHL	79	32	48	80	48	19	4	9	13	18
1992-93	Adirondack	AHL	47	24	53	77	66	....	....	....	....	....
	Los Angeles	**NHL**	**25**	**2**	**4**	**6**	**16**	**17**	**2**	**2**	**4**	**12**
	NHL Totals		**31**	**3**	**6**	**9**	**22**	**20**	**2**	**2**	**4**	**12**

a WCHA First All-Star Team (1990)
b WCHA Player of the Year (1990)
c NCAA West First All-American Team (1990)

Traded to **Los Angeles** by **Detroit** with Jimmy Carson and Marc Potvin for Paul Coffey, Sylvain Couturier and Jim Hiller, January 29, 1993.

SILLINGER, MIKE

Center. Shoots right. 5'10", 200 lbs. Born, Regina, Sask., June 29, 1971.
(Detroit's 1st choice, 11th overall, in 1989 Entry Draft).

			Regular Season					Playoffs				
Season	Club	Lea	GP	G	A	TP	PIM	GP	G	A	TP	PIM
1987-88	Regina	WHL	67	18	25	43	17	4	2	2	4	0
1988-89	Regina	WHL	72	53	78	131	52	....	....	....	....	....
1989-90a	Regina	WHL	70	57	72	129	41	11	12	10	22	2
	Adirondack	AHL	....	....	....	....	....	1	0	0	0	0
1990-91	**Detroit**	**NHL**	**3**	**0**	**1**	**1**	**0**	**3**	**0**	**1**	**1**	**0**
b	Regina	WHL	57	50	66	116	42	8	6	9	15	4
1991-92	**Detroit**	**NHL**	....	....	....	....	....	**8**	**2**	**2**	**4**	**2**
	Adirondack	AHL	64	25	41	66	26	15	9	*19	*28	12
1992-93	**Detroit**	**NHL**	**51**	**4**	**17**	**21**	**16**	....	....	....	....	....
	Adirondack	AHL	15	10	20	30	31	11	5	13	18	10
	NHL Totals		**54**	**4**	**18**	**22**	**16**	**11**	**2**	**3**	**5**	**2**

a WHL East Second All-Star Team (1990)
b WHL East First All-Star Team (1991)

SILVERMAN, ANDREW

Defense. Shoots left. 6'3", 210 lbs. Born, Beverly, MA, August 23, 1972.
(NY Rangers' 11th choice, 181st overall, in 1990 Entry Draft).

			Regular Season					Playoffs				
Season	Club	Lea	GP	G	A	TP	PIM	GP	G	A	TP	PIM
1991-92	U. of Maine	H.E.	30	2	9	11	18	....	....	....	....	....
1992-93	U. of Maine	H.E.	37	1	7	8	56	....	....	....	....	....

SIMARD, MARTIN

Right wing. Shoots right. 6'1", 215 lbs. Born, Montreal, Que., June 25, 1966.

			Regular Season					Playoffs				
Season	Club	Lea	GP	G	A	TP	PIM	GP	G	A	TP	PIM
1984-85	Granby	QMJHL	58	22	31	53	78	8	3	7	10	21
1985-86	Granby	QMJHL	54	32	28	60	129	....	....	....	....	....
	Hull	QMJHL	14	8	8	16	55	14	8	19	27	19
1986-87	Granby	QMJHL	41	30	47	77	105	8	3	7	10	21
1987-88	Salt Lake	IHL	82	8	23	31	281	19	6	3	9	100
1988-89	Salt Lake	IHL	71	13	15	28	221	14	4	0	4	45
1989-90	Salt Lake	IHL	59	22	23	45	151	11	5	8	13	12
1990-91	**Calgary**	**NHL**	**16**	**0**	**2**	**2**	**53**	....	....	....	....	....
	Salt Lake	IHL	54	24	25	49	113	4	3	0	3	20
1991-92	**Calgary**	**NHL**	**21**	**1**	**3**	**4**	**119**	....	....	....	....	....
	Salt Lake	IHL	11	3	7	10	51	....	....	....	....	....
	Halifax	AHL	10	5	3	8	26	....	....	....	....	....
1992-93	**Tampa Bay**	**NHL**	**7**	**0**	**0**	**0**	**11**	....	....	....	....	....
	Atlanta	IHL	19	5	5	10	77	....	....	....	....	....
	Halifax	AHL	13	3	4	7	17	....	....	....	....	....
	NHL Totals		**44**	**1**	**5**	**6**	**183**	....	....	....	....	....

Signed as a free agent by **Calgary**, May 19, 1987. Traded to **Quebec** by **Calgary** for Greg Smyth, March 10, 1992. Traded to **Tampa Bay** by **Quebec** to complete June 19, 1992 trade which sent Tim Hunter to Quebec for future considerations, September 14, 1992. Traded to **Quebec** by **Tampa Bay** with Steve Tuttle and Michel Mongeau for Herb Raglan, February 12, 1993.

SIMON, CHRIS

Left wing. Shoots left. 6'3", 230 lbs. Born, Wawa, Ont., January 30, 1972.
(Philadelphia's 2nd choice, 25th overall, in 1990 Entry Draft).

			Regular Season					Playoffs				
Season	Club	Lea	GP	G	A	TP	PIM	GP	G	A	TP	PIM
1988-89	Ottawa	OHL	36	4	2	6	31	....	....	....	....	....
1989-90	Ottawa	OHL	57	36	38	74	146	3	2	1	3	4
1990-91	Ottawa	OHL	20	16	6	22	69	17	5	9	14	59
1991-92	Ottawa	OHL	2	1	1	2	24	....	....	....	....	....
	S.S. Marie	OHL	31	19	25	44	143	11	5	8	13	49
1992-93	**Quebec**	**NHL**	**16**	**1**	**1**	**2**	**67**	**5**	**0**	**0**	**0**	**26**
	Halifax	AHL	36	12	6	18	131	....	....	....	....	....
	NHL Totals		**16**	**1**	**1**	**2**	**67**	**5**	**0**	**0**	**0**	**26**

Traded to **Quebec** by **Philadelphia** with Peter Forsberg, Steve Duchesne, Kerry Huffman, Mike Ricci, Ron Hextall, Philadelphia's first round choice in the 1993 (Jocelyn Thibault) and 1994 Entry Drafts and cash for Eric Lindros, June 30, 1992.

SIMON, DARCY

Defense. Shoots right. 6'1", 200 lbs. Born, North Battleford, Sask., January 21, 1970.

			Regular Season					Playoffs				
Season	Club	Lea	GP	G	A	TP	PIM	GP	G	A	TP	PIM
1987-88	Seattle	WHL	67	5	9	14	226	....	....	....	....	....
1988-89	Seattle	WHL	62	3	15	18	208	....	....	....	....	....
1989-90	Seattle	WHL	63	5	13	18	285	13	1	2	3	79
1990-91	Fredericton	AHL	29	0	3	3	183	9	2	0	2	45
1991-92	Fredericton	AHL	58	9	11	20	308	4	0	0	0	13
1992-93	Fredericton	AHL	57	2	7	9	257	2	0	0	0	6
	Wheeling	ECHL	3	0	1	1	26	....	....	....	....	....

Signed as a free agent by **Montreal**, October 3, 1990.

SIMON, TODD

Center. Shoots right. 5'10", 188 lbs. Born, Toronto, Ont., April 21, 1972.
(Buffalo's 9th choice, 203rd overall, in 1992 Entry Draft).

			Regular Season					Playoffs				
Season	Club	Lea	GP	G	A	TP	PIM	GP	G	A	TP	PIM
1990-91	Niagara Falls	OHL	65	51	74	125	35	14	7	8	15	12
1991-92a	Niagara Falls	OHL	66	53	93	*146	72	17	17	24	*41	36
1992-93	Rochester	AHL	68	27	66	93	54	12	3	14	17	15

a OHL First All-Star Team (1992)

SIMONOV, SERGEI

Defense. Shoots left. 6'1", 183 lbs. Born, Saratov, Soviet Union, May 20, 1974.
(Toronto's 11th choice, 221st overall, in 1992 Entry Draft).

			Regular Season					Playoffs				
Season	Club	Lea	GP	G	A	TP	PIM	GP	G	A	TP	PIM
1991-92	Saratov	CIS 2			UNAVAILABLE							
1992-93	Saratov	CIS	40	0	2	2	34	....	....	....	....	....

SIMPSON, CRAIG

Left wing. Shoots right. 6'2", 195 lbs. Born, London, Ont., February 15, 1967.
(Pittsburgh's 1st choice, 2nd overall, in 1985 Entry Draft).

			Regular Season					Playoffs				
Season	Club	Lea	GP	G	A	TP	PIM	GP	G	A	TP	PIM
1983-84	Michigan State	CCHA	46	14	43	57	38	....	....	....	....	....
1984-85ab	Michigan State	CCHA	42	31	53	84	33	....	....	....	....	....
1985-86	**Pittsburgh**	**NHL**	**76**	**11**	**17**	**28**	**49**	....	....	....	....	....
1986-87	**Pittsburgh**	**NHL**	**72**	**26**	**25**	**51**	**57**	....	....	....	....	....
1987-88	**Pittsburgh**	**NHL**	**21**	**13**	**13**	**26**	**34**	....	....	....	....	....
	Edmonton	**NHL**	**59**	**43**	**21**	**64**	**43**	**19**	**13**	**6**	**19**	**26**
1988-89	**Edmonton**	**NHL**	**66**	**35**	**41**	**76**	**80**	**7**	**2**	**0**	**2**	**10**
1989-90	**Edmonton**	**NHL**	**80**	**29**	**32**	**61**	**180**	**22**	***16**	**15**	***31**	**8**
1990-91	**Edmonton**	**NHL**	**75**	**30**	**27**	**57**	**66**	**18**	**5**	**11**	**16**	**12**
1991-92	**Edmonton**	**NHL**	**79**	**24**	**37**	**61**	**80**	**1**	**0**	**0**	**0**	**0**
1992-93	**Edmonton**	**NHL**	**60**	**24**	**22**	**46**	**36**	....	....	....	....	....
	NHL Totals		**588**	**235**	**235**	**470**	**625**	**67**	**36**	**32**	**68**	**56**

a CCHA First All-Star Team (1985)
b NCAA West First All-American Team (1985)

Traded to **Edmonton** by **Pittsburgh** with Dave Hannan, Moe Mantha and Chris Joseph for Paul Coffey, Dave Hunter and Wayne Van Dorp, November 24, 1987.

SIMPSON, GEOFF

Defense. Shoots right. 6'1", 180 lbs. Born, Victoria, B.C., March 6, 1969.
(Boston's 10th choice, 206th overall, in 1989 Entry Draft).

			Regular Season					Playoffs				
Season	Club	Lea	GP	G	A	TP	PIM	GP	G	A	TP	PIM
1989-90	N. Michigan	WCHA	39	4	19	23	40	....	....	....	....	....
1990-91	N. Michigan	WCHA	44	2	15	17	27	....	....	....	....	....
1991-92	N. Michigan	WCHA	25	1	3	4	20	....	....	....	....	....
1992-93	N. Michigan	WCHA	43	8	14	22	18	....	....	....	....	....

SIMPSON, REID

Left wing. Shoots left. 6'1", 211 lbs. Born, Flin Flon, Man., May 21, 1969.
(Philadelphia's 3rd choice, 72nd overall, in 1989 Entry Draft).

			Regular Season					Playoffs				
Season	Club	Lea	GP	G	A	TP	PIM	GP	G	A	TP	PIM
1987-88	Prince Albert	WHL	72	13	14	27	164	10	1	0	1	43
1988-89	Prince Albert	WHL	59	26	29	55	264	4	2	1	3	30
1989-90	Prince Albert	WHL	29	15	17	32	121	14	4	7	11	34
	Hershey	AHL	28	2	2	4	175	....	....	....	....	....
1990-91	Hershey	AHL	54	9	15	24	183	1	0	0	0	0
1991-92	**Philadelphia**	**NHL**	**1**	**0**	**0**	**0**	**0**	....	....	....	....	....
	Hershey	AHL	60	11	7	18	145	....	....	....	....	....
1992-93	**Minnesota**	**NHL**	**1**	**0**	**0**	**0**	**5**	....	....	....	....	....
	Kalamazoo	IHL	45	5	5	10	193	....	....	....	....	....
	NHL Totals		**2**	**0**	**0**	**0**	**5**	....	....	....	....	....

Signed as a free agent by **Minnesota**, December 14, 1992.

SINCLAIR, AL

Defense. Shoots right. 6'3", 210 lbs. Born, Mississauga, Ont., April 3, 1973.
(Ottawa's 6th choice, 121st overall, in 1992 Entry Draft).

			Regular Season					Playoffs				
Season	Club	Lea	GP	G	A	TP	PIM	GP	G	A	TP	PIM
1991-92	U. of Michigan	CCHA	22	0	4	4	40	....	....	....	....	....
1992-93	U. of Michigan	CCHA	20	0	3	3	26	....	....	....	....	....

SINISALO, ILKKA (sin-i-SAL-oh)

Right wing. Shoots left. 6', 185 lbs. Born, Hauho, Finland, July 10, 1958.

			Regular Season					Playoffs				
Season	Club	Lea	GP	G	A	TP	PIM	GP	G	A	TP	PIM
1977-78	HIFK	Fin.	36	9	3	12	18	....	....	....	....	....
1978-79	HIFK	Fin.	30	6	4	10	16	6	4	1	5	2
1979-80	HIFK	Fin.	35	16	9	25	16	7	1	3	4	4
1980-81	HIFK	Fin.	36	27	17	44	14	6	5	3	8	4
1981-82	**Philadelphia**	**NHL**	**66**	**15**	**22**	**37**	**22**	**4**	**0**	**2**	**2**	**0**
1982-83	**Philadelphia**	**NHL**	**61**	**21**	**29**	**50**	**16**	**3**	**1**	**1**	**2**	**0**
1983-84	**Philadelphia**	**NHL**	**73**	**29**	**17**	**46**	**29**	**2**	**2**	**0**	**2**	**0**
1984-85	**Philadelphia**	**NHL**	**70**	**36**	**37**	**73**	**16**	**19**	**6**	**1**	**7**	**0**
1985-86	**Philadelphia**	**NHL**	**74**	**39**	**37**	**76**	**31**	**5**	**2**	**2**	**4**	**2**
1986-87	**Philadelphia**	**NHL**	**42**	**10**	**21**	**31**	**8**	**18**	**5**	**1**	**6**	**4**
1987-88	**Philadelphia**	**NHL**	**68**	**25**	**17**	**42**	**30**	**7**	**4**	**2**	**6**	**0**
1988-89	**Philadelphia**	**NHL**	**13**	**1**	**6**	**7**	**2**	**8**	**1**	**1**	**2**	**0**
1989-90	**Philadelphia**	**NHL**	**59**	**23**	**23**	**46**	**26**	....	....	....	....	....
1990-91	**Minnesota**	**NHL**	**46**	**5**	**12**	**17**	**24**	....	....	....	....	....
	Los Angeles	**NHL**	**7**	**0**	**0**	**0**	**2**	**2**	**0**	**1**	**1**	**0**
1991-92	**Los Angeles**	**NHL**	**3**	**0**	**1**	**1**	**2**	....	....	....	....	....
	Phoenix	IHL	42	19	21	40	32	....	....	....	....	....
1992-93	HPK	Fin.	46	13	16	29	55	12	2	3	5	8
	NHL Totals		**582**	**204**	**222**	**426**	**208**	**68**	**21**	**11**	**32**	**6**

Signed as a free agent by **Philadelphia**, February 14, 1981. Signed as a free agent by **Minnesota**, July 3, 1990. Traded to **Los Angeles** by **Minnesota** for Los Angeles' eighth round choice (Michael Burkett) in 1991 Entry Draft, March 5, 1991.

SIREN, VILLE (SIH-rihn)

Defense. Shoots left. 6'2", 191 lbs. Born, Tampere, Finland, February 11, 1964.
(Hartford's 3rd choice, 23rd overall, in 1983 Entry Draft).

			Regular Season					Playoffs				
Season	Club	Lea	GP	G	A	TP	PIM	GP	G	A	TP	PIM
1982-83	Ilves	Fin.	29	3	2	5	42	8	1	3	4	8
1983-84	Ilves	Fin.	36	1	10	11	40	2	0	0	0	2
1984-85	Ilves	Fin.	36	11	13	24	24	9	0	2	2	10
1985-86	**Pittsburgh**	**NHL**	**60**	**4**	**8**	**12**	**32**	....	....	....	....	....
1986-87	**Pittsburgh**	**NHL**	**69**	**5**	**17**	**22**	**50**	....	....	....	....	....
1987-88	**Pittsburgh**	**NHL**	**58**	**1**	**20**	**21**	**62**	....	....	....	....	....
1988-89	**Pittsburgh**	**NHL**	**12**	**1**	**0**	**1**	**14**	....	....	....	....	....
	Minnesota	**NHL**	**38**	**2**	**10**	**12**	**58**	**4**	**0**	**0**	**0**	**4**
1989-90	**Minnesota**	**NHL**	**53**	**1**	**13**	**14**	**60**	**3**	**0**	**0**	**0**	**2**
1990-91	HPK	Fin.	44	4	9	13	90	8	1	1	2	37
1991-92	Ilves	Fin.	43	8	14	22	88	....	....	....	....	....
1992-93	Lulea	Swe.	37	3	11	14	84	11	0	0	0	22
	NHL Totals		**290**	**14**	**68**	**82**	**276**	**7**	**0**	**0**	**0**	**6**

Traded to **Pittsburgh** by **Hartford** for Pat Boutette, November 16, 1984. Traded to **Minnesota** by **Pittsburgh** with Steve Gotaas for Gord Dineen and Scott Bjugstad, December 17, 1988.

SIRKKA, JEFFREY

Defense. Shoots left. 6'1", 205 lbs. Born, Copper Cliff, Ont., June 17, 1968.

			Regular Season					Playoffs				
Season	Club	Lea	GP	G	A	TP	PIM	GP	G	A	TP	PIM
1986-87	Kingston	OHL	64	0	5	5	156	....	....	....	....	....
1987-88	Kingston	OHL	59	1	16	17	114	....	....	....	....	....
1988-89	North Bay	OHL	12	0	3	3	66	....	....	....	....	....
	Toronto	OHL	29	1	14	15	71	....	....	....	....	....
1989-90	Maine	AHL	56	0	9	9	110	....	....	....	....	....
	Binghamton	AHL	16	0	1	1	38	....	....	....	....	....
1990-91	Indianapolis	IHL	69	6	12	18	203	6	0	0	0	6
1991-92	Indianapolis	IHL	71	3	17	20	146	....	....	....	....	....
1992-93	Rochester	AHL	59	6	11	17	132	3	0	0	0	7

Rights traded to **Hartford** by **Boston** for Steve Dykstra, March 3, 1990. Signed as a free agent by **Chicago**, September 20, 1990.

SITTLER, RYAN

Left wing. Shoots left. 6'2", 185 lbs. Born, London, Ont., January 28, 1974.
(Philadelphia's 1st choice, 7th overall, in 1992 Entry Draft).

			Regular Season					Playoffs				
Season	Club	Lea	GP	G	A	TP	PIM	GP	G	A	TP	PIM
1991-92	Nicholls	HS	21	19	29	48	....	....	....	....	....	....
	Buffalo Regals	Midget	30	39	54	93	....	....	....	....	....	....
1992-93	U. of Michigan	CCHA	35	9	24	33	43	....	....	....	....	....

SJODIN, TOMMY (SHOH-deen)

Defense. Shoots right. 5'11", 190 lbs. Born, Timra, Sweden, August 13, 1965.
(Minnesota's 10th choice, 237th overall, in 1985 Entry Draft).

			Regular Season					Playoffs				
Season	Club	Lea	GP	G	A	TP	PIM	GP	G	A	TP	PIM
1983-84	Timra	Swe.2	16	4	4	8	6	6	0	....	....	4
1984-85	Timra	Swe.2	23	8	11	19	14	....	....	....	....	....
1985-86	Timra	Swe.2	32	13	12	25	40	....	....	....	....	....
1986-87	Brynas	Swe.	29	0	4	4	24	....	....	....	....	....
1987-88	Brynas	Swe.	40	6	9	15	28	....	....	....	....	....
1988-89	Brynas	Swe.	40	8	11	19	52	5	1	0	1	6
1989-90	Brynas	Swe.	40	14	14	28	46	5	0	0	0	2
1990-91	Brynas	Swe.	38	12	17	29	77	2	0	1	1	2
1991-92	Brynas	Swe.	40	6	16	22	46	5	0	3	3	4
1992-93	**Minnesota**	**NHL**	**77**	**7**	**29**	**36**	**30**	....	....	....	....	....
	NHL Totals		**77**	**7**	**29**	**36**	**30**	....	....	....	....	....

SKALDE, JARROD

Center. Shoots left. 6', 170 lbs. Born, Niagara Falls, Ont., February 26, 1971.
(New Jersey's 3rd choice, 26th overall, in 1989 Entry Draft).

			Regular Season					Playoffs				
Season	Club	Lea	GP	G	A	TP	PIM	GP	G	A	TP	PIM
1987-88	Oshawa	OHL	60	12	16	28	24	7	2	1	3	2
1988-89	Oshawa	OHL	65	38	38	76	36	6	1	5	6	2
1989-90	Oshawa	OHL	62	40	52	92	66	17	10	7	17	6
1990-91	**New Jersey**	**NHL**	**1**	**0**	**1**	**1**	**0**	....	....	....	....	....
	Utica	AHL	3	3	2	5	0	....	....	....	....	....
	Oshawa	OHL	15	8	14	22	14	....	....	....	....	....
a	Belleville	OHL	40	30	52	82	21	6	9	6	15	10
1991-92	**New Jersey**	**NHL**	**15**	**2**	**4**	**6**	**4**	....	....	....	....	....
	Utica	AHL	62	20	20	40	56	4	3	1	4	8
1992-93	**New Jersey**	**NHL**	**11**	**0**	**2**	**2**	**4**	....	....	....	....	....
	Utica	AHL	59	21	39	60	76	5	0	2	2	19
	Cincinnati	IHL	4	1	2	3	4	....	....	....	....	....
	NHL Totals		**27**	**2**	**7**	**9**	**8**	....	....	....	....	....

a OHL Second All-Star Team (1991)

Claimed by **Anaheim** from **New Jersey** in Expansion Draft, June 24, 1993.

SKARDA, RANDY

Defense. Shoots right. 6'1", 205 lbs. Born, St. Paul, MN, May 5, 1968.
(St. Louis' 8th choice, 157th overall, in 1986 Entry Draft).

			Regular Season					Playoffs				
Season	Club	Lea	GP	G	A	TP	PIM	GP	G	A	TP	PIM
1986-87	U. Minnesota	WCHA	43	3	10	13	77	....	....	....	....	....
1987-88ab	U. Minnesota	WCHA	42	19	26	45	102	....	....	....	....	....
1988-89	U. Minnesota	WCHA	43	6	24	30	91	....	....	....	....	....
1989-90	**St. Louis**	**NHL**	**25**	**0**	**5**	**5**	**11**	....	....	....	....	....
	Peoria	IHL	38	7	17	24	40	4	0	0	0	0
1990-91	Peoria	IHL	78	8	34	42	126	19	3	5	8	22
1991-92	**St. Louis**	**NHL**	**1**	**0**	**0**	**0**	**0**	....	....	....	....	....
	Peoria	IHL	57	8	24	32	64	7	0	0	0	14
1992-93	Milwaukee	IHL	54	3	9	12	104	....	....	....	....	....
	NHL Totals		**26**	**0**	**5**	**5**	**11**	....	....	....	....	....

a NCAA West Second All-American Team (1988)
b WCHA First All-Star Team (1988)

SKRIKO, PETRI (SKREE-koh)

Left wing. Shoots left. 5'10", 175 lbs. Born, Lappeenranta, Finland, March 12, 1962.
(Vancouver's 7th choice, 157th overall, in 1981 Entry Draft).

			Regular Season					Playoffs				
Season	Club	Lea	GP	G	A	TP	PIM	GP	G	A	TP	PIM
1979-80	SaiPa	Fin.2	36	25	20	45	8	....	....	....	....	....
1980-81	SaiPa	Fin.	36	20	13	33	14	....	....	....	....	....
1981-82	SaiPa	Fin.	33	19	27	46	24	....	....	....	....	....
1982-83	SaiPa	Fin.	36	23	12	35	12	....	....	....	....	....
1983-84	SaiPa	Fin.	32	25	26	51	13	....	....	....	....	....
1984-85	**Vancouver**	**NHL**	**72**	**21**	**14**	**35**	**10**	....	....	....	....	....
1985-86	**Vancouver**	**NHL**	**80**	**38**	**40**	**78**	**34**	**3**	**0**	**0**	**0**	**0**
1986-87	**Vancouver**	**NHL**	**76**	**33**	**41**	**74**	**44**	....	....	....	....	....
1987-88	**Vancouver**	**NHL**	**73**	**30**	**34**	**64**	**32**	....	....	....	....	....
1988-89	**Vancouver**	**NHL**	**74**	**30**	**36**	**66**	**57**	**7**	**1**	**5**	**6**	**0**
1989-90	**Vancouver**	**NHL**	**77**	**15**	**33**	**48**	**36**	....	....	....	....	....
1990-91	**Vancouver**	**NHL**	**20**	**4**	**4**	**8**	**8**	....	....	....	....	....
	Boston	**NHL**	**28**	**5**	**14**	**19**	**9**	**18**	**4**	**4**	**8**	**4**
1991-92	**Boston**	**NHL**	**9**	**1**	**0**	**1**	**6**	....	....	....	....	....
	Fin. Olympic	....	8	1	4	5	4	....	....	....	....	....
	Winnipeg	**NHL**	**15**	**2**	**3**	**5**	**4**	....	....	....	....	....
1992-93	**San Jose**	**NHL**	**17**	**4**	**3**	**7**	**6**	....	....	....	....	....
	Kiekko-Espoo	Fin.	18	5	4	9	8	....	....	....	....	....
	NHL Totals		**541**	**183**	**222**	**405**	**246**	**28**	**5**	**9**	**14**	**4**

Traded to **Boston** by **Vancouver** for Boston's second round choice (Mike Peca) in the 1992 Entry Draft, January 16, 1991. Traded to **Winnipeg** by **Boston** for Brent Ashton, October 29, 1991. Signed as a free agent by **San Jose**, August 27, 1992.

SKRUDLAND, BRIAN (SKROOD-luhnd)
Center. Shoots left. 6', 196 lbs. Born, Peace River, Alta., July 31, 1963.

			Regular Season					Playoffs				
Season	Club	Lea	GP	G	A	TP	PIM	GP	G	A	TP	PIM
1980-81	Saskatoon	WHL	66	15	27	42	97	....	....	....	....	....
1981-82	Saskatoon	WHL	71	27	29	56	135	5	0	1	1	2
1982-83	Saskatoon	WHL	71	35	59	94	42	6	1	3	4	19
1983-84	Nova Scotia	AHL	56	13	12	25	55	12	2	8	10	14
1984-85	Sherbrooke	AHL	70	22	28	50	109	17	9	8	17	23
1985-86	**Montreal**	**NHL**	65	9	13	22	57	20	2	4	6	76
1986-87	Montreal	NHL	79	11	17	28	107	14	1	5	6	29
1987-88	Montreal	NHL	79	12	24	36	112	11	1	5	6	24
1988-89	Montreal	NHL	71	12	29	41	84	21	3	7	10	40
1989-90	Montreal	NHL	59	11	31	42	56	11	3	5	8	30
1990-91	Montreal	NHL	57	15	19	34	85	13	3	10	13	42
1991-92	Montreal	NHL	42	3	3	6	36	11	1	1	2	20
1992-93	Montreal	NHL	23	5	3	8	55	....	....	....	....	....
	Calgary	NHL	16	2	4	6	10	6	0	3	3	12
	NHL Totals		**491**	**80**	**143**	**223**	**602**	**107**	**14**	**40**	**54**	**273**

Signed as a free agent by **Montreal**, September 13, 1983. Traded to **Calgary** by **Montreal** for Gary Leeman, January 28, 1993. Claimed by **Florida** from **Calgary** in Expansion Draft, June 24, 1993.

SKRYPEC, GERRY
Defense. Shoots left. 5'11", 186 lbs. Born, Kitchener, Ont., June 21, 1974.
(Chicago's 6th choice, 137th overall, in 1992 Entry Draft).

			Regular Season					Playoffs				
Season	Club	Lea	GP	G	A	TP	PIM	GP	G	A	TP	PIM
1990-91	Ottawa	OHL	62	2	7	9	53	17	0	4	4	2
1991-92	Ottawa	OHL	65	6	21	27	105	5	0	1	1	8
1992-93	Ottawa	OHL	20	1	3	4	20	....	....	....	....	....
	Newmarket	OHL	19	1	6	7	24	7	1	0	1	20

SLANEY, JOHN
Defense. Shoots left. 6', 185 lbs. Born, St. John's, Nfld., February 7, 1972.
(Washington's 1st choice, 9th overall, in 1990 Entry Draft).

			Regular Season					Playoffs				
Season	Club	Lea	GP	G	A	TP	PIM	GP	G	A	TP	PIM
1988-89	Cornwall	OHL	66	16	43	59	23	18	8	16	24	10
1989-90ab	Cornwall	OHL	64	38	59	97	68	6	0	8	8	11
1990-91c	Cornwall	OHL	34	21	25	46	28	....	....	....	....	....
1991-92d	Cornwall	OHL	34	19	41	60	43	6	3	8	11	0
	Baltimore	AHL	6	2	4	6	0	....	....	....	....	....
1992-93	Baltimore	AHL	79	20	46	66	60	7	0	7	7	8

a OHL First All-Star Team (1990)
b OHL and Canadian Major Junior Defenseman of the Year (1990)
c OHL Second All-Star Team (1991)
d OHL Third All-Star Team (1992)

SLEGR, JIRI (SLAYGUHR)
Defense. Shoots left. 6'1", 210 lbs. Born, Litvinov, Czechoslovakia, May 30, 1971.
(Vancouver's 3rd choice, 23rd overall, in 1990 Entry Draft).

			Regular Season					Playoffs				
Season	Club	Lea	GP	G	A	TP	PIM	GP	G	A	TP	PIM
1987-88	Litvinov	Czech.	4	1	1	2	0	....	....	....	....	....
1988-89	Litvinov	Czech.	8	0	0	0	4	....	....	....	....	....
1989-90	Litvinov	Czech.	51	4	15	19	....	....	....	....	....	....
1990-91	Litvinov	Czech.	47	11	36	47	26	....	....	....	....	....
1991-92	Litvinov	Czech.	42	9	23	32	38	....	....	....	....	....
1992-93	**Vancouver**	**NHL**	41	4	22	26	109	5	0	3	3	4
	Hamilton	AHL	21	4	14	18	42	....	....	....	....	....
	NHL Totals		**41**	**4**	**22**	**26**	**109**	**5**	**0**	**3**	**3**	**4**

SMAIL, DOUGLAS (DOUG)
Left wing. Shoots left. 5'9", 175 lbs. Born, Moose Jaw, Sask., September 2, 1957.

			Regular Season					Playoffs				
Season	Club	Lea	GP	G	A	TP	PIM	GP	G	A	TP	PIM
1978-79	North Dakota	WCHA	35	24	34	58	46	....	....	....	....	....
1979-80ab	North Dakota	WCHA	40	43	44	87	70	....	....	....	....	....
1980-81	Winnipeg	NHL	30	10	8	18	45	....	....	....	....	....
1981-82	Winnipeg	NHL	72	17	18	35	55	4	0	0	0	0
1982-83	Winnipeg	NHL	80	15	29	44	32	3	0	0	0	6
1983-84	Winnipeg	NHL	66	20	17	37	62	3	0	1	1	7
1984-85	Winnipeg	NHL	80	31	35	66	45	8	2	1	3	4
1985-86	Winnipeg	NHL	73	16	26	42	32	3	1	0	1	0
1986-87	Winnipeg	NHL	78	25	18	43	36	10	4	0	4	10
1987-88	Winnipeg	NHL	71	15	16	31	34	5	1	0	1	22
1988-89	Winnipeg	NHL	47	14	15	29	52	....	....	....	....	....
1989-90	Winnipeg	NHL	79	25	24	49	63	5	1	0	1	0
1990-91	Winnipeg	NHL	15	1	2	3	10	....	....	....	....	....
	Minnesota	NHL	57	7	13	20	38	1	0	0	0	0
1991-92	Quebec	NHL	46	10	18	28	47	....	....	....	....	....
1992-93	Ottawa	NHL	51	4	10	14	51	....	....	....	....	....
	San Diego	IHL	9	2	1	3	20	9	3	2	5	20
	NHL Totals		**845**	**210**	**249**	**459**	**602**	**42**	**9**	**2**	**11**	**49**

a WCHA Second All-Star Team (1980)
b Most Valuable Player, NCAA Tournament (1980)

Played in NHL All-Star Game (1990)

Signed as a free agent by **Winnipeg**, May 22, 1980. Traded to **Minnesota** by **Winnipeg** for Don Barber, November 7, 1990. Signed as a free agent by **Quebec**, August 30, 1991. Signed as a free agent by **Ottawa**, August 30, 1992.

SMART, JASON
Center. Shoots left. 6'4", 212 lbs. Born, Prince George, B.C., January 23, 1970.
(Pittsburgh's 13th choice, 247th overall, in 1989 Entry Draft).

			Regular Season					Playoffs				
Season	Club	Lea	GP	G	A	TP	PIM	GP	G	A	TP	PIM
1986-87	Prince Albert	WHL	57	9	22	31	62	8	3	3	6	8
1987-88	Prince Albert	WHL	72	16	29	45	77	10	1	2	3	11
1988-89	Prince Albert	WHL	12	1	3	4	31	....	....	....	....	....
	Saskatoon	WHL	36	6	17	23	33	8	1	6	7	16
1989-90	Saskatoon	WHL	66	27	48	75	187	10	1	5	6	19
1990-91	Albany	IHL	15	4	2	6	28	....	....	....	....	....
	Muskegon	IHL	36	12	27	39	55	5	0	3	3	11
1991-92	Muskegon	IHL	45	10	14	24	49	....	....	....	....	....
1992-93	Cleveland	IHL	78	12	36	48	151	3	0	0	0	6

SMEHLIK, RICHARD (SHMEH-lihk)
Defense. Shoots left. 6'3", 208 lbs. Born, Ostrava, Czechoslovakia, January 23, 1970.
(Buffalo's 3rd choice, 97th overall, in 1990 Entry Draft).

			Regular Season					Playoffs				
Season	Club	Lea	GP	G	A	TP	PIM	GP	G	A	TP	PIM
1988-89	TJ Vitkovice	Czech.	38	2	5	7	12	....	....	....	....	....
1989-90	TJ Vitkovice	Czech.	51	5	4	9	....	....	....	....	....	....
1990-91	Dukla Jihlava	Czech.	58	4	3	7	22	....	....	....	....	....
1991-92	TJ Vitkovice	Czech.	47	9	10	19	42	....	....	....	....	....
1992-93	**Buffalo**	**NHL**	80	4	27	31	59	8	0	4	4	2
	NHL Totals		**80**	**4**	**27**	**31**	**59**	**8**	**0**	**4**	**4**	**2**

SMITH, DERRICK
Left wing. Shoots left. 6'2", 215 lbs. Born, Scarborough, Ont., January 22, 1965.
(Philadelphia's 2nd choice, 44th overall, in 1983 Entry Draft).

			Regular Season					Playoffs				
Season	Club	Lea	GP	G	A	TP	PIM	GP	G	A	TP	PIM
1982-83	Peterborough	OHL	70	16	19	35	47	....	....	....	....	....
1983-84	Peterborough	OHL	70	30	36	66	31	8	4	4	8	7
1984-85	**Philadelphia**	**NHL**	77	17	22	39	31	19	2	5	7	16
1985-86	Philadelphia	NHL	69	6	6	12	57	4	0	0	0	10
1986-87	Philadelphia	NHL	71	11	21	32	34	26	6	4	10	26
1987-88	Philadelphia	NHL	76	16	8	24	104	7	0	0	0	6
1988-89	Philadelphia	NHL	74	16	14	30	43	19	5	2	7	12
1989-90	Philadelphia	NHL	55	3	6	9	32	....	....	....	....	....
1990-91	Philadelphia	NHL	72	11	10	21	37	....	....	....	....	....
1991-92	Minnesota	NHL	33	2	4	6	33	7	1	0	1	9
	Kalamazoo	IHL	6	1	5	6	4	....	....	....	....	....
1992-93	Minnesota	NHL	9	0	1	1	2	....	....	....	....	....
	Kalamazoo	IHL	52	22	13	35	43	....	....	....	....	....
	NHL Totals		**536**	**82**	**92**	**174**	**373**	**82**	**14**	**11**	**25**	**79**

Claimed on waivers by **Minnesota**, October 26, 1991.

SMITH, GEOFF
Defense. Shoots left. 6'3", 200 lbs. Born, Edmonton, Alta., March 7, 1969.
(Edmonton's 3rd choice, 63rd overall, in 1987 Entry Draft).

			Regular Season					Playoffs				
Season	Club	Lea	GP	G	A	TP	PIM	GP	G	A	TP	PIM
1987-88	North Dakota	WCHA	42	4	12	16	34	....	....	....	....	....
1988-89	North Dakota	WCHA	9	0	1	1	8	....	....	....	....	....
	Kamloops	WHL	32	4	31	35	29	6	1	3	4	12
1989-90a	**Edmonton**	**NHL**	74	4	11	15	52	3	0	0	0	0
1990-91	Edmonton	NHL	59	1	12	13	55	4	0	0	0	0
1991-92	Edmonton	NHL	74	2	16	18	43	5	0	1	1	6
1992-93	Edmonton	NHL	78	4	14	18	30	....	....	....	....	....
	NHL Totals		**285**	**11**	**53**	**64**	**180**	**12**	**0**	**1**	**1**	**6**

a NHL All-Rookie Team (1990)

SMITH, JASON
Defense. Shoots right. 6'3", 183 lbs. Born, Calgary, Alta., November 2, 1973.
(New Jersey's 1st choice, 18th overall, in 1992 Entry Draft).

			Regular Season					Playoffs				
Season	Club	Lea	GP	G	A	TP	PIM	GP	G	A	TP	PIM
1990-91	Regina	WHL	2	0	0	0	7	4	0	0	0	2
1991-92	Regina	WHL	62	9	29	38	168	....	....	....	....	....
1992-93a	Regina	WHL	64	14	52	66	175	13	4	8	12	39

a Canadian Major Junior First All-Star Team (1993).

SMITH, JASON
Defense. Shoots left. 6'4", 210 lbs. Born, Calgary, Alta., November 19, 1974.
(Calgary's 4th choice, 95th overall, in 1993 Entry Draft).

			Regular Season					Playoffs				
Season	Club	Lea	GP	G	A	TP	PIM	GP	G	A	TP	PIM
1991-92	Calgary	AJHL	58	4	28	32	203	....	....	....	....	....
1992-93	Princeton	ECAC	28	5	4	9	94	....	....	....	....	....

SMITH, MIKE
Defense. Shoots left. 6', 185 lbs. Born, Winnipeg, Man., January 17, 1971.
(Buffalo's 13th choice, 255th overall, in 1991 Entry Draft).

			Regular Season					Playoffs				
Season	Club	Lea	GP	G	A	TP	PIM	GP	G	A	TP	PIM
1989-90	Lake Superior	CCHA	41	4	10	14	6	....	....	....	....	....
1990-91	Lake Superior	CCHA	43	5	29	34	30	....	....	....	....	....
1991-92	Lake Superior	CCHA	39	6	16	22	28	....	....	....	....	....
1992-93abc	Lake Superior	CCHA	42	5	25	30	42	....	....	....	....	....
	Rochester	AHL	2	0	1	1	0	....	....	....	....	....

a CCHA Second All-Star Team (1993)
b NCAA West Second All-American Team (1993)
c NCAA Final Four All-Tournament Team (1993)

SMITH, ROBERT DAVID (BOBBY)

Center. Shoots left. 6'4", 210 lbs. Born, North Sydney, N.S., February 12, 1958.
(Minnesota's 1st choice, 1st overall, in 1978 Amateur Draft).

			Regular Season					Playoffs				
Season	Club	Lea	GP	G	A	TP	PIM	GP	G	A	TP	PIM
1976-77a	Ottawa	OHA	64	*65	70	135	52	19	16	16	32	29
1977-78bc	Ottawa	OHA	61	69	*123	*192	44	16	15	15	30	10
1978-79d	Minnesota	NHL	80	30	44	74	39	....	....	....	....	....
1979-80	Minnesota	NHL	61	27	56	83	24	15	1	13	14	9
1980-81	Minnesota	NHL	78	29	64	93	73	19	8	17	25	13
1981-82	Minnesota	NHL	80	43	71	114	82	4	2	4	6	5
1982-83	Minnesota	NHL	77	24	53	77	81	9	6	4	10	17
1983-84	Minnesota	NHL	10	3	6	9	9	....	....	....	....	....
	Montreal	NHL	70	26	37	63	62	15	2	7	9	8
1984-85	Montreal	NHL	65	16	40	56	59	12	5	6	11	30
1985-86	Montreal	NHL	79	31	55	86	55	20	7	8	15	22
1986-87	Montreal	NHL	80	28	47	75	72	17	9	9	18	19
1987-88	Montreal	NHL	78	27	66	93	78	11	3	4	7	8
1988-89	Montreal	NHL	80	32	51	83	69	21	11	8	19	46
1989-90	Montreal	NHL	53	12	14	26	35	11	1	4	5	6
1990-91	Minnesota	NHL	73	15	31	46	60	23	8	8	16	56
1991-92	Minnesota	NHL	68	9	37	46	109	7	1	4	5	6
1992-93	Minnesota	NHL	45	5	7	12	10	....	....	....	....	....
	NHL Totals		1077	357	679	1036	917	184	64	96	160	245

a OHA Second All-Star Team (1977)
b OHA First All-Star Team (1978)
c Named Canadian Major Junior Player of the Year (1978)
d Won Calder Memorial Trophy (1979)

Played in NHL All-Star Game (1981, 1982, 1989, 1991)

Traded to **Montreal** by **Minnesota** for Keith Acton, Mark Napier and Toronto's third round choice (previously acquired by Montreal — Minnesota selected Ken Hodge) in 1984 Entry Draft, October 28, 1983. Traded to **Minnesota** by **Montreal** for Minnesota's fourth round choice (Louis Bernard) in the 1992 Entry Draft, August 7, 1990.

SMITH, RYAN

Defense. Shoots left. 6'2", 200 lbs. Born, Lethbridge, Alta., June 28, 1974.
(San Jose's 8th choice, 171st overall, in 1992 Entry Draft).

			Regular Season					Playoffs				
Season	Club	Lea	GP	G	A	TP	PIM	GP	G	A	TP	PIM
1990-91	Lethbridge	AJHL	34	8	19	27	103	....	....	....	....	....
1991-92	Brandon	WHL	71	7	24	31	48	....	....	....	....	....
1992-93	Brandon	WHL	71	9	38	47	103	4	0	1	1	4

SMITH, SANDY

Right wing. Shoots right. 5'11", 200 lbs. Born, Brainerd, MN, October 23, 1967.
(Pittsburgh's 5th choice, 88th overall, in 1986 Entry Draft).

			Regular Season					Playoffs				
Season	Club	Lea	GP	G	A	TP	PIM	GP	G	A	TP	PIM
1986-87	Minn.-Duluth	WCHA	35	3	3	6	26	....	....	....	....	....
1987-88	Minn.-Duluth	WCHA	41	22	9	31	47	....	....	....	....	....
1988-89	Minn.-Duluth	WCHA	40	6	16	22	75	....	....	....	....	....
1989-90	Minn.-Duluth	WCHA	39	15	16	31	53	....	....	....	....	....
	Muskegon	IHL	3	1	0	1	0	....	....	....	....	....
1990-91	Muskegon	IHL	82	25	29	54	51	5	1	1	2	6
1991-92	Muskegon	IHL	64	15	18	33	109	14	7	2	9	4
1992-93	Cleveland	IHL	77	32	36	68	174	4	0	0	0	8

SMITH, STEVE

Defense. Shoots left. 6'4", 215 lbs. Born, Glasgow, Scotland, April 30, 1963.
(Edmonton's 5th choice, 111th overall, in 1981 Entry Draft).

			Regular Season					Playoffs				
Season	Club	Lea	GP	G	A	TP	PIM	GP	G	A	TP	PIM
1980-81	London	OHA	62	4	12	16	141	....	....	....	....	....
1981-82	London	OHL	58	10	36	46	207	4	1	2	3	13
1982-83	Moncton	AHL	2	0	0	0	0	....	....	....	....	....
	London	OHL	50	6	35	41	133	3	1	0	1	10
1983-84	Moncton	AHL	64	1	8	9	176	....	....	....	....	....
1984-85	Edmonton	NHL	2	0	0	0	2	....	....	....	....	....
	Nova Scotia	AHL	68	2	28	30	161	5	0	3	3	40
1985-86	Edmonton	NHL	55	4	20	24	166	6	0	1	1	14
	Nova Scotia	AHL	4	0	2	2	11	....	....	....	....	....
1986-87	Edmonton	NHL	62	7	15	22	165	15	1	3	4	45
1987-88	Edmonton	NHL	79	12	43	55	286	19	1	11	12	55
1988-89	Edmonton	NHL	35	3	19	22	97	7	2	2	4	20
1989-90	Edmonton	NHL	75	7	34	41	171	22	5	10	15	37
1990-91	Edmonton	NHL	77	13	41	54	193	18	1	2	3	45
1991-92	Chicago	NHL	76	9	21	30	304	18	1	11	12	16
1992-93	Chicago	NHL	78	10	47	57	214	4	0	0	0	10
	NHL Totals		539	65	240	305	1598	109	11	40	51	242

a WHL East First All-Star Team (1993)

Played in NHL All-Star Game (1991)

Traded to **Chicago** by **Edmonton** for Dave Manson and future considerations, October 2, 1991.

SMOLINSKI, BRYAN

Center. Shoots right. 6'1", 200 lbs. Born, Toledo, OH, December 27, 1971.
(Boston's 1st choice, 21st overall, in 1990 Entry Draft).

			Regular Season					Playoffs				
Season	Club	Lea	GP	G	A	TP	PIM	GP	G	A	TP	PIM
1989-90	Michigan State	CCHA	35	9	13	22	34	....	....	....	....	....
1990-91	Michigan State	CCHA	35	9	12	21	24	....	....	....	....	....
1991-92	Michigan State	CCHA	41	28	33	61	55	....	....	....	....	....
1992-93ab	Michigan State	CCHA	40	31	37	*68	93	....	....	....	....	....
	Boston	NHL	9	1	3	4	0	4	1	0	1	2
	NHL Totals		9	1	3	4	0	4	1	0	1	2

a CCHA First All-Star Team (1993)
b NCAA West First All-American Team (1993)

SMYTH, GREG (SMIHTH)

Defense. Shoots right. 6'3", 212 lbs. Born, Oakville, Ont., April 23, 1966.
(Philadelphia's 1st choice, 22nd overall, in 1984 Entry Draft).

			Regular Season					Playoffs				
Season	Club	Lea	GP	G	A	TP	PIM	GP	G	A	TP	PIM
1983-84	London	OHL	64	4	21	25	252	6	1	0	1	24
1984-85	London	OHL	47	7	16	23	188	8	2	2	4	27
1985-86	Hershey	AHL	2	0	1	1	5	8	0	0	0	60
a	London	OHL	46	12	42	54	199	4	1	2	3	28
1986-87	Philadelphia	NHL	1	0	0	0	0	1	0	0	0	2
	Hershey	AHL	35	0	2	2	158	2	0	0	0	19
1987-88	Philadelphia	NHL	48	1	6	7	192	5	0	0	0	38
	Hershey	AHL	21	0	10	10	102	....	....	....	....	....
1988-89	Quebec	NHL	10	0	1	1	70	....	....	....	....	....
	Halifax	AHL	43	3	9	12	310	4	0	1	1	35
1989-90	Quebec	NHL	13	0	0	0	57	....	....	....	....	....
	Halifax	AHL	49	5	14	19	235	6	1	0	1	52
1990-91	Quebec	NHL	1	0	0	0	0	....	....	....	....	....
	Halifax	AHL	56	6	23	29	340	....	....	....	....	....
1991-92	Quebec	NHL	29	0	2	2	138	....	....	....	....	....
	Halifax	AHL	9	1	3	4	35	....	....	....	....	....
	Calgary	NHL	7	1	1	2	15	....	....	....	....	....
1992-93	Calgary	NHL	35	1	2	3	95	....	....	....	....	....
	Salt Lake	IHL	5	0	1	1	31	....	....	....	....	....
	NHL Totals		144	3	12	15	567	6	0	0	0	40

a OHL Second All-Star Team (1986)

Traded to **Quebec** by **Philadelphia** with Philadelphia's third round choice (John Tanner) in the 1989 Entry Draft for Terry Carkner, July 25, 1988. Traded to **Calgary** by **Quebec** for Martin Simard, March 10, 1992.

SMYTH, KEVIN

Left wing. Shoots left. 6'2", 217 lbs. Born, Banff, Alta., November 22, 1973.
(Hartford's 4th choice, 79th overall, in 1992 Entry Draft).

			Regular Season					Playoffs				
Season	Club	Lea	GP	G	A	TP	PIM	GP	G	A	TP	PIM
1990-91	Moose Jaw	WHL	66	30	45	75	96	6	1	1	2	0
1991-92	Moose Jaw	WHL	71	30	55	85	114	4	1	3	4	6
1992-93	Moose Jaw	WHL	64	44	38	82	111	....	....	....	....	....

SNELL, CHRIS

Defense. Shoots left. 5'11", 200 lbs. Born, Regina, Sask., May 12, 1971.
(Buffalo's 8th choice, 145th overall, in 1991 Entry Draft).

			Regular Season					Playoffs				
Season	Club	Lea	GP	G	A	TP	PIM	GP	G	A	TP	PIM
1989-90a	Ottawa	OHL	63	18	62	80	36	3	2	4	6	4
1990-91	Ottawa	OHL	54	23	59	82	58	17	3	14	17	8
1991-92	Rochester	AHL	65	5	27	32	66	10	2	1	3	6
1992-93	Rochester	AHL	76	14	57	71	83	17	5	8	13	39

a OHL First All-Star Team (1990)

Signed as a free agent by **Toronto**, August 3, 1993.

SNUGGERUD, DAVE

Right wing. Shoots left. 6', 190 lbs. Born, Minnetonka, MN, June 20, 1966.
(Buffalo's 1st choice, 1st overall, in 1987 Supplemental Draft).

			Regular Season					Playoffs				
Season	Club	Lea	GP	G	A	TP	PIM	GP	G	A	TP	PIM
1985-86	U. Minnesota	WCHA	42	14	18	32	47	....	....	....	....	....
1986-87	U. Minnesota	WCHA	39	30	29	59	38	....	....	....	....	....
1987-88	U.S. National	....	51	14	21	35	26	....	....	....	....	....
	U.S. Olympic	....	6	3	2	5	4	....	....	....	....	....
1988-89ab	U. Minnesota	WCHA	45	29	20	49	39	....	....	....	....	....
1989-90	Buffalo	NHL	80	14	16	30	41	6	0	0	0	2
1990-91	Buffalo	NHL	80	9	15	24	32	6	1	3	4	4
1991-92	Buffalo	NHL	55	3	15	18	36	....	....	....	....	....
	San Jose	NHL	11	0	1	1	4	....	....	....	....	....
1992-93	San Jose	NHL	25	4	5	9	14	....	....	....	....	....
	Philadelphia	NHL	14	0	2	2	0	....	....	....	....	....
	NHL Totals		265	30	54	84	127	12	1	3	4	6

a WCHA Second All-Star Team (1989)
b NCAA West Second All-American Team (1989)

Traded to **San Jose** by **Buffalo** for Wayne Presley, March 9, 1992. Traded to **Philadelphia** by **San Jose** for Mark Pederson and future considerations, December 19, 1992.

SOCHA, GARY

Center. Shoots left. 6'4", 190 lbs. Born, North Attleboro, MA, December 30, 1969.
(Calgary's 3rd choice, 84th overall, in 1988 Entry Draft).

			Regular Season					Playoffs				
Season	Club	Lea	GP	G	A	TP	PIM	GP	G	A	TP	PIM
1989-90	Providence	H.E.	25	2	2	4	8	....	....	....	....	....
1990-91	Providence	H.E.	35	15	13	28	20	....	....	....	....	....
1991-92	Providence	H.E.	26	11	14	25	34	....	....	....	....	....
1992-93	Providence	H.E.	33	13	15	28	22	....	....	....	....	....
	Salt Lake	IHL	4	0	0	0	0	....	....	....	....	....

SOROCHAN, LEE

Defense. Shoots left. 5'11", 208 lbs. Born, Edmonton, Alta., September 9, 1975.
(NY Rangers' 2nd choice, 34th overall, in 1993 Entry Draft).

			Regular Season					Playoffs				
Season	Club	Lea	GP	G	A	TP	PIM	GP	G	A	TP	PIM
1991-92	Lethbridge	WHL	67	2	9	11	105	5	0	2	2	6
1992-93	Lethbridge	WHL	69	8	32	40	208	4	0	1	1	12

SOROKIN, SERGEI

Defense. Shoots left. 5'11", 187 lbs. Born, Gorky, Soviet Union, October 2, 1969.
(Winnipeg's 10th choice, 247th overall, in 1991 Entry Draft).

			Regular Season					Playoffs				
Season	Club	Lea	GP	G	A	TP	PIM	GP	G	A	TP	PIM
1985-86	Torpedo Gorky	USSR	3	0	0	0	0	....	....	....	....	....
1986-87	Torpedo Gorky	USSR	34	0	0	0	22	....	....	....	....	....
1987-88	Torpedo Gorky	USSR	19	2	0	2	20	....	....	....	....	....
1988-89	Torpedo Gorky	USSR	25	1	1	2	29	....	....	....	....	....
1989-90	Moscow D'amo	USSR	10	0	2	2	2	....	....	....	....	....
1990-91	Moscow D'amo	USSR	41	4	5	9	20	....	....	....	....	....
1991-92	Moscow D'amo	CIS	42	7	11	18	34	....	....	....	....	....
1992-93	Moscow D'amo	CIS	38	12	8	20	20	10	1	0	1	6

SPEER, MICHAEL

Defense. Shoots left. 6'2", 202 lbs. Born, Toronto, Ont., March 26, 1971.
(Chicago's 2nd choice, 27th overall, in 1989 Entry Draft).

			Regular Season					Playoffs				
Season	Club	Lea	GP	G	A	TP	PIM	GP	G	A	TP	PIM
1987-88	Guelph	OHL	53	4	10	14	60	....	....	....	....	....
1988-89	Guelph	OHL	65	9	31	40	185	7	2	4	6	23
1989-90	Owen Sound	OHL	61	18	39	57	176	12	3	7	10	21
1990-91	Owen Sound	OHL	32	13	19	32	86	....	....	....	....	....
	Windsor	OHL	25	8	28	36	40	11	2	7	9	15
	Indianapolis	IHL	1	0	1	1	0	1	0	0	0	5
1991-92	Indianapolis	IHL	54	0	6	6	67	....	....	....	....	....
1992-93	Indianapolis	IHL	38	1	1	2	109	5	1	0	1	26

SPITZIG, TIM

Right wing. Shoots right. 6', 195 lbs. Born, Goderich, Ont., April 15, 1974.
(Detroit's 7th choice, 152nd overall, in 1993 Entry Draft).

			Regular Season					Playoffs				
Season	Club	Lea	GP	G	A	TP	PIM	GP	G	A	TP	PIM
1991-92	Kitchener	OHL	62	8	13	21	89	4	0	0	0	2
1992-93	Kitchener	OHL	66	40	39	79	127	7	5	4	9	14

STAGG, BRIAN

Right wing. Shoots right. 6'2", 177 lbs. Born, North Bay, Ont., May 23, 1974.
(Washington's 9th choice, 215th overall, in 1992 Entry Draft).

			Regular Season					Playoffs				
Season	Club	Lea	GP	G	A	TP	PIM	GP	G	A	TP	PIM
1991-92	Kingston	OHL	65	17	14	31	23	....	....	....	....	....
1992-93	Kingston	OHL	20	4	5	9	17	....	....	....	....	....
	Belleville	OHL	9	1	0	1	2	....	....	....	....	....
	North Bay	OHL	42	16	13	29	27	5	2	0	2	0

STAIOS, STEVE

Defense. Shoots right. 6', 185 lbs. Born, Hamilton, Ont., July 28, 1973.
(St. Louis' 1st choice, 27th overall, in 1991 Entry Draft).

			Regular Season					Playoffs				
Season	Club	Lea	GP	G	A	TP	PIM	GP	G	A	TP	PIM
1990-91	Niagara Falls	OHL	66	17	29	46	115	12	2	3	5	10
1991-92	Niagara Falls	OHL	65	11	42	53	122	17	7	8	15	27
1992-93	Niagara Falls	OHL	12	4	14	18	30	....	....	....	....	....
	Sudbury	OHL	53	13	44	57	67	11	5	6	11	22

STAJDUHAR, NICK (STAD-joo-hahr)

Defense. Shoots left. 6'2", 194 lbs. Born, Kitchener, Ont., December 6, 1974.
(Edmonton's 2nd choice, 16th overall, in 1993 Entry Draft).

			Regular Season					Playoffs				
Season	Club	Lea	GP	G	A	TP	PIM	GP	G	A	TP	PIM
1990-91	London	OHL	66	3	12	15	51	7	0	0	0	2
1991-92	London	OHL	66	6	15	21	62	10	1	4	5	10
1992-93	London	OHL	49	15	45	60	58	12	4	11	15	10

STANTON, PAUL

Defense. Shoots right. 6'1", 200 lbs. Born, Boston, MA, June 22, 1967.
(Pittsburgh's 8th choice, 149th overall, in 1985 Entry Draft).

			Regular Season					Playoffs				
Season	Club	Lea	GP	G	A	TP	PIM	GP	G	A	TP	PIM
1985-86	U. Wisconsin	WCHA	36	4	6	10	16	....	....	....	....	....
1986-87	U. Wisconsin	WCHA	41	5	17	22	70	....	....	....	....	....
1987-88ab	U. Wisconsin	WCHA	45	9	38	47	98	....	....	....	....	....
1988-89c	U. Wisconsin	WCHA	45	7	29	36	126	....	....	....	....	....
1989-90	Muskegon	IHL	77	5	27	32	61	15	2	4	6	21
1990-91	**Pittsburgh**	**NHL**	**75**	**5**	**18**	**23**	**40**	**22**	**1**	**2**	**3**	**24**
1991-92	**Pittsburgh**	**NHL**	**54**	**2**	**8**	**10**	**62**	**21**	**1**	**7**	**8**	**42**
1992-93	**Pittsburgh**	**NHL**	**77**	**4**	**12**	**16**	**97**	**1**	**0**	**1**	**1**	**0**
	NHL Totals		**206**	**11**	**38**	**49**	**199**	**44**	**2**	**10**	**12**	**66**

a NCAA West First All-American Team (1988)
b WCHA Second All-Star Team (1988)
c WCHA First All-Star Team (1989)

STAPLETON, MIKE

Center. Shoots right. 5'10", 183 lbs. Born, Sarnia, Ont., May 5, 1966.
(Chicago's 7th choice, 132nd overall, in 1984 Entry Draft).

			Regular Season					Playoffs				
Season	Club	Lea	GP	G	A	TP	PIM	GP	G	A	TP	PIM
1983-84	Cornwall	OHL	70	24	45	69	94	3	1	2	3	4
1984-85	Cornwall	OHL	56	41	44	85	68	9	2	4	6	23
1985-86	Cornwall	OHL	56	39	64	103	74	6	2	3	5	2
1986-87	**Chicago**	**NHL**	**39**	**3**	**6**	**9**	**6**	**4**	**0**	**0**	**0**	**2**
	Cdn. Olympic	....	21	2	4	6	4	....	....	....	....	....
1987-88	**Chicago**	**NHL**	**53**	**2**	**9**	**11**	**59**	....	....	....	....	....
	Saginaw	IHL	31	11	19	30	52	10	5	6	11	10
1988-89	**Chicago**	**NHL**	**7**	**0**	**1**	**1**	**7**	....	....	....	....	....
	Saginaw	IHL	69	21	47	68	162	6	1	3	4	4
1989-90	Indianapolis	IHL	16	5	10	15	6	13	9	10	19	38
1990-91	**Chicago**	**NHL**	**7**	**0**	**1**	**1**	**2**	....	....	....	....	....
	Indianapolis	IHL	75	29	52	81	76	7	1	4	5	0
1991-92	**Chicago**	**NHL**	**19**	**4**	**4**	**8**	**8**	....	....	....	....	....
	Indianapolis	IHL	59	18	40	58	65	....	....	....	....	....
1992-93	**Pittsburgh**	**NHL**	**78**	**4**	**9**	**13**	**10**	**4**	**0**	**0**	**0**	**0**
	NHL Totals		**203**	**13**	**30**	**43**	**92**	**8**	**0**	**0**	**0**	**2**

Signed as a free agent by **Pittsburgh**, September 30, 1992.

STAROSTENKO, DMITRI (stahr-oh-STEN-koh)

Right wing. Shoots left. 6', 185 lbs. Born, Minsk, Soviet Union, March 18, 1973.
(NY Rangers' 5th choice, 120th overall, in 1992 Entry Draft).

			Regular Season					Playoffs				
Season	Club	Lea	GP	G	A	TP	PIM	GP	G	A	TP	PIM
1989-90	D'amo Minsk	USSR	7	0	0	0	2	....	....	....	....	....
1990-91	CSKA	USSR	20	2	1	3	4	....	....	....	....	....
1991-92	CSKA	CIS	32	3	1	4	12	....	....	....	....	....
1992-93	CSKA	CIS	42	15	12	27	22	....	....	....	....	....

STASIUK, JEREMY

Right wing. Shoots right. 5'11", 189 lbs. Born, Saskatoon, Sask., December 26, 1974.
(Dallas' 6th choice, 165th overall, in 1993 Entry Draft).

			Regular Season					Playoffs				
Season	Club	Lea	GP	G	A	TP	PIM	GP	G	A	TP	PIM
1991-92	Spokane	WHL	2	0	0	0	0	....	....	....	....	....
1992-93	Spokane	WHL	63	14	23	37	111	10	3	5	8	15

STASTNY, PETER (STAHST-nee)

Center. Shoots left. 6'1", 200 lbs. Born, Bratislava, Czechoslovakia, September 18, 1956.

			Regular Season					Playoffs				
Season	Club	Lea	GP	G	A	TP	PIM	GP	G	A	TP	PIM
1973-74	Bratislava	Czech.				UNAVAILABLE						
1974-75	Bratislava	Czech.				UNAVAILABLE						
1975-76	Bratislava	Czech.	32	19	9	28	....	....	....	....	....	....
1976-77	Bratislava	Czech.	44	25	27	52	....	....	....	....	....	....
1977-78	Bratislava	Czech.	42	29	24	53	28	....	....	....	....	....
1978-79	Bratislava	Czech.	39	32	23	55	21	....	....	....	....	....
1979-80a	Bratislava	Czech.	41	26	26	52	58	....	....	....	....	....
1980-81bcd	**Quebec**	**NHL**	**77**	**39**	**70**	**109**	**37**	**5**	**2**	**8**	**10**	**7**
1981-82	**Quebec**	**NHL**	**80**	**46**	**93**	**139**	**91**	**12**	**7**	**11**	**18**	**10**
1982-83	**Quebec**	**NHL**	**75**	**47**	**77**	**124**	**78**	**4**	**3**	**2**	**5**	**10**
1983-84	**Quebec**	**NHL**	**80**	**46**	**73**	**119**	**73**	**9**	**2**	**7**	**9**	**31**
1984-85	**Quebec**	**NHL**	**75**	**32**	**68**	**100**	**95**	**18**	**4**	**19**	**23**	**24**
1985-86	**Quebec**	**NHL**	**76**	**41**	**81**	**122**	**60**	**3**	**0**	**1**	**1**	**2**
1986-87	**Quebec**	**NHL**	**64**	**24**	**53**	**77**	**43**	**13**	**6**	**9**	**15**	**12**
1987-88	**Quebec**	**NHL**	**76**	**46**	**65**	**111**	**69**	....	....	....	....	....
1988-89	**Quebec**	**NHL**	**72**	**35**	**50**	**85**	**117**	....	....	....	....	....
1989-90	**Quebec**	**NHL**	**62**	**24**	**38**	**62**	**24**	....	....	....	....	....
	New Jersey	**NHL**	**12**	**5**	**6**	**11**	**16**	**6**	**3**	**2**	**5**	**2**
1990-91	**New Jersey**	**NHL**	**77**	**18**	**42**	**60**	**53**	**7**	**3**	**4**	**7**	**2**
1991-92	**New Jersey**	**NHL**	**66**	**24**	**38**	**62**	**42**	**7**	**3**	**7**	**10**	**19**
1992-93	**New Jersey**	**NHL**	**62**	**17**	**23**	**40**	**22**	**5**	**0**	**2**	**2**	**2**
	NHL Totals		**954**	**444**	**777**	**1221**	**820**	**89**	**33**	**72**	**105**	**121**

a Czechoslovakian League Player of the Year (1980)
b Won Calder Memorial Trophy (1981)
c NHL record for assists by a rookie (1981)
d NHL record for points by a rookie (1981)

Played in NHL All-Star Game (1981, 1982-84, 1986, 1988)

Signed as a free agent by **Quebec**, August 26, 1980. Traded to **New Jersey** by **Quebec** for Craig Wolanin and future considerations (Randy Velischek, August 13, 1990), March 6, 1990.

STAUBER, PETE

Left wing. Shoots left. 5'11", 185 lbs. Born, Duluth, MN, May 10, 1966.

			Regular Season					Playoffs				
Season	Club	Lea	GP	G	A	TP	PIM	GP	G	A	TP	PIM
1986-87	Lake Superior	CCHA	40	22	13	35	80	....	....	....	....	....
1987-88	Lake Superior	CCHA	45	25	33	58	103	....	....	....	....	....
1988-89	Lake Superior	CCHA	46	25	13	38	115	....	....	....	....	....
1989-90	Lake Superior	CCHA	46	25	31	56	90	....	....	....	....	....
1990-91	Adirondack	AHL	26	7	11	18	2	....	....	....	....	....
1991-92	Adirondack	AHL	25	2	5	7	14	....	....	....	....	....
	Toledo	ECHL	25	7	21	28	46	5	2	3	5	46
1992-93	Adirondack	AHL	12	2	2	4	8	....	....	....	....	....

Signed as a free agent by **Detroit**, June 21, 1990. Claimed by **Florida** from **Detroit** in Expansion Draft, June 24, 1993.

STAVJANA, ANTONIN (stahv-YAH-nah)

Defense. Shoots left. 6', 187 lbs. Born, Gottwaldov, Czechoslovakia, February 10, 1963.
(Calgary's 11th choice, 247th overall, in 1986 Entry Draft).

			Regular Season					Playoffs				
Season	Club	Lea	GP	G	A	TP	PIM	GP	G	A	TP	PIM
1980-81	TJ Gottwaldov	Czech.	41	1	3	4	14	....	....	....	....	....
1981-82	TJ Gottwaldov	Czech.	43	3	7	10	12	....	....	....	....	....
1982-83	Dukla Trencin	Czech.2				UNAVAILABLE						
1983-84	Dukla Trencin	Czech.	38	3	10	13	12	....	....	....	....	....
1984-85	TJ Gottwaldov	Czech.	43	5	6	11	10	....	....	....	....	....
1985-86	TJ Gottwaldov	Czech.	39	11	11	22	....	....	....	....	....	....
1986-87	TJ Gottwaldov	Czech.	40	12	9	21	10	....	....	....	....	....
1987-88	TJ Gottwaldov	Czech.	40	10	15	25	24	....	....	....	....	....
1988-89	TJ Gottwaldov	Czech.	43	11	12	23	10	....	....	....	....	....
1989-90	TJ Zlin	Czech.	46	7	14	21	....	....	....	....	....	....
1990-91	JoKP	Fin.2	42	13	35	48	10	....	....	....	....	....
1991-92	JoKP	Fin.	44	9	11	20	24	....	....	....	....	....
1992-93	HV-71	Swe.	39	2	11	13	14	....	....	....	....	....

STEEN, THOMAS (STEEN)

Center. Shoots left. 5'11", 185 lbs. Born, Grums, Sweden, June 8, 1960.
(Winnipeg's 5th choice, 103rd overall, in 1979 Entry Draft).

			Regular Season					Playoffs				
Season	Club	Lea	GP	G	A	TP	PIM	GP	G	A	TP	PIM
1976-77	Leksand	Swe.	2	1	1	2	2	....	....	....	....	....
1977-78	Leksand	Swe.	35	5	6	11	30	....	....	....	....	....
1978-79	Leksand	Swe.	23	13	4	17	35	2	0	0	0	0
1979-80	Leksand	Swe.	18	7	7	14	14	2	0	0	0	6
1980-81	Farjestad	Swe.	32	16	23	39	30	7	4	2	6	8
1981-82	**Winnipeg**	**NHL**	**73**	**15**	**29**	**44**	**42**	**4**	**0**	**4**	**4**	**2**
1982-83	**Winnipeg**	**NHL**	**75**	**26**	**33**	**59**	**60**	**3**	**0**	**2**	**2**	**0**
1983-84	**Winnipeg**	**NHL**	**78**	**20**	**45**	**65**	**69**	**3**	**0**	**1**	**1**	**9**
1984-85	**Winnipeg**	**NHL**	**79**	**30**	**54**	**84**	**80**	**8**	**2**	**3**	**5**	**17**
1985-86	**Winnipeg**	**NHL**	**78**	**17**	**47**	**64**	**76**	**3**	**1**	**1**	**2**	**4**
1986-87	**Winnipeg**	**NHL**	**75**	**17**	**33**	**50**	**59**	**10**	**3**	**4**	**7**	**8**
1987-88	**Winnipeg**	**NHL**	**76**	**16**	**38**	**54**	**53**	**5**	**1**	**5**	**6**	**2**
1988-89	**Winnipeg**	**NHL**	**80**	**27**	**61**	**88**	**80**	....	....	....	....	....
1989-90	**Winnipeg**	**NHL**	**53**	**18**	**48**	**66**	**35**	**7**	**2**	**5**	**7**	**16**
1990-91	**Winnipeg**	**NHL**	**58**	**19**	**48**	**67**	**49**	....	....	....	....	....
1991-92	**Winnipeg**	**NHL**	**38**	**13**	**25**	**38**	**29**	**7**	**2**	**4**	**6**	**2**
1992-93	**Winnipeg**	**NHL**	**80**	**22**	**50**	**72**	**75**	**6**	**1**	**3**	**4**	**2**
	NHL Totals		**843**	**240**	**511**	**751**	**707**	**56**	**12**	**32**	**44**	**62**

STEER, JAMIE

Right wing. Shoots right. 5'11", 180 lbs.   Born, Calgary, Alta., February 24, 1969.
(Buffalo's 1st choice, 19th overall, in 1991 Supplemental Draft).

			Regular Season					Playoffs				
Season	Club	Lea	GP	G	A	TP	PIM	GP	G	A	TP	PIM
1988-89	Michigan Tech	WCHA	42	13	16	29	22	....	....	....	....	....
1989-90	Michigan Tech	WCHA	40	21	21	42	26	....	....	....	....	....
1990-91	Michigan Tech	WCHA	39	14	14	28	20	....	....	....	....	....
1991-92	Michigan Tech	WCHA	39	26	24	50	30	....	....	....	....	....
1992-93	Greensboro	ECHL	35	16	14	30	8	....	....	....	....	....
	Louisville	ECHL	30	13	16	29	14	....	....	....	....	....

STEINER, ONDREJ

Center. Shoots left. 6'1", 176 lbs.   Born, Plzen, Czech., February 12, 1974.
(Buffalo's 3rd choice, 59th overall, in 1992 Entry Draft).

			Regular Season					Playoffs				
Season	Club	Lea	GP	G	A	TP	PIM	GP	G	A	TP	PIM
1991-92	Skoda Plzen	Czech.	4	0	1	1	0	....	....	....	....	....
1992-93	Skoda Plzen	Czech.	29	1	7	8	....	....	....	....	....	....

STERN, RONALD (RONNIE)

Right wing. Shoots right. 6', 195 lbs.   Born, Ste. Agathe, Que., January 11, 1967.
(Vancouver's 3rd choice, 70th overall, in 1986 Entry Draft).

			Regular Season					Playoffs				
Season	Club	Lea	GP	G	A	TP	PIM	GP	G	A	TP	PIM
1984-85	Longueuil	QMJHL	67	6	14	20	176	....	....	....	....	....
1985-86	Longueuil	QMJHL	70	39	33	72	317	....	....	....	....	....
1986-87	Longueuil	QMJHL	56	32	39	71	266	19	11	9	20	55
1987-88	**Vancouver**	**NHL**	15	0	0	0	52	....	....	....	....	....
	Fredericton	AHL	2	1	0	1	4	....	....	....	....	....
	Flint	IHL	55	14	19	33	294	16	8	8	16	94
1988-89	**Vancouver**	**NHL**	17	1	0	1	49	3	0	1	1	17
	Milwaukee	IHL	45	19	23	42	280	5	1	0	1	11
1989-90	**Vancouver**	**NHL**	34	2	3	5	208	....	....	....	....	....
	Milwaukee	IHL	26	8	9	17	165	....	....	....	....	....
1990-91	**Vancouver**	**NHL**	31	2	3	5	171	....	....	....	....	....
	Milwaukee	IHL	7	2	2	4	81	....	....	....	....	....
	Calgary	**NHL**	13	1	3	4	69	7	1	3	4	14
1991-92	**Calgary**	**NHL**	72	13	9	22	338	....	....	....	....	....
1992-93	**Calgary**	**NHL**	70	10	15	25	207	6	0	0	0	43
	NHL Totals		252	29	33	62	1094	16	1	4	5	74

Traded to **Calgary** by **Vancouver** with Kevan Guy for Dana Murzyn, March 5, 1991.

STEVENS, JOHN

Defense. Shoots left. 6'1", 195 lbs.   Born, Campbellton, N.B., May 4, 1966.
(Philadelphia's 5th choice, 47th overall, in 1984 Entry Draft).

			Regular Season					Playoffs				
Season	Club	Lea	GP	G	A	TP	PIM	GP	G	A	TP	PIM
1983-84	Oshawa	OHL	70	1	10	11	71	7	0	1	1	6
1984-85	Oshawa	OHL	44	2	10	12	61	5	0	2	2	4
	Hershey	AHL	3	0	0	0	0	....	....	....	....	....
1985-86	Kalamazoo	IHL	6	0	1	1	8	6	0	3	3	9
	Oshawa	OHL	65	1	7	8	146	6	0	2	2	14
1986-87	**Philadelphia**	**NHL**	6	0	2	2	14	....	....	....	....	....
	Hershey	AHL	63	1	15	16	131	3	0	0	0	7
1987-88	**Philadelphia**	**NHL**	3	0	0	0	0	....	....	....	....	....
	Hershey	AHL	59	1	15	16	108	....	....	....	....	....
1988-89	Hershey	AHL	78	3	13	16	129	12	1	1	2	29
1989-90	Hershey	AHL	79	3	10	13	193	....	....	....	....	....
1990-91	**Hartford**	**NHL**	14	0	1	1	11	....	....	....	....	....
	Springfield	AHL	65	0	12	12	139	18	0	6	6	35
1991-92	**Hartford**	**NHL**	21	0	4	4	19	....	....	....	....	....
	Springfield	AHL	45	1	12	13	73	11	1	3	4	27
1992-93	Springfield	AHL	74	1	19	20	111	15	0	1	1	18
	NHL Totals		44	0	7	7	44	....	....	....	....	....

Signed as a free agent by **Hartford**, July 30, 1990.

STEVENS, KEVIN

Left wing. Shoots left. 6'3", 217 lbs.   Born, Brockton, MA, April 15, 1965.
(Los Angeles' 6th choice, 108th overall, in 1983 Entry Draft).

			Regular Season					Playoffs				
Season	Club	Lea	GP	G	A	TP	PIM	GP	G	A	TP	PIM
1983-84	Boston College	ECAC	37	6	14	20	36	....	....	....	....	....
1984-85	Boston College	H.E.	40	13	23	36	36	....	....	....	....	....
1985-86	Boston College	H.E.	42	17	27	44	56	....	....	....	....	....
1986-87ab	Boston College	H.E.	39	35	35	70	54	....	....	....	....	....
1987-88	U.S. National	....	44	22	23	45	52	....	....	....	....	....
	U.S. Olympic	....	5	1	3	4	2	....	....	....	....	....
	Pittsburgh	**NHL**	16	5	2	7	8	....	....	....	....	....
1988-89	**Pittsburgh**	**NHL**	24	12	3	15	19	11	3	7	10	16
	Muskegon	IHL	45	24	41	65	113	....	....	....	....	....
1989-90	**Pittsburgh**	**NHL**	76	29	41	70	171	....	....	....	....	....
1990-91c	**Pittsburgh**	**NHL**	80	40	46	86	133	24	*17	16	33	53
1991-92d	**Pittsburgh**	**NHL**	80	54	69	123	254	21	13	15	28	28
1992-93c	**Pittsburgh**	**NHL**	72	55	56	111	177	12	5	11	16	22
	NHL Totals		348	195	217	412	762	68	38	49	87	119

a Hockey East First All-Star Team (1987)
b NCAA East Second All-American Team (1987)
c NHL Second All-Star Team (1991, 1993)
d NHL First All-Star Team (1992)
Played in NHL All-Star Game (1991-93)
Rights traded to **Pittsburgh** by **Los Angeles** for Anders Hakansson, September 9, 1983.

STEVENS, MIKE

Left wing. Shoots left. 6', 202 lbs.   Born, Kitchener, Ont., December 30, 1965.
(Vancouver's 5th choice, 58th overall, in 1984 Entry Draft).

			Regular Season					Playoffs				
Season	Club	Lea	GP	G	A	TP	PIM	GP	G	A	TP	PIM
1982-83	Kitchener	OHL	13	0	4	4	16	12	0	1	1	9
1983-84	Kitchener	OHL	66	19	21	40	109	16	10	7	17	40
1984-85	**Vancouver**	**NHL**	6	0	3	3	6	....	....	....	....	....
	Kitchener	OHL	37	17	18	35	121	4	1	1	2	8
1985-86	Fredericton	AHL	79	12	19	31	208	6	1	1	2	35
1986-87	Fredericton	AHL	71	7	18	25	258	....	....	....	....	....
1987-88	**Boston**	**NHL**	7	0	1	1	9	....	....	....	....	....
	Maine	AHL	63	30	25	55	265	7	1	2	3	37
1988-89	**NY Islanders**	**NHL**	9	1	0	1	14	....	....	....	....	....
	Springfield	AHL	42	17	13	30	120	....	....	....	....	....
1989-90	Springfield	AHL	28	12	10	22	75	....	....	....	....	....
	Toronto	**NHL**	1	0	0	0	0	....	....	....	....	....
	Newmarket	AHL	46	16	28	44	86	....	....	....	....	....
1990-91	Newmarket	AHL	68	24	23	47	229	....	....	....	....	....
1991-92	St. John's	AHL	30	13	11	24	65	....	....	....	....	....
	Binghamton	AHL	44	15	15	30	87	11	7	6	13	45
1992-93	Binghamton	AHL	68	31	61	92	230	14	5	5	10	63
	NHL Totals		23	1	4	5	29	....	....	....	....	....

Traded to **Boston** by **Vancouver** for cash, October 6, 1987. Signed as a free agent by **NY Islanders**, August 20, 1988. Traded to **Toronto** by **NY Islanders** with Gilles Thibaudeau for Jack Capuano, Paul Gagne and Derek Laxdal, December 20, 1989. Traded to **NY Rangers** by **Toronto** for Guy Larose, December 26, 1991.

STEVENS, SCOTT

Defense. Shoots left. 6'2", 215 lbs.   Born, Kitchener, Ont., April 1, 1964.
(Washington's 1st choice, 5th overall, in 1982 Entry Draft).

			Regular Season					Playoffs				
Season	Club	Lea	GP	G	A	TP	PIM	GP	G	A	TP	PIM
1980-81	Kitchener	OPJHL	39	7	33	40	82	....	....	....	....	....
	Kitchener	OHA	1	0	0	0	0	....	....	....	....	....
1981-82	Kitchener	OHL	68	6	36	42	158	15	1	10	11	71
1982-83a	**Washington**	**NHL**	77	9	16	25	195	4	1	0	1	26
1983-84	**Washington**	**NHL**	78	13	32	45	201	8	1	8	9	21
1984-85	**Washington**	**NHL**	80	21	44	65	221	5	0	1	1	20
1985-86	**Washington**	**NHL**	73	15	38	53	165	9	3	8	11	12
1986-87	**Washington**	**NHL**	77	10	51	61	283	7	0	5	5	19
1987-88b	**Washington**	**NHL**	80	12	60	72	184	13	1	11	12	46
1988-89	**Washington**	**NHL**	80	7	61	68	225	6	1	4	5	11
1989-90	**Washington**	**NHL**	56	11	29	40	154	15	2	7	9	25
1990-91	**St. Louis**	**NHL**	78	5	44	49	150	13	0	3	3	36
1991-92c	**New Jersey**	**NHL**	68	17	42	59	124	7	2	1	3	29
1992-93	**New Jersey**	**NHL**	81	12	45	57	120	5	2	2	4	10
	NHL Totals		828	132	462	594	2022	92	13	50	63	255

a NHL All-Rookie Team (1983)
b NHL First All-Star Team (1988)
c NHL Second All-Star Team (1992)
Played in NHL All-Star Game (1985, 1989, 1991-93)
Signed as a free agent by **St. Louis**, July 16, 1990. Acquired by **New Jersey** from **St. Louis** as compensation for St. Louis' signing of free agent Brendan Shanahan, September 3, 1991.

STEVENSON, JEREMY

Left wing. Shoots left. 6'1", 208 lbs.   Born, San Bernadino, CA, July 28, 1974.
(Winnipeg's 3rd choice, 60th overall, in 1992 Entry Draft).

			Regular Season					Playoffs				
Season	Club	Lea	GP	G	A	TP	PIM	GP	G	A	TP	PIM
1990-91	Cornwall	OHL	58	13	20	33	124	....	....	....	....	....
1991-92	Cornwall	OHL	63	15	23	38	176	6	3	1	4	4
1992-93	Newmarket	OHL	54	28	28	56	144	5	5	1	6	28

STEVENSON, SHAYNE

Right wing. Shoots right. 6'1", 190 lbs.   Born, Newmarket, Ont., October 26, 1970.
(Boston's 1st choice, 17th overall, in 1989 Entry Draft).

			Regular Season					Playoffs				
Season	Club	Lea	GP	G	A	TP	PIM	GP	G	A	TP	PIM
1986-87	London	OHL	61	7	15	22	56	....	....	....	....	....
1987-88	London	OHL	36	14	25	39	56	....	....	....	....	....
	Kitchener	OHL	30	10	25	35	48	4	1	1	2	4
1988-89	Kitchener	OHL	56	25	50	75	86	5	2	3	5	4
1989-90	Kitchener	OHL	56	28	61	89	225	17	16	21	37	31
1990-91	**Boston**	**NHL**	14	0	0	0	26	....	....	....	....	....
	Maine	AHL	58	22	28	50	112	....	....	....	....	....
1991-92	**Boston**	**NHL**	5	0	1	1	2	....	....	....	....	....
	Maine	AHL	54	10	23	33	150	....	....	....	....	....
1992-93	**Tampa Bay**	**NHL**	8	0	1	1	7	....	....	....	....	....
	Atlanta	IHL	53	17	17	34	160	6	0	2	2	21
	NHL Totals		27	0	2	2	35	....	....	....	....	....

Claimed by **Tampa Bay** from **Boston** in Expansion Draft, June 18, 1992.

STEVENSON, TURNER

Right wing. Shoots right. 6'3", 200 lbs.   Born, Prince George, B.C., May 18, 1972.
(Montreal's 1st choice, 12th overall, in 1990 Entry Draft).

			Regular Season					Playoffs				
Season	Club	Lea	GP	G	A	TP	PIM	GP	G	A	TP	PIM
1989-90	Seattle	WHL	62	29	32	61	276	....	....	....	....	....
1990-91	Seattle	WHL	57	36	27	63	222	6	1	5	6	15
	Fredericton	AHL	....	....	....	....	....	4	0	0	0	5
1991-92ab	Seattle	WHL	58	20	32	52	264	15	9	3	12	55
1992-93	**Montreal**	**NHL**	1	0	0	0	0	....	....	....	....	....
	Fredericton	AHL	79	25	34	59	102	5	2	3	5	11
	NHL Totals		1	0	0	0	0	....	....	....	....	....

a WHL West First All-Star Team (1992)
b Memorial Cup All-Star Team (1992)

STEWART, ALLAN

Left wing. Shoots left. 6', 195 lbs. Born, Fort St. John, B.C., January 31, 1964.
(New Jersey's 9th choice, 205th overall, in 1983 Entry Draft).

			Regular Season					Playoffs				
Season	Club	Lea	GP	G	A	TP	PIM	GP	G	A	TP	PIM
1982-83	Prince Albert	WHL	70	25	34	59	272	....	....	....	....	....
1983-84	Prince Albert	WHL	67	44	39	83	216	5	1	2	3	29
	Maine	AHL	....	....	....	....	....	3	0	0	0	0
1984-85	Maine	AHL	75	8	11	19	241	11	1	2	3	58
1985-86	**New Jersey**	**NHL**	**4**	**0**	**0**	**0**	**21**	....	....	....	....	....
	Maine	AHL	58	7	12	19	181	....	....	....	....	....
1986-87	**New Jersey**	**NHL**	**7**	**1**	**0**	**1**	**26**	....	....	....	....	....
	Maine	AHL	74	14	24	38	143	....	....	....	....	....
1987-88	**New Jersey**	**NHL**	**1**	**0**	**0**	**0**	**0**	....	....	....	....	....
	Utica	AHL	49	8	17	25	129	....	....	....	....	....
1988-89	**New Jersey**	**NHL**	**6**	**0**	**2**	**2**	**15**	....	....	....	....	....
	Utica	AHL	72	9	23	32	110	5	1	0	1	4
1989-90	Utica	AHL	....	....	....	....	....	1	0	0	0	11
1990-91	**New Jersey**	**NHL**	**41**	**5**	**2**	**7**	**159**	....	....	....	....	....
	Utica	AHL	9	2	0	2	9	....	....	....	....	....
1991-92	**New Jersey**	**NHL**	**1**	**0**	**0**	**0**	**5**	....	....	....	....	....
	Boston	**NHL**	**4**	**0**	**0**	**0**	**17**	....	....	....	....	....
1992-93	Moncton	AHL	45	3	8	11	118	2	1	0	1	20
	NHL Totals		**64**	**6**	**4**	**10**	**243**	....	....	....	....	....

Traded to **Boston** by **New Jersey** for future considerations, October 16, 1991. Signed as a free agent by **Winnipeg**, October 5, 1992.

STEWART, CAMERON

Center. Shoots left. 5'11", 190 lbs. Born, Kitchener, Ont., September 18, 1971.
(Boston's 2nd choice, 63rd overall, in 1990 Entry Draft).

			Regular Season					Playoffs				
Season	Club	Lea	GP	G	A	TP	PIM	GP	G	A	TP	PIM
1990-91	U. of Michigan	CCHA	44	8	24	32	122	....	....	....	....	....
1991-92	U. of Michigan	CCHA	44	13	15	28	106	....	....	....	....	....
1992-93	U. of Michigan	CCHA	39	20	39	59	69	....	....	....	....	....

STEWART, DAVE

Defense. Shoots right. 5'11", 195 lbs. Born, Norwood, Ont., January 11, 1972.

			Regular Season					Playoffs				
Season	Club	Lea	GP	G	A	TP	PIM	GP	G	A	TP	PIM
1990-91	Kingston	OHL	64	10	41	51	127	....	....	....	....	....
1991-92	Kingston	OHL	65	15	45	60	143	....	....	....	....	....
	Toledo	ECHL	3	0	2	2	2	....	....	....	....	....
1992-93	Phoenix	IHL	32	0	3	3	53	....	....	....	....	....

Signed as a free agent by **Los Angeles**, August 3, 1992.

STEWART, MICHAEL

Defense. Shoots left. 6'2", 210 lbs. Born, Calgary, Alta., May 30, 1972.
(NY Rangers' 1st choice, 13th overall, in 1990 Entry Draft).

			Regular Season					Playoffs				
Season	Club	Lea	GP	G	A	TP	PIM	GP	G	A	TP	PIM
1989-90	Michigan State	CCHA	40	2	6	8	39	....	....	....	....	....
1990-91	Michigan State	CCHA	37	3	12	15	58	....	....	....	....	....
1991-92	Michigan State	CCHA	8	1	3	4	6	....	....	....	....	....
1992-93	Binghamton	AHL	68	2	10	12	71	1	0	0	0	0

STICKNEY, BRETT

Center. Shoots left. 6'5", 205 lbs. Born, Hanover, NH, May 26, 1972.
(Chicago's 6th choice, 121st overall, in 1990 Entry Draft).

			Regular Season					Playoffs				
Season	Club	Lea	GP	G	A	TP	PIM	GP	G	A	TP	PIM
1991-92	Boston College	H.E.	29	1	2	3	10	....	....	....	....	....
1992-93	Boston College	H.E.	21	2	4	6	10	....	....	....	....	....

STIENBURG, TREVOR

Right wing. Shoots right. 6'1", 200 lbs. Born, Kingston, Ont., May 13, 1966.
(Quebec's 1st choice, 15th overall, in 1984 Entry Draft).

			Regular Season					Playoffs				
Season	Club	Lea	GP	G	A	TP	PIM	GP	G	A	TP	PIM
1983-84	Guelph	OHL	65	33	18	51	104	....	....	....	....	....
1984-85	Guelph	OHL	18	7	12	19	38	....	....	....	....	....
	London	OHL	22	9	11	20	45	8	1	3	4	22
1985-86	**Quebec**	**NHL**	**2**	**1**	**0**	**1**	**0**	**1**	**0**	**0**	**0**	**0**
	London	OHL	31	12	18	30	88	5	0	0	0	20
1986-87	**Quebec**	**NHL**	**6**	**1**	**0**	**1**	**12**	....	....	....	....	....
	Fredericton	AHL	48	14	12	26	123	....	....	....	....	....
1987-88	**Quebec**	**NHL**	**8**	**0**	**1**	**1**	**24**	....	....	....	....	....
	Fredericton	AHL	55	12	24	36	279	13	3	3	6	115
1988-89	**Quebec**	**NHL**	**55**	**6**	**3**	**9**	**125**	....	....	....	....	....
1989-90	Halifax	AHL	11	3	3	6	36	....	....	....	....	....
1990-91	Halifax	AHL	41	16	7	23	190	....	....	....	....	....
1991-92	New Haven	AHL	66	17	22	39	201	1	0	0	0	2
1992-93	Springfield	AHL	65	14	20	34	244	10	0	0	0	31
	NHL Totals		**71**	**8**	**4**	**12**	**161**	**1**	**0**	**0**	**0**	**0**

Signed as a free agent by **Hartford**, July 21, 1992.

STILLMAN, CORY

Center. Shoots left. 6', 174 lbs. Born, Peterborough, Ont., December 20, 1973.
(Calgary's 1st choice, 6th overall, in 1992 Entry Draft).

			Regular Season					Playoffs				
Season	Club	Lea	GP	G	A	TP	PIM	GP	G	A	TP	PIM
1990-91	Windsor	OHL	64	31	70	101	31	11	3	6	9	8
1991-92	Windsor	OHL	53	29	61	90	59	7	2	4	6	8
1992-93	Peterborough	OHL	61	25	55	80	55	18	3	8	11	18
	Cdn. National	....	1	0	0	0	0	....	....	....	....	....

STIVER, DAN

Right wing. Shoots right. 6', 185 lbs. Born, Chicoutimi, Que., September 14, 1971.
(Toronto's 7th choice, 157th overall, in 1990 Entry Draft).

			Regular Season					Playoffs				
Season	Club	Lea	GP	G	A	TP	PIM	GP	G	A	TP	PIM
1989-90	U. of Michigan	CCHA	40	9	10	19	6	....	....	....	....	....
1990-91	U. of Michigan	CCHA	41	14	15	29	26	....	....	....	....	....
1991-92	U. of Michigan	CCHA	41	8	8	16	8	....	....	....	....	....
1992-93	U. of Michigan	CCHA	36	23	20	43	22	....	....	....	....	....

STOJANOV, ALEK (stoh-YAN-ohv)

Right wing. Shoots left. 6'4", 220 lbs. Born, Windsor, Ont., April 25, 1973.
(Vancouver's 1st choice, 7th overall, in 1991 Entry Draft).

			Regular Season					Playoffs				
Season	Club	Lea	GP	G	A	TP	PIM	GP	G	A	TP	PIM
1989-90	Hamilton	OHL	37	4	4	8	91	....	....	....	....	....
1990-91	Hamilton	OHL	62	25	20	45	181	4	1	1	2	14
1991-92	Guelph	OHL	33	12	15	27	91	....	....	....	....	....
1992-93	Guelph	OHL	36	27	28	55	62	....	....	....	....	....
	Newmarket	OHL	14	9	7	16	26	7	1	3	4	26
	Hamilton	AHL	4	4	0	4	0	....	....	....	....	....

STONE, DONALD

Center. Shoots left. 5'11", 165 lbs. Born, Detroit, MI, May 6, 1969.
(Detroit's 11th choice, 248th overall, in 1988 Entry Draft).

			Regular Season					Playoffs				
Season	Club	Lea	GP	G	A	TP	PIM	GP	G	A	TP	PIM
1987-88	U. of Michigan	CCHA	38	18	19	37	22	....	....	....	....	....
1988-89	U. of Michigan	CCHA	40	24	17	41	19	....	....	....	....	....
1989-90	U. of Michigan	CCHA	42	20	24	44	12	....	....	....	....	....
1990-91	U. of Michigan	CCHA	47	21	27	48	20	....	....	....	....	....
1991-92	Toledo	ECHL	64	26	44	70	10	5	2	4	6	6
1992-93	Toledo	ECHL	10	3	5	8	4	....	....	....	....	....

STORM, JIM

Left wing. Shoots left. 6'2", 200 lbs. Born, Milford, MI, February 5, 1971.
(Hartford's 5th choice, 75th overall, in 1991 Entry Draft).

			Regular Season					Playoffs				
Season	Club	Lea	GP	G	A	TP	PIM	GP	G	A	TP	PIM
1990-91	Michigan Tech	WCHA	36	16	18	34	46	....	....	....	....	....
1991-92	Michigan Tech	WCHA	39	25	33	58	12	....	....	....	....	....
1992-93	Michigan Tech	WCHA	33	22	32	54	30	....	....	....	....	....

STRACHAN, WAYNE

Right wing. Shoots right. 5'10", 185 lbs. Born, Fort Frances, Ont., December 12, 1972.
(NY Rangers' 1st choice, 8th overall, in 1993 Supplemental Draft).

			Regular Season					Playoffs				
Season	Club	Lea	GP	G	A	TP	PIM	GP	G	A	TP	PIM
1991-92	Lake Superior	CCHA	42	12	18	30	35	....	....	....	....	....
1992-93	Lake Superior	CCHA	38	20	21	41	28	....	....	....	....	....

STRAKA, MARTIN

Center. Shoots left. 5'10", 178 lbs. Born, Plzen, Czech., September 3, 1972.
(Pittsburgh's 1st choice, 19th overall, in 1992 Entry Draft).

			Regular Season					Playoffs				
Season	Club	Lea	GP	G	A	TP	PIM	GP	G	A	TP	PIM
1989-90	Skoda Plzen	Czech.	1	0	3	3	....	....	....	....	....	....
1990-91	Skoda Plzen	Czech.	47	7	24	31	6	....	....	....	....	....
1991-92	Skoda Plzen	Czech.	50	27	28	55	20	....	....	....	....	....
1992-93	**Pittsburgh**	**NHL**	**42**	**3**	**13**	**16**	**29**	**11**	**2**	**1**	**3**	**2**
	Cleveland	IHL	4	4	3	7	0	....	....	....	....	....
	NHL Totals		**42**	**3**	**13**	**16**	**29**	**11**	**2**	**1**	**3**	**2**

STRAUB, BRIAN

Defense. Shoots left. 6'2", 195 lbs. Born, Bozeman, MT, July 2, 1968.

			Regular Season					Playoffs				
Season	Club	Lea	GP	G	A	TP	PIM	GP	G	A	TP	PIM
1989-90	U. of Maine	H.E.	43	7	14	21	18	....	....	....	....	....
1990-91	U. of Maine	H.E.	42	6	25	31	14	....	....	....	....	....
1991-92	San Diego	IHL	43	3	16	19	75	....	....	....	....	....
	Kalamazoo	IHL	29	2	12	14	45	11	0	5	5	6
1992-93	Kalamazoo	IHL	75	6	14	20	101	....	....	....	....	....

Signed as a free agent by **Minnesota**, August 19, 1992.

STROMBERG, MIKA

Defense. Shoots left. 5'11", 183 lbs. Born, Helsinki, Finland, February 28, 1970.
(Quebec's 10th choice, 211th overall, in 1990 Entry Draft).

			Regular Season					Playoffs				
Season	Club	Lea	GP	G	A	TP	PIM	GP	G	A	TP	PIM
1988-89	Jokerit	Fin.2	39	6	12	18	....	....	....	....	....	....
1989-90	Jokerit	Fin.	42	2	15	17	42	....	....	....	....	....
1990-91	Jokerit	Fin.	44	4	16	20	38	....	....	....	....	....
1991-92	Jokerit	Fin.	36	7	14	21	32	9	2	3	5	16
	Vantaa	Fin. 2	1	1	0	1	2	....	....	....	....	....
1992-93	Jokerit	Fin.	16	2	5	7	6	....	....	....	....	....

STRUCH, DAVID

Center. Shoots left. 5'10", 180 lbs. Born, Calgary, Alta., February 11, 1971.
(Calgary's 10th choice, 195th overall, in 1991 Entry Draft).

			Regular Season					Playoffs				
Season	Club	Lea	GP	G	A	TP	PIM	GP	G	A	TP	PIM
1990-91	Saskatoon	WHL	72	45	57	102	69	....	....	....	....	....
1991-92	Saskatoon	WHL	47	29	26	55	34	22	8	15	23	26
	Salt Lake	IHL	12	4	1	5	8	....	....	....	....	....
1992-93	Salt Lake	IHL	78	20	22	42	73	....	....	....	....	....

STUMPEL, JOZEF (STUM-puhl)

Right wing. Shoots right. 6'1", 190 lbs. Born, Nitra, Czechoslovakia, June 20, 1972.
(Boston's 2nd choice, 40th overall, in 1991 Entry Draft).

			Regular Season					Playoffs				
Season	Club	Lea	GP	G	A	TP	PIM	GP	G	A	TP	PIM
1989-90	Nitra	Czech.2	38	12	11	23	....	....	....	....	....	....
1990-91	Nitra	Czech.	49	23	22	45	14	....	....	....	....	....
1991-92	Koln	Ger.	37	20	19	39	35	....	....	....	....	....
	Boston	**NHL**	**4**	**1**	**0**	**1**	**0**	....	....	....	....	....
1992-93	**Boston**	**NHL**	**13**	**1**	**3**	**4**	**4**	....	....	....	....	....
	Providence	AHL	56	31	61	92	26	6	4	4	8	0
	NHL Totals		**17**	**2**	**3**	**5**	**4**	....	....	....	....	....

SUHY, ANDY

Defense. Shoots left. 6'1", 190 lbs. Born, Detroit, MI, March 9, 1970.
(Detroit's 8th choice, 158th overall, in 1989 Entry Draft).

			Regular Season					Playoffs				
Season	Club	Lea	GP	G	A	TP	PIM	GP	G	A	TP	PIM
1988-89	W. Michigan	CCHA	42	0	4	4	74	....	....	....	....	....
1989-90	W. Michigan	CCHA	34	3	5	8	52	....	....	....	....	....
1990-91	W. Michigan	CCHA	42	4	7	11	84	....	....	....	....	....
1991-92	W. Michigan	CCHA	36	3	9	12	89	....	....	....	....	....
1992-93	Toledo	ECHL	64	5	15	20	97	15	1	4	5	60

SULLIVAN, BRIAN

Right wing. Shoots right. 6'4", 195 lbs. Born, South Windsor, CT, April 23, 1969.
(New Jersey's 3rd choice, 65th overall, in 1987 Entry Draft).

			Regular Season					Playoffs				
Season	Club	Lea	GP	G	A	TP	PIM	GP	G	A	TP	PIM
1987-88	Northeastern	H.E.	37	20	12	32	18	....	....	....	....	....
1988-89	Northeastern	H.E.	34	13	14	27	65	....	....	....	....	....
1989-90	Northeastern	H.E.	34	24	21	45	54	....	....	....	....	....
1990-91	Northeastern	H.E.	32	17	23	40	75	....	....	....	....	....
1991-92	Utica	AHL	70	23	24	47	58	4	0	4	4	6
1992-93	**New Jersey**	**NHL**	**2**	**0**	**1**	**1**	**0**	....	....	....	....	....
	Utica	AHL	75	30	27	57	88	5	0	0	0	12
	NHL Totals		**2**	**0**	**1**	**1**	**0**	....	....	....	....	....

SULLIVAN, MICHAEL (MIKE)

Center. Shoots left. 6'2", 185 lbs. Born, Marshfield, MA, February 27, 1968.
(NY Rangers' 4th choice, 69th overall, in 1987 Entry Draft).

			Regular Season					Playoffs				
Season	Club	Lea	GP	G	A	TP	PIM	GP	G	A	TP	PIM
1986-87	Boston U.	H.E.	37	13	18	31	18	....	....	....	....	....
1987-88	Boston U.	H.E.	30	18	22	40	30	....	....	....	....	....
1988-89	Boston U.	H.E.	36	19	17	36	30	....	....	....	....	....
1989-90	Boston U.	H.E.	38	11	20	31	26	....	....	....	....	....
1990-91	San Diego	IHL	74	12	23	35	27	....	....	....	....	....
1991-92	**San Jose**	**NHL**	**64**	**8**	**11**	**19**	**15**	....	....	....	....	....
	Kansas City	IHL	10	2	8	10	8	....	....	....	....	....
1992-93	**San Jose**	**NHL**	**81**	**6**	**8**	**14**	**30**	....	....	....	....	....
	NHL Totals		**145**	**14**	**19**	**33**	**45**	....	....	....	....	....

Rights traded to **Minnesota** by **NY Rangers** with Paul Jerrard, the rights to Bret Barnett, and Los Angeles' third round choice (previously acquired by NY Rangers — Minnesota selected Murray Garbutt) in 1989 Entry Draft for Brian Lawton, Igor Liba and the rights to Eric Bennett, October 11, 1988. Signed as a free agent by **San Jose**, August 9, 1991.

SULLIVAN, MIKE

Center. Shoots left. 6'1", 190 lbs. Born, Woburn, MA, October 16, 1973.
(Detroit's 4th choice, 118th overall, in 1992 Entry Draft).

			Regular Season					Playoffs				
Season	Club	Lea	GP	G	A	TP	PIM	GP	G	A	TP	PIM
1991-92	Reading	HS	24	39	41	80	0	....	....	....	....	....
1992-93	N. Hampshire	H.E.	36	5	5	10	12	....	....	....	....	....

SUNDBLAD, NIKLAS

Right wing. Shoots right. 6'1", 196 lbs. Born, Stockholm, Sweden, January 3, 1973.
(Calgary's 1st choice, 19th overall, in 1991 Entry Draft).

			Regular Season					Playoffs				
Season	Club	Lea	GP	G	A	TP	PIM	GP	G	A	TP	PIM
1990-91	AIK	Swe.	39	1	3	4	14	....	....	....	....	....
1991-92	AIK	Swe.	33	9	2	11	20	3	3	1	4	0
1992-93	AIK	Swe.	22	5	4	9	56	....	....	....	....	....

SUNDIN, MATS (suhn-DEEN)

Center/Right wing. Shoots right. 6'2", 190 lbs. Born, Bromma, Sweden, February 13, 1971.
(Quebec's 1st choice, 1st overall, in 1989 Entry Draft).

			Regular Season					Playoffs				
Season	Club	Lea	GP	G	A	TP	PIM	GP	G	A	TP	PIM
1988-89	Nacka	Swe.2	25	10	8	18	18	....	....	....	....	....
1989-90	Djurgarden	Swe.	34	10	8	18	16	8	7	0	7	4
1990-91	**Quebec**	**NHL**	**80**	**23**	**36**	**59**	**58**	....	....	....	....	....
1991-92	**Quebec**	**NHL**	**80**	**33**	**43**	**76**	**103**	....	....	....	....	....
1992-93	**Quebec**	**NHL**	**80**	**47**	**67**	**114**	**96**	**6**	**3**	**1**	**4**	**6**
	NHL Totals		**240**	**103**	**146**	**249**	**257**	**6**	**3**	**1**	**4**	**6**

SUNDSTROM, NIKLAS

Left wing. Shoots left. 6', 183 lbs. Born, Ornskoldsvik, Sweden, June 6, 1975.
(NY Rangers' 1st choice, 8th overall, in 1993 Entry Draft).

			Regular Season					Playoffs				
Season	Club	Lea	GP	G	A	TP	PIM	GP	G	A	TP	PIM
1991-92	MoDo	Swe.	9	1	3	4	0	....	....	....	....	....
1992-93	MoDo	Swe.	40	7	11	18	18	3	0	0	0	0

SUOMALAINEN, JUKKA

Defense. Shoots left. 6'5", 198 lbs. Born, Helsinki, Finland, April 20, 1966.
(Minnesota's 10th choice, 250th overall, in 1991 Entry Draft).

			Regular Season					Playoffs				
Season	Club	Lea	GP	G	A	TP	PIM	GP	G	A	TP	PIM
1991-92	Springfield	AHL	46	1	5	6	55	9	1	0	1	12
1992-93	Springfield	AHL	61	1	9	10	78	10	0	0	0	26

Traded to **Hartford** by **Minnesota** to complete previous transaction of June 22, 1991, November 21, 1991.

SUTER, GARY

Defense. Shoots left. 6', 190 lbs. Born, Madison, WI, June 24, 1964.
(Calgary's 9th choice, 180th overall, in 1984 Entry Draft).

			Regular Season					Playoffs				
Season	Club	Lea	GP	G	A	TP	PIM	GP	G	A	TP	PIM
1983-84	U. Wisconsin	WCHA	35	4	18	22	32	....	....	....	....	....
1984-85	U. Wisconsin	WCHA	39	12	39	51	110	....	....	....	....	....
1985-86ab	**Calgary**	**NHL**	**80**	**18**	**50**	**68**	**141**	**10**	**2**	**8**	**10**	**8**
1986-87	**Calgary**	**NHL**	**68**	**9**	**40**	**49**	**70**	**6**	**0**	**3**	**3**	**10**
1987-88c	**Calgary**	**NHL**	**75**	**21**	**70**	**91**	**124**	**9**	**1**	**9**	**10**	**6**
1988-89	**Calgary**	**NHL**	**63**	**13**	**49**	**62**	**78**	**5**	**0**	**3**	**3**	**10**
1989-90	**Calgary**	**NHL**	**76**	**16**	**60**	**76**	**97**	**6**	**0**	**1**	**1**	**14**
1990-91	**Calgary**	**NHL**	**79**	**12**	**58**	**70**	**102**	**7**	**1**	**6**	**7**	**12**
1991-92	**Calgary**	**NHL**	**70**	**12**	**43**	**55**	**128**	....	....	....	....	....
1992-93	**Calgary**	**NHL**	**81**	**23**	**58**	**81**	**112**	**6**	**2**	**3**	**5**	**8**
	NHL Totals		**592**	**124**	**428**	**552**	**852**	**49**	**6**	**33**	**39**	**68**

a Won Calder Memorial Trophy (1986)
b NHL All-Rookie Team (1986)
c NHL Second All-Star Team (1988)

Played in NHL All-Star Game (1986, 1988, 1989, 1991)

SUTTER, BRENT COLIN (SUH-tuhr)

Center. Shoots right. 5'11", 180 lbs. Born, Viking, Alta., June 10, 1962.
(NY Islanders' 1st choice, 17th overall, in 1980 Entry Draft).

			Regular Season					Playoffs				
Season	Club	Lea	GP	G	A	TP	PIM	GP	G	A	TP	PIM
1979-80	Red Deer	AJHL	59	70	101	171	....	....	....	....	....	....
	Lethbridge	WHL	5	1	0	1	2	....	....	....	....	....
1980-81	**NY Islanders**	**NHL**	**3**	**2**	**2**	**4**	**0**	....	....	....	....	....
	Lethbridge	WHL	68	54	54	108	116	9	6	4	10	51
1981-82	**NY Islanders**	**NHL**	**43**	**21**	**22**	**43**	**114**	**19**	**2**	**6**	**8**	**36**
	Lethbridge	WHL	34	46	33	79	162	....	....	....	....	....
1982-83	**NY Islanders**	**NHL**	**80**	**21**	**19**	**40**	**128**	**20**	**10**	**11**	**21**	**26**
1983-84	**NY Islanders**	**NHL**	**69**	**34**	**15**	**49**	**69**	**20**	**4**	**10**	**14**	**18**
1984-85	**NY Islanders**	**NHL**	**72**	**42**	**60**	**102**	**51**	**10**	**3**	**3**	**6**	**14**
1985-86	**NY Islanders**	**NHL**	**61**	**24**	**31**	**55**	**74**	**3**	**0**	**1**	**1**	**2**
1986-87	**NY Islanders**	**NHL**	**69**	**27**	**36**	**63**	**73**	**5**	**1**	**0**	**1**	**4**
1987-88	**NY Islanders**	**NHL**	**70**	**29**	**31**	**60**	**55**	**6**	**2**	**1**	**3**	**18**
1988-89	**NY Islanders**	**NHL**	**77**	**29**	**34**	**63**	**77**	....	....	....	....	....
1989-90	**NY Islanders**	**NHL**	**67**	**33**	**35**	**68**	**65**	**5**	**2**	**3**	**5**	**2**
1990-91	**NY Islanders**	**NHL**	**75**	**21**	**32**	**53**	**49**	....	....	....	....	....
1991-92	**NY Islanders**	**NHL**	**8**	**4**	**6**	**10**	**6**	....	....	....	....	....
	Chicago	**NHL**	**61**	**18**	**32**	**50**	**30**	**18**	**3**	**5**	**8**	**22**
1992-93	**Chicago**	**NHL**	**65**	**20**	**34**	**54**	**67**	**4**	**1**	**1**	**2**	**4**
	NHL Totals		**820**	**325**	**389**	**714**	**858**	**110**	**28**	**41**	**69**	**146**

Played in NHL All-Star Game (1985)

Traded to **Chicago** by **NY Islanders** with Brad Lauer for Adam Creighton and Steve Thomas, October 25, 1991.

SUTTER, RICHARD (RICH) (SUH-tuhr)

Right wing. Shoots right. 5'11", 188 lbs. Born, Viking, Alta., December 2, 1963.
(Pittsburgh's 1st choice, 10th overall, in 1982 Entry Draft).

			Regular Season					Playoffs				
Season	Club	Lea	GP	G	A	TP	PIM	GP	G	A	TP	PIM
1980-81	Lethbridge	WHL	72	23	18	41	255	9	3	1	4	35
1981-82	Lethbridge	WHL	57	38	31	69	263	12	3	3	6	55
1982-83	**Pittsburgh**	**NHL**	**4**	**0**	**0**	**0**	**0**	....	....	....	....	....
	Lethbridge	WHL	64	37	30	67	200	17	14	9	23	43
1983-84	**Pittsburgh**	**NHL**	**5**	**0**	**0**	**0**	**0**	....	....	....	....	....
	Baltimore	AHL	2	0	1	1	0	....	....	....	....	....
	Philadelphia	**NHL**	**70**	**16**	**12**	**28**	**93**	**3**	**0**	**0**	**0**	**15**
1984-85	**Philadelphia**	**NHL**	**56**	**6**	**10**	**16**	**89**	**11**	**3**	**0**	**3**	**10**
	Hershey	AHL	13	3	7	10	14	....	....	....	....	....
1985-86	**Philadelphia**	**NHL**	**78**	**14**	**25**	**39**	**199**	**5**	**2**	**0**	**2**	**19**
1986-87	**Vancouver**	**NHL**	**74**	**20**	**22**	**42**	**113**	....	....	....	....	....
1987-88	**Vancouver**	**NHL**	**80**	**15**	**15**	**30**	**165**	....	....	....	....	....
1988-89	**Vancouver**	**NHL**	**75**	**17**	**15**	**32**	**122**	**7**	**2**	**1**	**3**	**12**
1989-90	**Vancouver**	**NHL**	**62**	**9**	**9**	**18**	**133**	....	....	....	....	....
	St. Louis	**NHL**	**12**	**2**	**0**	**2**	**22**	**12**	**2**	**1**	**3**	**39**
1990-91	**St. Louis**	**NHL**	**77**	**16**	**11**	**27**	**122**	**13**	**4**	**2**	**6**	**16**
1991-92	**St. Louis**	**NHL**	**77**	**9**	**16**	**25**	**107**	**6**	**0**	**0**	**0**	**8**
1992-93	**St. Louis**	**NHL**	**84**	**13**	**14**	**27**	**100**	**11**	**0**	**1**	**1**	**10**
	NHL Totals		**754**	**137**	**149**	**286**	**1265**	**68**	**13**	**5**	**18**	**129**

Traded to **Philadelphia** by **Pittsburgh** with Pittsburgh's second round (Greg Smyth) and third round (David McLay) choices in 1984 Entry Draft for Andy Brickley, Mark Taylor, Ron Flockhart, Philadelphia's first round (Roger Belanger) and third round (later traded to Vancouver — Vancouver selected Mike Stevens) choices in 1984 Entry Draft, October 23, 1983. Traded to **Vancouver** by **Philadelphia**, with Dave Richter and Vancouver's third round choice (previously acquired by Philadelphia — Vancouver selected Don Gibson) in 1986 Entry Draft for J.J. Daigneault and Vancouver's second round choice (Kent Hawley) in 1986 Entry Draft, June 6, 1986. Traded to **St Louis** by **Vancouver** with Harold Snepsts and St. Louis' second round choice (previously acquired by Vancouver — St. Louis selected Craig Johnson) in 1990 Entry Draft for Adrien Plavsic, Montreal's first round choice (previously acquired by St. Louis — Vancouver selected Shawn Antoski) in 1990 Entry Draft and St. Louis' second round choice (later traded to Montreal — Montreal selected Craig Darby) in 1991 Entry Draft, March 6, 1990.

SUTTER, RONALD (RON) (SUH-tuhr)

Center. Shoots right. 6', 180 lbs. Born, Viking, Alta., December 2, 1963.
(Philadelphia's 1st choice, 4th overall, in 1982 Entry Draft).

			Regular Season					Playoffs				
Season	Club	Lea	GP	G	A	TP	PIM	GP	G	A	TP	PIM
1980-81	Lethbridge	WHL	72	13	32	45	152	9	2	5	7	29
1981-82	Lethbridge	WHL	59	38	54	92	207	12	6	5	11	28
1982-83	Philadelphia	NHL	10	1	1	2	9	....	....	....	....	....
	Lethbridge	WHL	58	35	48	83	98	20	*22	*19	*41	45
1983-84	Philadelphia	NHL	79	19	32	51	101	3	0	0	0	22
1984-85	Philadelphia	NHL	73	16	29	45	94	19	4	8	12	28
1985-86	Philadelphia	NHL	75	18	42	60	159	5	0	2	2	10
1986-87	Philadelphia	NHL	39	10	17	27	69	16	1	7	8	12
1987-88	Philadelphia	NHL	69	8	25	33	146	7	0	1	1	26
1988-89	Philadelphia	NHL	55	26	22	48	80	19	1	9	10	51
1989-90	Philadelphia	NHL	75	22	26	48	104	....	....	....	....	....
1990-91	Philadelphia	NHL	80	17	28	45	92	....	....	....	....	....
1991-92	St. Louis	NHL	68	19	27	46	91	6	1	3	4	8
1992-93	St. Louis	NHL	59	12	15	27	99	....	....	....	....	....
	NHL Totals		682	168	264	432	1044	75	7	30	37	157

Traded to **St. Louis** by **Philadelphia** with Murray Baron for Dan Quinn and Rod Brind'Amour, September 22, 1991.

SUTTON, KENNETH

Defense. Shoots left. 6', 198 lbs. Born, Edmonton, Alta., May 11, 1969.
(Buffalo's 4th choice, 98th overall, in 1989 Entry Draft).

			Regular Season					Playoffs				
Season	Club	Lea	GP	G	A	TP	PIM	GP	G	A	TP	PIM
1988-89	Saskatoon	WHL	71	22	31	53	104	8	2	5	7	12
1989-90	Rochester	AHL	57	5	14	19	83	11	1	6	7	15
1990-91	Buffalo	NHL	15	3	6	9	13	6	0	1	1	2
	Rochester	AHL	62	7	24	31	65	3	1	1	2	14
1991-92	Buffalo	NHL	64	2	18	20	71	7	0	2	2	4
1992-93	Buffalo	NHL	63	8	14	22	30	8	3	1	4	8
	NHL Totals		142	13	38	51	114	21	3	4	7	14

SVARTVADET, PER

Center. Shoots left. 6'1", 180 lbs. Born, Solleftea, Sweden, May 17, 1975.
(Dallas' 5th choice, 139th overall, in 1993 Entry Draft).

			Regular Season					Playoffs				
Season	Club	Lea	GP	G	A	TP	PIM	GP	G	A	TP	PIM
1992-93	MoDo	Swe.	2	0	0	0	0	....	....	....	....	....

SVEHLA, ROBERT (SCHVE-khlah)

Defense. Shoots right. 6', 190 lbs. Born, Martin, Czech., January 2, 1969.
(Calgary's 4th choice, 78th overall, in 1992 Entry Draft).

			Regular Season					Playoffs				
Season	Club	Lea	GP	G	A	TP	PIM	GP	G	A	TP	PIM
1989-90	Dukla Trencin	Czech.	29	4	3	7	....	....	....	....	....	....
1990-91	Dukla Trencin	Czech.	52	16	9	25	62	....	....	....	....	....
1991-92	Dukla Trencin	Czech.	51	23	28	51	74	....	....	....	....	....
1992-93	Malmo	Swe.	40	19	10	29	86	6	0	1	1	14

SVENSSON, MAGNUS (SVEHN-suhn)

Defense. Shoots left. 5'11", 180 lbs. Born, Tranas, Sweden, March 1, 1963.
(Calgary's 13th choice, 250th overall, in 1987 Entry Draft).

			Regular Season					Playoffs				
Season	Club	Lea	GP	G	A	TP	PIM	GP	G	A	TP	PIM
1983-84	Leksand	Swe.	35	3	8	11	20	....	....	....	....	....
1984-85	Leksand	Swe.	35	8	7	15	22	....	....	....	....	....
1985-86	Leksand	Swe.	36	6	9	15	62	....	....	....	....	....
1986-87	Leksand	Swe.	33	8	16	24	42	....	....	....	....	....
1987-88	Leksand	Swe.	40	12	11	23	20	3	0	0	0	8
1988-89	Leksand	Swe.	39	15	22	37	40	9	3	5	8	8
1989-90	Leksand	Swe.	26	11	12	23	60	1	0	0	0	0
1990-91	Lugano	Switz.	33	16	20	36	....	11	3	2	5	....
1991-92	Leksand	Swe.	22	4	10	14	32	....	....	....	....	....
1992-93	Leksand	Swe.	37	10	17	27	36	2	0	2	2	0

SVOBODA, PETR (svah-BOH-duh)

Defense. Shoots left. 6'1", 174 lbs. Born, Most, Czechoslovakia, February 14, 1966.
(Montreal's 1st choice, 5th overall, in 1984 Entry Draft).

			Regular Season					Playoffs				
Season	Club	Lea	GP	G	A	TP	PIM	GP	G	A	TP	PIM
1982-83	Litvinov	Czech.	4	0	0	0	2	....	....	....	....	....
1983-84	Litvinov	Czech.	18	3	1	4	20	....	....	....	....	....
1984-85	Montreal	NHL	73	4	27	31	65	7	1	1	2	12
1985-86	Montreal	NHL	73	1	18	19	93	8	0	0	0	21
1986-87	Montreal	NHL	70	5	17	22	63	14	0	5	5	10
1987-88	Montreal	NHL	69	7	22	29	149	10	0	5	5	12
1988-89	Montreal	NHL	71	8	37	45	147	21	1	11	12	16
1989-90	Montreal	NHL	60	5	31	36	98	10	0	5	5	7
1990-91	Montreal	NHL	60	4	22	26	52	2	0	1	1	2
1991-92	Montreal	NHL	58	5	16	21	94	....	....	....	....	....
	Buffalo	NHL	13	1	6	7	52	7	1	4	5	6
1992-93	Buffalo	NHL	40	2	24	26	59	....	....	....	....	....
	NHL Totals		587	42	220	262	872	79	3	32	35	86

Traded to **Buffalo** by **Montreal** for Kevin Haller, March 10, 1992.

SWEENEY, DON

Defense. Shoots left. 5'10", 188 lbs. Born, St. Stephen, N.B., August 17, 1966.
(Boston's 8th choice, 166th overall, in 1984 Entry Draft).

			Regular Season					Playoffs				
Season	Club	Lea	GP	G	A	TP	PIM	GP	G	A	TP	PIM
1984-85	Harvard	ECAC	29	3	7	10	30	....	....	....	....	....
1985-86	Harvard	ECAC	31	4	5	9	12	....	....	....	....	....
1986-87	Harvard	ECAC	34	7	4	11	22	....	....	....	....	....
1987-88ab	Harvard	ECAC	30	6	23	29	37	....	....	....	....	....
	Maine	AHL	....	....	....	....	....	6	1	3	4	0
1988-89	Boston	NHL	36	3	5	8	20	....	....	....	....	....
	Maine	AHL	42	8	17	25	24	....	....	....	....	....
1989-90	Boston	NHL	58	3	5	8	58	21	1	5	6	18
	Maine	AHL	11	0	8	8	8	....	....	....	....	....
1990-91	Boston	NHL	77	8	13	21	67	19	3	0	3	25
1991-92	Boston	NHL	75	3	11	14	74	15	0	0	0	10
1992-93	Boston	NHL	84	7	27	34	68	4	0	0	0	4
	NHL Totals		330	24	61	85	287	59	4	5	9	57

a NCAA East All-American Team (1988)
b ECAC First All-Star Team (1988)

SWEENEY, ROBERT (BOB)

Center/Right wing. Shoots right. 6'3", 200 lbs. Born, Concord, MA, January 25, 1964.
(Boston's 6th choice, 123rd overall, in 1982 Entry Draft).

			Regular Season					Playoffs				
Season	Club	Lea	GP	G	A	TP	PIM	GP	G	A	TP	PIM
1982-83	Boston College	ECAC	30	17	11	28	10	....	....	....	....	....
1983-84	Boston College	ECAC	23	14	7	21	10	....	....	....	....	....
1984-85a	Boston College	ECAC	44	32	32	64	43	....	....	....	....	....
1985-86	Boston College	H.E.	41	15	24	39	52	....	....	....	....	....
1986-87	Boston	NHL	14	2	4	6	21	3	0	0	0	0
	Moncton	AHL	58	29	26	55	81	4	0	2	2	13
1987-88	Boston	NHL	80	22	23	45	73	23	6	8	14	66
1988-89	Boston	NHL	75	14	14	28	99	10	2	4	6	19
1989-90	Boston	NHL	70	22	24	46	93	20	0	2	2	30
1990-91	Boston	NHL	80	15	33	48	115	17	4	2	6	45
1991-92	Boston	NHL	63	6	14	20	103	14	1	0	1	25
	Maine	AHL	1	1	0	1	0	....	....	....	....	....
1992-93	Buffalo	NHL	80	21	26	47	118	8	2	2	4	8
	NHL Totals		462	102	138	240	622	95	15	18	33	193

a ECAC Second Team All-Star (1985)

Claimed on waivers by **Buffalo** from **Boston**, October 9, 1992.

SWEENEY, TIM

Left wing. Shoots left. 5'11", 185 lbs. Born, Boston, MA, April 12, 1967.
(Calgary's 7th choice, 122nd overall, in 1985 Entry Draft).

			Regular Season					Playoffs				
Season	Club	Lea	GP	G	A	TP	PIM	GP	G	A	TP	PIM
1985-86	Boston College	H.E.	32	8	4	12	8	....	....	....	....	....
1986-87	Boston College	H.E.	38	31	18	49	28	....	....	....	....	....
1987-88	Boston College	H.E.	18	9	11	20	18	....	....	....	....	....
1988-89ab	Boston College	H.E.	39	29	44	73	26	....	....	....	....	....
1989-90cd	Salt Lake	IHL	81	46	51	97	32	11	5	4	9	4
1990-91	Calgary	NHL	42	7	9	16	8	....	....	....	....	....
	Salt Lake	IHL	31	19	16	35	8	4	3	3	6	0
1991-92	U.S. National	....	21	9	11	20	10	....	....	....	....	....
	U.S. Olympic	....	8	3	4	7	6	....	....	....	....	....
	Calgary	NHL	11	1	2	3	4	....	....	....	....	....
1992-93	Boston	NHL	14	1	7	8	6	3	0	0	0	0
e	Providence	AHL	60	41	55	96	32	3	2	2	4	0
	NHL Totals		67	9	18	27	18	3	0	0	0	0

a Hockey East First All-Star Team (1989)
b NCAA East Second All-American Team (1989)
c IHL Second All-Star Team (1990)
d Won Ken McKenzie Trophy (Outstanding U.S.-born rookie—IHL) (1990)
e AHL Second All-Star Team (1993)

Signed as a free agent by **Boston**, September 16, 1992. Claimed by **Anaheim** from **Boston** in Expansion Draft, June 24, 1993.

SYCHRA, MARTIN

Center. Shoots left. 6'1", 180 lbs. Born, Brno, Czech., June 19, 1974.
(Montreal's 8th choice, 140th overall, in 1992 Entry Draft).

			Regular Season					Playoffs				
Season	Club	Lea	GP	G	A	TP	PIM	GP	G	A	TP	PIM
1991-92	Zetor Brno	Czech.	14	2	2	4	2	....	....	....	....	....
1992-93	Dukla Trencin	Czech.	4	0	1	1	....	....	....	....	....	....
	Dukla Jihlava	Czech.	14	1	2	3	....	....	....	....	....	....

SYDOR, DARRYL (CEE-der)

Defense. Shoots left. 6', 205 lbs. Born, Edmonton, Alta., May 13, 1972.
(Los Angeles' 1st choice, 7th overall, in 1990 Entry Draft).

			Regular Season					Playoffs				
Season	Club	Lea	GP	G	A	TP	PIM	GP	G	A	TP	PIM
1988-89	Kamloops	WHL	65	12	14	26	86	15	1	4	5	19
1989-90a	Kamloops	WHL	67	29	66	95	129	17	2	9	11	28
1990-91a	Kamloops	WHL	66	27	78	105	88	12	3	*22	25	10
1991-92	Los Angeles	NHL	18	1	5	6	22	....	....	....	....	....
a	Kamloops	WHL	29	9	39	48	43	17	3	15	18	18
1992-93	Los Angeles	NHL	80	6	23	29	63	24	3	8	11	16
	NHL Totals		98	7	28	35	85	24	3	8	11	16

a WHL West First All-Star Team (1990, 1991, 1992)

SYKORA, MICHAL (SEE-koh-ra)

Defense. Shoots left. 6'4", 210 lbs. Born, Pardubice, Czech., July 5, 1973.
(San Jose's 6th choice, 123rd overall, in 1992 Entry Draft).

			Regular Season					Playoffs				
Season	Club	Lea	GP	G	A	TP	PIM	GP	G	A	TP	PIM
1990-91	Pardubice	Czech.	2	0	0	0	....	....	....	....	....	....
1991-92	Tacoma	WHL	61	13	23	36	66	4	0	2	2	2
1992-93a	Tacoma	WHL	70	23	50	73	73	7	4	8	12	2

a WHL West First All-Star Team (1993)

SYLVESTER, DEAN

Right wing. Shoots right. 6'2", 185 lbs. Born, Hanson, MA, December 20, 1972.
(San Jose's 1st choice, 2nd overall, in 1993 Supplemental Draft).

			Regular Season					Playoffs				
Season	Club	Lea	GP	G	A	TP	PIM	GP	G	A	TP	PIM
1991-92	Kent State	CCHA	31	7	21	28	....	....	....	....	....	....
1992-93	Kent State	CCHA	38	33	20	53	28	....	....	....	....	....

TAGLIANETTI, PETER

Defense. Shoots left. 6'2", 200 lbs. Born, Framingham, MA, August 15, 1963.
(Winnipeg's 4th choice, 43rd overall, in 1983 Entry Draft).

			Regular Season					Playoffs				
Season	Club	Lea	GP	G	A	TP	PIM	GP	G	A	TP	PIM
1981-82	Providence	ECAC	2	0	0	0	2	....	....	....	....	....
1982-83	Providence	ECAC	43	4	17	21	68	....	....	....	....	....
1983-84	Providence	ECAC	30	4	25	29	68	....	....	....	....	....
1984-85	Winnipeg	NHL	1	0	0	0	0	1	0	0	0	0
a	Providence	H.E.	35	6	18	24	32	....	....	....	....	....
1985-86	Winnipeg	NHL	18	0	0	0	48	3	0	0	0	2
	Sherbrooke	AHL	24	1	18	9	75	....	....	....	....	....
1986-87	Winnipeg	NHL	3	0	0	0	12	....	....	....	....	....
	Sherbrooke	AHL	54	5	14	19	104	10	2	5	7	25
1987-88	Winnipeg	NHL	70	6	17	23	182	5	1	1	2	12
1988-89	Winnipeg	NHL	66	1	14	15	226	....	....	....	....	....
1989-90	Winnipeg	NHL	49	3	6	9	136	5	0	0	0	6
	Moncton	AHL	3	0	2	2	2	....	....	....	....	....
1990-91	Minnesota	NHL	16	0	1	1	14	....	....	....	....	....
	Pittsburgh	NHL	39	3	8	11	93	19	0	3	3	49
1991-92	Pittsburgh	NHL	44	1	3	4	57	....	....	....	....	....
1992-93	Tampa Bay	NHL	61	1	8	9	150	....	....	....	....	....
	Pittsburgh	NHL	11	1	4	5	34	11	1	2	3	16
	NHL Totals		378	16	61	77	952	44	2	6	8	85

a Hockey East First All-Star Team (1985)

Traded to **Minnesota** by **Winnipeg** for future considerations, September 30, 1990. Traded to **Pittsburgh** by **Minnesota** with Larry Murphy for Chris Dahlquist and Jim Johnson, December 11, 1990. Claimed by **Tampa Bay** from **Pittsburgh** in Expansion Draft, June 18, 1992. Traded to **Pittsburgh** by **Tampa Bay** for Pittsburgh's third round choice (later traded to Florida — Florida selected Steve Washburn) in 1993 Entry Draft, March 22, 1993.

TAMER, CHRIS

Defense. Shoots left. 6'2", 185 lbs. Born, Dearborn, MI, November 17, 1970.
(Pittsburgh's 3rd choice, 68th overall, in 1990 Entry Draft).

			Regular Season					Playoffs				
Season	Club	Lea	GP	G	A	TP	PIM	GP	G	A	TP	PIM
1989-90	U. of Michigan	CCHA	42	2	7	9	147	....	....	....	....	....
1990-91	U. of Michigan	CCHA	45	8	19	27	130	....	....	....	....	....
1991-92	U. of Michigan	CCHA	43	4	15	19	125	....	....	....	....	....
1992-93	U. of Michigan	CCHA	39	5	18	23	113	....	....	....	....	....

TAMMINEN, JOE

Center. Shoots left. 6'2", 187 lbs. Born, Virginia, MN, January 23, 1973.
(Pittsburgh's 4th choice, 82nd overall, in 1991 Entry Draft).

			Regular Season					Playoffs				
Season	Club	Lea	GP	G	A	TP	PIM	GP	G	A	TP	PIM
1991-92	Minn.-Duluth	WCHA	23	1	3	4	12	....	....	....	....	....
1992-93	Minn.-Duluth	WCHA	39	4	6	10	42	....	....	....	....	....

TANCILL, CHRIS (TAN-sihl)

Center. Shoots left. 5'10", 185 lbs. Born, Livonia, MI, February 7, 1968.
(Hartford's 1st choice, 15th overall, in 1989 Supplemental Draft).

			Regular Season					Playoffs				
Season	Club	Lea	GP	G	A	TP	PIM	GP	G	A	TP	PIM
1986-87	U. Wisconsin	WCHA	40	9	23	32	26	....	....	....	....	....
1987-88	U. Wisconsin	WCHA	44	13	14	27	48	....	....	....	....	....
1988-89	U. Wisconsin	WCHA	44	20	23	43	50	....	....	....	....	....
1989-90a	U. Wisconsin	WCHA	45	39	32	71	44	....	....	....	....	....
1990-91	Hartford	NHL	9	1	1	2	4	....	....	....	....	....
	Springfield	AHL	72	37	35	72	46	17	8	4	12	32
1991-92	Hartford	NHL	10	0	0	0	2	....	....	....	....	....
b	Springfield	AHL	17	12	7	19	20	....	....	....	....	....
	Detroit	NHL	1	0	0	0	0	....	....	....	....	....
	Adirondack	AHL	50	36	34	70	42	19	7	9	16	31
1992-93	Detroit	NHL	4	1	0	1	2	....	....	....	....	....
b	Adirondack	AHL	68	*59	43	102	62	10	7	7	14	10
	NHL Totals		24	2	1	3	8	....	....	....	....	....

a NCAA All-Tournament Team, Tournament MVP (1990)
b AHL First All-Star Team (1992, 1993)

Traded to **Detroit** by **Hartford** for Daniel Shank, December 18, 1991.

TANGUAY, MARTIN

Center. Shoots left. 5'11", 185 lbs. Born, Ste-Julie, Que., January 12, 1973.
(Tampa Bay's 6th choice, 122nd overall, in 1992 Entry Draft).

			Regular Season					Playoffs				
Season	Club	Lea	GP	G	A	TP	PIM	GP	G	A	TP	PIM
1989-90	Longueuil	QMJHL	69	11	16	27	35	7	1	4	5	9
1990-91	Longueuil	QMJHL	69	27	34	61	14	8	3	4	7	6
1991-92	Verdun	QMJHL	67	41	50	91	117	19	8	13	21	32
1992-93	St-Jean	QMJHL	72	53	58	111	78	4	1	2	3	21

TANTI, TONY (TAN-tee)

Right wing. Shoots left. 5'9", 180 lbs. Born, Toronto, Ont., September 7, 1963.
(Chicago's 1st choice, 12th overall, in 1981 Entry Draft).

			Regular Season					Playoffs				
Season	Club	Lea	GP	G	A	TP	PIM	GP	G	A	TP	PIM
1980-81a	Oshawa	OHA	67	81	69	150	197	11	7	8	15	41
1981-82	Chicago	NHL	2	0	0	0	0	....	....	....	....	....
b	Oshawa	OHL	57	62	64	126	138	12	14	12	26	15
1982-83	Chicago	NHL	1	1	0	1	0	....	....	....	....	....
	Oshawa	OHL	30	34	28	62	35	....	....	....	....	....
	Vancouver	NHL	39	8	8	16	16	4	0	1	1	0
1983-84	Vancouver	NHL	79	45	41	86	50	4	1	2	3	0
1984-85	Vancouver	NHL	68	39	20	59	45	....	....	....	....	....
1985-86	Vancouver	NHL	77	39	33	72	85	3	0	1	1	11
1986-87	Vancouver	NHL	77	41	38	79	84	....	....	....	....	....
1987-88	Vancouver	NHL	73	40	37	77	90	....	....	....	....	....
1988-89	Vancouver	NHL	77	24	25	49	69	7	0	5	5	4
1989-90	Vancouver	NHL	41	14	18	32	50	....	....	....	....	....
	Pittsburgh	NHL	37	14	18	32	22	....	....	....	....	....
1990-91	Pittsburgh	NHL	46	6	12	18	44	....	....	....	....	....
	Buffalo	NHL	10	1	7	8	6	5	2	0	2	8
1991-92	Buffalo	NHL	70	15	16	31	100	7	0	3	3	4
1992-93	Preussen Berlin	Ger.	34	14	17	31	73	....	....	....	....	....
	NHL Totals		697	287	273	560	661	30	3	12	15	27

a OHA First All-Star Team (1981)
b OHL Second All-Star Team (1982)

Played in NHL All-Star Game (1986)

Traded to **Vancouver** by **Chicago** for Curt Fraser, January 6, 1983. Traded to **Pittsburgh** by **Vancouver** with Rod Buskas and Barry Pederson for Dave Capuano, Andrew McBain and Dan Quinn, January 8, 1990. Traded to **Buffalo** by **Pittsburgh** for Ken Priestlay, March 5, 1991.

TARDIF, MARC

Left wing. Shoots left. 6'1", 199 lbs. Born, Montreal, Que., January 6, 1973.
(Tampa Bay's 10th choice, 218th overall, in 1992 Entry Draft).

			Regular Season					Playoffs				
Season	Club	Lea	GP	G	A	TP	PIM	GP	G	A	TP	PIM
1990-91	Shawinigan	QMJHL	66	11	26	37	174	6	0	2	2	38
1991-92	Shawinigan	QMJHL	55	25	34	59	214	10	0	8	8	57
1992-93	Sherbrooke	QMJHL	63	21	46	67	249	14	4	8	12	55

TARDIF, PATRICE

Center. Shoots left. 6'2", 185 lbs. Born, Thetford Mines, Que., October 30, 1970.
(St. Louis' 2nd choice, 54th overall, in 1990 Entry Draft).

			Regular Season					Playoffs				
Season	Club	Lea	GP	G	A	TP	PIM	GP	G	A	TP	PIM
1990-91	U. of Maine	H.E.	36	13	12	25	18	....	....	....	....	....
1991-92	U. of Maine	H.E.	31	18	20	38	14	....	....	....	....	....
1992-93	U. of Maine	H.E.	45	23	25	48	22	....	....	....	....	....

TATARINOV, MIKHAIL (tah-TAH-ree-nahf)

Defense. Shoots left. 5'10", 195 lbs. Born, Angarsk, Soviet Union, July 16, 1966.
(Washington's 10th choice, 225th overall, in 1984 Entry Draft).

			Regular Season					Playoffs				
Season	Club	Lea	GP	G	A	TP	PIM	GP	G	A	TP	PIM
1983-84	Sokol Kiev	USSR	38	7	3	10	46	....	....	....	....	....
1984-85	Sokol Kiev	USSR	34	3	6	9	54	....	....	....	....	....
1985-86	Sokol Kiev	USSR	37	7	5	12	41	....	....	....	....	....
1986-87	Moscow D'amo	USSR	40	10	8	18	43	....	....	....	....	....
1987-88	Moscow D'amo	USSR	30	2	2	4	8	....	....	....	....	....
1988-89	Moscow D'amo	USSR	4	1	0	1	2	....	....	....	....	....
1989-90	Moscow D'amo	USSR	44	11	10	21	34	....	....	....	....	....
1990-91	Moscow D'amo	USSR	11	5	4	9	6	....	....	....	....	....
	Washington	NHL	65	8	15	23	82	....	....	....	....	....
1991-92	Quebec	NHL	66	11	27	38	72	....	....	....	....	....
1992-93	Quebec	NHL	28	2	6	8	28	....	....	....	....	....
	NHL Totals		159	21	48	69	182	....	....	....	....	....

Traded to **Quebec** by **Washington** for Toronto's second round choice (previously acquired by Quebec – Washington selected Eric Lavigne) in 1991 Entry Draft, June 22, 1991. Signed as a free agent by **Boston**, July 30, 1993.

TAYLOR, CHRIS

Center. Shoots left. 6', 185 lbs. Born, Stratford, Ont., March 6, 1972.
(NY Islanders' 2nd choice, 27th overall, in 1990 Entry Draft).

			Regular Season					Playoffs				
Season	Club	Lea	GP	G	A	TP	PIM	GP	G	A	TP	PIM
1988-89	London	OHL	62	7	16	23	52	15	0	2	2	15
1989-90	London	OHL	66	45	60	105	60	6	3	2	5	6
1990-91a	London	OHL	65	50	78	128	50	7	4	8	12	6
1991-92	London	OHL	66	48	74	122	57	10	8	16	24	9
1992-93	Capital Dist.	AHL	77	19	43	62	32	4	0	1	1	2
	Roanoke	ECHL	5	2	1	3	0	....	....	....	....	....

a OHL Third All-Star Team (1991)

TAYLOR, DAVID ANDREW (DAVE)
Right wing. Shoots right. 6', 190 lbs.   Born, Levack, Ont., December 4, 1955.
(Los Angeles' 14th choice, 210th overall, in 1975 Amateur Draft).

			Regular Season					Playoffs				
Season	Club	Lea	GP	G	A	TP	PIM	GP	G	A	TP	PIM
1975-76	Clarkson	ECAC	....	....	....	....	....	....	....	....	....	....
1976-77	Clarkson	ECAC	34	41	67	108	....	....	....	....	....	....
	Fort Worth	CHL	7	2	4	6	6	....	....	....	....	....
1977-78	**Los Angeles**	**NHL**	64	22	21	43	47	2	0	0	0	5
1978-79	**Los Angeles**	**NHL**	78	43	48	91	124	2	0	0	0	2
1979-80	**Los Angeles**	**NHL**	61	37	53	90	72	4	2	1	3	4
1980-81a	**Los Angeles**	**NHL**	72	47	65	112	130	4	2	2	4	10
1981-82	**Los Angeles**	**NHL**	78	39	67	106	130	10	4	6	10	20
1982-83	**Los Angeles**	**NHL**	46	21	37	58	76	....	....	....	....	....
1983-84	**Los Angeles**	**NHL**	63	20	49	69	91	....	....	....	....	....
1984-85	**Los Angeles**	**NHL**	79	41	51	92	132	3	2	2	4	8
1985-86	**Los Angeles**	**NHL**	76	33	38	71	110	....	....	....	....	....
1986-87	**Los Angeles**	**NHL**	67	18	44	62	84	5	2	3	5	6
1987-88	**Los Angeles**	**NHL**	68	26	41	67	129	5	3	3	6	6
1988-89	**Los Angeles**	**NHL**	70	26	37	63	80	11	1	5	6	19
1989-90	**Los Angeles**	**NHL**	58	15	26	41	96	6	4	4	8	2
1990-91bc	**Los Angeles**	**NHL**	73	23	30	53	148	12	2	1	3	12
1991-92	**Los Angeles**	**NHL**	77	10	19	29	63	6	1	1	2	20
1992-93	**Los Angeles**	**NHL**	48	6	9	15	49	22	3	5	8	31
	NHL Totals		**1078**	**427**	**635**	**1062**	**1561**	**92**	**26**	**33**	**59**	**145**

a NHL Second All-Star Team (1981)
b Won Bill Masterton Memorial Trophy (1991)
c Won King Clancy Memorial Trophy (1991)
Played in NHL All-Star Game (1981, 1982, 1986)

TAYLOR, TIM
Center. Shoots left. 6'1", 180 lbs.   Born, Stratford, Ont., February 6, 1969.
(Washington's 2nd choice, 36th overall, in 1988 Entry Draft).

			Regular Season					Playoffs				
Season	Club	Lea	GP	G	A	TP	PIM	GP	G	A	TP	PIM
1986-87	London	OHL	34	7	9	16	11	....	....	....	....	....
1987-88	London	OHL	64	46	50	96	66	12	9	9	18	26
1988-89	London	OHL	61	34	80	114	93	21	*21	25	*46	58
1989-90	Baltimore	AHL	79	31	36	67	124	9	2	2	4	13
1990-91	Baltimore	AHL	79	25	42	67	75	5	0	1	1	4
1991-92	Baltimore	AHL	65	9	18	27	131	....	....	....	....	....
1992-93	Baltimore	AHL	41	15	16	31	49	....	....	....	....	....
	Hamilton	AHL	36	15	22	37	37	....	....	....	....	....

Traded to **Vancouver** by **Washington** for Eric Murano, January 29, 1993.

TEPPER, STEPHEN
Right wing. Shoots right. 6'4", 215 lbs.   Born, Santa Ana, CA, March 10, 1969.
(Chicago's 7th choice, 134th overall, in 1987 Entry Draft).

			Regular Season					Playoffs				
Season	Club	Lea	GP	G	A	TP	PIM	GP	G	A	TP	PIM
1988-89	U. of Maine	H.E.	26	3	9	12	32	....	....	....	....	....
1989-90	U. of Maine	H.E.	41	10	6	16	68	....	....	....	....	....
1990-91	U. of Maine	H.E.	38	6	11	17	58	....	....	....	....	....
1991-92	U. of Maine	H.E.	16	0	3	3	20	....	....	....	....	....
1992-93	**Chicago**	**NHL**	1	0	0	0	0	....	....	....	....	....
	Indianapolis	IHL	12	0	1	1	40	....	....	....	....	....
	Kansas City	IHL	32	4	10	14	51	4	0	1	1	6
	NHL Totals		**1**	**0**	**0**	**0**	**0**	....	....	....	....	....

THERIEN, CHRIS
Defense. Shoots left. 6'3", 205 lbs.   Born, Ottawa, Ont., December 14, 1971.
(Philadelphia's 7th choice, 47th overall, in 1990 Entry Draft).

			Regular Season					Playoffs				
Season	Club	Lea	GP	G	A	TP	PIM	GP	G	A	TP	PIM
1990-91	Providence	H.E.	36	4	18	22	36	....	....	....	....	....
1991-92	Providence	H.E.	36	16	25	41	38	....	....	....	....	....
1992-93a	Providence	H.E.	33	8	11	19	52	....	....	....	....	....
	Cdn. National	....	8	1	4	5	8	....	....	....	....	....

a Hockey East Second All-Star Team (1993)

THIESSEN, TRAVIS
Defense. Shoots left. 6'3", 203 lbs.   Born, North Battleford, Sask., July 11, 1972.
(Pittsburgh's 3rd choice, 67th overall, in 1992 Entry Draft).

			Regular Season					Playoffs				
Season	Club	Lea	GP	G	A	TP	PIM	GP	G	A	TP	PIM
1990-91	Moose Jaw	WHL	69	4	14	18	80	8	0	0	0	10
1991-92	Moose Jaw	WHL	72	9	50	59	112	4	0	2	2	8
1992-93	Cleveland	IHL	64	3	7	10	69	4	0	0	0	16

THOMAS, JOHN (SCOTT)
Right wing. Shoots right. 6'2", 195 lbs.   Born, Buffalo, NY, January 18, 1970.
(Buffalo's 2nd choice, 56th overall, in 1989 Entry Draft).

			Regular Season					Playoffs				
Season	Club	Lea	GP	G	A	TP	PIM	GP	G	A	TP	PIM
1989-90	Clarkson	ECAC	34	19	13	32	95	....	....	....	....	....
1990-91	Clarkson	ECAC	40	28	14	42	89	....	....	....	....	....
1991-92	Clarkson	ECAC	29	22	20	42	57	....	....	....	....	....
	Rochester	AHL	....	....	....	....	....	9	0	1	1	17
1992-93	**Buffalo**	**NHL**	7	1	1	2	15	....	....	....	....	....
	Rochester	AHL	66	32	27	59	38	17	8	5	13	6
	NHL Totals		**7**	**1**	**1**	**2**	**15**	....	....	....	....	....

THOMAS, STEVE
Left wing. Shoots left. 5'11", 185 lbs.   Born, Stockport, England, July 15, 1963.

			Regular Season					Playoffs				
Season	Club	Lea	GP	G	A	TP	PIM	GP	G	A	TP	PIM
1983-84	Toronto	OHL	70	51	54	105	77	....	....	....	....	....
1984-85	**Toronto**	**NHL**	18	1	1	2	2	....	....	....	....	....
ab	St. Catharines	AHL	64	42	48	90	56	....	....	....	....	....
1985-86	**Toronto**	**NHL**	65	20	37	57	36	10	6	8	14	9
	St. Catharines	AHL	19	18	14	32	35	....	....	....	....	....
1986-87	**Toronto**	**NHL**	78	35	27	62	114	13	2	3	5	13
1987-88	**Chicago**	**NHL**	30	13	13	26	40	3	1	2	3	6
1988-89	**Chicago**	**NHL**	45	21	19	40	69	12	3	5	8	10
1989-90	**Chicago**	**NHL**	76	40	30	70	91	20	7	6	13	33
1990-91	**Chicago**	**NHL**	69	19	35	54	129	6	1	2	3	15
1991-92	**Chicago**	**NHL**	11	2	6	8	26	....	....	....	....	....
	NY Islanders	**NHL**	71	28	42	70	71	....	....	....	....	....
1992-93	**NY Islanders**	**NHL**	79	37	50	87	111	18	9	8	17	37
	NHL Totals		**542**	**216**	**260**	**476**	**689**	**82**	**29**	**34**	**63**	**123**

a Won AHL Rookie of the Year (1985)
b AHL First All-Star Team (1985)
Signed as a free agent by **Toronto**, May 12, 1984. Traded to **Chicago** by **Toronto** with Rick Vaive and Bob McGill for Al Secord and Ed Olczyk, September 3, 1987. Traded to **NY Islanders** by **Chicago** with Adam Creighton for Brent Sutter and Brad Lauer, October 25, 1991.

THOMLINSON, DAVE
Left wing. Shoots left. 6'1", 196 lbs.   Born, Edmonton, Alta., October 22, 1966.
(Toronto's 3rd choice, 43rd overall, in 1985 Entry Draft).

			Regular Season					Playoffs				
Season	Club	Lea	GP	G	A	TP	PIM	GP	G	A	TP	PIM
1984-85	Brandon	WHL	26	13	14	27	70	....	....	....	....	....
1985-86	Brandon	WHL	53	25	20	45	116	....	....	....	....	....
1986-87	Brandon	WHL	2	0	1	1	9	....	....	....	....	....
	Moose Jaw	WHL	70	44	36	80	117	9	7	3	10	19
1987-88	Peoria	IHL	74	27	30	57	56	7	4	3	7	11
1988-89	Peoria	IHL	64	27	29	56	154	3	0	1	1	8
1989-90	**St. Louis**	**NHL**	19	1	2	3	12	....	....	....	....	....
	Peoria	IHL	59	27	40	67	87	5	1	1	2	15
1990-91	**St. Louis**	**NHL**	3	0	0	0	0	9	3	1	4	4
	Peoria	IHL	80	53	54	107	107	11	6	7	13	28
1991-92	**Boston**	**NHL**	12	0	1	1	17	....	....	....	....	....
	Maine	AHL	25	9	11	20	36	....	....	....	....	....
1992-93	Binghamton	AHL	54	25	35	60	61	12	2	5	7	8
	NHL Totals		**34**	**1**	**3**	**4**	**29**	**9**	**3**	**1**	**4**	**4**

Signed as a free agent by **St. Louis**, June 4, 1987. Signed as a free agent by **Boston**, July 30, 1991. Signed as a free agent by **NY Rangers**, September 4, 1992. Signed as a free agent by **Los Angeles**, July 22, 1993.

THOMPSON, BRENT
Defense. Shoots left. 6'2", 175 lbs.   Born, Calgary, Alta., January 9, 1971.
(Los Angeles' 1st choice, 39th overall, in 1989 Entry Draft).

			Regular Season					Playoffs				
Season	Club	Lea	GP	G	A	TP	PIM	GP	G	A	TP	PIM
1988-89	Medicine Hat	WHL	72	3	10	13	160	3	0	0	0	2
1989-90	Medicine Hat	WHL	68	10	35	45	167	3	0	1	1	14
1990-91a	Medicine Hat	WHL	51	5	40	45	87	12	1	7	8	16
	Phoenix	IHL	....	....	....	....	....	4	0	1	1	6
1991-92	**Los Angeles**	**NHL**	27	0	5	5	89	4	0	0	0	4
	Phoenix	IHL	42	4	13	17	139	....	....	....	....	....
1992-93	**Los Angeles**	**NHL**	30	0	4	4	76	....	....	....	....	....
	Phoenix	IHL	22	0	5	5	112	....	....	....	....	....
	NHL Totals		**57**	**0**	**9**	**9**	**165**	**4**	**0**	**0**	**0**	**4**

a WHL East Second All-Star Team (1991)

THOMPSON, MICHAEL
Right wing. Shoots right. 6', 202 lbs.   Born, Montreal, Que., February 1, 1971.
(Pittsburgh's 13th choice, 215th overall, in 1990 Entry Draft).

			Regular Season					Playoffs				
Season	Club	Lea	GP	G	A	TP	PIM	GP	G	A	TP	PIM
1989-90	Michigan State	CCHA	17	4	4	8	4	....	....	....	....	....
1990-91	Michigan State	CCHA	15	1	3	4	8	....	....	....	....	....
1991-92	Michigan State	CCHA	14	1	1	2	10	....	....	....	....	....
1992-93	Michigan State	CCHA				DID NOT PLAY						

THOMPSON, PAT
Defense. Shoots . 6'1", 185 lbs.   Born, Halifax County, N.S., January 16, 1972.
(Anaheim's 1st choice, 5th overall, in 1993 Supplemental Draft).

			Regular Season					Playoffs				
Season	Club	Lea	GP	G	A	TP	PIM	GP	G	A	TP	PIM
1991-92	Brown	ECAC	15	1	0	1	6	....	....	....	....	....
1992-93	Brown	ECAC	30	1	7	8	16	....	....	....	....	....

THOMSON, JIM

Right wing. Shoots right. 6'1", 205 lbs. Born, Edmonton, Alta., December 30, 1965.
(Washington's 8th choice, 185th overall, in 1984 Entry Draft).

			Regular Season					Playoffs				
Season	Club	Lea	GP	G	A	TP	PIM	GP	G	A	TP	PIM
1983-84	Toronto	OHL	60	10	18	28	68	9	1	0	1	26
1984-85	Toronto	OHL	63	23	28	51	122	5	3	1	4	25
	Binghamton	AHL	4	0	0	0	2	....	....	....	....	....
1985-86	Binghamton	AHL	59	15	9	24	195	....	....	....	....	....
1986-87	**Washington**	**NHL**	**10**	**0**	**0**	**0**	**35**	....	....	....	....	....
	Binghamton	AHL	57	13	10	23	360	10	0	1	1	40
1987-88	Binghamton	AHL	25	8	9	17	64	4	1	2	3	7
1988-89	**Washington**	**NHL**	**14**	**2**	**0**	**2**	**53**	....	....	....	....	....
	Baltimore	AHL	41	25	16	41	129	....	....	....	....	....
	Hartford	**NHL**	**5**	**0**	**0**	**0**	**14**	....	....	....	....	....
1989-90	Binghamton	AHL	8	1	2	3	30	....	....	....	....	....
	New Jersey	**NHL**	**3**	**0**	**0**	**0**	**31**	....	....	....	....	....
	Utica	AHL	60	20	23	43	124	4	1	0	1	19
1990-91	**Los Angeles**	**NHL**	**8**	**1**	**0**	**1**	**19**	....	....	....	....	....
	New Haven	AHL	27	5	8	13	121	....	....	....	....	....
1991-92	**Los Angeles**	**NHL**	**45**	**1**	**2**	**3**	**162**	....	....	....	....	....
	Phoenix	IHL	2	1	0	1	0	....	....	....	....	....
1992-93	**Ottawa**	**NHL**	**15**	**0**	**1**	**1**	**41**	....	....	....	....	....
	Los Angeles	**NHL**	**9**	**0**	**0**	**0**	**56**	**1**	**0**	**0**	**0**	**0**
	Phoenix	IHL	14	4	5	9	44	....	....	....	....	....
	NHL Totals		**109**	**4**	**3**	**7**	**411**	**1**	**0**	**0**	**0**	**0**

Traded to **Hartford** by **Washington** for Scot Kleinendorst, March 6, 1989. Traded to **New Jersey** by **Hartford** for Chris Cichocki, October 31, 1989. Signed as a free agent by **Los Angeles**, July 2, 1990. Claimed by **Minnesota** from **Los Angeles** in Expansion Draft, May 30, 1991. Traded to **Los Angeles** by **Minnesota** with Randy Gilhen, Charlie Huddy and NY Rangers' fourth round choice (previously acquired by Minnesota - Alexei Zhitnik) in 1991 Entry Draft for Todd Elik, June 22, 1991. Claimed by **Ottawa** from **Los Angeles** in Expansion Draft, June 18, 1992. Traded to **Los Angeles** by **Ottawa** with Marc Fortier for Bob Kudelski and Shawn McCosh, December 19, 1992. Claimed by **Anaheim** from **Los Angeles** in Expansion Draft, June 24, 1993.

THORNTON, SCOTT

Center. Shoots left. 6'2", 200 lbs. Born, London, Ont., January 9, 1971.
(Toronto's 1st choice, 3rd overall, in 1989 Entry Draft).

			Regular Season					Playoffs				
Season	Club	Lea	GP	G	A	TP	PIM	GP	G	A	TP	PIM
1987-88	Belleville	OHL	62	11	19	30	54	6	0	1	1	2
1988-89	Belleville	OHL	59	28	34	62	103	5	1	1	2	6
1989-90	Belleville	OHL	47	21	28	49	91	11	2	10	12	15
1990-91	**Toronto**	**NHL**	**33**	**1**	**3**	**4**	**30**	....	....	....	....	....
	Newmarket	AHL	5	1	0	1	4	....	....	....	....	....
	Belleville	OHL	3	2	1	3	2	6	0	7	7	14
1991-92	**Edmonton**	**NHL**	**15**	**0**	**1**	**1**	**43**	**1**	**0**	**0**	**0**	**0**
	Cape Breton	AHL	49	9	14	23	40	5	1	0	1	8
1992-93	**Edmonton**	**NHL**	**9**	**0**	**1**	**1**	**0**	....	....	....	....	....
	Cape Breton	AHL	58	23	27	50	102	16	1	2	3	35
	NHL Totals		**57**	**1**	**5**	**6**	**73**	**1**	**0**	**0**	**0**	**0**

Traded to **Edmonton** by **Toronto** with Vincent Damphousse, Peter Ing, Luke Richardson, future considerations and cash for Grant Fuhr, Glenn Anderson and Craig Berube, September 19, 1991.

THURESSON, MARCUS

Center. Shoots left. 6'1", 187 lbs. Born, Tyringe, Sweden, May 31, 1971.
(NY Islanders' 11th choice, 224th overall, in 1991 Entry Draft).

			Regular Season					Playoffs				
Season	Club	Lea	GP	G	A	TP	PIM	GP	G	A	TP	PIM
1989-90	Leksand	Swe.	28	8	7	15	18	3	2	0	2	12
1990-91	Leksand	Swe.	22	3	2	5	20	....	....	....	....	....
1991-92	Leksand	Swe.	21	2	4	6	22	....	....	....	....	....
1992-93	Leksand	Swe.	31	6	10	16	22	2	2	0	2	2

Rights traded to **San Jose** by **NY Islanders** for Brian Mullen, August 24, 1992.

TICHY, MILAN (TEE-hee)

Defense. Shoots left. 6'3", 198 lbs. Born, Plzen, Czechoslovakia, September 22, 1969.
(Chicago's 6th choice, 153rd overall, in 1989 Entry Draft).

			Regular Season					Playoffs				
Season	Club	Lea	GP	G	A	TP	PIM	GP	G	A	TP	PIM
1987-88	Skoda Plzen	Czech.	30	1	3	4	20	....	....	....	....	....
1988-89	Skoda Plzen	Czech.	36	1	12	13	44	....	....	....	....	....
1989-90	Dukla Trencin	Czech.	51	14	8	22	....	....	....	....	....	....
1990-91	Dukla Trencin	Czech.	41	9	12	21	72	....	....	....	....	....
1991-92	Indianapolis	IHL	49	6	23	29	28	....	....	....	....	....
1992-93	**Chicago**	**NHL**	**13**	**0**	**1**	**1**	**30**	....	....	....	....	....
	Indianapolis	IHL	49	7	32	39	62	4	0	5	5	14
	NHL Totals		**13**	**0**	**1**	**1**	**30**	....	....	....	....	....

Claimed by **Florida** from **Chicago** in Expansion Draft, June 24, 1993.

TIILIKAINEN, JUKKA

Right wing. Shoots left. 6', 174 lbs. Born, Espoo, Finland, April 4, 1974.
(Los Angeles' 8th choice, 255th overall, in 1992 Entry Draft).

			Regular Season					Playoffs				
Season	Club	Lea	GP	G	A	TP	PIM	GP	G	A	TP	PIM
1991-92	Kiekko	Fin.2	1	0	0	0	0	....	....	....	....	....
1992-93	Vantaa	Fin.2	18	7	3	10	10	....	....	....	....	....
	Kiekko	Fin.	5	0	0	0	4	....	....	....	....	....

TIKKANEN, ESA (TEE-kuh-nehn)

Left wing. Shoots left. 6'1", 200 lbs. Born, Helsinki, Finland, January 25, 1965.
(Edmonton's 4th choice, 80th overall, in 1983 Entry Draft).

			Regular Season					Playoffs				
Season	Club	Lea	GP	G	A	TP	PIM	GP	G	A	TP	PIM
1981-82	Regina	SJHL	59	38	37	75	216	....	....	....	....	....
	Regina	WHL	2	0	0	0	0	....	....	....	....	....
1982-83	HIFK	Fin. Jr.	30	34	31	65	104	4	4	3	7	10
	HIFK	Fin.	....	....	....	....	....	1	0	0	0	2
1983-84	HIFK	Fin. Jr.	6	5	9	14	13	4	4	3	7	8
	HIFK	Fin.	36	19	11	30	30	2	0	0	0	0
1984-85	HIFK	Fin.	36	21	33	54	42	....	....	....	....	....
	Edmonton	**NHL**	....	....	....	....	....	**3**	**0**	**0**	**0**	**2**
1985-86	**Edmonton**	**NHL**	**35**	**7**	**6**	**13**	**28**	**8**	**3**	**2**	**5**	**7**
	Nova Scotia	AHL	15	4	8	12	17	....	....	....	....	....
1986-87	**Edmonton**	**NHL**	**76**	**34**	**44**	**78**	**120**	**21**	**7**	**2**	**9**	**22**
1987-88	**Edmonton**	**NHL**	**80**	**23**	**51**	**74**	**153**	**19**	**10**	**17**	**27**	**72**
1988-89	**Edmonton**	**NHL**	**67**	**31**	**47**	**78**	**92**	**7**	**1**	**3**	**4**	**12**
1989-90	**Edmonton**	**NHL**	**79**	**30**	**33**	**63**	**161**	**22**	**13**	**11**	**24**	**26**
1990-91	**Edmonton**	**NHL**	**79**	**27**	**42**	**69**	**85**	**18**	**12**	**8**	**20**	**24**
1991-92	**Edmonton**	**NHL**	**40**	**12**	**16**	**28**	**44**	**16**	**5**	**3**	**8**	**8**
1992-93	**Edmonton**	**NHL**	**66**	**14**	**19**	**33**	**76**	....	....	....	....	....
	NY Rangers	**NHL**	**15**	**2**	**5**	**7**	**18**	....	....	....	....	....
	NHL Totals		**537**	**180**	**263**	**443**	**777**	**114**	**51**	**46**	**97**	**173**

Traded to **NY Rangers** by **Edmonton** for Doug Weight, March 17, 1993.

TILEY, BRAD

Defense. Shoots left. 6'1", 185 lbs. Born, Markdale, Ont., July 5, 1971.
(Boston's 4th choice, 84th overall, in 1991 Entry Draft).

			Regular Season					Playoffs				
Season	Club	Lea	GP	G	A	TP	PIM	GP	G	A	TP	PIM
1988-89	S.S. Marie	OHL	50	4	11	15	31	....	....	....	....	....
1989-90	S.S. Marie	OHL	66	9	32	41	47	....	....	....	....	....
1990-91a	S.S. Marie	OHL	66	11	55	66	29	14	4	15	19	12
1991-92	Maine	AHL	62	7	22	29	36	....	....	....	....	....
1992-93	Phoenix	IHL	46	11	27	38	35	....	....	....	....	....
	Binghamton	AHL	26	6	10	16	19	8	0	1	1	2

a Memorial Cup All-Star Team (1991)

Signed as a free agent by **NY Rangers**, September 4, 1992.

TILLEY, TOM

Defense. Shoots right. 6', 190 lbs. Born, Trenton, Ont., March 28, 1965.
(St. Louis' 13th choice, 196th overall, in 1984 Entry Draft).

			Regular Season					Playoffs				
Season	Club	Lea	GP	G	A	TP	PIM	GP	G	A	TP	PIM
1984-85	Michigan State	CCHA	37	1	5	6	58	....	....	....	....	....
1985-86	Michigan State	CCHA	42	9	25	34	48	....	....	....	....	....
1986-87	Michigan State	CCHA	42	7	14	21	48	....	....	....	....	....
1987-88a	Michigan State	CCHA	46	8	18	26	44	....	....	....	....	....
1988-89	**St. Louis**	**NHL**	**70**	**1**	**22**	**23**	**47**	**10**	**1**	**2**	**3**	**17**
1989-90	**St. Louis**	**NHL**	**34**	**0**	**5**	**5**	**6**	....	....	....	....	....
	Peoria	IHL	22	1	8	9	13	....	....	....	....	....
1990-91	**St. Louis**	**NHL**	**22**	**2**	**4**	**6**	**4**	....	....	....	....	....
b	Peoria	IHL	48	7	38	45	53	13	2	9	11	25
1991-92	Milan Devils	Italy	18	7	13	20	12	12	5	12	17	10
1992-93	Milan Devils	Alp.	32	5	17	22	21	....	....	....	....	....
	Milan Devils	Italy	14	8	3	11	2	8	1	5	6	4
	NHL Totals		**126**	**3**	**31**	**34**	**57**	**10**	**1**	**2**	**3**	**17**

a CCHA First All-Star Team (1988)
b IHL Second All-Star Team (1991)

TILTGEN, DEAN

Center. Shoots left. 5'11", 175 lbs. Born, Ponoka, Alta., February 3, 1974.
(Buffalo's 8th choice, 179th overall, in 1992 Entry Draft).

			Regular Season					Playoffs				
Season	Club	Lea	GP	G	A	TP	PIM	GP	G	A	TP	PIM
1990-91	Tri-City	WHL	53	5	6	11	11	2	0	0	0	2
1991-92	Tri-City	WHL	69	29	34	63	43	5	2	0	2	6
1992-93	Red Deer	WHL	72	50	61	111	33	4	1	2	3	0

TIMANDER, MATTIAS

Defense. Shoots left. 6'1", 194 lbs. Born, Solleftea, Sweden, April 16, 1974.
(Boston's 7th choice, 208th overall, in 1992 Entry Draft).

			Regular Season					Playoffs				
Season	Club	Lea	GP	G	A	TP	PIM	GP	G	A	TP	PIM
1991-92	MoDo Jrs.	Swe.				UNAVAILABLE						
1992-93	MoDo	Swe.	1	0	0	0	0	....	....	....	....	....

TINORDI, MARK

Defense. Shoots left. 6'4", 205 lbs. Born, Red Deer, Alta., May 9, 1966.

			Regular Season					Playoffs				
Season	Club	Lea	GP	G	A	TP	PIM	GP	G	A	TP	PIM
1982-83	Lethbridge	WHL	64	0	4	4	50	20	1	1	2	6
1983-84	Lethbridge	WHL	72	5	14	19	53	5	0	1	1	7
1984-85	Lethbridge	WHL	58	10	15	25	134	4	0	2	2	12
1985-86	Lethbridge	WHL	58	8	30	38	139	8	1	3	4	15
1986-87	Calgary	WHL	61	29	37	66	148	....	....	....	....	....
	New Haven	AHL	2	0	0	0	2	2	0	0	0	0
1987-88	**NY Rangers**	**NHL**	**24**	**1**	**2**	**3**	**50**	....	....	....	....	....
	Colorado	IHL	41	8	19	27	150	11	1	5	6	31
1988-89	**Minnesota**	**NHL**	**47**	**2**	**3**	**5**	**107**	**5**	**0**	**0**	**0**	**0**
	Kalamazoo	IHL	10	0	0	0	35	....	....	....	....	....
1989-90	**Minnesota**	**NHL**	**66**	**3**	**7**	**10**	**240**	**7**	**0**	**1**	**1**	**16**
1990-91	**Minnesota**	**NHL**	**69**	**5**	**27**	**32**	**189**	**23**	**5**	**6**	**11**	**78**
1991-92	**Minnesota**	**NHL**	**63**	**4**	**24**	**28**	**179**	**7**	**1**	**2**	**3**	**11**
1992-93	**Minnesota**	**NHL**	**69**	**15**	**27**	**42**	**157**	....	....	....	....	....
	NHL Totals		**338**	**30**	**90**	**120**	**922**	**42**	**6**	**9**	**15**	**105**

Played in NHL All-Star Game (1992)

Signed as a free agent by **NY Rangers**, January 4, 1987. Traded to **Minnesota** by **NY Rangers** with Paul Jerrard, the rights to Bret Barnett and Mike Sullivan, and Los Angeles' third round choice (previously acquired by NY Rangers — Minnesota selected Murray Garbutt) in 1989 Entry Draft for Brian Lawton, Igor Liba and the rights to Eric Bennett, October 11, 1988.

TIPPETT, DAVE (TIP-it)

Left wing. Shoots left. 5'10", 180 lbs.   Born, Moosomin, Sask., August 25, 1961.

			Regular Season					Playoffs			
Season	Club	Lea	GP	G	A	TP	PIM	GP	G	A	TP	PIM
1981-82	North Dakota	WCHA	43	13	28	41	20	....	....	....	....	....
1982-83	North Dakota	WCHA	36	15	31	46	24	....	....	....	....	....
1983-84	Cdn. Olympic	....	66	14	19	33	24	....	....	....	....	....
	Hartford	NHL	17	4	2	6	2	....	....	....	....	....
1984-85	Hartford	NHL	80	7	12	19	12	....	....	....	....	....
1985-86	Hartford	NHL	80	14	20	34	18	10	2	2	4	4
1986-87	Hartford	NHL	80	9	22	31	42	6	0	2	2	4
1987-88	Hartford	NHL	80	16	21	37	32	6	0	0	0	2
1988-89	Hartford	NHL	80	17	24	41	45	4	0	1	1	0
1989-90	Hartford	NHL	66	8	19	27	32	7	1	3	4	2
1990-91	Washington	NHL	61	6	9	15	24	10	2	3	5	8
1991-92	Washington	NHL	30	2	10	12	16	7	0	1	1	0
	Cdn. National	....	1	0	0	0	4	....	....	....	....	....
	Cdn. Olympic	....	7	1	2	3	10	....	....	....	....	....
1992-93	Pittsburgh	NHL	74	6	19	25	56	12	1	4	5	14
	NHL Totals		**648**	**89**	**158**	**247**	**279**	**62**	**6**	**16**	**22**	**34**

Signed as a free agent by **Hartford**, February 29, 1984. Traded to **Washington** by **Hartford** for future considerations, September 30, 1990. Signed as a free agent by **Pittsburgh**, August 25, 1992.

TJALLDEN, MIKAEL

Defense. Shoots left. 6'2", 194 lbs.   Born, Ornskoldsvik, Sweden, February 16, 1975.
(Florida's 4th choice, 67th overall, in 1993 Entry Draft).

			Regular Season					Playoffs			
Season	Club	Lea	GP	G	A	TP	PIM	GP	G	A	TP	PIM
1992-93	MoDo Jrs.	Swe.				UNAVAILABLE						

TKACHUK, KEITH (kuh-CHUK)

Left wing. Shoots left. 6'2", 215 lbs.   Born, Melrose, MA, March 28, 1972.
(Winnipeg's 1st choice, 19th overall, in 1990 Entry Draft).

			Regular Season					Playoffs			
Season	Club	Lea	GP	G	A	TP	PIM	GP	G	A	TP	PIM
1990-91	Boston U.	H.E.	36	17	23	40	70	....	....	....	....	....
1991-92	U.S. National	....	45	10	10	20	141	....	....	....	....	....
	U.S. Olympic	....	8	1	1	2	12	....	....	....	....	....
	Winnipeg	NHL	17	3	5	8	28	7	3	0	3	30
1992-93	Winnipeg	NHL	83	28	23	51	201	6	4	0	4	14
	NHL Totals		**100**	**31**	**28**	**59**	**229**	**13**	**7**	**0**	**7**	**44**

TOCCHET, RICK (TOK-iht)

Right wing. Shoots right. 6', 205 lbs.   Born, Scarborough, Ont., April 9, 1964.
(Philadelphia's 5th choice, 121st overall, in 1983 Entry Draft).

			Regular Season					Playoffs			
Season	Club	Lea	GP	G	A	TP	PIM	GP	G	A	TP	PIM
1981-82	S.S. Marie	OHL	59	7	15	22	184	11	1	1	2	28
1982-83	S.S. Marie	OHL	66	32	34	66	146	16	4	13	17	67
1983-84	S.S. Marie	OHL	64	44	64	108	209	16	*22	14	*36	41
1984-85	Philadelphia	NHL	75	14	25	39	181	19	3	4	7	72
1985-86	Philadelphia	NHL	69	14	21	35	284	5	1	2	3	26
1986-87	Philadelphia	NHL	69	21	26	47	288	26	11	10	21	72
1987-88	Philadelphia	NHL	65	31	33	64	301	5	1	4	5	55
1988-89	Philadelphia	NHL	66	45	36	81	183	16	6	6	12	69
1989-90	Philadelphia	NHL	75	37	59	96	196	....	....	....	....	....
1990-91	Philadelphia	NHL	70	40	31	71	150	....	....	....	....	....
1991-92	Philadelphia	NHL	42	13	16	29	102	....	....	....	....	....
	Pittsburgh	NHL	19	14	16	30	49	14	6	13	19	24
1992-93	Pittsburgh	NHL	80	48	61	109	252	12	7	6	13	24
	NHL Totals		**630**	**277**	**324**	**601**	**1986**	**97**	**35**	**45**	**80**	**342**

Played in NHL All-Star Game (1989-91, 1993)

Traded to **Pittsburgh** by **Philadelphia** with Kjell Samuelsson and Ken Wregget for Mark Recchi, Brian Benning and Los Angeles' first round choice (previously acquired by Pittsburgh — Philadelphia selected Jason Bowen) in 1992 Entry Draft, February 19, 1992.

TOCHER, RYAN

Defense. Shoots right. 6'1", 194 lbs.   Born, Hamilton, Ont., June 14, 1975.
(Quebec's 5th choice, 101st overall, in 1993 Entry Draft).

			Regular Season					Playoffs			
Season	Club	Lea	GP	G	A	TP	PIM	GP	G	A	TP	PIM
1991-92	Niagara Falls	OHL	58	4	8	12	53	16	0	0	0	2
1992-93	Niagara Falls	OHL	59	6	17	23	68	4	0	0	0	4

TODD, KEVIN

Center. Shoots left. 5'10", 180 lbs.   Born, Winnipeg, Man., May 4, 1968.
(New Jersey's 7th choice, 129th overall, in 1986 Entry Draft).

			Regular Season					Playoffs			
Season	Club	Lea	GP	G	A	TP	PIM	GP	G	A	TP	PIM
1985-86	Prince Albert	WHL	55	14	25	39	19	20	7	6	13	29
1986-87	Prince Albert	WHL	71	39	46	85	92	8	2	5	7	17
1987-88	Prince Albert	WHL	72	49	72	121	83	10	8	11	19	27
1988-89	New Jersey	NHL	1	0	0	0	0	....	....	....	....	....
	Utica	AHL	78	26	45	71	62	4	2	0	2	6
1989-90	Utica	AHL	71	18	36	54	72	5	2	4	6	2
1990-91	New Jersey	NHL	1	0	0	0	0	1	0	0	0	6
abc	Utica	AHL	75	37	*81	*118	75	....	....	....	....	....
1991-92d	New Jersey	NHL	80	21	42	63	69	7	3	2	5	8
1992-93	New Jersey	NHL	30	5	5	10	16	....	....	....	....	....
	Utica	AHL	2	2	1	3	0	....	....	....	....	....
	Edmonton	NHL	25	4	9	13	10	....	....	....	....	....
	NHL Totals		**137**	**30**	**56**	**86**	**95**	**8**	**3**	**2**	**5**	**14**

a AHL First All-Star Team (1991)
b Won Les Cunningham Plaque (MVP - AHL) (1991)
c Won John B. Sollenberger Trophy (Leading Scorer - AHL) (1991)
d NHL/Upper Deck All-Rookie Team (1992)

Traded to **Edmonton** by **New Jersey** with Zdeno Ciger for Bernie Nicholls, January 13, 1993.

TOK, CHRIS

Defense. Shoots left. 6'1", 185 lbs.   Born, Grand Rapids, MN, March 19, 1973.
(Pittsburgh's 10th choice, 214th overall, in 1991 Entry Draft).

			Regular Season					Playoffs			
Season	Club	Lea	GP	G	A	TP	PIM	GP	G	A	TP	PIM
1991-92	U. Wisconsin	WCHA	19	0	2	2	8	....	....	....	....	....
1992-93	U. Wisconsin	WCHA	41	3	12	15	68	....	....	....	....	....

TOMBERLIN, JUSTIN

Center. Shoots left. 6', 191 lbs.   Born, Grand Rapids, MN, November 15, 1970.
(Toronto's 11th choice, 192nd overall, in 1989 Entry Draft).

			Regular Season					Playoffs			
Season	Club	Lea	GP	G	A	TP	PIM	GP	G	A	TP	PIM
1989-90	U. of Maine	H.E.	35	10	7	17	6	....	....	....	....	....
1990-91	U. of Maine	H.E.	26	8	5	13	10	....	....	....	....	....
1991-92					DID NOT PLAY							
1992-93	U. of Maine	H.E.	34	13	9	22	22	....	....	....	....	....

TOMILIN, VITALI

Left wing. Shoots left. 6', 183 lbs.   Born, Elektrostal, Soviet Union, January 15, 1974.
(New Jersey's 4th choice, 90th overall, in 1992 Entry Draft).

			Regular Season					Playoffs			
Season	Club	Lea	GP	G	A	TP	PIM	GP	G	A	TP	PIM
1990-91	Soviet Wings	USSR	1	0	0	0	0	....	....	....	....	....
1991-92	Soviet Wings	CIS	37	1	1	2	8	....	....	....	....	....
1992-93	Soviet Wings	CIS	28	0	1	1	14	2	0	0	0	0

TOMLAK, MIKE

Center/Left wing. Shoots left. 6'3", 205 lbs.   Born, Thunder Bay, Ont., October 17, 1964.
(Toronto's 10th choice, 208th overall, in 1983 Entry Draft).

			Regular Season					Playoffs			
Season	Club	Lea	GP	G	A	TP	PIM	GP	G	A	TP	PIM
1982-83	Cornwall	OHL	70	18	49	67	26	....	....	....	....	....
1983-84	Cornwall	OHL	64	24	64	88	21	....	....	....	....	....
1984-85	Cornwall	OHL	66	30	70	100	9	....	....	....	....	....
1985-86	Western Ont.	OUAA	38	28	20	48	45	....	....	....	....	....
1986-87	Western Ont.	OUAA	38	16	30	46	10	....	....	....	....	....
1987-88	Western Ont.	OUAA	39	24	52	76		....	....	....	....	....
1988-89	Western Ont.	OUAA	35	16	34	50		....	....	....	....	....
1989-90	Hartford	NHL	70	7	14	21	48	7	0	1	1	2
1990-91	Hartford	NHL	64	8	8	16	55	3	0	0	0	2
	Springfield	AHL	15	4	9	13	15	....	....	....	....	....
1991-92	Hartford	NHL	6	0	0	0	0	....	....	....	....	....
	Springfield	AHL	39	16	21	37	24	....	....	....	....	....
1992-93	Springfield	AHL	38	16	21	37	56	5	1	1	2	2
	NHL Totals		**140**	**15**	**22**	**37**	**103**	**10**	**0**	**1**	**1**	**4**

Signed as a free agent by **Hartford**, November 14, 1988.

TOMLINSON, DAVE

Center. Shoots left. 5'11", 177 lbs.   Born, North Vancouver, B.C., May 8, 1969.
(Toronto's 1st choice, 3rd overall, in 1989 Supplemental Draft).

			Regular Season					Playoffs			
Season	Club	Lea	GP	G	A	TP	PIM	GP	G	A	TP	PIM
1987-88	Boston U.	H.E.	34	16	20	36	28	....	....	....	....	....
1988-89	Boston U.	H.E.	34	16	30	46	40	....	....	....	....	....
1989-90	Boston U.	H.E.	43	15	22	37	53	....	....	....	....	....
1990-91	Boston U.	H.E.	41	30	30	60	55	....	....	....	....	....
1991-92	Toronto	NHL	3	0	0	0	2	....	....	....	....	....
	St. John's	AHL	75	23	34	57	75	12	4	5	9	6
1992-93	Toronto	NHL	3	0	0	0	2	....	....	....	....	....
	St. John's	AHL	70	36	48	84	115	9	1	4	5	8
	NHL Totals		**6**	**0**	**0**	**0**	**4**					

Traded to **Florida** by **Toronto** for cash, July 30, 1993. Traded to **Winnipeg** by **Florida** for Jason Cirone, August 3, 1993.

TOMPKINS, DAN

Left wing. Shoots left. 6'2", 205 lbs.   Born, MN, January 31, 1975.
(Calgary's 3rd choice, 70th overall, in 1993 Entry Draft).

			Regular Season					Playoffs			
Season	Club	Lea	GP	G	A	TP	PIM	GP	G	A	TP	PIM
1991-92	Hopkins	HS	17	10	12	22	20	....	....	....	....	....
1992-93	Omaha	USHL	43	16	34	50	48	....	....	....	....	....

TOMS, JEFF

Left wing. Shoots left. 6'3", 180 lbs.   Born, Swift Current, Sask., June 4, 1974.
(New Jersey's 9th choice, 210th overall, in 1992 Entry Draft).

			Regular Season					Playoffs			
Season	Club	Lea	GP	G	A	TP	PIM	GP	G	A	TP	PIM
1991-92	S.S. Marie	OHL	36	9	5	14	0	16	0	1	1	2
1992-93	S.S. Marie	OHL	59	16	23	39	20	16	4	4	8	7

TOOKEY, TIMOTHY RAYMOND (TIM)

Center. Shoots left. 5'11", 185 lbs. Born, Edmonton, Alta., August 29, 1960.
(Washington's 4th choice, 88th overall, in 1979 Entry Draft).

			Regular Season					Playoffs				
Season	Club	Lea	GP	G	A	TP	PIM	GP	G	A	TP	PIM
1977-78	Portland	WHL	72	16	15	31	55	8	2	2	4	5
1978-79	Portland	WHL	56	33	47	80	55	25	6	14	20	6
1979-80	Portland	WHL	70	58	83	141	55	8	2	5	7	4
1980-81	**Washington**	**NHL**	**29**	**10**	**13**	**23**	**18**	....	....	....	....	....
	Hershey	AHL	47	20	38	58	129	....	....	....	....	....
1981-82	**Washington**	**NHL**	**28**	**8**	**8**	**16**	**35**	....	....	....	....	....
	Hershey	AHL	14	4	9	13	10	....	....	....	....	....
	Fredericton	AHL	16	6	10	16	16	....	....	....	....	....
1982-83	**Quebec**	**NHL**	**12**	**1**	**6**	**7**	**4**	....	....	....	....	....
	Fredericton	AHL	53	24	43	67	24	9	5	4	9	0
1983-84	**Pittsburgh**	**NHL**	**8**	**0**	**2**	**2**	**2**	....	....	....	....	....
	Baltimore	AHL	58	16	28	44	25	8	1	1	2	2
1984-85	Baltimore	AHL	74	25	43	68	74	15	8	10	18	13
1985-86ab	Hershey	AHL	69	35	*62	97	66	18	*11	8	19	10
1986-87	**Philadelphia**	**NHL**	**2**	**0**	**0**	**0**	**0**	**10**	**1**	**3**	**4**	**2**
cde	Hershey	AHL	80	51	*73	*124	45	5	5	4	9	0
1987-88	**Los Angeles**	**NHL**	**20**	**1**	**6**	**7**	**8**	....	....	....	....	....
	New Haven	AHL	11	6	7	13	2	....	....	....	....	....
1988-89	**Los Angeles**	**NHL**	**7**	**2**	**1**	**3**	**4**	....	....	....	....	....
	New Haven	AHL	33	11	18	29	30	....	....	....	....	....
	Muskegon	IHL	18	7	14	21	7	8	2	9	11	4
1989-90	Hershey	AHL	42	18	22	40	28	....	....	....	....	....
1990-91	Hershey	AHL	51	17	42	59	43	5	0	5	5	0
1991-92a	Hershey	AHL	80	36	69	105	63	6	4	2	6	4
1992-93	Hershey	AHL	80	38	70	108	63	....	....	....	....	....
	NHL Totals		**106**	**22**	**36**	**58**	**71**	**10**	**1**	**3**	**4**	**2**

a AHL Second All-Star Team (1986, 1992)
b AHL Playoff MVP (1986)
c AHL First All-Star Team (1987)
d Won Les Cunningham Plaque (MVP-AHL) (1987)
e Won John B. Sollenberger Trophy (Top Scorer–AHL) (1987)

Traded to **Quebec** by **Washington** with Washington's seventh round choice (later traded to Calgary — Calgary traded Daniel Poudrier) in 1982 Entry Draft for Lee Norwood and Quebec's sixth round choice (Mats Kilstrom) in 1982 Entry Draft, February 1, 1982. Signed as a free agent by **Pittsburgh**, September 12, 1983. Signed as a free agent by **Philadelphia,** July 23, 1985. Claimed by **Los Angeles** in NHL Waiver Draft, October 5, 1987. Traded to **Pittsburgh** by **Los Angeles** for Patrick Mayer, March 7, 1989. Signed as a free agent by **Philadelphia**, June 30, 1989.

TOPOROWSKI, KERRY

Defense. Shoots right. 6'2", 213 lbs. Born, Paddockwood, Sask., April 9, 1971.
(San Jose's 5th choice, 67th overall, in 1991 Entry Draft).

			Regular Season					Playoffs				
Season	Club	Lea	GP	G	A	TP	PIM	GP	G	A	TP	PIM
1989-90	Spokane	WHL	65	1	13	14	384	6	0	0	0	37
1990-91	Spokane	WHL	65	11	16	27	*505	15	2	2	4	*108
1991-92	Indianapolis	IHL	18	1	2	3	206	....	....	....	....	....
1992-93	Indianapolis	IHL	17	0	0	0	57	....	....	....	....	....

Traded to **Chicago** by **San Jose** with San Jose's second round choice (later traded to Winnipeg — Winnipeg selected Boris Mironov) in 1992 Entry Draft for Doug Wilson, September 6, 1991.

TOPOROWSKI, SHAYNE

Right wing. Shoots right. 6'2", 204 lbs. Born, Paddockwood, Sask., August 6, 1975.
(Los Angeles' 1st choice, 42nd overall, in 1993 Entry Draft).

			Regular Season					Playoffs				
Season	Club	Lea	GP	G	A	TP	PIM	GP	G	A	TP	PIM
1991-92	Prince Albert	WHL	6	2	0	2	2	7	2	1	3	6
1992-93	Prince Albert	WHL	72	25	32	57	235	....	....	....	....	....

TORREL, DOUGLAS

Center. Shoots right. 6'2", 200 lbs. Born, Hibbing, MN, April 29, 1969.
(Vancouver's 3rd choice, 66th overall, in 1987 Entry Draft).

			Regular Season					Playoffs				
Season	Club	Lea	GP	G	A	TP	PIM	GP	G	A	TP	PIM
1988-89	Minn.-Duluth	WCHA	40	4	6	10	36	....	....	....	....	....
1989-90	Minn.-Duluth	WCHA	39	11	11	22	48	....	....	....	....	....
1990-91	Minn.-Duluth	WCHA	40	17	18	35	78	....	....	....	....	....
1991-92	Minn.-Duluth	WCHA	37	22	22	44	84	....	....	....	....	....
1992-93	Hamilton	AHL	75	16	28	44	24	....	....	....	....	....

TOUPAL, RADEK (TOH-pahl)

Center. Shoots right. 5'11", 185 lbs. Born, Pisek, Czechoslovakia, August 16, 1966.
(Edmonton's 6th choice, 126th overall, in 1987 Entry Draft).

			Regular Season					Playoffs				
Season	Club	Lea	GP	G	A	TP	PIM	GP	G	A	TP	PIM
1982-83	Budejovice	Czech.	3	1	0	1	0	....	....	....	....	....
1983-84	Budejovice	Czech.	6	0	2	2	0	....	....	....	....	....
1984-85	Budejovice	Czech.	40	8	10	18	16	....	....	....	....	....
1985-86	Budejovice	Czech.	43	21	14	35	....	....	....	....	....	....
1986-87	Budejovice	Czech.	35	16	14	30	20	....	....	....	....	....
1987-88	Budejovice	Czech.	31	16	17	33	10	....	....	....	....	....
1988-89	Budejovice	Czech.	43	29	29	58	10	....	....	....	....	....
1989-90	Budejovice	Czech.	47	23	27	50	....	....	....	....	....	....
1990-91	Dukla Trencin	Czech.	56	22	60	82	32	....	....	....	....	....
1991-92	HPK	Fin.	44	17	29	46	10	....	....	....	....	....
1992-93	HPK	Fin.	48	16	37	53	14	12	4	5	9	2

TOWNSHEND, GRAEME

Right wing. Shoots right. 6'2", 225 lbs. Born, Kingston, Jamaica, October 2, 1965.

			Regular Season					Playoffs				
Season	Club	Lea	GP	G	A	TP	PIM	GP	G	A	TP	PIM
1985-86	RPI	ECAC	29	1	7	8	52	....	....	....	....	....
1986-87	RPI	ECAC	29	6	1	7	50	....	....	....	....	....
1987-88	RPI	ECAC	32	6	14	20	64	....	....	....	....	....
1988-89	Maine	AHL	5	2	1	3	11	....	....	....	....	....
	RPI	ECAC	31	6	16	22	50	....	....	....	....	....
1989-90	**Boston**	**NHL**	**4**	**0**	**0**	**0**	**7**	....	....	....	....	....
	Maine	AHL	64	15	13	28	162	....	....	....	....	....
1990-91	**Boston**	**NHL**	**18**	**2**	**5**	**7**	**12**	....	....	....	....	....
	Maine	AHL	46	16	10	26	119	2	2	0	2	4
1991-92	**NY Islanders**	**NHL**	**7**	**1**	**2**	**3**	**0**	....	....	....	....	....
	Capital Dist.	AHL	61	14	23	37	94	4	0	2	2	0
1992-93	**NY Islanders**	**NHL**	**2**	**0**	**0**	**0**	**0**	....	....	....	....	....
	Capital Dist.	AHL	67	29	21	50	45	2	0	0	0	0
	NHL Totals		**31**	**3**	**7**	**10**	**19**	....	....	....	....	....

Signed as a free agent by **Boston**, May 12, 1989. Signed as a free agent by **NY Islanders**, September 3, 1991.

TRAVERSE, PATRICK

Defense. Shoots left. 6'3", 173 lbs. Born, Montreal, Que., March 14, 1974.
(Ottawa's 3rd choice, 50th overall, in 1992 Entry Draft).

			Regular Season					Playoffs				
Season	Club	Lea	GP	G	A	TP	PIM	GP	G	A	TP	PIM
1991-92	Shawinigan	QMJHL	69	3	11	14	12	10	0	0	0	4
1992-93	St-Jean	QMJHL	68	6	30	36	24	4	0	1	1	2
	New Haven	AHL	2	0	0	0	2	....	....	....	....	....

TREBIL, DANIEL

Defense. Shoots right. 6'3", 185 lbs. Born, Edina, MN, April 10, 1974.
(New Jersey's 7th choice, 138th overall, in 1992 Entry Draft).

			Regular Season					Playoffs				
Season	Club	Lea	GP	G	A	TP	PIM	GP	G	A	TP	PIM
1991-92	Jefferson	HS	28	7	26	33	6	....	....	....	....	....
1992-93	U. Minnesota	WCHA	36	2	11	13	16	....	....	....	....	....

TRETOWICZ, DAVID

Defense. Shoots right. 5'11", 190 lbs. Born, Liverpool, NY, March 15, 1969.
(Calgary's 11th choice, 231st overall, in 1988 Entry Draft).

			Regular Season					Playoffs				
Season	Club	Lea	GP	G	A	TP	PIM	GP	G	A	TP	PIM
1987-88	Clarkson	ECAC	35	8	14	22	28	....	....	....	....	....
1988-89	Clarkson	ECAC	32	6	17	23	22	....	....	....	....	....
1989-90a	Clarkson	ECAC	35	15	24	39	34	....	....	....	....	....
1990-91b	Clarkson	ECAC	40	4	32	36	18	....	....	....	....	....
1991-92	U.S. National	....	57	1	7	8	4	....	....	....	....	....
	U.S. Olympic	....	8	0	0	0	0	....	....	....	....	....
	Phoenix	IHL	16	3	2	5	14	....	....	....	....	....
1992-93	Phoenix	IHL	79	1	15	16	22	....	....	....	....	....

a ECAC Second All-Star Team (1990)
b ECAC First All-Star Team (1991)

Signed as a free agent by **Los Angeles**, March 2, 1992.

TROTTIER, BRYAN JOHN (TRAH-chay)

Center. Shoots left. 5'11", 195 lbs. Born, Val Marie, Sask., July 17, 1956.
(NY Islanders' 2nd choice, 22nd overall, in 1974 Amateur Draft).

			Regular Season					Playoffs				
Season	Club	Lea	GP	G	A	TP	PIM	GP	G	A	TP	PIM
1972-73	Swift Current	WHL	67	16	29	45	10	....	....	....	....	....
1973-74	Swift Current	WHL	68	41	71	112	76	13	7	8	15	8
1974-75ab	Lethbridge	WHL	67	46	*98	144	103	6	2	5	7	14
1975-76c	**NY Islanders**	**NHL**	**80**	**32**	**63**	**95**	**21**	**13**	**1**	**7**	**8**	**8**
1976-77	**NY Islanders**	**NHL**	**76**	**30**	**42**	**72**	**34**	**12**	**2**	**8**	**10**	**2**
1977-78d	**NY Islanders**	**NHL**	**77**	**46**	***77**	**123**	**46**	**7**	**0**	**3**	**3**	**4**
1978-79defg	**NY Islanders**	**NHL**	**76**	**47**	***87**	***134**	**50**	**10**	**2**	**4**	**6**	**13**
1979-80h	**NY Islanders**	**NHL**	**78**	**42**	**62**	**104**	**68**	**21**	***12**	**17**	***29**	**16**
1980-81	**NY Islanders**	**NHL**	**73**	**31**	**72**	**103**	**74**	***18**	**11**	***18**	**29**	**34**
1981-82i	**NY Islanders**	**NHL**	**80**	**50**	**79**	**129**	**88**	**19**	**6**	***23**	***29**	**40**
1982-83	**NY Islanders**	**NHL**	**80**	**34**	**55**	**89**	**68**	**17**	**8**	**12**	**20**	**18**
1983-84i	**NY Islanders**	**NHL**	**68**	**40**	**71**	**111**	**59**	**21**	**8**	**6**	**14**	**49**
1984-85	**NY Islanders**	**NHL**	**68**	**28**	**31**	**59**	**47**	**10**	**4**	**2**	**6**	**8**
1985-86	**NY Islanders**	**NHL**	**78**	**37**	**59**	**96**	**72**	**3**	**1**	**1**	**2**	**2**
1986-87	**NY Islanders**	**NHL**	**80**	**23**	**64**	**87**	**50**	**14**	**8**	**5**	**13**	**12**
1987-88j	**NY Islanders**	**NHL**	**77**	**30**	**52**	**82**	**48**	**6**	**0**	**0**	**0**	**10**
1988-89k	**NY Islanders**	**NHL**	**73**	**17**	**28**	**45**	**44**	....	....	....	....	....
1989-90	**NY Islanders**	**NHL**	**59**	**13**	**11**	**24**	**29**	**4**	**1**	**0**	**1**	**4**
1990-91	**Pittsburgh**	**NHL**	**52**	**9**	**19**	**28**	**24**	**23**	**3**	**4**	**7**	**49**
1991-92	**Pittsburgh**	**NHL**	**63**	**11**	**18**	**29**	**54**	**21**	**4**	**3**	**7**	**8**
1992-93						DID NOT PLAY						
	NHL Totals		**1238**	**520**	**890**	**1410**	**876**	**219**	**71**	**113**	**184**	**277**

a WHL Most Valuable Player (1975)
b WHL First All-Star Team (1975)
c Won Calder Memorial Trophy (1976)
d NHL First All-Star Team (1978, 1979)
e Won Art Ross Trophy (1979)
f Won Hart Trophy (1979)
g NHL Plus/Minus Leader (1979)
h Won Conn Smythe Trophy (1980)
i NHL Second All-Star Team (1982, 1984)
j Named Budweiser/NHL Man of the Year (1988)
k Won King Clancy Memorial Trophy (1989)

Played in NHL All-Star Game (1976, 1978, 1980, 1982, 1983, 1985, 1986, 1992)

Signed as a free agent by **Pittsburgh**, July 20, 1990.

TSULYGIN, NIKOLAI (tsoo-LEE-gihn)

Defense. Shoots right. 6'3", 196 lbs. Born, Ufa, Soviet Union, May 29, 1975.
(Anaheim's 2nd choice, 30th overall, in 1993 Entry Draft).

			Regular Season					Playoffs				
Season	Club	Lea	GP	G	A	TP	PIM	GP	G	A	TP	PIM
1992-93	Yulayev	CIS	42	5	4	9	21	2	0	0	0	0

TSYGUROV, DENIS (tsih-GOO-rawv)

Defense. Shoots left. 6'3", 198 lbs. Born, Chelyabinsk, Soviet Union, February 26, 1971.
(Buffalo's 1st choice, 38th overall, in 1993 Entry Draft).

			Regular Season					Playoffs				
Season	Club	Lea	GP	G	A	TP	PIM	GP	G	A	TP	PIM
1988-89	Chelyabinsk	USSR	8	0	0	0	2	....	....	....	....	....
1989-90	Chelyabinsk	USSR	27	0	1	1	18	....	....	....	....	....
1990-91	Chelyabinsk	USSR	26	0	1	1	16	....	....	....	....	....
1991-92	Togliatti	CIS	29	3	2	5	6	....	....	....	....	....
1992-93a	Togliatti	CIS	37	7	13	20	29	10	1	1	2	6

a CIS All-Star Team (1993)

TUCKER, CHRIS

Center. Shoots left. 5'11", 183 lbs. Born, White Plains, NY, February 9, 1972.
(Chicago's 3rd choice, 79th overall, in 1990 Entry Draft).

			Regular Season					Playoffs				
Season	Club	Lea	GP	G	A	TP	PIM	GP	G	A	TP	PIM
1990-91	U. Wisconsin	WCHA	35	5	6	11	6	....	....	....	....	....
1991-92	U. Wisconsin	WCHA	34	12	8	20	23	....	....	....	....	....
1992-93	U. Wisconsin	WCHA	40	10	9	19	12	....	....	....	....	....

TUCKER, DARCY

Center. Shoots left. 5'10", 163 lbs. Born, Castor, Alta., March 15, 1975.
(Montreal's 8th choice, 151st overall, in 1993 Entry Draft).

			Regular Season					Playoffs				
Season	Club	Lea	GP	G	A	TP	PIM	GP	G	A	TP	PIM
1991-92	Kamloops	WHL	26	3	10	13	32	9	0	1	1	16
1992-93	Kamloops	WHL	67	31	58	89	155	13	7	6	13	34

TUCKER, JOHN

Center. Shoots right. 6', 200 lbs. Born, Windsor, Ont., September 29, 1964.
(Buffalo's 4th choice, 31st overall, in 1983 Entry Draft).

			Regular Season					Playoffs				
Season	Club	Lea	GP	G	A	TP	PIM	GP	G	A	TP	PIM
1981-82	Kitchener	OHL	67	16	32	48	32	15	2	3	5	2
1982-83	Kitchener	OHL	70	60	80	140	33	11	5	9	14	10
1983-84	**Buffalo**	**NHL**	**21**	**12**	**4**	**16**	**4**	**3**	**1**	**0**	**1**	**0**
ab	Kitchener	OHL	39	40	60	100	25	12	12	18	30	8
1984-85	**Buffalo**	**NHL**	**64**	**22**	**27**	**49**	**21**	**5**	**1**	**5**	**6**	**0**
1985-86	**Buffalo**	**NHL**	**75**	**31**	**34**	**65**	**39**	....	....	....	....	....
1986-87	**Buffalo**	**NHL**	**54**	**17**	**34**	**51**	**21**	....	....	....	....	....
1987-88	**Buffalo**	**NHL**	**45**	**19**	**19**	**38**	**20**	**6**	**7**	**3**	**10**	**18**
1988-89	**Buffalo**	**NHL**	**60**	**13**	**31**	**44**	**31**	**3**	**0**	**3**	**3**	**0**
1989-90	**Buffalo**	**NHL**	**8**	**1**	**2**	**3**	**2**	....	....	....	....	....
	Washington	**NHL**	**38**	**9**	**19**	**28**	**10**	**12**	**1**	**7**	**8**	**4**
1990-91	**Buffalo**	**NHL**	**18**	**1**	**3**	**4**	**4**	....	....	....	....	....
	NY Islanders	**NHL**	**20**	**3**	**4**	**7**	**4**	....	....	....	....	....
1991-92	Asiago	Italy	18	16	21	37	6	11	7	13	20	15
1992-93	**Tampa Bay**	**NHL**	**78**	**17**	**39**	**56**	**69**	....	....	....	....	....
	NHL Totals		**481**	**145**	**216**	**361**	**225**	**29**	**10**	**18**	**28**	**22**

a OHL First All-Star Team (1984)
b OHL Player of the Year (1984)

Traded to **Washington** by **Buffalo** for future considerations, January 5, 1990. Traded to **Buffalo** by **Washington** for cash, July 3, 1990. Traded to **NY Islanders** by **Buffalo** for future considerations, January 21, 1991. Signed as a free agent by **Tampa Bay**, August 5, 1992.

TUCKER, TRAVIS

Defense. Shoots right. 6'4", 205 lbs. Born, Hartford, CT, March 15, 1971.
(Detroit's 9th choice, 192nd overall, in 1990 Entry Draft).

			Regular Season					Playoffs				
Season	Club	Lea	GP	G	A	TP	PIM	GP	G	A	TP	PIM
1990-91	Lowell	H.E.	22	0	0	0	40	....	....	....	....	....
1991-92	Lowell	H.E.	32	1	7	8	77	....	....	....	....	....
1992-93	Lowell	H.E.	31	2	9	11	90	....	....	....	....	....

TULLY, BRENT

Defense. Shoots right. 6'3", 190 lbs. Born, Peterborough, Ont., March 26, 1974.
(Vancouver's 5th choice, 93rd overall, in 1992 Entry Draft).

			Regular Season					Playoffs				
Season	Club	Lea	GP	G	A	TP	PIM	GP	G	A	TP	PIM
1990-91	Peterborough	OHL	45	3	5	8	35	2	0	0	0	0
1991-92	Peterborough	OHL	65	9	23	32	65	10	0	0	0	2
1992-93a	Peterborough	OHL	59	15	45	60	81	21	8	24	32	32

a OHL Second All-Star Team (1993)

TUOMAINEN, MARKO

Right wing. Shoots right. 6'2", 190 lbs. Born, Kuopio, Finland, April 25, 1972.
(Edmonton's 10th choice, 205th overall, in 1992 Entry Draft).

			Regular Season					Playoffs				
Season	Club	Lea	GP	G	A	TP	PIM	GP	G	A	TP	PIM
1989-90	KalPa	Fin.	5	0	0	0	0	....	....	....	....	....
1990-91	KalPa	Fin.	30	2	1	3	2	8	0	0	0	6
1991-92	Clarkson	ECAC	28	11	12	23	32	....	....	....	....	....
1992-93a	Clarkson	ECAC	35	25	30	55	26	....	....	....	....	....

a ECAC First All-Star Team (1993)

TURCOTTE, DARREN

Center. Shoots left. 6', 185 lbs. Born, Boston, MA, March 2, 1968.
(NY Rangers' 6th choice, 114th overall, in 1986 Entry Draft).

			Regular Season					Playoffs				
Season	Club	Lea	GP	G	A	TP	PIM	GP	G	A	TP	PIM
1984-85	North Bay	OHL	62	33	32	65	28	....	....	....	....	....
1985-86	North Bay	OHL	62	35	37	72	35	10	3	4	7	8
1986-87	North Bay	OHL	55	30	48	78	20	18	12	8	20	6
1987-88	North Bay	OHL	32	30	33	63	16	4	3	0	3	4
	Colorado	IHL	8	4	3	7	9	6	2	6	8	8
1988-89	**NY Rangers**	**NHL**	**20**	**7**	**3**	**10**	**4**	**1**	**0**	**0**	**0**	**0**
	Denver	IHL	40	21	28	49	32	....	....	....	....	....
1989-90	**NY Rangers**	**NHL**	**76**	**32**	**34**	**66**	**32**	**10**	**1**	**6**	**7**	**4**
1990-91	**NY Rangers**	**NHL**	**74**	**26**	**41**	**67**	**37**	**6**	**1**	**2**	**3**	**0**
1991-92	**NY Rangers**	**NHL**	**71**	**30**	**23**	**53**	**57**	**8**	**4**	**0**	**4**	**6**
1992-93	**NY Rangers**	**NHL**	**71**	**25**	**28**	**53**	**40**	....	....	....	....	....
	NHL Totals		**312**	**120**	**129**	**249**	**170**	**25**	**6**	**8**	**14**	**10**

Played in NHL All-Star Game (1991)

TURGEON, PIERRE

Center. Shoots left. 6'1", 202 lbs. Born, Rouyn, Que., August 29, 1969.
(Buffalo's 1st choice, 1st overall, in 1987 Entry Draft).

			Regular Season					Playoffs				
Season	Club	Lea	GP	G	A	TP	PIM	GP	G	A	TP	PIM
1985-86	Granby	QMJHL	69	47	67	114	31	....	....	....	....	....
1986-87	Granby	QMJHL	58	69	85	154	8	7	9	6	15	15
1987-88	**Buffalo**	**NHL**	**76**	**14**	**28**	**42**	**34**	**6**	**4**	**3**	**7**	**4**
1988-89	**Buffalo**	**NHL**	**80**	**34**	**54**	**88**	**26**	**5**	**3**	**5**	**8**	**2**
1989-90	**Buffalo**	**NHL**	**80**	**40**	**66**	**106**	**29**	**6**	**2**	**4**	**6**	**2**
1990-91	**Buffalo**	**NHL**	**78**	**32**	**47**	**79**	**26**	**6**	**3**	**1**	**4**	**6**
1991-92	**Buffalo**	**NHL**	**8**	**2**	**6**	**8**	**4**	....	....	....	....	....
	NY Islanders	**NHL**	**69**	**38**	**49**	**87**	**16**	....	....	....	....	....
1992-93a	**NY Islanders**	**NHL**	**83**	**58**	**74**	**132**	**26**	**11**	**6**	**7**	**13**	**0**
	NHL Totals		**474**	**218**	**324**	**542**	**161**	**34**	**18**	**20**	**38**	**14**

a Won Lady Byng Memorial Trophy (1993)

Played in NHL All-Star Game (1990, 1993)

Traded to **NY Islanders** by **Buffalo** with Uwe Krupp, Benoit Hogue and Dave McLlwain for Pat Lafontaine, Randy Hillier, Randy Wood and future considerations, October 25, 1991.

TURGEON, SYLVAIN

Left wing. Shoots left. 6', 200 lbs. Born, Noranda, Que., January 17, 1965.
(Hartford's 1st choice, 2nd overall, in 1983 Entry Draft).

			Regular Season					Playoffs				
Season	Club	Lea	GP	G	A	TP	PIM	GP	G	A	TP	PIM
1981-82	Hull	QMJHL	57	33	40	73	78	14	11	11	22	16
1982-83a	Hull	QMJHL	67	54	109	163	103	7	8	7	15	10
1983-84b	**Hartford**	**NHL**	**76**	**40**	**32**	**72**	**55**	....	....	....	....	....
1984-85	**Hartford**	**NHL**	**64**	**31**	**31**	**62**	**67**	....	....	....	....	....
1985-86	**Hartford**	**NHL**	**76**	**45**	**34**	**79**	**88**	**9**	**2**	**3**	**5**	**4**
1986-87	**Hartford**	**NHL**	**41**	**23**	**13**	**36**	**45**	**6**	**1**	**2**	**3**	**4**
1987-88	**Hartford**	**NHL**	**71**	**23**	**26**	**49**	**71**	**6**	**0**	**0**	**0**	**4**
1988-89	**Hartford**	**NHL**	**42**	**16**	**14**	**30**	**40**	**4**	**0**	**2**	**2**	**4**
1989-90	**New Jersey**	**NHL**	**72**	**30**	**17**	**47**	**81**	**1**	**0**	**0**	**0**	**0**
1990-91	**Montreal**	**NHL**	**19**	**5**	**7**	**12**	**20**	**5**	**0**	**0**	**0**	**2**
1991-92	**Montreal**	**NHL**	**56**	**9**	**11**	**20**	**39**	**5**	**1**	**0**	**1**	**4**
1992-93	**Ottawa**	**NHL**	**72**	**25**	**18**	**43**	**104**	....	....	....	....	....
	NHL Totals		**589**	**247**	**203**	**450**	**610**	**36**	**4**	**7**	**11**	**22**

a QMJHL First All-Star Team (1983)
b NHL All-Rookie Team (1984)

Played in NHL All-Star Game (1986)

Traded to **New Jersey** by **Hartford** for Pat Verbeek, June 17, 1989. Traded to **Montreal** by **New Jersey** for Claude Lemieux, September 4, 1990. Claimed by **Ottawa** from **Montreal** in Expansion Draft, June 18, 1992.

TURNER, BART

Left wing. Shoots left. 6'3", 200 lbs. Born, Beaverton, OR, January 11, 1972.
(Detroit's 9th choice, 230th overall, in 1991 Entry Draft).

			Regular Season					Playoffs				
Season	Club	Lea	GP	G	A	TP	PIM	GP	G	A	TP	PIM
1990-91	Michigan State	CCHA	21	3	1	4	4	....	....	....	....	....
1991-92	Michigan State	CCHA	41	8	7	15	36	....	....	....	....	....
1992-93	Michigan State	CCHA	39	5	9	14	53	....	....	....	....	....

TURNER, BRAD

Defense. Shoots right. 6'2", 205 lbs. Born, Winnipeg, Man., May 25, 1968.
(Minnesota's 6th choice, 58th overall, in 1986 Entry Draft).

			Regular Season					Playoffs				
Season	Club	Lea	GP	G	A	TP	PIM	GP	G	A	TP	PIM
1986-87	U. of Michigan	CCHA	40	3	10	13	40	....	....	....	....	....
1987-88	U. of Michigan	CCHA	39	3	11	14	52	....	....	....	....	....
1988-89	U. of Michigan	CCHA	33	3	8	11	38	....	....	....	....	....
1989-90	U. of Michigan	CCHA	32	8	9	17	34	....	....	....	....	....
1990-91	Capital Dist.	AHL	31	1	2	3	8	....	....	....	....	....
	Richmond	ECHL	40	16	25	41	31	....	....	....	....	....
1991-92	**NY Islanders**	**NHL**	**3**	**0**	**0**	**0**	**0**	....	....	....	....	....
	Capital Dist.	AHL	35	3	6	9	17	....	....	....	....	....
	New Haven	AHL	32	6	11	17	58	....	....	....	....	....
1992-93	Capital Dist.	AHL	65	8	11	19	71	3	0	0	0	2
	NHL Totals		**3**	**0**	**0**	**0**	**0**	....	....	....	....	....

Signed as a free agent by **NY Islanders**, June 4, 1991.

TUTTLE, STEVE

Right wing. Shoots right. 6'1", 197 lbs. Born, Vancouver, B.C., January 5, 1966.
(St. Louis' 8th choice, 113th overall, in 1984 Entry Draft).

			Regular Season					Playoffs				
Season	Club	Lea	GP	G	A	TP	PIM	GP	G	A	TP	PIM
1984-85	U. Wisconsin	WCHA	28	3	4	7	0	....	....	....	....	....
1985-86	U. Wisconsin	WCHA	32	2	10	12	2	....	....	....	....	....
1986-87	U. Wisconsin	WCHA	42	31	21	52	14	....	....	....	....	....
1987-88ab	U. Wisconsin	WCHA	45	27	39	66	18	....	....	....	....	....
1988-89	**St. Louis**	**NHL**	**53**	**13**	**12**	**25**	**6**	**6**	**1**	**2**	**3**	**0**
1989-90	**St. Louis**	**NHL**	**71**	**12**	**10**	**22**	**4**	**5**	**0**	**1**	**1**	**2**
1990-91	**St. Louis**	**NHL**	**20**	**3**	**6**	**9**	**2**	**6**	**0**	**3**	**3**	**0**
	Peoria	IHL	42	24	32	56	8	....	....	....	....	....
1991-92c	Peoria	IHL	71	43	46	89	22	10	4	8	12	4
1992-93	Milwaukee	IHL	51	27	34	61	12	4	0	2	2	2
	Halifax	AHL	22	11	17	28	2	....	....	....	....	....
	NHL Totals		**144**	**28**	**28**	**56**	**12**	**17**	**1**	**6**	**7**	**2**

a NCAA West Second All-American Team (1988)
b WCHA Second All-Star Team (1988)
c IHL First All-Star Team (1992)

Traded to **Tampa Bay** by **St. Louis** with Pat Jablonski and Darin Kimble for future considerations, June 19, 1992. Traded to **Quebec** by **Tampa Bay** with Martin Simard and Michel Mongeau for Herb Raglan, February 12, 1993.

TWIST, TONY

Left wing/Defense. Shoots left. 6'1", 212 lbs. Born, Sherwood Park, Alta., May 9, 1968.
(St. Louis' 9th choice, 177th overall, in 1988 Entry Draft).

			Regular Season					Playoffs				
Season	Club	Lea	GP	G	A	TP	PIM	GP	G	A	TP	PIM
1987-88	Saskatoon	WHL	55	1	8	9	226	10	1	1	2	6
1988-89	Peoria	IHL	67	3	8	11	312	....	....	....	....	....
1989-90	**St. Louis**	**NHL**	**28**	**0**	**0**	**0**	**124**	....	....	....	....	....
	Peoria	IHL	36	1	5	6	200	5	0	1	1	8
1990-91	Peoria	IHL	38	2	10	12	244	....	....	....	....	....
	Quebec	**NHL**	**24**	**0**	**0**	**0**	**104**	....	....	....	....	....
1991-92	**Quebec**	**NHL**	**44**	**0**	**1**	**1**	**164**	....	....	....	....	....
1992-93	**Quebec**	**NHL**	**34**	**0**	**2**	**2**	**64**	....	....	....	....	....
	NHL Totals		**130**	**0**	**3**	**3**	**456**	....	....	....	....	....

Traded to **Quebec** by **St. Louis** with Herb Raglan and Andy Rymsha for Darin Kimble, February 4, 1991.

ULANOV, IGOR (oo-LAH-nov)

Defense. Shoots left. 6'2", 202 lbs. Born, Krasnokamsk, Soviet Union, October 1, 1969.
(Winnipeg's 8th choice, 203rd overall, in 1991 Entry Draft).

			Regular Season					Playoffs				
Season	Club	Lea	GP	G	A	TP	PIM	GP	G	A	TP	PIM
1990-91	Khimik	USSR	41	2	2	4	52	....	....	....	....	....
1991-92	Khimik	CIS	27	1	4	5	24	....	....	....	....	....
	Winnipeg	**NHL**	**27**	**2**	**9**	**11**	**67**	**7**	**0**	**0**	**0**	**39**
	Moncton	AHL	3	0	1	1	16	....	....	....	....	....
1992-93	**Winnipeg**	**NHL**	**56**	**2**	**14**	**16**	**124**	**4**	**0**	**0**	**0**	**4**
	Moncton	AHL	9	1	3	4	26	....	....	....	....	....
	Fort Wayne	IHL	3	0	1	1	29	....	....	....	....	....
	NHL Totals		**83**	**4**	**23**	**27**	**191**	**11**	**0**	**0**	**0**	**43**

USTORF, STEFAN

Center. Shoots left. 5'11", 180 lbs. Born, Kaufbeuren, Germany, January 3, 1974.
(Washington's 3rd choice, 53rd overall, in 1992 Entry Draft).

			Regular Season					Playoffs				
Season	Club	Lea	GP	G	A	TP	PIM	GP	G	A	TP	PIM
1991-92	Kaufbeuren	Ger.	41	2	22	24	46	5	2	7	9	6
1992-93	Kaufbeuren	Ger.	37	14	18	32	32	3	1	0	1	10

UVAYEV, VYACHESLAV (oo-VIH-ev)

Defense. Shoots left. 5'11", 189 lbs. Born, Moscow, Soviet Union, April 15, 1966.
(NY Rangers' 9th choice, 191st overall, in 1991 Entry Draft).

			Regular Season					Playoffs				
Season	Club	Lea	GP	G	A	TP	PIM	GP	G	A	TP	PIM
1988-89	Torpedo Yaro.	USSR	22	0	1	1	14	....	....	....	....	....
1989-90	Torpedo Yaro.	USSR	48	4	8	12	64	....	....	....	....	....
1990-91	Spartak	USSR	45	1	10	11	44	....	....	....	....	....
1991-92	Spartak	CIS	42	0	7	7	12	....	....	....	....	....
1992-93	Spartak	CIS	40	3	9	12	30	3	0	0	0	2

VACHON, NICK

Center. Shoots left. 5'10", 190 lbs. Born, Montreal, Que., July 20, 1972.
(Toronto's 11th choice, 241st overall, in 1990 Entry Draft).

			Regular Season					Playoffs				
Season	Club	Lea	GP	G	A	TP	PIM	GP	G	A	TP	PIM
1990-91	Boston U.	H.E.	8	0	1	1	4	....	....	....	....	....
1991-92	Boston U.	H.E.	16	6	7	13	10	....	....	....	....	....
	Portland	WHL	25	9	19	28	46	6	0	3	3	14
1992-93	Portland	WHL	66	33	58	91	100	16	11	7	18	34

VAIVE, RICHARD CLAUDE (RICK) (VIGHV)

Right wing. Shoots right. 6'1", 198 lbs. Born, Ottawa, Ont., May 14, 1959.
(Vancouver's 1st choice, 5th overall, in 1979 Entry Draft).

			Regular Season					Playoffs				
Season	Club	Lea	GP	G	A	TP	PIM	GP	G	A	TP	PIM
1976-77	Sherbrooke	QJHL	67	51	59	110	91	18	10	13	23	78
1977-78	Sherbrooke	QJHL	68	76	79	155	199	9	8	4	12	38
1978-79	Birmingham	WHA	75	26	33	59	*248	....	....	....	....	....
1979-80	**Vancouver**	**NHL**	**47**	**13**	**8**	**21**	**111**	....	....	....	....	....
	Toronto	**NHL**	**22**	**9**	**7**	**16**	**77**	**3**	**1**	**0**	**1**	**11**
1980-81	**Toronto**	**NHL**	**75**	**33**	**29**	**62**	**229**	**3**	**1**	**0**	**1**	**4**
1981-82	**Toronto**	**NHL**	**77**	**54**	**35**	**89**	**157**	....	....	....	....	....
1982-83	**Toronto**	**NHL**	**78**	**51**	**28**	**79**	**105**	**4**	**2**	**5**	**7**	**6**
1983-84	**Toronto**	**NHL**	**76**	**52**	**41**	**93**	**114**	....	....	....	....	....
1984-85	**Toronto**	**NHL**	**72**	**35**	**33**	**68**	**112**	....	....	....	....	....
1985-86	**Toronto**	**NHL**	**61**	**33**	**31**	**64**	**85**	**9**	**6**	**2**	**8**	**9**
1986-87	**Toronto**	**NHL**	**73**	**32**	**34**	**66**	**61**	**13**	**4**	**2**	**6**	**23**
1987-88	**Chicago**	**NHL**	**76**	**43**	**26**	**69**	**108**	**5**	**6**	**2**	**8**	**38**
1988-89	**Chicago**	**NHL**	**30**	**12**	**13**	**25**	**60**	....	....	....	....	....
	Buffalo	**NHL**	**28**	**19**	**13**	**32**	**64**	**5**	**2**	**1**	**3**	**8**
1989-90	**Buffalo**	**NHL**	**70**	**29**	**19**	**48**	**74**	**6**	**4**	**2**	**6**	**6**
1990-91	**Buffalo**	**NHL**	**71**	**25**	**27**	**52**	**74**	**6**	**1**	**2**	**3**	**6**
1991-92	**Buffalo**	**NHL**	**20**	**1**	**3**	**4**	**14**	....	....	....	....	....
	Rochester	AHL	12	4	9	13	4	16	4	4	8	10
1992-93	Hamilton	AHL	38	16	15	31	34	....	....	....	....	....
	NHL Totals		**876**	**441**	**347**	**788**	**1445**	**54**	**27**	**16**	**43**	**111**

Played in NHL All-Star Game (1982-84)

Traded to **Toronto** by **Vancouver** with Bill Derlago for Dave Williams and Jerry Butler, February 18, 1980. Traded to **Chicago** by **Toronto** with Steve Thomas and Bob McGill for Al Secord and Ed Olczyk, September 3, 1987. Traded to **Buffalo** by **Chicago** for Adam Creighton, December 26, 1988. Signed as a free agent by **Vancouver**, September 2, 1992.

VALICEVIC, ROBERT

Right wing. Shoots right. 6'2", 197 lbs. Born, Detroit, MI, January 6, 1971.
(NY Islanders' 6th choice, 114th overall, in 1991 Entry Draft).

			Regular Season					Playoffs				
Season	Club	Lea	GP	G	A	TP	PIM	GP	G	A	TP	PIM
1991-92	Lake Superior	CCHA	32	8	4	12	12	....	....	....	....	....
1992-93	Lake Superior	CCHA	43	21	20	41	28	....	....	....	....	....

VALILA, MIKA

Center. Shoots left. 6', 187 lbs. Born, Sodertalje, Sweden, February 20, 1970.
(Pittsburgh's 7th choice, 130th overall, in 1990 Entry Draft).

			Regular Season					Playoffs				
Season	Club	Lea	GP	G	A	TP	PIM	GP	G	A	TP	PIM
1988-89	Tappara	Fin.	14	2	5	7	8	3	1	0	1	2
1989-90	Tappara	Fin.	44	8	16	24	16	7	2	2	4	4
1990-91	Tappara	Fin.	41	10	9	19	16	3	0	1	1	0
1991-92	Jokerit	Fin.	30	4	3	7	4	8	1	1	2	2
1992-93	Lukko	Fin.	48	8	10	18	24	3	0	0	0	0

VALK, GARRY

Left wing. Shoots left. 6'1", 205 lbs. Born, Edmonton, Alta., November 27, 1967.
(Vancouver's 5th choice, 108th overall, in 1987 Entry Draft).

			Regular Season					Playoffs				
Season	Club	Lea	GP	G	A	TP	PIM	GP	G	A	TP	PIM
1987-88	North Dakota	WCHA	38	23	12	35	64	....	....	....	....	....
1988-89	North Dakota	WCHA	40	14	17	31	71	....	....	....	....	....
1989-90	North Dakota	WCHA	43	22	17	39	92	....	....	....	....	....
1990-91	**Vancouver**	**NHL**	**59**	**10**	**11**	**21**	**67**	**5**	**0**	**0**	**0**	**20**
	Milwaukee	IHL	10	12	4	16	13	3	0	0	0	2
1991-92	**Vancouver**	**NHL**	**65**	**8**	**17**	**25**	**56**	**4**	**0**	**0**	**0**	**5**
1992-93	**Vancouver**	**NHL**	**48**	**6**	**7**	**13**	**77**	**7**	**0**	**1**	**1**	**12**
	Hamilton	AHL	7	3	6	9	6	....	....	....	....	....
	NHL Totals		**172**	**24**	**35**	**59**	**200**	**16**	**0**	**1**	**1**	**37**

VALLIS, LINDSAY

Defense. Shoots right. 6'3", 207 lbs. Born, Winnipeg, Man., January 12, 1971.
(Montreal's 1st choice, 13th overall, in 1989 Entry Draft).

			Regular Season					Playoffs				
Season	Club	Lea	GP	G	A	TP	PIM	GP	G	A	TP	PIM
1987-88	Seattle	WHL	68	31	45	76	65	....	....	....	....	....
1988-89	Seattle	WHL	63	21	32	53	48	....	....	....	....	....
1989-90	Seattle	WHL	65	34	43	77	68	13	6	5	11	14
1990-91	Seattle	WHL	72	41	38	79	119	6	1	3	4	17
	Fredericton	AHL	....	....	....	....	....	7	0	0	0	6
1991-92	Fredericton	AHL	71	10	19	29	84	4	0	1	1	7
1992-93	Fredericton	AHL	65	18	16	34	38	5	0	2	2	10

VAN ALLEN, SHAUN

Center. Shoots left. 6'1", 200 lbs. Born, Shaunavon, Sask., August 29, 1967.
(Edmonton's 5th choice, 105th overall, in 1987 Entry Draft).

			Regular Season					Playoffs				
Season	Club	Lea	GP	G	A	TP	PIM	GP	G	A	TP	PIM
1984-85	Swift Current	WHL	61	12	20	32	136	....	....	....	....	....
1985-86	Saskatoon	WHL	55	12	11	23	43	13	4	8	12	28
1986-87	Saskatoon	WHL	72	38	59	97	116	11	4	6	10	24
1987-88	Milwaukee	IHL	40	14	28	42	34	....	....	....	....	....
	Nova Scotia	AHL	19	4	10	14	17	4	1	1	2	4
1988-89	Cape Breton	AHL	76	32	42	74	81	....	....	....	....	....
1989-90	Cape Breton	AHL	61	25	44	69	83	4	0	2	2	8
1990-91	**Edmonton**	**NHL**	**2**	**0**	**0**	**0**	**0**	....	....	....	....	....
a	Cape Breton	AHL	76	25	75	100	182	4	0	1	1	8
1991-92bc	Cape Breton	AHL	77	29	*84	*113	80	5	3	7	10	14
1992-93	**Edmonton**	**NHL**	**21**	**1**	**4**	**5**	**6**	....	....	....	....	....
	Cape Breton	AHL	43	14	62	76	68	....	....	....	....	....
	NHL Totals		**23**	**1**	**4**	**5**	**6**	....	....	....	....	....

a AHL Second All-Star Team (1991)
b Won John B. Sollenberger Trophy (Top Scorer-AHL) (1992)
c AHL First All-Star Team (1992)

Signed as a free agent by **Anaheim**, July 22, 1993.

VANDENBUSSCHE, RYAN

Right wing. Shoots right. 5'11", 187 lbs. Born, Simcoe, Ont., February 28, 1973.
(Toronto's 8th choice, 173rd overall, in 1992 Entry Draft).

			Regular Season					Playoffs				
Season	Club	Lea	GP	G	A	TP	PIM	GP	G	A	TP	PIM
1990-91	Cornwall	OHL	49	3	8	11	139	....	....	....	....	....
1991-92	Cornwall	OHL	61	13	15	28	232	6	0	2	2	9
1992-93	Newmarket	OHL	30	15	12	27	161	....	....	....	....	....
	Guelph	OHL	29	3	14	17	99	5	1	3	4	13

VAN DORP, WAYNE

Left wing. Shoots left. 6'4", 225 lbs. Born, Vancouver, B.C., May 19, 1961.

			Regular Season					Playoffs				
Season	Club	Lea	GP	G	A	TP	PIM	GP	G	A	TP	PIM
1979-80	Seattle	WHL	68	8	13	21	195	12	3	1	4	33
1980-81	Seattle	WHL	63	22	30	52	242	5	1	0	1	10
1981-82	Heerenveen	Neth.	22	11	7	18	44	12	1	4	5	34
1982-83	Heerenveen	Neth.	23	7	12	19	40	15	4	5	9	20
1984-85	GIJS Groningen	Neth.	29	38	46	84	112	6	6	2	8	23
	Erie	ACHL	7	9	8	17	21	10	0	2	6	2
1985-86a	GIJS Groningen	Neth.	29	19	24	43	81	8	9	*12	21	6
1986-87	Rochester	AHL	47	7	3	10	192	....	....	....	....	....
	Edmonton	**NHL**	**3**	**0**	**0**	**0**	**25**	**3**	**0**	**0**	**0**	**2**
	Nova Scotia	AHL	11	2	3	5	37	5	0	0	0	56
1987-88	**Pittsburgh**	**NHL**	**25**	**1**	**3**	**4**	**75**	....	....	....	....	....
	Nova Scotia	AHL	12	2	2	4	87	....	....	....	....	....
1988-89	Rochester	AHL	28	3	6	9	202	....	....	....	....	....
	Chicago	**NHL**	**8**	**0**	**0**	**0**	**23**	**16**	**0**	**1**	**1**	**17**
	Saginaw	IHL	11	4	3	7	60	....	....	....	....	....
1989-90	**Chicago**	**NHL**	**61**	**7**	**4**	**11**	**303**	**8**	**0**	**0**	**0**	**23**
1990-91	**Quebec**	**NHL**	**4**	**1**	**0**	**1**	**30**	....	....	....	....	....
1991-92	**Quebec**	**NHL**	**24**	**3**	**5**	**8**	**109**	....	....	....	....	....
	Halifax	AHL	15	5	5	10	54	....	....	....	....	....
1992-93	Milwaukee	IHL	19	1	4	5	57	....	....	....	....	....
	NHL Totals		**125**	**12**	**12**	**24**	**565**	**27**	**0**	**1**	**1**	**42**

a Named playoff MVP (1986)

Traded to **Edmonton** by **Buffalo** with Normand Lacombe and future consideration for Lee Fogolin and Mark Napier, March 6, 1987. Traded to **Pittsburgh** by **Edmonton** with Paul Coffey and Dave Hunter for Craig Simpson, Dave Hannan, Moe Mantha, and Chris Joseph, November 24, 1987. Traded to **Buffalo** by **Pittsburgh** for future considerations, September 30, 1988. Traded to **Chicago** by **Buffalo** for Chicago's seventh round choice (Viktor Gordijuk) in 1990 Entry Draft, February 16, 1989. Claimed by **Quebec** in NHL Waiver Draft, October 1, 1990.

VARGA, JOHN

Left wing. Shoots left. 5'9", 172 lbs. Born, Chicago, IL, January 31, 1974.
(Washington's 5th choice, 119th overall, in 1992 Entry Draft).

			Regular Season					Playoffs				
Season	Club	Lea	GP	G	A	TP	PIM	GP	G	A	TP	PIM
1991-92	Tacoma	WHL	72	25	34	59	93	4	1	2	3	0
1992-93	Tacoma	WHL	61	32	32	64	63	7	1	1	2	8

VARIS, PETRI

Left wing. Shoots left. 6'1", 200 lbs. Born, Varkaus, Finland, May 13, 1969.
(San Jose's 7th choice, 132nd overall, in 1993 Entry Draft).

			Regular Season					Playoffs				
Season	Club	Lea	GP	G	A	TP	PIM	GP	G	A	TP	PIM
1990-91	KooKoo	Fin.2	44	20	31	51	42	....	....	....	....	....
1991-92a	Assat	Fin.	36	13	23	36	24	....	....	....	....	....
1992-93	Assat	Fin.	46	14	35	49	42	8	2	2	4	12

a Finnish Rookie of the Year (1992)

VARVIO, JARKKO (VAHR-vee-oh, YAHR-koh)

Right wing. Shoots right. 5'9", 175 lbs. Born, Tampere, Finland, April 28, 1972.
(Minnesota's 1st choice, 34th overall, in 1992 Entry Draft).

			Regular Season					Playoffs				
Season	Club	Lea	GP	G	A	TP	PIM	GP	G	A	TP	PIM
1989-90	Ilves	Fin.	1	0	0	0	0	....	....	....	....	....
1990-91	Ilves	Fin.	37	10	7	17	6	....	....	....	....	....
1991-92	HPK	Fin.	41	25	9	34	6	....	....	....	....	....
1992-93	HPK	Fin.	40	29	19	48	16	12	3	2	5	8

VARY, JOHN

Defense. Shoots right. 6'1", 207 lbs. Born, Owen Sound, Ont., February 11, 1972.
(NY Rangers' 3rd choice, 55th overall, in 1990 Entry Draft).

			Regular Season					Playoffs				
Season	Club	Lea	GP	G	A	TP	PIM	GP	G	A	TP	PIM
1988-89	North Bay	OHL	45	2	7	9	38	3	0	0	0	0
1989-90	North Bay	OHL	59	7	39	46	79	5	0	2	2	8
1990-91	North Bay	OHL	39	5	21	26	108	....	....	....	....	....
	Kingston	OHL	31	5	15	20	16	....	....	....	....	....
1991-92	Kingston	OHL	54	11	38	49	102	....	....	....	....	....
	Binghamton	AHL	1	0	0	0	0	....	....	....	....	....
1992-93	Binghamton	AHL	12	0	2	2	8	....	....	....	....	....
	Phoenix	IHL	9	0	6	6	10	....	....	....	....	....
	Erie	ECHL	46	15	31	46	158	5	1	2	3	20

VASILJEV, ANDREI

Left wing. Shoots right. 5'9", 180 lbs. Born, Voskresensk, Soviet Union, March 30, 1972.
(NY Islanders' 11th choice, 248th overall, in 1992 Entry Draft).

			Regular Season					Playoffs				
Season	Club	Lea	GP	G	A	TP	PIM	GP	G	A	TP	PIM
1991-92	CSKA	CIS	28	7	2	9	2	....	....	....	....	....
1992-93	Khimik	CIS	34	4	8	12	20	....	....	....	....	....

VASKE, DENNIS (VAS-kee)

Defense. Shoots left. 6'2", 210 lbs. Born, Rockford, IL, October 11, 1967.
(NY Islanders' 2nd choice, 38th overall, in 1986 Entry Draft).

			Regular Season					Playoffs				
Season	Club	Lea	GP	G	A	TP	PIM	GP	G	A	TP	PIM
1986-87	Minn.-Duluth	WCHA	33	0	2	2	40	....	....	....	....	....
1987-88	Minn.-Duluth	WCHA	39	1	6	7	90	....	....	....	....	....
1988-89	Minn.-Duluth	WCHA	37	9	19	28	86	....	....	....	....	....
1989-90	Minn.-Duluth	WCHA	37	5	24	29	72	....	....	....	....	....
1990-91	**NY Islanders**	**NHL**	**5**	**0**	**0**	**0**	**2**	....	....	....	....	....
	Capital Dist.	AHL	67	10	10	20	65	....	....	....	....	....
1991-92	**NY Islanders**	**NHL**	**39**	**0**	**1**	**1**	**5**	....	....	....	....	....
	Capital Dist.	AHL	31	1	11	12	59	....	....	....	....	....
1992-93	**NY Islanders**	**NHL**	**27**	**1**	**5**	**6**	**32**	**18**	**0**	**6**	**6**	**14**
	Capital Dist.	AHL	42	4	15	19	70	....	....	....	....	....
	NHL Totals		**71**	**1**	**6**	**7**	**39**	**18**	**0**	**6**	**6**	**14**

VAUHKONEN, JONNI

Right wing. Shoots left. 6'2", 189 lbs. Born, Suonenjoki, Finland, January 1, 1975.
(Chicago's 7th choice, 128th overall, in 1993 Entry Draft).

			Regular Season					Playoffs				
Season	Club	Lea	GP	G	A	TP	PIM	GP	G	A	TP	PIM
1992-93	Reipas	Fin.	41	8	5	13	63	....	....	....	....	....

VEILLEUX, STEVE

Defense. Shoots right. 6', 190 lbs. Born, Lachenaie, Que., March 9, 1969.
(Vancouver's 2nd choice, 45th overall, in 1987 Entry Draft).

			Regular Season					Playoffs				
Season	Club	Lea	GP	G	A	TP	PIM	GP	G	A	TP	PIM
1985-86	Trois-Rivières	QMJHL	67	1	20	21	132	5	0	0	0	13
1986-87	Trois-Rivières	QMJHL	62	6	22	28	227	....	....	....	....	....
1987-88a	Trois-Rivières	QMJHL	63	7	25	32	150	....	....	....	....	....
1988-89a	Trois-Rivières	QMJHL	49	5	28	33	149	4	0	0	0	10
	Milwaukee	IHL	1	0	0	0	0	4	0	0	0	13
1989-90	Milwaukee	IHL	76	4	12	16	195	2	0	0	0	2
1990-91	Milwaukee	IHL	58	0	9	9	152	....	....	....	....	....
	Indianapolis	IHL	11	1	3	4	30	7	0	3	3	13
1991-92	Fredericton	AHL	53	3	7	10	122	....	....	....	....	....
1992-93	Fredericton	AHL	63	3	11	14	94	1	0	0	0	4

a QMJHL Second All-Star Team (1988, 1989)

Signed as a free agent by **Montreal**, August 6, 1991.

VELISCHEK, RANDY (VEHL-ih-shehk)

Defense. Shoots left. 6', 200 lbs. Born, Montreal, Que., February 10, 1962.
(Minneota's 3rd choice, 53rd overall, in 1980 Entry Draft).

			Regular Season					Playoffs				
Season	Club	Lea	GP	G	A	TP	PIM	GP	G	A	TP	PIM
1979-80	Providence	ECAC	31	5	5	10	20	....	....	....	....	....
1980-81	Providence	ECAC	33	3	12	15	26	....	....	....	....	....
1981-82a	Providence	ECAC	33	1	14	15	38	....	....	....	....	....
1982-83bc	Providence	ECAC	41	18	34	52	50	....	....	....	....	....
	Minnesota	**NHL**	**3**	**0**	**0**	**0**	**2**	**9**	**0**	**0**	**0**	**0**
1983-84	**Minnesota**	**NHL**	**33**	**2**	**2**	**4**	**10**	**1**	**0**	**0**	**0**	**0**
	Salt Lake	CHL	43	7	21	28	54	5	0	3	3	2
1984-85	**Minnesota**	**NHL**	**52**	**4**	**9**	**13**	**26**	**9**	**2**	**3**	**5**	**8**
	Springfield	AHL	26	2	7	9	22	....	....	....	....	....
1985-86	**New Jersey**	**NHL**	**47**	**2**	**7**	**9**	**39**	....	....	....	....	....
	Maine	AHL	21	0	4	4	4	....	....	....	....	....
1986-87	**New Jersey**	**NHL**	**64**	**2**	**16**	**18**	**52**	....	....	....	....	....
1987-88	**New Jersey**	**NHL**	**51**	**3**	**9**	**12**	**66**	**19**	**0**	**2**	**2**	**20**
1988-89	**New Jersey**	**NHL**	**80**	**4**	**14**	**18**	**70**	....	....	....	....	....
1989-90	**New Jersey**	**NHL**	**62**	**0**	**6**	**6**	**72**	**6**	**0**	**0**	**0**	**4**
1990-91	**Quebec**	**NHL**	**79**	**2**	**10**	**12**	**42**	....	....	....	....	....
1991-92	**Quebec**	**NHL**	**38**	**2**	**3**	**5**	**22**	....	....	....	....	....
	Halifax	AHL	16	3	6	9	0	....	....	....	....	....
1992-93	Halifax	AHL	49	6	16	22	18	....	....	....	....	....
	NHL Totals		**509**	**21**	**76**	**97**	**401**	**44**	**2**	**5**	**7**	**32**

a ECAC Second All-Star Team (1982)
b ECAC First All-Star Team (1983)
c Named ECAC Player of the Year (1983)

Claimed by **New Jersey** from **Minnesota** in NHL Waiver Draft, October 7, 1985. Traded to **Quebec** by **New Jersey** to complete March 6, 1990 trade which sent Peter Stastny to New Jersey for Craig Wolanin and future considerations, August 13, 1990.

VERBEEK, PATRICK (PAT) (vuhr-BEEK)

Right/Left wing. Shoots right. 5'9", 190 lbs. Born, Sarnia, Ont., May 24, 1964.
(New Jersey's 3rd choice, 43rd overall, in 1982 Entry Draft).

			Regular Season					Playoffs				
Season	Club	Lea	GP	G	A	TP	PIM	GP	G	A	TP	PIM
1981-82	Sudbury	OHL	66	37	51	88	180	....	....	....	....	....
1982-83	**New Jersey**	**NHL**	**6**	**3**	**2**	**5**	**8**	....	....	....	....	....
	Sudbury	OHL	61	40	67	107	184	....	....	....	....	....
1983-84	**New Jersey**	**NHL**	**79**	**20**	**27**	**47**	**158**	....	....	....	....	....
1984-85	**New Jersey**	**NHL**	**78**	**15**	**18**	**33**	**162**	....	....	....	....	....
1985-86	**New Jersey**	**NHL**	**76**	**25**	**28**	**53**	**79**	....	....	....	....	....
1986-87	**New Jersey**	**NHL**	**74**	**35**	**24**	**59**	**120**	....	....	....	....	....
1987-88	**New Jersey**	**NHL**	**73**	**46**	**31**	**77**	**227**	**20**	**4**	**8**	**12**	**51**
1988-89	**New Jersey**	**NHL**	**77**	**26**	**21**	**47**	**189**	....	....	....	....	....
1989-90	**Hartford**	**NHL**	**80**	**44**	**45**	**89**	**228**	**7**	**2**	**2**	**4**	**26**
1990-91	**Hartford**	**NHL**	**80**	**43**	**39**	**82**	**246**	**6**	**3**	**2**	**5**	**40**
1991-92	**Hartford**	**NHL**	**76**	**22**	**35**	**57**	**243**	**7**	**0**	**2**	**2**	**12**
1992-93	**Hartford**	**NHL**	**84**	**39**	**43**	**82**	**197**	....	....	....	....	....
	NHL Totals		**783**	**318**	**313**	**631**	**1857**	**40**	**9**	**14**	**23**	**129**

Played in NHL All-Star Game (1991)

Traded to **Hartford** by **New Jersey** for Sylvain Turgeon, June 17, 1989.

VERMETTE, MARK

Right wing. Shoots right. 6'1", 203 lbs. Born, Cochenour, Ont., October 3, 1967.
(Quebec's 8th choice, 134th overall, in 1986 Entry Draft).

			Regular Season					Playoffs				
Season	Club	Lea	GP	G	A	TP	PIM	GP	G	A	TP	PIM
1985-86	Lake Superior	CCHA	32	1	4	5	7	....	....	....	....	....
1986-87	Lake Superior	CCHA	38	19	17	36	59	....	....	....	....	....
1987-88abc	Lake Superior	CCHA	46	*45	30	75	154	....	....	....	....	....
1988-89	**Quebec**	**NHL**	**12**	**0**	**4**	**4**	**7**	....	....	....	....	....
	Halifax	AHL	52	12	16	28	30	1	0	0	0	0
1989-90	**Quebec**	**NHL**	**11**	**1**	**5**	**6**	**8**	....	....	....	....	....
	Halifax	AHL	47	20	17	37	44	6	1	5	6	6
1990-91	**Quebec**	**NHL**	**34**	**3**	**4**	**7**	**10**	....	....	....	....	....
	Halifax	AHL	46	26	22	48	37	....	....	....	....	....
1991-92	**Quebec**	**NHL**	**10**	**1**	**0**	**1**	**8**	....	....	....	....	....
	Halifax	AHL	44	21	18	39	39	....	....	....	....	....
1992-93	Halifax	AHL	67	42	37	79	32	....	....	....	....	....
	NHL Totals		**67**	**5**	**13**	**18**	**33**	....	....	....	....	....

a NCAA West All-American Team (1988)
b CCHA Player of the Year (1988)
c CCHA First All-Star Team (1988)

VESEY, JIM

Center/Right wing. Shoots right. 6'1", 202 lbs. Born, Columbus, MA, October 29, 1965.
(St. Louis' 11th choice, 155th overall, in 1984 Entry Draft).

			Regular Season					Playoffs				
Season	Club	Lea	GP	G	A	TP	PIM	GP	G	A	TP	PIM
1984-85	Merrimack	NCAA	33	19	11	30	28	....	....	....	....	....
1985-86	Merrimack	NCAA	32	29	32	61	67	....	....	....	....	....
1986-87	Merrimack	NCAA	35	22	36	58	57	....	....	....	....	....
1987-88	Merrimack	NCAA	33	33	50	83	....	....	....	....	....	....
1988-89	**St. Louis**	**NHL**	**5**	**1**	**1**	**2**	**7**	....	....	....	....	....
a	Peoria	IHL	76	47	46	93	137	4	1	2	3	6
1989-90	**St. Louis**	**NHL**	**6**	**0**	**1**	**1**	**0**	....	....	....	....	....
	Peoria	IHL	60	47	44	91	75	5	1	3	4	21
1990-91	Peoria	IHL	58	32	41	73	69	19	4	14	18	26
1991-92	**Boston**	**NHL**	**4**	**0**	**0**	**0**	**0**	....	....	....	....	....
	Maine	AHL	10	6	7	13	13	....	....	....	....	....
1992-93	Providence	AHL	71	38	39	77	42	6	2	5	7	4
	NHL Totals		**15**	**1**	**2**	**3**	**7**	....	....	....	....	....

a IHL First All-Star Team (1989)

Traded to **Winnipeg** by **St. Louis** to complete February 28, 1991 trade which sent Tom Draper to St. Louis for future considerations, May 24, 1991. Traded to **Boston** by **Winnipeg** for future considerations, June 20, 1991.

VIAL, DENNIS   (vee-AHL)

Defense. Shoots left. 6'1", 215 lbs.   Born, Sault Ste. Marie, Ont., April 10, 1969.
(NY Rangers' 5th choice, 110th overall, in 1988 Entry Draft).

			Regular Season					Playoffs				
Season	Club	Lea	GP	G	A	TP	PIM	GP	G	A	TP	PIM
1985-86	Hamilton	OHL	31	1	1	2	66	....	....	....	....	....
1986-87	Hamilton	OHL	53	1	8	9	194	8	0	0	0	8
1987-88	Hamilton	OHL	52	3	17	20	229	13	2	2	4	49
1988-89	Niagara Falls	OHL	50	10	27	37	227	15	1	7	8	44
1989-90	Flint	IHL	79	6	29	35	351	4	0	0	0	10
1990-91	**NY Rangers**	**NHL**	21	0	0	0	61	....	....	....	....	....
	Binghamton	AHL	40	2	7	9	250	....	....	....	....	....
	Detroit	**NHL**	9	0	0	0	16	....	....	....	....	....
1991-92	**Detroit**	**NHL**	27	1	0	1	72	....	....	....	....	....
	Adirondack	AHL	20	2	4	6	107	17	1	3	4	43
1992-93	**Detroit**	**NHL**	9	0	1	1	20	....	....	....	....	....
	Adirondack	AHL	30	2	11	13	177	11	1	1	2	14
	NHL Totals		**66**	**1**	**1**	**2**	**169**	....	....	....	....	....

Traded to **Detroit** by **NY Rangers** with Kevin Miller and Jim Cummins for Joey Kocur and Per Djoos, March 5, 1991. Traded to **Quebec** by **Detroit** with Doug Crossman for cash, June 15, 1992. Traded to **Detroit** by **Quebec** for cash, September 9, 1992. Traded to **Tampa Bay** by **Detroit** for Steve Maltais, June 8, 1993. Claimed by **Anaheim** from **Tampa Bay** in Expansion Draft, June 24, 1993. Claimed by **Ottawa** from **Anaheim** in Phase II of Expansion Draft, June 25, 1993.

VIITAKOSKI, VESA

Left wing. Shoots left. 6'2", 200 lbs.   Born, Lappeenranta, Finland, February 13, 1971.
(Calgary's 3rd choice, 32nd overall, in 1990 Entry Draft).

			Regular Season					Playoffs				
Season	Club	Lea	GP	G	A	TP	PIM	GP	G	A	TP	PIM
1988-89	SaiPa	Fin.	11	4	1	5	6	....	....	....	....	....
1989-90	SaiPa	Fin.	44	24	10	34	8	....	....	....	....	....
1990-91	Tappara	Fin.	41	17	23	40	14	3	2	0	2	4
1991-92	Tappara	Fin.	44	19	19	38	39	....	....	....	....	....
1992-93	Tappara	Fin.	48	27	27	54	28	....	....	....	....	....

VILGRAIN, CLAUDE

Right wing. Shoots right. 6'1", 205 lbs.   Born, Port-au-Prince, Haiti, March 1, 1963.
(Detroit's 6th choice, 107th overall, in 1982 Entry Draft).

			Regular Season					Playoffs				
Season	Club	Lea	GP	G	A	TP	PIM	GP	G	A	TP	PIM
1983-84	U. of Moncton	AUAA	20	11	20	31	8	....	....	....	....	....
1984-85	U. of Moncton	AUAA	24	35	28	63	20	....	....	....	....	....
1985-86	U. of Moncton	AUAA	19	17	20	37	25	....	....	....	....	....
1986-87	Cdn. Olympic	....	78	28	42	70	38	....	....	....	....	....
1987-88	Cdn. National	....	61	21	20	41	41	....	....	....	....	....
	Cdn. Olympic	....	6	0	0	0	0	....	....	....	....	....
	Vancouver	**NHL**	6	1	1	2	0	....	....	....	....	....
1988-89	Milwaukee	IHL	23	9	13	22	26	....	....	....	....	....
	Utica	AHL	55	23	30	53	41	5	0	2	2	2
1989-90	**New Jersey**	**NHL**	6	1	2	3	4	4	0	0	0	0
	Utica	AHL	73	37	52	89	32	....	....	....	....	....
1990-91	Utica	AHL	59	32	46	78	26	....	....	....	....	....
1991-92	**New Jersey**	**NHL**	71	19	27	46	74	7	1	1	2	17
1992-93	**New Jersey**	**NHL**	4	0	2	2	0	....	....	....	....	....
	Utica	AHL	22	6	8	14	4	5	0	1	1	0
	Cincinnati	IHL	57	19	26	45	22	....	....	....	....	....
	NHL Totals		**87**	**21**	**32**	**53**	**78**	**11**	**1**	**1**	**2**	**17**

Signed as a free agent by **Vancouver**, June 18, 1987. Traded to **New Jersey** by **Vancouver** for Tim Lenardon, March 7, 1989. Signed as a free agent by **Philadelphia**, August 3, 1993.

VINCELETTE, DANIEL

Left wing. Shoots left. 6'2", 202 lbs.   Born, Verdun, Que., August 1, 1967.
(Chicago's 3rd choice, 74th overall, in 1985 Entry Draft).

			Regular Season					Playoffs				
Season	Club	Lea	GP	G	A	TP	PIM	GP	G	A	TP	PIM
1984-85	Drummondville	QMJHL	64	11	24	35	124	12	0	1	1	11
1985-86	Drummondville	QMJHL	70	37	47	84	234	22	11	14	25	40
1986-87	Drummondville	QMJHL	50	34	35	69	288	8	6	5	11	17
	Chicago	**NHL**	....	....	....	....	....	3	0	0	0	0
1987-88	**Chicago**	**NHL**	69	6	11	17	109	4	0	0	0	0
1988-89	**Chicago**	**NHL**	66	11	4	15	119	5	0	0	0	4
	Saginaw	IHL	2	0	0	0	14	....	....	....	....	....
1989-90	**Chicago**	**NHL**	2	0	0	0	4	....	....	....	....	....
	Indianapolis	IHL	49	16	13	29	262	....	....	....	....	....
	Quebec	**NHL**	11	0	1	1	25	....	....	....	....	....
1990-91	**Quebec**	**NHL**	16	0	1	1	38	....	....	....	....	....
	Halifax	AHL	24	4	9	13	85	....	....	....	....	....
	Indianapolis	IHL	15	5	3	8	51	7	2	1	3	62
1991-92	**Chicago**	**NHL**	29	3	5	8	56	....	....	....	....	....
	Indianapolis	IHL	16	5	3	8	84	....	....	....	....	....
1992-93	Atlanta	IHL	30	5	5	10	126	....	....	....	....	....
	San Diego	IHL	6	0	0	0	6	....	....	....	....	....
	NHL Totals		**193**	**20**	**22**	**42**	**351**	**12**	**0**	**0**	**0**	**4**

Traded to **Quebec** by **Chicago** with Mario Doyon and Everett Sanipass for Greg Millen, Michel Goulet and Quebec's sixth round choice (Kevin St. Jacques) in 1991 Entry Draft, March 5, 1990. Traded to **Chicago** by **Quebec** with Paul Gillis for Ryan McGill and Mike McNeil, March 5, 1991. Claimed by **Tampa Bay** from **Chicago** in Expansion Draft, June 18, 1992. Traded to **Philadelphia** by **Tampa Bay** for Steve Kasper, December 8, 1992.

VINCENT, PAUL

Center. Shoots left. 6'4", 200 lbs.   Born, Utica, NY, January 4, 1975.
(Toronto's 4th choice, 149th overall, in 1993 Entry Draft).

			Regular Season					Playoffs				
Season	Club	Lea	GP	G	A	TP	PIM	GP	G	A	TP	PIM
1991-92	Cushing	HS	30	22	41	63	16	....	....	....	....	....
1992-93	Cushing	HS	25	30	32	62	62	....	....	....	....	....

VISHEAU, MARK

Defense. Shoots right. 6'5", 201 lbs.   Born, Burlington, Ont., June 27, 1973.
(Winnipeg's 4th choice, 84th overall, in 1992 Entry Draft).

			Regular Season					Playoffs				
Season	Club	Lea	GP	G	A	TP	PIM	GP	G	A	TP	PIM
1990-91	London	OHL	59	4	11	15	40	7	0	1	1	6
1991-92	London	OHL	66	5	31	36	104	10	0	4	4	27
1992-93	London	OHL	62	8	52	60	88	12	0	5	5	26

VITOLINSH, HARIJS   (VEE-toh-leensh)

Center. Shoots left. 6'3", 205 lbs.   Born, Riga, Soviet Union, April 30, 1968.
(Montreal's 10th choice, 188th overall, in 1988 Entry Draft).

			Regular Season					Playoffs				
Season	Club	Lea	GP	G	A	TP	PIM	GP	G	A	TP	PIM
1986-87	Dynamo Riga	USSR	17	1	1	2	8	....	....	....	....	....
1987-88	Dynamo Riga	USSR	30	3	3	6	24	....	....	....	....	....
1988-89	Dynamo Riga	USSR	36	3	2	5	16	....	....	....	....	....
1989-90	Dynamo Riga	USSR	45	7	6	13	18	....	....	....	....	....
1990-91	Dynamo Riga	USSR	46	12	19	31	22	....	....	....	....	....
1991-92	Riga	CIS	30	12	5	17	10	....	....	....	....	....
1992-93	Chur	Switz.	17	12	6	18	23	....	....	....	....	....
	Thunder Bay	Col.	8	6	7	13	12	....	....	....	....	....
	New Haven	AHL	7	6	3	9	4	....	....	....	....	....

Re-entered NHL Entry Draft. **Winnipeg's** 12th choice, 228th overall in 1993 Entry Draft.

VLASAK, TOMAS

Center. Shoots right. 5'10", 161 lbs.   Born, Prague, Czech., February 1, 1975.
(Los Angeles' 6th choice, 120th overall, in 1993 Entry Draft).

			Regular Season					Playoffs				
Season	Club	Lea	GP	G	A	TP	PIM	GP	G	A	TP	PIM
1992-93	Slavia Praha	Czech.2	31	17	6	23	....	....	....	....	....	....

VOLEK, DAVID   (VOH-lehk)

Left/Right wing. Shoots left. 6', 185 lbs.   Born, Prague, Czechoslovakia, June 18, 1966.
(NY Islanders' 11th choice, 208th overall, in 1984 Entry Draft).

			Regular Season					Playoffs				
Season	Club	Lea	GP	G	A	TP	PIM	GP	G	A	TP	PIM
1984-85	Sparta Praha	Czech.	32	5	5	10	14	....	....	....	....	....
1985-86	Sparta Praha	Czech.	35	10	7	17	....	....	....	....	....	....
1986-87	Sparta Praha	Czech.	39	27	25	52	38	....	....	....	....	....
1987-88	Sparta Praha	Czech.	42	29	18	47	58	....	....	....	....	....
1988-89a	**NY Islanders**	**NHL**	77	25	34	59	24	....	....	....	....	....
1989-90	**NY Islanders**	**NHL**	80	17	22	39	41	5	1	4	5	0
1990-91	**NY Islanders**	**NHL**	77	22	34	56	57	....	....	....	....	....
1991-92	**NY Islanders**	**NHL**	74	18	42	60	35	....	....	....	....	....
1992-93	**NY Islanders**	**NHL**	56	8	13	21	34	10	4	1	5	2
	NHL Totals		**364**	**90**	**145**	**235**	**191**	**15**	**5**	**5**	**10**	**2**

a   NHL All-Rookie Team (1989)

VOLKOV, MIKHAIL   (vohl-KOHV)

Right wing. Shoots left. 5'10", 174 lbs.   Born, Voronezh, Soviet Union, March 9, 1972.
(Buffalo's 12th choice, 233rd overall, in 1991 Entry Draft).

			Regular Season					Playoffs				
Season	Club	Lea	GP	G	A	TP	PIM	GP	G	A	TP	PIM
1989-90	Soviet Wings	USSR	24	0	2	2	4	....	....	....	....	....
1990-91	Soviet Wings	USSR	40	8	4	12	8	....	....	....	....	....
1991-92	Soviet Wings	CIS	37	3	6	9	16	....	....	....	....	....
1992-93	Soviet Wings	CIS	33	9	6	15	11	5	0	1	1	2

VOLOGZHANINOV, IVAN

Right wing. Shoots left. 6', 180 lbs.   Born, Kiev, Soviet Union, April 7, 1974.
(Winnipeg's 12th choice, 254th overall, in 1992 Entry Draft).

			Regular Season					Playoffs				
Season	Club	Lea	GP	G	A	TP	PIM	GP	G	A	TP	PIM
1990-91	Sokol Kiev	CIS	3	0	1	1	0	....	....	....	....	....
1991-92	Sokol Kiev	CIS	23	2	2	4	4	....	....	....	....	....
1992-93	Lethbridge	WHL	71	48	60	108	12	4	1	2	3	2

VON STEFENELLI, PHILIP

Defense. Shoots left. 6'1", 200 lbs.   Born, Vancouver, B.C., April 10, 1969.
(Vancouver's 5th choice, 122nd overall, in 1988 Entry Draft).

			Regular Season					Playoffs				
Season	Club	Lea	GP	G	A	TP	PIM	GP	G	A	TP	PIM
1987-88	Boston U.	H.E.	34	3	13	16	38	....	....	....	....	....
1988-89	Boston U.	H.E.	33	2	6	8	34	....	....	....	....	....
1989-90	Boston U.	H.E.	44	8	20	28	40	....	....	....	....	....
1990-91	Boston U.	H.E.	41	7	23	30	32	....	....	....	....	....
1991-92	Milwaukee	IHL	80	2	34	36	40	5	1	2	3	2
1992-93	Hamilton	AHL	78	11	20	31	75	....	....	....	....	....

VOPAT, JAN   (VOH-paht)

Defense. Shoots left. 6', 198 lbs.   Born, Most, Czech., March 22, 1973.
(Hartford's 3rd choice, 57th overall, in 1992 Entry Draft).

			Regular Season					Playoffs				
Season	Club	Lea	GP	G	A	TP	PIM	GP	G	A	TP	PIM
1990-91	Litvinov	Czech.	25	1	4	5	4	....	....	....	....	....
1991-92	Litvinov	Czech.	46	4	2	6	16	....	....	....	....	....
1992-93	Litvinov	Czech.	45	12	10	22	....	....	....	....	....	....

VOROBJEV, VLADIMIR

Left wing. Shoots right. 5'11", 185 lbs.   Born, Cherepovets, Soviet Union, October 2, 1972.
(NY Rangers' 10th choice, 240th overall, in 1992 Entry Draft).

			Regular Season					Playoffs				
Season	Club	Lea	GP	G	A	TP	PIM	GP	G	A	TP	PIM
1991-92	Cherepovets	CIS 2			UNAVAILABLE			....	....	....	....	....
1992-93	Cherepovets	CIS	42	18	5	23	18	....	....	....	....	....

VUJTEK, VLADIMIR (VOI-tek)

Left wing. Shoots left. 6', 190 lbs. Born, Ostrava, Czech., February 17, 1972.
(Montreal's 4th choice, 73rd overall, in 1991 Entry Draft).

			Regular Season					Playoffs				
Season	Club	Lea	GP	G	A	TP	PIM	GP	G	A	TP	PIM
1988-89	TJ Vitkovice	Czech.	3	0	1	1	0	....	....	....	....	....
1989-90	TJ Vitkovice	Czech.	29	7	7	14	....	....	....	....	....	....
1990-91	TJ Vitkovice	Czech.	26	7	4	11	....	....	....	....	....	....
	Tri-City	WHL	37	26	18	44	25	7	2	3	5	4
1991-92	**Montreal**	**NHL**	**2**	**0**	**0**	**0**	**0**	....	....	....	....	....
a	Tri-City	WHL	53	41	61	102	114	....	....	....	....	....
1992-93	**Edmonton**	**NHL**	**30**	**1**	**10**	**11**	**8**	....	....	....	....	....
	Cape Breton	AHL	20	10	9	19	14	1	0	0	0	0
	NHL Totals		**32**	**1**	**10**	**11**	**8**	....	....	....	....	....

a WHL West First All-Star Team (1992)

Traded to **Edmonton** by **Montreal** with Shayne Corson and Brent Gilchrist for Vincent Damphousse and Edmonton's fourth round choice (Adam Wiesel) in 1993 Entry Draft, August 27, 1992.

VUKONICH, MICHAEL

Center. Shoots left. 6'1", 190 lbs. Born, Duluth, MN, May 11, 1968.
(Los Angeles' 4th choice, 90th overall, in 1987 Entry Draft).

			Regular Season					Playoffs				
Season	Club	Lea	GP	G	A	TP	PIM	GP	G	A	TP	PIM
1987-88	Harvard	ECAC	32	9	14	23	24	....	....	....	....	....
1988-89	Harvard	ECAC	27	11	8	19	12	....	....	....	....	....
1989-90a	Harvard	ECAC	27	22	29	51	18	....	....	....	....	....
1990-91b	Harvard	ECAC	27	*31	23	54	28	....	....	....	....	....
1991-92	Phoenix	IHL	68	17	11	28	21	....	....	....	....	....
1992-93	Phoenix	IHL	70	25	15	40	27	....	....	....	....	....

a ECAC First All-Star Team (1990)
b ECAC Second All-Star Team (1991)

VUKOTA, MICK

Right wing. Shoots right. 6'2", 195 lbs. Born, Saskatoon, Sask., September 14, 1966.

			Regular Season					Playoffs				
Season	Club	Lea	GP	G	A	TP	PIM	GP	G	A	TP	PIM
1983-84	Winnipeg	WHL	3	1	1	2	10	....	....	....	....	....
1984-85	Kelowna	WHL	66	10	6	16	247	....	....	....	....	....
1985-86	Spokane	WHL	64	19	14	33	369	9	6	4	10	68
1986-87	Spokane	WHL	61	25	28	53	*337	4	0	0	0	40
1987-88	**NY Islanders**	**NHL**	**17**	**1**	**0**	**1**	**82**	**2**	**0**	**0**	**0**	**23**
	Springfield	AHL	52	7	9	16	375	....	....	....	....	....
1988-89	**NY Islanders**	**NHL**	**48**	**2**	**2**	**4**	**237**	....	....	....	....	....
	Springfield	AHL	3	1	0	1	33	....	....	....	....	....
1989-90	**NY Islanders**	**NHL**	**76**	**4**	**8**	**12**	**290**	**1**	**0**	**0**	**0**	**17**
1990-91	**NY Islanders**	**NHL**	**60**	**2**	**4**	**6**	**238**	....	....	....	....	....
	Capital Dist.	AHL	2	0	0	0	9	....	....	....	....	....
1991-92	**NY Islanders**	**NHL**	**74**	**0**	**6**	**6**	**293**	....	....	....	....	....
1992-93	**NY Islanders**	**NHL**	**74**	**2**	**5**	**7**	**216**	**15**	**0**	**0**	**0**	**16**
	NHL Totals		**349**	**11**	**25**	**36**	**1356**	**18**	**0**	**0**	**0**	**56**

Signed as a free agent by **NY Islanders**, March 2, 1987.

VYBORNY, DAVID

Center. Shoots left. 5'10", 172 lbs. Born, Jihlava, Czech., January 22, 1975.
(Edmonton's 3rd choice, 33rd overall, in 1993 Entry Draft).

			Regular Season					Playoffs				
Season	Club	Lea	GP	G	A	TP	PIM	GP	G	A	TP	PIM
1990-91	Sparta Praha	Czech.	3	0	0	0	0	....	....	....	....	....
1991-92a	Sparta Praha	Czech.	32	6	9	15	2	....	....	....	....	....
1992-93	Sparta Praha	Czech.	52	20	24	44	....	....	....	....	....	....

a Czech. Rookie of the Year (1992)

WAINWRIGHT, DAVID

Defense. Shoots left. 6', 193 lbs. Born, Boston, MA, January 17, 1974.
(NY Islanders' 10th choice, 224th overall, in 1992 Entry Draft).

			Regular Season					Playoffs				
Season	Club	Lea	GP	G	A	TP	PIM	GP	G	A	TP	PIM
1991-92	Thayer Academy	....	25	4	25	29	0	....	....	....	....	....
1992-93					UNAVAILABLE							

WALKER, JEFF

Defense. Shoots left. 6'4", 190 lbs. Born, Sudbury, Ont., February 6, 1974.
(Detroit's 9th choice, 214th overall, in 1992 Entry Draft).

			Regular Season					Playoffs				
Season	Club	Lea	GP	G	A	TP	PIM	GP	G	A	TP	PIM
1991-92	Peterborough	OHL	40	2	1	3	18	6	0	1	1	0
1992-93	Peterborough	OHL	53	3	5	8	21	20	0	3	3	14

WALKER, SCOTT

Defense. Shoots right. 5'9", 170 lbs. Born, Montreal, Que., July 19, 1973.
(Vancouver's 4th choice, 124th overall, in 1993 Entry Draft).

			Regular Season					Playoffs				
Season	Club	Lea	GP	G	A	TP	PIM	GP	G	A	TP	PIM
1991-92	Owen Sound	OHL	53	7	31	38	128	5	0	7	7	8
1992-93a	Owen Sound	OHL	57	23	68	91	110	8	1	5	6	16

a OHL Second All-Star Team (1993)

WALTER, RYAN WILLIAM

Center/Left wing. Shoots left. 6', 200 lbs. Born, New Westminster, B.C., April 23, 1958.
(Washington's 1st choice, 2nd overall, in 1978 Amateur Draft).

			Regular Season					Playoffs				
Season	Club	Lea	GP	G	A	TP	PIM	GP	G	A	TP	PIM
1974-75	Kamloops	WHL	9	8	4	12	2	2	1	1	2	2
1975-76	Kamloops	WHL	72	35	49	84	96	12	3	9	12	10
1976-77	Kamloops	WHL	71	41	58	99	100	5	1	3	4	11
1977-78abc	Seattle	WHL	62	54	71	125	148	....	....	....	....	....
1978-79	**Washington**	**NHL**	**69**	**28**	**28**	**56**	**70**	....	....	....	....	....
1979-80	**Washington**	**NHL**	**80**	**24**	**42**	**66**	**106**	....	....	....	....	....
1980-81	**Washington**	**NHL**	**80**	**24**	**44**	**68**	**150**	....	....	....	....	....
1981-82	**Washington**	**NHL**	**78**	**38**	**49**	**87**	**142**	....	....	....	....	....
1982-83	**Montreal**	**NHL**	**80**	**29**	**46**	**75**	**40**	**3**	**0**	**0**	**0**	**11**
1983-84	**Montreal**	**NHL**	**73**	**20**	**29**	**49**	**83**	**15**	**2**	**1**	**3**	**4**
1984-85	**Montreal**	**NHL**	**72**	**19**	**19**	**38**	**59**	**12**	**2**	**7**	**9**	**13**
1985-86	**Montreal**	**NHL**	**69**	**15**	**34**	**49**	**45**	**5**	**0**	**1**	**1**	**2**
1986-87	**Montreal**	**NHL**	**76**	**23**	**23**	**46**	**34**	**17**	**7**	**12**	**19**	**10**
1987-88	**Montreal**	**NHL**	**61**	**13**	**23**	**36**	**39**	**11**	**2**	**4**	**6**	**6**
1988-89	**Montreal**	**NHL**	**78**	**14**	**17**	**31**	**48**	**21**	**3**	**5**	**8**	**6**
1989-90	**Montreal**	**NHL**	**70**	**8**	**16**	**24**	**59**	**11**	**0**	**2**	**2**	**0**
1990-91	**Montreal**	**NHL**	**25**	**0**	**1**	**1**	**12**	**5**	**0**	**0**	**0**	**2**
1991-92d	**Vancouver**	**NHL**	**67**	**6**	**11**	**17**	**49**	**13**	**0**	**3**	**3**	**8**
1992-93	**Vancouver**	**NHL**	**25**	**3**	**0**	**3**	**10**	....	....	....	....	....
	NHL Totals		**1003**	**264**	**382**	**646**	**946**	**113**	**16**	**35**	**51**	**62**

a WHL Most Valuable Player (1978)
b WHL Player of the Year (1978)
c WHL First All-Star Team (1978)
d Won Bud Light/NHL Man of the Year Award (1992)

Played in NHL All-Star Game (1983)

Traded to **Montreal** by **Washington** with Rick Green for Rod Langway, Brian Engblom, Doug Jarvis and Craig Laughlin, September 9, 1982. Signed as a free agent by **Vancouver**, July 26, 1991.

WALZ, WES

Center. Shoots right. 5'10", 180 lbs. Born, Calgary, Alta., May 15, 1970.
(Boston's 3rd choice, 57th overall, in 1989 Entry Draft).

			Regular Season					Playoffs				
Season	Club	Lea	GP	G	A	TP	PIM	GP	G	A	TP	PIM
1988-89a	Lethbridge	WHL	63	29	75	104	32	8	1	5	6	6
1989-90	**Boston**	**NHL**	**2**	**1**	**1**	**2**	**0**	....	....	....	....	....
b	Lethbridge	WHL	56	54	86	140	69	19	13	*24	*37	33
1990-91	**Boston**	**NHL**	**56**	**8**	**8**	**16**	**32**	**2**	**0**	**0**	**0**	**0**
	Maine	AHL	20	8	12	20	19	2	0	0	0	21
1991-92	**Boston**	**NHL**	**15**	**0**	**3**	**3**	**12**	....	....	....	....	....
	Maine	AHL	21	13	11	24	38	....	....	....	....	....
	Philadelphia	**NHL**	**2**	**1**	**0**	**1**	**0**	....	....	....	....	....
	Hershey	AHL	41	13	28	41	37	6	1	2	3	0
1992-93	Hershey	AHL	78	35	45	80	106	....	....	....	....	....
	NHL Totals		**75**	**10**	**12**	**22**	**44**	**2**	**0**	**0**	**0**	**0**

a WHL Rookie of the Year (1989)
b WHL East First All-Star Team (1990)

Traded to **Philadelphia** by **Boston** with Garry Galley and future considerations for Gord Murphy, Brian Dobbin and Philadelphia's third round choice (Sergei Zholtok) in 1992 Entry Draft, January 2, 1992.

WARD, AARON

Defense. Shoots right. 6'2", 200 lbs. Born, Windsor, Ont., January 17, 1973.
(Winnipeg's 1st choice, 5th overall, in 1991 Entry Draft).

			Regular Season					Playoffs				
Season	Club	Lea	GP	G	A	TP	PIM	GP	G	A	TP	PIM
1990-91	U. of Michigan	CCHA	46	8	11	19	126	....	....	....	....	....
1991-92	U. of Michigan	CCHA	42	7	12	19	64	....	....	....	....	....
1992-93	U. of Michigan	CCHA	30	5	8	13	73	....	....	....	....	....
	Cdn. National	....	4	0	0	0	8	....	....	....	....	....

Traded to **Detroit** by **Winnipeg** with Toronto's fourth round choice (previously acquired by Winnipeg — later traded to Detroit — Detroit selected John Jakopin) in 1993 Entry Draft for Paul Ysebaert and future considerations (Alan Kerr, June 18, 1993), June 11, 1993.

WARD, DIXON

Right wing. Shoots right. 6', 200 lbs. Born, Leduc, Alta., September 23, 1968.
(Vancouver's 6th choice, 128th overall, in 1988 Entry Draft).

			Regular Season					Playoffs				
Season	Club	Lea	GP	G	A	TP	PIM	GP	G	A	TP	PIM
1988-89	North Dakota	WCHA	37	8	9	17	26	....	....	....	....	....
1989-90	North Dakota	WCHA	45	35	34	69	44	....	....	....	....	....
1990-91a	North Dakota	WCHA	43	34	35	69	84	....	....	....	....	....
1991-92a	North Dakota	WCHA	38	33	31	64	90	....	....	....	....	....
1992-93	**Vancouver**	**NHL**	**70**	**22**	**30**	**52**	**82**	**9**	**2**	**3**	**5**	**0**
	NHL Totals		**70**	**22**	**30**	**52**	**82**	**9**	**2**	**3**	**5**	**0**

a WCHA Second All-Star Team (1991, 1992)

WARD, EDWARD

Right wing. Shoots right. 6'3", 190 lbs. Born, Edmonton, Alta., November 10, 1969.
(Quebec's 7th choice, 108th overall, in 1988 Entry Draft).

			Regular Season					Playoffs				
Season	Club	Lea	GP	G	A	TP	PIM	GP	G	A	TP	PIM
1987-88	N. Michigan	WCHA	25	0	2	2	40	....	....	....	....	....
1988-89	N. Michigan	WCHA	42	5	15	20	36	....	....	....	....	....
1989-90	N. Michigan	WCHA	39	5	11	16	77	....	....	....	....	....
1990-91	N. Michigan	WCHA	46	13	18	31	109	....	....	....	....	....
1991-92	Greensboro	ECHL	12	4	8	12	21	....	....	....	....	....
	Halifax	AHL	51	7	11	18	65	....	....	....	....	....
1992-93	Halifax	AHL	70	13	19	32	56	....	....	....	....	....

WARRINER, TODD

Left wing. Shoots left. 6'1", 172 lbs. Born, Blenheim, Ont., January 3, 1974.
(Quebec's 1st choice, 4th overall, in 1992 Entry Draft).

			Regular Season					Playoffs				
Season	Club	Lea	GP	G	A	TP	PIM	GP	G	A	TP	PIM
1990-91	Windsor	OHL	57	36	28	64	26	11	5	6	11	12
1991-92a	Windsor	OHL	50	41	41	82	64	7	5	4	9	6
1992-93	Windsor	OHL	23	13	21	34	29	....	....	....	....	....
	Kitchener	OHL	32	19	24	43	35	7	5	14	19	14

a OHL First All-Star Team (1992)

WASHBURN, STEVE

Center. Shoots left. 6'2", 185 lbs.   Born, Ottawa, Ont., April 10, 1975.
(Florida's 5th choice, 78th overall, in 1993 Entry Draft).

				Regular Season					Playoffs			
Season	Club	Lea	GP	G	A	TP	PIM	GP	G	A	TP	PIM
1991-92	Ottawa	OHL	59	5	17	22	10	11	2	3	5	4
1992-93	Ottawa	OHL	66	20	38	58	54	....	....	....	....	....

WASLEY, CHARLIE

Defense. Shoots left. 6'2", 173 lbs.   Born, Minneapolis, MN, April 4, 1974.
(Quebec's 6th choice, 100th overall, in 1992 Entry Draft).

				Regular Season					Playoffs			
Season	Club	Lea	GP	G	A	TP	PIM	GP	G	A	TP	PIM
1991-92	St. Paul	USHL	44	3	6	9	144	....	....	....	....	....
1992-93	U. Minnesota	WCHA	35	2	5	7	42	....	....	....	....	....

WATTERS, TIMOTHY J. (TIM)

Defense. Shoots left. 5'11", 185 lbs.   Born, Kamloops, B.C., July 25, 1959.
(Winnipeg's 6th choice, 124th overall, in 1979 Entry Draft).

				Regular Season					Playoffs			
Season	Club	Lea	GP	G	A	TP	PIM	GP	G	A	TP	PIM
1978-79	Michigan Tech	WCHA	38	6	21	27	48	....	....	....	....	....
1979-80	Cdn. National	....	56	8	21	29	43	....	....	....	....	....
	Cdn. Olympic	....	6	1	1	2	0	....	....	....	....	....
1980-81ab	Michigan Tech	WCHA	43	12	38	50	36	....	....	....	....	....
1981-82	Tulsa	CHL	5	1	2	3	0	....	....	....	....	....
	Winnipeg	NHL	69	2	22	24	97	4	0	1	1	8
1982-83	Winnipeg	NHL	77	5	18	23	98	3	0	0	0	2
1983-84	Winnipeg	NHL	74	3	20	23	169	3	1	0	1	2
1984-85	Winnipeg	NHL	63	2	20	22	74	8	0	1	1	16
1985-86	Winnipeg	NHL	56	6	8	14	97	....	....	....	....	....
1986-87	Winnipeg	NHL	63	3	13	16	119	10	0	0	0	21
1987-88	Cdn. National	....	8	0	1	1	2	....	....	....	....	....
	Cdn. Olympic	....	2	0	2	2	0	....	....	....	....	....
	Winnipeg	NHL	36	0	0	0	106	4	0	0	0	4
1988-89	Los Angeles	NHL	76	3	18	21	168	11	0	1	1	6
1989-90	Los Angeles	NHL	62	1	10	11	92	4	0	0	0	6
1990-91	Los Angeles	NHL	45	0	4	4	92	7	0	0	0	12
1991-92	Los Angeles	NHL	37	0	7	7	92	6	0	0	0	8
	Phoenix	IHL	5	0	3	3	6	....	....	....	....	....
1992-93	Los Angeles	NHL	22	0	2	2	18	22	0	2	2	30
	Phoenix	IHL	31	3	3	6	43	....	....	....	....	....
	NHL Totals		**680**	**25**	**142**	**167**	**1222**	**82**	**1**	**5**	**6**	**115**

a   WCHA First All-Star Team (1981)
b   Named to NCAA All-Tournament Team (1981)
Signed as a free agent by **Los Angeles**, June 27, 1988.

WEIGHT, DOUG

Center. Shoots left. 5'11", 191 lbs.   Born, Warren, MI, January 21, 1971.
(NY Rangers' 2nd choice, 34th overall, in 1990 Entry Draft).

				Regular Season					Playoffs			
Season	Club	Lea	GP	G	A	TP	PIM	GP	G	A	TP	PIM
1989-90	Lake Superior	CCHA	46	21	48	69	44	....	....	....	....	....
1990-91ab	Lake Superior	CCHA	42	29	46	75	86	....	....	....	....	....
	NY Rangers	NHL	....	....	....	....	....	1	0	0	0	0
1991-92	NY Rangers	NHL	53	8	22	30	23	7	2	2	4	0
	Binghamton	AHL	9	3	14	17	2	4	1	4	5	6
1992-93	NY Rangers	NHL	65	15	25	40	55	....	....	....	....	....
	Edmonton	NHL	13	2	6	8	10	....	....	....	....	....
	NHL Totals		**131**	**25**	**53**	**78**	**88**	**8**	**2**	**2**	**4**	**0**

a   CCHA First All-Star Team (1991)
b   NCAA West Second All-American Team (1991)
Traded to **Edmonton** by **NY Rangers** for Esa Tikkanen, March 17, 1993.

WEINRICH, ALEXANDER

Defense. Shoots right. 6', 180 lbs.   Born, Lewiston, ME, March 12, 1969.
(Toronto's 12th choice, 238th overall, in 1987 Entry Draft).

				Regular Season					Playoffs			
Season	Club	Lea	GP	G	A	TP	PIM	GP	G	A	TP	PIM
1990-91	Merrimack	H.E.	38	2	12	14	16	....	....	....	....	....
1991-92	Merrimack	H.E.	34	2	18	20	40	....	....	....	....	....
1992-93	Merrimack	H.E.	24	1	5	6	28	....	....	....	....	....

WEINRICH, ERIC   (WIGHN-rick)

Defense. Shoots left. 6'1", 210 lbs.   Born, Roanoke, VA, December 19, 1966.
(New Jersey's 3rd choice, 32nd overall, in 1985 Entry Draft).

				Regular Season					Playoffs			
Season	Club	Lea	GP	G	A	TP	PIM	GP	G	A	TP	PIM
1985-86	U. of Maine	H.E.	34	0	15	15	26	....	....	....	....	....
1986-87ab	U. of Maine	H.E.	41	12	32	44	59	....	....	....	....	....
1987-88	U. of Maine	H.E.	8	4	7	11	22	....	....	....	....	....
	U.S. National	....	38	3	9	12	24	....	....	....	....	....
	U.S. Olympic	....	3	0	0	0	0	....	....	....	....	....
1988-89	New Jersey	NHL	2	0	0	0	0	....	....	....	....	....
	Utica	AHL	80	17	27	44	70	5	0	1	1	4
1989-90	New Jersey	NHL	19	2	7	9	11	6	1	3	4	17
cd	Utica	AHL	57	12	48	60	38	....	....	....	....	....
1990-91e	New Jersey	NHL	76	4	34	38	48	7	1	2	3	6
1991-92	New Jersey	NHL	76	7	25	32	55	7	0	2	2	4
1992-93	Hartford	NHL	79	7	29	36	76	....	....	....	....	....
	NHL Totals		**252**	**20**	**95**	**115**	**190**	**20**	**2**	**7**	**9**	**27**

a   Hockey East First All-Star Team (1987)
b   NCAA East Second All-American Team (1987)
c   AHL First All-Star Team (1990)
d   Won Eddie Shore Plaque (Outstanding Defenseman-AHL) (1990)
e   NHL/Upper Deck All-Rookie Team (1991)
Traded to **Hartford** by **New Jersey** with Sean Burke for Bobby Holik, Hartford's second round choice (Jay Pandolfo) in 1993 Entry Draft and future considerations, August 28, 1992.

WEINRICH, JASON

Defense. Shoots right. 6'2", 189 lbs.   Born, Lewiston, ME, February 13, 1972.
(NY Rangers' 8th choice, 118th overall, in 1990 Entry Draft).

				Regular Season					Playoffs			
Season	Club	Lea	GP	G	A	TP	PIM	GP	G	A	TP	PIM
1990-91	U. of Maine	H.E.	14	1	1	2	4	....	....	....	....	....
1991-92	U. of Maine	H.E.	36	1	15	16	18	....	....	....	....	....
1992-93	U. of Maine	H.E.	38	1	8	9	42	....	....	....	....	....

WEISBROD, JOHN

Center. Shoots right. 6'3", 215 lbs.   Born, Syosset, NY, October 8, 1968.
(Minnesota's 4th choice, 73rd overall, in 1987 Entry Draft).

				Regular Season					Playoffs			
Season	Club	Lea	GP	G	A	TP	PIM	GP	G	A	TP	PIM
1987-88	Harvard	ECAC	22	8	11	19	16	....	....	....	....	....
1988-89	Harvard	ECAC	31	22	13	35	61	....	....	....	....	....
1989-90	Harvard	ECAC	27	11	21	32	62	....	....	....	....	....
1990-91	Harvard	ECAC	5	2	8	10	8	....	....	....	....	....
1991-92					DID NOT PLAY – INJURED								
1992-93	Kansas City	IHL	16	6	2	8	6	....	....	....	....	....

Claimed by **San Jose** from **Minnesota** in Dispersal Draft, May 30, 1991.

WELLS, GORDON (JAY)

Defense. Shoots left. 6'1", 210 lbs.   Born, Paris, Ont., May 18, 1959.
(Los Angeles' 1st choice, 16th overall, in 1979 Entry Draft).

				Regular Season					Playoffs			
Season	Club	Lea	GP	G	A	TP	PIM	GP	G	A	TP	PIM
1977-78	Kingston	OHA	68	9	13	22	195	5	1	2	3	6
1978-79a	Kingston	OHA	48	6	21	27	100	11	2	7	9	29
1979-80	Los Angeles	NHL	43	0	0	0	113	4	0	0	0	11
	Binghamton	AHL	28	0	6	6	48	....	....	....	....	....
1980-81	Los Angeles	NHL	72	5	13	18	155	4	0	0	0	27
1981-82	Los Angeles	NHL	60	1	8	9	145	10	1	3	4	41
1982-83	Los Angeles	NHL	69	3	12	15	167	....	....	....	....	....
1983-84	Los Angeles	NHL	69	3	18	21	141	....	....	....	....	....
1984-85	Los Angeles	NHL	77	2	9	11	185	3	0	1	1	0
1985-86	Los Angeles	NHL	79	11	31	42	226	....	....	....	....	....
1986-87	Los Angeles	NHL	77	7	29	36	155	5	1	2	3	10
1987-88	Los Angeles	NHL	58	2	23	25	159	5	1	2	3	21
1988-89	Philadelphia	NHL	67	2	19	21	184	18	0	2	2	51
1989-90	Philadelphia	NHL	59	3	16	19	129	....	....	....	....	....
	Buffalo	NHL	1	0	1	1	0	6	0	0	0	12
1990-91	Buffalo	NHL	43	1	2	3	86	1	0	1	1	0
1991-92	Buffalo	NHL	41	2	9	11	157	....	....	....	....	....
	NY Rangers	NHL	11	0	0	0	24	13	0	2	2	10
1992-93	NY Rangers	NHL	53	1	9	10	107	....	....	....	....	....
	NHL Totals		**879**	**43**	**199**	**242**	**2133**	**69**	**3**	**13**	**16**	**183**

a   OHA First All-Star Team (1979)
Traded to **Philadelphia** by **Los Angeles** for Doug Crossman, September 29, 1988. Traded to **Buffalo** by **Philadelphia** with Philadelphia's fourth round choice (Peter Ambroziak) in 1991 Entry Draft for Kevin Maguire and Buffalo's second round choice (Mikael Renberg) in 1990 Entry Draft, March 5, 1990. Traded to **NY Rangers** by **Buffalo** for Randy Moller, March 9, 1992.

WERENKA, BRAD

Defense. Shoots left. 6'2", 205 lbs.   Born, Two Hills, Alta., February 12, 1969.
(Edmonton's 2nd choice, 42nd overall, in 1987 Entry Draft).

				Regular Season					Playoffs			
Season	Club	Lea	GP	G	A	TP	PIM	GP	G	A	TP	PIM
1986-87	N. Michigan	WCHA	30	4	4	8	35	....	....	....	....	....
1987-88	N. Michigan	WCHA	34	7	23	30	26	....	....	....	....	....
1988-89	N. Michigan	WCHA	28	7	13	20	16	....	....	....	....	....
1989-90	N. Michigan	WCHA	8	2	5	7	8	....	....	....	....	....
1990-91abc	N. Michigan	WCHA	47	20	43	63	36	....	....	....	....	....
1991-92	Cape Breton	AHL	66	6	21	27	95	5	0	3	3	6
1992-93	Edmonton	NHL	27	5	3	8	24	....	....	....	....	....
	Cdn. National		18	3	7	10	10	....	....	....	....	....
	Cape Breton	AHL	4	1	1	2	4	16	4	17	21	12
	NHL Totals		**27**	**5**	**3**	**8**	**24**	....	....	....	....	....

a   WCHA First All-Star Team (1991)
b   NCAA West First All-American Team (1991)
c   NCAA Final Four All-Tournament Team (1991)

WERENKA, DARCY

Defense. Shoots right. 6'1", 210 lbs.   Born, Edmonton, Alta., May 13, 1973.
(NY Rangers' 2nd choice, 37th overall, in 1991 Entry Draft).

				Regular Season					Playoffs			
Season	Club	Lea	GP	G	A	TP	PIM	GP	G	A	TP	PIM
1990-91	Lethbridge	WHL	72	13	37	50	39	16	1	7	8	4
1991-92	Lethbridge	WHL	69	17	58	75	56	5	2	1	3	0
1992-93	Brandon	WHL	55	8	42	50	31	3	0	0	0	2
	Binghamton	AHL	3	0	1	1	2	3	0	0	0	0

WERNBLOM, MAGNUS

Right wing. Shoots left. 6', 187 lbs.   Born, Kramfors, Sweden, February 3, 1973.
(Los Angeles' 6th choice, 207th overall, in 1992 Entry Draft).

				Regular Season					Playoffs			
Season	Club	Lea	GP	G	A	TP	PIM	GP	G	A	TP	PIM
1990-91	MoDo	Swe.	16	4	2	6	8	....	....	....	....	....
1991-92	MoDo	Swe.	35	7	6	13	50	....	....	....	....	....
1992-93	MoDo	Swe.	37	8	3	11	36	3	0	0	0	0

WESLEY, GLEN

Defense. Shoots left. 6'1", 201 lbs. Born, Red Deer, Alta., October 2, 1968.
(Boston's 1st choice, 3rd overall, in 1987 Entry Draft).

			Regular Season					Playoffs				
Season	Club	Lea	GP	G	A	TP	PIM	GP	G	A	TP	PIM
1983-84	Portland	WHL	3	1	2	3	0	....	....	....	....	....
1984-85	Portland	WHL	67	16	52	68	76	6	1	6	7	8
1985-86a	Portland	WHL	69	16	75	91	96	15	3	11	14	29
1986-87a	Portland	WHL	63	16	46	62	72	20	8	18	26	27
1987-88b	Boston	NHL	79	7	30	37	69	23	6	8	14	22
1988-89	Boston	NHL	77	19	35	54	61	10	0	2	2	4
1989-90	Boston	NHL	78	9	27	36	48	21	2	6	8	36
1990-91	Boston	NHL	80	11	32	43	78	19	2	9	11	19
1991-92	Boston	NHL	78	9	37	46	54	15	2	4	6	16
1992-93	Boston	NHL	64	8	25	33	47	4	0	0	0	0
	NHL Totals		456	63	186	249	357	92	12	29	41	97

a WHL West All-Star Team (1986, 1987)
b NHL All-Rookie Team (1988)

Played in NHL All-Star Game (1989)

WETHERILL, DARREN

Defense. Shoots left. 6', 180 lbs. Born, Regina, Sask., January 28, 1970.
(Boston's 8th choice, 189th overall, in 1990 Entry Draft).

			Regular Season					Playoffs				
Season	Club	Lea	GP	G	A	TP	PIM	GP	G	A	TP	PIM
1990-91	Lake Superior	CCHA	26	0	6	6	14	....	....	....	....	....
1991-92	Lake Superior	CCHA	27	1	4	5	42	....	....	....	....	....
1992-93	Lake Superior	CCHA	43	2	10	12	64	....	....	....	....	....

WHITE, PETER

Left wing. Shoots left. 5'11", 200 lbs. Born, Montreal, Que., March 15, 1969.
(Edmonton's 4th choice, 92nd overall, in 1989 Entry Draft).

			Regular Season					Playoffs				
Season	Club	Lea	GP	G	A	TP	PIM	GP	G	A	TP	PIM
1988-89	Michigan State	CCHA	46	20	33	53	17	....	....	....	....	....
1989-90	Michigan State	CCHA	45	22	40	62	6	....	....	....	....	....
1990-91	Michigan State	CCHA	37	7	31	38	28	....	....	....	....	....
1991-92	Michigan State	CCHA	41	26	49	75	32	....	....	....	....	....
1992-93	Cape Breton	AHL	64	12	28	40	10	16	3	3	6	12

WHITE, SCOTT

Defense. Shoots right. 6'1", 195 lbs. Born, Ormstown, Que., March 15, 1968.
(Quebec's 6th choice, 117th overall, in 1986 Entry Draft).

			Regular Season					Playoffs				
Season	Club	Lea	GP	G	A	TP	PIM	GP	G	A	TP	PIM
1985-86	Michigan Tech.	WCHA	40	3	15	18	58	....	....	....	....	....
1986-87	Michigan Tech.	WCHA	36	4	15	19	58	....	....	....	....	....
1987-88	Michigan Tech.	WCHA	40	7	25	32	32	....	....	....	....	....
1988-89	Michigan Tech.	WCHA	38	6	18	24	38	....	....	....	....	....
1989-90	Bergen	Nor.	29	10	21	31	76	....	....	....	....	....
	Greensboro	ECHL	30	9	13	22	67	14	4	10	14	24
1990-91	Kansas City	IHL	18	3	2	5	37	....	....	....	....	....
	Kalamazoo	IHL	6	0	1	1	8	....	....	....	....	....
	Greensboro	ECHL	42	8	29	37	93	13	2	11	13	10
1991-92ab	Greensboro	ECHL	57	21	63	84	204	....	....	....	....	....
	Fort Wayne	IHL	....	....	....	....	....	1	0	0	0	2
1992-93	New Haven	AHL	80	10	44	54	72	....	....	....	....	....

a Named ECHL's Best Defenceman (1992)
b ECHL First All-Star Team (1992)

Signed as a free agent by **Ottawa**, August 4, 1992.

WHITNEY, RAY

Center. Shoots right. 5'9", 160 lbs. Born, Fort Saskatchewan, Alta., May 8, 1972.
(San Jose's 2nd choice, 23rd overall, in 1991 Entry Draft).

			Regular Season					Playoffs				
Season	Club	Lea	GP	G	A	TP	PIM	GP	G	A	TP	PIM
1988-89	Spokane	WHL	71	17	33	50	16	....	....	....	....	....
1989-90	Spokane	WHL	71	57	56	113	50	6	3	4	7	6
1990-91abc	Spokane	WHL	72	67	118	*185	36	15	13	18	*31	12
1991-92	Koln	Ger.	10	3	6	9	4	....	....	....	....	....
	San Diego	IHL	63	36	54	90	12	4	0	0	0	0
	San Jose	NHL	2	0	3	3	0	....	....	....	....	....
1992-93	San Jose	NHL	26	4	6	10	4	....	....	....	....	....
	Kansas City	IHL	46	20	33	53	14	12	5	7	12	2
	NHL Totals		28	4	9	13	4	....	....	....	....	....

a WHL West First All-Star Team (1991)
b Memorial Cup All-Star Team (1991)
c Won George Parsons Trophy (Memorial Cup Most Sportsmanlike Player) (1991)

WHYTE, SEAN

Right wing. Shoots right. 6', 198 lbs. Born, Sudbury, Ont., May 4, 1970.
(Los Angeles' 7th choice, 165th overall, in 1989 Entry Draft).

			Regular Season					Playoffs				
Season	Club	Lea	GP	G	A	TP	PIM	GP	G	A	TP	PIM
1986-87	Guelph	OHL	41	1	3	4	13	....	....	....	....	....
1987-88	Guelph	OHL	62	6	22	28	71	....	....	....	....	....
1988-89	Guelph	OHL	53	20	44	64	57	....	....	....	....	....
1989-90	Owen Sound	OHL	54	23	30	53	90	3	0	1	1	10
1990-91	Phoenix	IHL	60	18	17	35	61	4	1	0	1	2
1991-92	Los Angeles	NHL	3	0	0	0	0	....	....	....	....	....
	Phoenix	IHL	72	24	30	54	113	....	....	....	....	....
1992-93	Los Angeles	NHL	18	0	2	2	12	....	....	....	....	....
	Phoenix	IHL	51	11	35	46	65	....	....	....	....	....
	NHL Totals		21	0	2	2	12	....	....	....	....	....

WIDMER, JASON

Defense. Shoots left. 6', 205 lbs. Born, Calgary, Alta., August 1, 1973.
(NY Islanders' 8th choice, 176th overall, in 1992 Entry Draft).

			Regular Season					Playoffs				
Season	Club	Lea	GP	G	A	TP	PIM	GP	G	A	TP	PIM
1990-91	Lethbridge	WHL	58	2	12	14	55	16	0	1	1	12
1991-92	Lethbridge	WHL	40	2	19	21	181	5	0	4	4	9
1992-93	Lethbridge	WHL	55	3	15	18	140	4	0	3	3	2

WIEMER, JAMES DUNCAN (JIM) (WEE-muhr)

Defense. Shoots left. 6'4", 216 lbs. Born, Sudbury, Ont., January 9, 1961.
(Buffalo's 5th choice, 83rd overall, in 1980 Entry Draft).

			Regular Season					Playoffs				
Season	Club	Lea	GP	G	A	TP	PIM	GP	G	A	TP	PIM
1978-79	Peterborough	OHA	61	15	12	27	50	18	4	4	8	15
1979-80	Peterborough	OHA	53	17	32	49	63	14	6	9	15	19
1980-81	Peterborough	OHA	65	41	54	95	102	5	1	2	3	15
1981-82	Rochester	AHL	74	19	26	45	57	9	0	4	4	2
1982-83	Rochester	AHL	74	15	44	59	43	15	5	15	20	22
	Buffalo	NHL	....	....	....	....	....	1	0	0	0	0
1983-84	Buffalo	NHL	64	5	15	20	48	....	....	....	....	....
	Rochester	AHL	12	4	11	15	11	18	3	13	16	20
1984-85	Buffalo	NHL	10	3	2	5	4	....	....	....	....	....
	Rochester	AHL	13	1	9	10	24	....	....	....	....	....
	NY Rangers	NHL	22	4	3	7	30	1	0	0	0	0
	New Haven	AHL	33	9	27	36	39	....	....	....	....	....
1985-86	NY Rangers	NHL	7	3	0	3	2	8	1	0	1	6
ab	New Haven	AHL	73	24	49	73	108	....	....	....	....	....
1986-87	New Haven	AHL	6	0	7	7	6	....	....	....	....	....
	Nova Scotia	AHL	59	9	25	34	72	5	0	4	4	2
1987-88	Edmonton	NHL	12	1	2	3	15	2	0	0	0	2
	Nova Scotia	AHL	57	11	32	43	99	5	1	1	2	14
1988-89	Cape Breton	AHL	51	12	29	41	80	....	....	....	....	....
	Los Angeles	NHL	9	2	3	5	20	10	2	1	3	19
	New Haven	AHL	3	1	1	2	2	7	2	3	5	2
1989-90	Boston	NHL	61	5	14	19	63	8	0	1	1	4
	Maine	AHL	6	3	4	7	27	....	....	....	....	....
1990-91	Boston	NHL	61	4	19	23	62	16	1	3	4	14
1991-92	Boston	NHL	47	1	8	9	84	15	1	3	4	14
	Maine	AHL	3	0	1	1	4	....	....	....	....	....
1992-93	Boston	NHL	28	1	6	7	48	1	0	0	0	4
	Providence	AHL	4	2	1	3	2	....	....	....	....	....
	NHL Totals		321	29	72	101	376	62	5	8	13	63

a AHL First All-Star Team (1986)
b AHL Defenseman of the Year (1986)

Traded to **NY Rangers** by **Buffalo** with Steve Patrick for Dave Maloney and Chris Renaud, December 6, 1984. Traded to **Edmonton** by **NY Rangers** with Reijo Ruotsalainen, Clark Donatelli and Ville Kentala for Don Jackson, Mike Golden, Miloslav Horvava and future considerations, October 23, 1986. Traded to **Los Angeles** by **Edmonton** with Alan May for Brian Wilks and John English, March 7, 1989. Signed as a free agent by **Boston**, July 6, 1989.

WIESEL, ADAM

Defense. Shoots right. 6'3", 201 lbs. Born, Holyoke, MA, January 25, 1975.
(Montreal's 4th choice, 85th overall, in 1993 Entry Draft).

			Regular Season					Playoffs				
Season	Club	Lea	GP	G	A	TP	PIM	GP	G	A	TP	PIM
1991-92	Springfield	NEJHL	47	6	13	19	25	....	....	....	....	....
1992-93	Springfield	NEJHL	41	11	20	31	34	....	....	....	....	....

WILKIE, BOB

Defense. Shoots right. 6'2", 200 lbs. Born, Calgary, Alta., February 11, 1969.
(Detroit's 3rd choice, 41st overall, in 1987 Entry Draft).

			Regular Season					Playoffs				
Season	Club	Lea	GP	G	A	TP	PIM	GP	G	A	TP	PIM
1985-86	Calgary	WHL	63	8	19	27	56	....	....	....	....	....
1986-87	Swift Current	WHL	65	12	38	50	50	4	1	3	4	2
1987-88	Swift Current	WHL	67	12	68	80	124	10	4	12	16	8
1988-89	Swift Current	WHL	62	18	67	85	89	12	1	11	12	47
1989-90	Adirondack	AHL	58	5	33	38	64	6	1	4	5	2
1990-91	Detroit	NHL	8	1	2	3	2	....	....	....	....	....
	Adirondack	AHL	43	6	18	24	71	2	1	0	1	2
1991-92	Adirondack	AHL	7	1	4	5	6	16	2	5	7	12
1992-93	Adirondack	AHL	14	0	5	5	20	....	....	....	....	....
	Hershey	AHL	28	7	25	32	18	....	....	....	....	....
	Fort Wayne	IHL	32	7	14	21	82	12	4	6	10	10
	NHL Totals		8	1	2	3	2	....	....	....	....	....

WILKIE, DAVID

Defense. Shoots right. 6'3", 210 lbs. Born, Ellensburgh, WA, May 30, 1974.
(Montreal's 1st choice, 20th overall, in 1992 Entry Draft).

			Regular Season					Playoffs				
Season	Club	Lea	GP	G	A	TP	PIM	GP	G	A	TP	PIM
1990-91	Seattle	WHL	25	1	1	2	22	....	....	....	....	....
1991-92	Kamloops	WHL	71	12	28	40	153	16	6	5	11	19
1992-93	Kamloops	WHL	53	11	26	37	109	6	4	2	6	2

WILKINSON, NEIL

Defense. Shoots right. 6'3", 180 lbs. Born, Selkirk, Man., August 15, 1967.
(Minnesota's 2nd choice, 30th overall, in 1986 Entry Draft).

			Regular Season					Playoffs				
Season	Club	Lea	GP	G	A	TP	PIM	GP	G	A	TP	PIM
1986-87	Michigan State	CCHA	19	3	4	7	18	....	....	....	....	....
1987-88	Medicine Hat	WHL	55	11	21	32	157	5	1	0	1	2
1988-89	Kalamazoo	IHL	39	5	15	20	96	....	....	....	....	....
1989-90	Minnesota	NHL	36	0	5	5	100	7	0	2	2	11
	Kalamazoo	IHL	20	6	7	13	62	....	....	....	....	....
1990-91	Minnesota	NHL	50	2	9	11	117	22	3	3	6	12
	Kalamazoo	IHL	10	0	3	3	38	....	....	....	....	....
1991-92	San Jose	NHL	60	4	15	19	107	....	....	....	....	....
1992-93	San Jose	NHL	59	1	7	8	96	....	....	....	....	....
	NHL Totals		205	7	36	43	420	29	3	5	8	23

Claimed by **San Jose** from **Minnesota** in Dispersal Draft, May 30, 1991. Traded to **Chicago** by **San Jose** as future considerations to complete June 18, 1993 trade for Jimmy Waite, July 9, 1993.

WILLIAMS, DARRYL

Left wing. Shoots left. 5'11", 185 lbs. Born, Mt. Pearl, Nfld., February 9, 1968.

			Regular Season					Playoffs				
Season	Club	Lea	GP	G	A	TP	PIM	GP	G	A	TP	PIM
1986-87	Belleville	OHL	58	9	10	19	108	....	....	....	....	....
1987-88	Belleville	OHL	63	29	39	68	169	....	....	....	....	....
1988-89	Belleville	AHL	46	24	21	45	137	....	....	....	....	....
	New Haven	AHL	15	5	5	10	24	....	....	....	....	....
1989-90	New Haven	AHL	51	9	13	22	124	....	....	....	....	....
1990-91	New Haven	AHL	57	14	11	25	278	....	....	....	....	....
	Phoenix	IHL	12	1	2	3	53	7	1	0	1	12
1991-92	Phoenix	IHL	48	8	19	27	219	....	....	....	....	....
	New Haven	AHL	13	0	2	2	69	....	....	....	....	....
1992-93	**Los Angeles**	**NHL**	**2**	**0**	**0**	**0**	**10**	....	....	....	....	....
	Phoenix	IHL	61	18	7	25	314	....	....	....	....	....
	NHL Totals		**2**	**0**	**0**	**0**	**10**	....	....	....	....	....

Signed as a free agent by **Los Angeles**, May 19, 1989.

WILLIAMS, DAVID

Defense. Shoots right. 6'2", 195 lbs. Born, Plainfield, NJ, August 25, 1967.
(New Jersey's 12th choice, 234th overall, in 1985 Entry Draft).

			Regular Season					Playoffs				
Season	Club	Lea	GP	G	A	TP	PIM	GP	G	A	TP	PIM
1986-87	Dartmouth	ECAC	23	2	19	21	20	....	....	....	....	....
1987-88	Dartmouth	ECAC	25	8	14	22	30	....	....	....	....	....
1988-89ab	Dartmouth	ECAC	25	4	11	15	28	....	....	....	....	....
1989-90	Dartmouth	ECAC	26	3	12	15	32	....	....	....	....	....
1990-91	Muskegon	IHL	14	1	2	3	4	....	....	....	....	....
	Knoxville	ECHL	38	12	15	27	40	3	0	0	0	4
1991-92	**San Jose**	**NHL**	**56**	**3**	**25**	**28**	**40**	....	....	....	....	....
	Kansas City	IHL	18	2	3	5	22	....	....	....	....	....
1992-93	**San Jose**	**NHL**	**40**	**1**	**11**	**12**	**49**	....	....	....	....	....
	Kansas City	IHL	31	1	11	12	28	....	....	....	....	....
	NHL Totals		**96**	**4**	**36**	**40**	**89**	....	....	....	....	....

a ECAC First All-Star Team (1989)
b NCAA East Second All-American Team (1989)

Signed as a free agent by **San Jose**, August 9, 1991. Claimed by **Anaheim** from **San Jose** in Expansion Draft, June 24, 1993.

WILLIAMS, SEAN

Center. Shoots left. 6'1", 182 lbs. Born, Oshawa, Ont., January 28, 1968.
(Chicago's 11th choice, 245th overall, in 1986 Entry Draft).

			Regular Season					Playoffs				
Season	Club	Lea	GP	G	A	TP	PIM	GP	G	A	TP	PIM
1984-85	Oshawa	OHL	40	6	7	13	28	5	1	0	1	0
1985-86	Oshawa	OHL	55	15	23	38	23	6	2	3	5	4
1986-87	Oshawa	OHL	62	21	23	44	32	25	7	5	12	19
1987-88a	Oshawa	OHL	65	*58	65	123	38	7	3	3	6	6
1988-89	Saginaw	IHL	77	32	27	59	75	6	0	3	3	0
1989-90	Indianapolis	IHL	78	21	37	58	25	14	8	5	13	12
1990-91	Indianapolis	IHL	82	46	52	98	59	7	1	2	3	12
1991-92	**Chicago**	**NHL**	**2**	**0**	**0**	**0**	**4**	....	....	....	....	....
	Indianapolis	IHL	79	29	36	65	89	....	....	....	....	....
1992-93	Indianapolis	IHL	81	28	37	65	66	5	0	1	1	4
	NHL Totals		**2**	**0**	**0**	**0**	**4**	....	....	....	....	....

a OHL First All-Star Team (1988)

WILLIS, RICK

Left wing. Shoots left. 6', 190 lbs. Born, Lynn, MA, January 12, 1972.
(NY Rangers' 5th choice, 76th overall, in 1990 Entry Draft).

			Regular Season					Playoffs				
Season	Club	Lea	GP	G	A	TP	PIM	GP	G	A	TP	PIM
1991-92	U. of Michigan	CCHA	32	1	4	5	42	....	....	....	....	....
1992-93	U. of Michigan	CCHA	39	3	8	11	67	....	....	....	....	....

WILLNER, BRADLEY

Defense. Shoots right. 6'3", 191 lbs. Born, Edina, MN, January 6, 1973.
(New Jersey's 4th choice, 77th overall, in 1991 Entry Draft).

			Regular Season					Playoffs				
Season	Club	Lea	GP	G	A	TP	PIM	GP	G	A	TP	PIM
1991-92	Lake Superior	CCHA	16	0	0	0	10	....	....	....	....	....
1992-93	Lake Superior	CCHA	37	2	4	6	28	....	....	....	....	....

WILSON, CAREY

Center. Shoots right. 6'2", 195 lbs. Born, Winnipeg, Man., May 19, 1962.
(Chicago's 8th choice, 67th overall, in 1980 Entry Draft).

			Regular Season					Playoffs				
Season	Club	Lea	GP	G	A	TP	PIM	GP	G	A	TP	PIM
1979-80	Dartmouth	ECAC	31	16	22	38	20	....	....	....	....	....
1980-81	Dartmouth	ECAC	24	9	13	22	52	....	....	....	....	....
1981-82	HIFK	Fin.	29	15	17	32	58	7	1	4	5	6
1982-83	HIFK	Fin.	36	16	24	40	62	9	1	3	4	12
1983-84	Cdn. Olympic	....	56	19	24	43	34	....	....	....	....	....
	Calgary	**NHL**	**15**	**2**	**5**	**7**	**2**	**6**	**3**	**1**	**4**	**2**
1984-85	**Calgary**	**NHL**	**74**	**24**	**48**	**72**	**27**	**4**	**0**	**0**	**0**	**0**
1985-86	**Calgary**	**NHL**	**76**	**29**	**29**	**58**	**24**	**9**	**0**	**2**	**2**	**2**
1986-87	**Calgary**	**NHL**	**80**	**20**	**36**	**56**	**42**	**6**	**1**	**1**	**2**	**6**
1987-88	**Calgary**	**NHL**	**34**	**9**	**21**	**30**	**18**	....	....	....	....	....
	Hartford	**NHL**	**36**	**18**	**20**	**38**	**22**	**6**	**2**	**4**	**6**	**2**
1988-89	**Hartford**	**NHL**	**34**	**11**	**11**	**22**	**14**	....	....	....	....	....
	NY Rangers	**NHL**	**41**	**21**	**34**	**55**	**45**	**4**	**1**	**2**	**3**	**2**
1989-90	**NY Rangers**	**NHL**	**41**	**9**	**17**	**26**	**57**	**10**	**2**	**1**	**3**	**0**
1990-91	**Hartford**	**NHL**	**45**	**8**	**15**	**23**	**16**	....	....	....	....	....
	Calgary	**NHL**	**12**	**3**	**3**	**6**	**2**	**7**	**2**	**2**	**4**	**0**
1991-92	**Calgary**	**NHL**	**42**	**11**	**12**	**23**	**37**	....	....	....	....	....
1992-93	**Calgary**	**NHL**	**22**	**4**	**7**	**11**	**8**	....	....	....	....	....
	NHL Totals		**552**	**169**	**258**	**427**	**314**	**52**	**11**	**13**	**24**	**14**

Rights traded to **Calgary** by **Chicago** for Denis Cyr, November 8, 1982. Traded to **Hartford** by **Calgary** with Neil Sheehy and the rights to Lane MacDonald for Dana Murzyn and Shane Churla, January 3, 1988. Traded to **NY Rangers** by **Hartford** with Hartford's fifth round choice (Lubos Rob) in 1990 Entry Draft for Brian Lawton, Norm MacIver and Don Maloney, December 26, 1988. Traded to **Hartford** by **NY Rangers** with NY Rangers' third round choice (Mikael Nylander) in 1991 Entry Draft for Jody Hull, July 9, 1990. Traded to **Calgary** by **Hartford** for Mark Hunter, March 5, 1991.

WILSON, DOUGLAS JR. (DOUG)

Defense. Shoots left. 6'1", 187 lbs. Born, Ottawa, Ont., July 5, 1957.
(Chicago's 1st choice, 6th overall, in 1977 Amateur Draft).

			Regular Season					Playoffs				
Season	Club	Lea	GP	G	A	TP	PIM	GP	G	A	TP	PIM
1975-76	Ottawa	OHA	58	26	62	88	142	12	5	10	15	24
1976-77a	Ottawa	OHA	43	25	54	79	85	19	4	20	24	34
1977-78	**Chicago**	**NHL**	**77**	**14**	**20**	**34**	**72**	**4**	**0**	**0**	**0**	**0**
1978-79	**Chicago**	**NHL**	**56**	**5**	**21**	**26**	**37**	....	....	....	....	....
1979-80	**Chicago**	**NHL**	**73**	**12**	**49**	**61**	**70**	**7**	**2**	**8**	**10**	**6**
1980-81	**Chicago**	**NHL**	**76**	**12**	**39**	**51**	**80**	**3**	**0**	**3**	**3**	**2**
1981-82bc	**Chicago**	**NHL**	**76**	**39**	**46**	**85**	**54**	**15**	**3**	**10**	**13**	**32**
1982-83	**Chicago**	**NHL**	**74**	**18**	**51**	**69**	**58**	**13**	**4**	**11**	**15**	**12**
1983-84	**Chicago**	**NHL**	**66**	**13**	**45**	**58**	**64**	**5**	**0**	**3**	**3**	**2**
1984-85d	**Chicago**	**NHL**	**78**	**22**	**54**	**76**	**44**	**12**	**3**	**10**	**13**	**12**
1985-86	**Chicago**	**NHL**	**79**	**17**	**47**	**64**	**80**	**3**	**1**	**1**	**2**	**2**
1986-87	**Chicago**	**NHL**	**69**	**16**	**32**	**48**	**36**	**4**	**0**	**0**	**0**	**0**
1987-88	**Chicago**	**NHL**	**27**	**8**	**24**	**32**	**28**	....	....	....	....	....
1988-89	**Chicago**	**NHL**	**66**	**15**	**47**	**62**	**69**	**4**	**1**	**2**	**3**	**0**
1989-90d	**Chicago**	**NHL**	**70**	**23**	**50**	**73**	**40**	**20**	**3**	**12**	**15**	**18**
1990-91	**Chicago**	**NHL**	**51**	**11**	**29**	**40**	**32**	**5**	**2**	**1**	**3**	**2**
1991-92	**San Jose**	**NHL**	**44**	**9**	**19**	**28**	**26**	....	....	....	....	....
1992-93	**San Jose**	**NHL**	**42**	**3**	**17**	**20**	**40**	....	....	....	....	....
	NHL Totals		**1024**	**237**	**590**	**827**	**830**	**95**	**19**	**61**	**80**	**88**

a OHA First All-Star Team (1977)
b Won James Norris Memorial Trophy (1982)
c NHL First All-Star Team (1982)
d NHL Second All-Star Team (1985, 1990)

Played in NHL All-Star Game (1982-86, 1990, 1992)

Traded to **San Jose** by **Chicago** for Kerry Toporowski and San Jose's second round choice (later traded to Winnipeg — Winnipeg selected Boris Mironov) in 1992 Entry Draft, September 6, 1991.

WILSON, LANDON

Right wing. Shoots right. 6'2", 202 lbs. Born, St. Louis, MO, March 13, 1975.
(Toronto's 2nd choice, 19th overall, in 1993 Entry Draft).

			Regular Season					Playoffs				
Season	Club	Lea	GP	G	A	TP	PIM	GP	G	A	TP	PIM
1991-92	California	Midget	48	21	47	68	130	....	....	....	....	....
1992-93	Dubuque	USHL	43	29	36	65	284	....	....	....	....	....

WILSON, MIKE

Defense. Shoots left. 6'4", 180 lbs. Born, Brampton, Ont., February 26, 1975.
(Vancouver's 1st choice, 20th overall, in 1993 Entry Draft).

			Regular Season					Playoffs				
Season	Club	Lea	GP	G	A	TP	PIM	GP	G	A	TP	PIM
1991-92	Georgetown	OHA Jr. B	41	9	13	22	65	....	....	....	....	....
1992-93	Sudbury	OHL	53	6	7	13	58	14	1	1	2	2

WILSON, RONALD LEE (RON)

Center. Shoots left. 5'9", 180 lbs. Born, Toronto, Ont., May 13, 1956.
(Montreal's 15th choice, 133rd overall, in 1976 Amateur Draft).

			Regular Season					Playoffs				
Season	Club	Lea	GP	G	A	TP	PIM	GP	G	A	TP	PIM
1974-75	Toronto	OMJHL	16	6	12	18	6	23	9	17	26	6
1975-76	St. Catharines	OHA	64	37	62	99	44	4	1	6	7	7
1976-77	Nova Scotia	AHL	67	15	21	36	18	6	0	0	0	0
1977-78	Nova Scotia	AHL	59	15	25	40	17	11	4	4	8	9
1978-79	Nova Scotia	AHL	77	33	42	75	91	10	5	6	11	14
1979-80	**Winnipeg**	**NHL**	**79**	**21**	**36**	**57**	**28**	....	....	....	....	....
1980-81	**Winnipeg**	**NHL**	**77**	**18**	**33**	**51**	**55**	....	....	....	....	....
1981-82	**Winnipeg**	**NHL**	**39**	**3**	**13**	**16**	**49**	....	....	....	....	....
	Tulsa	CHL	41	20	38	58	22	3	1	0	1	2
1982-83	**Winnipeg**	**NHL**	**12**	**6**	**3**	**9**	**4**	**3**	**2**	**2**	**4**	**2**
	Sherbrooke	AHL	65	30	55	85	71	....	....	....	....	....
1983-84	**Winnipeg**	**NHL**	**51**	**3**	**12**	**15**	**12**	....	....	....	....	....
	Sherbrooke	AHL	22	10	30	40	16	....	....	....	....	....
1984-85	**Winnipeg**	**NHL**	**75**	**10**	**9**	**19**	**31**	**8**	**4**	**2**	**6**	**2**
1985-86	**Winnipeg**	**NHL**	**54**	**6**	**7**	**13**	**16**	**1**	**0**	**0**	**0**	**0**
	Sherbrooke	AHL	10	9	8	17	9	....	....	....	....	....
1986-87	**Winnipeg**	**NHL**	**80**	**3**	**13**	**16**	**13**	**10**	**1**	**2**	**3**	**0**
1987-88	**Winnipeg**	**NHL**	**69**	**5**	**8**	**13**	**28**	**1**	**0**	**0**	**0**	**2**
1988-89a	Moncton	AHL	80	31	61	92	110	8	1	4	5	20
1989-90	Moncton	AHL	47	16	37	53	39	....	....	....	....	....
	St. Louis	**NHL**	**33**	**3**	**17**	**20**	**23**	**12**	**3**	**5**	**8**	**18**
1990-91	**St. Louis**	**NHL**	**73**	**10**	**27**	**37**	**54**	**7**	**0**	**0**	**0**	**28**
1991-92	**St. Louis**	**NHL**	**64**	**12**	**17**	**29**	**46**	**6**	**0**	**1**	**1**	**0**
1992-93	**St. Louis**	**NHL**	**78**	**7**	**11**	**19**	**44**	**11**	**0**	**0**	**0**	**12**
	NHL Totals		**784**	**107**	**206**	**314**	**403**	**59**	**10**	**12**	**22**	**64**

a AHL Second All-Star Team (1989)

Sold to **Winnipeg** by **Montreal**, October 4, 1979. Traded to **St. Louis** by **Winnipeg** for Doug Evans, January 22, 1990. Signed as a free agent by **Montreal**, August, 1993.

WILSON, ROSS

Right wing. Shoots right. 6'3", 197 lbs. Born, The Pas, Man., June 26, 1969.
(Los Angeles' 3rd choice, 43rd overall, in 1987 Entry Draft).

			Regular Season					Playoffs				
Season	Club	Lea	GP	G	A	TP	PIM	GP	G	A	TP	PIM
1986-87	Peterborough	OHL	66	28	11	39	91	12	3	5	8	16
1987-88	Peterborough	OHL	66	29	30	59	114	12	2	9	11	15
1988-89	Peterborough	OHL	64	48	41	89	90	15	10	13	23	23
1989-90	New Haven	AHL	61	19	14	33	39	....	....	....	....	....
1990-91	New Haven	AHL	68	29	17	46	28	....	....	....	....	....
1991-92	Phoenix	IHL	28	9	9	18	81	....	....	....	....	....
	Kalamazoo	IHL	31	18	6	24	38	11	9	1	10	6
1992-93	Kalamazoo	IHL	58	15	14	29	49	....	....	....	....	....

WINCH, JASON

Left wing. Shoots left. 6'1", 215 lbs. Born, Listowel, Ont., May 23, 1971.
(Buffalo's 8th choice, 187th overall, in 1990 Entry Draft).

			Regular Season					Playoffs				
Season	Club	Lea	GP	G	A	TP	PIM	GP	G	A	TP	PIM
1988-89	Toronto	OHL	66	33	50	83	8	6	3	3	6	0
1989-90	Niagara Falls	OHL	64	31	63	94	23	16	9	12	21	4
1990-91	Niagara Falls	OHL	66	40	82	122	16	14	14	12	26	6
1991-92	Rochester	AHL	73	23	35	58	24	12	2	6	8	0
1992-93	Rochester	AHL	31	1	13	14	29	....	....	....	....	....
	Fort Wayne	IHL	2	0	1	1	0	....	....	....	....	....
	Erie	ECHL	9	6	7	13	4	5	2	5	7	4

WINNES, CHRISTOPHER (CHRIS)

Right wing. Shoots right. 6', 170 lbs. Born, Ridgefield, CT, February 12, 1968.
(Boston's 9th choice, 161st overall, in 1987 Entry Draft).

			Regular Season					Playoffs				
Season	Club	Lea	GP	G	A	TP	PIM	GP	G	A	TP	PIM
1987-88	N. Hampshire	H.E.	30	17	19	36	28	....	....	....	....	....
1988-89	N. Hampshire	H.E.	30	11	20	31	22	....	....	....	....	....
1989-90	N. Hampshire	H.E.	24	10	13	23	12	....	....	....	....	....
1990-91	N. Hampshire	H.E.	33	15	16	31	24	....	....	....	....	....
	Maine	AHL	7	3	1	4	0	1	0	2	2	0
	Boston	**NHL**	....	....	....	....	....	**1**	**0**	**0**	**0**	**0**
1991-92	**Boston**	**NHL**	**24**	**1**	**3**	**4**	**6**	....	....	....	....	....
	Maine	AHL	45	12	35	47	30	....	....	....	....	....
1992-93	**Boston**	**NHL**	**5**	**0**	**1**	**1**	**0**	....	....	....	....	....
	Providence	AHL	64	23	36	59	34	4	0	2	2	5
	NHL Totals		**29**	**1**	**4**	**5**	**6**	**1**	**0**	**0**	**0**	**0**

Signed as a free agent by **Philadelphia**, August 4, 1993.

WISEMAN, BRIAN

Center. Shoots left. 5'6", 175 lbs. Born, Chatham, Ont., July 13, 1971.
(NY Rangers' 12th choice, 257th overall, in 1991 Entry Draft).

			Regular Season					Playoffs				
Season	Club	Lea	GP	G	A	TP	PIM	GP	G	A	TP	PIM
1990-91	U. of Michigan	CCHA	47	25	33	58	58	....	....	....	....	....
1991-92	U. of Michigan	CCHA	44	27	44	71	38	....	....	....	....	....
1992-93	U. of Michigan	CCHA	35	13	37	50	40	....	....	....	....	....

WITKOWSKI, BYRON

Left wing. Shoots left. 6'3", 197 lbs. Born, Edenwold, Sask., November 20, 1969.
(Quebec's 13th choice, 211th overall, in 1989 Entry Draft).

			Regular Season					Playoffs				
Season	Club	Lea	GP	G	A	TP	PIM	GP	G	A	TP	PIM
1989-90	W. Michigan	CCHA	36	1	2	3	36	....	....	....	....	....
1990-91	W. Michigan	CCHA	31	10	4	14	66	....	....	....	....	....
1991-92	W. Michigan	CCHA	34	9	9	18	36	....	....	....	....	....
1992-93	W. Michigan	CCHA	38	14	12	26	44	....	....	....	....	....

WITT, BRENDAN

Defense. Shoots left. 6'1", 205 lbs. Born, Humbolt, Sask., February 20, 1975.
(Washington's 1st choice, 11th overall, in 1993 Entry Draft).

			Regular Season					Playoffs				
Season	Club	Lea	GP	G	A	TP	PIM	GP	G	A	TP	PIM
1991-92	Seattle	WHL	67	3	9	12	212	15	1	1	2	84
1992-93a	Seattle	WHL	70	2	26	28	239	5	1	2	3	30

a WHL West First All-Star Team (1993)

WOLANIN, CRAIG **(wuh-LAN-ihn)**

Defense. Shoots left. 6'3", 205 lbs. Born, Grosse Pointe, MI, July 27, 1967.
(New Jersey's 1st choice, 3rd overall, in 1985 Entry Draft).

			Regular Season					Playoffs				
Season	Club	Lea	GP	G	A	TP	PIM	GP	G	A	TP	PIM
1984-85	Kitchener	OHL	60	5	16	21	95	4	1	1	2	2
1985-86	**New Jersey**	**NHL**	**44**	**2**	**16**	**18**	**74**	....	....	....	....	....
1986-87	**New Jersey**	**NHL**	**68**	**4**	**6**	**10**	**109**	....	....	....	....	....
1987-88	**New Jersey**	**NHL**	**78**	**6**	**25**	**31**	**170**	**18**	**2**	**5**	**7**	**51**
1988-89	**New Jersey**	**NHL**	**56**	**3**	**8**	**11**	**69**	....	....	....	....	....
1989-90	**New Jersey**	**NHL**	**37**	**1**	**7**	**8**	**47**	....	....	....	....	....
	Utica	AHL	6	2	4	6	2	....	....	....	....	....
	Quebec	**NHL**	**13**	**0**	**3**	**3**	**10**	....	....	....	....	....
1990-91	**Quebec**	**NHL**	**80**	**5**	**13**	**18**	**89**	....	....	....	....	....
1991-92	**Quebec**	**NHL**	**69**	**2**	**11**	**13**	**80**	....	....	....	....	....
1992-93	**Quebec**	**NHL**	**24**	**1**	**4**	**5**	**49**	**4**	**0**	**0**	**0**	**4**
	NHL Totals		**469**	**24**	**93**	**117**	**697**	**22**	**2**	**5**	**7**	**55**

Traded to **Quebec** by **New Jersey** with future considerations (Randy Velischek, August 13, 1990) for Peter Stastny, March 6, 1990.

WOOD, DODY

Center. Shoots left. 5'11", 181 lbs. Born, Chetwynd, B.C., March 10, 1972.
(San Jose's 4th choice, 45th overall, in 1991 Entry Draft).

			Regular Season					Playoffs				
Season	Club	Lea	GP	G	A	TP	PIM	GP	G	A	TP	PIM
1989-90	Ft. St. John	Tier II	44	51	73	124	270	....	....	....	....	....
	Seattle	WHL	....	....	....	....	....	5	0	0	0	2
1990-91	Seattle	WHL	69	28	37	65	272	6	0	1	1	2
1991-92	Seattle	WHL	37	13	19	32	232	....	....	....	....	....
	Swift Current	WHL	3	0	2	2	14	7	2	1	3	37
1992-93	**San Jose**	**NHL**	**13**	**1**	**1**	**2**	**71**	....	....	....	....	....
	Kansas City	IHL	36	3	2	5	216	6	0	1	1	15
	NHL Totals		**13**	**1**	**1**	**2**	**71**	....	....	....	....	....

WOOD, RANDY

Left wing/Center. Shoots left. 6', 195 lbs. Born, Princeton, NJ, October 12, 1963.

			Regular Season					Playoffs				
Season	Club	Lea	GP	G	A	TP	PIM	GP	G	A	TP	PIM
1982-83	Yale	ECAC	26	5	14	19	10	....	....	....	....	....
1983-84	Yale	ECAC	18	7	7	14	10	....	....	....	....	....
1984-85a	Yale	ECAC	32	25	28	53	23	....	....	....	....	....
1985-86bc	Yale	ECAC	31	25	30	55	26	....	....	....	....	....
1986-87	**NY Islanders**	**NHL**	**6**	**1**	**0**	**1**	**4**	**13**	**1**	**3**	**4**	**14**
	Springfield	AHL	75	23	24	47	57	....	....	....	....	....
1987-88	**NY Islanders**	**NHL**	**75**	**22**	**16**	**38**	**80**	**5**	**1**	**0**	**1**	**6**
	Springfield	AHL	1	0	1	1	0	....	....	....	....	....
1988-89	**NY Islanders**	**NHL**	**77**	**15**	**13**	**28**	**44**	....	....	....	....	....
	Springfield	AHL	1	1	1	2	0	....	....	....	....	....
1989-90	**NY Islanders**	**NHL**	**74**	**24**	**24**	**48**	**39**	**5**	**1**	**1**	**2**	**4**
1990-91	**NY Islanders**	**NHL**	**76**	**24**	**18**	**42**	**45**	....	....	....	....	....
1991-92	**NY Islanders**	**NHL**	**8**	**2**	**2**	**4**	**21**	....	....	....	....	....
	Buffalo	**NHL**	**70**	**20**	**16**	**36**	**65**	**7**	**2**	**1**	**3**	**6**
1992-93	**Buffalo**	**NHL**	**82**	**18**	**25**	**43**	**77**	**8**	**1**	**4**	**5**	**4**
	NHL Totals		**468**	**126**	**114**	**240**	**375**	**38**	**6**	**9**	**15**	**34**

a ECAC Second All-Star Team (1985)
b ECAC First All-Star Team (1986)
c NCAA East Second All-Star Team (1986)

Signed as a free agent by **NY Islanders**, September 17, 1986. Traded to **Buffalo** by **NY Islanders** with Pat Lafontaine, Randy Hillier and future considerations for Pierre Turgeon, Uwe Krupp, Benoit Hogue and Dave McLlwain, October 25, 1991.

WOODCROFT, CRAIG

Left wing. Shoots left. 6'1", 185 lbs. Born, Toronto, Ont., December 3, 1969.
(Chicago's 6th choice, 134th overall, in 1988 Entry Draft).

			Regular Season					Playoffs				
Season	Club	Lea	GP	G	A	TP	PIM	GP	G	A	TP	PIM
1987-88	Colgate	ECAC	29	7	10	17	28	....	....	....	....	....
1988-89	Colgate	ECAC	29	20	29	49	62	....	....	....	....	....
	Cdn. National	....	2	0	0	0	4	....	....	....	....	....
1989-90	Colgate	ECAC	37	20	26	46	108	....	....	....	....	....
1990-91	Colgate	ECAC	32	26	30	56	52	....	....	....	....	....
1991-92	Indianapolis	IHL	75	21	17	38	67	....	....	....	....	....
1992-93	Cdn. National	....	11	2	4	6	6	....	....	....	....	....
	Indianapolis	IHL	65	12	19	31	80	....	....	....	....	....

WOODWARD, ROBERT (ROB)

Left wing. Shoots left. 6'4", 225 lbs. Born, Evanston, IL, January 15, 1971.
(Vancouver's 2nd choice, 29th overall, in 1989 Entry Draft).

			Regular Season					Playoffs				
Season	Club	Lea	GP	G	A	TP	PIM	GP	G	A	TP	PIM
1989-90	Michigan State	CCHA	37	17	9	26	8	....	....	....	....	....
1990-91	Michigan State	CCHA	32	5	13	18	16	....	....	....	....	....
1991-92	Michigan State	CCHA	40	14	15	29	60	....	....	....	....	....
1992-93	Michigan State	CCHA	36	12	9	21	90	....	....	....	....	....

WOOLLEY, JASON

Defense. Shoots left. 6', 186 lbs. Born, Toronto, Ont., July 27, 1969.
(Washington's 4th choice, 61st overall, in 1989 Entry Draft).

			Regular Season					Playoffs				
Season	Club	Lea	GP	G	A	TP	PIM	GP	G	A	TP	PIM
1988-89	Michigan State	CCHA	47	12	25	37	26	....	....	....	....	....
1989-90	Michigan State	CCHA	45	10	38	48	26	....	....	....	....	....
1990-91ab	Michigan State	CCHA	40	15	44	59	24	....	....	....	....	....
1991-92	Cdn. National	....	60	14	30	44	36	....	....	....	....	....
	Cdn. Olympic	....	8	0	5	5	4	....	....	....	....	....
	Washington	**NHL**	**1**	**0**	**0**	**0**	**0**	....	....	....	....	....
	Baltimore	AHL	15	1	10	11	6	....	....	....	....	....
1992-93	**Washington**	**NHL**	**26**	**0**	**2**	**2**	**10**	....	....	....	....	....
	Baltimore	AHL	29	14	27	41	22	1	0	2	2	0
	NHL Totals		**27**	**0**	**2**	**2**	**10**	....	....	....	....	....

a CCHA First All-Star Team (1991)
b NCAA West First All-American Team (1991)

WORTMAN, KEVIN

Defense. Shoots right. 6', 200 lbs. Born, Sagus, MA, February 22, 1969.
(Calgary's 9th choice, 168th overall, in 1989 Entry Draft).

			Regular Season					Playoffs				
Season	Club	Lea	GP	G	A	TP	PIM	GP	G	A	TP	PIM
1990-91	American Int'l	NCAA	28	21	25	46	6	....	....	....	....	....
1991-92	Salt Lake	IHL	82	12	34	46	34	5	1	0	1	0
1992-93a	Salt Lake	IHL	82	13	50	63	24	....	....	....	....	....

a IHL Second All-Star Team (1993)

WOTTON, MARK

Defense. Shoots left. 5'11", 187 lbs. Born, Foxwarren, Man., November 16, 1973.
(Vancouver's 11th choice, 237th overall, in 1992 Entry Draft).

			Regular Season					Playoffs				
Season	Club	Lea	GP	G	A	TP	PIM	GP	G	A	TP	PIM
1990-91	Saskatoon	WHL	45	4	11	15	37	....	....	....	....	....
1991-92	Saskatoon	WHL	64	11	25	36	92	....	....	....	....	....
1992-93	Saskatoon	WHL	71	15	51	66	90	9	6	5	11	18

WREN, BOB

Left wing. Shoots left. 5'10", 174 lbs. Born, Preston, Ont., September 16, 1974.
(Los Angeles' 3rd choice, 94th overall, in 1993 Entry Draft).

			Regular Season					Playoffs				
Season	Club	Lea	GP	G	A	TP	PIM	GP	G	A	TP	PIM
1991-92	Detroit	OHL	62	13	36	49	58	7	3	4	7	19
1992-93a	Detroit	OHL	63	57	88	145	91	15	4	11	15	20

a OHL Second All-Star Team (1993)

WRIGHT, TYLER

Center. Shoots right. 5'11", 175 lbs. Born, Canora, Sask., April 6, 1973.
(Edmonton's 1st choice, 12th overall, in 1991 Entry Draft).

			Regular Season					Playoffs				
Season	Club	Lea	GP	G	A	TP	PIM	GP	G	A	TP	PIM
1989-90	Swift Current	WHL	67	14	18	32	139	4	0	0	0	12
1990-91	Swift Current	WHL	66	41	51	92	157	3	0	0	0	6
1991-92	Swift Current	WHL	63	36	46	82	295	8	2	5	7	16
1992-93	**Edmonton**	**NHL**	**7**	**1**	**1**	**2**	**19**	....	....	....	....	....
	Swift Current	WHL	37	24	41	65	76	17	9	17	26	*49
	NHL Totals		**7**	**1**	**1**	**2**	**19**	....	....	....	....	....

YAKE, TERRY

Center. Shoots right. 5'11", 175 lbs. Born, New Westminster, B.C., October 22, 1968.
(Hartford's 3rd choice, 81st overall, in 1987 Entry Draft).

			Regular Season					Playoffs				
Season	Club	Lea	GP	G	A	TP	PIM	GP	G	A	TP	PIM
1984-85	Brandon	WHL	11	1	1	2	0	....	....	....	....	....
1985-86	Brandon	WHL	72	26	26	52	49	....	....	....	....	....
1986-87	Brandon	WHL	71	44	58	102	64	....	....	....	....	....
1987-88	Brandon	WHL	72	55	85	140	59	3	4	2	6	7
1988-89	**Hartford**	**NHL**	**2**	**0**	**0**	**0**	**0**	....	....	....	....	....
	Binghamton	AHL	75	39	56	95	57	....	....	....	....	....
1989-90	**Hartford**	**NHL**	**2**	**0**	**1**	**1**	**0**	....	....	....	....	....
	Binghamton	AHL	77	13	42	55	37	....	....	....	....	....
1990-91	**Hartford**	**NHL**	**19**	**1**	**4**	**5**	**10**	**6**	**1**	**1**	**2**	**16**
	Springfield	AHL	60	35	42	77	56	15	9	9	18	10
1991-92	**Hartford**	**NHL**	**15**	**1**	**1**	**2**	**4**	....	....	....	....	....
	Springfield	AHL	53	21	34	55	63	8	3	4	7	2
1992-93	**Hartford**	**NHL**	**66**	**22**	**31**	**53**	**46**	....	....	....	....	....
	Springfield	AHL	16	8	14	22	27	....	....	....	....	....
	NHL Totals		**104**	**24**	**37**	**61**	**60**	**6**	**1**	**1**	**2**	**16**

Claimed by **Anaheim** from **Hartford** in Expansion Draft, June 24, 1993.

YAKOVENKO, VLADISLAV

Left wing. Shoots right. 5'11", 176 lbs. Born, Lipetsk, Soviet Union, February 15, 1974.
(New Jersey's 12th choice, 258th overall, in 1992 Entry Draft).

			Regular Season					Playoffs				
Season	Club	Lea	GP	G	A	TP	PIM	GP	G	A	TP	PIM
1991-92	Argus	CIS 3	16	4	0	4	18	....	....	....	....	....
1992-93	Spartak	CIS	21	1	2	3	4	2	0	0	0	2

YAKUBOV, RAVIL (yah-KOO-bohv, rah-VEEL)

Center. Shoots left. 6'1", 190 lbs. Born, Moscow, Soviet Union, July 26, 1970.
(Calgary's 6th choice, 126th overall, in 1992 Entry Draft).

			Regular Season					Playoffs				
Season	Club	Lea	GP	G	A	TP	PIM	GP	G	A	TP	PIM
1990-91	Moscow D'amo	USSR	31	4	4	8	6	....	....	....	....	....
1991-92	Moscow D'amo	CIS	39	14	1	15	29	....	....	....	....	....
1992-93	Moscow D'amo	CIS	40	7	13	20	26	10	1	2	3	6

YASHIN, ALEXEI (YAH-shin)

Center. Shoots right. 6'2", 196 lbs. Born, Sverdlovsk, Soviet Union, November 5, 1973.
(Ottawa's 1st choice, 2nd overall, in 1992 Entry Draft).

			Regular Season					Playoffs				
Season	Club	Lea	GP	G	A	TP	PIM	GP	G	A	TP	PIM
1990-91	Sverdlovsk	USSR	26	2	1	3	10	....	....	....	....	....
1991-92	Moscow D'amo	CIS	35	7	5	12	19	....	....	....	....	....
1992-93	Moscow D'amo	CIS	27	10	12	22	18	10	7	3	10	18

YAWNEY, TRENT

Defense. Shoots left. 6'3", 192 lbs. Born, Hudson Bay, Sask., September 29, 1965.
(Chicago's 2nd choice, 45th overall, in 1984 Entry Draft).

			Regular Season					Playoffs				
Season	Club	Lea	GP	G	A	TP	PIM	GP	G	A	TP	PIM
1982-83	Saskatoon	WHL	59	6	31	37	44	6	0	2	2	0
1983-84	Saskatoon	WHL	73	13	46	59	81	....	....	....	....	....
1984-85	Saskatoon	WHL	72	16	51	67	158	3	1	6	7	7
1985-86	Cdn. Olympic	....	73	6	15	21	60	....	....	....	....	....
1986-87	Cdn. Olympic	....	51	4	15	19	37	....	....	....	....	....
1987-88	Cdn. National	....	60	4	12	16	81	....	....	....	....	....
	Cdn. Olympic	....	8	1	1	2	6	....	....	....	....	....
	Chicago	**NHL**	**15**	**2**	**8**	**10**	**15**	**5**	**0**	**4**	**4**	**8**
1988-89	**Chicago**	**NHL**	**69**	**5**	**19**	**24**	**116**	**15**	**3**	**6**	**9**	**20**
1989-90	**Chicago**	**NHL**	**70**	**5**	**15**	**20**	**82**	**20**	**3**	**5**	**8**	**27**
1990-91	**Chicago**	**NHL**	**61**	**3**	**13**	**16**	**77**	**1**	**0**	**0**	**0**	**0**
1991-92	**Calgary**	**NHL**	**47**	**4**	**9**	**13**	**45**	....	....	....	....	....
	Indianapolis	IHL	9	2	3	5	12	....	....	....	....	....
1992-93	**Calgary**	**NHL**	**63**	**1**	**16**	**17**	**67**	**6**	**3**	**2**	**5**	**6**
	NHL Totals		**325**	**20**	**80**	**100**	**402**	**47**	**9**	**17**	**26**	**61**

Traded to **Calgary** by **Chicago** for Stephane Matteau, December 16, 1991.

YELLE, STEPHANE

Center. Shoots left. 6'1", 162 lbs. Born, Ottawa, Ont., May 9, 1974.
(New Jersey's 8th choice, 186th overall, in 1992 Entry Draft).

			Regular Season					Playoffs				
Season	Club	Lea	GP	G	A	TP	PIM	GP	G	A	TP	PIM
1991-92	Oshawa	OHL	55	12	14	26	20	7	2	0	2	1
1992-93	Oshawa	OHL	66	24	50	74	20	10	2	4	6	4

YLONEN, JUHA (YOU-leh-nin, YOU-hah)

Center. Shoots left. 6', 180 lbs. Born, Helsinki, Finland, February 13, 1972.
(Winnipeg's 5th choice, 91st overall, in 1991 Entry Draft).

			Regular Season					Playoffs				
Season	Club	Lea	GP	G	A	TP	PIM	GP	G	A	TP	PIM
1990-91	Espoo	Fin.2	40	12	21	33	4	....	....	....	....	....
1991-92	HPK	Fin.	43	7	11	18	8	....	....	....	....	....
1992-93	HPK	Fin.	48	8	18	26	22	12	3	5	8	2

YORK, JASON

Defense. Shoots right. 6'1", 192 lbs. Born, Ottawa, Ont., May 20, 1970.
(Detroit's 6th choice, 129th overall, in 1990 Entry Draft).

			Regular Season					Playoffs				
Season	Club	Lea	GP	G	A	TP	PIM	GP	G	A	TP	PIM
1989-90	Windsor	OHL	39	9	30	39	38	....	....	....	....	....
	Kitchener	OHL	25	11	25	36	17	17	3	19	22	10
1990-91a	Windsor	OHL	66	13	80	93	40	11	3	10	13	12
1991-92	Adirondack	AHL	49	4	20	24	32	5	0	1	1	0
1992-93	**Detroit**	**NHL**	**2**	**0**	**0**	**0**	**0**	....	....	....	....	....
	Adirondack	AHL	77	15	40	55	86	11	0	3	3	18
	NHL Totals		**2**	**0**	**0**	**0**	**0**	....	....	....	....	....

a OHL Third All-Star Team (1991)

YOUNG, C.J.

Right wing. Shoots right. 5'10", 180 lbs. Born, Waban, MA, January 1, 1968.
(New Jersey's 1st choice, 5th overall, in 1989 Supplemental Draft).

			Regular Season					Playoffs				
Season	Club	Lea	GP	G	A	TP	PIM	GP	G	A	TP	PIM
1986-87	Harvard	ECAC	34	17	12	29	30	....	....	....	....	....
1987-88	Harvard	ECAC	28	13	16	29	40	....	....	....	....	....
1988-89a	Harvard	ECAC	36	20	31	51	36	....	....	....	....	....
1989-90bc	Harvard	ECAC	28	21	28	49	32	....	....	....	....	....
1990-91	Salt Lake	IHL	80	31	36	67	43	4	1	2	3	2
1991-92	U.S. National	....	49	17	17	34	38	....	....	....	....	....
	U.S. Olympic	....	8	1	3	4	4	....	....	....	....	....
	Salt Lake	IHL	9	2	2	4	2	5	0	1	1	4
1992-93	**Calgary**	**NHL**	**28**	**3**	**2**	**5**	**20**	....	....	....	....	....
	Boston	**NHL**	**15**	**4**	**5**	**9**	**12**	....	....	....	....	....
	Providence	AHL	7	4	3	7	26	6	1	0	1	16
	NHL Totals		**43**	**7**	**7**	**14**	**32**	....	....	....	....	....

a ECAC Second All-Star Team (1989)
b ECAC First All-Star Team (1990)
c NCAA East Second All-American Team (1990)

Signed as a free agent by **Calgary**, October 5, 1990. Traded to **Boston** by **Calgary** for Brent Ashton, February 1, 1993.

YOUNG, JASON

Left wing. Shoots left. 5'10", 197 lbs. Born, Sudbury, Ont., December 16, 1972.
(Buffalo's 3rd choice, 57th overall, in 1991 Entry Draft).

			Regular Season					Playoffs				
Season	Club	Lea	GP	G	A	TP	PIM	GP	G	A	TP	PIM
1989-90	Sudbury	OHL	62	26	47	73	64	7	3	2	5	8
1990-91	Sudbury	OHL	37	21	38	59	22	5	0	4	4	10
1991-92	Sudbury	OHL	55	26	56	82	49	11	3	2	5	14
1992-93	Rochester	AHL	59	20	20	40	60	14	3	4	7	31

YOUNG, SCOTT

Right wing. Shoots right. 6', 190 lbs. Born, Clinton, MA, October 1, 1967.
(Hartford's 1st choice, 11th overall, in 1986 Entry Draft).

			Regular Season					Playoffs				
Season	Club	Lea	GP	G	A	TP	PIM	GP	G	A	TP	PIM
1985-86a	Boston U.	H.E.	38	16	13	29	31	....	....	....	....	....
1986-87	Boston U.	H.E.	33	15	21	36	24	....	....	....	....	....
1987-88	U.S. National	....	56	11	47	58	31	....	....	....	....	....
	U.S. Olympic	....	6	2	6	8	4	....	....	....	....	....
	Hartford	**NHL**	**7**	**0**	**0**	**0**	**2**	**4**	**1**	**0**	**1**	**0**
1988-89	**Hartford**	**NHL**	**76**	**19**	**40**	**59**	**27**	**4**	**2**	**0**	**2**	**4**
1989-90	**Hartford**	**NHL**	**80**	**24**	**40**	**64**	**47**	**7**	**2**	**0**	**2**	**2**
1990-91	**Hartford**	**NHL**	**34**	**6**	**9**	**15**	**8**	....	....	....	....	....
	Pittsburgh	**NHL**	**43**	**11**	**16**	**27**	**33**	**17**	**1**	**6**	**7**	**2**
1991-92	Bolzano	Italy	18	22	17	39	6	5	4	3	7	7
	U.S. National	....	10	2	4	6	21	....	....	....	....	....
	U.S. Olympic	....	8	2	1	3	2	....	....	....	....	....
1992-93	**Quebec**	**NHL**	**82**	**30**	**30**	**60**	**20**	**6**	**4**	**1**	**5**	**0**
	NHL Totals		**322**	**90**	**135**	**225**	**137**	**38**	**10**	**7**	**17**	**8**

a Hockey East Rookie of the Year (1986)

Traded to **Pittsburgh** by **Hartford** for Rob Brown, December 21, 1990. Traded to **Quebec** by **Pittsburgh** for Bryan Fogarty, March 10, 1992.

YSEBAERT, PAUL (IGHS-BAHRT)

Center. Shoots left. 6'1", 190 lbs. Born, Sarnia, Ont., May 15, 1966.
(New Jersey's 4th choice, 74th overall, in 1984 Entry Draft).

			Regular Season					Playoffs				
Season	Club	Lea	GP	G	A	TP	PIM	GP	G	A	TP	PIM
1984-85	Bowling Green	CCHA	42	23	32	55	54	....	....	....	....	....
1985-86a	Bowling Green	CCHA	42	23	45	68	50	....	....	....	....	....
1986-87a	Bowling Green	CCHA	45	27	58	85	44	....	....	....	....	....
	Cdn. Olympic	....	5	1	0	1	4	....	....	....	....	....
1987-88	Utica	AHL	78	30	49	79	60	....	....	....	....	....
1988-89	**New Jersey**	**NHL**	**5**	**0**	**4**	**4**	**0**	....	....	....	....	....
	Utica	AHL	56	36	44	80	22	5	0	1	1	4
1989-90	**New Jersey**	**NHL**	**5**	**1**	**2**	**3**	**0**	....	....	....	....	....
bcd	Utica	AHL	74	53	52	*105	61	5	2	4	6	0
1990-91	**New Jersey**	**NHL**	**11**	**4**	**3**	**7**	**6**	....	....	....	....	....
	Detroit	**NHL**	**51**	**15**	**18**	**33**	**16**	**2**	**0**	**2**	**2**	**0**
1991-92e	**Detroit**	**NHL**	**79**	**35**	**40**	**75**	**55**	**10**	**1**	**0**	**1**	**10**
1992-93	**Detroit**	**NHL**	**80**	**34**	**28**	**62**	**42**	**7**	**3**	**1**	**4**	**2**
	NHL Totals		**231**	**89**	**95**	**184**	**119**	**19**	**4**	**3**	**7**	**12**

a CCHA Second All-Star Team (1986, 1987)
b AHL First All-Star Team (1990)
c Won John B. Sollenberger Trophy (Top Scorer-AHL) (1990)
d Won Les Cunningham Trophy (MVP-AHL) (1990)
e Won Alka-Seltzer Plus Award (1992)

Traded to **Detroit** by **New Jersey** for Lee Norwood and future considerations, November 27, 1990. Traded to **Winnipeg** by **Detroit** with future considerations (Alan Kerr, June 18, 1993) for Aaron Ward and Toronto's fourth round choice (previously acquired by Winnipeg — later traded to Detroit — Detroit selected John Jakopin) in 1993 Entry Draft, June 11, 1993.

YUDIN, ALEXANDER (EW-din)

Defense. Shoots left. 6'1", 191 lbs. Born, Minsk, Soviet Union, April 1, 1969.
(Calgary's 12th choice, 231st overall, in 1989 Entry Draft).

			Regular Season					Playoffs				
Season	Club	Lea	GP	G	A	TP	PIM	GP	G	A	TP	PIM
1986-87	Dynamo Minsk	USSR 2	35	0	4	4	36	....	....	....	....	....
1987-88	Dynamo Minsk	USSR 2	33	2	7	9	28	....	....	....	....	....
1988-89	Moscow D'amo	USSR	21	2	2	4	27	....	....	....	....	....
1989-90	Moscow D'amo	USSR	36	4	5	9	36	....	....	....	....	....
1990-91	Moscow D'amo	USSR	36	1	7	8	78	....	....	....	....	....
1991-92	Moscow D'amo	CIS	30	7	7	14	22	....	....	....	....	....
1992-93	Salt Lake	IHL	16	3	7	10	85	....	....	....	....	....
	Moscow D'amo	CIS	16	7	2	9	48	9	1	0	1	12

YULE, STEVE

Defense. Shoots right. 6', 210 lbs. Born, Gleichen, Alta., May 27, 1972.
(Hartford's 8th choice, 163rd overall, in 1991 Entry Draft).

			Regular Season					Playoffs				
Season	Club	Lea	GP	G	A	TP	PIM	GP	G	A	TP	PIM
1990-91	Kamloops	WHL	66	7	16	23	141	6	0	1	1	8
1991-92	Kamloops	WHL	61	7	10	17	257	17	2	1	3	37
1992-93	Springfield	AHL	38	0	4	4	52	....	....	....	....	....

YUSHKEVICH, DMITRI (yoush-KAY-vich)

Defense. Shoots right. 5'11", 187 lbs. Born, Yaroslavl, Soviet Union, November 19, 1971.
(Philadelphia's 6th choice, 122nd overall, in 1991 Entry Draft).

			Regular Season					Playoffs				
Season	Club	Lea	GP	G	A	TP	PIM	GP	G	A	TP	PIM
1988-89	Torpedo Yaro.	USSR	23	2	1	3	8	....	....	....	....	....
1989-90	Torpedo Yaro.	USSR	41	2	3	5	39	....	....	....	....	....
1990-91	Torpedo Yaro.	USSR	43	10	5	15	22	....	....	....	....	....
1991-92	Moscow D'amo	CIS	41	6	7	13	14	....	....	....	....	....
1992-93	**Philadelphia**	**NHL**	**82**	**5**	**27**	**32**	**71**	....	....	....	....	....
	NHL Totals		**82**	**5**	**27**	**32**	**71**					

YZERMAN, STEVE (IGH-zuhr-muhn)

Center. Shoots right. 5'11", 180 lbs. Born, Cranbrook, B.C., May 9, 1965.
(Detroit's 1st choice, 4th overall, in 1983 Entry Draft).

			Regular Season					Playoffs				
Season	Club	Lea	GP	G	A	TP	PIM	GP	G	A	TP	PIM
1981-82	Peterborough	OHL	58	21	43	64	65	6	0	1	1	16
1982-83	Peterborough	OHL	56	42	49	91	33	4	1	4	5	0
1983-84a	**Detroit**	**NHL**	**80**	**39**	**48**	**87**	**33**	**4**	**3**	**3**	**6**	**0**
1984-85	**Detroit**	**NHL**	**80**	**30**	**59**	**89**	**58**	**3**	**2**	**1**	**3**	**2**
1985-86	**Detroit**	**NHL**	**51**	**14**	**28**	**42**	**16**	....	....	....	....	....
1986-87	**Detroit**	**NHL**	**80**	**31**	**59**	**90**	**43**	**16**	**5**	**13**	**18**	**8**
1987-88	**Detroit**	**NHL**	**64**	**50**	**52**	**102**	**44**	**3**	**1**	**3**	**4**	**6**
1988-89b	**Detroit**	**NHL**	**80**	**65**	**90**	**155**	**61**	**6**	**5**	**5**	**10**	**2**
1989-90	**Detroit**	**NHL**	**79**	**62**	**65**	**127**	**79**	....	....	....	....	....
1990-91	**Detroit**	**NHL**	**80**	**51**	**57**	**108**	**34**	**7**	**3**	**3**	**6**	**4**
1991-92	**Detroit**	**NHL**	**79**	**45**	**58**	**103**	**64**	**11**	**3**	**5**	**8**	**12**
1992-93	**Detroit**	**NHL**	**84**	**58**	**79**	**137**	**44**	**7**	**4**	**3**	**7**	**4**
	NHL Totals		**757**	**445**	**595**	**1040**	**476**	**57**	**26**	**36**	**62**	**38**

a NHL All-Rookie Team (1984)
b Won Lester B. Pearson Award (1989)
Played in NHL All-Star Game (1984, 1988-93)

ZALAPSKI, ZARLEY

Defense. Shoots left. 6'1", 211 lbs. Born, Edmonton, Alta., April 22, 1968.
(Pittsburgh's 1st choice, 4th overall, in 1986 Entry Draft).

			Regular Season					Playoffs				
Season	Club	Lea	GP	G	A	TP	PIM	GP	G	A	TP	PIM
1985-86	Cdn. Olympic	....	59	22	37	59	56	....	....	....	....	....
1986-87	Cdn. Olympic	....	74	11	29	40	28	....	....	....	....	....
1987-88	Cdn. National	....	47	3	13	16	32	....	....	....	....	....
	Cdn. Olympic	....	8	1	3	4	2	....	....	....	....	....
	Pittsburgh	**NHL**	**15**	**3**	**8**	**11**	**7**	....	....	....	....	....
1988-89a	**Pittsburgh**	**NHL**	**58**	**12**	**33**	**45**	**57**	**11**	**1**	**8**	**9**	**13**
1989-90	**Pittsburgh**	**NHL**	**51**	**6**	**25**	**31**	**37**	....	....	....	....	....
1990-91	**Pittsburgh**	**NHL**	**66**	**12**	**36**	**48**	**59**	....	....	....	....	....
	Hartford	**NHL**	**11**	**3**	**3**	**6**	**6**	**6**	**1**	**3**	**4**	**8**
1991-92	**Hartford**	**NHL**	**79**	**20**	**37**	**57**	**120**	**7**	**2**	**3**	**5**	**6**
1992-93	**Hartford**	**NHL**	**83**	**14**	**51**	**65**	**94**	....	....	....	....	....
	NHL Totals		**363**	**70**	**193**	**263**	**380**	**24**	**4**	**14**	**18**	**27**

a NHL All-Rookie Team (1989)
Played in NHL All-Star Game (1993)

Traded to **Hartford** by **Pittsburgh** with John Cullen and Jeff Parker for Ron Francis, Grant Jennings and Ulf Samuelsson, March 4, 1991.

ZAMUNER, ROB (ZAM-un-uhr)

Center. Shoots left. 6'2", 202 lbs. Born, Oakville, Ont., September 17, 1969.
(NY Rangers' 3rd choice, 45th overall, in 1989 Entry Draft).

			Regular Season					Playoffs				
Season	Club	Lea	GP	G	A	TP	PIM	GP	G	A	TP	PIM
1986-87	Guelph	OHL	62	6	15	21	8	....	....	....	....	....
1987-88	Guelph	OHL	58	20	41	61	18	....	....	....	....	....
1988-89a	Guelph	OHL	66	46	65	111	38	7	5	5	10	9
1989-90	Flint	IHL	77	44	35	79	32	4	1	0	1	6
1990-91	Binghamton	AHL	80	25	58	83	50	9	7	6	13	35
1991-92	**NY Rangers**	**NHL**	**9**	**1**	**2**	**3**	**2**	....	....	....	....	....
	Binghamton	AHL	61	19	53	72	42	11	8	9	17	8
1992-93	**Tampa Bay**	**NHL**	**84**	**15**	**28**	**43**	**74**	....	....	....	....	....
	NHL Totals		**93**	**16**	**30**	**46**	**76**					

a OHL Third All-Star Team (1989)
Signed as a free agent by **Tampa Bay**, July 13, 1992.

ZAVISHA, BRAD

Left wing. Shoots left. 6'2", 205 lbs. Born, Hines Creek, Alta., January 4, 1972.
(Quebec's 3rd choice, 43rd overall, in 1990 Entry Draft).

			Regular Season					Playoffs				
Season	Club	Lea	GP	G	A	TP	PIM	GP	G	A	TP	PIM
1988-89	Seattle	WHL	52	8	13	21	43	....	....	....	....	....
1989-90	Seattle	WHL	69	22	38	60	124	13	1	6	7	16
1990-91	Seattle	WHL	24	15	12	27	40	....	....	....	....	....
	Portland	WHL	48	25	22	47	41	....	....	....	....	....
1991-92a	Portland	WHL	11	7	4	11	18	....	....	....	....	....
	Lethbridge	WHL	59	44	40	84	160	5	3	1	4	18
1992-93			DID NOT PLAY – INJURED									

a WHL East First All-Star Team (1992)
Traded to **Edmonton** by **Quebec** with Ron Tugnutt for Martin Rucinsky, March 10, 1992.

ZELEPUKIN, VALERI (zeh-leh-POO-kin)

Left wing. Shoots left. 6', 190 lbs. Born, Voskresensk, Soviet Union, September 17, 1968.
(New Jersey's 13th choice, 221st overall, in 1990 Entry Draft).

			Regular Season					Playoffs				
Season	Club	Lea	GP	G	A	TP	PIM	GP	G	A	TP	PIM
1984-85	Khimik	USSR	5	0	0	0	2	....	....	....	....	....
1985-86	Khimik	USSR	33	2	2	4	10	....	....	....	....	....
1986-87	Khimik	USSR	19	1	0	1	4	....	....	....	....	....
1987-88	SKA MVO	USSR 2	18	18	6	24	....	....	....	....	....	....
	CSKA	USSR	19	3	1	4	8	....	....	....	....	....
1988-89	CSKA	USSR	17	2	3	5	2	....	....	....	....	....
1989-90	Khimik	USSR	46	17	14	31	26	....	....	....	....	....
1990-91	Khimik	USSR	34	11	6	17	38	....	....	....	....	....
1991-92	**New Jersey**	**NHL**	**44**	**13**	**18**	**31**	**28**	**4**	**1**	**1**	**2**	**2**
	Utica	AHL	22	20	9	29	8	....	....	....	....	....
1992-93	**New Jersey**	**NHL**	**78**	**23**	**41**	**64**	**70**	**5**	**0**	**2**	**2**	**0**
	NHL Totals		**122**	**36**	**59**	**95**	**98**	**9**	**1**	**3**	**4**	**2**

ZEMLAK, RICHARD ANDREW

Right wing. Shoots right. 6'2", 190 lbs. Born, Wynard, Sask., March 3, 1963.
(St. Louis' 9th choice, 209th overall, in 1981 Entry Draft).

			Regular Season					Playoffs				
Season	Club	Lea	GP	G	A	TP	PIM	GP	G	A	TP	PIM
1980-81	Spokane	WHL	72	19	19	38	132	4	1	1	2	6
1981-82	Spokane	WHL	26	9	20	29	113	....	....	....	....	....
	Winnipeg	WHL	2	1	2	3	0	....	....	....	....	....
	Medicine Hat	WHL	41	11	20	31	70	....	....	....	....	....
	Salt Lake	CHL	6	0	0	0	2	1	0	0	0	0
1982-83	Medicine Hat	WHL	51	20	17	37	119	....	....	....	....	....
	Nanaimo	WHL	18	2	8	10	50	....	....	....	....	....
1983-84	Montana	CHL	14	2	2	4	17	....	....	....	....	....
	Toledo	IHL	45	8	19	27	101	....	....	....	....	....
1984-85	Muskegon	IHL	64	19	18	37	223	17	5	4	9	68
	Fredericton	AHL	16	3	4	7	59	....	....	....	....	....
1985-86	Fredericton	AHL	58	6	5	11	305	3	0	0	0	49
	Muskegon	IHL	3	1	2	3	36	....	....	....	....	....
1986-87	**Quebec**	**NHL**	**20**	**0**	**2**	**2**	**47**	....	....	....	....	....
	Fredericton	AHL	29	9	6	15	201	....	....	....	....	....
1987-88	**Minnesota**	**NHL**	**54**	**1**	**4**	**5**	**307**	....	....	....	....	....
1988-89	**Minnesota**	**NHL**	**3**	**0**	**0**	**0**	**13**	....	....	....	....	....
	Kalamazoo	IHL	2	1	3	4	22	....	....	....	....	....
	Pittsburgh	**NHL**	**31**	**0**	**0**	**0**	**135**	**1**	**0**	**0**	**0**	**10**
	Muskegon	IHL	18	5	4	9	55	8	1	1	2	35
1989-90	**Pittsburgh**	**NHL**	**19**	**1**	**5**	**6**	**43**	....	....	....	....	....
	Muskegon	IHL	61	17	39	56	263	14	3	4	7	105
1990-91	Salt Lake	IHL	59	14	20	34	194	3	0	1	1	14
1991-92	**Calgary**	**NHL**	**5**	**0**	**1**	**1**	**42**	....	....	....	....	....
	Salt Lake	IHL	60	5	14	19	204	3	0	0	0	0
1992-93	Milwaukee	IHL	62	3	9	12	301	2	1	1	2	6
	NHL Totals		**132**	**2**	**12**	**14**	**587**	**1**	**0**	**0**	**0**	**10**

Rights sold to **Quebec** by **St. Louis** with rights to Dan Wood and Roger Hagglund, June 22, 1984. Claimed by **Minnesota** in NHL Waiver Draft, October 5, 1987. Traded to **Pittsburgh** by **Minnesota** for the rights to Rob Gaudreau, November 1, 1988. Signed as a free agent by **Calgary**, November 8, 1990.

ZEMLICKA, RICHARD (zhem-LEECH-kah)

Right/Left wing. Shoots left. 6'1", 189 lbs. Born, Prague, Czechoslovakia, April 13, 1964.
(Edmonton's 9th choice, 185th overall, in 1990 Entry Draft).

			Regular Season					Playoffs				
Season	Club	Lea	GP	G	A	TP	PIM	GP	G	A	TP	PIM
1986-87	Sparta Praha	Czech.	27	7	3	10	14	....	....	....	....	....
1987-88	Sparta Praha	Czech.	44	8	10	18	32	....	....	....	....	....
1988-89	Sparta Praha	Czech.	42	20	17	37	40	....	....	....	....	....
1989-90	Sparta Praha	Czech.	45	15	14	29	....	....	....	....	....	....
1990-91	Sparta Praha	Czech.	51	22	30	52	99	....	....	....	....	....
1991-92	Sparta Praha	Czech.	27	14	23	37	39	....	....	....	....	....
	TPS	Fin.	15	5	9	14	6	3	2	1	3	0
1992-93	Freiburg	Ger.	43	25	31	56	52	7	3	3	6	2

ZENT, JASON

Left wing. Shoots left. 5'11", 180 lbs. Born, Buffalo, NY, April 15, 1971.
(NY Islanders' 3rd choice, 44th overall, in 1989 Entry Draft).

			Regular Season					Playoffs				
Season	Club	Lea	GP	G	A	TP	PIM	GP	G	A	TP	PIM
1990-91	U. Wisconsin	WCHA	39	19	18	37	51	....	....	....	....	....
1991-92a	U. Wisconsin	WCHA	39	22	17	39	128	....	....	....	....	....
1992-93	U. Wisconsin	WCHA	40	26	12	38	92	....	....	....	....	....

a NCAA All-Tournament Team (1992)

ZETTLER, ROB

Defense. Shoots left. 6'3", 195 lbs.   Born, Sept Iles, Que., March 8, 1968.
(Minnesota's 5th choice, 55th overall, in 1986 Entry Draft).

				Regular Season					Playoffs			
Season	Club	Lea	GP	G	A	TP	PIM	GP	G	A	TP	PIM
1985-86	S.S. Marie	OHL	57	5	23	28	92	....	....	....	....	....
1986-87	S.S. Marie	OHL	64	13	22	35	89	4	0	0	0	0
1987-88	Kalamazoo	IHL	2	0	1	1	0	7	0	2	2	2
	S.S. Marie	OHL	64	7	41	48	77	6	2	2	4	9
1988-89	**Minnesota**	**NHL**	**2**	**0**	**0**	**0**	**0**	....	....	....	....	....
	Kalamazoo	IHL	80	5	21	26	79	6	0	1	1	26
1989-90	**Minnesota**	**NHL**	**31**	**0**	**8**	**8**	**45**	....	....	....	....	....
	Kalamazoo	IHL	41	6	10	16	64	7	0	0	0	6
1990-91	**Minnesota**	**NHL**	**47**	**1**	**4**	**5**	**119**	....	....	....	....	....
	Kalamazoo	IHL	1	0	0	0	2	....	....	....	....	....
1991-92	**San Jose**	**NHL**	**74**	**1**	**8**	**9**	**99**	....	....	....	....	....
1992-93	**San Jose**	**NHL**	**80**	**0**	**7**	**7**	**150**	....	....	....	....	....
	NHL Totals		**234**	**2**	**27**	**29**	**413**	....	....	....	....	....

Claimed by **San Jose** from **Minnesota** in Dispersal Draft, May 30, 1991.

ZEZEL, PETER   (ZEH-zuhl)

Center. Shoots left. 5'11", 200 lbs.   Born, Toronto, Ont., April 22, 1965.
(Philadelphia's 1st choice, 41st overall, in 1983 Entry Draft).

				Regular Season					Playoffs			
Season	Club	Lea	GP	G	A	TP	PIM	GP	G	A	TP	PIM
1982-83	Toronto	OHL	66	35	39	74	28	4	2	4	6	0
1983-84	Toronto	OHL	68	47	86	133	31	9	7	5	12	4
1984-85	**Philadelphia**	**NHL**	**65**	**15**	**46**	**61**	**26**	19	1	8	9	28
1985-86	**Philadelphia**	**NHL**	**79**	**17**	**37**	**54**	**76**	5	3	1	4	4
1986-87	**Philadelphia**	**NHL**	**71**	**33**	**39**	**72**	**71**	25	3	10	13	10
1987-88	**Philadelphia**	**NHL**	**69**	**22**	**35**	**57**	**42**	7	3	2	5	7
1988-89	**Philadelphia**	**NHL**	**26**	**4**	**13**	**17**	**15**	....	....	....	....	....
	St. Louis	**NHL**	**52**	**17**	**36**	**53**	**27**	10	6	6	12	4
1989-90	**St. Louis**	**NHL**	**73**	**25**	**47**	**72**	**30**	12	1	7	8	4
1990-91	**Washington**	**NHL**	**20**	**7**	**5**	**12**	**10**	....	....	....	....	....
	Toronto	**NHL**	**32**	**14**	**14**	**28**	**4**	....	....	....	....	....
1991-92	**Toronto**	**NHL**	**64**	**16**	**33**	**49**	**26**	....	....	....	....	....
1992-93	**Toronto**	**NHL**	**70**	**12**	**23**	**35**	**24**	20	2	1	3	6
	NHL Totals		**621**	**182**	**328**	**510**	**351**	**98**	**19**	**35**	**54**	**63**

Traded to **St. Louis** by **Philadelphia** for Mike Bullard, November 29, 1988. Traded to **Washington** by **St. Louis** with Mike Lalor for Geoff Courtnall, July 13, 1990. Traded to **Toronto** by **Washington** with Bob Rouse for Al Iafrate, January 16, 1991.

ZHAMNOV, ALEXEI   (zham-NOV)

Center. Shoots left. 6'1", 187 lbs.   Born, Moscow, Soviet Union, October 1, 1970.
(Winnipeg's 5th choice, 77th overall, in 1990 Entry Draft).

				Regular Season					Playoffs			
Season	Club	Lea	GP	G	A	TP	PIM	GP	G	A	TP	PIM
1988-89	Moscow D'amo	USSR	4	0	0	0	0	....	....	....	....	....
1989-90	Moscow D'amo	USSR	43	11	6	17	21	....	....	....	....	....
1990-91	Moscow D'amo	USSR	46	16	12	28	24	....	....	....	....	....
1991-92	Moscow D'amo	CIS	39	15	21	36	28	....	....	....	....	....
1992-93	**Winnipeg**	**NHL**	**68**	**25**	**47**	**72**	**58**	6	0	2	2	2
	NHL Totals		**68**	**25**	**47**	**72**	**58**	**6**	**0**	**2**	**2**	**2**

ZHITNIK, ALEXEI   (ZHIT-nik)

Defense. Shoots left. 5'11", 180 lbs.   Born, Kiev, Soviet Union, October 10, 1972.
(Los Angeles' 3rd choice, 81st overall, in 1991 Entry Draft).

				Regular Season					Playoffs			
Season	Club	Lea	GP	G	A	TP	PIM	GP	G	A	TP	PIM
1989-90	Sokol Kiev	USSR	31	3	4	7	16	....	....	....	....	....
1990-91	Sokol Kiev	USSR	46	1	4	5	46	....	....	....	....	....
1991-92	CSKA	CIS	44	2	7	9	52	....	....	....	....	....
1992-93	**Los Angeles**	**NHL**	**78**	**12**	**36**	**48**	**80**	24	3	9	12	26
	NHL Totals		**78**	**12**	**36**	**48**	**80**	**24**	**3**	**9**	**12**	**26**

ZHOLTOK, SERGEI   (ZHOL-tok)

Left wing. Shoots right. 6', 185 lbs.   Born, Riga, Soviet Union, December 2, 1972.
(Boston's 2nd choice, 55th overall, in 1992 Entry Draft).

				Regular Season					Playoffs			
Season	Club	Lea	GP	G	A	TP	PIM	GP	G	A	TP	PIM
1990-91	Dynamo Riga	USSR	39	4	0	4	16	....	....	....	....	....
1991-92	Riga	CIS	27	6	3	9	6	....	....	....	....	....
1992-93	**Boston**	**NHL**	**1**	**0**	**1**	**1**	**0**	....	....	....	....	....
	Providence	AHL	64	31	35	66	57	6	3	5	8	4
	NHL Totals		**1**	**0**	**1**	**1**	**0**	....	....	....	....	....

ZMOLEK, DOUG

Defense. Shoots left. 6'2", 225 lbs.   Born, Rochester, MN, November 3, 1970.
(Minnesota's 1st choice, 7th overall, in 1989 Entry Draft).

				Regular Season					Playoffs			
Season	Club	Lea	GP	G	A	TP	PIM	GP	G	A	TP	PIM
1989-90	U. Minnesota	WCHA	40	1	10	11	52	....	....	....	....	....
1990-91	U. Minnesota	WCHA	34	11	6	17	38	....	....	....	....	....
1991-92ab	U. Minnesota	WCHA	41	6	20	26	84	....	....	....	....	....
1992-93	**San Jose**	**NHL**	**84**	**5**	**10**	**15**	**229**	....	....	....	....	....
	NHL Totals		**84**	**5**	**10**	**15**	**229**	....	....	....	....	....

a   WCHA Second All-Star Team (1992)
b   NCAA West Second All-American Team (1992)
Claimed by **San Jose** from **Minnesota** in Dispersal Draft, May 30, 1991.

ZOLOTOV, ROMAN   (ZOH-loh-tov)

Defense. Shoots left. 6'1", 191 lbs.   Born, Moscow, USSR, February 13, 1974.
(Philadelphia's 5th choice, 127th overall, in 1992 Entry Draft).

				Regular Season					Playoffs			
Season	Club	Lea	GP	G	A	TP	PIM	GP	G	A	TP	PIM
1991-92	Moscow D'amo	CIS	1	0	0	0	0	....	....	....	....	....
1992-93	Mosc.D'amo Jr.	CIS			UNAVAILABLE							

ZOLOTOV, SERGEI   (ZOH-loh-tov)

Left wing. Shoots right. 5'10", 172 lbs.   Born, Kazan, Soviet Union, January 27, 1971.
(Calgary's 11th choice, 219th overall, in 1991 Entry Draft).

				Regular Season					Playoffs			
Season	Club	Lea	GP	G	A	TP	PIM	GP	G	A	TP	PIM
1988-89	Soviet Wings	USSR	34	5	1	6	4	....	....	....	....	....
1989-90	Soviet Wings	USSR	48	12	2	14	14	....	....	....	....	....
1990-91	Soviet Wings	USSR	42	9	6	15	12	....	....	....	....	....
1991-92	Soviet Wings	CIS	39	12	5	17	4	....	....	....	....	....
1992-93	Soviet Wings	CIS	42	15	6	21	14	7	3	3	6	0

ZOMBO, RICHARD (RICK)

Defense. Shoots right. 6'1", 195 lbs.   Born, Des Plaines, IL, May 8, 1963.
(Detroit's 6th choice, 149th overall, in 1981 Entry Draft).

				Regular Season					Playoffs			
Season	Club	Lea	GP	G	A	TP	PIM	GP	G	A	TP	PIM
1981-82	North Dakota	WCHA	45	1	15	16	31	....	....	....	....	....
1982-83	North Dakota	WCHA	35	5	11	16	41	....	....	....	....	....
1983-84	North Dakota	WCHA	34	7	24	31	40	....	....	....	....	....
1984-85	**Detroit**	**NHL**	**1**	**0**	**0**	**0**	**0**	....	....	....	....	....
	Adirondack	AHL	56	3	32	35	70	....	....	....	....	....
1985-86	**Detroit**	**NHL**	**14**	**0**	**1**	**1**	**16**	....	....	....	....	....
	Adirondack	AHL	69	7	34	41	94	17	0	4	4	40
1986-87	**Detroit**	**NHL**	**44**	**1**	**4**	**5**	**59**	7	0	1	1	9
	Adirondack	AHL	25	0	6	6	22	....	....	....	....	....
1987-88	**Detroit**	**NHL**	**62**	**3**	**14**	**17**	**96**	16	0	6	6	55
1988-89	**Detroit**	**NHL**	**75**	**1**	**20**	**21**	**106**	6	0	1	1	16
1989-90	**Detroit**	**NHL**	**77**	**5**	**20**	**25**	**95**	....	....	....	....	....
1990-91	**Detroit**	**NHL**	**77**	**4**	**19**	**23**	**55**	7	1	0	1	10
1991-92	**Detroit**	**NHL**	**3**	**0**	**0**	**0**	**15**	....	....	....	....	....
	St. Louis	**NHL**	**64**	**3**	**15**	**18**	**46**	6	0	2	2	12
1992-93	**St. Louis**	**NHL**	**71**	**0**	**15**	**15**	**78**	11	0	1	1	12
	NHL Totals		**488**	**17**	**108**	**125**	**566**	**53**	**1**	**11**	**12**	**114**

Traded to **St. Louis** by **Detroit** for Vincent Riendeau, October 18, 1991.

ZUBOV, SERGEI   (ZOO-bahf)

Defense. Shoots right. 6'1", 199 lbs.   Born, Moscow, Soviet Union, July 22, 1970.
(NY Rangers' 6th choice, 85th overall, in 1990 Entry Draft).

				Regular Season					Playoffs			
Season	Club	Lea	GP	G	A	TP	PIM	GP	G	A	TP	PIM
1988-89	CSKA	USSR	29	1	4	5	10	....	....	....	....	....
1989-90	CSKA	USSR	48	6	2	8	16	....	....	....	....	....
1990-91	CSKA	USSR	41	6	5	11	12	....	....	....	....	....
1991-92	CSKA	CIS	44	4	7	11	8	....	....	....	....	....
1992-93	CSKA	CIS	1	0	1	1	0	....	....	....	....	....
	NY Rangers	**NHL**	**49**	**8**	**23**	**31**	**4**	....	....	....	....	....
	Binghamton	AHL	30	7	29	36	14	11	5	5	10	2
	NHL Totals		**49**	**8**	**23**	**31**	**4**	....	....	....	....	....

ZWAKMAN, GREG

Defense. Shoots left. 6'2", 182 lbs.   Born, Edina, MN, September 23, 1973.
(Hartford's 9th choice, 201st overall, in 1992 Entry Draft).

				Regular Season					Playoffs			
Season	Club	Lea	GP	G	A	TP	PIM	GP	G	A	TP	PIM
1991-92	Edina	HS	25	5	8	13	12	....	....	....	....	....
1992-93	U. Minnesota	WCHA	36	0	1	1	30	....	....	....	....	....

ZYGULSKI, SCOTT

Defense. Shoots right. 6'1", 190 lbs.   Born, South Bend, IN, April 11, 1970.
(Detroit's 7th choice, 137th overall, in 1989 Entry Draft).

				Regular Season					Playoffs			
Season	Club	Lea	GP	G	A	TP	PIM	GP	G	A	TP	PIM
1989-90	Boston College	H.E.	14	0	1	1	6	....	....	....	....	....
1990-91	Boston College	H.E.	25	0	5	5	2	....	....	....	....	....
1991-92	Boston College	H.E.	32	0	4	4	24	....	....	....	....	....
1992-93	Boston College	H.E.	35	2	2	4	14	....	....	....	....	....

Late Additions to Player Register

BAKULA, MARTIN

Defense. Shoots left. 6'1", 190 lbs.   Born, Kladno, Czechoslovakia, June 23, 1970.
(Edmonton's 8th choice, 189th overall, in 1993 Entry Draft).

			Regular Season					Playoffs				
Season	Club	Lea	GP	G	A	TP	PIM	GP	G	A	TP	PIM
1987-88	Poldi Kladno	Czech.	30	0	1	1	4	....	....	....	....	....
1988-89	Poldi Kladno	Czech.	24	1	2	3	20	....	....	....	....	....
1989-90	Poldi Kladno	Czech.	17	0	1	1	....	....	....	....	....	....
1990-91						DID NOT PLAY						
1991-92	Alaska-Anch.	G.N.	28	5	14	19	24	....	....	....	....	....
1992-93	Alaska-Anch.	WCHA	35	9	15	24	62	....	....	....	....	....

BYAKIN, ILJA

Defense. Shoots left. 5'9", 183 lbs.   Born, Sverdlovsk, Soviet Union, February 2, 1963.
(Edmonton's 11th choice, 267th overall, in 1993 Entry Draft).

			Regular Season					Playoffs				
Season	Club	Lea	GP	G	A	TP	PIM	GP	G	A	TP	PIM
1983-84	Spartak	USSR	44	9	12	21	26	....	....	....	....	....
1984-85	Spartak	USSR	46	1	18	56		....	....	....	....	....
1985-86	Spartak	USSR	34	8	7	15	41	....	....	....	....	....
1986-87						DID NOT PLAY						
1987-88	Sverdlovsk	USSR	30	10	10	20	37	....	....	....	....	....
1988-89	Sverdlovsk	USSR	40	11	9	20	53	....	....	....	....	....
1989-90	Sverdlovsk	USSR	27	14	7	21	20	....	....	....	....	....
1990-91	CSKA	USSR	29	4	7	11	20	....	....	....	....	....
1991-92	Rapperswil	Switz.2	36	27	40	67	36	....	....	....	....	....
1992-93	Landshut	Ger.	44	12	19	31	43	6	5	6	11	6

CHIBIREV, IGOR

Center. Shoots left. 6'1", 170 lbs.   Born, Kiev, Soviet Union, April 19, 1968.
(Hartford's 8th choice, 266th overall, in 1993 Entry Draft).

			Regular Season					Playoffs				
Season	Club	Lea	GP	G	A	TP	PIM	GP	G	A	TP	PIM
1987-88	CSKA	USSR	29	5	1	6	8	....	....	....	....	....
1988-89	CSKA	USSR	34	7	9	16	16	....	....	....	....	....
1989-90	CSKA	USSR	46	8	2	10	12	....	....	....	....	....
1990-91	CSKA	USSR	40	10	9	19	4	....	....	....	....	....
1991-92	CSKA	CIS	38	21	17	38	46	....	....	....	....	....
1992-93	Fort Wayne	IHL	60	33	36	69	2	12	7	13	20	2

MALTSEV, OLEG

Left wing. Shoots left. 6'3", 224 lbs.   Born, Chelyabinsk, Soviet Union, April 15, 1963.
(Edmonton's 10th choice, 241st overall, in 1993 Entry Draft).

			Regular Season					Playoffs				
Season	Club	Lea	GP	G	A	TP	PIM	GP	G	A	TP	PIM
1980-81	Chelyabinsk	USSR	1	0	0	0	0	....	....	....	....	....
1981-82	Chelyabinsk	USSR	5	0	0	0	4	....	....	....	....	....
1982-83	SKA MVO	USSR 2				UNAVAILABLE						
1983-84	SKA MVO	USSR 2				UNAVAILABLE						
1984-85	CSKA	USSR	10	0	0	0	6	....	....	....	....	....
1985-86	Kazan	USSR 2				UNAVAILABLE						
1986-87	Kazan	USSR 2				UNAVAILABLE						
1987-88	Chelyabinsk	USSR	41	6	5	11	34	....	....	....	....	....
1988-89	Chelyabinsk	USSR	24	5	7	12	12	....	....	....	....	....
1989-90	Chelyabinsk	USSR	30	4	4	8	18	....	....	....	....	....
1990-91	Chelyabinsk	USSR	21	2	4	6	10	....	....	....	....	....
1991-92	Chelyabinsk	CIS	30	11	12	23	48	....	....	....	....	....
1992-93	Chelyabinsk	CIS	39	21	15	36	54	7	1	1	2	8

PETRENKO, SERGEI

Left wing. Shoots left. 6', 176 lbs.   Born, Kharkov, Soviet Union, September 10, 1968.
(Buffalo's 5th choice, 168th overall, in 1993 Entry Draft).

			Regular Season					Playoffs				
Season	Club	Lea	GP	G	A	TP	PIM	GP	G	A	TP	PIM
1987-88	Moscow D'amo	USSR	31	2	5	7	4	....	....	....	....	....
1988-89	Moscow D'amo	USSR	23	4	6	10	6	....	....	....	....	....
1989-90	Moscow D'amo	USSR	33	5	4	9	8	....	....	....	....	....
1990-91	Moscow D'amo	USSR	43	14	13	27	10	....	....	....	....	....
1991-92	Moscow D'amo	CIS	31	9	10	19	10	....	....	....	....	....
1992-93	Moscow D'amo	CIS	36	12	12	24	10	10	4	5	9	6

TITOV, GERMAN

Center. Shoots left. 6'1", 185 lbs.   Born, Borovsk, Soviet Union, October 16, 1965.
(Calgary's 10th choice, 252nd overall, in 1993 Entry Draft).

			Regular Season					Playoffs				
Season	Club	Lea	GP	G	A	TP	PIM	GP	G	A	TP	PIM
1982-83	Khimik	USSR	16	0	2	2	4	....	....	....	....	....
1983-84						DID NOT PLAY						
1984-85						DID NOT PLAY						
1985-86						DID NOT PLAY						
1986-87	Khimik	USSR	23	1	0	1	10	....	....	....	....	....
1987-88	Khimik	USSR	39	6	5	11	10	....	....	....	....	....
1988-89	Khimik	USSR	44	10	3	13	24	....	....	....	....	....
1989-90	Khimik	USSR	44	6	14	20	19	....	....	....	....	....
1990-91	Khimik	USSR	45	13	11	24	28	....	....	....	....	....
1991-92	Khimik	CIS	42	18	13	31	35	....	....	....	....	....
1992-93	TPS	Fin.	47	25	19	44	49	12	5	12	17	10

TOROPCHENKO, LEONID

Center. Shoots right. 6'2", 235 lbs.   Born, Moscow, Soviet Union, August 28, 1968.
(Pittsburgh's 10th choice, 260th overall, in 1993 Entry Draft).

			Regular Season					Playoffs				
Season	Club	Lea	GP	G	A	TP	PIM	GP	G	A	TP	PIM
1987-88	SKA Leningrad	USSR	6	2	0	2	0	....	....	....	....	....
1988-89	SKA Leningrad	USSR	33	7	4	11	11	....	....	....	....	....
1989-90	Khimik	USSR	42	6	2	8	24	....	....	....	....	....
1990-91	Khimik	USSR	46	6	4	10	24	....	....	....	....	....
1991-92	Khimik	CIS	42	14	4	18	34	....	....	....	....	....
1992-93	Springfield	AHL	71	31	30	61	59	13	4	4	8	8

Free Agent Signings

BENNING, BRIAN signed as a free agent by Florida, July 13, 1993.

DAY, JOE signed as a free agent by NY Islanders, August 24, 1993.

DUBOIS, ERIC signed as a free agent by Tampa Bay, June 2, 1993.

EAKINS, DALLAS signed as a free agent by Florida, July 8, 1993.

GOSSELIN, GUY signed as a free agent by San Jose, August 1993.

HULL, JODY signed as a free agent by Florida, August, 1993.

KIMBLE, DARRIN signed as a free agent by Florida, July 9, 1993.

KNIPSCHEER, FRED signed as a free agent by Boston, April 30, 1993.

LAMBERT, DENNY signed as a free agent by Anaheim, August 16, 1993.

LANGDON, DARREN signed as a free agent by NY Rangers, August 16, 1993.

LEBEAU, PATRICK signed as a free agent by Florida, July 26, 1993.

LEDYARD, GRANT signed as a free agent by Dallas, August 12, 1993.

LINDSAY, SCOTT signed as a free agent by Boston, July 13, 1993.

MAJOR, MARK signed as a free agent by Boston, July 22, 1993.

MURANO, ERIC signed as a free agent by NY Rangers, August 24, 1993.

NELSON, TODD signed as a free agent by Washington, August 15, 1993.

PEDERSON, MARK signed as a free agent by Detroit, August 24, 1993.

REDDICK, ELDON signed as a free agent by Florida, July 12, 1993.

SMYTH, GREG signed as a free agent by Florida, August 10, 1993.

STOLK, DARREN signed as a free agent by Boston, July 13, 1993

YOUNG, C.J. signed as a free agent by Florida, August, 1993.

Larry Robinson began his National Hockey League career in 1972-73 and went on play 20 seasons, 17 with the Montreal Canadiens and three with the Los Angeles Kings. During his years with Montreal, Robinson was a member of six Stanley Cup-winning teams. He also won numerous individual honors including the James Norris Memorial Trophy as the NHL's top defenseman in 1977 and 1980, the Conn Smythe Trophy as playoff MVP in 1978 and six selections to the NHL's First or Second All-Star Teams. In 1993-94, Robinson will serve as an assistant coach with the New Jersey Devils.

Retired NHL Player Index

Abbreviations: Teams/Cities: — **Ana.** – Anaheim, **Atl.** – Atlanta, **Bos.** – Boston; **Bro.** – Brooklyn; **Buf.** – Buffalo; **Cal.** – California; **Cgy.** – Calgary; **Chi.** – Chicago; **Cle.** – Cleveland; **Col.** – Colorado; **Dal.** – Dallas, **Det.** – Detroit; **Edm.** – Edmonton; **Fla.** – Florida, **Ham.** – Hamilton; **Hfd.** – Hartford; **K.C.** – Kansas City; **L.A.** – Los Angeles; **Min.** – Minnesota; **Mtl.** – Montreal; **Mtl.M.** – Montreal Maroons; **Mtl.W.** – Montreal Wanderers; **N.J.** – New Jersey; **NYA** – NY Americans; **NYI** – New York Islanders; **NYR** – New York Rangers; **Oak.** – Oakland; **Ott.** – Ottawa; **Phi.** – Philadelphia; **Pit.** – Pittsburgh; **Que.** – Quebec; **St.L.** – St. Louis; **S.J.** – San Jose, **T.B.** – Tampa Bay, **Tor.** – Toronto; **Van.** – Vancouver; **Wpg.** – Winnipeg; **Wsh.** – Washington.

Total seasons are rounded off to the nearest full season. **A** – assists; **G** – goals; **GP** – games played; **PIM** – penalties in minutes; **TP** – total points. * – deceased. Assists not recorded during 1917-18 season.

A

Name	NHL Teams	NHL Seasons	Regular Schedule GP	G	A	TP	PIM	Playoffs GP	G	A	TP	PIM	NHL Cup Wins	First NHL Season	Last NHL Season
Abbott, Reg	Mtl.	1	3	0	0	0	0	....	....	....	....	....		1952-53	1952-53
• Abel, Clarence	NYR, Chi.	8	333	18	18	36	359	38	1	1	2	58	2	1926-27	1933-34
Abel, Gerry	Det.	1	1	0	0	0	0	....	....	....	....	....		1966-67	1966-67
Abel, Sid	Det., Chi.	14	613	189	283	472	376	96	28	30	58	77	3	1938-39	1953-54
Abgrall, Dennis	L.A.	1	13	0	2	2	4	....	....	....	....	....		1975-76	1975-76
Abrahamsson, Thommy	Hfd.	1	32	6	11	17	16	....	....	....	....	....		1980-81	1980-81
Achtymichuk, Gene	Mtl., Det.	4	32	3	5	8	2	....	....	....	....	....		1951-52	1958-59
Acomb, Doug	Tor.	1	2	0	1	1	0	....	....	....	....	....		1969-70	1969-70
Adam, Douglas	NYR	1	4	0	1	1	0	....	....	....	....	....		1949-50	1949-50
Adam, Russ	Tor.	1	8	1	2	3	11	....	....	....	....	....		1982-83	1982-83
Adams, Greg C.	Phi., Hfd., Wsh., Edm., Van., Que., Det.	10	545	84	143	227	1173	43	2	11	13	153		1980-81	1989-90
Adams, Jack	Mtl.	1	42	6	12	18	11	3	0	0	0	0		1940-41	1940-41
• Adams, Jack J.	Tor., Ott.	7	173	82	29	111	307	10	3	0	3	12	2	1917-18	1926-27
• Adams, Stewart	Chi., Tor.	4	106	9	26	35	60	11	3	3	6	14		1929-30	1932-33
Adduono, Rick	Bos., Atl.	2	4	0	0	0	2	....	....	....	....	....		1975-76	1979-80
Affleck, Bruce	St.L., Van., NYI	7	280	14	66	80	86	8	0	0	0	0		1974-75	1983-84
Ahern, Fred	Cal., Cle., Col.	4	146	31	30	61	130	2	0	1	1	2		1974-75	1977-78
Ahlin,	Chi.	1	1	0	0	0	0	....	....	....	....	....		1937-38	1937-38
Ahrens, Chris	Min.	6	52	0	3	3	14	1	0	0	0	0		1973-74	1977-78
Ailsby, Lloyd	NYR	1	3	0	0	0	2	....	....	....	....	....		1951-52	1951-52
Aitken, Brad	Pit., Edm.	2	14	1	3	4	25	....	....	....	....	....		1987-88	1990-91
Albright, Clint	NYR	1	59	14	5	19	19	....	....	....	....	....		1948-49	1948-49
Aldcorn, Gary	Tor., Det., Bos.	5	226	41	56	97	78	6	1	2	3	4		1956-57	1960-61
Alexander, Claire	Tor., Van.	4	155	18	47	65	36	16	2	4	6	4		1974-75	1977-78
• Alexandre, Art	Mtl.	2	11	0	2	2	8	4	0	0	0	0		1931-32	1932-33
Allen, George	NYR, Chi., Mtl.	8	339	82	115	197	179	41	9	10	19	32		1938-39	1946-47
Allen, Jeff	Cle.	1	4	0	0	0	2	....	....	....	....	....		1977-78	1977-78
Allen, Keith	Det.	2	28	0	4	4	8	5	0	0	0	0	1	1953-54	1954-55
Allen, Viv	NYA	1	6	0	1	1	0	....	....	....	....	....		1940-41	1940-41
Alley, Steve	Hfd.	2	15	3	3	6	11	3	0	1	1	0		1979-80	1980-81
Allison, Dave	Mtl.	1	3	0	0	0	12	....	....	....	....	....		1983-84	1983-84
Allison, Mike	NYR, Tor., L.A.	10	499	102	166	268	630	82	9	17	26	135		1980-81	1989-90
Allison, Ray	Hfd., Phi.	7	238	64	93	157	223	12	2	3	5	20		1979-80	1986-87
Allum, Bill	NYR	1	1	0	1	1	0	....	....	....	....	....		1940-41	1940-41
• Amadio, Dave	Det., L.A.	3	125	5	11	16	163	16	1	2	3	18		1957-58	1968-69
Amodeo, Mike	Wpg.	1	19	0	0	0	2	....	....	....	....	....		1979-80	1979-80
Anderson, Bill	Bos.	1	....	....	....	....	....	1	0	0	0	0		1942-43	1942-43
Anderson, Dale	Det.	1	13	0	0	0	6	2	0	0	0	0		1956-57	1956-57
Anderson, Doug	Mtl.	1	....	....	....	....	....	2	0	0	0	0	1	1952-53	1952-53
Anderson, Earl	Det., Bos.	3	109	19	19	38	22	5	0	1	1	0		1974-75	1976-77
Anderson, Jim	L.A.	1	7	1	2	3	2	....	....	....	....	....		1967-68	1967-68
Anderson, Murray	Wsh.	1	40	0	1	1	68	....	....	....	....	....		1974-75	1974-75
Anderson, Ron C.	Det., L.A., St.L., Buf.	5	251	28	30	58	146	5	0	0	0	4		1967-68	1971-72
Anderson, Ron H.	Wsh.	1	28	9	7	16	8	....	....	....	....	....		1974-75	1974-75
Anderson, Russ	Pit., Hfd., L.A.	10	519	22	99	121	1086	10	0	3	3	28		1976-77	1984-85
• Anderson, Tom	Det., NYA, Bro.	8	319	62	127	189	190	16	2	7	9	62		1934-35	1941-42
Andersson, Kent-Erik	Min., NYR	7	456	72	103	175	78	50	4	11	15	4		1977-78	1983-84
Andersson, Peter	Wsh., Que.	3	172	10	41	51	80	7	0	2	2	2		1983-84	1985-86
Andrascik, Steve	NYR	1	....	....	....	....	....	1	0	0	0	0		1971-72	1971-72
Andrea, Paul	NYR, Pit., Cal., Buf.	4	150	31	49	80	12	....	....	....	....	....		1965-66	1970-71
Andrews, Lloyd	Tor.	4	53	8	5	13	10	7	2	0	2	5		1921-22	1924-25
Andruff, Ron	Mtl., Col.,	5	153	19	36	55	54	2	0	0	0	0		1974-75	1978-79
Angotti, Lou	NYR, Chi., Phi., Pit., St.L.	10	653	103	186	289	228	65	8	8	16	17		1964-65	1973-74
Anholt, Darrel	Chi.	1	1	0	0	0	0	....	....	....	....	....		1983-84	1983-84
Anslow, Bert	NYR	1	2	0	0	0	0	....	....	....	....	....		1947-48	1947-48
Antonovich, Mike	Min., Hfd., N.J.	5	87	10	15	25	37	....	....	....	....	....		1975-76	1983-84
Apps, Syl (Jr.)	NYR, Pit., L.A.	10	727	183	423	606	311	23	5	5	10	23		1970-71	1979-80
Apps, Syl (Sr.)	Tor.	10	423	201	231	432	56	69	25	28	53	16	3	1936-37	1947-48
Arbour, Al	Det., Chi., Tor., St.L.	14	626	12	58	70	617	86	1	8	9	92	3	1953-54	1970-71
• Arbour, Amos	Mtl., Ham., Tor.	6	109	51	13	64	66	....	....	....	....	....		1918-19	1923-24
Arbour, Jack	Det., Tor.	2	47	5	1	6	56	....	....	....	....	....		1926-27	1928-29
Arbour, John	Bos., Pit., Van., St.L.	5	106	1	9	10	149	5	0	0	0	0		1965-66	1971-72
Arbour, Ty	Pit., Chi.	5	207	28	28	56	112	11	2	0	2	6		1926-27	1930-31
Archambault, Michel	Chi.	1	3	0	0	0	0	....	....	....	....	....		1976-77	1976-77
Archibald, Jim	Min.	3	16	1	2	3	45	....	....	....	....	....		1984-85	1986-87
Areshenkoff, Ronald	Edm.	1	4	0	0	0	0	....	....	....	....	....		1979-80	1979-80
Armstrong, Bill	Phi.	1	1	0	1	1	0	....	....	....	....	....		1990-91	1990-91
• Armstrong, Bob	Bos.	12	542	13	86	99	671	42	1	7	8	28		1950-51	1961-62
Armstrong, George	Tor.	21	1187	296	417	713	721	110	26	34	60	88	4	1949-50	1970-71
Armstrong, Murray	Tor., NYA, Bro., Det.	8	270	67	121	188	62	30	4	6	10	2		1937-38	1945-46
• Armstrong, Red	Tor.	1	7	1	1	2	2	....	....	....	....	....		1962-63	1962-63
Armstrong, Tim	Tor.	1	11	1	0	1	6	....	....	....	....	....		1988-89	1988-89
Arnason, Chuck	Mtl., Atl., Pit., K.C., Col., Cle., Min., Wsh.	8	401	109	90	199	122	9	2	4	6	4		1971-72	1978-79
Arthur, Fred	Hfd., Phi.	3	80	1	8	9	49	4	0	0	0	2		1980-81	1982-83
Arundel, John	Tor.	1	3	0	0	0	0	....	....	....	....	....		1949-50	1949-50
• Ashbee, Barry	Bos., Phi.	5	284	15	70	85	291	17	0	4	4	22	1	1965-66	1973-74
• Ashby, Don	Tor., Col., Edm.	6	188	40	56	96	40	12	1	0	1	4		1975-76	1980-81
Ashworth, Frank	Chi.	1	18	5	4	9	2	....	....	....	....	....		1946-47	1946-47
Asmundson, Oscar	NYR, Det., St.L., NYA, Mtl.	5	112	11	23	34	30	9	0	2	2	4	1	1932-33	1937-38
Atanas, Walt	NYR	1	49	13	8	21	40	....	....	....	....	....		1944-45	1944-45
Atkinson, Steve	Bos., Buf., Wsh.	6	302	60	51	111	104	1	0	0	0	0		1968-69	1974-75
Attwell, Bob	Col.	2	22	1	5	6	0	....	....	....	....	....		1979-80	1980-81
Attwell, Ron	St.L., NYR	1	21	1	7	8	8	....	....	....	....	....		1967-68	1967-68
Aubin, Norm	Tor.	2	69	18	13	31	30	1	0	0	0	0		1981-82	1982-83
Aubry, Pierre	Que., Det.	5	202	24	26	50	133	20	1	1	2	32		1980-81	1984-85
Aubuchon, Ossie	Bos., NYR	2	50	19	12	31	4	6	1	0	1	0		1942-43	1943-44
Auge, Les	Col.	1	6	0	3	3	4	....	....	....	....	....		1980-81	1980-81
• Aurie, Larry	Det.	12	489	147	129	276	279	24	6	9	15	10	2	1927-28	1938-39
Awrey, Don	Bos., St.L., Mtl., Pit., NYR, Col.	16	979	31	158	189	1065	71	0	18	18	150	2	1963-64	1978-79
Ayres, Vern	NYA, Mtl.M., St.L., NYR	6	211	6	14	20	350	....	....	....	....	....		1930-31	1935-36

B

Name	NHL Teams	NHL Seasons	Regular Schedule GP	G	A	TP	PIM	Playoffs GP	G	A	TP	PIM	NHL Cup Wins	First NHL Season	Last NHL Season
Babando, Pete	Bos., Det., Chi., NYR	6	351	86	73	159	194	17	3	3	6	6	1	1947-48	1952-53
Babe, Warren	Min.	3	21	2	5	7	23	2	0	0	0	0		1987-88	1990-91
Babin, Mitch	St.L.	1	8	0	0	0	0	....	....	....	....	....		1975-76	1975-76

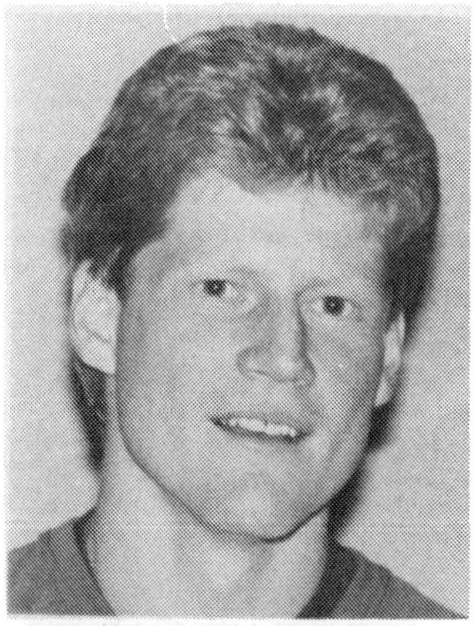

Mike Allison

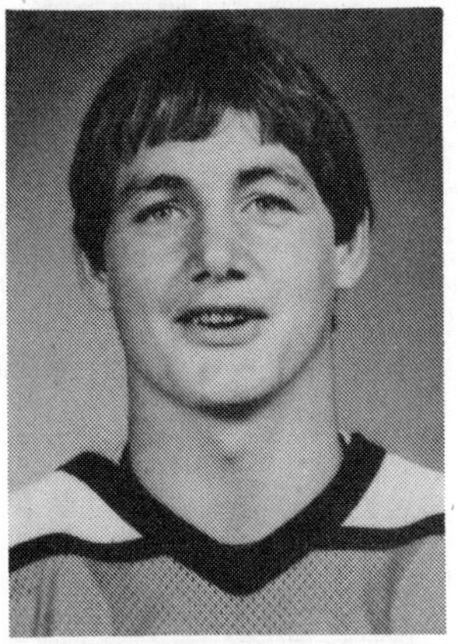

Ray Allison

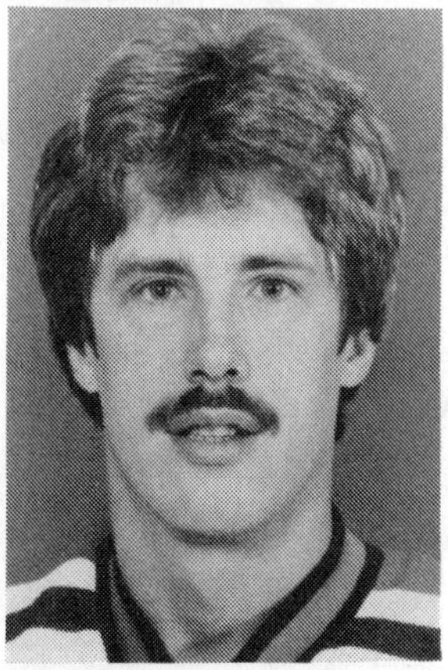

Mike Antonovich

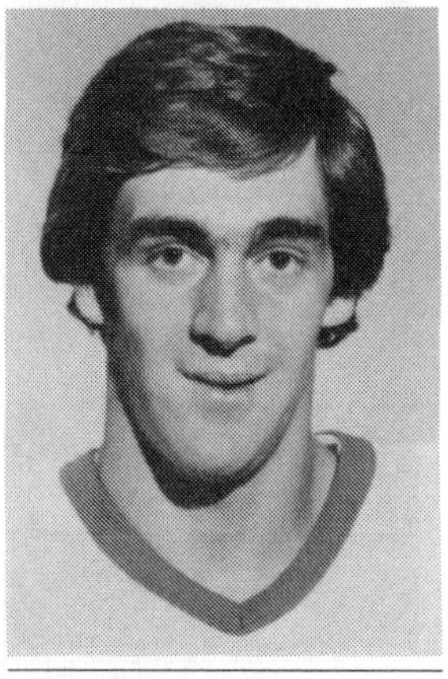

Pierre Aubrey

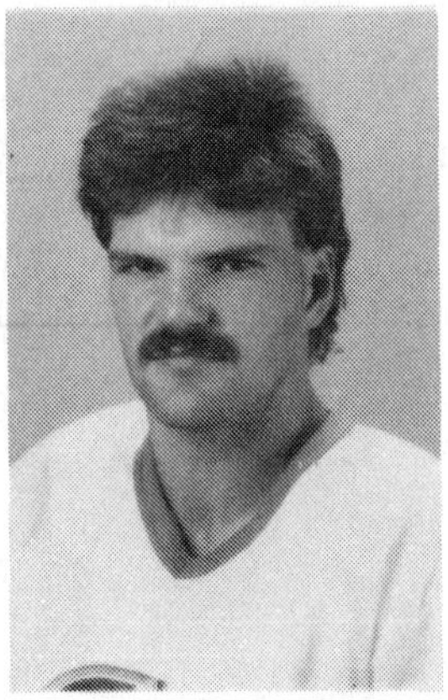

Joel Baillargeon

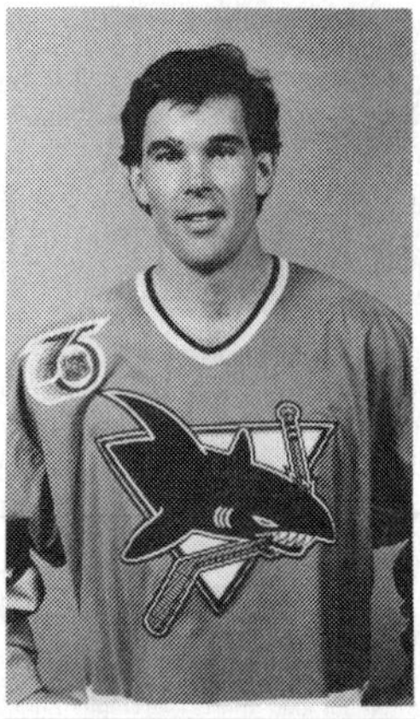

Don Barber

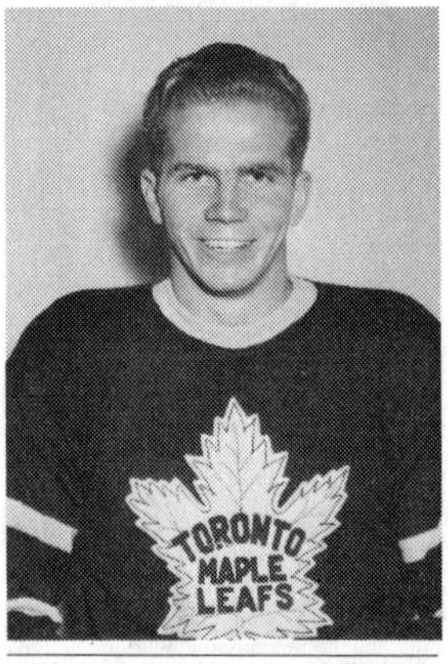

Bill Barilko

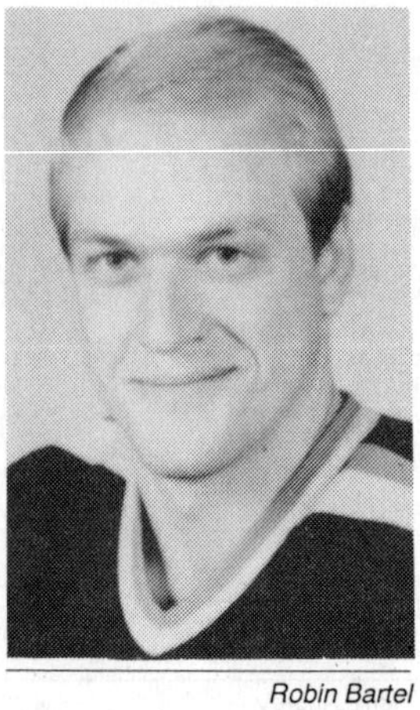

Robin Bartel

Name	NHL Teams	NHL Seasons	Regular Schedule					Playoffs					NHL Cup Wins	First NHL Season	Last NHL Season
			GP	G	A	TP	PIM	GP	G	A	TP	PIM			
Baby, John	Cle., Min.	2	26	2	8	10	26	....	....	....	....	....		1977-78	1978-79
Babych, Wayne	St.L., Pit., Que., Hfd.	9	519	192	246	438	498	41	7	9	16	25		1978-79	1986-87
Backman, Mike	NYR	3	18	1	6	7	18	10	2	2	4	2		1981-82	1983-84
Backor, Peter	Tor.	1	36	4	5	9	6	....	....	....	....	....	1	1944-45	1944-45
Backstrom, Ralph	Mtl., L.A., Chi.	17	1032	278	361	639	386	116	27	32	59	68	6	1956-57	1972-73
Bailey, Ace (G.)	Bos., Det., St.L., Wsh.	10	568	107	171	278	633	15	2	4	6	28	1	1968-69	1977-78
• Bailey, Ace (I.)	Tor.	8	313	111	82	193	472	21	3	4	7	12	1	1926-27	1933-34
Bailey, Bob	Tor., Det., Chi.	4	150	15	21	36	207	15	0	4	4	22		1953-54	1957-58
Bailey, Reid	Phi., Tor., Hfd.	4	40	1	3	4	105	16	0	2	2	25		1980-81	1983-84
Baillargeon, Joel	Wpg., Que.	3	20	0	2	2	31	....	....	....	....	....		1986-87	1988-89
Baird, Ken	Cal.	1	10	0	2	2	15	....	....	....	....	....		1971-72	1971-72
Baker, Bill	Mtl., Col., St.L., NYR	3	143	7	25	32	175	6	0	0	0	0		1980-81	1982-83
Bakovic, Peter	Van.	1	10	2	0	2	48	....	....	....	....	....		1987-88	1987-88
Balderis, Helmut	Min.	1	26	3	6	9	2	....	....	....	....	....		1989-90	1989-90
Baldwin, Doug	Tor., Det., Chi.	3	24	0	1	1	8	....	....	....	....	....		1945-46	1947-48
Balfour, Earl	Tor., Chi.,	7	288	30	22	52	78	26	0	3	3	4	1	1951-52	1960-61
• Balfour, Murray	Mtl., Chi., Bos.	8	306	67	90	157	393	40	9	10	19	45	1	1956-57	1964-65
Ball, Terry	Phi., Buf.	4	74	7	19	26	26	....	....	....	....	....		1967-68	1971-72
Balon, Dave	NYR, Mtl., Min., Van.	14	776	192	222	414	607	78	14	21	35	109	2	1959-60	1972-73
Baltimore, Byron	Edm.	1	2	0	0	0	4	....	....	....	....	....		1979-80	1979-80
Baluik, Stanley	Bos.	1	7	0	0	0	2	....	....	....	....	....		1959-60	1959-60
Bandura, Jeff	NYR	1	2	0	1	1	0	....	....	....	....	....		1980-81	1980-81
Barahona, Ralph J.	Bos.	2	6	2	2	4	0	....	....	....	....	....		1990-91	1991-92
Barbe, Andy	Tor.	1	1	0	0	0	2	....	....	....	....	....		1950-51	1950-51
Barber, Bill	Phi.	12	903	420	463	883	623	129	53	55	108	109	2	1972-73	1984-85
Barber, Don	Min., Wpg., Que., S.J.	4	115	25	32	57	64	11	4	4	8	10		1988-89	1991-92
• Barilko, Bill	Tor.	5	252	26	36	62	456	47	5	7	12	104	4	1946-47	1950-51
Barkley, Doug	Chi., Det.	6	253	24	80	104	382	30	0	9	9	63		1957-58	1965-66
Barlow, Bob	Min.	2	77	16	17	33	10	6	2	2	4	6		1969-70	1970-71
Barnes, Blair	L.A.	1	1	0	0	0	0	....	....	....	....	....		1982-83	1982-83
Barnes, Norm	Phi., Hfd.	4	156	6	38	44	178	12	0	0	0	8		1976-77	1981-82
Baron, Normand	Mtl., St.L.	2	27	2	0	2	51	3	0	0	0	22		1983-84	1985-86
Barrett, Fred	Min., L.A.	13	745	25	123	148	671	44	0	2	2	60		1970-71	1983-84
Barrett, John	Det., Wsh., Min.	8	488	20	77	97	604	16	2	2	4	50		1980-81	1987-88
Barrie, Doug	Pit., Buf., L.A.	3	158	10	42	52	268	....	....	....	....	....		1968-69	1971-72
Barry, Ed	Bos.	1	19	1	3	4	2	....	....	....	....	....		1946-47	1946-47
• Barry, Marty	NYA, Bos., Det., Mtl.	12	509	195	192	387	231	43	15	18	33	34	2	1927-28	1939-40
Barry, Ray	Bos.	1	18	1	2	3	6	....	....	....	....	....		1951-52	1951-52
Bartel, Robin	Cgy., Van.	2	41	0	1	1	14	6	0	0	0	16		1985-86	1986-87
Bartlett, Jim	Mtl., NYR, Bos.	5	191	34	23	57	273	2	0	0	0	0		1954-55	1960-61
• Barton, Cliff	Pit., Phi., NYR	3	85	10	9	19	22	....	....	....	....	....		1929-30	1939-40
Bathe, Frank	Det., Phi.,	9	224	3	28	31	542	27	1	3	4	42		1974-75	1983-84
Bathgate, Andy	NYR, Tor., Det., Pit.	17	1069	349	624	973	624	54	21	14	35	76	1	1952-53	1970-71
Bathgate, Frank	NYR	1	2	0	0	0	2	....	....	....	....	....		1952-53	1952-53
• Bauer, Bobby	Bos.	10	327	123	137	260	36	48	11	8	19	6	2	1935-36	1951-52
Baumgartner, Mike	K.C.	1	17	0	0	0	0	....	....	....	....	....		1974-75	1974-75
Baun, Bob	Tor., Oak., Det.	17	964	37	187	224	1493	96	3	12	15	171	4	1956-57	1972-73
Baxter, Paul	Que., Pit., Cgy.	8	472	48	121	169	1564	40	0	5	5	162		1979-80	1986-87
Beadle, Sandy	Wpg.	1	6	1	0	1	2	....	....	....	....	....		1980-81	1980-81
Beaton, Frank	NYR	2	25	1	1	2	43	....	....	....	....	....		1978-79	1979-80
Beattie, Red	Bos., Det., NYA	9	335	62	85	147	137	22	4	2	6	6		1930-31	1938-39
Beaudin, Norm	St.L., Min.	2	25	1	2	3	4	....	....	....	....	....		1967-68	1970-71
Beaudoin, Serge	Atl.	1	3	0	0	0	0	....	....	....	....	....		1979-80	1979-80
Beaudoin, Yves	Wsh.	3	11	0	0	0	5	....	....	....	....	....		1985-86	1987-88
Beck, Barry	Col., NYR, L.A.	10	615	104	251	355	1016	51	10	23	33	77		1977-78	1989-90
Beckett, Bob	Bos.	4	68	7	6	13	18	....	....	....	....	....		1956-57	1963-64
Bedard, James	Chi.	2	22	1	1	2	8	....	....	....	....	....		1949-50	1950-51
Bednarski, John	NYR, Edm.	4	100	2	18	20	114	1	0	0	0	0		1974-75	1979-80
Beers, Eddy	Cgy., St.L.	5	250	94	116	210	256	41	7	10	17	47		1981-82	1985-86
Behling, Dick	Det.	2	5	1	0	1	2	....	....	....	....	....		1940-41	1942-43
Beisler, Frank	NYA	2	2	0	0	0	0	....	....	....	....	....		1936-37	1939-40
Belanger, Alain	Tor.	1	9	0	1	1	6	....	....	....	....	....		1977-78	1977-78
Belanger, Roger	Pit.	1	44	3	5	8	32	....	....	....	....	....		1984-85	1984-85
Belisle, Danny	NYR	1	4	2	0	2	0	....	....	....	....	....		1960-61	1960-61
Beliveau, Jean	Mtl.	20	1125	507	712	1219	1029	162	79	97	176	211	10	1950-51	1970-71
• Bell, Billy	Mtl.W, Mtl., Ott.	6	61	3	1	4	4	9	0	0	0	0	1	1917-18	1923-24
Bell, Bruce	Que., St. L., NYR, Edm.	5	209	12	64	76	113	34	3	5	8	41		1984-85	1989-90
Bell, Harry	NYR	1	1	0	1	1	0	....	....	....	....	....		1946-47	1946-47
Bell, Joe	NYR	2	62	8	9	17	18	....	....	....	....	....		1942-43	1946-47
Belland, Neil	Van., Pit.	6	109	13	32	45	54	21	2	9	11	23		1981-82	1986-87
• Bellefeuille, Pete	Tor., Det.	4	92	26	4	30	58	....	....	....	....	....		1925-26	1929-30
Bellemer, Andy	Mtl.M.	1	15	0	0	0	0	....	....	....	....	....		1932-33	1932-33
Bend, Lin	NYR	1	8	3	1	4	2	....	....	....	....	....		1942-43	1942-43
Bennett, Bill	Bos., Hfd.	2	31	4	7	11	65	....	....	....	....	....		1978-79	1979-80
Bennett, Curt	St.L., NYR, Atl.	10	580	152	182	334	347	21	1	1	2	57		1970-71	1979-80
Bennett, Frank	Det.	1	7	0	1	1	2	....	....	....	....	....		1943-44	1943-44
Bennett, Harvey	Pit., Wsh., Phi., Min., St.L.	5	268	44	46	90	347	4	0	0	0	2		1974-75	1978-79
• Bennett, Max	Mtl.	1	1	0	0	0	0	....	....	....	....	....		1935-36	1935-36
Benning, Jim	Tor., Van.	9	605	52	191	243	461	7	1	1	2	2		1981-82	1989-90
Benoit, Joe	Mtl.	5	185	75	69	144	94	11	6	3	9	11	1	1940-41	1946-47
Benson, Bill	NYA, Bro.	2	67	11	25	36	35	....	....	....	....	....		1940-41	1941-42
Benson, Bobby	Bos.	1	8	0	1	1	4	....	....	....	....	....		1924-25	1924-25
• Bentley, Doug	Chi., NYR	13	566	219	324	543	217	23	9	8	17	8		1939-40	1953-54
• Bentley, Max	Chi., Tor., NYR	12	646	245	299	544	179	52	18	27	45	14	3	1940-41	1953-54
Bentley, Reggie	Chi.	1	11	1	2	3	2	....	....	....	....	....		1942-43	1942-43
Beraldo, Paul	Bos.	2	10	0	0	0	4	....	....	....	....	....		1987-88	1988-89
Berenson, Red	Mtl., NYR, St.L., Det.	17	987	261	397	658	305	85	23	14	37	49	2	1961-62	1977-78
Bergdinon, Fred	Bos.	1	2	0	0	0	0	....	....	....	....	....		1925-26	1925-26
Bergen, Todd	Phi.	1	14	11	5	16	4	17	4	9	13	8		1984-85	1984-85
Berger, Mike	Min.	2	30	3	1	4	67	....	....	....	....	....		1987-88	1988-89
Bergeron, Michel	Det., NYI, Wsh.	5	229	80	58	138	165	....	....	....	....	....		1974-75	1978-79
Bergeron, Yves	Pit.	2	3	0	0	0	0	....	....	....	....	....		1974-75	1976-77
Bergloff, Bob	Min.	1	2	0	0	0	5	....	....	....	....	....		1982-83	1982-83
Berglund, Bo	Que., Min., Phi.	3	130	28	39	67	40	9	2	0	2	6		1983-84	1985-86
Bergman, Gary	Det., Min., K.C.	12	838	68	299	367	1249	21	0	5	5	20		1964-65	1975-76
Bergman, Thommie	Det.	6	246	21	44	65	243	7	0	2	2	2		1972-73	1979-80
Bergqvist, Jonas	Cgy.	1	22	2	5	7	10	....	....	....	....	....		1989-90	1989-90
• Berlinquette, Louis	Mtl., Mtl.M., Pit.	8	193	44	29	73	111	16	1	1	2	0		1917-18	1925-26
Bernier, Serge	Phi., L.A., Que.	7	302	78	119	197	234	5	1	1	2	0		1968-69	1980-81
Berry, Bob	Mtl., L.A.	8	541	159	191	350	344	26	2	6	8	6		1968-69	1976-77
Berry, Doug	Col.	2	121	10	33	43	25	....	....	....	....	....		1979-80	1980-81
Berry, Fred	Det.	1	3	0	0	0	0	....	....	....	....	....		1976-77	1976-77
Berry, Ken	Edm., Van.	4	55	8	10	18	30	....	....	....	....	....		1981-82	1988-89
Besler, Phil	Bos., Chi., Det.	2	30	1	4	5	18	....	....	....	....	....		1935-36	1938-39
Bessone, Pete	Det.	1	6	0	1	1	6	....	....	....	....	....		1937-38	1937-38
Bethel, John	Wpg.	1	17	0	2	2	4	....	....	....	....	....		1979-80	1979-80
Bettio, Sam	Bos.	1	44	9	12	21	32	....	....	....	....	....		1949-50	1949-50
Beverley, Nick	Bos., Pit., NYR, Min., L.A., Col.	11	502	18	94	112	156	7	0	1	1	0		1966-67	1979-80
Bialowas, Dwight	Atl., Min.	4	164	11	46	57	46	....	....	....	....	....		1973-74	1976-77
Bianchin, Wayne	Pit., Edm.	7	276	68	41	109	137	3	0	1	1	6		1973-74	1979-80
Bidner, Todd	Wsh.	1	12	2	1	3	7	....	....	....	....	....		1981-82	1981-82
Biggs, Don	Min.	1	1	0	0	0	0	....	....	....	....	....		1984-85	1984-85
Bignell, Larry	Pit.	2	20	0	3	3	2	3	0	0	0	2		1973-74	1974-75
Bilodeau, Gilles	Que.	1	9	0	1	1	25	....	....	....	....	....		1979-80	1979-80
Bionda, Jack	Tor., Bos.	4	93	3	9	12	113	11	0	1	1	14		1955-56	1958-59
Bissett, Tom	Det.	1	5	0	0	0	0	....	....	....	....	....		1990-91	1990-91
Black, Stephen	Det., Chi.	2	113	11	20	31	77	13	0	0	0	13	1	1949-50	1950-51
Blackburn, Bob	NYR., Pit.	3	135	8	12	20	105	6	0	0	0	4		1968-69	1970-71
Blackburn, Don	Bos., Phi., NYR, NYI, Min.	6	185	23	44	67	87	12	3	0	3	10		1962-63	1972-73
Blade, Hank	Chi.	2	24	2	3	5	2	....	....	....	....	....		1946-47	1947-48
Bladon, Tom	Phi., Pit., Edm., Wpg., Det.	9	610	73	197	270	392	86	8	29	37	70	2	1972-73	1980-81
Blaine, Gary	Mtl.	1	1	0	0	0	0	....	....	....	....	....		1954-55	1954-55
• Blair, Andy	Tor., Chi.	9	402	74	86	160	323	38	6	6	12	32	1	1928-29	1936-37
Blair, Chuck	Tor.	2	3	0	0	0	0	....	....	....	....	....		1948-49	1950-51
Blair, George	Tor.	1	2	0	0	0	0	....	....	....	....	....		1950-51	1950-51

Name	NHL Teams	NHL Seasons	Regular Schedule GP	G	A	TP	PIM	Playoffs GP	G	A	TP	PIM	NHL Cup Wins	First NHL Season	Last NHL Season
Blaisdell, Mike	Det., NYR, Pit., Tor.	9	343	70	84	154	166	....	....	....	....	....		1980-81	1988-89
Blake, Mickey	St.L., Bos., Tor.	2	16	1	1	2	4	....	....	....	....	....		1934-35	1935-36
Blake, Toe	Mtl.M., Mtl.	15	578	235	292	527	272	57	25	37	62	23	3	1932-33	1947-48
Blight, Rick	Van., L.A.	7	326	96	125	221	170	5	0	5	5	2		1975-76	1982-83
Blinco, Russ	Mtl.M, Chi.	6	268	59	66	125	24	19	3	3	6	4	1	1933-34	1938-39
Block, Ken	Van.	1	1	0	0	0	0	....	....	....	....	....		1970-71	1970-71
Blomqvist, Timo	Wsh., N.J.	5	243	4	53	57	293	13	0	0	0	24		1981-82	1986-87
Bloom, Mike	Wsh., Det.	3	201	30	47	77	215	....	....	....	....	....		1974-75	1976-77
Blum, John	Edm., Bos., Wsh., Det.	8	250	7	34	41	610	20	0	2	2	27		1982-83	1989-90
Bodak, Bob	Cgy., Hfd.	2	4	0	0	0	29	....	....	....	....	....		1987-88	1989-90
Boddy, Gregg	Van.	5	273	23	44	67	263	3	0	0	0	0		1971-72	1975-76
Bodnar, Gus	Tor., Chi., Bos.	12	667	142	254	396	207	32	4	3	7	10	2	1943-44	1954-55
Boehm, Ron	Oak.	1	16	2	1	3	10	....	....	....	....	....		1967-68	1967-68
Boesch, Garth	Tor.	4	197	9	28	37	205	34	2	5	7	18	3	1946-47	1949-50
Boh, Rick	Min.	1	8	2	1	3	4	....	....	....	....	....		1987-88	1987-88
Boileau, Marc	Det.	1	54	5	6	11	8	....	....	....	....	....		1961-62	1961-62
Boileau, Rene	NYA	1	7	0	0	0	0	....	....	....	....	....		1925-26	1925-26
Boimistruck, Fred	Tor.	2	83	4	14	18	45	....	....	....	....	....		1981-82	1982-83
Boisvert, Serge	Tor., Mtl.	5	46	5	7	12	8	23	3	7	10	4	1	1982-83	1987-88
Boivin, Leo	Tor., Bos., Det., Pit., Min.	19	1150	72	250	322	1192	54	3	10	13	59		1951-52	1969-70
Boland, Mike A.	Phi.	1	2	0	0	0	0	....	....	....	....	....		1974-75	1974-75
Boland, Mike J.	K.C., Buf.	2	23	1	2	3	29	3	1	0	1	2		1974-75	1978-79
Boldirev, Ivan	Bos., Cal., Chi., Atl., Van., Det.	15	1052	361	505	866	507	48	13	20	33	14		1970-71	1984-85
Bolduc, Danny	Det., Cgy.	3	102	22	19	41	33	1	0	0	0	0		1978-79	1983-84
Bolduc, Michel	Que.	2	10	0	0	0	6	....	....	....	....	....		1981-82	1982-83
Boll, Buzz	Tor., NYA, Bro., Bos.	11	436	133	130	263	148	29	7	3	10	13		1933-34	1943-44
Bolonchuk, Larry	Van., Wsh.	4	74	3	9	12	97	....	....	....	....	....		1972-73	1977-78
Bolton, Hughie	Tor.	8	235	10	51	61	221	17	0	5	5	14		1949-50	1956-57
Bonar, Dan	L.A.	3	170	25	39	64	208	14	3	4	7	22		1980-81	1982-83
Bonin, Marcel	Det., Bos., Mtl.	9	454	97	175	272	336	50	11	14	25	51	4	1952-53	1961-62
Boo, Jim	Min.	1	6	0	0	0	22	....	....	....	....	....		1977-78	1977-78
Boone, Buddy	Bos.	2	34	5	3	8	28	22	2	1	3	25		1956-57	1957-58
Boothman, George	Tor.	2	58	17	19	36	18	5	2	1	3	2		1942-43	1943-44
Bordeleau, Chris	Mtl., St.L., Chi.,	4	205	38	65	103	82	19	4	7	11	17	1	1968-69	1971-72
Bordeleau, J.P.	Chi.	10	519	97	126	223	143	48	3	6	9	12		1969-70	1979-80
Bordeleau, Paulin	Van.	3	183	33	56	89	47	5	2	1	3	0		1973-74	1975-76
Borotsik, Jack	St.L.	1	1	0	0	0	0	....	....	....	....	....		1974-75	1974-75
Bossy, Mike	NYI	10	752	573	553	1126	210	129	85	75	160	38	4	1977-78	1986-87
Bostrom, Helge	Chi.	4	96	3	3	6	58	13	0	0	0	16		1929-30	1932-33
Botell, Mark	Phi.	1	32	4	10	14	31	....	....	....	....	....		1981-82	1981-82
Bothwell, Tim	NYR, St.L., Hfd.	11	502	28	93	121	382	49	0	3	3	56		1978-79	1988-89
Botting, Cam	Atl.	1	2	0	1	1	0	....	....	....	....	....		1975-76	1975-76
Boucha, Henry	Det., Min., K.C., Col.	6	247	53	49	102	157	....	....	....	....	....		1971-72	1976-77
Bouchard, Dick	NYR	1	1	0	0	0	0	....	....	....	....	....		1954-55	1954-55
Bouchard, Edmond	Mtl., Ham., NYA, Pit.	8	223	19	20	39	105	....	....	....	....	....		1921-22	1928-29
Bouchard, Emile (Butch)	Mtl.	15	784	49	144	193	863	113	11	21	32	121	4	1941-42	1955-56
Bouchard, Pierre	Mtl., Wsh.	12	595	24	82	106	433	76	3	10	13	56	5	1970-71	1981-82
• Boucher, Billy	Mtl., Bos., NYA	7	213	93	35	128	391	21	9	3	12	35	1	1921-22	1927-28
• Boucher, Frank	Ott., NYR	14	557	161	262	423	119	56	16	18	34	12	2	1921-22	1943-44
• Boucher, George	Ott., Mtl.M, Chi.	15	457	122	62	184	712	44	11	4	15	84	4	1917-18	1931-32
Boucher, Robert	Mtl.	1	12	0	0	0	0	....	....	....	....	....	1	1923-24	1923-24
Boudreau, Bruce	Tor., Chi.	8	141	28	42	70	46	9	2	0	2	0		1970-71	1985-86
Boudrias, Andre	Mtl., Min., Chi., St.L., Van.	12	662	151	340	491	218	34	6	10	16	12		1963-64	1975-76
Boughner, Barry	Oak., Cal.	2	20	0	0	0	11	....	....	....	....	....		1969-70	1970-71
Bourbonnais, Dan	Hfd.	2	59	3	25	28	11	....	....	....	....	....		1981-82	1983-84
Bourbonnais, Rick	St.L.	3	71	9	15	24	29	4	0	1	1	0		1975-76	1977-78
Bourcier, Conrad	Mtl.	1	6	0	0	0	0	....	....	....	....	....		1935-36	1935-36
Bourcier, Jean	Mtl.	1	9	0	1	1	0	....	....	....	....	....		1935-36	1935-36
• Bourgeault, Leo	Tor. NYR, Ott., Mtl.	8	307	24	20	44	269	24	1	1	2	18	1	1926-27	1934-35
Bourgeois, Charlie	Cgy., St.L., Hfd.	7	290	16	54	70	788	40	2	3	5	194		1981-82	1987-88
Bourne, Bob	NYI, L.A.	14	964	258	324	582	605	139	40	56	96	108	4	1974-75	1987-88
Boutette, Pat	Tor., Hfd., Pit.	10	756	171	282	453	1354	46	10	14	24	109		1975-76	1984-85
Boutilier, Paul	NYI, Bos., Min., NYR, Wpg.	8	288	27	83	110	358	41	1	9	10	45		1981-82	1988-89
Bowcher, Clarence	NYA	2	47	2	2	4	110	....	....	....	....	....		1926-27	1927-28
Bowman, Kirk	Chi.	3	88	11	17	28	19	7	1	0	1	0		1976-77	1978-79
• Bowman, Ralph	Ott., St.L., Det.	7	274	8	17	25	260	22	2	2	4	6	2	1933-34	1939-40
Bownass, Jack	Mtl., NYR	4	80	3	8	11	58	....	....	....	....	....		1957-58	1961-62
Bowness, Rick	Atl., Det., St. L, Wpg.	7	173	18	37	55	191	5	0	0	0	2		1975-76	1981-82
• Boyd, Bill	NYR, NYA	4	138	15	7	22	72	9	0	0	0	2	1	1926-27	1929-30
Boyd, Irwin	Bos., Det.	4	97	18	19	37	51	15	0	1	1	4		1931-32	1943-44
Boyd, Randy	Pit., Chi., NYI, Van.	8	257	20	67	87	328	13	0	2	2	26		1981-82	1988-89
Boyer, Wally	Tor., Chi., Oak. Pit.	7	365	54	105	159	163	15	1	3	4	0		1965-66	1971-72
Boyko, Darren	Wpg.	1	1	0	0	0	0	....	....	....	....	....		1988-89	1988-89
Bozek, Steve	L.A., Cgy., St. L., Van., S.J.	11	641	164	167	331	309	58	12	11	23	69		1981-82	1991-92
Brackenborough, John	Bos.	1	7	0	0	0	0	....	....	....	....	....		1925-26	1925-26
Brackenbury, Curt	Que., Edm., St.L.	4	141	9	17	26	226	2	0	0	0	0		1979-80	1982-83
Bradley, Barton	Bos.	1	1	0	0	0	0	....	....	....	....	....		1949-50	1949-50
Bradley, Lyle	Cal. Cle.	2	6	1	0	1	2	....	....	....	....	....		1973-74	1976-77
Bragnalo, Rick	Wsh.	4	145	15	35	50	46	....	....	....	....	....		1975-76	1978-79
Brannigan, Andy	NYA, Bro.	2	26	1	2	3	31	....	....	....	....	....		1940-41	1941-42
Brasar, Per-Olov	Min., Van.	5	348	64	142	206	33	13	1	2	3	0		1977-78	1981-82
Brayshaw, Russ	Chi.	1	43	5	9	14	24	....	....	....	....	....		1944-45	1944-45
Breitenbach, Ken	Buf.	3	68	1	13	14	49	8	0	1	1	4		1975-76	1978-79
Brennan, Dan	L.A.	2	8	0	1	1	9	....	....	....	....	....		1983-84	1985-86
Brennan, Doug	NYR	3	123	9	7	16	152	16	1	0	1	21	1	1931-32	1933-34
Brennan, Tom	Bos.	2	22	2	2	4	2	....	....	....	....	....		1943-44	1944-45
Brenneman, John	Chi., NYR, Tor., Det., Oak.	5	152	21	19	40	46	....	....	....	....	....		1964-65	1968-69
Bretto, Joe	Chi.	1	3	0	0	0	4	....	....	....	....	....		1944-45	1944-45
Brewer, Carl	Tor., Det., St.L.	12	604	25	198	223	1037	72	3	17	20	146	3	1957-58	1979-80
Briden, Archie	Det., Pit.	2	72	9	5	14	56	....	....	....	....	....		1926-27	1929-30
Bridgman, Mel	Phi., Cgy., N.J., Det., Van.	14	977	252	449	701	1625	125	28	39	67	298		1975-76	1988-89
• Briere, Michel	Pit.	1	76	12	32	44	20	10	5	3	8	17		1969-70	1969-70
Brindley, Doug	Tor.	1	3	0	0	0	0	....	....	....	....	....		1970-71	1970-71
Brink, Milt	Chi.	1	5	0	0	0	0	....	....	....	....	....		1936-37	1936-37
Brisson, Gerry	Mtl.	1	4	0	2	2	4	....	....	....	....	....		1962-63	1962-63
Britz, Greg	Tor., Hfd.	3	8	0	0	0	4	....	....	....	....	....		1983-84	1986-87
• Broadbent, Harry	Ott. Mt.M, NYA	11	302	122	45	167	553	41	13	1	14	69	4	1918-19	1928-29
Brochu, Stephane	NYR	1	1	0	0	0	0	....	....	....	....	....		1988-89	1988-89
Broden, Connie	Mtl.	3	6	2	1	3	2	7	0	1	1	0	2	1955-56	1957-58
Brooke, Bob	NYR, Min., N.J.	7	447	69	97	166	520	34	9	9	18	59		1983-84	1989-90
Brooks, Gord	St.L., Wsh.	3	70	7	18	25	37	....	....	....	....	....		1971-72	1974-75
• Brophy, Bernie	Mtl.M, Det.	3	62	4	4	8	25	2	0	0	0	2	1	1925-26	1929-30
Brossart, Willie	Phi., Tor., Wsh.	6	129	1	14	15	88	1	0	0	0	0		1970-71	1975-76
Broten, Aaron	Col., N.J., Min., Que., Tor., Wpg.	12	748	186	329	515	441	34	7	18	25	40		1980-81	1991-92
• Brown, Adam	Det. Chi. Bos.	10	391	104	113	217	358	26	2	14	6	14	1	1941-42	1951-52
Brown, Arnie	Tor. NYR, Det., NYI, Atl.	12	681	44	141	185	738	22	0	6	6	23		1961-62	1973-74
Brown, Connie	Det.	5	91	15	24	39	12	14	2	3	5	0		1938-39	1942-43
Brown, Fred	Mtl.M	1	19	1	0	1	0	9	0	0	0	0		1927-28	1927-28
Brown, George	Mtl.	3	79	6	22	28	34	7	0	0	0	2		1936-37	1938-39
Brown, Gerry	Det.	2	23	4	5	9	2	12	2	1	3	4		1941-42	1945-46
Brown, Harold	NYR	1	13	2	1	3	2	....	....	....	....	....		1945-46	1945-46
Brown, Jim	L.A.	1	3	0	1	1	5	....	....	....	....	....		1982-83	1982-83
Brown, Larry	NYR, Det., Phi., L.A.	9	455	7	53	60	180	35	0	4	4	10		1969-70	1977-78
Brown, Richard (Cam)	Van.	1	1	0	0	0	7	....	....	....	....	....		1990-91	1990-91
Brown, Stan	NYR, Det.	2	48	8	2	10	18	2	0	0	0	0		1926-27	1927-28
Brown, Wayne	Bos.	1	....	....	....	....	....	4	0	0	0	2		1953-54	1953-54
• Browne, Cecil	Chi.	1	13	2	0	2	4	....	....	....	....	....		1927-28	1927-28
Brownschidle, Jack	St.L., Hfd.	9	494	39	162	201	151	26	0	5	5	18		1977-78	1985-86
Brownschidle, Jeff	Hfd.	2	7	0	1	1	2	....	....	....	....	....		1981-82	1982-83
Brubaker, Jeff	Hfd., Mtl., Cgy., Tor., Edm., NYR, Det.	8	178	16	9	25	512	2	0	0	0	27		1979-80	1988-89
Bruce, Gordie	Bos.	3	28	4	9	13	13	7	2	3	5	4		1940-41	1945-46
Bruce, Morley	Ott.	4	72	8	1	9	27	12	0	0	0	3	2	1917-18	1921-22
Brumwell, Murray	Min., N.J.,	7	128	12	31	43	70	2	0	0	0	2		1980-81	1987-88
Bruneteau, Eddie	Det.	7	180	40	42	82	35	26	7	6	13	0		1940-41	1948-49
Bruneteau, Mud	Det.	11	411	139	138	277	80	77	23	14	37	22	3	1935-36	1945-46

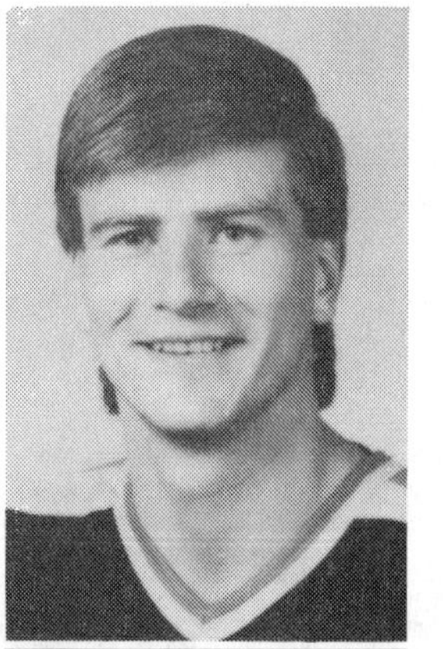
Jim Benning

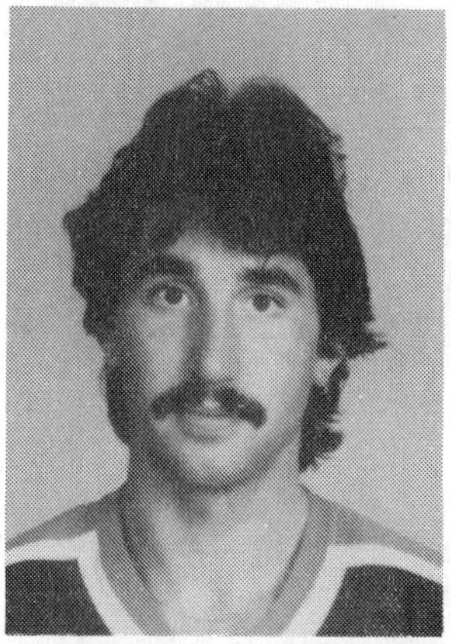
Todd Bidner

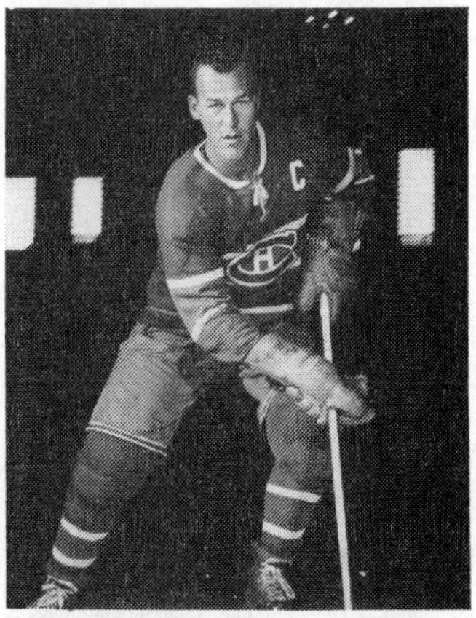
Emile "Butch" Bouchard

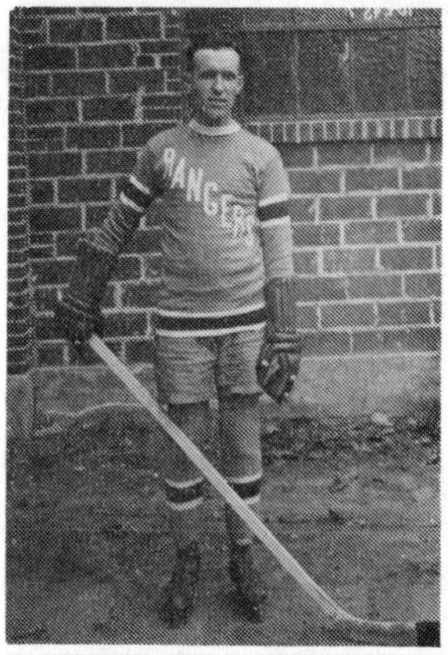

Frank Boucher

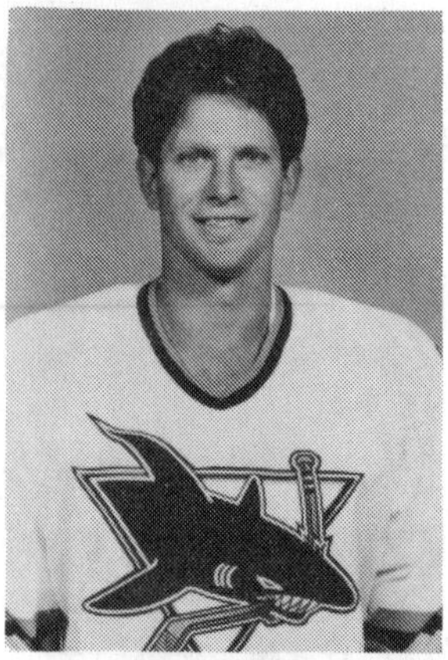

Steve Bozek

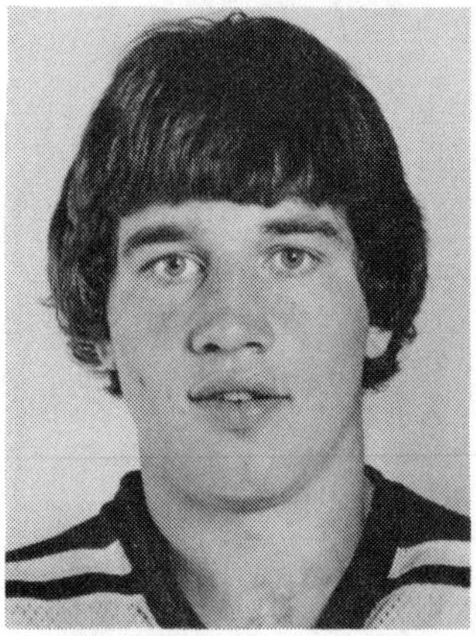

Aaron Broten

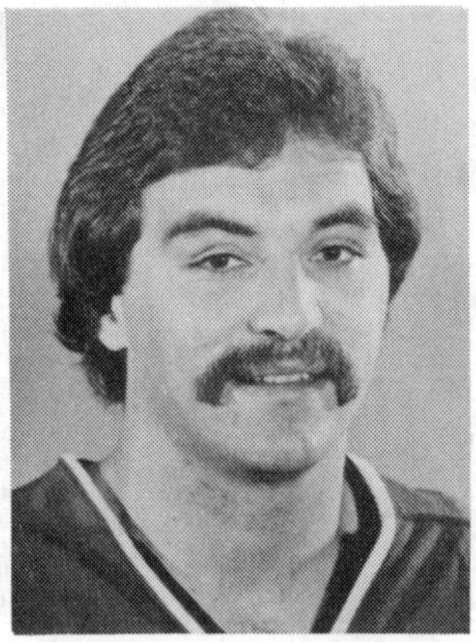

Ted Bulley

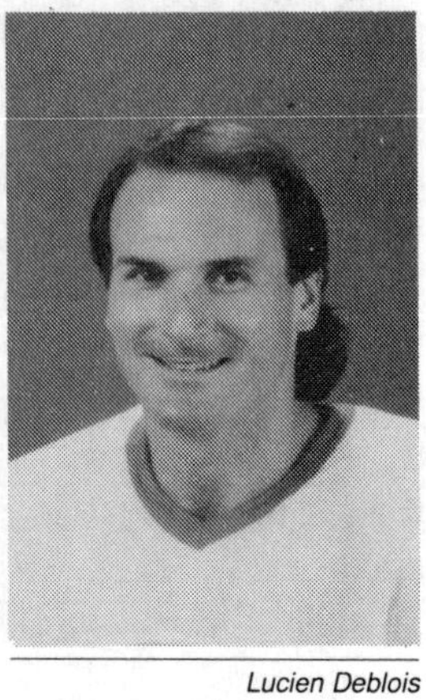

Lucien Deblois

			Regular Schedule					Playoffs							
Name	NHL Teams	NHL Seasons	GP	G	A	TP	PIM	GP	G	A	TP	PIM	NHL Cup Wins	First NHL Season	Last NHL Season
• Brydge, Bill	Tor., Det., NYA	9	368	26	52	78	506	2	0	0	0	4		1926-27	1935-36
Brydges, Paul	Buf.	1	15	2	2	4	6	....	....	....	....	....		1986-87	1986-87
Brydson, Glenn	Mtl.M, St.L., NYR, Chi.	8	299	56	79	135	203	11	0	0	0	8		1930-31	1937-38
Brydson, Gord	Tor.	1	8	2	0	2	8	....	....	....	....	....		1929-30	1929-30
Bubla, Jiri	Van.	5	256	17	101	118	202	6	0	0	0	7		1981-82	1985-86
Buchanan, Al	Tor.	2	4	0	1	1	2	....	....	....	....	....		1948-49	1949-50
Buchanan, Bucky	NYR	1	2	0	0	0	0	....	....	....	....	....		1948-49	1948-49
Buchanan, Mike	Chi.	1	1	0	0	0	0	....	....	....	....	....		1951-52	1951-52
Buchanan, Ron	Bos., St.L.	2	5	0	0	0	0	....	....	....	....	....		1966-67	1969-70
Bucyk, John	Det., Bos.,	23	1540	556	813	1369	497	124	41	62	103	42	2	1955-56	1977-78
Bucyk, Randy	Mtl., Cgy.	2	19	4	2	6	8	2	0	0	0	0		1985-86	1987-88
Buhr, Doug	K.C.	1	6	0	2	2	4	....	....	....	....	....		1974-75	1974-75
Bukovich, Tony	Det.	2	44	7	3	10	6	6	0	1	1	0		1943-44	1944-45
• Buller, Hy	Det., NYR	5	188	22	58	80	215	....	....	....	....	....		1943-44	1953-54
Bulley, Ted	Chi., Wsh., Pit.	8	414	101	113	214	704	29	5	5	10	24		1976-77	1983-84
• Burch, Billy	Ham., NYA, Bos., Chi.	11	390	137	53	190	251	2	0	0	0	0		1922-23	1932-33
Burchell, Fred	Mtl.	2	4	0	0	0	2	....	....	....	....	....		1950-51	1953-54
Burdon, Glen	K.C.	1	11	0	2	2	0	....	....	....	....	....		1974-75	1974-75
Burega, Bill	Tor.	1	4	0	1	1	4	....	....	....	....	....		1955-56	1955-56
Burke, Eddie	Bos., NYA	4	106	29	20	49	55	....	....	....	....	....		1931-32	1934-35
• Burke, Marty	Mtl., Pit., Ott., Chi.	11	494	19	47	66	560	31	2	4	6	44	2	1927-28	1937-38
Burmeister, Roy	NYA	3	67	4	3	7	2	....	....	....	....	....		1929-30	1931-32
Burnett, Kelly	NYR	1	3	1	0	1	0	....	....	....	....	....		1952-53	1952-53
Burns, Bobby	Chi.	3	20	1	0	1	8	....	....	....	....	....		1927-28	1929-30
Burns, Charlie	Det., Bos., Oak., Pit., Min.	11	749	106	198	304	252	31	5	4	9	4		1958-59	1972-73
Burns, Gary	NYR	2	11	2	2	4	18	5	0	0	0	6		1980-81	1981-82
Burns, Norm	NYR	1	11	0	4	4	2	....	....	....	....	....		1941-42	1941-42
Burns, Robin	Pit., K.C.	5	190	31	38	69	139	....	....	....	....	....		1970-71	1975-76
Burrows, Dave	Pit., Tor.	10	724	29	135	164	377	29	1	5	6	25		1971-72	1980-81
Burry, Bert	Ott.	1	4	0	0	0	0	....	....	....	....	....		1932-33	1932-33
Burton, Cummy	Det.	3	43	0	2	2	21	3	0	0	0	0		1955-56	1958-59
Burton, Nelson	Wsh.	2	8	1	0	1	21	....	....	....	....	....		1977-78	1978-79
• Bush, Eddie	Det.	2	27	4	6	10	50	12	1	6	7	23		1938-39	1941-42
Busniuk, Mike	Phi.	2	143	3	23	26	297	25	2	5	7	34		1979-80	1980-81
Busniuk, Ron	Buf.	2	6	0	3	3	4	....	....	....	....	....		1972-73	1973-74
• Buswell, Walt	Det., Mtl.	8	368	10	40	50	164	24	2	1	3	10		1932-33	1939-40
Butler, Dick	Chi.	1	7	2	0	2	0	....	....	....	....	....		1947-48	1947-48
Butler, Jerry	NYR, St.L., Tor., Van., Wpg.	11	641	99	120	219	515	48	3	3	6	79		1972-73	1982-83
Butters, Bill	Min.	2	72	1	4	5	77	....	....	....	....	....		1977-78	1978-79
Buttrey, Gord	Chi.	1	10	0	0	0	0	10	0	0	0	0		1943-44	1943-44
Buynak, Gordon	St. L	1	4	0	0	0	2	....	....	....	....	....		1974-75	1974-75
Byers, Gord	Bos.	1	1	0	1	1	0	....	....	....	....	....		1949-50	1949-50
Byers, Jerry	Min., Atl, NYR	4	43	3	4	7	10	....	....	....	....	....		1972-73	1977-78
Byers, Mike	Tor., Phi., Buf., L.A.	4	166	42	34	76	39	4	0	1	1	0		1967-68	1971-72
Byram, Shawn	NYI, Chi.	2	5	0	0	0	14	....	....	....	....	....		1990-91	1991-92

C

Caffery, Jack	Tor., Bos.	3	57	3	2	5	22	10	1	0	1	4		1954-55	1957-58
Caffery, Terry	Chi., Min.	2	14	0	0	0	0	1	0	0	0	0		1969-70	1970-71
Cahan, Larry	Tor., NYR, Oak., L.A.	13	665	38	92	130	700	29	1	1	2	38		1954-55	1970-71
Cahill, Chuck	Bos.	2	32	0	1	1	4	....	....	....	....	....		1925-26	1926-27
• Cain, Herb	Mtl.M, Mtl., Bos.	13	571	206	194	400	178	64	16	13	29	13	2	1933-34	1945-46
• Cain, Jim	Mtl.M, Tor.	2	61	4	0	4	35	....	....	....	....	....	1	1924-25	1925-26
Cairns, Don	K.C., Col.	2	9	0	1	1	2	....	....	....	....	....		1975-76	1976-77
Calder, Eric	Wsh.	2	2	0	0	0	0	....	....	....	....	....		1981-82	1982-83
Calladine, Norm	Bos.	3	63	19	29	48	8	....	....	....	....	....		1942-43	1944-45
Callander, Drew	Phi., Van.	4	39	6	2	8	7	....	....	....	....	....		1976-77	1979-80
Callighen, Brett	Edm.	3	160	56	89	145	132	14	4	6	10	8		1979-80	1981-82
Callighen, Patsy	NYR	1	36	0	0	0	32	9	0	0	0	0	1	1927-28	1927-28
Camazzola, James	Chi.	2	3	0	0	0	0	....	....	....	....	....		1983-84	1986-87
Camazzola, Tony	Wsh.	1	3	0	0	0	4	....	....	....	....	....		1981-82	1981-82
Cameron, Al	Det., Wpg.	6	282	11	44	55	356	7	0	1	1	2		1975-76	1980-81
Cameron, Billy	Mtl., NYA	2	39	0	0	0	2	6	0	0	0	0	1	1923-24	1925-26
Cameron, Craig	Det., St.L., Min., NYI	9	552	87	65	152	202	27	3	1	4	17		1966-67	1975-76
Cameron, Dave	Col., N.J.	3	168	25	28	53	238	....	....	....	....	....		1981-82	1983-84
• Cameron, Harry	Tor., Ott., Mtl.	6	127	90	27	117	120	20	7	3	10	29	3	1917-18	1922-23
Cameron, Scotty	NYR	1	35	8	11	19	0	....	....	....	....	....		1942-43	1942-43
Campbell, Bryan	L.A., Chi.	5	260	35	71	106	74	22	3	4	7	2		1967-68	1971-72
Campbell, Colin	Pit., Col., Edm., Van., Det.	11	636	25	103	128	1292	45	4	10	14	181		1974-75	1984-85
• Campbell, Dave	Mtl.	1	3	0	0	0	0	....	....	....	....	....		1920-21	1920-21
Campbell, Don	Chi.	1	17	1	3	4	8	....	....	....	....	....		1943-44	1943-44
Campbell, Scott	Wpg., St.L.	3	80	4	21	25	243	....	....	....	....	....		1979-80	1981-82
Campbell, Spiff	Ott., NYA	3	77	5	1	6	12	2	0	0	0	0		1923-24	1925-26
Campbell, Wade	Wpg., Bos.	6	213	9	27	36	305	10	0	0	0	20		1982-83	1987-88
Campeau, Tod	Mtl.	3	42	5	9	14	16	1	0	0	0	0		1943-44	1948-49
Campedelli, Dom	Mtl.	1	2	0	0	0	0	....	....	....	....	....		1985-86	1985-86
Capuano, Jack	Tor., Van., Bos.	0	6	0	0	0	0	....	....	....	....	....	3	1989-90	1991-92
Carbol, Leo	Chi.	1	6	0	1	1	4	....	....	....	....	....		1942-43	1942-43
Cardin, Claude	St.L.	1	1	0	0	0	0	....	....	....	....	....		1967-68	1967-68
Cardwell, Steve	Pit.	3	53	9	11	20	35	4	0	0	0	2		1970-71	1972-73
• Carey, George	Que, Ham., Tor.	5	72	22	8	30	14	....	....	....	....	....		1919-20	1923-24
Carleton, Wayne	Tor., Bos., Cal.	7	278	55	73	128	172	18	2	4	6	14	1	1965-66	1971-72
Carlin, Brian	L.A.	1	5	1	0	1	0	....	....	....	....	....		1971-72	1971-72
Carlson, Jack	Min., St.L.	6	236	30	15	45	417	25	1	2	3	72		1978-79	1986-87
Carlson, Kent	Mtl., St.L., Wsh.	5	113	7	11	18	148	8	0	0	0	13		1983-84	1988-89
Carlson, Steve	L.A.	1	52	9	12	21	23	4	1	1	2	7		1979-80	1979-80
Carlsson, Anders	N.J.	3	104	7	26	33	34	3	1	0	1	2		1986-87	1988-89
• Caron, Alain	Oak., Mtl.	2	60	9	13	22	18	....	....	....	....	....		1967-68	1968-69
• Carpenter, Eddie	Que, Ham.	2	44	10	4	14	23	....	....	....	....	....		1919-20	1920-21
Carr, Al	Tor.	1	5	0	1	1	4	....	....	....	....	....		1943-44	1943-44
Carr, Gene	St.L., NYR, L.A., Pit., Atl.	8	465	79	136	215	365	35	5	8	13	66		1971-72	1978-79
Carr, Lorne	NYR, NYA, Tor.	13	580	204	222	426	132	53	10	9	19	13	1	1933-34	1945-46
Carriere, Larry	Buf. Atl, Van., L.A., Tor.	7	366	16	74	90	463	27	0	3	3	42		1972-73	1979-80
• Carrigan, Gene	NYR, StL, Det.	3	37	2	1	3	13	4	0	0	0	0		1930-31	1934-35
Carroll, Billy	NYI, Edm., Det.	7	322	30	54	84	113	71	6	12	18	18	4	1980-81	1986-87
Carroll, George	Mtl.M, Bos.	1	15	0	0	0	9	....	....	....	....	....		1924-25	1924-25
Carroll, Greg	Wsh., Det., Hfd.	2	131	20	34	54	44	....	....	....	....	....		1978-79	1979-80
Carruthers, Dwight	Det. Phi.	2	2	0	0	0	0	....	....	....	....	....		1965-66	1967-68
Carse, Bill	NYR, Chi.	4	124	28	43	71	38	16	3	2	5	0		1938-39	1941-42
Carse, Bob	Chi., Mtl.	5	167	32	55	87	52	10	0	2	2	2		1939-40	1947-48
• Carson, Bill	Tor., Bos.	4	159	54	24	78	156	11	3	0	3	14	1	1926-27	1929-30
• Carson, Frank	Mtl.M., NYA, Det.	7	248	42	48	90	166	22	0	2	2	9	1	1925-26	1933-34
• Carson, Gerry	Mtl., NYR, Mtl.M.	6	261	12	11	23	205	22	0	0	0	12	1	1928-29	1936-37
Carson, Lindsay	Phi., Hfd.	7	373	66	80	146	524	49	4	10	14	56		1981-82	1987-88
Carter, Billy	Mtl., Bos.	3	16	0	0	0	6	....	....	....	....	....		1957-58	1961-62
Carter, Ron	Edm.	1	2	0	0	0	0	....	....	....	....	....		1979-80	1979-80
• Carveth, Joe	Det., Bos., Mtl.	11	504	150	189	339	81	69	21	16	37	28	2	1940-41	1950-51
Cashman, Wayne	Bos.	17	1027	277	516	793	1041	145	31	57	88	250	2	1964-65	1982-83
Cassidy, Bruce	Chi.	6	36	4	13	17	10	1	0	0	0	0		1983-84	1989-90
Cassidy, Tom	Pit.	1	26	3	4	7	15	....	....	....	....	....		1977-78	1977-78
Cassolato, Tony	Wsh.	3	23	1	6	7	4	....	....	....	....	....		1979-80	1981-82
Ceresino, Ray	Tor.	1	12	1	1	2	2	....	....	....	....	....		1948-49	1948-49
Cernik, Frantisek	Det.	1	49	5	4	9	13	....	....	....	....	....		1984-85	1984-85
Chad, John	Chi.	3	80	15	22	37	29	10	0	1	1	2		1939-40	1945-46
Chalmers, Bill	NYR	1	1	0	0	0	0	....	....	....	....	....		1953-54	1953-54
Chalupa, Milan	Det.	1	14	0	5	5	6	....	....	....	....	....		1984-85	1984-85
• Chamberlain, Murph	Tor., Mtl., Bro., Bos.	12	510	100	175	275	769	66	14	17	31	96	2	1937-38	1948-49
Champagne, Andre	Tor.	1	2	0	0	0	0	....	....	....	....	....		1962-63	1962-63
• Chapman, Art	Bos., NYA	10	438	62	176	238	140	25	1	5	6	9		1930-31	1939-40
Chapman, Blair	Pit., St.L.	7	402	106	125	231	158	25	4	6	10	15		1976-77	1982-83
Charbonneau, Jose (Joe)	Mtl., Van.	2	38	1	6	7	18	8	0	0	0	4		1987-88	1988-89
Charlebois, Bob	Min.	1	7	1	0	1	0	....	....	....	....	....		1967-68	1967-68

			Regular Schedule					Playoffs					NHL	First	Last
Name	NHL Teams	NHL Seasons	GP	G	A	TP	PIM	GP	G	A	TP	PIM	Cup Wins	NHL Season	NHL Season
Charlesworth, Todd	Pit., NYR	6	93	3	9	12	47	....	....	....	....	....		1983-84	1989-90
Charron, Guy	Mtl., Det., K.C., Wsh.	12	734	221	309	530	146	....	....	....	....	....		1969-70	1980-81
Chartier, Dave	Wpg.	1	1	0	0	0	0	....	....	....	....	....		1980-81	1980-81
Chartraw, Rick	Mtl., L.A., NYR, Edm.	10	420	28	64	92	399	75	7	9	16	80	4	1974-75	1983-84
Check, Lude	Det., Chi.	2	27	6	2	8	4	....	....	....	....	....		1943-44	1944-45
Chernoff, Mike	Min.	1	1	0	0	0	0	....	....	....	....	....		1968-69	1968-69
Cherry, Dick	Bos., Phi.	3	145	12	10	22	45	4	1	0	1	4		1956-57	1969-70
Cherry, Don	Bos.	1	....	....	....	....	....	1	0	0	0	0		1954-55	1954-55
• Chevrefils, Real	Bos., Det.	8	387	104	97	201	185	30	5	4	9	20		1951-52	1958-59
Chicoine, Dan	Cle. Min.	3	31	1	2	3	12	1	0	0	0	0		1977-78	1979-80
Chinnick, Rick	Min.	2	4	0	2	2	0	....	....	....	....	....		1973-74	1974-75
Chipperfield, Ron	Edm., Que.,	2	83	22	24	46	34	....	....	....	....	....		1979-80	1980-81
Chisholm, Art	Bos.	1	3	0	0	0	0	....	....	....	....	....		1960-61	1960-61
Chisholm, Colin	Min.	1	1	0	0	0	0	....	....	....	....	....		1986-87	1986-87
• Chisholm, Les	Tor.	2	54	10	8	18	19	3	1	0	1	0		1939-40	1940-41
Chorney, Marc	Pit. L.A.	4	210	8	27	35	209	7	0	1	1	2		1980-81	1983-84
Chouinard, Gene	Ott.	1	8	0	0	0	0	....	....	....	....	....		1927-28	1927-28
Chouinard, Guy	Atl, Cgy., St.L.	10	578	205	370	575	120	46	9	28	37	12		1974-75	1983-84
Christie, Mike	Cal., Cle., Col., Van.	7	412	15	101	116	550	2	0	0	0	0		1974-75	1980-81
Christoff, Steve	Min. Cgy., L.A.	5	248	77	64	141	108	35	16	12	28	25		1979-80	1983-84
Chrystal, Bob	NYR	2	132	11	14	25	112	....	....	....	....	....		1953-54	1954-55
Church, Jack	Tor., Bro., Bos.	6	145	5	22	27	164	25	1	1	2	18		1938-39	1945-46
• Ciesla, Hank	Chi., NYR	4	269	26	51	77	87	6	0	2	2	0		1955-56	1958-59
Clackson, Kim	Pit., Que.	2	106	0	8	8	370	8	0	0	0	70		1979-80	1980-81
• Clancy, Francis (King)	Ott., Tor.	16	592	137	143	280	904	61	9	8	17	92	3	1921-22	1936-37
Clancy, Terry	Oak., Tor.	4	93	6	6	12	39	....	....	....	....	....		1967-68	1972-73
• Clapper, Dit	Bos.	20	833	228	246	474	462	86	13	17	30	50	3	1927-28	1946-47
Clark, Andy	Bos.	1	5	0	0	0	0	....	....	....	....	....		1927-28	1927-28
Clark, Dan	NYR	1	4	0	1	1	6	....	....	....	....	....		1978-79	1978-79
Clark, Dean	Edm.	1	1	0	0	0	0	....	....	....	....	....		1983-84	1983-84
Clark, Gordie	Bos.	2	8	0	1	1	0	1	0	0	0	0		1974-75	1975-76
Clarke, Bobby	Phi.	15	1144	358	852	1210	1453	136	42	77	119	152	2	1969-70	1983-84
• Cleghorn, Odie	Mtl., Pit.	10	180	95	29	124	147	23	9	2	11	2	1	1918-19	1927-28
• Cleghorn, Sprague	Ott. Tor. Mtl., Bos.	10	256	84	39	123	489	37	7	8	15	48	3	1918-19	1927-28
Clement, Bill	Phi., Wsh., Atl., Cgy.	11	719	148	208	356	383	50	5	3	8	26	2	1971-72	1981-82
Cline, Bruce	NYR	1	30	2	3	5	10	....	....	....	....	....		1956-57	1956-57
Clippingdale, Steve	L.A., Wsh.	2	19	1	2	3	9	1	0	0	0	0		1976-77	1979-80
Cloutier, Real	Que. Buf.	6	317	146	198	344	119	25	7	5	12	20		1979-80	1984-85
Cloutier, Rejean	Det.	2	5	0	2	2	2	....	....	....	....	....		1979-80	1981-82
Cloutier, Roland	Det., Que.	3	34	8	9	17	2	....	....	....	....	....		1977-78	1979-80
Clune, Wally	Mtl.	1	5	0	0	0	6	....	....	....	....	....		1955-56	1955-56
Coalter, Gary	Cal., K.C.	2	34	2	4	6	2	....	....	....	....	....		1973-74	1974-75
Coates, Steve	Det.	1	5	1	0	1	24	....	....	....	....	....		1976-77	1976-77
Cochrane, Glen	Phi., Van., Chi., Edm.	10	411	17	72	89	1556	18	1	1	2	31		1978-79	1988-89
Coflin, Hughie	Chi.	1	31	0	3	3	33	....	....	....	....	....		1950-51	1950-51
Colley, Tom	Min.	1	1	0	0	0	2	....	....	....	....	....		1974-75	1974-75
Collings, Norm	Mtl.	1	1	0	1	1	0	....	....	....	....	....		1934-35	1934-35
Collins, Bill	Min., Mtl., Det., St. L, NYR, Phi., Wsh.	11	768	157	154	311	415	18	3	5	8	12		1967-68	1977-78
Collins, Gary	Tor.	1	....	....	....	....	....	2	0	0	0	0		1958-59	1958-59
Collyard, Bob	St.L.	1	10	1	3	4	4	....	....	....	....	....		1973-74	1973-74
Colville, Mac	NYR	9	353	71	104	175	130	40	9	10	19	14	1	1935-36	1946-47
• Colville, Neil	NYR	12	464	99	166	265	213	46	7	19	26	33	1	1935-36	1948-49
Colwill, Les	NYR	1	69	7	6	13	16	....	....	....	....	....		1958-59	1958-59
Comeau, Rey	Mtl., Atl, Col.	9	564	98	141	239	175	9	2	1	3	8		1971-72	1979-80
Conacher, Brian	Tor., Det.	5	154	28	28	56	84	12	3	2	5	21	1	1961-62	1971-72
• Conacher, Charlie	Tor., Det., NYA	12	460	225	173	398	523	49	17	18	35	53	1	1929-30	1940-41
Conacher, Jim	Det., Chi., NYR	8	328	85	117	202	91	19	5	2	7	4		1945-46	1952-53
• Conacher, Lionel	Pit., NYA, Mtl.M., Chi.	12	500	80	105	185	882	35	2	2	4	34	2	1925-26	1936-37
Conacher, Pete	Chi., NYR, Tor.	6	229	47	39	86	57	7	0	0	0	0		1951-52	1957-58
• Conacher, Roy	Bos., Det., Chi.	11	490	226	200	426	90	42	15	15	30	14	2	1938-39	1951-52
Conn, Hugh	NYA	2	96	9	28	37	22	....	....	....	....	....		1933-34	1934-35
Connelly, Wayne	Mtl., Bos., Min., Det., St. L, Van.	10	543	133	174	307	156	24	11	7	18	4		1960-61	1971-72
Connolly, Bert	NYR, Chi.	3	87	13	15	28	37	14	1	0	1	0	1	1934-35	1937-38
Connor, Cam	Mtl., Edm., NYR	5	89	9	22	31	256	20	5	0	5	6	1	1978-79	1982-83
Connor, Harry	Bos., NYA, Ott.	4	134	16	5	21	139	10	0	0	0	2		1927-28	1930-31
Connors, Bobby	NYA, Det.	3	78	17	10	27	110	2	0	0	0	10		1926-27	1929-30
Contini, Joe	Col., Min.	3	68	17	21	38	34	2	0	0	0	0		1977-78	1980-81
• Convey, Eddie	NYR	3	36	1	1	2	33	....	....	....	....	....		1930-31	1932-33
• Cook, Bill	NYR	11	452	229	138	367	386	46	13	12	25	66	2	1926-27	1936-37
Cook, Bob	Van., Det., NYI, Min.	4	72	13	9	22	22	....	....	....	....	....		1970-71	1974-75
Cook, Bud	Bos., Ott., St.L.	3	51	5	4	9	22	....	....	....	....	....		1931-32	1934-35
• Cook, Bun	NYR, Bos.	11	473	158	144	302	449	46	15	3	18	57	2	1926-27	1936-37
Cook, Lloyd	Bos.	1	4	1	0	1	0	....	....	....	....	....		1924-25	1924-25
• Cook, Tom	Chi., Mtl.M.	8	311	77	98	175	184	24	2	4	6	17	1	1929-30	1937-38
• Cooper, Carson	Bos., Mtl., Det.	8	278	110	57	167	111	4	0	0	0	2		1924-25	1931-32
Cooper, Ed	Col.	2	49	8	7	15	46	....	....	....	....	....		1980-81	1981-82
Cooper, Hal	NYR	1	8	0	0	0	2	....	....	....	....	....		1944-45	1944-45
• Cooper, Joe	NYR, Chi.	11	420	30	66	96	442	32	3	5	8	6		1935-36	1946-47
Copp, Bob	Tor.	2	40	3	9	12	26	....	....	....	....	....		1942-43	1950-51
• Corbeau, Bert	Mtl., Ham., Tor.,	10	257	64	31	95	501	14	2	0	2	10		1917-18	1926-27
Corbett, Michael	L.A.	1	....	....	....	....	....	2	0	1	1	2		1967-68	1967-68
Corcoran, Norm	Bos., Det., Chi.	4	29	1	3	4	21	4	0	0	0	6		1949-50	1955-56
Cormier, Roger	Mtl.	1	1	0	0	0	0	....	....	....	....	....		1925-26	1925-26
Corrigan, Charlie	Tor., NYA	2	19	2	2	4	2	....	....	....	....	....		1937-38	1940-41
Corrigan, Mike	L.A., Van., Pit.	10	594	152	195	347	698	17	2	3	5	20		1967-68	1977-78
Corriveau, Andre	Mtl.	1	3	0	1	1	0	....	....	....	....	....		1953-54	1953-54
Cory, Ross	Wpg.	2	51	2	10	12	41	....	....	....	....	....		1979-80	1980-81
Cossete, Jacques	Pit.	3	64	8	6	14	29	3	0	1	1	4		1975-76	1978-79
Costello, Les	Tor.	3	15	2	3	5	11	6	2	2	4	2	1	1947-48	1949-50
Costello, Murray	Chi., Bos., Det.	4	162	13	19	32	54	5	0	0	0	2		1953-54	1956-57
Costello, Rich	Tor.	2	12	2	2	4	2	....	....	....	....	....		1983-84	1985-86
Cotch, Charlie	Ham.	1	11	1	0	1	0	....	....	....	....	....		1924-25	1924-25
Cote, Alain	Que.	10	696	103	190	293	383	67	9	15	24	44		1979-80	1988-89
Cote, Ray	Edm.	3	15	0	0	0	4	14	3	2	5	0		1982-83	1984-85
• Cotton, Baldy	Pit., Tor., NYA	12	500	101	103	204	419	43	4	9	13	46	1	1925-26	1936-37
• Coughlin, Jack	Tor., Que, Mtl., Ham.	3	19	2	0	2	0	....	....	....	....	....	1	1917-18	1920-21
Coulis, Tim	Wsh., Min.	4	47	4	5	9	138	3	1	0	1	2		1979-80	1985-86
Coulson, D'arcy	Phi.	1	28	0	0	0	103	....	....	....	....	....		1930-31	1930-31
Coulter, Art	Chi., NYR	11	465	30	82	112	543	49	4	5	9	61	2	1931-32	1941-42
Coulter, Neal	NYI	3	26	5	5	10	11	1	0	0	0	0		1985-86	1987-88
Coulter, Tommy	Chi.	1	2	0	0	0	0	....	....	....	....	....		1933-34	1933-34
Cournoyer, Yvan	Mtl.	16	968	428	435	863	255	147	64	63	127	47	10	1963-64	1978-79
Courteau, Yves	Cgy., Hfd.	3	22	2	5	7	4	1	0	0	0	0		1984-85	1986-87
• Coutu, Billy	Mtl., Ham., Bos.	10	239	33	18	51	350	32	2	0	2	42	1	1917-18	1926-27
Couture, Gerry	Det., Mtl., Chi.,	10	385	86	70	156	89	45	9	7	16	4	1	1944-45	1953-54
• Couture, Rosie	Chi., Mtl.	8	304	48	56	104	184	23	1	5	6	15		1928-29	1935-36
Cowan, Tommy	Phi.	1	1	0	0	0	0	....	....	....	....	....		1930-31	1930-31
Cowick, Bruce	Phi., Wsh., St.L.	3	70	5	6	11	43	8	0	0	0	9	1	1973-74	1975-76
Cowley, Bill	St.L., Bos.	13	549	195	353	548	143	64	12	34	46	22	2	1934-35	1946-47
• Cox, Danny	Tor., Ott., Det., NYR, St.L.	9	329	47	49	96	110	10	0	1	1	6		1926-27	1934-35
Crashley, Bart	Det., K.C., L.A.	6	140	7	36	43	50	....	....	....	....	....		1965-66	1975-76
Crawford, Bob	St.L., Hfd., NYR, Wsh.	7	246	71	71	142	72	11	0	1	1	8		1979-80	1986-87
Crawford, Bobby	Col., Det.	2	16	1	3	4	6	....	....	....	....	....		1980-81	1982-83
• Crawford, John	Bos.	13	547	38	140	178	202	66	4	13	17	36	2	1937-38	1949-50
Crawford, Louis (Lou)	Bos.	2	26	2	1	3	29	....	....	....	....	....		1989-90	1991-92
Crawford, Marc	Van.	6	176	19	31	50	229	20	1	2	3	44		1981-82	1986-87
• Crawford, Rusty	Ott., Tor.,	2	38	10	3	13	51	2	2	1	3	0	1	1917-18	1918-19
Creighton, Dave	Bos., Chi., Tor., NYR	12	615	140	174	314	223	51	11	13	24	20		1948-49	1959-60
Creighton, Jimmy	Det.,	1	11	1	0	1	2	....	....	....	....	....		1930-31	1930-31
Cressman, Dave	Min.	2	85	6	8	14	37	....	....	....	....	....		1974-75	1975-76
Cressman, Glen	Mtl.	1	4	0	0	0	2	....	....	....	....	....		1956-57	1956-57
Crisofoli, Ed	Mtl.	1	9	0	1	1	4	....	....	....	....	....		1989-90	1989-90
Crisp, Terry	Bos., St.L., Phi., NYI	11	536	67	134	201	135	110	15	28	43	40	2	1965-66	1976-77
Croghen, Maurice	Mtl.M.	1	16	0	0	0	4	....	....	....	....	....		1937-38	1937-38
Crombeen, Mike	Cle., St.L., Hfd.	8	475	55	68	123	218	27	6	2	8	32		1977-78	1984-85

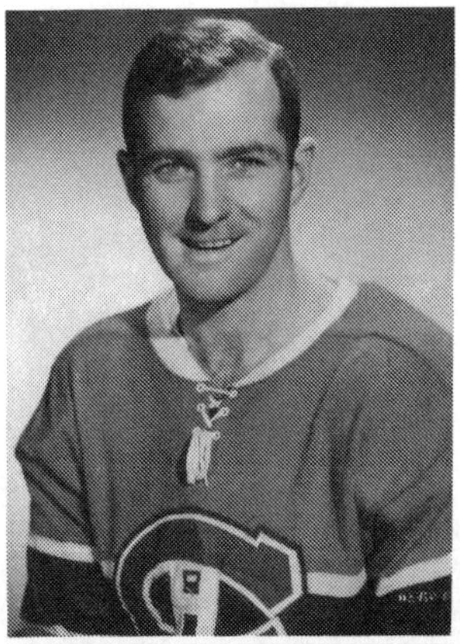

Dick Duff

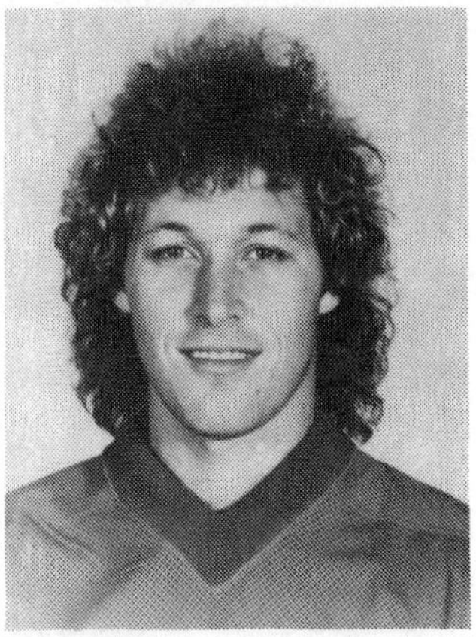

Ron Duguay

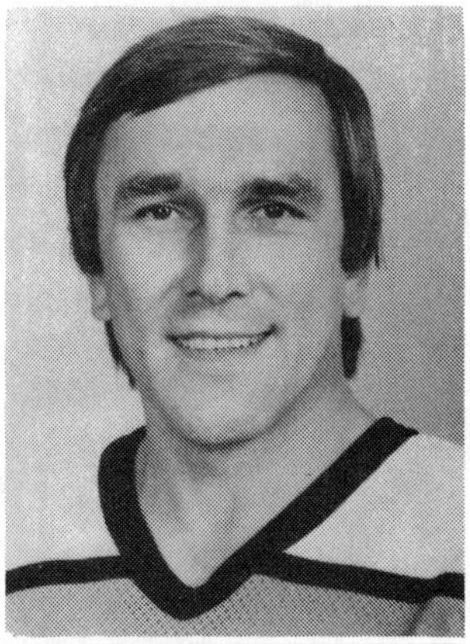

Miroslav Dvorak

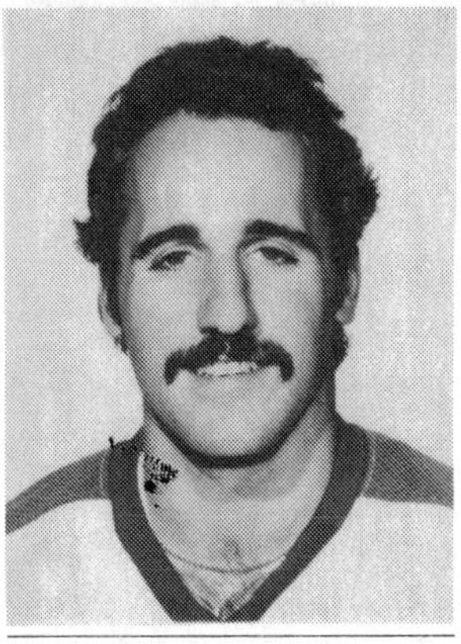

Daryl Evans

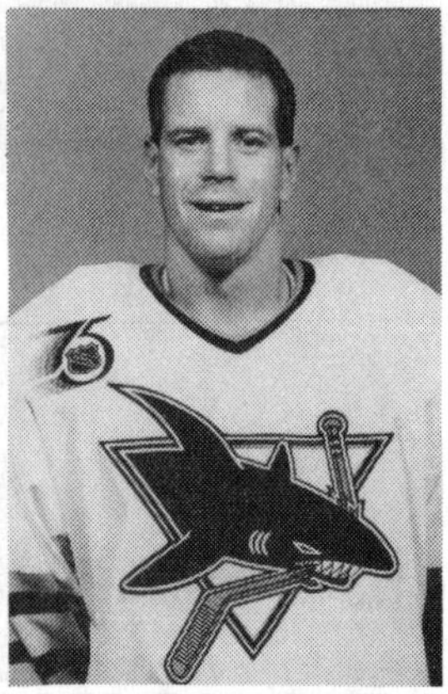

Paul Fenton

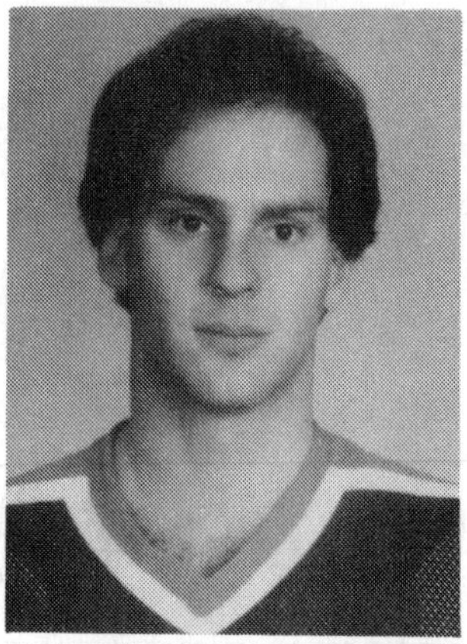

Lee Fogolin

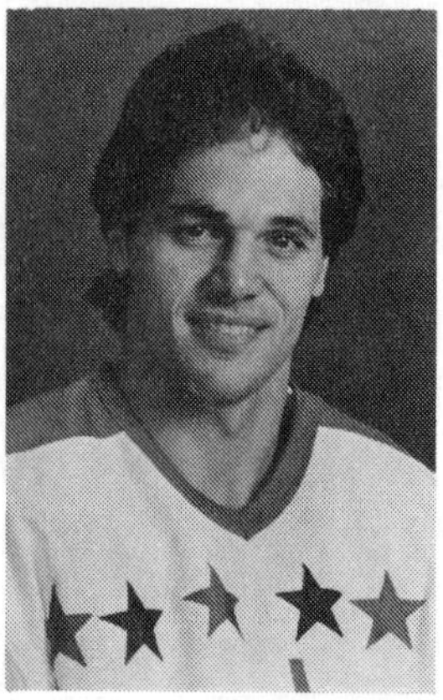

Lou Franceschetti

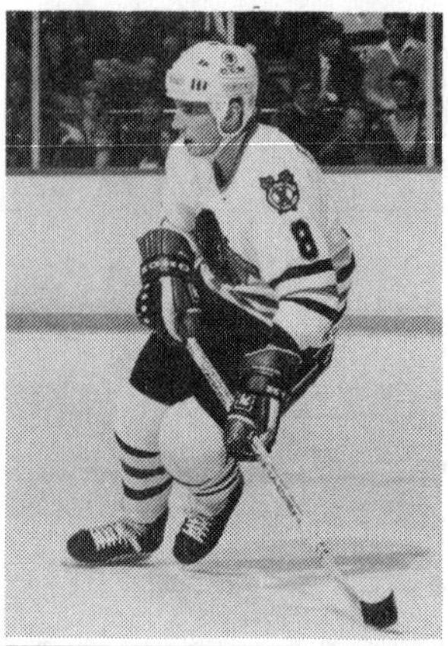

Curt Fraser

Name	NHL Teams	NHL Seasons	Regular Schedule GP	G	A	TP	PIM	Playoffs GP	G	A	TP	PIM	NHL Cup Wins	First NHL Season	Last NHL Season
Crossett, Stan	Phi.,	1	21	0	0	0	10	....	....	....	....	....		1930-31	1930-31
Croteau, Gary	L.A., Det., Cal., K.C., Col.	12	684	144	175	319	143	11	3	2	5	8		1968-69	1979-80
Crowder, Bruce	Bos., Pit.	4	243	47	51	98	156	31	8	4	12	41		1981-82	1984-85
Crowder, Keith	Bos., L.A.	10	662	223	271	494	1346	85	14	22	36	218		1980-81	1989-90
Crozier, Joe	Tor.,	1	5	0	3	3	2	....	....	....	....	....		1959-60	1959-60
Crutchfield, Nels	Mtl.	1	41	5	5	10	20	2	0	1	1	22		1934-35	1934-35
Culhane, Jim	Hfd.	1	6	0	1	1	4	....	....	....	....	....		1989-90	1989-90
Cullen, Barry	Tor., Det.	5	219	32	52	84	111	6	0	0	0	2		1955-56	1959-60
Cullen, Brian	Tor., NYR	7	326	56	100	156	92	19	3	0	3	2		1954-55	1960-61
Cullen, Ray	NYR, Det., Min., Van.	6	313	92	123	215	120	20	3	10	13	2		1965-66	1970-71
Cummins, Barry	Cal.	1	36	1	2	3	39	....	....	....	....	....		1973-74	1973-74
Cunningham, Bob	NYR	2	4	0	1	1	0	....	....	....	....	....		1960-61	1961-62
Cunningham, Jim	Phi.	1	1	0	0	0	4	....	....	....	....	....		1977-78	1977-78
Cunningham, Les	NYA, Chi.	2	60	7	19	26	21	1	0	0	0	2		1936-37	1939-40
Cupolo, Bill	Bos.	1	47	11	13	24	10	7	1	2	3	0		1944-45	1944-45
Currie, Glen	Wsh., L.A.	8	326	39	79	118	100	12	1	3	4	4		1979-80	1987-88
Currie, Hugh	Mtl.	1	1	0	0	0	0	....	....	....	....	....		1950-51	1950-51
Currie, Tony	St.L., Hfd., Van.	8	290	92	119	211	73	16	4	12	16	14		1977-78	1984-85
Curry, Floyd	Mtl.	11	601	105	99	204	147	91	23	17	40	38	4	1947-48	1957-58
Curtale, Tony	Cgy.	1	2	0	0	0	0	....	....	....	....	....		1980-81	1980-81
Curtis, Paul	Mtl., L.A., St.L.	4	185	3	34	37	151	5	0	0	0	2		1969-70	1972-73
Cushenan, Ian	Chi., Mtl., NYR, Det.	5	129	3	11	14	134	....	....	....	....	....		1956-57	1963-64
Cusson, Jean	Oak.	1	2	0	0	0	0	....	....	....	....	....		1967-68	1967-68
Cyr, Denis	Cgy., Chi., St.L.	6	193	41	43	84	36	4	0	0	0	0		1980-81	1985-86

D

Name	NHL Teams	NHL Seasons	Regular Schedule GP	G	A	TP	PIM	Playoffs GP	G	A	TP	PIM	NHL Cup Wins	First NHL Season	Last NHL Season
Dahlin, Kjell	Mtl.	3	166	57	59	116	10	35	6	11	17	6	1	1985-86	1987-88
Dahlstrom, Cully	Chi.	8	342	88	118	206	52	29	6	8	14	4	1	1937-38	1944-45
Daigle, Alain	Chi.	6	389	56	50	106	122	17	0	1	1	0		1974-75	1979-80
Dailey, Bob	Van., Phi.	9	561	94	231	325	814	63	12	34	46	106		1973-74	1981-82
Daley, Frank	Det.	1	5	0	0	0	0	2	0	0	0	0		1928-29	1928-29
Daley, Pat	Wpg.	2	12	1	0	1	13	....	....	....	....	....		1979-80	1980-81
Dallman, Marty	Tor.	2	6	0	1	1	0	....	....	....	....	....		1987-88	1988-89
Dallman, Rod	NYI, Phi.	4	6	1	0	1	26	1	0	1	1	0		1987-88	1991-92
Dame, Bunny	Mtl.	1	34	2	5	7	4	....	....	....	....	....		1941-42	1941-42
Damore, Hank	NYR	1	4	1	0	1	2	....	....	....	....	....		1943-44	1943-44
Daoust, Dan	Mtl., Tor.	8	522	87	167	254	544	32	7	5	12	83		1982-83	1989-90
Dark, Michael	St.L.	2	43	5	6	11	14	....	....	....	....	....		1986-87	1987-88
Darragh, Harry	Pit., Phi., Bos., Tor.	8	308	68	49	117	50	16	1	3	4	4	1	1925-26	1932-33
• Darragh, Jack	Ott.	6	120	68	21	89	84	21	14	2	16	7	3	1917-18	1923-24
David, Richard	Que.	3	31	4	4	8	10	1	0	0	0	0		1979-80	1982-83
Davidson, Bob	Tor.,	12	491	94	160	254	398	82	5	17	22	79	2	1934-35	1945-46
Davidson, Gord	NYR	2	51	3	6	9	8	....	....	....	....	....		1942-43	1943-44
• Davie, Bob	Bos.	3	41	0	1	1	25	....	....	....	....	....		1933-34	1935-36
Davies, Ken	NYR	1	....	....	....	....	....	1	0	0	0	0		1947-48	1947-48
Davis, Bob	Det.	1	3	0	0	0	0	....	....	....	....	....		1932-33	1932-33
Davis, Kim	Pit., Tor.	4	36	5	7	12	12	4	0	0	0	0		1977-78	1980-81
Davis, Lorne	Mtl., Chi., Det., Bos.	6	95	8	12	20	20	18	3	1	4	10	1	1951-52	1959-60
Davis, Mal	Det., Buf.	5	100	31	22	53	34	7	1	0	1	0		1980-81	1985-86
Davison, Murray	Bos.	1	1	0	0	0	0	....	....	....	....	....		1965-66	1965-66
Dawes, Robert	Tor., Mtl.	4	32	2	7	4	6	10	0	0	0	2	1	1946-47	1950-51
• Day, Hap	Tor., NYA	14	581	86	116	202	601	53	4	7	11	56	1	1924-25	1937-38
Dea, Billy	Chi., NYR, Det., Pit.	8	397	67	54	121	44	11	2	0	2	6		1953-54	1970-71
Deacon, Don	Det.	3	30	6	4	10	6	2	2	1	3	0		1936-37	1939-40
Deadmarsh, Butch	Buf., ATL, K.C.	5	137	12	5	17	155	4	0	0	0	17		1970-71	1974-75
Dean, Barry	Col., Phi.	3	165	25	56	81	146	....	....	....	....	....		1976-77	1978-79
Debenedet, Nelson	Det., Pit.	2	46	10	4	14	13	....	....	....	....	....		1973-74	1974-75
DeBlois, Lucien	NYR, Col., Wpg., Mtl., Que., Tor.	15	993	249	276	525	814	52	7	6	13	38		1977-78	1991-92
Debol, David	Hfd.	2	92	26	26	52	4	3	0	0	0	0		1979-80	1980-81
Defazio, Dean	Pit.	1	22	0	2	2	28	....	....	....	....	....		1983-84	1983-84
DeGray, Dale	Cgy., Tor. L.A., Buf.	5	153	18	47	65	195	13	1	3	4	28		1985-86	1989-90
Delmonte, Armand	Bos.	1	1	0	0	0	0	....	....	....	....	....		1945-46	1945-46
Delorme, Gilbert	Mtl., St. L., Que., Det., Pit.	9	541	31	92	123	520	56	1	9	10	56		1981-82	1989-90
Delorme, Ron	Col., Van.	9	524	83	83	166	667	25	1	2	3	59		1976-77	1984-85
Delory, Valentine	NYR	1	1	0	0	0	0	....	....	....	....	....		1948-49	1948-49
Delparte, Guy	Col.	1	48	1	8	9	18	....	....	....	....	....		1976-77	1976-77
Delvecchio, Alex	Det.	24	1549	456	825	1281	383	121	35	69	104	29	3	1950-51	1973-74
• DeMarco, Ab	Chi., Tor., Bos., NYR	7	209	72	93	165	53	11	3	0	3	2		1938-39	1946-47
DeMarco, Albert	NYR, St.L., Pit., Van., L.A., Bos.	9	344	44	80	124	75	25	1	2	3	17		1969-70	1978-79
DeMeres, Tony	Mtl., NYR	6	83	20	22	42	23	3	0	0	0	0		1937-38	1943-44
Denis, Johnny	NYR	2	10	0	2	2	2	....	....	....	....	....		1946-47	1949-50
Denis, Lulu	Mtl.	2	3	0	1	1	0	....	....	....	....	....		1949-50	1950-51
• Denneny, Corbett	Tor., Ham., Chi.	9	175	99	29	128	130	15	7	4	11	6	2	1917-18	1927-28
• Denneny, Cy	Ott., Bos.	12	326	246	69	315	176	37	18	3	21	31	5	1917-18	1928-29
Dennis, Norm	St.L.	4	12	3	0	3	11	5	0	0	0	2		1968-69	1971-72
Denoird, Gerry	Tor.	1	15	0	0	0	0	....	....	....	....	....		1922-23	1922-23
Derlago, Bill	Van., Bos., Wpg., Que., Tor.	9	555	189	227	416	247	13	5	0	5	8		1978-79	1986-87
• Desaulniers, Gerard	Mtl.	3	8	0	2	2	4	....	....	....	....	....		1950-51	1953-54
Desilets, Joffre	Mtl., Chi.	5	192	37	45	82	57	7	1	0	1	7		1935-36	1939-40
Desjardins, Martin		1	8	0	2	2	2	....	....	....	....	....		1989-90	1989-90
Desjardins, Vic	Chi., NYR	2	87	6	15	21	27	16	0	0	0	0		1930-31	1931-32
Deslauriers, Jacques	Mtl.	1	2	0	0	0	0	....	....	....	....	....		1955-56	1955-56
Devine, Kevin	NYI	1	2	0	1	1	8	....	....	....	....	....		1982-83	1982-83
Dewar, Tom	NYR	1	9	0	2	2	4	....	....	....	....	....		1943-44	1943-44
Dewsbury, Al	Det., Chi.	9	347	30	78	108	365	14	1	5	6	60	1	1946-47	1955-56
Deziel, Michel	Buf.	1	....	....	....	....	....	1	0	0	0	0		1974-75	1974-75
Dheere, Marcel	Mtl.	1	11	1	2	3	2	5	0	0	0	6		1942-43	1942-43
Diachuk, Edward	Det.	1	12	0	0	0	19	....	....	....	....	....		1960-61	1960-61
Dick, Harry	Chi.	1	12	0	1	1	12	....	....	....	....	....		1946-47	1946-47
Dickens, Ernie	Tor., Chi.	6	278	12	44	56	48	13	0	0	0	4	1	1941-42	1950-51
Dickenson, Herb	NYR	2	48	18	17	35	10	....	....	....	....	....		1951-52	1952-53
Dietrich, Don	Chi., N.J.	2	28	0	7	7	10	....	....	....	....	....		1983-84	1985-86
• Dill, Bob	NYR	2	76	15	15	30	135	....	....	....	....	....		1943-44	1944-45
Dillabough, Bob	Det., Bos., Pit., Oak.	7	283	32	54	86	76	17	3	0	3	0		1961-62	1969-70
• Dillon, Cecil	NYR, Det.	10	453	167	131	298	105	43	14	9	23	14	1	1930-31	1939-40
Dillon, Gary	Col.	1	13	1	1	2	29	....	....	....	....	....		1980-81	1980-81
Dillon, Wayne	NYR, Wpg.	4	229	43	66	109	60	3	0	1	1	0		1975-76	1979-80
Dineen, Bill	Det., Chi.	5	323	51	44	95	122	37	1	1	2	18	2	1953-54	1957-58
Dineen, Gary	Min.	1	4	0	1	1	0	....	....	....	....	....		1968-69	1968-69
Dineen, Peter	L.A., Det.	2	13	0	2	2	13	....	....	....	....	....		1986-87	1989-90
Dinsmore, Chuck	Mtl.M	4	100	6	2	8	44	12	1	0	1	6	1	1924-25	1929-30
Dionne, Marcel	Det., L.A., NYR	18	1348	731	1040	1771	600	49	21	24	45	17		1971-72	1988-89
Doak, Gary	Det., Bos., Van., NYR	16	789	23	107	130	908	78	2	4	6	121	1	1965-66	1980-81
Dobson, Jim	Min., Col.	3	11	0	0	0	6	....	....	....	....	....		1979-80	1981-82
• Doherty, Fred	Mtl.	1	3	0	0	0	0	....	....	....	....	....		1918-19	1918-19
Donaldson, Gary	Chi.	1	1	0	0	0	0	....	....	....	....	....	2	1973-74	1973-74
Donnelly, Babe	Mtl.M.	1	34	0	1	1	14	2	0	0	0	0		1926-27	1926-27
Donnelly, Dave	Bos., Chi., Edm.	5	137	15	24	39	150	5	0	0	0	0		1983-84	1987-88
Doran, Red (I.)	Det.	1	24	3	2	5	10	....	....	....	....	....		1946-47	1946-47
• Doran, Red (J.)	NYA., Det., Mtl.	5	98	5	10	15	110	3	0	0	0	0		1933-34	1939-40
• Doraty, Ken	Chi., Tor., Det.	5	103	15	26	41	24	15	7	2	9	2		1926-27	1937-38
Dore, Andre	NYR, St.L., Que.	7	257	14	81	95	261	23	1	2	3	32		1978-79	1984-85
Dorey, Jim	Tor., NYR	4	232	25	74	99	553	11	0	2	2	40		1968-69	1971-72
Dorion, Dan	N.J.	2	4	1	1	2	2	....	....	....	....	....		1985-86	1987-88
Dornhoefer, Gary	Bos., Phi.	14	787	214	328	542	1291	80	17	19	36	203	2	1963-64	1977-78
Dorohoy, Eddie	Mtl.	1	16	0	0	0	6	....	....	....	....	....		1948-49	1948-49
Douglas, Jordy	Hfd., Min., Wpg.	6	268	76	62	138	160	6	0	0	0	4		1979-80	1984-85
Douglas, Kent	Tor., Oak., Det.	7	428	33	115	148	631	19	1	3	4	33	1	1962-63	1968-69
Douglas, Les	Det.	4	52	6	12	18	8	10	3	2	5	0	1	1940-41	1946-47
Downie, Dave	Tor.	1	11	0	1	1	2	....	....	....	....	....		1932-33	1932-33
• Draper, Bruce	Tor.	1	1	0	0	0	0	....	....	....	....	....		1962-63	1962-63
• Drillon, Gordie	Tor., Mtl.	7	311	155	139	294	56	50	26	15	41	10	1	1936-37	1942-43

			Regular Schedule					Playoffs							
Name	NHL Teams	NHL Seasons	GP	G	A	TP	PIM	GP	G	A	TP	PIM	NHL Cup Wins	First NHL Season	Last NHL Season
Driscoll, Pete	Edm.	2	60	3	8	11	97	3	0	0	0	0		1979-80	1980-81
Drolet, Rene	Phi., Det.	2	2	0	0	0	0	....	....	....	....	....		1971-72	1974-75
Drouillard, Clarence	Det.	1	10	0	1	1	0	....	....	....	....	....		1937-38	1937-38
Drouin, Jude	Mtl., Min., NYI, Wpg.	12	666	151	305	456	346	72	27	41	68	33		1968-69	1980-81
• Drouin, Polly	Mtl.	6	173	23	50	73	80	5	0	1	1	5		1935-36	1940-41
Drummond, John	NYR	1	2	0	0	0	0	....	....	....	....	....		1944-45	1944-45
Drury, Herb	Pit., Phi.	6	213	24	13	37	203	4	1	1	2	0		1925-26	1930-31
Dube, Gilles	Mtl., Det.	2	12	1	2	3	2	2	0	0	0	0	1	1949-50	1953-54
Dube, Norm	K.C.	2	57	8	10	18	54	....	....	....	....	....		1974-75	1975-76
Dudley, Rick	Buf., Wpg.	6	309	75	99	174	292	25	7	2	9	69		1972-73	1980-81
Duff, Dick	Tor., NYR, Mtl., L.A., Buf.	18	1030	283	289	572	743	114	30	49	79	78	6	1954-55	1971-72
Dufour, Luc	Bos., Que., St.L.	3	167	23	21	44	199	18	1	0	1	32		1982-83	1984-85
Dufour, Marc	NYR, L.A.	3	14	1	0	1	2	....	....	....	....	....		1963-64	1968-69
Duggan, Jack	Ott.	1	27	0	0	0	0	2	0	0	0	0		1925-26	1925-26
Duggan, Ken	Min.	1	1	0	0	0	0	....	....	....	....	....		1987-88	1987-88
Duguay, Ron	NYR, Det., Pit., L.A.	12	864	274	346	620	582	89	31	22	53	118		1977-78	1988-89
• Duguid, Lorne	Mtl.M, Det., Bos.	6	135	9	15	24	57	2	0	0	0	4		1931-32	1936-37
Dumart, Woody	Bos.	16	771	211	218	429	99	82	12	15	27	23	2	1935-36	1953-54
Dunbar, Dale	Van., Bos.	2	2	0	0	0	2	....	....	....	....	....		1985-86	1988-89
• Duncan, Art	Det., Tor.	5	156	18	16	34	225	5	0	0	0	4		1926-27	1930-31
Dundas, Rocky	Tor.	1	5	0	0	0	14	....	....	....	....	....		1989-90	1989-90
Dunlap, Frank	Tor.	1	15	0	1	1	2	....	....	....	....	....		1943-44	1943-44
Dunlop, Blake	Min., Phi., St.L., Det.	11	550	130	274	404	172	40	4	10	14	18		1973-74	1983-84
Dunn, Dave	Van., Tor.	3	184	14	41	55	313	10	1	1	2	41		1973-74	1975-76
Dunn, Richie	Buf., Cgy., Hfd.	12	483	36	140	176	314	36	3	15	18	24		1977-78	1988-89
Dupere, Denis	Tor., Wsh., St.L., K.C., Col.	8	421	80	99	179	66	16	1	0	1	0		1970-71	1977-78
Dupont, Andre	NYR, St.L., Phi., Que.	13	810	59	185	244	1986	140	14	18	32	352	2	1970-71	1982-83
Dupont, Jerome	Chi., Tor.	6	214	7	29	36	468	20	0	2	2	56		1981-82	1986-87
Dupont, Norm	Mtl., Wpg., Hfd.	5	256	55	85	140	52	13	4	2	6	0		1979-80	1983-84
Durbano, Steve	St.L., Pit., K.C., Col.	6	220	13	60	73	1127	5	0	2	2	8		1972-73	1978-79
Duris, Vitezslav	Tor.	2	89	3	20	23	62	3	0	1	1	2		1980-81	1982-83
Dussault, Norm	Mtl.	4	206	31	62	93	47	7	3	1	4	0		1947-48	1950-51
Dutkowski, Duke	Chi., NYA, NYR	5	200	16	30	46	172	6	0	0	0	6		1926-27	1933-34
• Dutton, Red	Mtl.M, NYA	10	449	29	67	96	871	18	1	0	1	33		1926-27	1935-36
Dvorak, Miroslav	Phi.	3	193	11	74	85	51	18	0	2	2	6		1982-83	1984-85
Dwyer, Mike	Col., Cgy.	4	31	2	6	8	25	1	1	0	1	0		1978-79	1981-82
Dyck, Henry	NYR	1	1	0	0	0	0	....	....	....	....	....		1943-44	1943-44
• Dye, Babe	Tor., Ham., Chi., NYA	11	269	202	41	243	205	15	11	2	13	11	1	1919-20	1930-31
Dykstra, Steven	Buf., Edm., Pit., Hfd.	5	217	8	32	40	545	1	0	0	0	2		1985-86	1989-90
Dyte, John	Chi.	1	27	1	0	1	31	....	....	....	....	....		1943-44	1943-44
E															
Eakin, Bruce	Cgy., Det.	4	13	2	2	4	4	....	....	....	....	....		1981-82	1985-86
Eatough, Jeff	Buf.	1	1	0	0	0	0	....	....	....	....	....		1981-82	1981-82
Eaves, Mike	Min., Cgy.	8	324	83	143	226	80	43	7	10	17	14		1978-79	1985-86
Eaves, Murray	Wpg., Det.	8	57	4	13	17	9	4	0	1	1	2		1980-81	1989-90
Ecclestone, Tim	St.L., Det., Tor., Atl.	11	692	126	233	359	346	48	6	11	17	76		1967-68	1977-78
Edberg, Rolf	Wsh.	3	184	45	58	103	24	....	....	....	....	....		1978-79	1980-81
• Eddolls, Frank	Mtl., NYR	8	317	23	43	66	114	31	0	2	2	10	1	1944-45	1951-52
Edestrand, Darryl	St.L., Phi., Pit., Bos., L.A.	10	455	34	90	124	404	42	3	9	12	57		1967-68	1978-79
Edmundson, Garry	Mtl., Tor.	3	43	4	6	10	49	11	0	1	1	8		1951-52	1960-61
Edur, Tom	Col., Pit	2	158	17	70	87	67	....	....	....	....	....		1976-77	1977-78
Egan, Pat	Bro., Det., Bos., NYR	11	554	77	153	230	776	44	9	4	13	44		1939-40	1950-51
Egers, Jack	NYR, St.L., Wsh.	7	284	64	69	133	154	32	5	6	11	32		1969-70	1975-76
Ehman, Gerry	Bos., Det., Tor., Oak, Cal.	9	429	96	118	214	100	41	10	10	20	12	1	1957-58	1970-71
Eldebrink, Anders	Van., Que.	2	55	3	11	14	29	14	0	0	0	0		1981-82	1982-83
Elik, Boris	Det.	1	3	0	0	0	0	....	....	....	....	....		1962-63	1962-63
Elliot, Fred	Ott.	1	43	2	0	2	6	....	....	....	....	....		1928-29	1928-29
Ellis, Ron	Tor.	16	1034	332	308	640	207	70	18	8	26	20	1	1963-64	1980-81
Eloranta, Kari	Cgy., St.L.	5	267	13	103	116	155	26	1	7	8	19		1981-82	1986-87
Emberg, Eddie	Mtl.	1	....	....	....	....	....	2	1	0	1	0		1944-45	1944-45
• Emms, Hap	Mtl.M, NYA, Det., Bos.	10	320	36	53	89	311	14	0	0	0	12		1926-27	1937-38
Engblom, Brian	Mtl., Wsh., L.A., Buf., Cgy.	11	659	29	177	206	599	48	3	9	12	43	3	1976-77	1986-87
Engele, Jerry	Min.	3	100	2	13	15	162	2	0	1	1	0		1975-76	1977-78
English, John	L.A.	1	3	1	3	4	4	1	0	0	0	0		1987-88	1987-88
Ennis, Jim	Edm.	1	5	1	0	1	10	....	....	....	....	....		1987-88	1987-88
Erickson, Aut	Bos., Chi., Oak., Tor.	7	227	7	84	31	182	7	0	0	0	2	1	1959-60	1969-70
Erickson, Grant	Bos., Min.	2	6	1	0	1	4	....	....	....	....	....		1968-69	1969-70
Eriksson, Peter	Edm.	1	20	3	3	6	24	....	....	....	....	....		1989-90	1989-90
Eriksson, Rolie	Min., Van.	3	193	48	95	143	26	2	1	0	1	0		1976-77	1978-79
Eriksson, Thomas	Phi.	5	208	22	76	98	107	19	0	3	3	6		1980-81	1985-86
Esposito, Phil	Chi., Bos., NYR	18	1282	717	873	1590	910	130	61	76	137	137	2	1963-64	1980-81
Evans, Chris	Tor., Buf., St.L., Det., K.C.	5	241	19	42	61	143	12	1	1	2	8		1969-70	1974-75
Evans, Daryl	L.A., Wsh., Tor.	6	113	22	30	52	25	11	5	8	13	12		1981-82	1986-87
Evans, Jack	NYR, Chi.	14	752	19	80	99	989	56	2	2	4	97	1	1948-49	1962-63
Evans, John	Phi.	3	103	14	25	39	34	1	0	0	0	0		1978-79	1982-83
Evans, Paul	Tor.	2	11	1	1	2	21	2	0	0	0	0		1976-77	1977-78
Evans, Shawn	St. L., NYI	2	9	1	0	1	2	....	....	....	....	....		1985-86	1989-90
Evans, Stewart	Det., Mtl.M., Mtl.	8	367	28	49	77	425	26	0	0	0	20	1	1930-31	1938-39
Ezinicki, Bill	Tor., Bos., NYR	9	368	79	105	184	713	40	5	8	13	87	3	1944-45	1954-55
F															
Fahey, Trevor	NYR	1	1	0	0	0	0	....	....	....	....	....		1964-65	1964-65
Fairbairn, Bill	NYR, Min. St.L.	11	658	162	261	423	173	54	13	22	35	42		1968-69	1978-79
Falkenberg, Bob	Det.	5	54	1	5	6	26	....	....	....	....	....		1966-67	1971-72
Farrant, Walt	Chi.	1	1	0	0	0	0	....	....	....	....	....		1943-44	1943-44
Farrish, Dave	NYR, Que, Tor.	7	430	17	110	127	440	14	0	2	2	24		1976-77	1983-84
Fashoway, Gordie	Chi.	1	13	3	2	5	14	....	....	....	....	....		1950-51	1950-51
Faubert, Mario	Pit.	7	231	21	90	111	292	10	2	2	4	6		1974-75	1981-82
Faulkner, Alex	Tor., Det.	3	101	15	17	32	15	12	5	0	5	2		1961-62	1963-64
Fauss, Ted	Tor.	2	28	0	2	2	15	....	....	....	....	....		1986-87	1987-88
Feamster, Dave	Chi.	4	169	13	24	37	155	33	3	5	8	61		1981-82	1984-85
Featherstone, Tony	Oak., Cal., Min.	3	130	17	21	38	65	2	0	0	0	0		1969-70	1973-74
Federko, Bernie	St.L., Det.	14	1000	369	761	1130	487	91	35	66	101	83		1976-77	1989-90
Felix, Chris	Wsh.	4	35	1	12	13	10	2	0	1	1	0		1987-88	1990-91
Feltrin, Tony	Pit., NYR	4	48	3	3	6	65	....	....	....	....	....		1980-81	1985-86
Fenton, Paul	Hfd., NYR, L.A., Wpg., Tor., Cgy., S.J.	8	411	100	83	183	198	17	4	1	5	27		1984-85	1991-92
Ferguson,	Chi.	1	1	0	0	0	0	....	....	....	....	....		1939-40	1939-40
Ferguson, George	Tor., Pit, Min	12	797	160	238	398	431	86	14	23	37	44		1972-73	1983-84
Ferguson, John	Mtl.	8	500	145	158	303	1214	85	20	18	38	260	5	1963-64	1970-71
Ferguson, Lorne	Bos., Det., Chi.	8	422	82	80	162	193	31	6	3	9	24		1949-50	1958-59
Ferguson, Norm	Oak., Cal.	4	279	73	66	139	72	10	1	4	5	7		1968-69	1971-72
Fidler, Mike	Cle., Min, Hfd., Chi.	7	271	84	97	181	124	....	....	....	....	....		1976-77	1982-83
Field, Wilf	Bro., Mtl., Chi.	6	218	17	25	42	151	3	0	0	0	0		1936-37	1944-45
Fielder, Guyle	Det., Chi.	4	36	0	0	0	2	6	0	0	0	2		1950-51	1957-58
Fillion, Bob	Mtl.	7	327	42	61	103	84	33	7	4	11	10	2	1943-44	1949-50
Fillion, Marcel	Bos.	1	1	0	0	0	0	....	....	....	....	....		1944-45	1944-45
• Filmore, Tommy	Det., NYA, Bos.	4	116	15	12	27	33	....	....	....	....	....		1930-31	1933-34
Finkbeiner, Lloyd	NYA	1	1	0	0	0	0	....	....	....	....	....		1940-41	1940-41
Finney, Sid	Chi.	3	59	10	7	17	4	7	0	0	0	2		1951-52	1953-54
Finnigan, Ed	Bos.	1	3	0	0	0	0	....	....	....	....	....		1935-36	1935-36
• Finnigan, Frank	Ott., Tor., St.L.	14	555	115	88	203	405	39	6	9	15	22	2	1923-24	1936-37
Fischer, Ron	Buf.	2	18	0	7	7	6	....	....	....	....	....		1981-82	1982-83
Fisher, Alvin	Tor.	1	9	1	0	1	4	....	....	....	....	....		1924-25	1924-25
Fisher, Dunc	NYR, Bos., Det.	7	275	45	70	115	104	21	4	4	8	14		1947-48	1958-59
Fisher, Joe	Det.	4	66	8	12	20	13	15	2	1	3	6	1	1939-40	1942-43
Fitchner, Bob	Que	2	78	12	20	32	59	3	0	0	0	10		1979-80	1980-81
Fitzpatrick, Ross	Phi.	4	20	5	2	7	0	....	....	....	....	....		1982-83	1985-86
Fitzpatrick, Sandy	NYR, Min.	2	22	3	6	9	8	12	0	0	0	0		1964-65	1967-68
Flaman, Fern	Bos., Tor.	17	910	34	174	208	1370	63	4	8	12	93	1	1944-45	1960-61

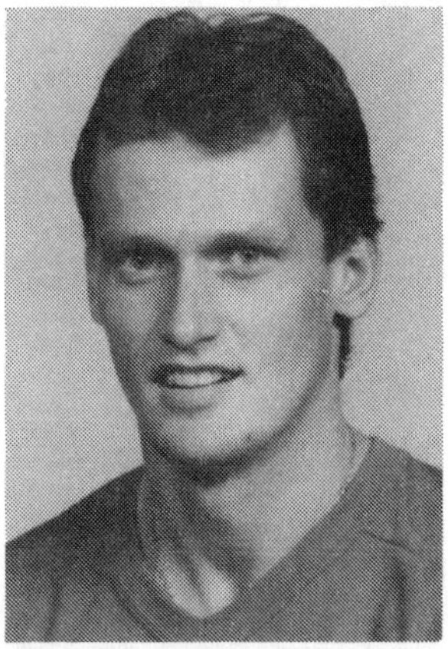

Miroslav Frycer

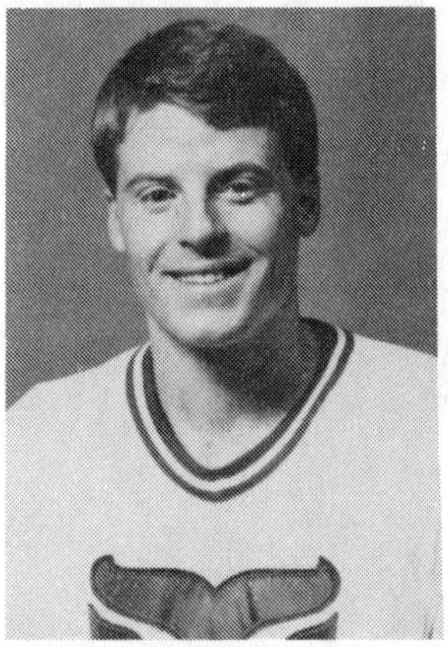

Mark Fusco

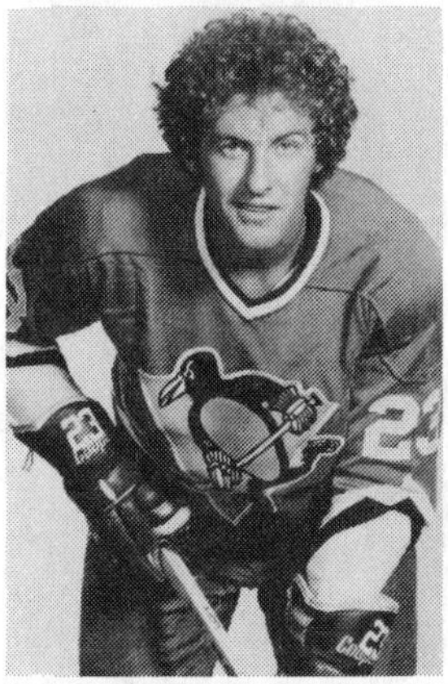

Ed Gilbert

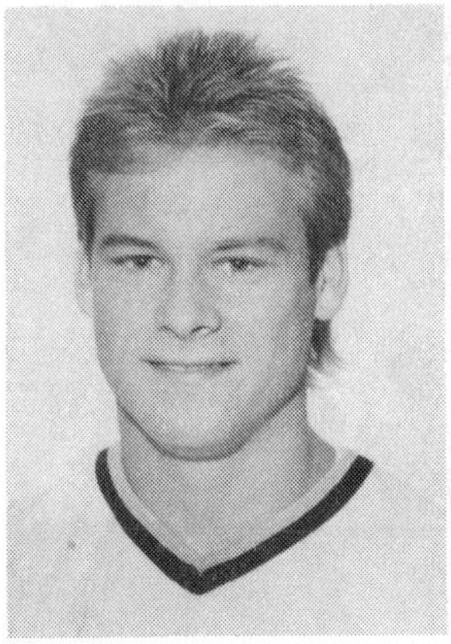

Dan Gratton

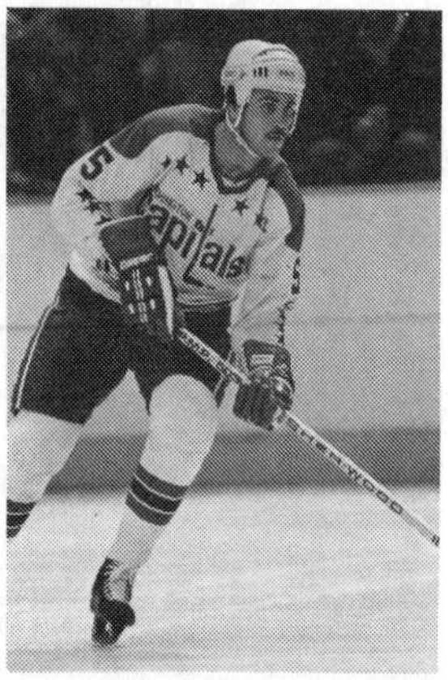

Rick Green

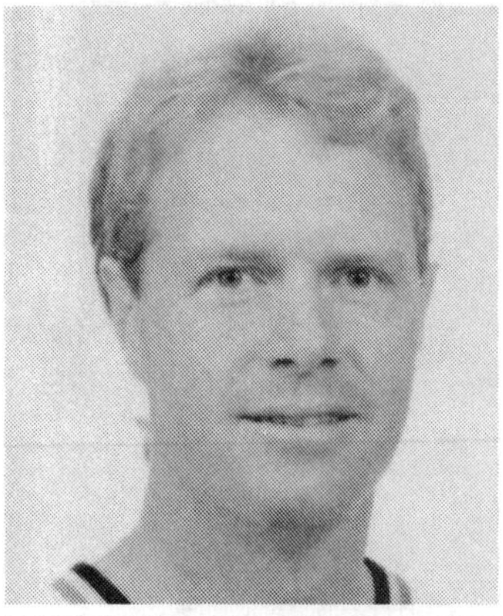

Randy Gregg

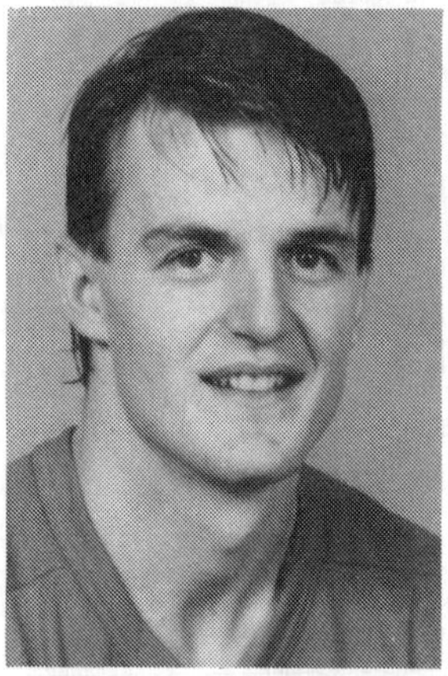

Marc Habscheid

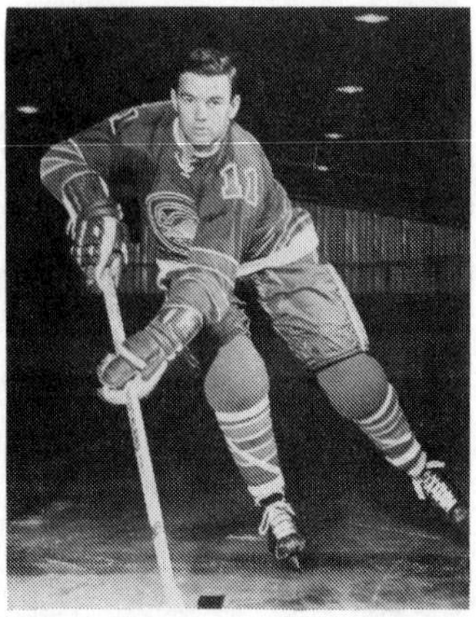

Ted Hampson

			Regular Schedule					Playoffs							
Name	NHL Teams	NHL Seasons	GP	G	A	TP	PIM	GP	G	A	TP	PIM	NHL Cup Wins	First NHL Season	Last NHL Season
Fleming, Reggie	Mtl., Chi., Bos., NYR, Phi., Buf.	12	749	108	132	240	1468	50	3	6	9	106	1	1959-60	1970-71
Flesch,	Ham.	1	1	0	0	0	0	....	....	....	....	....		1920-21	1920-21
Flesch, John	Min, Pit, Col.	4	124	18	23	41	117	....	....	....	....	....		1974-75	1979-80
Fletcher, Steven	Mtl., Wpg.	2	3	0	0	0	5	1	0	0	0	5		1987-88	1988-89
Flett, Bill	L.A., Phi., Tor., Atl, Edm.	11	689	202	215	417	501	52	7	16	23	42	1	1967-68	1979-80
Flichel, Todd	Wpg.	4	6	0	1	1	4	....	....	....	....	....		1987-88	1989-90
Flockhart, Rob	Van., Min	5	55	2	5	7	14	1	1	0	1	2		1976-77	1980-81
Flockhart, Ron	Phi., Pit., Mtl., St.L., Bos.	9	453	145	183	328	208	29	11	18	29	16		1980-81	1988-89
Floyd, Larry	N.J.	2	12	2	3	5	9	....	....	....	....	....		1982-83	1983-84
Floyd, Larry	N.J.	2	12	2	3	5	9	....	....	....	....	....		1982-83	1983-84
Fogolin, Lee	Buf., Edm.	13	924	44	195	239	1318	108	5	19	24	173	2	1974-75	1986-87
Fogolin, Lidio (Lee)	Det., Chi.	9	427	10	48	58	575	28	0	2	2	30	1	1947-48	1955-56
Folco, Peter	Van.	1	2	0	0	0	0	....	....	....	....	....		1973-74	1973-74
Foley, Gerry	Tor., NYR, L.A.	4	142	9	14	23	99	9	0	1	1	2		1954-55	1968-69
Foley, Rick	Chi., Phi., Det.	3	67	11	26	37	180	4	0	1	1	4		1970-71	1973-74
Folk, Bill	Det.	2	12	0	0	0	4	....	....	....	....	....		1951-52	1952-53
Fontaine, Len	Det.	2	46	8	11	19	10	....	....	....	....	....		1972-73	1973-74
Fontas, Jon	Min.	2	2	0	0	0	0	....	....	....	....	....		1979-80	1980-81
Fonteyne, Val	Det., NYR, Pit.	13	820	75	154	229	26	59	3	10	13	8		1959-60	1971-72
Fontinato, Louie	NYR, Mtl.	9	535	26	78	104	1247	21	0	2	2	42		1954-55	1962-63
Forbes, Dave	Bos., Wsh.	6	363	64	64	128	341	45	1	4	5	13		1973-74	1978-79
Forbes, Mike	Bos., Edm.	3	50	1	11	12	41	....	....	....	....	....		1977-78	1981-82
Forey, Connie	St.L.	1	4	0	0	0	2	....	....	....	....	....		1973-74	1973-74
Forsey, Jack	Tor.	1	19	7	9	16	10	3	0	1	1	0		1942-43	1942-43
Forslund, Gus	Ott.	1	48	4	9	13	2	....	....	....	....	....		1932-33	1932-33
Forsyth, Alex	Wsh.	1	1	0	0	0	0	....	....	....	....	....		1976-77	1976-77
Fortier, Charles	Mtl.	1	1	0	0	0	0	....	....	....	....	....	1	1923-24	1923-24
Fortier, Dave	Tor., NYI, Van.	4	205	8	21	29	335	20	0	2	2	33		1972-73	1976-77
Fortin, Ray	St.L.	3	92	2	6	8	33	6	0	0	0	8		1967-68	1969-70
Foster, Dwight	Bos., Col., N.J., Det.	10	541	111	163	274	420	35	5	12	17	4		1977-78	1986-87
Foster, Harry	NYR, Bos., Det.	4	83	3	2	5	32	....	....	....	....	....		1929-31	1934-35
Foster, Herb	NYR	2	5	1	0	1	5	....	....	....	....	....		1940-41	1947-48
Fotiu, Nick	NYR, Hfd., Cgy., Phi., Edm.	13	646	60	77	137	1362	38	0	4	4	67		1976-77	1988-89
• Fowler, Jimmy	Tor.	3	135	18	29	47	39	18	0	3	3	2		1936-37	1938-39
Fowler, Tom	Chi.	1	24	0	1	1	18	....	....	....	....	....		1946-47	1946-47
Fox, Greg	Atl, Chi., Pit.	8	494	14	92	106	637	44	1	9	10	67		1977-78	1984-85
Fox, Jim	L.A.	10	578	186	293	479	143	22	4	8	12	0		1980-81	1989-90
• Foyston, Frank	Det.	2	64	17	7	24	32	....	....	....	....	....		1926-27	1927-28
Frampton, Bob	Mtl.	1	2	0	0	0	0	3	0	0	0	0		1949-50	1949-50
Franceschetti, Lou	Wsh., Tor., Buf.	10	459	59	81	140	747	44	3	2	5	111		1981-82	1991-92
Francis, Bobby	Det.	1	14	2	0	2	0	....	....	....	....	....		1982-83	1982-83
Fraser, Archie	NYR	1	3	0	1	1	0	....	....	....	....	....		1943-44	1943-44
Fraser, Curt	Van., Chi., Min.	12	704	193	240	433	1306	65	15	18	33	198		1978-79	1989-90
Fraser, Gord	Chi., Det., Mtl., Pit., Phi.	5	144	24	12	36	224	2	1	0	1	6		1926-27	1930-31
Fraser, Harry	Chi.	1	21	5	4	9	0	....	....	....	....	....		1944-45	1944-45
Fraser, Jack	Ham.	1	1	0	0	0	0	....	....	....	....	....		1923-24	1923-24
Frawley, Dan	Chi., Pit.	6	273	37	40	77	674	1	0	0	0	0		1983-84	1988-89
• Frederickson, Frank	Det., Bos., Pit.	5	165	39	34	73	207	10	2	5	7	26	1	1926-27	1930-31
Frew, Irv	Mtl.M, St.L., Mtl.	3	95	2	5	7	146	4	0	0	0	6		1933-34	1935-36
Friday, Tim	Det.	1	23	0	3	3	6	....	....	....	....	....		1985-86	1985-86
Fridgen, Dan	Hfd.	2	13	2	3	5	2	....	....	....	....	....		1981-82	1982-83
Friest, Ron	Min.	3	64	7	7	14	191	6	1	0	1	7		1980-81	1982-83
Frig, Len	Chi., Cal., Cle., St.L.	7	311	13	51	64	479	14	2	1	3	0		1972-73	1979-80
Frost, Harry	Bos.	1	3	0	0	0	0	1	0	0	0	0		1938-39	1938-39
Frycer, Miroslav	Que., Tor., Det., Edm.	8	415	147	183	330	486	17	3	8	11	16		1981-82	1988-89
Fryday, Bob	Mtl.	2	5	1	0	1	0	....	....	....	....	....		1949-50	1951-52
Ftorek, Robbie	Det., Que, NYR	8	334	77	150	227	262	19	9	6	15	28		1972-73	1984-85
Fullan, Lawrence	Wsh.	1	4	1	0	1	0	....	....	....	....	....		1974-75	1974-75
Fusco, Mark	Hfd.	2	80	3	12	15	42	....	....	....	....	....		1983-84	1984-85

G

Gadsby, Bill	Chi., NYR, Det.	20	1248	130	437	567	1539	67	4	23	27	92		1946-47	1965-66
Gagne, Art	Mtl., Bos., Ott., Det.	6	228	67	33	100	257	11	2	1	3	20		1926-27	1931-32
Gagne, Paul	Col., N.J., Tor., NYI	8	390	110	101	211	127	....	....	....	....	....		1980-81	1989-90
Gagne, Pierre	Bos.	1	2	0	0	0	0	....	....	....	....	....		1959-60	1959-60
Gagnon, Germaine	Mtl., NYI, Chi., K.C.	5	259	40	101	141	72	19	2	3	5	2		1971-72	1975-76
• Gagnon, Johnny	Mtl., Bos., NYA	10	454	120	141	261	295	32	12	12	24	37	1	1930-31	1939-40
Gainey, Bob	Mtl.	16	1160	239	262	501	585	182	25	48	73	151	5	1973-74	1988-89
• Gainor, Dutch	Bos., NYR, Ott., Mtl.M	7	243	51	56	107	129	25	2	1	3	14	2	1927-28	1934-35
Galarneau, Michel	Hfd.	3	78	7	10	17	34	....	....	....	....	....		1980-81	1982-83
• Galbraith, Percy	Bos., Ott.	8	347	29	31	60	223	31	4	7	11	24		1926-27	1933-34
Gallagher, John	Mtl.M, Det., NYA	7	204	14	19	33	153	22	2	3	5	27	1	1930-31	1938-39
Gallimore, Jamie	Min.	1	2	0	0	0	0	....	....	....	....	....		1977-78	1977-78
Gallinger, Don	Bos.	5	222	65	88	153	89	23	5	5	10	19		1942-43	1947-48
Gamble, Dick	Mtl., Chi., Tor.	8	195	41	41	82	66	14	1	2	3	4	2	1950-51	1966-67
Gambucci, Gary	Min.	2	51	2	7	9	9	....	....	....	....	....		1971-72	1973-74
Ganchar, Perry	St. L., Mtl., Pit.	4	42	3	7	10	36	7	3	1	4	0		1983-84	1988-89
Gans, Dave	L.A.	2	6	0	0	0	2	....	....	....	....	....		1982-83	1985-86
• Gardiner, Herb	Mtl., Chi.	3	101	10	9	19	52	7	0	1	1	14		1926-27	1928-29
Gardner, Bill	Chi., Hfd.	9	380	73	115	188	68	45	3	8	11	17		1980-81	1988-89
Gardner, Cal	NYR, Tor., Chi., Bos.	12	696	154	238	392	517	61	7	10	17	20	2	1945-46	1956-57
Gardner, Dave	Mtl., St.L., Cal., Cle., Phi.	7	350	75	115	190	41	....	....	....	....	....		1972-73	1979-80
Gardner, Paul	Col., Tor., Pit., Wsh., Buf.	7	447	201	201	402	207	16	2	6	8	14		1976-77	1985-86
Gare, Danny	Buf., Det., Edm.	13	827	354	331	685	1285	64	25	21	46	195		1974-75	1986-87
Gariepy, Ray	Bos., Tor.	2	36	1	6	7	43	....	....	....	....	....		1953-54	1955-56
• Garland, Scott	Tor., L.A.	3	91	13	24	37	115	7	1	2	3	35		1975-76	1978-79
Garner, Bob	Pit.	1	1	0	0	0	0	....	....	....	....	....		1982-83	1982-83
• Garrett, Red	NYR	1	23	1	1	2	18	....	....	....	....	....		1942-43	1942-43
• Gassoff, Bob	St.L.	4	245	11	47	58	866	9	0	1	1	16		1973-74	1976-77
Gassoff, Brad	Van.	4	122	19	17	36	163	3	0	0	0	0		1975-76	1978-79
Gatzos, Steve	Pit.	4	89	15	20	35	83	1	0	0	0	0		1981-82	1984-85
Gaudreault, Armand	Bos.	1	44	15	9	24	27	7	0	2	2	8		1944-45	1944-45
• Gaudreault, Leo	Mtl.	3	67	8	4	12	30	....	....	....	....	....		1927-28	1932-33
Gaulin, Jean-Marc	Que.	4	26	4	3	7	8	1	0	0	0	0		1982-83	1985-86
Gaume, Dallas	Hfd.	1	4	1	1	2	0	....	....	....	....	....		1988-89	1988-89
Gauthier, Art	Mtl.	1	13	0	0	0	0	1	0	0	0	0		1926-27	1926-27
• Gauthier, Fern	NYR, Mtl., Det.	6	229	46	50	96	35	22	5	1	6	7		1943-44	1948-49
Gauthier, Jean	Mtl., Phi., Bos.	10	166	6	29	35	150	14	1	3	4	22	1	1960-61	1969-70
Gauvreau, Jocelyn	Mtl.	1	2	0	0	0	0	....	....	....	....	....		1983-84	1983-84
Geale, Bob	Pit.	1	1	0	0	0	2	....	....	....	....	....		1984-85	1984-85
• Gee, George	Chi., Det.	9	551	135	183	318	345	41	6	13	19	32	1	1945-46	1953-54
Geldart, Gary	Min.	1	4	0	0	0	5	....	....	....	....	....		1970-71	1970-71
Gendron, Jean-Guy	NYR, Mtl., Bos., Phi.	14	863	182	201	383	701	42	7	4	11	47		1955-56	1971-72
Geoffrion, Bernie	Mtl., NYR	16	883	393	429	822	689	132	58	60	118	88	6	1950-51	1967-68
Geoffrion, Danny	Mtl., Wpg.	3	111	20	32	52	99	2	0	0	0	7		1979-80	1981-82
• Geran, Gerry	Mtl.W., Bos.	2	37	5	1	6	6	....	....	....	....	....		1917-18	1925-26
• Gerard, Eddie	Ott.	6	128	50	30	80	94	26	7	3	10	51	4	1917-18	1922-23
Germain, Eric	L.A.	1	4	0	1	1	13	1	0	0	0	4		1987-88	1987-88
Getliffe, Ray	Bos., Mtl.	10	393	136	137	273	260	45	9	10	19	30	2	1935-36	1944-45
Giallonardo, Mario	Col.	2	23	0	3	3	6	....	....	....	....	....		1979-80	1980-81
Gibbs, Barry	Bos., Min., Atl., St.L., L.A.	13	797	58	224	282	945	36	4	2	6	67		1967-68	1979-80
Gibson, Don	Van.	1	14	0	3	3	20	....	....	....	....	....		1990-91	1990-91
Gibson, Doug	Bos., Wsh.	3	63	9	19	28	0	1	0	0	0	0		1973-74	1977-78
Gibson, John	L.A., Tor., Wpg.	3	48	0	2	2	120	....	....	....	....	....		1980-81	1983-84
Giesebrecht, Gus	Det.	4	135	27	51	78	13	17	2	3	5	0		1938-39	1941-42
Giffin, Lee	Pit.	2	27	1	3	4	9	....	....	....	....	....		1986-87	1987-88
Gilbert, Ed	K.C., Pit.	3	166	21	31	52	22	....	....	....	....	....		1974-75	1976-77
Gilbert, Jean	Bos.	2	9	0	0	0	4	....	....	....	....	....		1962-63	1964-65
Gilbert, Rod	NYR	18	1065	406	615	1021	508	79	34	33	67	43		1960-61	1977-78
Gilbertson, Stan	Cal., St.L., Wsh., Pit.	6	428	85	89	174	148	3	1	1	2	2		1971-72	1976-77
Gillen, Don	Phi., Hfd.	2	35	2	4	6	22	....	....	....	....	....		1979-80	1981-82
Gillie, Ferrand	Det.	1	1	0	0	0	0	....	....	....	....	....		1928-29	1928-29

			Regular Schedule					Playoffs					NHL	First	Last
Name	NHL Teams	NHL Seasons	GP	G	A	TP	PIM	GP	G	A	TP	PIM	Cup Wins	NHL Season	NHL Season
Gillies, Clark	NYI, Buf.	14	958	319	378	697	1023	164	47	47	94	287	4	1974-75	1987-88
Gillis, Jere	Que., Buf., Phi., Van., NYR	9	386	78	95	173	230	19	4	7	11	9		1977-78	1986-87
Gillis, Mike	Col., Bos.	6	246	33	43	76	186	27	2	5	7	10		1978-79	1983-84
Gingras, Gaston	Mtl., Tor., St.L.	10	476	61	174	235	161	52	6	18	24	20	1	1979-80	1988-89
Girard, Bob	Cal., Cle., Wsh.	5	305	45	69	114	140	....	....	....	....	....		1975-76	1979-80
Girard, Kenny	Tor.	3	7	0	1	1	2	....	....	....	....	....		1956-57	1959-60
Giroux, Art	Mtl., Bos., Det.	3	54	6	4	10	14	2	0	0	0	0		1932-33	1935-36
Giroux, Larry	St.L., K.C., Det., Hfd.	7	274	15	74	89	333	5	0	0	0	4		1973-74	1979-80
Giroux, Pierre	L.A.	1	6	1	0	1	17	....	....	....	....	....		1982-83	1982-83
Gladney, Bob	L.A., Pit.	2	14	1	5	6	4	....	....	....	....	....		1982-83	1983-84
Gladu, Jean	Bos.	1	40	6	14	20	2	7	2	2	4	0		1944-45	1944-45
Glennie, Brian	Tor., L.A.	10	572	14	100	114	621	32	0	1	1	66		1969-70	1978-79
Glennon, Matthew (Matt)	Bos.	1	3	0	0	0	2	....	....	....	....	....		1991-92	1991-92
Gloeckner, Lorry	Det.	1	13	0	2	2	6	....	....	....	....	....		1978-79	1978-79
Gloor, Dan	Van.	1	2	0	0	0	0	....	....	....	....	....		1973-74	1973-74
Glover, Fred	Det., Chi.	4	92	13	11	24	62	3	0	0	0	0		1948-49	1952-53
Glover, Howie	Chi., Det., NYR, Mtl.	5	144	29	17	46	101	11	1	2	3	2		1958-59	1968-69
Godden, Ernie	Tor.	1	5	1	1	2	6	....	....	....	....	....		1981-82	1981-82
Godfrey, Warren	Bos., Det.	16	786	32	125	157	752	52	1	4	5	42		1952-53	1967-68
Godin, Eddy	Wsh.	2	27	3	6	9	12	....	....	....	....	....		1977-78	1978-79
Godin, Sammy	Ott., Mtl.	3	83	4	3	7	36	....	....	....	....	....		1927-28	1933-34
Goegan, Peter	Det., NYR, Min.	11	383	19	67	86	365	33	1	3	4	61		1957-58	1967-68
Goertz, Dave	Pit.	1	2	0	0	0	2	....	....	....	....	....		1987-88	1987-88
• Goldham, Bob	Tor., Chi., Det.	12	650	28	143	171	400	66	3	14	17	53	4	1941-42	1955-56
Goldsworthy, Bill	Bos., Min., NYR	14	771	283	258	541	793	40	18	19	37	30		1964-65	1977-78
• Goldsworthy, Leroy	NYR, Det., Chi., Mtl., Bos., NYA	9	337	66	57	123	79	22	1	0	1	4	1	1929-30	1938-39
Goldup, Glenn	Mtl., L.A.	9	291	52	67	119	303	16	4	3	7	22		1973-74	1981-82
Goldup, Hank	Tor., NYR	6	181	63	80	143	97	26	5	1	6	6	1	1939-40	1945-46
Gooden, Bill	NYR	2	53	9	11	20	15	....	....	....	....	....		1942-43	1943-44
Goodenough, Larry	Phi., Van.	6	242	22	77	99	179	22	3	15	18	10	1	1974-75	1979-80
• Goodfellow, Ebbie	Det.	14	554	134	190	324	511	45	8	8	16	65	3	1929-30	1942-43
Gordon, Fred	Det., Bos.	2	77	8	7	15	68	1	0	0	0	0		1926-27	1927-28
Gordon, Jackie	NYR	3	36	3	10	13	0	9	1	1	2	7		1948-49	1950-51
Gorence, Tom	Phi., Edm.	6	303	58	53	111	89	37	9	6	15	47		1978-79	1983-84
Goring, Butch	L.A., NYI, Bos.	16	1107	375	513	888	102	134	38	50	88	32	4	1969-70	1984-85
Gorman, Dave	Atl.	1	3	0	0	0	0	....	....	....	....	....		1979-80	1979-80
• Gorman, Ed	Ott., Tor.	4	111	14	5	19	108	8	0	0	0	2	1	1924-25	1927-28
Gosselin, Benoit	NYR	1	7	0	0	0	33	....	....	....	....	....		1977-78	1977-78
Gosselin, Guy	Wpg.	1	5	0	0	0	6	....	....	....	....	....		1987-88	1987-88
Gotaas, Steve	Pit., Min.	3	49	6	9	15	53	3	0	1	1	5		1987-88	1990-91
• Gottselig, Johnny	Chi.	16	589	176	195	371	203	43	13	13	26	20	2	1928-29	1944-45
Gould, Bobby	Atl., Cgy., Wsh., Bos.	11	697	145	159	304	572	78	15	13	28	58		1979-80	1989-90
Gould, John	Buf., Van., Atl.	9	504	131	138	269	113	14	3	2	5	4		1971-72	1979-80
Gould, Larry	Van.	1	2	0	0	0	0	....	....	....	....	....		1973-74	1973-74
Goupille, Red	Mtl.	8	222	12	28	40	256	8	2	0	2	6		1935-36	1942-43
Goyer, Gerry	Chi.	1	40	1	2	3	4	3	0	0	0	2		1967-68	1967-68
Goyette, Phil	Mtl., NYR, St.L., Buf.	16	941	207	467	674	131	94	17	29	46	26	4	1956-57	1971-72
Graboski, Tony	Mtl.	3	66	6	10	16	18	2	0	0	0	0		1940-41	1942-43
• Gracie, Bob	Tor., Bos., NYA, Mtl.M., Mtl., Chi.	9	378	82	109	191	204	33	4	7	11	4	2	1930-31	1938-39
Gradin, Thomas	Van., Bos.	9	677	209	384	593	298	42	17	25	42	20		1978-79	1986-87
• Graham, Leth	Ott., Ham.	6	26	3	0	3	0	1	0	0	0	0	1	1920-21	1925-26
Graham, Pat	Pit., Tor.	3	103	11	17	28	136	4	0	0	0	2		1981-82	1983-84
Graham, Rod	Bos.	1	14	2	1	3	7	....	....	....	....	....		1974-75	1974-75
Graham, Ted	Chi., Mtl.M., Det., St.L., Bos., NYA	9	343	14	25	39	300	23	3	1	4	34		1927-28	1936-37
Grant, Danny	Mtl., Min., Det., L.A.	13	736	263	273	536	239	43	10	14	24	19	1	1965-66	1978-79
Gratton, Dan	L.A.	1	7	1	0	1	5	....	....	....	....	....		1987-88	1987-88
Gratton, Norm	NYR, Atl., Buf., Min.	5	201	39	44	83	64	6	0	1	1	2		1971-72	1975-76
Gravelle, Leo	Mtl., Det.	5	223	44	34	78	42	17	4	1	5	2		1946-47	1950-51
Graves, Hilliard	Cal., Atl., Van., Wpg.	9	556	118	163	281	209	2	0	0	0	0		1970-71	1979-80
Graves, Steve	Edm.	3	35	5	4	9	10	....	....	....	....	....		1983-84	1987-88
Gray, Alex	NYR, Tor.	2	50	7	0	7	30	13	1	0	1	0	1	1927-28	1928-29
Gray, Terry	Bos., Mtl., L.A., St.L.	6	147	26	28	54	64	35	5	5	10	22		1961-62	1970-71
Green, Red	Ham., NYA, Bos. Det.	6	195	59	13	72	261	....	....	....	....	....	1	1923-24	1928-29
Green, Rick	Wsh., Mtl., Det., NYI	15	845	43	220	263	588	100	3	16	19	73	1	1976-77	1991-92
Green, Ted	Bos.	11	620	48	206	254	1029	31	4	8	12	54	1	1960-61	1971-72
• Green, Wilf	Ham., NYA	4	103	33	8	41	151	....	....	....	....	....		1923-24	1926-27
• Gregg, Randy	Edm., Van.	10	474	41	152	193	333	137	13	38	51	127	6	1981-82	1991-92
Greig, Bruce	Cal.	2	9	0	1	1	46	....	....	....	....	....		1973-74	1974-75
Grenier, Lucien	Mtl., L.A.	4	151	14	14	28	18	2	0	0	0	0	1	1968-69	1971-72
Grenier, Richard	NYI	1	10	1	1	2	2	....	....	....	....	....		1972-73	1972-73
Greschner, Ron	NYR	16	982	179	431	610	1226	84	17	32	49	106		1974-75	1989-90
Grigor, George	Chi.	1	2	1	0	1	0	1	0	0	0	0		1943-44	1943-44
Grisdale, John	Tor., Van.	6	250	4	39	43	346	10	0	1	1	15		1972-73	1978-79
Gronsdahl, Lloyd	Bos.	1	10	1	2	3	0	....	....	....	....	....		1941-42	1941-42
Gronstrand, Jari	Min., NYR, Que., NYI	5	185	8	26	34	135	3	0	0	0	4		1986-87	1990-91
Gross, Llyod	Tor., NYA, Bos., Det.	3	62	11	5	16	20	1	0	0	0	0		1926-27	1934-35
• Grosso, Don	Det., Chi., Bos.	9	334	87	117	204	90	50	14	12	26	46	1	1938-39	1946-47
• Grosvenar, Len	Ott., NYA, Mtl.	6	147	9	11	20	78	4	0	0	0	2		1927-28	1932-33
Groulx, Wayne	Que.	1	1	0	0	0	0	....	....	....	....	....		1984-85	1984-85
Gruen, Danny	Det., Col.	3	49	9	13	22	19	....	....	....	....	....		1972-73	1976-77
Gryp, Bob	Bos., Wsh.	3	74	11	13	24	33	....	....	....	....	....		1973-74	1975-76
Guay, Francois	Buf.	1	117	11	23	34	92	9	0	1	1	12		1989-90	1989-90
Guerard, Stephane	Que.	2	34	0	0	0	40	....	....	....	....	....		1987-88	1989-90
Guevremont, Jocelyn	Van., Buf., NYR	9	571	84	223	307	319	40	4	17	21	18		1971-72	1979-80
Guidolin, Aldo	NYR	4	182	9	15	24	117	....	....	....	....	....		1952-53	1955-56
Guidolin, Bep	Bos., Det., Chi.	9	519	107	171	278	606	24	5	7	12	35		1942-43	1951-52
Guindon, Bobby	Wpg.	1	6	0	1	1	0	....	....	....	....	....		1979-80	1979-80
Gustafsson, Bengt	Wsh.	9	629	196	359	555	196	32	9	19	28	16		1979-80	1988-89
Gustavsson, Peter	Col.	1	2	0	0	0	0	....	....	....	....	....		1981-82	1981-82

H

Haanpaa, Ari	NYI	3	60	6	11	17	37	6	0	0	0	10		1985-86	1987-88
Habscheid, Marc Joseph	Edm., Min., Det., Cgy.	11	345	72	91	163	171	12	1	3	4	13		1981-82	1991-92
Hachborn, Len	Phi., L.A.	3	102	20	39	59	29	7	0	3	3	7		1983-84	1985-86
Haddon, Lloyd	Det.	1	8	0	0	0	2	1	0	0	0	0		1959-60	1959-60
Hadfield, Vic	NYR, Pit.	16	1002	323	389	712	1154	73	27	21	48	117		1961-62	1976-77
Haggarty, Jim	Mtl.	1	5	1	1	2	0	3	2	1	3	0		1941-42	1941-42
• Hagglund, Roger	Que.	1	3	0	0	0	0	....	....	....	....	....		1984-85	1984-85
Hagman, Matti	Bos., Edm.	4	237	56	89	145	36	20	5	2	7	6		1976-77	1981-82
Haidy, Gord	Det.	1	....	....	....	....	....	1	0	0	0	0	1	1949-50	1949-50
Hajdu, Richard	Buf.	2	5	0	0	0	4	....	....	....	....	....		1985-86	1986-87
Hajt, Bill	Buf.	14	854	42	202	244	43	80	2	16	18	70		1973-74	1986-87
Hakansson, Anders	Min., Pit., L.A.	5	330	52	46	98	141	6	0	0	0	2		1981-82	1985-86
• Halderson, Slim	Det., Tor.	1	44	3	2	5	65	....	....	....	....	....	1	1926-27	1926-27
Hale, Larry	Phi.	4	196	5	37	42	90	8	0	0	0	12		1968-69	1971-72
Haley, Len	Det.	2	30	2	2	4	14	6	1	3	4	6		1959-60	1960-61
Hall, Bob	NYA	1	8	0	0	0	0	....	....	....	....	....		1925-26	1925-26
Hall, Del	Cal.	3	9	2	0	2	2	....	....	....	....	....		1971-72	1973-74
• Hall, Joe	Mtl.	2	37	15	1	16	85	12	0	2	2	0		1917-18	1918-19
Hall, Murray	Chi., Det., Min., Van.	9	164	35	48	83	46	6	0	0	0	0		1961-62	1971-72
Hall, Taylor	Van., Bos.	5	41	7	9	16	29	....	....	....	....	....		1983-84	1987-88
Hall, Wayne	NYR	1	4	0	0	0	0	....	....	....	....	....		1960-61	1960-61
Halliday, Milt	Ott.	3	67	1	0	1	6	6	0	0	0	0	1	1926-27	1928-29
Hallin, Mats	NYI, Min.	5	152	17	14	31	193	15	1	0	1	13	1	1982-83	1986-87
Halward, Doug	Bos., L.A., Van., Det., Edm.	14	653	69	224	293	774	47	7	10	17	113		1975-76	1988-89
Hamel, Gilles	Buf., Wpg., L.A.	9	519	127	147	274	276	27	4	5	9	10		1980-81	1988-89
Hamel, Herb	Tor.	1	2	0	0	0	14	....	....	....	....	....		1930-31	1930-31
Hamel, Jean	St.L., Det., Que., Mtl.	12	699	26	95	121	766	33	0	2	2	44		1972-73	1983-84
• Hamill, Red	Bos., Chi.	12	418	128	94	222	160	13	1	2	3	12	2	1937-38	1950-51
Hamilton, Al	NYR, Buf., Edm.	7	257	10	78	88	258	7	0	0	0	2		1965-66	1979-80
Hamilton, Chuck	Mtl., St.L.	2	4	0	2	2	2	....	....	....	....	....		1961-62	1972-73

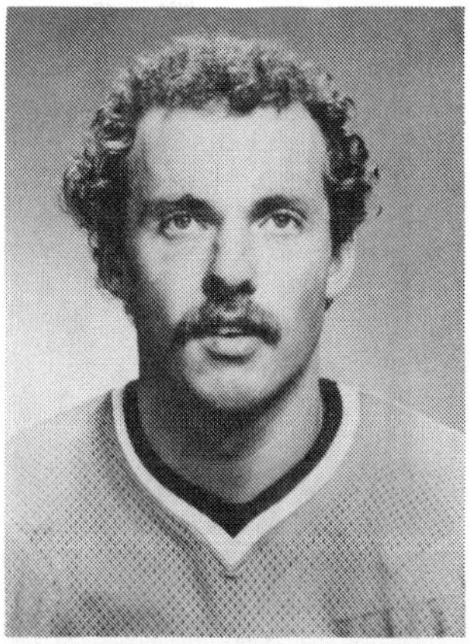
Al Hill

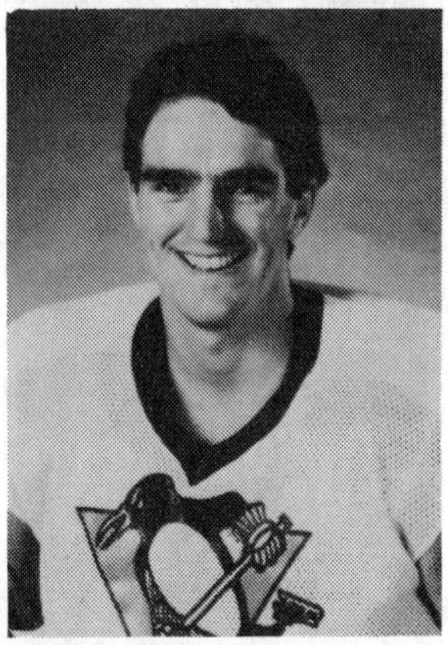
Randy Hillier

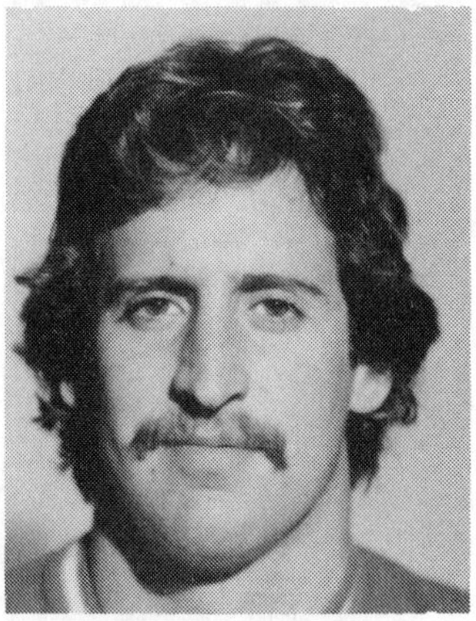
Dave Hindmarch

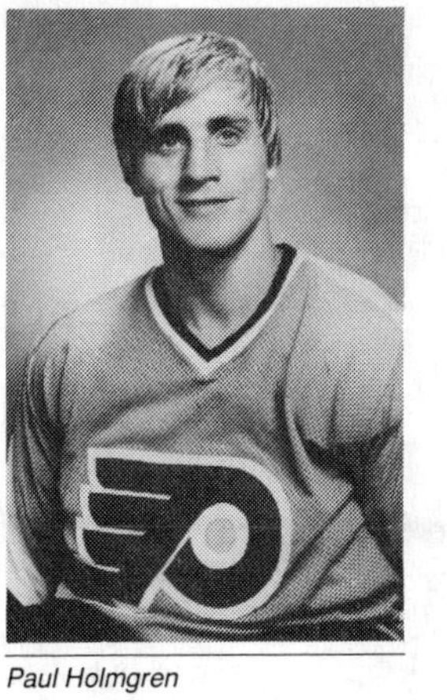
Paul Holmgren

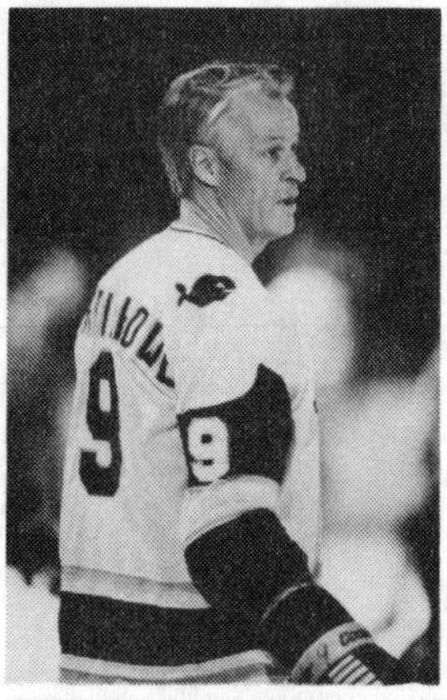

Gordie Howe

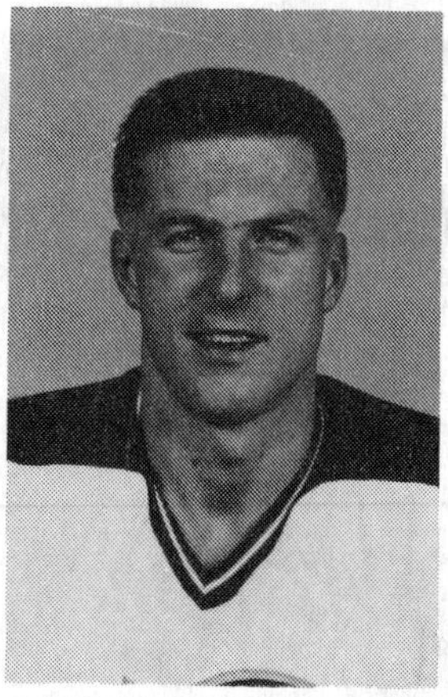

Jiri Hrdina

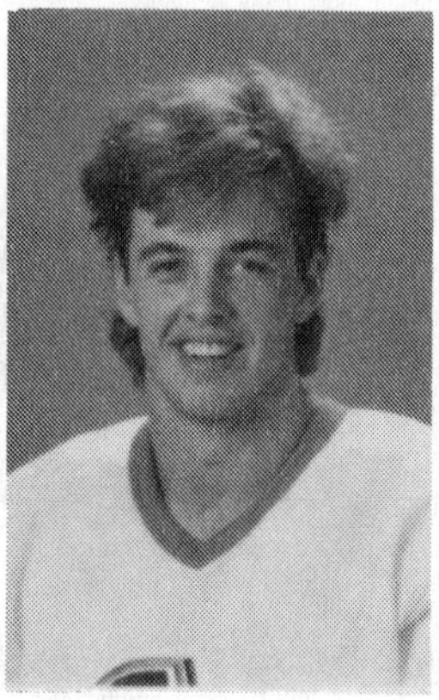

Jeff Jackson

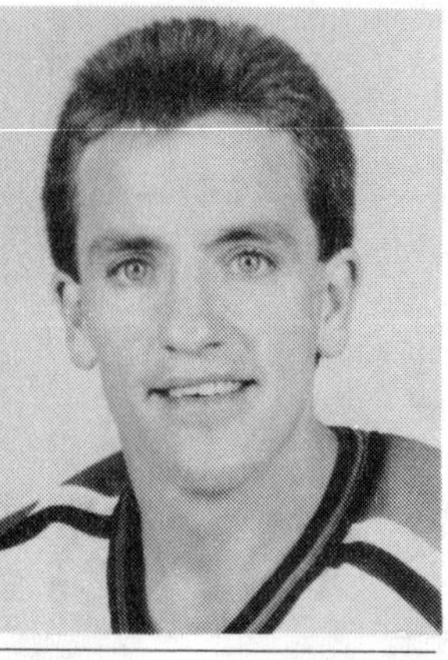

Mark Johnson

Name	NHL Teams	NHL Seasons	Regular Schedule					Playoffs					NHL Cup Wins	First NHL Season	Last NHL Season
			GP	G	A	TP	PIM	GP	G	A	TP	PIM			
Hamilton, Jack	Tor.	3	138	31	48	79	76	11	2	1	3	0		1942-43	1945-46
Hamilton, Jim	Pit.	8	95	14	18	32	28	6	3	0	3	0		1977-78	1984-85
• Hamilton, Reg	Tor., Chi.	12	387	21	87	108	412	64	6	6	12	54	2	1935-36	1946-47
Hammarstrom, Inge	Tor., St.L.	6	427	116	123	239	86	13	2	3	5	4		1973-74	1978-79
Hampson, Gord	Cgy.	1	4	0	0	0	5	....	....	....	....	....		1982-83	1982-83
Hampson, Ted	Tor., NYR, Det., Oak., Cal., Min.	12	676	108	245	353	94	35	7	10	17	2		1959-60	1971-72
Hampton, Rick	Cal., Cle., L.A.	6	337	59	113	172	147	2	0	0	0	0		1974-75	1979-80
Hamway, Mark	NYI	3	53	5	13	18	9	1	0	0	0	0		1984-85	1986-87
Handy, Ron	NYI, St.L.	2	14	0	3	3	0	....	....	....	....	....		1984-85	1987-88
Hangsleben, Al	Hfd., Wsh., L.A.	3	185	21	48	69	396	....	....	....	....	....		1979-80	1981-82
Hanna, John	NYR, Mtl., Phi.	5	198	6	26	32	206	....	....	....	....	....		1958-59	1967-68
• Hannigan, Gord	Tor.	4	161	29	31	60	117	9	2	0	2	8		1952-53	1955-56
Hannigan, Pat	Tor., NYR, Phi.	5	182	30	39	69	116	11	1	2	3	11		1959-60	1968-69
Hannigan, Ray	Tor.	1	3	0	0	0	2	....	....	....	....	....		1948-49	1948-49
Hansen, Ritchie	NYI, St.L.	4	20	2	8	10	6	....	....	....	....	....		1976-77	1981-82
Hanson, Dave	Det., Min.	2	33	1	1	2	65	....	....	....	....	....		1978-79	1979-80
Hanson, Emil	Det.	1	7	0	0	0	6	....	....	....	....	....		1932-33	1932-33
Hanson, Keith	Cgy.	1	25	0	2	2	77	....	....	....	....	....		1983-84	1983-84
Hanson, Ossie	Chi.	1	7	0	0	0	0	....	....	....	....	....		1937-38	1937-38
Harbaruk, Nick	Pit., St.L.	5	364	45	75	120	273	14	3	1	4	20		1969-70	1973-74
Harding, Jeff	Phi.	2	15	0	0	0	47	....	....	....	....	....		1988-89	1989-90
Hardy, Joe	Oak., Cal.	2	63	9	14	23	51	4	0	0	0	0		1969-70	1970-71
Hargreaves, Jim	Van.	2	66	1	7	8	105	....	....	....	....	....		1970-71	1972-73
Harlow, Scott	St.L.	1	1	0	1	1	0	....	....	....	....	....		1987-88	1987-88
Harmon, Glen	Mtl.	9	452	50	96	146	334	53	5	10	15	37	2	1942-43	1950-51
Harms, John	Chi.	2	44	5	5	10	21	3	3	0	3	2		1943-44	1944-45
Harnott, Happy	Bos.	1	6	0	0	0	6	....	....	....	....	....		1933-34	1933-34
Harper, Terry	Mtl., L.A., Det., St.L., Col.	19	1066	35	221	256	1362	112	4	13	17	140	5	1962-63	1980-81
Harrer, Tim	Cgy.	1	3	0	0	0	2	....	....	....	....	....		1982-83	1982-83
• Harrington, Hago	Bos., Mtl.	3	72	9	3	12	15	4	1	0	1	2		1925-26	1932-33
Harris, Billy	Tor., Det., Oak., Cal., Pit.	12	769	126	219	345	205	62	8	10	18	30	3	1955-56	1968-69
Harris, Billy	NYI, L.A., Tor.	12	897	231	327	558	394	71	19	19	38	48		1972-73	1983-84
Harris, Duke	Min., Tor.	1	26	1	4	5	4	....	....	....	....	....		1967-68	1967-68
Harris, Hugh	Buf.	1	60	12	26	38	17	3	0	0	0	0		1972-73	1972-73
Harris, Ron	Det., Oak., Atl., NYR	12	476	20	91	111	484	28	4	3	7	33		1962-63	1975-76
Harris, Smokey	Bos.	2	40	5	5	10	28	2	0	0	0	0		1924-25	1930-31
Harris, Ted	Mtl., Min., Det., St.L., Phi.	12	788	30	168	198	1000	100	1	22	23	230	5	1963-64	1974-75
Harrison, Ed	Bos., NYR	4	194	27	24	51	53	9	1	0	1	2		1947-48	1950-51
Harrison, Jim	Bos., Tor., Chi., Edm.	8	324	67	86	153	435	13	1	1	2	43		1968-69	1979-80
Hart, Gerry	Det., NYI, Que., St.L.	15	730	29	150	179	1240	78	3	12	15	175		1968-69	1982-83
• Hart, Gizzy	Det., Mtl.	3	100	6	8	14	12	8	0	1	1	0	1	1926-27	1932-33
Hartsburg, Craig	Min.	10	570	98	315	413	818	61	15	27	42	70		1979-80	1988-89
• Harvey, Doug	Mtl., NYR, Det., St.L.	20	1113	88	452	540	1216	137	8	64	72	152	6	1947-48	1968-69
Harvey, Fred	Min., Atl., K.C., Det.	7	407	90	118	208	131	14	0	2	2	8		1970-71	1976-77
Harvey, Hugh	K.C.	2	18	1	1	2	4	....	....	....	....	....		1974-75	1975-76
Hassard, Bob	Tor., Chi.	5	126	9	28	37	22	....	....	....	....	....		1949-50	1954-55
Hatoum, Ed	Det., Van.	3	47	3	6	9	25	....	....	....	....	....		1968-69	1970-71
Haworth, Alan	Buf., Wsh., Que.	8	524	189	211	400	425	42	12	16	28	28		1980-81	1987-88
Haworth, Alan	Buf., Wsh., Que.	8	524	189	211	400	425	42	12	16	28	28		1980-81	1987-88
Haworth, Gord	NYR	1	2	0	1	1	0	....	....	....	....	....		1952-53	1952-53
Hawryliw, Neil	NYI	1	1	0	0	0	0	....	....	....	....	....		1981-82	1981-82
Hay, Billy	Chi.	8	506	113	273	386	244	67	15	21	36	62		1959-60	1966-67
• Hay, George	Chi., Det.	7	242	74	60	134	84	8	2	3	5	14		1926-27	1933-34
Hay, Jim	Det.	3	75	1	5	6	22	9	1	0	1	2	1	1952-53	1954-55
Hayek, Peter	Min.	1	1	0	0	0	0	....	....	....	....	....		1981-82	1981-82
Hayes, Chris	Bos.	1	....	....	....	....	....	1	0	0	0	0	1	1971-72	1971-72
Haynes, Paul	Mtl.M., Bos., Mtl.	11	390	61	134	195	164	25	2	8	10	13		1930-31	1940-41
Hayward, Rick	L.A.	1	4	0	0	0	5	....	....	....	....	....		1990-91	1990-91
Hazlett, Steve	Van.	1	1	0	0	0	0	....	....	....	....	....		1979-80	1979-80
Head, Galen	Det.	1	1	0	0	0	0	....	....	....	....	....		1967-68	1967-68
Headley, Fern	Bos., Mtl.	1	27	1	1	2	6	5	0	0	0	0		1924-25	1924-25
Healey, Dick	Det.	1	1	0	0	0	2	....	....	....	....	....		1960-61	1960-61
Heaslip, Mark	NYR, L.A.	3	117	10	19	29	110	5	0	0	0	2		1976-77	1978-79
Heath, Randy	NYR	2	13	2	4	6	15	....	....	....	....	....		1984-85	1985-86
Hebenton, Andy	NYR, Bos.	9	630	189	202	391	83	22	6	5	11	8		1955-56	1963-64
Hedberg, Anders	NYR	7	465	172	225	397	144	58	22	24	46	31		1978-79	1984-85
• Heffernan, Frank	Tor.	1	17	0	0	0	4	....	....	....	....	....		1919-20	1919-20
Heffernan, Gerry	Mtl.	3	83	33	35	68	27	11	3	3	6	8	1	1941-42	1943-44
Heidt, Mike	L.A.	1	6	0	1	1	7	....	....	....	....	....		1983-84	1983-84
Heindl, Bill	Min., NYR	3	18	2	1	3	0	....	....	....	....	....		1970-71	1972-73
Heinrich, Lionel	Bos.	1	35	1	1	2	33	....	....	....	....	....		1955-56	1955-56
Heiskala, Earl	Phi.	3	127	13	11	24	294	....	....	....	....	....		1968-69	1970-71
Helander, Peter	L.A.	1	7	0	1	1	0	....	....	....	....	....		1982-83	1982-83
• Heller, Ott	NYR	15	647	55	176	231	465	61	6	8	14	61	2	1931-32	1945-46
Helman, Harry	Ott.	3	42	1	0	1	7	5	0	0	0	0	1	1922-23	1924-25
Helminen, Raimo	NYR, Min., NYI	3	117	13	46	59	16	2	0	0	0	0		1985-86	1988-89
Hemmerling, Tony	NYA	2	24	3	3	6	4	....	....	....	....	....		1935-36	1936-37
Henderson, Archie	Wsh., Min., Hfd.	3	23	3	1	4	92	....	....	....	....	....		1980-81	1982-83
Henderson, Murray	Bos.	8	405	24	62	86	305	41	2	3	5	23		1944-45	1951-52
Henderson, Paul	Det., Tor., Atl.	13	707	236	241	477	304	56	11	14	25	28		1962-63	1979-80
Hendrickson, John	Det.	3	5	0	0	0	4	....	....	....	....	....		1957-58	1961-62
Henning, Lorne	NYI	9	544	73	111	184	102	81	7	7	14	8	2	1972-73	1980-81
Henry, Camille	NYR, Chi., St.L.	14	727	279	249	528	88	47	6	12	18	7		1953-54	1969-70
Henry, Dale	NYI	6	132	13	26	39	263	....	....	....	....	....		1984-85	1989-90
Hepple, Alan	N.J.	3	3	0	0	0	7	....	....	....	....	....		1983-84	1985-86
Hepple, Alan	N.J.	3	3	0	0	0	7	....	....	....	....	....		1983-84	1985-86
• Herberts, Jimmy	Bos., Tor., Det.	6	206	83	29	112	250	9	3	0	3	35		1924-25	1929-30
Herchenratter, Art	Det.	1	10	1	2	3	2	....	....	....	....	....		1940-41	1940-41
Hergerts, Fred	NYA	2	19	2	4	6	2	....	....	....	....	....		1934-35	1935-36
Hergesheimer, Philip	Chi., Bos.	4	125	21	41	62	19	7	0	0	0	2		1939-40	1942-43
Hergesheimer, Wally	NYR, Chi.	7	351	114	85	199	106	5	1	0	1	0		1951-52	1958-59
Heron, Red	Tor., Bro., Mtl.	4	106	21	19	40	38	16	2	2	4	55		1938-39	1941-42
Hess, Bob	St.L., Buf., Hfd.	8	329	27	95	122	178	4	1	1	2	2		1974-75	1983-84
Heximer, Orville	NYR, Bos., NYA	3	85	13	7	20	28	5	0	0	0	2		1929-30	1934-35
Hextall, Bryan Jr.	NYR, Pit., Atl., Det., Min.	8	549	99	161	260	738	18	0	4	4	59		1962-63	1975-76
• Hextall, Bryan Sr.	NYR	11	447	187	175	362	227	37	8	9	17	19	1	1936-37	1947-48
Hextall, Dennis	NYR, L.A., Cal., Min., Det., Wsh.	13	681	153	350	503	1398	22	3	3	6	45		1968-69	1979-80
Heyliger, Vic	Chi.	2	34	2	3	5	2	....	....	....	....	....		1937-38	1943-44
Hicke, Bill	Mtl., NYR, Oak.	14	729	168	234	402	395	42	3	10	13	41	2	1958-59	1971-72
Hicke, Ernie	Cal., Atl., NYI, Min., L.A.	8	520	132	140	272	407	2	1	0	1	0		1970-71	1977-78
Hickey, Greg	NYR	1	1	0	0	0	0	....	....	....	....	....		1977-78	1977-78
Hickey, Pat	NYR, Col., Tor., Que., St.L.	10	646	192	212	404	351	55	5	11	16	37		1975-76	1984-85
Hicks, Doug	Min., Chi., Edm., Wsh.	9	561	37	131	168	442	....	....	....	....	....		1974-75	1982-83
Hicks, Glenn	Det.	2	108	6	12	18	127	....	....	....	....	....		1979-80	1980-81
• Hicks, Hal	Mtl.M., Det.	3	110	7	2	9	72	....	....	....	....	....		1928-29	1930-31
Hicks, Wayne	Chi., Bos., Mtl., Phi., Pit.	5	115	13	23	36	22	2	0	1	1	2	1	1959-60	1967-68
Hidi, Andre	Wsh.	2	7	2	1	3	9	2	0	0	0	0		1983-84	1984-85
Hiemer, Uli	N.J.	3	143	19	54	73	176	....	....	....	....	....		1984-85	1986-87
Higgins, Paul	Tor.	2	25	0	0	0	152	1	0	0	0	0		1981-82	1982-83
Higgins, Tim	Chi., N.J., Det.	11	706	154	198	352	719	65	5	8	13	77		1978-79	1988-89
Hildebrand, Ike	NYR, Chi.	2	41	7	11	18	16	....	....	....	....	....		1953-54	1954-55
Hill, Al	Phi.	8	221	40	55	95	227	51	8	11	19	43		1976-77	1987-88
Hill, Brian	Hfd.	1	19	1	1	2	4	....	....	....	....	....		1979-80	1979-80
Hill, Mel	Bos., Bro., Tor.	9	323	89	109	198	138	43	12	7	19	18	3	1937-38	1945-46
Hiller, Dutch	NYR, Det., Bos., Mtl.	9	385	91	113	204	163	48	9	8	17	21	2	1937-38	1945-46
Hillier, Randy	Bos., Pit., NYI, Buf.	11	543	16	110	126	906	28	0	2	2	93	1	1981-82	1991-92
Hillman, Floyd	Bos.	1	6	0	0	0	10	....	....	....	....	....		1956-57	1956-57
Hillman, Larry	Det., Bos., Tor., Min., Mtl., Phi., L.A., Buf.	19	790	36	196	232	579	74	2	9	11	30	4	1954-55	1972-73
• Hillman, Wayne	Chi., NYR, Min., Phi.	13	691	18	86	104	534	28	0	3	3	19	1	1960-61	1972-73
Hilworth, John	Det.	3	57	1	1	2	89	....	....	....	....	....		1977-78	1979-80
Himes, Normie	NYA	9	402	106	113	219	127	2	0	0	0	0		1926-27	1934-35
Hindmarch, Dave	Cgy.	4	99	21	17	38	25	10	0	0	0	6		1980-81	1983-84
Hinse, Andre	Tor.	1	4	0	0	0	0	....	....	....	....	....		1967-68	1967-68
Hinton, Dan	Chi.	1	14	0	0	0	16	....	....	....	....	....		1976-77	1976-77

Name	NHL Teams	NHL Seasons	Regular Schedule					Playoffs					NHL Cup Wins	First NHL Season	Last NHL Season
			GP	G	A	TP	PIM	GP	G	A	TP	PIM			
Hirsch, Tom	Min.	3	31	1	7	8	30	12	0	0	0	6		1983-84	1987-88
Hirschfeld, Bert	Mtl.	2	33	1	4	5	2	5	1	0	1	0		1949-50	1950-51
Hislop, Jamie	Que., Cgy.	5	345	75	103	178	86	28	3	2	5	11		1979-80	1983-84
• Hitchman, Lionel	Ott., Bos.	12	413	28	33	61	523	40	4	1	5	77	2	1922-23	1933-34
Hlinka, Ivan	Van.	2	137	42	81	123	28	16	3	10	13	8		1981-82	1982-83
Hodge, Ken	Chi., Bos., NYR	13	881	328	472	800	779	97	34	47	81	120	2	1965-66	1977-78
Hodgson, Dan	Tor., Van.	4	114	29	45	74	64	....	....	....	....	....		1985-86	1988-89
Hodgson, Rick	Hfd.	1	6	0	0	0	6	1	0	0	0	0		1979-80	1979-80
Hodgson, Ted	Bos.	1	4	0	0	0	0	....	....	....	....	....		1966-67	1966-67
Hoekstra, Cecil	Mtl.	1	4	0	0	0	0	....	....	....	....	....		1959-60	1959-60
Hoekstra, Ed	Phi.	1	70	15	21	36	6	7	0	1	1	0		1967-68	1967-68
Hoene, Phil	L.A.	3	37	2	4	6	22	....	....	....	....	....		1972-73	1974-75
Hoffinger, Vic	Chi.	2	28	0	1	1	30	....	....	....	....	....		1927-28	1928-29
Hoffman, Mike	Hfd.	3	9	1	3	4	2	....	....	....	....	....		1982-83	1985-86
Hoffmeyer, Bob	Chi., Phi., N.J.	6	198	14	52	66	325	3	0	1	1	25		1977-78	1984-85
Hofford, Jim	Buf., L.A.	3	18	0	0	0	47	....	....	....	....	....		1985-86	1988-89
Hogaboam, Bill	Atl., Det., Min.	8	332	80	109	189	100	2	0	0	0	0		1972-73	1979-80
Hoganson, Dale	L.A., Mtl., Que.	7	343	13	77	90	186	11	0	3	3	12		1969-70	1981-82
Holbrook, Terry	Min.	2	43	3	6	9	4	6	0	0	0	0		1972-73	1973-74
Holland, Jerry	NYR	2	37	8	4	12	6	....	....	....	....	....		1974-75	1975-76
Hollett, Frank	Tor., Ott., Bos., Det.	13	565	132	181	313	358	79	8	26	34	38	2	1933-34	1945-46
• Hollingworth, Gord	Chi., Det.	4	163	4	14	18	201	3	0	0	0	2		1954-55	1957-58
Holloway, Bruce	Van.	1	2	0	0	0	0	....	....	....	....	....		1984-85	1984-85
• Holmes, Bill	Mtl., NYA.	2	51	6	4	10	35	....	....	....	....	....		1925-26	1929-30
Holmes, Chuck	Det.	2	23	1	3	4	10	....	....	....	....	....		1958-59	1961-62
Holmes, Lou	Chi.	2	59	1	4	5	6	2	0	0	0	2		1931-32	1932-33
Holmes, Warren	L.A.	3	45	8	18	26	7	....	....	....	....	....		1981-82	1983-84
Holmgren, Paul	Phi., Min.	10	527	144	179	323	1684	82	19	32	51	195		1975-76	1984-85
• Holota, John	Det.	2	15	2	0	2	0	....	....	....	....	....		1942-43	1945-46
Holst, Greg	NYR	3	11	0	0	0	0	....	....	....	....	....		1975-76	1977-78
Holt, Gary	Cal., Clev., St.L.	5	101	13	11	24	183	....	....	....	....	....		1973-74	1977-78
Holt, Randy	Chi., Clev., Van., L.A., Cgy., Wsh., Phi.	10	395	4	37	41	1438	21	2	3	5	83		1974-75	1983-84
• Holway, Albert	Tor., Mtl.M., Pit.	5	117	7	2	9	48	8	0	0	0	2	1	1923-24	1928-29
Homenuke, Ron	Van.	1	1	0	0	0	0	....	....	....	....	....		1972-73	1972-73
Hopkins, Dean	L.A., Edm.	5	218	23	49	72	302	18	1	5	6	29		1979-80	1985-86
Hopkins, Dean	L.A., Edm., Que.	6	223	23	51	74	306	18	1	5	6	29		1979-80	1988-89
Hopkins, Larry	Tor., Wpg.	4	60	13	16	29	26	6	0	0	0	2		1977-78	1982-83
Horava, Miloslav	NYR	3	80	5	17	22	38	2	0	1	1	0		1988-89	1990-91
Horbul, Doug	K.C.	1	4	1	0	1	2	....	....	....	....	....		1974-75	1974-75
Hordy, Mike	NYI	2	11	0	0	0	7	....	....	....	....	....		1978-79	1979-80
Horeck, Pete	Chi., Det., Bos.	8	426	106	118	224	340	34	6	8	14	43		1944-45	1951-52
• Horne, George	Mtl.M, Tor.	3	54	9	3	12	34	4	0	0	0	4	1	1925-26	1928-29
Horner, Red	Tor.	12	490	42	110	152	1264	71	7	10	17	166	1	1928-29	1939-40
Hornung, Larry	St.L.	2	48	2	9	11	10	11	0	2	2	2		1970-71	1971-72
• Horton, Tim	Tor., NYR, Buf., Pit.	24	1446	115	403	518	1611	126	11	39	50	183	4	1949-50	1973-74
Horvath, Bronco	NYR, Mtl., Bos., Chi., Tor., Min.	9	434	141	185	326	319	36	12	9	21	18		1955-56	1967-68
Hospodar, Ed	NYR, Hfd., Phi., Min., Buf.	9	450	17	51	68	1314	44	4	1	5	206		1979-80	1987-88
Hotham, Greg	Tor., Pit.	6	230	15	74	89	139	5	0	3	3	6		1979-80	1984-85
Houck, Paul	Min.	3	16	1	2	3	2	....	....	....	....	....		1985-86	1987-88
Houde, Claude	K.C.	2	59	3	6	9	40	....	....	....	....	....		1974-75	1975-76
Houle, Rejean	Mtl.	11	635	161	247	408	395	90	14	34	48	66	5	1969-70	1982-83
Houston, Ken	Atl., Cgy., Wsh., L.A.	9	570	161	167	328	624	35	10	9	19	66		1975-76	1983-84
Howard, Frank	Tor.	1	2	0	0	0	0	....	....	....	....	....		1936-37	1936-37
Howatt, Garry	NYI, Hfd., N.J.	12	720	112	156	268	1836	87	12	14	26	289	2	1972-73	1983-84
Howe, Gordie	Det., Hfd.	26	1767	801	1049	1850	1685	157	68	92	160	220	4	1946-47	1979-80
Howe, Marty	Hfd., Bos.	6	197	2	29	31	99	15	1	2	3	9		1979-80	1984-85
• Howe, Syd	Ott., Phi., Tor., St.L., Det.	17	691	237	291	528	212	70	17	27	44	10	3	1929-30	1945-46
Howe, Vic	NYR	3	33	3	4	7	10	....	....	....	....	....		1950-51	1954-55
Howell, Harry	NYR, Oak., L.A.	21	1411	94	324	418	1298	38	3	3	6	32		1952-53	1972-73
Howell, Ron	NYR	2	4	0	0	0	4	....	....	....	....	....		1954-55	1955-56
Howse, Don	L.A.	1	33	2	5	7	6	2	0	0	0	0		1979-80	1979-80
Howson, Scott	NYI	2	18	5	3	8	4	....	....	....	....	....		1984-85	1985-86
Hoyda, Dave	Phi., Wpg.	4	132	6	17	23	299	12	0	0	0	17		1977-78	1980-81
Hrdina, Jiri	Cgy., Pit.	5	250	45	85	130	92	46	2	5	7	24		1987-88	1991-92
Hrechkosy, Dave	Cal., St.L.	4	140	42	24	66	41	3	1	0	1	2		1973-74	1976-77
Hrycuik, Jim	Wsh.	1	21	5	5	10	12	....	....	....	....	....		1974-75	1974-75
Hrymnak, Steve	Chi., Det.	2	18	2	1	3	4	2	0	0	0	0		1951-52	1952-53
Hrynewich, Tim	Pit.	2	55	6	8	14	82	....	....	....	....	....		1982-83	1983-84
Huard, Rolly	Tor.	1	1	1	0	1	0	....	....	....	....	....		1930-31	1930-31
Huber, Willie	Det., NYR, Van., Phi.	10	655	104	217	321	950	33	5	5	10	35		1978-79	1987-88
Hubick, Greg	Tor., Van.	2	77	6	9	15	10	....	....	....	....	....		1975-76	1979-80
Huck, Fran	Mtl., St.L.	3	94	24	30	54	38	11	3	4	7	2		1969-70	1972-73
Hucul, Fred	Chi., St.L.	5	164	11	30	41	113	6	1	0	1	10		1950-51	1967-68
Hudson, Dave	NYI, K.C., Col.	6	409	59	124	183	89	2	1	1	2	0		1972-73	1977-78
Hudson, Lex	Pit.	1	2	0	0	0	0	2	0	0	0	0		1978-79	1978-79
Hudson, Ron	Det.	2	34	5	2	7	2	....	....	....	....	....		1937-38	1939-40
Huggins, Al	Mtl.M	1	20	1	1	2	2	....	....	....	....	....		1930-31	1930-31
Hughes, Al	NYA	2	60	6	8	14	22	....	....	....	....	....		1930-31	1931-32
Hughes, Brent	L.A., Phi., St.L., Det., K.C.	8	435	15	117	132	440	22	1	3	4	53		1967-68	1974-75
Hughes, Frank	Cal.	1	5	0	0	0	0	....	....	....	....	....		1971-72	1971-72
Hughes, Howie	L.A.	3	168	25	32	57	30	14	2	0	2	2		1967-68	1969-70
Hughes, Jack	Col.	2	46	2	5	7	104	....	....	....	....	....		1980-81	1981-82
Hughes, John	Van., Edm., NYR	3	70	2	14	16	211	7	0	1	1	16		1979-80	1980-81
Hughes, Pat	Mtl., Pit., Edm., Buf., St.L., Hfd.	10	573	130	128	258	646	71	8	25	33	77	3	1977-78	1986-87
Hughes, Rusty	Det.	1	40	0	1	1	48	....	....	....	....	....		1929-30	1929-30
Hull, Bobby	Chi., Wpg., Hfd.	16	1063	610	560	1170	640	119	62	67	129	102	1	1957-58	1979-80
Hull, Dennis	Chi., Det.	14	959	303	351	654	261	104	33	34	67	30		1964-65	1977-78
• Hunt, Fred	NYA, NYR	2	59	15	14	29	6	....	....	....	....	....		1940-41	1944-45
Hunter, Dave	Edm., Pit., Wpg.	10	746	133	190	323	918	105	16	24	40	211	3	1979-80	1988-89
Huras, Larry	NYR	1	1	0	0	0	0	....	....	....	....	....		1976-77	1976-77
Hurlburt, Bob	Van.	1	1	0	0	0	2	....	....	....	....	....		1974-75	1974-75
Hurley, Paul	Bos.	1	1	0	1	1	0	....	....	....	....	....		1968-69	1968-69
Hurst, Ron	Tor.	2	64	9	7	16	7	3	0	2	2	4		1955-56	1956-57
Huston, Ron	Cal.	2	79	15	31	46	8	....	....	....	....	....		1973-74	1974-75
Hutchinson, Ronald	NYR	1	9	0	0	0	0	....	....	....	....	....		1960-61	1960-61
Hutchison, Dave	L.A., Tor., Chi., N.J.	10	584	19	97	116	1550	48	2	12	14	149		1974-75	1983-84
• Hutton, William	Bos., Ott., Phi.	2	64	3	2	5	8	2	0	0	0	0		1929-30	1930-31
• Hyland, Harry	Mtl.W, Ott.	1	16	14	0	14	0	....	....	....	....	....		1917-18	1917-18
Hynes, Dave	Bos.	2	22	4	0	4	2	....	....	....	....	....		1973-74	1974-75

I

Ihnacak, Miroslav	Tor., Det.	3	56	8	9	17	39	1	0	0	0	0		1985-86	1988-89
Ihnacak, Peter	Tor.	8	417	102	165	267	175	28	4	10	14	25		1982-83	1989-90
Imlach, Brent	Tor.	2	3	0	0	0	2	....	....	....	....	....		1965-66	1966-67
Ingarfield, Earl	NYR, Pit., Oak., Cal.	13	746	179	226	405	239	21	9	8	17	10		1958-59	1970-71
Ingarfield, Earl Jr.	Atl., Cgy., Det.	2	39	4	4	8	22	2	0	1	1	0		1979-80	1980-81
Inglis, Bill	L.A., Buf.	3	36	1	3	4	4	11	1	2	3	4		1967-68	1970-71
• Ingoldsby, Johnny	Tor.	2	29	5	1	6	15	....	....	....	....	....		1942-43	1943-44
Ingram, Frank	Bos., Chi.	4	102	24	16	40	69	11	0	1	1	2		1924-25	1931-32
Ingram, Ron	Chi., Det., NYR	4	114	5	15	20	81	2	0	0	0	0		1956-57	1964-65
• Irvin, Dick	Chi.	3	94	29	23	52	76	2	2	0	2	4		1926-27	1928-29
Irvine, Ted	Bos., L.A., NYR, St.L.	11	724	154	177	331	657	83	16	24	40	115		1963-64	1976-77
Irwin, Ivan	Mtl., NYR	5	155	2	27	29	214	5	0	0	0	8		1952-53	1957-58
Isaksson, Ulf	L.A.	1	50	7	15	22	10	....	....	....	....	....		1982-83	1982-83
Issel, Kim	Edm.	1	4	0	0	0	0	....	....	....	....	....		1988-89	1988-89

J

• Jackson, Art	Bos., Tor.	11	466	123	178	301	144	51	8	12	20	27	2	1934-35	1944-45
Jackson, Don	Min., Edm., NYR	10	311	16	52	68	640	53	4	5	9	147	2	1977-78	1986-87
Jackson, Hal	Chi., Det.	8	222	17	34	51	208	31	1	2	3	33	2	1936-37	1946-47

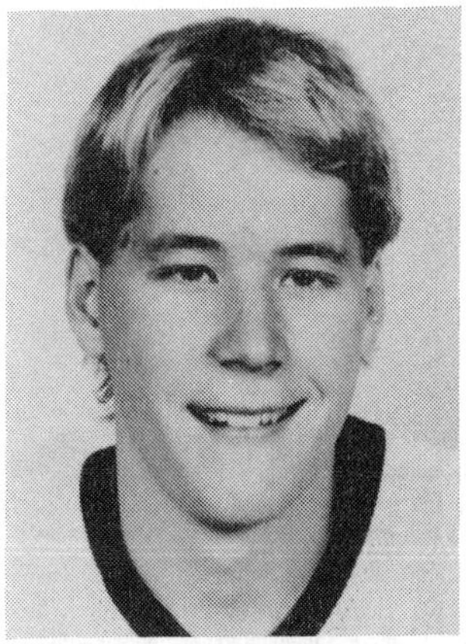

Greg Johnston

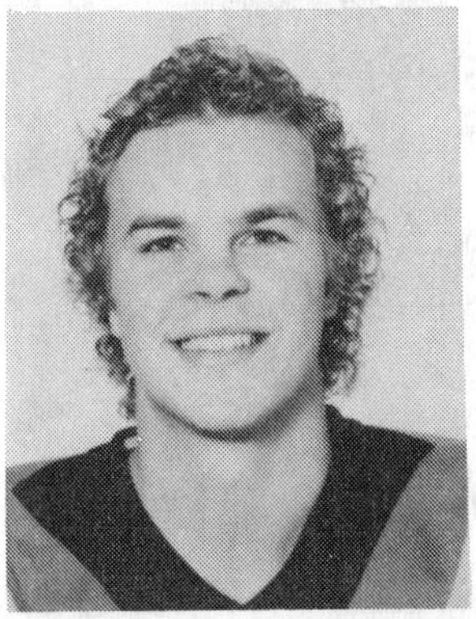

Mark Kirton

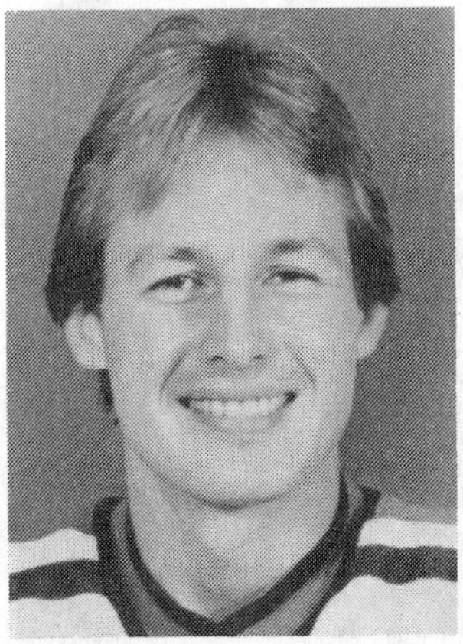

Mike Kitchen

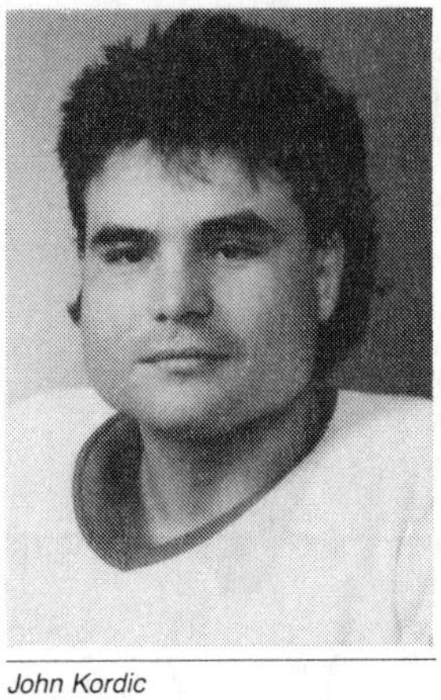

John Kordic

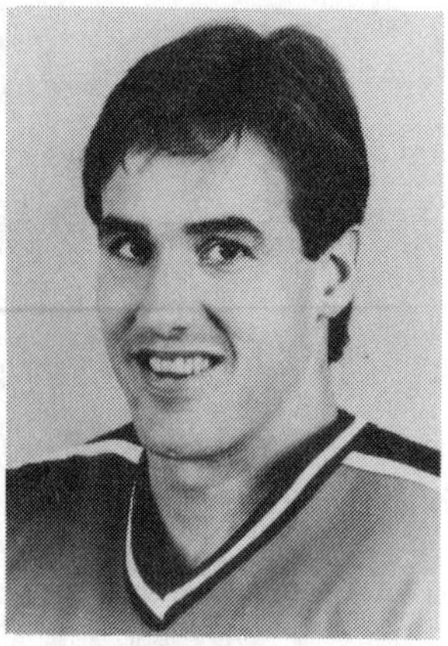

Jim Korn

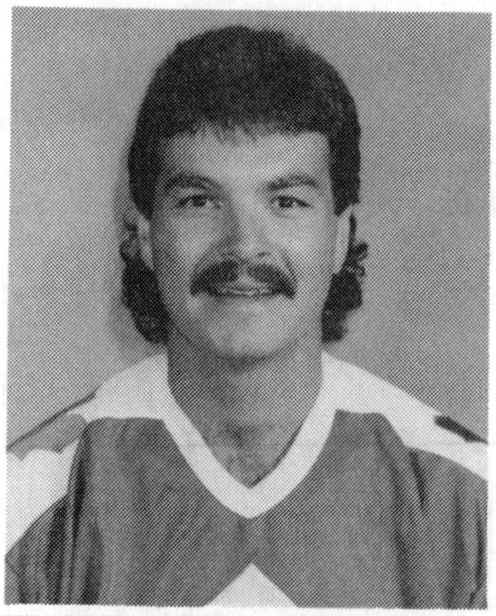

Chris Kotsopoulos

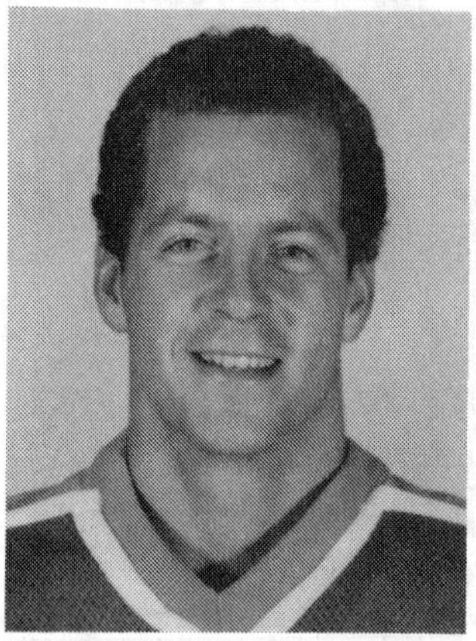

Normand Lacombe

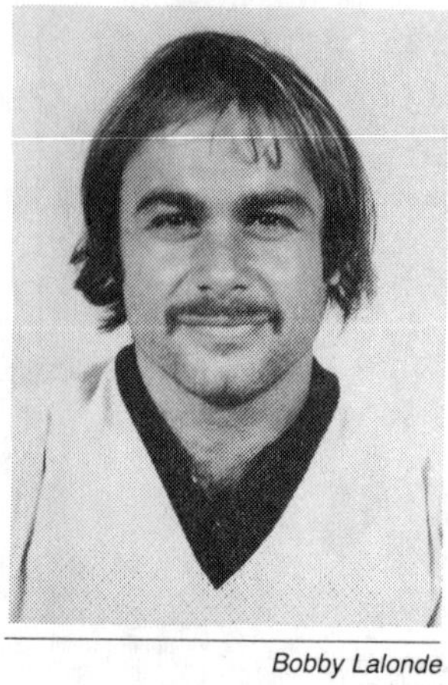

Bobby Lalonde

Name	NHL Teams	NHL Seasons	Regular Schedule					Playoffs					NHL Cup Wins	First NHL Season	Last NHL Season
			GP	G	A	TP	PIM	GP	G	A	TP	PIM			
• Jackson, Harvey	Tor., Bos., NYA	15	636	241	234	475	437	71	18	12	30	53	1	1929-30	1943-44
Jackson, Jeff	Tor., NYR, Que., Chi.	8	263	38	48	86	313	6	1	1	2	16		1984-85	1991-92
Jackson, Jim	Cgy., Buf.	4	112	17	30	47	20	14	3	2	5	6		1982-83	1987-88
Jackson, John	Chi.	1	48	2	5	7	38	....	....	....	....	....		1946-47	1946-47
Jackson, Lloyd	NYA	1	14	1	1	2	0	....	....	....	....	....		1936-37	1936-37
Jackson, Stan	Tor., Bos., Ott.	5	84	9	4	13	74	....	....	....	....	....	1	1921-22	1926-27
Jackson, Walt	NYA	3	82	16	11	27	18	....	....	....	....	....		1932-33	1934-35
• Jacobs, Paul	Tor.	1	1	0	0	0	0	....	....	....	....	....		1918-19	1918-19
Jacobs, Tim	Cal.	1	46	0	10	10	35	....	....	....	....	....		1975-76	1975-76
Jalo, Risto	Edm.	1	3	0	3	3	0	....	....	....	....	....		1985-86	1985-86
Jalonen, Kari	Cgy., Edm.	2	37	9	6	15	4	5	1	0	1	0		1982-83	1983-84
James, Gerry	Tor.	5	149	14	26	40	257	15	1	0	1	8		1954-55	1959-60
James, Val	Buf., Tor.	2	11	0	0	0	30	....	....	....	....	....		1981-82	1986-87
Jamieson, Jim	NYR	1	1	0	1	1	0	....	....	....	....	....		1943-44	1943-44
Jankowski, Lou	Det., Chi.	4	127	19	18	37	15	1	0	0	0	0		1950-51	1954-55
Jarrett, Doug	Chi., NYR	13	775	38	182	220	631	99	7	16	23	82		1964-65	1976-77
Jarrett, Gary	Tor., Det., Oak., Cal.	7	341	72	92	164	131	11	3	1	4	9		1960-61	1971-72
Jarry, Pierre	NYR, Tor., Det., Min.	7	344	88	117	205	142	5	0	1	1	0		1971-72	1977-78
Jarvenpaa, Hannu	Wpg.	3	114	11	26	37	83	....	....	....	....	....		1986-87	1988-89
Jarvi, Iiro	Que.	2	116	18	43	61	58	....	....	....	....	....		1988-89	1989-90
Jarvis, Doug	Mtl., Wsh., Hfd.	13	964	139	264	403	263	105	14	27	41	42	4	1975-76	1987-88
Jarvis, Jim	Pit., Phi., Tor.	3	108	17	15	32	62	....	....	....	....	....		1929-30	1936-37
Jarvis, Wes	Wsh., Min., L.A., Tor.	8	237	31	55	86	98	2	0	0	0	2		1979-80	1987-88
Javanainen, Arto	Pit.	1	14	4	1	5	2	....	....	....	....	....		1984-85	1984-85
Jeffrey, Larry	Det., Tor., NYR	8	368	39	62	101	293	38	4	10	14	42	1	1961-62	1968-69
Jenkins, Dean	L.A.	1	5	0	0	0	2	....	....	....	....	....		1983-84	1983-84
Jenkins, Roger	Tor., Chi., Mtl., Bos., Mtl.M., NYA	8	328	15	39	54	279	25	1	7	8	12	2	1930-31	1938-39
Jennings, Bill	Det., Bos.	5	108	32	33	65	45	20	4	4	8	6		1940-41	1944-45
Jensen, David A.	Hfd., Wsh.	4	69	9	13	22	22	11	0	0	0	2		1983-84	1987-88
Jensen, David H.	Min.	3	18	0	2	2	11	....	....	....	....	....		1983-84	1985-86
Jensen, Steve	Min., L.A.	7	438	113	107	220	318	12	0	3	3	9		1975-76	1981-82
• Jeremiah, Ed	NYA, Bos.	1	15	0	1	1	0	....	....	....	....	....		1931-32	1931-32
Jerwa, Frank	Bos.	1	28	4	5	9	12	....	....	....	....	....		1931-32	1931-32
Jerwa, Joe	NYR, Bos., St.L., NYA	9	293	36	69	105	338	17	2	3	5	20		1930-31	1938-39
Jirik, Jaroslav	St.L.	1	3	0	0	0	0	....	....	....	....	....		1969-70	1969-70
Joanette, Rosario	Mtl.	1	2	0	1	1	4	....	....	....	....	....		1944-45	1944-45
Jodzio, Rick	Col., Clev.	1	70	2	8	10	71	....	....	....	....	....		1977-78	1977-78
Johannesen, Glenn	NYI	1	2	0	0	0	0	....	....	....	....	....		1985-86	1985-86
Johannson, John	N.J.	1	5	0	0	0	0	....	....	....	....	....		1983-84	1983-84
Johansen, Trevor	Tor., Col., L.A.	5	286	11	46	57	282	13	0	3	3	21		1977-78	1981-82
Johansson, Bjorn	Clev.	2	15	1	1	2	10	....	....	....	....	....		1976-77	1977-78
Johns, Don	NYR, Mtl., Min.	6	153	2	21	23	76	....	....	....	....	....		1960-61	1967-68
Johnson, Al	Mtl., Det.	4	105	21	28	49	30	11	2	2	4	6		1956-57	1962-63
Johnson, Brian	Det.	1	3	0	0	0	5	....	....	....	....	....		1983-84	1983-84
• Johnson, Danny	Tor., Van., Det.	3	121	18	19	37	24	....	....	....	....	....		1969-70	1971-72
Johnson, Earl	Det.	1	1	0	0	0	0	....	....	....	....	....		1953-54	1953-54
• Johnson, Ivan	NYR, NYA	12	435	38	48	86	808	60	5	2	7	161	2	1926-27	1937-38
Johnson, Jim	NYR, Phi., L.A.	8	302	75	111	186	73	7	0	2	2	2		1964-65	1971-72
Johnson, Mark	Pit., Min., Hfd., St.L., N.J.	11	669	203	305	508	260	37	16	12	28	10		1979-80	1989-90
Johnson, Norm	Bos., Chi.	3	61	5	20	25	41	14	4	0	4	6		1957-58	1959-60
Johnson, Terry	Que., St.L., Cgy., Tor.	9	285	3	24	27	580	38	0	4	4	118		1979-80	1987-88
Johnson, Tom	Mtl., Bos.	17	978	51	213	264	960	111	8	15	23	109	6	1947-48	1964-65
Johnson, Virgil	Chi.	3	75	2	9	11	27	19	0	3	3	4	1	1937-38	1944-45
Johnson, William	Tor.	1	1	0	0	0	0	....	....	....	....	....		1949-50	1949-50
Johnston, Bernie	Hfd.	2	57	12	24	36	44	3	0	1	1	0		1979-80	1980-81
Johnston, George	Chi.	4	58	20	12	32	2	....	....	....	....	....		1941-42	1946-47
Johnston, Greg	Bos., Tor.	9	187	26	30	56	124	22	2	1	3	12		1983-84	1991-92
Johnston, Jay	Wsh.	2	8	0	0	0	13	....	....	....	....	....		1980-81	1981-82
Johnston, Joey	Min., Cal., Chi.	6	332	85	106	191	320	....	....	....	....	....		1968-69	1975-76
Johnston, Larry	L.A., Det., K.C., Col.	7	320	9	64	73	580	....	....	....	....	....		1967-68	1976-77
Johnston, Marshall	Min., Cal.	7	251	14	52	66	58	6	0	0	0	2		1967-68	1973-74
Johnston, Randy	NYI	1	4	0	0	0	4	....	....	....	....	....		1979-80	1979-80
Johnstone, Eddie	NYR, Det.	10	426	122	136	258	375	55	13	10	23	83		1975-76	1986-87
Johnstone, Ross	Tor.	2	42	5	4	9	14	3	0	0	0	0	1	1943-44	1944-45
• Joliat, Aurel	Mtl.	16	654	270	190	460	757	54	14	19	33	89	3	1922-23	1937-38
Joliat, Bobby	Mtl.	1	1	0	0	0	0	....	....	....	....	....		1924-25	1924-25
Joly, Greg	Wsh., Det.	9	365	21	76	97	250	5	0	0	0	8		1974-75	1982-83
Joly, Yvan	Mtl.	3	2	0	0	0	0	10	0	0	0	0		1979-80	1982-83
Jonathon, Stan	Bos., Pit.	8	411	91	110	201	751	63	8	4	12	137		1975-76	1982-83
Jones, Bob	NYR	1	2	0	0	0	0	....	....	....	....	....		1968-69	1968-69
Jones, Buck	Det., Tor.	4	50	2	2	4	36	12	0	1	1	18		1938-39	1942-43
Jones, Jim	Cal.	1	2	0	0	0	0	....	....	....	....	....		1971-72	1971-72
Jones, Jimmy	Tor.	3	148	13	18	31	68	19	1	5	6	11		1977-78	1979-80
Jones, Ron	Bos., Pit., Wsh.	5	54	1	4	5	31	....	....	....	....	....		1971-72	1975-76
Jonsson, Tomas	NYI	8	552	85	259	344	482	80	11	26	37	97	2	1981-82	1988-89
Joseph, Anthony	Wpg.	1	2	1	0	1	0	....	....	....	....	....		1988-89	1988-89
Joyal, Eddie	Det., Tor., L.A., Phi.	9	466	128	134	262	103	50	11	8	19	18		1962-63	1971-72
Juckes, Bing	NYR	2	16	2	1	3	6	....	....	....	....	....		1947-48	1949-50
Julien, Claude	Que.	2	14	0	1	1	25	....	....	....	....	....		1984-85	1985-86
Jutila, Timo	Buf.	1	10	1	5	6	13	....	....	....	....	....		1984-85	1984-85
Juzda, Bill	NYR, Tor.	9	393	14	54	68	398	42	0	3	3	46	2	1940-41	1951-52

K

Name	NHL Teams	NHL Seasons	GP	G	A	TP	PIM	GP	G	A	TP	PIM	NHL Cup Wins	First NHL Season	Last NHL Season
Kabel, Bob	NYR	2	48	5	13	18	34	....	....	....	....	....		1959-60	1960-61
Kachowski, Mark	Pit.	3	64	6	5	11	209	....	....	....	....	....		1987-88	1989-90
Kachur, Ed	Chi.	2	96	10	14	24	35	....	....	....	....	....		1956-57	1957-58
Kaese, Trent	Buf.	1	1	0	0	0	0	....	....	....	....	....		1988-89	1988-89
Kaiser, Vern	Mtl.	1	50	7	5	12	33	2	0	0	0	0		1950-51	1950-51
Kalbfleish, Walter	Ott., St.L., NYA, Bos.	4	36	0	4	4	32	5	0	0	0	2		1933-34	1936-37
• Kaleta, Alex	Chi., NYR	7	387	92	121	213	190	17	1	6	7	2		1941-42	1950-51
Kallur, Anders	NYI	6	383	101	110	211	149	78	12	23	35	32	4	1979-80	1984-85
• Kaminsky, Max	Ott., St.L., Bos., Mtl.M.	4	130	22	34	56	38	4	0	0	0	0		1933-34	1936-37
• Kampman, Bingo	Tor.	5	189	14	30	44	287	47	1	4	5	38	1	1937-38	1941-42
Kane, Frank	Det.	1	2	0	0	0	0	....	....	....	....	....		1943-44	1943-44
Kannegiesser, Gord	St.L.	2	23	0	1	1	15	....	....	....	....	....		1967-68	1971-72
Kannegiesser, Sheldon	Pit., NYR, L.A., Van.	8	366	14	67	81	292	18	0	2	2	10		1970-71	1977-78
Karlander, Al	Det.	4	212	36	56	92	70	4	0	1	1	0		1969-70	1972-73
Kaszycki, Mike	NYI, Wsh., Tor.	5	226	42	80	122	108	19	2	6	8	10		1977-78	1982-83
Kea, Ed	Atl., St.L.	10	583	30	145	175	508	32	2	4	6	39		1973-74	1982-83
Kearns, Dennis	Van.	10	677	31	290	321	386	11	1	2	3	8		1971-72	1980-81
• Keating, Jack	NYA	2	35	5	5	10	17	....	....	....	....	....		1931-32	1932-33
Keating, John	Det.	2	11	2	1	3	4	....	....	....	....	....		1938-39	1939-40
Keating, Mike	NYR	1	1	0	0	0	0	....	....	....	....	....		1977-78	1977-78
• Keats, Duke	Det., Chi.	3	80	3	19	49	113	....	....	....	....	....		1926-27	1928-29
• Keeling, Butch	Tor., NYR	12	528	157	63	220	331	47	11	11	22	32	1	1926-27	1937-38
Keenan, Larry	Tor., St.L., Buf., Phi.	6	233	38	64	102	28	46	15	16	31	12		1961-62	1971-72
Kehoe, Rick	Tor., Pit.	14	906	371	396	767	120	39	4	17	21	4		1971-72	1984-85
Keller, Ralph	NYR	1	3	1	0	1	6	....	....	....	....	....		1962-63	1962-63
Kellgren, Christer	Col.	1	5	0	0	0	0	....	....	....	....	....		1981-82	1981-82
Kelly, Bob	St.L., Pit., Chi.	6	425	87	109	196	687	23	6	3	9	40		1973-74	1978-79
Kelly, Bob	Phi., Wsh.	12	837	154	208	362	1454	101	9	14	23	172	2	1970-71	1981-82
Kelly, Dave	Det.	1	16	2	0	2	4	....	....	....	....	....		1976-77	1976-77
Kelly, John Paul	L.A.	7	400	54	70	124	366	18	1	1	2	41		1979-80	1985-86
Kelly, Pete	St.L., Det., NYA, Bro.	7	180	21	38	59	68	19	3	1	4	8	2	1934-35	1941-42
Kelly, Red	Det., Tor.	20	1316	281	542	823	327	164	33	59	92	51	8	1947-48	1966-67
• Kelly, Reg	Tor., Chi., Bro.	8	289	74	53	127	105	39	7	6	13	10		1934-35	1941-42
Kemp, Kevin	Hfd.	1	3	0	0	0	4	....	....	....	....	....		1980-81	1980-81
Kemp, Stan	Tor.	1	1	0	0	0	2	....	....	....	....	....		1948-49	1948-49
Kendall, William	Chi., Tor.	5	132	16	10	26	28	5	0	0	0	0	1	1933-34	1937-38
Kennedy, Forbes	Chi., Det., Bos., Phi., Tor.	11	603	70	108	178	988	12	2	4	6	64		1956-57	1968-69
Kennedy, Ted	Tor.	14	696	231	329	560	432	78	29	31	60	32	5	1942-43	1956-57
• Kenny, Eddie	NYR, Chi.	2	11	0	0	0	18	....	....	....	....	....		1930-31	1934-35

Name	NHL Teams	NHL Seasons	Regular Schedule GP	G	A	TP	PIM	Playoffs GP	G	A	TP	PIM	NHL Cup Wins	First NHL Season	Last NHL Season
Keon, Dave	Tor., Hfd.	18	1296	396	590	986	117	92	32	36	68	6	4	1960-61	1981-82
Kerr, Reg	Cle., Chi., Edm.	6	263	66	94	160	169	7	1	0	1	7		1977-78	1983-84
Kessell, Rick	Pit., Cal.	5	135	4	24	28	6	....	....	....	....	....		1969-70	1973-74
Ketola, Veli-Pekka	Col.	1	44	9	5	14	4	....	....	....	....	....		1981-82	1981-82
Ketter, Kerry	Atl.	1	41	0	2	2	58	....	....	....	....	....		1972-73	1972-73
Kharin, Sergei	Wpg.	1	7	2	3	5	2	....	....	....	....	....		1990-91	1990-91
Kidd, Ian	Van.	2	20	4	7	11	25	....	....	....	....	....		1987-88	1988-89
Kiessling, Udo	Min.	1	1	0	0	0	2	....	....	....	....	....		1981-82	1981-82
Kilrea, Brian	Det., L.A.	2	26	3	5	8	12	....	....	....	....	....		1957-58	1967-68
• Kilrea, Hec	Ott., Det., Tor.	15	633	167	129	296	438	48	8	7	15	18	3	1925-26	1939-40
Kilrea, Ken	Det.	5	88	16	23	39	8	10	2	2	4	4		1938-39	1943-44
Kilrea, Wally	Ott., Phi., NYA, Mtl.M., Det.	9	315	35	58	93	87	25	2	4	6	6		1929-30	1937-38
Kindrachuk, Orest	Phi., Pit., Wsh.	10	508	118	261	379	648	76	20	20	40	53	2	1972-73	1981-82
King, Frank	Mtl.	1	10	1	0	1	2	....	....	....	....	....		1950-51	1950-51
King, Wayne	Cal.	3	73	5	18	23	34	....	....	....	....	....		1973-74	1975-76
Kinsella, Brian	Wsh.	2	10	0	1	1	0	....	....	....	....	....		1975-76	1976-77
Kinsella, Ray	Ott.	1	14	0	0	0	0	....	....	....	....	....		1930-31	1930-31
Kirk, Bobby	NYR	1	39	4	8	12	14	....	....	....	....	....		1937-38	1937-38
Kirkpatrick, Bob	NYR	1	49	12	12	24	6	....	....	....	....	....		1942-43	1942-43
Kirton, Mark	Tor., Det., Van.	6	266	57	56	113	121	4	1	2	3	7		1979-80	1984-85
Kitchen, Bill	Mtl., Tor.	4	41	1	4	5	40	3	0	1	1	0		1981-82	1984-85
• Kitchen, Hobie	Mtl.M., Det.	2	47	5	4	9	58	....	....	....	....	....		1925-26	1926-27
Kitchen, Mike	Col., N.J.	8	474	12	62	74	370	2	0	0	0	2		1976-77	1983-84
Klassen, Ralph	Cal., Clev., Col., St.L.	9	497	52	93	145	120	26	4	2	6	12		1975-76	1983-84
Klein, Jim	Bos., NYA	8	169	30	24	54	68	5	0	0	0	2	1	1928-29	1937-38
Kleinendorst, Scot	NYR, Hfd., Wsh.	8	281	12	46	58	452	26	2	7	9	40		1982-83	1989-90
Klingbeil, Ike	Chi.	1	5	1	2	3	2	....	....	....	....	....		1936-37	1936-37
Klukay, Joe	Tor., Bos.	11	566	109	127	236	189	71	13	10	23	23	4	1942-43	1955-56
Kluzak, Gord	Bos.	7	299	25	98	123	543	46	6	13	19	129		1982-83	1990-91
Knibbs, Bill	Bos.	1	53	7	10	17	4	....	....	....	....	....		1964-65	1964-65
• Knott, Nick	Bro.	1	14	3	1	4	9	....	....	....	....	....		1941-42	1941-42
Knox, Paul	Tor.	1	1	0	0	0	0	....	....	....	....	....		1954-55	1954-55
Komadoski, Neil	L.A., St.L.	8	502	16	76	92	632	23	0	2	2	47		1972-73	1979-80
Konik, George	Pit.	1	52	7	8	15	26	....	....	....	....	....		1967-68	1967-68
Kopak, Russ	Bos.	1	24	7	9	16	0	....	....	....	....	....		1943-44	1943-44
Korab, Jerry	Chi., Van., Buf., L.A.	15	975	114	341	455	1629	93	8	18	26	201		1970-71	1984-85
• Kordic, John	Mtl., Tor., Wsh., Que.	7	244	17	18	35	997	41	4	3	7	131	1	1985-86	1991-92
Korn, Jim	Det., Tor., Buf., N.J., Cgy.	10	597	66	122	188	1801	16	1	2	3	109		1979-80	1989-90
Korney, Mike	Det., NYR	4	77	9	10	19	59	....	....	....	....	....		1973-74	1978-79
Koroll, Cliff	Chi.	11	814	208	254	462	376	85	19	29	48	67		1969-70	1979-80
Kortko, Roger	NYI	2	79	7	17	24	28	10	0	3	3	17		1984-85	1985-86
Kostynski, Doug	Bos.	2	15	3	1	4	4	....	....	....	....	....		1983-84	1984-85
Kotanen, Dick	Det., NYR	2	2	0	1	1	0	....	....	....	....	....		1948-49	1950-51
Kotsopoulos, Chris	NYR, Hfd.,Tor., Det.	10	479	44	109	153	827	31	1	3	4	91		1980-81	1989-90
Kowal, Joe	Buf.	2	22	0	5	5	13	2	0	0	0	0		1976-77	1977-78
Kozak, Don	L.A., Van.	7	437	96	86	182	480	29	7	2	9	69		1972-73	1978-79
Kozak, Les	Tor.	1	12	1	0	1	2	....	....	....	....	....		1961-62	1961-62
Kraftcheck, Stephen	Bos., NYR, Tor.	4	157	11	18	29	83	6	0	0	0	7		1950-51	1958-59
Krake, Skip	Bos., L.A., Buf.	7	249	23	40	63	182	10	1	0	1	17		1963-64	1970-71
Krentz, Dale	Det.	3	30	5	3	8	9	2	0	0	0	0		1986-87	1988-89
Krol, Joe	NYR, Bro.	3	26	10	4	14	8	....	....	....	....	....		1936-37	1941-42
Krook, Kevin	Col.	1	3	0	0	0	2	....	....	....	....	....		1978-79	1978-79
Krulicki, Jim	NYR, Det.	1	41	0	3	3	6	....	....	....	....	....		1970-71	1970-71
Krutov, Vladimir	Van.	1	61	11	23	34	20	....	....	....	....	....		1989-90	1989-90
Kryskow, Dave	Chi., Wsh., Det., Atl.	4	231	33	56	89	174	12	2	0	2	4		1972-73	1975-76
Kryznowski, Edward	Bos., Chi.	5	237	15	22	37	65	18	0	1	1	4		1948-49	1952-53
Kuhn, Gord	NYA	1	12	1	1	2	4	....	....	....	....	....		1932-33	1932-33
Kukulowicz, Adolph	NYR	2	4	1	0	1	0	....	....	....	....	....		1952-53	1953-54
Kulak, Stu	Van., Edm., NYR, Que., Wpg.	4	90	8	4	12	130	3	0	0	0	2		1982-83	1988-89
Kullman, Arnie	Bos.	2	13	0	1	1	11	....	....	....	....	....		1947-48	1949-50
Kullman, Eddie	NYR	6	343	56	70	126	298	6	1	0	1	2		1947-48	1953-54
Kumpel, Mark	Que., Det., Wpg.	6	288	38	46	84	113	39	6	4	10	14		1984-85	1990-91
Kuntz, Alan	NYR	2	45	10	12	22	12	6	1	0	1	2		1941-42	1945-46
Kuntz, Murray	St.L.	1	7	1	2	3	0	....	....	....	....	....		1974-75	1974-75
Kurtenbach, Orland	NYR, Bos., Tor., Van.	13	639	119	213	332	628	19	2	4	6	70		1960-61	1973-74
Kuryluk, Mervin	Chi.	1	....	....	....	....	....	2	0	0	0	0		1961-62	1961-62
Kuzyk, Ken	Clev.	2	41	5	9	14	8	....	....	....	....	....		1976-77	1977-78
Kwong, Larry	NYR	1	1	0	0	0	0	....	....	....	....	....		1947-48	1947-48
• Kyle, Bill	NYR	2	3	0	3	3	0	....	....	....	....	....		1949-50	1950-51
Kyle, Gus	NYR, Bos.	3	203	6	20	26	362	14	1	2	3	34		1949-50	1951-52
Kyllonen, Marku	Wpg.	1	9	0	2	2	2	....	....	....	....	....		1988-89	1988-89

L

Labadie, Mike	NYR	1	3	0	0	0	0	....	....	....	....	....		1952-53	1952-53
Labatte, Neil	St.L.	2	26	0	2	2	19	....	....	....	....	....		1978-79	1981-82
L'Abbe, Moe	Chi.	1	5	0	1	1	0	....	....	....	....	....		1972-73	1972-73
Labine, Leo	Bos., Det.	11	643	128	193	321	730	60	11	12	23	82		1951-52	1961-62
Labossierre, Gord	NYR, L.A., Min.	6	215	44	62	106	75	10	2	3	5	28		1963-64	1971-72
Labovitch, Max	NYR	1	5	0	0	0	4	....	....	....	....	....		1943-44	1943-44
Labraaten, Dan	Det., Cgy.	4	268	71	73	144	47	5	1	0	1	4		1978-79	1981-82
Labre, Yvon	Pit., Wsh.	9	371	14	87	101	788	....	....	....	....	....		1970-71	1980-81
Labrie, Guy	Bos., NYR	2	42	4	9	13	16	....	....	....	....	....		1943-44	1944-45
Lach, Elmer	Mtl.	14	664	215	408	623	478	76	19	45	64	36	3	1940-41	1953-54
Lachance, Earl	Mtl.	1	1	0	0	0	0	....	....	....	....	....		1926-27	1926-27
Lachance, Michel	Col.	1	21	0	4	4	22	....	....	....	....	....		1978-79	1978-79
Lacombe, Francois	Oak., Buf., Que.	4	78	2	17	19	54	3	1	0	1	0		1968-69	1979-80
Lacombe, Normand	Buf., Edm., Phi	7	319	53	62	115	196	26	5	1	6	49	1	1984-85	1990-91
Lacroix, Andre	Phi., Chi., Hfd.	6	325	79	119	198	44	16	2	5	7	0		1967-68	1979-80
Lacroix, Pierre	Que., Hfd.	4	274	24	108	132	197	8	0	2	2	10		1979-80	1982-83
Lafleur, Guy	Mtl., NYR, Que.	17	1126	560	793	1353	399	128	58	76	134	67	5	1971-72	1990-91
Lafleur, Rene	Mtl.	1	1	0	0	0	0	....	....	....	....	....		1924-25	1924-25
Laforce, Ernie	Mtl.	1	1	0	0	0	0	....	....	....	....	....		1942-43	1942-43
LaForest, Bob	L.A.	1	5	1	0	1	2	....	....	....	....	....		1983-84	1983-84
Laforge, Claude	Mtl., Det., Phi.	8	192	24	33	57	82	5	1	2	3	15		1957-58	1968-69
Laframboise, Pete	Cal., Wsh., Pit.	4	227	33	55	88	70	9	1	0	1	0		1971-72	1974-75
Lafrance, Adie	Mtl.	1	3	0	0	0	2	2	0	0	0	0		1933-34	1933-34
Lafrance, Leo	Mtl., Chi.	2	33	2	0	2	6	....	....	....	....	....		1926-27	1927-28
Lafreniere, Roger	Det., St.L.	2	13	0	0	0	4	....	....	....	....	....		1962-63	1972-73
Lagace, Jean-Guy	Pit., Buf., K.C.	6	187	9	39	48	251	....	....	....	....	....		1968-69	1975-76
Laidlaw, Tom	NYR, L.A.	10	705	25	139	164	717	69	4	17	21	78		1980-81	1989-90
Laird, Robbie	Min.	1	1	0	0	0	0	....	....	....	....	....		1979-80	1979-80
Lajeunesse, Serge	Det., Phi.	5	103	1	4	5	103	7	1	2	3	4		1970-71	1974-75
Lalande, Hec	Chi., Det.	4	151	21	39	60	120	....	....	....	....	....		1953-54	1957-58
Lalonde, Bobby	Van., Atl., Bos., Cgy.	11	641	124	210	334	298	16	4	2	6	6		1971-72	1981-82
• Lalonde, Edouard	Mtl., NYA	6	99	124	27	151	122	12	22	1	23	0	1	1917-18	1926-27
Lalonde, Ron	Pit., Wsh.	7	397	45	78	123	106	....	....	....	....	....		1972-73	1978-79
Lamb, Joe	Mtl.M., Ott., NYA, Bos., Mtl., St.L., Det.	11	444	108	101	209	601	18	1	1	2	51		1927-28	1937-38
Lambert, Lane	Det., NYR, Que.	6	283	58	66	124	521	17	2	4	6	40		1983-84	1988-89
Lambert, Yvon	Mtl., Buf.	10	683	206	273	479	340	90	27	22	49	67	4	1972-73	1981-82
Lamby, Dick	St.L.	3	22	0	5	5	22	....	....	....	....	....		1978-79	1980-81
• Lamirande, Jean-Paul	NYR, Mtl.	4	49	5	5	10	26	8	0	0	0	4		1946-47	1954-55
• Lamoureux, Leo	Mtl.	6	235	19	79	98	175	28	1	6	7	16	2	1941-42	1946-47
Lamoureux, Mitch	Pit., Phi.	3	73	11	9	20	59	....	....	....	....	....		1983-84	1987-88
Lampman, Mike	St.L., Van., Wsh.	4	96	17	20	37	34	....	....	....	....	....		1972-73	1976-77
Lancien, Jack	NYR	4	63	1	5	6	35	6	0	1	1	2		1946-47	1950-51
Landon, Larry	Mtl., Tor.	2	9	0	0	0	2	....	....	....	....	....		1983-84	1984-85
Lane, Gord	Wsh., NYI	10	539	19	94	113	1228	75	3	14	17	214	4	1975-76	1984-85
• Lane, Myles	NYR, Bos.	3	60	4	1	5	41	10	0	0	0	0	1	1928-29	1933-34
Langdon, Steve	Bos.	3	7	0	1	1	2	4	0	0	0	2		1974-75	1977-78
Langelle, Pete	Tor.	4	137	22	51	73	11	41	5	9	14	4	1	1938-39	1941-42
Langevin, Chris	Buf.	2	22	3	1	4	22	....	....	....	....	....		1983-84	1985-86
Langevin, Dave	NYI, Min., L.A.	8	513	12	107	119	530	87	2	15	17	106	4	1979-80	1986-87

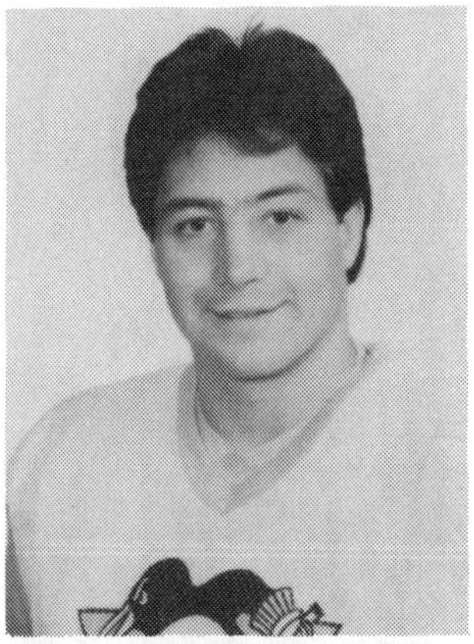

Mitch Lamoureaux

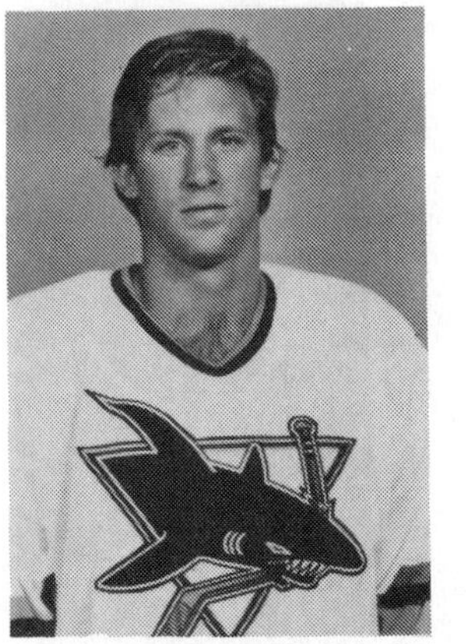

Peter Lappin

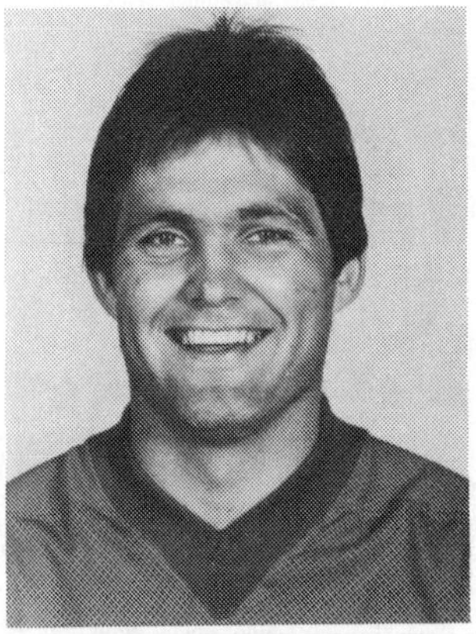

Reed Larson

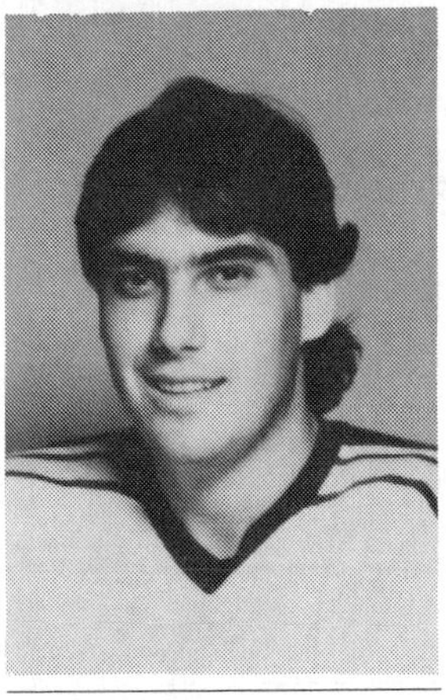

Alain Lemieux

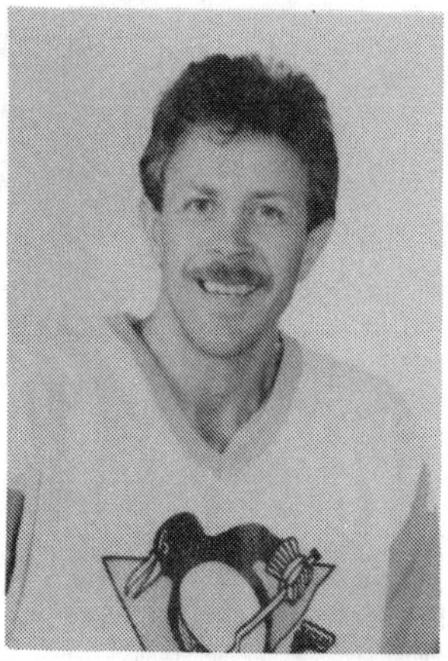

Willy Lindstrom

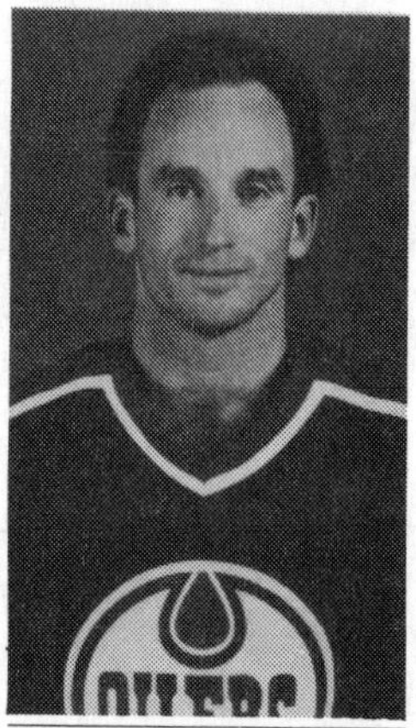

Ken Linseman

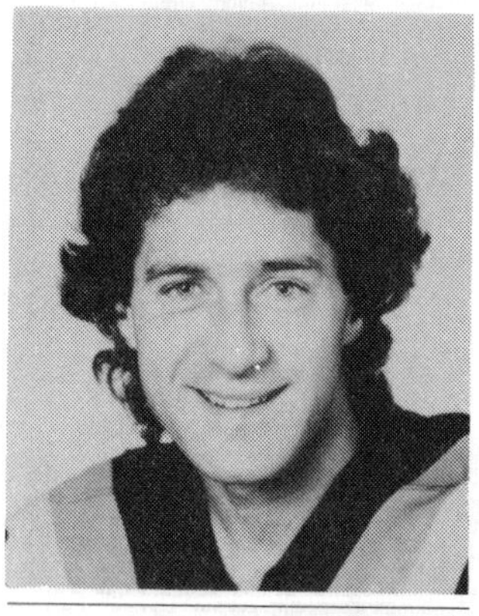

Blair MacDonald

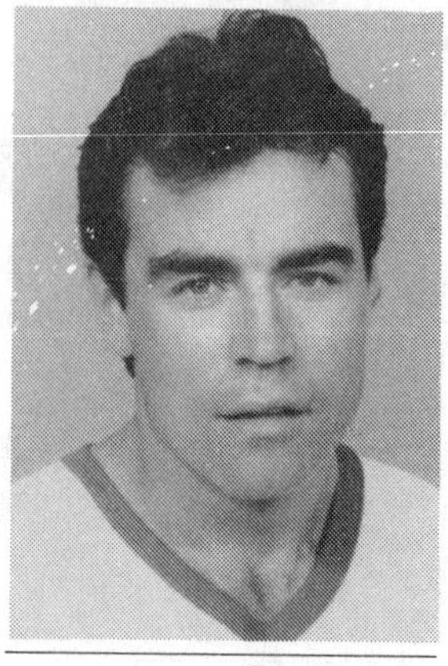

Brian MacLellan

			Regular Schedule					Playoffs							
Name	NHL Teams	NHL Seasons	GP	G	A	TP	PIM	GP	G	A	TP	PIM	NHL Cup Wins	First NHL Season	Last NHL Season
Langlais, Alain	Min.	2	25	4	4	8	10	....	....	....	....	....		1973-74	1974-75
Langlois, Al	Mtl., NYR, Det., Bos.	9	448	21	91	112	488	53	1	5	6	60	3	1957-58	1965-66
Langlois, Charlie	Ham., NYA., Pit., Mtl.	4	151	22	3	25	201	2	0	0	0	0		1924-25	1927-28
Lanthier, Jean-Marc	Van.	4	105	16	16	32	29	....	....	....	....	....		1983-84	1987-88
Lanyon, Ted	Pit.	1	5	0	0	0	4	....	....	....	....	....		1967-68	1967-68
Laperriere, Jacques	Mtl.	12	691	40	242	282	674	88	9	22	31	101	6	1962-63	1973-74
Lapointe, Guy	Mtl., St.L., Bos.	16	884	171	451	622	893	123	26	44	70	138	6	1968-69	1983-84
Lapointe, Rick	Det., Phi., St.L., Que., L.A.	11	664	44	176	220	831	46	2	7	9	64		1975-76	1985-86
Lappin, Peter	Min., S.J.	2	7	0	0	0	2	....	....	....	....	....		1989-90	1991-92
Laprade, Edgar	NYR	10	501	108	172	280	42	18	4	9	13	4		1945-46	1954-55
LaPrairie, Ben	Chi.	1	7	0	0	0	0	....	....	....	....	....		1936-37	1936-37
Lariviere, Garry	Que., Edm.	4	219	6	57	63	167	14	0	5	5	8		1979-80	1982-83
Larmer, Jeff	Col., N.J., Chi.	5	158	37	51	88	57	5	1	0	1	2		1981-82	1985-86
• Larochelle, Wildor	Mtl., Chi.	12	474	92	74	166	211	34	6	4	10	24	2	1925-26	1936-37
Larocque, Denis	L.A.	1	8	0	1	1	18	....	....	....	....	....		1987-88	1987-88
Larose, Charles	Bos.	1	6	0	0	0	0	....	....	....	....	....		1925-26	1925-26
Larose, Claude	NYR	2	25	4	7	11	2	2	0	0	0	0		1979-80	1981-82
Larose, Claude	Mtl., Min., St.L.	16	943	226	257	483	887	97	14	18	32	143	5	1962-63	1977-78
Larouche, Pierre	Pit., Mtl., Hfd., NYR	14	812	395	427	822	237	64	20	34	54	16	1	1974-75	1987-88
Larson, Norman	NYA., Bro., NYR	3	89	25	18	43	12	....	....	....	....	....		1940-41	1946-47
Larson, Reed	Det., Bos., Edm., NYI, Min., Buf.	14	904	222	463	685	1391	32	4	7	11	63		1976-77	1989-90
Larter, Tyler	Wsh.	1	1	0	0	0	0	....	....	....	....	....		1989-90	1989-90
Latal, Jiri	Phi.	2	92	12	36	48	24	....	....	....	....	....		1989-90	1990-91
Latos, James	NYR	1	1	0	0	0	0	....	....	....	....	....		1988-89	1988-89
Latreille, Phil	NYR	1	4	0	0	0	2	....	....	....	....	....		1960-61	1960-61
Latta, David	Que.	4	36	4	8	12	4	....	....	....	....	....		1985-86	1990-91
Lauder, Marty	Bos.	1	3	0	0	0	2	....	....	....	....	....		1927-28	1927-28
Lauen, Mike	Wpg.	1	3	0	1	1	0	....	....	....	....	....		1983-84	1983-84
Laughlin, Craig	Mtl., Wsh., L.A., Tor.	8	549	136	205	341	364	33	6	6	12	20		1981-82	1988-89
Laughton, Mike	Oak., Cal.	4	189	39	48	87	101	11	2	4	6	0		1967-68	1970-71
Laurence, Red	Atl., St.L.	2	79	15	22	37	14	....	....	....	....	....		1978-79	1979-80
LaVallee, Kevin	Cgy., L.A., St.L., Pit.	7	366	110	125	235	85	32	5	8	13	24		1980-81	1986-87
Lavarre, Mark	Chi.	3	78	9	16	25	58	1	0	0	0	2		1985-86	1987-88
Lavender, Brian	St.L., NYI, Det., Cal.	4	184	16	26	42	174	3	0	0	0	2		1971-72	1974-75
• Laviolette, Jack	Mtl.	1	18	2	0	2	0	2	0	0	0	0		1917-18	1917-18
Lawless, Paul	Hfd., Phi., Van., Tor.	7	239	49	77	126	54	3	0	2	2	2		1982-83	1989-90
Lawson, Danny	Det., Min., Buf.	5	219	28	29	57	61	16	0	1	1	2		1967-68	1971-72
Laxdal, Derek	Tor., NYI	6	67	12	7	19	90	1	0	2	2	2		1984-85	1990-91
Laycoe, Hal	NYR, Mtl., Bos.	11	531	25	77	102	292	40	2	5	7	39		1945-46	1955-56
Leach, Larry	Bos.	3	126	13	29	42	91	7	1	1	2	8		1958-59	1961-62
Leach, Reggie	Bos., Cal., Phi., Det.	13	934	381	285	666	387	94	47	22	69	22	1	1970-71	1982-83
Leavins, Jim	Det., NYR	2	41	2	12	14	30	....	....	....	....	....		1985-86	1986-87
Leavins, Jim	Det., NYR	2	41	2	12	14	30	....	....	....	....	....		1985-86	1986-87
LeBlanc, Fern	Det.	3	34	5	6	11	0	....	....	....	....	....		1976-77	1978-79
LeBlanc, J.P.	Chi., Det.	5	153	14	30	44	87	2	0	0	0	0		1968-69	1978-79
LeBrun, Al	NYR	2	6	0	2	2	4	....	....	....	....	....		1960-61	1965-66
Lecaine, Bill	Pit.	1	4	0	0	0	0	....	....	....	....	....		1968-69	1968-69
Leclair, Jackie	Mtl.,	3	160	20	40	60	56	20	6	0	7	6	1	1954-55	1956-57
Leclerc, Rene	Det.	2	87	10	11	21	105	....	....	....	....	....		1968-69	1970-71
Lecuyer, Doug	Chi., Wpg., Pit.	4	126	11	31	42	178	7	4	0	4	15		1978-79	1982-83
Ledingham, Walt	Chi., NYI	3	15	0	2	2	4	....	....	....	....	....		1972-73	1976-77
• LeDuc, Albert	Mtl., Ott., NYR	10	383	57	35	92	614	31	5	6	11	32	2	1925-26	1934-35
LeDuc, Rich	Bos., Que.	4	130	28	38	66	55	5	0	0	0	9		1972-73	1980-81
• Lee, Bobby	Mtl.	1	1	0	0	0	0	....	....	....	....	....		1942-43	1942-43
Lee, Edward	Que.	1	2	0	0	0	5	....	....	....	....	....		1984-85	1984-85
Lee, Peter	Pit.	6	431	114	131	245	257	19	0	8	8	4		1977-78	1982-83
Lefley, Bryan	N.Y.I., K.C., Col.	5	228	7	29	36	101	2	0	0	0	0		1972-73	1977-78
Lefley, Chuck	Mtl., St.L.	9	407	128	164	292	137	29	5	8	13	10		1970-71	1980-81
• Leger, Roger	NYR, Mtl.	5	187	18	53	71	71	20	0	7	7	14		1943-44	1949-50
Legge, Barry	Que., Wpg.	3	107	1	11	12	144	....	....	....	....	....		1979-80	1981-82
Legge, Randy	NYR	1	12	0	2	2	2	....	....	....	....	....		1972-73	1972-73
Lehmann, Tommy	Bos., Edm.	3	36	5	5	10	16	....	....	....	....	....		1987-88	1989-90
Lehto, Petteri	Pit.	1	6	0	0	0	4	....	....	....	....	....		1984-85	1984-85
Lehtonen, Antero	Wsh.	1	65	9	12	21	14	....	....	....	....	....		1979-80	1979-80
Lehvonen, Henri	K.C.	1	4	0	0	0	0	....	....	....	....	....		1974-75	1974-75
Leier, Edward	Chi.	2	16	2	1	3	2	....	....	....	....	....		1949-50	1950-51
Leinonen, Mikko	NYR, Wsh.	4	162	31	78	109	71	20	2	11	13	28		1981-82	1984-85
Leiter, Bobby	Bos., Pit., Atl.	10	447	98	126	224	144	8	3	0	3	2		1962-63	1975-76
Leiter, Ken	NYI, Min.	5	143	14	36	50	62	15	0	6	6	8		1984-85	1989-90
Lemaire, Jacques	Mtl.	12	853	366	469	835	217	145	61	78	139	63	8	1967-68	1978-79
Lemay, Moe	Van., Edm., Bos., Wpg.	8	317	72	94	166	442	28	6	3	9	55	1	1981-82	1988-89
Lemelin, Roger	K.C., Col.	4	36	1	2	3	27	....	....	....	....	....		1974-75	1977-78
Lemieux, Alain	St.L., Que., Pit.	6	119	28	44	72	38	19	4	6	10	0		1981-82	1986-87
Lemieux, Bob	Oak.	1	19	0	1	1	12	....	....	....	....	....		1967-68	1967-68
Lemieux, Jacques	L.A.	2	19	0	4	4	8	1	0	0	0	0		1967-68	1969-70
Lemieux, Jean	L.A., Atl., Wsh.	6	204	23	63	86	39	3	1	1	2	0		1969-70	1977-78
• Lemieux, Real	Det., L.A., NYR, Buf.	7	381	40	75	115	184	18	2	4	6	10		1966-67	1973-74
Lemieux, Richard	Van., K.C., Atl.	5	274	39	82	121	132	2	0	0	0	0		1971-72	1975-76
Lenardon, Tim	N.J., Van.	2	15	2	1	3	4	....	....	....	....	....		1986-87	1989-90
• Lepine, Hec	Mtl.	1	33	5	2	7	2	....	....	....	....	....		1925-26	1925-26
• Lepine, Pit	Mtl.	13	526	143	98	241	392	41	7	5	12	26	2	1925-26	1937-38
Leroux, Gaston	Mtl.	1	2	0	0	0	0	....	....	....	....	....		1935-36	1935-36
Lesieur, Art	Mtl., Chi.	4	100	4	2	6	50	14	0	0	0	4	1	1928-29	1935-36
Lesuk, Bill	Bos., Phi., L.A., Wsh., Wpg.	8	388	44	63	107	368	9	1	0	1	12	1	1968-69	1979-80
Leswick, Jack	Chi.	1	47	1	7	8	16	....	....	....	....	....	1	1933-34	1933-34
Leswick, Peter	NYA, Bos.	2	3	1	0	1	0	....	....	....	....	....		1936-37	1944-45
Leswick, Tony	NYR, Det., Chi.	12	740	165	159	324	900	59	13	10	23	91	3	1945-46	1957-58
Levandoski, Joseph	NYR	1	8	1	1	2	0	....	....	....	....	....		1946-47	1946-47
Leveille, Norm	Bos.	2	75	17	25	42	49	....	....	....	....	....		1981-82	1982-83
Lever, Don	Van., Atl., Cgy., Col., N.J., Buf.	15	1020	313	367	680	593	30	7	10	17	26		1972-73	1986-87
Levie, Craig	Wpg., Min., Van., St.L.	6	183	22	53	75	177	16	2	3	5	32		1981-82	1986-87
• Levinsky, Alex	Tor., Chi., NYR	9	367	19	49	68	307	34	2	1	3	2	2	1930-31	1938-39
Levo, Tapio	Col., N.J.,	2	107	16	53	69	36	....	....	....	....	....		1981-82	1982-83
Lewicki, Danny	Tor., NYR, Chi.	9	461	105	135	240	177	28	0	4	4	8	1	1950-51	1958-59
Lewis, Bob	NYR	1	8	0	0	0	0	....	....	....	....	....		1975-76	1975-76
Lewis, Dave	NYI, L.A., N.J., Det.	15	1008	36	187	223	953	91	1	20	21	143		1973-74	1987-88
Lewis, Douglas	Mtl.	1	3	0	0	0	0	....	....	....	....	....		1946-47	1946-47
• Lewis, Herbie	Det.	11	483	148	161	309	248	38	13	10	23	6	2	1928-29	1938-39
Ley, Rick	Tor., Hfd.	6	310	12	72	84	528	14	0	2	2	20		1968-69	1980-81
Liba, Igor	NYR, L.A.	1	37	7	18	25	36	2	0	0	0	2		1988-89	1988-89
Libett, Nick	Det., K.C., Pit.	14	982	237	268	505	472	16	6	2	8	2		1967-68	1980-81
Licari, Anthony	Det.	1	9	0	1	1	0	....	....	....	....	....		1946-47	1946-47
Liddington, Bob	Tor.	1	11	0	1	1	2	....	....	....	....	....		1970-71	1970-71
Lindgren, Lars	Van., Min.	6	394	25	113	138	325	40	5	6	11	20		1978-79	1983-84
Lindholm, Mikael	L.A.	1	18	2	2	4	2	....	....	....	....	....		1989-90	1989-90
Lindsay, Ted	Det., Chi.	17	1068	379	472	851	1808	133	47	49	96	194	4	1944-45	1964-65
Lindstrom, Willy	Wpg., Edm., Pit.	8	582	161	162	323	200	57	14	18	32	24	2	1979-80	1986-87
Linseman, Ken	Phi., Edm., Bos., Tor.	14	860	256	551	807	1727	113	43	77	120	325	1	1978-79	1991-92
Liscombe, Carl	Det.	9	383	137	140	277	117	59	22	19	41	20	1	1937-38	1945-46
Litzenberger, Ed	Mtl., Chi., Det., Tor.	12	618	178	238	416	283	40	5	13	18	34	4	1952-53	1963-64
• Locas, Jacques	Mtl.	2	59	7	8	15	66	....	....	....	....	....		1947-48	1948-49
Lochead, Bill	NYR, Det., Col.	6	330	69	62	131	180	7	3	0	3	6		1974-75	1979-80
Locking, Norm	Chi.	2	48	2	6	8	26	1	0	0	0	0		1934-35	1935-36
Lofthouse, Mark	Wsh., Det.	6	181	42	38	80	73	....	....	....	....	....		1977-78	1982-83
Logan, Dave	Chi., Van.	6	218	5	29	34	470	12	0	0	0	10		1975-76	1980-81
Logan, Robert	Buf., L.A.	3	42	10	5	15	0	....	....	....	....	....		1986-87	1988-89
Long, Barry	L.A., Det., Wpg.	5	280	11	68	79	250	5	0	1	1	18		1972-73	1981-82
Long, Stanley	Mtl.	1	....	....	....	....	....	3	0	0	0	0		1951-52	1951-52
Lonsberry, Ross	Phi., Pit., Bos., L.A.	15	968	256	310	566	806	100	21	25	46	87	2	1966-67	1980-81
Loob, Hakan	Cgy.	6	450	193	236	429	189	73	26	28	54	16	1	1983-84	1988-89
Loob, Peter	Que.	1	8	1	2	3	0	....	....	....	....	....		1984-85	1984-85
Lorentz, Jim	NYR, Buf., Bos., St.L.	10	659	161	238	399	208	54	12	10	22	30	1	1968-69	1977-78
Lorimer, Bob	NYI, Col., N.J.	10	529	22	90	112	431	49	3	10	13	83	2	1976-77	1985-86
Lorraine, Rod	Mtl.	6	179	28	39	67	30	11	0	3	3	0		1935-36	1941-42
Loughlin, Clem	Det., Chi.	3	101	8	6	14	77	....	....	....	....	....		1926-27	1928-29

Name	NHL Teams	NHL Seasons	Regular Schedule GP	G	A	TP	PIM	Playoffs GP	G	A	TP	PIM	NHL Cup Wins	First NHL Season	Last NHL Season
Loughlin, Wilf	Tor.	1	14	0	0	0	2	....	....	....	....	....		1923-24	1923-24
Lovsin, Ken	Wsh.	1	1	0	0	0	0	....	....	....	....	....		1990-91	1990-91
Lowdermilk, Dwayne	Wsh.	1	2	0	1	1	2	....	....	....	....	....		1980-81	1980-81
Lowe, Darren	Pit.	1	8	1	2	3	0	....	....	....	....	....		1983-84	1983-84
Lowe, Norm	NYR	2	4	1	1	2	0	....	....	....	....	....		1948-49	1949-50
• Lowe, Ross	Bos., Mtl.	3	77	6	8	14	82	2	0	0	0	0		1949-50	1951-52
• Lowery, Fred	Mtl.M., Pit.	2	54	1	0	1	10	2	0	0	0	6	1	1924-25	1925-26
• Lowrey, Eddie	Ott., Ham.	3	24	2	0	2	3	....	....	....	....	....		1917-18	1920-21
• Lowrey, Gerry	Chi., Ott., Tor., Phi., Pit.	6	209	48	48	96	168	2	1	0	1	2		1927-28	1932-33
Lucas, Danny	Phi.	1	6	1	0	1	0	....	....	....	....	....		1978-79	1978-79
Lucas, Dave	Det.	1	1	0	0	0	0	....	....	....	....	....		1962-63	1962-63
Luce, Don	NYR, Det., Buf., L.A., Tor.	13	894	225	329	554	364	71	17	22	39	52		1969-70	1981-82
Ludvig, Jan	N.J., Buf.	7	314	54	87	141	418	....	....	....	....	....		1982-83	1988-89
Ludzik, Steve	Chi., Buf.	9	424	46	93	139	333	44	4	8	12	70		1981-82	1989-90
Lukowich, Bernie	Pit., St.L.	2	79	13	15	28	34	2	0	0	0	0		1973-74	1974-75
Lukowich, Morris	Wpg., Bos., L.A.	8	582	199	219	418	584	11	0	2	2	24		1979-80	1986-87
Luksa, Charlie	Hfd.	1	8	0	1	1	4	....	....	....	....	....		1979-80	1979-80
Lumley, Dave	Mtl., Edm., Hfd.	9	437	98	160	258	680	61	6	8	14	131	2	1978-79	1986-87
Lund, Pentti	NYR, Bos.	7	259	44	55	99	40	18	7	5	12	0		1946-47	1952-53
Lundberg, Brian	Pit.	1	1	0	0	0	2	....	....	....	....	....		1982-83	1982-83
Lunde, Len	Min., Van., Det., Chi.	8	321	39	83	122	75	20	3	2	5	2		1958-59	1970-71
Lundholm, Bengt	Wpg.	5	275	48	95	143	72	14	3	4	7	14		1981-82	1985-86
Lundrigan, Joe	Tor., Wsh.	2	52	2	8	10	22	....	....	....	....	....		1972-73	1974-75
Lundstrom, Tord	Det.	1	11	1	1	2	0	....	....	....	....	....		1973-74	1973-74
Lundy, Pat	Det. Chi.	5	150	37	32	69	31	9	1	1	2	2		1945-46	1950-51
Lupien, Gilles	Mtl., Pit., Hfd.	5	226	5	25	30	416	25	0	0	0	21	2	1977-78	1981-82
Lupul, Gary	Van.	7	293	70	75	145	243	25	4	7	11	11		1979-80	1985-86
Lyle, George	Det., Hfd.	4	99	24	38	62	51	....	....	....	....	....		1979-80	1982-83
Lynch, Jack	Pit., Det., Wsh.	7	382	24	106	130	336	....	....	....	....	....		1972-73	1978-79
Lynn, Vic	Det., Mtl., Tor., Bos., Chi.	10	326	49	76	125	274	47	7	10	17	46	3	1943-44	1953-54
Lyon, Steve	Pit.	1	3	0	0	0	2	....	....	....	....	....		1976-77	1976-77
Lyons, Ron	Bos., Phi.	1	36	2	4	6	29	5	0	0	0	0		1930-31	1930-31
Lysiak, Tom	Atl., Chi.	13	919	292	551	843	567	78	25	38	63	49		1973-74	1985-86

M

Name	NHL Teams	NHL Seasons	Regular Schedule GP	G	A	TP	PIM	Playoffs GP	G	A	TP	PIM	NHL Cup Wins	First NHL Season	Last NHL Season
MacAdam, Al	Phi., Cal., Cle., Min., Van.	12	864	240	351	591	509	64	20	24	44	21	1	1973-74	1984-85
MacDonald, Blair	Edm., Van.	4	219	91	100	191	65	11	0	6	6	2		1979-80	1982-83
MacDonald, Brett	Van.	1	1	0	0	0	0	....	....	....	....	....		1987-88	1987-88
• MacDonald, Kilby	NYR	4	151	36	34	70	47	15	1	2	3	4	1	1939-40	1944-45
MacDonald, Lowell	Det., L.A., Pit.	13	506	180	210	390	92	30	11	11	22	12		1961-62	1977-78
MacDonald, Parker	Tor., NYR, Det., Bos., Min.	14	676	144	179	323	253	75	14	14	28	20		1952-53	1968-69
MacDougall, Kim	Min.	1	1	0	0	0	0	....	....	....	....	....		1974-75	1974-75
MacEachern, Shane	St.L.	1	1	0	0	0	0	....	....	....	....	....		1987-88	1987-88
Macey, Hubert	NYR, Mtl.	3	30	6	9	15	0	8	0	0	0	0		1941-42	1946-47
MacGregor, Bruce	Det., NYR	14	893	213	257	470	217	107	19	28	47	44		1960-61	1973-74
MacGregor, Randy	Hfd.	1	2	1	1	2	2	....	....	....	....	....		1981-82	1981-82
MacGuigan, Garth	NYI	1	2	0	0	0	0	....	....	....	....	....		1979-80	1979-80
MacIntosh, Ian	NYR	1	4	0	0	0	4	....	....	....	....	....		1952-53	1952-53
MacIver, Don	Wpg.	1	6	0	0	0	2	....	....	....	....	....		1979-80	1979-80
MacKasey, Blair	Tor.	1	1	0	0	0	2	....	....	....	....	....		1976-77	1976-77
MacKay, Calum	Det., Mtl.	8	237	50	55	105	214	38	5	13	18	20	1	1946-47	1954-55
Mackay, Dave	Chi.	1	29	3	0	3	26	5	0	1	1	2		1940-41	1940-41
• MacKay, Mickey	Chi., Pit., Bos.	4	151	44	19	63	79	11	0	0	0	6	1	1926-27	1929-30
MacKay, Murdo	Mtl.	3	19	0	3	3	0	15	1	2	3	0		1945-46	1947-48
Mackell, Fleming	Tor., Bos.	13	665	149	220	369	562	80	22	41	63	75	2	1947-48	1959-60
MacKenzie, Barry	Min.	1	6	0	1	1	6	....	....	....	....	....		1968-69	1968-69
• MacKenzie, Bill	Chi., Mtl.(M),Mtl., NYR	7	266	15	14	29	133	19	1	1	2	11	1	1932-33	1939-40
MacKey, Reggie	NYR	1	34	0	0	0	16	1	0	0	0	0		1926-27	1926-27
Mackie, Howie	Det.	2	20	1	0	1	4	8	0	0	0	0	1	1936-37	1937-38
MacKinnon, Paul	Wsh.	5	147	5	23	28	91	....	....	....	....	....		1979-80	1983-84
MacLean, Paul	St.L., Wpg., Det.	11	719	324	349	673	968	53	21	14	35	104		1980-81	1990-91
MacLeish, Rick	Phi., Hfd., Pit., Det.	14	846	349	410	759	434	114	54	53	107	38	2	1970-71	1983-84
MacLellan, Brian	L.A., NYR, Min., Cgy., Det.	10	606	172	241	413	551	47	5	9	14	42		1982-83	1991-92
MacMillan, Billy	Tor., Atl., NYI	7	446	74	77	151	184	53	6	6	12	40		1970-71	1976-77
MacMillan, Bob	NYR, St.L., Atl., Cgy., Col., N.J., Chi.	11	753	228	349	577	260	31	8	11	19	16		1974-75	1984-85
MacMillan, John	Tor., Det.	5	104	5	10	15	32	12	0	1	1	2	2	1960-61	1964-65
MacNeil, Al	Tor., Mtl., Chi., NYR, Pit.	11	524	17	75	92	617	37	0	4	4	67		1955-56	1967-68
MacNeil, Bernie	St.L.	1	4	0	0	0	0	....	....	....	....	....		1973-74	1973-74
• MacPherson, Bud	Mtl.	7	259	5	33	38	233	29	0	3	3	21	1	1948-49	1956-57
MacSweyn, Ralph	Phi.	5	47	0	5	5	10	8	0	0	0	6		1967-68	1971-72
Madigan, Connie	St.L.	1	20	0	3	3	25	5	0	0	0	4		1972-73	1972-73
Magee, Dean	Min.	1	7	0	0	0	4	....	....	....	....	....		1977-78	1977-78
Maggs, Daryl	Chi., Cal., Tor.	3	135	14	19	33	54	4	0	0	0	0		1971-72	1979-80
Magnan, Marc	Tor.	1	4	0	1	1	5	....	....	....	....	....		1982-83	1982-83
Magnuson, Keith	Chi.	11	589	14	125	139	1442	68	3	9	12	164		1969-70	1979-80
Maguire, Kevin	Tor., Buf., Phi.	6	260	29	30	59	782	11	0	0	0	86		1986-87	1991-92
Mahaffy, John	Mtl., NYR	3	37	11	25	36	4	1	0	1	1	0		1942-43	1944-45
Mahovlich, Frank	Tor., Det., Mtl.	18	1181	533	570	1103	1056	137	51	67	118	163	6	1956-57	1973-74
Mahovlich, Pete	Det., Mtl., Pit.	16	884	288	485	773	916	88	30	42	72	134	4	1965-66	1980-81
Mailhot, Jacques	Que.	1	5	0	0	0	33	....	....	....	....	....		1988-89	1988-89
Mailley, Frank	Mtl.	1	1	0	0	0	0	....	....	....	....	....		1942-43	1942-43
Mair, Jim	Phi., NYI, Van.	5	76	4	15	19	49	3	1	2	3	4		1970-71	1974-75
• Majeau, Fern	Mtl.	2	56	22	24	46	43	1	0	0	0	0	1	1943-44	1944-45
Major, Bruce	Que.	1	4	0	0	0	0	....	....	....	....	....		1990-91	1990-91
Maki, Chico	Chi.	15	841	143	292	435	345	113	17	36	53	43	1	1960-61	1975-76
• Maki, Wayne	Chi., St.L., Van.	6	246	57	79	136	184	2	1	0	1	2		1967-68	1972-73
Makkonen, Karl	Edm.	1	9	2	2	4	0	....	....	....	....	....		1979-80	1979-80
Malinowski, Merlin	Col., N.J., Hfd.	5	282	54	111	165	121	....	....	....	....	....		1978-79	1982-83
Malone, Cliff	Mtl.	1	3	0	0	0	0	....	....	....	....	....		1951-52	1951-52
Malone, Greg	Pit., Hfd., Que.	11	704	191	310	501	661	20	3	5	8	32		1976-77	1986-87
• Malone, Joe	Mtl., Que., Ham.	7	125	146	21	167	23	9	5	0	5	0	1	1917-18	1923-24
Maloney, Dan	Chi., L.A., Det., Tor.	11	737	192	259	451	1489	40	4	7	11	35		1970-71	1981-82
Maloney, Dave	NYR, Buf.	11	657	71	246	317	1154	49	7	17	24	91		1974-75	1984-85
Maloney, Don	NYR, Hfd., NYI	13	765	214	350	564	815	94	22	35	57	101		1978-79	1990-91
Maloney, Phil	Bos., Tor., Chi.	5	158	28	43	71	16	6	0	0	0	0		1949-50	1959-60
Maluta, Ray	Bos.	2	25	2	3	5	6	2	0	0	0	0		1975-76	1976-77
Manastersky, Tom	Mtl.	1	6	0	0	0	11	....	....	....	....	....		1950-51	1950-51
Mancuso, Gus	Mtl., NYR	4	42	7	9	16	17	....	....	....	....	....		1937-38	1942-43
Mandich, Dan	Min.	4	111	5	11	16	303	7	0	0	0	2		1982-83	1985-86
Manery, Kris	Van., Wpg., Clev., Min.	4	250	63	64	127	91	....	....	....	....	....		1977-78	1980-81
Manery, Randy	L.A., Det., Atl.	10	582	50	206	256	415	13	0	2	2	12		1970-71	1979-80
Mann, Jack	NYR	2	9	3	4	7	0	....	....	....	....	....		1943-44	1944-45
Mann, Jimmy	Wpg., Que., Pit.	8	293	10	20	30	895	22	0	0	0	89		1979-80	1987-88
Mann, Ken	Det.	1	1	0	0	0	0	....	....	....	....	....		1975-76	1975-76
Mann, Norm	Tor.	2	31	0	3	3	4	1	0	0	0	0		1938-39	1940-41
Manners, Rennison	Pit., Phi.	2	37	3	2	5	14	....	....	....	....	....		1929-30	1930-31
Manno, Bob	Van., Tor., Det.	8	371	41	131	172	274	17	2	4	6	12		1976-77	1984-85
Manson, Ray	Bos., NYR	2	2	0	1	1	0	....	....	....	....	....		1947-48	1948-49
• Mantha, Georges	Mtl.	13	498	89	102	181	148	36	6	2	8	16	2	1928-29	1940-41
Mantha, Moe	Wpg., Pit., Edm., Min., Phi.	12	656	81	289	370	501	17	5	10	15	18		1980-81	1991-92
• Mantha, Sylvio	Mtl., Bos.	14	543	63	72	135	667	46	5	4	9	66	3	1923-24	1936-37
Maracle, Buddy	NYR	1	11	1	3	4	4	4	0	0	0	0		1930-31	1930-31
Marcetta, Milan	Tor., Min.	3	54	7	15	22	10	17	7	7	14	4	1	1966-67	1968-69
March, Mush	Chi.	17	758	153	230	383	540	48	12	15	27	41	2	1928-29	1944-45
Marchinko, Brian	Tor., NYI	4	47	2	6	8	0	....	....	....	....	....		1970-71	1973-74
Marcon, Lou	Det.	3	70	0	4	4	42	....	....	....	....	....		1958-59	1962-63
Marcotte, Don	Bos.	15	868	230	255	485	317	.132	34	27	61	81	2	1965-66	1981-82
Marini, Hector	NYI, N.J.	5	154	27	46	73	246	10	3	6	9	14	2	1978-79	1983-84
Mario, Frank	Bos.	2	53	9	19	28	24	....	....	....	....	....		1941-42	1944-45
• Mariucci, John	Chi.	5	223	11	34	45	308	8	0	3	3	26		1940-41	1947-48
Mark, Gordon	N.J.	2	55	3	7	10	109	....	....	....	....	....		1986-87	1987-88
Markell, John	Wpg., St. L., Min.	4	55	11	10	21	36	....	....	....	....	....		1979-80	1984-85

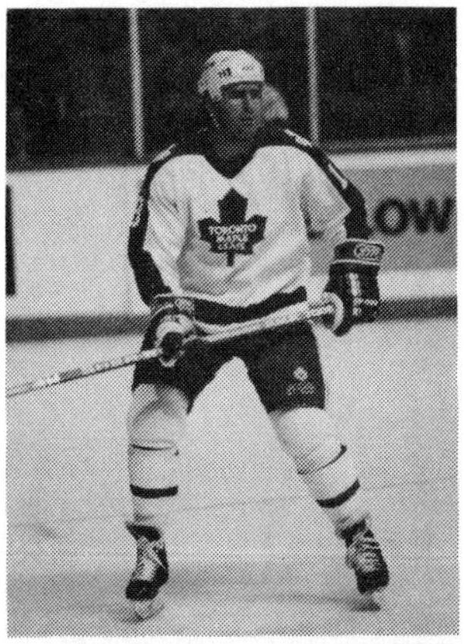

Kevin Maguire

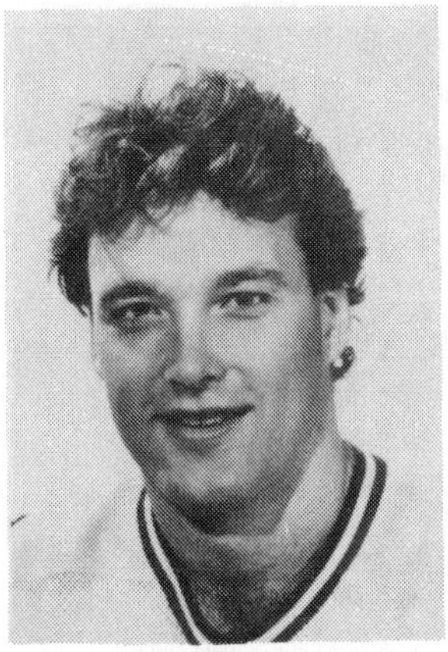

Dan Mandich

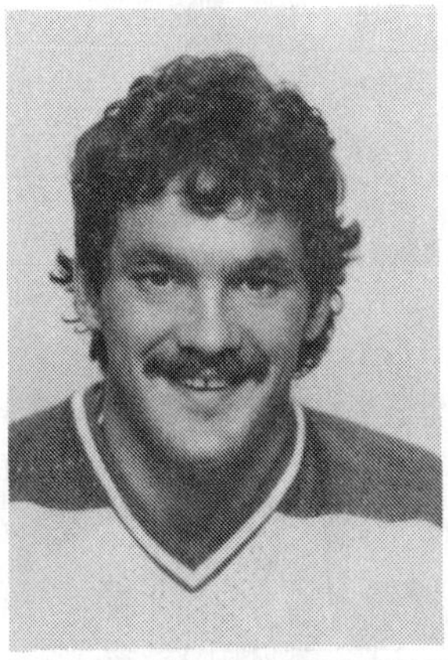

Jimmy Mann

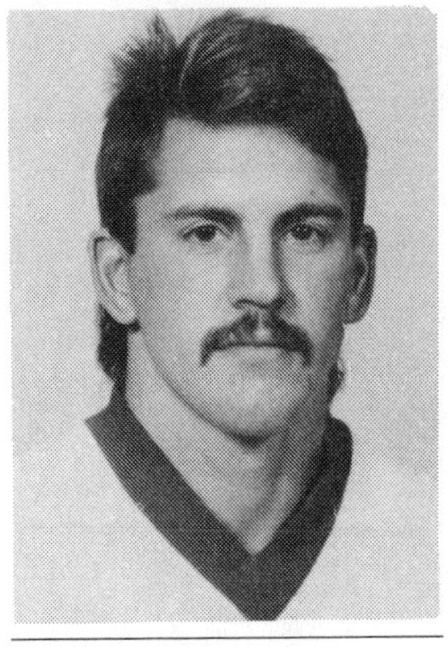

Steve Martinson

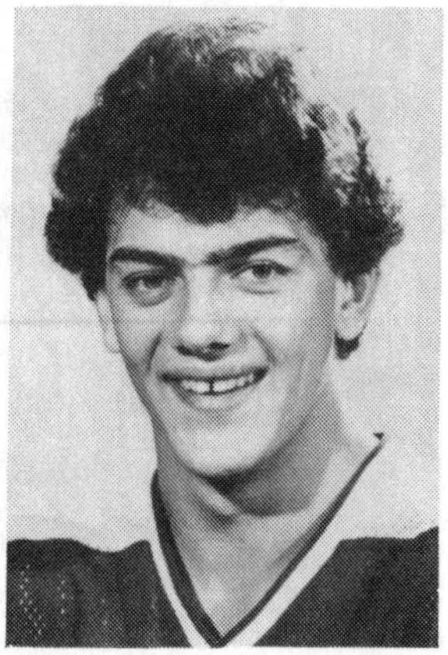

Tom McCarthy

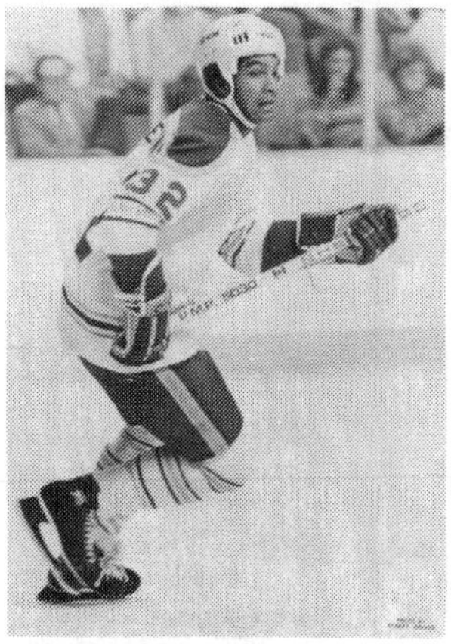

Tony McKegney

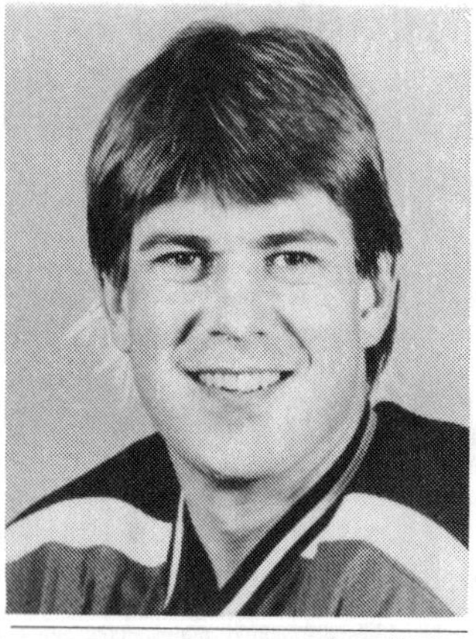

Peter McNab

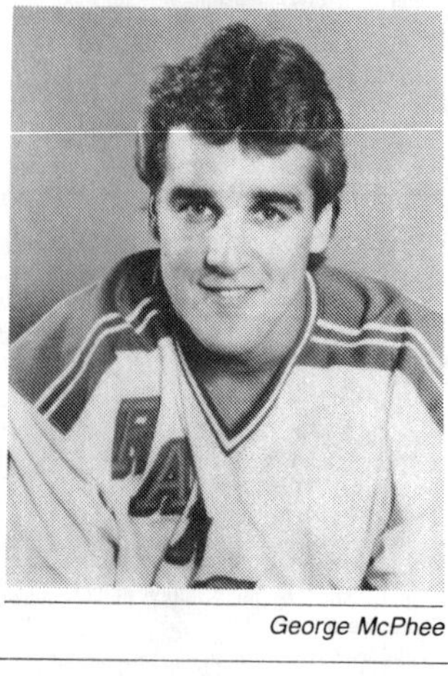

George McPhee

Name	NHL Teams	NHL Seasons	Regular Schedule GP	G	A	TP	PIM	Playoffs GP	G	A	TP	PIM	NHL Cup Wins	First NHL Season	Last NHL Season
Marker, Gus	Det., Mtl.M., Tor., Bro.	10	336	64	69	133	133	45	6	8	14	36	1	1932-33	1941-42
Markham, Ray	NYR	1	14	1	1	2	21	7	1	0	1	24		1979-80	1979-80
Markle, Jack	Tor.	1	8	0	1	1	0	....	....	....	....	....		1935-36	1935-36
• Marks, Jack	Mtl.W, Tor., Que.	2	7	0	0	0	4	....	....	....	....	....	1	1917-18	1919-20
Marks, John	Chi.	10	657	112	163	275	330	57	5	9	14	60		1972-73	1981-82
Markwart, Nevin	Bos., Cgy.	8	309	41	68	109	794	19	1	0	1	33		1983-84	1991-92
Marotte, Gilles	Bos., Chi., L.A., NYR, St.L.	12	808	56	265	321	872	29	3	3	6	26		1965-66	1976-77
Marquess, Mark	Bos.	1	27	5	4	9	27	4	0	0	0	0		1946-47	1946-47
Marsh, Gary	Det., Tor.	2	7	1	3	4	4	....	....	....	....	....		1967-68	1968-69
Marsh, Peter	Wpg., Chi.	5	278	48	71	119	224	26	1	5	6	33		1979-80	1983-84
Marshall, Bert	Det., Oak., Cal., NYR, NYI	14	868	17	181	198	926	72	4	22	26	99		1965-66	1978-79
Marshall, Don	Mtl., NYR, Buf., Tor.	19	1176	265	324	589	127	94	8	15	23	14	5	1951-52	1971-72
Marshall, Paul	Pit., Tor., Hfd.	4	95	15	18	33	17	1	0	0	0	0		1979-80	1982-83
Marshall, Willie	Tor.	4	33	1	15	16	2	....	....	....	....	....		1952-53	1958-59
Marson, Mike	Wsh., L.A.	6	196	24	24	48	233	....	....	....	....	....		1974-75	1979-80
Martin, Clare	Bos., Det., Chi., NYR	6	237	12	28	40	78	22	0	2	2	6	1	1941-42	1951-52
Martin, Frank	Bos., Chi.	6	282	11	46	57	122	10	0	1	1	2		1952-53	1957-58
Martin, Grant	Van., Wsh.	4	44	0	4	4	55	1	1	0	1	2		1983-84	1986-87
Martin, Jack	Tor.	1	1	0	0	0	0	....	....	....	....	....		1960-61	1960-61
Martin, Pit	Det., Bos., Chi., Van.	17	1101	324	485	809	609	100	27	31	58	56		1961-62	1978-79
Martin, Rick	Buf., L.A.	11	685	384	317	701	477	63	24	29	53	74		1971-72	1981-82
Martin, Ron	NYA	2	94	13	16	29	36	....	....	....	....	....		1932-33	1933-34
Martin, Terry	Buf., Que., Tor., Edm., Min.	10	479	104	101	205	202	21	4	2	6	26		1975-76	1984-85
Martin, Tom	Wpg., Hfd., Min.	6	92	12	11	23	249	4	0	0	0	6		1984-85	1989-90
Martin, Tom	Tor.	1	3	1	0	1	0	....	....	....	....	....		1967-68	1967-68
Martineau, Don	Atl., Min., Det.	4	90	6	10	16	63	....	....	....	....	....		1973-74	1976-77
Martinson, Steven	Det., Mtl., Min.	4	49	2	1	3	244	1	0	0	0	10		1987-88	1991-92
Maruk, Dennis	Cal., Clev., Min., Wsh.	14	888	356	522	878	761	34	14	22	36	26		1975-76	1988-89
Masnick, Paul	Mtl., Chi., Tor.	6	232	18	41	59	139	33	4	5	9	27	1	1950-51	1957-58
Mason, Charley	NYR, NYA, Det., Chi.	4	95	7	18	25	44	4	0	1	1	0		1934-35	1938-39
Massecar, George	NYA	3	100	12	11	23	46	....	....	....	....	....		1929-30	1931-32
Masters, Jamie	St.L.	3	33	1	13	14	2	2	0	0	0	0		1975-76	1978-79
• Masterton, Bill	Min.	1	38	4	8	12	4	....	....	....	....	....		1967-68	1967-68
Mathers, Frank	Tor.	3	23	1	3	4	4	....	....	....	....	....		1948-49	1951-52
Mathiasen, Dwight	Pit.	3	33	1	7	8	18	....	....	....	....	....		1985-86	1987-88
• Matte, Joe	Tor., Ham., Bos., Mtl.	4	64	18	14	32	43	....	....	....	....	....		1919-20	1925-26
Matte, Joe	Chi.	1	12	0	1	1	0	....	....	....	....	....		1942-43	1942-43
Matte, Roland	Det.	1	12	0	1	1	0	....	....	....	....	....		1929-30	1929-30
Mattiussi, Dick	Pit., Oak., Cal.	4	200	8	31	39	124	8	0	1	1	6		1967-68	1970-71
Matz, Johnny	Mtl.	1	30	3	2	5	0	5	0	0	0	2		1924-25	1924-25
Maxner, Wayne	Bos.	2	62	8	9	17	48	....	....	....	....	....		1964-65	1965-66
Maxwell, Brad	Min., Que., Tor., Van., NYR	10	612	98	270	368	1292	79	12	49	61	178		1977-78	1986-87
Maxwell, Bryan	Min., St.L., Wpg., Pit.	8	331	18	77	95	745	15	1	1	2	86		1977-78	1984-85
Maxwell, Kevin	Min., Col., N.J.	3	66	6	15	21	61	16	3	4	7	24		1980-81	1983-84
Maxwell, Wally	Tor.	1	2	0	0	0	0	....	....	....	....	....		1952-53	1952-53
Mayer, Jim	NYR	1	4	0	0	0	0	....	....	....	....	....		1979-80	1979-80
Mayer, Pat	Pit.	1	1	0	0	0	4	....	....	....	....	....		1987-88	1987-88
Mayer, Shep	Tor.	1	12	1	2	3	4	....	....	....	....	....		1942-43	1942-43
Mazur, Eddie	Mtl., Chi.	6	107	8	20	28	120	25	4	5	9	22	1	1950-51	1956-57
McAdam, Gary	Buf., Pit., Det., Cal., Wsh., N.J., Tor.	11	534	96	132	228	243	30	6	5	11	16		1975-76	1985-86
McAdam, Sam	NYR	1	5	0	0	0	0	....	....	....	....	....		1930-31	1930-31
McAndrew, Hazen	Bro.	1	7	0	1	1	6	....	....	....	....	....		1941-42	1941-42
McAneeley, Ted	Cal.	3	158	8	35	43	141	....	....	....	....	....		1972-73	1974-75
McAtee, Jud	Det.	3	46	15	13	28	6	14	2	1	3	0		1942-43	1944-45
McAtee, Norm	Bos.	1	13	0	1	1	0	....	....	....	....	....		1946-47	1946-47
McAvoy, George	Mtl.	1	....	....	....	....	....	4	0	0	0	0		1954-55	1954-55
McBride, Cliff	Mtl.M., Tor.	2	2	0	0	0	0	....	....	....	....	....		1928-29	1929-30
McBurney, Jim	Chi.	1	1	0	1	1	0	....	....	....	....	....		1952-53	1952-53
McCabe, Stan	Det., Mtl.M.	4	78	9	4	13	49	....	....	....	....	....		1929-30	1933-34
• McCaffrey, Bert	Tor., Pit., Mtl.	7	260	42	30	72	202	8	2	1	3	12		1924-25	1930-31
McCahill, John	Col.	1	1	0	0	0	0	....	....	....	....	....		1977-78	1977-78
McCaig, Douglas	Det., Chi.	7	263	8	21	29	255	17	0	1	1	8		1941-42	1950-51
• McCallum, Dunc	NYR, Pit.	5	187	14	35	49	230	10	1	2	3	12		1965-66	1970-71
McCalmon, Eddie	Chi., Phi.	2	39	5	0	5	14	....	....	....	....	....		1927-28	1930-31
McCann, Rick	Det.	6	43	1	4	5	6	....	....	....	....	....		1967-68	1974-75
McCarthy, Dan	NYR	1	5	4	0	4	4	....	....	....	....	....		1980-81	1980-81
McCarthy, Kevin	Phi., Van., Pit.	10	537	67	191	258	527	21	2	3	5	20		1977-78	1986-87
• McCarthy, Tom	Que., Ham.	2	34	19	3	22	10	....	....	....	....	....		1919-20	1920-21
McCarthy, Tom	Det., Bos.	4	60	8	9	17	8	....	....	....	....	....		1956-57	1960-61
McCarthy, Tom	Min., Bos.	9	460	178	221	399	330	68	12	26	38	67		1979-80	1987-88
McCartney, Walt	Mtl.	1	2	0	0	0	0	....	....	....	....	....		1932-33	1932-33
McCaskill, Ted	Min.	1	4	0	2	2	0	....	....	....	....	....		1967-68	1967-68
McClanahan, Rob	Buf., Hfd., NYR	5	224	38	63	101	126	34	4	12	16	31		1979-80	1983-84
McCord, Bob	Bos., Det., Min., St.L.	7	316	58	68	126	262	14	2	5	7	10		1963-64	1972-73
McCord, Dennis	Van.	1	3	0	0	0	0	....	....	....	....	....		1973-74	1973-74
McCormack, John	Tor., Mtl., Chi.	8	311	25	49	74	35	22	1	1	2	0	1	1947-48	1954-55
McCourt, Dale	Det., Buf., Tor.	7	532	194	284	478	124	21	9	7	16	6		1977-78	1983-84
McCreary, Bill	Tor.	1	12	1	0	1	4	....	....	....	....	....		1980-81	1980-81
McCreary, Bill E.	NYR, Det., Mtl., St.L.	10	309	53	62	115	108	48	6	16	22	14		1953-54	1970-71
McCreary, Keith	Mtl., Pit., Atl.	10	532	131	112	243	294	16	0	4	4	6		1961-62	1974-75
• McCreedy, Johnny	Tor.	2	64	17	12	29	25	21	4	3	7	16	2	1941-42	1944-45
McCrimmon, Jim	St.L.	1	2	0	0	0	0	....	....	....	....	....		1974-75	1974-75
McCulley, Bob	Mtl.	1	1	0	0	0	0	....	....	....	....	....		1934-35	1934-35
McCurry, Duke	Pit.	4	148	21	11	32	119	4	0	2	2	4		1925-26	1928-29
McCutcheon, Brian	Det.	3	37	3	1	4	7	....	....	....	....	....		1974-75	1976-77
McCutheon, Darwin	Tor.	1	1	0	0	0	0	....	....	....	....	....		1981-82	1981-82
McDill, Jeff	Chi.	1	1	0	0	0	0	....	....	....	....	....		1976-77	1976-77
McDonagh, Bill	NYR	1	4	0	0	0	2	....	....	....	....	....		1949-50	1949-50
McDonald, Ab	Mtl., Chi., Bos., Det., Pit., St.L.	15	762	182	248	430	200	84	21	29	50	42	4	1957-58	1971-72
McDonald, Brian	Chi., Buf.	2	12	0	0	0	29	8	0	0	0	2		1967-68	1970-71
• McDonald, Bucko	Det., Tor., NYR	11	448	35	88	123	206	63	6	1	7	24	3	1934-35	1944-45
McDonald, Butch	Det., Chi.	2	66	8	20	28	2	5	0	2	2	10		1939-40	1944-45
McDonald, Gerry	Hfd.	1	3	0	0	0	0	....	....	....	....	....		1981-82	1981-82
• McDonald, Jack	Mtl.W, Mtl., Que., Tor.	5	73	27	11	38	13	12	2	0	2	0		1917-18	1921-22
McDonald, John	NYR	1	43	10	9	19	6	....	....	....	....	....		1943-44	1943-44
McDonald, Lanny	Tor., Col., Cgy.	16	1111	500	506	1006	899	117	44	40	84	120	1	1973-74	1988-89
McDonald, Robert	NYR	1	1	0	0	0	0	....	....	....	....	....		1943-44	1943-44
McDonald, Terry	K.C.	1	8	0	1	1	6	....	....	....	....	....		1975-76	1975-76
McDonnell, Joe	Van., Pit.	3	50	2	10	12	34	....	....	....	....	....		1981-82	1985-86
• McDonnell, Moylan	Ham.	1	20	1	1	2	0	....	....	....	....	....		1920-21	1920-21
McDonough, Al	L.A., Pit., Atl., Det.	5	237	73	88	161	73	8	0	1	1	2		1970-71	1977-78
McDougal, Mike	NYR, Hfd.	4	61	8	10	18	43	....	....	....	....	....		1978-79	1982-83
McElmury, Jim	Min., K.C., Col.	5	180	14	47	61	49	....	....	....	....	....		1972-73	1977-78
McEwen, Mike	NYR, Col., NYI, L.A., Wsh., Det., Hfd.	12	716	108	296	404	460	78	12	36	48	48	3	1976-77	1987-88
McFadden, Jim	Det., Chi.	7	412	100	126	226	89	49	10	9	19	30	1	1947-48	1953-54
McFadyen, Don	Chi.	4	179	12	33	45	77	12	2	2	4	5	1	1932-33	1935-36
McFall, Dan	Wpg.	2	9	0	1	1	0	....	....	....	....	....		1984-85	1985-86
McFarland, George	Chi.	1	2	0	0	0	0	....	....	....	....	....		1926-27	1926-27
McGeough, Jim	Wsh., Pit.	4	57	7	10	17	32	....	....	....	....	....		1981-82	1986-87
McGibbon, John	Mtl.	1	1	0	0	0	2	....	....	....	....	....		1942-43	1942-43
McGill, Jack	Mtl.	3	134	27	10	37	71	3	2	0	2	0		1934-35	1936-37
McGill, Jack G.	Bos.	4	97	23	36	59	42	27	7	4	11	17		1941-42	1946-47
McGregor, Sandy	NYR	1	2	0	0	0	2	....	....	....	....	....		1963-64	1963-64
McGuire, Mickey	Pit.	2	36	3	0	3	6	....	....	....	....	....		1926-27	1927-28
McIlhargey, Jack	Phi., Van., Hfd.	8	393	11	36	47	1102	27	0	3	3	68		1974-75	1981-82
McInenly, Bert	Det., NYA, Ott., Bos.	6	166	19	15	34	144	4	0	0	0	2		1930-31	1935-36
McIntosh, Bruce	Min.	1	2	0	0	0	0	....	....	....	....	....		1972-73	1972-73
McIntosh, Paul	Buf.	2	48	0	0	2	66	2	0	0	0	7		1974-75	1975-76
McIntyre, Jack	Bos., Chi., Det.	11	499	109	102	211	173	29	7	6	13	4		1949-50	1959-60
McIntyre, Larry	Tor.	2	41	0	3	3	26	....	....	....	....	....		1969-70	1972-73
McKay, Doug	Det.	1	....	....	....	....	....	1	0	0	0	0	1	1949-50	1949-50
McKay, Ray	Chi., Buf., Cal.	6	140	2	16	18	102	....	....	....	....	....		1968-69	1973-74
McKechnie, Walt	Min., Cal., Bos., Det., Wsh., Clev., Tor., Col.	16	955	214	392	606	469	15	7	5	12	9		1967-68	1982-83
McKegney, Ian	Chi.	1	3	0	0	0	2	....	....	....	....	....		1976-77	1976-77

Name	NHL Teams	NHL Seasons	Regular Schedule					Playoffs					NHL Cup Wins	First NHL Season	Last NHL Season
			GP	G	A	TP	PIM	GP	G	A	TP	PIM			
McKegney, Tony	Buf., Que., Min., NYR, St. L., Det., Chi.	13	912	320	319	639	517	79	24	23	47	56		1978-79	1990-91
• McKell, Jack	Ott.	2	42	4	1	5	42	9	0	0	0	0	1	1919-20	1920-21
McKendry, Alex	NYI, Cgy.	4	46	3	6	9	21	6	2	2	4	0	1	1977-78	1980-81
McKenna, Sean	Buf., L.A., Tor.	9	414	82	80	162	181	15	1	2	3	2		1981-82	1989-90
McKenney, Don	Bos., NYR, Tor., Det., St.L.	13	798	237	345	582	211	58	18	29	47	10	1	1954-55	1967-68
McKenny, Jim	Tor., Min.	14	604	82	247	329	294	37	7	9	16	10		1965-66	1978-79
McKenzie, Brian	Pit.	1	6	1	1	2	4	....	....	....	....	....		1971-72	1971-72
McKenzie, John	Chi., Det., NYR, Bos.	12	691	206	268	474	917	69	15	32	47	133	2	1958-59	1971-72
McKinnon, Alex	Ham., NYA, Chi.	5	194	19	10	29	235	....	....	....	....	....		1924-25	1928-29
McKinnon, Bob	Chi.	1	2	0	0	0	0	....	....	....	....	....		1928-29	1928-29
• McKinnon, John	Mtl., Pit., Phi.	6	218	28	11	39	224	2	0	0	0	4		1925-26	1930-31
McLean, Don	Wsh.	1	9	0	0	0	6	....	....	....	....	....		1975-76	1975-76
• McLean, Fred	Que., Ham.	2	9	0	0	0	2	....	....	....	....	....		1919-20	1920-21
McLean, Jack	Tor.	3	67	14	24	38	76	13	2	2	4	8	1	1942-43	1944-45
• McLellan, John	Tor.	1	2	0	0	0	0	....	....	....	....	....		1951-52	1951-52
McLellan, Scott	Bos.	1	2	0	0	0	0	....	....	....	....	....		1982-83	1982-83
McLellan, Todd	NYI	1	5	1	1	2	0	....	....	....	....	....		1987-88	1987-88
McLenahan, Roly	Det.	1	9	2	1	3	10	2	0	0	0	0		1945-46	1945-46
McLeod, Al	Det.	1	26	2	2	4	24	....	....	....	....	....		1973-74	1973-74
McLeod, Jackie	NYR	5	106	14	23	37	12	7	0	0	0	0		1949-50	1954-55
McMahon, Mike	NYR, Min., Chi., Det., Pit., Buf.	8	224	15	68	83	171	14	3	7	10	4		1963-64	1971-72
• McMahon, Mike C.	Mtl., Bos.	3	57	7	18	25	102	13	1	2	3	30	1	1942-43	1945-46
McManama, Bob	Pit.	3	99	11	25	36	28	8	0	1	1	6		1973-74	1975-76
McManus, Sammy	Mtl.M., Bos.	2	26	0	1	1	8	1	0	0	0	0	1	1934-35	1936-37
McMurchy, Tom	Chi., Edm.	4	55	8	4	12	65	....	....	....	....	....		1983-84	1987-88
McNab, Max	Det.	4	128	16	19	35	24	25	1	0	1	4	1	1947-48	1950-51
McNab, Peter	Buf., Bos., Van., N.J.	14	954	363	450	813	179	107	40	42	82	20		1973-74	1986-87
McNabney, Sid	Mtl.	1	....	....	....	....	....	5	0	1	1	2		1950-51	1950-51
• McNamara, Howard	Mtl.	1	11	1	0	1	2	....	....	....	....	....		1919-20	1919-20
• McNaughton, George	Que.B.	1	1	0	0	0	0	....	....	....	....	....		1919-20	1919-20
McNeill, Billy	Det.	6	257	21	46	67	142	4	1	1	2	4		1956-57	1963-64
McNeill, Stu	Det.	3	10	1	1	2	2	....	....	....	....	....		1957-58	1959-60
McPhee, George	NYR, N.J.	7	115	24	25	49	257	29	5	3	8	69		1982-83	1988-89
McRae, Chris		0	21	1	0	1	122	....	....	....	....	....			
McReavy, Pat	Bos., Det.	4	55	5	10	15	4	20	3	3	6	9	1	1938-39	1941-42
McSheffrey, Bryan	Van., Buf.	3	90	13	7	20	44	....	....	....	....	....		1972-73	1974-75
McTaggart, Jim	Wsh.	2	71	3	10	13	205	....	....	....	....	....		1980-81	1981-82
McTavish, Gordon	St.L., Wpg.	2	11	1	3	4	2	....	....	....	....	....		1978-79	1979-80
McVeigh, Charley	Chi., NYA	9	397	84	88	172	138	4	0	0	0	2		1926-27	1934-35
McVicar, Jack	Mtl.M.	2	88	2	4	6	63	2	0	0	0	2		1930-31	1931-32
Meagher, Rick	Mtl., Hfd., N.J., St.L.	12	691	144	165	309	383	62	8	7	15	41		1979-80	1990-91
Meehan, Gerry	Tor., Phi., Buf., Van., Atl., Wsh.	10	670	180	243	423	111	10	0	1	1	0		1968-69	1978-79
Meeke, Brent	Cal., Clev.	5	75	9	22	31	8	....	....	....	....	....		1972-73	1976-77
Meeker, Howie	Tor.	8	346	83	102	185	329	42	6	9	15	50	4	1946-47	1953-54
Meeker, Mike	Pit.	1	4	0	0	0	5	....	....	....	....	....		1978-79	1978-79
• Meeking, Harry	Tor., Det., Bos.	3	63	18	3	21	42	14	4	2	6	0	1	1917-18	1926-27
Meger, Paul	Mtl.	6	212	39	52	91	112	35	3	8	11	16	1	1949-50	1954-55
Meighan, Ron	Min., Pit.	2	48	3	7	10	18	....	....	....	....	....		1981-82	1982-83
Meissner, Barrie	Min.	2	6	0	1	1	4	....	....	....	....	....		1967-68	1968-69
Meissner, Dick	Bos., NYR	5	171	11	15	26	37	....	....	....	....	....		1959-60	1964-65
Melametsa, Anssi	Wpg.	1	27	0	3	3	2	....	....	....	....	....		1985-86	1985-86
Melin, Roger	Min.	2	3	0	0	0	0	....	....	....	....	....		1980-81	1981-82
Mellor, Tom	Det.	2	26	2	4	6	25	....	....	....	....	....		1973-74	1974-75
Melnyk, Gerry	Det., Chi., St.L.	6	269	39	77	116	34	53	6	6	12	6		1955-56	1967-68
Melnyk, Larry	Bos., Edm., NYR, Van.	10	432	11	63	74	686	66	2	9	11	127	1	1980-81	1989-90
Melrose, Barry	Wpg., Tor., Det.	6	300	10	23	33	728	7	0	2	2	38		1979-80	1985-86
Menard, Hillary	Chi.	1	1	0	0	0	0	....	....	....	....	....		1953-54	1953-54
Menard, Howie	Det., L.A., Chi., Oak.	4	151	23	42	65	87	19	3	7	10	36		1963-64	1969-70
Mercredi, Vic	Atl.	1	2	0	0	0	0	....	....	....	....	....		1974-75	1974-75
Meredith, Greg	Cgy.	2	38	6	4	10	8	5	3	1	4	4		1980-81	1982-83
Merkosky, Glenn	Hfd., N.J., Det.	4	63	5	12	17	22	....	....	....	....	....		1981-82	1985-86
Merkosky, Glenn	Hfd., N.J., Det.	5	66	5	12	17	22	....	....	....	....	....		1981-82	1989-90
Meronek, Bill	Mtl.	2	19	5	8	13	0	1	0	0	0	0		1939-40	1942-43
Merrick, Wayne	St.L., Cal., Clev., NYI	12	774	191	265	456	303	102	19	30	49	30	4	1972-73	1983-84
• Merrill, Horace	Ott.	2	11	0	0	0	0	....	....	....	....	....	1	1917-18	1919-20
Messier, Paul	Col.	1	9	0	0	0	4	....	....	....	....	....		1978-79	1978-79
Metcalfe, Scott	Edm., Buf.	3	19	1	2	3	18	....	....	....	....	....		1987-88	1989-90
Metz, Don	Tor.	8	172	20	35	55	42	47	7	8	15	10	5	1939-40	1948-49
• Metz, Nick	Tor.	12	518	131	119	250	149	76	19	20	39	31	4	1934-35	1947-48
Michaluk, Art	Chi.	1	5	0	0	0	0	....	....	....	....	....		1947-48	1947-48
Michaluk, John	Chi.	1	1	0	0	0	0	....	....	....	....	....		1950-51	1950-51
Michayluk, Dave	Phi.	2	14	2	6	8	8	....	....	....	....	....		1981-82	1982-83
Micheletii, Pat	Min.	1	12	2	0	2	8	....	....	....	....	....		1987-88	1987-88
Micheletti, Joe	St.L., Col.	3	158	11	60	71	114	11	1	11	12	10		1979-80	1981-82
• Mickey, Larry	Chi., NYR., Tor., Mtl., L.A., Phi., Buf.	11	292	39	53	92	160	9	1	0	1	10		1964-65	1974-75
Mickoski, Nick	NYR, Chi., Det., Bos.	13	703	158	184	342	319	18	1	6	7	6		1947-48	1959-60
Middleton, Rick	NYR, Bos.	14	1005	448	540	988	157	114	45	55	100	19		1974-75	1987-88
Migay, Rudy	Tor.	10	418	59	92	151	293	15	1	0	1	20		1949-50	1959-60
Mikita, Stan	Chi.	22	1394	541	926	1467	1270	155	59	91	150	169	1	1958-59	1979-80
Mikkelson, Bill	L.A., N.Y.I., Wsh.	4	147	4	18	22	105	....	....	....	....	....		1971-72	1976-77
Mikol, Jim	Tor., NYR	2	34	1	4	5	8	....	....	....	....	....		1962-63	1964-65
Milbury, Mike	Bos.	12	754	49	189	238	1552	86	4	24	28	219		1975-76	1986-87
• Milks, Hib	Pit., Phi., NYR, Ott.	8	314	87	41	128	179	10	0	0	0	2		1925-26	1932-33
Millar, Hugh	Det.	1	4	0	0	0	0	1	0	0	0	0		1946-47	1946-47
Millar, Mike	Hfd., Wsh., Bos., Tor.	5	78	18	18	36	12	....	....	....	....	....		1986-87	1990-91
Miller, Bill	Mtl.M., Mtl.	3	95	7	3	10	16	12	0	0	0	0	1	1934-35	1936-37
Miller, Bob	Bos., Col., L.A.	6	404	75	119	194	220	36	4	7	11	27		1977-78	1984-85
• Miller, Earl	Chi., Tor.	5	116	19	14	33	124	10	1	0	1	6	1	1927-28	1931-32
Miller, Jack	Chi.	2	17	0	0	0	4	....	....	....	....	....		1949-50	1950-51
Miller, Jay	Bos., L.A.	7	446	40	44	84	1723	48	2	3	5	243		1985-86	1991-92
Miller, Paul	Col.	1	3	0	3	3	0	....	....	....	....	....		1981-82	1981-82
Miller, Perry	Det.	4	217	10	51	61	387	....	....	....	....	....		1977-78	1980-81
Miller, Tom	Det., NYI	4	118	16	25	41	34	....	....	....	....	....		1970-71	1974-75
Miller, Warren	NYR, Hfd.	4	262	40	50	90	137	6	1	0	1	0		1979-80	1982-83
Miner, John	Edm.	1	14	2	3	5	16	....	....	....	....	....		1987-88	1987-88
Minor, Gerry	Van.	5	140	11	21	32	173	12	1	3	4	25		1979-80	1983-84
Miszuk, John	Det., Chi., Phi., Min.	6	237	7	39	46	232	19	0	3	3	19		1963-64	1969-70
Mitchell, Bill	Det.	1	1	0	0	0	0	....	....	....	....	....		1963-64	1963-64
Mitchell, Herb	Bos.	2	53	6	0	6	38	....	....	....	....	....		1924-25	1925-26
Mitchell, Red	Chi.	3	83	4	5	9	67	....	....	....	....	....		1941-42	1944-45
Moe, Billy	NYR	5	261	11	42	53	163	1	0	0	0	0		1944-45	1948-49
Moffat, Lyle	Tor., Wpg.	3	97	12	16	28	51	....	....	....	....	....		1972-73	1979-80
Moffat, Ron	Det.	3	36	1	1	2	8	7	0	0	0	0		1932-33	1934-35
Moher, Mike	N.J.	1	9	0	1	1	28	....	....	....	....	....		1982-83	1982-83
Mohns, Doug	Bos., Chi., Min., Atl., Wsh.	22	1390	248	462	710	1250	94	14	36	50	122		1953-54	1974-75
Mohns, Lloyd	NYR	1	1	0	0	0	0	....	....	....	....	....		1943-44	1943-44
Mokosak, Carl	Cgy., L.A., Phi., Pit., Bos.	6	83	11	15	26	170	1	0	0	0	0		1981-82	1988-89
Mokosak, John	Det.	2	41	0	2	2	96	....	....	....	....	....		1988-89	1989-90
Molin, Lars	Van.	3	172	33	65	98	37	19	2	9	11	7		1981-82	1983-84
Moller, Mike	Buf., Edm.	7	134	15	28	43	41	3	0	1	1	0		1980-81	1986-87
Molloy, Mitch	Buf.	1	2	0	0	0	10	....	....	....	....	....		1989-90	1989-90
Molyneaux, Larry	NYR	2	45	0	1	1	20	3	0	0	0	8		1937-38	1938-39
Monahan, Garry	Mtl., Det., L.A., Tor., Van.	12	748	116	169	285	484	22	3	1	4	13		1967-68	1978-79
Monahan, Hartland	Cal., NYR, Wsh., Pit., L.A., St.L.	7	334	61	80	141	163	6	0	0	0	4		1973-74	1980-81
• Mondou, Armand	Mtl.	12	385	47	71	118	99	35	3	5	8	12	2	1928-29	1939-40
Mondou, Pierre	Mtl.	9	548	194	262	456	179	69	17	28	45	26	3	1976-77	1984-85
Mongrain, Bob	Buf., L.A.	6	83	13	14	27	14	11	1	2	3	2		1979-80	1985-86
Monteith, Hank	Det.	3	77	5	12	17	6	4	0	0	0	0		1968-69	1970-71
Moore, Dickie	Mtl., Tor., St.L.	14	719	261	347	608	652	135	46	64	110	122	6	1951-52	1967-68
Moran, Amby	Mtl., Chi.	2	35	1	1	2	24	....	....	....	....	....		1926-27	1927-28
• Morenz, Howie	Mtl., Chi., NYR	14	550	270	197	467	563	47	21	11	32	68	3	1923-24	1936-37
Moretto, Angelo	Clev.	1	5	1	2	3	2	....	....	....	....	....		1976-77	1976-77
Morin, Pete	Mtl.	1	31	10	12	22	7	1	0	0	0	0		1941-42	1941-42
Morris, Bernie	Bos.	1	6	2	0	2	0	....	....	....	....	....		1924-25	1924-25
Morris, Elwyn	Tor., NYR	4	135	13	29	42	58	18	4	2	6	16	1	1943-44	1948-49

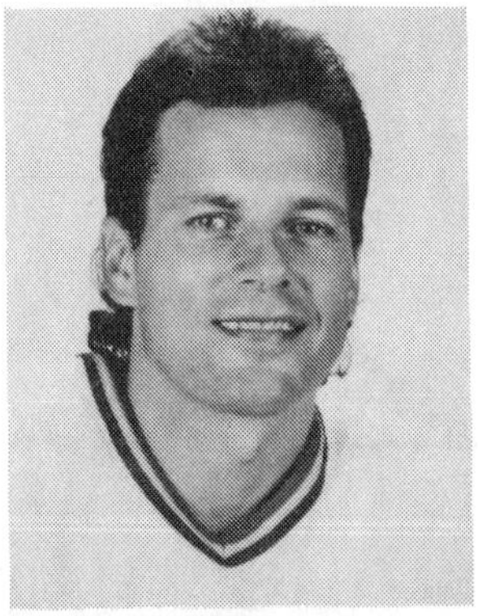

Rick Meagher

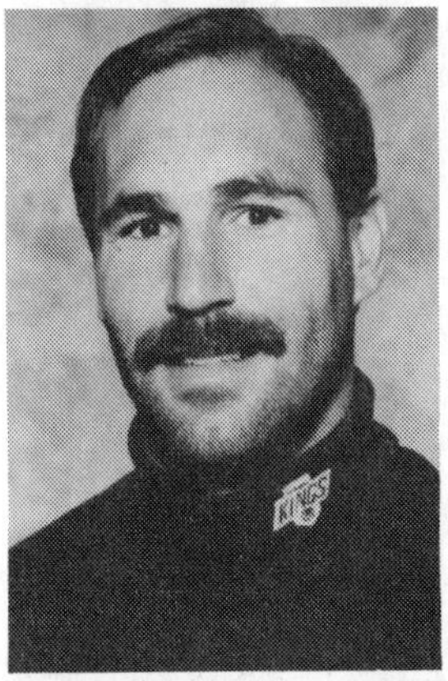

Jay Miller

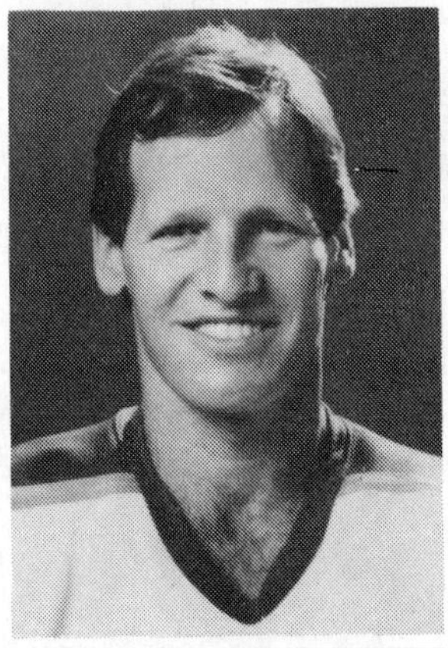

Mark Napier

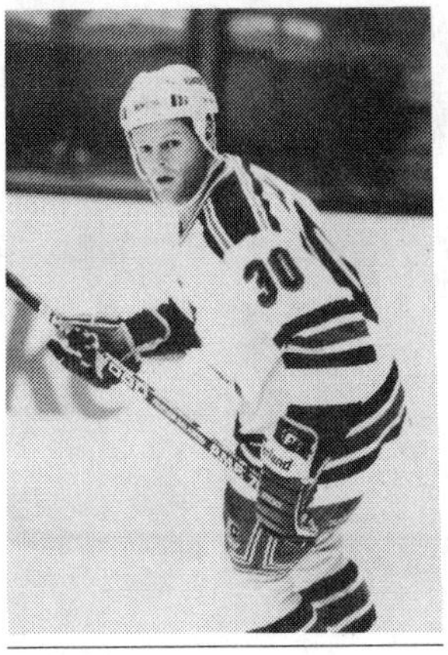

Chris Nilan

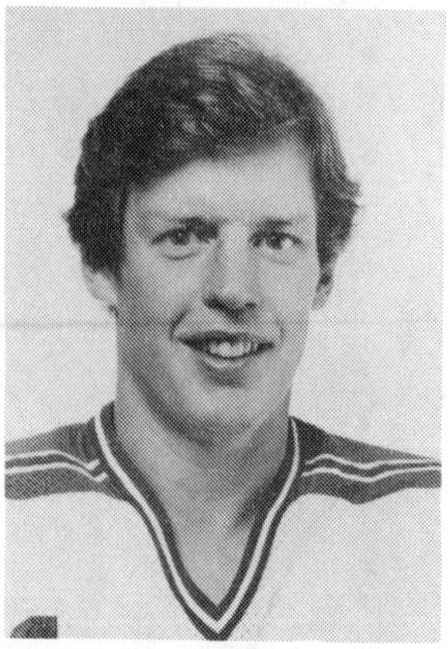
Ulf Nilsson

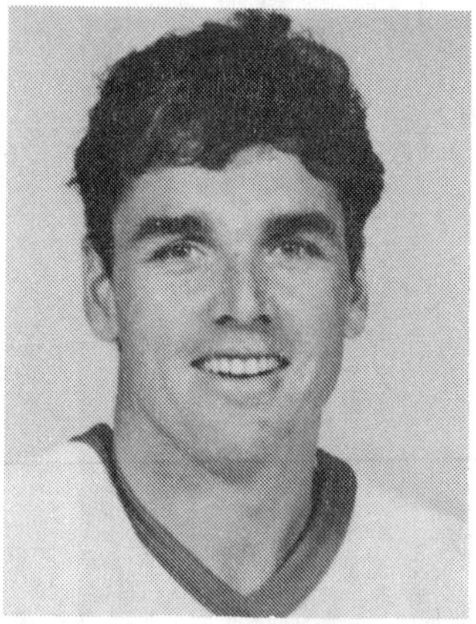
Mike O'Connell

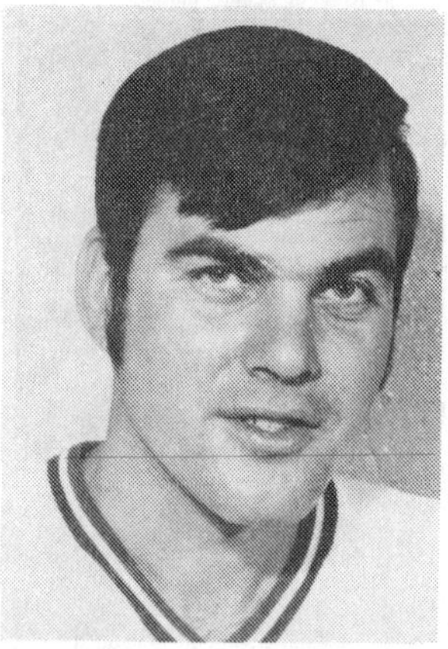
Rosaire Paiement

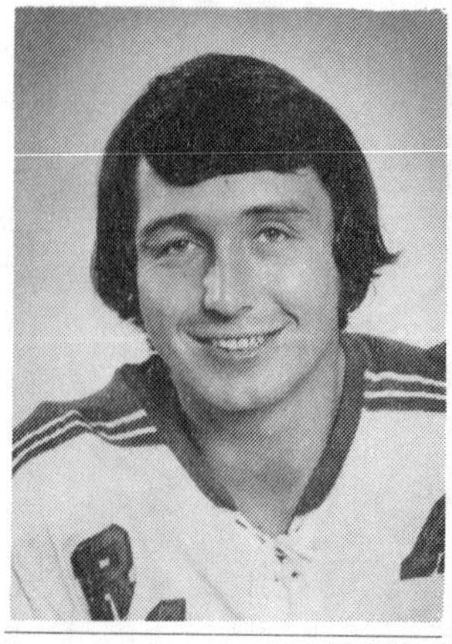
Brad Park

Name	NHL Teams	NHL Seasons	Regular Schedule GP	G	A	TP	PIM	Playoffs GP	G	A	TP	PIM	NHL Cup Wins	First NHL Season	Last NHL Season
Morrison, Dave	L.A., Van.	4	39	3	3	6	4	....	....	....	....	....		1980-81	1984-85
Morrison, Don	Det., Chi.	3	112	18	28	46	12	3	0	1	1	0		1947-48	1950-51
Morrison, Doug	Bos.	4	23	7	3	10	15	....	....	....	....	....		1979-80	1984-85
Morrison, Gary	Phi.	3	43	1	15	16	70	5	0	1	1	2		1979-80	1981-82
Morrison, George	St.L.	2	115	17	21	38	13	3	0	0	0	0		1970-71	1971-72
Morrison, Jim	Bos., Tor., Det., NYR, Pit.	12	704	40	160	200	542	36	0	12	12	38		1951-52	1970-71
Morrison, John	NYA	1	18	0	0	0	0	....	....	....	....	....		1925-26	1925-26
Morrison, Kevin	Col.	1	41	4	11	15	23	....	....	....	....	....		1979-80	1979-80
Morrison, Lew	Phi., Atl., Wsh., Pit.	9	564	39	52	91	107	17	0	0	0	2		1969-70	1977-78
Morrison, Mark	NYR	2	10	1	1	2	0	....	....	....	....	....		1981-82	1983-84
Morrison, Roderick	Det.	1	34	8	7	15	4	3	0	0	0	0		1947-48	1947-48
Morrow, Ken	NYI	10	550	17	88	105	309	127	11	22	33	97	4	1979-80	1988-89
Morton, Dean	Det.	1	1	1	0	1	2	....	....	....	....	....		1989-90	1989-90
Mortson, Gus	Tor., Chi., Det.	13	797	46	152	198	1380	54	5	8	13	68	4	1946-47	1958-59
Mosdell, Kenny	Bro., Mtl., Chi.	16	693	141	168	309	475	79	16	13	29	48	4	1941-42	1958-59
Mosienko, Bill	Chi.	14	711	258	282	540	117	22	10	4	14	15		1941-42	1954-55
Mott, Morris	Cal.	3	199	18	32	50	49	....	....	....	....	....		1972-73	1974-75
Motter, Alex	Bos., Det.	8	267	39	64	103	135	40	3	9	12	41	1	1934-35	1942-43
Moxey, Jim	Cal., Clev., L.A.	3	127	22	27	49	59	....	....	....	....	....		1974-75	1976-77
Mulhern, Richard	Atl., L.A., Tor., Wpg.	6	303	27	93	120	217	7	0	3	3	5		1975-76	1980-81
Muloin, Wayne	Det., Oak., Cal., Min.	3	147	3	21	24	93	11	0	0	0	2		1963-64	1970-71
Mulvey, Grant	Chi., N.J.	10	586	149	135	284	816	42	10	5	15	70		1974-75	1983-84
Mulvey, Paul	Wsh., Pit., L.A.	4	225	30	51	81	613	....	....	....	....	....		1978-79	1981-82
• Mummery, Harry	Tor., ue., Mtl., Ham.	6	106	33	13	46	161	7	1	4	5	0		1917-18	1922-23
• Munro, Dunc	Mtl.	8	239	28	18	46	170	25	3	2	5	24	1	1924-25	1931-32
Munro, Gerry	Mtl., Tor.	2	33	1	0	1	22	....	....	....	....	....		1924-25	1925-26
Murdoch, Bob J.	Mtl., L.A., Atl., Cgy.	12	757	60	218	278	764	69	4	18	22	92	2	1970-71	1981-82
Murdoch, Bob L.	Cal., Clev., St.L.	4	260	72	85	157	127	....	....	....	....	....		1975-76	1978-79
Murdoch, Don	NYR, Edm., Det.	5	320	121	117	238	155	24	10	8	18	16		1976-77	1981-82
Murdoch, Murray	NYR	11	507	84	108	192	197	55	9	12	21	28		1926-27	1936-37
Murphy, Brian	Det.	1	1	0	0	0	0	....	....	....	....	....		1974-75	1974-75
Murphy, Mike	St.L. NYR, L.A.	12	831	238	318	556	514	66	13	23	36	54		1971-72	1982-83
Murphy, Ron	NYR, Chi., Det., Bos.	18	889	205	274	479	460	53	7	8	15	26	1	1952-53	1969-70
Murray, Allan	NYA	7	277	5	9	14	163	14	0	0	0	8		1933-34	1939-40
Murray, Bob F.	Chi.	15	1008	132	382	514	873	112	19	37	56	0		1975-76	1989-90
Murray, Bob J.	Atl., Van.	4	194	6	16	22	98	9	1	1	2	15		1973-74	1976-77
Murray, Jim	L.A.	1	30	0	2	2	14	....	....	....	....	....		1967-68	1967-68
Murray, Ken	Tor., N.Y.I., Det., K.C.	5	106	1	10	11	135	....	....	....	....	....		1969-70	1975-76
Murray, Leo	Mtl.	1	6	0	0	0	2	....	....	....	....	....		1932-33	1932-33
Murray, Mike	Phi.	1	1	0	0	0	0	....	....	....	....	....		1987-88	1987-88
Murray, Randy	Tor.	1	3	0	0	0	2	....	....	....	....	....		1969-70	1969-70
Murray, Terry	Cal., Phi., Det., Wsh.	8	302	4	76	80	199	18	2	2	4	10		1972-73	1981-82
Myers, Hap	Buf.	1	13	0	0	0	6	....	....	....	....	....		1970-71	1970-71
Myles, Vic	NYR	1	45	6	9	15	57	....	....	....	....	....		1942-43	1942-43

N

Name	NHL Teams	NHL Seasons	Regular Schedule GP	G	A	TP	PIM	Playoffs GP	G	A	TP	PIM	NHL Cup Wins	First NHL Season	Last NHL Season
Nachbaur, Don	Hfd., Edm., Phi.	8	223	23	46	69	465	11	1	1	2	24		1980-81	1989-90
Nahrgang, Jim	Det.	3	57	5	12	17	34	....	....	....	....	....		1974-75	1976-77
Nanne, Lou	Min.	11	635	68	157	225	356	32	4	10	14	9		1967-68	1977-78
Nantais, Richard	Min.	3	63	5	4	9	79	....	....	....	....	....		1974-75	1976-77
Napier, Mark	Mtl., Min., Edm., Buf.	11	767	235	306	541	157	82	18	24	42	11	1	1978-79	1988-89
Naslund, Mats	Mtl.	8	617	243	369	612	107	97	34	57	91	33	1	1982-83	1989-90
Nattrass, Ralph	Chi.	4	223	18	38	56	308	....	....	....	....	....		1946-47	1949-50
Natyshak, Mike	Que.	1	4	0	0	0	0	....	....	....	....	....		1987-88	1987-88
Nechaev, Victor	L.A.	1	3	1	0	1	0	....	....	....	....	....		1982-83	1982-83
Nedomansky, Vaclav	Det., NYR, St.L.	6	421	122	156	278	88	7	3	5	8	0		1977-78	1982-83
Neely, Bob	Tor., Col.	5	283	39	59	98	266	26	5	7	12	15		1973-74	1977-78
Neilson, Jim	NYR, Cal., Clev.	16	1023	69	299	368	904	65	1	17	18	61		1962-63	1977-78
Nelson, Gordie	Tor.	1	3	0	0	0	11	....	....	....	....	....		1969-70	1969-70
Nemeth, Steve	NYR	1	12	2	0	2	2	....	....	....	....	....		1987-88	1987-88
Nesterenko, Eric	Tor., Chi.	21	1219	250	324	574	1273	124	13	24	37	127	1	1951-52	1971-72
Nethery, Lance	NYR, Edm.	2	41	11	14	25	14	14	5	3	8	9		1980-81	1981-82
Neufeld, Ray	Hfd., Win., Bos.	11	595	157	200	357	816	28	8	6	14	55		1979-80	1989-90
• Neville, Mike	Tor., NYA	4	62	6	3	9	14	2	0	0	0	0	1	1917-18	1930-31
Nevin, Bob	Tor., NYR, Min., L.A.	18	1128	307	419	726	211	84	16	18	34	24	2	1957-58	1975-76
Newberry, John	Mtl., Hfd.	4	22	0	4	4	6	2	0	0	0	0		1982-83	1985-86
Newell, Rick	Det.	2	7	0	0	0	0	....	....	....	....	....		1972-73	1973-74
Newman, Dan	NYR, Mtl., Edm.	4	126	17	24	41	63	3	0	0	0	4		1976-77	1979-80
Newman, John	Det.	1	8	1	1	2	0	....	....	....	....	....		1930-31	1930-31
Nicholson, Al	Bos.	2	19	0	1	1	4	....	....	....	....	....		1955-56	1956-57
Nicholson, Edward	Det.	1	1	0	0	0	0	....	....	....	....	....		1947-48	1947-48
Nicholson, Graeme	Bos., Col., NYR	3	52	2	7	9	60	....	....	....	....	....		1978-79	1982-83
Nicholson, John	Chi.	1	2	1	0	1	0	....	....	....	....	....		1937-38	1937-38
Nicholson, Neil	Oak., N.Y.I.	4	39	3	1	4	23	2	0	0	0	0		1969-70	1977-78
Nicholson, Paul	Wsh.	3	62	4	8	12	18	....	....	....	....	....		1974-75	1976-77
Niekamp, Jim	Det.	2	29	0	2	2	27	....	....	....	....	....		1970-71	1971-72
Nienhui, Kraig	Bos.	3	87	20	16	36	39	2	0	0	0	14		1985-86	1987-88
• Nighbor, Frank	Ott., Tor.	13	348	136	60	196	241	36	11	9	20	27	4	1917-18	1929-30
Nigro, Frank	Tor.	2	68	8	18	26	39	3	0	0	0	2		1982-83	1983-84
Nilan, Chris	Mtl., NYR, Bos.	13	688	110	115	225	3043	111	8	9	17	541	1	1979-80	1991-92
Nill, Jim	St.L., Van., Bos., Wpg., Det.	9	524	58	87	145	854	59	10	5	15	203		1981-82	1989-90
Nilsson, Kent	Atl., Cgy., Min., Edm.	8	547	263	422	685	116	59	11	41	52	14	1	1979-80	1986-87
Nilsson, Ulf	NYR	4	170	57	112	169	85	25	8	14	22	27		1978-79	1982-83
Nistico, Lou	Col.	1	3	0	0	0	0	....	....	....	....	....		1977-78	1977-78
• Noble, Reg	Tor., Mtl.M., Det.	16	526	167	79	246	807	32	4	5	9	39	3	1917-18	1932-33
Noel, Claude	Wsh.	1	7	0	0	0	0	....	....	....	....	....		1979-80	1979-80
Nolan, Pat	Tor.	1	2	0	0	0	0	....	....	....	....	....	1	1921-22	1921-22
Nolan, Ted	Det., Pit.	3	78	6	16	22	105	....	....	....	....	....		1981-82	1985-86
Nolet, Simon	Phi., K.C., Pit., Col.	10	562	150	182	332	187	34	6	3	9	8	1	1967-68	1976-77
Nordmark, Robert	St. L., Van.	4	236	13	70	83	254	7	3	2	5	8		1987-88	1990-91
Noris, Joe	Pit., St.L., Buf.	3	55	2	5	7	22	....	....	....	....	....		1971-72	1973-74
Norrish, Rod	Min.	2	21	3	3	6	2	....	....	....	....	....		1973-74	1974-75
• Northcott, Baldy	Mtl.M., Chi.	11	446	133	112	245	273	31	8	5	13	14	1	1928-29	1938-39
Norwich, Craig	Wpg., St.L., Col.	2	104	17	58	75	60	....	....	....	....	....		1979-80	1980-81
Novy, Milan	Wsh.	1	73	18	30	48	16	2	0	0	0	0		1982-83	1982-83
Nowak, Hank	Pit., Det., Bos.	4	180	26	29	55	161	3	1	0	1	8		1973-74	1976-77
Nykoluk, Mike	Tor.	1	32	3	1	4	20	....	....	....	....	....		1956-57	1956-57
Nyrop, Bill	Mtl., Min.	4	207	12	51	63	101	35	1	7	8	22	3	1975-76	1981-82
Nystrom, Bob	NYI	14	900	235	278	513	1248	157	39	44	83	236	4	1972-73	1985-86

O

Name	NHL Teams	NHL Seasons	Regular Schedule GP	G	A	TP	PIM	Playoffs GP	G	A	TP	PIM	NHL Cup Wins	First NHL Season	Last NHL Season
• Oatman, Russell	Det., Mtl.M., NYR	3	124	20	9	29	100	17	1	0	1	18		1926-27	1928-29
O'Brien, Dennis	Min., Col., Clev., Bos.	10	592	31	91	122	1017	34	1	2	3	101		1970-71	1979-80
O'Brien, Obie	Bos.	1	2	0	0	0	0	....	....	....	....	....		1955-56	1955-56
O'Callahan, Jack	Chi., N.J.	7	389	27	104	131	541	32	4	11	15	41		1982-83	1988-89
O'Connell, Mike	Chi., Bos., Det.	13	860	105	334	439	605	82	8	24	32	64		1977-78	1989-90
• O'Connor, Buddy	Mtl., NYR	10	509	140	257	397	34	53	15	21	36	6	2	1941-42	1950-51
Oddleifson, Chris	Bos., Van.	9	524	95	191	286	464	14	1	6	7	8		1972-73	1980-81
Odelin, Selmar	Edm.	3	18	0	2	2	35	....	....	....	....	....		1985-86	1988-89
O'Donnell, Fred	Bos.	2	115	15	11	26	98	5	0	1	1	5		1972-73	1973-74
O'Donoghue, Don	Oak., Cal.	3	125	18	17	35	35	3	0	0	0	0		1969-70	1971-72
Odrowski, Gerry	Det., Oak., St.L.	6	299	12	19	31	111	30	0	1	1	16		1960-61	1971-72
O'Dwyer, Bill	L.A., Bos.	5	120	9	13	22	113	10	0	0	0	2		1983-84	1989-90
O'Flaherty, Gerry	Tor., Van., Atl.	8	438	99	95	194	168	7	2	2	4	6		1971-72	1978-79
O'Flaherty, John	NYA, Bro.	2	21	5	1	6	0	....	....	....	....	....		1940-41	1941-42
Ogilvie, Brian	Chi., St.L.	6	90	15	21	36	29	....	....	....	....	....		1972-73	1978-79
O'Grady, George	Mtl.M.	1	4	0	0	0	0	....	....	....	....	....		1917-18	1917-18
Okerlund, Todd	NYI	1	4	0	0	0	2	....	....	....	....	....		1987-88	1987-88
• Oliver, Harry	Bos., NYA	11	473	127	85	212	147	35	10	6	16	22	1	1926-27	1936-37
Oliver, Murray	Det., Bos., Tor., Min.	17	1127	274	454	728	319	35	9	16	25	10		1957-58	1974-75

Name	NHL Teams	NHL Seasons	Regular Schedule GP	G	A	TP	PIM	Playoffs GP	G	A	TP	PIM	NHL Cup Wins	First NHL Season	Last NHL Season
Olmstead, Bert	Chi., Mtl., Tor.	14	848	181	421	602	884	115	16	42	58	1	5	1948-49	1961-62
Olson, Dennis	Det.	1	4	0	0	0	0	....	....	....	....	....		1957-58	1957-58
O'Neil, Paul	Van., Bos.	2	6	0	0	0	0	....	....	....	....	....		1973-74	1975-76
O'Neill, Jim	Bos., Mtl.	6	165	6	30	36	109	11	1	1	2	13		1933-34	1941-42
• O'Neill, Tom	Tor.	2	66	10	12	22	53	4	0	0	0	6	1	1943-44	1944-45
Orban, Bill	Chi., Min.	3	114	8	15	23	673	3	0	0	0	0		1967-68	1969-70
O'Ree, Willie	Bos.	2	45	4	10	14	26	....	....	....	....	....		1957-58	1960-61
O'Regan, Tom	Pit.	3	60	5	12	17	10	....	....	....	....	....		1983-84	1985-86
O'Reilly, Terry	Bos.	14	891	204	402	606	2095	108	25	42	67	335		1971-72	1984-85
Orlando, Gaetano	Buf.	3	98	18	26	44	51	5	0	4	4	14		1984-85	1986-87
Orlando, Jimmy	Det.	6	200	7	24	31	375	36	0	9	9	105	1	1936-37	1942-43
Orleski, Dave	Mtl.	2	2	0	0	0	0	....	....	....	....	....		1980-81	1981-82
Orr, Bobby	Bos., Chi.	12	657	270	645	915	953	74	26	66	92	107	2	1966-67	1978-79
Osburn, Randy	Tor., Phi.	2	27	0	2	2	0	....	....	....	....	....		1972-73	1974-75
O'Shea, Danny	Min., Chi., St.L.	5	369	64	115	179	265	39	3	7	10	62		1968-69	1972-73
O'Shea, Kevin	Buf., St.L.	3	134	13	18	31	85	12	2	1	3	10		1970-71	1972-73
Ouelette, Eddie	Chi.	1	43	3	2	5	11	1	0	0	0	0		1935-36	1935-36
Ouelette, Gerry	Bos.	1	34	5	4	9	0	....	....	....	....	....		1960-1	1960-61
Owchar, Dennis	Pit., Col.	6	288	30	85	115	200	10	1	1	2	8		1974-75	1979-80
• Owen, George	Bos.	5	192	44	33	77	151	21	2	5	7	25	1	1928-29	1932-33
P															
Pachal, Clayton	Bos., Col.	3	35	2	3	5	95	....	....	....	....	....		1976-77	1978-79
Paddock, John	Wsh., Phi., Que.	5	87	8	14	22	86	5	2	0	2	0		1975-76	1982-83
Paiement, Rosaire	Phi., Van.	5	190	48	52	100	343	3	3	0	3	0		1967-68	1971-72
Paiement, Wilf	K.C. Col., Tor., Que., NYR, Buf., Pit.	14	946	356	458	814	1757	69	18	17	35	185		1974-75	1987-88
Palangio, Peter	Mtl., Det., Chi.	5	71	13	10	23	28	7	0	0	0	0	1	1926-27	1937-38
Palazzari, Aldo	Bos., NYR	1	35	8	3	11	4	....	....	....	....	....		1943-44	1943-44
Palazzari, Doug	St.L.	4	108	18	20	38	23	2	0	0	0	0		1974-75	1978-79
Palmer, Brad	Min., Bos.	3	168	32	38	70	58	29	9	5	14	16		1980-81	1982-83
Palmer, Rob H.	Chi.	3	16	0	3	3	2	....	....	....	....	....		1973-74	1975-76
Palmer, Rob R.	L.A., N.J.	6	320	9	101	110	115	8	1	2	3	6		1977-78	1983-84
• Panagabko, Ed	Bos.	2	29	0	3	3	38	....	....	....	....	....		1955-56	1956-57
Papike, Joe	Chi.	3	21	3	3	6	4	5	0	2	2	0		1940-41	1944-45
Pappin, Jim	Tor., Chi., Cal., Clev.	14	767	278	295	573	667	92	33	34	67	101	2	1963-64	1976-77
Paradise, Bob	Min., Atl., Pit., Wsh.	8	368	8	54	62	393	12	0	1	1	19		1971-72	1978-79
Pargeter, George	Mtl.	1	4	0	0	0	0	....	....	....	....	....		1946-47	1946-47
Parise, J.P.	Bos., Tor., Min., NYI, Clev.	14	890	238	356	594	706	86	27	31	58	87		1965-66	1978-79
Parizeau, Michel	St.L., Phi.	1	58	3	14	17	18	....	....	....	....	....		1971-72	1971-72
Park, Brad	NYR, Bos., Det.	17	1113	213	683	896	1429	161	35	90	125	217		1968-69	1984-85
Parker, Jeff	Buf., Hfd.	5	141	16	19	35	163	5	0	0	0	26		1986-87	1990-91
Parkes, Ernie	Mtl.M.	1	17	0	0	0	2	....	....	....	....	....		1924-25	1924-25
Parsons, George	Tor.	3	64	12	13	25	17	7	3	2	5	11		1936-37	1938-39
Pasek, Dusan	Min.	1	48	4	10	14	30	2	1	0	1	0		1988-89	1988-89
Pasin, Dave	Bos., L.A.	2	76	18	19	37	50	3	0	1	1	0		1985-86	1988-89
Paterson, Joseph (Joe)	Det., Phi., L.A., NYR	9	291	19	37	56	829	22	3	4	7	77		1980-81	1988-89
Paterson, Mark	Hfd.	4	29	3	3	6	33	....	....	....	....	....		1982-83	1985-86
Paterson, Rick	Chi.	9	430	50	43	93	136	61	7	10	17	51		1978-79	1986-87
Patey, Doug	Wsh.	3	45	4	2	6	8	....	....	....	....	....		1976-77	1978-79
Patey, Larry	Cal., St.L., NYR	12	717	153	163	316	631	40	8	10	18	57		1973-74	1984-85
Patrick, Craig	Cal., St.L., K.C., Min. Wsh.	8	401	72	91	163	61	2	0	1	1	0		1971-72	1978-79
Patrick, Glenn	St.L., Cal., Clev.	3	38	2	3	5	72	....	....	....	....	....		1973-74	1976-77
• Patrick, Lester	NYR	1	1	0	0	0	2	....	....	....	....	....		1926-27	1926-27
• Patrick, Lynn	NYR	10	455	145	190	335	240	44	10	6	16	22	1	1934-35	1945-46
Patrick, Muzz	NYR	5	166	5	26	31	133	25	4	0	4	34	1	1937-38	1945-46
Patrick, Steve	Buf., NYR, Que.	6	250	40	68	108	242	12	0	1	1	12		1980-81	1985-86
Patterson, Dennis	K.C., Phi.	3	138	6	22	28	67	....	....	....	....	....		1974-75	1979-80
• Patterson, George	Bos., Det., St.L., Tor., Mtl., NYA	9	289	51	27	78	218	3	0	0	0	2		1926-27	1934-35
• Paul, Butch	Det.	1	3	0	0	0	0	....	....	....	....	....		1964-65	1964-65
Paulhus, Rollie	Mtl.	1	33	0	0	0	0	....	....	....	....	....		1925-26	1925-26
Pavelich, Mark	NYR, Min., S.J.	7	355	137	192	329	340	23	7	17	24	14		1981-82	1991-92
Pavelich, Mark	NYR, Min.	6	353	137	191	328	336	23	7	17	24	14		1981-82	1986-87
Pavelich, Marty	Det.	10	634	93	159	252	454	91	13	15	28	74	4	1947-48	1956-57
Pavese, Jim	St.L., NYR, Det., Hfd.	8	328	13	44	57	689	34	0	6	6	81		1981-82	1988-89
• Payer, Evariste	Mtl.	1	1	0	0	0	0	....	....	....	....	....		1917-18	1917-18
Payne, Steve	Min.	10	613	228	238	466	435	71	35	35	70	60		1978-79	1987-88
Pearson, Mel	NYR, Pit.	5	38	2	6	8	25	....	....	....	....	....		1949-50	1967-68
Pederson, Barry	Bos., Van., Pit., Hfd.	12	701	238	416	654	472	34	22	30	52	25		1980-81	1991-92
Peer, Bert	Det.	1	1	0	0	0	0	....	....	....	....	....		1939-40	1939-40
Peirson, Johnny	Bos.	11	545	153	173	326	315	49	9	17	26	26		1946-47	1957-58
Pelensky, Perry	Chi.	1	4	0	0	0	5	....	....	....	....	....		1983-84	1983-84
Pelletier, Roger	Phi.	1	1	0	0	0	0	....	....	....	....	....		1967-68	1967-68
Peloffy, Andre	Wsh.	1	9	0	0	0	2	....	....	....	....	....		1974-75	1974-75
Pelyk, Mike	Tor.	9	441	26	88	114	566	40	0	3	3	41		1967-68	1977-78
Pennington, Cliff	Mtl., Bos.	3	101	17	42	59	6	....	....	....	....	....		1960-61	1962-63
Peplinski, Jim	Cgy.	10	705	161	262	423	1456	99	15	31	46	382	1	1980-81	1989-90
Perlini, Fred	Tor.	2	8	2	3	5	0	....	....	....	....	....		1981-82	1983-84
Perreault, Fern	NYR	2	3	0	0	0	0	....	....	....	....	....		1947-48	1949-50
Perreault, Gilbert	Buf.	17	1191	512	814	1326	500	90	33	70	103	44		1970-71	1986-87
Perry, Brian	Oak., Buf.	3	96	16	29	45	24	8	1	1	2	4		1968-69	1970-71
Persson, Stefan	NYI	9	622	52	317	369	574	102	7	50	57	69	4	1977-78	1985-86
Pesut, George	Cal.	2	92	3	22	25	130	....	....	....	....	....		1974-75	1975-76
Peters, Frank	NYR	1	43	0	0	0	59	4	0	0	0	2		1930-31	1930-31
Peters, Garry	Mtl., NYR, Phi., Bos.	8	331	34	34	68	261	9	2	2	4	31	1	1964-65	1971-72
Peters, Jim	Det., Chi., Mtl., Bos.	9	574	125	150	275	186	60	5	9	14	22	3	1945-46	1953-54
Peters, Jimy	Det., L.A.	9	309	37	36	73	48	11	0	2	2	2		1964-65	1974-75
Peters, Steve	Col.	1	2	0	1	1	0	....	....	....	....	....		1979-80	1979-80
Peterson, Brent	Det., Buf., Van., Hfd.	10	620	72	141	213	484	31	4	4	8	65		1979-80	1988-89
Pettersson, Jorgen	St.L., Hfd., Wsh.	6	435	174	192	366	117	44	15	12	27	4		1980-81	1985-86
Pettinger, Eric	Ott., Bos., Tor.	3	97	7	12	19	83	4	1	0	1	8		1928-29	1930-31
Pettinger, Gord	Det., NYR, Bos.	8	292	42	74	116	77	49	4	5	9	11	4	1932-33	1939-40
Phair, Lyle	L.A.	3	48	6	7	13	12	1	0	0	0	0		1985-86	1987-88
Phillipoff, Harold	Atl., Chi.,	3	141	26	57	83	267	6	0	2	2	9		1977-78	1979-80
Phillips, Bat	Mtl.M.	1	27	1	1	2	6	4	0	0	0	2		1929-30	1929-30
• Phillips, Bill	Mtl.M., NYA.	8	302	52	31	83	232	28	6	2	8	19	1	1925-26	1932-33
Phillips, Charlie	Mtl.	1	17	0	0	0	6	....	....	....	....	....		1942-43	1942-43
Picard, Noel	Atl., Mtl., St.L.	7	335	12	63	75	616	50	2	11	13	167	1	1964-65	1972-73
Picard, Robert	Wsh. Tor., Mtl., Wpg., Que., Det.	13	899	104	319	423	1025	36	5	15	20	39		1977-78	1989-90
Picard, Roger	St.L.	1	15	2	2	4	21	....	....	....	....	....		1967-68	1967-68
Pichette, Dave	Que., St.L., N.J., NYR	7	322	41	140	181	348	28	3	7	10	54		1980-81	1987-88
Picketts, Hal	NYA.	1	48	3	1	4	32	....	....	....	....	....		1933-34	1933-34
Pidhirny, Harry	Bos.	1	2	0	0	0	0	....	....	....	....	....		1957-58	1957-58
Pierce, Randy	Col., N.J., Hfd.	8	277	62	76	138	223	2	0	0	0	0		1977-78	1984-85
Pike, Alf	NYR	6	234	42	77	119	145	21	4	2	6	12	1	1939-40	1946-47
Pilote, Pierre	Chi., Tor.	14	890	80	418	498	1251	86	8	53	61	102	1	1955-56	1968-69
Pinder, Gerry	Chi., Cal.	3	223	55	69	124	135	17	0	4	4	6		1969-70	1971-72
Pirus, Alex	Min., Det.	4	159	30	28	58	94	2	0	1	1	2		1976-77	1979-80
• Pitre, Didier	Mtl.	6	127	64	17	81	50	14	2	2	4	0		1917-18	1922-23
• Plager, Barclay	St.L.	10	614	44	187	231	1115	68	3	20	23	182		1967-68	1976-77
Plager, Bob	NYR, St.L.	14	644	20	126	146	802	74	2	17	19	195		1964-65	1977-78
Plager, William	Min., St.L., Atl.	9	263	4	34	38	292	31	0	2	2	26		1967-68	1975-76
Plamondon, Gerry	Mtl.	5	74	7	13	20	10	11	5	2	7	2	1	1945-46	1950-51
Plante, Cam	Tor.	1	2	0	0	0	0	....	....	....	....	....		1984-85	1984-85
Plante, Pierre	NYR, Que., Phi., St.L., Chi.	9	599	125	172	297	599	33	2	6	8	51		1971-72	1979-80
Plantery, Mark	Wpg.	1	25	1	5	6	14	....	....	....	....	....		1980-81	1980-81
Plaxton, Hugh	Mtl.M.	1	15	1	2	3	4	....	....	....	....	....		1932-33	1932-33
Playfair, Jim	Edm., Chi.	3	21	2	4	6	51	....	....	....	....	....		1983-84	1988-89
Playfair, Larry	Buf., L.A.	12	688	26	94	120	1812	43	0	6	6	111		1978-79	1989-90
Pleau, Larry	Mtl.	3	94	9	15	24	27	4	0	0	0	0		1969-70	1971-72
Plett, Willi	Atl., Cgy., Min., Bos.	13	834	222	215	437	2572	83	24	22	46	466		1975-76	1987-88
Plumb, Rob	Det.	1	7	2	1	3	0	....	....	....	....	....		1977-78	1977-78
Plumb, Ron	Hfd.	1	26	3	4	7	14	....	....	....	....	....		1979-80	1979-80

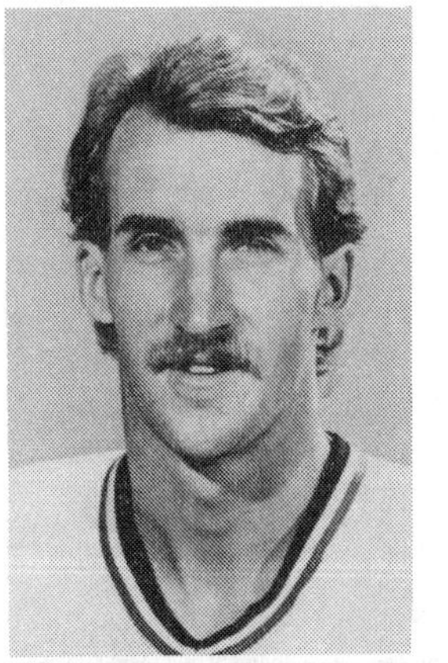
Steve Payne

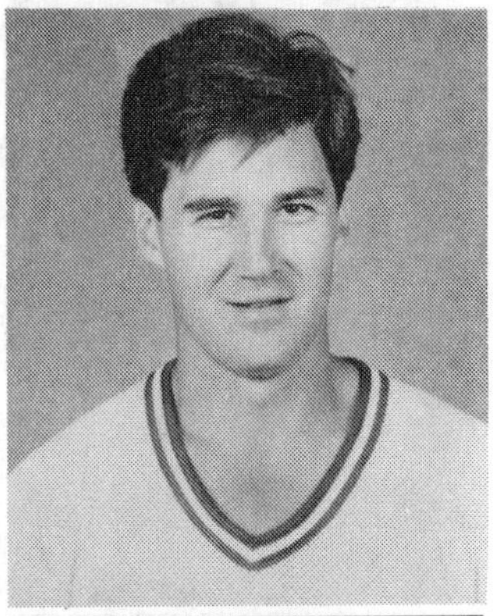
Barry Pederson

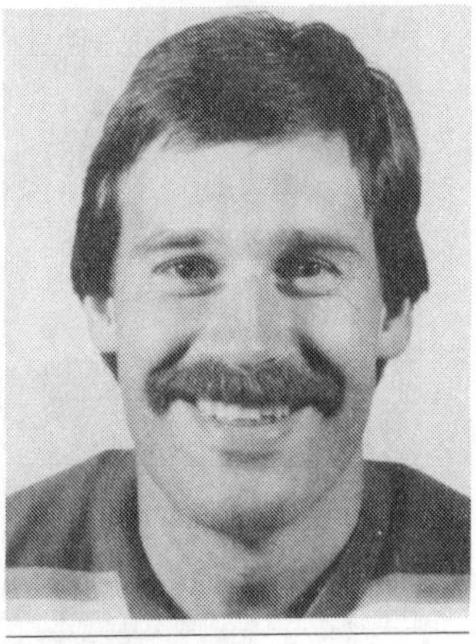
Brent Peterson

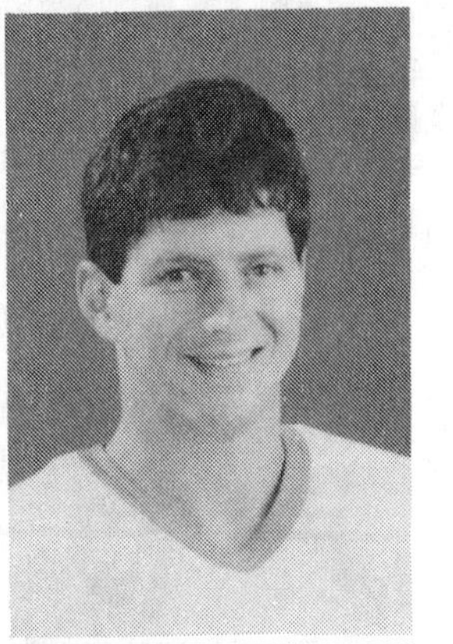
Robert Picard

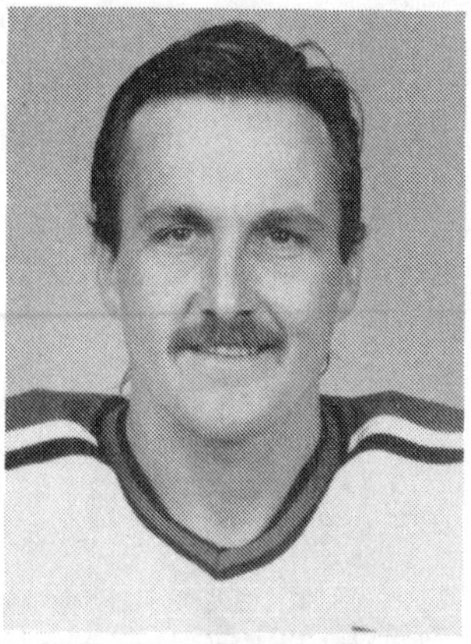
Walt Poddubny

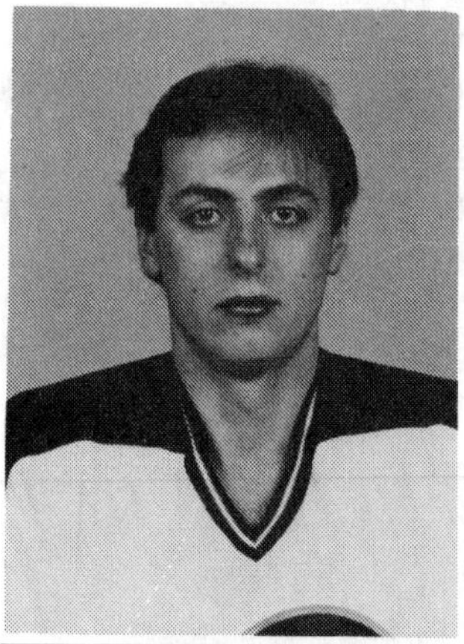
Sergei Priakin

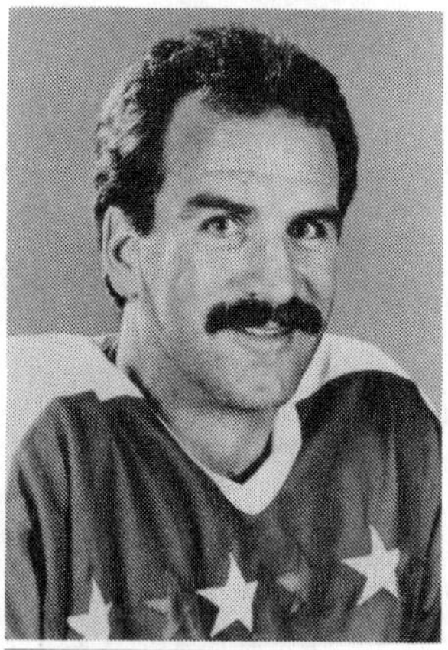
Joel Quenneville

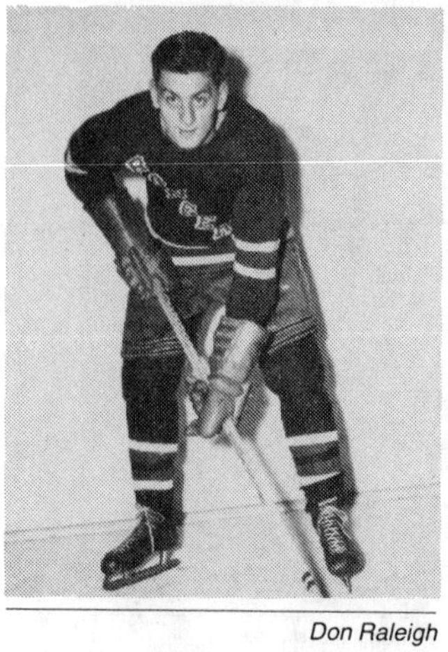
Don Raleigh

Name	NHL Teams	NHL Seasons	Regular Schedule GP	G	A	TP	PIM	Playoffs GP	G	A	TP	PIM	NHL Cup Wins	First NHL Season	Last NHL Season
Pocza, Harvie	Wsh.	2	3	0	0	0	0	....	....	....	....	....		1979-80	1981-82
Poddubny, Walt	Edm., Tor., NYR, Que., N.J.	11	468	184	238	422	454	19	7	2	9	12		1981-82	1991-92
Podloski, Ray	Bos.	1	8	0	1	1	22	....	....	....	....	....		1988-89	1988-89
Podolsky, Nels	Det.	1	1	0	0	0	0	7	0	0	0	4		1948-49	1948-49
Poeta, Anthony	Chi.	1	1	0	0	0	0	....	....	....	....	....		1951-52	1951-52
Poile, Bud	NYR, Bos., Det., Tor., Chi.,	7	311	107	122	229	91	23	4	4	8	8	1	1942-43	1949-50
Poile, Don	Det.	2	66	7	9	16	12	4	0	0	0	0		1954-55	1957-58
Poirer, Gordie	Mtl.	1	10	0	1	1	0	....	....	....	....	....		1939-40	1939-40
Polanic, Tom	Min.	2	19	0	2	2	53	5	1	1	2	4		1969-70	1970-71
Polich, John	NYR	2	3	0	1	1	0	....	....	....	....	....		1939-40	1940-41
Polich, Mike	Mtl., Min.	5	226	24	29	53	7	23	2	1	3	2	1	1976-77	1980-81
Polis, Greg	Pit., St.L., NYR, Wsh.	10	615	174	169	343	391	7	0	2	2	6		1970-71	1979-80
Poliziani, Daniel	Bos.	1	1	0	0	0	0	3	0	0	0	0		1958-59	1958-59
Polonich, Dennis	Det.	8	390	59	82	141	1242	7	1	0	1	19		1974-75	1982-83
Pooley, Paul	Wpg.	2	15	0	3	3	0	....	....	....	....	....		1984-85	1985-86
Popein, Larry	NYR, Oak.	8	449	80	141	221	162	16	1	4	5	6		1954-55	1967-68
Popiel, Paul	Bos., .A., Det., Van., Edm.	7	224	13	41	54	210	4	1	0	1	4		1965-66	1979-80
Portland, Jack	Chi., Mtl., Bos.	10	381	15	56	71	323	33	1	3	4	25	1	1933-34	1942-43
Porvari, Jukka	Col., N.J.	2	39	3	9	12	4	....	....	....	....	....		1981-82	1982-83
Posa, Victor	Chi.	1	2	0	0	0	2	....	....	....	....	....		1985-86	1985-86
Posavad, Mike	St.L.	2	8	0	0	0	0	....	....	....	....	....		1985-86	1986-87
Potvin, Denis	NYI	15	1060	310	742	1052	1356	185	56	108	164	253	4	1973-74	1987-88
Potvin, Jean	L.A., Min., Phi., NYI, Cle.	11	613	63	224	287	478	39	2	9	11	17	1	1970-71	1980-81
Poudrier, Daniel	Que.	1	25	1	5	6	10	....	....	....	....	....		1985-86	1987-88
Poulin, Dan	Min.	1	3	1	1	2	2	....	....	....	....	....		1981-82	1981-82
Pouzar, Jaroslav	Edm.	4	186	34	48	82	135	29	6	4	10	16	3	1982-83	1986-87
Powell, Ray	Chi.	1	31	7	15	22	2	....	....	....	....	....		1950-51	1950-51
Powis, Geoff	Chi.	1	2	0	0	0	0	....	....	....	....	....		1967-68	1967-68
Powis, Lynn	Chi., K.C.	2	130	19	33	52	25	1	0	0	0	0		1973-74	1974-75
Prajsler, Petr	L.A., Bos.	4	46	3	10	13	51	4	0	0	0	0		1987-88	1991-92
• Pratt, Babe	Bos., NYR, Tor.	12	517	83	209	292	473	63	12	17	29	90	2	1935-36	1946-47
Pratt, Jack	Bos.	2	37	2	0	2	42	4	0	0	0	0		1930-31	1931-32
Pratt, Kelly	Pit.	1	22	0	6	6	15	....	....	....	....	....		1974-75	1974-75
Pratt, Tracy	Van., Col., Buf., Pit. Tor., Oak.	10	580	17	97	114	1026	25	0	1	1	62		1967-68	1976-77
Prentice, Dean	Pit., Min., Det., NYR, Bos.	22	1378	391	469	860	484	54	13	17	30	38		1952-53	1973-74
Prentice, Eric	Tor.	1	5	0	0	0	4	....	....	....	....	....		1943-44	1943-44
Preston, Rich	Chi., N.J.	8	580	127	164	291	348	47	4	18	22	56		1979-80	1986-87
Preston, Yves	Phi.	2	28	7	3	10	4	....	....	....	....	....		1978-79	1980-81
Priakin, Sergei	Cgy.	3	46	3	8	11	2	1	0	0	0	0		1988-89	1990-91
• Price, Bob	Ott.	1	1	0	0	0	0	....	....	....	....	....		1919-20	1919-20
Price, Jack	Chi.	3	57	4	6	10	24	4	0	0	0	0		1951-52	1953-54
Price, Noel	Pit., L.A., Det., Tor., NYR, Mtl., Atl.	14	499	14	114	128	333	12	0	1	1	8	1	1957-58	1975-76
Price, Pat	NYI, Edm., Pit., Que., NYR, Min.	13	726	43	218	261	1456	74	2	10	12	195		1975-76	1987-88
Price, Tom	Cal., Clev., Pit.	5	29	0	2	2	12	....	....	....	....	....		1974-75	1978-79
• Primeau, Joe	Tor.	9	310	66	177	243	105	38	5	18	23	12	1	1927-28	1935-36
Primeau, Kevin	Van.	1	2	0	0	0	4	....	....	....	....	....		1980-81	1980-81
Pringle, Ellie	NYA	1	6	0	0	0	0	....	....	....	....	....		1930-31	1930-31
• Prodgers, Goldie	Tor., Ham.	6	110	63	22	85	33	....	....	....	....	....		1919-20	1924-25
Pronovost, Andre	Det., Min., Mtl., Bos.	10	556	94	104	198	408	70	11	11	22	58	4	1956-57	1967-68
Pronovost, Jean	Wsh., Pit., Atl.	14	998	391	383	774	413	35	11	9	20	14		1968-69	1981-82
Pronovost, Marcel	Det., Tor.	21	1206	88	257	345	851	134	8	23	31	104	5	1950-51	1969-70
• Provost, Claude	Mtl.	15	1005	254	335	589	469	126	25	38	63	86	9	1955-56	1969-70
Pryor, Chris	Min., NYI	6	82	1	4	5	122	....	....	....	....	....		1984-85	1989-90
Prystai, Metro	Chi., Det.	11	674	151	179	330	231	43	12	14	26	8	2	1947-48	1957-58
• Pudas, Al	Tor.	1	3	0	0	0	0	....	....	....	....	....		1926-27	1926-27
Pulford, Bob	Tor., L.A.	16	1079	281	362	643	792	89	25	26	51	126	4	1956-57	1971-72
Pulkkinen, Dave	NYI	1	2	0	0	0	0	....	....	....	....	....		1972-73	1972-73
Purpur, Cliff	Det., Chi., St.L.	5	144	26	34	60	46	16	1	2	3	4		1934-35	1944-45
• Pusie, Jean	Mtl., NYR, Bos.	5	61	1	4	5	28	7	0	0	0	0	1	1930-31	1935-36
Pyatt, Nelson	Det., Wsh., Col.	7	296	71	63	134	69	....	....	....	....	....		1973-74	1979-80

Q

Name	NHL Teams	NHL Seasons	Regular Schedule GP	G	A	TP	PIM	Playoffs GP	G	A	TP	PIM	NHL Cup Wins	First NHL Season	Last NHL Season
Quackenbush, Bill	Det., Bos.	14	774	62	222	284	95	80	2	19	21	8		1942-43	1955-56
Quackenbush, Max	Bos., Chi.,	2	61	4	7	11	30	6	0	0	0	4		1950-51	1951-52
Quenneville, Joel	Tor., Col., N.J., Hfd., Wsh.	13	803	54	136	190	705	32	0	8	8	22		1978-79	1990-91
Quenneville, Leo	NYR	1	25	0	3	3	10	3	0	0	0	0		1929-30	1929-30
• Quilty, John	Mtl., Bos.	4	125	36	34	70	81	13	3	5	8	9		1940-41	1947-48
Quinn, Pat	Tor., Van., Atl.	9	606	18	113	131	950	11	0	1	1	21		1968-69	1976-77

R

Name	NHL Teams	NHL Seasons	Regular Schedule GP	G	A	TP	PIM	Playoffs GP	G	A	TP	PIM	NHL Cup Wins	First NHL Season	Last NHL Season
Radley, Yip	NYA, Mtl.M.	2	18	0	1	1	13	....	....	....	....	....		1930-31	1936-37
Raglan, Clare	Det., Chi.	3	100	4	9	13	52	3	0	0	0	0		1950-51	1952-53
Raleigh, Don	NYR	10	535	101	219	320	96	18	6	5	11	6		1943-44	1955-56
• Ramsay, Beattie	Tor.,	1	43	0	2	2	10	....	....	....	....	....		1927-28	1927-28
Ramsay, Craig	Buf.	14	1070	252	420	672	201	89	17	31	48	27		1971-72	1984-85
Ramsay, Wayne	Buf.	1	2	0	0	0	0	....	....	....	....	....		1977-78	1977-78
Ramsey, Les	Chi.	1	11	2	2	4	2	....	....	....	....	....		1944-45	1944-45
• Randall, Ken	Tor., Ham., NYA	10	217	67	28	95	360	13	3	1	4	19	2	1917-18	1926-27
Ranieri, George	Bos.	1	2	0	0	0	0	....	....	....	....	....		1956-57	1956-57
Ratelle, Jean	NYR, Bos.	21	1281	491	776	1267	276	123	32	66	98	24		1960-61	1980-81
Rathwell, John	Bos.	1	1	0	0	0	0	....	....	....	....	....		1974-75	1974-75
Rausse, Errol	Wsh.	3	31	7	3	10	0	....	....	....	....	....		1979-80	1981-82
Rautakallio, Pekka	Atl., Cgy.	3	235	33	121	154	122	23	2	5	7	8		1979-80	1981-82
Ravlich, Matt	Bos., Chi., Det., L.A.	9	410	12	78	90	364	24	1	5	6	16		1962-63	1972-73
Raymond, Armand	Mtl.	2	22	0	2	2	10	....	....	....	....	....		1937-38	1939-40
Raymond, Paul	Mtl.	4	76	2	3	5	6	5	0	0	0	2		1932-33	1937-38
Read, Mel	NYR	1	1	0	0	0	0	....	....	....	....	....		1946-47	1946-47
Reardon, Ken	Mtl.	7	341	26	96	122	604	31	2	5	7	62	1	1940-41	1949-50
Reardon, Terry	Bos., Mtl.	7	193	47	53	100	73	30	8	10	18	12	1	1938-39	1946-47
Reaume, Marc	Tor., Det., Mtl., Van.	9	344	8	43	51	273	21	0	2	2	8		1954-55	1970-71
Reay, Billy	Det., Mtl.	10	479	105	162	267	202	63	13	16	29	43	2	1943-44	1952-53
Redahl, Gord	Bos.	1	18	0	1	1	2	....	....	....	....	....		1958-59	1958-59
Redding, George	Bos.	2	35	3	2	5	10	....	....	....	....	....		1924-25	1925-26
Redmond, Craig	L.A., Edm.	5	191	16	68	84	134	3	1	0	1	2		1984-85	1988-89
Redmond, Dick	Min., Cal., Chi., St.L., Atl., Bos.	13	771	133	312	445	504	66	9	22	31	27		1969-70	1981-82
Redmond, Mickey	Mtl., Det.	9	538	233	195	428	219	16	2	3	5	2	2	1967-68	1975-76
Reeds, Mark	St.L., Hfd.	8	365	45	114	159	135	53	8	9	17	23		1981-82	1988-89
Regan, Bill	NYR, NYA	3	67	3	2	5	67	8	0	0	0	2		1929-30	1932-33
Regan, Larry	Bos., Tor.,	5	280	41	95	136	71	42	7	14	21	18		1956-57	1960-61
Regier, Darcy	Clev., NYI	3	26	0	2	2	35	....	....	....	....	....		1977-78	1983-84
Reibel, Earl	Det., Chi., Bos.	6	409	84	161	245	75	39	6	14	20	4	2	1953-54	1958-59
Reid, Dave	Tor.	3	7	0	0	0	0	....	....	....	....	....		1952-53	1955-56
Reid, Gerry	Det.	1	....	....	....	....	....	2	0	0	0	2		1948-49	1948-49
Reid, Gordie	NYA	1	1	0	0	0	2	....	....	....	....	....		1936-37	1936-37
Reid, Reg	Tor.	2	40	2	0	2	4	2	0	0	0	0		1924-25	1925-26
Reid, Tom	Chi., Min.	11	701	17	113	130	654	42	1	13	14	49		1967-68	1977-78
Reierson, Dave	Cgy.	1	2	0	0	0	2	....	....	....	....	....		1988-89	1988-89
Reigle, Ed	Bos.	1	17	0	2	2	25	....	....	....	....	....		1950-51	1950-51
Reinhart, Paul	Atl., Cgy., Van.	11	648	133	426	559	277	83	23	54	77	42		1979-80	1989-90
Reinikka, Ollie	NYR	1	16	0	0	0	0	....	....	....	....	....		1926-27	1926-27
Reise, Leo Jr.	Chi., Det., NYR	9	494	28	81	109	399	52	8	5	13	68	2	1945-46	1953-54
• Reise, Leo Sr.	Ham., NYA, NYR	8	199	36	29	65	177	6	0	0	0	16		1920-21	1929-30
Renaud, Mark	Hfd., Buf.	5	152	6	50	56	86	....	....	....	....	....		1979-80	1983-84
Reynolds, Bobby	Tor.	1	7	1	1	2	0	....	....	....	....	....		1989-90	1989-90
Ribble, Pat	Atl., Chi., Tor., Wsh., Cgy.	8	349	19	60	79	365	8	0	1	1	12		1975-76	1982-83
Richard, Henri	Mtl.	20	1256	358	688	1046	928	180	49	80	129	181	11	1955-56	1974-75
Richard, Jacques	Alt., Buf., Que.	10	556	160	187	347	307	35	5	5	10	34		1972-73	1982-83
Richard, Maurice	Mtl.	18	978	544	421	965	1285	133	82	44	126	188	8	1942-43	1959-60
Richard, Mike	Wsh.	2	7	0	2	2	0	....	....	....	....	....		1987-88	1989-90
Richardson, Dave	NYR, Chi., Det.	4	45	3	2	5	27	....	....	....	....	....		1963-64	1967-68

Name	NHL Teams	NHL Seasons	Regular Schedule GP	G	A	TP	PIM	Playoffs GP	G	A	TP	PIM	NHL Cup Wins	First NHL Season	Last NHL Season
Richardson, Glen	Van.	1	24	3	6	9	19	....	....	....	....	....		1975-76	1975-76
Richardson, Ken	St.L.	3	49	8	13	21	16	....	....	....	....	....		1974-75	1978-79
Richer, Bob	Buf.	1	3	0	0	0	0	....	....	....	....	....		1972-73	1972-73
Richmond, Steve	NYR, Det., N.J., L.A.	5	159	4	23	27	514	4	0	0	0	12		1983-84	1988-89
Richter, Dave	Min., Phi., Van., St.L.	9	365	9	40	49	1030	22	1	0	1	80		1981-82	1989-90
Riley, Bill	sh., Wpg.	5	139	31	30	61	320	....	....	....	....	....		1974-75	1979-80
Riley, Jack	Det., Mtl., Bos.,	4	104	10	22	32	8	4	0	3	3	0		1932-33	1935-36
Riley, Jim	Det.	1	17	0	2	2	14	....	....	....	....	....		1926-27	1926-27
Riopellie, Howard	Mtl.	3	169	27	16	43	73	8	1	1	2	2		1947-48	1949-50
Rioux, Gerry	Wpg.	1	8	0	0	0	6	....	....	....	....	....		1979-80	1979-80
Rioux, Pierre	Cgy.	1	14	1	2	3	4	....	....	....	....	....		1982-83	1982-83
Ripley, Vic	Chi., Bos., NYR, St.L.	7	278	51	49	100	173	20	4	1	5	10		1928-29	1934-35
Risebrough, Doug	Mtl., Cgy.	14	740	185	286	471	1542	124	21	37	58	238	4	1974-75	1986-87
Rissling, Gary	Wsh., Pit.	7	221	23	30	53	1008	5	0	1	1	4		1978-79	1984-85
Ritchie, Bob	Phi., Det.	2	29	8	4	12	10	....	....	....	....	....		1976-77	1977-78
• Ritchie, Dave	Mtl.W, Ott., Tor., Que., Mtl.	6	54	15	3	18	27	1	0	0	0	0		1917-18	1925-26
Ritson, Alex	NYR	1	1	0	0	0	0	....	....	....	....	....		1944-45	1944-45
Rittinger, Alan	Bos.	1	19	3	7	10	0	....	....	....	....	....		1943-44	1943-44
Rivard, Bob	Pit.	1	27	5	12	17	4	....	....	....	....	....		1967-68	1967-68
• Rivers, Gus	Mtl.	3	88	4	5	9	12	16	2	0	2	2	2	1929-30	1931-32
Rivers, Wayne	Det., Bos., St.L., NYR	7	108	15	30	45	94	....	....	....	....	....		1961-62	1968-69
Rizzuto, Garth	Van.	1	37	3	4	7	16	....	....	....	....	....		1970-71	1970-71
• Roach, Mickey	Tor., Ham., NYA	8	209	75	27	102	41	....	....	....	....	....		1919-20	1926-27
Robert, Claude	Mtl.	1	23	1	0	1	9	....	....	....	....	....		1950-51	1950-51
Robert, Rene	Tor., Pit., Buf., Col.	12	744	284	418	702	597	50	22	19	41	73		1970-71	1981-82
• Robert, Sammy	Ott.	1	1	0	0	0	0	....	....	....	....	....		1917-18	1917-18
Roberto, Phil	Mtl., St.L., Det., K.C., Col., Clev.	8	385	75	106	181	464	31	9	8	17	69	1	1969-70	1976-77
Roberts, Doug	Det., Dak., Cal., Bos.	10	419	43	104	147	342	16	2	3	5	46		1965-66	1974-75
Roberts, Jim	Mtl., St.L.	15	1006	126	194	320	621	153	20	16	36	160	5	1963-64	1977-78
Roberts, Jimmy	Min.	3	106	17	23	40	33	2	0	0	0	0		1976-77	1978-79
Robertson, Fred	Tor., Det.,	2	34	1	0	1	35	7	0	0	0	0	1	1931-32	1933-34
Robertson, Geordie	Buf.	1	5	1	2	3	7	....	....	....	....	....		1982-83	1982-83
Robertson, George	Mtl.	2	31	2	5	7	6	....	....	....	....	....		1947-48	1948-49
Robertson, Torrie	Wsh., Hfd., Det.	10	442	49	99	148	1751	22	2	1	3	90		1980-81	1989-90
Robidoux, Florent	Chi.	3	52	7	4	11	75	....	....	....	....	....		1980-81	1983-84
Robinson, Doug	Chi., NYR, L.A.	7	239	44	67	111	34	11	4	3	7	0		1963-64	1970-71
Robinson, Douglas	Min.	1	1	0	0	0	2	....	....	....	....	....		1989-90	1989-90
Robinson, Douglas (Scott)	Min.	1	1	0	0	0	2	....	....	....	....	....		1989-90	1989-90
Robinson, Earl	Mtl.M., Chi., Mtl.	11	418	83	98	181	123	25	5	4	9	0	1	1928-29	1939-40
Robinson, Larry Clark	Mtl., L.A.	20	1384	208	750	958	793	227	28	116	144	211	6	1972-73	1991-92
Robinson, Moe	Mtl	1	1	0	0	0	0	....	....	....	....	....		1979-80	1979-80
Robitaille, Mike	NYR, Det., Buf., Van.	8	382	23	105	128	280	13	0	1	1	4		1969-70	1976-77
• Roche, Earl	Mtl.M., Bos., Ott., St.L., Det.	4	146	25	27	52	48	2	0	0	0	0		1930-31	1934-35
Roche, Ernest	Mtl.	1	4	0	0	0	2	....	....	....	....	....		1950-51	1950-51
Roche, Michel	Mtl.M., Ott., St.L., Mtl., Det.	4	112	20	18	38	44	....	....	....	....	....		1930-31	1934-35
Rochefort, Dave	Det	1	1	0	0	0	0	....	....	....	....	....		1966-67	1966-67
Rochefort, Leon	NYR, Mtl., Phi., L.A., Det., Atl., Van.	15	617	121	147	268	93	39	4	4	8	16	2	1960-61	1975-76
Rochefort, Normand	Que., NYR	12	592	39	119	158	560	69	7	5	12	82		1980-81	1991-92
Rockburn, Harvey	Det., Ott.	3	94	4	2	6	254	....	....	....	....	....		1929-30	1932-33
• Rodden, Eddie	Chi., Tor., Bos., NYR	4	98	6	14	20	152	2	0	1	1	0	1	1926-27	1930-31
Rogers, Alfred	Min.	2	14	2	4	6	0	....	....	....	....	....		1973-74	1974-75
Rogers, Mike	Hfd., NYR, Edm.	7	484	202	317	519	184	17	1	13	14	6		1979-80	1985-86
Rohlicek, Jeff	Van.	2	9	0	0	0	8	....	....	....	....	....		1987-88	1988-89
Rolfe, Dale	Bos., L.A., Det., NYR	9	509	25	125	150	556	71	5	24	29	89		1959-60	1974-75
Romanchych, Larry	Chi., Atl	6	298	68	97	165	102	7	2	2	4	4		1970-71	1976-77
Rombough, Doug	Buf., NYI, Min.	4	150	24	27	51	80	....	....	....	....	....		1972-73	1975-76
• Romnes, Doc	Chi., Tor., NYA	10	359	68	136	204	42	43	7	18	25	4	2	1930-31	1939-40
• Ronan, Skene	Ott.	1	11	0	0	0	0	....	....	....	....	....		1918-19	1918-19
Ronson, Len	NYR, Oak.	2	18	2	1	3	10	....	....	....	....	....		1960-61	1968-69
Ronty, Paul	Bos., NYR, Mtl.	8	488	101	211	312	103	21	1	7	8	6		1947-48	1954-55
Rooney, Steve	Mtl., Wpg., N.J.	5	154	15	13	28	496	25	3	2	5	86	1	1984-85	1988-89
Root, Bill	Mtl., Tor., St.L., Phi.	6	247	11	23	34	180	22	1	2	3	25		1982-83	1987-88
• Ross, Art	Mtl.W	1	3	1	0	1	0	....	....	....	....	....		1917-18	1917-18
Ross, Jim	NYR	2	62	2	11	13	29	....	....	....	....	....		1951-52	1952-53
Rossignol, Roland	Det., Mtl.	3	14	3	5	8	6	1	0	0	0	2		1943-44	1945-46
Rota, Darcy	Chi., Atl., Van.	11	794	256	239	495	973	60	14	7	21	147		1973-74	1983-84
Rota, Randy	Mtl., L.A., K.C., Col.	5	212	38	39	77	60	5	0	1	1	0		1972-73	1976-77
• Rothschild, Sam	Mtl.M., NYA	4	99	8	6	14	24	10	0	0	0	0	1	1924-25	1927-28
• Roulston, Rolly	Det.	3	24	0	6	6	10	....	....	....	....	....	1	1935-36	1937-38
Roulston, Tom	Edm., Pit.	6	195	47	49	96	74	21	2	2	4	2		1980-81	1985-86
Roupe, Magnus	Phi.	2	40	3	5	8	42	....	....	....	....	....		1987-88	1988-89
Rousseau, Bobby	Mtl., Min., NYR	15	942	245	458	703	359	128	27	57	84	69	4	1960-61	1974-75
Rousseau, Guy	Mtl.	2	4	0	1	1	0	....	....	....	....	....		1954-55	1956-57
Rousseau, Roland	Mtl.	1	2	0	0	0	0	....	....	....	....	....		1952-53	1952-53
Routhier, Jean-Marc	Que.	1	8	0	0	0	9	....	....	....	....	....		1989-90	1989-90
Rowe, Bobby	Bos.	1	4	1	0	1	0	....	....	....	....	....		1924-25	1924-25
Rowe, Mike	Pit.	3	11	0	0	0	11	....	....	....	....	....		1984-85	1986-87
Rowe, Ron	NYR	1	5	1	0	1	0	....	....	....	....	....		1947-48	1947-48
Rowe, Tom	Wsh., Hfd., Det.	7	357	85	100	185	615	3	2	0	2	0		1976-77	1982-83
Roy, Stephane	Min.	1	12	1	0	1	0	....	....	....	....	....		1987-88	1987-88
Rozzini, Gino	Bos.	1	31	5	10	15	20	6	1	2	3	6		1944-45	1944-45
Rucinski, Mike	Chi.	2	1	0	0	0	0	2	0	0	0	0		1987-88	1988-89
Ruelle, Bernard	Det.	1	2	1	0	1	0	....	....	....	....	....		1943-44	1943-44
Ruhnke, Kent	Bos.	1	2	0	1	1	0	....	....	....	....	....		1975-76	1975-76
Rundqvist, Thomas	Mtl.	1	2	0	1	1	0	....	....	....	....	....		1984-85	1984-85
• Runge, Paul	Bos., Mtl.M., Mtl.	7	143	18	22	40	57	7	0	0	0	6		1930-31	1937-38
Ruotsalainen, Reijo	NYR, Edm., N.J.	7	446	107	237	344	180	86	15	32	47	44	2	1981-82	1989-90
Ruotsalinen, Reijo	NYR, Edm.	6	405	104	225	329	160	64	13	21	34	32	2	1981-82	1986-87
Rupp, Duane	NYR, Tor., Min., Pit.	10	374	24	93	117	220	10	2	2	4	8		1962-63	1972-73
Ruskowski, Terry	Chi., L.A., Pit., Min.	10	630	113	313	426	1354	21	1	6	7	86		1979-80	1988-89
Russell, Churchill	NYR	3	90	20	16	36	12	....	....	....	....	....		1945-46	1947-48
Russell, Phil	Chi., Atl., Cgy., N.J., Buf.	15	1016	99	325	424	2038	73	4	22	26	202		1972-73	1986-87

S

Name	NHL Teams	NHL Seasons	Regular Schedule GP	G	A	TP	PIM	Playoffs GP	G	A	TP	PIM	NHL Cup Wins	First NHL Season	Last NHL Season
Saarinen, Simo	NYR	1	8	0	0	0	0	....	....	....	....	....		1984-85	1984-85
Sabol, Shaun	Phi.	1	2	0	0	0	0	....	....	....	....	....		1989-90	1989-90
Sabourin, Bob	Tor.	1	1	0	0	0	2	....	....	....	....	....		1951-52	1951-52
Sabourin, Gary	St.L., Tor., Cal., Clev.	10	627	169	188	357	397	62	19	11	30	58		1967-68	1976-77
Sacharuk, Larry	NYR, St.L.	5	151	29	33	62	42	2	1	1	2	2		1972-73	1976-77
Saganiuk, Rocky	Tor., Pit.	6	259	57	65	122	201	6	1	0	1	15		1978-79	1983-84
St. Laurent, Andre	NYI, Det., L.A., Pit.	11	644	129	187	316	749	59	8	12	20	48		1973-74	1983-84
St. Laurent, Dollard	Mtl., Chi.	12	652	29	133	162	496	92	2	22	24	87	5	1950-51	1961-62
St. Marseille, Frank	St.L., L.A.	10	707	140	285	425	242	88	20	25	45	18		1967-68	1976-77
St. Sauveur, Claude	Atl.	1	79	24	24	48	23	2	0	0	0	0		1975-76	1975-76
Saleski, Don	Phi., Col.	9	543	128	125	253	629	82	13	17	30	131	2	1971-72	1979-80
Salovaara, John	Det.	2	90	2	13	15	70	....	....	....	....	....		1974-75	1975-76
Salvian, Dave	NYI	1	....	....	....	....	....	1	0	1	1	2		1976-77	1976-77
Samis, Phil	Tor.	2	2	0	0	0	0	5	0	1	1	2	1	1947-48	1949-50
Sampson, Gary	Wsh.	4	105	13	22	35	25	12	1	0	1	0		1983-84	1986-87
Sandelin, Scott	Mtl., Phi., Min.	4	25	0	4	4	2	....	....	....	....	....		1986-87	1991-92
Sanderson, Derek	Bos., NYR, St.L., Van., Pit.	13	598	202	250	452	911	56	18	12	30	187	2	1965-66	1977-78
Sandford, Ed	Bos., Det., Chi.	9	502	106	145	251	355	42	12	11	24	27		1947-48	1955-56
• Sands, Charlie	Tor., Bos., Mtl., NYR	12	432	99	109	208	58	44	6	6	12	4	1	1932-33	1943-44
Sanipass, Everett	Chi., Que.	5	164	25	34	59	358	5	2	0	2	4		1986-87	1990-91
Sargent, Gary	L.A., Min.	8	402	61	161	222	273	20	5	7	12	8		1975-76	1982-83
Sarner, Craig	Bos.	1	7	0	0	0	0	....	....	....	....	....		1974-75	1974-75
Sarrazin, Dick	Phi.	3	100	20	35	55	22	4	0	0	0	0		1968-69	1971-72
Saskamoose, Fred	Chi.	1	11	0	0	0	6	....	....	....	....	....		1953-54	1953-54
Sasser, Grant	Pit.	1	3	0	0	0	0	....	....	....	....	....		1983-84	1983-84
Sather, Glen	Bos., Pit., NYR, St.L., Mtl., Min.	10	658	80	113	193	724	72	1	5	6	86		1966-67	1975-76
Saunders, Bernie	Que.	2	10	0	1	1	8	....	....	....	....	....		1979-80	1980-81
Saunders, Bud	Ott.	1	19	1	3	4	4	....	....	....	....	....		1933-34	1933-34

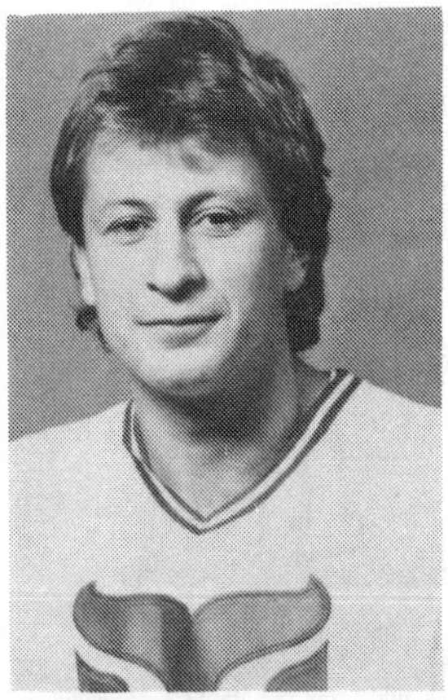

Torrie Robertson

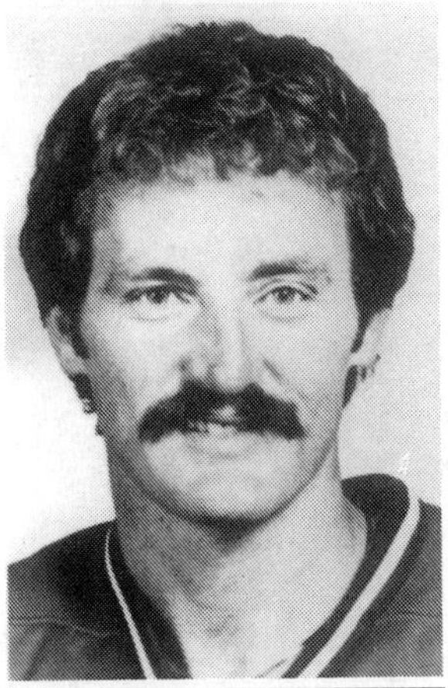

Larry Robinson

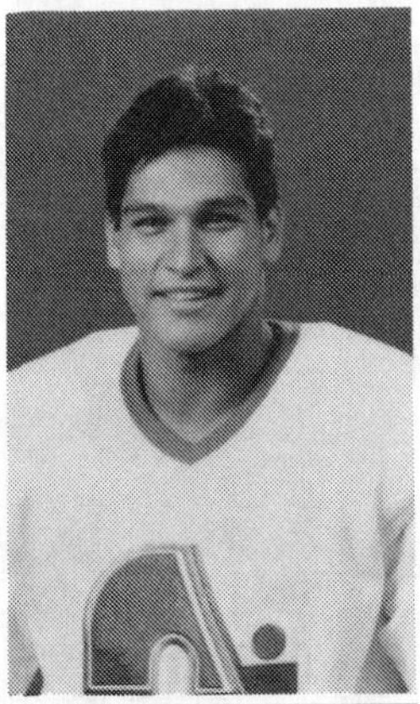

Everett Sanipass

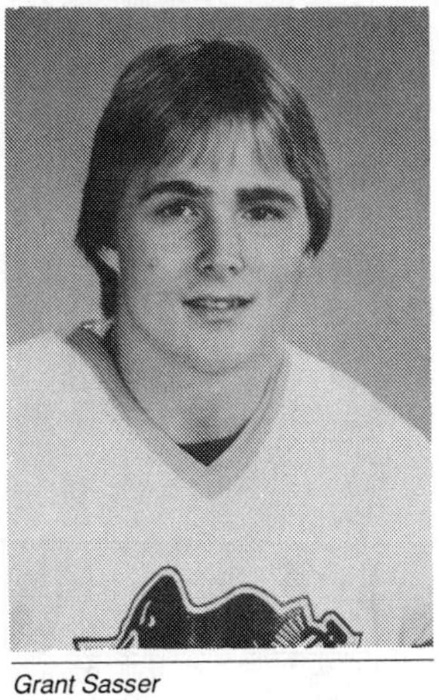

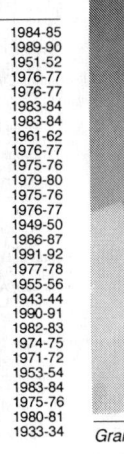

Grant Sasser

Milt Schmidt

Rod Schutt

Steve Seguin

Risto Siltanen

Name	NHL Teams	NHL Seasons	Regular Schedule GP	G	A	TP	PIM	Playoffs GP	G	A	TP	PIM	NHL Cup Wins	First NHL Season	Last NHL Season
Saunders, David	Van.	1	56	7	13	20	10	....	....	....	....	....		1987-88	1987-88
Sauve, Jenn F.	Buf., Que.	7	290	65	138	203	117	36	9	12	21	10		1980-81	1986-87
• Savage, Tony	Bos., Mtl.	1	49	1	5	6	6	2	0	0	0	0		1934-35	1934-35
Savard, Andre	Bos., Buf., Que.	12	790	211	271	482	411	85	13	18	31	77		1973-74	1984-85
Savard, Jean	Chi, Hfd.	3	43	7	12	19	29	....	....	....	....	....		1977-78	1979-80
Savard, Serge	Mtl., Wpg.	17	1040	106	333	439	592	130	19	49	68	88	7	1966-67	1982-83
Scamurra, Peter	Wsh.	4	132	8	25	33	59	....	....	....	....	....		1975-76	1979-80
Sceviour, Darin	Chi.	1	1	0	0	0	0	....	....	....	....	....		1986-87	1986-87
Schaeffer, Butch	Chi.,	1	5	0	0	0	6	....	....	....	....	....		1936-37	1936-37
Schamehorn, Kevin	Det., L.A.	3	10	0	0	0	17	....	....	....	....	....		1976-77	1980-81
Schella, John	Van.	2	115	2	18	20	224	....	....	....	....	....		1970-71	1971-72
Scherza, Chuck	Bos., NYR	2	56	6	6	12	35	....	....	....	....	....		1943-44	1944-45
Schinkel, Ken	NYR, Pit.	12	636	127	198	325	163	19	7	2	9	4		1959-60	1972-73
Schliebener, Andy	Van.	3	84	2	11	13	74	6	0	0	0	0		1981-82	1984-85
Schmautz, Bobby	Chi., Bos., Edm., Col., Van.	13	764	271	286	557	988	73	28	33	61	92		1967-68	1980-81
Schmautz, Cliff	Buf., Phi.	1	56	13	19	32	33	....	....	....	....	....		1970-71	1970-71
Schmidt, Clarence	Bos.,	1	7	1	0	1	2	....	....	....	....	....		1943-44	1943-44
Schmidt, Jackie	Bos.	1	45	6	7	13	6	5	0	0	0	0		1942-43	1942-43
Schmidt, Joseph	Bos.	1	2	0	0	0	0	....	....	....	....	....		1943-44	1943-44
Schmidt, Milt	Bos.	16	778	229	346	575	466	86	24	25	49	60	2	1936-37	1954-55
Schmidt, Norm	Pit.	4	125	23	33	56	73	....	....	....	....	....		1983-84	1987-88
Schnarr, Werner	Bos.	2	25	0	0	0	0	....	....	....	....	....		1924-25	1925-26
Schock, Danny	Bos., Phi.	2	20	1	2	3	0	1	0	0	0	0	1	1969-70	1970-71
Schock, Ron	Bos., St.L., Pit., Buf.	15	909	166	351	517	260	55	4	16	20	29		1963-64	1977-78
Schoenfeld, Jim	Buf., Det., Bos.	13	719	51	204	255	1132	75	3	13	16	151		1972-73	1984-85
Schofield, Dwight	Det., Mtl., St.L., Wsh., Pit., Wpg.	7	211	8	22	30	631	9	0	0	0	55		1976-77	1987-88
Schreiber, Wally	Min.	2	41	8	10	18	12	....	....	....	....	....		1987-88	1988-89
• Schriner, Sweeney	NYA, Tor.	11	484	201	204	405	148	60	18	11	29	54	2	1934-35	1945-46
Schultz, Dave	Phi., L.A., Pit., Buf.	9	535	79	121	200	2294	73	8	12	20	412	2	1971-72	1979-80
Schurman, Maynard	Hfd.	1	7	0	0	0	0	....	....	....	....	....		1979-80	1979-80
Schutt, Rod	Mtl., Pit., Tor.	8	286	77	92	169	177	22	8	6	14	26		1977-78	1985-86
Sclisizzi, Enio	Det., Chi.	6	81	12	11	23	26	13	0	0	0	6		1946-47	1952-53
Scott, Ganton	Tor., Ham., Mtl.M.	3	53	1	1	2	0	....	....	....	....	....		1922-23	1924-25
• Scott, Laurie	NYA, NYR	2	62	6	3	9	28	....	....	....	....	....	1	1926-27	1927-28
Scruton, Howard	L.A.	1	4	0	4	4	9	....	....	....	....	....		1982-83	1982-83
Seabrooke, Glen	Phi.	3	19	1	6	7	4	....	....	....	....	....		1986-87	1988-89
Secord, Al	Bos., Chi., Tor, Phi.	12	766	273	222	495	2093	102	21	34	55	382		1978-79	1989-90
Sedlbauer, Ron	Van., Chi., Tor.	7	430	143	86	229	210	19	1	3	4	27		1974-75	1980-81
Seftel, Steve	Wsh.	1	4	0	0	0	2	....	....	....	....	....		1990-91	1990-91
Seguin, Dan	Min., Van.	2	37	2	6	8	50	....	....	....	....	....		1970-71	1973-74
Seguin, Steve	L.A.	1	5	0	0	0	9	....	....	....	....	....		1984-85	1984-85
• Seibert, Earl	NYR, Chi., Det.	15	652	89	187	276	768	66	8	9	19	66	2	1931-32	1945-46
Seiling, Ric	Buf., Det.	10	738	179	208	387	573	62	14	14	28	36		1977-78	1986-87
Seiling, Rod	Tor., NYR, Wsh., St.L., Atl.	17	979	62	269	331	603	77	4	8	12	55		1962-63	1978-79
Sejba, Jiri	Buf.	1	11	0	2	2	8	....	....	....	....	....		1990-91	1990-91
Selby, Brit	Tor., Phi., St.L.	8	350	55	62	117	163	16	1	1	2	8		1964-65	1971-72
Self, Steve	Wsh.	1	3	0	0	0	0	....	....	....	....	....		1976-77	1976-77
Selwood, Brad	Tor., L.A.	3	163	7	40	47	153	6	0	0	0	4		1970-71	1979-80
Semenko, Dave	Edm., Hfd., Tor.	9	575	65	88	153	1175	73	6	6	12	208	2	1979-80	1987-88
Senick, George	NYR	1	13	2	3	5	8	....	....	....	....	....		1952-53	1952-53
Seppa, Jyrki	Wpg.	1	13	0	2	2	6	....	....	....	....	....		1983-84	1983-84
Serafini, Ron	Cal.	1	2	0	0	0	2	....	....	....	....	....		1973-74	1973-74
Servinis, George	Min.	1	5	0	0	0	0	....	....	....	....	....		1987-88	1987-88
Sevcik, Jaroslav	Que.	1	13	0	2	2	2	....	....	....	....	....		1989-90	1989-90
Shack, Eddie	NYR, Tor., Bos., L.A., Buf., Pit.	17	1047	239	226	465	1437	74	6	7	13	151	4	1958-59	1974-75
• Shack, Joe	NYR	2	70	23	13	36	20	....	....	....	....	....		1942-43	1944-45
Shakes, Paul	Cal.	1	21	0	4	4	12	....	....	....	....	....		1973-74	1973-74
Shanahan, Sean	Mtl., Col., Bos.	3	40	1	3	4	47	....	....	....	....	....		1975-76	1977-78
Shand, Dave	Atl., Tor., Wsh.	8	421	19	84	103	544	26	1	2	3	83		1976-77	1984-85
Shannon, Charles	NYA	1	4	0	0	0	2	....	....	....	....	....		1939-40	1939-40
Shannon, Gerry	Ott., St.L., Bos., Mtl.M.	5	183	23	29	52	121	9	0	1	1	2		1933-34	1937-38
Sharpley, Glen	Min., Chi.	6	389	117	161	278	199	27	7	11	18	24		1976-77	1981-82
Shaunessy, Scott	Que.	1	3	0	0	0	7	....	....	....	....	....		1986-87	1986-87
Shaunessy, Scott	Que.	2	7	0	0	0	23	....	....	....	....	....		1986-87	1988-89
Shay, Norman	Bos., Tor.	2	53	5	2	7	34	....	....	....	....	....		1924-25	1925-26
Shea, Pat	Chi.	1	14	0	1	1	0	....	....	....	....	....		1931-32	1931-32
Shedden, Doug	Pit., Det., Que., Tor.	8	416	139	186	325	176	....	....	....	....	....		1981-82	1990-91
Sheehan, Bobby	Mtl., Cal., Chi., Det., NYR, Col., L.A.	9	310	48	63	111	50	25	4	3	7	8	1	1969-70	1981-82
Sheehy, Neil	Cgy., Hfd., Wsh.	9	379	18	47	65	1311	54	0	3	3	241		1983-84	1991-92
Sheehy, Tim	Det., Hfd.	2	27	2	1	3	0	....	....	....	....	....		1977-78	1979-80
Shelton, Doug	Chi.	1	5	0	1	1	0	....	....	....	....	....		1967-68	1967-68
Sheppard, Frank	Det.	1	8	1	1	2	0	....	....	....	....	....		1927-28	1927-28
Sheppard, Gregg	Bos., Pit.	10	657	205	293	498	243	92	32	40	72	31		1972-73	1981-82
Sheppard, Johnny	Det., NYA, Bos., Chi.	8	311	68	58	126	224	10	0	0	0	0	1	1926-27	1933-34
Sherf, John	Det.	5	19	0	0	0	8	8	0	1	1	2	1	1935-36	1943-44
• Shero, Fred	NYR	3	145	6	14	20	137	13	0	2	2	8		1947-48	1949-50
Sherritt, Gordon	Det.	1	8	0	0	0	12	....	....	....	....	....		1943-44	1943-44
Sherven, Gord	Edm., Min., Hfd.	5	97	13	22	35	33	3	0	0	0	0		1983-84	1987-88
• Shewchuck, Jack	Bos.	6	187	9	19	28	160	20	0	1	1	19	1	1938-39	1944-45
Shibicky, Alex	NYR	8	317	110	91	201	159	40	12	12	24	12	1	1935-36	1945-46
Shields, Al	Ott., Phi., NYA, Mtl.M., Bos.	11	460	42	46	88	637	17	0	1	1	14	1	1927-28	1937-38
Shill, Bill	Bos.	3	79	21	13	34	18	7	1	2	3	2		1942-43	1946-47
• Shill, Jack	Tor., Bos., NYA, Chi.	6	163	15	20	35	70	27	1	6	7	13	1	1933-34	1938-39
Shinske, Rick	Clev., St.L.	3	63	5	16	21	10	....	....	....	....	....		1976-77	1978-79
Shires, Jim	Det., St.L., Pit.	3	56	3	6	9	32	....	....	....	....	....		1970-71	1972-73
Shmyr, Paul	Chi., Cal., Min., Hfd.	7	343	13	72	85	528	34	3	3	6	44		1968-69	1981-82
Shoebottom, Bruce	Bos.	4	35	1	4	5	53	14	1	2	3	77		1987-88	1990-91
• Shore, Eddie	Bos., NYA	14	553	105	179	284	1047	55	6	13	19	187	2	1926-27	1939-40
• Shore, Hamby	Ott.	1	18	3	0	3	0	....	....	....	....	....		1917-18	1917-18
Shores, Aubry	Phi.	1	1	0	0	0	0	....	....	....	....	....		1930-31	1930-31
Short, Steve	L.A., Det.	2	6	0	0	0	2	....	....	....	....	....		1977-78	1978-79
Shudra, Ron	Edm.	1	10	0	5	5	6	....	....	....	....	....		1987-88	1987-88
Shutt, Steve	Mtl., L.A.	13	930	424	393	817	410	99	50	48	98	65	5	1972-73	1984-85
• Siebert, Babe	Mtl.M., NYR, Bos., Mtl.	14	592	140	156	296	982	53	8	7	15	62	2	1925-26	1938-39
Silk, Dave	NYR, Bos., Wpg., Det.	7	249	54	59	113	271	13	2	4	6	13		1979-80	1985-86
Siltala, Mike	Wsh., NYR	3	7	1	0	1	2	....	....	....	....	....		1981-82	1987-88
Siltanen, Risto	Edm., Hfd., Que.	8	562	90	265	355	266	32	6	12	18	30		1979-80	1986-87
Sim, Trevor	Edm.	1	3	0	1	1	2	....	....	....	....	....		1989-90	1989-90
Simmer, Charlie	Cal., Cle., L.A., Bos., Pit.	14	712	342	369	711	544	24	9	9	18	32		1974-75	1987-88
Simmons, Al	Cal., Bos.	3	11	0	1	1	21	1	0	0	0	0		1971-72	1975-76
Simon, Cully	Det., Chi.	3	130	4	11	15	121	14	0	1	1	6	1	1942-43	1944-45
Simon, Thain	Det.	1	3	0	0	0	0	....	....	....	....	....		1946-47	1946-47
Simonetti, Frank	Bos.	4	115	5	8	13	76	12	0	1	1	8		1984-85	1987-88
Simpson, Bobby	Atl., St.L., Pit.	5	175	35	29	64	98	6	0	1	1	2		1976-77	1982-83
• Simpson, Cliff	Det.	2	6	0	1	1	0	2	0	0	0	0		1946-47	1947-48
• Simpson, Joe	NYA	6	228	21	19	40	156	2	0	0	0	0		1925-26	1930-31
Sims, Al	Bos., Hfd., L.A.	10	475	49	116	165	286	41	0	2	2	14		1973-74	1982-83
Sinclair, Reg	NYR, Det.	3	208	49	43	92	139	3	1	0	1	0		1950-51	1952-53
Singbush, Alex	Mtl.	1	32	0	5	5	15	3	0	0	0	4		1940-41	1940-41
Sirois, Bob	Phi., Wsh.	6	286	92	120	212	42	....	....	....	....	....		1974-75	1979-80
Sittler, Darryl	Tor., Phi., Det.	15	1096	484	637	1121	948	76	29	45	74	137		1970-71	1984-85
• Sjoberg, Lars-Erik	Wpg.	1	79	7	27	34	48	....	....	....	....	....		1979-80	1979-80
• Skaare, Bjorne	Det.	1	1	0	0	0	0	....	....	....	....	....		1978-79	1978-79
• Skilton, Raymie	Mtl.W	1	1	1	0	1	0	....	....	....	....	....		1917-18	1917-18
• Skinner, Alf	Tor., Bos., Mtl.M., Pit.	4	70	26	4	30	56	7	8	1	9	0	1	1917-18	1925-26
Skinner, Larry	Col.	4	47	10	12	22	8	2	0	0	0	0		1976-77	1979-80
Skov, Glen	Det., Chi., Mtl.	12	650	106	136	242	413	53	7	7	14	48	3	1949-50	1960-61
Sleaver, John	Chi.	2	24	2	0	2	6	....	....	....	....	....		1953-54	1956-57
Sleigher, Louis	Que., Bos.	6	194	46	53	99	146	17	1	1	2	64		1979-80	1985-86
Sloan, Tod	Tor., Chi.	13	745	220	262	482	781	47	9	12	21	47	2	1947-48	1960-61
Slobodzian, Peter	NYA	1	41	3	2	5	54	....	....	....	....	....		1940-41	1940-41
Slowinski, Eddie	NYR	6	291	58	74	132	63	16	2	6	8	6		1947-48	1952-53
Sly, Darryl	Tor., Min., Van.	4	79	1	2	3	20	....	....	....	....	....		1965-66	1970-71
Smart, Alex	Mtl.	1	8	3	5	8	0	....	....	....	....	....		1942-43	1942-43
Smedsmo, Dale	Tor.	1	4	0	0	0	0	....	....	....	....	....		1972-73	1972-73

Name	NHL Teams	NHL Seasons	Regular Schedule					Playoffs					NHL Cup Wins	First NHL Season	Last NHL Season
			GP	G	A	TP	PIM	GP	G	A	TP	PIM			
Smillie, Don	Bos.	1	12	2	2	4	4	....	....	....	....	....		1933-34	1933-34
• Smith, Alex	Ott., Det., Bos., NYA	11	443	41	50	91	643	19	0	2	2	40	1	1924-25	1934-35
• Smith, Arthur	Tor., Ott.	4	137	15	10	25	249	4	1	1	2	8		1927-28	1930-31
Smith, Barry	Bos., Col.	3	114	7	7	14	10	....	....	....	....	....		1975-76	1980-81
Smith, Brad	Van., Atl., Cgy., Det., Tor.	9	222	28	34	62	591	20	3	3	6	49		1978-79	1986-87
Smith, Brian D.	L.A., Min.	2	67	10	10	20	33	7	0	0	0	0		1967-68	1968-69
Smith, Brian S.	Det.	3	61	2	8	10	12	5	0	0	0	0		1957-58	1960-61
Smith, Carl	Det.	1	7	1	1	2	2	....	....	....	....	....		1943-44	1943-44
Smith, Clint	NYR, Chi.	11	483	161	236	397	24	44	10	14	24	2	1	1936-37	1946-47
Smith, Dallas	Bos., NYR	16	890	55	252	307	959	86	3	29	32	128	2	1959-60	1977-78
Smith, Dalton	NYA, Det.	2	11	1	2	3	0	....	....	....	....	....		1936-37	1943-44
Smith, Dennis	Wsh., L.A.	2	8	0	0	0	4	....	....	....	....	....		1989-90	1990-91
Smith, Derek	Buf., Det.	8	335	78	116	194	60	30	9	14	23	13		1975-76	1982-83
Smith, Des	Mtl.M., Mtl., Chi., Bos.	5	195	22	25	47	236	25	1	4	5	18	1	1937-38	1941-42
• Smith, Don	Mtl.	1	10	1	0	1	4	....	....	....	....	....		1919-20	1919-20
Smith, Don A.	NYR	1	11	1	1	2	0	1	0	0	0	0		1949-50	1949-50
Smith, Doug	L.A., Buf., Edm., Van., Pit.	9	535	115	138	253	624	....	....	....	....	....		1981-82	1989-90
Smith, Floyd	Bos., NYR, Det., Tor., Buf.	13	616	129	178	307	207	48	12	11	23	16		1954-55	1971-72
Smith, George	Tor.	1	9	0	0	0	0	....	....	....	....	....		1921-22	1921-22
Smith, Glen	Chi.	1	2	0	0	0	0	....	....	....	....	....		1950-51	1950-51
Smith, Glenn	Tor.	1	9	0	0	0	0	....	....	....	....	....		1922-23	1922-23
Smith, Gord	Wsh., Wpg.	6	299	9	30	39	284	....	....	....	....	....		1974-75	1979-80
Smith, Greg	Cal., Clev., Min., Det., Wsh.	13	829	56	232	288	1110	63	4	7	11	106		1975-76	1987-88
• Smith, Hooley	Ott., Mtl.M., Bos., NYA	17	715	200	215	415	1013	54	11	8	19	109	2	1924-25	1940-41
Smith, Kenny	Bos.	7	331	78	93	171	49	30	8	13	21	6		1944-45	1950-51
Smith, Randy		0	3	0	0	0	0	....	....	....	....	....			
Smith, Rick	Bos., Cal., St.L., Det., Wsh.	11	687	52	167	219	560	78	3	23	26	73	1	1968-69	1980-81
• Smith, Roger	Pit., Phi.	6	210	20	4	24	172	4	3	0	3	0		1925-26	1930-31
Smith, Ron	NYI	1	11	1	1	2	14	....	....	....	....	....		1972-73	1972-73
Smith, Sid	Tor.	12	601	186	183	369	94	44	17	10	27	2	3	1946-47	1957-58
Smith, Stan	NYR	2	9	2	1	3	0	....	....	....	....	....	1	1939-40	1940-41
Smith, Steve	Phi., Buf.	6	173	20	95	115	443	8	0	0	0	20		1981-82	1988-89
Smith, Stu E.	Mtl.	2	4	2	2	4	2	1	0	0	0	0		1940-41	1941-42
Smith, Stu G.	Hfd.	4	77	2	10	12	95	....	....	....	....	....		1979-80	1982-83
• Smith, Tommy	Que.B.	1	10	0	0	0	9	....	....	....	....	....		1919-20	1919-20
Smith, Vern	NYI	1	1	0	0	0	0	....	....	....	....	....		1984-85	1984-85
Smith, Wayne	Chi.	1	2	1	1	2	2	1	0	0	0	0		1966-67	1966-67
Smrke, John	St.L., Que.	3	103	11	17	28	33	....	....	....	....	....		1977-78	1979-80
• Smrke, Stan	Mtl.	2	9	0	3	3	0	....	....	....	....	....		1956-57	1957-58
Smyl, Stan	Van.	13	896	262	411	673	1556	41	16	17	33	64		1978-79	1990-91
• Smylie, Rod	Tor., Ott.	6	76	4	1	5	10	9	1	2	3	2	1	1920-21	1925-26
Snell, Ron	Pit.	2	7	3	2	5	6	....	....	....	....	....		1968-69	1969-70
Snell, Ted	Pit., K.C., Det.	2	104	7	18	25	22	....	....	....	....	....		1973-74	1974-75
Snepsts, Harold	Van., Min., Det., St.L.	17	1033	38	195	223	2009	93	1	14	15	231		1974-75	1990-91
Snow, Sandy	Det.	1	3	0	0	0	2	....	....	....	....	....		1968-69	1968-69
Sobchuk, Denis	Det., Que.	2	35	5	6	11	2	....	....	....	....	....		1979-80	1982-83
Sobchuk, Gene	Van.	1	1	0	0	0	0	....	....	....	....	....		1973-74	1973-74
Solheim, Ken	Chi., Min., Det., Edm.	5	135	19	20	39	34	3	1	1	2	2		1980-81	1985-86
Solinger, Bob	Tor., Det.	5	99	10	11	21	19	....	....	....	....	....		1951-52	1959-60
• Somers, Art	Chi., NYR	6	222	33	56	89	189	30	1	5	6	20	1	1929-30	1934-35
Sommer, Roy	Edm.	1	3	1	0	1	7	....	....	....	....	....		1980-81	1980-81
Songin, Tom	Bos.	3	43	5	5	10	22	....	....	....	....	....		1978-79	1980-81
Sonmor, Glen	NYR	2	28	2	0	2	21	....	....	....	....	....		1953-54	1954-55
• Sorrell, John	Det., NYA	11	490	127	119	246	100	42	12	15	27	10	2	1930-31	1940-41
Sparrow, Emory	Bos.	1	6	0	0	0	4	....	....	....	....	....		1924-25	1924-25
Speck, Fred	Det., Van.	3	28	1	2	3	2	....	....	....	....	....		1968-69	1971-72
• Speer, Bill	Pit., Bos.	4	130	5	20	25	79	8	1	0	1	4	1	1967-68	1970-71
Speers, Ted	Det.	1	4	1	1	2	0	....	....	....	....	....		1985-86	1985-86
• Spencer, Brian	Tor., NYI, Buf., Pit.	10	553	80	143	223	634	37	1	5	6	29		1969-70	1978-79
Spencer, Irv	NYR, Bos., Det.	8	230	12	38	50	127	16	0	0	0	8		1959-60	1967-68
Speyer, Chris	Tor., NYA	3	14	0	0	0	0	....	....	....	....	....		1923-24	1933-34
Spring, Don	Wpg.	4	259	1	52	55	80	6	0	0	0	10		1980-81	1983-84
Spring, Frank	Bos., St.L., Cal., Clev.	5	61	14	20	34	12	....	....	....	....	....		1969-70	1976-77
• Spring, Jesse	Ham., Pit., Tor., NYA	6	137	11	2	13	62	2	0	2	2	2		1923-24	1929-30
Spruce, Andy	Van., Col.	3	172	31	42	73	111	2	0	2	2	2		1976-77	1978-79
Srsen, Tomas	Edm.	1	2	0	0	0	0	....	....	....	....	....		1990-91	1990-91
Stackhouse, Ron	Cal., Det., Pit.	12	889	87	372	459	824	32	5	8	13	38		1970-71	1981-82
Stackhouse, Ted	Tor.	1	12	0	0	0	2	5	0	0	0	0	1	1921-22	1921-22
Stahan, Butch	Mtl.	1	....	....	....	....	....	3	0	1	1	2		1944-45	1944-45
Staley, Al	NYR	1	1	0	1	1	0	....	....	....	....	....		1948-49	1948-49
Stamler, Lorne	L.A., Tor., Wpg.	4	116	14	11	25	16	....	....	....	....	....		1976-77	1979-80
Standing, George	Min.	1	2	0	0	0	0	....	....	....	....	....		1967-68	1967-68
Stanfield, Fred	Chi., Bos., Min., Buf.	14	914	211	405	616	134	106	21	35	56	10	2	1964-65	1977-78
Stanfield, Jack	Chi.	1	....	....	....	....	....	1	0	0	0	0		1965-66	1965-66
Stanfield, Jim	L.A.	3	7	0	1	1	0	....	....	....	....	....		1969-70	1971-72
Stankiewicz, Edward	Det.	2	6	0	0	0	2	....	....	....	....	....		1953-54	1955-56
Stankiewicz, Myron	St.L., Phi.	1	35	0	7	7	36	1	0	0	0	0		1968-69	1968-69
Stanley, Allan	NYR, Chi., Bos., Tor., Phi.	21	1244	100	333	433	792	109	7	36	43	80	4	1948-49	1968-69
• Stanley, Barney	Chi.	1	1	0	0	0	0	....	....	....	....	....		1927-28	1927-28
Stanley, Daryl	Phi., Van.	6	189	8	17	25	408	17	0	0	0	30		1983-84	1989-90
Stanowski, Wally	Tor., NYR	10	428	23	88	111	160	60	3	14	17	13	4	1939-40	1950-51
Stapleton, Brian	Wsh.	1	1	0	0	0	0	....	....	....	....	....		1975-76	1975-76
Stapleton, Pat	Bos., Chi.	10	635	43	294	337	353	65	10	39	49	38		1961-62	1972-73
Starikov, Sergei	N.J.	1	16	0	1	1	8	....	....	....	....	....		1989-90	1989-90
Starr, Harold	Ott., Mtl.M., Mtl., NYR	7	203	6	5	11	186	17	1	0	1	2		1929-30	1935-36
Starr, Wilf	NYA, Det.	4	89	8	6	14	25	7	0	2	2	2	1	1932-33	1935-36
Stasiuk, Vic	Chi., Det., Bos.	14	745	183	254	437	669	69	16	18	34	40	2	1949-50	1962-63
Stastny, Anton	Que.	9	650	252	384	636	150	66	20	32	52	31		1980-81	1988-89
Stastny, Marian	Que., Tor.	5	322	121	173	294	110	32	5	17	22	7		1981-82	1985-86
Staszak, Ray	Det.	1	4	0	1	1	7	....	....	....	....	....		1985-86	1985-86
Steele, Frank	Det.	1	1	0	0	0	0	....	....	....	....	....		1930-31	1930-31
Steen, Anders	Wpg.	1	42	5	11	16	22	....	....	....	....	....		1980-81	1980-81
Stefaniw, Morris	Atl.	1	13	1	1	2	2	....	....	....	....	....		1972-73	1972-73
Stefanski, Bud	NYR	1	1	0	0	0	0	....	....	....	....	....		1977-78	1977-78
Stemkowski, Pete	Tor., Det., NYR, L.A.	15	967	206	349	555	866	83	25	29	54	136	1	1963-64	1977-78
Stenlund, Vern	Clev.	1	4	0	0	0	0	....	....	....	....	....		1976-77	1976-77
• Stephens, Phil	Mtl.W, Mtl.	2	8	1	0	1	0	....	....	....	....	....		1917-18	1921-22
Stephenson, Bob	Hfd., Tor.	1	18	2	3	5	4	....	....	....	....	....		1979-80	1979-80
Sterner, Ulf	NYR	1	4	0	0	0	0	....	....	....	....	....		1964-65	1964-65
Stevens, Paul	Bos.	1	17	0	0	0	0	....	....	....	....	....		1925-26	1925-26
Stewart, Bill	Buf., St.L., Tor., Min.	8	261	7	64	71	424	13	1	3	4	11		1977-78	1985-86
Stewart, Blair	Det., Wsh., Que.	7	229	34	44	78	326	....	....	....	....	....		1973-74	1979-80
Stewart, Gaye	Tor., Chi., Det., NYR, Mtl.	11	502	185	159	344	274	25	2	9	11	16	2	1941-42	1953-54
• Stewart, Jack	Det., Chi.	12	565	31	84	115	765	80	5	14	19	143	2	1938-39	1951-52
Stewart, John	Pit., Atl., Cal., Que.	6	260	58	60	118	158	4	0	0	0	10		1970-71	1979-80
Stewart, Ken	Chi.	1	6	1	1	2	2	....	....	....	....	....		1941-42	1941-42
• Stewart, Nels	Mtl.M., Bos., NYA	15	650	324	191	515	953	54	15	11	26	61	1	1925-26	1939-40
Stewart, Paul	Que.	1	21	2	0	2	74	....	....	....	....	....		1979-80	1979-80
Stewart, Ralph	Van., NYI	7	252	57	73	130	28	19	4	4	8	2		1970-71	1977-78
Stewart, Robert	Bos., Cal., Clev., St.L., Pit.	9	510	27	101	128	809	5	1	1	2	2		1971-72	1979-80
Stewart, Ron	Tor., Bos., St.L., NYR, Van., NYI	21	1353	276	253	529	560	119	14	21	35	60	3	1952-53	1972-73
Stewart, Ryan	Wpg.	1	3	1	0	1	0	....	....	....	....	....		1985-86	1985-86
Stiles, Tony	Cgy.	1	30	2	7	9	20	....	....	....	....	....		1983-84	1983-84
Stoddard, Jack	NYR	2	80	16	15	31	31	....	....	....	....	....		1951-52	1952-53
Stoltz, Roland	Wsh.	1	14	2	2	4	14	....	....	....	....	....		1981-82	1981-82
Stone, Steve	Van.	1	2	0	0	0	0	....	....	....	....	....		1973-74	1973-74
Stothers, Michael	Phi., Tor.	4	30	0	2	2	65	5	0	0	0	11		1984-85	1987-88
Stoughton, Blaine	Pit., Tor., Hfd., NYR	8	526	258	191	449	204	8	4	2	6	2		1973-74	1983-84
Stoyanovich, Steve	Hfd.	1	23	3	5	8	11	....	....	....	....	....		1983-84	1983-84
Strain, Neil	NYR	1	52	11	13	24	12	....	....	....	....	....		1952-53	1952-53
Strate, Gord	Det.	3	61	0	0	0	34	....	....	....	....	....		1956-57	1958-59
Stratton, Art	NYR, Det., Chi., Pit., Phi.	4	95	18	33	51	24	5	0	0	0	0		1959-60	1967-68
Strobel, Art	NYR	1	7	0	0	0	0	....	....	....	....	....		1943-44	1943-44
Strong, Ken	Tor.	3	15	2	2	4	6	....	....	....	....	....		1982-83	1984-85
Strueby, Todd	Edm.	3	5	0	1	1	2	....	....	....	....	....		1981-82	1983-84

Brad Smith

Stan Smyl

Dennis Sobchuk

Anton Stastny

Patrik Sundstrom

Steve Tambellini

John Tonelli

Garry Unger

			Regular Schedule					Playoffs							
Name	NHL Teams	NHL Seasons	GP	G	A	TP	PIM	GP	G	A	TP	PIM	NHL Cup Wins	First NHL Season	Last NHL Season
• Stuart, Billy	Tor., Bos.	7	193	30	17	47	145	17	1	0	1	12	1	1920-21	1926-27
Stumpf, Robert	St.L., Pit.	1	10	1	1	2	20	....	....	....	....	....		1974-75	1974-75
Sturgeon, Peter	Col.	2	6	0	1	1	2	....	....	....	....	....		1979-80	1980-81
Suikkanen, Kai	Buf.	2	2	0	0	0	0	....	....	....	....	....		1981-82	1982-83
Sulliman, Doug	NYR, Hfd., N.J., Phi.	11	631	160	168	328	175	16	1	3	4	2		1979-80	1989-90
Sullivan, Barry	Det.	1	1	0	0	0	0	....	....	....	....	....		1947-48	1947-48
Sullivan, Bob	Hfd.	1	62	18	19	37	18	....	....	....	....	....		1982-83	1982-83
Sullivan, Frank	Tor., Chi.	4	8	0	0	0	2	....	....	....	....	....		1949-50	1955-56
Sullivan, Peter	Wpg.	2	126	28	54	82	40	....	....	....	....	....		1979-80	1980-81
Sullivan, Red	Bos., Chi., NYR	11	557	107	239	346	441	18	1	2	3	7		1949-50	1960-61
Summanen, Raimo	Edm., Van.	5	151	36	40	76	35	10	2	5	7	0		1983-84	1987-88
• Summerhill, Bill	Mtl., Bro.	3	72	14	17	31	70	3	0	0	0	2		1938-39	1941-42
Sundstrom, Patrik	Van., N.J.	10	679	219	369	588	349	37	9	17	26	25		1982-83	1991-92
Sundstrom, Peter	NYR, Wsh., N.J.	6	338	61	83	144	120	23	3	3	6	8		1983-84	1989-90
Suomi, Al	Chi.	1	5	0	0	0	0	....	....	....	....	....		1936-37	1936-37
Sutherland, Bill	Mtl., Phi., Tor., St.L., Det.	6	250	70	58	128	99	14	2	4	6	0		1962-63	1971-72
Sutherland, Ron	Bos.	1	2	0	0	0	0	....	....	....	....	....		1931-32	1931-32
Sutter, Brian	St.L	12	779	303	333	636	1786	65	21	21	42	249		1976-77	1987-88
Sutter, Darryl	Chi.	8	406	161	118	279	288	51	24	19	43	26		1979-80	1986-87
Sutter, Duane	NYI, Chi.	11	731	139	203	342	1333	161	26	32	58	405	4	1979-80	1989-90
Suzor, Mark	Phi., Col.	2	64	4	16	20	60	....	....	....	....	....		1976-77	1977-78
Svensson, Leif	Wsh.	2	121	6	40	46	49	....	....	....	....	....		1978-79	1979-80
Swain, Garry	Pit.	1	9	1	1	2	0	....	....	....	....	....		1968-69	1968-69
Swarbrick, George	Oak., Pit., Phi.	4	132	17	25	42	173	....	....	....	....	....		1967-68	1970-71
• Sweeney, Bill	NYR	1	4	1	0	1	0	....	....	....	....	....		1959-60	1959-60
Sykes, Bob	Tor.	1	2	0	0	0	0	....	....	....	....	....		1974-75	1974-75
Sykes, Phil	L.A., Wpg.	10	456	79	85	164	519	26	0	3	3	29		1982-83	1991-92
Szura, Joe	Oak.	2	90	10	15	25	30	7	2	3	5	2		1967-68	1968-69
T															
Taft, John	Det.	1	15	0	2	2	4	....	....	....	....	....		1978-79	1978-79
Talafous, Dean	Atl., Min., NYR	8	497	104	154	258	163	21	4	7	11	11		1974-75	1981-82
Talakoski, Ron	NYR	2	9	0	1	1	33	....	....	....	....	....		1986-87	1987-88
Talbot, Jean-Guy	Mtl., Min., Det., St.L., Buf.	17	1056	43	242	285	1006	150	4	26	30	142	7	1954-55	1970-71
Tallon, Dale	Van., Chi., Pit.	10	642	98	238	336	568	33	2	10	12	45		1970-71	1979-80
Tambellini, Steve	NYI, Col., N.J., Cgy., Van.	10	553	160	150	310	105	2	0	1	1	0	1	1978-79	1987-88
Tanguay, Chris	Que.	1	2	0	0	0	0	....	....	....	....	....		1981-82	1981-82
Tannahill, Don	Van.	2	111	30	33	63	25	....	....	....	....	....		1972-73	1973-74
Tardif, Marc	Mtl., Que.	8	517	194	207	401	443	62	13	15	28	75	2	1969-70	1982-83
• Taylor, Billy	Tor., Det., Bos., NYR	7	323	87	180	267	120	33	6	18	24	13	1	1939-40	1947-48
• Taylor, Billy	NYR	1	2	0	0	0	0	....	....	....	....	....		1964-65	1964-65
Taylor, Bob	Bos.	1	8	0	0	0	6	....	....	....	....	....		1929-30	1929-30
Taylor, Harry	Tor., Chi.	3	66	5	10	15	30	1	0	0	0	0	1	1946-47	1951-52
Taylor, Mark	Phi., Pit., Wsh.	5	209	42	68	110	73	6	0	0	0	0		1981-82	1985-86
• Taylor, Ralph	Chi., NYR	3	99	4	1	5	169	4	0	0	0	10		1927-28	1929-30
Taylor, Ted	NYR, Det., Min., Van.	6	166	23	35	58	181	....	....	....	....	....		1964-65	1971-72
Teal, Jeff	Mtl.	1	6	0	1	1	0	....	....	....	....	....		1984-85	1984-85
Teal, Skip	Bos.	1	1	0	0	0	0	....	....	....	....	....		1954-55	1954-55
Teal, Victor	NYI	1	1	0	0	0	0	....	....	....	....	....		1973-74	1973-74
Tebbutt, Greg	Que., Pit.	2	26	0	3	3	35	....	....	....	....	....		1979-80	1983-84
Terbenche, Paul	Chi., Buf.	5	189	5	26	31	28	12	0	0	0	0		1967-68	1973-74
Terrion, Greg	L.A., Tor.	8	561	93	150	243	339	35	2	9	11	41		1980-81	1987-88
Terry, Bill	Min.	1	5	0	0	0	0	....	....	....	....	....		1987-88	1987-88
Tessier, Orval	Mtl., Bos.	3	59	5	7	12	6	....	....	....	....	....		1954-55	1960-61
Thatchell, Spence	NYR	1	1	0	0	0	0	....	....	....	....	....		1942-43	1942-43
Theberge, Greg	Wsh.	5	153	15	63	78	73	4	0	1	1	0		1979-80	1983-84
Thelin, Mats	Bos.	3	163	8	19	27	107	5	0	0	0	6		1984-85	1986-87
Thelven, Michael	Bos.	5	207	20	80	100	217	34	4	10	14	34		1985-86	1989-90
Therrien, Gaston	Que.	3	22	0	8	8	12	9	0	1	1	4		1980-81	1982-83
Thibaudeau, Gilles	Mtl., NYI, Tor.	5	119	25	37	62	40	8	3	3	6	2		1986-87	1990-91
Thibeault, Laurence	Det., Mtl.	2	5	0	2	2	0	....	....	....	....	....		1944-45	1945-46
Thiffault, Leo	Min.	1	....	....	....	....	....	5	0	0	0	0		1967-68	1967-68
Thomas, Cy	Chi., Tor.	1	14	2	2	4	12	....	....	....	....	....		1947-48	1947-48
Thomas, Reg	Que.	1	39	9	7	16	6	....	....	....	....	....		1979-80	1979-80
Thompson, Cliff	Bos.	2	13	0	1	1	2	....	....	....	....	....		1941-42	1948-49
Thompson, Errol	Tor., Det., Pit.	10	599	208	185	393	184	34	7	5	12	11		1970-71	1980-81
• Thompson, Kenneth	Mtl.W	1	1	0	0	0	0	....	....	....	....	....		1917-18	1917-18
Thompson, Paul	NYR, Chi.	13	586	153	179	332	336	48	11	11	22	54	3	1926-27	1938-39
• Thoms, Bill	Tor., Chi., Bos.	13	549	135	206	341	172	44	6	10	16	6		1932-33	1944-45
Thomson, Bill	Det., Chi.	2	10	2	2	4	0	2	0	0	0	0		1938-39	1943-44
Thomson, Floyd	St.L.	8	411	56	97	153	341	10	0	2	2	6		1971-72	1979-80
Thomson, Jack	NYA	3	15	1	1	2	0	2	0	0	0	0		1938-39	1940-41
• Thomson, Jimmy	Tor., Chi.	13	787	19	215	234	920	63	2	13	15	135	4	1945-46	1957-58
• Thomson, Rhys	Mtl., Tor.	2	25	0	2	2	38	....	....	....	....	....		1939-40	1942-43
Thornbury, Tom	Pit.	1	14	1	8	9	16	....	....	....	....	....		1983-84	1983-84
Thorsteinson, Joe	NYA	1	4	0	0	0	0	....	....	....	....	....		1932-33	1932-33
Thurier, Fred	NYA, Bro., NYR	3	80	25	27	52	18	....	....	....	....	....		1940-41	1944-45
Thurlby, Tom	Oak.	1	20	1	2	3	4	....	....	....	....	....		1967-68	1967-68
Thyer, Mario	Min.	1	5	0	0	0	0	1	0	0	0	2		1989-90	1989-90
Tidey, Alex	Buf., Edm.	3	9	0	0	0	8	2	0	0	0	0		1976-77	1979-80
Timgren, Ray	Tor., Chi.	6	251	14	44	58	70	30	3	9	12	6	2	1948-49	1954-55
Titanic, Morris	Buf.	2	19	0	0	0	0	....	....	....	....	....		1974-75	1975-76
Tkaczuk, Walt	NYR	14	945	227	451	678	556	93	19	32	51	119		1967-68	1980-81
Toal, Mike	Edm.	1	3	0	0	0	0	....	....	....	....	....		1979-80	1979-80
Tomalty, Glenn	Wpg.	1	1	0	0	0	0	....	....	....	....	....		1979-80	1979-80
Tomlinson, Kirk	Min.	1	1	0	0	0	0	....	....	....	....	....		1987-88	1987-88
Tonelli, John	NYI, Cgy., L.A., Chi., Que.	14	1028	325	511	836	911	172	40	75	115	200	4	1978-79	1991-92
Toomey, Sean	Min.	1	1	0	0	0	0	....	....	....	....	....		1986-87	1986-87
Toppazzini, Jerry	Bos., Chi., Det.	12	783	163	244	407	436	40	13	9	22	13		1952-53	1963-64
Toppazzini, Zellio	Bos., NYR, Chi.	5	123	21	22	43	49	2	0	0	0	0		1948-49	1956-57
Torkki, Jari	Chi.	1	4	1	0	1	0	....	....	....	....	....		1988-89	1988-89
Touhey, Bill	Mtl.M., Ott., Bos.	7	280	65	40	105	107	2	1	0	1	0		1927-28	1933-34
Toupin, Jaques	Chi.	1	8	1	2	3	0	4	0	0	0	0		1943-44	1943-44
Townsend, Art	Chi.	1	5	0	0	0	0	....	....	....	....	....		1926-27	1926-27
Trader, Larry	Det., St.L., Mtl.	4	91	5	13	18	74	3	0	0	0	0		1982-83	1987-88
Trainor, Wes	NYR	1	17	1	2	3	6	....	....	....	....	....		1948-49	1948-49
• Trapp, Bobby	Chi.	2	82	4	4	8	129	2	0	0	0	4		1926-27	1927-28
Trapp, Doug	Buf.	1	2	0	0	0	0	....	....	....	....	....		1986-87	1986-87
Traub, Percy	Chi., Det.	3	130	3	3	6	214	4	0	0	0	6		1926-27	1928-29
Tredway, Brock	L.A.	1	....	....	....	....	....	1	0	0	0	0		1981-82	1981-82
Tremblay, Brent	Wsh.	2	10	1	0	1	6	....	....	....	....	....		1978-79	1979-80
Tremblay, Gilles	Mtl.	9	509	168	162	330	161	48	9	14	23	4	2	1960-61	1968-69
Tremblay, J.C.	Mtl.	13	794	57	306	363	204	108	14	51	65	58	5	1959-60	1971-72
Tremblay, Marcel	Mtl.	1	10	0	2	2	0	....	....	....	....	....		1938-39	1938-39
Tremblay, Mario	Mtl.	12	852	258	326	584	1043	100	20	29	49	187	5	1974-75	1985-86
• Tremblay, Nels	Mtl.	2	3	0	1	1	0	2	0	0	0	0		1944-45	1945-46
Trimper, Tim	Chi., Wpg., Min.	6	190	30	36	66	153	2	0	0	0	2		1979-80	1984-85
• Trottier, Dave	Mtl.M., Det.	11	446	121	113	234	517	31	4	3	7	41	1	1928-29	1938-39
Trottier, Guy	NYR, Tor.	3	115	28	17	45	37	9	1	0	1	16		1968-69	1971-72
Trottier, Rocky	N.J.	2	38	6	4	10	2	....	....	....	....	....		1983-84	1984-85
• Trudel, Louis	Chi., Mtl.	8	306	49	69	118	122	24	1	3	4	6	2	1933-34	1940-41
Trudell, Rene	NYR	3	129	24	28	52	72	5	0	0	0	2		1945-46	1947-48
Tudin, Connie	Mtl.	1	4	0	1	1	4	....	....	....	....	....		1941-42	1941-42
Tudor, Rob	Van., St.L.	3	28	4	4	8	19	3	0	0	0	0		1978-79	1982-83
Tuer, Allan	L.A., Min., Hfd.	4	57	1	1	2	208	....	....	....	....	....		1985-86	1989-90
Turcotte, Alfie	Mtl., Wpg., Wsh.	7	112	17	29	46	49	5	0	0	0	0		1983-84	1990-91
Turlick, Gord	Bos.	1	2	0	0	0	2	....	....	....	....	....		1959-60	1959-60
Turnbull, Ian	Tor., L.A., Pit.	10	628	123	317	440	736	55	13	32	45	94		1973-74	1982-83
Turnbull, Perry	St.L., Mtl., Wpg.	9	608	188	163	351	1245	34	6	7	13	86		1979-80	1987-88
Turnbull, Randy	Cgy.	1	1	0	0	0	2	....	....	....	....	....		1981-82	1981-82
Turner, Bob	Mtl., Chi.	8	478	19	51	70	307	68	1	4	5	44	5	1955-56	1962-63
Turner, Dean	NYR, Col., L.A.	4	35	1	0	1	59	....	....	....	....	....		1978-79	1982-83

Name	NHL Teams	NHL Seasons	Regular Schedule GP	G	A	TP	PIM	Playoffs GP	G	A	TP	PIM	NHL Cup Wins	First NHL Season	Last NHL Season
Tustin, Norman	NYR	1	18	2	4	6	0	....	....	....	....	....		1941-42	1941-42
Tuten, Audley	Chi.	2	39	4	8	12	48	....	....	....	....	....		1941-42	1942-43
Tutt, Brian	Wsh.	1	7	1	0	1	2	....	....	....	....	....		1989-90	1989-90

U V

Name	NHL Teams	NHL Seasons	Regular Schedule GP	G	A	TP	PIM	Playoffs GP	G	A	TP	PIM	NHL Cup Wins	First NHL Season	Last NHL Season
Ubriaco, Gene	Pit., Oak., Chi.	3	177	39	35	74	50	11	2	0	2	4		1967-68	1969-70
Ullman, Norm	Det., Tor.	20	1410	490	739	1229	712	106	30	53	83	67		1955-56	1974-75
Unger, Garry	Tor., Det., St.L., Atl., L.A., Edm.	16	1105	413	391	804	1075	52	12	18	30	105		1967-68	1982-83
Vadnais, Carol	Mtl., Oak., Cal., Bos., NYR, N.J.	17	1087	169	418	587	1813	106	10	40	50	185	2	1966-67	1982-83
Vail, Eric	Atl, Cgy., Det.	9	591	216	260	476	281	20	5	6	11	6		1973-74	1981-82
Vail, Melville	NYR	2	50	4	1	5	18	10	0	0	0	2		1928-29	1929-30
Valentine, Chris	Wsh.	3	105	43	52	95	127	2	0	0	0	4		1981-82	1983-84
Valiquette, Jack	Tor., Col.	7	350	84	134	218	79	23	3	6	9	4		1974-75	1980-81
Van Boxmeer, John	Mtl., Col., Buf., Que.	11	588	84	274	358	465	38	5	15	20	37		1973-74	1983-84
Van Impe, Ed	Chi., Phi., Pit.	11	700	27	126	153	1025	66	1	12	13	131	2	1966-67	1976-77
Vasko, Elmer	Chi., Min.	13	786	34	166	200	719	78	2	7	9	73	1	1956-57	1969-70
Vasko, Rick	Det.	3	31	3	7	10	29	....	....	....	....	....		1977-78	1980-81
Vautour, Yvon	NYI, Col., N.J., Que.	6	204	26	33	59	401	....	....	....	....	....		1979-80	1984-85
Vaydik, Greg	Chi.	1	5	0	0	0	0	....	....	....	....	....		1976-77	1976-77
Veitch, Darren	Wsh., Det., Tor.	10	511	48	209	257	296	33	4	11	15	33		1980-81	1990-91
Venasky, Vic	L.A.	7	430	61	101	162	66	21	1	5	6	12		1972-73	1978-79
Veneruzzo, Gary	St.L.	2	7	1	1	2	0	9	0	2	2	2		1967-68	1971-72
Verret, Claude	Buf.	2	14	2	5	7	2	....	....	....	....	....		1983-84	1984-85
Verstraete, Leigh	Tor.	3	8	0	1	1	14	....	....	....	....	....		1982-83	1987-88
Ververgaert, Dennis	Van., Phi., Wsh.	8	583	176	216	392	247	8	1	2	3	6		1973-74	1980-81
Veysey, Sid	Van.	1	1	0	0	0	0	....	....	....	....	....		1977-78	1977-78
Vickers, Steve	NYR	10	698	246	340	586	330	68	24	25	49	58		1972-73	1981-82
Vigneault, Alain	St.L.	2	42	2	5	7	82	4	0	1	1	26		1981-82	1982-83
Vipond, Pete	Cal.	1	3	0	0	0	0	....	....	....	....	....		1972-73	1972-73
Virta, Hannu	Buf.	5	245	25	101	126	66	17	1	3	4	6		1981-82	1985-86
Viveiros, Emanuel	Min.	3	29	1	11	12	6	....	....	....	....	....		1985-86	1987-88
Vokes, Ed	Chi.	1	5	0	0	0	0	....	....	....	....	....		1930-31	1930-31
Volcan, Mickey	Hfd., Cgy.	4	162	8	33	41	146	....	....	....	....	....		1980-81	1983-84
Volmar, Doug	Det., L.A.	4	62	13	8	21	26	2	1	0	1	0		1969-70	1972-73
Voss, Carl	Tor., NYR, Det., Ott., St.L., Mtl.M., NYA, Chi.	8	261	34	70	104	50	24	5	3	8	0		1926-27	1937-38
Vyazmikin, Igor	Edm.	1	4	1	0	1	0	....	....	....	....	....		1990-91	1990-91

W

Name	NHL Teams	NHL Seasons	Regular Schedule GP	G	A	TP	PIM	Playoffs GP	G	A	TP	PIM	NHL Cup Wins	First NHL Season	Last NHL Season
Waddell, Don	L.A.	1	1	0	0	0	0	....	....	....	....	....		1980-81	1980-81
Waite, Frank	NYR	1	17	1	3	4	4	....	....	....	....	....		1930-31	1930-31
Walker, Gord	NYR, L.A.	4	31	3	4	7	23	....	....	....	....	....		1986-87	1989-90
Walker, Howard	Wsh., Cal.	3	83	2	13	15	133	....	....	....	....	....		1980-81	1982-83
• Walker, Jack	Det.	2	80	5	8	13	18	....	....	....	....	....		1926-27	1927-28
Walker, Kurt	Tor.	3	71	4	5	9	152	16	0	0	0	34		1975-76	1977-78
Walker, Russ	L.A.	2	17	1	0	1	41	....	....	....	....	....		1976-77	1977-78
Wall, Bob	Det., L.A., St.L.	8	322	30	55	85	155	22	0	3	3	2		1964-65	1971-72
Wallin, Peter	NYR	2	52	3	14	17	14	14	2	6	8	6		1980-81	1981-82
Walsh, Jim	Buf.	1	4	0	1	1	4	....	....	....	....	....		1981-82	1981-82
Walsh, Mike	NYI	2	14	2	0	2	4	....	....	....	....	....		1987-88	1988-89
Walton, Bobby	Mtl.	1	4	0	0	0	0	....	....	....	....	....		1943-44	1943-44
Walton, Mike	Tor., Bos., Van., Chi., St.L.	12	588	201	247	448	357	47	14	10	24	45	2	1965-66	1978-79
Wappel, Gord	Atl., Cgy.	3	20	1	1	2	10	2	0	0	0	4		1979-80	1981-82
Ward, Don	Chi., Bos.	2	34	0	1	1	16	....	....	....	....	....		1957-58	1959-60
• Ward, Jimmy	Mtl.M., Mtl.	12	532	147	127	274	465	31	4	4	8	18	1	1927-28	1938-39
Ward, Joe	Col.	1	4	0	0	0	2	....	....	....	....	....		1980-81	1980-81
Ward, Ron	Tor., Van.,	2	89	2	5	7	6	....	....	....	....	....		1969-70	1971-72
Ware, Michael	Edm.	2	5	0	1	1	15	....	....	....	....	....		1988-89	1989-90
Wares, Eddie	NYR, Det., Chi.	9	291	60	102	162	161	45	5	7	12	34	1	1936-37	1946-47
Warner, Bob	Tor.	2	10	1	1	2	4	4	0	0	0	0		1975-76	1976-77
Warner, Jim	Hfd.	1	32	0	3	3	10	....	....	....	....	....		1979-80	1979-80
Warwick, Bill	NYR	2	14	3	3	6	16	....	....	....	....	....		1942-43	1943-44
Warwick, Grant	NYR, Bos., Mtl.	9	395	147	142	289	220	16	2	4	6	6		1941-42	1949-50
• Wasnie, Nick	Chi., Mtl., NYA, Ott., St.L.	7	248	57	34	91	176	14	6	3	9	20	2	1927-28	1934-35
Watson, Bill	Chi.	4	115	23	36	59	12	6	0	2	2	0		1985-86	1988-89
Watson, Bryan	Mtl., Oak., Pit., Det., St.L., Wsh.	16	878	17	135	152	2212	32	2	0	2	70		1963-64	1978-79
Watson, Dave	Col.	2	18	0	1	1	10	....	....	....	....	....		1979-80	1980-81
Watson, Harry	Bro., Det., Tor., Chi.	14	805	236	207	443	150	62	16	9	25	27	5	1941-42	1956-57
Watson, Jim	Det., Buf.	7	221	4	19	23	345	....	....	....	....	....		1963-64	1971-72
Watson, Jimmy	Phi.	10	613	38	148	186	492	101	5	34	39	89	2	1972-73	1981-82
Watson, Joe	Bos., Phi., Col.	14	835	38	178	216	447	84	3	12	15	82	2	1964-65	1978-79
• Watson, Phil	NYR, Mtl.	13	590	144	265	409	542	45	10	25	35	67	2	1935-36	1947-48
Watts, Brian	Det.	1	4	0	0	0	0	....	....	....	....	....		1975-76	1975-76
Webster, Aubrey	Phi., Mtl.M.	2	5	0	0	0	0	....	....	....	....	....		1930-31	1934-35
• Webster, Don	Tor.	1	27	7	6	13	28	5	0	0	0	12		1943-44	1943-44
Webster, John	NYR	1	14	0	0	0	4	....	....	....	....	....		1949-50	1949-50
Webster, Tom	Bos., Det., Cal.	5	102	33	42	75	61	1	0	0	0	0		1968-69	1979-80
• Weiland, Cooney	Bos., Ott., Det.	11	508	173	160	333	147	45	12	10	22	12		1928-29	1938-39
Weir, Stan	Cal., Tor., Edm., Col., Det.	10	642	139	207	346	183	37	6	5	11	4		1972-73	1982-83
Weir, Wally	Que., Hfd., Pit.	6	320	21	45	66	625	23	0	1	1	96		1979-80	1984-85
• Wellington, Duke	Que.	1	1	0	0	0	0	....	....	....	....	....		1919-20	1919-20
Wensink, John	Bos., Que., Col., N.J., St.L.	8	403	70	68	138	840	43	2	6	8	86		1973-74	1982-83
• Wentworth, Cy	Chi., Mtl.M., Mtl.	13	578	39	68	107	355	35	5	6	11	22	1	1927-28	1939-40
Wesley, Blake	Phi., Hfd., Que., Tor.	7	298	18	46	64	486	19	2	2	4	30		1979-80	1985-86
Westfall, Ed	Bos., NYI	18	1227	231	394	625	544	95	22	37	59	41	2	1961-62	1978-79
Wharram, Kenny	Chi.	14	766	252	281	533	222	80	16	27	43	38	1	1951-52	1968-69
Wharton, Len	NYR	1	1	0	0	0	0	....	....	....	....	....		1944-45	1944-45
Wheeldon, Simon	NYR, Wpg.	3	15	0	2	2	10	....	....	....	....	....		1987-88	1990-91
• Wheldon, Donald	St.L.	1	2	0	0	0	0	....	....	....	....	....		1974-75	1974-75
Whelton, Bill	Wpg.	1	2	0	0	0	0	....	....	....	....	....		1980-81	1980-81
Whistle, Rob	NYR, St.L.	2	51	7	5	12	16	4	0	0	0	2		1985-86	1987-88
White, Bill	L.A., Chi.	9	604	50	215	265	495	91	7	32	39	76		1967-68	1975-76
White, Moe	Mtl.	1	4	0	1	1	2	....	....	....	....	....		1945-46	1945-46
White, Sherman	NYR	2	4	0	2	2	0	....	....	....	....	....		1946-47	1949-50
• White, Tex	Pit., NYA, Phi.	6	203	33	12	45	141	4	0	0	0	2		1925-26	1930-31
White, Tony	Wsh., Min.	5	164	37	28	65	104	....	....	....	....	....		1974-75	1979-80
Whitelaw, Bob	Det.	2	32	0	2	2	2	8	0	0	0	0		1940-41	1941-42
Whitlock, Bob	Min.	1	1	0	0	0	0	....	....	....	....	....		1969-70	1969-70
Wickenheiser, Doug	Mtl., St.L., Van., NYR, Wsh.	10	556	111	165	276	286	....	....	....	....	....		1980-81	1989-90
• Widing, Juha	NYR, L.A., Clev.	8	575	144	226	370	208	8	1	2	3	2		1969-70	1976-77
• Wiebe, Art	Chi.	11	411	14	27	41	209	31	1	3	4	8	1	1932-33	1943-44
Wilcox, Archie	Mtl.M., Bos., St.L.	6	212	8	14	22	158	12	1	0	1	10		1929-30	1934-35
Wilcox, Barry	Van.	2	33	3	2	5	15	....	....	....	....	....		1972-73	1974-75
Wilder, Arch	Det.	1	18	0	2	2	2	....	....	....	....	....		1940-41	1940-41
Wiley, Jim	Pit., Van.	5	63	4	10	14	8	....	....	....	....	....		1972-73	1976-77
Wilkins, Barry	Bos., Van., Pit.	9	418	27	125	152	663	6	0	1	1	4		1966-67	1975-76
Wilkinson, John	Bos.	1	9	0	0	0	3	....	....	....	....	....		1943-44	1943-44
Wilks, Brian	L.A.	4	48	4	8	12	27	....	....	....	....	....		1984-85	1988-89
Willard, Rod	Tor.	1	1	0	0	0	0	....	....	....	....	....		1982-83	1982-83
Williams, Burr	Det., St.L., Bos.	3	19	0	1	1	28	2	0	0	0	8		1933-34	1936-37
Williams, Dave	Tor., Van., Det., L.A., Hfd.	14	962	241	272	513	3966	83	12	23	35	455		1974-75	1987-88
Williams, Fred	Det.	1	44	2	5	7	10	....	....	....	....	....		1976-77	1976-77
Williams, Gord	Phi.	2	2	0	0	0	2	....	....	....	....	....		1981-82	1982-83
• Williams, Tom	Bos., Min., Cal., Wsh.	13	663	161	269	430	177	10	2	5	7	2		1961-62	1975-76
Williams, Tommy	NYR, L.A.	8	397	115	138	253	73	29	8	7	15	4		1971-72	1978-79
Williams, Warren	St.L., Cal.	3	108	14	35	49	131	....	....	....	....	....		1973-74	1975-76
Willson, Don	Mtl.	2	22	2	7	9	0	3	0	0	0	0		1937-38	1938-39
Wilson, Behn	Phi., Chi.	9	601	98	260	358	1480	67	12	29	41	190		1978-79	1987-88
• Wilson, Bert	NYR, L.A., St.L., Cgy.	8	478	37	44	81	646	21	0	2	2	42		1973-74	1980-81
Wilson, Bob	Chi.	1	1	0	0	0	0	....	....	....	....	....		1953-54	1953-54

Ed Van Impe

Blake Wesley

Mitch Wilson

Rik Wilson

Tim Young

![Warren Young]

Warren Young

Name	NHL Teams	NHL Seasons	GP	G	A	TP	PIM	GP	G	A	TP	PIM	NHL Cup Wins	First NHL Season	Last NHL Season
				Regular Schedule					Playoffs						
Wilson, Cully	Tor., Mtl., Ham., Chi.	5	125	60	23	83	232	2	1	0	1	6		1919-20	1926-27
Wilson, Gord	Bos.	1	....	....	....	....	....	2	0	0	0	0		1954-55	1954-55
Wilson, Hub	NYA	1	2	0	0	0	0							1931-32	1931-32
Wilson, Jerry	Mtl.	1	3	0	0	0	2							1956-57	1956-57
Wilson, Johnny	Det., Chi., Tor., NYR	13	688	161	171	332	190	66	14	13	27	11	4	1949-50	1961-62
• Wilson, Larry	Det., Chi.	6	152	21	48	69	75	4	0	0	0	0	1	1949-50	1955-56
Wilson, Mitch	N.J., Pit.	2	26	2	3	5	104							1984-85	1986-87
Wilson, Murray	Mtl., L.A.	7	386	94	95	189	162	53	5	14	19	32	4	1972-73	1978-79
Wilson, Rick	Mtl., St.L., Det.	4	239	6	26	32	165	3	0	0	0	0		1973-74	1976-77
Wilson, Rik	St.L., Cgy., Chi.	6	251	25	65	90	220	22	0	4	4	23		1981-82	1987-88
Wilson, Roger	Chi.	1	7	0	2	2	6							1974-75	1974-75
Wilson, Ron	Tor., Min.	7	177	26	67	93	68	20	4	13	17	8		1977-78	1987-88
Wilson, Wally	Bos.	1	53	11	8	19	18	1	0	0	0	0		1947-48	1947-48
Wing, Murray	Det.	1	1	0	1	1	0							1973-74	1973-74
• Wiseman, Eddie	Det., NYA, Bos.	10	454	115	164	279	137	45	10	10	20	16	1	1932-33	1941-42
Wiste, Jim	Chi., Van.	3	52	1	10	11	8							1968-69	1970-71
Witherspoon, Jim	L.A.	1	2	0	0	0	0							1975-76	1975-76
Witiuk, Steve	Chi.	1	33	3	8	11	14							1951-52	1951-52
Woit, Benny	Det., Chi.	7	334	7	26	33	170	41	2	6	8	18	3	1950-51	1956-57
Wojciechowski, Steven	Det.	2	54	19	20	39	17	6	0	1	1	0		1944-45	1946-47
Wolf, Bennett	Pit.	3	30	0	1	1	133							1980-81	1982-83
Wong, Mike	Det.	1	22	1	1	2	12							1975-76	1975-76
Wood, Robert	NYR	1	1	0	0	0	0							1950-51	1950-51
Woodley, Dan	Van.	1	5	2	0	2	17							1987-88	1987-88
Woods, Paul	Det.	7	501	72	124	196	276	7	0	5	5	4		1977-78	1983-84
• Woytowich, Bob	Bos., Min., Pit., L.A.	8	503	32	126	158	352	24	1	3	4	20		1964-65	1971-72
Wright, John	Van., St.L., K.C.	3	127	16	36	52	67							1972-73	1974-75
Wright, Keith	Phi.	1	1	0	0	0	0							1967-68	1967-68
Wright, Larry	Phi., Cal., Det.	5	106	4	8	12	19							1971-72	1977-78
Wycherley, Ralph	NYA, Bro.	2	28	4	7	11	6							1940-41	1941-42
• Wylie, Duane	Chi.	2	14	3	3	6	2							1974-75	1976-77
• Wylie, William	NYR	1	1	0	0	0	0							1950-51	1950-51
Wyrozub, Randy	Buf.	4	100	8	10	18	10							1970-71	1973-74

Y Z

Name	NHL Teams	NHL Seasons	GP	G	A	TP	PIM	GP	G	A	TP	PIM	NHL Cup Wins	First NHL Season	Last NHL Season
Yackel, Ken	Bos.	1	6	0	0	0	2	2	0	0	0	0		1958-59	1958-59
Yaremchuk, Gary	Tor.	4	34	1	4	5	28	....	....	....	....	....		1981-82	1984-85
Yaremchuk, Ken	Chi., Tor.	6	235	36	56	92	106	31	6	8	14	49		1983-84	1988-89
Yates, Ross	Hfd.	1	7	1	1	2	4							1983-84	1983-84
Young, Brian	Chi.	1	8	0	2	2	6							1980-81	1980-81
• Young, Doug	Mtl., Det.	10	391	35	45	80	303	28	1	5	6	16	2	1931-32	1940-41
Young, Howie	Det., Chi., Van.	8	336	12	62	74	851	19	2	4	6	46		1960-61	1970-71
Young, Tim	Min., Wpg., Phi.	10	628	195	341	536	438	36	7	24	31	27		1975-76	1984-85
Young, Warren	Min., Pit., Det.	7	236	72	77	149	472							1981-82	1987-88
Younghans, Tom	Min., NYR	6	429	44	41	85	373	24	2	1	3	21		1976-77	1981-82
Zabroski, Marty	Chi.	1	1	0	0	0	0							1944-45	1944-45
Zaharko, Miles	Atl., Chi.	4	129	5	32	37	84	3	0	0	0	0		1977-78	1981-82
Zaine, Rod	Pit., Buf.	2	61	10	6	16	25							1970-71	1971-72
Zanussi, Joe	NYR, Bos., St.L.	3	87	1	13	14	46	4	0	1	1	2		1974-75	1976-77
Zanussi, Ron	Min., Tor.	5	299	52	83	135	373	17	0	4	4	17		1977-78	1981-82
Zeidel, Larry	Det., Chi., Phi.	5	158	3	16	19	198	12	0	1	1	12	1	1951-52	1968-69
Zeniuk, Ed	Det.	1	2	0	0	0	0							1954-55	1954-55
Zetterstrom, Lars	Van.	1	14	0	1	1	2							1978-79	1978-79
Zuke, Mike	St.L., Hfd.	8	455	86	196	282	220	26	6	6	12	12		1978-79	1985-86
Zunich, Ruby	Det.	1	2	0	0	0	2							1943-44	1943-44

Retired Players and Goaltenders Research Project

THROUGHOUT THE RETIRED PLAYERS AND RETIRED GOALTENDERS SECTIONS of this book, you will notice many players with a bullet (•) by their names. These players, according to our records, are deceased. The editors recognize that our information on the death dates of NHLers is incomplete. If you have documented information on the passing of any player not marked with a bullet (•) in this edition, we would like to hear from you. Please send this information to:

Retired Player Research Project
c/o NHL Publishing
194 Dovercourt Road
Toronto, Ontario
M6J 3C8   Canada
Fax: 416/531-3939

Many thanks to the following contributors in 1992-93:

Fredrik Arntsen, Ric Browde, Curtis Burtt, Don Clahane, Paul Debbas, Raymond DeVillers, Francois Dupuis, Michael Gaschnitz, Peter Fillman, Marty Friedrich, Alex Goddard, Martin Harris, Nicolas Lacroix, Andre Lamirande, Lisette Lapointe, Scott Mercer, Scott Miller, Nabeel Nasir, Gary Pearce, Duff Sprague, Robert Stanton, Jin Tan, Sebastien Tremblay, Jason B. Young.

1993-94 Goaltender Register

Note: The 1993-94 Goaltender Register lists every goaltender who appeared in an NHL game in the 1992-93 season, every goaltender drafted in the first six rounds of the 1992 and 1993 Entry Drafts, and other goaltenders on NHL Reserve Lists.

Trades and roster changes are current as of August 16, 1993

To calculate a goaltender's goals-against-per-game average **(AVG)**, divide goals against **(GA)** by minutes played **(Mins)** and multiply this result by **60**.

Abbreviations: A list of league names can be found at the beginning of the Player Register. **Avg.** – goals against per game average; **GA** – goals against; **GP** – games played; **L** – losses; **Lea** – league; **SO** – shutouts; **T** – ties; **W** – wins.

Player Register begins on page 231.

ABEL, BRETT

Goaltender. Catches left. 6'2", 185 lbs. Born, Lynnfield, MA, June 10, 1970.
(Edmonton's 1st choice, 7th overall, in 1993 Supplemental Draft).

			Regular Season								Playoffs						
Season	Club	Lea	GP	W	L	T	Mins	GA	SO	Avg	GP	W	L	Mins	GA	SO	Avg
1991-92	N. Hampshire	H.E.	*35	20	13	2	*2030	111	0	3.28	....	....	....	....	....	....	....
1992-93	N. Hampshire	H.E.	32	15	15	2	1903	109	0	3.44	....	....	....	....	....	....	....

ALLAN, SANDY

Goaltender. Catches left. 6', 175 lbs. Born, Nassau, Bahamas, January 22, 1974.
(Los Angeles' 2nd choice, 63rd overall, in 1992 Entry Draft).

			Regular Season								Playoffs						
Season	Club	Lea	GP	W	L	T	Mins	GA	SO	Avg	GP	W	L	Mins	GA	SO	Avg
1991-92	North Bay	OHL	34	18	5	4	1747	112	0	3.85	3	0	0	18	2	0	6.67
1992-93	North Bay	OHL	39	8	19	4	1845	134	0	4.36	4	0	3	180	10	0	3.33

BACH, RYAN

Goaltender. Catches left. 6'1", 180 lbs. Born, Sherwood Park, Alta., October 21, 1973.
(Detroit's 11th choice, 262nd overall, in 1992 Entry Draft).

			Regular Season								Playoffs						
Season	Club	Lea	GP	W	L	T	Mins	GA	SO	Avg	GP	W	L	Mins	GA	SO	Avg
1991-92	Notre Dame	SJHL	33	....	....	....	1062	124	0	4.00	....	....	....	....	....	....	....
1992-93	Colorado	WCHA	4	1	3	0	239	11	0	2.76	....	....	....	....	....	....	....

BAILEY, SCOTT

Goaltender. Catches left. 6', 195 lbs. Born, Calgary, Alta., May 2, 1972.
(Boston's 3rd choice, 112th overall, in 1992 Entry Draft).

			Regular Season								Playoffs						
Season	Club	Lea	GP	W	L	T	Mins	GA	SO	Avg	GP	W	L	Mins	GA	SO	Avg
1990-91a	Spokane	WHL	46	33	11	0	2537	157	*4	3.71	....	....	....	....	....	....	....
1991-92a	Spokane	WHL	65	34	23	5	3798	206	1	3.30	10	5	5	605	43	0	4.26
1992-93	Johnstown	ECHL	36	13	15	3	1750	112	1	3.84	....	....	....	....	....	....	....

a WHL West Second All-Star Team (1991, 1992)

BALES, MICHAEL

Goaltender. Catches left. 6'1", 180 lbs. Born, Prince Albert, Sask., August 6, 1971.
(Boston's 4th choice, 105th overall, in 1990 Entry Draft).

			Regular Season								Playoffs						
Season	Club	Lea	GP	W	L	T	Mins	GA	SO	Avg	GP	W	L	Mins	GA	SO	Avg
1989-90	Ohio State	CCHA	21	6	13	2	1117	95	0	5.11	....	....	....	....	....	....	....
1990-91	Ohio State	CCHA	*39	11	24	3	*2180	184	0	5.06	....	....	....	....	....	....	....
1991-92	Ohio State	CCHA	36	11	20	5	2060	180	0	5.24	....	....	....	....	....	....	....
1992-93	**Boston**	**NHL**	**1**	**0**	**0**	**0**	**25**	**1**	**0**	**2.40**	....	....	....	....	....	....	....
	Providence	AHL	44	22	17	0	2363	166	1	4.21	2	0	2	118	8	0	4.07
	NHL Totals		**1**	**0**	**0**	**0**	**25**	**1**	**0**	**2.40**	....	....	....	....	....	....	....

BARRASSO, TOM (buh-RAH-soh)

Goaltender. Catches right. 6'3", 211 lbs. Born, Boston, MA, March 31, 1965.
(Buffalo's 1st choice, 5th overall, in 1983 Entry Draft).

			Regular Season								Playoffs						
Season	Club	Lea	GP	W	L	T	Mins	GA	SO	Avg	GP	W	L	Mins	GA	SO	Avg
1982-83	Acton-Boxboro	HS	23	....	....	....	1035	17	10	0.73	....	....	....	....	....	....	....
1983-84abcd	**Buffalo**	**NHL**	**42**	**26**	**12**	**3**	**2475**	**117**	**2**	**2.84**	**3**	**0**	**2**	**139**	**8**	**0**	**3.45**
1984-85ef	**Buffalo**	**NHL**	**54**	**25**	**18**	**10**	**3248**	**144**	***5**	***2.66**	**5**	**2**	**3**	**300**	**22**	**0**	**4.40**
	Rochester	AHL	5	3	1	1	267	6	1	1.35	....	....	....	....	....	....	....
1985-86	**Buffalo**	**NHL**	**60**	**29**	**24**	**5**	**3561**	**214**	**2**	**3.61**	....	....	....	....	....	....	....
1986-87	**Buffalo**	**NHL**	**46**	**17**	**23**	**2**	**2501**	**152**	**2**	**3.65**	....	....	....	....	....	....	....
1987-88	**Buffalo**	**NHL**	**54**	**25**	**18**	**8**	**3133**	**173**	**2**	**3.31**	**4**	**1**	**3**	**224**	**16**	**0**	**4.29**
1988-89	**Buffalo**	**NHL**	**10**	**2**	**7**	**0**	**545**	**45**	**0**	**4.95**	....	....	....	....	....	....	....
	Pittsburgh	**NHL**	**44**	**18**	**15**	**7**	**2406**	**162**	**0**	**4.04**	**11**	**7**	**4**	**631**	**40**	**0**	**3.80**
1989-90	**Pittsburgh**	**NHL**	**24**	**7**	**12**	**3**	**1294**	**101**	**0**	**4.68**	....	....	....	....	....	....	....
1990-91	**Pittsburgh**	**NHL**	**48**	**27**	**16**	**3**	**2754**	**165**	**1**	**3.59**	**20**	**12**	**7**	**1175**	**51**	***1**	***2.60**
1991-92	**Pittsburgh**	**NHL**	**57**	**25**	**22**	**9**	**3329**	**196**	**1**	**3.53**	***21**	***16**	**5**	***1233**	**58**	**1**	**2.82**
1992-93e	**Pittsburgh**	**NHL**	**63**	***43**	**14**	**5**	**3702**	**186**	**4**	**3.01**	**12**	**7**	**5**	**722**	**35**	***2**	**2.91**
	NHL Totals		**502**	**244**	**181**	**55**	**28948**	**1655**	**19**	**3.43**	**76**	**45**	**29**	**4424**	**230**	**4**	**3.12**

a NHL First All-Star Team (1984)
b Won Vezina Trophy (1984)
c Won Calder Memorial Trophy (1984)
d NHL All-Rookie Team (1984)
e NHL Second All-Star Team (1985, 1993)
f Shared William Jennings Trophy with Bob Sauve (1985)

Played in NHL All-Star Game (1985)

Traded to **Pittsburgh** by **Buffalo** with Buffalo's third round choice (Joe Dziedzic) in 1990 Entry Draft for Doug Bodger and Darrin Shannon, November 12, 1988.

BEAUBIEN, FREDERICK

Goaltender. Catches left. 6'1", 204 lbs. Born, Lauzon, Que., April 1, 1975.
(Los Angeles' 4th choice, 105th overall, in 1993 Entry Draft).

			Regular Season								Playoffs						
Season	Club	Lea	GP	W	L	T	Mins	GA	SO	Avg	GP	W	L	Mins	GA	SO	Avg
1991-92	Ste-Foy	Midget	26	....	....	....	1526	89	....	3.50	....	....	....	....	....	....	....
1992-93	St-Hyacinthe	QMJHL	33	8	16	3	1702	133	0	4.69	....	....	....	....	....	....	....

BEAUPRE, DONALD WILLIAM (DON) (boh-PRAY)

Goaltender. Catches left. 5'10", 172 lbs. Born, Waterloo, Ont., September 19, 1961.
(Minnesota's 2nd choice, 32nd overall, in 1980 Entry Draft).

			Regular Season								Playoffs						
Season	Club	Lea	GP	W	L	T	Mins	GA	SO	Avg	GP	W	L	Mins	GA	SO	Avg
1978-79	Sudbury	OHA	54	....	....	....	3248	260	2	4.78	10	....	....	600	44	0	4.20
1979-80a	Sudbury	OHA	59	28	29	2	3447	248	0	4.32	9	5	4	552	38	0	4.13
1980-81	**Minnesota**	**NHL**	**44**	**18**	**14**	**11**	**2585**	**138**	**0**	**3.20**	**6**	**4**	**2**	**360**	**26**	**0**	**4.33**
1981-82	**Minnesota**	**NHL**	**29**	**11**	**8**	**9**	**1634**	**101**	**0**	**3.71**	**2**	**0**	**1**	**60**	**4**	**0**	**4.00**
	Nashville	CHL	5	2	3	0	299	25	0	5.02	....	....	....	....	....	....	....
1982-83	**Minnesota**	**NHL**	**36**	**19**	**10**	**5**	**2011**	**120**	**0**	**3.58**	**4**	**2**	**2**	**245**	**20**	**0**	**4.90**
	Birmingham	CHL	10	8	2	0	599	31	0	3.11	....	....	....	....	....	....	....
1983-84	**Minnesota**	**NHL**	**33**	**16**	**13**	**2**	**1791**	**123**	**0**	**4.12**	**13**	**6**	**7**	**782**	**40**	**1**	**3.07**
	Salt Lake	CHL	7	2	5	0	419	30	0	4.30	....	....	....	....	....	....	....
1984-85	**Minnesota**	**NHL**	**31**	**10**	**17**	**3**	**1770**	**109**	**1**	**3.69**	**4**	**1**	**1**	**184**	**12**	**0**	**3.91**
1985-86	**Minnesota**	**NHL**	**52**	**25**	**20**	**6**	**3073**	**182**	**1**	**3.55**	**5**	**2**	**3**	**300**	**17**	**0**	**3.40**
1986-87	**Minnesota**	**NHL**	**47**	**17**	**20**	**6**	**2622**	**174**	**1**	**3.98**	....	....	....	....	....	....	....
1987-88	**Minnesota**	**NHL**	**43**	**10**	**22**	**3**	**2288**	**161**	**0**	**4.22**	....	....	....	....	....	....	....
1988-89	**Minnesota**	**NHL**	**1**	**0**	**1**	**0**	**59**	**3**	**0**	**3.05**	....	....	....	....	....	....	....
	Kalamazoo	IHL	3	1	2	0	179	9	1	3.02	....	....	....	....	....	....	....
	Washington	**NHL**	**11**	**5**	**4**	**0**	**578**	**28**	**1**	**2.91**	....	....	....	....	....	....	....
	Baltimore	AHL	30	14	12	2	1715	102	0	3.57	....	....	....	....	....	....	....
1989-90	**Washington**	**NHL**	**48**	**23**	**18**	**5**	**2793**	**150**	**2**	**3.22**	**8**	**4**	**3**	**401**	**18**	**0**	**2.69**
1990-91	**Washington**	**NHL**	**45**	**20**	**18**	**3**	**2572**	**113**	***5**	**2.64**	**11**	**5**	**5**	**624**	**29**	***1**	**2.79**
	Baltimore	AHL	2	2	0	0	120	3	0	1.50	....	....	....	....	....	....	....
1991-92	**Washington**	**NHL**	**54**	**29**	**17**	**6**	**3108**	**166**	**1**	**3.20**	**7**	**3**	**4**	**419**	**22**	**0**	**3.15**
	Baltimore	AHL	3	1	1	1	184	10	0	3.26	....	....	....	....	....	....	....
1992-93	**Washington**	**NHL**	**58**	**27**	**23**	**5**	**3282**	**181**	**1**	**3.31**	**2**	**1**	**1**	**119**	**9**	**0**	**4.54**
	NHL Totals		**532**	**230**	**205**	**64**	**30166**	**1749**	**13**	**3.48**	**62**	**28**	**29**	**3494**	**197**	**2**	**3.38**

a OHA First All-Star Team (1980)

Played in NHL All-Star Game (1981)

Traded to **Washington** by **Minnesota** for rights to Claudio Scremin, November 1, 1988.

BEAUREGARD, STEPHANE

Goaltender. Catches right. 5'11", 182 lbs. Born, Cowansville, Que., January 10, 1968.
(Winnipeg's 3rd choice, 52nd overall, in 1988 Entry Draft).

			Regular Season								Playoffs						
Season	Club	Lea	GP	W	L	T	Mins	GA	SO	Avg	GP	W	L	Mins	GA	SO	Avg
1986-87	St-Jean	QMJHL	13	6	7	0	785	58	0	4.43	5	1	3	260	26	0	6.00
1987-88ab	St-Jean	QMJHL	66	38	20	3	3766	229	2	3.65	7	3	4	423	34	0	4.82
1988-89	Moncton	AHL	15	4	8	2	824	62	0	4.51	....	....	....	....	....	....	....
	Fort Wayne	IHL	16	9	5	0	830	43	0	3.10	9	4	4	484	21	*1	*2.60
1989-90	**Winnipeg**	**NHL**	**19**	**7**	**8**	**3**	**1079**	**59**	**0**	**3.28**	**4**	**1**	**3**	**238**	**12**	**0**	**3.03**
	Fort Wayne	IHL	33	20	8	3	1949	115	0	3.54	....	....	....	....	....	....	....
1990-91	**Winnipeg**	**NHL**	**16**	**3**	**10**	**1**	**836**	**55**	**0**	**3.95**	....	....	....	....	....	....	....
	Moncton	AHL	9	3	4	1	504	20	1	2.38	1	1	0	60	1	0	1.00
	Fort Wayne	IHL	32	14	13	2	1761	109	0	3.71	*19	*10	9	*1158	57	0	2.95
1991-92	**Winnipeg**	**NHL**	**26**	**6**	**8**	**6**	**1267**	**61**	**2**	**2.89**	....	....	....	....	....	....	....
1992-93	**Philadelphia**	**NHL**	**16**	**3**	**9**	**0**	**802**	**59**	**0**	**4.41**	....	....	....	....	....	....	....
	Hershey	AHL	13	5	5	3	794	48	0	3.63	....	....	....	....	....	....	....
	NHL Totals		**77**	**19**	**35**	**10**	**3984**	**234**	**2**	**3.52**	**4**	**1**	**3**	**238**	**12**	**0**	**3.03**

a QMJHL First All-Star Team (1988)
b QMJHL and Canadian Major Junior Goaltender of the year (1988)

Traded to **Buffalo** by **Winnipeg** for Christian Ruuttu and future considerations, June 15, 1992. Traded to **Chicago** by **Buffalo** for Dominik Hasek and future considerations, August 7, 1992. Traded to **Winnipeg** by **Chicago** for Christian Ruuttu, August 10, 1992. Traded to **Philadelphia** by **Winnipeg** for Philadelphia's third round choice in 1993 Entry Draft and future considerations, October 1, 1992.

BELFOUR, ED

Goaltender. Catches left. 5'11", 182 lbs. Born, Carman, Man., April 21, 1965.

			Regular Season								Playoffs						
Season	Club	Lea	GP	W	L	T	Mins	GA	SO	Avg	GP	W	L	Mins	GA	SO	Avg
1986-87a	North Dakota	WCHA	34	29	4	0	2049	81	3	2.43	....	....	....	....	....	....	....
1987-88bc	Saginaw	IHL	61	32	25	0	*3446	183	3	3.19	9	4	5	561	33	0	3.53
1988-89	Chicago	NHL	23	4	12	3	1148	74	0	3.87	....	....	....	....	....	....	....
	Saginaw	IHL	29	12	10	0	1760	92	0	3.10	5	2	3	298	14	0	2.82
1989-90	Cdn. National	....	33	13	12	6	1808	93	0	3.08	....	....	....	....	....	....	....
	Chicago	NHL	....	....	....	....	....	....	....	....	9	4	2	409	17	0	2.49
1990-91 defghi	Chicago	NHL	*74	*43	19	7	*4127	170	4	*2.47	6	2	4	295	20	0	4.07
1991-92	Chicago	NHL	52	21	18	10	2928	132	*5	2.70	18	12	4	949	39	1	*2.47
1992-93deg	Chicago	NHL	*71	41	18	11	*4106	177	*7	2.59	4	0	4	249	13	0	3.13
	NHL Totals		220	109	67	31	12309	553	16	2.70	37	18	14	1902	89	1	2.81

a WCHA First All-Star Team (1987)
b IHL First All-Star Team (1988)
c Shared Garry F. Longman Memorial Trophy (Top Rookie - IHL) (1988)
d NHL First All-Star Team (1991, 1993)
e Won Vezina Trophy (1991, 1993)
f Won Calder Memorial Trophy (1991)
g Won William M. Jennings Trophy (1991, 1993)
h Won Trico Goaltender Award (1991)
i NHL/Upper Deck All-Rookie Team (1991)

Played in NHL All-Star Game (1992, 1993)

Signed as a free agent by **Chicago**, September 25, 1987.

BELLEY, ROCH

Goaltender. Catches left. 5'10", 170 lbs. Born, Hull, Que., August 12, 1971.
(Chicago's 8th choice, 176th overall, in 1991 Entry Draft).

			Regular Season								Playoffs						
Season	Club	Lea	GP	W	L	T	Mins	GA	SO	Avg	GP	W	L	Mins	GA	SO	Avg
1990-91	Niagara Falls	OHL	45	26	8	7	2499	151	1	3.68	14	7	5	743	49	....	3.96
1991-92	Indianapolis	IHL	25	4	12	3	1270	88	0	4.16	....	....	....	....	....	....	....
1992-93	Fort Worth	CHL	33	14	13	2	1782	141	0	4.75	....	....	....	....	....	....	....
	Indianapolis	IHL	7	1	2	1	289	25	0	5.19	2	0	0	33	2	0	3.64

BERGERON, JEAN-CLAUDE

Goaltender. Catches left. 6'2", 192 lbs. Born, Hauterive, Que., October 14, 1968.
(Montreal's 5th choice, 104th overall, in 1988 Entry Draft).

			Regular Season								Playoffs						
Season	Club	Lea	GP	W	L	T	Mins	GA	SO	Avg	GP	W	L	Mins	GA	SO	Avg
1987-88	Verdun	QMJHL	49	13	31	3	2715	265	0	5.86	....	....	....	....	....	....	....
1988-89	Verdun	QMJHL	44	8	34	1	2417	199	0	4.94	....	....	....	....	....	....	....
	Sherbrooke	AHL	5	4	1	0	302	18	0	3.58	....	....	....	....	....	....	....
1989-90abc	Sherbrooke	AHL	40	21	8	7	2254	103	2	*2.74	9	6	2	497	28	0	3.38
1990-91	Montreal	NHL	18	7	6	2	941	59	0	3.76	....	....	....	....	....	....	....
	Fredericton	AHL	18	12	6	0	1083	59	1	3.27	10	5	5	546	32	0	3.52
1991-92	Fredericton	AHL	13	5	7	1	791	57	0	4.32	....	....	....	....	....	....	....
	Peoria	IHL	27	14	9	3	1632	96	1	3.53	6	3	3	352	24	0	4.09
1992-93	Tampa Bay	NHL	21	8	10	1	1163	71	0	3.66	....	....	....	....	....	....	....
	Atlanta	IHL	31	21	7	1	1722	92	1	3.21	6	3	3	368	19	0	3.10
	NHL Totals		39	15	16	3	2104	130	0	3.71	....	....	....	....	....	....	....

a AHL First All-Star Team (1990)
b Shared Harry "Hap" Holmes Trophy (fewest goals-against-AHL) with Andre Racicot (1990)
c Won Baz Bastien Award (Top Goaltender-AHL) (1990)

Traded to **Tampa Bay** by **Montreal** for Frederic Chabot, June 19, 1992.

BERTHIAUME, DANIEL (bair-TYOHM)

Goaltender. Catches left. 5'9", 150 lbs. Born, Longueuil, Que., January 26, 1966.
(Winnipeg's 3rd choice, 60th overall, in 1985 Entry Draft).

			Regular Season								Playoffs						
Season	Club	Lea	GP	W	L	T	Mins	GA	SO	Avg	GP	W	L	Mins	GA	SO	Avg
1984-85	Chicoutimi	QMJHL	59	40	11	2	2177	149	0	4.11	14	8	6	770	51	0	3.97
1985-86	Chicoutimi	QMJHL	66	34	29	3	3718	286	1	4.62	9	4	5	580	36	0	3.72
	Winnipeg	NHL	....	....	....	....	....	....	....	....	1	0	1	68	4	0	3.53
1986-87	Winnipeg	NHL	31	18	7	3	1758	93	1	3.17	8	4	4	439	21	0	2.87
	Sherbrooke	AHL	7	4	3	0	420	23	0	3.29	....	....	....	....	....	....	....
1987-88	Winnipeg	NHL	56	22	19	7	3010	176	2	3.51	5	1	4	300	25	0	5.00
1988-89	Winnipeg	NHL	9	0	8	0	443	44	0	5.96	....	....	....	....	....	....	....
	Moncton	AHL	21	6	9	2	1083	76	0	4.21	3	1	2	180	11	0	3.67
1989-90	Winnipeg	NHL	24	10	11	3	1387	86	1	3.72	....	....	....	....	....	....	....
	Minnesota	NHL	5	1	3	0	240	14	0	3.50	....	....	....	....	....	....	....
1990-91	Los Angeles	NHL	37	20	11	4	2119	117	1	3.31	....	....	....	....	....	....	....
1991-92	Los Angeles	NHL	19	7	10	1	979	66	0	4.04	....	....	....	....	....	....	....
	Boston	NHL	8	1	4	2	399	21	0	3.16	....	....	....	....	....	....	....
1992-93	Graz	Alp.	28	....	....	....	....	110	0	4.07	....	....	....	....	....	....	....
	Ottawa	NHL	25	2	17	1	1326	95	0	4.30	....	....	....	....	....	....	....
	NHL Totals		214	81	90	21	11661	712	5	3.66	14	5	9	807	50	0	3.72

Traded to **Minnesota** by **Winnipeg** for future considerations, January 22, 1990. Traded to **Los Angeles** by **Minnesota** for Craig Duncanson, September 6, 1990. Traded to **Boston** by **Los Angeles** for future considerations, January 18, 1992. Traded to **Winnipeg** by **Boston** for Doug Evans, June 10, 1992. Signed as a free agent by **Ottawa**, December 15, 1992.

BESTER, ALLAN J.

Goaltender. Catches left. 5'7", 155 lbs. Born, Hamilton, Ont., March 26, 1964.
(Toronto's 3rd choice, 48th overall, in 1983 Entry Draft).

			Regular Season								Playoffs						
Season	Club	Lea	GP	W	L	T	Mins	GA	SO	Avg	GP	W	L	Mins	GA	SO	Avg
1981-82	Brantford	OHL	19	4	11	0	970	68	0	4.21	....	....	....	....	....	....	....
1982-83a	Brantford	OHL	56	29	21	3	3210	188	0	3.51	8	3	3	480	20	*1	*2.50
1983-84	Toronto	NHL	32	11	16	4	1848	134	0	4.35	....	....	....	....	....	....	....
	Brantford	OHL	23	12	9	1	1271	71	1	3.35	1	0	1	60	5	0	5.00
1984-85	Toronto	NHL	15	3	9	1	767	54	1	4.22	....	....	....	....	....	....	....
	St. Catharines	AHL	30	9	18	1	1669	133	0	4.78	....	....	....	....	....	....	....
1985-86	Toronto	NHL	1	0	0	0	20	2	0	6.00	....	....	....	....	....	....	....
	St. Catharines	AHL	50	23	23	3	2855	173	1	3.64	11	7	3	637	27	0	2.54
1986-87	Toronto	NHL	36	10	14	3	1808	110	2	3.65	1	0	0	39	1	0	1.54
	Newmarket	AHL	3	1	0	0	190	6	0	1.89	....	....	....	....	....	....	....
1987-88	Toronto	NHL	30	8	12	5	1607	102	2	3.81	5	2	3	253	21	0	4.98
1988-89	Toronto	NHL	43	17	20	3	2460	156	2	3.80	....	....	....	....	....	....	....
1989-90	Toronto	NHL	42	20	16	0	2206	165	0	4.49	4	0	3	196	14	0	4.29
	Newmarket	AHL	5	2	1	1	264	18	0	4.09	....	....	....	....	....	....	....
1990-91	Toronto	NHL	6	0	4	0	247	18	0	4.37	....	....	....	....	....	....	....
	Newmarket	AHL	19	7	8	4	1157	58	1	3.01	....	....	....	....	....	....	....
	Detroit	NHL	3	0	3	0	178	13	0	4.38	1	0	0	20	1	0	3.00
1991-92	Detroit	NHL	1	0	0	0	31	2	0	3.87	....	....	....	....	....	....	....
b	Adirondack	AHL	22	13	8	0	1268	78	0	3.69	*19	*14	5	1174	50	*1	*2.56
1992-93	Adirondack	AHL	41	16	15	5	2268	133	1	3.52	10	7	3	633	26	*1	2.46
	NHL Totals		209	69	94	16	11172	756	7	4.06	11	2	6	508	37	0	4.37

a OHL First All-Star Team (1983)
b Won Jack Butterfield Trophy (Playoff MVP-AHL) (1992)

Traded to **Detroit** by **Toronto** for Detroit's sixth round choice (Alexander Kuzminsky) in 1991 Entry Draft, March 5, 1991.

BILLINGTON, CRAIG

Goaltender. Catches left. 5'10", 170 lbs. Born, London, Ont., September 11, 1966.
(New Jersey's 2nd choice, 23rd overall, in 1984 Entry Draft).

			Regular Season								Playoffs						
Season	Club	Lea	GP	W	L	T	Mins	GA	SO	Avg	GP	W	L	Mins	GA	SO	Avg
1983-84	Belleville	OHL	44	20	19	0	2335	162	1	4.16	1	0	0	30	3	0	6.00
1984-85a	Belleville	OHL	47	26	19	0	2544	180	1	4.25	14	7	5	761	47	1	3.71
1985-86	New Jersey	NHL	18	4	9	1	901	77	0	5.13	....	....	....	....	....	....	....
	Belleville	OHL	3	2	1	0	180	11	0	3.67	20	9	6	1133	68	0	3.60
1986-87	New Jersey	NHL	22	4	13	2	1114	89	0	4.79	....	....	....	....	....	....	....
	Maine	AHL	20	9	8	2	1151	70	0	3.65	....	....	....	....	....	....	....
1987-88	Utica	AHL	*59	22	27	8	*3404	208	1	3.67	....	....	....	....	....	....	....
1988-89	New Jersey	NHL	3	1	1	0	140	11	0	4.71	....	....	....	....	....	....	....
	Utica	AHL	41	17	18	6	2432	150	2	3.70	4	1	3	220	18	0	4.91
1989-90	Utica	AHL	38	20	13	1	2087	138	0	3.97	....	....	....	....	....	....	....
1990-91	Cdn. National	....	34	17	14	2	1879	110	2	3.51	....	....	....	....	....	....	....
1991-92	New Jersey	NHL	26	13	7	1	1363	69	2	3.04	....	....	....	....	....	....	....
1992-93	New Jersey	NHL	42	21	16	4	2389	146	2	3.67	2	0	1	78	5	0	3.85
	NHL Totals		111	43	46	8	5907	392	4	3.98	2	0	1	78	5	0	3.85

a OHL First All-Star Team (1985)

Played in NHL All-Star Game (1993)

Traded to **Ottawa** by **New Jersey** with Troy Mallette and New Jersey's fourth round choice (Cosmo Dupaul) in 1993 Entry Draft for Peter Sidorkiewicz and future considerations (Mike Peluso, June 26, 1993), June 20, 1993.

BLUE, JOHN

Goaltender. Catches left. 5'10", 190 lbs. Born, Huntington Beach, CA, February 19, 1966.
(Winnipeg's 9th choice, 197th overall, in 1986 Entry Draft).

			Regular Season								Playoffs						
Season	Club	Lea	GP	W	L	T	Mins	GA	SO	Avg	GP	W	L	Mins	GA	SO	Avg
1984-85	U. Minnesota	WCHA	34	23	10	0	1964	111	2	3.39	....	....	....	....	....	....	....
1985-86a	U. Minnesota	WCHA	29	20	6	0	1588	80	2	3.02	....	....	....	....	....	....	....
1986-87	U. Minnesota	WCHA	33	21	9	1	1889	99	3	3.14	....	....	....	....	....	....	....
1987-88	Kalamazoo	IHL	15	3	8	4	847	65	0	4.60	1	0	1	40	6	0	9.00
	U.S. National	....	13	3	4	1	588	33	0	3.37	....	....	....	....	....	....	....
1988-89	Kalamazoo	IHL	17	8	6	0	970	69	0	4.27	....	....	....	....	....	....	....
	Virginia	ECHL	10	....	....	....	570	38	0	4.00	....	....	....	....	....	....	....
1989-90	Phoenix	IHL	19	5	10	3	986	92	0	5.65	....	....	....	....	....	....	....
	Knoxville	ECHL	19	6	10	1	1000	85	0	5.15	....	....	....	....	....	....	....
	Kalamazoo	IHL	4	2	1	1	232	18	0	4.65	....	....	....	....	....	....	....
1990-91	Maine	AHL	10	3	4	2	545	22	0	2.42	1	0	1	40	7	0	10.50
	Albany	IHL	19	11	6	0	1077	71	0	3.96	....	....	....	....	....	....	....
	Kalamazoo	IHL	1	1	0	0	64	2	0	1.88	....	....	....	....	....	....	....
	Peoria	IHL	4	4	0	0	240	12	0	3.00	....	....	....	....	....	....	....
	Knoxville	ECHL	3	1	1	0	149	13	0	5.23	....	....	....	....	....	....	....
1991-92	Maine	AHL	43	11	23	6	2168	165	1	4.57	....	....	....	....	....	....	....
1992-93	Boston	NHL	23	9	8	4	1322	64	1	2.90	2	0	1	96	5	0	3.13
	Providence	AHL	19	14	4	1	1159	67	0	3.47	....	....	....	....	....	....	....
	NHL Totals		23	9	8	4	1322	64	1	2.90	2	0	1	96	5	0	3.13

a WCHA First All-Star Team (1986)

Traded to **Minnesota** by **Winnipeg** for Winnipeg's seventh round choice (Markus Akerblom) in 1988 Entry Draft, March 7, 1988. Signed as a free agent by **Boston**, August 1, 1991.

BRADLEY, JOHN

Goaltender. Catches left. 6', 165 lbs. Born, Pawtucket, RI, February 6, 1968.
(Buffalo's 4th choice, 84th overall, in 1987 Entry Draft).

			Regular Season								Playoffs						
Season	Club	Lea	GP	W	L	T	Mins	GA	SO	Avg	GP	W	L	Mins	GA	SO	Avg
1987-88	Boston U.	H.E.	9	4	4	0	528	40	0	4.53	....	....	....	....	....	....	....
1988-89	Boston U.	H.E.	11	5	4	1	584	53	0	5.45	....	....	....	....	....	....	....
1989-90	Boston U.	H.E.	7	2	3	1	377	20	1	3.18	....	....	....	....	....	....	....
1990-91	Boston U.	H.E.	20	14	4	1	1177	62	*3	3.16	....	....	....	....	....	....	....
1991-92	Rochester	AHL	6	2	2	1	248	13	1	3.15	1	0	0	20	2	0	6.00
	Erie	ECHL	15	6	4	2	810	59	0	4.37	....	....	....	....	....	....	....
1992-93	Johnstown	ECHL	36	20	7	3	1910	127	1	3.99	5	2	3	307	17	0	3.32

BROCHU, MARTIN

Goaltender. Catches left. 5'11", 185 lbs. Born, Anjou, Que., March 10, 1973.

			Regular Season								Playoffs						
Season	Club	Lea	GP	W	L	T	Mins	GA	SO	Avg	GP	W	L	Mins	GA	SO	Avg
1991-92	Granby	QMJHL	52	15	29	2	2772	278	0	4.72	....	....	....	....	....	....	....
1992-93	Hull	QMJHL	29	9	15	1	1453	137	0	5.66	2	0	1	69	7	0	6.07

Signed as a free agent by **Montreal**, September 22, 1992.

BRODEUR, MARTIN

Goaltender. Catches left. 6'1", 205 lbs. Born, Montreal, Que., May 6, 1972.
(New Jersey's 1st choice, 20th overall, in 1990 Entry Draft).

			Regular Season								Playoffs						
Season	Club	Lea	GP	W	L	T	Mins	GA	SO	Avg	GP	W	L	Mins	GA	SO	Avg
1989-90	St-Hyacinthe	QMJHL	42	23	13	2	2333	156	0	4.01	12	5	7	678	46	0	4.07
1990-91	St-Hyacinthe	QMJHL	52	22	24	4	2946	162	2	3.30	4	0	4	232	16	0	4.14
1991-92	**New Jersey**	**NHL**	**4**	**2**	**1**	**0**	**179**	**10**	**0**	**3.35**	**1**	**0**	**1**	**32**	**3**	**0**	**5.63**
a	St-Hyacinthe	QMJHL	48	27	16	4	2846	161	2	3.39	5	2	3	317	14	0	2.65
1992-93	Utica	AHL	32	14	13	5	1952	131	0	4.03	4	1	3	258	18	0	4.19
	NHL Totals		**4**	**2**	**1**	**0**	**179**	**10**	**0**	**3.35**	**1**	**0**	**1**	**32**	**3**	**0**	**5.63**

a QMJHL Second All-Star Team (1992)

BROWN, CRAIG

Goaltender. Catches left. 5'11", 170 lbs. Born, Scarborough, Ont., February 29, 1972.
(Los Angeles' 9th choice, 196th overall, in 1991 Entry Draft).

			Regular Season								Playoffs						
Season	Club	Lea	GP	W	L	T	Mins	GA	SO	Avg	GP	W	L	Mins	GA	SO	Avg
1990-91	W. Michigan	CCHA	33	17	13	2	1898	111	0	3.51	....	....	....	....	....	....	....
1991-92	W. Michigan	CCHA	28	13	10	5	1668	89	0	3.20	....	....	....	....	....	....	....
1992-93	W. Michigan	CCHA	20	9	8	1	1125	72	....	3.84	....	....	....	....	....	....	....

BURKE, SEAN

Goaltender. Catches left. 6'4", 210 lbs. Born, Windsor, Ont., January 29, 1967.
(New Jersey's 2nd choice, 24th overall, in 1985 Entry Draft).

			Regular Season								Playoffs						
Season	Club	Lea	GP	W	L	T	Mins	GA	SO	Avg	GP	W	L	Mins	GA	SO	Avg
1984-85	Toronto	OHL	49	25	21	3	2987	211	0	4.24	5	1	3	266	25	0	5.64
1985-86	Toronto	OHL	47	16	27	3	2840	233	0	4.92	4	0	4	238	24	0	6.05
1986-87	Cdn. National	....	42	27	13	2	2550	130	0	3.05	....	....	....	....	....	....	....
1987-88	Cdn. National	....	37	19	9	2	1962	92	1	2.81	....	....	....	....	....	....	....
	Cdn. Olympic	....	4	1	2	1	238	12	0	3.02	....	....	....	....	....	....	....
	New Jersey	**NHL**	**13**	**10**	**1**	**0**	**689**	**35**	**1**	**3.05**	**17**	**9**	**8**	**1001**	**57**	***1**	**3.42**
1988-89	**New Jersey**	**NHL**	**62**	**22**	**31**	**9**	**3590**	**230**	**3**	**3.84**	....	....	....	....	....	....	....
1989-90	**New Jersey**	**NHL**	**52**	**22**	**22**	**6**	**2914**	**175**	**0**	**3.60**	**2**	**0**	**2**	**125**	**8**	**0**	**3.84**
1990-91	**New Jersey**	**NHL**	**35**	**8**	**12**	**8**	**1870**	**112**	**0**	**3.59**	....	....	....	....	....	....	....
1991-92	Cdn. National	....	31	18	6	4	1721	75	1	2.61	....	....	....	....	....	....	....
	Cdn. Olympic	....	7	....	....	....	429	17	0	2.37	....	....	....	....	....	....	....
	San Diego	IHL	7	4	2	1	424	17	0	2.41	3	0	3	160	13	0	4.88
1992-93	**Hartford**	**NHL**	**50**	**16**	**27**	**3**	**2656**	**184**	**0**	**4.16**	....	....	....	....	....	....	....
	NHL Totals		**212**	**78**	**93**	**26**	**11719**	**736**	**4**	**3.77**	**19**	**9**	**10**	**1126**	**65**	**1**	**3.46**

Played in NHL All-Star Game (1989)

Traded to **Hartford** by **New Jersey** with Eric Weinrich for Bobby Holik, Hartford's second round choice (Jay Pandolfo) in 1993 Entry Draft and future considerations, August 28, 1992.

BURNS, CHRIS

Goaltender. Catches left. 6'1", 185 lbs. Born, Sudbury, Ont., May 19, 1973.
(San Jose's 9th choice, 195th overall, in 1992 Entry Draft).

			Regular Season								Playoffs						
Season	Club	Lea	GP	W	L	T	Mins	GA	SO	Avg	GP	W	L	Mins	GA	SO	Avg
1991-92	Thunder Bay	USHL	26	....	....	....	1381	80	0	3.48	....	....	....	....	....	....	....
1992-93	U. of Denver	WCHA	12	1	2	0	433	35	0	4.85	....	....	....	....	....	....	....

BUTLER, JEROME

Goaltender. Catches left. 5'11", 165 lbs. Born, Roseau, MN, December 14, 1972.
(Calgary's 6th choice, 107th overall, in 1991 Entry Draft).

			Regular Season								Playoffs						
Season	Club	Lea	GP	W	L	T	Mins	GA	SO	Avg	GP	W	L	Mins	GA	SO	Avg
1991-92	Minn.-Duluth	WCHA	22	9	11	2	1325	91	0	4.12	....	....	....	....	....	....	....
1992-93	Minn.-Duluth	WCHA	21	12	6	2	1183	74	0	3.75	....	....	....	....	....	....	....

CALLINAN, JEFF

Goaltender. Catches left. 5'10", 169 lbs. Born, Minneapolis, MN, January 6, 1973.
(St. Louis' 5th choice, 109th overall, in 1991 Entry Draft).

			Regular Season								Playoffs						
Season	Club	Lea	GP	W	L	T	Mins	GA	SO	Avg	GP	W	L	Mins	GA	SO	Avg
1991-92	U. Minnesota	WCHA	6	2	1	0	209	15	0	4.32	....	....	....	....	....	....	....
1992-93	U. Minnesota	WCHA	21	8	5	5	1113	72	0	3.88	....	....	....	....	....	....	....

CAREY, JIM

Goaltender. Catches left. 6'2", 190 lbs. Born, Dorchester, MA, May 31, 1974.
(Washington's 2nd choice, 32nd overall, in 1992 Entry Draft).

			Regular Season								Playoffs						
Season	Club	Lea	GP	W	L	T	Mins	GA	SO	Avg	GP	W	L	Mins	GA	SO	Avg
1991-92	Catholic Mem.	HS	16	....	....	....	240	27	....	1.67	....	....	....	....	....	....	....
1992-93a	U. Wisconsin	WCHA	26	15	8	1	1525	78	1	3.07	....	....	....	....	....	....	....

a WCHA Second All-Star Team (1993)

CASEY, DENIS

Goaltender. Catches left. 5'10", 180 lbs. Born, Kelowna, B.C., March 5, 1971.
(Pittsburgh's 6th choice, 110th overall, in 1990 Entry Draft).

			Regular Season								Playoffs						
Season	Club	Lea	GP	W	L	T	Mins	GA	SO	Avg	GP	W	L	Mins	GA	SO	Avg
1989-90	Colorado	WCHA	19	7	9	1	1059	75	1	4.15	....	....	....	....	....	....	....
1990-91	Colorado	WCHA	11	3	7	0	607	43	0	4.25	....	....	....	....	....	....	....
1991-92	Colorado	WCHA	12	6	4	1	664	44	0	3.97	....	....	....	....	....	....	....
1992-93	Colorado	WCHA					DID NOT PLAY										

CASEY, JON

Goaltender. Catches left. 5'10", 155 lbs. Born, Grand Rapids, MN, March 29, 1962.

			Regular Season								Playoffs						
Season	Club	Lea	GP	W	L	T	Mins	GA	SO	Avg	GP	W	L	Mins	GA	SO	Avg
1980-81	North Dakota	WCHA	5	3	1	0	300	19	0	3.80	....	....	....	....	....	....	....
1981-82	North Dakota	WCHA	18	15	3	0	1038	48	1	2.77	....	....	....	....	....	....	....
1982-83	North Dakota	WCHA	17	9	6	2	1020	42	0	2.51	....	....	....	....	....	....	....
1983-84	North Dakota	WCHA	37	25	10	2	2180	115	2	3.13	....	....	....	....	....	....	....
	Minnesota	**NHL**	**2**	**1**	**0**	**0**	**84**	**6**	**0**	**4.29**	....	....	....	....	....	....	....
1984-85ab	Baltimore	AHL	46	30	11	4	2646	116	*4	*2.63	*13	8	3	689	38	0	3.31
1985-86	**Minnesota**	**NHL**	**26**	**11**	**11**	**1**	**1402**	**91**	**0**	**3.89**	....	....	....	....	....	....	....
	Springfield	AHL	9	4	3	1	464	30	0	3.88	....	....	....	....	....	....	....
1986-87	Springfield	AHL	13	1	8	0	770	56	0	4.36	....	....	....	....	....	....	....
	Indianapolis	IHL	31	14	15	0	1794	133	0	4.45	....	....	....	....	....	....	....
1987-88	**Minnesota**	**NHL**	**14**	**1**	**7**	**4**	**663**	**41**	**0**	**3.71**	....	....	....	....	....	....	....
	Kalamazoo	IHL	42	24	13	5	2541	154	2	3.64	7	3	3	382	26	0	4.08
1988-89	**Minnesota**	**NHL**	**55**	**18**	**17**	**12**	**2961**	**151**	**1**	**3.06**	**4**	**1**	**3**	**211**	**16**	**0**	**4.55**
1989-90	**Minnesota**	**NHL**	**61**	***31**	**22**	**4**	**3407**	**183**	**3**	**3.22**	**7**	**3**	**4**	**415**	**21**	**1**	**3.04**
1990-91	**Minnesota**	**NHL**	**55**	**21**	**20**	**11**	**3185**	**158**	**3**	**2.98**	***23**	***14**	**7**	***1205**	**61**	***1**	**3.04**
1991-92	**Minnesota**	**NHL**	**52**	**19**	**23**	**5**	**2911**	**165**	**2**	**3.40**	**7**	**3**	**4**	**437**	**22**	**0**	**3.02**
	Kalamazoo	IHL	4	2	1	1	250	11	....	2.64	....	....	....	....	....	....	....
1992-93	**Minnesota**	**NHL**	**60**	**26**	**26**	**5**	**3476**	**193**	**3**	**3.33**	....	....	....	....	....	....	....
	NHL Totals		**325**	**128**	**126**	**42**	**18089**	**988**	**12**	**3.28**	**41**	**21**	**18**	**2268**	**120**	**2**	**3.17**

a Won Baz Bastien Trophy (AHL Most Valuable Goaltender) (1985)
b AHL First All-Star Team (1985)

Played in NHL All-Star Game (1993)

Signed as a free agent by **Minnesota**, April 1, 1984. Traded to **Boston** by **Dallas** for Andy Moog to complete June 20, 1993 trade which sent Gord Murphy to **Dallas** for future considerations, June 25, 1993.

CASHMAN, SCOTT

Goaltender. Catches left. 6'2", 186 lbs. Born, Ottawa, Ont., September 20, 1969.
(Minnesota's 8th choice, 112th overall, in 1989 Entry Draft).

			Regular Season								Playoffs						
Season	Club	Lea	GP	W	L	T	Mins	GA	SO	Avg	GP	W	L	Mins	GA	SO	Avg
1989-90ab	Boston U.	H.E.	*39	*23	14	1	*2277	122	*2	3.27	....	....	....	....	....	....	....
1990-91	Boston U.	H.E.	22	14	7	1	1307	79	0	3.58	....	....	....	....	....	....	....
1991-92	Boston U.	H.E.	20	12	5	2	1149	73	0	3.81	....	....	....	....	....	....	....
1992-93	Boston U.	H.E.	17	11	4	0	888	44	0	2.97	....	....	....	....	....	....	....

a Hockey East Rookie of the Year (1990)
b Hockey East Second All-Star Team (1990)

Claimed by **San Jose** from **Minnesota** in Dispersal Draft, May 30, 1991.

CAVICCHI, TRENT

Goaltender. Catches left. 6'3", 190 lbs. Born, Dartmouth, N.S., March 20, 1974.
(Montreal's 10th choice, 236th overall, in 1992 Entry Draft).

			Regular Season								Playoffs						
Season	Club	Lea	GP	W	L	T	Mins	GA	SO	Avg	GP	W	L	Mins	GA	SO	Avg
1992-93	N. Hampshire	H.E.	9	3	2	1	391	32	0	4.91	....	....	....	....	....	....	....

CHABOT, FREDERIC (shah-BOH)

Goaltender. Catches right. 5'11", 177 lbs. Born, Hebertville-Station, Que., February 12, 1968.
(New Jersey's 10th choice, 192nd overall, in 1986 Entry Draft).

			Regular Season								Playoffs						
Season	Club	Lea	GP	W	L	T	Mins	GA	SO	Avg	GP	W	L	Mins	GA	SO	Avg
1986-87	Drummondville	QMJHL	62	31	29	0	3508	293	1	5.01	8	2	6	481	40	0	4.99
1987-88	Drummondville	QMJHL	58	27	24	4	3276	237	1	4.34	16	10	6	1019	56	*1	*3.30
1988-89a	Prince Albert	WHL	54	21	29	0	2957	202	2	4.10	4	1	1	199	16	0	4.82
1989-90	Sherbrooke	AHL	2	1	1	0	119	8	0	4.03	....	....	....	....	....	....	....
	Fort Wayne	IHL	23	6	13	3	1208	87	1	4.32	....	....	....	....	....	....	....
1990-91	**Montreal**	**NHL**	**3**	**0**	**0**	**1**	**108**	**6**	**0**	**3.33**	....	....	....	....	....	....	....
	Fredericton	AHL	35	9	15	5	1800	122	0	4.07	....	....	....	....	....	....	....
1991-92	Fredericton	AHL	30	17	9	4	1761	79	2	*2.69	7	3	4	457	20	0	2.63
	Winston-Salem	ECHL	24	15	7	2	1449	71	0	*2.94	....	....	....	....	....	....	....
1992-93	**Montreal**	**NHL**	**1**	**0**	**0**	**0**	**40**	**1**	**0**	**1.50**	....	....	....	....	....	....	....
	Fredericton	AHL	45	22	17	4	2544	141	0	3.33	4	1	3	261	16	0	3.68
	NHL Totals		**4**	**0**	**0**	**1**	**148**	**7**	**0**	**2.84**	....	....	....	....	....	....	....

a WHL East All-Star Team (1989)

Signed as a free agent by **Montreal**, January 16, 1990. Claimed by **Tampa Bay** from **Montreal** in Expansion Draft, June 18, 1992. Traded to **Montreal** by **Tampa Bay** for J.C. Bergeron, June 19, 1992.

CHARBONNEAU, PATRICK

Goaltender. Catches left. 5'11", 217 lbs. Born, St-Jean, Que., July 22, 1975.
(Ottawa's 3rd choice, 53rd overall, in 1993 Entry Draft).

			Regular Season								Playoffs						
Season	Club	Lea	GP	W	L	T	Mins	GA	SO	Avg	GP	W	L	Mins	GA	SO	Avg
1991-92	Victoriaville	QMJHL	37	9	23	2	1943	163	0	5.03	....	....	....	....	....	....	....
1992-93	Victoriaville	QMJHL	59	*35	22	0	3121	216	0	4.15	2	1	0	92	4	0	2.61

CHEVELDAE, TIM (SHE-vehl-day)

Goaltender. Catches left. 5'10", 195 lbs. Born, Melville, Sask., February 15, 1968.
(Detroit's 4th choice, 64th overall, in 1986 Entry Draft).

			Regular Season								Playoffs						
Season	Club	Lea	GP	W	L	T	Mins	GA	SO	Avg	GP	W	L	Mins	GA	SO	Avg
1985-86	Saskatoon	WHL	36	21	10	3	2030	165	0	4.88	8	6	2	480	29	0	3.63
1986-87	Saskatoon	WHL	33	20	11	0	1909	133	2	4.18	5	4	1	308	20	0	3.90
1987-88a	Saskatoon	WHL	66	44	19	3	3798	235	1	3.71	6	4	2	364	27	0	4.45
1988-89	**Detroit**	**NHL**	**2**	**0**	**2**	**0**	**122**	**9**	**0**	**4.43**	....	....	....	....	....	....	....
	Adirondack	AHL	30	20	8	0	1694	98	1	3.47	2	1	0	99	9	0	5.45
1989-90	**Detroit**	**NHL**	**28**	**10**	**9**	**8**	**1600**	**101**	**0**	**3.79**	....	....	....	....	....	....	....
	Adirondack	AHL	31	17	8	6	1848	116	0	3.77	....	....	....	....	....	....	....
1990-91	**Detroit**	**NHL**	**65**	**30**	**26**	**5**	**3615**	**214**	**2**	**3.55**	**7**	**3**	**4**	**398**	**22**	**0**	**3.32**
1991-92	**Detroit**	**NHL**	***72**	***38**	**23**	**9**	***4236**	**226**	**2**	**3.20**	**11**	**3**	**7**	**597**	**25**	***2**	**2.51**
1992-93	**Detroit**	**NHL**	**67**	**34**	**24**	**7**	**3880**	**210**	**4**	**3.25**	**7**	**3**	**4**	**423**	**24**	**0**	**3.40**
	NHL Totals		**234**	**112**	**84**	**29**	**13453**	**760**	**8**	**3.39**	**25**	**9**	**15**	**1418**	**71**	**2**	**3.00**

a WHL East All-Star Team (1988)

Played in NHL All-Star Game (1992)

CLOUTIER, JACQUES (clootz-YAY)

Goaltender. Catches left. 5'7", 168 lbs. Born, Noranda, Que., January 3, 1960.
(Buffalo's 4th choice, 55th overall, in 1979 Entry Draft).

			Regular Season								Playoffs						
Season	Club	Lea	GP	W	L	T	Mins	GA	SO	Avg	GP	W	L	Mins	GA	SO	Avg
1977-78	Trois-Rivières	QJHL	71	....	....	....	4134	240	*4	3.48	13	....	....	779	40	1	3.08
1978-79a	Trois-Rivières	QJHL	72	....	....	....	4168	218	*3	*3.14	13	....	....	780	36	0	*2.77
1979-80	Trois-Rivières	QJHL	55	27	20	7	3222	231	2	4.30	7	3	4	420	33	0	4.71
1980-81	Rochester	AHL	*61	27	27	6	*3478	209	1	3.61	....	....	....	....	....	....	....
1981-82	**Buffalo**	**NHL**	**7**	**5**	**1**	**0**	**311**	**13**	**0**	**2.51**	....	....	....	....	....	....	....
	Rochester	AHL	23	14	7	2	1366	64	0	2.81	....	....	....	....	....	....	....
1982-83	**Buffalo**	**NHL**	**25**	**10**	**7**	**6**	**1390**	**81**	**0**	**3.50**	....	....	....	....	....	....	....
	Rochester	AHL	13	7	3	1	634	42	0	3.97	16	12	4	992	47	0	2.84
1983-84	Rochester	AHL	*51	26	22	1	*2841	172	1	3.63	*18	9	9	*1145	68	0	3.56
1984-85	**Buffalo**	**NHL**	**1**	**0**	**0**	**1**	**65**	**4**	**0**	**3.69**	....	....	....	....	....	....	....
	Rochester	AHL	14	10	2	1	803	36	0	2.69	....	....	....	....	....	....	....
1985-86	**Buffalo**	**NHL**	**15**	**5**	**9**	**1**	**872**	**49**	**1**	**3.37**	....	....	....	....	....	....	....
	Rochester	AHL	14	10	2	2	835	38	1	2.73	....	....	....	....	....	....	....
1986-87	**Buffalo**	**NHL**	**40**	**11**	**19**	**5**	**2167**	**137**	**0**	**3.79**	....	....	....	....	....	....	....
1987-88	**Buffalo**	**NHL**	**20**	**4**	**8**	**2**	**851**	**67**	**0**	**4.72**	....	....	....	....	....	....	....
1988-89	**Buffalo**	**NHL**	**36**	**15**	**14**	**0**	**1786**	**108**	**0**	**3.63**	**4**	**1**	**3**	**238**	**10**	**1**	**2.52**
	Rochester	AHL	11	2	7	0	527	41	0	4.67	....	....	....	....	....	....	....
1989-90	**Chicago**	**NHL**	**43**	**18**	**15**	**2**	**2178**	**112**	**2**	**3.09**	**4**	**0**	**2**	**175**	**8**	**0**	**2.74**
1990-91	**Chicago**	**NHL**	**10**	**2**	**3**	**0**	**403**	**24**	**0**	**3.57**	....	....	....	....	....	....	....
	Quebec	**NHL**	**15**	**3**	**8**	**2**	**829**	**61**	**0**	**4.41**	....	....	....	....	....	....	....
1991-92	**Quebec**	**NHL**	**26**	**6**	**14**	**3**	**1345**	**88**	**0**	**3.93**	....	....	....	....	....	....	....
1992-93	**Quebec**	**NHL**	**3**	**0**	**2**	**1**	**154**	**10**	**0**	**3.90**	....	....	....	....	....	....	....
	NHL Totals		**241**	**79**	**100**	**23**	**12351**	**754**	**3**	**3.66**	**8**	**1**	**5**	**413**	**18**	**1**	**2.62**

a QMJHL First All-Star Team (1979)

Traded to **Chicago** by **Buffalo** for future considerations, September 28, 1989. Traded to **Quebec** by **Chicago** for Tony McKegney, January 29, 1991.

COUSINEAU, MARCEL

Goaltender. Catches left. 5'9", 180 lbs. Born, Delson, Que., April 30, 1973.
(Boston's 3rd choice, 62nd overall, in 1991 Entry Draft).

			Regular Season								Playoffs						
Season	Club	Lea	GP	W	L	T	Mins	GA	SO	Avg	GP	W	L	Mins	GA	SO	Avg
1990-91	Beauport	QMJHL	49	13	29	3	2739	196	1	4.29	....	....	....	....	....	....	....
1991-92	Beauport	QMJHL	*67	26	32	5	*3673	241	0	3.94	....	....	....	....	....	....	....
1992-93	Drummondville	QMJHL	60	20	32	2	3298	225	0	4.09	9	3	6	498	37	*1	4.45

CURRIE, JASON

Goaltender. Catches right. 5'10", 170 lbs. Born, Brampton, Ont., April 26, 1972.
(Hartford's 10th choice, 207th overall, in 1991 Entry Draft).

			Regular Season								Playoffs						
Season	Club	Lea	GP	W	L	T	Mins	GA	SO	Avg	GP	W	L	Mins	GA	SO	Avg
1990-91	Clarkson	ECAC	21	11	3	2	968	58	0	3.59	....	....	....	....	....	....	....
1991-92	Clarkson	ECAC	18	11	6	1	965	42	2	2.61	....	....	....	....	....	....	....
1992-93	Clarkson	ECAC	12	4	6	1	642	34	1	3.18	....	....	....	....	....	....	....

DAFOE, BYRON

Goaltender. Catches left. 5'11", 175 lbs. Born, Sussex, England, February 25, 1971.
(Washington's 2nd choice, 35th overall, in 1989 Entry Draft).

			Regular Season								Playoffs						
Season	Club	Lea	GP	W	L	T	Mins	GA	SO	Avg	GP	W	L	Mins	GA	SO	Avg
1988-89	Portland	WHL	59	29	24	3	3279	291	1	5.32	*18	10	8	*1091	81	*1	4.45
1989-90	Portland	WHL	40	14	21	3	2265	193	0	5.11	....	....	....	....	....	....	....
1990-91	Portland	WHL	8	1	5	1	414	41	0	5.94	....	....	....	....	....	....	....
	Prince Albert	WHL	32	13	12	4	1839	124	0	4.05	....	....	....	....	....	....	....
1991-92	New Haven	AHL	7	3	2	1	364	22	0	3.63	....	....	....	....	....	....	....
	Baltimore	AHL	33	12	16	4	1847	119	0	3.87	....	....	....	....	....	....	....
	Hampton Rds.	ECHL	10	6	4	0	562	26	0	2.78	....	....	....	....	....	....	....
1992-93	**Washington**	**NHL**	**1**	**0**	**0**	**0**	**1**	**0**	**0**	**0.00**	....	....	....	....	....	....	....
	Baltimore	AHL	48	16	20	7	2617	191	1	4.38	5	2	3	241	22	0	5.48
	NHL Totals		**1**	**0**	**0**	**0**	**1**	**0**	**0**	**0.00**	....	....	....	....	....	....	....

D'ALESSIO, CORRIE

Goaltender. Catches left. 5'11", 155 lbs. Born, Cornwall, Ont., September 9, 1969.
(Vancouver's 4th choice, 107th overall, in 1988 Entry Draft).

			Regular Season								Playoffs						
Season	Club	Lea	GP	W	L	T	Mins	GA	SO	Avg	GP	W	L	Mins	GA	SO	Avg
1987-88a	Cornell	ECAC	25	17	8	0	1457	67	0	2.76	....	....	....	....	....	....	....
1988-89	Cornell	ECAC	29	15	13	1	1684	96	1	3.42	....	....	....	....	....	....	....
1989-90	Cornell	ECAC	16	6	7	2	887	50	0	3.38	....	....	....	....	....	....	....
1990-91	Cornell	ECAC	24	10	8	3	1160	67	0	3.47	....	....	....	....	....	....	....
1991-92	Milwaukee	IHL	27	9	14	2	1435	96	0	4.01	2	0	2	119	12	0	6.05
1992-93	**Hartford**	**NHL**	**1**	**0**	**0**	**0**	**11**	**0**	**0**	**0.00**	....	....	....	....	....	....	....
	Springfield	AHL	23	3	13	2	1120	77	0	4.13	4	1	0	75	3	0	2.40
	NHL Totals		**1**	**0**	**0**	**0**	**11**	**0**	**0**	**0.00**	....	....	....	....	....	....	....

a ECAC All-Rookie Team (1988)

Traded to **Hartford** by **Vancouver** with future considerations for Kay Whitmore, October 1, 1992.

DAUBENSPECK, KIRK

Goaltender. Catches left. 6', 170 lbs. Born, Madison, WI, July 16, 1974.
(Philadelphia's 7th choice, 151st overall, in 1992 Entry Draft).

			Regular Season								Playoffs						
Season	Club	Lea	GP	W	L	T	Mins	GA	SO	Avg	GP	W	L	Mins	GA	SO	Avg
1991-92	Culver Acad.	HS						UNAVAILABLE									
1992-93	Sioux City	USHL	9	0	7	1	470	49	0	6.26	....	....	....	....	....	....	....
	Wisconsin	USHL	28	5	20	1	1542	123	....	4.79	....	....	....	....	....	....	....

DEGRACE, YANICK

Goaltender. Catches left. 5'11", 175 lbs. Born, Lameque, N.B., April 16, 1971.
(Philadelphia's 5th choice, 94th overall, in 1991 Entry Draft).

			Regular Season								Playoffs						
Season	Club	Lea	GP	W	L	T	Mins	GA	SO	Avg	GP	W	L	Mins	GA	SO	Avg
1990-91	Trois-Rivières	QMJHL	33	13	11	2	1726	97	1	3.37	4	1	0	129	11	0	5.12
1991-92	Hull	QMJHL	35	18	9	3	1970	112	0	3.41	2	0	2	31	4	0	7.64
	Hershey	AHL	2	0	1	1	125	6	0	2.88	....	....	....	....	....	....	....
1992-93	Hershey	AHL	30	10	15	2	1442	103	1	4.29	....	....	....	....	....	....	....

DELGUIDICE, MATT (del-GOO-dis)

Goaltender. Catches right. 5'9", 170 lbs. Born, West Haven, CT, March 5, 1967.
(Boston's 5th choice, 77th overall, in 1987 Entry Draft).

			Regular Season								Playoffs						
Season	Club	Lea	GP	W	L	T	Mins	GA	SO	Avg	GP	W	L	Mins	GA	SO	Avg
1988-89	U. of Maine	H.E.	20	16	4	0	1090	57	1	*3.14	....	....	....	....	....	....	....
1989-90	U. of Maine	H.E.	23	16	4	0	1257	68	0	3.25	....	....	....	....	....	....	....
1990-91	**Boston**	**NHL**	**1**	**0**	**0**	**0**	**10**	**0**	**0**	**0.00**	....	....	....	....	....	....	....
	Maine	AHL	52	23	18	9	2893	160	2	3.32	2	1	1	82	5	0	3.66
1991-92	**Boston**	**NHL**	**10**	**2**	**5**	**1**	**424**	**28**	**0**	**3.96**	....	....	....	....	....	....	....
	Maine	AHL	25	5	15	0	1369	101	0	4.43	....	....	....	....	....	....	....
1992-93	Providence	AHL	9	0	7	1	478	58	0	7.28	....	....	....	....	....	....	....
	San Diego	IHL	1	0	0	0	20	2	0	6.00	....	....	....	....	....	....	....
	NHL Totals		**11**	**2**	**5**	**1**	**434**	**28**	**0**	**3.87**	....	....	....	....	....	....	....

DENOMME, C. JAY

Goaltender. Catches left. 5'11", 180 lbs. Born, London, Ont., April 8, 1974.
(Detroit's 9th choice, 189th overall, in 1992 Entry Draft).

			Regular Season								Playoffs						
Season	Club	Lea	GP	W	L	T	Mins	GA	SO	Avg	GP	W	L	Mins	GA	SO	Avg
1991-92	Kitchener	OHL	21	4	5	4	881	63	0	4.29	1	0	0	20	2	0	6.00
1992-93	Kitchener	OHL	45	17	20	5	2497	189	0	4.54	2	0	2	65	7	0	6.46

DERKSEN, DUANE

Goaltender. Catches left. 6'1", 180 lbs. Born, St. Boniface, Man., July 7, 1968.
(Washington's 4th choice, 57th overall, in 1988 Entry Draft).

			Regular Season								Playoffs						
Season	Club	Lea	GP	W	L	T	Mins	GA	SO	Avg	GP	W	L	Mins	GA	SO	Avg
1988-89	U. Wisconsin	WCHA	11	4	5	0	561	37	1	3.96	....	....	....	....	....	....	....
1989-90ab	U. Wisconsin	WCHA	*41	*31	8	1	*2345	133	*2	*3.40	....	....	....	....	....	....	....
1990-91a	U. Wisconsin	WCHA	*42	24	15	3	*2474	133	3	3.23	....	....	....	....	....	....	....
1991-92cd	U. Wisconsin	WCHA	31	18	11	2	1825	100	0	3.29	....	....	....	....	....	....	....
1992-93	Baltimore	AHL	26	6	13	3	1247	86	0	4.14	4	1	1	188	7	0	2.23
	Hampton Rds.	ECHL	13	7	5	0	747	48	0	3.86	....	....	....	....	....	....	....

a WCHA Second All-Star Team (1990, 1991)
b NCAA All-Tournament Team, Tournament Top Goaltender (1990)
c NCAA West Second All-American Team (1992)
d WCHA First All-Star Team (1992)

DEROUVILLE, PHILIPPE

Goaltender. Catches left. 6'1", 183 lbs. Born, Victoriaville, Que., August 7, 1974.
(Pittsburgh's 5th choice, 115th overall, in 1992 Entry Draft).

			Regular Season								Playoffs						
Season	Club	Lea	GP	W	L	T	Mins	GA	SO	Avg	GP	W	L	Mins	GA	SO	Avg
1990-91	Longueuil	QMJHL	20	13	6	0	1030	50	0	2.91	....	....	....	....	....	....	....
1991-92	Verdun	QMJHL	34	20	6	3	1854	99	2	3.20	11	7	3	593	28	1	2.83
1992-93	Verdun	QMJHL	61	30	27	2	3491	210	1	3.61	4	....	4	256	18	....	3.61

a QMJHL Second All-Star Team (1993)

DONEGHEY, MICHAEL

Goaltender. Catches left. 6', 165 lbs. Born, Boston, MA, July 28, 1970.
(Chicago's 10th choice, 237th overall, in 1989 Entry Draft).

			Regular Season								Playoffs						
Season	Club	Lea	GP	W	L	T	Mins	GA	SO	Avg	GP	W	L	Mins	GA	SO	Avg
1989-90	Merrimack	H.E.	9	3	5	0	424	36	1	5.09	....	....	....	....	....	....	....
1990-91	Merrimack	H.E.	12	2	4	1	557	48	0	4.90	....	....	....	....	....	....	....
1991-92	Merrimack	H.E.	3	1	2	0	233	18	0	4.64	....	....	....	....	....	....	....
1992-93	Merrimack	H.E.	33	13	15	1	1822	147	1	4.84	....	....	....	....	....	....	....

DOPSON, ROBERT

Goaltender. Catches left. 6', 200 lbs. Born, Smiths Falls, Ont., August 21, 1967.

			Regular Season								Playoffs						
Season	Club	Lea	GP	W	L	T	Mins	GA	SO	Avg	GP	W	L	Mins	GA	SO	Avg
1989-90	Wilfred Laurier	OUAA	22	....	....	....	1319	57	0	2.59	....	....	....	....	....	....	....
1990-91	Muskegon	IHL	24	10	10	0	1243	90	0	4.34	....	....	....	....	....	....	....
	Louisville	ECHL	3	3	0	0	180	12	0	4.00	5	3	1	270	16	0	3.55
1991-92	Muskegon	IHL	28	13	12	2	1655	90	4	3.26	12	8	4	697	40	0	3.44
1992-93	Cleveland	IHL	50	26	15	3	2825	167	1	3.55	4	0	4	203	20	0	5.91

Signed as a free agent by **Pittsburgh**, July 6, 1991.

DRAPER, TOM

Goaltender. Catches left. 5'11", 185 lbs. Born, Outremont, Que., November 20, 1966.
(Winnipeg's 8th choice, 165th overall, in 1985 Entry Draft).

			Regular Season								Playoffs						
Season	Club	Lea	GP	W	L	T	Mins	GA	SO	Avg	GP	W	L	Mins	GA	SO	Avg
1983-84	U. of Vermont	ECAC	20	8	12	0	1205	82	0	4.08	....	....	....	....	....	....	....
1984-85	U. of Vermont	ECAC	24	5	17	0	1316	90	0	4.11	....	....	....	....	....	....	....
1985-86	U. of Vermont	ECAC	29	15	12	1	1697	87	1	3.08	....	....	....	....	....	....	....
1986-87a	U. of Vermont	ECAC	29	16	13	0	1662	96	2	3.47	....	....	....	....	....	....	....
1987-88	Tappara	Fin.	28	16	3	9	1619	87	0	3.22	....	....	....	....	....	....	....
1988-89	**Winnipeg**	**NHL**	**2**	**1**	**1**	**0**	**120**	**12**	**0**	**6.00**	....	....	....	....	....	....	....
b	Moncton	AHL	*54	27	17	5	*2962	171	2	3.46	7	5	2	419	24	0	3.44
1989-90	**Winnipeg**	**NHL**	**6**	**2**	**4**	**0**	**359**	**26**	**0**	**4.35**	....	....	....	....	....	....	....
	Moncton	AHL	51	20	24	3	2844	167	1	3.52	....	....	....	....	....	....	....
1990-91	Moncton	AHL	30	15	13	2	1779	95	1	3.20	....	....	....	....	....	....	....
	Fort Wayne	IHL	10	5	3	1	564	32	0	3.40	....	....	....	....	....	....	....
	Peoria	IHL	10	6	3	1	584	36	0	3.70	4	2	1	214	10	0	2.80
1991-92	**Buffalo**	**NHL**	**26**	**10**	**9**	**5**	**1403**	**75**	**1**	**3.21**	**7**	**3**	**4**	**433**	**19**	**1**	**2.63**
	Rochester	AHL	9	4	3	2	531	28	0	3.16	....	....	....	....	....	....	....
1992-93	**Buffalo**	**NHL**	**11**	**5**	**6**	**0**	**664**	**41**	**0**	**3.70**	....	....	....	....	....	....	....
	Rochester	AHL	5	3	2	0	303	22	0	4.36	....	....	....	....	....	....	....
	NHL Totals		**45**	**18**	**20**	**5**	**2546**	**154**	**1**	**3.63**	**7**	**3**	**4**	**433**	**19**	**1**	**2.63**

a ECAC First All-Star Team (1987)
b AHL Second All-Star Team (1989)

Traded to **St. Louis** by **Winnipeg** for future considerations (Jim Vesey, May 24, 1991), February 28, 1991. Traded to **Winnipeg** by **St. Louis** for future considerations, May 24, 1991. Traded to **Buffalo** by **Winnipeg** for future considerations, June 22, 1991.

DUFFUS, PARRIS

Goaltender. Catches left. 6'2", 192 lbs. Born, Denver, CO, January 27, 1970.
(St. Louis' 6th choice, 180th overall, in 1990 Entry Draft).

			Regular Season								Playoffs						
Season	Club	Lea	GP	W	L	T	Mins	GA	SO	Avg	GP	W	L	Mins	GA	SO	Avg
1990-91	Cornell	ECAC	4	0	0	0	37	3	0	4.86	....	....	....	....	....	....	....
1991-92ab	Cornell	ECAC	28	14	11	3	1677	74	1	2.65	....	....	....	....	....	....	....
1992-93	Hampton Rds.	ECHL	4	3	1	0	245	13	0	3.18	....	....	....	....	....	....	....
	Peoria	IHL	37	16	15	4	2149	142	0	3.96	1	0	1	59	5	0	5.08

a NCAA East First All-American Team (1992)
b ECAC Second All-Star Team (1992)

DUNHAM, MICHAEL

Goaltender. Catches left. 6'2", 170 lbs. Born, Johnson City, NY, June 1, 1972.
(New Jersey's 4th choice, 53rd overall, in 1990 Entry Draft).

			Regular Season								Playoffs						
Season	Club	Lea	GP	W	L	T	Mins	GA	SO	Avg	GP	W	L	Mins	GA	SO	Avg
1990-91	U. of Maine	H.E.	23	14	5	2	1275	63	0	*2.96	....	....	....	....	....	....	....
1991-92	U. of Maine	H.E.	7	6	0	0	382	14	1	2.20	....	....	....	....	....	....	....
	U.S. National	....	3	0	1	1	157	10	0	3.82	....	....	....	....	....	....	....
1992-93ab	U. of Maine	H.E.	25	*21	1	1	1429	63	0	2.65	....	....	....	....	....	....	....

a Hockey East First All-Star Team (1993)
b NCAA East First All-American Team (1993)

DYCK, LARRY

Goaltender. Catches left. 5'11", 180 lbs. Born, Winkler, Man., December 15, 1965.

			Regular Season								Playoffs						
Season	Club	Lea	GP	W	L	T	Mins	GA	SO	Avg	GP	W	L	Mins	GA	SO	Avg
1986-87	U. Manitoba	CWUAA	18	....	....	....	1019	61	*3	3.59	....	....	....	....	....	....	....
1987-88	U. Manitoba	CWUAA	19	....	....	....	1118	87	0	4.78	....	....	....	....	....	....	....
1988-89	Kalamazoo	IHL	42	17	20	2	2308	168	0	4.37	....	....	....	....	....	....	....
1989-90	Kalamazoo	IHL	36	20	12	0	1959	116	0	3.55	7	2	3	353	22	0	3.74
	Knoxville	ECHL	3	1	1	1	184	12	0	3.91	....	....	....	....	....	....	....
1990-91	Kalamazoo	IHL	38	21	15	0	2182	133	1	3.66	1	0	1	60	6	0	6.00
1991-92	Kalamazoo	IHL	*56	25	23	6	*3305	195	0	3.54	12	5	7	690	43	0	3.74
1992-93	Milwaukee	IHL	40	23	9	5	2329	131	0	3.37	3	1	2	180	10	0	3.33

Signed as a free agent by **Minnesota**, November 10, 1988.

ELLIS, AARON

Goaltender. Catches left. 6'1", 170 lbs. Born, Indianapolis, IN, May 13, 1974.
(Quebec's 11th choice, 244th overall, in 1992 Entry Draft).

			Regular Season								Playoffs						
Season	Club	Lea	GP	W	L	T	Mins	GA	SO	Avg	GP	W	L	Mins	GA	SO	Avg
1991-92	Culver	HS	13	....	....	....	....	....	4	2.32	....	....	....	....	....	....	....
1992-93	Bowling Green	CCHA	25	14	10	1	1479	94	0	3.81	....	....	....	....	....	....	....

ERICKSON, CHAD

Goaltender. Catches right. 5'10", 180 lbs. Born, Minneapolis, MN, August 21, 1970.
(New Jersey's 8th choice, 138th overall, in 1988 Entry Draft).

			Regular Season								Playoffs						
Season	Club	Lea	GP	W	L	T	Mins	GA	SO	Avg	GP	W	L	Mins	GA	SO	Avg
1988-89	Minn.-Duluth	WCHA	15	5	7	1	821	49	0	3.58	....	....	....	....	....	....	....
1989-90ab	Minn.-Duluth	WCHA	39	19	19	1	2301	141	0	3.68	....	....	....	....	....	....	....
1990-91	Minn.-Duluth	WCHA	40	14	19	7	2393	159	0	3.99	....	....	....	....	....	....	....
1991-92	**New Jersey**	**NHL**	**2**	**1**	**1**	**0**	**120**	**9**	**0**	**4.50**	....	....	....	....	....	....	....
	Utica	AHL	43	18	19	3	2341	147	2	3.77	2	0	2	127	11	0	5.20
1992-93	Utica	AHL	9	1	7	1	505	47	0	5.58	....	....	....	....	....	....	....
	Cincinnati	IHL	10	2	6	1	516	42	0	4.88	....	....	....	....	....	....	....
	Birmingham	ECHL	14	6	6	2	856	54	0	3.79	....	....	....	....	....	....	....
	NHL Totals		**2**	**1**	**1**	**0**	**120**	**9**	**0**	**4.50**	....	....	....	....	....	....	....

a WCHA Second All-Star Team (1990)
b NCAA West First All-American Team (1990)

ESSENSA, BOB (EH-sehn-sah)

Goaltender. Catches left. 6', 180 lbs. Born, Toronto, Ont., January 14, 1965.
(Winnipeg's 5th choice, 69th overall, in 1983 Entry Draft).

			Regular Season								Playoffs						
Season	Club	Lea	GP	W	L	T	Mins	GA	SO	Avg	GP	W	L	Mins	GA	SO	Avg
1983-84	Michigan State	CCHA	17	11	4	0	946	44	2	2.79	....	....	....	....	....	....	....
1984-85	Michigan State	CCHA	18	15	2	0	1059	29	2	1.64	....	....	....	....	....	....	....
1985-86a	Michigan State	CCHA	23	17	4	1	1333	74	1	3.33	....	....	....	....	....	....	....
1986-87	Michigan State	CCHA	25	19	3	1	1383	64	2	2.78	....	....	....	....	....	....	....
1987-88	Moncton	AHL	27	7	11	1	1287	100	1	4.66	....	....	....	....	....	....	....
1988-89	**Winnipeg**	**NHL**	**20**	**6**	**8**	**3**	**1102**	**68**	**1**	**3.70**	....	....	....	....	....	....	....
	Fort Wayne	IHL	22	14	7	0	1287	70	0	3.26	....	....	....	....	....	....	....
1989-90b	**Winnipeg**	**NHL**	**36**	**18**	**9**	**5**	**2035**	**107**	**1**	**3.15**	**4**	**2**	**1**	**206**	**12**	**0**	**3.50**
	Moncton	AHL	6	3	3	0	358	15	0	2.51	....	....	....	....	....	....	....
1990-91	**Winnipeg**	**NHL**	**55**	**19**	**24**	**6**	**2916**	**153**	**4**	**3.15**	....	....	....	....	....	....	....
	Moncton	AHL	2	1	0	1	125	6	0	2.88	....	....	....	....	....	....	....
1991-92	**Winnipeg**	**NHL**	**47**	**21**	**17**	**6**	**2627**	**126**	***5**	**2.88**	**1**	**0**	**0**	**33**	**3**	**0**	**5.45**
1992-93	**Winnipeg**	**NHL**	**67**	**33**	**26**	**6**	**3855**	**227**	**2**	**3.53**	**6**	**2**	**4**	**367**	**20**	**0**	**3.27**
	NHL Totals		**225**	**97**	**84**	**26**	**12535**	**681**	**13**	**3.26**	**11**	**4**	**5**	**606**	**35**	**0**	**3.47**

a CCHA Second All-Star Team (1986)
b NHL All-Rookie Team (1990)

FERNANDEZ, EMMANUEL

Goaltender. Catches left. 6', 173 lbs. Born, Etobicoke, Ont., August 27, 1974.
(Quebec's 4th choice, 52nd overall, in 1992 Entry Draft).

			Regular Season								Playoffs						
Season	Club	Lea	GP	W	L	T	Mins	GA	SO	Avg	GP	W	L	Mins	GA	SO	Avg
1991-92	Laval	QMJHL	31	14	13	2	1593	99	1	3.73	9	3	5	468	39	0	5.00
1992-93	Laval	QMJHL	43	26	14	2	2347	141	1	3.60	13	*12	1	818	42	0	3.08

FINCH, GEOFF

Goaltender. Catches left. 6', 180 lbs. Born, Oshawa, Ont., April 8, 1972.
(Minnesota's 7th choice, 137th overall, in 1991 Entry Draft).

			Regular Season								Playoffs						
Season	Club	Lea	GP	W	L	T	Mins	GA	SO	Avg	GP	W	L	Mins	GA	SO	Avg
1990-91	Brown	ECAC	22	9	9	1	1203	78	1	3.89	....	....	....	....	....	....	....
1991-92	Brown	ECAC	15	4	7	2	815	65	0	4.79	....	....	....	....	....	....	....
1992-93	Brown	ECAC	18	11	5	1	1020	56	0	3.29	....	....	....	....	....	....	....

FISET, STEPHANE (fih-SET)

Goaltender. Catches left. 6', 175 lbs. Born, Montreal, Que., June 17, 1970.
(Quebec's 3rd choice, 24th overall, in 1988 Entry Draft).

			Regular Season								Playoffs						
Season	Club	Lea	GP	W	L	T	Mins	GA	SO	Avg	GP	W	L	Mins	GA	SO	Avg
1987-88	Victoriaville	QMJHL	40	15	17	4	2221	146	1	3.94	2	0	2	163	10	0	3.68
1988-89a	Victoriaville	QMJHL	43	25	14	0	2401	138	1	*3.45	12	*9	2	711	33	0	*2.78
1989-90	**Quebec**	**NHL**	**6**	**0**	**5**	**1**	**342**	**34**	**0**	**5.96**	....	....	....	....	....	....	....
	Victoriaville	QMJHL	24	14	6	3	1383	63	1	*2.73	*14	7	6	*790	49	0	3.72
1990-91	**Quebec**	**NHL**	**3**	**0**	**2**	**1**	**186**	**12**	**0**	**3.87**	....	....	....	....	....	....	....
	Halifax	AHL	36	10	15	8	1902	131	0	4.13	....	....	....	....	....	....	....
1991-92	**Quebec**	**NHL**	**23**	**7**	**10**	**2**	**1133**	**71**	**1**	**3.76**	....	....	....	....	....	....	....
	Halifax	AHL	29	8	14	6	1675	110	*3	3.94	....	....	....	....	....	....	....
1992-93	**Quebec**	**NHL**	**37**	**18**	**9**	**4**	**1939**	**110**	**0**	**3.40**	**1**	**0**	**0**	**21**	**1**	**0**	**2.86**
	Halifax	AHL	3	2	1	0	180	11	0	3.67	....	....	....	....	....	....	....
	NHL Totals		**69**	**25**	**26**	**8**	**3600**	**227**	**1**	**3.78**	**1**	**0**	**0**	**21**	**1**	**0**	**2.86**

a QMJHL First All-Star Team (1989)

FITZPATRICK, MARK

Goaltender. Catches left. 6'2", 190 lbs. Born, Toronto, Ont., November 13, 1968.
(Los Angeles' 2nd choice, 27th overall, in 1987 Entry Draft).

			Regular Season								Playoffs						
Season	Club	Lea	GP	W	L	T	Mins	GA	SO	Avg	GP	W	L	Mins	GA	SO	Avg
1985-86a	Medicine Hat	WHL	41	26	6	1	2074	99	1	2.86	19	12	5	986	58	0	3.53
1986-87	Medicine Hat	WHL	50	31	11	4	2844	159	4	3.35	20	12	8	1224	71	1	3.48
1987-88	Medicine Hat	WHL	63	36	15	6	3600	194	2	3.23	16	12	4	959	52	*1	*3.25
1988-89	**Los Angeles**	**NHL**	**17**	**6**	**7**	**3**	**957**	**64**	**0**	**4.01**	....	....	....	....	....	....	....
	New Haven	AHL	18	10	5	1	980	54	1	3.31	....	....	....	....	....	....	....
	NY Islanders	**NHL**	**11**	**3**	**5**	**2**	**627**	**41**	**0**	**3.92**	....	....	....	....	....	....	....
1989-90	**NY Islanders**	**NHL**	**47**	**19**	**19**	**5**	**2653**	**150**	**3**	**3.39**	**4**	**0**	**2**	**152**	**13**	**0**	**5.13**
1990-91	**NY Islanders**	**NHL**	**2**	**1**	**1**	**0**	**120**	**6**	**0**	**3.00**	....	....	....	....	....	....	....
	Capital Dist.	AHL	12	3	7	2	734	47	0	3.84	....	....	....	....	....	....	....
1991-92b	**NY Islanders**	**NHL**	**30**	**11**	**13**	**5**	**1743**	**93**	**0**	**3.20**	....	....	....	....	....	....	....
	Capital Dist.	AHL	14	6	5	1	782	39	0	2.99	....	....	....	....	....	....	....
1992-93	**NY Islanders**	**NHL**	**39**	**17**	**15**	**5**	**2253**	**130**	**0**	**3.46**	**3**	**0**	**1**	**77**	**4**	**0**	**3.12**
	Capital Dist.	AHL	5	1	3	1	284	18	0	3.80	....	....	....	....	....	....	....
	NHL Totals		**146**	**57**	**60**	**20**	**8353**	**484**	**3**	**3.48**	**7**	**0**	**3**	**229**	**17**	**0**	**4.45**

a Named WHL's Top Goaltender (1986)
b Won Bill Masterton Memorial Trophy (1992)

Traded to **NY Islanders** by **Los Angeles** with Wayne McBean and future considerations (Doug Crossman, May 23, 1989) for Kelly Hrudey, February 22, 1989. Traded to **Quebec** by **NY Islanders** with NY Islanders' first round choice (Adam Deadmarsh) in 1993 Entry Draft for Ron Hextall and Quebec's first round choice (Todd Bertuzzi) in 1993 Entry Draft, June 20, 1993. Claimed by **Florida** from **Quebec** in Expansion Draft, June 24, 1993.

FITZSIMMONS, JASON

Goaltender. Catches left. 5'11", 185 lbs. Born, Regina, Sask., June 3, 1971.
(Vancouver's 11th choice, 227th overall, in 1991 Entry Draft).

			Regular Season								Playoffs						
Season	Club	Lea	GP	W	L	T	Mins	GA	SO	Avg	GP	W	L	Mins	GA	SO	Avg
1990-91	Moose Jaw	WHL	44	15	23	2	2170	179	0	4.95	8	4	4	481	27	....	3.37
1991-92	Moose Jaw	WHL	60	29	28	1	3286	222	0	4.05	4	0	4	186	27	0	8.71
1992-93	Hamilton	AHL	14	5	8	1	788	53	0	4.04	....	....	....	....	....	....	....
	Columbus	ECHL	23	10	9	3	1340	91	0	4.07	....	....	....	....	....	....	....

FLAHERTY, WADE

Goaltender. Catches right. 6', 170 lbs. Born, Terrace, B.C., January 11, 1968.
(Buffalo's 10th choice, 181st overall, in 1988 Entry Draft).

			Regular Season								Playoffs						
Season	Club	Lea	GP	W	L	T	Mins	GA	SO	Avg	GP	W	L	Mins	GA	SO	Avg
1988-89	Victoria	WHL	42	21	19	0	2408	180	4	4.49	....	....	....	....	....	....	....
1989-90	Greensboro	ECHL	27	12	10	0	1308	96	0	4.40	....	....	....	....	....	....	....
1990-91	Kansas City	IHL	*56	16	31	4	2990	224	0	4.49	....	....	....	....	....	....	....
1991-92	**San Jose**	**NHL**	**3**	**0**	**3**	**0**	**178**	**13**	**0**	**4.38**	....	....	....	....	....	....	....
	Kansas City	IHL	43	26	14	3	2603	140	1	3.23	1	0	0	1	0	0	0.00
1992-93	**San Jose**	**NHL**	**1**	**0**	**1**	**0**	**60**	**5**	**0**	**5.00**	....	....	....	....	....	....	....
	Kansas City	IHL	*61	*34	19	7	*3642	195	2	3.21	*12	6	6	733	34	*1	2.78
	NHL Totals		**4**	**0**	**4**	**0**	**238**	**18**	**0**	**4.54**	....	....	....	....	....	....	....

a IHL Second All-Star Team (1993)

Signed as a free agent by **San Jose**, September 3, 1991.

FOSTER, NORM

Goaltender. Catches left. 5'9", 175 lbs. Born, Vancouver, B.C., February 10, 1965.
(Boston's 11th choice, 222nd overall, in 1983 Entry Draft).

			Regular Season								Playoffs						
Season	Club	Lea	GP	W	L	T	Mins	GA	SO	Avg	GP	W	L	Mins	GA	SO	Avg
1984-85	Michigan State	CCHA	26	22	4	0	1531	67	0	2.63	....	....	....	....	....	....	....
1985-86	Michigan State	CCHA	24	17	5	1	1414	87	0	3.69	....	....	....	....	....	....	....
1986-87	Michigan State	CCHA	24	14	7	1	1383	90	1	3.90	....	....	....	....	....	....	....
1987-88	Milwaukee	IHL	38	10	22	1	2001	170	0	5.10	....	....	....	....	....	....	....
1988-89	Maine	AHL	47	16	17	6	2411	156	1	3.88	....	....	....	....	....	....	....
1989-90	Maine	AHL	*64	23	28	10	*3664	217	3	3.55	....	....	....	....	....	....	....
1990-91	**Boston**	**NHL**	**3**	**2**	**1**	**0**	**184**	**14**	**0**	**4.57**	....	....	....	....	....	....	....
	Maine	AHL	2	1	1	0	122	7	0	3.44	....	....	....	....	....	....	....
	Cape Breton	AHL	40	15	14	7	2207	135	1	3.67	2	0	2	128	8	0	3.75
1991-92	**Edmonton**	**NHL**	**10**	**5**	**3**	**0**	**439**	**20**	**0**	**2.73**	....	....	....	....	....	....	....
	Cape Breton	AHL	29	15	13	1	1699	119	0	4.20	3	1	2	193	14	0	4.35
1992-93	Cape Breton	AHL	10	5	5	0	560	53	0	5.68	....	....	....	....	....	....	....
	Kansas City	IHL	8	6	1	1	489	28	0	3.44	1	0	0	16	0	0	0.00
	NHL Totals		**13**	**7**	**4**	**0**	**623**	**34**	**0**	**3.27**	....	....	....	....	....	....	....

Traded to **Edmonton** by **Boston** for future considerations, September 11, 1991. Signed as a free agent by **Philadelphia**, August 4, 1993.

FOUNTAIN, MIKE

Goaltender. Catches left. 6', 176 lbs. Born, North York, Ont., January 26, 1972.
(Vancouver's 4th choice, 69th overall, in 1992 Entry Draft).

			Regular Season								Playoffs						
Season	Club	Lea	GP	W	L	T	Mins	GA	SO	Avg	GP	W	L	Mins	GA	SO	Avg
1990-91	S.S. Marie	OHL	7	5	2	0	380	19	....	3.00	....	....	....	....	....	....	....
	Oshawa	OHL	30	17	5	1	1483	84	....	3.40	8	1	4	292	26	0	5.34
1991-92a	Oshawa	OHL	40	18	13	6	2260	149	1	3.96	7	3	4	429	26	0	3.64
1992-93	Cdn. National	....	13	7	5	1	45	37	1	2.98	....	....	....	....	....	....	....
	Hamilton	AHL	12	2	8	0	618	46	0	4.47	....	....	....	....	....	....	....

a OHL First All-Star Team (1992)

FUHR, GRANT (FYOOR)

Goaltender. Catches right. 5'9", 190 lbs. Born, Spruce Grove, Alta., September 28, 1962.
(Edmonton's 1st choice, 8th overall, in 1981 Entry Draft).

			Regular Season								Playoffs						
Season	Club	Lea	GP	W	L	T	Mins	GA	SO	Avg	GP	W	L	Mins	GA	SO	Avg
1979-80ab	Victoria	WHL	43	30	12	0	2488	130	2	3.14	8	5	3	465	22	0	2.84
1980-81ac	Victoria	WHL	59	48	9	1	3448	160	*4	*2.78	15	12	3	899	45	*1	*3.00
1981-82d	**Edmonton**	**NHL**	**48**	**28**	**5**	**14**	**2847**	**157**	**0**	**3.31**	**5**	**2**	**3**	**309**	**26**	**0**	**5.05**
1982-83	**Edmonton**	**NHL**	**32**	**13**	**12**	**5**	**1803**	**129**	**0**	**4.29**	**1**	**0**	**0**	**11**	**0**	**0**	**0.00**
	Moncton	AHL	10	4	5	1	604	40	0	3.98	....	....	....	....	....	....	....
1983-84	**Edmonton**	**NHL**	**45**	**30**	**10**	**4**	**2625**	**171**	**1**	**3.91**	**16**	**11**	**4**	**883**	**44**	**1**	**2.99**
1984-85	**Edmonton**	**NHL**	**46**	**26**	**8**	**7**	**2559**	**165**	**1**	**3.87**	***18**	***15**	**3**	**1064**	**55**	**0**	**3.10**
1985-86	**Edmonton**	**NHL**	**40**	**29**	**8**	**0**	**2184**	**143**	**0**	**3.93**	**9**	**5**	**4**	**541**	**28**	**0**	**3.11**
1986-87	**Edmonton**	**NHL**	**44**	**22**	**13**	**3**	**2388**	**137**	**0**	**3.44**	**19**	**14**	**5**	**1148**	**47**	**0**	**2.46**
1987-88ef	**Edmonton**	**NHL**	***75**	***40**	**24**	**9**	***4304**	**246**	***4**	**3.43**	***19**	***16**	**2**	***1136**	**55**	**0**	**2.90**
1988-89	**Edmonton**	**NHL**	**59**	**23**	**26**	**6**	**3341**	**213**	**1**	**3.83**	**7**	**3**	**4**	**417**	**24**	**1**	**3.45**
1989-90	**Edmonton**	**NHL**	**21**	**9**	**7**	**3**	**1081**	**70**	**1**	**3.89**	....	....	....	....	....	....	....
	Cape Breton	AHL	2	2	0	0	120	6	0	3.01	....	....	....	....	....	....	....
1990-91	**Edmonton**	**NHL**	**13**	**6**	**4**	**3**	**778**	**39**	**1**	**3.01**	**17**	**8**	**7**	**1019**	**51**	**0**	**3.00**
	Cape Breton	AHL	4	2	2	0	240	17	0	4.25	....	....	....	....	....	....	....
1991-92	**Toronto**	**NHL**	**66**	**25**	**33**	**5**	**3774**	**230**	**2**	**3.66**	....	....	....	....	....	....	....
1992-93	**Toronto**	**NHL**	**29**	**13**	**9**	**4**	**1665**	**87**	**1**	**3.14**	....	....	....	....	....	....	....
	Buffalo	**NHL**	**29**	**11**	**15**	**2**	**1694**	**98**	**0**	**3.47**	**8**	**3**	**4**	**474**	**27**	**1**	**3.42**
	NHL Totals		**547**	**275**	**174**	**65**	**31043**	**1885**	**12**	**3.64**	**119**	**77**	**36**	**7002**	**357**	**3**	**3.06**

a WHL First All-Star Team (1980, 1981)
b WHL Rookie of the Year (1980)
c Named WHL's Top Goaltender (1981)
d NHL Second All-Star Team (1982)
e NHL First All-Star Team (1988)
f Won Vezina Trophy (1988)

Played in NHL All-Star Game (1982, 1984-86, 1988-89)

Traded to **Toronto** by **Edmonton** with Glenn Anderson and Craig Berube for Vincent Damphousse, Peter Ing, Scott Thornton, Luke Richardson, future considerations and cash, September 19, 1991. Traded to **Buffalo** by **Toronto** with future considerations for Dave Andreychuk, Daren Puppa and Buffalo's first round choice (Kenny Jonsson) in 1993 Entry Draft, February 2, 1993.

GAGE, JOAQUIN

Goaltender. Catches left. 6', 200 lbs. Born, Vancouver, B.C., October 19, 1973.
(Edmonton's 6th choice, 109th overall, in 1992 Entry Draft).

			Regular Season								Playoffs						
Season	Club	Lea	GP	W	L	T	Mins	GA	SO	Avg	GP	W	L	Mins	GA	SO	Avg
1990-91	Portland	WHL	3	0	3	0	180	17	0	5.70	....	....	....	....	....	....	....
1991-92	Portland	WHL	63	27	30	4	3635	269	2	4.44	6	2	4	366	28	0	4.59
1992-93	Portland	WHL	38	21	16	1	2302	153	2	3.99	8	5	2	427	30	0	4.22

GAGNON, DAVID

Goaltender. Catches left. 6', 185 lbs. Born, Windsor, Ont., October 31, 1967.

			Regular Season								Playoffs						
Season	Club	Lea	GP	W	L	T	Mins	GA	SO	Avg	GP	W	L	Mins	GA	SO	Avg
1987-88	Colgate	ECAC	13	6	4	2	743	43	1	3.47	....	....	....	....	....	....	....
1988-89	Colgate	ECAC	28	17	9	2	1622	102	0	3.77	....	....	....	....	....	....	....
1989-90ab	Colgate	ECAC	33	28	3	1	1986	93	0	2.88	....	....	....	....	....	....	....
1990-91	**Detroit**	**NHL**	**2**	**0**	**1**	**0**	**35**	**6**	**0**	**10.29**	....	....	....	....	....	....	....
	Adirondack	AHL	24	8	8	5	1356	94	0	4.16	....	....	....	....	....	....	....
c	Hampton Rds.	ECHL	10	7	1	2	606	26	2	2.57	11	*10	1	696	27	0	*2.32
1991-92	Fort Wayne	IHL	2	2	0	0	125	7	0	3.36	....	....	....	....	....	....	....
	Toledo	ECHL	7	4	2	0	354	18	0	3.05	....	....	....	....	....	....	....
1992-93	Adirondack	AHL	1	0	1	0	60	5	0	5.00	....	....	....	....	....	....	....
	Fort Wayne	IHL	31	15	11	2	1771	116	0	3.93	1	0	0	6	0	0	0.00
	NHL Totals		**2**	**0**	**1**	**0**	**35**	**6**	**0**	**10.29**	....	....	....	....	....	....	....

a ECAC First All-Star Team (1990)
b ECAC Player of the Year (1990)
c MVP in Playoffs — ECHL (Shared with Dave Flanagan) (1991)

Signed as a free agent by **Detroit**, June 11, 1990.

GAGNON, JOEL

Goaltender. Catches left. 6', 194 lbs. Born, Hearst, Ont., March 14, 1975.
(Anaheim's 4th choice, 82nd overall, in 1993 Entry Draft).

			Regular Season								Playoffs						
Season	Club	Lea	GP	W	L	T	Mins	GA	SO	Avg	GP	W	L	Mins	GA	SO	Avg
1991-92	Kapuskasing	Midget	20	....	....	....	1201	57	0	2.85	....	....	....	....	....	....	....
1992-93	Oshawa	OHL	48	19	19	1	2248	159	0	4.24	7	3	0	285	21	0	4.42

GAMBLE, TROY

Goaltender. Catches left. 5'11", 195 lbs. Born, New Glasgow, N.S., April 7, 1967.
(Vancouver's 2nd choice, 25th overall, in 1985 Entry Draft).

			Regular Season								Playoffs						
Season	Club	Lea	GP	W	L	T	Mins	GA	SO	Avg	GP	W	L	Mins	GA	SO	Avg
1984-85ab	Medicine Hat	WHL	37	27	6	2	2095	100	3	2.86	2	1	1	120	9	0	4.50
1985-86	Medicine Hat	WHL	45	28	11	0	2264	142	0	3.76	11	5	4	530	31	0	3.51
1986-87	**Vancouver**	**NHL**	**1**	**0**	**1**	**0**	**60**	**4**	**0**	**4.00**	....	....	....	....	....	....	....
	Medicine Hat	WHL	11	7	3	0	646	46	0	4.27	....	....	....	....	....	....	....
	Spokane	WHL	38	17	17	1	2155	163	0	4.54	5	0	5	298	35	0	7.05
1987-88c	Spokane	WHL	67	36	26	1	3824	235	0	3.69	15	7	8	875	56	1	3.84
1988-89	**Vancouver**	**NHL**	**5**	**2**	**3**	**0**	**302**	**12**	**0**	**2.38**	....	....	....	....	....	....	....
	Milwaukee	IHL	42	23	9	0	2198	138	0	3.77	11	5	5	640	35	0	3.28
1989-90	Milwaukee	IHL	*56	22	21	4	2779	160	2	4.21	5	2	2	216	19	0	5.28
1990-91	**Vancouver**	**NHL**	**47**	**16**	**16**	**6**	**2433**	**140**	**1**	**3.45**	**4**	**1**	**3**	**249**	**16**	**0**	**3.86**
1991-92	**Vancouver**	**NHL**	**19**	**4**	**9**	**3**	**1009**	**73**	**0**	**4.34**	....	....	....	....	....	....	....
	Milwaukee	IHL	9	2	4	2	521	31	0	3.57	....	....	....	....	....	....	....
1992-93	Hamilton	AHL	14	1	10	2	769	62	0	4.84	....	....	....	....	....	....	....
	Cincinnati	IHL	33	11	18	2	1762	134	0	4.56	....	....	....	....	....	....	....
	NHL Totals		**72**	**22**	**29**	**9**	**3804**	**229**	**1**	**3.61**	**4**	**1**	**3**	**249**	**16**	**0**	**3.86**

a WHL First All-Star Team, East Division (1985)
b Named WHL's Top Goaltender (1985)
c WHL First All-Star Team, West Division (1988)

GAUTHIER, SEAN

Goaltender. Catches left. 5'11", 202 lbs. Born, Sudbury, Ont., March 28, 1971.
(Winnipeg's 7th choice, 181st overall, in 1991 Entry Draft).

			Regular Season								Playoffs						
Season	Club	Lea	GP	W	L	T	Mins	GA	SO	Avg	GP	W	L	Mins	GA	SO	Avg
1990-91	Kingston	OHL	*59	16	36	3	3200	282	0	5.29	....	....	....	....	....	....	....
1991-92	Moncton	AHL	25	8	10	5	1415	88	1	3.73	2	0	0	26	2	0	4.62
	Fort Wayne	IHL	18	10	4	2	978	59	1	3.62	2	0	0	48	7	0	8.75
1992-93	Moncton	AHL	38	10	16	9	2196	145	0	3.96	2	0	1	75	6	0	4.80

GILMORE, MIKE

Goaltender. Catches left. 5'10", 173 lbs. Born, Detroit, MI, March 11, 1968.
(NY Rangers' 1st choice, 18th overall, in 1990 Supplemental Draft).

			Regular Season								Playoffs						
Season	Club	Lea	GP	W	L	T	Mins	GA	SO	Avg	GP	W	L	Mins	GA	SO	Avg
1988-89	Michigan State	CCHA	3	1	0	0	74	5	0	4.04	....	....	....	....	....	....	....
1989-90	Michigan State	CCHA	12	9	1	0	638	29	0	2.73	....	....	....	....	....	....	....
1990-91a	Michigan State	CCHA	22	9	8	3	1218	54	*2	2.66	....	....	....	....	....	....	....
1991-92	Michigan State	CCHA	33	14	9	7	1831	95	0	3.11	....	....	....	....	....	....	....
1992-93	Erie	ECHL	31	19	8	1	1762	134	0	4.56	5	2	3	300	24	0	4.80

a CCHA Second All-Star Team (1991)

GILMOUR, DARRYL

Goaltender. Catches left. 6', 171 lbs. Born, Winnipeg, Man., February 13, 1967.
(Philadelphia's 3rd choice, 48th overall, in 1985 Entry Draft).

			Regular Season								Playoffs						
Season	Club	Lea	GP	W	L	T	Mins	GA	SO	Avg	GP	W	L	Mins	GA	SO	Avg
1984-85	Moose Jaw	WHL	58	15	35	0	3004	297	0	5.93	....	....	....	....	....	....	....
1985-86a	Moose Jaw	WHL	62	19	34	3	3482	276	1	4.76	9	4	4	490	48	0	5.88
1986-87	Moose Jaw	WHL	31	14	13	2	1776	123	2	4.16	....	....	....	....	....	....	....
	Portland	WHL	24	15	7	1	1460	111	0	4.56	19	12	7	1167	83	1	4.27
1987-88	Hershey	AHL	25	14	7	0	1273	78	1	3.68	....	....	....	....	....	....	....
1988-89	Hershey	AHL	38	16	14	5	2093	144	0	4.13	....	....	....	....	....	....	....
1989-90	New Haven	AHL	23	10	11	2	1356	85	0	3.76	....	....	....	....	....	....	....
	Nashville	ECHL	10	6	3	0	529	43	0	4.87	....	....	....	....	....	....	....
1990-91	New Haven	AHL	26	5	14	3	1375	90	1	3.93	....	....	....	....	....	....	....
	Phoenix	IHL	4	2	0	0	180	13	0	4.33	....	....	....	....	....	....	....
1991-92	Phoenix	IHL	30	10	15	3	1774	120	0	4.06	....	....	....	....	....	....	....
1992-93	Phoenix	IHL	41	7	28	3	2281	168	0	4.42	....	....	....	....	....	....	....

a WHL First All-Star Team, East Division (1986)

Signed as a free agent by **Los Angeles**, December 15, 1989.

GOSSELIN, MARIO

Goaltender. Catches left. 5'8", 160 lbs. Born, Thetford Mines, Que., June 15, 1963.
(Quebec's 3rd choice, 55th overall, in 1982 Entry Draft).

			Regular Season								Playoffs						
Season	Club	Lea	GP	W	L	T	Mins	GA	SO	Avg	GP	W	L	Mins	GA	SO	Avg
1980-81	Shawinigan	QMJHL	21	4	9	0	907	75	0	4.96	1	0	0	20	2	0	6.00
1981-82a	Shawinigan	QMJHL	60	....	....	....	3404	230	0	4.05	14	....	....	788	58	0	4.42
1982-83	Shawinigan	QMJHL	46	32	9	1	2496	133	3	3.12	8	5	3	457	29	0	3.81
1983-84	Cdn. Olympic	....	36	....	....	....	2007	126	0	3.77	....	....	....	....	....	....	....
	Quebec	**NHL**	**3**	**2**	**0**	**0**	**148**	**3**	**1**	**1.21**	....	....	....	....	....	....	....
1984-85	**Quebec**	**NHL**	**35**	**19**	**10**	**3**	**1960**	**109**	**1**	**3.34**	**17**	**9**	**8**	**1059**	**54**	**0**	**3.06**
1985-86	**Quebec**	**NHL**	**31**	**14**	**14**	**1**	**1726**	**111**	**2**	**3.86**	**1**	**0**	**1**	**40**	**5**	**0**	**7.50**
	Fredericton	AHL	5	2	2	1	304	15	0	2.96	....	....	....	....	....	....	....
1986-87	**Quebec**	**NHL**	**30**	**13**	**11**	**1**	**1625**	**86**	**0**	**3.18**	**11**	**7**	**4**	**654**	**37**	**0**	**3.39**
1987-88	**Quebec**	**NHL**	**54**	**20**	**28**	**4**	**3002**	**189**	**2**	**3.78**	....	....	....	....	....	....	....
1988-89	**Quebec**	**NHL**	**39**	**11**	**19**	**3**	**2064**	**146**	**0**	**4.24**	....	....	....	....	....	....	....
	Halifax	AHL	3	3	0	0	183	9	0	2.95	....	....	....	....	....	....	....
1989-90	**Los Angeles**	**NHL**	**26**	**7**	**11**	**1**	**1226**	**79**	**0**	**3.87**	**3**	**0**	**2**	**63**	**3**	**0**	**2.90**
1990-91	Phoenix	IHL	46	24	15	4	2673	172	1	3.86	11	7	4	670	43	0	3.83
1991-92	Springfield	AHL	47	28	11	5	2606	142	0	3.27	6	1	4	319	18	0	3.39
1992-93	**Hartford**	**NHL**	**16**	**5**	**9**	**1**	**867**	**57**	**0**	**3.94**	....	....	....	....	....	....	....
	Springfield	AHL	23	8	7	7	1345	75	0	3.35	....	....	....	....	....	....	....
	NHL Totals		**234**	**91**	**102**	**14**	**12618**	**780**	**6**	**3.71**	**32**	**16**	**15**	**1816**	**99**	**0**	**3.27**

a QMJHL Second All-Star Team (1982)

Played in NHL All-Star Game (1986)

Signed as a free agent by **Los Angeles**, June 14, 1989. Signed as a free agent by **Hartford**, September 4, 1991.

GOVERDE, DAVID

Goaltender. Catches right. 6', 210 lbs. Born, Toronto, Ont., April 9, 1970.
(Los Angeles' 4th choice, 91st overall, in 1990 Entry Draft).

			Regular Season								Playoffs						
Season	Club	Lea	GP	W	L	T	Mins	GA	SO	Avg	GP	W	L	Mins	GA	SO	Avg
1989-90	Sudbury	OHL	52	28	12	7	2941	182	0	3.71	7	3	3	394	25	0	3.81
1990-91	Phoenix	IHL	40	11	19	5	2007	137	0	4.10	....	....	....	....	....	....	....
1991-92	**Los Angeles**	**NHL**	**2**	**1**	**1**	**0**	**120**	**9**	**0**	**4.50**	....	....	....	....	....	....	....
	Phoenix	IHL	35	11	19	3	1951	129	1	3.97	....	....	....	....	....	....	....
	New Haven	AHL	5	1	3	0	248	17	0	4.11	....	....	....	....	....	....	....
1992-93	**Los Angeles**	**NHL**	**2**	**0**	**2**	**0**	**98**	**13**	**0**	**7.96**	....	....	....	....	....	....	....
	Phoenix	IHL	45	18	21	3	2569	173	1	4.04	....	....	....	....	....	....	....
	NHL Totals		**4**	**1**	**3**	**0**	**218**	**22**	**0**	**6.06**	....	....	....	....	....	....	....

GRAVISTIN, SHAUN

Goaltender. Catches left. 5'7", 150 lbs. Born, Calgary, Alta., November 17, 1970.
(Hartford's 1st choice, 15th overall, in 1991 Supplemental Draft).

			Regular Season								Playoffs						
Season	Club	Lea	GP	W	L	T	Mins	GA	SO	Avg	GP	W	L	Mins	GA	SO	Avg
1989-90	Alaska-Anch.	G.N.	2	1	0	0	81	3	0	2.22	....	....	....	....	....	....	....
1990-91	Alaska-Anch.	G.N.	8	4	2	1	425	20	0	2.82	....	....	....	....	....	....	....
1991-92	Alaska-Anch.	G.N.	9	8	0	1	524	30	0	3.44	....	....	....	....	....	....	....
1992-93	Alaska-Anch.	WCHA	29	16	9	4	1679	90	1	3.22	....	....	....	....	....	....	....

GREENLAY, MIKE

Goaltender. Catches left. 6'3", 200 lbs. Born, Vitoria, Brazil, September 15, 1968.
(Edmonton's 9th choice, 189th overall, in 1986 Entry Draft).

			Regular Season								Playoffs						
Season	Club	Lea	GP	W	L	T	Mins	GA	SO	Avg	GP	W	L	Mins	GA	SO	Avg
1986-87	Lake Superior	CCHA	17	7	5	0	744	44	0	3.54	....	....	....	....	....	....	....
1987-88	Lake Superior	CCHA	19	10	3	3	1023	57	0	3.34	....	....	....	....	....	....	....
1988-89	Saskatoon	WHL	20	10	8	1	1128	86	0	4.57	6	2	0	174	16	0	5.52
	Lake Superior	CCHA	2	1	1	0	85	6	0	4.23	....	....	....	....	....	....	....
1989-90	**Edmonton**	**NHL**	**2**	**0**	**0**	**0**	**20**	**4**	**0**	**12.00**	....	....	....	....	....	....	....
	Cape Breton	AHL	46	19	18	5	2595	146	2	3.38	5	1	3	306	26	0	5.09
1990-91	Cape Breton	AHL	11	5	2	0	493	33	0	4.02	....	....	....	....	....	....	....
	Knoxville	ECHL	29	17	9	2	1725	108	2	3.75	....	....	....	....	....	....	....
1991-92	Cape Breton	AHL	3	1	1	1	144	12	0	5.00	....	....	....	....	....	....	....
	Knoxville	ECHL	27	8	12	2	1415	113	0	4.79	....	....	....	....	....	....	....
1992-93	Louisville	ECHL	27	12	11	2	1437	96	1	4.01	....	....	....	....	....	....	....
	Atlanta	IHL	12	5	3	2	637	40	0	3.77	....	....	....	....	....	....	....
	NHL Totals		**2**	**0**	**0**	**0**	**20**	**4**	**0**	**12.00**	....	....	....	....	....	....	....

Signed as a free agent by **Tampa Bay**, July 29, 1992.

HACKETT, JEFF

Goaltender. Catches left. 6'1", 180 lbs. Born, London, Ont., June 1, 1968.
(NY Islanders' 2nd choice, 34th overall, in 1987 Entry Draft).

			Regular Season								Playoffs						
Season	Club	Lea	GP	W	L	T	Mins	GA	SO	Avg	GP	W	L	Mins	GA	SO	Avg
1986-87	Oshawa	OHL	31	18	9	2	1672	85	2	3.05	15	8	7	895	40	0	2.68
1987-88a	Oshawa	OHL	53	30	21	2	3165	205	0	3.89	7	3	4	438	31	0	4.25
1988-89	**NY Islanders**	**NHL**	**13**	**4**	**7**	**0**	**662**	**39**	**0**	**3.53**	....	....	....	....	....	....	....
	Springfield	AHL	29	12	14	2	1677	116	0	4.15	....	....	....	....	....	....	....
1989-90b	Springfield	AHL	54	24	25	3	3045	187	1	3.68	*17	*10	5	934	60	0	3.85
1990-91	**NY Islanders**	**NHL**	**30**	**5**	**18**	**1**	**1508**	**91**	**0**	**3.62**	....	....	....	....	....	....	....
1991-92	**San Jose**	**NHL**	**42**	**11**	**27**	**1**	**2314**	**148**	**0**	**3.84**	....	....	....	....	....	....	....
1992-93	**San Jose**	**NHL**	**36**	**2**	**30**	**1**	**2000**	**176**	**0**	**5.28**	....	....	....	....	....	....	....
	NHL Totals		**121**	**22**	**82**	**3**	**6484**	**454**	**0**	**4.20**	....	....	....	....	....	....	....

a OHL Third All-Star Team (1988)
b Won Jack Butterfield Trophy (Playoff MVP-AHL) (1990)

Claimed by **San Jose** from **NY Islanders** in Expansion Draft, May 30, 1991. Traded to **Chicago** by **San Jose** for San Jose's third round choice (previously acquired by Chicago) in 1994 Entry Draft and future considerations, July 13, 1993.

HASEK, DOMINIK (HAH-shehk)

Goaltender. Catches left. 5'11", 165 lbs. Born, Pardubice, Czechoslovakia, January 29, 1965.
(Chicago's 11th choice, 199th overall, in 1983 Entry Draft).

			Regular Season								Playoffs						
Season	Club	Lea	GP	W	L	T	Mins	GA	SO	Avg	GP	W	L	Mins	GA	SO	Avg
1981-82	Pardubice	Czech.	12	....	....	....	661	34	....	3.09	....	....	....	....	....	....	....
1982-83	Pardubice	Czech.	42	....	....	....	2358	105	....	2.67	....	....	....	....	....	....	....
1983-84	Pardubice	Czech.	40	....	....	....	2304	108	....	2.81	....	....	....	....	....	....	....
1984-85	Pardubice	Czech.	42	....	....	....	2419	131	....	3.25	....	....	....	....	....	....	....
1985-86a	Pardubice	Czech.	45	....	....	....	2689	138	....	3.08	....	....	....	....	....	....	....
1986-87ab	Pardubice	Czech.	43	....	....	....	2515	103	....	2.46	....	....	....	....	....	....	....
1987-88ac	Pardubice	Czech.	31	....	....	....	1862	93	....	3.00	....	....	....	....	....	....	....
1988-89abc	Pardubice	Czech.	42	....	....	....	2507	114	....	2.73	....	....	....	....	....	....	....
1989-90abc	Dukla Jihlava	Czech.	40	....	....	....	2251	80	....	2.13	....	....	....	....	....	....	....
1990-91	**Chicago**	**NHL**	**5**	**3**	**0**	**1**	**195**	**8**	**0**	**2.46**	**3**	**0**	**0**	**69**	**3**	**0**	**2.61**
d	Indianapolis	IHL	33	20	11	1	1903	80	*5	*2.52	1	1	0	60	3	0	3.00
1991-92e	**Chicago**	**NHL**	**20**	**10**	**4**	**1**	**1014**	**44**	**1**	**2.60**	**3**	**0**	**2**	**158**	**8**	**0**	**3.04**
	Indianapolis	IHL	20	7	10	3	1162	69	1	3.56	....	....	....	....	....	....	....
1992-93	**Buffalo**	**NHL**	**28**	**11**	**10**	**4**	**1429**	**75**	**0**	**3.15**	**1**	**1**	**0**	**45**	**1**	**0**	**1.33**
	NHL Totals		**53**	**24**	**14**	**6**	**2638**	**127**	**1**	**2.89**	**7**	**1**	**2**	**272**	**12**	**0**	**2.65**

a Czechoslovakian Goaltender-of-the-Year (1986, 1987, 1988, 1989, 1990)
b Czechoslovakian Player-of-the-Year (1987, 1989, 1990)
c Czechoslovakian First-Team All-Star (1988, 1989, 1990)
d IHL First All-Star Team (1991)
e NHL/Upper Deck All-Rookie Team (1992)

Traded to **Buffalo** by **Chicago** for Stephane Beauregard and future considerations, August 7, 1992.

HAYWARD, BRIAN

Goaltender. Catches left. 5'10", 180 lbs. Born, Toronto, Ont., June 25, 1960.

			Regular Season								Playoffs						
Season	Club	Lea	GP	W	L	T	Mins	GA	SO	Avg	GP	W	L	Mins	GA	SO	Avg
1978-79	Cornell	ECAC	25	18	6	0	1469	95	0	3.88	3	2	1	179	14	0	4.66
1979-80	Cornell	ECAC	12	2	7	0	508	52	0	6.02	....	....	....	....	....	....	....
1980-81	Cornell	ECAC	19	11	4	1	967	58	1	3.54	4	2	1	181	18	0	4.50
1981-82ab	Cornell	ECAC	22	11	10	1	1320	68	0	3.09	....	....	....	....	....	....	....
1982-83	**Winnipeg**	**NHL**	**24**	**10**	**12**	**2**	**1440**	**89**	**1**	**3.71**	**3**	**0**	**3**	**160**	**14**	**0**	**5.24**
	Sherbrooke	AHL	22	6	11	3	1208	89	1	4.42	....	....	....	....	....	....	....
1983-84	**Winnipeg**	**NHL**	**28**	**7**	**18**	**2**	**1530**	**124**	**0**	**4.86**	....	....	....	....	....	....	....
	Sherbrooke	AHL	15	4	8	0	781	69	0	5.30	....	....	....	....	....	....	....
1984-85	**Winnipeg**	**NHL**	**61**	**33**	**17**	**7**	**3436**	**220**	**0**	**3.84**	**6**	**2**	**4**	**309**	**23**	**0**	**4.47**
1985-86	**Winnipeg**	**NHL**	**52**	**13**	**28**	**5**	**2721**	**217**	**0**	**4.79**	**2**	**0**	**1**	**68**	**6**	**0**	**5.29**
	Sherbrooke	AHL	3	2	0	1	185	5	0	1.62	....	....	....	....	....	....	....
1986-87c	**Montreal**	**NHL**	**37**	**19**	**13**	**4**	**2178**	**102**	**1**	***2.81**	**13**	**6**	**5**	**708**	**32**	**0**	**2.71**
1987-88c	**Montreal**	**NHL**	**39**	**22**	**10**	**4**	**2247**	**107**	**2**	**2.86**	**4**	**2**	**2**	**230**	**9**	**0**	**2.35**
1988-89c	**Montreal**	**NHL**	**36**	**20**	**13**	**3**	**2091**	**101**	**1**	**2.90**	**2**	**1**	**1**	**124**	**7**	**0**	**3.39**
1989-90	**Montreal**	**NHL**	**29**	**10**	**12**	**6**	**1674**	**94**	**1**	**3.37**	**1**	**0**	**0**	**33**	**2**	**0**	**3.64**
1990-91	**Minnesota**	**NHL**	**26**	**6**	**15**	**3**	**1473**	**77**	**2**	**3.14**	**6**	**0**	**2**	**171**	**11**	**0**	**3.86**
	Kalamazoo	IHL	2	2	0	0	120	5	0	2.50	....	....	....	....	....	....	....
1991-92	**San Jose**	**NHL**	**7**	**1**	**4**	**0**	**305**	**25**	**0**	**4.92**	....	....	....	....	....	....	....
	Kansas City	IHL	2	1	1	0	119	3	1	1.51	....	....	....	....	....	....	....
1992-93	**San Jose**	**NHL**	**18**	**2**	**14**	**1**	**930**	**86**	**0**	**5.55**	....	....	....	....	....	....	....
	NHL Totals		**357**	**143**	**156**	**37**	**20025**	**1242**	**8**	**3.72**	**37**	**11**	**18**	**1803**	**104**	**0**	**3.46**

a ECAC First All-Star Team (1982)
b NCAA All-American Team (1982)
c Shared William Jennings Trophy with Patrick Roy (1987, 1988, 1989)

Signed as a free agent by **Winnipeg**, May 5, 1982. Traded to **Montreal** by **Winnipeg** for Steve Penney and the rights to Jan Ingman, August 19, 1986. Traded to **Minnesota** by **Montreal** for Jayson More, November 7, 1990. Claimed by **San Jose** from **Minnesota** in Dispersal Draft, May 30, 1991.

HEALY, GLENN

Goaltender. Catches left. 5'10", 183 lbs. Born, Pickering, Ont., August 23, 1962.

			Regular Season								Playoffs						
Season	Club	Lea	GP	W	L	T	Mins	GA	SO	Avg	GP	W	L	Mins	GA	SO	Avg
1981-82	W. Michigan	CCHA	27	7	19	1	1569	116	0	4.44	....	....	....	....	....	....	....
1982-83	W. Michigan	CCHA	30	8	19	2	1732	116	0	4.01	....	....	....	....	....	....	....
1983-84	W. Michigan	CCHA	38	19	16	3	2241	146	0	3.90	....	....	....	....	....	....	....
1984-85	W. Michigan	CCHA	37	21	14	2	2171	118	0	3.26	....	....	....	....	....	....	....
1985-86	**Los Angeles**	**NHL**	**1**	**0**	**0**	**0**	**51**	**6**	**0**	**7.06**	....	....	....	....	....	....	....
	New Haven	AHL	43	21	15	4	2410	160	0	3.98	2	0	2	49	11	0	5.55
1986-87	New Haven	AHL	47	21	15	0	2828	173	1	3.67	7	3	4	427	19	0	2.67
1987-88	**Los Angeles**	**NHL**	**34**	**12**	**18**	**1**	**1869**	**135**	**1**	**4.33**	**4**	**1**	**3**	**240**	**20**	**0**	**5.00**
1988-89	**Los Angeles**	**NHL**	**48**	**25**	**19**	**2**	**2699**	**192**	**0**	**4.27**	**3**	**0**	**1**	**97**	**6**	**0**	**3.71**
1989-90	**NY Islanders**	**NHL**	**39**	**12**	**19**	**6**	**2197**	**128**	**2**	**3.50**	**4**	**1**	**2**	**166**	**9**	**0**	**3.25**
1990-91	**NY Islanders**	**NHL**	**53**	**18**	**24**	**9**	**2999**	**166**	**0**	**3.32**	....	....	....	....	....	....	....
1991-92	**NY Islanders**	**NHL**	**37**	**14**	**16**	**4**	**1960**	**124**	**1**	**3.80**	....	....	....	....	....	....	....
1992-93	**NY Islanders**	**NHL**	**47**	**22**	**20**	**2**	**2655**	**146**	**1**	**3.30**	**18**	**9**	**8**	**1109**	**59**	**0**	**3.19**
	NHL Totals		**259**	**103**	**116**	**24**	**14430**	**897**	**5**	**3.73**	**29**	**11**	**14**	**1612**	**94**	**0**	**3.50**

Signed as a free agent by **Los Angeles**, June 13, 1985. Signed as a free agent by **NY Islanders**, August 16, 1989. Claimed by **Anaheim** from **NY Islanders** in Expansion Draft, June 24, 1993. Claimed by **Tampa Bay** from **Anaheim** in Phase II of Expansion Draft, June 25, 1993. Traded to **NY Rangers** by **Tampa Bay** for Tampa Bay's third round choice (previously acquired by NY Rangers — Tampa Bay selected Allan Egeland) in 1993 Entry Draft, June 25, 1993.

HEBERT, GUY (HEE-buhrt, GIGH)

Goaltender. Catches left. 5'11", 180 lbs. Born, Troy, NY, January 7, 1967.
(St. Louis' 8th choice, 159th overall, in 1987 Entry Draft).

			Regular Season								Playoffs						
Season	Club	Lea	GP	W	L	T	Mins	GA	SO	Avg	GP	W	L	Mins	GA	SO	Avg
1986-87	Hamilton Coll.	NCAA	18	12	5	0	1070	40	0	2.19	....	....	....	....	....	....	....
1987-88	Hamilton Coll.	NCAA	8	5	3	0	450	19	0	2.53	....	....	....	....	....	....	....
1988-89	Hamilton Coll.	NCAA	25	18	7	0	1453	62	0	2.56	....	....	....	....	....	....	....
1989-90	Peoria	IHL	30	7	13	7	1706	124	1	4.36	2	0	1	76	5	0	3.95
1990-91a	Peoria	IHL	36	24	10	1	2093	100	2	2.87	8	3	4	458	32	0	4.19
1991-92	**St. Louis**	**NHL**	**13**	**5**	**5**	**1**	**738**	**36**	**0**	**2.93**	....	....	....	....	....	....	....
	Peoria	IHL	29	20	9	0	1731	98	0	3.40	4	3	1	239	9	0	2.26
1992-93	**St. Louis**	**NHL**	**24**	**8**	**8**	**2**	**1210**	**74**	**1**	**3.67**	**1**	**0**	**0**	**2**	**0**	**0**	**0.00**
	NHL Totals		**37**	**13**	**13**	**3**	**1948**	**110**	**1**	**3.39**	**1**	**0**	**0**	**2**	**0**	**0**	**0.00**

a IHL Second All-Star Team (1991)

Claimed by **Anaheim** from **St. Louis** in Expansion Draft, June 24, 1993.

HEINKE, MICHAEL

Goaltender. Catches left. 5'11", 165 lbs. Born, Denville, NY, January 11, 1971.
(New Jersey's 5th choice, 89th overall, in 1989 Entry Draft).

			Regular Season								Playoffs						
Season	Club	Lea	GP	W	L	T	Mins	GA	SO	Avg	GP	W	L	Mins	GA	SO	Avg
1990-91	Providence	H.E.	14	8	7	1	923	74	0	4.81	....	....	....	....	....	....	....
1991-92	Providence	H.E.	16	10	4	0	816	48	*2	3.53	....	....	....	....	....	....	....
1992-93	N. Hampshire	H.E.					DID NOT PLAY										

HENDERSON, TODD

Goaltender. Catches left. 6'1", 155 lbs. Born, Sault Ste. Marie, Ont., March 8, 1969.
(Buffalo's 11th choice, 224th overall, in 1989 Entry Draft).

			Regular Season								Playoffs						
Season	Club	Lea	GP	W	L	T	Mins	GA	SO	Avg	GP	W	L	Mins	GA	SO	Avg
1990-91	Alaska-Fair.	G.N.	20	10	9	1	1155	74	0	3.85	....	....	....	....	....	....	....
1991-92	Alaska-Fair.	G.N.	20	8	12	0	1111	80	0	4.32	....	....	....	....	....	....	....
1992-93	Alaska-Fair.	CCHA	5	1	1	0	179	10	0	3.34	....	....	....	....	....	....	....

HERLOFSKY, DEREK

Goaltender. Catches left. 6', 160 lbs. Born, Minneapolis, MN, October 1, 1971.
(Minnesota's 9th choice, 184th overall, in 1991 Entry Draft).

			Regular Season								Playoffs						
Season	Club	Lea	GP	W	L	T	Mins	GA	SO	Avg	GP	W	L	Mins	GA	SO	Avg
1991-92	Boston U.	H.E.	9	7	1	1	537	22	0	2.46	....	....	....	....	....	....	....
1992-93	Boston U.	H.E.	19	12	5	1	1060	50	*3	2.83	....	....	....	....	....	....	....

HEXTALL, RON

Goaltender. Catches left. 6'3", 192 lbs. Born, Brandon, Man., May 3, 1964.
(Philadelphia's 6th choice, 119th overall, in 1982 Entry Draft).

			Regular Season								Playoffs						
Season	Club	Lea	GP	W	L	T	Mins	GA	SO	Avg	GP	W	L	Mins	GA	SO	Avg
1981-82	Brandon	WHL	30	12	11	0	1398	133	0	5.71	3	0	2	103	16	0	9.32
1982-83	Brandon	WHL	44	13	30	0	2589	249	0	5.77	....	....	....	....	....	....	....
1983-84	Brandon	WHL	46	29	13	2	2670	190	0	4.27	10	5	5	592	37	0	3.75
1984-85	Hershey	AHL	11	4	6	0	555	34	0	3.68	....	....	....	....	....	....	....
	Kalamazoo	IHL	19	6	11	1	1103	80	0	4.35	....	....	....	....	....	....	....
1985-86ab	Hershey	AHL	*53	30	19	2	*3061	174	*5	3.41	13	5	7	780	42	*1	3.23
1986-87 cdef	**Philadelphia**	**NHL**	***66**	**37**	**21**	**6**	***3799**	**190**	**1**	**3.00**	***26**	**15**	**11**	***1540**	**71**	***2**	**2.77**
1987-88g	**Philadelphia**	**NHL**	**62**	**30**	**22**	**7**	**3561**	**208**	**0**	**3.51**	**7**	**2**	**4**	**379**	**30**	**0**	**4.75**
1988-89h	**Philadelphia**	**NHL**	***64**	**30**	**28**	**6**	***3756**	**202**	**0**	**3.23**	**15**	**8**	**7**	**886**	**49**	**0**	**3.32**
1989-90	**Philadelphia**	**NHL**	**8**	**4**	**2**	**1**	**419**	**29**	**0**	**4.15**	....	....	....	....	....	....	....
	Hershey	AHL	1	1	0	0	49	3	0	3.67	....	....	....	....	....	....	....
1990-91	**Philadelphia**	**NHL**	**36**	**13**	**16**	**5**	**2035**	**106**	**0**	**3.13**	....	....	....	....	....	....	....
1991-92	**Philadelphia**	**NHL**	**45**	**16**	**21**	**6**	**2668**	**151**	**3**	**3.40**	....	....	....	....	....	....	....
1992-93	**Quebec**	**NHL**	**54**	**29**	**16**	**5**	**2988**	**172**	**0**	**3.45**	**6**	**2**	**4**	**372**	**18**	**0**	**2.90**
	NHL Totals		**335**	**159**	**126**	**36**	**19226**	**1058**	**4**	**3.30**	**54**	**27**	**26**	**3177**	**168**	**2**	**3.17**

a AHL First All-Star Team (1986)
b AHL Rookie of the Year (1986)
c NHL First All-Star Team (1987)
d Won Vezina Trophy (1987)
e Won Conn Smythe Trophy (1987)
f NHL All-Rookie Team (1987)
g Scored a goal vs. Boston, December 8, 1987
h Scored a goal in playoffs vs. Washington, April 11, 1989

Played in NHL All-Star Game (1988)

Traded to **Quebec** by **Philadelphia** with Peter Forsberg, Steve Duchesne, Kerry Huffman, Mike Ricci, Chris Simon, Philadelphia's first choice in the 1993 (Jocelyn Thibault) and 1994 Entry Drafts and cash for Eric Lindros, June 30, 1992. Traded to **NY Islanders** by **Quebec** with Quebec's first round choice (Todd Bertuzzi) in 1993 Entry Draft for Mark Fitzpatrick and NY Islanders' first round choice (Adam Deadmarsh) in 1993 Entry Draft, June 20, 1993.

HILLEBRANDT, JON

Goaltender. Catches left. 5'10", 160 lbs. Born, Cottage Grove, WI, December 18, 1971.
(NY Rangers' 12th choice, 202nd overall, in 1990 Entry Draft).

			Regular Season								Playoffs						
Season	Club	Lea	GP	W	L	T	Mins	GA	SO	Avg	GP	W	L	Mins	GA	SO	Avg
1991-92a	Ill.-Chicago	CCHA	31	7	19	....	1754	121	0	4.14	....	....	....	....	....	....	....
1992-93	Ill.-Chicago	CCHA	33	8	22	2	1783	134	0	4.51	....	....	....	....	....	....	....

a CCHA Second All-Star Team (1992)

HIRSCH, COREY

Goaltender. Catches left. 5'10", 160 lbs. Born, Medicine Hat, Alta., July 1, 1972.
(NY Rangers' 8th choice, 169th overall, in 1991 Entry Draft).

			Regular Season								Playoffs						
Season	Club	Lea	GP	W	L	T	Mins	GA	SO	Avg	GP	W	L	Mins	GA	SO	Avg
1988-89	Kamloops	WHL	32	11	12	2	1516	106	....	4.20	5	3	2	....	....	....	4.65
1989-90	Kamloops	WHL	*63	*48	13	0	3608	230	*3	3.82	*17	*14	3	*1043	60	0	*3.45
1990-91a	Kamloops	WHL	38	26	7	1	1970	100	3	*3.05	11	5	6	623	42	....	4.04
1991-92																	
abcd	Kamloops	WHL	48	35	10	2	2732	124	5	*2.72	*16	*11	5	954	35	*2	*2.20
1992-93	**NY Rangers**	**NHL**	**4**	**1**	**2**	**1**	**224**	**14**	**0**	**3.75**	....	....	....	....	....	....	....
efg	Binghamton	AHL	46	*35	4	5	2692	125	1	*2.79	14	7	7	831	46	0	3.32
	NHL Totals		**4**	**1**	**2**	**1**	**224**	**14**	**0**	**3.75**	....	....	....	....	....	....	....

a WHL West First All-Star Team (1991, 1992)
b WHL and Canadian Major Junior Goaltender of the Year (1992)
c Memorial Cup All-Star Team (1992)
d Memorial Cup Tournament Top Goaltender (1992)
e Won Dudley "Red" Garrett Memorial Trophy (AHL Rookie of the Year)
f Shared Harry "Hap" Holmes Memorial Trophy (AHL's Top Goaltender) with Boris Rousson (1993)
g AHL First All-Star Team (1993)

HNILICKA, MILAN (hih-LEECH-kah, MEE-lahn)

Goaltender. Catches left. 6', 180 lbs. Born, Litomerice, Czech., June 25, 1973.
(NY Islanders' 4th choice, 70th overall, in 1991 Entry Draft).

			Regular Season								Playoffs						
Season	Club	Lea	GP	W	L	T	Mins	GA	SO	Avg	GP	W	L	Mins	GA	SO	Avg
1989-90	Kladno	Czech.	24	....	....	....	1113	70	....	3.77	....	....	....	....	....	....	....
1990-91	Kladno	Czech.	40	....	....	....	2122	98	0	2.80	....	....	....	....	....	....	....
1991-92	Kladno	Czech.	38	....	....	....	2066	128	0	3.73	....	....	....	....	....	....	....
1992-93	Swift Current	WHL	*65	*46	12	2	3679	206	2	3.36	*17	*12	5	*1017	54	*2	3.19

HODSON, KEVIN

Goaltender. Catches left. 6', 178 lbs. Born, Winnipeg, Man., March 27, 1972.

			Regular Season								Playoffs						
Season	Club	Lea	GP	W	L	T	Mins	GA	SO	Avg	GP	W	L	Mins	GA	SO	Avg
1990-91	S.S. Marie	OHL	30	18	11	0	1638	88	0	*3.22	10	*9	1	581	28	0	*2.89
1991-92	S.S. Marie	OHL	50	28	12	4	2722	151	0	3.33	18	12	6	1116	54	1	2.90
1992-93ab	S.S. Marie	OHL	26	18	5	2	1470	76	1	*3.10	14	11	2	755	34	0	2.70

a Memorial Cup All-Star Team (1993)
b Memorial Cup Tournament Top Goaltender (1993)

Signed as a free agent by **Chicago**, August 17, 1992. Signed as a free agent by **Detroit**, June 16, 1993.

HRIVNAK, JIM (RIV-NAK)

Goaltender. Catches left. 6'2", 195 lbs. Born, Montreal, Que., May 28, 1968.
(Washington's 4th choice, 61st overall, in 1986 Entry Draft).

			Regular Season								Playoffs						
Season	Club	Lea	GP	W	L	T	Mins	GA	SO	Avg	GP	W	L	Mins	GA	SO	Avg
1985-86	Merrimack	NCAA	21	12	8	0	1230	75	0	3.66	....	....	....	....	....	....	....
1986-87	Merrimack	NCAA	34	27	7	0	1618	58	3	2.14	....	....	....	....	....	....	....
1987-88	Merrimack	NCAA	37	31	6	0	2119	84	4	2.38	....	....	....	....	....	....	....
1988-89	Merrimack	NCAA	22	....	....	....	1295	52	4	2.41	....	....	....	....	....	....	....
	Baltimore	AHL	10	1	8	0	502	55	0	6.57	....	....	....	....	....	....	....
1989-90	**Washington**	**NHL**	**11**	**5**	**5**	**0**	**609**	**36**	**0**	**3.55**	....	....	....	....	....	....	....
a	Baltimore	AHL	47	24	19	2	2722	139	*4	3.06	6	4	2	360	19	0	3.17
1990-91	**Washington**	**NHL**	**9**	**4**	**2**	**1**	**432**	**26**	**0**	**3.61**	....	....	....	....	....	....	....
	Baltimore	AHL	42	20	16	6	2481	134	1	3.24	6	2	3	324	21	0	3.89
1991-92	**Washington**	**NHL**	**12**	**6**	**3**	**0**	**605**	**35**	**0**	**3.47**	....	....	....	....	....	....	....
	Baltimore	AHL	22	10	8	3	1303	73	0	3.36	....	....	....	....	....	....	....
1992-93	**Washington**	**NHL**	**27**	**13**	**9**	**2**	**1421**	**83**	**0**	**3.50**	....	....	....	....	....	....	....
	Winnipeg	**NHL**	**3**	**2**	**1**	**0**	**180**	**13**	**0**	**4.33**	....	....	....	....	....	....	....
	NHL Totals		**62**	**30**	**20**	**3**	**3247**	**193**	**0**	**3.57**	....	....	....	....	....	....	....

a AHL Second All-Star Team (1990)

Traded to **Winnipeg** by **Washington** with future considerations for Rick Tabaracci, March 22, 1993. Traded to **St. Louis** by **Winnipeg** for St. Louis' seventh round choice in 1994 Entry Draft and future considerations, July 29, 1993.

HRUDEY, KELLY STEPHEN (ROO-dee)

Goaltender. Catches left. 5'10", 189 lbs. Born, Edmonton, Alta., January 13, 1961.
(NY Islanders' 2nd choice, 38th overall, in 1980 Entry Draft).

			Regular Season								Playoffs						
Season	Club	Lea	GP	W	L	T	Mins	GA	SO	Avg	GP	W	L	Mins	GA	SO	Avg
1978-79	Medicine Hat	WHL	57	12	34	7	3093	318	0	6.17	....	....	....	....	....	....	....
1979-80	Medicine Hat	WHL	57	25	23	4	3049	212	1	4.17	13	6	6	638	48	0	4.51
1980-81a	Medicine Hat	WHL	55	32	19	1	3023	200	4	3.97	4	....	....	244	17	0	4.18
	Indianapolis	CHL	....	....	....	....	....	....	....	....	2	....	....	135	8	0	3.56
1981-82bc	Indianapolis	CHL	51	27	19	4	3033	149	1	*2.95	13	11	2	842	34	*1	*2.42
1982-83bcd	Indianapolis	CHL	47	*26	17	1	2744	139	2	3.04	10	*7	3	*637	28	0	*2.64
1983-84	**NY Islanders**	**NHL**	**12**	**7**	**2**	**0**	**535**	**28**	**0**	**3.14**	....	....	....	....	....	....	....
	Indianapolis	CHL	6	3	2	1	370	21	0	3.40	....	....	....	....	....	....	....
1984-85	**NY Islanders**	**NHL**	**41**	**19**	**17**	**3**	**2335**	**141**	**2**	**3.62**	**5**	**1**	**3**	**281**	**8**	**0**	**1.71**
1985-86	**NY Islanders**	**NHL**	**45**	**19**	**15**	**8**	**2563**	**137**	**1**	**3.21**	**2**	**0**	**2**	**120**	**6**	**0**	**3.00**
1986-87	**NY Islanders**	**NHL**	**46**	**21**	**15**	**7**	**2634**	**145**	**0**	**3.30**	**14**	**7**	**7**	**842**	**38**	**0**	**2.71**
1987-88	**NY Islanders**	**NHL**	**47**	**22**	**17**	**5**	**2751**	**153**	**3**	**3.34**	**6**	**2**	**4**	**381**	**23**	**0**	**3.62**
1988-89	**NY Islanders**	**NHL**	**50**	**18**	**24**	**3**	**2800**	**183**	**0**	**3.92**	....	....	....	....	....	....	....
	Los Angeles	**NHL**	**16**	**10**	**4**	**2**	**974**	**47**	**1**	**2.90**	**10**	**4**	**6**	**566**	**35**	**0**	**3.71**
1989-90	**Los Angeles**	**NHL**	**52**	**22**	**21**	**6**	**2860**	**194**	**2**	**4.07**	**9**	**4**	**4**	**539**	**39**	**0**	**4.34**
1990-91	**Los Angeles**	**NHL**	**47**	**26**	**13**	**6**	**2730**	**132**	**3**	**2.90**	**12**	**6**	**6**	**798**	**37**	**0**	**2.78**
1991-92	**Los Angeles**	**NHL**	**60**	**26**	**17**	**13**	**3509**	**197**	**1**	**3.37**	**6**	**2**	**4**	**355**	**22**	**0**	**3.72**
1992-93	**Los Angeles**	**NHL**	**50**	**18**	**21**	**6**	**2718**	**175**	**2**	**3.86**	**20**	**10**	**10**	**1261**	**74**	**0**	**3.52**
	NHL Totals		**466**	**208**	**166**	**59**	**26409**	**1532**	**15**	**3.48**	**84**	**36**	**46**	**5143**	**282**	**0**	**3.29**

a WHL Second All-Star Team (1981)
b CHL First All-Star Team (1982, 1983)
c Shared Terry Sawchuk Trophy (CHL's Leading Goaltender) with Rob Holland (1982, 1983)
d Won Tommy Ivan Trophy (CHL's Most Valuable Player) (1983)

Traded to **Los Angeles** by **NY Islanders** for Mark Fitzpatrick, Wayne McBean and future considerations (Doug Crossman, May 23, 1989) February 22, 1989.

ING, PETER

Goaltender. Catches left. 6'2", 170 lbs. Born, Toronto, Ont., April 28, 1969.
(Toronto's 3rd choice, 48th overall, in 1988 Entry Draft).

			Regular Season								Playoffs						
Season	Club	Lea	GP	W	L	T	Mins	GA	SO	Avg	GP	W	L	Mins	GA	SO	Avg
1986-87	Windsor	OHL	28	13	11	3	1615	105	0	3.90	5	4	0	161	9	0	3.35
1987-88	Windsor	OHL	43	30	7	1	2422	125	2	3.10	3	2	0	225	7	0	1.87
1988-89	Windsor	OHL	19	7	7	3	1043	76	*1	4.37	....	....	....	....	....	....	....
a	London	OHL	32	18	11	2	1848	104	*2	3.38	21	11	9	1093	82	0	4.50
1989-90	**Toronto**	**NHL**	**3**	**0**	**2**	**1**	**182**	**18**	**0**	**5.93**	....	....	....	....	....	....	....
	Newmarket	AHL	48	16	19	12	2829	184	0	3.90	....	....	....	....	....	....	....
	London	OHL	8	6	2	0	480	27	0	3.38	....	....	....	....	....	....	....
1990-91	**Toronto**	**NHL**	**56**	**16**	**29**	**8**	**3126**	**200**	**1**	**3.84**	....	....	....	....	....	....	....
1991-92	**Edmonton**	**NHL**	**12**	**3**	**4**	**0**	**463**	**33**	**0**	**4.28**	....	....	....	....	....	....	....
	Cape Breton	AHL	24	9	10	4	1411	92	0	3.91	1	0	1	60	9	0	9.00
1992-93	San Diego	IHL	17	11	4	1	882	53	0	3.61	4	2	2	183	13	0	4.26
	Detroit	Col.	3	2	1	0	136	6	0	2.65	....	....	....	....	....	....	....
	NHL Totals		**71**	**19**	**35**	**9**	**3771**	**251**	**1**	**3.99**	....	....	....	....	....	....	....

a OHL Third All-Star Team (1989)

Traded to **Edmonton** by **Toronto** with Vincent Damphousse, Scott Thornton, Luke Richardson, future considerations and cash for Grant Fuhr, Glenn Anderson and Craig Berube, September 19, 1991.

IRBE, ARTURS (EER-bay, AHR-turs)

Goaltender. Catches left. 5'8", 180 lbs. Born, Riga, Soviet Union, February 2, 1967.
(Minnesota's 11th choice, 196th overall, in 1989 Entry Draft).

			Regular Season								Playoffs						
Season	Club	Lea	GP	W	L	T	Mins	GA	SO	Avg	GP	W	L	Mins	GA	SO	Avg
1986-87	Dynamo Riga	USSR	2	....	....	....	27	1	0	2.22	....	....	....	....	....	....	....
1987-88a	Dynamo Riga	USSR	34	....	....	....	1870	86	4	2.69	....	....	....	....	....	....	....
1988-89	Dynamo Riga	USSR	40	....	....	....	2460	116	4	2.85	....	....	....	....	....	....	....
1989-90	Dynamo Riga	USSR	48	....	....	....	2880	115	2	2.42	....	....	....	....	....	....	....
1990-91	Dynamo Riga	USSR	46	....	....	....	2713	133	5	2.94	....	....	....	....	....	....	....
1991-92	**San Jose**	**NHL**	**13**	**2**	**6**	**3**	**645**	**48**	**0**	**4.47**	....	....	....	....	....	....	....
bc	Kansas City	IHL	32	24	7	1	1955	80	0	2.46	15	12	3	914	44	0	2.89
1992-93	**San Jose**	**NHL**	**36**	**7**	**26**	**0**	**2074**	**142**	**1**	**4.11**	....	....	....	....	....	....	....
	Kansas City	IHL	6	3	3	0	364	20	0	3.30	....	....	....	....	....	....	....
	NHL Totals		**49**	**9**	**32**	**3**	**2719**	**190**	**1**	**4.19**	....	....	....	....	....	....	....

a Soviet National League Rookie-of-the-Year (1988)
b IHL First All-Star Team (1992)
c Won James Norris Memorial Trophy (Top Goaltender-IHL) (1992)

Claimed by **San Jose** from **Minnesota** in Dispersal Draft, May 30, 1991.

JABLONSKI, PAT

Goaltender. Catches right. 6', 178 lbs. Born, Toledo, OH, June 20, 1967.
(St. Louis' 6th choice, 138th overall, in 1985 Entry Draft).

			Regular Season								Playoffs						
Season	Club	Lea	GP	W	L	T	Mins	GA	SO	Avg	GP	W	L	Mins	GA	SO	Avg
1985-86	Windsor	OHL	29	6	16	4	1600	119	1	4.46	6	0	3	263	20	0	4.56
1986-87	Windsor	OHL	41	22	14	2	2328	128	*3	3.30	12	8	4	710	38	0	3.21
1987-88	Peoria	IHL	5	2	2	1	285	17	0	3.58	....	....	....	....	....	....	....
	Windsor	OHL	18	14	3	0	994	48	2	*2.90	9	*8	0	537	28	0	3.13
1988-89	Peoria	IHL	35	11	20	0	2051	163	1	4.77	3	0	2	130	13	0	6.00
1989-90	**St. Louis**	**NHL**	**4**	**0**	**3**	**0**	**208**	**17**	**0**	**4.90**	....	....	....	....	....	....	....
	Peoria	IHL	36	14	17	4	2023	165	0	4.89	4	1	3	223	19	0	5.11
1990-91	**St. Louis**	**NHL**	**8**	**2**	**3**	**3**	**492**	**25**	**0**	**3.05**	**3**	**0**	**0**	**90**	**5**	**0**	**3.33**
	Peoria	IHL	29	23	3	2	1738	87	0	3.00	10	7	2	532	23	0	2.59
1991-92	**St. Louis**	**NHL**	**10**	**3**	**6**	**0**	**468**	**38**	**0**	**4.87**	....	....	....	....	....	....	....
	Peoria	IHL	8	6	1	1	493	29	1	3.53	....	....	....	....	....	....	....
1992-93	**Tampa Bay**	**NHL**	**43**	**8**	**24**	**4**	**2268**	**150**	**1**	**3.97**	....	....	....	....	....	....	....
	NHL Totals		**65**	**13**	**36**	**7**	**3436**	**230**	**1**	**4.02**	**3**	**0**	**0**	**90**	**5**	**0**	**3.33**

Traded to **Tampa Bay** by **St. Louis** with Steve Tuttle and Darin Kimble for future considerations, June 19, 1992.

JAKS, PAULI (YAHKS, POW-lee)

Goaltender. Catches left. 6', 191 lbs. Born, Schaffhausen, Switzerland, January 25, 1972.
(Los Angeles' 5th choice, 108th overall, in 1991 Entry Draft).

			Regular Season								Playoffs						
Season	Club	Lea	GP	W	L	T	Mins	GA	SO	Avg	GP	W	L	Mins	GA	SO	Avg
1990-91	Ambri-Piotta	Switz.	22	....	....	....	1247	100	0	4.81	....	....	....	....	....	....	....
1991-92	Ambri-Piotta	Switz.	33	25	7	1	1890	97	2	2.93	....	....	....	....	....	....	....
1992-93	Ambri-Piotta	Switz.	29	....	....	....	....	92	....	3.17	....	....	....	....	....	....	....

JOSEPH, CURTIS

Goaltender. Catches left. 5'10", 182 lbs. Born, Keswick, Ont., April 29, 1967.

			Regular Season								Playoffs						
Season	Club	Lea	GP	W	L	T	Mins	GA	SO	Avg	GP	W	L	Mins	GA	SO	Avg
1988-89abc	U. Wisconsin	WCHA	38	21	11	5	2267	94	1	2.49	....	....	....	....	....	....	....
1989-90	**St. Louis**	**NHL**	**15**	**9**	**5**	**1**	**852**	**48**	**0**	**3.38**	**6**	**4**	**1**	**327**	**18**	**0**	**3.30**
	Peoria	IHL	23	10	8	2	1241	80	0	3.87	....	....	....	....	....	....	....
1990-91	**St. Louis**	**NHL**	**30**	**16**	**10**	**2**	**1710**	**89**	**0**	**3.12**	....	....	....	....	....	....	....
1991-92	**St. Louis**	**NHL**	**60**	**27**	**20**	**10**	**3494**	**175**	**2**	**3.01**	**6**	**2**	**4**	**379**	**23**	**0**	**3.64**
1992-93	**St. Louis**	**NHL**	**68**	**29**	**28**	**9**	**3890**	**196**	**1**	**3.02**	**11**	**7**	**4**	**715**	**27**	***2**	**2.27**
	NHL Totals		**173**	**81**	**63**	**22**	**9946**	**508**	**3**	**3.06**	**23**	**13**	**9**	**1421**	**68**	**2**	**2.87**

a WCHA First All-Star Team (1989)
b WCHA Player of the Year (1989)
c WCHA Rookie of the Year (1989)

Signed as a free agent by **St. Louis**, June 16, 1989.

KETTERER, MARKUS

Goaltender. Catches left. 5'11", 167 lbs. Born, Helsinki, Finland, August 23, 1967.
(Buffalo's 6th choice, 107th overall, in 1992 Entry Draft).

			Regular Season								Playoffs						
Season	Club	Lea	GP	W	L	T	Mins	GA	SO	Avg	GP	W	L	Mins	GA	SO	Avg
1987-88	Jokerit	Fin.	21	....	....	....	....	61	0	....	....	....	....	....	....	....	....
1988-89	TPS	Fin.	34	....	....	....	2021	95	2	2.82	3	....	....	139	6	0	2.59
1989-90	TPS	Fin.	29	....	....	....	1709	68	1	2.38	7	....	....	422	15	1	2.13
1990-91	TPS	Fin.	36	....	....	....	2022	85	2	2.52	8	....	....	440	13	2	1.77
1991-92	Jokerit	Fin.	37	....	....	....	2128	97	1	2.73	10	7	3	634	20	3	1.89
1992-93	Jokerit	Fin.	37	....	....	....	2064	96	3	2.79	2	0	0	130	11	0	5.07

KHABIBULIN, NIKOLAI (khah-bee-BOO-lihn)

Goaltender. Catches left. 6', 176 lbs. Born, Sverdlovsk, Soviet Union, January 13, 1973.
(Winnipeg's 8th choice, 204th overall, in 1992 Entry Draft).

			Regular Season								Playoffs						
Season	**Club**	**Lea**	**GP**	**W**	**L**	**T**	**Mins**	**GA**	**SO**	**Avg**	**GP**	**W**	**L**	**Mins**	**GA**	**SO**	**Avg**
1988-89	Sverdlovsk	USSR	1	....	....	....	3	0	0	0.00	....	....	....	....	....	....	....
1989-90	Sverdlovsk Jrs.	USSR						UNAVAILABLE									
1990-91	Sputnik	USSR 3						UNAVAILABLE									
1991-92	CSKA	CIS	2	....	....	....	34	2	....	3.52	....	....	....	....	....	....	....
1992-93	CSKA	CIS	13	....	....	....	491	27	....	3.29	....	....	....	....	....	....	....

KIDD, TREVOR

Goaltender. Catches left. 6'2", 185 lbs. Born, Dugald, Man., March 29, 1972.
(Calgary's 1st choice, 11th overall, in 1990 Entry Draft).

			Regular Season								Playoffs						
Season	**Club**	**Lea**	**GP**	**W**	**L**	**T**	**Mins**	**GA**	**SO**	**Avg**	**GP**	**W**	**L**	**Mins**	**GA**	**SO**	**Avg**
1988-89	Brandon	WHL	32	....	....	....	1509	102	0	4.06	....	....	....	....	....	....	....
1989-90a	Brandon	WHL	*63	24	32	2	*3676	254	2	4.15	....	....	....	....	....	....	....
1990-91	Brandon	WHL	30	10	19	1	1730	117	0	4.06	....	....	....	....	....	....	....
	Spokane	WHL	14	8	3	0	749	44	0	3.52	15	*14	1	926	32	2	*2.07
1991-92	Cdn. National	....	28	18	4	4	1349	79	2	3.51	....	....	....	....	....	....	....
	Cdn. Olympic	....	1	1	0	0	60	0	1	0.00	....	....	....	....	....	....	....
	Calgary	**NHL**	**2**	**1**	**1**	**0**	**120**	**8**	**0**	**4.00**	....	....	....	....	....	....	....
1992-93	Salt Lake	IHL	29	10	16	1	1696	111	1	3.93	....	....	....	....	....	....	....
	NHL Totals		**2**	**1**	**1**	**0**	**120**	**8**	**0**	**4.00**	....	....	....	....	....	....	....

a WHL East First All-Star Team (1990)

KING, SCOTT

Goaltender. Catches left. 6'1", 185 lbs. Born, Thunder Bay, Ont., June 25, 1967.
(Detroit's 10th choice, 190th overall, in 1986 Entry Draft).

			Regular Season								Playoffs						
Season	**Club**	**Lea**	**GP**	**W**	**L**	**T**	**Mins**	**GA**	**SO**	**Avg**	**GP**	**W**	**L**	**Mins**	**GA**	**SO**	**Avg**
1986-87	U. of Maine	H.E.	21	11	6	1	1111	58	0	3.13	....	....	....	....	....	....	....
1987-88a	U. of Maine	H.E.	33	25	5	1	1761	91	0	3.10	....	....	....	....	....	....	....
1988-89a	U. of Maine	H.E.	27	13	8	0	1394	83	0	3.57	....	....	....	....	....	....	....
1989-90b	U. of Maine	H.E.	29	17	7	2	1526	67	1	2.63	....	....	....	....	....	....	....
1990-91	**Detroit**	**NHL**	**1**	**0**	**0**	**0**	**45**	**2**	**0**	**2.67**	....	....	....	....	....	....	....
	Adirondack	AHL	24	8	10	2	1287	91	0	4.24	1	0	0	32	4	0	7.50
	Hampton Rds.	ECHL	15	8	4	1	819	57	0	4.17	....	....	....	....	....	....	....
1991-92	**Detroit**	**NHL**	**1**	**0**	**0**	**0**	**16**	**1**	**0**	**3.75**	....	....	....	....	....	....	....
	Adirondack	AHL	33	14	14	3	1904	112	0	3.53	....	....	....	....	....	....	....
	Toledo	ECHL	7	4	2	1	424	25	0	3.54	....	....	....	....	....	....	....
1992-93	Adirondack	AHL	1	1	0	0	60	1	0	1.00	....	....	....	....	....	....	....
c	Toledo	ECHL	*45	*26	11	7	*2602	153	2	3.53	*14	*10	3	*823	52	0	3.79
	NHL Totals		**2**	**0**	**0**	**0**	**61**	**3**	**0**	**2.95**	....	....	....	....	....	....	....

a Hockey East Second All-Star Team (1988, 1989)
b Hockey East First All-Star Team (1990)
c ECHL Second All-Star Team (1993)

KNICKLE, RICHARD (RICK) (kuh-NIHK-uhl)

Goaltender. Catches left. 5'10", 155 lbs. Born, Chatham, N.B., February 26, 1960.
(Buffalo's 7th choice, 116th overall, in 1979 Entry Draft).

			Regular Season								Playoffs						
Season	**Club**	**Lea**	**GP**	**W**	**L**	**T**	**Mins**	**GA**	**SO**	**Avg**	**GP**	**W**	**L**	**Mins**	**GA**	**SO**	**Avg**
1977-78	Brandon	WHL	49	34	5	7	2806	182	0	3.89	8	....	....	450	36	0	4.82
1978-79ab	Brandon	WHL	38	26	3	8	2240	118	1	*3.16	16	12	3	886	41	*1	*2.78
1979-80	Brandon	WHL	33	11	14	1	1604	125	0	4.68	....	....	....	....	....	....	....
	Muskegon	IHL	16	....	....	....	829	52	0	3.76	3	....	....	156	17	0	6.54
1980-81c	Erie	EHL	43	....	....	....	2347	125	1	*3.20	8	....	....	446	14	0	*1.88
1981-82	Rochester	AHL	31	10	12	5	1753	108	1	3.70	3	0	2	125	7	0	3.37
1982-83	Flint	IHL	27	....	....	....	1638	92	2	3.37	3	....	....	193	10	0	3.11
	Rochester	AHL	4	....	....	....	143	11	0	4.64	....	....	....	....	....	....	....
1983-84d	Flint	IHL	60	32	21	5	3518	203	3	3.46	8	8	0	480	24	0	3.00
1984-85	Sherbrooke	AHL	14	7	6	0	780	53	0	4.08	....	....	....	....	....	....	....
	Flint	IHL	36	18	11	3	2018	115	2	3.42	7	3	4	401	27	0	4.04
1985-86	Saginaw	IHL	39	16	15	0	2235	135	2	3.62	3	2	1	193	12	0	3.73
1986-87	Saginaw	IHL	26	9	13	0	1413	113	0	4.80	5	1	4	329	21	0	3.83
1987-88	Flint	IHL	1	0	1	0	60	4	0	4.00	....	....	....	....	....	....	....
	Peoria	IHL	13	2	8	1	705	58	0	4.94	6	3	3	294	20	....	4.08
1988-89ef	Fort Wayne	IHL	47	22	16	0	2716	141	1	*3.11	4	1	2	173	15	0	5.20
1989-90	Flint	IHL	55	25	24	1	2998	210	1	4.20	2	0	2	101	13	0	7.72
1990-91	Albany	IHL	14	4	6	2	679	52	0	4.59	....	....	....	....	....	....	....
	Springfield	AHL	9	6	0	2	509	28	0	3.30	....	....	....	....	....	....	....
1991-92d	San Diego	IHL	46	*28	13	4	2686	155	0	3.46	2	0	1	78	3	0	2.31
1992-93g	San Diego	IHL	41	33	4	4	2437	88	*4	*2.17	....	....	....	....	....	....	....
	Los Angeles	**NHL**	**10**	**6**	**4**	**0**	**532**	**35**	**0**	**3.95**	....	....	....	....	....	....	....
	NHL Totals		**10**	**6**	**4**	**0**	**532**	**35**	**0**	**3.95**	....	....	....	....	....	....	....

a WHL First All-Star Team (1979)
b Named WHL's Top Goaltender (1979)
c EHL First All-Star Team (1981)
d IHL Second All-Star Team (1984, 1992)
e IHL First All-Star Team (1989, 1993)
f Won James Norris Memorial Trophy (Top Goaltender-IHL) (1989)
g Shared James Norris Memorial Trophy (Top Goaltender - IHL) with Clint Malarchuk (1993)

Signed as a free agent by **Montreal**, February 8, 1985. Signed as a free agent by **Los Angeles**, February 16, 1993.

KOCHAN, DIETER

Goaltender. Catches left. 6'1", 165 lbs. Born, Saskatoon, Sask., November 5, 1974.
(Vancouver's 3rd choice, 98th overall, in 1993 Entry Draft).

			Regular Season								Playoffs						
Season	**Club**	**Lea**	**GP**	**W**	**L**	**T**	**Mins**	**GA**	**SO**	**Avg**	**GP**	**W**	**L**	**Mins**	**GA**	**SO**	**Avg**
1992-93	Kelowna	BCJHL	44	....	....	....	2582	137	0	3.18	....	....	....	....	....	....	....

KOLZIG, OLAF

Goaltender. Catches left. 6'3", 205 lbs. Born, Johannesburg, South Africa, April 9, 1970.
(Washington's 1st choice, 19th overall, in 1989 Entry Draft).

			Regular Season								Playoffs						
Season	**Club**	**Lea**	**GP**	**W**	**L**	**T**	**Mins**	**GA**	**SO**	**Avg**	**GP**	**W**	**L**	**Mins**	**GA**	**SO**	**Avg**
1987-88	N. Westminster	WHL	15	6	5	0	650	48	1	4.43	3	....	....	149	11	0	4.43
1988-89	Tri-Cities	WHL	30	16	10	2	1671	97	1	*3.48	....	....	....	....	....	....	....
1989-90	**Washington**	**NHL**	**2**	**0**	**2**	**0**	**120**	**12**	**0**	**6.00**	....	....	....	....	....	....	....
	Tri-Cities	WHL	48	27	27	3	2504	250	1	4.38	6	4	0	318	27	0	5.09
1990-91	Baltimore	AHL	26	10	12	1	1367	72	0	3.16	....	....	....	....	....	....	....
	Hampton Rds.	ECHL	21	11	9	1	1248	71	2	3.41	3	1	2	180	14	0	4.66
1991-92	Baltimore	AHL	28	5	17	2	1503	105	1	4.19	....	....	....	....	....	....	....
	Hampton Rds.	ECHL	14	11	3	0	847	41	0	2.90	....	....	....	....	....	....	....
1992-93	**Washington**	**NHL**	**1**	**0**	**0**	**0**	**20**	**2**	**0**	**6.00**	....	....	....	....	....	....	....
	Rochester	AHL	49	25	16	4	2737	168	0	3.68	*17	9	8	*1040	61	0	3.52
	NHL Totals		**3**	**0**	**2**	**0**	**140**	**14**	**0**	**6.00**	....	....	....	....	....	....	....

KRAKE, PAUL

Goaltender. Catches left. 6', 175 lbs. Born, Lloydminster, Sask., March 25, 1969.
(Quebec's 10th choice, 148th overall, in 1989 Entry Draft).

			Regular Season								Playoffs						
Season	**Club**	**Lea**	**GP**	**W**	**L**	**T**	**Mins**	**GA**	**SO**	**Avg**	**GP**	**W**	**L**	**Mins**	**GA**	**SO**	**Avg**
1988-89	Alaska-Anch.	G.N.	19	....	....	....	1111	75	0	4.05	....	....	....	....	....	....	....
1989-90	Alaska-Anch.	G.N.	18	8	6	2	937	58	0	3.87	....	....	....	....	....	....	....
1990-91	Alaska-Anch.	G.N.	37	18	15	3	2183	123	4	3.38	....	....	....	....	....	....	....
1991-92	Alaska-Anch.	G.N.	27	19	7	0	1587	87	0	3.29	....	....	....	....	....	....	....
1992-93	Oklahoma City	CHL	17	13	3	1	1029	60	0	*3.50	....	....	....	....	....	....	....
	Halifax	AHL	17	8	6	1	916	57	1	3.73	....	....	....	....	....	....	....

KRUHLAK, ROB

Goaltender. Catches left. 5'11", 170 lbs. Born, Calgary, Alta., April 18, 1970.
(New Jersey's 1st choice, 17th overall, in 1991 Supplemental Draft).

			Regular Season								Playoffs						
Season	**Club**	**Lea**	**GP**	**W**	**L**	**T**	**Mins**	**GA**	**SO**	**Avg**	**GP**	**W**	**L**	**Mins**	**GA**	**SO**	**Avg**
1989-90	N. Michigan	WCHA	9	1	4	0	357	22	0	3.69	....	....	....	....	....	....	....
1990-91	N. Michigan	WCHA	11	5	2	0	428	18	0	*2.52	....	....	....	....	....	....	....
1991-92	N. Michigan	WCHA	7	2	2	2	367	30	0	4.90	....	....	....	....	....	....	....
1992-93	N. Michigan	WCHA	5	0	3	0	210	21	0	6.02	....	....	....	....	....	....	....

KUNTAR, LES

Goaltender. Catches left. 6'2", 195 lbs. Born, Elma, NY, July 28, 1969.
(Montreal's 8th choice, 122nd overall, in 1987 Entry Draft).

			Regular Season								Playoffs						
Season	**Club**	**Lea**	**GP**	**W**	**L**	**T**	**Mins**	**GA**	**SO**	**Avg**	**GP**	**W**	**L**	**Mins**	**GA**	**SO**	**Avg**
1987-88	St. Lawrence	ECAC	10	6	1	0	488	27	0	3.31	....	....	....	....	....	....	....
1988-89	St. Lawrence	ECAC	14	11	2	0	786	31	0	2.37	....	....	....	....	....	....	....
1989-90	St. Lawrence	ECAC	20	7	11	1	1136	80	0	4.23	....	....	....	....	....	....	....
1990-91ab	St. Lawrence	ECAC	*33	*19	11	1	*1797	97	*1	*3.24	....	....	....	....	....	....	....
1991-92	Fredericton	AHL	11	7	3	0	638	26	0	2.45	....	....	....	....	....	....	....
	U.S. National	....	2	0	1	0	100	4	0	2.40	....	....	....	....	....	....	....
1992-93	Fredericton	AHL	42	16	14	7	2315	130	0	3.37	1	0	1	64	6	0	5.63

a ECAC First All-Star Team (1991)
b NCAA East First All-American Team (1991)

LABRECQUE, PATRICK

Goaltender. Catches left. 6', 187 lbs. Born, Laval, Que., March 6, 1971.
(Quebec's 5th choice, 90th overall, in 1991 Entry Draft).

			Regular Season								Playoffs						
Season	**Club**	**Lea**	**GP**	**W**	**L**	**T**	**Mins**	**GA**	**SO**	**Avg**	**GP**	**W**	**L**	**Mins**	**GA**	**SO**	**Avg**
1990-91	St-Jean	QMJHL	59	17	34	6	3375	216	1	3.84	....	....	....	....	....	....	....
1991-92	Halifax	AHL	29	5	12	8	1570	114	0	4.36	....	....	....	....	....	....	....
1992-93	Greensboro	ECHL	11	6	3	2	650	31	0	2.86	1	0	1	59	5	0	5.08
	Halifax	AHL	20	3	12	2	914	76	0	4.99	....	....	....	....	....	....	....

LaFOREST, MARK ANDREW

Goaltender. Catches left. 5'11", 190 lbs. Born, Welland, Ont., July 10, 1962.

			Regular Season								Playoffs						
Season	**Club**	**Lea**	**GP**	**W**	**L**	**T**	**Mins**	**GA**	**SO**	**Avg**	**GP**	**W**	**L**	**Mins**	**GA**	**SO**	**Avg**
1981-82	Niagara Falls	OHL	24	10	13	1	1365	105	1	4.62	5	1	2	300	19	0	3.80
1982-83	North Bay	OHL	54	34	17	1	3140	195	0	3.73	8	4	4	474	31	0	3.92
1983-84	Adirondack	AHL	7	3	3	1	351	29	0	4.96	....	....	....	....	....	....	....
	Kalamazoo	IHL	13	4	5	2	718	48	1	4.01	....	....	....	....	....	....	....
1984-85	Adirondack	AHL	11	2	3	1	430	35	0	4.88	....	....	....	....	....	....	....
1985-86	**Detroit**	**NHL**	**28**	**4**	**21**	**0**	**1383**	**114**	**1**	**4.95**	....	....	....	....	....	....	....
	Adirondack	AHL	19	13	5	1	1142	57	0	2.99	*17	*12	5	*1075	58	0	3.24
1986-87	**Detroit**	**NHL**	**5**	**2**	**1**	**0**	**219**	**12**	**0**	**3.29**	....	....	....	....	....	....	....
a	Adirondack	AHL	37	23	8	0	2229	105	*3	2.83	....	....	....	....	....	....	....
1987-88	**Philadelphia**	**NHL**	**21**	**5**	**9**	**2**	**972**	**60**	**1**	**3.70**	**2**	**1**	**0**	**48**	**1**	**0**	**1.25**
	Hershey	AHL	5	2	1	2	309	13	0	2.52	....	....	....	....	....	....	....
1988-89	**Philadelphia**	**NHL**	**17**	**5**	**7**	**2**	**933**	**64**	**0**	**4.12**	....	....	....	....	....	....	....
	Hershey	AHL	3	2	0	0	185	9	0	2.92	12	7	5	744	27	1	2.18
1989-90	**Toronto**	**NHL**	**27**	**9**	**14**	**0**	**1343**	**87**	**0**	**3.89**	....	....	....	....	....	....	....
	Newmarket	AHL	10	6	4	0	604	33	1	3.28	....	....	....	....	....	....	....
1990-91ab	Binghamton	AHL	45	25	14	2	2452	129	0	3.16	9	3	4	442	28	1	3.80
1991-92	Binghamton	AHL	43	25	15	3	2559	146	1	3.42	11	7	4	662	34	0	3.08
1992-93	New Haven	AHL	30	10	18	1	1688	121	1	4.30	....	....	....	....	....	....	....
	Brantford	Col.	10	5	3	1	565	35	1	3.72	....	....	....	....	....	....	....
	NHL Totals		**98**	**25**	**52**	**4**	**4850**	**337**	**2**	**4.17**	**2**	**1**	**0**	**48**	**1**	**0**	**1.25**

a Won Baz Bastien Trophy (Top Goalie - AHL) (1987, 1991)
b AHL Second All-Star Team (1991)

Signed as a free agent by **Detroit**, April 29, 1983. Traded to **Philadelphia** by **Detroit** for Philadelphia's second round choice (Bob Wilkie) in 1987 Entry Draft, June 13, 1987. Traded to **Toronto** by **Philadelphia** for Toronto's sixth round choice in 1991 Entry Draft and its seventh round choice in 1991 Entry Draft, September 8, 1989. Traded to **NY Rangers** by **Toronto** with Tie Domi for Greg Johnston, June 28, 1990. Claimed by **Ottawa** from **NY Rangers** in Expansion Draft, June 18, 1992.

LAGRAND, SCOTT

Goaltender. Catches left. 6', 165 lbs. Born, Potsdam, NY, February 11, 1970.
(Philadelphia's 5th choice, 77th overall, in 1988 Entry Draft).

			Regular Season								Playoffs						
Season	**Club**	**Lea**	**GP**	**W**	**L**	**T**	**Mins**	**GA**	**SO**	**Avg**	**GP**	**W**	**L**	**Mins**	**GA**	**SO**	**Avg**
1989-90	Boston College	H.E.	24	17	4	0	1268	57	0	2.70	....	....	....	....	....	....	....
1990-91a	Boston College	H.E.	12	7	2	0	557	39	2	4.20	....	....	....	....	....	....	....
1991-92b	Boston College	H.E.	30	11	16	2	1750	108	1	3.70	....	....	....	....	....	....	....
1992-93	Hershey	AHL	32	8	17	4	1854	145	0	4.69	....	....	....	....	....	....	....

a Hockey East First All-Star Team (1991)
b NCAA East Second All-American Team (1992)

LALIME, PATRICK

Goaltender. Catches left. 6'2", 165 lbs. Born, St. Bonaventure, Que., July 7, 1974.
(Pittsburgh's 6th choice, 156th overall, in 1993 Entry Draft).

			Regular Season								Playoffs						
Season	Club	Lea	GP	W	L	T	Mins	GA	SO	Avg	GP	W	L	Mins	GA	SO	Avg
1992-93	Shawinigan	QMJHL	44	10	24	4	2467	192	0	4.67	....	....	....	....	....	....	....

LAMOTHE, MARC

Goaltender. Catches left. 6'2", 187 lbs. Born, New Liskeard, Ont., February 27, 1974.
(Montreal's 6th choice, 92nd overall, in 1992 Entry Draft).

			Regular Season								Playoffs						
Season	Club	Lea	GP	W	L	T	Mins	GA	SO	Avg	GP	W	L	Mins	GA	SO	Avg
1991-92	Kingston	OHL	42	10	25	2	2378	189	1	4.77	....	....	....	....	....	....	....
1992-93	Kingston	OHL	45	23	12	6	2489	162	1	3.91	15	8	5	753	48	1	3.82

LANG, CHAD

Goaltender. Catches left. 5'10", 188 lbs. Born, Newmarket, Ont., February 11, 1975.
(Dallas' 3rd choice, 87th overall, in 1993 Entry Draft).

			Regular Season								Playoffs						
Season	Club	Lea	GP	W	L	T	Mins	GA	SO	Avg	GP	W	L	Mins	GA	SO	Avg
1991-92	Peterborough	OHL	16	7	5	1	886	63	0	4.27	2	0	0	65	9	0	8.31
1992-93a	Peterborough	OHL	43	*32	6	4	2554	140	1	3.29	*21	*12	8	*1224	74	*1	3.63

a OHL Second All-Star Team (1993)

LANGKOW, SCOTT

Goaltender. Catches left. 5'11", 180 lbs. Born, Edmonton, Alta., April 21, 1975.
(Winnipeg's 2nd choice, 31st overall, in 1993 Entry Draft).

			Regular Season								Playoffs						
Season	Club	Lea	GP	W	L	T	Mins	GA	SO	Avg	GP	W	L	Mins	GA	SO	Avg
1991-92	Portland	WHL	1	....	....	....	33	2	0	3.46	....	....	....	....	....	....	....
1992-93	Portland	WHL	34	24	8	2	2064	119	2	3.46	9	....	....	535	31	0	3.48

LEBLANC, RAYMOND

Goaltender. Catches right. 5'10", 170 lbs. Born, Fitchburg, MA, October 24, 1964.

			Regular Season								Playoffs						
Season	Club	Lea	GP	W	L	T	Mins	GA	SO	Avg	GP	W	L	Mins	GA	SO	Avg
1983-84	Kitchener	OHL	54	....	....	....	2965	185	1	3.74	....	....	....	....	....	....	....
1984-85	Pinebridge	ACHL	40	....	....	....	2178	150	0	4.13	....	....	....	....	....	....	....
1985-86	Carolina	ACHL	42	....	....	....	2505	133	3	3.19	....	....	....	....	....	....	....
1986-87	Flint	IHL	64	....	....	....	3417	222	0	3.90	....	....	....	....	....	....	....
1987-88	Flint	IHL	62	27	19	8	3269	239	1	4.39	16	10	6	925	55	1	3.57
1988-89	Flint	IHL	15	5	9	0	852	67	0	4.72	....	....	....	....	....	....	....
	New Haven	AHL	1	0	0	0	20	3	0	9.00	....	....	....	....	....	....	....
	Saginaw	IHL	29	19	7	2	1655	99	0	3.59	1	0	1	5	9	0	3.05
1989-90	Indianapolis	IHL	23	15	6	2	1334	71	2	3.19	....	....	....	....	....	....	....
	Fort Wayne	IHL	15	3	3	3	680	44	0	3.88	3	0	2	139	11	0	4.75
1990-91	Fort Wayne	IHL	21	10	8	0	1072	69	0	3.86	....	....	....	....	....	....	....
	Indianapolis	IHL	3	2	0	0	145	7	0	2.90	1	0	0	19	1	0	3.20
1991-92	U.S. National	....	17	5	10	1	891	54	0	3.63	....	....	....	....	....	....	....
	U.S. Olympic	....	8	....	....	....	463	17	2	2.20	....	....	....	....	....	....	....
	Chicago	**NHL**	**1**	**1**	**0**	**0**	**60**	**1**	**0**	**1.00**	....	....	....	....	....	....	....
	Indianapolis	IHL	25	14	9	2	1468	84	2	3.43	....	....	....	....	....	....	....
1992-93	Indianapolis	IHL	56	23	22	7	3201	206	0	3.86	5	1	4	276	23	0	5.00
	NHL Totals		**1**	**1**	**0**	**0**	**60**	**1**	**0**	**1.00**	....	....	....	....	....	....	....

Signed as a free agent by **Chicago**, July 5, 1989.

LEHKONEN, TIMO (LEH-koh-nehn)

Goaltender. Catches left. 6'3", 183 lbs. Born, Helsinki, Finland, January 8, 1966.
(Chicago's 4th choice, 90th overall, in 1984 Entry Draft).

			Regular Season								Playoffs						
Season	Club	Lea	GP	W	L	T	Mins	GA	SO	Avg	GP	W	L	Mins	GA	SO	Avg
1983-84	Jokerit	Fin.	1	....	....	....	60	7	0	7.00	....	....	....	....	....	....	....
1984-85	Toronto	OHL	16	....	....	....	821	64	0	4.68	1	....	....	34	4	0	7.06
1985-86	Jokerit	Fin.	2	....	....	....	57	9	0	9.47	....	....	....	....	....	....	....
1986-87	Jokerit	Fin.	13	....	....	....	679	66	0	5.83	....	....	....	....	....	....	....
1987-88	TPS	Fin.	17	....	....	....	910	60	2	3.96	....	....	....	....	....	....	....
1988-89	TPS	Fin.	12	8	4	0	644	25	3	2.33	8	....	....	459	14	1	1.91
1989-90	HPK	Fin.	35	18	13	4	2032	123	0	3.63	....	....	....	....	....	....	....
1990-91	HPK	Fin.	35	....	....	....	2023	122	0	3.62	8	....	....	437	26	0	3.57
1991-92	HPK	Fin.	43	....	....	....	2493	164	0	3.95	....	....	....	....	....	....	....
1992-93	HPK	Fin.	43	....	....	....	2557	110	3	2.58	12	....	....	702	29	1	2.48

LEMBKE, JEFF

Goaltender. Catches left. 5'11", 175 lbs. Born, Pembina, ND, November 29, 1972.
(Pittsburgh's 9th choice, 192nd overall, in 1991 Entry Draft).

			Regular Season								Playoffs						
Season	Club	Lea	GP	W	L	T	Mins	GA	SO	Avg	GP	W	L	Mins	GA	SO	Avg
1991-92	North Dakota	WCHA	10	3	3	0	412	41	0	5.97	....	....	....	....	....	....	....
1992-93	North Dakota	WCHA	4	0	2	0	160	16	0	5.99	....	....	....	....	....	....	....

LEMELIN, REJEAN (REGGIE) (LEHM-uh-lihn)

Goaltender. Catches left. 5'11", 170 lbs. Born, Quebec City, Que., November 19, 1954.
(Philadelphia's 6th choice, 125th overall, in 1974 Amateur Draft).

			Regular Season								Playoffs						
Season	Club	Lea	GP	W	L	T	Mins	GA	SO	Avg	GP	W	L	Mins	GA	SO	Avg
1972-73	Sherbrooke	QJHL	28	....	....	....	1681	146	0	5.21	2	....	....	120	12	0	6.00
1973-74	Sherbrooke	QJHL	35	....	....	....	2061	158	0	4.60	1	....	....	60	3	0	3.00
1974-75	Philadelphia	NAHL	43	....	....	....	2277	131	3	3.45	....	....	....	....	....	....	....
1975-76	Philadelphia	NAHL	29	....	....	....	1601	97	1	3.63	3	....	....	171	15	0	5.26
1976-77	Springfield	AHL	3	2	1	0	180	10	0	3.33	....	....	....	....	....	....	....
	Philadelphia	NAHL	51	26	19	1	2763	170	1	3.61	3	....	....	191	14	0	4.40
1977-78a	Philadelphia	AHL	60	31	21	7	3585	177	4	2.96	2	0	2	119	12	0	6.05
1978-79	**Atlanta**	**NHL**	**18**	**8**	**8**	**1**	**994**	**55**	**0**	**3.32**	**1**	**0**	**0**	**20**	**0**	**0**	**0.00**
	Philadelphia	AHL	13	3	9	1	780	36	0	2.77	....	....	....	....	....	....	....
1979-80	**Atlanta**	**NHL**	**3**	**0**	**2**	**0**	**150**	**15**	**0**	**6.00**	....	....	....	....	....	....	....
	Birmingham	CHL	38	13	21	2	2188	137	0	3.76	2	0	1	79	5	0	3.80
1980-81	**Calgary**	**NHL**	**29**	**14**	**6**	**7**	**1629**	**88**	**2**	**3.24**	**6**	**3**	**3**	**366**	**22**	**0**	**3.61**
	Birmingham	CHL	13	3	8	2	757	56	0	4.44	....	....	....	....	....	....	....
1981-82	**Calgary**	**NHL**	**34**	**10**	**15**	**6**	**1866**	**135**	**0**	**4.34**	....	....	....	....	....	....	....
1982-83	**Calgary**	**NHL**	**39**	**16**	**12**	**8**	**2211**	**133**	**0**	**3.61**	**7**	**3**	**3**	**327**	**27**	**0**	**4.95**
1983-84	**Calgary**	**NHL**	**51**	**21**	**12**	**9**	**2568**	**150**	**0**	**3.50**	**8**	**4**	**4**	**448**	**32**	**0**	**4.29**
1984-85	**Calgary**	**NHL**	**56**	**30**	**12**	**10**	**3176**	**183**	**1**	**3.46**	**4**	**1**	**3**	**248**	**15**	**1**	**3.63**
1985-86	**Calgary**	**NHL**	**60**	**29**	**24**	**4**	**3369**	**229**	**1**	**4.08**	**3**	**0**	**1**	**109**	**7**	**0**	**3.85**
1986-87	**Calgary**	**NHL**	**34**	**16**	**9**	**1**	**1735**	**94**	**2**	**3.25**	**2**	**0**	**1**	**101**	**6**	**0**	**3.56**
1987-88	**Boston**	**NHL**	**49**	**24**	**17**	**6**	**2828**	**138**	**3**	**2.93**	**17**	**11**	**6**	**1027**	**45**	***1**	***2.63**
1988-89	**Boston**	**NHL**	**40**	**19**	**15**	**6**	**2392**	**120**	**0**	**3.01**	**4**	**1**	**3**	**252**	**16**	**0**	**3.81**
1989-90b	**Boston**	**NHL**	**43**	**22**	**15**	**2**	**2310**	**108**	**2**	**2.81**	**3**	**0**	**1**	**135**	**13**	**0**	**5.78**
1990-91	**Boston**	**NHL**	**33**	**17**	**10**	**3**	**1829**	**111**	**1**	**3.64**	**2**	**0**	**0**	**32**	**0**	**0**	**0.00**
1991-92	**Boston**	**NHL**	**8**	**5**	**1**	**0**	**407**	**23**	**0**	**3.39**	**2**	**0**	**0**	**54**	**3**	**0**	**3.33**
1992-93	**Boston**	**NHL**	**10**	**5**	**4**	**0**	**542**	**31**	**0**	**3.43**	....	....	....	....	....	....	....
	NHL Totals		**507**	**236**	**162**	**63**	**28006**	**1613**	**12**	**3.46**	**59**	**23**	**25**	**3119**	**186**	**2**	**3.58**

a AHL First All-Star Team (1978)
b Shared William Jennings Trophy with Andy Moog (1990)

Played in NHL All-Star Game (1989)

Signed as a free agent by **Atlanta**, August 17, 1978. Signed as a free agent by **Boston**, August 13, 1987.

LENARDUZZI, MIKE

Goaltender. Catches left. 6'1", 165 lbs. Born, London, Ont., September 14, 1972.
(Hartford's 3rd choice, 57th overall, in 1990 Entry Draft).

			Regular Season								Playoffs						
Season	Club	Lea	GP	W	L	T	Mins	GA	SO	Avg	GP	W	L	Mins	GA	SO	Avg
1989-90	Oshawa	OHL	12	6	3	1	444	32	0	4.32	....	....	....	....	....	....	....
1990-91a	S.S. Marie	OHL	35	19	8	3	1966	107	0	3.27	5	3	1	268	13	*1	2.91
1991-92	S.S. Marie	OHL	9	5	3	0	486	33	0	4.07	....	....	....	....	....	....	....
	Ottawa	OHL	18	5	12	1	986	60	1	3.65	....	....	....	....	....	....	....
	Sudbury	OHL	22	11	5	4	1201	84	2	4.20	11	4	7	651	38	0	3.50
	Springfield	AHL	....	....	....	....	....	....	....	....	1	0	0	39	2	0	3.08
1992-93	**Hartford**	**NHL**	**3**	**1**	**1**	**1**	**168**	**9**	**0**	**3.21**	....	....	....	....	....	....	....
	Springfield	AHL	36	10	17	5	1945	142	0	4.38	2	1	0	100	5	0	3.00
	NHL Totals		**3**	**1**	**1**	**1**	**168**	**9**	**0**	**3.21**	....	....	....	....	....	....	....

a OHL Third All-Star Team (1991)

LEVY, JEFF

Goaltender. Catches left. 5'11", 160 lbs. Born, Salt Lake City, UT, December 9, 1970.
(Minnesota's 7th choice, 134th overall, in 1990 Entry Draft).

			Regular Season								Playoffs						
Season	Club	Lea	GP	W	L	T	Mins	GA	SO	Avg	GP	W	L	Mins	GA	SO	Avg
1990-91abc	N. Hampshire	H.E.	24	15	7	2	1490	80	0	3.22	....	....	....	....	....	....	....
1991-92	N. Hampshire	H.E.	6	2	2	0	191	14	0	4.40	....	....	....	....	....	....	....
1992-93	Dayton	ECHL	1	0	0	1	65	3	0	2.77	2	0	2	139	9	0	3.88
	Kalamazoo	IHL	28	8	14	1	1512	115	0	4.56	....	....	....	....	....	....	....

a Hockey East Rookie of the Year (1991)
b Hockey East Second All-Star Team (1991)
c NCAA East Second All-American Team (1991)

LIBERTUCCI, ANGELO

Goaltender. Catches left. 5'10", 165 lbs. Born, Toronto, Ont., January 3, 1970.
(Philadelphia's 1st choice, 6th overall, in 1991 Supplemental Draft).

			Regular Season								Playoffs						
Season	Club	Lea	GP	W	L	T	Mins	GA	SO	Avg	GP	W	L	Mins	GA	SO	Avg
1989-90	Bowling Green	CCHA	28	16	10	1	1591	107	0	4.03	....	....	....	....	....	....	....
1990-91	Bowling Green	CCHA	29	12	15	1	1594	124	1	4.67	....	....	....	....	....	....	....
1991-92	Bowling Green	CCHA	18	3	8	4	1002	81	0	4.85	....	....	....	....	....	....	....
1992-93	Bowling Green	CCHA	5	0	2	0	165	16	....	5.83	....	....	....	....	....	....	....

LINDFORS, SAKARI (LIHND-fohrs)

Goaltender. Catches left. 5'7", 150 lbs. Born, Helsinki, Finland, April 27, 1966.
(Quebec's 9th choice, 150th overall, in 1988 Entry Draft).

			Regular Season								Playoffs						
Season	Club	Lea	GP	W	L	T	Mins	GA	SO	Avg	GP	W	L	Mins	GA	SO	Avg
1986-87	HIFK	Fin.	20	....	....	....	1009	65	0	3.86	....	....	....	....	....	....	....
1987-88	HIFK	Fin.	39	....	....	....	2346	....	....	....	6	....	....	340	....	....	....
1988-89	HIFK	Fin.	24	11	11	2	1433	89	1	3.75	2	....	....	118	7	....	3.53
1989-90	HIFK	Fin.	42	23	15	4	2518	146	2	3.48	....	....	....	....	....	....	....
1990-91	HIFK	Fin.	41	....	....	....	2445	142	2	3.48	3	....	....	180	14	0	4.67
1991-92	HIFK	Fin.	38	....	....	....	2222	127	4	3.43	9	....	....	538	28	0	3.12
1992-93	HIFK	Fin.	39	....	....	....	2293	123	0	3.22	4	....	....	236	12	0	3.04

LITTLE, NEIL

Goaltender. Catches left. 6'1", 175 lbs. Born, Medicine Hat, Alta., December 18, 1971.
(Philadelphia's 11th choice, 226th overall, in 1991 Entry Draft).

			Regular Season								Playoffs						
Season	Club	Lea	GP	W	L	T	Mins	GA	SO	Avg	GP	W	L	Mins	GA	SO	Avg
1990-91	RPI	ECAC	18	9	8	0	1032	71	0	4.13	....	....	....	....	....	....	....
1991-92	RPI	ECAC	28	11	11	3	1532	96	0	3.76	....	....	....	....	....	....	....
1992-93ab	RPI	ECAC	*31	*19	9	3	*1801	88	0	2.93	....	....	....	....	....	....	....

a ECAC First All-Star Team (1993)
b NCAA East Second All-American Team (1993)

LITTMAN, DAVID

Goaltender. Catches left. 6', 183 lbs. Born, Cranston, RI, June 13, 1967.
(Buffalo's 12th choice, 211th overall, in 1987 Entry Draft).

			Regular Season								Playoffs						
Season	Club	Lea	GP	W	L	T	Mins	GA	SO	Avg	GP	W	L	Mins	GA	SO	Avg
1985-86	Boston College	H.E.	7	4	0	1	312	18	0	3.46	....	....	....	....	....	....	....
1986-87	Boston College	H.E.	21	15	5	0	1182	68	0	3.45	....	....	....	....	....	....	....
1987-88a	Boston College	H.E.	30	11	16	2	1726	116	0	4.03	....	....	....	....	....	....	....
1988-89bc	Boston College	H.E.	*32	19	9	4	*1945	107	0	3.30	....	....	....	....	....	....	....
1989-90	Rochester	AHL	14	5	6	1	681	37	0	3.26	....	....	....	....	....	....	....
	Phoenix	IHL	18	8	7	2	1047	64	0	3.67	....	....	....	....	....	....	....
1990-91	Buffalo	NHL	1	0	0	0	36	3	0	5.00	....	....	....	....	....	....	....
d	Rochester	AHL	*56	*33	13	5	*3155	160	3	3.04	8	4	2	378	16	0	2.54
1991-92	Buffalo	NHL	1	0	1	0	60	4	0	4.00	....	....	....	....	....	....	....
ef	Rochester	AHL	*61	*29	20	9	*3558	174	*3	2.93	15	8	7	879	43	*1	2.94
1992-93	Tampa Bay	NHL	1	0	1	0	45	7	0	9.33	....	....	....	....	....	....	....
	Atlanta	IHL	44	23	12	4	2390	134	0	3.36	3	1	2	178	8	0	2.70
	NHL Totals		3	0	2	0	141	14	0	5.96	....	....	....	....	....	....	....

a Hockey East Second All-Star Team (1988)
b Hockey East First All-Star Team (1989)
c NCAA East Second All-American Team (1989)
d AHL First All-Star Team (1991)
e Won Harry "Hap" Holmes Memorial Trophy (Leading Goaltender-AHL) (1992)
f AHL Second All-Star Team (1992)

Signed as a free agent by **Tampa Bay**, August 27, 1992. Signed as a free agent by **Boston**, August 6, 1993.

LORENZ, DANNY

Goaltender. Catches left. 5'10", 183 lbs. Born, Murrayville, B.C., December 12, 1969.
(NY Islanders' 4th choice, 58th overall, in 1988 Entry Draft).

			Regular Season								Playoffs						
Season	Club	Lea	GP	W	L	T	Mins	GA	SO	Avg	GP	W	L	Mins	GA	SO	Avg
1986-87	Seattle	WHL	38	12	21	2	2103	199	0	5.68	....	....	....	....	....	....	....
1987-88	Seattle	WHL	62	20	37	2	3302	314	0	5.71	....	....	....	....	....	....	....
1988-89	Springfield	AHL	4	2	1	0	210	12	0	3.43	....	....	....	....	....	....	....
a	Seattle	WHL	*68	31	33	4	*4003	240	*3	3.60	....	....	....	....	....	....	....
1989-90a	Seattle	WHL	56	37	15	2	3226	221	0	4.11	13	6	7	751	40	0	3.21
1990-91	NY Islanders	NHL	2	0	1	0	80	5	0	3.75	....	....	....	....	....	....	....
	Capital Dist.	AHL	17	5	9	2	940	70	0	4.47	....	....	....	....	....	....	....
	Richmond	ECHL	20	6	9	2	1020	75	0	4.41	....	....	....	....	....	....	....
1991-92	NY Islanders	NHL	2	0	2	0	120	10	0	5.00	....	....	....	....	....	....	....
	Capital Dist.	AHL	53	22	22	7	3050	181	2	3.56	7	3	4	442	25	0	3.39
1992-93	NY Islanders	NHL	4	1	2	0	157	10	0	3.82	....	....	....	....	....	....	....
	Capital Dist.	AHL	44	16	17	5	2412	146	1	3.63	4	0	3	219	12	0	3.29
	NHL Totals		8	1	5	0	357	25	0	4.20	....	....	....	....	....	....	....

a WHL West First All-Star Team (1989, 1990)

LOUDER, GREG

Goaltender. Catches left. 6'1", 185 lbs. Born, Concord, MA, November 16, 1971.
(Edmonton's 5th choice, 101st overall, in 1990 Entry Draft).

			Regular Season								Playoffs						
Season	Club	Lea	GP	W	L	T	Mins	GA	SO	Avg	GP	W	L	Mins	GA	SO	Avg
1990-91	Notre Dame	NCAA	33	16	5	2	1958	134	1	4.11	....	....	....	....	....	....	....
1991-92	Notre Dame	NCAA	18	5	13	0	1055	88	0	5.00	....	....	....	....	....	....	....
1992-93	Notre Dame	CCHA	24	4	16	1	1177	95	....	4.84	....	....	....	....	....	....	....

LUKOWSKI, BRIAN

Goaltender. Catches left. 5'9", 180 lbs. Born, Buffalo, NY, January 8, 1971.
(St. Louis' 11th choice, 219th overall, in 1989 Entry Draft).

			Regular Season								Playoffs						
Season	Club	Lea	GP	W	L	T	Mins	GA	SO	Avg	GP	W	L	Mins	GA	SO	Avg
1989-90	Lake Superior	CCHA	4	1	0	0	114	8	0	4.20	....	....	....	....	....	....	....
1990-91	Lake Superior	CCHA	4	3	0	0	200	8	0	2.40	....	....	....	....	....	....	....
1991-92	Lake Superior	CCHA	1	0	0	0	30	2	0	4.00	....	....	....	....	....	....	....
	Geneseo State	NCAA	15	9	6	....	....	....	....	4.09	....	....	....	....	....	....	....
1992-93	Geneseo State	NCAA	15	5	8	0	745	60	0	4.83	....	....	....	....	....	....	....

MacDONALD, TODD

Goaltender. Catches left. 6', 155 lbs. Born, Charlottetown, P.E.I., July 5, 1975.
(Florida's 7th choice, 109th overall, in 1993 Entry Draft).

			Regular Season								Playoffs						
Season	Club	Lea	GP	W	L	T	Mins	GA	SO	Avg	GP	W	L	Mins	GA	SO	Avg
1991-92	Kingston	OHAJrA	28	....	....	....	1680	84	0	3.00	....	....	....	....	....	....	....
1992-93	Tacoma	WHL	19	6	6	0	823	59	0	4.30	....	....	....	....	....	....	....

MADELEY, DARRIN

Goaltender. Catches left. 5'11", 165 lbs. Born, Holland Landing, Ont., February 25, 1968.

			Regular Season								Playoffs						
Season	Club	Lea	GP	W	L	T	Mins	GA	SO	Avg	GP	W	L	Mins	GA	SO	Avg
1989-90	Lake Superior	CCHA	30	21	7	1	....	68	....	2.42	....	....	....	....	....	....	....
1990-91a	Lake Superior	CCHA	36	*29	3	3	....	93	....	*2.61	....	....	....	....	....	....	....
1991-92abc	Lake Superior	CCHA	36	23	6	4	....	69	....	2.05	....	....	....	....	....	....	....
1992-93	Ottawa	NHL	2	0	2	0	90	10	0	6.67	....	....	....	....	....	....	....
d	New Haven	AHL	41	10	16	9	2295	127	0	3.32	....	....	....	....	....	....	....
	NHL Totals		2	0	2	0	90	10	0	6.67	....	....	....	....	....	....	....

a NCAA West First All-American Team (1991, 1992)
b NCAA All-Tournament Team (1992)
c CCHA First All-Star Team (1992)
d AHL Second All-Star Team (1993)

Signed as a free agent by **Ottawa**, June 20, 1992.

MALARCHUK, CLINT

Goaltender. Catches left. 6', 185 lbs. Born, Grande Prairie, Alta., May 1, 1961.
(Quebec's 3rd choice, 74th overall, in 1981 Entry Draft).

			Regular Season								Playoffs						
Season	Club	Lea	GP	W	L	T	Mins	GA	SO	Avg	GP	W	L	Mins	GA	SO	Avg
1979-80	Portland	WHL	37	21	10	0	1948	147	0	4.53	1	0	0	40	3	0	4.50
1980-81	Portland	WHL	38	28	8	0	2235	142	3	3.81	4	....	....	307	21	0	4.10
1981-82	Quebec	NHL	2	0	1	1	120	14	0	7.00	....	....	....	....	....	....	....
	Fredericton	AHL	51	15	34	2	2906	247	0	5.10	....	....	....	....	....	....	....
1982-83	Quebec	NHL	15	8	5	2	900	71	0	4.73	....	....	....	....	....	....	....
	Fredericton	AHL	25	....	....	....	1506	78	0	3.11	....	....	....	....	....	....	....
1983-84	Quebec	NHL	23	10	9	2	1215	80	0	3.95	....	....	....	....	....	....	....
	Fredericton	AHL	11	5	5	1	663	40	0	3.62	....	....	....	....	....	....	....
1984-85	Fredericton	AHL	*56	26	25	4	*3347	198	2	3.55	6	2	4	379	20	0	3.17
1985-86	Quebec	NHL	46	26	12	4	2657	142	4	3.21	3	0	2	143	11	0	4.62
1986-87	Quebec	NHL	54	18	26	9	3092	175	1	3.40	3	0	2	140	8	0	3.43
1987-88	Washington	NHL	54	24	20	4	2926	154	*4	3.16	4	0	2	193	15	0	4.66
1988-89	Washington	NHL	42	16	18	7	2428	141	1	3.48	1	0	1	59	5	0	5.08
	Buffalo	NHL	7	3	1	1	326	13	1	2.39	....	....	....	....	....	....	....
1989-90	Buffalo	NHL	29	14	11	2	1596	89	0	3.35	....	....	....	....	....	....	....
1990-91	Buffalo	NHL	37	12	14	10	2131	119	1	3.35	4	2	2	246	17	0	4.15
1991-92	Buffalo	NHL	29	10	13	3	1639	102	0	3.73	....	....	....	....	....	....	....
	Rochester	AHL	2	2	0	0	120	3	1	1.50	....	....	....	....	....	....	....
1992-93a	San Diego	IHL	27	17	3	3	1516	72	3	2.85	*12	6	4	668	34	0	3.05
	NHL Totals		338	141	130	45	19030	1100	12	3.47	15	2	9	781	56	0	4.30

a Shared James Norris Memorial Trophy (Top Goaltender - IHL) with Rick Knickle (1993)

Traded to **Washington** by **Quebec** with Dale Hunter for Gaetan Duchesne, Alan Haworth and Washington's first round choice (Joe Sakic) in 1987 Entry Draft, June 13, 1987. Traded to **Buffalo** by **Washington** with Grant Ledyard and Washington's sixth round choice (Brian Holzinger) in 1991 Entry Draft for Calle Johansson and Buffalo's second round choice (Byron Dafoe) in 1989 Entry Draft, March 7, 1989.

MARACLE, NORM

Goaltender. Catches left. 5'9", 175 lbs. Born, Belleville, Ont., October 2, 1974.
(Detroit's 6th choice, 126th overall, in 1993 Entry Draft).

			Regular Season								Playoffs						
Season	Club	Lea	GP	W	L	T	Mins	GA	SO	Avg	GP	W	L	Mins	GA	SO	Avg
1991-92	Saskatoon	WHL	29	13	6	3	1529	87	1	3.41	15	9	5	860	37	0	3.38
1992-93a	Saskatoon	WHL	53	27	18	3	1939	160	1	3.27	9	4	5	569	33	0	3.48

a WHL East Second All-Star Team (1993)

MASON, BOB

Goaltender. Catches right. 6'1", 180 lbs. Born, International Falls, MN, April 22, 1961.

			Regular Season								Playoffs						
Season	Club	Lea	GP	W	L	T	Mins	GA	SO	Avg	GP	W	L	Mins	GA	SO	Avg
1981-82	Minn.-Duluth	WCHA	26	....	....	....	1401	115	0	4.45	....	....	....	....	....	....	....
1982-83	Minn.-Duluth	WCHA	43	....	....	....	2593	151	1	3.49	....	....	....	....	....	....	....
1983-84	U.S. National	....	33	....	....	....	1895	89	0	2.82	....	....	....	....	....	....	....
	U.S. Olympic	....	3	....	....	....	160	10	0	3.75	....	....	....	....	....	....	....
	Washington	NHL	2	2	0	0	120	3	0	1.50	....	....	....	....	....	....	....
	Hershey	AHL	5	1	4	0	282	26	0	5.53	....	....	....	....	....	....	....
1984-85	Washington	NHL	12	8	2	1	661	31	1	2.81	....	....	....	....	....	....	....
	Binghamton	AHL	20	10	6	1	1052	58	1	3.31	....	....	....	....	....	....	....
1985-86	Washington	NHL	1	1	0	0	16	0	0	0.00	....	....	....	....	....	....	....
	Binghamton	AHL	34	20	11	2	1940	126	0	3.90	3	1	1	124	9	0	4.35
1986-87	Washington	NHL	45	20	18	5	2536	137	0	3.24	4	2	2	309	9	1	1.75
	Binghamton	AHL	2	1	1	0	119	4	0	2.02	....	....	....	....	....	....	....
1987-88	Chicago	NHL	41	13	18	8	2312	160	0	4.15	1	0	1	60	3	0	3.00
1988-89	Quebec	NHL	22	5	14	1	1168	92	0	4.73	....	....	....	....	....	....	....
	Halifax	AHL	23	11	7	1	1278	73	1	3.43	2	0	2	97	9	0	5.57
1989-90	Washington	NHL	16	4	9	1	822	48	0	3.50	....	....	....	....	....	....	....
	Baltimore	AHL	13	9	2	2	770	44	0	3.43	6	2	4	373	20	0	3.22
1990-91	Vancouver	NHL	6	2	4	0	353	29	0	4.93	....	....	....	....	....	....	....
	Milwaukee	IHL	22	8	12	1	1199	82	0	4.10	....	....	....	....	....	....	....
1991-92	Milwaukee	IHL	51	27	18	4	3024	171	1	3.39	3	1	2	179	15	0	5.03
1992-93	Hamilton	AHL	44	20	19	3	2601	159	0	3.67	....	....	....	....	....	....	....
	NHL Totals		145	55	65	16	7988	500	1	3.76	5	2	3	369	12	1	1.95

Signed as a free agent by **Washington**, February 21, 1984. Signed as a free agent by **Chicago**, June 12, 1987. Traded to **Quebec** by **Chicago** for Mike Eagles, July 5, 1988. Traded to **Washington** by **Quebec** for future considerations, June 17, 1989. Signed as a free agent by **Vancouver**, December 1, 1990.

MAZZOLI, PAT

Goaltender. Catches left. 5'10", 172 lbs. Born, Toronto, Ont., March 16, 1970.
(Quebec's 8th choice, 169th overall, in 1990 Entry Draft).

			Regular Season								Playoffs						
Season	Club	Lea	GP	W	L	T	Mins	GA	SO	Avg	GP	W	L	Mins	GA	SO	Avg
1990-91	Ferris State	CCHA	22	13	8	1	1265	66	0	3.13	....	....	....	....	....	....	....
1991-92	Ferris State	CCHA	18	5	7	3	939	71	0	4.54	....	....	....	....	....	....	....
1992-93	Ferris State	CCHA	24	10	9	2	1297	79	....	3.65	....	....	....	....	....	....	....

McKERSIE, JOHN

Goaltender. Catches left. 6', 210 lbs. Born, Madison, WI, January 23, 1972.
(Minnesota's 12th choice, 239th overall, in 1990 Entry Draft).

			Regular Season								Playoffs						
Season	Club	Lea	GP	W	L	T	Mins	GA	SO	Avg	GP	W	L	Mins	GA	SO	Avg
1991-92	Boston U.	H.E.	8	3	2	1	396	23	1	3.48	....	....	....	....	....	....	....
1992-93	Boston	HE	9	6	....	1	466	31	1	3.99	....	....	....	....	....	....	....
1992-93	Boston	HE	9	6	0	1	466	31	1	3.99	....	....	....	....	....	....	....

McLEAN, KIRK

Goaltender. Catches left. 6', 195 lbs. Born, Willowdale, Ont., June 26, 1966.
(New Jersey's 6th choice, 107th overall, in 1984 Entry Draft).

			Regular Season								Playoffs						
Season	Club	Lea	GP	W	L	T	Mins	GA	SO	Avg	GP	W	L	Mins	GA	SO	Avg
1983-84	Oshawa	OHL	17	5	9	0	940	67	0	4.28	....	....	....	....	....	....	....
1984-85	Oshawa	OHL	47	23	17	2	2581	143	1	*3.32	5	1	3	271	21	0	4.65
1985-86	New Jersey	NHL	2	1	1	0	111	11	0	5.95	....	....	....	....	....	....	....
	Oshawa	OHL	51	24	21	2	2830	169	1	3.58	4	1	2	201	18	0	5.37
1986-87	New Jersey	NHL	4	1	1	0	160	10	0	3.75	....	....	....	....	....	....	....
	Maine	AHL	45	15	23	4	2606	140	1	3.22	....	....	....	....	....	....	....
1987-88	Vancouver	NHL	41	11	27	3	2380	147	1	3.71	....	....	....	....	....	....	....
1988-89	Vancouver	NHL	42	20	17	3	2477	127	4	3.08	5	2	3	302	18	0	3.58
1989-90	Vancouver	NHL	*63	21	30	10	*3739	216	0	3.47	....	....	....	....	....	....	....
1990-91	Vancouver	NHL	41	10	22	3	1969	131	0	3.99	2	1	1	123	7	0	3.41
1991-92a	Vancouver	NHL	65	*38	17	9	3852	176	*5	2.74	13	6	7	785	33	*2	2.52
1992-93	Vancouver	NHL	54	28	21	5	3261	184	3	3.39	12	6	6	754	42	0	3.34
	NHL Totals		312	130	136	33	17949	1002	13	3.35	32	15	17	1964	100	2	3.05

a NHL Second All-Star Team (1992)

Played in NHL All-Star Game (1990)

Traded to **Vancouver** by **New Jersey** with Greg Adams for Patrik Sundstrom and Vancouver's fourth round choice (Matt Ruchty) in 1988 Entry Draft, September 15, 1987.

McLENNAN, JAMIE

Goaltender. Catches left. 6', 190 lbs. Born, Edmonton, Alta., June 30, 1971.
(NY Islanders' 3rd choice, 48th overall, in 1991 Entry Draft).

			Regular Season								Playoffs						
Season	Club	Lea	GP	W	L	T	Mins	GA	SO	Avg	GP	W	L	Mins	GA	SO	Avg
1989-90	Lethbridge	WHL	34	20	4	2	1690	110	1	3.91	13	6	5	677	44	0	3.90
1990-91a	Lethbridge	WHL	56	32	18	4	3230	205	0	3.81	*16	8	8	*970	56	0	3.46
1991-92	Capital Dist.	AHL	18	4	10	2	952	60	1	3.78	....	....	....	....	....	....	....
	Richmond	ECHL	32	16	12	2	1837	114	0	3.72	....	....	....	....	....	....	....
1992-93	Capital Dist.	AHL	38	17	14	6	2171	117	1	3.23	1	0	1	20	5	0	15.00

a WHL East First All-Star Team (1991)

MICHAUD, MARK

Goaltender. Catches left. 5'10", 175 lbs. Born, Quebec, Que., August 15, 1967.

			Regular Season								Playoffs						
Season	Club	Lea	GP	W	L	T	Mins	GA	SO	Avg	GP	W	L	Mins	GA	SO	Avg
1990-91	Miami-Ohio	CCHA	19	2	13	1	929	91	0	5.87	....	....	....	....	....	....	....
1991-92	Miami-Ohio	CCHA	31	14	12	4	1577	112	0	4.26	....	....	....	....	....	....	....
1992-93	New Haven	AHL	12	2	7	1	550	51	0	5.56	....	....	....	....	....	....	....
	Thunder Bay	Col.	22	12	7	2	1280	82	1	3.84	....	....	....	....	....	....	....

Signed as a free agent by **Ottawa**, October 8, 1992.

MIGNACCA, SONNY

Goaltender. Catches left. 5'8", 178 lbs. Born, Winnipeg, Man., January 4, 1974.
(Vancouver's 10th choice, 213th overall, in 1992 Entry Draft).

			Regular Season								Playoffs						
Season	Club	Lea	GP	W	L	T	Mins	GA	SO	Avg	GP	W	L	Mins	GA	SO	Avg
1990-91	Medicine Hat	WHL	33	....	....	....	1743	121	0	4.17	1	0	0	13	2	0	9.23
1991-92a	Medicine Hat	WHL	56	....	....	....	3207	189	2	3.54	4	0	4	240	17	0	4.25
1992-93	Medicine Hat	WHL	50	18	25	2	2724	210	1	4.63	10	5	5	605	36	0	3.57

a WHL East Second All-Star Team (1992)

MIKLENDA, JAROSLAV

Goaltender. Catches left. 6'1", 176 lbs. Born, Uherske Hradiste, Czech., March 7, 1974.
(Ottawa's 7th choice, 146th overall, in 1992 Entry Draft).

			Regular Season								Playoffs						
Season	Club	Lea	GP	W	L	T	Mins	GA	SO	Avg	GP	W	L	Mins	GA	SO	Avg
1991-92	Olomouc	Czech.	1	....	....	....	36	6	0	9.99	....	....	....	....	....	....	....
1992-93	Olomouc	Czech.	5	....	....	....	285	22	....	4.63	....	....	....	....	....	....	....

MOEN, JEFFREY

Goaltender. Catches left. 6'1", 170 lbs. Born, Roseville, MN, February 9, 1974.
(Minnesota's 11th choice, 250th overall, in 1992 Entry Draft).

			Regular Season								Playoffs						
Season	Club	Lea	GP	W	L	T	Mins	GA	SO	Avg	GP	W	L	Mins	GA	SO	Avg
1990-91	Roseville	HS	13	....	....	....	585	49	0	3.80	....	....	....	....	....	....	....
1991-92	Roseville	HS						UNAVAILABLE									
1992-93	U. Minnesota	WCHA	6	0	3	1	303	20	0	3.96	....	....	....	....	....	....	....

MOOG, DONALD ANDREW (ANDY) (MOHG)

Goaltender. Catches left. 5'8", 170 lbs. Born, Penticton, B.C., February 18, 1960.
(Edmonton's 6th choice, 132nd overall, in 1980 Entry Draft).

			Regular Season								Playoffs						
Season	Club	Lea	GP	W	L	T	Mins	GA	SO	Avg	GP	W	L	Mins	GA	SO	Avg
1978-79	Billings	WHL	26	13	5	4	1306	90	4	4.13	5	1	3	229	21	0	5.50
1979-80a	Billings	WHL	46	23	14	1	2435	149	1	3.67	3	2	1	190	10	0	3.16
1980-81	Edmonton	NHL	7	3	3	0	313	20	0	3.83	9	5	4	526	32	0	3.65
	Wichita	CHL	29	14	13	1	1602	89	0	3.33	5	3	2	300	16	0	3.20
1981-82	Edmonton	NHL	8	3	5	0	399	32	0	4.81	....	....	....	....	....	....	....
b	Wichita	CHL	40	23	13	3	2391	119	1	2.99	7	3	4	434	23	0	3.18
1982-83	Edmonton	NHL	50	33	8	7	2833	167	1	3.54	16	11	5	949	48	0	3.03
1983-84	Edmonton	NHL	38	27	8	1	2212	139	1	3.77	7	4	0	263	12	0	2.74
1984-85	Edmonton	NHL	39	22	9	3	2019	111	1	3.30	2	0	0	20	0	0	0.00
1985-86	Edmonton	NHL	47	27	9	7	2664	164	1	3.69	1	1	0	60	1	0	1.00
1986-87	Edmonton	NHL	46	28	11	3	2461	144	0	3.51	2	2	0	120	8	0	4.00
1987-88	Cdn. National	....	27	10	7	5	1438	86	0	3.58	....	....	....	....	....	....	....
	Cdn. Olympic	....	4	4	0	0	240	9	1	2.25	....	....	....	....	....	....	....
	Boston	NHL	6	4	2	0	360	17	1	2.83	7	1	4	354	25	0	4.24
1988-89	Boston	NHL	41	18	14	8	2482	133	1	3.22	6	4	2	359	14	0	2.34
1989-90c	Boston	NHL	46	24	10	7	2536	122	3	2.89	20	13	7	1195	44	*2	*2.21
1990-91	Boston	NHL	51	25	13	9	2844	136	4	2.87	19	10	9	1133	60	0	3.18
1991-92	Boston	NHL	62	28	22	9	3640	196	1	3.23	15	8	7	866	46	1	3.19
1992-93	Boston	NHL	55	37	14	3	3194	168	3	3.16	3	....	3	161	14	....	5.22
	NHL Totals		496	279	128	57	27957	1549	17	3.32	107	59	41	6006	304	3	3.04

a WHL Second All-Star Team (1980)
b CHL Second All-Star Team (1982)
c Shared William Jennings Trophy with Rejean Lemelin (1990)

Played in NHL All-Star Game (1985, 1986, 1991)

Traded to **Boston** by **Edmonton** for Geoff Courtnall, Bill Ranford and Boston's second choice (Petro Koivunen) in 1988 Entry Draft, March 8, 1988. Traded to **Dallas** by **Boston** for Jon Casey to complete June 20, 1993 trade which sent Gord Murphy to Dallas for future considerations, June 25, 1993.

MOSS, TYLER

Goaltender. Catches right. 6', 168 lbs. Born, Ottawa, Ont., June 29, 1975.
(Tampa Bay's 2nd choice, 29th overall, in 1993 Entry Draft).

			Regular Season								Playoffs						
Season	Club	Lea	GP	W	L	T	Mins	GA	SO	Avg	GP	W	L	Mins	GA	SO	Avg
1991-92	Nepean	OHAJrA	26	....	....	....	1335	109	0	4.90	....	....	....	....	....	....	....
1992-93	Kingston	OHL	31	13	7	5	1537	97	0	3.79	6	....	....	228	19	0	5.00

MULLAHY, BRAD

Goaltender. Catches left. 5'10", 185 lbs. Born, North Easton, MA, February 12, 1970.
(Winnipeg's 1st choice, 5th overall, in 1991 Supplemental Draft).

			Regular Season								Playoffs						
Season	Club	Lea	GP	W	L	T	Mins	GA	SO	Avg	GP	W	L	Mins	GA	SO	Avg
1989-90	Providence	H.E.	5	2	1	0	207	13	0	3.77	....	....	....	....	....	....	....
1990-91	Providence	H.E.	22	14	5	1	1257	65	0	3.10	....	....	....	....	....	....	....
1991-92	Providence	H.E.	22	11	9	2	1291	80	2	3.72	....	....	....	....	....	....	....
1992-93	Providence	H.E.	25	8	8	1	1169	82	1	4.16	....	....	....	....	....	....	....

MURRAY, SHAWN

Goaltender. Catches left. 5'9", 160 lbs. Born, St. Paul, MN, September 3, 1971.
(Calgary's 9th choice, 167th overall, in 1990 Entry Draft).

			Regular Season								Playoffs						
Season	Club	Lea	GP	W	L	T	Mins	GA	SO	Avg	GP	W	L	Mins	GA	SO	Avg
1990-91	Colgate	ECAC	6	2	2	0	311	21	0	4.06	....	....	....	....	....	....	....
1991-92	Colgate	ECAC	15	7	7	0	904	71	0	4.71	....	....	....	....	....	....	....
1992-93	Colgate	ECAC	15	5	7	1	723	50	0	4.15	....	....	....	....	....	....	....

MUZZATTI, JASON (mew-ZA-tee)

Goaltender. Catches left. 6'1", 190 lbs. Born, Toronto, Ont., February 3, 1970.
(Calgary's 1st choice, 21st overall, in 1988 Entry Draft).

			Regular Season								Playoffs						
Season	Club	Lea	GP	W	L	T	Mins	GA	SO	Avg	GP	W	L	Mins	GA	SO	Avg
1987-88a	Michigan State	CCHA	33	19	9	3	1915	109	0	3.41	....	....	....	....	....	....	....
1988-89	Michigan State	CCHA	42	32	9	1	2515	127	3	*3.03	....	....	....	....	....	....	....
1989-90bc	Michigan State	CCHA	33	*24	6	0	1976	99	0	3.01	....	....	....	....	....	....	....
1990-91	Michigan State	CCHA	22	8	10	2	1204	75	1	3.74	....	....	....	....	....	....	....
1991-92	Salt Lake	IHL	52	24	22	5	3033	167	2	3.30	4	1	3	247	18	0	4.37
1992-93	Cdn. National	....	16	6	9	0	880	53	0	3.84	....	....	....	....	....	....	....
	Indianapolis	IHL	12	5	6	1	707	48	0	4.07	....	....	....	....	....	....	....
	Salt Lake	IHL	13	5	6	1	747	52	0	4.18	....	....	....	....	....	....	....

a CCHA Second All-Star Team (1988)
b CCHA First All-Star Team (1990)
c NCAA West Second All-American Team (1990)

NEWMAN, THOMAS

Goaltender. Catches left. 6'1", 185 lbs. Born, Golden Valley, MN, February 23, 1971.
(Los Angeles' 4th choice, 103rd overall, in 1989 Entry Draft).

			Regular Season								Playoffs						
Season	Club	Lea	GP	W	L	T	Mins	GA	SO	Avg	GP	W	L	Mins	GA	SO	Avg
1989-90	U. Minnesota	WCHA	35	19	13	2	1982	127	0	3.84	....	....	....	....	....	....	....
1990-91	U. Minnesota	WCHA	22	12	2	2	942	54	2	3.44	....	....	....	....	....	....	....
1991-92	U. Minnesota	WCHA	11	5	1	0	399	15	0	2.26	....	....	....	....	....	....	....
1992-93	U. Minnesota	WCHA	22	14	4	2	1172	61	3	3.12	....	....	....	....	....	....	....

O'NEILL, MICHAEL (MIKE)

Goaltender. Catches left. 5'7", 160 lbs. Born, LaSalle, Que., November 3, 1967.
(Winnipeg's 1st choice, 15th overall, in 1988 Supplemental Draft).

			Regular Season								Playoffs						
Season	Club	Lea	GP	W	L	T	Mins	GA	SO	Avg	GP	W	L	Mins	GA	SO	Avg
1985-86	Yale	ECAC	6	3	1	0	389	17	0	3.53	....	....	....	....	....	....	....
1986-87a	Yale	ECAC	16	9	6	1	964	55	2	3.42	....	....	....	....	....	....	....
1987-88	Yale	ECAC	24	6	17	0	1385	101	0	4.37	....	....	....	....	....	....	....
1988-89ab	Yale	ECAC	25	10	14	1	1490	93	0	3.74	....	....	....	....	....	....	....
1989-90	Tappara	Fin.	41	23	13	5	2369	127	2	3.22	....	....	....	....	....	....	....
1990-91	Fort Wayne	IHL	8	5	2	1	490	31	0	3.80	....	....	....	....	....	....	....
	Moncton	AHL	30	13	7	6	1613	84	0	3.12	8	3	4	435	29	0	4.00
1991-92	Winnipeg	NHL	1	0	0	0	13	1	0	4.62	....	....	....	....	....	....	....
	Moncton	AHL	32	14	16	2	1902	108	1	3.41	11	4	7	670	43	*1	3.85
	Fort Wayne	IHL	33	22	6	3	1858	97	*4	3.13	....	....	....	....	....	....	....
1992-93	Winnipeg	NHL	2	0	0	1	73	6	0	4.93	....	....	....	....	....	....	....
	Moncton	AHL	30	13	10	4	1649	88	1	3.20	....	....	....	....	....	....	....
	NHL Totals		3	0	0	1	86	7	0	4.88	....	....	....	....	....	....	....

a ECAC First All-Star Team (1987, 1989)
b NCAA East First All-American Team (1989)

OSGOOD, CHRIS

Goaltender. Catches left. 5'10", 156 lbs. Born, Peace River, Alta., November 26, 1972.
(Detroit's 3rd choice, 54th overall, in 1991 Entry Draft).

			Regular Season								Playoffs						
Season	Club	Lea	GP	W	L	T	Mins	GA	SO	Avg	GP	W	L	Mins	GA	SO	Avg
1989-90	Medicine Hat	WHL	57	24	28	2	3094	228	0	4.42	3	0	3	173	17	0	5.91
1990-91a	Medicine Hat	WHL	46	23	18	3	2630	173	2	3.95	12	7	5	712	42	0	3.54
1991-92	Medicine Hat	WHL	15	10	3	0	819	44	0	3.22	....	....	....	....	....	....	....
	Brandon	WHL	16	3	10	1	890	60	1	4.04	....	....	....	....	....	....	....
	Seattle	WHL	21	12	7	1	1217	65	1	3.20	15	9	6	904	51	0	3.38
1992-93	Adirondack	AHL	45	19	19	4	2438	159	0	3.91	1	0	1	59	2	0	2.03

a WHL East Second All-Star Team (1991)

PASSMORE, STEVE

Goaltender. Catches left. 5'9", 165 lbs. Born, Thunder Bay, Ont., January 29, 1973.
(Quebec's 9th choice, 196th overall, in 1992 Entry Draft).

			Regular Season								Playoffs						
Season	Club	Lea	GP	W	L	T	Mins	GA	SO	Avg	GP	W	L	Mins	GA	SO	Avg
1990-91	Victoria	WHL	35	3	25	1	1838	190	0	6.20	....	....	....	....	....	....	....
1991-92	Victoria	WHL	*71	15	50	5	*4228	347	0	4.92	....	....	....	....	....	....	....
1992-93a	Victoria	WHL	43	14	24	2	2402	150	1	3.75	....	....	....	....	....	....	....

a WHL West First All-Star Team (1993)

PIETRANGELO, FRANK (PEE-tuhr-AN-jehl-oh)

Goaltender. Catches left. 5'10", 185 lbs. Born, Niagara Falls, Ont., December 17, 1964.
(Pittsburgh's 4th choice, 63rd overall, in 1983 Entry Draft).

			Regular Season								Playoffs						
Season	Club	Lea	GP	W	L	T	Mins	GA	SO	Avg	GP	W	L	Mins	GA	SO	Avg
1982-83	U. Minnesota	WCHA	25	15	6	1	1348	80	1	3.55	....	....	....	....	....	....	....
1983-84	U. Minnesota	WCHA	20	13	7	0	1141	66	0	3.47	....	....	....	....	....	....	....
1984-85	U. Minnesota	WCHA	17	8	3	3	912	52	0	3.42	....	....	....	....	....	....	....
1985-86	U. Minnesota	WCHA	23	15	7	0	1284	76	0	3.55	....	....	....	....	....	....	....
1986-87	Muskegon	IHL	35	23	11	0	2090	119	2	3.42	15	10	4	923	46	0	2.99
1987-88	**Pittsburgh**	**NHL**	**21**	**9**	**11**	**0**	**1207**	**80**	**1**	**3.98**	....	....	....	....	....	....	....
	Muskegon	IHL	15	11	3	1	868	43	2	2.97	....	....	....	....	....	....	....
1988-89	**Pittsburgh**	**NHL**	**15**	**5**	**3**	**0**	**669**	**45**	**0**	**4.04**	....	....	....	....	....	....	....
	Muskegon	IHL	13	10	1	0	760	38	1	3.00	9	*8	1	566	29	0	3.07
1989-90	**Pittsburgh**	**NHL**	**21**	**8**	**6**	**2**	**1066**	**77**	**0**	**4.33**	....	....	....	....	....	....	....
	Muskegon	IHL	12	9	2	1	691	38	0	3.30	....	....	....	....	....	....	....
1990-91	**Pittsburgh**	**NHL**	**25**	**10**	**11**	**1**	**1311**	**86**	**0**	**3.94**	**5**	**4**	**1**	**288**	**15**	***1**	**3.13**
1991-92	**Pittsburgh**	**NHL**	**5**	**2**	**1**	**0**	**225**	**20**	**0**	**5.33**	....	....	....	....	....	....	....
	Hartford	**NHL**	**5**	**3**	**1**	**1**	**306**	**12**	**0**	**2.35**	**7**	**3**	**4**	**425**	**19**	**0**	**2.68**
1992-93	**Hartford**	**NHL**	**30**	**4**	**15**	**1**	**1373**	**111**	**0**	**4.85**	....	....	....	....	....	....	....
	NHL Totals		**122**	**41**	**48**	**5**	**6157**	**431**	**1**	**4.20**	**12**	**7**	**5**	**713**	**34**	**1**	**2.86**

Traded to **Hartford** by **Pittsburgh** for future considerations, March 10, 1992.

POTVIN, FELIX

Goaltender. Catches left. 6'1", 183 lbs. Born, Anjou, Que., June 23, 1971.
(Toronto's 2nd choice, 31st overall, in 1990 Entry Draft).

			Regular Season								Playoffs						
Season	Club	Lea	GP	W	L	T	Mins	GA	SO	Avg	GP	W	L	Mins	GA	SO	Avg
1988-89	Chicoutimi	QMJHL	*65	25	31	1	*3489	271	*2	4.66	....	....	....	....	....	....	....
1989-90a	Chicoutimi	QMJHL	*62	*31	26	2	*3478	231	*2	3.99	....	....	....	....	....	....	....
1990-91																	
bcde	Chicoutimi	QMJHL	54	33	15	4	3216	145	*6	*2.70	*16	*11	5	*992	46	0	*2.78
1991-92	**Toronto**	**NHL**	**4**	**0**	**2**	**1**	**210**	**8**	**0**	**2.29**	....	....	....	....	....	....	....
fgh	St. John's	AHL	35	18	10	6	2070	101	2	2.93	11	7	4	642	41	0	3.83
1992-93i	**Toronto**	**NHL**	**48**	**25**	**15**	**7**	**2781**	**116**	**2**	***2.50**	***21**	**11**	**10**	***1308**	**62**	**1**	**2.84**
	St. John's	AHL	5	3	0	2	309	18	0	3.50	....	....	....	....	....	....	....
	NHL Totals		**52**	**25**	**17**	**8**	**2991**	**124**	**2**	**2.49**	**21**	**11**	**10**	**1308**	**62**	**1**	**2.84**

a QMJHL Second All-Star Team (1990)
b QMJHL First All-Star Team (1991)
c Canadian Major Junior Goaltender of the Year (1991)
d Memorial Cup All-Star Team (1991)
e Won Hap Emms Memorial Trophy (Memorial Cup Top Goalie) (1991)
f Won Baz Bastien Trophy (Top Goalie-AHL) (1992)
g Won Dudley "Red" Garrett Memorial Trophy (Top Rookie-AHL) (1992)
h AHL First All-Star Team (1992)
i NHL/Upper Deck All-Rookie Team (1993)

PUPPA, DAREN (POO-puh)

Goaltender. Catches right. 6'3", 205 lbs. Born, Kirkland Lake, Ont., March 23, 1965.
(Buffalo's 6th choice, 74th overall, in 1983 Entry Draft).

			Regular Season								Playoffs						
Season	Club	Lea	GP	W	L	T	Mins	GA	SO	Avg	GP	W	L	Mins	GA	SO	Avg
1983-84	RPI	ECAC	32	24	6	0	....	....	....	2.94	....	....	....	....	....	....	....
1984-85	RPI	ECAC	32	31	1	0	1830	78	0	2.56	....	....	....	....	....	....	....
1985-86	**Buffalo**	**NHL**	**7**	**3**	**4**	**0**	**401**	**21**	**1**	**3.14**	....	....	....	....	....	....	....
	Rochester	AHL	20	8	11	0	1092	79	0	4.34	....	....	....	....	....	....	....
1986-87	**Buffalo**	**NHL**	**3**	**0**	**2**	**1**	**185**	**13**	**0**	**4.22**	....	....	....	....	....	....	....
a	Rochester	AHL	57	*33	14	0	3129	146	1	2.80	*16	*10	6	*944	48	*1	3.05
1987-88	**Buffalo**	**NHL**	**17**	**8**	**6**	**1**	**874**	**61**	**0**	**4.19**	**3**	**1**	**1**	**142**	**11**	**0**	**4.65**
	Rochester	AHL	26	14	8	2	1415	65	2	2.76	2	0	1	108	5	0	2.78
1988-89	**Buffalo**	**NHL**	**37**	**17**	**10**	**6**	**1908**	**107**	**1**	**3.36**	....	....	....	....	....	....	....
1989-90b	**Buffalo**	**NHL**	**56**	***31**	**16**	**6**	**3241**	**156**	**1**	**2.89**	**6**	**2**	**4**	**370**	**15**	**0**	**2.43**
1990-91	**Buffalo**	**NHL**	**38**	**15**	**11**	**6**	**2092**	**118**	**2**	**3.38**	**2**	**0**	**1**	**81**	**10**	**0**	**7.41**
1991-92	**Buffalo**	**NHL**	**33**	**11**	**14**	**4**	**1757**	**114**	**0**	**3.89**	....	....	....	....	....	....	....
	Rochester	AHL	2	0	2	0	119	9	0	4.54	....	....	....	....	....	....	....
1992-93	**Buffalo**	**NHL**	**24**	**11**	**5**	**4**	**1306**	**78**	**0**	**3.58**	....	....	....	....	....	....	....
	Toronto	**NHL**	**8**	**6**	**2**	**0**	**479**	**18**	**2**	**2.25**	**1**	**0**	**0**	**20**	**1**	**0**	**3.00**
	NHL Totals		**223**	**102**	**70**	**28**	**12243**	**686**	**7**	**3.36**	**12**	**3**	**6**	**613**	**37**	**0**	**3.62**

a AHL First All-Star Team (1987)
b NHL Second All-Star Team (1990)

Played in NHL All-Star Game (1990)

Traded to **Toronto** by **Buffalo** with Dave Andreychuk and Buffalo's first round choice (Kenny Jonsson) in 1993 Entry Draft for Grant Fuhr and future considerations, February 2, 1993. Claimed by **Florida** from **Toronto** in Expansion Draft, June 24, 1993. Claimed by **Tampa Bay** from **Florida** in Phase II of Expansion Draft, June 25, 1993.

PYE, BILL

Goaltender. Catches left. 5'9", 180 lbs. Born, Canton, MI, April 9, 1969.
(Buffalo's 5th choice, 107th overall, in 1989 Entry Draft).

			Regular Season								Playoffs						
Season	Club	Lea	GP	W	L	T	Mins	GA	SO	Avg	GP	W	L	Mins	GA	SO	Avg
1987-88	N. Michigan	WCHA	13	....	....	....	654	49	0	4.49	....	....	....	....	....	....	....
1988-89	N. Michigan	WCHA	43	26	15	2	2533	133	1	3.15	....	....	....	....	....	....	....
1989-90	N. Michigan	WCHA	36	20	14	1	2035	149	1	4.39	....	....	....	....	....	....	....
1990-91abc	N. Michigan	WCHA	39	*32	3	4	2300	109	*4	2.84	....	....	....	....	....	....	....
1991-92	Rochester	AHL	7	0	4	0	272	13	0	2.87	1	1	0	60	2	0	2.00
	New Haven	AHL	4	0	3	1	200	19	0	5.70	....	....	....	....	....	....	....
	Fort Wayne	IHL	8	5	2	1	451	29	0	3.86	....	....	....	....	....	....	....
	Erie	ECHL	5	5	0	0	310	22	0	4.26	4	1	3	220	15	0	4.09
1992-93	Rochester	AHL	26	9	14	2	1427	107	0	4.50	....	....	....	....	....	....	....

a WCHA First All-Star Team (1991)
b NCAA West Second All-American Team (1991)
c NCAA Final Four All-Tournament Team (1991)

RACICOT, ANDRE

Goaltender. Catches left. 5'11", 165 lbs. Born, Rouyn-Noranda, Que., June 9, 1969.
(Montreal's 5th choice, 83rd overall, in 1989 Entry Draft).

			Regular Season								Playoffs						
Season	Club	Lea	GP	W	L	T	Mins	GA	SO	Avg	GP	W	L	Mins	GA	SO	Avg
1986-87	Longueuil	QMJHL	3	1	2	0	180	19	0	6.33	....	....	....	....	....	....	....
1987-88	Granby	QMJHL	30	15	11	1	1547	105	1	4.07	5	1	4	298	23	0	4.63
1988-89a	Granby	QMJHL	54	22	24	3	2944	198	0	4.04	4	0	4	218	18	0	4.95
1989-90	**Montreal**	**NHL**	**1**	**0**	**0**	**0**	**13**	**3**	**0**	**13.85**	....	....	....	....	....	....	....
b	Sherbrooke	AHL	33	19	11	2	1948	97	1	2.99	5	0	4	227	18	0	4.76
1990-91	**Montreal**	**NHL**	**21**	**7**	**9**	**2**	**975**	**52**	**1**	**3.20**	**2**	**0**	**1**	**12**	**2**	**0**	**10.00**
	Fredericton	AHL	22	13	8	1	1252	60	1	2.88	....	....	....	....	....	....	....
1991-92	**Montreal**	**NHL**	**9**	**0**	**3**	**3**	**436**	**23**	**0**	**3.17**	**1**	**0**	**0**	**1**	**0**	**0**	**0.00**
	Fredericton	AHL	28	14	8	5	1666	86	0	3.10	....	....	....	....	....	....	....
1992-93	**Montreal**	**NHL**	**26**	**17**	**5**	**1**	**1433**	**81**	**1**	**3.39**	**1**	**0**	**0**	**18**	**2**	**0**	**6.67**
	NHL Totals		**57**	**24**	**17**	**6**	**2857**	**159**	**2**	**3.34**	**4**	**0**	**1**	**31**	**4**	**0**	**7.74**

a QMJHL Second All-Star Team (1989)
b Shared Harry "Hap" Holmes Trophy (fewest goals-against-AHL) with J.C. Bergeron (1990)

RACINE, BRUCE

Goaltender. Catches left. 6', 178 lbs. Born, Cornwall, Ont., August 9, 1966.
(Pittsburgh's 3rd choice, 58th overall, in 1985 Entry Draft).

			Regular Season								Playoffs						
Season	Club	Lea	GP	W	L	T	Mins	GA	SO	Avg	GP	W	L	Mins	GA	SO	Avg
1984-85	Northeastern	H.E.	26	11	14	1	1615	103	1	3.83	....	....	....	....	....	....	....
1985-86	Northeastern	H.E.	32	17	14	1	1920	147	0	4.56	....	....	....	....	....	....	....
1986-87ab	Northeastern	H.E.	33	12	18	3	1966	133	0	4.06	....	....	....	....	....	....	....
1987-88b	Northeastern	H.E.	30	15	11	4	1808	108	1	3.58	....	....	....	....	....	....	....
1988-89	Muskegon	IHL	51	*37	11	0	*3039	184	*3	3.63	5	4	1	300	15	0	3.00
1989-90	Muskegon	IHL	49	29	15	4	2911	182	1	3.75	9	5	4	566	32	1	3.34
1990-91	Albany	IHL	29	7	18	1	1567	104	0	3.98	....	....	....	....	....	....	....
	Muskegon	IHL	9	4	4	1	516	40	0	4.65	....	....	....	....	....	....	....
1991-92	Muskegon	IHL	27	13	10	3	1559	91	1	3.50	1	0	1	60	6	0	6.00
1992-93	Cleveland	IHL	35	13	16	6	1949	140	1	4.31	2	0	0	37	2	0	3.24

a Hockey East First All-Star Team (1987)
b NCAA East First All-American Team (1987, 1988)

Signed as a free agent by **Toronto**, August 11, 1993.

RAM, JAMIE

Goaltender. Catches left. 5'11", 164 lbs. Born, Scarborough, Ont., January 18, 1971.
(NY Rangers' 10th choice, 213th overall, in 1991 Entry Draft).

			Regular Season								Playoffs						
Season	Club	Lea	GP	W	L	T	Mins	GA	SO	Avg	GP	W	L	Mins	GA	SO	Avg
1990-91	Michigan Tech	WCHA	14	5	9	0	826	57	0	4.14	....	....	....	....	....	....	....
1991-92	Michigan Tech	WCHA	23	9	9	1	1144	83	0	4.35	....	....	....	....	....	....	....
1992-93ab	Michigan Tech	WCHA	*36	16	14	5	*2078	115	0	3.32	....	....	....	....	....	....	....

a WCHA First All-Star Team (1993)
b NCAA West First All-American Team (1993)

RANFORD, BILL

Goaltender. Catches left. 5'10", 170 lbs. Born, Brandon, Man., December 14, 1966.
(Boston's 2nd choice, 52nd overall, in 1985 Entry Draft).

			Regular Season								Playoffs						
Season	Club	Lea	GP	W	L	T	Mins	GA	SO	Avg	GP	W	L	Mins	GA	SO	Avg
1983-84	N. Westminster	WHL	27	10	14	0	1450	130	0	5.38	1	0	0	27	2	0	4.44
1984-85	N. Westminster	WHL	38	19	17	0	2034	142	0	4.19	7	2	3	309	26	0	5.05
1985-86	**Boston**	**NHL**	**4**	**3**	**1**	**0**	**240**	**10**	**0**	**2.50**	**2**	**0**	**2**	**120**	**7**	**0**	**3.50**
	N. Westminster	WHL	53	17	29	1	2791	225	0	4.84	....	....	....	....	....	....	....
1986-87	**Boston**	**NHL**	**41**	**16**	**20**	**2**	**2234**	**124**	**3**	**3.33**	**2**	**0**	**2**	**123**	**8**	**0**	**3.90**
	Moncton	AHL	3	3	0	0	180	6	0	2.00	....	....	....	....	....	....	....
1987-88	Maine	AHL	51	27	16	6	2856	165	1	3.47	....	....	....	....	....	....	....
	Edmonton	**NHL**	**6**	**3**	**0**	**2**	**325**	**16**	**0**	**2.95**	....	....	....	....	....	....	....
1988-89	**Edmonton**	**NHL**	**29**	**15**	**8**	**2**	**1509**	**88**	**1**	**3.50**	....	....	....	....	....	....	....
1989-90a	**Edmonton**	**NHL**	**56**	**24**	**16**	**9**	**3107**	**165**	**1**	**3.19**	***22**	***16**	**6**	***1401**	**59**	**1**	**2.53**
1990-91	**Edmonton**	**NHL**	**60**	**27**	**27**	**3**	**3415**	**182**	**0**	**3.20**	**3**	**1**	**2**	**135**	**8**	**0**	**3.56**
1991-92	**Edmonton**	**NHL**	**67**	**27**	**26**	**10**	**3822**	**228**	**1**	**3.58**	**16**	**8**	**8**	**909**	**51**	***2**	**3.37**
1992-93	**Edmonton**	**NHL**	**67**	**17**	**38**	**6**	**3753**	**240**	**1**	**3.84**	....	....	....	....	....	....	....
	NHL Totals		**330**	**132**	**136**	**34**	**18405**	**1053**	**7**	**3.43**	**45**	**25**	**20**	**2688**	**133**	**3**	**2.97**

a Won Conn Smythe Trophy (1990)

Played in NHL All-Star Game (1991)

Traded to **Edmonton** by **Boston** with Geoff Courtnall and future considerations for Andy Moog, March 8, 1988.

REDDICK, ELDON

Goaltender. Catches left. 5'8", 170 lbs. Born, Halifax, N.S., October 6, 1964.

			Regular Season								Playoffs						
Season	Club	Lea	GP	W	L	T	Mins	GA	SO	Avg	GP	W	L	Mins	GA	SO	Avg
1982-83	Nanaimo	WHL	66	19	38	1	3549	383	0	6.46	....	....	....	....	....	....	....
1983-84	N. Westminster	WHL	50	24	22	2	2930	215	0	4.40	9	4	5	542	53	0	5.87
1984-85	Brandon	WHL	47	14	30	1	2585	243	0	5.64	....	....	....	....	....	....	....
1985-86	Ft. Wayne	IHL	29	15	11	0	1674	86	*3	3.00	....	....	....	....	....	....	....
1986-87	**Winnipeg**	**NHL**	**48**	**21**	**21**	**4**	**2762**	**149**	**0**	**3.24**	**3**	**0**	**2**	**166**	**10**	**0**	**3.61**
1987-88	**Winnipeg**	**NHL**	**28**	**9**	**13**	**3**	**1487**	**102**	**0**	**4.12**	....	....	....	....	....	....	....
	Moncton	AHL	9	2	6	1	545	26	0	2.86	....	....	....	....	....	....	....
1988-89	**Winnipeg**	**NHL**	**41**	**11**	**17**	**7**	**2109**	**144**	**0**	**4.10**	....	....	....	....	....	....	....
1989-90	**Edmonton**	**NHL**	**11**	**5**	**4**	**2**	**604**	**31**	**0**	**3.08**	**1**	**0**	**0**	**2**	**0**	**0**	**0.00**
	Cape Breton	AHL	15	9	4	1	821	54	0	3.95	....	....	....	....	....	....	....
	Phoenix	IHL	3	2	1	0	185	7	0	2.27	....	....	....	....	....	....	....
1990-91	**Edmonton**	**NHL**	**2**	**0**	**2**	**0**	**120**	**9**	**0**	**4.50**	....	....	....	....	....	....	....
	Cape Breton	AHL	31	19	10	0	1673	97	2	3.48	2	0	2	124	10	0	4.84
1991-92	Cape Breton	AHL	16	5	3	3	765	45	0	3.53	....	....	....	....	....	....	....
	Ft. Wayne	IHL	14	6	5	2	787	40	1	3.05	7	3	4	369	18	0	2.93
1992-93a	Ft. Wayne	IHL	54	33	16	4	3043	156	3	3.08	12	12	0	723	18	0	1.49
	NHL Totals		**130**	**46**	**57**	**16**	**7082**	**435**	**0**	**3.69**	**4**	**0**	**2**	**168**	**10**	**0**	**3.57**

a Won "Bud" Poile Trophy (IHL Playoff MVP) (1993)

Signed as a free agent by **Winnipeg**, September 27, 1985. Traded to **Edmonton** by **Winnipeg** for future considerations, September 28, 1989.

REESE, JEFF

Goaltender. Catches left. 5'9", 170 lbs. Born, Brantford, Ont., March 24, 1966.
(Toronto's 3rd choice, 67th overall, in 1984 Entry Draft).

			Regular Season								Playoffs						
Season	Club	Lea	GP	W	L	T	Mins	GA	SO	Avg	GP	W	L	Mins	GA	SO	Avg
1983-84	London	OHL	43	18	19	0	2308	173	0	4.50	6	3	3	327	27	0	4.95
1984-85	London	OHL	50	31	15	1	2878	186	1	3.88	8	5	2	440	20	1	2.73
1985-86	London	OHL	57	25	26	3	3281	215	0	3.93	5	0	4	299	25	0	5.02
1986-87	Newmarket	AHL	50	11	29	0	2822	193	1	4.10	....	....	....	....	....	....	....
1987-88	Toronto	NHL	5	1	2	1	249	17	0	4.10	....	....	....	....	....	....	....
	Newmarket	AHL	28	10	14	3	1587	103	0	3.89	....	....	....	....	....	....	....
1988-89	Toronto	NHL	10	2	6	1	486	40	0	4.94	....	....	....	....	....	....	....
	Newmarket	AHL	37	17	14	3	2072	132	0	3.82	....	....	....	....	....	....	....
1989-90	Toronto	NHL	21	9	6	3	1101	81	0	4.41	2	1	1	108	6	0	3.33
	Newmarket	AHL	7	3	2	2	431	29	0	4.04	....	....	....	....	....	....	....
1990-91	Toronto	NHL	30	6	13	3	1430	92	1	3.86	....	....	....	....	....	....	....
	Newmarket	AHL	3	2	1	0	180	7	0	2.33	....	....	....	....	....	....	....
1991-92	Toronto	NHL	8	1	5	1	413	20	1	2.91	....	....	....	....	....	....	....
	Calgary	NHL	12	3	2	2	587	37	0	3.78	....	....	....	....	....	....	....
1992-93	Calgary	NHL	26	14	4	1	1311	70	1	3.20	4	1	3	209	17	0	4.88
	NHL Totals		112	36	38	12	5577	357	3	3.84	6	2	4	317	23	0	4.35

Traded to **Calgary** with Craig Berube, Alexander Godynyuk, Gary Leeman and Michel Petit for Doug Gilmour, Jamie Macoun, Ric Natress, Rick Wamsley and Kent Manderville, January 2, 1992.

RHODES, DAMIAN

Goaltender. Catches left. 6', 165 lbs. Born, St. Paul, MN, May 28, 1969.
(Toronto's 6th choice, 112th overall, in 1987 Entry Draft).

			Regular Season								Playoffs						
Season	Club	Lea	GP	W	L	T	Mins	GA	SO	Avg	GP	W	L	Mins	GA	SO	Avg
1987-88	Michigan Tech	WCHA	29	16	10	1	1625	114	0	4.20	....	....	....	....	....	....	....
1988-89	Michigan Tech	WCHA	37	15	22	0	2216	163	0	4.41	....	....	....	....	....	....	....
1989-90	Michigan Tech	WCHA	25	6	17	0	1358	119	0	6.26	....	....	....	....	....	....	....
1990-91	Toronto	NHL	1	1	0	0	60	1	0	1.00	....	....	....	....	....	....	....
	Newmarket	AHL	38	8	24	3	2154	144	1	4.01	....	....	....	....	....	....	....
1991-92	St. John's	AHL	43	20	16	5	2454	148	0	3.62	6	4	1	331	16	0	2.90
1992-93	St. John's	AHL	*52	27	16	8	*3074	184	1	3.59	9	4	5	538	37	0	4.13
	NHL Totals		1	1	0	0	60	1	0	1.00	....	....	....	....	....	....	....

RICHARDS, MARK A.

Goaltender. Catches left. 5'8", 179 lbs. Born, Jamison, PA, July 24, 1969.
(Winnipeg's 1st choice, 19th overall, in 1990 Supplemental Draft).

			Regular Season								Playoffs						
Season	Club	Lea	GP	W	L	T	Mins	GA	SO	Avg	GP	W	L	Mins	GA	SO	Avg
1988-89	Lowell	H.E.	18	1	12	1	918	83	0	5.42	....	....	....	....	....	....	....
1989-90	Lowell	H.E.	32	11	19	2	1773	149	0	5.04	....	....	....	....	....	....	....
1990-91	Lowell	H.E.	22	5	13	1	1149	91	0	4.75	....	....	....	....	....	....	....
1991-92a	Lowell	H.E.	23	8	11	4	1393	97	0	4.18	....	....	....	....	....	....	....
1992-93	Moncton	AHL	13	6	6	1	736	49	0	3.99	4	1	3	231	19	0	4.94
	Toledo	ECHL	11	5	4	1	612	28	1	2.75	....	....	....	....	....	....	....
	Fort Wayne	IHL	3	1	0	0	139	11	0	4.75	....	....	....	....	....	....	....

a Hockey East First All-Star Team (1992)

RICHTER, MIKE

Goaltender. Catches left. 5'11", 182 lbs. Born, Abington, PA, September 22, 1966.
(NY Rangers' 2nd choice, 28th overall, in 1985 Entry Draft).

			Regular Season								Playoffs						
Season	Club	Lea	GP	W	L	T	Mins	GA	SO	Avg	GP	W	L	Mins	GA	SO	Avg
1985-86a	U. Wisconsin	WCHA	24	14	9	0	1394	92	1	3.96	....	....	....	....	....	....	....
1986-87b	U. Wisconsin	WCHA	36	19	16	1	2136	126	0	3.54	....	....	....	....	....	....	....
1987-88	Colorado	IHL	22	16	5	0	1298	68	1	3.14	10	5	3	536	35	0	3.92
	U.S. National	....	29	17	7	2	1559	86	0	3.31	....	....	....	....	....	....	....
	U.S. Olympic	....	4	2	2	0	230	15	0	3.91	....	....	....	....	....	....	....
1988-89	Denver	IHL	*57	23	26	0	3031	217	1	4.30	4	0	4	210	21	0	6.00
	NY Rangers	NHL	....	....	....	....	....	....	....	....	1	0	1	58	4	0	4.14
1989-90	NY Rangers	NHL	23	12	5	5	1320	66	0	3.00	6	3	2	330	19	0	3.45
	Flint	IHL	13	7	4	2	782	49	0	3.76	....	....	....	....	....	....	....
1990-91	NY Rangers	NHL	45	21	13	7	2596	135	0	3.12	6	2	4	313	14	*1	2.68
1991-92	NY Rangers	NHL	41	23	12	2	2298	119	3	3.11	7	4	2	412	24	1	3.50
1992-93	NY Rangers	NHL	38	13	19	3	2105	134	1	3.82	....	....	....	....	....	....	....
	Binghamton	AHL	5	4	0	1	305	6	0	1.18	....	....	....	....	....	....	....
	NHL Totals		147	69	49	17	8319	454	4	3.27	20	9	9	1113	61	2	3.29

a WCHA Rookie of the Year (1986)
b WCHA Second All-Star Team (1987)

Played in NHL All-Star Game (1992)

RIENDEAU, VINCENT (ree-EHN-doh)

Goaltender. Catches left. 5'10", 181 lbs. Born, St. Hyacinthe, Que., April 20, 1966.

			Regular Season								Playoffs						
Season	Club	Lea	GP	W	L	T	Mins	GA	SO	Avg	GP	W	L	Mins	GA	SO	Avg
1985-86a	Drummondville	QMJHL	57	33	20	3	3336	215	2	3.87	23	10	13	1271	106	1	5.00
1986-87b	Sherbrooke	AHL	41	25	14	0	2363	114	2	2.89	13	8	5	742	47	0	3.80
1987-88	Montreal	NHL	1	0	0	0	36	5	0	8.33	....	....	....	....	....	....	....
cd	Sherbrooke	AHL	44	27	13	3	2521	112	*4	*2.67	2	0	2	127	7	0	3.31
1988-89	St. Louis	NHL	32	11	15	5	1842	108	0	3.52	....	....	....	....	....	....	....
1989-90	St. Louis	NHL	43	17	19	5	2551	149	1	3.50	8	3	4	397	24	0	3.63
1990-91	St. Louis	NHL	44	29	9	6	2671	134	3	3.01	13	6	7	687	35	*1	3.06
1991-92	St. Louis	NHL	3	1	2	0	157	11	0	4.20	....	....	....	....	....	....	....
	Detroit	NHL	2	2	0	0	87	2	0	1.38	2	1	0	73	4	0	3.29
	Adirondack	AHL	3	2	1	0	179	8	0	2.68	....	....	....	....	....	....	....
1992-93	Detroit	NHL	22	13	4	2	1193	64	0	3.22	....	....	....	....	....	....	....
	NHL Totals		147	73	49	18	8537	473	4	3.32	23	10	11	1157	63	1	3.27

a QMJHL Second All-Star Team (1986)
b Won Harry "Hap" Holmes Memorial Trophy (AHL Leading Goaltender) (1987)
c Shared Harry "Hap" Holmes Memorial Trophy (AHL Leading Goaltender) with Jocelyn Perreault (1988)
d AHL Second All-Star Team (1988)

Signed as a free agent by **Montreal**, October 9, 1985. Traded to **St. Louis** by **Montreal** with Sergio Momesso for Jocelyn Lemieux, Darrell May and St. Louis' second round choice (Patrice Brisebois) in 1989 Entry Draft, August 9, 1988. Traded to **Detroit** by **St. Louis** for Rick Zombo, October 18, 1991.

RISDALE, MIKE

Goaltender. Catches left. 5'9", 150 lbs. Born, Tofield, Alta., June 18, 1972.

			Regular Season								Playoffs						
Season	Club	Lea	GP	W	L	T	Mins	GA	SO	Avg	GP	W	L	Mins	GA	SO	Avg
1990-91	Regina	WHL	33	....	....	....	1566	100	3	3.83	3	....	....	100	10	0	6.00
1991-92	Regina	WHL	61	24	29	3	3521	232	1	3.95	2	....	....	60	3	0	3.00
1992-93	Regina	WHL	62	29	24	1	3252	214	2	3.95	....	....	....	....	....	....	....

RONNQVIST, PETTER

Goaltender. Catches left. 5'10", 154 lbs. Born, Stockholm, Sweden, February 7, 1973.
(Ottawa's 12th choice, 264th overall, in 1992 Entry Draft).

			Regular Season								Playoffs						
Season	Club	Lea	GP	W	L	T	Mins	GA	SO	Avg	GP	W	L	Mins	GA	SO	Avg
1991-92	Nacka	Swe.2						UNAVAILABLE									
1992-93	Djurgarden	Swe.	7	....	....	....	380	20	0	3.15	1	....	....	60	5	0	5.00

ROUSSEL, DOMINIC (roo-SEHL)

Goaltender. Catches left. 6'1", 185 lbs. Born, Hull, Que., February 22, 1970.
(Philadelphia's 4th choice, 63rd overall, in 1988 Entry Draft).

			Regular Season								Playoffs						
Season	Club	Lea	GP	W	L	T	Mins	GA	SO	Avg	GP	W	L	Mins	GA	SO	Avg
1987-88	Trois-Rivières	QMJHL	51	18	25	4	2905	251	0	5.18	....	....	....	....	....	....	....
1988-89	Shawinigan	QMJHL	46	24	15	2	2555	171	0	4.02	10	6	4	638	36	0	3.39
1989-90	Shawinigan	QMJHL	37	20	14	1	1985	133	0	4.02	2	1	1	120	12	0	6.00
1990-91	Hershey	AHL	45	20	14	7	2507	151	1	3.61	7	3	4	366	21	0	3.44
1991-92	Philadelphia	NHL	17	7	8	2	922	40	1	2.60	....	....	....	....	....	....	....
	Hershey	AHL	35	15	11	6	2040	121	1	3.56	....	....	....	....	....	....	....
1992-93	Philadelphia	NHL	34	13	11	5	1769	111	1	3.76	....	....	....	....	....	....	....
	Hershey	AHL	6	0	3	3	372	23	0	3.71	....	....	....	....	....	....	....
	NHL Totals		51	20	19	7	2691	151	2	3.37	....	....	....	....	....	....	....

ROUSSON, BORIS

Goaltender. Catches left. 6'2", 195 lbs. Born, Val D'or, Que., June 14, 1970.

			Regular Season								Playoffs						
Season	Club	Lea	GP	W	L	T	Mins	GA	SO	Avg	GP	W	L	Mins	GA	SO	Avg
1988-89	Laval	QMJHL	22	12	7	0	....	....	....	4.44	....	....	....	....	....	....	....
1989-90	Granby	QMJHL	39	10	26	0	....	....	....	4.56	....	....	....	....	....	....	....
1990-91a	Granby	QMJHL	*63	28	25	6	*3693	190	0	3.09	....	....	....	....	....	....	....
1991-92	Binghamton	AHL	38	16	15	6	2261	123	1	3.26	....	....	....	....	....	....	....
1992-93b	Binghamton	AHL	31	18	9	4	1847	115	0	3.74	1	0	0	20	2	0	6.00

a QMJHL Second All-Star Team (1991)
b Shared Harry "Hap" Holmes Memorial Trophy (AHL's Top Goaltender) with Corey Hirsch (1993)

Signed as a free agent by **NY Rangers**, March 31, 1991.

ROY, ALLAIN (WAH)

Goaltender. Catches left. 5'10", 170 lbs. Born, Campbellton, N.B., February 6, 1970.
(Winnipeg's 6th choice, 69th overall, in 1989 Entry Draft).

			Regular Season								Playoffs						
Season	Club	Lea	GP	W	L	T	Mins	GA	SO	Avg	GP	W	L	Mins	GA	SO	Avg
1988-89	Harvard	ECAC	16	14	2	0	952	40	0	2.46	....	....	....	....	....	....	....
1989-90	Harvard	ECAC	15	7	8	0	867	54	1	3.74	....	....	....	....	....	....	....
1990-91	Harvard	ECAC	14	7	5	2	821	45	*1	3.29	....	....	....	....	....	....	....
1991-92	Harvard	ECAC	15	9	4	2	919	39	1	*2.55	....	....	....	....	....	....	....
1992-93	Cdn. National	....	36	16	15	2	2055	120	1	3.50	....	....	....	....	....	....	....

ROY, PATRICK (WAH)

Goaltender. Catches left. 6', 182 lbs. Born, Quebec City, Que., October 5, 1965.
(Montreal's 4th choice, 51st overall, in 1984 Entry Draft).

			Regular Season								Playoffs						
Season	Club	Lea	GP	W	L	T	Mins	GA	SO	Avg	GP	W	L	Mins	GA	SO	Avg
1982-83	Granby	QMJHL	54	....	....	....	2808	293	0	6.26	....	....	....	....	....	....	....
1983-84	Granby	QMJHL	61	29	29	1	3585	265	0	4.44	4	0	4	244	22	0	5.41
1984-85	Montreal	NHL	1	1	0	0	20	0	0	0.00	....	....	....	....	....	....	....
	Granby	QMJHL	44	16	25	1	2463	228	0	5.55	....	....	....	....	....	....	....
	Sherbrooke	AHL	1	1	0	0	60	4	0	4.00	13	10	3	*769	37	0	*2.89
1985-86ab	Montreal	NHL	47	23	18	3	2651	148	1	3.35	20	*15	5	1218	39	*1	1.92
1986-87c	Montreal	NHL	46	22	16	6	2686	131	1	2.93	6	4	2	330	22	0	4.00
1987-88cd	Montraal	NHL	45	23	12	9	2586	125	3	2.90	8	3	4	430	24	0	3.35
1988-89 cefg	Montreal	NHL	48	33	5	6	2744	113	4	*2.47	19	13	6	1206	42	2	*2.09
1989-90efg	Montreal	NHL	54	*31	16	5	3173	134	3	2.53	11	5	6	641	26	1	2.43
1990-91d	Montreal	NHL	48	25	15	6	2835	128	1	2.71	13	7	5	785	40	0	3.06
1991-92efh	Montreal	NHL	67	36	22	8	3935	155	*5	*2.36	11	4	7	686	30	1	2.62
1992-93a	Montreal	NHL	62	31	25	5	3595	192	2	3.20	20	*16	4	1293	46	0	*2.13
	NHL Totals		418	225	129	48	24225	1126	20	2.79	108	67	39	6589	269	5	2.45

a Won Conn Smythe Trophy (1986, 1993)
b NHL All-Rookie Team (1986)
c Shared William Jennings Trophy with Brian Hayward (1987, 1988, 1989)
d NHL Second All-Star Team (1988, 1991)
e Won Vezina Trophy (1989, 1990, 1992)
f NHL First All-Star Team (1989, 1990, 1992)
g Won Trico Goaltending Award (1989, 1990)
h Won William M. Jennings Award (1992)

Played in NHL All-Star Game (1988, 1990-93)

RYDER, DAN

Goaltender. Catches left. 6'1", 190 lbs. Born, Kitchener, Ont., October 24, 1972.
(San Jose's 5th choice, 89th overall, in 1991 Entry Draft).

			Regular Season								Playoffs						
Season	Club	Lea	GP	W	L	T	Mins	GA	SO	Avg	GP	W	L	Mins	GA	SO	Avg
1990-91	Hamilton	OHL	1	0	0	0	40	1	0	1.50	....	....	....	....	....	....	....
	Sudbury	OHL	37	18	9	4	2089	126	....	3.62	2	0	0	26	1	0	2.31
1991-92	Sudbury	OHL	23	9	11	1	1157	91	0	4.72	....	....	....	....	....	....	....
	Ottawa	OHL	24	16	6	0	1380	55	3	*3.29	11	5	6	625	38	0	3.64
1992-93	Johnstown	ECHL	4	1	1	1	214	15	0	4.21	....	....	....	....	....	....	....
	Columbus	ECHL	1	0	1	0	60	6	0	6.00	....	....	....	....	....	....	....
	Kansas City	IHL	10	3	3	2	514	35	0	4.09	....	....	....	....	....	....	....

SAAL, JASON

Goaltender. Catches left. 5'9", 165 lbs. Born, Detroit, MI, February 1, 1975.
(Los Angeles' 5th choice, 117th overall, in 1993 Entry Draft).

			Regular Season								Playoffs						
Season	Club	Lea	GP	W	L	T	Mins	GA	SO	Avg	GP	W	L	Mins	GA	SO	Avg
1992-93	Detroit	OHL	23	11	8	1	1289	85	0	3.96	3	0	0	42	2	0	2.86

SALO, TOMMY

Goaltender. Catches left. 5'11", 161 lbs. Born, Surahammar, Sweden, February 1, 1971.
(NY Islanders' 5th choice, 118th overall, in 1993 Entry Draft).

			Regular Season								Playoffs						
Season	Club	Lea	GP	W	L	T	Mins	GA	SO	Avg	GP	W	L	Mins	GA	SO	Avg
1990-91	Vasteras	Swe.	2	....	....	....	100	11	0	6.60	....	....	....	....	....	....	....
1991-92	Vasteras	Swe.	....	....	....	....	....	....	....	....	....	....	....	....	....	....	....
1992-93	Vasteras	Swe.	24	....	....	....	1431	59	2	2.47	2	....	....	120	6	0	3.00

SALZMAN, WADE

Goaltender. Catches right. 6'3", 195 lbs. Born, Duluth, MN, May 30, 1974.
(St. Louis' 12th choice, 259th overall, in 1992 Entry Draft).

			Regular Season								Playoffs						
Season	Club	Lea	GP	W	L	T	Mins	GA	SO	Avg	GP	W	L	Mins	GA	SO	Avg
1991-92	Duluth East	HS	22	....	....	....	990	60	....	2.73	....	....	....	....	....	....	....
1992-93	Notre Dame	CCHA						DID NOT PLAY									

SARJEANT, GEOFF

Goaltender. Catches left. 5'9", 180 lbs. Born, Newmarket, Ont., November 30, 1969.
(St. Louis' 1st choice, 17th overall, in 1990 Supplemental Draft).

			Regular Season								Playoffs						
Season	Club	Lea	GP	W	L	T	Mins	GA	SO	Avg	GP	W	L	Mins	GA	SO	Avg
1988-89	Michigan Tech	WCHA	6	0	3	2	329	22	0	4.01	....	....	....	....	....	....	....
1989-90	Michigan Tech	WCHA	19	4	13	0	1043	94	0	5.41	....	....	....	....	....	....	....
1990-91	Michigan Tech	WCHA	23	5	15	3	1540	97	0	3.78	....	....	....	....	....	....	....
1991-92	Michigan Tech	WCHA	23	7	13	0	1201	90	1	4.50	....	....	....	....	....	....	....
1992-93	Peoria	IHL	41	22	14	3	2356	130	0	3.31	3	0	3	179	13	0	4.36

SAURDIFF, CORWIN

Goaltender. Catches left. 5'11", 168 lbs. Born, Warroad, MN, October 17, 1972.
(San Jose's 9th choice, 177th overall, in 1991 Entry Draft).

			Regular Season								Playoffs						
Season	Club	Lea	GP	W	L	T	Mins	GA	SO	Avg	GP	W	L	Mins	GA	SO	Avg
1991-92	N. Michigan	WCHA	34	22	9	1	1926	110	0	3.43	....	....	....	....	....	....	....
1992-93	N. Michigan	WCHA	29	13	12	3	1629	101	1	3.72	....	....	....	....	....	....	....

SCHOEN, BRYAN

Goaltender. Catches left. 6'2", 180 lbs. Born, St. Paul, MN, September 9, 1970.
(Minnesota's 6th choice, 91st overall, in 1989 Entry Draft).

			Regular Season								Playoffs						
Season	Club	Lea	GP	W	L	T	Mins	GA	SO	Avg	GP	W	L	Mins	GA	SO	Avg
1989-90	U. of Denver	WCHA	18	8	9	0	1040	81	0	4.67	....	....	....	....	....	....	....
1990-91	U. of Denver	WCHA	19	4	13	2	1103	94	0	5.11	....	....	....	....	....	....	....
1991-92	U. of Denver	WCHA	36	9	25	2	2039	167	0	4.91	....	....	....	....	....	....	....
1992-93	U. of Denver	WCHA	35	*18	15	2	1860	121	0	3.90	....	....	....	....	....	....	....

Claimed by **San Jose** from **Minnesota** in Dispersal Draft, May 30, 1991.

SCHWAB, COREY

Goaltender. Catches left. 6', 180 lbs. Born, Battleford, Sask., November 4, 1970.
(New Jersey's 12th choice, 200th overall, in 1990 Entry Draft).

			Regular Season								Playoffs						
Season	Club	Lea	GP	W	L	T	Mins	GA	SO	Avg	GP	W	L	Mins	GA	SO	Avg
1988-89	Seattle	WHL	10	2	2	0	386	31	0	4.82	....	....	....	....	....	....	....
1989-90	Seattle	WHL	27	15	2	1	1150	69	0	3.60	....	....	....	....	....	....	....
1990-91	Seattle	WHL	*58	32	18	3	*3289	224	0	4.09	6	1	5	382	25	0	3.93
1991-92	Utica	AHL	24	9	12	1	1322	95	0	4.31	....	....	....	....	....	....	....
	Cincinnati	ECHL	8	6	0	1	450	31	0	4.13	9	6	3	540	29	0	3.22
1992-93	Utica	AHL	40	18	16	5	2387	169	*2	4.25	1	0	1	59	6	0	6.10
	Cincinnati	IHL	3	1	2	0	185	17	0	5.51	....	....	....	....	....	....	....

SHARPLES, SCOTT

Goaltender. Catches left. 6', 180 lbs. Born, Montreal, Que., March 1, 1968.
(Calgary's 8th choice, 184th overall, in 1986 Entry Draft).

			Regular Season								Playoffs						
Season	Club	Lea	GP	W	L	T	Mins	GA	SO	Avg	GP	W	L	Mins	GA	SO	Avg
1986-87	U. of Michigan	CCHA	32	12	16	1	1720	148	1	5.14	....	....	....	....	....	....	....
1987-88	U. of Michigan	CCHA	33	18	15	0	1930	132	0	4.10	....	....	....	....	....	....	....
1988-89	U. of Michigan	CCHA	33	17	11	2	1887	116	0	3.69	....	....	....	....	....	....	....
1989-90	U. of Michigan	CCHA	*39	20	10	0	*2165	117	0	3.24	....	....	....	....	....	....	....
	Salt Lake	IHL	3	0	3	0	178	13	0	4.38	....	....	....	....	....	....	....
1990-91	Salt Lake	IHL	37	21	11	1	2097	124	2	3.55	4	0	3	188	14	0	4.47
1991-92	**Calgary**	**NHL**	**1**	**0**	**0**	**1**	**65**	**4**	**0**	**3.69**	....	....	....	....	....	....	....
	Salt Lake	IHL	35	9	18	4	1936	121	0	3.75	1	0	1	60	7	0	7.00
1992-93	St. John's	AHL	25	9	8	3	1168	80	0	4.11	1	0	0	7	0	0	0.00
	Brantford	Col.	7	5	1	0	400	27	0	4.05	....	....	....	....	....	....	....
	NHL Totals		**1**	**0**	**0**	**1**	**65**	**4**	**0**	**3.69**	....	....	....	....	....	....	....

SHIELDS, STEVE

Goaltender. Catches left. 6'3", 210 lbs. Born, Toronto, Ont., July 19, 1972.
(Buffalo's 5th choice, 101st overall, in 1991 Entry Draft).

			Regular Season								Playoffs						
Season	Club	Lea	GP	W	L	T	Mins	GA	SO	Avg	GP	W	L	Mins	GA	SO	Avg
1990-91	U. of Michigan	CCHA	37	26	6	3	1963	106	0	3.24	....	....	....	....	....	....	....
1991-92	U. of Michigan	CCHA	*37	*27	7	2	*2090	99	1	2.84	....	....	....	....	....	....	....
1992-93ab	U. of Michigan	CCHA	*39	*30	6	2	2027	75	....	*2.22	....	....	....	....	....	....	....

a CCHA First All-Star Team (1993)
b NCAA West Second All-American Team (1993)

SHTALENKOV, MIKHAIL

Goaltender. Catches left. 6'2", 180 lbs. Born, Moscow, Soviet Union, October 20, 1965.
(Anaheim's 5th choice, 108th overall, in 1993 Entry Draft).

			Regular Season								Playoffs						
Season	Club	Lea	GP	W	L	T	Mins	GA	SO	Avg	GP	W	L	Mins	GA	SO	Avg
1986-87a	Moscow D'amo	USSR	17	....	....	....	893	36	1	2.41	....	....	....	....	....	....	....
1987-88	Moscow D'amo	USSR	25	....	....	....	1302	72	1	3.31	....	....	....	....	....	....	....
1988-89	Moscow D'amo	USSR	4	....	....	....	80	3	0	2.25	....	....	....	....	....	....	....
1989-90	Moscow D'amo	USSR	6	....	....	....	20	1	0	3.00	....	....	....	....	....	....	....
1990-91	Moscow D'amo	USSR	31	....	....	....	1568	56	2	2.14	....	....	....	....	....	....	....
1991-92	Moscow D'amo	CIS	27	....	....	....	1268	45	1	2.12	....	....	....	....	....	....	....
1992-93	Milwaukee	IHL	47	26	14	5	2669	135	2	3.03	3	1	2	209	11	....	3.16

a Soviet Rookie of the Year (1987)

SHULMISTRA, RICHARD

Goaltender. Catches right. 6'2", 186 lbs. Born, Sudbury, Ont., April 1, 1971.
(Quebec's 1st choice, 4th overall, in 1992 Supplemental Draft).

			Regular Season								Playoffs						
Season	Club	Lea	GP	W	L	T	Mins	GA	SO	Avg	GP	W	L	Mins	GA	SO	Avg
1990-91	Miami-Ohio	CCHA	20	2	12	2	920	80	0	5.21	....	....	....	....	....	....	....
1991-92	Miami-Ohio	CCHA	19	3	5	2	850	67	0	4.72	....	....	....	....	....	....	....
1992-93a	Miami-Ohio	CCHA	33	22	6	4	1949	88	....	2.71	....	....	....	....	....	....	....

a CCHA Second All-Star Team (1993)

SIDORKIEWICZ, PETER (sih-DOHR-kuh-vihch)

Goaltender. Catches left. 5'9", 180 lbs. Born, Dabrowa Bialostocka, Poland, June 29, 1963.
(Washington's 5th choice, 91st overall, in 1981 Entry Draft).

			Regular Season								Playoffs						
Season	Club	Lea	GP	W	L	T	Mins	GA	SO	Avg	GP	W	L	Mins	GA	SO	Avg
1980-81	Oshawa	OHA	7	3	3	0	308	24	0	4.68	5	2	2	266	20	0	4.52
1981-82	Oshawa	OHL	29	14	11	1	1553	123	*2	4.75	1	0	0	13	1	0	4.62
1982-83	Oshawa	OHL	60	36	20	3	3536	213	0	3.61	17	15	1	1020	60	0	3.53
1983-84a	Oshawa	OHL	52	28	21	1	2966	250	1	4.15	7	3	4	420	27	*1	3.86
1984-85	Binghamton	AHL	45	31	9	5	2691	137	3	3.05	8	4	4	481	31	0	3.87
	Fort Wayne	IHL	10	4	4	2	590	43	0	4.37	....	....	....	....	....	....	....
1985-86	Binghamton	AHL	49	21	22	3	2819	150	2	*3.19	4	1	3	235	12	0	3.06
1986-87b	Binghamton	AHL	57	23	16	0	3304	161	4	2.92	13	6	7	794	36	0	*2.72
1987-88	**Hartford**	**NHL**	**1**	**0**	**1**	**0**	**60**	**6**	**0**	**6.00**	....	....	....	....	....	....	....
	Binghamton	AHL	42	19	17	3	2345	144	0	3.68	3	0	2	147	8	0	3.27
1988-89c	**Hartford**	**NHL**	**44**	**22**	**18**	**4**	**2635**	**133**	**4**	**3.03**	**2**	**0**	**2**	**124**	**8**	**0**	**3.87**
1989-90	**Hartford**	**NHL**	**46**	**19**	**19**	**7**	**2703**	**161**	**1**	**3.57**	**7**	**3**	**4**	**429**	**23**	**0**	**3.22**
1990-91	**Hartford**	**NHL**	**52**	**21**	**22**	**7**	**2953**	**164**	**1**	**3.33**	**6**	**2**	**4**	**359**	**24**	**0**	**4.01**
1991-92	**Hartford**	**NHL**	**35**	**9**	**19**	**6**	**1995**	**111**	**2**	**3.34**	....	....	....	....	....	....	....
1992-93	**Ottawa**	**NHL**	**64**	**8**	**46**	**3**	**3388**	**250**	**0**	**4.43**	....	....	....	....	....	....	....
	NHL Totals		**242**	**79**	**125**	**27**	**13734**	**825**	**8**	**3.60**	**15**	**5**	**10**	**912**	**55**	**0**	**3.62**

a OHL Third All-Star Team (1984)
b AHL Second All-Star Team (1987)
c NHL All-Rookie Team (1989)

Played in NHL All-Star Game (1993)

Traded to **Hartford** by **Washington** with Dean Evason for David Jensen, March 12, 1985. Claimed by **Ottawa** from **Hartford** in Expansion Draft, June 18, 1992. Traded to **New Jersey** by **Ottawa** with future considerations (Mike Peluso, June 26, 1993) for Craig Billington, Troy Mallette and New Jersey's fourth round choice (Cosmo Dupaul) in 1993 Entry Draft, June 20, 1993.

SNOW, GARTH

Goaltender. Catches left. 6'3", 200 lbs. Born, Wrentham, MA, July 28, 1969.
(Quebec's 6th choice, 114th overall, in 1987 Entry Draft).

			Regular Season								Playoffs						
Season	Club	Lea	GP	W	L	T	Mins	GA	SO	Avg	GP	W	L	Mins	GA	SO	Avg
1988-89	U. of Maine	H.E.	5	2	2	0	241	14	1	3.49	....	....	....	....	....	....	....
1989-90								DID NOT PLAY									
1990-91	U. of Maine	H.E.	25	*18	4	0	1290	64	2	2.98	....	....	....	....	....	....	....
1991-92a	U. of Maine	H.E.	31	*25	4	2	1792	73	*2	*2.44	....	....	....	....	....	....	....
1992-93b	U. of Maine	H.E.	23	*21	0	1	1210	42	1	*2.08	....	....	....	....	....	....	....

a Hockey East Second All-Star Team (1992)
b NCAA Final Four All-Tournament Team (1993)

SODERSTROM, TOMMY (SOH-der-strom)

Goaltender. Catches left. 5'9", 165 lbs. Born, Stockholm, Sweden, July 17, 1969.
(Philadelphia's 14th choice, 214th overall, in 1990 Entry Draft).

			Regular Season								Playoffs						
Season	Club	Lea	GP	W	L	T	Mins	GA	SO	Avg	GP	W	L	Mins	GA	SO	Avg
1989-90	Djurgarden	Swe.	4	....	....	....	240	14	0	3.50	....	....	....	....	....	....	....
1990-91	Djurgarden	Swe.	39	....	....	....	2340	104	3	2.67	7	....	....	423	10	2	1.42
1991-92	Djurgarden	Swe.	39	....	....	....	2340	109	4	2.79	10	....	....	635	28	0	2.65
1992-93	**Philadelphia**	**NHL**	**44**	**20**	**17**	**6**	**2512**	**143**	**5**	**3.42**	....	....	....	....	....	....	....
	Hershey	AHL	7	4	1	0	373	15	0	2.41	....	....	....	....	....	....	....
	NHL Totals		**44**	**20**	**17**	**6**	**2512**	**143**	**5**	**3.42**	....	....	....	....	....	....	....

STAUBER, ROBB

Goaltender. Catches left. 5'11", 180 lbs. Born, Duluth, MN, November 25, 1967.
(Los Angeles' 5th choice, 107th overall, in 1986 Entry Draft).

			Regular Season								Playoffs						
Season	Club	Lea	GP	W	L	T	Mins	GA	SO	Avg	GP	W	L	Mins	GA	SO	Avg
1986-87	U. Minnesota	WCHA	20	13	5	0	1072	63	0	3.53	....	....	....	....	....	....	....
1987-88abcd	U. Minnesota	WCHA	44	34	10	0	2621	119	5	2.72	....	....	....	....	....	....	....
1988-89e	U. Minnesota	WCHA	34	26	8	0	2024	82	0	2.43	....	....	....	....	....	....	....
1989-90	**Los Angeles**	**NHL**	**2**	**0**	**1**	**0**	**83**	**11**	**0**	**7.95**	....	....	....	....	....	....	....
	New Haven	AHL	14	6	6	2	851	43	0	3.03	5	2	3	302	24	0	4.77
1990-91	New Haven	AHL	33	13	16	4	1882	115	1	3.67	....	....	....	....	....	....	....
	Phoenix	IHL	4	1	2	0	160	11	0	4.13	....	....	....	....	....	....	....
1991-92	Phoenix	IHL	22	8	12	1	1242	80	0	3.86	....	....	....	....	....	....	....
1992-93	**Los Angeles**	**NHL**	**31**	**15**	**8**	**4**	**1735**	**111**	**0**	**3.84**	**4**	**3**	**1**	**240**	**16**	**0**	**4.00**
	NHL Totals		**33**	**15**	**9**	**4**	**1818**	**122**	**0**	**4.03**	**4**	**3**	**1**	**240**	**16**	**0**	**4.00**

a Won Hobey Baker Memorial Award (Top U.S. Collegiate Player) (1988)
b NCAA West First All-American Team (1988)
c WCHA Player of the Year (1988)
d WCHA First All-Star Team (1988)
e WCHA Second All-Star Team (1989)

STOLP, JEFFREY

Goaltender. Catches left. 6', 180 lbs. Born, Nashwauk, MN, June 20, 1970.
(Minnesota's 4th choice, 64th overall, in 1988 Entry Draft).

			Regular Season								Playoffs						
Season	Club	Lea	GP	W	L	T	Mins	GA	SO	Avg	GP	W	L	Mins	GA	SO	Avg
1988-89	U. Minnesota	WCHA	16	7	2	3	742	45	0	3.64	....	....	....	....	....	....	....
1989-90	U. Minnesota	WCHA	10	5	1	0	417	33	1	4.75	....	....	....	....	....	....	....
1990-91	U. Minnesota	WCHA	32	18	8	3	1766	82	2	2.79	....	....	....	....	....	....	....
1991-92a	U. Minnesota	WCHA	33	25	7	0	1858	88	0	2.84	....	....	....	....	....	....	....
1992-93	Dayton	ECHL	27	12	13	2	1550	99	0	3.83	....	....	....	....	....	....	....
	Kalamazoo	IHL	14	2	11	1	733	62	0	5.08	....	....	....	....	....	....	....

a WCHA Second All-Star Team (1992)

TABARACCI, RICHARD (RICK)

Goaltender. Catches left. 5'11", 179 lbs. Born, Toronto, Ont., January 2, 1969.
(Pittsburgh's 2nd choice, 26th overall, in 1987 Entry Draft).

			Regular Season								Playoffs						
Season	Club	Lea	GP	W	L	T	Mins	GA	SO	Avg	GP	W	L	Mins	GA	SO	Avg
1986-87	Cornwall	OHL	59	23	32	3	3347	290	1	5.20	5	1	4	303	26	0	3.17
1987-88a	Cornwall	OHL	58	*33	18	6	3448	200	*3	3.48	11	5	6	642	37	0	3.46
	Muskegon	IHL	....	....	....	....	....	....	....	....	1	0	0	13	1	0	4.62
1988-89	**Pittsburgh**	**NHL**	**1**	**0**	**0**	**0**	**33**	**4**	**0**	**7.27**	....	....	....	....	....	....	....
b	Cornwall	OHL	50	24	20	5	2974	210	1	4.24	18	10	8	1080	65	*1	3.61
1989-90	Moncton	AHL	27	10	15	2	1580	107	2	4.06	....	....	....	....	....	....	....
	Fort Wayne	IHL	22	8	9	1	1064	73	0	4.12	3	1	2	159	19	0	7.17
1990-91	**Winnipeg**	**NHL**	**24**	**4**	**9**	**4**	**1093**	**71**	**1**	**3.90**	....	....	....	....	....	....	....
	Moncton	AHL	11	4	5	2	645	41	0	3.81	....	....	....	....	....	....	....
1991-92	**Winnipeg**	**NHL**	**18**	**6**	**7**	**3**	**966**	**52**	**0**	**3.23**	**7**	**3**	**4**	**387**	**26**	**0**	**4.03**
	Moncton	AHL	23	10	11	1	1313	80	0	3.66	....	....	....	....	....	....	....
1992-93	**Winnipeg**	**NHL**	**19**	**5**	**10**	**0**	**959**	**70**	**0**	**4.38**	....	....	....	....	....	....	....
	Moncton	AHL	5	2	1	2	290	18	0	3.72	....	....	....	....	....	....	....
	Washington	**NHL**	**6**	**3**	**2**	**0**	**343**	**10**	**2**	**1.75**	**4**	**1**	**3**	**304**	**14**	**0**	**2.76**
	NHL Totals		**68**	**18**	**28**	**7**	**3394**	**207**	**3**	**3.66**	**11**	**4**	**7**	**691**	**40**	**0**	**3.47**

a OHL First All-Star Team (1988)
b OHL Second All-Star Team (1989)

Traded to **Winnipeg** by **Pittsburgh** with Randy Cunneyworth and Dave McLlwain for Jim Kyte, Andrew McBain and Randy Gilhen, June 17, 1989. Traded to **Washington** by **Winnipeg** for Jim Hrivnak and future considerations, March 22, 1993.

TAKKO, KARI (TAH-koh)

Goaltender. Catches left. 6'2", 189 lbs. Born, Uusikaupunki, Finland, June 23, 1962.
(Minnesota's 5th choice, 97th overall, in 1984 Entry Draft).

			Regular Season								Playoffs						
Season	Club	Lea	GP	W	L	T	Mins	GA	SO	Avg	GP	W	L	Mins	GA	SO	Avg
1978-79	Assat	Fin.	2	....	....	....	....	2	....	....	....	....	....	....	....	....	....
1979-80	Assat	Fin.	2	....	....	....	....	8	....	....	....	....	....	....	....	....	....
1980-81	Assat	Fin.	4	....	....	....	....	16	....	....	....	....	....	....	....	....	....
1981-82	Assat	Fin.	14	....	....	....	....	60	....	....	....	....	....	....	....	....	....
1982-83	Assat	Fin.	21	....	....	....	....	77	0	....	....	....	....	....	....	....	....
1983-84	Assat	Fin.	32	....	....	....	....	102	3	....	9	....	....	....	37	0	....
1984-85	Assat	Fin.	35	....	....	....	....	123	3	....	8	....	....	....	32	0	....
1985-86	**Minnesota**	**NHL**	**1**	**0**	**1**	**0**	**60**	**3**	**0**	**3.00**	....	....	....	....	....	....	....
	Springfield	AHL	43	18	19	3	2286	161	1	4.05	....	....	....	....	....	....	....
1986-87	**Minnesota**	**NHL**	**38**	**13**	**18**	**4**	**2075**	**119**	**0**	**3.44**	....	....	....	....	....	....	....
	Springfield	AHL	5	3	2	0	300	16	1	3.20	....	....	....	....	....	....	....
1987-88	**Minnesota**	**NHL**	**37**	**8**	**19**	**6**	**1919**	**143**	**1**	**4.47**	....	....	....	....	....	....	....
1988-89	**Minnesota**	**NHL**	**32**	**8**	**15**	**4**	**1603**	**93**	**0**	**3.48**	**3**	**0**	**1**	**105**	**7**	**0**	**4.00**
1989-90	Kalamazoo	IHL	1	0	1	0	59	5	0	5.08	....	....	....	....	....	....	....
	Minnesota	**NHL**	**21**	**4**	**12**	**0**	**1012**	**68**	**0**	**4.03**	**1**	**0**	**0**	**4**	**0**	**0**	**0.00**
1990-91	**Minnesota**	**NHL**	**2**	**0**	**2**	**0**	**119**	**12**	**0**	**6.05**	....	....	....	....	....	....	....
	Kalamazoo	IHL	5	4	1	0	300	10	1	2.00	....	....	....	....	....	....	....
	Edmonton	**NHL**	**11**	**4**	**4**	**0**	**529**	**37**	**0**	**4.20**	....	....	....	....	....	....	....
1991-92	Assat	Fin.	28	....	....	....	1628	98	1	3.61	6	....	....	359	17	1	2.84
1992-93	Assat	Fin.	45	....	....	....	2723	138	3	3.04	7	....	....	430	29	0	4.05
	NHL Totals		**142**	**37**	**71**	**14**	**7317**	**475**	**1**	**3.90**	**4**	**0**	**1**	**109**	**7**	**0**	**3.85**

Traded to **Edmonton** by **Minnesota** for Bruce Bell, November 22, 1990.

TANNER, JOHN

Goaltender. Catches left. 6'3", 182 lbs. Born, Cambridge, Ont., March 17, 1971.
(Quebec's 4th choice, 54th overall, in 1989 Entry Draft).

			Regular Season								Playoffs						
Season	Club	Lea	GP	W	L	T	Mins	GA	SO	Avg	GP	W	L	Mins	GA	SO	Avg
1987-88a	Peterborough	OHL	26	18	4	3	1532	88	0	3.45	2	1	0	98	3	0	1.84
1988-89a	Peterborough	OHL	34	22	10	0	1923	107	2	*3.34	8	4	3	369	23	0	3.74
1989-90	**Quebec**	**NHL**	**1**	**0**	**1**	**0**	**60**	**3**	**0**	**3.00**	....	....	....	....	....	....	....
	Peterborough	OHL	18	6	8	2	1037	70	0	4.05	....	....	....	....	....	....	....
	London	OHL	19	12	5	1	1097	53	1	2.90	6	2	4	341	24	0	4.22
1990-91	**Quebec**	**NHL**	**6**	**1**	**3**	**1**	**228**	**16**	**0**	**4.21**	....	....	....	....	....	....	....
	London	OHL	7	3	3	1	427	29	0	4.07	....	....	....	....	....	....	....
	Sudbury	OHL	19	10	8	0	1043	60	0	3.45	5	1	4	274	21	0	4.60
1991-92	**Quebec**	**NHL**	**14**	**1**	**7**	**4**	**796**	**46**	**1**	**3.47**	....	....	....	....	....	....	....
	Halifax	AHL	12	6	5	1	672	29	2	2.59	....	....	....	....	....	....	....
	New Haven	AHL	16	7	6	2	908	57	0	3.77	....	....	....	....	....	....	....
1992-93	Halifax	AHL	51	20	18	7	2852	199	0	4.19	....	....	....	....	....	....	....
	NHL Totals		**21**	**2**	**11**	**5**	**1084**	**65**	**1**	**3.60**	....	....	....	....	....	....	....

a Won Dave Pinkney Trophy (Top Team Goaltending, OHL) shared with Todd Bojcun (1988, 1989)

TERRERI, CHRIS

Goaltender. Catches left. 5'8", 160 lbs. Born, Providence, RI, November 15, 1964.
(New Jersey's 3rd choice, 87th overall, in 1983 Entry Draft).

			Regular Season								Playoffs						
Season	Club	Lea	GP	W	L	T	Mins	GA	SO	Avg	GP	W	L	Mins	GA	SO	Avg
1982-83	Providence	ECAC	11	7	1	0	528	17	2	1.93	....	....	....	....	....	....	....
1983-84	Providence	ECAC	10	4	2	0	391	20	0	3.07	....	....	....	....	....	....	....
1984-85abc	Providence	H.E.	33	15	13	5	1956	116	1	3.35	....	....	....	....	....	....	....
1985-86	Providence	H.E.	22	6	16	0	1320	84	0	3.74	....	....	....	....	....	....	....
1986-87	**New Jersey**	**NHL**	**7**	**0**	**3**	**1**	**286**	**21**	**0**	**4.41**	....	....	....	....	....	....	....
	Maine	AHL	14	4	9	1	765	57	0	4.47	....	....	....	....	....	....	....
1987-88	Utica	AHL	7	5	1	0	399	18	0	2.71	....	....	....	....	....	....	....
	U.S. National	....	26	17	7	2	1430	81	0	3.40	....	....	....	....	....	....	....
	U.S. Olympic	....	3	1	1	0	128	14	0	6.56	....	....	....	....	....	....	....
1988-89	**New Jersey**	**NHL**	**8**	**0**	**4**	**2**	**402**	**18**	**0**	**2.69**	....	....	....	....	....	....	....
	Utica	AHL	39	20	15	3	2314	132	0	3.42	2	0	1	80	6	0	4.50
1989-90	**New Jersey**	**NHL**	**35**	**15**	**12**	**3**	**1931**	**110**	**0**	**3.42**	**4**	**2**	**2**	**238**	**13**	**0**	**3.28**
1990-91	**New Jersey**	**NHL**	**53**	**24**	**21**	**7**	**2970**	**144**	**1**	**2.91**	**7**	**3**	**4**	**428**	**21**	**0**	**2.94**
1991-92	**New Jersey**	**NHL**	**54**	**22**	**22**	**10**	**3186**	**169**	**1**	**3.18**	**7**	**3**	**3**	**386**	**23**	**0**	**3.58**
1992-93	**New Jersey**	**NHL**	**48**	**19**	**21**	**3**	**2672**	**151**	**2**	**3.39**	**4**	**1**	**3**	**219**	**17**	**0**	**4.66**
	NHL Totals		**205**	**80**	**83**	**26**	**11447**	**613**	**4**	**3.21**	**22**	**9**	**12**	**1271**	**74**	**0**	**3.49**

a Hockey East All-Star Team (1985)
b Hockey East Player of the Year (1985)
c NCAA All-American Team (1985)

THIBAULT, JOCELYN

Goaltender. Catches left. 5'11", 170 lbs. Born, Montreal, Que., January 12, 1975.
(Quebec's 1st choice, 10th overall, in 1993 Entry Draft).

			Regular Season								Playoffs						
Season	Club	Lea	GP	W	L	T	Mins	GA	SO	Avg	GP	W	L	Mins	GA	SO	Avg
1991-92	Trois Rivieres	QMJHL	30	14	7	1	1496	77	0	2.99	3	....	....	110	4	0	2.19
1992-93abc	Sherbrooke	QMJHL	56	34	14	5	3190	159	3	3.09	15	9	6	882	57	0	3.87

a QMJHL First All-Star Team (1993)
b Canadian Major Junior First All-Star Team (1993)
c Canadian Major Junior Goaltender of the Year (1993)

TKACHENKO, SERGEI

Goaltender. Catches left. 6'2", 198 lbs. Born, Kiev, Soviet Union, June 6, 1971.
(Vancouver's 9th choice, 280th overall, in 1993 Entry Draft).

			Regular Season								Playoffs						
Season	Club	Lea	GP	W	L	T	Mins	GA	SO	Avg	GP	W	L	Mins	GA	SO	Avg
1989-90	Sokol Kiev	USSR	1	....	....	....	10	0	0	0.00	....	....	....	....	....	....	....
1990-91	Sokol Kiev	USSR	14	....	....	....	220	14	0	3.37	....	....	....	....	....	....	....
1991-92	Sokol Kiev	CIS	24	....	....	....	1305	91	0	4.18	....	....	....	....	....	....	....
1992-93	Brantford	Col.	4	0	1	0	96	11	0	6.88	....	....	....	....	....	....	....
	Hamilton	AHL	1	1	0	0	60	3	0	3.00	....	....	....	....	....	....	....

TORCHIA, MIKE (TOR-chee-ah)

Goaltender. Catches left. 5'11", 215 lbs. Born, Toronto, Ont., February 23, 1972.
(Minnesota's 2nd choice, 74th overall, in 1991 Entry Draft).

			Regular Season								Playoffs						
Season	Club	Lea	GP	W	L	T	Mins	GA	SO	Avg	GP	W	L	Mins	GA	SO	Avg
1988-89	Kitchener	OHL	30	14	9	4	1472	102	0	4.02	2	0	2	126	8	0	3.81
1989-90a	Kitchener	OHL	40	25	11	2	2280	136	1	3.58	*17	*11	6	*1023	60	0	3.52
1990-91	Kitchener	OHL	57	25	24	7	*3317	219	0	3.95	6	2	4	382	30	0	4.71
1991-92	Kitchener	OHL	55	25	24	3	3042	203	1	4.00	14	7	7	900	47	0	3.13
1992-93	Cdn. National	....	5	5	0	0	300	11	1	2.20	....	....	....	....	....	....	....
	Kalamazoo	IHL	48	19	17	9	2729	173	0	3.80	....	....	....	....	....	....	....

a Memorial Cup All-Star Team, Top Goaltender (1990)

TREFILOV, ANDREI (treh-FEE-lohv)

Goaltender. Catches left. 6', 180 lbs. Born, Kirovo-Chepetsk, Soviet Union, August 31, 1969.
(Calgary's 14th choice, 261st overall, in 1991 Entry Draft).

			Regular Season								Playoffs						
Season	Club	Lea	GP	W	L	T	Mins	GA	SO	Avg	GP	W	L	Mins	GA	SO	Avg
1990-91	Moscow D'amo	USSR	20	....	....	....	1070	36	0	2.01	....	....	....	....	....	....	....
1991-92	Moscow D'amo	CIS	28	....	....	....	1326	35	0	1.58	....	....	....	....	....	....	....
1992-93	**Calgary**	**NHL**	**1**	**0**	**0**	**1**	**65**	**5**	**0**	**4.62**	....	....	....	....	....	....	....
	Salt Lake	IHL	44	23	17	3	2536	135	0	3.19	....	....	....	....	....	....	....
	NHL Totals		**1**	**0**	**0**	**1**	**65**	**5**	**0**	**4.62**	....	....	....	....	....	....	....

TROFIMENKOFF, DAVE

Goaltender. Catches right. 6', 177 lbs. Born, Calgary, Alta., January 20, 1975.
(NY Rangers' 6th choice, 138th overall, in 1993 Entry Draft).

			Regular Season								Playoffs						
Season	Club	Lea	GP	W	L	T	Mins	GA	SO	Avg	GP	W	L	Mins	GA	SO	Avg
1991-92	Lethbridge	WHL	21	10	8	1	1080	67	0	3.72	....	....	....	....	....	....	....
1992-93	Lethbridge	WHL	27	14	9	0	1419	103	0	4.36	....	....	....	....	....	....	....

TUGNUTT, RON

Goaltender. Catches left. 5'11", 155 lbs. Born, Scarborough, Ont., October 22, 1967.
(Quebec's 4th choice, 81st overall, in 1986 Entry Draft).

			Regular Season								Playoffs						
Season	Club	Lea	GP	W	L	T	Mins	GA	SO	Avg	GP	W	L	Mins	GA	SO	Avg
1984-85	Peterborough	OHL	18	7	4	2	938	59	0	3.77	....	....	....	....	....	....	....
1985-86	Peterborough	OHL	26	18	7	0	1543	74	1	2.88	3	2	0	133	6	0	2.71
1986-87a	Peterborough	OHL	31	21	7	2	1891	88	2	*2.79	6	3	3	374	21	1	3.37
1987-88	**Quebec**	**NHL**	**6**	**2**	**3**	**0**	**284**	**16**	**0**	**3.38**	....	....	....	....	....	....	....
	Fredericton	AHL	34	20	9	4	1964	118	1	3.60	4	1	2	204	11	0	3.24
1988-89	**Quebec**	**NHL**	**26**	**10**	**10**	**3**	**1367**	**82**	**0**	**3.60**	....	....	....	....	....	....	....
	Halifax	AHL	24	14	7	2	1368	79	1	3.46	....	....	....	....	....	....	....
1989-90	**Quebec**	**NHL**	**35**	**5**	**24**	**3**	**1978**	**152**	**0**	**4.61**	....	....	....	....	....	....	....
	Halifax	AHL	6	1	5	0	366	23	0	3.77	....	....	....	....	....	....	....
1990-91	**Quebec**	**NHL**	**56**	**12**	**29**	**10**	**3144**	**212**	**0**	**4.05**	....	....	....	....	....	....	....
	Halifax	AHL	2	0	1	0	100	8	0	4.80	....	....	....	....	....	....	....
1991-92	**Quebec**	**NHL**	**30**	**6**	**17**	**3**	**1583**	**106**	**1**	**4.02**	....	....	....	....	....	....	....
	Halifax	AHL	8	3	3	1	447	30	0	4.03	....	....	....	....	....	....	....
	Edmonton	**NHL**	**3**	**1**	**1**	**0**	**124**	**10**	**0**	**4.84**	**2**	**0**	**0**	**60**	**3**	**0**	**3.00**
1992-93	**Edmonton**	**NHL**	**26**	**9**	**12**	**2**	**1338**	**93**	**0**	**4.17**	....	....	....	....	....	....	....
	NHL Totals		**182**	**45**	**96**	**21**	**9818**	**671**	**1**	**4.10**	**2**	**0**	**0**	**60**	**3**	**0**	**3.00**

a OHL First All-Star Team (1987)

Traded to **Edmonton** by **Quebec** with Brad Zavisha for Martin Rucinsky, March 10, 1992. Claimed by **Anaheim** from **Edmonton** in Expansion Draft, June 24, 1993.

TUREK, ROMAN (TOOR-ehk)

Goaltender. Catches right. 6'3", 190 lbs. Born, Strakonice, Czechoslovakia, May 21, 1970.
(Minnesota's 6th choice, 113th overall, in 1990 Entry Draft).

			Regular Season								Playoffs						
Season	Club	Lea	GP	W	L	T	Mins	GA	SO	Avg	GP	W	L	Mins	GA	SO	Avg
1990-91	Budejovice	Czech.	26	....	....	....	1244	98	0	4.70	....	....	....	....	....	....	....
1991-92	Budejovice	Czech.2	....	....	....	....	....	....	....	....	....	....	....	....	....	....	....
1992-93	Budejovice	Czech.	43	....	....	....	2555	121	....	2.84	....	....	....	....	....	....	....

VANBIESBROUCK, JOHN (van-BEES-bruhk)

Goaltender. Catches left. 5'8", 172 lbs. Born, Detroit, MI, September 4, 1963.
(NY Rangers' 5th choice, 72nd overall, in 1981 Entry Draft).

			Regular Season								Playoffs						
Season	Club	Lea	GP	W	L	T	Mins	GA	SO	Avg	GP	W	L	Mins	GA	SO	Avg
1980-81a	S.S. Marie	OHA	56	31	16	1	2941	203	0	4.14	11	3	3	457	24	1	3.15
1981-82	NY Rangers	NHL	1	1	0	0	60	1	0	1.00	....	....	....	....	....	....	....
	S.S. Marie	OHL	31	12	12	2	1686	102	0	3.62	7	1	4	276	20	0	4.35
1982-83b	S.S. Marie	OHL	62	39	21	1	3471	209	0	3.61	16	7	6	944	56	*1	3.56
1983-84	NY Rangers	NHL	3	2	1	0	180	10	0	3.33	1	0	0	1	0	0	0.00
cde	Tulsa	CHL	37	20	13	2	2153	124	*3	3.46	4	4	0	240	10	0	*2.50
1984-85	NY Rangers	NHL	42	12	24	3	2358	166	1	4.22	1	0	0	20	0	0	0.00
1985-86fg	NY Rangers	NHL	61	*31	21	5	3326	184	3	3.32	16	8	8	899	49	*1	3.27
1986-87	NY Rangers	NHL	50	18	20	5	2656	161	0	3.64	4	1	3	195	11	1	3.38
1987-88	NY Rangers	NHL	56	27	22	7	3319	187	2	3.38	....	....	....	....	....	....	....
1988-89	NY Rangers	NHL	56	28	21	4	3207	197	0	3.69	2	0	1	107	6	0	3.36
1989-90	NY Rangers	NHL	47	19	19	7	2734	154	1	3.38	6	2	3	298	15	0	3.02
1990-91	NY Rangers	NHL	40	15	18	6	2257	126	3	3.35	1	0	0	52	1	0	1.15
1991-92	NY Rangers	NHL	45	27	13	3	2526	120	2	2.85	7	2	5	368	23	0	3.75
1992-93	NY Rangers	NHL	48	20	18	7	2757	152	4	3.31	....	....	....	....	....	....	....
	NHL Totals		449	200	177	47	25380	1458	16	3.45	38	13	20	1940	105	2	3.25

a OHA Third All-Star Team (1981)
b OHL Second All-Star Team (1983)
c CHL First All-Star Team (1984)
d Shared Terry Sawchuk Trophy (CHL's Leading Goaltender) with Ron Scott (1984)
e Shared Tommy Ivan Trophy (CHL's Most Valuable Player) with Bruce Affleck of Indianapolis (1984)
f Won Vezina Trophy (1986)
g NHL First All-Star Team (1986)

Traded to **Vancouver** by **NY Rangers** for future considerations (Doug Lidster, June 25, 1993), June 20, 1993. Claimed by **Florida** from **Vancouver** in Expansion Draft, June 24, 1993.

VEISOR, MIKE (VIGH-awr)

Goaltender. Catches right. 6'2", 195 lbs. Born, Dallas, TX, December 7, 1972.
(St. Louis' 12th choice, 263rd overall, in 1991 Entry Draft).

			Regular Season								Playoffs						
Season	Club	Lea	GP	W	L	T	Mins	GA	SO	Avg	GP	W	L	Mins	GA	SO	Avg
1991-92	Springfield	US Jr.	46	....	....	....	2226	153	0	4.12	....	....	....	....	....	....	....
1992-93	Northeastern	H.E.	30	8	19	1	1699	151	0	5.33	....	....	....	....	....	....	....

VERNER, ANDREW

Goaltender. Catches left. 6', 194 lbs. Born, Weston, Ont., November 20, 1972.
(Edmonton's 3rd choice, 34th overall, in 1991 Entry Draft).

			Regular Season								Playoffs						
Season	Club	Lea	GP	W	L	T	Mins	GA	SO	Avg	GP	W	L	Mins	GA	SO	Avg
1989-90	Peterborough	OHL	13	7	3	0	624	38	1	3.65	2	....	....	121	6	0	2.98
1990-91a	Peterborough	OHL	46	22	14	7	2523	148	0	3.52	3	0	3	185	15	0	4.86
1991-92a	Peterborough	OHL	53	*34	13	6	3123	190	1	3.65	10	5	5	539	30	0	3.34
1992-93	Cape Breton	AHL	36	17	10	6	1974	126	1	3.83	....	....	....	....	....	....	....

a OHL Second All-Star Team (1991, 1992)

VERNON, MICHAEL (MIKE)

Goaltender. Catches left. 5'9", 165 lbs. Born, Calgary, Alta., February 24, 1963.
(Calgary's 2nd choice, 56th overall, in 1981 Entry Draft).

			Regular Season								Playoffs						
Season	Club	Lea	GP	W	L	T	Mins	GA	SO	Avg	GP	W	L	Mins	GA	SO	Avg
1980-81	Calgary	WHL	59	33	17	1	3154	198	1	3.77	22	....	....	1271	82	1	3.87
1981-82abc	Calgary	WHL	42	22	14	2	2329	143	3	3.68	9	....	....	527	30	0	3.42
	Oklahoma City	CHL	....	....	....	....	....	....	....	....	1	0	1	70	4	0	3.43
1982-83	Calgary	NHL	2	0	2	0	100	11	0	6.59	....	....	....	....	....	....	....
abc	Calgary	WHL	50	19	18	2	2856	155	3	3.26	16	9	7	925	60	0	3.89
1983-84	Calgary	NHL	1	0	1	0	11	4	0	22.22	....	....	....	....	....	....	....
d	Colorado	CHL	46	30	13	2	2648	148	1	*3.35	6	2	4	347	21	0	3.63
1984-85	Moncton	AHL	41	10	20	4	2050	134	0	3.92	....	....	....	....	....	....	....
1985-86	Calgary	NHL	18	9	3	3	921	52	1	3.39	*21	12	*9	1229	60	0	2.93
	Moncton	AHL	6	3	1	2	374	21	0	3.37	....	....	....	....	....	....	....
	Salt Lake	IHL	10	....	....	....	600	34	1	3.40	....	....	....	....	....	....	....
1986-87	Calgary	NHL	54	30	21	1	2957	178	1	3.61	5	2	3	263	16	0	3.65
1987-88	Calgary	NHL	64	39	16	7	3565	210	1	3.53	9	4	4	515	34	0	3.96
1988-89e	Calgary	NHL	52	*37	6	5	2938	130	0	2.65	*22	*16	5	*1381	52	*3	2.26
1989-90	Calgary	NHL	47	23	14	9	2795	146	0	3.13	6	2	3	342	19	0	3.33
1990-91	Calgary	NHL	54	31	19	3	3121	172	1	3.31	7	3	4	427	21	0	2.95
1991-92	Calgary	NHL	63	24	30	9	3640	217	0	3.58	....	....	....	....	....	....	....
1992-93	Calgary	NHL	64	29	26	9	3732	203	2	3.26	4	1	1	150	15	0	6.00
	NHL Totals		419	222	138	46	23780	1323	6	3.34	74	40	29	4307	217	3	3.02

a WHL First All-Star Team (1982, 1983)
b WHL Most Valuable Player (1982, 1983)
c Named WHL's Top Goaltender (1982, 1983)
d CHL Second All-Star Team (1984)
e NHL Second All-Star Team (1989)

Played in NHL All-Star Game (1988-91, 1993)

WAITE, JIMMY (WAYT)

Goaltender. Catches left. 6'1", 182 lbs. Born, Sherbrooke, Que., April 15, 1969.
(Chicago's 1st choice, 8th overall, in 1987 Entry Draft).

			Regular Season								Playoffs						
Season	Club	Lea	GP	W	L	T	Mins	GA	SO	Avg	GP	W	L	Mins	GA	SO	Avg
1986-87a	Chicoutimi	QMJHL	50	23	17	3	2569	209	2	4.48	11	4	6	576	54	1	5.63
1987-88	Chicoutimi	QMJHL	36	17	16	1	2000	150	0	4.50	4	1	2	222	17	0	4.59
1988-89	Chicago	NHL	11	0	7	1	494	43	0	5.22	....	....	....	....	....	....	....
	Saginaw	IHL	5	3	1	0	304	10	0	1.97	....	....	....	....	....	....	....
1989-90	Chicago	NHL	4	2	0	0	183	14	0	4.59	....	....	....	....	....	....	....
bc	Indianapolis	IHL	54	*34	14	5	*3207	135	*5	*2.53	*10	*9	1	*602	19	*1	*1.89
1990-91	Chicago	NHL	1	1	0	0	60	2	0	2.00	....	....	....	....	....	....	....
	Indianapolis	IHL	49	*26	18	4	2888	167	3	3.47	6	2	4	369	20	0	3.25
1991-92	Chicago	NHL	17	4	7	4	877	54	0	3.69	....	....	....	....	....	....	....
	Indianapolis	IHL	13	4	7	1	702	53	0	4.53	....	....	....	....	....	....	....
	Hershey	AHL	11	6	4	1	631	44	0	4.18	6	2	4	360	19	0	3.17
1992-93	Chicago	NHL	20	6	7	1	996	49	2	2.95	....	....	....	....	....	....	....
	NHL Totals		53	13	21	6	2610	162	2	3.72	....	....	....	....	....	....	....

a QMJHL Second All-Star Team (1987)
b IHL First All-Star Team (1990)
c Won James Norris Memorial Trophy (Top Goaltender-IHL) (1990)

Traded to **San Jose** by **Chicago** for future considerations (Neil Wilkinson, July 9, 1993), June 19, 1993.

WAKALUK, DARCY (WAHK-uh-luhk)

Goaltender. Catches left. 5'11", 180 lbs. Born, Pincher Creek, Alta., March 14, 1966.
(Buffalo's 7th choice, 144th overall, in 1984 Entry Draft).

			Regular Season								Playoffs						
Season	Club	Lea	GP	W	L	T	Mins	GA	SO	Avg	GP	W	L	Mins	GA	SO	Avg
1983-84	Kelowna	WHL	31	....	....	....	1555	163	0	6.29	....	....	....	....	....	....	....
1984-85	Kelowna	WHL	54	19	30	4	3094	244	0	4.73	5	1	4	282	22	0	4.68
1985-86	Spokane	WHL	47	21	22	1	2562	224	1	5.25	7	3	4	419	37	0	5.30
1986-87	Rochester	AHL	11	2	2	0	545	26	0	2.86	5	2	0	141	11	0	4.68
1987-88	Rochester	AHL	55	27	16	3	2763	159	0	3.45	6	3	3	328	22	0	4.02
1988-89	Buffalo	NHL	6	1	3	0	214	15	0	4.21	....	....	....	....	....	....	....
	Rochester	AHL	33	11	14	0	1566	97	1	3.72	....	....	....	....	....	....	....
1989-90	Rochester	AHL	56	31	16	4	3095	173	2	3.35	*17	*10	6	*1001	50	0	*3.01
1990-91	Buffalo	NHL	16	4	5	3	630	35	0	3.33	2	0	1	37	2	0	3.24
	Rochester	AHL	26	10	10	3	1363	68	4	*2.99	9	6	3	544	30	0	3.31
1991-92	Minnesota	NHL	36	13	19	1	1905	104	1	3.28	....	....	....	....	....	....	....
	Kalamazoo	IHL	1	1	0	0	60	7	0	7.00	....	....	....	....	....	....	....
1992-93	Minnesota	NHL	29	10	12	5	1596	97	1	3.65	....	....	....	....	....	....	....
	NHL Totals		87	28	39	9	4345	251	2	3.47	2	0	1	37	2	0	3.24

Traded to **Minnesota** by **Buffalo** for Minnesota's eighth round choice (Jiri Kuntos) in 1991 Entry Draft, May 26, 1991.

WAMSLEY, RICHARD (RICK) (WAHMS-lee)

Goaltender. Catches left. 5'11", 185 lbs. Born, Simcoe, Ont., May 25, 1959.
(Montreal's 5th choice, 58th overall, in 1979 Entry Draft).

			Regular Season								Playoffs						
Season	Club	Lea	GP	W	L	T	Mins	GA	SO	Avg	GP	W	L	Mins	GA	SO	Avg
1977-78	Hamilton	OHA	25	....	....	....	1495	74	2	2.97	....	....	....	....	....	....	....
1978-79	Brantford	OHA	24	....	....	....	1444	128	0	5.32	....	....	....	....	....	....	....
1979-80	Nova Scotia	AHL	40	19	16	2	2305	125	2	3.25	3	1	1	143	12	0	5.03
1980-81	Montreal	NHL	5	3	0	1	253	8	1	1.90	....	....	....	....	....	....	....
	Nova Scotia	AHL	43	17	19	3	2372	155	0	3.92	4	2	1	199	6	*1	1.81
1981-82a	Montreal	NHL	38	23	7	7	2206	101	2	2.75	5	2	3	300	11	0	*2.20
1982-83	Montreal	NHL	46	27	12	5	2583	151	0	3.51	3	0	3	152	7	0	2.77
1983-84	Montreal	NHL	42	19	17	3	2333	144	2	3.70	1	0	0	32	0	0	0.00
1984-85	St. Louis	NHL	40	23	12	5	2319	126	0	3.26	2	0	2	120	7	0	3.50
1985-86	St. Louis	NHL	42	22	16	3	2517	144	1	3.43	10	4	6	569	37	0	3.90
1986-87	St. Louis	NHL	41	17	15	6	2410	142	0	3.54	2	1	1	120	5	0	2.50
1987-88	St. Louis	NHL	31	13	16	1	1818	103	2	3.40	....	....	....	....	....	....	....
	Calgary	NHL	2	1	0	0	73	5	0	4.11	1	0	1	33	2	0	3.64
1988-89	Calgary	NHL	35	17	11	4	1927	95	2	2.96	1	0	1	20	2	0	6.00
1989-90	Calgary	NHL	36	18	8	6	1969	107	2	3.26	1	0	1	49	9	0	11.02
1990-91	Calgary	NHL	29	14	7	5	1670	85	0	3.05	1	0	0	2	1	0	30.00
1991-92	Calgary	NHL	9	3	4	0	457	34	0	4.46	....	....	....	....	....	....	....
	Toronto	NHL	8	4	3	0	428	27	0	3.79	....	....	....	....	....	....	....
1992-93	Toronto	NHL	3	0	3	0	160	15	0	5.63	....	....	....	....	....	....	....
	St. John's	AHL	2	0	1	0	112	8	0	4.29	....	....	....	....	....	....	....
	NHL Totals		407	204	131	46	23123	1287	12	3.34	27	7	18	1397	81	0	3.48

a Shared Williams Jennings Trophy with Denis Herron (1982)

Traded to **St. Louis** by **Montreal** with Hartford's second round choice (previously acquired by Montreal — St. Louis selected Brian Benning), Montreal's second round choice (Tony Hrkac) and third round choice (Robert Dirk), in the 1984 Entry Draft, for St. Louis' first (Shayne Corson) and second round (Stephane Richer) choices in the 1984 Entry Draft, June 9, 1984. Traded to **Calgary** by **St. Louis** with Rob Ramage for Brett Hull and Steve Bozek, March 7, 1988. Traded to **Toronto** by **Calgary** with Doug Gilmour, Jamie Macoun, Kent Manderville and Ric Nattress for Gary Leeman, Alexander Godynyuk, Jeff Reese, Michel Petit and Craig Berube, January 2, 1992.

WEEKES, KEVIN

Goaltender. Catches left. 6', 158 lbs. Born, Toronto, Ont., April 4, 1975.
(Florida's 2nd choice, 41st overall, in 1993 Entry Draft).

			Regular Season								Playoffs						
Season	Club	Lea	GP	W	L	T	Mins	GA	SO	Avg	GP	W	L	Mins	GA	SO	Avg
1991-92	St. Michael's	Jr. A	2	....	....	....	127	11	0	5.20	....	....	....	....	....	....	....
1992-93	Owen Sound	OHL	29	9	12	5	1645	143	0	5.22	1	0	0	26	5	0	11.50

WEEKS, STEPHEN (STEVE)

Goaltender. Catches left. 5'11", 170 lbs. Born, Scarborough, Ont., June 30, 1958.
(NY Rangers' 12th choice, 176th overall, in 1978 Amateur Draft).

			Regular Season								Playoffs						
Season	Club	Lea	GP	W	L	T	Mins	GA	SO	Avg	GP	W	L	Mins	GA	SO	Avg
1977-78	N. Michigan	CCHA	19	....	....	....	1015	56	1	3.31	....	....	....	....	....	....	....
1978-79	N. Michigan	CCHA	25	....	....	....	1437	82	0	3.42	....	....	....	....	....	....	....
1979-80	N. Michigan	CCHA	36	29	6	1	2133	105	0	2.95	....	....	....	....	....	....	....
1980-81	NY Rangers	NHL	1	0	1	0	60	2	0	2.00	1	0	0	14	1	0	4.29
	New Haven	AHL	36	14	17	3	2065	142	1	4.04	....	....	....	....	....	....	....
1981-82	NY Rangers	NHL	49	23	16	9	2852	179	1	3.77	4	1	2	127	9	0	4.25
1982-83	NY Rangers	NHL	18	9	5	3	1040	68	0	3.92	....	....	....	....	....	....	....
	Tulsa	CHL	19	8	10	0	1116	60	0	3.23	....	....	....	....	....	....	....
1983-84	NY Rangers	NHL	26	10	11	2	1361	90	0	3.97	....	....	....	....	....	....	....
	Tulsa	CHL	3	3	0	0	180	7	0	2.33	....	....	....	....	....	....	....
1984-85	Hartford	NHL	23	9	12	2	1397	91	2	3.91	....	....	....	....	....	....	....
	Binghamton	AHL	5	5	0	0	303	13	0	2.57	....	....	....	....	....	....	....
1985-86	Hartford	NHL	27	13	13	0	1544	99	1	3.85	3	1	2	169	8	0	2.84
1986-87	Hartford	NHL	25	12	8	2	1367	78	1	3.42	1	0	0	36	1	0	1.67
1987-88	Hartford	NHL	18	6	7	2	918	55	0	3.59	....	....	....	....	....	....	....
	Vancouver	NHL	9	4	3	2	550	31	0	3.38	....	....	....	....	....	....	....
1988-89	Vancouver	NHL	35	11	19	5	2056	102	0	2.98	3	1	1	140	8	0	3.43
1989-90	Vancouver	NHL	21	4	11	4	1142	79	0	4.15	....	....	....	....	....	....	....
1990-91	Vancouver	NHL	1	0	1	0	59	6	0	6.10	....	....	....	....	....	....	....
	Milwaukee	IHL	37	16	19	0	2014	127	0	3.78	3	1	2	210	13	0	3.71
1991-92	NY Islanders	NHL	23	9	4	2	1032	62	0	3.60	....	....	....	....	....	....	....
	Los Angeles	NHL	7	1	3	0	252	17	0	4.05	....	....	....	....	....	....	....
1992-93	Ottawa	NHL	7	0	5	0	249	30	0	7.23	....	....	....	....	....	....	....
	New Haven	AHL	6	0	6	0	323	32	0	5.94	....	....	....	....	....	....	....
	NHL Totals		290	111	119	33	15879	989	5	3.74	12	3	5	486	27	0	3.33

Traded to **Hartford** by **NY Rangers** for future considerations, September, 1984. Traded to **Vancouver** by **Hartford** for Richard Brodeur, March 8, 1988. Traded to **Buffalo** by **Vancouver** for future considerations, March 5, 1991. Signed as a free agent by **NY Islanders**, September 16, 1991. Traded to **Los Angeles** by **NY Islanders** for Los Angeles' seventh round choice (Steve O'Rourke) in 1992 Entry Draft, February 18, 1992. Signed as a free agent by **Washington**, June 16, 1992. Traded to **Ottawa** by **Washington** for future considerations, August 13, 1992.

WHITMORE, KAY

Goaltender. Catches left. 5'11", 175 lbs.   Born, Sudbury, Ont., April 10, 1967.
(Hartford's 2nd choice, 26th overall, in 1985 Entry Draft).

Season	Club	Lea	GP	W	L	T	Mins	GA	SO	Avg	GP	W	L	Mins	GA	SO	Avg
1983-84	Peterborough	OHL	29	17	8	0	1471	110	0	4.49	....	....	....	....	....	....	....
1984-85a	Peterborough	OHL	53	*35	16	2	3077	172	*2	3.35	17	10	4	1020	58	0	3.41
1985-86b	Peterborough	OHL	41	27	12	2	2467	114	*3	2.77	14	8	5	837	40	0	2.87
1986-87	Peterborough	OHL	36	14	17	5	2159	118	1	3.28	7	3	3	366	17	1	2.79
1987-88	Binghamton	AHL	38	17	15	4	2137	121	*3	3.40	2	0	2	118	10	0	5.08
1988-89	**Hartford**	**NHL**	3	2	1	0	180	10	0	3.33	2	0	2	135	10	0	4.44
	Binghamton	AHL	*56	21	29	4	*3200	241	1	4.52	....	....	....	....	....	....	....
1989-90	**Hartford**	**NHL**	9	4	2	1	442	26	0	3.53	....	....	....	....	....	....	....
	Binghamton	AHL	24	3	19	2	1386	109	0	4.72	....	....	....	....	....	....	....
1990-91	**Hartford**	**NHL**	18	3	9	3	850	52	0	3.67	....	....	....	....	....	....	....
c	Springfield	AHL	33	22	9	1	1916	98	1	3.07	*15	*11	4	*926	37	0	*2.40
1991-92	**Hartford**	**NHL**	45	14	21	6	2567	155	3	3.62	1	0	0	19	1	0	3.16
1992-93	**Vancouver**	**NHL**	31	18	8	4	1817	94	1	3.10	....	....	....	....	....	....	....
	NHL Totals		**106**	**41**	**41**	**14**	**5856**	**337**	**4**	**3.45**	**3**	**0**	**2**	**154**	**11**	**0**	**4.29**

a OHL Third All-Star Team (1985)
b OHL First All-Star Team (1986)
c Won Jack A. Butterfield Trophy (MVP in Playoffs - AHL) (1991)
Traded to **Vancouver** by **Hartford** for Corrie D'Alessio and future considerations, October 1, 1992.

WILKINSON, DEREK

Goaltender. Catches left. 6', 160 lbs.   Born, Lasalle, Que., July 29, 1974.
(Tampa Bay's 7th choice, 145th overall, in 1992 Entry Draft).

Season	Club	Lea	GP	W	L	T	Mins	GA	SO	Avg	GP	W	L	Mins	GA	SO	Avg
1991-92	Detroit	OHL	38	16	17	1	1943	138	1	4.26	7	3	2	313	28	0	5.37
1992-93	Detroit	OHL	4	1	2	1	245	18	0	4.41	....	....	....	....	....	....	....
	Belleville	OHL	*59	21	24	11	*3370	237	0	4.22	7	3	4	434	29	0	4.01

WREGGET, KEN

Goaltender. Catches left. 6'1", 195 lbs.   Born, Brandon, Man., March 25, 1964.
(Toronto's 4th choice, 45th overall, in 1982 Entry Draft).

Season	Club	Lea	GP	W	L	T	Mins	GA	SO	Avg	GP	W	L	Mins	GA	SO	Avg
1981-82	Lethbridge	WHL	36	19	12	0	1713	118	0	4.13	3	....	....	84	3	0	2.14
1982-83	Lethbridge	WHL	48	26	17	1	2696	157	0	3.49	20	14	5	1154	58	1	3.02
1983-84	**Toronto**	**NHL**	3	1	1	1	165	14	0	5.09	....	....	....	....	....	....	....
ab	Lethbridge	WHL	53	32	20	0	3053	161	0	*3.16	4	1	3	210	18	0	5.14
1984-85	**Toronto**	**NHL**	23	2	15	3	1278	103	0	4.84	....	....	....	....	....	....	....
	St. Catharines	AHL	12	2	8	1	688	48	0	4.19	....	....	....	....	....	....	....
1985-86	**Toronto**	**NHL**	30	9	13	4	1566	113	0	4.33	10	6	4	607	32	*1	3.16
	St. Catharines	AHL	18	8	9	0	1058	78	1	4.42	....	....	....	....	....	....	....
1986-87	**Toronto**	**NHL**	56	22	28	3	3026	200	0	3.97	13	7	6	761	29	1	2.29
1987-88	**Toronto**	**NHL**	56	12	35	4	3000	222	2	4.44	2	0	1	108	11	0	6.11
1988-89	**Toronto**	**NHL**	32	9	20	2	1888	139	0	4.42	....	....	....	....	....	....	....
	Philadelphia	**NHL**	3	1	1	0	130	13	0	6.00	5	2	2	268	10	1	2.24
1989-90	**Philadelphia**	**NHL**	51	22	24	3	2961	169	0	3.42	....	....	....	....	....	....	....
1990-91	**Philadelphia**	**NHL**	30	10	14	3	1484	88	0	3.56	....	....	....	....	....	....	....
1991-92	**Philadelphia**	**NHL**	23	9	8	3	1259	75	0	3.57	....	....	....	....	....	....	....
	Pittsburgh	**NHL**	9	5	3	0	448	31	0	4.15	1	0	0	40	4	0	6.00
1992-93	**Pittsburgh**	**NHL**	25	13	7	2	1368	78	0	3.42	....	....	....	....	....	....	....
	NHL Totals		**341**	**115**	**169**	**28**	**18573**	**1245**	**2**	**4.02**	**31**	**15**	**13**	**1784**	**86**	**3**	**2.89**

a WHL First All-Star Team, East Division (1984)
b Named WHL's Top Goaltender (1984)
Traded to **Philadelphia** by **Toronto** for Philadelphia's first round choice (Rob Pearson) and Calgary's first round choice (previously acquired by Philadelphia — Toronto selected Steve Bancroft) in 1989 Entry Draft, March 6, 1989. Traded to **Pittsburgh** by **Philadelphia** with Rick Tocchet and Kjell Samuelsson for Mark Recchi, Brian Benning and Los Angeles' first round choice (previously acquired by Pittsburgh — Philadelphia selected Jason Bowen) in 1992 Entry Draft, February 19, 1992.

YOUNG, WENDELL

Goaltender. Catches left. 5'9", 181 lbs.   Born, Halifax, N.S., August 1, 1963.
(Vancouver's 3rd choice, 73rd overall, in 1981 Entry Draft).

Season	Club	Lea	GP	W	L	T	Mins	GA	SO	Avg	GP	W	L	Mins	GA	SO	Avg
1980-81	Kitchener	OHA	42	19	15	0	2215	164	1	4.44	14	9	1	800	42	*1	3.15
1981-82	Kitchener	OHL	60	38	17	2	3470	195	1	3.37	15	12	1	900	35	*1	2.33
1982-83a	Kitchener	OHL	61	41	19	0	3611	231	1	3.84	12	6	5	720	43	0	3.58
1983-84	Fredericton	AHL	11	7	3	0	569	39	1	4.11	....	....	....	....	....	....	....
	Milwaukee	IHL	6				339	17	0	3.01	....	....	....	....	....	....	....
	Salt Lake	CHL	20	11	6	0	1094	80	0	4.39	4	0	2	122	11	0	5.42
1984-85	Fredericton	AHL	22	7	11	3	1242	83	0	4.01	....	....	....	....	....	....	....
1985-86	**Vancouver**	**NHL**	22	4	9	3	1023	61	0	3.58	1	0	1	60	5	0	5.00
	Fredericton	AHL	24	12	8	4	1457	78	0	3.21	....	....	....	....	....	....	....
1986-87	**Vancouver**	**NHL**	8	1	6	1	420	35	0	5.00	....	....	....	....	....	....	....
	Fredericton	AHL	30	11	16	0	1676	118	0	4.22	....	....	....	....	....	....	....
1987-88	**Philadelphia**	**NHL**	6	3	2	0	320	20	0	3.75	....	....	....	....	....	....	....
bcd	Hershey	AHL	51	*33	15	1	2922	135	1	2.77	12	*12	0	*767	28	*1	2.19
1988-89	**Pittsburgh**	**NHL**	22	12	9	0	1150	92	0	4.80	1	0	0	39	1	0	1.54
	Muskegon	IHL	2				125	7	0	3.36	....	....	....	....	....	....	....
1989-90	**Pittsburgh**	**NHL**	43	16	20	3	2318	161	1	4.17	....	....	....	....	....	....	....
1990-91	**Pittsburgh**	**NHL**	18	4	6	2	773	52	0	4.04	....	....	....	....	....	....	....
1991-92	**Pittsburgh**	**NHL**	18	7	6	0	838	53	0	3.79	....	....	....	....	....	....	....
1992-93	**Tampa Bay**	**NHL**	31	7	19	2	1591	97	0	3.66	....	....	....	....	....	....	....
	Atlanta	IHL	3	3	0	0	183	8	0	2.62	....	....	....	....	....	....	....
	NHL Totals		**168**	**54**	**77**	**11**	**8433**	**571**	**1**	**4.06**	**2**	**0**	**1**	**99**	**6**	**0**	**3.64**

a OHL Third All-Star Team (1983)
b AHL First All-Star Team (1988)
c Won Baz Bastien Award (AHL Most Valuable Goaltender) (1988)
d Won Jack Butterfield Trophy (AHL Playoff MVP) (1988)
Traded to **Philadelphia** by **Vancouver** with Vancouver's third round choice (Kimbi Daniels) in 1990 Entry Draft for Daryl Stanley, August 28, 1987. Traded to **Pittsburgh** by **Philadelphia** with Philadelphia's seventh round choice (Mika Valila) in 1990 Entry Draft for Pittsburgh's third round choice (Chris Therien) in 1990 Entry Draft, September 1, 1988. Claimed by **Tampa Bay** from **Pittsburgh** in Expansion Draft, June 18, 1992.

Ken Broderick

Gary Inness

Alex Connell

Mike Liut

Dave Dryden

Johnny Mowers

Ken Dryden

Glenn Resch

Retired NHL Goaltender Index

Abbreviations: Teams/Cities:—**Ana.**-Anaheim, **Atl.**-Atlanta; **Bos.**-Boston; **Bro.**-Brooklyn; **Buf.**-Buffalo; **Cal.**-California; **Cgy.**-Calgary; **Chi.**-Chicago; **Cle.**-Cleveland; **Col.**-Colorado; **Dal.**-Dallas, **Det.**-Detroit; **Edm.**-Edmonton; **Fla.**-Florida, **Ham.**-Hamilton; **Hfd.**-Hartford; **K.C.**-Kansas City; **L.A.**-Los Angeles; **Min.**-Minnesota; **Mtl.**-Montreal; **Mtl. M.**-Montreal Maroons; **Mtl. W.**-Montreal Wanderers; **N.J.**-New Jersey; **NY**-New York; **NYA**-NY Americans; **NYI**-New York Islanders; **NYR**-New York Rangers; **Oak.**-Oakland; **Ott.**-Ottawa; **Phi.**-Philadelphia; **Pit.**-Pittsburgh; **Que.**-Quebec; **St. L.**-St. Louis; **S.J.**-San Jose, **T.B.**-Tampa Bay, **Tor.**-Toronto; **Van.**-Vancouver; **Wpg.**-Winnipeg; **Wsh.**-Washington.

Avg – goals against per 60 minutes played; **GA** – goals against; **GP** – games played; **Mins** – minutes played; **SO** – shutouts.

			Regular Schedule								Playoffs										
Name	NHL Teams	NHL Seasons	GP	W	L	T	Mins	GA	SO	Avg	GP	W	L	T	Mins	GA	SO	Avg	NHL Cup Wins	First NHL Season	Last NHL Season
Abbott, George	Bos.	1	1	0	1	0	60	7	0	7.00	....	....	....	....	....	....	....	....		1943-44	1943-44
Adams, John	Bos., Wsh.	2	22	9	10	1	1180	85	1	4.32	....	....	....	....	....	....	....	....		1972-73	1974-75
Aiken, Don	Mtl.	1	1	0	1	0	34	6	0	10.59	....	....	....	....	....	....	....	....		1957-58	1957-58
Aitkenhead, Andy	NYR	3	106	47	43	16	6570	257	11	2.35	10	6	3	1	608	15	3	1.48	1	1932-33	1934-35
Almas, Red	Det., Chi.	3	3	0	2	1	180	13	0	4.33	5	1	3	0	263	13	0	2.97		1946-47	1952-53
• Anderson, Lorne	NYR	1	3	1	2	0	180	18	0	6.00	....	....	....	....	....	....	....	....		1951-52	1951-52
Astrom, Hardy	NYR, Col.	3	83	17	44	12	4456	278	0	3.74	....	....	....	....	....	....	....	....		1977-78	1980-81
Baker, Steve	NYR	4	57	20	20	11	3081	190	3	3.70	14	7	7	0	826	55	0	4.00		1979-80	1982-83
Bannerman, Murray	Van., Chi.	8	289	116	125	33	16470	1051	8	3.83	40	20	18	0	2322	165	0	4.26		1977-78	1986-87
Baron, Marco	Bos., L.A., Edm.	6	86	34	39	9	4822	292	1	3.63	1	0	1	0	20	3	0	9.00		1979-80	1984-85
Bassen, Hank	Chi., Det., Pit.	9	157	47	66	31	8829	441	5	3.00	5	1	4	0	274	11	0	2.41		1954-55	1967-68
• Bastien, Baz	Tor.	1	5	0	4	1	300	20	0	4.00	....	....	....	....	....	....	....	....		1945-46	1945-46
Bauman, Gary	Mtl., Min.	3	35	6	18	6	1718	102	0	3.56	....	....	....	....	....	....	....	....		1966-67	1968-69
Bedard, Jim	Wsh.	2	73	17	40	13	4232	278	1	3.94	....	....	....	....	....	....	....	....		1977-78	1978-79
Behrend, Marc	Wpg.	3	38	12	19	3	1991	164	1	4.94	7	1	3	0	312	19	0	3.65		1983-84	1985-86
Belanger, Yves	St.L., Atl., Bos.	6	78	27	36	6	4134	259	2	3.76	....	....	....	....	....	....	....	....		1974-75	1979-80
Belhumeur, Michel	Phi., Wsh.	3	65	9	36	7	3306	254	0	4.61	1	0	0	0	10	1	0	6.00		1972-73	1975-76
• Bell, Gordie	Tor., NYR	2	8	3	5	0	480	31	0	3.88	2	1	1	0	120	9	0	4.50		1945-46	1955-56
• Benedict, Clint	Ott., Mtl.M.	13	362	190	43	28	22321	863	57	2.32	48	25	18	4	2907	87	15	1.80	4	1917-18	1929-30
Bennett, Harvey	Bos.	1	24	10	12	2	1470	103	0	4.20	....	....	....	....	....	....	....	....		1944-45	1944-45
Bernhardt, Tim	Cgy., Tor.	4	67	17	36	2	3748	267	0	4.27	....	....	....	....	....	....	....	....		1982-83	1986-87
Beveridge, Bill	Det., Ott., St.L., Mtl.M., NYR	9	297	87	166	42	18375	879	18	2.87	5	2	3	0	300	11	0	2.20		1929-30	1942-43
• Bibeault, Paul	Mtl., Tor., Bos., Chi.	7	214	68	82	21	12890	785	10	3.65	20	6	14	0	1237	71	2	3.44		1940-41	1946-47
Binette, Andre	Mtl.	1	1	1	0	0	60	4	0	4.00	....	....	....	....	....	....	....	....		1954-55	1954-55
Binkley, Les	Pit.	5	196	58	94	34	11046	575	11	3.12	7	5	2	0	428	15	0	2.10		1967-68	1971-72
Bittner, Richard	Bos.	1	1	0	0	1	60	3	0	3.00	....	....	....	....	....	....	....	....		1949-50	1949-50
Blake, Mike	L.A.	3	40	13	5	15	2117	150	0	4.25	....	....	....	....	....	....	....	....		1981-82	1983-84
Boisvert, Gilles	Det.	1	3	0	3	0	180	9	0	3.00	....	....	....	....	....	....	....	....		1959-60	1959-60
Bouchard, Dan	Atl., Cgy., Que., Wpg.	14	655	286	232	113	37919	2061	27	3.26	43	13	30	0	2549	147	1	3.46		1972-73	1985-86
• Bourque, Claude	Mtl., Det.	2	62	16	38	8	3830	192	5	3.01	3	1	2	0	188	8	1	2.55		1938-39	1939-40
Boutin, Rollie	Wsh.	3	22	7	10	1	1137	75	0	3.96	....	....	....	....	....	....	....	....		1978-79	1980-81
Bouvrette, Lionel	NYR	1	1	0	1	0	60	6	0	6.00	....	....	....	....	....	....	....	....		1942-43	1942-43
Bower, Johnny	NYR, Tor.	15	552	251	196	90	32077	1347	37	2.52	74	34	35	0	4350	184	5	2.54	4	1953-54	1969-70
Brannigan, Andy	NYA	1	1	0	0	0	7	0	0	0.00	....	....	....	....	....	....	....	....		1940-41	1940-41
Brimsek, Frank	Bos., Chi.	10	514	252	182	80	31210	1404	40	2.70	68	32	36	0	4365	186	2	2.56	2	1938-39	1949-50
• Broda, Turk	Tor.	14	629	302	224	101	38173	1609	62	2.53	101	58	42	1	6389	211	13	1.98	5	1936-37	1951-52
Broderick, Ken	Min., Bos.	3	27	11	12	1	1464	74	2	3.03	....	....	....	....	....	....	....	....		1969-70	1974-75
Broderick, Len	Mtl.	1	1	1	0	0	60	2	0	2.00	....	....	....	....	....	....	....	....		1957-58	1957-58
Brodeur, Richard	NYI, Van., Hfd.	9	385	131	176	62	21968	1410	6	3.85	33	13	20	0	2009	111	1	3.32		1979-80	1987-88
Bromley, Gary	Buf., Van.	6	136	54	44	28	7427	425	7	3.43	7	2	5	0	360	25	0	4.17		1973-74	1980-81
• Brooks, Arthur	Tor.	1	4	2	1	0	220	23	0	6.27	....	....	....	....	....	....	....	....		1917-18	1917-18
Brooks, Ross	Bos.	3	54	37	7	6	3047	134	4	2.64	1	0	0	0	20	3	0	9.00		1972-73	1974-75
• Brophy, Frank	Que.	1	21	3	18	0	1247	148	0	7.12	....	....	....	....	....	....	....	....		1919-20	1919-20
Brown, Andy	Det., Pit.	3	62	22	26	9	3373	213	1	3.79	....	....	....	....	....	....	....	....		1971-72	1973-74
Brown, Ken	Chi.	1	1	0	0	0	18	1	0	3.33	....	....	....	....	....	....	....	....		1970-71	1970-71
Brunetta, Mario	Que.	3	40	12	17	1	1967	128	0	3.90	....	....	....	....	....	....	....	....		1987-88	1989-90
Bullock, Bruce	Van.	3	16	3	9	3	927	74	0	4.79	....	....	....	....	....	....	....	....		1972-73	1976-77
Buzinski, Steve	NYR	1	9	2	6	1	560	55	0	5.89	....	....	....	....	....	....	....	....		1942-43	1942-43
Caley, Don	St.L.	1	1	0	0	0	30	3	0	6.00	....	....	....	....	....	....	....	....		1967-68	1967-68
Caprice, Frank	Van.	6	102	31	40	11	5589	391	1	4.20	....	....	....	....	....	....	....	....		1982-83	1987-88
Caron, Jacques	L.A., St.L., Van.	5	72	24	29	11	3846	211	2	3.29	12	4	7	0	639	34	0	3.19		1967-68	1973-74
Carter, Lyle	Cal.	1	15	4	7	0	721	50	0	4.16	....	....	....	....	....	....	....	....		1971-72	1971-72
• Chabot, Lorne	NYR, Tor., Mtl., Chi., Mtl.M., NYA	11	411	206	140	65	25309	861	73	2.04	37	13	17	6	2558	64	5	1.50	2	1926-27	1936-37
Chadwick, Ed	Tor., Bos.	6	184	57	92	35	10980	551	14	3.01	....	....	....	....	....	....	....	....		1955-56	1961-62
Champoux, Bob	Det., Cal.	2	17	2	11	3	923	80	0	5.20	1	0	0	0	55	4	0	4.36		1963-64	1973-74
Cheevers, Gerry	Tor., Bos.	13	418	230	94	74	24394	1175	26	2.89	88	47	35	0	5396	242	8	2.69	2	1961-62	1979-80
Chevrier, Alain	N.J., Wpg., Chi., Pit., Det.	6	234	91	100	14	12202	845	2	4.16	16	9	7	0	1013	44	0	2.61		1985-86	1990-91
Clancy, Frank	Tor.	1	1	0	0	0	1	0	0	0.00	....	....	....	....	....	....	....	....		1931-32	1931-32
Cleghorn, Odie	Pit.	1	1	1	0	0	60	2	0	2.00	....	....	....	....	....	....	....	....		1925-26	1925-26
Clifford, Chris	Chi.	2	2	0	0	0	24	0	0	0.00	....	....	....	....	....	....	....	....		1984-85	1988-89
Colvin, Les	Bos.	1	1	0	1	0	60	4	0	4.00	....	....	....	....	....	....	....	....		1948-49	1948-49
Conacher, Charlie	Tor., Det.	13	3	0	0	0	9	0	0	0.00	....	....	....	....	....	....	....	....		1929-30	1940-41
• Connell, Alex	Ott., Det., NYA, Mtl.M.	12	417	199	155	59	26030	830	81	1.91	21	9	5	7	1309	26	4	1.19	2	1924-25	1936-37
Corsi, Jim	Edm.	1	26	8	14	3	1366	83	0	3.65	....	....	....	....	....	....	....	....		1979-80	1979-80
Courteau, Maurice	Bos.	1	6	2	4	0	360	33	0	5.50	....	....	....	....	....	....	....	....		1943-44	1943-44
Cox, Abbie	Mtl.M., Det., NYA, Mtl.	3	5	1	1	2	263	11	0	2.51	....	....	....	....	....	....	....	....		1929-30	1935-36
Craig, Jim	Atl., Bos., Min.	3	30	11	10	7	1588	100	0	3.78	....	....	....	....	....	....	....	....		1979-80	1983-84
Crha, Jiri	Tor.	2	69	28	27	11	3942	261	0	3.97	5	0	4	0	186	21	0	6.77		1979-80	1980-81
Crozier, Roger	Det., Buf., Wsh.	14	518	206	197	74	28567	1446	30	3.04	31	14	15	0	1769	82	1	2.78		1963-64	1976-77
• Cude, Wilf	Phi., Bos., Chi., Det., Mtl.	10	282	100	129	49	17486	796	24	2.73	19	7	11	1	1317	51	1	2.32		1930-31	1940-41
Cutts, Don	Edm.	1	6	1	2	1	269	16	0	3.57	....	....	....	....	....	....	....	....		1979-80	1979-80
• Cyr, Claude	Mtl.	1	1	0	0	0	20	1	0	3.00	....	....	....	....	....	....	....	....		1958-59	1958-59
Dadswell, Doug	Cgy.	2	27	8	8	3	1346	99	0	4.41	....	....	....	....	....	....	....	....		1986-87	1987-88
Daley, Joe	Pit., Buf., Det.	4	105	34	44	19	5836	326	3	3.35	....	....	....	....	....	....	....	....		1968-69	1971-72
Damore, Nick	Bos.	1	1	0	1	0	60	3	0	3.00	....	....	....	....	....	....	....	....		1941-42	1941-42
D'Amour, Marc	Cgy., Phi.	2	16	2	4	2	579	32	0	3.32	....	....	....	....	....	....	....	....		1985-86	1988-89
Daskalakis, Cleon	Bos.	3	12	3	4	1	506	41	0	4.86	....	....	....	....	....	....	....	....		1984-85	1986-87
Davidson, John	St.L., NYR	10	301	123	124	39	17109	1004	7	3.52	31	16	14	0	1862	77	1	2.48		1973-74	1982-83
Decourcy, Robert	NYR	1	1	0	1	0	29	6	0	12.41	....	....	....	....	....	....	....	....		1947-48	1947-48
Defelice, Norman	Bos.	1	10	3	5	2	600	30	0	3.00	....	....	....	....	....	....	....	....		1956-57	1956-57
DeJordy, Denis	Chi., L.A., Mtl., Det.	11	316	124	127	51	17798	929	15	3.13	18	6	9	0	946	55	0	3.49		1962-63	1973-74
Desjardins, Gerry	L.A., Chi., NYI, Buf.	10	331	122	153	44	19014	1042	12	3.29	35	15	15	0	1874	108	0	3.46		1968-69	1977-78
Dickie, Bill	Chi.	1	1	1	0	0	60	3	0	3.00	....	....	....	....	....	....	....	....		1941-42	1941-42
Dion, Connie	Det.	2	38	23	11	4	2280	119	0	3.13	5	1	4	0	300	17	0	3.40		1943-44	1944-45
Dion, Michel	Que., Wpg., Pit.	6	227	60	118	32	12695	898	2	4.24	5	2	3	0	304	22	0	4.34		1979-80	1984-85
Dolson, Clarence	Det.	3	93	35	44	13	5820	192	16	1.98	2	0	2	0	120	7	0	3.50		1928-29	1930-31
Dowie, Bruce	Tor.	1	2	0	1	0	72	4	0	3.33	....	....	....	....	....	....	....	....		1983-84	1983-84
Dryden, Dave	NYR, Chi., Buf., Edm.	9	203	48	57	24	10424	555	9	3.19	3	0	2	0	133	9	0	4.06		1961-62	1979-80
Dryden, Ken	Mtl.	8	397	258	57	74	23352	870	46	2.24	112	80	32	0	6846	274	10	2.40	6	1970-71	1978-79
Dumas, Michel	Chi.	2	8	2	1	2	362	24	0	3.98	1	0	0	0	19	1	0	3.16		1974-75	1976-77
Dupuis, Bob	Edm.	1	1	0	1	0	60	4	0	4.00	....	....	....	....	....	....	....	....		1979-80	1979-80
• Durnan, Bill	Mtl.	7	383	208	112	62	22945	901	34	2.36	45	27	18	0	2851	99	2	2.08	2	1943-44	1949-50
Dyck, Ed	Van.	3	49	8	28	5	2453	178	1	4.35	....	....	....	....	....	....	....	....		1971-72	1973-74
Edwards, Don	Buf., Cgy., Tor.	10	459	208	155	77	26181	1449	16	3.32	42	16	21	0	2302	132	1	3.44		1976-77	1985-86
Edwards, Gary	St.L., L.A., Clev., Min., Edm., Pit.	13	286	88	125	43	16002	973	10	3.65	11	5	4	0	537	34	0	3.80		1968-69	1981-82
Edwards, Marv	Pit., Tor., Cal.	4	61	15	34	7	3467	218	2	3.77	....	....	....	....	....	....	....	....		1968-69	1973-74
Edwards, Roy	Det., Pit.	7	236	92	88	38	13109	637	12	2.92	4	0	3	0	206	11	0	3.20		1967-68	1973-74
Eliot, Darren	L.A., Det., Buf.	5	89	25	41	12	4931	377	1	4.59	1	0	0	0	40	7	0	10.50		1984-85	1988-89
Ellacott, Ken	Van.	1	12	2	3	4	555	41	0	4.43	....	....	....	....	....	....	....	....		1982-83	1982-83
Esposito, Tony	Mtl., Chi.	16	886	423	307	151	52585	2563	76	2.92	99	45	53	0	6017	308	6	3.07	1	1968-69	1983-84
• Evans, Claude	Mtl., Bos.	2	5	2	2	1	280	16	0	3.43	....	....	....	....	....	....	....	....		1954-55	1957-58
Exelby, Randy	Mtl., Edm.	2	2	0	1	0	63	5	0	4.76	....	....	....	....	....	....	....	....		1988-89	1989-90

			Regular Schedule								Playoffs										
Name	NHL Teams	NHL Seasons	GP	W	L	T	Mins	GA	SO	Avg	GP	W	L	T	Mins	GA	SO	Avg	NHL Cup Wins	First NHL Season	Last NHL Season
Farr, Rocky	Buf.	3	19	2	6	3	722	42	0	3.49	....	....	....	....	....	....	....	....		1972-73	1974-75
Favell, Doug	Phi., Tor., Col.	12	373	123	153	69	20771	1096	18	3.17	21	5	16	0	1270	66	1	3.12		1967-68	1978-79
• Forbes, Jake	Tor., Ham., NYA, Phi.	13	210	84	114	11	12922	594	19	2.76	2	0	2	0	120	7	0	3.50		1919-20	1932-33
Ford, Brian	Que., Pit.	2	11	3	7	0	580	61	0	6.31	....	....	....	....	....	....	....	....		1983-84	1984-85
Fowler, Hec	Bos.	1	7	1	6	0	420	43	0	6.14	....	....	....	....	....	....	....	....		1924-25	1924-25
Francis, Emile	Chi., NYR	6	95	31	52	11	5660	355	1	3.76	....	....	....	....	....	....	....	....		1946-47	1951-52
Franks, Jim	Det., NYR, Bos.	4	43	12	23	7	2580	185	1	4.30	1	0	1	0	30	2	0	4.00	1	1936-37	1943-44
Frederick, Ray	Chi.	1	5	0	4	1	300	22	0	4.40	....	....	....	....	....	....	....	....		1954-55	1954-55
Friesen, Karl	N.J.	1	4	0	2	1	130	16	0	7.38	....	....	....	....	....	....	....	....		1986-87	1986-87
Froese, Bob	Phi., NYR	9	242	128	72	20	13451	694	13	3.10	18	3	9	0	830	55	0	3.98		1982-83	1990-91
• Gamble, Bruce	NYR, Bos., Tor., Phi.	10	327	109	139	47	18442	992	22	3.23	5	0	4	0	206	25	0	7.28		1958-59	1971-72
Gardiner, Bert	NYR, Mtl., Chi., Bos.	6	144	49	68	27	8760	554	3	3.79	9	4	5	0	647	20	0	1.85		1935-36	1943-44
• Gardiner, Chuck	Chi.	7	316	112	152	52	19687	664	42	2.02	21	12	6	3	1532	35	5	1.37	1	1927-28	1933-34
Gardner, George	Det., Van.	5	66	16	30	6	3313	207	0	3.75	....	....	....	....	....	....	....	....		1965-66	1971-72
Garrett, John	Hfd., Que., Van.	6	207	68	91	37	11763	837	1	4.27	9	4	3	0	461	33	0	4.30		1979-80	1984-85
Gatherum, Dave	Det.	1	3	2	0	1	180	3	1	1.00	....	....	....	....	....	....	....	....		1953-54	1953-54
Gauthier, Paul	Mtl.	1	1	0	0	1	70	2	0	1.71	....	....	....	....	....	....	....	....		1937-38	1937-38
Gelineau, Jack	Bos., Chi.	4	143	46	64	33	8580	447	7	3.13	4	2	2	0	260	7	1	1.62		1948-49	1953-54
Giacomin, Ed	NYR, Det.	13	610	289	206	97	35693	1675	54	2.82	65	29	35	0	3834	180	1	2.82		1965-66	1977-78
Gilbert, Gilles	Min., Bos., Det.	14	416	182	148	60	23677	1290	18	3.27	32	17	15	0	1919	97	3	3.03		1969-70	1982-83
Gill, Andre	Bos.	1	5	3	2	0	270	13	1	2.89	....	....	....	....	....	....	....	....		1967-68	1967-68
• Goodman, Paul	Chi.	3	52	23	20	9	3240	117	6	2.17	3	0	3	0	187	10	0	3.21	1	1937-38	1940-41
Gordon, Scott	Que.	2	23	2	16	0	1082	101	0	5.60	....	....	....	....	....	....	....	....		1989-90	1990-91
Grahame, Ron	Bos., L.A., Que.	4	114	50	43	15	6472	409	5	3.79	4	2	1	0	202	7	0	2.08		1977-78	1980-81
Grant, Ben	Tor., NYA., Bos.	6	50	17	26	4	2990	188	4	3.77	....	....	....	....	....	....	....	....		1928-29	1943-44
Grant, Doug	Det., St.L.	7	77	27	34	8	4199	280	2	4.00	....	....	....	....	....	....	....	....		1973-74	1979-80
Gratton, Gilles	St.L., NYR	2	47	13	18	9	2299	154	0	4.02	....	....	....	....	....	....	....	....		1975-76	1976-77
Gray, Gerry	Det., NYI	2	8	1	5	1	440	35	0	4.77	....	....	....	....	....	....	....	....		1970-71	1972-73
Gray, Harrison	Det.	1	1	0	0	0	40	5	0	7.50	....	....	....	....	....	....	....	....		1963-64	1963-64
Guenette, Steve	Pit., Cgy.	5	35	19	16	0	1958	122	1	3.74	....	....	....	....	....	....	....	....		1866-87	1990-91
• Hainsworth, George	Mtl., Tor.	11	465	246	145	74	29415	937	94	1.91	52	21	26	5	3486	112	8	1.93	2	1926-27	1936-37
Hall, Glenn	Det., Chi., St.L.	18	906	407	327	165	53484	2239	84	2.51	115	49	65	0	6899	321	6	2.79	1	1952-53	1970-71
Hamel, Pierre	Tor., Wpg.	4	69	13	41	7	3766	276	0	4.40	....	....	....	....	....	....	....	....		1974-75	1980-81
Hanlon, Glen	Van., St.L., NYR, Det.	14	477	167	202	61	26037	1561	13	3.60	35	11	15	0	1756	92	4	3.14		1977-78	1990-91
Harrison, Paul	Min., Tor., Pit., Buf.	7	109	28	53	8	5806	408	2	4.22	4	0	1	0	157	9	0	3.44		1975-76	1981-82
Head, Don	Bos.	1	38	9	26	3	2280	161	2	4.24	....	....	....	....	....	....	....	....		1961-62	1961-62
• Hebert, Sammy	Tor., Ott.	2	4	1	3	0	200	19	0	5.70	....	....	....	....	....	....	....	....	1	1917-18	1923-24
Heinz, Rick	St.L., Van.	5	49	14	19	5	2356	159	2	4.05	1	0	0	0	8	1	0	7.50		1980-81	1984-85
Henderson, John	Bos.	2	46	15	15	15	2700	113	5	2.51	2	0	2	0	120	8	0	4.00		1954-55	1955-56
• Henry, Gord	Bos.	4	3	1	2	0	180	5	1	1.67	5	0	4	0	283	21	0	4.45		1948-49	1952-53
Henry, Jim	NYR, Chi., Bos.	9	404	159	178	67	24240	1166	28	2.89	29	11	18	0	1741	81	2	2.79		1941-42	1954-55
Herron, Denis	Pit., K.C., Mtl.	14	462	146	203	76	25608	1579	10	3.70	15	5	10	0	901	50	0	3.33		1972-73	1985-86
Highton, Hec	Chi.	1	24	10	14	0	1440	108	0	4.50	....	....	....	....	....	....	....	....		1943-44	1943-44
Himes, Normie	NYA	2	2	0	0	1	79	3	0	2.28	....	....	....	....	....	....	....	....		1927-28	1928-29
Hodge, Charlie	Mtl., Oak., Van.	13	358	152	124	60	20593	927	24	2.70	16	6	8	0	803	32	2	2.39	4	1954-55	1970-71
Hoffort, Bruce	Phi.	2	9	4	0	3	368	22	0	3.59	....	....	....	....	....	....	....	....		1989-90	1990-91
Hoganson, Paul	Pit.	1	2	0	1	0	57	7	0	7.37	....	....	....	....	....	....	....	....		1970-71	1970-71
Hogosta, Goran	NYI, Que.	2	22	5	12	3	1208	83	1	4.12	....	....	....	....	....	....	....	....		1977-78	1979-80
Holden, Mark	Mtl., Wpg.	4	8	2	2	1	372	25	0	4.03	....	....	....	....	....	....	....	....		1981-82	1984-85
Holland, Ken	Hfd.	1	1	0	1	0	60	7	0	7.00	....	....	....	....	....	....	....	....		1980-81	1980-81
Holland, Robbie	Pit.	2	44	11	22	9	2513	171	1	4.08	....	....	....	....	....	....	....	....		1979-80	1980-81
• Holmes, Harry	Tor., Det.	4	105	41	54	10	6510	264	17	2.43	7	4	3	0	420	26	0	3.71		1917-18	1927-28
Horner, Red	Tor.	1	1	0	0	0	1	1	0	60.00	....	....	....	....	....	....	....	....		1932-33	1932-33
Inness, Gary	Pit., Phi., Wsh.	7	162	58	61	27	8710	494	2	3.40	9	5	4	0	540	24	0	2.67		1973-74	1980-81
Ireland, Randy	Buf.	1	2	0	0	0	30	3	0	6.00	....	....	....	....	....	....	....	....		1978-79	1978-79
Irons, Robbie	St.L.	1	1	0	0	0	3	0	0	0.00	....	....	....	....	....	....	....	....		1968-69	1968-69
• Ironstone, Joe	NYA, Tor.	2	2	1	1	0	110	3	0	1.64	....	....	....	....	....	....	....	....		1925-26	1927-28
Jackson, Doug	Chi.	1	6	2	3	1	360	42	0	7.00	....	....	....	....	....	....	....	....		1947-48	1947-48
Jackson, Percy	Bos., NYA, NYR	4	7	1	3	1	392	26	0	3.98	....	....	....	....	....	....	....	....		1931-32	1935-36
Janaszak, Steve	Min., Col.	2	3	0	1	1	160	15	0	5.62	....	....	....	....	....	....	....	....		1979-80	1981-82
Janecyk, Bob	Chi., L.A.	6	110	43	47	13	6250	432	2	4.15	3	0	3	0	184	10	0	3.26		1983-84	1988-89
Jenkins, Roger	NYA	1	1	0	1	0	30	7	0	14.00	....	....	....	....	....	....	....	....		1938-39	1938-39
Jensen, Al	Det., Wsh., L.A.	7	179	95	53	18	9974	557	8	3.35	12	5	5	0	598	32	0	3.21		1980-81	1986-87
Jensen, Darren	Phi.	2	30	15	10	1	1496	95	2	3.81	....	....	....	....	....	....	....	....		1984-85	1985-86
Johnson, Bob	St.L., Pit.	2	24	9	9	1	1059	66	0	3.74	....	....	....	....	....	....	....	....		1972-73	1974-75
Johnston, Eddie	Bos., Tor., St.L., Chi.	16	592	236	256	87	34209	1855	32	3.25	18	7	10	0	1023	57	1	3.34	2	1962-63	1977-78
Junkin, Joe	Bos.	1	1	0	0	0	8	0	0	0.00	....	....	....	....	....	....	....	....		1968-69	1968-69
Kaarela, Jari	Col.	1	5	2	2	0	220	22	0	6.00	....	....	....	....	....	....	....	....		1980-81	1980-81
Kampurri, Hannu	N.J.	1	13	1	10	1	645	54	0	5.02	....	....	....	....	....	....	....	....		1984-85	1984-85
• Karakas, Mike	Chi., Mtl.	8	336	114	169	53	20616	1002	28	2.92	23	11	12	0	1434	72	3	3.01	1	1935-36	1945-46
Keans, Doug	L.A., Bos.	9	210	96	64	26	11388	666	4	3.51	9	2	6	0	432	34	0	4.72		1979-80	1987-88
Keenan, Don	Bos.	1	1	0	1	0	60	4	0	4.00	....	....	....	....	....	....	....	....		1958-59	1958-59
• Kerr, Dave	Mtl.M., NYA, NYR	11	426	203	148	75	26519	960	51	2.17	40	18	19	3	2616	76	8	1.74	1	1930-31	1940-41
Kleisinger, Terry	NYR	1	4	0	2	0	191	14	0	4.40	....	....	....	....	....	....	....	....		1985-86	1985-86
Klymkiw, Julian	NYR	1	1	0	0	0	19	2	0	6.32	....	....	....	....	....	....	....	....		1958-59	1958-59
Kurt, Gary	Cal.	1	16	1	7	5	838	60	0	4.30	....	....	....	....	....	....	....	....		1971-72	1971-72
Lacroix, Al	Mtl.	1	5	1	4	0	280	16	0	3.43	....	....	....	....	....	....	....	....		1925-26	1925-26
LaFerriere, Rick	Col.	1	1	0	0	0	20	1	0	3.00	....	....	....	....	....	....	....	....		1981-82	1981-82
• Larocque, Michel	Mtl., Tor., Phi., St.L.	11	312	160	89	45	17615	978	17	3.33	14	6	6	0	759	37	1	2.92	4	1973-74	1983-84
Laskowski, Gary	L.A.	2	59	19	27	5	2942	228	0	4.65	....	....	....	....	....	....	....	....		1982-83	1983-84
Laxton, Gord	Pit.	4	17	4	9	0	800	74	0	5.55	....	....	....	....	....	....	....	....		1975-76	1978-79
LeDuc, Albert	Mtl.	1	1	0	0	0	2	1	0	30.00	....	....	....	....	....	....	....	....		1931-32	1931-32
Legris, Claude	Det.	2	4	0	1	1	91	4	0	2.64	....	....	....	....	....	....	....	....		1980-81	1981-82
• Lehman, Hugh	Chi.	2	48	20	24	4	3047	136	6	2.68	2	0	1	1	120	10	0	5.00		1926-27	1927-28
Lessard, Mario	L.A.	6	240	92	97	39	13529	843	9	3.74	20	6	12	0	1136	83	0	4.38		1978-79	1983-84
Levasseur, Louis	Min.	1	1	0	1	0	60	7	0	7.00	....	....	....	....	....	....	....	....		1979-80	1979-80
Levinsky, Alex	Tor.	1	1	0	0	0	1	1	0	60.00	....	....	....	....	....	....	....	....		1932-33	1932-33
• Lindbergh, Pelle	Phi.	5	157	87	49	15	9151	503	7	3.30	23	12	10	0	1214	63	3	3.11		1981-82	1985-86
• Lindsay, Bert	Mtl.W., Tor.	2	20	6	14	0	2219	118	0	3.19	....	....	....	....	....	....	....	....		1917-18	1918-19
Liut, Mike	St. L., Hfd., Wsh.	13	663	293	271	74	38155	2219	25	3.49	67	29	32	0	3814	215	2	3.38		1979-80	1991-92
Lockett, Ken	Van.	2	55	13	15	8	2348	131	2	3.35	1	0	1	0	60	6	0	6.00		1974-75	1975-76
• Lockhart, Howie	Tor., Que., Ham., Bos.	5	57	17	39	0	3371	282	1	5.02	....	....	....	....	....	....	....	....		1919-20	1924-25
LoPresti, Pete	Min., Edm.	6	175	43	102	20	9858	668	5	4.07	2	0	2	0	77	6	0	4.68		1974-75	1980-81
• LoPresti, Sam	Chi.	2	74	30	38	6	4530	236	4	3.13	8	3	5	0	530	17	1	1.92		1940-41	1941-42
Loustel, Ron	Wpg.	1	1	0	1	0	60	10	0	10.00	....	....	....	....	....	....	....	....		1980-81	1980-81
Low, Ron	Tor., Wsh., Det., Que., Edm., NJ	11	382	102	203	37	20502	1463	4	4.28	7	1	6	0	452	29	0	3.85		1972-73	1984-85
Lozinski, Larry	Det.	1	30	6	11	7	1459	105	0	4.32	....	....	....	....	....	....	....	....		1980-81	1980-81
Lumley, Harry	Det., NYR, Chi., Tor., Bos.	16	804	332	324	143	48107	2210	71	2.76	76	29	47	0	4759	199	7	2.51	1	1943-44	1959-60
MacKenzie, Shawn	N.J.	1	4	0	1	0	130	15	0	6.92	....	....	....	....	....	....	....	....		1982-83	1982-83
Maneluk, George	NYI	1	4	1	1	0	140	15	0	6.43	....	....	....	....	....	....	....	....		1990-91	1990-91
Maniago, Cesare	Tor., Mtl., NYR, Min., Van.	15	568	189	261	96	32570	1774	30	3.27	36	15	21	0	2245	100	3	2.67		1960-61	1977-78
Marios, Jean	Tor., Chi.	2	3	1	2	0	180	15	0	5.00	....	....	....	....	....	....	....	....		1943-44	1953-54
Martin, Seth	St.L.	1	30	8	10	7	1552	67	1	2.59	2	0	0	0	73	5	0	4.11		1967-68	1967-68
Mattson, Markus	Wpg., Min., L.A.	4	92	21	46	14	5007	343	6	4.11	....	....	....	....	....	....	....	....		1979-80	1983-84
May, Darrell	St. L.	2	6	1	5	0	364	31	0	5.11	....	....	....	....	....	....	....	....		1985-86	1987-88
Mayer, Gilles	Tor.	4	9	1	7	1	540	25	0	2.78	....	....	....	....	....	....	....	....		1949-50	1955-56
McAuley, Ken	NYR	2	96	17	64	15	5740	537	1	5.61	....	....	....	....	....	....	....	....		1943-44	1944-45
McCartan, Jack	NYR	2	12	3	7	2	680	43	1	3.79	....	....	....	....	....	....	....	....		1959-60	1960-61
• McCool, Frank	Tor.	2	72	34	31	7	4320	242	4	3.36	13	8	5	0	807	30	4	2.23	1	1944-45	1945-46
McDuffe, Pete	St.L., NYR, K.C., Det.	5	57	11	36	6	3207	218	0	4.08	1	0	1	0	60	7	0	7.00		1971-72	1975-76
McGrattan, Tom	Det.	1	1	0	0	0	8	0	0	0.00	....	....	....	....	....	....	....	....		1947-48	1947-48
McKay, Ross	Hfd.	1	1	0	0	0	35	3	0	5.14	....	....	....	....	....	....	....	....		1990-91	1990-91
McKenzie, Bill	Det., K.C., Col.	6	91	18	49	13	4776	326	2	4.10	....	....	....	....	....	....	....	....		1973-74	1979-80
McKichan, Steve	Van.	1	1	0	0	0	20	2	0	6.00	....	....	....	....	....	....	....	....		1990-91	1990-91
McLachlan, Murray	Tor.	1	2	0	1	0	25	4	0	9.60	....	....	....	....	....	....	....	....		1970-71	1970-71

			Regular Schedule								Playoffs										
Name	NHL Teams	NHL Seasons	GP	W	L	T	Mins	GA	SO	Avg	GP	W	L	T	Mins	GA	SO	Avg	NHL Cup Wins	First NHL Season	Last NHL Season
McLelland, Dave	Van.	1	2	1	1	0	120	10	0	5.00	....	....	....	....	....	....	....	....		1972-73	1972-73
McLeod, Don	Det., Phi.	2	18	3	10	1	879	74	0	5.05	....	....	....	....	....	....	....	....		1970-71	1971-72
McLeod, Jim	St.L.	1	16	6	6	4	880	44	0	3.00	....	....	....	....	....	....	....	....		1971-72	1971-72
McNamara, Gerry	Tor.	2	7	2	2	1	323	15	0	2.79	....	....	....	....	....	....	....	....		1960-61	1969-70
McNeil, Gerry	Mtl.	7	276	119	105	52	16535	650	28	2.36	35	17	18	0	2284	72	5	1.89	3	1947-48	1956-57
McRae, Gord	Tor.	5	71	21	32	10	3799	221	1	3.49	8	2	5	0	454	22	0	2.91		1972-73	1977-78
Melanson, Roland	NYI, Min., L.A., N.J., Mtl.	11	291	129	106	33	16452	995	6	3.63	23	4	9	0	801	59	0	4.42		1980-81	1991-92
Meloche, Gilles	Chi., Cal., Cle., Min., Pit.	18	788	270	351	131	45401	2756	20	3.64	45	21	19	0	2464	143	2	3.48		1970-71	1987-88
Micalef, Corrado	Det.	5	113	26	59	15	5794	409	2	4.24	3	0	0	0	49	8	0	9.80		1981-82	1985-86
Middlebrook, Lindsay	Wpg., Min., N.J., Edm.	4	37	3	23	6	1845	152	0	4.94	....	....	....	....	....	....	....	....		1979-80	1982-83
Millar, Joe	Bos.	1	6	1	3	2	360	25	0	4.17	....	....	....	....	....	....	....	....		1957-58	1957-58
Millen, Greg H.	Pit., Hfd., St. L., Que., Chi., Det.	14	604	215	284	89	35377	2281	17	3.87	59	27	29	0	3383	193	0	3.42		1978-79	1991-92
• Miller, Joe	NYA, NYR, Pit., Phi.	4	130	24	90	16	7981	386	16	2.90	3	2	1	0	180	3	1	1.00		1927-28	1930-31
Mio, Eddie	Edm., NYR, Det.	7	192	83	85	31	12299	822	6	4.01	17	9	7	0	986	63	0	3.83		1979-80	1985-86
• Mitchell, Ivan	Tor.	3	21	11	9	0	1232	93	0	4.53	....	....	....	....	....	....	....	....	1	1919-20	1921-22
Moffatt, Mike	Bos.	3	19	7	7	2	979	70	0	4.29	11	6	5	0	663	38	0	3.44		1981-82	1983-84
Moore, Alfie	NYA, Det., Chi.,	4	21	7	14	0	1290	81	1	3.77	3	1	2	0	180	7	0	2.33	1	1936-37	1939-40
Moore, Robbie	Phi., Wsh.	2	6	3	1	1	257	8	2	1.87	5	3	2	0	268	18	0	4.03		1978-79	1982-83
Morisette, Jean	Mtl.	1	1	0	1	0	36	4	0	6.67	....	....	....	....	....	....	....	....		1963-64	1963-64
Mowers, Johnny	Det.	4	152	65	55	25	9350	399	15	2.56	32	19	13	0	2000	85	2	2.55	1	1940-41	1946-47
Mrazek, Jerry	Phi.	1	1	0	0	0	6	1	0	10.00	....	....	....	....	....	....	....	....		1975-76	1975-76
• Mummery, Harry	Que., Ham.	2	4	2	1	0	191	20	0	6.28	....	....	....	....	....	....	....	....		1919-20	1921-22
• Murphy, Hal	Mtl.	1	1	1	0	0	60	4	0	4.00	....	....	....	....	....	....	....	....		1952-53	1952-53
Murray, Tom	Mtl.	1	1	0	1	0	60	4	0	4.00	....	....	....	....	....	....	....	....		1929-30	1929-30
Myllys, Jarmo	Min., S.J.	4	39	4	27	1	1846	161	0	5.23	....	....	....	....	....	....	....	....		1988-89	1991-92
Mylnikov, Sergei	Que.	1	10	1	7	2	568	47	0	4.96	....	....	....	....	....	....	....	....		1989-90	1989-90
Myre, Phil	Mtl., Atl., St.L., Phi., Col., Buf.	14	439	149	198	76	25220	1482	14	3.53	12	6	5	0	747	41	1	3.29		1969-70	1982-83
Newton, Cam	Pit.	2	16	4	7	1	814	51	0	3.76	....	....	....	....	....	....	....	....		1970-71	1972-73
Norris, Jack	Bos., Chi., L.A.	4	58	19	26	4	3119	202	2	3.89	....	....	....	....	....	....	....	....		1964-65	1970-71
Oleschuk, Bill	K.C., Col.	4	55	7	28	10	2835	188	1	3.98	....	....	....	....	....	....	....	....		1975-76	1979-80
• Olesevich, Dan	NYR	1	1	0	0	1	40	2	0	3.00	....	....	....	....	....	....	....	....		1961-62	1961-62
Ouimet, Ted	St.L.	1	1	0	1	0	60	2	0	2.00	....	....	....	....	....	....	....	....		1968-69	1968-69
Pageau, Paul	L.A.	1	1	0	1	0	60	8	0	8.00	....	....	....	....	....	....	....	....		1980-81	1980-81
Paille, Marcel	NYR	7	107	33	52	21	6342	362	2	3.42	....	....	....	....	....	....	....	....		1957-58	1964-65
Palmateer, Mike	Tor., Wsh.	8	356	149	138	52	20131	1183	17	3.53	29	12	17	0	1765	89	2	3.03		1976-77	1983-84
Pang, Darren	Chi.	3	81	27	35	7	4252	287	0	4.05	6	1	3	0	250	18	0	4.32		1984-85	1988-89
Parent, Bernie	Bos., Tor., Phi.	13	608	270	197	121	35136	1493	55	2.55	71	38	33	0	4302	174	6	2.43	2	1965-66	1978-79
Parent, Bob	Tor.	2	3	0	2	0	160	15	0	5.62	....	....	....	....	....	....	....	....		1981-82	1982-83
Parro, Dave	Wsh.	4	77	21	36	10	4015	274	2	4.09	....	....	....	....	....	....	....	....		1980-81	1983-84
• Patrick, Lester	NYR	1	....	....	....	....	....	....	....	....	1	1	0	0	46	1	0	1.30		1927-28	1927-28
Peeters, Pete	Phi., Bos., Wsh.	13	489	246	155	51	27699	1424	21	3.08	71	35	35	0	4200	232	2	3.31		1978-79	1990-91
Pelletier, Marcel	Chi., NYR	2	8	1	6	1	395	33	0	5.01	....	....	....	....	....	....	....	....		1950-51	1962-63
Penney, Steve	Mtl., Wpg.	5	91	35	38	12	5194	313	1	3.62	27	15	12	0	1604	72	4	2.69		1983-84	1987-88
• Perreault, Robert	Mtl., Det., Bos.	3	31	8	16	6	1833	106	2	3.47	....	....	....	....	....	....	....	....		1955-56	1962-63
Pettie, Jim	Bos.	3	21	9	7	2	1157	71	1	3.68	....	....	....	....	....	....	....	....		1976-77	1978-79
• Plante, Jacques	Mtl., NYR, St.L., Tor., Bos.	18	837	434	246	137	49553	1965	82	2.38	112	71	37	0	6651	241	14	2.17	6	1952-53	1972-73
Plasse, Michel	St.L., Mtl., K.C., Pit., Col., Que.	11	299	92	136	54	16760	1058	2	3.79	4	1	2	0	195	9	1	2.77	1	1970-71	1981-82
Plaxton, Hugh	Mtl.M.	1	1	0	1	0	59	5	0	5.08	....	....	....	....	....	....	....	....		1932-33	1932-33
Pronovost, Claude	Bos., Mtl.	2	3	1	1	0	120	7	1	3.50	....	....	....	....	....	....	....	....		1955-56	1958-59
Pusey, Chris	Det.	1	1	0	0	0	40	3	0	4.50	....	....	....	....	....	....	....	....		1985-86	1985-86
Raymond, Alain	Wsh.	1	1	0	1	0	40	2	0	3.00	....	....	....	....	....	....	....	....		1987-88	1987-88
Rayner, Chuck	NYA, Bro., NYR	10	424	138	209	77	25491	1294	25	3.05	18	9	9	0	1134	46	1	2.43		1940-41	1952-53
Reaugh, Daryl	Edm., Hfd.	3	27	8	9	1	1246	72	1	3.47	....	....	....	....	....	....	....	....		1984-85	1990-91
Redquest, Greg	Pit.	1	1	0	0	0	13	3	0	13.85	....	....	....	....	....	....	....	....		1977-78	1977-78
Reece, Dave	Bos.	1	14	7	5	2	777	43	2	3.32	....	....	....	....	....	....	....	....		1975-76	1975-76
Resch, Glenn	NYI, Col., N.J., Phi.	14	571	231	224	82	32279	1761	26	3.27	41	17	17	0	2044	85	2	2.50	1	1973-74	1986-87
Rheaume, Herb	Mtl.	1	31	10	19	1	1889	92	0	2.92	....	....	....	....	....	....	....	....		1925-26	1925-26
Ricci, Nick	Pit.	4	19	7	12	0	1087	79	0	4.36	....	....	....	....	....	....	....	....		1979-80	1982-83
Richardson, Terry	Det., St.L.	5	20	3	11	0	906	85	0	5.63	....	....	....	....	....	....	....	....		1973-74	1978-79
Ridley, Curt	NYR, Van., Tor.	6	104	27	47	16	5498	355	1	3.87	2	0	2	0	120	8	0	4.00		1974-75	1980-81
Riggin, Denis	Det.	2	18	5	10	2	985	54	1	3.29	....	....	....	....	....	....	....	....		1959-60	1962-63
Riggin, Pat	Atl., Cgy., Wsh., Bos., Pit.	9	350	153	120	52	19872	1135	11	3.43	25	8	13	0	1336	72	0	3.23		1979-80	1987-88
Ring, Bob	Bos.	1	1	0	0	0	34	4	0	7.06	....	....	....	....	....	....	....	....		1965-66	1965-66
Rivard, Fern	Min.	4	55	9	20	7	2865	190	2	3.98	....	....	....	....	....	....	....	....		1968-69	1974-75
• Roach, John	Tor., NYR, Det.	14	491	218	204	69	30423	1246	58	2.46	34	15	16	3	2206	69	8	1.88	1	1921-22	1934-35
• Roberts, Moe	Bos., NYA, Chi.	4	10	2	5	0	506	31	0	3.68	....	....	....	....	....	....	....	....		1925-26	1951-52
• Robertson, Earl	NYA, Bro., Det.	6	190	60	95	34	11820	575	16	2.92	15	6	7	0	995	29	2	1.75	1	1936-37	1941-42
Rollins, Al	Tor., Chi., NYR	9	430	138	205	84	25717	1196	28	2.79	13	6	7	0	755	30	0	2.38	1	1949-50	1959-60
Romano, Roberto	Pit., Bos.	5	125	45	64	7	7046	474	4	4.04	....	....	....	....	....	....	....	....		1982-83	1986-87
Rupp, Pat	Det.	1	1	0	1	0	60	4	0	4.00	....	....	....	....	....	....	....	....		1963-64	1963-64
Rutherford, Jim	Det., Pit., Tor., L.A.	13	457	150	227	59	25895	1576	14	3.65	8	2	5	0	440	28	0	3.82		1970-71	1982-83
Rutledge, Wayne	L.A.	3	82	22	30	5	4325	241	2	3.34	8	2	2	0	378	20	0	3.17		1967-68	1969-70
St. Laurent, Sam	N.J., Det.	5	34	7	12	4	1572	92	1	3.51	1	0	0	0	10	1	0	6.00		1985-86	1989-90
Sands, Charlie	Mtl.	1	1	0	0	0	25	5	0	12.00	....	....	....	....	....	....	....	....		1939-40	1939-40
Sands, Mike	Min.	2	6	0	5	0	302	26	0	5.17	....	....	....	....	....	....	....	....		1984-85	1986-87
Sauve, Bob	Buf., Det., Chi., N.J.	12	405	178	149	53	22991	1321	8	3.45	34	15	16	0	1850	95	4	3.08		1976-77	1987-88
• Sawchuk, Terry	Det., Bos., Tor., L.A., NYR	21	971	435	337	188	57205	2401	103	2.52	106	54	48	0	6291	267	12	2.55	4	1949-50	1969-70
Schaefer, Joe	NYR	2	2	0	1	0	86	8	0	5.58	....	....	....	....	....	....	....	....		1959-60	1960-61
Scott, Ron	NYR, L.A.	5	28	8	13	4	1450	91	0	3.77	1	0	0	0	32	4	0	7.50		1983-84	1989-90
Sevigny, Richard	Mtl., Que.	8	176	90	44	20	9485	507	5	3.21	6	0	3	0	208	13	0	3.75	1	1979-80	1986-87
Shields, Al	NYA	1	2	0	0	0	41	9	0	13.17	....	....	....	....	....	....	....	....		1931-32	1931-32
Simmons, Don	Bos., Tor., NYR	11	247	100	104	39	14436	705	20	2.93	24	13	11	0	1436	64	3	2.67	2	1956-57	1968-69
Simmons, Gary	Cal., Clev., L.A.	4	107	30	57	15	6162	366	5	3.56	1	0	0	0	20	1	0	3.00		1974-75	1977-78
Skidmore, Paul	St.L.	1	2	1	1	0	120	6	0	3.00	....	....	....	....	....	....	....	....		1981-82	1981-82
Skorodenski, Warren	Chi., Edm.	5	35	12	11	4	1732	100	2	3.46	2	0	0	0	33	6	0	10.91		1981-82	1987-88
Smith, Al	Tor., Pit., Det., Buf., Hfd., Col.	10	233	68	99	36	12752	735	10	3.46	6	1	4	0	317	21	0	3.97		1965-66	1980-81
Smith, Billy	L.A., NYI	18	680	305	233	105	38431	2031	22	3.17	132	88	36	0	7645	348	5	2.73	4	1971-72	1988-89
Smith, Gary	Tor., Oak., Cal., Chi., Van., Min., Wsh., Wpg.	14	532	152	237	67	29619	1675	26	3.39	20	5	13	0	1153	62	1	3.23		1965-66	1979-80
• Smith, Norman	Mtl.M., Det.	8	199	81	83	35	12297	475	17	2.32	12	9	2	0	880	18	3	1.23	2	1931-32	1944-45
Sneddon, Bob	Cal.	1	5	0	2	0	225	21	0	5.60	....	....	....	....	....	....	....	....		1970-71	1970-71
Soetaert, Doug	NYR, Wpg., Mtl.	12	284	110	103	44	15583	1030	6	3.97	5	1	2	0	180	14	0	4.67	1	1975-76	1986-87
Spooner, Red	Pit.	1	1	0	1	0	60	6	0	6.00	....	....	....	....	....	....	....	....		1929-30	1929-30
St.Croix, Rick	Phi., Tor.	8	129	49	54	18	7275	450	2	3.71	11	4	6	0	562	29	1	3.10		1977-78	1984-85
Staniowski, Ed	St.L., Wpg., Hfd.	10	219	67	104	21	12075	818	2	4.06	8	1	6	0	428	28	0	3.93		1975-76	1984-85
Starr, Harold	Mtl.M.	1	1	0	0	0	3	0	0	0.00	....	....	....	....	....	....	....	....		1931-32	1931-32
Stefan, Greg	Det.	9	299	115	127	30	16333	1068	5	3.92	30	12	17	0	1681	99	1	3.53		1981-82	1989-90
Stein, Phil	Tor.	1	1	0	0	1	70	2	0	1.71	....	....	....	....	....	....	....	....		1939-40	1939-40
Stephenson, Wayne	St.L., Phi., Wsh.	10	328	146	93	46	18343	937	14	3.06	26	11	12	0	1522	79	2	3.11	1	1971-72	1980-81
Stevenson, Doug	NYR, Chi.	2	8	2	6	0	480	39	0	4.88	....	....	....	....	....	....	....	....		1944-45	1945-46
Stewart, Charles	Bos.	3	77	31	41	5	4737	194	10	2.46	....	....	....	....	....	....	....	....		1924-25	1926-27
Stewart, Jim	Bos.	1	1	0	1	0	20	5	0	15.00	....	....	....	....	....	....	....	....		1979-80	1979-80
Stuart, Herb	Det.	1	3	0	1	0	180	5	0	1.67	....	....	....	....	....	....	....	....		1926-27	1926-27
Sylvestri, Don	Bos.	1	3	0	0	2	102	6	0	3.53	....	....	....	....	....	....	....	....		1984-85	1984-85
Tataryn, Dave	NYR	1	2	1	1	0	80	10	0	7.50	....	....	....	....	....	....	....	....		1976-77	1976-77
Taylor, Bobby	Phi., Pit.	5	46	15	17	6	2268	155	0	4.10	....	....	....	....	....	....	....	....	1	1971-72	1975-76
Teno, Harvey	Det.	1	5	2	3	0	3	15	0	300.0	....	....	....	....	....	....	....	....		1938-39	1938-39
Thomas, Wayne	Mtl., Tor., NYR	8	243	103	93	34	13768	766	10	3.34	15	6	8	0	849	50	1	3.53		1972-73	1980-81
• Thompson, Tiny	Bos., Det.	12	553	284	194	75	34174	1183	81	2.08	44	20	22	0	2970	93	7	1.88	1	1928-29	1939-40
Tremblay, Vince	Tor., Pit.	5	58	12	26	8	2785	223	1	4.80	....	....	....	....	....	....	....	....		1979-80	1983-84
Tucker, Ted	Cal.	1	5	1	1	1	177	10	0	3.39	....	....	....	....	....	....	....	....		1973-74	1973-74
Turner, Joe	Det.	1	1	0	0	1	60	3	0	3.00	....	....	....	....	....	....	....	....		1941-42	1941-42
Vachon, Rogatien	Mtl., L.A., Det., Bos.	16	795	355	291	115	46298	2310	51	2.99	48	23	23	0	2876	133	2	2.77	3	1966-67	1981-82
Veisor, Mike	Chi., Hfd., Wpg.	10	139	41	62	26	7806	532	5	4.09	4	0	2	0	180	15	0	5.00		1973-74	1983-84
• Vezina, Georges	Mtl.	9	191	105	80	5	11564	633	13	3.28	26	19	6	0	1596	74	4	2.78	2	1917-18	1925-26

Name	NHL Teams	NHL Seasons	Regular Schedule								Playoffs								NHL Cup Wins	First NHL Season	Last NHL Season
			GP	W	L	T	Mins	GA	SO	Avg	GP	W	L	T	Mins	GA	SO	Avg			
Villemure, Gilles	NYR, Chi.	10	205	98	65	27	11581	542	13	2.81	14	5	5	0	656	32	0	2.93		1963-64	1976-77
Wakely, Ernie	Mtl., St.L.	5	113	41	42	17	6344	290	8	2.74	10	2	6	0	509	37	1	4.36		1962-63	1971-72
• Walsh, James	Mtl.M., NYA	7	108	48	43	16	6461	250	12	2.32	8	2	4	2	570	16	2	1.68		1926-27	1932-33
Watt, Jim	St.L.	1	1	0	0	0	20	2	0	6.00	....									1973-74	1973-74
Wetzel, Carl	Det., Min.	2	7	1	3	1	302	22	0	4.37	....									1964-65	1967-68
Wilson, Dunc	Phi., Van., Tor., NYR, Pit.	10	287	80	150	33	15851	988	8	3.74	....									1969-70	1978-79
Wilson, Lefty	Det., Tor., Bos.	3	3	0	0	1	85	1	0	0.71	....									1953-54	1957-58
• Winkler, Hal	NYR, Bos.	2	75	35	26	14	4739	126	21	1.60	10	2	3	5	640	18	2	1.69		1926-27	1927-28
Wolfe, Bernie	Wsh.	4	120	20	61	21	6104	424	1	4.17	....									1975-76	1978-79
Woods, Alec	NYA	1	1	0	1	0	70	3	0	2.57	....									1936-37	1936-37
Worsley, Gump	NYR, Mtl., Min.	21	862	335	353	150	50232	2432	43	2.90	70	41	25	0	4081	192	5	2.82	4	1952-53	1973-74
• Worters, Roy	Pit., NYA, Mtl.	12	484	171	233	68	30175	1143	66	2.27	11	3	6	2	690	24	3	2.09		1925-26	1936-37
Worthy, Chris	Oak., Cal.	3	26	5	10	4	1326	98	0	4.43	....									1968-69	1970-71
Young, Doug	Det.	1	1	0	0	0	21	1	0	2.86	....									1933-34	1933-34
Zanier, Mike	Edm.	1	3	1	1	1	185	12	0	3.89	....									1984-85	1984-85

1992-93 Transactions

August, 1992

4 – **Collin Bauer** traded from Edmonton to Minnesota for future considerations.

7 – **Dominik Hasek** traded from Chicago to Buffalo for **Stephane Beauregard** and future considerations.

10 – **Christian Ruuttu** traded from Winnipeg to Chicago for **Stephane Beauregard.**

13 – **Steve Weeks** traded from Washington to Ottawa for future considerations.

14 – **Mike McPhee** traded from Montreal to Minnesota for Minnesota's 5th round choice in 1993 Entry Draft.

20 – **Sylvain Lefebvre** traded from Montreal to Toronto for Toronto's 3rd round choice in 1994 Entry Draft.

20 – **Yvon Corriveau** traded from Hartford to Washington to complete earlier transaction of June 16, 1992.

24 – **Brian Mullen** traded from San Jose to NY Islanders for the rights to **Markus Thuresson.**

25 – **Shawn Cronin** traded from Winnipeg to Quebec for **Dan Lambert.**

27 – **Shayne Corson, Brent Gilchrist** and **Vladimir Vujtek** traded from Montreal to Edmonton for **Vincent Damphousse** and Edmonton's 4th round choice in 1993 Entry Draft.

28 – **Bobby Holik,** Hartford's 2nd round choice in 1993 Entry Draft and future considerations traded from Hartford to New Jersey for **Sean Burke** and **Eric Weinrich.**

28 – **Hubie McDonough** traded from NY Islanders to San Jose for cash.

31 – **Russ Courtnall** traded from Montreal to Minnesota for **Brian Bellows.**

September

2 – **David Shaw** traded from Minnesota to Boston for future considerations.

3 – **Mark Janssens** traded from Minnesota to Hartford for **James Black.**

3 – **Neil Brady** traded from New Jersey to Ottawa for future considerations.

3 – **Pat Conacher** traded from New Jersey to Los Angeles for future considerations.

4 – **Matt Hervey** and **Ken Hodge** traded from Boston to Tampa Bay for **Darin Kimble** and future considerations.

8 – **Jeff Riccardi** traded from Winnipeg to Boston for future considerations.

9 – **Dennis Vial** traded from Quebec to Detroit for cash.

14 – **Martin Simard** traded from Quebec to Tampa Bay to complete earlier transaction of June 19, 1992.

25 – **Jeff Bloemberg** traded from Tampa Bay to Edmonton for future considerations.

October

1 – **Stephane Beauregard** traded from Winnipeg to Philadelphia for Philadelphia's 3rd round choice in 1993 Entry Draft and future considerations.

1 – **Brent Fedyk** traded from Detroit to Philadelphia for Philadelphia's 4th round choice in 1993 Entry Draft.

1 – **John Druce** and future considerations traded from Washington to Winnipeg for **Pat Elynuik.**

1 – **Corrie D'Alessio** and future considerations traded from Vancouver to Hartford for **Kay Whitmore.**

4 – 1992 Waiver Draft

Adam Creighton to Tampa Bay from NY Islanders

Norm Maciver to Ottawa from Edmonton

Yvon Corriveau to San Jose from Washington

Chris Dahlquist to Calgary from Minnesota

Shawn Cronin to Philadelphia from Quebec

Igor Larionov to San Jose from Vancouver

Doug Evans to Philadelphia from Boston

Dave Christian to Chicago from St. Louis

5 – **Patrick Lebeau** traded from Montreal to Calgary for future considerations.

5 – Tampa Bay's 5th round choice in 1994 Entry Draft traded from Tampa Bay to NY Islanders for future considerations.

9 – **Michel Picard** traded from Hartford to San Jose for future considerations.

13 – **John Mokosak** traded from NY Rangers to Los Angeles for future considerations.

16 – **Paul Holden** traded from Los Angeles to Calgary for **Kevin Grant.**

22 – **Joe Crowley** traded from Edmonton to Chicago for **Justin Lafayette.**

27 – **Bryan Deasley** traded from Calgary to Quebec for future considerations.

28 – **Bob Beers** traded from Boston to Tampa Bay for **Stephane J.G. Richer.**

November

2 – **Paul Cavallini** traded from St. Louis to Washington for **Kevin Miller.**

3 – **Anatoli Semenov** traded from Tampa Bay to Vancouver for **Dave Capuano** and Vancouver's 4th round choice in 1994 Entry Draft.

5 – **David Archibald** traded from NY Rangers to Ottawa for Ottawa's 5th round choice in 1993 Entry Draft.

6 – **Peter Ahola** traded from Los Angeles to Pittsburgh for **Jeff Chychrun.**

24 – **John Cullen** traded from Hartford to Toronto for future considerations.

December

11 – **Kevin Lowe** traded from Edmonton to NY Rangers for NY Rangers' 3rd round choice in 1993 Entry Draft and **Roman Oksyuta.**

15 – **Rick Lessard** traded from San Jose to Vancouver for **Robin Bawa.**

16 – **Ken Sabourin** traded from Washington to Calgary for future considerations.

19 – **Bob Kudelski** and **Shawn McCosh** traded from Los Angeles to Ottawa for **Marc Fortier** and **Jim Thomson.**

19 – **Dave Snuggerud** traded from San Jose to Philadelphia for **Mark Pederson** and future considerations.

28 – **Tie Domi** and **Kris King** traded from NY Rangers to Winnipeg for **Ed Olczyk.**

January, 1993

13 – **Bernie Nicholls** traded from Edmonton to New Jersey for **Zdeno Ciger** and **Kevin Todd.**

16 – **Brian Benning** traded from Philadelphia to Edmonton for **Greg Hawgood** and **Josef Beranek.**

21 – **Yvon Corriveau** traded from San Jose to Hartford to complete earlier transaction of October 9, 1992.

22 – **Brian Lawton** traded from San Jose to New Jersey for future considerations.

28 – **Gary Leeman** traded from Calgary to Montreal for **Brian Skrudland.**

28 – **Jason Ruff** and future considerations traded from St. Louis to Tampa Bay for **Doug Crossman, Basil McRae,** and Tampa Bay's 4th choice in 1996 Entry Draft.

29 – **Tim Taylor** traded from Washington to Vancouver for **Eric Murano.**

29 – **Jimmy Carson, Marc Potvin** and **Gary Shuchuk** traded from Detroit to Los Angeles for **Paul Coffey, Sylvain Couturier** and **Jim Hiller.**

February

1 – **C.J. Young** traded from Calgary for Boston for **Brent Ashton.**

2 – **Grant Fuhr** and future considerations traded from Toronto to Buffalo for **Dave Andreychuk, Daren Puppa** and Buffalo's 1st choice in 1993 Entry Draft.

2 – **Bob Wilkie** traded from Detroit to Philadelphia for future considerations.

12 – **Martin Simard, Steve Tuttle** and **Michel Mongeau** traded from Tampa Bay to Quebec for **Herb Raglan.**

21 – **Troy Murray** traded from Winnipeg to Chicago for **Steve Bancroft** and future considerations.

22 – **Rick Hayward** traded from Winnipeg to NY Islanders for future considerations.

24 – **Igor Kravchuk** and **Dean McAmmond** traded from Chicago to Edmonton for **Joe Murphy.**

25 – **Brad Miller** traded from Ottawa to Toronto for Toronto's 9th round choice in 1993 Entry Draft.

26 – **Peter Ahola** traded from Pittsburgh to San Jose for future considerations.

March

5 – **Todd Elik** traded from Minnesota to Edmonton for **Brent Gilchrist.**

14 – The rights to **Dmitri Filimonov** traded from Winnipeg to Ottawa for Ottawa's 4th round choice in 1993 Entry Draft.

17 – **Esa Tikkanen** traded from Edmonton to NY Rangers for **Doug Weight.**

18 – **Greg Paslawski** traded from Philadelphia to Calgary for Calgary's 9th round choice in 1993 Entry Draft.

18 – **Daniel Marois** traded from NY Islanders to Boston for future considerations.

20 – **Mark Osiecki** and Winnipeg's 10th round choice in 1993 Entry Draft traded from Winnipeg to Minnesota for Minnesota's 9th round choice in 1993 Entry Draft.

20 – **Rob Ramage** traded from Tampa Bay to Montreal for **Eric Charron, Alain Cote** and future considerations.

22 – **Mark Hardy** and Ottawa's 5th round choice in 1993 Entry Draft (previously acquired from Ottawa) traded from NY Rangers to Los Angeles for **John McIntyre.**

22 – **Jim Hrivnak** and future considerations traded from Washington to Winnipeg for **Rick Tabaracci.**

22 – **Peter Taglianetti** traded from Tampa Bay to Pittsburgh for Pittsburgh's 3rd round choice in 1993 Entry Draft.

22 – **Steve Konroyd** traded from Hartford to Detroit for Detroit's 6th round choice in 1993 Entry Draft.

22 – Vancouver's 9th round choice in 1993 Entry Draft traded from Vancouver to Winnipeg for **Dan Ratushny.**

22 – **Mike Hartman** traded from Tampa Bay to NY Rangers for **Randy Gilhen.**

22 – **Murray Craven** and Vancouver's 5th round choice in 1993 Entry Draft (previously acquired from Vancouver) traded from Hartford to Vancouver for **Robert Kron,** Vancouver's 3rd round choice in 1993 Entry Draft and future considerations.

22 – **Mike Ramsey** traded from Buffalo to Pittsburgh for **Bob Errey.**

22 – **Craig Muni** traded from Edmonton to Chicago for **Mike Hudson.**

May

7 – **Robert Burakowski** traded from NY Rangers to Ottawa for future considerations.

17 – **Jim Sandlak** traded from Vancouver to Hartford to complete earlier transaction of March 22, 1993.

June

1 – **Brad McCrimmon** traded from Detroit to Hartford for Detroit's 6th round choice in 1993 Entry Draft (previously acquired by Detroit).

8 – **Dennis Vial** traded from Detroit to Tampa Bay for **Steve Maltais.**

11 – **Paul Ysebaert** traded from Detroit to Winnipeg for **Aaron Ward,** Toronto's 4th round choice in 1993 Entry Draft (previously acquired by Winnipeg) and future considerations.

11 – **Stephane Beauregard** traded from Philadelphia to Winnipeg for Philadelphia's 3rd round choice in 1993 Entry Draft (previously acquired by Winnipeg, later traded to Pittsburgh) and Winnipeg's 5th round choice in 1994 Entry Draft.

15 – **Kevin Kaminski** traded from Quebec to Washington for **Mark Matier.**

16 – **Petr Klima** traded from Edmonton to Tampa Bay for future considerations.

18 – **Alan Kerr** traded from Winnipeg to Detroit to complete previous transaction of June 11, 1993.

18 – **Donald Dufresne** traded from Montreal to Tampa Bay to complete previous transaction of March 20, 1993.

19 – **Jim Waite** traded from Chicago to San Jose for future considerations.

19 – **Peter Ahola** traded from San Jose to Tampa Bay for **Dave Capuano.**

20 – **Greg Johnson** and future considerations traded from Philadelphia to Detroit for **Jim Cummins** and Philadelphia's 4th round choice in 1993 Entry Draft (previously acquired from Philadelphia).

20 – **Reggie Savage** and **Paul MacDermid** traded from Washington to Quebec for **Mike Hough.**

20 – **Ron Hextall** and Quebec's 1st round choice in 1993 Entry Draft traded from Quebec to NY Islanders for **Mark Fitzpatrick** and NY Islanders' 1st round choice in 1993 Entry Draft.

20 – **Jeff Norton** traded from NY Islanders to San Jose for San Jose's 3rd round choice in 1994 Entry Draft and future considerations.

20 – **Gaetan Duchesne** traded from Dallas to San Jose for San Jose's 6th round choice in 1993 Entry Draft.

20 – **Gord Murphy** traded from Boston to Dallas for future considerations.

20 – **Paul Cavallini** traded from Washington to Dallas for future considerations.

20 – **Martin Gelinas** and Edmonton's 6th round choice in 1993 Entry Draft traded from Edmonton to Quebec for **Scott Pearson.**

20 – **Craig Billington, Troy Mallette** and New Jersey's 4th round choice in 1993 Entry Draft traded from New Jersey to Ottawa for **Peter Sidorkiewicz** and future considerations.

20 – **Sergei Makarov** traded from Calgary to Hartford for future considerations.

20 – **John Vanbiesbrouck** traded from NY Rangers to Vancouver for future considerations.

25 – **Doug Lidster** traded from Vancouver to NY Rangers as future considerations in previous transaction of June 20, 1993.

25 – **Glenn Healy** traded from Tampa Bay to NY Rangers for Tampa Bay's 3rd round choice in 1993 Entry Draft (previously acquired by NY Rangers).

25 – **Enrico Ciccone** traded from Dallas to Washington as future considerations in previous transaction of June 20, 1993.

25 – **Andy Moog** traded from Boston to Dallas for **Jon Casey** to complete previous transaction of June 20, 1993.

25 – **NHL Supplemental Draft**

Ottawa	**Eric Fenton** (U. of New Hampshire)
San Jose	**Dean Sylvester** (Kent State)
Tampa Bay	**Brent Peterson** (Michigan State)
Florida	**Chris Imes** (U. of Maine)
Anaheim	**Pat Thompson** (Brown U.)
Hartford	**Kent Fearns** (Colorado College)
Edmonton	**Brett Able** (U. of New Hampshire)
NY Rangers	**Wayne Strachan** (Lake Superior)
Dallas	**Jacques Joubert** (Boston U.)
Philadelphia	**Shannon Finn** (U. of Illinois-Chicago)

26 – Winnipeg's 11th round choice in 1993 Entry Draft traded from Winnipeg to St. Louis as future considerations in previous transaction of June 22, 1992.

26 – **Craig Berube** traded from Calgary to Washington

for Washington's 5th round choice in 1993 Entry Draft.

26 – San Jose's 1st round choice in 1993 Entry Draft traded from San Jose to Hartford for Hartford's 1st and 3rd round choices in 1993 Entry Draft and Toronto's 2nd round choice in 1993 Entry Draft (acquired previously by Hartford).

26 – Winnipeg's 2nd and 3rd round choices in 1993 Entry Draft traded from Winnipeg to Florida for Florida's 2nd round choice in 1993 Entry Draft.

26 – **Dean Evason** traded from San Jose to Dallas for San Jose's 6th round choice in 1993 Entry Draft (acquired previously by Minnesota/Dallas).

26 – **Corey Millen** traded from Los Angeles to New Jersey for New Jersey's 5th round choice in 1993 Entry Draft.

26 – Pittsburgh's 3rd round choice in 1993 Entry Draft (acquired previously by Tampa Bay) traded from Tampa Bay to Florida for future considerations.

26 – **Mike Peluso** traded from Ottawa to New Jersey as future considerations in previous transaction.

26 – Washington's 4th round choice in 1993 Entry Draft (previously acquired by Hartford) traded from Hartford to Calgary as future considerations in Sergei Makarov trade of June 20, 1993

26 – **Brad Schlegel** traded from Washington to Calgary for Calgary's 7th round choice in 1993 Entry Draft.

26 – Boston's 11th round choice in 1993 Entry Draft (acquired previously by Chicago) traded from Chicago to Winnipeg for future considerations.

30 – **Chris Luongo** traded from Ottawa to NY Islanders for **Jeff Finley.**

30 – **Kris Draper** traded from Winnipeg to Detroit for future considerations.

July

9 – **Neil Wilkinson** traded from San Jose to Chicago to complete previous transaction of June 18, 1993.

13 – **Jeff Hackett** traded from San Jose to Chicago for San Jose's 3rd round choice in 1994 Entry Draft and future considerations.

29 – **Jim Hrivnak** traded from Winnipeg to St. Louis for St. Louis' 7th round choice in 1994 Entry Draft and future considerations.

30 – **Dave Tomlinson** traded from Toronto to Florida for cash.

August

3 – **Dave Tomlinson** traded from Florida to Winnipeg for **Jason Cirone.**

5 – **Shawn Cronin** traded from Philadelphia to San Jose for cash.

5 – **Sergei Makarov** traded from Hartford to San Jose to complete earlier trade of June 26, 1993.

10 – **Patrik Carnback** and **Todd Ewen** traded from Montreal to Anaheim for Anaheim's 3rd round choice in 1994 Entry Draft.

12 – **Kevin McClelland** traded from Toronto to Winnipeg for cash.

THREE STAR SELECTION...

NHL PUBLICATIONS
ORDER FORM

Please send

☐ copies of next year's
NHL Guide & Record Book/94-95 (available Sept. 94)

☐ copies of this year's
NHL Guide & Record Book/93-94 (available now)

☐ copies of next year's
NHL Yearbook 1995 magazine (available Sept. 94)

☐ copies of this year's
NHL Yearbook 1994 magazine (available Sept. 93)

☐ copies of the
NHL Rule Book/93-94 (available Sept. 93)

PRICES:	CANADA	U.S.A.	OVERSEAS
Guide & Record Book	$18.95	$16.95	$18.95 CDN
Handling (per copy)	$ 3.48	$ 7.00	$ 8.00 CDN
7% GST	$ 1.57	—	—
Total (per copy)	**$24.00**	**$23.95**	**$26.95** CDN
Add Extra for airmail	$ 8.00	$ 9.00	$18.00 CDN
Yearbook	$ 7.95	$ 6.95	$ 6.95 CDN
Handling (per copy)	$ 2.94	$ 3.50	$ 5.00 CDN
7% GST	$ .76	—	—
Total (per copy)	**$11.65**	**$10.45**	**$11.95** CDN
Rule Book	$ 9.95	$ 7.95	$ 9.95 CDN
Handling (per copy)	$ 1.95	$ 3.00	$ 4.00 CDN
7% GST	$ .83	—	—
Total (per copy)	**$12.73**	**$10.95**	**$13.95** CDN

◯ Enclosed is my cheque or money order.

Charge my ◯ Visa ◯ MasterCard ◯ Am Ex

_____
Credit Card #   Expiry Date

_____
Signature

_____
Name

_____
Address

_____

_____
Province/State   Postal/Zip Code

IN CANADA
Mail completed form to:
NHL Publishing
194 Dovercourt Rd.
Toronto, Ontario
M6J 3C8

IN U.S.A.
Mail completed form to:
NHL Publishing
194 Dovercourt Rd.
Toronto, Ontario
M6J 3C8
Remit in U.S. funds

OVERSEAS
Mail completed form to:
NHL Publishing
194 Dovercourt Rd.
Toronto, Ontario
CANADA M6J 3C8
**Money order or
credit card only
No cheques please.**

Please allow up to five weeks for delivery.

NHL PUBLISHING IS PLEASED TO OFFER THREE OF THE GAME'S LEADING ANNUAL PUBLICATIONS

1. The NHL Official Guide & Record Book

*is the NHL's authoritative
information source.
62st year in print.
432 pages.
The "Bible of Hockey".
Read worldwide.*

2. The NHL Yearbook

*200-page, full- color magazine
with features on each club.
Award winners, All-Stars
and special statistics.*

3. The NHL Rule Book

*Complete playing rules,
including all changes for 1993-94.
New expanded format*

**Free Book List and NHL Schedule
included with each order**